# THE
# ALL ENGLAND
# LAW REPORTS
# 1985

## Volume 1

*Editor*
PETER HUTCHESSON LL M
Barrister, New Zealand

*Assistant Editor*
BROOK WATSON
of Lincoln's Inn, Barrister
and of the New South Wales Bar

*Consulting Editor*
WENDY SHOCKETT
of Gray's Inn, Barrister

London
BUTTERWORTHS

| | |
|---|---|
| ENGLAND | Butterworth & Co (Publishers) Ltd, 88 Kingsway, **London** WC2B 6AB |
| AUSTRALIA | Butterworths Pty Ltd, **Sydney, Melbourne, Brisbane, Adelaide, Perth, Canberra** and **Hobart** |
| CANADA | Butterworth & Co (Canada) Ltd, **Toronto** and **Vancouver** |
| NEW ZEALAND | Butterworths of New Zealand Ltd, **Wellington** and **Auckland** |
| SINGAPORE | Butterworth & Co (Asia) Pte Ltd, **Singapore** |
| SOUTH AFRICA | Butterworth Publishers (Pty) Ltd, **Durban** and **Pretoria** |
| USA | Butterworth Legal Publishers, **Seattle**, Washington, **Boston**, Massachusetts, **Austin**, Texas and **St Paul**, Minnesota D & S Publishers, **Clearwater**, Florida |

©

Butterworth & Co (Publishers) Ltd

1985

ISBN 0 406 85154 9

Typeset by CCC, printed and bound in Great Britain by William Clowes Limited, Beccles and London

# House of Lords

The Lord High Chancellor: Lord Hailsham of St Marylebone

## Lords of Appeal in Ordinary

Lord Fraser of Tullybelton
Lord Scarman
Lord Diplock
Lord Keith of Kinkel
Lord Roskill

Lord Bridge of Harwich
Lord Brandon of Oakbrook
Lord Brightman
Lord Templeman

# Court of Appeal

The Lord High Chancellor

The Lord Chief Justice of England: Lord Lane
(President of the Criminal Division)

The Master of the Rolls: Sir John Francis Donaldson
(President of the Civil Division)

The President of the Family Division: Sir John Lewis Arnold

The Vice-Chancellor: Sir Robert Edgar Megarry

## Lords Justices of Appeal

Sir John Frederick Eustace Stephenson
(retired 23 February 1985)
Sir Frederick Horace Lawton
Sir James Roualeyn Hovell-Thurlow-
Cumming-Bruce
(retired 14 April 1985)
Sir Edward Walter Eveleigh
(retired 21 December 1984)
Sir Desmond James Conrad Ackner
Sir Peter Raymond Oliver
Sir Tasker Watkins VC
Sir Patrick McCarthy O'Connor
Sir William Hugh Griffiths
Sir Michael John Fox
Sir Michael Robert Emanuel Kerr

Sir John Douglas May
Sir Christopher John Slade
Sir Francis Brooks Purchas
Sir Robert Lionel Archibald Goff
Sir George Brian Hugh Dillon
Sir Stephen Brown
Sir Roger Jocelyn Parker
Sir Nicolas Christopher Henry Browne-
Wilkinson
Sir David Powell Croom-Johnson
Sir Anthony John Leslie Lloyd
Sir Brian Thomas Neill
(appointed 11 January 1985)
Sir Michael John Mustill
(appointed 25 February 1985)

# Chancery Division

The Lord High Chancellor

The Vice-Chancellor

Sir John Norman Keates Whitford
Sir Ernest Irvine Goulding
Sir Raymond Henry Walton
Sir John Evelyn Vinelott
Sir Martin Charles Nourse
Sir Douglas William Falconer

Sir Jean-Pierre Frank Eugene Warner
Sir Peter Leslie Gibson
Sir David Herbert Mervyn Davies
Sir Jeremiah LeRoy Harman
Sir Donald James Nicholls
Sir Richard Rashleigh Folliott Scott

# Queen's Bench Division

The Lord Chief Justice of England

Sir Joseph Donaldson Cantley
Sir Hugh Eames Park
Sir Bernard Caulfield
Sir William Lloyd Mars-Jones
Sir Peter Henry Rowley Bristow
Sir Hugh Harry Valentine Forbes
Sir Leslie Kenneth Edward Boreham
Sir Alfred William Michael Davies
Sir John Dexter Stocker
Sir Kenneth George Illtyd Jones
Sir Haydn Tudor Evans
Sir Peter Richard Pain
Sir Kenneth Graham Jupp
Sir Ralph Brian Gibson
Sir Walter Derek Thornley Hodgson
Sir James Peter Comyn
Sir Frederick Maurice Drake
Sir Brian Thomas Neill
   (appointed Lord Justice of Appeal,
   11 January 1985)
Sir Michael John Mustill
   (appointed Lord Justice of Appeal,
   25 February 1985)
Sir Barry Cross Sheen
Sir David Bruce McNeill
Sir Harry Kenneth Woolf
Sir Christopher James Saunders French
Sir Thomas Patrick Russell
Sir Peter Edlin Webster
Sir Thomas Henry Bingham

Sir Iain Derek Laing Glidewell
Sir Henry Albert Skinner
Sir Peter Murray Taylor
Sir Murray Stuart-Smith
Sir Christopher Stephen Thomas Jonathan
   Thayer Staughton
Sir Donald Henry Farquharson
Sir Anthony James Denys McCowan
Sir Iain Charles Robert McCullough
Sir Hamilton John Leonard
Sir Alexander Roy Asplan Beldam
Sir David Cozens-Hardy Hirst
Sir John Stewart Hobhouse
Sir Michael Mann
Sir Andrew Peter Leggatt
Sir Michael Patrick Nolan
Sir Oliver Bury Popplewell
Sir William Alan Macpherson
Sir Philip Howard Otton
Sir Paul Joseph Morrow Kennedy
Sir Michael Hutchison
Sir Simon Denis Brown
Sir David William Tudor Price
Sir Anthony Howell Meurig Evans
Sir Mark Oliver Saville
   (appointed 18 January 1985)
Sir Johan van Zyl Steyn
   (appointed 8 February 1985)
Sir Christopher Dudley Roger Rose
   (appointed 17 April 1985)

# Family Division

The President of the Family Division

Sir John Brinsmead Latey
Sir Alfred Kenneth Hollings
Sir Charles Trevor Reeve
Dame Rose Heilbron
Sir Brian Drex Bush
Sir Alfred John Balcombe
Sir John Kember Wood
Sir Ronald Gough Waterhouse

Sir John Gervase Kensington Sheldon
Sir Thomas Michael Eastham
Dame Margaret Myfanwy Wood Booth
Sir Anthony Leslie Julian Lincoln
Dame Ann Elizabeth Oldfield Butler-Sloss
Sir Anthony Bruce Ewbank
Sir John Douglas Waite
Sir Anthony Barnard Hollis

# CITATION

## These reports are cited thus:

## [1985] 1 All ER

## REFERENCES

These reports contain references to the following major works of legal reference described in the manner indicated below.

## Halsbury's Laws of England

The reference 26 Halsbury's Laws (4th edn) para 577 refers to paragraph 577 on page 296 of volume 26 of the fourth edition of Halsbury's Laws of England.

## Halsbury's Statutes of England and Wales

The reference 4 Halsbury's Statutes (4th edn) 105 refers to page 105 of volume 4 of the fourth edition of Halsbury's Statutes of England and Wales, and the reference 39 Halsbury's Statutes (3rd edn) 895 refers to page 895 of volume 39 of the third edition of Halsbury's Statutes of England.

## The Digest

References are to the green band reissue volumes and the blue band replacement volumes of The Digest (formerly the English and Empire Digest).

The reference 36(2) Digest (Reissue) 764, *1398* refers to case number 1398 on page 764 of Digest Green Band Reissue Volume 36(2).

The reference 47 Digest (Repl) 781, *25* refers to case number 25 on page 781 of Digest Blue Band Replacement Volume 47.

## Halsbury's Statutory Instruments

The reference 20 Halsbury's Statutory Instruments (4th reissue) 302 refers to page 302 of the fourth reissue of volume 20 of Halsbury's Statutory Instruments; references to other reissues are similar.

# Cases reported in volume 1

# Digest of cases reported in volume 1

# CORRIGENDA

**[1985] 1 All ER**

p 130. **Gatoil International Inc v Arkwright-Boston Manufacturers Mutual Insurance Co.** Counsel for the appellants should read '*Gordon Pollock QC, A C M Johnston QC* (of the Scottish Bar) and *Julian Cooke*'.

p 216. **W A Sherratt Ltd v John Bromley (Church Stretton) Ltd.** Line *e*2 should read '. . . the company *since* the payment . . .'; line *e*3 should read '. . . the moneys, *because* otherwise . . .'

p 367. **Meah v McCreamer.** Line *b*3 should read 'In August *1978* the plaintiff . . .'

p 431. **BICC plc v Burndy Corp.** Line *f*3. The phrase 'consistent with legal principle' should conclude the sentence on that line and a new paragraph should then begin, reading 'There is little authority on the point of principle, but we were helpfully . . .'

# McKee v Chief Constable for Northern Ireland

HOUSE OF LORDS

LORD SCARMAN, LORD ELWYN-JONES, LORD DIPLOCK, LORD ROSKILL AND LORD BRIGHTMAN

22 OCTOBER, 22 NOVEMBER 1984

*Arrest – Arrest without warrant – Terrorist – Suspicion of being a terrorist – Constable arresting person on suspicion of being a terrorist – Constable acting on instructions of superior officer – Whether arresting officer's own state of mind only relevant consideration in deciding whether arrest lawful – Whether arresting officer entitled to derive honest suspicion that person a terrorist from instructions of superior officer – Whether arresting officer's suspicion must be reasonable as well as honest – Northern Ireland (Emergency Provisions) Act 1978, s 11(1).*

The respondent was arrested by a police officer under s 11(1)[a] of the Northern Ireland (Emergency Provisions) Act 1978 on suspicion of being a terrorist. In making the arrest the officer acted on the instructions of a superior officer, and as a result of what he had been told by his superior officer he suspected the respondent of being a terrorist. The respondent was released after 18 hours. He then sued the chief constable for trespass, assault and unlawful arrest and imprisonment. In his defence the chief constable relied on the fact that the arresting officer had been exercising the power conferred on a constable by s 11(1) of the 1978 Act to 'arrest without warrant any person whom he suspects of being a terrorist'. The judge held that the arrest was lawful, on the grounds that the officer's genuine suspicion that the respondent was a terrorist was sufficient for the purposes of a lawful arrest under s 11(1). The Court of Appeal in Northern Ireland reversed that decision, on the grounds that the arresting officer's only suspicion was that the respondent was a member of a proscribed organisation and that he had not inquired of his superiors the nature of the respondent's involvement in terrorism. The chief constable appealed.

**Held** – On the true construction of s 11(1) of the 1978 Act a constable made a lawful arrest if he had an honest, though not necessarily a reasonable, suspicion that the person being arrested was a terrorist. What was relevant in deciding whether the arrest was lawful was the arresting officer's state of mind, rather than the state of mind of his superior officer when he issued instructions to the arresting officer. Furthermore, the arresting officer was entitled to have an honest suspicion merely from the fact of the instructions given by his superior, since an arresting officer was not bound and indeed might not even be entitled to question those instructions or to ask on what information they were founded. Accordingly, since the arresting officer had honestly suspected the respondent of being a terrorist, the arrest was lawful and the chief constable's appeal would therefore be allowed (see p 2 d to f and p 3 j to p 4 e and g h, post).

### Notes

For a constable's power to arrest a suspected terrorist, see 11 Halsbury's Laws (4th edn) para 847.

For the Northern Ireland (Emergency Provisions) Act 1978, s 11, see 48 Halsbury's Statutes (3rd edn) 982.

---

*a* Section 11(1) is set out at p 2 j, post

**Case referred to in opinions**
*McElduff, Re* [1972] NI 1.

**Appeal**
The Chief Constable for Northern Ireland appealed with leave of the Appeal Committee of the House of Lords granted on 1 March 1984 against the decision of the Court of Appeal in Northern Ireland (O'Donnell LJ and Kelly J, Jones LJ dissenting) on 15 November 1981 allowing an appeal by the respondent, Gerard McKee, against a decision of MacDermott J sitting in the Queen's Bench Division of the High Court of Justice in Northern Ireland on 9 and 25 March 1983 in which he found that the arrest and detention of the respondent were lawful and that there had been no actionable assault or trespass proved against the appellant and ordered that judgment be entered in the appellant's favour. The facts are set out in the opinion of Lord Roskill.

*W A Campbell QC, P D Smith QC* and *R N H Hanna* (all of the Northern Ireland Bar) for the appellant.
*R C Hill QC* and *Barry Macdonald* (both of the Northern Ireland Bar) for the respondent.

Their Lordships took time for consideration.

22 November. The following opinions were delivered.

**LORD SCARMAN.** My Lords, I have had the advantage of reading in draft the speech to be delivered by my noble and learned friend Lord Roskill. I agree with it, and for the reasons he gives I would allow the appeal and restore the order of MacDermott J.

**LORD ELWYN-JONES.** My Lords, I have had the advantage of reading in draft the speech of my noble and learned friend Lord Roskill. For the reasons he has given I would allow this appeal and restore the order of MacDermott J dismissing this action.

**LORD DIPLOCK.** My Lords, I have had the advantage of reading in draft the speech of my noble and learned friend Lord Roskill. For the reasons he has given I too would allow this appeal and restore the order of MacDermott J dismissing this action.

**LORD ROSKILL.** My Lords, early in the morning of 8 September 1981 Pc Graham of the Royal Ulster Constabulary was sent with another police officer and a soldier to the respondent's home in Theodore Street in Belfast. Pc Graham's instructions, given earlier that night by his superior officer, Sgt Jackson, were to arrest the respondent as a 'suspected terrorist'. Pc Graham's evidence, which the trial judge, MacDermott J, accepted in preference to that of the respondent, was that Sgt Jackson had told him that the respondent 'was a suspect terrorist and from what he told me about that person I was firmly convinced that this was correct'. Pc Graham also said that when he arrested the respondent he told him:

'I am arresting you under s 11 of the Emergency Powers Act 1978 and am taking you to Castlereagh. Just then he said, "What for?" I told him it was as a suspect terrorist.'

The respondent having been so arrested was detained and questioned. At about 10.00 pm on the same day he was released, having been in custody for some 18 hours. The respondent then sued the appellant as the police authority responsible for the actions of Pc Graham and others for damages for trespass, assault and unlawful arrest and imprisonment. The appellant by way of defence relied on s 11 of the Northern Ireland (Emergency Provisions) Act 1978. Section 11(1) of that statute reads: 'Any constable may arrest without warrant any person whom he suspects of being a terrorist.'
Section 31(1) defines 'terrorism' and 'terrorist' in the following terms:

'"terrorism" means the use of violence for political ends and includes any use of violence for the purpose of putting the public or any section of the public in fear; "terrorist" means a person who is or has been concerned in the commission or attempted commission of any act of terrorism or in directing, organising or training persons for the purpose of terrorism.'

MacDermott J dismissed the respondent's action. Two findings of the judge's judgment are crucial. First:

'I am satisfied . . . that the officer when he went to Theodore Street was convinced in his own mind that the [respondent] was suspected of being a terrorist and that he himself suspected him of being a terrorist.'

Second:

'. . . I accept that Pc Graham genuinely suspected that the [respondent] was a terrorist. As can be seen from the definition, "terrorist" and "terrorism" are defined in wide terms. In my judgment the arresting constable does not have to know or even suspect the nature of the involvement in terrorism which his superior attributes to the person who is being arrested.'

It was for this reason that the trial judge held that the respondent's arrest was lawful and dismissed the action.

The respondent appealed to the Court of Appeal in Northern Ireland (Jones, O'Donnell LJJ and Kelly J). The Court of Appeal on 5 December 1983 by a majority, Jones LJ dissenting, allowed the appeal, held the arrest unlawful and awarded the respondent £500 damages against the appellant. By the same majority leave to appeal to this House was refused but subsequently your Lordships granted leave to appeal. The reasoning of Jones LJ was in substance that of the trial judge. But the majority in the judgment given by Kelly J thought otherwise. After stating that the statute 'required a suspicion of being a terrorist in narrower terms than popular usage of the word "terrorist" might connote to a police officer or a layman', the judge went on to say:

'Neither limb brings into its definition the person for example who is merely a member of a proscribed or paramilitary organisation, nor one whose activity is no more than soliciting support for such an organisation. So, if a police officer suspects a person of membership of a proscribed organisation and nothing more, he has no lawful power of arrest under s 11(1) of the 1978 Act because such membership does not make him a terrorist under the Act.'

Later in his judgment, the judge asked:

'Was there evidence before the trial judge to enable a finding to be made that Pc Graham suspected the appellant of being a terrorist within the definition of s 31?'

He concluded that there was not, because of the later questioning of the respondent by Det Con Moody after the respondent's arrest with a view to establishing that the respondent was a member of the Provisional IRA. I quote the judge's words:

'Therefore the [respondent's] deepest involvement in terrorism as suspected by the interviewing detectives and their file was membership of the Provisional IRA. I would find it surprising if Sgt Jackson, a uniformed section sergeant, knew or suspected more. It is possible that he did but he was not called to give evidence. If he did not, then the most he could communicate to Pc Graham was that the [respondent] was a suspected member of the Provisional IRA. If the officer accepted this and this was his suspicion, then that suspicion fell short of that required by s 11(1) and s 31 of the Act.'

My Lords, with profound respect to the majority of the Court of Appeal, I cannot agree. Nor do I agree that the two definitions in s 31 are narrow. On the contrary, in common with the trial judge, I think they are wide. There was never any suggestion

throughout Pc Graham's evidence that the reason for his being of the firm opinion that
the respondent was a suspect terrorist was that he was or was believed to be a member of    a
the Provisional IRA. Indeed, that organisation is nowhere mentioned from beginning to
end of Pc Graham's evidence. On the true construction of s 11(1) of the statute, what
matters is the state of mind of the arresting officer and of no one else. That state of mind
can legitimately be derived from the instruction given to the arresting officer by his
superior officer. The arresting officer is not bound and indeed may well not be entitled
to question those instructions or to ask on what information they are founded. It is, in    b
my view, not legitimate in the light of the trial judge's findings as to Pc Graham's state
of mind at the time of the arrest to seek to go behind that finding and deduce from Det
Con Moody's evidence as to questioning which took place some time after the arrest what
Sgt Jackson's state of mind may have been when he gave Pc Graham his instructions. It
is Pc Graham's state of mind that matters and that alone. In my view the matter is
concluded in favour of the appellant by the trial judge's findings to which I have already    c
referred.

My Lords, I do not doubt that the burden is on the appellant to justify the respondent's
arrest. In my view he has amply done so. I have already said that I reached this conclusion
simply on the trial judge's findings as to Pc Graham's state of mind. That Pc Graham
honestly had that belief was not challenged and, if it be relevant, the existence of that
honest belief seems to me to be well established by the fact that Pc Graham said in    d
evidence that Sgt Jackson had told him to be careful and that after knocking on the door
of the respondent's house he, Pc Graham, was 'standing back against the wall because I
suspected he [the respondent] might have guns'.

In conclusion I would mention two other matters. First, I respectfully agree with all
the judges below that on the true construction of the statute the powers of arrest under
s 11 are not qualified by any words of 'reasonableness'. The suspicion has to be honestly    e
held but it need not be a reasonable suspicion as well. I also agree with what was said on
this topic by McGonigal J in Re McElduff [1972] NI 1 at 19, in the passage quoted by Kelly
J.

Second, the respondent in his printed case claimed that it was conceded below 'that
mere membership of the Provisional IRA does not necessarily amount to being a
"terrorist" as defined'.    f

Counsel who conducted the appellant's case in the Court of Appeal said that neither he
nor his junior had any recollection of making any such concession. In these circumstances,
counsel for the respondent properly felt unable to press the point. I will only say that, if
any such concession had been made, I find it difficult to understand how O'Donnell LJ,
on the application for leave to appeal to this House, would have said that the question
was 'a hypothetical one since no evidence was given to raise its factual basis'.    g

For my part, I decline to express any view whatever on the question whether suspicion
of membership of the Provisional IRA would without more justify arrest under s 11(1).
There is no evidence to suggest that suspicion of such membership was a factor in any
way operating on Pc Graham's mind at the time he effected the arrest.

In the result I would allow this appeal and restore the order of MacDermott J dismissing
this action.    h

**LORD BRIGHTMAN.** My Lords, I agree with the speech of my noble and learned
friend Lord Roskill, and would allow this appeal for the reasons given by him.

*Appeal allowed.*

Solicitors: *Treasury Solicitor,* agents for *Crown Solicitor,* Belfast; *Robin Thompson & Partners,*
agents for *Madden & Finucane,* Belfast (for the respondent).

Mary Rose Plummer    Barrister.

a

# Insurance Officer v McCaffrey

HOUSE OF LORDS

LORD SCARMAN, LORD ELWYN-JONES, LORD DIPLOCK, LORD ROSKILL AND LORD BRIGHTMAN

24 OCTOBER, 22 NOVEMBER 1984

b
*National insurance – Non-contributory invalidity pension – Entitlement – Whether claim a necessary precondition to entitlement – Social Security (Northern Ireland) Act 1975, ss 36(1), 79(1).*

c
On the true construction of s 79(1)[a] of the Social Security (Northern Ireland) Act 1975, the requirement that 'it shall be a condition of a person's right to any benefit that he makes a claim for it in the prescribed manner and within the prescribed time' is a reference merely to a person's right to be paid the benefit, and not a reference to a person's entitlement to that benefit. Accordingly, entitlement to a non-contributory invalidity pension under s 36(1)[b] of the 1975 Act is governed solely by the terms of s 36, and the making of a claim in accordance with s 79(1) is not one of the necessary preconditions to entitlement to such a pension (see p 6 c to p 7 d and g to j, post).

d
### Notes
For entitlement to non-contributory invalidity pension, see 33 Halsbury's Laws (4th edn) para 450.

Sections 36 and 79 of the Social Security (Northern Ireland) Act 1975 correspond to ss 36 and 79 of the Social Security Act 1975. For ss 36 and 79 of the Social Security Act 1975, see 45 Halsbury's Statutes (3rd edn) 1122, 1177.

e

### Case referred to in opinions
*Pearson v Secretary of State for Social Services* 1983 SLT 73.

### Appeal
f
The insurance officer appealed with leave of the Court of Appeal in Northern Ireland against the decision of that court (Lord Lowry LCJ and Gibson LJ) dated 13 March 1984 dismissing his appeal against the decision of the social security commissioner (Mr R W B McConnell) on 30 June 1983 dismissing his appeal against the decision of the local tribunal, Enniskillen, on 2 November 1981 reversing his decision on 25 June 1981 that non-contributory invalidity pension was not payable to the respondent, Margaret McCaffrey, from 15 April 1980 because the respondent had attained pensionable age on that date and had not been entitled, and could not be treated as having been entitled, to such a pension immediately before that age. The facts are set out in the opinion of Lord Scarman.

g

*W A Campbell QC* and *C A McKay* (both of the Northern Ireland Bar) for the appellant.
*Patrick Markey QC* and *F J Farrelly* (both of the Northern Ireland Bar) for the respondent.

h
Their Lordships took time for consideration.

22 November. The following opinions were delivered.

j
**LORD SCARMAN.** My Lords, on 10 February 1981 the respondent made a claim for a non-contributory invalidity pension (the pension). She was then in her 61st year, having attained pensionable age on her 60th birthday, which fell on 15 April 1980. The insurance officer, who is the appellant, decided against her claim. He did so because in

a   Section 79(1) is set out at p 6 j, post
b   Section 36(1) is set out at p 6 d, post

his view she had failed to show that she was entitled to the pension immediately, or
indeed at any time, before she attained pensionable age. He accepted that she had shown      a
that she had met the statutory condition of entitlement in that she had been incapable of
work for the required minimum period before 15 April 1980. But she had made no
claim before that date, and in his view the making of a claim before reaching pensionable
age was a condition precedent to her entitlement.

The respondent's claim falls to be considered under the Northern Ireland legislation,
which is, however, in substantially the same terms as the legislation which governs social      b
security elsewhere in the United Kingdom. She appealed to her local tribunal against the
insurance officer's decision, and was successful. Since then, the insurance officer has taken
the case without success to the social security commissioner and to the Court of Appeal
in Northern Ireland. Undaunted he now appeals to your Lordships' House.

Section 36 of the Social Security (Northern Ireland) Act 1975 makes provision for the
non-contributory invalidity pension. The section contains no hint of the point taken by      c
the appellant: nowhere does it suggest that the making of a claim is necessary to the
establishment of entitlement. Section 36(1) sets out what has to be shown in order that a
person shall be entitled to the pension. It makes no reference to the need for a claim. The
subsection is in these terms:

> 'Subject to the provisions of this section, a person shall be entitled to a non-
> contributory invalidity pension for any day on which he is incapable of work, if he      d
> has been so incapable for a period of not less than 196 consecutive days ending
> immediately before that day.'

It will be observed that the entitlement is 'subject to the provisions of this section'. A
number of conditions are imposed by the succeeding subsections on entitlement; they
do not include the making of a claim. Only one of them is relevant to this appeal. It is      e
contained in sub-s (4), the terms of which are as follows:

> 'Subject to subsection (5) below, a person who has attained pensionable age shall
> not be entitled to a pension under this section unless he was so entitled (or is treated
> by regulations as having been so entitled) immediately before attaining that age.'

Subsection (5) is not relevant and may be disregarded for the purposes of this appeal.      f

There can be no doubt that the respondent has satisfied the conditions set out in sub-ss
(1) and (4). The evidence is that by 1 January 1980 she had been incapable of work for a
period of not less than 196 consecutive days immediately before that date and that she
continued to be incapable of work up to the date on which she attained pensionable age,
and indeed thereafter up to the date of her claim. If there be no guide to entitlement
other than s 36, the respondent succeeds: she has met the conditions set by the section.      g

The appellant recognises that unless he can find elsewhere in the statute a condition
not mentioned in s 36 restricting entitlement to the pension he fails. He finds such a
condition in s 79(1) of the Act.

Section 79 is the first section in Pt II of Ch VI of the Act. Chapter VI deals with the
administration of social security benefit. Section 36 does not: it deals with entitlement,
and is in Ch II, which makes provision for non-contributory benefits. Chapter II precedes      h
Ch VI logically as well as structurally: for entitlement to benefit must exist in order that
the benefit can be administered. Section 79(1) is, therefore, an unlikely place in which to
find rules governing entitlement to benefit. Section 79, in fact, deals with the business of
claims and awards. Briefly and subject to certain exceptions its effect is that no award
may be made unless a benefit is claimed. The making of a claim is, therefore, a condition
of the right to be paid the benefit. Section 79(1) is in these terms:      j

> 'Subject to the following provisions of this Chapter, and, in the case of retirement
> pensions, to section 27(6), it shall be a condition of a person's right to any benefit
> that he makes a claim for it in the prescribed manner and within the prescribed
> time.'

The appellant submits that the subsection modifies the effect of s 36(1) so that there is

a  no entitlement until a claim is made; since the respondent failed to make a claim before
she attained pensionable age, she cannot, he submits, show, as s 36(4) requires that she
should show, that she was entitled to the pension immediately before she attained that
age.

The submission is, in my view, totally misconceived. First, entitlement is governed by
s 36. The section does not define entitlement by reference to the making of a claim or
require a claim as a condition precedent to entitlement. Second, s 79(1) has to be
b  construed so as to be consistent with the entitlement which is created by s 36, and not
vice versa. Any other approach makes nonsense of s 36. A government department,
faced with the complexities of administering social security, may perhaps be forgiven for
putting the cart before the horse. But a judge can have no excuse. The logic of entitlement
and claim is clear: claim is based on the existence of entitlement. Third, s 79(1) does not
speak of 'entitlement'. It merely declares it to be 'a condition of a person's right to any
c  benefit that he makes a claim'. These words do not have to be construed as a reference to
entitlement. They can equally well, as a matter of ordinary English, be a reference to the
right to be paid. And this is the meaning appropriate to a section dealing with the
administration of benefit. Accordingly, I read the subsection as having this effect: a
claimant not only has to show the existence of an entitlement but has also to make a
claim in the prescribed manner and within the prescribed time in order that he may be
d  paid. This construction avoids introducing a restriction on entitlement not to be found
in s 36 and makes sense of s 79(1) as a provision dealing with the administration of
benefit.

Your Lordships were referred to a decision of the Court of Session, Second Division,
*Pearson v Secretary of State for Social Services* 1983 SLT 73. The case was concerned with
attendance allowance, for which s 35 of the Social Security Act 1975 makes provision,
e  and with para 10 of Sch 1 to the Supplementary Benefits Act 1976, which provides for
the increase of the allowance to meet certain attendance requirements of a severely
disabled person. The court was not concerned with the statutory provision which the
House has to consider in this appeal. I prefer, therefore, to express no opinion as to the
correctness or otherwise of the decision save to observe that I am not persuaded that it
supports the construction of s 36 for which the appellant contends. If it does, that would
f  seem to me to be no ground for questioning the construction of s 36 which has been
accepted in this case by every tribunal, other than the insurance officer himself, which
has considered it.

Finally, the department responsible for administering social security need fear no
opening of the floodgates to a rush of stale claims. Section 82(2)(c) provides that in respect
of most non-contributory benefits including the invalidity pension no sum shall be paid
g  to any person for any period more than 12 months before the date of the claim. The
respondent therefore is limited, so far as payment is concerned, to the 12 months
immediately preceding the date of her claim. I would dismiss the appeal with costs.

**LORD ELWYN-JONES.** My Lords, I have had the advantage of reading in draft the
speech prepared by my noble and learned friend Lord Scarman. For the reasons which
h  he has given I would dismiss this appeal with costs.

**LORD DIPLOCK.** My Lords, I have had the advantage of reading in draft the speech
of my noble and learned friend Lord Scarman. I agree with it, and for the reasons which
he gives I would dismiss this appeal.

j  **LORD ROSKILL.** My Lords, I have had the advantage of reading in draft the speech
delivered by my noble and learned friend Lord Scarman. I agree with it, and for the
reasons which he gives I would dismiss this appeal.

**LORD BRIGHTMAN.** My Lords, I agree that this appeal should be dismissed for the
reasons given by my noble and learned friend Lord Scarman.

*Appeal dismissed.*

Solicitors: *Solicitor to the Department of Health and Social Security,* agents for *Solicitor, Health and Social Services Division,* Belfast; *Hylton-Potts,* agents for *Vincent B Maguire & Co,* Enniskillen (for the respondent).

Mary Rose Plummer    Barrister.

# R v Dudley Justices, ex parte Gillard

QUEEN'S BENCH DIVISION
STEPHEN BROWN LJ AND KENNEDY J
16 JULY 1984

*Magistrates – Summary trial – Offence triable summarily or on indictment – Discontinuance of summary trial and committal to Crown Court – Discontinuance at any time before conclusion of prosecution evidence – Magistrates accepting jurisdiction over offence and accused electing summary trial – Accused entering unequivocal plea of guilty – Magistrates accepting plea – Prosecution not calling further evidence – Magistrates then deciding to discontinue summary proceedings and act as examining justices in committal proceedings – Whether magistrates having power to discontinue summary proceedings – Magistrates' Courts Act 1980, s 25(2).*

The applicant appeared before a magistrates' court charged with an offence which was triable either summarily or on indictment. The prosecution opposed a summary trial but the magistrates decided to accept summary jurisdiction and the applicant was put to his election. He elected summary trial before the magistrates and entered an unequivocal plea of guilty. He was remanded in custody pending sentence. When he appeared before the magistrates for sentence, however, the prosecution applied for the summary proceedings to be discontinued and for the applicant to be committed to the Crown Court for trial on indictment. The magistrates agreed to take that course. The applicant applied for judicial review of the magistrates' decision, seeking orders of prohibition restraining the magistrates from committing him for trial in the Crown Court and mandamus requiring the magistrates to continue with the summary hearing. The applicant contended that, since under s 25(2)[a] of the Magistrates' Courts Act 1980 magistrates could only discontinue summary proceedings and act as examining justices in committal proceedings 'at any time before the conclusion of the evidence for the prosecution', they had no power to commit the applicant for trial once they had accepted his plea of guilty in the summary proceedings.

**Held** – On the true construction of s 25(2) of the 1980 Act, where a magistrates' court accepted jurisdiction over an offence which was triable either summarily or on indictment, and the defendant elected summary trial, entered an unequivocal plea of guilty which was accepted by the magistrates and, as normally happened, the prosecution indicated that it did not wish to tender evidence, the court had no power to divest itself of summary jurisdiction and commit the defendant for trial in the Crown Court, since if it were to do so it would be acting after 'the conclusion of the evidence for the prosecution'. It followed that the magistrates had had no power to discontinue the summary proceedings and embark on committal proceedings, and accordingly orders of prohibition and mandamus would be granted (see p 10 *d e* and p 13 *d f* and *j* to p 14 *d*, post).

*R v Sheridan* [1936] 2 All ER 883 and *R v Grant* [1936] 2 All ER 1156 applied.

*S (an infant) v Manchester City Recorder* [1969] 3 All ER 1230 considered.

---

a   Section 25(2), so far as material, is set out at p 10 c, post

**Notes**

*a* For changing the mode of trial in proceedings before a magistrates' court, see 29 Halsbury's Laws (4th edn) para 306.

For the Magistrates' Courts Act 1980, s 25, see 50(2) Halsbury's Statutes (3rd edn) 1466.

**Cases referred to in judgments**

*R v Gordon* [1983] Crim LR 735, Crown Ct at Inner London Sessions.

*b R v Gore Justices, ex p N (an infant)* [1966] 3 All ER 991, [1966] 1 WLR 1522, DC.

*R v Grant* [1936] 2 All ER 1156, 26 Cr App R 8, CCA.

*R v Guest, ex p Anthony* [1964] 3 All ER 385, [1964] 1 WLR 1273, DC.

*R v Midhurst Justices, ex p Thompson, R v Midhurst Justices, ex p Mattesons Meats Ltd* [1973] 3 All ER 1164, [1974] QB 137, [1973] 3 WLR 715, DC.

*R v Norfolk Justices, ex p DPP* [1950] 2 All ER 42, [1950] 2 KB 558, DC.

*c R v Sheridan* [1936] 2 All ER 883, [1937] 1 KB 223, CCA.

*S (an infant) v Manchester City Recorder* [1969] 3 All ER 1230, [1971] AC 481, [1970] 2 WLR 21, HL.

*Simms v Moore* [1970] 3 All ER 1, [1970] 2 QB 327, [1970] 2 WLR 1099, DC.

**Application for judicial review**

*d* David Horace Gillard applied, with the leave of Glidewell J granted on 12 April 1984, for judicial review of a decision of the respondents, the Dudley justices, made on 13 February 1984, to discontinue the summary hearing of an information charging the applicant with assault occasioning actual bodily harm to which on 6 February 1984 he had pleaded guilty and to commit him for trial at the Crown Court. The relief sought was (1) an order of prohibition to restrain the magistrates' court from purporting to commit the *e* applicant to the Crown Court for trial of the offence in question and (2) an order of mandamus requiring the magistrates' court to continue the summary hearing. The grounds on which the relief was sought were (i) that the magistrates had no power to commit the applicant for trial in the Crown Court once they had decided to hear the information summarily, had accepted the applicant's plea of guilty and he had not sought to change that plea and (ii) that if the applicant was committed to the Crown Court for *f* trial he would be entitled to plead autrefois convict. The facts are set out in the judgment of Kennedy J.

*Simon Brand* for the applicant.
*R D H Smith* for the respondents.

*g* **KENNEDY J** (delivering the first judgment at the invitation of Stephen Brown LJ). This is an application for judicial review of a decision of the Dudley justices who decided to proceed it commit for trial a man who on an earlier occasion they had permitted to elect summary trial and who had on that earlier occasion pleaded guilty.

The circumstances of this matter are that on 6 February 1984 David Horace Gillard and a co-accused appeared before the justices charged with an offence of assault *h* occasioning actual bodily harm and a further offence of possessing an offensive weapon, that latter offence being one which was laid before the justices apparently on the morning of the hearing. The prosecution opposed the summary trial, but the bench decided to accept jurisdiction and they then invited Gillard to elect whether or not he was prepared to have a summary trial. He elected, in the event, to be tried by the magistrates. His plea was then taken and he pleaded guilty to the offence of assault occasioning actual bodily *j* harm but not guilty to the offence of possessing an offensive weapon. His co-accused elected to be tried at the Crown Court, and the bench then agreed to hear the remaining charge against Gillard on a subsequent occasion. Both men were remanded in custody.

A week later, on 13 February 1984, the case was relisted before the magistrates, and on this second occasion the prosecution invited the court to discontinue the summary proceedings and to commit both men for trial. Despite objections which were raised by the solicitor who was representing Gillard, the bench agreed to take that course.

The events which followed after that hearing on 13 February are not for our purposes relevant, save that it should be said that on 27 February the prosecution, it seems, offered *a* no evidence on the charge of possessing an offensive weapon.

What is said before us is that, having regard to what had taken place on 6 February 1984 when the applicant was permitted to elect summary trial and his plea of guilty was accepted, the magistrates had no power to commit him on 13 February for trial in respect of the offence of assault occasioning actual bodily harm. In order to consider that matter we have to have regard to the statutory powers which the magistrates purported to *b* exercise, and those are to be found in the Magistrates' Courts Act 1980, s 25(2), which reproduces for present purposes in the same words what appeared in s 18(5) of the Magistrates' Courts Act 1952. Section 25(2) reads as follows:

'Where the court has . . . begun to try the information summarily, the court may, at any time before the conclusion of the evidence for the prosecution, discontinue the summary trial and proceed to inquire into the information as examining justices *c* and, on doing so, may adjourn the hearing without remanding the accused.'

The material words for present purposes clearly are 'at any time before the conclusion of the evidence for the prosecution'. Where there has been a plea of guilty, normally speaking no evidence is called on behalf of the prosecution, but counsel for the applicant, who appears before us, submits that on the wording of s 25(2) the magistrates lose their *d* power to commit for trial when there is an unequivocal plea of guilty tendered and that plea is in fact accepted, as unquestionably happened on this occasion.

In support of that submission he relies on the decision of the Court of Criminal Appeal in *R v Grant* [1936] 2 All ER 1156, 26 Cr App R 8. The headnote in that case reads as follows (26 Cr App R 8):

'A magistrate decided to deal summarily with an indictable offence, and the *e* prisoner pleaded guilty. The magistrate did not, however, pass sentence forthwith, but remanded the prisoner on bail until he had obtained a report. On obtaining the report, the magistrate altered his mind and decided to commit the prisoner for trial at quarter sessions. . .'

The decision of the court in that case was given by Humphreys J and he said (26 Cr App *f* R 8 at 11–12; cf [1936] 2 All ER 1156 at 1158):

'In SHERIDAN ([1936] 2 All ER 883, [1937] 1 KB 223) [to which he had already referred] this Court decided that, while a Court of summary jurisdiction has power to deal summarily with an indictable offence at any stage of the case and to commit for trial an accused person whom it has commenced to deal with summarily up to *g* the time when the Court has either convicted or acquitted, it has no power, once it has arrived at a decision on the case, to alter that decision and commit for trial, because by that time the accused person has been either convicted or acquitted, and, if the Court has registered a conviction, the only matter remaining for the Court is that of sentence. The only difference between SHERIDAN and the present case is that in that case the prisoner pleaded not guilty and the trial proceeded and at the close *h* of the case the magistrates convicted, whereas in the present case the appellant pleaded guilty. There is no distinction in law between a conviction by the verdict of a jury or the finding of a Court and a conviction on a prisoner's own confession. The decision in SHERIDAN would be binding on the present Court, even if the Court entertained any doubt as to its correctness, which it does not.'

That decision in *R v Grant* was criticised in the speech of Lord Upjohn in *S (an infant) v* *j* *Manchester City Recorder* [1969] 3 All ER 1230, [1971] AC 481. It is material to observe at the outset that *S (an infant) v Manchester City Recorder* was concerned with an application by a defendant to change his plea which the magistrates felt they were unable to entertain. It was therefore a problem which differed in kind from that with which we are concerned. It is also material to observe that the majority of their Lordships did not in fact come to a conclusion about whether or not the decisions in *R v Sheridan* and *R v Grant* were correct. Lord Reid, with whom Lord Guest agreed, said ([1969] 3 All ER 1230 at 1233–1234, [1971] AC 481 at 490):

> 'I do not think it necessary to enter on the technicalities of autrefois convict. Other authorities cited to us strongly suggest that this is not a good plea unless the earlier case was carried to a conclusion. But even if *Sheridan's* case was rightly decided and a "conviction" in the narrower sense will support a plea of autrefois convict that does not appear to me to lead to the conclusion that a "conviction" in the narrower sense must end the power of the court to allow a plea to be changed. No one has ever suggested that the decision of *Sheridan's* case conflicts with the power of a trial judge to allow a plea of guilty on an indictment to be changed, so why should it conflict with a similar power in magistrates' courts?'

I observe in passing that Lord Reid there uses the term 'conviction in the narrower sense'. It may be that that has some application to the facts with which we are concerned. Lord MacDermott also considered the decision in *R v Sheridan*. He said ([1969] 3 All ER 1230 at 1239, [1971] AC 481 at 497):

> 'Before your Lordships issue was joined on whether the cases of *R. v. Sheridan* and *R. v. Grant* were properly decided, the contention against the decisions being that a plea of autrefois convict only lies where there has been a conviction in the broader sense of the word, that is to say, a finding of guilt followed by an adjudication on what should be done with the convicted person by way of punishment, or otherwise. This raised a debatable point, but one which I do not find it necessary to decide in the present appeal.'

Lord Morris said ([1969] 3 All ER 1230 at 1244–1245, [1971] AC 481 at 503–504):

> 'It was laid down in the Divisional Court that a magistrate cannot entertain an application by an accused person to change his plea once the magistrate has convicted under s. 13(3) of the Act of 1952. I cannot accept this conclusion. Support for it was said to be found in *R. v. Sheridan*. But no question of the withdrawal of a plea arose in *Sheridan's* case. In that case there had been a plea of not guilty, but after hearing evidence the magistrates found the accused guilty. When they learned of his previous convictions they did not pass sentence but committed him for trial at quarter sessions. At such trial he raised a plea of autrefois convict. That plea was overruled and he was convicted by quarter sessions. That conviction was set aside by the Court of Criminal Appeal who held that in order to support a plea of autrefois convict it is not necessary that a conviction should have been followed by sentence; they held that the plea of autrefois convict should have been accepted at sessions. I do not find the case very helpful for present purposes. Nor was it a very satisfactory case. It seemed doubtful whether the correct procedure had been followed before summary trial had been embarked on. It may be that the case could have been decided on the basis that once magistrates had made a finding in the case, they had no jurisdiction (as the statutory provisions then stood) to commit to quarter sessions. But in any event it seems to me to be unnecessary for present purposes to consider whether *Sheridan's* case was rightly decided or to consider whether a conviction in the narrow sense (i.e., of a finding of guilt not followed by some appropriate order) is sufficient to support a plea of autrefois convict. *Sheridan's* case was followed and applied in *R. v. Grant*. Again, in that case (where there had been a plea of guilty before a magistrate) no question arose concerning the withdrawal of a plea. In that case there was a committal for trial which was quite unwarranted. Both cases were referred to without disapproval by LORD GODDARD, C.J., in his judgment in *R. v. Norfolk Justices, ex parte Director of Public Prosecutions* ([1950] 2 All ER 42, [1950] 2 KB 558). In that case magistrates decided to convict and then decided to commit to quarter sessions for sentence. That committal, however (for reasons which need not be elaborated) was invalid. Quarter sessions quite properly declined to deal

substantively with the case. It was held that a mandamus must issue directing the justices (who had convicted) to proceed to impose a sentence. They were not functi *a* officio. There had been no judgment or final adjudication. Again, in that case no question arose as to the withdrawal of a plea but the case is important as showing that (leaving out of account the procedure where s. 29 of the Act of 1952 is applicable and is properly followed) magistrates who try a case are not functi officio until they have passed a sentence or have otherwise finally adjudicated. I do not think either *Sheridan's* case or *Grant's* case compelled the decision in *Guest's* case [*R v Guest, ex p* *b* *Anthony* [1964] 3 All ER 385, [1964] 1 WLR 1273]. In neither of those cases did the point arise whether a plea of guilty could be withdrawn after acceptance of it and before a case is disposed of by a sentence or by some appropriate order.'

Lord Upjohn, whose speech is relied on by the applicant before us, dealt with this matter in two passages, in the first of which he says that the problem which was concerning their Lordships in *S (an infant) v Manchester City Recorder* stemmed from a mis- *c* understanding of the word 'conviction' in *R v Sheridan*. He goes on ([1969] 3 All ER 1230 at 1246, [1971] AC 481 at 506):

'The primary meaning of the word "conviction" denotes the judicial determination of a case; it is a judgment which involves two matters, a finding of guilt or the acceptance of a plea of guilty followed by sentence. Until there is such a judicial *d* determination the case is not concluded, the court is not functus officio and a plea of autrefois convict cannot be entertained. This has been the law from the earliest times: see HALES PLEAS OF THE CROWN (2 Hale PC 251) and it is equally applicable in a court of summary jurisdiction . . .'

Again Lord Upjohn says ([1969] 3 All ER 1230 at 1248, [1971] AC 481 at 507):
                                                                                *e*
'My Lords, it seems to me clear that the law plainly took the wrong turning in *Sheridan's* case. The court, whether High Court, quarter sessions or a court of summary jurisdiction retains full jurisdiciton over all matters before it until sentence, that is, until the final adjudication of the matter; and the reasoning in *Sheridan's* case and the cases of *R. v. Grant, R. v. Guest* and *R. v. Gore Justices* which followed that reasoning must be treated as overruled. In future it will be quite *f* unnecessary to accept a provisional plea or to resort to the "guilty but . . ." artifice. If the court, on all the facts before it, thinks that it is proper to accept a plea of guilty then the court may permit that plea to be withdrawn and a plea of not guilty accepted at a later stage up to sentence, that is until the complete adjudication of conviction.'

Our attention has also been invited to *R v Gordon* [1983] Crim LR 735. I need not cite *g* from that case in detail. Suffice it to say that the judge at the Crown Court at Inner London Sessions in that case appears to have taken the view that the decision in *R v Grant* was no longer binding on the court because of what was decided by the House of Lords in *S (an infant) v Manchester City Recorder*.

We were also referred to the decision of this court in *R v Midhurst Justices, ex p* *h* *Thompson, R v Midhurst Justices, ex p Mattesons Meats Ltd* [1973] 3 All ER 1164 esp at 1166, [1974] 1 QB 137 esp at 139–140 per Bridge J. *R v Midhurst Justices* was concerned with an application for an order of certiorari to quash a conviction where the justices had in error pronounced a conviction immediately after there had been a defence submission of no case to answer. Bridge J at the point which I have indicated said that the court had had drawn to its attention *S (an infant) v Manchester City Recorder*. He went on to say ([1973] *j* 3 All ER 1164 at 1166, [1974] QB 137 at 140):

'The essence of the decision, so far as material for our purposes, can be collected very shortly from a single sentence towards the end of the speech of Lord Upjohn. Having considered a series of decisions, mostly of this court, some of them of some antiquity, in which a distinction had hitherto been drawn between courts of assize and quarter sessions on the one hand, and courts of summary jurisdiction on the other, as to the circumstances in which those courts respectively become functi officio, Lord Upjohn said: "The court, whether High Court, quarter sessions or a court of summary jurisdiction retains full jurisdiction over all matters before it until sentence, that is, until the final adjudication of the matter; and the reasoning in *Sheridan's* case and the cases of *R. v. Grant, R. v. Guest* and *R. v. Gore Justices* which followed that reasoning must be treated as overruled.'"

This court then went on to apply that observation to the facts which it was considering in *R v Midhurst Justices*.

It seems to us, having looked at the authorities to which our attention has been invited, that there is nothing in the decision in *S (an infant) v Manchester City Recorder* which would enable us to say that the decision of the Court of Criminal Appeal in *R v Grant* has been overruled. What happened so far as we can discover in *S (an infant) v Manchester City Recorder* was that four of their Lordships declined to express a concluded view on the matter, and Lord Upjohn alone took the view that it was no longer possible for that decision to stand.

That leaves us in the position that, as is conceded by counsel before us, if the decision in *R v Grant* is applicable to the facts with which we are concerned we are bound by it and nothing which is said by the judge either in *R v Gordon* or in *R v Midhurst Justices* can release us from the binding effect of that earlier decision.

Counsel who appears before us on behalf of the respondent makes a number of submissions which are helpful. It is suggested by counsel that when one looks at s 25(2) of the Magistrates' Courts Act 1980 one should come to the conclusion, first of all, that where the section refers to trial it intends to embrace both a contested hearing and the hearing where the accused pleads guilty. No doubt that is right.

He then invites us to look at certain other parts of the 1980 Act in order to reach the conclusion that where there is a plea of guilty, for example in s 9(3), there is still power in the court to hear evidence. That is a course which is on occasions taken where there is an application for compensation or where the Crown is alleging that there were aggravating circumstances of which the magistrates should hear from the mouth of some witness.

No doubt again that is correct, but none of that in our view bears on the decision to which we have referred already in *R v Grant* and which in our judgment is binding on us in relation to the facts with which we have to deal.

Finally it was submitted to us that the magistrates' court has an inherent jurisdiction to regulate its own procedure and that therefore, whatever may be said in s 25(2) and whatever may be the proper interpretation of that statutory power, the court has a right if it considers it proper to act as the magistrates did on this occasion.

In support of that fairly bold submission our attention was invited to the decision in *Simms v Moore* [1970] 3 All ER 1, [1970] 2 QB 327. In that case the clerk to the justices examined the prosecution witnesses because the police officer who would normally have acted as the advocate on behalf of the prosecution was, it seems, a possible witness on behalf of the prosecution, who was likely to be called to give evidence. Complaint was made about that procedure having been adopted. The decision which was arrived at in that case was that the court had an inherent jurisdiction to regulate its own procedure, but it is noteworthy that the case was only concerned with the way in which evidence should be adduced. It was not concerned with whether or not, a point having been reached in the course of the hearing where an accused had pleaded guilty unequivocally, and that plea equally unequivocally had been accepted, the court still retained the power, having initially accepted jurisdiction itself, to divest itself of that jurisdiction and commit the accused for trial. That is the issue with which we are concerned. Having regard to the decision in *R v Grant*, by which we consider ourselves to be bound, we have come to the conclusion that the magistrates here had no power to adopt the course which they did in fact adopt on 13 February 1984. We are asked now to arrive at the decision that a writ of prohibition should be issued and in our judgment that writ should go.

**STEPHEN BROWN LJ.** I agree. The powers of the magistrates are clearly laid down
in s 25(2) of the Magistrates' Courts Act 1980. The subsection gives a clear deadline for    *a*
the time when a summary trial, once embarked on, may be discontinued and the court
may proceed to act as examining justices with a view to committal to the Crown Court.
It is quite clear that on the facts of this case the prosecution case had been completed.
There had been an adjournment, a remand, and a different view was taken apparently de
novo by a different prosecuting officer. That explains apparently the course which was
then set in motion. It is plain that applying strictly the terms of s 25(2), and bearing in    *b*
mind the authority of *R v Grant* [1936] 2 All ER 1156, this was not a course which was
open to the magistrates at that particular juncture. It must be borne in mind that s 38 of
the Magistrates' Courts Act 1980 gives the magistrates' courts the residual power
nevertheless to commit to the Crown Court for sentence should facts emerge after the
evidence of the prosecution has been given which suggest that that is the appropriate
course, having regard to the facts known about the particular offender and the need for    *c*
greater powers for sentence. That power would be unnecessary, it would appear, if the
view of the respondent were to be accepted.

In my judgment the magistrates were in error on this occasion in acceding to the
request to discontinue the summary proceedings and to embark on a committal for trial.
Accordingly, the application for judicial review succeeds and the appropriate orders
would be an order of prohibition to restrain the court from committing the applicant to    *d*
the Crown Court and an order of mandamus requiring the magistrates' court to continue
the summary hearing. That writ will go.

*Orders of prohibition and mandamus issued.*

*The court refused leave to appeal to the House of Lords but certified, under s 1(2) of the*    *e*
*Administration of Justice Act 1960, that the following point of law of general public importance*
*was involved in the decision: in the case of an offence triable either summarily or on indictment,*
*where a magistrates' court has allowed an accused to elect summary trial and he has pleaded*
*guilty and his plea has been accepted, can the court thereafter commit the case for trial on*
*indictment?*

*f*

*18 December. The Appeal Committee of the House of Lords granted the applicant leave to appeal.*

Solicitors: *Tanfields*, Dudley (for the applicant); *I S Manson*, Birmingham (for the
respondent).

N P Metcalfe Esq    Barrister.

# Coates (Inspector of Taxes) v Arndale Properties Ltd

HOUSE OF LORDS

LORD KEITH OF KINKEL, LORD EDMUND-DAVIES, LORD BRIDGE OF HARWICH, LORD BRANDON OF OAKBROOK AND LORD TEMPLEMAN

2, 3 OCTOBER, 22 NOVEMBER 1984

*Income tax – Company – Group relief – Appropriation of assets to trading stock – Transfer between members of group – Property dealing company acquiring lease at slightly less than market value from development company in same group – Lease not part of trading stock of development company – Market value of lease at acquisition substantially less than costs incurred by development company on lease – Property dealing company disposing of lease to another member of group for market value – Property dealing company electing to have lease brought into its trading account – Whether property dealing company acquired lease as trading stock – Finance Act 1965, Sch 7, para 1(3) – Income and Corporation Taxes Act 1970, s 274(1).*

The taxpayer was a property dealing company and was a member of the same group of companies as a development company and an investment company. On 30 March 1973 the taxpayer acquired a lease for £3,090,000 from the development company and on the same day assigned it to the investment company for its then market value of £3,100,000. By that date the development company's expenditure in connection with the lease amounted to £5,313,822. The taxpayer had previously acted as a property dealer within the group, buying properties from and selling properties to other members of the group for the purposes of its trade. It was not disputed that the transactions were genuine. The taxpayer claimed that it had acquired the lease as trading stock for the purposes of the Income and Corporation Taxes Act 1970, s 274(1)ᵃ and made an election to have the property brought into its trading account at £5,313,822 under the Finance Act 1965, Sch 7, para 1(3)ᵇ. The taxpayer admitted that the companies' motive for engaging in the transaction was the expectation that favourable tax consequences would ensue for one or more of the companies in the group. The Crown contended that the taxpayer had not acquired the lease from the development company as trading stock in the normal course of its business and that therefore s 274(1) did not apply and the taxpayer was not entitled to take advantage of the right of election under Sch 7, para 1(3). The General Commissioners allowed an appeal by the taxpayer, holding that the transaction was a proper transaction in the course of the taxpayer's trade and that the lease had been acquired by the taxpayer as trading stock. The Crown appealed, contending further that the motive of the companies for entering into the transaction deprived it of its trading character. The judge dismissed the appeal, holding that the transaction was genuine and that the fiscal motive for it did not deprive it of its trading character. The Court of Appeal reversed the judge's decision, holding that since the taxpayer had acquired the lease not for a commercial purpose but only to obtain a fiscal benefit the lease had not been acquired as 'trading stock'. The taxpayer appealed to the House of Lords.

**Held** – On the facts the group had procured the transfer of the lease from the development company to the taxpayer and from the taxpayer to the investment company with the object of obtaining group relief of £2·2m trading loss without in fact changing the lease from a capital asset to a trading asset. The group sought the advantage of treating the lease as trading stock while ensuring that the group retained the lease as a capital asset at all times. The taxpayer followed instructions and lent to the transaction its name and description as a property dealing company. However, the taxpayer did not

---

*a Section 274(1) is set out at p 18 c d, post*
*b Paragraph 1(3), so far as material, is set out at p 18 h j, post*

trade and had never had any intention of trading with the lease and it never acquired the lease as its trading stock within s 274(1) of the 1970 Act. Accordingly, the taxpayer was not entitled to exercise the election provided by para 1(3) of Sch 7 to the 1965 Act. The appeal would therefore be dismissed (see p 16 g to j, p 19 e to j and p 20 a to c, post).

**Notes**
For transfer of trading stock between members of groups of companies, see 5 Halsbury's Laws (4th edn) para 206.
    For the Finance Act 1965, Sch 7, para 1, see 34 Halsbury's Statutes (3rd edn) 949.
    For the Income and Corporation Taxes Act 1970, s 274, see 33 ibid 375.
    With effect from 6 April 1979 para 1 of Sch 7 to the 1965 Act was replaced by s 122 of the Capital Gains Tax Act 1979.

**Cases referred to in opinions**
Furniss (Inspector of Taxes) v Dawson [1984] 1 All ER 530, [1984] AC 474, [1984] 2 WLR 226, HL.
Griffiths (Inspector of Taxes) v J P Harrison (Watford) Ltd [1962] 1 All ER 909, [1963] AC 1, [1962] 2 WLR 909, HL.
IRC v Burmah Oil Co Ltd [1982] STC 30, HL.
Sharkey (Inspector of Taxes) v Wernher [1955] 3 All ER 493, [1956] AC 58, [1955] 3 WLR 671, HL.

**Appeal**
Arndale Properties Ltd (Arndale) appealed, with the leave of the Court of Appeal, against the decision of the Court of Appeal (Lawton, Fox and Kerr LJJ) ([1984] STC 124) on 6 December 1983 allowing an appeal by the Crown against a decision of Goulding J ([1982] STC 573) dated 24 March 1982 dismissing the Crown's appeal by way of case stated (set out at [1982] STC 575–577) from the decision of the Commissioners for the General Purposes of the Income Tax whereby the commissioners found that Arndale had acquired assets in the course of its trade as trading stock and qualified for stock relief pursuant to para 1 of Sch 7 to the Finance Act 1965. The facts are set out in the opinion of Lord Templeman.

*Andrew Park QC* and *Michael Flesch QC* for Arndale.
*Jonathan Parker QC, John Mummery* and *Peter Goldsmith* for the Crown.

Their Lordships took time for consideration.

22 November. The following opinions were delivered.

**LORD KEITH OF KINKEL.** My Lords, I have had the opportunity of reading in advance the speech to be delivered by my noble and learned friend Lord Templeman. I agree with it and for the reasons he gives would dismiss the appeal.

**LORD EDMUND-DAVIES.** My Lords, I am in respectful and complete agreement with the views expressed in the speech prepared by the noble and learned Lord Templeman. I accordingly concur in holding that this appeal should be dismissed.

**LORD BRIDGE OF HARWICH.** My Lords, for the reasons given in the speech of my noble and learned friend Lord Templeman, with which I agree, I would dismiss this appeal.

**LORD BRANDON OF OAKBROOK.** My Lords, I have had the advantage of reading in draft the speech prepared by my noble and learned friend Lord Templeman. I agree with it and for the reasons which he gives I would dismiss the appeal.

**LORD TEMPLEMAN.** My Lords, Town and City Properties Ltd is the parent of a
*a* group of companies which includes the three wholly-owned subsidiary companies
featured in this appeal. The first subsidiary, Sovereign Property Investments (Newport)
Ltd (SPI), carries on business as a property developer. SPI acquired a lease for 125 years of
land at Newport in Gwent and developed the site at a total cost of £5·3m. The market
value of the lease on 30 March 1973, according to the group, was £3·1m. SPI thus faced
a potential capital loss of £2·2m which might be reduced or eliminated by an increase in
*b* the value of the land prior to its eventual disposal. Any loss in fact suffered on disposal
would then rank as an allowable loss which could only be set off for corporation tax
purposes against chargeable gains, if any, made by SPI. The second subsidiary, the
appellant Arndale Properties Ltd (Arndale), carries on business as a property dealer; any
losses incurred by Arndale in carrying on that business are trading losses which can be
set off in any year against trading profits made by Arndale or by any other member of
*c* the group. There were therefore sound commercial reasons for converting the potential
capital loss of SPI into a trading loss suffered by Arndale and there is express statutory
provision which enables this to be done for corporation tax purposes. By an assignment
dated 30 March 1973 SPI assigned the lease to Arndale for £3·1m. According to the
accounts of SPI and Arndale the price in fact paid was £3,090,000 and in these proceedings
it has been assumed that the accounts, supported as they were by the auditors, are more
*d* accurate than the assignment. The object of the assignment was to enable Arndale to
convert the potential capital loss of £2·2m which threatened SPI into a trading loss for
corporation tax purposes of £2·2m to be suffered by Arndale and then to be available for
distribution between all members of the group to set off against trading profits. This
conversion is made possible by the legislation but only if Arndale acquired the lease 'as
trading stock' for the purposes of its property dealing business.
*e*        The third subsidiary of the group, Arndale Property Trust Ltd (APTL), carries on
business as an investment company. By an assignment also dated 30 March 1973 Arndale
assigned the lease to APTL for £3·1m. Arndale could then proceed to complete the
conversion of the potential capital loss of £2·2m into an actual trading loss for corporation
tax purposes and to distribute that trading loss between the companies of the group,
provided that Arndale had acquired the lease 'as trading stock'. The effect of the
*f* assignment to APTL was to ensure that the lease became a capital asset of APTL and thus
remained a capital asset of the group.
        The legislation which confers power on a group of companies to procure the conversion
of a potential capital loss into a trading loss provided certain conditions are fulfilled must
now be considered.
        By s 238 of the Income and Corporation Taxes Act 1970 a company is chargeable to
*g* corporation tax in respect of income and in respect of chargeable gains. By s 265
chargeable gains are to be included in the total profits of a company assessable to
corporation tax after deducting any allowable losses accruing to that company. Chargeable
gains to be included for corporation tax purposes are computed in accordance with the
principles applying to capital gains tax subject to any express provisions enacted with
regard to companies. Thus, as I have already indicated, if SPI, having acquired and
*h* developed land at a cost of £5·3m, had sold it on the open market for £3·1m, the sale
would have produced an allowable loss of £2·2m deductible in computing the chargeable
gains, if any, liable to corporation tax of SPI.
        Sections 272 to 281 make express provisions for corporation tax in connection with a
group of companies and each member of that group. In particular, s 273(1) provides:

*j*        '... where a member of a group of companies disposes of an asset to another
        member of the group, both members shall ... be treated, so far as relates to
        corporation tax on chargeable gains, as if the asset ... were acquired for a
        consideration of such amount as would secure that ... neither a gain nor a loss
        would accrue ...'

        Thus, although the lease was in fact assigned by SPI to Arndale for £3,090,000, the

lease is deemed for corporation tax purposes to have been assigned for £5·3m. If that
provision had stood alone, then the assignment by one member of the group, SPI, to   **a**
another member of the group, Arndale, would have had no effect on the corporation tax
liability of either company save that when Arndale eventually sold the lease a chargeable
gain or allowable loss would result to Arndale depending on the difference between the
price obtained by Arndale and the original cost to SPI, namely £5·3m.

Where, however, a member of a group transfers an asset to a trading member,
difficulties arise. These difficulties are similar to those which arise when an individual   **b**
who carries on a trading business appropriates property to or from his business activities
as trading stock. In *Sharkey (Inspector of Taxes) v Wernher* [1955] 3 All ER 493, [1956] AC
58, for example, a transfer of a horse from a stud farm carried on as a business to a racing
stable carried on as a recreation, produced tax consequences for the business similar to
those which would have been produced by a sale of the horse at market value.

By s 274(1) of the Income and Corporation Taxes Act 1970:   **c**

'Where a member of a group of companies acquires an asset as trading stock from
another member of the group, and the asset did not form part of the trading stock
of any trade carried on by the other member, the member acquiring it shall be
treated for purposes of paragraph 1 of Schedule 7 to the Finance Act 1965 as having
acquired the asset otherwise than as trading stock and immediately appropriated it
for the purposes of the trade as trading stock.'   **d**

The lease did not form part of the trading stock of SPI. Provided that Arndale acquired
the lease 'as trading stock' of the property dealing business carried on by Arndale, then
Arndale is deemed to have acquired the lease otherwise than as trading stock and
immediately appropriated it for the purposes of the trade as trading stock. Paragraph 1
of Sch 7 to the Finance Act 1965 makes provisions, similar in some respects to the results   **e**
achieved in the case of individuals by the decision in *Sharkey v Wernher*, in the event of
the appropriation of an asset as trading stock.

Paragraph 1(1) of Sch 7 to the 1965 Act, as amended, provides:

'Subject to sub-paragraph (3) below, where an asset acquired by a person otherwise
than as trading stock of a trade carried on by him is appropriated by him for the
purposes of the trade as trading stock . . . and, if he had then sold the asset for its   **f**
market value, a chargeable gain or allowable loss would have accrued to him, he shall
be treated as having thereby disposed of the asset by selling it for its then market
value.'

The confusing result is that if Arndale acquired the lease as trading stock it is treated as
having first acquired the lease for £5·3m otherwise than as trading stock, then as having   **g**
appropriated the lease as trading stock, then as having sold the lease for its market value,
namely £3·1m, thus as having made an allowable loss of £2·2m. Paragraph 1(3) of Sch 7
however confers an option on the trading company to convert the allowable loss of £2·2m
into a trading loss of £2·2m. By para 1(3):

'Sub-paragraph (1) above shall not apply in relation to a person's appropriation of   **h**
an asset for the purposes of a trade if he is chargeable to income tax in respect of the
profits of the trade . . . and elects that instead the market value of the asset at the time
of the appropriation shall, in computing the profits of the trade for purposes of tax,
be treated as reduced by the amount of the chargeable gain or increased by the amount
of the allowable loss referred to in that sub-paragraph, and where that sub-paragraph
does not apply by reason of such an election, the profits of the trade shall be computed   **j**
accordingly . . .'

Thus, if Arndale purchased the lease from SPI 'as trading stock' for the purposes of the
property dealing trade of Arndale then Arndale may elect that the acquisition cost of the
lease shall be entered in its trading accounts as £5·3m and not £3·1m and thus when
Arndale sold the lease to APTL for £3·1m Arndale for corporation tax purposes would
suffer a trading loss of £2·2m.

Provision is made for such a trading loss to be applied for the benefit of the group. By
*a* s 258 of the Income and Corporation Taxes Act 1970, headed 'Group relief':

'(1) Relief for trading losses . . . may . . . be surrendered by a company . . . which
is a member of a group of companies and, on the making of a claim by another
company . . . which is a member of the same group, may be allowed to the claimant
company by way of a relief from corporation tax called "group relief". . .'

*b*    Arndale claimed that it acquired the lease 'as trading stock' and pursuant to that claim
elected that para 1(3) of Sch 7 to the 1965 Act, as amended, should apply, and surrendered
to other members of the group relief from the alleged trading loss of £2·2m.
    The conversion of a potential capital loss into a trading loss for corporation tax purposes
and the distribution of the benefit of that trading loss by way of group relief cannot,
however, be achieved unless an asset is transferred from a non-trading member of the
*c* group to a trading member and is acquired by the trading member as 'trading stock' of
the business carried on by the trading member. If this were not the case the practical
distinction between chargeable gains and profits for the purposes of calculation of
corporation tax could be largely eliminated by including at least one trading company in
a group. The extent to which such distinction is desirable is not a matter for present
discussion. For the conversion of a capital loss into a trading loss it must be shown that a
*d* capital asset has been appropriated as trading stock.
    On behalf of Arndale it was submitted that Arndale was carrying on its trade as a
property dealer when it bought and sold the lease. A trader may buy and sell
simultaneously; a trader may even sell in anticipation of buying. One subsidiary
company may trade with another subsidiary company in the same group. Arndale traded
and made a profit of £10,000. If, in addition, Arndale was able to make available group
*e* relief amounting to £2·2m so much the better. The purchase from SPI and the sale to
APTL were no different in substance from a purchase from or sale to a third party having
no connection with the group. Arndale bought the lease as trading stock and traded with
it.
    In my opinion Arndale never decided to acquire, and never did acquire, the lease as
trading stock. The group's advisers procured the transfer of the lease from SPI to Arndale
*f* and from Arndale to APTL with the object of obtaining group relief of £2·2m trading
loss without in fact changing the lease from a capital asset to a trading asset. The group
seeks the advantage of treating the lease as trading stock while ensuring that the group
retains the lease as a capital asset at all times. Arndale followed instructions and lent to
the transaction its name and its description as a property dealing company. Arndale did
not trade and never had any intention of trading with the lease. In order to give the
*g* whole transaction a faint air of commercial verisimilitude, the trading company Arndale
was awarded the modest sum of £10,000 for entering into two assignments of property
worth over £3m. The award of £10,000 was ostensibly made at the expense of APTL,
which paid Arndale for the lease £10,000 more than the price paid by Arndale to SPI. In
reality the award of £10,000 was made at the expense of SPI which sold for £10,000 less
than the market value assessed by the group. The profit of £10,000 did not represent the
*h* difference between the price at which Arndale negotiated the purchase and the price at
which Arndale negotiated the sale. The profit of £10,000 did not represent the difference
between the value of the lease to SPI and the value of the lease to APTL. The profit of
£10,000 was a timid veil designed to conceal the fact that the lease was not being traded.
Moreover, all three companies being wholly-owned subsidiaries of the same parent, the
£10,000 was a book entry which had no material effect on the overall financial position
*j* of the group.
    I conclude, therefore, that, while Arndale acquired the lease, it did not acquire the
lease as 'trading stock' within s 274(1) of the 1970 Act and, therefore, never was in a
position to exercise the election provided by para 1(3) of Sch 7 to the 1965 Act. In these
circumstances it is unnecessary to consider the application of the principles enunciated
by your Lordships' House in *IRC v Burmah Oil Co Ltd* [1982] STC 30 and *Furniss (Inspector
of Taxes) v Dawson* [1984] 1 All ER 530, [1984] AC 474 to a case where the legislature has

made express provision for the mitigation of tax by the conversion of a capital loss into a
trading loss provided certain conditions are fulfilled. It is also unnecessary to consider    *a*
whether the dividend-stripping cases since 1963 have finally stripped the decision in
*Griffiths (Inspector of Taxes) v J P Harrison (Watford) Ltd* [1962] 1 All ER 909, [1963] AC 1
of its value to the tax-avoider. In the present case the legislature has expressly provided a
method of tax mitigation designed no doubt to ensure that a group of companies is in no
worse position than an individual whose activities embrace all the activities of a group of
companies. The taxing statutes allow a potential capital loss to be converted into a trading    *b*
loss in respect of an asset which becomes part of the stock-in-trade of the trading activities
of the group. The lease never became part of the trading assets of any company in the
group. The Court of Appeal reached the same conclusion and the appeal must be
dismissed.

*Appeal dismissed.*
                                                                                              *c*

Solicitors: *Speechly Bircham* (for Arndale); *Solicitor of Inland Revenue.*

                                                           Gnana Mott    Barrister.


                                                                                              *d*
# Basildon District Council v
# J E Lesser (Properties) Ltd and others

QUEEN'S BENCH DIVISION (OFFICIAL REFEREES' BUSINESS)
HIS HONOUR JUDGE JOHN NEWEY QC
11, 12, 16, 17, 18, 19 JANUARY, 6 FEBRUARY 1984                                                *e*

*Building contract – Construction – Implied term – Fitness for purpose – Dwelling – Builder
responsible for erection and design of dwelling – Whether implied term in contract as to fitness for
habitation – Whether implied term as to standard of skill and care to be adopted in design of
dwelling.*
                                                                                              *f*

*Contract – Damages for breach – Contributory negligence – Whether plea of contributory
negligence a defence to action for breach of contract – Law Reform (Contributory Negligence) Act
1945, ss 1(1), 4.*

In December 1967 the first defendants, who were system builders, submitted a tender,    *g*
including design drawings, to complete site works and sub-structures for a number of
dwellings for the plaintiff council. In March 1968 the plaintiffs entered into a standard-
term contract with the first defendants for the construction of the dwellings. The contract
contained recitals which referred, inter alia, to design drawings, stating that they had
been prepared under the direction of the plaintiffs' engineer or architect. By a deed of
assignment executed in January 1969 the first defendants assigned the benefit of the    *h*
building contract to the second defendants. By a deed of indemnity made on the same
day the third defendants agreed to indemnify the plaintiffs against any breach of the
building contract by the second defendants. Subsequently, defects developed in some of
the buildings, necessitating repairs. The plaintiffs brought an action against the first,
second and third defendants claiming damages, or alternatively an indemnity from the
second and third defendants. The action proceeded only against the third defendants and    *j*
by consent it was agreed that preliminary issues should be tried on the questions, inter
alia, (i) whether it was an implied term of the building contract that the buildings when
completed would be fit for habitation by the plaintiffs' tenants, (ii) whether it was an
implied term of the building contract that the first defendants would design the buildings
with all proper professional skill and care and (iii) whether the third defendants were

able to rely on a plea of contributory negligence in answer to the plaintiffs' claim for
a damages for breach of contract.

**Held** – (1) It was an implied term of the building contract that the buildings designed as
dwellings by the first defendants were to be fit for habitation on completion,
notwithstanding that the parties had entered into a standard-term contract. The design
of the dwellings was, both before and at the time of the signing of the building contract,
b in reality the exclusive work of the first defendants, so that the first defendants'
responsibility for the design continued after their drawings had become incorporated
into that contract and, furthermore, the plaintiffs had relied on the expertise of the first
defendants as system builders to produce habitable dwellings. In any event, if such a
term had not been implied, there would have been implied a lesser term, namely that
the first defendants were to design the buildings with the skill and care to be expected of
c system builders (see p 27 e to j, post); *Lynch v Thorne* [1956] 1 All ER 744 distinguished.
  (2) On the true construction of ss 1(1)$^a$ and 4$^b$ of the Law Reform (Contributory
Negligence) Act 1945 that Act applied only if there was negligence on the part of both
the plaintiff and the defendant. Accordingly, the 1945 Act did not apply unless the
plaintiff's cause of action was founded on an act or omission of the defendant which gave
rise to liability in tort. Furthermore, no act or omission of the plaintiff entitled the
d defendant to a reduction of damages on the grounds of contributory negligence unless
the plaintiff's conduct amounted to negligence. If the defendant's conduct gave rise to
liability in tort the 1945 Act could apply irrespective of whether the same conduct was
also actionable in contract. It followed that the third defendants were not able to rely on
a plea of contributory negligence in answer to the plaintiff's claim for damages based on
breach of contract (see p 29 g to p 30 c and f to h, post); dictum of Prichard J in *Rowe v
e Turner Hopkins & Partners* [1980] 2 NZLR at 555–556 adopted.

**Notes**
For implied terms as to fitness and quality in building contracts, see 4 Halsbury's Laws
(4th edn) para 1159, and for cases on the subject, see 7 Digest (Reissue) 330–333, 2228–
2234.
f     For contributory negligence in relation to claims in contract, see 34 Halsbury's Laws
(4th edn) para 68.
  For the Law Reform (Contributory Negligence) Act 1945, ss 1, 4, see 23 Halsbury's
Statutes (3rd edn) 789, 791.

**Cases referred to in judgment**
g *Bolam v Friern Hospital Management Committee* [1957] 2 All ER 118, [1957] 1 WLR 582.
  *Butterfield v Forrester* (1809) 11 East 60, 103 ER 926.
  *Davies v Swan Motor Co (Swansea) Ltd (Swansea Corp and James, third parties)* [1949] 1 All
    ER 620, [1949] 2 KB 291, CA.
  *De Meza & Stuart v Apple Van Straten Shena & Stone* [1975] 1 Lloyd's Rep 498, CA; *affg*
    [1974] 1 Lloyd's Rep 508.
h *Greaves & Co (Contractors) Ltd v Baynham Meikle & Partners* [1975] 3 All ER 99, [1975] 1
    WLR 1095, CA.
  *Grein v Imperial Airways Ltd* [1936] 2 All ER 1258, [1937] 1 KB 50, CA.
  *Hancock v B W Brazier (Anerley) Ltd* [1966] 2 All ER 901, [1966] 1 WLR 1317, CA; *affg*
    [1966] 2 All ER 1, [1966] 1 WLR 1317.
  *Independent Broadcasting Authority v EMI Electronics Ltd and BICC Construction Ltd* (1980)
j     14 Build LR 1, HL; *rvsg* (1978) 11 Build LR 29, CA.
  *James (A S) Pty Ltd v Duncan* [1970] VR 705.
  *Lynch v Thorne* [1956] 1 All ER 744, [1956] 1 WLR 303, CA.

---

a   Section 1(1), so far as material, is set out at p 28 c d, post
b   Section 4, so far as material, is set out at p 28 e, post

*Miller v Cannon Hill Estates Ltd* [1931] 2 KB 113, [1931] All ER Rep 93, DC.
*Perry v Sharon Development Co Ltd* [1937] 4 All ER 390, CA.
*Quinn v Burch Bros (Builders) Ltd* [1966] 2 All ER 283, [1966] 2 QB 370, [1966] 2 WLR
  1017, CA; *affg* [1965] 3 All ER 801, [1966] 2 QB 370, [1966] 2 WLR 430.
*Rowe v Turner Hopkins & Partners* [1980] 2 NZLR 550.
*Samuels v Davis* [1943] 2 All ER 3, [1943] 1 KB 526, CA.
*Sayers v Harlow UDC* [1958] 2 All ER 342, [1958] 1 WLR 623, CA.
*Simonius Vischer & Co v Holt & Thompson* [1979] 2 NSWLR 322, NSW, CA.
*Young v Grote* (1827) 4 Bing 253, 130 ER 764.
*Young & Marten Ltd v McManus Childs Ltd* [1968] 2 All ER 1169, [1969] 1 AC 454, [1968]
  3 WLR 630, HL.

### Preliminary issue

By a reamended statement of claim issued on 25 June 1981 the plaintiffs, Basildon
District Council, claimed damages for breach of contract against the first defendants, J E
Lesser (Properties) Ltd, the second defendants, Springfield (Builders) Ltd, and the third
defendants, J E Lesser & Sons (Holdings) Ltd (the holding company). By an order dated
29 January 1981 proceedings against the first and second defendants were stayed pursuant
to s 4 of the Arbitration Act 1950 and the action proceeded against the holding company
only. By agreement six issues arising between the council and the holding company were
tried as preliminary issues, namely (1) whether the first defendants became ultimately
responsible for the stability of all the buildings, (1A) whether it was a term of the building
contract made on 18 March 1968 between the council and the first defendants that the
first defendants comply with the Building Regulations 1965, SI 1965/1373, (2) whether
it was an implied term of the building contract that the first defendants would design
the building with all proper professional skill and care, (3) whether it was an implied
term of the building contract that the buildings when completed would be fit for
habitation by tenants of the council, (4) whether the first defendants owed duties of care
to the council in negligence, (5) whether the holding company's obligation to indemnify
the council under a deed of indemnity made between the council and the holding
company on 20 January 1969 related only to losses, damages, costs and expenses caused
by breaches of the building contract occurring after the deed of the indemnity was
signed, (6) whether the holding company were able to rely on the defence of contributory
negligence in relation to the council's claim for damages for breach of contract. During
the course of the hearing the council expressly abandoned the allegation giving rise to
issue (4). The case is only reported on issues (2), (3) and (6). The facts are set out in the
judgment.

*John Uff QC* and *John Marrin* for the council.
*Colin Reese* and *Andrew Burr* for the holding company.

*Cur adv vult*

6 February. The following judgment was delivered.

**HIS HONOUR JUDGE JOHN NEWEY QC.** In this case the plaintiffs, Basildon
District Council, have brought an action as successors to the Basildon Urban District
Council. I will refer to the two councils collectively as 'the council'. The defendants are
J E Lesser (Properties) Ltd, Springfield (Builders) Ltd and J E Lesser & Sons (Holdings)
Ltd, whom I will refer to respectively as the contractors, the assignees and the holding
company. The action has been stayed against the contractors and the assignees under s 4
of the Arbitration Act 1950. I am dealing, therefore, only with the council's claim against
the holding company, which is based on the terms of a deed of indemnity.

In the mid-1960s the then government was concerned to encourage local authorities
to build residential accommodation for letting. On 1 April 1965 the Ministry of Housing
and Local Government issued circular, 21/65, which, inter alia, encouraged local
authorities to make use of industrialised methods, informed them that a National

Building Agency had been set up which was arranging for appraisals of new systems of
*a* building and advised them to rely on the appraisals undertaken by the agency and not to
carry out investigations and make evaluations of their own. The main characteristic of
industrialised (otherwise known as system) building is that large parts of a building are
made in factory conditions off the building site and are then fitted together with parts
made on the site.

The council undertook various housing schemes and employed the contractors, who
*b* were system builders, in connection with four of them. In April 1967 the council wished
to develop an area known as Fryerus XI by the formation of roads, provision of sewers
and the construction of houses and maisonettes. The council arranged an exhibition to
illustrate their requirements, obtained answers from the contractors to a questionnaire
concerning their system, passed to them information obtained from Le Grand Adsco
Sutcliff & Gell Ltd, as to site conditions and provided them with design criteria for
*c* dwellings. The latter stated in respect of building regulations that formal approval of the
council would not be required, but that the contractor must satisfy himself that the
buildings to be erected would comply with them.

There were various meetings between members of the council's architect's department
and representatives of the contractors. In substance the council was seeking from the
contractors proposals how dwellings built in accordance with their system, which had
*d* been appraised by the National Building Agency and found suitable, could be used to
meet the council's requirements. The contractors submitted proposals, mainly in the
form of drawings, on which the architect's department commented. The contractors
were also asked to prepare foundation designs; they did so and the architect's department
commented on them.

On 8 December 1967 the contractors submitted a tender to complete site works and
*e* sub-structures of all dwellings, which by letter of 5 January 1968 the council accepted,
subject, among other things, to completion of a formal contract. There were further
exchanges of a technical nature and also as to the wording of contractual documents.

On 18 March 1968 an agreement under seal was made between the council and the
contractors. The agreement contained recitals which referred to drawings, bills of
quantities, bills of rates and specifications, stated to have been prepared by or under the
*f* direction of the council's engineer or architect.

By the agreement, the contractors undertook to carry out and complete the works
shown on the drawings, bills and specifications referred to in the recitals. The documents
relating to dwellings were: bills of quantities, marked 'A1', drafted by the council and
relating to garages, stores and external works; a schedule of rates, marked 'A2', drafted
by the council with information provided by the contractors and concerned with sub-
structural works; a specification, marked 'A3', drafted by the contractors, which related
*g* to the dwellings and was subject to an addendum 2¼ pages long, which was the result of
correspondence between the council and the contractors; and nine drawings, all drawn
by the contractors and bearing their name and references.

The agreement was subject to conditions marked 'O' and 'P'. Conditions marked 'O'
related to works above the structural slab level of buildings and were in the RIBA
*h* Standard Form of Building Contract (Local Authorities' Edition without Quantities, 1963
edn). Conditions marked 'P' related to works including and below the structural level of
the buildings, external works and the site works and were in the RIBA Standard Form of
Building Contract (Local Authorities' Edition with Quantities). In 'P', conditions 11 and
12, relating to variations and bills, stood so far as dwellings were concerned, but were
deleted for the purposes of site works.

*j* The agreement named two supervising officers who were to exercise the powers and
perform the functions of the 'Architect' provided for in the conditions, namely the
council's architect and the council's engineer and surveyor.

On or about 25 March 1968 work started on site. The work force rose from 150 to
200. One of the council's group architects, a Mr Vanezis, was job architect on Fryerus XI
and other sites. Mr Tearle was the council's clerk of works on site; he spent half his time

on it until September 1968, and afterwards all of it. After September also Mr Tearle was joined first by Mr Summerhayes, then by Mr Brunker and after an interval by Mr Hawes, all clerks of works. Among other duties Mr Tearle inspected foundations when asked to do so by the site agent and he checked that they were in accordance with drawings which were in his possession. Unfortunately, he did not have a copy of a drawing prepared by the contractors, which was not a contract drawing, and which bore a note warning that because of the highly shrinkable nature of the clay soil if houses were built in close proximity to trees the foundations should be taken down below the level of the roots. As contemplated in the design criteria the council's building inspectors did not attend the site.

On 7 May 1968 the contractors requested the council to agree that 'in accordance with clause 17 of the RIBA contract' the contract be assigned to the assignees, who were also members of the Lesser group of companies. It may be that from that time onwards the workforce were employed by the assignees, but it was not until 20 January 1969 that what was at any rate called a deed of assignment was executed. By that time, according to Mr Randall, who was then the council's deputy architect, most of the foundations for the new houses had been laid, but only a small proportion of those for the new maisonettes. Very little work had been done on superstructures.

The parties to the deed of assignment were the contractors, the assignees and the council. On the same day as it was executed, the holding company entered into the deed of indemnity on which the council are not relying. I will return to the wording and effect of the deed of assignment later. The deed of indemnity began with recitals which referred to the agreement of 18 March 1968 and to the deed assigning 'the agreement' to the assignees and by stating that it was in consideration of the council consenting to the assignment that the holding company agreed to indemnify the council. The deed of indemnity then read:

'If the Assignee . . . shall in any respect fail to carry out the terms of the Agreement or commit any breach of its obligation thereunder then the Holding Company will indemnify the Council against all losses damages costs and expenses which may be incurred by the Council by reason of any default on the part of the Assignee in performing and observing the agreements and provisions on the Contractors part contained in the Agreement.'

Subsequently defects developed in some of the houses and in some of the maisonettes. The council attribute the defects to movement of foundations and also, in maisonettes, inadequate support to cross walls. The cost of repairs to date is said to be of the order of £$\frac{3}{4}$m.

In an endeavour to save time and costs the council and the holding company have agreed that I should try a number of preliminary issues. At the commencement of the hearing there were seven issues, but during the course of it counsel for the council expressly abandoned any allegation that the contractors owed duties of care to the council in negligence, so that there are now only six.

[His Honour dealt with issues 1 and 1A and held that the contractors were under an obligation to ensure that the buildings were stable and were required to comply with the Building Regulations 1965, SI 1965/1373. His Honour continued:]

I will take issues 2 and 3 together, stating them in the reverse order to their numbering.

*Issue 3. Whether it was an implied term of the 1968 agreement that the buildings when completed would be fit for habitation by tenants of the council.*

*Issue 2. Whether it was an implied term of the 1968 agreement that the contractors would design the building with all proper professional skill and care.*

Counsel for the council submitted that whenever an employer makes known to a builder, who holds himself out as being capable of carrying out skilled work, the purpose for which work is required, so as to show reliance on him, a term as to fitness for purpose is to be implied, unless there is an express term in the contract to the contrary. He said that in the present case the factual requirements for the implication of such a term were a fulfilled in respect of the system-built dwellings and that there was nothing in the agreement to preclude it. He said that, if a term requiring that dwellings be fit for habitation were not be implied, then a term requiring that the contractors should have designed with proper care and skill should be.

Counsel for the holding company submitted that only when necessary should a term be implied and that there had been no necessity for one in this case. In any event the council had not relied on the contractors, but on an appraisal of the contractors' system b by the National Building Agency and on the advice of their own architect's department. He said that the elaborate express terms of the agreement were wholly inconsistent with either of the terms for which the council contended.

I was referred to numerous authorities, but all of comparatively recent date. It is clear that, whereas terms as to fitness for purpose were well recognised in the sale of goods and in some other branches of the law in the nineteenth century and the early part of this c century, none was even considered in connection with the building of houses.

In *Miller v Cannon Hill Estates Ltd* [1931] 2 KB 113, [1931] All ER Rep 93, in which the defendants had agreed to build a house for sale for the plaintiff and had expressly warranted that the best materials would be used and the best workmanship applied to them, the Divisional Court held that there was also an implied warranty that the house would be fit for human habitation. Swift J said ([1931] 2 KB 113 at 121, [1931] All ER d Rep 93 at 96):

'... the whole object, as both parties know, is that there shall be erected a house in which the intended purchaser shall come to live. It is the very nature and essence of the transaction between the parties that he will have a house put up there which is fit for him to come into as a dwelling-house. It is plain that in those circumstances there is an implication of law that the house shall be reasonably fit for the purpose e for which it is required, that is for human dwelling.'

In *Perry v Sharon Development Co Ltd* [1937] 4 All ER 390, in which the facts were similar to those in *Miller v Cannon Hill Estates Ltd* except that there were no express warranties, the Court of Appeal reached the same conclusion as the Divisional Court had in *Miller's* case. Greene MR (at 394) referred with approval to the words of Swift J which f I have quoted.

In *Lynch v Thorne* [1956] 1 All ER 744, [1956] 1 WLR 303 a builder had agreed to complete a partially erected house in accordance with a plan and specification and did so, but a wall then leaked because it was of 9 inches brickwork only. The owner claimed against the builder, but lost in the Court of Appeal. Lord Evershed MR said ([1956] 1 All ER 744 at 746, [1956] 1 WLR 303 at 306):

g 'Where there is a written contract expressly setting forth the bargain between the parties, it is, as a general rule ... well established that terms are to be implied only under the compulsion of some necessity ... I am, however, prepared to assume for the purposes of this judgment that, whether or not it can be said that any necessity so compels ... prima facie there is an implied covenant on the ... builder's part that he will complete the house so as to make it habitable. Nevertheless, although such a h term is prima facie to be implied, it must, according to well-established principle, always yield to the express letter of the bargain.'

In *Hancock v B W Brazier (Anerley) Ltd* [1966] 2 All ER 1, [1956] 1 WLR 1317 the defendants had agreed to erect houses in a proper and workmanlike manner each in accordance with a plan and specification. Two to four years later the floors and walls cracked due to the deleterious effects on concrete of sodium sulphate which unknown to j the defendant was in hardcore used by them. The specification had merely referred to 'hardcore' without further particularity. Diplock LJ (sitting at first instance) held that since there had been no definite specification concerning the hardcore to be used, as there had been with regard to the brickwork in *Lynch's* case, there was room for an implied condition that the hardcore should be fit, proper and suitable and that the defendants were in breach of that condition. The Court of Appeal upheld Diplock LJ, Lord Denning MR saying ([1966] 2 All ER 901 at 903, [1966] 1 WLR 1317 at 1332):

*a*

'... when a purchaser buys a house from a builder who contracts to build it, there is a threefold implication: that the builder will do his work in a good and workmanlike manner; that he will supply good and proper materials; and that it will be reasonably fit for human habitation.'

In *Young & Marten Ltd v McManus Childs Ltd* [1968] 2 All ER 1169, [1969] 1 AC 454 *b* sub-contractors had agreed with builders that they would roof houses with specified tiles which could only be bought from one manufacturer. They did so and the tiles cracked, because of defects which the sub-contractors could not have discovered. The House of Lords held that the builders' selection of tiles did not prevent there having been an implied warranty as to their quality, so that the sub-contractors were liable. Lord Reid said that it would have made a difference if the manufacturer had only been willing to *c* sell on terms which excluded liability by him (see [1968] 2 All ER 1169 at 1172, [1969] 1 AC 454 at 467).

In *Independent Broadcasting Authority v EMI Electronics Ltd and BICC Construction Ltd* (1978) 11 Build LR 29 the IBA had employed EMI under the terms of a written contract as main contractors for the design, construction and erection of a television mast, but had insisted that they sub-contract much of the work to BICC. The mast collapsed due to *d* defects in design and IBA sued EMI for breach of contract and negligence and BICC for negligence. At first instance O'Connor J held EMI liable for breach of contract and BICC liable both in contract and negligence.

The Court of Appeal upheld the findings of breach of contract, but decided that BICC had not been negligent. The judgment of the court was given by Roskill LJ who said (11 Build LR 29 at 50–51):

*e*

'... in relation to contracts for work and labour done and materials supplied corresponding obligations have long been implied as to the quality of the workmanship and the materials which would be used.' ·

and, in respect of *Miller v Cannon Hill Estates Ltd* and *Hancock v B W Brazier (Anerley) Ltd* and *Greaves & Co (Contractors) Ltd v Baynham Meikle & Partners* [1975] 3 All ER 99, [1975] *f* 1 WLR 1095 (a case to which I will return), that:

'It is not easy to see why if, in any of those cases, the builder had been guilty of bad design rather than of the supply of bad materials or bad workmanship, the result should have been different on the ground that, as has been contended, the matter of design should always be regarded as involving no higher duty than that of reasonable care ...'

*g*

Roskill LJ said (11 Build LR 29 at 52), giving the basis of the decision:

'We see no good reason ... for not importing an obligation as to reasonable fitness for the purpose into these contracts or for importing a different obligation in relation to design from the obligation which plainly exists in relation to materials.'

The *IBA* case went to the House of Lords (see (1981) 14 Build LR 1). The House of *h* Lords restored O'Connor J's finding that BICC had been negligent and did not find it necessary to decide whether EMI and BICC had each impliedly undertaken to provide a mast which was fit for its purpose, but Viscount Dilhorne (at 26) and Lord Fraser (at 44) each said words to the effect that they probably would have done so.

The implication of a term that a builder should provide a building which is fit for *j* purposes imposes on him a higher duty than is ordinarily implied in a contract for the design of a building by an architect. The latter, like the engineer, solicitor, doctor and other professionally qualified persons, has only to use reasonable care and skill: see *Bolam v Friern Hospital Management Committee* [1957] 2 All ER 118, [1957] 1 WLR 582 and *Greaves & Co (Contractors) Ltd v Baynham Meikle & Partners*.

However, it would seem that if the professional person does not merely design, but
a makes something, it is to be implied that what he has made will be fit for purpose: see
*Samuels v Davis* [1943] 2 All ER 3, [1943] 1 KB 526, a case concerning the supply of false
teeth by a dentist. Even where the professional man has merely designed, the
circumstances may be such as to require that he take what Lord Denning MR in *Greaves
& Co's* case ([1975] 3 All ER 99 at 105, [1975] 1 WLR 1095 at 1101) described as 'special
steps . . . in order to fulfil the duty of care'. In *Greaves & Co's* case an engineer had been
b engaged to design a warehouse, knowing that it was intended for the storage and
movement of oil drums, and he was held liable when it cracked under the weight of
drums.

In the light of the authorities to which I have referred, if in the present case the council
and the contractors had entered into a contract with a minimum of terms providing for
the contractors to build system-dwellings for the council it would, I think, have been
c very easy to imply that the dwellings should be fit for habitation. The council would, I
think, have been placing reliance on the contractors, despite an earlier appraisal of the
contractors' system by the National Building Agency.

The conclusion between the council and the contractors of an agreement incorporating
standard conditions made the position much less clear. Terms as to workmanship and
materials are invariably implied in standard construction contracts and other terms are
d obviously possible, but an implied term as to design is unheard of, since a principal
feature of such contracts is that there is a division of function: the employer's architect
undertakes design, while the contractor is responsible for workmanship and materials.
The specification A3 and the nine drawings prepared by the contractors became part of
the contract drawings, showing the contract works.

Since the third recital stated only that A3 and the drawings had been prepared by or
e under the direction of a council officer and not that he had prepared them, the council
are not precluded from asserting their true authorship. The reality is that the design of
the dwellings was, apart from such small contribution as was made by the addendum to
A3, the exclusive work of the contractors. As the contractors well knew, the council
wanted dwellings, the contractors were the experts in their system and the council were
relying on them to apply it properly, so as to produce habitable dwellings. The case was
f quite unlike the usual standard contract case, in which the architect has, as contemplated
by the contract, designed the works. The contractors had I think a continuing
responsibility for the design of the dwellings, even after their drawings had become
contract drawings.

The case can I think be distinguished from *Lynch v Thorne* [1956] 1 All ER 744, [1956]
1 WLR 303, in which the court concentrated its attention on the agreed defective plan
g and did not consider whether if the builder was its author he was in breach of an implied
term either on account of its faults or in failing to warn against the use of it.

I hold that it was an implied term of the agreement that the buildings designed by the
contractors as dwellings should be fit for habitation on completion. There was no
comparable implied term in relation to the garages and the civil engineering works
which were designed by the council's officers.

h     If I had not decided that there was an implied term as to fitness for habitation in
respect of the dwellings, I should have decided that a lesser term, namely that the
contractors should have designed them with the skill and care to be expected of system
builders, should have been implied.

[His Honour dealt with issue 5 and held that it was sufficient that the assignee had not
fulfilled the requirements of the 1968 agreement and that the council had suffered loss
j as a result for the holding company to be liable. His Honour further held that whether
breaches of the 1968 agreement occurred before or after the date of the deeds of
assignment and of indemnity was immaterial. His Honour continued:]

*Issue 6. Whether the holding company are able to rely on the defence of contributory negligence
in relation to the council's claim for damages for breach of contract.*

The holding company wish to be able to rely on contributory negligence in answer to

the council's allegations of breach of contract concerning foundations by claiming that
the council's job architect and clerks of works should have ensured that they were taken    *a*
down to appropriate depths and in answer to the council's allegations of breach of
contract by failing to provide natural support by asserting that the council's architect's
department should have detected the lack of provision on seeing the contractors' initial
drawings.

Counsel for the holding company contended that defendants have a general right to
set up contributory negligence against a claim in contract, or alternatively that, where a    *b*
breach of contract involves a failure to take care, contributory negligence may be relied
on under the Law Reform (Contributory Negligence) Act 1945. Counsel for the council
submitted that contributory negligence could never be a defence in contract. Both
counsel agreed that there was no clear English authority on the subject, but they made
submissions with regard to the construction of the 1945 Act and referred me to various
textbooks and cases.                                                                          *c*

Section 1(1) of the 1945 Act reads (omitting the last proviso):

> 'Where any person suffers damage as the result partly of his own fault and partly
> of the fault of any other person or persons, a claim in respect of that damage shall
> not be defeated by reason of the fault of the person suffering the damage, but the
> damages recoverable in respect thereof shall be reduced to such extent as the court
> thinks just and equitable having regard to the claimant's share in the responsibility    *d*
> for the damage: Provided that—(a) this subsection shall not operate to defeat any
> defence arising under a contract . . .'

In s 4, the interpretation section, the expression 'fault' is assigned the meaning:

> 'negligence, breach of statutory duty or other act or omission which gives rise to
> a liability in tort or would, apart from this Act, give rise to the defence of    *e*
> contributory negligence.'

Professor Glanville Williams in *Joint Torts and Contributory Negligence* (1951) pp 216–
222, published only six years after the 1945 Act, contended that in substance contributory
negligence had been recognised as a defence in contract before the Act. His best
authorities were *Young v Grote* (1827) 4 Bing 253, 130 ER 764 and other cases in which    *f*
customers who had written cheques in such manner as to facilitate fraud were held
unable to recover moneys which they had lost from their banks. Professor Glanville
Williams wrote that the Act should be applied to both tort and contract and that was
required by broad considerations of justice and equity (at p 328). He expressed the view
that the definition of 'fault' enabled the Act to be applied at least when a breach of
contract occurs through the 'negligence' of the defendant (at p 329). He submitted that,    *g*
where the same act or omission constitutes both a tort and a breach of contract, the Act
should be applied (at p 330).

Other textbook writers take a more guarded view. In particular, 34 Halsbury's Laws
(4th edn) para 68, note 4, *Chitty on Contracts* (25th edn, 1983) paras 1, 6, 8, 9 and *McGregor
on Damages* (14th edn, 1980) all regard the question of whether the 1945 Act can apply to
contract as undecided.                                                                        *h*

In *Sayers v Harlow UDC* [1958] 2 All ER 342, [1958] 1 WLR 623 the plaintiff, who had
found herself locked in the cubicle of a public lavatory and had suffered injury as a result
of attempting to climb out, claimed damages on the grounds that the defendants had
warranted that the cubicle was safe or, in the alternative, on the grounds of negligence.
The county court judge found the defendants had been guilty of a breach of duty, but,
attaching importance to a decision of the Court of Common Pleas in a negligence case of    *j*
the 1860s, he held the plaintiff had embarked on a dangerous manoeuvre and must bear
the consequences. The Court of Appeal held that the plaintiff was entitled to recover, but
reduced her damages by 25% on account of her contributory negligence. Lord Evershed
MR mentioned that the plaintiff was suing for breach of duty 'whether or not arising
under the implied contract' (see [1958] 2 All ER 342 at 344, [1958] 1 WLR 623 at 625),

but afterwards his judgment reads as if her claim were only in negligence and so do the
a  judgments of Morris and Ormerod LJJ.

In *Quinn v Burch Bros (Builders) Ltd* [1965] 3 All ER 801, [1966] 2 QB 370 the plaintiff,
an independent sub-contractor, brought an action against contractors, alleging that,
because they had failed to provide him with a ladder, he had stood on a trestle and fallen
and suffered injuries. Paull J, having referred to cases in contract in which the plaintiff's
conduct had broken the chain of causation, stated that he regretted that the phrase
b  'negligent breach of contract' used by the Court of Appeal in *Grein v Imperial Airways Ltd*
[1936] 2 All ER 1258, [1937] 1 KB 50 had crept into legal language, because, as he said
([1965] 3 All ER 801 at 807, [1966] 2 QB 370 at 379): 'I cannot think that in contract it
matters whether the breach is brought about deliberately or negligently or per incuriam',
and, after quoting from Professor Glanville Williams, he concluded that the 1945 Act
applied where a contract contained a term which imported a duty not to be negligent
c  (see [1965] 3 All ER 801 at 808, [1966] 2 QB 370 at 380). However, Paull J went on to
decide that the contractors had not been negligent. The Court of Appeal dismissed the
plaintiff's appeal without even referring to contributory negligence (see [1966] 2 All ER
283, [1966] 2 QB 370).

In *De Meza & Stuart v Apple Van Straten Shena & Stone* [1974] 1 Lloyd's Rep 508, in an
action by solicitors against their auditors, Brabin J said that he considered himself bound
d  by *Sayers v Harlow UDC* [1958] 2 All ER 342, [1958] 1 WLR 623 and by what was said in
*Grein v Imperial Airways Ltd* [1936] 2 All ER 1258, [1937] 1 KB 50 to hold, but would in
any event have held, that the 1945 Act applies when a contract imposes a duty of care.
The Court of Appeal stated that they expressed no view as to the correctness or otherwise
of the conclusion reached by Brabin J (see [1975] 1 Lloyd's Rep 498).

Statutes identical in wording to the 1945 Act have been enacted with various names in
e  each of the Australian jurisdictions and in New Zealand: see Jane Swanton 'Contributory
Negligence as a Defence to Actions for Breach of Contract' (1981) 55 ALJ 278.

In *A S James Pty Ltd v Duncan* [1970] VR 705 McInerney J said, obiter, but after a very
careful examination of the law in England and Australia, that the equivalent of the 1945
Act did not apply to contract. A similar conclusion was reached by the Court of Appeal
of New South Wales in *Simonius Vischer & Co v Holt & Thompson* [1979] 2 NSWLR 322.
f  In *Rowe v Turner Hopkins & Partners* [1980] 2 NZLR 550 Prichard J, who was trying a
solicitor's negligence case in the New Zealand High Court, referred to the English and
Australian cases and to the textbooks and then concluded (at 555–556) (in quoting him I
will substitute for the numbers of the sections in the New Zealand Act the corresponding
English section numbers):

g  'To my mind, the Act provides its own interpretation if it is acceptable to regard
the definition of "fault" in s [4] as comprising two limbs—the first referable to the
defendant's conduct, the second to the plaintiff's conduct. Section [4] defines "fault"
as meaning "negligence, breach of statutory duty, or other act or omission which
gives rise to a liability in tort" (the first limb). It then goes on to include any act or
omission which "would, apart from this Act, give rise to the defence of contributory
h  negligence" (the second limb). In my view, the first limb of the definition is plainly
directed to defining "fault" as it relates to the conduct of the defendant—in other
words, as it relates to the plaintiff's cause of action. This phrase is qualified by the
expression "which gives rise to a liability in tort". It follows that no negligence,
breach of statutory duty and no other act or omission of the defendant will bring s
[1] into play unless it is one which gives rise to liability in tort. In other words, the
j  Act applies only when the plaintiff's cause of action is in respect of some act or
omission for which the defendant is liable in tort. Conceivably, the defendant may
be concurrently liable in contract—but that is immaterial—the sine qua non is
conduct creating liability in tort. The second limb of the definition is concerned
with and is referable only to the conduct of the plaintiff. It relates not to any cause
of action but to conduct which, prior to the Act, would give rise to the defence of

contributory negligence and which is now to be regarded as that conduct on the part of a plaintiff which will lead not to a complete defence but to a reduction in damages. Before the enactment of the Contributory Negligence Act, the defence of contributory negligence was a complete defence in tort: it was not a defence in contract—where the issue was more likely to be simply causation. I therefore conclude, in the absence of any clear authority to the contrary, that the first limb of the definition of s [4] determines the meaning of the word "fault" as it relates to the plaintiff's cause of action: that accordingly, the Contributory Negligence Act cannot apply unless the cause of action is founded on some act or omission on the part of the defendant which gives rise to liability in tort: that if the defendant's conduct meets that criterion, the Act can apply—whether or not the same conduct is also actionable in contract. By the same token—the second limb of the definition means simply and logically that no act or omission of the plaintiff will entitle the defendant to a reduction of damages unless it amounts to the sort of conduct which, prior to the enactment of the Contributory Negligence Act, would have afforded a defence of contributory negligence.'

My approach to the question of whether contributory negligence was a defence to a claim in contract at common law is historical. Only gradually, beginning in the late seventeenth century, did negligence come to be recognised as a basis of civil liability. Involved in it was an element of 'fault', of 'blameworthiness': the defendant had acted 'carelessly'. It was logical, therefore, that, when the plaintiff had also been careless and so blameworthy, his conduct should be brought into account. If, notwithstanding the defendant's negligence, the plaintiff could with reasonable care have avoided injury, he could not succeed: see *Butterfield v Forrester* (1809) 11 East 60, 103 ER 926 and many other cases. Contributory negligence came to be applied to other, older, stricter forms of liability in tort, such as those based on status.

The 1945 Act retained the concept of blameworthiness, for under s 1(1) the plaintiff's damages are not to be reduced on the basis of causation, but 'to such extent as the court thinks just and equitable': see Denning LJ in *Davies v Swan Motor Co (Swansea) Ltd (Swansea Corp and James, third parties)* [1949] 1 All ER 620 at 632, [1949] 2 KB 291 at 326.

In contract blameworthiness was irrelevant. The defendant had entered into a contract under seal or given an undertaking for which he had received or become entitled to receive valuable consideration and if he acted in breach of it he had to pay damages. There was no room for contributory negligence, although, in the assessment of damages, causation and the plaintiff's duty to mitigate his loss were very relevant. I do not think that the banking cases referred to by Professor Glanville Williams affect this position.

Whether the 1945 Act changed the common law so as to make contributory negligence a defence, or rather a ground for reducing damages, in contract must depend on its wording, but it would be surprising if Parliament when limiting the effect of contributory negligence in tort introduced it into contract.

I think that Prichard J in *Rowe's* case analysed the wording of ss 1 and 4 of the 1945 Act with admirable clarity and exactness and I cannot do better than to adopt his words which I have set out above. The 1945 Act does not apply to contract.

In my judgment the holding company are not able to rely on the defence of contributory negligence in answer to the council's claims for damages for breach of contract.

*Judgment for the council on preliminary issues.*

Solicitors: *J L Knight*, Basildon (for the council); *McKenna & Co* (for the holding company).

K Mydeen Esq    Barrister.

# Morley-Clarke v Jones (Inspector of Taxes)

CHANCERY DIVISION

ANTHONY LINCOLN J

5, 6 JULY, 24 SEPTEMBER 1984

*Husband and wife – Maintenance – Order – Effect of order – Order requiring husband to pay maintenance for child to wife – Whether payments under order income of wife or of child.*

*Husband and wife – Variation or discharge of maintenance order – Power of court – Power to order retrospective variation – Order requiring husband to pay maintenance for child to wife – Order varied directing husband to pay maintenance to child – Variation to take effect from date of original order – Whether court having power to vary maintenance order retrospectively – Whether order as varied valid.*

In 1969, in the course of divorce proceedings, the taxpayer's husband was ordered by the High Court to pay to the taxpayer 'maintenance for [their] child . . . until further order at [a specified rate] payable weekly'. During 1973 the taxpayer began to receive earned income, and she consulted the Revenue regarding her tax position. By 1979 she had been made aware of the disadvantage of her former husband making the maintenance payments to her rather than to their child. Accordingly, she made an application to the court and in 1980 obtained by consent a variation of the 1969 order requiring her former husband to make the maintenance payments direct to the child. The variation was ordered to be backdated so as to take effect from 1969. The taxpayer was subsequently assessed to income tax under Sch D, Case III on the basis that the maintenance payments were her income and assessable as such. Her appeal against the assessments for the years from 1975–76 to 1979–80 was dismissed by the General Commissioners. They determined that, notwithstanding the retrospective variation of the 1969 maintenance order, the payments from her former husband in respect of their son were, for tax purposes, the taxpayer's income and not that of the child. The taxpayer appealed.

**Held** – (1) Although no formal words were required to create a resulting or other trust, on its true construction the 1969 maintenance order did not create a trust for the purpose of maintaining the taxpayer's child. Instead the money paid under the order was income paid into the hands of the taxpayer to which the child was not entitled in his own right (see p 35 *c* to *g* and p 36 *d*, post); dictum of Clauson LJ in *Stevens (Inspector of Taxes) v Tirard* [1939] 4 All ER at 190 followed.

(2) The limits on the power of the High Court to vary a maintenance order were commensurate and coterminous with those imposed on the order it was sought to vary. Accordingly, the court could order a variation of payee, retrospectively as well as prospectively, where the person intended to be the beneficiary of the payment remained the same, and could specify a date, being not earlier than the date of the original order, from which any variation was to take effect. It followed that the court could vary a maintenance order and backdate the variation to the date of the original order. The 1980 order was therefore a valid order (see p 37 *d* to *f*, post).

(3) The effect of the 1980 order was to substitute the obligations and rights under it for those of the 1969 order and thus determine retrospectively the nature and the quality of the maintenance payments for the purposes of income tax. Accordingly, from 1969 onwards the maintenance payments made by the husband represented income in the hands of the son and were not to be assessed as the income of the taxpayer. The appeal would therefore be allowed (see p 39 *j* to p 40 *a*, post).

## Notes

For the liability to income tax of small maintenance payments, see 22 Halsbury's Laws (4th edn) para 1177.

For variation of maintenance orders, see 13 ibid paras 1168–1170.

**Cases referred to in judgment**

Anderton & Halstead Ltd v Birrell (Inspector of Taxes) [1932] 1 KB 271, [1931] All ER Rep 796.
Dodworth (Inspector of Taxes) v Dale [1936] 2 All ER 440.
Macdonald v Macdonald [1963] 2 All ER 857, [1964] P 1, [1963] 3 WLR 350, CA.
Quistclose Investments Ltd v Rolls Razor Ltd [1967] 1 All ER 864, [1967] Ch 910, [1967] 2 WLR 1064; rvsd [1968] 1 All ER 613, [1968] Ch 540, [1968] 2 WLR 478, CA; affd sub nom Barclays Bank Ltd v Quistclose Investments Ltd [1968] 3 All ER 651, [1970] AC 567, [1968] 3 WLR 1097, HL.
Slocock's Will Trusts, Re [1979] 1 All ER 358.
Spence v IRC (1941) 24 TC 311, CS.
Stevens (Inspector of Taxes) v Tirard [1939] 4 All ER 186, [1940] 1 KB 204, CA; affg [1939] 3 All ER 154, [1939] 2 KB 410.
Warden v Warden [1981] 3 All ER 193, [1982] Fam 10, [1981] 3 WLR 435, CA.
Yates (Inspector of Taxes) v Starkey [1951] 1 All ER 732, [1951] Ch 465, CA; affg [1950] 2 All ER 614, [1951] Ch 45.
Young v Young (No 2) [1961] 3 All ER 793, [1962] P 218, [1961] 3 WLR 1041.

**Cases also cited**

Gardner Mountain & D'Ambrumenil Ltd v IRC [1947] 1 All ER 650, HL.
Hatton v Harris [1892] AC 547, HL.
IRC v Plummer [1979] 3 All ER 775, [1980] AC 896, HL.
Paul v Constance [1977] 1 All ER 195, [1977] 1 WLR 527, CA.
Robinson v Robinson [1982] 2 All ER 699n, [1982] 1 WLR 786n, CA.
Vestey v IRC (Nos 1 and 2) [1979] 3 All ER 976, [1980] AC 1148, HL.

**Case stated**

1. At a meeting of the Commissioners for the General Purposes of the Income Tax for the division of Woking in the County of Surrey held on 27 October 1982 Mrs Morley-Clarke (the taxpayer) appealed against assessments for income tax under Case III of Sch D made on her by the inspector of taxes for the years and for the respective sums set out below, namely:

| Period of assessment | Amount of assessment (£) |
| --- | --- |
| 1975–76 | 120 |
| 1976–77 | 120 |
| 1977–78 | 120 |
| 1978–79 | 120 |
| 1979–80 | 80 |

2. The question for the commissioners' determination was whether the income the subject of the respective assessments was income of the taxpayer and assessable under Case III of Sch D or income of her child John Robert.

3. The taxpayer appeared in person before the commissioners and the inspector was represented by Mr A Wheaten, Solicitor's Office, Inland Revenue.

[Paragraph 4 listed the documents proved or admitted before the commissioners, which included, inter alia, a copy order of the High Court made on 18 April 1969 (the first order), a copy order of the High Court in the same matter made on 14 November 1979 (the second order) and a copy amended order of the High Court in the same matter dated 26 February 1980 (the third order). There was also produced to the commissioners a statement of agreed facts marked 'amended draft'.]

5. The commissioners found the following facts proved or admitted: (a) those facts set out in the statement of agreed facts and (b) the taxpayer had been informed by the Revenue that a variation to the first order to provide that the maintenance be paid 'to'

the child John Robert and stated to have effect from the date of the first order would have a retrospective effect to the date of the first order and that tax already paid by the taxpayer in respect thereof would be repaid.

6. The following authorities were cited to the commissioners by the solicitor for the inspector: *Dodworth (Inspector of Taxes) v Dale* [1936] 2 All ER 440; *Stevens (Inspector of Taxes) v Tirard* [1939] 4 All ER 186, [1940] 1 KB 204 and *Yates (Inspector of Taxes) v Starkey* [1951] 1 All ER 732, [1951] Ch 465, CA; *affg* [1950] 2 All ER 614, [1951] Ch 45.

7. It was contended by the taxpayer as follows: (a) it had always been the intention of the taxpayer and her former husband that all payments of maintenance for the said child should be paid to the child and not form part of the income of the taxpayer; (b) on her first becoming aware of the apparent defect in the first order the taxpayer sought the advice of the Revenue by correspondence and telephone with the offices at Woking and Public Departments 2 in Cardiff; (c) as a result of these discussions the taxpayer took steps to have the first order varied and this was effected by the second order on 14 November 1979; (d) the taxpayer became aware that the variation had not been stated to be of retrospective effect by means of backdating the second order to the date of the making of the first order and she took steps to obtain a further variation to the first order to provide for this omission by means of the third order; and (e) in 1979 and prior to the date of the second order the taxpayer's former husband had ceased making the maintenance payments in favour of the taxpayer and had commenced paying them by means of cheques drawn in favour of the child. The taxpayer contended that she should not in any event have been charged to income tax on those payments.

8. It was contended on the part of the inspector: (a) that the authority of *Dodworth v Dale* was persuasive that a taxpayer could not treat a court order as having retrospective operation for all fiscal purposes; (b) that the other two authorities cited demonstrated different methods in which a court order in favour of a child might be drawn and their respective effect on the taxation position; (c) that in the instant case the first order created no trust for the child and the income could only be that of the taxpayer prior to the date of the second order; and (d) that, although the inspector accepted that subsequent to that date the maintenance payments were income of the child, the payment of any maintenance due prior to the date of the second order direct to the child would not in any way alter the effect of the first order to make the payment the income of the child for income tax purposes.

9. The commissioners who heard the appeal found: (a) the first order provided that maintenance be paid to the taxpayer for the child and that would have been the income of the taxpayer for income tax purposes; (b) the second order provided that maintenance thenceforth be paid to the child and payments made thereunder would have been the income of the child; (c) the third order purported to make the effect of the second order retrospective but in view of the persuasive authority cited above it could not have had effect for the purposes of assessment to income tax; and (d) from 18 April 1969 until 14 November 1979 all maintenance payments made under the terms of the first order were the income of the taxpayer for income tax purposes.

10. The commissioners accordingly concluded that the inspector's contentions were correct and they confirmed the assessments for the several years subject to the recalculation of the final year of assessment in the light of the agreed facts. That conclusion was reached by the commissioners with great reluctance as they were of the opinion that the taxpayer had suffered an injustice in the light of the previous assurances given by or on behalf of the inspector that the tax already paid by the taxpayer on the assessments would be repaid once the court order of 14 November 1979 had been rectified and the commissioners urged the inspector to deal with the matter sympathetically.

11. Immediately after giving their decision, the taxpayer declared her dissatisfaction therewith as being erroneous in point of law and the commissioners were in due course required to state a case for the opinion of the High Court pursuant to s 56 of the Taxes Management Act 1970.

12. The question of law for the opinion of the court was whether, on the facts as found

by the commissioners, the commissioners were correct in their decision that the amounts of the assessments of the several years represented income in the hands of the taxpayer and were accordingly assessable as her income under Case III of Sch D.

*T Scott Baker QC* and *Andrew Thornhill* for the taxpayer.
*Robert Carnwath* for the Crown.

*Cur adv vult*

24 September. The following judgment was delivered.

**ANTHONY LINCOLN J.** The taxpayer, Mrs Morley-Clarke, is the mother of John Robert. She appeals by way of case stated from the General Commissioners of the Income Tax who upheld certain assessments raised between 1975 and 1980 under Sch D, Case III. These assessments determined the tax payable on sums ordered to be paid to the taxpayer for the maintenance of her son by his father, Mr Morley-Clarke. The first order was made in 1969 and no complaint would have been made about the assessments if that order had stood alone. But it was varied in 1979 and in 1980 the variation was itself varied and backdated. It is the last backdated order which gives rise to the problem as to the correctness of the assessments.

The general question formulated by the commissioners is whether, on the facts as found by them, they were correct in deciding that the amounts of the assessments represented income in the hands of the taxpayer and were correctly assessable as her income under Case III. The specific questions on which the answer to the general question is dependent are: (i) what is the true construction of the maintenance orders; (ii) what are the limits on the power of the High Court to backdate a maintenance order; and (iii) what are the tax consequences of such backdating.

The circumstances giving rise to these questions aroused the sympathy of the commissioners for the taxpayer and are certainly disquieting. On behalf of the Commissioners of Inland Revenue regret was expressed for what had occurred.

In 1969 the taxpayer was engaged in divorce proceedings against her husband, the father of John Robert. On 18 April 1969 his Honour Judge Baxter, sitting in the Probate, Divorce and Admiralty Division, granted her a decree nisi and thereupon ordered her husband 'to pay to [the taxpayer] maintenance for herself . . . and with effect from today maintenance for the child John Robert until further order at the rate of £2. 10s. od. per week payable weekly'.

In the years of assessment 1969–70 to 1979–80 her husband made the payments as ordered. In 1973 the taxpayer began receiving earned income on which she was liable to tax. Now, if the maintenance were ordered to be paid directly to her son, her tax liability would be reduced. The taxpayer became aware of the disadvantage of the 1969 order and sought the advice of the Revenue and the outcome was that on 7 November 1979 she applied to the court for a variation of the 1969 order amending the order so far as it related to John Robert. On 14 November 1979 Mr Registrar Rowe made a consent order 'that the order herein dated the 18th April 1969 . . . be varied' and that Mr Morley-Clarke should make to the child 'as from the 14th November 1979' periodical payments for the child at the rate of £2·50 per week.

This order did not give effect to the taxpayer's intention. She wanted the variation order to be made retrospective by backdating the variation to the date of the first order in 1969. So yet a third order was obtained to correct the mistake: on 12 February 1980 Mr Registrar Rowe made a further consent order that the order dated 18 April 1969 be varied and that Mr Morley-Clarke should make to the child as from 18 April 1969 periodical payments at the rate of £2·50 payable weekly.

The circumstances in which the taxpayer came to apply for these variation orders were these. She consulted the Revenue authorities and received an assurance that if she applied for and obtained a retrospective variation order she would be repaid any tax overpaid on the basis of such variation. She did so, but the Revenue authorities refused to honour their assurance and so this litigation arose. It may well be that legal advice was belatedly taken and given to the effect that the taxpayer was not entitled to repayment as indeed is now contended. But it is deplorable that the taxpayer, having been led to believe that only formalities stood between her and an expected improvement in her financial position, should find herself involved in a possibly prolonged lawsuit.

First as to the construction of the 1969 order. It was argued for the taxpayer that its terms created a trust in favour of John Robert with the consequence that the income was income to which the child was entitled. Although there is no express reference to a trust as such it is said that the words 'payment to [the taxpayer] for the maintenance of the child' imposed on the taxpayer the obligation to hold the moneys paid as trustee for her child. It is certainly true that in some circumstances money paid to a person for a specific purpose may impose on that person a fiduciary obligation to carry out the purpose. It requires no formal words to create a resulting or other trust. Counsel for the taxpayer relied on *Quistclose Investments Ltd v Rolls Razor Ltd* [1967] 1 All ER 864 at 867, [1967] Ch 910 at 927–928 for this proposition. He then argued that the words 'payment to [the taxpayer] for the maintenance of the child' mean (and as I see it must always mean) 'for the purpose of maintaining the child' and so, he says, the taxpayer holds the money in trust.

But there is a very sizeable obstacle in the path of counsel for the taxpayer, namely the decision in *Stevens (Inspector of Taxes) v Tirard* [1939] 4 All ER 186, [1940] 1 KB 204, CA; *affg* [1939] 3 All ER 154, [1939] 2 KB 410. The wording of the maintenance order in that case was identical with the instant one. It was held there that the money was paid to the mother as income paid into her hands to which the child was not entitled in his own right. Clauson LJ said ([1939] 4 All ER 186 at 190, [1940] 1 KB 204 at 213):

> 'As a matter of construction of this order, it appears to me abundantly clear that the scheme of the order is not at all to create an income to which the infant is in any way entitled. The scheme of the order is to increase the income of the mother so as to enable her to discharge the duty of maintenance laid upon her by the court in view of her having the infant's custody.'

Counsel for the taxpayer urges me to circumvent the decision. He argues that in the changed legislative context of today, namely the enactment of s 3 of the Matrimonial Proceedings and Property Act 1970, which empowers the court to make orders for payment direct to the child, a more flexible approach is desirable and that the decision in *Stevens v Tirard* is no longer binding. I cannot accept that. Clauson LJ continued ([1939] 4 All ER 186 at 190, [1940] 1 KB 204 at 213):

> 'I feel very much fortified in construing the order in that way, because I should have the gravest doubts whether, under sect. 193 [of the Supreme Court of Judicature (Consolidation) Act 1925], there would be any jurisdiction in the court at all to take income away from the father and make it the infant's income, though the court has full jurisdiction to take money from the father and make it available for the benefit of the infant by putting it in the hands of the mother, in whom, under the whole scheme which is completed by this order, are vested the rights of custody and the duty of maintenance of the infant.'

Clauson LJ first construed the order according to its ordinary and plain meaning and then tested his construction in the light of the court's jurisdiction at the time, as he saw it. His doubts as to the extent of the then jurisdiction were not, as I see it, any part of the ratio decidendi: s 3 of the 1970 Act has simply widened the choice of orders that can be made by adding payments to or for the benefit of the child.

Nor is it desirable, even had I the power to do so, to circumvent this long-standing decision of the Court of Appeal. There are now many ways in which maintenance orders can be formulated and it is important that each formula should enjoy an enduring and certain meaning, whatever may be the fiscal changes which the formula with that meaning may suffer. At the time of *Stevens v Tirard* the power of the court was to make such provision as appears just with respect to the maintenance of children (see s 193 of the Supreme Court of Judicature (Consolidation) Act 1925). Under s 25 of the Matrimonial Causes Act 1950 there was the same power. Nothing was expressly said of trusts or of payments to the child. The Matrimonial Causes Act 1955, s 34(1) empowered the court to make orders 'for the maintenance of children', which wording is echoed in the 1969 order in the instant case, and it is clear that that order adopted the descriptive phrase of the Act. It is unlikely that the registrar would have attempted, by the use of these words, to establish a trust as between the taxpayer and her child (which would not in any case have helped the taxpayer owing to double aggregation) or that, if he were trying to do that, he would not have used some express reference to a trust. Finally, as I have mentioned, by the Matrimonial Proceedings and Property Act 1970, s 3 the court was given the power to order payment to a person for the benefit of a child or to such a child.

I derive no assistance from *Yates (Inspector of Taxes) v Starkey* [1951] 1 All ER 732, [1951] Ch 465, CA; *affg* [1950] 2 All ER 614, [1951] Ch 45, which left unresolved the question whether at that time the court had power to create a trust when ordering maintenance. The case does not seem to me to impugn or throw doubt on the validity of *Stevens v Tirard*.

I conclude that, of the many formulae which may today be adopted so as to secure fiscal advantages for the parties, the formula used in the 1969 order continues to have the consequences that money paid under the order is income in the hands of the immediate payee: in this case the taxpayer mother.

I turn now to the powers of the court with regard to backdating, about the limits of which I am informed that there is great uncertainty. The Matrimonial Causes Act 1973, s 28 imposes a limit on the date at which a periodical payments order may be ordered to begin, namely not earlier than the date of the making of an application for the order. The same limit applies to secured periodical payments. Section 31 of the same Act provides for the power to vary such orders. There are two observations to be made about this section. First, it contains no express term as to the period from which it may retrospectively take effect, some three sections later than the one in which the legislature has expressly sanctioned retrospective orders. Second, the section is, as it were, parasitic on s 28. An order under the later section cannot be made unless an order under the earlier one exists. If the earlier and original order is made to take retroactive effect, and requires variation in any part of its effect, retroactive or prospective, the varying order will require to be retroactive to that extent. I cannot understand why, if there is a power to vary the original order, any period during which that order takes effect should be beyond the reach of the variation power.

In *Macdonald v Macdonald* [1963] 2 All ER 857, [1964] P 1 the Court of Appeal adopted an unrestrictive approach to the variation power (then contained in the Matrimonial Causes Act 1950, s 28(1)). The court was not impressed by the argument that courts of summary jurisdiction were given express sanction to remit arrears but that no express sanction for the High Court could be found in the relevant Acts. A similar but not identical argument was put in this case in the following way: (i) that a variation order creates an obligation to make periodical payments; (ii) that orders for periodical payments are limited under s 28 of the Matrimonial Causes Act 1973 to the date of application; (iii) that therefore the variation order is limited to the date of application for variation; and (iv) that this brings the High Court's jurisdiction into line with the courts of summary jurisdiction (see the Domestic Proceedings and Magistrates' Courts Act 1978, s 65(9)). My response to the fourth argument is an echo of the passage in *Macdonald v Macdonald* [1963] 2 All ER 857 at 858, [1964] P 1 at 4. Express power of a limited character had to be given to the justices for the very reason that they had no jurisdiction to make retrospective orders. The High Court's jurisdiction stemming from s 31 of the 1973 Act, which contains no express limitation, is limited only by the extent of the original order. As to the first argument, and those which are pendant on it, of course it is true that a variation order may impose an obligation to make periodical payments. So may an interim order or an order for

maintenance pending suit. But, as a matter of phraseology, the Act has attached the term
*a* 'periodical payments order' not to an interim nor to a variation order but to a substantive
order which is intended to endure unless varied. It is with reference to this latter category
of order alone that s 28 of the Act has imposed time limits on backdating.

*Warden v Warden* [1981] 3 All ER 193, [1982] Fam 10 was also cited, a decision relating
to the variation of maintenance agreements. A passage in that case lends some support in a
different but related context for an unrestricted approach (see [1981] 3 All ER 193 at 195,
*b* [1982] Fam 10 at 14). The Crown reserve the right, if necessary, to argue that this case was
wrongly decided.

Finally, in *Young v Young (No 2)* [1961] 3 All ER 793, [1962] P 218 Karminski J stated
that under s 28 of the Matrimonial Causes Act 1950 the court had power to go back in date
beyond the date of application. It was not the ratio decidendi but the judge stated and
reiterated that he had no doubt of the extent of the court's power (see [1961] 3 All ER 793
*c* at 795, [1962] P 218 at 222–223).

It may be said it is one thing to vary the amount of an order and to make that order
retroactive in effect but quite another to vary an order retroactively by changing the
beneficiary of the order. And this is what the 1980 order purported to do, substituting
John Robert for the taxpayer as the payee under the order. There may be objections to the
introduction of a wholly unrelated adult payee into an order on an application to vary a
*d* substantive periodical payments order. On that I express no view. But here the purpose of
the payment remained the same in the original and in the varied order: the maintenance
of John Robert. The method of achieving that objective was altered by the final order, John
Robert being designated the recipient but the taxpayer effectively and ultimately receiving
the payments. I consider that there is power to make such a variation of payee,
retrospectively as well as prospectively, where the person intended to be the beneficiary of
*e* the payment remains the same.

In my judgment the limits on the power to vary are commensurate and coterminous
with those imposed on the order which it is sought to vary. The High Court has power to
specify a term in a variation order beginning not earlier than the date at which the term of
the original order was specified to begin. In the present case the third order reaching back
to 1969 was in my view a valid one.

*f* Finally, what are the tax consequences of a retrospective order? When an interim order
is made it is very often a provisional decision arrived at after cursory investigation of the
parties' resources. There follows the main periodical payments order. If the circumstances
justify a retrospective order the court may specify a term starting from the time of the
original application. The later order usually results from a fuller investigation than the
interim inquiry. Then there is the contrasting situation. A periodical payments order may
*g* be varied under s 31. The investigations leading to both orders are equally full and
thorough. But fresh circumstances create the need for changed obligations and, to the
extent that the later order supersedes the earlier by its retroactive effect, the need for past
changes is also demonstrated. So far as the tax consequences of each situation is concerned
I can see no principle justifying differing treatment.

An example of the former situation would be a provisional order for payment of £10
*h* per week. After fuller investigation a periodical payments order is made for the payment
of £15 per week for a term which is made to start within the period when the interim
order was in force. At first sight the intention of such a retroactive order is to supplant the
provisional figure of £10 and replace it correctively with the final figure of £15, so that
the order is to be regarded as having been in force (though delayed by the need for fuller
investigation) at the time of and in the place of the interim and provisional order. By the
*j* same token if a variation order entrenches on an earlier substantive periodical payment
order retroactively the same considerations should arise. The Crown argues that this is not
the true effect of such orders. The variation order does not redefine the obligation created
by the earlier order (be it interim or a substantive periodical payments order). Tax arises
not out of the order but out of the fact of payment. Nothing can undo the fact that
payment has taken place. That fact and the time at which the event occurred remains

unchanged by the variation order, which does not purport to rewrite history. The Crown argues that the tax properly to be assessed in relation to such retrospective orders is related to and arises out of payments pursuant to the order as and when they occur. Accordingly, payments by way of adjustment (eg repayments under s 33 of the Act) have to be considered and assessed as and when they occur within the relevant year of assessment, not written back into the history of the earlier orders and payments thereunder so as to reopen past assessments. The Crown, therefore, contends that in this case the 1980 order did not affect the validity of the 1969 order or the character of the payments already made; and, if that is right, in one sense the change of payee and of amount is of no retrospective effect whatsoever. It is the future that is changed by reference to the past.

Alternatively it is contended that the court had no power to make a retrospective order which could affect the validity of the 1969 order or the character of payments made under it. Thirdly it is said that the 1980 order cannot alter tax liability if it was properly determined at the time.

If these contentions, or any of them, are correct hardship must result and in recognition and mitigation of this the Revenue have issued a statement of practice, a non-statutory concession which is invariably observed. The Crown asserts that registrars, when determining the amount of an order and how far it should be backdated, take into account such concessions and should continue to do so without difficulty.

For the taxpayer it is argued that the 1973 Act equips the court with the widest possible and the most flexible powers to do justice between the spouses. In most cases there are not sufficient funds to maintain two families. Parliament cannot have intended that the beneficiary of a variation order should be put in a worse position fiscally than if his initial order, eg an interim order, had been fully and correctly determined in the first place so that no variation would then have been necessary.

The question should be capable of resolution by construing the terms of s 28 of the Act to the extent that they expressly create the power to backdate. But the words of sub-s (1) 'the term to be specified shall begin not earlier than the date of the making of an application' are sparing in the guidance they offer. The wording is consistent with the contentions of either party.

Counsel have therefore turned for support to a number of decisions, which provide guidance if they do not directly resolve the question in issue. The decision in *Spence v IRC* (1941) 24 TC 311 puts it beyond doubt that assessments will be reopened within the statutory limits in certain circumstances, eg where there is a clear intention to 'put the clock back', as in the case of the remedy of restitutio in integrum or an order for rescission by the court. In *Spence v IRC* a sale of shares was rescinded and the defrauded vendor was awarded a lump sum representing dividends he ought to have received if he had not been improperly dispossessed. The vendor was held to have been rightly assessed as having received the dividends though in the relevant years of assessment he had not in fact received them. The tax liability in that case arose not by virtue of the historical receipt in the first place of the dividends but by virtue of the subsequent receipt of the lump sum under the compulsion of a court order. Nor was the date of the subsequent receipt regarded as the point of time at which the liability arose. So there was a complete reconstruction of history, a restitutio in integrum not only between the parties but also against the Crown. If the 1980 variation order has the same effect as an order for rescission, then the taxpayer must succeed.

An order for rectification has the same effect. An erroneous contractual document is reconstructed by the court ab initio to give effect to the common intention of the contractual parties and it matters not that this reconstruction may give tax advantages (see *Re Slocock's Will Trusts* [1979] 1 All ER 358). But a taxpayer seeking to reopen an assessment has to show that the court order (the event which is subsequent to the assessment) has the effect of redisposing matters ab initio. A decree of nullity on the ground of incapacity does not reach back to the beginning of the marriage. It takes effect from the date of the decree. Until such time the parties are treated as husband and wife and an assessment raised in respect of the period when the marriage had not been nullified is not invalidated by the

subsequent decree (see *Dodworth (Inspector of Taxes) v Dale* [1936] 2 All ER 440). If the
*a* 1980 order has the same effect as this nullity decree the Crown must succeed.

It was suggested by the Crown that events which take place after an assessment has been
completed should, in such circumstances as prevail here, be disregarded. Reliance was
placed on *Anderton & Halstead Ltd v Birrell (Inspector of Taxes)* [1932] 1 KB 271, [1931] All
ER Rep 796. If there is any such rule, in my view, *Anderton & Halstead Ltd v Birrell* does
not establish it. A company's estimate that certain debts were bad and should be written
*b* off was accepted by the inspector and an assessment was raised accordingly. Subsequent
events cast doubt on the accuracy of the estimate. Additional assessments on the basis that
the debts were later shown to be good were refused. The decision seems to me to have
turned on the terms of reference of the commissioners at the time. The statute in that case
required that bad debts proved to be such to the satisfaction of the commissioners should
be deducted. In the words of Rowlatt J an estimate of a bad debt is not a prophecy to be
*c* judged as to its truth by after events but a valuation of an asset de praesenti on an uncertain
future to be judged as to its soundness as an estimate on the then facts and probabilities (see
[1932] 1 KB 271 at 282, [1931] All ER Rep 796 at 802). The decision throws no light on
the question whether a retrospective maintenance order rearranges obligations so that
though subsequent they come into force in replacement of earlier ones.

The case most directly in point could be said to be *Young v Young (No 2)* [1961] 3 All ER
*d* 793, [1962] P 218. If the effect of backdating an order is the reconstruction not only of the
earlier obligations but also of their consequences, whether fiscal or of any other description,
a kind of restitutio in integrum, it would surely follow that sums which can be seen to be
overpaid, having regard to the dispositions of the backdated order, should as a matter of
course be repaid. Yet Karminski J found himself powerless to make any such order for
repayment. If that was how matters stood today the case for the Crown would be difficult
*e* to fault. But the decision has been overtaken by statutory intervention. By s 33 of the 1973
Act the court was given the power it thought it lacked. Sections 28 to 35 are to be read
together as a single code equipping the court with wide and flexible maintenance powers.
Section 33 may be a newcomer to the group, but it takes its place with them, correcting
*Young v Young (No 2)* and completing the court's range of powers. Read as a whole, this
group of sections seem to me to have included in their range of remedies the power to
*f* rearrange or even eliminate past obligations, to determine from a future point of time a
past entitlement or liability as if the latter had been in force at the time to which it relates.
The code thus provides a remedy akin to restitutio in integrum and the consequences of
that remedy are the same as those which, in *Spence v IRC*, flowed from rescission, such as
the reopening of an assessment.

The Crown foresees difficulties arising out of such a conclusion. For example, there
*g* could be a collusive agreement to obtain a maintenance order unacceptable to the Revenue
authorities (unlike, I emphasise, the facts of this case). It is said that the Crown could, and
usually would, be unaware of the imminence of such a consent order and would be
powerless (as a matter of fact, not law) to intervene. But this is to underestimate the
astuteness of the relevant tribunals such as registrars experienced in these matters in
looking at the wider implications of consent orders and protecting the public interest. For
*h* example, they are habitually on the watch for orders likely to defeat the Law Society charge
in legally-aided litigation.

It is further argued that the Revenue are not joined as parties in maintenance applications
and are accordingly not bound by the result. This is right in theory. But the argument
could be directed at all litigation involving an adjustment of financial resources and
resulting in an in personam judgment. The Department of Health and Social Security, the
*j* Law Society and other bodies not directly involved are obliged to act on the basis of these
judgments. So, too, should the Revenue. A maintenance order when implemented gives
rise to a tax liability and the form of the order determines the nature and quality of the
payment. A retrospective order is no different.

I would accordingly hold that the 1980 order substituted its obligations and rights for
those of the 1969 order as if the former had been in force under the 1969 order. The

question could arise whether the discretion to make the consent variation order was properly exercised. I have no doubt that it was. I answer the general question by holding that the amounts of the assessments represented income in the hands of the child John Robert and assessable as such, contrary to the decision of the commissioners.

*Appeal allowed. Assessments reduced to nil. No order as to costs.*

Solicitors: *Potter & Kempson*, Farnham (for the taxpayer); *Solicitor of Inland Revenue*.

Vivian Horvath Barrister.

# R v Secretary of State for the Home Department, ex parte Khan

COURT OF APPEAL, CIVIL DIVISION

DUNN, WATKINS AND PARKER LJJ

I MARCH, 4 APRIL 1984

*Natural justice – Hearing – Duty to hear parties etc – Legitimate expectation – Immigration – Secretary of State issuing circular setting out criteria and procedure for certain entrants – Secretary of State applying different criteria and procedure to applicant – Whether circular creating legitimate expectation that Secretary of State would apply criteria and procedure set out in it – Whether Secretary of State entitled to apply different criteria.*

*Immigration – Leave to enter – Adoption – Entry of child for purposes of adoption – Secretary of State issuing circular setting out criteria and procedure for entry of children for purposes of adoption – Whether circular creating legitimate expectation that Secretary of State would apply criteria and procedure set out in it – Whether Secretary of State entitled to apply different criteria and procedure.*

A Home Office circular giving guidance to persons in the United Kingdom who wished to adopt a child from abroad stated that, although the immigration rules did not permit a foreign child to enter the United Kingdom for the purposes of adoption, the Secretary of State would in exceptional circumstances exercise a discretion to allow a child to enter the United Kingdom for adoption if certain specified criteria were met. The circular set out the procedural steps to be taken when such an application was made and stated, inter alia, that when an application was referred to the Secretary of State he would make certain inquiries within the Department of Health and Social Security whether there were any reasons for an adoption order to be refused by the court. The applicant and his wife, who were settled in England, wished to adopt a relative's child who lived with its natural mother in Pakistan. The applicant obtained a copy of the Home Office circular and applied for an entry clearance certificate for the child. The application together with the entry clearance officer's report on the child was referred to the Secretary of State. There was nothing in the report to indicate that the criteria set out in the circular would not be met. However, the Secretary of State did not make any inquiries within the Department of Health and Social Security or apply the criteria set out in the circular, but instead decided the application by applying different criteria, namely the criteria for deciding whether to admit for settlement children who were already adopted by persons settled in the United Kingdom, and applying those criteria he decided that the child should not be given leave to enter. The applicant applied for judicial review by way of an order of certiorari to quash the Secretary of State's decision refusing entry clearance for the child, contending that he had a legitimate expectation arising out of the terms of the circular that the criteria and procedure there set out would be followed. The Secretary of State contended that he had an unfettered discretion regarding the grant of leave to a child to enter for the purpose of adoption and in exercising that discretion he was entitled to take into account considerations other than those stated in the circular.

**Held** (Watkins LJ dissenting) – Where a member of the public affected by a decision of a
*a* public authority had a legitimate expectation based on a statement or undertaking by the
authority that it would apply certain criteria or follow certain procedures in making its
decision, the authority was under a duty to follow those criteria or procedures in reaching
its decision, provided that the statement or undertaking in question did not conflict with
the authority's statutory duty. Thus, where the Secretary of State undertook to allow
persons to enter the United Kingdom if certain conditions were met he could not resile
*b* from that undertaking without affording interested persons a hearing and then only if
the overriding public interest required it. Accordingly, since a recipient of the Home
Office circular, such as the applicant, would have a reasonable expectation that the criteria
and procedures there set out would be followed and since (per Dunn LJ) those criteria
and procedures in effect constituted rules made by the Secretary of State for deciding
applications for entry, it followed that, vis-à-vis a recipient of the circular, the Secretary
*c* of State could only apply different criteria and procedures in regard to granting leave to a
child to enter for the purpose of its adoption if he first gave the recipient of the circular a
full opportunity of making representations why in his particular case criteria and
procedures different from those set out in the circular ought not to be followed. In the
circumstances the Secretary of State had acted unfairly and unreasonably in deciding the
applicant's application for entry clearance for the child by applying different criteria
*d* from those set out in the circular. Accordingly, the appeal would be allowed and the
refusal of entry clearance quashed (see p 46 *a b g h*, p 47 *h*, p 48 *d* to *g*, p 49 *a b* and p 52 *c*
to *h*, post).

*A-G of Hong Kong v Ng Yuen Shiu* [1983] 2 All ER 346 applied.

**Notes**
*e* For the admission of children into the United Kingdom, see 4 Halsbury's Laws (4th edn)
para 994.

**Cases referred to in judgments**
*A-G of Hong Kong v Ng Yuen Shiu* [1983] 2 All ER 346, [1983] 2 AC 629, [1983] 2 WLR
735, PC.
*f* *Amin v Entry Clearance Officer, Bombay* [1983] 2 All ER 864, [1983] 2 AC 818, [1983] 3
WLR 258, HL.
*Associated Provincial Picture Houses Ltd v Wednesbury Corp* [1947] 2 All ER 680, [1948] 1
KB 225, CA.
*Liverpool Taxi Owners' Association, Re* [1972] 2 All ER 589, [1972] 2 QB 299, [1972] 2
WLR 1262, CA.
*g* *O'Reilly v Mackman* [1982] 3 All ER 1124, [1983] 2 AC 237, [1982] 3 WLR 1096, HL; *affg*
[1982] 3 All ER 680, [1983] 2 AC 237, [1982] 3 WLR 604, CA.

**Case also cited**
*R v IRC, ex p Preston* [1983] 2 All ER 300.

*h* **Appeal**
Asif Mahmood Khan (the applicant) appealed against the decision of Stephen Brown J,
hearing the Crown Office list on 18 May 1983, whereby he dismissed an application by
the applicant for judicial review by way of an order of certiorari to quash the decision of
the entry clearance officer at Islamabad, notified on 28 February 1982, refusing an
application made by the applicant on behalf of Shehzad Asif Khan, a child, for an entry
*j* clearance certificate to allow Shehzad Asif Khan to enter the United Kingdom for the
purposes of being adopted by the applicant. The respondent to the application was the
Secretary of State for the Home Department. The facts are set out in the judgment of
Parker LJ.

*Malcolm Knott* for the applicant.
*David Latham* for the Secretary of State.

*Cur adv vult*

4 April. The following judgments were delivered.

**PARKER LJ** (giving the first judgment at the invitation of Dunn LJ). The applicant is
by birth a citizen of Pakistan. He is settled in this country; having been given indefinite
leave to remain, notwithstanding his original illegal entry in October 1972, under an
amnesty of 28 February 1975. His wife was given indefinite leave to remain on her
arrival in February 1976. He and his wife have been married for some six years and have
been informed that for medical reasons they are incapable of having a child of their own.
They desire to adopt one Shehzad who was born in Pakistan on 10 October 1978 and is
thus some 5½ years of age. He is the third and youngest child of the applicant's brother
and sister-in-law.

In the autumn of 1981 the applicant, whose brother and sister-in-law were willing for
their child to be adopted, went to the Dalston citizens' advice bureau to seek advice about
the procedure for adoption. He was there handed a letter issued by the Home Office
explaining the system. That letter is the foundation of the applicant's case and it is
necessary to set out certain parts of it. It begins:

'Dear . . .
    Thank you for your letter of . . . the following information may be of help to you.'

It is clearly a letter used by the Home Office to answer inquiries from those such as the
applicant and is supplied to advice bureaux so that they may use it when inquiries are
made of them. The letter then continues:

'There is no provision in the Immigration Rules for a child to be brought to the
United Kingdom for adoption. The Home Secretary may, however, exercise his
discretion and exceptionally allow a child to be brought here for adoption where he
is satisfied that the intention to adopt under United Kingdom law is genuine and
not merely a device for gaining entry; that the child's welfare in this country is
assured; and that the court here is likely to grant an adoption order. It is also
necessary for one of the intending adopters to be domiciled here.'

Anyone reading this paragraph would have no difficulty in understanding that a child
could not be brought in for adoption under the Immigration Rules and that if a child
was to be allowed in for such a purpose it would only be at the discretion of the Home
Secretary and in exceptional cases. Such cases would arise only where the Home Secretary
was satisfied of the four matters specified, namely: (1) that there was a genuine intention
to adopt; (2) that the child's welfare in this country was assured; (3) that the court here
would be likely to grant an adoption order; (4) that one of the intending adopters was
domiciled here. The paragraph does not say that on the Home Secretary being satisfied
as to such four matters the child *will* be allowed in, although a reader might well infer
that this would be the likely result.

In the following paragraph the seriousness of adoption is pointed out. It is unnecessary
to set out that paragraph but the next paragraph thereafter is of importance. It reads:

'It is particularly important that the adoption law in this country, which is
designed to safeguard the interests of the child and the natural parents and to ensure
that the intending adopters are suitable persons to adopt a particular child, is fully
satisfied. Also, the law specifically requires that in reaching any decision relating to
the adoption of a child, a court must give first consideration to the need to safeguard
and promote the welfare of the child throughout his childhood. Because the welfare
of a child is at stake, the Department concerned must be satisfied that there are no
apparent reasons why a court would refuse to grant an adoption order. They have
therefore devised the following procedure which is designed to act as a safeguard for
everyone concerned.'

This paragraph is clearly in amplification of the third of the requirements mentioned
in the first paragraph. It rightly stresses that the welfare of the child is the paramount
consideration for the court when considering whether to make an adoption order.

The devised procedure is in two parts, the first relating to the steps to be taken in the country in which the prospective adoptee is living. That first part reads as follows:

'The procedure is for the representatives of the intending adopters in the country where the child is living to apply to the nearest British Government representative for an entry clearance for the child to come here. He will require the documentation and information outlined in Appendix 1 attached to this letter. He will also need to ascertain the child's wishes and feelings having regard to his age and understanding and to see evidence that the child's parents or guardians fully understand what is involved and unconditionally agree to the child coming to the United Kingdom for adoption. He will also be required to confirm that the relevant authorities in the child's present country of residence do not object to the proposal. Further he will be required to prepare, attest and certify documents confirming the information he has given and in some cases will need to translate original documents. The intending adopters will be charged consular fees for this service, which may be substantial.'

The applicant did not appoint representatives to carry out his part of this phase of the procedure, but himself went to the immigration section at the British Embassy at Islamabad to apply for an entry clearance for the child to come to this country. There the necessary documentation was completed. It is important to note that the letter does not state that the government representative will require to be satisfied that the original parents are incapable of caring for the child, merely that he will require evidence that they fully understand what is involved and unconditionally agree to the child coming to the United Kingdom for adoption. It is also important to note that there is nothing in App 1 to the letter which seeks information whether the parents are or are not capable of looking after the child.

The entry clearance officer at Islamabad, having interviewed the applicant, the natural mother and the child on 22 October 1981, sent a report with the necessary documentation attached to the Home Office on 11 November 1981. No complaint is made about that report. It includes certain statements which must be mentioned. They are (a) that the applicant had stated that the child lived with his mother, two brothers and paternal grandparents in the grandparents' brick built modern house with electricity and water on tap and the family enjoyed a good standard of living, the natural father remitting funds from Iran, (b) that although legal adoption was not permitted in Pakistan it was not unknown for parents to hand over children to childless close relatives and that this was certainly such a case, (c) that the application was made for the benefit of the childless sponsors rather than the child, which enjoyed a comfortable standard of living in Pakistan.

The applicant, having been told that his application for entry clearance would be referred to the Home Office, returned to this country on 7 November 1981 and waited.

I now return to the Home Office letter which sets out, or purports to set out, what would happen when the entry clearance application was referred to the department. It is in the following terms:

'When the application is referred to this Department for decision we will require the intending adopters to give an undertaking that as soon as the child arrives here they will inform the Social Services Department of their local authority of their intention to apply to the court for an adoption order. They must also give an undertaking that they will take financial responsibility for the child, including the cost of repatriating the child if for any reason this becomes necessary, for example, the child is not adopted by them. A suitable form specifying the undertakings is attached at Appendix 2. We will then ask the Department of Health and Social Security (or in the case of intending adopters living in Northern Ireland, Scotland or Wales, the relevant Department there) if there are any apparent reasons why a court would refuse to grant an adoption order. The relevant Department will then arrange for appropriate enquiries to be made through the intending adopters' local authority social services department, establish that a suitable home is being offered and ensure that the placement would be in the interests of the child's welfare. It may, in some cases, instigate enquiries into the child's background through a social work agency operating in his country of residence. It is emphasised that these enquiries are necessary to safeguard both the child's and public interest and are likely to be protracted. It is therefore important that the application for the entry clearance is made as soon as details of the child are known. It is also important that *intending adopters do not make arrangements to travel to collect the child or for his journey here or enter any commitments with regard to the child, until they have been informed by this Department that the entry clearance has been authorised.*' (Emphasis as in letter.)

In fact the undertakings in App 2 had been duly signed on the visit to Pakistan and were forwarded by the entry clearance officer with his report. According to the Home Office letter the procedure to be adopted on receipt of the report was therefore as follows: (1) the Home Office would inquire of the Department of Health and Social Security if there were any apparent reasons why a court would refuse to grant an adoption order; (2) that department would then arrange for appropriate inquiries to be made through the applicant's local authority's social services department with a view to establishing that a suitable home was being offered and ensuring that the placement would be in the interests of the child's welfare; (3) in some cases inquiries in the country of origin might be made.

In the case of the applicant the above procedure was not however initiated. It appears that there was a postal or administrative muddle which resulted in a delay until 28 February when the Islamabad entry clearance officer issued a refusal of the application made on behalf of the child in the following terms:

'You have applied to enter the United Kingdom for adoption by Asif Mahmood Khan but you have no claim to admission for this purpose under the Immigration Rules. Furthermore the Secretary of State is not satisfied that serious and compelling family or other considerations make exclusion undesirable.'

In the light of the Home Office letter the terms of the second sentence are a little surprising. The applicant took legal advice. An appeal on behalf of the child was launched but it is common ground that this must fail because it is clear that no case under the Immigration Rules can be made out. The applicant, however, also applied for judicial review of the refusal of the application for entry clearance and an order of certiorari to quash it. That application was dismissed by Stephen Brown J on 23 May 1983 and the applicant now appeals against that decision.

In opposition to the application an affidavit sworn by a senior executive in the Home Office, one Daphne Hewett, was filed on behalf of the Secretary of State. She deposed that the discretion of the Secretary of State to allow entry to a child for adoption is exercised on closely analogous principles to those laid down in the Statement of Changes in Immigration Rules (HC Paper (1979-80) no 394), para 46, and that guidance in very general terms for prospective adopters is given in the Home Office letter to which I have referred.

The relevant part of para 46 reads as follows:

'... children under 18 ... are to be admitted for settlement ... (f) if one parent or a relative other than a parent is settled ... in the United Kingdom and there are serious and compelling family or other considerations which make exclusion undesirable ... and suitable arrangements have been made for the child's care. In this paragraph "parent" includes ... an adoptive parent, but only where there has been a genuine transfer of parental responsibility on the ground of the original parents' inability to care for the child, and the adoption is not one of convenience arranged to facilitate the child's admission.'

According to Mrs Hewett the Secretary of State when exercising his discretion treats 'would-be adoptive parents' on a par with adoptive parents.

If this was the policy, the 'guidance' given in the Home Office letter is grossly
misleading, as was frankly accepted by counsel on behalf of the Secretary of State. There
is not a word to suggest that in exercising his discretion the Secretary of State requires to
be satisfied that the natural parents are incapable of looking after the prospective adoptee,
or even that their ability or inability to do so was considered relevant. Furthermore,
there is no evidence that entry clearance officers were instructed to inquire as to this
matter, which of course does not depend only on the standard of living enjoyed in the
natural home. The whole tenor of the letter is that, if the application was genuine, if the
child's welfare was assured, if a court would be likely to grant an order and if the natural
parents gave a real consent, the child would be let in and its ultimate fate left to the court
here. If an adoption order was made it would remain. If an order was refused it would
be returned.

The applicant relies on three authorities on the basis of which he contends that the
refusal of entry clearance should be quashed. The first of these cases is *Re Liverpool Taxi
Owners' Association* [1972] 2 All ER 589, [1972] 2 QB 299. In that case the corporation
had statutory powers to license such numbers of Hackney carriages or coaches as they
thought fit. The corporation gave public and private undertakings that no licences in
addition to the existing number (300) would be issued until proposed legislation had
been enacted and come into force. Notwithstanding the undertakings, which were given
on 4 and 11 August 1971, the corporation in December resolved to increase the number
of licences to 350 from 1 January 1972, to 400 from 1 July 1972 and thereafter without
limit. The proposed legislation was expected to be in force in early 1973. The Court of
Appeal prohibited the corporation from acting on the resolution to increase the numbers
without first hearing any representations which might be made by interested persons
and any other matters relevant thereto including the undertaking of 11 August.

The form of the order was the result of the decision that the undertaking was binding
so long as the performance of it was compatible with the corporation's public duty. Lord
Denning MR said ([1972] 2 All ER 589 at 594, [1972] 2 QB 299 at 308):

> '... they ought not to depart from it [the undertaking] except after the most
> serious consideration and hearing what the other party has to say; and then only if
> they are satisfied that the overriding public interest requires it. The public interest
> may be better served by honouring their undertaking than by breaking it. . . . they
> broke their undertaking without any sufficient cause or excuse.'

Reference may also be made to the judgment of Roskill LJ where he said ([1972] 2 All
ER 589 at 596–597, [1972] 2 QB 299 at 311):

> 'It seems to me, therefore, that now to allow the council to resile from that
> undertaking without notice to and representations from the applicants is to condone
> unfairness in a case where the duty was to act fairly.'

Also to Sir Gordon Wilmer where he said ([1972] 2 All ER 589 at 598, [1972] 2 QB 299
at 313):

> 'As has been pointed out by Lord Denning MR, what is now sought to be done
> can only be regarded as being in flat defiance of the undertaking publicly given by
> the chairman of the sub-committee at the meeting of the city council, and repeated
> privately to the applicants through the town clerk's letter. It seems to me that in
> these very special circumstances, having regard to the history of how this matter
> had been dealt with in the past, and having regard especially to the giving of the
> undertaking, the applicants are justified in regarding themselves as "aggrieved" by
> what I can only describe as unfair treatment on the part of Liverpool Corporation.
> Accordingly, it seems to me that this is indeed a proper case in which this court can
> and should interfere, in order to ensure that a decision should be arrived at only
> after fair discussion and after hearing all proper representations of the parties
> interested.'

In that case there was a specific undertaking, whereas here there is not; the corporation had a statutory power, whereas here the power of the Secretary of State is a common law power; and the matter complained of was a positive act, whereas here the complaint is a refusal to act. There can, however, be no doubt that the Secretary of State has a duty to exercise his common law discretion fairly. Furthermore, just as, in the *Liverpool Taxi Owners* case, the corporation was held not to be entitled to resile from an undertaking and change its policy without giving a fair hearing so, in principle, the Secretary of State, if he undertakes to allow in persons if certain conditions are satisfied, should not in my view be entitled to resile from that undertaking without affording interested persons a hearing and then only if the overriding public interest demands it.

The second of the authorities relied on by the applicant is *O'Reilly v Mackman* [1982] 3 All ER 1124, [1983] 2 AC 237. The case is relied on solely for a statement of principle in the speech of Lord Diplock with which all members of the House of Lords agreed. It is therefore necessary to state the facts only to the limited extent necessary to render that statement understandable. Four prisoners had been awarded forfeiture of remission by the board of visitors. They sought to challenge the decision of the board on the ground that there had been a failure to observe the rules of natural justice, the relief sought being declaratory only.

Lord Diplock said ([1982] 3 All ER 1124 at 1126–1127, [1983] 2 AC 237 at 275):

'It is not, and it could not be, contended that the decision of the board awarding him forfeiture of remission had infringed or threatened to infringe any right of the appellant derived from private law, whether a common law right or one created by a statute. Under the Prison Rules remission of sentence is not a matter of right but of indulgence. So far as private law is concerned all that each appellant had was a legitimate expectation, based on his knowledge of what is the general practice, that he would be granted the maximum remission, permitted by r 5(2) of the Prison Rules, of one-third of his sentence if by that time no disciplinary award of forfeiture or remission had been made against him. So the second thing to be noted is that none of the appellants had any remedy in private law. In public law, as distinguished from private law, however, such legitimate expectation gave to each appellant a sufficient interest to challenge the legality of the adverse disciplinary award made against him by the board on the ground that in one way or another the board in reaching its decision had acted outwith the powers conferred on it by the legislation under which it was acting; and such grounds would include the board's failure to observe the rules of natural justice: which means no more than to act fairly towards him in carrying out their decision-making process, and I prefer so to put it.'

Here it is contended that the applicant, by virtue of the terms of the Home Office letter, had a legitimate expectation that the procedures set out in the letter would be followed and that such legitimate expectation gave him sufficient interest to challenge the admitted failure of the Secretary of State to observe such procedures. I agree and the contrary was not suggested by counsel for the Secretary of State. But to have a sufficient interest to afford a locus standi to challenge is a long way from being entitled to succeed in such challenge.

The applicant, however, contends that on the basis of the third authority on which he relies, coupled with his first which I have already considered, he is so entitled. That authority is a Privy Council case, *A-G of Hong Kong v Ng Yuen Shiu* [1983] 2 All ER 346, [1983] 2 AC 629, which at the time of the hearing before the judge had been reported only in The Times. The advice of their Lordships was delivered by Lord Fraser. The other members of the Judicial Committee were Lord Scarman, Lord Bridge, Lord Brandon and Sir John Megaw. For some years prior to 23 October 1980 the government of Hong Kong had adopted a policy under which illegal immigrants from China were not repatriated if they managed to reach the urban areas without being arrested. This was known as the 'reached base' policy. On 23 October 1980 the government announced that this policy would be discontinued forthwith and at the same time issued a new

ordinance which, inter alia, gave the Director of Immigration power to make removal
*a* orders in respect of illegal immigrants. There was no statutory provision for a hearing or
inquiry before a removal order was made. Subsequent to the change of policy there were
a series of television announcements stating that all illegal immigrants from China would
be liable to be repatriated. Mr Ng, like many others in the colony, although they had
entered illegally from Macau, was of Chinese origin. They were accordingly worried and
on 28 October 1980 a group, not including Mr Ng, went to Government House and
*b* submitted a petition. There, there were read out a series of questions and answers
prepared in the office of the Secretary for Security which dealt with the position of such
persons and the action they should take. One of such questions, with its answer, was:

> 'Q. Will we be given identity cards? A. Those illegal immigrants from Macau will
> be treated in accordance with procedures for illegal immigrants from anywhere
> other than China. They will be interviewed in due course. No guarantee can be
*c* > given that you may not subsequently be removed. Each case will be treated on its
> merits.'

Although Mr Ng was not present he did see a television programme on the subject on
the evening of the same day.

On 31 October a removal order was made against him. This he challenged and
*d* eventually on 13 May 1981 the Court of Appeal of Hong Kong made an order of
prohibition prohibiting the Director of Immigration from executing the removal order
before an opportunity had been given to Mr Ng of putting all the circumstances of his
case before the director. The Attorney General of Hong Kong appealed to the Privy
Council.

The High Court and the Court of Appeal in Hong Kong had both held that Mr Ng had
*e* no general right to a fair hearing before a removal order was made against him and the
Judicial Committee assumed, without deciding, that they had rightly so decided. It was
concerned only with the narrow question whether what had been said outside
Government House entitled Mr Ng to such a hearing. It is necessary to cite four passages
from Lord Fraser's judgment:

*f* > '. . . "legitimate expectations" in this context are capable of including expectations
> which go beyond enforceable legal rights, *provided they have some reasonable basis . . .*'
> (My emphasis.)

(See [1983] 2 All ER 346 at 350, [1983] 2 AC 629 at 636.)

> 'The expectations may be based on some *statement* or undertaking by, or on behalf
> of, the public authority which has the duty of making the decision, if the authority
*g* > has, through its officers, acted *in a way that would make in unfair or inconsistent with
> good administration for him to be denied such* an inquiry.' (My emphasis.)

(See [1983] 2 All ER 346 at 350, [1983] 2 AC 629 at 637.)

> 'Their Lordships see no reason why the principle should not be applicable when
> the person who will be affected by the decision is an alien, just as much as when he
*h* > is a British subject. The justification for it is primarily that, *when a public authority
> has promised to follow a certain procedure, it is in the interest of good administration that it
> should act fairly and should implement its promise, so long as implementation does not
> interfere with its statutory duty.* The principle is also justified by the further
> consideration that, when the promise was made, *the authority must have considered
> that it would be assisted in discharging its duty fairly* by any representations from
*j* > interested parties and as a general rule that is correct. In the opinion of their
> Lordships the principle that a public authority is bound by its undertakings as to
> the procedure it will follow, provided they do not conflict with its duty, is applicable
> to the undertaking given by the government of Hong Kong to the respondent,
> along with other illegal immigrants from Macau, in the announcement outside

Government House on 28 October 1980, that each case would be considered on its merits. The only ground on which it was argued before the Board that the undertaking had not been implemented was that the respondent had not been given an opportunity to put his case for an exercise of discretion, which the director undoubtedly possesses, in his favour before a decision was reached.' (My emphasis.)

(See [1983] 2 All ER 346 at 351–352, [1983] 2 AC 629 at 638.)

'Their Lordships consider that this is a very narrow case on its facts, but they are not disposed to differ from the view expressed by both the courts below, to the effect that the government's promise to the respondent has not been implemented. Accordingly the appeal ought to be dismissed. But in the circumstances their Lordships are of opinion that the order made by the Court of Appeal should be varied. The appropriate remedy is not the conditional order of prohibition made by the Court of Appeal, but an order of certiorari to quash the removal order made by the director on 31 October against the respondent. That order of certiorari is of course entirely without prejudice to the making of a fresh removal order by the Director of Immigration after a fair inquiry has been held at which the respondent has been given an opportunity to make such representations as he may see fit as to why he should not be removed.'

(See [1983] 2 All ER 346 at 352, [1983] 2 AC 629 at 639.)

That case is, of course, not binding on this court but is of high persuasive authority. In my view it correctly sets out the law of England and should be applied.

· I have no doubt that the Home Office letter afforded the applicant a reasonable expectation that the procedures it set out, which were just as certain in their terms as the question and answer in Mr Ng's case, would be followed, that if the result of the implementation of those procedures satisfied the Secretary of State of the four matters mentioned a temporary entry clearance certificate would be granted and that the ultimate fate of the child would then be decided by the adoption court of this country. I have equally no doubt that it was considered by the department at the time the letter was sent out that if those procedures were fully implemented they would be sufficient to safeguard the public interest. The letter can mean nothing else. This is not surprising. The adoption court will apply the law of this country and will thus protect all the interests which the law of this country considers should be protected. The Secretary of State is, of course, at liberty to change the policy but in my view, vis-à-vis the recipient of such a letter, a new policy can only be implemented after such recipient has been given a full and serious consideration whether there is some overriding public interest which justifies a departure from the procedures stated in the letter.

I refer to the policy of refusing entry save where the natural parents are incapable of looking after the child as a new policy for, without specific evidence, which is not present, that such policy existed at the time, I am not prepared to assume that the Home Office would have issued a letter in the terms which they did or have failed both to mention that the sponsors would be required to satisfy the Home Secretary on the point and to have instructed officers to make inquiries as to the position.

There are two further matters which I should mention. In the first place the applicant can have no complaint, and indeed made none, that he was led to expend money on the faith of the letter. Secondly, counsel for the Secretary of State raised the point that it would be very strange if a child which had already been adopted could be let in only where the adoption was on the ground that the natural parents were incapable of looking after the child but a prospective adoptee could be let in even if this were not so. At first sight this argument appears to have considerable force and it may account for the new policy, but it appears to me on further examination to be based on a failure to distinguish between two quite separate situations. Where an existing adoptee seeks entry, the adoption will in many cases have been effected pursuant to laws very different from our own which fail to afford the safeguards afforded by our own laws and the question is

whether he should be admitted for settlement. Where, however, a prospective adoptee is
a concerned, the question is different. It is whether he should be allowed in *temporarily*
and allowed to remain permanently only after a court of this country has made an
adoption order.

I would allow the appeal and quash the refusal of entry clearance. This will leave the
Secretary of State free either to proceed on the basis of the letter or, if he considers it
desirable to operate the new policy, to afford the applicant a full opportunity to make
b representations why, in his case, it should not be followed.

I would only add this. If the new policy is to continue in operation, the sooner the
Home Office letter is redrafted and false hopes cease to be raised in those who may have
a deep emotional need to adopt, the better it will be. To leave it in its present form is not
only bad and grossly unfair administration but, in some instances at any rate, positively
cruel.

c **WATKINS LJ.** The applicant's complaint, his counsel said, was essentially of unfairness.
He was told his case would be dealt with by the Secretary of State in one way. It was in
fact dealt with in another way. The applicant is an intending adopter of a child who can
lawfully enter this country from his native Pakistan only if in his discretion the Secretary
of State exercising a common law power decides to allow him to enter for the purpose of
being legally adopted here. In his discretion the Secretary of State has denied him entry.
d That discretion was, so counsel for the applicant contends, wrongly exercised.

In a circular letter issued to intending adopters of children of a foreign state the
Secretary of State, it is submitted, undertook, on receiving an application for leave to
bring a child into this country to be adopted, (1) to carry out a procedure involving the
taking of a number of steps so as to acquaint himself with relevant information and (2)
to be guided in the exercise of his discretion solely by clearly stated criteria. In this case
e the Secretary of State in breach of his undertakings has failed to take an important step
in the procedure: he did not ask the Department of Health and Social Security if there
was an apparent reason why a court here would not make the adoption order to be
applied for and he was not guided only by the stated criteria in exercising his discretion.
The criteria referred to are said to appear in the first paragraph of the letter, which states:

f      'There is no provision in the Immigration Rules for a child to be brought to the
      United Kingdom for adoption. The Home Secretary may, however, exercise his
      discretion and exceptionally allow a child to be brought here for adoption where he
      is satisfied that the intention to adopt under United Kingdom law is genuine and
      not merely a device for gaining entry; that the child's welfare in this country is
      assured; and that the court here is likely to grant an adoption order. It is also
g      necessary for one of the intending adopters to be domiciled here.'

It is not in doubt, so it seems to me, that the Secretary of State was satisfied that the
intention to adopt by an intending adopter domiciled here was genuine and that the
child's welfare in this country was assured. It is true that he did not inquire whether a
court here would be likely to grant an adoption order but it is equally true that there is
no evidence to suggest that he at any time thought that a court would be unlikely to
h grant an adoption order. It was a matter which did not influence him one way or the
other.

He exercised his discretion, as was customary in a case such as this, states Mrs Hewett
in her affidavit, by analogy with the terms of the Statement of Changes in Immigration
Rules (HC Paper (1979–80) no 394), para 46. These terms include the following:

j      '... children under 18 ... are to be admitted for settlement . . . (f) if one parent
      or a relative other than a parent is settled . . . in the United Kingdom *and there are
      serious and compelling family or other considerations which make exclusion undesirable* . . .
      and suitable arrangements have been made for the child's care. In this paragraph
      "parent" includes . . . an adoptive parent, but only where there has been a genuine
      transfer of parental responsibility on the ground of the original parents' inability to

care for the child, and the adoption is not one of convenience arranged to facilitate the child's admission.' (My emphasis.)

In this case the Secretary of State, in refusing entry, and having stated that the child has no claim to admission under the Immigration Rules, declared that he was not satisfied that serious and compelling family or other considerations made exclusion undesirable.

This, in the light of the undertaking to apply only the stated criteria is, it is argued, obviously the wrong test. The Secretary of State took account of matters he was not entitled to. Thus he was classically in error in exercising a discretion. This court is, therefore, left with no alternative but to quash the decision, leaving the Secretary of State to reconsider the matter, adopting the procedures and applying the criteria in his undertakings. This would involve no far-reaching implications. All the Secretary of State has to do is to deal with this case as he should have done and did not do, and simply reword appropriately the letter.

Much of the argument addressed to this court on behalf of the applicant was submitted to Stephen Brown J in the court below. His general conclusions in response to them were these:

'The submission which [counsel for the applicant] makes is that the letter to which I have referred which gives advice and guidance to prospective adoptive parents ought to be considered as setting out something in the nature of a rule. He submits that in this case all the procedures which that letter envisages have not been carried out. I say at once that I cannot accept that the entry clearance officer did not give proper consideration to the matter on the basis of his affidavit and on the basis of the information which clearly was considered by Mrs Hewett. It seems to me that the most careful consideration was given to this case, not only by the entry clearance officer, but ultimately by Mrs Hewett who in fact made the decision. I am unable to accept the argument that this letter offering guidance could or should be considered as giving any right to, or laying down any rule for, prospective adopters. This is, as it indicates, a letter designed to help as to how to go about seeking the exercise of the Secretary of State's "exceptional discretion". The letter emphasises in the first paragraph: "The Home Secretary may, however," (although there is no provision in the Immigration Rules) "exercise his discretion and exceptionally allow a child to be brought here for adoption". In this case it seems to me that it is impossible to point to any failure on the part of the Secretary of State to consider any relevant matter. It is not for this court to seek to tell the Secretary of State how to exercise his discretion; this court has the function of judicially reviewing the exercise of discretion, but in this particular sphere the court cannot express its own view as to what ought to be done having regard to the facts of any particular case. I am quite unable to find any ground on which this application can succeed. It seems to me to indicate what may be a general misapprehension and a growing misunderstanding of the function and powers of the court in relation to these matters. Where there are no rules, it can only be in extreme cases (of bad faith for example) that the court could possibly intervene in the exercise of the Secretary of State's discretion. I am quite unable to find that he has failed to apply correct principles or that he has applied incorrect principles. Indeed, it seems to me that this matter has received fair consideration on its merits.'

Although, having regard to the arguments addressed to this court by counsel for the applicant and counsel for the Secretary of State, I would express my reasons somewhat differently, I agree with the judge. There has, in my judgment, been a fundamental misconception by counsel for the applicant of the status of the whole contents of the letter and a misunderstanding of the first paragraph of it which has caused him to endeavour to create an edifice of an argument on a basis which does not in reality exist. Hence his striving to rely erroneously, in my view, for support on the principles said to emerge from *Re Liverpool Taxi Owners' Association* [1972] 2 All ER 589, [1972] 2 QB 299, a  *O'Reilly v Mackman* [1982] 3 All ER 1124, [1983] 2 AC 237 and *A-G of Hong Kong v Ng Yuen Shiu* [1983] 2 All ER 346, [1983] 2 AC 629.

In two of those cases, the first and third, the facts in which differ vastly from those in the present case, it could not be gainsaid that the successful applicants for the various kinds of relief which they succeeded in obtaining were either given undertakings or promises which to their detriment were breached or broken or they had been denied natural justice, or both. The second of them involved issues of private and public law

b  and the rules of natural justice.

Returning to the letter which is the centrepiece of this appeal, I do not think it could properly be said that undertakings were therein given of the kind referred to in the cases I have mentioned. I take the letter to be no more than a helpful guide to an intending adopter from the Secretary of State on whom there is no legal obligation to allow into this country a child who it is sought legally to adopt here. Even if it could be said that

c  undertakings which the Secretary of State was bound to honour were by the letter given to an intending adopter in relation to procedural steps, I would totally reject the suggestion that that undertaking was in any circumstance broken. All the steps referred to in the letter, save one, were taken. That one, namely the inquiry of the Department of Health and Social Security as to adoption was, in the circumstances in which the Secretary of State made his decision, wholly irrelevant to it. His rejection of the application to

d  bring the child into this country was not in any way influenced by his failure to secure a satisfactory answer to such an inquiry.

As for the undertaking to exercise discretion on stated criteria, I am unable to understand how it can possibly be said on a fair reading of the first paragraph of the letter to which I have referred that the Secretary of State was therein informing an intending adopter that he would allow the child to be admitted into this country merely on being

e  satisfied that the intention to adopt that child under United Kingdom law was genuine and not merely a device for gaining entry; that the child's welfare in this country was assured; and that the court here would be likely to grant an adoption order on the application of an intending adopter domiciled here. I take it to be clear from the whole of that paragraph that the Secretary of State was informing the intending adopter that, once those conditions were demonstrated to him to have been satisfied, he would then

f  proceed to exercise his discretion and in an exceptional case allow a child to be brought here for adoption. A failure to satisfy him on one or more of those essential prerequisites would effectively prevent him from even beginning the process of exercising that discretion.

It is apparent from that paragraph and from the remainder of the letter that the Secretary of State did not explain how he would exercise his discretion. In other words, he did not set out the matters that he either would, or would not, take into consideration.

g  I do not in that respect regard him as having behaved in the least unfairly. He was under no legal or other obligation to do otherwise.

There is, in my judgment, no material before this court which would enable it to judicially review the exercise of the discretion of the Secretary of State in this case. He was, I think, fully entitled to exercise it, provided he acted in good faith, by analogy with

h  para 46 of the Statement of Changes in Immigration Rules, or in any other manner deemed by him to be appropriate in the interests of everyone concerned with this kind of immigration.

I reject the submission that this applicant has been in any way unfairly or unjustly treated and would dismiss this appeal.

j  **DUNN LJ.** The Home Office circular letter states, with accuracy, that there is no provision in the Immigration Rules for a child to be brought into the United Kingdom for adoption. The letter goes on to assert that the Home Secretary may in the exercise of his discretion, allow children to be brought here for that purpose. Thus, it appears that the Home Secretary was assuming an administrative discretion the exercise of which is subject to judicial review on the principles which were stated by Lord Greene MR in the well-known case of *Associated Provincial Picture Houses Ltd v Wednesbury Corp* [1947] 2 All ER 680 at 682, [1948] 1 KB 223 at 228. Such review is concerned not with the merits of a decision but with the manner in which the decision was made (see *Amin v Entry Clearance Officer, Bombay* [1983] 2 All ER 864 at 868, [1983] AC 818 at 829 per Lord Fraser). If the manner of making the decision is unreasonable, the courts can intervene to quash the decision. As Lord Greene MR said in the *Wednesbury* case [1948] 1 KB 223 at 229, cf [1947] 2 All ER 680 at 682–683:

> 'It is true the discretion must be exercised reasonably. Now what does that mean? Lawyers familiar with the phraseology commonly used in relation to exercise of statutory discretions often use the word "unreasonable" in a rather comprehensive sense. It has frequently been used and is frequently used as a general description of the things that must not be done. For instance, a person entrusted with a discretion must, so to speak, direct himself properly in law. He must call his own attention to the matters which he is bound to consider. He must exclude from his consideration matters which are irrelevant to what he has to consider. If he does not obey those rules, he may truly be said, and often is said, to be acting "unreasonably".'

So, if there are statutory provisions or rules which the minister has failed to follow, or if he has taken into account matters outside such provisions or rules, then the court may intervene, because he will have misdirected himself and so acted unreasonably. Counsel for the Secretary of State submitted that there were no statutory provisions or rules, that the Secretary of State had an unfettered discretion, and that he was entitled to take into account a pre-eminent policy consideration, namely that leave would only be granted to bring a child here for adoption where there was to be a genuine transfer of parental responsibility on the ground of the natural parents' inability to care for the child.

If the Home Secretary had done no more than to state that it was a matter for his discretion whether or not the child could be brought here for adoption, I should find great force in that submission. But the Home Secretary did not do that. He caused the circular letter in common form to be sent to all applicants setting out the four criteria to be satisfied before leave could be given. Thereby, in my judgment, he in effect made his own rules, and stated those matters which he regarded as relevant and would consider in reaching his decision. The letter said nothing about the natural parents' inability to care for the child as being a relevant consideration, and did not even contain a general 'sweeping up clause' to include all the circumstances of the case which might seem relevant to the Home Secretary.

The categories of unreasonableness are not closed, and in my judgment an unfair action can seldom be a reasonable one. The cases cited by Parker LJ show that the Home Secretary is under a duty to act fairly, and I agree that what happened in this case was not only unfair but unreasonable. Although the circular letter did not create an estoppel, the Home Secretary set out therein for the benefit of applicants the matters to be taken into consideration, and then reached his decision on a consideration which on his own showing was irrelevant. In so doing in my judgment he misdirected himself according to his own criteria and acted unreasonably.

I would allow the appeal and quash the refusal of entry clearance.

*Appeal allowed.*

Solicitors: *Seifert Sedley & Co* (for the applicant); *Treasury Solicitor*.

Frances Rustin   Barrister.

# X County Council v A and another

FAMILY DIVISION

BALCOMBE J

12, 13, 20, 30 JULY 1984

*Ward of court – Jurisdiction – Protection of ward – Freedom of publication – Publication of matter likely to be harmful to ward – Jurisdiction of court to restrain publication – Jurisdiction of court to make order against world at large – Factors to be considered by court before exercising jurisdiction – Enforcement of order.*

In wardship proceedings the High Court has jurisdiction to make an order which operates against the world at large restraining the publication of any information about the ward which the court considers might be harmful to the ward, but that jurisdiction will only be exercised if the court is satisfied that the right to freedom of publication is outweighed by the court's duty to protect the ward, eg where the information might identify the whereabouts and name of a ward of court who is the child of a woman once convicted of child manslaughter, thereby adversely affecting the ward's welfare. An order binding on the world at large will, however, be binding only on those who have notice of its existence. A person who has no knowledge of the order and who in good faith publishes prohibited information about the ward cannot be guilty of contempt of court (see p 55 *h j*, p 56 *c* to *j* and p 57 *b* to *d* and *g h*, post).

*Re X (a minor)* [1975] 1 All ER 697 and *Z Ltd v A* [1982] 1 All ER 556 applied.

*Scott v Scott* [1911–13] All ER Rep 1 and *Re F (a minor)* [1977] 1 All ER 114 considered.

### Notes

For the court's jurisdiction over wards of court see 24 Halsbury's Laws (4th edn) para 594, and for cases on subject, see 28(2) Digest (Reissue) 911–916, *2220–2248*.

### Cases referred to in judgment

*A-G v Leveller Magazine Ltd* [1979] 1 All ER 745, [1979] AC 440, [1979] 2 WLR 247, HL.

*F (a minor) (publication of information), Re* [1977] 1 All ER 114, [1977] Fam 58, [1976] 3 WLR 813, CA.

*Iveson v Harris* (1802) 7 Ves 251, 32 ER 102, LC.

*Scott v Scott* [1913] AC 417, [1911–13] All ER Rep 1, HL.

*X (a minor) (wardship: restriction on publication), Re* [1975] 1 All ER 697, [1975] Fam 47, [1975] 2 WLR 335, CA.

*Z Ltd v A* [1982] 1 All ER 556, [1982] QB 558, [1982] 2 WLR 288, CA.

### Cases also cited

*Brydges v Brydges and Wood* [1909] P 187, CA.

*De Beaujeu, Re* [1949] 1 All ER 439, [1949] Ch 230.

*Marengo v Daily Sketch and Sunday Graphic Ltd* [1948] 1 All ER 406, HL.

*Martindale, Re* [1894] 3 Ch 193, [1891–4] All ER Rep 1248.

*R v Socialist Worker Printers and Publishers Ltd, ex p A-G* [1975] 1 All ER 142, [1975] QB 637, DC.

### Summons

The parents of a baby who had been made a ward of court at the request of a county council applied by summons in the wardship proceedings for an order restraining the respondents, News Group Newspapers Ltd, by themselves, their servants or agents, from (i) publishing the name or identity of the ward or the parents of the ward or any information which would lead to their identification, (ii) publishing the address, locality or area of the ward or the parents or any information which could lead to the identification of its location, (iii) publishing the identity, name or address or any information by which the same could be established of the ward's maternal grandmother, until the ward reached 18 years of age or further order. On an opposed ex parte hearing of an application by the parents on 12 and 13 July 1984 for an injunction restraining the respondents from publishing a story about the ward on 15 July 1984, the respondents stated that they had no intention of identifying the ward or the parents and submitted, inter alia, that it would be unjust if the order were made against them because there would be nothing to prevent someone else publishing the information, and, on the basis of undertakings given by the respondents to that effect, Balcombe J made no order. On 13 July 1984 the Court of Appeal (Cumming-Bruce and Purchas LJJ) dismissed an appeal by the parents against Balcombe J's refusal to make an order. On 20 July 1984, the return date for inter partes hearing of the summons, Balcombe J indicated that he wished to hear argument on the extent of his power in wardship proceedings to make an order in the interests of the ward which was directed not just against the respondents but against the world at large, and the matter was adjourned to 30 July 1984. The hearing was in chambers but judgment was given by Balcombe J in open court. The facts are set out in the judgment.

*Jacqueline Davies* for the county council.
*Christopher Knox* for the parents.
*Richard Parkes* for the respondents.

**BALCOMBE J.** In December 1968 Mary Bell, then aged 11, was found guilty of the manslaughter of two boys aged four and three respectively. She was sentenced to detention for life. In 1980 she was released on licence. She is now aged 27, and in May 1984 a daughter was born to her.

The local authority for the area in which she is now living applied to have that child made a ward of court. That case came before me; and without opposition from either the mother or father of the child, indeed with their active co-operation, I made an order making the child a ward of court, giving care and control to her parents and making a supervision order in favour of the probation service so that the same probation officer, who already supervised Mary Bell under the terms of her licence, was responsible for the supervision of that child.

In July 1984 the fact of the child's birth became known to the News of the World newspaper in certain circumstances which, let me say at once, reflect no discredit on that newspaper. Thereupon Mary Bell, and also the local authority concerned, made an application to me ex parte, because I have retained this case, for an order to restrain the News of the World from publishing any material which could identify the present name and whereabouts of the child and her parents. The News of the World was prepared to give an undertaking to that effect, but the mother then applied for an order restraining publication of any articles relating to the fact that the young woman, originally known as Mary Bell, had had a child on the grounds that any publicity could harm the stability of the home she has now made for herself and child. But, after being referred to the decision of the Court of Appeal in *Re X (a minor) (wardship: restriction on publication)* [1975] 1 All ER 697, [1975] Fam 47, I took the view that the balancing act which the majority of the Court of Appeal held that the court has to perform in these circumstances required me not to impose a complete ban on publication, and I did not. I understand that my decision in that respect was subsequently affirmed by the Court of Appeal. In due course, on 15 July 1984, an article did appear in the News of the World, setting out the fact that Mary Bell had had a child, and certain other facts which I have already mentioned, and that article was in turn followed by similar articles in the daily press.

The application has now been renewed inter partes by summons in the wardship, to which the proprietor of the News of the World, the editor and the reporter concerned have been made respondents. Evidence has been put in on behalf of the News of the World, which of course I accept, indicating that they have no present intention of publishing any further article relating to Mary Bell, but maintaining, first, that they should be free to publish any further article should that in due course be justifiable and, second, through their counsel, submitting that it would be unjust if I were to make an

order restraining publication which could identify the ward by her relationship to the
*a* mother, if that order were binding only on the News of the World and did not affect any
other newspaper or other medium of publication.

I have considerable sympathy with that submission, both because it seems to me that
it would be unfair to injunct one newspaper and not others, but more especially because
the harm to the ward which prohibition of publication is intended to prevent would be
caused by publication in any other newspaper or other medium. It is not just publication
*b* in the News of the World which could harm the ward. It is clearly any form of
publication which could identify, under her present name, Mary Bell, thereby upset the
stability of the home she has now formed and in which her infant child is being raised,
and thereby possibly affect the welfare of the court's ward.

So, in those circumstances, I invited counsel to address me on the question of
jurisdiction, namely whether the court has jurisdiction to prevent publication by the
*c* world at large of any material which could identify Mary Bell by her present name, and
hence her infant child.

I am satisfied that, without an order of the court, there is nothing which would prevent
a newspaper, television station or radio station, or any other medium from publishing
the present identity of Mary Bell, or of the child or of the child's father. The authority
for that general proposition is to be found in the decision of the Court of Appeal in *Re F*
*d* *(a minor) (publication of information)* [1977] 1 All ER 114 at 122, [1977] Fam 58 at 88,
where Lord Denning MR said:

> 'But none of those old cases considered the publication of information relating to
> a ward of court. There is no suggestion anywhere that it was a contempt of court to
> publish information about *the ward herself*, be it favourable or adverse, helpful or
> injurious to her. But there are cases to show that it was a contempt of court to
*e* > publish information relating to the *proceedings in court* about a ward.' (Lord
> Denning's emphasis.)

Scarman LJ said ([1977] 1 All ER 114 at 126, [1977] Fam 58 at 93):

> 'It is, I think, a necessary implication in all the speeches in *Scott v Scott* [1913] AC
> 417, [1911–13] All ER Rep 1 that the cloak of secrecy was available to conceal from
*f* > the world not the life story of the ward, but only so much of it as was properly to be
> regarded as the subject of the proceedings.'

He followed that up, after referring to a statutory provision, with these words ([1977]
1 All ER 114 at 130, [1977] Fam 58 at 99):

> 'As I read the section [s 12 of the Administration of Justice Act 1960], what is
*g* > protected from publication is the proceedings of the court: in all other respects the
> ward enjoys no greater protection against unwelcome publicity than other children.'

Geoffrey Lane LJ is to the same effect.

So I am satisfied on that authority that it is necessary, if publication of Mary Bell's
present identity, and hence the ward's identity, is to be prevented, that there should be
*h* an order of the court. The question then arises: has this court jurisdiction to make an
order binding on the world at large, when persons who are potentially subject to that
order have not been parties to the proceedings in which the order was obtained?

Let me say at once that, if it were not an exercise of the wardship jurisdiction, I am
satisfied that there would be no such power.

Counsel for the respondents, who very helpfully has acted not merely in this instance
*j* to represent the News of the World but has assisted the court by adducing authority
dealing with the whole question, has invited my attention to a line of authorities which
make it clear that the court cannot in general make an order good against the world at
large or against anyone who is not a party to proceedings, or an application made in those
proceedings. He referred me to *Iveson v Harris* (1802) 7 Ves 251, 32 ER 102 and
subsequent authorities. He has also referred me to some exceptions to that general rule,
and in particular to cases where in the course of court proceedings which would normally

be in public the court makes an order prohibiting publication of the identity of witnesses. He referred me to the decision of the House of Lords in *A-G v Leveller Magazine Ltd* [1979] 1 All ER 745, [1979] AC 440 and the provisions of the Contempt of Court Act 1981 which in part, at any rate, were clearly intended to deal with the decision in the *Leveller Magazine* case.

However, I am exercising what is conceded to be a very peculiar jurisdiction. In *Scott v Scott* [1913] AC 417 at 437, [1911–13] All ER Rep 1 at 9 Viscount Haldane LC said:

'In the two cases of wards of Court and of lunatics the Court is really sitting primarily to guard the interests of the ward or the lunatic. Its jurisdiction is in this respect parental and administrative, and the disposal of controverted questions is an incident only in the jurisdiction.'

He then went on to deal with the question of excluding the public from hearings, which is of course now common form because all wardship cases are heard in chambers.

It is because of this peculiar administrative responsibility that it seems to me that I have jurisdiction in this case to make an order which has the effect of prohibiting publication by anybody of details which would enable the present identity of Mary Bell and her child to become known. There is nothing, it seems to me, particularly remarkable about this when one considers some of the other incidents of wardship. It is well established that the very act of making a child a ward of court has certain automatic consequences. For example, it then becomes a contempt of court to marry the ward or to remove him or her from the jurisdiction of the court without the court's prior leave. As it is put correctly in Lowe and White *Wards of Court* (1979) p 139, in each case the embargo arises as soon as the child becomes a ward and is not dependent on any specific restraining order. I believe it is also the case that if the court, in the exercise of its wardship jurisdiction, makes an order committing the care and control of the ward to a particular individual, it is a contempt of court to remove the child from the care of the person to whom the court has committed it to the care of some other person, provided at any rate that the person who is guilty of removing the child is aware of the existence of the order.

Let me say at once that I do not believe, whatever the theoretical jurisdiction may be, that if, as I intend to do, I make an order prohibiting publication of the identity of Mary Bell and her child, it would be a contempt of court punishable in the usual way if someone who has no knowledge at all of the existence of this order and in perfectly good faith publishes the prohibited information. Indeed, that is one of the reasons why I thought it right and proper to give this judgment in open court.

But, subject to that qualification (that the existence of the order must be brought to the attention of anybody who is subsequently charged with having committed a contempt of court by breaking it), I can see nothing in the cases which have been cited to me which precludes the court from having jurisdiction to make the order proposed. Indeed, it would be rather a remarkable thing if, in the exercise of this parental administrative jurisdiction, the court's powers were so limited that it could not in an appropriate case make an order of this nature.

I think there is advantage to be gained by considering those cases where the court in other jurisdictions makes orders in rem. A well-known example is, of course, the exercise of the Admiralty jurisdiction where an order is made arresting a ship; and in the more recent development of the Mareva injunction in *Z Ltd v A* [1982] 1 All ER 556, [1982] QB 558 the Court of Appeal made it clear that there are cases in which an order, although made in proceedings inter partes, does operate against the world at large or, at any rate, those members of the public at large who have notice of the existence of the order. Thus Lord Denning MR said ([1982] 1 All ER 556 at 562, [1982] QB 558 at 572–573):

'What then is the principle? It seems to me to be this. As soon as the judge makes his order for a Mareva injunction restraining the defendant from disposing of his assets, the order takes effect at the very moment that it is pronounced ... Even though the order has not then been drawn up, even though it has not then been served on the defendant, it has immediate effect on every asset of the defendant covered by the injunction. Every person who has knowledge of it must do what he reasonably can to preserve the asset. He must not assist in any way in the disposal of it. Otherwise he is guilty of a contempt of court . . . The reason is because a Mareva injunction is a method of attaching the asset itself. It operates in rem just as the arrest of a ship does.'

Kerr LJ also made it clear that third parties are bound by the terms of the Mareva injunction as soon as they have notice of it, even though the defendant himself has not yet been served and does not know that the order has been made (see [1982] 1 All ER 556 at 572, [1982] QB 558 at 586).

If the court can protect proprietary interests in that way, as it clearly can, how much more should it be able to protect the interests of its wards if it is satisfied in a proper case that the interests of the ward require protection in this form? So I am satisfied that I have the jurisdiction to make an order which is binding on the world at large.

I turn now to the only remaining question, whether in the circumstances of this case it is appropriate that I should exercise that jurisdiction. In this context, I do bear in mind what was said by the Court of Appeal in Re X (a minor) [1975] 1 All ER 697, [1975] Fam 47, and in particular by the two members of the court, Roskill LJ and Sir John Pennycuick, who in that case made it clear that the court is concerned to hold a proper balance between the protection of the ward and the rights of outside parties. Sir John Pennycuick said ([1975] 1 All ER 697 at 706–707, [1975] Fam 47 at 61):

'Specifically, it seems to me, the court must hold a proper balance between the protection of the ward and the right of free publication enjoyed by outside parties and should hesitate long before interfering with that right of free publication. It would be impossible and not, I think, desirable to draw any rigid line beyond which the protection of a ward should not be extended. The distinction between direct and indirect interference with a ward is valuable, though the borderline may be blurred. I am not prepared to say that the court should never interfere with the publication of matter concerning a ward. On the contrary, I think in exceptional circumstances the court should do so.'

I have had evidence put in front of me, particularly by the probation officer concerned, of the harm which publicity identifying Mary Bell by her present name could do to the ward. It requires only a very small exercise of the imagination to appreciate that the original case rightly stirred up very strong feelings; but the criminal law has taken its course, Mary Bell is out on licence, she has this child, and I am concerned with the welfare of the child. It must be apparent, particularly with a child who is still only a little over two months old, that any disturbance to the fragile stability which her mother has achieved must rebound on that child's welfare. Although, as I said previously, I did not think it right to prohibit any reference to the fact that Mary Bell has grown up and has had a child, equally I am satisfied that it is a proper exercise of this jurisdiction, for the protection of the welfare of the two-month-old ward, that I should make an order, and I do make an order, which prohibits any publication which could identify Mary Bell by the name which she is now known, or the child as the child of Mary Bell, or the identity of the child's father.

*Order accordingly.*

Bebe Chua   Barrister.

# Gadd v Gadd

COURT OF APPEAL, CIVIL DIVISION
DUNN AND BROWNE-WILKINSON LJJ
19, 20 JULY 1984

*Divorce – Practice – Stay of proceedings – Discretionary stay – Balance of fairness and convenience – Relevant factors – Deprivation of remedies available in England – Husband and wife British nationals resident in Monaco – Wife petitioning for divorce in England – Husband commencing divorce proceedings in Monaco – Husband applying for stay of English proceedings – Wife likely to receive much greater financial relief if proceedings conducted in England – Whether balance of fairness and convenience in favour of stay of English proceedings – Domicile and Matrimonial Proceedings Act 1973, Sch 1, para 9.*

The husband and wife were married in the Bahamas in 1967 and lived there until 1973, when they moved to France. Both were British nationals. In 1979 they moved to Monaco. In 1983, after the breakdown of the marriage, the wife returned to England and in November of that year she filed a petition for divorce. A month later the husband filed a petition for divorce in Monaco on the grounds of desertion. Under Monégasque law the wife would not be entitled to any financial provision or maintenance if the husband succeeded on his petition, whereas under English law she would have available the full range of remedies under the English matrimonial causes legislation and would be in a much more advantageous position as regards financial relief. The husband applied for, and was granted, an order under para 9[a] of Sch 1 to the Divorce and Matrimonial Proceedings Act 1973 staying the wife's proceedings in England, on the grounds that 'the balance of fairness and convenience' required the husband to be allowed to proceed in Monaco. The wife appealed.

**Held** – When considering 'the balance of fairness and convenience' for the purpose of determining whether English divorce proceedings should be stayed under para 9 of Sch 1 to the 1973 Act in favour of concurrent proceedings in another jurisdiction, the relevant factors to be considered by the court included any personal or juridical advantage which the petitioner in properly constituted English proceedings might lose if those proceedings were stayed. Since the financial remedies afforded by the English matrimonial causes legislation were an important personal or juridical advantage which the wife would lose if the English proceedings were not permitted to continue, the appeal would be allowed and the stay granted to the husband would be lifted (see p 63 *f* to p 64 *a* and *d* to *f*, post).

Dicta of Lord Diplock in *MacShannon v Rockware Glass Ltd* [1978] 1 All ER at 630 and of Lord Diplock in *The Abidin Daver* [1984] 1 All ER at 476 applied.

### Notes

For staying of matrimonial proceedings, see 13 Halsbury's Laws (4th edn) paras 896–899, and for cases on the subject, see 27(2) Digest (Reissue) 711–714, 5486–5512.

For the Domicile and Matrimonial Proceedings Act 1973, Sch 1, para 9, see 43 Halsbury's Statutes (3rd edn) 630.

### Cases referred to in judgments

*Abidin Daver, The* [1984] 1 All ER 470, [1984] AC 398, [1984] 2 WLR 196, HL.
*Atlantic Star, The, Atlantic Star (owners) v Bona Spes (owners)* [1973] 2 All ER 175, [1974] AC 436, [1973] 2 WLR 795, HL.
*MacShannon v Rockware Glass Ltd* [1978] 1 All ER 625, [1978] AC 795, [1978] 2 WLR 362, HL.

---

*a*   Paragraph 9, so far as material, is set out at p 61 *g* to *j*, post

*Mytton v Mytton* (1977) 7 Fam Law 244, CA.
*St Pierre v South American Stores (Gath & Chaves) Ltd* [1936] 1 KB 382, [1935] All ER Rep
    408, CA.
*Sealey (orse Callan) v Callan* [1953] 1 All ER 942, [1953] P 135, [1953] 2 WLR 910.
*Shemshadfard v Shemshadfard* [1981] 1 All ER 726.
*Wilson v Wilson* (1872) LR 2 P & D 435.

**Interlocutory appeal**
Ann Honour Gadd (the wife) appealed against the order of his Honour Judge Watts
sitting as a judge of the High Court on 25 May 1984 whereby on the application of
Bernard Gadd (the husband) he ordered that the wife's petition for divorce in England be
stayed until after the trial of the husband's petition for divorce and ancillary matters in
Monaco. The facts are set out in the judgment of Dunn LJ.

*Richard Hayward* for the wife.
*Paul Focke QC* and *H Jonathan Barnes* for the husband.

*Cur adv vult*

20 July. The following judgments were delivered.

**DUNN LJ.** This is an appeal from an order of his Honour Judge Watts, sitting as a judge
of the Family Division on 25 May of this year, whereby he stayed a petition which had
been filed by the wife on 18 November 1983 on the ground that the balance of fairness
required that the husband should be allowed to proceed with his petition, which he had
filed in Monaco on 21 December 1983.

The facts of the matter are that the parties were married in the Bahamas in 1967; there
are no children and both the husband and the wife are British nationals. They lived in
the Bahamas from the date of the marriage until 1973, when they moved to France. The
husband is described as an international accountant. They lived in France from 1973
until 1979 and then, for probably perfectly legitimate tax reasons, they took up residence
in Monaco.

The wife has been suffering from cancer for some years and from time to time has had
treatment for that disease in this country but, as I have said, their matrimonial residence
has always been outside this country.

In October 1983 the marriage broke down and the wife returned to this country to
live with her mother. On 19 October English solicitors, who had an office in Monte
Carlo, wrote to the wife on behalf of the husband recording that she had left the
matrimonial home, that her husband considered her act as one of desertion and that he
reserved his rights to take such steps as he considered appropriate, and they asked for the
name of the wife's solicitor. Thereafter the wife filed her petition under s 1(2)(b) of the
Matrimonial Causes Act 1973, basing jurisdiction on her domicile here. The husband in
his answer put the question of domicile in issue, but his counsel in this court very
properly conceded that he could not suggest that, by returning to this country, as the
wife says in an affidavit, with the intention of residing here permanently, she had not
thereby reverted to her domicile of origin. So the issue of domicile, so far as the wife is
concerned, goes out of the case.

The husband, in his proceedings in Monaco, effectively relies on desertion; those
proceedings have been adjourned until a date in October.

There was no evidence of Monégasque law led by the wife in the proceedings in the
court below. In an affidavit she said that she had been advised that she would have
difficulty in proving her case in Monaco because neither she nor her husband were
competent witnesses, and she also pointed out that there was no discovery or cross-
examination in Monaco, which would be a disadvantage to her. These procedural matters
were dealt with in an affidavit by Mr Picarda, who is a member of the English Bar
qualified in French and also Monégasque law, and the judge accepted Mr Picarda's

affidavit as being the only expert evidence. On the basis of that affidavit the judge held that there was nothing to support the wife's suggestion that she would be less able to make out her case in Monaco than in England, and accordingly that the balance of fairness and convenience fell in favour of all issues being determined in Monaco, since the parties had lived in France or in Monaco for the past 11 years. There was no evidence before the judge as to the difference in remedies, especially in relation to financial provision, between the English and Monégasque courts. The judge offered the wife's solicitor an adjournment to enable him to file expert evidence but that offer was declined, so the judge was obliged to proceed with the matter on the basis of the evidence which was before him.

In those circumstances, at the outset of the appeal counsel for the wife applied in this court for leave to file evidence of Monégasque law; after hearing argument we granted that application under RSC Ord 15, r 10(2), and we also granted leave to the husband to file further evidence by Mr Picarda in answer to the wife's evidence.

The affidavit of Mrs Sparrow, the wife's expert, raises a question as to the jurisdiction of the Monégasque court which is dealt with by Mr Picarda in his affidavit in answer. No issue as to jurisdiction was raised by the wife's lawyers in Monaco and I am content to assume that the courts of Monaco would have jurisdiction to hear, and adjudicate on, the husband's petition, just as the English courts have jurisdiction based on domicile to adjudicate on the wife's petition.

Mrs Sparrow's affidavit goes on to contrast the financial remedies available to a wife in Monacao as compared with the remedies available to her in England. The position on the two affidavits is not seriously in dispute; since the parties were married in the Bahamas the regime of community property does not apply in Monaco and the matrimonial regime accordingly is that of separate estates.

Accordingly the position can be summarised as follows. If the husband obtains a decree against the wife in Monaco on the ground of desertion, the wife will not receive any maintenance at all and will not be entitled to any financial provision. Moreover, she will be liable to return a house in Monaco which was given to her by the husband during the marriage. Counsel for the husband told us that it would not be the intention of the husband to claim the return of that house; the wife says that it is of little value in any event, but he has the right to claim its return. It appears, although this is not dealt with by Mr Picarda, that if the court in Monaco were to grant cross-decrees, since both parties would be deemed to have been guilty of a matrimonial offence on which the divorce law of Monaco still depends, then once again the wife would not be entitled to any financial provision. If the wife successfully defends the divorce proceedings in Monaco and obtains a decree against the husband, then, subject to one matter to which I shall refer in a moment, she will not be entitled to any capital provision or any property adjustment, but she would be entitled to maintenance not exceeding one-third of the husband's income.

According to Mr Picarda's affidavit there is provision, not under the matrimonial law of Monaco but under the general law contained in art 1229 of the Civil Code, whereby any act of any person which causes to any other person a loss obligates the person through whose fault the loss arose to make good such loss, and Mr Picarda suggests that under art 1229 the wife could apply for compensation if the husband had been found to have caused her any loss by his conduct. But that is not a provision of the matrimonial law, it is simply a general provision of the Civil Code and Mr Picarda in his affidavit is very cautious as to the chances of the wife's obtaining any compensation under that particular article.

That summary of the law of Monaco, so far as it is relevant, makes it plain that the wife would have an important advantage from the point of view of financial relief if the English proceedings were allowed to continue, because she would have the full range of remedies afforded to her under ss 23 and 24 of the Matrimonial Causes Act 1973, including lump sum payment, adjustment of property and periodical payments.

The question in this appeal is how far that advantage is decisive in considering an

application for a stay, or indeed whether it is relevant at all and if it is, what weight
should be attached to it. In matrimonial proceedings, unlike other proceedings, the
power of the court to stay the English proceedings where there are concurrent proceedings
elsewhere in respect of the same marriage derives now not from the inherent jurisdiction
but from statute. Historically, the English court always accepted jurisdiction when, and
only when, the husband, and consequently by reason of her dependent domicile, the
wife, was domiciled in England (see *Wilson v Wilson* (1872) LR 2 P & D 435 per Lord
Penzance).

By the Matrimonial Causes Act 1950 a provision was inserted whereby, even though
the husband was not domiciled here, the court had jurisdiction to adjudicate on a petition
filed by a wife who had been ordinarily resident here for at least three years immediately
preceding the petition. That provision naturally gave rise to the possibility of concurrent
proceedings in this country and in a foreign country where the husband was domiciled
abroad.

In *Sealey (orse Callan) v Callan* [1953] 1 All ER 942, [1953] P 135 the wife filed a
petition in England based on three years' residence immediately preceding the
presentation of the petition. The husband was domiciled in South Africa; he subsequently
filed a petition there and then applied for the wife's petition to be stayed. The matter
came before Davies J, who dealt with it under the inherent jurisdiction and, having
recited the authorities that were then relevant, said ([1953] 1 All ER 942 at 950, [1953] P
135 at 149):

> 'In view of all the circumstances in this case, in view of the undoubted possibility
> that the wife may be able to derive advantages from exercising the right which she
> has to proceed here, in view of the fact to which I cannot shut my eyes that there
> has been at least some delay by the husband in setting the machinery of the law
> moving in South Africa when he had ground for thinking that he had a cause for
> complaint against his wife, I am not satisfied that the husband has here made out
> his case for a stay.'

So the judge took into account all the circumstances of the case including, in particular,
the possibility that the petitioner might be able to derive advantages from proceeding in
this country.

In 1973 the wife's dependent domicile was abolished by s 1 of the Domicile and
Matrimonial Proceedings Act 1973, so that the possibilities of concurrent divorce
proceedings in this country and abroad became even more likely. Schedule 1 to that Act
has effect in relation to cases where there are concurrent proceedings elsewhere in respect
of the same marriage. Paragraph 9 of Sch 1, which deals with the discretionary power to
grant a stay, provides—

> '(1) Where before the beginning of the trial or first trial in any matrimonial
> proceedings which are continuing in the court it appears to the court—(a) that any
> proceedings in respect of the marriage in question, or capable of affecting its validity
> . . . are continuing in another jurisdiction; and (b) that the balance of fairness
> (including convenience) as between the parties to the marriage is such that it is
> appropriate for the proceedings in that jurisdiction to be disposed of before further
> steps are taken in the proceedings in the court or in those proceedings so far as they
> consist of a particular kind of matrimonial proceedings, the court may then, if it
> thinks fit, order that the proceedings in the court be stayed or, as the case may be,
> that those proceedings be stayed so far as they consist of proceedings of that kind.
> (2) In considering the balance of fairness and convenience for the purposes of
> sub-paragraph (1)(b) above, the court shall have regard to all factors appearing to be
> relevant, including the convenience of witnesses and any delay or expense which
> may result from the proceedings being stayed, or not being stayed . . .'

Counsel for the husband submitted that although the wife was domiciled in England
the husband was not, and that from the very start of the marriage the parties had lived

outside the jurisdiction of the English court. For the last five years they had lived in Monaco, and, for six years before that, in France. The law most closely associated with the marriage was certainly not English law, but French or Monégasque law, which for all practical purposes are the same, and which the parties must be taken to have accepted as the law governing the marriage, and he submitted accordingly that it would be unfair to the husband to force him to submit to English law.

He relied on an observation made by Ormrod LJ in *Mytton v Mytton* (1977) 7 Fam Law 244 at 245. The report is not expressed in oratio recta, and is in these terms:

'It was not, his Lordship thought, a very attractive exercise to compare the remedies offered by one jurisdiction with those offered by another. Nor was it very helpful in terms of fairness, because what was fair for one party may seem to have an equal and opposite effect on the other.'

Unfortunately we have not been provided with a transcript of the judgment of Ormrod LJ (who gave the only judgment, Bridge and Stamp LJJ agreeing), so that we are in the position of not knowing the precise phraseology in which Ormrod LJ expressed himself and that may be important. In any event, the observation was obiter because in that case the stay was refused on the ground that the wife, and indeed the children, had come to England with the full agreement of the husband. As reported, Ormrod LJ continued:

'Secondly, it seemed, as Lord Justice Bridge had indicated in the course of argument, equally clear that the onus must be on the party applying for a stay to show that the balance of fairness favoured a stay.'

We were also referred to *Shemshadfard v Shemshadfard* [1981] 1 All ER 726 at 734, where Purchas J, considering Sch 1 to the Domicile and Matrimonial Proceedings Act 1973, refused a stay of English proceedings where the husband had taken proceedings in Iran, the family being Iranian, but who had lived in this country. The judge, having recited the statutory provisions which I have just cited, said:

'There is no doubt that in the exercise of its discretion under these provisions the court must have regard to all relevant factors and that the area of this inquiry ought to be defined liberally. This must include, where relevant, the broad question of remedies including the possibility of the dissolution of the marriage itself and custody of children besides ancillary relief as matters of general fairness between the parties.'

In considering the factors to be taken into account and the weight to be attached to them, I derive assistance from the decisions of the House of Lords in cases decided under the inherent jurisdiction. In *MacShannon v Rockware Glass Ltd* [1978] 1 All ER 625 at 630, [1978] AC 795 at 811 Lord Diplock referred to Scott LJ's statement of the rule in *St Pierre v South American Stores (Gath & Chaves) Ltd* [1936] 1 KB 382 at 398, [1935] All ER Rep 408 at 414 and said:

'If these expressions are eliminated from Scott LJ's statement of the rule, the gist of the three speeches of Lord Reid, Lord Wilberforce and Lord Kilbrandon, in my opinion, enables the second part of it to be restated thus: "In order to justify a stay two conditions must be satisfied, one positive and the other negative: (a) the defendant must satisfy the court that there is another forum to whose jurisdiction he is amenable in which justice can be done between the parties at substantially less inconvenience or expense, and (b) the stay must not deprive the plaintiff of a legitimate personal or juridical advantage which would be available to him if he invoked the jurisdiction of the English court"....'

In *The Abidin Daver* [1984] 1 All ER 470 at 476, [1984] AC 398 at 411–412, another case relating to a stay of English proceedings where proceedings had already been started in a foreign jurisdiction, Lord Diplock said:

'Where a suit about a particular subject matter between a plaintiff and a defendant is already pending in a foreign court which is a natural and appropriate forum for the resolution of the dispute between them, and the defendant in the foreign suit seeks to institute as plaintiff an action in England about the same matter to which the person who is plaintiff in the foreign suit is made defendant, then the additional inconvenience and expense which must result from allowing two sets of legal proceedings to be pursued concurrently in two different countries where the same facts will be in issue and the testimony of the same witnesses required can only be jusified if the would-be plaintiff can establish objectively by cogent evidence that there is some personal or juridical advantage that would be available to him only in the English action that is of such importance that it would cause injustice to him to deprive him of it.'

In the instant case the English proceedings were started first in point of time, but that is not a decisive consideration. What is interesting is that Lord Diplock regarded the loss of an important personal or juridical advantage as amounting to an injustice, which I equate with unfairness for the purpose of the statute that we are considering.

Lord Brandon, having cited the reformulation of the test laid down by Scott LJ which had been made by Lord Diplock in *MacShannon v Rockware Glass Ltd*, and having observed that clause (b) of the formulation omits any reference to burden of proof, whereas clause (a) puts the burden on the defendant to satisfy the court that there is another forum in which justice can be done, went on to say ([1984] 1 All ER 470 at 482, [1984] AC 398 at 419):

'Third, and this concept emerges most clearly from the speech of Lord Wilberforce in *The Atlantic Star* [1973] 2 All ER 175, [1974] AC 436, the exercise of the court's discretion in any particular case necessarily involves the balancing of all the relevant factors on either side, those favouring the grant of a stay on the one hand, and those militating against it on the other. Such balancing may be a difficult process and some cases may be very near the line.'

That language is very close to the words of the Domicile and Matrimonial Proceedings Act 1973, Sch 1, para 9, and very similar to the language that was used by Purchas J when considering the statute in *Shemshadfard v Shemshadfard*.

In considering the balance of fairness under the Domicile and Matrimonial Proceedings Act 1973 in matrimonial proceedings, the court should take all relevant circumstances into account, including the loss of any important personal or juridical advantage which the petitioner, in properly constituted English proceedings, might lose if the proceedings were stayed. I put it in that way because there is no dispute in this case that the English court has jurisdiction and the proceedings are properly constituted. The wife is domiciled in England; it is not suggested that she came here simply in order to invoke the jurisdiction of the English court; she came here as the natural place to come when her marriage broke down, in order to live with her mother and obtain treatment for her illness in England. If the stay is upheld she will lose the advantage of the English remedies for financial provision to which I have referred, and perhaps also her house in France. If she is obliged to rely on the financial remedies in Monaco, she will be likely to be less well provided for financially in Monaco even if she is successful in those proceedings, and if she fails to obtain a decree she will get nothing. If the English proceedings continue it is unlikely that they will be contested since it is accepted that the marriage has broken down, so it is unlikely that there will be any need to call witnesses from Monaco on the issue of matrimonial conduct which would not appear to be relevant in this case to the issue of financial provision.

On the other side of the coin, if the English proceedings continue the husband is likely to be ordered to make more generous financial provision for his wife than he would be ordered to make in Monaco and this could be said to be unfair to him since the parties have never lived together permanently in England. But the Domicile and Matrimonial

Proceedings Act 1973 does not provide that the law of the country which has the closest connection with the marriage should determine the choice of forum for its dissolution. The question is one of balance of fairness; and where, as here, there is a domiciled English woman who has started proceedings in England it would in my judgment be most unfair if she were not to have the important advantages of the remedies, particularly the financial remedies, afforded by the English courts.

Counsel for the husband drew our attention to the Matrimonial and Family Proceedings Act 1984, which was assented to on 12 July and which is due to become law this autumn. Part III of the Act provides machinery whereby where a marriage has been dissolved abroad either party who is domiciled in England may apply to the English court for leave to apply for financial relief. On such an application the court is bound to consider certain specific matters under s 16 of the Act, and if it is not satisfied that it would be appropriate to make an order for financial provision, the court shall dismiss the application. The onus would therefore be on the wife to satisfy the court that it would be appropriate to make an order, whereas in an application for financial relief ancillary to English divorce proceedings the wife has an absolute right to apply for financial relief.

It is impossible to say how the new Act will be interpreted by the courts, or what meaning will be put on the word 'appropriate', but even if the Act is in force by the time a decree is granted in Monaco the wife would still be at a juridical disadvantage in having to apply for financial relief in England. Whether she would be likely to succeed in such an application can at this stage be no more than speculative.

In my judgment, therefore, the provisions of the Matrimonial and Family Proceedings Act 1984, though relevant and a factor to be taken into account, should not be given any great weight in the circumstances of this case.

In the absence of any evidence before the judge as to the difference between the financial remedies in England and Monaco, he did not direct his mind to any of the considerations which I have set out in this judgment; hence he did not take into account an important factor in exercising his discretion, namely the loss to the wife of her financial remedies in England if the proceedings were stayed. Having seen the evidence and having heard full argument on it, I have come to the conclusion that the balance of fairness requires that the English proceedings should be allowed to continue.

I would therefore allow the appeal and lift the stay.

**BROWNE-WILKINSON LJ.** For the reasons that have been given by Dunn LJ, I agree that the appeal should be allowed; there is nothing that I can usefully add.

*Appeal allowed.*

Solicitors: *Lee Bolton & Lee* (for the wife); *Goodman Derrick & Co* (for the husband).

Patricia Hargrove   Barrister.

# Nurcombe v Nurcombe and another

COURT OF APPEAL, CIVIL DIVISION
LAWTON, BROWNE-WILKINSON LJJ AND SIR DENYS BUCKLEY
5, 6, 7, 11 JUNE, 24 JULY 1984

*Company – Minority shareholder – Action by minority shareholder – Nature of action – Locus standi of plaintiff to bring minority shareholder's action – Inequitable conduct on part of plaintiff – Whether plaintiff prevented by inequitable conduct from suing by way of minority shareholder's action notwithstanding that proceedings vested in company and not in plaintiff.*

The husband and the wife were respectively the majority and minority shareholders in a company. They were divorced in 1974 and in matrimonial proceedings in 1977 it was disclosed that the husband had breached the fiduciary duty which he owed as a director to the company by wrongfully diverting from it to another company in which he had a controlling interest an opportunity to enter into a lucrative transaction involving the purchase and resale of land. The wife continued with the matrimonial proceedings after that information came to light and the improper profit made by the husband was taken into account when the wife was awarded a lump sum in the proceedings. Subsequently, after receiving two instalments of the lump sum which the husband had been ordered to pay, the wife commenced a minority shareholder's action claiming that the husband should pay to the company the improper profit which he had made from the breach of the fiduciary duty which he owed to the company. The judge dismissed the action on the grounds that the wife, by continuing with the matrimonial proceedings after discovering the husband's wrongdoing, had elected to treat the profit as belonging to the husband and therefore could not thereafter allege that it belonged to the company. The wife appealed, contending that since she was suing for the benefit of the company, her personal interest in the outcome of the action was irrelevant.

**Held** – The appeal would be dismissed for the following reasons—

(1) (Per Lawton and Browne-Wilkinson LJJ) Since a minority shareholder's action in which the plaintiff shareholder sued on behalf of the company was a procedural device for the purpose of doing justice for the benefit of the company where it was controlled by miscreant directors or shareholders, the court was entitled to look at the conduct of the plaintiff to satisfy itself that the plaintiff was a proper person to bring the action. Thus, if the plaintiff's conduct was so tainted as to bar equitable relief or if there was an unacceptable delay in bringing the action, the plaintiff might well be held not to be a proper person to bring the action. It followed that a defendant in a minority shareholder's action was entitled to raise against the plaintiff any defence which could have been raised had the action been brought by the plaintiff personally. Since the wife had been made aware in the course of the matrimonial proceedings of the husband's wrongdoing but nevertheless chose to continue with the proceedings rather than commence a separate minority shareholder's action, and since the judge in the matrimonial proceedings had, in making his award, taken into consideration the improper profit made by the husband, it would be inequitable to allow the wife to bring her action (see p 69 *f g*, p 70 *e* to *h* and p 71 *e f* and *j* to p 72 *a*, post); *Towers v African Tug Co* [1904] 1 Ch 558 applied.

(2) (Per Sir Denys Buckley) By continuing with the matrimonial proceedings after she had discovered the husband's wrongdoing, the wife had elected to pursue that particular avenue of redress rather than bring a minority shareholder's action. Since the husband had acted to his detriment on the basis of the wife's election, it would be inequitable to allow the wife to sue by way of a minority shareholder's action, notwithstanding that the cause of action in such proceedings was vested in the company and not in the wife (see p 72 *j* to p 73 *a* and *d* to *h*, post); *Towers v African Tug Co* [1904] 1 Ch 558 applied.

**Notes**
For actions brought by companies, see 7 Halsbury's Laws (4th edn) paras 767–772, and
for cases on the subject, see 9 Digest (Reissue) 747–753, 4434–4483.

**Cases referred to in judgments**
*Prudential Assurance Co Ltd v Newman Industries Ltd (No 2)* [1982] 1 All ER 354, [1982] Ch
204, [1982] 2 WLR 31, CA.
*Towers v African Tug Co* [1904] 1 Ch 558, CA.

**Cases also cited**
*Attwool v Merryweather* (1867) LR 5 Eq 464n.
*Clinch v Financial Corp* (1868) LR 5 Eq 450.
*Foss v Harbottle* (1843) 2 Hare 461, 67 ER 189.
*Kammin's Ballrooms Co v Zenith Investments (Torquay) Ltd* [1970] 2 All ER 871, [1971] AC
850, HL.
*Knipe v British Rlys Board* [1972] 1 All ER 673, [1972] 1 QB 361, CA.
*Regal (Hastings) Ltd v Gulliver* [1942] 1 All ER 378, [1967] 2 AC 134n, HL.
*Seaton v Grant* (1867) LR 2 Ch App 459, LJJ.
*Whitwam v Watkin* (1898) 78 LT 188.

**Appeal**
The plaintiff, Mrs Miriam Evelyn Nurcombe, appealed against the judgment of Vinelott
J given on 25 May 1983 whereby he dismissed her claim as a minority shareholder that
the first defendant, Crawford Harvey Nurcombe, her former husband and the majority
shareholder in, and director of, the second defendant, CHN Investment Co Ltd, should
pay the company a profit of £293,925 which she alleged the first defendant had diverted
from the company to another company in which he had a controlling interest, in breach
of his fiduciary duty as a director. The facts are set out in the judgment of Lawton LJ.

*Augustus Ullstein* for the plaintiff.
*Hywel Moseley* for the defendants.

*Cur adv vult*

24 July. The following judgments were delivered.

**LAWTON LJ.** This is an appeal by the plaintiff, Mrs Miriam Evelyn Nurcombe, against
a judgment of Vinelott J, delivered on 25 May 1983, whereby he dismissed with costs
her claim as a minority shareholder that the first defendant, her former husband and the
majority shareholder in, and a director of, the second defendant company (CHN), should
pay to CHN a profit of £293,925 which, so she alleged, in breach of his fiduciary duty as
a director, he had diverted from CHN to another company in which he had a controlling
interest. The judge decided as he did on the ground that, when, in proceedings against
the first defendant under the Matrimonial Causes Act 1973 for periodical payments and
a lump sum, she learned of his breach of fiduciary duty to CHN with its consequence of
loss to it and potential loss to her, she elected to continue with those proceedings and,
through her counsel, she invited the judge to take into consideration when assessing
what, if anything, the first defendant should pay her by way of a lump sum the profit
which had accrued to him as a result of his breach of that duty.

The first defendant is a property dealer. At all material times he worked as such in
South Wales. He married the plaintiff on 21 July 1951. On 30 September 1964 CHN was
incorporated: 99 shares were allotted to the first defendant, one to the plaintiff. At some
date before 31 October 1968 the first defendant transferred another 33 shares to the
plaintiff. She was the registered holder of 34 shares when the writ in this action was
issued on 20 December 1978. On 15 April 1966 another company, Maidsfield Property
Ltd (Maidsfield) was incorporated. A solicitor named Biggs was allotted 99 shares and a

Mr Francis one share. On 30 July 1976 Mr Biggs transferred his shares to Mrs Gerda Nurcombe, whom the first defendant had married on 12 June 1974 after a decree absolute in favour of the plaintiff had been pronounced on 14 May 1974. In the matrimonial proceedings to which I have referred Rees J decided in a judgment delivered on 3 October 1977 that Mrs Gerda Nurcombe held these shares as nominee for the first defendant.

The plaintiff and the first defendant separated in 1969. She started matrimonial proceedings in 1971, at first for judicial separation and later for divorce. After the decree absolute she asked the court to make financial provision for her and later, as a result of learning something about the first defendant's property dealings, for an order under s 37 of the Matrimonial Causes Act 1973 to set aside dispositions of moneys and shares alleged to have been made by the first defendant.

When the plaintiff started the proceedings for financial provision she did not know much about the first defendant's financial position and she did not get much reliable information from his affidavit of capital and income. Some time in the spring of 1977 she learned from a magazine called 'Rebecca' that in 1966 he had been concerned with the purchase and development of some land at Pontypridd. It was alleged in that magazine that the first defendant had made a substantial profit, alleged to be at least £128,000, out of his property dealing activities in respect of that land.

The proceedings for financial provision started before Rees J at Cardiff on 4 April 1977. The plaintiff was represented by Mr Joseph Jackson QC. On 5 April 1977 the first defendant gave evidence. In his examination-in-chief he said that he had no beneficial interest in Maidsfield. He was merely a consultant, entitled to fees. He claimed that he had been frank with the court about his assets. Under cross-examination it became clear that he had not been frank and had not made full discovery of the relevant documents in his possession. He was asked questions about his dealings with regard to the land at Pontypridd and gave unsatisfactory answers. He had to admit that he had been concerned with the making of a contract for the purchase of this land on behalf of CHN. He claimed that it had proved impossible for GHN to take advantage of its contract and that it had lapsed. He also had to admit that Maidsfield had entered into a contract for the purchase of part of the land. He said that he had no interest in Maidsfield save to the extent that he was entitled to fees as its consultant.

On 6 April 1977 Rees J adjourned the proceedings until 2 May 1977. By that date the plaintiff, by her advisers, had reason to suspect that the first defendant might have been in breach of his fiduciary duty to CHN but there was no firm evidence to prove a breach.

The hearing was resumed on 2 May 1977. The first defendant's solicitor, Mr Biggs, gave evidence. He was cross-examined by Mr Jackson about the first defendant's connection with the dealings over the land at Pontypridd and his connection with Maidsfield. At the end of that day's proceedings it was clear that between 31 March 1976 and 30 July 1976 CHN had had a contractual right to purchase the land, that it had not done so, that Maidsfield had bought part of the land and had made a substantial profit as a result of a further sale to Tesco Stores.

The next day, 3 May, Mr Biggs returned to the witness box for further cross-examination. He then produced a number of contracts relating to the purchase of the land, to two of which CHN was a party, and to three of which Maidsfield was a party. For the purposes of this appeal I do not find it necessary to deal in detail with these contracts. It suffices to record that by a contract dated 29 January 1976 CHN agreed to buy from Ninian Property Investment Co Ltd 38·8 acres of land at Pontypridd at a price of £10,000 per acre. The contract was not well drafted. The parties to it decided to substitute for it another contract dated 31 March 1976. This provided for the purchase by CHN of the same land at the same price. Under it CHN had to use its best endeavours to get planning permission within 12 months for a specified development, the vendors to have the right to rescind if planning permission was not obtained within this period. The first defendant expected to be able to get planning permission. Once it was obtained CHN could have expected to make a substantial profit on any resale. At all material times the first defendant was the sole director of CHN. It was his duty to get for CHN, not for himself, all the profit he reasonably could out of this contract. He did not do so. He negotiated with the owners a contract for the purchase by Maidsfield of 13·073 acres of the same land at a price of £125,000. It was this land which was sold to Tesco Stores for £500,000. In acting as he did the first defendant was in breach of his duty to CHN: and on Rees J's finding as to his beneficial interests in the 99 shares in Maidsfield registered in Mrs Gerda Nurcombe's name he did what he did in order to get the profit for himself. Mr Biggs's explanation for the first defendant's conduct, namely that there were tax advantages in letting Maidsfield buy part of the land rather than CHN, did not provide the first defendant with any defence to a charge of breach of duty to CHN. Such tax advantages as there may have been would have been for his benefit, not CHN's.

At the end of Mr Biggs's evidence the plaintiff, by her advisers, knew, first, that the first defendant, for his own purposes but not for CHN's, had so arranged matters that Maidsfield was put into a position to make a profit which could have been made by CHN, and second, that Maidsfield's profit had been large and, subject to some of it which went elsewhere because of a third party's interest in the negotiations with Tesco Stores, most of it had gone to the first defendant. On 3 May the exact amount of this profit was not known but the plaintiff's advisers would have appreciated that it would have been at least £125,000. At that stage of the proceedings, with more witnesses to be heard, Mr Jackson could not have been expected to consider the legal implications of what had been revealed; but he had an opportunity of doing so a few days later when Rees J adjourned the hearing until 22 July 1977. During this adjournment the plaintiff's advisers had an opportunity of evaluating the evidence and considering the legal consequences of it. The first defendant, as a result of his dealings with the Pontypridd land, had acquired assets out of which Rees J could and probably would order him to pay a substantial lump sum to the plaintiff. But what the first defendant had acquired should have gone to CHN in which the plaintiff had one-third of the shares. As a shareholder she could expect one day to get the benefit of any sum which the first defendant had to pay CHN for breach of his duty to it. It was doubtful, however, what that benefit would be or when she would get it. It was probable that CHN would be liable for a substantial amount of corporation tax once the first defendant had repaid CHN the profit which Maidsfield had made. On repayment there would be no certainty, as Browne-Wilkinson LJ pointed out during argument, as to when, if ever, CHN would distribute the profit by way of dividend. The first defendant controlled CHN and might for his own purposes decide not to procure the declaration of a dividend. If the plaintiff's advisers considered these factors, and it is likely that they did, there were advantages in going on with the matrimonial proceedings for both periodic payments and a lump sum. That which was almost certain to be obtained soon was better than that which might be obtained later. The plaintiff went on with the matrimonial proceedings. On 3 October 1977 Rees J, by a reserved judgment, ordered the first defendant to make periodic payments to the plaintiff of £1,500 per annum and to pay her a lump sum of £25,000. In assessing this sum he took into account the profit which the first defendant had made from the Maidsfield transaction. By later orders the first defendant was allowed to discharge his liability for this sum by paying it in three instalments, each of £8,000. After being paid two of these instalments the plaintiff issued her writ in this action. The third and final instalment was paid and accepted soon after.

By their amended defence, both defendants alleged, inter alia, that the plaintiff had no locus standi to complain of the breaches of duty which she alleged and that the statement of claim disclosed no cause of action by the plaintiff. By a further amendment made at the beginning of the trial the two defendants alleged that, before starting this action, the plaintiff knew all the material facts on which she based her claim in this action and had accepted two instalments of £8,000 before the issue of the writ. The defendants applied to have the statement of claim struck out as showing no cause of action. Fox J on 21 January 1981 refused the application.

On the trial of the action Vinelott J adjudged that, when the plaintiff discovered what had happened, she—

'had to elect to bring an action as minority shareholder on behalf of CHN or to abandon her right to bring such an action and in the application for financial provision to take the substitution of Maidsfield and Perignon [the third party in the negotiations with Tesco Stores] for CHN as valid and effective and to claim against Mr Nurcombe that the profit made by Maidsfield and its potential profit from the remainder of the [Pontypridd] land were assets which ought to be treated as available to him and that he should not be treated as under any corresponding liability to CHN. She chose the latter course and, having obtained the benefit of the judgment and orders of Rees J, she cannot now assert a right as shareholder of and on behalf of CHN. Even if it is in principle open to a party in these circumstances to disgorge a benefit and to assert an inconsistent right, the benefit or advantage obtained by the plaintiff clearly cannot in this case be restored.'

The plaintiff in this court submitted, first, that she did not know the material facts until after the conclusion of the matrimonial proceedings and, second, that, as the plaintiff was suing for the benefit of the company, her personal interest in the outcome of the action was irrelevant.

The first of the grounds required us to examine the transcript of the evidence given at the trial before Rees J. I am satisfied that, by 22 July 1977 when the evidence was concluded, the plaintiff, by her advisers, had had enough information about the first defendant's activities to appreciate that he had been in breach of his fiduciary duty to CHN to its grave financial disadvantage. Her advisers would have known what she could do as a shareholder to help CHN to recover the loss it had suffered. She was then able to make an election as to her remedies if the law required her to make one.

In the common law sense of choosing between two remedies for the same unlawful act, she did not have to elect. In the matrimonial proceedings she was seeking to enforce for her own benefit rights she had as a wife. In this action she is suing for the benefit of CHN. She cannot be said to have suffered any personal loss as a result of the first defendant's breach of duty. Her shares in CHN have diminished in value because of the first defendant's wrongdoing. But this is because of the diminution in the value of CHN's net assets. Her shares, as such, were not affected by the wrongdoing: see *Prudential Assurance Co Ltd v Newman Industries Ltd (No 2)* [1982] 1 All ER 354 at 367, [1982] Ch 204 at 223.

It is pertinent to remember, however, that a minority shareholder's action is in form nothing more than a procedural device for enabling the court to do justice to a company controlled by miscreant directors or shareholders. Since the procedural device has evolved so that justice can be done for the benefit of the company, whoever comes forward to start the proceedings must be doing so for the benefit of the company and not for some other purpose. It follows that the court has to satisfy itself that the person coming forward is a proper person to do so. In *Gower's Principles of Modern Company Law* (4th edn, 1979) p 652 the law is stated, in my opinion correctly, in these terms:

'The right to bring a derivative action is afforded the individual member as a matter of grace. Hence the conduct of a shareholder may be regarded by a court of equity as disqualifying him from appearing as plaintiff on the company's behalf. This will be the case, for example, if he participated in the wrong of which he complains.'

The authority which is said to establish this proposition is the decision of the Court of Appeal in *Towers v African Tug Co* [1904] 1 Ch 558. Beyond this case, there seems to be a scarcity of reliable English authority. There are more American authorities: see Fletcher *Cyclopaedia of Corporations* (1970) vol 13, paras 5859–5950. In *Towers v African Tug Co* for one year the directors honestly but illegally applied a profit made in the earlier part of 1900 in payment of an interim dividend instead of in reduction of a debit balance on the previous year's trading, thus in effect paying a dividend out of capital. The balance sheet for 1900 showing the debit balance and the payment of the dividend was submitted to and approved by the shareholders in general meeting. In 1903 two of the shareholders who had themselves received portions of the dividend, and concurred in passing the balance sheet, commenced an action 'on behalf of themselves and all the other shareholders of the company' against the company and the directors to compel the directors to repay to the company the amount of the dividend. The claim succeeded at first instance. On appeal this court adjudged that the plaintiffs were not entitled to succeed. Vaughan Williams LJ said (at 567):

'I think that an action cannot be brought by an individual shareholder complaining of an act which is ultra vires if he himself has in his pocket at the time he brings the action some of the proceeds of that very ultra vires act. Nor, in my opinion, does it alter matters that he represents himself as suing on behalf of himself and others.'

He also adjudged that, on the facts of that case, the action was not for the benefit of the company. Cozens-Hardy LJ said (at 571):

'An action in respect of or arising out of an ultra vires transaction ought properly to be brought by the company; but it has long been well established that there are cases in which such an action may be maintained by a shareholder suing on behalf of himself and all other shareholders against the company as defendants. I will not pause to consider under what particular circumstances such an action may be maintained, but I assume that this is one of those cases in which such an action may be maintained—I mean in point of form. But I think it is equally clear that the action cannot be maintained by a common informer. A plaintiff in an action in this form must be a person who is really interested. When you get that fact clearly established it seems to me impossible to avoid taking the next step—that all personal objections against the individual plaintiff must be gone into and considered before relief can be granted.'

My understanding of these judgments is that the court is entitled to look at the conduct of a plaintiff in a minority shareholder's action in order to satisfy itself that he is a proper person to bring the action on behalf of the company and that the company itself will benefit. A particular plaintiff may not be a proper person because his conduct is tainted in some way which under the rules of equity may bar relief. He may not have come with 'clean hands' or he may have been guilty of delay.

Applying these principles to the facts of this case the plaintiff took her chance of persuading Rees J that she should benefit from the ill-gotten gains which the first defendant had made. She succeeded and by the time this action started she had received two-thirds of the fruits of her victory. When she received these fruits she knew how the first defendant had got them and at whose expense: CHN's. In this action she is in effect saying: 'Although I have shared with the first defendant his ill-gotten gains, I want the court to order that he should pay over to CHN his share of them plus my share so that I can have a chance of getting some more because of my status as a shareholder.' In my judgment, the court should not countenance such conduct. I would dismiss the appeal for the reasons given by Vinelott J.

If my brethren agree that Vinelott J's judgment should stand, it will be unnecessary for us to consider the further grounds for upholding the judgment set out in the defendants' cross notice of appeal.

**BROWNE-WILKINSON LJ.** I have read the judgment of Lawton LJ, with which I agree. I only add a few words of my own because this case raises a principle of some importance in relation to minority shareholder's actions.

Vinelott J held that, as a result of the proceedings in the Family Division, the plaintiff had sufficient information to put her to her election whether to pursue the claim for a lump sum payment in the matrimonial proceedings (the anticipated profit to the first defendant from the property transaction being taken into account) or to pursue the claim of CHN by a minority shareholder's action against the first defendant. For the reasons given by Lawton LJ I agree that, if this were strictly a case of election, the plaintiff had sufficient information by 22 July 1977 to put her to her election. Moreover, she made *a*  her election by persisting in her claim for a lump sum payment on the basis that the profit from the property dealing was to be taken into account as part of the first defendant's assets.

But this is not strictly a case of election. A duty to elect only arises where someone has two alternative rights both of which belong to him. In this case, although the right to claim a lump sum payment was the plaintiff's, the right to complain of the wrong done to CHN belonged to CHN, not to her: in a minority shareholder's action the shareholder
*b*  who is the plaintiff is asserting not the shareholder's individual right but the right of the company. The question is whether this technical objection precludes the court from giving effect to the elementary concepts of justice on which the doctrine of election is founded.

The judge found the answer in the decision of this court in *Towers v African Tug Co* [1904] 1 Ch 558. He apparently treated that as being a case in which the plaintiffs had
*c*  been put to their election whether to accept the ultra vires dividend (in which case they could not thereafter bring a minority shareholder's action) or refuse the dividend and bring the minority shareholder's action. For myself, I think that case was treated by the Court of Appeal as a case of acquiescence by the plaintiffs and not one of election. But, whether the judge's or my own view on the matter is correct, it does not affect the principle established by the case. The Court of Appeal relied on the fact that only a
*d*  person having a personal interest could bring a minority shareholder's action and (at 571 per Cozens-Hardy LJ):

> 'When you get that fact clearly established it seems to me impossible to avoid taking the next step—that all personal objections against the individual plaintiff must be gone into and considered before relief can be granted.'

*e*  In my judgment that case establishes that behaviour by the minority shareholder, which, in the eyes of equity, would render it unjust to allow a claim brought by the company at his instance to succeed, provides a defence to a minority shareholder's action. In practice, this means that equitable defences which would have been open to defendants in an action brought by the minority shareholder personally (if the cause of action had been
*f*  vested in him) would also provide a defence to those defendants in a minority shareholder's action brought by him.

The juristic basis of this principle (which is applicable in many jurisdictions in the United States of America) is not clear. In the United States it has apparently been rationalised by saying that a minority shareholder's action is in fact two actions, one a personal action by the minority shareholder against the company for its failure to enforce
*g*  the company's right, the other by the company against the wrongdoer. Without expressing any view on the correctness of this analysis (which was not fully examined in argument), I do not think it is necessary to adopt such analysis in the present case. Since the wrong complained of is a wrong to the company, not to the shareholder, in the ordinary way the only competent plaintiff in an action to redress the wrong would be the company itself. But, where such a technicality would lead to manifest injustice, the
*h*  courts of equity permitted a person interested to bring an action to enforce the company's claim. The case is analogous to that in which equity permits a beneficiary under a trust to sue as plaintiff to enforce a legal right vested in trustees (which right the trustees will not themselves enforce), the trustees being joined as defendants. Since the bringing of such an action requires the exercise of the equitable jurisdiction of the court on the grounds that the interests of justice require it, the court will not allow such an action to
*j*  be used in an inequitable manner so as to produce an injustice. *Towers v African Tug Co* shows that 'all personal objections against the individual plaintiff' must be considered. It is for this reason that, in my judgment, a court of equity will not allow a minority shareholder to succeed in a minority shareholder's action where there are equitable defences which, as between the shareholder personally and the defendants, the defendants could properly rely on in equity, eg the duty to elect between conflicting rights, acquiescence or laches of the minority shareholders.

For these reasons, in my judgment, the judge's decision was correct and the appeal should be dismissed.

**SIR DENYS BUCKLEY.** Sacrificing contemporary accuracy (for they are no longer married to one another) for the sake of simplicity I shall call the plaintiff 'the wife' and the first defendant 'the husband'. I shall call the second defendant 'CHN' and Maidsfield Property Ltd I shall call 'Maidsfield'.

At all material times the wife held and owned beneficially 34% of the issued share capital of CHN and the husband held and owned the remaining 66%, as they still do; and, at all material times, the husband, as Rees J held in the matrimonial proceedings between the husband and the wife, was the beneficial owner of the 99% of the issued share capital of Maidsfield registered in the name of Mrs Gerda Nurcombe, to whom he is now married.

I need not recapitulate the facts which Lawton LJ has already stated. Vinelott J dismissed the action on the ground that the wife was barred from success in it by the course which she had elected to follow on her application for financial provision in the matrimonial proceedings.

The doctrine of election is formulated in Spencer Bower and Turner *The Law Relating to Estoppel by Representation* (3rd edn, 1977) para 310 thus:

'Where A, dealing with B, is confronted with two alternative and mutually exclusive courses of action in relation to such dealing, between which he may make his election, and A so conducts himself as reasonably to induce B to believe that he is intending definitely to adopt one course, and definitely to reject or relinquish the other, and B in such belief alters his position to his detriment, A is precluded, as against B, from afterwards resorting to the course which he has thus deliberately declared his intention of rejecting.'

The wife propounded her claim against the husband for financial provision on the express basis that her shares in CHN were valueless, and that the assets of Maidsfield were at the husband's disposition; and there is no ground for supposing that she did not then believe that this was the case. In the course of the evidence adduced on that application, it became apparent that, in breach of his duty to CHN, the husband had abandoned CHN's valuable contract for the purchase by CHN of the Pontypridd land and had renegotiated the purchase for the benefit not of CHN but of Maidsfield. It also became apparent that Maidsfield had realised a large profit on the resale of part of the land to Tesco Stores. It is clear from the cross-examination of Mr Biggs that the wife's legal advisers then appreciated that there was at least a likelihood that a judgment for very substantial damages could be obtained against the husband for the benefit of CHN in a misfeasance action. The consequence of such a judgment, if it could be successfully enforced, as it presumably could have been, would have been substantially to enhance the value of the wife's shares in CHN. While it is true that, as a minority shareholder, she could not control the use of any moneys which might have thus become available to CHN, she could have prevented the husband from sterilising the money in CHN or using it in any way which would oppressively exclude her, a minority shareholder, from a proper participation in any benefits arising from such use.

The circumstances were such that a misfeasance action against the husband could not have been brought in the name of CHN as plaintiff. The wife, as the only minority shareholder in CHN, was the only person capable of launching a minority shareholder's action against the husband and CHN to recover damages for the misfeasance.

In these circumstances, the wife was confronted with two alternative and mutually exclusive courses of action, the choice of either of which would be likely substantially to affect both her financial position and the husband's. She could embark on a minority shareholder's misfeasance action against the husband, which would probably delay the outcome of her application for financial provision in the matrimonial proceedings pending the trial of the action, or result in her getting no lump sum or a much reduced lump sum on that application; or she could proceed with that application, which was then already at the stage of hearing by the court, on the basis that the husband's conduct in relation to dealing with the Pontypridd land would remain unchallenged, and that her shares in CHN were consequently valueless. She could not, in my opinion, do what she has sought to do, that is pursue both courses.

The wife's advisers had plenty of time between 4 May 1977, when the facts relating to the misfeasance became known, and 3 October 1977, when Rees J delivered his judgment, to advise the wife how she should elect between the two courses open to her. In fact, she chose to let the financial provision application before Rees J proceed to judgment without seeking any adjournment or attempting to amend in any way the statement of her financial resources and those of the husband on which that application was based. In other words, she elected to adopt the second of the two alternatives to which I have referred, and made clear to the husband that she had done so. As Lawton LJ has indicated, there were considerations which may well have seemed to the wife and her advisers to make that the more attractive alternative.

In his very careful judgment in which he assessed the amount of the lump sum which he ordered the husband to pay to the wife, Rees J explicitly took into consideration as available to the husband the profits realised by Maidsfield as the result of its dealings with the Pontypridd land.

If *Spencer Bower and Turner* is correct in suggesting, in the passage which I have read, that it is a necessary element of a binding election that the other party has altered his position to his detriment on the faith of the elector's election (as to which I express no opinion), the husband has, in the present case, clearly acted to his detriment: before issue of the writ in the present action he had paid £16,000 to the wife under Rees J's order. In my judgment, the wife's election became binding on her at the latest when she received the first instalment of that sum. Consequently, in my view, at the date of the issue of the writ, she was as effectively barred from commencing the action as she would have been if she had entered into a binding obligation not to sue. A minority shareholder, who is under a disability of that nature, is not, in my judgment, qualified or competent to sue as a plaintiff in a minority shareholder's action, notwithstanding that, in such an action, the plaintiff sues on behalf of the company and in right of a cause of action vested in the company: see in this connection *Towers v African Tug Co* [1904] 1 Ch 558, where shareholders, who had participated in a dividend which had been innocently but illegally paid out of capital, were held in this court incompetent to sue the directors of the company in a representative action for repayment to the company of the amount of the dividend because they had received and retained their share of the dividend. The present case is, in my view, a stronger case because of the binding effect of the wife's election.

It was suggested in the course of the argument that the wife might repay the lump sum which she has received as a condition of her being allowed to continue the action. This would not, in my view, be an admissible course because, for reasons which I have already given, she was not competent to bring the action.

I also would dismiss this appeal.

*Appeal dismissed.*

*3 1 October. Leave to appeal to the House of Lords refused.*

Solicitors: *Clintons* (for the plaintiff); *Morgan Bruce & Nicholas*, Cardiff (for the defendants).

Mary Rose Plummer    Barrister.

# R v Brent Health Authority, ex parte Francis

QUEEN'S BENCH DIVISION (CROWN OFFICE LIST)
FORBES J
24 SEPTEMBER 1984

*Public authority – Meeting – Admission of public – Power to exclude public – Prevention of disorderly conduct – Whether public body having power to prevent public from entering meeting if public likely to disrupt meeting – Whether power exercisable only at meeting itself – Public Bodies (Admission to Meetings) Act 1960, s 1(1)(8).*

Three meetings of a local health authority, which by s 1(1)[a] of the Public Bodies (Admissions to Meetings) Act 1960 were required to be open to the public, were seriously disrupted by members of the public when the subject of expenditure cuts was discussed. The authority, purporting to act under s 1(8)[b] of the 1960 Act, which preserved to public bodies 'any power of exclusion to suppress or prevent disorderly conduct or other misbehaviour at a meeting', decided to exclude the public from its next meeting on that subject. The applicant, a member of the public, applied for an order of certiorari to quash the authority's decision to exclude the public, contending that it was ultra vires because s 1(8) merely preserved the authority's power to remove, in the course of a meeting, members of the public who disrupted or threatened to disrupt its proceedings and did not extend to preventing the public from entering and in effect holding the meeting in camera.

**Held** – On its true construction s 1(8) of the 1960 Act merely preserved the common law power of public bodies to prevent members of the public entering a meeting if the public body had reasonable grounds for believing that they would disrupt the meeting by disorderly conduct and make it impossible for the public body to conduct its business properly. Furthermore, such a power could in urgent cases be exercised by the chairman of the public body in advance of any meeting, provided it was exercised bona fide, since otherwise the power would be useless. On the facts, the health authority had been justified in exercising that power and therefore the application for an order of certiorari would be dismissed (see p 78 e to g and p 80 c to e and j to p 81 e and j to p 82 a, post).

Doyle v Falconer (1866) LR 1 PC 328 and Lucas v Mason (1875) LR 10 Exch 251 considered.

## Notes

For the power of local authorities to exclude the public from meetings, see 28 Halsbury's Laws (4th edn) para 1137, and for a case on the subject, see 33 Digest (Reissue) 20, 64.

For the Public Bodies (Admission to Meetings) Act 1960, s 1, see 19 Halsbury's Statutes (3rd edn) 835.

## Cases referred to in judgment

Associated Provincial Picture Houses Ltd v Wednesbury Corp [1947] 2 All ER 680, [1948] 1 KB 223, CA.

Doyle v Falconer (1866) LR 1 PC 328.

Lucas v Mason (1875) LR 10 Exch 251.

R v Liverpool City Council, ex p Liverpool Taxi Fleet Operators' Association [1975] 1 All ER 379, [1975] 1 WLR 701, DC.

## Cases also cited

Albert v Lavin [1981] 3 All ER 879, [1982] AC 546, HL.

Harrison v Duke of Rutland [1893] 1 QB 142, [1891–4] All ER Rep 514, CA.

John v Rees [1969] 2 All ER 274, [1970] Ch 345.

Lovelock v Secretary of State for Transport (1979) 39 P & CR 468, CA.

---

a   Section 1(1) is set out at p 77 e, post
b   Section 1(8) is set out at p 78 d e, post

**Application for judicial review**

Eileen Doris Francis applied, with the leave of Woolf J granted on 19 January 1984, (1) for an order of certiorari (a) to quash the decision of the chairman of the Brent Health Authority, in advance of a meeting of that authority on 5 December 1983, to exclude members of the public (other than accredited, invited members of the press and a representative of Brent Community Health Council) from the meeting in view of the likelihood that members of the public would disrupt the meeting, and (b) to quash all the resolutions passed at that meeting; (2) for an order of mandamus requiring the health authority to hold all future meetings in accordance with the law and allow the public admittance. The facts are set out in the judgment.

*Richard Drabble* for the applicant.
*James Goudie QC* and *Adrian Lynch* for the health authority.

**FORBES J.** Originally this was an application by Eileen Doris Francis and an organisation known as the Community Rights Project Ltd. Leave was given to both those persons to pursue an application for judicial review in January 1984, but the Community Rights Project have dropped out and the application is pursued only by Eileen Doris Francis. It is another chapter in the saga of the Brent Health Authority. I do not think that I need to go into the background too closely but, as everybody knows, this government has enjoined local health authorities to cut their spending. The fact that they have done so has provoked a vociferous political reaction, nowhere more so than in the Brent area.

The situation is, and I take this from the unchallenged affidavit of Mrs Nina Talmage who, at the time, was the chairman of the Brent Health Authority, that the question of implementing the cuts in the budget required by the government was to be debated at a meeting which took place on 19 September 1983. Owing to the provisions of the Public Bodies (Admission to Meetings) Act 1960, a statute to which I will refer in a moment, the meetings of this particular body are to be open to the public. On this occasion something like 200 people turned up, although there was only seating for about 100 members. The chairman tried to keep some order but was unable to do so. The public who were admitted were shouting: 'No cuts, no cuts'. Every time members of the authority in the course of the debate attempted to speak in favour of implementing the cuts, they were shouted down amidst rowdy behaviour and stamping feet, while the members who spoke against the cuts were heard in silence. At that meeting the members of the authority passed a resolution against implementing the cuts. Most of the public then left.

The difficulty was that the health authorities had to conform with government directions. Another meeting had to be called, again on the question of the implementation of the cuts. Mrs Talmage, the chairman, considered the matter with the district administrator of the health authority and thought of bringing in the local police, but decided against that on the grounds that it might cause more harm than good. The cuts came up for consideration again on 17 October 1983. That was a meeting which was even rowdier than the September meeting. There were television cameras. There were about 300 people. There were some well behaved people but most of the crowd were hostile, stamping on the floor and shouting, cheering the authority members of whose views they approved and booing the members of whose views they disapproved. Mrs Talmage said that it was almost impossible to hear what was being said by members of the authority. She also said that the atmosphere was most unpleasant and that the public behaved just like a mob. the more militant members of the public stood up, turned their backs on the authority, faced the public and shouted various slogans. She said that it was a frightening experience and that the members came away in a very nervous state. Mrs Talmage said: 'It was very difficult to transact business in such circumstances because we could not hear anything that the other members said.' Once again, at that meeting, the authority voted against the cuts.

Following that, again the question of implementing the cuts had once more to be decided. The matter clearly had to come back on the agenda and the question of inviting the police to attend was again taken up. There was a dialogue with the police about this. There were difficulties. The police considered that it was impossible effectively to police the meeting as the hospital in which the meeting was to be held was private property and so, although there were some police officers about the grounds, there was no police presence at the meeting itself.

The meeting took place on 21 November 1983. In order to attempt to control the public a somewhat smaller meeting hall or room was found and a system of tickets was operated. The system of tickets did not work because people just barged in without tickets. There were about 100 people and the room was very tightly packed. People were using cameras and they continued to take photographs despite the chairman's insistence that photographs should not be taken. At this stage it became apparent that a majority of the members would, at this meeting, vote in favour of the cuts. When it came to take the votes, and I quote from the affidavit:

> 'Councillor Durham, who is very much the focus of the opposition to the cuts and a member of the health authority as well as a Labour member of the Brent local authority, stood up and said: "You know what to do, go to it". At this point one member of the public rushed up to the tables where the authority members were seated with a loud hailer and a number of other members of the public moved in also. A large part of the audience rose to their feet, and some people jumped on to the tables and started shouting.'

The authority members had to leave very quickly and no business was properly done.

After that meeting a number of the members of the authority went to the chairman's office and said that an emergency meeting was definitely required to complete the business of the meeting, because most of the business of the authority had been unable to be concluded, including the long-term and short-term plans for the future. The result of that was that the chairman and the district administrator sought legal advice. They were advised that they could exclude the public from the meeting in order to prevent disorderly conduct. Taking that legal advice the chairman telephoned round to all the members of the authority. It is quite clear from her affidavit that the situation had been reached in which it would be impossible, in the view of the chairman, to get the business of the authority going without excluding the public from the meeting. She puts it in this way:

> 'We believed that, if the public came, most would not come merely to listen, but with the intention of creating disorder, as we had experienced at the previous meetings, and if the vote appeared unlikely to go their way, of breaking up the meeting before a vote could take place. Obviously, there were those members of the public who were genuinely interested in observing the proceedings, but it was not possible to decide in advance which individuals would cause trouble and which would not. Nor was there any practical means of excluding those who might be identified as intending to disrupt the proceedings. In the light of our experience of previous meetings, there was likewise no practicable way of ensuring that the public would leave if they became disruptive and were asked to leave in the course of the meeting. We did not believe that they would act upon any such instruction, and it would not have been practicable for the police to expel forcibly such a large number of people.'

Those are the reasons for coming to the conclusion that, without excluding the public, the business of the authority could not go on. The chairman telephoned all the members of the authority who could be found, finding out the dates on which they could attend, whether the member wished the meeting to be open to the general public or not and whether he or she wished the press to be there or not. One member could not be contacted but 12 out of the 16 who were contacted decided that they wanted to exclude the public. All the members decided not to exclude the press.

The result was that on 5 December a meeting took place at which the public were excluded. The press were admitted and so was one member of the community health council. In those circumstances the meeting was held without the public apart from the representatives of the press, the community health councillor and one elderly lady who was let in because she was in some difficulty because of the howling mob outside. The business of the meeting proceeded and the first item on the agenda was an item to approve the chairman's action of excluding members of the public other than accredited invited members of the press, and so on. That resolution was debated and passed; not, however, before the particular councillor who had invited the public to take over the meeting in October had, in fact, stated that the meeting was improperly constituted, announced that he would take over the chair, advanced to the chair and placed his hands on the chairman's shoulders. The police had to be called and the councillor removed.

The fact that this particular gentleman had invited the public to take over the previous meeting is duly recorded in the minutes:

'He called on the public present at the meeting to take over the meeting. At this point the authority's proceedings became so badly disrupted that the meeting had to be abandoned. No further business was transacted.'

That is the history of the previous meetings, giving an indication of how political tempers had got into such a state on this contentious issue that neither the members of the public nor, indeed, it appears, even the councillors, could be trusted to behave themselves properly. It is in those circumstances that the applicant in this case applies for judicial review on the grounds that the meeting of 5 December was invalidly convened, that the whole of its deliberations were invalid and asks the court for an order of certiorari to quash it.

Section 1(1) of the Public Bodies (Admission to Meetings) Act 1960, reads:

'Subject to subsection (2) below, any meeting of a local authority or other body exercising public functions, being an authority or other body to which this Act applies, shall be open to the public.'

It is not suggested that this authority is a body to which the Act applies. Section 1(2) and (3) reads:

'(2) A body may, by resolution, exclude the public from a meeting (whether during the whole or part of the proceedings) whenever publicity would be prejudicial to the public interest by reason of the confidential nature of the business to be transacted or for other special reasons stated in the resolution and arising from the nature of that business or of the proceedings; and where such a resolution is passed, this Act shall not require the meeting to be open to the public during proceedings to which the resolution applies.

(3) A body may under subsection (2) above treat the need to receive or consider recommendations or advice from sources other than members, committees or sub-committees of the body as a special reason why publicity would be prejudicial to the public interest, without regard to the subject or purport of the recommendations or advice; but the making by this subsection of express provision for that case shall not be taken to restrict the generality of subsection (2) above in relation to other cases (including in particular cases where the report of a committee or sub-committee of the body is of a confidential nature).'

I shall deal with counsel for the health authority's second submission first, and that is that the actions taken by the chairman and the subsequent ratification of her action by resolution were validly taken under s 1(2). In order to substantiate that he relied on *R v Liverpool City Council, ex p Liverpool Taxi Fleet Operators' Association* [1975] 1 All ER 379, [1975] 1 WLR 701. I am not, in fact, going to read very much of that case for the reason that it became clear, during the course of argument, that counsel was not prepared to argue that it would be right to take that case as concluding the matter, but there are passages in the judgment of Lord Widgery CJ which seem to indicate that in his view, or in the view of the court, that the other special reasons mentioned in s 1(2) could be reasons unconnected with the fact that publicity would be prejudicial to the public interest. I think that it is sufficient for me to say that this point was not argued, as I understand it, in the *Liverpool Taxi* case. When one looks at s 1(2) and, particularly, when one looks at the words in s 1(3), where it is stated that 'A body may under subsection (2) above treat the need to receive or consider recommendations or advice from sources other than members, committees or sub-committees of the body as *a special reason why publicity would be prejudicial to the public interest*', I would be prepared to say that, in my view, that subsection can only apply to some reason which is connected with the fact that publicity would be prejudicial to the public interest. There is no suggestion in this case that the public could have been excluded for that reason so I do not propose to go any further with that argument, as it was not advanced with any particular liking by counsel for the health authority. I shall leave it at that.

Section 1(4) of the Act provides for various matters which should take place when a meeting of a body required by the Act to be open to the public takes place, including public notice of the time and place, the transmission of the agenda to the members, and so on. Paragraph (c) of that subsection is in these terms:

'while the meeting is open to the public, the body shall not have power to exclude members of the public from the meeting . . .'

One then goes on to s 1(8), which reads:

'The provisions of this section shall be without prejudice to any power of exclusion to suppress or prevent disorderly conduct or other misbehaviour at a meeting.'

I do not think that there is anything between counsel for the health authority's argument and counsel for the applicant's argument about the meaning of that subsection. It is quite plain, and indeed both counsel accept it, that this subsection does not create a power. It merely preserves one, and the power it preserves, if it exists, must be looked for elsewhere.

The sort of power it preserves is any *power*, and I emphasise the word, 'of exclusion to suppress or prevent disorderly conduct or other misbehaviour at a meeting'. Although it seems to me quite clear that the word 'exclusion' cannot be taken too widely, it must clearly include the idea of expelling somebody who has already been admitted. It must also, it seems to me, be taken in its primary meaning of preventing somebody coming in at all in the first place. In the words 'power of exclusion to suppress' this sort of conduct, I suppose the word 'exclusion' is used in both senses. When you add the words 'prevent disorderly conduct', it seems to me that the word is there used in its primary meaning as to prevent somebody coming in in the first place. So one of the powers, if it exists, which this subsection preserves is the power to prevent the public or some part of it from coming into the meeting in order to avoid disorderly conduct or other misbehaviour. I do not understand that counsel for the applicant dissents from that proposition because his main proposition is that there is no power in that subsection. There is only one to be preserved. What he says is that, of course, before 1960, meetings of public bodies were not open to the public; at least, they did not have to be open to the public and the power to exclude the public was a power derived not from any statute but from the position that the meetings were normally held on private property. The owner of the property was therefore entitled to exclude the public if he wished to and he was further entitled, if he allowed the public to come in, to revoke any licence to enter that might have been given.

When one is looking at the position before 1960, it must be, it seems to me, that you cannot expect a power, such as the one contended for by counsel for the health authority, to have been exercised before 1960 because the situation did not arise. What one is looking for, if it exists, is a power to prevent the entry of the public in circumstances where disruption or disorderly conduct is apprehended. Counsel says that there is such a common law power and that reference to it can be found in *Doyle v Falconer* (1866) LR 1

PC 328, 16 ER 293. That case was a long way away from this one. It was a case which, put in a nutshell, decided that whilst a colonial legislative house might have the power to expel people from the assembly if they were misbehaving themselves, the assembly had no power to punish for contempt. There is a general statement of law by Sir James Colville which I shall read (at 340–341):

> 'The learned Counsel for the Appellants invoked the principles of the Common Law, and as it must be conceded that the Common Law sanctions the exercise of the prerogative by which the Assembly has been created, the principle of the Common Law, which is embodied in the maxim, *"Quando lex aliquid concedit, concedere videtur et illud, sine quo res ipsa esse non potest,"* applies to the body so created. The question, therefore, is reduced to this: Is the power to punish and commit for contempts committed in its presence one necessary to the existence of such a body as the Assembly of *Dominica*, and the proper exercise of the functions which it is intended to execute? It is necessary to distinguish between a power to punish for a contempt, which is a judicial power, and a power to remove any obstruction offered to the deliberations or proper action of a Legislative body during its sitting, which last power is necessary for self-preservation. If a Member of a Colonial House of Assembly is guilty of disorderly conduct in the House whilst sitting, he may be removed, or excluded for a time, or even expelled; but there is a great difference between such powers and the judicial power of inflicting a penal sentence for the offence. The right to remove for self-security is one thing, the right to inflict punishment is another. The former is, in their Lordships' judgment, all that is warranted by the legal maxim that has been cited, but the latter is not its legitimate consequence ... If the good sense and conduct of the members of Colonial Legislatures prove, as in the present case, insufficient to secure order and decency of debate, the law would sanction the use of that degree of force which might be necessary to remove the person offending from the place of meeting, and to keep him excluded. The same rule would apply, *à fortiori*, to obstructions caused by any person not a member. And whenever the violation of order amounts to a breach of the peace, or other legal offence, recourse may be had to the ordinary tribunals ... But their Lordships, sitting as a Court of Justice, have to consider not what privileges the House of Assembly of *Dominica* ought to have, but what by law it has.'

I do not think that I need, in fact, refer to the other cases. Counsel for the health authority relied on a passage in the judgment of Pollock B in *Lucas v Mason* (1875) LR 10 Exch 251 at 254:

> 'It is no doubt the duty of the chairman of a meeting, where a large body of people are gathered together, to do his best to preserve order, and it is equally the duty of those who are acting as stewards or managers to assist him in so doing, but the nature and extent of this duty on both sides cannot be very closely defined à priori, and must necessarily arise out of, and in character and extent depend upon, the events and emergencies which may from time to time arise.'

Really counsel for the health authority places his argument on those two passages, the first indicating that where, in effect, Parliament has entrusted a statutory duty to a statutory body, it must be assumed that that body has the power to do those things which may be necessary to carry out the duty entrusted to them. Counsel would go on to say that if it becomes apparent that the opening of the meeting to the public means that the business of the authority simply cannot be carried on, because the public is continually disrupting them, then their duty to carry out their statutory duties overrides their duty under the Act to keep meetings open, because there exists in this case the power in a statutory body of that kind to exclude persons in order to prevent such disruption. If the situation comes to such a point that the only practical way of carrying on the business of the authority is to exclude the public then there is the power so to do. Counsel relies on the general statement I have read out that you cannot define a priori the circumstances in which the power can be exercised, in Pollock B's words (at 254)—

'but the nature and extent of this duty on both sides cannot be very closely defined à priori, and must necessarily arise out of, and in character and extent depend upon, the events and emergencies which may from time to time arise.'

When Parliament passed the 1960 Act they had assumed, and had every right to assume, that if the public were granted admission to meetings of public bodies the public would behave themselves. The purpose of giving the public the right to attend meetings is so that they can inform themselves of what is going on. They are not given the right to disrupt meetings and, of course, the right is not a right to participate in anything that is going on, merely to observe and hear what is going on. It is since 1960 that the all too prevalent habit has grown up of political opponents of one kind or another getting their supporters to descend on public meetings to disrupt them by rowdy and noisy behaviour, and shouting down all the arguments which the opponents do not wish to hear. I have come to the conclusion that there simply must exist such a common law power. If this statutory body has a duty to perform it must perform its duty. If it becomes apparent that it cannot perform its duty without excluding the public then, it seems to me, there is a general power such as that referred to by Sir James W Colvile in *Doyle v Falconer*, to exclude the public despite the other words of s 1 of the 1960 Act. Of course, as far as the requirements of public notice and so on are concerned, those only apply to a meeting of a body required by this Act to be open to the public. If the power exists to exclude the public, and it was rightly exercised on this occasion, it is not a meeting of a body required by this Act to be open to the public. It falls within the exception, and notice and so on is not in my view necessary. But that such a power does exist seems to me without question.

There is the second question and that is that this was a power not exercised by the body itself directly in the first place, but by the chairman. There is a number of cases concerned with the powers of chairmen of meetings to maintain order and control discipline at such meetings. The chairman of this authority was not, as I understand it, purporting to act in that fashion. She was purporting to act in her capacity as chairman of the authority, not as chairman of the meeting. Indeed, as chairman of the authority, she is required by statute to abide by the regulations to convene the meetings. Of course, the business she was about when she had the other members telephoned to find out their views about the exclusion of the public was the business of convening a meeting as chairman of the authority. The meeting had not yet occurred so she could not be acting as chairman of the meeting. Counsel for the applicant says that in those circumstances she has no power to do anything on behalf of the authority even though the authority might subsequently indorse or ratify what she has done.

Standing Order No 42 of the standing orders of the authority provides that (and it is headed 'Urgent decisions'):

'Where the Chairman of the Authority (or, in his absence, the Vice-Chairman) authorises urgent action in respect of a matter on behalf of the Authority which would have normally been considered by the Authority itself, such action shall be reported to the next meeting of the Authority.'

Counsel for the applicant maintains that this standing order does not of itself give the chairman any authority to act in between meetings of the health authority itself. He points out that there is nothing in the rest of the standing orders and nothing in the regulations or the schedule to the regulations (which govern the proceedings of these authorities), which entitles the chairman of the authority to act in that way in between meetings of the authority. In fact, no authority can function unless the chairman in between meetings, and in conjunction with the officers, does things which are urgently necessary for the carrying on of the business of the authority. I have no doubt that in many authorities there may well be standing orders delimiting precisely the powers of

the chairmen in those circumstances, but I decline to take the view that Standing Order
No 42, when properly read, does not and was not intended to give the chairman such
authority. It seems to me plain that the standing order is entirely useless unless it was
intended to imply that the chairman of the authority was empowered to authorise urgent
action which would normally have been considered by the authority itself. In this case
this chairman not only considered, as I understand it, that urgent action was required,
but went further and consulted 16 out of the 17 members of the authority about that
urgent action. That urgent action was subsequently ratified by the authority when the
meeting was held. It seems to me clear that the chairman in this case, on this occasion,
was acting as the authority and she was entitled so to do. The action which she took was
properly authorised and confirmed by the authority at its next meeting. In all those
circumstances it seems to me that this is a case where, faced with a difficult situation in
the health authority, the chairman of that authority took the right decision and cannot, I
think, be faulted. There must exist, as I indicated, a power to enable the business of the
authority to be carried on in circumstances where it reasonably appears that, if the
requirements of keeping the meeting open to the public were followed, no business
could possibly be transacted by the authority because the meeting would be disrupted.
Of course, that is a power, it seems to me, which must be exercised bona fide on proper
grounds. The power, if abused, would be subject to judicial review on the *Wednesbury*
principles, just like any other power (see *Associated Provincial Picture Houses Ltd v
Wednesbury Corp* [1947] 2 All ER 680, [1948] 1 KB 223). That the power exists in extreme
circumstances such as these, I have no doubt. The question is whether it exists and not
whether it can be shown to have been exercised in the past. As I say, the general power
exists to see that the business of a statutory authority is carried on, with a power to
exclude the public if that is necessary for the carrying on of the business of the authority.
I find it was necessary in this case.

Had I not come to that conclusion there would still be another question. I have a
supplementary affidavit from the district administrator in which it is said that following
the decisions of the meeting of 5 December a whole lot of matters were implemented,
and properly implemented, about the future of the authority. The question about the
planned level of expenditure, the closure of certain hospitals, the provision of facilities at
other hospitals to take their place, the capital expense involved in those matters, and so
on, have all gone on since 5 December on the basis of the resolutions passed at that
meeting. The only thing complained of by the applicant, in this case, is not that those
resolutions are wrongful. She has declined to take up a position on the merits, as it were,
of the decisions taken. In fact, apart from the fact that it is argued that the meeting itself
was invalid, there has not been any suggestion that the resolutions passed at that meetings
were themselves invalid, illegal or irregular, or anything of that kind. The only complaint
this applicant has, and can possibly have, is not that the resolution were passed, or that
following those resolutions actions were taken, but that she has been, as it were, deprived
of the opportunity of hearing the debate take place before those resolution were passed.

In the circumstances it seems to me that, if this court were faced with a decision
whether or not to quash the meeting and all the resolutions which were passed there, the
balance of convenience, if that is a sensible way of looking at it, seems to me to lie on the
side of the authority. It would be quite wrong, in my view, for this court to exercise its
discretion and grant the relief sought, in that it would result in what could only be
described as a completely irregular situation about the future of the health service in
Brent on the one hand, and merely restoring, to the applicant, on the other hand, the
opportunity to hear the debate about these resolutions. Had I taken a different view
about the existence of these powers I should inevitably have come to the conclusion that
the discretion of the court should be exercised in such a way that while one might have
held that the power did not exist or had not been properly exercised, or something of
that kind, nevertheless no relief could be granted.

As it is, I have come to the conclusion, as I have indicated, that this power exists and that there is nothing wrong with the exclusion of the public in these special circumstances, that the meeting of 5 December, and the resolutions which were passed that day, was a valid meeting and were valid resolutions and that accordingly this application is dismissed. *a*

*Application dismissed.*

Solicitors: *Hallmark Carter & Atkinson* (for the applicant); *Capstick Hamer & Co* (for the *b* health authority).

Raina Levy    Barrister.

# Gaimster v Marlow

*c*

QUEEN'S BENCH DIVISION
LORD LANE CJ, WATKINS LJ AND MACPHERSON J
8 DECEMBER 1983

*Road traffic – Breath test – Device – Print-out produced by device – Admissibility as evidence – Lion Intoximeter 3000 device – Whether print-out contains a 'statement' admissible as evidence – *d* Road Traffic Act 1972, s 10(3)(a).*

*Case stated – Form – Document subject of appeal by case stated – Original document or photocopy to be appended to case.*

The test record print-out issued by an automatic breath-testing device (such as the Lion *e* Intoximeter 3000) used to ascertain the proportion of alcohol in a specimen of breath is a 'statement' of the measurement of alcohol within the meaning of s 10(3)(a)[a] of the Road Traffic Act 1972, since it contains a formal written account of the facts which the accused is entitled to know, even though it may not be immediately intelligible without further explanation. Accordingly, it is admissible as evidence of the proportion of alcohol in an accused's breath on a charge of driving after consuming alcohol in excess of the limit, *f* contrary to s 6(1)[b] of the 1972 Act. In any event, the court is entitled to hear evidence from the police officer who operated the device at the time of the test, if he was a trained operator of the device, in order to explain or interpret the print-out (see p 85 *h j* and p 86 *a* to *c* and *e* to *h*, post).

Where a document such as a computer print-out or other record produced by a mechanical device is the subject of an appeal by way of a case stated, the original *g* document, or a photostat copy of the whole of the original document, should be appended to the case (see p 84 *j* and p 86 *g h*, post).

## Notes
For evidence of the proportion of alcohol in specimens of breath, see 40 Halsbury's Laws (4th edn) para 496.

For the Road Traffic Act 1972, ss 6, 10 (as substituted by the Transport Act 1981, *h* s 25(3), Sch 8), see 51 Halsbury's Statutes (3rd edn) 1427, 1434.

## Cases cited
*Chatenay v Brazilian Submarine Telegraph Co Ltd* [1891] 1 QB 79, CA.
*R v Oakley* (1979) 70 Cr App R 7, CA.
*R v Pettigrew* (1980) 71 Cr App R 39, CA. *j*
*Wetherall v Harrison* [1976] 1 All ER 241, [1976] QB 773, DC.

---

*a*    Section 10(3), so far as material, is set out at p 84 *f g*, post
*b*    Section 6(1), so far as material, provides: 'If a person—(a) drives or attempts to drive a motor vehicle on a road . . . after consuming so much alcohol that the proportion of it in his breath . . . exceeds the prescribed limit he shall be guilty of an offence.'

**Case stated**

Rhona Elizabeth Gaimster, a police officer, appealed by way of case stated by justices for the county of Hampshire, acting in and for the petty sessional division of Basingstoke, in respect of their adjudication as a magistrates' court on 12 September 1983 whereby they dismissed an information against the respondent, Russell John Gary Marlow, of driving after consuming alcohol in excess of the prescribed limit, contrary to s 6(1) of the Road Traffic Act 1972, as substituted by s 25(3) of and Sch 8 to the Transport Act 1981. The facts are set out in the judgment of Lord Lane CJ.

*John Spokes QC* and *Guy Boney* for the appellant.
*Michael Dineen* for the respondent.

**LORD LANE CJ.** This is an appeal by way of case stated by justices for the county of Hampshire in the petty sessional division of Basingstoke. The respondent to the appeal is Russell John Gary Marlow.

The circumstances which gave rise to this case are these. On 18 May 1983 an information was preferred by the appellant, a police officer, against Marlow, the respondent, alleging that he at Basingstoke on 11 May 1983 drove a motor car on a public road after consuming so much alcohol that the proportion of it in his breath was 111 microgrammes of alcohol in 100 ml of breath, which exceeds the prescribed limit of 35 microgrammes per 100 ml of breath. That offence was contrary to s 6(1) of the Road Traffic Act 1972 (as substituted by s 25(3) of and Sch 8 to the Transport Act 1981).

The case was heard by the justices on 12 September 1983. The evidence called on behalf of the prosecution was that of a Sgt Younghusband. He gave evidence that on 11 May at Basingstoke he had carried out a test of the respondent's breath using an automatic breath-testing device known as the Lion Intoximeter 3000. He produced a document headed 'Test Record' and he identified that as having been issued by the Intoximeter and signed in two places by himself on that date, 11 May 1983.

Objection at that point was taken by counsel for the respondent, on the basis that the document headed 'Test Record' was not 'a statement' within the meaning of s 10(3)(a) of the Road Traffic Act 1972 (as substituted by s 25(3) of and Sch 8 to the Transport Act 1981) and therefore was inadmissible as evidence of the proportion of alcohol in the respondent's breath.

The justices having set out the contentions of each side in their case, then set out the basis on which they upheld that submission made by the respondent's counsel. It is necessary in this case that I should set out those reasons from the case as given:

'(a) The word "statement" had to be given its ordinary meaning and . . . the words "automatically produced by the machine" in section 10(3)(a) were simply descriptive of the means by which statements had to be produced so as to gain admissibility under section 10(3)(a). Production by an automatic device could not presuppose that "a statement" must result. (b) "A statement" must be understandable or comprehensible by an ordinary person. In the normal course, explanation of the meaning of an otherwise incomprehensible statement could be given by the person who made the statement but not by others without infringing the rule against hearsay. Words or symbols could be interpreted by a person qualified, but this [was] limited to literal translation. (c) The "Test Record" document identified by Sergeant Younghusband was not capable of being understood or comprehended by an ordinary person without explanation. In particular, nowhere was there any clear indication that the letters and figures in the document referred to the proportion of alcohol in the respondent's breath, the only evidence made admissible by section 10(3). (d) The words "purporting to be a statement" in section 10(3) referred to the document itself and were not to be read as allowing for a different standard of evidence in the contents of the document. If this were not so, any data, no matter how incomprehensible, would have been made admissible by section 10(3). (e) We had to discount special knowledge obtained during demonstrations at the local police station at the time of the introduction of the automatic breath testing devices. This knowledge was not available to an ordinary person, [was] not evidence before us and [was] not facts of which judicial notice could be taken. (f) A statement under section 10(3)(a) had to contain all the facts necessary to prove the entire matters set out in section 10(3) i.e. "the proportion of alcohol in a specimen of (the respondent's) breath . . .". We considered that section 10(3) also had an exclusionary effect in that, once the appellant had chosen to prove the requisite matters by way of the statement, it was not open to her to cure defects in it by calling extraneous evidence. (g) Even if wrong in this last conclusion, we considered that evidence by the police officer who had conducted the breath test as to the meaning of the "statement" would have been inadmissible hearsay. It would have gone beyond a literal reiteration of the letters and numbers, thus purporting to supplement or explain the contents. Viewed as a question of "interpretation", we considered that the police officer would not have been able to interpret the "statement" without repeating what others had told him about the meaning of it. (h) The supposed purpose of the legislation could not be taken into account if that purpose had not been met.'

The justices then go on to point out that since the appellant was offering no further evidence, they on that basis acceded to the respondent's submission that there was no case for him to answer.

The justices now ask two questions of this court:

'(i) Were we correct in law in treating the "Test Record" document as inadmissible as evidence of the proportion of alcohol in the respondent's breath in that it was not "a statement" within the meaning of section 10(3)(a) of the Road Traffic Act 1972? (ii) Were we correct in law in excluding the evidence of the police officer who conducted the test to explain or interpret the meaning of the contents of the document?'

It is necessary first of all to set out the terms of s 10 of the 1972 Act, as substituted by the Transport Act 1981. The material part of s 10, as already indicated, is s 10(3)(a) and it reads as follows:

'Evidence of the proportion of alcohol . . . in a specimen of breath . . . may, subject to subsections (5) and (6) below, be given by the production of a document or documents purporting to be whichever of the following is appropriate, that is to say—(a) a statement automatically produced by the device by which the proportion of alcohol in a specimen of breath was measured and a certificate signed by a constable (which may but need not be contained in the same document as the statement) that the statement relates to a specimen provided by the accused at the date and time shown in the statement . . .'

The only other part of the statute to which it is necessary to make reference is s 12 (as substituted by s 25(3) of and Sch 8 to the Transport Act 1981), which is the definition section, and there the words 'the prescribed limit' are defined, and they mean, as far as we are concerned, '35 microgrammes of alcohol in 100 millilitres of breath'.

The first point taken by counsel on behalf of the respondent is that the only part of the piece of paper, to use a neutral term, issued by the machine called the 'Test Record', to which it is proper to have regard when considering the analysis of breath, in other words the only part which can be considered as 'the statement', is the part which ends immediately above the operator's name. All that the court can have regard to are the figures produced of the test, that is to say, 'Test UG% Time' down to, in this particular case, 'STD 33 01·40 GMT'. We note that in the case stated the magistrates confined their reference to the document to that part of it only. Whether they had regard to the rest of the document is not clear.

I should like to say in general that it is essential in cases of this sort that where a document as material as this is going to be the subject of a case stated, the original document, or a photostat copy of the whole of the original document, should be appended to the case.

We have now been supplied with the full document, and it is important that this court should make clear what the rest of the document, not cited by the magistrates, contains:

'Operator Name = Younghusband PS 187 I certify that in this statement reading one relates to the first specimen of breath provided by the subject named above, and reading two to the second, at the date and time shown herein.'

Then comes the signature of Sgt Younghusband and the word 'signature' underneath. Before the part cited by the magistrates in their case, and the only part, come these words:

'Test Record Lion Intox 3000/5920 Basingstoke Police Hampshire Constab. Wed May 11, 1983 Subject name = Marlow Russell John DOB = 26 10 57',

then plainly in the sergeant's handwriting, 'Refused to sign', and then once again Sgt Younghusband's signature. That is the document which was, or should have been, before the magistrates and the whole of it should have been the subject of their deliberation and their decision.

The submission made by counsel for the respondent, and his principal submission in this case, is that it is only the part which the magistrates set out, and not the second half of the document which I have read, which can be considered as being 'the statement'. He goes on that if one considers that particular document and that part of it only, that is not intelligible and is therefore not a 'statement'. Consequently, he submits, the magistrates were correct in the conclusion at which they arrived.

It is necessary, before I turn to consider the technical aspect of that argument, to look at reality. We are dealing with the real world and not some fanciful world. The subject of such a case as this, the respondent here, Mr Marlow, knows that he has been breathalysed at the roadside and presumably knows why. He is being taken to the police station. His car has presumably been left behind, or other arrangements made with regard to that. He knows he has had two tests in the police station. He knows, if he is compos mentis, that it is all to do with the alcohol in his breath and the percentage of alcohol in his breath. He has been standing, necessarily, alongside or in front of the machine while he delivers his breath sample into it, and he has been there watching it operate. He knows that he has given two breath samples. Presumably he has seen the piece of paper come out of the machine. He has been handed a copy. He has been asked to sign it. In this case he has refused to sign it.

He is told he is going to be charged and if at that stage he is not capable of reading the document, or if, possibly, he is unable to read it at all, then he can put it in his pocket and go away and get help, if necessary, or, when he recovers his senses, can read it for himself. He then looks at the document, and if he looks at the document it seems to us, taken as a whole, that the document is plainly intelligible. Indeed although the justices say, looking at the part they looked at, it is not intelligible without explanation, we would beg leave to question that, although of course we are bound by their finding of fact on that particular issue.

Is it then to be said that this document can be split in two halves, and has to be rigidly compartmentalised, so that you are not allowed to look at the second half, but only at the first half, that part only being a statement? I think not. It seems to me that, as the Act allows, this document as a whole contains both a statement and a certificate. It contains the certificate that the specimen has been provided by the respondent as the Act requires. It also contains an explanation, so far as one is required, of the meaning of the figures. I read it again: 'reading one relates to the first specimen of breath provided by the subject named above, and reading two to the second, at the date and time shown herein.' That comprises the statutory certificate and, if necessary, an explanation of what the document means.

Having read that, the holder of the document looks at it, and where he sees 'One', against 'One' he sees the figure '114'. He casts his eye up to the top of that column and sees percentage at the top, and the same with 'Two'. Against that is '111'. He casts his eye up again and sees percentage at the top. In my judgment it is abundantly clear, or would be abundantly clear to anyone in his senses, precisely what that document meant, namely that he was being tested against the statutory limit of 35 microgrammes in the definition section which I have read, and, it is to be observed, that in the first test exceeded it, at 114, and in the second test exceeded it rather less, at 111. This seems to me perfectly plainly to be a document purporting to be a statement automatically produced and it is also a certificate signed by the constable, the statement relating to a specimen provided by the respondent. The one document contains in its second part the explanation and meaning of the first part. That is all part of the document and part of the statement.

So far as the first point of counsel for the respondent is concerned, namely rigid separation of what he says to be the statement and what he says to be the certificate, that fails. I would, if necessary, go further. It seems to me that a statement in the circumstances of this particular case is a formal written account of facts providing the subject with information that he is entitled to have. The fact that to some people, or even to most people, it may not be immediately intelligible without explanation does not prevent it being a statement.

There are further subsidiary points taken by counsel for the respondent. The first point is that there is no reference in the statement to 'alcohol'. But once again against the reality of the matter, it is perfectly plain to everyone, even if the words 'Lion Intoximeter' mean nothing to the person tested, that the whole object of the exercise is to test the percentage of alcohol in his breath. There is nothing to my mind in that point.

Secondly, it is objected that the 'UG%', which is the heading of a column, is again unintelligible. The English 'U' is the nearest the machine can get to the Greek 'μ', and 'UG' is an abbreviation for microgramme. But even if that is not known, alongside that is the percentage sign which is perfectly plain. If he does not know 35 is the limit imposed by the law, then he ought to know. There is nothing in that point.

The final point with which I feel it necessary to deal, because the reference to s 182 of the Road Traffic Act 1972 does not seem to take this matter any further forward or backward, is the question whether the justices would be entitled to have evidence as to the meaning of these signs explained to them by a police officer. The answer to that is the answer to any question of this sort: if the officer is shown to be a trained operator of the machine and knows what the meaning of these signs is, and that is proved by way of evidence, then it seems to me there is no reason why he should not give evidence, if required (it seldom will be required as I see it) to explain the meaning of these signs.

It follows from what I have said that the answers to the two questions posed by the justices are that they were not correct in law in treating the 'Test Record' document as inadmissible; and so far as the second question is concerned, 'Were we correct in law in excluding the evidence of the police officer who conducted the test to explain or interpret the meaning of the contents of the document?', the answer to that is that if he had been shown to be a trained operator of the machine, they were wrong in that conclusion too.

Consequently I would allow this appeal.

**WATKINS LJ.** I agree and have nothing to add.

**MACPHERSON J.** I agree and have nothing to add.

*Appeal allowed. Case remitted to justices to continue hearing. Leave to appeal to the House of Lords refused.*

*16 December. The court refused to certify under s 1(2) of the Administration of Justice Act 1960 that a point of law of general public importance was involved in its decision.*

Solicitors: *R J Gwilliam*, Winchester (for the appellant); *Emersons*, Basingstoke (for the respondent).

N P Metcalfe Esq     Barrister.

# Castle v Cross

QUEEN'S BENCH DIVISION
STEPHEN BROWN LJ AND KENNEDY J
17 JULY 1984

*Road traffic – Breath test – Device – Analysis of breath specimen by approved device – Whether print-out produced by device at conclusion of analysis admissible evidence of failure to provide proper specimen – Whether print-out product of a mechanical device constituting real evidence at common law – Road Traffic Act 1972, s 8(7).*

On the trial of an information alleging an offence under s 8(7)[a] of the Road Traffic Act 1972 of failing without reasonable excuse to provide a specimen of breath when required to do so, the test record print-out of an automatic breath-testing device (such as the Lion Intoximeter 3000) used to ascertain the proportion of alcohol in specimens of breath is admissible as evidence, since the print-out constitutes the product of a mechanical device which, at common law, falls into the category of real evidence (see p 91 *c d j* and p 92 *a b* and *d* to *f*, post).

Dicta of Simon P in *The Statue of Liberty* [1968] 2 All ER at 196 and of Lord Lane CJ in *R v Wood* (1982) 76 Cr App R at 27 applied.

### Notes

For failure to provide specimen, see 40 Halsbury's Laws (4th edn) para 493.

For evidence of the proportion of alcohol in a specimen of breath, see ibid para 496.

For admissibility of statements produced by computers, see 17 ibid para 59.

For the Road Traffic Act 1972, s 8 (as substituted by the Transport Act 1981, s 25(3), Sch 8), see 51 Halsbury' Statutes (3rd edn) 1432.

### Cases referred to in judgments

*Myers v DPP* [1964] 2 All ER 881, [1965] AC 1001, [1964] 3 WLR 145.

*R v Wood* (1982) 76 Cr App R 23, CA.

*Statue of Liberty, The, Sapporo Maru (owners) v Statue of Liberty (owners)* [1968] 2 All ER 195, [1968] 1 WLR 739.

### Case stated

Douglas Castle appealed by way of a case stated by the justices for the county of Hertford acting for the petty sessional division of Welwyn in respect of their adjudication as a magistrates' court sitting at Hatfield on 2 March 1984. On 11 November 1983 the appellant preferred an information against the respondent, Nicholas Sidney Cross, alleging that on 25 October 1983 at Welwyn Garden City police station the respondent, being a person who had been driving a motor vehicle on a road in Welwyn Garden City and having been required, pursuant to s 8 of the Road Traffic Act 1972 (as substituted by s 25 of and Sch 8 to the Transport Act 1981), to provide a specimen of breath for analysis by means of the Lion Intoximeter 3000 device, failed without reasonable excuse to provide such a specimen, contrary to s 8(7) of the 1972 Act (as so substituted). At the close of the prosecution's case the justices upheld a submission of no case to answer made on behalf of the respondent and dismissed the information. The question for the opinion of the High Court was whether, on the trial of an information alleging an offence under s 8(7) of the 1972 Act of failing without reasonable excuse to provide a specimen when required to do so, pursuant to s 8(1)(a) of that Act, for analysis by the Lion Intoximeter 3000 device, the 'test record' print-out from that device was admissible in evidence. The facts are set out in the judgment of Stephen Brown LJ.

_____

*a* Section 8(7), provides: 'A person who, without reasonable excuse, fails to provide a specimen when required to do so in pursuance of this section shall be guilty of an offence.'

*J P Wadsworth QC* and *Neill Stewart* for the appellant.
*Alan Beaven* for the respondent.

**STEPHEN BROWN LJ.** This is a prosecutor's appeal by way of case stated from the
decision of the justices acting for the petty sessional division of Welwyn sitting at Hatfield
in the county of Hertford on 2 March 1984 when they dismissed, on finding no case to
answer, a charge against the respondent of failing to provide a specimen of breath for
analysis without reasonable excuse, contrary to s 8 of the Road Traffic Act 1972 (as
substituted by s 25(3) of and Sch 8 to the Transport Act 1981).

The short facts which gave rise to that summons are set out in the statement of the
justices' case. The respondent was the driver of a motor car in Welwyn Garden City on
Tuesday night, 25 October 1983. The car was seen by a police officer to be travelling fast
and it braked harshly on the approach to a roundabout. The car was stopped and the
respondent, who was the driver, was requested by the police constable to provide breath
for a roadside breath test, administered by an Alcotest 80 device. He failed fully to inflate
the bag. Some of the crystals, apparently, had changed colour and the officer came to the
conclusion that he had failed to provide the sample for that test. He was arrested and
taken to the police station. There, after the facts leading to his arrest had been reported
to the station sergeant, Sgt Martin, he was required to provide two specimens of breath
on an approved Intoximeter 3000 breath-testing machine in accordance with the
provisions of the Road Traffic Act 1972, s 8. It is to be observed that, when specimens are
required at a police station, they are referred to as 'specimens' to distinguish them from
the sample which is requested at the roadside under s 7.

The facts as found by the justices were that, on being required to provide two
specimens of breath on the approved Intoximeter 3000 breath-testing machine, the
respondent agreed to do so, and the sergeant then instructed him to blow into the
mouthpiece of the machine with one breath until he was told to stop. He was allowed
four attempts. On the first attempt the respondent blew air through the mouthpiece
into the machine but it plainly did not produce any result. A second test was then
administered with the same result. A third and fourth attempt were then made by the
respondent. The justices record: '. . . in the third the result was inconclusive and on the
fourth air went through the mouthpiece into the machine', but no result, it would
appear, was achieved.

The justices found that the machine was 'fitted with a visual display panel' but that no
clear evidence was adduced before them 'as to the precise state of the visual display panel
during each of the respondent's attempts'. They record: 'The Intoximeter 3000 produced
a print out at the conclusion of the test being a test record of the tests carried out on the
machine.'

Following that, Sgt Martin reported the respondent with a view to prosecution for an
offence under s 8(7) of the 1972 Act of having 'without reasonable excuse, [failed] to
provide a specimen when required to do so in pursuance of [the] section'.

On behalf of the respondent it was submitted that the print-out from the machine
which came forth at the conclusion of the fourth attempt was not admissible in evidence,
that it was hearsay and should not be admitted in evidence. The court has before it the
certificate with the print-out which, in accordance with the procedure, is affixed to that
particular certificate recording the test. It specifies, in accordance with the requirements,
the operating instructions of this machine, the date of the test, the subject, a signature
and the time when the test took place. It records: 'One no sample.' That means, as the
court understands it, that the machine did not have a sufficient sample of breath of the
deep kind, from the deep lung, which is required to enable it to perform an analysis.
But, as I have already said, the magistrates upheld a submission made on behalf of the
respondent to this appeal that that certificate was inadmissible.

The justices found the following:

'(a) We were of the opinion that the statement produced by the Intoximeter 3000
was a statement made by a machine akin to a computer. (b) The machine was

required to assess sufficiency of breath, analyse the quantity of alcohol in the breath and convert that information into figures in statement form. (c) In our submission therefore the Intoximeter contributes to its own knowledge. (d) We noted that Parliament had specifically legislated to overcome this evidential difficulty by a specific statutory authorisation in Section 10(3) of the Road Traffic Act, 1972 (as amended) but that the Section only applied to proceedings under Section 5 and Section 6 of the Act and not to proceedings under Section 8(7). (e) We had our attention drawn to Section 12(3) of the Act dealing with sufficiency of breath for analysis but felt on the facts found by us that the appellant was unable to satisfy any reasonable Bench of Magistrates that the specimen was not sufficient to enable the test or analysis to be carried out. (f) Accordingly, we upheld a submission of no case to answer made on behalf of the respondent and dismissed the information.'

They ask the following question for the opinion of this court:

'On the trial of an information alleging an offence under Section 8(7) Road Traffic Act, 1972 (as substituted by Section 25(3) of, and Schedule 8 to, Transport Act, 1981) of failing without reasonable excuse to provide a specimen when required to do so in pursuance of Section 8 of the said Act where the defendant had been required by a Constable under Section 8(1)(a) of the said Act to provide two specimens of breath for an analysis by means of a Lion Intoximeter 3000, whether the "test record" print out from that device is admissible in evidence?'

By the agreement of both counsel, the court has had placed before it the Lion Intoximeter 3000 Operator Handbook produced by the manufacturers. Our attention has been drawn to the breath test procedure, which sets out very clearly the sequence of events which has to take place if the correct procedure is to be adopted:

'Step 1—Press "Start" Button; Step 2—Enter Operator Name; Step 3—Enter Operator Code; Step 4—Enter Subject's Name; Step 5—Enter Subject's Date of Birth; Step 6—Stand By; Step 7—Purge and Blank Cycle; Step 8—First Calibration Check; Step 9—Purge and Blank Cycle; Step 10—Attach Mouthpiece; Step 11— Subject's First Breath Sample [and so on].'

It is clear that the procedure is set in motion and supervised by a person trained as an operator for that particular purpose, ie a police officer. There is no suggestion in this case, and indeed no finding, to suggest that the correct procedure was not adopted. It is also clear that the justices' case does not record any finding or indeed submission that the Intoximeter machine was in any way defective.

Counsel on behalf of the appellant prosecutor reminds us of the passage in *Cross on Evidence* (5th edn, 1979) p 47 headed 'Mechanical Instruments' which states:

'A presumption which serves the same purpose of saving the time and expense of calling evidence as that served by the maxim *omnia praesumuntur rite esse acta* is the presumption that mechanical instruments were in order when they were used. In the absence of evidence to the contrary, the courts will presume that stopwatches and speedometers and traffic lights were in order at the material time; but the instrument must be one of a kind as to which it is common knowledge that they are more often than not in working order.'

The last sentence is not adopted by *Phipson on Evidence* (13th edn, 1982) p 209, para 12–34, but the principle which is there accurately set out in the view of this court is that, 'In the absence of evidence to the contrary, the courts will presume that [mechanical instruments] were in order at the material time'. As I have already observed, there is no evidence recorded in the magistrates' case and certainly no finding to suggest that this Intoximeter 3000 was defective or might have been defective at the relevant time.

Counsel for the appellant submits that the justices were in error in ruling that the statement on the print-out 'One no sample' was inadmissible. He submits that there is no logical distinction between the position in this case and that in many cases where sophisticated and less sophisticated mechanical devices or instruments are used. He cites *The Statue of Liberty* [1968] 2 All ER 195, [1968] 1 WLR 739 for the proposition that the results of mechanical devices and electrical devices which are achieved without human intervention are admissible in evidence, that they are real evidence.

It is relevant to cite the final paragraph of the judgment of Simon P, when he stated his view that in the case which he was deciding, which related to a record made by a radar set at a shore radar station, the record was admissible in that case concerning liability for a collision at sea. He cited *Cockle's Cases and Statutes on Evidence* (10th edn, 1963) p 348 (see [1968] 2 All ER 195 at 196, [1968] 1 WLR 739 at 740):

> '"Real evidence is evidence afforded by the production of physical objects for inspection or other examination by the court." If tape recordings are admissible, it seems that a photograph of radar reception is equally admissible—or, indeed, any other type of photograph. It would be an absurd distinction that a photograph should be admissible if the camera were operated manually by a photographer, but not if it were operated by a trip or clock mechanism. Similarly, if evidence of weather conditions were relevant, the law would affront common sense if it were to say that those could be proved by a person who looked at a barometer from time to time, but not by producing a barograph record. So, too, with other types of dial recordings. Again, cards from clocking-in-and-out machines are frequently admitted in accident cases. The law is bound now to take cognisance of the fact that mechanical means replace human effort.'

Counsel for the appellant submits that that is the correct basis on which to approach consideration of the status of the print-out from this particular machine. He submits that the fact that it is a sophisticated machine which depends for part of its operation on what has been described as computer control does not set it in a different class from other sophisticated mechanical devices and instruments of the kind referred to by Simon P in *The Statue of Liberty*.

Counsel for the appellant further relies on *R v Wood* (1982) 76 Cr App R 23. That was a case dealing with a different set of circumstances and was in fact considering the application of s 1(1) of the Criminal Evidence Act 1965. It was a case of handling stolen goods. The point was consideration of the method of proof of the origin of certain processed metals which had been stolen in transit from the processors and to tie up the original processed metals with metals found in the possession of the appellant, Mr Wood. Part of the method by which the Crown attempted to prove that chain, and to relate the metals found in the possession of the appellant with those actually stolen from the processors, was by certain records achieved by computer calculations. It involved an elaborate analysis of the various metals in order to seek to identify them and marry them up. The contention was that the computer print-outs produced in that case were inadmissible as hearsay evidence at common law and not authorised under the Criminal Evidence Act 1965.

The court decided (at 23–24) that whilst—

> 'the printouts were inadmissible under section 1(1) of the Criminal Evidence Act 1965 because they had been prepared for the purpose of the prosecution of the appellant and not in the course of a trade or business as required by subsection (1)(a); nevertheless . . . the computer in the instant case had been used as a calculator—it was a tool and did not contribute to its own knowledge, and was properly treated as a piece of real evidence the actual proof of which depended upon the testimony of the witnesses; thus, the answers produced by the computer were in principle admissible at common law and were properly proved . . .'

In the course of giving the judgment of the court, Lord Lane CJ said (at 27):

> '[Counsel for the appellant] submitted that there was a difference in kind between the measuring device (even a sophisticated one) and this computer. He also suggested that there was a difference in kind between a mathematician who used a slide rule

and one who used a calculating computer. We do not agree. This computer was rightly described as a tool. It did not contribute its own knowledge. It merely did a sophisticated calculation which could have been done manually by the chemist and was in fact done by the chemists using the computer programmed by Mr. Kellie whom the Crown called as a witness. The fact that the efficiency of a device is dependent on more than one person does not make any difference in kind. Virtually every device will involve the persons who made it, the persons who calibrated, programmed or set it up (for example with a clock the person who set it to the right time in the first place) and the person who uses or observes the device. In each particular case how many of these people it is appropriate to call must depend on the facts of, and the issues raised and concessions made in that case.'

In point of fact, Myers v DPP [1964] 2 All ER 881, [1965] AC 1001 was distinguished in that judgment.

It seems to this court that in this case the Intoximeter was in terms a tool, albeit a sophisticated tool, which was operated by the police sergeant who was trained in the appropriate procedure. There has been no challenge recorded in the case to the efficiency of the machine or instrument and there is no finding that it was in any way defective. Accordingly, it seems to this court that the result in the form of the print-out was the product of a mechanical device which falls into the same category of real evidence as that indicated by Simon P in The Statue of Liberty [1968] 2 All ER 195, [1968] 1 WLR 739.

Sophisticated arguments were addressed to the justices and it may be, if I may say so, that they were blinded by science. They used the phrase in para 6(c) of the case: 'In our submission therefore the Intoximeter contributes to its own knowledge.' That phrase is not explained. It seems to this court that it may be a misunderstanding of the headnote in R v Wood (1982) 76 Cr App R 23 at 23–24, to which I have referred.

Quite plainly the position in this particular instance was that this respondent was correctly required to give two specimens of breath for the purpose of analysis by the approved instrument, the Intoximeter 3000, and that he went through the motions of so doing but in fact failed to give a sufficient sample. That was observed by the police sergeant but apparently he was prevented from giving that evidence because of an objection made by the respondent's counsel that such evidence would be hearsay. But it seems to this court quite plain that he was in a position to say, as the trained operator of the machine, that the result of the respondent's attempt was a failure to deliver sufficient breath into the machine to permit it to carry out the required analysis. The justices held that there was no case to answer. It seems to this court that this was a misunderstanding of the position.

Counsel for the respondent has argued forcefully that the potential for computer error renders the consideration of evidence stemming from a computer particularly sensitive and places it into a separate class in relation to its admissibility. He has referred to the relevant statute in Australia and to a case heard in the courts of the State of South Australia. It does not seem to this court that they can substantially assist in this problem, which is essentially whether this evidence which was sought to be given was admissible at common law.

The question of computer error does not enter into the ambit of this appeal. As I have already indicated, the justices made no finding which would permit the inference that the Intoximeter was in any way defective or not in proper working order. It has to be assumed, certainly for the purposes of the submission of no case to answer, that it was in proper working order and that the proper procedure was followed.

I, for my part, am unable to accept the submissions made by counsel for the respondent. They were extremely wide in their ambit but, in my judgment, did not go to the central issue, which was simply one of admissibility. Other authorities were referred to by counsel for the appellant which in fact are in line with The Statue of Liberty [1968] 2 All ER 195, [1968] 1 WLR 739 and with what I have indicated can be derived from R v Wood (1982) 76 Cr App R 23.

In my judgment, this print-out was admissible and, furthermore, the controlling, operating station sergeant ought to have been permitted to give evidence as to what he had observed and as to the result of what he observed, interpreting if necessary the print-out and supplementing it by saying that it meant no sufficient sample, just as if he had been looking at a dial where the pressure and degree of effort was recorded.

The justices, in my judgment, were in error and I would allow this appeal. I would answer the question which they pose: '. . . whether the "test record" print out from [the] device is admissible in evidence' with the word Yes. I would, therefore, allow the appeal and remit the case to the justices for them to continue to hear the case.

I should add that, because the case was stopped at the close of the evidence for the prosecution, the respondent was not given the opportunity of developing any reasonable cause which there might or might not have been for failing to provide the specimen of breath. All that the court at that stage had to consider was whether a specimen of breath had been provided. In s 12(3) of the Road Traffic Act 1972 (as substituted by the Transport Act 1981, s 25(3), Sch 8, and amended by the Transport Act 1982, s 59), the test which they should have applied is set out:

> 'A person does not provide a specimen of breath for a breath test or for analysis unless the specimen is sufficient to enable the test or the analysis to be carried out and provided in such a way as to enable the objective of the test or analysis to be satisfactorily achieved.'

In my judgment that was what they had to consider at that stage of the case and plainly there was a case for them to consider. It follows furthermore that I regard the reference to s 10(2) of the 1972 Act to be irrelevant to considerations in this case.

I have dealt with this matter on the basis of common law principles. That, in my judgment, is what this matter amounts to.

**KENNEDY J.** I agree. The central issue here is whether the police sergeant, who was called as a witness and who invited this respondent to provide a specimen of breath, was entitled to rely on the indications he obtained from the Intoximeter 3000 machine when he said that the respondent had not provided the specimen. In my judgment also he was entitled to rely on those indications because they amounted to real evidence.

This machine, as it was used in relation to this respondent, was indistinguishable in principle from, for example, a speedometer or a calculator. Of course, where a computer is used in respect of its memory function, it is possible to envisage cases where it it might fall foul of the rule against hearsay. But that is not this case.

I observe in looking at the form (with a copy of which we have been provided) that it says, in handwriting which may be that of the sergeant: 'The accused made a very poor attempt to blow into the machine. He would blow for approximately two seconds and this he kept repeating.' As I understand it, what was said to us by counsel during the course of this case was that that evidence of the sergeant was not in fact given because counsel for the respondent was able to persuade the lower court that the evidence of the sergeant, as to his own observations, was objectionable. That submission made by him was upheld.

Speaking for myself, if the sergeant was able to say what appears on the face of the form, it seems to me that that is evidence which he plainly could have given without any reference whatsoever to the Intoximeter and that is evidence which he should have been allowed to give.

*Appeal allowed. Case remitted to justices to continue hearing.*

Solicitors: *Wynter Davies & Lee*, Hertford (for the appellant); *Breeze & Wyles*, Enfield (for the respondent).

Hilary Kindelan    Barrister.

# Allen v Allen

FAMILY DIVISION
BOOTH J
15 NOVEMBER 1983, 16 APRIL, 25 JUNE 1984

*Husband and wife – Variation or discharge of maintenance order – Variation of order registered in magistrates' court – Application by husband for variation of order and remission of sums due under it – Refusal of justices to vary order and remit arrears – Husband having right of appeal by way of notice of motion against refusal 'to vary the order' – Appeal by notice of motion against refusal to vary order and remit arrears – Whether court having jurisdiction to entertain appeal against refusal to remit arrears – Whether magistrates' power to vary order including power to remit arrears – Maintenance Orders Act 1958, s 4(7) – Magistrates' Courts Act 1980, ss 95, 111 – RSC Ords 55, 56, r 5(2).*

When the husband fell into arrears of periodical payments under an order made in divorce proceedings and registered under the Maintenance Orders Act 1958 the wife applied, by way of complaint under s 1 of that Act, to a magistrates' court for enforcement of the order. By a separate complaint the husband requested the magistrates to vary the order under s 1 of the 1958 Act, by reducing the amount payable under it, and to exercise their power under s 95[a] of the Magistrates' Courts Act 1980 to remit the arrears. The magistrates dismissed his complaint and on the wife's complaint ordered him to pay the arrears in addition to the current periodical payments. He appealed under s 4(7)[b] of the 1958 Act, by way of notice of motion under RSC Ord 55[c], against the magistrates' refusal to vary the order or to remit the arrears. Since s 4(7) of the 1958 Act only conferred a right of appeal against a magistrates' court's refusal 'to vary a registered order', the question arose whether the court could also consider the magistrates' refusal to remit the arrears or whether the only method of appeal on that matter was by way of a case stated under s 111[d] of the 1980 Act and RSC Ord 56, r 5(2)[e].

**Held** – A magistrates' court's power under the 1958 Act to vary a maintenance order registered under that Act included by implication the power which the court had under s 95 of the 1980 Act to remit arrears owing under the order. Consequently, the right of appeal given by s 4(7) of the 1958 Act covered not only an appeal against a refusal to vary the order itself but also an appeal against a refusal to remit arrears under s 95 of the 1980 Act. Since the magistrates had refused to remit the arrears when refusing to vary the order and not when considering the wife's complaint to enforce the order, it followed that the husband was entitled to appeal under s 4(7) by way of notice of motion against both the refusal to vary the order and the refusal to remit the arrears. The court therefore had jurisdiction to deal with both aspects of the appeal (see p 98 *a b* and *h* to p 99*d*, post).

### Notes
For the variation or discharge or registered order, see 13 Halsbury's Laws (4th edn) para 1238, and for cases on the subject, see 27(2) Digest (Reissue) 1015–1022, 8126–8160.

For the Maintenance Orders Act 1958, ss 1, 4, see 17 Halsbury's Statutes (3rd edn) 294, 297.

For the Magistrates' Courts Act 1980, ss 95, 111, see 50(2) ibid 1525, 1538.

---

*a*   Section 95 is set out at p 96 *c*, post
*b*   Section 4(7), so far as material, is set out at p 96 *f*, post
*c*   Order 55, so far as material, provides:
'1.—(1) . . . this Order shall apply to every appeal which by or under any enactment lies to the High Court from any court . . .
3.—(1) An appeal to which this Order applies shall be by way of rehearing and must be brought by originating motion . . .'
*d*   Section 111, so far as material, is set out at p 96 *h j*, post
*e*   Rule 5(2), so far as material, is set out at p 97 *a b*, post

**Cases referred to in judgment**
*Michael v Gowland* [1977] 2 All ER 328, [1977] 1 WLR 296, DC.
*Miller v Miller* [1960] 3 All ER 115, [1961] P 1, [1960] 3 WLR 658.
*Mills v Mills* (1982) 12 Fam Law 174.

**Cases also cited**
*Blackedge v Blackedge* [1913] P 9, DC.
*Grocock v Grocock* [1920] 1 KB 1, DC.
*Manders v Manders* [1897] 1 QB 474, DC.
*O'Kelly v Trust House Forte plc* [1983] 3 All ER 456, [1984] QB 90, CA.
*Peagram v Peagram* [1926] 2 KB 165, [1926] All ER Rep 261, DC.
*Pilcher v Pilcher (No 2)* [1956] 1 All ER 463, DC, [1956] 1 WLR 298.
*Ruther v Ruther* [1903] 2 KB 270, DC.
*Snape v Snape* (1983) 13 Fam Law 210.

**Appeal**
Douglas John Allen (the husband) appealed, by way of notice of motion, against an order
of the Wirral Borough Magistrates' Court, dated 21 February 1983, whereby it dismissed
his application for an order (i) varying down an order made by that court on 28 April
1971 (which was itself a variation of an order made by the Birkenhead County Court and
registered in the Wirral Borough Magistrates' Court) whereby he was required to pay
periodical payments to the respondent, Phyllis Mary Allen (the wife), at the rate of £4
weekly, and (ii) remitting the sums due under that order. On 15 November 1983 Booth
J allowed the appeal in so far as it related to the refusal of the magistrates' court to vary
the periodical payments order and reduced the amount payable under it to 5p per
annum. She adjourned for further argument the appeal in so far as it related to the
magistrates' refusal to remit the arrears, and the report is concerned only with that aspect
of the appeal. The facts are set out in the judgment.

*Martyn Bennett* for the husband.
*Nicholas Jarman* as amicus curiae.
The wife did not appear.

*Cur adv vult*

25 June. The following judgment was delivered.

**BOOTH J.** This is an appeal from an order of the Wirral Borough magistrates of 21
February 1983. It arises from an application by the husband to vary by reducing a
maintenance order originally made in a county court in divorce proceedings between
himself and his wife, and thereafter registered in a magistrates' court, by which he was
to pay the sum of £4 a week to the wife. Arrears had accrued under the order which
amounted to £632 and the husband also asked the justices to remit them. Having heard
the matter, the justices dismissed the husband's application that the order should be
varied and refused to remit the arrears. On the wife's complaint to enforce the arrears
the husband was ordered to pay them at the rate of £2 a week in addition to paying the
periodical payments of £4 a week.
    The husband appealed to the Divisional Court by way of notice of motion under RSC
Ord 90, r 16. Sitting as a single judge I allowed his appeal against the refusal of the
justices to vary the order and I reduced it to a nominal sum. But I adjourned for further
argument his appeal against the refusal of the justices to remit the arrears. This judgment
is concerned only with that latter aspect of the husband's appeal. The wife has not
appeared on this part of the appeal and has not been represented in this court, but counsel
instructed by the Official Solicitor has appeared as amicus curiae and I am grateful both
to him and to counsel who has appeared on behalf of the husband for their submissions.
    The husband and wife were married in 1954 and have two children of their family

now both over the age of 18. In 1969 they separated and in 1971 the marriage was dissolved. In the course of the divorce proceedings on 28 April 1971 in the Birkenhead County Court the husband was ordered to make periodical payments at the rate of £3·50 to each child, while a nominal order was made in favour of the wife. On 15 July 1971 an order was made for periodical payments for the wife at the rate of £3 a week pending suit and that order was registered in the Liverpool Magistrates' Court on 22 October 1971. The order for the children was subsequently varied on 14 December, 1973 and by a further order of 5 November 1975 the payments for the children ceased altogether but the order for the wife was continued in the sum of £4 a week. That was the subsisting order under which the arrears had accrued and which the husband sought to vary.

In 1972 the husband remarried and he now has one child of his present family who is aged 13. He earned his living as a tool setter but in June 1981 he was made redundant and he remained unemployed until September 1982 when he succeeded in obtaining part-time work as a petrol pump attendant. In that same month on the wife's complaint to enforce the arrears, which by then were said to have amounted to £570, a warrant was issued for the husband's arrest, but he was not brought before the magistrates until January 1983. The matter was then adjourned to enable him to apply for variation of the order. It was finally heard on 21 February 1983 when the justices made the order against which the husband appeals.

The evidence before the justices was given very briefly by the husband and wife, neither of whom was represented. The justices found that the husband had an income of £28·32 per week, that his present wife was earning £49 per week, that they had child benefit of £5·80 per week, and that their basic outgoings amounted to £84 per week. They found that the wife was earning £58 per week with basic outgoings of £42 per week. The justices further found that in June 1981 the husband had received a redundancy payment of £4,000. The accrued arrears under the order were stated at £632, a figure which was not challenged by the husband. But, as counsel who has appeared for him in this court has pointed out, the method by which the arrears appear to have been assessed was manifestly unsatisfactory. A schedule was produced which was kept by the magistrates' court of payments made by the husband between June 1977 and April 1981, and again between January 1982 and March 1983. There was otherwise no documentary evidence as to the payments made by him prior to June 1977 or during the period from the middle of April 1981 until the end of that year. Further, there was no certificate or statutory declaration of the accrued arrears and the schedule itself was not certificated. Nevertheless the justices considered that there were no grounds for remitting the arrears since the husband had not made regular payments during the time he was in full-time employment and earning as much as £130 per week, and that when he received his substantial redundancy payment he made no attempt to pay off any of the arrears then outstanding.

I gave leave to the husband to appeal out of time and I reduced the periodical payments order to a nominal order of 5p a year. As to the merits of the husband's case for the remission of the arrears, I am satisfied that it would be right to allow his appeal from the justices' refusal to remit all or any part of them, subject to the question of the jurisdiction of this court to do so. Not only was the method of their assessment unsatisfactory but it is also clear from the facts found by the justices that the wife's income now exceeds that of the husband by the sum of £20 per week and that he has financial obligations to his new family and in particular to the child of that family. There was no evidence that the husband now has any capital or other resources from which to pay the arrears. In those circumstances I would consider it right to remit all the outstanding arrears. But before I can do so I have to decide whether this court has the jurisdiction to entertain the husband's appeal against the justices' refusal to remit the arrears. The question to be decided is whether that aspect of the husband's appeal should have come to the Divisional Court by way of case stated and not by way of notice of motion which is the procedure that the husband has followed.

The original maintenance order was made by a divorce county court, but when it was registered in the magistrates' court under the provisions of the Maintenance Orders Act 1958 it became enforceable in the same way as an order made by a magistrates' court and it became variable by a magistrates' court (see s 1 of the 1958 Act). With regard to the enforcement of such an order, s 3(2) of that Act provides:

> '... an order registered in a magistrates' court shall be enforceable as if it were an affiliation order; and the provisions of any enactment with respect to the enforcement of affiliation orders (including enactments relating to the accrual of arrears and the remission of sums due) shall apply accordingly.'

The relevant statutory provisions relating to the enforcement of affiliation orders are now contained in Pt III of the Magistrates' Courts Act 1980. Section 93 of that Act provides that a sum payable under an affiliation order or an order enforceable as such, shall not be enforced except by an order made on complaint. Section 95 deals with the justices' powers to remit arrears and provides:

> 'On the hearing of a complaint for the enforcement, revocation, revival, variation or discharge of an affiliation order or an order enforceable as an affiliation order, the court may remit the whole or any part of the sum due under the order.'

That same power to remit arrears on a warrant of enforcement is also contained in s 17(6) of the 1958 Act and in this case a warrant had been issued on the wife's complaint.

So the wife in this case issued her complaint to enforce the order under the 1958 Act and the magistrates undoubtedly had the statutory power on that complaint to vary the order and to remit the arrears without the necessity of the husband himself issuing a complaint. But this husband did in fact issue a separate complaint to vary the order as under s 1 of the 1958 Act he was entitled to do. I shall consider that complaint and the powers of the justices to vary the order on it at a later stage.

I turn now to the procedure for appeals. The right to appeal any order of the magistrates' courts is governed by statute and in relation to maintenance orders there are two ways of appealing, either by way of notice of motion or by way of case stated. In respect of an application to vary an order registered in a magistrates' court, s 4(7) of the 1958 Act provides:

> 'Where a magistrates' court ... varies or refuses to vary a registered order, an appeal from the variation or refusal shall lie to the High Court ...'

The procedure for such an appeal is governed by the provisions of RSC Ord 55 and in consequence it is an appeal which is by way of rehearing and it must be brought to the appellate court by an originating motion. The powers of the appellate court are set out in r 7 of the order and include the power to—

> '(5) ... give any judgment or decision or make any order which ought to have been given or made by the court ... and make such further or other order as the case may require or may remit the matter ... for rehearing ...'

The second procedure for appeal is by way of case stated. This is governed by s 111 of the Magistrates' Courts Act 1980 and by RSC Ord 56. The material part of s 111 reads as follows:

> '(1) Any person who was party to any proceedings before a magistrates' court or is aggrieved by the conviction, order, determination or other proceedings of the court may question the proceeding on the ground that it is wrong in law or is in excess of jurisdiction by applying to the justices composing the court to state a case for the opinion of the High Court on the question of the law or jurisdiction involved; but a person shall not make an application under this section in respect of a decision against which he has a right of appeal to the High Court ...'

The section further provides that an application to justices to state a case must be made within 21 days after the day on which the decision complained of was given. But otherwise the procedure for an appeal by way of case stated is contained in Ord 56, r 5(2) of which provides:

> 'An appeal by way of case stated against an order or determination of a magistrates' court shall be heard and determined by a single judge or, if the Court so directs, a Divisional Court of the Family Division if the order or determination appealed against was made or given in affiliation proceedings, or in care proceedings under the Children and Young Persons Act 1969, or on an application under section 35 of the Matrimonial Causes Act 1973 or if it relates to the enforcement of . . . (c) an order for periodical or other payments made, or having effect as if made, under Part II of the Matrimonial Causes Act 1973 and registered in a magistrates' court under the Maintenance Orders Act 1958.'

In this case if the only complaint before the justices had been the wife's complaint to enforce the arrears under the maintenance order, then in my judgment the only means by which the husband could have appealed against their refusal to remit all or any part of the sum due would have been on a question of law or jurisdiction by way of case stated. There is no other statutory right of appeal in such circumstances. Had that been the case, the husband would have been bound to have failed in this court because he has come by way of notice of motion and this court has no jurisdiction to extend the time within which justices must be asked to state a case (see *Michael v Gowland* [1977] 2 All ER 328, [1977] 1 WLR 296).

I now return to the husband's complaint which was also before the justices asking them to vary the periodical payments order. Counsel for the husband contends that the husband's application to remit the arrears came within the ambit of that complaint by virtue of the provisions of s 95 of the Magistrates' Courts Act 1980. The gravamen of his argument is that the husband's complaint to vary the registered order was supplemented by those provisions which gave the justices power to remit the arrears on the hearing of a complaint for the enforcement, revocation, revival, variation or discharge of an affiliation order or an order enforceable as an affiliation order. So, counsel for the husband argues, the husband's appeal, including the appeal against the refusal to remit the arrears, relates to the question of the variation of the order and lies under s 4(7) of the 1958 Act. If this is so, it is properly constituted before this court. The question is whether s 4(7) of that Act can be construed so as to enable an appeal to lie to the High Court not only against the justices' refusal to vary the maintenance order itself but also against their refusal to remit the arrears. Are the enabling provisions of s 95 of the 1980 Act to be read into s 4 of the 1958 Act?

One of the purposes of the Maintenance Orders Act 1958 was to enable maintenance orders of the High Court and county court to be registered in a magistrates' court so that they could be there enforced and varied, no doubt with the intention of saving the parties the time and expense of having to go back to the higher court. An order which is registered remains the order of the original court which made it. But the 1958 Act specifically provides that while it remains so registered, an order may be enforced in the magistrates' court 'in like manner as an order made by the court of registration'. The powers of the justices to vary a registered order are contained in s 4(2)(a) of the Act, which provides that—

> 'the court of registration may exercise the same jurisdiction to vary any rate of payments specified by a registered order . . . as is exercisable . . . by the original court . . .'

Provision is also made to enable the justices to remit an application for variation to the original court. But there is otherwise nothing in the terms of that statute which empowers the magistrates to do other than to vary the rate of payment of a registered order. So, on an application to vary a registered order the powers of the justices under the 1958 Act are limited to varying the rate of payment and do not extend to the suspension or revocation of the order itself. This was the construction placed on s 4 by

Marshall J in *Miller v Miller* [1960] 3 All ER 115, [1961] P 1, with which, with respect, I agree.

But the question remains whether s 95 of the Magistrates' Courts Act 1980 nevertheless supplements the justices' powers on an application to vary to enable them to remit any arrears. The application of that section is not limited to the hearing of a complaint brought under the 1980 Act or any other specific statute. It applies wherever there is a complaint before the justices for the enforcement, revocation, revival, variation or discharge of an affiliation order or an order enforceable as an affiliation order. An order registered under the 1958 Act is an order enforceable as if it were an affiliation order and in my judgment the provisions of s 95 of the 1980 Act clearly apply to an application to vary such an order.

The next question is whether it is proper to regard the justices' refusal to remit the arrears as part of their order made in relation to the application to vary the order and in respect of which there is a statutory right of appeal to the High Court under s 4(7) of the 1958 Act. Can the words in that subsection, 'an appeal from the variation or refusal shall lie to the High Court', be constructed to include an appeal against the refusal to remit the arrears? Or because that part of the justices' decision relates to arrears, must it therefore be regarded as relating to the enforcement of the order?

The consequences of a narrow construction of s 4(7) of the 1958 Act which would exclude the ability to appeal to the High Court against the refusal to remit the arrears are several and serious. The appellant, as in this case, would be then compelled to follow two quite separate and distinct procedures if he wished to appeal both against the refusal to vary the order and against the refusal to remit the arrears, despite the fact that both those decisions were made on a single complaint. If the appellant failed to follow both procedures the appellate court, as would happen in this case, would have no jurisdiction to deal fully with the subject matter of the appeal. As in this case, it could not be considered satisfactory that while the husband's appeal in respect of the variation may be considered and dealt with, the appellate court has no power to consider the position with regard to the arrears. Further, an appeal by way of case stated is not an appeal by way of rehearing when questions of fact and of law are before the appellate court. It is instead an appeal which is limited to questions of law and jurisdiction. In this case, as counsel as amicus has observed, it might well have been open to the husband to have applied for a case to be stated in relation to the schedule of payments and the proof of the arrears, but that is by no means always the situation. The remission of arrears is frequently a matter for the exercise of the magistrates' discretion against which no appeal lies by way of case stated.

There is no provision either in the Maintenance Orders Act 1958 or in the Magistrates' Courts Act 1980 or in any other statute which requires appeals relating to the enforcement of orders to be by way of case stated. It is only if there is no other right of appeal given by statute that an appeal now lies by this procedure. So it is only by virtue of the fact that there is no other statutory right of appeal in relation to the enforcement of certain orders that an appeal lies by way of case stated. Order 56 is not of itself mandatory and does not require such appeals to be by way of case stated, but deals only with the procedure for that method of appeal and with the courts by which such appeals must be heard.

Counsel as amicus has supported counsel for the husband's submissions that the husband's appeal is properly constituted under s 4(7) of the 1958 Act. He adopts the argument that the power to remit the arrears should be read into the power of the magistrates under the 1958 Act to vary the registered order and so must be covered by the statutory right of appeal given by s 4(7) of that Act.

I accept the submissions of counsel. In my judgment, the refusal by the justices to remit the arrears may properly be regarded as not having been made on the complaint of the wife to enforce that registered order but as having been made on the husband's application and that it was a part of his complaint to vary the order. To require the husband to pursue two different courses of appeal against the two decisions made on that one complaint would be to impose on him, and on other litigants in the same position, a cumbersome and costly procedure quite contrary to the spirit and intention of the 1958 Act itself. Such a construction should only be placed on the relevant statutes by this court if it is compelled by their clear language so to hold. I do not think I am so compelled. The order of the justices which enforced the registered order for periodical payments was that which was made on the wife's complaint and which assessed the arrears and directed the husband to pay them off at a weekly rate. That order, as counsel concede and I accept, could only be appealed on a question of law or jurisdiction by way of case stated. There is no other statutory right of appeal. The refusal of the justices to remit the arrears, in my judgment, was part of their refusal to vary the order itself, both their orders being made on the application of the husband and on his complaint to vary the registered order, the justices' power to vary the registered order having been clearly supplemented by statute to enable them also to remit the arrears. Therefore, I conclude that the right of appeal given by s 4(7) of the 1958 Act from the justices' variation or refusal to vary the order must be held to cover appeals against decisions made in the exercise of their supplementary statutory powers. I am satisfied that the right of appeal to the High Court given by s 4(7) of the 1958 Act enables the husband to appeal by way of notice of motion both against the justices' refusal to vary the order and their refusal to remit the arrears.

I wish to add only this. The ability of the court to enforce a periodical payments order is a matter of importance to many litigants, a substantial number of whom appear in person both in the courts below and on appeal. It is in the public interest that the procedures to be followed both at first instance and on appeal should be straightforward and as expeditious as possible. Unfortunately, as this case has illustrated, this has not always been achieved by the relevant statutes. In *Mills v Mills* (1982) 12 Fam Law 174 I took the view that in a similar situation which had arisen under the Domestic Proceedings and Magistrates' Courts Act 1978 I did not have the power to remit arrears and in that case the only way that the husband could have proceeded was by way of case stated. But, as counsel in this case have submitted, in *Mills v Mills* I was dealing with a different statute as well as with different facts and so it has not been necessary for me to consider that decision or the statutory provisions which were relevant to it. Under the provisions of the 1958 Act I have been able to reach a different conclusion, but it is unfortunate, to say the least, that the statutory procedures for appeals against such orders may vary from one statute to another in a jurisdiction where the need for clarity and simplicity is paramount.

So my order will be that I will remit the arrears.

*Order accordingly.*

Solicitors: *Cuff Roberts North Kirk*, Liverpool (for the husband); *Official Solicitor.*

Bebe Chua    Barrister.

# R v West Yorkshire Coroner, ex parte Smith (No 2)

QUEEN'S BENCH DIVISION

STEPHEN BROWN LJ AND KENNEDY J

18, 19 JULY, 28 SEPTEMBER 1984

*Coroner – Inquest – Contempt of court – Contempt in face of court – Jurisdiction of coroner's court to punish contempt – Whether coroner's court a court of record – Whether coroner's court having jurisdiction to fine for contempt.*

During the course of an inquest into the death of a nurse who died in Saudi Arabia in 1979, the applicant, who was the nurse's father, accused one of the witnesses of murdering her. The following day the press published details of the allegations. The coroner took the view that the applicant's conduct had been a serious contempt of court and fined him £50. The applicant applied for judicial review of the coroner's order on the ground that the coroner had had no jurisdiction to impose a fine for contempt because a coroner's court was not a court of record but an inferior court or tribunal in respect of which no contempt was possible.

**Held** – A coroner's court was an inferior court of record which had the power to impose a fine for contempt committed in the face of the court. Moreover, having regard to the feelings which could be generated at an inquest, that was a necessary power which enabled the coroner to keep order during the proceedings. Accordingly, the application for judicial review would be refused (see p 105 *a* and *j* to p 106 *d*, post).

**Note**

For a coroner's jurisdiction to punish for contempt, see 9 Halsbury's Laws (4th edn) para 1103.

**Cases referred to in judgments**

A-G v BBC [1980] 3 All ER 161, [1981] AC 303, [1980] 3 WLR 109, HL.
Beecher's Case (1608) 8 Co Rep 58a, 77 ER 559.
Garnett v Ferrand (1827) 6 B & C 611, [1824–34] All ER Rep 244, 108 ER 576.
Godfrey's Case (1614) 11 Co Rep 42a, 77 ER 1199.
Griesley's Case (1588) 8 Co Rep 38a, 77 ER 530.
Jewison v Dyson (1842) 9 M & W 540, 152 ER 228.
R v Lefroy (1873) LR 8 QB 134.
Royal Aquarium and Summer and Winter Gardens Society v Parkinson [1892] 1 QB 431, [1891–4] All ER Rep 429, CA.

**Cases also cited**

Balogh v Crown Court at St Albans [1974] 3 All ER 283, [1975] QB 73.
Bird v Keep [1918] 2 KB 692, CA.
Chippett v Thompson (1868) 7 NSWSCR (2) 349.
Davidson v Garrett (1899) 30 OR 653.
Grenville v College of Physicians (1700) 12 Mod Rep 386, 88 ER 1398.
Guilfoyle v Home Office [1981] 1 All ER 943, [1981] QB 309, CA.
Kemp v Neville (1861) 10 CBNS 523, 142 ER 556.
R v Almon (1765) Wilm 243, 97 ER 94.
R v Clarke, ex p Crippen (1910) 103 LT 636, [1908–10] All ER Rep 915, DC.
R v Clement (1821) 4 B & Ald 218, 106 ER 918.
R v Cotton (1733) 2 Barn KB 313, 94 ER 523.
R v St Edmundsbury and Ipswich Diocese (Chancellor), ex p White [1947] 2 All ER 170, [1948] 1 KB 195, CA.
Sparks v Martyn (1668) 1 Vent 1, 86 ER 1.
Thomas v Churton (1862) 2 B & S 475, 121 ER 1150.

**Application for judicial review**

Ronald Smith, the father of Helen Smith deceased, applied, with the leave of Mann J granted on 17 February 1984, for (i) an order of certiorari to bring up and quash the decision of Philip S Gill, HM Coroner for the eastern district of the county of West Yorkshire, on 25 November 1982 whereby he imposed a £50 fine for contempt of court on the applicant, and (ii) a further order prohibiting enforcement of the fine against him. The facts are set out in the judgment of Stephen Brown LJ.

*Stephen Sedley QC* and *Philip Sapsford* for the applicant.
*Simon D Brown* as amicus curiae.

*Cur adv vult*

28 September. The following judgments were delivered.

**STEPHEN BROWN LJ.** This is an application for judicial review by Mr Ronald Smith, who seeks the following relief by his notice of motion. He seeks an order to bring up into this court and to quash the decision of Her Majesty's Coroner for the eastern district of the metropolitan county of West Yorkshire to impose a fine of £50 on the applicant for contempt on 25 November 1982, and a further order to prohibit the stipendiary magistrate for the City of Leeds from accepting jurisdiction to enforce the fine. He claims that the coroner had no jurisdiction to impose a fine for contempt; further, or alternatively, that the conduct which allegedly gave rise to the coroner's order did not amount to a contempt. He claims further that the magistrate had no power in any event to collect the fine.

The incident which gave rise to the coroner's decision to impose the fine for contempt on the applicant occurred during an inquest held at Leeds town hall in November 1982 into the death of the applicant's daughter, Helen Smith, in Saudi Arabia. The circumstances of her death have been, and continue to be, the subject of allegations and of speculation of a sensational nature. Following her death in May 1979 the applicant has been relentless in his pursuit of the truth surrounding the circumstances of her death. Allegations and suggestions of the gravest nature were made against a number of persons. Eventually, after the applicant had overcome a number of legal obstacles, an inquest into the circumstances of the death of his daughter, Helen Smith, opened at the Leeds town hall on 18 November 1982 and continued until 9 December 1982, when the jury returned an open verdict.

The inquest attracted a great deal of publicity and the evidence engendered an emotional atmosphere, for the applicant had made no secret of his belief that his daughter's death was not an accident. A number of the witnesses called by the coroner fell into the category of interested persons and were represented at the inquest. These included a Dr Arnot and one Manfred Schlaefer.

The incident which gave rise to the coroner's action in imposing a fine on the applicant for contempt occurred shortly before the midday adjournment on 24 November 1982. The witness Schlaefer was answering questions in the course of his evidence put to him by his solicitor. In the course of this the solicitor sought to question Mr Schlaefer on a letter which had been written to him by the applicant. Apparently the letter contained serious imputations against Mr Schlaefer in relation to the death of the applicant's daughter.

The shorthand transcript of the proceedings shows that the applicant's counsel objected to the line of questioning which was about to be conducted by Mr Schlaefer's solicitor. The solicitor asked the witness: 'Would you look at that letter? Is that a letter addressed to you from Mr Smith?' At that point the applicant's counsel objected saying, 'Well, if we are going to have that sort of thing . . .' The coroner said, 'I was just wondering whether this was going to take some time and whether we should adjourn. It is 1 o'clock', and the solicitor said, 'All right, very well', and at that point the applicant turned to face the gallery where the press were assembled and shouted words which the coroner says in his affidavit he did not clearly hear but which the shorthand transcript shows were: 'I'm accusing Arnot of murdering my daughter and Texier.' At that point the court adjourned until 2 o'clock, when the proceedings resumed.

Next morning, after the press had published the details of the outbursts under sensational headlines, the solicitor representing Dr Arnot raised the matter with the coroner. He expressed his concern and the concern of his client at the allegation which had resulted in banner headlines, saying, 'Ron Smith accused Dr Arnot of MURDER' and similar headlines in a number of papers. Dr Arnot's solicitor submitted that it had constituted a gross contempt of the court.

The coroner then raised the matter with Mr Smith's counsel, saying that it had given him a lot of concern overnight. In particular he expressed the concern which he felt that an allegation had been made against a M Texier who was not present at the proceedings. Counsel for Mr Smith indicated to the coroner that it would be desirable if in due course his client went into the witness box and explained the course of the investigations he had made and said that it was not an angry outburst that had taken place but was a statement of fact; he submitted that it was not a deliberate attempt to make headlines and that it was not a contempt of court.

The coroner, after hearing counsel for Mr Smith, expressed the view that the manner in which the allegation of murder had been made was done in a wholly unacceptable way and had constituted a contempt. He expressed sympathy for the distress which Mr Smith undoubtedly felt about the whole subject matter of the inquest but said that he could not tolerate conduct of that kind and must indicate the court's displeasure, and he imposed a fine of £50.

In his affidavit the coroner says that the full record of the statement made by Mr Smith disclosed that it was not a spontaneous outburst of an opinion but was designed to distract attention from the potentially damaging evidence which the letter constituted and which denied the witness giving evidence the opportunity of effectively refuting the serious and damaging allegations that were made against him. He further said that he had intended to take action at the commencement of the sitting on the day following the outburst but that the solicitor representing Dr Arnot had forestalled him by addressing him on the subject before he had initiated consideration of the matter.

He then says in para 10 of his affidavit:

'After consideration of all the circumstances and the submission of Counsel I regarded Mr. Smith's behaviour as having been a serious contempt of the Court both in seeking to disrupt the orderly consideration of the evidence and . . . in attempting to frustrate the rights of an interested party to answer grievous charges levelled against him and of uttering fresh serious allegations in front of the jury in a wholly improper and unacceptable way.'

In para 13 of his affidavit the coroner says:

'. . . I was, however, concerned with the interference with the proceedings within the Court. I considered that it was in the interests of the proper administration of justice that such behaviour should not pass unadmonished. In the absence of any indication of contrition on the part of Mr. Smith, after the serious view which I held had been made clear to him, I felt it to be necessary that the Court's disapproval should be demonstrated by the imposition of an appropriate penalty.'

In para 15 of the affidavit he says: 'Pursuant to the provisions of the Contempt of Court Act 1981 I imposed a fine of £50. Subsequently I delivered a Certificate to that effect to the Clerk of Leeds Magistrates Court.'

The applicant did not take any step to appeal pursuant to the provisions of s 13 of the Administration of Justice Act 1960, and he took no step of any kind with regard to the matter until the Leeds stipendiary magistrate stated that he would proceed to enforce and collect the fine on 24 October 1983. It appears from the affidavit of the applicant's solicitor that the applicant had been sent a notice of the fine on 9 December 1982 but that nothing further was heard subsequently, and it was believed that nothing further would be heard because of the doubt that the coroner had the ability to impose the fine and the magistrates' court had the ability to enforce it. The affidavit concludes with the following passage: 'It seemed idle to take steps to quash the purported fine at that stage unless an attempt was made to enforce it. Such attempt was not made as stated above until the 12th October 1983 . . .'

Counsel for the applicant opened his case by saying that there were two principal issues: (1) was what occurred a contempt? and (2) if it was, had the coroner any jurisdiction to try and punish it? He added a third subsidiary issue: has the magistrate any power to collect the fine? I believe that counsel subsequently felt unable seriously to pursue the first matter, ie was what occurred a contempt? in the light of the failure on the part of his client to take any steps to appeal from the order under the provisions of s 13 of the 1960 Act. It seems to me, having regard to the transcript of the proceedings made contemporaneously by the shorthand writer and to the affidavit of the coroner, that what took place plainly could amount to a contempt. I do not consider that it is open to the applicant in these proceedings to pursue the ground that what occurred was not a contempt.

The real and principal issue raised in these proceedings is the matter concerning the jurisdiction of the coroner to try and punish conduct allegedly amounting to contempt. In 9 Halsbury's Laws (4th edn) para 1103 it is stated:

'As the judge of a court of record the coroner has power at common law to commit for contempt of court, but, as his court is an inferior court of record, his power is limited in this respect to contempt committed in the face of the court, and does not extend to contempt committed out of court . . .'

In the same volume of Halsbury's Laws it is stated that 'The coroner's court is a court of record' (at para 1002).

In the 1797 edition of Coke's Institutes, (4 Co Inst 271) under the title of 'The Court of the Coroner' it is stated: '. . . the court which he holdeth is a court of record.'

In *Jervis on the Office and Duties of Coroners* (9th edn, 1957) p 23, the author says of the office of coroner:

'Borough coroners and, analogously it seems, county coroners, are to be regarded as having offices under the Crown and not under the local authorities appointing them. The coroner's court is an inferior court of record. A court of record is one of which the acts and judicial proceedings are enrolled in its archives and are conclusive evidence of what is required. Amongst the incidents pertaining to a court of record is the power to commit a person to prison for contempt of court. As the coroner's court is an inferior court of record, the power to commit for contempt is limited to contempt committed in facie and not to cases of contempt committed out of court.'

In *Borrie and Lowe's Law of Contempt* (2nd edn, 1983) p 314 the authors say:

'The power that courts of record enjoy to punish contempts is part of their *inherent* jurisdiction. The juridical basis of the inherent jurisdiction has been well described by Master Jacob as being: "the authority of the judiciary to uphold, to protect and to fulfil the judicial function of administering justice according to law in a regular, orderly and effective manner." Such a power is not derived from statute nor truly from the common law but instead flows from the very concept of a court of law. The major significance of the contempt power being part of the inherent jurisdiction of courts of record is that because it has not been derived from statute, courts should be slow to hold that the power has been abrogated or restricted by Parliament. It has been repeatedly held that Parliament can only restrict or abrogate the contempt power if it does so in the clearest terms.' (The authors' emphasis.)

In the same work the authors refer to coroners' courts and say (p 351):

'The status of Coroner's courts is not definitely settled but the better view is that it is a court of record, and as such has jurisdiction to punish all contempts committed in its face. Such a view is strengthened by the wording of the Coroners Act 1887, s 19(3): "Any power by this Act vested in a Coroner of imposing a fine on a juror or witness shall be deemed to be in addition to and not in derogation of any power the coroner may possess independently of this Act, for compelling any person to appear and give evidence before him on any inquest or other proceedings, *or punishing any person for contempt of court* in not so appearing and giving evidence with this qualification, that a person shall not be fined by the coroner under this Act, and also be punished under the power of a coroner independently of this Act." [The authors' emphasis.] The wording of this provision clearly assumes that coroners can punish offenders for contempt and furthermore states that any powers vested by the Act do not derogate from such powers. It accordingly must be accepted that a coroners' court can punish contempts committed in its face.'

Section 19 contains specific provisions for the coroner to fine witnesses and jurors for non-attendance.

In the course of his judgment in *Garnett v Ferrand* (1827) 6 B & C 611 at 625, [1824–34] All ER Rep 244 at 245 Lord Tenterden CJ said:

'The court of the coroner is a court of record of which the coroner is the judge; and it is a general rule of very great antiquity, that no action will lie against a judge of record for any matter done by him in the exercise of his judicial functions . . .'

However in *Jewison v Dyson* (1842) 9 M & W 540 at 586, 152 ER 228 at 247 Lord Abinger CB said:

'It has been said that the coroner's is a court of record. I am very unwilling to enter into that discussion; but I must own, if it were *res integra*, I think it would be wise to consider whether that extra-judicial opinion, delivered by the Lord Chief Justice of the Queen's Bench in the case that has been cited [*Garnett v Ferrand*], is a sufficient authority for saying that the coroner's court is a court of record.'

All the reported cases are to the effect that it is only courts of record which can fine or commit for contempt. These authorities commence with *Griesley's Case* (1588) 8 Co Rep 38a, 77 ER 530, *Beecher's Case* (1608) 8 Co Rep 58a, 77 ER 559 and *Godfrey's Case* (1614) 11 Co Rep 42a, 77 ER 1199.

More recently, in *R v Lefroy* (1873) LR 8 QB 134 at 137 Cockburn CJ said:

'It is perfectly true that it is laid down by authority, and reason shews the correctness of the rule, that all courts of record have power to fine and imprison for any contempt committed in the face of the Court; for the power is necessary for the due administration of justice, to prevent the Court being interrupted. But it is quite another thing to say that every inferior court of record shall have power to fine or imprison for contempt of court when that contempt is committed out of court, as the writing or publication of articles reflecting on the conduct of the judge. There are other remedies for such proceedings.'

On behalf of the applicant counsel recognises the weight of these authorities and the weight of opinion expresssed by learned authors, but he submits the coroner's court is not a court of record. It is, he submits, an inferior court, or alternatively a tribunal in respect of which no contempt is possible. He says that the argument with regard to the power to punish for contempt deriving from a court of record is in effect a circular argument, for it can be said that only if there is the power to commit or punish for contempt can the court be a court of record. All that the authorities propound are self-supporting arguments, he claims: that is to say the court of record has the power to fine and the power to fine makes it a court of record. In modern times, says counsel for the applicant, the coroner's court has lost most of its ancient jurisdiction. It no longer has power to make a decision to bind anybody; it does not try any issue; the coroner has no power to determine anybody's rights or liabilities, and furthermore, if it is a court of record, it must be for some reason other than the type of the decisions which are made in a coroner's court. Accordingly he submits that today it is no longer realistic to call the coroner's court a court of record. The county court did not have a power to commit for contempt at common law but had to be given that power by statute. Also the magistrates' courts have had to be given power by statute.

Counsel appearing as amicus submits that there are two well-founded propositions: one that the coroner's court is an inferior court of record and, two, that an inferior court of record can punish by fine or imprisonment for contempt in the face of the court.

I am satisfied that an overwhelming body of judicial opinion and learned academic opinion supports the view that the coroner's court is an inferior court of record which has the power to commit for contempt in the face of the court. This has been recognised inferentially in more recent times in *A-G v BBC* [1980] 3 All ER 161, [1981] AC 303. In that case the House of Lords had to consider whether a local valuation court was a court for the purposes of the powers of the High Court relating to contempt. The House in reversing the decision of the Court of Appeal held that a local valuation court, although having some of the attributes of the long-established inferior courts, did not constitute a court for the purposes of the powers relating to contempt.

In the course of his speech Lord Salmon said ([1980] 3 All ER 161 at 169, [1981] AC 303 at 342):

'There is today a plethora of such tribunals which may well resemble the old "inferior courts". In my view, it does not by any means follow that the modern inferior courts need the umbrella of contempt of court or that they come under it. Indeed, in my opinion, public policy requires that most of the principles relating to contempt of court which have for ages necessarily applied to the long-established inferior courts such as county courts, magistrates' courts, courts-martial, coroners' courts and consistory courts shall not apply to valuation courts and the host of other modern tribunals which may be regarded as inferior courts . . .'

Lord Scarman commented on certain parts of the judgment of Fry LJ in *Royal Aquarium and Summer and Winter Garden Society Ltd v Parkinson* [1892] 1 QB 431, [1891–4] All ER Rep 429. Lord Scarman, referring to the judgment of Fry LJ in which the judge had examined the relevant legislation to determine the character in which the London County Council had acted when hearing applications for licences and had concluded that the proceeding was administrative and not judicial, said ([1980] 3 All ER 161 at 179, [1981] AC 303 at 355–356):

'He [ie Fry LJ] considered that the word "court" had an ascertainable meaning in this branch of English law, but refrained from telling us what it is (see [1892] 1 QB 431 at 446, [1891–4] All ER Rep 429 at 433). He remarked that Parliament itself was a court, even though its duties as a whole were deliberative and legislative, because the duties of a part of it were judicial. He recognised the existence of courts, which "though not courts of justice, are nevertheless courts according to our law", eg a court of investigation such as the coroner's court, which is of ancient royal origin. This led him to the view, which is, I think, constitutionally correct and true to the historical origins of our court system, that the existence of immunity from suit for defamation, which participants in a court's proceedings enjoy—". . . does not depend upon the question whether the subject-matter of consideration is a Court of Justice, but whether it is a Court in law. Wherever you find a Court in law, to that the law attaches certain privileges, among which is the immunity in question." (See [1892] 1 QB 431 at 447, [1891–4] All ER Rep 429 at 434.) I would add that, though a court in law will also have the protection of the doctrine of contempt of court, it does not follow that because an institution enjoys the protection for its proceedings of absolute privilege it necessarily follows it has also the protection of the law relating to contempt of court. Nevertheless "a court in law" will have the two protections.'

Although not directly in issue, it is clear from those passages that both Lord Salmon and Lord Scarman were not questioning but were assuming that the coroner's court was a court in law which did have the protection which Lord Scarman referred to. I am further satisfied that the terms of the Coroners Act 1887 necessarily assume the continuance of the coroner's court as a court which has powers of committal for contempt in the face of the court. Accordingly in my judgment the applicant's submission that the coroner in this case did not have jurisdiction to impose a fine for contempt committed in the face of the court must fail. In my judgment the coroner's court clearly does have that power. Moreover, today it may still be regarded as being a necessary power, having regard to the emotions generated by certain inquests. It is very necessary that the coroner should be able to keep order in the proceedings which he has the duty of conducting. Unless and until the power which has existed, in my judgment from early times, is removed by statute, it must be understood to continue to exist.

The question raised as to the power of the stipendiary magistrate to collect the fine imposed has not been argued before this court because, amongst other reasons, it is said that the fine has in fact been paid by some person or persons other than the applicant. I feel it right to add that it would be remarkable indeed if a fine having been properly imposed by the coroner there should not be machinery to collect it.

The essential issue in this application has been that of the jurisdiction of the coroner to fine for contempt committed in the face of the court. For the reasons which I have given the application should fail.

**KENNEDY J.** I agree.

*Application dismissed.*

Solicitors: *Howard Cohen & Co*, Leeds (for the applicant); *Treasury Solicitor.*

Richard Willett Esq    Barrister.

# Livesey (formerly Jenkins) v Jenkins

HOUSE OF LORDS

LORD HAILSHAM OF ST MARYLEBONE LC, LORD SCARMAN, LORD KEITH OF KINKEL, LORD BRIDGE OF HARWICH AND LORD BRANDON OF OAKBROOK

12, 13 NOVEMBER, 13 DECEMBER 1984

*Divorce – Financial provision – Consent order – Disclosure – Duty to make full and frank disclosure – Wife becoming engaged to remarry between date when terms of consent order agreed and date when order made – Wife failing to disclose her engagement – Whether wife under duty to disclose engagement – Whether failure to make disclosure affecting validity of consent order.*

*Divorce – Financial provision – Consent order – Form – Terms of order to be limited to those within power of court to order – Other terms to be incorporated as undertakings given to court.*

The husband and wife married in 1957 and separated in 1981. After negotiations between their respective solicitors the parties agreed that the wife would seek a divorce on the basis of a written confession of adultery provided by the husband, that the wife would be entitled to custody of the two children of the marriage and that the parties would seek a consent order embodying agreed terms in settlement of claims for financial provision and property adjustment under ss 23 and 24 of the Matrimonial Causes Act 1973. In April 1982 the marriage was dissolved. On 12 August the parties' solicitors reached final agreement about the form and terms of the consent order whereby in consideration of the wife agreeing to relinquish all her claims for periodical payments the husband agreed to transfer to the wife his half share in the matrimonial home, for the express purpose of providing the wife with a home of her own for herself and the two children. On 18 August the wife became engaged to be married to another man but she failed to disclose that fact either to her own solicitors or to the husband or his solicitors. On 19 August the parties made a joint application to the registrar for a consent order on the terms agreed. The order was made on 2 September. On 24 September the wife remarried and two months later advertised the matrimonial home for sale. The husband learnt of the marriage in October 1982 and thereupon appealed against the consent order and applied for it to be set aside on the ground that he had been induced to agree to its being made by a misrepresentation by the wife as to her true position. The judge dismissed his appeal. On appeal, the Court of Appeal held that the wife had been under no duty to disclose her engagement and that therefore the husband was not entitled to have the consent order set aside. The husband appealed to the House of Lords.

**Held** – Where the parties to a marriage wished the court to exercise its discretion under ss 23 and 24 of the 1973 Act to make orders for financial provision and property adjustment following a divorce they were under a duty, in both contested and consent proceedings, to make full and frank disclosure to the court and the other party of all material facts, including matters (such as those specified in s 25(1)(a) and (b)) to which the court was statutorily required to have regard when deciding whether to exercise its discretion, since otherwise the court was not equipped to exercise its discretion properly. However, because of the importance of encouraging the parties to make a clean break after a divorce, a financial provision and property adjustment order ought not to be set aside lightly. Accordingly, if, but only if, the absence of full and frank disclosure led the court, whether in contested or consent proceedings, to make an order which was substantially different from that which would have been made if there had been full and frank disclosure, the order would be set aside. Since the wife's engagement was a material circumstance and was directly relevant to the parties' agreement on financial provision and property adjustment she had been under a duty to disclose that fact before the parties' agreement was put into effect by means of the consent order and her failure to disclose that fact invalidated the order, which would accordingly be set aside. The husband's appeal would therefore be allowed and the proceedings for financial provision and property adjustment remitted for rehearing (see p 108 c d and f to p 109 a, p 113 d to g, p 114 b to g, p 115 g to j, p 116 e to g, p 117 j to p 118 a and p 119 g to j, post).

*Robinson v Robinson* [1982] 2 All ER 699n applied.

*Wales v Wadham* [1977] 2 All ER 125 overruled in part.

*Tommey v Tommey* [1982] 3 All ER 385 overruled.

Per curiam. When a consent order is drafted it is essential that all its terms should come clearly within the powers conferred on the court by ss 23 and 24 of the 1973 Act. The proper procedure for incorporating into a consent order terms which are not within those powers is to formulate them as undertakings given to the court. Such undertakings are then enforceable as effectively as direct orders (see p 108 c d g and j to p 109 a, p 118 j and p 119 a b, post).

**Notes**

For consent orders embodying the spouses' agreement on financial provisions, see 13 Halsbury's Laws (4th edn) para 1158.

For the Matrimonial Causes Act 1973, ss 23, 24, 25, see 43 Halsbury's Statutes (3rd edn) 564, 566, 567.

As from 12 October 1984, s 25 of the 1973 Act was substituted by s 3 of the Matrimonial and Family Proceedings Act 1984.

**Cases referred to in opinions**

*de Lasala v de Lasala* [1979] 2 All ER 1146, [1980] AC 546, [1979] 3 WLR 390, PC.

*Minton v Minton* [1979] 1 All ER 79, [1979] AC 593, [1979] 2 WLR 31, HL.

*Robinson v Robinson* [1982] 2 All ER 699n, [1982] 1 WLR 786n, 4 FLR 102, CA.

*Tommey v Tommey* [1982] 3 All ER 385, [1983] Fam 15, [1982] 3 WLR 909.

*Wales v Wadham* [1977] 2 All ER 125, [1977] 1 WLR 199.

*Wells v Wells* [1980] CA Transcript 526.

**Interlocutory appeal**

David Henry Jenkins (the husband) appealed by leave of the Court of Appeal against the decision of that court (Sir John Arnold P and Heilbron J) on 21 December 1983 dismissing the husband's appeal from the decision of his Honour Judge Anthony Cox sitting in the

Plymouth County Court on 5 May 1983 whereby the judge dismissed the husband's appeal from an order made by consent by Mr Registrar Carder on 22 September 1982 in the Plymouth County Court whereby it was ordered, inter alia, that the husband transfer his half interest in the former matrimonial home, namely Peach Tree Cottage, Higher Tremar, St Cleer, near Liskeard, Cornwall, to Beryl Livesey (formerly Jenkins) (the wife) and that the wife's claims for other financial relief including periodical payments be dismissed. The facts are set out in the opinion of Lord Brandon.

*Robert L Johnson QC* and *A C Myer* for the husband.
*Swinton Thomas QC* and *Jean H Ritchie* for the wife.

Their Lordships took time for consideration.

13 December. The following opinions were delivered.

**LORD HAILSHAM OF ST MARYLEBONE LC.** My Lords, I have had the advantage of reading in draft the speech about to be delivered by my noble and learned friend Lord Brandon. I agree with every word of it and am in consequence of the opinion that this appeal must be allowed, the order set aside and the proceedings remitted for rehearing by a judge of the Family Division in the form suggested by my noble and learned friend.

There is, therefore, nothing useful that I can add on the merits of the appeal. Since, however, the advisers to the respondent clearly attached importance to my doing so I wish to add that they acted in perfect good faith throughout, since, at the material time, that is at the time the consent order was perfected, they were not aware of the essential fact of which there had been non-disclosure.

I would also wish to add that though, for the reasons given by my noble and learned friend, I do not agree with it I fully understand the position of the respondent. A former wife is naturally reticent about any plan she may have to remarry, and I do not think she was fully aware (though she should have been) of the vital nature of the information she was withholding from the other side and from the court.

I would also wish to underscore the warning with which my noble and learned friend is concluding his speech. Consent orders which effect a clean break between former spouses are, when there has been full relevant disclosure, much to be encouraged, and, properly negotiatied, greatly reduce the pain and trauma of divorce. They are, therefore, not lightly to be overthrown.

**LORD SCARMAN.** My Lords, I have had the advantage of reading in draft the speech to be delivered by my noble and learned friend Lord Brandon. I agree with it, and for the reasons he gives I would allow the appeal. I agree that the consent order made on 2 September 1982 should be set aside and the proceedings for financial provision and property adjustment remitted to the Family Division of the High Court for rehearing by a judge of that division.

Before leaving the case I wish to express my firm support for the emphatic word of warning with which my noble and learned friend concludes his speech. The principle of the 'clean break' as formulated in *Minton v Minton* [1979] 1 All ER 79 at 81, 87–88, [1979] AC 593 at 601, 608 by Viscount Dilhorne and myself retains its place of importance in the law. The justice of the clean break depends on the full and frank disclosure of all material matters by the parties. But orders, whether made by consent or in proceedings which are contested, are not to be set aside on the ground of non-disclosure if the disclosure would not have made any substantial difference to the order which the court would have made.

**LORD KEITH OF KINKEL.** My Lords, I have had the advantage of reading in draft the speech to be delivered by my noble and learned friend Lord Brandon. I agree with it, and for the reasons he gives I too would allow the appeal.

**LORD BRIDGE OF HARWICH.** My Lords, for the reasons given in the speech of my noble and learned friend Lord Brandon, with which I fully agree, I would allow the appeal and remit the proceedings for rehearing by a judge of the Family Division of the High Court.

**LORD BRANDON OF OAKBROOK.** My Lords, this appeal arises in the field of family law and concerns the making by the court of consent orders for financial provision and property adjustment following a divorce.

On the facts of the present case two important questions of principle require to be decided by your Lordships. The first question is this. Where a compromise in respect of claims for financial provision and property adjustment made by either or both of the former spouses has been reached by two firms of solicitors acting on their respective behalf, with the intention that the terms of such compromise shall subsequently be given effect to by a consent order of the court, is each of the former spouses under a remaining duty to disclose to the other, or to the other's solicitors, the occurrence of a material change in his or her situation which has taken place after the compromise has been reached but before effect has been given to it by the making of a consent order by the court? The second question is this. Assuming that the remaining duty referred to above exists, and is not complied with by one of the two former spouses, so that a consent order is made by the court without such material change having been taken into account, is the other former spouse entitled, in proceedings before a judge of first instance, to have the order so made set aside?

As will appear, a circuit judge and the Court of Appeal have held, in effect, in the present case, in favour of a former wife and against a former husband, that there is no remaining duty of disclosure of the kind mentioned in the first question above, and that, since there is no such duty, the second question referred to above does not arise. The former husband now brings a further appeal with regard to these matters, with the leave of the Court of Appeal, to your Lordships' House.

The appellant is David Henry Jenkins and the respondent is Beryl Livesey (formerly Jenkins). In what follows I shall for convenience refer to them as 'the husband' and 'the wife' respectively, despite the fact that, by reason of the divorce which I shall mention shortly, they are no longer married to each other.

The husband and the wife were married on 20 February 1957. There are two children of the family, both boys: Matthew, now aged 15, and Nicholas, now aged 13. Prior to 15 October 1981 the husband and the wife, with their two children, were living in a house near Liskeard in Cornwall. That house, to which I shall refer from now on as 'the matrimonial home', was owned jointly by the husband and the wife, subject to a mortgage on it. On 15 October 1981, following marital disagreements apparently arising from the husband's association with another woman, the husband left the matrimonial home, since when he has never returned to live in it.

Before the husband left both he and the wife had consulted different firms of solicitors about their marital troubles. As a result an exchange of letters between these two firms, relating to the affairs of the husband and the wife and the two children, had begun on 9 September 1981 and continued for a long time afterwards. In the course of that correspondence the two firms of solicitors succeeded in reaching agreement on a number of matters on behalf of their respective clients.

The first agreement was that, since the marriage had broken down irretrievably, the wife should divorce the husband on the basis of a written confession of adultery to be provided by him. The second agreement was that the wife should have custody of the two children, with reasonable access for the husband. The third agreement was that, following the proposed divorce, there should be a consent order of the court in respect of financial provision and property adjustment, which would dispose finally of all claims by both the husband and the wife in respect of such matters.

In accordance with these agreements the wife presented a petition for divorce in the Plymouth County Court, and on 1 March 1982 was granted a decree nisi in an undefended suit. That decree was made absolute on 14 April 1982. Meanwhile, negotiations with regard to the proposed consent order for financial provision and property adjustment were continuing, and on or about 12 August 1982 the solicitors on either side reached final agreement about the form and terms of such order.

The proposed consent order so agreed contained two essential provisions material to this appeal. The first such provision was that the husband should transfer to the wife his half share in the matrimonial home, subject to the mortgage on it, for which the wife would, after such transfer, have sole responsibility. The expressed purpose of this transfer was to provide the wife with a home entirely of her own, in which she could live with the two children. The second essential provision was that, with the wife's consent, all her claims for financial provision for herself should be finally dismissed.

It is apparent from the correspondence between the solicitors on either side that these two essential provisions of the proposed form of consent order were interdependent, that is to say that, in substance, the consideration for the transfer by the husband to the wife of his half share in the matrimonial home was the wife's final abandonment of all claims by her for financial provision for herself, and vice versa.

The proposed consent order contained a number of other provisions in addition to the two essential provisions referred to above. These are not, however, directly relevant to the appeal, and it will therefore be convenient to defer setting them out in full until a later stage. The possibility of the wife deciding to remarry another man at any time, and more particularly of her doing so in the near future, before the proposed consent order came to be put into effect by the court, was never once mentioned in the correspondence between the solicitors on either side, or between the parties themselves.

On 18 August 1982 the wife became engaged to be married to another man, Thomas Livesey, whom she had first met on 12 July 1982. She did not disclose the fact of this engagement either to the husband or his solicitors or even to her own solicitors.

On 19 August 1982 the solicitors for the husband and the wife issued jointly on behalf of their respective clients in the Plymouth County Court a registrar's summons applying for a consent order in the form and terms previously agreed between them. On 2 September 1982, the wife still not having disclosed the fact of her engagement to Thomas Livesey either to the husband or his solicitors or to her own solicitors, Mr Registrar Carder made the consent order which had been jointly applied for in the summons of 19 August 1982. The registrar, in accordance with common practice at that time, did not make any inquiries of his own about the nature or basis of the proposed consent order, but, relying on the fact that the husband and the wife were both represented by solicitors, made an order on 2 September 1982 in the form and terms sought.

The full terms of the order so made were as follows:

'UPON THE JOINT APPLICATION OF The Petitioner and Respondent IT IS ORDERED: 1. That the Respondent do within 28 days of the granting of the Order transfer to the Petitioner his interest in the former matrimonial home situate and known as Peach Tree Cottage, Higher Tremar, St. Cleer Near Liskeard in the County of Cornwall. 2. That the petitioner shall be solely responsible for the mortgage, insurance, general and water rates and all other outgoings in respect of the said Peach Tree Cottage as from the date of the transfer of the Respondent's interest in the property to the Petitioner. 3. That the Respondent do pay or cause to be paid as from the date of the Order hereunder periodical payments to the children Matthew Charles Jenkins (born 4.10.69) and Nicholas Robert Jenkins (born 20.1.71) at the rate of £7·50 per week each until they shall attain the age of 17 years or further order. 4. That the Respondent do accept sole responsibility for payment of the overdraft (if any) on the parties' current account with the Midland Bank PLC and the overdraft (if any) on the parties' budget account with the Midland Bank PLC. 5. That the Respondent do accept sole responsibility for discharging the loan account with the Midland Bank PLC in respect of his motorcycle and the Petitioner shall release any interest she may have in the said motorcycle to the Respondent. 6. That the Petitioner do accept sole responsibility for discharging the loan account with the Midland Bank PLC in respect of the wood-burning stove and insulation. 7. That the Petitioner do retain and the Respondent do transfer to the Petitioner all his interest in the "H" registration

Hillman Avenger motor car. 8. That the Petitioner and Respondent each retain such items forming part of the contents of the former matrimonial home as held by them on or before 14th December 1981, save that the Respondent be at liberty to collect and retain as his sole property the tools (other than the gardening tools) at the former matrimonial home. 9. That all other claims of the Petitioner and the Respondent against each other for periodical payments, maintenance pending suit, lump sums, secured provision and property adjustment or settlement are hereby dismissed. 10. That neither party shall upon the death of the other apply for an Order under S. 2 of the Inheritance (Provision for Family and Dependants) Act 1975. 11. That there should be no order as to costs.'

My Lords, the form of this order is open to criticism in a number of respects. These criticisms, however, have no direct bearing on the substance of the appeal, and I shall, therefore, defer reference to them until later.

On 22 September 1982 the husband, in accordance with para 1 of the consent order, executed a conveyance to the wife of his half share in the matrimonial home. That home had a value of about £28,000, subject to a mortgage of £3,646, so that the value of the transfer was somewhat over £12,000.

Two days later, on 24 September 1982, the wife married Thomas Livesey. The husband later learned of the marriage and further correspondence relating to it then ensued between the solicitors on either side. In a letter dated 21 October 1982 the husband's solicitors complained that the husband had been induced to agree to the making of the consent order by a misrepresentation by the wife as to her true position. In a letter dated 1 November 1982 the wife's solicitors denied any misrepresentation by the wife, asserted that the husband's solicitors must have taken into account the possibility of the wife remarrying when advising the husband about the consent order, and said that it had in any case been for the husband to make any necessary inquiries with regard to the matter.

My Lords, the suggestion that the wife had made any misrepresentation to the husband or his solicitors, which induced him to agree to the making of the consent order, cannot be supported. The true position was that the wife, having become engaged to be married to Thomas Livesey on 19 August 1982, failed to disclose that fact at any time before the consent order was made on 2 September 1982. The importance of that non-disclosure lay in this: that, by s 28 of the Matrimonial Causes Act 1973, the wife would, on remarriage, have lost permanently any right to any financial provision from the husband. That being so, if the husband or his solicitors had been informed of the intended remarriage at any time before the consent order was made, it is clear that the husband would have withdrawn his consent to the making of that order, under which, in substance, the consideration for the transfer by him to the wife of his half share in the matrimonial home was, as I indicated earlier, her agreement to the final dismissal of all her claims for financial provision for herself.

About two months after the wife had been remarried, she arranged for the publication in the Cornish Times of 26 November 1982 of an advertisement for the sale of the matrimonial home at a price of £28,000. In view, however, of the further proceedings to which I shall now refer, the wife did not proceed with the intended sale.

On 3 April 1983 the husband's solicitors issued in the Plymouth County Court a registrar's summons applying, first, for leave to appeal out of time against the consent order made by Mr Registrar Carder on 2 September 1982 and, second, for that order to be set aside. The grounds of the application stated in the summons were, first, that the wife had failed to disclose a material fact, namely that she intended to remarry, and, second, the fact of her remarriage. The husband's solicitors filed two affidavits by him in support of his application, in which he stated that he had first learnt of the wife's remarriage in the middle of October 1982. The wife's solicitors filed an affidavit by her in answer, in which she admitted that the husband did not learn of her remarriage until 10 October 1982. There was further available at the hearing of the husband's application an agreed bundle containing copies of all the material letters which has passed between the solicitors on either side from beginning to end.

The husband's summons dated 3 April 1983 was heard on 5 May 1983, not by a registrar, but by a circuit judge, his Honour Judge Anthony Cox. The judge, in his judgment, after discussing the delay by the husband in making his application, exercised his discretion to allow the husband's appeal against the consent order to be brought out of time. Having done so, he proceeded to deal with the substantive appeal. He said that he was not satisfied that there had been full disclosure by the wife before the consent order was made, but considered himself bound, by an earlier decision of the Family Division of the High Court, to refuse to set aside the consent order on that ground. The decision concerned was that of Tudor Evans J in *Wales v Wadham* [1977] 2 All ER 125, [1977] 1 WLR 199.

By notice of appeal dated 14 June 1983 the husband appealed to the Court of Appeal against the decision of Judge Anthony Cox. The appeal was heard on 21 December 1983 by a two-judge court, consisting of Sir John Arnold P and Heilbron J. That court dismissed the appeal, but gave the husband leave to bring a further appeal to your Lordships' House.

My Lords, there can be no doubt that this appeal raises important questions of principles in family law. None of the authorities which have any bearing on those questions are binding on your Lordships' House, and I propose, therefore, to consider the questions first from the point of view of principle, and to examine and comment on some of the relevant authorities later.

In considering the questions from the point of view of principle, there are four matters which I think that it is necessary to state and emphasise from the beginning. The first matter is that the powers of a judge of the Family Division of the High Court or of a judge of a divorce county court to make orders for financial provision and property adjustment following a divorce are conferred on them, and conferred on them solely, by statute, the relevant statute at the time of the proceedings out of which this appeal arises being the Matrimonial Causes Act 1973. The second matter is that there is no difference in this respect between a judge's powers to make such orders after a disputed hearing involving evidence on both sides and his powers to make such orders by the consent of the parties without having heard any evidence at all. The third matter is that the powers of registrars to make such orders, when delegated to them by rules of court, are exactly the same as those of judges, whether the proceedings concerned are in the principal registry of the Family Division or in the registry of a divorce county court. The fourth matter is that, when parties agree the provisions of a consent order, and the court subsequently gives effect to such agreement by approving the provisions concerned and embodying them in an order of the court, the legal effect of those provisions is derived from the court order itself, and does not depend any longer on the agreement between the parties: see *de Lasala v de Lasala* [1979] 2 All ER 1146 at 1155, [1980] AC 546 at 560 per Lord Diplock.

The powers to make orders for financial provision following a divorce were at the material time, and are still, conferred by s 23 of the 1973 Act. The kinds of orders for financial provision authorised by s 23(1) include orders for the making by one of the former spouses to the other, or by either of such former spouses to a specified person for the benefit of any children of the family, or to such children themselves, of, first, unsecured periodical payments, second, secured periodical payments and, third, lump sums.

The powers to make orders for property adjustment following a divorce were at the material time, and are still, conferred by s 24 of the 1973 Act. The kinds of orders for property adjustment authorised by s 24(1) include orders for the transfer of property of any kind by either or each of the former spouses to the other, or to a specified person for the benefit of any children of the family, orders for the settlement by either of the former spouses of property of any kind for the benefit either of the other former spouse, or of any children of the family, orders varying, for the benefit of the two former spouses and any children of the family, any ante-nuptial or post-nuptial settlements and orders extinguishing or reducing the interest of either of the former spouses under any such settlements.

The powers conferred by ss 23 and 24, which I have summarised above, are essentially discretionary powers, and s 25 of the 1973 Act prescribed at the material time the criteria by reference to which courts should exercise the discretion so given to them. That section has since been repealed and replaced by a new and different s 25 by s 3 of the Matrimonial and Family Proceedings Act 1984.

Section 25(1) of the 1973 Act, as originally enacted, so far as material, provided as follows:

> 'It shall be the duty of the court in deciding whether to exercise its powers under section 23(1)(a), (b) or (c) or 24 above in relation to a party to the marriage and, if so, in what manner, to have regard to all the circumstances of the case including the following matters, that is to say—(a) the income, earning capacity, property and other financial resources which each of the parties to the marriage has or is likely to have in the foreseeable future; (b) the financial needs, obligations and responsibilities which each of the parties to the marriage has or is likely to have in the foreseeable future . . .'

The references to the powers under s 23(1)(a), (b) or (c) are references to the powers to order financial provision to be made by one former spouse to the other in the form of unsecured periodical payments, secured periodical payments and lump sums.

My Lords, the terms of s 25(1) of the 1973 Act which I have set out above are, in my opinion, of crucial importance in relation to the questions raised by this appeal. The scheme which the legislature enacted by ss 23, 24 and 25 of the 1973 Act was a scheme under which the court would be bound, before deciding whether to exercise its powers under ss 23 and 24, and, if so, in what manner, to have regard to all the circumstances of the case, including, inter alia, the particular matters specifed in paras (a) and (b) of s 25(1). It follows that, in proceedings in which parties invoke the exercise of the court's powers under ss 23 and 24, they must provide the court with information about all the circumstances of the case, including, inter alia, the particular matters so specified. Unless they do so, directly or indirectly, and ensure that the information provided is correct, complete and up to date, the court is not equipped to exercise, and cannot therefore lawfully and properly exercise, its discretion in the manner ordained by s 25(1).

In contested cases relating to the exercise of the court's powers under ss 23 and 24 the requirement that it should have the prescribed information is met by rules of court with which both parties must comply. The relevant rules are the Matrimonial Causes Rules 1977, SI 1977/344. Rules 73 to 76 deal with affidavit evidence to be filed. Rule 77 deals with the investigation by a registrar of applications, in the course of which one party may be compelled to give further information to the other on any material matter; orders may be made for lists or affidavits of documents and for the inspection and production of documents referred to in them, for the hearing of oral evidence, for the cross-examination of deponents on their affidavits and for the filing of further affidavits. Only when the registrar has before him all the material which he considers to be necessary for the exercise of his discretion under s 25(1) (and there may have to be more than one hearing before him in order that this should be achieved) does he go on to make such orders, if any, as he thinks right under ss 23 and 24. If the contested claims come before a judge instead of a registrar, as often happens in more difficult cases, the procedure is the same. Any changes in the situation of either party occurring between the filing of the original affidavits and the final disposition of the claims by the court must be brought to the notice of the other party and the court by further affidavits or otherwise. In this way, so far as contested claims are concerned, the court should normally be provided directly with adequate information on all the matters to which it is bound to have regard under s 25(1).

The situation with regard to consent orders, especially where no affidavits are filed at all and reliance is placed entirely on the exchange of information between the solicitors of the parties, was at the material time less satisfactory. There were at the time of the proceedings out of which this appeal arises no statutory provisions or rules of court relating specifically to the making of consent orders. It was, as I indicated earlier, common practice for registrars to make such orders without making any inquiries themselves, but relying simply on the fact that both parties were represented by solicitors, and that these could be relied on to have inquired adequately into all the matters to which regard has to be had under s 25(1) before advising their respective clients to agree to the making of consent orders by the court. In this way the court considered that it was indirectly, through the medium of the solicitors concerned, having regard to all such matters before making the consent orders sought. I do not suggest that this practice was wholly satisfactory, and, as I shall show later, it has since been improved.

I stated earlier that, unless a court is provided with correct, complete and up-to-date information on the matters to which, under s 25(1), it is required to have regard, it cannot lawfully or properly exercise its discretion in the manner ordained by that subsection. If follows necessarily from this that each party concerned in claims for financial provision and property adjustment (or other forms of ancillary relief not material in the present case) owes a duty to the court to make full and frank disclosure of all material facts to the other party and the court. This principle of full and frank disclosure in proceedings of this kind has long been recognised and enforced as a matter of practice. The legal basis of that principle, and the justification for it, are to be found in the statutory provisions to which I have referred.

My Lords, once it is accepted that this principle of full and frank disclosure exists, it is obvious that it must apply not only to contested proceedings heard with full evidence adduced before the court, but also to exchanges of information between parties and their solicitors leading to the making of consent orders without further inquiry by the court. If that were not so, it would be impossible for a court to have any assurance that the requirements of s 25(1) were complied with before it made such consent orders.

Applying this principle to the facts of the present case, there can be no doubt whatever that the fact that the wife had, on 18 August 1982, become engaged to be remarried shortly to Thomas Livesey was a matter which she was under a duty to disclose before the agreement with regard to financial provision and property adjustment previously reached between the solicitors on either side was put into effect, as it was on 2 September 1982, by the making of a consent order in the form and terms so agreed. This is because the fact of the wife's engagement was one of the circumstances of the case referred to in s 25(1), and was further of direct relevance to the particular matters specified in paras (a) and (b) of that subsection. Such disclosure should have been made by the wife to her own solicitors, and through them to the husband's solicitors, and the husband himself, as soon as the engagement to remarry took place. Since it was not made, the consent order was invalid, and the husband should be entitled, in order to prevent injustice, to have it set aside.

My Lords, I have until now discussed the two questions raised by this appeal, namely whether the wife was under a duty to disclose her engagement as soon as it occurred and whether her failure to do so entitled the husband to have the consent order set aside, from the point of view of principle only. I turn now to examine and comment on such recent authorities as have a bearing on these matters.

The most important of such authorities is Wales v Wadham [1977] 2 All ER 125, [1977] 1 WLR 199, which, as I indicated earlier, was an authority against the existence of any duty of disclosure, by which Judge Anthony Cox rightly considered himself to be bound, and which the Court of Appeal approved and applied.

The essential facts of that case were these. It was agreed between the husband and the wife that a consent order should be made following a divorce under which the husband should pay to the wife, out of his half share of the former matrimonial home, the sum of £13,000 in full and final settlement of any claims which she might otherwise have for financial provision for herself. Both parties consulted solicitors and the agreement was reached without any affidavits having been filed. The agreed terms were subsequently embodied in a court order made under ss 23 and 25 of the 1973 Act. In the course of the negotiations both parties failed to disclose matters relevant to the making of an order for financial provision. The wife failed to disclose the fact that she intended to remarry soon after decree absolute. The husband failed to disclose the resources available to him and another woman with whom he was living.

The wife having remarried shortly after decree absolute, the husband brought an action in the Bristol district registry of the Queen's Bench Division, in which he claimed rescission of the agreement and a declaration that the consent order be set aside on four main grounds. These were, first, that the wife had fraudulently misrepresented to him that she did not intend to remarry, second, that the agreement had been made in such circumstances that the doctrine of uberrima fides applied to it at common law, third, that the established practice of the Family Division imposed a duty on parties to proceedings for financial provision and other forms of ancillary relief a duty to make a full and frank disclosure of all material facts before any order was made, and, fourth, that the husband had entered into the agreement under a unilateral mistake in that he believed that the wife did not intend to remarry.

The action, having been begun in the Queen's Bench Division of the High Court, was subsequently transferred to the Family Division and tried there by Tudor Evans J. The judge decided the action in favour of the wife. He dealt with the husband's four grounds of claim in this way. First, with regard to fraudulent misrepresentation, he found that the case failed on the facts. Second, with regard to the agreement being one to which the doctrine of uberrima fides applied at common law, he held that, in the circumstances in which the negotiations for the agreement took place and the agreement was ultimately made, the common law doctrine relied on did not apply. Third, with regard to the practice of the Family Division under which parties to proceedings for financial provision or other ancillary relief were required to make full and frank disclosure of all material facts, he held that, since no affidavits had been filed, and the parties were bargaining at arm's length with the help of their respective solicitors, the usual requirement for such disclosure did not apply. Fourth, with regard to unilateral mistake, he held that, since the husband had had in mind the possibility that the wife might remarry when he made the offer to pay £13,000 in settlement of all her claims, it was impossible to find that the husband's mind was affected by a fundamental mistake of fact such at to entitle him to rescind the agreement on that ground.

My Lords, I do not consider that the manner in which Tudor Evans J disposed of the first, second and fourth of the husband's grounds of claim are open to criticism in any way. With regard to the manner in which he disposed of the third ground of claim, however, I am clearly of opinion that he erred in law. That he did so is understandable, because the husband's attack was directed primarily at the agreement between the parties, and only secondarily at the consent order made pursuant to it, whereas what really mattered was that consent order, from which, once it had been made, the rights of the parties were derived to the exclusion of the earlier agreement itself.

When the question of the validity of the consent order, as distinct from that of the earlier agreement, is looked at, it becomes apparent that the principle of full and frank disclosure of all material facts, depending as it does, for the reasons which I gave earlier, on the terms of s 25(1) of the 1973 Act, could not in any circumstances be rendered inapplicable by the manner in which the earlier agreement was negotiated and reached. The principle concerned does not depend in any way on the concept that the parties must, in reaching an agreement for a consent order, show uberrima fides in the contractual connotation of that expression. It depends rather on the statutory requirement imposed by s 25(1), that the court must exercise its discretion to make orders under ss 23 and 24 in accordance with the criteria prescribed by that subsection, and that, unless the parties make full and frank disclosure of all material matters, the court cannot lawfully or properly exercise such discretion.

In my judgment, therefore, Tudor Evans J was wrong in *Wales v Wadham* to reject so much of the husband's claim as was based on the need for full and frank disclosure in ancillary proceedings in the Family Division, and the Court of Appeal in the present case was wrong to approve and apply that decision.

In *Tommey v Tommey* [1982] 3 All ER 385, [1983] Fam 15 a wife applied to set aside a consent order under which she was to transfer to the husband her half share in the former matrimonial home and the husband was to pay to her £8,000 in full and final settlement of all her claims for financial provision for herself. The main ground on which she claimed to have the consent order set aside was that, in the negotiations leading up to the agreement pursuant to which the consent order was made, the husband had exercised undue influence on the wife. Balcombe J held, as a matter of law, that undue influence, even if proved, was not a good ground for setting aside a consent order. The question of the effect of undue influence in circumstances of this kind does not arise on this appeal, and, that being so, it would be undesirable to express even a provisional opinion on it. I think it right to say, however, that I am not persuaded that Balcombe J's decision on the question was necessarily correct.

The wife in that case, however, had relied on another ground for setting aside the consent order, namely that, because the husband had filed no affidavit, the judge had made the consent order without having full knowledge of all the material facts. With regard to this contention Balcombe J said ([1982] 3 All ER 385 at 390, [1983] Fam 15 at 21):

> 'Nor is there any substance in another ground, namely ignorance of relevant facts on the part of the judge. A judge who is asked to make a consent order cannot be compelled to do so: he is no mere rubber stamp. If he thinks there are matters about which he needs to be more fully informed before he makes the order, he is entitled to make such inquiries and require such evidence to be put before him, as he considers necessary. But, per contra, he is under no obligation to make inquiries or require evidence. He is entitled to assume that parties of full age and capacity know what is in their own best interests, more especially when they are represented before him by counsel or solicitors. The fact that he was not told facts which, had he known them, might have affected his decision to make a consent order cannot of itself be a ground for impeaching the order. Accordingly, the wife is not entitled on this ground to have the order of 18 February 1975 set aside.'

Having regard to the practice with regard to the making of consent orders existing at the time when this judgment of Balcombe J was given, there is a great deal of practical common sense in the paragraph from that judgment set out above. But, if Balcombe J was saying, as I think that he was by necessary implication, that, in the case of consent orders made without affidavits having been filed, between parties of full age and capacity and represented by counsel or solicitors, the principles of full and frank disclosure of all material facts was not applicable, I cannot agree with that view. For the reasons of principle which I discussed earlier, the requirement of full and frank disclosure always exists in proceedings for financial provision and other ancillary relief. It is, as I have sought to stress, a requirement founded on the terms of s 25(1) of the 1973 Act, and, for reasons of public policy, it is not open to parties, whether represented by lawyers or not, to disregard, or to contract out of, such requirement. To the extent which I have indicated, I am of opinion that, in *Tommey v Tommey*, Balcombe J erred in law.

In *Robinson v Robinson* [1982] 2 All ER 699n, [1982] 1 WLR 786n the requirement of full and frank disclosure in relation to a consent order was forcefully upheld by the Court of Appeal. In that case the parties had been divorced in 1973, at which time the husband was ordered to make periodical payments for the wife and children. The amount of those payments was increased by the Court of Appeal later in the same year. In 1976, on an application by the husband for the periodical payments to the wife herself to be suspended or reduced, the judge discharged the order for such payments in her favour, and made an order, to which the wife consented, under which she accepted a lump sum in full and final settlement of all her claims against the husband. In 1983 the wife applied to a judge at first instance for the two previous orders of 1973 and 1976 to be set aside on the ground that the husband had, on each occasion, misrepresented or inadequately represented his financial position. The judge having dismissed her claim, the wife brought an appeal to the Court of Appeal. That court allowed the appeal and set aside both orders. Its reasons for doing so appear from the headnote of the report (as reported in 4 FLR 102). The first ground was that, in proceedings for ancillary relief, there was a duty, both under the rules and by authority, on the parties to make full and frank disclosure of their property and financial resources; accordingly, the power to set aside orders was not limited to cases of fraud or mistake, but extended to cases of material non-disclosure; where it could be said that, on the true facts, the orders should not have been made, then the orders could be set aside. The second ground was that, although intensive research might have revealed to the wife the husband's financial position, it was clear that, both in 1973 and in the proceedings leading up to his application in 1976, the husband had not provided the wife with the full and frank disclosure to which she was entitled; accordingly, the orders would be set aside, so that the parties could either settle their differences or go to court for a settlement based on the position in 1982.

The principal judgment setting out these reasons for allowing the appeal was that of Templeman LJ. Ormrod LJ and Wood J agreed with his judgment. The former said ([1982] All ER 699n at 700, [1982] 1 WLR 786n at 786–787):

'There is no doubt that both the Court of Appeal and the judge at first instance have jurisdiction in the situation with which we are faced in this case, where the application is to set aside a final order. Lord Diplock said so in *de Lasala v de Lasala* [1979] 2 All ER 1146 at 1155, [1980] AC 546 at 561: "Where a party to an action who seeks to challenge, on the ground that it was obtained by fraud or mistake, a judgment or order that finally disposes of the issues raised between the parties, the only ways of doing it that are open to him are by appeal from the judgment or order to a higher court or by bringing a fresh action to set it aside." There are many references in the books to separate actions to set aside a judgment on the ground of fraud. In the Family Division, as has been said many times, this power to set aside final orders is not limited to cases when fraud or mistake can be alleged. It extends, and has always extended, to cases of material non-disclosure ... A distinction has to be drawn between the restrictions imposed by the Matrimonial Causes Act 1973 on varying lump sum orders or property adjustment orders which cannot be varied, and the power to set aside an order which has been obtained by fraud or mistake, or by material non-disclosure. The essence of the distinction is that the power to vary usually reflects changes of circumstances subsequent to the date of the order, whereas the power to set aside arises when there has been fraud, mistake or material non-disclosure as to the facts *at the time the order was made*. From the point of view of convenience, there is a lot to be said for proceedings of this kind taking place before a judge at first instance, because there will usually be serious and often difficult issues of fact to be determined before the power to set aside can be exercised. These can be determined more easily, as a rule, by a judge at first instance. Moreover he can go on to make the appropriate order which we cannot do in this court. I think that these proceedings should normally be started before a judge at first instance, although there may be special circumstances which make it better to proceed by way of appeal.' (My emphasis.)

Then, after referring to the well-known principle of the 'clean break' discussed extensively by Lord Scarman in *Minton v Minton* [1979] 1 All ER 79, [1979] AC 593, Ormrod LJ continued ([1982] 2 All ER 699n at 700–701, [1982] 1 WLR 786n at 787):

'It is essential in these case that the court retains its power to protect both parties against injustice which may arise from failure to comply with their obligations to disclose. In other words there is a lot to be said for the principle of the clean break but I have no doubt that Lord Scarman, when he used the phrase in *Minton v Minton*, had in mind the break should be clean in more senses than one.'

My Lords, this decision of the Court of Appeal in *Robinson v Robinson* fully supports, on the basis of long-established authority, the opinion with regard to the duty on parties to make full and frank disclosure of material matters before an order for ancillary relief, including a consent order, is made under ss 23, 24 and 25(1) of the 1973 Act at which I arrived earlier, on the basis of principle, by an examination of the terms of s 25(1).

Both on principle and on authority, therefore, I am of opinion that the wife was in this case under a duty to disclose the facts of her engagement as soon as it took place, and that her failure to do so is relevant to the validity of the consent order. I am further of the opinion that, since the fact which was not disclosed undermined, as it were, the whole basis on which the consent order was agreed, that order should be set aside and the proceedings for financial provision and property adjustment remitted to the Family Division of the High Court for rehearing by a judge of that division. I would, therefore, allow the appeal and remit the case in the manner indicated.

My Lords, there are several subsidiary matters with which I consider that it is appropriate for me to deal before parting from this appeal.

The first matter is that, following the decision of the Court of Appeal in this case, the President of the Family Division, with the concurrence of the Lord Chancellor, issued a Practice Direction dated 13 April 1984 ([1984] 2 All ER 256, [1984] 1 WLR 674) relating to the procedure to be followed in applications for financial provision or property adjustment. That practice direction provided, inter alia, as follows:

'The decision of the Court of Appeal in *Jenkins v Livesey* (*formerly Jenkins*) is a reminder that in all cases where application is made for financial provision or property adjustment order the court is required to have before it an agreed statement of the general nature of the means of each party signed by the parties or their solicitors. If affidavits of means have been filed it will be sufficient if the statement is in the form of a certificate that there has been no change of substance since the date of the affidavit or, if there has, what changes there have been. If no such evidence has been filed the statement should include a summary of the amount or value of the capital and income resources of each of the spouses . . . and any special features which require to be considered under s 25 of the Matrimonial Causes Act 1973 . . .'

This Practice Direction was clearly a step in the right direction so far as the making of consent orders for financial provision or property adjustment is concerned.

The second matter is that, by s 7 of the 1984 Act, a new s 33A has been inserted to follow s 33 in the 1973 Act. This new section deals expressly with consent orders for financial relief, an expression which, by the terms of s 37 of the 1973 Act, includes, inter alia, both financial provision and property adjustment. It provides:

'(1) Notwithstanding anything in the preceding provisions of this Part of this Act, on an application for a consent order for financial relief the court may, unless it has reason to think that there are other circumstances into which it ought to inquire, make an order in the terms agreed on the basis only of the prescribed information furnished with the application . . .
(3) In this section . . . "prescribed" means prescribed by rules of court.'

Relevant rules of court have been made and are to be found in the Matrimonial Causes (Amendment) Rules 1984, SI 1984/1511. Rule 8 of those rules inserts after r 76 of the Matrimonial Causes Rules 1977 a new r 76A, dealing with the procedure to be followed on applications for consent orders for financial relief. The procedure so laid down includes the lodging of a statement containing the kind of information which the court needs to have before making an order in accordance with the revised criteria contained in the new s 25, substituted by s 3 of the 1984 Act for the original s 25 of the 1973 Act.

These further provisions, by statute and rules of court, represent a further step in the right direction, following on the Practice Direction referred to above. It must not be thought, however, that these further provisions alter in any way at all the basic principle of the need for full and frank disclosure by the parties before a consent order is made.

The third matter relates to the form of the consent order made in this case. I said earlier that its form was open to a number of criticisms, and it is right that I should now indicate what these criticisms are. When a consent order is drafted it is essential that all its terms should come clearly within the court's powers conferred on it by ss 23 and 24 of the 1973 Act. In the present case there are several terms which are not within those powers. These are para 2, which directs that the wife shall be solely responsible, after the transfer to her of the husband's half share in the matrimonial home, for the mortgage on it and all other outgoings relating to it, and paras 4, 5 and 6, which direct that the husband and the wife are to be solely responsible for certain specified bank overdrafts and loan accounts. There is nothing in s 23 or s 24 of the 1973 Act which directly empowers the court to make orders of these kinds. That being so, the proper procedure for incorporating the obligations concerned into a consent order is by formulating them as undertakings given to the court. Such undertakings are, needless to say, enforceable as effectively as direct orders.

The fourth and final matter arises out of certain observations made by Sir John Arnold P in the present case with regard to the judgment of a two-judge Court of Appeal, consisting of Ormrod LJ and myself, in *Wells v Wells* [1980] CA Transcript 526. Sir John Arnold P expressed the view that this case was decided per incuriam and should not be followed. Since I gave the only judgment in the case, with which Ormrod LJ agreed, I feel some diffidence in questioning the learned President's observations. Despite such diffidence, however, I think that I should, in defence both of Ormrod LJ and of myself, express my firm view that *Wells v Wells* was in no way decided per incuriam. The history of the case is simple. On 2 October 1979 Booth J had made an order in contested proceedings for financial provision and property adjustment. In December 1979 the wife began to associate with another man whom she had known before; later she began living with him; and on 19 April 1980 she married him. Four days earlier, on 15 April 1980, the husband applied to a division of the Court of Appeal, in which to the best of my recollection I myself was not sitting, for leave to appeal out of time from the order of Booth J dated 2 October 1979, on the ground of a radical change of circumstances occurring after that order had been made. Leave to appeal out of time was given, and later the substantive appeal came before a different division of the Court of Appeal, consisting of Ormrod LJ and myself. It was apparent that the whole basis on which Booth J had made her order had been falsified by events occurring within about three months of the date on which it had been made. Ormrod LJ and I accordingly took the view that, in order that justice should be done, Booth J's order, based on a state of affairs falsified by later events, should be set aside, and that a different order, based on the true state of affairs by then existing, should be substituted for it. I can see that two views might be taken of the prior decision to give the husband leave to appeal out of time at all. That decision having been made, however, I cannot see that the court hearing the substantive appeal could have done otherwise than allow it and substitute a just order for what, in the events which had since occurred, was plainly an unjust order.

My Lords, I hope that I have not taken up too much time with these subsidiary matters, since they do not bear directly on the decision of this appeal. As to that, I have indicated earlier the order which I have concluded should be made on the appeal, and my reasons for reaching that conclusion.

I would end with an emphatic word of warning. It is not every failure of frank and full disclosure which would justify a court in setting aside an order of the kind concerned in this appeal. On the contrary, it will only be in cases when the absence of full and frank disclosure has led to the court making, either in contested proceedings or by consent, an order which is substantially different from the order which it would have made if such disclosure had taken place that a case for setting aside can possibly be made good. Parties who apply to set aside orders on the ground of failure to disclose some relatively minor matter or matters, the disclosure of which would not have made any substantial difference to the order which the court would have made or approved, are likely to find their applications being summarily dismissed, with costs against them, or, if they are legally aided, against the legal aid fund.

*Appeal allowed.*

Solicitors: *Gregory Rowcliffe & Co,* agents for *G & I Chisholm,* Bodmin (for the husband); *Bower Cotton & Bower,* agents for *Bond Pearce,* Liskeard (for the wife).

Mary Rose Plummer    Barrister.

# Meng Leong Development Pte Ltd v Jip Hong Trading Co Pte Ltd

PRIVY COUNCIL

LORD KEITH OF KINKEL, LORD BRIDGE OF HARWICH, LORD BRANDON OF OAKBROOK, LORD TEMPLEMAN AND SIR ROBIN COOKE

13, 14 JUNE, 15 OCTOBER 1984

*Estoppel – Election – Litigation – Election to accept particular remedy – Action by purchaser for specific performance of contract – Purchaser awarded damages instead – Purchaser accepting award – Purchaser later wishing to appeal in order to seek specific performance – Whether purchaser estopped from seeking specific performance on appeal.*

The purchaser brought an action against the vendor seeking specific performance of a contract for the sale of a property in Singapore or alternatively damages for breach of contract. At the trial the judge refused specific performance in the mistaken belief that it was not open to him to grant that relief because the vendor had, after the date of the contract, sold the property to a third party who was not before the court. The judge accordingly awarded the purchaser damages in lieu of specific performance. The vendor appealed against the amount of damages awarded and in the mean time, at the purchaser's insistence and in order to forestall the purchaser levying execution, the vendor paid the damages awarded into a bank account in the name of the purchaser's solicitors to be held by them as stakeholders to await the outcome of the appeal. When the appeal came on for hearing by the Singapore Court of Appeal the court pointed out that the purchaser's right to specific performance at the date of the trial could not be affected by any sale to a third party with notice and gave leave to the purchaser to cross-appeal for specific performance. The vendor's appeal was accordingly adjourned. At the resumed hearing of the appeal the court dismissed the vendor's appeal as to quantum and allowed the purchaser's cross-appeal for specific performance. At no time was the court informed of the deposit of damages into a bank account. The vendor appealed to the Privy Council. At the hearing before the Board the vendor was given leave to argue for the first time that the purchaser was estopped from seeking specific performance after electing to enforce the order for damages.

**Held** (Sir Robin Cooke dissenting) – The purchaser's action in demanding and accepting the deposit of the damages awarded to it was consistent with an election on its part to accept the trial judge's award of damages and abandon its right of appeal seeking specific performance. Since the vendor had altered its position to its detriment by raising and paying over the damages when it would not have been required to do so if the purchaser had sought specific performance on appeal, the purchaser was estopped from seeking specific performance on appeal. The appeal would therefore be allowed and the Court of Appeal's order for specific performance set aside (see p 123 *j* to p 124 *c* and *g* to *j*, p 125 *d* to *j* and p 126 *b* to *e* and *h* to p 127 *d* and *h j*, post).

## Notes

For estoppel by election, see 16 Halsbury's Laws (4th edn) para 1508, and for cases on the subject, see 21 Digest (Reissue) 17, 77–82.

## Cases referred to in judgment

*Adamson, Ex p, re Collie* (1878) 8 Ch D 807.
*Ajayi v R T Briscoe (Nigeria) Ltd* [1964] 3 All ER 556, [1964] 1 WLR 1326, PC.
*Cannan v Reynolds* (1855) 5 E & B 301, 119 ER 493.
*Johnson v Agnew* [1979] 1 All ER 883, [1980] AC 367, [1979] 2 WLR 487, HL.
*Kaprow (S) & Co Ltd v Maclelland & Co Ltd* [1948] 1 All ER 264, [1948] 1 KB 618, CA.
*Lagunas Nitrate Co v Lagunas Syndicate* [1899] 2 Ch 392.
*United Australia Ltd v Barclays Bank Ltd* [1940] 2 All ER 20, [1941] AC 1, HL.

**Appeal**

By a writ issued on 26 September 1979 the plaintiff, Jip Hong Trading Co Pte Ltd (the purchaser), claimed, inter alia, against the defendant, Meng Leong Development Pte Ltd (the vendor), (1) specific performance of a contract for sale and purchase of a two-storey terrace house now known as 27A Jalan Chengkek, Singapore, constituted by the exercise of an option to purchase in writing dated 21 March 1979 at a price of $152,000, (2) an injunction to restrain the vendor from selling, mortgaging or otherwise dealing with the property and (3) further or alternatively, damages for breach of contract. On 8 September 1981 Rajah J in the High Court of Singapore awarded the purchaser damages of $297,000 and refused a stay of execution pending appeal for reasons given on 16 October 1981. On 16 September 1982 the Court of Appeal of Singapore (Kulasekaram, Lai Kew Chai and Chua JJ), for reasons given on 22 April 1983, dismissed an appeal by the vendor on quantum and allowed a cross-appeal by the purchaser by setting aside the award of damages and in lieu thereof ordering specific performance of the contract. On 22 November 1982 the Court of Appeal gave the vendor leave to appeal to the Judicial Committee of the Privy Council but refused to stay the order for specific performance. On 9 December 1982 the Judicial Committee gave special leave to the vendor to appeal against the refusal of the Court of Appeal to grant a stay of execution and granted a stay against the order for specific performance pending the appeal to the Board. The facts are set out in the judgment of the Board.

*Gerald Godfrey QC* and *Molly Lim* (of the Singapore Bar) for the vendor.
*Edward Nugee QC* and *John Trenhaile* for the purchaser.

15 October. The following judgment of the Board and opinion were delivered.

**LORD TEMPLEMAN.** This appeal arises out of a purchaser's specific performance action. The purchaser is the respondent Jip Hong Trading Co Pte Ltd. The defendant vendor is the appellant Meng Leong Development Pte Ltd. The action was tried by Rajah J in the High Court of Singapore. On behalf of the vendor it was submitted at the trial that specific performance could not be granted because the vendor had, since the date of the purchaser's contract, sold the contractual property to a third party who was not before the court. The judge accepted that submission and awarded damages in lieu of specific performance. The purchaser's contract price was $152,500, the vendor had spent $38,000 on improvements and there was evidence that at the date of the trial the property was worth $488,000. Accordingly, by an order dated 8 September 1981, Rajah J awarded the purchaser $297,500 damages; he refused a stay of execution. By notice dated 23 September 1981 the vendor gave notice of appeal for the purpose of obtaining a reduction in the damages of $297,500 ordered by the judge. The purchaser did not give notice of appeal or cross-appeal against the decision of the judge to deny the purchaser specific performance and to award damages instead. The purchaser shared the mistaken view of the law of specific performance accepted by the judge. The time allowed by the operative rules of court for the service of notice of appeal expired in October 1981, subject to the power of the court to grant an extension of time.

By a letter dated 23 October 1981 the vendor's solicitors wrote to the purchaser's solicitors saying that the purchaser's solicitors had proposed that the vendor pay the $297,500 damages to the Overseas Chinese Banking Corp on fixed deposit on a three-month basis in the name of the purchaser's solicitors to be held by them as stakeholders and to pay over the deposit to the party who succeeded in the pending appeal together with all accrued interest. By a letter dated 28 October 1981 the purchaser's solicitors confirmed these arrangements but added:

> '... the agreement was reached on the strict understanding that the said sum of $297,500/– was to be paid to us immediately without any further delay. Therefore kindly let us have your clients' cheque of $297,500/– on receipt of this letter.'

The plain implication was that if the vendor did not deposit the damages of $297,500 the purchaser would proceed to levy execution for this sum. With a letter dated 12 November 1981 the vendor's solicitors sent to the purchaser's solicitors the vendor's cheque for $297,500 pursuant to the agreement:

> '... that in the event that our clients succeed in the pending appeal and damages payable to your clients are reduced, your clients will only be entitled to a proportionate sum of the interest accrued under the fixed deposit. The balance of the interest is to be paid out to our clients ...'

The vendor's appeal against the quantum of damages came before the Court of Appeal (Kulasekaram, Lai Kew Chai and Chua JJ) on 20 August 1982. The court pointed out that the purchaser's right to specific performance at the date of the trial could not have been affected by any sale to a third party with notice and suggested that the purchaser should cross-appeal asking for specific performance. The Court of Appeal gave leave to the purchaser to do so and adjourned the vendor's appeal. The Court of Appeal was not on that occasion, or any subsequent occasion, informed by either party that the damages of $297,500 ordered by the judge had already been raised by the vendor and placed on deposit awaiting the outcome of the vendor's appeal as to quantum. By notice of cross-appeal dated 8 September 1982 the purchaser asked that the order of Rajah J should be varied and that specific performance be substituted therefor. On 16 September 1982 the Court of Appeal dismissed the vendor's appeal on quantum, allowed the purchaser's cross-appeal and made an order for specific performance. By a letter dated 17 September 1982 the vendor's solicitors wrote to the purchaser's solicitors saying:

> 'As your cross-appeal for specific performance ... has been allowed, kindly release to us our clients' monies held by you as stakeholders together with interest immediately.'

The purchaser declined to release the deposited damages of $297,500 but by a summons dated 5 November 1982 applied for an order giving directions for the conveyance of the property to the purchaser, the delivery up of vacant possession and for the damages of $297,500 to be retained until specific performance had been completed and all moneys and costs due to the purchaser had been accounted for. In support of this application the purchaser's managing director swore an affidavit on 3 November 1982 to which he exhibited all the correspondence between 23 October 1981 and 16 November 1981 which related to the deposit of the damages of $297,500. By an order dated 12 November 1982 Lai Kew Chai J made the order sought by the purchaser's summons. By a notice of motion dated 17 November 1982 the vendor sought leave to appeal to the Judicial Committee against the order for specific performance made by the Court of Appeal and on 22 November 1982 the Court of Appeal gave that leave but refused to stay the order for specific performance. Subsequently, the Court of Appeal refused leave to appeal against their order refusing a stay of specific performance. On 9 December 1982 the Board gave special leave to the vendor to appeal against the refusal of the Court of Appeal to grant a stay of execution and granted a stay against the order for specific performance pending the hearing by the Board of the vendor's appeal.

In the appellant's case to the Board, the vendor alleged that the purchaser was not entitled to an order for specific performance because at the trial before Rajah J the purchaser had elected to accept damages in lieu of specific performance. The vendor sought leave to adduce before the Board evidence as to what had happened at the trial. Their Lordships declined to give such leave; no such election appears from the judgment of Rajah J or from his notes of evidence.

The documents placed before the Board by the vendor in connection with this appeal properly included the affidavit and exhibits of the purchaser's managing director which disclosed the deposit of the damages of $297,500 and the agreement which had been reached with regard thereto. It was suggested by a member of the Board that the Court of Appeal might not have made an order for specific performance if it had been aware of the deposit of the damages and the agreement. The vendor's counsel therefore applied for leave to argue that the purchaser was estopped from seeking specific performance after electing to enforce the order for damages made by the trial judge Rajah J.

The vendor's application to rely on this estoppel by election was opposed by counsel for the purchaser. All the evidence relevant to estoppel was before the Board and there were no material disputes of fact. After a short adjournment counsel for the purchaser was in a position to make submissions concerning estoppel. Accordingly, the Board was in a position to decide whether, as a matter of law, the purchaser was estopped from obtaining specific performance but, as counsel for the purchaser pointed out, the Board will not, save in exceptional circumstances, permit a point to be taken which has been conceded or not taken before the Court of Appeal, especially if, as in the present case, the point is not adumbrated in the relevant case and is put forward for the first time at the oral hearing before the Board. The Board decided to allow the vendor to rely on the argument of estoppel by election.

These proceedings have been bedevilled with mistakes on both sides. The purchaser had been allowed to cross-appeal on grounds which were suggested by the Court of Appeal, in ignorance of the facts. There was then admittedly a month's adjournment, but the attention of the vendor's advisers then, and subsequently, was directed to the problem of whether the purchaser had elected at the trial to accept damages, not to the question whether the purchaser's conduct after the trial gave rise to an estoppel.

The crucial circumstances in the present case were that, if the Board ignored admitted facts which were not made available to the Court of Appeal and which were subsequently put in evidence by the purchaser, and if the estoppel point was good in law, then the Board was in danger of upholding the order of the Court of Appeal for specific performance made per incuriam and of approving a result which was unjust and should never have been reached. Any prejudice to the purchaser caused by the fact that estoppel was not adumbrated until the hearing of this appeal can be corrected by an appropriate order for costs. Their Lordships consider that the proper course is to decide the issue of estoppel by considering whether it would have been proper for the Court of Appeal to have granted the purchaser an order for specific performance in September 1982 if the Court of Appeal had been aware of all the facts relating to the deposit of damages on the terms imposed by the purchaser.

Counsel for the vendor submitted that after the award of damages by the trial judge, Rajah J, the purchaser had a choice. The purchaser could either enforce the judgment for damages or appeal to the Court of Appeal to set aside the order for damages and to substitute an order for specific performance. The purchaser elected to take the benefit of the judge's order and force the vendor to provide the damages. The purchaser thereby abandoned the right to appeal and was estopped from asserting any such right thereafter.

Spencer Bower and Turner *The Law Relating to Estoppel by Representation* (3rd edn, 1977) p 313, para 310 summarises the doctrine of election as applied to the law of estoppel in these terms:

'Where A, dealing with B, is confronted with two alternative and mutually exclusive courses of action in relation to such dealing, between which he may make his election, and A so conducts himself as reasonably to induce B to believe that he is intending definitely to adopt the one course, and definitely to reject or relinquish the other, and B in such belief alters his position to his detriment, A is precluded, as against B, from afterwards resorting to the course which he has thus deliberately declared his intention of rejecting. It is of the essence of election that the party electing shall be "confronted" with two mutually exclusive courses of action between which he must, in fairness to the other party, make his choice.'

In the present case the purchaser could not take the damages and obtain specific performance. By demanding and accepting the deposit of the damages the purchaser chose to adopt the order of the trial judge and relinquished the right to appeal for that order to be set aside and for specific performance to be substituted. The vendor altered its position to its detriment by raising and paying $297,500 on 12 November 1981. The vendor has been deprived of that sum ever since. After the judgment of Rajah J the purchaser was indeed confronted with two alternative and mutually exclusive courses of action, namely to enforce the award of damages or to seek to persuade the Court of Appeal to set aside the award of damages and to substitute the remedy of specific performance.

By procuring the payment of the damages of $297,500 the purchaser accepted the judge's order. If the purchaser had served a notice of appeal seeking specific performance or had informed the vendor that the purchaser intended to seek an order for specific performance from the Court of Appeal, the vendor would have been able to refuse to place the damages on deposit and would have been entitled to renew and to succeed in an application for a stay of execution with regard to the damages pending the hearing of the purchaser's appeal seeking specific performance.

*Spencer Bower and Turner* p 334, para 322, relating to election in the conduct of litigation, is in these terms:

> 'Where a litigant has taken the benefit, in whole or in part, of a decision in his favour, he is precluded from setting up in any subsequent proceedings between the same parties, by way of appeal or otherwise, that such decision was erroneous, or, though correct as to the part which was in his favour, was wrongly decided as to the residues.'

Counsel for the purchaser submitted that this statement is not justified by authority, but it appears to be good law and good sense. Here the purchaser, by obtaining the deposit of the damages of $297,500, took the benefit of the decision in its favour made by Rajah J and thereby precluded the purchaser from arguing that his decision was erroneous.

With commendable speed, counsel for the purchaser and those assisting him prepared and submitted a supplemental case for the respondent denying that the purchaser was estopped by election from appealing against the order of the trial judge. From the thoroughness of that supplemental case and from the detailed oral arguments put forward by counsel for the purchaser, for which their Lordships are indebted, it appears that the purchaser's advisers were able to consider and to deal fully with the arguments of the vendor relating to estoppel, despite the tardy appearance of the claim. Counsel for the purchaser submitted that no election arose. He said that the demand by the purchaser for the deposit of the damages of $297,500 ordered by the trial judge was only a prudent method of obtaining security for those damages and did not imply or necessitate abandonment by the purchaser of its right to appeal against that order out of time and to obtain an order for specific performance from the Court of Appeal.

If the Court of Appeal dismissed the purchaser's appeal, then the purchaser would remain entitled to the damages awarded by the trial judge and in the mean time was entitled to security for the payment of those damages. The argument is misconceived. If the purchaser had appealed against the order of the trial judge and sought specific performance, the vendor would have been entitled as of right to a stay of the order for damages and would have refused to raise and deposit those damages pending the appeal. This follows from the fact that, if the purchaser had appealed, the property comprised in the contract would have remained security for the obtaining by the purchaser of specific performance and for the alternative and mutually exclusive remedy of damages. The purchaser would not be entitled to a further $297,500 in cash as well as the contractual property by way of security. If the purchaser had appealed the vendor and any person claiming through the vendor would not have been able to dispose of the property pending the appeal. If, in due course, the Court of Appeal were otherwise minded to refuse specific performance, the Court could and would have declined to do so unless the vendor secured payment to the purchaser of the damages of $297,500 by a charge on the property or payment into court or by some other method.

The property was worth $488,000 at the date of trial and the damages were only

$297,500. Counsel for the purchaser said that property values might have fallen between 8 September 1981, the date of the trial, and 20 August 1982, the date of the hearing of the appeal The purchaser's present eagerness for specific performance indicates that the property did not in fact fall below $297,500 in value. But in any event the risk of loss between 8 September 1981 and 20 August 1982 would have been created by the purchaser's appeal and that risk would have been borne and suffered by the vendor and not by the purchaser. If the property became or was likely to become worth less than $297,500 the purchaser could at any time abandon the appeal and enforce against the property and any other assets of the vendor the order for damages of $297,500. The purchaser, by appealing, would automatically deprive the vendor, and any other person asserting an interest in the property, of the power to dispose of the property at an advantageous time at the advantageous price of $488,000 while the purchaser retained the right to abandon the appeal if the property became less valuable than the damages. The vendor in those circumstances would be left with the property at its reduced value of less than $297,500 and would still be liable to pay the full damages. Thus, the purchaser by appealing, could ensure that the property then worth $488,000 could not be sold or otherwise turned to advantage pending the appeal.

The purchaser was secured by the forced retention of the property. In these circumstance a demand by the purchaser for the vendor to provide a further $297,500 in cash by way of additional security would have been mere impudence. The purchaser was only entitled to enforce the order for damages in lieu of specific performance if the purchaser abandoned the right to appeal against that order. The purchaser elected to enforce the order for damages by procuring payment from the vendor of the full amount of the damages. It is true that the damages were placed on deposit in the name of the purchaser's solicitors but this was due to the fact that the vendor was pursuing an appeal against the quantum of damages.

The purchaser relied and could only rely on the order of Rajah J to enforce payment of the damages of $297,500 by the vendor to the purchaser's solicitors as stakeholders. By relying on that order the purchaser lost the right to dispute it. By demanding and procuring payment of the damages of $297,500 the purchaser abandoned any claim to specific performance. Counsel for the purchaser submitted that the vendor never even alleged any belief that the purchaser had abandoned a claim for specific performance. But actual intentions and beliefs are irrelevant to the raising of an estoppel in the present case. The facts which raise an estoppel are that the purchaser demanded and accepted payment of the damages, and thus acted in a manner which was only consistent with acceptance of the decision of the trial judge and only consistent with abandonment of the right to appeal against that decision. Factually, it is plain that the purchaser did accept the decision of the trial judge and had no intention of appealing until the Court of Appeal, in ignorance of any estoppel by election, suggested that the purchaser was labouring under a mistake of law in accepting that decision. The vendor had already altered its position by raising and paying $297,500 and the essential requirements for estoppel by election were satisfied.

Next, counsel for the purchaser argued that, subject to the purchaser releasing the deposited damages and interest and possibly paying damages to the vendor for any loss caused to the vendor by raising and placing the money on deposit in the first place, the purchaser could reverse the election made in November 1981 and resume the claim to specific performance. But, in the absence of any misconduct on the part of the vendor, the court could not permit the purchaser to escape from the consequences of the election constituted by the demand made and enforced for payment of the damages payable pursuant to the order made by the trial judge. There is no equity which assists the purchaser to forgo that demand and to cancel that election freely exercised in a manner which the purchaser subsequently regretted.

In a detailed and careful argument counsel for the purchaser referred to a number of cases on which he relied by way of analogy for his submission that the purchaser, notwithstanding any earlier election, could restore the right to appeal against the order for damages made by the trial judge by offering to release the damages on deposit together with interest and possibly damages. But, on examination, the cases on which counsel for the purchaser relied did not support the submission.

First, counsel for the purchaser referred to the jurisdiction of the court to set aside a judgment on the application of the person by whom it has been obtained, before or after the time for appealing has expired, and before or after execution. The authorities cited, namely *Cannan v Reynolds* (1855) 5 E & B 301, 119 ER 493, *S Kaprow & Co Ltd v Maclelland & Co Ltd* [1948] 1 All ER 264, [1948] 1 KB 618 and *Ex p Adamson, re Collie* (1878) 8 Ch D 807, are instances where judgment was obtained or action was taken under a mistake and where that mistake could be corrected without injustice. In the present case the purchaser did not make any mistake, except a mistake of law as to the grounds of specific performance and that mistake cannot now be corrected without injustice to the vendor. The authorities do not support the view that a litigant who has elected to enforce a judgment for damages and to abandon the right to appeal against that judgment may change his mind after the damages have been paid.

Second, counsel for the purchaser relied on the principle of promissory estoppel and, in particular, on *Ajayi v R T Briscoe (Nigeria) Ltd* [1964] 3 All ER 556, [1964] 1 WLR 1326. But in that case, and in similar cases, the promise was not intended to be irrevocable and the recipient of the promise did not act to his detriment.

Third, counsel for the purchaser relied on the fact that in ordering rescission of a contract for misrepresentation or undue influence the court only insists on substantial restitution accompanied, if necessary, by payment of compensation: see *Lagunas Nitrate Co v Lagunas Syndicate* [1899] 2 Ch 392. There must, however, be substantial restitution even in such a case where the court is striving by the order of rescission to protect an innocent party against a wrongdoer. In the present case the purchaser exercised an unfettered election to accept the damages payable pursuant to the order of Rajah J or to appeal against that order. Moreover, substantial restitution is impossible because no one knows what would have happened to the vendor's assets if the vendor had not been compelled by the purchaser to raise and deposit $297,500 by way of damages. It was said that there was no evidence that the vendor had any difficulty in finding the money or that the rate of interest earned on the deposit was any less than the interest which might have been earned by the vendor. If necessary, it was said, there could be an inquiry as to the damages suffered by the vendor in raising and paying and being deprived of the use of $297,500. But it is impossible to put the clock back: the damages would be imponderable and any inquiry would inflict on the vendor uncertainty, delay and expense merely to relieve the purchaser against the consequences of the purchaser's own voluntary conduct in insisting on payment of the damages and enforcing the order of the trial judge.

Counsel for the purchaser submitted that in any event no election could arise until a final order, not subject to appeal, had been made: '... on a question of alternative remedies, no question of election arises until one or other claim has been brought to judgment': see *United Australia Ltd v Barclays Bank Ltd* [1940] 4 All ER 20 at 38, [1941] AC 1 at 30 per Lord Atkin, cited with approval by Lord Wilberforce in *Johnson v Agnew* [1979] 1 All ER 883 at 892, [1980] AC 367 at 396.

It is true, of course, that the purchaser was not bound to make an election: the purchaser could have appealed against that order of the judge and retained the right to elect between specific performance and damages until after any final appeal. But in that case the vendor could not have been compelled to raise and deposit $297,500. The purchaser chose to elect to enforce the order made by Rajah J immediately after the date of that order and thereby abandoned the right to appeal against that order.

Accordingly, their Lordships conclude that, if the Court of Appeal had been aware of the payment of damages of $297,500, the Court of Appeal would have been bound either to refuse the purchaser leave to cross-appeal or to dismiss that cross-appeal.

Finally, counsel for the purchaser submitted that a cross-estoppel arose because the day after the Court of Appeal gave judgment for specific performance the vendor's solicitors asked for the release of the damages held on deposit. It was said that the purchaser assumed that the vendor was accepting the decision of the Court of Appeal and therefore issued a summons for implementation of the decree for specific performance. However, the purchaser insisted on retaining the damages while pursuing implementation of the order for specific performance and knew full well from the date when the vendor sought leave to appeal to the Board that the decision of the Court of Appeal was under challenge. There was no election by the vendor, no estoppel, and the purchaser by seeking to implement the order for specific performance did not act to its detriment in reliance on any act or omission by the vendor or at all. The purchaser sought to implement the order for specific performance in reliance on the order made by the Court of Appeal. Indeed, the events which happened after the judgment of the Court of Appeal only illustrate the justification for the application of the principle of estoppel by election which prevented the purchaser from appealing against the order of Rajah J once the purchaser had enforced that order and procured the deposit of the damages. By retaining the damages and also seeking to enforce the order for specific performance the purchaser was enabled to pursue inconsistent and alternative claims. The vendor was only liable to pay damages or to perform the contract and was not bound to suffer the infliction of both remedies, even with the hope of recovering from the effect of one of them in due course, subject to any order the court might care to make about costs or delay. The vendor having been obliged by the purchaser to comply with the order to pay damages was harassed by the order for specific performance. Once the damages had been raised and paid and accepted the purchaser was estopped by election from appealing against the order for the payment of those damages.

On behalf of the vendor, counsel argued that the damages awarded by Rajah J were excessive and should be reduced. The vendor's appeal to the Court of Appeal for such a reduction had not been heard on its merits. He asked that the issue as to the quantum of damages should be referred back to the Court of Appeal or should be made the subject of an inquiry. He said that the written judgment of Rajah J did not explain the basis on which the damages were calculated. Examination of the record, however, makes the matter quite plain. The judge rightly decided that damages should be assessed as at the date of trial. Counsel for the vendor said that it was arguable that damages should have been assessed at an earlier date when the vendor repudiated the contract. But that repudiation was not accepted: the purchaser issued a writ for specific performance. There is nothing in this point.

As to the quantum of damages, there was one expert witness called by the purchaser who gave evidence of value at the date of trial. He assessed that value at $488,000. Counsel for the vendor frankly conceded that the judge must have accepted that evidence, deducted from the value of $488,000 the value, namely $38,000, of certain improvements carried out by the vendor, deducted the contract price of $152,500 payable by the purchaser pursuant to their contract of purchase and thus arrived at the damage award of $297,500. The only evidence of value on behalf of the vendor was given by the managing director of the vendor, who, inter alia, said that adjoining property had been sold for much less than $488,000. The judge must have rejected this evidence and preferred the evidence of the expert valuer. The judge was entitled so to do. There are no grounds on which the Court of Appeal or the Board could interfere with the amount of damages awarded by the trial judge.

In the result, their Lordships will allow the appeal from the Court of Appeal. The order for specific performance made by the Court of Appeal and any consequential orders must be set aside and the order of Rajah J restored.

There remains the question of costs. If the vendor had produced to the Court of Appeal the facts relating to the deposit, then the Court of Appeal would have been bound either to refuse to allow the purchaser to cross-appeal or, if the facts had been revealed after leave had been granted, to dismiss the cross-appeal and to refuse to grant specific performance. The vendor's appeal against quantum of damages would have been dismissed. Before the Board, the vendor has succeeded, but only on a ground raised for the first time on the day when the appeal was opened. In the circumstances, their Lordships consider that the orders made by the Court of Appeal with regard to costs should be set aside and that there should be no order for any costs incurred by either party after the trial before Rajah J.

Dissenting opinion of **SIR ROBIN COOKE.** Not being persuaded that this case should be decided on a point never mentioned in its long history until stated by one of their Lordships at the hearing of the final appeal, I have the signal misfortune to differ from the majority and would dismiss the appeal.

At first sight the course taken by the Court of Appeal in suggesting specific performance and giving the purchaser liberty to cross-appeal seems unusual; but that course was apparently not opposed on behalf of the vendor, and the court records in its reasons for judgment that counsel for the vendor frankly admitted that he saw no reason why specific performance could not have been ordered.

At the lowest, it is a reasonable inference that the parties and their legal advisers in Singapore did not regard the arrangement for payment of the damages to a stakeholder as an election. Indeed, even in the vendor's case before the Judicial Committee, settled by leading counsel in London, the arrangement was nowhere mentioned, and notwithstanding that the subject of election (allegedly at the trial) was by then in the forefront. Such relevant evidence as there is may be incomplete. The Judicial Committee does not have the benefit of any opinion from the Court of Appeal about the significance of the arrangement as between the parties. In all these circumstances it is difficult to see any firm basis for concluding that, by insisting that the deposit arrangement be carried out, the purchaser induced the vendor to believe that the purchaser had relinquished any claim to specific performance. Moreover, counsel for the vendor accepted before their Lordships that it was too late to contend that the arrangement amounted to an agreement to forgo specific performance.

All this might not matter if there were an overriding rule of law that in no circumstances can a purchaser who has been awarded damages at first instance require, as a term of some arrangement, that the damages be deposited with a stakeholder, or paid into court, without ipso facto electing against specific performance. With the greatest respect to those who may favour such a rule, I cannot help thinking that it would go too far.

In the present case, after the initial judgment the vendor applied for a stay, which was refused by the High Court. Next the vendor filed a notice of motion in the Court of Appeal for a stay. The correspondence (letters of 23, 28, 30 October and 4, 12 and 16 November 1981) shows that a bargain was then reached that, if the damages were paid to a stakeholder, execution of the judgment would be stayed pending the outcome of the vendor's appeal. By previously opposing a stay, except on such terms, the purchaser did not commit itself to executing the judgment. Evidently the purchaser in fact took no step towards execution, nor does there even appear to be evidence of a clear threat of execution. What the vendor gained by the bargain was that the purchaser no longer had the *option* of taking any steps to enforce the judgment (as by winding-up proceedings).

I agree that the principles are correctly stated in the chapter on election in Spencer Bower and Turner *The Law Relating to Estoppel by Representation* (3rd edn, 1977) ch 13, a chapter which may be said to be of special authority, having been substantially rewritten by Sir Alexander Turner. But a theme of the chapter is that election must be unequivocal, the alternative courses of action in truth mutually exclusive. Looking at the known facts of the present case in the light of those tests, I think that to be satisfied that the doctrine applied one should require, like Hamlet, 'grounds more relative than this'.

*Appeal allowed. No order for costs after trial before Rajah J.*

Solicitors: *Coward Chance* (for the vendor); *Freshfields* (for the purchaser).

Mary Rose Plummer   Barrister.

# Gatoil International Inc v Arkwright-Boston Manufacturers Mutual Insurance Co and others

HOUSE OF LORDS

LORD FRASER OF TULLYBELTON, LORD SCARMAN, LORD WILBERFORCE, LORD KEITH OF KINKEL AND LORD ROSKILL

29 OCTOBER, 13 DECEMBER 1984

*Admiralty – Jurisdiction – Action in rem – Claim arising out of agreement relating to carriage of goods in a ship or to use or hire of a ship – Agreement – Claim for payment of premiums on insurance policy over cargo – Whether claim for premiums arising out of 'any agreement relating to the carriage of goods in any ship' – Administration of Justice Act 1956, s 47(2)(e).*

The respondents, six insurance companies and an insurance broker, brought an action against the appellants in a sheriff court in Scotland claiming payment of premiums on a policy of insurance effected with them by the appellants, a Panamanian company, over a cargo of oil shipped from Iran to various destinations. In order to found jurisdiction over the appellants and also to obtain security for their claim, the respondents arrested a vessel owned by the appellants lying in the Shetland Islands, although that vessel was not concerned with the carriage of the oil cargo which was the subject of the insurance policy. The appellants commenced an action in the sheriff court against the respondents seeking discharge of the arrest, contending, inter alia, that the respondents were not entitled to arrest the vessel since their claim did not fall within s 47(2)ᵃ of the Administration of Justice Act 1956, which Act was passed to enable the United Kingdom to ratify and comply with the International Convention Relating to the Arrest of Sea-going Ships signed by the United Kingdom in 1952. The sheriff held that a claim for payment of premiums on a policy of insurance over goods to be carried by sea fell within the terms of s 47(2)(e), which provided that a ship could be arrested in respect of a maritime claim arising out of 'any agreement relating to the carriage of goods in any ship whether by charterparty or otherwise', and accordingly held that the arrest was valid. On appeal, the Court of Session affirmed the sheriff's decision. The appellants appealed to the House of Lords, contending that an insurance policy over cargo could not be an 'agreement relating to the carriage of goods in any ship whether by charterparty or otherwise'.

**Held** – The appeal would be allowed for the following reasons—

(1) On the true construction of s 47(2)(e) of the 1956 Act the words 'any agreement relating to the carriage of goods in any ship whether by charterparty or otherwise' did not cover an agreement to pay premiums on a policy of insurance on cargo. It followed that the respondents' claim against the appellants for payment of insurance premiums was not a claim which fell within the provisions of s 47(2) and accordingly the arrest of the appellants' vessel was not valid (see p 130 *j* to p 131 *b*, p 132 *b*, p 133 *d* and p 137 *e* and *h j*, post); *West of Scotland Ship Owners Mutual Protection and Indemnity Association (Luxembourg) v Aifanourios Shipping SA, The Aifanourios* [1980] 2 Lloyd's Rep 403 considered; *The Sonia S* [1983] 2 Lloyd's Rep 63 overruled.

(2) (Per Lord Fraser, Lord Scarman, Lord Wilberforce and Lord Roskill) Furthermore, since the 1956 Act had been enacted with the primary purpose of enabling the United Kingdom to ratify and comply with the 1952 convention, regard could be had to the travaux préparatoires of the 1952 convention in order to resolve any ambiguity in s 47(2)(e) of the 1956 Act and, in particular, regard could be had to the fact that a proposal for claims for premiums on policies of maritime insurance to be included in the list of maritime claims was specifically not adopted when the convention was drafted because

---

*a*    Section 47(2), so far as material, is set out at p 133 *f g*, post

as a matter of policy it was considered unnecessary to provide for the protection of such premiums by means of arrest, and s 47(2)(e) should be construed to give effect to that intention. It followed that s 47(2)(e) did not cover claims in respect of an agreement to pay premiums on a policy of insurance on cargo (see p 130 j to p 131 b, p 132 b ĉ, p 133 a to d and p 137 j, post); *Fothergill v Monarch Airlines Ltd* [1980] 2 All ER 696 applied.

**Notes**
For Admiralty jurisdiction in the High Court, see 1 Halsbury's Laws (4th edn) paras 307–312, and for cases on the subject, see 1(1) Digest (Reissue) 219–223, *1240–1251.*
     Section 47(2)(e) of the Administration of Justice Act 1956, which applies to Scotland only, corresponds to s 20(2)(h) of the Supreme Court Act 1981. For s 20 of the 1981 Act, see 51 Halsbury's Statutes (3rd edn) 612.

**Cases referred to in opinions**
*Alina, The* (1880) 5 Ex D 227, CA.
*Antonis P Lemos, The* [1984] 2 All ER 353, [1984] 2 WLR 825, CA.
*Beldis, The* [1936] P 51, [1935] All ER Rep 760, CA.
*Fothergill v Monarch Airlines Ltd* [1980] 2 All ER 696, [1981] AC 251, [1980] 3 WLR 209, HL.
*Gunnestad v Price, Fullmore v Wait* (1875) LR 10 Exch 65.
*Jade, The, The Eschersheim, Erkowit (owners) v Jade (owners), Erkowit (cargo owners) v Eschersheim (owners)* [1976] 1 All ER 920, [1976] 1 WLR 430, HL.
*Queen of the South, The, Corps v Queen of the South (owners) (Port of London Authority intervening)* [1968] 1 All ER 1163, [1968] P 449, [1968] 2 WLR 973.
*R v City of London Court Judge* (1883) 12 QBD 115.
*R v City of London Court Judge* [1892] 1 QB 273, CA.
*Sonia S, The* [1983] 2 Lloyd's Rep 63.
*Tesaba, The* [1982] 1 Lloyd's Rep 397.
*West of Scotland Ship Owners Mutual Protection and Indemnity Association (Luxembourg) v Aifanourios Shipping SA, The Aifanourios* [1980] 2 Lloyd's Rep 403.
*Zeus, The* (1888) 13 PD 188.

**Appeal**
Gatoil International Inc appealed, with leave of the Second Division of the Court of Session, against the judgment of that court (the Lord Justice Clerk (Lord Wheatley), Lord Stott and Lord Robertson) given on 23 March 1984 whereby they dismissed the appellants' appeal from the interlocutors of the Sheriff Court of Aberdeen made on 5 March 1984, and held that the claim of the respondents, Arkwright-Boston Manufacturers Mutual Insurance Co, New York Managers Inc, St Paul Mercury Insurance Co, Highlands Insurance Co, American Motorists Insurance Co, Texas Marine Underwriters Agency Inc and Marsh & McLennan Middle East Ltd, against the appellants for payment of certain marine insurance premiums was a claim which fell within the provisions of s 47(2) of the Administration of Justice Act 1956 and accordingly a warrant to arrest on the dependence obtained by the respondents and used against the vessel Sandrina allegedly owned by the appellants was a valid arrestment. The facts are set out in the opinion of Lord Keith.

*Gordon Pollock QC* and *Alan Johnson* for the appellants.
*John Murray QC* and *M G Clarke* (both of the Scottish Bar) for the respondents.

Their Lordships took time for consideration.

13 December. The following opinions were delivered.

**LORD FRASER OF TULLYBELTON.** My Lords, I have had the advantage of reading in draft the speeches prepared by my noble and learned friends Lord Keith and

Lord Wilberforce. I agree with both of them and, for the reasons stated in their speeches, I would allow the appeal.

**LORD SCARMAN.** My Lords, I agree with the speech to be delivered by my noble and learned friend Lord Keith. For the reasons he gives I would allow the appeal.

I have also had the advantage of reading in draft the speech to be delivered by my noble and learned friend Lord Wilberforce. I agree with his view that the interpretation of the Administration of Justice Act 1956 is legitimately aided by consideration of the travaux préparatoires to which he refers and that we should not deny ourselves the reinforcement which they provide to the interpretation which for the reasons given by Lord Keith we hold to be correct.

**LORD WILBERFORCE.** My Lords, I have had the benefit of reading in advance the speech to be delivered by my noble and learned friend Lord Keith. I take the benefit of his full statement of the issue in this appeal which, briefly, concerns the interpretation of s 47(2)(e) of the Administration of Justice Act 1956. Do the words 'any agreement relating to the carriage of goods in any ship whether by charterparty or otherwise' cover an agreement to pay premiums on a policy of insurance under a war risk open cover on cargo? If so, the arrestment of the appellants' ship Sandrina, by order of the Sheriff at Lerwick, was valid; if not, it must be discharged.

Taking the statutory words by themselves, it is obvious enough that they are, in a legal sense, ambiguous, or as I would prefer to state it, loose textured. It is not possible to ascribe a precise or certain meaning to words denoting relationships without an indication what the criterion of relationship is to be. Must the agreement be directly 'for' carriage of goods in a ship, or is it enough that it involves directly or indirectly or that the parties contemplated that there would be, such carriage as a consequence of the agreement? How close, in such a case, must the relationship be between the agreement and the carriage? Is any connection of a factual character between the agreement and some carriage in a ship sufficient? If not, what is the test of relevant connection? Even when para (e) is read in conjunction with the other paragraphs in s 47(2), the statute provides no guidance: the courts are left with a choice of a broad or a narrow interpretation.

Decided authorities show that this choice is inevitable and difficult; they are analysed by my noble and learned friend Lord Keith. It is no doubt true that earlier cases, based on similar words occurring in s 2 of the County Courts Admiralty Jurisdiction Amendment Act 1869, may have been influenced by a reluctance to attribute to county courts a wider jurisdiction than was then possessed by the Admiralty Court, but at least they show that the words were capable of being narrowly construed.

After 1956, when the provision appeared (substantially) in s 1(1) of the 1956 Act, as regards English cases a more liberal approach was preferred. The relationship accepted in *The Queen of the South, Corps v Queen of the South (owners) (Port of London Authority intervening)* [1968] 1 All ER 1163, [1968] P 449 was quite loose: the agreement for mooring etc of a ship was held to fall within s 1(1)(h) of the 1956 Act (in which paras (d) and (e) of s 47(2) were combined for the purposes of Scottish Admiralty jurisdiction), because it involved the use of motor boats, ie ships. As for salvage agreements, although in *The Jade, The Eschersheim, Erkowit (owners) v Jade (owners), Erkowit (cargo owners) v Eschersheim (owners)* [1976] 1 All ER 920, [1976] 1 WLR 430 an agreement for salvage services was held to be within para (h) as involving the use of a salvage vessel, in *The Tesaba* [1982] 1 Lloyd's Rep 397 a claim on a salvage agreement for damages for breach of an undertaking to obtain security from cargo owners was held to be outside it. In *The Sonia S* [1983] 2 Lloyd's Rep 63 the judge held to be within para (h) (now in s 20(2) of the Supreme Court Act 1981) an agreement for the hire by shipowners of containers to be carried on a ship. My noble and learned friend Lord Keith considers this decision to be wrong and the relationship to be too remote, and I agree with him, but the case well illustrates the looseness of the provision and the spectral character of the boundary between claims within and those outwith the subsection. Finally, we may note that in Scotland in *West of Scotland Ship Owners Mutual Protection and Indemnity Association*

(*Luxembourg*) v *Aifanourios Shipping SA, The Aifanourios* [1980] 2 Lloyd's Rep 403 Lord
Wylie held that a claim for release calls under a policy of marine insurance was outwith
both para (*d*) and para (*e*) of s 47(2), but the Second Division in the present case held to
the contrary and declined to follow *The Aifanourios*.

My Lords, there is here, no doubt, no more than a degree of doubt as to the meaning
of statutory words not significantly greater than often arises, particularly in such cases as
reach this House. They can be, and are, solved by a judicial process of interpretation. My
noble and learned friend Lord Keith has followed this path, and if there were no other
material to help us, I would be content to follow him. However, I believe that
contentment can be converted to conviction by legitimate reinforcement ab extra,
namely by resort to the travaux préparatoires of the International Convention Relating
to the Arrest of Sea-going Ships (Brussels, 10 May 1952; TS 47 (1960); Cmnd 1128).

The case for a cautious use of travaux préparatoires in aid of the interpretation of
conventions or treaties of private law received some acceptance in this House in *Fothergill
v Monarch Airlines Ltd* [1980] 2 All ER 696, [1981] AC 251. I there suggested that two
conditions must be fulfilled before they can be used: first, that the material is public and
accessible; second, that it clearly and indisputably points to a definite legislative intention.

The case for resort to them here is, in my opinion, a strong one. The Administration
of Justice Act 1956, Pt V (which included s 47) was enacted to give effect to the obligations
of the United Kingdom consequent on its accession to the 1952 convention (see *The Jade,
The Eschersheim* [1976] 1 All ER 920 at 923, [1976] 1 WLR 430 at 434 per Lord Diplock),
and in particular to displace, in Scotland, the wide common law powers of arrestment in
favour of statutory provisions which were narrower and precisely defined. The situation
is slightly more complex in that the list of maritime claims set out in art 1 of the 1952
convention was, in fact, based on the list of such claims then applicable in *England* under
s 22 of the Supreme Court of Judicature (Consolidation) Act 1925 (see particularly sub-
s (1)(*a*)(xii)). This list was adopted, as part of a compromise, in the 1952 convention, and
was then made applicable (with minor variations) to England and to Scotland by ss 1 and
47 of the 1956 Act respectively. This derivation provides a clear justification for
attributing to the provisions in the Scottish portion of the 1956 Act the meaning which
they ought to receive under the convention, if that can be ascertained.

The proceedings of the conference which led to the 1952 convention are public and
accessible: they have been published by the International Maritime Committee as regards
the preparatory conference at Naples held in 1951, and as regards the Diplomatic
Conference of 1952 by the Foreign Ministry of Belgium. They show the following:

1. As regards the list of maritime claims in art 1 the report of the Naples conference
(Bulletin No 105) states as follows:

'This enumeration is based on the types of claims specifically assigned under
English law to the Admiralty Jurisdiction of the High Court of Justice (Supreme
Court of Judicature (Consolidation) Act 1925.) The International Commission thinks
that the types of claims mentioned in this paragraph cover practically every
maritime claim in respect of which a ship should be arrested, whilst on the other
hand there seem to be no other claims of a maritime character which should, under
the Convention, justify such arrest.'

2. A decision was made by a committee of the Netherlands Maritime Law Association
to propose the addition to the list of maritime claims of a new subsection reading (Naples
report, p 59):

'(q) premiums of insurance due to underwriters and contributions due to mutual
insurance associations for cover granted in connection with the operation of a ship.'

This was put forward at the Brussels conference (Brussels report, p 96).

3. The addition of this new paragraph was opposed by the British delegation on the
ground that the policy of insurance itself was sufficient protection for insurers (pp 101-
102).

4. The Netherlands delegation maintained its proposal claiming that the claims in
question were essentially maritime claims (p 103).

5. The British delegation claimed that the clause was unnecessary in the United Kingdom but understood that elsewhere it might be of use (p 104).

6. The French delegation considered there was no 'absolute necessity', to include insurance premiums in the list of maritime claims (p 106).

7. Article 1 of the convention was agreed without the addition of the new paragraph.

The conclusion from the above is clear. The conference decided not to include premiums on policies of insurance among the maritime claims justifying arrest. It did so, moreover, not because it thought that these premiums were already covered (so that explicit reference was unnecessary) but because it considered it unnecessary as a matter of policy to provide for their protection by means of arrestment. The legislative intention is manifest: not by any provision in art 1 to provide for the inclusion of premiums among arrestable maritime claims.

In the face of this legislative intention the adoption of the provisions of art 1 of the convention in the 1956 Act must be treated as carrying the same meaning as that evidently placed on them in the convention and as not extending to premiums on insurance policies.

My Lords, I respectfully think that the interpretation of the 1956 Act is legitimately aided by consideration of this extrinsic material, and that we should not deny ourselves this reinforcement to our conclusions. With that reinforcement I am of opinion that this appeal must be allowed and the arrestment recalled.

**LORD KEITH OF KINKEL.** My Lords, this appeal, which arises out of certain proceedings in the Sheriff Court at Lerwick, is concerned with the proper construction of s 47(2)(e) of the Administration of Justice Act 1956. Section 47 provides, so far as material:

> '(1) Subject to the provisions of this section and section fifty of this Act, no warrant issued after the commencement of this Part of this Act for the arrest of property on the dependence of an action or in rem shall have effect as authority for the detention of a ship unless the conclusion in respect of which it is issued is appropriate for the enforcement of a claim to which this section applies, and, in the case of a warrant to arrest on the dependence of an action, unless either—(a) the ship is the ship with which the action is concerned, or (b) all the shares in the ship are owned by the defender against whom that conclusion is directed.
>
> (2) This section applies to any claim arising out of one or more of the following, that is to say—[and there follow 19 paragraphs lettered (a) to (s), para (e) being in these terms] (e) any agreement relating to the carriage of goods in any ship whether by charterparty or otherwise . . .'

The respondents, six insurance companies and an insurance broker, raised an action against the appellants in the Sheriff Court at Lerwick claiming payment of premiums on a policy of insurance which they say was effected with them by the appellants over a cargo of oil shipped from Kharg Island in Iran to various destinations. In order to found jurisdiction over the appellants, a Panamanian company, and also in order to obtain security for their claim, the respondents on 24 February 1984 arrested at Sullom Voe in the Shetland Islands a ship, the Sandrina, at the time lying there. There is a dispute whether or not the Sandrina was then owned by the appellants, but the House is not concerned with that issue in the instant appeal, it being required to be assumed for present purposes that they were in fact the owners. It is to be remarked that there is no question of the Sandrina or any other ship owned by the appellants having been concerned with the carriage from Kharg Island of the oil cargo which was the subject of the insurance policy.

The appellants then raised an action against the respondents in the Lerwick Sheriff Court seeking recall of the arrestments. That is the action in which this appeal arises. They denied ownership of the Sandrina and in addition pleaded that the arrestment was incompetent because the respondents' claim was not one of those specified in s 47(2) of the 1956 Act. A debate on relevancy was heard by Sheriff Russell sitting at Aberdeen. He allowed a proof on the matter of ownership of the Sandrina, and held that on a proper construction of para (e) of s 47(2), which I have quoted above, the respondents' claim for payment of premiums on a policy of insurance over goods to be carried by sea fell within its terms. The appellants appealed to the Court of Session, and on 23 March 1984 the Second Division of the Inner House (the Lord Justice Clerk (Lord Wheatley), Lord Stott and Lord Robertson) affirmed the decision of the sheriff and dismissed the appeal, but gave leave to appeal to your Lordships' House.

It is common knowledge that the 1956 Act, though its long title does not express this, was passed for the principal purpose of enabling the United Kingdom to ratify and to comply with the international obligations accepted by states which became parties to the International Convention relating to the Arrest of Sea-going Ships (Brussels, 10 May 1952; TS 47 (1960); Cmnd 1128) (see The Jade, The Eschersheim, Erkowit (owners) v Jade (owners), Erkowit (cargo owners) v Eschersheim (owners) [1976] 1 All ER 920 at 923, [1976] 1 WLR 430 at 434 per Lord Diplock). Before the passing of the 1956 Act the maritime claims falling within the Admiralty jurisdiction of the High Court in England were limited to those listed in s 22 of the Supreme Court of Judicature (Consolidation) Act 1925. This list was substantially reproduced in s 1 of the 1956 Act, which is in Pt I of the Act relating to England. Section 3(4) of the Act provided that the jurisdiction might be invoked by action in rem against a ship in connection with which the claim arose, or a sister ship. This liberty to take proceedings against a sister ship was new. It was provided for by art 3(1) of the 1952 convention. In Scotland, before the 1956 Act, the right to arrest a ship did not depend on any particular Admiralty jurisdiction provided for by statute, but on the general common law under which any movable property within the jurisdiction of an intended defender might be arrested ad fundandam jurisdictionem and on the dependence of an action against him. Section 47 limited this right, as respects maritime claims, to the list of such claims there set out, which follows very closely the list in art 1(1) of the convention. However, s 47(1)(b) is so worded that it is competent to arrest any ship wholly owned by the defender, even though neither that ship nor a sister ship had any connection whatever with the claim against him, which is the position in the present case.

Paragraph (e) of s 47(2) follows verbatim (except for the opening word 'any') the terms of the corresponding paragraph in the English language version of the convention, as does para (d): 'any agreement relating to the use or hire of a ship whether by charterparty or otherwise'. In s 1(1)(h), however, these two heads of claim are rolled up together: 'any claim arising out of any agreement relating to the carriage of goods in any ship or to the use or hire of a ship'. A very similar form of words was used in s 2(1) of the County Courts Admiralty Jurisdiction Amendment Act 1869, which gave jurisdiction to county courts appointed to have Admiralty jurisdiction to try and determine, inter alia, causes—

> 'As to any claim arising out of any agreement made in relation to the use or hire of any ship, or in relation to the carriage of goods in any ship, and also as to any claim in tort in respect of goods carried in any ship, provided the amount claimed does not exceed £300 . . .'

The proper construction of this provision came under consideration in a number of cases, and it may well be that the draftsman of s 1(1) of the 1956 Act had these cases in mind. In Gunnestad v Price (1875) LR 10 Ex 65 it was held that a claim by the owner of a ship against a charterer for demurrage did not fall within s 2 of the 1869 Act. This was a claim over which the High Court of Admiralty itself did not at the time have jurisdiction, and the ratio decidendi was that, reading the 1869 Act along with the County Courts Admiralty Jurisdiction Act 1868, it appeared that the legislature did not intend to invest county courts with any more than a portion of the then existing jurisdiction of the Admiralty Court, to a limited monetary amount. This decision was disapproved of in The Alina (1880) 5 Ex D 227, where a Court of Appeal presided over by Jessel MR held that the county court had jurisdiction over a claim for damages for breach of a charterparty. In R v City of London Court Judge [1892] 1 QB 273 it was held by the Court of Appeal that, since the Admiralty Court had no jurisdiction over a claim against a pilot for damages on the ground of his negligence in causing a collision on the high seas, the county court had no such jurisdiction either by virtue of s 2 of the 1869 Act. Lord Esher MR expressed strong criticism of *The Alina*. He said (at 291): 'I will, therefore, follow *The Alina* so far as it actually goes, but not one inch further.' In the mean time, in *R v City of London Court Judge* (1883) 12 QBD 115 Day J, in the course of holding that a passenger's luggage was not 'goods' within the meaning of s 2, had expressed the view that the first part of the material passage in that section ('use or hire of a ship') had reference to a charterparty and the second part ('carriage of goods in a ship') had reference to a bill of lading. Finally, in the nineteenth century, in *The Zeus* (1888) 13 PD 188, a Divisional Court consisting of Hannen P and Butt J held that an agreement by a colliery owner to load a ship with coal within 48 hours and to pay 'demurrage for each hour exceeded' was not an agreement made in relation to the use or hire of a ship or in relation to the carriage of goods in a ship within s 2, and that the county court therefore had no jurisdiction.

Turning to more modern English cases, in *The Beldis* [1936] P 51, [1935] All ER Rep 760 an action to enforce an arbitrator's award under a charterparty was held not to arise out of an agreement made in relation to the use or hire of a ship and therefore not to be within s 2. The reported cases since then have been under s 1(1) of the 1956 Act and its re-enactment as s 20(1) of the Supreme Court Act 1981. In *The Queen of the South, Corps v Queen of the South (owners)* [1968] 1 All ER 1163, [1968] P 449 Brandon J decided that an agreement for the mooring and unmooring and other servicing of a ship fell within s 1(1)(h) because it involved the use of motor boats for providing the agreed services, and motor boats were ships within the definition in s 8(1) of the Act. Likewise in *The Jade, The Eschersheim* [1976] 1 All ER 920, [1976] 1 WLR 430 this House held that an agreement for salvage services fell within s 1(1)(h) because the rendering of these services involved the use of a salvage vessel. The claims were for negligence in the manner of carrying out the salvage services. Lord Diplock after having considered *R v City of London Court Judge* and *The Alina*, said in relation to the former case:

'My Lords, this was not a decision which ascribed a specific and precise meaning to the words "an agreement relating to the use or hire of a ship". The reasons given in the judgment for giving a restricted meaning to words conferring admiralty jurisdiction on county courts, in the context in which they appeared in the 1869 Act, have no application in the context of Part I of the Administration of Justice Act 1956, which is dealing with the jurisdiction of the High Court itself. I see no reason in that context for not giving to them their ordinary wide meaning. That would include the salvage agreement in the present case.'

(See [1976] 1 All ER 920 at 926, [1976] 1 WLR 430 at 438):

*The Tesaba* [1982] 1 Lloyd's Rep 397 was another case concerned with a salvage agreement. There was provision for security, and the shipowners agreed to use their best endeavours to ensure that the cargo owners provided security before the cargo was released. The vessel having been safely salved, the owners in breach of that undertaking allowed the cargo to be discharged without security being given. The salvors' claim against the shipowners for damage for breach of the undertaking was held by Sheen J not to fall within para (h). He said (at 401):

'If the ordinary businessman were to be asked "Is that an agreement relating to the carriage of goods in *Tesaba*?", the answer would undoubtedly be "No".'

In *The Sonia S* [1983] 2 Lloyd's Rep 63, however, the same judge held that an agreement for the hire by shipowners of containers intended to be used by customers of the latter for packing goods to be carried on their ships was within para (h) of s 20(2) of the 1981 Act. The claim was by the owners of the containers for non-payment of hire. Sheen J said (at 65):

'It seems to me that the claim arises out of an agreement which relates to the carriage of goods by sea. It relates to it, as I have said, because the only purpose of the agreement was for the shipowners to provide for their customers the facility for packing their own goods, and for no purpose other than to have those goods carried in a ship.'

The most recent English case is *The Antonis P Lemos* [1984] 2 All ER 353, [1984] 2 WLR 825. The defendants were owners of a ship of which the plaintiffs were sub-charterers, under a time charter. The plaintiffs in turn entered into a voyage charter with a third party for the carriage of grain from Houston to Alexandria, and undertook that the vessel's draught on arrival would not exceed 32 feet. The defendants loaded the vessel to a greater draught, so that the plaintiffs sustained loss for which they claimed against the defendants in negligence. The Court of Appeal held that the claim fell within para (*h*) of s 20(2) on the ground that it arose out of the plaintiffs' time charter or their voyage sub-charter or both, it not being essential that it should arise out of an agreement between the plaintiffs and the defendants.

There is one Scottish decision directly in point. That is *West of Scotland Ship Owners Mutual Protection and Indemnity Association (Luxembourg) v Aifanourios Shipping SA, The Aifanourios* [1980] 2 Lloyd's Rep 403, where an insurance association had arrested the defenders' ship on the dependence of an action claiming payment of release calls under a contract of marine insurance over the ship and its cargo. Lord Wylie held that such a contract did not come within the provisions of either para (*d*) or para (*e*) of s 47(1) of the 1956 Act, and that the arrestment was therefore incompetent. He said (at 407):

> 'Counsel for the pursuers submitted that the provisions of these two paragraphs fell to be broadly interpreted. "Any agreement relating to the use . . . of a ship" was any agreement connected with the use of a ship. The provision was not confined to an agreement "for" the use of a ship, and it could not be said that an agreement for the insurance of a ship, or for the insurance of its cargo, did not come within the broad terms of the statutory provisions. Put in these simple terms the agreement is attractive, but these provisions have to be construed in the light of other provisions of the subsection as a whole. In addition to claims arising out of damage done to or by any ship, claims in respect of salvage, towing or pilotage, they include claims arising out of the supply of goods or materials to a ship for her operation or maintenance, the construction, repair or equipment of a ship, liability for dock charges and master's disbursements, to take but a few examples of the kind of claims covered by the subsection. If the provisions of para (d) fell to be as broadly construed as was contended for, it is difficult to see how any of these provisions could fail to come within the ambit of the provision. A claim, for example, arising out of the supply of goods to a ship for her operation or maintenance or arising out of her repair would certainly appear to arise from an agreement relating to the use of a ship. I am accordingly driven to the view that a more restricted construction is called for than that which, in isolation, the words might otherwise bear. Moreover, it is clear that the insurance of a vessel is a matter directed to the convenience or protection of the owner, and is not essential for the operation of the vessel as such.'

That concludes the review of the authorities. It is to be observed that, while some divergences from the provisions of the 1952 convention can be seen both in the provisions of the 1956 Act relating to England and in those relating to Scotland, it is desirable that such provisions for both jurisdictions as can be identified as having a common derivation from particular provisions of the convention should be interpreted alike in each of these jurisdictions, if that can be done without undue straining of language. Paragraph (*h*) of s 1(1) of the 1956 Act and paras (*d*) and (*e*) of s 47(2) are in this category, deriving as they all clearly do from art 1(1)(*d*) and (*e*) of the convention. In the English cases under s 2 of the County Courts Admiralty Jurisdiction Amendment Act 1869 there prevailed a tendency to give a restricted interpretation to words almost identical to those of para (*h*) of s 1(1) of the 1956 Act. Lord Diplock in *The Jade, The Eschersheim* attributed this to a disinclination on the part of the judges to attribute to Parliament an intention to give a wider jurisdiction to the county court than was possessed by the Admiralty Court itself, and said that since similar considerations did not apply to the 1956 Act there was no reason for not giving to para (*h*) its ordinary wide meaning. The agreement in issue in *The Jade, The Eschersheim* was, however, one which was concerned in a very direct sense with the use of the salvage vessel involved, and as I have mentioned it may well be that the draftsman of para (*h*) had in mind the cases under s 2 of the 1869 Act and the restricted interpretation which had there been placed on the words which he was using. *The Zeus* (1888) 13 PD 188 is perhaps a particularly important decision in this connection. It did not purport to proceed on a consideration of the unlikelihood of Parliament having intended to confer on the county court a jurisdiction which the Admiralty Court itself did not possess. There is no doubt that the agreement there in issue, to load a ship with coals within a time limit, had some connection with the carriage of goods by a ship and also with the use of a ship. But Hannen P said (at 190):

> 'We should disturb the natural meaning of the words of the statute if we said that the agreement has relation to the use or hire of the ship. It is merely an engagement to deliver coals at a particular place.'

It is necessary to attribute due significance to the circumstance that the words of the relevant paragraphs speak of an agreement 'in relation to' not 'for' the carriage of goods in a ship and the use or hire of a ship. The meaning must be wider than would be conveyed by the particle 'for'. It would, on the other hand, be unreasonable to infer from the expression actually used, 'in relation to', that it is intended to be sufficient that the agreement in issue should be in some way connected, however remotely, with the carriage of goods in a ship or with the use or hire of a ship, and I think there is much force in the view expressed by Lord Wylie in *The Aifanourios* [1980] 2 Lloyd's Rep 403 as to the inference to be drawn from the presence of certain other paragraphs in s 47(2). There must, in my opinion, be some reasonably direct connection with such activities. An agreement for the cancellation of a contract for the carriage of goods in a ship or for the use or hire of a ship would, I think, show a sufficiently direct connection. It is unnecessary to speculate what other cases might be covered. Each case would require to be decided on its own facts. As regards the contract of insurance founded on in the instant appeal, I am of opinion that it is not connected with the carriage of goods in a ship in a sufficiently direct sense to be capable of coming within para (e).

I consider that in *The Sonia S* there was likewise an insufficiently direct connection between the agreement for the hire of containers and the carriage of goods in a ship. There is clear fallacy in the reasoning of Sheen J in the latter part of his judgment, where he equates the use to which the containers were to be put with the use to which the salvage vessel was to be put in *The Jade, The Eschersheim*. The salvage vessel there was a ship which was to be used under the salvage agreement. The containers were not a ship. In my opinion that decision was wrong and should be overruled.

The appellants argued that, should the House conclude that the provisions of para (e) were ambiguous, regard should be had, for the purpose of resolving that ambiguity, to a certain aspect of the travaux préparatoires for the 1952 convention. The particular aspect in question was that, as published records show, the Dutch representative in the course of the negotiation of the convention proposed that claims for premiums on policies of marine insurance should be specifically included in the list of maritime claims, that this proposal was opposed by other representatives, and that in the event it was not adopted. Since I am of opinion that any ambiguity in s 47(2)(e) can be resolved to the effect of holding that it does not, on a proper construction, cover the respondents' claim, it is unnecessary to deal with this branch of the appellants' argument.

My Lords, for these reasons I would allow the appeal, to the effect of sustaining the third plea-in-law for the pursuers, repelling the third plea-in-law for the defenders, and granting decree in terms of the conclusions of the summons. The appellants must have their costs in this House and their expenses of the proceedings in the courts below.

**LORD ROSKILL.** My Lords, I have had the advantage of reading in draft the speeches delivered by my noble and learned friends Lord Keith and Lord Wilberforce. I agree with them, and for the reasons which they give I would allow this appeal.

*Appeal allowed.*

Solicitors: *Ince & Co*, agents for *Maclay Murray & Spens*, Edinburgh (for the appellants); *Sinclair Roche & Temperley*, agents for *A C Bennett & Fairweather WS*, Edinburgh, agents for *Anderson Fyfe Stewart & Young*, Glasgow (for the respondents).

Mary Rose Plummer        Barrister.

# Anderton v Ryan

QUEEN'S BENCH DIVISION
PARKER LJ AND FORBES J
4 APRIL 1984

*Criminal law – Attempt – Impossible offence – Belief of accused that his acts constitute an offence – Uncompleted offence – Handling stolen goods – No evidence that goods were stolen – Whether accused guilty of attempt to handle stolen goods – Criminal Attempts Act 1981, s 1(1)(2).*

The defendant bought a video recorder believing it to have been stolen. She was subsequently charged with dishonestly attempting to handle the video recorder knowing or believing it to be stolen, contrary to s 1(1)[a] of the Criminal Attempts Act 1981. The prosecution adduced no evidence whether the video recorder was in fact stolen and the magistrates dismissed the charge on the ground that the defendant's mere belief that the video recorder was stolen was insufficient for a conviction under s 1 of the 1981 Act. The prosecutor appealed. At the hearing of the appeal the defendant contended that, since the prosecutor had been unable to prove one way or the other whether the video recorder was stolen, she could not be guilty under s 1(1) of an attempt to commit the full offence of handling stolen goods or under s 1(2) of an attempt to commit an offence which was impossible, since if the video recorder had been stolen then for the purposes of s 1(1) she would have done every act required on her part to commit the full offence rather than an attempt, and for the purposes of s 1(2) would not have been attempting an impossible offence.

**Held** – Since it could not be supposed that Parliament intended that a person who could be charged with an attempt if he failed to complete a particular act could not be charged with an offence if he did in fact complete it, it was to be assumed for the purposes of s 1(1) and (2) of the 1981 Act that, if an attempt to do a particular act was an offence but the completed act was not, a person doing the completed act was nevertheless chargeable with attempt. Alternatively, where a full offence remained uncompleted because all the facts necessary to establish the full offence could not be proved, the accused was nevertheless guilty of an attempt if, with intent, he had done acts which were 'more than merely preparatory' to the commission of the full offence. Accordingly, since the defendant had committed all the acts necessary for the full offence of handling stolen goods it followed that she was guilty of an attempt, notwithstanding that the full offence was either uncompleted or impossible (see p 141 *e* to p 142 *f*, post).

## Notes

For attempts to commit an offence and acts constituting an attempt, see 11 Halsbury's Laws (4th edn) paras 63–65.

For the Criminal Attempts Act 1981, s 1, see 51 Halsbury's Statutes (3rd edn) 736.

## Cases referred to in judgments

*Haughton v Smith* [1973] 3 All ER 1109, [1975] AC 476, [1974] 2 WLR 1, HL.
*R v Donnelly* [1970] NZLR 980, CA.

## Cases also cited

*R v Hack* [1978] Crim LR 359.
*R v Marshall* [1977] Crim LR 196.

## Case stated

The prosecutor, Cyril James Anderton, Chief Constable of Greater Manchester, appealed

---

*a*   Section 1, so far as material, is set out at p 140 *h j* and p 141 *a*, post

by way of a case stated by the justices for the county of Greater Manchester, acting in and for the petty sessional division of Manchester, in respect of their adjudication as a magistrates' court sitting at Manchester on the trial of an information preferred on 10 April 1983 by the prosecutor against the defendant, Bernadette Ryan, charging that she between 6 and 10 April 1983 at Manchester did dishonestly handle stolen goods, namely a video recorder, knowing or believing them to be stolen, contrary to s 22 of the Theft Act 1968. On 6 June 1983 at the hearing of the information the prosecutor preferred a further information charging that the defendant between 6 and 10 April 1983 at Manchester did dishonestly attempt to handle a video recorder, value £500, knowing or believing it to be stolen, contrary to s 1(1) of the Criminal Attempts Act 1981. The defendant consented to be tried summarily and pleaded not guilty. At the outset of the proceedings the prosecutor indicated that he wished to offer no evidence on the allegation of handling and invited the court to dismiss that charge, which the justices did. On the charge of attempted handling the justices were of the opinion that the mere fact that the defendant believed the goods to be stolen was inconclusive in the absence of any evidence tending to show that the goods were, in fact, worth more than the £110 which the defendant paid for them. They were further of the opinion that the defendant's mere belief that the goods were stolen was insufficient to make out a charge of attempted handling. Accordingly they dismissed the charge against the defendant. The questions for the opinion of the court were (a) whether the court was right to dismiss the information and (b) whether the failure of the prosecutor to prove that the goods in question had been or were stolen goods was fatal to a charge of attempted handling of stolen goods. The facts are set out in the judgment of Parker LJ.

*David A Poole* for the prosecutor.
*Peter Crichton-Gold* for the defendant.

**PARKER LJ.** This is an appeal by case stated from the justices in the county of Greater Manchester in respect of an adjudication made by them on 6 June 1983. On that day the defendant appeared to answer two informations. The first was that she between 6 and 10 April 1983 at Manchester did dishonestly handle stolen goods, namely a video recorder, knowing or believing them to be stolen contrary to s 22 of the Theft Act 1968. The second information, which was preferred on the same day as the hearing which had been fixed for the first, was that the defendant, between 6 and 10 April 1983 in the city of Manchester did dishonestly attempt to handle a video recorder knowing or believing it to be stolen, value £500, contrary to s 1(1) of the Criminal Attempts Act 1981.

The prosecution, for reasons which will shortly be clear, tendered no evidence on the charge of receiving or dishonest handling, but proceeded only with the charge of attempt. In the result, the charge of handling was dismissed. The case finds the following facts. A police officer visited the home of the defendant at her request on 6 April 1983 in respect of an alleged burglary. During the course of the inquiries that he then made his suspicions were aroused when the defendant admitted that she had bought a video recorder for £110 from some person whom she declined to name. On further questioning the defendant said: 'I may as well be honest, it was a stolen one I bought, I should not have phoned you.' When the police officer said to the defendant that to pay £110 for a video recorder was well below the price of the video, 'You obviously knew it was stolen, didn't you?', the defendant replied: 'Yes, I knew, but it was damaged at the back. I had to fix it before it would work.' When further questioned why she had bought it if she knew it to be stolen the defendant replied: 'Well everyone's at it. I didn't think I'd get discovered.' The police officer did not see the video recorder and thus could give no evidence about its condition or value.

There then follows a paragraph in the case stated which is somewhat oddly drafted, but which is fully understandable in the circumstances. It reads as follows:

'We [the justices] formed the view at the end of the Prosecution case that there was evidence upon which we could find as a matter of fact that the [defendant] had received into her possession a video cassette recorder and that at the time of her receipt into her possession she was of the belief that it was stolen goods.'

There clearly was evidence on which the justices could so find and since there was a submission of no case at the end of the prosecution case the justices were clearly looking at the question to see whether they should uphold the submission rather than that they should find specific facts on the very issue which was before the court. No evidence was adduced that the goods had been stolen or as to the value of the goods.

The point which is raised before this court is one which has apparently not been ventilated previously and arises under the Criminal Attempts Act 1981. What is submitted on behalf of the defendant is that no offence under s 1 of that Act has been committed and that the justices were entirely right to uphold the submission that was made, it being, so it is contended, essential that the prosecution should prove that the goods were stolen goods. Alternatively, it is submitted that if they remained in doubt whether or not the goods were stolen, it would be impossible for an offence under s 1 to be made out.

The prosecution appeal and they appeal on a very simple basis. They say that the wording of s 1 is clear and that it was designed to deal with the very sort of cases to which *Haughton v Smith* [1973] 3 All ER 1109, [1975] AC 476 referred. The law as it then stood was stated in Lord Hailsham LC's speech in the following terms ([1973] 3 All ER 1109 at 1112, [1975] AC 476 at 490):

> 'In my view, it is plain that, in order to constitute the offence of handling, the goods specified in the particulars of offence must not only be believed to be stolen, but actually continue to be stolen goods at the moment of handling. Once this is accepted as the true construction of the section, I do not think that it is possible to convert a completed act of handling, which is not itself criminal because it was not the handling of stolen goods, into a criminal act by the simple device of alleging that it was an attempt to handle stolen goods on the gound that at the time of handling the accused falsely believed them still to be stolen. In my opinion, this would be for the courts to manufacture a new criminal offence not authorised by the legislature.'

Further on in his speech, quoting from Turner J in the New Zealand case of *R v Donnelly* [1970] NZLR 980 at 990–991, Lord Hailsham LC sets out the six categories mentioned by that learned judge, of which the sixth is as follows ([1973] 3 All ER 1109 at 1115, [1975] AC 476 at 493):

> '... he may without interruption efficiently do every act which he set out to do, but may be saved from criminal liability by the fact that what he has done, contrary to his own belief at the time, does not after all amount in law to a crime.'

It would be quite plain that on the state of the law prior to the Criminal Attempts Act 1981 what had occurred in this case was insufficient to amount to an attempt. The only question is whether the 1981 Act has converted it into an attempt.

The offence itself is described as follows in s 1(1):

> 'If, with intent to commit an offence to which this section applies, a person does an act which is more than merely preparatory to the commission of the offence, he is guilty of attempting to commit the offence.'

Section (4) provides:

> 'This section applies to any offence which, if it were completed, would be triable in England and Wales as an indictable offence, other than ...'

and then there are certain exceptions which are not immediately relevant. Then come the two vital subsections, sub-ss (2) and (3):

'(2) A person may be guilty of attempting to commit an offence to which this section applies even though the facts are such that the commission of the offence is impossible.

(3) In any case where—(a) apart from this subsection a person's intention would not be regarded as having amounted to an intent to commit an offence; but (b) if the facts of the case had been as he believed them to be, his intention would be so regarded, then, for the purposes of subsection (1) above, he shall be regarded as having had an intent to commit that offence.'

In the present case, the prosecution were unable to prove one way or the other whether these goods were stolen or were not, but the defendant believed them to be so. What is submitted on behalf of the defendant is this: that it cannot be said that the facts in this case are such that the commission of the offence is impossible, therefore there is no room for the application of sub-s (2). It is also submitted that, since the defendant had committed every act which on her part fell to be committed, this cannot be regarded as coming within the words '[doing] an act which is more than merely preparatory to the commission of the offence'. Finally, it is submitted that, since sub-s (1) is dealing with attempts and sub-s (4) refers to uncompleted offences, it cannot be supposed that Parliament intended to cover a case where the accused had done every act which on her part or his part would have constituted the commission of the offence but for the fact that, in the case of handling, the goods were not or could not be shown to be stolen. The draftsmanship of this section clearly caused considerable difficulty at the time. The difficulties are mentioned in Smith and Hogan *Criminal Law* (5th edn 1983) p 264. It is not possible entirely to reconcile the wording of every bit of every subsection, but one thing would appear to be plain and that is this. If it had been possible to prove positively that the goods in this case were not stolen goods, then the case would have fallen straight within s 1(2), because the facts would then have been such that the commission of the offence was impossible. That would mean that if the prosecution had gone or been able to go as far as to show that it was quite impossible for any criminal act in the nature of the full offence to be committed they would succeed in finding the defendant guilty by virtue of s 1(1) and (2). But it is said that if the position remains open and therefore there might have been the commission of the full offence the position is such that there must be an acquittal. This appears to me so bizarre that I cannot attribute to it parliamentary intent.

There are further results which I find it impossible to attribute to Parliament. Suppose, for example, that an accused attempts to have intercourse with a girl whom he believes to be below the age of consent albeit that is not the case. The offence is impossible, because the girl is over the age of consent. If he has only attempted to have intercourse but has not succeeded there would clearly be an attempt and s 1 would apply. It is impossible to suppose that Parliament intended that if he had not only attempted intercourse but succeeded he should then be found not to have committed any offence. It may be that the way to reconcile such matters is this. If somebody (and sticking to the example that I have already given) finally succeeds in the act of intercourse, he must, prior to that, have committed acts which were more than merely preparatory and therefore the final act must have been preceded by acts which were themselves chargeable.

An alternative is that the acts which are required to be proved to have been done by an accused are only part of the offence and an offence is uncompleted unless all the facts exist which the prosecution would need to prove to establish the commission of the full offence. If that be so, then, since to prove the full offence it is necessary to show that the goods were stolen, an inability to prove that ingredient means that the facts do not exist or cannot be shown to exist which constitute the full offence. Whichever way the matter is approached it appears to me that the present case can be brought fairly within and should be brought fairly within the wording of s 1(1) and (2) of the 1981 Act, s 1(3) being, as it seems to me, largely superfluous, and that the justices in this case were wrong to dismiss the information. So the question 'Was the court right to dismiss the information?' must be answered in the negative. As to the question 'Is the failure of the prosecution to prove that the goods in question are or were stolen goods fatal to a charge of attempted handling of stolen goods?' the answer must also be in the negative. If it were so fatal it appears to me that it would rob s 1 of the 1981 Act of all content and I am not prepared to attribute to Parliament either (a) a useless exercise or (b) an exercise so bizarre that the guiltier you are the less likely you are to be convicted. The position that where there is a partial advance up the road to an intended crime the result will be a conviction, but that arrival at the destination, apart from the impossibility envisaged in this case, results in acquittal does not appear to me at all acceptable.

Accordingly, I would allow this appeal. The submission having been made and succeeded the case must, I think, but I am prepared to hear argument about it, go back to the justices with a direction to convict.

**FORBES J.** I agree. At one time in the course of argument I was attracted by the view that this section was concerned solely with inchoate crime. Section 1(1) has two elements: an intent and the doing of an act. There is no doubt that in this case the defendant had the intent to commit the offence of handling. The section requires that the person charged should do an act which is more than merely preparatory. Of course, an act which completes the offence must, in one sense, be more than merely preparatory to its commission. In a section, however, which is devoted to attempts and which in sub-s (4) refers to an offence which 'if it were completed' would be triable as an indictable offence, it occurs to me that it might be forcibly argued that the words 'more than merely preparatory' were not intended to include the final act which would amount to the commission of an offence if an offence were committed. However, if this were the proper interpretation of s 1, it would have most remarkable effects, such as, for instance, the example given by Parker LJ.

I would respectfully therefore accept his suggestion that in the circumstances he has outlined there must have been a stage where an act properly to be described as amounting to more than merely preparatory was committed and therefore, despite my initial doubt, that this charge was in this case properly proved.

*Appeal allowed. Case remitted with direction to convict.*

*The court refused leave to appeal to the House of Lords but certified, under s 1(2) of the Administration of Justice Act 1960, that the following point of law of general public importance was involved in the decision: does a person commit an offence under s 1 of the Criminal Attempts Act 1981 where if the facts were as that person believed them to be the full offence would have been committed by him but where on the true facts the offence which that person set out to commit was in law impossible, e g because the goods handled and believed to be stolen were not stolen or because the substance imported and believed to be heroin was not heroin but harmless white powder or because a girl with whom he had sexual intercourse was not under the age of consent although he believed her to be under such age?*

*12 July. The Appeal Committee of the House of Lords granted the defendant leave to appeal.*

Solicitors: *D S Gandy*, Manchester (for the prosecutor); *Ollier Wilner & Jones*, Manchester (for the defendant).

N P Metcalfe Esq    Barrister.

# R v Shivpuri

COURT OF APPEAL, CRIMINAL DIVISION
ACKNER LJ, STUART SMITH AND LEGGATT JJ
18 OCTOBER, 5 NOVEMBER 1984

*Criminal law – Attempt – Impossible offence – Belief of accused that his acts constitute an offence – Impossible for accused to commit full offence – Accused attempting to deal with and harbour a substance he believed to be a prohibited drug – Substance not in fact a prohibited drug – Whether accused guilty of attempt to deal with and harbour prohibited drug – Customs and Excise Management Act 1979, s 170(1)(b) – Criminal Attempts Act 1981, s 1.*

The appellant was arrested by customs officials while in possession of a suitcase which he believed contained prohibited drugs. After his arrest he told the officials that he knew he was dealing with prohibited drugs. Analysis, however, revealed that the substances in the suitcase were not drugs but a vegetable material akin to snuff. The appellant was convicted of attempting to be knowingly concerned in dealing with and harbouring a prohibited drug, contrary to s 1(1)[a] of the Criminal Attempts Act 1981 and s 170(1)(b)[b] of the Customs and Excise Management Act 1979. He appealed, contending that, because the substance found in his possession was not a drug, he could not be guilty of attempting to be knowingly concerned in either dealing with or harbouring a prohibited drug, and that s 1(2) of the 1981 Act, which provided that a person could be convicted of an attempt even though the commission of the full offence was impossible, only applied where a person was prevented from committing the full offence by reason of some supervening physical impossibility imposed by events and did not apply where an essential ingredient of the full offence was missing from the outset.

**Held** – If a person had the requisite intent and did acts which were more than merely preparatory to the commision of an offence, he could be convicted under s 1 of the 1981 Act of an attempt to commit that offence even though commission of the full offence was impossible because the facts were such that an essential ingredient of the full offence was missing. Accordingly, since the appellant had had the intention to deal with and harbour a prohibited drug and his conduct had been more than merely preparatory to the commission of that offence, he was guilty of attempting to be knowingly concerned in dealing with and harbouring a prohibited drug and it was irrelevant that the substance was not in fact a drug. His appeal would therefore be dismissed (see p 147 c to j and p 148 b, post).

*Anderton v Ryan* [1985] 1 All ER 138 approved.
*Haughton v Smith* [1973] 3 All ER 1109 considered.

## Notes

For attempts to commit an offence and acts constituting an attempt, see 11 Halsbury's Laws (4th edn) paras 63–65.

For the Customs and Excise Management Act 1979, s 170, see 49 Halsbury's Statutes (3rd edn) 443.

For the Criminal Attempts Act 1981, s 1, see 51 ibid 736.

## Cases referred to in judgment

*Anderton v Ryan* [1985] 1 All ER 138, [1985] 2 WLR 23, DC.
*Haughton v Smith* [1973] 3 All ER 1109, [1975] AC 477, [1974] 2 WLR 1, HL.

---

a   Section 1 is set out at p 146 c to f, post
b   Section 170(1), so far as material, provides: '. . . if any person . . . (b) is in any way knowingly concerned in . . . harbouring . . . or in any manner dealing with any . . . goods [the importation of which, inter alia, is prohibited], and does so with intent . . . to evade . . . such prohibition . . . with respect to the goods he shall be guilty of an offence . . .'

*Police v Jay* [1974] 2 NZLR 204, SC.
*R v Donnelly* [1970] NZLR 980, CA.

**Appeal and application**
On 23 February in the Crown Court at Reading before his Honour Judge Pigot QC and a
jury the appellant, Pyare Shivpuri, was convicted of (1) attempting to be knowingly
concerned in dealing with a controlled drug, the importation of which was prohibited
and (2) attempting to be knowingly concerned in harbouring a controlled drug the
importation of which was prohibited, both offences being contrary to s 1(1) of the
Criminal Attempts Act 1981 and s 170(1)(b) of the Customs and Excise Management Act
1979. He was sentenced to three years' imprisonment concurrent on each count. He
appealed against conviction on the ground that, in view of the fact that the substances
found in the possession of the appellant were not drugs, he could not be guilty of
attempting to be knowingly concerned in either dealing with or harbouring a controlled
drug the importation of which is prohibited, contrary to s 1(1) of the 1981 Act and
s 170(1)(b) of the 1979 Act. He also applied for leave to appeal against the sentence
imposed on him. The facts are set out in the judgment of the court.

*Louis Blom-Cooper QC* and *Samuel H Colgan* (assigned by the Registrar of Criminal Appeals)
for the appellant.
*Alan Suckling QC* and *Tony Docking* for the Crown.

*Cur adv vult*

5 November. The following judgment of the court was delivered.

**ACKNER LJ.** On 23 February 1984, after a trial lasting some nine days, the appellant
was convicted at the Crown Court at Reading and was sentenced as follows: attempting
to be knowingly concerned in dealing with a controlled drug, the importation of which
is prohibited, contrary to s 1(1) of the Criminal Attempts Act 1981 and s 170(1)(b) of the
Customs and Excise Management Act 1979. This was count 1. He was also charged with
attempting to be knowingly concerned in harbouring a controlled drug, the importation
of which is prohibited, also contrary to the same sections of the same Acts. This was
count 2. He was sentenced to three years' imprisonment on each count concurrent. He
now appeals against conviction, his appeal being based on a short point of law, to which
we will refer in some detail hereafter.
   The circumstances out of which the prosecution arose and the nature of the factual
issues that had to be determined at the trial was simple enough. It was the prosecution's
case that when the appellant was in India in 1982 he agreed with a man called Desai that
when he, the appellant, returned to England he would receive and look after a suitcase
containing packages of drugs. He would pass on the drugs in accordance with instructions
which would be given to him and for this service he would receive £1,000. In due course
a case was delivered to his flat in Cambridge. On 30 November 1982, between 6.45 pm
and 7.00 pm, the appellant met his co-accused, Bath, at Southall station. The meeting
appeared to be prearranged and they left the station together and walked towards Bath's
car. They were arrested by customs officers who had been watching. The appellant
attempted to run away but was restrained and arrested. Inside his shoulder bag was a
package containing a powdered substance. He was taken to the customs office at New
Fetter Lane, Cambridge.
   During the journey he was asked how he became involved in drugs, and he said it was
because of money. He said there were more drugs around at his house in Cambridge and
he was looking after them for Desai. After being searched and given some refreshment
he was interviewed in a car and, according to the prosecution, a contemporaneous note
was taken. He repeated that he was looking after drugs for Desai, who had told him to
take the packages of drugs from the linings of the suitcase. He had arranged to take one
of the packages of drugs to Mr Surrinder Singh at Southall station. He knew it was illegal

to be involved in the supply of drugs. He did not think the package contained heroin, but cannabis which he described as 'dried hash'. Desai had told him that the stuff was 'maal' which the appellant thought meant drugs.

At his flat in Cambridge the appellant produced an empty suitcase, the lining of which was ripped. He also gave the officers a package containing a substance which had been in his desk drawer. He was asked if he wished to make a statement and he typed out his own statement, under caution. He described how and when he met Desai, the financial problems that he, the appellant, was experiencing, Desai's proposal that a friend of his would contact him in Cambridge and leave him with a suitcase and that there would be some 'maal' hidden in the suitcase, which he was to keep until he received instructions to make the delivery or until someone, giving him the appropriate reference, arranged to take the delivery. For these services he was to receive £1,000. He further described how he came to receive the suitcase which he was told contained 'maal' packed in the linings of the case. He mentioned his misgivings, but said he found the consideration of £1,000 too tempting. He explained how he had ripped the lining of the suitcase and taken out the packets and the subsequent telephone call from a Mr Surrinder Singh on 27 November, which mentioned Desai's name, and arranged to meet him a few days later outside Southall station, bringing one of the packets with him.

The appellant was interviewed again and he confirmed that he knew he was dealing with drugs, but that he did not know what kind, but that he thought the value was some £50,000. He asked for mercy.

There were further interviews and in a final interview, after an analysis had revealed that the substances were not drugs, but were some vegetable material akin to snuff, he told the interviewers that he had suspected very deeply that it was heroin.

One of the most significant features of the prosecution's case was that at none of the many interviews had the appellant ever said that he knew the substance was not drugs because he had himself tested the material and discovered this to be the case.

So much for the prosecution case. The appellant gave evidence. He was a man aged 47, of good character and worked as a journalist. He said that when he was in India Desai had asked him to look after a suitcase containing 'maal' at his home in England. He was told that a greenish brown powder would be hidden in the case and he would be paid £1,000. When he took delivery of the case, he tested the powder and found that it did not contain any drugs. The appellant thought that, if he agreed to do as requested, Desai would in due course give him the names of contacts and he, the appellant, would 'get a good story' out of it. He agreed that he had received a telephone call from a Surrinder Singh arranging the meeting described above. When he saw the officers approaching him, he ran away because he feared that this was a racial attack, in his words a 'Paki-bashing'.

As to the interviews, he denied making any admissions about drugs, told the officers in terms about his tests on the substance and that he thought it was 'grass powder'. As regards his typed statement, he denied that this amounted to a confession because he knew that the substance was not drugs.

No complaint is made that the appellant's defence was not fully and fairly put before the jury. The point of law which is raised is simply this: in view of the fact that the substances found in the possession of the appellant were not drugs, he could not be guilty of *attempting* to be knowingly concerned in either dealing with or harbouring a controlled drug, the importation of which is prohibited, contrary to s 1(1) of the Criminal Attempts Act 1981 and s 170(1)(b) of the Customs and Excise Management Act 1979.

His Honour Judge Pigot QC gave the jury the following direction:

'The prosecution have not charged the defendants with the offence itself, but with an attempt to commit the offence. The reason for that is that all the packages (that is to say the one package in the bag which was with [the appellant] at Southall and the 15 found in the desk at his flat in Cambridge) did not contain prohibited drugs (you may think, on the evidence, that they were snuff or some other vegetable material) and therefore the offence was not committed. But if either accused thought or believed that the goods were heroin or knew they were heroin and knew they had been imported, despite the prohibition, and they were playing a part in the actual disposal of those goods in this country, they can be found guilty of an attempt to commit the offence, although the offence itself is strictly impossible because the substance itself was not a prohibited drug. A person may be guilty of attempting to commit the offence, even though the facts are such that the commission of the offence is impossible. That is as a result of an Act of Parliament passed quite recently in 1981, called the Criminal Attempts Act. It was passed to rectify a gap in the law. So if you are sure that either accused believed the facts to be such that the offence would have been committed, if either thought the package contained heroin, he can be convicted of an attempt, provided you are sure that there was participation.'

It is convenient at this stage to set out in its entirety s 1 of the Criminal Attempts Act 1981:

'(1) If, with intent to commit an offence to which this section applies, a person does an act which is more than merely preparatory to the commission of the offence, he is guilty of attempting to commit the offence.

(2) A person may be guilty of attempting to commit an offence to which this section applies even though the facts are such that the commission of the offence is impossible.

(3) In any case where—(a) apart from this subsection a person's intention would not be regarded as having amounted to an intent to commit an offence; but (b) if the facts of the case had been as he believed them to be, his intention would be so regarded, then, for the purposes of subsection (1) above, he shall be regarded as having had an intent to commit that offence.

(4) This section applies to any offence which, if it were completed, would be triable in England and Wales as an indictable offence, other than—(a) conspiracy (at common law or under section 1 of the Criminal Law Act 1977 or any other enactment); (b) aiding, abetting, counselling, procuring or suborning the commission of an offence; (c) offences under section 4(1) (assisting offenders) or 5(1) (accepting or agreeing to accept consideration for not disclosing information about an arrestable offence) of the Criminal Law Act 1967.'

It is, of course, common ground that before the Criminal Attempts Act 1981 the appellant could not have been indicted for attempting to commit an offence under s 170(1)(b) of the Customs and Excise Management Act 1979, since, contrary to his own belief at the time, what he set out to do did not amount in law to the offence under that section: see Haughton v Smith [1973] 3 All ER 1109, [1975] AC 477. In that case the defendant was charged with and convicted of attempting to handle stolen goods, albeit that at the time of the alleged offence the goods, being in the lawful custody of the police, ceased to be stolen goods by virtue of s 24(3) of the Theft Act 1968. That conviction was quashed, not because the acts of the accused, who took a leading part in arranging for the future disposal of the goods, were not sufficiently proximate or because he lacked the necessary intention, but because—

'[his] acts are not part of a series "which would constitute the actual commission of the offence if it were not interrupted" . . . steps on the way to do something which is thereafter not completed, but which if done would not constitute a crime cannot be indicted as attempts to commit that crime.'

(See [1973] 3 All ER 1109 at 1118, [1975] AC 477 at 496–497 per Lord Hailsham LC; his emphasis.)

Counsel for the appellant submits that the Criminal Attempts Act 1981 does not alter the decision in Haughton v Smith, which continues to be good law. The Act only makes indictable the attempts in the fifth class of case in the sixfold classification of Turner J in the New Zealand case of R v Donnelly [1970] NZLR 980, to which Lord Hailsham LC made detailed reference in Haughton v Smith. This category of attempt arises where the defendant is prevented from committing the crime which he intended by reason of some supervening physical impossibility imposed by events. It does not apply, he submits, where some essential ingredient of the substantive offence is missing, as was the case in *Haughton v Smith*.

To illustrate the artificiality of this distinction we can take the well-known example of the frustrated pickpocket, who fails to steal because the pocket into which he has put his hand is empty. Counsel for the appellant accepts that, on his approach, if there had been money in the pocket when the defendant's activity had gone beyond mere acts of preparation but it had disappeared, e g because of falling through a hole in that pocket just before the defendant had placed his hand in it, he could be properly indicted for an attempt. In such a case there had been a supervening physical impossibility. However, if there never had been any money in that pocket, or if it had fallen through the hole when the defendant's acts were merely preparatory, he could not be indicted for an attempt to steal. There is no difficulty in providing further illustrations of the anomalous situation which counsel's submission produces. However, whether or not it was Parliament's intention to produce such a situation must be decided by construing the words of the statute.

Section 1(1) is a general statement of the necessary ingredients of an attempt, s 6(1) having abolished the offence of attempt at common law. The alleged attempt must relate to an offence to which the section applies and the conduct must consist of an act which is more than merely preparatory to the commission of such an offence.

Subsection (4) provides that s 1 applies 'to any offence which, *if it were completed*, would be triable in England and Wales as an indictable offence' other than offences which it specifies. The phrase 'any offence which, if it were completed' clearly suggests that the prosecution no longer have to establish that the substantive offence would have been committed if the acts of the accused had not been interrupted.

Subsection (2) provides that a person may be guilty of attempting to commit an offence in a special situation. That situation exists where the facts are such that the commission of the offence is impossible. However, having regard to the terms of s 1(1), not only must the conduct of the accused be more than merely preparatory, he must have the requisite intent. Subsection (3) makes a special provision in relation to the accused's state of mind by providing that the facts of the case are to be taken as he believed them to be and his intention judged accordingly and it matters not that the offence was not completed (s 1(4)).

Applying the relevant subsections to the facts of this case, we have the following situation. (a) Section 1 applies to the offence because it is not one of the excepted offences and it matters not that the offence would not have been completed if the acts of the accused had not been interrupted (s 1(4)). (b) The acts of the appellant were more than merely preparatory to the commission of the offence (s 1(1)). (c) The fact that the substance was not a drug and thus the commission of the offence was impossible is irrelevant (s 1(2)). (d) The appellant had the requisite intent because he believed that the substance was a controlled drug, the importation of which was prohibited (s 1(3)). (e) The appellant did not, and indeed could not, achieve his purpose only because the facts were such that the commission of the offence was impossible.

In our judgment, the Criminal Attempts Act 1981 reverses the decision in *Haughton v Smith* by providing that a person may be guilty of attempting to commit an offence where the facts are such that an essential ingredient of the substantive offence is missing. We use the word 'may', as it is used in s 1(2), because the conduct of the accused must go beyond mere acts of preparation and he must have the requisite intent.

Thus, to return to the much discussed example, the would-be pickpocket who fails in his endeavour to steal because there was nothing in the pocket before he decided to steal or before he had proceeded further than acts of mere preparation or at the moment when he inserted his hand is guilty in each instance of an attempt to steal. Similarly, to take another such example, a man who intends to kill is guilty of attempted murder although the body in the bed which he attempts to strangle is a dummy placed there by his forewarned intended victim.

Finally, we should add that we carefully considered s 9 of the Act, strongly relied on by counsel for the appellant, but we find it is of no assistance in interpreting s 1. The interference necessary to constitute the offence may well, and often will, amount to only an act or acts that are merely preparatory and could not therefore constitute an attempt to commit any of the offences mentioned in that section. Hence the need for a special provision. We therefore conclude that *Anderton v Ryan* [1985] 1 All ER 138 was correctly decided and we do not accept the criticisms of the recent New Zealand decision, *Police v Jay* [1974] 2 NZLR 204. Accordingly, the appeal against conviction is dismissed.

Counsel for the appellant applied for, and we granted, leave to appeal against the sentence of three years. Counsel submitted that an immediate sentence of imprisonment was not appropriate since his client was of previous good character and, as matters had ultimately turned out, had never placed the public at risk. Alternatively, he submitted that the sentence was excessive.

We consider the judge was wholly justified in imposing an immediate sentence of imprisonment. It was clear from the very statement which the appellant had typed out that he believed that he was involved in handling drugs of considerable value and was prepared to accept instructions for their distribution. His attempt to pull the wool over the jury's eyes deprived him of the discount which the judge would certainly have given him if he had pleaded guilty. However, in view of the appellant's age and previous good character, we consider that the appropriate sentence in all the circumstances was that of two years, and we reduce his sentence accordingly. To that extent, the appeal against sentence is allowed.

*Appeal dismissed. Appeal against sentence allowed.*

*13 November. The court granted leave to appeal to the House of Lords and certified, under s 33(2) of the Criminal Appeal Act 1968, that the following point of law of general public importance was involved in the decision: does a person commit an offence under s 1 of the Criminal Attempts Act 1981 where, if the facts were as that person believed them to be, the full offence would have been committed by him, but on the true facts the offence which that person had set out to commit was in law impossible, e g because the substance imported and believed to be heroin was not heroin but a harmless substance?*

Solicitors: *Solicitor for the Customs and Excise.*

N P Metcalfe Esq    Barrister.

# R v Allen

COURT OF APPEAL, CRIMINAL DIVISION
WATKINS LJ, BOREHAM AND STUART-SMITH JJ
12 MARCH, 16 MAY 1984

*Criminal law – Theft – Making off without payment – Intent to avoid payment – Intent required – Whether intent to avoid payment permanently a necessary ingredient of offence – Whether intent to delay or defer payment temporarily sufficient – Theft Act 1978, s 3(1).*

The defendant was charged with making off without payment of an hotel bill, contrary to s 3(1)[a] of the Theft Act 1978. His defence was that he genuinely expected to pay the bill and had intended merely to delay or defer payment until he received the proceeds from certain business ventures. The judge directed the jury that a person made off 'with intent to avoid payment' for the purposes of s 3(1) if he intended to avoid payment at the

a    Section 3(1), so far as material, provides: '. . . a person who, knowing that payment on the spot for any goods supplied or service done is required or expected from him, dishonestly makes off without having paid as required or expected and with intent to avoid payment of the amount due shall be guilty of an offence.'

time the bill was due, which in the defendant's case was when he left the hotel, and that the Crown did not have to show that the defendant intended permanently to avoid payment of the bill. The defendant was convicted. He appealed, contending that the words 'intent to avoid payment' in s 3(1) meant intent permanently to avoid payment.

**Held** – On the true construction of s 3(1) of the 1978 Act 'intent to avoid payment' required more than mere intent at the time payment was due to delay or defer payment, and meant an intent to evade payment altogether. Accordingly, the offence of making off without payment under s 3(1) was not established if the defendant may have intended no more than to delay or defer payment when it fell due. It followed that the judge had misdirected the jury, and the appeal would accordingly be allowed and the conviction quashed (see p 151 h and p 154 d–h, post).

Corbyn v Saunders [1978] 2 All ER 697 and R v Brooks (Edward) (1982) 76 Cr App R 66 considered.

**Notes**
For making off without payment, see Supplement to 11 Halsbury's Laws (4th edn) para 1279A(3).
For the Theft Act 1978, s 3, see 48 Halsbury's Statutes (3rd edn) 314.

**Cases referred to in judgment**
Corbyn v Saunders [1978] 2 All ER 697, [1978] 1 WLR 400, DC.
R v Brooks (Edward) (1982) 76 Cr App R 66, CA.

**Appeal against conviction**
On 24 November 1983 in the Crown Court at Southwark before his Honour Judge Solomon and a jury the appellant, Christopher Allen, was convicted on count 2 of an indictment with making off without payment, contrary to s 3(1) of the Theft Act 1978. He was sentenced to 12 months' imprisonment of which 6 months were suspended and on 6 February 1984 the judge recommended that he should be deported. He appealed against the conviction on the grounds that the judge erred (1) in directing the jury that the words 'with intent to avoid payment' in s 3(1) of the 1978 Act did not require an intent permanently to avoid payment and (2) in directing the jury that they could convict the appellant if they were satisfied that he intended only a temporary default on the payment due from him. The facts are set out in the judgment of the court.

Elikkos Georghiades (assigned by the Registrar of Criminal Appeals) for the appellant.
Sonia Woodley for the Crown.

*Cur adv vult*

16 May. The following judgment of the court was delivered.

**BOREHAM J.** On 24 November 1983 in the Crown Court at Southwark before his Honour Judge Solomon and a jury the appellant was convicted of making off without payment, contrary to s 3 of the Theft Act 1978. He was sentenced to 12 months' imprisonment of which 6 months were suspended. On 6 February 1984 before the same court it was recommended that he be deported. He appeals against conviction on a point of law and against sentence by leave of the single judge.

We heard the appeals on 12 March 1984. We reserved judgment on the appeal against conviction. We gave our reasons for allowing the appeal against sentence should the conviction be upheld; we quashed the recommendation for deportation and reduced the sentence of imprisonment to such a term as would allow the appellant's immediate release.

The case against the appellant was that, having stayed at the London Embassy Hotel from 15 January to 11 February 1983, and run up a bill for £1,286·94, he dishonestly made off without paying. The facts were these. Through a third party the appellant reserved a double room at the hotel for ten nights from 15 January 1983, in the name of Mrs Johnson, his American girlfriend. Mrs Johnson registered at the hotel on 15 January, giving as her date of departure 24 January. The appellant stayed with her. On 16 January he attempted to cash a cheque for £30. This was initially refused, because he was not registered as a guest, but after explaining to the duty manager that he was in fact a guest and after registering as such, the cheque was cashed.

Mrs Johnson left, as she had predicted, on 24 January. The appellant stayed on. Early in February he was asked to pay part of the bill, which then exceeded £1,000. He accepted the account and told the receptionist that he would see her later. By 8 February it was suspected that he had left without paying, although he had left some personal effects in his room and retained the key. On 8 February the appellant telephoned the assistant manager and gave the impression that he would return to the hotel. He was told that the cheque he had cashed had been returned marked 'Refer to drawer'. He said that he would settle his account and repay the £30 in cash. A day or so later he telephoned again and said that he intended to return on 11 February. He failed to do so, but telephoned to say that he had been delayed in Northampton by bad weather. Two days later he telephoned to say that disappointing results of certain business transactions had caused him financial embarrassment. He said that he would return on 18 February when he would leave his passport as security for the debt and remove his belongings.

The police were informed and were in attendance when the appellant arrived at the hotel on 18 February. He was arrested. At interview he denied that he intended not to pay the bill. He was released on bail until 2 March when, in the course of a further interview, he gave the police details of his financial problems.

He was charged in an indictment containing three counts. In count 1 with evasion of a liability by deception, contrary to s 2(1)(b) of the Theft Act 1978. In count 2 with making off without payment, contrary to s 3 of the 1978 Act. In count 3 with obtaining services by deception, contrary to s 1 of the 1978 Act.

His defence on each count was that he had acted honestly and that he genuinely expected to pay the hotel bill from the proceeds of various business ventures. He gave details of those ventures and he called two witnesses who confirmed some of them. The jury convicted on count 2 (making off without payment); they were then discharged from returning verdicts on counts 1 and 3.

The appellant now complains of the judge's direction in law on count 2. The issues were whether the appellant had been dishonest and whether he intended to avoid payment. His case was that he had acted honestly, that he genuinely expected to pay and that he intended at most to defer or delay payment. The judge's direction in law is to be found first in the transcript of his summing up:

'How do you decide that? Is [the appellant] right in saying that he thought that ordinary people will not consider what he did to be dishonest? Is the Crown right in saying that he knew that ordinary people will regard what he did was dishonest? That is your function: you are the ordinary people, and you must answer that question. You see, in count 1, it is very clear: it speaks of an intent to make permanent default by inducing the hotel to wait for payment, by deception, namely by falsely representing that it was then his intention to pay for the said accommodation and services and he was able to pay. Count 2 is alleging that he made off without payment. The basis of this count is that payment is required on the spot. When a person checks out of a hotel, he has got to pay then; you cannot give yourself time. Your contract is on that basis; it is implied, and you cannot argue about that. You have got to pay. It is said that on the day between 8 and 11 February 1983, knowing that payment on the spot for goods supplied and services done was required or expected from him he dishonestly made off without having paid as required or expected and with intent to avoid payment of £1,286·94. He did not tell anybody that he was going on 11 February. What he did was he had his last telephone call for £10 and left. It is for you to say whether there is dishonesty there.

Look at the circumstances in which he left, when he did not check out in the normal way: he vanished just like that.'

That direction makes clear that in respect of count 1 an intent to make permanent default was required. In respect of count 2 it failed to direct whether an intent to avoid payment meant that the appellant intended never to pay or that he intended to defer or delay payment. That omission was picked up by the jury. They retired at 1 pm. Immediately after the short adjournment they sent a note to the judge with this question:

'Regarding count 2 of the indictment, the words "and with intent to avoid payment of the £1,286·94", do you refer to permanent intention or one applying only to the dates mentioned in the charge?'

The judge answered it thus:

'The answer is; one applying only to 8 and 11 February 1983. You see it says in count 2: "knowing that payment on the spot for goods supplied and services done was required or expected from him . . ." "On the spot" means the day you leave. There was no payment on the spot when he should have paid. It contrasts sharply with count 1 where the intent there is permanent: that is not so in count 2 where he was required to pay on the spot; and there has been a failure to do that. Will you please, once more, retire to consider your verdict.'

The jury retired again at 2.20 pm and within five minutes returned their verdict of guilty on count 2.

Counsel for the appellant submits that that last direction was wrong and that the error was so fundamental to the main issue that the conviction cannot stand. He contends that the words 'with intent to avoid payment' in s 3 are to be construed as meaning an intention never to pay. The Crown submits that the judge's direction was correct.

One of the main planks in the argument of counsel for the appellant is that the interpretation for which he contends accords with the intention of the Criminal Law Revision Committee who first drafted s 3 of the 1978 Act. Their intentions are expressed in their working paper of August 1974 and in their 13th report (Cmnd 6733, 1977). We venture to doubt the propriety of relying on such aids to construction. First, it is not the intention of the committee that we have to determine; it is the intention of Parliament. It may very well be that they coincide. It is conceivable, however, that they do not. Second, our duty, as we see it, is to judge the intention of the legislature from the words used and their context.

For the Crown, counsel takes two main points. First, that the construction of the material words is governed by the opening words of the section, namely 'a person who, knowing that payment on the spot for any goods supplied or service done is required or expected from him'. She contends that it is payment on the spot which is required or expected and the later reference to payment of the amount due relates to such payment, namely payment on the spot. This is a cogent argument, but we find no reason to conclude from the grammatical structure of the section that it was the intention that the payment sought to be avoided is necessarily payment on the spot. Indeed, if that had been the intention one is entitled to wonder why in the later phrase the payment was not more particularly identified as 'such payment' or the like.

Second, counsel for the Crown draws attention to the markedly different wording of s 2(1)(b) of the 1978 Act, namely 'with intent to make permanent default in whole or in part, etc'. Her point is that had it been the intention of Parliament that the intent in s 3 should be permanently to avoid payment it would have been simple enough to say so in explicit terms. At first sight this, too, is a cogent argument. However, on examination we doubt if it throws any light on the interpretation of s 3. In s 2(1)(b) what is dealt with is an intention to make default, a word which, unless qualified, would cover the mere delaying or deferment of payment. On the other hand, the expression 'to avoid payment' is not so readily susceptible of meaning no more than to delay or to defer and thus does not necessarily require the adverb 'permanently' to convey the meaning contended for by the appellant.

So far as we have been able to discover there is no decision directly in point. Our attention has been drawn to two cases. The first, *Corbyn v Saunders* [1978] 2 All ER 697, [1978] 1 WLR 400, was an appeal by way of case stated from the decision of a Metropolitan stipendiary magistrate. The appellant had been charged under s 5(3) of the Regulation of Railways Act 1889, which provides, so far as it is material, that 'if any person travels or attempts to travel on a railway without having previously paid his fare and with intent to avoid payment thereof he shall be liable' etc. The facts, as stated in the headnote ([1978] 2 All ER 697), were these:

> 'C purchased a 10p ticket for a journey on the London Underground intending to travel further than his ticket entitled him to go. On arrival at his destination he handed the ticket collector the ticket and a form detailing his journey, giving his name and address and inviting the railway authorities to recover the balance of the fare at a later date.'

The magistrate was of the opinion that, as the appellant commenced each journey intending not to pay the proper fare at any time before reaching or at the time of leaving the railway property, but only on request at some future date, he was guilty of each offence.

The question for the opinion of the High Court was whether the intent to avoid payment referred to in s 5(3) of the 1889 Act was an intention permanently to avoid payment as the appellant maintained or whether an intention to avoid 'previous payment' of the fare was sufficient. It is very similar to the issue in this case.

In his considered judgment, with which the other members of the court agreed, Cumming-Bruce LJ said ([1978] 2 All ER 697 at 699, [1978] 1 WLR 400 at 403):

> 'It was contended on his behalf that in order to prove an offence under s 5(3)(a) the prosecution had to prove an intention never to pay the proper fare, ie an intent permanently to avoid payment. There is no reason for importing into the section the adverb "permanently". It is clear on the facts that he did not intend to pay the proper fare unless and until the railway authorities tracked him down and requested payment. That is quite enough to constitute an intent to avoid payment. It is perfectly plain that he had no intention of paying unless the London Transport pursued him for the money. His intention was not an unqualified intention to make the prescribed payment, but an intention not to pay unless later requested to pay. That is an intention to avoid payment.'

He is there saying that, where a person did not intend to pay the proper fare unless and until the railway authority tracked him down and requested payment, that was quite enough to constitute an intent to avoid payment. This is very far from the instant case. However, Cumming-Bruce LJ continued ([1978] 2 All ER 697 at 699, [1978] 1 WLR 400 at 403):

> 'That is enough to dispose of this appeal, but the same result is reached by another route. It is clear from the first clause of s 5(3)(a) that the traveller is not to travel on the railway without paying the fare for the intended journey before he begins that journey. The intention that has to be proved is intention to avoid that obligation, ie payment of the proper fare before he begins his journey. Likewise, if he buys a ticket which is the prescribed fare to a destination, but when he travels he intends to travel beyond that destination without previously paying for the additional distance, he travels that additional distance with intent to avoid the required payment therefor. In that case, if he fails to tender the outstanding balance of the fare, at the latest when passing the ticket collector on the station of destination, the requisite intent to avoid payment is proved.'

That is very close indeed to the proposition urged by the Crown in this appeal. It is a decision which, although not binding on us, is of powerful persuasive authority. It is, of course, a decision on a different statute, one significant difference being the absence of the word 'dishonestly' in the 1889 Act. Thus the appellant's state of mind had to be judged entirely by reference to the specific intent to avoid payment and to nothing else.

The second case is *R v Brooks (Edward)* (1982) 76 Cr App R 66, a case decided in this court and one concerned with s 3 of the 1978 Act. The facts were that the appellants, father and daughter, with one S had a meal together one evening in the upstairs room of a restaurant. At 10.30 pm the daughter was seen leaving the premises in haste. The manager went upstairs and saw the two men were not there but found S downstairs waiting outside the men's lavatory. Nearby was a door inside the premises which led into the yard. S made no comment when asked about the unpaid bill but, after entering the lavatory, later made off through the outer door. The manager chased after him and asked him to come back. While they were re-entering the restaurant, the father came out of it. All three then went back inside. All the father could offer for payment for the bill of £8·52 was a cheque for £130 in his favour, which later turned out to be valueless. S said in the father's hearing that the payment was not due from him, S. When the daughter was later interviewed by the police she maintained that S had met them earlier that night for the first time and had generously offered to treat her and her father to a meal. Both father and daughter were charged with making off without payment contrary to s 3(1) of the Theft Act 1978. The prosecution case was that the father and daughter jointly and severally intended to avoid payment and separately made off from the spot which, it was said, was the restaurant as a whole. The recorder read out in full s 3(1) of the 1978 Act and said the whole essence of the offence was that people left intending, if they could, to get away without paying. But he never told the jury that on the evidence the daughter had left earlier and in haste; that she said she went to the restaurant at the invitation of S believing he would pay; and that they would have to draw the inference that at the time she left she dishonestly intended to evade payment before she could be convicted. Both father and daughter were convicted.

A number of points arose for decision. Among them was this (at 69):

> 'The second ground put forward, i.e. that the recorder failed adequately or at all to direct the jury that the prosecution had to prove that the accused had either made off or was about to do so when challenged and second that the making off was with intent to avoid payment. But the recorder had immediately before the passage cited, read out in full the words of the subsection which are remarkably clear and simple. He then summarised the effect of the subsection in succinct fashion in the sentence "Here the whole essence of the offence is that the people left intending, if they could, to get away without paying". The matter could not have been put better than that. So the jury could not have been left in any doubt.'

Before taking up a further passage in the judgment it is pertinent to observe that in *R v Brooks* there was no evidence of an intention to pay later or, put another way, of an intention to defer or delay payment. The question that arises in this appeal did not arise in *R v Brooks*. The inference in *R v Brooks* was that once payment on the spot had been avoided, payment would have been avoided for good.

Kilner Brown J returned to the question of intent to avoid payment in the following terms (at 70):

> 'In the case of the appellant Julie Brooks, there is a further and different consideration. It is submitted on her behalf that a clear direction was required to the effect that it must be proved that at the time she left the premises she knew that no payment was intended and that there was an intention on her part to participate in a dishonest evasion of the cost of the meal. All that the judge said as to this was the general direction which was given in the passage previously cited and, earlier to that, he had directed the jury in these words: "There are two defendants and you will bring in separate verdicts in respect of each. You may find one guilty and one not guilty or both guilty. Their cases must be considered separately." That was all right as far as it went, but the jury were never told that upon the evidence that she left earlier and in haste and her defence that she went to the restaurant at the other man's invitation believing that he would pay, they would have to draw the inference that at the time she left she intended dishonestly to evade payment, before she could be convicted. If the jury had been alerted to this necessity, it is quite possible that they may not have been satisfied of her guilt.'

We conclude that *R v Brooks* sheds no light on the question we have to resolve. The question did not then present itself for decision.

The textbook writers are not unanimous (compare Professor J C Smith in his book *The Law of Theft* (5th edn, 1984) para 249 and Professor Griew in his book *The Theft Acts 1968 and 1978* (4th edn, 1982) paras 11–14 with Professor Glanville Williams's *Textbook of Criminal Law* (2nd edn, 1983) p 878), although there is a preponderance of opinion in favour of the view expressed by Judge Solomon in his direction to the jury in the present case.

In these circumstances we approach the matter in this way. The verb 'to avoid' is capable of meaning to escape completely or evade permanently. Indeed, the modern dictionary definition 'to escape or evade' when related to payment suggests a permanent rather than a temporary default. Nevertheless, in modern parlance, in some contexts, it might be used to denote no more than default in making payment at due time. In short, we believe the verb itself to be capable of the meaning contended for by both the appellant and the Crown.

We turn, therefore, for assistance from the context in which it is used in the relevant section. To secure a conviction under s 3 of the 1978 Act the following must be proved: (1) that the defendant in fact made off without making payment on the spot; (2) the following mental elements: (a) knowledge that payment on the spot was required or expected of him; and (b) dishonesty; and (c) intent to avoid payment. If (c) means, or is taken to include, no more than an intention to delay or defer payment of the amount due, it is difficult to see what it adds to the other elements. Anyone who knows that payment on the spot is expected or required of him and who then dishonestly makes off without paying as required or expected must have at least the intention to delay or defer payment. It follows, therefore, that the conjoined phrase 'and with intent to avoid payment of the amount due' adds a further ingredient: an intention to do more than delay or defer, an intention to evade payment altogether.

Finally, we can see no reason why, if the intention of Parliament was to provide, in effect, that an intention to delay or defer payment might suffice, Parliament should not have said so in explicit terms. This *might* have been achieved by the insertion of the word 'such' before payment in the phrase in question. It *would* have been achieved by a grammatical reconstruction of the material part of s 3(1) thus, 'dishonestly makes off without having paid and with intent to avoid payment of the amount due as required or expected'.

To accede to the Crown's submission would be to read the section as if it were constructed in that way. That we cannot do. Had it been intended to relate the intention to avoid 'payment' to 'payment as required or expected' it would have been easy to say so. The section does not say so. At the very least it contains an equivocation which should be resolved in favour of the appellant.

For these reasons we conclude that the judge was wrong in his final direction to the jury and that the appeal against conviction must be allowed and the conviction quashed. In saying this we wish to emphasise that we infer no criticism of the judge. This is not an easy section to construe.

*Appeal allowed ; conviction quashed.*

Solicitors: *D M O'Shea* (for the Crown).

*23 July. The court refused leave to appeal to the House of Lords but certified, under s 33(2) of the Criminal Appeal Act 1968, that the following point of law of general public importance was involved in the decision: on a construction of the words 'with intent to avoid payment' in section 3(1) of the Theft Act 1978, namely whether an intention to make permanent default on payment is required.*

*25 October. The Appeal Committee of the House of Lords granted the Crown leave to appeal.*

N P Metcalfe Esq    Barrister.

# Carreras Rothmans Ltd v Freeman Mathews Treasure Ltd (in liq) and another

CHANCERY DIVISION
PETER GIBSON J
14, 15, 16, 17, 18, 21, 22, 23, 24, 25 MAY 1984

*Trust and trustee – Constructive trust – Fiduciary relationship – Debtor and creditor – Agreement between plaintiff and company whereby plaintiff providing company with funds paid into special bank account for sole purpose of paying particular debts owed by company to third parties – Company going into voluntary liquidation – Liquidator claiming money in special bank account an asset of company available for distribution to general body of creditors – Plaintiff claiming money in special bank account held by company on primary trust for third parties – Whether money a company asset or held by company on trust for particular creditors.*

*Company – Voluntary winding up – Distribution of company's property – Assets available for distribution – Agreement between plaintiff and company whereby plaintiff providing company with funds paid into special bank account for sole purpose of paying particular debts owed by company to third parties – Company going into voluntary liquidation – Liquidator claiming money in special bank account an asset of company available for distribution to general body of creditors – Whether agreement between plaintiff and company violating principle of equal distribution between creditors – Whether agreement constituting an unregistered charge on book debts in favour of particular creditors and therefore void – Companies Act 1948, ss 95, 302.*

The plaintiff was a manufacturer of cigarettes which advertised extensively in the United Kingdom. In 1979 the plaintiff employed the defendant company, an advertising agency, to manage its advertising, which involved the defendant in employing the services of production agencies and buying advertising space in the media. In the course of doing that work the defendant contracted as principal with production agencies and advertising media (the agency and media creditors) and paid accounts submitted by them for work done on the plaintiff's advertising. Each month the plaintiff paid the defendant a monthly fee for its services and also a sum equal to that which the defendant owed the agency and media creditors for invoices submitted that month for work done on the plaintiff's advertising. By 1983 the defendant was in financial difficulties and the plaintiff, which was worried about the damage to its business interests if the defendant collapsed, proposed that it pay a monthly sum into a special bank account at the defendant's bank on which the defendant could draw for the sole purpose of settling invoices submitted by the agency and media creditors. The defendant agreed to that arrangement and on 26 July the plaintiff paid the first cheque into the special account to cover the defendant's debts to the agency and media creditors incurred in June. On 29 July the defendant sent cheques drawn on the special account to the agency and media creditors, but later that day the defendant went into voluntary liquidation and the money in the special account was frozen before any of the cheques had been cleared. The plaintiff felt obliged for commercial reasons to pay the agency and media creditors for debts incurred by the defendant in June and July, but refused to meet certain outstanding debts incurred in May on the grounds that it had already paid the defendant in respect of that month and it was up to the agency and media creditors to pursue that matter with the defendant. When it also became clear that the liquidator would not pay any money out of the special account, the plaintiff began proceedings against the defendant and the liquidator claiming that the money in the special account was held on trust for the sole purpose of paying the debts owed to the agency and media creditors and sought an order that the money be so applied. The defendant and the liquidator contended by way of defence that the July agreement was unenforceable because it was entered into to avoid the provisions of s 302[a] of the Companies Act 1948, which required that a company's assets at the time of liquidation were to be shared between the general body of creditors pari passu. The defendant and the liquidator further contended that the agreement was a charge on the defendant's book debts in favour of the agency and media creditors which was void under s 95(1)[b] of the 1948 Act for non-registration, and also counterclaimed for payment of £780,000, being the defendant's monthly fee and expenditure on the plaintiff's advertising incurred during July. By way of reply the plaintiff contended that since the defendant had acted in breach of the July agreement in not paying certain of the May and June debts promptly, the plaintiff was entitled to set off against the amount counterclaimed the payments made by the plaintiff in respect of the June and July debts.

**Held** – (1) On the principle that a trust arose whenever money was transferred from one person to another for a specific purpose which was made known to that other person, a trust was created by the July agreement, because the money had not been paid to the defendant beneficially, and it had never been entitled to use the money for anything other than the intended purpose. Instead, the common intention to be drawn from the arrangement whereby the money was paid directly into the special bank account solely for the purpose of paying the media and agency creditors was that the account would be merely a conduit and that while in the conduit the money would be protected, and that if that purpose was not carried out the defendant would not be entitled to keep the money. The money paid into the special account was therefore held by the defendant on trust (see p 164 *e* to *j*, p 165 *a b* and *g* to *j*, p 167 *b c* and p 172 *g h*, post); *Barclays Bank Ltd v Quistclose Investments Ltd* [1968] 3 All ER 651 applied.

(2) Where a contract had the effect that an asset actually owned by a company at the beginning of its liquidation would not be applied in satisfaction of its liabilities pari passu in accordance with s 302 of the 1948 Act, then to that extent the contract would be declared void as a matter of public policy even if the contract was entered into for bona fide commercial reasons. However, since the money in the special account was subject to a trust it did not form part of the defendant's assets and was therefore not available for distribution to the general body of creditors (see p 168 *j* to p 169 *a*, post); *British Eagle International Airlines Ltd v Cie Nationale Air France* [1975] 2 All ER 390 distinguished.

(3) The July agreement was not a charge under s 95 of the 1948 Act on the defendant's book debts in favour of the agency and media creditors, because the agency and media creditors' rights to the money in the special account were those of beneficiaries and only arose when the money was in fact paid in, at which time the book debt owed by the plaintiff to the defendant in respect of each month's expenditure on the plaintiff's advertising was discharged by the payment into the special account. Furthermore, the rights of the agency and media creditors to enforce the carrying out of the trust by the defendant as trustee were wholly different from the rights of a chargee, and even if the rights of the agency and media creditors did amount to charges that did not prevent the plaintiff from exercising its equitable right to enforce the trust relating to the money in the special account. Accordingly, the plaintiff was entitled to an order that the defendant

---

*a*    Section 302, so far as material, provides: 'Subject to the provisions of this Act as to preferential payments, the property of a company shall, on its winding up, be applied in satisfaction of its liabilities pari passu . . .'

*b*    Section 95, so far as material, provides:

'(1) Subject to the provisions of this Part of this Act, every charge created . . . by a company registered in England and being a charge to which this section applies shall, so far as any security on the company's property or undertaking is conferred thereby, be void against the liquidator and any creditor of the company, unless the prescribed particulars of the charge together with the instrument, if any, by which the charge is created or evidenced, are delivered to or received by the registrar of companies for registration in manner required by this Act within twenty-one days after the date of its creation . . .

(2) This section applies to the following charges . . . (*e*) a charge on book debts of the company . . .'

carry out the terms of the trust and pay the money in the special account to the agency and media creditors (see p 166 *f* to *h* and p 169 *c* and *e* to *g*, post).

(4) However, the defendant was entitled to payment of the £780,000 counterclaimed, because the July agreement did not discharge or replace the defendant's book debt, which remained an asset of the defendant until the debt was discharged by the plaintiff making payment into the special account. The payment made by the plaintiff in July had been in respect of expenditure for June and did not cover debts incurred in July, which remained owing to the defendant under the normal debtor/creditor relationship. Accordingly, the July agreement did not effectively appropriate to the agency and media creditors money which the plaintiff had not yet paid into the special account to discharge its debt to the defendant (see p 170 *c* to *g* and p 172 *h*, post); *British Eagle International Airlines Ltd v Cie Nationale Air France* [1975] 2 All ER 390 considered.

(5) Furthermore, the defendant was entitled to the £780,000 free of any set-off, because, although a contractual obligation on the part of the defendant to pay the agency and media creditors duly and promptly once it was put in funds by the plaintiff could be implied from the nature of the parties' mutual dealings, the defendant's failure to pay those creditors by the time it went into liquidation on 3 August 1983 after having received funds from the plaintiff on 26 July did not amount to a breach of that obligation (see p 171 *e* and *j* to p 172 *b* and *f*, post).

### Notes

For property available for distribution in a winding up, see 7 Halsbury's Laws (4th edn) para 1180, and for cases on the subject, see 10 Digest (Reissue) 1009–1012, 6133–6158.

For the Companies Act 1948, ss 95, 302, see 5 Halsbury's Statutes (3rd edn) 189, 337.

### Cases referred to in judgment

*Barclays Bank Ltd v Quistclose Investments Ltd* [1968] 3 All ER 651, [1970] AC 567, [1968] 3 WLR 1097, HL.
*British Eagle International Airlines Ltd v Cie Nationale Air France* [1975] 2 All ER 390, [1975] 1 WLR 758, HL.
*Daintrey, Re, ex p Mant* [1900] 1 QB 546, [1895–9] All ER Rep 657, CA.
*Debtor (No 66 of 1955), Re a, ex p the debtor v Trustee of the property of Waite (a bankrupt)* [1956] 3 All ER 225, [1956] 1 WLR 1226, CA.
*Northern Developments (Holdings) Ltd, Re* (6 October 1978, unreported), Ch D.
*Oriental Bank Corp, Re, ex p Guillemin* (1884) 28 Ch D 634.
*Wiltshire Iron Co, Re, ex p Pearson* (1868) LR 3 Ch App 443.

### Cases also cited

*Ayerst (Inspector of Taxes) v C & K (Construction) Ltd* [1975] 2 All ER 537, [1976] AC 167, HL.
*B & S Contracts and Design Ltd v Victor Green Publications Ltd* [1984] CA Bound Transcript 52.
*Churchill (Lord) v Hunt* (1819) 2 B & Ald 685, 106 ER 515.
*Edwards v Glyn* (1859) 2 E & E 29, 121 ER 12.
*FLE Holdings Ltd, Re* [1967] 3 All ER 553, [1967] 1 WLR 1409.
*Foaminol Laboratories Ltd v British Artid Plastics Ltd* [1941] 2 All ER 393.
*Hanak v Green* [1958] 2 All ER 141, [1958] 2 QB 9, CA.
*Kayford Ltd, Re* [1975] 1 All ER 604, [1975] 1 WLR 279.
*Kent and Sussex Sawmills Ltd, Re* [1946] 2 All ER 638, [1947] Ch 177.
*Lobb (Alec) (Garages) Ltd v Total Oil GB Ltd* [1983] 1 All ER 944, [1983] 1 WLR 87.
*Pao On v Lau Yiu* [1979] 3 All ER 65, [1980] AC 614, PC.
*Rogers, Re, ex p Holland & Hannen* (1891) 8 Morr 243, CA.
*Saunderson & Co v Clark* (1913) 29 TLR 579.
*Sharp v Jackson* [1899] AC 419, [1895–9] All ER Rep 755, HL.
*Toovey v Milne* (1819) 2 B & Ald 683, 106 ER 514.

*Tout & Finch Ltd, Re* [1954] 1 All ER 127, [1954] 1 WLR 178.
*Universe Tankships Inc of Monrovia v International Transport Workers Federation* [1982] 2
   All ER 67, [1983] 1 AC 366, HL.
*X Co Ltd, Re* [1907] 2 Ch 92.

**Action and counterclaim**
By a writ indorsed with a statement of claim dated 26 August 1983 the plaintiff, Carreras
Rothmans Ltd (CR), sought as against the first defendant, Freeman Mathews Treasure
Ltd (in liq) (FMT), and the second defendant, Laurence Gerrard (the liquidator), (1) a
declaration that moneys in a special bank account were held by FMT for CR on trust for
the sole purpose of applying the same in meeting the accounts of the media and
production fees of third parties directly attributable to CR's involvement with FMT and
in default of such purpose being carried into effect on resulting trust to repay to CR the
full amount and/or any remaining balance thereof, (2) an order that FMT and the
liquidator forthwith apply the moneys in carrying out that purpose and in default thereof
that they repay the same to CR, (3) such injunctions as might be necessary, (4) all other
necessary accounts, inquiries and directions. By a defence and counterclaim dated 21
October 1983 FMT and the liquidator sought, inter alia, (1) a declaration that if CR was
entitled to repayment of the moneys in the account, they were entitled to a corresponding
payment for services rendered to CR and (2) for payment of £649,639·93 plus interest
for further services provided. The facts are set out in the judgment of Peter Gibson J.

*Peter Millett QC* and *John Higham* for CR.
*Robin Potts QC* and *John Vallat* for FMT and the liquidator.

*Cur adv vult*

25 May. The following judgment was delivered.

**PETER GIBSON J.** By this action and counterclaim the plaintiff, Carreras Rothmans
Ltd (CR), and the defendants, Freeman Mathews Treasure Ltd (FMT), now in creditors'
voluntary liquidation, and its liquidator, Mr Laurence Gerrard, seek the determination
of certain questions as to the consequences in law of an arrangement entered into by CR
and FMT shortly before FMT's liquidation whereby moneys payable by CR to FMT were
to be paid, and some moneys were paid, into a special bank account for the payment of
certain of FMT's creditors.
   CR is the manufacturer of several well-known brands of cigarettes and pipe tobacco.
In carrying on its business it advertises extensively in the United Kingdom to promote
its products. Because of restrictions agreed with the government the advertising is
confined to newspapers, periodicals and posters, but the amounts expended are enormous.
CR allocated approximately £5m to its UK advertising for 1983. CR had in 1983 a UK
advertising manager, Miss Pauline Moore, who reported to Mr Ray Higgs, the UK
marketing director of CR, who in turn reported to Mr John Webb, CR's managing
director. CR employs advertising agencies to carry out its advertising. The advertising
work is in two parts. First there is the creative work, that is to say the work of advising
CR what its advertisements should look like and, when that is approved, of producing
the artwork for the advertisements. Second, there is the placement work, that is to say in
producing from that artwork all that is needed (such as negatives and proofs) for the
printing of the advertisements in the newspapers and periodicals or for the production
of the posters and then buying the space for the advertisements. Placement work is
skilled work, in particular in negotiating with the media and assessing the quality of the
media whose space is being bought for the advertisements.
   FMT was for many years until its liquidation one of the advertising agencies employed
by CR. It was founded shortly after the war and at one time had the reputation of being
the most profitable of all advertising agencies. In 1979 CR appointed FMT to handle all
CR's placement work in the UK. FMT also thereafter did some creative work in

connection with two of CR's brands but this part of its association with CR is irrelevant to the issues in the case. CR was throughout satisfied with the placement work done by FMT. For this work FMT had a team of five headed by Mr Sydney Shephard. However, Mr Shephard appears to have been dissatisfied with FMT and for some time prior to FMT's liquidation, and in particular in the period leading up to that liquidation, had openly voiced his desire to leave FMT either to set up on his own or to join another agency but in either case taking the CR placement work with him.

The appointment in 1979 of FMT to do CR's placement work was contained in a letter from CR to FMT and covered the financial arrangements between them. Unhappily neither CR nor FMT has been able to find the original or a copy of that letter, but the pattern of their financial dealings in relation to placement work was from 1979 until July 1983 very largely consistent. CR paid FMT an annual fee payable by monthly instalments for the services performed by FMT on that work. The amount of the fee was fixed several months in advance of the calendar year to which it related. Thus on 17 August 1982 Mr Higgs met and agreed with Mr Shephard the amount to be paid in 1983. The monthly fee was £20,416·67. In addition CR paid FMT a sum equal to all expenditure incurred by FMT on the placement work which it carried out for CR, such payment being limited to debts incurred to third parties. Any work done by FMT itself was paid for by the annual fee.

The third parties were newspapers and periodicals in whose publications CR's advertisements appeared and what have been described as production agencies who performed technical services to enable FMT to supply the newspapers and periodicals with the actual advertisements to be printed. The obligations incurred to such third parties were incurred by FMT as principal and not as agent of CR, although the third parties would be well aware that they were working on advertisements for CR. To obtain payment from CR for the debts incurred by FMT to third parties, FMT supplied invoices each month to CR. Thus the invoices for May would be supplied by 22 May and, after being checked and the details entered in CR's computer, CR supplied FMT with a cheque for the sum claimed by means of the invoices and accepted by CR. That cheque would then be paid by 23 or 24 June. The evidence as to when FMT would pay the third parties and when such payments from FMT were due is not wholly satisfactory, and CR complains of a failure by FMT to give proper discovery of invoices and bank statements to establish any dates of payment. But the unchallenged evidence of Mr Higgs was that it was his understanding that the payments were regularly made by CR a few days before debts owed by FMT became due. It appears from the standard conditions of the Newspaper Publishers Association that in respect of advertisements placed with their members the due date was the last business day of the month following that to which the invoices related, and it appears from the standard conditions of the Periodical Publishers Association that the due date was the end of the month following the month in which the advertisement appeared. All this supports an inference that in general the debts incurred by FMT one month would become payable at about the end of the following month and the payment system operated by CR was designed to put FMT in funds to enable it to pay shortly afterwards the debts incurred to third parties. There were provisions for surcharges for late payment in the standard terms of the two publishers associations. CR in the words of Mr Laurie Duskwick, FMT's managing director in the period immediately before liquidation, always paid on the nail.

CR was by far FMT's most important client, providing FMT with 70% of its turnover. But in 1982 FMT began to be subject to financial pressures. It lost one of its larger accounts, Amoco, and in February 1983 Mr Brian Mathews and in May 1983 Dr John Treasure, both leading figures in FMT, left. Mr Duskwick then took over as managing director. He caused independent business consultants to investigate FMT's financial position and that investigation confirmed that FMT was not in a healthy position. It was estimated by Mr Duskwick that FMT had lost £150,000 in the first quarter of 1983. Mr Duskwick decided that overheads had to be cut down drastically and many employees were made redundant in June. Desparate attempts were made to find further capital.

There were merger discussions with a number of other agencies and with a financier, but all in the end came to nothing.

CR in the mean time had become aware that FMT was being subjected to financial pressures and the departure of Mr Mathews, who had long been associated with the CR account, caused concern. But Mr Shephard and his team were still working satisfactorily on CR's placement business. Nevertheless in June and July Mr Higgs had been considering what the attitude of FMT's third party creditors would be if FMT ceased trading and Mr Higgs was of the view that they would look to CR for payment even if there was no legal obligation on CR to pay. In July 1983 two press reports also gave him concern. One, in Marketing Weekly for 8 July and headed 'Troubled FMT finds new partner', referred to FMT calling off negotiations which it had been holding with various agencies and signing a deal with an unnamed financial partner. The other in the Daily Express for 12 July referred to a financier by name as having acquired a 76% holding in FMT. Both reports were inaccurate in suggesting that the agreement with the financier had been completed.

At this time Mr Duskwick was worried about Mr Shephard, who by reason of his dissatisfaction with FMT and his hope of taking the CR account with him if he left might have prejudiced any merger that FMT might have been able to arrange. Mr Duskwick felt he should try to reassure CR about FMT and at the same time he would try to find out if CR was ready to support Mr Shephard if he left FMT. On 13 July Mr Duskwick arranged that he and another director who had worked for FMT with CR for many years, Mr Dick Wellbourne, should go to see Mr Higgs and Miss Moore the next day. The meeting between them on 14 July was a cordial one. Mr Duskwick and Mr Wellbourne told Mr Higgs and Miss Moore that FMT had financial difficulties but a new board had been constituted, they had taken a number of steps to cut overheads and were living within their means and they were determined to make a go of the business. They expressed anxiety about the possibility of CR removing its account from FMT, in particular because of Mr Shephard's talk of setting up on his own, but Mr Higgs reassured them that CR was very satisfied with FMT and had no wish to change the status quo. However, Mr Higgs sought agreement on two matters. First he asked if CR's financial controller, Mr Mallinder, could visit FMT so as to be able to report to CR on FMT's financial situation. Mr Duskwick and Mr Wellbourne agreed to that. Second, Mr Higgs said that he wanted to explore whether the very large sums of money that CR was putting through FMT could be protected. It is clear that in putting forward that suggestion Mr Higgs was concerned at the damage to CR if FMT ceased trading through insolvency leaving the third party creditors with their debts unpaid. Mr Higgs had the idea that there might be a different way of treating payments made by CR to FMT to pay third parties and he wanted FMT's approval for the suggestion that he should explore ways and means to protect such payments. Mr Wellbourne said that was no problem. Mr Higgs said it would be ideal if the arrangements could be in place before the July payment became due. Again there was no objection by FMT.

Mr Higgs the next day asked Mr Mallinder to visit FMT and this was arranged for 26 July. Mr Higgs also instructed CR's employee solicitor, Mr Osborn-King, to devise the protection scheme. Mr Osborn-King devised such a scheme incorporating it in a letter (the contract letter) which he drafted for Mr Higgs's signature. Mr Higgs thought the wording rather legalistic but signed the contract letter and both telephoned Mr Wellbourne, for whose attention the letter was addressed, and wrote an informal letter to accompany the contract letter. In the telephone conversation on 19 July he told Mr Wellbourne that CR had come up with a scheme to protect third parties and that a letter was on its way. He said that FMT's directors would probably wish to take legal advice and if there were any problems they could come back to him. In the informal letter he referred to the contract letter as describing the banking arrangements CR would like to set up in order to protect the interests of CR and the media creditors and he apologised that the letter was rather cold and legalistic, but that, he said, was a function of the way it had been drafted. He said he trusted that their relationship would continue on a new and improved basis from that point onwards. The contract letter was in this form:

'Dear Mr. Wellbourne

I write in view of the present uncertainty about your company as disclosed in recent newspaper reports. We have no wish to create further difficulties for you, yet at the same time are under a positive obligation to protect the Company's interests to the full. Accordingly, I am pleased to confirm that all accounts representing your fees will be paid direct as before. However, as regards payments made to you for purely onwards transmission (in effect) to the media and production agencies by way of reimbursement for past services, we require the following arrangements to be approved and implemented by you before we are prepared to make further payments. In essence, we require such payments to be paid to a special account to be opened by you at your bank for the purposes only of meeting the accounts of media and production agencies incurred on your behalf for Carreras Rothmans. The bare bones of the arrangement are as follows—1. Your agreement to setting up a special account at your bank under the title of "FMT/Carreras Rothmans Client Account". 2. All monies received by you from us for such account will be clearly marked "FMT/Carreras Rothmans Client Account Only" and payable only into such account. 3. The monies in the account will be used only for the purposes of meeting the accounts of the media and production fees of third parties directly attributable to Carreras Rothmans involvement with the Agency. 4. The account will be used only for the purposes in (3) above and no other monies will be paid in or out of such account. 5. In the event of any balance occurring in the account after the payment as in (3) then such sum will be repaid to us (obviously this should never occur in the usual course of things). 6. We are supplied with fortnightly statements in respect of the account through your goodselves as supplied by the bank. 7. We receive written confirmation from the bank that they are aware of the conditions and purpose of this account prior to our cheque (shortly due to be paid) being sent to you and that such an account has been opened. 8. In consideration for your meeting the above arrangements, we pay a one-off fee of £150 plus VAT against receipt of the appropriate invoice. Upon receiving your written confirmation of the above, we foresee no delay in making future payments to you in respect of placements charges etc. I believe that it is also appropriate for us to seek your confirmation that all placements and forward media options obtained by you on our instructions are held for us on trust subject only to payment by us of your fee and our paying for the expenditure on the placements so incurred. Equally, I hope that your and our present anxieties are soon resolved to the satisfaction of all and I have no intention of permitting these precautionary arrangements to be divulged to anyone apart from the bank through your goodselves.

Yours sincerely

R. D. HIGGS.'

Whether legal advice was taken on the letter neither Mr Duskwick nor Mr Wellbourne was able to say. Certainly FMT had solicitors then acting for it, but I think it unlikely that FMT did consult them, as Mr Wellbourne's attitude to the letter was that the matter had already been agreed in principle at the meeting on 14 July while Mr Duskwick considered that the letter was obviously very carefully thought out, this was what CR wanted and FMT would have done anything to comply with CR's wishes. On 20 or 21 July Mr Wellbourne told Mr Higgs by telephone that an acceptance letter was being signed. On 25 July the manager of FMT's bankers, Midland Bank, Pall Mall branch, wrote to Mr Higgs confirming the opening of the special account and his knowledge of the purposes of the account. On the morning of 26 July My Mallinder visited FMT. He was given information about FMT's financial position and a profit forecast for 1983–84 which showed that after losses for April, May, June and July FMT would move back to profitability for six out of the following eight months. An unaudited balance sheet prepared as at 31 March 1983 showed current liabilities exceeding current assets, but net assets exceeding liabilities. FMT's overdraft facility with its bank was said to be £175,000, but the current overdraft was said to be in the region of £25,000. Mr Mallinder reported the same afternoon to Mr Webb and Mr Higgs. The result of his review indicated that the action that had been taken by FMT to reduce overheads would probably enable FMT to survive in the short term provided the bank supported FMT and no client pulled out, but that unless FMT could obtain additional business the action it had taken would provide only a temporary reprieve.

Still later on 26 July at 4 pm Mr Freeman, the chairman of FMT, met Mr Webb. Mr Freeman handed Mr Webb a letter signed by Mr Freeman on behalf of the board of directors of FMT and addressed to Mr Higgs. In it he referred to the contract letter, to the setting up of the special account and he said:

> 'We totally accept and agree with the conditions set out in your letter and the Board thank you for the consideration your Company has shown to us whilst in this difficult time.'

Thus an agreement (the July agreement) on the terms of the contract letter was thereby concluded. Mr Webb handed Mr Freeman a letter (the cheque letter) dated 26 July from Mr Higgs referring to a cheque for £597,128·72 made payable to FMT/Carreras Rothmans Client Account. The cheque was handed to Mr Freeman against his signature acknowledging receipt of and agreement with the contract letter and was said in the cheque letter to be in payment of the invoices shown on an attached remittance advice. The invoices were those supplied by FMT relating to the debts incurred to third parties in June. Thus the amount paid corresponded precisely to the aggregate of the amounts shown as due to particular third party creditors of FMT.

Within CR discussions thereafter ensued whether CR should continue to use FMT after the end of that year. Mr Higgs suggested a decision be taken to appoint a replacement agency. It is, I think, common ground that six months' notice would have had to be given to terminate the contract of FMT. However, no decision was taken as in the mean time events had taken a turn for the worse in FMT.

FMT had set about paying the third party creditors for June promptly after receiving CR's cheque, and cheques were sent off on or by 29 July. But on the afternoon of 29 July Midland Bank informed FMT that it would not lend FMT money to support a merger which FMT had been arranging with another agency. FMT's board took the advice of its solicitors on fraudulent trading. On 3 August FMT went into a creditors' voluntary winding up and the moneys in the special account were frozen at the instigation of the liquidator, before any cheque drawn on that account had been cleared.

The news of the liquidation surprised CR. It promptly arranged for another agency to carry on with the placement work but the immediate problem that arose was what to do about the third party creditors. On 4 August Mr Higgs and Miss Moore were telephoned by practically every advertising manager of a newspaper which had carried CR's advertisements in June. The cheques drawn on the special account had bounced and the newspapers sought an undertaking from CR that CR would be responsible for the June debts. A meeting was arranged for 5 August and was attended by Mr Higgs and Miss Moore and by representatives of nearly all the major newspapers. The mood of the representatives was very angry. Mr Higgs attempted to reassure the representatives by explaining the special account arrangement, but they were not satisfied with that and they indicated that unless CR was prepared to undertake responsibility for the debts incurred by FMT in respect of CR's advertisements they would cancel the unfulfilled orders and would refuse to take further advertisements of CR save on a renegotiated basis. The very good discounts negotiated by FMT would be lost and Mr Higgs and Miss Moore estimated that this could have increased CR's advertising costs by 24%.

At this time the second phase of CR's huge advertising campaign had not yet commenced. CR decided that that campaign was too important to jeopardise and accordingly it should pay FMT's debts to third parties, including production agencies which were considered to be in the like position to the newspapers and whose goodwill CR wished to keep. Further, such agencies were less able than the newspapers to withstand a bad debt. The aggregate of the debts incurred to third parties, subsequent to the June debts, is £759,583·33. The payments made by CR to third parties were made against assignments by the third parties to CR, thereby enabling CR to stand in the shoes of the third parties so far as any claim can be made against the moneys in the special account or to prove in the liquidation. In all a total of £1,290,673·02 has been paid by CR for June and July debts totalling £1,308,124·22. The second phase of the advertising campaign was duly completed.

In the course of communications with the third parties to ascertain the amounts owed by FMT, CR discovered that FMT had failed to pay some of its third party debts incurred in May notwithstanding that it had been put in funds by CR in June to pay such creditors. The unpaid May debts amounted to £101,306·29. CR refused to pay those debts on the footing that CR had already paid FMT for them and it was the creditors' own fault in failing to pursue FMT promptly.

On 12 August 1983 CR's solicitors wrote to the liquidator's firm claiming that the moneys in the special account were trust moneys and asking for confirmation that those moneys would be applied in meeting the third party debts or that it would be repaid forthwith. On 15 August the liquidator's solicitors replied, expressing the view that for payment to be made to the third parties would be a fraudulent preference and they said they had advised the liquidator that no payment should be made out of the account. Accordingly these proceedings were commenced with commendable promptness by CR on 26 August 1983.

The facts that I have narrated are a summary of the evidence, documentary and oral, that was presented to me. I heard oral evidence from Mr Webb, Mr Higgs and Miss Moore for CR and from Mr Duskwick and Mr Wellbourne for FMT and the liquidator. Happily this is a case where there is no irreconcilable conflict of evidence and all the witnesses gave their evidence truthfully.

By its statement of claim CR claims that the sum of £597,128·72 in the special account is and was since 26 July 1983 held by FMT for CR on trust for the sole purpose of applying the same in meeting the debts owed to third parties and in default of that purpose being carried into effect on a resulting trust to repay the same to CR. CR seeks a declaration to that effect and an order that FMT and the liquidator forthwith apply those moneys in carrying out that purpose and in default thereof an order that they repay the same to CR. In their defence FMT and the liquidator deny that the moneys in the special account were or are held in trust and they allege four grounds on which the July agreement was unenforceable and a fifth was added by amendment at the commencement of the trial: (1) no consideration for the agreement; (2) the July agreement was procured by economic duress; (3) the July agreement constituted a fraudulent preference; (4) the July agreement was contrary to public policy being entered into to avoid the provisions of s 302 of the Companies Act 1948 (providing for pari passu distribution to unsecured creditors of an insolvent company in voluntary liquidation); (5) the July agreement constituted an unregistered charge on book debts and was void under s 95 of the 1948 Act. FMT and the liquidator also claim that the court should not order specific performance of the July agreement. FMT and the liquidator counterclaim that if CR is entitled to repayment of the moneys in the account they are entitled to a corresponding payment for FMT's services provided to CR. Further they counterclaim for payment of £780,000 for further services provided by FMT (in effect those provided in July). Of that sum £20,416·67 is the monthly fee for July which was payable to FMT itself and was left unaffected by the July agreement and the balance represents the amounts payable by CR in respect of the third party July debts. In its reply and defence to counterclaim CR raises two defences to the counterclaim: (1) after the date of the July agreement CR was not obliged to make payments to FMT otherwise than pursuant to and in accordance with the July agreement; (2) it was an implied term of the contract between CR and FMT, alternatively of the July agreement, that FMT should pay the third parties duly and promptly on being put in funds by CR for that purpose; there were breaches of that term in relation to the May and June debts and an anticipatory breach in relation to the July debts, from which breach loss and damage resulted; CR reasonably mitigated that loss and damage by paying third party creditors in respect of June and July debts and CR is entitled to treat that expenditure as part of the recoverable loss and damage and to set that off against FMT's claim.

After the oral evidence and at the start of the sixth day of the trial counsel for FMT and the liquidator abandoned the defences to the statement of claim which were based on absence of consideration, economic duress and fraudulent preference, and in my opinion he was right to do so. The remaining issues can therefore be classified under five heads (in respect of the statement of claim): (1) trust; (2) s 302; (3) s 95; and (in respect of the counterclaim) (4) CR's obligations; (5) set-off.

### (1) *Trust*

Counsel for CR contended that the language of the contract letter was apt to create a trust and that such trust was fully constituted as to the moneys in the special account when FMT agreed to the terms of the contract letter and received the moneys from CR. They relied on the line of cases of which *Barclays Bank Ltd v Quistclose Investments Ltd* [1968] 3 All ER 651, [1970] AC 567 is the highest authority. Counsel for FMT and the liquidator denied that any enforceable trust was created. He submitted that the language of the contract letter was apt to create obligations of a contractual nature only in relation to the moneys to be paid into the special account, that the *Quistclose* line of cases was distinguishable, that if there were a trust it was an illusory trust and that in any event the court should not order specific performance of the July agreement to perform any trust that was created.

The July agreement was plainly intended to vary the contractual position of the parties as to how, as the contract letter put it, payments made by CR to FMT for purely onwards transmission, in effect, to the third party creditors would be dealt with. If one looks objectively at the genesis of the variation, CR was concerned about the adverse effect on it if FMT, which CR knew to have financial problems, ceased trading and third party creditors of FMT were not paid at a time when FMT had been put in funds by CR. The objective was accurately described by Mr Higgs in his informal letter of 19 July as to protect the interests of CR and the third parties. For this purpose a special account was to be set up with a special designation. The moneys payable by CR were to be paid not to FMT beneficially but directly into that account so that FMT was never free to deal as it pleased with the moneys so paid. The moneys were to be used only for the specific purpose of paying the third parties and, as the cheque letter indicated, the amount paid matched the specific invoices presented by FMT to CR. The account was intended to be little more than a conduit pipe, but the intention was plain that whilst in the conduit pipe the moneys should be protected. There was even a provision covering the possibility (though what actual situation it was intended to meet it is hard to conceive) that there might be a balance left after payment and in that event the balance was to be paid to CR and not kept by FMT. It was thus clearly intended that the moneys once paid would never become the property of FMT. That was the last thing CR wanted in view of its concern about FMT's financial position. As a further precaution the bank was to be put on notice of the conditions and purpose of the account. I infer that this was to prevent the bank attempting to exercise any rights of set-off against the moneys in the account.

Only two matters were relied on as indicating that no trust was intended. One was the consideration fee; but the presence of consideration does not negative a trust. The other was the express reference in the penultimate sentence in relation to placements and forward media options with which was contrasted the absence of the words 'trust' in relation to the moneys in the account. But I regard that as of minimal significance when I consider all the other indications as to the capacity in which FMT was to hold any moneys in the account. In my judgment even in the absence of authority it is manifest that FMT was intended to act in relation to those moneys in a fiduciary capacity only.

There is of course ample authority that moneys paid by A to B for a specific purpose which has been made known to B are clothed with a trust. In the *Quistclose* case [1968] 3 All ER 651 at 654, [1970] AC 567 at 580, Lord Wilberforce referred to the recognition, in a series of cases over some 150 years, that arrangements for the payment of a person's creditors by a third person gives rise to 'a relationship of a fiduciary character or trust, in favour, as a primary trust, of the creditors, and secondarily, if the primary trust fails, of the third person'. Lord Wilberforce in describing the facts of the *Quistclose* case said a little earlier that the mutual intention of the provider of the moneys and of the recipient of the moneys, and the essence of the bargain, was that the moneys should not become part of the assets of the recipient but should be used exclusively for payment of a particular class of its creditors. That description seems to me to be apt in relation to the facts of the present case too.

Counsel for FMT and the liquidator sought to distinguish the *Quistclose* case in this way. He submitted that for any trust one needed (i) a settlor conveying property to a trustee or declaring a trust of property in his own hands, (ii) trust property and (iii) a beneficiary. He said that in the *Quistclose* case the settlor was the provider of the moneys, who did so by way of loan. In the present case, he submitted, the settlor was not CR but FMT, to which CR owed a debt to reimburse FMT for the June debts owed to the third parties and he pointed out that CR made no claim that there was a trust of the book debt. In the *Quistclose* case [1968] 3 All ER 651 at 656, [1970] AC 567 at 581, Lord Wilberforce, in rejecting an argument that the lender only had contractual rights in a transaction of loan, said:

> 'There is surely no difficulty in recognising the co-existence in one transaction of legal and equitable rights and remedies: when the money is advanced, the lender acquires an equitable right to see that it is applied for the primary designated purpose . . .'

Counsel for FMT and the liquidator submitted that there was no recognition in the *Quistclose* case that anyone else had an enforceable right and that in particular a person in the position of CR discharging a debt had no right to enforce any trust.

It is of course true that there are factual differences between the *Quistclose* case and the present case. The transaction there was one of loan with no contractual obligation on the part of the lender to make payment prior to the agreement for the loan. In the present case there is no loan but there is an antecedent debt owed by CR. I doubt if it is helpful to analyse the *Quistclose* type of case in terms of the constituent parts of a conventional settlement, though it may of course be crucial to ascertain in whose favour the secondary trust operates (as in the *Quistclose* case itself) and who has an enforceable right. In my judgment the principle in all these cases is that equity fastens on the conscience of the person who receives from another property transferred for a specific purpose only and not therefore for the recipient's own purposes, so that such person will not be permitted to treat the property as his own or to use it for other than the stated purpose. Most of the cases in this line are cases where there has been an agreement for consideration, so that in one sense each party has contributed to providing the property. But, if the common intention is that property is transferred for a specific purpose and not so as to become the property of the transferee, the transferee cannot keep the property if for any reason that purpose cannot be fulfilled. I am left in no doubt that the provider of the moneys in the present case was CR. True it is that its own witnesses said that if FMT had not agreed to the terms of the contract letter CR would not have broken its contract but would have paid its debt to FMT, but the fact remains that CR made its payment on the terms of that letter and FMT received the moneys only for the stipulated purpose. That purpose was expressed to relate only to the moneys in the account. In my judgment therefore CR can be equated with the lender in the *Quistclose* case as having an enforceable right to compel the carrying out of the primary trust.

Counsel for FMT and the liquidator also submitted that the third party creditors had no enforceable rights and that where the beneficiaries under the primary trust have no enforceable right no trust is created. Counsel for CR also submitted that the third party creditors had no enforceable rights, though that submission was made primarily with an eye to an argument relevant to the s 95 point that the beneficial interest in the moneys paid into the special account always remained in CR. In none of the many reported cases in the *Quistclose* line of cases, so far as I am aware, had any consideration been given to the question whether the person intended to benefit from the carrying out of the specific purpose which created the trust has enforceable rights. Thus the existence of enforceable rights in such persons has not been treated as crucial to the existence of a trust. Further, in the one case in which so far as I am aware the question who, in addition to the provider of the property, had enforceable rights was determined by the court, it was held that the persons intended to benefit from the carrying out of the primary trust did have enforceable rights. That case is the unreported decision on 6 October 1978 of Sir Robert Megarry V-C in *Re Northern Developments (Holdings) Ltd*. In that case the eponymous company (Northern ) was the parent company of a group of companies including one (Kelly) which was in financial straits. Seventeen banks agreed to put up a fund in excess of half a million pounds in an attempt to rescue Kelly. The banks already had other companies in the group as customers. They paid the moneys into an account in Northern's name for the express purpose of providing moneys for Kelly's unsecured creditors and for no other purpose, the amounts advanced being treated as advances to the banks' other customers in the group. The fund was used to sustain Kelly for a time, but then Kelly was put into receivership at a time when a little over half the fund remained unexpended. One of the questions for the court was who was entitled to that balance. The Vice-Chancellor held that there was a *Quistclose* type of trust attaching to the fund, that trust was a purpose trust but enforceable by identifiable individuals, namely the banks as lenders, Kelly, for whose immediate benefit the fund was established, and Kelly's creditors. The reason given by the Vice-Chancellor for holding that Kelly's creditors had enforceable rights were the words of Lord Wilberforce in the *Quistclose* case which I have already cited, describing the *Quistclose* type of trust as giving rise to a relationship of a fiduciary character or trust in favour of the creditors. However, the Vice-Chancellor went on to describe the interests of the creditors in this way:

> 'The fund was established not with the object of vesting the beneficial interest in them, but in order to confer a benefit on Kelly (and so, consequentially, on the rest of the group and the bankers) by ensuring that Kelly's creditors would be paid in an orderly manner. There is perhaps some parallel in the position of a beneficiary entitled to a share of residue under a will. What he has is not a beneficial interest in any asset forming part of residue, but a right to compel the executor to administer the assets of the deceased properly. It seems to me that it is that sort of right which the creditors of Kelly had.'

The interest of the banks was held to be under the secondary trust if the primary trust failed. In the light of that authority I cannot accept the joint submission that the third party creditors for the payment of whose debts CR had paid the moneys into the special account had no enforceable rights. In any event I do not comprehend how a trust which on no footing could CR revoke unilaterally and which was expressed as a trust to pay third parties and was still capable of performance could nevertheless leave the beneficial interest in CR which had parted with the moneys. On the Vice-Chancellor's analysis the beneficial interest is in suspense until the payment is made.

I can dispose of the remaining arguments of counsel for FMT and the liquidator under this head more briefly. In my judgment the doctrine of illusory trusts has no application to the facts of the present case. That doctrine applies where a debtor for his own convenience settles property in favour of his creditors, the court treating the trust as a revocable one. In the present case, although FMT agreed to the discharge of an asset, its book debt, by payment by its debtor, CR, in such a way that the moneys paid would be held on trust to pay its creditors, FMT did not enter into the arrangement for its convenience but for good commercial reasons on the insistence of CR and the trust was not for its creditors generally but for a particular class of creditor. It cannot be said in the circumstances that the July agreement was intended to be revocable by FMT alone. Nor can I accept the argument of counsel for FMT and the liquidator on specific performance. He submitted that, where, as here, the beneficial interest in the moneys in the account has not yet become vested in the third party creditors, the court should not order payment. His argument was based on a suggested analogy with cases like *Re Wiltshire Iron Co, ex p Pearson* (1868) LR 3 Ch App 443 and *Re Oriental Bank Corp, ex p Guillemin* (1884) 28 Ch D 634 in which the court refused to allow the completion of contracts after the commencement of a winding up where the property the subject of the contracts remained in the company's ownership at the commencement of the winding up. In the present case CR seeks, an order not for specific performance but for the carrying out of the primary trust in respect of moneys which not only are not the property of FMT but never have been. At the commencement of the liquidation its previous asset, the book debt, had been discharged. I see no reason why the court should not so order.

In my judgment therefore a trust was created by the July agreement, that trust was completely constituted by the payment of moneys into the special account and CR as the provider of the moneys has an equitable right to an order for the carrying out by FMT of the trust.

### (2) *Section 302*

Counsel for FMT and the liquidator submitted that the July agreement was an agreement to contract out of s 302 of the Companies Act 1948 and as such was contrary to public policy. Prior to the July agreement, counsel said, FMT had an asset in the form of the debt owed to it by CR in respect of the debts incurred to third parties by FMT. But for the July agreement, that asset would have been available to meet the debts of its general body of creditors. As a result of the July agreement, that debt could no longer be discharged by payment to it beneficially but was appropriated for the benefit of particular creditors. Those particular creditors remained creditors at the time of the commencement of the liquidation. The principle which he submitted was applicable was this: an arrangement which is entered into by a company in contemplation of its insolvency and which has the effect that an asset of the company is not available at the commencement of its liquidation, not having been disposed of in a manner recognised as legitimate by law, but is available only for particular creditors is avoided as a matter of public policy as an attempt to contract out of the provisions of s 302.

Two points should be noted on this formulation. First, it is not necessary that the asset in question affected by the arrangement should be an asset of the company at the date of the commencement of the winding up; instead a comparison must be made between what the actual contractual position was at that date and what would have been the position but for the arrangement. That seems to me to involve a highly unsatisfactory hypothesis for what is suggested as a principle of public policy. How does one know what a company might have done with the asset but for the arrangement? Second, there is an exception for what is a legitimate disposition and counsel for FMT and the liquidator gave as an example the discharge of a debt, to which he added the qualification that such discharge must not be a fraudulent preference. Again this exception seems to me to be unsatisfactory. What is a legitimate disposition? Counsel for FMT and the liquidator submitted that the arrangement would be struck down even if entered into for consideration and for bona fide commercial reasons. Take a case where a company issues a debenture charging its property by way of security, the company and the debenture holder thereby plainly contemplating that the company might become insolvent. So commonplace a transaction might be vulnerable if counsel for FMT and the liquidator were right. Further it would appear that the statutory provisions relating to fraudulent preference were quite unnecessary. Considerations such as these seem to me to cast the gravest doubts on the correctness of counsel's proposition. However, he submits that that is the effect of the decision of the House of Lords in *British Eagle International Airlines Ltd v Cie Nationale Air France* [1975] 2 All ER 390, [1975] 1 WLR 758. To that I now turn.

The essential facts of that case were these. British Eagle and Air France were airline operators and members of IATA (the International Air Transport Association) along with many other airlines. Airlines perform services for each other constantly. IATA established a clearing house system under which there was a mandatory monthly settlement of debits and credits. But, instead of each member settling with any other who was in debit or credit on their mutual dealings, the scheme provided that no member could claim payment from another member but could only claim from IATA the balance due under the scheme and likewise IATA alone could claim from the member the net amount due from that member. The scheme therefore provided for a form of set-off internal to the members of the clearing house system. There were good commercial reasons for the clearing house arrangements. When British Eagle went into liquidation, the aggregate amount it owed to other members exceeded the aggregate amount that other members owed it. One member owing British Eagle at the commencement of the liquidation on their mutual dealings was Air France. British Eagle by its liquidator sought to recover from Air France the sum so owed, claiming that the clearing house arrangements were not binding on him in respect of those moneys. Templeman J at first instance, the Court of Appeal and Lord Morris and Lord Simon (who dissented from the majority in the House of Lords) did not, as I understand them, dissent as to the applicable principles. They accepted that it is not possible to contract out of s 302. Where they differed from the majority in the House of Lords was in their view as to what was the property of British Eagle at the commencement of the liquidation. Their view was that the property of British Eagle did not include any debt recoverable from, or chose in action against, Air France by reason of the bona fide commercial arrangements by which British Eagle and its liquidator were bound. But Lord Cross, with whom Lord Diplock and Lord Edmund-Davies agreed, found that on the true interpretation of the provisions of the arrangement British Eagle did have an asset at the commencement of the liquidation, that asset being described by Lord Cross as an innominate chose in action having some but not all the characteristics of debts (see [1975] 2 All ER 390 at 409, [1975] 1 WLR 758 at 778). That Lord Cross was looking to the actual assets of British Eagle at the date of liquidation is, I think, clear from his statement where he said ([1975] 2 All ER 390 at 404, [1975] 1 WLR 758 at 772):

> 'The question to be decided in this appeal is whether if a member of such a group becomes insolvent the clearing house system continues to apply to its credits and debits which have not been cleared at the date of the insolvency or whether they should be dealt with in the general liquidations on the same footing as its "non-clearing house" assets and liabilities.'

The answer he gave was ([1975] 2 All ER 390 at 411, [1975] 1 WLR 758 at 780–781):

> 'But what Air France are saying here is that the parties to the "clearing house" arrangements by agreeing that simple contract debts are to be satisfied in a particular way have succeeded in "contracting out" of the provisions contained in s 302 of the 1948 Act for the payment of unsecured debts "pari passu". In such a context it is to my mind irrelevant that the parties to the "clearing house" arrangements had good business reasons for entering into them and did not direct their minds to the question how the arrangements might be affected by the insolvency of one or more of the parties. Such a "contracting out" must, to my mind, be contrary to public policy. The question is, in essence, whether what was called in argument the "mini liquidation" flowing from the clearing house arrangements is to yield or to prevail over the general liquidation. I cannot doubt that on principle the rules of the general liquidation should prevail.'

Thus the principle that I would extract from that case is that, where the effect of a contract is that an asset which is actually owned by a company at the commencement of its liquidation would be dealt with in a way other than in accordance with s 302, then to that extent the contract as a matter of public policy is avoided, whether or not the contract was entered into for consideration and for bona fide commercial reasons and whether or not the contractual provision affecting that asset is expressed to take effect only on insolvency.

When that principle is sought to be applied to the facts of the present case, it is clear that the moneys in the special account were not assets of FMT at the date of liquidation.

The book debt which had been its asset was discharged no later than the date when the moneys were paid into the special account. Accordingly the principle has no application to those moneys and this defence fails.

### (3) Section 95

Counsel for FMT and the liquidator submitted that the agreement constituted a charge by FMT on its book debts, being a charge on moneys due or to become due to FMT from CR, and that the charge was in favour of the third party creditors; such charge was not registered within 21 days or at all and so, counsel says, it was void under s 95 of the Companies Act 1948. To this submission counsel for CR responded with a large number of arguments. One, that the third party creditors had no enforceable interests and hence nothing that could come within the description of a charge, I have already rejected in the light of *Re Northern Developments (Holdings) Ltd* case. But others of their submissions seem to me to be manifestly correct and I shall not extend a lengthy judgment by going through them all. To come within s 95 counsel for FMT and the liquidator must show that the creditors have a charge on FMT's book debts, such that in the absence of registration the security conferred on the company's property or undertaking is avoided. 'Charge' is not defined for the purpose of s 95 (save to extend its meaning to include a mortgage) and so must, in the absence of any indication to the contrary (and none is suggested), bear its ordinary meaning. The type of charge which it is said was created is an equitable charge. Such a charge is created by an appropriation of specific property to the discharge of some debt or other obligation without there being any change in ownership either at law or in equity, and it confers on the chargee rights to apply to the court for an order for sale or for the appointment of a receiver, but no right to foreclosure (so as to make the property his own) or take possession (see, for example, Megarry and Wade *The Law of Real Property* (4th edn, 1975) pp 902, 925). I do not see how the rights of the third party creditors to enforce the primary trust, relating as it does to the moneys in the special account, can be said to amount to a charge on any book debt of FMT. The book debt of FMT owed to it by CR is discharged no later than on payment of the moneys into the account and only on such payment do the rights of the third parties arise. Their rights to enforce against FMT as trustee the carrying out of the primary trust seem to me to be wholly different from the rights of a chargee. There is no equity of redemption in FMT. In reality what was created by the July agreement was a method of settling CR's debt to FMT and FMT's corresponding debts to the third party creditors' without any intention to create a charge in favour of the third party creditors who knew nothing of the July agreement until the newspapers' representatives were told of it after the commencement of the liquidation. Further, even if the rights of the third parties were charges, and the security were avoided, that would not in my judgment prevent CR from exercising its equitable right to enforce the primary trust. In my judgment this defence also fails.

### (4) CR's obligations

In the light of my conclusions that the primary trust can and should be carried out in relation to the moneys in the special account, that part of the counterclaim which relates to those moneys has no application. That leaves the claim to £780,000. It is common ground that, subject to the question of set-off, there is no defence to the claim that the fee for July in the sum of £20,416·67 is payable.

In respect of the balance, the claim of FMT and the liquidator is very simple. FMT performed its contractual obligations by its services and incurred debts in July to third parties for which it is entitled to be paid by CR. Not so, says CR: by the July agreement CR's only obligation to FMT was to pay its debt into the special account, that is to say to constitute the trust by paying FMT as trustee and any outstanding debt on 26 July and any further debts incurred thereafter became owed to FMT only as trustee; FMT's counterclaim to receive the moneys beneficially must, CR says, fail. To that FMT replies that that is an incorrect analysis of the position: FMT was owed a debt by CR which it had not discharged at the commencement of the liquidation; that was an asset of FMT and, to the extent that the July agreement purported to provide for the appropriation of that asset to the third party creditors, it is avoided as contrary to public policy (see *British Eagle International Airlines Ltd v Cie Nationale Air France* [1975] 2 All ER 390, [1975] 1 WLR 758).

In short, therefore, the issue between the parties is very similar to the crucial issue in the *British Eagle* case. Again there is no dispute in principle. Junior counsel for CR accepted that, if the debt of CR was an asset of FMT at the date of the commencement of the liquidation, the July agreement could not cause that asset to be taken away from FMT. Just as in the *British Eagle* case the issue turned on the identification of what, having regard to the clearing house arrangement, was the property of British Eagle, so in the present case the issue turns on the identification of what, having regard to the July agreement, was the property of FMT.

Counsel for FMT and the liquidator submitted that the position here was even clearer than in the *British Eagle* case, where Lord Cross described the relevant assets of British Eagle as not, strictly speaking, 'debts' owing by Air France (because the contract under which the right to be paid arose did not permit British Eagle to sue Air France for payment but provided for payment exclusively through the medium of the clearing house). In contrast, here there is no bar on FMT suing CR. Counsel for FMT and the liquidator submitted that notwithstanding the July agreement the debtor/creditor relationship subsisted between CR and FMT; on its true construction it provided merely for the discharge of the debt owed to FMT in a particular manner.

In my judgment counsel for FMT and the liquidator is correct in that submission. Immediately before the July agreement FMT had a book debt owed to it by CR. Immediately after the July agreement FMT (as junior counsel for CR accepted) still had a valuable right against CR which it could enter in its books. Junior counsel for CR said that that right was not a debt but the contractual right to enforce CR's obligation to constitute the trust by paying the moneys owed into the special account. He accepted that, if the July agreement had provided for payment to a trustee other than FMT, the trustee would have had no right to enforce payment. Similarly only when the trust was constituted did the third parties acquire any rights. No debt in any sense of the term was owing to FMT as trustee. The position would of course be different if FMT had constituted itself trustee of its book debt, but CR does not contend for that result. In my judgment, on a proper analysis of the July agreement, it did not discharge or replace FMT's book debt, which remained an asset of FMT until that debt was discharged by payment by CR into the special account. That did not occur in respect of the July debts and accordingly the July agreement is ineffective in purporting to appropriate to the third parties any moneys which CR might pay FMT to discharge its debt. Therefore the whole of the sum of £780,000 is payable by CR to FMT.

## (5) Set-off

CR claims that it is entitled to set off certain sums against FMT's and the liquidator's right to receive £780,000. Its argument proceeds thus: (1) CR and FMT had mutual dealings pursuant to its agreement with FMT in August 1982 for the calendar year 1983 and the variation thereof in the form of the July agreement; (2) it was an implied term of the 1982 agreement, alternatively of the July agreement, that to the extent to which FMT was put in funds by CR to pay third parties it would pay the third parties duly and promptly; (3) in breach of that term it failed to make due and prompt payment of the outstanding May debts, the June debts and the July debts; (4) CR thereby suffered loss and damage; (5) in reasonable mitigation of the loss and damage CR incurred expenses, in that it paid the June and July debts, and it is therefore entitled to recover those expenses subject to giving credit for any recoveries made by it by reason of the assignments which it took from the third parties. For completeness I should add that there is also a novel claim for interest on those expenses and a claim for management and administrative expenses, but the latter claim was never proved.

The riposte of counsel for FMT and the liquidator was that for a valid set-off CR must show that moneys were due from FMT to CR at the commencement of the liquidation and that CR could not show this because (i) there was no such implied term, (ii) if there was, the only breach that had occurred by the time of the commencement of the liquidation was the failure to pay the May debts and no loss was thereby caused, (iii) no damage for any breach has in any event been proven and consequently no mitigation is possible, (iv) it is not legitimate to treat the mitigation as part of the sum due at the commencement of the liquidation.

There is no doubt that there have been mutual dealings between CR and FMT. Section 31 of the Bankruptcy Act 1914 states explicitly:

'. . . an account shall be taken of what is due from the one party to the other in respect of such mutual dealings, and the sum due from the one party shall be set off against any sum due from the other party . . .'

There is also no doubt that a liability existing at the relevant date but which cannot be quantified till after the relevant date is nevertheless a sum due at the relevant date for the purposes of the section: see *Re Daintrey, ex p Mant* [1900] 1 QB 546, [1895–9] All ER Rep 657. There is also no doubt that a contingent obligation to pay is not a debt due even though the contingency subsequently occurs and the obligation to pay arises under the contract entered into before the due date: see *Re a debtor (No 66 of 1955), ex p the debtor v Trustee of the property of Waite (a bankrupt)* [1956] 3 All ER 225, [1956] 1 WLR 1226. Junior counsel for CR submitted that damages for a breach of contract occurring after the date of the commencement of the liquidation where there have been mutual dealings and the contractual obligation which was subsequently broken existed at that date were the proper subject of a set-off. But he was unable to cite any authority which supported this proposition and in my judgment it is contrary to principle. Unless and until the breach of contract occurs, no damages could arise and hence nothing was due at the date relevant for set-off. Accordingly I am only concerned with breaches of contract that have occurred at the commencement of the liquidation.

Was there an implied term in the August 1982 contract between FMT and CR when Messrs Higgs and Shephard agreed the fee for 1983 that FMT would pay the third party creditors duly and promptly to the extent to which it was put in funds by CR? There are two matters to be shown: an obligation to pay the creditors and if so an obligation to pay duly and promptly. The meeting on 17 August 1982 was only to discuss the question of the fee and so there was no express agreement on payment of creditors. It was mutually understood that in all other respects the business relationship of the parties would continue as it had since 1979. Counsel for FMT and the liquidator rightly points out that it is not enough for the implication of a term to say that it would be a reasonable term for the parties to have agreed. It must be a matter of necessity to give business efficacy to the contractual relations between the parties. He says that as FMT already had its own obligation to the third parties such a term was not necessary. However I am satisfied on the evidence before me that such a term which CR could enforce against FMT is to be implied. CR plainly regarded advertising as an important part of its business, hence the huge sums spent on its advertising campaign, as FMT as an experienced agency well knew. It was obvious to the third parties that the advertisements were those of CR and CR had regular meetings with the media. As Mr Higgs said, because the media channels open to a cigarette and tobacco manufacturing company were very restricted, CR was highly dependent on the press and needed to preserve its goodwill with the press. Any delay in payment by FMT or other action to undermine that goodwill was regarded by him as very damaging to CR. Mr Duskwick was also aware of the consequences of failing to pay promptly. He said that a failure to pay a bill to a newspaper could cause a total blacking of CR's advertisements by that paper. He also confirmed that the third party creditors expected that the bills they presented to FMT would be passed on to CR. The payment system operated by FMT and CR was designed to ensure and was operated in such a way that FMT would be put in funds to enable it to pay the third party creditors about the end of the month following that in which FMT incurred liabilities to the third parties. Mr Higgs and Miss Moore both regarded the failure by FMT to pay the May debts as a breach of the contract with CR and in my judgment they were right to do so. I would add that in any event there was an express obligation on FMT in the July agreement for FMT to make payment to the third party creditors, and, if one then asks the question when was FMT to perform that obligation, the obvious answer is that it should do so duly and promptly once the moneys had been received.

However, an obligation to pay duly and promptly once put in funds does not in my judgment mean that the obligation must necessarily be performed by the end of the month in which payment is made by CR. Indeed it is to be noted that CR itself pleads that its own obligation to pay FMT was to pay by the last day of the month. If it exercised its right to delay payment until the last day of the month, FMT had to have time to make payments, the total of which each month in the material period was many hundreds of thousands of pounds.

Were there any breaches that occurred on or before the commencement of the winding up? Counsel for FMT and the liquidator concedes that there was such a breach in respect of the May debts, but denies that there was any such breach in respect of the June and July debts. The cheque for the June debts was not handed over until after banking hours on 26 July, that is to say effectively three or four days later than CR's normal practice. I am not satisfied that by 3 August a breach had already occurred. Indeed it is clear that, even though FMT appears to have sent off the cheque drawn on the special account on or before 29 July, there had not been time for the cheque to be cleared before 3 August. In my judgment therefore there was no breach in respect of the June debts. A fortiori there was no breach in respect of the July debts as FMT had not been put in funds by CR. It is also pleaded by CR that the liquidation itself caused a breach, but that seems to me to be fundamentally wrong. It is not liquidation which causes a breach of unperformed contracts but actions taken thereafter, as in this case by the liquidator in causing the cheques to be stopped.

What damage was caused to CR by the breach in respect of the May debts? Junior counsel for CR concedes that no damage can be shown as resulting from that breach alone, and that concession was in my view rightly made in view of the evidence that no creditor acted on the failure to pay the May debts until in August or September that failure was brought to the attention of CR.

It follows that the claim to a set-off fails. However, in case this case goes further and I am held to be wrong in the views expressed on this head, I should add that I am satisfied that the failure to pay the June debts by itself or coupled with any anticipatory breach of the obligation to pay the July debts did cause loss and damage to CR in that it would either have had to stop its advertising campaign with consequent damage, which I am prepared to infer, to its business or it would have had to pay increased advertising charges. Further I am satisfied that CR acted reasonably in seeking to mitigate its loss by paying the June and July debts. As Mr Webb put it, 'We had no alternative.'

In the result I shall make the following orders: (on the statement of claim) (1) a declaration that the moneys now and since 27 July 1983 standing to the credit of the special account are and were held by FMT on trust for the sole purpose of applying the sums in meeting the debts of the third parties to which the invoices attached to the cheque letter related; (2) an order that FMT and the liquidator do forthwith apply the said moneys in carrying out that purpose; (on the counterclaim) (3) an order for payment by CR to FMT of £780,000.

In conclusion I would like to pay tribute to counsel on both sides for their admirably presented arguments, and in particular to junior counsel for CR who in the absence of his leader had the conduct of CR's reply and performed his duties with conspicuous ability.

*Orders accordingly.*

Solicitors: *Linklaters & Paines* (for CR); *Fielder Le Riche* (for FMT and the liquidator).

Vivian Horvath   Barrister.

# Hasselblad (GB) Ltd v Orbinson

COURT OF APPEAL, CIVIL DIVISION
SIR JOHN DONALDSON MR, O'CONNOR AND MAY LJJ
9, 10, 11, 12 JULY, 10 OCTOBER 1984

*Privilege – Absolute privilege – Tribunal recognised by law – EC Commission – Complaint made to Commission – Complaint containing defamatory remarks – Commission investigating and adjudicating on complaint – Company complained about suing complainant for libel – Whether voluntary complaint to EC Commission protected by absolute privilege – Whether in public interest for complaint not to be produced in libel proceedings – EEC Council Regulation 17, arts 11, 20.*

*European Economic Community – Restrictive trade practices – Investigation of undertakings – Privilege relating to documents produced in connection with investigation – Documents voluntarily produced to Commission containing defamatory material – Whether documents produced to Commission protected by privilege – EEC Council Regulation 17, arts 11, 20.*

The plaintiffs were the United Kingdom subsidiary of a well-known Swedish camera manufacturer and were the sole United Kingdom distributors of the camera. C Ltd was one of a number of authorised dealers for the camera, but in 1978 the plaintiffs terminated C Ltd's dealership. In 1979 C Ltd complained to the EC Commission that the plaintiffs had engaged in conduct which was monopolistic and an abuse of a dominant position, contrary to arts 85 and 86 of the EEC Treaty, by refusing to repair cameras manufactured by the plaintiffs' parent company which had not been imported and sold by the plaintiffs. By virtue of EEC Council Regulation 17 the Commission had special powers in relation to the investigation of breaches and the enforcement of arts 85 and 86. In particular, art 11[a] of Regulation 17 provided, inter alia, that, in carrying out its duties in relation to investigating anti-competition practices, the Commission could obtain all necessary information from undertakings, including private companies, by requiring such information to be provided on pain of a substantial fine. Article 20[b] of Regulation 17 provided that information so acquired was to be used only for the purpose of the relevant investigation and that the Commission was not to disclose such information acquired by it under Regulation 17 if it was covered by the obligation of professional secrecy. In 1980 the Commission began proceedings against the plaintiffs and in the course of those proceedings C Ltd sent to the Commission a letter signed by the defendant, who had purchased a camera manufactured by the plaintiffs' parent company from a dealer in the United Kingdom who had not been authorised by the plaintiffs. The letter alleged that the camera had developed a fault and that the plaintiffs had refused to repair it on the ground that it had been purchased from an unauthorised dealer. The Commission, as required under its procedure, sent a copy of the letter to the plaintiffs in order to afford them the opportunity of answering the allegations. The plaintiffs denied the allegations and also wrote to the defendant stating that, unless he withdrew his allegations, they would institute proceedings for defamation. The defendant refused to withdraw the allegations or to apologise, and the plaintiffs commenced proceedings against him alleging that the letter was defamatory in that it implied that the plaintiffs had refused to repair the camera for an ill-founded reason and had breached arts 85 and 86 of the EEC Treaty. At the trial of the defamation action the question arose whether the defendant's letter was privileged. The trial judge held (i) that the Commission was a quasi-judicial body by virtue of the treaty and accordingly the rule that absolute privilege attached to words spoken or written in the course of giving evidence in judicial proceedings applied, and (ii) that because of art 20(1) of Regulation 17 the letter could not be used for the purposes of a libel action or for any other purpose. The plaintiffs appealed, contending that absolute privilege did not attach to the letter and that they

---

*a*   Article 11 is set out at p 182 *g* to p 183 *b*, post
*b*   Article 20 is set out at p 183 *b* to *d*, post

should be allowed to use it in the libel proceedings. The Commission was permitted to attend the hearing of the appeal and to present argument. It contended that the prohibition in art 20 against information 'acquired' under art 11 being used for any purpose other than the Commission's investigation extended to information supplied voluntarily as well pursuant to a formal request made under art 11, since voluntary information was nevertheless 'acquired', and therefore the prohibition in art 20 extended to the defendant's letter.

**Held** – (1) (Per Sir John Donaldson MR and O'Connor LJ) On the facts, since the Commission's proceedings relied heavily on written communications to provide the foundation for its decision, the letter was to be regarded as being sufficiently closely connected to the process of giving evidence for it to be covered by absolute privilege if absolute privilege attached to written or oral evidence to the like effect given by the defendant directly to or before the Commission (see p 177 j to p 178 b, p 179 j to p 180 a and p 187 c d, post).

(2) In order to decide whether the Commisision was a quasi-judicial tribunal to which the rule of absolute privilege applied, the court had to consider (a) the authority under which the Commission acted, (b) the nature of the question into which it was the duty of the Commission to inquire, (c) the legal consequences of its conclusions and (d) the procedure adopted by the Commission. Although the Commission's duties in relation to anti-competition practices under arts 85 and 86 of the EEC Treaty required it to investigate infringements of the principles enshrined in those articles and to take appropriate measures to bring them to an end, and although its decision were enforceable by the High Court under the provisions contained in RSC Ord 71 for the reciprocal enforcement of European Community judgments, the procedure adopted by the Commission, and in particular the fact that its decisions were reached by commissioners (who had not attended the hearing) on the basis of advice from representatives of member states (who were not directly concerned), indicated that the Commission acted in a manner dissimilar to that of a court of justice, under either civil or common law. It followed that the Commission and its procedures were administrative rather than judicial or quasi-judicial in character and evidence given to it did not attract the absolute privilege attaching to evidence given to a court. Accordingly, absolute privilege did not attach to the letter (see p 181 e to h, p 182 a, p 187 c d and p 188 a to c, post); dictum of Lord Diplock in Trapp v Mackie [1979] 1 All ER 492 applied; dictum of Lord Wilberforce in Rio Tinto Zinc Corp v Westinghouse Electric Corp [1978] 1 All ER at 444–445, van Landewyck Sàrl v EC Commission [1980] ECR 3125 and SA Musique Diffusion Française v EC Commission [1983] ECR 1825 considered.

(3) Even if the letter could be said to contain anything which was a professional secret, art 20(1) of Regulation 17, although expressly linked to arts 11 to 14 which gave the Commission power to compel the disclosure of information, made no reference to art 3, which made provision for the Commission to receive complaints, ie information which was volunteered. Accordingly, on its true construction art 20(1) did not apply to information acquired otherwise than by the application or threat of compulsion contained in arts 11 to 14. It followed that since the letter had been acquired by the Commission voluntarily and not by the use of the Commission's powers to compel the disclosure of information it was not protected by art 20(1) from use in the libel action (see p 183 g to j and p 187 c d and f, post).

(4) (May LJ dissenting) However, the public interest in allegations (eg of libel) by citizens concerning the infringement of their private rights being investigated and, if proved, redressed by the law had to be weighed against the public interest in ensuring that the Commission, as a primary authority of the Community, should not be frustrated in its duty under the EEC Treaty and Regulation 17 to enforce compliance with arts 85 and 86. On balance, the public interest in favour of assisting the Commission to carry out its duties required the court to refuse to allow the letter to be produced in the libel action, having regard to the facts that the only reason which prevented the court from

holding that the letter was subject to absolute privilege was the procedure adopted by the Commission, in particular the injection of the commissioners as the decision-takers when the investigation was by others, and the only reason which prevented the letter being protected by the rule relating to the misuse of documents obtained on discovery was that under the Commission's procedure the obligation to disclose the letter lay on the Commission rather than the defendant. The appeal would therefore be dismissed (see p 183 *j* to p 184 *a* and p 186 *j* to p 187 *c*, post); dictum of Lord Reid in *Rogers v Secretary of State for the Home Dept* [1972] 2 All ER at 1060 considered.

Per May LJ. Absolute privilege attaches to statements made in any proceedings by the Court of Justice of the European Communities reviewing a decision of the Commission regarding alleged infringements of arts 85 and 86 of the treaty (see p 189 *a* to *c*, post).

### Notes

For the defence of absolute privilege and tribunals to which the doctrine extends, see 28 Halsbury's Laws (4th edn) paras 98–100, and for cases on the subject, see 32 Digest (Reissue) 216–219, *1840–1862*.

For the defence of qualified privilege to actions for libel and slander generally, see 28 Halsbury's Laws (4th edn) paras 108–118, and for cases on the subject, see 32 Digest (Reissue) 228–232, *1934–1958*.

For implied undertaking not to use documents produced on discovery for a collateral or ulterior purpose, see 13 Halsbury's Laws (4th edn) para 66, and for cases on the subject, see 18 Digest (Reissue) 62, 70, 102, *426, 492–495, 756*.

For investigation and hearing of suspected infringements of EEC competition rules, see Supplement to 38 Halsbury's Laws (3rd edn) para 185G.6.

For the EEC Treaty, arts 85, 86, see 42A Halsbury's Statutes (3rd edn) 1178, 1183.

For EEC Council Regulation 17, arts 3, 11, 12, 13, 14, 20, see ibid 1191, 1195, 1196, 1199.

### Cases referred to in judgments

*Barratt v Kearns* [1905] 1 KB 504, CA.
*Crompton (Alfred) Amusement Machines Ltd v Customs and Excise Comrs (No 2)* [1973] 2 All ER 1169, [1974] AC 405, [1973] 3 WLR 268, HL.
*D v National Society for the Prevention of Cruelty to Children* [1977] 1 All ER 589, [1978] AC 171, [1977] 2 WLR 201, HL.
*Dawkins v Lord Rokeby* (1873) LR 8 QB 255, Ex Ch; *affd* (1875) LR 7 HL 744, [1874–80] All ER Rep 994, HL.
*Home Office v Harman* [1982] 1 All ER 532, [1983] 1 AC 280, [1982] 2 WLR 338, HL.
*Lincoln v Daniels* [1961] 3 All ER 740, [1962] 1 QB 237, [1961] 3 WLR 866, CA.
*Munster v Lamb* (1883) 11 QBD 588, [1881–5] All ER Rep 791, CA.
*O'Connor v Waldron* [1935] AC 76, [1934] All ER Rep 281, PC.
*Riddick v Thames Board Mills Ltd* [1977] 3 All ER 677, [1977] QB 881, [1977] 3 WLR 63, CA.
*Rio Tinto Zinc Corp v Westinghouse Electric Corp, RTZ Services Ltd v Westinghouse Electric Corp* [1978] 1 All ER 434, [1978] AC 547, [1978] 2 WLR 81, HL.
*Rogers v Secretary of State for the Home Dept, Gaming Board for Great Britain v Rogers* [1972] 2 All ER 1057, [1973] AC 388, [1972] 3 WLR 279, HL.
*Roy v Prior* [1970] 2 All ER 729, [1971] AC 470, [1970] 3 WLR 202, HL.
*Royal Aquarium and Summer and Winter Garden Society Ltd v Parkinson* [1892] 1 QB 431, [1891–4] All ER Rep 429, CA.
*SA Musique Diffusion Française v EC Commission* Joined Cases 100-103/80 [1983] ECR 1825.
*Shell Co of Australia Ltd v Federal Comr of Taxation* [1931] AC 275, [1930] All ER Rep 671, PC.
*Shufflebottom v Allday* (1857) 28 LTOS 292.
*Trapp v Mackie* [1979] 1 All ER 489, [1979] 1 WLR 377, HL.

*van Landewyck Sàrl v EC Commission* Joined Cases 209-215/78 [1980] ECR 3125.
*Watson v M'Ewan, Watson v Jones* [1905] AC 480, [1904–7] All ER Rep 1, HL.

**Cases also cited**
*Collins v Henry Whiteway & Co* [1927] 2 KB 378.
*Conway v Rimmer* [1968] 1 All ER 874, [1968] AC 910, HL.
*Copartnership Farms v Harvey-Smith* [1918] 2 KB 405.
*Garden Cottage Foods Ltd v Milk Marketing Board* [1983] 2 All ER 770, [1984] AC 130, HL.
*Gerhold v Baker* (1918) 35 TLR 102, CA.
*Hodson v Pare* [1899] 1 QB 455, CA.
*Pergamon Press Ltd, Re* [1970] 3 All ER 535, [1971] 1 Ch 388, CA.
*Smith v National Meter Co Ltd* [1945] 2 All ER 35, [1945] KB 543.

**Appeal**
Hasselblad (GB) Ltd appealed against the judgment of Comyn J given on 1 March 1984
whereby he held that a letter dated 16 February 1981 sent by the respondent, Kenneth
Orbinson, to the Commission of the European Communities was covered by absolute
privilege and ordered that judgment be entered for Mr Orbinson in the action brought
against him by Hasselblad for damages for libel. On 24 May 1984 Mr Registrar Adams
ordered that Hasselblad's notice of appeal be served on the Commission pursuant to RSC
Ord 59, r 8. On 2 July 1984 the Court of Appeal (Sir John Donaldson MR, O'Connor and
May LJJ) dismissed an appeal by Hasselblad against the order of Mr Registrar Adams.
The facts are set out in the judgment of Sir John Donaldson MR.

*Michael Burton QC, Richard Slowe* and *Geoffrey Mott* for Hasselblad.
*Christopher Carr QC* and *Richard Behar* for Mr Orbinson.
*Alan Tyrrell QC* and *Ian Carlson* for the EC Commission.

*Cur adv vult*

10 October. The following judgments were delivered.

**SIR JOHN DONALDSON MR.** Hasselblad (GB) Ltd are the sole United Kingdom
distributors of Hasselblad cameras, which are made in Sweden. At one time Camera Care
Ltd, a Belfast company, had a sub-distributorship, but this was terminated by Hasselblad.
Subsequently, in July 1979, Camera Care complained to the Commission of the European
Communities (the Commission) that Hasselblad were carrying on their business in
breach of art 85 of the EEC Treaty. In 1980 the Commission began proceedings against
Hasselblad and in the course of those proceedings Camera Care sent to the Commission a
letter dated 16 February 1981. This letter was signed by the respondent, Mr Orbinson,
and addressed to a Mr Hodes, the proprietor of Amateurs Nook Ltd, from whom Mr
Orbinson said that he had bought a Hasselblad camera, the camera having been obtained
by Amateurs Nook from Camera Care. The letter alleged that the camera developed a
fault and that Hasselblad refused to repair it on the grounds that it was a 'grey' or 'parallel'
import, having been purchased from an unauthorised dealer. The Commission sent a
copy of this letter to Hasselblad and invited its comments. Hasselblad, by a letter dated 5
May 1981, replied that the allegations were untrue. However, it also wrote to Mr
Orbinson telling him that unless he withdrew his allegations and apologised, proceedings
for defamation would be instituted. Mr Orbinson did not withdraw his allegation or
apologise and these proceedings were begun.
  Comyn J ruled that a defence of absolute privilege was available to Mr Orbinson. From
that decision Hasselblad now appeal. Mr Orbinson contends, as was contended below,
that he is entitled to rely (a) on the defence of absolute privilege, (b) on the principle that
documents which are disclosed in the course of Commission proceedings cannot be used
for any ulterior purpose and (c) on EEC regulations as prohibiting the use of the letter as

a basis for a libel action. Hasselblad concede that the defence of qualified privilege and justification are open to Mr Orbinson, if he can establish them, but deny that any of the defences put forward by Mr Orbinson are available.

This is a completely novel issue and one which is of very considerable importance in the light of our increasing involvement with the Commission.

*Absolute privilege*

The last occasion on which the House of Lords considered this defence was in the case of *Trapp v Mackie* [1979] 1 All ER 489, [1979] 1 WLR 377. Mr Trapp had been dismissed from his post as headmaster of a Scottish school and a local inquiry was held before a commissioner appointed by the Secretary of State for Scotland pursuant to statutory powers. In the course of the inquiry Mr Mackie gave evidence which Mr Trapp alleged to be both false and malicious. The House of Lords held that the evidence was protected by absolute privilege, but the importance of the decision lies in the guidance given by Lord Diplock and Lord Fraser on the approach which should be adopted by courts charged with the duty of deciding whether this defence is available. Lord Diplock said ([1979] 1 All ER 489 at 491–492, [1979] 1 WLR 377 at 378):

> 'That absolute privilege attaches to words spoken or written in the course of giving evidence in proceedings in a court of justice is a rule of law, based on public policy, that has been established since earliest times. That the like privilege extends to evidence given before tribunals which, although not courts of justice, nevertheless act in a manner similar to that in which courts of justice act was established more than a hundred years ago by the decision of this House in *Dawkins v Lord Rokeby* (1875) LR 7 HL 744, [1974–80] All ER Rep 994, where the unanimous answer of the judges to the question asked them by the House was adopted and the ratio decidendi of the judgment of the Court of Exchequer Chamber ((1873) LR 8 QB 255) was approved. The kind of tribunal in which the evidence of witnesses is entitled to absolute privilege was described by Lord Atkin in *O'Connor v Waldron* [1935] AC 76 at 81, [1934] All ER Rep 281 at 283 as a tribunal which "has similar attributes to a court of justice or acts in a manner similar to that in which such courts act". That the "or" in this phrase is not intended to be disjunctive is apparent from the fact that Lord Atkin was confirming the accuracy of the law as it had been stated by Lord Esher MR in *Royal Aquarium and Summer and Winter Garden Society Ltd v Parkinson* [1892] 1 QB 431 at 422, [1891–4] All ER Rep 429 at 432. Lord Esher MR, having spoken of "an authorised inquiry which, though not before a Court of justice, is before a tribunal which has similar attributes", went on to explain that what he meant by similar attributes was "acting . . . in a manner as nearly as possible similar to that in which a Court of justice acts in respect of an inquiry before it". In the course of the hearing which, as in both courts below, has been conducted by the appellant in person with skill and erudition, your Lordships' attention has been drawn to what must be nearly every reported case on this topic in Scotland, and in England where most of the authorities are to be found. I do not find it necessary to refer to them. They provide examples of inquiries and tribunals which have been held to fall on one or other side of a line which as Lord Atkin said in *O'Connor v Waldron* [1935] AC 76 at 81, [1934] All ER Rep 281 at 283 "is not capable of very precise limitation". No single touchstone emerges from the cases; but this is not surprising, for the rule of law is one which involves the balancing of conflicting public policies, one general: that the law should provide a remedy to the citizen whose good name and reputation is traduced by malicious falsehoods uttered by another; the other particular: that witnesses before tribunals recognised by law should, in the words of the answer of the judges in *Dawkins v Lord Rokeby* (1875) LR 7 HL 744 at 753, [1874–80] All ER Rep 994 at 995, "give their testimony free from any fear of being harassed by an action of an allegation, *whether true or false*, that they acted from malice" [Lord Diplock's emphasis]. So, to decide whether a tribunal acts in a manner similar to courts of justice and thus is of such a kind as will attract

absolute, as distinct from qualified, privilege for witnesses when they give testimony before it, one must consider first, under what authority the tribunal acts, secondly, the nature of the question into which it is its duty to inquire, thirdly, the procedure adopted by it in carrying out the inquiry and, fourthly, the legal consequences of the conclusion reached by the tribunal as a result of the inquiry. To attract absolute privilege for the testimony of witnesses the tribunal, by whatever name it is described, must be "recognised by law", a phrase first used by the Court of Exchequer Chamber in *Dawkins v Lord Rokeby* (1873) LR 8 QB 255 at 263. This is a sine qua non; the absolute privilege does not attach to purely domestic tribunals. Although the description "recognised by law" is not necessarily confined to tribunals constituted or recognised by Act of Parliament (see *Lincoln v Daniels* [1961] 3 All ER 740, [1962] 1 QB 237) it embraces all that are, and so includes the local inquiry in the instant case . . .'

Lord Fraser said ([1979] 1 All ER 489 at 496–497, [1979] 1 WLR 377 at 385):

'It will be convenient first to consider the legal principles to be applied. It is, and has long been, well settled that no action will lie against a witness for words spoken in giving evidence in a court even if the evidence is falsely and maliciously given. In *Watson v M'Ewan* [1905] AC 480 at 486, cf [1904–7] All ER Rep 1 at 3, Lord Halsbury LC said that was "settled law and cannot be doubted". He went on thus: "The remedy against a witness who has given evidence which is false and injurious to another is to indict him for perjury; but for very obvious reasons, the conduct of legal procedure by Courts of justice, *with the necessity of compelling witnesses to attend*, involves as one of the necessitites of the administration of justice the immunity of witnesses from action being brought against them in respect of evidence they have given." [Lord Fraser's emphasis.] That case decided that the same immunity attached to statements made on precognition with a view to giving evidence. The rule was reaffirmed recently in *Roy v Prior* [1970] 2 All ER 729, [1971] AC 470 and its justification was explained by Lord Wilberforce thus ([1970] 2 All ER 729 at 736, [1971] AC 470 at 480): "The reasons why immunity is traditionally (and for this purpose I accept the tradition) conferred on witnesses in respect of evidence given in court, are in order that they may give their evidence fearlessly and to avoid a multiplicity of actions in which the value or truth of their evidence would be tried over again. Moreover, the trial process contains in itself, in the subjection to cross-examination and confrontation with other evidence, some safeguard against careless, malicious or untruthful evidence." The rule has been extended beyond courts of justice and has been held to apply to authorised inquiries before tribunals which, though not courts of justice, have similar attributes: see *Royal Aquarium and Summer and Winter Garden Society Ltd v Parkinson* [1892] 1 QB 431 at 442, [1891–4] All ER Rep 429 at 432, per Lord Esher MR. In *O'Connor v Waldron* [1935] AC 76 at 81, [1934] All ER Rep 281 at 283 Lord Atkin giving the advice of the Judicial Committee said this: "In their Lordships' opinion the law on the subject was accurately stated by Lord Esher in *Royal Aquarium etc Ltd v Parkinson*, where he says that the privilege 'applies wherever there is an authorised inquiry which, though not before a Court of justice, is before a tribunal which has similar attributes . . . This doctrine has never been extended further than to courts of justice and tribunals acting in a manner similar to that in which such Courts act'. The question therefore in every case is whether the tribunal in question has similar attributes to a court of justice or acts in a manner similar to that in which such courts act? This is of necessity a differentia which is not capable of very precise limitation."'

Lord Fraser later said ([1979] 1 All ER 489 at 499, [1979] 1 WLR 377 at 388):

'Consideration of the cases shows that, provided the tribunal is one recognised by law, there is no single element the presence or absence of which will be conclusive in showing whether it has attributes sufficiently similar to those of a court of law to create absolute privilege. It is not essential that the tribunal itself should have power to determine the issue before it, and a statement by Lord Sankey LC in *Shell Co of Australia Ltd v Federal Comr of Taxation* [1931] AC 275 at 295, [1930] All ER Rep 671 at 679, which at first sight appears to indicate the contrary, is not truly in pari materia. It was directed to the different question of the meaning of "judicial power" in s 71 of the Australian Constitution. Cases such as *Dawkins v Lord Rokeby* (1875) LR 7 HL 744, [1874–80] All ER Rep 994 and *Barratt v Kearns* [1905] 1 KB 504 show that absolute privilege may apply if the inquiry is a step leading directly toward determination of an issue by the authority who appointed it. In each case the object of the tribunal, its constitution and its manner of proceeding must all be considered before the question can be answered.'

In *Watson v M'Ewan* [1905] AC 480 at 487, cf [1904–7] All ER Rep 1 at 4, absolute privilege was accorded to a precognition, or witness's proof, on the grounds expressed in the speech of the Lord Halsbury LC when he said:

'If it were otherwise, I think what one of the learned counsel has with great cogency pointed out would apply—that from time to time in these various efforts which have been made to make actual witnesses responsible in the shape of an action against them for the evidence they have given, the difficulty in the way of those who were bringing the action would have been removed at once by saying, "I do not bring the action against you for what you said in the witness-box, but I bring the action against you for what you told the solicitor you were about to say in the witness-box." If that could be done the object for which the privilege exists is gone, because then no witness could be called; no one would know whether what he was going to say was relevant to the question in debate between the parties. A witness would only have to say, "I shall not tell you anything; I may have an action brought against me tomorrow if I do; therefore I shall not give you any information at all." It is very obvious that the public policy which renders the protection of witnesses necessary for the administration of justice must as a necessary consequence involve that which is a step towards and is part of the administration of justice—namely, the preliminary examination of witnesses to find out what they can prove. It may be that to some extent it seems to impose a hardship, but after all the hardship is not to be compared with that which would arise if it were impossible to administer justice, because people would be afraid to give their testimony.'

The first question which arises is whether this letter is to be regarded as sufficiently closely connected to the process of giving evidence, for it to be necessary to extend absolute privilege to it, assuming always that absolute privilege would attach to evidence to the like effect given to the Commission.

The precise way in which the letter came into existence was not investigated by Comyn J. However, for present purposes I shall assume, as did counsel appearing for Hasselblad, that at the oral hearing before the Commission it was alleged for the first time that Hasselblad were restricting the servicing of cameras which were 'grey' or 'parallel' imports. Mr Ferry, who had conducted the hearing, then said that the Commission would write to Hasselblad giving them an opportunity to answer and that all parties could make written submissions within 15 days. Thereafter Mr Robert Hodes, the father of Mr Emmanuel Hodes who owned Amateurs Nook, remembered a complaint made by Mr Orbinson. He told his son and thereafter drafted the letter of 16 February 1981 for Mr Orbinson to sign. Once it was signed, it was passed to Camera Care who forwarded it to the Commission on 25 February 1981.

Assuming these facts and bearing in mind the fact that the proceedings of the Commission rely heavily on written communications as providing a foundation for its decisions, I consider that the letter should be treated as being sufficiently closely connected with giving evidence to the Commission to be absolutely privileged if written or oral evidence to the like effect given by Mr Orbinson directly to or before the Commission would have been so privileged.

I therefore turn to the criteria identified by Lord Diplock in *Trapp v Mackie* [1979] 1 All ER 489, [1979] 1 WLR 377 as aids to deciding whether a body which is not a court of justice is a tribunal which acts in a manner similar to courts of justice.

(a)  *The authority under which the Commission acts*

It is conceded, as it must be, that the Commission is recognised by the law of this country. Its general duties are laid down by art 155 of the EEC Treaty. More specifically in relation to competition and arts 85 and 86, art 89 requires it to investigate suspected infringements of the principles enshrined in those articles and to take appropriate measures to bring them to an end. Article 87 arms the Commission with the power to impose fines and periodic penalty payments. In addition to these provisions, the Council has legislated (EEC Council Regulation 17 of 6 February 1962) giving the Commission special powers and the Commission itself has made regulations governing its hearings (EEC Regulation 99/63). Finally the decisions of the Commission are subject to review by the Court of Justice of the European Communities under art 173.

(b)  *The nature of the question into which it is the duty of the Commission to inquire*

The Commission is charged with the duty of inquiring whether there have been infringements of arts 85 or 86 of the treaty, not with a view to reporting the facts to others, but with a view to reaching a definitive decision, subject to any review by the Court of Justice, and imposing penalties, again subject to any such review.

(c)  *The legal consequences of its conclusion*

Decisions of the Commission enforceable under art 192 of the EEC Treaty are known as 'Community judgments' and are enforceable by the High Court under RSC Ord 71 without further proof, other than of authenticity.

Thus far I can detect nothing which indicates that the Commission in its role in relation to alleged breaches of arts 85 and 86 is other than a tribunal which could be said to be one which, though not a court of justice, had similar attributes (see Lord Fraser's speech in *Trapp v Mackie* [1979] 1 All ER 489 at 499, [1979] 1 WLR 377 at 388). However the picture changes when one comes to look at the remaining criterion listed by Lord Diplock.

(d)  *The procedure adopted by the Commission*

The starting point is either a complaint from outside the Commission or the Commission being put on inquiry by published materials, but it is simpler to consider an investigation which begins with a complaint, this being the more usual situation and the one which obtained in the present instance.

The complaint is considered within the Commission by an examiner and a case team. They can and do make further inquiries including, in an appropriate case, making use of the Commission's right to enter and search the premises of the alleged infringer on the lines of the Anton Piller jurisdiction (see art 14(3) of Regulation 17). Once the Commission's own preliminary investigations are complete, a decision is made whether to take no further action or to serve a statement of objections on the alleged infringer. If the decision is that no further action be taken, the complainant is informed and can, if he wishes, seek judicial review from the Court of Justice. If a statement of objections is served, it is accompanied by a letter setting out the alleged infringer's time for reply, rights of defence and rights of access to the Commission's file. The letter ends by inviting the alleged infringer to a hearing, if he requires it.

The next stage consists of the hearing. The chairman is now an officer of the Commission who is to some extent independent, but, at the time with which we are concerned, the chairman or hearing officer was Mr Ferry, who had been involved in evaluating the complaint at an earlier stage. The parties present at the hearing are the alleged infringer, the complainant, third parties with a sufficient interest and representatives of the Commission. All these can have legal advisers. Member states of the European Community also send representatives.

The hearing begins with a brief outline of the matter by the hearing officer of the Commission. The alleged infringer then presents his case and is free to call witnesses. The hearing officer can ask questions and he can and does permit questions by representatives of the competition department of the Commission and on occasion by those of other directorates, e g agriculture, industrial policy, etc. Unlike the position of the Commission, the other parties are not allowed to ask questions. The complainant and third parties then present their case by calling evidence and making submissions. Finally the hearing officer closes the proceedings and, in an appropriate case, can invite the parties, but not the Commission, to submit any further evidence in writing within a time limit. The fact that the Commission is not invited to submit further evidence is both significant and easily explicable. The hearing is a hearing by or on behalf of the Commission and it is open to it to take account of such new evidence as it may acquire at any time before a decision is reached. No formal procedures are necessary.

After the hearing has been concluded, the hearing officer presents his conclusions to the director general. If his recommendation is that the case proceed no further, the matter is considered by the director general. The hearing officer has direct access to the commissioners. If a decision is taken to drop the case, the complainant is informed and given the opportunity to comment and may seek judicial review of the decision in some circumstances. If, on the other hand, the decision is that the case should proceed, then a preliminary draft decision is prepared for approval and forwarded to an advisory committee consisting of representatives of the ten member states. This advisory committee considers the draft and issues a confidential opinion for consideration by the Commission itself. That draft is scrutinised by the legal service. Thereafter it is submitted to the Commission with the opinion of the advisory committee and any opinion of the hearing officer. The commissioner to whom the draft is submitted places it before his fellow commissioners for adoption. The decision, once adopted, is promulgated and thereupon becomes fully enforceable throughout the European Community.

This procedure is wholly dissimilar to that of any court or judicial tribunal operating under the common law system, but I do not think that that is the test. When in *Trapp v Mackie* [1979] 1 All ER 489, [1979] 1 WLR 377 Lord Diplock referred to a tribunal acting in a manner similar to courts of justice and Lord Fraser to tribunals having similar attributes to courts of justice, I think that they must have had a wider concept in mind which would embrace courts of justice operating both under common law and under civil law procedures. The fact that the Commission quite clearly has regard to the rules of natural justice, as shown, inter alia, by the procedure which gives the alleged infringer a right to an oral hearing, does not advance the matter, because those who take purely administrative decisions are often required to have regard to those rules. However, the fact that the decision is reached by commissioners, who have not attended the hearing, on the basis of advice from representatives of the European Community nations, who are not directly concerned, seems to me to show that the Commission is acting in a manner which is dissimilar to that of either civil or common law courts of justice and that its attributes are dissimilar to such courts. This is not a criticism of the Commission and its procedures. It is merely an acceptance that the Commission and its procedures fall into a different category, better labelled as administrative rather than judicial or quasi-judicial.

I find that my reaction is not wholly unsupported by that of others. Thus Lord Wilberforce in *Rio Tinto Zinc Corp v Westinghouse Electric Corp, RTZ Services Ltd v Westinghouse Electric Corp* [1978] 1 All ER 434 at 444–445, [1978] AC 547 at 612 regarded penalties imposed by the Commission as being imposed by administrative, rather than judicial or quasi-judicial, action. The same view has been expressed by the Commission itself in paras 47 and 48 of its 1980 report on competition policy. And in para 49, basing itself on the decision of the Court of Justice in *van Landewyck Sàrl v EC Commission* Joined Cases 209-215/78 [1980] ECR 3125, the Commission expressed the view that, since its proceedings were administrative rather than judicial in nature, it was not obliged to organise its procedure in the manner of court proceedings. The Commission has maintained the same stance in para 169 of its 1983 report on competition policy, basing itself on the decision of the Court of Justice in *SA Musique Diffusion Française v EC Commission* Joined Cases 100–103/80 [1983] ECR 1825.

Accordingly, I am quite satisfied that absolute privilege does not, as such, attach to the letter signed by Mr Orbinson.

*Confidentiality*

This defence is based primarily on *Riddick v Thames Board Mills Ltd* [1977] 3 All ER 677, [1977] QB 881. The defendant company had disclosed a document in an action in which Mr Riddick claimed damages for wrongful arrest and false imprisonment. That action was settled, but thereafter Mr Riddick began a new action claiming damages for libel based on this document. This court held that where a party disclosed a document on discovery, it was entitled to protection against any use of that document, otherwise than in the action in which it was disclosed. Lord Denning MR based his decision on a balancing of competing public interests in (a) privacy and confidence and (b) the administration of justice (see [1977] 3 All ER 677 at 686–687, [1977] QB 881 at 895–896). In doing so he pointed out that the document was obtained by compulsion. Stephenson LJ regarded the use of the document for a purpose other than that for which it was disclosed as an abuse of the process of the court (see [1977] 3 All ER 677 at 694–695, [1977] QB 881 at 902) and Waller LJ based himself on the public interest in there being no disincentives to full and frank disclosure (see [1977] 3 All ER 677 at 702, [1977] QB 881 at 912).

Whilst I shall have to return to public interest as a basis for refusing to allow Hasselblad to make use of Mr Orbinson's letter as a basis for a libel action, *Riddick's* case is plainly distinguishable in that, as counsel for Hasselblad pointed out, the letter was not sent to Camera Care or by Camera Care to the Commission under any form of compulsion.

*EEC regulations*

Following the decision of Comyn J and the institution of this appeal by Hasselblad, the Commission successfully applied for a direction under RSC Ord 59, r 8(1) that the notice of appeal be served on them and we have invited counsel who has appeared on behalf of the Commission to assist us on the workings of the Commission and its view of the construction of the regulations. He also, as amicus, drew our attention to a possible argument based on public interest privilege to which I will return hereafter. This is apparently the first occasion on which the Commission has felt impelled to seek rights of audience in national proceedings and I am most grateful to them for an intervention which I have found most helpful.

So far as the EEC regulations are concerned, both counsel for Mr Orbinson and counsel for the Commission rely on arts 11 and 20 of Regulation 17. These are in the following terms:

'*Article 11. Requests for information*

1. In carrying out the duties assigned to it by Article 89 and by provisions adopted under Article 87 of the Treaty, the Commission may obtain all necessary information from the Governments and competent authorities of the Member States and from undertakings and associations of undertakings.

2. When sending a request for information to an undertaking or association of undertakings, the Commission shall at the same time forward a copy of the request to the competent authority of the Member State in whose territory the seat of the undertaking or association of undertakings is situated.

3. In its request the Commission shall state the legal basis and the purpose of the request and also the penalties provided for in Article 15(1)(*b*) for supplying incorrect information.

4. The owners of the undertakings or their representatives and, in the case of legal persons, companies or firms, or of associations having no legal personality, the persons authorised to represent them by law or by their constitution shall supply the information requested.

5. Where an undertaking or association of undertakings does not supply the information requested within the time limit fixed by the Commission, or supplies incomplete information, the Commission shall by decision require the information to be supplied. The decision shall specify what information is required, fix an appropriate time limit within which it is to be supplied and indicate the penalties provided for in Article 15(1)(b) and Article 16(1)(c) and the right to have the decision reviewed by the Court of Justice.

6. The Commission shall at the same time forward a copy of its decision to the competent authority of the Member State in whose territory the seat of the undertaking or association of undertakings is situated.

*Article 20. Professional secrecy*

1. Information acquired as a result of the application of Articles 11, 12, 13 and 14 shall be used only for the purpose of the relevant request or investigation.

2. Without prejudice to the provisions of Articles 19 and 21, the Commission and the competent authorities of the Member States, their officials and other servants shall not disclose information acquired by them as a result of the application of this Regulation and of the kind covered by the obligation of professional secrecy.

3. The provisions of paragraphs 1 and 2 shall not prevent publication of general information or surveys which do not contain information relating to particular undertakings or associations of undertakings.'

Counsel for the Commission submits that the letter was acquired as a result of the application of art 11, since, in the view of the Commission, art 11(1) empowered the Commission to acquire information from Camera Care in carrying out its duties under art 89. In other words, the article applies to information which is volunteered as well as to information which is supplied pursuant to a formal request under para 2 or to a formal decision under para 5. He supports this submission by reference to the use of the words 'request or investigation' in art 20(1). This latter point, however, loses much of its force when it is remembered that art 11 refers to requests and arts 12, 13 and 14 refer expressly or impliedly to investigations.

Counsel for Mr Orbinson submits that if a formal request is a prerequisite to the application of art 20(1), then he can rely on such a request made on 1 April 1980 long before the statement of objections was issued. I am quite unpersuaded that this is correct. The request of 1 April 1980 was made at an early stage in the investigatory phase of the proceedings and gave a three-week period for a reply. Furthermore, the issue to which the letter of 16 February 1981 is relevant only emerged in or at about the time of the oral hearing at the beginning of that month.

I can well understand why the Commission should want these regulations to have the effect which it submits that they have, but even applying a purposive approach to their construction as contrasted with the more literal approach which is traditional in English courts, I am unable to get over the striking fact that, even if the letter could be said to contain anything which was a professional secret, art 20(1) is expressly linked to arts 11, 12, 13 and 14, all of which give the Commission power to compel the disclosure of information, but makes no reference to art 3, pursuant to which it receives complaints, ie information which is volunteered. I am therefore unable to construe art 20(1) as applying to information acquired otherwise than by the application, or at least the threat of the application, of the compulsory powers contained in arts 11, 12, 13 and 14.

*The public interest as a defence*

As always, this involves a balancing of one interest against another. Hasselblad have a potential cause of action in libel against Mr Orbinson. This is a private interest, but it is supported by a public interest, namely that allegations by citizens that their private rights have been infringed shall be investigated and, if the allegation is made good, that the citizen and his rights shall be supported by the law and the courts. On the other hand, since this country is a member of the European Community, there is a public interest in ensuring that the Commission, as a primary authority of the Community, shall not be frustrated in the duty imposed on it by the EEC Treaty and EEC Council Regulation 17 of enforcing compliance with arts 85 and 86 of the treaty. This balancing operation is very similar to that which was performed by the House of Lords in *Rogers v Secretary of State for the Home Dept, Gaming Board for Great Britain v Rogers* [1972] 2 All ER 1057, [1973] AC 388.

The Commission's original request for information pursuant to arts 11 and 15 of Regulation 17 informed Camera Care that its answers would be subject to the provisions concerning professional secrecy. It produced a reply from Camera Care dated 20 April 1980, which included the following paragraph:

'We feel that, given suitable assurances of total secrecy, we can provide the Commission with names and addresses of people who collectively, should be able to confirm our complaint beyond doubt, and possibly some very malicious practices against us in pursuance of this policy. However, to a man, everyone is scared stiff of reprisals by Hasselblad. Should this total secrecy not be available, Hasselblad, and for that matter any other firm, has effective means to enforce such practices as we allege without fear of recrimination.'

Now total secrecy is impossible, because art 19 of Regulation 17 requires the Commission to give the alleged informer an opportunity of being heard before it takes decisions and this, we are told, is construed by the Commission, on the basis of decisions by the Court of Justice, as requiring it to reveal to an alleged infringer the full text of any written evidence on which it may rely and, if it does not do so, it cannot rely on that evidence. In the instant case, the Commission was minded to rely and, in the event, did rely on Mr Orbinson's letter. That the Advocate-General advised that this and other unspecified evidence had insufficient probative value to justify a conclusion that Hasselblad was guilty of anti-competitive conduct by discriminating against parallel imports in its repair service and that the Court of Justice accepted this advice is nothing to the point. The Commission had either to ignore Mr Orbinson's letter or to disclose it to Hasselblad.

Mr Orbinson's letter of 16 February 1981 with two other letters was sent by the Commission to Hasselblad on 24 April 1981. Hasselblad's solicitor replied by a letter dated 5 May 1981 categorically denying that Hasselblad ever refused to service any Hasselblad camera or accessory or refused to honour the manufacturer's one year guarantee or gave any different service to 'parallel imported equipment' as compared to that given to equipment purchased by Hasselblad, with the exception of the 'Silver Service Guarantee' which applied only to purchasers from Hasselblad. Hasselblad's solicitor then referred to the three letters as 'the evidence supplied by Camera Care', thus leaving no doubt as to the role played by Mr Orbinson's letter or as to Hasselblad's recognition of this fact. After commenting on the other two letters, Hasselblad's solicitor turned to Mr Orbinson's letter and wrote:

'2.3 The contents of Mr. Orbinson's letter are untrue and defamatory. I enclose a copy of my letter of today to Mr. Orbinson threatening libel proceedings unless the comments are withdrawn. The contents of the letter are self-explanatory. I also enclose for your information a copy of Mr. Orbinson's registration card, which may or may not relate to the equipment about which Mr. Orbinson is complaining. It is noticeable that Mr. Orbinson states that the matters took place "in or around mid-1978" and yet the registration card for new equipment purchased from one of my client's dealers was dated 14th October, 1978.'

The letter to Mr Orbinson, also dated 5 May, which is referred to, was in the following terms:

'The allegation that my clients refused to repair a camera purchased by yourself is untrue and libellous. Indeed, my clients are in possession of a registration card in respect of a lens purchased by yourself on 14th October, 1978 from Arthur Hobson, Belfast. If the complaint to which you are referring related to that lens, then of course the whole allegation is irrelevant, because the lens was purchased from a dealer who had in turn purchased it from my clients. If your statement relates to some other lens, then it is strictly denied that my clients have ever refused to execute guarantee repairs in respect thereof, but there is no record of your having ever made any application to my clients for such guarantee repair. Unless within 14 days from the date hereof I receive your written withdrawal of the allegations contained in your letter of 16th February, 1981 together with an apology, proceedings will immediately be instituted against you for defamation.'

Earlier I referred to the fears expressed by Camera Care in their letter of 20 April 1980 as to the consequence if evidence furnished by them to the Commission was revealed to Hasselblad. I did so not because I have any evidence on which I could form any conclusion whether Camera Care at that time in fact had, or were justified in having, such fears. I did so because it seems to me to illustrate the sort of fears which might reasonably be entertained by potential sources of evidence for the Commission. What is being investigated in such circumstances is an abuse or unlawful use of economic power. If there is any substance in the complaint which is under investigation, the likelihood is that there will be very high stakes involved and that, unless and until the Commission strikes down the anti-competitive practice, it will be the less powerful victim who will be the probable source of evidence of the practice. It would therefore be in no way surprising if the alleged infringer's economic and other power were turned to the suppression of this evidence.

It is against this background that Hasselblad's letter to Mr Orbinson falls to the considered. Counsel for Hasselblad seeks to enlist my sympathy for Hasselblad on the footing that only a libel action would enable Hasselblad to retrieve its reputation by testing the probative value of the letter, bearing in mind that the procedures of the Commission do not permit of cross-examination. This might be slightly more convincing if Hasselblad had waited to see what the Commission's reactions to its denial would be. It would have been even more convincing if the action had been withdrawn when the Court of Justice accepted the Advocate-General's view that the letter had little probative value. But, on the contrary, Hasselblad have continued with the action with the greatest vigour. In the circumstances I am left in no doubt whatever that, whether Mr Orbinson's letter was true or false, Hasselblad intended to do everything it could to force him to withdraw his evidence and to ensure that no one else had the temerity to give evidence against them.

In a sense it matters not what were Hasselblad's motives. As Lord Reid said in *Rogers v Secretary of State for the Home Dept* [1972] 2 All ER 1057 at 1060, [1973] AC 388 at 400, if production is to be withheld or, in this context, if the letter is to be treated as inadmissible in a libel action based on it, it must be on grounds which have nothing to do with the merits or demerits of Hasselblad or Mr Orbinson and, like Lord Reid, I am content to put aside my clear view of the realities and proceed on the footing that Hasselblad has a legitimate interest in vindicating its reputation. What matters is the likely effect on potential suppliers of evidence to the Commission.

Counsel for Hasselblad submits, correctly, that the defence of qualified privilege will be available to Mr Orbinson, provided that he has not been activated by malice. So it will, eventually. But before then, on Hasselblad making good its plea that the letter bears a defamatory meaning, Mr Orbinson will be likely to wish to prove that it is true, since this would be a complete defence, whether or not he would otherwise succeed on the issue of malice. It is only the very rich, the very foolish, the very malicious or the very dedicated who will knowingly put themselves in a position in which they have to defend a libel action, even with the benefit of qualified privilege as a possible defence. The anxieties would be enormous and, even if ultimately successful, the difference between actual and recoverable costs would be very substantial indeed.

And the matter does not stop at the potential disincentive to tendering evidence to the Commission. Under its procedures written matter is clearly a major source of evidence. If written matter tends to show that the alleged infringer is acting in breach of arts 85 and 86, it is likely to be defamatory. It would follow that, certainly in England and possibly in other countries, evidence given to the Commission would be tested and weighed by the Commission and reviewed by the Advocate-General of the Court of Justice and by that court, whilst simultaneously it was being weighed and tested by national courts in the context of a libel jurisdiction. The possibility of inconsistent conclusions seems to me to be a very real one.

Counsel for Hasselblad takes the point that an informer in England has only the benefit of qualified privilege (see *Shufflebottom v Allday* (1857) 28 LTOS 292). Bringing the matter more up to date and relating it to an inquiry similar to that undertaken by the Commission, counsel submits, rightly, that if Mr Orbinson's letter had been addressed to the Director-General of Fair Trading, he could have been sued for libel and would have had to be content with the defence of qualified privilege. However, this ignores the fact that the Director-General would have been under no obligation to disclose the letter to Hasselblad and would have been most unlikely to have done so. If he regarded Mr Orbinson's information as sufficiently cogent, it would almost certainly have emerged in the witness box and been subject to absolute privilege.

Next it is said that, if the public interest requires that suppliers of evidence to the Commission shall have a greater degree of protection, this is a matter for the legislature rather than the courts and it is suggested that power exists to provide this by means of an order in council under s 5 of the International Organisations Act 1968. I am not satisfied that the Commission is in law an 'international tribunal', because I am not sure whether it exercises its jurisdiction or performs its function of inquiry in pursuance of any agreement to which the United Kingdom is a party. It seems to me to be arguable that, following the United Kingdom's accession to the European Community and the enactment of the European Communities Act 1972, the authority of the Commission in relation to the United Kingdom and those subject to United Kingdom law rests on statute rather than agreement. However that may be, it is undoubtedly true that in one way or another Parliament and the Community could legislate so as to prevent the use of Mr Orbinson's letter as a basis for a claim in libel. But, omitting the reference to the Community, the same retort could have been made in the *Rogers* case. The House of Lords, however, decided that it was for the courts to determine where the balance of public interest lay in the context of the threat of proceedings for defamation, in that case criminal libel.

Lastly, counsel for Hasselblad submits that in all such cases as the *Rogers* case, *Alfred Crompton Amusement Machines Ltd v Customs and Excise Comrs (No 2)* [1973] 2 All ER 1169, [1974] AC 405, *D v National Society for the Prevention of Cruelty to Children* [1977] 1 All ER 589, [1978] AC 171 and others, the courts were concerned with the public interest to prevent disclosure, whereas in this case what the court is invited to do is to restrict the use which can be made of a document which has already been disclosed. This is, of course, to ignore *Riddick v Thames Board Mills Ltd* [1977] 3 All ER 677, [1977] QB 881. It does not apply directly, because Mr Orbinson did not have to disclose the evidence contained in the letter to the Commission, but the Commission did have to disclose it to Hasselblad and did so for a very limited purpose, namely to allow Hasselblad to answer it.

In the end the court has to balance competing public interests. As Lord Reid put it in the *Rogers* case [1972] 2 All ER 1057 at 1060, [1973] AC 388 at 400:

'The real question is whether the public interest requires that the letter shall not be [used as the basis of a libel action] and whether that public interest is so strong as to override the ordinary right and interest of a litigant that he shall be able to lay before a court of justice all relevant evidence.'

I think that the public interest does so require and that it is sufficiently strong. It is really only the procedure adopted by the Commission and, in particular, the injection of the Commissioners as the decision-takers when the investigation is by others, which prevents my holding that the letter is subject to absolute privilege. Again, it is only the fact that the compulsion to disclose operates on the Commission and not on Mr Orbinson which prevents my holding that the letter is subject to the rule in *Riddick's* case. Its disclosure to

Hasselblad was for a very limited purpose and Hasselblad propose to use it for a very different purpose. The obstacles which will, in future, be in the way of the Commission in investigating breaches of arts 85 and 86 of the treaty if Hasselblad can proceed with this action are obvious. Either the Commission will be unable to make any use of volunteered evidential material, because it dare not disclose it to the alleged infringer, or it will disclose this material in the certain knowledge that if the informer is sued for libel, the supply of information will be severely reduced. Furthermore, it cannot be right that national courts and Community institutions should independently both weigh the force of particular evidence with the possibility of inconsistent results. Hasselblad are already in a position to say that it denies and has always denied Mr Orbinson's allegations and that the Court of Justice has held that those allegations cannot be relied on by the Commission. This, in my judgment, must and should suffice.

I would dismiss the appeal, albeit for slightly different reasons from those which appealed to the judge.

**O'CONNOR LJ.** I have had the opportunity to read the judgments prepared by Sir John Donaldson MR and May LJ. I agree with Sir John Donaldson MR that the appeal should be dismissed for the reasons given by him.

**MAY LJ.** It is with regret that I find myself unable to reach the same conclusion as Sir John Donaldson MR and O'Connor LJ in this appeal. The former has not only set out the facts of this case in his judgment but he has also described the procedure adopted by the Commission of the European Community when investigating alleged infringements of arts 85 and 86 of the EEC Treaty. I need not therefore repeat them herein. As will have appeared, the issue in this case is whether Mr Orbinson is entitled to any further protection than that of qualified privilege in respect of a letter dated 16 February 1981 signed by him and which was sent to the Commission by Camera Care Ltd in the course of the investigation by the former of alleged infringements of arts 85 and 86 by the Hasselblad organisation generally and Hasselblad (GB) Ltd in particular.

I respectfully agree with the views expressed by Sir John Donaldson MR about arts 11 and 20 of EEC Council Regulation 17 of 6 February 1962. In my opinion, however one approaches them they cannot bear the construction sought to be put on them either by counsel on behalf of Mr Orbinson or by counsel on behalf of the Commission.

The argument before us ranged widely. However, I respectfully think that we should not forget that the instant litigation is a defamation action for damages for libel. In that context, on the assumption that Mr Orbinson's letter of 16 February 1981 was defamatory, the only defence available to him which is wider than qualified privilege is that of absolute privilege. Thus I think that the question in this appeal, notwithstanding the width of the argument, is simply whether the judge was correct in holding that absolute privilege did attach to Mr Orbinson's letter.

It follows in my opinion that the concept of public interest which was under consideration in such cases as *Rogers v Secretary of State for the Home Dept, Gaming Board for Great Britain v Rogers* [1972] 2 All ER 1057, [1973] AC 388, *Alfred Crompton Amusement Machines Ltd v Customs and Excise Comrs (No 2)* [1973] 2 All ER 1169, [1974] AC 405 and *D v National Society for the Prevention of Cruelty to Children* [1977] 1 All ER 589, [1978] AC 171 is not directly in point in this case, though it may be of help by way of analogy. Each of those cases was concerned with the question of disclosure of documents and whether a party to litigation was entitled to rely on what had earlier been called 'Crown privilege' but which is now clearly a principle much wider in its scope. It involves balancing the public interest in requiring the full disclosure of documents for the proper conduct of litigation, on the one hand, against the public interest in permitting a person or body to refuse to disclose documents, or the identity of informers, where to disclose these would prevent the effective functioning of that person or organisation, on the other. Thus, although I respectfully think that these cases are of substantial assistance when a court is indeed called on to conduct a balancing exercise between two similar competing public interests, I do not think that they are, at least directly, in point in the instant appeal.

In English law as it stands at the moment the only basis for holding that Mr Orbinson was protected by absolute privilege in the circumstances of this case is that the letter which he signed was either a statement made in the course of judicial or quasi-judicial proceedings, or at the least was intimately connected with them, such as the precognition held to be protected in *Watson v M'Ewan* [1905] AC 480, [1904-7] All ER Rep 1. However, for the reasons given by Sir John Donaldson MR in his judgment, and with which I respectfully agree, I think that it would be wrong to consider the proceedings of the Commission to have that necessary judicial or quasi-judicial nature which could give rise to the protection of absolute privilege on such authorities as *Watson v M'Ewan* and *Trapp v Mackie* [1979] 1 All ER 489, [1979] 1 WLR 377. Still using English legal terminology for the moment, I think that the Commission's procedure in investigating alleged infringements of arts 85 and 86 has to be described as administrative rather than judicial or quasi-judicial. Indeed both the Commission itself and the Court of Justice of the European Communities have clearly taken the same view in *van Landewyck Sárl v EC Commission* Joined Cases 209-215/78 [1980] ECR 3125 and in *SA Musique Diffusion Française v EC Commission* Joined Cases 100-103/80 [1983] ECR 1825.

However, in none of the many authorities to which we were referred was it necessary to consider the defence in an English court of absolute privilege in the European context with which we are concerned in the present appeal. I accept that English courts are having increasingly to apply European Community law and to remember that the common law procedures so familiar to us are very different in many respects from the procedures under the civil law which obtain in most, if not all, of the other members of the European Community. It is also true that the basis of the rule which gives absolute privilege to communications in judicial or quasi-judicial proceedings was succinctly stated by Fry LJ in *Munster v Lamb* (1883) 11 QBD 588 at 607, cf [1881-5] All ER Rep 791 at 797 (quoted in full and with approval by Sellers LJ in another case to which we were referred, *Lincoln v Daniels* [1961] 3 All ER 740 at 743, [1962] 1 QB 237 at 247):

> 'The rule of law exists, not because the conduct of those persons ought not of itself to be actionable, but because if their conduct was actionable, actions would be brought against judges and witnesses in cases in which they had not spoken with malice, in which they had not spoken with falsehood. It is not a desire to prevent actions from being brought in cases where they ought to be maintained that has led to the adoption of the present rule of law; but it is the fear that if the rule were otherwise, numerous actions would be brought against persons who were merely discharging their duty. It must always be borne in mind that it is not intended to protect malicious and untruthful persons, but that it is intended to protect persons acting bonâ fide, who under a different rule would be liable, not perhaps to verdicts and judgments against them, but to the vexation of defending actions.'

In other words, where there is a serious risk that numerous actions may be brought against people who are merely doing their duty, that people acting bona fide may nevertheless be put to the vexation of defending defamation proceedings, it may be necessary to grant absolute and not merely qualified privilege to such people in respect of a particular class of communication.

*Riddick v Thames Board Mills Ltd* [1977] 3 All ER 677, [1977] 1 QB 881 is plainly distinguishable from the instant case on its facts. In it the document on which the plaintiff sought to sue had been compulsorily disclosed by the defendant in earlier litigation between the same parties. No question of absolute privilege could arise; indeed this was accepted in argument by counsel for Mr Orbinson. In *Riddick's* case this court allowed the defendant's appeal and held that it was entitled to protection, but as Sir John Donaldson MR has pointed out, each member of the court based his decision on a different ground. Lord Denning MR held that the public interest in the privacy and confidence that a person should have in his own documents outweighed the public interest in the full discovery of documents in litigation, once this has taken place. However, I think that the real ratio of his judgment was that when a party to litigation discloses documents he does so on the implied condition that his opponent may only make use of such documents for the purpose of that litigation: cf *Home Office v Harman*

[1982] 1 All ER 532, [1983] 1 AC 280. Stephenson LJ regarded the use of the document disclosed for another purpose as an abuse of the process of the court, which could be restrained. Waller LJ also thought that the ulterior use of the document was an abuse of the process of the court, basing himself on the public interest in full and frank disclosure in litigation. On this analysis, apart entirely from the factual difference between the two cases, I do not think that *Riddick's* case can help Mr Orbinson in this appeal.

Before returning to what in my opinion is the fundamental issue in this appeal, I think that to complete the picture we should note that clearly absolute privilege would attach to statements made in any review proceedings before the Court of Justice of the European Communities of any decision of the Commission on alleged infringements of arts 85 and 86 of the treaty. Further, any perjury by an English citizen in his evidence before the Court of Justice is indictable in this country by virtue of s 11 of the European Communities Act 1972.

In the end, therefore, I come back to what I think is the only point in this appeal, namely are we prepared to extend the scope of absolute privilege in defamation litigation in this country and hold that it attaches to Mr Orbinson's letter of 16 February 1981?

This is the first time in which this particular and important point has come before the English courts: indeed, we were told that this is the first time that the point has arisen in any of the national courts in any of the members of the European Community. As I have said, Community law is now part of English law and we with our common law traditions must remember that very different procedures under the civil law obtain at least in the majority of the other members of the European Community. I accept therefore that we should look at the problem in the instant appeal with the assistance of, but not restricted by the common law decisions to which we have been referred. Nevertheless, I ask myself whether it is presently relevant or appropriate to carry out a balancing exercise similar to that done by the House of Lords in the public interest decisions to which I have referred and whether it is either necessary or desirable that we should substantially extend the scope of absolute privilege in defamation litigation in this country and hold that it attaches to Mr Orbinson's letter of 16 February 1981 which is sued on herein. Sir John Donaldson MR has set out many of the relevant considerations in his judgment and I need not repeat them. I respectfully think that the likely economic imbalance between complainants and alleged infringers of arts 85 and 86 of the treaty is the most important consideration. On the other hand, I do not think that we should lightly extend the scope of absolute privilege in respect of alleged defamatory matter. If communications to the Commission such as Mr Orbinson's letter are not malicious, then they will be protected by qualified privilege. I bear fully in mind the vexation of having to defend actions referred to in the passage from the judgment of Fry LJ in *Munster v Lamb* which I quoted earlier in this judgment. However, the fact that this is the first time that this point has arisen for decision in any court in the European Community does make me wonder whether the public interest in protecting complainants from vexatious litigation is as strong as has been suggested. When infringement proceedings reach the Court of Justice, the protection for both complainants on the one hand and infringers against whom false evidence may be given on the other is in my opinion quite sufficient. It may be that in time, when we have more experience of the workings of the Commission, that that unruly horse of public policy will lead me to accord absolute privilege to communications to the Commission such as Mr Orbinson's letter. At the moment I do not see the need for any such substantial extension of this defence beyond the presently decided cases in this country. Further, if it were necessary or desirable so to extend the defence, I think that it would be essential carefully to define and limit any such extension. Clearly the privilege cannot attach to every communication to the Commission relating to an alleged infringement of arts 85 or 86.

Finally, although I have carefully considered the several submissions founded on the International Organisations Act 1968 and what has or has not been done thereunder, I hope I shall not be considered discourteous if I say that I do not think that they are relevant to the single issue which arises in this appeal. Neither the European Commission nor the Court of Justice are international organisations for the purposes of the 1968 Act.

Further and in any event, the privileges and immunities with which the 1968 Act is concerned are those set out in Sch 1 to the 1968 Act, none of which has any relation to the common law defence of absolute privilege in defamation actions.

For these reasons I am regretfully driven to a conclusion different from Sir John Donaldson MR and O'Connor LJ and the judge below. For my part, I would allow this appeal.

*Appeal dismissed. No order for costs below. Respondent to have costs in the Court of Appeal. No order for costs of European Commission. Leave to appeal granted to Hasselblad to include costs. Leave to appeal granted to Mr Orbinson on costs only. European Commission to be served with any petition.*

Solicitors: *William T Stockler* (for Hasselblad); *Pollard Scott Winter* (for Mr Orbinson); *Freshfields* (for the EC Commission).

Frances Rustin　Barrister.

# Practice Note

CHANCERY DIVISION (NORTHERN AREA)

*Practice – Chancery Division – Northern Area – Lists – Fixed dates – Motion days – Papers for judge – Urgent matters.*

The following memorandum, issued by the Lord Chancellor's Department as a press notice, was approved by his Honour Judge Blackett-Ord V-C on 3 December 1984 and is to apply from 2 January 1985.

| R POTTER | C W PRATLEY |
|---|---|
| Administrator of the | Circuit Administrator |
| Northern Circuit | North Eastern Circuit |

5 December 1984.

1. From 2 January 1985 the Senior Chancery Clerk (the clerk) in the district registries at Leeds, Liverpool, Manchester, Newcastle upon Tyne and Preston will each maintain separate lists of cases in the Chancery Division of the High Court proceeding in that registry or intended to be tried at that centre, namely: (a) a *setting down list* comprising all cases for hearing by the judge except cases entered in the Motion Day lists. In this list cases will be identified as 'witness' cases (involving the oral examination of witnesses or deponents) or 'non-witness' cases (not involving oral evidence); (b) a list for each motion day at that centre, comprising motions, company petitions and all cases estimated to occupy the time of the court for two hours or less; (c) a *warned list* of cases from (a) above.

2. *The Setting Down List*
   (a) Cases will be entered when they are set down, adjourned into court or otherwise ready for hearing or when transferred from a Motion Day list and will be deleted when disposed of.
   (b) Each case will be given an identifying number. The plaintiff's solicitor will be sent a letter enclosing a blank counsel's certificate of estimated hearing time and giving a date (which will normally be one month ahead) by which the certificate is required to be returned signed by all counsel in the case.
   (c) On receipt of counsel's certificate the case will be entered in the Warned List.

3. *The Warned List*

(a) Any case in the Warned List which has not been given a fixed date for trial will be liable to be called on for trial at seven days' notice if a date becomes available.

(b) From amongst these cases the clerk will on Thursday of each week prepare a list of cases liable to be called on for trial during the following week and will notify the parties or their solicitors by telephone.

(c) Before finalising such list, the clerk will try to ascertain through the solicitors concerned and counsel's chambers the convenience of the parties and the availability of counsel concerned. The court, however, has a discretion to include a case against the wishes of a party or parties and notwithstanding the unavailability of the counsel originally instructed; it may, in exceptional circumstances and at the direction of the judge, be necessary to call on such a case.

(d) Parties or their solicitors in any case in the list referred to in sub-para (b) above will be notified as soon as practicable that their case will be called on. Although at least one full day's notice will normally be given, shorter notice may be unavoidable on occasion.

4. *Fixed dates*

(a) The present practice of allotting fixed dates for all cases expected to last for a day or more will continue, the clerk in Manchester keeping the judges' diaries and acting as co-ordinator. But, now that there are usually three judges sitting to hear Chancery cases in the area, more cases are required at short notice to fill the gaps caused by settlements and it is hoped to use these gaps to expedite the hearing of shorter cases. Accordingly, to make the system more flexible, the clerk will have a discretion whether or not to give a fixed date for any case with an estimated length of three days or less and any fixed date given for such a case will usually be not more than two months ahead. Any party dissatisfied with a decision of the clerk may apply (on one clear day's notice to all other parties) to the judge.

(b) Any case with a fixed date will remain in the warned list and the date and estimated hearing length will be noted in the list. If the date is vacated, para 3 above will apply. A date may be vacated by the clerk if a revised certificate lengthening counsel's estimate of the length of hearing is lodged but otherwise his Honour Judge Blackett-Ord V-C's direction dated 14 July 1980 ([1980] 3 All ER 831) will apply with the addition of the words 'or his Honour Judge O'Donoghue' after each reference to his Honour Judge FitzHugh QC.

5. If counsel's certificate is not lodged within the period specified or if it appears to the clerk that through the default of any party the trial of the case may be delayed he will communicate with the party concerned. In the absence of a satisfactory reply the case will be referred to the district registrar (under RSC Ord 34, r 5 or Ord 28, r 10) or to the judge for directions.

6. *Motion Day lists*

(a) Any case falling within para 1(b) above may be entered on the list for any motion day at any centre, but motions and petitions with a time estimate of over two hours may (at the discretion of the judge) be adjourned to another motion day or other date to be fixed as seems appropriate. In exercising his discretion the judge will take into account the state of the lists generally and the relative urgency of the case.

(b) Subject to the above, motions will continue to be heard on any motion day and at any centre named in the notice of motion and may be stood over or saved for hearing at any other centre.

7. *Papers for the judge*

(1) In addition to any documents in the court file legible copies must be provided as follows:

(a) *Writ actions*   On setting down, copies of the pleadings and other documents specified in RSC Ord 34, r 3(1) and complying with Ord 66.

(b) *Originating summonses* and other cases involving affidavit evidence (other than simple creditors' winding-up petitions) when listed under para 2(a) above: (i) the originating summons or other originating process; (ii) the affidavits and exhibits, which must comply with the practice direction of the Lord Chief Justice dated 21 July 1983 (see *Practice Note* [1983] 3 All ER 33, [1983] 1 WLR 922). Copies of exhibits which do not lend themselves to photographic reproduction may be omitted; (iii) any orders of the district registrar which have been drawn up; (iv) any requisite legal aid documents.

(c) *Motions*: (i) the writ and any subsequent pleadings; (ii) the notice of motion; (iii) the affidavits and exhibits (see sub-para (b)(ii) above which applies); (iv) in the case of motions for judgment, the documents referred to in *The Supreme Court Practice 1985* p 328, para 19/7/8 (with the exception of Form E26 praecipe).

(2) The provision of these documents is the responsibility of the solicitor for the plaintiff, the petitioner or the party moving the court (as the case may be) except that (a) the court will provide copies of writs and orders on request, (b) the solicitor for any defendant or respondent is responsible for copies of affidavits on which he relies and of their exhibits.

8. *Urgent matters*

On a certificate of urgency (oral or in writing) by a solicitor or (if possible) counsel, arrangements will be made to communicate with the judge without delay, by telephone if necessary.

# Practice Direction

CHANCERY DIVISION

*Patent – Rectification of register – Application for rectification of register of patents or designs – Agreed directions – Procedure – RSC Ord 104, r 17.*

By para 9 of the Practice Direction dated 23 June 1980 ([1980] 2 All ER 750, [1980] 1 WLR 751), as set out in an updated form in *The Supreme Court Practice 1985* vol 2, para 826, p 225, a procedure for obtaining agreed directions out of court was made applicable to certain proceedings commenced by originating motion and specified in that paragraph. As from 1 January 1985 this procedure will also apply to applications for rectification of the register of patents or designs to which RSC Ord 104, r 17 applies.

By direction of the Vice-Chancellor.

EDMUND HEWARD
10 December 1984                                                  Chief Master.

# R v Mansfield Justices, ex parte Sharkey
# and other applications

QUEEN'S BENCH DIVISION
LORD LANE CJ, STUART-SMITH AND LEGGATT JJ
8, 12 OCTOBER 1984

*Criminal law – Bail – Condition – Validity – Bail granted to striking miner on condition that he did not picket except at his place of employment – Condition imposed to prevent defendant committing offence while on bail – Whether necessary for magistrates to be satisfied that there were 'substantial grounds for believing' defendant likely to commit offence if released on bail – Whether condition valid – Bail Act 1976, s 3(6), Sch 1, Pt I, paras 2, 8(1).*

In the course of an industrial dispute between the miners' union and the National Coal Board large numbers of striking miners from South Yorkshire regularly picketed working collieries in the East Midlands in an attempt to persuade working miners to join the strike. It was well known that the confrontation at the picket lines between striking and working miners had led to outbreaks of violence and disorder. The nine applicants were striking miners from South Yorkshire who had regularly picketed the East Midlands collieries. They were each arrested while picketing and charged with threatening behaviour, contrary to s 5 of the Public Order Act 1936, or obstructing a police officer, contrary to s 51(3) of the Police Act 1964. When they were brought before magistrates to be remanded the magistrates, mindful of the violence on the picket lines and notwithstanding the good character of the applicants, imposed a condition when granting bail that each applicant was 'not to visit any premises or place for the purpose of picketing or demonstrating in connection with the current trade dispute between [the union and the coal board] other than peacefully to picket or demonstrate at his usual place of employment'. Magistrates were empowered by s 3(6)[a] of the Bail Act 1976 to impose conditions when granting bail in order to secure that the person bailed did not commit an offence while on bail, while para 8(1)[b] of Pt I of Sch 1 to the 1976 Act provided that a condition was not to be imposed under s 3(6) unless it appeared to be 'necessary . . . for the purpose of preventing the occurrence of any of the events mentioned in paragraph 2[c]' of Pt I of Sch 1. The applicants applied for judicial review of the magistrates' decision to attach the condition to the grant of bail, on the ground that the reference in para 8(1) to para 2 (which related to the refusal of bail) imported into the exercise of the discretion under para 8(1) the requirement that the court had to be 'satisfied that there are substantial grounds for believing' that, inter alia, the person bailed would 'commit an offence while on bail' before a condition could be attached when bail was granted. The applicants contended that before imposing the condition when granting bail the magistrates had not considered whether there were substantial grounds for believing that each applicant would commit an offence while on bail.

**Held** – Although when refusing a person bail magistrates were required by para 2 of Pt I of Sch 1 to the 1976 Act to have 'substantial grounds' for believing that he might, for example, commit an offence when on bail, the requirement of having 'substantial grounds' did not apply to the grant of bail on conditions under s 3(6) and para 8(1), since all that was required of magistrates before they imposed conditions when granting bail was that they perceived a real and not a fanciful risk of the person bailed committing an offence while on bail. In deciding whether to impose a particular condition magistrates

---

*a*    Section 3(6) is set out at p 200 *d*, post
*b*    Paragraph 8(1) is set out at p 200 *h j*, post
*c*    Paragraph 2 is set out at p 200 *g h*, post

had a wide discretion to inquire whether the condition was necessary and were entitled to use their knowledge of local events and conditions. Accordingly, against the background that the picketing was no longer peaceful but was part of intimidation and the threat of violence directed to working miners and having regard to the fact that the applicants would, if released unconditionally, immediately rejoin the picketing, the magistrates had been entitled to conclude that if the applicants' bail was not made conditional they would commit offences while on bail. The applications for judicial review would accordingly be refused (see p 201 c to f and j to p 202 a and j to p 203 a and d to j and p 204 h j, post).

Per curiam. The practice of putting into the dock together defendants who have been arrested on different occasions or at different places is to be discouraged because it may give the impression of 'group justice' (see p 203 j, post).

**Notes**

For conditions of granting bail generally, see Supplement to 11 Halsbury's Laws (4th edn) para 165A. 1–2.

For the exercise of discretion in granting bail by magistrates, see ibid para 167, and for cases on the subject, see 14(1) Digest (Reissue) 251, 1828–1829.

For the Public Order Act 1936, s 5, see 8 Halsbury's Statutes (3rd edn) 332.

For the Police Act 1964, s 51, see 25 ibid 364.

For the Bail Act 1976, s 3, Sch 1, Pt I, paras 1, 8, see 46 Halsbury's Statutes (3rd edn) 293, 308, 309.

**Cases referred to in judgment**

Associated Provincial Picture Houses Ltd v Wednesbury Corp [1947] 2 All ER 680, [1948] 1 KB 223, CA.

Moles, Re [1981] Crim LR 170, DC.

Short v Poole Corp [1926] Ch 66, [1925] All ER Rep 74, CA.

**Applications for judicial review**

*R v Mansfield Justices, ex p Sharkey*

Stephen James Sharkey applied, with the leave of Hutchison J granted on 17 August 1984, for (i) an order of certiorari to quash a decision of the justices sitting at Mansfield Magistrates' Court on 25 July 1984 to grant him bail only on condition that he was 'not to visit any premises or place for the purpose of picketing or demonstrating in connection with the current trade dispute between the NUM and NCB other than peacefully to picket or demonstrate at his usual place of employment', (ii) an order of mandamus requiring the justices to grant him unconditional bail, (iii) a declaration that he was entitled to unconditional bail and (iv) such other order or relief as the court thought fit. The facts are set out in the judgment of the court.

*R v Mansfield Justices, ex p Hunt and Barron*

Peter David Hunt and Geoffrey Barron each applied, with the leave of Hutchison J granted on 17 August 1984, for (i) an order of certiorari to quash a decision of a justice sitting at Mansfield Magistrates' Court on 25 July 1984 to grant him bail only on condition that he was 'not to visit any premises or place for the purpose of picketing or demonstrating in connection with the current trade dispute between the NUM and NCB other than peacefully to picket or demonstrate at his usual place of employment'; (ii) an order of mandamus requiring the justices to grant him unconditional bail, (iii) a declaration that he was entitled to unconditional bail and (iv) such other order or relief as the court thought fit. The facts are set out in the judgment of the court.

*R v Mansfield Justices, ex p Fretwell*

Brian Fretwell applied, with the leave of Hutchison J granted on 17 August 1984, for (i) an order of certiorari to quash an order of the justices sitting at Mansfield Magistrates' Court on 11 July 1984, and an order of the justices sitting at Worksop Magistrates' Court on 2 August 1984, granting him bail only on condition that he was 'not to visit any premises or place for the purpose of picketing or demonstrating in connection with the current trade dispute between the NUM and NCB other than peacefully to picket or demonstrate at his usual place of employment', (ii) an order of mandamus requiring the justices to grant him unconditional bail, (iii) a declaration that he was entitled to unconditional bail and (iv) such other order or relief as the court thought fit. The facts are set out in the judgment of the court.

### R v Mansfield Justices, ex p Robinson

Paul Robinson applied, with the leave of Hutchison J granted on 17 August 1984, for (i) an order of certiorari to quash a decision of the justices sitting at Mansfield Magistrates' Court on 2 August 1984 to grant him bail only on condition that he was 'not to visit any premises or place for the purpose of picketing or demonstrating in connection with the current trade dispute between the NUM and NCB other than peacefully to picket or demonstrate at his usual place of employment', an order of mandamus requiring the justices to grant him unconditional bail, (iii) a declaration that he was entitled to unconditional bail and (iv) such other order or relief as the court thought fit. The facts are set out in the judgment of the court.

### R v Mansfield Justices, ex p Swatten

Martin Swatten applied, with the leave of Hutchison J granted on 17 August 1984, for (i) an order of prohibition and/or (ii) an order of certiorari to quash a decision of the justices sitting at Mansfield Magistrates' Court on 27 June 1984 to grant him bail only on condition that he was 'not to visit any premises or place for the purpose of picketing or demonstrating in connection with the current trade dispute between the NUM and NCB other than peacefully to picket or demonstrate at his usual place of employment' or (iii) such further or other order as seemed just to the court. The facts are set out in the judgment of the court.

### R v Mansfield Justices, ex p Grove

John Grove applied, with the leave of Hutchison J granted on 17 August 1984, for (i) an order of prohibition and/or (ii) an order of certiorari to quash a decision of the justices sitting at Mansfield Magistrates' Court on 26 June 1984 to grant him bail only on condition that he was 'not to visit any premises or place for the purpose of picketing or demonstrating in connection with the current trade dispute between the NUM and NCB other than peacefully to picket or demonstrate at his usual place of employment' or (iii) such further or other order as seemed just to the court. The facts are set out in the judgment of the court.

### R v Mansfield Justices, ex p Fellows

Graham Paul Fellows applied, with the leave of Hutchison J granted on 17 August 1984, (i) for an order of prohibition and/or (ii) for an order of certiorari to quash a decision of the justices sitting at Mansfield Magistrates' Court on 29 June 1984 to grant him bail only on condition that he was 'not to visit any premises or place for the purpose of picketing or demonstrating in connection with the current trade dispute between the NUM and NCB other than peacefully to picket or demonstrate at his usual place of employment' or (iii) for such further or other order as seemed just to the court. The facts are set out in the judgment of the court.

### R v Mansfield Justices, ex p Anderson

James George Anderson applied, with the leave of Hutchison J granted on 17 August 1984, for (i) an order of prohibition and/or (ii) an order of certiorari to quash a decision of the justices sitting at Mansfield Magistrates' Court on 14 June 1984 to grant him bail only on condition that he was 'not to visit any premises or place for the purpose of picketing or demonstrating in connection with the current trade dispute between the NUM and NCB other than peacefully to picket or demonstrate at his usual place of employment' or (iii) such further or other order as seemed just to the court. The facts are set out in the judgment of the court.

*John R Macdonald QC* and *James Wood* for the applicants.
*Brian Appleby QC* and *Alexandra Scott* for the Nottinghamshire police.
*John Laws* as amicus curiae.

*Cur adv vult*

12 October. The following judgment of the court was delivered.

**LORD LANE CJ.** These applications for judicial review by way of certiorari and mandamus directed to the justices sitting at Mansfield in the county of Nottingham arise out of the current troubles at various collieries in the East Midlands. There are nine applicants. All of them are coal miners. There are on strike. All are of good character. Some have been charged with offences against the Public Order Act 1936 and some with obstructing the police and other offences. All were remanded on bail by the justices. In each case a condition was imposed in the following terms:

'not to visit any premises or place for the purpose of picketing or demonstrating in connection with the current trade dispute between the NUM and NCB other than peacefully to picket or demonstrate at his usual place of employment'.

Counsel for on behalf of the applicants bases his arguments on the following submissions. (1) The condition was imposed without any proper consideration of the individual circumstances of the applicants. (2) The condition was imposed when there was insufficient material before the justices to justify it. (3) Whilst accepting that a bail application is an informal inquiry and no strict rules of evidence are to be applied, nevertheless the justices must take relevant considerations into account and these justices did not. (4) On the evidence, although the justices deny that they are applying a policy, it appears that it is their practice to impose this condition on striking miners brought before them after arrest and that they have therefore fettered the exercise of their discretion. In other words, they have made a practice of imposing this condition without a proper consideration of the individual cases.

This court is accordingly asked to rule that the justices failed to exercise their discretion judicially and that the condition which was imposed should be quashed and the justices should be directed to admit the applicants to bail unconditionally.

We turn now to the individual cases.

Two of the applicants are no longer on bail, the charges against them having been tried and determined. Those two are James George Anderson and John Grove. Mr Anderson was convicted on 6 September 1984 of obstructing the police and given a conditional discharge for one year and ordered to pay certain costs and witness expenses. Mr Grove was on 26 June 1984 convicted of threatening behaviour under the Public Order Act 1936 and fined £50 and £75 costs. There is accordingly no need to consider their cases further except as part of the general picture where relevant.

The remaining seven are as follows.

Mr Stephen James Sharkey. He appeared before the Mansfield justices on 25 July 1984 charged with threatening behaviour contrary to s 5 of the Public Order Act 1936 and also wilful obstruction of the highway. He was a member of the South Yorkshire branch of the National Union of Mineworkers. He was one of 4,000 pickets who attempted to enter the county of Nottingham on that date. Approximately half of that number were prevented from doing so because of interception by the police en route.

The target of the pickets was Babbington pit, where some 150 miners were reporting for work. There was a rapid build up of pickets shortly before midday. In the initial stages five windscreens were smashed and stone throwing damaged five cars belonging to working miners. The pickets were marshalled by the police into containment areas. As a result of the police action the miners who wished to work were able to enter the colliery but the pickets became violent and aggressive. The police alleged that Mr Sharkey was seen to lead a charge against a police cordon and that he was seen to strike out with his boot shouting and waving his fist. He was then arrested.

The police officer presenting the case to the justices asked for the condition already referred to to be imposed on any bail granted to the applicant. The policeman said that his reasons for asking for the condition was that during the past few months there had been numerous outbreaks of disorder and if this condition were not imposed it was likely that further offences would be committed by the applicant.

The solicitor appearing on behalf of the applicant submitted that no evidence had been adduced with regard to the particular circumstances of the applicant which could justify any condition being imposed on bail and that bail conditions had to be justified by reference to the individual circumstances of each case. The police officer repeated that having regard to the general situation of the strike it was felt likely that this particular applicant would return to commit further offences unless a condition was imposed. It was admitted, and indeed asserted, that the applicant had been on strike and actively picketing since the strike began some 21 weeks previously. It was said that he rejected all forms of violence, but believed in his right as a miner on strike to engage in peaceful picketing.

The bench retired to consider their decision, and on their return the chairman made the following statement:

> 'We in this court are mindful of the present position and the lawlessness it has created. We feel that unless the evidence has been concocted by the officers there must be some substance to it and some foundation. We feel that there are substantial grounds for believing that the defendant without conditional bail would be likely to commit further offences whilst on bail.'

Mr Barron and Mr Hunt were arrested on the same occasion as Mr Sharkey. According to the police Mr Barron was arrested during a concerted push which was accompanied by shouts and gestures and kicking out at police officers. The prosecution apparently alleged that he surged forward within a police cordon, shouting 'Sieg heil', as working miners entered Babbington colliery. Mr Hunt is similarly said to have been arrested when instigating a push against the police as miners were entering the colliery. According to his solicitor he was described, when first released on bail, as having pushed and shoved other demonstrators in order to get at the working miners.

Mr Barron comes from Barnsley. He says that before his arrest he has picketed on numerous occasions and at various locations both inside and outside Nottinghamshire. He asserted that his sole intention in doing so was to picket peacefully, to communicate with miners going to work and to persuade them to join the strike. He says that he has never picketed in an aggressive manner, but has seen much provocative behaviour from police officers. According to Mr Barron at most (in fact nearly all) of the pickets he has been to there has been a jovial atmosphere of co-operation with the police. He would not join others in intimidating working miners and he regards the additional charge against him of unlawful assembly as disgraceful.

Despite having been arrested when he was one of between 1,500 and 2,000 pickets, Mr Hunt, who comes from Rotherham, illustrates his desire to talk to working miners by reference to occasions when there were about ten pickets present. By arrangement with the police they operated two at a time, accosting working miners. Up to the time of his arrest Mr Hunt had been picketing every day for five days a week. He says that the vast majority of pickets he attended were peaceful, though he has seen 'a lot of intimidation' by police. Mr Hunt deplores violence. Were he able he would picket again. He too denies the allegations against him.

The same solicitor appeared for Mr Barron and Mr Hunt. She applied first for bail for Mr Hunt, submitting that there was no evidence against him and that he was a man of good character with nothing in his previous history to suggest that he would commit any further offences. She also submitted that a condition of bail should only be imposed after careful consideration of individual circumstances. She answered comments about the violent nature of the crowd at Babbington by contending, first, that it is no offence for a person, not himself engaged in any unlawful activity, to be present at scenes of violence and, second, that there is nothing intrinsically intimidatory or unlawful about large gatherings of people. The magistrates nevertheless imposed the standard condition of bail, saying:

'We feel that there are stringent grounds for believing that the defendant without conditional bail would be likely to commit further offences whilst on bail.'

On behalf of Mr Barron his solicitor asked the magistrate to give guidance if there were any circumstances in which he would be prepared to grant unconditional bail, remarking that it was becoming increasingly apparent that the imposition of conditions was automatic in such case. The magistrate replied that he would not prejudge what might be said, and refused to disqualify himself from sitting. The application that he should do so had been made 'on the grounds that it appeared to the court that he believed that striking miners arrested on the picket line would commit further offences simply because they were miners on strike'. The same conditions of bail were imposed on Mr Barron, and for the same reasons, as in relation to Mr Hunt.

Mr Fretwell is charged with threatening behaviour and obstructing police. It is alleged that on 10 July 1984 he was one of a group of some 150 men who gathered near the entrance to Harworth colliery, who were said to be hostile to both police and working miners. Amidst shouting, threats and abuse, when the police attempted to cordon the group, Mr Fretwell is said to have exacerbated the situation by standing his ground and shouting excitably: 'Fuck off you bastards, why don't you move.' Mr Fretwell is 37 years old and lives in Doncaster. He has been a miner ever since he left school and has never been in trouble with the police before. Only one other person was arrested when he was. He himself, after being photographed, was taken to Mansfield police station, where he was kept in a cell overnight before being taken to the magistrates' court.

According to his solicitor, the prosecuting officer outlined the circumstances in which Mr Fretwell had been arrested, and applied for him to be granted conditional bail because of the officer's fear of the likelihood of further offences being committed. When he indicated that he was not going to call any evidence, Mr Fretwell's solicitor called first his co-accused and then him. Both gave evidence that they had been on strike for 18 weeks, that they had not been arrested in relation to the dispute and in Mr Fretwell's case that he was of good character. This evidence was not controverted.

The solicitor submitted that before imposing a condition of bail the court must be satisfied that in the individual circumstances of each case that was necessary. She referred to the charges, which then were of threatening behaviour, as being for 'essentially minor offences'. She remarked that in an earlier case the bench had granted unconditional bail to a defendant (not a striking miner) who was charged with inflicting grievous bodily harm. In Mr Fretwell's case the prosecution had called no evidence to substantiate the fear of the commission of further offences. In the light of the defendant's own evidence it was submitted that the grant of unconditional bail was 'the only appropriate decision'. The solicitor asked the bench to indicate, if imposing conditional bail, what factors relating to each individual had led them to conclude that it was necessary.

After a retirement of 25 minutes the bench granted bail in both cases subject to a condition, which was in terms identical to that typed on slips of paper already available to be affixed to bail forms.

When Mr Fretwell was further charged with obstructing a police officer, application was made for his bail to be unconditional. His solicitor said that, if the bench had a policy that any striking miner who was arrested in connection with the dispute was to be placed on bail with the usual condition, then they should say so. The chairman of the bench assured her that the imposing of the usual condition had never been his policy and that he would deal with Mr Fretwell's case individually.

The solicitor thereupon submitted that if ever there was a case for unconditional bail this was it and indicated that, if bail was to remain conditional, it would be helpful if the magistrates, though they need not, would indicate what factors were taken into consideration in arriving at this conclusion. The bench retired for 15 minutes before imposing the usual condition of bail on the ground that Mr Fretwell, as it was put, 'may' commit further offences, without giving further explanation.

Mr Robinson is 18 years old. On 1 August 1984 he was one of four men arrested out of a total of 1,000 men who were picketing the entrance to Bentinck colliery. According to the police, abuse was shouted at them by pickets and stones thrown at them by a man who was thereupon arrested. It is alleged that Mr Robinson took hold of the arrested man and attempted strongly to pull him back into the crowd, with the result that the situation was exacerbated. He was arrested only after a violent struggle, and, perhaps in consequence, was handcuffed before being put into a police van. He was charged with obstructing a police officer and kept in custody overnight. On the following day he was brought before the court with two other men.

They were placed in the dock together and the prosecuting officer gave brief details of the charge against each of them, asking for the imposition of a condition of bail because of the likelihood of further offences. In doing so he reminded the bench that arising out of the dispute there had been repeated incidents of serious and violent public disorder in which considerable damage had been done and as a result of which two men had died.

In applying for the bail of one of Mr Robinson's co-accused to be unconditional his solicitor urged the bench to deal with the case individually. Although it was accepted that since the beginning of the dispute there had been several incidents of serious disorder involving violence and damage, these acts were not caused by the co-accused. It was accordingly submitted that they should not be quoted unless the prosecution was alleging that in some way the co-accused had been responsible for those incidents. The bench was concerned with individual justice, not with group justice.

After a retirement of ten minutes the magistrates imposed the standard condition on the bail of the co-accused, stating that they considered it necessary to prevent the commission of further offences. Mr Robinson's solicitor then told the magistrates that, because they had imposed a condition without indicating why they had decided it was necessary, there was nothing further that she could say on behalf of Mr Robinson or his other co-accused save their ages, their good character and the length of time for which they had been on strike. Mr Robinson's bail, which was granted at once, was conditional.

The solicitor has made many applications for bail. She says that magistrates, 'while strenuously denying that they are making decisions on the imposition of the usual condition of bail pursuant to a policy, and are dealing with every case on its own merits, will impose the condition requested when the only information they have about the individual defendant is that he is a miner on strike and therefore involved in the present dispute'.

Mr Robinson has made his own comment on affidavit:

'I wasn't surprised because they treat us all the same, don't they? They are not bothered about us. They just think we are all the same, just miners on strike.'

Mr Swatten lives near Doncaster. He had gathered with others to demonstrate at Bilsthorpe colliery at midnight on 27 June 1984. He says he was picketing peacefully when he was tripped up and arrested by one of several police officers who ran into the crowd of pickets. According to the police version he was one of 250 men who were confronted by a cordon of police officers. Mr Swatten is said to have been one of the instigators of a sudden and concerted effort to breach the police cordon by shoving against it in the manner of a rugby forward. The police claim that in a renewed incident Mr Swatten was again seen shouting and pushing against the police as before.

When he was taken to court he was one of eight miners in the dock at the same time, although they had been arrested at different locations in Nottinghamshire. Since the dispute started Mr Swatten had been picketing regularly in Nottinghamshire without having previously been arrested. The charge against him was one of threatening behaviour. The solicitor says that the court clerk continued, during his application for unconditional bail, to prepare bail sheets on the basis that the bail granted would be conditional, despite the solicitor's objection.

On this occasion all the defendants were remanded on conditional bail. It has the effect of preventing Mr Swatten from picketing, as he would have wished to do. The picketing which he has witnessed on countless occasions when taking part himself has been, as he described it, 'usually peaceful'. He regards the affidavits sworn on behalf of the police, in so far as they suggest that miners are trying to stop pits working by violence, as 'a complete load of rubbish'.

It is now necessary to consider the statutory background against which the justices reached their decision. That is contained in the Bail Act 1976. Section 1(1) of the Act provides:

'In this Act "bail in criminal proceedings" means—(a) bail grantable in or in connection with proceedings for an offence to a person who is accused or convicted of the offence, or (b) bail grantable in connection with an offence to a person who is under arrest for the offence or for whose arrest for the offence a warrant (endorsed for bail) is being issued.'

Section 3, so far as is material, runs as follows:

'(1) A person granted bail in criminal proceedings shall be under a duty to surrender to custody, and that duty is enforceable in accordance with section 6 of this Act.
(2) No recognizance for his surrender to custody shall be taken from him.
(3) Except as provided by this section—(a) no security for his surrender to custody shall be taken from him, (b) he shall not be required to provide a surety or sureties for his surrender to custody, and (c) no other requirement shall be imposed on him as a condition of bail . . .
(6) He may be required (but only by a court) to comply, before release on bail or later, with such requirements as appear to the court to be necessary to secure that—(a) he surrenders to custody, (b) he does not commit an offence while on bail, (c) he does not interfere with witnesses or otherwise obstruct the course of justice whether in relation to himself or any other person, (d) he makes himself available for the purpose of enabling inquiries or a report to be made to assist the court in dealing with him for the offence . . .'

Section 4, so far as material, provides:

'(1) A person to whom this section applies shall be granted bail except as provided in Schedule 1 to this Act . . .
(5) Schedule 1 to this Act also has effect as respects conditions of bail for a person to whom this section applies . . .'

Paragraph 1 of Pt I of Sch 1 provides as follows:

'Where the offence or one of the offences of which the defendant is accused or convicted in the proceedings is punishable with imprisonment the following provisions of this Part of this Schedule apply.'

Paragraph 2 reads as follows:

'The defendant need not be granted bail if the court is satisfied that there are substantial grounds for believing that the defendant, if released on bail (whether subject to conditions or not) would—(a) fail to surrender to custody, or (b) commit an offence while on bail, or (c) interfere with witnesses or otherwise obstruct the course of justice, whether in relation to himself or any other person.'

Paragraph 8(1) provides as follows:

'Subject to sub-paragraph (3) below, where the defendant is granted bail, no conditions shall be imposed under subsections (4) to (7) of section 3 of this Act unless it appears to the court that it is necessary to do so for the purpose of preventing the occurrence of any of the events mentioned in paragraph 2 of this Part of this Schedule or, in the case of a condition under subsection (6)(d) of that section, that it is necessary to impose it to enable inquiries or a report to be made into the defendant's physical or mental condition.'

Paragraph 9 reads:

'In taking the decisions required by paragraph 2 of this Part of this Schedule, the court shall have regard to such of the following considerations as appear to it to be relevant, that is to say—(a) the nature and seriousness of the offence or default (and the probable method of dealing with the defendant for it), (b) the character, antecedents, associations and community ties of the defendant, (c) the defendant's record as respects the fulfilment of his obligations under previous grants of bail in criminal proceedings, (d) except in the case of a defendant whose case is adjourned for inquiries or a report, the strength of the evidence of his having committed the offence or having defaulted, as well as to any others which appear to be relevant.'

The effect of these provisions is not altogether clear. Counsel for the applicants submits that there should be two stages in the magistrates' process of thought. First they should determine whether there are substantial grounds for believing that an offence will be committed. Second, if so, does it appear to the court to be necessary to impose a condition to prevent such commission? That is to say, if and only if you believe he will commit an offence will it be necessary to impose a condition. Counsel bases that argument on the words of Sch 1, para 8. He suggests that 'the events mentioned in paragraph 2' of the schedule include the words 'if the court is satisfied that there are substantial grounds for believing'.

We do not accept that contention. The magistrates, when the defendant is going to be bailed, are not concerned with para 2 of the schedule, which deals with the refusal of bail. They are concerned with s 3(6) and with para 8(1) of the schedule. The reference to 'any of the events mentioned in paragraph 2' is to sub-paras (a), (b) and (c), namely failure to surrender, commit an offence on bail or interfere with witnesses etc. There is a duplication between para 8 and s 3(6) due to indifferent drafting, but the intention of the legislature emerges as the logical wish to impose less rigorous requirements when a defendant is being admitted to bail than when an unconvicted man is being refused bail altogether.

In the present circumstances the question the magistrates should ask themselves is a simple one: is this condition necessary for the prevention of the commission of an offence by the defendant when on bail? They are not obliged to have substantial grounds. It is enough if they perceive a real and not a fanciful risk of an offence being committed. Thus s 3(6) and para 8 give the court a wide discretion to inquire whether the condition is necessary.

That discretion is only limited by the principles enunciated by Lord Greene MR in *Associated Provincial Picture Houses Ltd v Wednesbury Corp* [1947] 2 All ER 680 at 682–683, [1948] 1 KB 223 at 229:

'It is true the discretion must be exercised reasonably. What does that mean? Lawyers familiar with the phraseology commonly used in relation to the exercise of statutory discretions often use the word "unreasonable" in a rather comprehensive sense. It is frequently used as a general description of the things that must not be done. For instance, a person entrusted with a discretion must direct himself properly in law. He must call his own attention to the matters which he is bound to consider. He must exclude from his consideration matters which are irrelevant to the matter that he has to consider. If he does not obey those rules, he may truly be said, and often is said, to be acting "unreasonably". Similarly, you may have something so absurd that no sensible person could ever dream that it lay within the powers of the authority. WARRINGTON, L.J., I think it was, gave the example of the red-haired teacher, dismissed because she had red hair [see *Short v Poole Corp* [1926] Ch 66 at 90–91, [1925] All ER Rep 74 at 80]. That is unreasonable in one sense. In another sense it is taking into consideration extraneous matters. It is so unreasonable that it might almost be described as being done in bad faith. In fact, all these things largely fall under one head.'

It is conceded that there is no requirement for formal evidence to be given (see *Re Moles* [1981] Crim LR 170). It was for example sufficient for the facts to be related to the magistrates at secondhand by a police officer.

The nub of the problem is how far, if at all, the magistrates were entitled to have regard to what was described by counsel as the matrix of events which brought these defendants before the court. The answer in our judgment is that they were certainly entitled to use their knowledge of events at local collieries during the preceding weeks, because it was only on the basis of that knowledge, inter alia, that they could properly reach a conclusion as to the necessity of imposing a condition. What those events comprised has already been touched on, but there were before us affidavits sworn by certain police officers which gave more detailed information about those local events.

Edward Griffith, Assistant Chief Constable in the Nottinghamshire Constabulary, deposes that from the earliest days of the dispute it was apparent that a determined effort was being made to close the Nottinghamshire coalfield. Large numbers of miners travelled down from South Yorkshire and attempted by weight of numbers to physically block the entrances to pits in the north of the county. Working miners were abused, threatened with violence and expulsion from the union. Large groups of striking miners moved in a concerted fashion from one pit to another following the wind-downs where angry scenes, violence and intimidation were repeated.

Chief Superintendent Holford of the Nottinghamshire Constabulary has this to say:

> 'I have on a number of occasions during the period taken command at the scenes of mass picketing at demonstrations at Mansfield NUM offices, various collieries and power stations within the county. On all of these occasions I have observed at close quarters the tactics and behaviour of the pickets. I have yet to attend a mass picket where violence and intimidation of working miners has not been the sole intention of those present . . . It has been physically impossible to arrest all the persons who have perpetrated criminal acts during mass picketing at collieries in the county.'

Chief Inspector Sheppard sets out a list of some 19 separate instances between March and the end of July 1984. The numbers of pickets or demonstrators at collieries on those occasions vary between some 900 at the lowest and some 19,000 at the highest. He adds that on many occasions numbers of demonstrators at specific pits have exceeded 500, and concludes:

> 'Levels of activity at different locations vary from day to day but it is apparent that specific collieries are designated as a main target and demonstrators are orchestrated to reach that location in large numbers.'

Thus, for months before the magistrates reached their decisions, a bitter dispute had raged and indeed still rages between the NUM and the NCB. We are not concerned with the rights and the wrongs of the unhappy matter, only with the situation which has resulted from it. Some miners are on strike as a result of the dispute. Some miners, however, particularly in the East Midlands area, wished and continue to wish to go to work. Striking miners, and particularly in this case members of the South Yorkshire NUM, not only wished to remain on strike but also wished to persuade the working miners to cease work and come out on strike. This they have endeavoured to achieve by descending on working collieries in the manner described in order to prevent by one means or another the men employed at those collieries from going to work. It is clear from the affidavits, and must have been obvious to the magistrates, that the defendants would, if released unconditionally on bail, have resumed their picketing activities in the East Midlands coalfields at the first opportunity. That much is in effect conceded.

Now there is of course nothing criminal in bodies of men, even large bodies of men, congregating together to carry out lawful activities. What is not lawful is for bodies of men to foregather in order to prevent others who wish to work from working by means of intimidation, by threats of violence or by violence itself. Whatever offences, common law or statutory, may be committed in these cases, there is no need to go beyond the provisions of the Public Order Act 1936, s 5, which reads, so far as material:

> 'Any person who in any public place . . . (a) uses threatening, abusive or insulting words or behaviour . . . whereby a breach of the peace is likely to be occasioned, shall be guilty of an offence . . .'

By the time these defendants appeared in court, it must have been clear to everyone, and to the magistrates in particular, that any suggestion of peaceful picketing was a colourable pretence and that it was a question of picketing by intimidation and threat. It must have been obvious to all those participating in the picketing that their presence in large numbers was part of the intimidation and threats. It must have been clear to them that their presence would, at the least, encourage others to threats and/or violence even if they themselves said nothing.

One of the first requirements of any civilised society is that bullying should not succeed, that mere physical strength or strength of numbers should not be permitted to coerce the weaker or the fewer in number. This requirement is exemplified, inter alia, by the common law offence of assault. An assault is any act by which the defendant intentionally, or recklessly, causes the victim to apprehend immediate unlawful violence. There is no need for it to proceed to physical contact. If it does, it is an assault and a battery. Assault is a crime independent of battery and it is important to remember that fact.

Where large numbers of pickets assemble (as they have been doing in the East Midlands coalfields) with the intention of trying to prevent working miners from going to work by threats of violence and the force of numbers, there is no doubt that each of the picketing miners who is proved to be party to such intimidation (or bullying, if you like) is guilty at least of an offence under s 5 of the 1936 Act.

Against that background, the magistrates, in our judgment, were right to conclude that, if no condition were imposed, offences would be committed by these defendants whilst on bail. They were right to conclude therefore that such a condition was necessary.

We revert to counsel for the applicants' particular complaints. The individual circumstances of each defendant were, for the reasons already stated, not material, save in so far as they showed that unless restrained each defendant would rejoin the mass picketing operation at the first opportunity. The fact that they were men of good character and other personal considerations did not affect the likelihood of their committing public order offences when on bail. There was ample material before the magistrates on which they could reach their conclusion. The magistrates took relevant considerations into account and did not have regard to anything irrelevant.

There is no doubt on the evidence that in 90% or more of the cases before them the magistrates acceded to the submissions of the police that the conditions should be imposed. It is however a far cry from that to saying that the magistrates were not exercising their discretion properly. If they were of the view that the condition was necessary to prevent any defendant from committing crime whilst on bail, they were entitled to impose it. In each case the defendant was alleged to have committed an offence against the public order; in each case he was a striking miner from outside the area; in each case he was, so to speak, a regular picket; in each case the practical certainty was that, unless restrained, he would be back picketing again in the same way almost immediately.

Enough has already been said about the nature of the so-called 'peaceful picketing' to show that it inevitably gave rise to large numbers of public order offences at least. The high proportion of cases where the condition was imposed indicates not the adoption of a policy by the magistrates or a fettering in advance of their discretion so much as the fact that in almost every case the police applied for the condition to be imposed, because the likelihood of the defendant committing an offence if bailed without the condition was very high.

Applying all the foregoing considerations to the individual cases of the applicants, it follows, in our judgment, that the exercise of their discretion by the magistrates cannot be properly criticised in any of the cases except that of Mr Fellows, to whom different considerations apply.

However, before dealing with the case of Mr Fellows, we would like to make these observations. Putting into the dock together defendants who have been arrested on different occasions or at different places makes it difficult to avoid the appearance of 'group justice'. We appreciate that these magistrates faced the uphill task of dealing with literally hundreds of cases over and above their normal list. We sympathise with them in their task. However, whatever pressures a court is subject to, the practice is one to be discouraged. Nor does it do the bench credit if their clerk continues to affix standard conditions to bail forms even while applications are being made for unconditional bail, as happened in some of the instant cases. But the fact that the outcome of the application was correctly anticipated does not vitiate the decision.

We have anxiously considered the case of Mr Fellows. He lives in Sheffield. He is charged with threatening behaviour. The prosecution say that he was one of 400 men who on 28 June 1984 assembled at Rufford colliery and directed abuse at miners as they entered for work. As a car carrying working miners drove past, Mr Fellows is said to have shouted at them, 'Get away you scabbing bastards.' Later he is said to have shouted at another miner as he made his way to work on foot, 'Get away, you scabbing twat.'

After being held in custody overnight he was brought before the court with five other miners who had been arrested at different places in Nottinghamshire. On this occasion the prosecuting officer merely indicated to the court that the six defendants had been arrested as a result of their activities in connection with the dispute and asked for the court to remand them on bail with the usual condition. Mr Fellows's solicitor asked that the police be required to give at least an outline of the allegations against each defendant individually. Counsel for two of the six defendants supported this application.

During the argument the court clerk, as he has admitted on affidavit, referred to what he called 'the analogy of deterrent sentences being imposed on defendants being involved in similar cases and comparing that with similar conditions for bail being imposed in remand cases'. He says that this was 'not stated as categorical advice' to the magistrates, although Mr Fellows's solicitor says that it was expressed in that way. The solicitor repudiated the supposed analogy and asked for a decision on the issue of principle, namely whether the fact that men had been arrested by the police in connection with an industrial dispute was a proper basis for the magistrates to remand on conditional bail without hearing any details of the circumstances surrounding the arrest or of their personal circumstances.

The magistrates retired and on their return remanded all six defendants on conditional bail. Mr Fellows's solicitor did not regard himself as having had the opportunity to address the court on reasons why this should not have been done in relation to his individual clients. But he does not appear to have protested at the time that the opportunity was denied him. If it was, that can only have come about through misunderstanding, because the magistrates believed, and it would appear reasonably believed, that the solicitor had said all that he wished to say. The magistrates imposed a condition on Mr Fellows's bail despite the chairman's assertion on affidavit to this court that in the majority of cases in which he has been concerned he and his colleagues have granted unconditional bail. In the light of that it is difficult to see what consideration was before the magistrates which could have moved them not to do so in Mr Fellows's case.

It is plain that there were, to say the least, unsatisfactory features about this hearing. This is a case where the magistrates have failed to take relevant matters into consideration. Their decision therefore becomes liable to be quashed.

This is, however, plainly a case where we would remit the matter for rehearing under the powers contained in the Supreme Court Act 1981, s 31(5). If the matter were to be reheard, and if the magistrates then took into account all the considerations which they ought in the light of this judgment to take into account, they could not fail to impose the same or a similar condition on any grant of bail. Accordingly, it would be a waste of time to order certiorari and in our discretion we decline so to do. All these applications are accordingly dismissed.

*Applications refused.*

Solicitors: *Seifert Sedley & Co* (for the applicants Sharkey, Hunt and Barron); *Saunders & Co* (for the applicants Fretwell and Robinson); *Brian Thompson & Partners*, Sheffield (for the applicants Swatten, Grove, Fellows and Anderson); *David Ritchie*, Nottingham (for the Nottinghamshire police); *Treasury Solicitor*.

N P Metcalfe Esq    Barrister.

# Kowloon Stock Exchange Ltd v Inland Revenue Commissioner

PRIVY COUNCIL

LORD KEITH OF KINKEL, LORD BRANDON OF OAKBROOK, LORD BRIGHTMAN, LORD TEMPLEMAN
AND SIR ROBIN COOKE

23, 24 JULY, 2 OCTOBER 1984

*Club – Trading association – Stock exchange – Mutual association assisting members to make profits for themselves – Whether stock exchange a club.*

*Income tax – Trade – Trade association – Stock exchange – Stock exchange providing premises for transaction of members' business – Stock exchange's income consisting of founders' contributions, members' entrance fees and monthly subscriptions – Whether stock exchange a club or a trading association – Whether founders' contributions and members' entrance fees qualifying as 'subscriptions' – Inland Revenue Ordinance (Hong Kong), s 24(1)(2)*

The taxpayer was incorporated in Hong Kong in March 1970 as a company limited by guarantee and began operating as a stock exchange in January 1972. The objects of the taxpayer were, inter alia, to furnish premises and other facilities for the transaction of business by its members and to occupy and to take up a role with similar organisations in the financing of Hong Kong industry. Under its articles of association, the management and control of the taxpayer's affairs were vested in a committee of the founder members and ten elected members. The taxpayer was assessed to profits tax in respect of its receipts, which consisted almost entirely of founders' contributions, members' entrance fees and monthly subscriptions. The assessments were made under s 24(2)ᵃ of the Hong Kong Inland Revenue Ordinance on the basis that the taxpayer was a trade association and that neither the founders' contributions nor the members' entrance fees were 'subscriptions'. The taxpayer appealed, contending (i) that it was a club and in the circumstances was deemed by s 24(1) not to carry on a business or, alternatively, (ii) that, if it was a trade association, the entrance fees and founders' contributions ranked as 'subscriptions' and were, as such, exempt from profits tax. The Board of Review rejected the taxpayer's contention and the Hong Kong Court of Appeal upheld their decision. The taxpayer appealed to the Privy Council.

**Held** – The appeal would be dismissed for the following reasons—

(1) No distinction could be drawn between a mutual association whose purpose was to make profits for itself and a mutual association whose purpose was to assist its members to make profits for themselves: neither qualified for the status of a club. The taxpayer existed to aid the profit-making activities of its members, its principal object being to provide a place where its members could carry on their business. Accordingly, it could not properly be described as a club (see p 207 *b*, p 209 *h j* and p 211 *a*, post).

(2) 'Trade' meant not only the buying and selling of goods but also the buying and selling of land and, in an appropriate context, the buying and selling of choses in action. In a stock exchange brokers traded in stocks and shares and were therefore traders. The taxpayer was an association formed by traders to hold and manage premises for the purposes of their trade and was, therefore, a trade association (see p 210 *a b e f* and p 211 *a*, post).

(3) On its true construction the word 'subscriptions' in the Inland Revenue Ordinance was not used in a sense wide enough to include 'entrance fees': the word 'subscriptions' was used in s 24(2) both on its own and in conjunction with the words 'entrance fees', while 'entrance fees' were distinguished from 'subscriptions' in s 24(1). Likewise, since founders' contributions possessed no characteristics which distinguished them from entrance fees, they also did not qualify as subscriptions (see p 210 *g* to *j* and p 211 *a*, post).

---

*a*   Section 24 is set out at p 208 *d* to *f*, post

**Notes**

For the definition of a club, see 6 Halsbury's Laws (4th edn) para 201, and for cases on the subject, see 8(2) Digest (Reissue) 612, 1–8.

For what constitutes trading, see 23 Halsbury's Laws (4th edn) paras 212–225, and for cases on the subject, see 28(1) Digest (Reissue) 24–57, 85–226.

For payments to trade associations, see 23 Halsbury's Laws (4th edn) paras 314–317, and for cases on the subject, see 28(1) Digest (Reissue) 147–148, 451–455.

For trading by clubs, see 23 Halsbury's Laws (4th edn) para 224.

**Cases referred to in judgment**

Fletcher v Income Tax Comr [1971] 3 All ER 1185, [1972] AC 414, [1972] 2 WLR 14, PC.

Ransom (Inspector of Taxes) v Higgs [1974] 3 All ER 949, [1974] 1 WLR 1594, HL.

**Appeal**

Kowloon Stock Exchange Ltd (the taxpayer) appealed against an order of the Court of Appeal of Hong Kong (Leonard V-P, Cons and Barker JJA) dated 13 July 1983 dismissing the taxpayer's appeal against a decision of the Hong Kong Board of Review that the taxpayer was not a club but a trade association and that neither the members' entrance fees nor the founders' contributions ranked as 'subscriptions' within s 24 of the Inland Revenue Ordinance (Hong Kong). The facts are set out in the judgment of the Board.

George Newman QC and Mark Strachan for the taxpayer.
D C Potter QC and H J Somerville (of the Hong Kong bar) for the Inland Revenue Commissioner.

2 October. The following judgment of the Board was delivered.

**LORD BRIGHTMAN.** This appeal from the Court of Appeal of Hong Kong concerns the assessment of profits tax on Kowloon Stock Exchange Ltd (the taxpayer). Three questions are raised by the stated case: whether the taxpayer is a club; if not, whether it is a trade association; if a trade association, whether entrance fees and so-called founders' contributions are properly to be described as subscriptions.

The taxpayer was incorporated under the Companies Ordinance on 10 March 1970 as a company limited by guarantee without a share capital. The objects of the taxpayer are set out in the first seven paragraphs of cl 3 of the memorandum of association, the remaining paragraphs being of the nature of powers exercisable in furtherance of those objects. The objects are as follows:

'(a) To furnish, purchase, take on lease, hire or otherwise acquire, exchange rooms, security market places, meeting places, and other facilities for the convenient transaction of business by stock brokers, share brokers, exchange brokers and brokers in gold and silver and other precious metals, commodities, foreign ex change [sic] and money of all kinds and to obtain licences in that behalf for members where required.

(b) To maintain high standards of commercial honour and integrity among its members and to promote and maintain just and equable principles of trade and business.

(c) To protect the interests of such brokers, and to promote honourable practices.

(d) To record transactions between such brokers and to furnish reliable quotations of the price of shares and stocks, gold and silver and other precious metals, commodities and foreign exchange and money of all kinds.

(e) To occupy and take up a role with similar organisations and associations in the vital delicate and rapidly changing aspect of the Hong Kong economy, the finance of Hong Kong industry and the provision of necessary safeguards of the investors who directly and indirectly entrust their savings to the stock and shares markets.

(f) To act as arbitrators in the settlement of all disputes and differences between member brokers or between member brokers and their clients arising in the course of business and of those between any parties.

(g) To make rules for any of the above purpose [sic] and to make and from time to time alter a scale of charges for brokerage in share and other transactions . . .'

The facts are not extensively set out in the stated case and there is little evidence of the activities of the taxpayer. No doubt the memorandum of association generally reflects what the taxpayer does. There is a finding of fact that the principal object of the taxpayer is to provide a place where its members can carry on their business.

The articles of association of the taxpayer at the relevant time included the following provisions, stated shortly. Article 2: the number of members is limited to 150. Article 3: any person who desires to carry on the business of a stockbroker, or of a broker as described in the memorandum of association, shall subject to there being a vacancy be eligible for membership. Article 4: a candidate for membership must sign an application form. His name is then submitted to a ballot. Three adverse votes are sufficient to exclude him. Article 5: on election and payment of the prescribed subscription and entrance fee, the candidate becomes a member of the taxpayer, and is entitled to the benefit of a seat on the exchange. Article 9: the subscription payable to the taxpayer is a sum not exceeding $500 per month as the committee may from time to time determine. Article 11: the entrance fee is also to be decided by the committee. Article 16: a member who has given notice of resignation may nominate another person for election as a member in his place. Such nominee is not required to pay an entrance fee. Article 17: a similar right is vested in the personal representative of a deceased member. Article 28: the eight subscribers to the memorandum and articles of association, and six others, are expressed to be 'founders of the [taxpayer]'. Article 28 (wherein 'Exchange' means the taxpayer) then provides as follows:

'(b) Each of the Founders shall contribute a sum of not exceeding HK$40,000·00 towards the establishment of the Exchange.

(c) A Founder shall be entitled to nominate a respectable person to be a member of the Exchange and such nominated member shall not be required to pay any Entrance Fee for his admission. In the absence of and until such nomination, a Founder shall be entitled to a seat in the Exchange.

(d) A Founder is a Member of the Exchange and a Member of the Committee for life whether the right of nomination above mentioned shall have been exercised. A Founder who has exercised his aforesaid right of nomination shall not be required to pay any further subscriptions.

(e) The Founders shall be entitled to be paid such remuneration as the Committee shall from time to time decide.

(f) A Founder may nominate a successor who shall be entitled to all the benefits of the Founder. Such nomination must be approved by the Committee and it shall not take effect during the life of the Founder.'

Article 29: the management and control of the taxpayer is vested in the committee, which consists of all the founders and not more than ten other members. Article 33: the members of the committee are entitled to such remuneration as the committee shall from time to time decide. Article 47: the committee have power—

'(b) To make and from time to time alter as they may think fit a scale of charges for brokerage on all transactions for the sale and purchase of stocks, shares, bonds, debentures and other securities and gold and silver and other precious metals, commodities, foreign exchange and money of all kinds.'

Article 52 to 63: these articles deal with general meetings of the taxpayer. There is to be found a clear implication that every member of the taxpayer is entitled to vote at a general meeting.

On 16 November 1971 the taxpayer took a lease of the premises which it intended to use for its activities. On or before 28 December 1971 the taxpayer compiled rules embodying 'Board Trading Rules'. On 5 January 1972 the taxpayer was authorised to begin operations as a stock exchange, and monthly subscriptions began to be payable.

Part IV of the Inland Revenue Ordinance (1971) contains a number of sections under the cross-heading 'Profits Tax'. Section 14 is in the following terms:

> 'Subject to the provisions of this Ordinance, profits tax shall be charged for each year of assessment at the standard rate on every person carrying on a trade, profession or business in the Colony in respect of his assessable profits arising in or derived from the Colony for that year from such trade, profession or business (excluding profits arising from the sale of capital assets) as ascertained in accordance with this Part.'

Section 16 provides that in ascertaining the profits in respect of which a person is chargeable to tax under this part for any year of assessment there shall be deducted all outgoings and expenses to the extent to which they are incurred in the production of profits, with certain specific inclusions. Section 24, on which this appeal hinges, is in the following terms:

> '(1) Where a person carries on a club or similar institution which receives from its members not less than half of its gross receipts on revenue account (including entrance fees and subscriptions), such person shall be deemed not to carry on a business; but where less than half of its gross receipts are received from members, the whole of the income from transactions both with members and others (including entrance fees and subscriptions) shall be deemed to be receipts from a business, and such person shall be chargeable in respect of the profits therefrom.
>
> (2) Where a person carries on a trade association in such circumstances that more than half its receipts by way of subscriptions are from persons who claim or would be entitled to claim that such sums were allowable deductions for the purposes of section 16, such person shall be deemed to carry on a business, and the whole of the income of such association from transactions both with members and others (including entrance fees and subscriptions) shall be deemed to be receipts from business, and such person shall be chargeable in respect of the profits therefrom.
>
> (3) In this section, "members" means those persons entitled to vote at a general meeting of the club, or similar institutions, or trade association.'

In the period which is relevant for the purpose of computing the liability, if any, of the taxpayer to profits tax, the taxpayer received the following moneys from its members:

|  | $ |
|---|---|
| monthly subscriptions | 130,660 |
| other receipts on revenue account | 54,773 |
| total | 185,433 |
| founders' contributions (at $25,000 per founder) | 350,000 |
| members' entrance fees | 5,745,000. |

It is common ground that the monthly subscriptions of $130,660 were paid by persons who were entitled to claim that such sums were allowable deductions for the purposes of s 16; also that founders' contributions and members' entrance fees were not allowable deductions. It follows that, in the context of sub-s (1) of s 24, if applicable, the taxpayer received from its members not less than half of its gross receipts on revenue account, including entrance fees and subscriptions, whatever might be the true status of founders' contributions; so that, if the association is a club, it would be deemed *not* to carry on a business and that, in the context of sub-s (2), if applicable, more than half its receipts by way of subscriptions were allowable deductions, unless founders' contributions or entrance fees, or both, had the status of 'subscriptions'; so that, if a trade association, it *would* be deemed to carry on a business unless either of these payments were subscriptions.

On 6 September 1973 the taxpayer was assessed to profits tax on the basis that it was not a club but was a trade association and that neither founders' contributions nor entrance fees were subscriptions. The taxpayer appealed to the Board of Review against the determination of the Inland Revenue Commissioner. The board decided that the taxpayer carried on a trade and was therefore a trade association and that founders' contributions and entrance fees were not subscriptions, with the result that sub-s (2) of s 24 applied and that the taxpayer had not established a claim to exemption based on the fact that it was a 'club or similar institution' within the meaning of sub-s (1).

On 22 October 1980 the Board of Review stated the following questions of law for the opinion of the High Court, but with leave under s 69A of the ordinance (1981) the taxpayer appealed directly to the Court of Appeal against the board's decision: (i) whether, on a proper construction of the provisions of s 24(2), having regard to the evidence adduced before the Board of Review, the taxpayer could be said to have been carrying on a trade association; (ii) whether the words 'receipts by way of subscriptions' in s 24(2) excluded the sums subscribed by members by way of founders' contributions and entrance fees; and (iii) whether, on a proper construction of the provisions of s 24(1), having regard to the evidence adduced before the Board of Review, the taxpayer was carrying on a 'club or similar institution'.

The judgment of the court, delivered by Cons JA on 13 July 1983, decided, first, that the taxpayer was not carrying on a club or similar institution but, second, that the taxpayer was carrying on a trade association and, third, that neither entrance fees nor founders' contributions ranked with the monthly subscriptions as 'subscriptions', with the consequence that more than half (in fact the whole of) its receipts by way of subscriptions were from persons who could claim such sums as allowable deductions and therefore the taxpayer was caught by sub-s (2).

Their Lordships will address themselves, first, to the claim that the taxpayer 'carries on a club or similar institution'. The Court of Appeal denied the taxpayer the status of a club because it was the common understanding, supported by a number of authorities, that a club was an association formed for other than business purposes. It was of crucial importance that the association should not exist for the financial advantage of its members (except merely as incidental to the general purpose) and a predominant intention to benefit members financially was by itself sufficient to prevent an association ranking as a club.

In *Fletcher v Income Tax Comr* [1971] 3 All ER 1185 at 1190, [1972] AC 414 at 422 the Board accepted that a voluntary association of persons who agree, under their own committee of management, to maintain an establishment for their common personal benefit and not for profit, and to defray the expenses thereof by contributions of amounts sufficient for that purpose could properly be described as a club. It was the taxpayer's contention that it fulfilled all these conditions. It did not operate for profit. It was not a purpose of the taxpayer to make a profit for itself. The 'personal benefit of members' could include the assistance of members in the advancement of their own business interests. The fact that the taxpayer helped its members to make profits for themselves was immaterial to the status of the taxpayer as a club or similar institution.

Their Lordships are in agreement with the Court of Appeal that the taxpayer cannot properly be described as a club for the reason which they gave, namely that the taxpayer exists to aid the profit-making activities of its members. As found by the Board of Review its principal object is to provide a place where its members can carry on their business. There is no justification for drawing a distinction between a mutual association the purpose of which is to make profits for itself and a mutual association the purpose of which is to assist members to make profits for themselves and while denying the status of a club to the former to accord such status to the latter. Their Lordships therefore answer the third question in the negative.

Their Lordships turn to the first question, whether the taxpayer 'carries on a trade association'. This is not an expression defined in the ordinance, nor is 'trade' defined in an adjectival sense. In a substantive sense it is defined by s 2 as including 'every trade and manufacture, and every adventure and concern in the nature of trade'. Part IV of the ordinance makes liberal use of the threefold expression 'trade, profession or business', and sometimes of 'trade or business' alone, but in the opinion of their Lordships these uses throw no light on the meaning to be given to the composite expression 'trade association'.

The word 'trade' is no doubt capable of bearing a variety of meanings according to the context in which it is used. In its most restricted sense it means the buying and selling of goods; in a slightly wider sense, it includes the buying and selling of land; there is no reason to exclude, in an appropriate context, the buying and selling of choses in action. It is commonly used '. . . to denote operations of a commercial character by which the trader provides to customers for reward some kind of goods or services' (see *Ransom (Inspector of Taxes) v Higgs* [1974] 3 All ER 949 at 955, [1974] 1 WLR 1594 at 1600).

The taxpayer advanced the following argument against its classification as a trade association. It is apparent from the wording of the ordinance that a distinction is to be drawn between a trade on the one hand and a profession or business on the other hand. The taxpayer answers more naturally to the title of a professional or business association than to the title of a trade association. The word 'trade' in the context of s 24(2) should be restricted to the buying and selling of goods. Although a stockbroker is engaged in the buying and selling of shares, he does so only as an agent for his clients. He does not buy or sell on his own account. Furthermore, his involvement in buying and selling shares is only one of the functions which he performs for his clients. Of equal importance is his role as a person exercising specialist professional skills in giving advice to his clients. For these reasons stockbrokers are properly to be regarded as carrying on a business or a profession rather than carrying on a trade, and the taxpayer is therefore a business or professional association and not a trade association.

The Court of Appeal rejected these submissions, rightly in the opinion of their Lordships. A stock exchange is unquestionably a market. It is frequently so described. The expression 'stock market' is in common use. Stocks and shares are traded in that market. The trading in that market is done by brokers, who are therefore traders. An association which is formed by traders to hold and manage premises for the purposes of their trade is a trade association. Their Lordships answer the first question in the affirmative.

The final question is whether either or both the entrance fees ($5,745,000) and founders' contributions ($350,000), neither of which are tax deductible, can be grouped with the monthly subscriptions ($130,660), which are tax deductible, so as to raise the non-deductible proportion of the 'receipts by way of subscriptions' above the halfway level.

It is not arguable that the legislature used the word 'subscription' in a sense wide enough to include 'entrance fee'. The word 'subscriptions' is used on its own in the opening words of s 24(2). In the later part of the subsection it is used in conjunction with 'entrance fees' as a separate and distinct ingredient of 'the whole of the income of such association from transactions'. It is also distinguished from 'subscriptions' in sub-s (1). It inevitably follows that 'subscriptions' does not include 'entrance fees', by virtue of the dictionary which the section itself provides.

'Founders' contributions' are a similar case. They, like entrance fees, are once-for-all payments. They lack the recurrent quality of 'subscriptions'. If, as is clear beyond argument, the subsection uses the word 'subscriptions' in a sense which excludes entrance fees, it must logically follow that 'founders' contributions' are also excluded. A 'founders' contribution' entitles the founder to a seat on the exchange. It bears all the hallmarks of an entrance fee, with certain additional characteristics: it is paid by only 14 named founders; it confers certain rights of nomination and a seat on the committee; it is expressed as a contribution towards the establishment of the taxpayer and it exempts the founder from the payment of monthly subscriptions. None of these special characteristics which distinguish a founders' contribution from an entrance fee are apt to detach it from its affinity to an entrance fee and to qualify it as a subscription. For these and similar reasons stated in the judgment of the Court of Appeal their Lordships answer the second question in the affirmative.

Their Lordships will humbly advise Her Majesty that this appeal should be dismissed. The appellant must pay the costs.

*Appeal dismissed.*

Solicitors: *Philip Conway Thomas & Co* (for the taxpayer); *Macfarlanes* (for the Inland Revenue Commissioner).

Clare Mainprice    Barrister.

# Clarke and others v Chadburn and others

CHANCERY DIVISION
SIR ROBERT MEGARRY V-C
10, 17, 18 JULY 1984

*Injunction – Breach of injunction – Effect of breach – Wilful disobedience or disregard of injunction – Resolution changing union rules passed in defiance of injunction – Effect on rules – Whether resolution and changes in rules illegal and invalid.*

*Declaration – Jurisdiction – Interlocutory proceedings – Final declaration affecting party's rights – Whether court having jurisdiction to make final declaration in interlocutory proceedings – When jurisdiction will be exercised.*

Officials of a trade union intended to propose at a conference of the union that the union's rules be altered by inserting in the rules wide-ranging disciplinary powers over members of the union. On the day before the conference the plaintiffs, who were members of the union opposed to the rule changes, applied ex parte for an order restraining the defendants, namely the president and secretary of the union and the union itself, from putting, proposing, allowing to be put or proposed, voting on or passing at the conference any resolution proposing an alteration to the union's rules. The court granted the order but gave the defendants liberty to apply to discharge or vary it. Without doing so, and in disregard of the order, the defendants put to the vote at the conference resolutions proposing alterations to the union's rules which gave the union extra disciplinary powers over its members. The resolutions were carried by the two-thirds majority required to effect a change in the rules. The plaintiffs applied for a declaration that the resolutions were void and not binding on the plaintiffs and an injunction restraining the defendants from enforcing the disciplinary powers contained in the resolutions.

**Held** – (1) An act done in wilful disobedience of an injunction or court order was not only a contempt of court but also an illegal and invalid act which could not, therefore, effect any change in the rights and liabilities of others. It followed that the resolutions passed at the union conference purporting to alter the union's rules in disregard of the court order were void for illegality (see p 213 *h* to p 214 *a*, post).

(2) The court had jurisdiction in interlocutory proceedings to make a final, and not merely an interim, declaration affecting the rights of a party, but that jurisdiction would only be exercised sparingly and infrequently. Since the plaintiffs' motion raised an issue which was a matter of public concern affecting the rights of members of the union, the court was justified in making a final declaration in the terms sought by the motion. Furthermore, because it was unlikely that the defendants would observe the terms of the declaration the court would also grant the plaintiffs an injunction restraining the defendants from acting on the powers contained in the altered rules (see p 214 *b* to *j*, post); dictum of Upjohn LJ *International General Electric Co of New York Ltd v Customs and Excise Comrs* [1962] 2 All ER at 400 applied.

Per curiam. Where neither the litigant nor the Attorney General seeks to enforce an order of the court which is not performed, the court will act of its own volition to punish the contempt only in exceptional cases of clear contempt where it is urgent and imperative for the court to act immediately (see p 215 c d, post).

**Notes**
For disobedience to a court order, see 9 Halsbury's Laws (4th edn) para 52.

**Cases referred to in judgment**
*International General Electric Co of New York Ltd v Customs and Excise Comrs* [1962] 2 All ER 398, [1962] Ch 784, [1962] 3 WLR 20, CA.
*Balogh v Crown Court at St Albans* [1974] 3 All ER 283, [1975] QB 73, [1974] 3 WLR 314, CA.

**Motion**
By a notice of motion dated 12 July 1984 the plaintiffs, Colin Patrick Clarke, John Bonser, George Liddel, Arthur Lyons, Eric Flint, Albert Gallent, Jim Else, John Allsop, Albert Tanswell, David Betts, Keith Harrison, Stuart Davis, Dennis Langley, Alan Bingham, John Allen, Ron Bradley and Trevor Marlow, members of the National Union of Mineworkers (Nottingham area) sought certain relief as against the defendants, Raymond Chadburn, T Henry Richardson, Arthur Scargill (the president of the National Union of Mineworkers (the NUM)), Peter Heathfield (the secretary of the NUM) and the NUM itself which included, as against the last three named defendants, the following relief, namely a declaration that each and every resolution of the conference of delegates of the NUM purported to have been passed at the conference held on 11 and 12 July 1984 and which would, if valid, have the effect of altering the NUM's rules in disobedience to the order of Sir Robert Megarry V-C made on 10 July 1984 be declared void and of no effect and not binding on the plaintiffs or any of them and (2) an injunction restraining the last three defendants and each of them by themselves their servants or agents or otherwise howsoever from seeking to enforce or otherwise act on any purported rule as altered or new rule so declared to be void and of no effect. The facts are set out in the judgment.

*Michael Burton QC* and *Richard Slowe* for the plaintiffs.
The defendants did not appear.

**SIR ROBERT MEGARRY V-C.** This is a motion. The plaintiffs are 17 members of the National Union of Mineworkers (Nottingham Area); I shall call this the 'Nottingham union'. The defendants are the president and secretary of the Nottingham union, the president and secretary of the National Union of Mineworkers, and the National Union of Mineworkers itself; I shall call this the 'NUM'. Counsel appeared for the plaintiffs. The defendants are not represented, though they have been duly served with the notice of motion and it is therefore an inter partes motion.

Under the notice of motion, dated 12 July 1984, relief is claimed under five heads. Counsel for the plaintiffs moves only under paras 4 and 5, and then only against the third, fourth and fifth defendants, namely the president and secretary of the NUM and the NUM itself. Putting it shortly, what he seeks is, first, a declaration that every resolution of the NUM conference held on 11 and 12 July 1984 which purported to alter the rules of the NUM in contravention of an order of this court made on 10 July 1984 is void and of no effect, and does not bind any of the plaintiffs. Second, he moves for an injunction against the third, fourth and fifth defendants, restraining them from seeking to enforce or otherwise act on any rule so declared to be void. The first and second defendants, I should say, were notified that no relief against them would be sought on this motion.

The order of the court in question was the second order that I made on 10 July 1984. In the morning, on an ex parte application by the present plaintiffs, I made an order designed to ensure that a meeting of the area council of the Nottingham union should be held in time for the delegate to an extraordinary annual conference of the NUM that was to be held the next day to be mandated by the area council as to how they should vote on proposed changes to the rules of the NUM that were to be considered at that conference. A day or two earlier a forcible occupation of the Nottingham union premises had prevented the area council from meeting. There was a residuary provision in the order requiring the second defendant to cast the votes of the Nottingham union against the proposed changes in the rules if the meeting of the area council was not held in time, since the plaintiffs constitute the majority of that area council, and they, and others, opposed the changes in rules. The main change that was proposed was the insertion of wide-ranging disciplinary powers into the NUM rules.

In the evening of 10 July 1984 a further ex parte application was made by the plaintiffs. No meeting of the area council had been held, but there were grounds for fearing that the order requiring the second defendant to vote against the rule changes would not be obeyed. As a result, an ex parte order was made restraining the third, fourth and fifth defendants from 'putting proposing allowing to be put or proposed or discussed or voted upon or passing' at any conference (including the impending extraordinary annual conference) any resolution proposing an alteration to the NUM rules. The order gave the defendants liberty to apply to discharge or vary the order on giving the plaintiffs notice of their intention to do so, no length of notice being required; and the liberty to apply was expressly made applicable if the Nottingham union meeting was held and enabled the delegates of that union to be mandated as to their votes at the conference.

It is plain that the third, fourth and fifth defendants (who, for brevity, I shall now simply call 'the defendants') had due notice of the order, and equally plain that they nevertheless decided to hold the meeting and proceed to a vote. In the event, the second defendant complied with the order made in the morning and voted against the change in the rules; but the resolution was carried by, as it now appears, 162 votes to 66, thus attaining the two-thirds majority required for a change in the rules. The purpose of the morning order having been achieved, it seems at least probable that prompt application for the discharge of the evening order would have succeeded, though counsel for the plaintiffs said that this would have been opposed on the ground that there were other irregularities or illegalities affecting the voting strength. I need not go into these allegations, as counsel for the plaintiffs does not seek to rely on them on this application. What he does contend is that a resolution passed in defiance of an order of the court is illegal and void, and ought so to be declared.

The point seems to be wholly devoid of any direct authority. Counsel for the plaintiffs could cite none, and although I took a little time to consider the matter, I could find none. Counsel for the plaintiffs says that the change of rules altered the contract between the NUM and the plaintiffs, and an alteration of a contract, like the making of a contract, is liable to be invalidated by illegality; and to do something in breach of an order of the court must inevitably be illegal. Counsel for the plaintiffs cited various authorities on illegality as affecting contracts, but I did not find them of much help. I have to consider the point as a matter of principle.

I need not cite authority for the proposition that it is of high importance that orders of the court should be obeyed. Wilful disobedience to an order of the court is punishable as a contempt of court, and I feel no doubt that such disobedience may properly be described as being illegal. If by such disobedience the persons enjoined claim that they have validly effected some change in the rights and liabilities of others, I cannot see why it should be said that although they are liable to penalties for contempt of court for doing what they did, nevertheless those acts were validly done. Of course, if an act is done, it is not undone merely by pointing out that it was done in breach of the law. If a meeting is held in breach of an injunction, it cannot be said that the meeting has not been held. But the legal consequences of what has been done in breach of the law may plainly be very much affected by the illegality. It seems to me on principle that those who defy a prohibition ought not to be able to claim that the fruits of their defiance are good, and not tainted by the illegality that produced them. Accordingly, I think that in their essentials the contentions of counsel for the plaintiffs are right, and the resolutions of the NUM changing their rules at their conference held on 11 and 12 July last are void for illegality. Even if the defendants thought that the injunction was improperly obtained or too wide in its terms, that provides no excuse for disobeying it; the remedy is to apply to vary or discharge it (see, e g, 9 Halsbury's Laws (4th edn) para 55).

The question, then, is whether the court can properly make the declaration sought by the plaintiffs on this motion. Counsel for the plaintiffs was not satisfied with an injunction against enforcing the new rule about discipline because that would require application to the court to enforce it, whereas a declaration did not. One difficulty is that in modern practice there appears to be no such thing as an interim declaration: but counsel for the plaintiffs said that what he wanted was a final declaration, and not an interim declaration. For this, he relied on *International General Electric Co of New York Ltd v Customs and Excise Comrs* [1962] 2 All ER 398, [1962] Ch 784. There, Upjohn LJ, with the concurrence of Diplock LJ, rejected the concept of an interim declaration, but envisaged the possibility that in certain cases it might be proper to make a declaration of rights in interlocutory proceedings, though this jurisdiction would be infrequently and sparingly exercised. Such a declaration would finally determine the point, and would not operate only as a declaration for the interim. This statement, I think, was plainly made obiter. Even if one accepts to the full that it correctly states the law, as I do, there is still the question whether the case before me is one which justifies me in exercising this jurisdiction. I also bear in mind that although this motion is inter partes, all five defendants have chosen to be absent and unrepresented, the first and second for good reason, and so I have been deprived of the advantage of hearing what could be said on the other side.

After some hesitation I have come to the conclusion that the circumstances of this case are such that I ought to make the declaration sought. I need not expand on the bitter divisions that now exist in the coal mining industry, on the acts of violence that are common knowledge, or on the attempts made by the majority to intimidate the minority and to prevent them voting. If the NUM chooses to conduct itself fairly and properly in accordance with its own rules, then of course the proposed changes in the rules could be made and would be upheld by the courts. But as long as it disregards its own rules and the democratic process for which the rules provide, it must not be surprised if it finds that any changes of rules made by these means are struck with invalidity. Membership of a union is a matter of high importance to very large numbers of working men and women, and the hurried imposition of a disciplinary process that may affect the rights of membership is something that must be scrutinised with care. What is at issue in this motion is a matter of such public concern to so many people that it seems to me to fall within the category of infrequent cases in which the sparing exercise of this jurisdiction is fully justified. If the defendants had wished to contend to the contrary, they could have attended or asked for an adjournment. I shall therefore make the declaration sought: the precise wording is for consideration. I propose to consider whether it should be confined to the new disciplinary rule, r 51. I would only add that it may be no bad thing if to the recognised remedies available for breach of an order of the court there comes to be added a power to declare invalid acts done contrary to the order. Of course, it may prove to be expensive to hold meetings which produce no valid results; but in time the defendants may learn that to adopt a policy of ignoring the courts and their orders may result in the waste of much of their money, if nothing more.

The injunction is primarily claimed as being ancillary to the declaration. In many cases in which declarations are granted, there is a justifiable expectation that the declaration will be honoured and observed. There is no such expectation here, and so it seems to me right to reinforce the declaration by restraining the defendants from acting on a rule that has been declared to be void. Subject to any question that there may be on the wording, I shall grant the injunction as prayed, to run until judgment at the trial or further order. I should make it plain that even if I had not made the declaration I would have granted the injunction on the simple ground that the defendants ought to be restrained from acting on amendments to the NUM rules which in my judgment are void.

I should add this. Counsel for the plaintiffs made it explicit that he was not seeking to have any penalty imposed on any of the five defendants in respect of disobedience to any of the orders made on 10 July, even though he was founding the present application on a plain breach of one of those orders. Not surprisingly, there has been some comment on the inactivity of the courts in cases where an order of the court is being openly flouted and contemned. There are some who ask why the courts stand by and do nothing.

It is perhaps not generally realised that where the party who has obtained an order from the court is content that it should not be performed, the court, generally speaking, has no interest in interfering so as to enforce what the litigant does not want enforced. The order is made so as to assist the litigant in obtaining his rights, and he may consult his own interests in deciding whether or not to enforce it. If he decides not to, there may in some cases be a public element involved, and the Attorney General will judge whether the public interest requires him to intervene in order to enforce the order. If neither the litigant nor the Attorney General seeks to enforce the order, the court will act of its own volition in punishing the contempt only in exceptional cases of clear contempts which cannot wait to be dealt with, cases in which, in the words of Lord Denning MR, 'it is urgent and imperative to act immediately' (see *Balogh v Crown Court at St Albans* [1974] 3 All ER 283 at 288, [1975] QB 73 at 85, where, however, the facts were very different). The present case, I may say, does not seem to me to fall into this category. I should add that I speak only of disobedience to orders, and not, for example, of contempts committed in the face of the court.

Whether this is a satisfactory state of the law is a matter of debate. In cases where (as in this case) there are political overtones, if not more, there are obvious difficulties in requiring it to be the Attorney General who determines whether the public interest requires him to intervene; for however strictly unpolitical a mind he brings to the decision, the opportunities for misrepresentation are almost unlimited. There seems to me to be a clear case for considering whether there should be some relaxation by the courts of their present restraint on themselves in enforcing their orders in cases where these are being openly flouted and the administration of justice is being brought into disrespect. For the courts to say, as they often say, that 'Orders of the court must be obeyed', becomes idle if there are daily instances of open and notorious disobedience remaining unpunished. If the courts became more ready to enforce orders of their own motion, no doubt consideration should be given to the machinery by which this might be done. But I have to apply the law as it stands.

I would add this. A variety of critical and abusive comments, many of them made with considerable publicity, have come to my attention. I need only say that most of these are too stupid to deserve comment; but if the public interest is thought to require that any of them should be the subject of proceedings, whether for contempt or otherwise, I am well content to leave the matter to the Attorney General. For my part I have been little affected by any such comments, apart from feeling a somewhat mild curiosity about what will be said next.

*Declaration and injunction accordingly.*

Solicitors: *Ellis-Fermor*, Ripley (for the plaintiffs).

Vivian Horvath    Barrister.

# W A Sherratt Ltd v John Bromley (Church Stretton) Ltd

COURT OF APPEAL, CIVIL DIVISION

SIR JOHN DONALDSON MR, OLIVER AND ROBERT GOFF LJJ

19, 22 OCTOBER, 2 NOVEMBER 1984

*Practice — Payment into court — Withdrawal of payment in — Discretion of court to allow withdrawal — Circumstances in which discretion exercisable — Change in circumstances — Defendant company paying in sum representing difference between plaintiffs' claim and company's counterclaim — Receiver of company subsequently appointed and company later going into liquidation — Whether plaintiffs secured creditors to extent of payment in — Whether company's insolvency a change of circumstance justifying withdrawal of payment in — RSC Ord 22, r 1(3).*

The plaintiffs began an action against the defendant company claiming some £36,000. The company counterclaimed, and paid into court £13,000 in satisfaction of the plaintiffs' claim after taking into account the counterclaim. Subsequently a receiver was appointed under the terms of a debenture created by the company in favour of a third party, and the company later went into liquidation with an estimated large deficiency regarding unsecured creditors. The company applied under RSC Ord 22, r 1(3)[a] for leave to withdraw the moneys paid into court on the grounds, inter alia, that as a result of the insolvency the plaintiffs would, in respect of the moneys held in court, be accorded an unfair preference over other unsecured creditors. The plaintiffs cross-applied for the moneys in court to be paid out to them. The district registrar dismissed the company's claim. The company appealed to the judge in chambers, who held that the insolvency was a sufficient change in the circumstances of the company because the payment into court to justify granting it leave to withdraw the moneys, since otherwise the plaintiffs would be unfairly promoted from the status of unsecured creditors. The plaintiffs appealed.

**Held** — (1) Since there were conflicting decisions of the Court of Appeal concerning whether a plaintiff was a secured or an unsecured creditor in regard to moneys paid into court in satisfaction of his claim, the court was required to choose, in accordance with established guidelines, which authority it would follow. Since the previous rules of court regarding the court's power to order payment out did not differ materially from the rules currently in force there was nothing to displace the long line of authority which clearly established that a plaintiff was a secured creditor to the extent of moneys paid into court (see p 225 c d, p 226 e to g and j, p 227 d g, p 228 c e and p 229 c to f and j, post); *Re Gordon, ex p Navalchand* [1897] 2 QB 576, *Dessau v Rowley* [1916] WN 238 and *Young v Bristol Aeroplane Co Ltd* [1944] 2 All ER 293 applied; *Peal Furniture Co Ltd v Adrian Share (Interiors) Ltd* [1977] 2 All ER 211 disapproved.

(2) In exercising its discretion to allow a defendant to withdraw a payment into court made by him, the court had to consider whether there had been a sufficient change of circumstances since the payment in to justify granting him leave to do so. Since the plaintiffs' position was that of secured creditors, the company's supervening insolvency did not of itself constitute a change in the circumstances of the company following the payment in. Accordingly, the court would not grant the company leave to withdraw the money paid in. The appeal would therefore be allowed and the order of the district registrar restored (see p 222 e, p 228 c to e and p 229 b to e and j, post); dictum of Goddard LJ in *Cumper v Pothecary* [1941] 2 All ER at 522 applied.

---

*a*   Rule 1(3) provides: 'A defendant may, with leave, give notice of an increase in a payment made under this Rule but, subject to that and without prejudice to paragraph (5) a notice of payment may not be withdrawn or amended without leave of the Court which may be granted on such terms as may be just.'

**Notes**

For payment into and out of court, see 37 Halsbury's Laws (4th edn) para 285, and for cases on the subject, see 37(2) Digest (Reissue) 422–428, 2584–2613.

For the position of secured creditors generally, see 3 Halsbury's Laws (4th edn) paras 318, 785–793, and for cases on the subject, see 4 Digest (Reissue) 392–404, 3499–3576.

For conflicting decisions of the Court of Appeal, see 26 Halsbury's Laws (4th edn) para 578, and for cases on the subject, see 30 Digest (Reissue) 270–273, 772–793.

**Cases referred to in judgments**

Brown v Feeny [1906] 1 KB 563, CA.
Colyer v Selby (1840) cited in Archbold's Practice of the Queen's Bench (9th edn, 1856) Vol 2, p 1282.
Cumper v Pothecary [1941] 2 All ER 516, [1941] 2 KB 58, CA.
Davies v Rustproof Metal Window Co Ltd [1943] 1 All ER 248, [1943] 1 KB 299, CA.
Debtor (No 5 of 1932), Re a, ex p the petitioning creditors (1932) 101 LJ Ch 372, DC.
Dessau v Rowley [1916] WN 238, CA.
Evans v Philippides (1963) 107 SJ 632.
Ford, Re, ex p the trustee [1900] 2 QB 211.
Frazer & Haws Ltd v Burns (1934) 49 Ll L Rep 216, CA.
Gordon, Re, ex p Navalchand [1897] 2 QB 516.
Keyworth, Re, ex p Banner (1874) LR 9 Ch App 379, CA.
Maple v Earl of Shrewsbury and Talbot (1887) 19 QBD 463, CA.
Maxwell v Viscount Wolseley [1907] 1 KB 274, CA.
Miliangos v George Frank (Textiles) Ltd [1975] 3 All ER 801, [1976] AC 443, [1975] 3 WLR 758, HL.
Moojen, Re, ex p Bouchard (1879) 12 Ch D 26, CA.
Peal Furniture Co Ltd v Adrian Share (Interiors) Ltd [1977] 2 All ER 211, [1977] 1 WLR 464, CA.
Powell v Vickers Sons & Maxim Ltd [1907] 1 KB 71, [1904–7] All ER Rep 390, CA.
Spurr v Hall (1877) 2 QBD 615.
Williams v Boag [1940] 4 All ER 246, [1941] 1 KB 1, CA.
Young v Bristol Aeroplane Co Ltd [1944] 2 All ER 293, [1944] KB 718, CA; affd [1946] 1 All ER 98, [1946] AC 163, HL.

**Cases also cited**

Garner v Cleggs [1983] 2 All ER 398, [1983] 1 WLR 862, CA.
Schroeder v Accountant General [1980] 2 All ER 648, [1980] 1 WLR 1314.

**Interlocutory appeal**

The plaintiffs, W A Sherratt Ltd, appealed with leave from the order of Hutchison J made in chambers at Birmingham on 18 April 1984 whereby he allowed an appeal by the defendants, John Bromley (Church Stretton) Ltd, from an order dated 4 November 1983 made by Mr District Registrar Freeman at the Shrewsbury District Registry refusing the defendants leave to withdraw the sum of £13,000 paid into court by them on 29 October 1981. The facts are set out in the judgment of Oliver LJ.

*David Ritchie* for the plaintiffs.
*Richard Adkins* for the defendants.

*Cur adv vult*

2 November. The following judgments were delivered.

**OLIVER LJ** (giving the first judgment at the invitation of Sir John Donaldson MR). This is an appeal from an order of Hutchison J made on 18 April 1984 by which he reversed a decision of the district registrar refusing the defendants' application for payment out to them of a sum of £13,000 in court and adjourning the plaintiffs' application to accept that sum out of time in satisfaction of their claim.

The relevant facts can be very briefly stated. The plaintiffs (the present appellants) commenced an action against the defendants on 21 September 1981 claiming some £36,000 as due to them under the terms of an agreement under which certain business assets were sold to the defendants. They sought a judgment under RSC Ord 14 but were met by an affidavit which exhibited a defence and counter-claim said to overtop the claim. Shortly after this affidavit was sworn the defendants paid into court a sum of £13,000 stated in the notice of payment in to be in satisfaction of the plaintiffs' claim after taking into account the counterclaim. The plaintiffs did not proceed with their Ord 14 summons, but, equally, they did not accept the payment in. The action accordingly proceeded and, no doubt, further costs were incurred by the plaintiffs in the comfortable knowledge that there was a substantial sum in court.

The defendants had, in July 1981, created a debenture in favour of the Midland Bank and in February 1983 a Mr Dawes, of Touche Ross & Co, was appointed to be the receiver and manager of the defendants' business under the terms of that document. On 12 April 1983 the defendants went into liquidation with an estimated deficiency as regards unsecured creditors of over £370,000. In June 1983 the defendants applied to the court for payment out to themselves of the moneys in court, the affidavit in support specifying two grounds, namely that the defendants were heavily insolvent so that if the money in court were paid out to the plaintiffs it would give them a preference over the general body of unsecured creditors and that the amount of the counterclaim had increased so as to render the moneys in court excessive. That application was met by a cross-application by the plaintiffs for the money in court to be paid out to them. The defendants' claim having failed before the district registrar, they appealed to the judge in chambers and at the hearing before Hutchison J it was conceded on their behalf for the purposes of the argument that the plaintiffs had a good prospect of obtaining judgment in the proceedings for at least £13,000, taking into account any valid counterclaim. Thus the only question before the judge was whether the defendants' insolvency and the alleged preference which would be accorded to the plaintiffs if the money in court were paid out to them constituted a sufficient ground for reversing the decision of the district registrar.

In a careful judgment in which he extensively reviewed the relevant authorities, the judge concluded that it did. Adopting what was said in this court by Roskill LJ in *Peal Furniture Co Ltd v Adrian Share (Interiors) Ltd* [1977] 2 All ER 211 at 215–216, [1977] 1 WLR 464 at 468, he held that the court had, under the provisions of RSC Ord 22, r 1(3), a complete discretion to allow payment out to be made to a defendant, and continued:

> 'Approaching the matter in this way, and making full allowance for the fact that the plaintiffs' claim is to be regarded for present purposes as being an extremely strong one, it nevertheless seems to me that I ought to give very great weight to the desirability of allowing the rules of insolvency to determine the destiny of the debtor's assets. I think that comparatively little weight should be given to the strength of the plaintiffs' claim because many unsecured creditors have undisputed claims. Why should the plaintiffs, merely because they have begun an action in which money has been paid into court, be regarded in a different light from a plaintiff who has not taken that course but, nevertheless, has an undisputed claim? In the end, there is no escape from the conclusion that if I were to refuse the defendants' application I should, effectively, be promoting the plaintiffs from the status of an unsecured to the status of a secured creditor.'

Accordingly he allowed the appeal and ordered that the sum of £13,000 be paid out to the defendants. From that the plaintiffs now appeal to this court.

Counsel's primary submission on behalf of the plaintiffs is that in describing the plaintiffs as unsecured creditors the judge misdirected himself in law and that this, accordingly, vitiates the exercise of his discretion on well-accepted principles. Counsel has drawn the court's attention to a number of authorities which support the proposition that where a defendant pays money into court in satisfaction of the plaintiff's claim, the plaintiff, albeit he has not taken the money out, is nevertheless treated as a secured creditor to the extent of the moneys in court in the ensuing bankruptcy of the defendant. The proposition, which is stated as still being the law in *Williams and Muir Hunter on*

*Bankruptcy* (19th edn, 1979) pp 54, 77 and in 3 Halsbury's Laws (4th edn) para 318, is based on a line of cases starting with *Re Gordon, ex p Navalchand* [1897] 2 QB 516. That was a case in which, the defendant having been adjudicated bankrupt and his trustees having refused to agree to payment out to the plaintiff of the moneys in court, the plaintiff moved in the Bankruptcy Court for a declaration of his entitlement and for liberty to prove in the bankruptcy for the balance of his debt over and above the sum in court. Vaughan Williams J said (at 519–520):

> '. . . I am clearly of opinion that if the proof is admitted, or to the extent to which it is admitted, the plaintiff is a secured creditor by reason of the payment into court. The money paid into court, even with a plea denying liability, has become subject to the plaintiff's claim by the act of the defendant, who thereby agrees that the sum paid in shall remain in court subject to the conditions of Order XXII., r. 6.'

To the same effect is *Re Ford, ex p the trustee* [1900] 2 QB 211. That was in fact not a case of a voluntary payment in, but of a payment under order of the court under Ord 14 as a condition of leave to defend. Wright J observed (at 213):

> '. . . it is settled that where money is ordered to be paid into court to abide the event it must be treated as a security that the plaintiff shall not lose the benefit of the decision of the Court in his favour . . . The very object of such an order is that the plaintiff shall be in as good a position, so far as the money paid in extends, against contingencies such as bankruptcy as if he had got an immediate judgment . . .'

A somewhat similar point, though in very unusual circumstances, arose in *Dessau v Rowley* [1916] WN 238. That, like *Re Gordon*, was a case of a voluntary payment in. The plaintiff had declined to accept the payment in and proceeded with the case to the point of giving notice of trial. No further step was taken, however, for several months and the defendant was adjudicated bankrupt, a fact which escaped the plaintiff's notice. Subsequently a scheme of arrangement was approved by the court and the bankruptcy was annulled. The effect was thus that the defendant was released from debts proveable in the bankruptcy so that the plaintiff, not having proved, was unable to proceed with the action. The defendant applied to strike out the action for want of prosecution and the only question before the court was the disposition of the money in court. The argument on the plaintiff's behalf was, in reliance on the cases already referred to, that he was a secured creditor and thus entitled to rest on his security outside the bankruptcy. The contrary argument was that, there being a denial of liability, the money remained the defendant's subject to the provisions of Ord 22. In this court the leading judgment was delivered by Swinfen Eady LJ. He distinguished the case from one where liability had been admitted, but said that the court had no material before it to enable it to determine to whom the money ought now to be paid. Accordingly he directed that there should be an inquiry before the master whether there was at the date of payment in any sum due from the defendant to the plaintiff as alleged in the pleadings. The master was then to deal with the fund according to the event.

Phillimore and Bankes LJJ concurred, the former observing that he thought the plaintiff a secured creditor and that nothing that had happened in the bankruptcy ought to deprive him of the right to have the money appropriated to meet his claim.

Finally, we have been referred to *Re a debtor (No 5 of 1932), ex p the petitioning creditors* (1932) 101 LJ Ch 372, a decision of a Divisional Court in bankruptcy consisting of Luxmoore and Farwell JJ, where it was held that a plaintiff who had declined to accept money paid into court with a denial of liability had an interest in it in the nature of a lien and was thus a secured creditor within the meaning of s 167 of the Bankruptcy Act 1914. The result was that if he wished to present a bankruptcy petition against the defendant, he had either to state in his petition that he abandoned his security for the benefit of the defendant's creditors or to value his security and base his petition on the unsecured balance.

These authorities, whose correctness, so far as appears, has never been questioned, provide on the face of them powerful support for the submissions of counsel for the plaintiffs. The judge, however, whilst not doubting their correctness, was not persuaded that they could any longer be relied on, since they were decided in relation to the provisions of the Rules of the Supreme Court as they existed at the time, which, he considered, were materially different from the provisions of the present Ord 22. In those circumstances, he felt bound to prefer the reasoning of this court in *Peal Furniture Ltd v Adrian Share (Interiors) Ltd* [1977] 2 All ER 211, [1977] 1 WLR 464, which in any event accorded with his own inclination and which was decided under the present Ord 22. In that case the plaintiffs had instituted proceedings in September 1975 for a sum of some £13,500 for services rendered. The defendants in their defence and counterclaim admitted part of the claim but counterclaimed a sum of some £4,500 as special damage in the form of loss of profit caused by delay in carrying out the work. A little over a year after the commencement of the action they paid into court a sum of £3,967 under the provisions of Ord 22, r 1. Subsequently they got into financial difficulties and their bankers, who were secured by a debenture, appointed a receiver.

It does not appear that they were at any material time in liquidation or, indeed, that they were necessarily insolvent. The receiver having recalculated the amount of the counterclaim, the defendants then applied for leave to amend their defence and counterclaim and at the same time sought to withdraw their notice of payment into court under the provisions of Ord 22, r 1(3). Reeve J having acceded to that application, the plaintiffs appealed to this court which dismissed the appeal. It did so on two grounds. The first was that the defendants had now received advice which indicated that they were entitled to counterclaim for a larger sum than they had previously supposed was sustainable: a circumstance which, it was held, afforded a good reason for resiling from the step of making a payment into court and thus justified the court in exercising its discretion to permit the notice of payment in, and the money in court, to be withdrawn.

The second, and it is this that is the material one for the present purposes, was that if it turned out that the defendants were insolvent the plaintiffs would, by obtaining judgment and taking the money out of court, be in a better position than the general body of creditors. It does not appear that the court was referred to any of the cases to which counsel for the plaintiffs has drawn our attention and it seems to have been assumed throughout that a plaintiff in an action in which money has been paid into court was in no different position from that of an ordinary unsecured creditor if the defendant became insolvent. The argument appears from the judgments to have centred round the question whether it was necessary to show a change of circumstance which had 'put a wholly different complexion on the case' (as was suggested in the headnote to the report in *Cumper v Pothecary* [1941] 2 All ER 516) or whether, as a result of the introduction into Ord 22 (in 1965) of the present r 1(3), a wider discretion was conferred on the court.

*Cumper v Pothecary* was not in fact a case in which the defendant was seeking to withdraw the money in court. His application was to amend his notice of payment in, as a result of a recent decision of the House of Lords regarding the measure of damages for loss of expectation of life, by reducing the amount allocated in satisfaction of the plaintiff's claim under the Law Reform (Miscellaneous Provisions) Act 1934. This court did, however, consider the principles on which money paid into court in satisfaction ought to be permitted to be reduced or withdrawn. The judgment of the court was delivered by Goddard LJ who said this ([1941] 2 All ER 516 at 522–523, [1941] 2 KB 58 at 69):

'We think it right to say what we conceive to be the proper procedure to adopt when a defendant desires to obtain leave to withdraw or reduce his payment into court. In our opinion, if he wishes to withdraw the whole payment, he should ask for an order that he be at liberty to withdraw his notice of payment in and that the sum in court should be paid out to him, or be otherwise dealt with as the court may direct. Then, if the court grants the application, it will consider whether the money should still remain in court as a security, as in *Frazer & Haws, Ltd. v. Burns* ((1934) 49 Ll L Rep 216), or whether it should be returned to the defendant, as in *Williams*

v. *Boag* ([1940] 4 All ER 246, [1941] 1 KB 1). . . we think it is desirable to say that it must not be thought that a defendant who has paid a sum into court is entitled as of right to resile from that step. He must, in our opinion, show that there are good reasons for his application—for instance, the discovery of further evidence which puts a wholly different complexion on the case, as in *Frazer & Haws, Ltd.* v. *Burns* and *Williams* v. *Boag*, or a change in the legal outlook brought about by a new judicial decision, as in the present case, and there may be others. Having once put a valuation on the plaintiff's case, the defendant ought not to be allowed to alter it without good reason. . . [Apart] from matters such as fraud or mistake affecting the original payment [the court] should consider whether there is a sufficient change of circumstance since the money was paid in to make it just that the defendant should have an opportunity of withdrawing or reducing his payment.'

In his judgment in the *Peal Furniture* case Shaw LJ quoted from the passage cited above and then went on to consider the new r 1(3), new, that is, in the sense that it had been introduced since *Cumper v Pothecary* was decided. That provides as follows:

'A defendant may, without leave, give notice of an increase in a payment made under this rule but, subject to that and without prejudice to paragraph (5), a notice of payment may not be withdrawn or amended without the leave of the court which may be granted on such terms as may be just.'

It is not clear, however, whether Shaw LJ regarded this rule as extending the scope of the court's discretion. He observed that prior to the introduction of the rule there was no express provision enabling a notice of payment to be withdrawn and that the court relied on its inherent jurisdiction, but he does not appear to have contemplated that there was any difference in the approach to be adopted. He was in fact of the view that the receiver's recalculation of the amount which could be counterclaimed did, to use Goddard LJ's words, put 'a wholly different complexion' on the case. Shaw LJ continued ([1977] 2 All ER 211 at 215, [1977] 1 WLR 464 at 468):

'But there is yet another factor. The receiver in his affirmation says that whereas the financial position of the defendant company had at one time seemed sound, it now was apparent that it was financially weak. Accordingly, if the money were allowed to remain in court, and the plaintiffs succeeded in recovering a judgment in excess of anything to which the defendants might be entitled on the counterclaim, they would be able to satisfy that judgment, in whole or in part, by taking money out of court. To that extent, if it turned out that the defendant company were indeed insolvent, they would be given a preference over the general body of creditors, which would produce a result which in a general sense would be inequitable.'

Roskill LJ in his judgment does appear to have considered that r 1(3) in its present form introduced a new principle. He pointed out that *Cumper v Pothecary* was decided at a time when there was no such provision in the rules, and continued ([1977] 2 All ER 211 at 215–216, [1977] 1 WLR 464 at 468):

'Caution must always be exercised in applying decisions on rules long since abolished to other rules now in force; and it is quite clear, when one looks at the Annual Practice 1940, that the payment into court rules were quite different in form from those in force at the present time. In particular, as I understand it, there was nothing comparable to the latter part of RSC Ord 22, r 1(3) . . . It seems to me, therefore, that the court has a complete discretion, which of course has to be exercised properly and judicially—whether to allow payment out to be made back to the defendant and, if so, on what terms.'

Roskill LJ then considered the reformulation of the counterclaim and concluded that that made the facts very different from what they were when the defendants made their payment in. He continued ([1977] 2 All ER 211 at 216, [1977] 1 WLR 464 at 469):

'Secondly (and for my part I attach a good deal of importance to this), the receiver is acting as receiver on behalf of Lloyds Bank, who are the debenture-holders and have a fixed and floating charge on the whole of the defendants' assets. Any money, therefore, that comes into the hands of the receiver will be applied in accordance with his obligations towards those who appointed him. If this money is allowed to remain in court, and if the plaintiffs recover upwards of £4,000, it is likely that that money would be paid out to the plaintiffs in pro tanto satisfaction of what would be recoverable under the judgment. They would thus become in the position of secured creditors, or preferred creditors, and thus in a far better position than that in which they would be as judgment creditors. I am not saying that this consideration applies in all cases; but for my part, in the present case I think that it would be wrong to allow the plaintiffs to take advantage of this payment into court in order to give themselves preferential rights, in events which might happen, beyond those to which they would be entitled if they were ordinary judgment creditors.'

Megaw LJ did not expressly deal with this point in his judgment. He was content to assume that the statement of principle in *Cumper v Pothecary* [1941] 2 All ER 516, [1941] 2 KB 58 was no more than a reflection of the way in which discretion should be exercised under the new rule and he was unpersuaded that the judge had erred in exercising his discretion.

I have quoted from the judgments of the majority in some detail because they do, as it seems to me, demonstrate beyond doubt that, as Hutchison J found when the matter was before him, the position of the plaintiff as an unsecured but potentially preferred creditor was a part of the ratio as regards the exercise of discretion, although there appears to be some difference of emphasis, Shaw LJ looking to the position of creditors generally in a possible future liquidation and Roskill LJ apparently considering the interest of a particular secured creditor. But, however it is expressed, the concept of the plaintiff as an unsecured creditor who ought not to be allowed to become secured is totally inconsistent with the line of authority to which reference has been made above.

One of those authorities, *Dessau v Rowley* [1916] WN 238, although not very fully reported, is a decision of this court and if, as counsel for the plaintiff submits, the ratio of the decision is the same as that in *Re Gordon* [1897] 2 QB 516, namely that a payment into court results in the plaintiff becoming a secured creditor in the subsequent bankruptcy of the debtor, then we are faced with two directly conflicting decisions of this court, unless there is some reasonable ground for distinguishing them.

Now it is true that in *Dessau v Rowley* the court was faced with a very unusual situation, where there was money in court but where the cause of action in respect of which it had been paid in had gone by reason of the plaintiff's inadvertent failure to prove in the bankruptcy. In a sense, therefore, it may be said that the decision was sui generis and colourless: the court had somehow to deal with the money and took the course of ordering that it depended on the outcome of a reference to the master. This, indeed, seems to have been the submission which was made by counsel in *Re a debtor* (1932) 101 LJ Ch 372 and which was rejected. If one looks, however, at the argument before the court and particularly at the rather scanty report of the judgment of Phillimore LJ, it appears to me irresistible that the underlying basis of the decision was that the plaintiff was a secured creditor in respect of his contingent debt at the time of the payment in, for, his cause of action having now gone, there could be no other basis for the order for payment out to him which it was contemplated that the master would make if satisfied of the validity of his claim.

Counsel for the plaintiffs, therefore, submits first that the judge was wrong to distinguish *Dessau v Rowley* and what I may call the *Re Gordon* line of cases on the ground that they were decided under earlier rules of court and had therefore no application to an exercise of the court's discretion under the current rule. Certain it is that they were decided under earlier rules but the differences between those rules and the present rule are, he submits, immaterial.

Second, he submits that there is a direct conflict between *Dessau v Rowley* and the *Peal*

*Furniture* case and that we should prefer the earlier line of authority which, on this hypothesis, we are free to do in the light of *Young v Bristol Aeroplane Co Ltd* [1944] 2 All ER 293, [1944] KB 718.

If necessary, he boldly submits that the *Peal Furniture* case was a decision reached per incuriam because the relevant authorities were not brought to the court's attention. Thus, in the ultimate, he invites us to hold that the judge in exercising his discretion misdirected himself.

In examining these submissions, the first question to be answered is whether there is, as counsel for the plaintiffs would submit, a direct conflict between the *Re Gordon* line of cases and the *Peal Furniture* case or whether, as counsel for the defendants submits, those cases are distinguishable. It is counsel for the defendants' submission that they are clearly distinguishable for reasons which are elaborated below, and that they can have no application to the case of a voluntary payment under Ord 22, r 1 of the current rules. If that is right, then the judge was not only entitled but bound to follow the guidance given by this court in the *Peal Furniture* case and it cannot possibly be said that the judge exercised his discretion on any wrong principle.

Counsel for the defendants' argument proceeds in two stages. To begin with, he distinguishes a voluntary from an involuntary payment in. The latter, which is dealt with by different rules, may indeed still constitute the plaintiff a secured creditor. He points out that *Re Ford* [1900] 2 QB 211 and a number of other cases in which the plaintiff was held to be a secured creditor (see e g *Re Keyworth, ex p Banner* (1874) LR 9 Ch App 379, *Re Moojen, ex p Bouchard* (1879) 12 Ch D 26, *Evans v Philippides* (1963) 107 SJ 632) were cases in which the payment in had been made under order as a condition of obtaining leave to defend. The judgment of Wright J in *Re Ford* which has already been referred to is particularly in point in this context.

If reference is made to the rules, counsel for the defendants submits, it becomes apparent that there are significant differences between the voluntary and involuntary payment as regards the conditions on which orders can be made for payment out before the conclusion of the proceedings. An involuntary payment cannot be accepted by the plaintiff, and although both types of payment are subject (in the case of a voluntary payment after the expiration of the period prescribed for acceptance) to the restriction that they 'shall not be paid out except in pursuance of an order of the court' (see rr 5 and 8(1)), r 5 expressly provides in the case of a voluntary payment that an order 'may be made at any time before, at, or after the trial or hearing of the action', although subject to the restriction that, if made before trial, the money can be paid out only in satisfaction of the cause of action in respect of which it was paid in. Further, although r 1(3) enables the court to give leave for the withdrawal of a notice of payment in under the voluntary procedure, there is no similar provision allowing the repayment of an involuntary payment.

Counsel for the defendants meets the twin difficulties that the distinction which he draws is one which was argued in *Re Gordon* [1897] 2 QB 516 and distinctly rejected and that no such distinction has been adverted to in any of the subsequent cases, by the submission that, on the rules as they then stood, no distinction needed to be drawn. In substance the submission is that, whilst under the present rules these authorities remain good so far as involuntary payments are concerned, the introduction into the rules of the present r 1(3) has the effect of nullifying their authority as regards voluntary payments. In order to clarify this submission, it is necessary to look back to the rules as they stood at the time when these cases were decided.

They changed from time to time but until 1933 there were no alterations of any materiality, so far as the present point is concerned, in the rules as they stood when *Re Gordon* was decided in 1897. At that time the framework of the rules was rather different from the present, but there was not much difference in substance. They may be summarised for relevant purposes as follows. Under r 1 a defendant in an action for debt or damages had a choice if he wanted to pay in. He could pay in a sum in satisfaction without more, which had the effect of admitting the cause of action, or he could pay in (except in cases of defamation) with a defence denying liability in which case the payment became subject to r 6. If he pleaded a tender, the sum tendered had to be brought into court. He was not, however, bound to wait for a defence. He could, before defence, pay into court and serve a notice specifying the payment and the claim in respect of which it was paid. If money was paid in before defence, or with a defence not denying liability, or under a plea of tender, the plaintiff was entitled to take it out 'unless the Court or a Judge shall otherwise order' (see r 5). Where, however, liability was denied, then the plaintiff could accept the sum in satisfaction, in which case he became entitled to the money in court and proceedings were stayed, or he could refuse, in which case 'the money shall remain in court subject to the provisions hereinafter mentioned'.

The consequences of refusal and acceptance were dealt with in r 6(*b*) and (*c*). In the case of acceptance, the plaintiff was entitled to have the money paid out to him 'unless the Court or a Judge shall otherwise order', as in the case of a payment before defence. In the case of non-acceptance, 'the money shall remain in Court and be subject to the order of the Court or a Judge, and shall not be paid out of Court except in pursuance of an order', words to which counsel for the defendants attaches great significance in his submissions. There followed provisions as to payment out to the parties in accordance with the result of the action.

Involuntary payment was dealt with in r 11 where it was provided that it should not be paid out of court 'except in pursuance of an order of the Court or a Judge'. There followed a provision enabling a defendant who had paid in before defence pursuant to an order under Ord 14 to appropriate by his pleading (unless the court or a judge should otherwise order) the whole or part of the money to the plaintiff's claim or a specified part of it—

'and the money so appropriated shall thereupon be deemed to be money paid into Court pursuant to the preceding Rules of this Order relating to money paid into Court, and shall be subject in all respects thereto.'

Counsel for the defendants' submission rests in substance on the meaning which, in an earlier decision of this court, had been attributed to the words 'order of the Court' in r 6(*c*). That case was *Maple v Earl of Shrewsbury* (1887) 19 QBD 463. In that case a sum of £15,000 had been paid in under order as a condition of leave to defend, i e an involuntary payment. The defendant, however, delivered a defence denying liability but at the same time paid in a further £3,000 and pleaded that the aggregate sum in court was sufficient to satisfy the plaintiffs' claim. They refused to accept and proposed to proceed with the claim but nevertheless applied for payment out to them of the sum in court. A Divisional Court, to whom the master referred the application, considered that the rules enabled the sum to be paid out to the plaintiffs, even though proceeding with the action, subject to a liability to repay if the action went against them or if they recovered less than the sum in court. The defendant, perhaps not surprisingly, appealed, and it is, I think, important to observe that the question before the court was whether it was right that the plaintiffs, in a case where liability was in issue, should both be entitled to refuse to take the money in satisfaction and have it paid to them on account of a liability which remained to be litigated. Lord Esher MR observed (at 465–466):

'. . . if a plaintiff is not willing to do that [i e accept the money paid into court], then the rule provides that the money shall remain in court and be subject to the order of the court or a judge, and shall not be paid out of court except in pursuance of an order. I think that the order there referred to means a final order of the Court with regard to the money after the action has been tried or in some other way disposed of, as for example by the withdrawal of the defence; for even if the defence is withdrawn, I think an order would be necessary.'

Lindley LJ agreed, saying (at 466):

'I do not think it is essential in all cases that there should have been a trial in order that the money may be ordered to be paid out; but, as long as the question of liability remains undetermined, it seems to me that it is contrary to the terms of Order XXII, r. 6, to allow it to be paid out.'

To similar effect is Lopes LJ, who thought that the order admitted of only one construction, 'viz. that the order therein mentioned is an order to be made after the trial or other determination of the action' (at 466).

Now counsel for the defendants points to this case as supplying the explanation of why in the *Re Gordon* line of cases a voluntary payment in was regarded as constituting the plaintiff a secured creditor. He was secured because, once the money had been paid in, there was no possibility of it being paid out to the defendant before the termination of the proceedings. But that, he submits, was totally changed by the introduction into the rules in 1965 of the present r 1(3) which was in force at the time of the *Peal Furniture* case. Once that rule had been introduced, and it is a rule which applies only to a voluntary payment, the plaintiff could no longer be classified as 'secured' because it was always open to the defendant, pursuant to the rule, to apply for, and, at the discretion of the court, to obtain, a payment out.

Speaking for myself, I have not felt able to accept this submission, which rests on the proposition that prior to the introduction of the present r 1(3) there was no way in which the money paid into court could be ordered to be repaid to the defendant until the final determination of the proceedings. *Cumper v Pothecary* [1941] 2 All ER 516, [1941] 2 KB 58 shows that this was not so. It had been long established that if the defendant could show, for instance, that he had paid money into court under a mistake or if he was compelled to amend his pleading so as to render the payment inappropriate, the court in the exercise of its inherent jurisdiction could order it to be repaid (see eg *Spurr v Hall* (1877) 2 QBD 615). That proposition appears, from the notes to *Archbold's Practice of the Queen's Bench* (Chitty ed) (9th edn, 1856) vol 2, p 1282, to have been of long standing, reference there being made to a decision of Parke B in chambers in 1840 in *Colyer v Selby* (unreported, 5 December 1840).

It is also supported by *Fraser & Haws Ltd v Burns* (1934) 49 Ll L Rep 216 (where the defendant was allowed to withdraw his pleas of payment in, although the money was directed to remain in court) and by the later authority of *Williams v Boag* [1940] 4 All ER 246, [1941] 1 KB 1, where money had been paid in in the erroneous belief (based on a mistake of fact) that there was no defence to the action. In that case MacKinnon LJ, who delivered the leading judgment, with which Goddard and du Parcq LJJ agreed, observed ([1940] 4 All ER 246 at 248, [1941] 1 KB 1 at 3):

> '. . . if, in such a case as this, it is admitted that the amendment of the pleadings raises an insuperable obstacle to any possible success by the plaintiff, I think that there must be inherent power in the court, on that state of facts being established, to order payment out of the money to the defendant, notwithstanding the fact that R.S.C., Ord. 22, r. 3, does not in terms contemplate such a possibility.'

The rule there referred to was the predecessor to the present r 5, which incorporated the substance of the original r 6(c) which had been the subject matter of the decision in *Maple v Shrewsbury*. Certainly nothing that was said in *Cumper v Pothecary* suggests that the court considered that it was effecting any change in the law. That case clearly proceeded on the footing that, quite independently of the rules, the court had an inherent jurisdiction in appropriate circumstances, which included both mistake and a material change in the position of the parties, to order repayment to the defendant of moneys paid in. It is, of course, true that when *Cumper v Pothecary* was decided the rules were in a different form from that in which they stood at the date of *Maple v Shrewsbury*. Their form was radically altered in 1933, but the principal material effects of the changes were to eliminate references to payment in the pleadings and to allow payment in at any time on notice, and it is, perhaps, worth noting that the notes to Ord 22, r 1 in the 1940 *Yearly Practice* include under the heading 'General principles still applicable' the decisions in *Re Gordon* [1897] 2 QB 516 and *Dessau v Rowley* [1916] WN 238. Certainly Goddard LJ noted that 'decisions on statutes and rules which formerly obtained are of no material assistance' but in that part of the judgment which dealt with payment out to the defendant the court was not applying any provision of the rules (see [1941] 2 All ER 516 at 519, [1941] 2 KB 58 at 66). An order for payment out to the defendant was, in fact, directly contrary to the provision of the then r 3, which provided that the money should not be paid out 'except in satisfaction of the claim . . . in respect of which it was paid in'.

Moreover it is worth observing that the original r 6(c) as it stood in 1887 was modified in 1913 by the insertion of an express provision enabling an order to be made 'at any time before, or at or after the trial of the action'. That was the form of the order in force at the time when *Dessau v Rowley* was decided. The notes to r 6(c) in the 1913 *Yearly Practice of the Supreme Court* indicate some doubt as to the universal accuracy of what was said in *Maple v Shrewsbury* as to the occasion on which an order could be made. The text reads:

'. . . but it is submitted that an order could be made on proper terms for payment out in the event of a plaintiff electing to accept the money after he had delivered a reply refusing to accept it, though possibly in this case the safer course would be to give leave to deliver an amended reply, or to give the plaintiff leave to withdraw his reply and to give a notice accepting the money paid in in satisfaction of his claim. . .'

Reference is there made to a decision of this court in *Powell v Vickers Sons & Maxim Ltd* [1907] 1 KB 71 at 77, [1904–7] All ER Rep 390 at 394 in which Farwell LJ said:

'I think it impossible to construe Order xxii, r. 6 (c), so as to make the Court a mere machine, without any discretion to refuse an order for the payment out of money paid into Court by a defendant with a denial of liability. The provision that money is not to be paid out of Court except in pursuance of an order of a Court or a judge is intended to give a discretion to be exercised on proper occasions and materials.'

*Brown v Feeney* [1906] 1 KB 563 and *Maxwell v Wolseley* [1907] 1 KB 274, albeit concerned with payments in in defamation suits with an admission of liability, also support the existence of a general discretion.

For my part I do not find, in the alterations effected in the rules prior to 1965, anything which detracts from the authority of the *Re Gordon* line of cases or which indicates that they no longer apply. Was there, then, anything in the alterations which were affected in 1965, when the rules were again recast, which had that effect? Nothing has been suggested, other than the introduction of the express power to sanction a withdrawal of a notice of payment in, which is now contained in r 1(3). The former r 3, which forbade payment out before the trial except in satisfaction of a claim in respect of which the money was paid in, remains, although in a slightly altered form, in the present r 5.

Speaking for myself, I cannot see that this effected any alteration to the previous position as regards the ability of the court to order payment out. In terms it does no more than enable a defendant to withdraw his notice with leave so that the moneys in court are no longer capable of being accepted by the plaintiff. It has been said that, by implication, it also authorises the court to order payment out, but whether this is so or whether the court's power to order payment out rests on the inherent jurisdiction which, as *Cumper v Pothecary* [1941] 2 All ER 516, [1941] 1 KB 58 shows, was previously exercisable is immaterial. At its highest it seems to do no more than to state in express terms the previous position, but in fact it seems likely that it was designed primarily with a view simply to enable the defendant to alter the terms of his notice in response to the suggestion which had been made by this court in *Davies v Rustproof Metal Window Co Ltd* [1943] 1 All ER 248 at 250, [1943] 1 KB 299 at 302.

In the *Peal Furniture* case [1977] 2 All ER 211, [1977] 1 WLR 464 neither Shaw LJ nor Megaw LJ appears to have founded himself on the supposition that the new rule had enlarged the court's discretion, and indeed it is not entirely clear from Roskill LJ's judgment whether, when he spoke of the court having a 'complete' discretion, he regarded the discretion which previously existed as more circumscribed.

For my part, therefore, I am unable to see why it should be suggested that the introduction of this rule should, by a sidewind, hence destroy the authority of the *Re Gordon* line of cases which has stood unchallenged for over 80 years.

On one view of the matter it can, I suppose, be argued that *Peal Furniture* does not necessarily conflict with them, since they were concerned with the same position as obtains here, namely the bankruptcy of the defendant while the money remains in court. In *Peal Furniture* the question was whether, there being no present bankruptcy or liquidation, or, indeed, for aught that appears, any existing insolvency, the plaintiff should be deprived of the opportunity of asserting a security in circumstances which had not yet arisen. But that cannot, I think, be a valid ground of distinction. If the effect of the payment in is that the plaintiff becomes a secured creditor, that effect cannot in itself and at the same time be a good ground for depriving him of his security whether it has or has not matured. So far, therefore, as *Peal Furniture* decides that this is a ground, even if not a universal ground, for ordering payment out to the defendant, it cannot stand alongside the previous authorities.

I have considerable sympathy with the judge, who was faced with conflicting decisions, but I cannot but feel that, inasmuch as the court's attention in *Peal Furniture* was never drawn, so far as appears, to the bankruptcy line of authorities, it was, so far as the decision rests on the plaintiffs' position as unsecured creditors, decided per incuriam. The judge felt able to disregard those authorities on the ground that they were decided under different rules. So they were, but for the reasons which I have endeavoured to express I cannot find in the previous rules differences of such materiality as to deprive the earlier cases of continuing authority.

We are, therefore, as it seems to me, faced with two conflicting decisions of this court which cannot stand together, and are compelled to choose which we should follow. As I read the classical judgment of Lord Greene MR in *Young v Bristol Aeroplane Co Ltd* [1944] 2 All ER 293 at 298, [1944] KB 718 at 725–726, that choice is open on either the first or the third grounds which he there enumerates. It has certainly been said (in particular by Lord Simon in *Miliangos v George Frank (Textiles) Ltd* [1975] 3 All ER 801 at 821, [1976] AC 443 at 477) that the exception to the rule of stare decisis on the ground that a previous decision was per incuriam should be most modestly invoked and then only if two conditions are satisfied, namely that the judgment was given in advertence of some authority apparently binding and that if the court giving such judgment had been advertent of such authority, it would have decided otherwise than it did. The mere fact, of course, that prior authority is not referred to in a judgment is not of itself a demonstration that it was not considered, but it is impossible to believe that if the court in *Peal Furniture* had had its attention directed to the bankruptcy cases, it would not have mentioned them and equally impossible to believe that if its attention had been so drawn, it would not have affected the judgment. But in any event, for the reasons given, I am driven to the conclusion that there is a direct conflict between *Dessau v Rowley* and *Peal Furniture* and this court is not merely entitled but bound to decide which to follow.

*Peal Furniture* seems to have been based on the supposition, with which Hutchison J obviously sympathised, that there was something inequitable or unfair in a plaintiff achieving a preference in the event of his obtaining judgment. For myself, I do not see why this should be. Subject to the bankruptcy rules relating to fraudulent preferences, there has never been any restriction on a debtor preferring a particular creditor if he wishes to do so, and I am not clear why it should be thought desirable that a creditor who has a valid claim but is kept out of his money by a defence which ultimately fails should be deprived of the advantage which he gains by a payment into court. In the ordinary way, his claim ought to have been dealt with and discharged when payment was demanded and if this had been done no question would arise. Why, because he has been made to wait for payment as a result of an unsuccessful defence until the defendant has gone into liquidation, his position in the mean time being secure to the extent of the money in court, should he be put in a worse position than the creditor of equal degree whose claim has been admitted and paid?

*Peal Furniture* proceeds on two propositions which, if I may respectfully say so, appear to me to be open to doubt. The first is that in exercising the discretion as to payment out to a defendant it is right to have regard to matters occurring right outside and having no connection with the litigation, that is to say the interests of some person who is a stranger to the litigation and whose relationship with the defendant in no way affects the dispute between plaintiff and defendant. The second is that the money in court remains, as it were, an asset of the defendant which, on his bankruptcy, forms part of his property available for distribution. Speaking entirely for myself, I question this approach. That the money in court may become such an asset is unquestionable if an order is made for payment out. But in my judgment a defendant paying into court under Ord 22, r 1 parts outright with his money. I doubt whether it can be said that the Accountant General is a trustee in whose hands his money can be traced. Nor is there a 'debt' or chose in action in the accepted sense of the word. The money becomes subject entirely to whatever order the court may see fit to make and to treat it as the defendant's property available for distribution in his bankruptcy is to assume, for the purpose of exercising the court's discretion, the very situation which will only arise if the court exercises its discretion in a particular way.

In my judgment the principles emerging from the *Re Gordon* line of cases are still applicable to money paid in under the current rules. The plaintiff is therefore a secured creditor to the extent of those moneys in the defendant's liquidation and that event cannot, by itself, constitute a change of circumstances which can properly be regarded as justifying the court in exercising its discretion to order repayment. Whilst, therefore, I appreciate the dilemma with which the judge was faced, I am forced to the conclusion that in adopting the starting position that the plaintiffs were unsecured creditors, he misdirected himself. I would allow the appeal and restore the order of the district registrar.

**ROBERT GOFF LJ.** I entirely agree with the judgment delivered by Oliver LJ, and I only add a few words because we are differing from the conclusion reached by the judge.

It is plain that there is an established line of authority, stemming from *Re Gordon, ex p Navalchand* [1897] 2 QB 516, that a plaintiff is treated as a secured creditor to the extent of money paid into court, whether that money has been paid in involuntarily, ie as a condition of defending the action, or voluntarily. In particular, I am satisfied that the decision of this court in *Dessau v Rowley* [1916] WN 238 was made on that basis. It is true that in the judgments in that case only Phillimore LJ expressly refers to the plaintiff as a secured creditor; but I do not see how the court could have made the order it did unless it proceeded on the basis that the plaintiff was indeed a secured creditor. Ever since *Re Gordon* this has been regarded as established law; and, so far as I am aware, it has never been questioned. It has been treated as such in successive editions of *The Supreme Court Practice*, and is still treated as such in, for example, 3 Halsbury's Laws (4th edn) para 318 and *Williams and Muir Hunter on Bankruptcy* (19th edn, 1979) pp 55, 77.

It has been suggested that the position of the plaintiff as a secured creditor used to be dependent on the provisions of the old Ord 22, r 6(c), and in particular on the interpretation based on that rule by this court in *Maple v Earl of Shrewsbury* (1887) 19 QBD 463; and that the position is different now, because of the provision in the present Ord 22, r 1(3) that a notice of payment into court may be withdrawn by the defendant with the leave of the court. However, having seen the manner in which Ord 22 has developed over the years, and having regard to the authorities to which Oliver LJ has referred, I am satisfied that the court has always had a discretion to permit a defendant to withdraw money paid into court. The earliest reference which I have been able to find is the reference in *Archbold's Practice of the Queen's Bench* (Chitty ed) (9th edn, 1856) vol 2, p 1282 to the decision of Parke B in chambers in 1840 in *Colyer v Selby* (unreported, 5 December 1840); but from time to time there has appeared in successive editions of *The Yearly Practice of the Supreme Court*, under the rubric mistake, the proposition that the court has power to permit a defendant to withdraw money paid into court under fraud or mistake, and that proposition has appeared in editions of *The Yearly Practice* published after the decision in *Maple v Shrewsbury* and before the introduction of the present Ord 22, r 1(3). Indeed, I find it inconceivable that the court should not have jurisdiction to permit a defendant to withdraw a payment made into court when, for example, he has been fraudulently induced to make the payment in; and I do not read *Maple v Shrewsbury* as precluding the exercise of that discretion. It is moreover of some interest that the present Ord 22, r 1(3) does not in terms refer to the court having power to permit a defendant to withdraw a *payment in*, but only to permit him to withdraw his *notice of payment in*; and the rule may well have been so drawn because it presupposes the existence of the long-standing discretionary power which the court has to permit a defendant to withdraw his payment in.

It is plain to me that none of the earlier authorities, and in particular *Dessau v Rowley*, can have been drawn to the attention of this court in *Peal Furniture Co Ltd v Adrian Share (Interiors) Ltd* [1977] 2 All ER 211, [1977] 1 WLR 464. Furthermore, it must follow that if the plaintiff is a secured creditor to the extent of the payment in, then the supervening insolvency of the defendant cannot of itself be a material factor for the court to take into account in exercising its discretion whether to allow a defendant to withdraw his notice of payment in, or indeed the payment itself. It follows that this is one of those very rare cases where we are faced with two conflicting decisions of this court, and, on the principles stated by Lord Greene MR in *Young v Bristol Aeroplane Co Ltd* [1944] 2 All ER 293 at 298, [1944] KB 718 at 725–726, we are free, and indeed compelled, to choose which we should follow. I have no doubt that we should follow the long-established line of authority of which *Dessau v Rowley* forms part; and, like Oliver LJ, I see nothing objectionable in holding that the plaintiff should not be deprived of the benefit of a payment into court simply because the defendant has become insolvent.

The judge, faced as he was with conflicting authorities, was placed in a difficult position, and I have considerable sympathy with him in his dilemma. But I have come to the conclusion that, in exercising his discretion as he did, he misdirected himself in law in that he took into account an immaterial consideration, and that that misdirection was not merely influential, but decisive, with regard to the manner in which he exercised his discretion. For these reasons I too would allow the appeal and restore the order of the district registrar.

**SIR JOHN DONALDSON MR.** I agree that the decisions of this court in *Dessau v Rowley* [1916] WN 238 and *Peal Furniture Co Ltd v Adrian Share (Interiors) Ltd* [1977] 2 All ER 211, [1977] 1 WLR 464 are inconsistent with one another and that we are required to choose between them. I also agree, for the reasons given by Oliver and Robert Goff LJJ, that we should not follow *Peal's* case.

This disposes of the second ground for the decision in *Peal's* case, which is the only ground applicable to the facts of this appeal. However, I entertain grave doubts as to the correctness of the first ground, namely that on the facts it was appropriate to allow the defendant to withdraw his notice. In *Cumper v Pothecary* [1941] 2 All ER 516 at 523, [1941] 2 KB 2 KB 58 at 69 Goddard LJ, giving the judgment of this court, said:

> '[Apart] from matters such as fraud or mistake affecting the original payment [the court] should consider whether there is a sufficient change of circumstance since the money was paid in to make it just that the defendant should have an opportunity of withdrawing or reducing his payment.'

In *Peal's* case shop premises were temporarily unusable and the plaintiffs assessed their loss at 10% of the normal level of takings. Later they, or the receiver appointed by the bank, revised that figure to 43% on the basis, no doubt, that overhead expenses continued to be incurred. This does not seem to me to be a change of circumstances, either objectively or as reasonably known the plaintiffs. It amounted simply to a misappreciation of circumstances well known to the plaintiffs. If this were a ground for permitting a reduction in the amount of money in court, it seems to me that there could be applications whenever counsel reviewed the case and took a more favourable view than he had hitherto taken.

For the reasons given by Oliver and Robert Goff LJJ, I would allow the appeal.

*Appeal allowed. Leave to appeal to the House of Lords refused.*

Solicitors: *Garrard Mitchell & Co*, Shrewsbury (for the plaintiffs); *Edge & Ellison Hatwell Pritchett & Co*, Birmingham (for the defendants).

Diana Procter    Barrister.

# Fox v Chief Constable of Gwent

QUEEN'S BENCH DIVISION
ROBERT GOFF LJ AND MANN J
9 MAY, 19 JUNE 1984

*Road traffic – Breath test – Arrest – Arrest for failure to provide specimen of breath – Validity – Constable a trespasser at time of request for specimen of breath – Request for breath specimen made at defendant's home after police unlawfully entering house – Whether defendant's non-compliance with request an offence – Whether defendant's subsequent arrest lawful – Road Traffic Act 1972, s 7(4)(6).*

*Criminal evidence – Exclusion of evidence – Discretion – Evidence unfairly obtained by police – Defendant wrongfully arrested for failure to provide breath specimen – Defendant taken to police station where he provided breath specimen – Whether breath specimen at police station obtained unfairly – Whether evidence relating to breath specimen should be excluded – Road Traffic Act 1972, s 10.*

The defendant was the driver of a motor car which was involved in an accident. The defendant had had a passenger with him but by the time the police arrived they had both left the scene of the accident. The police officers, who had no reason to suspect that the defendant or his passenger were injured, went to the defendant's house, knocked on the front door and, when there was no response, opened the door and entered the house, where they found the defendant. They asked him to provide a specimen of breath for testing for alcohol and when he refused he was arrested and taken to the police station. He was then requested to provide two breath specimens, which he did and which showed that the amount of alcohol in his breath exceeded the prescribed limit. He was charged (i) in respect of the refusal to provide a breath test at his home, with failing without reasonable cause to provide a breath specimen, contrary to s 7(4)[a] of the Road Traffic Act 1972, and (ii) with driving after consuming alcohol in excess of the prescribed limit, contrary to s 6(1)[b] of the 1972 Act. He was convicted on both counts. He appealed, contending (i) in relation to the charge of failing to provide a breath specimen, that the police officers had entered his house unlawfully and that therefore their request for a breath specimen had been unlawful and (ii) in relation to the drink driving charge, that the evidence obtained at the police station of the alcohol content of his breath, although relevant and admissible, ought to have been excluded because it had been unfairly obtained following his unlawful arrest.

**Held** – (1) Since under s 7(6) of the 1972 Act a police officer could enter 'any place' for the purpose of requiring a person to provide a specimen of breath only if he had 'reasonable cause to suspect that the accident involved injury to another person' and since, on the facts, the police officers had had no reasonable cause to suspect that the defendant's accident had involved injury to another person, they had entered the defendant's house as trespassers and their unlawful entry meant that their request to the defendant to supply a breath specimen was not a lawful requirement. It followed that the defendant's failure to comply with that request did not constitute an offence under s 7(4) and, further, that the police officers had unlawfully arrested the defendant at his house for failing to provide a breath specimen. Accordingly, the defendant's conviction for refusing to supply a breath specimen at his home would be quashed and to that extent the appeal would be allowed (see p 233 e f, p 234 a and p 237 a, post); *Morris v Beardmore* [1980] 2 All ER 753 applied.

(2) Magistrates had a discretion to exclude evidence which, although relevant and admissible, had been obtained by unfair means from an accused after the commission of an offence. However, the evidence obtained at the police station, on which the drink

---

a Section 7, so far as material, is set out at p 232 j and p 233 b, post
b Section 6(1), so far as material, is set out at p 232 h, post

driving conviction was based, had been obtained in accordance with the procedure laid down in the 1972 Act and without any inducement, threat, trick or other impropriety, and had therefore been fairly obtained. The fact that the defendant had been at the police station only because he had been wrongfully arrested was irrelevant in considering whether the evidence had been fairly obtained. It followed that the magistrates would not have been entitled to exercise their discretion to exclude the evidence. Accordingly, the defendant's appeal against his conviction on the drink driving charge would be dismissed (see p 236 c to h and p 237 a, post); dicta of Lord Diplock, Lord Fraser and Lord Scarman in *R v Sang* [1979] 2 All ER at 1228–1229, 1239, 1247 and *R v Trump* (1979) 70 Cr App R 300 applied.

Semble. The 'evidence' of the proportion of alcohol or drugs in a specimen of breath which must, by s 10ᶜ of the 1972 Act, be taken into account in proceedings under s 5 or s 6 of that Act does not include evidence which is excluded by the court in the exercise of its discretion (see p 236 h j, post).

### Notes

For failure to provide a specimen, see 40 Halsbury's Laws (4th edn) para 493.

For evidence of the proportion of alcohol in specimens of breath, see ibid para 496.

For the court's discretion to reject evidence wrongfully obtained, see 17 ibid para 12.

For the Road Traffic Act 1972, s 5, see 42 Halsbury's Statutes (3rd edn) 1646, and for ss 6, 7, 10 of that Act (as substituted by the Transport Act 1981, s 25(3), Sch 8), see 51 ibid 1427, 1429, 1434.

### Cases referred to in judgment

*Callis v Gunn* [1963] 3 All ER 677, [1964] 1 QB 495, [1963] 3 WLR 931, DC.
*Harris v DPP* [1952] 1 All ER 1044, [1952] AC 694, HL.
*Jeffrey v Black* [1978] 1 All ER 555, [1978] QB 490, [1977] 3 WLR 895, DC.
*Kuruma Son of Kaniu v R* [1955] 1 All ER 236, [1955] AC 197, [1955] 2 WLR 223, PC.
*Morris v Beardmore* [1980] 2 All ER 753, [1981] AC 446, [1980] 3 WLR 283, HL.
*Noor Mohamed v R* [1984] 1 All ER 365, [1949] AC 182, PC.
*R v Barker* [1941] 3 All ER 33, [1941] 2 KB 381, CCA.
*R v Payne* [1963] 1 All ER 848, [1963] 1 WLR 637, CCA.
*R v Sang* [1979] 2 All ER 1222, [1980] AC 402, [1979] 3 WLR 263, HL.
*R v Trump* (1979) 70 Cr App R 300, CA.

### Case stated

Leslie Raymond Gerald Fox appealed by way of case stated by justices for the county of Gwent, acting in and for the petty sessional division of Usk, in respect of their adjudication as a magistrates' court on 14 July 1983 whereby they convicted the appellant on informations laid by the respondent, the Chief Constable of Gwent, namely (1) that on 8 May 1983 at Raglan in the county of Gwent the appellant drove a motor vehicle on a road after consuming alcohol in excess of the prescribed limit, contrary to s 6(1) of the Road Traffic Act 1972, as substituted by s 25(3) of and Sch 8 to the Transport Act 1981, and (2) that at Raglan on 8 May 1983 the appellant, a person driving a motor vehicle, having been required to provide a specimen of breath for a breath test there or nearby by a constable in uniform who had reasonable cause to suspect him of having committed a traffic offence while the vehicle was in motion, failed without reasonable excuse to provide a specimen of breath, contrary to s 7(4) of the 1972 Act, as substituted by s 25(3) of and Sch 8 to the 1981 Act. The justices ordered the appellant to be fined and to be disqualified in respect of the first information. The facts are set out in the judgment of the court.

*Peter A Jones* for the appellant.
*Gavyn Arthur* for the respondent.

*Cur adv vult*

---

c    Section 10, so far as material, is set out at p 233 d, post

19 June. The following judgment of the court was delivered.

**MANN J.** There is before the court an appeal by way of case stated against a decision of justices of the peace for the county of Gwent sitting for the petty sessional division of Usk on 14 July 1983. The justices had before them two informations each of which had been laid by the respondent against the appellant. The informations were that:

'(a) on the 8th May, 1983 at Raglan in the County of Gwent the Appellant drove a motor vehicle on a road after consuming so much alcohol that the proportion of it in his breath was 57 microgrammes of alcohol in 100 millilitres of breath, the limit being 35 microgrammes of alcohol in 100 millilitres of breath, contrary to Section 6(1) of the Road Traffic Act, 1972 as substituted by the Transport Act, 1981;
(b) that the Appellant at Raglan on the 8th May, 1983, being a person driving a motor vehicle and having been required to provide a specimen of breath for a breath test there or nearby by a Constable in uniform who had reasonable cause to suspect him of having committed a traffic offence whilst the vehicle was in motion, did without reasonable excuse fail to do so, contrary to Section 8(3) and Part I of Schedule 4 to the Road Traffic Act, 1972.'

The reference in the second information to 'Section 8(3) and Part I of Schedule 4 to the Road Traffic Act 1972' was a slip and should have read 'Section 7(4) of the Road Traffic Act 1972 as substituted by the Transport Act 1981.' The appellant did not take any point on the slip and the argument before us proceeded on the basis that the error had been corrected.

The facts of the case can shortly be stated. On 8 May 1983 the appellant was the driver of a motor vehicle when it met with an accident. There was a passenger in the vehicle. No other person and no other vehicle was involved in the accident. When police officers arrived at the scene they found that the appellant and his passenger had left. The justices found that the officers 'had no information about the Appellant or his passenger' which was a finding treated in this court as meaning that they 'had no information about the physical condition of the appellant or his passenger'. The officers left the scene and went directly to the appellant's house and knocked. The door was shut but not locked. There was no response to the knock, but after hearing voices within the officers entered the house and required the appellant to provide a specimen of breath for a breath test. He refused. He was arrested and taken to a police station where he was required to provide specimens of breath. A specimen contained 57 microgrammes of alcohol in 100 ml of breath, that is to say 22 microgrammes above the prescribed limit (see the Road Traffic Act 1972, s 12(2) (as substituted by s 25(3) of and Sch 8 to the Transport Act 1981)).

On those facts the justices convicted the appellant on each information. In this court it was argued that the conviction on the first information was wrong because the justices ought to have excluded from their consideration the evidence of the proportion of alcohol in the specimen provided at the police station. The conviction on the second information was said to be wrong because the request to provide a specimen of breath at the appellant's house was not a lawful request.

The relevant statutory provisions are in the Road Traffic Act 1972 and are provisions which were substituted with effect from 6 May 1983 by s 25(3) of and Sch 8 to the Transport Act 1981 (see the Transport Act 1981 (Commencement No 9) Order 1983, SI 1983/576). Those provisions are hereinafter referred to by section number alone and are:

'**6.**—(1) If a person—(a) drives or attempts to drive a motor vehicle on a road or other public place . . . after consuming so much alcohol that the proportion of it in his breath, blood or urine exceeds the prescribed limit he shall be guilty of an offence . . .

**7.** . . . (2) If an accident occurs owing to the presence of a motor vehicle on a road or other public place a constable may require any person who he has reasonable cause to believe was driving or attempting to drive or in charge of the vehicle at the time of the accident to provide a specimen of breath for a breath test . . .
(3) A person may be required under . . . subsection (2) of this section to provide a specimen either at or near the place where the requirement is made . . .

(4) A person who, without reasonable excuse, fails to provide a specimen of breath when required to do so in pursuance of this section shall be guilty of an offence.

(5) A constable may arrest a person without warrant if . . . (b) that person has failed to provide a specimen of breath for a breath test when required to do so in pursuance of this section and the constable has reasonable cause to suspect that he has alcohol in his body . . .

(6) For the purpose of requiring a person to provide a specimen of breath under subsection (2) above in a case where he has reasonable cause to suspect that the accident involved injury to another person . . . a constable may enter (if need be by force) any place where that person is or where the constable, with reasonable cause, suspects him to be . . .

8.—(1) In the course of an investigation whether a person has committed an offence under . . . section 6 of this Act a constable may, subject to the following provisions of this section . . . require him—(a) to provide two specimens of breath for analysis by means of a device of a type approved by the Secretary of State . . .

(2) A requirement under this section to provide specimens of breath can only be made at a police station . . .

(7) A person who, without reasonable excuse, fails to provide a specimen when required to do so in pursuance of this section shall be guilty of an offence . . .

10.—(1) The following provisions apply with respect to proceedings for an offence under . . . section 6 of this Act.

(2) Evidence of the proportion of alcohol or any drug in a specimen of breath, blood or urine provided by the accused shall, in all cases, be taken into account, and it shall be assumed that the proportion of alcohol in the accused's breath, blood or urine at the time of the alleged offence was not less than in the specimen . . .'

We find it convenient to deal first with the offence of having failed without reasonable excuse to provide a specimen of breath. The failure occurred in the appellant's house which the police officers had entered without his consent. If they had any power so to do it can have been derived only from s 7(6), but on the facts as found the officers could not have had reasonable cause to suspect that the accident had involved injury to another person in that they had no information about the passenger's condition. Accordingly s 7(6) had no application and the police officers were trespassers. In that circumstance was the requirement for a specimen a lawful requirement? Unless it was a lawful requirement the offence of failing to provide a specimen could not have been committed. The answer to the question must be No. It is sufficient to refer to *Morris v Beardmore* [1980] 2 All ER 753 at 757, [1981] AC 446 at 455 where Lord Diplock said:

'I have considered whether, even if it must be accepted in accordance with this presumption that Parliament did not "authorise" a constable to enter a person's home against his will in order to require him to take a breath test, it nevertheless intended the requirement made in such circumstances to be a lawful one, so that non-compliance with it would constitute a criminal offence, leaving as the sole remedy for the unlawful conduct of the constable a civil action for tort against him. My Lords, if this be right it must apply not only to comparatively venial trespasses such as that committed in the instant case, but also to cases where entry to the private house of the person sought to be breathalysed has been obtained by the police by forcing doors or windows or overcoming reasonable force lawfully exerted by that person or on his behalf to remove them from the premises. I find it quite impossible to suppose that Parliament intended that a person whose common law right to keep his home free from unauthorised intruders had been violated in this way should be bound under penal sanctions to comply with a demand which only the violation of that common law right had enabled the constable to make to him. In my opinion, in order to constitute a valid requirement the constable who makes it must be acting lawfully towards the person whom he requires to undergo a breath test at the moment that he makes the requirement. He is not acting lawfully if he is then committing the tort of trespass on that person's property, for s 8(2) of the 1972 Act gives him no authority to do so.'

The decision and the speech concerned the legislation which was superseded on 6 May 1983 but they apply equally to the present legislation. The conviction on information (b) must be quashed.

We turn to the offence of driving after consuming excess alcohol. The critical piece of evidence against the appellant was the evidence of the proportion of alcohol in a specimen of breath supplied by the appellant at the police station in response to a requirement under s 8(1). Counsel for the appellant accepted that that evidence was both relevant and admissible but argued that the justices should have excluded it from their consideration. Justices, said counsel, have a discretion to exclude relevant and admissible evidence if it is evidence which has been unfairly obtained from an accused after the commission of the offence with which he is charged. Counsel said the specimen of breath was unfairly obtained because the requirement under s 8(1) had to be made at a police station (see s 8(2)) and the appellant was at the police station solely because he had been wrongfully arrested. That the arrest was wrongful must follow from our earlier conclusion that the requirement to supply a specimen at the appellant's house was an unlawful requirement.

The nature and extent of a judge's discretion to exclude relevant and admissible evidence in a criminal trial was considered by members of the House of Lords in *R v Sang* [1979] 2 All ER 1222, [1980] AC 402. All members of the House identified a discretion to exclude relevant and admissible evidence which would be likely to have a prejudicial effect out of proportion to its probative value (see [1979] 2 All ER 1222 at 1228, 1231–1232, 1237, 1238–1239, 1243, [1980] AC 402 at 434, 438, 445, 446–447, 452). Such a discretion is not germane to the present case. Three members of the House seem to have recognised a further discretion to exclude relevant and admissible evidence where that evidence is obtained from an accused after the commission of the crime with which he is charged and is evidence which was unfairly obtained as by a trick, oppression or inducement.

Lord Diplock said ([1979] 2 All ER 1222 at 1228–1229, [1980] AC 402 at 434–435):

'What has been regarded as the fountain-head of all subsequent dicta on this topic is the statement by Lord Goddard CJ delivering the advice of the Privy Council in *Kuruma Son of Kaniu v R* [1955] 1 All ER 236 at 239, [1955] AC 197 at 204. That was a case in which the evidence of unlawful possession of ammunition by the accused was obtained as a result of an illegal search of his person. The Board held that this evidence was admissible and had rightly been admitted; but Lord Goddard CJ, although he had earlier said that if evidence is admissible "the court is not concerned with how the evidence was obtained", nevertheless went on to say ([1955] 1 All ER 236 at 239, [1955] AC 197 at 204): "No doubt in a criminal case the judge always has a discretion to disallow evidence if the strict rules of admissibility would operate unfairly against the accused. This was emphasised in the case before this Board of *Noor Mohamed* v. *Regem* ([1949] 1 All ER 365 at 370, [1949] AC 182 at 192), and in the recent case in the House of Lords of *Harris* v. *Director of Public Prosecutions* ([1952] 1 All ER 1044 at 1048, [1952] AC 694 at 707). *If, for instance, some admission of some piece of evidence, e.g., a document, had been obtained from a defendant by a trick, no doubt the judge might properly rule it out.*" Up to the sentence that I have emphasised there is nothing in this passage to suggest that when Lord Goddard CJ spoke of admissible evidence operating "unfairly" against the accused he intended to refer to any wider aspect of unfairness than the probable prejudicial effect of the evidence on the minds of the jury outweighing its true evidential value; though he no doubt also had in mind the discretion that had long been exercised in England under the Judges' Rules to refuse to admit confessions by the accused made after the crime even though strictly they may be admissible. The instance given in the passage I have italicised appears to me to deal with a case which falls within the latter category since the document "obtained from a defendant by a trick" is clearly analogous to a confession which the defendant has been unfairly induced to make, and had, indeed, been so treated in *R v Barker* ([1941] 3 All ER 33, [1941] 2 KB 381) where an incriminating document obtained from the defendant by a promise of favours was held to be inadmissible.'

In a later passage in his speech Lord Diplock again referred to the statement by Lord Goddard CJ, and continued ([1979] 2 All ER 1222 at 1229–1230, [1980] AC 402 at 436):

'That statement was not, in my view, ever intended to acknowledge the existence of any wider discretion than to exclude (1) admissible evidence which would probably have a prejudicial influence on the minds of the jury that would be out of proportion to its true evidential value and (2) evidence tantamount to a self-incriminatory admission which was obtained from the defendant, after the offence had been committed, by means which would justify a judge in excluding an actual confession which had the like self-incriminating effect.'

Lord Fraser said ([1979] 2 All ER 1222 at 1239, [1980] AC 402 at 447):

'The important question is whether the discretion (a) is limited to excluding evidence which is likely to have prejudicial value out of proportion to its evidential value or (b) extends to excluding other evidence which might operate unfairly against the accused and, if so, how far it extends. On the best consideration that I can give to the authorities, I have reached the opinion that the discretion is not limited to excluding evidence which is likely to have prejudicial effects out of proportion to its evidential value.'

His Lordship concluded ([1979] 2 All ER 1222 at 1241, [1980] AC 402 at 450):

'On the other hand, I doubt whether they were ever intended to apply to evidence obtained from sources other than the accused himself or from premises occupied by him. Indeed it is not easy to see how evidence obtained from other sources, even if the means for obtaining it were improper, could lead to the accused being denied a fair trial. I accordingly agree with my noble and learned friends that the various statements with regard to the discretion to which I have referred should be treated as applying only to evidence and documents obtained from an accused person or from premises occupied by him. That is enough to preserve the important principle that the judge has an overriding discretion to exclude evidence, the admission of which would prevent the accused from having a fair trial.'

Lord Scarman said ([1979] 2 All ER 1222 at 1247, [1980] AC 402 at 456):

'The question remains whether evidence obtained from an accused by deception, or a trick, may be excluded at the discretion of the trial judge. Lord Goddard CJ thought it could be: *Kuruma Son of Kaniu v R* [1955] 1 All ER 236 at 239, [1955] AC 197 at 204. Lord Parker CJ and Lord Widgery CJ thought so too: see *Callis v Gunn* [1963] 3 All ER 677 at 681, [1964] 1 QB 495 at 502 and *Jeffrey v Black* [1978] 1 All ER 555, [1978] QB 490. The dicta of three successive Lord Chief Justices are not to be lightly rejected. It is unnecessary, for the purposes of this appeal, to express a conclusion on them. But, always provided that these dicta are treated as relating exclusively to the obtaining of evidence from the accused, I would not necessarily dissent from them. If an accused is misled or tricked into providing evidence (whether it be an admission or the provision of fingerprints or medical evidence or some other evidence), the rule against self-incrimination, nemo tenetur se ipsum prodere, is likely to be infringed. Each case must, of course, depends on its circumstances. All I would say is that the principle of fairness, though concerned exclusively with the use of evidence at trial, is not susceptible to categorisation or classification, and is wide enough in some circumstances to embrace the way in which, after the crime, evidence has been obtained from the accused.'

Lord Salmon declined to categorise the cases in which a discretion could arise (see [1979] 2 All ER 1222 at 1237, [1980] AC 402 at 445), but Viscount Dilhorne seems to have doubted the existence of a further discretion and reserved his position on the correctness of *R v Payne* [1963] 1 All ER 848, [1963] 1 WLR 637 (see [1979] 2 All ER 1222 at 1233, [1980] AC 402 at 440), which, as Lord Diplock observed, is the only case in which an appellate court has 'come across conduct so unfair, so tricky or so oppressive as to justify [it] in holding that the discretion ought to have been exercised in favour of exclusion' (see [1979] 2 All ER 1222 at 1229, [1980] AC 202 at 435). Viscount Dilhorne did however formulate an answer to the question certified by the Court of Appeal, Criminal Division which was the answer adopted by the four other members of the House (see [1979] 2 All ER 1222 at 1231, [1980] AC 402 at 437 per Lord Diplock):

> '(1) A trial judge in a criminal trial has always a discretion to refuse to admit evidence if in his opinion its prejudicial effect outweighs its probative value. (2) Save with regard to admissions and confessions and generally with regard to evidence obtained from the accused after commission of the offence, he has no discretion to refuse to admit relevant admissible evidence on the ground that it was obtained by improper or unfair means.'

The dicta and the answer seem to us to indicate the existence of a limited but further discretion in cases of opprobrious conduct. It is not necessary for us to justify our opinion because in *R v Trump* (1979) 70 Cr App R 300 at 302 the Court of Appeal, Criminal Division held that 'a limited exception in cases analogous to improperly obtained admissions was recognised by the House of Lords to exist'.

That decision is binding on us. We therefore proceed on the basis that a trial judge has a discretion to exclude relevant and admissible evidence being evidence which was unfairly obtained from an accused after the commission of the offence with which he is charged. Lord Diplock, Lord Fraser and Lord Scarman observed in *R v Sang* [1979] 2 All ER 1222 at 1225, 1242, 1246, [1980] AC 402 at 431, 450, 456 that the discretion given to a judge of the Crown Court is possessed also by justices. Accordingly, the justices in the present case had a discretion to exclude evidence unfairly obtained from the appellant.

The evidence obtained from the appellant was a specimen of breath which he was required to provide by a police officer who was investigating whether the appellant had committed an offence under s 6. The appellant did not suggest that the officer was not entitled to make the requirement which he did or that the statutory warning under s 8(8) had not been given. There is no suggestion that any of the police officers who were at any stage concerned with the appellant acted otherwise than in good faith. In these circumstances the only point which can be made in relation to unfairness was that made by counsel for the appellant, viz the appellant was at the place at which a specimen could be required solely because he had been wrongfully arrested. However, the evidence is the specimen. The specimen was obtained without inducement, threat (apart from the statutory warning), trick or other impropriety. There was nothing opprobrious. The historical fact that the appellant was at the police station because of a wrongful arrest, which might be the subject of a civil remedy, does not bear on the question of whether the specimen was unfairly obtained. In our judgment if the justices had excluded the evidence of the proportion of alcohol in the specimen they would have improperly exercised their discretion. The conviction of an offence under s 6 must stand.

We should record that the respondent conceded that the word 'Evidence' where it occurs in s 10(2) means evidence which is for consideration, that is relevant, admissible evidence which is not excluded by an exercise of discretion. We do not have to decide the point but the concession seems to be correct.

We return to the case stated. The questions posed by the justices for the opinion of this court are:

> 'Were we correct in Law in finding that (i) the procedure at the Police Station was not dependent for its legality upon the lawfulness of the arrest; and (ii) even if the subsequent procedure *was* so dependent, on the facts of this particular case the entry and arrest were lawful.'

The answer to the first question is Yes. The second question must be reformulated in order to accommodate information (b) as follows: 'On the facts as found by us were the entry and the arrest lawful?' The answer is No.

*Appeal against conviction on second information allowed and conviction quashed. Appeal against conviction on first information dismissed.*

*The court refused leave to appeal to the House of Lords but certified, under s 1(2) of the Administration of Justice Act 1960, that the following point of law of general public importance was involved in the decision: were the justices correct in convicting the appellant under s 6(1) of the Road Traffic Act 1972 (as substituted by the Transport Act 1981) on the basis of the proportion of alcohol in a specimen of breath which he had been required to provide at a police station when the appellant was present at that police station because he had been wrongfully arrested?*

*15 November. The Appeal Committee of the House of Lords allowed a petition by the appellant for leave to appeal.*

Solicitors: *Wedlake Bell,* agents for *Gabb & Co,* Abergavenny (for the appellant); M L Boland, Cwmbran (for the respondent).

Hilary Kindelan    Barrister.

# R & H Green & Silley Weir Ltd v British Railways Board (Kavanagh, third party)

CHANCERY DIVISION
DILLON J
2 OCTOBER 1980

*Limitation of action – Indemnity – Accrual of cause of action – Third party granted right to tip material onto land owned by defendants – Third party agreeing to indemnify defendants against all consequent liabilities – Plaintiffs alleging damage to neighbouring land from third party's activities – Whether defendants' claim against third party for indemnity statute-barred – Whether general indemnity an indemnity against liabilities arising under principal claim or against payment and discharge of those liabilities – Whether time not beginning to run against person claiming indemnity until he is called on to pay principal claim.*

In 1970 the third party and the defendants made an agreement under which the third party was permitted to tip material onto land owned by the defendants on condition that the third party agreed to indemnify the defendants against liability for loss or damage arising as a result of the agreement. In 1971 the plaintiffs complained that their property had been damaged by the tipping and in 1974 they commenced an action against the defendants. The statement of claim was not served until December 1977 and in January 1978 the defendants issued a summons to dismiss the action for want of prosecution. When the summons came on for hearing it was agreed that, if the defendants commenced proceedings against the third party and if the third party alleged that those proceedings were statute-barred under the Limitation Act 1939, the question whether the defendants' claim to an indemnity under the 1970 agreement was so barred would be tried as a preliminary issue. On the trial of the preliminary issue the defendants, arguing in favour of the indemnity being statute-barred, contended that time ran against a person seeking to enforce an indemnity from the date of the event giving rise to his liability to pay the claimant and not from the date when he was called on by the claimant to make payment.

**Held** – Having regard to the general rule that a person entitled to an indemnity under a contract of indemnity had no cause of action against the person giving the indemnity until the fact and extent of the obligations of the person entitled to the indemnity had been ascertained or established (because a general indemnity was an indemnity not against liabilities arising under the principal claim but against the payment and discharge of those liabilities), it followed that time ran against a person seeking to enforce an indemnity from the date when he was called on to pay the principal claim and not from the date of the event giving rise to his liability to pay. Accordingly, time did not begin to run against the defendants in respect of their claim to be indemnified by the third party until the defendants' liability, if any, to the plaintiffs had been established and ascertained and they had been called on to pay the plaintiffs. The defendants' claim against the third party for an indemnity was therefore not statute-barred (see p 240 *a* to *c* and p 242 *d* to *g*, post).

County and District Properties Ltd v C Jenner & Son Ltd [1976] 2 Lloyd's Rep 728 followed.

Bosma v Larsen [1966] 1 Lloyd's Rep 22 not followed.

**Notes**

For the accrual of cause of action when claiming indemnification, see 28 Halsbury's Laws (4th edn) para 622 and 20 ibid 315, and for cases on the subject, see 32 Digest (Reissue) 495–496, 3794–3800.

For the Limitation Act 1939, see 19 Halsbury's Statutes (3rd edn) 60.

As from 1 May 1981 the 1939 Act has been replaced by the Limitation Act 1980.

**Cases referred to in judgment**

Bosma v Larsen [1966] 1 Lloyd's Rep 22.
Collinge v Heywood (1839) 9 Ad & El 633, 112 ER 1352.
County and District Properties Ltd v C Jenner & Son Ltd [1976] 2 Lloyd's Rep 728.
Hood's Trustees v Southern Union General Insurance Co [1928] Ch 793.
Richardson, Re, ex p St Thomas's Hospital Governors [1911] 2 KB 705, CA.
Spark v Heslop (1859) 1 E & E 563, 120 ER 1020.
Post Office v Norwich Union Fire Insurance Society Ltd [1967] 1 All ER 577, [1967] 2 QB 363, [1967] 2 WLR 709, CA.

**Preliminary issue**

Pursuant to (i) an undertaking given to the court by the British Railways Board, the defendants to an action commenced by the plaintiffs, R & H Green & Silley Weir Ltd, by a statement of claim dated 14 February 1974, and (ii) an order of Brightman J dated 8 March 1979, the defendants (a) served a third party notice dated 29 March 1979 claiming an indemnity against Sean Michael Kavanagh and (b) sought the determination as a preliminary issue of the question whether the defendant's claim against the third party was statute-barred under the Limitation Act 1939. The facts are set out in the judgment.

*Richard Fowler* for the plaintiffs.
*D Gidley Scott* for the defendants.
The third party appeared in person.

**DILLON J.** In June 1970 the third parties in these proceedings, Mr Kavanagh and Mr Taffe, who carried on in partnership a business called Integrated Reclamation and Dredging Co, made an agreement with the defendants, the British Railways Board, whereby in consideration of making a payment to the defendants, the third parties were given permission to tip approved excavated material on a former railway cutting of the defendants' extending east from Blackwall Way bridge. By cl 3 of the letter, the terms of which were accepted by the third parties, the third parties agreed that, notwithstanding any supervision given or approval expressed by the defendants, they would be responsible for, and release and indemnify the defendants, their servants or agents, from and against all liability for personal injury (whether fatal or otherwise) loss of or damage to property and any other loss, damage, costs and expenses which might arise in consequence of the grant or existence of the agreement or of anything done as a result of its grant or existence howsoever such injury, loss, damage, costs or expenses be caused whether by the negligence of the defendants, their servants or agents or otherwise and whether in the carrying out by the third parties and the defendants of the arrangements set out in the letter or otherwise.

It seems that the tipping works envisaged were carried out later in 1970 and in the course of 1971, and the plaintiffs, R & H Green & Silley Weir Ltd, complain that, as the filling was carried out without first providing alternative support to their adjoining premises, they have suffered damage for which the defendants are responsible. The complaints of the plaintiffs were raised in correspondence in 1971 and were referred by the defendants to the third parties, and in the correspondence the third parties by a letter of February 1972, repudiated all claims that any damage had been caused by their operations. On 12 September 1972, the defendants' legal adviser and solicitor wrote to the third parties, drawing attention to cl 3 of the letter, and saying that this was a contract which afforded the defendants a complete defence to any claim, and suggesting that the third parties should take the matter up direct with the plaintiffs. In a further letter of 4 January 1973 the defendants' legal adviser and solicitor wrote to the third parties, saying that it seemed likely that the plaintiffs would shortly be commencing proceedings to recover the damage allegedly caused to their property by the filling, and the writer intimated that the third parties would if necessary be joined, as he puts it, as co-defendants in any action that might result.

On 14 February 1974 the plaintiffs started the present action against the defendants alone, but they did not proceed very fast with it. The statement of claim was not served until 7 December 1977, and on 4 January 1978 the defendants issued a summons to dismiss the action for want of prosecution. That summons came before Brightman J in May 1978, and, finally, on 8 March 1979, when he made an order by consent of the plaintiffs and the defendants. By that order, the defendants undertook that, in the event of (1) the action being allowed to continue and (2) the defendants commencing third party proceedings against the third parties and (3) the third parties alleging that the defendants' claim against them is statute-barred under the Limitation Act 1939, then the defendants will seek to have determined as a preliminary issue the question whether the defendants' proposed claim against the third parties is statute-barred; and they undertook also that on any hearing of that issue the plaintiffs should be at liberty to argue on behalf of the defendants that the defendants' proposed claim is not statute-barred. Conversely, the plaintiffs, by their counsel, undertook that, in the event of the issue being determined against the defendants, that is in the event of a determination that the proposed claim is statute-barred, the plaintiffs would discontinue the action or consent to it being dismissed.

Following that order, a third party notice was served on Mr Kavanagh on 29 March 1979 (Mr Taffe has not been served), and third party directions were given on 11 June 1979, as a result of which a third party defence was served on behalf of Mr Kavanagh in October 1979 asserting that the claim of the defendants against the third party is in any event barred under s 2(1) of the Limitation Act 1939 in that these third party proceedings were brought after the expiration of six years from the date on which the cause of action, if any, thereon accrued. Whether that claim against the third party is statute-barred has now been set down for determination as a preliminary issue, and that is the issue which I have to resolve.

The argument has, because of the terms of Brightman J's order, taken a somewhat unusual course. Counsel for the plaintiffs has been arguing that the claim against the third party is not statute-barred. The third party has been present in person. He has assisted me by reference to dates and facts, but, not unnaturally, has not plunged into the authorities. Counsel for the defendants, having regard to the defendants' interest under Brightman J's order, has presented the argument that the defendants' third party claim is statute-barred.

Counsel for the plaintiffs draws my attention to a general statement in 20 Halsbury's Laws (4th edn) para 315, where, under the headings 'Enforcement of Indemnity. When Right to enforce Indemnity arises', there appears the general statement:

'In the absence of a contractual term to the contrary, time runs against a person seeking to enforce an indemnity from the date when he is called upon to pay, not from the date of the event giving rise to his liability to do so.'

The authority cited for that proposition is *Collinge v Heywood* (1839) 9 Ad & El 633, 112 ER 1352. I think the particular passage that counsel for the plaintiffs has relied on has to be read in the light of the preceding section, where it is pointed out that in law an action on a contract of indemnity does not normally lie until the promisee has paid the third person's claim but that the former rules of equity enable a person entitled to an indemnity to obtain relief as soon as his liability to the third person has arisen and before he has made payment, and he may, where appropriate, obtain an order compelling the person giving the indemnity to set aside a fund out of which liability may be met or to pay the amount due directly to the third person. It is, however, further pointed out that the equitable right to enforce an indemnity does not constitute a debt.

In *County and District Properties Ltd v C Jenner & Son Ltd* [1976] 2 Lloyd's Rep 728 Swanwick J had occasion to consider the previous authorities. In *Jenner's* case there had been a contract in RIBA form between building owners (the plaintiffs) and main contractors (the defendants), and there had been various sub-contracts with sub-contractors (the third parties), and these sub-contracts had contained agreements by the sub-contractors to indemnify and save harmless the contractors against and from any breach, non-observance or non-performance of the provisions of the main contract, or any act or omission of the sub-contractor which involved the contractor in any liability and any claim, damage, loss or expense resulting from any breach of duty on the part of the sub-contractor. A procedural situation somewhat akin to that in the case before me came about because the writ had been issued at a very late stage before the expiration of the limitation period as between the plaintiffs and the defendants, and the statement of claim had been served just over six years after the date of practical completion of the work. There had then been a summons to stay the action pending arbitration, but the judge had declined to grant such a stay because, had there been an arbitration, the claims of the plaintiffs would have been statute-barred, whereas they were not statute-barred under the writ that had been issued. He therefore made an order allowing the action to proceed on terms that the defendants should issue third party proceedings as advised and if any defence of limitation should be raised to any claim of the defendants against the third parties for an indemnity the defendants should apply for that to be tried as a preliminary issue, and if an order for the trial of such a preliminary issue should be made the plaintiffs should have liberty to take part therein, and, if the issue should be determined against the defendants, then the plaintiffs undertook to discontinue the action.

Swanwick J, in his judgment, accepted the submission that a cause of action first accrued when there arose a factual situation the existence of which entitled one person to obtain from the court a remedy against another person, and he accepted the submission that that stage would be reached when the defendants were damnified. It was submitted there that at common law the damnification of a person indemnified under a contract never occurred until he had to pay and had paid money, but in equity the rule was relaxed to the extent that time started to run when the fact and extent of the liability of the person to be indemnified was ascertained or established. In support of that, reference was made to a number of authorities, including *Collinge v Heyward* and *Re Richardson, ex p St Thomas's Hospital Governors* [1911] 2 KB 705 at 709–710 where Cozens-Hardy MR said:

'It is settled at common law that, given a contract of indemnity, no action could be maintained until actual loss had been incurred. The common law view was first pay and then come to the Court under your agreement to indemnify. In equity that was not the view taken. Equity has always recognised the existence of a larger and wider right in the person entitled to indemnity. He was entitled, in a Court of Equity, if he was a surety whose liability to pay had become absolute, to maintain an action against the principal debtor and to obtain an order that he should pay off the creditor and relieve the surety . . . So that in the view of the Court of Equity it was not necessary for the person entitled to the indemnity to be ruined by having to pay the full amount in the first instance. He had full power to take proceedings under which that fate might be averted, and he might substantially protect himself and secure his position by coming to the Court.'

Fletcher Moulton LJ (at 712–713) summarised the law in substantially similar terms, saying, after referring to the rule in Chancery, that to his mind it emphasised the fundamental common law principle that you must have paid before you had a right to indemnity because the remedy which equity gave was a declaration of a right, ie a declaration of the right to be indemnified. Then he said (at 713):

'I do not think that equity ever compelled a surety to pay money to the person to whom he was surety before the latter had actually paid.'

Applying those principles, Swanwick J in *Jenner's* case [1976] 2 Lloyd's Rep 728 at 734 concluded—

'that the general rule in cases of indemnity is that while equity will safeguard the position pending the ascertainment of the fact and extent of liability of the person to be indemnified, he has no cause of action until such ascertainment. There is thus a strong body of authority not only in favour of [the] proposition as to when the cause of action for an indemnity arises at common law as modified by equity but also to the effect that these rules . . . are universal.'

Swanwick J referred to *Spark v Heslop* (1859) 1 E & E 563, 120 ER 1020, but I do not think that that really helps because the particular contract in that case was construed by the court as not being a contract of indemnity in the ordinary sense; it was a contract not merely to repay but also to take care that the plaintiff should not be called on to pay. Swanwick J had further to consider a decision of McNair J in *Bosma v Larsen* [1966] 1 Lloyd's Rep 22, and that case Swanwick J felt unable to follow. He consequently held in *Jenner's* case that the third parties, who were sub-contractors who had entered into the agreements of indemnity which I have mentioned, could be sued and the causes of action against them were not statute-barred because the causes of action did not arise until the ascertainment of the fact and extent of liability of the main contractor who was to be indemnified.

*Bosma v Larsen* was concerned with the position as between shipowners and charterers. One of the provisions of the charterparty was that the master of the ship was to be under the orders of the charterers. In consequence, the master had signed bills of lading on the charterers' orders in respect of a cargo which arrived damaged and in consequence the shipowners were held liable in damages to the cargo owners. Under the charterparty, however, the charterers had agreed to indemnify the owners against all consequences of liabilities arising from the master signing bills of lading or other documents or otherwise complying with the orders of the charterers. The owners, therefore, claimed indemnity from the charterers, and the question that arose was whether the cause of action of the owners against the charterers arose when the master signed the bills of lading for the damaged goods, or, alternatively, when they were delivered damaged at the port of delivery, or whether the cause of action only arose when the cargo owners established their claim against the shipowners in legal proceedings abroad, or when a compromise payment was made in satisfaction of that claim. McNair J held that the shipowners' cause

of action arose long before the claim against them by the cargo owners was established
and that consequently that the claim against the charterers was statute-barred. The nub
of his decision, as I understand it (apart from a reference to *Spark v Heslop*, which he
regarded as not being a contract of indemnity in the ordinary sense but turning on the
exact language of the undertaking given) was that the particular contract whereby the
charterers had agreed to indemnify the shipowners meant that the obligation was an
obligation to indemnify against the incurring of the liability, and not merely against the
discharge of that liability by payment or the determination of that liability by judicial
process. He said that indemnity against a liability seemed to him to be different from
reimbursement against sums paid in pursuance of a legal liability. A shipowner is
damnified as soon as he comes under a liability. The damnification contemplated by the
clause is the incurring of the liability and not the payment (see [1966] 1 Lloyd's Rep 22
at 28).

It is common ground that the view taken by McNair J is not reconcilable with the
view taken by Swanwick J. I have been referred, to assist me in resolving this, to certain
other authorities, in particular, *Post Office v Norwich Union Fire Insurance Society Ltd* [1967]
1 All ER 577, [1967] 2 QB 363. That case, as it seems to me, indicates that, where there is
an insurance against liability to third parties, while there may be rights as soon as events
happen which may lead to a claim being made, there is no enforceable liability to sue the
insurers until the liability has been established and ascertained. I refer in particular to the
judgment of Harman LJ, where he also refers to the earlier decision of Tomlin J and the
Court of Appeal in *Hood's Trustees v Southern Union General Insurance Co* [1928] Ch 793.

I think it follows from Swanwick J's approach and the approach in *Post Office v Norwich
Union Fire Insurance Society Ltd* that, in the present case, time did not run against the
defendants in favour of the third party until the liability, if any, of the defendants to the
plaintiffs had been established and ascertained. The wording of cl 3 of the letter of
agreement is very general:

'You will be responsible for, and release and indemnify the [defendants] from and
against, all liability for loss or damage to property and any other loss, damage, costs
and expenses which may arise.'

That, as I read it, is a general indemnity within the general rule as enunciated by
Swanwick J.

Accordingly, on this preliminary issue, I prefer Swanwick J's approach to that of
McNair J, and I read the indemnity as being an indemnity not against liabilities arising
so much as against the payment and determination of the liabilities. That leads to the
consequence that the third party claim against Mr Kavanagh is not barred by the 1939
Act.

*Order accordingly.*

Solicitors: *Ashurst Morris Crisp & Co* (for the plaintiffs); *Evan Harding* (for the defendants).

Evelyn M C Budd    Barrister.

# Telfair Shipping Corp v Inersea Carriers SA
# The Caroline P

QUEEN'S BENCH DIVISION (COMMERCIAL COURT)

NEILL J

13, 14, 15 FEBRUARY, 3 JULY 1984

*Limitation of action – Indemnity – Accrual of cause of action – Charterparty requiring master to sign bills of lading as presented – Bills of lading containing more onerous terms than charterparty and exposing owners to greater liability to consignees of cargo – Charterers owing implied indemnity to owners – Whether implied indemnity against incurring of liability or against consequences of master signing more onerous bills – Whether owners' right to indemnity arising when damage occurring or when owners' liability to consignees ascertained – Whether owners' claim against charterers for indemnity time-barred.*

The shipowners chartered a vessel to the charterers under a charterparty in New York Produce Exchange form which provided, by cl 8, that the charterers would load, stow, trim and discharge the cargo under the supervision of the master, who would sign bills of lading for cargo as presented. A cargo of rice was loaded in Houston and two bills of lading dated 31 December 1974 and 12 January 1975 were issued and signed on behalf of the master when loading was completed. The bills of lading imposed on the shipowners obligations in respect of the cargo which were more onerous than those stipulated in the charterparty. When the cargo was discharged at the port of destination in Iraq between 2 and 21 April 1975 it was found to be badly damaged as the result of bad stowage. The consignees of the cargo brought an action under the bills of lading against the shipowners in Iraq and in December 1978 the consignees were awarded damages by an Iraqi court against the shipowners' agents. The damages were paid by the shipowners, who then claimed an indemnity from the charterers on the ground that it was to be implied from the terms of cl 8 of the charterparty making the charterers responsible for stowage that they would indemnify the shipowners against any liability for bad stowage incurred by the shipowners under the bills of lading. The charterers contended, inter alia, that the action was time-barred. The matter was referred to a sole arbitrator whose appointment was confirmed on 30 March 1981. The arbitrator held that the action was not time-barred, on the ground that the earliest date on which the shipowners' cause of action under the implied indemnity arose was when discharge of the cargo was completed (ie April 1975), which was less than six years from the date of his appointment, and he awarded the shipowners damages against the charterers. The charterers appealed, contending that any indemnity implied under cl 8 was against liability to the consignees, and as such the right to claim that indemnity arose as soon as the breach of the charterparty occurred, which was when the cargo was badly stowed and the bills of lading issued in December 1974 and January 1975, which was more than six years before the appointment of the arbitrator. The shipowners contended that the indemnity was a general indemnity against the consequences of the master signing more onerous bills of lading than provided for in the charterparty, the consequences being the award of damages against the shipowners in 1978, which was when their cause of action against the charterers arose.

**Held** – An indemnity which was implied from the terms of a contract or the conduct of the potential indemnifier was to be construed as being an implied general indemnity against the consequences of certain action when those consequences occurred and not as an indemnity against the incurring of liability. Accordingly, what the shipowners were entitled to be indemnified against by the charterers by reason of the indemnity implied under cl 8 of the charterparty was the consequences of the master signing the bills of lading in terms more onerous than the terms of the charterparty. Since the indemnity in respect of those consequences did not become enforceable until the shipowners' liability to the consignees had been ascertained by the award of damages against the shipowners in 1978, which was when time began to run for the purposes of the limitation period, the shipowners' action against the charterers was not time-barred. Moreover, even if the indemnity was construed as an indemnity against the incurring of liability, it was an indemnity against the incurring of actual rather than contingent liability to the consignees and since the actual liability had been incurred when the cargo was discharged in April 1975 the shipowners' action was still not time-barred. The appeal would accordingly be dismissed (see p 247 c d, p 248 f, p 254 f to j, p 255 c to j and p 256 b, post).

*Krüger & Co Ltd v Moel Tryvan Ship Co* [1907] AC 272, *Elder Dempster & Co v C G Dunn & Co (Ltd)* (1909) 15 Com Cas 49, *Re Richardson, ex p St Thomas's Hospital Governors* [1911] 2 KB 705, *Dawson Line Ltd v AG Adler für Chemische Industrie of Berlin* [1931] All ER Rep 546, *Strathlorne Steamship Co Ltd v Andrew Weir & Co* (1934) 50 Ll L Rep 185, *Bosma v Larsen* [1966] 1 Lloyd's Rep 22, *County and District Properties Ltd v C Jenner & Son Ltd* [1976] 2 Lloyd's Rep 728 and *R & H Green & Silley Weir Ltd v British Rlys Board (Kavanagh, third party)* [1985] 1 All ER 237 considered.

## Notes
For accrual of cause of action when claiming indemnification, see 28 Halsbury's Laws (4th edn) para 622 and 20 ibid 315, and for cases on the subject, see 32 Digest (Reissue) 495–496, 3794–3800.

## Cases referred to in judgment
*Birmingham and District Land Co v London and North Western Rly Co* (1886) 34 Ch D 261, [1886–90] All ER Rep 620, CA.
*Bosma v Larsen* [1966] 1 Lloyd's Rep 22.
*Collinge v Heywood* (1839) 9 Ad & El 633, 112 ER 1352.
*County and District Properties Ltd v C Jenner & Son Ltd* [1976] 2 Lloyd's Rep 728.
*Dawson Line Ltd v Adler für Chemische Industrie of Berlin* [1932] 1 KB 433, [1931] All ER Rep 546, CA.
*Elder Dempster & Co v C G Dunn & Co (Ltd)* (1909) 15 Com Cas 49, HL.
*Forster v Outred & Co (a firm)* [1982] 2 All ER 753, [1982] 1 WLR 86, CA.
*Green (R & H) & Silley Weir Ltd v British Rlys Board (Kavanagh, third party)* (1980) [1985] 1 All ER 237.
*Hadley v Baxendale* (1854) 9 Exch 341, [1843–60] All ER Rep 461, 156 ER 145.
*Krüger & Co Ltd v Moel Tryvan Ship Co* [1907] AC 272, HL; affg [1907] KB 809, CA.
*Littlewood v George Wimpey & Co Ltd, British Overseas Airways Corp (second defendants and third parties)* [1953] 2 All ER 915, [1953] 2 QB 501, [1953] 3 WLR 553, CA; affd [1954] 3 All ER 661, [1956] AC 169, [1954] 3 WLR 932, HL.
*M'Gillivray v Hope* [1935] AC 1, HL.
*Richardson, Re, ex p St Thomas's Hospital Governors* [1911] 2 KB 705, CA.
*Robinson v Harkin* [1896] 2 Ch 415.
*Sheffield Corp v Barclay* [1905] AC 392, [1904–7] All ER Rep 703, HL.
*Strathlorne Steamship Co Ltd v Andrew Weir & Co* (1934) 50 Ll L Rep 185.
*Toplis v Grane* (1839) 5 Bing NC 636, [1835–42] All ER Rep 592, 133 ER 1245, CP.
*Wolmershausen v Gullick* [1893] 2 Ch 514, [1891–4] All ER Rep 740.

## Appeal
Pursuant to leave granted by Parker J on 26 November 1983 the plaintiffs, Telfair Shipping Corp (the charterers), appealed against an award made by Mr John L Potter as sole arbitrator in an arbitration between the charterers and the respondents, Inersea Carriers SA (the owners), in which the arbitrator held that the owners were entitled as a matter of indemnity to recover from the charterers £25,660·57 and $US1,378·00, and awarded that the charterers pay to the owners £25,660·57 and $US1,378·00 plus interest, and declared that the charterers should indemnify the owners in respect of all further sums and expenses reasonably paid in connection with the cargo claim. The facts are set out in the judgment.

*Jeremy Cooke* for the charterers.
*Jonathan Hirst* for the owners.

*Cur adv vult*

3 July. The following judgment was delivered.

**NEILL J.** The appellants (the charterers) bring this appeal pursuant to the order giving leave to appeal made by Parker J on 26 November 1983. The appeal is against the award of Mr John L Potter dated 13 September 1983. The appeal raises difficult questions as to the nature and extent of an implied indemnity.

By a charterparty dated and concluded in London on 5 November 1974, on a New York Produce Exchange form, the present respondents (the owners) chartered their motor vessel Caroline P to the charterers for trading for a time charter trip on the terms and conditions set out in the charterparty. On 11 November 1974 the charterers concluded a sub-charter on similar terms with another company, who themselves further sublet the vessel on a voyage charterparty to Tradax SA.

The charterparty between the owners and the charterers provided in cl 8 as follows:

'That the Captain shall prosecute his voyages with the utmost despatch, and shall render all customary assistance with ship's crew and boats. The Captain (although appointed by the Owners), shall be under the orders and directions of the Charterers as regards employment and agency; and Charterers are to load, stow, trim and discharge the cargo at their expense under the supervision of the Captain, who is to sign Bills of Lading for cargo as presented, in conformity with Mate's or Tally Clerk's Receipts without prejudice to this Charterparty.'

In due course the Caroline P was ordered to Houston, where she loaded a cargo of about 14,600 metric tons of rice in bags. Two bills of lading, dated respectively 31 December 1974 and 12 January 1975, were issued and signed by the agents for the charterers on behalf of the master. Both bills of lading had typed in after the name of the discharge port the words 'Free out'. According to the arbitrator's reasons the vessel arrived at Surabaya, the first discharge port, on 8 March 1975, and sailed from there to Basrah, where she berthed on or about 31 March. The cargo was discharged during the course of the next three weeks, discharge being completed at 0040 hrs on 21 April 1975. In his reasons the arbitrator stated that 'in all probability no rice [which was the cargo with which the arbitration was concerned] was discharged before 2nd April'.

As the discharge of the rice proceeded it was found that many bags had been badly damaged and subsequently a substantial amount of rebagging took place. The damage to the bags and the resulting shortages led to claims being made by the consignees and proceedings were instituted before the Court of First Instance in Basrah against the owners' agents.

On 11 December 1978 the Court of First Instance gave judgment against the owners' agents in the sum of 79,490·444 Iraqi dinars plus legal fees and expenses of 500 Iraqi dinars. The owners appealed to the Court of Appeal in Basrah, which on 8 May 1979 reduced the damages payable to 57,107·609 Iraqi dinars, but on the owners' further appeal to the Cassation Court and on the charterers' cross-appeal the damages were increased to 79,341·412 Iraqi dinars.

The judgment of the Cassation Court was given on 5 June 1981. All the courts held that the loss and damage were due to bad stowage. According to the surveyor who attended on board the vessel on the instructions of the Court of First Instance in Basrah, however, the damage was caused by a number of factors as set out by the arbitrator in his reasons.

It is now common ground that of these factors four concerned loading or stowage, one concerned discharge and the sixth factor could be connected with loading or discharge.

Faced with the judgment of the Court of Appeal in Basrah, the owners decided to make a claim against the charterers. The parties agreed to Mr John Potter acting as sole arbitrator and his appointment was perfected on 30 March 1981. On 22 July 1981 the owners served their points of claim, claiming the sum awarded by the Court of Appeal in Basrah. On 8 November 1982 the points of claim were amended to increase the sum claimed to correspond with the figure awarded by the Cassation Court in Baghdad.

In para 7 of their pleading, the owners put their claim as follows:

'By Clauses 2 and 8 of the Time Charter, the responsibility for bad stowage is upon the Charterers and there is to be implied from Clause 8 that the Charterers will indemnify the Owners in respect of any liability incurred by the Owners under Bills of Lading in respect of matters for which the Charterers are responsible under the Charterparty.'

The charterers served a defence which was later amended in which they raised a number of defences including a defence that the claim was time-barred. In para 3 of the amended defence, it was pleaded as follows:

'Further the Charterers received notice of the appointment of the Owners' Arbitrator on 9th April 1981. As discharge of the cargo at Basrah took place in March 1975 the appointment was made more than six years after the claim arose. In the premises the Owners' claim is time-barred.'

Despite this plea, however, it is now accepted that the relevant date for the purpose of calculating the limitation period is 30 March 1981.

The matter came on for hearing before the arbitrator on 15 August 1983. By that stage the owners had subdivided their claim under four headings as follows: (a) £22,808·56, being the sum which was equivalent to the amount they had to provide in Iraqi dinars under a guarantee plus interest, (b) $US1,378 for legal expenses in Baghdad, (c) £2,852·01, being the bank charges incurred in servicing the guarantee until 19 July 1983 plus interest, and (d) a declaration that they should be indemnified by the charterers in respect of all further sums and expenses reasonably paid in connection with the cargo claim.

The reason why a declaration was sought was that, although the Cassation Court had given judgment in June 1981, it was still hoped that negotiations might result in a settlement at a lower figure than that awarded. By his award, the arbitrator awarded the owners the sums claimed and made the declaration which they sought. He also adjudged that the charterers should pay the owners' costs of the reference and of the award.

In the course of the hearing before the arbitrator he was referred to some of the authorities to which my attention has been drawn and in particular he had to consider conflicting submissions as to the date when the cause of action on the indemnity arose. In his reasons, he expressed his opinion as follows:

'The cases are difficult to reconcile but on the time-bar point it seems to me that I need go no further than finding that the earliest date for the cause of action arose on completion of discharge of the damaged cargo, for only then can it be said the facts came into existence to create the liability ... In the present case a liability was not established against the Owners under the bill of lading until the judgment of the Iraqi Court in December 1978 and logically, in my view, it cannot be said that before then a liability had been established against the Owners in excess of those undertaken in the charterparty contract. I cannot accept the Charterers' contention that the cause of action arose when the breach occurred. Clearly, all the damage complained of was not wholly attributable to the method of stowage but if it were, the existence of any breach regarding that method of stowage would only become apparent at the time of discharge. The Charterers' argument on this point appeared to me to be artificial.'

Accordingly, the arbitrator found that the claim by the owners was not barred by effluxion of time because discharge was not completed until 21 April 1975, whereas his appointment had been perfected a little less than six years later, on 30 March 1981.

In the course of the argument before me a number of questions were raised which I can summarise as follows. (1) What is the nature of the indemnity to be implied when an owners' agent is required under the terms of the charterparty to sign bills of lading 'as presented'? (2) At what point does time begin to run for the purpose of a period of limitation where the person who has the benefit of such an indemnity seeks to enforce it? (3) What is the extent of the indemnity and in particular does it cover such matters as legal costs and expenses and other expenses including bank charges? (4) Does the indemnity in the present case include sums payable to consignees in respect of claims arising from negligent discharge of the cargo notwithstanding the fact that the bills of lading were marked 'Free out'? I shall deal with the first two questions together.

It was common ground that the bills of lading dated 31 December 1974 and 12 January 1975 imposed obligations on the owners which were more onerous than those stipulated in the charterparty. Thus, by cl 8 of the charterparty, the charterers were responsible for loading, stowing, trimming and discharge. It was also common ground that, though the charterparty contained no express indemnity, the owners were entitled to the benefit of an implied indemnity. There was an issue between the parties, however, as to the nature and extent of this implied indemnity.

On behalf of the charterers it was contended that the indemnity was against liability, whereas on behalf of the owners it was contended that the indemnity was against the consequences of signing more onerous bills of lading. The distinction, which at first sight may appear academic, is of importance when one comes to examine the time at which the period of limitation began to run.

Counsel for the charterers placed great reliance on the language used in the speeches in the House of Lords in *Krüger & Co Ltd v Moel Tryvan Ship Co Ltd* [1907] AC 272 and in *Elder Dempster & Co v C G Dunn & Co (Ltd)* (1909) 15 Com Cas 49. It is necessary to consider these cases in turn.

In the *Krüger* case the charterparty contained a clause exempting the owners from liability for stranding and other accidents of navigation even when occasioned by the negligence of the master. It also contained a clause to the effect that the master was to sign clean bills of lading without prejudice to the charter. By mistake the master signed bills of lading presented by the charterers which did not give the owners the exemption provided for in the charterparty. Subsequently, owing to the negligent navigation of the master, there was a total loss of the cargo and the holders of the bills of lading recovered damages against the owners. It was held that the owners were entitled to be indemnified by the charterers. It is important, however, to examine what was said as to the basis for this entitlement.

In the Court of Appeal both Barnes P, and Farwell LJ based the indemnity on the fact that the charterers had been in breach of contract. At the end of his judgment Barnes P used these words ([1907] 1 KB 809 at 825):

'I base my judgment on this broad ground, that there was a breach of contract on the part of the charterers which has resulted in the loss to the shipowner.'

Farwell LJ said (at 828):

'Now in the present case the bill of lading tendered is entirely different from the charterparty, and the charterer has therefore committed a breach of contract in preparing and tendering and obtaining the execution of such a contract as that.'

Buckley LJ, however, held that the owners were also entitled to recover on the basis that the charterers had requested the owners' agent to sign the bills and the owners were therefore entitled to an indemnity. He said (at 832):

'The right in law seems to me to follow from this, that he requests him to do an act, and then the law implies that if liability results from the act there will be an indemnity given by the one party to the other.'

Counsel for the charterers submitted that in the House of Lords the right to an indemnity appears to have been based on a breach of contract. I should set out the relevant passages. Lord Loreburn LC said (at 276):

'When bills of lading are given they may give rise to rights in persons other than the charterers and on conditions other than those contained in the charterparty; and therefore it is the duty of the charterers who have to present these bills, to provide that they shall not expose the shipowners to risks from which by contract they are to be exempt . . . It is not a case of warranty. It is a case in which, by contract, the shipowners undertook to carry a cargo on the footing that they were not to be liable for the master's negligent navigation, and the charterers have made them so liable by the bills of lading. Hence arises a duty to give adequate indemnity.'

Lord Halsbury said (at 277):

'I agree with Sir Gorell Barnes that the defendants were bound by their contract to tender a bill of lading if they thought proper to do so, and that such bill of lading ought to have incorporated in terms what has been called the negligence clause. I think it is their breach of contract that has occasioned the loss. I think there was a contract by them that if the master signed a bill of lading at their request it should not be in the form of a contract which would strike out the negligence clause . . . As different reasons have been discussed and assigned for the ground upon which the charterers ought to be made liable, I wish to say, inasmuch as I do not concur in some of the reasons given, that I am of opinion that the liability arises from the contract relations between the shipowners and the charterers . . .'

Lord James said (at 281):

'By contract and by course of business the charterers undertook that the bills of lading they presented to the master should be in accordance with the charterparty. They failed in this respect, and by that failure the respondents were rendered liable for the loss occasioned by the negligence of the master.'

Lord Atkinson concurred (at 282).

Having considered these passages I have come to the conclusion that counsel for the charterers' submission is well founded. I shall return later to consider the significance of this conclusion. Before I do so, however, I must examine some of the later cases, starting with *Elder Dempster & Co v C G Dunn & Co (Ltd)* (1909) 15 Com Cas 49.

In the *Elder Dempster* case, as in the *Krüger* case, the House of Lords was concerned with a vessel chartered under a voyage charterparty. The charterparty provided that the charterers were 'to load, stow and trim the cargo at their own expense, under the direction of the Master' and that the master should 'sign bills of lading as presented, without prejudice' to the charterparty. At the conclusion of the loading, in a port in Texas, of the cargo consisting of bales of cotton the charterers presented bills of lading to the master for signature. Some of the bales which had been loaded, however, were not marked in a way which corresponded with the terms of the bills of lading. On arrival at Le Havre some of the consignees refused to accept the wrongly-marked bales and claimed their value from the owners. As by French law the bills of lading constituted conclusive evidence against the owners of the receipt of the goods by them, the owners paid the claims and sought to recover what they had paid from the charterers.

They put the case in two ways: (a) they asserted that the charterers, by presenting the bills of lading with the marks specified in them, requested the master to sign them and therefore that the charterers were liable to indemnify the owners 'from the consequent liability incurred by them'; (b) in the alternative, they asserted that by presenting the bills the charterers 'represented and warranted' to the master that the marks specified therein correctly specified the marks on the bales, and they made this representation and warranty intending that the master should sign the bills and that the owners 'should thereby incur liabilities thereunder'. The speeches in the House of Lords were very short. Lord Loreburn LC said that in his opinion both the relevant paragraphs were fully proved. The Earl of Halsbury concurred with the judgment of the Lord Chancellor, but appears to have founded his decision mainly on the fact that it was the duty of the charterers under the charter to have loaded the vessel and taken care that the proper marks were there. Lord Gorell (as Barnes P had by then become) expressed his concurrence, but then went on to say that he thought that the evidence established the cause of action 'set out in paragraph 11 of the Points of Claim', ie the cause of action based on a representation and warranty. Lord Shaw, too, seems to have taken the view that the charterers were in breach of their obligations under the charterparty relating to the loading of the vessel. Lord Atkinson merely concurred.

I should turn next to the decision of the Court of Appeal in *Dawson Line Ltd v AG Adler für Chemische Industrie of Berlin* [1932] 1 KB 433, [1931] All ER Rep 546. This was another voyage charter case where the charterparty required the master to sign the bill of lading as presented by the charterers. The bills of lading which were signed by the master understated the weight of the cargo and the question which arose in the subsequent arbitration was whether the charterers, who, under the charterparty, would ordinarily have been entitled to pay freight 'on bill of lading weight less 2 per cent in lieu of weighing', were entitled to deduct 2% from the out-turn weight.

Scrutton LJ referred to the *Elder Dempster* and the *Krüger* cases in his judgment and continued ([1932] 1 KB 433 at 439, [1931] All ER Rep 546 at 549–550):

> 'In those cases I was counsel for the successful parties, and I remember that considerable discussion took place as to the lines upon which the claim to indemnity should be put. Some of the judges and law lords said that the charterers were liable on two grounds. The first of these was that a right to indemnity followed from the terms of the charterparty, because it required the master to sign bills of lading in a particular form, and consequently that the charterers must be liable if loss followed in consequence of presenting inaccurate bills of lading. The second ground—and this has nothing to do with the charterparty but turns on the principle stated in *Sheffield Corporation v. Barclay* ([1905] AC 392, [1904–7] All ER Rep 703) and *Birmingham and District Land Co. v. London and North Western Ry. Co.* ((1886) 34 Ch D 261 at 272, [1886–90] All ER 620)—that a mere request from the charterers, involving, as it did, the shipowners in a liability in which otherwise they would not have been involved, raised the implication of an indemnity against those consequences. Some of the judges and law lords took one view, some the other, and some both. In this case it is sufficient to say that as the master was required to sign the bill of lading as presented to him, the charterers were bound to present an accurate bill of lading as to the weight shipped. The shippers were the charterers' agent to supply the cargo and present the bill of lading; they presented an inaccurate bill of lading with consequent loss. The charterers must therefore make good that loss.'

Greer LJ put the matter as follows ([1932] 1 KB 433 at 440, [1931] All ER Rep 546 at 550):

> '... I regard the two cases [*Elder Dempster* and *Krüger*] as meaning this and no more, that if the charterer or some person for whom he is responsible, presents a bill of lading to the master which the latter is bound to sign as part of the terms of the contract, there may be implied from the act in presenting the bill of lading, taken together with the terms of the contract, a warranty of the correctness of the figures, description, or marks stated in the bill of lading.'

Slesser LJ agreed with the reasons given by Greer LJ.

I come next to *Strathlorne Steamship Co Ltd v Andrew Weir & Co* (1934) 50 Ll L Rep 185. In that case the owners had chartered the vessel to the charterers under a time charterparty. By cl 16 of the charterparty, the charterers agreed—

> 'to indemnify the owners from all consequences or liabilities that may arise from the captain signing bills of lading by the orders of charterers or of their agents, or in otherwise complying with the same.'

The charterers sub-chartered the vessel by a voyage charterparty for a voyage from Rangoon to China. On arrival in China some of the goods were delivered without the production of the bills of lading but against letters of guarantee. This was done on the instructions of the charterers' agents. In proceedings in Scotland the owners were found liable to the pledgees of the bills of lading for misdelivery and they claimed an indemnity from the charterers. The owners relied on cl 16 of the charterparty, but they also based their case on a right to an indemnity at common law, relying on a letter dated 5 August 1924 from the charterers' agents instructing the master to deliver against bills of lading or in the absence of bills against guarantees. The points of claim included these words:

'. . . as the said goods . . . were released or delivered by the master on the orders or directions or at the request of the respondents' [charterers'] agents, the respondents [charterers] were and are bound to pay the said claim and to indemnify the claimants [owners] against the same.'

Lord Hanworth MR (at 193) considered the claim based on the letter of 5 August, and applied the words of Tindal CJ in *Toplis v Grane* (1839) 5 Bing NC 636 at 649, [1835–42] All ER Rep 592 at 596:

'. . . where an act has been done by the Plaintiff under the express directions of the Defendant which occasions an injury to the rights of third persons, yet if such act is not apparently illegal in itself, but is done honestly and bonâ fide in compliance with the Defendant's directions, he shall be bound to indemnify the Plaintiff against the consequences thereof.'

Slesser LJ agreed and cited the same passage from the judgment of Tindal CJ. He added (50 Ll L Rep 185 at 194):

'. . . as it seems to me, in the facts of this case all the constituents of an implied promise to indemnify arise.'

Romer LJ agreed too, but he also considered the matter on the basis that the ship's agents had wrongly delivered the cargo at the instigation of the charterers. He said (at 195):

'Now, if the agents for the ship do a wrong to their own principals at the instigation of the time charterers, then plainly in accordance with the principle which was applied in the case of Kruger & Co., Ltd. v. Moel Tryvan Ship Company, Ltd. ([1907] AC 272), the time charterers became liable to indemnify the principals against the consequences of the agents acting on their direction. For these reasons, as well as those given by the other members of the Court, I think this appeal fails.'

Finally I come to three cases decided in the last 20 years in which the court gave specific consideration to the question whether a claim under an indemnity was statute-barred. In each of these cases the indemnity was an express indemnity.

The first of these cases, and the one on which counsel for the charterers placed particular reliance, is *Bosma v Larsen* [1966] 1 Lloyd's Rep 22. In that case the owners chartered a motor vessel to the charterers on time charter. Clause 9 of the charterparty provided:

'The Master to be under the orders of the Charterers as regards employment, agency, or other arrangements. The Charterers to indemnify the Owners against all consequences or liabilities arising from the Master . . . signing Bills of Lading or other documents or otherwise complying with such orders . . .'

Subsequently a bill of lading was signed by agents on behalf of the master and as ordered by the charterers. On arrival, part of the cargo was found to be damaged. It was accepted for the purpose of the action that under the bill of lading the owners were liable to the receivers for that damage but that they were not liable under the terms of the charterparty.

In those circumstances the owners claimed to be indemnified by the charterers for the sum they had to pay. The charterers admitted that the indemnity in cl 9 applied to the case but set up the defence that the claim was barred by statute under the Limitation Act 1939.

I should refer to parts of the judgment of McNair J, who said (at 25):

> 'Admittedly the cause of action for an indemnity under Clause 9 of the charterparty is an action founded on simple contract. The writ having been issued on Mar. 12, 1965, the defence succeeds if the cause of action accrued before Mar. 12, 1959. If as the plaintiff contends the cause of action accrued after that date, it fails. In summary, the plaintiff contends that the cause of action accrued at the earliest when judgment was entered against him on Mar. 10, 1962, or alternatively on Dec. 17, 1963, when he paid under the compromise settlement. The defendant on the other hand contends that the cause of action accrued at the latest when the goods were discharged damaged at Naples in July, 1956, and therefore accrued at a date outside the six-year limitation period ... as it seems to me, the material question in this case is: When, on the facts stated above, did a factual situation arise which, subject to the effect of the Limitation Act 1939, would have entitled the plaintiff to have obtained from the Court a judgment against the defendant in respect of the indemnity relied on?'

McNair J then referred to some of the authorities to which his attention had been drawn, and continued (at 27):

> 'Accordingly, in my judgment, the first task of the Court is to construe the document and it is not proper or consistent with the authorities to apply a label to an obligation in a document and then to deduce from that label the legal consequences which may flow from other contracts to which the same label can be attached ... Accordingly the issue in this case which I have to decide depends on my view of the proper construction of Clause 9 ... Though the range of the protection afforded by clauses of this nature to the shipowners has not yet been fully worked out by the decisions of the Courts there have been a number of decisions on the question which are noted in Scrutton on Charterparties ((17th edn, 1964) art 154) which have established certain instances of incidents which are within or without the protection of the Clause; but so far as I know it has never been held that payment by the shipowner of a claim or determination of his liability by a judicial decision was a condition precedent to the shipowner's rights of recovery. It seems to me that the plain meaning of the expression to indemnify against "all liabilities" is that it imposes the obligation to indemnify against the incurring of a liability, not the discharge of that liability by payment or the determination of that liability by judicial process. Indemnity against liability seems to me to be different from reimbursement against sums paid in pursuance of a legal liability. The shipowner is damnified as soon as he comes under a liability. The damnification contemplated by the Clause is the incurring of the liability not the payment ... I accordingly conclude that on the agreed facts of this case the plaintiff's cause of action under Clause 9 of the charter-party arose at the date when the facts came into existence which created their liability to the cargo-owners or their insurers which facts came into existence before the date when the six-year period of limitation began and was not dependent upon either the determination of liability by the Italian Court on Mar. 10, 1962 or the plaintiff's payment under the compromise settlement on Dec. 17, 1963.'

The judge then considered an argument that since the fusion of law and equity the cause of action on a true indemnity arises as soon as there comes into existence a right to seek equitable relief. The judge expressed no concluded opinion on this point.

In 1974 *Bosma v Larsen* was considered by Swanwick J in *County and District Properties Ltd v C Jenner & Son Ltd* [1976] 2 Lloyd's Rep 728. In that case Swanwick J was concerned with express indemnities contained in contracts between building contractors and their sub-contractors. By the relevant clause, sub-contractors agreed to indemnify and save harmless the contractors against and from—

'(i) any breach non-observance or non-performance by the subcontractor his servants or agents of the said provisions of the main contract or any of them; (ii) any act or omission of the subcontractor, his servants or agents which involves the contractor in any liability to the employer under the main contract; (iii) any claim damage loss or expense due to or resulting from any negligence or breach of duty on the part of the subcontractor his servants or agents.'

There was an additional sub-cl (iv) to which I do not need to refer.

Work on the building site was completed on 28 October 1964. In 1969 the building owners brought proceedings against the main contractors claiming damages for breach of contract. In May 1971 the main contractors issued third party notices against the sub-contractors. The sub-contractors contended that the claims by the main contractors were barred because six years had elapsed since the completion of the work. Swanwick J summarised the arguments of counsel (at 732):

'It was common ground that the claim of the defendants against all third parties was for an indemnity under a simple contract; that the period of limitation was therefore six years from when the cause of action first accrued; that this must be the date when there arose . . . "A factual situation, the existence of which entitles one person to obtain from the Court a remedy against another person . . ." and that this stage would be reached when the defendants were damnified.'

Swanwick J next referred to the argument on behalf of the main contractors:

'Counsel . . . contends firstly that at common law the damnification of a person indemnified under a contract never occurred until he had had to pay, and had paid, money. He submitted that in equity the rule was relaxed to the extent that time started to run when the fact and extent of the liability of the person to be indemnified was ascertained or established.'

The judge then considered the authorities to which he had been referred and the arguments put forward on behalf of the sub-contractors, including an argument that, because equity could grant relief by means of a declaration or the setting up of a fund, the cause of action arose immediately on a breach by the sub-contractor. Swanwick J continued (at 734):

'These authorities satisfy me that . . . the general rule in cases of indemnity is that while equity will safeguard the position pending the ascertainment of the fact and extent of liability of the person to be indemnified, he has no cause of action until such ascertainment. There is thus a strong body of authority not only in favour of [the main contractors'] proposition as to when the cause of action for an indemnity arises at common law as modified by equity but also to the effect that these rules . . . are universal.'

The judge then turned his attention to the decision in *Bosma v Larsen*, which he described as the only authority which had been cited to him which was contrary to the rule which he had just formulated, and continued (at 735):

'From this case, as I understood it, all the third parties invited me to deduce the principle that the propositions put forward by [the main contractors] were not of general, and certainly not of universal, application and that every contract of indemnity should be scrutinized to determine from its wording whether . . . the event to be indemnified is a loss or damage or expense . . . or a breach of contract act or omission of the indemnifier . . . If I were untrammelled by authority, I could see some attractions in this distinction; I can also see some dangers, for it could mean a multiplicity of writs in respect of defects observed by the contractor, which might or might not result in a claim against him . . . Having regard to the authorities to which I have referred, I do not feel at liberty to accept the distinction contended for by the third parties; it may be that the case of *Bosma* v. *Larsen* can be distinguished on its special facts; if not, I fear that I must differ from it, and reaffirm the principles for which [the main contractors] contend. After all, an indemnity against a breach, or an act, or an omission, can only be an indemnity against the harmful consequences that may flow from it, and I take the law to be that the indemnity does not give rise to a cause of action until those consequences are ascertained.'

The third of the three cases in which a limitation defence was considered is *R & H Green & Silley Weir Ltd v British Rlys Board (Kavanagh, third party)* (1980) [1985] 1 All ER 237. In that case the third parties carried out tipping in 1970 and 1971 in a railway cutting owned by the board. The work was done under an agreement whereby, inter alia, the third parties agreed to indemnify the board—

'from and against all liability for personal injury (whether fatal or otherwise) loss of or damage to property and any other loss damage costs and expenses which might arise in consequence of the grant or existence of this Agreement or of anything done as a result of its grant or existence . . .'

In 1974 adjoining landowners brought an action against the board complaining of damage. The action made slow progress but eventually, in 1979, the board joined the third parties. The third parties asserted that the claim was time-barred. On the trial of a preliminary issue Dillon J held that the relevant clause in the agreement constituted a general indemnity in favour of the board and that time did not run against the board until the liability, if any, of the board to the plaintiffs in the action had been established and ascertained. Dillon J supported the decision of Swanwick J in the *Jenner* case and declined to follow *Bosma v Larsen*.

From a consideration of these cases and other authorities to which my attention was directed it seems to me that it is possible to identify at least three ways in which a person A who has become liable to B may be able to obtain redress from C.

The first way is by an action for damages for breach of contract (or warranty). In such a case A will be in a position to claim that the incurring of his liability to B flowed directly from an act of C which constituted a breach of a contract between A and C or of a warranty given by C to A. The damages will be assessed in accordance with *Hadley v Baxendale* (1854) 9 Exch 341, [1843–60] All ER Rep 461 principles. The cause of action will date from the date of breach.

The second way is by a claim on an express indemnity. In such a case the extent of the indemnity and the time at which the cause of action arises will depend on the construction of the contract. If the indemnity is an indemnity against liability, as it was held to be in *Bosma v Larsen*, the cause of action will come into existence when A incurs a liability to B. It may be that in certain circumstances a liability may be incurred for this purpose when the liability is still merely contingent (see *Forster v Outred & Co (a firm)* [1982] 2 All ER 753, [1982] 1 WLR 86). If, however, the indemnity is a general indemnity, as the relevant clause was held to be in *R & H Green & Silley Weir Ltd v British Rlys Board* then time will not begin to run against A for the purpose of pursuing his indemnity against C until A's liability to B has been established and ascertained: see below. One may notice in passing that, as the arbitrator pointed out in his reasons, McNair J did not deal separately with the words 'all consequences' in the contractual indemnity in *Bosma v Larsen*.

The third way in which A may claim against C in respect of sums which he has had to pay to B is under an implied indemnity. As I understand the matter, such an implied indemnity would prima facie be a general indemnity of the kind recognised by the common law. The rules relating to what I have described as a general indemnity were explained by Fletcher Moulton LJ as follows in *Re Richardson, ex p St Thomas's Hospital Governors* [1911] 2 KB 705 at 712–713:

'If, for instance, B. was bound to pay a sum to A. and C. was bound to indemnify B. . . . then B could not sue C. unless he could aver payment to A. It was the same thing whether it was a case of suretyship, indemnity, or contribution. In all cases before you could make a guarantor pay you must prove that you had actually paid the money. No better example of this could be given than the case of *Collinge* v.

*Heywood* ((1839) 9 Ad & El 633, 112 ER 1352). That was a contract to indemnify a plaintiff against costs, and it was decided that the cause of action arose when he paid the costs, not when the costs were incurred or the attorney's bill was delivered to him; and it happened that it was a point of cardinal importance in that case to decide the moment when the cause of action arose, because it was a question there of the date from which the Statute of Limitations began to run. There the Court applied the well-known common law principle that before you can avail yourself of your right of indemnity you must shew that you have paid the money . . . the rule in Chancery was somewhat different, and yet, to my mind, it emphasizes the fundamental principle that you must have paid before you have a right to indemnity, because the remedy which equity gave was a declaration of a right. You could file a bill against the principal debtor to make him pay the debt so that you would not be called upon to pay it, and then you obtained a declaration that you were entitled to an indemnity. You could in certain cases have a fund set aside in order that you might be indemnified, to avoid the necessity of your having to pay and then to sue for the money you had paid, which perhaps would not repair your loss and credit even if it discharged the debt. But I do not think that equity ever compelled a surety to pay money to the person to whom he was surety before the latter had actually paid. He might be ordered to set a fund aside, but I do think that he could be ordered to pay.'

It seems clear, however, that even in equity time does not begin to run for the purposes of any limitation period until the liability of the person to be indemnified has been ascertained. I can see no satisfactory distinction on this point between claims on an indemnity and claims between sureties or trustees (cf *Wolmershausen v Gullick* [1893] 2 Ch 514, [1891–4] All ER Rep 740, *Robinson v Harkin* [1896] 2 Ch 415, *Littlewood v George Wimpey & Co Ltd* [1953] 2 All ER 915 at 923–924, [1953] 2 QB 501 at 519).

With this introduction I return to the facts of the instant case.

It will be remembered that in para 7 of the points of claim in the arbitration the indemnity was put forward as an indemnity against liability to be implied from cl 8 of the charterparty, in other words an implied contractual indemnity against liability. Before me, however, the arguments as to the true basis of the indemnity were wide-ranging and I do not propose to decide the matter on any point of pleading.

The owners' right to recover can, as I see it, be formulated in a number of different ways as follows. (a) As a claim on a breach of an implied term of the charterparty, the breach consisting of the presentation of the bills of lading for signature. On this basis the cause of action arose at the moment of breach. (b) As a claim based on an implied indemnity against liability. On this basis the cause of action arose when a liability to the receivers was incurred. Counsel for the charterers argued that a contingent liability to the receivers was incurred as soon as the bills of lading were signed and he relied on *Forster v Outred & Co* [1982] 2 All ER 753, [1982] 1 WLR 86. If such a contingent liability is not enough it seems clear that, as to the majority of the claim at any rate which was a claim for shortages, the cause of action did not arise until the cargo was discharged in the period between 2 and 21 April 1975. (c) As a claim based on an implied general indemnity. Such an indemnity would, as counsel for the owners put it, indemnify the owners from the 'consequences' of the master signing the bills of lading in terms which were more onerous than the charterparty.

I have had to consider whether the true view of this case is that the charterers were in breach of an implied term of the charterparty in putting the bills of lading before the master for signature and that the subsequent losses suffered by the owners flowed from that breach. Such a solution would not seem out of line with some of the speeches in the *Krüger* case. But the case has been argued on the basis of an implied indemnity, the issue being as to the nature of such indemnity. Furthermore, it appears that where a person is entitled to rely on an implied indemnity he can make a claim on such an indemnity in addition to making a claim based on some express provision of his contract with the indemnifier or (semble) a claim for damages for breach of contract. I turn therefore to the implied indemnity.

It seems to me that there is great force in the argument that as a matter of principle an indemnity which is to be implied from the terms of a contract or from the conduct of the potential indemnifier should be an indemnity against the *incurring* of liability. But a long line of cases establishes that at common law a person who is entitled to an indemnity cannot enforce it until he has made a payment to the third party. In M'*Gillivray v Hope* [1935] AC 1 at 10, Lord Tomlin set out the common law rule succinctly:

> '. . . where one who is liable to pay a sum of money to another is entitled against a third party to be indemnified in whole or in part against what he has so to pay, he cannot recover on the indemnity against this party where he himself has made no payment in respect of his own liability (see *Collinge* v. *Heywood*) . . .'

This common law rule has now been modified because in equity the person to be indemnified can seek relief as soon as his liability has been ascertained (cf *Littlewood v George Wimpey & Co Ltd* and the cases there cited).

I have therefore come to the conclusion, though not without hesitation, that the implied indemnity to which the owners are entitled in the present case is of the kind suggested by counsel for the owners, namely an indemnity against the consequences of the master signing the bills of lading, and that such an indemnity did not become enforceable by action until at the earliest the liability of the owners to the receivers had been ascertained by the Court of First Instance in Basrah in December 1978.

In reaching this conclusion I have not overlooked an argument that the owners might have been entitled to invoke the assistance of a court of equity to obtain declaratory relief or the setting up of a fund before the Iraqi court had reached its decision. I very much doubt, however, on the facts of this case whether a court of equity would have given any relief before December 1978, but, even if it had, I do not consider that such an action would have affected the time at which the cause of action for the recovery of any moneys from the charterers would have begun to run: see above.

I should, however, also express a view on the alternative hypothesis that time began to run for the purposes of the indemnity from the moment when the owners first incurred a liability to the consignees. As counsel for the owners pointed out, the major part of the claims by the consignees was in respect of shortages. I do not see how the consignees could have brought a claim in respect of these shortages before the completion of the period of discharge or, at the very earliest, the commencement of the discharge. Discharge commenced on 2 April 1975, and even on this basis the appointment of the arbitrator was just in time. Moreover, even in respect of the damaged bags, the claim by the consignees would have been formulated as a claim in respect of the bags discharged in a damaged condition. Accordingly, as I see it, no *actual* liability was incurred to the consignees before 2 April 1975.

It will be remembered, however, that counsel for the charterers argued that, for the purpose of a claim under the implied indemnity, the relevant date was the date when a *contingent* liability to the receivers was incurred. This date, or these dates, were in December 1974 or January 1975, when the bags were badly stowed and when the bills of lading were signed. I see the force of the argument on this point based on the decision of the Court of Appeal in *Forster v Outred & Co*, but I have come to the conclusion that, even if the indemnity is to be construed as an indemnity against the incurring of liability, such an indemnity could not have been invoked by the owners until they had incurred some *actual* liability to the consignees.

For these reasons I am satisfied that the arbitrator was correct in his decision that the claim by the owners was not time-barred.

I can deal with the two remaining arguments very shortly.

It seems to me that once it is established that the owners are entitled to an indemnity then that indemnity should be an adequate indemnity. The owners were found liable by the Iraqi courts in the sums and to the extent claimed in the arbitration. It has not been suggested that the owners failed to conduct the case properly in Iraq and it is to be observed that the case was taken on appeal to the Cassation Court.

In my judgment they are entitled to the relief which they obtained from the arbitrator.

It is to be observed that in *Strathlorne Steamship Co Ltd v Andrew Weir & Co* (1935) 50 Ll L Rep 185 at 187 the express indemnity was held to cover claims for costs including the costs of the claimants' own solicitors.

The final argument concerned the effect of the words 'Free out' in the bills of lading. It is uncertain how far this point was canvassed before the Iraqi courts. It seems to me, however, on the facts of this case that the court cannot reopen the issue of the liability of the owners to the receivers. I see no ground for interfering with the decision of the arbitrator on this point.

For these reasons I have come to the conclusion that this appeal must be dismissed.

*Appeal dismissed.*

Solicitors: *Richards Butler & Co* (for the charterers); *Clyde & Co* (for the owners).

K Mydeen Esq   Barrister.

# Practice Direction

CHANCERY DIVISION

*Practice – Chancery Division – Proceedings outside London – Excepted Chancery jurisdiction – Order for trial – Standard directions – Pleadings to be lodged – Transfer between district registries.*

1. A circuit judge exercising the powers of a judge of the Chancery Division has been sitting at Birmingham, Bristol and Cardiff since 4 October 1982. He exercises a general Chancery jurisdiction with certain specific exceptions. These exceptions are the same as those for Liverpool, Manchester and the other northern districts, as set out in *The Supreme Court Practice 1985* vol 1, para 34/4/8. Put shortly, these exceptions are: revenue, bankruptcy and patents; certain statutory jurisdictions, namely proceedings under Pt VII of the Mental Health Act 1983, or under the Defence Contracts Act 1958 or the Registered Designs Acts 1949 to 1961; appeals to the Divisional Court of the Chancery Division; and appeals, cases stated and questions referred for the opinion of the court which fall within RSC Ord 93, r 10(2).

2. If an action or originating summons is proceeding in the Birmingham, Bristol or Cardiff district registries, the district registrar will in a clear case make the order for trial either in Birmingham, Bristol or Cardiff, or else in London, as the case requires. In case of difficulty he will consult the judge, who may hear the matter himself or deal with it informally.

3. When standard directions under RSC Ord 25, r 9(1) are required and all the parties wish the case to be tried in Birmingham, Bristol or Cardiff, one copy of the pleadings must be lodged in the appropriate district registry with the written consent of all parties indorsed thereon, indicating the place of trial desired and the estimated length of hearing. Another copy must be lodged at the same time in order to comply with the provisions for setting down under RSC Ord 34, r 3(1), which requires two bundles to be lodged.

4. If a Chancery action is proceeding on the Midland and Oxford, Western, or Wales and Chester circuits in any district registry other than Birmingham, Bristol or Cardiff, and trial at Birmingham, Bristol or Cardiff is desired, the action should be transferred to the Birmingham, Bristol or Cardiff district registry (as the case may be) on the first hearing of the summons for directions. This direction applies also to an originating summons.

By direction of the Vice-Chancellor.

EDMUND HEWARD
Chief Master.

18 December 1984

# Payne (Inspector of Taxes) v Barratt Developments (Luton) Ltd

HOUSE OF LORDS
LORD SCARMAN, LORD KEITH OF KINKEL, LORD BRIDGE OF HARWICH, LORD BRANDON OF
OAKBROOK AND LORD BRIGHTMAN
14 NOVEMBER, 13 DECEMBER 1984

*Statute – Construction – Word – Word occurring more than once in enactment – Consistency in meaning – Contrary intention – Rule that word should be given consistent meaning – Rule to give way where contrary intention indicated – Land – Finance Act 1976, Sch 5, para 29(2)(b)(3) – Interpretation Act 1978, Sch 2, para 5(b).*

*Income tax – Computation of profits – Stock-in-trade – Valuation – Land – Taxpayer carrying on business of building houses for sale – Taxpayer accepting customers' existing properties in satisfaction or part-satisfaction of purchase price of houses – Taxpayer selling properties in their existing condition – Whether properties 'land' – Whether properties can be included in taxpayer's stock-in-trade – Whether taxpayer entitled to stock relief in respect of any increase in value of properties – Finance Act 1976, Sch 5, para 29(2)(b)(3).*

The rule that a word which occurs more than once in an enactment should be given the same meaning whenever it occurs is a guide which must yield to indications of contrary intention. Paragraph 29[a] of Sch 5 to the Finance Act 1976 does indicate such a contrary intention in respect of the word 'land' where it occurs in sub-paras (2)(b) and (3), so that, although 'land' in sub-para (2)(b) is to be given the meaning assigned to that word by para 5(b)[b] of Sch 2 to the Interpretation Act 1978 and therefore includes any buildings on the land in question, 'land' in sub-para (3) in its context is necessarily required to be limited to such land as is capable of being developed by the construction or reconstruction of buildings on it. Accordingly a taxpayer which carries on business as a builder of houses for sale and which accepts customers' existing properties in satisfaction or part-satisfaction of the purchase price of its houses cannot include the properties acquired from its customers in its stock-in-trade so as to claim stock relief under Sch 5 to the 1976 Act in respect of any increase in the value in those properties if it intends merely to sell them as soon as possible in their existing condition (see p 258 e and p 260 b to p 261 a, post).

*IRC v Clydebridge Properties Ltd* [1980] STC 68 overruled.

## Notes

For consistency in the meaning of a word in a statute, see 44 Halsbury's Laws (4th edn) para 873, and for cases on the subject, see 44 Digest (Repl) 219–220, 354–357.

For relief for increases in value of trading stock for income tax purposes, see 23 Halsbury's Laws (4th edn) para 275.

For the Finance Act 1976, Sch 5, para 29, see 49 Halsbury's Statutes (3rd edn) 1782.

For the Interpretation Act 1978, Sch 2, para 5, see 48 ibid 1325.

With effect in relation to any period of account beginning after 14 November 1980 a new scheme of stock relief was introduced by Sch 9 to the Finance Act 1981, and paras 28 to 30 of that schedule define 'trading stock'.

## Case referred to in opinions

*IRC v Clydebridge Properties Ltd* [1980] STC 68, 53 TC 313, CS.

---

a  Paragraph 29, so far as material, is set out at p 258 h to p 259 b, post
b  Paragraph 5, so far as material, provides: '. . . (b) in any Act passed before [1 January 1979] and after the year 1850, "land" includes messuages, tenements and hereditaments, houses and buildings of any tenure . . .'

**Appeal**

In the accounting period ended 30 June 1979 Barratt Developments (Luton) Ltd (the company) acquired five old houses from their customers in exchange or part-exchange for its new homes sold to them. The company claimed that the old properties were its stock-in-trade and claimed stock relief pursuant to para 29(1) of Sch 5 to the Finance Act 1976. The Revenue rejected the company's claim on the ground that the old properties, being 'land', were excluded from the definition of trading stock under para 29(2)(b). The Commissioners for the Special Purposes of the Income Tax Acts allowed the company's appeal holding that 'land' in the context meant undeveloped land and did not include buildings and disallowed stock relief only in respect of the gardens. On 18 November 1983 Vinelott J ([1984] STC 65) dismissed the Crown's appeal, but granted a certificate under s 12 of the Administration of Justice Act 1969 to apply to the House of Lords for leave to appeal direct to the House. On 20 February 1984 leave was given by the House for the appeal to be heard. The facts are set out in the opinion of Lord Keith.

*Nicholas Phillips QC* and *Robert Carnwath* for the Crown
*Stephen Oliver QC* for the company.

Their Lordships took time for consideration.

13 December. The following opinions were delivered.

**LORD SCARMAN.** My Lords, I have had the advantage of reading in draft the speech to be delivered by my noble and learned friend Lord Keith. I agree with it and for the reasons he gives I would allow the appeal.

**LORD KEITH OF KINKEL.** My Lords, the principal trade of Barratt Developments (Luton) Ltd (the company) is the building of houses for sale. They found that potential buyers were often inhibited because they encountered difficulty in selling their existing dwellings in order to raise the funds necessary for their intended purchases. So they adopted a scheme whereby they accepted customers' properties in satisfaction or part-satisfaction of the purchase price of houses which they had for sale. The properties so acquired were sold as soon as possible in their existing condition.

At the end of their accounting year to 30 June 1979 the company had on their books five properties acquired under this scheme, namely two freehold semi-detached houses with gardens, a freehold terraced house with garden, a ground-floor leasehold flat without exclusive garden rights and a second-floor leasehold flat with no garden rights. They claimed stock relief in respect of all five properties under s 37 of and Sch 5 to the Finance Act 1976. By virtue of para 9 of that schedule a trading company, where the value of its trading stock at the end of an accounting period exceeds its value at the beginning of that period, is entitled to relief against corporation tax assessed on Case I, Sch D income tax principles. The amount of the relief is the amount of the increase in stock value during any accounting period less 15% of the relevant income of the trade for that period.

'Trading stock' is defined in para 29 of the schedule, which, so far as material, provides:

'(1) Subject to the provisions of this paragraph, in this Schedule "trading stock" means property of any description, whether real or personal, being either—(a) property such as is sold in the ordinary course of the trade, profession or vocation in question, or would be so sold if it were mature or if its manufacture, preparation or construction were complete; or (b) materials such as are used in the manufacture, preparation or construction of any such property as is referred to in paragraph (a) above, and includes work in progress.

(2) Sub-paragraph (1) above does not apply to—(a) securities, which for this

purpose includes stocks and shares; or (b) land, other than such as is ordinarily sold in the course of the trade, profession or vocation only—(i) after being developed by the person carrying on the trade, profession or vocation, or (ii) in the case of a company which is a member of a group, for the purpose of being developed by another company in that group; or (c) goods which the person carrying on the trade, profession or vocation has let on hire or hire-purchase.

(3) In sub-paragraph (2) above, references to development are references to the construction or substantial reconstruction of buildings on the land in question and "group" shall be construed in accordance with section 272 of the [Income and Corporation Taxes Act 1970]...'

The Revenue accepted that the five properties were such as were sold in the ordinary course of the company's trade, but rejected the claim on the ground that they were excluded by sub-para (2) as being land other than such as was ordinarily sold only after being developed by the company. The company appealed to the Special Commissioners, who held that they were entitled to relief except in respect of the gardens of the three freehold properties. The Revenue in turn appealed to the High Court. On 18 November 1983 Vinelott J ([1984] STC 65) dismissed the appeal, but granted a certificate under s 12(1) and (3)(b) of the Administration of Justice Act 1969. Leave to appeal direct to this House was given on 20 February 1984. The principal reason why the certificate and the leave to appeal were granted was the existence of a previous decision directly in point by the Inner House of the Court of Session, namely *IRC v Clydebridge Properties Ltd* [1980] STC 68, which Vinelott J felt constrained, somewhat reluctantly, to follow.

That case was decided under s 54 of and Sch 10 to the Finance (No 2) Act 1975, which were reproduced by s 37 of and Sch 5 to the 1976 Act, para 16 of the former schedule corresponding to para 29 of the latter. The facts were that the company carried on the trade of buying and selling small residential flats in tenement properties. Apparently its stock of such flats during the material period did not include any ground-floor flats. The First Division (the Lord President (Emslie), Lord Cameron and Lord Avonside) held that the flats were trading stock of the company, not being excluded by sub-para (2) of para 16. The opinion of the court was delivered by Lord Avonside (not, as stated in the report at 53 TC 313, by the Lord President). Having referred to the definition of 'land' in s 3 of the Interpretation Act 1889, viz 'In every Act ... unless the contrary intention appears ... The expression "land" shall include messuages, tenements, and hereditaments, houses, and buildings of any tenure...' he said ([1980] STC 68 at 71–72):

'The argument appears to be that s 3 of the Interpretation Act 1889 should be applied, therefore a flat is "land" and that "land" is taken out of para 16(1)(a) by the provisions of sub-para (2)(b)(i) unless it is "developed". In the first place it is more than doubtful whether it is permissible to take from the definition of "land" in the 1889 Act only one of the terms used. If an attempt is made to apply the whole definition to para 16(2)(b) it becomes completely meaningless. If it is permissible to extract the word "building" and use it as "land" then para 16(2)(b) as necessarily construed together with para 16(3) reads as follows: "(2) Sub-paragraph (1) above does not apply to a building other than such as is ordinarily sold in the course of the trade only after the construction or substantial reconstruction of buildings on the building in question" and that result is plainly inoperable. It illustrates that there is obviously an intention in the 1975 Act contrary to the application of s 3 of the 1889 Act and that therefore the extended definition of "land" in that Act does not apply. Further it is clear the wording of para 16 of Sch 10 does recognise the existence of land with a building on it. This alone demonstrates the futility of attempting to apply s 3 of the 1889 Act. That section if once applied to interpret the word "land" must be consistent in its application. It cannot be used in one sense in para 16 of the schedule and used in another sense, or departed from, to suit the convenience of argument. Unless selective meanings could be permitted the argument for the Crown fails.'

So in the result it was held that the only kind of heritable property which was excluded from the definition of trading stock by sub-para (2)(b) was land in a completely undeveloped state, ie such as had no buildings or structures on it of any kind. That was supported by the company in the instant appeal and sought by them to be applied in a corresponding situation in England. Counsel for the Crown, on the other hand, argued that the definition of land in para 5(b) of the Interpretation Act 1978 was to be read into sub-para (2).

It is clear that the proper construction of sub-para (2)(b) would present no difficulty if it were not for the presence of sub-para (3). Applying the Interpretation Act meaning of 'land' to that word in sub-para (2)(b) would have the result of demonstrating that no land, in that wide sense, was intended to have the benefit of stock relief unless it was such as was not ordinarily sold in the course of the trade by the person carrying on the trade except after development by that person. That would evince an entirely reasonable and intelligible policy. The fact that land can embrace various species of property which by their nature, are not capable of being developed would not present any problem. It would only be such species as were capable of being developed that would fall into the privileged class if they were not ordinarily sold in an undeveloped state. The purpose of sub-para (3) is to define the meaning of references to development in sub-para (2), and it prescribes a more limited meaning than would, in a planning context, be applicable to such references. Here again the definition can only have relevance in connection with such species of land as are capable of being developed. Having regard to what is the clear purpose of sub-para (3), it cannot, in my opinion, be relied on so as to attribute to 'land' in sub-para (2)(b) a special limited meaning, excluding the application of the Interpretation Act. If it had been the intention of the draftsman to limit the meaning to land which is unbuilt on, one would have expected him to say so expressly. Further, it seems to me that the references to 'reconstruction of buildings on the land in question' recognises that some land which is within the ambit of sub-para (2) may be land with buildings on it. Obviously the land and the buildings on it form one hereditament. The Interpretation Act does not require an artificial separation between land and a building erected on it, contrary to the maxim quiquid plantatur solo, solo cedit. For these reasons I am of opinion that there is nothing in the context to exclude the application of the Interpretation Act definition to the word 'land' in sub-para (2)(b), whereas the context of sub-para (3) necessarily requires its limitation there to such land as is capable of being developed by the construction or reconstruction of buildings on it. The rule that the same word occurring more than once in an enactment should be given the same meaning wherever it occurs is a guide which must yield to indications of contrary intention, and such an intention must necessarily be inferred here. A further consideration in favour of that view is that the contrary one would require a separation of the site of a building from the building itself, with relief being available in respect of the latter but not in respect of the former. This would involve an apportionment of value, for which no machinery is provided.

The fallacy in the reasoning contained in the opinion of the court in *IRC v Clydebridge Properties Ltd* appears to me, with respect, to have been a failure to appreciate that sub-para (2), in creating an exception within an exception, carved out from the generality of the meaning of the word 'land' a particular limited category of land, namely such as was capable of being developed. I conclude that the case was wrongly decided and should be overruled.

My Lords, for these reasons I would allow the appeal.


**LORD BRIDGE OF HARWICH.** My Lords, for the reasons given in the speech of my noble and learned friend Lord Keith, with which I agree, I would allow this appeal.


**LORD BRANDON OF OAKBROOK.** My Lords, I have had the advantage of reading in draft the speech prepared by my noble and learned friend Lord Keith. I agree with it, and for the reasons which he gives I would allow the appeal.

**LORD BRIGHTMAN.** My Lords, I also would allow this appeal for the reasons given in the speech of my noble and learned friend Lord Keith.

*Appeal allowed.*

Solicitors: *Solicitor of Inland Revenue*; *Slaughter & May* (for the company).

Rengan Krishnan Esq    Barrister.

# Harvela Investments Ltd v Royal Trust Co of Canada (CI) Ltd and others

COURT OF APPEAL, CIVIL DIVISION

WALLER, OLIVER AND PURCHAS LJJ

18, 19, 20, 21, 22 JUNE, 18 JULY 1984

*Contract – Offer and acceptance – Invitation to treat – Contract for sale of shares – Invitation to make bids for shares – Party inviting bids stating that it bound itself to accept highest bid – Whether invitation to bid an offer or invitation to treat.*

*Contract – Implied term – Bids – Sealed bids – Contract for sale of shares – Invitation to make sealed competitive bids for shares – Bid of '$101,000 in excess of any other offer' – Whether implied term in invitation to bid excluding bids framed by reference to other bids.*

*Interest – Sale of shares – Interest on unpaid purchase money – Vendor not entitled to interest if 'delay on our part' – Vendor prevented by third party's injunction from completing – Whether purchaser liable to interest during period of delay.*

The plaintiff and the second defendant were rival offerors for a parcel of shares which would give effective control of a company to the plaintiff or to the second defendant and his family, whichever was the successful offeror. The parcel of shares was held by the first defendants, the trustees of a settlement, who invited both parties to submit by sealed offer or confidential telex a 'single offer' for the whole parcel by a stipulated date. The trustees stated in the invitation to bid that 'we bind ourselves to accept [the highest] offer'. The invitation to bid further stated that interest was payable by the purchaser in the event of delay in completing the purchase, unless completion was unable to take place 'by reason of any delay on our [the trustees'] part'. The plaintiff tendered a bid of $2,175,000. The second defendant tendered a bid of '$2,100,000 or ... $101,000 in excess of any other offer ... which is expressed as a fixed monetary amount, whichever is the higher'. The trustees accepted the second defendant's bid, as being a bid of $2,276,000, and entered into a contract with the second defendant for the sale of the parcel of shares. The trustees also informed the plaintiff of the terms of the second defendant's bid, whereupon the plaintiff commenced proceedings against the trustees and the second defendant, contending that the second defendant's bid was invalid because (i) it was not a 'single offer' within the terms of the invitation to bid and (ii) it was an implied term of the invitation to bid that referential bids (ie bids framed by reference to other bids) would be excluded from the bidding. The plaintiff obtained an interlocutory injunction preventing the trustees from accepting the second defendant's bid and in its action sought (i) a declaration that there was a binding contract between the trustees and the plaintiff for the sale of the shares for the sum of $2,175,000 and (ii) specific performance of that contract. The judge upheld the plaintiff's claim on the ground that it was an implied term of the trustees' invitation to bid that referential bids would be excluded. The second defendant appealed. The trustees cross-appealed, contending that if the second defendant's bid was held to be the successful bid the second defendant was liable to pay interest from the stipulated completion date.

**Held** – (1) The trustees' invitation to bid constituted a contractual offer rather than a mere invitation to treat, because the statement by the trustees that they bound themselves to accept the highest offer made it clear that it was to have contractual effect when it was accepted by either party submitting the highest bid which conformed with the stipulated terms (see p 265 e to j, p 268 a b and p 277 a to d, post).

(2) Furthermore, the second defendant's bid was a 'single offer' because although it contained two figures the actual offer was of only one of those figures, namely the higher of the two, and in any event (per Oliver LJ) the term 'single offer' referred to an offer embracing all the shares of whatever class in one parcel as opposed to an offer which could be accepted piecemeal as regards different classes (see p 267 c d, p 268 b to d and p 277 c, post).

(3) Since the transaction between the trustees, the plaintiff and the second defendant concerned a private negotiation between a fiduciary vendor and two potential purchasers in which the vendor fixed his own terms and therefore had the opportunity to exclude referential bids if he so wished and since the actual terms stipulated could sensibly be read as setting out fully the terms proposed by the trustees, a term excluding referential bids could not be implied into the trustees' invitation to bid. The second defendant's referential bid was therefore the highest offer and the trustees were bound to accept it. The second defendant's appeal would accordingly be allowed and he would be granted specific performance and an inquiry into damages for the delay in completing the contract, during which time he and his family had been deprived of control of the company (see p 267 a to j, p 268 d to f, p 269 a to d, p 270 h j, p 272 e to h, p 273 c, p 276 a b and j, p 277 f to j and p 278 d, post); *Liverpool City Council v Irwin* [1976] 2 All ER 39 distinguished; dicta of Lindley MR in *South Hetton Coal Co v Haswell Shotton and Easington Coal and Coke Co* [1898] 1 Ch at 469 and *SSI Investors Ltd v Korea Tungsten Mining Co Ltd* (1982) 449 NYS 2d 173 not followed.

(4) Since the trustees, in a document prepared by themselves, had stipulated that no interest was payable by the successful bidder in the event of 'any delay on our part' in completion, which was to be construed as denoting a failure, from whatever cause, to complete within the stipulated time, the fact that the trustees had been prevented by the plaintiff's injunction from completing within the stipulated time meant that the delay had occurred on the part of the trustees, albeit not through their fault, and accordingly they were not entitled to claim interest from the second defendant. The trustees' cross-appeal would therefore be dismissed (see p 267 h j, p 275 b to h, p 276 a b and p 278 a to d, post).

Decision of Peter Gibson J [1984] 2 All ER 65 reversed.

## Notes

For implied terms in a contract, see 9 Halsbury's Laws (4th edn) paras 351–362, and for cases on the subject, see 12 Digest (Reissue) 750–757, 5390–5425.

For offer and acceptance generally and for the difference between an offer and an invitation to treat, see 9 Halsbury's Laws (4th edn) paras 226–230, and for cases on the subject, see 12 Digest (Reissue) 63–66, 328–338.

For interest on purchase money in proceedings for specific performance, see 44 Halsbury's Laws (4th edn) paras 541–545.

## Cases referred to in judgments

*Bennett v Stone* [1903] 1 Ch 509, CA.
*Carlill v Carbolic Smoke Ball Co* [1893] 1 QB 256, [1891–4] All ER Rep 127, CA.
*Hewitt's Contract, Re* [1963] 3 All ER 419, [1963] 1 WLR 1298.
*Hillas & Co Ltd v Arcos Ltd* (1932) 147 LT 503, [1932] All ER Rep 494, HL.
*Liverpool City Council v Irwin* [1976] 2 All ER 39, [1977] AC 239, [1976] 2 WLR 562, HL.
*Moorcock, The* (1889) 14 PD 64, [1886–90] All ER Rep 530, CA.

R v Paddington and St Marylebone Rent Tribunal, ex p Bedrock Investments Ltd [1947] 2 All
    ER 15, [1947] 1 KB 984, DC; affd [1948] 2 All ER 528, [1948] 2 KB 413, CA.
South Hetton Coal Co v Haswell Shotton and Easington Coal and Coke Co [1898] 1 Ch 465, CA.
SSI Investors Ltd v Korea Tungsten Mining Co Ltd (1982) 449 NYS 2d 173.
Williams v Glenton (1866) LR 1 Ch App 200.
Woods and Lewis's Contract, Re [1898] 2 Ch 211, CA.
Young and Harston's Contract, Re (1886) 31 Ch D 168, CA.

**Cases also cited**
Bartlett v Barclays Bank Trust Co Ltd (No 2) [1980] 2 All ER 92, [1980] Ch 515.
Beesly v Hallwood Estates Ltd [1961] 1 All ER 90, [1960] 1 WLR 549.
Bushwall Properties Ltd v Vortex Properties Ltd [1976] 2 All ER 283, [1976] 1 WLR 591,
    CA.
Daulia Ltd v Four Millbank Nominees Ltd [1978] 2 All ER 557, [1978] Ch 231, CA.
Esdaile v Stephenson (1822) 1 Sim & St 122, 57 ER 49.
Harbutt's Plasticine Ltd v Wayne Tank and Pump Co Ltd [1970] 1 All ER 225, [1970] 1 QB
    447, CA.
Rightside Properties Ltd v Gray [1974] 2 All ER 1169, [1975] Ch 72.
Saltzburg and Rubin v Hollis Securities Ltd (Sweet, third party) (1964) 48 DLR (2d) 344, NS
    SC.

**Appeal and cross-appeal**
The second defendant, Sir Leonard Outerbridge, appealed against the judgment of Peter
Gibson J ([1984] 2 All ER 65, [1984] 2 WLR 884) given on 29 November 1983 whereby
he granted specific performance of a contract between the plaintiff, Harvela Investments
Ltd (Harvela), and the first defendants, Royal Trust Co of Canada (CI) Ltd (Royal Jersey),
for the sale of 825 common shares, 311 6% voting preference shares and 24,337 non-
voting redeemable preference shares in A Harvey & Co Ltd, which shares were held by
Royal Jersey on behalf of itself and its London-based associated company, Royal Trust of
Canada, as trustees of a settlement. The judge also dismissed a counterclaim by Sir
Leonard for specific performance of a contract between himself and Royal Jersey on
behalf of the trustees for the sale of the shares to him. The trustees cross-appealed
claiming, inter alia, that in the event of Sir Leonard's appeal succeeding Sir Leonard was
liable to pay interest on the purchase price of the shares from 30 days after 16 September
1981 until the date of the completion of the sale. The facts are set out in the judgment of
Waller LJ.

Leolin Price QC and James Denniston for Sir Leonard Outerbridge.
Michael Essayan QC and Michael Driscoll for Harvela.
Edward Nugee QC and Oliver Weaver for the trustees.

                                                                    Cur adv vult

18 July. The following judgments were delivered.

**WALLER LJ.** This is an appeal from a decision of Peter Gibson J ([1984] 2 All ER 65,
[1984] 2 WLR 884) making an order for specific performance of a contract between the
plaintiff, Harvela Investments Ltd (Harvela), and the first defendants, Royal Trust
Company of Canada (CI) Ltd (Royal Jersey). The appellant is Sir Leonard Outerbridge,
who claims specific performance of a contract to sell the shares to him. There is also a
cross-appeal by Royal Jersey on the question of interest payable by the purchaser, but it is
first necessary to decide which party is the purchaser.
    The shares are in a company called A Harvey & Co Ltd (Harveys), who were third
defendants in the court below. Approximately 43% of the shares are held by Harvela,
representing members of the Harvey family, and approximately 40% of the shares are
held by members of the Outerbridge family. The shares in issue in this case represent
approximately 12% of the voting strength and are held by Royal Jersey on behalf of the

trustees of a settlement made in 1962. If Harvela purchases the shares in issue the Harvey family will have the majority holding in Harveys and if Sir Leonard purchases the shares the Outerbridge family will have the majority holding. I do not need to set out all the facts leading up to the events of September 1981; they are fully set out in the judgment of Peter Gibson J. It is sufficient to say that in August 1981, in response to an invitation from the trustees, Harvela and Sir Leonard each made bids which, though similar in size, were different in content. I now take up the narrative by quoting from the judge ([1984] 2 All ER 65 at 69–70, [1984] 2 WLR 884 at 889–890):

'The trustees then decided that they should invite both Harvela and Sir Leonard to submit revised offers on identical terms and conditions. They sent a telex (the invitation telex) to each of Harvela and Sir Leonard asking each to continue its or his existing offer to 3 pm on 16 September 1981 and containing (so far as material) the following terms and conditions: "We have before us two similar offers but subject to differing terms and conditions and value. Accordingly we invite you to submit to [Royal Jersey] any revised offer which you may wish to make by sealed tender or confidential telex to be submitted to our London solicitors, Messrs. Bischoff and Co. ... by 3 p.m. London time Wednesday 16th September 1981, attention J. Jowitt who has undertaken not to disclose any details of any revised offer to any party before that time ... Tenders are to be submitted on the following terms:—1. That tenders are a single offer for all shares held by us ... 5. In the event that closing shall not take place within 30 days interest shall be payable by the purchaser on the full purchase price at a rate higher by 4 per cent. than the Bank of Montreal prime rate from time to time for Canadian dollar loans. We hereby agree subject to acceptance by us of any offer made by you:— ... C) We confirm that if any offer made by you is the highest offer received by us we bind ourselves to accept such offer provided that such offer complies with the terms of the telex." Two amendments to those terms were made by the trustees by a telex dated 16 September 1981 and sent to each of Harvela and Sir Leonard before either had responded to the invitation telex. I need refer only to the amendment to term 5, the words "other than by reason of any delay on our part" being inserted after the words "within 30 days". Further on 16 September Royal Jersey orally confirmed to Sir Leonard and Harvela that the promise in para C to accept the highest offer was not qualified by the words "subject to acceptance by us of any offer made by you". Thus each of Harvela and Sir Leonard knew that the other had already bid a sum of an amount similar to its or his bid of $1¾m without knowing which of the earlier bids was the higher. Each knew that it was likely that it or he would have to increase its or his previous bid to be successful but each had the assurance that the trustees were promising to be bound to accept the highest offer made in accordance with the terms of the invitation telex. On 16 September 1981 before 3 pm Mr Chalker telexed to Mr Jowitt Harvela's revised offer; this was in the sum of $2,175,000. Also on 16 September before 3 pm the London solicitors of Sir Leonard sent his written revised offer to Mr Jowitt. That offer was expressed as follows: "The amount of our client's tender is C$2,100,000 or C$101,000 in excess of any other offer which you may receive which is expressed as a fixed monetary amount, whichever is the higher." At 4.47 pm the same afternoon Mr Broughton, the assistant manager of Royal Jersey's trust department, telexed Mr Chalker that Harvela's tender was unsuccessful. Royal London however decided not to notify Sir Leonard of acceptance of his offer unless Mr Nugee [leading counsel] advised that the offer was valid and satisfied the conditions of Royal Jersey's invitation and that Royal Jersey was bound to accept. Mr Nugee advised orally on 22 September and in writing on 29 September. Whilst confessing to a feeling of unease regarding the form of the offer, Mr Nugee advised that Sir Leonard's offer was a valid offer of $2,276,000 which Royal Jersey was bound to accept. Mr Nugee further advised that Royal Jersey should advise both parties of the tenders which it had received, that it proposed to complete with Sir

Leonard and that if Harvela wished to dispute the validity of Sir Leonard's offer it would have to do so by proceeding against both Royal Jersey and Sir Leonard. On 18 September Mr Chalker asked that the details of the successful tender should be telexed to him and that request was repeated on 27 September. On 29 September Royal Jersey in accordance with advice from Mr Jowitt telexed each of Sir Leonard and Harvela, giving the details of each bid, and concluded: "In the circumstances our clients are bound to accept and do hereby accept the offer received from Sir Leonard Outerbridge and give notice that they propose and require the purchase of the shares to be completed on the 15th October next."'

Harvela, having thus been put on notice, started proceedings in Jersey but by agreement between the parties the present proceedings were started in the Chancery Division and the Jersey action was not proceeded with.

As I have already said Peter Gibson J gave judgment for Harvela, deciding that they had made the highest bid. He came to this conclusion because he found that, in contracts where sealed bids were made, a term had to be implied that referential bidding was not allowed. Accordingly, the bid of Sir Leonard remained at the fixed price and was lower than that of Harvela. The main ground of this appeal is that the judge was in error in this conclusion.

The first question to consider is what is the proper construction to put on the telex sent by the trustees inviting Harvela and Sir Leonard to submit revised offers. Only two of the terms in the telex are important for the decision on this part of the case. The first is: 'Tenders are to be submitted on the following terms:—(1) That tenders are a single offer for all shares held by us', and then later in the telex: 'We confirm that if any offer made by you is the highest offer received by us we bind ourselves to accept such offer provided that such offer complies with the terms of this telex.' This court has to consider whether this telex was an invitation to treat or a binding offer to enter into a contract with the highest bidder or an offer which the bidder who was highest could accept. In my judgment the clause confirming that the trustees bound themselves to accept the highest offer received by them made it clear that it was not a mere invitation to treat. It emphasised that, if the offer complied with the terms of the telex, the trustees would accept the highest offer and therefore it was either an offer which when the highest bid was received completed a contract of sale or at least completed a contract to enter into a contract of sale (see e g *Carlill v Carbolic Smoke Ball Co* [1893] 1 QB 256, [1891–4] All ER Rep 127). The question of whether it would be a complete contract of sale or a contract to enter into a contract of sale is, as it seems to me, purely a question of words: the effect is a contract of sale. I find support for this view in the speech of Lord Wright in *Hillas & Co Ltd v Arcos Ltd* (1932) 147 LT 503 at 515, [1932] All ER Rep 494 at 505 where he says:

> 'A contract *de præsenti* to enter into what, in law, is an enforceable contract, is simply that enforceable contract, and no more and no less; and if what may, not very accurately, be called the "second contract" is not to take effect till some future date, but is otherwise an enforceable contract, the position is as in the preceding illustration, save that the operation of the contract is postponed. But in each case there is *eo instanti* a complete obligation.'

If it were not for the words 'We bind ourselves to accept', this would have been a mere invitation to treat; but those words in my opinion make it an offer which the bidder being highest accepted.

The next question is whether the bid of Sir Leonard was the highest bid, or whether the referential part had to be rejected thereby making Harvela's bid the highest bid. The submission on Harvela's part was that a term had to be implied that a bid which depended on reference to the bid of another was not a valid bid. The argument for implying such a term was that to have a referential bid defeated the whole purpose of sealed bidding.

Sir Leonard submits that the judge was wrong to imply a term prohibiting referential bidding. The case against referential bidding was that it could lead to very unfortunate results, e g where more than one bidder made a referential bid the final result might be that the vendor having bound himself to accept the highest bid would have to accept an offer which was below that which should have been achieved. However, we were also given examples of more than one referential bid which would not have any unfortunate effect. We were informed that there was no difficulty in the vendor making it a condition that there should be no referential bids and were given examples of this being done. Furthermore, we were informed that only in some cases did vendors bind themselves to accept the highest offer. In many cases of sealed bidding the vendor retained the right to decide and it would only be in cases where the vendor had bound himself to accept the highest offer that there could be any untoward effect. In *Liverpool City Council v Irwin* [1976] 2 All ER 39 at 43, [1977] AC 239 at 253–254 Lord Wilberforce said:

> 'To say that the construction of a complete contract out of these elements involves a process of "implication" may be correct: it would be so if implication means the supplying of what is not expressed. But there are varieties of implications which the courts think fit to make and they do not necessarily involve the same process. Where there is, on the face of it, a complete, bilateral contract, the courts are sometimes willing to add terms to it, as implied terms; this is very common in mercantile contracts where there is an established usage; in that case the courts are spelling out what both parties know and would, if asked, unhesitatingly agree to be part of the bargain. In other cases, where there is an apparently complete bargain, the courts are willing to add a term on the ground that without it the contract will not work— this is the case, if not of *The Moorcock* (1889) 14 PD 64, [1886–90] All ER Rep 530 itself on its facts, at least of the doctrine of *The Moorcock* as usually applied. This is, as was pointed out by the majority in the Court of Appeal, a strict test—though the degree of strictness seems to vary with the current legal trend, and I think that they were right not to accept it as applicable here. There is a third variety of implication, that which I think Lord Denning MR favours, or at least did favour in this case, and that is the implication of reasonable terms. But though I agree with many of his instances, which in fact fall under one or other of the preceding heads, I cannot go so far as to endorse his principle; indeed, it seems to me, with respect, to extend a long, and undesirable, way beyond sound authority. The present case, in my opinion, represents a fourth category, or I would rather say a fourth shade on a continuous spectrum. The court here is simply concerned to establish what the contract is, the parties not having themselves fully stated the terms. In this sense the court is searching for what must be implied.'

That was a case of landlord and tenant where the tenant had to sign 'Conditions of Tenancy' but where there were no express undertakings by the landlord. The House of Lords held that although there were no express undertakings it was nevertheless implied in the relationship of landlord and tenant that in blocks of high-rise flats there was an obligation to take reasonable care on the part of the landlord to keep the means of access in reasonable repair and usability. In that case there was the example of the mother and child in a flat on the tenth floor who would not be able to go to and from the flat were it not for an efficient lift. Furthermore, the implication in that case was for a term imposing a duty on the landlord who had no written obligation, all the written obligations being imposed on the tenant. In this case the vendor has set out all his conditions in the telex and the purchaser simply has to make a bid. Yet the argument seeks to imply that there was another condition to be added to those already in the vendor's offer. Are there any similar inferences to be drawn in the present case? No evidence was called on this particular issue. Examples of some strange possible results were given and it was said that to allow referential bids defeated the purpose of sealed bids. We were also referred to two cases where observations had been made by the court of the undesirability of referential bidding. In *South Hetton Coal Co v Haswell Shotton and Easington Coal and Coke Co* [1898] 1 Ch 465 the vendor proposed to receive sealed tenders from two parties and undertook to accept the 'highest net money tender'. One of the parties offered 'such a sum as will exceed by £200 the amount offered' by the other party. The court held that it was not a net money tender because it was not a tender at all if other people did not tender. 'It does not answer the description in a business sense, and it does not answer the description in a legal sense,' said Lindley MR (at 469). He made some observations about possible trickery, but they were obiter.

There was also an American case, *SSI Investors Ltd v Korea Tungsten Mining Co Ltd* (1982) 449 NYS 2d 173, a decision of the New York Court of Appeals. There the offer was: '1. The total price of . . . $556,000 and/or 2. $1 more than the highest bidding price you receive.' The court held that the offer was not definite and certain and did not specify which alternative was to be taken. The majority expressed views obiter about sealed bids dependent on the bids of another but one member of the court reserved his opinion on this topic. It is quite clear that the facts of those two cases are quite different from the present case. Only the obiter remarks give any support to the submission that referential bids are undesirable.

The offer made in this case is free from the main faults shown in the above two cases. There was a firm offer exceeding by a considerable margin the previous offers which had been made so that it did not depend on there being other bids. If that was less than the other bid then the offer was $101,000 greater than the other offer, a very substantial increase. I agree with the judge that on the plain wording of Sir Leonard's bid there was only one offer by Sir Leonard, that is to say the higher of the amounts specified in the two bids (see [1984] 2 All ER 65 at 71, [1984] 2 WLR 884 at 892). If a term is to be implied in this contract it must be the implication of a term in the trustees' offer. I do not see how this can be done. Considering the four groups set out by Lord Wilberforce, this clearly is not in the first group of established usage. Nor, in my judgment, can it be put in the second group, namely adding a term on the ground that the contract without it will not work. His third group is really a repetition of the first two, leaving his last group, namely where the court is concerned to establish what the contract is, the parties not having themselves fully stated the terms. In this case, unlike *Irwin*'s case, which was seeking to imply obligations on the party which had no obligations in writing, this involves implying an extra condition in an offer which set out a number of conditions which had to be complied with. Where conditions have been set out in detail there would have to be very strong grounds indeed, in my opinion, to imply another condition. This is more particularly so when there is no need to state that the offeror intends to be bound by a particular bid and when some offers actually contain a prohibition on referential bidding. In my judgment the facts of this case do not fit into any of Lord Wilberforce's categories. *Irwin*'s case concerned a widespread group, namely landlords and tenants of high-rise flats. This case concerns a very small group, namely those vendors who have bound themselves to accept the highest bid and have not in their offer excluded referential bidding. If one considers the position of the reasonable man receiving this offer, would he immediately think that a referential bid would not be allowed? If not, are there any other compelling reasons for implying such a term? In my judgment there are not. If the offeror wishes to rule out referential bids, he should say so. I respectfully disagree with the judge on this point. In my opinion there is no implication of a ban on referential bidding which should be made. On this issue, therefore, I would allow the appeal against the judge's order and grant an order of specific performance to Sir Leonard and an inquiry as to damages.

On the cross-appeal by Royal Jersey in relation to interest I have had the advantage of reading Oliver LJ's judgment on this part of the case in draft and I agree with it.

Accordingly, I would allow the appeal of Sir Leonard and decree specific performance and order an inquiry as to damages. I would discharge the orders for specific performance and damages in Harvela's favour and I would dismiss the cross-appeal of the first defendants, Royal Jersey.

**OLIVER LJ.** I agree that this appeal should be allowed. Essentially the principal issue between the parties is one purely of the proper construction to be placed on what has been referred to throughout as 'the invitation telex' (as modified by the amending telex of 16 September 1981). So far as the contractual analysis of the invitation telex is concerned, that is whether it constituted itself a contractual offer or an invitation to treat, I am in entire agreement with the judge. It seems to me perfectly plain that it was what it purported to be, namely an offer intended to have contractual effect on acceptance by one or the other party sending a bid which conformed with the terms stipulated and which, in the event, was the highest such bid received by the offerors. The only question (and it is not one which, speaking for myself, I have found an easy one to answer) is what, in the context of the document as a whole, is meant by the expression 'revised offer' and 'highest offer'. There is no doubt that, as a pure matter of language and arithmetic, the highest bid received by the trustees was that of Sir Leonard Outerbridge and there is equally no doubt that, if that bid was an offer within the terms of the invitation telex and was a 'single offer', it otherwise complied with the terms stipulated. As regards the question first decided by the judge, was it a 'single offer'? I am, for my part, entirely in agreement with his conclusion. This seems to me right for two reasons. In the first place, although no doubt it was necessary to look at two figures in order to ascertain what the offer was, it was an offer of only one of those figures, that is to say whichever was the higher. But secondly, and in any event, the meaning of the term 'single offer' must take its colour from the correspondence as a whole. It derives from an earlier offer from Sir Leonard's solicitors dated 14 September 1984, and it is quite evident that what it was intended to signify was an offer which embraced all the shares, of whatever class, in one parcel and not one which could be accepted piecemeal as regards different classes.

Thus the only arguable point appears to me to be whether it was an offer at all within the terms of the telex, and looking at the matter purely as one of the ordinary use of language one's immediate reaction is to ask simply, 'Why not?' What is there in the invitation telex which points to the conclusion that an offer of this sort was not, as a matter of objective interpretation, an 'offer' within the meaning of the language used? No such indication can be found from the words themselves, used in the ordinary primary sense, and it is necessary, therefore, for Harvela to convince the court that the circumstances are such that the ordinary primary meaning is compulsively displaced in favour of some secondary and more restricted meaning. Now there is nothing either in the language or in reason which necessarily precludes a bid which involves an arithmetical calculation of the price offered by reference to some other figure, such a bid being conveniently spoken of as 'a referential bid'.

For instance, if these had been shares with a public quotation, there would have been no objection that I can see or that counsel for Harvela can suggest to a bid on the basis of a price per share of, say, $2 above whatever is the market price of the shares as published in a certain newspaper on the closing day. It is said, however, that what is precluded is a certain type of referential bid only, that is to say a bid framed by reference to the figure offered by another interested bidder.

There being nothing in the language itself to lead to this conclusion, it can, as I see it, be reached by one or other of only three possible routes.

First, it may be said that the transaction is one of such a familiar nature or that the surrounding circumstances (including previous negotiations) are such that no reasonable offeree receiving the invitation telex could construe the offer made in any other way than as an offer which precluded acceptance by a bid of the type in fact submitted by Sir Leonard. Second, it may be said that in order to make the transaction work at all it is necessary to imply into the invitation telex a term that no bid in response to the offer made shall be in a form which is referential to any other bid. Third, it may be said that the transaction in which the parties were engaged is one in which the law precludes the formation of a contract by a bid of this nature.

The first two of these suggested approaches come to pretty much the same thing, differing as they do only in the source from which the implication is to be derived. Each depends on the presumed intention of the parties to the transaction on a matter as to which they have not expressed themselves, whether that intention be derived from the usual course of dealing in the market or the factual background of their negotiations or from the necessity to give business efficacy to those negotiations. It is, of course, not difficult to see that, if all bidders have resort to certain forms of referential bid, the offer could be entirely stultified. Equally, if a different type of referential bid is resorted to, that is one in which the incremental element in each is related to the fixed element in the other, no such result would necessarily ensue. There is, however, nothing that I can see in the background here nor in the necessity of the case judged by the officious bystander test which would, in my judgment, justify the implied restriction on which counsel for Harvela is compelled to rely. Nor does it appear that the transaction is one of a type where, as a matter of public notoriety, a restriction of this sort is so generally accepted as applying that anyone entering into such a transaction would assume as a matter of ordinary business dealing that it would apply. There was not, so far as I am aware, any evidence before the judge, and certainly none before this court, whether sales by means of sealed bids are a regular feature of the market in modern conditions. Certainly invitations for tenders are familiar in the field of building contracts, as are invitations for subscription for shares by tender, and I understand that sales of real estate by sealed offer are regularly carried out in Scotland. There does not appear, however, in such cases to be any reasonable objection to referential bids, because in the ordinary way the seller does not bind himself in advance to accept them. That, as it seems to me, is the feature which distinguishes the present case from the ordinary case of an invitation to submit sealed bids, which is in truth no more than an invitation to treat, and it is this which leads me to approach the general submission of counsel for Harvela with some caution. His submission is that in sealed competitive bidding referential bids are inconsistent with what he describes as 'the very essence' of the transaction and that even though parties must be presumed to frame their offers in the way which best suits their intentions the general law requires a term to be implied into the offer inviting competitive bids to the effect that any bid expressed by reference to another's bid is to be invalid and ineffective.

It was this submission which persuaded the judge. He accepted, as I read his judgment, that it was not possible to imply any such term by reference to the officious bystander test and thus he rejected the *Moorcock* type of implication (see *The Moorcock* (1889) 14 PD 64, [1886–90] All ER Rep 530); but in reliance on *Liverpool City Council v Irwin* [1976] 2 All ER 39, [1977] AC 239 he held that the relationship between the parties, that is the relationship between one who invites sealed competitive bids and the potential bidders, was such that the general law would imply such a term even in a case in which, if the parties had been asked, they might not all have assented to such a term. In doing so he relied on the only two reported decisions which counsel have been able to discover which have any relation to this type of transaction. The first was the decision of this court in *South Hetton Coal Co v Haswell Shotton and Easington Coal and Coke Co* [1898] 1 Ch 465, a case where the vendor liquidator had at any rate purported to bind himself to accept the highest tender, although it was qualified by the words 'all other things being equal and satisfactory'. What the vendor there had bound himself to accept, however, was 'the highest net money tender I receive'. The plaintiff's tender was for an unspecified sum which would exceed by £200 the amount offered by another potential bidder. His claim for specific performance failed, but on the grounds that it did not correspond with the offer. It bid no sum of money, but depended entirely on whether there were other bids, and it did not therefore comply with the description of a 'net money tender'. Lindley MR in the course of his judgment did, however, observe (at 469):

'I think that we should be encouraging trickery and making a very bad precedent if we held that this was, in any fair sense of the word, the highest net money tender which the liquidator had bound himself to accept. I do not accuse these gentlemen of trickery; but if we said that this letter answered the description of the highest net money tender, we should open the door to gross fraud, not only on purchasers, but on vendors also.'

This was, of course, obiter but the judge observed that it gave some support to the suggestion that the law should 'require the exclusion of referential bids'.

The other case referred to by the judge and relied on by Harvela is the decision of the New York Court of Appeals in *SSI Investors Ltd v Korea Tungsten Mining Co Ltd* (1982) 449 NYS 2d 173 affirming a decision of the Appellate Division of the New York Supreme Court (438 NYS 2d 96). That was a case of an offer of real estate by public advertisement which fixed a minimum price and invited 'sealed written bids'. The advertisement indicated that the property would be awarded to the highest bidder. The plaintiff, the unsuccessful appellant, bid $556,000 'and/or . . . $1 more than the highest bidding price you have received for the above property'. The New York Court of Appeals held that this failed for uncertainty in any event because it simply stated two alternative prices, but the majority went on to express the view that, even if certain, such a bid could not be permitted, observing (449 NYS 2d 173 at 174):

> 'Although in some circumstances a bid which by itself is incomplete may properly be made definite and certain by reference to external objective facts, in the context of sealed competitive bidding the necessary certainty cannot be imported by cross reference to the bids of others participating in the same competitive bidding over the objection of the owner or another bidder . . . The very essence of sealed competitive bidding is the submission of independent, self-contained bids to the fair compliance with which not only the owner but the other bidders are entitled . . . to give effect to . . . any . . . practice in which the . . . amount of one bid was tied to the bid or bids of another or others in the same bidding would be to recognise means whereby effective sealed competitive bidding could be wholly frustrated. In the context of such bidding, therefore, a submission by one bidder of a bid dependent for its definition on the bids of others is invalid and unacceptable as inconsistent with and potentially destructive of the very bidding in which it is submitted.'

This again was no more than an obiter view and it was one not shared by Fuchsberg J, who concurred in the result but observed (at 175) that he did not see—

> 'any reason, in the absence of illegality, and in the context of a private sector business transaction in our relatively free enterprise society, to concern ourselves with the possible or potential effect of appellant's novel offer on commercial competitive bidding. This problem, if it turns out to be one, could easily be abated by appropriate conditions imposed by those who invite bids, or, if the Legislature thought it of sufficient interest, by statutory enactment.'

Peter Gibson J in the instant case was, in fact, referred to two examples of invitations to tender where this type of bid was specifically excluded.

It is worth noting, moreover, that the majority opinion in the New York case refers throughout to 'sealed competitive bidding' as if this were a term of art or at least a familiar commercial practice, and there is, as I have mentioned, no evidence of any familiar practice in this country of this type of publicly advertised bidding where the vendor binds himself in advance to accept the highest offer submitted. What the instant appeal is concerned with is a private negotiation between a fiduciary vendor and two potential purchasers in which the vendor fixes his own terms and imposes on himself this very unusual obligation. Persuasive, therefore, though the two decisions referred to are, they represent only obiter views which were expressed in relation to very different transactions.

At highest they seem to me to be merely pointers at the possibility of some sort of implied term if there exist the conditions in which, as a matter of law, such a term can be implied. Now speaking for myself, once one discards a secondary meaning for the term used in the offer as a matter purely of construction, I find some difficulty in the concept of the implication of a term, not for the purpose of finding what the parties have agreed on a matter on which their written or proven oral exchanges are silent, but for the purpose of ascertaining whether they have entered into an agreement at all. That difficulty is not ameliorated by the fact that the vendor, into whose written offer it is sought to imply the term, has throughout shown himself quite content to treat his offer as meaning exactly what, on its face, it said. Harvela's argument is that the term that it seeks, namely that any bid expressed by reference to the amount of another bid is to be invalid although the offer says nothing about it, is one which is to be implied by the general law from the relationship assumed by a vendor when he invited sealed offers to be submitted. It is, in other words, an incident of the type of transaction in which he has chosen to engage and which attaches regardless of his actual wishes and intentions unless he expressly excludes it. The sheet-anchor of counsel for Harvela's case here is the decision of the House of Lords in *Liverpool City Council v Irwin* [1976] 2 All ER 39, [1977] AC 239, where their lordships were prepared to imply a term imposing a limited repairing covenant on a landlord in circumstances where there was no established usage and no ground for its implication either on the officious bystander test or under the doctrine of *The Moorcock* (1889) 14 PD 64, [1886–90] All ER Rep 530. In approaching the decision in *Irwin's* case, however, it is I think important to bear in mind the circumstances and the limitations within which the term was implied. It was a case where the landlord of a high-rise block had let the flats but retained the common parts, including the lifts, rubbish chutes etc. The only evidence of the terms of the tenancies was a document headed 'Conditions of Tenancy' which imposed a number of obligations on the tenant but which imposed no obligation whatever on the landlord, although some of the terms recognised the existence of the facilities (lifts, rubbish disposal, lighting of common parts and so on) which were in issue. Thus the court was faced with what by definition was a bilateral transaction and one where the statutory obligations incidental to the relationship of landlord and tenant could not, as a matter of reason, be the sum total of the landlord's obligations. Lord Wilberforce observed ([1976] 2 All ER 39 at 43, [1977] AC 239 at 253):

> 'On the landlords' side there is nothing, no signature, no demise, no covenant: the contract takes effect as soon as the tenants sign the form and are let into possession. We have then a contract which is partly, but not wholly, stated in writing. In order to complete it, in particular to give it a bilateral character, it is necessary to take account of the actions of the parties and the circumstances . . .'

I pause to observe that the instant case is very different. We are not concerned here with a contract which is only partly written but where there are clearly and necessarily terms beyond the written document, but with the construction of a contractual offer wholly reduced to writing in words chosen by the offeror.

Lord Wilberforce continued with a consideration of the process of implication ([1976] 2 All ER 39 at 43, [1977] AC 239 at 254):

> 'To say that the construction of a complete contract out of these elements [that is to say actions and circumstances] involves a process of "implication" may be correct; it would be so if implication means the supplying of what is not expressed. But there are varieties of implications which the courts think fit to make and they do not necessarily involve the same process. Where there is, on the face of it, a complete, bilateral contract, the courts are sometimes willing to add terms to it, as implied terms: this is very common in mercantile contracts where there is an established usage . . . In other cases, where there is an apparently complete bargain, the courts are willing to add a term on the ground that without it the contract will not work . . . The present case, in my opinion, represents a fourth category, or I would rather say a fourth shade on a continuous spectrum. The court here is simply concerned to establish what the contract is, the parties not having themselves fully stated the terms. In this sense the court is searching for what must be implied.'

A little later, Lord Wilberforce propounded the test for this fourth category in these words ([1976] 2 All ER 39 at 44, [1977] AC 239 at 254):

'In my opinion such obligation should be read into the contract as the nature of the contract itself implicitly requires, no more, no less: a test in other words of necessity.'

Finally Lord Wilberforce defines the standard as follows ([1976] 2 All ER 39 at 45, [1977] AC 239 at 256): 'My Lords, if, as I think, the test of the existence of the term is necessity the standard must surely not exceed what is necessary having regard to the circumstances.'

This emphasis on the necessity of implying a term and of limiting the term implied to what is necessary is found again in the speech of Lord Salmon (with whom Lord Cross agreed), who quoted with approval Lord Goddard CJ's observation in *R v Paddington and St Marylebone Rent Tribunal, ex p Bedrock Investments Ltd* [1947] 2 All ER 15 at 17, [1947] 1 KB 984 at 990 that no covenant—

'ought ever to be implied unless there is such a necessary implication that the court can have no doubt what covenant or undertaking they ought to write into the agreement.'

(See [1976] 2 All ER 39 at 51, [1977] AC 239 at 262.)

Lord Fraser agreed with Lord Wilberforce. Lord Edmund-Davies put the matter slightly differently. He based the matter rather on the legal incidents of the type of contract with which the court was concerned (in that case the letting of a block with access only by lifts in the control of the landlord) which the landlords must be assumed to know about as well as anyone else. This comes rather nearer the established user test suggested by Lord Wilberforce. But, whether one adopts this view or the majority view of the test of necessity, the case does not appear to me to support the implication of a term in the circumstances of the instant case. The court is here concerned only with the construction of a contractual offer which on its face purported to set out, and can sensibly be read as setting out, fully the terms which the offeror was proposing. There is no established usage proved from which it can be contended that it should be read as meaning anything other than it says. It would, no doubt, be reasonable for an offeror in these circumstances, if he wished to, to exclude the crudest form of referential bid which might result in the whole exercise being stultified, to name a reserve price, or to specify expressly what sort of offers he will or will not entertain. But I cannot, for my part, see why it should be said that the exclusion of the type of bid made by Sir Leonard is 'necessary' or that it strikes at the 'very essence' of the transaction. It was for the trustees as vendors to frame whatever transaction they wished. It follows that I have not found myself able to take the same view as the judge took on this part of the case. In my judgment there is no ground on which it can be said that Sir Leonard's bid did not comply with the contractual offer on the footing on which it was submitted or that the trustees as vendors, by making their offer, assumed some undefined obligation to Harvela not to accept an offer expressed in a referential form. Sir Leonard's offer was the highest offer and in my judgment the trustees were right in their view that they were bound to accept it. Thus, on Sir Leonard's appeal I would allow the appeal, decree specific performance of that contract and dismiss Harvela's claim for specific performance.

This means that many of the subsidiary questions fall away, but there remain two to be dealt with. In the first place, Sir Leonard asks also for damages for delay in carrying out the contract which he claimed. The judge found in fact that he had a contract as a result of correspondence after the receipt of his bid, but one which was, as the judge held, subject to the prior rights of Harvela. The judge refused an inquiry as to damages, however, on the ground that Sir Leonard had shown no damage at all which would justify an inquiry and there were no facts before him from which he could infer that any damage had been sustained. Now I agree that it is necessary for a plaintiff seeking an inquiry to prove that he has suffered some damage, but the circumstances may be such that damage is self-evident or that there is at least an inference that some damage has resulted, although it may not be readily quantifiable. The fact is that Sir Leonard was always ready and willing to complete. He has not had the shares the subject matter of the contract to deal with in the interim, and he has not had them because the trustees were, albeit not through any conscious volition on their part, in breach of the obligation which they had assumed to complete on the closing date.

On the footing that the trustees had contracted to sell to Harvela the judge found a sufficient indication of damage in the fact that they had not had the control of the company which the shares would have given them and he ordered an inquiry accordingly. That does not, of course, apply in Sir Leonard's case, since his own shareholding did not carry control, but he has over the period of delay been deprived of the opportunity of enlisting the support of other family shareholders so as, with the shares the subject matter of the sale, to exercise control at general meetings and he has, of course, not had the freedom which he would otherwise have had to dispose of the shares in accordance with his own wishes or any advice he might have been given. In my judgment there is sufficient here for an inference that at least *some* damage has been sustained and I, for my part, would order an inquiry, the costs of which will have to be reserved. If and so far as any damage can be shown to have been sustained as a result of the inability of the trustees to complete the contract, it may, in the ultimate analysis be recoverable from Harvela under the cross-undertaking in damages given on the grant of the injunction which produced the trustees' inability.

The other outstanding matter is that raised by the trustees' cross-appeal. On the basis of the decision at which the judge arrived, the question arose whether Harvela were responsible for the payment of interest on the purchase money as a term of specific performance. The failure to perform the contract found by the judge was due to the trustees' decision to affirm a contract with Sir Leonard and the judge accordingly declined to award them interest either under the contract or on general principles. In my judgment he was, on the basis on which he decided the main claim, entirely right to do so. The trustees' notice of appeal, however, raises also the question of whether, in the event of this court finding that there was no concluded contract with Harvela but a contract with Sir Leonard on the terms of the invitation telex, interest becomes payable by Sir Leonard as from the date on which the contract ought to have been completed, and that raises slightly different questions. What is claimed in the notice of appeal is a declaration that the trustees are not entitled to retain the dividends or interest payable on the shares down to the date of completion (so that those have to be accounted for to Sir Leonard) but that they are bound to transfer the shares to Sir Leonard against payment of the sum of $2,276,000 together with interest from 16 October 1981 down to the date of payment, at a rate equal to the one month fixed Canadian dollar LIBOR rate quoted at 11.00 am London time on 16 October 1981 and each renewal date thereafter, such interest to be compounded. This is not in fact the contractual rate of interest and the claim to compound interest is a startling one. Counsel for the trustees, however, justifies it by pointing out that simple interest at the contractual rate would produce a greater sum than compound interest at the lower rate claimed, and suggests the addition of a proviso that the total sum claimed by way of interest should not exceed the aggregate amount of simple interest over the relevant period calculated at the contract rate.

Counsel for Sir Leonard argues that in the circumstances the trustees are not entitled to any interest at all any more than they would have been entitled to interest against Harvela if this court had concluded that Harvela's was the highest bid within the terms of the invitation telex.

The starting point of any inquiry must be to look at the terms of the contract. What the invitation telex provided (as amended by a further telex on the following day) was this:

'In the event that closing shall not take place within 30 days (other than by reason of any delay on our part) interest shall be payable by the purchaser on the full purchase price at a rate higher by 4 per cent. than the Bank of Montreal prime rate from time to time for Canadian dollar loans.'

It will be appreciated that, having regard to the very considerable lapse of time since the anticipated closing date, the sum now payable by way of interest (if any is payable) is very substantial indeed. It amounted at the date of trial to something over $650,000, as against dividends received by the trustees of $1,866, although the shares themselves must by now be significantly more valuable than they were, having regard to substantial retained earnings which have accrued to the company in the interim.

It is, of course, fair to say that if the contract had been completed in due time Sir Leonard would have had to find, either by borrowing or by realisation, a sum of $2,276,000 on 16 October 1981 and would thus either have been deprived of or would have had to pay interest on that sum over the ensuing three years. He argues, however, that because of the exception introduced by the amending telex, in the words 'other than by reason of delay on our part', no interest at all is payable, either under the contract or general equitable principles. So far as the latter are concerned, I am for my part disposed to agree, for it seems to me that, where the contract itself regulates what interest is to be paid and then goes on to provide for a particular event in which that interest is not to be payable, that must almost of necessity import a term that if that event occurs not only is interest not payable at the contract rate but that no interest is to be payable at all. If the contract is so construed, there does not appear to me to be any equitable principle which justifies a departure from what the parties have agreed even though the delay may have been more extended than they contemplated. But equally if, as a matter of construction, interest is payable under the contract the mere fact that there had been little benefit receivable in fact from the property contracted to be sold or that the delay has been extended does not alter the fact that the purchaser affirming the contract has, as I see it, to affirm it with all the consequences which the contractual terms involve. The submission of counsel for Sir Leonard is simply that the exception inserted by the amending telex in fact occurred. The delay in completing the contract was 'on the part' of the trustees in the sense that it was not on Sir Leonard's part. The contract could not be completed because the trustees were enjoined by court order from completing it. That was not their fault, but, if one asks the question 'Did the failure to complete result from the purchaser's or the vendor's inability?', counsel for Sir Leonard submits that the answer is that it was the vendor's and that, therefore, the delay was 'on his part' (ie on the vendor's side of the contract).

Counsel for the trustees, on the other hand, has referred us to a number of authorities, such as *Re Young and Harston's Contract* (1886) 31 Ch D 168, *Re Woods and Lewis's Contract* [1898] 2 Ch 211 and *Bennett v Stone* [1903] 1 Ch 509, in which it has been held that a clause exempting the purchaser from interest on the wilful default of the vendor imports the necessity for some conscious act or omission of the vendor and some want of reasonable care on his part. Speaking for myself, however, I have not derived a great deal of assistance from these cases, for we are not here concerned with a formula such as 'default' or 'wilful default' but merely with 'delay' (which I take to mean no more than a failure to complete, from whatever cause on the due date) 'on the *part* of the vendors', an expression which, so far as the industry of counsel has been able to discover, has not fallen to be construed apart from a reference to default. Counsel for Sir Leonard, relying on a quotation from Turner LJ in *Williams v Glenton* (1866) LR 1 Ch App 200 at 210 in which he used the expression 'there has been so much delay on the part of the vendor as to amount to a wilful default', submits that the formula 'on the part of the vendor' is apt, purely as a matter of grammar, to signify no more than the factual inability of the vendor to complete and that, accordingly, if the vendor is unable to complete for any cause at all, there is delay 'on his part'. It is perhaps not without significance that, although the wilful default formula is a very familiar one, the trustees did not choose to adopt it. One must, however, look at the phrase 'delay on our part' in the context of the contract as a whole and, in particular, in the light of the circumstance that this was an amendment inserted for the purpose of qualifying an otherwise absolute obligation to pay interest in the event of delay, by whomsoever caused and however arising.

Counsel for trustees argues that 'on our part' imports the concept of some fault or responsibility and does not naturally comprehend some circumstance which is forced on the vendor as a result of matters entirely outside his control, but his support for this rests ultimately on the construction which the courts have consistently put on 'default' and 'wilful default', which expressions are conspicuously absent here. He also argues that the construction of conditions of sale has to be approached having regard to the normal rules of equity (see *Re Hewitt's Contract* [1963] 3 All ER 419 at 422, [1963] 1 WLR 1298 at 1301) and, in particular, the normal rule that a purchaser pays interest from the date fixed for completion and, in the absence of express stipulation, can excuse himself only by showing default on the part of the vendor. Accepting this, however, one still has to bear in mind that the terms were the trustees' terms, set out in a document prepared by them. There is, therefore, no context for a benevolent construction in the trustees' favour beyond that which the words bear as a matter of their ordinary meaning. 'Delay' in my judgment is not a word which signifies necessarily any default on anyone's part. It is apt merely to describe a failure, from whatever cause, to complete on the due date. It may occur as a matter of mutual agreement, but in the ordinary way it is the result of a breach of contract on one side or the other, not necessarily a wilful breach but an inability or failure of one party or the other to perform his side of the bargain. Here the trustees were engaging to complete on a particular date and, in my judgment, a clause which exonerates the purchaser from payment of the agreed interest in the event of the contract not being then completed 'as a result of delay on our part' means no more than 'as a result of a breach by us of our contractual obligation'. I cannot for my part treat it as importing some notion of neglect or default. It recognises, as it seems to me, only that some circumstances may occur in which the vendor will be in breach of his obligation to complete on the due date and for that reason the contract will not then be completed. In that event the purchaser is exonerated from his obligation to pay interest.

One asks then: what was it that prevented the completion of this contract on the due date? What occurred in fact was that Harvela, on 12 October 1981, obtained an injunction in Jersey against Royal Jersey preventing them from completing the contract. At the same time, Harvela obtained another injunction against Sir Leonard, in case the contract had already been completed, from lodging any transfer of the shares for registration. That, in fact, never operated, but the injunction against Royal Jersey was subsequently confirmed on 23 October 1981 and has operated, either in terms or by extension by undertaking, ever since. Now it is perfectly true that this was something imposed entirely from without and for which Royal Jersey was in no way responsible.

It is also true that, once the trustees had been disabled from completing by the injunction, any attempt by Sir Leonard to persuade them to complete might have involved him in proceedings for contempt of court. Nevertheless, it seems to me that it is inescapable that the injunction put the trustees in breach of contract. They had engaged to complete and they were unable to do so, although Sir Leonard was able and willing to fulfil his obligations; and, if one once arrives at that conclusion, then it seems to me equally inescapable that the failure to complete was a breach of contract 'on their part'. It was that breach which resulted in the delay and it is nihil ad rem to say that the breach was forced on them by a third party. For my part, therefore, I would dismiss the cross-appeal of the trustees. It may seem hard that they should be deprived of a substantial sum in interest through no fault on their part but that, as it seems to me, is what they contracted for and it is, of course, open to them to claim any loss of interest which would otherwise have fallen to be paid by Sir Leonard as damages recoverable against Harvela under the cross-undertaking given as the price of the injunction. I express no view as to the possible result of such a claim, if made, which would have to be the subject matter of an inquiry.

As regards the small sum of income received by the trustees in the interim, it would not appear to me right that Sir Leonard should be entitled to treat that as his from the date of completion while at the same time disclaiming any liability for interest which would have been earned by the purchase money if the contract had then been completed and I would take the same course in relation to that as the judge proposed in relation to specific performance of the contract which he found to have been concluded with Harvela.

I would therefore allow the appeal of the second defendant, Sir Leonard, and concur in the order which has been proposed by Waller LJ.

**PURCHAS LJ.** I agree that the appeal of the second defendant, Sir Leonard, succeeds and that the cross-appeal of the first defendants, Royal Jersey, fails. As we are differing from the trial judge I add a few words of my own.

The circumstances leading up to the issue by the trustees of the telex messages inviting revised tenders on the evening of 15 September 1981 have already been fully described in the preceding judgments and in the judgment of the trial judge ([1984] 2 All ER 65, [1984] 2 WLR 884) and need not be repeated. The effect of the invitation telex was to invite both Sir Leonard and the plaintiff, Harvela, to make a revised offer in the form of a 'sealed tender or confidential telex' to be submitted to the trustees' London solicitors by 3 pm on Wednesday, 16 September 1981. In their invitation telex the trustees confirmed to each of the recipients that if their respective bid was the highest offer received they bound themselves to accept it provided only that the offer complied with the terms of the telex. It is not necessary to detail these terms except to say that there were four specifically detailed stipulations; but none of them restricted in any way the nature of the tender to be offered apart from providing that the tender must be 'a single offer for all shares held by [Royal Jersey]'. On the cross-appeal by Royal Jersey it is important to notice that one of the terms provided that, should closing not take place within 30 days, interest should be payable by the purchaser at a set rate geared to the Bank of Montreal prime rate for Canadian dollar loans. This was varied by a subsequent telex to insert the qualification, 'other than by reason of any delay on our part', namely on the part of the trustees.

The central issue on the appeal was whether the tender made by Sir Leonard, which was undoubtedly the highest bid, complied with the terms of the telex. If it did not, then the highest tender complying with the terms of the offer was that made by Harvela. Harvela's contention was that a term had to be implied in the telex to the effect that referential bids were excluded. As has been stated, Sir Leonard's bid was in the following terms, which for convenience I repeat here:

> 'The amount of our client's tender is C$2,100,000 or C$101,000 in excess of any other offer which you may receive which is expressed as a fixed monetary amount, whichever is the higher.'

On the main issue, therefore, the judge was concerned to decide the single question whether Sir Leonard's bid complied with the terms of the invitation telex. Before him, counsel for Harvela relied on the implication of a term under the principle stated in *Liverpool City Council v Irwin* [1976] 2 All ER 39, [1977] AC 239. In my view the judge set out the proper principles to be derived from that authority ([1984] 2 All ER 65 at 73, [1984] 2 WLR 884 at 894):

> 'Counsel for Sir Leonard submitted that there was no reason why the law should intervene by implying a term in relation to sealed competitive bidding and he contrasted the relationship relied on by counsel for Harvela with the two relationships providing the established examples of this type of implied term (namely landlord and tenant, and master and servant). But I do not see why the categories of relationship need be so limited and provided *that I can be satisfied that the term contended for is a term required by the relationships relied on*, I would be prepared to imply that term.' (My emphasis.)

With great respect to the judge it is in the application of that correctly stated principle that I have reluctantly come to the conclusion that he fell into error in the particular circumstances surrounding sealed bids. A little later the judge again repeated the question correctly ([1984] 2 All ER 65 at 73, [1984] 2 WLR 884 at 895):

> 'In my judgment the question that I must determine is whether in sealed competitive bidding a bid framed by reference to another's bid is excluded as a

necessary incident of the relationship between vendor and bidder and between bidder and bidder. A vendor is free to choose the method by which he sells his property, but a vendor who opts for sealed competitive bidding must be presumed to have done so deliberately.'

The judge then proceeded to consider in detail the purpose of sealed bids. Having reminded himself that the way in which the invitation is couched is entirely a matter for the vendor and that he may, if he wishes, exclude specifically referential bidding, a practice of which there was evidence before him, the judge appears to have placed little, if any, weight on the fact that what precipitated the evil of a referential bid in the circumstances of the instant case was the fact that the trustees had taken the exceptional course of binding themselves to accept the highest offer. They may well have been advised that they should accept the offer most advantageous to the class of beneficiaries as a whole; obviously this would normally (but not inevitably) be the highest fixed monetary figure. However, I find it difficult to see why this should be a mandate for binding themselves to accept the highest fixed monetary offer.

As Waller LJ has said, it was the promise to accept the highest bid that converted the invitation telex from an invitation to treat into an offer capable of acceptance by anyone making the highest offer within the terms of the telex. In this way the trustees abandoned any residuary discretion otherwise available to them to choose between any tenders they received, which in turn distinguished the present invitation to submit sealed tenders from the usual one in which the common practice of vendors is to leave open to themselves the option of accepting any particular bid or none. It may be that when trustees come to select the sealed tender they might be under a duty to select one rather than the other, but for my part, as I have just said, I do not see the necessity of including in the invitation to tender a binding undertaking to accept the highest bid. Happily, however, this is not a matter with which we are concerned other than with its impact, if any, on the interpretation of the invitation telex. Without the specific stipulation to accept the highest bid, then in the ordinary case of sealed tenders there is no evil such as that described by counsel for Harvela and accepted by the judge in referential bids in such a process. The vendor can either invite a further definition of the referential bid or reject it or accept it as he wishes. For my part, therefore, I cannot see that the implication of a term excluding referential bids necessarily arises out of the relationship between a vendor and bidder where sealed tenders are involved, which was the test which the judge accepted on the authority of *Irwin's* case. With great respect to the judge it is at this point that I have to part company with him. The two authorities cited, namely *South Hetton Coal Co v Haswell Shotton and Easington Coal and Coke Co* [1898] 1 Ch 465 and the American case of *SSI Investors Ltd v Korea Tungsten Mining Co Ltd* (1982) 449 NYS 2d 173, are clearly distinguishable from the instant case and are not authority, as the judge seemed to consider they were, for the implication of a term inhibiting referential bidding in the form made by Sir Leonard in this case. In my judgment, the highest bid, which the trustees were bound to accept, was that made by Sir Leonard.

I now turn to the questions of the claim for an inquiry as to damages by Sir Leonard and the claim for interest raised by Royal Jersey in their cross-appeal. For the reasons given by Oliver LJ, I agree that there is evidence of some injury suffered by Sir Leonard which would justify an inquiry into damages arising out of the failure by the trustees to complete the transfer of shares in accordance with the contract. I agree that such an inquiry should be ordered on the terms suggested by Waller and Oliver LJJ.

The judge came to the conclusion that the wording of cl 5 of the invitation telex as qualified by the subsequent telex and set out in the extract from the judgment of Peter Gibson J quoted by Waller LJ, meant that any delay in completing for whatever reason on the part of the trustees was sufficient to exclude the liability otherwise imposed on the purchaser to pay interest after 30 days. I agree that the wording of cl 5 must be construed as being wider than default. At the same time can it be said that the delay in completion was 'on the part of the trustees'? In fact it was caused in the first place by the injunction obtained by Harvela in the courts of the Channel Islands but subsequently continued as a result of undertakings given and the order made by Walton J.

Although Harvela obtained an injunction preventing Sir Leonard from registering the transfer of the shares, Sir Leonard was not enjoined from completing his contract with the trustees to purchase those shares. As between Sir Leonard and the trustees, on the due date the former was ready, willing and able to complete the contract, while the latter were ready and willing but unable to do so. In my judgment, the trustees, through no fault of theirs, were in 'de facto' breach of their contract to complete on time; but of course they have the protection of the undertaking as to damages by Harvela as a term of obtaining the injunction. The terms of the contract called for completion by both parties on the due date and this did not come to pass, with the consequent delay in completion which is now a matter of history. There are, in my view, only four alternatives. The delay was on the part of one or other of the parties or on the part of both of them or it was caused by some supervening frustrating event. The last named alternative is not relevant here, and the clear cause was delay on the part of the trustees, within the meaning of cl 5 of the invitation telex as amended.

In these circumstances I have come to the conclusion that although Sir Leonard is affirming the contract, notwithstanding the breach by the trustees, he is not under the provisions of cl 5 obliged to pay interest from 30 days after 16 September 1981. I would, therefore, dismiss the cross-appeal by Royal Jersey.

Accordingly I agree with the orders proposed by Waller and Oliver LJJ.

*Appeal allowed. Cross-appeal dismissed. Leave to appeal refused.*

*18 December. The Appeal Committee of the House of Lords granted Harvela leave to appeal.*

Solicitors: *McKenna & Co* (for Sir Leonard Outerbridge); *Slaughter & May* (for Harvela); *Bischoff & Co* (for the trustees).

Diana Procter    Barrister.

# Halton Borough Council v Cawley and another

CHANCERY DIVISION AT LIVERPOOL
HIS HONOUR JUDGE BLACKETT-ORD V-C SITTING AS A JUDGE OF THE HIGH COURT
11, 12 JULY 1984

*Markets and fairs – Disturbance – Levying of rival market – Rival market within common law distance – Statutory market – Defendant holding rival market within common law distance of plaintiff local authority's market but outside plaintiff's district – Whether local authority's market entitled to protection from rival market.*

A local authority held two markets within its district. Both markets were of statutory origin and both were held on Saturdays. The defendants also held a market on Saturdays, at a place less than 6⅔ miles from the local authority's markets, but which was outside the local authority's district. The local authority brought an action against the defendants, contending that since the defendants' market was held within the distance of 6⅔ miles from its markets the defendants' market was an actionable nuisance at common law and accordingly it sought an injunction restraining the defendants from holding their market. The defendants contended that, although the local authority would be entitled to protect its markets from competition by rival markets within 6⅔ miles if its markets were common law markets, the fact that the local authority's markets had been created by statute, rather than by Crown grant, meant that the local authority's right to protect its markets was limited to its own district.

**Held** – Whether a market was created by statute or by Crown grant, prima facie the normal rights of market attached to it, including the common law right to protection by the restraining of a rival market from competing within a distance of $6\frac{2}{3}$ miles of it, and accordingly that right applied to a market created by statute unless the statute expressly or by necessary implication excluded it. Since the statutes creating the local authority's markets did not vary or take away the common law right to protection, the local authority's markets had a right to protection from rival markets within the distance of $6\frac{2}{3}$ miles even though the rival markets were outside the local authority's district. Accordingly, the local authority was entitled to an injunction restraining the defendants from holding their rival market (see p 281 *h* to p 282 *a*, post).

### Notes

For markets created by or under statute, see 29 Halsbury's Laws paras 609–617, and for cases on the subject, see 33 Digest (Reissue) 206–207, *1648–1660*.

For the rights and duties of the owner of a market, see 29 Halsbury's Laws (4th edn) para 620, and for cases on the subject, see 33 Digest (Reissue) 208–209, *1664–1666*.

For levying a rival market within the common law distance, see 29 Halsbury's Laws (4th edn) paras 653–658, and for cases on the subject, see 33 Digest (Reissue) 227–228, *1890–1895*.

### Cases referred to in judgment

*Birmingham Corp v Foster* (1894) 70 LT 371.
*Birmingham Corp v Perry Barr Stadium Ltd* [1972] 1 All ER 725.
*East Lindsey DC v Hamilton* (29 March 1984, CA Unbound Transcript 1297).
*IRC v Dowdall O'Mahoney & Co Ltd* [1952] 1 All ER 531, [1952] AC 401, HL.
*Leicester City Council v Oxford and Bristol Stores Ltd* (21 December 1978, unreported), Ch D.
*Sevenoaks DC v Pattullo & Vinson Ltd* [1984] 1 All ER 544, [1984] Ch 211, [1984] 2 WLR 479, CA.

### Cases also cited

*Birmingham City Corp v West Midland Baptist (Trust) Association (Inc)* [1969] 3 All ER 172, [1970] AC 874.
*Hailsham Cattle Market Co v Tolman* [1915] 2 Ch 1, CA.
*Northampton BC v Midland Development Group of Cos Ltd* (1978) 76 LGR 750.
*Wakefield City Council v Box* [1982] 3 All ER 506.

### Action

By a writ and statement of claim dated 7 November 1983 and subsequently amended the plaintiffs, Halton Borough Council, sought as against the defendants, John Kenneth Cawley and Hawsley Co Ltd, (i) a declaration that the plaintiffs were entitled to statutory markets in Widnes on Monday, Friday and Saturday in every week and in Runcorn on Tuesday, Thursday and Saturday in every week and to the tolls, stallage, pickage and other profits appertaining to those markets under the provisions of the Runcorn Improvement Act 1852 and the Food and Drugs Act 1955, (ii) a declaration that the plaintiffs had exclusive market rights within a distance of $6\frac{2}{3}$ miles from those markets, (iii) a declaration that the defendants had levied a rival market in disturbance of the plaintiffs' rights, and (iv) an injunction restraining the defendants from holding a market at the Hawsley Garden Centre, Frodsham, or on land adjoining or adjacent thereto on Saturday in any week or otherwise using or permitting to be used any portion of their property in such a manner as to interfere with or prejudicially affect the market rights of the plaintiffs at Widnes and at Runcorn. The facts are set out in the judgment.

*Konrad Schiemann QC* and *John Morgan* for the plaintiffs.
*Nigel Hague QC* and *Nicholas Orr* for the defendants.

**HIS HONOUR JUDGE BLACKETT-ORD V-C.** This case raises an interesting question on the law of markets, which I am told has not yet been the subject of a decision. The facts are not in dispute and no evidence has been called.

The plaintiffs are a local authority. The Borough of Halton includes the townships of Runcorn and Widnes, where the plaintiffs hold markets on, amongst other days, Saturdays. These markets are all of statutory origin. At Runcorn a market is held under the Runcorn Improvement Act 1852 (15 & 16 Vict c lxviii) (which incorporates the Markets and Fairs Clauses Act 1847), and at Widnes various markets are held under the provisions of Pt III of the Food and Drugs Act 1955 (which replaced earlier Acts).

Section 4 of the 1852 Act lays down what are called the 'limits of this Act' which, not surprisingly, include the whole of the township of Runcorn, and so on. Section 44 provides that the improvement commissioners, who, for the present purposes are the predecessors of the plaintiff council 'shall hold the markets within the limits of this Act on Tuesday and Saturday . . .' and so on. Similarly, though not in mandatory terms, s 49(1) of the 1955 Act provides:

> 'Subject to the provisions of this section, the council of a borough or urban district and, with the consent of the Minister of Housing and Local Government, the council of a rural district may—(a) establish a market within their district . . .'

and para (b) says that they can acquire an existing market by agreement.

Both the 1847 Act and the 1955 Act contain provisions, a sort of code in each case, concerning the running of the markets held subject to their respective provisions. In particular, for present purposes, s 13 of the 1847 Act says this:

> 'After the market place is opened for public use every person other than a licensed hawker who shall sell or expose for sale in any place within the prescribed limits, except in his own dwelling place or shop, any articles in respect of which tolls are by the special Act authorised to be taken in the market, shall for such offence be liable to a penalty not exceeding £2.'

Section 55 of the 1955 Act contains a comparable provision (which I will not read), also imposing a fine of £2. Section 55 does not apply automatically, but can be brought into force by the passing of a byelaw by a council acting under the provisions of the Act.

The defendants hold a market on Saturdays at a place called Frodsham, which is agreed to be 5⅔ miles from the plaintiffs' Runcorn market and 6¼ miles from their Widnes markets. But the defendants' market is outside the plaintiffs' district, and also outside the limits of the 1852 Act.

On the authority of the recent case of *Sevenoaks DC v Pattullo & Vinson Ltd* [1984] 1 All ER 544, [1984] Ch 211 (a decision of the Court of Appeal), the defendants' counsel conceded, although reserving the right to argue the point in higher courts, that if the plaintiffs' markets had been created not by statute but by the grant of a franchise by the Crown, as markets used to be granted long ago, then, as the defendants' market is held within the radius of 6⅔ miles from the plaintiffs' markets, the defendants' market would have been an actionable nuisance without proof of damage. As such, injunctive relief to restrain the defendant's from holding their market would have been appropriate. I refer to the observations of Slade LJ and Sir John Donaldson MR ([1984] 1 All ER 544 at 546–547, 554, [1984] Ch 211 at 214, 224).

But, says the counsel for the defendants, the plaintiffs' markets are statutory and not created by grant from the Crown, and that makes all the difference. The remedy to protect the plaintiffs' market is, the defendants concede, the same, the plaintiffs are entitled to protect their markets by obtaining the grant of an injunction in appropriate cases. But not in this case, the defendants say, because their market is outside the district, and as the plaintiffs' markets are the creatures of statute and vested in a local authority then, say the defendants, the plaintiffs are only entitled to restrain the holding of the markets within their own local authority district and are not, so to speak, to trespass into an adjoining district and stop the defendants holding a market there.

Counsel for the defendants relies on certain dicta in the cases. They are only dicta, because this particular point has not yet been decided in any case and, indeed, I have not been referred to any case in which the alleged market disturbance (that is to say, the equivalent of the defendants' market) has been held outside the plaintiffs' area. But in *Birmingham Corp v Foster* (1894) 70 LT 371 at 372 Romer J said:

> 'Now I agree that, treating as I do, the plaintiffs' market as a statutory market [and then he refers to the relevant local Act] the plaintiffs cannot be heard to say that their market rights are infringed, or their market disturbed, merely because any person is selling or exposing for sale within the borough [and he refers to the subject matter of the action, and goes on] But, subject to those statutory provisions, no person, as I have said, within the plaintiffs' borough has a right to attempt to set up a rival market, or to disturb the plaintiffs' statutory market.'

So there the judge is referring to a disturbance within the plaintiffs' borough; but I observe that that is where the disturbance in question was. It is said that he should have said 'within the plaintiffs' borough or within 6⅔ miles of' somewhere. But it was not a point which was before him and I do not think that dictum carries very much weight in the defendants' favour.

The same applies to a rather similar dicta by Pennycuick V-C in *Birmingham Corp v Perry Barr Stadium Ltd* [1972] 1 All ER 725. Again, the judge speaks of disturbances within the corporation's area, but that was the point with which he was concerned. The point with which I am now concerned did not arise.

The defendants also rely on the fact that the 1852 Act was a local Act and they say that the provisions of Pt III of the 1955 Act are similar to a local Act, being provisions which can be adopted by a particular council in its area, and they say that rights granted by a local Act are normally to be construed as applying only within the area of the Act. If I may say so, I take the point, but in my judgment it is not applicable in the present case.

If the plaintiffs' markets had been granted by the Crown in the distant past, perhaps to the lord of a manor, or to a borough (probably a smaller territorial area), it would have carried with it the right to stop anyone else carrying on a market within the common law distance which I take to be 6⅔ miles. That would normally have affected the rights of people outside the manor or borough. That being the position of common law, I cannot see any difference if, as is the case, the plaintiffs' markets are statutory.

Counsel for the defendants, in his argument, raised an interesting question of whether the relevant distance is 6⅔ miles radius from the actual site of the market or whether there is a sort of cordon sanitaire of that width round the permitted market area, and what is the position where you have a large district which extends in some direction, perhaps, more than 6⅔ miles away from the market? But counsel for the plaintiffs wisely confined themselves to the facts of the present case, and I propose to do the same.

Counsel for the defendants also rely on what I may call the criminal provisions (which I have already referred to), s 13 of the 1847 Act and s 55 of the 1955 Act, which apply criminal sanctions, that is to say a fine of £2 within and only within the council's area. They say that as the protection of the council's markets by a criminal law is confined to their area, then that provided by the civil law should be no more extensive. But those sanctions are concerned with selling within the market area and not with what is complained of here, the carrying on of a rival market, which is quite a different thing.

This leads me to the plaintiffs' submissions. They say that prima facie a market is a market, whether granted by the Crown or created by statute. However created it has, prima facie, the normal characteristics of a market or right of market, and a very important one of those characteristics is a right to stop anyone else competing within a certain area. It is not much use being granted a right of market if several other people can set up rival markets two or three hundred yards away.

This territorial restriction on competition is, in my judgment, clearly a very important matter, and the plaintiffs say, and I accept, that it is one of the normal characteristics of a market. They go on to say that for this reason the restriction applies to a market created by statute just as it applies to a franchise market, unless the statute expressly or by necessary implication excludes it. This, in my judgment, is also right.

Then they go on to say that there is no exclusion in the present case. I have already dealt with what I called the criminal sections of the Acts, which I think do not affect the position. The plaintiffs rely on the proviso to s 49(3) of the 1955 Act, which is in these terms. I read from the beginning of sub-s (3) because it is not a particularly elegant piece of drafting and it may be easier to understand if I do so:

'Without the consent of the person concerned, no market shall be established in pursuance of this section so as to interfere with any rights, powers or privileges enjoyed within the district in respect of a market by any person: Provided that, for the purposes of this subsection, another local authority shall not be deemed to be enjoying any rights, powers or privileges within the district by reason only of the fact that they have established a market within their own district either under paragraph (a) of subsection (1) of this section [or under the previous legislation]...'

and I need not read the rest.

Counsel for the defendants concedes that the meaning of the proviso is that Parliament contemplated something like the present situation, that is to say the competing market outside the district. But he is compelled to say that this is one of the cases where Homer has nodded and, as sometimes happens, Parliament has legislated on the mistaken view of the law. In such a case the mistaken legislation is not to be taken to have changed the substance of the law.

He relied on *IRC v Dowdall O'Mahoney & Co Ltd* [1952] 1 All ER 531, [1952] AC 401. I accept the principle of that case, but I do not accept that it is applicable in the present case. In my judgment, the principle is correctly stated by Sir Robert Megarry V-C in his judgment in *Leicester City Council v Oxford and Bristol Stores Ltd* (21 December 1978, unreported), of which I have been shown a transcript, and which was quoted with approval by Oliver LJ in *East Lindsey DC v Hamilton* (29 March 1984, CA Unbound Transcript 1297), a case, I should say, which was not fully argued and, perhaps, may not be reported. Nevertheless, Oliver LJ in the *East Lindsey* case approved this passage from the judgment of Sir Robert Megarry V-C in the *Leicester City Council* case:

'When statute authorises the creation of a 'market' simpliciter, then unless the Act contains some indication to the contrary, I would on principle take it that what Parliament intended to authorise was the creation of a market with all the attributes of a franchise market, including the right to protection against disturbance by the holding of rival markets. I cannot see why Parliament should be taken to have intended to have authorised the creation of a market shorn of one of the most important attributes of a franchise market, its right to protection against rivals. *Pease and Chitty's Law of Markets and Fairs* (2nd edn, 1958) p 18 says that the better view is that a statutory market has all the attributes of a common law market, except so far as the statutes vary them or take them away. Apart from cases where all that is done is merely an offence against a statute (see, for example, the Food and Drugs Act 1955, s 55), the disturbance of a statutory market by levying a rival market accordingly gives rise to an action for damages and an injunction...'

In the present case, in my judgment, the statutes do not vary or take away the common law protection, that common law protection being within a radius of 6⅔ miles. That protection is applicable even though part of the circle, as in the present cases, may be outside the district of the plaintiff council. Accordingly, in my judgment, the plaintiffs are entitled to the injunction which they seek.

*Order accordingly.*

Solicitors: *M F McNaughton*, Widnes (for the plaintiffs); *J L Cottrell*, Northwich (for the defendants).

M Denise Chorlton    Barrister.

# Buckbod Investments Ltd v Nana-Otchere and another

CHANCERY DIVISION
SIR ROBERT MEGARRY V-C
14 NOVEMBER 1984

*Practice – Appeal – Withdrawal of appeal – Appeal from order of master – Appeal not to be withdrawn without leave of court – Application to judge necessary – Distinction between withdrawal of appeal and dismissal of appeal by consent.*

Since it is normally in the interests of litigants that matters should be finally disposed of, the courts are in general reluctant to allow an appeal to be withdrawn, as opposed to being dismissed by consent, because (amongst other reasons) whereas the dismissal of an appeal is final an appellant might, provided he is in time or he obtains an extension of time, change his mind and launch the appeal again. Accordingly, where an appellant wishes to withdraw an appeal from a Chancery master, he must apply to a judge for that purpose, since Chancery Chambers have no power to allow such a withdrawal. It is often possible, however, for an appeal from a Chancery master to be dismissed by consent without any hearing by a judge, on making a written application in proper form (see p 284 *a b* and *d* to *h*, post).

*Tod-Heatley v Barnard* [1890] WN 130 applied.

## Notes
For dismissal of an appeal by consent, see 38 Halsbury's Laws (4th edn) para 692, and for cases on withdrawal of an appeal, see 37(3) Digest (Reissue) 169–170, 3870–3876.

## Case referred to in judgment
*Tod-Heatley v Barnard* [1890] WN 130, CA.

## Application
The plaintiffs, Buckbod Investments Ltd, applied to withdraw an appeal lodged by a notice dated 17 July 1984 against the decision of Master Cholmondeley-Clarke on 12 July 1984 extending the time for completion of the purchase by the first defendant, George Nana-Otchere, of certain freehold property in conformity with a notice to complete served by the plaintiff's solicitors on the first defendant dated 6 July 1983 and ordering that the first defendant's mortgagees' surveyors be permitted to inspect and survey the property. The second defendants, Barnard Marcus & Co, a firm of estate agents, took no part in the application.

*Peter Wulwik* for the plaintiffs.
*Ashitey K N Ollennu* for the first defendant.

**SIR ROBERT MEGARRY V-C.** This is a case in which the plaintiffs set down an appeal from a decision made by Master Cholmondeley-Clarke on 12 July 1984. I do not think I need to go into the substance of the case, beyond saying that it is a case between vendor and purchaser and the purchaser has not completed.

As a result of other steps that have been taken in the proceedings, the plaintiffs came to the conclusion that they did not wish to proceed with their appeal against the order of the master. Accordingly, they wrote to the court saying: 'We now withdraw that appeal.' The officers of Chancery Chambers then informed the plaintiffs that without an application to a judge, the appeal could not be removed from the list unless the defendant consented; and this consent was refused. The matter now comes before me in the form of an application by the plaintiffs for the withdrawal of the appeal from the list.

Now the court is in general somewhat reluctant (and certainly the Court of Appeal is somewhat reluctant) to allow an appeal to be withdrawn, as opposed to the appeal being dismissed by consent. One reason for this is that once an appeal has been dismissed, that is an end of the matter, whereas if an appeal is merely withdrawn, then it may be that the appellant, if he is in time or obtains an extension of time, could subsequently change his mind again and launch the appeal again; and it is normally in the interests of litigants that matters should be finally disposed of. However, in this case, in view of the tangle that has arisen, counsel for the plaintiffs is anxious to prevent himself from being met by some argument that the dismissal of his appeal by consent would debar him from contending that a consent order made before Goulding J on 19 June 1984 should not be the subject of an appeal. I think that the reasoning is somewhat thin, but on the whole, and in the circumstances of this case, I think that it is a proper case in which to allow the withdrawal of the appeal, rather than requiring it to be the subject of an application by the plaintiffs to dismiss it.

On behalf of the first defendant, counsel put forward a contention that the appeal ought not to be allowed to be withdrawn. However, nothing that he has said has convinced me that any benefit that maintaining the life of the appeal would bring him could not be achieved by a separate application on his part. Accordingly, his objection to the withdrawal of the appeal is one that I would reject. On the facts of this case, I therefore hold that the plaintiffs should be allowed to withdraw the appeal.

For the benefit of the profession, I think that I should say something further in general terms about the distinction between the withdrawal of an appeal and an appeal being dismissed by consent. *Tod-Heatley v Barnard* [1890] WN 130 still stands as authority for the proposition that an appeal cannot be withdrawn without the leave of the court. Accordingly, it seems to me that if on an appeal from a Chancery master the appellant wishes to withdraw the appeal, he must apply to a judge for that purpose. The withdrawal cannot be achieved merely by making a written application to Chancery Chambers, since Chancery Chambers have no power to allow such a withdrawal. On the other hand, bearing in mind the practice of the Court of Appeal (see *Practice Direction* [1983] 1 All ER 448, [1983] 1 WLR 85), it is often possible for an appeal from a Chancery master to be dismissed by consent without any hearing by a judge. For this purpose, a document signed by the solicitors for all parties, and by any litigant in person, or an equivalent exchange of letters, must be lodged with the Clerk of the Lists in room 163, requesting the dismissal of the appeal, certifying that all parties are sui juris, and specifying the order for costs required, including any legal aid taxation. The documents will then be put before a judge for consideration, and if he is satisfied he will initial the appropriate document and the appeal will thereupon stand dismissed without any hearing. The same procedure may be followed where an appeal has been settled, and is to be dismissed on agreed terms set out in the application, provided the judge sees no objection to any terms which are to be included in the order. Where, however, the appeal is simply to be dismissed, with costs to be taxed, an application signed by the appellant's solicitors alone (or by the appellant, if he is in person) will suffice. All other applications for the dismissal of an appeal will be listed and dealt with by a judge in chambers.

*Application allowed.*

Solicitors: *Blatchfords* (for the plaintiffs); *Martin Potter & Co* (for the first defendant).

Vivian Horvath    Barrister.

# Re Pittortou (a bankrupt), ex parte the trustee of the property of the bankrupt v The bankrupt and another

CHANCERY DIVISION
SCOTT J
23 JULY 1984

*Bankruptcy – Property available for distribution – Matrimonial home – Home in joint names of husband and wife – Home charged to bank by husband and wife to secure husband's business debts – Husband using bank account both for business and household payments and to support another woman – Shares in which home beneficially owned by wife and husband's trustee in bankruptcy – Whether equity of exoneration applying – Whether wife entitled to require husband's debt to bank to be met out of his interest in matrimonial home.*

*Equity – Exoneration – Husband and wife – Husband's debt to bank secured by joint charge over matrimonial home – Whether equity of exoneration applying – Whether wife entitled to require husband's debt to bank to be met out of his interest in matrimonial home.*

In 1979 the husband and wife purchased a home in their joint names using the proceeds of sale of their former matrimonial home (which had also been in their joint names). The new home was made subject to a first mortgage in respect of the balance of the purchase price and a second mortgage to the husband's bank to secure his indebtedness to the bank on an account which he used not only for his business but also for the payment of the joint household expenses. In 1981 he left the matrimonial home and went to live with another woman whom he was supporting. In 1982 he became bankrupt and subsequently his trustee in bankruptcy applied for an order for the sale of the matrimonial home and the division of the proceeds according to the shares in the property which the court declared the wife and the trustee to have. The question arose how, as between the trustee's share and the wife's share, the secured indebtedness on the husband's bank account should be met.

**Held** – Where jointly owned property was charged to secure the debts of only one of the joint owners, then, under the equitable doctrine of exoneration and in the absence of evidence of the parties having a contrary intention, the other joint owner, being in the position of a surety, was entitled, not only as between the two joint owners but also as between himself and the creditor, to have the secured indebtedness discharged so far as possible out of the debtor's interest in the property, thereby enhancing the value of the other joint owner's share of the property. Applying that principle and having regard to the parties' intentions, the wife was entitled to insist that the husband's debts to the bank incurred in running the business and in supporting the other woman be met primarily out of his interest in the matrimonial home, since those debts were not the wife's debts. On the other hand, that part of the husband's debt to the bank which represented payments made by him for the benefit of the joint family expenses was a debt which fell on the property as a whole. Accordingly, the respective shares of the trustee in bankruptcy and the wife were dependent on the amounts of the husband's business and personal debts (which were deductible only from his share of the property) on the one hand and of the joint family debt (which were deductible from both parties' shares) on the other (see p 287 *j*, p 288 *b* to *d* and *f g* and p 289 *a* to *h*, post).

*Paget v Paget* [1895–9] All ER Rep 1150 and *Re a debtor (No 24 of 1971), ex p Marley (J) v Trustee of the property of the debtor* [1976] 2 All ER 1010 applied.

**Notes**

For the equity of exoneration, see 22 Halsbury's Laws (4th edn) paras 1071–1076, and for cases on the subject, see 27(1) Digest (Reissue) 169–174, 1126–1168.

**Cases referred to in judgment**

Cronmire, Re, ex p Cronmire [1901] 1 KB 480, CA.
Debtor, A (No 24 of 1971), Re, ex p Marley (J) v Trustee of the property of the debtor [1976] 2 All ER 1010, [1976] 1 WLR 952, DC.
Gee v Liddell [1913] 2 Ch 62.
Hall v Hall [1911] 1 Ch 487.
Paget v Paget [1898] 1 Ch 470, [1895–9] All ER Rep 1150, CA.
Woodstock (a bankrupt), Re (19 November 1979, unreported), Ch D.

**Motion**

By a notice of motion dated 13 December 1983 the trustee in bankruptcy of Christopher Louis Pittortou, the first respondent to the motion (the bankrupt), applied for (1) a declaration that the trustee and the second respondent to the motion, Orsalia Pittortou, the bankrupt's former wife, were each entitled beneficially to a one-half share in the equity of the freehold property known as 23 Kilvinton Drive, Clay Hill, Enfield, Middlesex, (2) an order that the property be sold with vacant possession, (3) an order that the conduct of the sale be given to the trustee, (4) an order that the bankrupt and the second respondent concur in the sale and take all necessary steps to convey the property as the trustee might direct, (5) an order that the bankrupt and the second respondent deliver up vacant possession of the property to the trustee and (6) an order that one-half of the net proceeds of the sale be paid to the second respondent. The facts are set out in the judgment.

*Richard Sheldon* for the trustee in bankruptcy.
The second respondent appeared in person.
The bankrupt did not appear.

**SCOTT J.** The application before me today in this case is an application by the trustee of the bankrupt, Christopher Louis Pittortou, asking for a declaration as to the beneficial ownership of the property, 23 Kilvinton Drive, Clay Hill, Enfield, Middlesex, which formerly represented the matrimonial home of the bankrupt and his wife, Orsalia Pittortou, the second respondent to this motion and of their daughter. The trustee asks for the usual relief in respect of the sale of the property and the steps necessary to effect a sale.

The act of bankruptcy in the case was committed by the bankrupt on 15 June 1982, a receiving order was made on 22 November 1982 and he was adjudicated bankrupt on 13 December 1982. The application before me was made by the trustee in bankruptcy on 13 December 1983. It has been before the court on two or three previous occasions, and has been adjourned for the purposes of enabling discussions to take place between the trustee and the second respondent, Mrs Pittortou, and to enable evidence for the purposes of the application to be completed.

The property, as I have said, formerly was the matrimonial home. However, in 1981 the bankrupt left his wife and daughter, as I understand it, to live with another woman whom he had for some time previously been supporting in her own establishment. The second respondent and the bankrupt have since been divorced. The property, 23 Kilvinton Drive, was purchased by the bankrupt and his wife, the second respondent, in April 1979 in their joint names. The purchase price was £30,000, of which £14,000 was found by Mr and Mrs Pittortou from the proceeds of sale of a previous matrimonial home, 261 North Circular Road, which also had stood in their joint names. The balance of £16,000 required to meet the purchase price was obtained by an advance from the Guardian Building Society secured by a first charge on the property. The building society charge remains outstanding, and there is currently just under £19,000 secured by that charge. There is a second charge on the property in favour of National Westminster Bank. The history of the National Westminster Bank's second charge goes back to the time when Mr and Mrs Pittortou owned and lived in 261 North Circular Road.

The bankrupt comes, as I understand it, of a family whose main business is the conduct of restaurants. In about 1972 it was proposed in the family that he should take over the conduct of a particular restaurant which had previously been run by the family, a restaurant known as Naples Restaurant. In 1972, on the occasion when the bankrupt took over on his own account the conduct of Naples Restaurant, he and his wife went to the National Westminster Bank offices and signed a charge of their then matrimonial home, 261 North Circular Road, to secure any indebtedness on the bank account of the bankrupt with the National Westminster Bank that he proposed to use for, among other things, the purposes of the business of that restaurant. In her affidavit, sworn for the purposes of this application, the wife has said that, when she went along to the bank for the purpose of signing that legal charge, the bank manager endeavoured to explain to her the meaning of the legal charge and its significance to her so far as her proprietary interest in 261 North Circular Road was concerned, but that her husband and her brother-in-law, who was associated with him in the conduct of the various family restaurants, had told the bank manager that it was none of her business and that she was just there to sign. In consequence she did then sign without having the significance of the legal charge explained to her.

However, she said very frankly in the witness box that, after that legal charge had been signed, her husband did explain to her the significance of it, and she did become aware that their then matrimonial home was charged to the National Westminster Bank to secure her husband's bank account used, among other things, for the trading purposes of the restaurant.

In 1979, when 261 North Circular Road was sold and the property with which I am concerned, 23 Kilvinton Drive, Enfield, was purchased, the National Westminster Bank's legal charge over 261 North Circular Road must have been discharged (although I have not seen the documentation in that regard) and a new legal charge, this time of 23 Kilvinton Drive, was executed by the bankrupt and his wife. This legal charge was executed by the parties in the offices of the solicitors who were dealing with their sale of 261 North Circular Road and their purchase of 23 Kilvinton Drive.

The bank account, which was secured by the second charge on 23 Kilvinton Drive and which had been earlier secured by the second charge on 261 North Circular Road, was not only used to enable the necessary banking transactions in regard to the conduct of the restaurant to be effected, but was also used by the bankrupt to some extent for payment of expenses in connection with the matrimonial home.

There has been evidence put before me that he paid a number of mortgage instalments to the Guardian Building Society out of this account. There has been evidence that he drew cheques on this account for such matters as electricity and rates, and for other expenses in connection with the joint occupation of the property by himself, his wife and daughter.

The question for me is how, as between the trustee in bankruptcy on the one hand, in whom the bankrupt's equitable interest in 23 Kilvinton Drive has vested, and the wife on the other hand, the secured indebtedness of the National Westminster Bank should be met.

The wife is in the position of a surety so far as her own proprietory interest in 23 Kilvinton Drive is concerned. The bank's charge is a charge to secure the husband's indebtedness and not her own, but that indebtedness is secured on property of which she is in part the beneficial owner. As a general proposition, if there is found a charge on property jointly owned to secure the debts of one only of the joint owners, the other joint owner, being in the position of a surety, is entitled as between the two joint owners to have the secured indebtedness discharged so far as possible out of the equitable interest of the debtor. The principle is expressed in 22 Halsbury's Laws (4th edn) paras 1071–1076, under the general heading 'Equity of Exoneration'. Paragraph 1071 begins:

'If the property of a married woman is mortgaged or charged in order to raise money for the payment of her husband's debts, or otherwise for his benefit, it is presumed, in the absence of evidence showing an intention to the contrary, that she meant to charge her property merely by way of security, and in such case she is in the position of surety and is entitled to be indemnified by the husband, and to throw the debt primarily on his estate to the exoneration of her own . . .'

But the entitlement of the wife to be indemnified by the husband, the bankrupt, in respect of the debt owing to the National Westminster Bank that is charged on the matrimonial home is a right of very little value since he is bankrupt. A right which would be of real value to her would be the right to have the National Westminster Bank indebtedness thrown primarily on his half share. That would have the effect of enhancing the size of her own proprietary beneficial interest in the property.

It is, I think, clear that the effect of the equity of exoneration in a case such as this is indeed to enhance the proprietary interest of the surety/joint mortgagor and not simply to give the surety a personal right to an indemnity from the debtor who is the other joint mortgagor. *Re Cronmire, ex p Cronmire* [1901] 1 KB 480 establishes the entitlement of a wife, whose property has been charged to secure her husband's debts, to prove in his bankruptcy in respect of the indemnity which he owes her. A subsequent case, *Re a debtor (No 24 of 1971), ex p Marley (J) v Trustee of the property of the debtor* [1976] 2 All ER 1010, [1976] 1 WLR 952, establishes that in addition to the right to claim an indemnity the surety can claim an enhanced proprietary interest. In that case Foster J, with whose judgment Fox J agreed, said ([1976] 2 All ER 1010 at 1013, [1976] 1 WLR 952 at 955):

'As between the bankrupt's father and the bankrupt, and bearing in mind that the father is admittedly only a surety, it should be implied that their intention was that the bankrupt's beneficial interest should bear the burden. If that is so, it seems to me that the bankrupt's interest vested in his trustee in bankruptcy, subject to an inchoate right of indemnity, if the surety were called on to pay, or the debt fell to be discharged, as it would have to be, out of the proceeds of sale of the property. Alternatively, I think that the father could be regarded as having an actual charge on the bankrupt's interest within the principle discussed by Warrington J in *Gee v Liddell* [1913] 2 Ch 62 at 72 . . .'

However, the equity of exoneration is a principle of equity which depends on the presumed intention of the parties. If the circumstances of a particular case do not justify the inference, or indeed if the circumstances negate the inference, that it was the joint intention of the joint mortgagors that the burden of the secured indebtedness should fall primarily on the share of that of them who was the debtor, then that consequence will not follow. In *Paget v Paget* [1898] 1 Ch 470, [1895–9] All ER Rep 1150 the Court of Appeal so found in a case where the indebtedness had been incurred in order to finance the luxurious living of the family, and had been taken advantage of and had been to the benefit of both joint mortgagors, notwithstanding that it was in law the debt of only one of them. And Walton J in *Re Woodstock (a bankrupt)* (19 November 1979, unreported) drew attention in his judgment to the need for the courts, in considering how the equity of exoneration should work as between a husband and a wife, to take into account the relationship which husbands and wives bear, or ought to bear, to one another in their family affairs in current times. The guide that Victorian cases can provide to the inferences which should be drawn from the dealings with one another of husbands and wives today is often not very valuable. Walton J, commenting on *Hall v Hall* [1911] 1 Ch 487, said:

'I do not think I have to go into the interesting question whether that case is now good law in view of completely changed social conditions. It appears to me that that case was decided in the days when the wife did nothing except sit at home and run the household and boss the servants about, and the husband was expected to be, and indeed was, the provider. Times have now changed, and I am very far from saying that if that case were to be heard on precisely the same facts tomorrow, the decision would necessarily be the same.'

I respectfully adopt that approach. The present is a case in which, as is plain from the evidence, the family, until the sad departure of the bankrupt in 1981, acted as a family unit in its family and business affairs. The wife worked in the restaurants which the Pittortou family conducted, and which later her husband on his own account conducted, for long hours and without pay. In that respect, her conduct was similar to the conduct of many wives assisting their husbands in the conduct of the business on which the livelihood and support of the family depend. In my view, payments made out of the bankrupt's National Westminster Bank account for the benefit of the Pittortou family are of a character as to make it impossible to impute to the parties the intention that as between the husband and the wife the payments should be regarded as falling only on the share in the mortgaged property of the husband. In my view the equity of exoneration should be confined to payments out of the account which do not have the character of payments made for the joint benefit of the household.

On the other hand, save for payments made for the joint benefit of the household, it does not seem to me that the equity of exoneration has any less part to play now than it had in the days when the equitable doctrine was being formulated. Accordingly, payments made by the bankrupt purely for business purposes and, a fortiori, any payments made by him for the purposes of the second establishment it seems he was supporting, should as between the bankrupt and the wife be treated as charged primarily on the bankrupt's half share in the mortgaged property.

In the notice of motion the trustee in bankruptcy asks, first, for a declaration as to the beneficial interests of the parties in 23 Kilvinton Drive. In my judgment, the beneficial interests are these. To start with, when the property was purchased, the bankrupt and his wife were each entitled beneficially to a half share subject to the building society mortgage. The second charge, securing the debt owing to the National Westminster Bank, secured a debt of the bankrupt; the debt was not a debt of the wife. Prima facie, therefore, in my judgment the equity of exoneration applies to entitle the wife to require that indebtedness to be met primarily out of her husband's share in the net proceeds of sale. But, to the extent that that indebtedness represents payments which can be shown to have been made by the bankrupt for the benefit of the household, the indebtedness should be discharged out of the proceeds of sale before division. There is no doubt that into that category will fall the building society instalments that were paid out of the National Westminster Bank account. Also, in my judgment, into that category would fall payments made for the purposes of the occupation of the property by the bankrupt, the wife and their daughter or otherwise for the benefit of the joint household.

The trustee, in my judgment rightly but in the circumstances with some generosity, does not seek to claim that any other payments than those to which I have already referred should be treated as coming out of the proceeds of sale before division. Any other payments accordingly will be treated as charged primarily on the bankrupt's half share in the property.

I now come to the question of sale. There will have to be an inquiry, which I hope will be an inexpensive inquiry and which ought to be an inexpensive inquiry, as to what are the payments that fall to be discharged out of the proceeds of sale before division. Until that inquiry has taken place, it is not possible to know exactly the extent of the respective beneficial interests in the property of the wife on the one hand and the trustee in bankruptcy, standing in the bankrupt's shoes, on the other hand. It is not therefore at present possible for the wife to make a fully informed offer to the trustee to purchase his interest in the property.

If the wife is not able to make an offer to the trustee which properly reflects the value of the trustee's interest in the property, the property will have to be sold, and ought to be sold. Nevertheless there ought not to be a sale until she is in a position to make such an offer. She will not be in that position until the extent of the respective beneficial interests has been ascertained.

*Order accordingly.*

Solicitors: *Goodman Derrick & Co* (for the trustee in bankruptcy).

Jacqueline Metcalfe    Barrister.

# Watson v Holland (Inspector of Taxes)

CHANCERY DIVISION
PETER GIBSON J
15, 16 MARCH 1984

*Settlement – Disposition – Resulting trust – Settlor making separate settlements in favour of each of his children as principal beneficiary – Trusts in favour of principal beneficiary not exhaustive – Gift to children other than principal beneficiary inconsistent with trusts in favour of principal beneficiary – Whether absolute gift in favour of principal beneficiary – Whether resulting trust for taxpayer – Income and Corporation Taxes Act 1970, s 457.*

The taxpayer had two children, T, born in 1968, and N, born in 1971. In 1977 the taxpayer made two irrevocable settlements, one in favour of T and the other in favour of N. The settlements were in identical form mutatis mutandis. Clause 2 of each settlement contained the trusts for the particular child's benefit. The trusts were not exhaustive and the principal beneficiary under each settlement had no right to capital. Clause 3, which was expressly made subject 'to all the trusts hereinbefore declared', required the trust fund and the income thereof to be held in trust (in equal shares if more than one) 'for the Settlor's children other than the [principal beneficiary] . . . and so that each such other child's share shall be held upon the same trusts and with and subject to the same powers and provisions' as those set out in cl 2. Clauses 8 and 11 provided, in effect, that the taxpayer and his wife were to receive no benefit from the settlement in any way whatsoever. In 1982 the Revenue raised assessments on the taxpayer under s 457[a] of the Income and Corporation Taxes Act 1970 in respect of the income arising under the settlements for the years of assessments 1977–78 to 1979–80 on the grounds that under each settlement there was a resulting trust in favour of the taxpayer as settlor. The taxpayer appealed, contending that s 457 did not apply because under each settlement the principal beneficiary had an absolute gift onto which were engrafted trusts which failed because they did not exhaust the beneficial interests, with the result that the absolute gift took effect so far as the trusts failed to the exclusion of a resulting trust for the taxpayer. The Crown contended that cl 3, read as a whole, did not confer an initial absolute gift but created a single system of trusts and accordingly there was a resulting trust to the taxpayer. The Special Commissioners decided that cl 3, read as a whole, did not confer an absolute gift but a gift on prescribed trusts and that, the trusts not being exhaustive, there was a resulting trust in favour of the taxpayer. They accordingly confirmed the assessments. The taxpayer appealed.

**Held** – The language of the first part of cl 3 was unambiguously that of an absolute gift, ie an outright disposition of the entirety of both capital and income of the trust fund. The referential trusts relating to 'each such other child's share' which followed were, however, inconsistent with an initial absolute gift, and were not exhaustive of the beneficial interest in the trust fund. Accordingly, the trust took effect as an absolute disposition to the exclusion of any resulting trust of capital or income of the trust fund in favour of the taxpayer, who was therefore not liable to tax on the income accruing to

---

*a* Section 457, so far as material, is set out at p 293 *j* to p 294 *b*, post

the trust fund by virtue of s 457 of the 1970 Act. The appeal would therefore be allowed (see p 300 *h* to p 301 *d*, p 302 *g h* and p 303 *a* to *d*, post).

*Lassence v Tierney* [1843–60] All ER Rep 47 followed.

*Fyfe v Irwin* [1939] 2 All ER 271 applied.

### Notes

For the rule in *Lassence v Tierney*, see 50 Halsbury's Laws (4th edn) para 416, and for cases on the subject, see 50 Digest (Reissue) 505–507, 4922–4932.

For the absolute divesting of property by a settlor, see 23 Halsbury's Laws (4th edn) para 1459.

For the Income and Corporation Taxes Act 1970, s 457, see 33 Halsbury's Statutes (3rd edn) 587.

### Cases referred to in judgment

*A-G v Lloyds Bank Ltd* [1935] AC 382, [1935] All ER Rep 518, HL.

*Burton's Settlement Trusts, Re, Public Trustee v Montefiore* [1955] 1 All ER 433, [1955] Ch 348, [1955] 2 WLR 452, CA; *rvsg* [1954] 3 All ER 231, [1955] Ch 60, [1954] 3 WLR 574.

*Cohen's Will Trusts, Re, Cullen v Westminster Bank Ltd* [1936] 1 All ER 103.

*Fyfe v Irwin* [1939] 2 All ER 271, HL.

*Goold's Will Trusts, Re, Lloyds Bank Ltd v Goold* [1967] 3 All ER 652.

*Hancock v Watson* [1902] AC 14, [1900–3] All ER Rep 87, HL.

*Johnson's Settlement Trusts, Re, McClure v Johnson* [1943] 2 All ER 499, [1943] Ch 341.

*Lassence v Tierney* (1849) 1 Mac & G 551, [1843–60] All ER Rep 47, 41 ER 1379.

*Litt's Will Trusts, Re, Parry v Cooper* [1946] 1 All ER 314, [1946] Ch 154, CA.

*Marshall, Re, Graham v Marshall* [1928] Ch 661, [1928] All ER Rep 694.

*Norton, Re, Wyatt v Bain* [1949] WN 23, CA.

*Payne, Re, Taylor v Payne* [1927] 2 Ch 1, [1927] All ER Rep 223.

*Rucker v Scholefield* (1862) 1 Hem & M 36, 71 ER 16.

### Case also cited

*Warren's Trusts, Re* (1884) 26 Ch D 208.

### Case stated

1. At a meeting of the Commissioners for the Special Purposes of the Income Tax Acts held on 29 March 1983 Peter Charles Watson (the taxpayer) appealed against the following assessments to income tax:

| Year | £ |
|---|---|
| 1977–78 | 2,050 |
| 1978–79 | 8,003 |
| 1979–80 | 8,149 |

2. Shortly stated the question for the commissioners' decision was whether the income of two settlements made by the taxpayer in favour of his children was assessable on him under the provisions of Pt XVI of the Income and Corporation Taxes Act 1970, by virtue of the possibility of a resulting trust in favour of the taxpayer.

3. The commissioners who heard the appeals took time to consider their decision and gave it in writing on 9 May 1983. A copy of that decision setting out the relevant facts, the contentions of the parties and the grounds on which they disallowed the appeals and confirmed the assessments is annexed hereto and forms part of this case.

[Paragraph 4 listed the documents proved or admitted before the commissioners.]

5. The taxpayer immediately after the determination of the appeal declared his dissatisfaction therewith as being erroneous in point of law and on 27 May 1983 required the commissioners to state a case for the opinion of the High Court pursuant to s 56 of the Taxes Management Act 1970.

6. The question of law for the opinion of the court was whether the commissioners, were correct in holding that there was under each of the settlements a possible resulting trust in favour of the taxpayer.

DECISION

1. The question for determination is whether the income of two settlements made by the taxpayer in favour of his children is assessable on him under the provisions of Pt XVI of the Income and Corporation Taxes Act 1970 by virtue of the possibility of a resulting trust in favour of the taxpayer. 2. The following facts are agreed between the parties. 2.1. The taxpayer is 42 years of age, having been born on 23 January 1941. He has been married once only, in 1966, and has had two children only, both sons: (i) Timothy Peter Watson (Timothy) born on 21 August 1968 and (ii) Neil George Watson (Neil) born on 13 January 1971. 2.2. The taxpayer's two settlements were both dated 9 March 1977 and both were made between the taxpayer (as settlor) of the one part and the taxpayer, Jonathan Charles Vivian Hunt and Brian Curson (as trustees) of the other part. The settlements were in identical form except that the principal beneficiary (defined as 'the Child') was Timothy in one case and Neil in the other case. 2.3. On 11 May 1982 the inspector of taxes raised assessments on the taxpayer in respect of the income arising under the settlements for the years of assessment 1977–78 (£2,050), 1978–79 (£8,003) and 1979–80 (£8,149), relying on the provisions of s 457 of the Income and Corporation Taxes Act 1970. On 7 June 1982 the taxpayer, through his solicitors, appealed against the assessments, and contended that s 457 does not apply.

3. We set out below the provisions (taken from Neil's settlement) to which we were expressly referred.

Recitals:

'1. The [taxpayer] being desirous of making such provision as is hereinafter contained for the benefit of [Neil] . . . has transferred to the Original Trustees the sum of One thousand pounds to be held by them upon the Trusts hereinafter declared. 2. The [taxpayer] intends that this Settlement shall be absolutely irrevocable in all circumstances.'

Clause 2:

'(a) So long as the Child is living and under the age of Twenty-five years the Trustees may pay or apply the whole or any part of the income of the Trust Fund for or towards the maintenance or education or otherwise for the benefit of the Child in such manner as the Trustees think fit and shall accumulate the balance of such income by investing or laying out the same in the acquisition of any investments or property hereby authorised and shall hold such accumulations as an accretion to the capital of the Trust Fund (but with power to pay or apply accumulations of income of any preceding year as if the same were income arising in the current year)

(b) The Trustees shall also have power exerciseable [sic] at any time or times during the lifetime of the Child and before the Vesting Day [9 March 2057] to pay transfer or apply any capital of the Trust Fund to or for the benefit of the Child but so that any capital applied for the benefit of the Child under this power shall be applied so that the Child becomes entitled thereto or to an interest in possession therein either forthwith or on or before attaining the age specified in the preceding sub-clause of this clause

(c) Subject as aforesaid the Trust Fund shall be held in trust for the Child during his lifetime

(d) The Child shall have power exerciseable [sic] by Deed revocable or irrevocable executed before the Vesting Day and not revocable thereafter or (in the event of his death before the Vesting Day) by Will or Codicil to appoint that the income of the Trust Fund or such part thereof as he may appoint shall from and after the Child's death be payable to his surviving spouse (being the person to whom the Child is married at the date of such Deed, Will or Codicil) during the remainder of the spouse's life or for any shorter period

(e) *Subject* as aforesaid the Trust Fund and the income thereof shall be held upon such trusts for the benefit of the Child's children and remoter issue or any one or more of them in such shares and with and subject to such powers and provisions (including if thought fit discretionary trusts and powers exerciseable [sic] at the discretion of any person or persons) as the Child by Deed revocable or irrevocable executed before the Vesting Day and not revocable thereafter or (in the event of his death before the Vesting Day) by Will or Codicil without transgressing the rule against perpetuities appoints

(f) *Subject* to and in default of any such appointment the Trust Fund shall be held as to both capital and income for such of the Child's children as attain the age of Eighteen years or marry under that age or are living and unmarried and under that age on the Vesting Day and if more than one in equal shares.'

Clause 3:

'*Subject* to all the trusts hereinbefore declared and to the powers hereby or by law conferred the Trustees shall hold the Trust Fund and the income thereof in trust (in equal shares if more than one) for the Settlor's children other than the Child (whether living at the date hereof or born thereafter) and so that each such other child's share shall be held upon the same trusts and with and subject to the same powers and provisions as are set out in Clause 2 hereof but with the substitution of a reference to such other child of the Settlor for every reference to the Child.'

Clause 8:

'*Any* Trustee (other than the Settlor or any wife of his) being a Solicitor Accountant or other person engaged in any profession or business shall be entitled to be paid all usual professional or proper charges for business transacted time expended and acts done by him or his firm or any partner of his in connection with the trusts hereof including acts which a trustee not being in any profession or business could have done personally.'

Clause 11:

'*Notwithstanding* anything to the contrary hereinbefore expressed or implied no discretion or power by this settlement conferred on any person or on the Trustees or any of them shall be exercised and no provision of this Settlement shall operate so as to cause any part of the income or capital of the Trust Fund to become payable to or applicable for the benefit of the Settlor or any wife of the Settlor.'

4. It is conceded on behalf of the taxpayer that the trusts of cl 2 do not exhaust the whole benefit of the trust fund, since they make no provision in relation thereto if the child were to die under the age 25 without issue. It is common ground that there will be no resulting trust for the taxpayer so long as the principal beneficiary lives, or if even one child of Timothy or Neil attains 18. What is in issue is what would happen if neither son were to have a child who married, or attained the age of 18, or survived until the vesting day. The resolution of this question turns on the interpretation of cl 3, which contains the ultimate trusts of capital and income.

5. Section 457, so far as relevant to these appeals, reads:

'(1) Where, during the life of the settlor, income arising under a settlement made on or after 7th April 1965 is, under the settlement and in the events that occur, payable to or applicable for the benefit of any person other than the settlor, then, unless, under the settlement and in the said events, the income . . . (d) is income from property of which the settlor has divested himself absolutely by the settlement . . . the income shall, for the purposes of excess liability, be treated as the income of the settlor and not as the income of any other person. In this subsection "excess liability" means the excess of liability to income tax over what it would be if all income tax not charged at a lower rate were charged at the basic rate to the exclusion of any higher or additional rate . . .'

*Submissions of the parties*

6.1. Counsel for the taxpayer relied on the rule commonly referred to as the rule in *Lassence v Tierney* (1849) 1 Mac & G 551, [1843–60] All ER Rep 47 and stated by Lord Romer in *Fyfe v Irwin* [1939] 2 All ER 271 at 281–282, and more particularly on *Hancock v Watson* [1902] AC 14, [1900–3] All ER Rep 87, where (as was not the case in *Lassence v Tierney*) the rule was applied. The draftsman of the settlements had, he said, made use of *Hancock v Watson* to write in neatly trusts which would exclude the possibility of a resulting trust. Counsel for the taxpayer advanced six propositions in relation to the rule: 6.1.1. The rule applies to deeds as well as to wills (see *A-G v Lloyds Bank Ltd* [1935] AC 382 at 394, [1935] All ER Rep 518 at 524 per Lord Tomlin). 6.1.2. If the court is in doubt whether there is an initial absolute gift within the rule the court will look at the whole trust instrument to seek indications of the testator's intention (see *Lassence v Tierney* 1 Mac & G 551 at 562, [1843–60] All ER Rep 47 at 51–52 per Lord Cottenham LC, *Hancock v Watson* [1902] AC 14 at 22, [1900–3] All ER Rep 87 at 91–92 per Lord Davey, *Fyfe v Irwin* [1939] 2 All ER 271 at 282–283, *Re Burton's Settlement Trusts, Public Trustee v Montefiore* [1955] 1 All ER 433 at 439–440, [1955] Ch 348 at 360 per Jenkins LJ). 6.1.3. Although the authorities and textbooks contain references to the possible significance of engrafted trusts being contained in a separate sentence from the initial gift, the existence or otherwise of separate clauses or sentences is not decisive either way as to the application of the rule. Examples of the wording in cl 3 are to be found in *Re Marshall, Graham v Marshall* [1928] Ch 661, [1978] All ER Rep 694, *Re Johnson's Settlement Trusts, McClure v Johnson* [1943] 2 All ER 499, [1943] Ch 341, *Re Norton, Wyatt v Bain* [1949] WN 23 and *A-G v Lloyds Bank Ltd*. 6.1.4. Where the rule is held not to apply, it will be found on analysis that it does not apply for one of three reasons: 1. although there is an initial gift, it is not a beneficial gift but a gift on trusts (see *Lassence v Tierney*); 2. there is no separate initial gift, the initial gift and the trusts running together so as to form one disposition (see *Rucker v Scholefield* (1862) 1 Hem & M 36 at 41, 71 ER 16 at 18, *Re Cohen's Will Trusts, Cullen v Westminster Bank Ltd* [1939] 1 All ER 103 at 105, *Re Payne, Taylor v Payne* [1927] 2 Ch 1 at 2); 3. there is no initial gift, merely an enumeration of shares (see *Re Cohen's Will Trusts*). 6.1.5. Where, in the engrafted trusts, there is a reference to a beneficiary's share, that is an indication that the rule applies and that there is an absolute initial gift. 6.1.6. Although the application of the rule may produce unexpected results (as in *Re Burton's Settlement Trusts*), there are cases in which the draftsman deliberately uses the rule as a tool of draftsmanship; where the engrafted trusts may not exhaust the beneficial interests because future events are not known, there is no element of surprise if the initial gift stands.

6.2. Counsel for the taxpayer then submitted that the decisions in those cases where there was held to be no absolute gift are to be explained either by reason of the particular language of the instrument under consideration (see *Lassence v Tierney*) or because the words of the disposition were so interrelated or interwoven that the gift and the trusts could not be separated without doing violence to the fabric of the whole (see *Rucker v Scholefield*, *Re Cohen's Will Trusts* and *Re Payne*). The wording in *Re Norton* bore no resemblance to cl 3 of the taxpayer's settlements.

6.3. Among those cases where it was held that the rule applied, *Hancock v Watson* demonstrates the need for there to be an absolute gift from which engrafted trusts can be struck off leaving the plinth intact. In *Re Marshall*, notwithstanding that the initial gift and the engrafted trusts were contained in a single sentence, the words 'pay or transfer' pointed to an absolute gift. *Re Johnson's Settlement Trusts* was close to the line at which the rule ceased to apply, but the gift in question was held to be severable from the engrafted trusts, and therefore absolute, because another gift which was beyond doubt an absolute one was comprised in the same gift as that which was in issue. Counsel for the taxpayer relied most strongly on *Re Burton's Settlement Trusts* [1955] 1 All ER 433 at 434, [1955] Ch 348 at 353 and *A-G v Lloyds Bank Ltd*; the trusts in the latter case, and the wording, came closest to the wording of cl 3 of the taxpayer's settlements. There is, too, reference to a share as indicating ownership (see *A-G v Lloyds Bank Ltd* [1935] AC 382 at 395, [1935] All ER Rep 518 at 525).

6.4. The strongest case for the application of the rule is where, as in the present case, it is obvious that the engrafted trusts do not exhaust the beneficial interests.

6.5 It was improbable that in a settlement professionally prepared as a tax-efficient instrument, with irrevocable trusts, and expressly excluding any benefit to the settlor (vide cll 8 and 11) there should be a resulting trust for the settlor. Clause 3 is a classic example of a *Hancock v Watson* case: it starts with a beneficial disposition; it satisfies the requirement that there should be a gift; it is not an example of a single system of trusts; there is a clear break between the gift and the trusts, so that the gift stands on its own. The recitals and cll 8 and 11 indicate beyond a shadow of doubt that the child was to own its share.

6.6. The appeals should be allowed.

7. Mr S Bousher, of the Office of the Solicitor of Inland Revenue, made the following submission on behalf of the inspector of taxes.

7.1. Properly construed cl 3 does not confer an initial absolute gift; in the absence of such a gift the rule cannot apply.

7.2. None of the cases cited is identical with the wording of cl 3 of the taxpayer's settlements.

7.3. The purpose of the rule is not to correct errors of drafting; it does not matter that the existence of resulting trust arrives through inadvertence. Inadvertence will not serve to convert into an absolute gift something which is not such.

7.4. Clauses 8 and 11 are standard clauses; they are indicative not of an intention to make a gift, but of an intention that nothing should revert to the settlor. At their highest these clauses are neutral in relation to the question in issue.

7.5. In an inter vivos settlement the court will be less reluctant to find a resulting trust than in the case of a will (see *Re Norton* [1949] WN 23 per Lord Greene MR).

7.6. Clause 3 is a referential clause incorporating cl 2; because cl 2 does not exhaust the beneficial interests neither does cl 3. Clause 3 was not designed to confer a gift but to determine the number of shares on which the trust fund was to be held in the event of cl 2 failing; it 'enumerates the shares'.

7.7. Clause 3 is designed to ensure that if the principal beneficiary has no children trusts for his siblings and their children are substituted; its purpose is to take the capital away from the principal beneficiary. The reference to 'each such other child's share' may, but need not, denote ownership (see *Re Payne* [1927] 2 Ch 1 at 2, *Re Cohen's Will Trusts* [1936] 1 All ER 103 at 104; *Re Goold's Will Trusts, Lloyds Bank Ltd v Goold* [1967] 3 All ER 652). That phrase is consistent with a gift to stirpes: providing a formula rather than conferring a gift on the siblings.

7.8. Although there is no direct authority on the issue, accruer clauses offer analogies. In *Re Atkinson's Will Trusts, Prescott v Child* [1957] Ch 117 at 120–121, 124 the accruer was not to the person but to the share, and is to be contrasted with *Re Litt, Parry v Cooper* [1946] 1 All ER 314, [1946] Ch 154, where it was held (adversely to the Crown's case here) that the accruer provision contained a further absolute gift to an individual. *Re Goold's Will Trusts* [1967] 3 All ER 652 at 657 supports the Crown's submission that cl 3 does not give a vested interest to the children other than the principal beneficiary. Clause 3 provides, as in *Re Atkinson's Will Trusts* for an accruer to the share rather than the individual. The cases show that a distinction is to be made between gifts to named beneficiaries and gifts to prescribed shares.

7.9. The words used in cases where the rule was held to apply, viz 'pay or transfer' (see *Re Marshall*), 'give' (see *Hancock v Watson*), a trust 'to divide . . . and appropriate' (see *A-G v Lloyds Bank Ltd*), are absent from cl 3.

8. Counsel for the taxpayer made the following points in reply:

8.1. *Re Goold's Will Trusts* is a difficult, and surprising, decision but it need not concern us because the language of cl 3 is entirely different.

8.2. *Re Litt* was concerned with the complications of an accruer clause. The present case is much simpler. The taxpayer relies on the passage from the judgment of Morton LJ relating to the words introducing the engrafted trusts (see [1946] 1 All ER 314 at 318, [1946] Ch 154 at 161).

8.3. Because in *Re Atkinson's Will Trusts* the accruer was to the share rather than to the individual there was no absolute gift. The language of cl 3 is different.

8.4. The two parts of cl 3 are not so interwoven that they cannot be looked at separately. The second half of cl 3, looked at on its own, takes in the cl 2 trusts. The two limbs of cl 3 are then irreconcilable, so the rule applies. The draftsman deliberately made use of *Hancock v Watson*.

*Conclusions*

9. The cases cited to us lead to no clear answer. The decisions reached in them depend partly on the particular words used, sometimes on the surrounding circumstances, always on the instrument looked at as a whole. It will not be enough to fix on a particular phrase or phrases and deduce an answer from the similarity or otherwise of words employed elsewhere to words employed in the taxpayer's settlements. There is no direct authority on the question we have to decide and the authorities can serve only as a guide to how we should approach the search for an answer. We accept the first three propositions put forward by counsel for the taxpayer in para 6. As to his sixth proposition, we have no evidence that the draftsman of these settlements deliberately used the rule as a tool of draftsmanship, as suggested by him. In any event, we should still have to decide whether the device was effective for the purpose alleged. We do not accept the suggestion that the strongest case for the application of the rule is where the engrafted trusts clearly do not exhaust the beneficial interests. That begs the question of whether there are engrafted trusts, or whether there is a single system of trusts so interrelated that they cannot be separated (para 6.4). Nor do we accept the submission in para 6.5. The improbability or otherwise of a resulting trust is irrelevant to the question of whether there was in fact such a trust. The settlements clearly were prepared with the intention that they should be tax-efficient instruments; the form of the trusts enumerated therein suggest, however, that the predominating purposes was to prepare an instrument which was efficient for the purposes of capital transfer tax. On cll 8 and 11, we accept the Crown's submission that the exclusion of the taxpayer from benefit under these clauses is no more than neutral for present purposes.

10. The essence of the approach of counsel for the taxpayer to the interpretation of cl 3 is summarised in para 8.4. The substantive case for the Crown is set out in para 7.1.

11. The authorities cited to us were, we were told, a selection of the much larger number that might have been examined. That suggests that the best guidance in a particular case is to consider the instrument as a whole. As we understand the settlements before us, after reciting the taxpayer's desire to make provision for the principal beneficiary (Timothy or Neil) by transferring to the trustees a sum of money to be held 'upon the Trusts hereinafter declared', they go on to provide a series of limitations which may be summarised thus: power to pay maintenance coupled with a trust for accumulation (cl 2(*a*)); power to pay, transfer or apply capital to the principal beneficiary on or before he attains the age of 25 (cl 2(*b*)); subject thereto in trust for him during his lifetime (cl 2(*c*)); power for the principal beneficiary to appoint income to a surviving spouse (cl 2(*d*)); subject as aforesaid on trusts (including discretionary trusts) for the

principal beneficiary's children and remoter issue as the principal beneficiary may appoint (cl 2(*e*)); subject to and in default of any such appointment the trust fund is to be held in trust as to both capital and income for such of the principal beneficiary's children as attain 18 (cl 2(*f*)). Clause 2 envisages the possibility of four different kinds of trust: for accumulation, a life interest for the principal beneficiary, a life interest for a surviving spouse, and discretionary or other trusts for the principal beneficiary's issue. The possibility of transferring capital to the principal beneficiary arises (like the widow's life interest) under a power, not under a trust. It is common ground that the provisions of cl 2 do not, despite the diverse possibilities they provide for, exhaust the beneficial interests under the settlement. This lacuna is intended to be filled by cl 3.

12. Clause 3, which is expressly made subject 'to all the trusts hereinbefore declared', requires the trust fund and the income thereof to be held in trust for the settlor's children other than the principal beneficiary (that is what counsel for the taxpayer asks us to regard as the initial absolute gift) and continues 'and so that each such other child's share shall be held upon the same trusts and with and subject to the same powers and provisions as are set out in Clause 2' with appropriate substitutions for every reference in cl 2 to the principal beneficiary. If, as the Crown would have us do, we read cl 3 as a whole, it sends us back to the succession of possibilities set out in the six sub-clauses of cl 2, and, because cl 2 did not itself exhaust the beneficial interests, cl 3 does not do so either; accordingly events may occur in which the taxpayer will be found not to have divested himself absolutely of property comprised in the settlement. Counsel for the taxpayer says that we should not read cl 3 as a whole, but should break it up into two separate parts. Read separately, the second part of cl 3, which directs the children's shares to be held on similar trusts to those set out in cl 2, is incompatible with the first part of cl 3, which bestows an absolute gift. We think that is a wrong approach. The right approach, it seems to us, is first to read cl 3 as a whole, and only if there is any ambiguity, lack of clarity or other difficulty, would it be appropriate to dissect the clause. The approach of counsel for the taxpayer requires us to read the clause in such a way as to produce ambiguity. Clause 3 was intended to fill the gap arising from the incompleteness of the trusts in cl 2, and to dispose of both the capital and the income of the trust fund. That end would have been achieved if cl 3 had stopped at the end of the first part. We infer that in adding the second part of the clause the draftsman must have had an additional purpose in mind. In the absence of direct evidence as to what that purpose was, we are entitled to look at the instrument as a whole. On 9 March 1977, when the settlements were executed, Timothy and Neil were aged eight and six respectively. The provisions of cl 2 were designed, as it seems to us, to leave open the question of their absolute entitlement to capital on or before attaining 25. (Had they had an absolute right to capital at 25 they would have come within the exemption in s 457(6)(*d*) of the Income and Corporation Taxes Act 1970.) It seems to us compatible with that approach that the settlor should have wished to adopt a similar approach in relation to those who might take in default under cl 3. If that is right, the correct way to read cl 3 is as a whole, ie not as an absolute gift (as in cl 2(*f*)) but as a gift on prescribed trusts. We incline to the Crown's submission that the reference in cl 3 to 'shares' (a reference which, when it first appears, is in parenthesis and is to be contrasted with the context in which the word appears in cl 2(*f*)) points to enumeration of the interests rather than to ownership. There are no other words in cl 3 suggesting an outright gift.

13. We hold that cl 3 of each settlement constitutes a single disposition, and is a gift on trusts. We hold, accordingly, that the rule does not apply.

14. We confirm the assessments.

*Robert Walker QC* for the taxpayer.
*Christopher McCall* for the Crown.

**PETER GIBSON J.** This is an appeal by the taxpayer from the decision of the Special Commissioners, who confirmed assessments made on the taxpayer for the years of assessment 1977–78, 1978–79 and 1979–80 in respect of income arising under two settlements made by the taxpayer. The inspector of taxes raised those assessments under s 457 of the Income and Corporation Taxes Act 1970, on the footing that the income arising under each settlement was in the years of assessment income from property of which the taxpayer has not divested himself absolutely by the settlement. This appeal turns on a short question of construction of each settlement. If, as counsel for the Crown contends, the trusts thereby declared were not exhaustive, so that there was the possibility of a resulting trust in those years, then the taxpayer was rightly assessed to income tax at the higher and additional rates, and this appeal fails; if, as counsel for the taxpayer contends, there was no such possibility, then the appeal succeeds.

The settlements were made on 9 March 1977. The taxpayer was then 36 and had two children, Timothy aged 8½ and Neil aged 6. One settlement was for the primary benefit of Timothy, the other for the primary benefit of Neil.

Timothy's settlement recited the taxpayer's desire to make such provision for the benefit of Timothy (defined as 'the Child') as was thereinafter contained and the taxpayer's intention that the settlement should be absolutely irrevocable in all circumstances.

In the operative part of the deed, cl 2 contained the trusts which might be described as being for Timothy's benefit, that is to say, in summary: (a) whilst Timothy is under 25 the trustees have a power to pay or apply income for his maintenance, education or benefit, and are obliged to accumulate the balance of that income; (b) the trustees have a power during Timothy's lifetime and before the expiration of 80 years from the date of the settlement to pay, transfer or apply capital to or for the benefit of Timothy subject to a qualification that any capital so applied should be applied so that Timothy becomes entitled thereto or to an interest in possession therein either forthwith or on or before attaining 25; (c) subject thereto the trust fund is to be held in trust for Timothy during his life; (d) Timothy has a power to appoint income to a surviving spouse; (e) subject thereto Timothy has a power to appoint capital and income in favour of his children and remoter issue; (f) subject thereto and in default of appointment the capital and income are to be held in trust for such of Timothy's children as attain 18 or marry under that age or are living at the end of 80 years from the date of the settlement, and if more than one in equal shares. Pausing there, I would observe that Timothy is given no right to capital and that the trusts are not exhaustive. Timothy may not have children who attain vested interests in the trust fund.

Clause 3 contains the provision that is central to this case:

> 'Subject to all the trusts hereinbefore declared and to the powers hereby or by law conferred the Trustees shall hold the Trust Fund and the income thereof in trust (in equal shares if more than one) for the Settlor's children other than the Child (whether living at the date hereof or born thereafter) and so that each such other child's share shall be held upon the same trusts and with and subject to the same powers and provisions as are set out in Clause 2 hereof but with the substitution of a reference to such other child of the Settlor for every reference to the Child.'

Clause 8 contains a professional charging clause in conventional modern form excluding the taxpayer or any wife of his from any entitlement to charge. Clause 11 contains another normal provision of modern settlements preventing the exercise of any discretion or power and the operation of any provision of the settlement in such a way as to cause any part of the income or capital of the trust fund to become payable or applicable for the benefit of the taxpayer or his wife. It is not suggested by counsel for the taxpayer that this clause would prevent a resulting trust from coming into being.

The settlement for the benefit of Neil was in identical form mutatis mutandis.

The sole issue in this case is whether what is usually called the rule in *Lassence v Tierney* (1849) 1 Mac & G 551, [1843–60] All ER Rep 47 applies to cl 3. Counsel for the taxpayer submits that it does; counsel for the Crown submits that it does not. That rule was stated by Lord Davey in *Hancock v Watson* [1902] AC 14 at 22, [1900–3] All ER Rep 87 at 91–92 in the following terms:

> '... if you find an absolute gift to a legatee in the first instance, and trusts are engrafted or imposed on that absolute interest which fail, either from lapse or invalidity or any other reason, then the absolute gift takes effect so far as the trusts have failed to the exclusion of the residuary legatee or next of kin as the case may be.'

Though Lord Davey refers to a legatee, it is common ground that the rule applies to deeds as well as to wills (see *A-G v Lloyds Bank Ltd* [1935] AC 382 at 394, [1935] All ER Rep 518 at 524 per Lord Tomlin).

The purpose of the rule was explained by Lord Romer in *Fyfe v Irwin* [1939] 2 All ER 271 at 281–282:

> 'My Lords, it sometimes happens that a will contains two dispositions of the same property which, if literally construed, are inconsistent with one another. In such cases, the court always endeavours to reconcile the dispositions, and will, if it be possible, so construe them that neither has to be rejected altogether.'

He then gives an example of the application of the rule, and continues:

> 'My Lords, it is, I conceive, this principle of construction that lies at the root of what is commonly referred to as the rule in *Lassence* v. *Tierney*. In that case, the rule was stated by LORD COTTENHAM, L.C., in these words ((1849) 1 Mac & G 551 at 561, [1843–60] All ER Rep 47 at 51): "If a testator leave a legacy absolutely as regards his estate, but restricts the mode of the legatee's enjoyment of it to secure certain objects for the benefit of the legatee—upon failure of such objects, the absolute gift prevails. . . ." This, however, is to state the rule far too narrowly. The restriction upon the legatee's enjoyment is inconsistent with the gift of the legacy in absolute terms, and the restriction will, therefore, be treated, in accordance with the principle to which I have referred, as only affecting the absolute gift so far as is necessary to give effect to the restriction. It is immaterial, however, whether the restriction be imposed by the testator for the benefit of the legatee or for the benefit of third parties. The restriction is inconsistent with the absolute gift in both cases. In the latter case, indeed, the inconsistency is perhaps the more glaring of the two. However, that can be no reason for excluding it from the rule, which is only invoked for the purpose of reconciling inconsistent provisions. The rule, moreover, has been applied over and over again in cases where the subsequent restrictions were not imposed merely for the benefit of the legatee.'

He then refers to *Hancock v Watson* [1902] AC 14, [1900–3] All ER Rep 87 and to Lord Davey's classic statement, which I have already cited, and continues:

> 'In other words, the court endeavours to reconcile the two inconsistent [dispositions] made by the absolute gift on the one hand and by the trust on the other hand, and it does so by imputing to the testator the intention to modify the absolute gift only so far as is necessary to give effect to the trusts, whatever those trusts may be.'

In the course of the persuasive arguments admirably presented by each of counsel for the taxpayer and counsel for the Crown, I was referred to 12 cases on the applicability of the rule, and those cases are only a selection from the numerous cases on the subject. This demonstrates the fact that the application of the rule to the particular words of an instrument is often a matter of difficulty. As the Special Commissioners rightly observed in relation to the cases cited to them (many of them being the same as those cited to me):

> 'The cases cited to us lead to no clear answer. The decisions reached in them depend partly upon the particular words used, sometimes on the surrounding circumstances, always on the instrument looked at as a whole. It will not be enough to fix on a particular phrase or phrases and deduce an answer from the similarity or otherwise of words employed elsewhere to words employed in the [taxpayer's]

settlements. There is no direct authority on the question we have to decide and the authorities can serve only as a guide to how we should approach the search for an answer.'

I would summarise the guidance to be obtained from the cases so far as material as follows. (1) In each case the court must ascertain from the language of the instrument as a whole whether there has been an initial absolute beneficial gift onto which inconsistent trusts have been engrafted (see, for example, *Lassence v Tierney* 1 Mac & G 551 at 562, [1843–60] All ER Rep 47 at 51–52 and *Re Burton's Settlement Trusts, Public Trustee v Montefiore* [1955] 1 All ER 433 at 439–440, [1955] Ch 348 at 360). (2) If the instrument discloses no separate initial gift but merely a gift coupled with a series of limitations over so as to form one system of trusts, then the rule will not apply (see *Rucker v Scholefield* (1862) 1 Hem & M 36, 71 ER 16). (3) In most of the cases where the rule has been held to apply, the engrafted inconsistent trusts have been separated from the absolute gift either by being placed in a separate clause or sentence or by being introduced by words implying a contrast, such as a proviso or words such as 'but so that' (see, for example, *Hancock v Watson, A-G v Lloyds Bank Ltd* and *Re Litt's Will Trusts, Parry v Cooper* [1946] 1 All ER 314, [1946] Ch 154). But this is not an essential requirement, and in an appropriate context the engrafted trusts may be introduced by the word 'and' or the words 'and so that' (see *Re Johnson's Settlement Trusts, McClure v Johnson* [1943] 2 All ER 499, [1943] Ch 341 and *Re Norton, Wyatt v Bain* [1949] WN 23). I add in parenthesis that although counsel for the taxpayer at one stage prayed in aid the remarks of Morton LJ in *Re Litt* [1946] 1 All ER 314 at 318, [1946] Ch 154 at 161 on 'and so that' as properly introducing a qualification in the form of engrafted trusts, counsel for the Crown satisfied me that properly construed those remarks related to the precise wording of the instrument in question, where there were two qualifying clauses of which the second was introduced by 'and so that' and was only a further proviso additional to the first qualifying clause introduced by 'but so that'. (4) References in parts of the instrument other than the initial gift claimed to be absolute to the share of the donee are usually treated as indicative that the share is owned by the donee (see *A-G v Lloyds Bank Ltd* [1932] AC 382 at 395, [1935] All ER Rep 518 at 525, *Fyfe v Irwin* [1939] 2 All ER 271 at 282–283 and *Re Burton's Settlement Trusts* [1955] 1 All ER 433 at 437, 440, [1955] Ch 348 at 356, 361), though in an appropriate context even a reference to a share given to a beneficiary will not be treated as belonging to the beneficiary (see *Re Goold's Will Trusts, Lloyds Bank Ltd v Goold* [1967] 3 All ER 652; in that case Buckley J held that an express provision that the share was not to be held in trust for a beneficiary absolutely was decisive). (5) If a donor, by the trusts which follow the initial gift, has sought to provide for every eventuality by creating what prima facie are exhaustive trusts, it is the more difficult to construe the initial gift as an absolute gift (see *Lassence v Tierney* 1 Mac & G 551 at 567, [1843–60] All ER Rep 47 at 53–54 and *A-G v Lloyds Bank Ltd* [1935] AC 382 at 395, [1935] All ER Rep 518 at 525).

With that guidance in mind, I turn to the settlements. Each is expressed to be for the benefit of the defined child. At the time of the settlement it could not be predicted that such a very young child would marry and have children. The benefit which the settlement was intended to confer on the child was contained in cl 2. That clause gives the child no right to capital, and plainly its trusts are not exhaustive. That is recognised by the draftsman in providing for cl 3. The opening words of cl 3, 'Subject to all the trusts hereinbefore declared and to the powers hereby or by law conferred the Trustees shall hold the Trust Fund and the income thereof', are language which to the trust lawyer is familiar in an ultimate trust intended to dispose of the entirety of the trust property, including the income thereof, so far as not otherwise disposed of; but whether such complete disposition was effected must depend on the trusts on which the trustees are to hold the capital and income. One then finds a trust '(in equal shares if more than one) for the Settlor's children other than the Child (whether living at the date hereof or born thereafter)'.

Pausing there for the moment, I do not think that it can be doubted that the language thus far used is unambiguously that of absolute gift. The language is not that of mere division or appropriation or of a gift equally amongst certain beneficiaries such as led the court in some cases to hold that there was no initial absolute gift (see *Lassence v Tierney, Re Payne, Taylor v Payne* [1927] 2 Ch 1, [1927] All ER Rep 223, *Re Cohen's Will Trusts, Cullen v Westminster Bank Ltd* [1936] 1 All ER 103 and the decision of Roxburgh J at first instance in *Re Burton's Settlement Trusts* [1954] 3 All ER 231, [1955] Ch 60, though he was reversed by the Court of Appeal). It is the clear language of outright disposition of the entirety of both capital and income.

I shall come back in a moment to the rather strange possible consequences of such a disposition, but confining myself for the time being to the language of the settlement I then move on to the second part of cl 3. This is introduced by the words 'and so that', and there follow referential trusts concerning what is described as 'each such other child's share' to be held on the like trusts for the benefit of each other child as were declared in cl 2 in favour of 'the Child'.

There are three features of those referential trusts. First, they relate to 'each such other child's share', language that normally indicates that the child owns a share. Second, the trusts are inconsistent with any initial absolute gift. Third, they are not exhaustive of the beneficial interest in the share for the same reason as cl 2 was not exhaustive of the beneficial interest in the trust fund. Subject only to the effect of the words 'and so that', the language used points strongly to the application of the rule; but, of course, one cannot ignore 'and so that'. Those words are found in two other places in the settlement (cll 1(3) and 5(6)), as counsel for the Crown pointed out, in each case in a manner indicating that the words following expand or explain the immediately preceding words, whereas there are three places in the settlement (cll 1(4)(b), 2(b) and 5(3)(i)) where 'but so that' and one place (cl 4) where 'provided always that' are used to introduce words of qualification cutting down what has been stated immediately before.

I would accept that 'but so that' would have been more appropriate language than 'and so that' if the intention was to introduce engrafted trusts inconsistent with the prior absolute gift, and I agree that 'and so that' is suitable language to introduce trusts which explain what will happen to an appropriated share if such appropriation is all that the trusts for the other children signify. But I bear in mind three things: first, both 'and' and 'but' are conjunctions; second, as I have already stated, there are two reported cases where the rule has been held applicable despite the use of the conjunction 'and'; and, third, whilst some engrafted trusts are in no way for the benefit of the beneficiary but confer benefits on strangers, so that the inconsistency with the absolute gift is very glaring and the engrafted trusts are appropriately introduced by a word such as 'but', in the present case what are said to be the engrafted trusts are for the benefit of the beneficiary said to have been given an absolute interest, and so the conjunction 'and' may be rather less inappropriate.

Each of counsel for the Crown and counsel for the taxpayer also urged on me to take account of the practical consequences if the rule did and did not apply. Counsel for the Crown rightly laid stress on the odd consequence, if the rule applied, that, whereas the person for whose benefit the settlement is expressed to have been made is given no right to capital, not only his brother existing at the date of the settlement but also any other brother or sister born after the date of the settlement to his father, then a man of only 36, would take an absolute interest even if he or she predeceased the primary beneficiary. Counsel for the Crown submitted that this could not have been intended and that it was a strong pointer in favour of the inapplicability of the rule. He pointed out that in *Re Payne* one of the matters which weighed with Astbury J in holding that there was no initial absolute gift in that case was that under the wording of the relevant disposition a share was to be appropriated to each of a specified class of beneficiaries whether that beneficiary survived the testator or not. Of course, in *Re Payne*, where the language of the initial gift was more dubiously to be interpreted as conferring an absolute gift, the instrument in question was a will, and it would have been surprising if a share was to belong absolutely to a beneficiary who died before the instrument took effect. The present case is not on all fours with *Re Payne* either in the language of the initial gift or in effect, in that, if there is an absolute gift in the first part of cl 3 and the beneficiary died, he or she must die after the settlement comes into effect.

Counsel for the Crown also submitted that there was no case of the rule applying to confer an interest on a beneficiary who had never taken an interest in possession. For my part, I cannot see why in principle that should matter. For example, if in *Re Marshall, Graham v Marshall* [1928] Ch 661, [1928] All ER Rep 694 the testator's widow had had a life interest, as the testator had originally directed, instead of the annuity she was given under a codicil, I cannot think that the decision that the rule applied to the gift to a beneficiary who took subject to the widow's interest would have been any different. Counsel for the taxpayer, on the other hand, submitted that, in the light of the evidence provided by cll 8 and 11 as to the taxpayer's intention to exclude himself from any interest in the settlement, it would be very odd if cl 3 did not exclude the possibility of a resulting trust. Counsel for the taxpayer puts the evidence of those clauses as being no more than straws in the wind, and counsel for the Crown accepted them to be such. The Special Commissioners themselves say that the lacuna from the non-exhaustive provisions of cl 2 was intended to be filled by cl 3. It would be surprising if the taxpayer had intended merely to impose referential trusts which were plainly not exhaustive for the same reason as the provisions of cl 2 were on their face non-exhaustive, and that must have been obvious to the draftsman. But given the inevitable nature of a resulting trust, I would regard this point as being only of slight weight.

Counsel for the Crown urged on me the words of Lord Cottenham LC in *Lassence v Tierney* (1849) 1 Mac & G 551 at 562, [1843–60] All ER Rep 47 at 52:

'It is, however, obvious that the intention that the gift should be absolute as between the legatee and the estate, is, as in all cases of construction, to be collected from the whole of the will, and not from there being words which, standing alone, would constitute an absolute gift.'

He submitted that for that reason the Special Commissioners were right to criticise the approach of counsel for the taxpayer as requiring one to stop half way through cl 3, before the words 'and so that'. Of course it is right to look at the whole of cl 3, but it does not follow that a clause like cl 3 cannot contain both an absolute gift and engrafted trusts in one and the same sentence.

The Special Commissioners said this in rejecting the approach of counsel for the taxpayer:

'The right approach, it seems to us, is first to read clause 3 as a whole, and only if there is any ambiguity, lack of clarity, or other difficulty, would it be appropriate to dissect the clause. [Counsel for the taxpayer's] approach requires us to read the clause in such a way as to produce ambiguity.'

In my judgment that criticism goes wide of the mark. As *Fyfe v Irwin* shows, where there is an initial absolute gift with engrafted trusts there will be an inconsistency which the rule is intended to resolve. I do not see that the approach of counsel for the taxpayer does produce ambiguity.

The Special Commissioners go on to say that cl 3 was intended to fill the gap arising from the incompleteness of the trusts in cl 2, and that the end of disposing of both the capital and income of the trust fund would have been achieved if cl 3 had stopped at the end of the first part. They go on to infer therefrom that in adding the second part of cl 3 the draftsman must have had an additional purpose in mind, and this they infer to be to leave open the question of a child other than the primary beneficiary becoming absolutely entitled to capital on or before attaining 25, that being, they suggest, the purpose of cl 2 in relation to the primary beneficiary. Counsel for the taxpayer criticised this part of the reasoning of the Special Commissioners as speculative, and I agree with him. I doubt that it is possible to limit the purpose of the draftsman in that way. Of course the draftsman must have had an additional purpose in mind in adding the second part of cl 3, but the purposes of the referential trusts, if they be engrafted trusts, can be taken at their face value. I do not see that they lead to the conclusion that in cl 3 one finds not an absolute gift with engrafted trusts but a single gift on prescribed trusts.

I must set on one side of the scale the points urged on me by counsel for the taxpayer in favour of the application of the rule, that is to say (1) the clear words of absolute gift in the first part of cl 3, (2) the existence of trusts inconsistent with any such absolute gift in the second part of cl 3, (3) the use of the phrase 'each such other child's share' as indicative of ownership, and (4) the straws in the wind provided by cll 8 and 11 of an intention on the part of the taxpayer to avoid retaining any interest, coupled with the manifestly non-exhaustive nature of the referential trusts. On the other side of the scale I must set the points urged on me by counsel for the Crown in favour of there being a single system of trusts excluding the application of the rule, that is to say (1) the use of the words 'and so that' instead of words of qualification, and (2) the unlikelihood of the taxpayer intending to make an absolute gift to any other child of his.

In my judgment, the submissions of counsel for the taxpayer are to be preferred. The strong impression made on me by the words of the first part of cl 3 as being an absolute gift, supported as it is by the reference to the other child's share, followed by the inconsistent referential trusts, reconcilable as they are by the application of the rule, to my mind outweigh the points of counsel for the Crown, neither of which seems to me to be decisive for the reasons that I have already given. Accordingly, I shall allow the appeal and discharge the assessments.

*Appeal allowed.*

Solicitors: *Wake Smith & Co,* Sheffield (for the taxpayer); *Solicitor of Inland Revenue.*

Clare Mainprice   Barrister.

# Alec Lobb (Garages) Ltd and others v Total Oil GB Ltd

COURT OF APPEAL, CIVIL DIVISION
WALLER, DUNN AND DILLON LJJ
22, 23, 24, 25, 26 OCTOBER, 8 NOVEMBER 1984

*Restraint of trade by agreement – Petrol filling station – Solus agreement – Mortgage – Agreement between owner of garage and petrol supplier for exclusive purchase and resale of supplier's products – Company which owned filling station facing insolvency – Company agreeing to solus agreement in lease and lease-back transaction designed to raise finance from supplier to prevent company's insolvency – Company leasing garage to supplier for 51 years in return for premium – Supplier immediately leasing back garage to proprietor of company – Whether tie in lease-back void as being in unreasonable restraint of trade.*

*Equity – Unconscionable bargain – Contract – Matters to be established to render contract harsh and unconscionable bargain – Contract between insolvent garage company and petrol supplier to raise further finance for company – Contract consisting of lease of garage for 51 years to supplier and lease-back for 21 years to proprietor of company – Transaction amounting to acquisition by supplier of interest in equity of redemption – Whether harsh and unconscionable bargain – Whether supplier taking unfair advantage of company's financial situation – Whether terms of contract unfair.*

*Restraint of trade by agreement – Separate agreements – Lease and underlease – Single transaction – Void covenant in underlease – Whether void covenant severable – Whether sufficient consideration to support agreement apart from void covenant.*

The plaintiffs were a company and a mother and her son, who were the shareholders and directors of the company, which in 1964 borrowed £15,000 from the defendant, a petrol company, on the security of a legal charge on the premises created by the plaintiff company in favour of the defendant. The charge contained a covenant (a tie covenant) by the plaintiff company to purchase the defendant's petrol exclusively during the continuance of the loan (which was repayable by instalments over 18 years) and for a further period thereafter, and made the charge irredeemable during the period of the loan. By November 1968 the plaintiff company, though trading profitably, was under financial pressure from other creditors. The mother and son stood to lose their livelihood and face personal bankruptcy if the plaintiff company was wound up due to insolvency. The son felt unable to resort to any other petrol company for finance because of the tie with the defendant and negotiations took place between the parties in which the plaintiffs were separately and independently advised by solicitors and accountants. The defendant, although reluctant to enter into any further transaction with the plaintiffs, wished to preserve the garage as an outlet for sales of its petrol. Accordingly, it agreed to put further capital into the plaintiff company by means of a lease and lease-back transaction, comprising a lease of the garage premises to the defendants for 51 years in return for the payment to the plaintiff company of a premium of £35,000 (based on a fair valuation of the premises as a tied site) and the immediate lease-back of the premises by an underlease to the son personally for a term of 21 years at a rent of £2,250, which represented an adequate return on the premium paid by the defendant. The underlease contained a tie covenant by the son to purchase the defendant's petrol exclusively for the 21-year term of the underlease and provisions for a mutual break of the underlease at the end of the seventh and fourteenth years and an absolute prohibition on assignment of the underlease. The transaction extinguished the existing charges. Completion of the transaction took place in July 1969, by which time the current tie covenant under the charges was treated as having three years to run. Payment of the plaintiff company's debts and costs absorbed most of the premium received from the defendant, leaving little of the premium left over for use as working capital. The transaction thus failed in its object of rescuing the company from the constraints of inadequate working capital. However, the plaintiffs took no steps to have the transaction set aside until June 1979, when they issued a writ against the defendant seeking to have the transaction set aside on the grounds, inter alia, that the bargain was harsh and unconscionable, or alternatively that the tie covenant was void as being an unreasonable restraint of trade which rendered the whole transaction invalid. The judge held, inter alia, (i) that although the tie provision was void as being an unreasonable restraint of trade it was severable from the rest of the transaction which was valid and enforceable, (ii) that on the facts the transaction was not harsh and unconscionable and (iii) that, in any event, the plaintiffs' claim to set aside the transaction was barred by laches. The plaintiffs appealed. The defendant cross-appealed, contending that the underlease was not an agreement in restraint of trade because (i) the underlease derived from the disposal by the company of substantially all its interest in the property by the grant of the 51-year lease to the defendant and (ii) the underlease was granted to the mother and son, and not to the company, or alternatively that, even if the underlease was an agreement in restraint of trade, the restrictions on trading in the underlease were, in all the circumstances, reasonable and were therefore valid.

**Held** – (1) The doctrine of restraint of trade did not apply to an agreement where a person deprived himself of all right to trade as he wished on a parcel of land by selling all his interest in that land, or to an agreement where restraints were imposed on persons who prior to the relevant transaction had no right to trade on the particular site. However, although the mother and son were not the original lessors of the defendants, the reality of the transaction was that the company had raised finance on its land by way of a lease and underlease rather than a mortgage, and the whole object was that the plaintiffs should continue to trade on the property. The lease and the underlease had to be taken together as two essential parts of the one transaction and the agreement constituted by the lease and the underlease was an agreement to which the doctrine of restraint of trade applied inasmuch as it subjected the company for a longer period to a continuation of the restraint of trade which had been validly imposed for a much shorter period before 25 July 1969 (see p 309 *c* to *h*, p 314 *e* to *h* and p 318 *b*, post); *Esso Petroleum Co Ltd v Harper's Garage (Stourport) Ltd* [1967] 1 All ER 699 applied.

(2) Although as a general rule a petrol supply restraint which required a dealer to take all his petrol from one company was reasonable and valid if it was stipulated to last for no more than five years, but was unreasonable and invalid if it was to last for significantly longer, eg for 21 years, unless the petrol company could prove that a tie for the longer period was an economic necessity, each case depended on its own facts, and the adequacy of the consideration received by the party subjected to the restraint was relevant to the question of the reasonableness of the restraint. Having regard to the nature of the overall transaction, in particular (a) that it was a rescue operation benefiting all three plaintiffs, as well as providing an outlet for the defendant's petrol, (b) that there was ample consideration for the grant of the lease to the defendant, (c) that there were break clauses in the underlease which could be invoked at the end of seven or fourteen years and (d) that there was a public interest in encouraging a transaction which enabled a plaintiff to continue trading, the restraint was not unreasonable, and was accordingly valid. It followed that the cross-appeal would be allowed (see p 309 *h j*, p 310 *b* to *j*, p 315 *c* to *h*, p 318 *b* and p 319 *h j*, post); dicta of Lord Macnaghten in *Nordenfelt v Maxim Nordenfelt Guns and Ammunition Co Ltd* [1891–4] All ER Rep at 18 and of Lord Reid in *Esso Petroleum Co Ltd v Harper's Garage (Stourport) Ltd* [1967] 1 All ER at 708–709 applied.

(3) Where one party had acted extortionately, oppressively or coercively towards the other, the court would in fairness set aside a transaction so made. However, a transaction was not rendered harsh or unconscionable merely because the parties were of unequal bargaining power and the stronger party had not shown that the terms of agreement were fair, just and reasonable. Furthermore, a transaction was not unconscionable merely because a party was forced by economic necessity to make it. On the facts, although the plaintiffs had no realistic alternative, no pressure had been exerted on them by the defendant, which was reluctant to enter into the transaction, and furthermore the plaintiffs themselves had sought the defendant's assistance to avert financial collapse and had sought the prior advice of their solicitors and accountant, which they had chosen to ignore. Accordingly, the judge had been right to find that the defendant's conduct was not unconscionable or oppressive. In any event the plaintiffs' claim in equity was barred by laches. The plaintiffs' appeal would therefore be dismissed (see p 312 *b* to *e* and *j* to p 313 *f*, p 314 *b c* and p 317 *j* to p 318 *b*, post); dictum of Lord Selborne LC in *Earl of Aylesford v Morris* [1861–73] All ER Rep at 302–303 applied; *Multiservice Bookbinding Ltd v Marden* [1978] 2 All ER 489 approved; *Lloyds Bank Ltd v Bundy* [1974] 3 All ER 757 distinguished.

Per curiam. The question whether a void covenant can be severed from the rest of an agreement depends on whether there is sufficient consideration to support the agreement apart from the void covenant. Where there is sufficient consideration, even though that consideration also supports the void covenant, the transaction can be severed and the remainder of the agreement is enforceable (see p 311 *d* to *h*, p 317 *d* and p 318 *b*, post); dictum of Lord Wilberforce in *Stenhouse Australia Ltd v Phillips* [1974] 1 All ER at 124, *Amoco Australia Pty Ltd v Rocco Bros Motor Engineering Co Pty Ltd* [1975] 1 All ER 968 and dictum of Buckley LJ in *Chemidus Wavin Ltd v Société pour la Transformation et l'Exploitation des Resines Industrielles SA* [1978] CMLR at 520 considered.

Decision of Peter Millett QC sitting as a deputy judge of the High Court [1983] 1 All ER 944 affirmed in part and reversed in part.

## Notes

For contracts entered into under duress, see 9 Halsbury's Laws (4th edn) para 297, and for cases on the subject, see 12 Digest (Reissue) 118–120, 640–651.

For setting aside unconscionable bargains, see 16 Halsbury's Laws (4th edn) para 1233.

For equitable relief in cases of fiduciary relationship, see ibid para 1454.

For agreements in restraint of trade, see 47 Halsbury's Laws (4th edn) para 13, and for cases on the subject, see 45 Digest (Repl) 443–449, 271–297.

### Cases referred to in judgments

*Amoco Australia Pty Ltd v Rocco Bros Motor Engineering Co Pty Ltd* [1975] 1 All ER 968, [1975] AC 561, [1975] 2 WLR 779, PC.
*Attwood v Lamont* [1920] 3 KB 571, [1920] All ER Rep 55, CA.
*Aylesford (Earl) v Morris* (1873) LR 8 Ch App 484, [1861–73] All ER Rep 300, CA.
*Bennett v Bennett* [1952] 1 All ER 413, [1952] 1 KB 249, CA.
*Chemidus Wavin Ltd v Société pour la Transformation et l'Exploitation des Resines Industrielles SA* [1978] 3 CMLR 514, CA.
*Cleveland Petroleum Co Ltd v Dartstone Ltd* [1969] 1 All ER 201, [1969] 1 WLR 116, CA.
*DHN Food Distributors Ltd v Tower Hamlets London Borough* [1976] 3 All ER 462, [1976] 1 WLR 852, CA.
*Esso Petroleum Co Ltd v Harper's Garage (Stourport) Ltd* [1967] 1 All ER 699, [1968] AC 269, [1967] 1 WLR 871, HL.
*Foley v Classique Coaches Ltd* [1934] 2 KB 1, [1934] All ER Rep 88, CA.
*Gilford Motor Co Ltd v Horne* [1933] Ch 935, [1933] All ER Rep 109, CA.
*Goldsoll v Goldman* [1915] 1 Ch 292, [1914–15] All ER Rep 257, CA.
*Goodinson v Goodinson* [1954] 2 All ER 255, [1954] 2 QB 118, [1954] 2 WLR 1121, CA.
*Horwood v Millar's Timber and Trading Co Ltd* [1917] 1 KB 305, [1916–17] All ER Rep 847, CA.
*Kearney v Whitehaven Colliery Co* [1893] 1 QB 700, [1891–4] All ER Rep 556, CA.
*Kelly v Kosuga* (1959) 358 US 516.
*Kingsway Investments (Kent) Ltd v Kent CC, Kenworthy v Kent CC* [1969] 1 All ER 601, [1969] 2 QB 332, [1969] 2 WLR 249, CA; *rvsd* [1970] 1 All ER 70, [1971] AC 72, [1970] 2 WLR 297, HL.
*Lloyds Bank Ltd v Bundy* [1974] 3 All ER 757, [1975] QB 326, [1974] 3 WLR 501, CA.
*Mason v Provident Clothing and Supply Co Ltd* [1913] AC 724, [1911–13] All ER Rep 400, HL.
*Multiservice Bookbinding Ltd v Marden* [1978] 2 All ER 489, [1979] Ch 84, [1978] 2 WLR 535.
*Nordenfelt v Maxim Nordenfelt Guns and Ammunition Co Ltd* [1894] AC 535, [1891–4] All ER Rep 1, HL.
*Pigot's Case* (1614) 11 Co Rep 26b, [1558–1774] All ER Rep 50, 77 ER 1177.
*Putsman v Taylor* [1927] 1 KB 637, [1927] All ER Rep 365.
*Stenhouse Australia Ltd v Phillips* [1974] 1 All ER 117, [1974] AC 391, [1974] 2 WLR 134, PC.
*Vancouver Malt and Sake Brewing Co Ltd v Vancouver Breweries Ltd* [1934] AC 181, [1934] All ER Rep 38, PC.

### Cases also cited

*Baker v Monk* (1864) 4 De GJ & S 388, 46 ER 968.
*Blomley v Ryan* (1954) 99 CLR 362.
*British Reinforced Concrete Engineering Co Ltd v Schelff* [1921] 2 Ch 563, [1921] All ER Rep 202.
*Bulley v Bulley* (1878) LR 8 Ch App 479, CA.
*Burmah Oil Co Ltd v Bank of England* [1979] 3 All ER 700, [1980] AC 1090, HL.
*Burmah Oil Co Ltd v Governor of the Bank of England* (1981) Times, 4 July.
*Chapman v Michealson* [1908] 2 Ch 612; *affd* [1909] 1 Ch 238, CA.
*Knight v Majoribanks* (1849) 2 Mac & G 10, 42 ER 4.
*Kasumu v Baba-Egbe* [1956] 3 All ER 266, [1956] AC 539, PC.
*Lucas (T) & Co Ltd v Mitchell* [1972] 3 All ER 689, [1974] Ch 129, CA.
*Miller v Cook* (1870) LR 10 Eq 641.
*Pao On v Lau Yiu* [1979] 3 All ER 65, [1980] AC 614, PC.

*Thames Water Authority v Elmbridge BC* [1983] 1 All ER 836, [1983] QB 570, CA.
*Wallis v Day* (1837) 2 M & W 273, [1835–42] All ER Rep 426, 150 ER 759.
*Waters v Donnelly* (1884) 9 OR 391.

**Appeal and cross-appeal**

Geoffrey Alec Lobb and Stephen John Lobb, the personal representatives of the third plaintiff, Bertha Alexandra Lobb, who died on 10 February 1984, appealed against the judgment of Peter Millett QC sitting as a deputy judge of the High Court ([1983] 1 All ER 944, [1983] 1 WLR 87) given on 24 June 1982 whereby he held that a transaction of lease and underlease, both dated 25 July 1969, which the plaintiffs, Alec Lobb (Garages) Ltd, Alec Thomas Lobb and Bertha Alexandra Lobb, sought to have set aside, was valid and enforceable by the defendant, Total Oil GB Ltd, after the excision of certain clauses contained in the underlease which were held to be in unreasonable restraint of trade and contrary to public policy. By a respondent's notice, Total cross-appealed against the judge's decision that the clauses in the underlease were void as an unreasonable restraint of trade. The facts are set out in the judgment of Dillon LJ.

*T L G Cullen QC* and *E W H Christie* for the appellants.
*John Peppitt QC, Peter Cresswell QC* and *Michael Kay* for Total.

*Cur adv vult*

8 November. The following judgments were delivered.

**DILLON LJ** (giving the first judgment at the invitation of Waller LJ). This is an apppeal from a decision of Mr Peter Millett QC, sitting as a deputy High Court judge in the Chancery Division ([1983] 1 All ER 944, [1983] 1 WLR 87). There is also a cross-appeal. They raise questions as to the validity of a lease/lease-back arrangement entered into in July 1969 in relation to a garage and petrol filling station (the property) in South Street, Braintree, Essex. The facts are set out with admirable clarity in the judgment of the deputy judge, and I do not need for the moment to do more than briefly summarise what happened in a very general way in order to make the issues intelligible.

In 1968 a company, Alec Lobb (Garages) Ltd (the company), which was the first plaintiff in the action as originally constituted, was the owner of the freehold of the property and carried on the business of a garage and petrol filling station there. It was the company's only garage. The company was a private company whose only directors and shareholders were Mr Alec Lobb and his mother Mrs Bertha Lobb, the second and third plaintiffs in the action as originally constituted. The company had since 1964 obtained its supplies of petrol exclusively from the respondent (Total). By the latter part of 1968 there were a number of agreements outstanding between the company and Total including mortgages on the property, guaranteed by Mr and Mrs Lobb personally, to secure moneys advanced by Total to the company which were either interest free or carried interest at relatively low rates, and including also various hire or hire-purchase agreements in respect of fuel tanks and other equipment, under one of which certain underground petrol tanks provided by Total, would at the end of 20 years from 1964, become the property of the company without more than nominal further payment. One effect of the mortgages was, as is not disputed, to impose a valid petrol tie on the company in respect of the property, obliging the company to take all petrol supplies for the property from Total and to keep the filling station on the property open at all reasonable times for the sale of petrol and to provide a proper and efficient service to the public for a period of which some four years remained unexpired by the end of 1968.

The company was seriously under-capitalised. Though it traded at a small profit in the six months to 30 November 1968, there had been substantial earlier losses. Cheques given to Total for the supply of petrol had been dishonoured on presentation, and Total very early in 1969 insisted that supplies could only be continued on the basis of payment by banker's draft for each load against delivery. Apart from indebtedness to Total, by November 1968 the company was in serious difficulties with its bankers who also had a charge on the property, and was under pressure to reduce its overdraft.

Against that background, Mr Lobb wrote to Total on 28 November 1968 proposing that in order to solve the company's financial difficulties the forecourt of the property should, for a premium, be leased to Total for a number of years and leased back to the company. Discussions followed. Separate solicitors were instructed by each party, and ultimately on 25 July 1969 a lease and lease-back were executed. The lease was a lease of the whole of the property, and not merely the forecourt, by the company to Total for a term of 51 years at a peppercorn rent in consideration of a premium of £35,000 paid by Total. The lease-back was a sublease granted by Total to Mr and Mrs Lobb, rather than to the company, for a term of 21 years, with a right for either party to terminate the lease-back at the end of the seventh or fourteenth years, at an initial rent of £2,250 per annum with upwards only rent reviews at the end of the eighth and fifteenth years of the term. The lease-back also contained an absolute prohibition on assignment and tie provisions throughout the term requiring the lessees to take all supplies of petrol from Total exclusively and to keep the filling station open at all reasonable times and provide a proper and efficient service to the public.

In the action, commenced on 11 June 1979, the company and Mr and Mrs Lobb (the plaintiffs) claimed to set aside the lease and lease-back on a variety of allegations, including an allegation that the 21-year tie provision in the lease-back constituted an unreasonable restraint of trade with, it was alleged, the result that the lease and lease-back were wholly void. The deputy judge held that the tie provisions in the lease-back were indeed void as an unreasonable restraint of trade but that they were severable from the remaining provisions of the lease-back. He rejected all the other allegations of the plaintiffs and accordingly held that the lease and the remaining provisions of the lease-back, other than the tie provisions which he identified, were valid.

I should at this juncture mention certain changes among the plaintiffs in the action. In the first place the company has been put into creditors' voluntary liquidation. In the next place, Mr Lobb died in July 1979; his personal representatives were added as plaintiffs by order to carry on before the trial. Finally, Mrs Lobb has died since the decision of the deputy judge. The appellants to this court are her personal representatives, but no argument was advanced to the effect that they have no locus standi to pursue an appeal which, if successful, would enure to the benefit, primarily, of the company which has not appealed.

Several arguments which were pressed in the court below are not raised on this appeal. In particular the appellants do not rely in this court on the tort of economic duress or on any allegations of undue influence and they do not submit that the lease and lease-back are, despite their form, in reality a mortgage and to be treated as such. In addition the appellants have accepted the judge's identification of the provisions of the lease-back which are struck down if only the tie provisions of the lease-back are invalid.

The appellants therefore put their case in this court on two grounds only. They say firstly that the tie provisions of the lease-back, which the judge held to be void as an unreasonable restraint of trade, are not severable and that the lease and lease-back, which have to be taken together as parts of one transaction, are therefore wholly void. They say alternatively that the lease and lease-back, taken together as one transaction, ought to be set aside in equity because at the material time in 1969 there was inequality of bargaining power as between Total on the one hand and the company and Mr and Mrs Lobb on the other hand, and Total has not established that the terms of the transaction were in point of fact, fair, just, and reasonable.

Total disputes both these contentions of the appellants. Total further submits that any claim to set aside the lease and lease-back on equitable grounds ought to be held to be barred by laches on the part of the company and Mr and Mrs Lobb. The deputy judge held that a somewhat different formulation of the plaintiffs' claim, namely that Total exercised coercive pressure on Mr Lobb and the company, was indeed barred by laches and delay on the part of the plaintiffs. In addition, however, by the cross-appeal Total challenges the findings of the deputy judge that the tie provisions of the lease-back are void as an unreasonable restraint of trade. Total advances three submissions on the cross-appeal, viz: (1) that the lease-back is not an agreement in restraint of trade at all because the restrictions on trading in the lease-back derive from the disposal by the company of substantially all its interest in the property by the grant of the 51 years' lease to Total, (2) that the lease-back is not an agreement in restraint of trade at all because the lease-back was granted to Mr and Mrs Lobb and not to the company, and (3) alternatively, that even if the lease-back is an agreement in restraint of trade the restrictions on trading in the lease-back are, in all the circumstances, reasonable and are therefore valid.

It is logical to consider the cross-appeal first, and I can deal very shortly with the second of the above arguments. In *Esso Petroleum Co Ltd v Harper's Garage (Stourport) Ltd* [1967] 1 All ER 699, [1968] AC 269 it was held that the doctrine of restraint of trade had no application to restraints imposed on persons who, before the transaction by which the restraints were imposed, had no right whatsoever to trade at all on the land in question. Their Lordships had in mind in particular the case where the owner of land grants a lease of the land to a person who had no previous right to occupy the land, and imposes by the lease restraints on the lessee's power to trade as he likes on the land. Such a lease would ordinarily not be regarded as an agreement in restraint of trade. In the present case however the granting of the lease-back to Mr and Mrs Lobb rather than to the company was a palpable device in an endeavour to evade the doctrine of restraint in trade. Mr and Mrs Lobb were only selected as lessees because they were the proprietors of the company previously in occupation. The court has ample power to pierce the corporate veil, recognise a continued identity of occupation and hold, as it should, that Total can be in no better position quoad restraints of trade by granting the lease-back to Mr and Mrs Lobb than if it had granted the lease-back to the company. See generally *Gilford Motor Co Ltd v Horne* [1933] Ch 935 at 961–962, [1933] All ER Rep 109 at 117 and *DHN Food Distributors Ltd v Tower Hamlets London Borough* [1976] 3 All ER 462, [1976] 1 WLR 852.

As for the argument that the lease-back is not an agreement in restraint of trade because the restrictions on the lease-back derive from a disposal by the company of a large part of its interest in the property, I have had considerable difficulty in understanding the argument. It is of course clear that there is no agreement in restraint of trade where a person deprives himself of all right to trade as he wishes on land by selling all his interest in that land. In the present case, however, that is not what the company did and the whole object was that trade should continue in the property. The lease and lease-back have to be taken together as two essential parts of one transaction, and in my judgment it follows from the reasoning of their Lordships in *Esso v Harper's Garage* that the agreement constituted by the lease and lease-back is an agreement in restraint of trade in as much as it subjects the company to a continuation for a longer period of the restraints on trading which had validly been imposed for a much shorter period before 25 July 1969.

I turn then to consider the third argument on the cross-appeal, that the restrictions on trading in the lease-back are reasonable, since it is clear law that a term in restraint of trade will not be enforced unless it is reasonable.

The decision in *Esso v Harper's Garage* has been generally taken as laying down a rule of thumb that a petrol supply restraint, requiring a dealer to take all his petrol from one petrol company, is reasonable and valid if it will last for no more than 5 years, but if it will last for significantly more than 5 years, eg for 21 years, it is unreasonable and invalid unless the petrol company can prove that a tie for the longer period is an economic necessity for it. No such evidence of economic necessity has been put forward by Total in the present case, but the contention that the longer tie is in all the circumstances reasonable has been urged on a different ground.

In *Esso v Harper's Garage* [1967] 1 All ER 699 at 708–709, 723, [1968] AC 269 at 300, 323 both Lord Reid and Lord Pearce referred with approval to the statement of Lord

Macnaghten in *Nordenfelt v Maxim Nordenfelt Guns and Ammunition Co Ltd* [1894] AC 535 at 565, [1891–4] All ER Rep 1 at 18 that 'of course the quantum of consideration may enter into the question of the reasonableness of the contract'. Moreover, in *Amoco Australia Pty Ltd v Rocca Bros Motor Engineering Co Ltd* [1975] 1 All ER 968 at 978, [1975] AC 561 at 579 Lord Cross commented that the fact that a covenantor had obtained and would continue to enjoy benefits under the relevant agreement which he claimed to be unenforceable was pro tanto a reason for holding that the covenant was not in unreasonable restraint of trade.

In the present case the consideration for the grant of the lease and thus the consideration for the restraint, since the lease-back was part of the same transaction as the lease, was the payment by Total to the company of the premium of £35,000. That figure was arrived at by a professional valuation as being the value of the 51-year lease, subject to the lease-back, the initial rent under which (£2,250 per annum) was significantly below a full market rent. The lease-back thus had a capital value, but the real value of the property was in the value of the lease, and, because the lease was for such a long term at a peppercorn rent, the value of the reversion on the lease, the company's underlying freehold interest subject to the lease, was of the very slight value of some £600 to £1,000 only.

The choice of 51 years as the term of the lease came about originally because it was common ground that if the term of the lease had not exceeded 50 years the premium of £35,000 would have been taxable as income in the company's hands, and that would have defeated the object of the whole transaction, viz recapitalising the business of the company in an endeavour to keep it afloat. But despite its provenance the 51-year length of the term is a very real factor in the case, firstly because that is what Total paid for by the premium and secondly because, despite some pressure, Total refused to grant the lease-back for more than 21 years with the mutual breaks which I have mentioned.

Against this background certain factors are clear. The first is that for planning reasons the property is most unlikely to be used, during the 21-year term of the lease-back, for any purpose other than that of a garage and filling station. The next is that it can make no significant difference to the public at large whether the petrol sold there comes from Total or from Esso or Shell or any other major oil company. The next point is that the lessees under the lease-back are not locked into trading in Total's products from the property for 21 years. If they find this unattractive, they are free to exercise the break clause under the lease-back at the end of the seventh or fourteenth years of the term and leave; if it seems harsh that the company may be compelled by adverse conditions to leave the property which it formerly owned the answer is that it has already received the substantial value of the property in the shape of the premium of £35,000 for the grant to Total of the 51-year lease of the property at a peppercorn rent.

Finally, if the lease-back had been granted for 5 years only, with the result that the tie in it would have been unquestionably valid, the lessees would have been left at the end of the 5 years with the choice of either leaving the property or applying for a new tenancy under the Landlord and Tenant Act 1954. But any new tenancy would, like any new tenancy which might be granted under the Act at the end of the 21-year term of the lease-back, have been likely to have been for a maximum of 5 or 7 years only (subject to the possibility of application for a further new tenancy under the 1954 Act) subject to the same tie provisions as are to be found in the lease-back. It was the lessee's interest that required that the lease and lease-back arrangement should be for a significantly long term since the premium payable by Total for a short term, such as a mere 5-year term, could not conceivably have been enough to recapitalise the company and solve the company's financial difficulties.

In the circumstances of this case, and not least because at the time of the grant of the lease and lease-back the company was subject to a valid tie for a term of three to four years, I can see no real significance in the difference between a tie for 5 years and the term of 7 years to the first break under the lease-back.

In the light of these factors the restraints on trading in the lease-back were in my judgment reasonable. Accordingly, I would allow the cross-appeal.

It follows that the question of severence which is sought to be raised by the appellants' first ground of appeal does not arise. None the less, in deference to the argument and in case this dispute goes further it may be appropriate that I should express my view.

The appellants support their case by reference to the *Amoco* case, a petrol case where because of the restraints by way of tie to Amoco in the lease-back the whole of a lease/lease-back transaction was held to be void. The case is the less helpful, however, in that Lord Cross did not find it necessary to lay down any clear test for whether invalid covenants in restraint of trade could be severed from the rest of the agreement or composite agreement in which they appeared; he merely referred to several possible tests, and held that by any of them the whole of the lease/lease-back arrangment in the *Amoco* case was void.

In the *Amoco* case, however, the invalid tie was the sole object or subject matter of the contract, as was also the case in *Vancouver Malt and Sake Brewing Co Ltd v Vancouver Breweries Ltd* [1934] AC 181, [1934] All ER Rep 38. In such a case the whole contract, or in the case of a lease/lease-back the whole of the composite contract, must fall within the tie. That is not however the present case. I find the most helpful test in the judgments of Somervell LJ in *Bennett v Bennett* [1952] 1 All ER 413 at 417, [1952] 1 KB 249 at 254, and in *Goodinson v Goodinson* [1954] 2 All ER 255 at 258, [1954] 2 QB 118 at 123–124. In the former case he posed the question whether the invalid promise was the whole or main consideration for the agreement moving from the plaintiff, and, finding that it was, he held the whole agreement void. In the latter case he held that there was ample consideration to support the agreement apart from the void covenant and so other covenants in the agreement could be enforced. The judgment of Goff LJ in *Chemidus Wavin Ltd v Société Pour la Transformation et l'Exploitation des Resines Industrielles SA* [1978] 3 CMLR 514 at 523 approves a test to the same effect.

In the present case, in July 1969 Total had no particular need to impose a petrol tie on the property since they already held a valid tie with, as I have mentioned, several years unexpired. The main object of the lease/lease-back transaction was to refinance the company by the payment of the £35,000. The tie provisions were, no doubt, in the eyes of Total an inevitable consequence but they were not either the sole consideration for the tie or the sole object of the transaction. The important consideration for Total was the grant of the 51-year lease, on the value of which the amount of the premium had been calculated, and with this went the agreement to pay rent under the lease-back which provided Total with an essential financial return on its outlay. I have no doubt therefore that in this case the tie provisions, if invalid, would, as the deputy judge held, be severable from the remaining provisions of the lease-back; these remaining provisions and the lease itself remain valid.

The contract is of course changed by the excision of the tie, and obviously Total would not have granted a lease-back which did not contain such a tie. But I do not think that is good enough to prevent severance and lead to the conclusion that the whole of the lease and lease-back is void. A mortgage to a petrol company containing a tie would, in my judgment, remain in all other respects valid despite the invalidity of the tie as an unreasonable restraint of trade, although the petrol company would not have contemplated making any advance on mortgage to a dealer without a tie.

I turn therefore to the appellants' case on equitable grounds.

The basis of the contention that the transaction of the lease and lease-back ought to be set aside in equity is that it is submitted, and in the court below was accepted on behalf of Total, that during the negotiations for the lease and lease-back the parties did not have equal bargaining power, and it is therefore further submitted that a contract between parties who had unequal bargaining power can only stand and be enforced by the stronger if he can prove that the contract was in point of fact fair, just and reasonable. The concept of unequal bargaining power is taken particularly from the judgment of Lord Denning MR in *Lloyds Bank Ltd v Bundy* [1974] 3 All ER 757, [1975] QB 326. The reference to a contract only standing if it is proved to have been in point of fact fair, just and reasonable is taken from the judgment of Lord Selborne LC in *Earl of Aylesford v Morris* (1873) LR 8 Ch App 484 at 490–491, [1861–73] All ER Rep 300 at 302–303. Lord

Selborne LC was not there seeking to generalise: he was dealing only with what he regarded as one of the oldest heads of equity, relieving against fraud practised on heirs or expectants, particularly fraud practised on young noblemen of great expectations, considerable extravagance and no ready money. It is none the less submitted that the logic of the development of the law leads to the conclusion that Lord Selborne's test should now be applied generally to any contract entered into between parties who did not have equal bargaining power.

In fact Lord Denning MR's judgment in *Lloyds Bank Ltd v Bundy* merely laid down the proposition that where there was unequal bargaining power the contract could not stand if the weaker did not have separate legal advice. In the present case Mr Lobb and the company did have separate advice from their own solicitor. On the facts of this case, however, that does not weaken the appellants' case if the general proposition of law which they put forward is valid. Total refused to accept any of the modifications of the transaction as put forward by Total which the solicitor for the company and Mr Lobb suggested, and in the end the solicitor advised them not to proceed. Mr Lobb declined to accept that advice because his and the company's financial difficulties were so great, and, it may be said, their bargaining power was so small, that he felt he had no alternative but to accept Total's terms. Because of the existing valid tie to Total which had, as I have said, three to four years to run, he had no prospect at all of raising finance on the scale he required from any source other than Total. There is no suggestion that there was any other dealer readily available who could have bought the property from him subject to the tie. The only practical solutions to him were to accept the terms of the lease and lease-back as put forward by Total on which Total was not prepared to negotiate, or to sell the freehold of the property to Total and cease trading. In these circumstances, it would be unreal, in my judgment, to hold that if the transaction is otherwise tainted it is cured merely because Mr Lobb and the company had independent advice.

But on the deputy judge's findings can it be said that the transaction is tainted? Lord Selborne LC in *Earl of Aylesford v Morris* (1873) LR 8 Ch App 484 at 490–491, [1861–73] All ER Rep 300 at 302–303 dealt with the case before him as a case of fraud. He said:

> 'The usury laws, however, proved to be an inconvenient fetter upon the liberty of commercial transactions; and the arbitrary rule of equity as to sales of reversions was an impediment to fair and reasonable, as well as to unconscionable, bargains. Both have been abolished by the Legislature; but the abolition of the usury laws still leaves the nature of the bargain capable of being a note of fraud in the estimation of this Court; and the Act as to sales of reversions (31 Vict. c. 4) is carefully limited to purchases "made *bonâ fide* and without fraud or unfair dealing," and leaves under-value still a material element in cases in which it is not the sole equitable ground for relief. These changes of the law have in no degree whatever altered the *onus probandi* in those cases, which, according to the language of Lord *Hardwicke*, raise "from the circumstances or conditions of the parties contracting—weakness on one side, usury on the other, or extortion, or advantage taken of that weakness"—a presumption of fraud. Fraud does not here mean deceit or circumvention; it means an unconscientious use of the power arising out of these circumstances and conditions; and when the relative position of the parties is such as *primâ facie* to raise this presumption, the transaction cannot stand unless the person claiming the benefit of it is able to repel the presumption by contrary evidence, proving it to have been in point of fact fair, just, an reasonable.'

The whole emphasis is on extortion, or undue advantage taken of weakness, an unconscientious use of the power arising out of the inequality of the parties' circumstances, and on unconscientious use of power which the court might in certain circumstances be entitled to infer from a particular, and in these days notorious, relationship unless the contract is proved to have been in fact fair, just and reasonable. Nothing leads me to suppose that the course of the development of the law over the last 100 years has been such that the emphasis on unconscionable conduct or unconscientious use of power has gone and relief will now be granted in equity in a case such as the present if there has been unequal bargaining power, even if the stronger has not used his strength unconscionably. I agree with the judgment of Browne-Wilkinson J in *Multiservice Bookbinding Ltd v Marden* [1978] 2 All ER 489, [1979] Ch 84, which sets out that to establish that a term is unfair and unconscionable it is not enough to show that it is, objectively, unreasonable.

In the present case there are findings of fact by the deputy judge that the conduct of Total was not unconscionable, coercive or oppressive. There is ample evidence to support those findings and they are not challenged by the appellants. Their case is that the judge applied the wrong test; where there is unequal bargaining power, the test is, they say, whether its terms are fair, just and reasonable and it is unnecessary to consider whether the conduct of the stronger party was oppressive or unconscionable. I do not accept the appellants' proposition of law. In my judgment the findings of the judge conclude this ground of appeal against the appellants.

Inequality of bargaining power must anyhow be a relative concept. It is seldom in any negotiation that the bargaining powers of the parties are absolutely equal. Any individual wanting to borrow money from a bank, building society or other financial institution in order to pay his liabilities or buy some property he urgently wants to acquire will have virtually no bargaining power; he will have to take or leave the terms offered to him. So, with house property in a seller's market, the purchaser will not have equal bargaining power with the vendor. But Lord Denning MR did not envisage that any contract entered into in such circumstances would, without more, be reviewed by the courts by the objective criterion of what was reasonable: see *Lloyds Bank Ltd v Bundy* [1974] 3 All ER 757 at 763, [1975] QB 326 at 336. The courts would only interfere in exceptional cases where as a matter of common fairness it was not right that the strong should be allowed to push the weak to the wall. The concepts of unconscionable conduct and of the exercise by the stronger of coercive power are thus brought in, and in the present case they are negatived by the deputy judge's findings.

Even if, contrary to my view just expressed, the company and Mr and Mrs Lobb had initially in 1969 a valid claim in equity to have the lease and lease-back set aside as a result of the inequality of bargaining power, that claim was, in my judgment, barred by laches well before the issue of the writ in this action.

The rescue operation by way of recapitalisation of the company was never successfully achieved. The £35,000 paid by Total was almost entirely absorbed in satisfying the company's existing liabilities, and the company was left still without working capital. Moreover, Mr Lobb did not take into account, and was not advised, that the grant of the 51-year lease to Total at a premium was likely to amount to a disposal of the property for capital gains tax purposes and to involve liability for that tax. That the premium did not go far enough was partly due to the actions of other creditors; the company's bankers insisted on the company's secured overdraft being cleared and on its account being kept in credit thereafter, without overdraft facilities, and United Dominions Trust Ltd insisted on a stocktaking loan being reduced to within its agreed limit. Total contributed to these difficulties partly because Total did not proceed very expeditiously to completion (primarily because Total was reluctant to enter into a transaction which it never found particularly attractive) and partly because Total insisted on deducting from the premium the full amount required to clear all subsisting hire-purchase agreements on plant and equipment including a capital sum in respect of the underground tanks. The judge regarded this insistence as unreasonable, though not oppressive.

All this, however, apart from the substantial capital gains tax liability, became known to the company and Mr and Mrs Lobb in 1969 very soon after the grant of the lease and lease-back. But the writ was not issued until June 1979, and the first intimation of a possible claim that the lease could, on unspecified grounds, be set aside on repayment of the premium was not given to Total until 22 July 1976.

In the mean time, however, trading from the property had continued and in 1973 Total, with the concurrence of the company and Mr Lobb, had spent £19,000 on the property in converting it to a self-service filling station. The rent under the lease-back was consequently increased, but Total would of course never have spent that money on the property if it had previously been made clear that the validity of the lease/lease-back arrangement was to be disputed. Even after the intimation of a possible claim on 22 July 1976 the Lobbs continued to negotiate with Total and alternative terms were put forward by Total which are described by the deputy judge in his judgment, but no writ was issued for nearly three years.

Counsel submits on behalf of the appellants that there can be no laches so long as the company's and Mr Lobb's financial difficulties continued, and they did continue up to the issue of the writ and afterwards. I do not accept this. Even though the company's cheques were again being dishonoured by December 1969, the immediate pressure was removed in July. Apart from that the company and Mr and Mrs Lobb were at all times free to consult solicitors and accountants. This is a clear case of laches.

I would dismiss the appeal and allow the cross-appeal.

**DUNN LJ.** The following questions appear to arise for decision in this appeal and cross-appeal. (1) Did the underlease contain covenants in unreasonable restraint of trade? (2) If so, are both the lease and the underlease to be regarded as unenforceable, or can the offending covenants be severed leaving the lease, and so much of the underlease as is valid, to stand? (3) In any event can both the lease and underlease be set aside in equity? (4) If so, are the plaintiffs barred from relief by laches?

The deputy judge answered question (1) in the affirmative. He held that the offending covenants could be severed, and answered question (3) in the negative. He did not find it necessary to deal with question (4). Questions (1) and (4) accordingly arise on the cross-appeal, and questions (2) and (3) on the appeal.

*Unreasonable restraint of trade*
The judge held: (1) that the lease and underlease formed the component elements of a single transaction; (2) that in the circumstances of this case the doctrine of restraint of trade applied to such a transaction since, although the underlessees were not the original lessors of the lease, the reality of the transaction was that the plaintiff company raised finance on its land by a lease and underlease rather than by a mortgage, and that the business continued to be carried on by and for the benefit of Mr and Mrs Lobb who were the sole proprietors of the company. The underlease to Mr and Mrs Lobb was no more than a device to avoid the application of the restraint of trade; (3) that the doctrine of restraint of trade was applicable when the restraint was imposed as a term of the rescue of an insolvent trader. He relied on *Vancouver Malt and Sake Brewing Co Ltd v Vancouver Breweries Ltd* [1934] AC 181 at 191–192, [1934] All ER Rep 38 at 42 per Lord Macmillan.

With respect to the arguments of counsel for Total to the contrary, in my judgment the judge was right to come to the conclusion which he did on those matters in holding that the doctrine of restraint of trade applied to the transaction. The remaining question on the cross-appeal is whether the respondent, Total, on whom the onus lies, had proved that the restraint was reasonable.

The judge felt unable to distinguish the case from *Esso Petroleum Co Ltd v Harper's Garage (Stourport) Ltd* [1967] 1 All ER 699, [1968] AC 269. He held ([1983] 1 All ER 944 at 966, [1983] 1 WLR 87 at 100):

'In the present case, [Total] has not attempted to call evidence to justify the length of the tie; nor has [it] relied on the existence of the mutual break clause to argue that the tie was only for a period of seven years. Mr and Mrs Lobb could of course have freed themselves from the tie after the expiry of that period, but only by ridding themselves of the underlease and losing the right to trade altogether from the site.'

Counsel for Total agreed that he had not attempted to justify the length of the tie as such, but said that he had submitted that there were special circumstances in this case on which the restrictions could be justified, and which distinguished the case from *Harper's* case.

n *Harper's* case the House of Lords was careful not to find that a 21-year tie was unreasonable in all circumstances. Each case depended on its own facts, and all their Lordships emphasised that it was ultimately public policy which prohibited the enforcement of covenants in restraint of trade (see [1967] 1 All ER 699 esp at 723–724, [1968] AC 269 esp at 323–324 per Lord Pearce). In *Amoco Australia Pty Ltd v Rocco Bros Motor Engineering Co Pty Ltd* [1975] 1 All ER 968 at 978, [1975] AC 561 at 579 Lord Cross, giving the advice of the Board, emphasised that the adequacy of the consideration received by the covenantor for the benefits which he obtained from the agreement, was relevant to the question of the reasonableness of a restraint imposed by the agreement. In *Foley v Classique Coaches Ltd* [1934] 2 KB 1, [1934] All ER Rep 88 the fact that the petrol was to be purchased by the covenantor at a reasonable price was held to be relevant to the question of the reasonableness of the covenant.

The special circumstances relied on by counsel for Total as justifying the covenants in restraint of trade may be summarised as follows. Total had paid the market price for a 51-year lease, which was for all practical purposes equivalent to a freehold. The company was insolvent, and the sum of £35,000 was designed to enable it to pay its debts, and to save the Lobbs from personal bankruptcy. Fifty-one years was the shortest term which would justify a payment sufficient to discharge the debts of the company. Without such a sum there was no realistic prospect that the company would be able to continue in business for any length of time. The company was independently advised with regard to the transaction by its solicitors and accountants, and insisted on proceeding contrary to their advice. By reason of the underlease, Mr and Mrs Lobb were able to continue to trade and to pass on the business to their sons. In July 1969, by reason of the terms of certain mortgages the company was already bound to buy all its petrol from Total for a number of years. Hence the company's freedom to trade was already restricted, and the further restrictions imposed by the underlease were illusory. The term of 21 years was the maximum term Total was prepared to grant, although Mr Lobb would have preferred a longer underlease.

In my judgment the transaction in question amounted to a rescue operation for the benefit of the company and the Lobbs which Total was reluctant to undertake, but which it undertook in order to preserve the site as an outlet for its petrol. The break clauses in the underlease enabled the company to cease to trade if the rescue operation should fail. The transaction was of advantage to the plaintiffs since it enabled the company to continue to trade from the site, which it did for another ten years, and was of advantage to Total since it preserved an outlet.

In *Harper's* case none of these circumstances existed. There was a loan to the dealer of £7,000 secured by a mortgage, and there was no special reason for a tie as long as 21 years. In the instant case Total paid a fair price for the 51-year lease and the covenants in restraint of trade only lasted for 21 years. There was ample consideration for the grant of the lease, and the underlease was necessary if the Lobbs were to continue trading from the site. In my judgment public policy does not require that such arrangements should be unenforceable. On the contrary, it seems to me that public policy should encourage a transaction which enabled trading by the plaintiff to continue, and preserved an outlet for the defendant's products. I would hold that in the special circumstances of this case Total has established that the covenants in restraint of trade were reasonable.

*Severance*

On the view that I have formed of the reasonableness of the covenants, the question of severance does not arise for decision. But since the question was fully argued, and since the cases on the subject are not easily reconcilable, I will state my views on it on the basis that the covenants were, as the judge held, in unreasonable restraint of trade.

We are not here concerned with severance in the sense of the reduction or modification of an objectionable covenant, as in such cases as *Mason v Provident Clothing and Supply Co Ltd* [1913] AC 724, [1911–13] All ER Rep 400, *Goldsoll v Goldman* [1915] 1 Ch 292, [1914–15] All ER Rep 257 or *Attwood v Lamont* [1920] 3 KB 571, [1920] All ER Rep 55. We are concerned here with the question whether the objectionable covenants can be cut

out altogether from the underlease, leaving the lease and the rest of the underlease vali(
and enforceable. As Lord Denning MR said in *Kingsway Investments Ltd v Kent CC* [1969]
1 All ER 601 at 611, [1969] 2 QB 332 at 354: 'This question of severance has vexed th(
law for centuries.' He followed the notes to *Pigot's Case* (1614) 77 ER 1177 at 1179:

> 'The general principle is, that if any clause, etc. void by statute or by the commoi
> law be mixed up with good matter which is entirely independent of it, the goo(
> part stands, the rest is void . . . but if the part which is good depends upon tha
> which is bad, the whole instrument is void.'

In *Kearney v Whitehaven Colliery Co* [1893] 1 QB 700 at 713, [1891–4] All ER Rep 55(
at 562 Lopes LJ held:

> '. . . where there is no illegality in the consideration, and some of the provisions
> are legal and others illegal, the illegality of those which are bad does not communicate
> itself to, or contaminate, those which are good, unless they are inseparable from anc
> dependent upon one another.'

In *Horwood v Millars Timber and Trading Co Ltd* [1917] 1 KB 305, [1916–17] All ER
Rep 847 the Court of Appeal held that the good and bad obligations were so closely
linked that there could be no severance. In *Bennett v Bennett* [1952] 1 All ER 413, [1952]
1 KB 249 Somervell LJ held that where the main consideration for the deed was an illega
covenant the whole deed was void. Denning LJ said ([1952] 1 All ER 413 at 421, [1952]
1 KB 249 at 261):

> 'If the void covenant goes only to part of the consideration, so that it can be
> ignored and yet leave the rest of the deed a reasonable arrangement between the
> parties, then the deed stands and can be enforced in every respect save in regard to
> the void covenant.'

In *Goodinson v Goodinson* [1954] 2 All ER 255 at 258, [1954] 2 QB 118 at 124 Somervell LJ
held that there was ample consideration to support the agreement apart from the illegal
covenant. Romer LJ also decided the question as being one of consideration.

In *Stenhouse Australia Ltd v Phillips* [1974] 1 All ER 117 at 124, [1974] AC 391 at 403
Lord Wilberforce said:

> 'Clause 4 is in no way dependant on other clauses declared to be unenforceable
> and since the effect of a holding that a contractual provision is in unreasonable
> restraint of trade is merely to render that provision unenforceable, without
> destroying the rest of the contract, there is no reason against enforcement of cl 4
> alone.'

In the *Amoco* case [1975] 1 All ER 968 at 977, [1975] AC 561 at 578 Lord Cross, having
referred to various tests as to severability which might not in every case lead to the same
result, said:

> '. . . whatever test be applied the answer must, their Lordships think, be the same
> in this case. It is inconceivable that any petrol company would grant a dealer a lease
> at a nominal rent of a site on which it had spent a substantial sum in installing
> pumps and other equipment without imposing on the dealer any obligation to buy
> petrol from it or even to carry on the business of a petrol station on the demised
> premises. [The restrictive covenants were] the heart and soul of the underlease.'

Hence no severance.

In *Chemidus Wavin Ltd v Société pour la Transformation et l'Exploitation des Resines
Industrielles SA* [1978] CMLR 514 at 520 Buckley LJ said:

> 'Applying article 85 to an English contract, one may well have to consider
> whether, after the excisions required by the Article of the Treaty had been made
> from the contract, the contract could be said to fail from lack of consideration or on

any other ground, or whether the contract would be so changed in its character as not to be the sort of contract that the parties intended to enter into at all.'

Goff LJ quoted (at 523) from Salter LJ in *Putsman v Taylor* [1927] 1 KB 637 at 639, 1927] All ER Rep 356 at 359:

'If a promisee claims the enforcement of a promise, and the promise is a valid promise and supported by consideration, the Court will enforce the promise, notwithstanding the fact that the promisor has made other promises, supported by the same consideration, which are void, and has included the valid and invalid promises in one document.'

The deputy judge in the instant case held that since, even without the restrictive covenants, the lease and underlease constituted 'a recognisable and commercially intelligible transaction' severance of the restrictive covenant was permissible leaving the lease and the remainder of the underlease valid. In adopting that test he followed the US case of *Kelly v Kosuga* (1959) 358 US 516 at 521. With respect to the deputy judge, although that case was referred to as providing a possible test by Lord Cross in the *Amoco* case, I do not think its adoption is warranted by the English authorities to which I have referred.

The preponderance of those authorities seems to me to indicate that, if the valid promises are supported by sufficient consideration, then the invalid promise can be severed from the valid even though the consideration also supports the invalid promise. On the other hand if the invalid promise is substantially the whole or main consideration for the agreement then there will be no severance.

In the *Amoco* case the lease and underlease were coterminous at a nominal rent. In the instant case a premium representing full consideration was paid for the lease. There remained a reversion of 29 years in the lessor. The underlease was near a rack rent and, because of the break and rent review clauses, a full rack rent was payable after eight years. Ample consideration was given for the transaction as a whole, though no doubt part of the consideration was applicable to the restrictive covenants. But the main consideration was that given for the lease and the transaction was not dependent on the unenforceable clauses in the underlease. For those reasons in my judgment the deputy judge was right to sever the unobjectionable clauses from the underlease.

*Equitable relief*

Counsel for the appellants conceded that he could not bring himself within any of the established categories of equitable relief, but relied on the dictum of Lord Denning MR in *Lloyds Bank Ltd v Bundy* [1974] 3 All ER 757 at 765, [1975] QB 326 at 339 and submitted that the circumstances of this case disclosed a classic case of inequality of bargaining power of which the defendants had taken advantage by entering into the transaction, although he did not suggest any pressure or other misconduct on their part. He submitted that if it was necessary to categorise the grant of relief sought, it was an unconscionable bargain. He reminded us that the categories of unconscionable bargains are not closed (per Browne-Wilkinson J in *Multiservice Bookbinding Ltd v Marden* [1978] 2 All ER 489 at 502, [1979] Ch 84 at 110) and sought to distinguish the instant case from that case by submitting that here the plaintiffs were under a compelling necessity to accept the loan, so that misconduct by Total was unnecessary. The fact of their impecuniosity, that they were already tied to Total by mortgages, that there was no other source of finance, and that they could not sell the equities of redemption under the mortgages without giving up trading, coupled with the knowledge of Total of those facts rendered the transaction unconscionable, and placed the onus on Total to show that its terms were fair and reasonable.

I find myself unable to accept those arguments. Mere impecuniosity has never been held a ground for equitable relief. In this case no pressure was placed on the plaintiffs. On the contrary Total was reluctant to enter into the transaction. The plaintiffs took independent advice from their solicitors and accountants. They went into the transaction with their eyes open, and it was of benefit to them because they were enabled to continue trade from the site for a number of years. In my view the judge was right to refuse equitable relief.

*Laches*

If I am wrong, and the plaintiffs are entitled to equitable relief, I would hold that they are barred by laches for the reasons given by Dillon LJ.

Accordingly I would allow the cross-appeal and dismiss the appeal.

**WALLER LJ.** I agree. I will however briefly express my own view of the two main issues. The first is whether or not there was an unreasonable restraint of trade in the agreements made between the parties and the second one is whether or not, if there was unreasonable restraint of trade, the tie provisions can be severed from the rest of the contract.

In this case one of the parties to the lease was different from one of the parties to the sublease. The effect is that the sub-tenants are strictly not giving up any right which they had enjoyed before. But since they controlled the company which had enjoyed unrestrained rights of trade, in my opinion the lease and the lease-back have to be considered as though they were made between the same parties. I say this reluctantly because it is the party which is not before the court that would benefit if the court came to the conclusion that the tie for 21 years was in unreasonable restraint of trade. However, counsel for the appellant sought to meet this by giving certain undertakings to Total.

The deputy judge found in favour of Total save in respect of the length of the tie in the lease-back. He came to the conclusion that, having regard to the fact that the defendant, Total, did not call evidence to justify the length of the tie and the decision in *Esso Petroleum Co Ltd v Harper's Garage (Stourport) Ltd* [1967] 1 All ER 699, [1968] AC 269, he had to find that the tie in this case was an unreasonable restraint of trade. Counsel for Total accepted that he did not call evidence to justify the length of the tie. He relied on the 51 year-lease which granted to Total an outlet for 51 years. The 21 years with a tie and break at 7 and 14 years was the most Total was prepared to grant and it did not require evidence to justify this. Counsel for Total further submitted that the facts in this case were very different from either *Cleveland Petroleum Co Ltd v Dartstone Ltd* [1969] 1 All ER 201, [1969] 1 WLR 116 or the *Harper's Garage* case. In *Esso Petroleum Co Ltd v Harper's Garage (Stourport) Ltd* [1967] 1 All ER 699 at 708–709, [1968] AC 269 at 299 Lord Reid said:

> 'It is now generally accepted that a provision in a contract which is to be regarded as in restraint of trade must be justified if it is to be enforceable, and that the law on this matter was correctly stated by LORD MACNAGHTEN in the *Nordenfelt* case ([1894] AC 535 at 565, [1891–94] All ER Rep 1 at 18). He said: "Restraints of trade and interference with individual liberty of action, may be justified by the special circumstances of a particular case. It is a sufficient justification, and indeed, it is the only justification, if the restriction is reasonable—reasonable, that is, in reference to the interests of the parties concerned and reasonable in reference to the interests of the public, so framed and so guarded as to afford adequate protection to the party in whose favour it is imposed, while at the same time it is in no way injurious to the public." So in every case it is necessary to consider, first whether the restraint went farther than to afford adequate protection to the party in whose favour it was granted, secondly whether it can be justified as being in the interests of the party restrained, and thirdly whether it must be held contrary to the public interest. I find it difficult to agree with the way in which the court has in some cases treated the interests of the party restrained. Surely it can never be in the interest of a person to agree to suffer a restraint unless he gets some compensating advantage, direct or indirect; and LORD MACNAGHTEN said "of course the quantum of consideration may enter into the question of the reasonableness of the contract".'

The circumstances which existed in the months immediately before and at the time when the lease and lease-back were executed were fully set out in the judgment of the deputy judge and are set out in the judgment of Dillon LJ. I will summarise those facts which are relevant when seeking to answer the three questions posed by Lord Reid. Alec Lobb (Garages) Ltd (the company) was in serious financial trouble. Not only had it borrowed £24,000 from Total which had a charge with a tie as security for the loan but the company had also borrowed from the bank. Furthermore, its trading position was not satisfactory. Because of its loans from Total the company was not in a position to raise money elsewhere. In these circumstances Mr Lobb approached Total for help suggesting a lease and lease-back of the forecourt. Mr Story of Total was not enthusiastic. Total suggested a purchase of the freehold, but Mr Lobb would not agree. Finally it was agreed that there should be a lease of 51 years. This was at Mr Lobb's request to avoid income tax but the premium of £35,000 was based on the market value and anything less would not have begun to solve the company's financial difficulties. From Total's point of view it was providing £35,000 which would be sufficient to pay the debts which it knew about and leave Alec Lobb Ltd with some spare capital. Total knew he was advised by his solicitor and by an accountant. Total did not know what the advice was. Total was acquiring an outlet for 51 years at a price based on market value. The lease-back was for 21 years which was the most Total would grant. No pressure whatever was put on by Total. In fact, Mr Lobb had other debts unknown to Total and he was soon in trouble again. Total was making a decision to help Mr Lobb to save him from bankruptcy which would have been the almost certain alternative. Did the restraint go further than to afford adequate protection to Total? The restraint was for 21 years with a break at 7 and 14 years. As a result of the lease and lease-back Total was virtually the freeholder, saving one of its customers and one of its outlets which might be lost in the event of bankruptcy of the company. In *Amoco Australia Pty Ltd v Rocco Bros Motor Engineering Co Pty Ltd* [1975] 1 All ER 968 at 978, [1975] AC 561 at 579 Lord Cross said:

> 'The fact that a covenantor has obtained and will continue to enjoy benefits under the relevant agreement which formed part of the consideration for the covenant which he claims to be unenforceable is no doubt pro tanto a reason for holding that the covenant is not in unreasonable restraint of trade.'

And Lord Reid, in the passage I have cited, quotes Lord Macnaghten to the same effect. Having regard to all the circumstances and in particular the amount of the consideration in my opinion the restraint did not go farther than was necessary to afford adequate protection. Could this be justified in the interests of Mr Lobb? The bargain has to be examined and judged at the time it was struck and if the facts were only those known to Total it was saving Mr Lobb from bankruptcy. There were however other circumstances, other liabilities unknown to Total which produced a different result. These other liabilities meant that although Mr Lobb was saved from immediate bankruptcy he did not have the working capital which Total had expected. Judged by the facts known to Total at the time of making the contract the existence of the tie can, in my opinion, be justified in the interests of Mr Lobb. In the words of the deputy judge it was not 'in any way unfair or unreasonable'. Without it or some other arrangement the consequences would have been early trouble.

Must the contract be held to be contrary to the public interest? In my judgment the answer is No. It is clearly in the public interest to save a firm from bankruptcy provided that the terms are not unfair and that improper pressure has not been exerted. No improper pressure, indeed no pressure, was exerted by Total. The initiative came from Mr Lobb. When Total suggested a sale of the freehold and a lease-back Mr Lobb said, 'No.' Total accepted his suggestion of a 51-year lease and paid for it at market value. Total was then not prepared to grant more than 21 years with a break at 7 and 14 years. In my judgment, although it is unusual to have a tie of this length this tie was not contrary to the public interest. Accordingly, I am of opinion that the restraint of trade imposed was reasonable.

If I am wrong in my conclusion that there was no unreasonable restraint of trade, it is submitted by counsel for appellants that the deputy judge was in error in finding that the clauses enforcing a restraint of trade were severable and that the contract remained enforceable when those clauses were severed. When Dunn LJ asked counsel what test had to be applied we were not only referred to a number of authorities setting out tests which varied in some degree the one from the other but also certain textbooks (eg *Cheshire and Fifoot on the Law of Contract* (10th edn, 1981) p 373, *Treitel on the Law of Contract* (6th edn, 1983) pp 382ff and *Chitty on Contracts* (25th edn, 1983) p 644). I do not here set out these cases save to say that there is a clear distinction between the severability of a convenant, ie whether a covenant itself can be divided leaving part of it effective, and those cases where the whole covenant is struck out and the decision then has to be made whether that which is left is enforceable or not. The instant case is, of course, in the latter category and in my opinion the test to be applied is best set out in the judgment of Buckley LJ in a Common Market case in the English Court of Appeal, *Chemidus Wavin Ltd v Société pour la Transformation et l'Exploitation des Resines Industrialles SA* [1978] CMLR 514 at 519:

> '(18) So, the position appears clearly to be this, that where in a contract there are certain clauses which are annulled by reason of their being in contravention of Article 85, paragraph (1), of the Treaty, one must look at the contract with those clauses struck out and see what the effect of that is in the light of the domestic law which governs the particular contract. In the present case, we have to consider what effect the invalidity, if any, of the clauses in the licence agreement by reason of Article 85 would have upon that contract as a whole. Whether it is right to regard the matter as one of severance of the contract or not, I do not think it is necessary for us to consider now. I doubt whether it is really a question of severance in the sense in which we in these courts are accustomed to use that term in considering whether covenants contained in contracts of employment and so forth are void as being in restraint of trade, and, if they are to any extent void, whether those covenants can be severed so as to save part of the covenant, although another part may be bad. It seems to me that, in applying Article 85 to an English contract, one may well have to consider whether, after the excisions required by the Article of the Treaty have been made from the contract, the contract could be said to fail for lack of consideration or on any other ground, or whether the contract would be so changed in its character as not to be the sort of contract that the parties intended to enter into at all.'

Can this contract be said to be so changed in its character as not to be the sort of contract that the parties intended to enter into at all? In my judgment the consideration was twofold. There was the 51-year term for which a sum based on the market price was paid and there was the tie. If the tie is removed there is a lease for which a substantial sum was paid and there is a lease-back at a rent which is not nominal. While the purpose of the contract included a tie, the contract was a contract for letting a petrol station. With the tie removed it is still a contract for letting a petrol station. Even though Total would not have entered into the contract without the tie it remained a contract for letting a petrol station and it was at a rent which was not nominal. It was therefore the sort of contract which the parties intended to enter into.

*Appeal dismissed. Cross-appeal allowed. Leave to appeal to the House of Lords refused.*

Solicitors: *Holmes & Hills,* Braintree (for the appellants); *Denton Hall & Burgin* (for Total).

Diana Procter    Barrister.

# Corby District Council v Holst & Co Ltd and others

COURT OF APPEAL, CIVIL DIVISION
OLIVER LJ AND NEILL J
21, 22 NOVEMBER 1984

*Practice – Payment into court – Offer of settlement – Effect of offer – Discretion – Trial judge's discretion to treat offer as payment in – Banker's bond – Defendant providing security for damages by way of banker's bond – Defendant offering amount secured to plaintiff in settlement of claim – Whether offer could be treated as equivalent to payment in for purposes of costs – Whether court could order in advance of trial that offer to be treated as payment in – Whether fetter on trial judge's discretion – RSC Ord 22, r 1.*

In 1980 the plaintiff property owners paid the defendant contractors an agreed sum in settlement of a claim by the contractors arising out of a building contract which had been referred to arbitration. Under that settlement the contractors were required to provide security for the repayment of the agreed sum paid by the owners if the owners succeeded in a counterclaim against the contractors which they were in the mean time proceeding with in the High Court. The contractors provided security by way of a banker's bond for the agreed amount. In October 1984, prior to the trial of the High Court action, the contractors offered in a 'without prejudice' letter to pay to the owners a secured sum by banker's bond in settlement of the claim against them. The contractors also applied to the court for an order that the offer be treated as if the secured sum had been paid into court under RSC Ord 22, r 1(1)[a] for the purposes of awarding costs at the trial. The judge refused to make the order and the contractors appealed, contending that, by analogy with the procedure under Ord 22, r 8(2)[b] whereby a sum paid into court by a defendant to an Ord 14 summons was treated not merely as security but as an offer and as if it had in fact been paid into court under Ord 22, r 1, the court should use its inherent jurisdiction to devise an equivalent procedure where security was provided other than by payment into court.

**Held** – There was no express jurisdiction under the Rules of the Supreme Court to make an order that an offer of settlement contained in a 'without prejudice' letter was to be treated for the purposes of awarding costs as though payment into court had been made pursuant to RSC Ord 22, r 1, and, although the court had an inherent jurisdiction to control its own proceedings, its power under that jurisdiction was limited to the doing of acts necessary to maintain its essential character as a court, and the order sought by the contractors did not fall within that category. Furthermore, since costs in legal proceedings were a matter for the discretion of the trial judge, where a sum secured by a banker's bond was offered by way of settlement in a 'without prejudice' letter it was for the trial judge to determine, in the exercise of his discretion, whether that offer was to be treated for all purposes, including costs, as though the sum so secured had been paid into court under Ord 22, r 1 and what weight was to be given to it, and it would be improper to usurp and so fetter his discretion by directing, in advance of the trial, that the bond be treated by the judge in a particular way. The appeal would therefore be dismissed (see p 326 c to e and g to p 327 a d and g to j, post).

---

a   Rule 1(1), so far as material, provides: 'In any action for a debt or damages any defendant may at any time pay into Court a sum of money in satisfaction of the cause of action in respect of which the plaintiff claims ...'
b   Rule 8(2), so far as material, provides: '... a party who has paid money into court in pursuance of an order made under Order 14—(a) may by notice to the other party appropriate the whole or any part of the money ... to any particular claim ... and money appropriated in accordance with this rule shall be deemed to be money paid into court in accordance with rule 1 ...'

Dictum of Lord Diplock in *Bremer Vulkan Schiffbau Und Maschinenfabrik v South India Shipping Corp* [1981] 1 All ER at 295 and *Rosengrens Ltd v Safe Deposit Centres Ltd* [1984] 3 All ER 198 considered.

**Notes**

For 'without prejudice' communications, see 17 Halsbury's Laws (4th edn) paras 212–213, and for cases on the subject, see 22 Digest (Reissue) 407–410, 4082–4108.

**Cases referred to in judgments**

*Bremer Vulkan Schiffbau Und Maschinenfabrik v South India Shipping Corp* [1981] 1 All ER 289, [1981] AC 909, [1981] 2 WLR 141, HL.
*Calderbank v Calderbank* [1975] 3 All ER 333, [1976] Fam 93, [1975] 3 WLR 586, CA.
*Cutts v Head* [1984] 1 All ER 597, [1984] Ch 290, [1984] 2 WLR 349, CA.
*Rosengrens Ltd v Safe Deposit Centres Ltd* [1984] 3 All ER 198, [1984] 1 WLR 1334, CA.

**Cases also cited**

*Siebe Gorman & Co Ltd v Pneupac Ltd* [1982] 1 All ER 377, [1982] 1 WLR 185, CA.
*Williams v Boag* [1940] 4 All ER 246, [1941] 1 KB 1, CA.

**Interlocutory appeal**

Holst & Co Ltd, the first defendants in an action brought by the plaintiffs, the Corby District Council, appealed against the decision of Mr Recorder Cripps QC, hearing official referee's business in chambers on 15 November 1984, whereby he refused to make any order on a summons issued by the first defendants on 19 October 1984 for an order that a letter from the first defendants' solicitors to the plaintiffs' solicitors dated 19 October 1984 be treated for all purposes as though payment into court in the sum stated therein had been made jointly by the first defendants and the third defendants pursuant to RSC Ord 22, r 1. The second defendants were Bruun & Sorensen (GB) Ltd and the third defendants were Young Austen Young Ltd. The facts are set out in the judgment of Oliver LJ.

*John Dyson QC* and *John Male* for the plaintiffs.
*Anthony Thornton* for the first defendants.
The second and third defendants were not represented.

**OLIVER LJ.** This is a very unusual case. It is an appeal from an interlocutory order of Mr Recorder Cripps QC made on 15 November 1984 by which he made no order except that the parties should be at liberty to bring a certain letter from the first defendants' solicitors to the plaintiffs' solicitors to the attention of the trial judge after all questions of liability and quantum have been decided.

The matter arises in this way. The plaintiffs are the owners of a housing estate in the construction of which the first defendants were, as I understand it, employed as main contractors under a building contract of 20 October 1970. The estate incorporated what seems to have been a fairly sophisticated communal heating system, in the construction of which the second defendants were nominated sub-contractors. They are now, I gather, in liquidation. The third defendants were sub-sub-contractors.

The position was this, that claims were made by the first defendants against the plaintiffs in respect of delay and disruption in the carrying out of the contract. Those claims were submitted to arbitration in 1975, but in 1979 the plaintiffs obtained leave to counterclaim in the arbitration for damages for faulty construction of the heating system. The arbitrator decided that the claim and the counterclaim should be separated. In April 1980 the defendants' claim was settled for an agreed sum and costs, and it was also agreed that the counterclaim should be removed from the arbitration and pursued through the courts, the first defendants being desirous to bring in, as they subsequently did, the third defendants and the supervising heating engineers as third parties.

Since the trial has yet to take place, in case any report of this appeal becomes public, I think perhaps it would be advisable that I should not mention the figures. One of the terms of settlement was that the first defendants should provide security for the repayment of the agreed sum, or the appropriate part of it, if the counterclaim against them, now, of course, the plaintiffs' claim in the action, succeeds. A banker's bond for this amount was provided conditional on non-payment of an agreed sum by way of settlement or of an amount adjudged due on the claim. That bond was provided on 13 April 1980 and the sum by way of settlement was duly paid by the plaintiffs to the first defendants.

The action proceeded, but in October 1984 the first defendants, wishing to protect themselves as regards costs in what promised to be a very expensive action, wrote a letter offering a sum by way of compromise. Having gone to the expense of providing the bond to which I have referred, which provided the security for the plaintiffs for the sum they had expended by way of settlement of the first defendants' claim, they did not want to pay the sum which they were prepared to offer into court. That would have provided, as they considered, a double security. So they wrote what has become known as a *Calderbank* letter (see *Calderbank v Calderbank* [1975] 3 All ER 333, [1976] Fam 93), although perhaps in this case it was a very unusual one. It was in these terms. It was headed 'Without Prejudice'. It said:

'Dear Sirs [and it gives the title of the action]
    Our clients Holst & Co, and Young Austen Young [the third defendants], who are separately represented, have decided to make an unconditional joint offer of [£X] in full and final settlement of all claims your clients have against them, including any claims for interest, on the understanding that your clients' costs to date excluding any costs/fees particularised by your clients in their claim—to be taxed if not agreed—will also be discharged. Please refer to the enclosed letter from Young Austen Young's solicitors. This offer will remain open for 21 days from today's date and our clients' wish and that of Young Austen Young is that in all other respects also this offer will have the same effect as a payment into Court. When the arbitration proceedings between Holst and The Council were settled, Holst provided a bond for [£Y] against your clients' claim in the present proceedings. Our clients and Young Austen Young propose that the sum which is subject to the bond shall be treated as though [£X] thereof has been allocated to Holst's and Young Austen Young's joint offer. In the event of your clients' accepting [£X] in full and final settlement within 21 days of the date of this letter, Holst and Young Austen Young will jointly pay that sum, and subsequent to that your clients' taxed/agreed costs, as stipulated above, to your clients and the bond will be released, no claim on it being made by your clients. Clause 1 of the contingencies set out in the bond gives your clients the right to call upon the bond should Holst for any reason fail to honour its obligations under the terms of this letter. The terms of this offer include a term that if your clients decline to accept the offer, and at the trial of this action recover less than [£X] from either Holst or Young Austen Young or from both: (1) your clients will not be entitled to any costs to be paid by either Holst or Young Austen Young after the date of this letter and (2) that your clients will be liable to pay the taxed costs of both Holst and Young Austen Young after the date of this letter. We enclose by way of service a copy summons seeking an order of the Court that the proposal set out in this letter be treated for all purposes as a payment into Court pursuant to Order 22 Rule 1. [Then there is a reference to an affidavit which I need not read.] We invite you to endorse your consent and return the Summons to us. Save for the purpose of the hearing of the Summons served herewith, which is to be dealt with by another Official Referee to the one assigned for the trial of this matter in January, this letter must not of course be drawn by any party to the attention of the Court (because it is marked "without prejudice") except for the purpose of dealing with costs once all matters of liability and damages have been disposed of.'

The summons enclosed with that letter was, so far as material, in these terms. It sought—

'an order that the First Defendants' solicitors' letter to the Plaintiffs' solicitors of the 19th October 1984 a copy of which is annexed hereto be treated for all purposes as if a payment into Court in the sum of [£X] inclusive of interest had been made jointly by the First and Third Defendants pursuant to Order 22 Rule 1 on 19th October 1984 and on the terms set out in the said letter.'

Counsel for the first defendants says they made it clear that, in seeking to incorporate in the form of the court's order the terms of the letter, he was not seeking to fetter the court's discretion as to costs, which of course exists as much where there has been a payment in as where there has not, but merely to reflect the normal consequences which usually flow from a payment in of a sum greater than that which is achieved by the plaintiff on the trial of the action.

The letter to which I have referred was answered on 30 October, when the plaintiffs' solicitors replied seeking clarification of a number of points regarding both the make-up of the sum offered and the costs which it was envisaged should be dealt with and asking for the 21-day period to be extended until those queries were dealt with. They concluded, however, by returning the summons which had been enclosed with this consent indorsed on it: 'We Wilson and Wilson, Solicitors for the Plaintiffs hereby consent to an Order being made in the terms set out in this Summons.'

However, before the summons came on for hearing, the plaintiffs were advised by counsel that the court had no jurisdiction to make such an order. That advice was communicated to the first defendants' solicitors and was confirmed by telex in these terms:

'We write to confirm our Mr. Ellam's conversation with your Miss Dimsdale-Gill of this morning when we informed you that with regard to the hearing before his Honour Judge Stabb next Monday 12th November, leading counsel has now advised that he is of the opinion that the court has no jurisdiction to make an order in terms applied for, but if it has, it cannot be right for the court to bind itself as to the payment of costs at this stage. For these reasons leading counsel advised that the application should be opposed and we have instructed junior counsel to attend the hearing on Monday.'

What in fact occurred, as I understand it, was that the matter came on for hearing before his Honour Judge Hawser QC, one of the official referees, and it was stood over because it was felt that an affidavit ought to be obtained giving the reasons why the consent which had been indorsed on the summons was now being withdrawn. As a result of that adjournment, the matter came on before Mr Recorder Cripps QC, when the order now appealed against was made.

On making the order appealed against, the recorder delivered a short judgment which was in these terms:

'This is an application by the first and third defendants to have their joint letter dated 19 October 1984 treated for all purposes as though a payment in on the terms contained therein had been made pursuant to RSC Ord 22, r 1. In my view the letter of 19 October 1984, which is without prejudice, makes an offer in the normal contractual sense, referring as it does to the summons enclosed therewith and the making of an application for an order in the terms sought today. By indorsing their consent on the summons the plaintiffs' solicitors accepted that offer and agreed to the order asked for, subject to the question of whether their agreement has true contractual effect, given that their letter dated 30 October 1984 refers to certain matters remaining outstanding. I am assuming without deciding that there was a valid offer and acceptance and that the plaintiffs have consented to the order sought on the summons. I also assume without deciding that I have jurisdiction to make this order as asked for. However, I take the view that I should exercise my discretion not to make such an order. Certainly, this attempt by the first and third defendants so to dispose of these proceedings is a good idea and should be encouraged. Their letter should be brought to the attention of the trial judge after the issues of liability and quantum have been decided. There is no question of it fettering the court's discretion. I therefore make no order on the summons. Either party can apply further.'

He reserved the costs to the trial judge and accordingly made the order to which I have referred.

From that order the first defendants now appeal to this court. I confess at first to having been mystified about what their complaint was because, under the order appealed from, the letter can be brought to the attention of the trial judge, indeed, it can be brought to the attention of the trial judge quite properly without any order at all. If brought to his attention, it could clearly be considered by him in exercising his discretion as to the incidence of the costs of the action. The complaint, however, is this. In the case of a payment into court which has to be taken into account on the question of costs, on the express terms of RSC Ord 62, r 5, there is a well-recognised practice which, whilst leaving the judge's discretion unfettered, nevertheless is normally followed, and that is that, if the amount recovered is less than the sum in court, the consequence is that the plaintiff pays the defendant's costs after the payment in. The defendants could secure that result by actually paying money into court, but they do not see why they should do that when the plaintiffs already are secured by the bond to which I have referred.

It may be that, on the trial, the trial judge might well consider that the offer, particularly in the circumstances that the plaintiffs were at first disposed to agree to its being treated as a good payment in, was to be treated for the purposes of the discretion as to costs in exactly the same way as if payment in had in fact been made, but, as counsel for the first defendants points out, they are taking a risk and he might not think that, particularly having regard to what was said in the last paragraphs of the two judgments in *Cutts v Head* [1984] 1 All ER 597, [1984] Ch 290. At the close of my judgment in that case, which dealt with the use of what has become known as a *Calderbank* letter in proceedings other than proceedings in the Family Division, I said ([1984] 1 All ER 597 at 610, [1984] Ch 290 at 312):

> 'I would add only one word of caution. The qualification imposed on the without prejudice nature of the *Calderbank* letter is, as I have held, sufficient to enable it to be taken into account on the question of costs; but it should not be thought that this involves the consequence that such a letter can now be used as a substitute for a payment into court, where a payment into court is appropriate. In the case of the simple money claim, a defendant who wishes to avail himself of the protection afforded by an offer must, in the ordinary way, back his offer with cash by making a payment in and, speaking for myself, I should not, as at present advised, be disposed in such a case to treat a *Calderbank* offer as carrying the same consequences as payment in.'

Fox LJ, who was sitting with me, added this at the end of his judgment ([1984] 1 All ER 597 at 613, [1984] Ch 290 at 317):

> 'I should add that I agree with the concluding observations in his [ie my] judgment as to attempts to use the *Calderbank* form as a substitute for payment into court in the case of a simple money claim.'

So the first defendants want it cleared up at this stage, otherwise they may, they say, incur a great many costs which in the event they might have saved if they had gone ahead and actually paid into court. Hence they seek not just an assurance that the letter can properly be brought to the attention of the judge at trial, but a positive order that, when it is brought to his attention, it will be treated exactly as if a payment in had been made.

Counsel for the first defendants argues that such an order is not only sensible but is consistent with recent developments; and, if I may say so, I agree that it may be a very sensible course to take. He has drawn our attention to the decision of this court in *Rosengrens Ltd v Safe Deposit Centres Ltd* [1984] 3 All ER 198, [1984] 1 WLR 1334, where

Sir John Donaldson MR and Parker LJ concurred in holding that, where a defendant was given leave to defend in RSC Ord 14 proceedings on giving security for the plaintiff's claim, such security, so long as adequately provided, ought to be provided in a way which suited the defendant, for instance by an acceptable bond or guarantee, and there was no hard and fast rule that the money must be brought into court. Counsel for the first defendants points out that under RSC Ord 22, r 8 a defendant who has paid in a sum under Ord 14 is enabled to give subsequently a notice to appropriate the payment to particular causes of action so that it then becomes, not merely security, but also an offer, and is to be treated as if it had in fact been paid in not pursuant to Ord 14 but under Ord 22, r 1; and thus, the argument runs, where the security is provided otherwise than by payment in, for instance, as in this case, by a bond, there ought to be devised, and he asks this court to devise for him, an equivalent procedure enabling the defendant to appropriate it and to produce exactly the same consequences as a payment into court under Ord 22, r 1.

For my part, I agree, respectfully, that this might be a very sensible procedure, and it may be that the Rules of Supreme Court are deficient in not providing for this particular case. But the fact is that they do not provide for it, and I cannot think that it is for this court to usurp the function of the Rule Committee by doing without debate and consultation what the Rules of the Supreme Court have not in fact sought to do. I question whether the court has any jurisdiction to make the order which is now sought, which constitutes a sort of interlocutory declaration as to the effect of the letter. Counsel for the first defendants himself accepts that there is certainly no jurisdiction under the rules in express terms, but he relies on an inherent jurisdiction in the court to control its own proceedings. He points to the fact that Ord 33, r 4(a) to some extent has introduced a greater degree of flexibility in relation to pre-trial offers.

I myself do not in fact see why there should be an inherent jurisdiction to make the order of the type he seeks to make. Counsel for the plaintiffs has drawn our attention to the House of Lords decision in *Bremer Vulkan Schiffbau Und Maschinenfabrik v South India Shipping Corp* [1981] 1 All ER 289 at 295, [1981] AC 909 at 977, in which Lord Diplock said:

> 'The power to dismiss a pending action for want of prosecution in cases where to allow the action to continue would involve a substantial risk that justice could not be done is thus properly described as an "inherent power" the exercise of which is within the "inherent jurisdiction" of the High Court. It would I think be conducive to legal clarity if the use of these two expressions were confined to the doing by the court of acts which it needs must have power to do in order to maintain its character as a court of justice.'

I cannot, for my part, see that the sort of order which counsel for the first defendants seeks in this case falls within that classification.

But, even assuming that there is jurisdiction and the court can make such an order, there seems to me to be a very good reason why the recorder was right to decline to exercise it in the case before him. The costs of legal proceedings are by statute left to the discretion of the court, and that discretion is to be exercised in accordance with the rules. One of the matters which may be taken into account, and, indeed, ordinarily would be, is an open offer by the defendant of everything to which the plaintiff ultimately shows himself entitled. Whether, however, such an offer is to be treated for all purposes in the same way as a payment into court must itself be a matter on which the judge of trial will have to make up his own mind in the exercise of his discretion. So far as payment in is concerned, that is specifically dealt with in RSC Ord 62, r 5, which merely provides that such a payment shall to such extent, if any, as may be appropriate in the circumstances be taken into account. But, whether what the judge has before him is an offer or a payment in, the effect of it is left to his discretion. In my judgment, it cannot be right at this stage of the proceedings to direct that the trial judge shall treat a particular transaction as something which it is not in fact. How the transaction is to be treated and what weight should be given to it is a matter for his discretion, and to seek to legislate in advance that it should be treated in a particular way is, as I see it, to usurp that discretion and to usurp it at a time when the circumstances of its exercise have not yet arisen. In my judgment, therefore, the recorder was right in declining to make the order sought by counsel for the first defendants on the grounds of convenience and analogy.

It remains to consider whether his discretion is open to attack on some other ground. We have heard some argument about whether the indorsement of the summons by the plaintiffs' solicitors amounted simply to an intimation of non-opposition or to a binding contract. For my part, I cannot see that it matters, and I am content to assume, as indeed was the recorder, that it did constitute a contract. That, no doubt, may be a material matter for the judge of trial when considering how the costs of the trial should be borne. It no doubt, if substantiated, makes the case for the defendants, assuming that they succeed in resisting the award beyond the sum offered, that much stronger. But it cannot, as I see it, be prayed in aid as conferring on the court some jurisdiction which it does not now have or, assuming such jurisdiction to exist, as compelling the court to make an order which takes the decision of the way in which the transaction is actually to be treated out of the hands of the trial judge.

For these reasons, therefore, I am of the opinion that the recorder came to the right decision. I do not think in fact that the order that he did make for the letter to be brought to the attention of the judge at trial was necessary. As I see it, that could be done in any case, the weight to be attributed to it being simply a matter for that judge's discretion. It seems to me that in rejecting counsel for the first defendants' claim for an order in the terms sought by the summons the recorder was perfectly right, and I would therefore dismiss this appeal.

That leaves only the question of the plaintiffs' cross-notice. Counsel for the plaintiffs seeks an order that the costs of the hearing below should be dealt with in this way, that, the summons being, as he contends, misconceived, those costs should be ordered to be paid by the first defendants in any event. Speaking for myself, I would have much sympathy with that course had it not been for the original hearing which was adjourned as a result of the withdrawal of the consent which had been given, the reasons for which had not been supported by an affidavit by the plaintiffs' solicitors. I think, for my part, that the right order as regards the costs below would have been this, that the first defendants should have in any event the costs of the first hearing, but the costs of the second hearing should be the plaintiffs' in any event. I do not think it is a convenient course for those costs to be reserved to the trial judge, because that merely clutters up the matter when the trial is over and when the circumstances surrounding the summons have largely been lost in the mists of time, and I would therefore propose to vary the judge's order to that extent by ordering that the costs be dealt with in the way I have suggested.

**NEILL J.** I agree. Counsel for the first defendants has rightly drawn our attention to recent developments in the practice of the court which are designed to encourage the settlement of actions. The recognition of what have come to be called *Calderbank* letters (see *Calderbank v Calderbank* [1975] 3 All ER 333, [1976] Fam 93), and the introduction in 1980 of the new RSC Ord 33, r 4(a) are examples. But I share Oliver LJ's doubt whether the court has any power under its inherent jurisdiction to make the order which is sought in the summons in this case. Even if that jurisdiction does exist, however, it seems to me to be quite wrong to make an order which in effect would fetter the discretion of the judge at the trial how the letter of 19 October 1984 should be treated.

I agree that this appeal should be dismissed.

*Appeal dismissed.*

Solicitors: *Wilson & Wilson*, Rushden (for the plaintiffs); *Lovell White & King* (for the first defendants).

Diana Procter    Barrister.

# Thyssen-Bornemisza v Thyssen-Bornemisza

COURT OF APPEAL, CIVIL DIVISION
WALLER, DUNN AND DILLON LJJ
8 NOVEMBER 1984

*Divorce – Practice – Stay of proceedings – Discretionary stay – Jurisdiction to stay proceedings – Wife petitioning for divorce in England – Husband cross-petitioning in England – Ancillary orders made in English proceedings – Wife commencing divorce proceedings in Switzerland and applying for dismissal of petition and stay of cross-petition in English proceedings – Jurisdiction of English court to stay proceedings – Whether 'trial or first trial in any matrimonial proceedings' including proceedings for ancillary relief – Domicile and Matrimonial Proceedings Act 1973, Sch 1, para 9(1).*

*Divorce – Practice – Stay of proceedings – Discretionary stay – Balance of fairness and convenience – Husband petitioning for divorce in Switzerland – Wife commencing divorce proceedings in England – Parties consenting to continue English proceedings – Husband cross-petitioning in England and discontinuing Swiss proceedings – Wife subsequently moving to Switzerland and commencing Swiss proceedings – Wife applying for dismissal of English proceedings and stay of husband's cross-petition – Whether balance of fairness and convenience in favour of stay of English proceedings – Domicile and Matrimonial Proceedings Act 1973, Sch 1, para 9(1).*

*Estoppel – Issue estoppel – Matrimonial proceedings – Husband petitioning for divorce in Switzerland – Wife commencing divorce proceedings in England – Husband applying for stay of English proceedings – Parties consenting to continue English proceedings – Husband cross-petitioning in England and withdrawing Swiss proceedings – Wife subsequently moving to Switzerland and commencing Swiss proceedings – Wife applying for stay of English proceedings – Whether wife estopped from applying for stay of English proceedings.*

The husband commenced divorce proceedings in Switzerland and the wife petitioned for divorce in England. The husband applied for a stay of the wife's English proceedings but in October 1983 the stay was dismissed by consent. The husband then filed an answer and cross-petition in the English proceedings. Subsequently, on the husband's application, the Swiss court struck out his Swiss divorce proceedings. In November 1983, after the wife and the child of the family had left England to reside in Switzerland, the wife applied by summons to stay or dismiss her English petition and her husband's cross-petition. In December interim orders were made in the English proceedings in relation to, inter alia, ancillary relief and the custody and education of the child. In February 1984 the wife commenced divorce proceedings in Switzerland. In April 1984 the wife's summons in the English proceedings was heard. The judge held (i) that she was estopped by the October 1983 order dismissing the husband's application for a stay of her petition from applying for the stay or dismissal of the English proceedings and (ii) that, since the wife had not shown that on the balance of fairness and convenience it was appropriate for her Swiss proceedings to be disposed of before further steps were taken on the husband's cross-petition, he would not exercise his discretion under para 9(1)[a] of Sch 1 to the Domicile and Matrimonial Proceedings Act 1973 to stay the husband's cross-petition. The wife appealed, contending (i) that she was not estopped from applying for dismissal

---

a   Paragraph 9(1), so far as material, provides: 'Where before the beginning of the trial or first trial in any matrimonial proceedings which are continuing in the court it appears to the court—(*a*) that any proceedings in respect of the marriage in question ... are continuing in another jurisdiction; and (*b*) that the balance of fairness (including convenience) as between the parties to the marriage is such that it is appropriate for the proceedings in that jurisdiction to be disposed of before further steps are taken in the proceedings in the court ... the court may then, if it thinks fit, order that the proceedings in the court be stayed ...'

of the English proceedings by reason of the October 1983 order and (ii) that the judge had wrongly exercised his discretion under para 9 of Sch 1 by failing to have regard to the change in circumstances existing in April 1983, in particular her change of residence. The husband contended (i) that in any event the court had no jurisdiction under para 9 of Sch 1 to stay his cross-petition because the discretion to do so was only exercisable 'before ... the trial or first trial in any matrimonial proceedings', which proceedings were to be taken to include the trial of an issue relating to custody or financial relief and therefore the December 1983 hearing, being a first trial in the proceedings, barred the judge from exercising his discretion under para 9, and (ii) that the wife was prevented by the doctrine of election and/or promissory estoppel from seeking to prevent the husband from continuing his cross-petition, since following the wife's election in October 1983 to continue her English proceedings the husband had acted to his detriment by agreeing not to proceed with his application to stay her proceedings in England and in discontinuing his own Swiss proceedings.

**Held** – (1) On the true construction of para 9(1) of Sch 1 to the 1973 Act the words 'trial or first trial in any matrimonial proceedings' related only to the trial of issues in the main suit and not to a hearing relating to custody or ancillary relief. Accordingly, the court had jurisdiction under para 9 to stay the English proceedings if the trial of the main issues between the parties had not commenced, irrespective of whether there had been any proceedings for ancillary relief. Since the main action between the parties had not commenced, and the only proceedings that had taken place in the English court at the time the wife's summons was heard were those for custody and ancillary relief, the judge had had jurisdiction to stay the proceedings in the English court (see p 332 c to g and p 334 e, post).

(2) As a general rule of public policy, where an identifiable issue had been raised and decided against one party, even though by consent, that party was estopped from raising the same issue in subsequent proceedings. On the facts, the issue in the husband's application for a stay in October 1983 was whether, as a matter of discretion, the wife's English petition should be stayed, and that depended on the facts and circumstances as they existed in October 1983, which was the basis on which the order by consent had been made. However, there had been a subsequent change of circumstances in that the wife had left England to reside in Switzerland and her application to stay the English proceedings had been made when she was resident in Switzerland. Accordingly, her application fell to be decided in the light of circumstances different from those existing at the time of the husband's application in October 1983. It followed that there was no issue estoppel barring the wife from making an application to stay (see p 332 h j, p 333 a to c and p 334 e, post); dicta of Diplock LJ in *Thoday v Thoday* [1964] 1 All ER at 352 and of Lord Maugham in *New Brunswick Rly Co v British and French Trust Corp* [1938] 4 All ER at 756 considered.

(3) The doctrines of election and promissory estoppel were not appropriate in opposing an application under para 9(1) of Sch 1 to the 1973 Act for a stay of proceedings in the English courts since all the issues raised as being relevant to those doctrines were equally relevant to the exercise of the court's discretion under para 9, and they were better dealt with as factors affecting the exercise of the court's discretion than as giving rise to those doctrines. Furthermore, the wife had not made an election to continue her English proceedings in October 1983 and nor was there a promissory estoppel (see p 333 f to j and p 334 e, post); *Castanho v Brown & Root (UK) Ltd* [1981] 1 All ER 143 considered.

(4) Since the judge had taken into account all the circumstances of the case and had concluded that fairness required that the English proceedings should continue, there were no grounds for disturbing the judge's exercise of his discretion. The wife's appeal would therefore be dismissed (see p 334 d e, post).

**Notes**

For stay of matrimonial proceedings, see 13 Halsbury's Laws (4th edn) paras 896–899, and for cases on the subject, see 27(2) Digest (Reissue) 711–714, 5486–5512.

For issue estoppel, see 16 Halsbury's Laws (4th edn) para 1530, and for cases on the subject, see 21 Digest (Reissue) 37–64, 232–403.

For the Domicile and Matrimonial Proceedings Act 1973, Sch 1, para 9, see 43 Halsbury's Statutes (3rd edn) 630.

**Cases referred to in judgments**

*Abidin Daver, The* [1984] 1 All ER 470, [1984] 1 AC 398, [1984] 2 WLR 196, HL.

*B (MAL) v B (NE)* [1968] 1 WLR 1109.

*Castanho v Brown & Root (UK) Ltd* [1981] 1 All ER 143, [1981] AC 557, [1980] 3 WLR 991, HL.

*King (formerly Kureishy) v Kureishy* (1982) 13 Fam Law 82, CA.

*New Brunswick Rly Co v British and French Trust Corp* [1938] 4 All ER 747, [1939] AC 1, HL.

*Schira v Schira and Sampajo* (1868) LR 1 P & D 466.

*Shemshadfard v Shemshadfard* [1981] 1 All ER 726.

*Somportex Ltd v Philadelphia Chewing Gum Corp* [1968] 3 All ER 26, CA.

*Thoday v Thoday* [1964] 1 All ER 341, [1964] P 181, [1964] 2 WLR 371, CA.

*Wachtel v Wachtel* [1973] 1 All ER 829, [1973] Fam 72, [1973] 2 WLR 266, CA.

**Cases also cited**

*Bryant v Bryant* (1980) 11 Fam Law 85.

*Carl-Zeiss-Stiftung v Rayner & Keeler Ltd (No 2)* [1966] 2 All ER 536, [1967] 1 AC 853, HL.

*Mytton v Mytton* (1977) 7 Fam Law 244, CA.

*Sennar, The, (No 2)* [1984] 2 Lloyd's Rep 142.

*Volkers v Volkers (Wingate cited)* [1935] P 33.

**Interlocutory appeal**

The petitioner, Baroness Lilian Denise Thyssen-Bornemisza (the wife), appealed against the order of Eastham J dated 9 April 1984 whereby he (i) dismissed the wife's summons dated 30 November 1983 for the petition to be dismissed, (ii) dismissed the wife's summons dated 17 February 1984 for the cross-petition of the respondent, Baron Hans Heinrich Thyssen-Bornemisza (the husband), to be stayed, and (iii) ordered that the wife be restrained from taking any step in any proceedings in respect of or arising out of the marriage of the husband and the wife (save in the English proceedings) either in Switzerland or elsewhere without the prior leave of the court. The facts are set out in the judgment of Dunn LJ.

*Leonard Hoffmann QC, T Scott Baker QC* and *B N Singleton* for the wife.
*Robert Alexander QC, Robert L Johnson QC* and *Paul Coleridge* for the husband.

**DUNN LJ** (giving the first judgment at the invitation of Waller LJ). This is an appeal from an order of Eastham J made on 9 April 1984, whereby he dismissed applications by the wife for her petition to be dismissed, and for the cross-petition to be stayed or dismissed, and ordered that the wife be restrained from taking any step in any proceedings in respect of or arising out of the marriage (save in the English proceedings) either in Switzerland or elsewhere without leave of the court. In order to understand the basis of the judge's findings, it is necessary to set out the principal steps taken by both parties in the proceedings both in England and Switzerland.

11 April 1983: application by husband in Lugano for attempt at reconciliation.

17 June: wife petitions for divorce in London.

21 June: petition by husband in Lugano for provisional financial etc arrangements.

8 July: husband's summons for stay of wife's English petition.

25 October: husband's summons for stay dismissed by consent by Eastham J. Husband files answer and cross-petition. Husband's summons for directions as to education and

custody of child (a boy aged 9). Husband's application for delivery up or transfer of jewellery and other property.

26 October: husband's application to Lugano court to withdraw divorce proceedings.

28 October: order of Lugano court striking out husband's petition.

26 November: wife and child to Zurich.

30 November: wife's application to dismiss her English petition and to stay cross-petition.

1 December: wife commences proceedings for 'protection of the marriage' in Zurich.

2 December: child becomes ward of court by order of Wood J.

6 December: husband's summons for injunction to restrain continuation of 'protection of marriage' proceedings.

15 December: hearing before Eastham J begins.

16 December: interim orders of Eastham J concerning jewellery, directions for hearing wife's summons to dismiss, injunction restraining Swiss 'protection of marriage' proceedings, and as to education of child. Order made continuing wardship and granting care and control to wife.

7 February 1984: wife commences divorce proceedings in Switzerland by filing application for reconciliation.

15 February: wife files divorce petition in Switzerland.

16 February: hearing before Eastham J. Orders concerning jewellery, directions for evidence on summons to dismiss, and injunction restraining wife from continuing divorce proceedings in Switzerland.

3 April: hearing of summons to dismiss begins before Eastham J.

9 April: judgment of Eastham J.

24 May: order of District Court at Meilen that wife's divorce proceedings in Switzerland be discontinued.

The judge held on 9 April that the wife was estopped, by reason of the order of 25 October 1983 dismissing by consent the husband's application for a stay of the English proceedings, from applying for those proceedings to be dismissed. Alternatively he held in the exercise of his discretion that the balance of fairness (including convenience) was not such that it was appropriate for the wife's divorce proceedings in Switzerland to be disposed of before further steps were taken in the husband's cross-petition in England. Accordingly, he refused a stay of the husband's cross-petition, and also refused to dismiss the wife's English petition. In accordance with established practice, since the jurisdiction of the English court depends on the wife's residence in England, he ordered a stay of the wife's petition so that the court might retain jurisdiction and the cause proceed on the husband's cross-petition.

The judge rejected a submission made on behalf of the husband that there was no jurisdiction to grant a stay under para 9 of Sch 1 to the Domicile and Matrimonial Proceedings Act 1973, and this decision is the subject of a respondent's notice. I deal with the point first since it goes to jurisdiction. The question turns on the meaning of the words in para 9 '... before the beginning of the trial or first trial in any matrimonial proceedings'. It was submitted that those words were not confined to a trial or first trial of the suit itself, but were apt to cover the trial of any issue in the proceedings, including the trial of an issue of custody or financial relief. It was said that the hearing in December 1983 of the wife's application for custody, and for directions as to the education of the child, extending as it did over two days with oral evidence, constituted a first trial in the matrimonial proceedings. Accordingly, it was said that since the wife's application to dismiss her petition and stay the husband's cross-petition did not come before the court until after the beginning of that trial, the court had no jurisdiction to consider it.

This is at first sight an attractive submission, especially since there are now very few contested divorce suits, and the issues of children and finance frequently involve contested hearings which have all the characteristics of trials, as that word is commonly understood. It would, on the face of it, be strange if a party could seek the intervention of the court in matters of children or finance, which experience shows are the main subjects of dispute in matrimonial proceedings, and then be entitled to apply to the court under para 9 unless there had been a trial or first trial of the suit itself.

However the question to be decided is what, in 1973, did Parliament mean by the phrase 'trial or first trial in matrimonial proceedings'? I remind myself that the reforms in divorce law were, in 1973, only of comparatively recent date, that *Wachtel v Wachtel* [1973] 1 All ER 829, [1973] Fam 72 had not been decided and that defended divorce suits were still not uncommon. The Matrimonial Causes Rules 1971, SI 1971/953, distinguished, as do the Matrimonial Causes Rules 1977, SI 1977/344, as amended, between 'trial' of the cause and hearing of applications for ancillary relief and custody. The word 'trial' was and is used exclusively in relation to the former. Moreover, the court had power, now contained in r 45 of the 1977 rules, to give directions 'for the separate trial of an issue'. These words are picked up in para 4(1) of Sch 1, which provides that: 'References to the trial or first trial in any proceedings do not include references to the separate trial of an issue as to jurisdiction only.' Preliminary issues as to the validity of marriage, or as to paternity, are not uncommon in divorce proceedings, and were even more common in 1973.

But in my judgment the decisive factor which leads me to the conclusion that the words in question relate only to trials of issues in the main suit, and not to hearings relating to custody or ancillary relief, is the wording of para 11, which was strongly relied on by counsel for the wife. The effect of that paragraph is that orders for maintenance pending suit, periodical payments for children, custody of children, and orders restraining the removal of children (relevant orders) made in connection with stayed proceedings, shall cease to have effect on the expiration of three months from the date of the stay. Paragraph 11 therefore envisages that such orders may have been made before the imposition of the stay, and the implication is irresistible that the hearing of an application for a relevant order cannot have been intended to be a 'trial or first trial' within the meaning of para 9. If it were otherwise, the court would have had no power to impose a stay, and para 11 would be otiose.

Counsel for the wife submitted, and I accept, that this construction of the words is not only in accordance with the provisions of Sch 1 read as a whole, but is also good sense. There may be cases in which, as a matter of urgency, the party opposing the stay applies for an order relating to children. Such application might involve a contested hearing. The party seeking a stay would be gravely prejudiced if, by opposing the application, he was held to be debarred from his application for a stay because there had been a 'first trial' in the proceedings. For those reasons in my judgment the judge was right to accept jurisdiction under para 9.

The wife appeals against the judge's finding that she was estopped from applying for dismissal of the husband's cross-petition by reason of his withdrawal in October 1983 of his application for a stay of her petition in England. The judge held that the real issue before the court in October 1983 was whether Switzerland or England was the appropriate forum, that that issue was decided by consent in favour of England, and that the wife's unilateral decision to leave England in November did not entitle her to avoid the estoppel in relation to her application before him, which raised precisely the same issue.

As Diplock LJ said in *Thoday v Thoday* [1964] 1 All ER 341 at 352, [1964] P 181 at 197–198, issue estoppel is an extension of the rule of public policy expressed by the Latin maxim nemo debet bis vexari pro una et eadem causa. So where an identifiable issue has been raised and decided against one party, even though by consent, that party cannot raise the same issue in subsequent proceedings. He is estopped from so doing (see *B (MAL) v B (NE)* [1968] 1 WLR 1109). In *New Brunswick Rly Co v British and French Trust Corp* [1938] 4 All ER 747 at 756, [1939] AC 1 at 21 Lord Maugham said:

'The true principle in such a case [a default judgment] would seem to be that the defendant is estopped from setting up in a subsequent action a defence which was necessarily and with complete precision decided by the previous judgment.'

In the instant case, the broad question was whether, as a matter of discretion, the wife's English petition should be stayed. That question depended on the facts and circumstances as they existed in October (see *Shemshadfard v Shemshadfard* [1981] 1 All ER 726 at 735 per Purchas J). The order was made by consent on that basis. Thereafter there was a change of circumstances. The wife left England in November 1983 and went to live in Switzerland. The judge found that in April 1984 she genuinely desired to live in Switzerland, and that it was her intention to reside there. In those circumstances it seems to me, with respect to the judge, that there was no issue estoppel. All that had been decided in October was that in the circumstances as they then existed the proceedings should continue in England. That was the only issue that was decided necessarily and with complete precision, to paraphrase the words of Lord Maugham in the *New Brunswick Rly Co* case. In April 1984 the wife's application fell to be decided in the light of the different circumstances which then existed. Accordingly in my judgment the wife succeeds on the question of issue estoppel.

By the respondent's notice it was alleged that if issue estoppel had no application, then the wife was prevented by the doctrine of election and/or promissory estoppel from seeking to prevent the husband from continuing his cross-petition in England. Counsel for the husband referred us to *Somportex Ltd v Philadelphia Chewing Gum Corp* [1968] 3 All ER 26, *King (formerly Kureishy) v Kureishy* (1982) 13 Fam Law 82 and *Schira v Schira and Sampajo* (1865) LR 1 P & D 466. He submitted that in this case the wife, after competent legal advice which distinguished the case from *Castanho v Brown & Root (UK) Ltd* [1981] 1 All ER 143, [1981] AC 557, had made the deliberate election to seek continuance of her English proceedings. As a result of that election, the husband had acted to his detriment in agreeing not to proceed with his application to stay the proceedings here, and in obtaining a 'desistement' of his own proceedings in Switzerland. It mattered not, said counsel for the husband, whether the case was one of election or promissory estoppel, or whether her application to stay the husband's cross-petition was an abuse of the process of the court. Whatever jurisprudential label was attached, the wife ought not to be allowed to change her mind.

In my judgment there was no election in this case in the sense in which the word has been used in the cases cited by counsel for the husband, that is to say, an election between inconsistent remedies, and there was no promissory estoppel. I find the case indistinguishable in principle from *Castanho v Brown & Root*. The wife commenced proceedings here and then, as in *Castanho*'s case, sought to discontinue those proceedings and proceed in another jurisdiction. The ratio decidendi of *Castanho*'s case was that to restrain the plaintiff from proceeding in Texas would deprive him of a legitimate personal juridical advantage, notwithstanding that he had originally commenced proceedings in England, and had received interim payments here. *King v Kureishy* could have been decided on the ground of issue estoppel, since in the previous proceedings the husband had withdrawn his assertion that the marriage had been dissolved by talaq, and had consented to the wife obtaining a decree on her cross-petition. No such precise issue had been decided in the instant case.

With respect to the submissions of counsel for the husband on this part of the case, I do not think that notions of estoppel or election are appropriate in opposing applications under para 9. All the issues raised as being relevant to those matters are equally relevant to the exercise of the judge's discretion under the paragraph. And they are better dealt with as factors affecting the exercise of discretion than as giving rise to doctrines of estoppel or election.

I turn finally to the wife's appeal against the exercise by the judge of his discretion under para 9. Counsel for the wife submitted that in reaching his decision, and refusing a stay of the husband's cross-petition, the judge erred in principle because he failed to have regard to the circumstances as they existed in April 1984, which was the relevant date, although he conceded that the history was also relevant. Since the wife was now living in Switzerland, counsel for the wife said that this was a case of a Swiss marriage, with a principal matrimonial home in Switzerland during the marriage, both parties now being mainly resident in Switzerland and of Swiss nationality, the child being educated in Switzerland, and a case in which Swiss law as to the disposition of chattels would be relevant. Counsel said that the judge was plainly wrong in holding, notwithstanding all those factors, that the balance of fairness tipped in favour of the husband because he had abandoned his application to stay the English proceedings, and had allowed 'desistement' of his Lugano proceedings, and had thereby suffered prejudice in Switzerland and loss of time and money.

The circumstances in which this court can interfere with the discretion of a judge are well established, and have been recently stated by Lord Brandon in *The Abidin Daver* [1984] 1 All ER 470 at 482–483, [1984] 1 AC 398 at 420–421. It was not suggested that the judge did not properly direct himself by reference to para 9. He considered with care the submission that Switzerland was the matrimonial home of the parties, taking into account that the wife's connection with England had gone, and thereby considering the situation as it stood in April 1984. But taking all those matters into account, he reached the firm conclusion that fairness required that the English proceedings should continue on the cross-petition, having regard to the acceptance by the husband in 1983 of the wife's preference for England as a forum, and the prejudice which he had suffered as a result. The judge also emphasised the time which would be lost if the English proceedings were now stayed, and the husband was, some 18 months after his original application in Lugano, obliged to commence proceedings again in Switzerland.

I find it quite impossible to be satisfied that in carrying out the balancing exercise in the way in which he did, the judge fell into error. He took into account all the relevant factors and there was ample evidence, which it is unnecessary to recite, to support the view which he formed. I would accordingly dismiss this appeal.

**DILLON LJ.** I agree.

**WALLER LJ.** I also agree.

*Appeal dismissed. Leave to appeal to the House of Lords refused.*

Solicitors: *Norton Rose Botterell & Roche* (for the wife); *Herbert Smith & Co* (for the husband).

Frances Rustin    Barrister.

# London Congregational Union Inc v Harriss & Harriss (a firm)

QUEEN'S BENCH DIVISION (OFFICIAL REFEREES' BUSINESS)
HIS HONOUR JUDGE JOHN NEWEY QC
14, 15, 16, 17 NOVEMBER 1983

*Limitation of action – When time begins to run – Actions in tort – Accrual of cause of action – Negligence – Damage – Lapse of time between negligent act and occurrence of damage – Action against architects in respect of negligent design and supervision of construction of buildings – Buildings completed outside limitation period – Damage occurring within limitation period – Whether buildings doomed from the start – Whether limitation period running from date when damage occurred or date when buildings completed.*

*Damages – Assessment – Date at which damages assessed – Repairs to buildings – Negligent design and supervision of construction of buildings – Material difference between cost of repairs at date of defendants' negligent act and date when plaintiffs could reasonably have carried out repairs – Plaintiffs not carrying out repairs after damage occurring because of financial difficulties and defendants' non-admission of liability – Whether reasonable for plaintiffs not to have carried out repairs earlier.*

In 1969 the plaintiffs employed the defendants, a firm of architects, to design and supervise the construction of a church and church hall, which the plaintiffs planned to use to hold meetings and to let out to other bodies. Practical completion of the buildings was achieved in January 1970 and final completion by the end of 1970. On 3 August 1971 the buildings were flooded when heavy rainfall caused the sewer in the street adjacent to the church hall to overflow, with resulting damage to the buildings. Further damage was caused by damp penetrating through the brickwork of the basement of the hall to the surface plaster because the defendants had failed to insert damp-proof courses. By mid-1975 flooding of the hall had occurred on eleven occasions and the plaintiffs ceased to use the hall after 4 August 1978. The plaintiffs did not consider themselves in a position to undertake repairs, and in fact did not do so, because of financial difficulties and the fact that the defendants were denying liability. The plaintiffs issued a writ against the defendants on 18 February 1977 claiming damages for negligence in the design and supervision of the construction of the buildings. The damages claimed included economic loss stemming from the loss of rental income as well as the cost of carrying out remedial works to the buildings. By their defence the defendants denied negligence and pleaded that the building was 'doomed from the start' and therefore the plaintiffs' cause of action had accrued when it was erected, which was more than six years before the writ was issued, and that accordingly their action was statute-barred by the Limitation Act 1939.

**Held** – (1) The defendants, by failing to apply their minds properly either to the safety of the drainage system they adopted or to the consideration of possible alternative methods of drainage, had failed to exercise the proper skill and care expected of professional architects and were accordingly liable to the plaintiffs for the damage to the buildings caused by their negligence (see p 31 *f* to *j*, post)

(2) The plaintiffs' cause of action, so far as it related to the flooding of the buildings, accrued when damage occurred to the buildings, which was on 3 August 1971 when the first flooding occurred. The buildings were not 'doomed from the start', since it could not be said that the situation was one in which there was never any hope for the buildings, or in which nothing could be done to save them. Although the sewer was capable of causing damage, the buildings remained and action could be taken to prevent the flooding (see p 343 *c d*, post); dictum of Diplock LJ in *Bagot v Stevens Scanlan & Co* [1964] 3 All ER at 579, *Batty v Metropolitan Property Realizations Ltd* [1978] 2 All ER 445 and

dicta of Lord Fraser in *Pirelli General Cable Works Ltd v Oscar Faber & Partners (a firm)* [1983] 1 All ER at 70, 72 considered.

(3) The damage caused by the lack of provision of damp-proof courses would not have occurred until damp reached the surface plaster and, since the evidence was inconclusive whether that damage occurred within or outside the limitation period, it followed that the defendants had failed to discharge the burden resting on them of proving that the plaintiffs' claim was statute-barred. Accordingly, the plaintiffs' claim was not statute-barred in relation to the lack of provision of damp-proof courses (see p 343 g to j, post).

(4) Although as a general rule damages fell to be assessed as at the date of the defendant's wrongful act, since there was a material difference between the cost of repairs at the date of the defendants' negligent act and the date when repairs could first reasonably have been undertaken, the plaintiffs' damages fell to be assessed at the rates prevailing at the latter date. Having regard to all the circumstances, the plaintiffs had acted reasonably in deciding not to have repairs carried out during the years 1977 to 1982 because of internal financial difficulties and the fact that the defendants were denying liability. However, the plaintiffs had been guilty of 18 months' delay in bringing the case to trial, and damages would therefore be assessed on the basis that the case should have been tried in 1982 and at the rates for repair current at that time (see p 344 a b and g to j, post); *Dodd Properties (Kent) Ltd v Canterbury City Council* [1980] 1 All ER 928 applied.

### Notes

For when a limitation period begins to run, see 28 Halsbury's Laws (4th edn) paras 622–623, and for cases on the subject, see 32 Digest (Reissue) 486–487, 503–509, 3737–3745, 3842–3869.

For the Limitation Act 1939, see 19 Halsbury's Statutes (3rd edn) 60.

As from 1 May 1981 the 1939 Act has been replaced by the Limitation Act 1980.

### Cases referred to in judgement

*Bagot v Stevens Scanlan & Co* [1964] 3 All ER 577, [1966] 1 QB 197, [1964] 3 WLR 1162.

*Batty v Metropolitan Property Realizations Ltd* [1978] 2 All ER 445, [1978] 1 QB 554, [1978] 2 WLR 500, CA.

*Cavendish Land (Metropolitan) Ltd v Tozer Kemsley Millbourne (Holdings) Ltd* (5 May 1983, unreported), QBD.

*Chelmsford DC v J J Evers Ltd* [1983] Construction Industry Law Letter 39.

*Dodd Properties (Kent) Ltd v Canterbury City Council* [1980] 1 All ER 928, [1980] 1 WLR 433, CA.

*Pirelli General Cable Works Ltd v Oscar Faber & Partners (a firm)* [1983] 1 All ER 65, [1983] 2 AC 1, [1983] 2 WLR 6, HL.

### Action

By a writ issued on 18 February 1977 the plaintiffs, London Congregational Union Inc, claimed against the defendants, Harriss & Harriss (a firm), damages for breach of contract and/or negligence in respect of the inadequate and deficient design of a church and hall which the defendants, as architects, had been employed by the plaintiffs to design and supervise during contruction. The facts are set out in the judgment.

*Richard Fernyhough* for the plaintiffs.
*Bruce Coles* for the defendants.

**HIS HONOUR JUDGE JOHN NEWEY QC.** In this case the plaintiffs by their statement of claim alleged that in 1969 they employed the defendants to design and supervise the construction of the new Congregational church and hall at East Finchley, that it was a term of the contract that the defendants would exercise the care and skill to be expected of an ordinary, competent architect, and that in breach of contract and/or negligently the defendants produced a design which was inadequate and defective, so that since August 1971 the hall and the church have suffered from damp, the basements have flooded and the plaintiffs have not been able to use the hall. The plaintiffs claimed continuing loss of rental in respect of the hall and the cost of carrying out remedial works. The defendants by their defence admitted that they were employed by the plaintiffs and the term alleged by the plaintiffs but they made no other admissions. The defendants pleaded that the action is statute-barred and, inter alia, they alleged that any damp penetration was due to the inadequacy of the local borough council's main sewer.

Although the plaintiffs bear the title London Congregational Union, they are in fact the members of the East Finchley United Reformed Church, previously the East Finchley Congregational Church. It is a church which has, so I have been told by Mr Meur, its treasurer, about 40 members and average attendances at services on a Sunday of about 20.

The defendants are a firm of architects and, most unfortunately, both of the partners who were in the firm at material times are dead. This action has been defended in their names with the consent of their insurers.

The plaintiffs used to own land to the north of East End Road in East Finchley, on which there stood a church and a church hall, both of them, judging from a plan which is before me, substantial buildings. It would seem that early in the 1960s the plaintiffs decided that they would demolish their existing church and hall, that they would sell part of their land and that on what remained they would build a new church and new hall with ancillary accommodation and make provision for car parking. They hoped that after paying for the new buildings out of the proceeds of sale of the land sold they would still be left with a largish sum and that interest on it would help to support the church. By a letter of 5 May 1962 the plaintiffs requested the defendants to act as architects for the redevelopment of the plaintiffs' premises, and the defendants replied, agreeing to act. Various meetings took place between representatives of the plaintiffs and the defendants and various plans were prepared; there were discussions with the local planning authority.

In order to be able to sell as much land as possible the plaintiffs decided to concentrate their new buildings and a scheme was prepared for them by the defendants, which provided for the new church to be placed on top of the new hall. This involved excavation to a depth of about six feet, the building of the new hall and ancillary buildings, and on top of them the church with ancillary buildings. Three small areas on the north side of the hall and a larger area on its south side would not be built on, but would be paved, and there would be a wall all round the whole of the excavated area.

The hall and church were to be substantial buildings. The hall was to be 60 ft by 30 ft and 12 ft high and the church was to be of similar dimensions. The church would be reached by going up a short flight of steps and the hall would be reached by going down short flights of steps. Four flights down were contemplated, three on the north side and one on the south side. The details of the design which the defendants prepared and which the plaintiffs approved are shown on two plans which are before me and which are dated 1968. In fact, before those plans were prepared, namely on 15 November 1967, Barnet Borough Council gave outline planning permission for the new buildings. On the day after Barnet gave their premission the borough planning officer wrote a letter to the defendants, the last paragraph of which reads:

> 'The lower ground floor of the proposed hall may be critical if gravity drainage of surface water is envisaged and you are advised to consult the borough engineer and surveyor thereon.'

The paragraph is not clearly written: 'may be critical' might have meant 'may be in a critical position if gravity drainage is envisaged', or might have meant simply that the distance between the buildings and the sewer would be relatively short. I do not think that too much importance should be attached to that letter, but it contained a note of warning given to the defendants.

The defendants wrote to the borough engineer on 18 December 1967:

'We shall be obliged if you will kindly let us know the depths of the soil and surface water sewers in East End Road at its approximate junction with Market Place. Perhaps you will also inform us if the sewers are on the church side of the road or on the opposite side.'

The borough engineer replied on 15 January 1968 enclosing a sketch plan of the sewers in the vicinity of the Congregational Church and bearing the usual disclaimer as to the accuracy of the information provided. The plan showed a sewer in East End Road on the side nearest to the Congregational Church. By 'sewer' I mean surface water sewer. There were a number of manholes in it and the invert of the one nearest to the church was at a depth of eight feet. There were other manholes to east and west of that manhole which each went down to a depth of nine feet. It is clear that on the last day of January 1968 one of the defendants went to see the borough engineer. I say that because there is a letter of 1 February 1968 in which one of the defendants wrote to the borough engineer saying:

'It was kind of you to see me at short notice yesterday and very helpful. I am enclosing a set of plans [presumably an earlier edition of the 1968 plans] as arranged and would appreciate your informal advice as to whether any radical amendments are necessary before their submission formally for bylaw approval.'

Then the letter went on to ask about road widths and the possibility of road widening.

On 13 February the borough engineer replied. He had obviously examined the plans and he raised various questions with regard to them. One asked that sections should be given through the drains or else the invert at ground level of each manhole shown. The gradient of the drains should be indicated on the plan. He went on to say that the gulley should be of a roddable type and there was also a reference to foul sewage.

The defendants replied to the engineer's queries on 16 May and there followed a grant of building regulation permission for the proposed new buildings and for the connections which the defendants proposed to the public sewer, or I should say sewers, though I am concerned only with the surface water sewer in this case. The defendants did not ask in writing specifically whether the sewer was adequate, but it is possible that they may have done so at their meeting with the borough engineer. When I say 'adequate' I mean 'unlikely to surcharge' or at least 'unlikely to surcharge very often'.

I have had expert evidence from two admirable witnesses: Mr Allerton, called by the plaintiffs, and Mr Melvin, called by the defendants. Mr Allerton said in effect that all or practically all sewers surcharge sometimes because the cost of providing sewers so large as never to surcharge would be excessive. Mr Melvin thought that a sewer should be regarded as adequate if it surcharged, say, once in every five to ten years.

If the defendants did ask orally whether the surface water sewer was adequate or, if by applying for permission to connect to it, they should be regarded as having done so by implication there is no direct evidence that they asked anything more, such as 'Is this sewer so satisfactory that the chance of its surcharging really are minute, or very slight indeed?' and I do not think that I can infer that they did.

The actual proposal which the defendants had submitted to the borough for dealing with the surface water which collected on the open staircases leading down to the areas six feet below ground level and in the areas themselves consisted of gulleys connected by pipes to the sewer. Originally the pipe size proposed was four inches while the sewer itself had a nine inch diameter. The depth of the sewer below the lowest point of the areas was about 3 ft 6 in. The fall from the gulleys to the sewer was conventional and no one has suggested that it was other than satisfactory.

It seems to me that the defendants' plans for the hall and church were of an imaginative character. I have seen photographs of the building and they certainly indicate that it was pleasing in appearance, while the plans of them show a building which would I think have been functionally satisfactory. Unhappily there was one defect in the design about which there is no doubt at all, as during the course of the trial it was admitted by the defendants, and that is that the staircases leading down to the lower level were set into the walls of the building, which were made of 14-inch brickwork with cement mortar in between and had on their inner faces, in the hall for instance, carlite plaster. There was no damp-proof course provided between the staircases and the brickwork, so that moisture could penetrate.

What is not agreed is that the method of disposing of surface water from the steps and areas to the sewer was in any way defective, although it is clear that that method of disposing of surface water contained no safeguard against the sewer surcharging. In other words, if the sewer became overloaded the water, instead of flowing from the areas into the sewer, would flow from the sewer back through the pipes, and there was nothing to prevent that water, having reached the areas and flooded them to the height of the step to the hall, about six inches, from entering the hall. The hall floor was of wood blocks and beneath the floor was electrical under floor heating. As I have already said the plaster was carlite and that is, of course, a type of plaster which holds water.

The plans were generally approved by the plaintiffs but the technical details were not their concern. Builders were instructed, but shortly after they had commenced work, the defendants varied the plans by enlarging the size of the drains leading to the sewer from four inches to six inches. It would seem that the builders were slow about their work. At any rate, it was not till January 1970 that what might be described as practical completion was achieved. On 11 January 1970 a Miss Nichol, the lady who dealt with the building works on behalf of the plaintiffs, wrote an appreciative letter to the defendants. On 26 January 1970 a letter was written apparently on behalf of the plaintiffs (I have only part of it and I do not know who signed it) to the defendants listing incomplete works and complaints. One item read: 'Efflorescence on the walls of the toilet off church vestibule.' Since the church vestibule was up in the air, because the church is six feet above ground level, the entry was I think of no significance for present purposes.

On 17 February Miss Nichol sent to the defendants what she described as a rather formidable list of items, which had been found to require attention. Among these were four to which I will refer. One of them, numbered 16, reads: 'Very bad dampness in church toilet and hall cloakroom and toilets.' Number 17 reads: 'Dampness in minister's vestry.' Number 18 reads: 'Dampness on outside wall at steps down to hall.' Number 28 reads: 'Large puddle forms in front of main church doors. Puddles also on side steps.' 'Very bad dampness in church toilet' must in substance be a repetition of the complaint contained in the letter of 26 January. The remainder of no 16 is complaining of damp in rooms at the hall level six feet down, which, as I can see from looking at the plans, are adjacent to staircases. Number 17 concerned the minister's vestry, which was at church level, and was apparently due to some trouble with a downpipe. Item 18 refers to a part of the wall, which had steps against it. 'Puddles . . . on side steps' is an indication that there was, as might be expected, water on the stairs.

Miss Nichol is alive and is preaching this Sunday, so I have been told. She was not called as a witness and I have therefore no evidence whether the damp disappeared, whether it remained or what happened in the various locations.

The plaintiffs hoped that they would be able to let their church hall when they did not require it for use themselves and so obtain substantial profits. Mr Meur, the treasurer, told me that they were hopeful of letting not just to charities, from whom they exact little or no hiring charge, but also to commercial concerns, who might want to mount exhibitions and the like, and for wedding receptions to people who were not members of their own church and from whom they would feel justified in exacting very substantial hiring fees. He said that they had been able to let their previous hall for these purposes and they were anxious to do the same with the new hall, but that by August 1971 they had not worked out a letting policy and no lettings had taken place, other than a letting to a play group run on commercial lines. That was a letting for use during mornings four or five days a week.

On 3 August 1971 disaster occurred. There had been some fairly heavy rain. The sewer in the street had obviously filled with water and it surcharged, water came up the pipes into the areas round the church hall, rose higher and flowed into the hall. On 4 August the water went down a certain amount, but then it came up again and there was something like a fountain at one of the gulleys. The result was that the wood block floors of the hall lifted and shrank and were otherwise seriously affected. The under-floor heating was put out of action, at least temporarily, and the plaster was damaged. As might be expected in the circumstances the plaintiffs called the defendants back to find out what had happened and to do something about it. The defendants obtained information as to the rainfall and they complained to the borough about the sewer. The borough replied in a letter on 18 January 1972 which read:

'I would refer to your letter of 22 December 1971. An examination of the surface water sewers in that area is being carried out, but the drain outlet from the church hall is at a low level with very little fall to the sewer, consequently a slight surcharge during a severe storm is likely to affect the basement.'

That was pointing out what I suppose must have been obvious all along, namely that if the sewer was going to surcharge, so that water had to escape from it, the water was going to escape by the easiest route. Water would rise in the manholes, but because of their depth, would have to rise to eight feet or more before it would flow out of the tops of them, but, on the other hand, the gulleys were only 3 ft 6 in above the sewer and would so provide an exit for water from it long before the manholes would do so. In effect what the defendants had created was really a large tank in which the church hall was situated, which could act as a relief area, a sort of balancing tank for the sewer in the event of it surcharging.

In the months that followed the defendants seem to have gone on pressing the borough to do something about it. They do not seem to have put forward any proposals of their own. Fortunately, the plaintiffs' insurers, who were apparently closely linked with the Congregational Church (the amalgamation of the Congregational and Presbyterian Churches to form the United Reformed Church had not then occurred), were sympathetic and they paid out in respect of all this damage, so that the hall was made good. The costs paid by the insurance company are not part of the claim which is before me today. The insurance company have not sought indemnification.

Further flooding occurred from time to time. A serviette found in one of the defendants' files bears references to the surcharging and also to silting in the sewer, but the dates are not clear. At any rate, by mid-1975 it would seem that there had been flooding of the hall on eleven occasions. The flooding of 1975 was the worst and it was to a depth of two feet and the plaster within the hall was damaged to a height of about three feet.

The borough ceased to be the sewerage authority. A water board became the authority, but the borough acted as its agent. As agent the borough installed what are called non-return valves in manholes at the sewer ends of the plaintiffs' pipes. The purpose of such valves is to prevent water from flowing back through them. It is a sort of one-way street provision for water. Unfortunately, so I was told, such valves can easily become wedged open by material which gets into the surface water sewer and, being at the bottom of the manholes, the tops of which were in the street, the plaintiffs had no right to maintain the valves; in any event it is unlikely that members of the congregation would have welcomed clambering down manholes. At any rate the non-return valves did not work and further flooding occurred. The plaintiffs made gates to the doors of the hall, which they fitted before leaving the hall unattended. The gates were to a height of two feet, were wedged in position, and were not able to keep out water effectively, but at least they helped. Since 1975, apart from the play group, the hall has not been used at all. Fairly recently some members of the congregation have themselves carried out some redecoration of the hall, but apart from that nothing much has been done to it.

In 1976 the plaintiffs went to solicitors and on 18 February 1977 a writ was issued against the defendants. It follows that the relevant date for the purpose of deciding whether the plaintiffs' claims are barred or not by the Limitation Act 1939 is 18 February 1971. The defendants denied liability and, until this trial began, the denial of negligence extended to the lack of damp-proof course adjacent to the stairs, as well as to what I will call the flooding. The plaintiffs have not taken any positive steps to have remedial work carried out or to prevent flooding at any time since 1977. I will deal with their reasons for not taking action later in this judgment.

This case has been before me on a previous occasion, when an application was made to strike out the plaintiffs' writ on the ground that there had been inordinate delay in the conduct of the proceedings. On that occasion I decided that the culpable delay amounted to 18 months and I declined to dismiss the plaintiffs' action. I understand there was an application to the Court of Appeal for leave to appeal from my decision, but that it was rejected.

The defendant's contractual obligations to the plaintiffs in respect of the building of the hall lasted until the hall was completed, and the hall must have reached practical completion early in 1970 and final completion at some date towards the end of 1970. The defendants' contractual obligations must therefore have come to an end well before 18 February 1971 and there is no possibility of the plaintiffs being able to succeed in claims that the defendants were guilty of breach of contract. Indeed, counsel for the plaintiffs has not sought to persuade me to the contrary.

I think the first issue for me to consider is whether or not the defendants were negligent in respect of the arrangements, or lack of arrangements, which gave rise to the flooding. The position has to be considered as it was at the time when the defendants were designing and superintending the building of the church and church hall. It is easy to be wise with hindsight, but what I have got to do is to consider whether they failed to exercise reasonable care at that time. Their design provided for the hall to be placed at a depth of six feet below ground level. It provided for areas surrounding the hall from which water could not flow away save through gulleys. The design made the hall a vulnerable building; the wood blocks, the under-floor heating, even the plaster were peculiarly vulnerable to water damage. The sewer into which they were proposing to drain was only 3ft 6in below the level of the areas. The nearest manhole was eight feet deep, others were nine feet deep. In those circumstances it seems to me that the defendants should have applied their minds to the question whether they could safely drain water which accumulated on the steps and the areas into the sewer in the manner which they did, or whether some other method of dealing with drainage should have been adopted, or whether they should have revised their whole design and perhaps put the hall at ground level with the church on top of it, or adopted some other design approach altogether. It seems to me obvious that they did not apply their minds to the problem at all or as fully as they should.

I am willing to assume in their favour (because, after all, they are both dead and I do not know what was said between one of them and the borough engineer) that he asked: 'Will a surcharge occur from this sewer?' and received a reply to the effect: 'Well, it does not happen very often', but I cannot possibly assume in their favour that they obtained an assurance that the capacity of a nine-inch sewer was such that there would never be surcharging from it. East Finchley is a residential area, built up to a large degree, with a substantial amount of land covered by impervious surfaces, and the run-off into the surface water sewers is bound to be substantial. I think that the defendants should have given thought to the problem and that if they had done so they could not possibly have adopted the method of dealing with the drainage which they did. They did not even insert non-return valves.

I have mentioned some of the alternatives open to them. Yet another would have been, as is now proposed, to have covered the stairs and areas with some form of roofing, so that water could not collect on them. If, contrary to my belief, they did consider the problem, they were the more at fault in adopting the solution which they did. I have no hesitation in holding that the defendants failed to exercise proper skill and care and must be held liable in negligence in respect of the flooding.

The second issue is whether the plaintiffs' action is statute-barred. I am going to take first 'flooding'. Counsel for the defendants submitted that time began to run in relation to the drainage from the date when the building was completed, which, as I have already said, was before 18 February 1971. He referred me to the very well-known case of *Pirelli General Cable Works Ltd v Oscar Faber & Partners (a firm)* [1983] 1 All ER 65, [1983] 2 AC 1, in which the House of Lords laid down the general rule that the date of accrual of a cause of action in tort for damage caused by the negligent design or construction of a building is the date when the damage came into existence, and not the date when the damage was discovered or should with reasonable diligence have been discovered. Counsel for the defendants referred in particular to two passages in the speech of Lord Fraser, with which all the other members of the House of Lords agreed. The first passage reads ([1983] 1 All ER 65 at 70, [1983] 2 AC 1 at 16):

'There may perhaps be cases where the defect is so gross that the building is doomed from the start, and where the owner's cause of action will accrue as soon as it is built, but it seems unlikely that such a defect would not be discovered within the limitation period. Such cases, if they exist, would be exceptional.'

The other passage is ([1983] 1 All ER 65 at 72, [1983] 2 AC 1 at 18):

'It seems to me that, except perhaps where the advice of an architect or consulting engineer leads to the erection of a building which is so defective as to be doomed from the start, the cause of action accrues only when physical damage occurs to the building.'

On the basis of those passages counsel for the defendants submitted that as an exception to the general rule time begins to run from completion of a building when it is such as to be doomed from the start.

Counsel for the defendants also referred me to a dictum of Diplock LJ in *Bagot v Stevens Scanlan & Co* [1964] 3 All ER 577 at 579, [1966] 1 QB 197 at 203. In his judgment Diplock LJ, who was sitting at first instance on that occasion, said, obiter:

'I said at the outset that I found some difficulty in that admission, because it seems to me that, having regard to the nature of the duty which is alleged to have been breached in this case, in effect, to see that the drains were properly designed and built, the damage from any breach of that duty must have occurred at the time when the drains were improperly built, because the plaintiff at that time was landed with property which had bad drains when he ought to have been provided with property which had good drains, and the damage, accordingly, occurred on that date.'

Counsel for the defendants submitted that this is a case in which time began to run from the completion of the building because it was 'doomed from the start'.

Counsel for the plaintiffs agreed that buildings doomed from the start constituted an exception to the general rule, but submitted that the exception was a very narrow one. He said that the source of the description 'doomed' was to be found in *Batty v Metropolitan Property Realizations Ltd* [1978] 2 All ER 445, [1978] 1 QB 554. In that case a house had been built on a hill which was subject to landslip so that, although the house was wholly unaffected at the time when the action was brought, it was plain from the evidence that within ten years it would have slipped down the hill and been totally destroyed, so that, although unaffected, it was quite unsaleable. Megaw LJ said ([1978] 2 All ER 445 at 449–450, [1978] 1 QB 554 at 562):

'The gravity of that litigation, its seriousness for the parties, will become apparent when I recount that it was held by Crichton J, from whose judgment this appeal is brought, that the plaintiffs' house is doomed; and the finding on that issue, although it was the subject of much conflicting evidence at the trial, is not now disputed or challenged.'

In fact *Batty* was not mentioned in any of the speeches in *Pirelli*, but it was cited in argument and Lord Fraser may well have had it in mind.

Certainly I think that by 'doomed from the start' Lord Fraser meant what might be described as a '*Batty* situation': one in which there was never any hope for the building or the part of it the subject of the action; nothing practicable could be done to save it. This was the view I took in an interlocutory matter, *Chelmsford DC v J J Evers Ltd* [1983] Construction Industry Law Letter 39, in which roofs were liable to blow off at any moment. I think it accords with the decision of his Honour Judge Sir William Stabb QC in *Cavendish Land (Metropolitan) Ltd v Tozer Kemsley Millbourne (Holdings) Ltd* (5 May 1983, unreported) which concerned an air-conditioning system, so defective that it never worked. I doubt whether today *Bagot* would be regarded as a 'doomed from the start' case.

I do not think that in this present case the church and hall, with ancillary buildings, various pipes and the like, could possibly be described as doomed from the start. At worst, surcharging of the sewer could cause water to enter the areas and hall, and cause damage. But the building itself remained and action could and can be taken to prevent the sort of flooding which has occurred. I think that in this case the plaintiffs' cause of action must have accrued at the date when the first flooding took place, namely on 3 August 1971. So, so far as the plaintiffs' claim relates to flooding, I do not think it is statute-barred.

I turn to the lack of damp proof-course. The letter of 26 January 1970 referred to efflorescence on the walls of the toilet and the church vestibule, locations which could not be affected by the lack of damp-proof courses. In the list of 17 February, there was reference to 'very bad dampness' but at the same places.

Disregarding the minister's vestry, dampness in the other places referred to in the list, namely the hall, cloakroom and toilets and the outside wall of the steps down to the hall, could be attributed to lack of damp-proof courses, but could equally well be due to the drying process which occurs with all new buildings. The fact that there was damp unconnected with the stairs indicates the latter.

The experts gave evidence that it might take one to two years for moisture to penetrate the brick walls, which were 14 inches thick.

There is nothing wrong with water entering bricks. Bricks are permeable things and they admit and extrude water. So damage resulting from the lack of damp-proof courses would not occur until the damp reached the plaster. The expert evidence makes it peculiarly difficult for me in this case, since a year from practical completion might be outside the limitation period, but two years would be within it.

Somewhat reluctantly I am driven to consider where the burden of proof lies. It is for the plaintiffs to prove their case, but at common law there was no such thing as a limitation period and, therefore, initially the plaintiffs do not have to prove that their cause of action accrued after any particular date. The Limitation Acts have, perfectly properly, been raised by the defendants. They are putting forward a positive case that the plaintiffs' action is statute-barred and, although I know of no authority dealing with the point and, if there is one, it has escaped the vigilance of counsel, I think it must follow that the burden of proof is on them. When I am left, as I am here, in the situation where I am uncertain whether the damp could have reached the plaster before the crucial date for limitation purposes, or whether it was afterwards, I think it must follow that the defendants have not discharged the legal burden. So I hold that the plaintiffs' claim is not statute-barred in relation to the lack of damp-proof course any more than in relation to the drainage arrangements.

The third issue is as to the damages the plaintiffs should recover. [His Honour dealt with the question of the measure of the plaintiffs' loss, and continued:]

I come now to the principle which must govern this assessment of damages. In *Dodd Properties (Kent) Ltd v Canterbury City Council* [1980] 1 All ER 928, [1980] 1 WLR 433 the Court of Appeal laid down that the fundamental principle as to damages was that the measure was that sum of money which would put the injured party in the same position as that in which he would have been if he had not sustained the injury and that, although as a general rule damages were assessed as at the date of the breach, that rule was subject to many exceptions and qualifications and that in a case in 'which there is a material difference between the cost of repair at the date of the wrongful act and the cost when the repairs could, having regard to all the relevant circumstances, first reasonably have been undertaken the damages were to be assessed by reference to the latter date.

Counsel for the defendants submitted to me that in this case the plaintiffs could reasonably have carried out the remedial action which was required at the very latest in 1977, and he says that that is the date at which the damages should be assessed. He says that because (and now I deal with matters of fact which I postponed dealing with earlier) the evidence given by Mr Meur is that the plaintiffs realised by the sale of their land, and after paying for the new buildings, £66,000, that that sum was handed to the trustees to the Congregational Church as a whole who held it as part of a large portfolio, and that, although some interest on the money has been used to enable the plaintiffs to continue, part of it should have been taken in 1977 to finance remedial works. The plaintiffs would then have been able to obtain income from lettings of the hall.

Counsel for the plaintiffs on the other hand invited me to consider the general accounts of the plaintiffs which are available from 1975 until 1982, and he pointed to the fact that in every single year the plaintiffs have had to draw on the interest in order to keep the church in existence. Counsel submitted that in 1977 and subsequently the plaintiffs were in no position to take capital moneys in order to finance work, because by doing so they would have reduced their income to such an extent that the church could not have been kept in existence.

Looking at the general accounts there can be no doubt that the plaintiffs would have had a deficit each year but for the fact that they were able to withdraw interest which would otherwise have accumulated in the hands of the trustees. In 1981, for instance, the amount which had to be withdrawn was £7,428. In 1982, the last year for which the accounts were available, the amount withdrawn was £5,450. Mr Meur told me that the church took the view that they could not reduce their income without impairing the continued viability of the church. I have no doubt that the plaintiffs took that view perfectly genuinely.

I think that I have to consider the situation as it was in about 1977. The church's income from collections and other sources was insufficient to finance their expenditure. They had to draw money from the trustees. They were not however having to draw capital money from the trustees. They are a charity and it is not just the position of the existing members of the church which has to be taken into account, but the continued existence of the church into the future. The income which it was expected could be derived from the letting of the hall would obviously have been substantially less than the amount which the plaintiffs were having to withdraw from the trustees each year. I think that the plaintiffs were faced with a difficult decision in 1977, and no doubt at other dates too, whether they should have the repairs carried out or whether they should go on putting up with a hall which was out of action to a large degree and subject to periodical flooding and wait till the action came to trial. The defendants of course were denying liability. I think that, bearing in mind that the defendants were denying liability altogether and given the parlous state of the church's finances, the plaintiffs acted reasonably in not having the work carried out in 1977. I think the same goes for each subsequent year.

On the other hand, I have held in the previous proceedings that the plaintiffs were guilty of 18 months' delay in bringing this case to trial. I think therefore it is right that I should approach the assessment of their damages on the basis that this case could have been tried early last year. If it had been tried early last year and I had decided in favour of the plaintiffs, as no doubt I would since I am doing so today, they could not have started building work immediately. There would have had to have been some interval before builders could have arrived at the site and started work. I should have thought that might have taken about four to five months. So that it seems to me that the right date at which to assess the plaintiffs' damages is mid-1982.

There has been an increase in building costs between 1982 and 1983. Doubtless there will be a further increase within the next year, when work could be carried out. The actual increase I can derive from a schedule of increased costs attached to a supplemental report of Mr Melvin. These increases were agreed by Mr Allerton as being correct. Unfortunately, I do not know what the datum year was, so that I cannot readily work it out, but as between 1982 and 1983 the increase as compared with the datum year in 1982 was 84·17 and in 1983 is 95·20. So I think that the money which the plaintiffs recover in respect of remedial works must be discounted by the difference between 95·20 and 84·17. That is a calculation which I do not propose making at this moment.

Another consideration is whether there should be a further reduction in the estimated costs of the remedial works, because they are based on a single quotation obtained by Mr Allerton from a single builder, admitted to be a good and sound builder, in East Finchley. Ought the work to go out to tender, three builders, say, being invited to tender? Certainly as anybody sitting in these courts knows, there is not a great deal of building work about and tenders may be expected to be fairly keen. Mr Melvin thinks that if this work was put out to tender a reduction of, say, 10% could probably be achieved on the prices which Mr Melvin obtained, and counsel for the defendants invites me to deduct from all these prices 10%. Counsel for the plaintiffs says, however, that there is no actual evidence that that would happen, it is pure speculation. The defendants could, if they had liked, have gone out into the market and got a price themselves for this work and then we could have judged whether in fact Mr Allerton's prices are right or not.

I think that the matter is a difficult one and I am going to approach it fairly arbitrarily, and I hope justly, and discount the figures put forward by Mr Allerton, on which I based my assessments a little while ago, by 5% throughout. So, in other words, the remedial figures have got to be discounted on account of the difference in year taken as the year in which the work should be done and again on account of the lack of tender, something to be calculated, but not by me at this moment. With regard to the loss of profits I think that the 18-month period of delay has to be taken into account again and I will not allow any loss of profit for this year, so it is 1971 to 1982 inclusive and the plaintiffs may recover two-thirds of whatever the total of that sum is, as appears in the document produced by Mr Meur.

There is no claim here for general damages, for inconvenience or distress, or anything of that sort. I think there remains only the question of interest. I am in fact assessing these various items of damages on a 1981 basis. That being so, it seems to me that the plaintiffs are entitled to interest but only for a period from, I will say, August 1982 until now.

*Judgment for the plaintiffs accordingly.*

Solicitors: *Kingsford Dorman* (for the plaintiffs); *Reynolds Porter Chamberlain* (for the defendants).

K Mydeen Esq   Barrister.

# Kensington and Chelsea and Westminster Area Health Authority v Wettern Composites Ltd and others

QUEEN'S BENCH DIVISION (OFFICIAL REFEREES' BUSINESS)
HIS HONOUR JUDGE DAVID SMOUT QC
14, 17, 21–24, 28–30 NOVEMBER, I DECEMBER 1983, 30 JANUARY 1984

*Limitation of action – When time begins to run – Actions in tort – Accrual of cause of action – Negligence – Damage – Lapse of time between negligent act and occurrence of damage – Action against architects in respect of negligent supervision of the fixing of stone mullions to facade of building – Cracks occurring within six years before action brought – Inevitability of damage at date of erection of mullions – Whether mullions doomed from the start – Whether limitation period running from date when damage occurred or date works completed.*

The plaintiffs were the occupiers and executive authority in charge of a hospital. In 1964 and 1965 an extension for the hospital was built according to plans prepared by the defendant architects and structural engineers. The plaintiffs employed their own clerk of works to inspect works on the site. The erection of the extension involved cladding, in the form of stone mullions, being attached to the main structure of the extension, but in September 1976 the plaintiffs discovered cracks in one of the mullions which gave cause for concern. The cracks were monitored and in 1980 the mullions were all removed and replaced. In September 1978 the plaintiffs issued a writ claiming damages for negligent supervision of the erection of the cladding against the architects and the structural engineers. The architects and structural engineers contended that it was inevitable that the mullions would have to be replaced and that therefore the cladding was 'doomed from the start', so that the plaintiffs' cause of action had accrued when the cladding was erected, which was more than six years before the commencement of proceedings, with the result that the action was time-barred by the Limitation Act 1939.

**Held** – (1) On the facts, the damage to the mullions had been caused by their movement vertically and horizontally after having been attached to the frame of the building, that movement having been caused by inadequate fixing of the mullions due to negligent supervision by the architects and the plaintiffs' clerk of works. Furthermore, it was unlikely that such movement had occurred prior to 1975 (see p 349 e f and p 350 d, post).

(2) The general rule was that time began to run for limitation purposes from the date when damage occurred. Since the damage which had occurred consisted of the physical harm resulting from the movement of the mullions rather than the absence of adequate fixing of the mullions to the building, time began to run not from the date of the erection of the mullions but from the date the damage occurred in 1975. Furthermore, the defects in fixing the mullions at the time of erection were not such as to render the cladding doomed from the start, since for that to be the case the defects would have had to give rise not just to an inevitability but to an impending inevitability of damage. The plaintiffs' claim, having been brought within six years of the occurrence of the damage, was therefore not time-barred and judgment would be given for the plaintiffs against the architects for the total amount of the claim, less 20% in respect of the contributory negligence of the plaintiffs' clerk of works (see p 349 f g, p 350 b and p 351 a to d, post); *Pirelli General Cable Works Ltd v Oscar Faber & Partners (a firm)* [1983] 1 All ER 65 applied; dicta of Lord Fraser in *Pirelli General Cable Works Ltd v Oscar Faber & Partners (a firm)* [1983] 1 All ER at 70, 72 considered.

**Notes**
For when a limitation period begins to run, see 28 Halsbury's Laws (4th edn) paras 622–

623, and for cases on the subject, see 32 Digest (Reissue) 486–487, 503–509, 3737–3745, 3842–3869.

For the Limitation Act 1939, see 19 Halsbury's Statutes (3rd edn) 60.

As from 1 May 1981 the 1939 Act has been replaced by the Limitation Act 1980.

**Cases referred to in judgment**

Batty v Metropolitan Property Realizations Ltd [1978] 2 All ER 445, [1978] 1 QB 554, [1978] 2 WLR 500, CA.

Cartledge v E Jopling & Sons Ltd [1963] 1 All ER 341, [1963] AC 758, [1963] 2 WLR 210, HL.

Dove v Banhams Patent Locks Ltd [1983] 2 All ER 833, [1983] 1 WLR 1436.

Junior Books Ltd v Veitchi Co Ltd [1982] 3 All ER 201, [1983] 1 AC 520, [1982] 3 WLR 477, HL.

Pirelli General Cable Works Ltd v Oscar Faber & Partners (a firm) [1983] 1 All ER 65, [1983] 2 AC 1, [1983] 2 WLR 6, HL.

**Action**

By a writ issued on 6 September 1978 the plaintiffs, Kensington and Chelsea and Westminster Area Health Authority, claimed damages for breach of contract and negligence against the first defendants, Wettern Composites Ltd, and the second defendants, Adams Holden & Pearson (a firm) (the architects). By a third party notice dated 12 January 1979 the architects brought proceedings against R Travers Morgan & Partners (a firm) (the structural engineers) for contribution or indemnity to the full extent of the plaintiffs' claim. By an amended writ issued on 20 November 1980 the structural engineers and Kendell's Stone and Paving Co Ltd were joined respectively as third and fourth defendants to the action, the plaintiffs claiming against them damages for negligence. The trial proceeded as against the architects and structural engineers only. The facts are set out in the judgment.

Donald Keating QC and Christopher Lewsley for the plaintiffs.
Michael Ogden QC and Timothy Elliott for the architects.
W R H Crowther QC and Howard Palmer for the structural engineers.

*Cur adv vult*

30 January. The following judgment was delivered.

**HIS HONOUR JUDGE DAVID SMOUT QC.** This action arises from the discovery in 1976 of certain defects relating to artificial stone mullions which had been erected in 1964 and 1965 as part of the outer cladding to an extension built for the Westminster Hospital. The plaintiffs are the occupiers and successors in title to the board of governors. The second defendants, Adams Holden & Pearson, are architects and the third defendants, Travers Morgan & Partners, are structural engineers. Their services were retained in respect of the extension and they were for that purpose appointed by the board of governors in 1961 or thereabouts. They are the effective defendants. The first and the fourth defendants have, as it has been put, fallen by the wayside. The first defendants were the sub-contractors who were engaged as specialists for the supply and erection of the mullions; at the material time they were known as Cooper Wettern & Co Ltd. They are now in liquidation. The fourth defendants were the manufacturers of the mullions, and they had also been involved in their erection: however the plaintiffs have withdrawn their claim against them. The main contractors, Tersons Ltd, for reasons with which the court is not concerned, were never joined in the action; nor was Mr Scott, the clerk of works.

The writ was issued against the architects on 6 September 1978. A third party notice was served by the architects against the structural engineers on 12 January 1979. Leave to amend the writ so as to join the structural engineers was given on 11 November 1980. The writ was so amended on 20 November 1980.

It is common ground that, if there was any material breach of contract by either the architects or the structural engineers, such breach must have occurred at the time of the erection of the mullions in 1964 and 1965. Thus any claim in contract is barred by the Limitation Acts.

The action has proceeded to trial on the basis of allegations of negligence. The plaintiffs contend that the architects and the structural engineers each failed to exercise the skill and care of competent practitioners in their respective fields, as judged by the standards prevailing at the time, and further that such negligence was an effective or subtantive cause of damage. The negligence alleged is in respect of the supervision by the architects and the structural engineers in the erection of the cladding. Whatever be set out in the pleadings no allegations have been pursued at trial against the architects or the structural engineers in respect of any matter of design.

The architects and the structural engineers deny negligence: they challenge causation: they assert that the plaintiffs' claim is in any event statute-barred, and by later amendments they allege that any loss was wholly or in part caused by the negligence of the plaintiffs' clerk of works. In the third party proceedings the architects claim that if found liable to the plaintiffs they are entitled to damages from the structural engineers equivalent to an indemnity or to contribution, and allege in effect that certain duties as to supervision were entrusted to the structural engineers and that the structural engineers failed to carry out that supervision with all proper professional skill.

The issues raise complex questions both of fact and of law. It is convenient to consider first the nature and purpose of the mullions, and the design as to the manner of their attachment to the building. The mullions have been variously referred to in the course of the case as units or panels. They were of pre-cast concrete. Each mullion measured 14 inches wide, 5 inches thick, 12 ft 6 inches long, and weighed 750 lb. They had the appearance of Portland stone and were arranged in lines of five, one mullion above another; between each vertical line of mullions were windows beneath which were rough exposed aggregate panels of a different texture as to which no complaint is made in these proceedings. Each line of mullions was five storeys high, extending from the first floor level to the top of the fifth storey, one mullion per storey. The mullions were not designed for structural strength, they were decorative and weatherproof and intended to be durable, and of course safe.

The separate mullions were designed to sit on projections extending from the structural frame, which constituted the skeleton of the building. The frame was of reinforced concrete. The projections, known as corbels, were intended originally also to be of concrete and to form part of the frame, but as in many instances such concrete corbels were omitted, so metal angle corbels were bolted to the frame and used instead. As a matter of design no criticism is made of that. A recess in the back of the mullion enabled it to fit onto and sit on the corbel. There was also incorporated in the design in respect of each mullion a form of lateral attachment to the frame by means of cramps and dowels. The arrangement was this: masonry slots (also known as abbey or anchor slots) were to be inserted in the reinforced concrete column of the frame at appropriate intervals; in each slot was to be fitted the dovetail of a non-ferrous cramp. The cramp was thus to be secured and to project outwards at right angles from the frame. It was then to be attached to the mullion by means of a dowel, which is a three-inch long bolt, that was to run vertically through a hole in the cramp and inserted in appropriate sockets at the top of a lower mullion and at the bottom of an upper mullion. Thus the cramps and dowels were to secure the mullion to the structural frame. The dowels so secured and fitting into the upper and lower mullions were to form the attachment between each mullion in the vertical plane one to the other. There were to be two such dowels and cramps at the top and at the bottom of each mullion. The design was such that it was not intended that the mullions should rest on each other. The vertical support to be provided to each mullion was the corbel on which it sat.

The design provided for soft joints between each of the mullions, that is to say, $\frac{1}{4}$ inch gaps. A soft joint is in effect a gap of air, surrounded by an outer edge of soft mastic to keep out the damp. It is of the essence of a soft joint that it is not to be filled in with mortar. Its purpose, if I may be forgiven a generalisation, is to enable the structural frame when it shrinks, particularly in the first few months after construction, to continue to accommodate the mullions without risk of undue stress. As the frame shrinks, the mullions would thus be free to follow the corbels downwards. Similarly, such soft joints would counteract the effect of elasticity or creep in the concrete of the frame.

In September 1976 it was noted that there had been cracking in one of the mullions on a corner of the building. It was of such a nature as to indicate that it had been subjected to stress for which the mullions were not designed. Closer examination gave cause for concern. Certain restraints were imposed. On 11 November 1976 it was noted that the mullion had moved outwards by one inch. The movement and cracking of the mullion was monitored, various investigations were undertaken and eventually in 1980 the mullions were all taken down and replaced. A representative of Sandbergs Ltd was on site and recorded on a set of standard forms the many defects that he found, some of which are illustrated by photographs. Mr Malcolm, the expert called for the structural engineers, depicts the findings from various inspections of the mullions in the period 1976–80, including that of Sandbergs.

The defects in the mullions fall into three groups: (i) there were defects in manufacture; (ii) there were defects in the manner of fixing the mullions to the frame; (iii) there were further defects in the nature of the joints between the individual mullions.

The defects in manufacture were not the responsibility of the architects or of the structural engineers.

[His Honour, having reviewed the evidence and having found that the defective fixing of the mullions was solely responsible for their movement, continued:]

I am readily convinced that movement of substance had taken place by the end of the summer of 1976. In my view it is likely to have taken place a few months or a year earlier. I accept that it is possible, but do not consider in all the circumstances that it is likely that there was any movement of the mullions, other than negligible movement, prior to the summer of 1975.

Such a finding does not dispose of the limitation point though it restricts the field of argument. It is convenient to deal with the limitation point now against the background of the facts so far as I have been able to determine them.

In actions alleging negligence in regard to the erection of a building time ordinarily begins to run not from the date of the alleged negligence, nor from the date when the damage was discovered, nor from when it ought to have been discovered, but from the date that the damage occurred. That proposition is established by the House of Lords in *Pirelli General Cable Works Ltd v Oscar Faber & Partners (a firm)* [1983] 1 All ER 65, [1983] 2 AC 1. It will be remembered that that case related to a tall factory chimney built with unsuitable lining material in 1969 whereby cracks developed in April 1970, but which were not reasonably discoverable before October 1972 and were not in fact discovered until November 1977. The defendants in that case were negligent in their design. There are two well-known passages in the speech of Lord Fraser to which one returns time and again. In the first passage he said ([1983] 1 All ER 65 at 70, [1983] 2 AC 1 at 16):

'The plaintiffs' cause of action will not accrue until *damage* occurs, which will commonly consist of cracks coming into existence as a result of the defect even though the cracks or the defect may be undiscovered and undiscoverable. There may perhaps be cases where the defect is so gross that the building is doomed from the start, and where the owner's cause of action will accrue as soon as it is built, but it seems unlikely that such a defect would not be discovered within the limitation period. Such cases, if they exist, would be exceptional.' (Lord Fraser's emphasis.)

In the second passage he said ([1983] 1 All ER 65 at 72, [1983] 2 AC 1 at 18):

'It seems to me that, except perhaps where the advice of an architect or consulting engineer leads to the erection of a building which is so defective as to be doomed from the start, the cause of action accrues only when physical damage occurs to the building. In the present case that was April 1970 when, as found by the judge, cracks must have occurred at the top of the chimney, even though that was before the date of discoverability.'

It follows from this that damage does not mean economic loss, it means physical damage. I note, in passing, that the decision in the *Pirelli* case was subsequent to that in *Junior Books Ltd v Veitchi Co Ltd* [1982] 3 All ER 201, [1983] 1 AC 520, in which Lord Fraser also participated.

It will be noted also that damage does not mean defects. If it did, then in the *Pirelli* case time would have run from the moment of construction, for the lining was as defective in the *Pirelli* chimney as was the fixing in the instant case. The absence of adequate fixing constitutes defects in the instant case and not damage, and I reject counsel for the structural engineer's argument to the contrary. The damage occurred in the *Pirelli* case when the cracks came into existence. It may be right in the context of the *Pirelli* case to construe damage as meaning harm, physical harm. Counsel on behalf of the plaintiffs suggested that one of the factors to be considered must be the purpose intended to be fulfilled by the object said to be damaged. Certainly, if it fails to fulfil its purposes then the object must be damaged. In my view the damage occurred in this case when movement occurred, for by then the mullions were no longer safe and no longer keeping the building weatherproof. But the movement if it is to constitute damage must be more than negligible, and if authority were needed for that it is to be found in the speech of Lord Reid in *Cartledge v E Jopling & Sons Ltd* [1963] 1 All ER 341 at 343, [1963] AC 758 at 771–772.

Accordingly, if the general test is to be applied, and if it be right that the damage did not occur prior to 1975, it would follow that the plaintiffs are not time-barred in pursuance of their claim. But does the general test apply? The defendants draw attention to Lord Fraser's possible exception in his references to a building that is so defective as to be 'doomed from the start'. It will, however, be noted that in the relevant passages whilst Lord Fraser leaves open the possibility of such an exception he calls in question its very existence.

In the course of counsel for the architect's cross-examination, Mr Coffin, the expert consulting engineer called by the plaintiffs, conceded that in the instant case if the defects of fixing had been known at the time of construction then it would have been obvious that at some time in the future what had to be done would have had to be done. Likewise, Mr Malcolm, the structural engineers' expert, agreed that, if he had known of the defects just after erection, his advice would be that the mullions would have to come down in due course. Asked by counsel for the architects 'if the building was doomed from the start', he stated that 'all the circumstances were there, and eventually replacement would have had to be done'. Counsel for the architects argues that for the purpose of the limitation period a distinction must be drawn between a defect which will and a defect which may cause damage, but I do not find it as straightforward as that. The House of Lords in the *Pirelli* case despite the defects which made damage inevitable did not regard that chimney as doomed from the start. In *Dove v Banhams Patent Locks Ltd* [1983] 2 All ER 833 Hodgson J expressed difficulty in understanding the exception, and counsel for the plaintiffs has not felt able to put forward any illustration in which he has confidence. The use of the phrase may stem from *Batty v Metropolitan Property Realizations Ltd* [1978] 2 All ER 445 at 450, [1978] 1 QB 554 at 562, where Megaw LJ referred to a house built on the side of a hill subject to landslip, as one which 'by its instability was, from the outset, doomed'. He added that 'for that reason, and for that reason alone, the house was unfit for human habitation, because in a foreseeable, and short, time it would collapse, through the movement of the hillside'. In a later passage Megaw LJ referred to 'the instability of the hillside which spelled the not far distant doom of the house from the outset of its life' (see [1978] 2 All ER 445 at 451, [1978] 1 QB 554 at 564). *Batty's* case, however, was not a limitation point case and turned on the construction of a warranty of fitness for habitation.

I respectfully suggest that there has to be not merely an inevitability but an impending inevitability to come within reach of Lord Fraser's dictum. But, be that as it may, I keep on stubbing my toe against this same obstacle: the cracks in the *Pirelli* chimney were the product of faulty materials and developed within a year of construction, yet the chimney was not regarded by the House of Lords as 'doomed from the start'; in those circumstances I ask myself by what reasoning could this court conclude that the poor fixing of the mullions in the hospital extension could render that extension 'doomed from the start' when the movement of the mullions developed 11 or 12 years after construction. I have to say that if the *Pirelli* chimney was not so doomed, nor was the Westminster Hospital extension. Accordingly, in my view this case is no exception to the ordinary rule. The proceedings against each of the defendants were brought within six years of the occurrence of the damage. The plaintiffs' claim is not time-barred.

[His Honour reviewed the evidence on liability and found that the architects had been negligent in the supervision of the fixing of the mullions, while the structural engineers had not been negligent. His Honour then dealt with the question of the plaintiffs' vicarious liability for the contributory negligence of their clerk of works, and continued:]

I assess responsibility as to the clerk of works 20%, as to the architects 80%. By reason of the vicarious liability of the plaintiffs I make a finding of contributory negligence of 20%. Accordingly I give judgment for the plaintiffs as against the architects, as to 80% of £250,000, ie in the sum of £200,000. The claim against the structural engineers is dismissed.

Junior counsel for the architects advanced an interesting argument in respect of the difficulties in determining when the limitation period applied in respect of contribution proceedings where, as here, the writ was amended so as to join additional defendants. In view of my findings that argument is not now directly in point and whilst acknowledging the care with which that argument was presented I excuse myself from dealing with it. If my findings are subsequently varied, then counsel's points remain and are, of course, open for further consideration as may be appropriate.

*Judgment for the plaintiffs against the architects as to 80% of plaintiffs' claim; plaintiffs' contributory negligence assessed at 20%; plaintiffs' claim against the structural engineers dismissed.*

Solicitors: *Radcliffes & Co* (for the plaintiffs); *Hewitt Woollacott & Chown* (for the architects); *Beale & Co* (for the structural engineers).

K Mydeen Esq    Barrister.

# Ketteman and others v Hansel Properties Ltd

COURT OF APPEAL, CIVIL DIVISION

LAWTON, STEPHEN BROWN AND PARKER LJJ

18, 19, 20, 21, 22, 25, 26 JUNE, 25 JULY 1984

*Limitation of action – When time begins to run – Actions in tort – Accrual of cause of action – Negligence – Damage – Lapse of time between negligent act and occurrence of damage – Action against builder brought within limitation period – Subsequent joinder of architects and local authority as defendants to action outside limitation period – Action against architects alleging negligence in siting houses and in design of foundations – Action against local authority for breach of duty in failing to ensure that builder complied with building regulations – Cracks in walls of houses occurring requiring underpinning of foundations – Economic loss suffered by occupiers but no deleterious effects on health – Whether actions against local authority and architects statute-barred – Whether houses doomed from the start.*

*Practice – Parties – Adding defendant – Amendment of writ – Date from when added defendant becomes party to proceedings – Writ not amended and re-served until outside limitation period – Judge declaring defendants made parties from date within limitation period – Whether judge having jurisdiction to declare when defendants became parties – Whether defendants joined as parties from date when writ first issued.*

In 1975 the five plaintiffs bought houses from the first defendants, who were builders and developers. The foundations of the houses had been laid between June 1973 and June 1975 in accordance with the designs and plans of the third defendants, a firm of architects, and had been inspected by the second defendants, the local authority which approved the designs and plans. The foundations were faulty and in August and September 1976 cracks appeared in the walls of the houses caused by the settling of the foundations. The houses required underpinning, but rather than incur the considerable expense which that entailed the plaintiffs instead sold their houses at a considerable loss. Prior to the sale of the houses the plaintiffs suffered inconvenience, some discomfort and mental distress but no deleterious effects on their health or that of their families. On 27 May 1980 the plaintiffs issued a writ against the builders claiming damages for breach of contract and negligence. On 25 June 1982 the plaintiffs were granted an order joining the architects and the local authority as defendants to the action but because they failed to amend and re-serve the writ within the time required by RSC Ord 15, r 8(4) the order was ineffective. The amended writ was served on the second and third defendants on 30 July 1982 and reissued on 9 September 1982. In the course of the trial the judge granted the architects and the local authority leave to amend their defences in order to plead that the claims against them were outside the limitation period because (i) the faulty plans and siting were bound to cause the foundations to settle thereby causing structural damage and therefore the houses were 'doomed from the start' so that the plaintiffs' cause of action accrued as soon as the houses were built and (ii) they had not been effectively joined until 9 September, which was more than six years after the cracks in the walls occurred. The judge also granted an application by the plaintiffs for the order of 25 June 1982 (which had been made by another judge) to be amended to provide for the joinder of the architects and local authority as defendants to take effect from 30 July 1982, which was less than six years after the cracks in the walls appeared. Following the trial the judge gave judgment for three of the plaintiffs against the architects but dismissed all claims against the local authority, on the ground that in accordance with House of Lords authority, proof of 'present or imminent danger to health or safety' was essential to establish the plaintiffs' claims and the plaintiffs, although able to establish discomfort, inconvenience and mental distress, had not established present or imminent danger. The architects appealed and the plaintiffs cross-appealed.

**Held** – The architects' appeal would be dismissed and the plaintiffs' cross-appeal allowed for the following reasons—

(1) A person could not be declared to have become a defendant on a date before he became a defendant by operation of the rules of court. Accordingly, when the order of 25 June 1982 was ineffective to make the architects and the local authority defendants to the action because the plaintiffs failed to amend the writ and re-serve it within the time required by RSC Ord 15, r 8, the trial judge had no power to declare that the architects and the local authority had become defendants on 30 July 1982 when the amended writ was served on them, since under the rules of court the architects and the local authority did not become defendants until 9 September when the amended writ was reissued. Furthermore, a judge at first instance could not amend another judge's order except by way of appeal or under the slip rule, which did not apply, and therefore the trial judge had had no power to amend the order of 25 June in any case (see p 360 g to p 361 a, p 365 f g and p 366 g to j, post).

(2) However, applying the principle that when a person was joined unconditionally as a defendant in an action he became a party to that action from the date when the writ was first issued, the action against the architects and the local authority was deemed to have been commenced when the writ was first issued against the builders in 1980, ie within the six-year limitation period, and therefore the plaintiffs' claims against the architects and the local authority were not statute-barred (see p 361 b c, p 362 f and p 365 f g, post); dicta of Greer LJ in Mabro v Eagle Star and British Dominions Insurance Co Ltd [1932] All ER Rep at 413, of Megaw LJ in Lucy v W T Henleys Telegraph Works Co Ltd [1969] 3 All ER at 467–468 and of Brandon LJ in Liff v Peasley [1980] 1 All ER at 642 considered.

(3) Furthermore, the plaintiffs' claims against the architects and the local authority were not statute-barred on the ground that the houses were doomed from the start, because the plaintiffs' cause of action had accrued when the physical damage to their houses occurred, which was when the cracks in the walls appeared in August and September 1976, ie within the six-year limitation period which began on 27 May 1974. It was only in exceptional cases that a building could be said to be 'doomed from the start'. Furthermore, the defendants could not raise a limitation defence based on economic loss stemming from the faulty foundations, because any economic loss resulting from the laying of defective foundations could not give rise to a cause of action before the occurrence of physical damage to the houses, unless the houses had been doomed from the start (see p 362 j to p 363 a c to e and g to j, p 365 f g and p 366 d, post); Pirelli General Cable Works Ltd v Oscar Faber & Partners (a firm) [1983] 1 All ER 65 applied; dicta of Lord Fraser in Pirelli General Cable Works Ltd v Oscar Faber & Partners (a firm) [1983] 1 All ER at 70, 72 considered.

(4) An occupier of a building which was structurally unsound as the result of a local authority's negligence and likely to become a danger to health or safety unless remedial action was taken did not have to wait until the building was about to collapse before his right of action against the local authority accrued. There was an 'imminent' danger to the health and safety of the occupier if the danger was likely to arise soon, that being a matter of fact and degree. Having regard to the nature and extent of the structural damage to the foundations and walls and the likelihood that it would get progressively worse, there was an imminent danger to the safety of the occupiers of the plaintiffs' houses which thereby afforded the plaintiffs a cause of action against the local authority (see p 364 j to p 365 a and f g, post); dictum of Lord Wilberforce in Anns v Merton London Borough [1977] 2 All ER at 505 explained.

Per Lawton and Stephen Brown LJJ. The court has a discretion under RSC Ord 15, r 6(2)(b)(ii) to allow a new defendant to be joined on terms that the joinder takes effect only from the date of the amendment of the writ (see p 362 g h and p 365 f, post); Liptons Cash Registers and Business Equipment Ltd v Hugin (GB) Ltd [1982] 1 All ER 595 approved.

## Notes

For when a limitation period begins to run, see 28 Halsbury's Laws (4th edn) paras 622–623, and for cases on the subject, see 32 Digest (Reissue) 486–487, 503–509, 3737–3745, 3842–3869.

**Cases referred to in judgments**

*Anns v Merton London Borough* [1977] 2 All ER 492, [1978] AC 728, [1977] 2 WLR 1024, HL.

*Byron v Cooper* (1844) 2 Cl & Fin 556, 8 ER 1212.

*Forster v Outred & Co (a firm)* [1982] 2 All ER 753, [1982] 1 WLR 86, CA.

*Howell v Young* (1826) 5 B & C 259, [1824–34] All ER Rep 377.

*Junior Books Ltd v Veitchi Co Ltd* [1982] 3 All ER 201, [1983] 1 AC 520, [1982] 3 WLR 477, HL.

*Liff v Peasley* [1980] 1 All ER 623, [1980] 1 WLR 781, CA.

*Liptons Cash Registers and Business Equipment Ltd v Hugin (GB) Ltd* [1982] 1 All ER 595.

*Lucy v W T Henleys Telegraph Works Co Ltd (ICI Ltd, third party)* [1969] 3 All ER 456, [1970] 1 QB 393, [1969] 3 WLR 588, CA.

*Mabro v Eagle Star and British Dominions Insurance Co Ltd* [1932] 1 KB 485, [1932] All ER Rep 411, CA.

*Pirelli General Cable Works Ltd v Oscar Faber & Partners (a firm)* [1983] 1 All ER 65, [1983] 2 AC 1, [1983] 2 WLR 6, HL.

*Sparham-Souter v Town and Country Developments (Essex) Ltd* [1976] 2 All ER 65, [1976] QB 858, [1976] 2 WLR 493, CA.

*Weldon v Neal* (1887) 19 QBD 394, CA.

**Cases also cited**

*A-G v Pontypridd Waterworks Co* [1908] 1 Ch 388.

*Aronson v Liverpool Corp* (1913) 29 TLR 325.

*Bagot v Stevens Scanlan & Co Ltd* [1964] 3 All ER 577, [1966] 1 QB 197.

*Battersby v Anglo-American Oil Co Ltd* [1944] 2 All ER 387, [1945] KB 23, CA.

*Batty v Metropolitan Property Realizations Ltd* [1978] 2 All ER 445, [1978] QB 554, CA.

*Bluett v Woodsprung DC* (1982) 266 EG 220.

*Bowden, Re, Andrew v Cooper* (1890) 45 Ch D 444.

*Braniff v Holland & Hannen and Cubitts (Southern) Ltd* [1969] 3 All ER 959, [1960] 1 WLR 1533, CA.

*Brickfield Properties Ltd v Newton* [1971] 3 All ER 328, [1971] 1 WLR 862, CA.

*Cartledge v E Jopling & Sons Ltd* [1963] 1 All ER 341, [1963] AC 758, HL.

*Covell Matthews & Partners v French Wools Ltd* [1978] 2 All ER 800, [1978] 1 WLR 1477, CA.

*Crump v Torfaen BC* (1981) 19 Build LR 84.

*Darley Main Colliery Co v Mitchell* (1886) 11 App Cas 127, [1886–90] All ER Rep 449, HL.

*Dawson v Hill* [1934] WN 218, CA.

*Dennis v Charnwood BC* [1982] 3 All ER 486, [1983] QB 409, CA.

*Dismore v Milton* [1938] 3 All ER 762, CA.

*Dove v Banhams Patent Locks Ltd* [1983] 2 All ER 833, [1983] 1 WLR 1436.

*Dutton v Bognor Regis United Building Co Ltd* [1972] 1 All ER 462, [1972] 1 QB 373, CA.

*Edevain v Cohen* (1889) 43 Ch D 187, CA.

*Gawthrop v Boulton* [1978] 3 All ER 615, [1979] 1 WLR 268.

*Hall v Meyrick* [1957] 2 All ER 722, [1957] 2 QB 455, CA.

*Harnett v Fisher* [1927] AC 573, HL.

*Heaven v Road and Rail Wagons Ltd* [1965] 2 All ER 409, [1965] 2 QB 355.

*Hewett v Barr* [1891] 1 QB 98, CA.

*Higgins v Arfon BC* [1975] 2 All ER 589, [1975] 1 WLR 524.

*Holman v George Elliot & Co Ltd* [1944] 1 All ER 639, [1944] KB 591, CA.

*Kensington and Chelsea and Westminster Area Health Authority v Wettern Composites Ltd* [1985] 1 All ER 346.

*Keystone Knitting Mills' Trade Mark, Re* [1929] 1 Ch 92, [1928] All ER Rep 276, CA.

*Lee v Bude and Torrington Junction Rly Co, ex p Stevens, ex p Fisher* (1871) LR 6 CP 576.

*Marshall v London Passenger Transport Board* [1936] 3 All ER 83, CA.

*Marubeni Corp v Pearlstone Shipping Corp* [1978] 1 Lloyd's Rep 38, CA.

*Mitchell v Harris Engineering Co Ltd* [1967] 2 All ER 682, [1967] 2 QB 703, CA.

*Pontin v Wood* [1962] 1 All ER 294, [1962] 1 QB 594, CA.
*Seabridge v H Cox & Son (Plant Hire) Ltd* [1968] 1 All ER 570, [1968] 2 QB 46, CA.
*Sneade v Wotherton Barytes and Lead Mining Co Ltd* [1904] 1 KB 295, CA.
*Sterman v E W & W J Moore Ltd (a firm)* [1970] 1 All ER 581, [1970] 1 QB 596, CA.
*UBAF Ltd v European American Banking Corp* [1984] 2 All ER 226, [1984] QB 713, CA.

**Appeal and cross-appeal**
By a writ issued on 27 May 1980 the plaintiffs, (1) David Michael Ketteman and Hilary
Judith Ketteman, (2) Clifford Christopher Janes Hollebon and Rita Cecilia Hollebon, (3)
Brian Henry Griffin and Mary Bernadette Griffin, (4) John Shepherd and Joan Janet
Shepherd, and (5) Ronald Victor Grover and Josephine Rosemary Grover, brought an
action against Hansel Properties Ltd (the first defendants) claiming damages for breach
of contract and negligence and breach of statutory duty arising from the building of five
houses by the first defendants which were bought by the plaintiffs in 1975. By a third
party notice issued on 28 April 1981 pursuant to the order of his Honour Judge Hawser
QC dated 9 September 1981 and statement of claim served on 30 June 1981 the first
defendants claimed against the Mid-Sussex District Council (as successors of Burgess Hill
Urban District Council) an indemnity or contribution in respect of the plaintiffs' claim
alleging breach of duty or breach of statutory duty by the third party. By a fourth party
notice issued pursuant to leave of Master Bickford Smith dated 18 August 1981 the third
party claimed against Jamieson Greene Associates (a firm) an indemnity in respect of the
plaintiffs' claim against the third party alleging that they were in breach of duty to the
plaintiffs. On 25 June 1982 his Honour Judge Sir William Stabb QC granted the plaintiffs
leave to join the third and fourth parties as defendants to the action. On 9 September
1982 the writ, having been amended, was reissued. On 10 December 1982 his Honour
Judge Hayman hearing official referees' business gave the second and third defendants
leave to amend their respective defences. On 18 January 1983 he amended the order of
25 June 1982 by providing that joinder of the third and fourth parties as defendants
should take effect from 30 July 1982. On 14 February 1983 the judge ordered that
judgment should be entered for the plaintiffs against the first defendants, that the first,
second and fifth plaintiffs should have judgment against the third defendants and that
the third and fourth plaintiffs' claims against the third defendants should be dismissed
and also all the plaintiffs' claims against the second defendants. The judge apportioned
the blame for the damage to the houses as follows: the first defendants, 60%; the third
defendants, 40%. If he had to apportion liability as between the three defendants he
would have done so as follows: the first defendants, 50%; the third defendants, 35%; the
second defendants, 15%. The third defendants appealed against so much of the order of
14 February 1983 as granted the plaintiffs leave to join the third defendants in the action
with effect from 30 July 1982 and from so much of the judgment of 14 February 1983
as adjudged the third defendants liable in damages to the first, second and fifth plaintiffs.
The third and fourth plaintiffs cross-appealed against the orders of the judge made on 18
January and 14 February 1983 and applied for leave to appeal from the judgment given
by the judge on 10 December 1982. The first defendants who were in liquidation took
no part in the appeal. The facts are set out in the judgment of Lawton LJ.

*Michael Ogden QC* and *Mark Smith* for the third defendants.
*John Owen QC* and *Adrian Brunner* for the second defendants.
*Robin Auld QC* and *Christopher Symons* for the plaintiffs.

*Cur adv vult*

25 July. The following judgments were delivered.

**LAWTON LJ.** These appeals are from judgments of his Honour Judge Hayman, sitting
as an official referee, given on 18 January and 14 February 1983 whereby he adjudged,
inter alia, that all the plaintiffs should have judgment against the first defendants, that

the first, second and fifth plaintiffs should have judgment against the third defendants for varying sums, together with interest thereon, and that the claims of the third and fourth plaintiffs against the third defendants should be dismissed, as should be the claims of all the plaintiffs against the second defendants. The third defendants, who are architects, have appealed against that part of the judgment which was in favour of the first, second and fifth plaintiffs. The third and fourth plaintiffs have appealed against that part of the judgment which dismissed their claims against the third defendants. All the plaintiffs have appealed against that part of the judgment which dismissed their claims against the second defendants, who are the Mid-Sussex District Council. Both the plaintiffs and the second defendants have given notice that they seek to support such parts of the judgment as were in their favour on grounds additional to those given by the judge.

*The issues*

The following were the main issues raised in these appeals. (1) When a building has faulty foundations due to negligence, giving rise either to subsequent structural damage or the need to take remedial action to avoid such damage, when does the cause of action accrue? (2) When a building has faulty foundations due to negligence, so that its value as a building is diminished, does a cause of action in tort arise and, if so, when? (3) When after action brought a new party is added as a defendant, is the date of joinder the material date for deciding whether a claim is statute-barred for the purposes of the Limitation Acts or is it the date of the issue of the writ? (4) When, if a local authority negligently fails to ensure compliance with building regulations so that a building has faulty foundations causing subsequent structural damage, is damage proved by evidence of a potential danger to health or safety?

*The facts*

The first defendants, who have taken no part in these appeals, from 1970 onwards began building houses on some land at Burgess Hill, Sussex. That land at all material times came within the jurisdiction of the second defendants. Between June 1973 and June 1975 the first defendants built some semi-detached four-bedroomed houses in Marle Avenue. Five, numbered 32, 34, 36, 38 and 42, were bought by the plaintiffs; 32, 34, 36 and 38 in the early part of 1975, 42 in November 1975. They all occupied their houses soon after purchase. The houses had been designed by the third defendants. The first defendants had laid the foundations in accordance with the third defendants' designs and plans, shortly before the following dates, which were those on which the second defendants inspected them: nos 32 and 34 on June 1973, nos 36 and 38 on May 1974 and no 42 on June 1975.

The foundations of all five houses were faulty. They were too shallow; the in-filling was of the wrong kind; and they had been laid too near some trees. For the purposes of these appeals it was accepted that the third defendants had been negligent in siting the houses too near the trees and in the design of the foundations and that the second defendants had been negligent in failing to ensure that the first defendants complied with reg D3 of the Building Regulations 1972, SI 1972/317 which prescribe standards for foundations.

The summer of 1976 in Burgess Hill was hot and dry. These conditions were likely to cause shrinking of ground under and around the foundations of houses. Between 11 August and 9 September 1976 cracks in the walls of the houses were noticed on the following dates: no 32 on 14 August 1976, nos 34 and 36 on 11 August 1976, no 38 on 3 September 1976 and no 42 on 9 September 1976.

The judge found that the cracks in the walls of nos 32, 34 and 42 had occurred not more than about a week before they were noticed. He said that he was unable to find when the cracks in the walls of nos 36 and 38 had occurred and that the third and fourth plaintiffs had not satisfied him that they had occurred on or after 30 July 1976, a date which he regarded as important for reasons which will be stated later in this judgment.

The cracks in all the walls had been caused by the settling of the faulty foundations. Expert evidence given by a Dr Weeks, on behalf of the plaintiffs, and accepted by the judge, established that the houses were at risk from further growth of the roots of some of the trees and that underpinning would be necessary to safeguard the houses for the future. Whilst underpinning was being done the plaintiffs and their families would have to move out.

All the plaintiffs decided to sell their houses rather than incur the considerable expense and the inconvenience of underpinning. On sale they all sustained substantial losses of about £15,000 each. Between the dates when the cracks occurred and the sales the plaintiffs sustained inconvenience, some discomfort and much worry; but there was no evidence of any deleterious effects on their health or that of their families.

*The litigation*

The plaintiffs decided to sue the first defendants. They issued their writ, indorsed with the statement of claim, on 27 May 1980. By their statement of claim they alleged breach of contract and negligence. Both were denied. On 28 April 1981 the first defendants issued a third party notice against the second defendants, asking for an indemnity or, alternatively, contribution. By their third party statement of claim the first defendants alleged that the second defendants had been in breach of duty to them and to each of the plaintiffs in approving plans which failed to comply with the Building Regulations 1972 and in failing to ensure that the foundations were properly laid. The third party denied these allegations. On 18 August 1981 they issued a fourth party notice against the architects. Their fourth party statement of claim alleged that the architects had been in breach of their duty to the first defendants and to each of the plaintiffs in failing to use all reasonable care and skill in designing and siting the houses and ensuring that the building works designed by them complied with the building regulations.

The plaintiffs' advisers appreciated that the three parties before the court were blaming each other for what had happened. Nevertheless, they decided not to add the third and fourth parties as defendants as they could have done. When the third and fourth parties were brought in, the plaintiffs had reason to think that the first defendants were sound financially. Later, they doubted whether they were. This was in June 1982. They decided to apply to the court for leave to join the third and fourth parties as defendants. They did not anticipate any opposition to their application because, as the law was then understood to be following the judgment of this court in *Sparham-Souter v Town and Country Developments (Essex) Ltd* [1976] 2 All ER 65, [1976] QB 858, the plaintiffs' causes of action did not accrue until the damage caused by the third and fourth parties' negligence first manifested itself, and the persons who then had interests in the houses first discovered it, or should with reasonable diligence have discovered it. It followed that all the claims were probably within the periods of limitation. The third and fourth parties' experienced solicitors were of the same opinion. The plaintiffs issued a summons which was heard by his Honour Judge Sir William Stabb QC on 25 June 1982. The third and fourth parties were represented by counsel who, so we were told, raised no objection to the order being made, the relevant parts of which were in this form:

'IT IS ORDERED THAT:

1. The First Third party and the Fourth party be joined as Defendants to the Action.

2. A Statement of Claim to be served on the First Third Party and the Fourth Party within 21 days.

3. Defences to be served 14 days thereafter . . .

7. The trial date for the 12 July to be vacated and that the date for the trial to be fixed for the 22nd November 1982 with an estimated length of 10 days . . .'

This order did not state explicitly that the specially indorsed writ should be amended. Counsel for the plaintiffs was instructed to settle an amended statement of claim. This he did. On or about 26 July 1982 a court clerk employed by the plaintiffs' solicitors went to the Central Office to get the amended specially indorsed writ stamped. A clerk there refused to apply the stamp on the ground that the order of 25 June 1982 did not provide for the writ indorsed with the statement of claim to be amended. It did so by implication because it provided that the third and fourth parties should be joined as defendants to the action. It is to be regretted that the clerk decided as he did. By letters dated 30 July 1982 the plaintiffs' solicitors sent the third and fourth parties an amended specially indorsed writ together with a draft consent order to put right that which the clerk in the Central Office had said was wrong. The fourth parties' solicitors returned the draft consent order duly indorsed on 4 August 1982. The third parties did the same on 9 August. The plaintiffs' solicitors returned to court on 8 September 1982. His Honour Judge Newey QC then made an order in these terms:

'UPON READING the parties' agreed terms IT IS ORDERED that:—The Plaintiffs have leave to amend the Statement of Claim in the form annexed hereto.'

On 9 September 1982 the writ was reissued. On 17 September 1982 the plaintiffs' solicitors sent the third and fourth parties a copy of the order dated 8 September, but they did not serve them with a copy of the reissued amended writ, as they should have done. Thereafter, the third and fourth parties behaved as if they were the second and third defendants.

The trial started on 23 November 1982 and lasted some days. The second and third defendants appeared by counsel and contested the claims on their merits. The third defendants called evidence. The second defendants did not do so. At the close of the evidence the third defendants' counsel made his closing submissions. This was probably on 9 December 1982. The plaintiffs' counsel then began his. Whilst he was doing so, on 10 December, counsel became aware of the judgment of the House of Lords in *Pirelli General Cable Works Ltd v Oscar Faber & Partners (a firm)* [1983] 1 All ER 65, [1983] 2 AC 1, which had been delivered on 9 December 1982. This judgment disapproved the judgment of this court in the *Sparham-Souter* case and held that the date of accrual of a cause of action in tort for damage caused by the negligent design or construction of a building is the date when the damage comes into existence and not the date when the damage is discovered or should with reasonable diligence have been discovered. The leading speech was delivered by Lord Fraser. The other members of the appellate committee agreed with it. Lord Fraser said ([1983] 1 All ER 65 at 70, [1983] 2 AC 1 at 16):

'The plaintiff's cause of action will not accrue until *damage* occurs, which will commonly consist of cracks coming into existence as a result of the defect even though the cracks or the defect may be undiscovered and undiscoverable. There may perhaps be cases where the defect is so gross that the building is doomed from the start, and where the owner's cause of action will accrue as soon as it is built, but it seems unlikely that such a defect would not be discovered within the limitation period. Such cases, if they exist, would be exceptional.'

Counsel for the second and third defendants appreciated that it might be possible to argue on the evidence called that the houses had been 'doomed from the start'. If this were so, it was arguable that all the claims were statute-barred. They applied for leave to amend their defences so as to add pleas in these terms:

'If, which is denied, the Second Defendant was guilty of negligence or breach of statutory or other duty whether as alleged or at all, time for the purposes of the Limitation Acts began to run on the occurrence of one of the following events: (a) the submissions to and/or approval by the Local Authority for Building Regulations purposes of the plans drawn by the Third Defendant and/or the approval by such authority of the excavations and/or foundations of the Plaintiffs' premises allegedly constructed in reliance upon the said plans, whereby the homes were negligently designed and/or built as alleged by the Plaintiffs. (b) The defective construction and/

or completion of the houses and/or their foundations, as alleged by the Plaintiffs. (c) The purchase by the Plaintiffs and each of them of their respective houses designed/ or constructed defectively as alleged by the Plaintiffs. (d) The settlement of the foundations wholly or in part or other movement or damage at the said houses caused or contributed to by the defective design and/or construction as alleged by the Plaintiffs.'

Each of the second and third defendants will contend that each of the events above mentioned occurred more than six years prior to the joinder of such defendants. Paragraphs (a), (b) and (c) of the proposed amendments were intended to raise the 'doomed from the start' defence. Paragraph (d) reflected the actual date as fixed by the *Pirelli* case; but, on the evidence which had been called, it was likely that the foundations had settled when, or shortly before, the cracks had appeared in the walls of the houses, that is to say more than six years before 9 September 1982 when the writ was reissued. After considering the well-known authorities about the amendment of pleadings (see the notes to RSC Ord 20, rr 5 to 8 in *The Supreme Court Practice 1982*), the judge gave the second and third defendants leave to amend as they had requested. The plaintiffs' counsel had opposed the application for leave to amend but the defendants did not appeal forthwith against the order. After judgment the plaintiffs were advised that the amendments ought not to have been allowed. They have appealed to this court against the order allowing the amendments and we granted them an extension of time in which to do so.

When allowing the amendments the judge asked counsel for all parties whether they wished to call further evidence. Although, when the amendments were allowed, all the counsel reserved their positions about calling further evidence, later they decided not to do so.

Understandably, on 10 December 1982 counsel then appearing had not appreciated all the ways in which the *Pirelli* case affected this case, particularly as to the procedural steps which had been taken on and after 25 June 1982. A weekend intervened after 10 December. On 13 December defending counsel told the judge that they wished to argue that the claims were statute-barred in any event, as the cracks had appeared over six years before the date of joinder which they now appreciated had been on 9 September 1982. The judge decided to adjourn the case until after the Christmas vacation. During the adjournment counsel for the plaintiffs appreciated the difficulties which faced them if the effective date for joinder was 9 September 1982. He also appreciated that no application had ever been made to extend the time for the joinder of the second and third defendants pursuant to the order made on 25 June 1982. That order had been made under RSC Ord 15, r 6. By r 8 of that order the amendment to the writ had to be made within 14 days, which it was not, and served on any defendant who was to be joined. As a result of counsel's appreciation of the procedural and limitation problems which arose, a summons was issued on 7 January 1982, returnable before the trial judge, asking for a declaration that proceedings against the second and third defendants had been commenced, or were deemed to have been commenced, on or before 30 July 1982, and for an order that the time limited for the joinder of the second and third defendants, pursuant to the order of his Honour Judge Sir William Stabb QC be extended to permit joinder on 9 September 1982. No application was made to extend time for the service of the amended writ, which was reissued on 9 September 1982.

In this court counsel for the third defendants submitted that the omission to serve the amended reissued writ meant that his clients had never been effectively made parties to the action; and, if they had been, it was not until after the date of the January 1983 order. There is nothing in that point. By serving defences and taking part in the trial both the second and third defendants had waived such rights as they had to have the amended reissued writ served on them.

On the hearing of the summons issued on 7 January 1983, the trial judge extended the time for joinder to 9 September 1982 without, as he said, the defendants' counsel raising any real objection to his doing so. He went on to consider that part of the plaintiffs' application asking for a declaration that the proceedings against the second and third defendants had been commenced or should be deemed to have been commenced on 30 July 1982. Defending counsel submitted that a direction in these terms would deprive their clients of their right to plead that the claims were statute-barred. The plaintiffs' counsel relied on what has come to be known as the 'relation back' principle, that is to say, when defendants are properly and unconditionally joined as parties, the action against them is deemed to have started when the writ was first issued. The second and third defendants also argued that as they had been joined at a time when the claims against them were statute-barred, they should be dismissed forthwith from the action. After considering a number of authorities, the judge decided on 18 January 1983 to amend the order made on 25 June 1982 by providing that the joinder should have effect as from 30 July 1982. The third defendants submitted to this court that the judge had no jurisdiction to amend that order and, even if he had, he should not have done so in the terms he did. Judge Hayman delivered judgment in the action on 14 February 1983.

### The procedural issues

It would be convenient, in my opinion, to start the unravelling of this surprising mish-mash of legal issues by considering the procedural ones. The first in point of time, and importance, is that raised by the amendments which were allowed on 10 December 1982. On that date the second and third defendants learned that they might have a limitation defence which they had not known about before, that is to say the houses might have been 'doomed from the start'. This is what they then wanted to plead. Nothing more. They told the judge that they did not want to plead that the claims had been statute-barred when they were joined as defendants. They could have done so and, as I have already commented, if they had, on the evidence, they could have argued that the foundations had settled when or shortly before the cracks appeared. Paragraph (d) of the amendments which were allowed was in substance nothing more than what could have been put into the defences served but which was not. In my judgment, an amendment in terms of para (d) should not have been allowed. The amendments allowed in paras (a), (b) and (c) were of a different kind. The second and third defendants and their advisers had had no reason to think before 10 December that a cause of action could accrue if a house were erected which, due to negligent design or construction, was 'doomed from the start'. They wanted that issue tried and, in my judgment, they were entitled to have it tried, provided that the plaintiffs were not prejudiced by a late amendment. They were not because they were given an opportunity of adducing more evidence. They decided not to take advantage of that opportunity.

### The backdating of the order

The order joining the second and third defendants was made on 25 June 1982. Because the writ was not amended and re-served within the time required by RSC Ord 15, r 8(4) the order was ineffective to make the third and fourth parties defendants. It follows that they were not defendants on 30 July 1982, the date referred to in the trial judge's order of 18 January 1983. The reissue of the writ on 9 September 1982 and the subsequent course of events to which I have already referred made them defendants as from that date but, in my judgment, not before then. It is pertinent to note that the third defendants' notice of appeal assumes that they were parties as from 9 September. It follows that the trial judge had no jurisdiction to declare that the second and third parties were defendants to the action before they were so under the Rules of Court. The judge thought that he had power to make the declaration he did under Ord 15, r 6(2). That rule cannot be used to declare parties to have been joined as defendants before they have been. Apart altogether from these general considerations, a judge at first instance cannot amend another judge's order, save by way of appeal or under the slip rule, and the slip rule did not apply in this case. It follows, in my judgment, that the joinder of the second and third defendants was effected on 9 September and not before. What are the consequences in law of fixing this date?

*Limitation and the doctrine of relation back*
    The plaintiffs, both before the judge and in this court, have submitted that, when a person is joined unconditionally as a defendant in an action, he becomes a party in that action, the starting date of which is the date when the writ was issued. The consequence in law, so it was submitted, is that the period of limitation in actions founded on tort is to be calculated, not from the date of joinder, but six years back from the date when the action started, that is when the writ was issued. Counsel for the plaintiffs invited our attention to a long line of authority starting with *Weldon v Neal* (1887) 19 QBD 394 and ending with *Liptons Cash Registers and Business Equipment Ltd v Hugin (GB) Ltd* [1982] 1 All ER 595.
    I do not consider it necessary to consider this line of cases in detail. It was done by Stephenson and Brandon LJJ in *Liff v Peasley* [1980] 1 All ER 623, [1980] 1 WLR 781 and by his Honour Judge Hawser QC, sitting as a judge of the High Court, in the *Liptons* case. What these cases clearly establish is that a party who asserts, and on the known facts correctly asserts, that the plaintiff's proposed claim against him is statute-barred ought not, in the absence of fraud or other special circumstances, to be joined in the action as a defendant. What is not so clear is the reason why he should not be joined. I have to admit that, until my attention was invited to these cases, I had assumed that the reason was that no useful purpose would be served by the joinder because the proposed defendant could raise a limitation plea. Counsel for the plaintiffs submitted that this was not so, notwithstanding that Brandon LJ in some comments in the *Liff* case was firmly of the opinion that it was.
    In *Mabro v Eagle Star and British Dominions Insurance Co Ltd* [1932] 1 KB 485 at 489, [1932] All ER Rep 411 at 413, which was concerned with an application to join a person as a plaintiff, Greer LJ stated the reason for refusing the application as follows:

'The objection to joining him was that if he were joined and treated as a plaintiff as from the time the writ was issued the defendants would be deprived of the benefit of the Statute of Limitations.'

    In *Lucy v W T Henleys Telegraph Works Co Ltd (ICI Ltd, third party)* [1969] 3 All ER 456, [1970] 1 QB 393 this court had to consider a situation not unlike the present. The plaintiff issued a writ in tort against the defendants (Henleys) who brought in ICI as a third party. Later, she applied to join ICI as a defendant. By this time, ICI could plead that a claim against them was statute-barred. The court held (Lord Denning MR dissenting) that ICI should not be added as a defendant, because to do so would deprive them of a limitation defence. Megaw LJ said ([1969] 3 All ER 456 at 467–468, [1970] 1 QB 393 at 410, 411):

'There is, then, a stark fact which counsel for [the plaintiff] did not seek to deny. If [the plaintiff] were now to seek to issue a writ against the proposed new defendant, I.C.I. she would be faced with an unanswerable plea of limitation, and the Act of 1963 would not provide any escape. She might escape from that position if the court were able to permit, and did permit, the amendment of her existing writ against Henleys so as to join I.C.I., as second defendants. Once new defendants were joined, the action to which they would then have become parties would be one single action, although against two different defendants on two different causes of action. It would have been commenced on the date when the original writ against Henleys was issued, namely 18th November 1965. That it would be one single action, and would be treated as having been commenced at the date of the original writ, is clear in principle and authority. It is the very reason why this court in *Mabro v. Eagle, Star and British Dominions Insurance Co., Ltd.* refused leave to amend a writ by joining an additional plaintiff. So here, if leave were given to amend the writ and to join I.C.I. as additional defendants, "the action" in s. 1(1) and s. 1(3)(b) and s. 3(4) of the Act of 1963 would be the action commenced in November 1965; and "the relevant action" for the purposes of s. 2 of the Act would be the selfsame action, so commenced; being an action to which the second defendants, by leave of the court, had been, or had been allowed to be, made parties. If leave were given to amend the writ and join the proposed new defendants, no recondite argument or subtlety of construction would be required . . . I did not understand counsel for the plaintiff to contend that *Mabro's* case was wrong. Let it be accepted, however, that, since it was a decision of a court consisting only of two members, SCRUTTON and GREER, L.JJ., it is not binding on this court. So far as I am aware, the principle enunciated in that case has never been challenged; and, with all respect, I think the principle is right, as much now as it was 37 years ago. In any event, would it be appropriate to overrule that longstanding authority in an application which is, at least in some respects, ex parte, and in which the court has not had the advantage of full argument on it? With all deference, I think not.'

*Liff v Peasley* brought forward for consideration, seemingly for the first time in a line of authority going back over 90 years, a House of Lords case, *Byron v Cooper* (1844) 2 Cl & Fin 556, 8 ER 1212. A bill for an account of tithes was filed against five defendants before the expiration of the time limited by the Tithe Act 1832, s 3. After the expiration of that time four other persons were introduced as defendants. The House of Lords adjudged that the suit as against these latter defendants must be taken to have been commenced at the date at which they were actually introduced into the bill; and that they could not, by relation back, be treated as defendants to the original bill and that they were consequently entitled to the protection of the statute. The only speech was that of Lord Brougham. I have found difficulty in following his reasoning, largely because the subject matter of the case, tithes, and the procedure to which he referred is outside my professional experience. Brandon LJ thought this case was inconsistent in principle with the 'relation back' theory. The mystery is why it was never referred to before 1980 and was overlooked when the 'relation back' theory was developing. Had there not been a long line of authority, which includes a number of decisions of this court which are binding on us, I would have adopted the reasoning of Brandon LJ, albeit it was obiter; but binding precedents oblige me to accept the 'relation back' theory. It follows that the action against the second and third defendants must be deemed to have started when the writ was issued.

In *Liff v Peasely* [1980] 1 All ER 623 at 642, [1980] 1 WLR 781 at 803 Brandon LJ invited attention to the difficulties which the 'relation back' theory creates when there is an arguable question whether the claim against the person added, or sought to be added, as a defendant is statute-barred or not. In September 1982, when the second and third defendants were added, there could have been an argument whether the plaintiffs' claims against them were statute-barred. This is what Judge Hawser had to consider in the *Liptons* case. He adjudged, in my opinion rightly, that the court has a discretion under Ord 15, r 6(2)(b)(ii) to allow a joinder of a new defendant on terms that it takes effect only from the date of the amendment of the writ.

*The 'doomed from the start' argument*

I turn now to the third defendants' submission that, notwithstanding the application of the 'relation back' theory, all the plaintiffs' claims were statute-barred because their houses were 'doomed from the start'. The plans and siting being faulty, the foundations were bound to settle, thereby causing structural damage. The first question to be decided might perhaps be, what was the 'start'? The depositing of the plans with the second defendants? The completion of the foundations? The completion of the houses? I do not find it necessary to decide when the start was because I am satisfied that this case, on its facts, must be decided in the same way as the *Pirelli* case was, namely that the plaintiffs' causes of action accrued when the physical damage to their houses occurred. In the *Pirelli* case the subject matter of the dispute was a chimney, 160 feet high, for which the defendants accepted responsibility for the way it had been designed. Unsuitable materials had been used in its construction. Damage in the form of cracks near the top of the chimney must have occurred within about ten months of the building work being finished and about eight years before a writ was issued. The damage could, with reasonable diligence, have been discovered about two years after it occurred, but was not discovered until seven years later. The issue was, when did Pirelli's cause of action accrue? The trial judge found that, as a consequence of the use of unsuitable materials, 'cracks were . . . bound to occur'. Nevertheless, it is clear that Lord Fraser did not consider this finding was such as to justify his adjudging that the chimney was 'doomed from the start'. In the two passages in which he referred to buildings which were doomed from the start (see [1983] 1 All ER 65 at 70, 72, [1983] 2 AC 1 at 16, 18), he used the word 'perhaps' in relation to their existence. He said: 'Such cases, if they exist, would be exceptional.' The facts out of which the plaintiffs' claims arise are broadly similar to those in *Pirelli*'s case. They are not exceptional; if anything, all too common. Lord Fraser's reference to buildings which were doomed from the start was not necessary for the decision he made. I would regard it as a cautionary dictum so as to leave for future consideration problems which might arise in exceptional cases.

There remains a further problem arising out of the plaintiffs' claims against the third defendants. The trial judge dismissed the third and fourth plaintiffs' claims. He found that they had noticed the cracks when they returned from holiday which, in the case of the third plaintiff, was on 11 August 1976, and in that of the fourth plaintiff on, or a few days before, 3 September 1976. As they had not said how long they had been away, they had not proved that the cracks had occurred on or after 30 July 1976 which he had, in my judgment wrongly, fixed as the beginning of the limitation period. Having regard to the operation of the 'relation back' theory, the limitation period began on 27 May 1974.

*Economic loss*

Counsel for the third defendants submitted that, even if physical damage to the houses had occurred during the limitation period, economic loss had been suffered by the first defendants when the faulty foundations were laid and that the plaintiffs were in no better position than they were. This meant that all the claims, except that of the fifth plaintiff, were statute-barred. This submission was based on *Junior Books Ltd v Veitchi Co Ltd* [1982] 3 All ER 201, [1983] 1 AC 520. There are a number of answers to this submission; a short one will suffice. The *Junior Books* case was cited in *Pirelli*. It was not a limitation case at all. Their Lordships did not have to consider when a cause of action accrued. Both Lord Fraser and Lord Brandon (who agreed with Lord Fraser's speech in *Pirelli*) had been members of the Appellate Committee when the *Junior Books* case was decided. In *Pirelli* [1983] 1 All ER 65 at 70, [1983] 2 AC 1 at 16 Lord Fraser rejected the notion that a person could recover for diminution in the value of a building by reason of defective foundations which had not yet led to physical damage to it, unless possibly the work could be said to have been doomed from the start. He also considered inapplicable submissions based on *Howell v Young* (1826) 5 B & C 259, [1824–34] All ER Rep 377 and *Forster v Outred & Co* (*a firm*) [1982] 2 All ER 753, [1982] 1 WLR 86 that a client who receives negligent advice suffers damage when he acts on that advice. He said ([1983] 1 All ER 65 at 72, [1983] 2 AC 1 at 18):

'It seems to me that, except perhaps where the advice of an architect or consulting engineer leads to the erection of a building which is so defective as to be doomed from the start, the cause of action accrues only when physical damage occurs to the building.'

I am satisfied that *Pirelli* governs this case.

*Present or imminent danger to health or safety*

I turn now to the plaintiffs' appeal against the dismissal of their claims against the second defendants. The trial judge found that the plaintiffs had not proved that the second defendants' negligence in failing to enforce the building regulations had caused them or their families any 'present or imminent danger to their health or safety' and that such proof was essential to establish their claims. He accepted that they had all suffered discomfort, inconvenience and mental distress. The judge decided, however, that this was not enough. Counsel for the plaintiffs submitted that these findings were wrong and arose from the judge misdirecting himself as to the effect of *Anns v Merton London Borough* [1977] 2 All ER 492, [1978] AC 728. I find it convenient to go at once to the main point in these submissions, namely that the judge should have decided that there was a present or imminent danger to safety, if not health. There was structural damage to the foundations and walls. This was likely to get progressively worse and required remedial action to stop it doing so. The facts of this case were substantially the same as those on which the House of Lords in the *Anns* case decided that a local authority could be in breach of duty to occupiers of buildings, the foundations of which had been negligently inspected (see [1978] AC 728 at 733, where the 'alleged and agreed' facts in that case are set out). There was no allegation that, at any material time, the occupants of the flats had been in present or imminent danger to their health or safety. Paragraph (h) of the statement of facts was in these terms:

> 'No remedial works to the block had as yet been undertaken by the plaintiffs nor had the damage claimed against the second defendants been specified in the pleadings. Such damage would apparently include the cost of work to remedy structural damage to the block, to underpin the foundations to prevent further structural movement, and the plaintiffs' expenses in connection with vacating their maisonettes temporarily while such works were undertaken.'

Their Lordships must, so submitted counsel for the plaintiffs, have decided that the structural damage alleged was of such a kind as to be likely to cause danger to health or safety of those occupying the flats if remedial work were not done. One of the items of damage recoverable was adjudged to be—

> 'the amount of expenditure necessary to restore the dwelling to a condition in which it is no longer a danger to the health or safety of persons occupying and possibly (depending on the circumstances) expenses arising from necessary displacement.'

(See [1977] 2 All ER 492 at 505, [1978] AC 728 at 759 per Lord Wilberforce.)

An absurd situation, said counsel for the plaintiffs, would arise if the occupiers of a building which was structurally unsound due to a local authority's negligence and which was likely to become a danger to health or safety unless remedial action were taken had to wait until it was about to collapse before his right of action against the local authority was accrued. Counsel for the second defendants submitted that the occupier did have to wait until there was a present or imminent danger to health or safety because that is what Lord Wilberforce had said ([1977] 2 All ER 492 at 505, [1978] AC 728 at 760):

> 'It [the cause of action] can only arise when the state of the building is such that there is present or imminent danger to the health or safety of persons occupying it.'

Lord Diplock and Lord Simon said that they agreed with his speech. Having regard to the absurdity to which counsel for the plaintiffs invited our attention, it seems to me that Lord Wilberforce's use of the word 'imminent' should be understood to mean a danger which was likely to arise soon, and how long soon was in any case would depend on the facts and would be a matter of degree. The trial judge did not consider the factor of the likelihood of danger arising soon. He should have done so. Having regard to the nature and extent of the cracks and the likelihood that the damage would be progressive, I would adjudge that there was an imminent danger to the safety of the occupiers of all five houses.

Counsel for the plaintiffs also submitted that Lord Wilberforce's speech should not be understood in a restrictive sense based on the words 'present or imminent danger'. When considered as a whole, its true ratio is that a cause of action lies against a local authority when its breach of duty has failed to prevent harm being caused to the occupiers of property in accordance with the ordinary principles of damage in negligence actions. This approach enabled him to submit that danger to health or safety was only one form of harm. Other forms of harm could be proved such as the discomfort, inconvenience and mental distress which the trial judge found had been caused to the plaintiffs. He pointed out that s 61 of the Public Health Act 1936, as amended by the Public Health Act 1961, empowered the minister to make regulations for purposes which had no connection with health and little, if any, with safety; for example, he could make regulations, as regards buildings, relating to the space around them, their lighting, ventilation and height: see s 61(1)(i)(b) and (c). The building regulations applicable to these claims were made under these powers. Since the passing of the Health and Safety at Work Act 1974, which by s 61 substituted a new s 61 in the Public Health Act 1936, building regulations may be made for the purpose of securing the health, safety, welfare and convenience of persons in or about buildings. Existing regulations were to have effect as if made under s 61 of the 1936 Act as substituted by the 1974 Act. The 1974 Act, however, had not come into force when the plaintiffs first occupied their houses. If the House of Lords in the *Anns* case had had the benefit of the argument of counsel for the plaintiffs as set out above, their Lordships might not have confined their attention to dangers to health or safety. Counsel for the respondents in that case did suggest that the local authority's duty related to health, safety and comfort (see [1978] AC 728 at 744). The fact is, however, that their Lordships decided that the duty owed by the local authority only arises when the state of the building is such that there is present or imminent danger to the health or safety of persons occupying it. It is not for this court to alter the ratio decidendi of *Anns* case.

I would dismiss the third defendants' appeal against the first, second and fifth plaintiffs. I would allow the third and fourth plaintiffs' appeal against the third defendants and the appeal of all the plaintiffs against the second defendants. As between the second and third defendants the apportionment of damage should be that which the trial judge said he would have awarded had he found against the second defendants.

**STEPHEN BROWN LJ.** I agree with Lawton LJ's judgment.

**PARKER LJ.** I agree with the orders proposed by Lawton LJ. On the special point raised on the appeal of the plaintiffs against the second defendants I have nothing to add. For the remainder, I can express my views shortly.

*The date of joinder*

Having regard to the facts (1) that the writ was reissued on 9 September, (2) that the second and third defendants delivered defences to the amended statement of claim enclosed thereon, (3) that thereafter they defended the claims made against them during a trial which occupied several days, (4) that they sought and obtained leave to amend their defences during closing speeches, (5) that, during the argument in January, they sought to have the claims against them dismissed on the basis that they were statute-barred by the time of joinder on 9 September, and finally (6) that in grounds 1, 2, 4, 5, 6 and 7 of their notice of appeal they repeatedly asserted that date of joinder was 9 September, it is not, in my judgment, open to them now to contend either that they have never been joined at all or that, if they have been joined, joinder did not take place until after the extension of time granted in January. Whatever technical points might be advanced on the basis of the Rules of the Supreme Court, it is now much too late to take them. The date of joinder must be taken to be 9 September.

*Amendment of the defences to plead limitation*

If, on joinder, there is a relation back as, in common with the judgment given by Lawton LJ and for his reasons, I hold that there is, any amendment seeking to raise limitation in respect of any cause of action accruing after 26 May 1974 ought to be and to have been refused, because any such amendment would be purposeless. It would inevitably fail. Since none of the plaintiffs purchased until 1975, it follows that sub-paras (c) and (d) of the amendments should not, in any event, have been allowed.

On the face of it, it would appear that no cause of action could arise before purchase, for until purchase no purchaser can have suffered any damage, physical or economic, but in *Pirelli General Cable Works Ltd v Oscar Faber & Partners (a firm)* [1983] 1 All ER 65 at 71, [1983] 2 AC 1 at 18 Lord Fraser said that the relevant duty was owed to owners as a class and that, if time begins to run against one owner, it also runs against his successors in title. Counsel for the third defendants contends that the cause of action arises in the original building owner and that time begins to run against him and all subsequent owners from as early as the submission of plans for approval or at various later stages down to completion of construction. This contention is based on the combination of the class duty already mentioned, the 'doomed from the start' references cited by Lawton LJ in his judgment and the economic damage argument based on the *Junior Books Ltd v Veitchi Co Ltd* [1982] 3 All ER 201, [1983] 1 AC 520. Unless driven by authority I would not be prepared to hold that time would begin to run against anyone other than the original building owner prior to completion of the building. I am not so driven. Indeed, it follows, in my judgment, from *Pirelli* that, on the facts of his case, there was no cause of action prior to actual damage. Accordingly, none of the plaintiffs are time-barred.

I desire to leave open the question whether a defendant should be permitted to amend to set up limitation where there is 'a change in the law' as in the present case, and thus whether the defendants should or should not have been permitted to rely on the cause of action arising earlier than the date on which it had hitherto been held to arise. In general, a defendant should, no doubt, be given leave to amend, on appropriate terms, to rely on the law as it stands up to judgment, but limitation may be a different case. If, for example, a plaintiff in such a case as this has, in the course of negotiations, taken care to issue a protective writ shortly before the limitation period would, on plain Court of Appeal authority, expire, it is, on the face of it, unjust if, perhaps years later, and just before judgment, the House of Lords overrules the Court of Appeal authority and he is then held to be statute-barred. This is no doubt why, when limitation periods are changed by statute, Parliament takes care to say that the change shall not affect any existing action. An even more extreme case would be where the House of Lords overruled a previous decision of its own. This would, on any view, be a change in the law, not merely the correction of the Court of Appeal's understanding as to the state of the law.

As a result of the foregoing, it is unnecessary for me to deal with any of the other points advanced. I should, however, add, first, that I agree that the judge had no jurisdiction to amend the order of 25 June and, second, that, even if the relation back principle is not right and the correct date for the purposes of limitation is 9 September, I would allow the appeal as to sub-para (d) of the amendment. It was clearly granted by the judge on a mistaken view of the situation and the fact that leave to amend is discretionary is therefore of no significance. In the circumstances of the case, no amendment should be allowed. Accordingly, even if the relation back principle is wrong, I would have reached the same conclusion.

*Appeal dismissed. Cross-appeal allowed.*

Solicitors: *Hewitt Woollacott & Chown* (for the third defendants); *Barlow Lyde & Gilbert* (for the second defendants); *Herbert Smith & Co* (for the plaintiffs).

Mary Rose Plummer    Barrister.

# Meah v McCreamer

QUEEN'S BENCH DIVISION
WOOLF J
25, 26, 27, 28, 29 JUNE 1984

*Damages – Personal injury – Brain damage – Severe personality change – Personality change resulting in plaintiff's imprisonment – Plaintiff committing serious sexual offences on women resulting in life imprisonment – Whether plaintiff entitled to damages for imprisonment.*

In August 1982 the plaintiff was a passenger in a car driven by the defendant, who was drunk at the time. The car was involved in an accident, which was caused by the defendant's negligence, and the plaintiff sustained serious head injuries and brain damage which resulted in him undergoing a marked personality change. Prior to the accident the plaintiff had been convicted of various criminal offences such as theft and burglary and had a poor employment record but he had had a number of successful relationships with women and there was no evidence of his being violent towards women. In February 1982 the plaintiff sexually assaulted and maliciously wounded two women and in September of that year raped and maliciously wounded a third woman. He was sentenced to life imprisonment for those offences and was classed as a category A (ie highly dangerous) prisoner. The plaintiff claimed damages against the defendant on the grounds, inter alia, that but for the brain damage caused in the accident and the resulting personality change he would not have committed the offences for which he was imprisoned.

**Held** – Since but for the injuries received in the accident, and the resulting personality change, the plaintiff would not have committed the criminal acts for which he was serving a sentence of life imprisonment, he was entitled to damages to compensate him for being imprisoned. However, in assessing those damages it was necessary to take into account the plaintiff's previous criminal tendencies, which would probably have resulted in him spending periods in prison, and the fact that, having regard to his previous poor employment record and the free board he would receive in prison, there would be no continuing financial loss. In all the circumstances, the appropriate damages were a round figure of £60,000 to compensate the plaintiff for pain and suffering, his injuries, including the physical after-effects of his brain injury, and his imprisonment. That figure would be reduced by 25% to take into account the plaintiff's contributory negligence in travelling as a passenger with a driver whom he knew to be drunk (see p 371 c d, p 382 f to j and p 383 b to j, post).

## Notes
For the general principles of damages for personal injury, see 12 Halsbury's Laws (4th edn) para 1146.

## Cases referred to in judgment
*Groom v Crocker* [1938] 2 All ER 394, [1939] 1 KB 194.
*Jones v Jones* [1984] 3 All ER 1003, [1984] 3 WLR 862, CA.
*Owens v Brimmell* [1976] 3 All ER 765, [1977] QB 859, [1977] 2 WLR 943.

## Action
The plaintiff, Christopher Brenty Meah, issued a writ dated 28 August 1981 against the defendant, Kenneth McCreamer, claiming damages for injuries suffered as a result of an accident on 9 August 1978 involving a car driven by the defendant in which the plaintiff was travelling as a passenger. The facts are set out in the judgment.

*David Kemp QC* and *Simon Levene* for the plaintiff.
*Julian Priest QC* and *Timothy Nash* for the defendant.

**WOOLF J.** This is a claim for damages in respect of an accident which took place on 9 August 1978 on High Road, Chigwell at about 2.30 am. On that occasion the plaintiff was travelling in a Jaguar motor car that left the road and crashed into a tree. There is no doubt that the plaintiff sustained serious injuries.

The case before me involved determination of the following issues: first of all, was the defendant the driver of the Jaguar car? He disappeared. Nobody has been able to get in touch with him and the solicitors and counsel who have been acting on his behalf are instructed by his insurers under his insurance policy.

The second issue is whether the plaintiff was sitting in the front passenger seat. That issue was relevant because of an allegation of contributory negligence arising out of alleged failure to use a safety belt. It would only apply if he was the passenger sitting in the front passenger seat.

The third issue is whether the solicitors acting for the defendant are entitled to allege contributory negligence arising out of the fact that the plaintiff is alleged to have agreed to be driven by a driver who was under the influence of alcohol without any specific instructions from the defendant. The matter was raised in the amended reply in the following terms: referring to an allegation which is contained in the amended defence suggesting that the plaintiff was negligent in causing or permitting himself to be driven in a motor car by a driver who he knew or ought to have known was unfit to drive by reason of excessive consumption of alcohol, it is stated in the amended reply that those allegations were made without the authority of the defendant and are contrary to his interests, and accordingly they should be struck out under RSC Ord 18, r 19, or alternatively under the inherent jurisdiction of the court, and furthermore, the plea cannot be relied on by the defendant to reduce the plaintiff's damages.

Finally, I have to deal with the question of the damages to which the plaintiff is entitled. Here the most significant issue is an allegation which was included for the first time in the amended statement of claim which was reserved in March 1984. As part of the particulars of the plaintiff's damages it alleges that:

'On 10 February 1982 the plaintiff sexually assaulted and maliciously wounded Janice Sullivan in her home in Hackney ... on the same day the plaintiff sexually assaulted Eileen Walsh in her home in Homerton ... on 25 September 1982 the plaintiff raped and maliciously wounded Christine Dashwood in her home in Bow ...'

It then states: 'It is averred that had the plaintiff not suffered the brain damage aforesaid [and this is referring to brain damage caused in the accident] it is unlikely that he would have committed' those acts. It then recites the fact that having pleaded guilty to offences in respect of those matters on 4 August 1983 he was sentenced as follows: in respect of the attack on Mrs Sullivan, three years' imprisonment; in respect of offences associated with that attack, 18 months' imprisonment consecutive; in respect of the assault on Mrs Walsh, 18 months' imprisonment, which was consecutive to the previous sentences; and in relation to the rape and wounding of Mrs Dashwood he was sentenced to life imprisonment.

I will deal with the issues I have identified in turn.

So far as the first issue is concerned: was the defendant the driver? I can record straight away that, having regard to the evidence which was called in the case, counsel for the defendant realistically accepted that although he would contend, with some justification, that the plaintiff was an unreliable witness the evidence which he gave that the defendant was the driver is supported by other evidence and, in the circumstances, he accepted that it was inevitable that I would find the defendant to be the driver of the Jaguar car in the early hours of 9 August 1978 when the accident occurred. I do so find, and accordingly the first issue is resolved.

With regard to the second issue, on the balance of probabilities on the evidence which is before me, again without argument being strongly addressed to the contrary before me by counsel for the defendant, I come to the conclusion that at the time of the accident the plaintiff was sitting in one of the rear seats of the Jaguar motor car. In those circumstances, the relevant allegation of contributory negligence fails. I come to that conclusion notwithstanding the fact that the plaintiff did make a statement at one stage saying that he was travelling in the front passenger seat. That statement, however, was made substantially after an earlier statement which he made to the police indicating that he was in the rear seat, and having heard his evidence on this point, on the balance of probabilities, I am prepared to find in his favour.

So far as the third issue is concerned, there was an agreed statement of facts put before me, to which I should refer and which is in these terms:

'Neither Insurers nor Solicitors were ever able to find the defendant, nor were the Police, nor were the plaintiff's solicitors. Neither Insurers nor Solicitors ever had any communication oral or written with the defendant. The defendant never submitted accident report or claim form or gave any explanation or information to Insurers or Solicitors regarding the accident.'

Having regard to those facts the submissions advanced by counsel for the plaintiff can be summarised shortly as follows: first, that the defendant's solicitors were acting and are acting, and indeed counsel are acting, as an agent of the defendant and, therefore, they are not allowed to act inconsistent with the duty they owe to him not to do anything which is in conflict with his interests.

Counsel for the plaintiff then refers to the terms of the policy in question which, so far as relevant, states:

'The Insurers shall be entitled if they so desire, to take over and conduct in the name of the insured the defence or settlement of any claim or to prosecute in the name of the insured for its own benefit any claim for indemnity or damages or otherwise, and shall have full discretion in the conduct of any proceedings or in the settlement of any claim.'

Notwithstanding the wide terms of that clause of the policy, counsel for the plaintiff submits it does not allow the insurers or the solicitors they have instructed to depart from the general duty to which I have made reference. So far I agree with and accept counsel for the plaintiff's submission.

In support of it he refers to *Groom v Crocker* [1938] 2 All ER 394, [1939] 1 KB 194. I do not need to refer to the facts of that case because they were very different from those in this case, but I do refer to a passage in the judgment in that case, one of the passages relied on by counsel for the plaintiff, where in referring to a similar policy to the policy in this case, Greene MR said ([1938] 2 All ER 394 at 400, [1939] 1 KB 194 at 203):

'The effect of the provisions in question is, I think, to give to the insurers the right to decide upon the proper tactics to pursue in the conduct of the action, provided that they do so in what they *bona fide* consider to be the common interest of themselves and their insured.'

There are other passages in the judgment which make it clear that the solicitors acting under the terms of a policy of this sort must not do acts which are inconsistent with the interest of the insured, they must not exercise their powers arbitrarily, and they must not fail to exercise a real discretion taking into account the insured's interests.

Counsel for the plaintiff then submits that the allegation of contributory negligence, based on the fact that the defendant may have been under the influence of drink, is a positive allegation being made by his assured that he was so obviously drunk that it was not only negligent for him to drive, it actually amounted to a criminal offence. What is more, the only evidence that this was the situation, so far as the insurers were concerned, was provided by a statement which the defendant made to the police, which included the fact that he was suggesting he was not even driving. There could be no implied authority to make this allegation which amounts to an admission of a serious offence and therefore it should be struck out.

I do not accept counsel for the plaintiff's contentions. It seems to me that it is in no way inconsistent with the duty which the solicitors undoubtedly owed to the defendant for them to make this allegation of contributory negligence. It was not a positive case that the defendant was guilty of a criminal offence, it amounted to this: if the court on the facts came to the conclusion that he was driving under the influence of drink, then, in those circumstances, there would be a breach of duty on the part of the plaintiff to take proper care for his own safety in agreeing to travel in the motor car with him. It seems to me for the defendant's solicitors not to have made an allegation of that sort, on the facts of this case, would have been inconsistent with the duty which they owed to the defendant to ensure that he was not under an obligation to pay more damages than was required. On the basis of the case which has been put forward by the plaintiff, this was something which they were entitled to rely on as a partial defence and, accordingly, it seems to me that it was a perfectly proper plea and the criticisms which are made of it are without substance.

I turn, therefore, to consider the allegation that the plaintiff was guilty of contributory negligence in agreeing to travel in the car in the circumstances which exist here. Guidance is provided by a previous decision of this court given by Watkins J in *Owens v Brimmell* [1976] 3 All ER 765, [1977] 1 QB 859. Dealing with the facts of that case, which were not dissimilar from those here, as is made clear by the headnote, part of the decision of the judge was ([1977] 1 QB 859 at 860):

> 'A person who accepted a lift in a car might be guilty of contributory negligence if he either knew that the driver had consumed alcohol in such quantity as was likely to impair to a dangerous degree the driver's capacity to drive properly and safely or, knowing that he would be given a lift in the car, accompanied the driver on a bout of drinking which had the effect eventually of affecting the passenger's clear thought and perception and diminished the driver's capacity to drive carefully. [So] the probabilities were that, at the time the plaintiff accepted the lift home, his powers of thought and perception were affected by drink, [or], if the plaintiff was not so affected by drink, he should have foreseen the danger of accepting a lift in the defendant's car and therefore, although the defendant had to take the greater responsibility, the plaintiff had been guilty of contributory negligence . . .'

Which in that case resulted in the damages being reduced by 20%.

So far as this case is concerned, there was evidence put before the court by a former Pc Fennell, who had been a police officer for 24 years, as to the condition of the defendant. He described him as manifesting what I call the conventional symptoms of a driver who had been drinking excessively. He also gave evidence that at the time of his attendance at the scene of the accident a sample of blood was taken which, when analysed, indicated that half an hour after the accident the defendant had a quantity of alcohol in his blood which was equivalent to 143mg per 100ml of blood. That was well in excess of the legal limit which is, of course, based on a figure of 80, and that clearly supports the view of the police officer that the defendant was not in a fit condition to drive a vehicle because of the amount he had been drinking.

The circumstances of the accident also support that view. As far as is known, there is no explanation for the defendant going off the road in the way he did apart from his inability to control the vehicle through drink.

What is the position with regard to the plaintiff's knowledge of this? The plaintiff himself gave evidence about the matter and he indicated that he had been driving a minicab on the day in question; that his last fare was a passenger who in fact accompanied him later on his drinking, and his drinking started at about 10 pm with a visit to a public house. The defendant was already there at the public house and had clearly been there for some time before he arrived. They had then gone off to the Epping Country Club which was some fifteen miles away. They had stayed there for approximately 2½ hours. During that period the plaintiff had taken six to eight Scotch and Coke drinks and the defendant had had about the same amount of drinks, although the plaintiff did not know precisely what he was drinking. The plaintiff said he did not think the defendant was drunk when they came to leave at about 2 15 to 2 30 am. However, he himself was tipsy but not drunk. What is more, it was elicited from him under cross-examination that he had left his car behind and travelled in the defendant's car because he knew they were going drinking; that he assumed that the defendant had had more to drink at the pub before he arrived, and that he believed the defendant was drinking the same shorts and drinking about the same pace as he had drunk himself. He said he paid little attention to the condition of the defendant and, although he described him as being happy earlier in the evening, he accepted under cross-examination that he supposed the defendant was in about the same condition as he was.

I have no doubt at all, on that evidence, that if the plaintiff had not himself been affected by drink it would have been quite obvious to him that the defendant was not in a fit state to drive, that there was an obvious risk in accompanying the defendant in that motor car, and that this is an appropriate case, therefore, in which there should be a finding of contributory negligence against the plaintiff on the basis of the approach indicated by Watkins J. Although urged by the defendant to take the view that this was a case which was considerably worse than that described by Watkins J and to treat it on the same basis as Watkins J by counsel for the plaintiff, I have come to the conclusion that the plaintiff is entitled to succeed in this case because there was clear negligence on the part of the defendant but that he was also negligent, and that the appropriate proportion of blame which he should bear is 25%. It accordingly follows that any damages I award will be reduced by that amount.

Turning now to the next issue which I have got to deal with, there was a claim for special damages in this case, but the evidence was difficult and unsatisfactory and that claim was not made out, except in part in relation to a claim for loss of earnings in respect of a poor work record. With regard to the claim for loss of earnings, the plaintiff might have been in difficulty but for the fact that, having regard to the totality of the evidence, the defendant's insurers were prepared to accept that the special damages should be agreed at £1,000.

I turn next to the remaining question of damages. It is with regard to these that the difficulty in this case arises.

There is, first of all, the entitlement of the plaintiff to be compensated for the pain and suffering in regard to what I will call the conventional injuries apart from the personality change which he seeks to allege to have been the result of the accident.

Then there is the damages that he is entitled to recover in respect of the consequences of the accident which he alleges to be due to the personality defect, which he says results from the accident. This in turn has two elements: first of all, there is the normal consequences of the sort of brain injury which the plaintiff undoubtedly suffered, which give rise to minor irritability and matters of that sort. Second, there is the much more fundamental claim which has been put forward on the basis of the plaintiff's allegation that his criminal conduct to which I have already made reference was in fact due to the accident.

So far as the last head of damage is concerned, as is made apparent by *Jones v Jones* [1984] 3 All ER 1003, [1984] 3 WLR 862, there can be claims for damages in head injury cases which at first sight appear surprising. And I indicate straight away that if it can be shown on the balance of probabilities that but for the accident and the injuries the plaintiff suffered as a result, he would not have committed the crimes referred to in the amended statement of claim and, therefore, would not be now serving a sentence of life imprisonment, it was not argued on behalf of the defendant that the plaintiff is not entitled to be compensated for that and, indeed, entitled to receive substantial damages in respect of that matter. Of course the cases in which a plaintiff would be able to put forward such a claim successfully will be few indeed, and it is not without significance that neither counsel, or indeed the very distinguished medical witnesses who gave evidence before me, were able to point to any precedent for the claim which the plaintiff has put forward in this case and which I must now consider, not on the basis of any issue of public policy or remoteness of damage, but as a question of fact on the basis of the medical evidence before me.

However, before doing so I will refer to his more conventional injuries and his more conventional claims in respect of them.

The plaintiff first of all had certain orthopaedic injuries. After the accident he was taken to hospital and it was then found that there was a fracture of the shaft of the right clavicle; there were also fractures of both the right and left ankle; there were abrasions and lacerations to the left side of the head and face; and also, and this is not unimportant and should be borne in mind when considering the medical evidence with regard to later issues, a laceration to the right side of the tongue. An operation was carried out in respect of both of the ankle injuries for internal fixation, and so far as those orthopaedic injuries are concerned the plaintiff made an extremely good recovery. Mr Monty, the orthopaedic consultant surgeon, in his report dated 19 July 1983, indicates that in the right shoulder there is a lump in the centre of the clavicle but no tenderness. So far as the left ankle is concerned there is no swelling, the circumferential measurement being equivalent to that on the opposite side; no pain was elicited on palpation of the bone round the ankle; movements of the left ankle, however, were limited, and while flexion was full, extension was 10° below though neither movements caused any particular pain. So far as the left foot was concerned there was a full range of movements. So far as the right ankle was concerned there was no swelling, there was no tenderness, there was a well healed scar and movements were full. The conclusion that Mr Monty came to was that the situation I have just described should be regarded as a permanent one subject to this, that there is a risk that in the future the plaintiff would develop osteo-arthritic changes in the left ankle joint which might require medical or even surgical intervention. So far as the right ankle is concerned, this was much less likely but also possible. However, apart from that, so far as the orthopaedic injuries are concerned there is unlikely to be any further sequelae.

There is one further matter I should add with regard to those injuries. The final certificate so far as his being off work is concerned was given on 27 May 1980.

The picture with regard to his head injuries, however, is much more serious. A computerised brain scan took place on his brain and the results of that appear most satisfactorily in the report of 11 June 1984 of Dr Gooddy, the consultant neuro-physician who holds many appointments, among them one at the National Hospital for Nervous Diseases. He says that the brain scan taken on 3 February 1983 which he has examined indicated 'a clear cut area of left anterior frontal damage extending from the inner surface of the skull to or almost to the anterior end of the left lateral ventricle'. Dr Gooddy was of the opinion that 'both lateral ventricles . . . are larger than normal, the left being larger than the right' and that there was also local damage.

To illustrate what is shown by the results of the scan which he had examined he put before me a diagram which illustrates the area of injury very clearly.

In addition to that evidence I have abundance of other medical evidence. I had a report from Mr King, who is the consultant neuro-surgeon at the London Hospital, dated 18 September 1981. There was also a report from Mr Offen, who was a consultant at the Whipps Cross Hospital, dated 10 August 1982. I can conveniently just refer to a short passage which is relevant. Dealing with the progress of the plaintiff, Mr Offen indicates that by 12 September 1978 he 'was still a little aggressive but this is common after such a severe head injury', and that the plaintiff was 'rather "thalamic" in his approach with a tendency to agitation and aggression'. I should say that the doctor also indicates that on 12 September 1978 the plaintiff took his own discharge from hospital, which was clearly before he was considered fit to be discharged by the doctors.

Then I had reports by a consultant psychiatrist, Dr Cookson, dated 30 November 1982 and 11 March 1983; reports by Dr Noble, who is also a consultant psychiatrist, dated 7 February and 18 June 1984, who has among his appointments the Bethlem Royal and Maudsley Hospital. I have an additional report by Dr Gooddy dated 22 May 1984. I have got reports from Dr Roberts which are dated 4 April and 15 June 1984. Dr Roberts is a consultant neuro-physician. Finally, I have got a report by the well-known consultant psychiatrist Dr Leigh who has great experience in these matters.

All the last four doctors whom I mentioned gave evidence before me. As I understand it, the other reports which are available are put before me as part of the material which was available to the doctors who did give evidence; that their reports are not agreed but are merely evidence of background matters which were part of the basis on which the doctors who did give oral evidence founded their opinion. There, of course, I am confining my remarks to the reports dealing with the neurological problems in this case and was not referring to the agreed orthopaedic reports.

First of all, adding to the description of the injuries to that provided by the results of the scan, I turn to the report from Mr King, who says that in his opinion the plaintiff—

'suffered quite a severe head injury characterised by loss of consciousness probably for a period of about a month and bleeding into the left frontal lobe. He seems to have made a good physical recovery so far as the brain injury is concerned and notes no alteration in his mentality.'

However, Mr King did refer to the fact that the plaintiff had had probably one generalised fit. This referred to a fit which took place on a not clearly specified date in about 1980 in a public house, of which there is no independent evidence but which I accept did take place in roughly the manner described by the plaintiff to the doctor. So far as the future was concerned, Mr King indicated that the risk of epilepsy was the principal disability. He said the patient had not been continued to be followed up in out-patients, but he was attempting to get him up for an EEG and for review, and added, 'but it seems likely that, if he has had one fit, he may well have more in the future and that he should probably be regarded as being epileptic'.

All the doctors whose evidence was given before me with regard to this head of damage agreed that the plaintiff was undoubtedly affected in his personality to some degree as a result of the accident. What was in issue was the extent of the personality change which followed. In order to assess this, it is most important to have in mind the evidence which was available to the court as to the plaintiff's general personality before the accident.

So far as this is concerned, he was born in January 1952, so he is now 32. It is clear that he had a poor background. He did not do well at school. He was bullied, as he says and I accept. He indulged in stealing while at school. He left at 15, probably semi-illiterate. He then had a period of time during which he accepts himself in evidence he acted in an irresponsible and at times violent way. He was, as he has put it, a 'skinhead'. Some support as to the extent of his violent behaviour at that time is to be found from his own medical record, which indicates that he was attending the London Hospital from time to time during this period of his life. Apparently in 1969, when he would have been 17, he was at the hospital being attended to for multiple cuts after being attacked with a bottle. In 1970 he was there having been hit over the head with a poker. In 1970, according to the medical records, he was attending the hospital because he had been kicked in the jaw and had a fractured mandible, but he says in fact he was punched with a knuckle duster when he had been on an outing to Southend-on-Sea on this occasion and the record is wrong. Then in 1971 he was being attended to for a cut head, knocking it through a window according to the medical notes, but his description of this incident is perhaps revealing. He says that he was provoked in some way by someone who was the other side of a plate-glass window, that he tried to butt that person through the window with his head and it was in the process of seeking to do that that he cut his head in this way. In 1971 he received injuries to his back.

However, it is fair to say in his favour that that pattern of violence which is indicated by those incidents did in fact take place over a limited period of time when it may well be that he was going through a skinhead phase which other young men grow out of.

More information is provided as to the sort of background the plaintiff had from his criminal record, to which I should now turn. This shows that he first appeared before the courts, a juvenile court, for housebreaking when he was 15, that was in June 1967, and for similar offences in February 1968. That he was before a juvenile court for theft in 1969 on two occasions, one from a woman's handbag. We then go to 1972 when he was before the Crown Court for theft. He had certain driving offences, and this was followed in December 1973, with his coming before the court for a driving offence, driving with alcohol above the prescribed limit, and also assault on the police. As far as that is concerned, he contended that the officer who was arresting him was too aggressive; he said he was high with amphetamines and he butted the police officer. He was sent for borstal training. Having been for borstal training, he was again before the court for driving offences, for attempting to steal a handbag in 1977; in 1978 two cases of burglary. That completes his record up to the time of the accident.

Now I do not want to diminish in any way the record of crime that this man has, but it is by no means a record which indicates serious or grave criminal offences of the sort that sometimes are disclosed when one is dealing with a person who subsequently commits the sort of offences which this man was to commit in the later years. He could be described, as he was described by a number of the doctors, as a criminally aggressive psycopath. However, the term 'psycopath' is a very wide one and, looking at the record to which I have just referred, notwithstanding other material which is provided by the medical records, one would not have regarded the plaintiff as being someone who had a record which indicated that he was committed to serious crime at the time of his accident in 1978.

So far as work is concerned, the pattern is much what one would expect having regard to what I have already said about him. He was in and out of work. He had worked as a sheet metal worker, a labourer. He did not keep jobs long. He was out of work for long periods of time. He worked as a minicab driver. The only record that we really have of any permanent employment is that as a railman between 3 October 1977 and 20 June 1978 with London Transport. His former wife, when she gave evidence, described him, rightly, as not being a good worker. Certainly it is of significance that if he found a job arduous that was a good ground, in his view, for giving up employment. Furthermore, from about 1975 he was taking drugs. He dealt with this in his own evidence. He described, in the course of cross-examination, that he had been using drugs from about 1975, cannabis and amphetamine or speed, and that he had been injecting himself from time to time with dephanol. He said he was not drinking heavily, but he was averaging about 15 to 20 pints of beer a week and, in addition, he would have a whisky or two. He thought he would have the amphetamine once every three weeks, but with regard to this I am sure there were times when the plaintiff indulged in drugs and drink to a greater extent than he was prepared to concede in the course of his evidence. What is more, he agreed that before the accident at times he had been depressed and this had continued for a period of ten years, and that he had been an in-patient at St Clement's Hospital for two or three weeks in the early 1970s for excess of amphetamines and he had also been drinking at that time.

If, however, the plaintiff had shortcomings so far as his employment and record of honesty is concerned, apparently he was nonetheless attractive to the opposite sex. There is no doubt that prior to the accident he had a considerable success with a number of ladies. In particular he met the lady who became his wife when she was 16 and they were married in August 1974. She gave evidence before me. She is still called Gloria Meah although she has since been divorced, and her evidence (which I scrutinised with care, conscious that she could have interests which meant that, notwithstanding she was divorced, she would be anxious to assist the plaintiff) I thought was reasonably impressive. She described that initially she regarded him as somebody who was concerned and, as she put it, 'had a heart'. She agreed that the marriage had gone wrong, but the main reason that she put this down to was his adultery, because he was undoubtedly carrying on with other women during the course of the marriage, and also what she described as mental cruelty. Because of his conduct she obtained a separation order in January 1977 from the magistrates. That was based on his desertion. But she said he did not use direct violence o her at any time prior to the accident. He broke the door down on one occasion when he was anxious to get into the house, on an occasion when her sister was present, and he pushed past her, but there was no actual violence. And there is no evidence before me to indicate that this description of their married life, with its ups and downs, was in any way inaccurate.

I also had evidence from a lady I am going to call 'Josephine'. She was a lady who had had various misfortunes in her life. She was nervous and unstable and had at times tried to take her own life. There is no doubt that she was, and, astonishingly in view of what I am going to have to relate hereafter, is still, fond of the plaintiff. She says that she loved him and still does love him. They met in 1976 and from then on, from time to time, the plaintiff would be spending periods living with her during the time with which I am concerned. She described him as being considerate in their sexual activities and she said that, although he was more experienced in sexual matters than she was, he would not insist on her indulging in sexual practices that she was not prepared to adopt. It is not necessary to go into the details of those sexual practices in this judgment, but there is no doubt about it that there was a certain amount of experimentation of a nature which some would regard as unusual occurring between the plaintiff and Josephine prior to the accident. But she says that nothing took place with which she was not in agreement, and she clearly, during this period, was attached to the plaintiff and it is right I should say that at a later date she bore a child, among the other children which she had, of which he was the father.

So far as the other ladies in his life are concerned, I did not hear evidence from them. Their identities were known and statements have been taken from certain of those ladies and the plaintiff was asked limited questions about them in cross-examination.

That was the position prior to the accident. So far as the position after the accident is concerned, both Gloria, his former wife, and Josephine described a very marked change in his behaviour in relation to them. Gloria said that when he first came out of hospital he was really rather childlike and followed her about and manifested some of the obvious features which are indicated by persons who have had a severe brain injury and who are affected by it. But she said as he got over his initial symptoms he became more demanding and aggressive. She described how he would insist on oral sex; that he treated her rougher and rougher, and she described one incident where he pulled her out of bed and then insisted on sexual activity. There is no doubt, if her account is right, the plaintiff was considerably more aggressive shortly after they resumed married life after the accident than he had been before, and eventually they separated and divorce proceedings took place.

As his marriage broke down so far as Gloria was concerned the plaintiff resumed his relationship with Josephine. It began again in 1980, already a substantial period after the accident, and she described a series of incidents thereafter which occurred up to the time when he left her for the last time. She in particular described herself as being held down and being forced to do things of a sexual nature to which she objected. She described being kicked in the face. She described also being held over a balcony with threats of having her throat cut. She also referred to other incidents which she said resulted in her receiving hospital treatment. At my instigation her medical records for this period were obtained, because I have already indicated that she was an unstable person and it seemed to me desirable, before giving full credence to what she said, to see whether there was any independent support. As a result, at a late stage in the case her medical records have been produced and whereas, so far as I have seen, there is nothing indicating any form of aggression by the plaintiff to her prior to the accident, from 1980 onwards there is a difference. In particular on 11 September 1980 she turned up alleging assault. She said that she had been punched five days previously (the medical records state: 'Injury to the mandible and nose. X-ray of mandible showed double factures. There was also a fracture of the nose') and she was then referred to St Bartholomew's Hospital. Josephine said that when she returned to the home at which she was then living with the plaintiff with her jaw wired up, the plaintiff then hit her on the jaw and she had to have further treatment.

That I do not see confirmed in the medical record, but there is another matter that she gave evidence about referred to and that resulted in her going to Hackney Hospital on 27 March 1981 when she had a crush injury to the right hand and she again alleged this was due to an assault. Then she came back again, and again this fitted in with her evidence, on 20 August 1982 when she was five months pregnant and she again was complaining of assault (the medical records state: 'Injury to the mandible and a broken incisor tooth' and no fracture was shown. Having regard to the support provided by the medical records, again on the balance of probabilities, I have come to the conclusion that the general description that Josephine gave of her relationship with the plaintiff after the accident is one which is true and that he was, as she said, very aggressive, he would fly off the handle and get himself in a state, that he was making increasing sexual demands on her and insisting on sexual conduct that she was not agreeable to, and that she was in a situation where, as she put it, 'she had to do what Chris said or else', and that he was insisting on things which she regarded as perverted and matters of a sexual nature which were not indulged in prior to the accident.

There is, therefore, on that evidence, strong support for saying that the plaintiff had become more aggressive after the accident than he had been before, and that he was certainly more callous and had less regard to the feelings of his partner in his sexual relations.

It is next necessary to turn to the attacks which he made on Mrs Sullivan, Mrs Walsh and Mrs Dashwood. I regret having to do so, but it is important that I refer to these matters as part of the evidence in this case because what the defendant says is that they indicate features which are quite different from the features which you would normally see as part of the result which can be expected from a head injury of this sort. In particular, so far as the defendant is concerned, it is important to have in mind whether there was any prior planning, whether there was any degree of foresight as to the consequences of the conduct in which the plaintiff was indulging, and what part other factors apart from his head injury may have played, in particular in relation to the attacks it is important to note the extent to which he was, or could have been, affected by drugs and drink.

In relation to these matters I find the descriptions of the victims much more helpful than the descriptions given by the plaintiff. It seems to me that so far as he was concerned, in so far as he was capable of doing so, he was seeking to try and minimise the gravity of what he had done.

The first victim, Mrs Sullivan, was well known to the plaintiff, and indeed on the day of the attack, 10 February 1982, the plaintiff had in fact been upstairs with her husband and another man, Tony Rogers. It seems that they came downstairs at one stage and then they went out. She noted when the plaintiff came downstairs and was playing with her children that 'he appeared drugged up and had been drinking'. It seems that one of the sources of his drugs was the Tony Rogers who was in the house. They went out at about 10 pm and after about 15 to 20 minutes the plaintiff returned and rang the door bell. He was admitted into the home. He told the woman concerned that he fancied her and tried to kiss her, and when she turned away he stood up in front of her and pulled out her carving knife from behind him and put it to her throat. She said she could not understand him, his speech was slurred, he was prodding her with the knife. She said that she put her hand up to protect herself and he cut her across the hand. He went on prodding her in the face and she put her hand up and he stabbed her in the middle of the hand. She tried to grab the knife and push it away and he then unzipped his trousers and got hold of her hair and pulled her head towards his penis. With some courage in the circumstances, she then said that she would bite it off before she did that and he then asked her where her bedroom was. She said she did not have one and then he tried to pull her jumper off and she pushed him away. She said that he told her to take her tights off and then went mad and went into a frenzied attack, cut her face and side and the right leg, and that she started screaming and he panicked and ran out with the knife. She thought that he had taken the knife earlier, because her impression was that he could not have had time during the visit when the attack took place to have got hold of that knife.

Having left that woman he turned his attention to Mrs Walsh, whom he also knew and whose husband was then in prison. She was disturbed at about 11 pm. She let him in. She said she had never really spoken to him much and she said he then pulled out a knife and said he had just had a fight in a pub and he had stabbed someone. She said that she noticed the knife was a kitchen knife; that he had been taking drugs, and he said he still had some on him. She went into the living room and she was with her young child and she said she sat on the sofa with the child in her arms. The plaintiff came back into the living room with the knife in his hand and she told him not to hurt her, and she says he leant over her and said, 'Just do as I say,' and she said, 'What do you want me to do?' He said, 'You know,' and she said, 'I haven't been with other men, I don't know what you want me to do' and she was extremely frightened, and she thought he might try to kill her. He then indulged in the sort of conduct which he had started to indulge in with Mrs Sullivan, again pulled her head towards his penis and she was threatened with a knife and she then took part in a number of sexual activities which she was forced to take part in because of his threat that he used against her. It is true that sexual intercourse did not take place, but the activities were certainly such that, in my view, they were every bit as serious as if that had taken place, if not more serious. Eventually he left, but before he had gone she told him he was wicked and he said to her that he was 'stoned' when he did it.

There is no doubt, with regard to those activities, they occurred with the plaintiff using very considerable violence, showing no consideration whatsoever for his victims, and it occurred at a time when he was affected both by drugs and drink.

I turn to Mrs Dashwood. She was a lady who lived nearby the plaintiff at that time whom he had only met on one previous occasion but whom he agreed in evidence he fancied as a result of seeing her, and that he fancied her in a sexual manner. She describes how he came to the door on 24 September 1982 at about 6 pm. We know from his evidence that earlier during the afternoon he had been at a public house and had some drink, but there is nothing to suggest that he had had any drugs and it is to be noted that we are talking about a time of about 6 pm when the attack took place when one would not expect the sort of drinking that the plaintiff normally indulged in at lunchtime to be affecting him in any marked way. He entered the house by making an excuse, inquiring whether his daughter had left a work book in Mrs Dashwood's home. In that way he was invited in and he said that he went in, having made that excuse, deliberately with a view to having sexual contact with Mrs Dashwood.

Mrs Dashwood described how shortly after the plaintiff had entered her home he put one of his hands across her mouth and said, 'Don't scream and I won't hurt you.' He then told her he was on the run and needed some money and she told him there was no money there. She said that she tried to calm him down, and she described how she made coffee and for a time appeared to cause him to quieten down. She indicates they had a cigarette and that he kept saying, 'I'm sorry I had to do that. Don't tell Tina [that is the lady with whom he was then living], she'll go mad', and she said she kept saying 'alright'. She said he then produced a knife from somewhere, and she said she thought it was from his back trouser pocket. This was a sizeable penknife which apparently the plaintiff said he normally carried but which he agreed he had gone home to collect before coming to Mrs Dashwood's house. He held the knife in front of her and told her to go into the bedroom. Having got her into the bedroom he made her undress but when she was in the bedroom he did not initially have the knife with him because she had gone to the bedroom on his agreeing to leave the knife behind in the living room. After she had gone into the bedroom she was subjected to a considerable number of sexual indignities. She was raped. This having occurred and the plaintiff apparently having obtained sexual relief, he then told her to lie on her side and he tied up her hands behind her back with a cord which he took either from a lamp or from an electric blanket in the room. He tied her feet together, but he said he was not going to hurt her. She says he then slowly got dressed, walked out of the bedroom door and came back with the knife in his hand, walked over to her and she started to scream. He then sat over her with a knee either side of her waist and started to stab her in the chest. She says that he kept stabbing her in the chest using the knife in a dagger-like movement. She was stabbed five times in the chest and she also had other injuries, some of which were to her right hand and to her left hand and to her right leg caused by that knife. She tried to defend herself. She managed to get one hand free and she clawed his face, and she said she thought that is what caused him to panic and he left, and it was after that that she was able to obtain assistance from the police.

Quite clearly this was a horrendous attack on this poor woman and, what is more, it is clear it could well have had more serious consequences than it in fact did. That lady could easily have been killed as a result of that attack.

When he was arrested the police asked the plaintiff about his reasons for this matter and he was asked, 'Can you recall why you stabbed her?' and his answer was, 'To hush her up so as I won't have to go to court.' He also made a statement to the police in which he said that he had been to the pub for a couple of pints; he had stayed there till about 2.30 pm and that he went home, and on the way home he had seen Christine Dashwood's door open. He did not know what came over him, 'but I just wanted to go to the house', and then he described graphically what happened. He went on to say:

'After the sex I got up and got dressed, tied her up with some electrical wire, binding her arms and legs. Then I walked into the living room picked up the knife and walked back to the bedroom again where I thrusted the knife several times into her chest. Then I ran.'

That offence was committed at a time when the plaintiff was on bail in respect of the earlier offences. That offence was committed on someone, like his other victims, who knew him and could identify him. Of course the question arises whether the purpose of the stabbing was to kill his victim so that she could not report on him. Having regard to those offences which I have set out there can be no surprise that the plaintiff was sentenced to life imprisonment, and indeed is regarded now as a category A prisoner so that when he gave evidence before the court he was handcuffed and is clearly regarded by the prison authorities as someone who can be very dangerous indeed.

I have indicated one reason why it was necessary to set out the circumstances of the offence. There is another reason, and that is the question as to how long the plaintiff is likely to serve having regard to the nature of the offences. He of course has been sentenced to life imprisonment, but he can be eligible for parole. The policy with regard to the circumstances in which parole is granted can vary, but clearly no Home Secretary is going to allow the plaintiff back into society without being satisfied as to the safety of the public, and having regard to the nature of the attacks to which I have made reference, I can well understand that extreme caution will be exercised before the plaintiff is released. Some medical evidence was given before me as to the likely date on which a doctor might be able to advise that the plaintiff was someone who was safe to be released. The evidence was limited and really amounted to no more than this, that, in the doctor's view, it would be a minimum of at least ten years before any advice could be given which could lead to the release of the plaintiff. I certainly take that view. I approach this case on the basis that the probabilities are that the plaintiff will spend substantially longer than ten years in prison under a life sentence; indeed, I consider that this is a case where if he is to be released he is going to be someone whose sexual urges, because of his age, will have then been substantially reduced. He is therefore going to spend a long time indeed in prison.

Having described the attacks, I return to the medical evidence. The consultant psychiatrist who did not give evidence before me was the consultant who first raised the question of a personality change being responsible for these attacks. That was Dr Cookson. Dr Cookson, although he did not give evidence, was indicated by other doctors to be someone who is regarded, as one would expect having regard to his appointments, as a sound practitioner whose judgment carried weight with his colleagues. He indicated in his second report his conclusions in these terms:

'The traits in his personality before his head injury do not seem sufficient to account for the behaviour for which he is charged. His personality was altered by the head injury in 1978 in the direction of a coarsening and an exaggeration of pre-existing traits, and a loss of emotional control. This change in itself does not seem sufficient to account for the alleged offences. It is likely, however, that the alleged offences would not have occurred had he not suffered the head injury in 1978.'

This view of Dr Cookson was considerably expanded by Dr Noble. Dr Noble has made a considerable study of cases where personality change is alleged to have occurred after head injury, though his experience has not been in connection with persons who have committed offences of this sort. However, he is responsible for a secure ward at a well-known London hospital. He says, first of all, with regard to the type of injury that the plaintiff has suffered that it is well known that it can produce deleterious personality changes in the absence of dementia. He says that injuries of the sort the plaintiff suffered are:

'... characterised by blunting of emotional and moral sensitivity. There is a tendency to be bland and even callous. There is often apathy and irresponsibility. Control is weakened and there may be aggressiveness. The person becomes irresponsible and without adequate regard for the welfare of others or their own welfare, except on an immediate basis. Any anti-social tendency is likely to be enhanced.'

He accepts that changes can improve, but he says people do not recover fully. He said with regard to the plaintiff:

'The major change would seem to have been in the pattern of his sexual feelings and behaviour. Prior to the accident his sexual relationships had been promiscuous and self-indulgent, but otherwise normal. Subsequent to the accident he remained capable of normal intercourse as in the relationship with Christina. [The woman with whom he was living at the time of the attacks.] There was, however, a very considerable coarsening of sexual sensitivity. Aggressive sexual fantasies developed. His post accident sexual behaviour with Josephine displayed insensitivity, callousness, and demands for immediate gratification which were followed by serious aggression if thwarted.'

He does make, in his report to which I am referring, a suggestion that he was neither drunk or intoxicated on either occasion. I am not sure that I would accept that (indeed I do not) in relation to the earlier two attacks which were the subject of the criminal proceedings. Dr Noble says:

'From the point of view of society the most serious aspect of his personality change has been a tendency to the unleashing of perverted and aggressive sexual desires in certain circumstances.'

As I understand the evidence of Dr Noble, which he amplified before me, what he was saying in regard to the plaintiff was this, that he was someone who had underlying tendencies to sexual aggressiveness. Before the accident he had not given effect to these, but that the consequence of the accident was to reduce his inhibitions so that from time to time he did give effect to them. In his second report, in support of his view that the plaintiff would not have committed these offences if he had not had his accident and the resultant brain injury, Dr Noble cites extensively from various textbooks and in particular the work of Professor Lishman. That work indicates that there are well-known sequelae from injuries of the type which the plaintiff had involving aggressiveness. The work makes it clear that one of the features of this sort of conduct is 'lack of foresight, tact and concern, inability to plan ahead or judge the consequences of actions' and that there are often symptoms of 'reduced control over aggression' and that requires special consideration.

By the time Dr Noble made his second report he had before him a report from Dr Leigh, which had indicated, accurately, that the sort of damage which the plaintiff had

had to his brain was similar to the sort of damage which could be caused deliberately in the course of carrying out a leucotomy, and with regard to that Dr Noble goes on to explain how there are certain people who have characteristics which were recognised by those who carried out the operation of leucotomy when that operation was in vogue and which were known to be contra-indications of their suitability for that operation, and in particular he refers again to a well-known work which makes it clear 'any social disinhibition after operation may bring people with sexually abnormal tendencies into conflict with society' and that symptoms denoting constitutional aggressiveness are of the worst omens in considering their suitability for the operation. In fact the editors of that work say, and Dr Noble adopts this, 'Markedly aggressive personalities should never be operated on', and the only tragic results, which have included persons committing murder, are those which have resulted from ignoring this prohibition of operating on persons who have constitutional aggressiveness.

Dr Noble went on to say that, in his view, the plaintiff is a man with—

'an unstable background with a history of irresponsibility, aggressiveness, and petty criminality. He was not perverted sexually, but he was promiscuous. Although not brutal or illegal his pre-accident sexual conduct showed self-indulgence and lack of restraint and lack of morality.'

The doctor adds:

'He is just the sort of person who is likely to react very badly to frontal damage and in particular to display abnormal sexual behaviour, aggressiveness, or antisocial conduct. His previous personality displayed traits which would exclude him from consideration for leucotomy . . .'

The doctor accepted that there was a considerable gap in time between the accident and the assaults in February and September 1982, but he does say that there was evidence of a continued changed behaviour after the accident up to that time. He says as his view that what had happened here is that this man had had his inhibitions removed which would have restrained his conduct as a result of the accident, and thus the brain damage is responsible for those attacks.

I turn, then, to consider the evidence given by Dr Gooddy. Dr Gooddy is a neuro-physician of very considerable experience and standing, and I say straight away I attach particular importance to his evidence. Dr Gooddy when he gave his report expressed himself with care. In addition to indicating that he regarded there as being a high rate of risk of epilepsy in this case, of which he put the percentage risk at 10%, went on to say:

'In summary, I consider that Mr Meah has made a very fair degree of recovery from a serious head injury . . . I believe that he has sustained permanent brain damage, with an increased epileptic risk. He does have, in my opinion, some degree of personality change; this problem being made more obvious, perhaps, because Mr Meah appears not to have been a very stable person even before he was injured. He will never be the same man again.'

In his reports, which were made before he gave evidence, Dr Gooddy had not indicated that he shared Dr Noble's view that the accident was responsible for the brutal attack and thus the sentence of imprisonment which the plaintiff is now serving. However, when he gave evidence, partly being questioned by me and partly being cross-examined, he expressed himself rather more firmly than he had before. Indeed, as I understand his evidence, he had been persuaded by the evidence that he had heard during the course of the period that he had been sitting in this court that the probabilities were in this case that but for his brain injury the attack which I have described would not have occurred. First of all, before being cross-examined, he described the plaintiff as a psychopath, and he used that word with reluctance, 'the worst possible person to sustain an injury of this kind', and he said that he felt the injury must have played a part in the change in the behaviour of the plaintiff. He said he regarded the changed behaviour as being an extension of the tendency which he had shown before the accident: it was an exaggeration of the tendencies. He went on to say that he thought that the lack of inhibition due to the injury to the man's brain caused this man to put into operation a plan in relation to Mrs Dashwood which he would not have put into effect before the accident. And he went on to say that the injury was of a kind which would lead you to expect this sort of thing. He agreed that drink has a similar disabilitating effect, as do drugs, but he thought the head injury was another element, and he said, 'I can't be sure about it', but this feeling was that he probably would not have gone ahead with regard to the Dashwood attack without his injury, and he based that on the well-known association between this kind of head injury and abnormal conduct and he said that there was a real possibility that the head injury was responsible.

When asked about the other attacks, where there was a much more marked element of drink or drugs, he went on to say with regard to these that, notwithstanding this, he saw them as fitting within the neurological pattern or, as he put it earlier, principle.

So with some hesitation, having heard the evidence, this eminent neuro-physician had come to the conclusion, to which he had not come earlier, that there was a pattern of conduct of this man, committing these vicious attacks, which was attributable to the head injury and which, as I understand it, the doctor was saying probably would not have happened, because the plaintiff would not have gone ahead, but for the injury.

Now I turn to the doctors called by the defendant. The first of those is Dr Roberts. Dr Roberts has in fact made a study of closed head injuries and he has made one finding as a result of his research which is not accepted by the other medical men, namely that if you are going to have serious anti-social behaviour as a result of a closed head injury there will normally be signs of dementia as well. There are no signs of dementia in this case, and that clearly coloured Dr Roberts's views. Furthermore, rather surprisingly, Dr Roberts had not himself examined the scans but had relied on the report which he had received about them.

Dr Leigh, in the politest possible manner, was critical about both these matters so far as Dr Roberts's evidence was concerned, which he had heard, but Dr Roberts is someone who must be listened to with respect in a matter of this sort and I do consider that it would be wrong to dismiss his evidence. However, I do not accept Dr Roberts's evidence in so far as it is in conflict with that of Dr Noble and Dr Gooddy. I understand their difference to be one of degree. Dr Roberts could not accept that a crime of the nature carried out to Mrs Dashwood could be attributable to an injury of this sort, largely because of his view that it shows the putting into operation of a fantasy which the plaintiff actually had and which indicated that the plaintiff must be someone who had constitutionally a tendency to fantasise in the way the attack indicated, and of course the fantasy would not be related to the brain injury. However, Dr Roberts did go quite a considerable way to share the views of the doctors to whom I have already made reference. He did say that he had no doubt head injuries of this kind can make persons more aggressive and more psychopathic, and he was not prepared to say that the injury played no part at all. He agreed that the injury could have had a disinhibiting effect and he said he was quite prepared to accept that the behaviour of the plaintiff had changed after the accident. It did, however, remain his view that you could not, on the balance of probabilities, relate the attacks to the injury and say that but for the injuries the attacks would not have occurred.

He furthermore indicated that he was very impressed by the period of time which had elapsed between the attacks and the injury. Of course, the significance of that time gap is greatly reduced if you accept the descriptions given by Gloria and Josephine of the change in the plaintiff's conduct. He put the future epilepsy risk as being nearer to 6% whereas, as I have indicated, Dr Gooddy put it as 10%. On balance I prefer to take the epilepsy risk as being somewhere between Dr Gooddy's and Dr Roberts's figure.

I turn finally to Dr Leigh's evidence. I have already paid respect to the standing of Dr Leigh in matters of this sort. Dr Leigh, having described the case originally as medically straightforward, said in evidence that it had become medico-legally difficult, and he was then dealing with the problem as to the extent to which this injury had affected this man's conduct at the time of the attacks. He pointed out the fact that rapists may or may not have a record of aggressive criminal activity prior to the rape, and he said that he did not consider that Mr Meah's previous history was in any way unusual for a man who committed these kind of offences. He finished up his report by saying:

'The fact that 3½ years had gone by before Mr Meah was involved in this serious anti-social behaviour, although he had continued in his less serious anti-social behaviour over the same period, suggests that the frontal lobe damage, itself, was not responsible for this serious anti-social behaviour. Surely, if it had been, he would have manifested dangerous aggressive activity certainly within 6 months of the head injury.'

Under cross-examination he modified the six months of the head injury because, of course, the plaintiff was still recovering during the six months from the initial symptoms of the head injury, but he still, when he was giving evidence, adhered to his view subject to that.

Now it became apparent when Dr Leigh was examined orally before me that Dr Leigh had felt it right in this case not to take into account matters that could not be established by independent records. In particular, he had not attached weight to the accounts given by Gloria or Josephine. He indicated that evaluation of their evidence was a matter for me, and there, of course, he was absolutely right, and having regard to their evidence he accepted that if their evidence was correct, that would certainly fill in, to some extent, the time gap to which he attached so much significance. And he accepted that if in fact this man had been behaving aggressively in a markedly changed manner towards these ladies after the accident and up to the time of the attacks, that would make it more likely that the accident was connected with the attacks.

I paid the greatest attention to Dr Leigh's evidence, in particular I was impressed by the fact that he knew in all of his experience of no precedent for a head injury resulting in this sort of attack. But as Dr Leigh himself pointed out, modern science has now made available to us much more material which scientifically establishes brain damage than was discernible previously, and it may be that cases which were not diagnosed as being partly due to brain injury have occurred which in fact if modern scientific equipment had been available could have been shown to be due to brain damage. Furthermore, there is always going to be a case where you have someone who is a particularly susceptible victim for an injury of this sort. Both Dr Gooddy and Dr Noble regarded the plaintiff, to use Dr Gooddy's words, as 'the worst possible person to sustain an injury of this kind', because he had inherent tendencies which could be triggered off.

I have come to the conclusion that, notwithstanding Dr Leigh's eminence in this field, I should in this case prefer the evidence of Dr Noble and Dr Gooddy to that of Dr Leigh. On that basis it seems to me it follows, first of all that it can be said that but for the accident the plaintiff would have probably resisted the inclination to embark on a sexual attack on Mrs Dashwood, and that that attack would not have taken place but for his accident.

I find it easier to form a view about that attack than I do with regard to the earlier attacks. It seems to me that just as the brain injury can have the effect of reducing the plaintiff's inhibitions, so could the drugs and drink which the plaintiff had had on the earlier occasions have reduced his inhibitions. But with less certainty, having regard to Dr Gooddy's reference to the neurological pattern of conduct, I have come to the conclusion that, again on the balance of probabilities, it has been shown that the plaintiff would not have committed those attacks but for his head injury. He may have committed monstrous attacks, therefore, but it is right that the court should say, on the balance of probabilities, that to some extent he is not to be blamed for that because but for an unfortunate road accident he would not have been turned into the sort of individual who could commit those attacks.

He now faces a future which at all times will be affected by the fact that he is not someone who can safely be left in society. The fact that the accident may have led to his being that sort of individual does not alter the position. He must be kept in a secure environment for the foreseeable future. Hospitals which will provide the security which he needs are not a place to which he would be sent because his condition is not one which would respond to treatment. The result is that he will remain in prison and, for the time being, be treated as a category A prisoner. One knows that those who are in prison for sexual offences are treated with contempt by their fellow inmates. One knows that somebody who is a category A prisoner is subject to very considerable restraints on their activities beyond those that are normally placed on prisoners. The plaintiff's future, and he is still a relatively young man, is one which, from his point of view, must be depressing and without hope, and that is a matter which I have got to take into account very fully in considering the appropriate figure by way of damages.

I also, however, take into account the fact that the plaintiff is someone who had underlying tendencies which could in any event result in his committing crimes, crimes of the same sort that he committed before, but what is more important from the point of view of considering what his future would have been but for the accident, crimes which could have resulted in periods of imprisonment if they were committed when he was affected by drugs or drink so as to give way to the tendencies to which the doctors referred. It seems to me, from what I have heard about the plaintiff, that he is the sort of individual who would have gone on being part of the criminal sub-culture, would have gone on taking drink and drugs, and gone on indulging in crime from time to time. He probably would not have committed offences of the gravity of those for which he is now in prison, but he could well have committed offences of a sort that whereas they did not demand life imprisonment, did involve periods of imprisonment. Notwithstanding the fact that in some cases the criminal pattern of behaviour terminates early, I do not think, on the balance of probabilities, this would be the situation with the plaintiff. I think the probability is that this pattern of behaviour would in any event have continued, certainly well into his forties and perhaps into his fifties. So that is a matter which must be taken into account in assessing what this man has lost as a result of the accident.

In addition, this case is unusual because it is not suggested that he has suffered any financial loss as a result of going into prison. He is a person who might have worked from time to time, but the money that he has been saved as a result of being boarded in prison has apparently been regarded as outweighing his loss. So I approach this case on the basis that there is no continuing financial loss as a result of his being in prison, that being the manner in which, as I understand it, the case was presented by counsel for the plaintiff.

Neither of the very experienced counsel who appeared before me were able to provide any case to give me guidance as to what was the appropriate head of damages. Clearly I start off, in dealing with this, by dividing the damages into categories. I start off with his orthopaedic injuries, I then go on to consider the injuries to the brain without considering the personality change and, finally, I consider the personality change. However, having come to the conclusion that the personality change was responsible for these crimes and therefore the plaintiff's present predicament, it seems to me that it would not be helpful for me to try to divide up the damages now because one has got to look at the damages in this case for the results of his accident as a whole and make the appropriate allowance from the figures which one would arrive at if one added up each of the single elements.

Looking at the matter in the best way that I can, bearing in mind the sort of compensation which is provided by the courts in the case of the worst type of injury (I am here thinking of people who suffer from injuries that cause them to be mere vegetables) bearing in mind that the plaintiff's insight into his predicament is in no way diminished, bearing in mind the sort of compensation that is provided in cases where people are wrongly imprisoned, though I emphasise that with regard to those cases there is usually compensation for loss of employment as well and that factor plays a part in the amount which is given as compensation, I think the appropriate sum to award by way of general damages is a sum of £60,000. So I will award here, subject to the reduction that I have to make for the contributory negligence, the sum of £60,000 by way of general damages to which must be added the sum of £1,000 for the agreed special damages.

One further matter arises out of this case which I am afraid I was responsible for raising. It may have been inappropriate for me to do so, but having carefully considered the matter I came to the conclusion it was my duty to do so, and that was the question of possible claims by the victims of these assaults. No such claim, as far as I know, has yet been made, but, of course, the plaintiff's position has now been dramatically changed as a result of the decision which I have come to. It seemed to me that there was at least a risk, so far as the plaintiff is concerned, that there would be a claim against him. They may, I hope, have received compensation in the meantime from the Criminal Injuries Compensation Board, but there could be possible claims in the future, subject to difficulties in relation to limitation of the action, and therefore I indicated that I was prepared to hear argument, if necessary, as to the appropriateness of making a declaration in this case that in the event of the plaintiff being under any liability to the victims, that he should be indemnified in the appropriate proportion by the defendant.

*Judgment for the plaintiff.*

*Solicitors:* Reynolds Porter Chamberlain (for the plaintiff); H R Pearce, Worthing (for the defendant).

K Mydeen Esq     Barrister.

# Practice Direction

CHANCERY DIVISION

*Practice – Motion – Notice of motion – Lodging of notice of motion and other documents – Chancery Division – Change in procedure.*

Under the present Practice Direction governing motions (see Practice Direction dated 23 June 1980 ([1980] 2 All ER 750, [1980] 1 WLR 751), the necessary papers have to be lodged with the clerk to the motions judge not later than 12 noon on the day before the date for which notice of motion has been given, or on the preceding Friday if the notice has been given for a Monday.

From 11 February 1985 the notice of motion and other documents must instead be lodged at the office of the Clerk of the Lists, room 163, Chancery Chambers, Royal Courts of Justice, and para 4(b) of the Practice Direction is amended accordingly.

By direction of the Vice-Chancellor.

EDMUND HEWARD
18 January 1985                                                                          Chief Master.

# Barclays Bank plc and others v Bank of England

BINGHAM J AS ARBITRATOR UNDER S 4 OF THE ADMINISTRATION OF JUSTICE ACT 1970
10, 11, 12, 13 SEPTEMBER, 3 OCTOBER 1984

*Bank – Cheque – Collection – Presenting bank's responsibility to its customer – Discharge of responsibility – Cheque dealt with through inter-bank clearing system – Whether responsibility not discharged until cheque physically delivered to paying bank for decision on payment.*

Where bank A (the presenting bank) receives from a customer for collection a cheque drawn on bank B (the paying bank) by a person having an account at a branch of the paying bank and the cheque is dealt with through the inter-bank system for clearing cheques, the presenting bank's responsibility to its customer in respect of the collection of the cheque is discharged only when the cheque is physically delivered to that branch of the paying bank for decision whether it should be paid or not (see p 387 *d*, p 391 *c* to *e* and *h j*, p 392 *a g h*, p 393 *h j* and p 394 *a* to *f*, post).

Hare v Henty (1861) 10 CBNS 65, Prideaux v Criddle (1869) LR 4 QB 455, *Bank of British North America v Haslip* (1914) 31 OLR 442, *Riedell v Commercial Bank of Australia Ltd* [1931] VLR 382 and *H H Dimond (Rotorua 1966) Ltd v Australia and New Zealand Banking Group Ltd* [1979] 2 NZLR 739 followed.

Dictum of Mann J in *Riedell v Commercial Bank of Australia Ltd* [1931] VLR at 389 applied.

*Reynolds v Chettle* (1811) 2 Camp 596 not followed.

## Notes

For the time for presentment of cheques, see 4 Halsbury's Laws (4th edn) para 421, and for cases on the subject, see 6 Digest (Reissue) 214–219, 1465–1512.

For the duties of a collecting banker, see 3 Halsbury's Laws (4th edn) para 100, and for cases on the subject, see 3 Digest (Reissue) 601–603, 3815–3825.

## Cases referred to in award

Bailey v Bodenham (1864) 16 CBNS 288, 143 ER 1139.
Bank of British North America v Haslip (1914) 30 OLR 299; affd 31 OLR 442.
Dimond (H H) (Rotorua 1966) Ltd v Australia and New Zealand Banking Group Ltd [1979] 2 NZLR 739, NZ SC.
Hare v Henty (1861) 10 CBNS 65, 142 ER 374.
Harris v Packer (1833) 3 Tyr 370.
Prideaux v Criddle (1869) LR 4 QB 455.
Prince v Oriental Bank Corp (1878) 3 App Cas 325, [1874–80] All ER Rep 769, PC.
Reynolds v Chettle (1811) 2 Camp 596, 170 ER 1263, NP.
Riedell v Commercial Bank of Australia Ltd [1931] VLR 382, Vict SC.
Royal Bank of Ireland Ltd v O'Rourke [1962] IR 159.

## Arbitration

By an agreement made on 9 May 1984 between Barclays Bank plc, Coutts & Co (an unlimited company), Lloyds Bank plc, Midland Bank plc, National Westminster Bank plc and Williams & Glyn's Bank plc, who were the member banks of the Committee of London Clearing Bankers, as claimants, and the Governor and Company of the Bank of England, as respondents, an issue (set out at p 386 *h* to p 387 *c*, post) was referred to arbitration before a sole arbitrator who was a named judge of the Commercial Court in accordance with s 4 of the Arbitration Act 1970. Bingham J accepted appointment as sole arbitrator on 21 May 1984. By an agreement dated 13 August 1984 as modified by a letter dated 13 September 1984 the parties agreed to exclude any right of appeal or application to the Court of Appeal with respect to any award made or in connection with any question of law arising in the course of the arbitration. The arbitration is reported with the consent of Bingham J and the approval of the parties. The facts are set out in the award.

*Peter Scott QC* and *Nicholas Strauss QC* for the claimants.
*Leonard Hoffmann QC* and *Andrew Smith* for the respondent.

3 October. **BINGHAM J** made the following award.

1. By an agreement made on 9 May 1984 it was agreed by the claimants, being the member banks of the Committee of London Clearing Bankers, and the respondent: (1) that the issue set out in para 5 below should be referred to the award, order and final determination of myself, a named judge of the Commercial Court, as sole arbitrator in accordance with s 4 of the Administration of Justice Act 1970; (2) that, as such arbitrator, I should have full jurisdiction in respect of the issue and should make my award in writing and give my reasons for the same; (3) that I might make different findings and reach different conclusions in respect of each of the claimants as if there were before me six separate references to each of which one of the claimants and the respondent were the parties; (4) that the claimants should be the claimants in the reference and the respondent should be the respondent; (5) that there should be an oral hearing before me; (6) that the parties should accept my award as final and binding on them and, pursuant to s 3(1) of the Arbitration Act 1979, would expressly exclude any right of appeal or application to the High Court under ss 1 and 2 of that Act with respect to any award made or in connection with any question of law arising in the course of the arbitration; (7) that the parties should enter into an exclusion agreement after the commencement of the arbitration, immediately after my acceptance of appointment; (8) that the parties should maintain the confidentiality of the arbitration proceedings and of all documentation therein; (9) that each party should bear its own legal costs of and in connection with the arbitration in any event; (10) that the claimants and the respondent should each bear one-half of my fees and the common administrative costs of the arbitration proceedings.

2. On 21 May 1984 I accepted appointment as sole arbitrator on the terms summarised above and in accordance with s 4 of the Administration of Justice Act 1970.

3. A hearing took place between 10 and 13 September 1984 when evidence was given orally and adduced in documentary form and submissions were made by counsel representing the claimants and the respondents respectively. In addition, at the invitation of the claimants and with the consent of the respondent, and in the presence of representatives of both parties, I paid a brief visit to the Clearing Department of Barclays Bank and to the London Clearing House.

4. By a further agreement made on 14 September 1984 the parties agreed that the reference to the High Court in para 1(6) above should be read as referring to the Court of Appeal.

AWARD
5. The issue referred to me for determination was framed by the parties in these terms:

'1. It is agreed that the issue in the arbitration shall be as follows:
Where Bank A ("the Presenting Bank") receives from a customer for collection a cheque drawn upon Bank B ("the Paying Bank") by a person having an account at a branch of the Paying Bank and the cheque is dealt with through the inter-bank system for clearing cheques (1) Is the Presenting Bank's responsibility to its customer in respect of the collection of the cheque discharged: (a) only when the cheque is physically delivered to the said branch; or (b) when the Presenting Bank so delivers it to the Clearing House, or in cases where this occurs when the Presenting Bank so delivers it to the Clearing Department in London of the Paying Bank; or (c) when the Paying Bank takes it away from the Clearing House; or (d) at some other time

and place and, if so, when and where (2) If the answer to question (1) is other than (a), is the Presenting Bank's responsibility so discharged: (a) on the grounds that such discharge is provided for by the general or mercantile law or the custom, usage and practices of bankers and is not procured pursuant to any contract, licence or other arrangement which is terminable on notice; or (b) (not being discharged on the grounds set out in (a) above), on the ground that it has an obligation to its customer to take steps physically to deliver the cheque to the said branch which obligation the Presenting Bank is entitled to discharge by entrusting or delegating it to a competent third party including the Paying Bank itself; or (c) on some other, and if so what, ground

    2. It is further agreed that the responsibility referred to in paragraph 1(1) does not include any responsibility of the Presenting Bank to its customer that may arise following payment or non-payment of the cheque by the Paying Bank.

    3. It is further agreed that the arbitration shall not cover the consequences of the answers to the above questions and, in particular, the period of notice required to terminate the present arrangements (if such are found to be terminable) for the clearing of cheques and other items through the inter-bank system for clearing cheques.'

    6. Having carefully considered the said evidence and submissions I hereby award as follows:

Where bank A (the presenting bank) receives from a customer for collection a cheque drawn on bank B (the paying bank) by a person having an account at a branch of the paying bank and the cheque is dealt with through the inter-bank system for clearing cheques, the presenting bank's responsibility to its customer in respect of the collection of the cheque is discharged only when the cheque is physically delivered to the said branch for decision whether it should be paid or not.

REASONS

A. *The facts*

    7. The claimants are, by their appointed representatives, the members of the Committee of London Clearing Bankers. They own the shares in the Bankers Clearing House Ltd, a private company which owns the premises of the Clearing House at 10 Lombard Street in the City of London (the clearing house). They, with the respondent, Co-operative bank plc, Central Trustee Savings Bank Ltd and National Girobank, are the banks fully and directly participating in the operations of the clearing house.

    8. The origins of the clearing house as it exists today can be traced back to a device adopted by bank employees in the eighteenth century, largely (as it would seem) for their own convenience. During the early years of the eighteenth century the banks employed walk clerks whose task it was to call at other banks in the City and the West End of London to present cheques for payment and obtain cash in exchange. As the use of cheques increased so this task became increasingly laborious. As a result a practice grew whereby, instead of visiting other banks on foot, the clerks would meet at a central point, exchange cheques and settle the difference between the total exchanged. To begin with, the meeting place was unofficial and unrecognised, but the advantages of this central exchange were obvious and in due course a room was hired and, in 1833, a building erected on the present site. The respondent entered the clearing house in 1864.

    9. The clearing house is only one part, although a central part, of the complex and sophisticated clearing system which now operates in this country. This arbitration was concerned with debit clearing only, and effectively with the general clearing and the town clearing. On the operation of these, I heard oral evidence from Mr Frost (head of the Clearing Department, National Westminster Bank) and Mr Hunt (clearing manager, Barclays Bank) for the claimants and Mr Nendick (deputy chief of the Banking Department, Bank of England) for the respondent. There were also admitted into evidence by consent written proofs of evidence of Mr Hunt, Mr Otterson (assistant general manager, Barclays Bank) (to the extent that his proof was incorporated into the

proof of Mr Hunt), Mr Marshall (deputy head of Branch Banking Division, Coutts & Co), Mr Harvey (assistant general manager, Management Services Division, Lloyds Bank), Mr Eaton (clearing manager, Midland Bank) and Mr Wilkinson (clearing manager, Williams & Glyn's Bank). During the hearing it became clear that the modus operandi of the general clearing and the town clearing, which were very fully described in the written evidence, was not the subject of controversy between the parties. It further became clear that, while there are, as one would expect, differences between the internal procedures of the various claimants, these were not relied on as suggesting different answers to the issues submitted for determination as between the respondent and individual claimants. For these reasons, and because the operation of these clearings is extremely familiar to all parties to this arbitration, I need not attempt to give any comprehensive account of the system in practice, nor need I identify the differences between the procedures of the various claimants where these exist. I shall confine myself to the bare summary needed to make sense of the discussion which follows.

10. I start with the case where a customer of a bank (the presenting or collecting bank) delivers to the presenting bank for collection and credit to his account a cheque drawn on another bank (the paying bank) by a person having an account at a branch of the paying bank, the cheque being eligible for handling through the general clearing but ineligible for handling through the town clearing. The steps which will normally follow are these. (1) The cheque will be stamped (crossed) on receipt by the branch which receives it. The amount will normally be credited to the customer's account forthwith. The customer will not, however, receive value for the cheque on that date: thus the customer cannot without agreement withdraw the sum prior to clearance, he will not earn interest or (if overdrawn) be relieved of his obligation to pay interest and it will not rank as a credit for purposes of calculating bank charges. The credit is provisional in the sense that it will be reversed if the cheque is dishonoured or not satisfactorily cleared and there is in any event a delay before it will become fully effective. (2) The branch which receives the cheque will in most cases encode it, by adding the sum payable under it in magnetisible ink to the cheque number, branch reference number and account number which are already printed on the bottom of it. At the end of the banking day the branch will sort out the cheques received during the day into bundles, one bundle for each bank whose cheques have been received. (3) These bundles will be collected from the branch during the evening of that day or early in the morning of the following day and taken to the clearing department of the presenting bank. If the encoding has not for any reason been done at the branch it will be done there, early on the day following receipt of the cheque at the branch. All the bundles received by the presenting bank from all its branches will then be amalgamated and placed in boxes labelled with the name of the bank on which they are drawn, the paying bank. They will also be checked to ensure that the cheques are all facing the same way, have the magnetisable ink characters at the bottom, are free of staples and are unfolded. They will be subject to no other inspection. (4) The cheques so sorted will then be taken in closed boxes to the clearing house, where they are either handed over to employees of the various paying banks or placed in racks reserved for those banks. The boxes are not opened and the cheques themselves are not the subject of consideration or inspection, which would be quite impracticable given that the cheques so handled run to several millions each day. (Sometimes the exchange or delivery may take place not at the clearing house but at the clearing department of the paying bank, but it is not suggested that this variation of practice gives rise to any difference of principle). (5) From the clearing house the cheques will be taken to the clearing department of the paying bank, whose employees then feed all the cheques received for payment into reader-sorter machines. This process performs a number of functions. First, it sorts the cheques received into bundles for each of the paying bank's branches on which cheques have been drawn (and, for some branches, further sorts the cheques according to account number or customer's name). Second, it checks the totals charged against the paying bank in the clearing by the various presenting banks which have delivered cheques for payment, making necessary corrections. Third, it records the

magnetisable references on the cheques sorted, so that this information can be transmitted to the computer centre where branch accounts are maintained. From this information a computer projection is (or is in some cases) made showing the state of customers' accounts at the end of the next day if the cheques are paid and no further transactions occur, but no alteration is made to the accounts themselves. No consideration is given to the validity or payability of a cheque at this stage. Thus a cheque obviously defective, for example because unsigned, will not be weeded out but will be treated in the same way as all other cheques. (6) Having been sorted, the cheques drawn on each branch will be delivered to that branch, so as to arrive during the night of the day on which they were received from the presenting bank or early the following morning. On the opening of the branch each cheque received overnight for payment will be inspected and considered by an officer of the branch to determine whether the cheque is technically in order (properly signed and dated, with numbers and figures corresponding, without unsigned alteration, and so on) and whether there is any reason (such as lack of funds, countermand or injunction) why the cheque should not be honoured. In the case of cheques for small amounts, or large and respected customers issuing large numbers of cheques, the process of inspection and consideration may be abbreviated, but the process described is the norm. If the cheque is to be paid, it is cancelled and the drawer's account is debited at the end of that working day. The debit projected by the computer will then take effect. If the cheque is not to be paid, it will be sent by first class post at the end of that working day to the branch at which it was delivered for collection and the computer projection entry will be reversed. Under rules agreed between the banks with seats in the clearing house, to which I must return, this step must be taken on the day the cheque is received at the branch, save in the case of inadvertence, when a delay until the next day is permitted. A telephone call will in that case be made to the branch at which the cheque was received for collection. (7) At the end of each working day the claimants settle between themselves by paying net balances between them. This is done by means of daily transfers to and from accounts maintained by each of them with the respondent. Such settlements comprise differences established in the general clearing carried out by their clearing departments on the preceding day and in the town clearing on that day, in each case on the assumption that all the cheques received for payment will be honoured. Dishonoured or unpaid cheques are the subject of later adjustment.

11. The town clearing handles cheques for more than £10,000 drawn on a City branch of a participating bank and received for collection by another such branch. In terms of volume the cheques so handled account for less than 1% of the total, but this relatively small number of cheques accounts for more than 90% in value of all cheques drawn. The procedure is in essence a streamlined version of that already described. (1) A cheque is received by a City branch for collection and credit to the customer's account. It is crossed with the branch stamp and, if eligible for the town clearing, is sorted (according to paying bank) into a batch prepared for the town clearing. The cheques for each paying bank are 'add-listed' and taken to the clearing house. (2) At the clearing house all the participating banks have desks, which are manned for the short period each afternoon when the town clearing takes place. The presenting banks will deliver their batches of cheques and listings to the desks of the respective paying banks. (3) Employees of the paying banks at the clearing house 'add-list' the cheques received, reconcile the totals with those on the presenting banks' listings and sort the cheques into bundles by branches of the paying bank. (4) The cheques are at once taken to the branches of the paying bank, where they are considered by bank staff to determine whether they are technically in order and whether there is any reason why they should not be paid. If a cheque is to be paid, it is debited to the drawer's account at once. If not, it is physically returned to the presenting bank in the clearing house the same afternoon. (5) The banks make payments of net balances between themselves for the town clearing as part of that day's clearing settlements by means of transfers to and from accounts maintained by each of them with the respondent. (6) The payee's account with the presenting bank is credited with the value of the cheque as part of that day's work. (7) The value of town clearing cheques

returned unpaid is repaid to the paying bank the following day as part of that day's settlement. (8) As in the general clearing, cheques are the subject of no banking decision at the clearing house stage of this process. To this there is one limited exception. The respondent has a procedure under which it rejects, in the clearing house, a cheque for £5m or more where payment has been countermanded, its understandable object being to avoid paying interest on so large a sum even for 24 hours. None of the claimants has a comparable procedure, although any cheque found to have been delivered to the wrong desk at the clearing house will be handed on to the right desk. The normal rule is that the consideration whether cheques should on technical and banking grounds be paid takes place at the drawee branch of the paying bank.

12. Many banks which have no seat in the clearing house, and hence cannot participate directly in the clearing system, are none the less able to take advantage of its facilities, by means of agency arrangements with the participating banks. In the absence of such an arrangement a cheque drawn on a non-participating bank cannot be processed through the system; the proceeds of such a cheque can be collected by a presenting bank only if it physically presents the cheque to the relevant branch of the paying bank with a request for settlement with a payment drawn on the branch of a participating bank or cash.

B. *The law*

13. The factual premise on which issue (1) is founded envisages at least three contracts, and in my opinion four: a contract between the payee of the cheque and the presenting bank to which he delivers it for collection; a contract between the drawer of the cheque and the paying bank on which it is drawn; a contract between the drawer and the payee arising by virtue of the cheque itself; and (as I think) a contract between the presenting bank and the paying bank as members of the clearing house. Of these contracts, the issue is concerned, at any rate primarily, with the first, 'the Presenting Bank's responsibility to its customer in respect of the collection of the cheque'.

14. A cheque may for present purposes be adequately defined as an unconditional order in writing addressed by a customer to his banker, signed by the customer, requiring the banker to pay on demand a sum certain in money to or to the order of a specified person (see the Bills of Exchange Act 1882, ss 3, 73). The respondent contended that 'the duty of a banker entrusted with a cheque for collection is to take reasonable steps to obtain payment of the cheque and credit the proceeds to the customer's account or notify the customer that payment has been refused'. This formulation is in my judgment correct but must be read subject to the overriding statutory rule that the appropriate way to obtain payment under the cheque is (subject to any relevant statutory exception) to present it for payment as prescribed by s 45 of the 1882 Act.

15. Section 45 is in these terms, so far as material:

'*Rules as to presentment for payment.*—(1) Subject to the provisions of this Act a bill must be duly presented for payment. If it be not so presented the drawer and indorsers shall be discharged. A bill is duly presented for payment which is presented in accordance with the following rules . . .

(2) Where the bill is payable on demand, then, subject to the provisions of this Act, presentment must be made within a reasonable time after its issue in order to render the drawer liable, and within a reasonable time after its indorsement, in order to render the indorser liable. In determining what is a reasonable time, regard shall be had to the nature of the bill, the usage of trade with regard to similar bills, and the facts of the particular case.

(3) Presentment must be made by the holder or by some person authorised to receive payment on his behalf at a reasonable hour on a business day, at the proper place as herein-after defined, either to the person designated by the bill as payer, or to some person authorised to pay or refuse payment on his behalf if with the exercise of reasonable diligence such person can there be found.

(4) A bill is presented at the proper place:—(*a*) Where a place of payment is

specified in the bill and the bill is there presented. (*b*) Where no place of payment is specified, but the address of the drawee or acceptor is given in the bill, and the bill is there presented. (*c*) Where no place of payment is specified and no address given, and the bill is presented at the drawee's or acceptor's place of business if known, and if not, at his ordinary residence if known. (*d*) In any other case if presented to the drawee or acceptor wherever he can be found, or if presented at his last known place of business or residence.

(5) Where a bill is presented at the proper place, and after the exercise of reasonable diligence no person authorised to pay or refuse payment can be found there, no further presentment to the drawee or acceptor is required . . .

(8) Where authorised by agreement or usage a presentment through the post office is sufficient.'

16. If one pauses at that point, the answer to issue (1) would appear plain. The presenting banker's admitted duty is to take reasonable steps to obtain payment. To obtain payment the cheque must be duly presented for payment, otherwise the drawer will be discharged. Presentation must be to the drawer or, as is usual, to 'some person authorised to pay or refuse payment on his behalf' at the place of payment specified in the cheque, which can only mean to the staff of the branch on which the cheque is drawn at the address shown on the face of the cheque. The cumulative effect of these provisions, standing alone, would indicate that 'the clear duty imposed upon the collecting bank to present the cheque for payment and obtain an answer without delay' (see *Riedell v Commercial Bank of Australia Ltd* [1931] VLR 382 at 389 per Mann J), even if only a duty to take reasonable steps to achieve this result, involves presentation for payment at the drawee branch.

17. But s 45 of the 1882 Act does not stand alone. Section 46(2) provides: 'Presentment for payment is dispensed with . . . (*e*) By waiver of presentment, express or implied.' This brings one close to the heart of the respondent's case. It contends that the established usage and practice of bankers participating in the clearing house is to treat delivery of cheques at the clearing house as the effective presentation to the paying bank. Thereafter the cheques are in the custody of the paying bank, the presenting bank receives credit in the clearing and the presenting bank has no further control of them. Nor has it any further interest, save in receiving notice of dishonour if the cheque is not paid. It is of no interest to the presenting bank whether cheques are sent to the paying bank branches or not. At any time the process of physical delivery could be truncated. Even before the cheques reach the branches the central computer is recording the sums to be debited. 'A man who employs a banker is bound by the usage of bankers' (per Willes J in *Hare v Henty* (1861) 10 CBNS 65 at 77, 142 ER 374 at 379) and for a customer of a participating bank this involves acceptance of the clearing system under which for all practical purposes presentation takes place at the clearing house. Whether as a result of usage, waiver or estoppel by convention between the banks, delivery at the clearing house is to be treated as equivalent to presentation, with the result that the collecting bank's duty to its customer is discharged on delivery of the cheque to the clearing house.

18. To test this argument I return to the prima facie duty on the presenting bank to take reasonable steps to obtain payment of the cheque by presenting it for payment at the drawee branch (s 45) unless the requirement of presentment has been expressly or impliedly waived (s 46). In the ordinary case with which this arbitration is concerned, no express waiver by the drawer of the cheque can be relied on. Implied waiver can be found only in the drawer's employment of a bank which is a member of the clearing house in circumstances such that he can be taken to know of and assent to the established usage and practice of banks participating in the clearing house. In other words, to establish waiver it must be shown (1) that the participating banks have expressly or impliedly agreed to treat delivery at the clearing house as equivalent to presentation *and* (2) that the customer knows of and expressly or impliedly assents to this arrangement.

19. My attention has been drawn in some detail to the agreed rules governing the

general clearing and the town clearing. I find there no express or implied agreement to the effect for which the respondent contends. The General Clearing Rules are prefaced by a general statement that a clearing is to be held each working day for the 'interchange' among the London Clearing Bankers of articles placed in their hands for collection. Despite occasional references to cheques being 'presented' in the clearing, the tendency of the rules is to refer to 'exchange' or 'delivery'. The most unequivocal reference is, however, to be found in r 12: 'the day of presentation' is there used to mean, on the practice clearly understood and operated by all the banks, the day on which the cheque arrives for payment at the drawee branch. In the Town Clearing Rules the respondent relied in particular on r 14:

> 'All crossed clean articles, cheques, etc. drawn on Town Clearing Offices must be presented through the Clearing and may not be presented for payment direct to the Office of the Paying Banker by another Clearing Banker (see Rule 3(g)), except for clean bills, presented by Offices outside the Town Clearing area, which may be sent direct.'

While the administrative purpose of this rule is clear, its language is in my view unhelpful to the respondent: by implication the rule requires indirect presentation *through* the clearing rather than direct presentation to the paying branch.

20. I therefore turn to consider the conduct of the banks to determine whether an agreement should be implied, and I start with the general clearing. It would on the face of it seem surprising if the handing of a closed box by one porter to another were treated as presentation for payment, but an issue of this importance cannot be resolved on mere grounds of superficial impression. The crucial features of the procedure outlined above are, in my opinion (1) that as a matter of invariable routine all cheques for collection are physically delivered to the branch on which they are drawn, (2) that the decision whether or not to pay the cheque is invariably taken at the drawee branch, whatever the routine adopted by the branch in making the decision, and (3) that until expiry of the primary period allowed for the decision by the branch under the rules the payee will not receive value for the cheque and the drawer will not be debited. Points (1) and (2) apply to the town clearing also, subject to the rare case where a cheque drawn on the respondent for £5m or more has been stopped. Point (3) also applies, but on the abbreviated time-scale of the town clearing cannot be regarded as significant. While it is true that the paying bank uses the reader-sorter to record information from cheques being sorted, and uses this information for accounting purposes (a function entirely extraneous to any collecting function), I regard this as a fact of little weight compared with the features I have mentioned.

21. The respondent was factually correct in its contention that from the moment of delivery at the clearing house cheques for payment were in the sole custody and control of the paying bank. I do not, however, judge this fact to pose any conceptual obstacle to the claimants' contention that the presenting bank's responsibility to its customer is discharged only when the cheque is presented for payment at the drawee branch. It is only necessary to regard the paying bank as being, from the time of receiving the cheque until the time of presenting it, a sub-agent of the presenting bank, which is itself the agent of the payee. This relationship has been readily accepted in the past: see *Bailey v Bodenham* (1864) 16 CBNS 288 at 296, 143 ER 1139 at 1142, *Prince v Oriental Bank Corp* (1878) 3 App Cas 325 at 328, [1874–80] All ER Rep 769 at 771, *Bank of British North America v Haslip* (1914) 30 OLR 299 at 301–302, opinion of Mr Arthur Cohen QC and Mr Mackenzie Chalmers (1879) 1 Journal of the Institute of Bankers 233–234, *Paget's Law of Banking* (9th edn, 1982) p 372. This interpretation is consistent with the rule, agreed between the banks, that a cheque lost between the clearing house and the branch is debited to the presenting bank. It may very well be that this rule is underpinned by practical considerations, but the rule would be very hard to reconcile with principle if the presenting bank were understood to have discharged its responsibility by delivering the cheque to the clearing house.

22. The respondent naturally relied strongly on a statement in *Chalmers on Bills of Exchange* (13th edn, 1964) p 148 to the effect that, if a bill is presented to a clerk or agent of a bank at the clearing house, that is a presentment to the bank and sufficient. A statement to substantially this effect has appeared in all editions of the work since the first in 1878, including all the early editions prepared by Sir Mackenzie Chalmers himself. A similar statement is to be found in a number of other textbooks. Despite the high authority of *Chalmers*, it is necessary to examine the foundation of the proposition.

23. The first authority relied on is *Reynolds v Chettle* (1811) 2 Camp 596, 170 ER 1263. In that case a bill of exchange was accepted payable at Messrs Harrison & Co's. No address was, it seems, specified, although they carried on business in the City of London. It appears from the brief headnote of the report that the bill, when due, was presented at the clearing house 'to the clerks of Messrs. *Harrison & Co.*, who said, it would not be paid'. The defence was that no presentation was shown at the banking house of Messrs Harrison & Co. The judgment of Lord Ellenborough was (2 Camp 596, 170 ER 1263 at 1264): 'I think a presentment to the banker's clerks in the *Clearing House*, was a presentment *at* Messrs. *Harrison & Co.*'s within the meaning of the acceptance.' Since the bankers in question evidently kept clerks at the clearing house authorised and able to make the banking decision whether the bill should be paid or not, and since no address for payment was specified, I find this decision entirely understandable and one that would cause no surprise even after the 1882 Act. Where neither of these conditions is satisfied, however, the same result could not in my view properly follow in the light of the Act and the duty of the presenting banker as I have found it to be.

24. The second case relied on by *Chalmers* is *Harris v Packer* (1833) 3 Tyr 370. In that case a bill was accepted by the drawee 'payable at *Ladbroke's* & Co.' The bill was presented to Ladbroke & Co at the clearing house, whence it was taken to Ladbroke's banking house, where a decision to pay was first made and then reversed. The defence appears to have been a pleading point that no presentment was averred to have taken place at Ladbroke's, the place where it was made payable, and an evidential point that no presentment at Ladbroke's was proved. The plaintiff relied on *Reynolds v Chettle*. Parke J ruled, in a briefly reported judgment, that 'the bill is shown to have been presented at the place where *T.* and *G.*, the acceptors, made it payable, and Messrs. *Ladbroke's* were agents to the acceptors for that purpose'. It is not clear whether the judge was treating the presentation as having occurred at the clearing house or at Ladbroke's, but since on the facts found there plainly was a presentation at one place if not the other it is hard to see how this could have been a very live legal issue.

25. These two cases and the statement in *Chalmers* were relied on by the Irish Supreme Court in *Royal Bank of Ireland Ltd v O'Rourke* [1962] IR 159. The case is in some ways an odd one since the plaintiff bank alleged presentation to have occurred on the day before the cheque was delivered to the Irish clearing house. It was also the case that both the clearing house and the drawee branch were situated in College Green, Dublin, so that the gap between delivery to the clearing house and delivery to the branch was very slight. Murnaghan J at first instance treated the date of presentation for payment as being that on which a decision was first taken at the branch whether the cheque should be paid or not. The Supreme Court unanimously reversed him, holding (in reliance on the cases quoted but without analysis of them) that the presentation to a clerk or agent of a bank at the clearing house was a presentment to the bank and was sufficient. Although the case was concerned with the time and not the place of presentation, the questions were very closely connected. In my judgment the approach of the judge below was to be preferred. There are other, more numerous, cases in which cheques have passed through a clearing house but presentation has been treated as taking place in the drawee branch where the effective banking decision was taken: see *Hare v Henty* (1861) 10 CBNS 65 at 89, 142 ER 374 at 383, *Prideaux v Criddle* (1869) LR 4 QB 455, *Bank of British North America v Haslip* (1914) 30 OLR 299; *affd* 31 OLR 442, *Riedell v Commercial Bank of Australia Ltd* [1931] VLR 382. It is also of interest to observe that in *H H Dimond (Rotorua 1966) Ltd v Australia and New Zealand Banking Group* [1972] 2 NZLR 739, where a cheque

passed through a centralised data processing system used by all the banks which led to provisional debit and credit entries in customers' accounts but without involving 'any banking decision whatsoever', it was common ground that the delivery of the cheque to the branch was the physical presentment to the banker for his decision whether to honour the cheque or not.

26. Since I conclude that the banks have not expressly or impliedly agreed to treat delivery at the clearing house as amounting to or dispensing with the need for presentation at the drawee branch, it is strictly futile and unnecessary for me to consider whether the drawer is to be taken as knowing of and assenting to such an arrangement. I would none the less make two observations. (1) Despite discovery by the claimants of their promotional literature directed to customers, I can find no trace of a suggestion by them that they regard presentation as taking place at the clearing house. If anything the implication is to the contrary, since the banks are at pains to stress that a cheque paid in for collection is not to be treated as a credit until the expiry of a period which is in fact the period allowed under the rules for consideration by the paying branch. (2) The drawer of a cheque has a clear statutory right under s 45 of the 1882 Act (subject to s 46) to be discharged from liability if the cheque is not duly presented to him or his branch of the paying bank for payment. If it is to be said that the drawer loses that right as the result of a private agreement made between the banks for their own convenience, the very strongest proof of his knowledge and assent would be needed, not only because of the general rule that an individual's rights are not to be cut down by an agreement made between others but also because, in this particular case, the rights of additional parties (such as indorsers) could be affected. In deciding whether presentation in a given way, as through the clearing house, is a proper and reasonable discharge of the presenting banker's duty to his customer, reference to the ordinary usage and practice of bankers is very relevant, and likely in most cases to be decisive (see, for example, *Hare v Henty* (1861) 10 CBNS 65, 142 ER 374, *Prideaux v Criddle* (1869) LR 4 QB 455), but the usage and practice contended for here, even if proved, could not without more derogate from the presenting bank's duty owed to its customer.

27. For these reasons I conclude as set out in para 6 above. The parties were agreed that if I should reach this conclusion I should not express my opinion on issue (2).

Solicitors: *Coward Chance* (for the claimants); *Freshfields* (for the respondent).

K Mydeen Esq    Barrister.

# Altertext Inc v Advanced Data Communications Ltd and others

CHANCERY DIVISION
SCOTT J
22, 23, 24, 29 OCTOBER 1984

*Practice – Inspection of property – Property subject matter of action or in respect of which question arising – Interlocutory motion – Ex parte application – Foreign defendant – Order against foreign defendant in respect of foreign premises – Jurisdiction to grant order against foreign defendant in respect of foreign premises – Execution of order where leave for service out of the jurisdiction granted.*

An Anton Piller order should not be made against a party over whom the court does not have jurisdiction. Accordingly, if such an order is sought against a foreign defendant in respect of foreign premises, it is essential that the case is one in which leave under RSC Ord 11 for service out of the jurisdiction ought to be given, since otherwise the court has no jurisdiction over the defendant. Where, however, an Anton Piller order has been accompanied by leave under Ord 11 for service out of the jurisdiction, the order should not be executed until the foreign defendant has been given the opportunity to apply to set aside the leave for service out of the jurisdiction, because until then the assumption of jurisdiction by the court is only provisional (see p 398 *a* to *c* and *j* to p 399 *g*, post).

## Notes

For Anton Piller orders, see 37 Halsbury's Laws (4th edn) para 372, and for cases on the subject, see 28(2) Digest (Reissue) 1125, 1234–1242.

For jurisdiction in actions in personam, see 8 Halsbury's Laws (4th edn) para 406.

For service out of the jurisdiction with leave, see 37 ibid paras 171–172.

## Cases referred to in judgment

*Anton Piller KG v Manufacturing Processes Ltd* [1976] 1 All ER 779, [1976] Ch 55, [1976] 2 WLR 162, CA.
*Cook Industries Inc v Galliher* [1978] 3 All ER 945, [1979] Ch 439, [1978] 3 WLR 637.
*Protector Alarms Ltd v Maxim Alarms Ltd* [1978] FSR 442.

## Application

The plaintiff, Altertext Inc, applied ex parte for interlocutory orders, including Anton Piller orders, against six defendants, of which the sixth was a company incorporated in Belgium with business premises in Belgium and which did not carry on any business in England. The application was heard in camera but judgment was given by Scott J in open court. The facts are set out in the judgment.

*Hugh Laddie* and *John P Baldwin* for the plaintiff.

At the conclusion of the hearing Scott J granted the bulk of the relief sought, but refused to grant an Anton Piller order against the sixth defendant for reasons to be given later.

29 October. The following judgment was delivered.

**SCOTT J.** On Monday, 22 October 1984 the plaintiff applied ex parte in camera for a variety of interlocutory orders, including Anton Piller orders (see *Anton Piller KG v Manufacturing Processes Ltd* [1976] 1 All ER 779, [1976] Ch 55), against all the six defendants. The sixth defendant, Advanced Data Communications (Europe) SA, is a company incorporated in Belgium and with business premises in Belgium. The sixth defendant does not carry on business in England.

So far as the sixth defendant was concerned, an Anton Piller order was sought by the plaintiff requiring the sixth defendant to allow the plaintiff and its solicitors to enter on the sixth defendant's premises in Belgium and to photograph or remove therefrom documentary and other material relevant to the action. It was implicit in the order that the documents and material removed from the premises would be taken by the plaintiff's solicitors out of Belgium and brought to England.

On Wednesday, 24 October I declined to grant the Anton Piller order against the sixth defendant. The question whether the court could or should make an Anton Piller order against a foreign defendant in respect of its foreign premises, seemed to me to raise considerations of general application so I indicated to counsel that I proposed, at a suitable time, to give judgment in open court.

The plaintiff carries on a highly specialised business in connection with word-processing machines. There are a large number of manufacturers servicing the word-processing market. Their respective systems are computer based and are not compatible with each other, that is to say the discs of one system on which information has been recorded cannot be used in the system of another manufacturer. If that information is to be used in another system it must first be translated into the language used by, and onto discs compatible with, that other system. The plaintiff has evolved a technique for translating information recorded on the disc of one system onto a disc of another system. The technique requires the use both of hardware and software designed and produced by the plaintiff, and the plaintiff's business is to supply the requisite hardware and software to customers.

The development of the plaintiff's complex technique required, according to the plaintiff's affidavit evidence (and I find it easy to believe), many months of highly skilled and difficult hard work by a number of persons. The cost of the development was very considerable indeed. It is not surprising in these circumstances that the plaintiff regards it as a matter of prime importance that it should protect its technique, the design of the requisite hardware and its software from unauthorised copying or other misuse.

By an agreement dated 6 August 1982, made between the plaintiff and the first defendant, Advanced Data Communications Ltd, the plaintiff granted the first defendant an exclusive licence to sell and distribute its software in a specified territory which comprised most of Western Europe and included the United Kingdom and Belgium. Under this agreement the first defendant agreed to use its best endeavours to promote the sale of the plaintiff's system in the specified territory. The first defendant also entered into contractual obligations designed to secure the protection and confidentiality of the plaintiff's system.

Pursuant to this agreement the first defendant began to market the system in Europe. The first defendant is an English company of which the principal directors and shareholders are the second and third defendants. The fourth defendant, also an English company, is controlled by the second defendant and has facilities for the formatting and duplicating of discs. The fifth defendant appears to be a firm of which the third defendant is a member; it carries on business from premises at 116 Cleveland Street, London W1, the address given for the first defendant in the agreement. The sixth defendant is, as I have said, a company incorporated and with its registered office in Belgium. The second and third defendants are directors of the sixth defendant and its principal shareholders are the first defendant, the second defendant and the third defendant.

On 22 October 1984 the plaintiff issued the writ in this action, claiming against the six defendants injunctions restraining them from infringing the plaintiff's copyright in its computer software, from passing off of various descriptions, from breaching, or procuring the breach of, the agreement and from misusing the plaintiff's confidential or secret information regarding the system. I have described merely the substance of the injunctions sought. In addition, the writ claims damages and the usual ancillary relief common in breach of copyright passing off and misuse of confidential information cases.

The writ was not, however, served on any of the defendants. Instead, the plaintiff moved the court ex parte for Anton Piller orders, Mareva injunctions and certain negative injunctions. The bulk of the relief sought I granted, including Anton Piller orders against the first five defendants in respect of their respective London premises. But, as I have said, I refused to make an Anton Piller order against the sixth defendant in respect of its Belgian premises. The justification put forward by counsel on behalf of the plaintiff for the grant of Anton Piller orders at a stage before service of the proceedings on, or any notice of the proceedings to, the defendants was that the facts of the case gave rise to a fear that, if free to do so the defendants, or some of them, might take steps to destroy or conceal the documentary and other evidence of the wrongdoing on which the plaintiff's action was based. Copied discs, it was said, could easily be scrubbed clean leaving no trace of the copying. Documentary evidence of improper sales of hardware or software to customers could be destroyed leaving no evidence of the transactions.

Very considerable affidavit evidence and very many exhibits were placed before me in support of the plaintiff's application. This evidence was, obviously, at the stage at which the application was made, unanswered. The defendants may have a complete answer to every allegation made against them. Nevertheless, on the basis of the evidence before me and for the purposes of the application being made, I was satisfied that the plaintiff's fear was a reasonable one and that the plaintiff ought to be protected by the grant of an appropriate Anton Piller order. I, therefore, made against the first five defendants, Anton Piller orders in respect of their respective premises.

The plaintiff's omission to serve the writ, or give any notice to the defendants of the proceedings, follows the usual practice where Anton Piller orders are to be sought. On the plaintiff's evidence the whole point of the Anton Piller order would otherwise have been lost. The plaintiff proposed that the writ, notice of motion and affidavit evidence should be served on the defendants, together with the Anton Piller order itself which would then immediately be executed.

In the case of English defendants, service presents no legal difficulty. The writ and other documents can be served in England. But where service abroad is necessary, leave of the court, under RSC Ord 11, must first be obtained and the case brought within one or other of the paragraphs of r 1(1) of that order. Since the sixth defendant is a Belgian company with no place of business in England, service on the sixth defendant required leave under Ord 11.

Accordingly, the plaintiff applied for such leave and relied on r 1(1)(j) of Ord 11 as covering the case. Paragraph (j) enables leave to be given—

'if the action begun by the writ being properly brought against a person duly served within the jurisdiction, a person out of the jurisdiction is a necessary or proper party thereto.'

That paragraph only applies if some defendant has been duly served within or outside the jurisdiction. In the present case, no one had yet been served. But, if the facts are otherwise appropriate for leave to be given under para (j), I do not see why, in a case such as the present, leave should not be given but expressed to be conditional on service first being duly effected on some proper defendant within the jurisdiction.

The plaintiff's evidence satisfied me, if the allegations in the affidavits are correct, that the sixth defendant represented one of the means whereby the two principal individual defendants combined to misuse the copyright material and the secret information of the plaintiff, and one of the means whereby the first defendant committed breaches of the agreement under which that material and information was put at its disposal. I was, therefore, satisfied that this was, or would be after service on an English defendant had been effected, a proper case for leave to be given for service abroad on the sixth defendant. Accordingly, I gave leave conditional on service first being duly effected on the first defendant. But the conclusion that the requisite leave under Ord 11 should be granted does not dispose, to my mind, of the difficulty of granting an Anton Piller order against the sixth defendant intended to be executed against that company's premises in Belgium before any service of process has been effected on that defendant.

There are difficulties both of jurisdiction and of discretion.

I will deal first with the jurisdiction. The High Court has a territorial jurisdiction. It has jurisdiction to make orders in respect of goods or land within the jurisdiction, or against persons subject to its jurisdiction. It frequently exercises such jurisdiction ex parte and before service of process on the relevant defendant. It often, on appropriate undertakings being given for the issue of a writ, exercises such jurisdiction before any action has actually been commenced. In these cases the question whether the desired ex parte order should or should not be made is generally one of discretion, not of jurisdiction.

But a foreign defendant is, prima facie, not subject to the jurisdiction of the court. Such a defendant may become subject to the jurisdiction of the court if service of process can be effected on the defendant in England, or if the defendant submits to the jurisdiction (as, for instance, by instructing solicitors to accept service), or if the court assumes jurisdiction by authorising service under Ord 11. But until service has been effected the foreign defendant does not become subject to the jurisdiction of the court. The remedy of a foreign defendant against whom an order under Ord 11 for service abroad has been made is to apply to set aside that order. It is well established that such an application is not a submission to the jurisdiction. If the application succeeds, and the order is set aside, the court is, in effect, declining to assume jurisdiction over that foreign defendant.

But an Anton Piller order is a mandatory order intended for immediate execution. The effect of execution of an Anton Piller order cannot, in practice, wholly be reversed by the setting aside of that order or, in the case of foreign defendants, by the setting aside of the leave given under Ord 11. The foreign premises will have been entered into, the documents in those premises will have been copied or taken away by the plaintiff's solicitors. The documents taken away are likely to have been taken out of the jurisdiction of the foreign country and brought into this country. They can all be returned but the plaintiff and his solicitors will already have seen their contents. And all this will have happened at a time when the propriety of the assumption by the court of jurisdiction has not been tested at any inter partes hearing.

In *Cook Industries Inc v Galliher* [1978] 3 All ER 945, [1979] Ch 439 an order was made by Templeman J against a foreign defendant requiring the foreign defendant to permit the plaintiff to enter his flat in Paris and to take an inventory of the furniture in the flat. But the foreign defendant had already been properly served in England, had entered an appearance and, indeed, was represented by counsel at the hearing before Templeman J. The question was raised before Templeman J whether the English court had jurisdiction to entertain the action at all involving, as it did, title to a flat in Paris and to the furniture in that flat. The judge held that the court did have jurisdiction since the plaintiff's claim was based on an equity and sought in personam relief against the defendants. But there is nothing in the judgment of Templeman J to indicate whether he would have felt able to make the interlocutory order he did if the plaintiff's application had been made before service of the proceedings on the foreign defendant.

Counsel for the plaintiff referred me also to *Protector Alarms Ltd v Maxim Alarms Ltd* [1978] FSR 442, a decision of Goulding J. The defendant in that case was a company incorporated in Scotland. Goulding J was asked to grant an Anton Piller order against the Scottish company in respect of its business premises in Scotland. He declined to do so, treating the case as one in which the plaintiff ought to have commenced its action in Scotland. It is plain, however, from the judge's judgment that he had very grave reservations about the propriety of granting, in any circumstances, Anton Piller orders against foreign defendants in respect of premises outside the jurisdiction of the court. Counsel for the plaintiff distinguished the case on the ground that the defendant's business activity to which exception was taken was carried on mainly in Scotland and that the ratio of the case was that the action ought not to have been commenced in England. That may be so, but the manner in which the judge expressed himself suggests that he would have declined to grant the Anton Piller order on the broader ground that such orders ought not to be made against foreign defendants in respect of foreign premises.

An Anton Piller order is an in personam order. It is an order which it is within the power of the court to make in an action in which the court has jurisdiction. It ought not, however, in my view, to be made except against a party over whom the court does have jurisdiction. If the order is sought ex parte, before service of the writ, and against a foreign defendant in respect of foreign premises, an essential requirement must be that the case is one in which leave under Ord 11 for service outside the jurisdiction ought to be given. Otherwise the court has no jurisdiction over that defendant. But since the initial application is ex parte, and since the foreign defendant may seek to have the leave under Ord 11 set aside, the assumption by the court of jurisdiction is, in a sense, provisional only. In my view, where an Anton Piller order against a foreign defendant has to be accompanied by leave under Ord 11 for service abroad, the Anton Piller order ought not to be executed until the foreign defendant has been given the opportunity to apply to set aside the Ord 11 leave. The assumption by the court of jurisdiction over foreign defendants is, under Ord 11, strictly controlled. It would be wrong, in my view, for the court to assume jurisdiction over a foreign defendant on an ex parte application, and then require a mandatory order of an Anton Piller character to be executed on the foreign defendant before he has had an opportunity to challenge the court's assumption of jurisdiction over him.

Accordingly, I indicated to counsel for the plaintiff that, having granted leave for service on the sixth defendant outside the jurisdiction, I was prepared to grant an Anton Piller order against that defendant in respect of its premises in Belgium but with a proviso that execution of the Anton Piller order was to be suspended for a short period sufficient to enable the sixth defendant to apply to set aside the Ord 11 leave. Counsel for the plaintiff took the view that that proviso would render the Anton Piller order valueless against the sixth defendant and pressed his application for that order without any such proviso. For the reasons I have given I declined to make it. I indicated to counsel for the plaintiff that I doubted my jurisdiction to do so. On reflection I am not sure that, strictly, the point is one of jurisdiction. The court has, I think, jurisdiction arising out of the leave given under Ord 11 and the service abroad of the writ pursuant to that leave. As I have said, the plaintiff's intention was to serve the writ and the Anton Piller order together. The point is rather, I think, one of discretion. The court is not, in my view, justified in acting on an assumed jurisdiction in order to make against a foreign defendant in respect of foreign premises a mandatory order required to be executed before the foreign defendant has had a chance of contesting the jurisdiction.

It does not follow that persons in the position of the plaintiff are without alternative remedy. Counsel for the plaintiff accepted that it might have been possible for effective concurrent proceedings to have been commenced in Belgium for the purpose of obtaining or preserving any relevant evidence situated in the sixth defendant's Belgian premises. But Anton Piller orders to be executed in respect of foreign premises ought not be granted, in my view, except against defendants over whom the courts have unquestionable jurisdiction.

I should add, finally, that counsel for the plaintiff invited me, as an alternative, to make an Anton Piller order in respect of the sixth defendant's Belgian premises, not against the sixth defendant itself but against the second and third defendants. His reasoning was that the court has unquestionable jurisdiction over those two defendants both of whom live and carry on business in England, that they control the sixth defendant, and that since an Anton Piller order is an in personam order they can be required to execute the order in respect of the Belgian premises. I can see the attraction of that approach but it cannot be right for me to do indirectly what I do not think it right to do directly, and I therefore decline to follow it.

*Orders accordingly.*

Solicitors: *Bristows Cooke & Carpmael* (for the plaintiffs).

Jacqueline Metcalfe    Barrister.

# R v Morris-Lowe

COURT OF APPEAL, CRIMINAL DIVISION
LORD LANE CJ, STOCKER AND FARQUHARSON JJ
26 OCTOBER 1984

*Criminal law – Prostitution – Procuring woman to become a common prostitute – Procure – Offer of reward – Man procuring woman to commit lewd acts on him in return for reward – Whether relevant that man had no intention to give reward – Sexual Offences Act 1956, s 22(1)(a).*

*Criminal law – Prostitution – Common prostitute – Common – Whether single act of lewdness with a man for reward constituting woman a 'common' prostitute – Whether to be a 'common' prostitute woman must be prepared to offer herself for lewdness for reward with all and sundry or with anyone who may hire her for that purpose – Sexual Offences Act 1956, s 22(1)(a).*

The offence of attempting to procure a woman to become a 'common prostitute', ie a woman who offers herself commonly for lewdness in return for reward, contrary to s 22(1)(a)[a] of the Sexual Offences Act 1956, is made out if it is proved that the accused attempted to procure the woman to commit lewd acts on him by offering her a reward in the form of well-paid employment, whether the offer of employment was genuine or not, and accordingly it is irrelevant that the accused never had any intention of employing the woman. Likewise, a man who persuades a woman to offer herself for lewd purposes for payment, even though he has no intention of paying her, is guilty of 'procuring' her, contrary to s 22(1)(a), provided that the other elements of the offence are present. However, the performance by a woman of a single act of lewdness with a man on one occasion for reward does not of itself make her a woman who offers herself 'commonly' for lewdness for reward, since for that to be the case she must be someone who is prepared for reward to engage in acts of lewdness with all and sundry or with anyone who may hire her for that purpose (see p 401 g to j and p 402 a to f, post).

*R v De Munck* [1918–19] All ER Rep 499 and *R v Broadfoot* [1976] 3 All ER 753 applied.

## Notes

For procuring a woman to become a common prostitute, see 11 Halsbury's Laws (4th edn) para 1064, and for cases on the subject, see 15 Digest (Reissue) 1225–1227, 10474–10490.

For the Sexual Offences Act 1956, s 22, see 8 Halsbury's Statutes (3rd edn) 429.

## Cases referred to in judgment

*R v Broadfoot* [1976] 3 All ER 753, CA.
*R v De Munck* [1918] 1 KB 635, [1918–19] All ER Rep 499, CCA.

## Appeal

On 23 November 1983 in the Crown Court at St Albans before Stuart-Smith J and a jury the appellant, Brian John Morris-Lowe, pleaded not guilty to three counts of attempting to procure a woman to become a common prostitute, contrary to s 1(1) of the Criminal Attempts Act 1981 and s 22(1)(a) of the Sexual Offences Act 1956. On 24 November 1983, following a ruling by the trial judge, he changed his pleas to guilty and was convicted of the offences and sentenced to concurrent terms of three months' imprisonment on each count, suspended for two years. He was also ordered to contribute a sum not exceeding £700 towards the prosecution costs and to pay £181 towards his legal aid costs. He appealed against conviction on the ground that the judge erred in law in ruling that the Crown did not have to prove that he actually intended to provide a reward or payment for the sexual services which he attempted to obtain for himself from

a Section 22(1), so far as material, is set out at p 402 c d, post

the women in question, and that his attempt to persuade the women to provide such services to him without any intention of rewarding or paying for those services, and without any intention that they should provide such services to anyone other than himself, could amount to attempt by him to procure the women to become common prostitutes. The facts are set out in the judgment of the court.

*Robert Purves* (assigned by the Registrar of Criminal Appeals) for the appellant.
*Richard Carver Wilson* (who did not appear below) for the Crown.

**LORD LANE CJ** delivered the following judgment of the court. The appellant was charged in the Crown Court at St Albans on 23 November 1983 before Stuart-Smith J and a jury on three counts of attempting to procure a woman for the purposes of common prostitution under the terms of s 1 of the Criminal Attempts Act 1981. He pleaded not guilty.

The facts of the case as put forward by the Crown were these. The appellant placed advertisements in a local paper in the Bedfordshire area for young women to train as masseuses for what he described as 'excellent pay'. He gave a telephone number to which aspirants for the job should call. He then hired a room in a hotel at Bedford and in that room carried out interviews, so called, of some of the girls who had responded to these advertisements.

Each woman was told that the appellant was going to set up a massage business locally in Bedford. Some of them were told that he already operated a similar business in Cambridge. Each girl was told that she would be expected to perform on male clients what he described as 'relief massage', for anyone who might request it. He left no doubt at all as to what he meant by relief massage, and that was of course masturbation. On each of the occasions represented by these three counts in respect of three separate girls, he also in effect invited the girl in question to masturbate him then and there in the hotel room.

The appellant's defence to these charges was to have been that he never had any intention at all of setting up a massage business, that he certainly had no massage business already in existence at Cambridge or anywhere else, and that he had no intention of employing any young woman to provide relief massage or any other form of entertainment for other men. The whole system of advertisement and interview and so on was an elaborate, and admittedly disgraceful, scheme to entice each of these young women who made their way to the hotel room into engaging in some sort of indecent sexual behaviour with him in the hotel room which he had hired.

At the end of the Crown case the judge was invited to rule whether, if the jury were to come to the conclusion that the appellant's version of events, which I have endeavoured to describe, might be correct, he would be entitled to a verdict of not guilty. The judge, as appears from the transcript of his short judgment which is before us, ruled that the offence would be made out if he, the appellant, was attempting to procure them to commit lewd acts on him in the hope of reward or in exchange for reward, the reward being the expectation of employment for substantial sums of money. The fact that the appellant himself may or may not have had any such intention of so employing them was irrelevant.

That ruling having been given, the appellant thereupon, on the advice of his counsel, changed his plea to one of guilty and was sentenced on the three counts to concurrent terms of three months' imprisonment on each count suspended for two years, and he was ordered to pay a sum of money towards the costs of the prosecution.

The sole question before this court is whether the judge's ruling which I have described was correct.

We say straight away that the judge, on the arguments advanced before him, was correct to rule as he did. Counsel for the appellant had submitted before the judge first that there was no element of reward, because the appellant had no intention of employing these girls despite what he told them. The second point advanced before the judge was that the word 'procure' should have its old common law meaning and should not, accordingly, apply as between the appellant and the woman if the appellant was present at the time of the acts in question.

As to the former point, it was plainly the prospect of well-paid and easy employment which was to be the reward, whether that offer was genuine or bogus. It is equally plain, it seems to us, that a man who persuades a woman to offer herself for lewd purposes for payment, even though he knows she is not going to get that payment in the end, is guilty of procuring provided that the other elements of that offence are present. As to the second point, the meaning of the word 'procure', the decision in R v Broadfoot [1976] 3 All ER 753 is authority, amongst other things, for saying that the word 'procure' in these particular circumstances may simply mean to persuade, which is plainly what the appellant in the present case attempted to do.

However, before this court an entirely fresh argument has been mounted by counsel for the appellant. This argument never saw the light of day before Stuart-Smith J. The offence which the appellant was alleged to have attempted to commit is to be found in s 22(1) of the Sexual Offences Act 1956, which, so far as material, provides: 'It is an offence for a person—(a) to procure a woman to become, in any part of the world, a common prostitute ...' The word 'procure', as already indicated, on the basis of the decision in R v Broadfoot, has no special meaning. An offer of large sums of money for undertaking certain tasks may amount to persuasion.

A common prostitute is any woman who offers herself commonly for lewdness for reward. This appellant on his own version plainly attempted to persuade the woman in each case to offer herself for lewdness for reward. What about the word 'common', or its adverbial form? Is it a meaningless word which adds nothing to the word 'prostitute', or does it have some effect? That really is the only point in this appeal.

It is clear to us that the word is not mere surplusage. We do not pause to consider whether the performance by a woman of a single act of lewdness with a man on one occasion for reward constitutes the woman a prostitute. But we are of the view that it does not make her a woman who offers herself commonly for lewdness. That must be someone who is prepared for reward to engage in acts of lewdness with all and sundry, or with anyone who may hire her for that purpose.

We are fortified in that view by the decision of the Court of Criminal Appeal in R v De Munck [1918] 1 KB 635, [1918–19] All ER Rep 499. It is true that the ratio of that decision was that to constitute prostitution there was no necessity for the prosecution to prove actual sexual intercourse. But there are other observations by the court, whose judgment was delivered by Darling J, which make it clear that that court was taking the same view on the instant question as that which we are expressing.

Let me quote what Darling J said ([1918] 1 KB 635 at 637–638, cf [1918–19] All ER Rep 499 at 500):

> 'We have to decide what is a prostitute or what is prostitution. The argument advanced on behalf of the appellant practically was that the offering by a woman of her body for the gratification of the sexual passions of men, even if it is done as a regular trade, indiscriminately and for gain, is not prostitution unless the men's passions are gratified by the act of sexual connection and not otherwise. We have come to the conclusion that that contention is not well founded. It was advanced before the learned commissioner at the Central Criminal Court and he laid down the law practically as we are now going to lay it down, and we, therefore, uphold his decision. The Court is of opinion that the term "common prostitute" in the statute is not limited so as to mean only one who permits acts of lewdness with all and sundry, or with such as hire her, when such acts are in the nature of ordinary sexual connection. We are of opinion that prostitution is proved if it be shown that a woman offers her body commonly for lewdness for payment in return. There was ample evidence that this girl did that, and that the appellant knew what she was doing and procured her for this particular conduct.'

That court consisted of Darling, Lord Coleridge and Salter JJ.

Consequently we are of the view that on the basis of what the appellant in the present case said was to be his defence, that is not an attempt to procure a woman to become a common prostitute. Accordingly for those reasons this appeal must be allowed and the conviction quashed.

*Appeal allowed ; conviction quashed.*

Solicitors: *Williams & Co*, Bedford (for the Crown).

N P Metcalfe Esq    Barrister.

# Re K (deceased)

CHANCERY DIVISION
VINELOTT J
16, 17, 19 OCTOBER 1984

*Will – Benefit – Exclusion from benefit – Public policy – Manslaughter – Beneficiary convicted of manslaughter of testator – Whether beneficiary precluded by forfeiture rule from benefiting under will and from interests accruing on survivorship – Whether moral culpability attending killing relevant in determining whether forfeiture rule applying – Whether court having jurisdiction to modify effect of forfeiture rule – Whether moral culpability attending killing relevant in determining whether effect of forfeiture rule should be modified in particular case – Forfeiture Act 1982, ss 2(7), 7(4).*

The deceased and the first defendant, his widow, were married in 1974. Throughout the marriage the widow had been subjected to violent physical attacks from the deceased, but had nevertheless remained loyal to him. In September 1982 the deceased was killed during an altercation by the discharge of a shotgun held by the widow, who was subsequently convicted of manslaughter. By his will the deceased bequeathed his residuary estate on trust to his widow for life and, after her death, to four residuary beneficiaries. The estate was worth some £412,000, and in addition the widow was entitled, as joint tenant, to succeed to the deceased's half share of the matrimonial home, valued at some £80,000. The questions arose whether the forfeiture rule (the rule of public policy which precluded a person who had unlawfully killed another from gaining a benefit in consequence of the killing) applied to prevent the widow from taking under the will and from succeeding to the deceased's half share in the matrimonial home, and whether, if that rule did apply, the court had jurisdiction under s 2[a] of the Forfeiture Act 1982, which came into force on 13 October 1982, to modify the effect of the rule. The residuary beneficiaries contended that, notwithstanding s 7(4)[b] of the 1982 Act, which enabled an order modifying the forfeiture rule to be made whether the unlawful killing occurred before or after the 1982 Act came into force, s 2(7) of that Act, which stated that such an order could not be made 'in respect of any interest in property which, in consequence of the rule, had been acquired before the coming into force of this section', precluded the court from making an order, since the forfeiture rule had applied on the death of the deceased two weeks before the 1982 Act came into force, thereby bringing into effect their residuary interests and a right on their part to have the estate administered in their favour, which right was an 'interest in property' within s 2(7), and since that right had been acquired before the Act came into force the court could not make an order modifying the effect of forfeiture rule.

---

*a*    Section 2, so far as material, is set out at p 405 *h* to p 406 *b*, post
*b*    Section 7(4) is set out at p 406 *e*, post

**Held** – (1) On the true construction of s 2(7) of the 1982 Act, an interest in property 'acquired' before the coming into force of the Act denoted property which had actually been transferred to the person entitled to it as a result of the operation of the forfeiture rule, or who had acquired an indefeasible right to have it transferred to him, and did not include property which, at the time s 2(7) came into force, was held by a personal representative who had not completed the administration of the estate (see p 414 *c* to *e*, post).

(2) Since the widow had been guilty of a deliberate threat of violence towards the deceased, and his death, although wholly unintended, was the consequence of her conduct, the forfeiture rule applied; it was not for the court to go further and evaluate the degree of moral culpability to be attributed to her in order to see whether the forfeiture rule applied to preclude her from benefiting under the deceased's will. However, the very purpose of the 1982 Act was to require the court to form a view of the moral culpability attending the killing in order to see whether, in the particular case, the effect of the rule should be modified. On the facts, since the widow had been a loyal wife who had suffered grave violence at the hands of the deceased, and having regard to the fact that there were no other persons for whom he had been under any moral duty to provide, it would be unjust for the widow to be deprived of the benefits which the deceased had conferred on her by his will or which accrued to her by survivorship, and the effect of the forfeiture rule would accordingly be modified to allow her to take under the will (see p 413 *c* to *g* and p 415 *b c* and *h* to p 416 *c*, post); *Gray v Barr (Prudential Assurance Co Ltd, third party)* [1971] 2 All ER 949 applied; *Re Giles (decd), Giles v Giles* [1971] 3 All ER 1141 considered.

**Notes**
For the rule against benefitting from a criminal act, see 11 Halsbury's Laws (4th edn) para 572.

For the Forfeiture Act 1982, ss 2, 7, see 52 Halsbury's Statutes (3rd edn) 526, 530.

**Cases referred to in judgment**
*DPP v Newbury, DPP v Jones* [1976] 2 All ER 365, [1977] AC 500, [1976] 2 WLR 918, HL.
*Giles (decd), Re, Giles v Giles* [1971] 3 All ER 1141, [1972] Ch 544, [1971] 3 WLR 640.
*Gray v Barr (Prudential Assurance Co Ltd, third party)* [1971] 2 All ER 949, [1971] 2 QB 554, [1971] 2 WLR 1334, CA; *affg* [1970] 2 All ER 702, [1970] 2 QB 626, [1970] 3 WLR 108.
*Pechar (decd), Re, re Cirbic (decd)* [1969] NZLR 574.
*R v National Insurance Comr, ex p Connor* [1981] 1 All ER 769, [1981] QB 758, [1981] 2 WLR 412, DC.
*Royse (decd), Re, Royse v Royse* [1984] 3 All ER 339, [1984] 3 WLR 784, CA.
*Schobelt v Barber* (1967) 60 DLR (2d) 519.

**Cases also cited**
*Comr of Stamp Duties v Livingston* [1964] 3 All ER 692, [1965] AC 694, PC.
*Jennings v US Government* [1982] 3 All ER 104, [1983] 1 AC 624, HL.
*Kent CC v Kingsway Investments (Kent) Ltd, Kent CC v Kenworthy* [1970] 1 All ER 70, [1971] AC 72, HL.
*Luke v IRC* [1963] 1 All ER 655, [1963] AC 557, HL.
*Pye v Minister for Lands for New South Wales* [1954] 3 All ER 514, [1954] 1 WLR 1410, PC.
*R v Lawrence* [1981] 1 All ER 974, [1982] AC 510, HL.

**Originating summons**
By an originating summons dated 25 July 1983 the plaintiff, the executor of the will dated 9 November 1978 of the deceased, sought the determination of the court on the questions (i) whether the first defendant, the widow of the deceased, who was entitled under the will to, inter alia, a life interest and legacy of £1,000, was precluded by the

forfeiture rule from acquiring any interest under the will or any beneficial interest in other property by way of survivorship, and (ii) whether, if the forfeiture rule applied, the court could under the Forfeiture Act 1982 modify the effect of that rule. The second defendant was the deceased's surviving sister and was entitled, as one of the deceased's next of kin, to share in the deceased's estate if it devolved as on an intestacy. The third to sixth defendants were nieces and nephews of the deceased and were the residuary beneficiaries under the will. The summons was heard in chambers but judgment was given by Vinelott J in open court. The facts are set out in the judgment.

*R W Ham* for the plaintiff.
*R F D Barlow* for the widow.
*Andrew Simmonds* for the second defendant.
*Brian Jubb* for the third defendant.
*William Henderson* for the fourth, fifth and sixth defendants.

*Cur adv vult*

19 October. The following judgment was delivered.

**VINELOTT J.** This is an application under the Forfeiture Act 1982. It is, I understand, the first application under that Act to come before the court. A number of questions of general importance relating to the scope and construction of this Act have been raised. I have accordingly decided to give my judgment in open court. To avoid distress to the person who seeks relief from forfeiture I shall not refer to the parties by name and I trust that in any report their names will not be mentioned.

On 30 September 1982 the deceased was killed by the discharge at short range of one barrel of a 12-bore shotgun held by his wife. I shall refer to her as 'the widow'. The widow was charged with his murder. At the trial the Crown did not press the charge of murder. The widow pleaded guilty to the lesser charge of manslaughter. The trial judge, a judge of great experience, having heard oral evidence from amongst others the court probation officer who had prepared a report on the case and having read the depositions and statements did not impose a custodial sentence. He made a probation order for two years with the added condition that if the widow should commit a criminal offence during the term of the probation order she would be punished for the offence of manslaughter as well as for the further offence, although he added, 'I am quite sure in your case that there is no question of that happening again.'

The first question that arises in this case is whether, in the circumstances in which the deceased met his death, the rule of public policy (commonly referred to as the forfeiture rule) which prevents a person guilty of another's death from taking a benefit which would otherwise accrue from the death applies to preclude the widow from taking any benefit under the deceased's will.

The second question that arises is whether, if the forfeiture rule applies, the court has jurisdiction under the Forfeiture Act 1982 to modify the effect of that rule. The second question arises in this way.

The Act received the royal assent on 13 July 1982. Subsections (1) and (2) of s 2 read as follows:

'(1) Where a court determines that the forfeiture rule has precluded a person (in this section referred to as "the offender") who has unlawfully killed another from acquiring any interest in property mentioned in subsection (4) below, the court may make an order under this section modifying the effect of that rule.

(2) The court shall not make an order under this section modifying the effect of the forfeiture rule in any case unless it is satisfied that, having regard to the conduct of the offender and of the deceased and to such other circumstances as appear to the court to be material, the justice of the case requires the effect of the rule to be so modified in that case.'

Subsection (3) provides that where a person is convicted of an offence of which unlawful killing is an element the court shall not make an order unless an application is made within three months after the conviction. Subsection (7) I should again read in full:

'The court shall not make an order under this section modifying the effect of the forfeiture rule in respect of any interest in property which, in consequence of the rule, has been acquired before the coming into force of this section by a person other than the offender or a person claiming through him.'

Section 3 provides that the forfeiture rule is not to preclude a person from making an application under, amongst other statutes, the Inheritance (Provision for Family and Dependants) Act 1975.

Section 4 provides that when a question arises whether a person is precluded from receiving an advantage under any relevant enactment therein defined (which includes the enactment conferring a right in given circumstances to a widow's pension) that question is to be determined by a commissioner. It does not give the commissioner or the court, as I understand it, power to modify the rule as regards any such advantage or right. I understand that the Chief Social Security Commissioner has been invited to find that the widow is not precluded by her conviction for the manslaughter of her husband from entitlement to a widow's pension but that he has reserved his decision, pending judgment in these proceedings.

Section 5 provides that the Act is not to affect the application of the rule in the case of a person convicted of murder.

Section 7(2) provides that ss 1 to 3 and 5 are to come into force on the expiry of the period of three months from the day when the Act received the royal assent. Section 7(4) I should read in full:

'Subject to section 2(7) of this Act, an order under section 2 of this Act or an order referred to in section 3(1) of this Act and made in respect of a person who has unlawfully killed another may be made whether the unlawful killing occurred before or after the coming into force of those sections.'

The second question is whether, notwithstanding s 7(4), s 2(7) precludes the court from making any order in this case under s 2.

The estate of the deceased is a large one. It was valued for purposes of probate at just under £285,000. That figure included a half share in the matrimonial home which was valued at £65,000, which was its cost a little over a year before the death. The value of the estate has since increased substantially. On 11 October 1984 the estate apart from the half share in the matrimonial home was valued at approximately £412,000. The matrimonial home is now thought to be worth some £80,000 to £85,000. It was conveyed to the deceased and the widow as joint tenants on 14 August 1981. It is common ground that they were also entitled as joint tenants in equity. By his will which is dated 9 November 1978 the deceased gave his personal and domestic effects to his executors and trustees on trust to permit his widow to have the use of them during her life with remainder on the trusts of his residuary estate; he gave to each of his widow and a niece (the third defendant) and a named godson a legacy of £1,000 free of capital transfer tax; he then settled his residuary estate on trust for his widow for life and, after her death, as to one-third to the third defendant, as to one-third to the fourth defendant, as to one-sixth for the fifth defendant and as to one-sixth for the sixth defendant, subject, in each case, to a proviso substituting the child or children living at the death of the widow who should attain 21 of any residuary legatee who should die during the widow's lifetime. He also gave his trustees power to raise £10,000 out of residue and to pay it to the widow. I should mention that the third and fourth defendants are the only surviving children of a sister of the deceased who predeceased him; the fifth and sixth defendants are the children of another sister of the deceased who is the second defendant. The second, third and fourth defendants are, with the widow, the deceased's only next of kin. If the forfeiture rule does not apply, or if the widow is wholly or substantially relieved from its operation, no capital transfer tax will be payable in respect of the estate; if it applies and is not modified, the capital transfer tax payable will be of the order of £105,000.

I turn now to the circumstances which are relied on in support of the claim that the forfeiture rule does not apply, or that the court should relieve the widow wholly or in part from the application of the rule.

The deceased and the widow married in November 1974. He was then 63 years old. He had been a commander in the navy. He retired when he was 50. He had not been married before. He lived with his mother and cared for her until she died at an advanced age in 1972. The widow was 52 years old. She had been married once before when she was aged 29. That marriage failed and was dissolved after seven years. There were no children. She and her first husband worked in the catering trade. For four years after the divorce she worked as a catering manageress. Then she went into the fashion trade, where she had a very successful career ending up as chief buyer for a large concern in Guernsey where she was responsible for a staff of 30. The deceased, who had known her for many years, started to court her very shortly after his mother's death. Her account is that she was at first very reluctant to give up a successful and satisfying career but that he persisted until ultimately she yielded. She was aware when she married that he was a man of quick temper. However he never showed any signs of violence during their courtship or during the first two years of their marriage. After two or three years there was a change. In the course of a friendly conversation she said something that upset him. He struck her without warning across her face with such violence that she was thrown to the floor. He carried her upstairs. He said nothing then or thereafter about the incident. She said nothing because he says she was afraid of further violence. Not long afterwards he approached her from behind, grabbed her by the hair, pulled her to the ground and proceeded to kick her. Again nothing was said then or subsequently by either of them. These attacks continued with greater or less severity thereafter. I do not find it necessary to go into further detail. It is sufficient to say that the widow has kept and produced her diaries for 1978 and for 1980 and subsequent years and in them details of assaults in those years are recorded. In the summer of 1978 she went to stay in the Channel Islands. She was contemplating leaving her husband. Letters written to her by him at the time corroborate her story that he was subject to fits of uncontrollable rage leading to violence towards her.

In a letter dated 4 June 1978 he said:

'I am proposing to make an appointment with [a named doctor] about Thursday or Friday, but am not very hopeful that he can help. I hope you will accept my assurance that it will not be with the object of putting the blame on you, but of getting treatment for myself if, as you suggest, I need it.'

A few days later he wrote to say that he had made an appointment to see the doctor and that his main object in seeing him—

'is to enable me to retain my self-control, whatever the provocation, so that I never again attack you. It distresses me, as well as you, to recall the last two dreadful occasions. I will let you know what he prescribes.'

Then on 10 June he reported on that visit. He said that he had 'told [the doctor] everything about "these women" and about my violence to you, including your belief that I caused your arm trouble. How is it now, I hope it is not being troublesome.' I pause to observe that the widow says that on one occasion he twisted her arm with such violence that she had to see a doctor about it. The arm continued to give her pain for some months. Later in this letter the deceased said that the doctor had arranged for him to see a psychiatrist, though it seems that he did not in fact do so. Then in another letter in the same month he said:

'One thing I want to say is when I recall the occasions when I have been violent towards you, I feel so horrified, so utterly disgusted and ashamed of myself that I feel literally sick. In spite of your provocation, with your untrue accusations, I should be able to control myself, and shall do my utmost to do so in the future.'

Again I pause to say that the reference there to untrue accusations and the earlier reference to accusations about women relate on the widow's evidence to the fact that the deceased behaved on occasions in a foolish and embarrassing way towards other women. There is no suggestion that he had an affair or was guilty of adultery.

The widow returned to live with the deceased. They moved to a new house. The violent attacks continued. The deceased's behaviour deteriorated in other ways. He began to abuse her in public. He punished her for some trivial offences, on one occasion by refusing to allow her to have friends to stay, on another by refusing to allow her to drive his car for a period of a year. In 1979 there was a particularly severe incident when he struck her with such violence that blood spurted from her nose onto the rug in the sitting room. He refused to allow her to use the telephone and stood by it in a menacing way. Later, for the first time, he apologised. The widow thought of leaving him. She did not do so, first, she says, because she thought his violent outbursts were the consequence of some illness such as a brain tumour and that he needed her to look after him, second, because he constantly said that if she left him he would commit suicide or drink himself to death and, third, because she thought that if he saw her packing her bags he would lose control again. Further, before her father died in February 1981 he stayed with the deceased and the widow for three to four months in each year and when he was there the deceased was more restrained and did nothing worse than slap her face.

In the summer of 1980 the deceased bought a 12-bore shotgun to keep down rabbits which despite the erection of rabbit fences were ravaging the garden. He kept it loaded in a corner of the kitchen. He showed the widow how to use it so, he said, that she could protect herself from marauders.

At about this time in July 1980 the widow for the first time consulted their joint doctor (not the doctor who the deceased saw in June 1978, who had retired) and gave him for the first time a full account of the attacks to which she had been subjected over the preceding four years. Thereafter she consulted him regularly for treatment following further attacks. An affidavit sworn by the doctor in this application exhibits attendance notes which corroborate the widow's account of violent attacks after July 1980 and her diary entries. The doctor expressed the view that the deceased showed signs of paranoid schizophrenia. He suggested that she should persuade the deceased to come and see him. The deceased refused to do so. This doctor did not at any time treat the deceased and his opinion was founded on what he had been told by the widow and on occasions when he had met the deceased, who was a neighbour, casually or socially.

After the widow's father died the attacks continued and if not more frequent were on occasions even more severe. In August 1981 he attacked her with great violence, kicking her while she lay on the ground. On the following day her head was a mass of bruises. Not long afterwards in February 1982 she moved from the bedroom they had theretofore shared to the spare bedroom, where she felt safer. At about this time, following another attack, she recorded in her diary: 'One cannot speak to him without his imagining everyone is getting at him as Dr E predicted.'

At the end of July 1982 she went to spend a holiday with a brother and his family in Canada. She went alone. While she was there she found her affection for the deceased revived and her fears evaporated. They exchanged affectionate letters. On her return in mid-August he met her aeroplane and they had an affectionate reunion. But violence erupted again on 23 September. She retired to her room and locked herself in.

The situation on 30 September 1982 was therefore this. The widow had for many years been subjected to violent and unprovoked attacks. The doctor to whose affidavit I have referred and the probation officer who gave evidence at the trial both described her as a 'battered wife'. But she was fond of and loyal to the deceased. She attributed his violence to illness, a brain tumour or paranoid schizophrenia. I should add also that he was a persistent and heavy drinker and may well have suffered in his intellectual capacity and power of self-control as a result. The widow had what she considered to be a refuge in the spare room which could be locked until a violent outburst had blown over.

On 30 September the deceased returned from a visit to the post office to collect his pension. The couple had a snack lunch. The widow's version of the events which followed in her evidence in this court is as follows. There was a disagreement over a trivial incident, a request that he guarantee the bank account of a friend of hers. He lost his temper and grabbed her hair, calling her a 'stupid bitch'. There was a lull but she feared a resumption of his attack as had happened before. She decided to escape to her bedroom. As she got to the kitchen door she decided on the spur of the moment to pick up the gun. She thought that if he saw the gun in her hands he would be deterred from following her. At that precise moment his back was towards her. He had turned towards the kitchen sink, but he could still have turned back and caught her before she reached the bedroom. That had happened before. To attract his attention and make sure that he would see that she had the gun she released the safety catch. It made an audible click. He started to turn towards her. The gun went off. She says that she has no recollection of touching, far less pulling, the trigger. She telephoned a friend in an hysterical state and then telephoned the ambulance service, but the deceased was dead when the ambulance arrived. That is the widow's evidence given in a statement verified by affidavit in this court. The other defendants have not adduced evidence on these matters nor have they sought leave to cross-examine the widow on her evidence.

In view of certain submissions made by counsel for the fourth, fifth and sixth defendants, I should say that there are some discrepancies between this account and other accounts which the widow gave shortly after the death and moreover discrepancies between those several statements. Immediately after the death she telephoned a friend in a distraught state and said: 'He was taunting me.' In a statement to one of two ambulance-men who arrived shortly thereafter in response to her telephone call she repeated this statement. She said to the other ambulance driver who asked what had happened: 'He was standing at the sink taunting me about his girlfriend. He's done this several times. I picked the gun up and pointed it at him. He turned to me and said, "Go on, why don't you shoot?" I don't remember pulling the trigger but I fiddled with the gun and shot him.' Two policemen arrived shortly after the ambulance crew. The short account of her husband's death which she gave to one of them does not differ significantly from the account she has given in her evidence in this court. To the other she said: 'We had a bit of a contretemps this morning and I saw the gun there. I picked it up in fun and clicked the thing back on top. It went off. I don't remember touching the trigger.' Later in the evening of the same day at the police station after being cautioned she told a detective sergeant that after lunch, when her husband was washing the dishes, 'I walked towards the door of the kitchen leading to the hall. The gun was just inside the door so I picked it up and turned round and clicked the safety catch which made my husband turn round which I knew it would do. I pointed at him and made a sort of face at him and he turned round, just raised his eyebrows at me and the next thing I knew he was lying slumping on the floor. I don't remember pulling the trigger at all.' However on 7 October when the widow made a statement under caution in the presence of her solicitor she gave an account of the events which had led to her husband's death which is in all material respects the same as the account which she has given in her evidence in this court.

Counsel for the fourth, fifth and sixth defendants stressed these discrepancies. He submitted that the court should look with caution at the evidence of a person who seeks relief from the consequences of a killing which has been found to be manslaughter where there are no other eye-witnesses and that I should bear these discrepancies in mind in evaluating the extent to which the widow should be relieved from the consequences of forfeiture. I do not think that any adverse inference can be drawn from these discrepancies. When the widow spoke to the ambulance-men and to the police officers who first arrived on the scene and to the detective sergeant the same evening she was clearly in a hysterical state. She may well have elided her recollection of the events of that day with other occasions when the deceased had goaded her about relationships with other women and have been in some confusion as to his precise movements immediately before the gun went off. What is important is that in every statement she has made the widow has always insisted that she did not intend to pull the trigger and indeed was not conscious of doing so.

At the trial an eminent gunmaker was called to give evidence on her behalf. His evidence was that the accident could easily have occurred in the way she described, and indeed he expressed the opinion that the cause of the discharge of the gun was the involuntary pressure of the finger of the widow caused by the emotional stress under which she suffered at the time when she released the safety catch. The pull required to fire a single trigger shotgun in good order is some 4 to 5 lb.

Counsel for the fourth, fifth and sixth defendants also placed some reliance on what was said by the trial judge. In opening the case for the prosecution counsel first informed the judge that the Crown would be content with a plea of manslaughter on the ground that 'the evidence available tends to show that as a result of provocation or recklessness in pointing a loaded gun a few feet from someone and releasing the safety catch may well tend to reduce the charge of murder to manslaughter'. It is I think clear that this passage has suffered in transcription. It seems more probable that what counsel for the prosecution intended to say was that while provocation might reduce the charge of murder to manslaughter it would be no defence to a charge of manslaughter and that the widow's recklessness in pointing a loaded gun at her husband and releasing the safety catch made a conviction for manslaughter inevitable. Counsel for the prosecution then addressed the judge and drew attention to the several statements to which I have referred. In sentencing the widow the judge said:

'I am satisfied that this is a very exceptional case, that you were subjected to very considerable pressure, that on the day this happened you were not yourself, that you picked up this gun, that you knew it was loaded, and because of the pressures to which I have referred and to which counsel has referred, you pointed it at your husband and shot and killed him.'

Counsel for the fourth, fifth and sixth defendants submitted that the inference from these passages is that the judge while satisfied that there had been sufficient provocation to reduce the charge to manslaughter was not satisfied that the discharge of the gun was unintentional. I do not think that it would be right to draw any inference from this passage in the transcript. The judge clearly accepted that, in the light of the history of violence and of the probation officer's report and evidence, the prosecution were justified in not persisting in the charge of murder and that the case was not one which called for a custodial sentence. He made no other finding or decision.

I must therefore form my own conclusion on this point on the basis of the evidence adduced before this court. Like the trial judge I have not had the advantage of hearing the oral evidence of the widow. Counsel for the fourth, fifth and sixth defendants stressed, rightly I think, that I must approach the widow's evidence as to the circumstances in which her husband was killed, inevitably uncorroborated as it is by any other eyewitness account, with some caution. I have done so. On the evidence before the court the salient facts which to my mind emerge clearly even from the written evidence are these. First, until her husband's death the widow's conduct towards him was beyond reproach. She stayed with him despite repeated and serious assaults which she attributed to mental or physical illness. She was loyal to him and told no one of the attacks to which she was subjected except at a late stage her doctor and on one occasion a solicitor. The probation officer in his oral evidence at the trial described the widow's situation in these terms:

'She appeared to be unable to find any channel for escape from it [ie the violence]. She was very much on her own. She has this very high level of respectability, if I can use the word, and what went on within closed doors in the house was something that traditionally she felt she ought to keep between herself and her husband. She had no avenue of escape from it and had she had different personal values, it may well be that she may have been able to have done something about it. She felt very isolated even though she had friends and neighbours. She impresses me very much as somebody who gave here a most accurate account of herself and her feelings as she could and her temperament was one which would not normally bring about behaviour of this sort.'

That leads me to my second point. The widow was clearly reduced by these repeated unpredictable and savage attacks to a state in which she was terrified of the possibility of a recurrence. She had sought some measure of protection by moving into a bedroom of her own which had a door which she could lock. That was the background to the tragic event on 30 September 1982. On that occasion her husband lost his temper. He began to lose his self-control. She knew how easily the situation could slip into serious violence towards her. She picked up the gun in the hope that it would deter him. It was a most foolish and dangerous thing to do. But on the evidence before me I do not think that it is possible to doubt that she did not intend to fire it when she picked it up or when she released the safety catch.

Counsel for the widow submits that in these circumstances the conviction for manslaughter does not carry with it as a necessary consequence the forfeiture of the widow's interest under the will or of the interest in the matrimonial home, which, apart from forfeiture, accrued to her as beneficial joint tenant. He founded these submissions on a decision of the Court of Appeal and on a decision of the Divisional Court. Before turning to these decisions I must briefly refer to the well-known decision of Pennycuick V-C in *Re Giles (decd), Giles v Giles* [1971] 3 All ER 1141, [1972] Ch 544. In that case the wife of the testator struck him a blow with a domestic chamber-pot from which he later died. She was charged with his murder. A plea of not guilty to murder but guilty to manslaughter under s 2 of the Homicide Act 1957 by reason of diminished responsibility was accepted. She was sentenced to be detained in Broadmoor. The Vice-Chancellor accepted the submission of counsel for those entitled under the will in the event of forfeiture that the rule applied to any person convicted of culpable homicide, that is of murder or manslaughter. He rejected the argument of counsel for the widow (see [1971] 3 All ER 1141 at 1145, [1972] Ch 544 at 552) that—

'the principle only applies to crime deserving of punishment or, to use another phrase, crime carrying a degree of moral culpability, and that where the crime does not deserve punishment and carries no degree of moral culpability, then the principle does not apply.'

Later Pennycuick V-C said ([1971] 3 All ER 1141 at 1146, [1972] Ch 544 at 553):

'I was referred to a number of insurance cases in which the broad principle which I have been discussing was held to be displaced by some other principle or consideration of public policy. It seems to me that a contract of insurance, particularly motor insurance, is in an entirely different sphere from that of succession on death and I do not think there is anything in what is said in those cases that could properly be held as modifying the principle which has been laid down in the sphere of succession on death. I do not think it would be useful for me to quote those cases.'

Pennycuick V-C was not referred to an earlier decision of the Court of Appeal which had not I think been reported when he gave his judgment. That was *Gray v Barr (Prudential Assurance Co Ltd, third party)* [1971] 2 All ER 949, [1971] 2 QB 554; *affg* [1970] 2 All ER 702, [1970] 2 QB 626. The facts are very striking. Mr Barr was living apart from his wife. Mr Gray was her lover. One evening Mr Barr took his wife out to dinner. She promised to give up Mr Gray and to return to live with her husband. He drove her home. He made up the boiler and did some other domestic chores and went to the bedroom expecting to find her there, but she was not there. In a state of great distress he went to Mr Gray's home, taking with him a loaded shotgun. When he arrived Mr Gray came to the top of the stairs. Mr Barr thought his wife was in the bedroom. He started to mount the stairs, carrying the gun at the high port and threatening Mr Gray with it to make him get out of the way. He fired one shot into the ceiling to frighten him. Then, according to Mr Barr's account, there was a struggle in the course of which Mr Barr slipped and the second barrel was accidentally discharged killing Mr Gray. He was tried for murder and acquitted both of murder and of manslaughter. Mrs Gray then sued him for damages. He joined the insurance company claiming an indemnity under a hearth and home policy covering liability to others resulting from accidental injury. Mrs Gray recovered damages. The trial judge, Geoffrey Lane J, dismissed the claim for indemnity on the ground of public policy, having found that on Mr Barr's own evidence he was clearly guilty of manslaughter. He distinguished the cases of what are commonly described as 'motor manslaughter' where an insured has been held entitled to recover under a policy in respect of injuries caused otherwise than deliberately in these terms ([1970] 2 All ER 702 at 710, [1970] 2 QB 626 at 640):

'The logical test [ie the test to be applied in deciding whether a person guilty of manslaughter can recover under a policy of indemnity] . . . is whether the person seeking the indemnity was guilty of deliberate, intentional and unlawful violence or threats of violence. If he was, and death resulted therefrom, then, however unintended the final death of the victim may have been, the court should not entertain a claim for indemnity.'

*Gray v Barr* was an insurance case. As I have pointed out Pennycuick V-C in *Re Giles* held the motor manslaughter cases at least to be inapplicable to a case concerning succession on death. However there are dicta in the Court of Appeal in *Gray v Barr* [1971] 2 All ER 949, [1971] 2 QB 554, where the decision of Geoffrey Lane J ([1970] 2 All ER 702, [1970] 2 QB 626) was upheld, which support the view that not all cases of manslaughter involve the consequence that the person convicted forfeits all rights of inheritance from the person killed. Salmon LJ said ([1971] 2 All ER 949 at 964, [1971] 2 QB 554 at 581):

'Although public policy is rightly regarded as an unruly steed which should be cautiously ridden, I am confident that public policy undoubtedly requires that no one who threatens unlawful violence with a loaded gun should be allowed to enforce a claim for indemnity against any liability he may incur as a result of having so acted. I do not intend to lay down any wider proposition. In particular, I am not deciding that a man who has committed manslaughter would, in any circumstances, be prevented from enforcing a contract of indemnity in respect of any liability he may have incurred for causing death *or from inheriting under a will or on the intestacy* of anyone whom he has killed. Manslaughter is a crime which varies infinitely in its seriousness. It may come very near to murder or amount to little more than inadvertence, although in the latter class of case the jury only rarely convicts.' (My emphasis.)

A little later he referred to the motor manslaughter cases as possibly 'sui generis'.

Moreover the later decision of the Divisional Court in *R v National Insurance Comr, ex p Connor* [1981] 1 All ER 769, [1981] 1 QB 758 did not concern a claim for indemnity under a policy of insurance. There the applicant stabbed her husband and was charged with murder. The trial judge withdrew the charge of murder from the jury and, on a direction that the only issue was whether the defendant had used the knife with intention to injure or accidentally, she was convicted of manslaughter and sentenced to two years' probation. Her claim to a widow's pension to which she would otherwise have been entitled was refused and on appeal the Chief National Insurance Commissioner upheld the refusal. She appealed by way of judicial review to the High Court. Lord Lane CJ, having cited the passage from the judgment of Salmon LJ which I have cited, continued ([1981] 1 All ER 769 at 774, [1981] 1 QB 758 at 765):

'I would respectfully agree with that dictum, and I would agree that in each case it is not the label which the law applies to the crime which has been committed but the nature of the crime itself which in the end will dictate whether public policy demands the court to drive the applicant from the seat of justice. Where that line is to be drawn may be a difficult matter to decide, but what this court has to determine is whether in the present case what this applicant did was sufficient to disentitle her to her remedy.'

It is, I think, impossible to draw any distinction between a claim to inherit under a will or intestacy and a claim to a provision to which, if the requisite conditions are satisfied, a widow is entitled as of right. The decision of the Divisional Court in *R v National Insurance Comr, ex p Connor* is accordingly in my judgment authority for the proposition that a conviction for manslaughter will not necessarily entail the consequence that the person convicted will be barred from all succession to any benefit under the will or intestacy of the person whom he or she has killed and from succession to any interest of the deceased in property held jointly. The question is where the line is to be drawn.

Counsel for the widow submitted that the forfeiture rule should apply (apart from cases of murder) only to cases of voluntary manslaughter, ie to cases where what would otherwise be murder is reduced to manslaughter by provocation or diminished responsibility or because the death occurred in pursuance of a suicide pact, and not to cases of involuntary manslaughter, ie where an unlawful killing is reduced to manslaughter because there was no intent to kill or to do grievous bodily harm. He submitted in the alternative that the rule should only apply to cases of voluntary manslaughter and to cases of involuntary manslaughter where there is something more than a threat sufficient to raise a fear of violence, that is to cases where actual force is employed. I do not think that that is a possible view. In *Gray v Barr* [1971] 2 All ER 949, [1971] 2 QB 554 on the evidence of Mr Barr, which was held sufficient to found the conclusion that he had been guilty of manslaughter (though acquitted at the trial), he did not intend to use the gun to injure Mr Gray but the Court of Appeal clearly thought that the forfeiture rule applied. In my judgment the facts of this case fall clearly within the test propounded by Geoffrey Lane J in the passage which I have cited from his judgment in *Gray v Barr* [1970] 2 All ER 702 at 710, [1970] 2 QB 626 at 640. The widow, like Mr Barr, was guilty of a threat of violence which was deliberate in that she intended to frighten and so deter the deceased. The death, though I accept wholly unintended, was the unfortunate consequence of her conduct in threatening the deceased with a loaded gun and disengaging the safety catch. Given that the death was the consequence, albeit unintended, of that deliberate threat the court cannot go further and evaluate the degree of moral culpability to be attributed to her conduct in order to say whether the forfeiture rule applies or not.

I turn therefore to the question whether the court has jurisdiction to modify the forfeiture rule. The case for the fourth, fifth and sixth defendants is shortly as follows. The interests in property to which s 2(1) applies are widely defined in sub-s (4) read in conjunction with sub-s (5) and extend to any chose in action. The right of a legatee, including a residuary legatee, during administration to have the estate duly administered is a chose in action. Accordingly in consequence of the forfeiture rule a right of action was acquired either by each residuary legatee by way of acceleration of his or her interests in remainder or, alternatively, by the next of kin, the second, third and fourth defendants, who took the interests forfeited by the widow. That right was acquired at the death two weeks before the 1982 Act came into force, though it could not be known with certainty that it had been acquired until the operation of the rule had been decided by the court. The court cannot therefore make an order modifying the effect of the rule in respect of those interests. Similarly the right of the widow in the matrimonial home which would otherwise have accrued by survivorship was divested by the forfeiture rule and vested in the deceased's next of kin or in the residuary legatees and in either case was an interest in property acquired by them on his death under s 2(7). Faced with the fact that s 7(4) expressly preserves a right (subject to s 2(7) and to the time limit in s 2(3)) to apply for an order under s 2 where the unlawful killing occurred before the coming into force of s 2, counsel for the fourth, fifth and sixth defendants submitted that s 7(4) only applies where an interest in property is divested by the forfeiture rule and is not acquired by anybody else. He instanced two possible cases. First, a person to whom the forfeiture rule applies might have an interest apart from the forfeiture rule in a pension fund vested in trustees under which on the death a pension or capital sum would otherwise have been payable to him or to her. The forfeiture might not then confer an interest in property on anybody else, though it might enhance the benefits payable to others with entitlements under the scheme, or relieve the employer from an obligation to contribute to the fund to ensure its solvency. Second, if such a person was interested as a discretionary beneficiary under a trust of income or as an object of a power to apply income or capital his or her removal as an object of the trust or power, while it might enhance the interests of other beneficiaries, would not confer any separate interest in property on them. I cannot believe that the framers of the 1982 Act had these recondite possibilities in mind. The Act is not in all respects very carefully drawn. It was, I understand, a private member's bill and may not have been drafted by parliamentary counsel. It is not couched in technical language but in language intended to be understood by persons other than lawyers specialising in property and trust matters. It is very wide in its scope. I think the word 'acquired' in s 2(7) is used in a quite intelligible sense to denote property which has actually been transferred to a person entitled thereto by virtue of the operation of the rule or who has thereby acquired an indefeasible right to have it transferred to him or to her. Whether it extends to a present or future interest in property settled by a will which on completion of administration has vested either in the executors or others as trustees is a question which does not arise and on which I express no opinion. In my judgment it clearly does not extend to property which, when the section came into force, was held by personal representatives who had not completed the administration of the estate.

Before turning to the substantial question whether the court should make an order relieving the widow in whole or in part from the operation of the rule, there are two other matters which I should mention.

I have already read sub-ss (1) and (2) of s 2. Subsection (5) reads as follows:

> 'An order under this section may modify the effect of the forfeiture rule in respect of any interest in property to which the determination referred to in subsection (1) above relates and may do so in either or both of the following ways, that is—(a) where there is more than one such interest, by excluding the application of the rule in respect of any (but not all) of those interests; and (b) in the case of any such interest in property.'

Literally construed para (a) gives the court power to modify the effect of the forfeiture rule where more than one interest in property is affected by it in respect of some but not all of those interests; and under para (b) in relation to any given interest in property the court can modify the rule in respect of part of it. So it is said that the court cannot relieve the applicant from the consequence of the rule altogether. The most the court can do is to relieve against the operation of the rule if there is more than one interest in property in respect of all the interests except one (under para (a)); and then under para (b) relieve against the operation of the rule in respect of a part, however large, of the remaining interest (or the only interest if there is only one). The court, like the donee of a non-exclusive power of appointment before the passing of the Illusory Appointments Act 1830 and before the absurdities created by that Act were cured by the Powers of Appointment Act 1874 can cut off the person entitled by the operation of the forfeiture rule with a shilling but cannot cut him off altogether. I cannot believe that the framers of the 1982 Act intended a result as bizarre as that. The answer to this submission in my judgment is that sub-s (5) is intended to enlarge the power conferred by sub-s (1) by making it clear that the court is not bound either to relieve against the operation of the forfeiture rule altogether or not to relieve against the operation of the rule at all. The draftsman assumed that sub-s (1) alone conferred power to relieve an applicant from the operation of the rule in respect of the entirety of all interests affected by the rule. Subsection (5) then in effect enlarges the court's powers.

As I have mentioned, the matrimonial home (which is registered land) was vested in the deceased and the widow as joint tenants at law and in equity. Counsel for the widow accepts that the forfeiture rule, unless modified under the 1982 Act, applies in effect to sever the joint tenancy in the proceeds of sale and in the rent and profits until sale. I think that concession is rightly made. There is curiously no reported case on the point in England but it has been held in other jurisdictions where the law is similar to English law before 1925 that where one of two joint tenants murders the other, while the entire interest vests in the survivor, the law imports a constructive trust of an undivided one-half share for the benefit of the next of kin of the deceased other than the offender (see *Schobelt v Barber* (1967) 60 DLR (2d) 519 and *Re Pechar (decd), re Cirbic (decd)* [1969] NZLR 574). Under English law since 1925 the result is more simply reached by treating the beneficial interest as vesting in the deceased and the survivor as tenants in common.

I turn therefore to the substantial question. Section 2(2) requires that before making any order under that section modifying the effect of the forfeiture rule the court must be satisfied that, having regard to the conduct of the offender and of the deceased and to such other circumstances as appear to the court to be material, the justice of the case requires the effect of the rule to be so modified in that case.

The only evidence as to the conduct of the deceased and the widow is that filed on behalf of the widow which I have already summarised. However, evidence has been filed by the widow and by the fourth and sixth defendants in this application and in a concurrent application by the widow under the Inheritance (Provision for Family and Dependants) Act 1975 as to their respective means. Apart from her interest in the matrimonial home the widow has capital of some £2,000 and a car worth £2,500 and personal jewellery worth £1,500. She owes her solicitors £13,800 for costs incurred in relation to her defence which her solicitors have generously not pressed her to pay. On the footing that she is not entitled to a widow's pension, her only income is a national insurance pension and a supplementary pension amounting to £41 per week in all. The sixth defendant lives at home and manages small properties for her mother for which she is paid some remuneration. Apart from savings of some £2,000 to £3,000 she has no other capital or income. The fourth defendant is in very reduced circumstances indeed. Though trained as a teacher he is unemployed and dependent on social security.

It is clear, I think, that the relative financial position of a person claiming relief under the 1982 Act and of others with claims under the testator's will or intestacy are circumstances which the court is entitled to take into account in the exercise of its discretion. I was referred by counsel to a case in the Court of Appeal, *Re Royse (decd)*, *Royse v Royse* [1984] 3 All ER 339, [1984] 3 WLR 784. The Court of Appeal held that a person for whom reasonable provision is made by the deceased's will but who forfeits the benefits conferred cannot make a claim under the 1975 Act, notwithstanding s 3 of the 1982 Act, because he or she cannot satisfy the precondition in s 2(1) of the 1975 Act. Such a person can therefore claim, if at all, only under s 2 of the 1982 Act. But, in entertaining a claim by a person who apart from the interest forfeited would have had a claim under the joint effect of the 1975 Act and of s 3 of the 1982 Act, the court must, I think, be entitled to have regard to the principles and the considerations set out in the 1975 Act. Such a person cannot be in a worse position than one for whom no provision is made in the deceased's will or by virtue of his intestacy, and who accordingly can only claim under the 1975 Act as applied by s 3 of the 1982 Act.

However, in a case where reasonable provision is made by the will, the first question is whether, having regard to the conduct of the deceased and of the claimant in particular in relation to the unlawful killing, justice requires that the claimant should be relieved against forfeiture in respect of all or any interests accruing on the death. The 1982 Act was clearly passed with the decision of Pennycuick V-C and earlier decisions in mind. In *Re Giles (decd), Giles v Giles* [1971] 3 All ER 1141, [1972] Ch 544 Pennycuick V-C declined to enter into any investigation of the degree of moral culpability attending the killing. The purpose of the 1982 Act as I see it is to entitle and indeed require the court to form a view on that very matter.

I have reached the conclusion after anxious consideration that in the very unusual circumstances of this case it would be unjust that the widow should be deprived of any of the benefits which the deceased chose to confer on her by his will or which accrued to her by survivorship. As Lord Salmon observed in *DPP v Newbury, DPP v Jones* [1976] 2 All ER 365 at 367, [1977] AC 500 at 507, it being unnecessary in cases of manslaughter to prove that the accused knew that the act causing death was unlawful or dangerous, cases of manslaughter necessarily vary infinitely in their gravity. Despite the revulsion which any person must feel at conduct which leads to the death of another human being it is impossible in the tragic circumstances of this case not to feel sympathy for the widow. If cases vary infinitely in their gravity, this is, I think, one of the cases which weighs least heavily. The widow, as I have said, was a loyal wife who suffered grave violence at the hands of the deceased. When she took hold of the gun and released the safety catch she was in a state of great distress and feared further violence. She must accept the blame for what happened but she should not, in my judgment, suffer the further punishment of being deprived of the provision which her husband made for her which was, it seems to me, wholly appropriate having regard to the fact that the widow gave up a worthwhile and satisfying career when she married him, to her conduct towards him to the very end of his life and to the fact that there were no other persons for whom he was under any moral duty to provide.

There is one other consideration which has weighed with me in reaching this conclusion. Shortly after the death one of the executors, the widow herself being the only other executor, wrote to all the members of the husband's family. He pointed out that he was also the widow's solicitor. He referred to the forfeiture rule and to the power of the court to relieve against it and he said that in the event of the widow being convicted he, if he acted as executor, felt that there might be some conflict between him as the widow's solicitor and other members of the family. He asked the members of the family to say whether they were willing that he should none the less act as executor. All the members of the family agreed that he should. They also, all of them, expressed their loyalty to the widow. In particular the fourth defendant generously expressed the view that if the widow were to be convicted the family should find a way of carrying out the deceased's testamentary expenses 'as though no court conviction had been made at all, in other words that [the widow] should receive what is stated in the will regardless'. If the attitude of some of the defendants has changed since it is not because any new fact relating to the death or to the conduct of the parties has emerged but because those defendants have had second thoughts in the light of what they have since learned as to the size of the estate and the comparative affluence of the widow if she retains all benefits conferred on her by the will. I do not say this in any way critically. The fourth and the sixth defendants have no means and in the case of the fourth defendant no employment. He feels that even a modest distribution of capital to him would enable him to regain his position in the world. But that cannot in fact be done without benefiting others, including those who wish the widow to be wholly relieved from the operation of the rule. Moreover, though not without sympathy for the position of the fourth defendant, it cannot be said that he had any moral claim on the bounty of the testator. I think that the attitude of the fourth defendant and of the other defendants when originally asked, namely that the widow should not suffer further than she has already suffered from her own conscience and from the experience of a criminal trial, was the right one.

I will ask counsel for the plaintiff to draft a minute of order embodying the effect of this judgment. The costs of the defendants will be taxed on a common fund basis, in the case of the plaintiff as trustee, and paid out of the residuary estate in due course of administration. There will be the usual order for legal aid taxation of any of the defendants who may be legally aided.

*Declaration accordingly.*

Solicitors: *Cripps Harries Hall & Co*, Tunbridge Wells (for the plaintiff); *Thomson Snell & Passmore*, Tunbridge Wells (for the widow); *Keene Marsland*, Tunbridge Wells (for the second defendant); *Proctor Gillett* (for the third defendant); *George Coleman & Son*, Haywards Heath (for the fourth, fifth and sixth defendants).

Jacqueline Metcalfe   Barrister.

# BICC plc v Burndy Corp and another

COURT OF APPEAL, CIVIL DIVISION
ACKNER, KERR AND DILLON LJJ
21, 22, 23, 24, 25 MAY, 13 JULY 1984

*Set-off – Cross-claim – Legal right of set-off – Claim for specific performance – Plaintiff having right to require defendant to assign patent rights for non-payment of fees – Defendant not paying fees – Plaintiff owing defendant more than outstanding fees in respect of other transactions – Whether plaintiff entitled to specific performance of assignment because of defendant's non-payment – Whether right of set-off available against claim for equitable relief based on money claim.*

*Equity – Forfeiture – Relief – Jurisdiction of court – Forfeiture of proprietary right in personal property – Forfeiture clause in commercial agreement – Enforcement of clause involving forfeiture of interest in patent rights – Whether jurisdiction to grant relief against forfeiture.*

The plaintiff and defendant companies, which had been in business together for 20 years, decided to dissolve their partnership and to allow each other to compete freely in international markets. The dissolution involved the parties entering into a series of closely related interlocking agreements, including a 'commercial agreement' which provided for the continued sale of goods between them, and an 'assignment agreement' regarding their joint rights (such as patent rights), which provided that such rights were to be vested in the parties jointly with freedom for each to use and exploit them. Clause 10(ii) of the assignment agreement provided that the plaintiff was to be primarily responsible for processing and maintaining, and paying the costs and fees relating to, the parties' joint patent rights, subject to the defendant reimbursing the plaintiff for half such costs and fees. Clause 10(iii) provided that, if the defendant failed to reimburse the plaintiff within 30 days of the plaintiff's written request to do so, the plaintiff was entitled to require the defendant to assign to the plaintiff all its interest in the patent rights concerned. The plaintiff incurred costs and fees in respect of a large number of joint patents and patent applications and sent the defendant ordinary commercial invoices for the defendant's half share of those expenses without insisting on payment within 30 days. When the defendant, under the impression that there was no urgency and at a time when the plaintiff's indebtedness to the defendant under the commercial agreement was well in excess of the amount of the invoices, failed to pay the invoices the plaintiff invoked its right under cl 10(iii) to require the defendant to assign its interest in the patent rights concerned. The value of the defendant's interest in the patent rights greatly exceeded the amount due to the plaintiff under the invoices. When the defendant refused to assign its interest the plaintiff brought an action against the defendant seeking specific performance of the assignment. The defendant contended, inter alia, (i) that any liability of the defendant to assign under cl 10(iii) depended on the defendant being in default, which it was not because of its right to set off the amounts owing by the plaintiff against the amounts due under the invoices, and (ii) that cl 10(iii) was a forfeiture clause and the defendant was entitled to seek relief against forfeiture. The judge held that a right of set-off was no defence to an action for specific performance, that he had no jurisdiction to grant relief against forfeiture because cl 10(iii) did not affect property but was instead a commercial agreement, and that even if he had jurisdiction he would not exercise his discretion to grant relief. The judge accordingly granted the plaintiff specific performance. The defendant appealed.

**Held** – (1) (Kerr LJ dissenting) The defence of set-off, whether legal or equitable, was available not only against a monetary claim but also where the claim in the proceedings was for relief other than money, including equitable relief such as specific performance, if the other relief was dependent on the non-payment of a money claim to which there

was a legal or equitable right of set-off. Since the plaintiff's claim for specific performance
depended on the defendant's non-payment of the plaintiff's money claim for the unpaid
costs and fees and since the defendant would have had a complete defence by way of set-
off against the plaintiff's money claim because of the amounts owed by the plaintiff to
the defendant under the commercial agreement, it followed that the defendant's right of
set-off was a good defence against the plaintiff's claim for specific performance (see p
425 *d* to p 426 *d* and *j* to p 427 *d* and p 433 *h*, post); dictum of Lord Denning MR in
*Federal Commerce and Navigation Ltd v Molena Alpha Inc, The Nanfri, The Benfri, The Lorfri*
[1978] 3 All ER at 1077 and *British Anzani (Felixstowe) Ltd v International Marine
Management (UK) Ltd* [1979] 2 All ER 1063 applied.

(2) In any event, although relief against forfeiture was only available in respect of
proprietary or possessory rights, it was not restricted to interests in real property but
extended to interests in personal property. The fact that a right to forfeiture arose under
a commercial agreement did not go to jurisdiction but merely to the exercise of
discretion. Since cl 10(iii) was a forfeiture clause involving the forfeiture by the defendant
of its proprietary rights in personal property (ie the patent rights) the court had
jurisdiction to grant the defendant relief against forfeiture. Furthermore, having regard
to the previous dealings between the parties, and the facts that the plaintiff invoked cl
10(iii) suddenly and without warning at a time when it owed to the defendant much
more than was owed to it and that the defendant would lose valuable property rights for
non-payment of a relatively small sum, the court would exercise its discretion to grant
the defendant relief against forfeiture. The appeal would accordingly be allowed (see
p 427 *e g* and *j* to p 428 *f* and *j*, p 429 *a* and *c* to *h* and p 433 *g h*, post); *Scandinavian
Trading Tanker Co AB v Flota Petrolera Ecuatoriana, The Scaptrade* [1983] 2 All ER 763 and
*Sport International Bussum BV v Inter-Footwear Ltd* [1984] 2 All ER 321 considered.

**Notes**

For availability of set-off in general, and for claims which may not be pleaded by way of
set-off, see 42 Halsbury's Laws (4th edn) paras 432, 440–441, and for cases on the subject,
see 40 Digest (Repl) 407–418, 13–123.

For relief against forfeiture, see 16 Halsbury's Laws (4th edn) paras 1447–1451, and
for cases on the subject, see 20 Digest (Reissue) 898–899, 6695–6703.

**Cases referred to in judgment**

*Bankruptcy notice (No 171 of 1934), Re a* [1934] Ch 431, sub nom *Judgment debtor (No 171
of 1934), Re a, ex p Judgment creditor* [1934] All ER Rep 688.
*Barton Thompson & Co Ltd v Stapling Machines Co* [1966] 2 All ER 222, [1966] Ch 499,
[1966] 2 WLR 1429.
*British Anzani (Felixstowe) Ltd v International Marine Management (UK) Ltd* [1979] 2 All ER
1063, [1980] QB 137, [1979] 3 WLR 451.
*Federal Commerce and Navigation Ltd v Molena Alpha Inc, The Nanfri, The Benfri, The Lorfri*
[1978] 3 All ER 1066, [1978] QB 927, [1978] 3 WLR 309, CA; *affd in part* [1979] 1 All
ER 307, [1979] AC 757, [1978] 3 WLR 991, HL.
*Gilbert-Ash (Northern) Ltd v Modern Engineering (Bristol) Ltd* [1973] 3 All ER 195, [1974]
AC 689, [1973] 3 WLR 421, HL.
*Hanak v Green* [1958] 2 All ER 141, [1958] 2 QB 9, [1958] 2 WLR 755, CA.
*Hughes v Metropolitan Rly Co* (1877) 2 App Cas 439, [1874–80] All ER 187, HL.
*Mondel v Steel* (1841) 8 M & W 858, [1835–42] All ER Rep 511, 151 ER 1288.
*Phipps v Child* (1857) 3 Drew 709, 61 ER 1074.
*Rawson v Samuel* (1841) Cr & Ph 161, 41 ER 451, LC.
*Rickards (Charles) Ltd v Oppenheim* [1950] 1 All ER 420, [1950] 1 KB 616.
*Scandinavian Trading Tanker Co AB v Flota Petrolera Ecuatoriana, The Scaptrade* [1983] 2
All ER 763, [1983] 2 AC 694, [1983] 3 WLR 203, HL; *affg* [1983] 1 All ER 301, [1983]
QB 529, [1983] 2 WLR 248, CA.
*Shiloh Spinners Ltd v Harding* [1973] 1 All ER 90 [1973] AC 691, [1973] 2 WLR 28, HL.
*Sport International Bussum BV v Inter-Footwear Ltd* [1984] 2 All ER 321, [1984] 1 WLR
776, HL; *affg* [1984] 1 All ER 376, [1984] 1 WLR 776, CA.

*Starside Properties Ltd v Mustapha* [1974] 2 All ER 567, [1974] 1 WLR 816, CA.
*Stocklosser v Johnson* [1954] 1 All ER 630, [1954] 1 QB 476, [1954] 2 WLR 439, CA.
*Stooke v Taylor* (1880) 5 QBD 569, DC.
*United Scientific Holdings Ltd v Burnley BC* [1977] 2 All ER 62, [1978] AC 904, [1977] 2
    WLR 806, HL.

**Appeal**
The first defendant, Burndy Corp, appealed against the decision of Falconer J on 27 July
1983 granting the plaintiff, BICC plc, (1) specific performance of an assignment dated 2
November 1981, made between BICC and Burndy and the second defendant, BICC-
Burndy Ltd, and the execution by Burndy of all necessary documents and the taking of
all necessary steps to assign to BICC all Burndy's rights and benefits in the patents and
patent applications listed in the schedule to the writ of summons, (2) a declaration that
the assignment be free of any licence to Burndy Electra SA or any other licence granted
by Burndy, (3) that pending specific performance of the assignment Burndy be restrained
from assigning or mortgaging the patents or patent applications and from granting any
licence or other right under the patents or patent application, and (4) that accounts and
inquiries be taken and made. The facts are set out in the judgment of Dillon LJ.

*T L G Cullen QC* and *Peter Prescott* for Burndy.
*Stephen Gratwick QC* and *Simon Thorley* for BICC.
The second defendant was not represented.

*Cur ad vult*

13 July. The following judgments were delivered.

**DILLON LJ** (giving the first judgment at the invitation of Ackner LJ). This is an appeal
against a decision of Falconer J given on 27 July 1983. The appellants, Burndy Corp who
are the first defendants in the action, are a substantial United States company particularly
concerned in the manufacture and sale of electrical and electronic connectors. The
respondents, BICC plc who are the plaintiffs in the action, are a substantial British
company particularly concerned with the manufacture and sale of cables and wires.
    In 1959, at a time when Burndy, though substantially established in the United States
and elsewhere, had no significant position in the United Kingdom market, and BICC had
not been concerned with electrical or electronic connectors, the two companies decided
to form a fifty-fifty company in the United Kingdom, essentially, as it is put in the
evidence, to exploit the know-how and rights which Burndy had in the connector field
by the involvement in the United Kingdom and certain parts of the British
Commonwealth of the extensive existing marketing force of BICC. The company so
formed was called initially BICC-Burndy Ltd (BBL); though formally joined in the action
as a second defendant, BBL has played no part in the trial or at the hearing of this appeal.
    In or about 1979 BICC and Burndy decided to dissolve their joint relationship so that
both companies would be left to compete freely throughout the world in the connector
business. Such an unscrambling of a joint relationship which had lasted for about 20
years raised a considerable number of practical problems, and to resolve these a series of,
as the judge put it, closely related interlocking and detailed agreements running to some
120 pages was entered into. Basically, there was an offer by BBL to sell its manufacturing
business to BICC for a substantial sum and, in the event which happened, that that offer
was accepted, four other agreements were to have effect, which are referred to as: (1) the
principal agreement, (2) the commercial agreeement, (3) the assignment, and (4) the
ancillary agreement. On this appeal we are concerned especially with the assignment,
but it is relevant to note that the commercial agreement provided, among other things,
for the continued sale of goods by Burndy to BICC and by BICC to Burndy on terms
which were fixed in considerable detail by the commercial agreement.

The assignment, which is dated 2 November 1981 and was made between (1) BBL, (2) BICC and (3) Burndy, was concerned with patent and other rights included in the definition of 'the joint rights' hereinafter mentioned. The background to the assignment was that, during the continuation of the joint relationship, numerous patent applications had been made and patents had been acquired in the name of BBL, mainly in the United Kingdom but also elsewhere. Since these patents and patent applications depended in large part on the know-how and experience of Burndy and on research done by Burndy, it was not appropriate that they should be acquired by BICC absolutely, with the manufacturing activities of BBL, to the entire exclusion of Burndy. What was arranged was therefore, basically, that these various rights should be vested in BICC and Burndy jointly with complete freedom for each of them to use and exploit the rights. It was for this purpose that the assignment was entered into. The important clauses for the purposes of this appeal are cll 9 and 10, particularly cl 10, but it is convenient to summarise all the major provisions of the document.

Clause 1 contains a definition of 'the joint rights' as meaning, in brief, all United Kingdom and overseas patents and registered designs and applications therefor, copyright in literary and artistic work and all other rights in inventions and discoveries, including information as to improvements, processes, formulae, trade secrets and other know-how relating thereto which were part of the assets of BBL and used by it for the purposes of its business.

By cl 3.1 in consideration of a payment by BICC which appears to have been of no special significance, BBL assigned to BICC and Burndy jointly and absolutely all BBL's right title and interest to and in the joint rights. By cl 7 these were to be held by BICC and Burndy in equal undivided shares.

By cl 8 BICC and Burndy agreed that each of them should be entitled: (a) to assign its share in or grant non-exclusive licences in respect of any of the joint rights to any person or persons without the consent of the other of them, and (b) to exercise or exploit in any other manner any of the joint rights for its own profit without accounting to the other of them.

Clause 9 contained mutual covenants between BICC and Burndy as follows: (a) not to do or omit to do or permit any act or thing whereby the protection granted by the law of any jurisdiction in which any of the joint rights subsisted should be in any way lessened or avoided; (b) (i) to notify the other of any infringement or threatened infringement by a third party of or of any proceedings for revocation, cancellation or rectification of the register affecting any of the joint rights; (ii) to consult with the other regarding mutual commencement of proceedings to prevent such infringement or to defend such proceedings for revocation, cancellation or rectification and if agreed to institute or defend such proceedings at their joint expense and for their joint benefit, but so that if they did not agree on the joint institution or joint defence of proceedings either might act at its own expense and retain for its own benefit any damages costs and other compensation recovered; (c) not to make any application or motion to amend the specification of any patent comprised in the joint rights without the other and that the costs of any such joint application or motion should be borne by the parties in equal shares; and (d) to consult with the other regarding the registration of or the extension of the term of any of the joint rights and if agreed to take any proceedings for such registration or extension at their joint expense but so that, if one of the parties should be unwilling to take such proceedings, it should assign to the other without payment all its right title and interest to and in such of the joint rights to which such proceedings would relate and should do all other things required by the other party to obtain and enjoy such registration or extension and the full sole and exclusive benefit thereof.

Clause 10 provided by para (i) that BICC should hold all documents relating to the joint rights, and there was the usual acknowledgment for production and undertaking for safe custody. Paragraphs (ii) and (iii) of cl 10 then provided as follows:

'(ii) BICC shall be primarily responsible for the processing and maintaining of applications and patents forming part of the Joint Rights and the making of payment of costs and fees in respect thereof (including the normal and reasonable charges of BICC's Patent and Licensing Department) subject to reimbursement of one half thereof by Burndy and BICC shall give Burndy sufficient notice of any application or motion which it may be necessary or desirable to make under sub-clauses (c) or (d) of Clause 9 hereof.

(iii) If BICC shall fail to pay all or Burndy fail to reimburse BICC one half of the costs and fees incurred by BICC under paragraph (ii) above in the case of BICC when payment is due and in the case of Burndy within 30 days of a written request therefor the other party not in default shall be entitled to require the party in default to assign to it all the rights and benefits in any patent or application in respect of which such payments were due and at the request and cost of such other party the assigning party shall if necessary furnish such information and execute and do all such documents and acts as may reasonably be required to enable such other party to obtain and enjoy the full sole and exclusive benefit thereof.'

It is BICC's case in this action, which the judge has upheld, that Burndy failed to reimburse one-half of the costs and fees incurred by BICC under cl 10(ii) in respect of a large number of patents and patent applications included in the joint rights within 30 days of written request as prescribed by cl 10(iii) and that BICC is accordingly entitled under cl 10(iii) to an assignment of all Burndy's rights and benefits in such patents and applications. It is common ground and not in doubt that Burndy never intended to give up any of its rights in any of the patents or patent applications, but it is claimed by BICC, and was held by the judge, that Burndy has irrevocably lost its rights by failing to pay timeously the relatively small amounts of costs and fees involved.

Before, however, I attempt to summarise the arguments on each side, I must briefly set out the remaining facts.

During the subsistence of the joint relationship before the assignment was entered into, there had been fees and expenses incurred by BICC for the maintenance of certain overseas patents and it had been the practice of BICC to invoice Burndy for Burndy's half share of those fees and expenses. The person in Burndy responsible for dealing with those invoices was Mr Reiter, Burndy's patent counsel, and the man in BICC with whom he dealt was Mr Ross-Gower, a chartered patent agent. Mr Reiter considered it his duty to check the invoices as far as he could, because apparently, on one occasion, a charge had been raised which had been withdrawn when challenged; the details do not matter.

When the assignment took effect, BICC continued, in respect of the costs and fees incurred by it under cl 10(ii), the practice of submitting periodic invoices to Burndy, and it remained the duty of Mr Reiter to deal with those invoices. Details of the invoices submitted are as follows:

| Number of invoice | Date | Amount |
|---|---|---|
| PS 27 | 25 January 1982 | £ 728 |
| PS 81 | 21 April 1982 | £2,701·68 |
| PS 125 | 19 July 1982 | £3,519·74 |
| PS 165 | 18 October 1982 | £2,181·29 |

None of these invoices was paid or commented on in any way by Burndy, save for an early comment by Mr Reiter to Mr Ross-Gower that there did not seem to be enough information in the invoices for them to be checked. The reason for this inactivity on the part of Burndy was that Mr Reiter, who was unaware of the terms of cl 10(iii), was heavily occupied with other matters and did not make time available to deal with BICC's invoices. Follow-up letters asking for prompt settlement of the invoices were sent by BICC on 19 May, 6 and 20 July and 18 August 1982, but it is a matter of fact, whether relevant or not, that these letters did not suggest any special urgency or refer to cl 10(iii). On the personal level as between Mr Ross-Gower and Mr Reiter, the relationship was very cordial.

In October 1982 Mr Reiter found that he would have an opportunity to come to London in relation to some other business and so by a telex of 12 October he proposed a meeting with Mr Ross-Gower on Tuesday 19 October 'to meet and resolve outstanding billing questions'. That meeting was accepted by BICC and on 18 October Mr Reiter arrived in London. On the same day BICC sent to Burndy a telex and a confirmatory letter invoking cl 10(iii) and calling on Burndy to assign to BICC all Burndy's interest in all the patents and applications to which the costs and fees the subject of the earlier invoices related. On the same day BICC sent to Burndy a further invoice, noted above, in respect of further costs and fees incurred by BICC under cl 10(iii) in the previous three months; some of these related to the same patents as some of the earlier invoices.

The meeting arranged between Mr Reiter and Mr Ross-Gower for 19 October did not, in the event, take place, because Mr Reiter was ill on that day. Instead, he spoke to Mr Ross-Gower by telephone and gave a somewhat nebulous assurance that he expected to authorise paying the invoices when he returned to his office, and would complain about them later if he later found out that they were wrong. In fact, nothing further was done on Mr Reiter's return to the United States. On 22 November 1982 BICC wrote to Burndy again, invoking cl 10(iii) and calling for an assignment of Burndy's interest in the patents and patent applications to which the invoice of 18 October related. Mr Reiter then telephoned Mr Ross-Gower, but was told by him that the matter was out of his, Mr Ross-Gower's, hands, and on 20 December 1982 the writ in this action was issued by BICC.

By the time of the trial of the action it was accepted by Burndy that all the invoices of BICC listed above were correct and that the sums claimed in these invoices were properly claimed. Conversely, it is accepted by BICC that Burndy was at all times in a position, financially, to pay those invoices. More importantly, it is expressly admitted by BICC that, at all material times, BICC owed Burndy liquidated sums very substantially in excess of the total amount of the invoices for goods sold to BICC by Burndy under the commercial agreement; a total indebtedness of BICC exceeding £100,000 was mentioned.

The differences between the parties as to the issues of law involved in this case start with a difference as to the purpose and effect of cl 10(iii) of the assignment.

Counsel on behalf of BICC submits, and the judge accepted, that the purpose of cl 10(iii) was to provide a simple mechanism whereby, if either party should not be interested in proceeding with a particular patent application in a particular country, or in maintaining a particular patent in a particular country and, therefore, was unwilling to pay towards the cost thereof, that party could divest itself of the responsibility therefor by doing nothing and the particular patent application or patent would go to the other, and interested, party wholly. In the court below counsel for BICC pointed to cl 10(iii) as a simple mechanism that avoided any need for consultation between the parties concerning any particular right. He further submitted that to claim an assignment of Burndy's rights under cl 10(iii) was the only remedy available to BICC in the event of failure by Burndy to pay its half share of any costs and fees incurred by BICC under cl 10(iii) because, as he submitted, there was no express or implied obligation on Burndy under cl 10(ii) or elsewhere in the assignment to pay the half share to BICC. So, it was submitted, BICC could not have brought an action for the money.

By contrast, counsel on behalf of Burndy submitted that there was an obligation on Burndy to reimburse to BICC Burndy's half share of the costs and fees paid by BICC and, if all other things had been equal, an action to recover the money would have lain against Burndy. From this, counsel for Burndy sought to make three main points in the court below and in this court (and I do not list the points in the order in which he put them).

1. The purpose of cl 10(iii) was merely to provide a sanction for the non-payment of the half-share of costs and fees due from Burndy, and so cl 10(iii) ought to be regarded as a penalty clause, and ought not to be enforced by a court of equity, because the value to Burndy of the patent rights involved could, and probably would, be very great compared with the amount of the unpaid costs and fees. The judge held that the clause was not a penalty clause.

2. Liability to execute an assignment of rights under cl 10(iii) depended on Burndy being in default, and Burndy never was in default in payment of the share of costs and fees because, at all times, Burndy had available a right of legal set-off in view of the much

higher sums due from BICC to Burndy under the commercial agreement. As to this, the judge held that, as the claim in the action against Burndy is for specific performance of an agreement to execute an assignment, no defence of set-off can lie; but this does not completely answer counsel for Burndy's point, which is that, because of the right to a legal set-off of a larger liquidated sum, the *right* to specific performance and to have the assignment never arose.

3. In the alternative, counsel for Burndy submitted that cl 10(iii) was a forfeiture clause, the enforcement of which would deprive Burndy of property rights, viz its undivided half interest in the relevant joint rights, and he asked for relief against forfeiture by the extension of time for payment. As to this, the judge held, in reliance on the judgment of the Court of Appeal in *Scandinavian Trading Tanker Co AB v Flota Petrolera Ecuatoriana, The Scaptrade* [1983] 1 All ER 301, [1983] QB 529, that he had no jurisdiction to grant relief against forfeiture because cl 10(iii) was part of a commercial agreement entered into between commercial parties bargaining at arm's length. He further held that, even if he had had jurisdiction, he would, in the exercise of his discretion, have refused relief. I refer to his reasoning below.

Finally, there is a separate point which counsel for Burndy takes if he fails on all other points. This is that any assignment ordered against Burndy should be subject to a licence under all relevant patents granted by Burndy in 1961 to its Belgian subsidiary, Burndy-Electra SA, and since extended (but before the execution of the principal agreement and not by any express exercise of Burndy's power to grant licences under cl 8 of the assignment). This point raises two issues. The first, as to which it is not clear whether the judge came to a conclusion or not, is whether any licence granted to Burndy-Electra SA survived the execution of the principal agreement and the assignment; this depends on the effect of certain provisions of those documents which I have not so far set out. The second issue is whether the judge was right in holding that BICC is entitled to the protection of s 33 of the Patents Act 1977 against any claims of Burndy-Electra SA since BICC had no notice of any licence to Burndy-Electra SA when BICC called for the assignment of the joint rights under cl 10(iii), although BICC did have notice of the licence (assuming it to subsist) from the pleadings and from the course of the trial before the execution of any assignment of the rights by Burndy, or the making of any order of the court vesting those rights in BICC.

*The construction and effect of cl 10 of the assignment*

I do not accept the submission of counsel for BICC that the purpose of cl 10(iii) was to provide a simple mechanism whereby any party not interested in proceedings with a particular patent or application could divest himself of all responsibility by doing nothing. Equally, I do not accept his submission that cl 10(iii) is the only remedy available to BICC if Burndy fails to pay its half share of fees and costs, and BICC has no right of action to recover the money.

If BICC had failed to pay the fees required to maintain a patent in force and Burndy, learning of the failure, had paid to the Patent Office the sum required to restore the patent, Burndy would clearly, in my judgment, have been entitled to recover one-half of the sum from BICC as damages for breach, as I see it, of BICC's obligation under cl 10(ii) or, as I think counsel for BICC would accept, for breach of BICC's obligation under cl 9(a). The right of Burndy to claim an assignment under cl 10(iii) would be an additional or alternative remedy. It would be startling, therefore, if the right to claim an assignment under cl 10(iii), which was merely an additional or alternative remedy in the event of a default by BICC, was the sole remedy available to BICC in the event of a default on the part of Burndy.

The obligation on BICC under cl 10(ii) to pay the requisite costs and fees is expressly subject to reimbursement of one-half of the amount by Burndy. That, in my judgment, imports an implied contract by Burndy under cl 10(ii) to pay BICC one-half of the amount of the costs and fees. Alternatively, the one half of the amount could be recovered by BICC from Burndy in quasi-contract as money paid to the use of Burndy on the basis that Burndy, having taken the benefit of the payment by accepting that the patent concerned is maintained in force, is bound, under the words 'subject to reimbursement', to bear the burden and can be sued for one-half of the costs and fees.

As to the purpose of cl 10(iii), the clause, in my judgment, plays a sensible part, even though that part has not been fully thought out in all details, in the scheme of the assignment in dealing with the joint rights. The joint rights are to be jointly owned and each party is to have a full independent right to exploit them. But, just as under cl 9(d) a party who is not prepared to pay its share of the costs of obtaining an extension or registration of a particular patent is to assign all its interest to the other party, so equally it is commercial sense that under cl 10(iii) a party who fails to pay its share of the costs and fees required to process a patent application or keep a patent alive may be required to give up to the other party all the first party's interest in the particular patent or application.

It may be that, in a particular set of circumstances, cl 10(iii) will operate as a simple mechanism to enable a party to divest itself of all rights and liabilities in respect of a patent or application in which that party is not, or is no longer, interested. That is not, however, either the purpose or the limitation on the operation of cl 10(iii).

Counsel for BICC urges that the conclusion that the amount of fees can be sued for leads to the conclusion that the party who no longer desires the continuation of a particular patent or application cannot, as of right, absolve himself from liability. That may be so. If it is so, it is because the draftsman of the clause, relying, no doubt, on a certain commercial common sense in the parties, had not thought of the difficulty. Had he thought of the difficulty, the answer would have been some form of put option to counterbalance cl 10(iii).

*Penalty*

It follows from the views expressed above as to the sensible purpose of cl 10(iii) that the clause is no more a penalty clause than is the ordinary power of re-entry in a lease or the ordinary provision in a patent licence to enable the patentee to determine the licence, however valuable, in the event of non-payment of royalties by the licensee. It is unnecessary to elaborate this point, which is separate from the questions whether relief against forfeiture can, or should, be granted.

*Set-off*

At the outset of his authoritative exposition of the law of set-off in *Hanak v Green* [1958] 2 All ER 141 at 145, [1958] 2 QB 9 at 16 Morris LJ cited the statement by Lord Hanworth MR in *Re a bankruptcy notice (No 171 of 1934)* [1934] Ch 431 at 437, [1934] All ER Rep 688 at 692 that the word 'set-off'—

'is a word well known and established in its meaning; it is something which provides a defence because the nature and quality of the sum so relied upon are such that it is a sum which is proper to be dealt with as diminishing the claim which is made, and against which the sum so demanded can be set off.'

Morris LJ went on to explain that there are three forms of set-off recognised by the law. The first is set-off at law, or legal set-off as it is sometimes called, of mutual debts under the Statutes of Set-off, where the claims on both sides have to be liquidated debts or money demands which can be ascertained with certainty at the time of pleading. This is the form of set-off relied on in the present case. The second form of set-off arose as explained by Parke B in *Mondel v Steel* (1841) 8 M & W 858, [1835–42] All ER Rep 511 and was a development of the common law: where an action was brought for an agreed price of a specific chattel sold with a warranty or a work which was to be performed according to contract, the defendant was allowed to plead by way of defence in reduction of the claim that the chattel, by reason of non-compliance with the warranty, or the work in consequence of the non-performance of the contract, was diminished in value. The third form of set-off, often referred to as equitable set-off, arose in cases in which a court of equity would have regarded the cross-claims as entitling the defendant to be protected in one way or another against the plaintiff's claims; these were particularly cases where the cross-claim was related to the subject matter of the claim and there were factors which would have rendered it unjust in the eyes of equity that the claim should be enforced without regard to the cross-claim.

These various forms of set-off arise by operation of law or equity. They do not depend on finding any express or implied contract between the parties that there shall be set-off; the position is the other way round. As Lord Diplock observed in *Gilbert-Ash (Northern) Ltd v Modern Engineering (Bristol) Ltd* [1973] 3 All ER 195 at 215, [1974] AC 689 at 717, a case of the second class:

> 'It is, of course open to parties to a contract for sale of goods or for work and labour or for both to exclude by express agreement a remedy for its breach which would otherwise arise by operation of law or such remedy may be excluded by usage binding on the parties . . . But in construing such a contract one starts with the presumption that neither party intends to abandon any remedies for its breach arising by operation of law, and clear express words must be used in order to rebut this presumption.'

These words seem to me, equally, if not a fortiori, applicable to legal set-off of the first class, which originally arose by statute.

In discussing legal set-off of the first class in *Hanak v Green* [1958] 2 All ER 141 at 149, [1958] 2 QB 9 at 23, Morris LJ approved the explanation of the basis of the doctrine given by Cockburn CJ in *Stooke v Taylor* (1880) 5 QBD 569 at 576 that the existence and amount of such a set-off must be taken to be known to a plaintiff who should give credit for it in his action against the defendant. In the present case, therefore (as counsel for BICC accepts), if BICC had sued Burndy for the unpaid amount of Burndy's half share of the fees and costs incurred by BICC under cl 10(ii) of the assignment, Burndy would have had a cast-iron defence of legal set-off in respect of the amounts due from BICC to Burndy under the commercial agreement and BICC's action would have been dismissed with costs.

The crucial question is then, as I see it, whether, even though a claim for payment would fail because of a defence of set-off, a claim for other relief dependent on non-payment can succeed. I cannot see that it can make any difference in substance whether procedurally the claim for the other relief is joined in one action with the claim for payment to which the set-off is a valid defence, or whether only the other relief is claimed, leaving the claim for payment to be raised in a subsequent action or to be resolved by the application of the set-off.

There are two reported cases which I find helpful on this point of law. Both were concerned with equitable set-off, ie set-off of the third class.

In *Federal Commerce and Navigation Ltd v Molena Alpha Inc, The Nanfri, The Benfri, The Lorfri* [1978] 3 All ER 1066 at 1077, [1978] QB 927 at 974 Lord Denning MR said:

> 'Again take the case where the contract gives a creditor a right to take the law into his own hands, to take a particular course of action if a sum is not paid: such as to forfeit a lease for non-payment of rent, or to withdraw a vessel for non-payment of hire. There the distinction between set-off and cross-claim is crucial. When the debtor has a true set-off it goes in reduction of the sums owing to the creditor. If the creditor does not allow it to be deducted, he is in peril. He will be liable in damages if he exercises his contractual right of withdrawal wrongly.'

From this passage, which I am happy to take as a correct statement of the law (although, despite the generality of the wording, I take it as referring to equitable set-off only, since equitable set-off was the only class of set-off under consideration in *Federal Commerce*), it clearly follows, in my judgment, that, if in the present case Burndy had had an equitable rather than a legal set-off against BICC, BICC would not have been entitled to call under cl 10(iii) of the assignment for an assignment of Burndy's patent rights.

Similarly, in *British Anzani (Felixstowe) Ltd v International Marine Management (UK) Ltd* [1979] 2 All ER 1063, [1980] QB 137 where there was a claim for unpaid rent and for forfeiture of leasehold premises for non-payment of the rent, it seems to have been common ground that an equitable set-off against the rent, if established, would have been a defence to both claims. I cannot think that it would in principle have made any difference if the claim had been made for forfeiture and possession of the premises only, without including in the same writ a claim for the unpaid rent; the claim for forfeiture and possession depended on the rent being unpaid, just as the claim for an assignment of patent rights under cl 10(iii) in the present case depends on Burndy's half share of the fees and costs under cl 10(ii) not having been paid.

I cannot see that it makes any difference in principle that the set-off in the present case is a legal set-off of the first class and not an equitable set-off. The would-be plaintiff, here BICC, is, as Cockburn CJ and Morris LJ explained, to be taken to know the existence and amount of liquidated money claims against it, and that must be equally applicable whether the plaintiff is seeking to claim payment of a sum or some other relief which is dependent on non-payment of that sum.

Counsel for BICC submits that in modern conditions it would be commercially impracticable for a multinational company to know what claims, which could be the basis of legal set-off, an apparent debtor may have against it. They may be claims through different branches in different countries and not merely, as here, claims under another of a group of interlocking agreements. But the argument, if valid, would apply to money claims of BICC against Burndy as much as to claims for other relief, and in relation to any money claim for the half share of costs and fees under cl 10(ii) it is accepted that set-off would, on the admitted facts, be a complete defence.

In my judgment, therefore, on the point of set-off Burndy has a valid and complete defence to this action.

I have had the opportunity of reading in draft the judgment of Kerr LJ and I note that he does not agree with my conclusion that Burndy has a defence to this action on the point of set-off. He takes the view that a right to set-off, whether legal or equitable, does not operate as a bar to a claim for equitable relief, such as BICC's claim for specific performance, as it would in relation to a monetary claim; it is only relevant if the claim to set-off provides equitable grounds for equity to intervene on a discretionary basis, as by refusing the equitable relief claimed or granting some other equitable relief, eg by way of relief against forfeiture.

Before the Supreme Court of Judicature Acts 1873 and 1875, set-off of any sort would almost invariably only have arisen in relation to claims in the common law courts for payment of money. Equitable relief would only have come in in a rather different, and purely procedural, context, namely that in the form of set-off known as equitable set-off, to which Lord Cottenham LC referred in *Rawson v Samuel* (1841) Cr & Ph 161, 41 ER 451, where set-off at law, ie under the statutes, was not available, but the court of equity felt that the defendant to an action at law ought, because of a cross-claim, to be protected against the action at law, that court would have granted the equitable relief of an injunction to restrain the claimant at law from enforcing his claim at law.

It seems that the only case in the books in which a plea of set-off was sought to be raised by a defendant to a claim for equitable relief in the Court of Chancery was *Phipps v Child* (1857) 3 Drew 709, 61 ER 1074, where a purchaser, who was defendant to an action for specific performance of a contract for the sale of an interest in land, sought unsuccessfully to reduce the purchase money due from him by setting off the unquantified balance allegedly due to him from the vendor in respect of other dealings, and sought equally unsuccessfully to resist specific performance of the contract until that balance had been established. The judgment does not, however, as I read it, lay down any general principle which is relevant now, and the set-off asserted by the purchaser would not have fallen within any of Morris LJ's three categories (see the comments in Spry *Equitable Remedies* (2nd edn, 1980) p 171.)

It is now clear that, since the Judicature Acts, equitable set-off can, like the first and second of Morris LJ's three categories, be pleaded as a defence where appropriate to proceedings, whether at law or in Chancery. Equally, since the Judicature Acts, equitable forms of relief, such as a decree for specific performance or an injunction, can be obtained in any division of the High Court and can be combined in one action with a claim for payment of money.

It seems to me right that, under the present practice, a set-off should be a defence, as in such a case as *British Anzani (Felixstowe) Ltd v International Marine Management (UK) Ltd* [1979] 2 All ER 1063, [1980] QB 137, not only to a money claim for unpaid rent but also to a claim for forfeiture or other relief for non-payment of the rent. It would make no difference if the re-entry clause had been backed by an agreement by the tenant to surrender the lease in the event of non-payment of rent, and the landord had sought specific performance of that agreement.

The essence of an equitable set-off is that equity considered it unjust that a claimant should seek to enforce a claim without giving credit for a related cross-claim which the defendant had against him. The logic of the argument makes the defence of equitable set-off equally applicable, under modern procedure, whatever form of relief, legal or equitable, the plaintiff is claiming, provided that that relief depends on the non-payment of the money claim to which the equitable set-off is a complete defence. That, as I understand him, is what Lord Denning MR was saying in the passage in his judgment in *Federal Commerce* quoted above.

But, if the equitable set-off can be a good defence to a claim for equitable relief, then I cannot see why legal set-off should not also be a good defence, since legal set-off was authorised by statute and equitable set-off was developed from it.

*Relief against forfeiture*

If I am wrong in my view on Burndy's defence of set-off, it becomes necessary to consider Burndy's claim for relief against forfeiture. Even though, as indicated above, I take the view that cl 10(iii) of the assignment is not a penalty clause, it is a forfeiture clause in that its enforcement would involve the forfeiture to BICC of Burndy's half share in the relevant patent or other joint rights.

There are here two questions, namely has the court jurisdiction to grant Burndy relief against forfeiture by an extension of time and, if so, is it appropriate that the court should exercise that jurisdiction in Burndy's favour?

The judge decided, in reliance especially on the judgment of the Court of Appeal in *The Scaptrade* [1983] 1 All ER 301, [1983] QB 529, that the court had no such jurisdiction, because the assignment was a commercial agreement between commercial parties. The decision of the Court of Appeal in *The Scaptrade* was, as the judge noted, affirmed by the House of Lords (see [1983] 2 All ER 763, [1983] 2 AC 694). As I understand the decision of the House of Lords, however, and the decision of the House of Lords in the subsequent case of *Sport International Bussum BV v Inter-Footwear Ltd* [1984] 2 All ER 321, [1984] 1 WLR 776, their effect was to confine the court's jurisdiction to grant relief against forfeiture to contracts concerning the transfer of proprietary or possessory rights (see [1984] 2 All ER 321 at 325, [1984] 1 WLR 776 at 794 per Lord Templeman). The present case, however, is distinguishable from those cases in that cl 10(iii) of the assignment is concerned with a transfer of property rights.

In *Shiloh Spinners Ltd v Harding* [1973] 1 All ER 90, [1975] AC 691 the House of Lords held that the court had jurisdiction to grant relief against forfeiture of proprietary rights in circumstances outside the ordinary landlord and tenant relationship; but the case was concerned with a claim for relief against a right of re-entry on land, and the speeches do not cast light on the extent to which jurisdiction exists to grant relief against forfeiture of property other than an interest in land. In *Barton Thompson & Co Ltd v Stapling Machines Co* [1966] 2 All ER 222, [1966] Ch 499 Pennycuick J considered it to be arguable that relief could be granted against forfeiture of a lease of chattels. That view seems to have been approved by Edmund Davies LJ in *Starside Properties Ltd v Mustapha* [1974] 2 All ER 567, [1974] 1 WLR 816, and in *Stockloser v Johnson* [1954] 1 All ER 630 at 644–645, [1954] 1 QB 476 at 502 Romer LJ apparently considered that the court would have power in an appropriate case to grant relief by way of extension of time to a purchaser of a diamond necklace who had failed to pay the final instalment of the price in due time.

There is no clear authority, but for my part I find it difficult to see why the jurisdiction of equity to grant relief against forfeiture should only be available where what is liable to forfeiture is an interest in land and not an interest in personal property. Relief is only available where what is in question is forfeiture of proprietary or possessory rights, but I see no reason in principle for drawing a distinction as to the type of property in which the rights subsist. The fact that the right to forfeiture arises under a commercial agreement is highly relevant to the question whether relief against forfeiture should be granted, but I do not see that it can preclude the existence of the jurisdiction to grant relief, if forfeiture of proprietary or possessory rights, as opposed to merely contractual rights, is in question. I hold, therefore, that the court has jurisdiction to grant Burndy relief.

The judge was of the view that, even if there was jurisdiction, relief should not be granted. He considered it inappropriate to grant relief, primarily, as I read his judgment, because Mr Reiter had not been told of cl 10(iii) and had not been given any instructions relating to it. The judge said that he was not satisfied that he had been told the whole story in that regard; for my part, however, I have great difficulty in seeing what else he could have expected to be told. I do not find anything sinister in the failure to give Mr Reiter proper instructions. The management of Burndy acted very incompetently, but I cannot see that incompetence is necessarily a bar to the grant of relief against forfeiture.

In my judgment, it is necessary to consider all the circumstances, including what was happening on BICC's side. I remind myself that there is not, and has never been, any plea against BICC of waiver or equitable estoppel, on the basis of *Hughes v Metropolitan Rly Co* (1877) 2 App Cas 439, [1874–80] All ER Rep 187 in respect of BICC's exercise of its right under cl 10(iii). The facts remain, however, that BICC, having initially sent in ordinary commercial invoices for the half share of the costs and fees, and having plainly not insisted on the 30 days' time limit when the invoices were rendered, invoked cl 10(iii) out of the blue on 18 October 1982, when there had been no relevant correspondence between the parties for two months, and at a time when a meeting had been set up between Mr Reiter and Mr Ross-Gower to resolve outstanding billing questions, and at a time when BICC in truth owed Burndy more under the commercial agreement than Burndy owed BICC under the assignment. In my judgment, the case for relief is made out and, if I had not taken the view that Burndy had a good defence to the action on the ground of set-off, I would grant Burndy relief, by way of an extension of time, against forfeiture of its rights under cl 10(iii).

*The licence to Burndy-Electra SA*

Since, for the foregoing reasons, Burndy is, in my judgment, entitled to succeed on this appeal, the question whether any assignment of rights which Burndy may be ordered to make under cl 10(iii) should be expressed to be subject to some licence in favour of Burndy-Electra SA does not arise. It is, therefore, unnecessary for me to express any concluded opinion on that question. I would merely say that, as at present advised, I have considerable difficulty in accepting the judge's views as to the application and effect of s 33 of the 1977 Act but, conversely, I am attracted by the submissions of junior counsel for BICC that any licence previously subsisting in favour of Burndy-Electra SA was brought to an end by the principal agreement and that it is not open to Burndy to set up any such previous licence against BICC now, as Burndy agreed by cl 2.3 of the principal agreement to procure that its subsidiaries should waive all rights under certain previously existing agreements including the existing agreement through which Burndy-Electra SA claims title.

I would allow this appeal.

**KERR LJ.** I have had the advantage of reading the judgment of Dillon LJ and agree that this appeal should be allowed for the reasons stated by him under the heading 'Relief against forfeiture'. The way in which Burndy's case was pleaded in their defence did not enable them to rely on the principles laid down in authorities such as *Hughes v Metropolitan Rly Co* (1877) 2 App Cas 439, [1874–80] All ER Rep 187 and *Charles Rickards Ltd v Oppenheim* [1950] 1 All ER 420, [1950] 1 KB 616, although they might well have been raised on the facts. But the pleading is sufficient to raise a defence for the intervention of equity as an answer to BICC's claim and entitles the court to have regard to all the circumstances in that connection. In my view, this defence is made out.

BICC's primary claim is for an order for specific performance of cl 10(iii) of the assignment by requiring Burndy to transfer all rights and benefits in the patents and applications listed in the schedule. BICC are therefore themselves claiming an equitable remedy. However, having regard to the course of dealing between the parties and the events to which Dillon LJ has already referred, I do not think that BICC are entitled to invoke the assistance of equity. I do not find it necessary to lengthen this judgment by a full analysis of the various invoices which they sent and the communications between the parties about them, save to say that this clearly shows that BICC's conduct throughout was wholly inconsistent with the applicability of cl 10(iii) which they then suddenly sought to impose without any warning. In addition, there is the question of set-off to which I refer later. I would accordingly refuse an order for specific performance in the circumstances of this case, with the result that on this basis BICC would, in any event, only succeed to the extent of any remedy by way of damages which they may be able to establish.

However, for the reasons stated by Dillon LJ, I also agree that this is a case where the court's equitable jurisdiction goes further. It entitles the court to grant an extension of time to Burndy to comply with cl 10(iii) in order to relieve them from the forfeiture of their proprietary share in 'the joint rights'. The relevant authorities have been discussed by Dillon LJ and I agree with his conclusions about their effect on the court's jurisdiction where, as here, the failure to make a timeous payment results in the forfeiture of property and not merely in the loss of contractual rights. I also agree that this is a case in which this court should differ from the views expressed by Falconer J as to how he would have exercised his discretion if he had concluded that this fell to be done. The judge does not mention, and does not appear to have had in mind, any of the important circumstances which clearly call for the intervention of equity in all the circumstances of this case. The only considerations mentioned by him in this connection are (1) the fact that the value of the patents etc was many times greater than the payment due from Burndy under cl 10(iii), and (2) the fact that Mr Reiter was unaware of the terms of cl 10(iii) and that no explanation had been given for this, a point with which Dillon LJ has already dealt. He makes no mention of the course of dealing between the parties, the conduct of BICC in suddenly invoking cl 10(iii) without warning against this background, and the fact that, when BICC invoked this provision, there were outstanding invoices from Burndy to BICC which were due and payable and which greatly exceeded the amounts due from Burndy under cl 10(iii).

The latter point must weigh heavily in Burndy's favour in the exercise of the court's equitable jurisdiction, particularly where the basis of this jurisdiction is capable of including the grant of relief against forfeiture. It would obviously be inequitable to allow a plaintiff to insist on the forfeiture of a defendant's valuable right of property for non-payment of a relatively small sum when the plaintiff is at that time himself indebted to the defendant in a far larger sum. However, with the greatest respect for the views of Dillon LJ stated in his judgment under the heading 'Set-off', I cannot agree that the existence of a right of set-off in itself provides a defence to BICC's claim for specific performance under cl 10(iii), and that BICC's action therefore fails in limine on this ground. This does not affect the outcome of the present appeal, but it raises a point of some general importance.

I bear in mind the passage from the speech of Lord Diplock in *Gilbert-Ash (Northern) Ltd v Modern Engineering (Bristol) Ltd* [1973] 3 All ER 195 at 215, [1974] AC 689 at 717, which Dillon LJ has already quoted. The context in that case was the entitlement of a debtor to rely on a right of set-off arising in connection with a contract under which the creditor was claiming payment from the debtor. The latter was held to be entitled to rely on an unliquidated cross-claim which arose under the same contract. This entitlement had not been excluded by the terms of the contract, with the result that the amount of the creditor's claim fell to be abated by the amount by which the debtor was held entitled to a set-off against it. To that extent he could withhold payment in response to the

creditor's demand. The creditor's claim was for the payment of money and he had no
other contractual right; the sole issue was what could be set-off against a monetary claim.

The position under cl 10(iii) is in my view very different, although I respectfully agree
with the judgment of Dillon LJ under the heading 'The construction and effect of cl 10
of the assignment'. On receiving a valid written request for payment of half the sums
expended by BICC in processing and maintaining the parties' 'joint rights', Burndy were
obliged to pay this amount or risk the forfeiture of their half share in these rights.
Following the decision in *Gilbert-Ash*, Burndy would therefore have been entitled to
respond to such a request by claiming to set-off an equal amount of the debts owed to
them by BICC so as to extinguish BICC's claim for payment. If they had done so, they
would not have been in default under this provision and BICC would have had no basis
for contending that a right of forfeiture of Burndy's share in 'the joint rights' had arisen.
Further, following *Stooke v Taylor* (1880) 5 QBD 569, and a fortiori *Gilbert-Ash*, proceedings
by BICC to recover the sums due from Burndy would have failed on a plea of set-off by
Burndy, as counsel for BICC rightly conceded.

However, I cannot accept that, on the proper construction of the assignment as a whole
and of cl 10(iii) in particular, Burndy were simply entitled to do nothing in response to a
valid claim for payment by BICC and then to rely on the overall state of accounts between
the parties, not arising under the terms of the assignment, as an answer to BICC's claim
to invoke the next provision of this clause by requiring Burndy to transfer their share of
'the joint rights'. Such a conclusion does not follow from the decision in *Gilbert-Ash* or of
any other authority of which I am aware. It would imply that BICC were not entitled to
make a valid request for payment by Burndy under cl 10(iii) of the assignment at any
time when BICC owed an equal or greater amount to Burndy by reason of transactions
which had nothing to do with the assignment, as is the position in the present case.
Although Burndy were overall creditors of BICC, the dictum of Cockburn CJ in *Stooke v
Taylor* (1880) 5 QBD 569 at 576, to which Dillon LJ has referred, cannot, in my view, be
applied to cl 10(iii) of the assignment: BICC were nevertheless entitled to invoice Burndy
under this provision without at that stage having to give credit for Burndy's invoices
under other contracts. The dictum would only operate if and when BICC thereafter
sought to enforce payment by action. In my view, any other construction of provisions
such as cl 10(iii) would fly in the face of commercial sense and would be wrong. They
might require an ex post facto determination of the overall consolidated state of accounts
on a particular earlier date, which no one was then in a position to oversee, as between
different branches or departments of the contestant legal entities engaged in different
commercial transactions.

Similarly, the remarks of Lord Denning MR in *Federal Commerce and Navigation Ltd v
Molena Alpha Inc, The Nanfri, The Benfri, The Lorfri* [1978] 3 All ER 1066 at 1077, [1978]
QB 927 at 974 which Dillon LJ has also quoted, do not, in my view, detract from this
conclusion in any way when they are considered in their context. The charterparty
required the charterer to pay the monthly hire 'in cash, in Montreal'. The full text of the
particular clause in that case does not appear from the report (see [1978] 3 All ER 1066 at
1071, [1978] QB 927 at 966), but it may well have specified a particular bank in Montreal
where the hire was to be paid into the shipowners' account, as is frequently done. The
issue was solely the extent to which the charterers could validly abate the amount of any
such monthly payment by deductions which were sufficiently connected with the off-
hire clause to permit them to do so. To the extent that such deductions could be claimed
as an equitable set-off against the owners' right to the hire they were held to be
permissible. In so far as they went beyond this, no deduction could be made and the
shipowners were entitled to exercise their right of withdrawal under the hire clause (see
[1978] 3 All ER 1066 at 1078–1080, 1083–1090, [1978] QB 927 at 974–977, 981–989
per Lord Denning MR and Goff LJ). It would be out of the question, in my view, for
charterers to pay nothing, or less than the hire with the permissible deductions, and then
to seek to rely on the owners' indebtedness to them on general account unconnected with
the charterparty; at any rate without first having claimed a right of set-off.

This is the context in which Lord Denning MR's remarks fall to be placed, and I return to his judgment again in a moment. If the shipowners had owed moneys to the charterers on grounds which were unconnected with the off-hire clause, let alone unconnected with the charterparty, I think that the decision would clearly have gone the other way. Lord Denning MR's remarks do not support the contention that the charterers would have been entitled to rely on any sum owed to them by the owners which could not have been validly deducted under the off-hire clause. On the contrary, the reasoning of the judgment in the passages mentioned above clearly shows that it was only to this extent that the charterers could invoke a right of set-off. Similarly, in *British Anzani (Felixstowe) Ltd v International Marine Management (UK) Ltd* [1979] 2 All ER 1063, [1980] QB 137, the claimed set-off arose out of the agreement and underleases on which the plaintiffs' claim was based and not out of some unconnected transaction.

Burndy's right to rely on a set-off against BICC's invoices under cl 10(iii) of the assignment by reason of the overall accountability between them under other unconnected contracts can, in my view, only arise in two ways. Firstly, if BICC had sought to enforce payment of their invoices by action, Burndy would have had a right at law to set off the debts owed by BICC under other invoices so as to extinguish BICC's claim and defeat the action. The position would be the same if BICC's liability had not arisen under mutual debts which gave right to a legal set-off but under any right recognised as giving rise to an equitable set-off (see e g *Hanak v Green* [1958] 2 All ER 141, [1958] 2 QB 9 and *Gilbert-Ash (Northern) Ltd v Modern Engineering (Bristol) Ltd* [1973] 3 All ER 195, [1974] AC 689). Secondly, if BICC seek to enforce cl 10(iii) by demanding the transfer by Burndy of their share in 'the joint rights', as they do, then Burndy can invoke the protection of the court's discretionary jurisdiction in equity. For that purpose, the existence of a right of set-off may carry great weight, but the intervention of equity must then depend on all the circumstances. In the present case, the protection of equity can be invoked in two respects: to refuse an order of specific performance in favour of BICC and to grant Burndy relief from the forfeiture of their proprietary 'joint rights'. But the right to a set-off, whether legal or equitable, does not, in my view, in itself operate as a bar to BICC's claim for specific performance, as it would in relation to a monetary claim; its only relevance is that equity may intervene on a discretionary basis. In my view, this conclusion stems from the true construction and effect of cl 10(iii) within the frame of the assignment as a contract which is unlinked to any other transaction out of which BICC's overall indebtedness arises, and it is also consistent with legal principle, but we were helpfully referred by counsel for Burndy to the discussion in Spry *Equitable Remedies* (2nd edn, 1980) pp 168–171. I would merely refer to two passages. First, the author states (at p 169) that—

'where a right to a set-off exists at law its existence will be recognized in equitable proceedings, unless circumstances arise such as to render reliance on it unjust.'

Then he says (at p 171):

'It should be noted that it has sometimes been said that equitable set-offs cannot arise in cases of specific performance [quoting 34 Halsbury's Laws (3rd edn) 400, para 683 (see now 42 Halsbury's Laws (4th edn) para 440)], but there is no reason in principle why this proposition should be correct, and, indeed, cases relied upon in support of it [quoting *Phipps v Child* (1857) 3 Drew 709, 61 ER 1074, cited in 42 Halsbury's Laws (4th edn) para 440] are found to depend in truth on the absence of a sufficient equity to relief.'

This must apply equally to legal rights of set-off pleaded as a defence to a claim grounded in equity, such as a claim for specific performance. *Spry* refers to *Rawson v Samuel* (1841) Cr & Ph 161, 41 ER 451 in support of this passage. In that case the issue was whether an injunction should be granted to the plaintiffs in the Court of Chancery to restrain the defendants from enforcing a judgment for damages for breach of contract pending the decision on the plaintiffs' claim for an account in the Court of Chancery. In rejecting this, Lord Cottenham LC said (Cr & Ph 161 at 178–180, 41 ER 451 at 458–459):

'We speak familiarly of equitable set-off, as distinguished from the set-off at law; but it will be found that this equitable set-off exists in cases where the parties seeking the benefit of it can shew some equitable ground for being protected against his adversary's demand. The mere existence of cross-demands is not sufficient ... Is there, then, any equity in preventing a party who has recovered damages at law from receiving them, because he may be found to be indebted, upon the balance of an unsettled account, to the party against whom the damages have been recovered? ... What equity have the Plaintiffs in the suit for an account to be protected against the damages awarded against them? If they have no such equity, there can be no good ground for the injunction. Several cases were cited in support of the injunction; but in every one of them ... it will be found that the equity of the bill impeached the title to the legal demand ... None of these cases furnish any ground for the injunction in the case before me.'

Similarly, I think, in agreement with the passage quoted from *Spry*, that the application of equitable principles is the explanation of the decision in *Phipps v Child*, although in that case the plaintiff was successful in his equitable claim. This was for specific performance of an agreement for the sale of part of a colliery which the defendant resisted, inter alia, on the ground that sums were due to him under a separate contract which he claimed to be entitled to set-off against the purchase price. Kindersley V-C rejected this, saying (3 Drew 709 at 714–715, 61 ER 1074 at 1076):

'Then the question is whether there is anything in the extrinsic circumstances to justify me in refusing to decree specific performance, and I think there is none ... Next, it is said that, if an account were taken, it would appear that something would be due from the Plaintiff to the Defendant, which ought to be set off against the demand on the Defendant. I think that is not a ground for me to refuse specific performance ... There may be a right in the Defendant to bring an action against the Plaintiff. But, if there is such a right, that is not a reason for non-performance of the contract.'

My reason for citing these passages is because they support the conclusion that a claim for an equitable remedy, such as the claim for specific performance in this case, can only be resisted on equitable grounds. To adapt the well-known phrase of Lord Cottenham LC, the defence must impeach the title to the plaintiff's demand. If it does not do so, then it depends on the application of the rules of equity whether the plaintiff's equitable claim will be enforced or not. But the existence of a right of set-off, whether legal or equitable, does not per se provide a defence to the equitable claim for specific performance so as to defeat it in limine. Its effect on the outcome of the action will depend on the circumstances and the application of the principles of equity. In my view this is clearly implicit in the judgment of Lord Denning MR in *Federal Commerce and Navigation Ltd v Molena Alpha Inc* [1978] 3 All ER 1066 at 1077–1078, [1978] QB 927 at 974–975 in the passage immediately following that quoted by Dillon LJ, as follows:

'In making the distinction between set-off and cross-claim, the courts of common law had their own special rules. For instance in a series of cases they formulated rules saying when there could be an abatement of rent or an abatement of the sums due for work and labour done, or an abatement of the price of goods sold and delivered. So that the defendant could make deductions accordingly. But the courts of equity, as was their wont, came in to mitigate the technicalities of the common law. They allowed deductions, by way of equitable set-off, whenever there were good equitable grounds for directly impeaching the demand which the creditor was seeking to enforce: see *Rawson v Samuel* (1841) Cr & Ph 161 at 178–179, 41 ER 451 at 458–459 per Lord Cottenham LC. These grounds were never precisely formulated before the Supreme Court of Judicature Act 1873. It is now far too late to search through the old books and dig them out. Over 100 years have passed since the Supreme Court of Judicature Act 1873. During that time the streams of common law and equity have flown together and combined so as to be indistinguishable the one from the other. We have no longer to ask ourselves: what would the courts of common law or the courts of equity have done before the Supreme Court of Judicature Act 1873? We have to ask ourselves: what should we do now so as to ensure fair dealing between the parties? (see *United Scientific Holdings Ltd v Burnley Borough Council* [1977] 2 All ER 62 at 68, [1978] AC 904 at 924–925 per Lord Diplock). This question must be asked in each case as it arises for decision; and then, from case to case, we shall build up a series of precedents to guide those who come after us. But one thing is quite clear: it is not every cross-claim which can be deducted. It is only cross claims that arise out of the same transaction or are closely connected with it. And it is only cross-claims which go directly to impeach the plaintiff's demands, that is, so closely connected with his demands that it would be manifestly unjust to allow him to enforce payment without taking into account the crossclaim.'

Similarly, Goff LJ said ([1978] 3 All ER 1066 at 1083, [1978] QB 927 at 981):

'The circumstances must be such as to make it unfair for the creditor to be paid his claim without allowing that of the debtor if and so far as well-founded, and thus to raise an equity against the creditor, or, as it has been expressed, impeach his title to be paid.'

I appreciate that, in that case, no question of discretion arose. The shipowners had already withdrawn the ships and were not claiming any equitable remedy. There was equally no question of a claim for relief from forfeiture, and any such claim would have been misconceived (see *Scandinavian Trading Tanker Co AB v Flota Petrolera Ecuatoriana, The Scaptrade* [1983] 2 All ER 763, [1983] 2 AC 694). The court was concerned solely with the extent to which an equitable set-off could be relied on by way of deduction from monthly hire payable under a time charter. My main reason for citing these passages is to show that Lord Cottenham LC's analysis is still applicable: leaving aside the third category of set-off mentioned in *Hanak v Green* [1958] 2 All ER 141 at 149, [1958] 2 QB 9 at 23 (matters of equity which formerly might have called for injunction or prohibition, which does not arise here) the test is whether the defence of set-off impeaches the plaintiff's demand. In the present case Burndy's right to a legal set-off would provide a complete defence if they were sued for the amounts due under cl 10(iii), because these would impeach and extinguish BICC's claim. But the existence of this right of set-off does not impeach BICC's claim for specific performance. It only raises an equity in favour of Burndy which, together with all the other circumstances to which I have already referred, calls for the exercise of the court's discretionary equitable jurisdiction (a) to refuse an order of specific performance in favour of BICC and (b) to grant Burndy relief from the forfeiture of their share of 'the joint rights' by extending their time for complying with cl 10(iii). I would accordingly allow this appeal on these grounds.

**ACKNER LJ.** I have had the benefit of reading the judgments of both Kerr and Dillon LJJ. I also agree that the appeal be allowed and, for the reasons set out in the judgment of Dillon LJ in so far as they differ from those of Kerr LJ.

*Appeal allowed. Leave to appeal to the House of Lords refused.*

*8 November. The Appeal Committee of the House of Lords allowed a petition by BICC for leave to appeal.*

Solicitors: *Allison & Humphreys* (for Burndy); *Bird & Bird* (for BICC).

Carolyn Toulmin    Barrister.

# Pocock v Steel

COURT OF APPEAL, CIVIL DIVISION
CUMMING-BRUCE, DILLON LJJ AND SIR DENYS BUCKLEY
14, 15, 16 NOVEMBER 1984

*Rent restriction – Possession – House required by landlord for own use – Recovery of possession by person who 'occupied' house as own residence and 'let' it on regulated tenancy – Whether person who last occupied house several years before relevant tenancy an 'owner-occupier' – Whether occupation as residence must immediately precede relevant letting to qualify person as 'owner-occupier' – Rent Act 1977, Sch 15, Case 11.*

To qualify as an 'owner-occupier' who is entitled to recover possession of a dwelling on satisfying the conditions specified in Case 11[a] in Sch 15 to the Rent Act 1977 a person must have 'occupied' the dwelling as his residence immediately before he 'let' it on the regulated tenancy he seeks to terminate, since the words 'occupied' and 'let' in Case 11 refer to substantially the same point of time. Accordingly, neither an owner who last occupied a dwelling some years before the commencement of the relevant tenancy nor an owner who grants a succession of regulated tenancies without going back into occupation before the grant of each tenancy qualifies as an 'owner-occupier' entitled to recover possession under Case 11 (see p 436 *a c d,* p 437 *b* to *e* and *j* and p 438 *b,* post).

Dicta of Shaw and Eveleigh LJJ in *Tilling v Whiteman* [1979] 1 All ER at 1109, 1111 applied.

### Notes

For the right to a possession order where a dwelling house is required as a residence for the owner occupier, see 27 Halsbury's Laws (4th edn) para 679.

For the Rent Act 1977, Sch 15, Case 11, see 47 Halsbury's Statutes (3rd edn) 607.

### Cases referred to in judgments

*Stratford v Syrett* [1957] 3 All ER 363, [1958] 1 QB 107, [1957] 3 WLR 733, CA.
*Tilling v Whiteman* [1979] 1 All ER 737, [1980] AC 1, [1979] 2 WLR 401, HL; *rvsg* [1978] 3 All ER 1103, [1980] AC 1, [1978] 3 WLR 137, CA.

### Appeal

Mrs Rosemary Ann Pocock appealed against the decision of his Honour Judge Galpin sitting in the Portsmouth County Court on 31 May 1984 whereby he allowed the appeal of the respondent, Miss Karen Nicola Steel, against an order made by Mr Registrar Bailey Cox on 25 April 1984 granting the appellant recovery of possession of a dwelling house in Petersfield, Hants which had been let to the respondent under a regulated tenancy by an agreement dated 7 December 1982. The facts are set out in the judgment of Dillon LJ.

*John Lofthouse* for the appellant.
*John R Davies* for the respondent.

**DILLON LJ** (delivering the first judgment at the invitation of Cumming-Bruce LJ). This is an appeal by the appellant in the action, Mrs Rosemary Pocock, against a decision of his Honour Judge Galpin given in the Portsmouth County Court on 31 May 1984. The appeal raises a question under the Rent Act 1977. By an agreement in writing dated 7 December 1982 the appellant granted the respondent, Miss Karen Nicola Steel, a furnished tenancy of a dwelling house known as Little Bushy, Steep, near Petersfield, for

---

*a*    Case 11, so far as material, is set out at p 435 *c d,* post

a term of one year less one day from 12 December 1982. That tenancy agreement created a regulated tenancy within the meaning of the Rent Acts. However, in the tenancy agreement the appellant gave notice to the respondent by cl 7 claiming to be the owner occupier of the dwelling house within the meaning of Case 11 in Sch 15 to the Rent Act 1977, and stating that possession of the property might be recovered by her under Case 11. The precise wording of cl 7 is not material.

The tenancy was extended by agreement for a further three months from 12 December 1983 but, after the extended term had expired, the respondent refused to give up possession, and the appellant now requires possession so that the property can be occupied as their residence by her daughter and son now aged 19 and 17. The question is therefore whether the appellant makes out her claim within Case 11 in Sch 15 to the 1977 Act. So far as material that case reads, as amended and currently in force, as follows:

'Where a person who occupied the dwelling-house as his residence (in this Case referred to as "the owner-occupier") let it on a regulated tenancy and—(a) not later than the relevant date the landlord gave notice in writing to the tenant that possession might be recovered under this Case, and (b) the dwelling-house has not, since . . . (ii) 14 August 1974, in the case of a regulated furnished tenancy . . . been let by the owner-occupier on a protected tenancy with respect to which the condition mentioned in paragraph (a) above was not satisfied, and (c) the court is of the opinion that of the conditions set out in Part V of this Schedule one of those in paragraphs (a) and (c) to (f) is satisfied . . .'

The conditions set out in Part V of the schedule include as para (a):

'. . . the dwelling-house is required as a residence for the owner or any member of his family who resided with the owner when he last occupied the dwelling-house as a residence . . .'

The importance of Case 11 is that if the facts to bring a particular situation within Case 11 are established, the court has no discretion to withhold an order for possession. If Case 11 is made out, an order for possession must be made.

The present case came originally before the county court registrar. The respondent at that time had no legal representation, apparently because her application for legal aid was still pending. The registrar decided in favour of the appellant and made an order for possession, but the respondent appealed to the judge. He allowed the appeal and dismissed the appellant's claim for possession. Although various other grounds were argued before the judge which are the subject of a respondent's notice, his decision in favour of the respondent was on one ground only, and that arises on the opening words of Case 11, which I quote again: 'Where a person who occupied the dwelling-house as his residence . . . let it on a regulated tenancy . . .' In point of fact, the appellant's occupation of the property ended 17 years ago. The legal title to the property has, since October 1963, been vested in the trustees of the appellant's marriage settlement on trust for sale. She herself has been one of the trustees, with her brother, since December 1976. She is entitled under the marriage settlement to the income from the proceeds of sale and to the net rents and profits until sale of the property, and from 1963 to 1967 she occupied the property under a power in the marriage settlement. Her son and daughter, who were then young children, lived with her in the property then. However, she went to live elsewhere in 1967 and has not occupied the property herself since then. Instead, it has been left furnished to a succession of tenants either by the trustees or by the appellant herself.

In relation to each of the tenancies granted since 14 August 1974, it is asserted (though this question only arises in relation to the respondent's notice) that not later than the relevant date, which is the date of the commencement of the tenancy, the appellant gave notice in writing to the tenant that possession might be recovered under Case 11 (or its predecessor). The question, therefore, on the appeal is whether it is sufficient to satisfy Case 11 if the owner-occupier occupied the property at some time, however long ago and however long before the grant of the relevant regulated tenancy, or whether the words 'occupied' and 'let' in the opening words of Case 11 are to be taken to refer to substantially the same point of time. On the cross-notice various questions are raised stemming from the fact that the appellant is not herself the owner of an estate in the property but merely has the possession and interests in relation to her marriage settlement which I have mentioned.

The practical objection to the construction of Case 11 that the words 'occupied' and 'let' refer to substantially the same point of time is that, if an owner-occupier quits a dwelling house, for instance to take up an appointment elsewhere for a period of years, and grants a tenancy which is, on any view, within Case 11, then, if the tenant dies or goes away, the landlord owner-occupier will have to go back into occupation of the property before he can safely grant a new tenancy to someone else which will be within the protection of Case 11. The question is whether it is permissible for an owner-occupier, provided appropriate statements are made to satisfy condition (b), to grant a succession of tenancies which will be protected by Case 11, however long the owner-occupier may remain out of occupation of the property.

This difficulty was clearly appreciated by Judge Galpin, and his own inclination was, therefore, to adopt the appellant's construction of Case 11. However, he decided against the appellant on the basis of obiter dicta by Shaw and Eveleigh LJJ in *Tilling v Whiteman* [1978] 3 All ER 1103, [1980] AC 1. The question at issue in *Tilling v Whiteman* was a different question not relevant to the point on the appeal and, in fact, more relevant to the points taken by the respondent's notice. In *Tilling v Whiteman* there had been joint owners of the property, one of whom had remained in occupation up to the grant of the tenancy to the defendant, and possession was sought so that one of them but not the other could resume occupation of the property as her residence. The dictum of Shaw LJ quoted by the judge was as follows ([1978] 3 All ER 1103 at 1109, [1980] AC 1 at 10):

'It is apparent that the characteristics which serve to identify an owner-occupier in this context are (i) that he owned the interest out of which the regulated tenancy was granted, and (ii) that he had occupied the dwelling-house as his residence at the time that he let it on a regulated tenancy.'

The dictum of Eveleigh LJ is as follows ([1978] 3 All ER 1103 at 1111, [1980] AC 1 at 12):

'We are not concerned in this present appeal to decide whether the occupation must be immediately before the letting or whether occupation at any previous time will do. However, as the past perfect tense is used for both verbs, there is much to be said for the contention that the occupation has to be the last occupation of the dwelling-house before the letting.'

In this court the inconvenience and illogicality of a construction which would prevent a landlord who, for instance, went abroad on a three-year basis granting successive tenancies under Case 11, without having come back to resume actual occupation himself, is strongly stressed by counsel for the appellant. He also advances an argument based on the legislative history of the enactment. He refers first to s 14(1) of the Rent Act 1965, which, it seems, introduced this type of exception to rent control. There the wording used is:

'Where a person who has occupied a dwelling-house as his residence (in this section referred to as the owner-occupier) has let the dwelling house on a regulated tenancy and the conditions mentioned in subsection (2) of this section are satisfied . . .'

The words used are 'has occupied' and 'has let'. On that wording *Megarry on the Rent Acts* (10th edn, 1967) p 311 commented:

'Despite the statutory phrase "owner-occupier", there seems to be nothing to require ownership in fee simple, so that a tenant who has sub-let a dwelling-house may satisfy the condition. Nor is there any limitation of time or capacity in the requirement of occupation as a residence, so that it might be satisfied, *e.g.*, by occupation for a few months *qua* licensee twenty years before becoming owner.'

The present wording 'occupied' and 'let' came in with the Rent Act 1968: see the 1968 Act, Sch 3, Case 10, where the wording is:

'Where a person who occupied the dwelling-house as his residence (in this Case referred to as "the owner-occupier") let it on a regulated tenancy . . .'

The 1968 Act is expressed to be a consolidating Act and the wording in the 1968 Act is taken from that Act into the 1977 Act with which we are concerned. So, it is said that the dicta of Shaw and Eveleigh LJJ were wrong; they failed to appreciate that they were concerned with a consolidating Act which ought to be construed by reference to the wording in the original Act, if the words 'has occupied' and 'has let' are looked at, then, it is said, it does not really appear that there is any link in time between the two.

For my part, I see the force of these arguments, but I regard the wording of Case 11 in the 1977 Act as clear: 'Where a person who occupied the dwelling-house . . . let it on a regulated tenancy'. The change of tense has removed any real ambiguity there might have been under the 1965 Act. The court has to construe the 1977 Act as it stands. It is not appropriate, just because the 1968 Act was a consolidating Act, to treat the 1977 Act as if it contained the wording of the 1965 Act which is not its actual wording. Neither the reference to past legislative history nor the anomaly of the inability to grant successive tenancies within Case 11 without an intermediate period of actual occupation can prevail against the clear wording of Case 11. Accordingly, I would, for my part, affirm the judge's decision and dismiss this appeal.

I have considered whether the condition in para (b) in Case 11 is a pointer to a different result. That envisages that the condition in para (a), as to giving notice in writing to a tenant that possession might be recovered under Case 11, must have been complied with on previous tenancies granted by the owner-occupier. It thus envisages that there may have been several tenancies granted by the owner-occupier; but I do not, for my part, find that enough, nor did counsel for the appellant seek to regard it as anything other than neutral. It could apply if, for instance, the owner-occupier goes away and grants one tenancy, comes back, and then goes away again and grants another tenancy, possibly on another posting to a different place of work.

The respondent's notice raises points which, on the view I take on the appeal, do not arise. Essentially, the main point taken is that, if the previous tenancy agreements granted from 1974 onwards before the tenancy to the respondent, and the notices given in relation to those tenancy agreements, are looked at, the proper conclusion is that the appellant herself, in entering into the tenancy agreement with the respondent, was doing so as an agent for the trustees and not on her own behalf, and the trustees have not as such ever occupied the property as their residence. The short answer to this is, in my judgment, that which the judge gave by reference to *Stratford v Syrett* [1957] 3 All ER 363, [1958] 1 QB 107, a decision of this court; and I apprehend that that conclusion is fortified by the observations of Eveleigh LJ in his judgment in *Tilling v Whiteman*, which was approved by the House of Lords (see [1979] 1 All ER 737 at 741, [1980] AC 1 at 21). But it is unnecessary to elaborate these points.

I would dismiss this appeal.

**SIR DENYS BUCKLEY.** I agree with the judgment delivered and the reasons adopted by Dillon LJ, and I do not think that I can usefully add anything to it.

**CUMMING-BRUCE LJ.** I also agree. I would only add to the reasons stated in the judgment of Dillon LJ that, in my approach to the instant problem of construction, I am assisted by the observations of Lord Fraser at the end of his dissenting speech in *Tilling v Whiteman* [1979] 1 All ER 737 at 744, [1980] AC 1 at 24 where he said:

'I do not find any assistance in the policy of s 10 of the 1968 Act, which is the section authorising Sch 3. No doubt s 10 is intended to benefit owners, and to increase the supply of houses for letting, but it is an exception to the main policy of Part II of the Act, which evidently is to give security of tenure to tenants. The question is what are the limits of the exception, and the answer must, I think, be found simply in the words used by Parliament.'

I can find nothing in the speeches of the majority which indicate that their Lordships are approaching the question of construction in a different way.

So, for the reasons explained by Dillon LJ, on the language of Case 11 in Sch 15 to the Rent Act 1977 there is a reasonable correspondence in point of time contemplated as the date of occupation and the date for the letting. I agree that the appeal should be dismissed.

*Appeal dismissed.*

Solicitors: *Burley & Geach*, Petersfield (for the appellant); *Mackarness & Lunt*, Petersfield (for the respondent).

Bebe Chua    Barrister.

# Carney v Herbert and others

PRIVY COUNCIL

LORD FRASER OF TULLYBELTON, LORD SCARMAN, LORD DIPLOCK, LORD ROSKILL AND LORD BRIGHTMAN

2, 3, 29 OCTOBER 1984

*Contract – Illegality – Severability of illegal term – Agreement for sale of company to defendant's nominee – Payment secured by defendant's guarantee and mortgages given by subsidiary of company being purchased – Mortgages illegal – Whether mortgages severable – Whether sale agreement and guarantee enforceable against defendant – Companies Act 1961 (NSW), s 67.*

The appellant and the three respondents between them owned the issued share capital of a company, A Ltd, and were directors of the company and its subsidiary, N Ltd. In 1980 the respondents agreed to sell all their shares in A Ltd to I Ltd, a company controlled by the appellant. The purchase price was to be paid by I Ltd by cash or bank cheques in three instalments secured by a guarantee by the appellant and a guarantee by N Ltd secured by mortgages of land owned by it. The respondents were paid the agreed purchase price by three cheques, two of which were postdated, drawn by A Ltd on its bankers. The sales agreements, mortgages and guarantee were then executed and the shares transferred to I Ltd. However, the postdated cheques in respect of the second and third instalments were not honoured. The appellant was called on to pay under his guarantee but failed to do so. The respondents then commenced actions against the appellant in the Supreme Court of New South Wales claiming, under the guarantee, the unpaid instalments. The appellant contended that he was not liable on the guarantee, since the sale agreements were illegal and unenforceable because the mortgages amounted to the provision of security by a subsidiary of the company whose shares were being purchased, which was contrary to s 67[a] of the New South Wales Companies Act 1961. The judge held the appellant to his guarantee on the ground that although the mortgages were illegal by virtue of the 1961 Act they could be severed from the sale agreements and guarantee. The appellant appealed to the Privy Council.

**Held** – The appeal would be dismissed for the following reasons—

(1) The sale agreements, guarantee and mortgages were concurrent steps in a single though composite transaction. Whether the illegal mortgages could be severed from the

_____

a    Section 67, so far as material, is set out at p 442 *a* to *c*, post

overall transaction leaving intact the respondents' rights of action against I Ltd on the sale agreements and against the appellant on the guarantee was a matter of construction and did not depend on whether the respondents would have entered into the contract if the mortgages had not been forthcoming at the time the contract was concluded. Since the contract was essentially concerned with the sale by the respondents to the appellant or his nominated company of shares in A Ltd and since the mortgages, like the guarantee, were ancillary to that contract and were for the sole purpose of ensuring due performance of the contract by the purchaser, the mortgages could not be said to go to the heart of the transaction and their elimination would not alter the subject matter and primary obligations of the parties thereto. Accordingly, the mortgages could be severed from the remainder of the contract. Furthermore, there was no public policy arising from the nature of the illegality which prevented the enforcement of the severed contract (see p 442 *e* to *j*, p 443 *j* to p 444 *a*, p 446 *b* to *d*, p 447 *e* to *j* and p 448 *a b* and *h j*, post); *Netherseal Colliery Co Ltd v Bourne* (1889) 14 App Cas 228, *Kearney v Whitehaven Colliery Co* [1891–4] All ER Rep 556, *McFarlane v Daniell* (1938) 38 SR (NSW) 337, *Thomas Brown & Sons Ltd v Fazal Deen* (1962) 108 CLR 391, *South Western Mineral Water Co Ltd v Ashmore* [1967] 2 All ER 953, *Niemann v Smedley* [1973] VR 769 and *Firman v Gray & Co Pty Ltd* (1984) 2 ACLC 338 applied.

(2) The financing of the purchase price by A Ltd out of its own bank account was not a breach of the 1961 Act and did not prevent the respondents from enforcing any of the provisions of the sale, because the sale agreements did not stipulate that payment of the purchase price would be made by A Ltd out of its own moneys but merely by cash or bank cheque, and the fact that the defendant used A Ltd's cheques did not necessarily denote any illegality since the appellant could have provided A Ltd with the requisite funds before the cheques were presented. It followed therefore that the appellant was liable on his guarantee to the respondents (see p 442 *e f* and p 448 *b* to *j*, post).

## Notes

For severance of illegal and void provisions in a contract, see 9 Halsbury's Laws (4th edn) para 430.

For assisting purchase of own or holding company's shares, see 7 ibid para 208.

Section 67 of the Companies Act 1961 (NSW) corresponds to s 54 of the Companies Act 1948. For s 54 of the 1948 Act, see 5 Halsbury's Statutes (3rd edn) 163. As from 3 December 1981 s 54 of the 1948 Act was superseded by s 42 of the Companies Act 1981.

## Cases referred to in judgment

*Brew v Whitlock (No 2)* [1967] VR 803, Vic Full Ct.
*Brooks v Burns Philp Trustee Co Ltd* (1969) 121 CLR 432, Aust HC.
*Brown (Thomas) & Sons Ltd v Fazal Deen* (1962) 108 CLR 391, Aust HC.
*DJE Constructions Pty Ltd v Maddocks* [1982] 1 NSWLR 5, NSW CA.
*Firmin v Gray & Co Pty Ltd* (1984) 2 ACLC 338, Qld SC.
*Kearney v Whitehaven Colliery Co* [1893] 1 QB 700, [1891–4] All ER Rep 556, CA.
*McFarlane v Daniell* (1938) 38 SR (NSW) 337, NSW Full Ct.
*Miller v Karlinski* (1945) 62 TLR 85, CA.
*Netherseal Colliery Co Ltd v Bourne* (1889) 14 App Cas 228, HL.
*Niemann v Smedley* [1973] VR 769, Vic Full Ct.
*South Western Mineral Water Co Ltd v Ashmore* [1967] 2 All ER 953, [1967] 1 WLR 1110.

## Consolidated appeals

Philip William Carney appealed pursuant to leave of the Supreme Court of New South Wales, Common Law Division, against the judgment of Rogers J sitting in that court on 31 March 1983 giving judgment for the respondents, John Edward Herbert, Darrell Bruce Arnett and Karlo Jehnic, in three consolidated actions brought by them, in the sums claimed on a guarantee made between the appellant and the respondents dated 24 March 1980. The facts are set out in the judgment of the Board.

*Raymond Jack QC* and *Keith Rewell* (of the New South Wales Bar) for the appellant.
*Alexander Shand QC* and *Robert McDougall* (both of the New South Wales Bar) for the
respondents.

29 October. The following judgment of the Board was delivered.

**LORD BRIGHTMAN.** These three consolidated appeals are from a decision of
Rogers J sitting in the Supreme Court of New South Wales, pursuant to leave granted by
that court. The case is concerned with the right of a transferee of shares, under a contract
for the purchase thereof, to avoid paying for the shares on the ground that the contract
involved illegal acts, namely the giving by a holding company and its subsidiary of
financial assistance in connection with a purchase of shares in the holding company,
contrary to s 67 of the Companies Act 1961 (NSW). In consequence of the illegality, it is
said, the purchaser is entitled to retain the shares without paying for them. Rogers J
rejected this defence, and the purchaser now appeals to Her Majesty in Council.

The company whose shares formed the subject matter of the contract is Airfoil
Registers Pty Ltd (Airfoil). At the relevant time there were 111 shares in issue: 93 shares
were held by Mr Carney, the appellant, whose company Ilerain Pty Ltd (Ilerain)
contracted to purchase the remainder of the shares; 5 shares were held by the respondent
Mr Herbert; 8 shares were held by the respondent Mr Jehnic; the remaining 5 shares
were held by the respondent Mr Arnett. The appellant and the respondents were the
directors of Airfoil.

A further company involved in the story is Newbridge Industries Pty Ltd (Newbridge).
This was a subsidiary of Airfoil. The appellant and the respondents were also the directors
of Newbridge.

At the beginning of 1980, when it had become apparent to the shareholders that their
continued association in Airfoil was undesirable, Mr Carney informed his colleagues that
he was prepared to buy their shares at a price based on the net value of the assets of the
company, the purchase to be taken in the name of a company which would be notified
to them. After some negotiation on the purchase price, agreement was reached on 17
March. The price payable to Mr Herbert was to be $114,800. As, however, he was
indebted to Airfoil on a loan account in the sum of $5,000, the sum payable to him
would be reduced to $109,800. The price payable to Mr Arnett was to be $106,500. The
price payable to Mr Jehnic was to be $183,700, but as he was indebted to Airfoil on a loan
account in the sum of $7,000, the sum payable to him would be reduced to $176,700.
Mr Carney made it clear that he would not be able to pay the whole of the purchase price
at once. Moreover, he did not want any documentation at all. With this in mind, he
wrote out nine cheques for the agreed purchase prices, and handed them to the proposed
vendors. The cheques were as follows:

| Date of cheque | Mr Herbert | Mr Jehnic | Mr Arnett |
| --- | --- | --- | --- |
| 24 March 1980 | $41,000 | $68,000 | $41,000 |
| 31 July 1980 | $23,000 | $37,000 | $28,000 |
| 15 August 1980 | $45,800 | $71,700 | $37,500 |

Each cheque was drawn on the account of Airfoil at the Padstow branch of the
Commercial Bank of Australia Ltd and signed by Mr Carney on behalf of Airfoil.

The vendors then sought advice from their accountant. As a result of the advice given
to them, a further meeting was held on the following day with Mr Carney to discuss the
question of securing payment of the purchase price. Rogers J summarised the evidence
of that meeting as follows:

'According to Mr Arnett he told the defendant: "We will require some sort of
security to ensure that we get paid." Mr Carney replied: "Everything I have is
mortgaged. The only other thing I have is my interest in Airfoil." Mr Arnett replied
to Mr Carney: "If everything you have is mortgaged, could we consider a mortgage

over the factory?" Mr Carney said: "Yes, but you will have to arrange for it and you will have to pay for it." There was then a discussion about the consent to the mortgage. Still in his evidence-in-chief Mr Arnett said that on that occasion he also made the statement, not quite the one ascribed to him by the defendant but the following: "If we don't get security we will not proceed." The significant omission is the word "the". As I say, I accept Mr Arnett's evidence about what transpired and have to consider the consequences of that arrangement on that basis.'

The factory referred to belonged to Newbridge.

In the mean time Mr Simpson, the solicitor for the vendors, had been consulted. He drew up certain documents. They consisted of three sale agreements and three mortgages, each of which was dated 21 March 1980. They were handed to the vendors, who passed them on to Mr Carney for his consideration. Their Lordships will take the Arnett documents as representative.

The sale agreement was in the form of a deed expressed to be made between Mr Arnett (the vendor) of the first part and Ilerain (the purchaser) of the second part, Ilerain being the purchasing company notified by Mr Carney. After brief recitals it went as follows:

'1. The Purchaser shall pay to the Vendor the sum of one hundred and six thousand five hundred dollars ($106,500·00) such amount to be made by cash or bank cheque as follows:—(a) As to the sum of $41,000·00 such sum to be paid on 24th March, 1980. (b) As to the sum of $28,000·00 such sum to be paid on 31st July, 1980. (c) As to the sum of $37,500·00 such sum to be paid on 15th August, 1980.

2. Upon receipt of the payment of the said $41,000·00 the Vendor shall execute a Transfer of the said shares in favour of the Purchaser in appropriate form and shall hand such Transfer to the Purchaser.

3. Should any payment due by the Purchaser to the Vendor under Clause (1) hereunder be in arrears exceeding fourteen (14) days from the due date then the Vendor shall be at liberty to immediately commence proceedings to recover the amount due as a liquidated sum.'

In the case of Mr Herbert and Mr Jehnic, the purchase price expressed in each sale agreement was the reduced amount.

The mortgage document was to be executed by Newbridge, and was in the form of a mortgage to secure payment to Mr Arnett of the purchase price due to him. It charged certain property of Newbridge expressed to be subject to two prior incumbrances. The mortgage also contained a covenant by Newbridge for the payment of such sum to Mr Arnett.

On 24 March a final meeting took place which was attended by the vendors, Mr Carney, Mr Carney's accountant and Mr Simpson. At this meeting a seventh document was produced by Mr Simpson, namely a guarantee. The guarantee was expressed to be made between Mr Carney of the first part and the three vendors of the second part. In consideration of each of the vendors entering into the sale agreement with Ilerain, Mr Carney agreed that, if Ilerain should make default in payment of the money due thereunder, he would pay the amount to the vendor. The seven documents were then executed, the shares were transferred to Ilerain and the cheques dated 24 March were presented and cleared.

The second instalments of the purchase price were due to be paid on 31 July. By that date the shares in Airfoil had been sold at what the judge described as an immense profit. The banking account on which the cheques had been drawn was closed, so that the cheques were worthless. New cheques were not tendered by Mr Carney. Ilerain defaulted in the payment of the second and third instalments of the purchase price. On 1 September Mr Simpson called on Mr Carney to implement his guarantee. He failed to do this.

In October 1980 the vendors commenced proceedings against Mr Carney on the guarantee. He defended the claim on the ground that the sale agreements were illegal and unenforceable by reason of the provisions of s 67 of the Companies Act 1961. Ilerain therefore had no obligations thereunder, and accordingly nothing was due from Mr Carney under his guarantee.

Section 67 of the 1961 Act is in the following terms:

'(1) Except as is otherwise expressly provided by this Act no company shall, whether directly or indirectly and whether by means of a loan guarantee or the provision of security or otherwise, give any financial assistance for the purpose of or in connection with a purchase or subscription made or to be made by any person of or for any shares in the company or, where the company is a subsidiary, in its holding company or in any way purchase, deal in or lend money on its own shares . . .

(3) If there is any contravention of this section, the company and every officer of the company who is in default shall be guilty of an offence against this Act. Penalty: Imprisonment for three months or one thousand dollars.'

The section is not significantly different from the comparable provisions of the legislation prevailing in England.

It is claimed on behalf of Mr Carney that the transactions contravened s 67 in three respects, with the happy result, for Mr Carney, that he and his company became entitled to retain the benefit of the shareholding in Airfoil which had been purchased without any liability for payment of the outstanding $243,000. The illegalities were said to be: (1) the fact that security was provided by Newbridge, a subsidiary of Airfoil; (2) the fact that the purchase price was tendered by cheques drawn on Airfoil's bank account; and (3) the fact that Airfoil released Mr Herbert and Mr Jehnic from liability on their loan accounts.

The judge held Mr Carney to his guarantee, and entered judgment for the vendors accordingly. The mortgages, though illegal and of no effect, could be severed from the sale agreements and the guarantee. The sale agreements required payment by cash or bank cheque, ie what in England, their Lordships were told, would be called a bank draft; the alternative accepted by the vendors of payment by Airfoil cheques did not necessarily involve any breach of s 67. The release of the loan accounts was not, on the facts of the case, a breach of s 67. With all these conclusions their Lordships agree.

*The mortgage point*

The vendors do not dispute that the mortgages were illegal and void. The mortgages amounted to the provision of security by a subsidiary of the company whose shares were purchased and thus offended s 67. The vendors were therefore implicated, together with Mr Carney, Airfoil, Ilerain and Newbridge, in an illegal act, namely a breach of statute law which amounted to a criminal offence.

The sale agreements, the guarantee and the mortgages are rightly to be viewed as concurrent steps in a single though composite transaction. The provision of the mortgages by Newbridge was a term forming part of the overall agreement reached between Mr Carney, on behalf of himself and Ilerain, and the vendors. That term was illegal. A plaintiff cannot sue on an illegal agreement. The question therefore arises whether the illegality of the mortgages taints the whole transaction and prevents the vendors suing Ilerain on the sale agreements and suing Mr Carney on the guarantee, or whether the illegal mortgages can be severed for the purposes of the action from the overall transaction, leaving intact the rights of action against Ilerain and Mr Carney because, by reason of such severance, a plaintiff would not need to sue on any illegal agreement.

Questions of severability are often difficult. There are no set rules which will decide all cases. As was said by Kitto J in *Brooks v Burns Philp Trustee Co Ltd* (1969) 121 CLR 432 at 438, tests for deciding questions of severability that have been formulated as useful in particular cases are not always satisfactory for cases of other kinds.

To some extent each case must depend on its own circumstances, and in particular on the nature of the illegality. The colliery cases, *Netherseal Colliery Co Ltd v Bourne* (1889) 14

App Cas 228 and *Kearney v Whitehaven Colliery Co* [1893] 1 QB 700, [1891–4] All ER Rep 556, provide a useful starting point for a consideration of this branch of the law.

In the *Netherseal* case two miners were suing for the balance of their wages. In the *Kearney* case the colliery was suing a miner for damages for his failure to give the contractual period of notice before leaving his employment. In the latter case the miner sought to defeat the claim by relying on the illegality of a term in the contract which, it was said, rendered the entire contract of employment void. The same illegal term was present in both cases. It was a term, illegal by statute, which purported to authorise the colliery owner to make a deduction from a miner's wages in respect of coal brought to the surface of the mine which was so small as to pass through a screening device known as 'Billy Fairplay'. Neither the House of Lords nor the Court of Appeal had difficulty in upholding the claims of the respective plaintiffs despite the presence of this illegal term. It was not argued in the *Netherseal* case that the illegal term vitiated the whole contract, so severability was not an issue. It was nevertheless raised and disposed of by Lord Halsbury LC in his concluding observation (14 App Cas 228 at 236):

> '. . . as the whole contract is not illegal but the deductions are not enforceable, the plaintiffs had a right to sue for the wages due to them without any such deduction.'

Severability was directly in issue in the second case, and it may be helpful to quote from the judgment of Lopes LJ ([1893] 1 QB 700 at 713; cf [1981–4] All ER Rep 556 at 562):

> 'The law is clear that where the consideration for a promise or promises contained in the contract is unlawful, the whole agreement is void. The reason is that it is impossible to discriminate between the weight to be given to different parts of the consideration, and therefore you cannot sever the legal from the illegal part. But where there is no illegality in the consideration, and some of the provisions are legal and others illegal, the illegality of those which are bad does not communicate itself to, or contaminate, those which are good, unless they are inseparable from and dependent upon one another. Here the consideration moving from the master to the men is the employment and the payment of wages. The consideration moving from the men to the master is the services rendered by them. Both are good and lawful considerations. Then we come to the stipulation with respect to deductions. I am of opinion that the stipulation is altogether separable from and independent of the consideration.'

This approach was echoed by Jordan CJ in *McFarlane v Daniell* (1938) 38 SR (NSW) 337. That was a case in which an actor sued for his remuneration under a contract of employment which contained a restrictive covenant which was void as being in unreasonable restraint of trade. The employer boldly contended that the actor could not recover his remuneration because the contract was wholly void. Jordan CJ said (at 345):

> 'When valid promises supported by legal consideration are associated with, but separate in form from, invalid promises, the test of whether they are severable is whether they are in substance so connected with the others as to form an indivisible whole which cannot be taken to pieces without altering its nature . . . If the elimination of the invalid promises changes the extent only but not the kind of contract, the valid promises are severable . . . If the substantial promises were all illegal or void, merely ancillary promises would be inseverable.'

He added later (at 346):

> 'The exact scope and limits of the doctrine that a legal promise associated with, but severable from, an illegal promise is capable of enforcement, are not clear. It can hardly be imagined that a Court would enforce a promise, however inherently valid and however severable, if contained in a contract one of the terms of which provided for assassination.'

Their Lordships agree with both observations. There are therefore two matters to be considered where a contract contains an illegal term: first, whether as a matter of construction the lawful part of the contract can be severed from the unlawful part, thus enabling the plaintiff to sue on a promise unaffected by any illegality; second, whether, despite severability, there is a bar to enforceability arising out of the nature of the illegality.

*Miller v Karlinski* (1945) 62 TLR 85 was a case before the English Court of Appeal which might have been decided against the plaintiff on the second ground instead of the first. An employee sued for his salary under an oral contract which provided for a fixed weekly salary plus 'travelling expenses', such 'travelling expenses' to include the income tax payable by the employee. It was held that, as the plaintiff was to be paid according to a scheme devised so as to defraud the Revenue, the fraudulent element could not be severed from the remainder of the contract. Alternatively, it might have been said that, although as a matter of construction the obligation of the employer to pay travelling expenses, or alternatively the right of the employee to include income tax in such expenses, was severable from the remainder of the contract as a matter of construction, nevertheless it was contrary to public policy to allow the plaintiff to sue. However, it seems unnecessary to decide whether in this type of case public policy should be regarded as barring the right to sever or as barring the right to enforce despite severability, as the end result will be the same.

The classic case where a contract containing an illegal provision was severed into its lawful and unlawful parts, and the lawful part enforced, was decided in 1962 by the High Court of Australia, *Thomas Brown & Sons Ltd v Fazal Deen* 108 CLR 391. In that case the plaintiff Fazal Deen had lodged with the defendant in 1943 a safe containing gold and gems under a contract of bailment. The bailment was illegal as regards the gold, which ought to have been delivered to the Commonwealth Bank under exchange control regulations. The contents of the safe disappeared in unexplained circumstances at some time during the ensuing 16 years, whereupon the plaintiff sued the company in detinue. The company resisted the claim on the ground, inter alia, that the entire contract of bailment was tainted by the illegality of the bailment of the gold. The High Court (at 411) approved the observation of Jordan CJ in *McFarlane*'s case (1938) 38 SR (NSW) 337 at 345 that 'If the elimination of the invalid promises changes the extent only but not the kind of contract, the valid promises are severable'. That test was clearly passed, because under the contract of bailment the plaintiff was entitled at any time to demand the return of part only of the property bailed without thereby affecting the bailment of the residue. Accordingly, the plaintiff could sue in detinue on the contract of bailment in respect of the safe and the gems. The High Court rejected the submission of the company's counsel (at 393) that 'If any part of the contract is illegal, public policy will not allow any part of the contract to be enforced'.

These principles were applied by the Supreme Court of Victoria in *Niemann v Smedley* [1973] VR 769. In that case employees were given the right to an allotment to shares on terms that the company would if desired finance their acquisition over a five-year period. The company became insolvent three years later, and the question arose whether the allottees, whose names had been entered on the register, were personally liable for the amounts unpaid on their shares, or whether they could claim that the allotments were illegal and void. One question which arose was whether the illegal provision for company finance was severable from the remainder of the contract constituted by the employee's application for shares (the offer) and notice to him of the allotment (the acceptance). It was held that the promise of the company to finance the acquisition of the shares was not the whole or the main consideration to support the promise of the applicants to pay for the shares, but was subsidiary to the main purpose of the contract, a contract to acquire fully paid shares in the company. Accordingly, the term by which the company agreed to provide finance was severable from the rest of the agreement, which remained valid, and accordingly the liquidator could recover capital unpaid on the shares. In the course of their decision, the Full Court said (at 778):

'An illegal term, as distinct from one merely void [for uncertainty], may raise different considerations for if it is of a kind involving a serious element of moral turpitude or is obviously inimical to the interest of the community so as to offend almost any concept of public policy it will so infect the rest of the contract that the courts will refuse to give any recognition at all to the contract, e.g. a promise to commit a burglary or to defraud the revenue or one *contra bonos mores*. But such class of cases apart, where the illegality has no such taint, the other terms will stand if the illegal portion can be severed . . .'

It is necessary to refer briefly to a recent decision of the Court of Appeal of New South Wales, *DJE Constructions Pty Ltd v Maddocks* [1982] 1 NSWLR 5, in which the *Niemann* case was distinguished. The company, which had in issue only two $1 shares, needed to increase its issued capital by $5,998 in order to qualify for a licence from the Builders' Licensing Board. In order to achieve this result Reilly, who did not however possess the requisite funds, drew a cheque on her bank account in favour of the company for $5,998 to pay for an allotment of shares in favour of Maddocks. In order to cover Reilly's cheque, the company then drew a cheque on its banking account in favour of Logan for the same amount, which Logan deposited in Reilly's bank account. This sum was shown in the company's account as a loan to Logan. The 5,998 shares intended to be issued appeared in the company's statutory returns as allotted to Maddocks, but only an unsealed share certificate in his name existed and his name was not entered on the register of members. Maddocks took proceedings against the company for rectification of the register by the entry of his name as the holder of 5,998 shares. His claim failed. In the course of his judgment Street CJ said (at 10):

'Whilst the doctrine of severance can be applied in proceedings brought in the context of a contract illegal and void by reason of an infringement of a statutory provision (*Thomas Brown and Sons Ltd v Fazal Deen*), I know of no case in which it has been applied in a claim for the actual enforcement of such a contract. The principles relating to severability were developed in connection with contractual clauses void for uncertainty and for restraint of trade, and not in cases involving contracts *illegal and void*.'

He then considered the *Niemann* case and added (at 11–12):

'With the greatest respect I do not consider that the doctrine of severability is available to save an integral term of an agreement such as the method of paying for shares that are being agreed to be issued in contravention of a section such as is presently under consideration. The distinction to be observed in the operation of the doctrine of severability as between contracts that are merely void and those that are *illegal* and void is adequately noted in *Halsbury* [9 Halsbury's Laws (4th edn) paras 386, 429]. In the light of the long-standing distinctions between a clause which is purely void and a clause which is illegal and void, I have some difficulty in accepting the correctness of applying the doctrine of severability in a situation such as existed in *Niemann v Smedley*.'

The approach of Samuels JA was somewhat different. He said (at 21):

'It is arguable that a contractual term cannot be severed if it involves the doing of an act which is contra bonos mores or illegal at common law . . . or by statute . . . and the company's loan to Mr Logan amounted to a criminal offence under s 67(3) punishable by imprisonment. It appears, however, that this limitation cannot stand with the decision of the High Court in *Thomas Brown & Sons Ltd v Fazal Deen* (1962) 108 CLR 391, where one term of a contract was severed from the rest, although its performance necessarily contravened a provision of the *National Security (Exchange Control) Regulations* and was thus subject to any penalty prescribed by the regulations, or constituted an indictable misdemeanour at common law . . .'

He came, however, to the same conclusion as Street CJ on the ground that—

'the allotment was dependent upon the loan, and the illegality of the loan infected the whole of the contract. This was not an ordinary contract to take shares. Its fundamental objective was to enable the company to satisfy the requirements of the Builders' Licensing Board. It was a device to achieve that purpose; and an unsuccessful one as it turned out, because the shares never were paid up in cash . . .'

Glass JA, who was the third member of the court, agreed with the result, but did not express a preference between the two approaches.

With great respect to Street CJ, their Lordships consider that the approach of Samuels JA was correct. Furthermore, so far as the Court of Appeal was concerned, the *Fazal Deen* case was a decision of the High Court and concluded the matter; in that case the plaintiff sued to enforce a contract of bailment a part of which contract was illegal, but he was allowed to succeed in relation to the lawful part of the contract.

In the light of the law as it has been developed in Australia and England, and also in Scotland though their Lordships have not been referred to the Scottish case law, their Lordships feel no doubt in the instant case that the illegal provision of the debentures can be severed from the composite transaction, leaving the vendors free to enforce the sale agreements against Ilerain and the guarantee against Mr Carney, and that the nature of the illegality is not such as to preclude the vendors on the ground of public policy from enforcing their rights under those documents. Before, however, their Lordships further elaborate their reasons, they will refer to two cases which bear a close resemblance to the present case.

The first of these cases is *South Western Mineral Water Co Ltd v Ashmore* [1967] 2 All ER 953, [1967] 1 WLR 1110, decided by Cross J in the Chancery Division of the English High Court. Ashmore had entered into a somewhat odd agreement with the Mineral Water Co (in effect) to buy the shareholding of its subsidiary Solent Products Ltd. A part of the purchase price was to be paid at once, and the balance at the end of eight years, secured by a debenture to be charged on the assets of Solent and guaranteed by Ashmore. Ashmore paid the first instalment of the purchase price and was let into possession of certain assets which were intended to be the effective subject matter of the purchase. A number of matters were in dispute between the parties, and Ashmore declined to pay the first half-year's interest due under the intended debenture (which had not been issued) until the Mineral Water Co had completed certain conveyances. Thereupon the Mineral Water Co issued proceedings against Ashmore to recover possession of the premises and to rescind the contract or, alternatively, for specific performance. It is unnecessary to narrate the course of the action. The importance of the case lies in this passage from the judgment of Cross J ([1967] 1 WLR 1110 at 1120; cf [1967] 2 All ER 953 at 958):

'I cannot take the view and do not take the view that the fact that the granting of this debenture would be a criminal offence by Solent made the whole of this agreement absolutely null and void so that the courts will not allow anybody to rely on any of its provisions. No case that has been cited to me suggests that I am obliged to arrive at so ridiculous a conclusion. The position was this, I think, that if the company were prepared to waive the obligation of Solent to provide the debenture and were prepared to complete the transaction on the footing that they merely had the personal undertaking of Mr. Ashmore to pay the £36,500 over eight years with 8 per cent interest secured only by the £9,000 securities and without any charge on the assets taken over by Solent, they were at liberty to enforce the contract on that basis. But, in fact, the company are not prepared to do that. They say that it is an integral part of the arrangement that there should be a debenture. I think that they are right on that point. It was so substantial a part of the consideration that though they could waive it and enforce the contract without it if they liked, Mr. Ashmore could not compel them to complete on that basis. Alternatively, I think that Mr. Ashmore, if he was willing to waive the period of eight years for the payment of the purchase-money, which was inserted obviously for his convenience, and pay the £36,500 down, he was at liberty to do that, and I do not think the company could have refused to accept the money and, quite clearly, they would not have refused. However, Mr. Ashmore was unwilling to pay it.'

Their Lordships agree entirely with what fell from Cross J. It should however be observed that, when Cross J spoke of the right of the company to 'waive' the obligation of Solent to provide the debenture, he did not mean waiver in the strict sense. The company had nothing to waive, because the obligation to provide the debenture was void for all purposes. The sense of the passage is that, if the company were content to continue with the contract notwithstanding that no debenture could be granted by Solent, it was at liberty to do so and to enforce it on that basis.

The second of the cases is *Firmin v Gray & Co Pty Ltd* (1984) 2 ACLC 338, decided earlier this year by the Supreme Court of Queensland on appeal. By a written contract Firmin and his co-plaintiffs agreed to sell their shares in Firmin & Co Pty Ltd to Gray & Co Pty Ltd. The contract, which provided for payment of a 10% deposit, contained a term (cl 22) that the purchasing company should arrange for Firmin & Co to execute a mortgage to secure the payment of the balance of the purchase money to the vendors. A little later it was realised that cl 22 contravened s 67. The purchasing company claimed the right to rescind and to recover its deposit. The vendors claimed that cl 22 was severable and capable of being 'waived' by them and it was thereby 'waived'. The vendors then called on the purchasing company to complete. The purchasing company failed to complete, whereupon the vendors brought an action for a declaration that the deposit was forfeited. They succeeded at the trial and on appeal. It is unnecessary for their Lordships to refer to the judgments in the Supreme Court, which are based on the same line of reasoning as is to be found in the *Mineral Water* case.

The contract in the present case was basically one for the sale by the respondents to Mr Carney or his nominated company of shares in Airfoil. The mortgages, like the guarantee, were ancillary to that contract for the sole purpose of ensuring the due performance of the contract by the purchaser. Mr Carney wanted only the shares in Airfoil. The respondents wanted only the purchase money. It made no difference to the respondents, or to the nature of the transaction, what security was provided so long as it was satisfactory security. The mortgage did not go to the heart of the transaction, and its elimination would leave unchanged the subject matter of the contract and the primary obligations of the vendors and the purchaser. The debenture is therefore capable of being severed from the remainder of the transaction, and its illegality does not taint the whole contract. There is no public policy objection to the enforcement of the contract from which the debenture has been divorced. The *Mineral Water* case is an authority that there is no public policy objection to such a course so far as the law of England and Wales is concerned. The *Firmin* case is a like authority so far as the State of Queensland is concerned. There is no reason to suppose that the public policy of the State of New South Wales is any different.

There is one final point on this aspect of the case to which their Lordships wish to allude. It was argued by the appellant that on the true interpretation of the evidence the vendors, at the time when the contract was made, required a mortgage on the property of Newbridge as an essential security for the payment of the purchase money, and that they would have declined to enter into the contract at all if they had been told that such a mortgage would not be forthcoming. Therefore, it is said, the mortgage is not severable from the remainder of the transaction, since severability must be judged at the moment when the contract is concluded according to the then intentions of the parties. There are observations by the Supreme Court of Victoria in *Brew v Whitlock (No 2)* [1967] VR 803 at 811–812 which might be read as giving some support to this proposition. In the opinion of their Lordships there is no such principle applicable to the instant type of case. Furthermore, it is manifest in the *Mineral Water* case that at the date when the contract was made, had the point then arisen, the vendor company would have declined to conclude the contract without the benefit of the offending debenture, because it did in fact so decline during the trial. Nor in the *Firmin* case did the court ask itself the question whether at the date of the contract the vendors would have been content to conclude the contract without cl 22. Their Lordships do not accept the relevance of any such inquiry.

Subject to a caveat that it is undesirable, if not impossible, to lay down any principles which will cover all problems in this field, their Lordships venture to suggest that, as a general rule, where parties enter into a lawful contract of, for example, sale and purchase, and there is an ancillary provision which is illegal but exists for the exclusive benefit of the plaintiff, the court may and probably will, if the justice of the case so requires, and there is no public policy objection, permit the plaintiff, if he so wishes, to enforce the contract without the illegal provision.

*The Airfoil cheques*

It is said by the appellant that it was at all times the intention of the parties that Airfoil cheques should be used to effect payment of the purchase price, that the financing by Airfoil of the purchase price out if its own banking account was a breach of s 67 and that the intention of the parties that the sale should be concluded in this illegal manner, and the part performance thereof in that way, has the consequence that the respondents cannot enforce any of the provisions of the sale.

The sale agreements themselves did not stipulate for payment of the purchase price out of the moneys of Airfoil, but by cash or bank cheque. In regard to the Airfoil cheques, the judge said:

'As it happened, the defendant chose to discharge the obligation which Ilerain Pty Ltd had by means of cheques drawn by the company [Airfoil]. However, that is not necessarily inconsistent with a number of ways in which that could have been effected legally. Why should I assume that it was to be done illegally? I do not intend to do so.'

In their Lordships' view that is plainly right. Over a week elapsed between the writing out of the first instalment cheques and their presentation for payment. There was ample time for the state of account between Mr Carney and Airfoil to be organised, if that were necessary, so as to justify such payments; likewise in the case of the later cheques had they been honoured.

*The loan accounts*

The release of liability on the loan accounts involved no breach of s 67. At the date of the contract Mr Herbert owed $5,000 to Airfoil and Mr Jehnic owed $7,000. Clearly Mr Carney would not have wished to hand over to them the full purchase money for their shares without requiring them to discharge their debts to Airfoil. This could have been achieved by requiring them to pay $5,000 and $7,000 to Airfoil at the same time as the first instalments of the purchase price were paid to them. Mr Carney merely short-circuited such an arrangement by causing the respective purchase prices to be reduced by $5,000 and $7,000, and agreeing that Mr Herbert and Mr Jehnic should be released from their liability to Airfoil. Mr Carney could properly do this, because his own loan account was in credit to an amount well in excess of $12,000. His loan account therefore could be, and in default of any other arrangement with Airfoil ought to have been, reduced to the like extent, and in the result the financial position of Airfoil would be totally unaffected by the releases.

Their Lordships will humbly advise Her Majesty that the appeals should be dismissed. The appellant will pay the costs of the respondents.

*Appeals dismissed.*

Solicitors: *Macfarlanes* (for the appellant); *Charles Russell & Co* (for the respondents).

Mary Rose Plummer    Barrister.

# Cooper v Motor Insurers' Bureau

COURT OF APPEAL, CIVIL DIVISION
CUMMING-BRUCE, DILLON LJJ AND EWBANK J
26, 27 NOVEMBER 1984

*Motor insurance – Compulsory insurance against third party risks – Liabilities required to be covered – Permitted driver – Owner of vehicle permitting another person to drive it – Permitted driver injured because of defective brakes – Whether owner's liability to permitted driver required to be covered by third party insurance – Whether injury to permitted driver an injury to 'any person . . . arising out of' use of vehicle – Road Traffic Act 1972, ss 143(1), 145(3)(a).*

*Motor insurance – Rights of third parties against insurers – Motor Insurers' Bureau – Liability of bureau to satisfy judgment against uninsured driver – Liability required to be covered by insurance – Owner of vehicle permitting another person to drive it – Permitted driver injured because of defective brakes – Owner not insured – Whether bureau obliged to satisfy judgment against owner – Whether owner's liability to permitted driver required to be covered by insurance – Whether injury to permitted driver an injury to 'any person . . . arising out of' use of vehicle – Road Traffic Act 1972, ss 143(1), 145(3)(a).*

K asked the plaintiff to road test K's motor cycle. During the road test the brakes on the motor cycle failed and the plaintiff collided with a car and was seriously injured. He brought an action against K claiming damages for negligence in respect of K's failure to warn him that the brakes were defective and obtained judgment for £214,207. K was unable to satisfy the judgment. Furthermore, he was not insured against third party risks as required by s 143(1)[a] of the Road Traffic Act 1972. The plaintiff brought an action against the Motor Insurers' Bureau seeking a declaration that by virtue of the bureau's undertaking given to the Secretary of State to compensate victims of uninsured drivers the bureau was liable to satisfy the judgment since it was a judgment in respect of a liability required to be covered by insurance, within the undertaking, because insurance against third party risks was required by s 145(3)(a)[b] of the 1972 Act to cover injury to 'any person . . . arising out of' the use of a vehicle on a road, which, it was contended, included a person who was permitted to use the vehicle and who was injured while using it. The plaintiff further contended that the third party risks required to be covered by s 143(1) were not confined to risks which were extraneous to the vehicle but included risks within the vehicle. The judge dismissed the plaintiff's action, holding (i) that the term 'any person' in s 145(3) of the Act was restricted to any person other than the user of the vehicle at the time the damage was caused, and the plaintiff, being the user of the vehicle at the material time, was not covered by that term, and (ii) that the only liability which fell to be covered by ss 145(3) and 143(1) was liability to persons injured by the use of the vehicle by the insured or a permitted driver. The plaintiff appealed.

**Held** – In construing s 145(3) of the 1972 Act, the court was required to have regard to s 143(1), which imposed an obligation on the owner of a vehicle to abstain from using or from causing or permitting any other person to use the vehicle unless there was, in respect of himself or the other driver, a policy of insurance against third party risks. That obligation clearly did not include insuring against an accident occurring to the actual driver of the vehicle at the time the accident occurred. It followed that on its true construction s 145(3) restricted the scope of the term 'any person' by excluding the actual driver of the vehicle from being a third party who was required to be covered by third party insurance. Accordingly, the plaintiff's claim did not arise out of a liability covered

a   Section 143(1) is set out at p 452 d e, post
b   Section 145(3), so far as material, is set out at p 451 j to p 452 a, post

under the 1972 Act and his appeal would therefore be dismissed (see p 452 e to b and p 453 a-b, post).

Decision of Barry Chedlow QC sitting as a deputy judge of the High Court [1983] 1 All ER 353 affirmed.

**Notes**

For compulsory insurance in relation to motor vehicles, see 25 Halsbury's Laws (4th edn) paras 756, 759–760.

For the Motor Insurers' Bureau, see ibid paras 784–785.

For the Road Traffic Act 1972, ss 143, 145, see 42 Halsbury's Statutes (3rd edn) 1786, 1790. .

**Case referred to in judgments**

Hughes v Metropolitan Rly Co (1877) 2 App Cas 439, [1874–80] All ER Rep 187, HL.

**Cases also cited**

Barnet Group Hospital Management Committee v Eagle Star Insurance Co Ltd [1959] 3 All ER 210, [1960] 1 QB 107.

Digby v General Accident Fire and Life Assurance Corp Ltd [1942] 2 All ER 319, [1943] AC 121, HL.

**Appeal**

By a writ issued on 23 July 1981 the plaintiff, Clifford George Cooper, claimed against the Motor Insurers' Bureau, the defendant, a declaration or order that the bureau was liable to satisfy a judgment obtained by the plaintiff on 5 December 1980 in the High Court against Mr Brendon Killacky for damages of £214,207·89 for personal injuries sustained by the plaintiff when testing Mr Killacky's motor cycle on a road, such injuries being caused by Mr Killacky's negligence in failing to warn the plaintiff that the brakes of the motor cycle were defective. Mr Killacky was not insured against third party risks as required by s 143(1) of the Road Traffic Act 1972, and was unable himself to satisfy the judgment. On 12 July 1982 Mr Barry Chedlow QC sitting as a deputy judge of the High Court ([1983] 1 All ER 353, [1983] 1 WLR 592) ordered that judgment be entered for the bureau. The plaintiff appealed. On 18 January 1984 Mr Registrar Adams ordered that Percy Ernest George Cooper, the administrator of the plaintiffs' estate, be given leave to carry on the appeal against the bureau. The fact are set out in the judgment of Cumming-Bruce LJ.

Michael Wright QC and Stephen Waine for the plaintiff.
Piers Ashworth QC and Andrew Prynne for the Motor Insurers' Bureau.

**CUMMING-BRUCE LJ.** On 9 January 1973 Mr Killacky asked the now deceased plaintiff, Mr Cooper, to road test Killacky's motor cycle. During the course of that test the brakes failed and the plaintiff collided with a motor car on the highway. The plaintiff was seriously injured. He sued Killacky in negligence and on 5 December 1980 the plaintiff recovered judgment against Killacky in the sum, including interest, of £214,207·89. Killacky was quite unable to satisfy the judgment and this litigation is concerned with an endeavour to cause the Motor Insurers' Bureau to satisfy the judgment.

The deputy judge ([1983] 1 All ER 353, [1983] 1 WLR 592) held that, as a matter of construction of the two relevant sections of the Road Traffic Act 1972, ie ss 143 and 145, the Motor Insurers' Bureau were under no obligation to satisfy the judgment because it did not arise out of a liability which fell to be covered under the relevant part of the 1972 Act. That was enough to decide the case in favour of the Motor Insurers' Bureau, but the bureau had also argued that they had a complete and independent defence arising out of the terms of the MIB agreement (the Motor Insurers' Bureau (Compenssation of Victims of Uninsured Drivers) Agreement dated 22 November 1972 between the Secretary of State for the Environment and the bureau). Under cl 5(1) of the agreement the bureau—

'shall not incur any liability under Clause 2 of this agreement unless—(a) notice of the bringing of the proceedings is given before or within seven days after the commencement of the proceedings—(i) to M.I.B. in the case of proceedings in respect of a relevant liability which is either not covered by a contract of insurance or covered by a contract of insurance with an insurer whose identity cannot be ascertained . . .'

It was common ground that notice of proceedings was not given for some 18 months after the date of their commencement but the plaintiff sought to overcome that difficulty by pleading waiver by the Motor Insurers' Bureau of the bureau's rights under cl 5(1) of the MIB agreement.

The deputy judge, for reasons that he stated, held that there was no waiver and that the defence available under cl 5(1) was available to the Motor Insurers' Bureau and, had it been necessary, itself defeated any right that the plaintiff might otherwise have against the bureau.

The plaintiff appeals by his administrator, who carries on the proceedings in the place of the deceased plaintiff.

The first ground of appeal is:

'That the Learned Deputy Judge erred in holding that the words "any person" in Section 145(3)(a) of the Road Traffic Act, 1972 . . . are restricted to any person other than the user of the vehicle at the material time, and that the Plaintiff who was the user of the vehicle at the material time was not covered by the term "any person".'

That is elaborated in the second ground of appeal:

'That the Learned Judge erred in holding that Section 145(3)(a) of the said Act, and in particular the words "any person", were to be construed within the limited context of Section 143(1) of the Act, and that the only liability which fell to be covered under the said Sections was the Plaintiff's liability to others.'

Counsel for the plaintiff has developed his argument on construction. As he recognises, it is a concise submission and can be readily encapsulated in a few words. The submission begins with consideration of cl 2 of the MIB agreement, which is headed 'Satisfaction of Claims by Motor Insurers' Bureau' and reads as follows:

'If judgment in respect of any relevant liability is obtained against any person or persons in any Court in Great Britain whether or not such a person or persons be in fact covered by a contract of insurance and any such judgment is not satisfied in full within seven days from the date upon which the person or persons in whose favour the judgment was given became entitled to enforce it, then M.I.B will, subject to the provisions of Clauses 4, 5 and 6 hereof, pay or satisfy or cause to be paid or satisfied to or to the satisfaction of the person or persons in whose favour the judgment was given, any sum payable or remaining payable thereunder in respect of the relevant liability including any sum awarded by the Court in respect of interest on that sum and any taxed costs or any costs awarded by the Court without taxation (or such proportion thereof as is attributable to the relevant liability) whatever may be the cause of the failure of the judgment debtor to satisfy the judgment.'

Relevant liability is there defined as any liability in respect of which a policy of insurance must insure a person in order to comply with Pt VI of the 1972 Act. That leads counsel for the plaintiff immediately to s 145 of the 1972 Act which sets out what an insured has to do in order to comply with the requirements of Pt VI of the Act, and which states in sub-s (2) the conditions of the policy of insurance required in order so to comply:

'(2) The policy must be issued by an authorised insurer, that is to say, a person or body of persons carrying on motor vehicle insurance business in Great Britain.
(3) Subject to subsection (4) below, the policy—(a) must insure such person,

persons or classes of persons as may be specified in the policy in respect of any liability which may be incurred by him or them in respect of the death of or bodily injury to any person caused by, or arising out of, the use of the vehicle on a road . . .'

The short proposition is this. On a consideration of s 145(3)(a) the policy will satisfy the requirements of the Act provided that it insures a person, persons or classes of persons specified in the policy in respect of liability that may be incurred by him or them in respect of damage to any person caused or arising out of the use of the vehicle on the road. To consider the facts, Mr Cooper was driving the motor vehicle on a road, namely the motor cycle. While he was thus driving it the brakes failed by reason of a defect in the braking system of which he knew nothing and which was the responsibility and liability of Mr Killacky, the owner of the vehicle. Therefore all the necessary requirements of s 145(3)(a) are fulfilled and Mr Cooper can claim to be, and is, 'any person suffering damage caused by or arising out of the use of the vehicle on a road'.

Had that been a complete statement of the relevant context of s 145(3)(a), that would no doubt be the end of the story. But it is not. I have no doubt that the deputy judge was right in deciding that the correct approach was to consider the first section in Pt VI, which is the relevant part of the Road Traffic Act 1972. That is introduced by the words, 'Compulsory insurance or security against third-party risks' and reads:

'**143.**—(1) Subject to the provisions of this Part of this Act, it shall not be lawful for a person to use, or to cause or permit any other person to use, a motor vehicle on a road unless there is in force in relation to the use of the vehicle by that person or that other person, as the case may be, such a policy of insurance or such a security in respect of third-party risks as complies with the requirements of this Part of this Act; and if a person acts in contravention of this section he shall be guilty of an offence . . .'

The obligation imposed by s 143(1), breach whereof constitutes a criminal offence, is an obligation to abstain from use or from causing or permitting any other person to use a motor vehicle on the road unless there is in force in relation to the use of the vehicle by that person or that other person such a policy of insurance in respect of third party risks as complies with the requirements of that Part of the Act, and, having regard to the content of that subsection, it is clear that that obligation on the insured is to take out a policy covering him in respect of third party risks which, whatever ambiguity the phrase may have, clearly does not include the actual driver of the vehicle at the time of the use of the vehicle which gives rise to the damage. When one comes to the construction of s 145(3) it is necessary to give a meaning to that subsection which has regard to the intention of s 143(1) in relation to the obligation which Pt VI of the Act imposes. As the judge found, although taken by itself the words of s 145(3) in the reference to 'any person' are unrestricted in any respect, as soon as s 143 and the obligation therein imposed is considered, it necessarily follows that there must be an intention to restrict the scope of the phrase 'any person' in s 145(3)(a) so as to exclude the driver of the vehicle at the time of the imagined risk.

The deputy judge so held. I agree with him. It is one of those comparatively rare, short questions of construction which can be determined shortly. I add nothing to the reasons given by the deputy judge, which I have, in my own language, concisely indorsed. In the circumstances it becomes unnecessary to say anything about the answer which the plaintiff raises to the Motor Insurers' Bureau's defence founded on the failure of the plaintiff to give notice of proceedings before or within seven days after commencement thereof. I ventured in argument to describe that defence as meritorious but unattractive. But there is no answer to it. However eager one may be, and there have been great judges in the Queen's Bench Division who have demonstrated that eagerness and enthusiasm over the last 20 years, to extend as far as possible the doctrine of forbearance stated in *Hughes v Metropolitan Rly Co* (1877) 2 App Cas 439, [1874–80] All ER Rep 187, I am quite unable to accept the invitation of counsel for the plaintiff to extend it to include the doctrine of forbearance by silence to be collected from the correspondence that has been laid before us.

For those reasons, which I again find unnecessary to elaborate (and I hope that counsel for the plaintiff will not be aggrieved by the conciseness of this part of my judgment) I would hold that the forbearance argument was also bound to fail. For those reasons I would move that the appeal be dismissed.

**DILLON LJ.** I agree.

**EWBANK J.** I agree.

*Appeal dismissed.*

Solicitors: *Robbins Olivey & Blake Lapthorn*, agents for *Horwood & James*, Aylesbury (for the plaintiff); *L Bingham & Co* (for the Motor Insurers' Bureau).

Bebe Chua      Barrister.

# R v Kirk
## (Case 63/83)

COURT OF JUSTICE OF THE EUROPEAN COMMUNITIES
JUDGES LORD MACKENZIE STUART (PRESIDENT), KOOPMANS, BAHLMANN, GALMOT (PRESIDENTS OF CHAMBERS), PESCATORE, O'KEEFFE, BOSCO, DUE AND KAKOURIS
ADVOCATE GENERAL M DARMON[1]
28 FEBRUARY, 3 APRIL, 10 JULY 1984

*European Economic Community – Fishing rights – Common fishing policy – Derogation from principle of non-discrimination – Maintenance of derogation regime – Derogation regime expiring before Council agreeing to continuation – Member state adopting conservation measure for interim period – Council subsequently authorising continuation of derogation regime with retroactive effect – Whether member state's conservation measure valid – Act of Accession (1972), art 100 – Sea Fish (Specified United Kingdom Waters) (Prohibition of Fishing) Order 1982.*

*Statute – Retrospective operation – Penal statute – Principle that penal provision may not have retroactive effect – Whether principle will be enforced by Court of Justice of European Communities – Sea Fish (Specified United Kingdom Waters) (Prohibition of Fishing) Order 1982.*

By art 100(1)[a] of the Act of Accession (1972) under which the United Kingdom became a member of the European Economic Community, member states were authorised, until 31 December 1982, to restrict fishing in waters under their sovereignty or jurisdiction to vessels which traditionally fished there (the derogation regime). In exercise of that power the United Kingdom adopted a measure which recognised that certain other member states, not including Denmark, held certain special fishing rights. In June 1982 the EC Commission submitted to the EC Council proposals intended to authorise member states to maintain the derogation regime until 31 December 1992. The proposals were discussed at the Community's Fisheries Council on 21 December 1982 but, as a result of the opposition of Denmark, no agreement was reached. On the same day the Commission declared that member states had a duty to take conservation measures and called on them to notify it of the measures they planned to adopt. On 22 December the United Kingdom adopted and submitted to the Commission for approval the Sea Fish (Specified United Kingdom Waters) (Prohibition of Fishing) Order 1982[b], which was to come into force for

_____

a  Article 100(1), so far as material, is set out at p 456 d e, post
b  The 1982 order, so far as material, is set out at p 458 a b, post

one year from 1 January 1983 and which, subject to certain conditions, would prohibit fishing boats registered in Denmark fishing within the United Kingdom's 12-mile coastal zone. On 5 January 1983 the Commission authorised, inter alia, the 1982 order provisionally for a period to expire not later than 26 January 1983. On 25 January the Fisheries Council adopted Regulation 170/83, which came into force on 27 January and which continued the derogation regime for a further ten years. By art 6 member states were authorised to maintain the previous arrangements 'as from 1 January 1983'. On 6 January the master of a Danish vessel fished within the United Kingdom 12-mile coastal zone. He was charged with contravening the 1982 order and on 7 January was convicted in a magistrates' court. He appealed to the Crown Court, contending that the United Kingdom had not been entitled to bring the 1982 order into force and that, consequently, no offence had been committed. The Crown Court referred the question of the 1982 order's compatibility with Community law to the Court of Justice of the European Communities for a preliminary ruling. The master of the vessel contended that, on the expiration on 31 December 1982 of the derogations permitted by the 1972 Act of Accession, the Community principle of non-discrimination became fully applicable, and accordingly the 1982 order was contrary to Community law.

**Held** – National measures derogating from the fundamental principle of Community law of non-discrimination were limited by art 100 of the 1972 Act of Accession to the transitional period which expired on 31 December 1982 and the power to bring into force any provisions thereafter was entrusted to the Community authorities, in particular the Council. The fact that the Council failed to adopt such provisions before 31 December 1982 did not give member states the power to act in place of the Council by extending the derogation beyond the prescribed time limit, and accordingly Community rules abolishing all discrimination based on nationality against nationals of member states then became fully applicable. Although rules relating to access to national waters could in certain cases constitute a response to a concern to conserve fishery resources, it was clear that the 1982 order had not been intended to achieve such an objective, and national rules which prohibited access to national waters and were not intended to achieve an objective of conservation could not be covered by the power of member states to take temporary conservation measures. Furthermore, although art 6(1) of Regulation 170/83 authorised retroactively the retention of the derogation regime defined in art 100 of the 1972 Act of Accession, that retroactivity could not have the effect of validating ex post facto a national measure of a penal nature which imposed a penalty for an act which, in fact, had not been punishable at the time at which it was committed and such an act would not be punishable where, at that time, the national measure was invalid because it was incompatible with Community law. It followed that Community law regarding fishing did not authorise a member state, at the time of the adoption of the 1982 order, to prohibit vessels registered in another member state from fishing within a coastal zone specified by that order and not covered by conservation measures (see p 461 *e* to *g j* and p 462 *b d e g*, post).

*EC Commission v UK* Case 804/79 [1981] ECR 1045 distinguished.

Per curiam. The principle that penal provisions may not have retroactive effect is one which is common to all the legal orders of the member states of the European Community, and takes its place among the general principles of law whose observance is ensured by the Court of Justice of the European Communities (see p 462 *c*, post).

**Notes**

For fishing rights in the European Economic Community, see 18 Halsbury's Laws (4th edn) para 608.

For the presumption against retroactivity of penal legislation, see 44 ibid para 923 and 18 ibid para 1686.

For the Act of Accession (1972), art 100, see 42A Halsbury's Statutes (3rd edn) 801.

**Cases cited**
*EC Commission v UK* Case 32/79 [1980] ECR 240.
*EC Commission v UK* Case 804/79 [1981] ECR 1045.

**Reference**
The Crown Court at Newcastle upon Tyne referred a question (set out at letter *h*, below, post) as to the right of the United Kingdom to bring into force the Sea Fish (Specified United Kingdom Waters) (Prohibition of Fishing) Order 1982, SI 1982/1849, to the extent that it prohibited only vessels registered in Denmark from fishing as specified in the order. The question arose following the conviction in the North Shields Magistrates' Court on 7 January 1983 of Kent Kirk, the master of the Danish fishing boat Sandkirk E550, for fishing on 6 January 1983 in certain waters in contravention of the 1982 order and contrary to the Sea Fish Conservation Act 1967, s 5(1), as amended by the Fisheries Act 1981. The magistrates' court fined Mr Kirk £30,000 and ordered him to pay £400 costs. On an appeal by Mr Kirk against both conviction and sentence the Crown Court at Newcastle upon Tyne referred the question to the Court of Justice of the European Communities for a preliminary ruling under art 177 of the EEC Treaty. The Commission of the European Communities, the governments of the Netherlands, the United Kingdom and Denmark and Mr Kirk submitted written observations to the court. The language of the case was English. The facts are set out in the opinion of the Advocate General.

*David Vaughan QC* for Mr Kirk.
*The Solicitor General (Sir Patrick Mayhew QC)* for the United Kingdom.
*Per Lachmann* for the government of Denmark.
*Richard Wainwright* for the EC Commission.

3 April. **The Advocate General (M Darmon)** delivered the following opinion[1]. Mr President, Members of the Court,

1. On 6 January 1983 Kent Kirk, the master of the Danish vessel the Sandkirk, set out to fish within 12 miles of the British coastline. In so doing he was clearly acting in contravention of the Sea Fish (Specified United Kingdom Waters) (Prohibition of Fishing) Order 1982, SI 1982/1849, clearly and, indeed, deliberately. On board with Mr Kirk, who is a Danish member of the European Parliament, were a number of journalists. The object of the exercise was, as he again pointed out in the course of argument, to challenge the validity under Community law of the 1982 order.

Mr Kirk was charged on the same day and on 7 January 1983 appeared before the North Shields Magistrates' Court, where he was fined £30,000 and ordered to pay costs of £400. He appealed against that judgment to the Crown Court at Newcastle upon Tyne and by order of 9 March 1983 that court referred the following question to the Court of Justice for a preliminary ruling:

'Having regard to all the relevant provisions of Community law did the United Kingdom have the right after 31 December 1982 to bring into force the Sea Fish (Specified United Kingdom Waters) (Prohibition of Fishing) Order 1982 to the extent that that Order prohibits only vessels registered in Denmark from fishing as specified in that Order?'

That is exactly the sort of question which, as it stands, may not be answered within the framework of art 177 of the EEC Treaty. The national court fails to cite any Community provision which is to be interpreted or whose validity is to be assessed. At the same time it asks the court whether a clearly specified national provision is in conformity with Community law.

As is customary in such cases it is therefore necessary to establish which Community rules were applicable so that the national court may decide whether the national measure

---
1 Translated from the French

to which it refers was indeed in conformity with those Community rules and if not, declare it inapplicable.

2. In a recent article, 'La Nouvelle Politique Commune de la Pêche' [1983] Cahiers de Droit Européen 437ff, Jörn Sack describes the fisheries policy as 'a "new problem" for which the Community was ill-prepared'.

Initially the fisheries question was merely an element of the common agriculture policy (see art 38(1) of the EEC Treaty) but it acquired a new dimension and considerable importance on the accession to the European Community of Denmark, Ireland and the United Kingdom.

In the light of the general development of the fishing industry and the importance of that sector to the new member states it was difficult to apply strictly and immediately the general prohibition of discrimination on grounds of nationality laid down in art 7 of the EEC Treaty and reaffirmed with regard to the fishing industry in art 2 of EC Council Regulation 2141/70 of 20 October 1970 laying down a common structural policy for the fishing industry.

Thus art 4 of that regulation provided:

'1. By way of derogation from the provisions of Article 2, access to certain fishing grounds ... may be limited, for certain types of fishing and for a period not exceeding five years ... to the local population of the coastal regions concerned if that population depends primarily on inshore fishing ...'

Similarly, art 100(1) of the Act of Accession (1972) authorised the member states—

'until 31 December 1982, to restrict fishing in waters under their sovereignty or jurisdiction ... to vessels which fish traditionally in those waters ...'

Any provisions adopted under that derogation were however required to be 'less restrictive than those applied in practice at the time of accession'.

Under art 103 of the Act of Accession, the Commission was required to present 'Before 31 December 1982 ... a report to the Council on the economic and social development of the coastal areas of the Member States and the state of stocks ...' It was stated that—

'On the basis of that report, and of the objectives of the common fisheries policy, the Council, acting on a proposal from the Commission, shall examine the provisions which could follow the derogations in force until 31 December 1982.'

In the exercise of its power under art 100 of the Act of Accession, the United Kingdom adopted the Fishing Boats (European Economic Community) Designation Order 1972, SI 1972/2026, which came into force on 1 January 1973, recognising that certain other member states, not including Denmark, held certain special fishing rights.

EC Council Regulation 2141/70 was repealed by EC Council Regulation 101/76 of 19 January 1976, art 2 of which reproduced in full the wording of art 2 of the earlier regulation.

3. On 11 June 1982 the Commission submitted to the Council a 'modified proposal for a Council Regulation establishing a Community system for the conservation and management of fishery resources' (see OJ C228, p 1 (a proposal had previously been submitted on 8 October 1976 and was published in OJ C255, p 3)).

It is emphasised in the recitals of that proposal that—

'in view of the over-fishing of stocks of the main species, it is essential that the Community, in the interests of both fisherman and consumers, ensure by an appropriate policy for the protection of fishing ground that stocks are conserved and reconstituted ... it is therefore desirable that the provisions of Council Regulation (EEC) No 101/76 of 19 January 1976 laying down a common structural policy for the fishing industry be supplemented by the establishment of a Community system for the conservation and management of fishery resources that will ensure balanced exploitation;
... conservation and management of resources must contribute to a greater

stability of fishing activities and must be appraised on the basis of a reference allocation reflecting the orientations given by the Council;

... that stability, in consideration of the temporary biological situation of stocks, must safeguard the particular needs of regions where local populations are especially dependent on fisheries and related industries as decided by the Council in its resolution of 3 November 1976 and in particular Annex VII thereof;

... There should be special provisions for inshore fishing to enable this sector to cope with the new fishing conditions resulting from the institution of 200 mile fishing zones ... to this end, Member States should be authorized to maintain in a first stage until 31 December 1992 the derogation regime defined in Article 100 of the Act of Accession and to generalize up to 12 miles the limit of six miles prescribed in that article;

... these measures constitute, pursuant to the Act of Accession, the arrangements succeeding those provided for up to 31 December 1982 ... this regime, after possible adjustments, will be applicable for a further period of 10 years and after this period the Council is asked to decide upon the provisions which could follow the regime referred to in Articles 6 and 7 ...'

The proposal contains 16 articles including the following:

'*Article 1*

In order to ensure the protection of fishing grounds, the conservation of the biological resources of the sea and their balanced exploitation on a lasting basis and appropriate economic and social conditions, a Community system for the conservation and management of fishery resources is hereby established.

For these purposes, the system will consist, in particular, of conservation measures, rules for the use and distribution of resources, special provisions for coastal fishing and supervisory measures ...

*Article 6*

1. From 1 January 1983 to 31 December 1992 Member States are authorized to maintain the regime defined in Article 100 of the Act of Accession annexed to the Treaty establishing the European Communities and to generalize up to 12 nautical miles for all waters under their sovereignty or jurisdiction the limit of six miles prescribed in that Article ...'

4. Those proposals were discussed at the Fisheries Council of 21 December 1982 which, as a result of the opposition of the Danish government, failed to reach an agreement.

On the same day the Commission addressed to the Council a declaration in the following terms (OJ C343, p 2; the emphasis is as in the original):

'... the Commission recalls that the Member States not only have the *right* to adopt the necessary measures, subject to their approval by the Commission, but also have the *duty* to take these measures in the collective interest, this being a duty which the Commission can ask them to accept ...

The Commission consequently calls upon all Member States: —to notify it without delay of the national measures of conservation they plan to adopt; —to confirm at the same time their intention to take the necessary action, at national level, to ensure that national measures of conservation planned, which the Commission approves, are complied with ...

... the Commission will, in carrying out its responsibilities, and particularly when approving national conservation measures, act on the basis of the proposals that it has submitted to the Council;

The Commission will ensure that the different national measures of conservation are as well coordinated as possible and requests the Member States' cooperation in this. The national measures must constitute a temporary system that is at once practicable, effective and non-discriminatory ...'

On 22 December 1982 the United Kingdom adopted the Sea Fish (Specified United Kingdom Waters) (Prohibition of Fishing) Order 1982, SI 1982/1849, which entered into force for one year as from 1 January 1983, and according to which, subject to certain conditions—

> 'fishing within such part of British fishery limits as lies within 12 miles from the baselines adjacent to the United Kingdom by any fishing boat registered in Denmark is hereby prohibited.'

On the same day the United Kingdom expressed its disappointment at the failure of the negotiations which had taken place the previous day and submitted the measure that it had just adopted to the Commission for approval. It confirmed that it would naturally be prepared to amend or revoke that measure—

> 'To avoid discrimination among fishermen from different Member States, when the Government of Denmark is able to give satisfactory assurances that this objective can be achieved in respect of Danish vessels.'

By Decision 83/3 of 5 January 1983 the Commission, while reserving its decision on the substance of the measures, authorised the national measures which had been notified to it by certain member states including the United Kingdom order adopted on 22 December 1982.

That authorisation was given 'for reasons of public order to avoid conflicts arising' during the period when the measures in question were being examined 'in the absence of any provision applying to fishing in Community waters' and was given 'provisionally ... for a period to expire not later than 26 January 1983'.

The Fisheries Council met on 25 January 1983. In the words of Mr Sack it produced 'results beyond all expectations' (see 'La Nouvelle Politique Commune de la Pêche' [1983] Cahiers de Droit Européen at 444). In particular the Council adopted Regulation 170/83, which incorporated the substance of the proposal submitted by the Commission on 11 June 1982 and, almost word for word, the provisions which are cited above.

That then is the 'Community context' of the case which is before the court. Clearly it follows that the maintenance, for a further period of ten years, of the derogatory rules based on art 100 of the Act of Accession (1972) is an integral part of the common fisheries policy.

5. The question is therefore whether that objective was achieved by proper means.

There would be no difficulty if Regulation 170/83 had been adopted and had entered into force before 1 January 1983. That is not the case. The regulation is dated 25 January and, under art 16 thereof, it entered into force on 27 January, the day of its publication in the Official Journal of the European Communities.

There has been some discussion as to the retroactive effect of the regulation or, more specifically, of art 6 thereof which, it may be recalled, authorises member states to maintain the previous arrangements 'as from 1 January 1983'. That discussion has been concerned in particular with the effects of such retroactivity in criminal law. Provisions relating to criminal law cannot be retroactive. However, it does not seem that the question arises in those terms in this instance.

What then was the situation shortly before 1 January 1983? The regulation that was then in the course of preparation could not yet apply. The court has already ruled that 'The effect of the Council's inability to reach a decision ... has not been to deprive the Community of its powers' in the conservation of fishery resources (see *EC Commission v UK* Case 32/79 [1980] ECR 2403 at 2434, para 15). The court stated:

> 'In such a situation, it was for the Member States, as regards the maritime zones coming within their jurisdiction, to take the necessary conservation measures in the common interest and in accordance with both the substantive and the procedural rules arising from Community law ...'

The court further developed that principle, which has now become established, in its other judgment in *EC Commission v UK* Case 804/79 [1981] ECR 1045 at 1075–1076, paras 27–31, stating that art 5 of the treaty—

> 'imposes on Member States special duties of action and abstention in a situation in which the Commission, in order to meet urgent needs of conservation, has submitted to the Council proposals which, although they have not been adopted by the Council, represent the point of departure for concerted Community action.'

It also pointed out that as 'trustees of the common interest' the member states are under 'an obligation to undertake detailed consultations with the Commission and to seek its approval in good faith'.

It would seem that those principles laid down in respect of the conservation of fishery resources may be applied to the question of access to the 12-mile coastal zone, first, because regulation of access is one of the preconditons for conservation and, second, because of the need to 'safeguard the particular needs of regions where local populations are especially dependent on fisheries and related industries' (see EC Council Regulation 170/83 of 25 January 1983, 6th recital).

The Commission's declaration to the Council of 21 December 1982 expressly drew attention to the court's decisions which are cited above. In accordance with those principles, the United Kingdom complied with the Commission's request and submitted the measure in question to the Commission for approval. The Commission authorised the measure on a provisional basis on 5 January 1983.

6. It remains to consider the substance of the contested order and its conformity with the relevant requirements of Community law. That raises the question of the discriminatory effect alleged both by Mr Kirk and by the Danish and Netherlands governments. It must be recalled that the 1982 order prohibited from fishing in British coastal waters only fishing vessels registered in Denmark.

Such a measure, although perhaps maladroit in form, is discriminatory only in appearance. From the point of view of Community law it was possible lawfully to exclude the Danish vessels, which did not traditionally fish in the waters concerned, on the basis of the authorisation contained in art 100 of the Act of Accession. The Commission's proposals, approved by the Council on 25 January 1983, did not create new rights for such vessels in this respect.

The matter in point in this case, therefore, is not discrimination but a derogation which is based on the respective situations of the two states concerned and which the United Kingdom has extended by adopting the contested order.

Indeed it might be thought that there was a particular need for that measure since, in contrast to most of the other member states, Denmark had refused at the time to give the United Kingdom assurances that it would respect the status quo pending the adoption of a Council regulation.

I am therefore of the opinion that the court should rule as follows: given that the authority that would normally have been responsible for laying down Community rules for the conservation and management of fishery resources had failed to act and in view of the state of the Community law, a member state was entitled, provided that it complied with the relevant procedural rules, to bring into force after 31 December 1982 a measure maintaining on a temporary basis a prohibition of fishing within 12 miles of its coast by vessels registered in another member state.

10 July. **THE COURT OF JUSTICE** delivered its judgment which, having summarised the facts, procedure and submissions of the parties, dealt with the law as follows.

1. By order of 9 March 1983, received at the court on 20 April 1983, the Crown Court at Newcastle upon Tyne referred a question to the court for a preliminary ruling pursuant to art 177 of the EEC Treaty on the interpretation of the Community law on fisheries in order to enable it to determine whether a measure adopted by the United Kingdom

prohibiting vessels registered in Denmark from fishing within its 12-mile coastal zone was compatible with that law.

2. By the Sea Fish (Specified United Kingdom Waters) (Prohibition of Fishing) Order 1982, SI 1982/1849, the United Kingdom prohibited 'fishing within such part of British fishery limits as lies within 12 miles from the baselines adjacent to the United Kingdom by any fishing boat registered in Denmark . . .' Kent Kirk, the master of a Danish fishing vessel, was intercepted in that vessel on 6 January 1983 by a ship of the Royal Navy whilst he was engaged in fishing within the coastal zone and was fined £30,000 by North Shields Magistrates' Court. He appealed to the Crown Court at Newcastle upon Tyne, where he claimed that the United Kingdom was not entitled to bring into force the 1982 order and that, consequently, no offence had been committed.

3. The Crown Court at Newcastle upon Tyne took the view that in order to enable it to determine whether the 1982 order was compatible with Community law a preliminary ruling from the Court of Justice was necessary. It therefore stayed the proceedings and referred the following question to the court:

'Having regard to all the relevant provisions of Community law did the United Kingdom have the right after 31 December 1982 to bring into force the Sea Fish (Specified United Kingdom Waters) (Prohibition of Fishing) Order 1982 to the extent that the Order prohibits only vessels registered in Denmark from fishing as specified in that Order?'

4. The purpose of that question is essentially to establish whether, at the time when the 1982 order was adopted, it was permissible for a member state, under Community law in the matter of fishing, to prohibit vessels registered in another named member state from fishing within a coastal zone specified by that order.

5. Mr Kirk takes the view, and is supported in that respect by the governments of Denmark and the Netherlands, that the rules which applied prior to the 1972 Act of Accession became fully applicable on the expiry of the derogations permitted during the transitional period, which ended on 31 December 1982. Those rules, codified in EC Council Regulation 101/76, include the principle of non-discrimination and therefore the exclusion of Danish vessels under the 1982 order is contrary to Community law.

6. It should be borne in mind, in this respect, that art 7 of the EEC Treaty provides that within the scope of application of the treaty, and without prejudice to any special provisions contained therein, any discrimination on grounds of nationality is prohibited.

7. Council Regulation 101/76 laying down a common structural policy for the fishing industry, which replaced EC Council Regulation 2141/70 of 20 October 1970, provides, in art 2(1), which is identical to article 2(1) of Regulation 2141/70, that rules applied by each member state in respect of fishing in the maritime waters coming under its sovereignty or within its jurisdiction must not lead to differences in treatment of other member states. Member states must ensure in particular equal conditions of access to and use of the fishing grounds situated in the waters referred to for all fishing vessels flying the flag of a member state and registered in Community territory.

8. Article 100(1) of the 1972 Act of Accession authorised a derogation from those principles for a period expiring on 31 December 1982, so that the member states could restrict fishing by nationals of other member states in waters under their sovereignty or jurisdiction, situated within a limit which was fixed in principle at six nautical miles.

9. Under art 103 of the 1972 Act of Accession, before 31 December 1982 the Council, acting on a proposal from the Commission, was to examine the provisions which could follow the derogations in force until 31 December 1982.

10. The modified proposal for a Council regulation establishing a Community system for the conservation and management of fishery resources, submitted by the Commission to the Council on 11 June 1982 (OJ C228, p 1) proposed that the zone covered by the derogation defined in art 100 of the 1972 Act of Accession should be extended to 12 nautical miles and should remain in force for a period expiring on 31 December 1982.

11. Following the Council's failure to adopt the proposed provisions at its meeting on 21 December 1982, the Commission that same day made a declaration (OJ C343, p 2), in

which it pointed out that the conservation of fishery resources had been the exclusive responsibility of the Community since 1 January 1979 but that the Community had still not succeeded in adopting a comprehensive conservation system. It further stated that member states not only had the right to adopt the necessary measures but also had the duty to take those measures in the collective interest. The Commission therefore called on all member states to notify it without delay of the national measures of conservation they planned to adopt, subject to approval by the Commission, and requested member states' cooperation in order to ensure that the different national measures of conservation were coordinated and that they constituted a temporary system that was at once practicable, effective and non-discriminatory.

12. On 22 December 1982 the United Kingdom notified the 1982 order to the Commission, which approved it by decision of 5 January 1983 (OJ L12, p 50). In that decision the Commission stated that the authorisation was only provisional until 26 January 1983, subject to a subsequent assessment of the substance of the measure. In the preamble, the Commission referred to the fact that 'whereas certain Member States have notified to the Commission national measures . . . Belgium, Denmark and Greece have not notified any such measures . . .' and emphasised that the decision had been adopted 'for reasons of public order to avoid conflicts arising during this period in the absence of any provision applying to fishing in Community waters'.

13. On 25 January 1983 the Council adopted Regulation 170/83 establishing a Community system for the conservation and management of fishery resources, art 6(1) of which authorises retroactively, as from 1 January 1983, the retention of the derogation regime defined in art 100 of the 1972 Act of Accession for a further ten years, and extends the coastal zones from six to twelve nautical miles. The events at issue in the main proceedings occurred in the intervening period between 1 January and 25 January 1983.

14. It follows from the above-mentioned provisions of arts 100 and 103 of the 1972 Act of Accession that the measures derogating from a fundamental principle of Community law, namely non-discrimination, were limited to the transitional period and that the power to bring into force any provisions thereafter was entrusted to the Community authorities, in particular to the Council.

15. It cannot be concluded from the fact that the Council failed to adopt such provisions within the period provided for in art 103 that the member states had the power to act in the place of the Council, in particular by extending the derogation beyond the prescribed time limits.

16. It follows that at the time of the events at issue before the national court, art 2(1) of Regulation 101/76, which provided for equal conditions of access to waters coming within the jurisdiction of member states and, in consequence, the abolition of all discrimination based on nationality against nationals of member states, was fully applicable.

17. The United Kingdom and the Commission claim that the fact that after the end of the transitional period the measures prescribed by art 103 of the 1972 Act of Accession were not adopted created a legal vacuum which the member states were entitled to fill as 'trustees' of the common interest by measures approved by the commission, as was recognised by the court in *EC Commission v UK* Case 804/79 [1981] ECR 1045.

18. In that judgment the court stated that, in the absence of Community rules, member states had the power to take temporary measures for the conservation of fishery resources in order to avoid irreparable damage contrary to the objectives of the common conservation policy.

19. Although, as the United Kingdom points out, rules relating to access may in certain cases constitute a response to a concern to conserve fishery resources, it is clear that in this instance the disputed measure was not intended to achieve such an objective. National rules which prohibit access to national waters and which are not intended to achieve an objective of conservation can not be covered by the power of member states, recognised in the aforementioned judgment of 5 May 1981, to take temporary conservation measures.

20. The Commission nevertheless contends that the member states were empowered

to adopt measures such as the 1982 order by art 6(1) of Regulation 170/83 of 25 January 1983, which authorises retroactively, as from 1 January 1983, the retention of the derogation regime defined in art 100 of the 1972 Act of Accession for a further ten years, and which extends the coastal zones from six to twelve nautical miles. In the Commission's view, the 1982 order constituted a proper exercise of the authorisation under Regulation 170/83 in view of the particular circumstances prevailing at that time.

21. Without embarking on an examination of the general legality of the retroactivity of art 6(1) of that regulation, it is sufficient to point out that such retroactivity may not, in any event, have the effect of validating ex post facto national measures of a penal nature which impose penalties for an act which, in fact, was not punishable at the time at which it was committed. That would be the case where, at the time of the act entailing a criminal penalty, the national measure was invalid because it was incompatible with Community law.

22. The principle that penal provisions may not have retroactive effect is one which is common to all the legal orders of the member states and is enshrined in art 7 of the European Convention for the Protection of Human Rights and Fundamental Freedoms (Rome, 4 November 1950; TS 71 (1953); Cmd 8969) as a fundamental right; it takes its place among the general principles of law whose observance is ensured by the Court of Justice.

23. Consequently the retroactivity provided for in art 6(1) of Regulation 170/83 cannot be regarded as validating ex post facto national measures which imposed criminal penalties, at the time of the conduct at issue, if those measures were not valid.

24. It follows from the foregoing considerations that Community law regarding fishing did not authorise a member state, at the time of the adoption of the 1982 order, to prohibit vessels registered in another named member state from fishing within a coastal zone specified by that order and not covered by conservation measures.

*Costs*

25. The costs incurred by the governments of Denmark and the Netherlands, by the United Kingdom and by the Commission of the European Communities, which have submitted observations to the court, are not recoverable. As these proceedings are, in so far as the parties to the main proceedings are concerned, in the nature of a step in the proceedings pending before the national court, costs are a matter for that court.

On those grounds, the court, in answer to the question referred to it by the Crown Court at Newcastle upon Tyne, by order of 9 March 1983, hereby rules: Community law regarding fishing did not authorise a member state, at the time of the adoption of the Sea Fish (Specified United Kingdom Waters) (Prohibition of Fishing) Order 1982, to prohibit vessels registered in another named member state from fishing within a coastal zone, specified by that order and not covered by conservation measures.

Agents: *Bawtree & Sons*, Witham (for Mr Kirk); *W H Godwin*, Treasury Solicitor's Department (for the United Kingdom); *Per Lachmann*, Legal Adviser, Ministry for Foreign Affairs (for the government of Denmark); *Richard Wainwright*, Legal Service of the EC Commission (for the Commission).

Mary Rose Plummer     Barrister.

# Collin v Duke of Westminster and others

COURT OF APPEAL, CIVIL DIVISION
OLIVER, MAY LJJ AND SIR ROGER ORMROD
28, 29, 30 NOVEMBER, 21 DECEMBER 1984

*Landlord and tenant – Leasehold enfranchisement – Tenant's notice – Tenant giving notice to landlords of desire to acquire freehold – Landlords opposing claim and citing current legal authority under which tenant's lease not qualifying as at low rent – Five years later legal decision defining letting value and thereby tenant becoming entitled to claim enfranchisement – Whether notice by tenant abandoned – Whether abandonment by conduct – Leasehold Reform Act 1967, s 20.*

*Landlord and tenant – Leasehold enfranchisement – Limitation of action – Tenant giving notice of desire to acquire freehold – Landlord opposing claim and citing current legal authority under which tenant's lease not qualifying as at low rent – Five years later legal decision defining letting value and thereby tenant becoming entitled to claim enfranchisement – Over six years after original notice tenant seeking to proceed on original notice – Whether cause of action statute-barred – Whether cause of action a statutory cause of action – Whether statutory cause of action a 'specialty' and accordingly limitation period of 12 years – Leasehold Reform Act 1967, s 8 – Limitation Act 1980, s 8.*

In December 1946 the tenant's predecessor in title was granted a lease of a house for a term of 48½ years at a rent of £125 per annum. In 1960 the lease was assigned to the tenant, who resided in the house from October 1960. In January 1975 he gave notice to the landlords under the Leasehold Reform Act 1967 that he wished to acquire the freehold on the basis that he had a long tenancy at a low rent and fell within the appropriate rateable value. In March the landlords gave notice opposing the claim, on the grounds that under the proviso to s 4(1)[a] of the 1967 Act a tenancy granted between August 1939 and April 1963 could not be regarded as being at a 'low rent' if at the commencement of the tenancy the rent payable under the tenancy exceeded two-thirds of the 'letting value' of the property, which value, on the basis of then current legal authority, could not exceed the amount lawfully exigible under the Rent Acts. Thereafter the tenant did not institute proceedings to enforce his right but entered into correspondence with the landlords as to the possibility of their selling the freehold to tenants not entitled to enfranchise and as to the possibility of an extension of his lease. In March 1977 the negotiations terminated without any agreement being reached. As a result of a legal decision in 1980 in which it was held that the 'letting value' fell to be determined according to not only the rental limit imposed by the Rent Acts but also the addition of the decapitalised value of any premium lawfully obtainable in lettings for terms not less than 14 years, the tenant became entitled to claim enfranchisement of his property. Accordingly, in July 1981, 6½ years after the original notice, he wrote to the landlords seeking to proceed on his notice, and also issuing a new notice. In December 1982 he applied to the county court for a declaration under s 20 of the 1967 Act that he was entitled to acquire the freehold of the property. The landlords contended (i) that the original notice of January 1975, if valid, had been abandoned, (ii) that the 1975 notice in conjunction with the 1967 Act created a contract for sale, and accordingly by virtue of s 5 of the Limitation Act 1980 the claim was barred in 1981, ie six years after receipt of the landlords' notice opposing the claim, and (iii) that the contract, if it still existed, was no longer capable of specific performance, and that in any event the court should exercise its discretion to refuse to grant a declaration. The judge held that there had been no abandonment of the claim and declared that the tenant was entitled to acquire the freehold under the 1967 Act. The landlords appealed.

---

*a*   Section 4(1), so far as material, is set out at p 466 *f*, post

**Held** – The appeal would be dismissed for the following reasons—

(1) In the law of contract there was no room for the concept of unilateral abandonment. In order to establish abandonment there had to be some representation or promise, whether express or by conduct, which had been relied on by the other party so as to found an estoppel, or material from which there could be inferred mutual release or mutual promises. However, although a tenant who was entitled to enfranchisement under the 1967 Act could not contract out of his entitlement, there was nothing in that Act which prevented him, once his right of franchisement had accrued, from contractually releasing the immediate right of enfranchisement acquired when he served notice under the 1967 Act. On the facts, it was not possible to infer from the tenant's failure to pursue a claim which was plainly disputed and which at the time appeared to be disputed on sustainable grounds a promise not to pursue the claim further. Furthermore, the abandonment on which the landlords claimed to rely was entirely unilateral and unsupported by any consideration on their part. It followed that there was no conduct which could properly be treated as justifying any assumption of mutual promises necessary to support abandonment. Moreover, the subsequent inquiry by the tenant as to the landlords' willingness to treat with tenants not entitled to enfranchise was not of a promissory nature (see p 468 *b* to *h*, p 469 *h* to p 470 *a* and *f* to *h*, p 471 *b c* and p 474 *h*, post); *James v Heim Gallery (London) Ltd* (1980) 41 P & CR 269 followed; dicta of Lord Bramwell in *Tiverton and North Devon Rly Co v Loosemore* (1884) 9 App Cas at 506, of Upjohn J in *Grice v Dudley Corp* [1957] 2 All ER at 679 and of Upjohn LJ in *Simpsons Motor Sales (London) Ltd v Hendon Corp* [1962] 3 All ER at 81–82 considered.

(2) Any cause of action which the tenant had was derived from statute alone, since the rights and duties of the respective parties stemmed from the obligation to enfranchise arising under s 8(1)[b] of the 1967 Act, and any claim which fell to be adjudicated by the court would be a claim arising under s 8(1). It followed that the tenant's claim was a claim on a specialty and not in contract and accordingly the six-year period of limitation did not apply. Furthermore, on the true construction of s 8[c] of the 1980 Act (which provided that an action on a specialty was limited to 12 years) a 'specialty' was not confined to specialty debts or to obligations arising specifically under contracts of sale, but included causes of action based on statute. Accordingly, in so far as the 1980 Act applied to a cause of action arising out of the enfranchisement provisions of the 1967 Act, the limitation period which applied was the 12-year limitation period specified in s 8 of the 1980 Act. It followed that the tenant's claim was not barred (see p 472 *d* to *g* and p 473 *b* to *d* and *j* to p 474 *b* and *h*, post); *Cork and Bandon Rly Co v Goode* [1843–60] All ER Rep 671 and *Aylott v West Ham Corp* [1927] 1 Ch 30 applied; *Leivers v Barber Walker & Co Ltd* [1943] 1 All ER 386 considered.

## Notes

For the right to enfranchisement or extension generally, see 27 Halsbury's Laws (4th edn) paras 1001–1003, and for cases on the subject, see 31(1) Digest (Reissue) 175–178, 1486–1497.

For the exercise of right of enfranchisement or extension, see 27 Halsbury's Laws (4th edn) paras 1019–1021.

For the Leashold Reform Act 1967, ss 4, 8, 20, see 18 Halsbury's Statutes (3rd edn) 640, 648, 674.

For the Limitation Act 1980, ss 5, 8, see 50(1) ibid 1258, 1260.

## Cases referred to in judgments

*Amherst v James Walker Goldsmith and Silversmith Ltd* [1983] 2 All ER 1067, [1983] 1 Ch 305, [1983] 3 WLR 334, CA.

*Aylott v West Ham Corp* [1927] 1 Ch 30, CA.

*Cork and Bandon Rly Co v Goode* (1853) 13 CB 826, [1843–60] All ER Rep 671, 138 ER 1427.

---

*b*   Section 8(1) is set out at p 472 *c d*, post
*c*   Section 8 is set out at p 472 *g*, post

*Cornwall Minerals Rly Co, Re* [1897] 2 Ch 74.
*Gidlow-Jackson v Middlegate Properties Ltd* [1974] 1 All ER 830, [1974] QB 361, [1974] 2
    WLR 116, CA.
*Grice v Dudley Corp* [1957] 2 All ER 673, [1958] Ch 329, [1957] 3 WLR 314.
*Gutsell v Reeve* [1936] 1 KB 272, [1935] All ER Rep 117, CA.
*James v Heim Gallery (London) Ltd* (1980) 41 P & CR 269, CA.
*Leivers v Barber Walker & Co Ltd* [1943] 1 All ER 386, [1943] 1 KB 385, CA.
*Manson v Duke of Westminster* [1981] 2 All ER 40, [1981] QB 323, [1981] 2 WLR 428, CA.
*Paal Wilson & Co A/S v Partenreederei Hannah Blumenthal, The Hannah Blumenthal* [1983] 1
    All ER 34, [1983] 1 AC 854, [1982] 3 WLR 1149, HL.
*Pratt v Cook & Co (St Paul's) Ltd* [1940] 1 All ER 410, [1940] AC 437, HL.
*R v Williams* [1942] 2 All ER 95, [1942] AC 541, PC.
*Shepherd v Hills* (1855) 11 Exch 55, 156 ER 743.
*Simpsons Motor Sales (London) Ltd v Hendon Corp* [1962] 3 All ER 75, [1963] Ch 57, [1962]
    3 WLR 666, CA; *affd* [1963] 2 All ER 484, [1964] AC 1088, [1963] 2 WLR 1187, HL.
*Tiverton and North Devon Rly Co v Loosemore* (1884) 9 App Cas 480, HL.

### Cases also cited

*Allied Marine Transport Ltd v Vale do Rio Doce Navegacao SA, The Leonidas D* [1983] 3 All
    ER 737, [1984] 1 WLR 1.
*Andre & Cie SA v Marine Transocean Ltd, The Splendid Sun* [1981] 2 All ER 993, [1981] 1
    QB 694, CA.
*Banco de Bilbao v Rey, Banco de Bilbao v Sancha* [1938] 2 All ER 253, [1938] 2 KB 176, CA.
*Beauchamp (Earl) v Winn* (1873) LR 6 HL 223, HL.
*Byrnlea Property Investments Ltd v Ramsay* [1969] 2 All ER 311, [1969] 2 QB 253, CA.
*Central Electricity Generating Board v Halifax Corp* [1962] 3 All ER 915, [1963] AC 785,
    HL.
*Cia de Electricidad de la Provincia de Buenos Aires Ltd, Re* [1978] 3 All ER 668, [1980] Ch
    146.
*Cooper v Phibbs* (1867) LR 2 HL 149, HL.
*Frost v Knight* (1872) LR 7 Exch 111, [1861–73] All ER Rep 221, Ex Ch.
*Grist v Bailey* [1966] 2 All ER 875, [1967] Ch 532.
*Heath v Pugh* (1881) 6 QBD 345, CA; *affd* (1882) 7 App Cas 235, HL.
*Heyman v Darwins Ltd* [1942] 1 All ER 337, [1942] AC 356, HL.
*Ibeneweka v Egbuna* [1964] 1 WLR 219, PC.
*Jackson v Hall, Williams v Thompson* [1980] 1 All ER 177, [1980] AC 854, HL.
*Mills v Haywood* (1877) 6 Ch D 196, CA.
*Moschi v LEP Air Services Ltd* [1972] 2 All ER 393, [1973] AC 331, HL.
*Pearl Mill Co Ltd v Ivy Tannery Co Ltd* [1919] 1 KB 78, [1918–19] All ER Rep 702, DC.
*Pollock v Brook-Shepherd* (1983) 45 P & CR 357, CA.
*Reeves v Butcher* [1891] 2 QB 509, [1891–4] All ER Rep 943, CA.
*Royal Trust Co v A-G for Alberta* [1930] AC 144, PC.
*Solle v Butcher* [1949] 2 All ER 1107, [1950] 1 KB 671, CA.
*Walters v Webb* (1870) LR 5 Ch App 531, LC & LJ.
*Williams v Thomas* [1909] 1 Ch 713, CA.

### Appeal

The respondents, the present trustees of the Grosvenor Estates, being the sixth Duke of
Westminster, the Hon Gerald Cavendish, John Nigel Courtenay James and Sir Richard
Baker Wilbraham, appealed against the judgment of his Honour Judge Harris QC made
on 27 February 1984 whereby it was adjudged that the applicant, Francis Spencer Collin,
was entitled by virtue of Pt I of the Leasehold Reform Act 1967 to acquire the freehold
and premises at 30 Eaton Terrace, Eaton Square, London SW1. The facts are set out in
the judgment of Oliver LJ.

*Simon Berry* for the respondents.
*J B W McDonnell QC* for the applicant.

*Cur adv vult*

21 December. The following judgments were delivered.

**OLIVER LJ.** This is an appeal by the trustees of the Westminster estate (the respondents) who are the owners of the freehold of certain properties in and around Eaton Square, from an order made by his Honour Judge Harris QC on 27 February 1984 in the West London County Court declaring that the applicant in proceedings under the Leasehold Reform Act 1967, Mr Francis Spencer Collin, was entitled under the Act to acquire from the estate the freehold of a house at 30 Eaton Terrace. Mr Collin (to whom I will refer as 'the applicant') is the present lessee by assignment in occupation of the house in question under a lease granted on 8 December 1948 for a term of 48½ years expiring on Lady Day 1997. The lease, which reserved a rent of £125 per annum, was assigned to the applicant and he was registered as the proprietor with good leasehold title under the Land Registration Acts on 21 October 1960.

Section 1 of the 1967 Act confers on the tenant of a leasehold house occupying the house as his residence (which the applicant does) a right to acquire the freehold where (a) his tenancy is a long tenancy at a low rent and the rateable value of the house on the appropriate day is not more than £400 in Greater London and (b) at the time when he gives notice requiring the freehold he has been a tenant of the house under a long tenancy at a low rent and occupying as his residence for the last five years.

The appropriate day was originally 23 March 1965 on which date the rateable value of the premises was £572, so that it was then outside the statutory limits. However, the 1967 Act underwent some amendment by virtue of s 118 of the Housing Act 1974. For relevant purposes the ambit of the enfranchisement provision was, in cases where the tenancy was created before February 1966, extended to houses the rateable value of which on 1 April 1973 did not exceed £1,500. The lease under which the applicant holds the house is, beyond dispute, a long lease for the purposes of the 1967 Act but prior to 1980 it was open to question whether the rent reserved by the lease was, at the material time, a low rent. Although that is statutorily defined as a rent of less than two-thirds of the rateable value on the appropriate day, that definition is subject to an important qualification under the proviso to s 4(1) of the 1967 Act, which is in these terms (so far as material):

'Provided that a tenancy granted between the end of August 1939 and the beginning of April 1963 otherwise than by way of building lease ... shall not be regarded as a tenancy at a low rent if at the commencement of the tenancy the rent payable under the tenancy exceeded two-thirds of the letting value of the property ...'

In 1939 the rateable value of the property had been less than £100 and the standard rent under the Rent Acts which was payable at the time of the grant of the lease was less than the £125 rent reserved. In *Gidlow-Jackson v Middlegate Properties Ltd* [1974] 1 All ER 830, [1974] QB 361 this court decided that the 'letting value' of property referred to in the proviso could not exceed the amount lawfully exigible under the Rent Acts. What occurred in this case was that the applicant, undeterred by that decision (which was widely thought to be open to challenge if anyone was hardy enough to take the question to the House of Lords) gave notice on the proper statutory form that he desired to acquire the freehold. It is not contested that, apart from the question whether the applicant could then avail himself of the provisions of the 1967 Act, that was a proper notice. A counter-notice denying the claim was duly served by the respondents and a letter accompanied it, referring to the case mentioned, and claiming that the proviso to s 4(1) applied. They appeared at that time to be on fairly firm ground because, despite a dissenting judgment of Lord Denning MR in this court, the Appeal Committee of the House of Lords had refused leave to appeal in *Gidlow-Jackson's* case. It is perhaps, therefore, not altogether surprising that the applicant did not seek to take the matter any further. There matters rested until 1981. In 1980, however, there was heard an appeal to this court in the case of *Manson v Duke of Westminster* [1981] 2 All ER 40, [1981] QB 323. That case raised a doubt at least whether the *Gidlow-Jackson* case was rightly decided, in other words, whether it was right to refer to the limits imposed by the Rent Acts at all for the purpose of a proviso referring simply to letting value. But, more importantly, it was held as a matter of decision that in any event, where the standard rent at the material time was payable under a tenancy which had been granted in consideration of a lawful premium, the letting value in the proviso fell to be determined having regard not merely to the rental limit imposed by the Rent Acts but also to the addition of the decapitalised value of any premium lawfully obtainable (premiums being lawful in the case of lettings for terms of not less than 14 years).

The respondents do not dispute that having regard to that decision, this property must now be considered a property in respect of which the applicant is qualified to claim enfranchisement under the 1967 Act. A fresh notice of enfranchisement has been given and accepted without prejudice to the original notice and the respondents have intimated that they will not dispute this. But of course the issue of which notice is the operative one crucially affects the question of the value of the property for enfranchisement purposes, because that is to be fixed at the date of the effective notice of enfranchisement and nearly 10 years have elapsed since the original notice, during which there has been an enormous inflation in property values. The difference in value between the date of the two notices is said to exceed £100,000.

So, accordingly, on 6 July 1981, some 6½ years after the original notice, the applicant's agents wrote to the respondents seeking to proceed on the original notice. That claim having been challenged, the originating application in these proceedings was issued on 23 December 1982. In it the applicant sought an order, pursuant to s 20 of the 1967 Act that he is entitled to acquire the freehold in the property. That section authorises proceedings in the county court 'for determining whether a person is entitled to acquire the freehold or an extended lease of a house and premises'.

By their reamended answer the respondents raised three points. First, they claimed that the original claim by the notice of 17 January 1975 (if valid) had been abandoned or must be taken to have been abandoned. Second, they said that if that notice gave rise to a cause of action, it was a cause of action in contract which accrued on 12 March 1975 as a result of para 7(5) of Pt II of Sch 3 to the 1967 Act and was therefore statute-barred on 12 March 1981 by virtue of the Limitation Act 1980. That paragraph provides that the tenant shall not institute proceedings to enforce his right to have the freehold before either the landlord has given his notice in reply (which was posted on 11 March 1975) or two months after the tenant's notice. The cause of action is, it was argued, a cause of action in contract by virtue of s 5 of the 1967 Act which provides that the rights and obligations arising from the tenant's notice are enforceable 'to the like extent . . . as rights and obligations arising under a contract for a sale or lease freely entered into between the landlord and tenant'. An alternative way of putting this limitation point is that the applicant's rights accrued as a result of one or other of two letters from the applicant dated 24 November 1976 and 2 December 1976 which, it is claimed, constituted acceptance by the applicant of the respondents' repudiation of the contract. Third, and in any event, it was said that by reason of delay the contract, if it still existed, was no longer capable of specific performance. Finally, by way of an additional point raised at the hearing, the respondents claimed that since, in effect, what the applicant was seeking was a declaration, and since a declaration is a discretionary remedy, this was a case in which the judge had to be satisfied that it was proper to exercise his discretion and it was argued that it was not a proper case.

The judge, in a most helpful and detailed judgment, rejected all four of the respondents' claims. As regards abandonment he held (and in my judgment he was clearly right in this) that in order to succeed the respondents had to show either some reliance and change of position amounting to an estoppel (of which there was no suggestion) or what amounted in effect to a contract for mutual release. Quite clearly there was no question of an express contract and what he had, therefore, to look for was whether there was material from which mutual promises could be implied. On the facts, he found himself unable to find any mutual release but, perhaps even more importantly, he held that the 1967 Act and the regulations provided, as it were, a complete statutory code which regulated exclusively how the statutory contract of sale was to be either completed or discharged and that there was no room for the application of the common law concept of inferred abandonment by mutual consent.

With respect to the judge, I doubt whether this latter conclusion can be right. In his judgment, the judge referred extensively to the speeches of Lord Brandon, Lord Diplock and Lord Brightman in *Paal Wilson & Co A/S v Partenreederei Hannah Blumenthal, The Hannah Blumenthal* [1983] 1 All ER 34, [1983] 1 AC 854, and to the principles to be deduced from that case. As he rightly pointed out there is, in the law of contract, no room for a concept of unilateral abandonment. What the court has to look for is either some representation or promise, whether express or by conduct, which has been relied on by the other party so as to ground an estoppel, or material from which there can be inferred mutual releases or mutual promises not to proceed. In other words, short of estoppel, and it is not contended that the facts in the instant case give rise to an estoppel, there has to be established, if only by inference, a fresh contract which has the effect of dissolving the relationship originally entered into by the parties and on which one party still seeks to rely. Now tenants who are entitled to enfranchise under the 1967 Act are not permitted to contract out of their entitlement, but there is nothing in the Act which prevents them, once their right of enfranchisement has accrued, from releasing contractually the immediate right of enfranchisement which they have acquired by serving a notice under the Act. Once such a notice has been served, there comes into being under s 8 of the 1967 Act (to which I will have to refer in a little more detail later) a statutory obligation on the landlord to transfer the freehold which, by s 5, is accorded incidents similar to those inherent in a contract freely entered into. Section 23(1) of the 1967 Act avoids agreements so far as they purport to exclude or modify the right to acquire the freehold or an extended lease conferred by the Act, but sub-s (2) of s 23 specifically provides that this shall not—

'where the tenant has given notice of his desire to have the freehold or an extended lease under this Part of this Act, invalidate any agreement between the landlord and the tenant that that notice shall cease to be binding . . .'

Nothing in this subsection carries, in my judgment, any necessary implication that the agreement there referred to has to be an express agreement and I can see no reason why, if the facts are such that the court is able to infer on both sides the necessary agreement to release the parties' respective rights arising from the service of a notice, that agreement should not be effective as an express agreement to that effect.

The principal ground for the judge's decision, however, was that on the facts there simply was no material from which he could infer the mutual release necessary to support a successful plea of abandonment. Although expressed in slightly different terms in the three speeches in the *The Hannah Blumenthal* case to which the judge referred, the essential concept is contained in the following passage from the speech of Lord Diplock ([1983] 1 All ER 34 at 48, [1983] 1 AC 854 at 915):

'To the formation of the contract of abandonment, the ordinary principles of the English law of contract apply. To create a contract by exchange of promises between two parties where the promise of each party constitutes the consideration for the promise of the other what is necessary is that the intention of each *as it has been communicated to and understood by the other* (even though that which has been communicated does not represent the actual state of mind of the communicator) should coincide.' (Lord Diplock's emphasis.)

In support of the respondents' contention that the applicant's notice under the Act and such rights as he had acquired under it had been abandoned the estate relied on two things, that is to say, first, the failure of the applicant to pursue the matter further after the initial landlord's notice of non-admission in March 1975 and, second, certain correspondence which passed between the applicant and Mr Lingren, the respondents' surveyor, in November 1976. As regards the former, following the landlord's notice and the covering letter on 11 March unequivocally declining to proceed and referring to the *Gidlow-Jackson* case, no further communication was received by them save for a letter from the applicant's solicitors saying that they were taking instructions. There the matter rested until 24 November 1976 when the applicant himself wrote to Mr Lingren inquiring whether the estate was 'selling freeholds to tenants who do *not* have the right to claim them' and 'whether the Estate is prepared . . . to grant an extension to a lease'.

Mr Lingren's reply made it clear that the estate, while unwilling to sell the freehold, would contemplate the grant of an extension to the existing lease, and thereafter a negotiation, if such it can be called, ensued in the course of which the estate quoted terms for an extension which involved not only an immediate and substantial increase in rent but also a substantial premium. That proved wholly unacceptable to the applicant, who broke off the correspondence in March 1977, whereafter nothing further was heard from him until, on 6 July 1981, his agents sought to revive the 1975 notice. In his evidence, Mr Lingren (who was the only person on behalf of the estate who applied his mind to the matter at all) made it quite clear that at the material time, that is in 1975, he thought that the estate was undeniably right in its contention and that the applicant had no claim at all under the Act. At the time when he received the letter of 24 November 1976, which, when he gave his evidence, he thought impliedly amounted to the applicant's giving up his rights, his view was that the applicant did not have any rights. He said:

'I cannot put it any clearer. The claim was made and refused. I thought he was evincing a view that he accepted the position in 1975, the position was that claim had been made and properly refused. Our view was Estate had no obligations.'

Counsel for the respondents rightly recognised that, in the light of the estate's refusal to proceed, it was a matter of no little difficulty for him to rely simply on the applicant's inactivity, although, for what it is worth, he points out that the procedural provisions set out in Pt II of Sch 3 to the 1967 Act contemplate (in para 7) the possibility of a notice by the landlord not admitting a tenant's claim to enfranchisement, indeed, they impose an obligation on the landlord to give a notice saying whether or not he admits the claim, and lay down a minimum period before the expiry of which the tenant is disabled from applying to the court to enforce his right. But it would, I think, be very difficult to infer merely from the tenant's failure to pursue a claim which was plainly disputed and which, at the time, appeared to be disputed on sustainable grounds, a promise not to pursue it further. He couples this, however, with the subsequent correspondence in which the applicant clearly implies that he does not put himself in the category of tenants having a right to enfranchise and with the abortive negotiations for the grant of an extension of the existing lease which, he submits, were clearly inconsistent with a continuing intention to proceed with the acquisition of the freehold under the 1975 notice.

This would, no doubt, be a formidable point if the estate had in some way altered its position in reliance on the negotiations. Nothing of that sort, however, is or can be alleged and the judge found himself quite unable to spell out of the inactivity and the correspondence the necessary contract for abandonment. For my part, I entirely agree with him. Even granted, for the moment, that the applicant's conduct would justify the inference that he was, as it were, making an offer of a promise to release the estate from any rights which might have accrued from the notice (or, if one prefers it, a promise to release the estate from any obligation to enfranchise as a result of the notice) I find it quite impossible to find anything from which any counter-promise or release on the part of the estate can be inferred. If it is suggested (and there is a measure of justification in the assertion) that the inferences of mutual promises which the court can draw objectively from the conduct of parties are somewhat artificial, at least they must be inferences which do not fly in the face of the proved facts. It seems to me quite impossible to infer from Mr Lingren's conduct any sort of promise or release of any kind. Quite apart from his own evidence that he never for a moment thought that the applicant ever had any rights, nobody looking at the correspondence could, in my judgment, draw any inference beyond this that the estate had rejected the claim, that it thought throughout that it had rightly rejected the claim and that it never departed from that position. Essentially, the abandonment on which counsel for the respondents is compelled to rely is, by the very nature of the case, entirely unilateral and unsupported by any consideration in the form of any inferential counter-promise or release on the part of his clients.

We have been referred by counsel for the respondents to the judgment of Upjohn J in *Grice v Dudley Corp* [1957] 2 All ER 673 at 679, [1958] Ch 329 at 339 in which it might, at first sight, appear that he contemplated the possibility of an effective unilateral abandonment. Dealing, as he was there, with the position of a promoter under the Lands Clauses (Consolidation) Act 1845 he observed: '... the [promoter] may evince an intention to abandon [his] rights given to [him] by the notice to treat, in which case the owner is entitled to treat those rights as abandoned.'

It is, however, clear from *Simpsons Motor Sales (London) Ltd v Hendon Corp* [1962] 3 All ER 75 at 81–82, [1963] Ch 57 at 83–84, in this court, in which the same judge delivered the judgment of the court that the term 'abandonment' was being used by him to comprehend a number of different concepts. In the context of compulsory purchase orders it is used to express the special rule peculiar to such cases that unreasonable delay in proceedings with the purchase may bar the promoter from proceeding under a notice to treat. Secondly it is used as describing a proposal to proceed with the purchase for a purpose other than that for which it was originally authorised. Thirdly it is used in the sense of evincing an intention not to proceed at all, and in this latter context, Upjohn LJ made it clear that he had no different contemplation of the operation of the concept from that subsequently expressed by the House of Lords in *The Hannah Blumenthal* case, for he quoted from the judgment of Lord Bramwell in *Tiverton and North Devon Rly Co v Loosemore* (1884) 9 App Cas 480 at 506 where he said:

> 'I quite agree that they might abandon their notice to purchase. If they had said so in so many words, and the respondent had assented, no doubt the notice would have ceased to have any effect. It would have operated like an agreement to rescind a contract. And no doubt what can be done in words can be done by conduct; and further it can be done unintentionally by conduct such that those to be affected by it reasonably infer the intention.'

For the reasons which I have endeavoured to express I can find no conduct here which could, in my judgment, properly be treated as justifying any assumption of the mutual promises necessary to support an abandonment. But I question in any event whether it is permissible on the facts to infer even a unilateral promise on the part of the applicant. The position with which he was faced is the not unfamiliar one in which one claiming a right is met by a challenge to its existence which appears to be based on unassailable legal grounds. It is very difficult in those circumstances to see how the reasonable man, looking at the position objectively, could infer from a reluctant acquiescence in the validity of the objection any sort of promise not to proceed with the claim if in fact the objection turns out to be ill-founded. Counsel for the applicant has referred us to two cases in this court, *James v Heim Gallery (London) Ltd* (1980) 41 P & CR 269, and *Amherst v James Walker Goldsmith and Silversmith Ltd* [1983] 2 All ER 1067, [1983] 1 Ch 305, in which it has been sought unsuccessfully to rely on a grudging acceptance of what was thought on both sides to be the legal position as constituting an abandonment by a landlord of his right to seek a rent review.

The following passages from the judgment of Buckley LJ in *James v Heim Gallery (London) Ltd* (at 277) seems particularly appropriate to the facts of the instant case:

> 'It seems to me that the plaintiffs, although they formally reserved their position for a short time, accepted that the point taken by the defendants was a valid point, or at least was a point which the plaintiffs would be unwise to contest in the light of the law as then understood. That, in my view, would involve nothing in the nature of a promise. To bow to the inevitable, or the near inevitable, is quite different from agreeing to forgo a right. Even assuming that the plaintiffs did always regard the

point as of doubtful validity, it seems to me that the mere fact that they did not pursue it imports no promise or representation that they would not do so at any later time. As the authorities then stood, it would have been very probable that no conclusive decision would have been reached short of the House of Lords. In these circumstances a potential plaintiff might very justifiably and reasonably choose to hold his hand in the hope that the point might be cleared up in litigation between other litigants before deciding whether to press his claim.'

All that seems equally applicable in the circumstances of the instant case and I cannot, for my part, attribute to the subsequent inquiry by the applicant as to the estate's willingness to treat with tenants not entitled to enfranchise any promissory quality. It shows, in my judgment, no more than the grudging acceptance of what everyone then thought was the legal position.

In my judgment, therefore, reliance on the concept of abandonment is of no assistance to the respondents and the judge was right in so holding.

I turn, therefore, to the issue of limitation. The way in which counsel for the respondents puts his case is this. Section 5(1) of the 1967 Act provides that, once a tenant entitled to enfranchise has given notice of his desire to have the freehold—

> 'the rights and obligations of the landlord and the tenant arising from the notice shall inure for the benefit of and be enforceable against them, their executors, administrators and assigns to the like extent (but no further) as rights and obligations arising under a contract for a sale . . . freely entered into between the landlord and tenant . . .'

By sub-s (3) of the same section it is provided that:

> 'In the event of any default by the landlord or the tenant in carrying out the obligations arising from any such notice, the other of them shall have the like rights and remedies as in the case of a contract freely entered into.'

Thus, counsel for the respondents argues, the 1967 Act, in conjunction with the notice, creates statutorily a perfectly ordinary simple contract for sale and s 5 of the Limitation Act 1980 applies. That provides that 'an action founded on simple contract shall not be brought after the expiration of six years from the date on which the cause of action accrued'. Accordingly, counsel for the respondents submits that on the receipt of the respondents notice of non-admission in March 1975 there accrued to the applicant a right to reply to the county court to enforce the landlords' obligations and that equally includes an application for the declaration sought in this case. Thus the claim became barred in March 1981. Alternatively, he claims that the refusal of the estate to proceed constituted a repudiation of the subsisting contract created by the notice which was accepted by the applicant's letter of 24 November 1976, thus giving rise to a cause of action which became barred at latest by November 1982. As regards this latter point, the judge rejected this as a correct analysis of the position and I agree with him. He also rejected the first contention of counsel for the respondents on two alternative grounds. In the first place, he held that if and so far as the 1967 Act gave rise to a cause of action enabling the applicant to apply to the court for a declaration as to his rights, it was not a cause of action to which the Limitation Act 1980 applied. The Act and the regulations made under it constituted, he thought, a special statutory code regulating the procedure of enfranchisement to which the provisions of the Limitation Act 1980 do not apply. But, secondly, and in any event, he held that there had never been any acceptance of the respondent's repudiation of the statutory contract from which time could run.

In seeking to uphold the judge's decision on the former point, counsel for the applicant draws attention to the terms of the Limitation Act 1980. As he points out, the limitation of actions is entirely statutory and an action will be barred only if there is some period of limitation applicable to it under the statute. The right to apply to the county court under s 20(2) of the 1967 Act for the determination of 'whether a person is entitled to acquire the freehold of a house and premises' is, he submits, not one which fits easily within any of the headings of the 1980 Act. It is not 'founded on a simple contract' but on a statutory procedure which produces incidents akin to but not precisely the same as those produced by a simple contract. For instance, s 5(2) of the 1967 Act imposes statutory restrictions on the assignability of the tenant's rights and indeed provides that the notice shall cease to have any effect if the tenant assigns his tenancy but without the benefit of the notice. While it is true that sub-s (3) of s 5 confers 'the like rights and remedies as in the case of a contract freely entered into' that subsection does not make the statutory rights into contractual rights and does not purport to subject the rights and remedies conferred to the period of limitation prescribed by the Limitation Act. Speaking for myself, I find some difficulty in treating the statutory rights as if they were in all respects the same as a simple contract. The purpose of s 5 of the 1967 Act appears to be simply to regulate the way in which and the persons by and against whom claims can be pursued. The obligation to enfranchise stems not from this section but from s 8(1) of the 1967 Act, which provides as follows:

> 'Where a tenant of a house has under this Part of this Act a right to acquire the freehold, and gives to the landlord written notice of his desire to have the freehold, then except as provided by this Part of this Act the landlord shall be bound to make to the tenant, and the tenant to accept, (at the price and on the conditions so provided) a grant of the house and premises for an estate in fee simple absolute, subject to the tenancy and to tenant's incumbrances, but otherwise free of incumbrances.'

It is, in my judgment, from this section that the rights and duties of the respective parties stem and any claims which fall to be adjudicated on by the court are claims arising from those statutory rights and obligations and not from s 5, which merely applies to them the remedies appropriate to a simple contract. My inclination therefore is to say that the judge was certainly right to reject the submission that in so far as any period of limitation applies it was the period of six years prescribed by s 5 of the 1980 Act. But, that said, the more general question of whether the 1980 Act applies at all becomes academic if counsel for the applicant's further point is a good one. His point, which was rejected by the judge, is simply this, that assuming that there is any appropriate period of limitation applicable, it is the period of 12 years prescribed either by s 8 or by s 15 of the 1980 Act. The latter section relates to actions to recover land and, for my part, I am wholly unpersuaded that an action to enforce the statutory right of enfranchisement falls within that category. The point which counsel for the applicant makes in relation to s 8 of the 1980 Act, however, is a more formidable one. That provides as follows:

> '(1) An action upon a specialty shall not be brought after the expiration of twelve years from the date on which the cause of action accrued.
> (2) Subsection (1) above shall not affect any action for which a shorter period of limitation is prescribed by any other provision of this Act.'

The obvious and most common case of an action on a specialty is an action based on a contract under seal, but it is clear that 'specialty' was not originally confined to such contracts but extended also to obligations imposed by statute. Under the Statute of Limitations 1623 no limit was prescribed for actions on a specialty and it was not until the Civil Procedure Act 1833 that a time limit of 20 years was introduced for 'actions for debt on any bond or other specialty'. There was no statutory definition of a specialty but it was established in *Cork and Bandon Rly Co v Goode* (1853) 13 CB 826, [1843–60] All ER Rep 671 that (to adopt the words of Lord Hanworth MR in *Aylott v West Ham Corp* [1927] 1 Ch 30 at 50)—

> 'where a plaintiff relies and has to rely upon the terms of a statute so that his claim is under the statute the nature of the claim is one of specialty and the twenty years applies.'

*Goode's* case was an action for calls and a similar principle was applied to an action for interest on debenture stock (see *Re Cornwall Minerals Rly Co* (1897) 2 Ch 74) and to an action for recovery of rates and duties imposed by statute (see *Shepherd v Hills* (1855) 11 Exch 55, 155 ER 743). A distinction, however, was drawn between the case where all that the statute did was to make binding a contract which otherwise would not be binding or to vary one term of a contract (see *Aylott's* case and *Gutsell v Reeve* [1936] 1 KB 272, [1935] All ER Rep 117) and the case where the action rested on the statute and only on the statute (see, for instance, *Pratt v Cook & Co (St Paul's) Ltd* [1940] 1 All ER 410, [1940] AC 437). Broadly the test is whether any cause of action exists apart from the statute (see *Pratt's* case [1940] 1 All ER 410 at 413, [1940] AC 437 at 446 per Lord Atkin).

It seems to me to be quite clear that in the instant case any cause of action which the applicant has derives from the statute and from the statute alone. Apart from the statutory provisions he could have no claim and it is only by virtue of the statute and the regulations made thereunder that there can be ascertained the amount of the price to be paid under the statutory contract the terms of which can be gathered only from the sections of the 1967 Act and the schedules. Subject, therefore, to one question, namely whether the word 'specialty' as used in the Limitation Act 1939 and the 1980 Act has assumed a more limited meaning than it originally bore, I have no doubt at all that the applicant's claim is a claim on a specialty.

The doubt, if it be a doubt, arises from the way in which sums recoverable under statute were dealt with in the 1939 Act and from certain observations of Goddard LJ and Lord Maugham in two cases referred to below. The provisions which now appear as s 8 of the 1980 Act were contained in substantially the same form in s 2(3) of the 1939 Act save that what is now sub-s (2) of s 8 there appeared as a proviso. Sums of money payable under statute were however dealt with specifically in s 2(1)(*d*) which provided a period of six years for 'actions to recover any sum recoverable by virtue of any enactment, other than a penalty or forfeiture or sum by way of penalty or forfeiture'. Now on the face of it this did not and could not affect the meaning of the word 'specialty' in s 2(3). Indeed the reference to an action for which a shorter period of limitation is prescribed in the proviso rather underlines that such an action *is* an action on a specialty but one for which a special limitation period is prescribed elsewhere in the Act. However, in *Leivers v Barber Walker & Co Ltd* [1943] 1 All ER 386 at 397, [1943] KB 385 at 398 Goddard LJ, in the course of reviewing the history of the statutory provisions and referring to *Goode's* case, observed:

> 'The Act of 1939 has, however, effected a material change in the law in this respect. Debts recoverable by virtue of an enactment are now subject to the same period of limitation as those arising from simple contracts, while a different period is prescribed for specialties. In my opinion, therefore, "specialties" must now be confined to deeds or contracts under seal.'

These observations were obiter but they have been adopted by textbook writers as an authoritative exposition of the meaning of the word in s 2(3) of the 1939 Act (see *Stroud's Judicial Dictionary* (4th edn, 1974) vol 5, p 2593). Undoubtedly the effect of the combination of sub-ss (1)(*d*) and (3) of s 2 of the 1939 Act was that the period of limitation of 12 years for the recovery of debts or sums of money was restricted to contracts under seal, so that to that extent what Goddard LJ said was not inaccurate; but with respect, I do not for my part see that it follows that the ancient and accepted meaning of 'specialty' as including causes of action based on statute was in any way altered. Undoubtedly the word immediately suggests a contract under seal and, no doubt, the word is used loosely as connoting a specialty debt. Thus in *R v Williams* [1942] 2 All ER 95 at 101, [1942] AC 541 at 551 Lord Maugham observed:

> 'The word "specialty" is sometimes used to denote any contract under seal, but it is more often used in the sense of a specialty debt, that is, an obligation under seal securing a debt, or a debt due from the Crown or under statute . . .'

Nevertheless it would, in my judgment, be wrong to deduce from this that the word 'specialty' where it is used in the Limitation Acts is, as a matter of construction, confined to specialty debts much less to obligations arising specifically under contracts under seal and in no other way.

Speaking for myself, I have found counsel for the applicant's argument on this point persuasive. In my judgment, if and so far as the 1980 Act applies to a cause of action arising out of the enfranchisement provisions of the 1967 Act, the applicable provisions are those contained in s 8 and the appropriate period of limitation is 12 years.

It follows, therefore, that the judge was right in concluding that the applicant's claim was not barred by limitation.

Counsel for the respondents has not sought to argue before us the third ground which he urged on the judge for refusing the applicant the relief which he sought, namely that the contract created by the statute was not, in the circumstances, any longer capable of specific performance. The judge rejected the respondents' contentions on this point, but in any event the question appears to me to be largely irrelevant to the only question which the judge was called on to decide, namely whether the applicant had lost or still retained his entitlement under the 1967 Act. If his entitlement remained, the question of whether the appropriate relief was specific performance or damages was immaterial to the declaration sought.

I turn, therefore, to counsel for the respondents' final point, which is that, inasmuch as a lengthy period has elapsed during which, if the statutory contract had been implemented, his clients would have had the purchase money and earned interest on it and inasmuch as the value of the land has increased greatly, there is a degree of hardship which renders it inequitable that the applicant should be granted the declaration which he seeks. A declaration, he points out, is a discretionary remedy and he relies on the hardship and lapse of time as a reason for saying that that discretion should not be exercised in the applicant's favour. I confess to having been puzzled at first not only as to the basis of but also as to the reason for this submission. The applicant's entitlement undoubtedly came into existence on the giving of notice in 1975. If it was not either discharged or barred by limitation it must still exist, whether the court so declares or not. It transpired, however, that what counsel for the respondents was suggesting was that a declaration should be withheld so that, in any subsequent proceedings based on the undoubted entitlement, the refusal of a declaration and the consequent dimissal of the application (since that is the only relief claimed) could be relied on as raising an issue estoppel which would effectively bar the applicant from claiming any other relief. Speaking for myself, I can hardly imagine any less meritorious reason for declining to declare the applicant entitled to the rights which he has established in the proceedings. The judge took the view that once the applicant had established his rights he did not, in any real sense, have any discretion to exercise about whether he declared them to be established, but he also held that, if and so far as he had any discretion, there was no good reason why it should not be exercised in favour of the applicant. I have to declare myself unsurprised by this conclusion, with which I entirely agree.

Accordingly, I would dismiss this appeal.

**MAY LJ.** I agree.

**SIR ROGER ORMROD.** I agree and have nothing further to add.

*Appeal dismissed. Leave to appeal to the House of Lords refused.*

Solicitors: *Boodle Hatfield & Co* (for the respondents); *Taylor Garrett* (for the applicant).

Frances Rustin    Barrister.

# Damon Cia Naviera SA v Hapag-Lloyd International SA
# The Blankenstein, The Bartenstein, The Birkenstein

COURT OF APPEAL, CIVIL DIVISION
STEPHENSON, FOX AND ROBERT GOFF LJJ
24, 25, 26, 27 JULY, 1 NOVEMBER 1984

*Contract – Offer and acceptance – Acceptance – Execution of memorandum of agreement – Payment of deposit – Terms agreed by exchange of telexes – Parties agreeing that 10% deposit payable on signing of memorandum of agreement – Memorandum not signed and deposit not paid – Whether contract validly concluded by telexes – Whether payment of deposit a condition precedent to conclusion of contract.*

*Contract – Damages for breach – Deposit – Sale of ships – Purchaser agreeing to pay deposit as security – Purchaser failing to pay deposit and to complete purchase – Vendor reselling ships for less than contract price – Vendor's actual loss less than amount of unpaid deposit – Whether vendor entitled to recover amount of deposit – Whether vendor limited to recovering actual loss as damages.*

In 1977 negotiations for the sale of three ships took place between the sellers and the intending buyers, whose identity was not disclosed to the sellers. Instead the buyers were represented in the negotiations by two brothers, who indicated their intention to nominate a company as a subsequent purchaser. By 8 July 1977 the principal terms of the sale had been agreed by exchanges of telexes between brokers acting for the parties except that the name of the purchasing company had not been disclosed. By the terms of the sale the purchase price was to be $US2,365,000 and a deposit of 10% was to be paid by the buyers. The sellers' broker forwarded a memorandum of agreement dated 8 July 1977, incorporating the agreed terms, to the buyers' broker for execution by the brothers for and on behalf of companies to be nominated later. Clause 2 of the memorandum provided for payment of a deposit of 10% on the execution of the contract and cl 13 provided that in the event of the buyers failing to pay the purchase price the sellers could cancel the contract and retain the deposit. On 1 August by telex to the sellers' broker the buyers' broker nominated a Panamanian company as the purchaser and requested that a new memorandum of agreement be prepared on that basis. A few hours later the brothers acquired shares in the nominated company and were made directors; one brother was appointed chairman and the other treasurer of the company. Under Panamanian law a chairman had power to negotiate, conclude, ratify and affirm contracts made in the company's name. A further memorandum of agreement was sent to the buyer's broker immediately and on 3 and 5 August the buyers' broker sent telexes which indicated the chairman's intention to continue with the purchase. On 9 August the sellers by telex gave the buyers until 12 August to sign the agreement and pay the deposit, failing which the contract would be rescinded. On 15 August, after a final telex to the buyers, the sellers sold the ships to another purchaser for $US2,295,000. The sellers claimed to be entitled to receive the deposit from the company, but it refused to pay. The dispute was referred to arbitration. The arbitrator held that the parties had concluded an enforceable agreement on 8 July 1977 which anticipated the later nomination of the company as purchaser and further held that, although the company's failure to execute the memorandum and pay the deposit was a repudiatory breach which entitled the sellers to withdraw from the sale, the fact that payment of the deposit was conditional on the signing of the memorandum meant that the company was only liable to pay the damage suffered by the sellers, which he assessed at $US60,000. At the request of the company the arbitrator stated a special case for the court to determine whether there was a binding contract concluded between the sellers and the company and whether the sellers were entitled to recover the amount of the deposit from the company. The judge held that a valid contract had been concluded by the exchange of telex messages and that the sellers were entitled to recover the amount of the deposit as damages for breach of the obligation to pay the deposit incurred under the contract. The company appealed contending, inter alia, that no contract had been entered into, since no memorandum of agreement was ever signed and no deposit had been paid, and that the sellers could not recover the amount of the unpaid deposit, since cl 2 of the memorandum of agreement provided for payment of the deposit 'on signing' the contract and the contract had never been signed.

**Held** – The company's appeal would be dismissed for the following reasons—

(1) The execution of a memorandum of agreement was not contemplated by the parties as being a prerequisite to the conclusion of the contract, since it was open to the parties to agree to execute a formal document incorporating terms which they had previously agreed and that agreement would be a binding contract. In the circumstances there was no indication that the agreed terms of sale were intended to be subject to the execution of a memorandum. Furthermore, actual payment of the deposit was not necessarily a condition precedent to the formation of a contract. The parties had entered into an executory sale agreement, all the terms of which had been finalised, and there was no reason to infer that a contract did not arise until the deposit was paid, since the provision for such payment was a fundamental term of the contract itself. Accordingly, since all the terms for the sale had been agreed by 8 July, the fact that the company failed to sign the memorandum of agreement and failed to pay the deposit did not prevent a binding contract from arising. The company was bound by that contract since the chairman had full power to make and ratify contracts on behalf of the company and by his conduct, including the authorising of certain telexes indicating the company's desire to preform the contract, he was to be taken as accepting and ratifying the contract on behalf of the company (see p 481 *e f* and *h* to p 482 *a*, p 484 *a* to *f*, p 485 *f* to *h*, p 488 *j*, p 489 *c* to *j*, p 490 *e* to p 491 *b* and p 492 *g*, post); dictum of Goulding J in *Myton Ltd v Schwab-Morris* [1974] 1 All ER at 331 and *Millichamp v Jones* [1983] 1 All ER 267 applied; *Myton Ltd v Schwab-Morris* [1974] 1 All ER 326 disapproved in part.

(2) (Goff LJ dissenting) Prior to accepting the company's repudiation of the contract on 15 August, the sellers had a vested right to sue the company for breach of its obligation to sign the memorandum of agreement within a reasonable time. Since the object of requiring the company to sign the memorandum was to oblige it to pay the deposit, the sellers were entitled to damages which would place them in the same position as if the company's contractual obligation to sign the memorandum had been performed. Had the company signed the memorandum, the sellers could have sued it for the amount of the deposit, and accordingly that fact should be reflected in the damages recoverable for the breach of the obligation. Furthermore, since the right to sue for breach of contract had accrued before the sellers accepted the company's repudiation of the contract, the sellers' right to damages in the amount of the deposit was unaffected by that repudiation (see p 486 *d* to p 487 *b* and *f* to p 488 *a h j* and p 492 *g h*, post); *Dewar v Mintoft* [1912] 2 KB 373 applied; *Lowe v Hope* [1969] 3 All ER 605 considered.

Decision of Leggatt J [1983] 3 All ER 510 affirmed.

**Notes**

For novation of contractual rights, see 9 Halsbury's Laws (4th edn) paras 580–584, and for cases on the subject, see 12 Digest (Reissue) 735–745, 5301–5370.

**Cases referred to in judgments**

*Beck v Box* (1973) 231 EG 1295.
*Casson v Roberts* (1862) 32 LJ Ch 105.
*Dewar v Mintoft* [1912] 2 KB 373.

*Hinton v Sparkes* (1868) LR 3 CP 161.
*Johnson v Agnew* [1979] 1 All ER 883, [1980] AC 367, [1979] 2 WLR 487, HL.
*Lowe v Hope* [1969] 3 All ER 605, [1970] Ch 94, [1969] 3 WLR 582.
*McDonald v Dennys Lascelles Ltd* (1933) 48 CLR 457, Aust HC.
*Millichamp v Jones* [1983] 1 All ER 267, [1982] 1 WLR 1422.
*Myton Ltd v Schwab-Morris* [1974] 1 All ER 326, [1974] 1 WLR 331.
*Pollway Ltd v Abdullah* [1974] 2 All ER 381, [1974] 1 WLR 493, CA.
*Portaria Shipping Co v Gulf Pacific Navigation Co Ltd, The Selene G* [1981] 2 Lloyd's Rep 180.
*Rugg (C H) & Co Ltd v Street* [1962] 1 Lloyd's Rep 364.
*Sociedade Portuguesa de Navios Tanques Ltda v Hvalfsisk Polaris A/S* [1952] 1 Lloyd's Rep 71; affd [1952] 1 Lloyd's Rep 407, CA.

**Appeal**
The appellant, Damon Cia Naviera SA (Damon), and the respondents, Hapag-Lloyd International SA (the sellers), by consent appointed Robert William Reed as sole arbitrator to determine a dispute between the parties whereby the sellers claimed against Damon $US236,500, being 10% of the purchase price for the motor vessels Blankenstein, Bartenstein and Birkenstein which Damon failed to pay as a deposit pursuant to cl 2 of a memorandum of agreement dated 8 July 1977 which was not executed by Damon, or alternatively damages in the sum of $US67,500 representing the loss suffered by the sellers on the resale of the vessels. The arbitrator held that Damon had been in breach of the sale contract and that the sellers were entitled to damages of $US60,000 representing the loss suffered by them on the resale of the vessels. At the request of Damon the arbitrator stated a special case for the decision of the High Court pursuant to s 21(1) of the Arbitration Act 1950 to determine, inter alia, (1) whether there was a binding contract concluded between the sellers and Damon for the sale of the motor vessels, (2) whether the sellers were entitled to damages from Damon and if so in what amount, and (3) whether the sellers were entitled to recover from Damon the amount of the deposit provided for in cl 2 of the memorandum of agreement. On 26 May 1983 Leggatt J held ([1983] 3 All ER 510) that there was a binding agreement concluded between the sellers and Damon for the sale of the ships and that the sellers were entitled to damages in the amount of the deposit, being $US236,500. Damon appealed. The facts are set out in the judgment of Fox LJ.

*Bernard Eder* for Damon
*Martin Moore-Bick* for the sellers.

*Cur adv vult*

1 November. The following judgments were delivered.

**FOX LJ** (giving the first judgment at the invitation of Stephenson LJ). This is an appeal from a decision of Leggatt J ([1983] 3 All ER 510) on a special case stated by an arbitrator, Mr Robert Reed, pursuant to s 21(1) of the Arbitration Act 1950.
  The case is concerned with an agreement for the sale of three ships called Blankenstein, Bartenstein and Birkenstein which were owned by the respondents, Hapag-Lloyd International SA (the sellers). The arbitrator decided that there was a concluded contract for the sale of the ships to the appellant, Damon Cia Naviera SA (Damon) and he awarded the sellers $US60,000 damages for breach of that contract. The sellers contended that they were entitled instead to the sum of $US236,000, being the amount of the deposit which Damon failed to pay. That contention was accepted by Leggatt J. Damon now appeal. The appeal raises questions on the law of contract which are, to some extent, the subject of conflicting authorities.
  I come to the facts of the case in more detail. The sellers decided to sell the three ships at about the end of 1976. They were small general cargo vessels built in 1955 or thereabouts. With the introduction of containers they had become of limited use. They

did not prove very easy to sell; there were a number of inquiries and offers which came
to nothing. Then in mid-April 1977 Mr Nebelsiek, one of the brokers acting for the
sellers, made contact with a broker in the Piraeus, Mr Panos, who was acting for two
Greek businessmen, Mr Menelaos Raftopoulos and his brother Mr George Raftopoulos.
Some negotiations between Mr Panas and Mr Nebelsiek then ensued, and in June 1977
Mr George Raftopoulos made an inspection of two of the ships at Amsterdam and found
them acceptable. Thereafter (I quote from the award)—

> 'formal negotiations commenced with a telex dated 4th July 1977 from Mr. Panas
> to Mr. Nebelsiek containing "an Official firm offer" for all three vessels at a price of
> $2,250,000. The offer was expressed to be made . . . for and on behalf of Messrs.
> Raftopoulos of Athens and for company or companies to be nominated by them in
> due course . . .'

Mr Panas had, it seems, earlier informed Mr Nebelsiek that, as is commonly the
practice when secondhand ships are bought and sold, those conducting the negotiations,
in this case the Raftopoulos brothers, did not intend to buy the vessels personally but
would (as the arbitrator found)—

> 'eventually nominate one or more companies in their control whose name(s)
> would be inserted into the contract as the real purchaser.'

Negotiations proceeded by means of telex messages until 8 July 1977. By that date, so the
arbitrator found—

> 'all the terms and conditions of the sale were agreed save that the name of the
> purchasing company or companies had yet to be disclosed.'

With one exception none of those telex messages is set out in the special case. Neither
side, however, takes any point on that. It is common ground that the agreement reached
by 8 July incorporated the terms of the Norwegian Shipbrokers' Association's Sale Form
agreement. The exception to which I have referred is a telex of 8 July 1977 from Mr
Nebelsiek to Mr Panas which is in the following terms:

> '. . . I AM VERY PLEASED TO RECONFIRM THE DEAL AT USD 2,365,000—CASH FOR THE
> THREE VESSELS EN BLOC. RE PARAGRAPH 7 AS PER YOUR STIPULATION, ALL OTHER TERMS
> HAVE BEEN AGREED. SELLERS SUPERVISORY BOARD APPROVAL HAS BEEN OBTAINED. I AM
> DRAWING UP MEMORANDUM OF AGREEMENT ON MONDAY AND KINDLY ASKING TO LET US
> KNOW EXACT STYLE AND ADDRESS OF BUYING COMPANY.'

As regards the position as it stood immediately after the conclusion of negotiations on 8
July 1977, the arbitrator makes the following finding:

> 'It was quite evident at this stage as confirmed at the hearing orally by Mr.
> Nebelsiek and in statement form by Mr. Panas, that both these experienced brokers
> were convinced that they had concluded a valid sale contract between their respective
> principals and all that remained was the performance by the Sellers and the
> Respondents of their respective obligations.'

After 8 July there followed an exchange of telexes between the brokers over a period of
some days. On 11 July Mr Panas telexed:

> 'SORRY FOR DELAY IN TELEXING DETAILS FOR M.O.A. BUT UNDERSTAND BUYERS ARE IN
> CONSULTATION WITH THEIR SOLICITORS AS TO THE EXACT STYLE THEY WILL OFFICIALLY USE
> . . .'

On 12 July Mr Panas replied:

> 'IN ORDER SAVE TIME AND EXPEDITE SIGNATURES AND DEPOSIT OF 10% SHOULD SUGGEST
> YOU ISSUE M.O.A. IN THE NAME OF MESSRS. MENELAOS RAFTOPOULOS AND GEORGE
> RAFTOPOULOS OF 10, EUPOLIDOS STREET, ATHENS AND URGE MAIL IT SIGNED BY SELLERS.
> SHOULD FARTHER SUGGEST YOU MAKE A NOTE THAT PRIOR OF DELIVERY OF EACH SHIP THE

OFFICIALLY PURCHASING COMPANY SHOULD HAVE TO BE NOMINATED BY BUYERS FOR BILL OF SALE PURPOSES.'

On 12 July Mr Panas telexed:

'HAD JUST NOW A PHONE CONVERSATION WITH MR. MENELAOS RAFTOPOULOS (WHO IS THE SENIOR ONE) AND WHO CONFIRMED THAT FORMATION OF THE PANAMANIAN COMPANIES WHO WILL OFFICIALLY APPEAR AS BUYERS PER EACH SHIP IN DUE COURSE AND THAT HE IS PRESSING PANAMANIAN CONSULATE TO EXPEDITE FORMALITIES. HOWEVER PERSONALLY MAINTAIN VIEW EXPRESSED IN MY PREVIOUS TELEX (WITH ONLY ONE EVENTUAL ALTERATION, ONE NAME TO BE INSERTED ONLY THAT OF MR. MENELAOS RAFTOPOULOS) . . .'

Also on 12 July Mr Nebelsiek replied to Mr Panas that he had prepared the memorandum of agreement and had inserted as buyers: 'MESSRS. MENELAOS RAFTOPOULOS AND GEORGE RAFTOPOULOS . . . FOR AND ON BEHALF OF COMPANIES STILL TO BE NOMINATED.' A copy of the memorandum of agreement was sent to Mr Panas by Mr Nebelsiek on 15 July. It was dated 8 July. The memorandum used was the Norwegian sale form. It recited that the sellers were Hapag-Lloyd and the buyers Messrs Menelaos and George Raftopoulos for and on behalf of companies still to be nominated. There are two clauses in the memorandum of agreement to which I should specifically refer. They are cll 2 and 13. Clause 2 provides:

'As a security for the correct fulfilment of this contract, the Buyers shall pay a deposit of 10% . . . of the Purchase Money on signing this contract. This amount shall be deposited with Bremer Bank . . . and held by them in a joint account for the sellers and the Buyers . . .'

Clause 13 provides:

'Should the Purchase Money not be paid as per cl 16 [which provided for payment of specified sums on the delivery of each ship], the Sellers have the right to cancel this contract, in which case the amount deposited shall be forfeited to the Sellers. If the deposit does not cover the Sellers' loss, they shall be entitled to claim further compensation for any loss and for all expenses together with interest at the rate of 5% per annum.'

The memorandum, though received by Mr Panas, was never signed by Messrs Raftopoulos or either of them or any company nominated by them.

On 19 July Mr Panas telexed to Mr Nebelsiek as follows:

'M.O.A. IN HAND HANDED OVER TO BUYERS BY SATURDAY MORNING (17TH JULY) HAVE SEEN THEM TODAY AND EXPECT TO HAVE M.O.A. RETURNED TO ME SIGNED EITHER THIS AFTERNOON OR TOMORROW MORNING. MEANTIME FROM CONVERSATION I HAD WITH THEM TODAY GOT FEELING THAT SOME INTERNAL FORMALITIES OF THEM MIGHT [sic] ARE NOT AS YET FULLY SETTLED. HOWEVER AM FOLLOWING EVERYTHING VERY CLOSE INDEED FURTHERMORE HAVE TO REPORT THAT MOST PROBABLY ALL THREE VESSELS WILL BE OFFICIALLY PURCHASED UNDER THE STYLE OF ONE COMPANY ONLY.'

The buyers having failed to sign the memorandum, Mr Panas on 27 July telexed to Mr Nebelsiek:

'OFFICIAL STATEMENT OF BUYERS SHOULD READ AS FOLLOWS QUOTE BUYERS REGRET FOR INCONVENIENCE AND ANXIETY THEY MIGHT CAUSE TO SELLERS BUT THEY CONSCIOUSLY DECLARE THAT DELAY HAS BEEN ENTIRELY UNFORSEEABLE AND BEYOND THEIR CONTROL. BUYERS OFFICIALLY DECLARE THAT THEY FULLY MAINTAIN DEAL ALREADY STIPULATED DURING NEGOTIATIONS CONFIRMED ON 8TH INSTANT AND ASSURE SELLERS THERE HAS NEVER BEEN ANY INTENTION OF STEPPING OUT OF SAME. BUYERS FURTHERMORE DECLARE THAT THE WHOLE INCONVENIENCE WAS CAUSED BECAUSE OF AN UNFORESEEN COMPLICATION WITH BANKERS INVOLVED. SUCH COMPLICATIONS HAVE BEEN NOW SOLVED PRACTICALLY BUT OFFICIALLY WILL BE CONFIRMED BY TUESDAY 2ND AUGUST, WHEN BUYERS WILL PROCEED WITHOUT ANY OTHER DELAYS IN COMPLETE FULFILMENT OF ALL THEIR CONTRACTUAL OBLIGATIONS TOWARDS SELLERS.'

On 28 July Mr Nebelsiek telexed that the sellers agreed to an alteration of the agreement so that the deposit might be lodged by 3 August.

On 1 August Mr Panas telexed to Mr Nebelsiek:

'BUYERS HEREBY NOMINATE AS PURCHASING COMPANY MESSRS. DAMON COMPANIA NAVIERA S.A. . . . THEY FURTHER REQUEST SELLERS TO ISSUE AND URGE FORWARD HERE A NEW M.O.A. (DATED OF COURSE 8TH JULY) BUT IN WHICH DAMON . . . WILL APPEAR AS PURCHASING COMPANY, AGAIN WITH OPTION OF NOMINATION OF FURTHER COMPANIES PRIOR OF DELIVERY OF 2ND AND 3RD UNIT. DO NOT FEEL KEEN ANYMORE TO SOLICIT SUCH REQUESTS ON THEIR BEHALF, BUT AS HAVE BEEN TOLD THAT UPON RECEIPT OF SUCH A M.O.A. THEY WILL TELEX REMIT DEPOSIT ETC., I FEEL COMPELLED TO SUGGEST TO GRANT THEM EVEN THAT, SO THAT FORECLOSE ANY FURTHER ALLEGATION FROM THEIR SIDE THAT THEY MIGHT NEED THAT FOR BANKING FORMALITIES ETC. PLEASE KINDLY CONFIRM ACCORDINGLY AND TRY UTMOST EXPRESS MAIL NEW M.O.A. STILL TODAY.'

On 1 August Mr Nebelsiek sent to Mr Panas by express post a new first page of the memorandum of agreement showing Damon as the buyers.

The facts found by the arbitrator regarding Damon are these. It is incorporated in Panama on 25 May 1977 and was registered there on 1 June 1977. It was created as an 'off the shelf' company. Some time in June or July 1977 the Raftopoulos brothers agreed to acquire Damon from the original subscribers. Pursuant to that agreement at a meeting of the subscribers held in Panama City on 1 August 1977, which took place a few hours after the company had been nominated to the sellers as the buyers, Messrs Raftopoulos were made directors of the company, and Mr Menelaos was made chairman and Mr George was made treasurer. There was, it seems, no discovery regarding the acquisition of the company. As from 1 August 1977 Damon's board of directors consisted of two other persons, Messrs Moschonas. The arbitrator found that it was 'more probable than not' that they knew of Messrs Raftopoulos' intention to nominate Damon as purchaser of the three ships and that they approved of this course. One of the objects of the company as set out in its instrument of incorporation was '. . . acquiring ownership or the use of or operating as Owners . . . any type of vessel'.

The arbitrator made the following finding regarding the Panamanian law as to the powers of the chairman of a company:

'The Chairman of a Panamanian company holds a position equivalent to that of a Managing Director of an English company. It is within his usual authority to negotiate and conclude contracts on the company's behalf or to ratify or affirm contracts made in the company's name. So far as Mr. Menelaos Raftopoulos was concerned, the Sellers were not aware of any limitation on his authority to represent or act on behalf of the Respondents and ostensibly, he was authorised to act on their behalf.'

From the office of Messrs Raftopoulos on 3 August Mr Panas sent the following telex to Mr Nebelsiek:

'IN CONFIRMATION OF MY TELEPHONE CONVERSATION REPEAT THAT: MR. RAFTOPOULOS HAS TWO WAYS THROUGH WHICH HAS ARRANGED THE FINANCING OF THE PRESENT DEAL: ONE THROUGH A BANK IN LONDON FROM WHICH HE IS EXPECTING OFFICIAL RECONFIRMATION EITHER STILL TODAY OR ANYHOW TOMORROW, AND A SECOND ONE THROUGH A BANK IN GREECE IN THE FORM OF A BANK GUARANTEE; THE BANK GUARANTEE FROM GREECE IS FROM ERGOBANK, 36 PANEPISTIMIOU STREET, ATHENS AND FOR THE SUM OF 3,250,000 DOLLARS OVER FIVE YEARS . . .'

On 5 August Mr Panas telexed that the Ergobank guarantee had still not arrived and suggested that the sellers 'should put matters on a legal footing'.

On 9 August Mr Panas telexed a notification on behalf of the sellers that—

'WE ARE GIVING YOU A FINAL LIMIT TO SETTLE MATTERS IN ACCORDANCE WITH THE AGREEMENT REACHED AND CONSEQUENTLY REQUEST YOU TO LET US KNOW BY FRIDAY THE

12TH AUGUST—5 P.M. GERMAN TIME THAT YOU SIGN THE MEMORANDUM OF AGREEMENT WITH HAPAG-LLOYD INTERNATIONAL S.A. AND LODGE THE 10% DEPOSIT. IN CASE YOU DO NOT ACCORDINGLY WITHIN THE TIME LIMIT HAPAG-LLOYD WILL RESCIND THE CONTRACT AND RESERVE ALL THEIR RIGHTS FOR COMPENSATION OF LOSSES CAUSED BY YOU . . .'

Damon failed to sign the memorandum of agreement or pay the deposit and on 15 August Damon was notified that the sellers had 'withdrawn from the contract and reserve all their rights for compensation or losses'.

On 15 August 1977 the sellers sold all three ships for $US2,295,000.

The arbitrator made a further finding to which I should refer, and which was as follows:

> 'Following the exchange of offers between the parties, the clean acceptance by the Sellers of the purchase offer of 15.10 hours 8th July, made without any "subjects" would be regarded in the Shipping Market as a binding contract of sale not requiring a signed memorandum of agreement to validate it.'

There are now three questions to be determined. First, was any binding contract concluded at all? Second, if there was a binding contract, is it binding on Damon? Third, if the answer to the first two questions is affirmative, can the sellers recover the amount of the unpaid deposit?

The special case contains no findings as to any relevant foreign law save in respect of the powers under Panamanian law of a chairman of a Panamanian company.

Save as aforesaid both sides have proceeded on the basis that any relevant law is the same as that of England.

I come then to the three questions.

*Was there any binding contract?*

The arbitrator concluded that there was and in my opinion he was right to do so. He found that on 8 July all the terms and conditions of the sale, including the price, were agreed save that the name of the purchasing company or companies had yet to be disclosed. So far as the latter point is concerned, I see no reason to suppose that it prevented the conclusion of a binding contract. The arbitrator found that Mr Panas had previously made it clear to Mr Nebelsiek that, as was common practice on the sale of secondhand ships, the Raftopoulos brothers did not intend to buy the ships personally but would eventually nominate one or more companies in their control as the real purchaser.

Counsel for Damon presses on us two objections to the proposition that a contract was entered into. The first is that no memorandum was ever signed. I would agree with counsel for Damon that—

> 'in each case the court has got to make up its mind on the construction of the documents and on the general surrounding circumstances whether the negotiations were not to have contractual force until a formal document was signed.'

(See *C H Rugg & Co Ltd v Street* [1962] 1 Lloyd's Rep 364 at 369 per McNair J.)

But I see nothing in the present case to lead me to the conclusion that the parties contemplated the execution of the memorandum of agreement as a prerequisite to the conclusion of a contract. That they contemplated and indeed agreed on the execution of a written memorandum I accept. But that, of itself, is not conclusive. It is open to parties to agree to execute a formal document incorporating terms which they have previously agreed. That is a binding contract. In the present case, on 8 July all the terms of the sale were agreed. And it seems to me that all the indications are that they were not intended to be subject to the execution of the memorandum. Thus, the arbitrator found (i) that the agreement was without any 'subjects', (ii) that the two experienced brokers, Mr Panas and Mr Nebelsiek, were convinced that they had concluded a valid contract between their principals and (iii) that the agreement would be regarded in the shipping market as a binding contract not requiring a signed memorandum to validate it.

I therefore reject the argument based on the absence of a signed document.

Counsel for Damon's next objection is based on the failure by the purchaser to pay the deposit. That, he says, prevented any contract of sale from coming into existence at all because the payment of the deposit was a condition precedent to the formation of the contract. At this point I must refer to certain authorities.

*Dewar v Mintoft* [1912] 2 KB 373 was an action before Horridge J. It was a case of a sale of a farm by auction. The farm was knocked down to the defendant. The conditions of sale provided for the payment of a deposit. The defendant refused to pay; he also refused to sign the memorandum of agreement. The plaintiff elected to treat the contract as discharged and sued for damages including the amount of the deposit. The main question was whether there was, on the correspondence after the auction, a sufficient memorandum to satisfy the Statute of Frauds. Horridge J held that there was a sufficient memorandum and that the plaintiff was entitled to damages as claimed. It does not appear to have been suggested that the failure to pay the deposit prevented the contract from coming into existence.

In *Lowe v Hope* [1969] 3 All ER 605, [1970] Ch 94 there was a written agreement providing for the payment of a deposit which was not paid. The vendor by his statement of claim sought recission and not specific performance. However he then moved for judgment, in default of defence, for the amount of the deposit. Pennycuick J refused that application on the ground that, the vendor having elected to rescind the contract, he could not seek to enforce a term of it. In that respect the judge was of opinion that *Dewar v Mintoft*, in which the plaintiff had elected to treat the contract as discharged, was wrongly decided. He does not, however, seem to have doubted that, if the vendor had not elected to rescind, he could have obtained specific performance notwithstanding that the deposit had not been paid.

*Myton Ltd v Schwab-Morris* [1974] 1 All ER 326, [1974] 1 WLR 331 is a direct decision on the matter in relation to sales of land. In that case there was a written agreement for the grant of an underlease. The agreement required the payment of a deposit by the purchaser on the signing of the agreement. The purchaser gave a cheque for the deposit but it was dishonoured. The vendor then informed the purchaser that the contract was rescinded because of the failure to pay the deposit. Subsequently, the purchaser registered a caution against the land to protect its alleged interest under the agreement. The vendor applied for the removal of the caution and put his case, in the alternative, as follows: first, that the requirement in the agreement for the payment of the deposit was a condition precedent to the operation of the agreement as a contract; alternatively, if it was not a condition precedent, it was at any rate a fundamental term of the contract the breach of which entitled the other party to renounce the contract. *Lowe v Hope* was not cited but *Dewar v Mintoft* was.

Goulding J accepted the vendor's first contention and held that, the deposit not having been paid, no contract existed. His view of the matter was stated thus ([1974] 1 All ER 326 at 330, [1974] 1 WLR 331 at 336):

'Speaking in quite general terms for the moment of contracts to sell land or grant a lease of land at a premium, without reference to the particular language of this document, it is well established that a deposit is demanded and paid on the signing of the contract as an earnest of the purchaser's ability and intention to complete the purchase in due course. The vendor, in the normal case, never intends to be bound by the contract without having the deposit in his own or his stakeholder's possession as a protection against possible loss from default by the purchaser. No doubt, it may be thought that where building operations are in progress and still unfinished, the vendor is even more concerned to have such a protection than in other cases. In any ordinary case where a deposit on signing is demanded, if the purchaser says, "I am sorry, I cannot find the deposit", the vendor would naturally reply, "I do not propose to hand over the contract signed by me until I am paid". In the circumstances of the present case, payment by cheque was made and received in the ordinary way as a conditional payment. The cheque not having been met, the plaintiff company can assert that its original rights remain. Accordingly, in my judgment, counsel for the plaintiff company is right to say that cl 2 of the contract stated a condition precedent to the contract taking effect as one of lease or sale, and that the cheque having been returned unpaid the plaintiff company is not bound by the document. There is nothing, in my view, in the language of the document or the special circumstances of the present case to produce a different result from that which I have reached by considering the general nature of the deposit on a contract of sale.'

Goulding J went on to hold that if he was wrong on that point the vendor's alternative argument was correct and that the provision for payment of a deposit was a fundamental term of the contract.

The next case is *Pollway Ltd v Abdullah* [1974] 2 All ER 381, [1974] 1 WLR 493. In that case the vendor had employed auctioneers to sell land. The conditions of sale provided for a deposit to be paid to the auctioneer as agents for the vendors. The property was knocked down to the defendant, who signed a memorandum of purchase. The defendant gave the auctioneer a cheque for the deposit but subsequently stopped payment of the cheque. The purchaser was given time to comply with the obligation but refused. It was held by the Court of Appeal that the auctioneers were entitled to judgment on the cheque. *Myton Ltd v Schwab-Morris* was not cited. Roskill LJ, whose judgment was concurred in by the other members of the court, said ([1974] 2 All ER 381 at 384, [1974] 1 WLR 493 at 496):

'The case appears to have been argued before the learned judge on the footing that the consideration for the cheque was the vendors' obligation to complete the sale. I will assume for the moment that this is correct. On this assumption, the contract of sale . . . still subsisted when the cheque was stopped. The vendors then still remained obliged to complete. True, the vendors became entitled to rescind immediately the cheque was stopped. But they did not immediately exercise that right. So long as they refrained from so doing their obligation to perform the sale contract remained.'

That passage cannot be reconciled with the view that, the deposit not having been paid, no contract existed, though I accept that the point does not seem to have been argued.

In *Millichamp v Jones* [1983] 1 All ER 267, [1982] 1 WLR 1422 there was a written agreement for the purchase of land. It included a provision for payment of a deposit. The purchaser failed to pay the deposit. Warner J held that the payment of the deposit was not a condition precedent to the creation of a contract. Having referred to the authorities which I have mentioned he said ([1983] 1 All ER 267 at 274, [1982] 1 WLR 1422 at 1430):

'. . . it seems to me that unless a distinction is to be made between sales by auction and sales by private treaty, the weight of authority is in favour of the view that a requirement in a contract for the sale of land that a deposit should be paid by the purchaser does not constitute a condition precedent, failure to fulfil which prevents the contract from coming into existence, but is in general to be taken as a fundamental term of the contract, breach of which entitles the vendor, if he so elects, to treat the contract as at an end and to sue for damages including the amount of the unpaid deposit. Nor do I see that anything, either in the authorities or in principle, calls for a distinction to be made in that respect between sales by auction and sales by private treaty.'

In *Portaria Shipping Co v Gulf Pacific Navigation Co Ltd, The Selene G* [1981] 2 Lloyd's Rep 180 the written agreement followed the Norwegian sale form but with some amendments. Clause 2 provided:

'As security for the correct fulfilment of this contract the Buyers shall pay a deposit of 10% . . . of the Purchase Money within 48 hours . . . after signing this Memorandum of Agreement . . .'

The buyers did not pay the deposit and the sellers rescinded. It was held by Robert Goff J that the obligation to pay the deposit was an essential term of the contract. It was not suggested that the payment of the deposit was a condition precedent to the existence of the contract.

Of the cases to which I have referred the condition precedent question was only directly in issue in *Myton Ltd v Schwab-Morris* and *Millichamp v Jones*. While I differ with hesitation from the view of Goulding J, who has much experience in matters relating to the sale of land, I do not feel able to agree that in general, where the agreement provides for the payment of a deposit, such payment is necessarily a prerequisite to the formation of a contract. It may well be that in practice a vendor's solicitors would refuse to exchange contracts until the deposit was in their hands or that of a stakeholder. But in my view, if the parties, as in the present case, actually enter into an executory agreement for sale all the terms of which are finalised, one of them being that a deposit shall be paid, and which objectively is a contractual agreement, I see no reason for inferring that no contract arises until the deposit is paid. The provision for the payment of a deposit is simply a term of the contract. In the absence of special provision it does not seem to me to carry with it any implication that it is a condition precedent to the existence of contractual relations. And in none of the cases to which I have referred, except *Myton Ltd v Schwab-Morris* and *Millichamp v Jones* (in which it failed), does such a suggestion appear to have been advanced at all. It seems also to have been raised before Goulding J in *Beck v Box* (1973) 231 EG 1295 but he did not have to decide it.

Accordingly, I prefer the view of Warner J in *Millichamp v Jones* and hold that the provision for payment of the deposit was not a condition precedent to the formation of a contract. It was in my view a fundamental term of the contract. I entirely agree with the view of Goulding J in *Myton Ltd v Schwab-Morris* [1974] 1 All ER 326 at 331, [1974] 1 WLR 331 at 337 (expressed on the alternative basis that he was wrong as to the condition precedent) that the provision for payment of the deposit was 'a term of so radical a nature that the defendant's failure to comply with it would entitle the plaintiff company to renounce further performance'. (See also *Millichamp v Jones* and *The Selene G.*) The result, in my opinion, is that the provision for payment of the deposit was not a condition precedent to the formation of the contract but was a fundamental term of a concluded contract.

### Was the contract binding on Damon?

It was always understood that the Raftopoulos brothers were not buying the ships in their own name but that they would eventually nominate a company or companies of their own choosing as the purchasers. On 1 August the Raftopoulos brothers nominated Damon as the purchaser. The brothers were as between themselves and the sellers entitled to do that. But a contract cannot be forced on Damon without its agreement. The question is whether, at some time between the nomination of Damon on 1 August and the acceptance of the repudiation of the contract by the sellers on 9 August, there was a novation of the contract in favour of Damon.

Since, as it seems to me, the contractual agreement between the sellers and the brothers entitled the latter to substitute Damon, the issue in the end is whether Damon accepted such substitution.

The nomination of Damon was at 1200 hrs on 1 August. Some time in June, the brothers had entered into an agreement to acquire the company. We do not know at what time that acquisition was effected. Let it be accepted that the Raftopoulos brothers had no authority to nominate Damon at the time the nomination was made. On that assumption the question is whether the nomination was subsequently ratified by Damon. As to that the material facts, in my view, are as follows. (i) Mr Menelaos Raftopoulos became chairman of Damon a few hours after the nomination of Damon. As such he had full power to conclude contracts on Damon's behalf and to ratify and affirm contracts. It is found by the arbitrator that ostensibly he had power to act on Damon's behalf. (ii) The nomination of Damon must have been made with the knowledge and approval of both the Raftopoulos brothers. Thus the telex containing the nomination was in the form 'Buyers hereby nominate . . .' The brothers never resiled from that telex. There is indeed no suggestion that Mr Panas sent any telex without authority. (iii) The arbitrator found that both the other directors of Damon, i e the Messrs Moschonas, probably knew of and approved the intention to nominate. Messrs Moschonas were directors 'as from 1st August'. (iv) The telexes sent by Mr Panas on 3 and 5 August (i e after the nomination) indicate that the Raftopoulos brothers were asserting that the contract, which by then they had sought to novate in favour of Damon, was still on foot and that active steps were being taken to provide the finance to secure its completion. In this respect the arbitrator found:

> 'Although Mr. Panas began to express his pesonal doubts of the Respondents to Mr. Nebelsiek from about 20th July, he continued to receive and put forward instructions received from the Raftopoulos Brothers up to and after 1st August, which gave the impression that the Respondents themselves still expected to perform the contract.'

The respondents were Damon. (v) While we do not know precisely when the Raftopoulos brothers acquired Damon, we know that, when the nomination was made, they had 'already made all the necessary arrangements to acquire the company and knew that they were to become Directors that day'. That being so, I think that, on the balance of probabilities, when, on 1 August, Mr Menelaos was appointed chairman and his brother a director, they in fact owned the company and that their appointment was in consequence of that. (vi) It can properly be inferred that the 'Mr. Raftopoulos' referred to in the telex of 3 August and the 'Raftopoulos' referred to in the telex of 5 August was Mr Menelaos. The only previous reference in the telexes which we have to a brother individually is the reference to Mr Menelaos in Mr Panas's telex of 12 July. Mr Panas went out of his way to add '(who is the senior one)'. It seems to me that when, in the telexes of 3 and 5 August, Mr Panas referred to 'Mr. Raftopoulos' and 'Raftopoulos' he was again referring to Mr Menelaos. In any event I cannot suppose that the telexes were sent without the authority of Mr Menelaos.

In the end one comes, I think, to the following situation. The Raftopoulos brothers had nominated Damon with the ultimate object of novating the contract with Damon as purchaser. On and after 1 August they were anxious to preserve the contract and to that end were, it seems, actively seeking finance and explaining their position to the sellers so as to preserve the contract. It is found by the arbitrator that after 1 August the telexes gave the impression that Damon 'still expected to perform the contract'. Mr Menelaos had full power to make and ratify contracts on behalf of Damon. He and his three co-directors knew and approved of the nomination of Damon. In authorising the telexes of 3 and 5 August which indicated Damon's wish to perform the contract, Mr Menelaos, in my view, must be taken as accepting and ratifying the contract on behalf of Damon. He had full power to do that and there can, I think, be no doubt that it was a result which he wished to achieve. And it is a result which is consistent with the content of the telexes themselves. In my view the contract is binding on Damon.

*Can the sellers recover the amount of the unpaid deposit?*

The contract which I have held existed incorporated the terms of the Norwegian sale form memorandum of agreement, cl 2 of which required the payment by the purchaser of a deposit of 10% purchase money 'on signing this contract'. Clause 13 provides that, if the purchase money is not paid as provided by cl 16, the vendors may cancel the contract and forfeit the deposit.

There are two matters which have to be considered. First, what rights did the sellers have under the contract, in relation to the deposit, immediately prior to the acceptance by the sellers of the repudiation? Second, what was the effect on those rights of the acceptance of the repudiation?

As to the first of those matters counsel for the Damon contends that there is a short answer to any claim for the amount of deposit. Clause 2, he says, provides for payment of the deposit 'on signing' the contract. The contract was never signed and accordingly, he says, the deposit never became payable. That was accepted by the arbitrator. Counsel for the sellers' answer is broadly as follows. On 8 July the parties entered into a binding contract all the terms of which had been agreed. Those terms included an agreement to sign a memorandum incorporating the Norwegian sale form terms. The signing of that memorandum was not a condition precedent to the formation of a contract. Nor was the signing of the memorandum a condition precedent to the payment of the deposit. The signing and the payment were both provisions of a concluded contract which fell due for performance simultaneously. The contract having been concluded on 8 July, those two terms were to be carried out as soon as reasonably possible. The difficulty which I feel about that argument is that, as a matter of language, the provision is not drafted in terms of simultaneous obligations but rather of postponement of the obligation to pay until the signing of the memorandum. It is true that the provision was not, as drafted, directed to the situation which has arisen in the present case where there is a concluded contract before signature of the memorandum. Clause 2 assumes that the memorandum is itself the contract. That however rather emphasises that the clause is contemplating payment after signature since if there is no contract until signature it is probable that the parties would not contemplate payment of the deposit until after signature. On the whole, therefore, I conclude, contrary to the view of the judge, that counsel for the sellers' argument on this point should be rejected. That, however, is not the end of the matter. By 8 July the parties had entered into a binding contract for sale of the ships. The contract incorporated the Norwegian sale form agreement and, as I have already indicated, the parties must have intended that the sale form memorandum of agreement should be signed. It seems to me therefore that, on the contract being entered into on 8 July, (i) the parties became bound to sign the memorandum of agreement incorporating the agreed terms, within a reasonable time, and (ii) the purchaser became bound, on signing the memorandum, to pay the deposit. The purchaser, no doubt, was only under an obligation to sign an accurate memorandum, but it is not suggested that the memorandum sent to Mr Panas by Mr Nebelsiek on 13 July was inaccurate. I think, therefore, that prior to 15 August, when the sellers accepted the repudiation of the contract, a reasonable time for the signing of the memorandum by Damon had expired. Two weeks had elapsed since the nomination of Damon and ten days since Mr Panas's telex of 5 August.

Prior to 15 August, therefore, Damon had become bound to sign the memorandum. Whether, if Damon had been sued for the deposit as such, it could have avoided liability by pleading its own breach of contract in failing to sign the memorandum, I express no view. The matter was not investigated before us. On the view which I take of the case it is not of consequence. Assuming that the sellers had no right to sue for the deposit as such, it is counsel for the sellers' submission that, prior to 15 August, the sellers were entitled to maintain an action for damages against Damon for failure to sign the memorandum and that the damages recoverable must include the value of the right to recover and retain the deposit and hence the value of the deposit itself. In my view that is correct. I accept that in a seller's action against the buyer for non-acceptance of goods and failure to pay the price the measure of damages would normally be the difference between the price under the contract and the market or current price for the goods. The postulated action in the present case, however, is of a different kind. It is not an action for failure to take delivery but an action on a particular term of the contract. That term, I suppose, had a practical use in that it required the terms of the contract to be recorded. But its principal, if not its only, legal consequence was that, on the construction which I have adopted, it was the event which obliged the purchaser to pay the deposit. Damages for breach of contract are a compensation for the loss which the plaintiff has suffered through the breach. Accordingly, the plaintiff is entitled to be placed in the same position as if the contractual obligation had been performed. In the present case, if the obligation had been performed, the sellers could have sued Damon in debt for the amount of the deposit and it seems to me that that should be reflected in the damages recoverable for breach of the obligation. The fact that the sellers would thus recover an amount of damages greater than the general loss of the bargain for sale does not seem to me to be a conclusive answer. The purpose of the deposit was to protect the sellers against the event which actually happened, namely the failure by Damon to complete. In that event the sellers were intended to have secured to it, by forfeiture of the deposit, an amount of money which could well exceed the amount of the general damages recoverable against the purchaser for failure to take delivery and pay the purchase price. Consequently to allow a claim for damages for failure to sign the memorandum, in an amount equal to the amount of the deposit, does not seem to me to distort the intention of the parties but merely to place the sellers in the position which they would be in if Damon had complied with the obligation to sign the memorandum.

Thus far, therefore, I accept counsel for the sellers' contention.

I come to the second question, namely the effect of the acceptance of the repudiation.

The general position I take to be as stated by Dixon J in *McDonald v Dennys Lascelles Ltd* (1933) 48 CLR 457 at 476–477:

'When a party to a simple contract, upon a breach by the other contracting party of a condition of the contract, elects to treat the contract as no longer binding upon him, the contract is not rescinded as from the beginning. Both parties are discharged from the further performance of the contract, but rights are not divested or discharged which have already been unconditionally acquired. Rights and obligations which arise from the partial execution of the contract and causes of action which have accrued from its breach alike continue unaffected. When a contract is rescinded because of matters which affect its formation, as in the case of fraud, the parties are to be rehabilitated and restored, so far as may be, to the position they occupied before the contract was made. But when a contract, which is not void or voidable at law, or liable to be set aside in equity, is dissolved at the election of one party because the other has not observed an essential condition or has committed a breach going to its root, the contract is determined so far as it is executory only and the party in default is liable for damages for its breach.'

This was approved by the House of Lords in *Johnson v Agnew* [1979] 1 All ER 883 at 892, [1980] AC 367 at 396.

This is not a case where the contract was rescinded because of something affecting its formation. It was put an end to by the sellers because of breach of contract by Damon. I should add that the use of the expression 'withdraw' from the contract in the telex of 15 August does not in my view affect that position.

The acceptance by the sellers of Damon's repudiation, therefore, did not affect any rights to which they were entitled under the contract and which had already accrued. The right to damages for failure to sign the memorandum was, it seems to me, such a right. Thus, in my view there was a promise to sign the memorandum; on signature by Damon the deposit was payable; and the deposit was forfeitable if the purchaser wrongfully failed to complete. Because of Damon's failure to sign, the sellers suffered damage because the deposit was not payable. I should mention that cl 13 provides that, if the purchase money is not paid in accordance with cl 16, ie in specified amounts on the delivery of the vessels, the deposit shall be forfeited to the sellers. I do not think that cl 13 does anything more than make it clear that prompt payment of the specified amounts of the purchase price on delivery of each vessel is essential and failure will involve forfeiture of the deposit. But cl 13 does not, it seems to me, detract from cl 2, which states that the deposit is 'security for the correct fulfilment of this contract'. That is in wide terms which are in no way restricted to the circumstances stated in cl 13 and are wholly in accord with the general purposes for which a deposit is given. It is, I think, a matter of necessary implication from the language of cl 2 that if the buyers were in default and refused to complete the contract the deposit might be forfeited. The agreement to forfeit may be implied as well as express (see *Hinton v Sparkes* (1868) LR 3 CP 161 at 165 in the passage there cited from *Casson v Roberts* (1862) 32 LJ Ch 105 at 106). And it normally will be implied unless the contract as a whole shows an intention to exclude forfeiture (see 42 Halsbury's Laws (4th edn) para 244). Thus far, therefore, I would conclude that the sellers are entitled to recover the amount of the deposit by way of damages for breach of contract even though the amount of the deposit exceeds the amount of the general damages. It is said, however, that such a conclusion is inconsistent with *Lowe v Hope* [1969] 3 All ER 605, [1970] Ch 94, which was, in fact, a more straightforward case than the present because under the contract the obligation to pay the deposit had clearly arisen. Before coming to *Lowe v Hope* I should mention *Dewar v Mintoft* [1912] 2 KB 373. In allowing the claim for damages for failure to pay the deposit, Horridge J in that case directed the jury (at 387–388):

'. . . the defendant could not put himself in a better position by refusing to pay the deposit than if the deposit had in fact been paid, in which case it could be retained by the seller . . .'

However, Pennycuick J in *Lowe v Hope* rejected that and said that *Dewar v Mintoft* was wrong. The vendor in *Lowe v Hope* having sought rescission by his statement of claim, then claimed the amount of the unpaid deposit. Pennycuick J said ([1969] 3 All ER 605 at 608, [1970] Ch 94 at 98):

'. . . it seems to me that the vendor, having elected to bring the contract to an end by rescission, is not entitled to insist on the performance of the contract in relation to the deposit. This is admittedly so, insofar as the deposit bears the character of part of the unpaid purchase price. It seems to me that it must equally be so, insofar as the deposit bears the character of a pledge; for once the vendor has rescinded the contract there are no outstanding obligations on the purchaser in respect of which the vendor can be entitled to be protected by a pledge.'

As regards the view of Horridge J that the defendant could not put himself into a better position by refusing to pay the deposit, Pennycuick J said that he did not think that there was any place for such a rule in the present context.

Counsel for the sellers contends that *Dewar v Mintoft* is to be preferred to *Lowe v Hope* because rescission by the injured party only releases the party in breach from future obligations. I think that is right. In deciding *Lowe v Hope* Pennycuick J did not have the advantage of the decision in *Johnson v Agnew* and the clarification of the law which it contained. Pennycuick J remarked that it was admittedly the case that, if the vendor has accepted the purchaser's repudiation, there can thereafter be no recovery in respect of money bearing simply the character of purchase price. That is correct but it is dealing with a different problem. A purchase price is payable in return for a conveyance and if the obligation to convey has gone because of the acceptance of the repudiation there is no longer a purchase and sale to which a purchase price can be related. The right of the vendor to forfeit the deposit is not, however, dependent on completion of the purchase. The right to forfeit arises out of the breach and is, therefore, something quite different from the right to receive the purchase money in return for a conveyance.

The result, in my view, is that *Dewar v Mintoft* was rightly decided. We were referred by counsel for the sellers to *Hinton v Sparkes* (1868) LR 3 CP 161, but I am not sure that the case is of assistance. The deposit was not paid in cash but an IOU was given and Bovill CJ proceeded on the basis that the IOU was for all purposes of the case to be treated as money (at 164–165). The case is not inconsistent with the view which I have taken of the present case and I need not examine it further.

It seems to me therefore that the sellers were at the time when they accepted the repudiation already entitled to a vested right to sue Damon for damages for breach of its obligation to sign the memorandum and that the measure of damages is the amount of the deposit.

Accordingly, I think that Leggatt J came to the right conclusion and I would dismiss the appeal.

**ROBERT GOFF LJ.** The first question which arises in this case is whether any binding contract was concluded. The judge, in agreement with the arbitrator, concluded that a binding contract came into existence on 8 July 1977, on the clean acceptance by the sellers (the respondents before this court) of the purchase offer made on that day by the

Raftopoulos brothers through their broker Mr Panas. At that date, of course, the appellant, Damon Cia Naviera SA, had not yet been nominated as buyer by the Raftopoulos brothers; and so the contract which the judge and the arbitrator held to have been made on 8 July was a contract between the sellers and the Raftopoulos brothers.

Before us, as before the judge, counsel for Damon challenged this conclusion on two grounds. First, he submitted that it was the intention of the parties that there should be no binding contract until the memorandum of agreement in the Norwegian sale form was signed; and, second, he submitted that on a true construction of the contract it was not binding on the parties until the deposit was paid. As neither event occurred, it was his submission that the contract never became binding, even on the Raftopoulos brothers.

I am, like the judge, unable to accept either of these submissions. The first I can deal with shortly. I agree with counsel for Damon that, in accordance with the law as stated by McNair J in *Sociedade Portuguesa de Navios Tanques Ltda v Hvalfsisk Polaris A/S* [1952] 1 Lloyd's Rep 71 at 74–75, the court has to decide on the construction of the relevant documents, considered in the light of the surrounding circumstances, whether it was the intention of the parties that the negotiations were not to have contractual force until a formal document was signed. In agreement with Fox LJ, I cannot discern any such intention from the telex messages which passed between the brokers, considered in the light of the circumstances set out in the special case. The mere facts that the parties intended, as is no doubt usual, that there should be a formal contract in the agreed standard form signed by the parties and that a company was to be nominated as purchaser do not of themselves reveal any such intention; and I feel fortified in this conclusion by the fact that the same view was formed by the two experienced brokers who negotiated the transaction, and by the arbitrator (Mr Robert Reed) who stated in his award that the clean acceptance on 8 July would be regarding in the shipping market as giving rise to a binding contract of sale, not requiring a signed memorandum of agreement to validate it.

Counsel for Damon's second submission under this head raised a more intricate question, though I cannot help commenting that, if it is right, any buyer under this form of agreement who subsequently feels doubts about it has only to drag his feet and then decline to pay the deposit to escape from the consequences of his misjudgment or of any subsequent adverse movement of the market. I approach the matter as follows. The clean acceptance on 8 July was on the terms of the Norwegian sale form. In cl 2 of that form, it is provided that:

'As a security for the correct fulfilment of this contract, the Buyers shall pay a deposit of 10%—ten per cent—of the Purchase Money on signing this contract.'

I am satisfied that in these circumstances, the parties having plainly evinced an intention to be bound on the clean acceptance on 8 July, (i) they became bound to sign a memorandum of agreement in the Norwegian sale form incorporating the terms agreed and (ii) the buyers became bound, on the signature of the memorandum of agreement, to pay the 10% deposit. It may well be that the appropriate form of memorandum of agreement would be prepared by the sellers' brokers, and forwarded by them to the buyers, through their brokers, for signature. If so, then on its receipt, if it was properly drawn up, the buyers would be bound to sign it, and thereupon to pay the 10% deposit. This is the conclusion I would reach as a simple matter of construction of the documents set out in, or exhibited to, the special case; and I am comforted to find that the same view was formed by the arbitrator. It seems that a short leeway may in practice be allowed between the signature of the contract and the payment of the deposit (see *Portaria Shipping Co v Gulf Pacific Navigation Co Ltd, The Selene G* [1981] 2 Lloyd's Rep 180 at 185); and sometimes, as appears from that case, there may be an express agreement that the deposit need not be paid until a specified time after the signature of the memorandum of agreement. But it would be most strange if, the parties having reached agreement through brokers in the ordinary way, the buyers should have a means of escape simply by failing to pay the deposit on signature of the memorandum of agreement.

We were referred to a number of authorities relating to deposits payable under contracts concerning land. In the last analysis, everything must depend on the construction of the terms agreed; and it is not to be forgotten that, in cases concerning land, the transaction is very frequently expressed to be 'subject to contract', and will not be enforceable unless the requirements of s 40 of the Law of Property Act 1925 are fulfilled. Furthermore, in the case of a sale of land not only will the contract usually not be binding until formal contracts are exchanged, but, if the deposit is not available at the time fixed for exchange, the seller will simply decline to exchange contracts and so no binding contract will come into existence. A problem can arise if the seller accepts a cheque from the buyer for the deposit and exchanges contracts on that basis, as appears to have happened in Myton Ltd v Schwab-Morris [1974] 1 All ER 326, [1974] 1 WLR 331, a case concerned with a lease. But, if that should occur, then, unless it is agreed expressly or impliedly that the exchange of contracts should not take effect until the cheque is cleared, a binding contract will, in my judgment, come into existence on the exchange of contracts. However, if the cheque is dishonoured, the vendor will in all probability be entitled to rescind the contract by reason of a misrepresentation of the purchaser, implicit in the giving of the cheque, that there are funds available in his account to meet the cheque and that he has no intention to stop payment of the cheque. Alternatively, if rescission is for any reason not possible, the term as to payment of the deposit having been incorporated in the contract so made and being a fundamental term, the dishonouring of the cheque will result in non-payment of the deposit on the exchange of contracts, entitling the vendor to bring the contract of sale to an end; this conclusion is, I consider, consistent with the approach of the Court of Appeal in Pollway Ltd v Abdullah [1974] 2 All ER 381, [1974] 1 WLR 493. In so far as Goulding J decided in Myton Ltd v Schwab-Morris that as a matter of construction the contract had not become binding until the deposit was paid, I myself would not, with all respect, be disposed to agree with him; in expressing that opinion, I find myself in agreement with the view expressed by Warner J in Millichamp v Jones [1983] 1 All ER 267 at 274, [1982] 1 WLR 1422 at 1430. In all the circumstances, therefore, I do not regard the authorities as requiring me to reach a conclusion in the present case different from that which I have reached as a matter of construction of the relevant documents.

For these reasons, in agreement with the judge, I am satisfied that a binding contract came into existence on 8 July as between the sellers and the Raftopoulos brothers, though the intention was clearly that there should be a novation on the nomination by the Raftopoulos brothers of a company or companies as purchasers, whose name or names would be inserted in the memorandum of agreement in due course.

I turn then to the next submission advanced by counsel for Damon, which was that, even if such a contract came into existence, there never was any novation whereby Damon became bound by the contract. I must confess that, although the Raftopoulos brothers were not appointed directors of Damon until a few hours after Damon had on 1 August 1977 been nominated to the sellers as the purchaser of the ships, I think it highly likely that, at the time of the nomination, since they had already agreed at some time in June or July to acquire the shares in Damon from the original subscribers, the Raftopoulos brothers had actual authority to make the nomination. However, even if that is not correct, I am satisfied that, by the telex sent to the sellers by Mr Panas on 3 August, Mr Menelaos Raftopoulos as chairman of Damon ratified the previous nomination of Damon as purchasers. Mr Panas's telex of 3 August was sent from the office of Messrs Raftopoulos, and there is no suggestion that it was not sent with their authority. The telex referred to 'Mr Raftopoulos'; this was obviously Mr Menelaos Raftopoulos, who is described by Mr Panas as the senior of the brothers and whose name had been put forward for entry in the memorandum of agreement pending the nomination of the company. The telex of 3 August refers to the financing of 'The present deal'; that must mean the deal as agreed between the parties, which then included the nomination of Damon as purchaser. It was within the usual authority of Mr Menelaos Raftopoulos as chairman of Damon to ratify the nomination of Damon as purchaser; in the absence of any evidence to the contrary, we are entitled to infer that he was actually authorised to do so. Following the purported nomination of Damon on 1 August, it is plain that Mr Menelaos Raftopoulos, in authorising Mr Panas to send the telex on 3 August, was proceeding on the basis of the contract binding Damon, and so acting on Damon's behalf, and I am satisfied that he thereby ratified the earlier nomination of Damon if it was not expressly authorised at the time that it was made. Further evidence of ratification is, in my judgment, provided by the finding of the arbitrator that Mr Panas telexed the sellers' broker at 1415 hrs on 5 August stating that 'MOMENT TO MOMENT' undertakings had been given by the respondents, ie by Damon. In these circumstances, in agreement with the arbitrator and the judge, I am satisfied that the contract became binding on Damon.

I come then to the third and final point in the case, which is this. Given that the contract became binding on Damon, and that Damon repudiated the contract, are the sellers entitled to recover the deposit payable by Damon under cl 2 of the Norwegian sale form, or are they only entitled to recover damages for the repudiation of the contract? The point is of importance in the case because, if the sellers are entitled to recover the deposit, they can recover $US236,500, being 10% of the purchase price; but, if they are only entitled to recover damages, they can recover only $US60,000, being the sum assessed by the arbitrator as the damages suffered by them.

The arbitrator held that the sellers were not entitled to the deposit, because the payment of the deposit was conditional on Damon signing the memorandum of agreement and it had not done so. The judge however formed a different view. He considered that the signing of the contract and the payment of the deposit by Damon were concurrent obligations, the performance of both of which had fallen due before the acceptance by the sellers of Damon's repudiation. Accordingly, the sellers were entitled to recover the deposit as an accrued debt owing under the contract; but, since the deposit exceeded the amount of the damages, no damages were recoverable in addition to the deposit.

On this point, I find myself to be in agreement with the arbitrator. No doubt under this form of contract it is contemplated that on signature of the contract the deposit will be paid. Accordingly, if a binding contract is entered into on the terms of the Norwegian sale form before signature of the memorandum of agreement, it will be contemplated that, when the buyer or his broker delivers back the memorandum of agreement duly signed to the seller, the deposit will then be paid. In such a case, however, there are two distinct obligations resting on the buyer. The first is the obligation to sign the memorandum of agreement; if no time is specified for the performance of this obligation, it must be performed in a reasonable time, but that must usually mean very shortly after receipt of the memorandum of agreement from the seller or his broker, in due form. The second obligation is the obligation to pay the deposit. This obligation is, however, to be performed not within a reasonable time, but on signature of the memorandum of agreement. The fact that the practical effect is that the deposit must be paid within a reasonable time, or even that the deposit may be paid simultaneously with the handing over of the memorandum of agreement signed by the buyer, does not in my judgment alter the fact that the two obligations are separate and distinct, and that the obligation to pay the deposit does not accrue until the memorandum of agreement is signed.

The point can be tested in this way. Let it be supposed that parties enter into a contract on the Norwegian sale form, which is not binding until the memorandum of agreement is signed. Under the sale form, the deposit is payable 'on signing this contract': that must there mean that it is payable immediately after the memorandum of agreement is signed, and not that it is payable concurrently with the signature of the contract. If, as in the present case, a contract is entered on the Norwegian sale form which is binding before signature, I do not see that any different meaning should be attached to the words 'on signing this contract'. I realise that the effect is that the seller does not get the protection of the deposit until signature, and that the buyer, by repudiating the contract before signature of the memorandum of agreement, can escape from the consequence of forfeiture of the deposit. That may not be very satisfactory from the seller's point of view; but it is, in my judgment, what he has agreed. The security of the deposit is not due until after signature of the memorandum of agreement; and so, if the buyer repudiates the contract before signature, the seller is without the benefit of the deposit.

Nor is it, in my judgment, an answer for the sellers to say that they are entitled to recover the amount of the deposit as damages. Their argument on this point runs as follows: (i) Damon was bound to sign the contract within a reasonable time; (ii) in breach and repudiation of its contract, it failed to do so; (iii) had it performed its obligations and signed the contract, the deposit would then have become payable and should have been paid; (iv) by reason of its breach, the sellers have lost the benefit of the deposit; (v) accordingly, the sellers can recover the amount of the deposit as damages. I am however unable to accept this argument. So far as the deposit is concerned, the position of the sellers in the event of the repudiation of the contract by Damon was as follows. If the repudiation occurred after Damon had paid the deposit, the sellers would be safe: they would have the deposit and could keep it. If the repudiation occurred after the obligation to pay the deposit had accrued due, but before Damon had paid it, the sellers could sue Damon for the deposit as a debt; whether they could get it or not would depend on whether they could enforce that right and in particular would depend on the solvency of Damon. But, if the repudiation occurred before Damon's obligation to pay the deposit had fallen due, then the sellers could only recover damages for the repudiation, which would fall to be assessed on the usual basis of compensating the sellers for the loss of their bargain. To assess those damages, it is necessary to compare what the sellers' position would have been if the contract had been performed with the position as it was following the repudiation. The normal measure, in a contract of sale of goods, is of course the difference between the contract and market prices for the goods. I can see no reason for departing from that ordinary measure of damages in the present case. To award the sellers damages assessed on the basis of the amount of the deposit would be to compare their present position with what their position would have been if the contract had only been partially performed (ie the deposit paid), and not with their position if the contract had been performed in full; if damages were assessed in that way, they would be over-compensated for the loss of their bargain. In truth, the inability of the sellers to obtain the protection of the deposit, in the circumstances of the present case, flows from their contracting on such terms that the deposit was not payable forthwith on the making of the contract.

To this extent, therefore, I would allow the appeal. I would answer the third question posed by the arbitrator, which is whether the sellers are entitled to recover from Damon the amount of the deposit provided for in cl 2 of the memorandum of agreement, in the negative, and I would answer the second question to the effect that the sellers are entitled to damages in the sum of $US60,000.

**STEPHENSON LJ.** I agree with Fox LJ that this appeal should be dismissed for the reasons which he gives.

On the last point I am attracted by the logic of Robert Goff LJ's contrary opinion. But the measure of damages resulting from Damon's repudiatory breach is, in my opinion, the loss directly and naturally resulting from the breach in the ordinary course of events, and I agree with Fox LJ that that loss is the amount of the deposit which was not paid or payable in consequence of Damon's wrongful refusal to sign the contract. It seems to me unreal and unfair to the sellers to exclude the deposit from the court's estimate of their loss.

*Appeal dismissed. Leave to appeal to the House of Lords refused.*

*4 February 1985. The Appeal Committee of the House of Lords granted Damon leave to appeal.*

Solicitors: *Lloyd Denby Neal* (for Damon); *Richards Butler & Co* (for the sellers).

Diana Brahams   Barrister.

# R v Exeter City Council, ex parte Gliddon and another

QUEEN'S BENCH DIVISION (CROWN OFFICE LIST)

WOOLF J

30 JANUARY 1984

*Housing – Homeless person – Person becoming homeless intentionally – Person obtaining accommodation by deception and landlord requiring surrender of lease on discovering deception – Whether person becoming homeless intentionally – Whether housing authority under duty to provide accommodation – Whether reasonable for person to continue to occupy accommodation against landlord's wishes – Housing (Homeless Persons) Act 1977, s 17(1).*

*Housing – Homeless person – Person becoming homeless intentionally – Duty to house person intentionally homeless for such period as will give him reasonable opportunity to secure accommodation – Standard of accommodation – Whether housing authority under duty to provide accommodation of same standard as that provided where person not homeless intentionally – Housing (Homeless Persons) Act 1977, s 4(3).*

In February 1983 the applicants, who were living together, obtained a short-term tenancy of a flat by representing to the landlord that they were both employed. In fact they were unemployed and were unable to pay the rent. On learning of the deception, the landlord sought the surrender of the lease and subsequently obtained an order for possession of the flat in uncontested proceedings. The applicants applied to the local housing authority for accommodation under the Housing (Homeless Persons) Act 1977 claiming to be persons who had a priority need under that Act because the female applicant was pregnant. The authority decided that it was not under a duty to provide permanent accommodation for the applicants because the applicants had become homeless 'intentionally' within s 17[a] of the 1977 Act by voluntarily surrendering the lease of the flat, despite being advised by the authority to take legal advice before doing so, and by failing to contest the proceedings for possession. Accordingly, pursuant to s 4(3)[b] of the 1977 Act the authority merely provided the applicants with temporary accommodation until they had an opportunity to secure accommodation for themselves. The applicants applied for judicial review of the authority's decision, seeking, inter alia, certiorari quashing the authority's decision that they had become homeless intentionally and a declaration that the authority was in breach of its duty under s 4(3) by providing temporary accommodation which was of an unsatisfactory standard of repair and maintenance.

**Held** – (1) On the true construction of s 17(1) of the 1977 Act a person was homeless intentionally only if (a) he did something or failed to do something which caused him to cease occupying accommodation and (b) the accommodation was such that it was reasonable for him to continue to occupy the premises. Where a person obtained accommodation by deception and the landlord discovered that deception, that person had no possible justification for refusing to surrender the lease and in those circumstances it would be unreasonable for the person to continue to occupy the accommodation

---

*a*    Section 17, so far as material, is set out at p 496 *d* to *g*, post

*b*    Section 4(3) provides: 'Where—(*a*) [a housing authority] are satisfied that [a person who has applied to them for accommodation] is homeless, and (*b*) they are subject to a duty towards him by virtue of subsection (2)(*b*) above, they shall secure that accommodation is made available for his occupation for such period as they consider will give him a reasonable opportunity for himself securing accommodation for his occupation.'

against the landlord's wishes. Since the local housing authority had never taken into account that the applicants could not have reasonably continued to occupy the flat, certiorari would be granted quashing the authority's decision that the applicants were homeless intentionally (see p 495 a, p 497 d to p 498 d and p 499 c, post).

(2) A local housing authority only had a limited obligation under s 4(3) of the 1977 Act to a homeless applicant who had a priority need but who had become homeless or threatened with homelessness intentionally. Furthermore, having regard to the fact that the authority was only required to make accommodation available for the period necessary to give the applicant a reasonable opportunity of securing accommodation for himself, the accommodation did not have to be of the same standard as that required to be provided for an applicant who was homeless or threatened with homelessness unintentionally. Since it could not be said that the accommodation provided for the applicants was of such a standard that it amounted to a failure by the council to fulfil its obligation under s 4(3), it followed that the declaration would accordingly be refused (see p 498 d to f and p 499 a to c, post).

### Notes

For a housing authority's duties to a homeless person, see 22 Halsbury's Laws (4th edn) para 513.

For the Housing (Homeless Persons) Act 1977, ss 4, 17, see Halsbury's Statutes (3rd edn) 318, 330.

### Cases cited

*Associated Provincial Picture Houses Ltd v Wednesbury Corp* [1947] 2 All ER 680, [1947] 1 KB 223, CA.
*Din v Wandsworth London Borough* [1981] 3 All ER 881, [1983] 1 AC 657, [1981] 3 WLR 918, HL.
*Lambert v Ealing London BC* [1982] 2 All ER 394, [1982] 1 WLR 550, CA.
*Lewis v North Devon DC* [1981] 1 All ER 27, [1981] 1 WLR 328.
*R v Basingstoke and Deane DC, ex p Bassett* (1983) Times, 18 July.
*R v Eastleigh BC, ex p Beattie* (1983) Times, 11 July.
*R v Hillingdon London BC, ex p Wilson* (1983) Times, 14 July.
*R v Portsmouth City Council, ex p Knight* (1984) 82 LGR 184.

### Application for judicial review

Clarence Michael Gliddon and Karen Draper applied, with the leave of Glidewell J granted on 22 August 1983, for, inter alia, (i) an order of certiorari quashing the decision of the respondent, the Exeter City Council, dated 6 May 1983 that the applicants were threatened with homelessness intentionally, (ii) an order of mandamus directing the council to accommodate the applicants as homeless persons with a priority need, and (iii) a declaration that the council was in breach of its obligations under s 4(3) of the Housing (Homeless Persons) Act 1977 to secure accommodation for the applicants' occupation for such period as would give them a reasonable opportunity of themselves securing accommodation for their occupation, in that such accommodation as the council did provide for the applicants was of an entirely unsatisfactory standard of repair and maintenance. The facts are set out in the judgment.

*Christopher Naish* for the applicants.
*William Birtles* for the council.

**WOOLF J.** This is an application for judicial review founded on the fact that a council, on this occasion Exeter City Council, has come to the conclusion that the two applicants have rendered themselves homeless, and they are in the words of the Housing (Homeless Persons) Act 1977 'intentionally homeless'.

The case illustrates the difficulties that are faced by a council when trying to administer the 1977 Act and trying to act fairly, not only to the applicants but also to the many other homeless persons for whom the council has a responsibility. For reasons which I will seek to explain hereafter, I have come to the conclusion that in this case the applicants are entitled to relief by way of certiorari. Although I have come to that conclusion, I would like to make it clear that I am very conscious of the fact that this particular council has taken very considerable care in investigating this matter and has sought to come to a conclusion which was a proper one and in accordance with the law.

The background of the matter is as follows. At all material times the two applicants were living together as man and wife. The female applicant was pregnant and because of that, for the purposes of the Act, the applicants were persons who had a priority need. Up until 22 February 1983 the applicants were living with one of their parents. The home in which they were living was very overcrowded and, although this matter has not been the subject of any finding by the council, according to the applicants the male applicant's parents required them to leave the house; and this they then did. For one or two nights they stayed in a car, and then on the following day they obtained accommodation in a flat at 1 Grosvenor Place in Exeter, the landlord of which was a Mr King. The tenancy was a short-term tenancy, which was due to expire on 18 October 1983, and it was at a rent of £50 per week plus £2 for colour television. The £2 for the television can be ignored for the purposes of this judgment.

There were difficulties with regard to the payment of rent and the rent went into arrear. In addition, Mr King contended that the applicants had obtained this tenancy by deception. They had represented to him that they were both employed, that they could afford to pay the rent, that they were not in receipt of supplementary benefit and, in addition (and this may be due to a misunderstanding), that the name of the male applicant was Blidden rather than Gliddon. On account of the situation which had arisen the applicants surrendered their tenancy and received instead a licence. The licence was one for an extremely limited period and in due course it was terminated by Mr King. The applicants did not leave the premises voluntarily and in due course an order for possession was made on 26 April 1983, that order taking effect on 10 May, but in fact possession was obtained on 23 May. An application was made for accommodation under the Housing (Homeless Persons) Act 1977 by the applicants. It came before the council, which initially by a letter dated 6 May informed the applicants that they had become homeless intentionally. They gave as the reason for their decision:

'You voluntarily surrendered your right to occupy [the flat at Grosvenor Place] despite prior advice to both of you to seek a legal opinion. In addition you failed to contest the possession proceedings that ensued.'

Having been notified of that decision, an application was made for judicial review, and leave was granted by this court. The relief which was sought was, first of all, an order of certiorari to quash the decision to which I have just referred, secondly, an order of mandamus directing the Exeter City Council to accommodate the applicants as homeless persons with a priority need, thirdly, a declaration that the Exeter City Council is in breach of its obligation under s 4(3) of the Housing (Homeless Persons) Act 1977 to secure accommodation for the applicants' occupation for such period as would give them a reasonable opportunity of themselves securing accommodation for their occupation, in that such accommodation as the council did provide for the applicants is of an entirely unsatisfactory standard of repair and maintenance, and, fourthly, damages in respect of the above breach.

The relief which was sought in respect of the alleged breach of s 4(3) arises out of the fact that while the council was pursuing its inquiries it had, as it was required to do, provided temporary accommodation, and that was provided at 4 Weirfield House. Leave having been granted by this court, the matter was further investigated by the council. That was a perfectly proper course for the council to take because it could well, if the matter had been considered in a manner which was unobjectionable, have led to the first two grounds of relief no longer being pursued. Evidence on this occasion was given before the council by both applicants, but the matter having been considered by the housing sub-committee on 17 November 1983, the fresh decision of the council was notified to the applicants by a letter dated 24 November 1983 and was in these terms (the emphasis is that in the letter itself):

'(1) That on 23 February 1983, you gave false information to Mr R G King, the landlord of Flat A, 1 Grosvenor Place, Exeter, about (a) your employment status and (b) whether or not you were in receipt of Social Security payments; (2) That Mr Gliddon deceived Mr King about his name by using the false surname "Blidden"; (3) That Mr King was deceived by that false information into granting you a tenancy of Flat A, 1 Grosvenor Place, Exeter; (4) That when Mr King subsequently discovered the deception, you agreed to surrender the security of your lease for a licence. (5) That before surrendering the lease, you were advised by a member of the City Housing Department that you should *not* surrender the lease without taking legal advice. You did not take such legal advice until *after* you had surrendered the lease; (6) You were, therefore, made homeless as a direct result of your own actions, knowing full well what the consequences of those actions would be.'

When one looks at those reasons, one notices that the deception plays a prominent role in the matter and that in addition to the deception there is reference to surrendering without taking legal advice. With regard to the question of whether or not the council was entitled to come to those decisions, the terms of s 17(1) and (2) of the 1977 Act must be borne in mind. Those subsections provide:

'(1) Subject to subsection (3) below, for the purposes of this Act a person becomes homeless intentionally if he deliberately does or fails to do anything in consequence of which he ceases to occupy accommodation which is available for his occupation and which it would have been reasonable for him to continue to occupy.

(2) Subject to subsection (3) below, for the purposes of this Act a person becomes threatened with homelessness intentionally if he deliberately does or fails to do anything the likely result of which is that he will be forced to leave accommodation which is available for his occupation and which it would have been reasonable for him to continue to occupy.'

Subsection (4), which is also relevant, provides:

'Regard may be had, in determining for the purposes of subsections (1) and (2) above whether it would have been reasonable for a person to continue to occupy accommodation, to the general circumstances prevailing in relation to housing in the area of the housing authority to whom he applied for accommodation or for assistance in obtaining accommodation.'

Having regard to the fact that the council have already reconsidered the matter, it seems to me that the appropriate course for this court to adopt is to concentrate on the second set of reasons which have been given by the council since, even if the first were flawed, this court would not grant relief by way of certiorari if satisfied that the matter had properly been reconsidered by the council and the council had come to the same conclusion. However, the reasoning of the court based on the second set of reasons would apply with the same effect to the first reasons given by the council, although they were not as extensive as the second set of reasons and did not deal with the question of deception in the same way that it was dealt with in the second set of reasons.

Considerable evidence is before the court with regard to the question of non-payment of rent and in his submissions counsel for the council stressed the fact that a factor certainly in Mr King requiring possession of this accommodation was the non-payment of rent. Furthermore, it was contended on behalf of the applicants by their counsel that because of the very limited means of the applicants it could not have been reasonable for them to continue to occupy the accommodation, because they could not afford the rent, and not being able to afford the rent, if they had remained there, that would only have resulted in the landlord being faced with having ever-increasing claims against the applicants which they could not hope to meet.

Counsel for the applicants supplements this argument by drawing attention to the amount of benefit which the applicants were in receipt of and submits that it is self-evident, having regard to their limited means, that they could not afford a rent of £50 per week.

I am by no means satisfied that if the council had come to the conclusion that the only reason why the applicants had ceased to occupy the accommodation was because they had not kept up their rental obligations, that would not, in the circumstances of this case, be a decision which it would not have been entitled to make. However, it is apparent from the reasons to which I have referred, that the decision of the council did not turn on non-payment of rent. The council was not saying that that was the cause of the applicants being rendered intentionally homeless and it is not necessary, therefore, for me to go into that matter or to make any final determination with regard to it.

What I regard as the crucial finding of the council is that Mr King was deceived and that when Mr King discovered the deception the applicants agreed to surrender the security of their lease for a licence. I have no doubt that counsel for the council is right in saying that on the reasoning of the council the homelessness of the applicants was caused, at least in part, by the deception which they practised on Mr King. However, it does not follow that as they were rendered homeless by that conduct on their part it would have been reasonable for them to continue to occupy the accommodation. For the purposes of s 17(1) an applicant is only homeless intentionally if he not only does something or fails to do something which is the cause of his ceasing to occupy the accommodation but, in addition, the accommodation is accommodation which it is reasonable for that person to continue to occupy. Where you have a situation where a person has only obtained accommodation, on the findings of the council, by deception, and the landlord on discovering that deception requires the person concerned to surrender his lease, the consequence must be that that person has no possible justification for refusing to do so. In my view, it is almost inevitable that, if this is required by the landlord, it would be unreasonable for him to continue to occupy the accommodation against the wishes of the landlord. He would have no defence in law to a claim to possession by the landlord. It would be adding to the harm which has already been done to the landlord to require the landlord to bring proceedings to obtain possession in those circumstances, and, notwithstanding s 17(4), which as counsel points out is there to protect the council, the needs of the council cannot in the ordinary way make it reasonable for the applicants to continue to occupy the accommodation.

In this case, the landlord did not demand immediate possession. He was content that there should be a temporary licence. However, if the landlord could require possession, he must also be entitled to require a licence; and, if it would be unreasonable for the tenant to continue to occupy the premises if the landlord required possession, so must it, in my view, in the normal way be unreasonable for the tenant to continue to insist on retaining the lease if the landlord is prepared to grant an indulgence and accept a licence. The situation here was therefore one where, in my view, there was almost an overwhelming if not irresistible case that the applicants could not reasonably continue to occupy the flat at 1 Grosvenor Place. The reasons given by the council in its letter of 24 November 1983 make it clear that it never considered this aspect of the application. If it had done so, then in my view the proper way for it to have proceeded, if it came to the conclusion that the applicants could not be regarded as intentionally homeless because of what occurred in relation to the flat at 1 Grosvenor Place, would have been to look at the circumstances prior to the applicants obtaining possession of those premises. If it had approached the matter in that way, it may or may not have come to the conclusion that the applicants were entitled to be treated as being outside s 17 because of what happened when they were required to leave the male applicant's home. I make no comment with regard to what conclusion it could have come to about that. If it approaches the matter in that way, there will be no question of the applicants benefiting by their deception:

they will be in exactly the same position as they would have been if they had not obtained temporary accommodation in consequence of their deception. Their conduct, on the findings of the council, are reprehensible in relation to that deception but what they obtained by the deception would neither make their position better or worse than it would have been if they had not embarked on that reprehensible conduct.

On this aspect of the case, it is only necessary for me to add that I apprehend that it will be rare for a council or other housing authority to have the same problem in the future. Whereas here the applicants are alleging that they were not guilty of deception and the landlord is alleging that they were, normally the answer of the council will be what apparently was originally the answer of the City Housing Department: 'Take legal advice and let the courts determine whether or not the landlord is entitled to possession.' In any case where the council is not satisfied that there was deception, that would be a reasonable course for the council to adopt, because the courts are clearly better equipped to determine issues of that sort, and if despite being provided with that advice an applicant voluntarily vacates premises and a council comes to the conclusion that the applicant is intentionally homeless, where it is not satisfied that there has been deception, the outcome will be different from that in this application.

There remains the second ground of application based on the condition of the temporary accommodation provided by the council under s 4(3) of the 1977 Act. The obligation of the council under that subsection is a limited one and in deciding whether or not it has been fulfilled, the period for which the obligation continues has to be borne in mind. The obligation arises where a council is satisfied that an applicant is homeless and that it is subject to a duty to him pursuant to s 4(2)(b). That is a situation where it is satisfied that he has a priority need but it is also satisfied that he has become homeless or threatened with homelessness intentionally. The duty is to ensure that accommodation is made available for such period as it considers will give him a reasonable opportunity of himself securing accommodation for his occupation. The accommodation which has to be provided pursuant to that duty certainly does not have to be of the same standard as would be required in a case where it came to the conclusion that the applicant was not homeless or threatened with homelessness intentionally. It must, however, be capable of being regarded as accommodation.

In this case, there is conflicting evidence before me as to the quality of the accommodation which was provided. It clearly, on any showing, was not of a high standard. In support of the applicants' case their counsel referred me in particular to the report of Mr Armitt, who has considerable experience and qualifications in this matter. In his first report, he concludes in this way:

> 'The standard of repair and management and maintenance, however, fall short of any standard which could be considered satisfactory. The extensive damage to wall and ceiling plaster throughout the letting and the common parts combined with a poor standard of decoration and other individual items of disrepair would warrant the intervention of a local authority and the application of the management regulations to this property. The absence of lighting on the common parts and entrance would also be included in such a management programme. The items of disrepair (as opposed to decoration) would also be appropriate for action under section 9(1A) of the Housing Act 1957 as amended and although the property is not considered to be either prejudicial to health or a statutory nuisance (section 93 Public Health Act 1936–section 4 Housing Act 1957) the circumstances are such that additional items of disrepair could bring about a deterioration of standards which would rapidly make the house unfit or a statutory nuisance.'

It is clear from that part of Mr Armitt's report and the reference to s 9(1A) of the Housing Act 1957 that the property could not be described as unfit for human habitation. It was, however, in a state, according to Mr Armitt, where substantial repairs were required to bring it up to a reasonable standard, having regard to its age, character and locality. (I am there referring to the terms of s 9(1A) of the Housing Act 1959, inserted by s 72 of the Housing Act 1969.)

There is a conflict with regard to Mr Armitt's evidence but, even assuming that Mr Armitt's evidence is accurate, in my view it could not be said on the basis of his evidence that this accommodation was of such a standard that it amounted to a failure by the council of its obligation to fulfil its duty under s 4(3) of the Act. In relation to that duty, it is important to bear in mind that here the council, as I have already indicated, like many others, has very many calls on its stock of accommodation and that being the position it would be wrong for the court to be too ready to come to a conclusion that the limited requirements of s 4(3) of the 1977 Act have not been met.

It therefore follows that I do not find that there has been a breach of s 4(3). I am not prepared to grant a declaration or to grant any damages in respect of the alleged breach of s 4(3). I am, however, for the reasons I have indicated, prepared to quash the decision of the council in respect of its second decision in relation to the question of intentional homelessness, so that that matter can be reconsidered by the council, having regard to the reasoning which I have sought to set out in this decision.

*Order accordingly.*

Solicitors: *Crosse & Crosse*, Exeter (for the applicants); *Michael C Brainsby*, Exeter (for the council).

N P Metcalfe Esq    Barrister.

# Giles (Electrical Engineers) Ltd v Plessey Communications Systems Ltd

COURT OF APPEAL, CIVIL DIVISION
SIR JOHN DONALDSON MR, SLADE AND LLOYD LJJ
5 DECEMBER 1984

*Court of Appeal – Leave to appeal – Requirement of leave – Official referee – Appeal from interlocutory order of official referee – Whether leave to appeal required – Supreme Court Act 1981, s 18(1)(h) – RSC Ord 58, r 4(2).*

Since in relation to any decision of an official referee from which an appeal lies to the Court of Appeal, RSC Ord 58, r 4(2)[a] provides that s 18 of the Supreme Court Act 1981 shall apply as if the official referee were a judge of the High Court, it follows that by virtue of s 18(1)(h)[b] leave is required to appeal against an interlocutory order made by an official referee (see p 500 *f* to *h*, post).

*Technistudy Ltd v Kelland* [1976] 3 All ER 632 not followed.

**Notes**
For the Supreme Court Act 1981, s 18, see 51 Halsbury's Statutes (3rd edn) 608.

**Case referred to in judgments**
*Technistudy Ltd v Kelland* [1976] 3 All ER 632, [1976] 1 WLR 1042, CA.

**Application for leave to appeal**
The defendants, Plessey Communications Systems Ltd, sought leave to appeal against the

---

a   Rule 4(2) is set out at p 500 *e f*, post
b   Section 18(1), so far as material, provides: 'No appeal shall lie to the Court of Appeal . . . (h) without the leave of the court or tribunal in question or of the Court of Appeal, from any interlocutory order or interlocutory judgment made or given by the High Court or any other court or tribunal . . .'

order of his Honour Judge Lewis Hawser QC hearing official referees' business on 25 May 1984 whereby he dismissed the defendants' application that action 1981 G no 2624 between the plaintiffs, Giles (Electrical Engineers) Ltd, and the defendants be struck out and ordered that the action be consolidated with action 1977 G no 507 between the same parties.

*Frederick A Philpott* for the defendants.
*Richard Fernyhough* for the plaintiffs.

**SIR JOHN DONALDSON MR.** Problems have arisen recently concerning the need for leave to appeal from interlocutory decisions of official referees. I should perhaps make it clear that the right of appeal from an official referee is limited by RSC Ord 58, r 4, and anything that I say on this topic is of course subject to that rule. Where there is a right of appeal under that rule, the question then arises whether a party needs leave to appeal.

The origin of the problem is the decision of this court in *Technistudy Ltd v Kelland* [1976] 3 All ER 632, [1976] 1 WLR 1042. It was there held that leave to appeal from an official referee was not required where the appeal was on a point of law even though the order sought to be appealed was interlocutory in nature. When the *Technistudy* case was decided s 31 of the Supreme Court of Judicature (Consolidation) Act 1925 was in force. Section 31(1)(i) provided that there was no appeal to the Court of Appeal 'without the leave of the judge or of the Court of Appeal from any interlocutory order'.

It seems to me that the reason why the Court of Appeal in the *Technistudy* case decided that leave to appeal against an interlocutory order made by an official referee was not required was because an official referee was not a 'judge' within the meaning of that particular subsection. But the court in the *Technistudy* case invited the Rules Committee to look into the matter since this was clearly anomalous; and in 1977 Ord 58, r 5 (now renumbered r 4) was amended by the addition at the beginning of para (1) of the words 'subject to paragraph (2)', and there was added a new para (2) which provided:

> 'In relation to any decision of an official referee referred to in paragraph (1) section 31 of the Act shall apply as if the official referee were a judge of the High Court.'[1]

In my judgment the effect of those amendments was to render the decision of this court in the *Technistudy* case no longer applicable. If there were any doubts about that, they have been removed by the enactment of s 18(1)(h) of the Supreme Court Act 1981, which does not confine the subject matter to a judge but expands it using the words 'court or tribunal'. Whatever else may be said about official referees, they are plainly a court or tribunal. Accordingly, leave to appeal is required in exactly the same type of cases as is required on an appeal from a judge of the High Court. This is, as is conceded, an interlocutory matter sought to be appealed in the present case and, as is conceded, leave to appeal is required.

For the avoidance of doubt, let me also make it clear that if leave to appeal is not required from a High Court judge, a party does not require it to appeal from an official referee, subject of course to the application of Ord 58, r 4 which may deprive a party of any right of appeal from an official referee. I trust that makes the position clear.

**SLADE LJ.** I agree.

**LLOYD LJ.** I agree.

*Leave to appeal refused.*

Solicitors: *Herbert Oppenheimer Nathan & Vandyk* (for the defendants); *Masons* (for the plaintiffs).

Diana Procter    Barrister.

---

1    By RSC (Amendment No 2) 1982, SI 1982/1111, r 101(2), for the reference in para (2) to 'section 31 of the Act', ie s 31 of the Supreme Court of Judicature (Consolidation) Act 1925, there was substituted a reference to 'section 18 of the Act', ie s 18 of the Supreme Court Act 1981

# Attorney General's Reference (No 3 of 1983)

COURT OF APPEAL, CRIMINAL DIVISION

LORD LANE CJ, BOREHAM AND TUDOR PRICE JJ

10, 21 DECEMBER 1984

*Criminal law – Affray – Public place – Elements of offence – Whether necessary to prove actual or likely presence of bystander at scene – Whether an innocent victim of an affray can constitute a bystander.*

The essence of the offence of affray in a public place is participation in unlawful fighting or violence of a kind calculated to cause any person of reasonable firmness who might have witnessed the scene to be terrified, e g by fearing for his safety. What is required to establish the offence is proof (i) that there was unlawful fighting or violence by one or more persons against another or others, or an unlawful display of force by one or more persons without actual violence, and (ii) that the unlawful fighting, violence or display of force was such that a bystander of reasonable firmness and courage (whether or not present or likely to be present) might reasonably have been expected to be terrified. Furthermore, if the presence of a bystander is necessary to prove the offence, an innocent victim of an affray can constitute a bystander (see p 505 *a* to *d* and *h* to p 506 *b*, post).

Dicta of Paull J in *R v Mapstone* [1963] 3 All ER at 931 and of Lord Hailsham LC in *Taylor v DPP* [1973] 2 All ER at 1112–1113 applied.

## Notes

For the offence of affray, see 11 Halsbury's Laws (4th edn) para 855, and for cases on the subject, see 15 Digest (Reissue) 906–908, 7780–7796.

## Cases referred to in opinion

*Button v DPP, Swain v DPP* [1965] 3 All ER 587, [1966] AC 591, [1965] 3 WLR 1131, HL.
*Kamara v DPP* [1973] 2 All ER 1242, [1974] AC 104, [1973] 3 WLR 198, HL.
*R v Mapstone* [1963] 3 All ER 930, [1964] 1 WLR 439.
*R v Scarrow* (1968) 52 Cr App R 591, CA.
*R v Sharp* [1957] 1 All ER 577, [1957] 1 QB 552, [1957] 2 WLR 472, CCA.
*R v Summers* (1972) 56 Cr App R 604, CA.
*Taylor v DPP* [1973] 2 All ER 1108, [1973] AC 964, [1973] 3 WLR 140, HL.

## Case also cited

*R v Pitchley* (1972) 57 Cr App R 30, CA.

## Reference

In September 1981 in the Crown Court at Leeds before his Honour Judge Hurwitz and a jury, five youths (the defendants) were indicted on an indictment which included a count of affray against them. At the end of the Crown's case the trial judge ruled, after hearing legal argument, that there was no case for any of the defendants to answer on the count of affray. The Attorney General referred the case, under s 36 of the Criminal Justice Act 1972 to the Court of Appeal, Criminal Division for its opinion on related points of law (set out at p 502 *b c*, post) regarding the essential elements of the offence of affray in a public place. The points of law, and the facts are set out in the opinion of the court.

*Allan Green* and *David Gripton* for the Attorney General.
*Andrew Collins* as amicus curiae.
The defendants were not represented.

*Cur adv vult*

21 December. The following opinion of the court was delivered.

**LORD LANE CJ.** The Court of Appeal is asked to give its opinion on the following related points of law:

'(i) On a charge of affray, where the unlawful fighting or violence occurred in a public place, do the prosecution have to prove not only (a) that it would have (or might reasonably be expected to have) terrified a bystander or person within earshot of reasonable firm character, but also either (b) the presence of a bystander or person within earshot, or (c) a reasonable likelihood of a member of the public coming within sight or earshot?

(ii) In what circumstances, if any, may an innocent victim or intended victim of fighting or violence or an innocent participant in it constitute a "bystander" for the purposes of (i)(b) above?'          •

In September 1981 five defendants appeared before the Crown Court at Leeds charged with affray, and certain other offences which are immaterial to the present argument. Submissions (with which we deal in detail hereafter), were made by defending counsel that there was no case for the defendants to answer so far as the affray was concerned; the judge upheld those submissions and the defendants were accordingly acquitted of affray.

On 29 June 1983 the present reference was filed with the Registrar of Criminal Appeals by the Attorney General.

The facts, in so far as they are material, were as follows. The incident took place in a public place, namely the car park at the rear of a public house at night shortly after the end of 'drinking-up time'. The defendants attacked a group of innocent youths. The ensuing mêlée was undoubtedly such as would have terrified a bystander of reasonably firm character.

There was no evidence that there was anybody in the car park or within earshot of it apart from the two groups of youths, and it is said that there was no reasonable likelihood of any other person coming within sight or earshot of the fighting. G was a member of the group of innocent youths. He himself was not attacked. However he did pull one of the defendants off a companion of his; he also collided with another defendant who was kicking a further companion of his; this was as he, G, ran off to telephone to the police.

The submission made by counsel for the defence was based on the following grounds: (i) The prosecution had to prove *not only* (a) that the fighting would have (or might reasonably be expected to have) terrified a bystander or person within earshot of reasonably firm character, *but also* either (b) the actual presence of a bystander or person within earshot or (c) the reasonable likelihood of a member of the public coming within sight or earshot. (ii) Since G and the other members of the 'innocent group' were victims and/or participants in the fighting, none of them could constitute a 'bystander' for the purpose of completing proof of the offence. Therefore, since the prosecution had failed to adduce any evidence of the actual presence of a bystander and no sufficient evidence of the likelihood of one appearing, their case must fail.

Prosecuting counsel submitted that (i) since the fighting took place in a public place, the prosecution only had to prove that it would have (or might reasonably be expected to have) terrified a bystander or person within earshot of reasonably firm character and did not have to prove the actual presence of a bystander or the reasonable likelihood of one materialising. (ii) Alternatively, if the prosecution did have to prove actual or likely presence, (1) G could constitute a bystander and (2) there was enough evidence of the likelihood of a member of the public coming within sight or earshot to constitute a prima facie case.

Counsel for the Attorney General has taken us through the recent history of the offence of affray to demonstrate how the courts have gradually defined and refined it. We think it may be useful to set out in summary form the various cases.

*R v Sharp* [1957] 1 All ER 577, [1957] 1 QB 552 decided firstly that on a charge of making an affray in a public place there is no necessity to call direct evidence of any person having been put in fear; it is sufficient to prove such circumstances that reasonable people might have been intimidated or frightened by the fighting and/or violence. (But see Lord Hailsham LC in *Taylor v DPP* [1973] 2 All ER 1108 at 1112, [1973] AC 964 at 987:

> '. . . it is essential to stress that the degree of violence required to constitute the offence of affray must be such as to be calculated to terrify a person of reasonably firm character. This should not be watered down. Thus it is arguable that the phrase "*might* be frightened or intimidated" may be too weak. The violence must be such as to be *calculated* to terrify (that is, might reasonably be expected to terrify) not simply such as *might* terrify a person of the requisite degree of firmness.')

Secondly, a person who merely defends himself against the attack of another and does not himself attack is not guilty of affray.

*Button v DPP, Swain v DPP* [1965] 3 All ER 587, [1966] AC 591, apart from containing a very useful and detailed history by McKenna J of the offence of affray from earliest times, decided that there was no requirement that the affray should be committed in a public place, despite decisions to the contrary over the previous century. These had crept into the law by error.

In *R v Scarrow* (1968) 52 Cr App R 591 it was decided that there is no requirement for the prosecution to prove that one defendant has fought with another. The offence may be committed though the persons attacked did not resist or retaliate. Lord Parker CJ said (at 596):

> 'It may well be that if two people fight and one is acting in self-defence, that man cannot be said to be guilty of an affray, but it would appear to this court that there is no reason why his attacker, whether acting alone or jointly with another attacker, should not be held guilty of the affray.'

*R v Summers* (1972) 56 Cr App R 604 covered much of the same ground as *R v Scarrow*, but in addition is authority for the proposition that one of the innocent parties attacked by the defendant is capable of being regarded as a member of the public, a potential subject of the necessary terror.

The questions raised by this reference however have been the subject of direct consideration in only one case, namely a charge to the jury by Paull J in *R v Mapstone* [1963] 3 All ER 930, [1964] 1 WLR 439. This was a case where a fight had taken place in a public house during opening hours. The judge directed the jury that they had to be satisfied that the particular defendant took part in a fight in a public place or road in such a way as might well frighten any members of the public who might be present. He went on ([1963] 3 All ER 930 at 931)

> ' "Affray" is an old English word, not one we use very often today, but what it means is this that a number of people, two will do, start fighting in a public road or place in such a way that people who may be present may well get frightened. The old English word used to be "terrified". So what the prosecution has to prove . . . is, first of all, that that accused person took part in a fight in a public place . . . Secondly, that the fighting that went on was such as might well frighten any ordinary person passing by. The prosecution has not got to prove that anyone *was* frightened; the prosecution has not got to prove that someone was passing by; but the prosecution must prove that the character of the fighting which was going on was such that it might well frighten.' (Our emphasis.)

This direction has now of course to be read in the light of *Button v DPP, Swain v DPP* in that the fighting may be in a private place, and also of Lord Hailsham LC's observations in *Taylor v DPP*, to both of which we have referred.

Counsel appearing as amicus curiae submits primarily that affray is a well-defined common law offence which should be kept within its historical bounds and should not be allowed, so to speak, to overflow into areas more properly covered by the offence of riot. His suggestion is that if there is no requirement for the prosecution to prove the actual or likely presence of a bystander available to be terrified, then the whole basis of the offence, namely fighting to the terror of the public, is lost. He does however concede that presence or likely presence does not have to be proved by direct evidence. It may be by inference. He gives the example of a fight in a public street in a town, where it would, he suggests, be proper to draw the inference that some member of the public was there or likely to be there to witness the fight.

We deal first with that proposition, namely that the actual or likely presence of a bystander is one of the essential elements which the prosecution must prove.

We have had our attention drawn to the following obiter dicta. *Taylor v DPP* was a case which was primarily concerned with the question whether one person fighting unlawfully could properly be convicted of an affray. It was held that he could, and that if one person was acting unlawfully it was not necessary to inquire whether others participating were acting lawfully or not. However in the course of his speech Lord Reid had this to say about the problem with which we are here concerned ([1973] 2 All ER 1108 at 1114–1115, [1973] AC 964 at 989–990):

'The question of terror does not arise in this case but as it was much referred to in argument and is an essential element in the offence, I think that I must say a word about it. Undoubtedly if people are present it is not necessary to prove by their evidence that they were terrified. It is enough if the circumstances are such that ordinary people like them would have been terrified. I say "would" not "might" have been. But I am much more doubtful about suggestions in some cases that no one but the combatants need be present at all or even within earshot: that it is enough that if someone had been present he would have been terrified. As terror is an essential ingredient of the offence I think that there can be no difference in principle between violence in a public or a private place. But that is a matter which can be decided when it arises.'

Lord Hailsham LC on the other hand said ([1973] 2 All ER 1108 at 1112–1113, [1973] AC 964 at 987–988):

'We were invited to express an opinion as to the extent to which persons must be proved to have been present in order to satisfy the ingredient of terror. I do not think that, on the facts of the present case, where many persons were in fact present and some were in fact terrified, it is desirable to explore this in depth. It is possible that where the fight takes place in a public street it is not necessary to prove the actual presence of bystanders, of persons within earshot or that they were actually terrified. It may be enough to show that the violence used was of such a kind to render the street unusable by persons of reasonable firmness by reason of the terror it was liable to cause. I am not, for example, prepared to say that a fight between rival gangs on the front of a seaside resort, or a duel with lethal weapons on Putney Heath, would not be an affray if the prosecution failed to establish the presence of bystanders or their actual terror. But in a private place it would be surprising if affray could be complete without the actual presence of onlookers or audience to be frightened by the sight or sound of what was occurring. This must clearly be considered of importance since the decision in *Button* [1965] 3 All ER 587, [1966] AC 591. These are matters which must be canvassed in the light of cases where the facts are such as to raise the issues.'

*Kamara v DPP* [1973] 2 All ER 1242, [1974] AC 104 was concerned with unlawful assembly rather than affray, but Lord Hailsham LC had this to say ([1973] 2 All ER 1242 at 1248, [1974] AC 104 at 116):

'No doubt unlawful assembly differs from an affray, because, unlike affray, it implies a common purpose, and because, unlike affray, actual violence is unnecessary provided the public peace is endangered, but in my view it is analogous to affray in that (1) it need not be in a public place and (2) that the essential requisite in both is the presence or likely presence of innocent third parties, members of the public not participating in the illegal activities in question. It is their presence, or the likelihood of it, and the danger to their security in each case which constitutes the threat to public peace and the public element necessary to the commission of each offence.'

We respectfully agree with the dictum of Lord Hailsham LC in *Taylor v DPP* [1973] 2 All ER 1108 at 1112–1113, [1973] AC 964 at 987–988, and, in so far as they are relevant, the terms of the directions to the jury by Paull J in *R v Mapstone*. Certainly, so far as fighting in a public place is concerned, it would be wrong to allow guilt or innocence to depend on the chance presence or absence of an uninvolved member of the public. The essence of affray is participation in unlawful violence in fighting of such a kind as is calculated to cause any person of reasonable firmness who might witness it to be terrified, for example by reason of fear for his or her own safety. There will in most cases be evidence available from actual uninvolved bystanders as to the nature and degree of the violence being exhibited, but the absence of such evidence does not mean that the prosecution must fail. It would be strange were it otherwise, because uninvolved members of the public are likely, if they are wise, to make themselves scarce at the first signs of trouble. It would scarcely be just if this fact allowed defendants to escape conviction.

Nor do we consider it necessary for the prosecution to prove the reasonable likelihood that members of the public might come on the scene. Quite apart from the practical difficulties of proving a 'likelihood' of that nature, it involves the jury in what is little more than a guessing game. As the Law Commission say in Working Paper no 82 (Offences against Public Order) para 4.27:

'... Furthermore, it may be argued that a "public place" is by definition a place where a member of the public may be, and that the extra requirement of reasonable likelihood of the presence of others therefore involves an arbitrary qualification of the scope of that term ...'

If counsel appearing as amicus curiae is right in his concession that in some cases the jury may properly infer the presence of a bystander from the nature of the place, and in some cases they may not, that would involve the court or jury in the task of deciding whether the public place was or was not sufficiently public for the inference to be drawn. This would, to say the least, be a difficult exercise.

In the light of those conclusions it is not strictly necessary for us to tackle the question of whether, assuming the bystander to be necessary for proof of the offence, G in the present case can be regarded as a bystander. However a simple example serves to demonstrate the absurdity of the situation if he could not be so regarded. G stands terrified, the sole spectator of the fighting and having nothing to do with either batch of contestants. At that point he is undoubtedly a bystander and the offence of affray is complete. The fighting then becomes more widespread and G is himself attacked. If the arguments put forward by defending counsel in the present case are correct, the affray then ceases because there is no uninvolved spectator/bystander. The attack on G then ceases and the situation becomes less serious but fighting continues, does the offence of affray then start again?

It seems to us clear that in any event the innocent victims of an affray may themselves fill the role of the so-called bystander. The opposite conclusion would lead to absurdity.

We have employed the word 'bystander' throughout this judgment as a convenient abbreviation and in deference to what seems to have become common usage. The word has however connotations which make it not altogether apt. We use it in the sense of 'innocent member of the public within sight or earshot of the fighting'.

We reject as impracticable the distinction which counsel appearing as amicus curiae seeks to draw between persons who are the intended victims of those unlawfully fighting on the one hand and those on the other hand who are, as he describes it, 'merely sucked into the mêlée'.

We summarise our views as follows. In order to establish the offence of affray in a public place, the Crown must establish that: (i) there was unlawful fighting or unlawful violence used by one or more than one person against another or others, or there was an unlawful display of force by one or more than one person without actual violence, and (ii) the unlawful fighting, violence or display of force was such that a bystander of reasonable firmness and courage (whether or not present or likely to be present) might reasonably be expected to be terrified.

We do not consider it either necessary or desirable in this opinion to embark on any discussion about fighting in places which are not public.

The answers to the questions posed are therefore as follows: (i) No. (ii) In all circumstances, so far as we are able to see.

*Opinion accordingly.*

Solicitors: *Director of Public Prosecutions*; *Treasury Solicitor*.

N P Metcalfe Esq    Barrister.

# Lawrence v Lawrence

FAMILY DIVISION
ANTHONY LINCOLN J
27, 28, 29 JUNE, 12 JULY 1984

*Conflict of laws – Marriage – Validity – Essential validity – Capacity to marry – Choice of law – Law with which marriage had most real and substantial connection – Law of intended matrimonial residence – Parties intending England to be matrimonial home – Husband having English domicile – Wife not having capacity to marry by law of her ante-nuptial domicile – Husband and wife having capacity to marry by English law – Whether validity of marriage to be governed by marriage's real and substantial connection with England or by wife's ante-nuptial domicile.*

In 1944 the wife, a Brazilian national whose domicile of origin was Brazil, married there a United States national who, at about that time, acquired a Brazilian domicile of choice. The parties lived in Brazil, so that the wife retained her Brazilian domicile. The marriage broke down and the parties separated. In 1970 the wife wished to marry the petitioner, who was domiciled in England. They agreed that when they were free to marry their matrimonial home would be in England. The wife could not obtain a divorce from her existing husband in Brazil but only a decree of separation. Furthermore, Brazilian law recognised foreign decrees of divorce only as decrees of separation and not as decrees of divorce. The wife therefore went to Nevada to obtain a divorce. On 11 September 1970, having resided there for the period required to give the Nevada court jurisdiction, the wife obtained a decree of divorce. The following day, while still in Nevada, the wife and the petitioner were married. Shortly afterwards they went to England and purchased a house there as their matrimonial home. In 1972 their marriage broke down and the wife went back to Brazil leaving the petitioner in England. In proceedings by the petitioner in England, the wife sought a decree that the Nevada marriage was null and void. She contended that under English conflict of law rules capacity to contract a marriage was governed by the law of each party's ante-nuptial domicile and accordingly, because her domicile prior to the Nevada marriage had been Brazil and Brazilian law did not recognise her foreign divorce decree as a decree of divorce but merely as a decree of separation, it followed that she had not had capacity to contract the marriage with the petitioner.

**Held** – When faced with the choice of upholding the validity of a foreign marriage by applying the doctrine of the law with which the marriage had the most real and substantial connection or invalidating it by applying the dual domicile doctrine (ie that both parties had to have capacity to marry under the law of their ante-nuptial domicile), an English court ought to apply the former doctrine and so uphold the marriage. Accordingly, the court would apply English law rather than Brazilian law in determining the wife's capacity to marry the petitioner and whether their consequent marriage in Nevada was valid, because the marriage had a real and substantial connection with England by virtue of that being where they intended to make their home and the choice of English law as the law governing the wife's capacity to marry the petitioner resulted in the validation of their marriage. The wife was therefore not entitled to a decree that her marriage to the petitioner was a nullity (see p 511 j to p 512 c and e, post).

*Perrini v Perrini* [1972] 2 All ER 323 and dictum of Lord Simon in *Vervaeke v Smith (Messina and A-G intervening)* [1982] 2 All ER at 159 applied.

Quaere. Whether the doctrine of the law with which the marriage has the most real and substantial connection should be chosen in preference to the dual domicile doctrine if the former doctrine results in the marriage being invalidated when the latter doctrine would not, or where the most real and substantial connection arising out of an intended matrimonial home is a domicile other than England (see p 512 c d, post).

### Notes
For the law governing capacity to marry, see 8 Halsbury's Laws (4th edn) para 466.

### Cases referred to in judgment
*De Reneville v De Reneville* [1948] 1 All ER 56, [1948] P 100, CA.
*Furse (decd), Re* [1980] 3 All ER 838.
*Indyka v Indyka* [1967] 2 All ER 689, [1969] 1 AC 33, [1967] 3 WLR 510, HL.
*Ingham ( falsely called Sachs) v Sachs* (1886) 56 LT 920.
*IRC v Bullock* [1976] 3 All ER 353, [1976] 1 WLR 1178, CA.
*Padolecchia v Padolecchia (orse Leis)* [1967] 3 All ER 863, [1968] P 314, [1968] 2 WLR 173.
*Paine, Re, re Williams, Griffith v Waterhouse* [1940] Ch 46.
*Perrini v Perrini* [1979] 2 All ER 323, [1979] Fam 84, [1979] 2 WLR 472.
*R v Brentwood Superintendent Registrar of Marriages, ex p Arias* [1968] 3 All ER 279, [1968] 2 QB 956, [1968] 3 WLR 531, DC.
*Vervaeke v Smith (Messina and A-G intervening)* [1982] 2 All ER 144, [1983] 1 AC 145, [1982] 2 WLR 855, HL.

### Petition
The petitioner, Norman Lawrence, sought a declaration that the marriage celebrated on 12 September 1970 between him and the respondent, Helena Lawrence, then Helena Harley, in Las Vegas in the State of Nevada in the United States of America was a valid and subsisting marriage. The respondent by her amended answer sought a declaration that the marriage was null and void. The facts are set out in the judgment.

*Ian Karsten* for the petitioner.
*Jonathan Cole* for the respondent.

*Cur adv vult*

12 July. The following judgment was delivered.

**ANTHONY LINCOLN J.** In these proceedings the petitioner seeks a declaration that his marriage in Nevada to the respondent following on her divorce in that state was and is a valid one, while the respondent by her amended answer seeks a decree that the marriage is null and void. In order to resolve the issues raised the court has to consider some of the uncertainties in the conflict of law rules governing the recognition of foreign divorces and the capacity of the parties to marry.

Somewhat illogically, at the close of the very full and helpful argument my attention was drawn to the possibility that the court had no jurisdiction to grant the declaration as formulated by the petitioner. But both parties are anxious to have their status resolved and there is no doubt that I have jurisdiction to grant or refuse the decree sought by the respondent. It raises exactly the same questions and I therefore readily gave leave for the amended answer claiming such a decree to be filed. The issue remains: is the petitioner the respondent's husband or not?

Some of the facts were in issue, some were conceded. First as to the husband. He was born in Seattle and lived in the United States until 1948. He then travelled widely but finally decided to settle in England. It is conceded that he was domiciled in England at the time of his marriage to the respondent in 1970 and remains so to this day.

The domicile of the respondent wife at the time of her divorce and remarriage in 1970 is more contentious. She was born in Brazil in 1921, the daughter of a prosperous Brazilian factory owner and one of his factory workers. There is ample documentary evidence showing that her nationality was Brazilian. Equally it is beyond doubt that her domicile of origin was Brazilian. In 1944 she married Robert Harley at Recife in Brazil. He was a national of the United States, having been born in Philadelphia, Pennsylvania in 1920. He went to Brazil early in his life and served there continuously as vice-consul. After the marriage in 1944 he gave up his consular work to become a director and subsequently managing director of one of his father-in-law's companies. He lived in Recife and travelled a great deal in Brazil. He continued to retain his United States passport and much reliance was placed by counsel for the petitioner on the entries made by Mr Harley when applying for a renewal. For my part I do not consider such entries a reliable indication of Mr Harley's true intentions at the time. I prefer the evidence of Jose de Barros, a Brazilian lawyer who worked closely with the respondent and her family companies and who knew Mr Harley well. He satisfied me that Mr Harley adopted Brazil as his permanent home. Mr Harley loved Brazil. He was in all but nationality a Brazilian with a Brazilian life-style. He spoke Brazilian perfectly and adopted all the ways of Brazil. He lived not as an expatriate but as if he were indigenous. His matrimonial home was there. It is true that he retained his United States passport and his United States nationality in case he should need to move to the United States if there were to be a revolution in Brazil. It was his method of leaving an escape route available to him should he be compelled by a serious and dangerous revolution to leave the country to which he was so devoted. It is also true that in 1977, by which time all signs of instability had faded, he renounced his American nationality and became a Brazilian national. But, as Buckley LJ said in *IRC v Bullock* [1976] 3 All ER 353 at 358, [1976] 1 WLR 1178 at 1184, the intention of establishing a permanent home in a new country does not have to be shown to be immutable; the decision to live there need not be irrevocable. Mr Harley, as I see it, meant to live in Brazil permanently. He kept his passport just in case things got out of hand: if badly out of hand, he might or might not have to leave; if less than badly, he would not. It was a matter of degree. The circumstances in which he might consider using the escape route were wholly indefinite, unpredictable and indefinable. The contingency was a vague one: see *Re Furse (decd)* [1980] 3 All ER 838. Whatever be the evidentiary burden, whether beyond reasonable doubt or on a balance of probabilities, the respondent wife, on whom the burden lay, has satisfied me that on or about the time of Mr Harley's marriage to her in 1944 he acquired a domicile of choice in Brazil.

By 1968 when the respondent wife first met the petitioner in Switzerland, she and Mr Harley were separated. In early 1970 the petitioner and the respondent decided to marry if and when she obtained a divorce and they agreed that their matrimonial home would be in England, where the petitioner was now well entrenched.

But there were difficulties in the way of the respondent if she were to be free to marry. She could not obtain a divorce in Brazil, only a decree of separation (desquite). And as to foreign decrees of divorce Brazilian law recognises them in the following way: in relation to the respondent wife, because she was a Brazilian national the foreign decree was recognised only as a decree of separation (personal and proprietary) so that she was not free to marry. In relation to a foreigner (and Mr Harley was in 1970 still a United States national), the decree of divorce was fully valid but he was prohibited from remarrying in Brazil.

In July 1970, under the guidance of legal advice, the petitioner and respondent went to Las Vegas in Nevada and resided there for seven weeks. The law of Nevada required six weeks' residence, regarded there as domicile, to found its jurisdiction. On 11 September 1970 at the Las Vegas court the respondent obtained a decree of divorce. Mr Harley was represented by his attorney.

The next day, still in Las Vegas, the petitioner and respondent married and there was a wedding reception. After a brief stay in the United States they went to London in accordance with their agreed plans. The freehold of a house was purchased at Godalming in Surrey and this was to be and became their matrimonial home. The respondent did not sever her links with Brazil. She always meant to visit the country and keep contact with the family companies, doing so from her base in England. She set up a company in England for the importation of goods from Brazil. I am satisfied that if the marriage had prospered the petitioner and the respondent would have remained at the matrimonial home or its successor, always in England.

But in June 1972 the marriage was in trouble. The petitioner moved out, leaving the respondent at the matrimonial home. Then the respondent left for Brazil in September. In June 1973 the petitioner moved back to the matrimonial home to look after the house and there he has remained, while the respondent for her part has remained in the country of her birth, Brazil.

The decree of divorce was pronounced in the District Court of Nevada in Clark County. It recites that the plaintiff (the respondent here) is and has been an actual and bona fide resident of the county, actually domiciled therein for more than six weeks immediately preceding the commencement of the proceedings. Under s 5 of the Recognition of Divorces and Legal Separations Act 1971 those findings of fact are conclusive evidence so far as I am concerned, since both spouses took part in the proceedings in Las Vegas, Mr Harley by appearing through his attorney. Mr Harley was at the time still a national of the United States, and so under s 3 of the 1971 Act the divorce decree is enjoined to be recognised by this court as being an effective decree.

Ideally the conflict laws relating to the status of married and divorced persons should be simple and easily understood. In a period of international mobility and frequent divorce, people should not find themselves bigamously married because of the complexity of the laws. One of the obvious consequences of a recognised freedom from one marriage would appear to the plain man to be the authorised freedom to enter into another marriage. That is precisely what the petitioner and respondent (and possibly Mr Harley) intended at the time. It is at least an arguable construction of the words in s 3(1) of the 1971 Act, 'The validity of an overseas divorce . . . shall be recognised', that Parliament also intended such consequences to flow from recognition. But case law and the divided opinions of academic lawyers rule out such simple solutions.

On my findings of fact the respondent wife, whose domicile of origin was Brazil, remained domiciled there when she married Mr Harley, his domicile in Brazil having been acquired by choice. Then after the Nevada divorce her domicile of origin prevailed alone. Her ante-nuptial domicile was Brazilian and that law withheld recognition of the divorce decree. The question then arises: did she have capacity to marry the petitioner? If the law of her ante-nuptial domicile is alone the governing law under English conflict rules, then she had no such capacity. If the law of the place of her intended matrimonial home determines the question, then under English law she had such capacity. The petitioner had the necessary capacity whichever law is to be applied.

The authorities have been reviewed on many occasions, but I must refer to certain aspects of the relevant decisions and the criticisms that have been levelled at them.

*Ingham ( falsely called Sachs) v Sachs* (1886) 56 LT 920 is a decision which is rarely cited. The facts were very similar to the present case. A domiciled Austrian whose law did not recognise divorce married in Berlin. He subsequently obtained a divorce decree in Berlin. He then married in England. Butt J refused to withhold recognition of the Berlin decree. He was not impressed by the fact that the Austrian's ante-nuptial domicile refused recognition. He held that the personal status resulting from the marriage in Berlin was to be determined by the law of the country in which the contract was made and refused to nullify the marriage. I do not accept that the case turned on a pleading point. The principle of the decision is a good deal closer to the principle of the intended matrimonial home than it is to the dual domicile principle.

In *R v Brentwood Superintendent Registrar of Marriages, ex p Arias* [1968] 3 All ER 279, [1968] 2 QB 956 the ante-nuptial and post-nuptial domicile of the parties was Swiss. Sachs LJ cited two passages from *Dicey and Morris on the Conflict of Laws* (8th edn, 1967) pp 254, 257 (r 31): '. . . a person's capacity to marry is a matter of public concern to the country of his domicile' and 'Capacity to marry is governed by the law of each party's ante-nuptial domicile' (see [1968] 3 All ER 279 at 282, [1968] 2 QB 956 at 958). It was not necessary to argue and was not argued that the domicile of the intended matrimonial home could provide the governing law. The rule as stated in *Dicey and Morris* was accepted as the starting point and the issue in the case was whether the discriminatory nature of Swiss law so offended the conscience that the English courts could not give effect to it. That argument was rejected. There are many allusions in the judgment to the post-nuptial domicile of the intending spouses (see [1968] 3 All ER 279 at 281–283, [1968] 2 QB 956 at 967–969). The decision, though it could have been based on that fact (the fact of post-nuptial domicile), was not.

*Re Paine, re Williams, Griffith v Waterhouse* [1940] Ch 46 was a decision which expressly adopted the ante-nuptial domicile. But as in the *Brentwood* case the spouses intended to live in England and did so until their deaths. Since this was also the country of their domicile before the marriage, there was no argument before the court in favour of the post-nuptial doctrine and no need for one.

*Padolecchia v Padolecchia (orse Leis)* [1967] 3 All ER 863, [1968] P 314 and *Perrini v Perrini* [1979] 2 All ER 323, [1979] Fam 84 were both concerned with nullity decrees. Each raised similar and separate questions, namely the recognition of such decrees and capacity to marry. In the first case Simon P took as his starting point that each party must be capable of marrying by the law of his and her respective ante-nuptial domicile, citing r 31 in *Dicey and Morris on the Conflict of Laws* (8th edn, 1967) p 254 (now r 33 in the 10th edn, 1980, p 285) (see [1967] 3 All ER 863 at 873, [1968] P 314 at 336). On that basis the law of Italy refused recognition to a Mexican decree and consequently the Italian-domiciled husband was not free to marry a second wife. He accordingly nullified the second marriage. It is to be noted that the husband's domicile of origin in Italy subsisted at all material times, but it was not argued that the law of the intended matrimonial domicile could be held in the alternative to govern the capacity or incapacity of the parties, nor is it easy to discern with what country the impugned marriage had the most real and substantial connection.

In *Perrini v Perrini* [1979] 2 All ER 323, [1979] Fam 84 Baker P reached the opposite conclusion on facts which in some respects were not the same. He recognised a decree of nullity as freeing each party to enter into another marriage and upheld the later marriage. Taking his cue from speeches in *Indyka v Indyka* [1967] 2 All ER 689, [1969] 1 AC 33 which encouraged departure from the tyranny of domicile, but emphasising that he was acting independently of anything said in *Indyka v Indyka*, Baker P held that the quality of the wife's residence in the state where the decree was granted was such as to entitle the decree to recognition. He thus applied the common law principles applicable to the recognition of foreign divorces in upholding the nullity decree. So much for the first question. Then as to the second question, capacity to marry, the husband had none if his domiciliary law governed the matter. Italian law did not recognise the foreign decree. Baker P was urged to apply the dual domicile test and to hold that each party must be capable of marrying by the law of his ante-nuptial domicile. He rejected the argument, holding the second marriage valid because the husband had in English law (the law with which in fact the marriage had a real and substantial connection) capacity to marry.

The facts in the case before me are to be distinguished. First this case concerns a foreign decree of divorce, the recognition of which is good by the terms of the 1971 Act. In the hours between the divorce and the second marriage the wife (the respondent) resumed or continued (it matters not which) her domicile of origin. The marriage was a foreign one, but the parties intended that their married years would be spent in England, the domicile of the petitioner. If guidance is to be derived from either *Padolecchia v Padolecchia* or *Perrini v Perrini*, those facts must be borne in mind.

My examination of these authorities persuades me that, while the dual domicile test has been applied over and over again, there is no case relating to a foreign divorce and subsequent marriage in which the courts have been confronted with a choice between the competing doctrines: dual domicile or intended matrimonial domicile (I use this latter phrase to refer to the law of the country with which the marriage has the most real and substantial connection). In *Ingham ( falsely called Sachs) v Sachs* (1886) 56 LT 920 the competing claims were between the dual domicile and (probably though this is not clear) the lex loci celebrationis. *Perrini v Perrini* concerned a foreign nullity decree.

In moving through this uncharted territory I find some guidance in the speech of Lord Simon in *Vervaeke v Smith (Messina and A-G intervening)* [1982] 2 All ER 144 at 159, [1983] 1 AC 145 at 166, where he said:

> 'The second test is the application to choice of law of the criterion which your Lordships proposed in *Indyka v Indyka* [1967] 2 All ER 689, [1969] 1 AC 33 in considering recognition of the jurisdiction of a foreign divorce court. The criterion of a real and substantial connection seems to me to be useful and relevant in considering the choice of law for testing, if not all questions of essential validity, at least the question of the sort of quintessential validity in issue in this appeal, the question which law's public policy should determine the validity of the marriage. The territorial law with which a marriage has the most real and substantial connection will often be the law of the prospective matrimonial home; this was the law favoured to govern all questions of essential validity by [*Cheshire and North on Private International Law* (10th edn, 1979)], and by Lord Greene MR (Somervell LJ concurring) in *De Reneville v De Reneville* [1948] 1 All ER 56 at 61–62, [1948] P 100 at 114. The test of the most real and substantial connection may obviate some of the objections to the test of the prospective matrimonial home, eg that the latter gives no guidance where no matrimonial home is clearly indicated or, as here, no cohabitation at all is proposed. Undoubtedly, in the instant case, England was the territory with which the marriage had the most real and substantial connection . . .'

His dictum was directed at circumstances in which the public policy of two legal systems pulled in opposite directions. The context was a little different from the present case, but it concerned a facet of the law of personal capacity. The question in the instant case, whether the petitioner and respondent were free to marry, appears to me directly to involve 'the quintessential validity' of the marriage contract into which they purported to enter. I am encouraged to adopt the same approach and apply the criterion of real and substantial connection not only by this dictum in a similar though not identical context, but also by Baker P's approach in relation to nullity decrees. In the instant case the criterion is a sensible one: when the petitioner and the respondent were marrying they were looking to the future, to a married life in England and to an established matrimonial home in this country, not backwards to the period in which Brazil had played a very important part in the respondent's life and scarcely any in the life of the petitioner. So the future domicile of their joint home and of themselves personally is at least as important in determining their status as the past domiciles of each of them. The domicile of the respondent of course became English at the moment of the conclusion of their marriage contract.

The virtue and vices of both criteria have been fully and fairly canvassed in *Cheshire and North on Private International Law* (10th edn) pp 332ff and the opposed academic factions seem entrenched in their positions. For my part I consider it desirable that contracts of marriage entered into in circumstances such as occurred in the instant case (where the domiciles became English) should be upheld rather than destroyed. If the application of the criterion of real and substantial connection results in the marriage being held valid and the application of the dual domicile criterion results in invalidation, in my view the former should prevail. I leave open the question whether the vice versa proposition should also hold good. Nor is it necessary to resolve the question whether, where the intended domicile is other than that of England, the criterion should apply, though I see no grounds for such chauvinistic distinctions.

Now such a principle if it be correct is an extension by analogy of s 7 of the 1971 Act (a fact which has disturbed at least one juristic author writing in the Cambridge Law Journal about the decision in *Perrini v Perrini* (see J G Collier (1979) 38 CLJ 289)). But the conclusion I have reached at least fulfils the hopes expressed by the Law Commission in their consultation paper on Recognition of Foreign Nullity Decrees and Related Matters (April 1983).

I accordingly hold that in the eyes of our law the Nevada divorce is to be fully recognised and that the Nevada marriage had a real and substantial connection with England and is valid by the law of this country. Thus I refuse to grant the respondent a decree of nullity.

*Declaration accordingly.*

Solicitors: *Clintons* (for the petitioner); *Gamlens* (for the respondent).

Bebe Chua     Barrister.

# South West Water Authority v Rumble's

HOUSE OF LORDS

LORD SCARMAN, LORD DIPLOCK, LORD ROSKILL, LORD BRANDON OF OAKBROOK AND LORD TEMPLEMAN

16 JANUARY, 14 FEBRUARY 1985

*Water supply – Charges – Power of water authority to make charges – Charges for services performed – Liability of person who has not received services – Power of water authority to make such charges for services performed, facilities provided or rights made available by them as they think fit – Sewerage services – Roof drainage – Occupier of shop – Shop not connected to public sewers – Occupier not receiving sewerage services – Surface water from roof on hereditament above occupier's shop draining into water authority's sewer – Whether water authority having power to impose charge on occupier for sewerage and drainage services provided by authority – Water Act 1973, s 30(1)(1A).*

The respondents were the rateable occupiers of ground floor shop premises situated in the area of the appellant water authority. The premises, which formed part of a separate hereditament within the meaning of s 30(11) of the Water Act 1973, had no separate water supply and there were no water appliances or facilities within the shop and no water therefore drained from inside the shop to the sewer. There was a separate hereditament above the respondents' premises containing facilities connected to a sewer, and above which was a roof from which surface water was drained by gutters emptying into two downpipes which discharged into the water authority's sewer. The water authority sought to charge the respondents for water services under s 30<sup>a</sup> of the 1973 Act in respect of the provision of a sewer into which the drainage system of the roof discharged but the respondents refused to pay. The registrar held that the respondents were liable for the water charges but on appeal the judge held that they were not. The water authority appealed to the Court of Appeal, which dismissed the appeal. The water authority appealed to the House of Lords, contending, inter alia, (i) that the drainage of water by a sewer from the building as a whole constituted for the purposes of s 30(1)(b) and (1A)(a) 'drainage' from a hereditament because the respondents' shop was structurally an integral part of the building, which enjoyed as a whole the protection of the roof and its drainage facilities, and (ii) that the drainage of water falling on the roof of the premises above the shop amounted to 'use', for the benefit of the hereditament, 'of facilities which drain to a sewer' for the purposes of s 30(1)(b) and (1A)(b).

**Held** – Whether the rateable owner or occupier of a hereditament had the 'use' of drainage facilities within s 30(1A)(b) of the 1973 Act was a question of fact in each case. Where a structure had a roof which covered and protected a separate hereditament on the ground floor as well as other hereditaments above it, it was a realistic and proper use of language to describe the situation as one in which the occupier of the ground floor had the use of the roof and its drainage facilities. Since the respondents' shop clearly enjoyed the benefit of that facility, the respondents were liable to pay the water charges in respect of that benefit. The appeal would therefore be allowed (see p 518 *a* to *e* and p 519 *c* to *g*).

Decision of the Court of Appeal [1984] 2 All ER 240 reversed.

## Notes

For the power of a water authority to make charges for services performed, facilities provided or rights made available, see 49 Halsbury's Laws (4th edn) para 762.

For the Water Act 1973, s 30(1) and (1A) (as substituted by the Water Charges Act 1976, s 2(1)) and for s 30(11) of the 1973 Act (as added by s 2(2) of the 1976 Act), see 46 Halsbury's Statutes (3rd edn) 2099.

---

*a*   Section 30, so far as material, is set out at p 515 *f* to p 516 *b*, post

**Case referred to in opinions**

*Daymond v South West Water Authority* [1976] 1 All ER 39, [1976] AC 609, [1975] 3 WLR 865, HL.

**Appeal**

The South West Water Authority appealed with leave of the Court of Appeal against the decision of that court (Ackner and O'Connor LJJ) ([1984] 2 All ER 240, [1984] 1 WLR 800) on 12 March 1984 dismissing an appeal by the appellants against the decision of his Honour Judge Chope given on 25 August 1983 in the Truro County Court whereby he allowed an appeal by the respondents, A B & P J Rumble, a partnership trading as Rumble's, against an order of Mr Registrar Lyne dated 9 June 1983 that the respondents pay to the water authority the sum of £196·84 in respect of water charges levied pursuant to s 30 of the Water Act 1973 as amended by s 2 of the Water Charges Act 1976 on the respondents' shop at 5 Fore Street, Newquay. The facts are set out in the opinion of Lord Scarman.

*Gerard Ryan QC* and *Roger Toulson* for the appellants.
*John Stuart Colyer QC* and *Timothy Scott* for the respondents.

Their Lordships took time for consideration.

14 February. The following opinions were delivered.

**LORD SCARMAN.** My Lords, the appellants are a regional water authority established pursuant to s 2 of the Water Act 1973. The respondents are the rateable occupiers of ground floor shop premises at 5 Fore Street, Newquay. The water authority seek to recover from the respondents a water charge for sewerage services in respect of the shop premises. The water authority rely on a charges scheme made by them pursuant to s 31 of the 1973 Act as entitling them to demand and recover the charge which they claim. The power to charge for sewerage services arises under s 30(1) of the 1973 Act as amended by s 2 of the Water Charges Act 1976. Put very briefly, the case for the authority is that they have the power to charge because the respondents are persons for whom sewerage services were provided during the financial year 1981–82 in respect of the shop. The respondents deny that the authority performed any services for them for the benefit of their shop: the shop is not drained to a sewer, and the respondents do not, in their submission, have the use for the benefit of the shop of any sewerage service or facility. The point is primarily one of construction of the relevant statutory provisions, the facts being agreed. If the authority are, as they submit, empowered to make the charge, a further question calls for consideration, namely whether on the true construction of the charges scheme the authority have validly and effectually fixed the charge so as to impose on the respondents liability to pay it.

*The facts*

The shop is a separate hereditament for rating purposes, its rateable value being £930. It has no water supply. There are no water appliances or facilities within the shop; no water therefore, drains from inside the shop to a sewer. But the shop does enjoy the protection of the roof of the building of which it is structurally the lower part; and surface water is drained off the roof by a gutter and pipe system discharging into a public sewer.

The building, known as 5 Fore Street, consists of the shop on the ground floor and above it a flat which is separate from the shop and is in separate occupation. No satisfactory evidence was received at the trial as to tenure, but it appears from what the judge in the county court said in his judgment that the respondents' interest in the shop is leasehold and that their landlord is under an obligation to keep the roof of the building in good repair.

The roof, which protects the shop as well as the flat, is drained of surface water by gutters emptying into two downpipes. One downpipe, which is fixed to the street front of the building, discharges onto the footpath over which the water passes into a gulley connected to the public sewer; the other is fixed to the back of the building and its discharge is channelled into the sewer.

The authority claim the sum of £196·84, being the balance of a charge which they say is due for sewerage services performed during the year beginning 1 April 1981. The sewerage services for which they seek to charge are the provision of a sewer into which the drainage system of the roof discharges in the manner which I have described. The charge being unpaid, the authority began proceedings in the Truro County Court. The registrar gave judgment for the sum claimed. On the respondents' appeal, the county court judge reversed the decision of the registrar, holding that on the true construction of the statutory provisions the water authority were not entitled to make a charge against the respondents in respect of the shop. He added on a point initially raised by himself and thereafter pursued by the respondents that, if the authority were entitled to make a charge, the charges scheme constituted an undue discrimination against persons in the situation of the respondents (i e occupiers of premises having no connection with a sewer) and was illegal under s 30(5) of the 1973 Act.

The water authority appealed. Dismissing the appeal, the Court of Appeal (Ackner and O'Connor LJJ) ([1984] 2 All ER 240, [1984] 1 WLR 800) held that the statute did not empower the authority to recover the charge. In the view of the court the shop was not drained to a public sewer; nor did the respondents, the rateable occupiers, have the use for the benefit of the shop of the drainage facility attached to the roof. The court did not deal with the discrimination point save only to order a retrial of the issue in the county court on the ground that there had been insufficient material to enable the judge to reach a decision. The court granted the water authority leave to appeal to your Lordships' House.

*The statute*

For the purposes of the appeal the critical statutory provision is the amendment to s 30 of the 1973 Act made by s 2 of the 1976 Act. The effect of the amendment, so far as material to the appeal, was to substitute three new subsections for the original sub-s (1) of s 30. This substitution resulted in sub-s (1) being replaced by sub-s (1), (1A) and (1B) so that the amended law reads:

'(1) Subject to the provisions of this Act, a water authority shall have power to fix such charges for the services performed, facilities provided or rights made available by them (including separate charges for separate services, facilities or rights or combined charges for a number of services, facilities or rights) as they think fit, and to demand, take and recover such charges—(a) for services performed, facilities provided or rights made available in the exercise of any of their functions, from persons for whom they perform the services, provide the facilities or make the rights available, and (b) without prejudice to paragraph (a) above,—(i) for services performed, facilities provided or rights made available in the exercise of functions under section 14 above, from persons liable to be rated in respect of hereditaments to which this sub-paragraph applies, and (ii) for services performed, facilities provided or rights made available in the exercise of functions specified in subsection (1B) below, from all persons liable to be rated in respect of hereditaments in their area or particular classes of such persons.

(1A) Subsection (1)(b)(i) above applies to a hereditament if—(a) it is drained by a sewer or drain connecting, either directly or through an intermediate sewer or drain, with a public sewer provided for foul water or surface water or both, or (b) the person liable to be rated in respect of the hereditament has the use, for the benefit of the hereditament, of facilities which drain to a sewer or drain so connecting, or (c) it is subject to special rating.

(1B)  The functions mentioned in subsection (1)(b)(ii) above are functions under—
(a) the Rivers (Prevention of Pollution) Acts 1951 to 1961; (b) sections 20, 21 and 22
of the Water Act 1973 (recreation, nature conservation and amenity); (c) the Control
of Pollution Act 1974; (d) the Salmon and Freshwater Fisheries Act 1975; (e) any
local statutory provision conferring functions analogous to those mentioned in
paragraphs (a) to (d) above; and (f) any local statutory provision conferring functions
with respect to navigation.'

It will be observed that these provisions, first, declare a general rule, namely that
charges may be demanded, taken and recovered from persons for whom services are
performed (I shall use these words as a shorthand for services, facilities and rights made
available) by a water authority in the exercise of their statutory functions, and, second,
without prejudice to the general rule, they specify certain classes of persons by reference
to rateability of their premises as persons from whom charges may be recovered. The
appellant authority's submission rests on two propositions: first, that the respondents are
persons liable to be rated in respect of the shop, as to which there is no challenge; and,
second, that the shop is a hereditament to which either para (a) or para (b) of sub-s (1A)
applies. The respondents challenge the second proposition. The issue turns, therefore, on
the construction which it is proper to put on the two paragraphs. It is not, however,
possible to determine their true meaning save in the context of the legislation read as a
whole. I turn first, therefore, to a consideration of the Water Act 1973 and its amendment
by the Water Charges Act 1976.

The 1973 Act introduced great changes of policy and organisation into the management
of the nation's water resources. It established a central and local organisation for the
exercise of functions relating to the supply, abstraction and use of the country's water
resources. These functions included water conservation and supply, sewerage services
and sewage disposal, action against river pollution, the protection of fisheries, land
drainage and the promotion of recreation, nature conservation and amenity. Section 2 of
the 1973 Act established regional water authorities, one of which is the appellant
authority. Part II of the Act sets out the functions of these authorities. This appeal is
concerned with the sewerage and sewerage disposal function. Section 14(1) provides that
it shall be the duty of a water authority to provide such public sewers as may be necessary
for effectually draining their area and to make provision for effectually dealing with the
contents of the sewers; sub-s (4) provides that the owner or occupier of premises shall be
entitled to have his drains made to communicate with a public sewer and thereby to
discharge foul and surface water from his premises to a public sewer.

Section 30 appears in Pt III of the 1973 Act, which contains the financial provisions. As
originally formulated, sub-s (1) empowered a water authority to fix and to require
payment of such charges as the authority should think fit for services performed in the
exercise of the functions imposed on water authorities by the 1973 Act. The subsection
was, as indeed was the rest of the Act, silent as to the persons, or classes of persons, from
whom such charges could be demanded, taken and recovered, save only that by sub-s (5)
of the section the charges were to be fixed so as to avoid any undue preference to, or
discrimination against, any class of persons made chargeable. This silence fell to be
considered by your Lordships' House in *Daymond v South West Water Authority* [1976] 1
All ER 39, [1976] AC 609. Mr Daymond was the rateable owner and occupier of a house
400 yards from the nearest public sewer and not connected to it. The water authority
sought to impose on him a 'general services charge', 95% of which was referable to
sewerage and sewage disposal services. The charge was comparable to the old water rate
which existed before the far-reaching changes introduced by the 1973 Act. A contention
advanced by the authority was that the test of chargeability under the 1973 Act was
benefit derived from the sewerage services provided in their area. The majority of their
Lordshops rejected the contention, holding that the omission of any mention in the Act
of those from whom sewerage charges could be recovered must be repaired by implying
a provision to the effect that sewerage charges could be recovered only from those persons

who availed themselves of such services, eg by connection of their premises to a sewer. Mr Daymond was not, therefore, liable.

Section 2 of the Water Charges Act 1976, which introduced the new provision which is the subject of this appeal and which I have already set out in full, was the legislature's answer to the mischief of omission exposed by your Lordships' House sitting judicially in *Daymond's* case. Clearly Parliament has formulated a different test of chargeability from that which was formulated in that case. Basically it is a test of benefit derived from services performed subject to such limitations as are to be found in the three new subsections.

The benefit test is stated as the governing rule in sub-s (1)(*a*): the authority may recover charges for services etc performed 'from persons for whom they [ie the authority] perform the services'. Nothing in the succeeding two subsections derogates from the general rule, for sub-s (1)(*b*), which introduces the concept of recovery of charges from persons liable to be rated in respect of hereditaments to which the sub-ss (1A) and (1B) apply, is expressed to be 'without prejudice to paragraph (*a*) above'.

The appellant authority made, but soon abandoned, a submission that they could rely on para (*a*) of sub-s (1) and did not have to undertake the task of showing that the shop is a hereditament to which sub-s (1A) applies. The submission failed for the simple reason that the authority's charges scheme, in so far as it relates to sewerage charges, is, with one exception, limited in its application to hereditaments and no person can be charged under the scheme save in respect of a hereditament which is drained to a sewer as set out in para (*a*) of sub-s (1A) or which has the benefit of facilities which drain to a sewer as set out in para (*b*) of that subsection. The exception having no application to the present case, the authority's attempt to rely on the general rule in sub-s (1)(*a*) is defeated by the terms of their own scheme. For a charge can be levied only under a scheme duly made or by agreement: see s 30(2). There was no agreement; and no persons other than those liable to be rated in respect of the hereditaments specified are chargeable under the scheme, if, indeed, they are (a point to which it will be necessary to return when I deal with the case against the scheme itself).

Driven off the general rule, the appellant authority put their case on sub-s (1A). They submitted that the shop meets the conditions specified by paras (*a*) and (*b*), or at the very least by one or other of them. The argument at the bar centred on the true meaning of the word 'drained' in para (*a*) and of the words 'has the use, for the benefit of the hereditament, of facilities which drain to a sewer' in para (*b*).

Save for the technical but well-understood term 'hereditament', the language of the two paragraphs consists of ordinary English words which possess by their very imprecision the flexibility which is the hallmark of the English language, and which is one of the reasons for the survival of English as a living and worldwide tongue. I have no doubt that it would be contrary to the legislative purpose of the enactment to restrict or refine their breadth and flexibility in the context of this legislation, which has to cover a wide range of circumstances and situations present and future. A restrictive interpretation of the legislature's language would defeat the broad purpose of this innovative and reforming statute.

With these general observations very much in mind, I turn to sub-s (1A). The authority's submission is that the word 'drained' in para (*a*) has a broad meaning and must be construed in the light of their duty under s 14(1) of the 1973 Act to drain their area effectually. They argue that the provision of a sewer connected to the roof drainage system does drain the building of water collected on the roof; if the roof were not drained, the shop would be at risk of roof water finding its way into it; removal of that risk is included within the word 'drained' if it be given a broad meaning. The respondents say simply, and with some force, that the verb 'to drain' connotes the removal of water from the premises drained and is not apt to cover the benefit premises may derive from the drainage of other premises. They point to the possibility of absurd results, viz that premises downhill of other premises could be said to be drained merely because the presence of a drainage system higher up the hill prevented them from being flooded.

For myself, I am unimpressed by the argument based on absurdity. It may well be that the shop can be said to be drained by the roof system because structurally it is an integral part of the building which enjoys as a whole the protection of the roof and its drainage facility. It is possible, therefore, that para (*a*) should be given a construction broad enough to cover separate hereditaments comprised in a structure which have the common benefit of the structure's roof and its drainage facility. It is, however, unnecessary to decide the question in this appeal, since, if para (*a*) does not apply, para (*b*) certainly does. Bearing in mind the omission in the original s 30(1) which was discussed in *Daymond's* case [1976] 1 All ER 39, [1976] AC 609, I think that it cannot be doubted that para (*b*) was introduced to cover a hereditament which was not physically drained (in either of the two senses discussed above). In such a case, para (*b*) requires two conditions to be satisfied: (1) that the person liable to be rated has the use of drainage facilities (of the roof in the present case); and (2) that these facilities are a benefit to the hereditament (the shop). A semantic argument developed over the meaning of the words 'has the use'. Their presence in the paragraph is because it was necessary to state in broad terms that the facilities must be those of which the rateable owner or occupier has the use. Whether he does or does not have the use is a question of fact. Where a structure has a roof which covers and protects a separate hereditament on the ground floor as well as other hereditaments above it, it is a realistic and proper use of language to describe the situation as one in which the occupier of the ground floor has the use of the roof and its drainage facility. As for the second condition, the shop plainly enjoys the benefit of the roof's drainage facilities.

My Lords, the one difficulty with the statutory provision in the three subsections which now replace s 30(1) of the 1973 Act, is their complex, over elaborate structure. The words used are simple enough and in their context provide an aspect of the test of benefit which the legislature by sub-s (1)(*a*) clearly intended to introduce. Accordingly, I would hold that the respondents are chargeable in respect of the benefit to their shop of the roof's drainage facility discharging to a public sewer.

*The charges scheme*

The scheme came into force on 1 April 1981. It was made pursuant to the power conferred on the water authority by s 31(1) of the 1973 Act. Subsection (2) of that section provides that the charges to be paid to an authority 'shall be those for which the scheme provides'.

The scheme is poorly drafted, at least in so far as its Part Two, section A is concerned. This part of the scheme sets out the formula for charges in respect of sewerage and sewage disposal. With one immaterial exception, the scheme limits liability to charge for sewerage services to hereditaments defined by reference to the conditions set out in paras (*a*) and (*b*) of s 30(1A) of the 1973 Act. It is, however, woefully inaccurate. It refers not to a person having the use of the drainage facility but to the hereditament having the use. The respondents submit that the slipshod and inaccurate drafting of the scheme, which makes liability to charge to depend, inter alia, on the *hereditament's* use of the drainage facility, fails to reflect the statute which looks to the occupier's use. This failure, it is said, renders the scheme so far as it imposes liability to charge for sewerage services null and void. The intention of the scheme is, however, clear: to incorporate as the test of chargeability the conditons set out in sub-s (1)(*b*) and (1A); and I have no hesitation in so construing it. It is accepted by the respondents that the scheme, in so far as it relates to sewerage charges, is within the statute in all other respects save only that it constitutes, in their submission, an undue discrimination against persons such as the respondents, whose hereditament is chargeable because it has the benefit of facilities which belong to another. This, the judge's point on s 30(5) of the 1973 Act, is the subject of the Court of Appeal's order for a retrial which neither party has asked the House to disturb. For myself, I have the gravest doubts whether this subsection has any application whatever to this charges scheme or to the charge which the authority seeks to levy. But, as your

Lordships have heard no argument on the point, it is right that I should reserve my opinion.

Subject, therefore, to the retrial of the discrimination issue, I would hold that the scheme is a valid scheme in so far as it fixes charges for sewerage services and that it imposes liability to charge on those whose premises comply with one or other of the sets of conditions specified in s 30(A) of the 1973 Act. The argument to the contrary advanced by the respondents was based on a fallacy. It assumed that a charges scheme must spell out those for whom sewerage services are performed. A close scrutiny of s 30(1) in its amended form reveals that a scheme fixes charges for services: it is a price list only. The persons from whom the charges may lawfully be demanded, taken or recovered are set out not in the scheme but in the Act itself: in paras (a) and (b) of sub-s (1). Subsections (1A) and (1B) merely spell out the hereditaments to which para (b) of sub-s (1) applies.

For these reasons, I would allow the authority's appeal, and remit the case to the Truro County Court. The appellants do not seek to disturb the orders for costs made in the courts below and have undertaken to pay the respondents' costs in your Lordships' House in any event. It therefore suffices to order that the appeal be allowed and that the case be remitted to the county court with the following directions: (1) that the discrimination issue arising under s 30(5) of the Water Act 1973 be tried by a judge other than the judge who dealt with the case in the county court; (2) that, if the appellant authority succeed on that issue, judgment for the sum claimed be entered in favour of the appellants; (3) that, if the respondents succeed on that issue, judgment be entered for them; (4) that the costs of the retrial be in the discretion of the judge who hears it.

**LORD DIPLOCK.** My Lords, I have had the advantage of reading in draft the speech of my noble and learned friend Lord Scarman. I agree with it, and for the reasons which he gives I would allow the appeal.

**LORD ROSKILL.** My Lords, I have had the advantage of reading in draft the speech delivered by my noble and learned friend Lord Scarman. I agree that, for the reasons which he states, the appeal should be allowed and an order made in the terms which he proposes.

**LORD BRANDON OF OAKBROOK.** My Lords, I have had the advantage of reading in draft the speech prepared by my noble and learned friend Lord Scarman. I agree with it, and for the reasons which he gives I would allow the appeal and remit the case to the Truro County Court with the directions proposed by him.

**LORD TEMPLEMAN.** My Lords, for the reasons given by my noble and learned friend Lord Scarman, I agree that the appeal should be allowed.

*Appeal allowed.*

Solicitors: *Sherwood & Co*, agents for *I A D Todd*, Exeter (for the appellants); *Radcliffes & Co* (for the respondents).

Mary Rose Plummer    Barrister.

# Mutual Shipping Corp of New York v Bayshore Shipping Co of Monrovia

# The Montan

COURT OF APPEAL, CIVIL DIVISION

SIR JOHN DONALDSON MR, ROBERT GOFF LJ AND SIR ROGER ORMROD

8 NOVEMBER, 21 DECEMBER 1984

*Arbitration – Award – Remission – Grounds for remission – Error – Arbitrator accidentally attributing evidence to wrong parties thereby awarding wrong figure as final sum due – Whether grounds for remission – Arbitration Act 1950, s 22.*

*Arbitration – Award – Confidentiality – Confidential reasons – Arbitrator making accidental slip in figure to be calculated between parties – Arbitrator admitting slip in communications to parties – Whether breach of confidentiality in referring to 'confidential reasons' of arbitrator – Whether court entitled to look at confidential reasons.*

*Arbitration – Award – Arbitrator making accidental slip by attributing evidence to wrong parties thereby giving rise to incorrect final account between them – Whether arbitrator having jurisdiction to correct error without reference to court – Arbitration Act 1950, s 17.*

A dispute arose between the owners and the charterers of a vessel, regarding, inter alia, the amount of fuel used by the vessel. The dispute was referred to arbitration, where the owners contended that the actual fuel consumption was 7·176 tons per day and the charterers contended that it was 4·5 tons per day. The arbitrator accepted the charterers' figure but by mistake transposed the names of the parties thereby incorporating the owners' figure. Accordingly, in calculating the final account, he determined that the charterers were required to pay the owners (on the basis of the higher figure of 7·146 tons) whereas he should have determined that the owners were required to pay the charterers. The arbitrator set out the reasons for his award in a separate document which he marked 'confidential'. Subsequently, in response to the charterers' inquiries, the arbitrator acknowledged that he had made an error and the charterers then applied to the court for an order that the award be remitted to the arbitrator under s 22(1)[a] of the Arbitration Act 1950 so that he could correct the error. The owners contended, inter alia, that there was no evidence of the error since it appeared in the document of reasons and communications between the parties which were confidential, and not on the face of the award. The judge ordered that the award be remitted to the arbitrator, holding that the error could be detected from the communications between the charterers and the arbitrator which, although they referred to the reasons, were not themselves confidential, and therefore it was unnecessary to look at the reasons. The owners appealed.

**Held** – (1) Although s 22 of the 1950 Act did not enable the arbitrator to correct errors of judgment, whether of law or of fact, or to have second thoughts about his decision, it provided the ultimate safeguard to prevent injustice by giving the court a wide power to remit an award to the arbitrator where he had made either a clerical mistake or an error arising from an accidental slip or omission. Accordingly, the question for the court was whether the error made by the arbitrator arose from an accidental slip or omission. In the circumstances, (per Sir John Donaldson MR) in order to ascertain the nature and effect of the error it was necessary to look at the reasons given by the arbitrator, although the cases in which the court would do so were extremely limited since there was a public

---

a    Section 22(1), so far as material, provides: 'In all cases of reference to arbitration the High Court or a judge thereof may . . . remit the matters referred . . . to the reconsideration of the arbitrator or umpire'

interest in preserving the finality of arbitral awards, or alternatively (per Robert Goff LJ) it was unnecessary to refer to the reasons since the existence and nature of the error was sufficiently apparent, without breaching the confidentiality of the reasons, from the arbitrator's admission of his error and the parties' rival contentions and the evidence adduced (see p 524 j, p 525 c to f, p 528 d, p 529 d e, p 531 b c and p 532 a, post).

(2) On the facts, the arbitrator, by mistakenly attributing evidence to the wrong parties, had made an accidental error which seriously affected the award, and since the award was before the court it would be unjust to allow it to remain uncorrected. Accordingly, the judge had been right to exercise his power under s 22 to remit the award to the arbitrator. The appeal would therefore be dismissed (see p 525 c f g, p 526 a b, p 527 a, p 530 b c j, p 531 c to f and p 532 a to e and h, post).

Per curiam. The power of an arbitrator under s 17[b] of the 1950 Act is the same as that of a High Court judge under RCS Ord 20, r 11 (the 'slip rule'), in that he can correct clerical errors or accidental slips, although he cannot reconsider his award. It follows that where an error arises from an accidental slip the arbitrator can himself correct the error under s 17 of the 1950 Act without reference to the court (see p 526 h to p 527 d, p 529 h j, p 531 h j and p 532 b, post); R v Cripps, ex p Muldoon [1984] 2 All ER 705 applied.

Per Sir John Donaldson MR and Robert Goff LJ. (1) Where an arbitrator has made an accidental error, he can himself apply to the court for the award to be remitted to him (see p 525 h, p 530 g to j and p 531 e f, post).

(2) An admission of error by the arbitrator is not a prerequisite to the exercise of the court's jurisdiction to remit, although (per Robert Goff LJ) as a general rule the court should not interfere in cases of simple mistakes unless there has been a clear admission by the arbitrator of his error (see p 525 j and p 530 e f and j, post); Dinn v Blake (1875) LR 10 CP 388 and dictum of Moulton LJ in Re Baxters and Midland Rly Co (1906) 95 LT at 23 applied.

### Notes
For alteration of an arbitration award, see 2 Halsbury's Laws (4th edn) para 613, and for cases on the subject; see 3 Digest (Reissue) 260–261, 1707–1719.

For the Arbitration Act 1950, ss 17, 22, see 2 Halsbury's Statutes (3rd edn) 447, 451.

### Cases referred to in judgments
Adam & Harvey Ltd v International Maritime Supplies Co Ltd [1967] 1 All ER 533, [1967] 1 WLR 445, CA.
Ainsworth v Wilding [1896] 1 Ch 673.
Antaios Cia Naviera SA v Salen Rederierna AB, The Antaios [1984] 3 All ER 229, [1984] 3 WLR 592, HL.
Armitage v Parsons [1908] 2 KB 410, CA.
Barker v Purvis (1888) 56 LT 131, CA.
Baxters and Midland Rly Co, Re (1906) 95 LT 20, CA.
Chessum & Sons v Gordon [1901] 1 KB 694, [1900–3] All ER Rep 260, CA.
Czarnikow v Roth Schmidt & Co [1922] 2 KB 478, [1922] All ER Rep 45, CA.
Dinn v Blake (1875) LR 10 CP 388, DC.
Fritz v Hobson (1880) 14 Ch D 542, [1874–80] All ER Rep 75.
Fuga AG v Bunge AG [1975] 2 Lloyd's Rep 192.
Inchcape, Re, Craigmyle v Inchcape [1942] 2 All ER 157, [1942] Ch 394.
Intermare Transport GmbH v International Copra Export Corp, The Ross Isle and Ariel [1982] 2 Lloyd's Rep 589.
Lawrie v Lees (1881) 7 App Cas 19, HL.
MacCarthy v Agard [1933] 2 KB 417, [1933] All ER Rep 991, CA.
Mello, The, The Nereus (1948) 81 Ll L Rep 230.
Mordue v Palmer (1870) LR 6 Ch App 22.

---

b   Section 17 provides: 'Unless a contrary intention is expressed in the arbitration agreement, the arbitrator or umpire shall have power to correct in an award any clerical mistake or error arising from any accidental slip or omission.'

*Oxley v Link* [1914] 2 KB 734, CA.
*Pioneer Shipping Ltd v BTP Tioxide Ltd, The Nema* [1981] 2 All ER 1030, [1982] AC 724, [1981] 3 WLR 292, HL.
*Preston Banking Co v William Allsup & Sons* [1895] 1 Ch 141, [1891–4] All ER Rep 688, CA.
*R v Cripps, ex p Muldoon* [1984] 2 All ER 705, [1984] QB 686, [1984] 3 WLR 53, CA.
*St Nazaire Co, Re* (1879) 12 Ch D 88, CA.
*Sutherland & Co v Hannevig Bros Ltd* [1921] 1 KB 336, [1920] All ER Rep 670, DC.
*Swire, Re, Mellor v Swire* (1885) 30 Ch D 239, CA.

**Case also cited**
*Flynn v Robertson* (1869) LR 4 CP 324.

**Appeal**
The respondents, Bayshore Shipping Co of Monrovia (the owners), appealed against that part of the order of Hobhouse J made on 12 December 1983 whereby it was ordered (i) that the award of the arbitrator, Mr Clifford Clark, dated 1 August 1983 adjudging that the applicants, Mutual Alliance Co of New York (the charterers), pay to the owners the sum of $US62,402·13 together with interest and costs be set aside, and (ii) that the matter be remitted to the arbitrator for reconsideration. The charterers cross-appealed.

*Roger Buckley QC* and *Peter Irvin* for the owners.
*Jeffrey Gruder* for the charterers.

*Cur adv vult*

21 December. The following judgments were delivered.

**SIR JOHN DONALDSON MR.** In this case Homer has nodded and we have to decide what we can and should do about it. Homer, in this instance, was disguised as Mr Clifford Clark, the doyen of the London maritime arbitrators. Sitting as sole arbitrator he had to resolve a number of individual disputes on specific items appearing in the final accounts between owners and time charterers of the vessel Montan after about 12 months' service. Having done so, he had to make an award of the balance due from one to the other.

By his award dated 1 August 1983 Mr Clark ordered the charterers to pay to the owners $US62,402·13 with costs and to bear the cost of the award. It was now clear that he should have ordered the owners to pay to the charterers $US27,527·87 and in such circumstances he might well have made different orders as to costs. I say that this is now clear and it is. However, the owners submit that they are entitled to retain this windfall benefit, because the court should not have looked at the documents which reveal the truth. This is a submission which is as important and far-reaching as, on one view, it is unmeritorious.

Mr Clark was not asked to give reasons for his award, because the issues were purely matters of fact. His award, in essence, consisted of a bare determination that a sum was owing by the charterers to the owners with consequential orders as to costs. However, in accordance with the practice of London maritime arbitrators, he also provided the parties with a document headed:

'REASONS of Mr Clifford A L Clark, not issued contemporaneously with or forming part of or to be used in any way in connection with his Award dated LONDON, the 1st August 1983.'

It was this document which revealed to the charterers that Mr Clark had made a mistake and the nature of that mistake. Amongst other items in dispute had been an adjustment in the hire to take account of fuel oil saved, as compared with a standard daily rate of consumption. The parties were not agreed on how much fuel had in fact been used. A Mr Sinclair was called by the owners to give evidence that the actual consumption was 7·146 tons per day, a figure which was more favourable to the owners than 4·5 tons per day, which was put forward by a Mr Ferryman, called by the charterers.

In para (4) of his reasons, Mr Clark set out the relevant charterparty clause and added 'Charterers calculated a saving of 1429 tons based on 7·146 m.t. per day against the owners' calculation of 900 tons'. This was a patent error, since 1,429 tons (based on 7·146 tons) would have rendered the charterers liable to pay the owners a very much larger sum than 900 tons (based on 4·5 tons). 'Charterers' should have read 'owners' and vice versa. We have all made such errors. My pupil master once suggested that it would save both of us a deal of trouble if we included a standard paragraph in our pleadings reading: 'In this pleading "plaintiff" means "defendant" and vice versa, unless the context otherwise requires.' However it is a type of error which normally has no adverse consequences.

Mr Clark then went on in para (8) to say that he preferred the evidence of Mr Ferryman. This involved accepting the charterers' figures. When, in para (19), he came to reconstitute the final account between the parties on the basis of his findings, he meant to accept the charterers' figures but incorporated the figure of 1,429 tons 'because of the unintentional transposition of the parties in paragraph (4)'. The quotation is from a letter dated 31 August 1983 which Mr Clark sent to the parties following a flurry of telex messages.

The charterers have applied to the court for an order under s 22 of the Arbitration Act 1950 remitting the award to Mr Clark for reconsideration. Hobhouse J made such an order and the owners now appeal.

I think that it is important to remember why the practice of giving 'claused' or 'restricted' reasons grew up. They are sometimes described as 'confidential' reasons, but this is a misnomer since the only restriction is on using them 'in connection with' the award. The reason for adopting this course was simple. Under the law as it existed before the Arbitration Act 1979 came into force, it was possible to set aside an award on the grounds that it disclosed an error of fact or law 'on its face', but it was not permissible to rely on any such error if its existence required evidence not appearing on the face of the award. There was much learning as to what constituted the face of the award and the first part of Mr Clark's rubric is designed to prevent his reasons being in some way linked with and becoming part of the face of his award.

The situation has been changed dramatically by s 1 of the 1979 Act, which abolished all right to set aside or remit an award for error of fact or law on its face and substituted a limited right of appeal on questions of law, based on the arbitrator's reasons for his award. Unless ordered to do so, arbitrators are not required to give reasons, but the Commercial Court Committee in paras 25 and 26 of the report (Cmnd 7284 (1978)) on which the 1979 Act is based said this:

'25. The existing obstacle to a judicial review based upon reasoned awards is the power and the duty of the court to set aside awards for error on their face. This obstacle could easily be removed and this system would have considerable attractions.
26. In every case an arbitrator would be free to give reasons for his award. This would in itself be an improvement, if arbitrators took advantage of the facility. The making of an award is, or should be, a rational process. Formulating and recording the reasons tends to accentuate its rationality. Furthermore, unsuccessful parties will often, and not unreasonably, wish to know why they have been unsuccessful. This change in the law would make this possible.'

The present position is that an arbitrator can (a) give reasons for his award without any restriction on the use to be made of those reasons, (b) give no reasons or (c) give reasons subject to a restriction, as Mr Clark has done. But whether any reasons are or are not issued contemporaneously with or do or do not form part of the award is now quite irrelevant for any purpose. Probably Mr Clark used this formula before the passing of the 1979 Act and has never revised it.

Unrestricted reasons can form the basis of an application for leave to appeal on a question of law, but the burden of persuading the court to grant leave is a heavy one (see *Pioneer Shipping Ltd v BTP Tioxide Ltd, The Nema* [1981] 2 All ER 1030, [1982] AC 724 and *Antaios Cia Naviera SA v Salen Rederierna AB, The Antaios* [1984] 3 All ER 229, [1984] 3 WLR 592.) Where an arbitrator gives no reasons, the court has power to order him to supply them in sufficient detail to enable it, if leave to appeal is granted, to consider the question of law under appeal (see the 1979 Act, s 1(5), subject to s 3(1)(*b*)). However it will not normally make such an order, unless one of the parties requested such reasons before the award was made (see s 1(6)). The courts have not yet been asked to order an arbitrator to remove the restriction on restricted reasons, but I have no doubt that they could do so in circumstances in which, if no reasons had been given, the courts would have ordered them to be given. The court could achieve this result by wholly ignoring the restricted reasons, treating the arbitrator as having given no reasons and ordering new reasons. It must therefore be able to simply 'open' the restrictions. That is not, however, this case.

Hobhouse J expressed his view on the status of restricted reasons (which he referred to as 'confidential reasons') in the following passage from his judgment:

'(A) *Confidential reasons*  The status of confidential reasons was discussed by Staughton J in *Intermare Transport GmbH v International Copra Export Corp, The Ross Isle and Ariel* [1982] 2 Lloyd's Rep 589. I agree with him that as a matter of contract the parties have agreed with each other and the arbitrator or arbitrators to treat such confidential reasons as confidential. This, as a matter of contract, precludes any party, except by agreement, from referring to them on any application to the court. The contract which imposes and accepts the obligation of confidence is a contract which comes into existence either when the parties concur in asking the arbitrator for such reasons or, when an arbitrator, where there has been no request for reasons, follows the usual practice of London Maritime arbitrators and supplies the parties with confidential reasons and the parties accept such reasons from the arbitrator . . . If I was of the opinion that the charterers' case before me depended on their referring me to the arbitrator's reasons, I would have peremptorily dismissed the motion. But this is not the correct analysis of the application before me. The application is founded on the letter of 31 August 1983 of the arbitrator. That letter is not itself confidential. It was written in the context of a possible application of charterers to the court and does not contain any restriction on its use. It admits an error in the arbitrator's calculations. It is open to Mr Maskell [the solicitor who represented the charterers at the arbitration] to supplement from his own knowledge of the issues in the arbitration the fact that this admitted error must have affected the net sum awarded by the arbitrator in the award. He would not be able to put a precise figure on it because he would not know the fuel oil price which the arbitrator has chosen, but the admitted error can be proved without actually placing the confidential reasons before the court. In some cases it might be possible to detect an arithmetical error simply from a knowledge of the issues and a process of reasoning starting from the actual figure appearing in the award. In other cases such an error might be suspected and the arbitrator, having consulted his own private notes, might admit he had made an error. In the present case the confidential reasons were referred to by Mr Maskell in communications to his opposite number and to the arbitrator to draw their attention to the probability that an error had been made in arriving at the figure used for the award. Such an exercise did not involve any breach of confidence. It is not a breach of confidence to refer to a confidential document in communications between the parties to whom it is confidential.'

I do not think that I would myself have felt able to say whether or not there had been an error by Mr Clark which affected the final award, without referring to the restricted reasons. I say that because I do not think that Mr Maskell could, without referring to those reasons, have been able to say that the build-up to the figure awarded included a figure based on 7·146 tons. Without a sight of para (19) I could not have been certain of the significance of the passage in Mr Clark's letter of 31 August which reads: 'I am, therefore, satisfied that the figure of 7·146 m.t. in paragraph (19) was used because of the unintentional transposition of the parties in paragraph (4).' This certainly reveals an admitted error, but not necessarily in the figure awarded. It is consistent with para (19) being a narrative rather than an operative paragraph.

However this is of no consequence. I agree with Hobhouse J that, where restricted reasons are given and accepted by the parties, the parties must be deemed to have agreed that the reasons cannot be placed before the court. Such an agreement purports to oust the jurisdiction of the court and is void as being contrary to public policy (see *Czarnikow v Roth Schmidt & Co* [1922] 2 KB 478, [1922] All ER Rep 45). Were it otherwise the court would be powerless in the face of misconduct or even fraud revealed by the restricted reasons. We can therefore look at Mr Clark's reasons, although I hasten to add that no question of misconduct and still less of fraud arises or has ever been suggested.

That said, it is important that there shall be no misunderstanding of the purposes for which reasons can be used. They are extremely limited. Few nations are prepared to lend the power of the state to enforcing arbitration awards without retaining some right to review the awards themselves. This is reflected in the New York Convention (the Convention on the Recognition and Enforcement of Foreign Arbitral Awards (10 June 1958; TS 20 (1976); Cmnd 6419)), which has been incorporated into English domestic law by the Arbitration Act 1975. Section 5 of that Act sets out circumstances which would justify the courts of the convention country in refusing to enforce an award. The reasons for an award can certainly be referred to in order to demonstrate that such circumstances exist. On the other hand, it cannot be over-emphasised that the parties, having chosen their tribunal, have to accept it 'with all faults'. Accordingly, even if the reasons show an error of fact or of law, the court will take no action, unless, in the case of an error of law, the reasons are 'open' or 'unrestricted' and leave to appeal is obtained under s 1 of the 1979 Act.

The principal supervisory review powers of the English courts are contained in ss 22 and 23 of the 1950 Act. Section 23 empowers the court to set an award aside if the arbitrator has misconducted himself or the reference. Section 22 empowers the court to remit an award to an arbitrator for reconsideration. It provides the ultimate safety net whereby injustice can be prevented, but it is subject to the consideration that it cannot be used merely to enable the arbitrator to correct errors of judgment, whether of fact or law, or to have second thoughts, even if they would be better thoughts.

In the instant case, Mr Clark has accidentally made a major error, which, if uncorrected, would lead to the charterers paying the owners, when it is the owners who should be paying the charterers. No court could lend the power of the state to the enforcement of such an award and no court should stand by when it has power to correct such an accidental error, and I stress the word 'accidental'. The only matter which has caused me any surprise or concern, and surprise is an understatement, is that the owners have sought desperately to take advantage of this accidental error in order to secure a windfall profit to which they have no claim whatsoever in law or justice. Such conduct does them no credit whatsoever.

Mr Clark, for his part, must be very unhappy at the situation which has arisen and it may assist other arbitrators in a similar situation (mistakes will occur even in the practices of the best of arbitrators) to be told that he could himself have applied to the court to have the award remitted to him, in order that he might correct the error. In the light of the owners' conduct, I hesitate to assert that it would not have been resisted, but it would have succeeded without the slightest difficulty.

In the instant case, as in *Fuga AG v Bunge AG* [1975] 2 Lloyd's Rep 192, the arbitrator admits that he made an accidental error, but I should not like it to be thought that such an admission is a prerequisite to the exercise of the court's jurisdiction to remit. If the arbitrator says nothing and there is a strong prima facie case that there has been an accidental error, the award could be remitted to him with a direction to reconsider it and to revise it if, but only if, there was such an error. If the arbitrator denies that he made any error or that the error was accidental, there would still be jurisdiction to remit, but I cannot think that any court would consider it appropriate to do so, unless there were other factors present.

Much of the argument turned on whether Mr Clark could himself have corrected his error in the exercise of the powers conferred on him by s 17 of the 1950 Act, the slip rule. Since he did not do so and since the award is now before this court, it should, in my judgment, be remitted to Mr Clark for reconsideration whether or not he could have achieved this result without judicial intervention. However, in deference to that argument, I shall express my own view.

Its predecessor, s 7(c) of the Arbitration Act 1889, was considered by a Divisional Court in *Sutherland & Co v Hannevig Bros Ltd* [1921] 1 KB 336, [1920] All ER Rep 670. Rowlatt J pointed out that it covers two quite distinct situations, namely (a) a clerical error (a slip of the pen or something of that kind) and (b) an error arising from an accidental slip or omission. In the latter context he said ([1921] 1 KB 336 at 341, [1920] All ER Rep 670 at 672):

> 'Here we get upon ground which is almost metaphysical. An accidental slip occurs when something is wrongly put in by accident, and an accidental omission occurs when something is left out by accident. What is an accident in this connection, an accident affecting the expression of a man's thought? It is a very difficult thing to define, but I am of opinion that this was not an accident within the meaning of the clause. I cannot pretend to give a formula which will cover every case, but in this case there was nothing omitted by accident: the arbitrator wrote down exactly what he intended to write down, thought it is doubtful what that really meant when considered from a legal point of view . . . I do not think that inadvertence is the right word. A man may inadvertently put down a word which if he had thought more about the matter he would have put down differently, but that means that he has merely gone wrong.'

The High Court slip rule (RSC Ord 20, r 11), which is similarly worded, was considered only recently by this court in *R v Cripps, ex p Muldoon* [1984] 2 All ER 705, [1984] QB 686. We there pointed out the width of the power, but also drew attention to the fact that it does not enable the court to have second thoughts (see [1984] 2 All ER 705 at 711–712, [1984] QB 686 at 697).

It is the distinction between having second thoughts or intentions and correcting an award of judgment to give true effect to first thoughts or intentions, which creates the problem. Neither an arbitrator nor a judge can make any claim to infallibility. If he assesses the evidence wrongly or misconstrues or misappreciates the law, the resulting award or judgment will be erroneous, but it cannot be corrected either under s 17 or under Ord 20, r 11. It cannot normally even be corrected under s 22. The remedy is to appeal, if a right of appeal exists. The skilled arbitrator or judge may be tempted to describe this as an accidental slip, but this is a natural form of self-exculpation. It is not an accidental slip. It is an intended decision which the arbitrator or judge later accepts as having been erroneous.

Into which category does Mr Clark's action fall? Counsel for the owners argued that Mr Clark intended to make an award in favour of the owners and that that is the end of the matter. But I do not think that it is. Section 17 is directed to clerical mistakes in the award, which this was not, and to errors in the award, which this was. It is then necessary to consider carefully why the award was erroneous. Was it due to a mistaken appreciation of the evidence or of the law? Or was it due to an accidental slip or omission? Section 17 of the 1950 Act applies to the latter, but not to the former. Mr Clark correctly recorded the competing views of the expert witnesses, but accidentally and erroneously attributed the views of the owners' expert to that of the charterers' expert and vice versa. As an exercise in judgment, he accepted the evidence of the charterers' expert and he does not have any second thoughts about having done so. Having accepted that evidence, he sought to give effect to his acceptance in his award. That he did not succeed was due solely to the accidental attribution of the evidence to the wrong parties in his reasons which he used as a tool in constructing his award. This seems to me to be a classic case of 'error [in an award] arising from . . . accidental slip [in the recording of material contained in the reasons]'. I therefore think that Mr Clark could have himself corrected the error by issuing an amendment to his award.

Counsel for the owners pressed on us that this would lead to dissatisfied disputants scanning reasons with a microscope in order to detect accidental slips or omissions leading to error. I regard this as quite fanciful. Such situations are extremely rare, but where they occur the arbitrator will be the first to wish to correct them. Section 17 gives him the power to do so without resort to the courts. Where he is minded to exercise this power, he should notify the parties and give them an opportunity to make respresentations and, if so minded, to challenge in the courts the applicability of the power to the facts of the particular situation.

I would dismiss the appeal.

**ROBERT GOFF LJ.** I first ask myself whether the arbitrator's mistake was one which he could himself correct in the exercise of his powers under s 17 of the Arbitration Act 1950. Under that section, he has 'power to correct in an award any clerical mistake or error arising from any accidental slip or omission'. Although the wording is slightly different, I do not think that there is any material distinction between an arbitrator's power under s 17, and the court's power under RSC Ord 20, r 11 (the so-called slip rule) which provides that—

'Clerical mistakes in judgments or orders, or errors arising therein from any accidental slip or omission, may at any time be corrected by the court on motion or summons without an appeal.'

It follows that authorities on the slip rule may assist us in considering the scope of an arbitrator's power under s 17; and I turn first to those authorities for guidance.

The slip rule, in the form in which we know it, now embodied in Ord 20, r 11, came from the old Chancery General Orders. It was first introduced, with a number of other orders, on 3 April 1828 (numbered Ord 45): under the Consolidated General Orders of 1859 it became Ord 23, r 21. It provided as follows:

'Clerical mistakes in decrees or orders, or errors arising from any accidental slip or omission, may at any time before inrolment be corrected upon motion or petition, without the form and expense of a rehearing.'

However, as the words of the rule betray, there also existed in the Court of Chancery a jurisdiction in the judges of the court to rehear not only their own decrees, but also the decrees of their predecessors. Under that jurisdiction, after a decree or order had been passed and entered, any error could be put right by an application to rehear, unless the order had been enrolled; even after enrolment, there was power to vacate the enrolment on proper grounds, and when that had been done the court again had power over its own decree (see Re St Nazaire Co (1879) 12 Ch D 88 at 97 per Jessel MR and Re Swire, Mellor v Swire (1885) 30 Ch D 239 at 246 per Lindley LJ). So there was, in the Court of Chancery, the most ample procedure for correcting errors in judgments and orders. It is understandable that, in that court, concerned as it was with property matters which can generate orders of considerable complexity, there should have developed a more complex procedure for correcting errors in orders than in the courts of common law. But, in the courts of common law, there has existed a power, exercised for hundreds of years before the passing of the Supreme Court of Judicature Acts of 1873 and 1875, under which the court could rectify an order, even when passed and entered, so as to make it carry out the intention and express the meaning of the court at the time when the order was made, provided that the amendment could be made without injustice or on terms which precluded injustice (see Lawrie v Lees (1881) 7 App Cas 19 at 34–35 per Lord Penzance and Re Swire 30 Ch D 239 at 247 per Bowen LJ). Following the Judicature Acts, the jurisdiction in the Court of Chancery to rehear ceased to exist, being absorbed in the appellate jurisdiction of the Court of Appeal (see *Re St Nazaire Co*), and enrolment had become obsolete. The slip rule in Consolidated General Ord 23, r 21 was not included among the new Rules of the Supreme Court enacted under the Supreme Court of Judicature Act 1875, Sch 1; but a slip rule in almost exactly its present form, based very closely on the old Ord 23, r 21, was added as Ord 41A in December 1879 (see [1880] WN (Pt II) 16). (It was later to become Ord 28, r 11, and is now Ord 20, r 11.) Since 1879 it has been recognised that there existed in the High Court two parallel jurisdictions: first, the jurisdiction to correct errors in judgments or orders under the slip rule; and second, the inherent jurisdiction of the court, which always existed in the courts of common law before the Judicature Acts, and has since been recognised as always having existed in the Court of Chancery (see *Lawrie v Lees* 7 App Cas 19 at 34–35 per Lord Penzance and *Re Swire* 30 Ch D 239 at 246 per Lindley LJ), to rectify an order so as to make it carry out the intention and express the meaning of the court when the order was made (see *Ainsworth v Wilding* [1896] 1 Ch 673 at 677 per Romer J). It is probable that the inherent jurisdiction to rectify survived the Judicature Acts by virtue of the note to Sch 1 to the 1875 Act, setting out the new Rules of the Supreme Court, that, where no other provision was made by the Act or the new rules, the present procedure and practice remained in force.

Now, it is to be observed that these two jurisdictions, though they may overlap, are not the same. The jurisdiction under the slip rule is concerned with (1) *clerical* mistakes in judgments or orders, and (2) errors arising in judgments or orders from any *accidental* slip or omission; whereas the inherent jurisdiction is concerned with ensuring that the judgment or order does give effect to the intention of the court at the time when it was made, whether the failure of the judgment or order to do so is the result of a clerical mistake in it, or of an error arising from an accidental slip or omission, or otherwise. No doubt, the inherent jurisdiction will not be invoked except in cases which do not fall within the slip rule. The inherent jurisdiction has been invoked on a number of occasions since *Re Swire* in 1885. But the question has arisen whether that part of the slip rule which is concerned with the correction of errors arising in a judgment or order from an accidental slip or omission could be wider than the inherent jurisdiction. As a matter of construction of the rule, this must depend on whether the words 'errors arising *therein*' are interpreted as meaning errors in the judgment or order, in the sense that the effect of such error is that the judgment or order does not give effect to the intention of the court at the time when it was made. There are statements in the cases which appear to impose this limited meaning on the latter part of the slip rule. Thus in *MacCarthy v Agard* [1933] 2 KB 417 at 424–425, [1933] All ER Rep 991 at 995 Greer LJ stated that:

> '. . . the true view is that where the Court has intentionally given a judgment and there is no mistake in drawing it up—no mistake in words—the only way to correct it is either by appeal, or, in certain cases, by an action brought to have it set aside.'

That case was concerned with the question whether the court, in the exercise of its power under the slip rule or its inherent jurisdiction, could correct a judgment drawn up in the wrong form by reason of a misrepresentation by the defendant. Such a case is not generally concerned with an error arising from an *accidental* slip or omission (see *Preston Banking Co v William Allsup & Sons* [1895] 1 Ch 141, [1891–4] All ER Rep 688). Greer LJ's statement of the law was wider than was necessary for the decision of the case before him; and there is a long line of authority which shows that errors arising from accidental slips or omissions may be corrected under the slip rule, even though the judgment or order as drawn does in fact represent the intention of the court at that time. In *Fritz v Hobson* (1880) 14 Ch D 542, [1874–80] All ER Rep 75 Fry J exercised the power to correct an order to award certain costs to the plaintiff which his counsel had accidentally omitted to draw to the attention of the court. In *Barker v Purvis* (1887) 56 LT 131 a judgment was drawn up on the basis that certain payments of interest had been made from a certain date. This was due to the accidental slip of one of the parties. The Court of Appeal held that the judgment could be corrected under the slip rule. In *Chessum & Sons v Gordon*

[1901] 1 KB 694, [1900–3] All ER Rep 260 one of the parties 'by a pure slip' did not include in his bill of costs for taxation an item which obviously ought to have been included. The Court of Appeal held that the order could be corrected under the slip rule by including the relevant item. In *Armitage v Parsons* [1908] 2 KB 410 the plaintiff signed a judgment in default of appearance by the defendant, and through a slip his solicitor's clerk included in the sum in respect of which judgment was signed costs on too high a scale, so that the judgment was signed for a sum which was too high by 12s. The Court of Appeal held, by a majority, that the defendant was not entitled to have the judgment set aside, but the judgment should be amended under the slip rule. In *Re Inchcape, Craigmyle v Inchcape* [1942] 2 All ER 157, [1942] Ch 394 Morton J corrected an order to add costs which had been omitted as the result of the accidental omission of counsel to ask for them to be included.

In none of the last five cases I have cited did the judgment or order as drawn fail to give effect to the intention of the court at the time when it was drawn. In each case there was, however, an error in the judgment or order arising from an accidental slip or omission, by a party, or by his counsel, or by his solicitor. Furthermore, there is authority that if a court makes an order in certain words which do not have the effect which the court intended them to have, that order may be corrected under the slip rule to make it accord with the court's actual intention: see *Adam & Harvey Ltd v International Maritime Supplies Co Ltd* [1967] 1 All ER 533, [1967] 1 WLR 445. I, for my part, can see no reason why, if a court gives judgment in, for example, a certain sum, and the order is then drawn up and perfected, and it is afterwards discovered that the court has, by accident, miscalculated the figure or omitted an item from it, the error in the order should not be corrected under the slip rule. That is just as much an error in the order arising from an accidental slip or omission as was the error in the cases I have referred to. The crucial question, under this part of the slip rule, is whether the error does indeed arise from an *accidental* slip or omission. Rowlatt J once observed, in *Sutherland & Co v Hannevig Bros Ltd* [1921] 1 KB 336 at 341, [1920] All ER Rep 670 at 672: 'Here we get upon ground which is almost metaphysical.' That case itself and *Oxley v Link* [1914] 2 KB 734 provide examples of the limits within which the courts have confined the concept of accident in this context. Plainly, as Sir John Donaldson MR observed in *R v Cripps, ex p Muldoon* [1984] 2 All ER 705 at 710, [1984] 1 QB 686 at 695, the power under the slip rule cannot be exercised to enable a tribunal 'to reconsider a final and regular decision once it has been perfected'. I do not think that it would be right for me to attempt in this judgment to define what is meant by 'accidental slip or omission': the animal is, I suspect, usually recognisable when it appears on the scene.

A slip rule in terms which, though not identical to, are of the same effect as, the slip rule in Ord 20, r 11, was included in the Arbitration Act 1889, s 7(c), probably following on decisions such as *Mordue v Palmer* (1870) LR 6 Ch App 22, in which it was held that an arbitrator could not even correct a mistake by a clerk in copying his draft award, the proper course being to ask the court to remit the award to the arbitrator for reconsideration. That slip rule is now embodied in s 17 of the 1950 Act, which I have already quoted. I have no doubt that an arbitrator has the same power to correct errors under s 17 as the High Court has to correct errors under Ord 20, r 11. The difference between the powers of an arbitrator and the powers of the High Court is that the former lacks the inherent jurisdiction of the court to rectify an order, so as to make it accord with the intention of the court. As, however, an arbitrator draws up his own award, the only mistake in the actual drawing up of the award is likely to be a clerical error, which he can himself correct under s 17. It is true that, when a judge of the High Court makes an obvious error, counsel may observe it and draw the matter to the attention of the court for correction before the order is drawn up, whereas, since an arbitrator becomes functus officio at the moment when he publishes his award, that opportunity is not available in arbitrations; furthermore, there is in many cases (though not in all) the possibility of an appeal from a court on a question of fact, whereas no such appeal lies from an arbitrator. Even so, apart from the arbitrator's power to correct errors under s 17 of the 1950 Act, the court has a wide power of remission under s 22 of the 1950 Act, which it can exercise in cases of mistake, a power which I shall refer to again in a moment. Since the enactment of the slip rule in s 7(c) of the 1889 Act, the need to exercise the power of remission in cases of error by arbitrators is far less likely to arise. But it still has a useful function in that, if an arbitrator is in any doubt whether he has power to correct an error under s 17, the matter can be brought before the court which can deal with the matter by an order of remission under s 22, if that is thought appropriate.

In the present case it is plain that the arbitrator, by transposing the parties, made an accidental slip which gave rise to an error in his award. For the reasons which I have already given, and in agreement with Sir John Donaldson MR, I am satisfied that this is an error which, if made by the High Court, could have been corrected under Ord 20, r 11; and it could likewise have been corrected by the arbitrator in the present case under s 17 of the 1950 Act. However, he has not done so; and I turn therefore to consider whether this is an appropriate case for the court to exercise its power to remit the award to the arbitrator, under s 22 of the 1950 Act.

As I have already indicated, it is plain on the authorities that there is power to remit an award to an arbitrator in a case where he has made a mistake. It is however stated in Mustill and Boyd *Commercial Arbitration* (1982) p 503 that 'There is no doubt that an admission of the mistake by the arbitrator himself is essential'. On this point, the authorities are not entirely consistent. It has been authoritatively stated that—

'it must not be supposed that reported decisions prevent the court from deciding whether in the interests of justice it ought to send the matter back to the arbitrator.'

(See *Re Baxters and Midland Rly Co* (1906) 95 LT 20 at 23 per Moulton LJ.)

I do not wish to depart from that statement. But, as a general rule, the mistake must be admitted by the arbitrator: see, in particular, *Dinn v Blake* (1875) LR 10 CP 388. For more recent examples where, in such circumstances, the court has remitted the award for the mistake to be rectified, see *The Mello, The Nereus* (1948) 81 Ll L Rep 230 and *Fuga AG v Bunge AG* [1975] 2 Lloyd's Rep 192. Without laying down any hard and fast rule, I think that as a general rule the court should not intervene in cases of simple mistake unless there is a clear admission by the arbitrator that he has made a mistake. Nowadays, arbitrators should be able to correct any clerical mistakes in their awards, or any mistakes in their awards arising from accidental errors or omissions, under s 17. The most likely case which may arise in which the court may be asked to exercise its power to remit an award on grounds of error will be where an arbitrator, having made a mistake, is not certain whether he has power to correct his award under s 17, as he may not be when one party disputes his power to do so. In such a case, or if the arbitrator otherwise declines to exercise his power, the aggrieved party may apply to the court for a remission. Such cases apart, I cannot but think that the court's power of remission will be very rarely exercised in cases of mistake; but, as I have said, I do not wish to restrict the width of the power to order remission in the interests of justice.

In the present case, if the arbitrator, being in doubt whether he had power to correct his error under s 17, had explained his error and asked the court to remit the award to him to enable him to correct it, I have no doubt that the court would have done so. I myself think that, in a case such as this, that is the best course for the arbitrator to take. He does not have to refer to the document called his reasons, and so no question of confidentiality arises. He simply has to explain the nature of his mistake, and its effect on his award; and his own evidence (which would normally be on affidavit) would supply the best evidence of his mistakes and its consequences. But it is not suggested that such a request by the arbitrator is a prerequisite of the exercise by the court of its power to remit; if that were so, then, if the arbitrator had died after admitting his error, the court could not correct it. Nor is it any longer suggested by the owners in the present case that an affidavit by the arbitrator is necessary. So, subject to one argument, this appears to be an appropriate case for the exercise by the court of its power to remit.

That one argument relates to the use which has been made of the arbitrator's reasons.

It was pointed out by the owners that Mr Maskell, the charterers' solicitor, had to make
use of the reasons in order to extract from the arbitrator an admission of his mistake; and
he also made reference to the reasons in his affidavit in support of the charterers'
application to remit, in order to explain the mistake which had been made. Furthermore,
it is submitted that the arbitrator's letter, in which he admits his mistake, cannot properly
be understood without reference to the reasons.

For my part, I cannot see why Mr Maskell should not, in communications with the
arbitrator, have referred to the reasons in order to point out what has proved to be an
obviously accidental mistake of substance in his final award. I do not see how any
confidentiality in the reasons can inhibit any such conduct. Furthermore, I find myself
in agreement with the judge that the existence and nature of the arbitrator's mistake is
sufficiently apparent from his letter for the purpose of the court's exercise of its power to
remit, without reference to the reasons. The nature of the dispute between the parties on
the relevant point, their rival contentions and the evidence called on behalf of each can
be revealed without breaking the confidentiality of the reasons. Once those matters are
known, and the arbitrator's letter is read in the light of that knowledge, it becomes
apparent that the unintentional transposition of the parties by the arbitrator has resulted
in the figure of 7·146 tons per day being attributed to the charterers rather than to the
owners, whereas the charterers were in fact contending for a saving of only 4·5 tons per
day. It is apparent also from the arbitrator's letter that this was (as one would expect) a
material error, which must have affected the amount of his award. The precise monetary
consequence is not revealed; but it is enough, in my judgment, for present purposes that
the nature of the mistake should be known and that it should be known to have affected
the amount of the award. For these reasons I conclude, in agreement with the judge, that
this is an appropriate case for remission to the arbitrator under s 22.

In these circumstances, I need not express any opinion about the nature of the
confidentiality which attaches to reasons given by arbitrators, and in particular by
maritime arbitrators, with a rider attached in the form used by Mr Clark in the present
case. I only wish to underline that, if an arbitrator makes a mistake and admits that he
has done so, then if he himself draws the matter to the attention of the court and asks the
court to correct it, he can do so without reference to the document containing his reasons
and so no question of the confidentiality of that document need arise.

I too would dismiss the appeal.

**SIR ROGER ORMROD.** In this appeal the court is faced with a remarkable situation.
The owners concede that they are the beneficiaries of a gross (and now obvious)
miscarriage of justice. They concede that the award of $US62,402·13 in their favour is
erroneous and that, on the arbitrator's findings of fact, the charterers should have been
awarded a sum of $US27,527·87, but they contend that the court (and the arbitrator) are
impotent. This is a bold challenge which becomes even bolder when, as counsel for the
owners has made plain in his submissions, it rests, ultimately, on public policy: the vital
need to preserve intact the finality of arbitrators' awards.

The question should never have reached the courts because it could and ought to have
been resolved by the parties themselves as honest business people. But, the challenge has
been made and must be taken up.

There are two possible ways of approaching the problem. The first is under s 17 of the
Arbitration Act 1950, which is the arbitrators' equivalent of RSC Ord 20, r 11 (the 'slip
rule'). The second is under s 22 of the same Act which gives the court power to remit an
award to the arbitrator for reconsideration.

My immediate reaction to the first approach was to think that it was not open to the
arbitrator on the facts of this case. The error which is at the root of the trouble arose
during the preparation of the award and consisted in the arbitrator, in a momentary
lapse, confusing, and thereby transposing in his mind, the identity of the parties which
led him in his calculations to credit (or debit) the wrong party with an important item.
This is not the type of mistake or error which one normally associates with the slip rule.

Reading it and s 17 (which is in almost identical terms) one tends to run together 'clerical mistake' and 'error due to an accidental slip or omission'. But it is common ground that s 17 must be considered disjunctively, so that it is directed at two quite different situations, clerical mistake on the one hand and accidental error on the other. No question of clerical mistake arises in this case, but there has undoubtedly been an error which, in my judgment, was due to an 'accidental slip' within the section, the accident being the mental lapse which caused the arbitrator to transpose in his mind the parties which led him to refer to the one when he plainly intended to refer to the other. My conclusion therefore is that this case falls within s 17 and it was open to the arbitrator to amend his award to bring it into line with his findings of fact.

I also think that the charterers succeed on the s 22 point and that Hobhouse J was entitled to remit this award for reconsideration.

The section gives the court an entirely unfettered discretion but it is accepted that the overriding importance of preserving the finality of awards imposes severe constraints on its exercise. The section and its predecessors were, presumably, inserted to preserve the powers of the court at common law or, perhaps more accurately, the practice adopted by the courts before the law was codified. Codification converts a practice into a discretion and subtly changes its complexion.

Just as under the common law the court, in its prerogative jurisdiction, interfered with the decisions of inferior tribunals in strictly limited circumstances, so it interfered with arbitral awards, if the interest of justice demanded and the circumstances permitted.

I find it impossible to imagine that the court, on facts like those before us in this case, would not have intervened under the old practice and I can see no justification for not intervening now under s 22.

Counsel for the owners, however, has submitted that this case would never have come before the court had not the charterers deliberately breached the confidentiality of the reasons for his award which were provided by the arbitrator and which disclosed his accidental error.

The exact status of these reasons may be a matter for discussion. To an inexperienced eye it looks difficult to derive their quality of confidentiality from contract, particularly where, as in this case, they were supplied on the initiative of the arbitrator himself, labelled, as they were, 'confidential'. Perhaps it would be safer to regard confidentiality as a matter of practice which is generally accepted by all concerned and recognised by the court which will support it to the extent of usually in its discretion refusing to look at such reasons, in order to preserve the finality of awards.

Whichever way of looking at this problem is correct it is clear to my mind that the parties themselves cannot blindfold the court, only the court itself can do that and in the vast majority of cases it will do so. But in those rare cases where an error occurs of the kind which we are considering in this case, the court cannot decline to interfere without gravely prejudicing in the eyes of the lay world the machinery of justice. For my part I do not think that either conclusion will significantly endanger the finality of arbitral awards. Section 17 is limited to *clerical* mistakes or *accidental* errors. Section 22 is limited by the discretion being subject to the constraints imposed by the overriding importance of preserving finality in all but the most exceptional situations.

I would therefore dismiss this appeal.

*Appeal dismissed. Leave to appeal to the House of Lords refused.*

Solicitors: *Lloyd Denby Neal* (for the owners); *Norton Rose Botterell & Roche* (for the charterers).

Diana Procter    Barrister.

# Gillick v West Norfolk and Wisbech Area Health Authority and another

COURT OF APPEAL, CIVIL DIVISION
EVELEIGH, FOX AND PARKER LJJ
19, 20, 21, 22 NOVEMBER, 20 DECEMBER 1984

*National health service – Family planning clinics – Contraception – Circular containing guidance to area health authorities – Legality of advice contained in circular – Advice given regarding contraception for girls under 16 – Whether doctor may give advice and treatment on contraception to girl under 16 without parental consent – Whether doctor committing criminal offence or acting unlawfully by giving advice on contraception to girl under 16 – Whether doctor interfering with parental rights – Sexual Offences Act 1956, ss 6(1), 28(1).*

*Minor – Medical treatment – Consent – Nature of consent which minor can give to medical treatment without obtaining parental consent.*

The Department of Health and Social Security, in the exercise of its statutory functions, issued a circular to area health authorities containing, inter alia, advice to the effect that a doctor consulted at a family planning clinic by a girl under 16 would not be acting unlawfully if he prescribed contraceptives for the girl, so long as in doing so he was acting in good faith to protect her against the harmful effects of sexual intercourse. The circular further stated that, although a doctor should proceed on the assumption that advice and treatment on contraception should not be given to a girl under 16 without parental consent and that he should try to persuade the girl to involve her parents in the matter, nevertheless the principle of confidentiality between doctor and patient applied to a girl under 16 seeking contraceptives and therefore in exceptional cases the doctor could prescribe contraceptives without consulting the girl's parents or obtaining their consent if in the doctor's clinical judgment it was desirable to prescribe contraceptives. The plaintiff, who had five daughters under the age of 16, sought an assurance from her local area health authority that her daughters would not be given advice and treatment on contraception without the plaintiff's prior knowledge and consent while they were under 16. When the authority refused to give such an assurance the plaintiff brought an action against the authority and the department seeking (i) as against both defendants a declaration that the advice contained in the circular was unlawful, because it amounted to advice to doctors to commit the offence of causing or encouraging unlawful sexual intercourse with a girl under 16, contrary to s 28(1)[a] of the Sexual Offences Act 1956, or the offence of being an accessory to unlawful sexual intercourse with a girl under 16, contrary to s 6(1)[b] of that Act, and (ii) as against the area health authority a declaration that a doctor or other professional person employed by it in its family planning service could not give advice and treatment on contraception to any child of the plaintiff below the age of 16 without the plaintiff's consent, because to do so would be unlawful as being inconsistent with the plaintiff's parental rights. The plaintiff conceded that, in order to be entitled to the first declaration sought, she was required to show that a doctor who followed the advice contained in the circular would necessarily be committing a criminal offence or acting unlawfully. The judge held (i) that a doctor prescribing contraceptives to a girl under 16 in accordance with the advice contained in the department's circular would not thereby be committing an offence of causing or encouraging unlawful sexual

---

a    Section 28(1), so far as material, provides: 'It is an offence for a person to cause or encourage . . . the commission of unlawful sexual intercourse with . . . a girl under the age of sixteen for whom he is responsible.'

b    Section 6(1), so far as material, provides: 'It is an offence . . . for a man to have unlawful sexual intercourse with a girl under the age of sixteen.'

intercourse with the girl, contrary to s 28(1) of the 1956 Act, and (ii) that a parent's interest in his or her child did not amount to a 'right' but was more accurately described as a responsibility or duty, and accordingly giving advice to a girl under 16 on contraception without her parent's consent was not unlawful interference with parental 'rights'. He accordingly dismissed the plaintiff's action. The plaintiff appealed.

**Held** – The appeal would be allowed for the following reasons—

(1) (Per Eveleigh LJ) Since the authority to make major decisions in relation to a child's upbringing rested with the person having custody of the child, it followed that a parent's decisions prevailed unless displaced by the child's welfare. Where a parent's decision was not circumscribed by statute, it would be treated as being prima facie in the child's best interests, and a person who interfered with the parent's decision had to demonstrate that the decision was not in the child's best interests. Each case depended on its own facts, and, although it could not be said that it was never permissible to act in spite of the parent's wishes to the contrary, it would be extremely rare where the parents were responsible persons (see p 557 d to g and p 559 e f, post).

(2) (Per Fox and Parker LJJ) A parent or guardian had a parcel of rights in relation to a child in his custody including the right to control the manner in which and the place at which the child spent his or her time, and in general such rights could not be abandoned or transferred. Those parental rights would be enforced by the court, subject always to the court's right to override them in the interests of the child. There was no basis on which anyone other than the court could interfere with those rights otherwise than by resort to the court, or pursuant to specific statutory powers or exceptions. Furthermore, it was clearly recognised that there was some age below which a child was incapable as a matter of law of giving a valid consent or making a valid decision for itself in regard to its custody or upbringing, and the provisions of the criminal law showed that in the matter of sexual intercourse that age was 16 for a girl. It followed that a girl under 16 could not give a valid consent to contraceptive or abortion treatment without her parents' consent and that a doctor who afforded contraceptive or abortion treatment to a girl of 16 without the knowledge and consent of the parents infringed the legal rights of the parent, except in an emergency (which rendered the parents' consent unnecessary) or where the leave of the court was obtained (see p 540 j, p 547 b, p 550 h to p 551 d, p 544 e to j, p 556 b to e and p 557 b, post); R v Howes (1860) 3 E & E 332, Re Agar-Ellis, Agar-Ellis v Lascelles (1883) 24 Ch D 317 and Hewer v Bryant [1969] 3 All ER 578 considered.

(3) It followed that the circular issued by the department stating that a doctor could prescribe contraceptives for a girl under 16 without first informing her parents was contrary to law, and declarations to that effect would be granted (see p 551 d to f, p 556 j, p 557 b and p 558 j, post).

Decision of Woolf J [1984] 1 All ER 365 reversed.

**Notes**

For causing or encouraging the commission of unlawful sexual intercourse with a girl under 16, see 11 Halsbury's Laws (4th edn) para 1066, and for cases on the subject, see 15 Digest (Reissue) 1228, 10493–10496.

For unlawful sexual intercourse with a girl under 16, see 11 Halsbury's Laws (4th edn) para 1234, and for cases on the subject, see 15 Digest (Reissue) 1222–1224, 10454–10466.

For the Sexual Offences Act 1956, ss 6, 28, see 8 Halsbury's Statutes (3rd edn) 420, 432.

**Cases referred to in judgments**

Agar-Ellis, Re, Agar-Ellis v Lascelles (1878) 10 Ch D 49, CA.

Agar-Ellis, Re, Agar-Ellis v Lascelles (1883) 24 Ch D 317, CA.

Associated Provincial Picture Houses Ltd v Wednesbury Corp [1947] 2 All ER 680, [1948] 1 KB 223, CA.

Carroll, Re [1931] 1 KB 317, [1930] All ER Rep 192, CA.

D (a minor) (wardship: sterilisation), Re [1976] 1 All ER 326, [1976] Fam 185, [1976] 2 WLR 279.

*Hewer v Bryant* [1969] 3 All ER 578, [1970] 1 QB 357, [1969] 3 WLR 425, CA.
*J v C* [1969] 1 All ER 788, [1970] AC 668, [1969] 2 WLR 540, HL.
*N (minors) (parental rights), Re* [1974] 1 All ER 126, [1974] Fam 40, [1973] 3 WLR 866, DC.
*P (a minor), Re* (1982) 80 LGR 301, CA.
*People, The (A-G) v Edge* [1943] IR 115, Eire SC.
*R v D* [1984] 2 All ER 449, [1984] AC 778, [1984] 3 WLR 186, HL.
*R v De Manneville* (1804) 5 East 221, 102 ER 1054.
*R v Gyngall* [1893] 2 QB 232, CA.
*R v Howes* (1860) 3 E & E 332, 121 ER 467.
*R v Webster* (1885) 16 QBD 134.
*Sykes v DPP* [1961] 3 All ER 33, [1962] AC 528, [1961] 3 WLR 371, HL.
*Thomasset v Thomasset* [1894] P 295, [1891–4] All ER Rep 308, CA.
*Wellesley v Duke of Beaufort* (1827) 2 Russ 1, 38 ER 236, LC; *affd sub nom Wellesley v Wellesley* (1828) 2 Bli NS 124, [1824–34] All ER Rep 189, 4 ER 1078, HL.

**Cases also cited**

*A-G v Able* [1984] 1 All ER 277, [1984] QB 795.
*B (a minor) (wardship; medical treatment), Re* [1981] 1 WLR 1421, CA.
*BRB v JB* [1968] 2 All ER 1023, [1968] P 466, CA.
*City of Akron v Akron Center for Reproductive Health Inc* (1983) 103 S Ct 2481, US.
*Curtis, Re* (1859) 28 LJ Ch 458.
*H v Lambeth London BC* (1984) Times, 5 April.
*Johnston v Wellesley Hospital* [1971] 2 OR 103.
*Khaliq v HM Advocate* 1984 SLT 137.
*National Coal Board v Gamble* [1958] 3 All ER 203, [1959] 1 QB 11, DC.
*O'Reilly v Mackman* [1982] 3 All ER 1124, [1983] 2 AC 237, HL.
*R v Bourne* (1952) 36 Cr App R 125, CCA.
*R v Drury* (1974) 60 Cr App R 195, CA.
*R v Fretwell* (1862) 9 Cox CC 152, CA.
*R v Harling* [1938] 1 All ER 307, CCA.
*R v Howard* [1965] 3 All ER 684, [1966] 1 WLR 13, CCA.
*R v Tyrrell* [1894] 1 QB 710, [1891–4] All ER Rep 1215, CCR.

**Appeal**

Victoria Gillick appealed against the order of Woolf J ([1984] 1 All ER 365, [1984] QB 581) hearing the Crown Office list on 26 July 1983 whereby he held that the appellant was not entitled to declarations (i) as against the defendants, Norfolk Area Health Authority (subsequently amended to West Norfolk and Wisbech Area Health Authority) and the Department of Health and Social Security, a declaration that on its true construction a Health Service notice (HN (80) 46) issued by the department had no authority in law and gave advice which was unlawful, wrong and adversely affected or might adversely affect the welfare of the appellant's children and/or the rights of the appellant as parent and custodian of the children, and/or the ability of the appellant properly and effectively to discharge her duties as parent and custodian, and (ii) as against the area health authority alone a declaration that no doctor or other professional person employed by them in the family planning service or otherwise might give any contraceptive and/or abortion advice and/or treatment to any child of the appellant below the age of 16 without the appellant's prior knowledge and consent. The facts are set out in the judgment of Parler LJ.

*Gerard Wright QC, David Poole QC* and *Patrick Field* for the appellant.
*John Laws* for the department.
The area health authority was not represented.

*Cur adv vult*

20 December. The following judgments were delivered.

**PARKER LJ** (giving the first judgment at the invitation of Eveleigh LJ). By s 1 of the National Health Service (Family Planning) Act 1967 local health authorities in England and Wales were empowered, with the approval of the Minister of Health and to such extent as he might direct, to make arrangements for the giving of advice on contraception, the medical examination of persons seeking advice on contraception for the purpose of determining what advice to give and the supply of contraceptive substances and contraceptive appliances. This was, so far as is known, the first occasion on which Parliament had made any provision for what may be described simply as contraceptive advice and treatment. The 1967 Act was repealed by the National Health Service Reorganisation Act 1973, which Act, by s 4, replaced the power of local health authorities to provide for such advice and treatment with a duty on the Secretary of State to do so. Section 4 has now been replaced in like terms by s 5(1)(b) of the National Health Service Act 1977, which provides that it is the Secretary of State's duty—

> 'To arrange, to such extent as he considers necessary to meet all reasonable requirements in England and Wales, for the giving of advice on contraception, the medical examination of persons seeking advice on contraception, the treatment of such persons and the supply of contraceptive substances and appliances.'

It is to be noted in passing that neither the original power of the local health authority nor the subsequent duty of the Secretary of State to provide for contraceptive advice and treatment was subject to any limitation on the age of the persons to whom such service was to be accorded.

In pursuance of his duty under s 5(1)(b), the Secretary of State made arrangements, and in May 1974 the Department of Health and Social Security, which is the second respondent in this appeal, issued an explanatory circular concerning such arrangements to which was attached a memorandum of guidance (Health Service circular (interim series) (HSC (IS) 32)), section G of which was entitled 'The Young'. The relevant parts of it are set out in full in the judgment of Woolf J presently under appeal (see [1984] 1 All ER 365 at 367–368, [1984] QB 581 at 588–589). In view of that and the fact that section G was amended in 1980 it is unnecessary to do more here than mention that it states (1) that in the light of the fact that there were 1,490 births and 2,804 induced abortions among girls under 16 there was a clear need for contraceptive services to be available for and accessible to young people at risk of pregnancy *irrespective of age*, (2) that it was *for the doctor to decide* whether to provide contraceptive advice and treatment, (3) that the Medical Defence Union had advised that *the parents of a child, of whatever age, should not be contacted by any staff without his or her permission.*

The memorandum of guidance with its plain acceptance, if not encouragement, of the idea that contraceptive advice and treatment could be given to girls, not merely under 16 but well under 16, without the consent or even the knowledge of parents, not unnaturally provoked much concern and in December 1980 the department issued a notice (HN (80) 46) containing section G, the terms of which are directly challenged in the appeal and which I therefore quote in full:

> 'Clinic sessions should be available for people of all ages, but it may be helpful to make separate, less formal arrangements for young people. The staff should be experienced in dealing with young people and their problems. There is widespread concern about counselling and treatment for children under 16. Special care is needed not to undermine parental responsibility and family stability. The Department would therefore hope that in any case where a doctor or other professional worker is approached by a person under the age of 16 for advice on these matters, the doctor, or other professional, will always seek to persuade the child to involve the parent or guardian (or other person in loco parentis) at the earliest stage of consultation, and will proceed from the assumption that it would be

most unusual to provide advice about contraception without parental consent. It is, however, widely accepted that consultations between doctors and patients are confidential, and the Department recognises the importance which doctors and patients attach to this principle.  It is a principle which applies also to the other professions concerned. To abandon this principle for children under 16 might cause some not to seek professional advice at all. They could then be exposed to the immediate risks of pregnancy and of sexually-transmitted disease, as well as other long-term physical, psychological and emotional consequences which are equally a threat to stable family life. This would apply particularly to young people whose parents are, for example, unconcerned, entirely unresponsive, or grossly disturbed. Some of these young people are away from their parents and in the care of local authorities or voluntary organisations standing in loco parentis. The Department realises that in such exceptional cases the nature of any counselling must be a matter for the doctor or other professional worker concerned and that the decision whether or not to prescribe contraception must be for the clinical judgment of a doctor.'

This revised text is, no doubt, less forthright than its predecessor in its acceptance of the position that the young can be advised and treated without the knowledge or consent of their parents, but that position is plainly still accepted.

As a result of the issue of the revised text Mrs Gillick, the appellant, a Roman Catholic who then had four, but now has five, daughters under the age of 16, wrote on 21 January 1981 to the local health authority in the following terms:

'Concerning the *new* D.H.S.S. Guidelines on the contraceptive and abortion treatment of children under both the legal and medical age of consent, *without* the knowledge or consent of the parents, can I please ask you for a written assurance that in no circumstances whatsoever will any of my daughters ... be given contraceptive or abortion treatment whilst they are under *sixteen*, in any of the Family Planning Clinics under your control, without my prior knowledge, and irrefutable evidence of my consent? Also, should any of them seek advice in them, can I have your assurance that I would be automatically contacted in the interests of my children's safety and welfare? If you are in any doubt about giving me such assurances, can I please ask you to seek legal medical advice.

Yours faithfully,
Mrs. Victoria Gillick

She received the following reply on 27 January 1981:

'Thank you for your letter of 21st January addressed to the Chairman and he has asked me to reply to you on his behalf. I enclose for your information a copy of the official guidance issued in May 1980, together with a copy of a recent press statement made by the Minister of Health on this important matter. You will see that the Minister emphasises that it would be most unusual to provide advice about contraception without parental consent, but it does go on to say that the final decision must be for the doctor's clinical judgment. We would expect our doctors to work within these guidelines but, as the Minister has stated, the final decision in these matters must be one of clinical judgment.'

This did not satisfy the appellant and further correspondence ensued until on 3 March 1981 the appellant wrote a final letter making her position clear as follows:

'... I formally FORBID any medical staff employed by Norfolk A.H.A. to give any contraception or abortion advice or treatment whatsoever to my four daughters, while they are under 16 years, without my consent. Will you please acknowledge this letter and agree wholeheartedly to advise your doctors etc. to abide by my forbidding ...'

This produced no change in attitude and eventually on 5 August 1982 the appellant commenced proceedings against both the local health authority and the department. By her specially indorsed writ she claimed two declarations, the first against the local health authority and the department and the second against the local authority only. The declarations sought are:

'(i) a declaration against the [area health authority] and the [department] on a true construction of the said Notice and in the events which have happened, including and in particular the publication and the circulation of the said Notice, the said Notice has no authority in law and gives advice which is unlawful and wrong, and which adversely affects or which may adversely affect the welfare of the [appellant's] said children, *and/or the rights of the [appellant] as parent and custodian of the said children, and/or the ability of the [appellant] properly and effectively to discharge her duties as such parent and custodian*; (ii) a declaration against the [area health authority] that no doctor or other professional person employed by the [area health authority] either in the Family Planning Service or otherwise may give any contraceptive and/ or abortion advice and/or treatment to any child of the [appellant] below the age of 16 without the prior *knowledge and/or consent* of the said child's parent or guardian.'

On 26 July 1983 the appellant's action was dismissed by Woolf J and she now appeals to this court.

It must be stated at the outset that the appellant's purpose in bringing the action is to establish the extent of parental rights and duties in respect of girls under 16, for there is not the slightest suggestion that any of her daughters is likely, when under 16, to need contraceptive or abortion advice or treatment much less to seek it and accept it without her knowledge and consent. Indeed only her three eldest daughters can realistically be regarded as being at risk of pregnancy and capable of seeking and accepting contraceptive advice or treatment even if they did form a sudden desire to indulge in sexual activity and yielded to it. These three were aged respectively 13, 12 and 10 at the date of the writ. The fourth daughter was then aged 5 and the fifth not yet born.

It is however clear that even in the best of families something may go suddenly and badly wrong and that, if and when it does, a parent may either be unaware of the fact or left with little time in which to act. She has therefore in my opinion ample interest to justify her attempt to establish the extent of her rights and duties and to do so by way of action for a declaration rather than by way of judicial review. Neither of the respondents indeed contended to the contrary and counsel for the department conceded that if the appellant could establish the right which she asserted it must follow that the department's notice was contrary to law and must be struck down on one or other of the heads recognised in *Associated Provincial Picture Houses Ltd v Wednesbury Corp* [1947] 2 All ER 680, [1948] 1 KB 223.

It is clear that respectable and responsible people may hold different, strong and sincere views whether and if so in what circumstances doctors should on medical, social, moral, religious or ethical grounds either (i) fail to inform a parent that a child under 16 had sought contraceptive advice or (ii) provide contraceptive advice or treatment without the parents' knowledge and consent.

This appeal, however, is concerned only with the legal position, albeit that in the course of ascertaining the legal position the court may resort to established public policy which itself may be based on some social, moral or other non-legal judgment. Accordingly this court does not seek to determine, and indeed has no material on which it could determine, whether, for example, it is 'better' on some such ground (1) that mothers of young children should be kept in ignorance of what their children are doing lest young girls be deterred from seeking contraceptive advice and treatment with, so it is said, increased risks of pregnancy, more unwanted babies, more backstreet abortions and so on, or (2) that mothers should always be informed and their consent obtained despite the alleged disadvantages mentioned above and possible family friction, because otherwise the stability of families will be threatened, the parents' ability to carry out their rights and obligations will be impaired etc.

Whether the appellant is right or wrong in her contentions such matters will have to be determined in another forum and the law if necessary altered by Parliament. Such matters are not for this court.

Although the contentions advanced on behalf of the appellant were divided under a number of heads and are clearly set out in a most helpful skeleton argument, there were before Woolf J and in this court in essence two matters to be investigated, namely (a) the extent of a parents' rights and duties with respect to the medical treatment of a girl under 16, (b) the extent to which, if at all, the provisions of the criminal law assist in the determination of the extent of the parents' rights and duties in relation specifically to contraceptive or abortion advice and treatment.

In relation to the first of these two matters it is contended for the appellant that a parent has a right to determine whether advice shall be given or not and a further right to determine whether, if treatment is recommended, it shall be given. This is in effect a right to withhold consent and it is contended that this right cannot be overridden by anyone save the court. If a doctor disagrees with a parent he must, it is submitted, seek the ruling of the court. This is quite apart from the question of trespass. If however the treatment would, apart from consent, constitute a trespass no consent given by a child under 16 will prevent it being such.

In relation to the second of the two matters the appellant contends that in the specific case of contraception the provisions of the criminal law are such that any doctor giving contraceptive advice or treatment will either commit a criminal offence or will be acting against a clearly defined public policy.

With this preliminary I turn to these two matters considering, in relation to each of them, first the statutory background and then any relevant case law.

*The extent of a parent's right and duties with respect to the medical treatment of a child*
(a) *The statutory background*
Until the Family Law Reform Act 1969, by s 1 of which the age of majority was reduced from 21 to 18, there was no statutory provision with regard to a minor's consent to surgical, medical or dental treatment, but s 8 of that Act provided:

> '(1) The consent of a minor who has attained the age of sixteen years to any surgical, medical or dental treatment which, in the absence of consent, would constitute a trespass to his person, shall be as effective as it would be if he were of full age; and where a minor has by virtue of this section given an effective consent to any treatment it shall not be necessary to obtain any consent for it from his parent or guardian.
>
> (2) In this section "surgical, medical or dental treatment" includes any procedure undertaken for the purposes of diagnosis, and this section applies to any procedure (including, in particular, the administration of an anaesthetic) which is ancillary to any treatment as it applies to that treatment.
>
> (3) Nothing in this section shall be construed as making ineffective any consent which would have been effective if this section had not been enacted.'

The construction of this section is the subject of dispute. For the appellant it is contended that, but for s 8, no consent could be given by a minor, and that the effect of sub-s (1) is to lower the age of consent in the particular case to 16 but that at any lesser age, if consent is required, it can only be given by a parent or guardian.

Subsection (3) is, it is submitted, merely to make it clear that, where a parent's consent has been obtained, it is not made ineffective because a consent from the minor could be or could have been obtained under sub-s (1).

For the respondents, however, it is contended that all that the section was doing was to make it clear (1) that in the case of a person who had attained the age of 16 the doctor had no need to satisfy himself that the minor was of sufficient understanding to give consent and (2) that the purpose of sub-s (3) was merely to ensure that a consent by a minor under 16 which would have been valid prior to the Act could still be relied on.

There is no decided case that, prior to the Act, the consent of a minor under the age of 16 would have been effective and there are many indications that it would not, as I shall in due course show.

Although prior to 1969 there was no statutory provision relating to consent to treatment, the National Health Service (General Medical and Pharmaceutical Service Regulations 1962, SI 1962/2248, gave to a person who had attained the age of 16 th right to choose his own doctor by providing that until such age the right should be exercised on his behalf by a parent, guardian or other person who had the care of the child, and the Mental Health Act 1959, s 5(2) (which deals with the informal admission of patients requiring treatment for a mental disorder) provides:

> 'In the case of an infant who has attained the age of sixteen years and is capable of expressing his own wishes, any such arrangements as are mentioned in the foregoing subsection may be made, carried out and determined notwithstanding any right of custody or control vested by law in his parent or guardian.'

This last provision plainly proceeds on the basis that the right of custody or control vested in a parent or guardian carried with it the right to prevent a minor submitting to treatment for mental disorder or admitting himself to a hospital or nursing home therefor and qualifies that right in respect, but only in respect, of minors who have attained the age of 16 years *and* are capable of expressing their own wishes. This as it seems to me is but one aspect of what is inherent in the right to custody or control. In this connection certain provisions of the Children Act 1975 are of some assistance:

> '**85.**—(1) In this Act, unless the context otherwise requires, "the parental rights and duties" means as respects a particular child (whether legitimate or not), all the rights and duties which by law the mother and father have in relation to a legitimate child and his property; and references to a parental right or duty shall be construed accordingly and shall include a right of access and any other element included in a right or duty.
> (2) Subject to section 1(2) of the Guardianship Act 1973 (which relates to separation agreements between husband and wife), a person cannot surrender or transfer to another any parental right or duty he has as respects a child . . .'

It will be observed that there is a recognition that the father and mother have both rights and duties in respect of the child himself and his property and that, subject to the specific exception, a person is incapable of surrendering or transferring any parental right or duty. Under this provision therefore a parent cannot opt out of his rights and duties whatever they may be.

Sections 86 and 87(2) then deal with the question of legal custody and actual custody:

> '**86.** In this Act, unless the context otherwise requires, "legal custody" means, as respect a child, so much of the parental rights and duties as relate to the person of the child (*including the place and manner in which his time is spent*) but a person shall not by virtue of having legal custody of a child be entitled to effect or arrange for his emigration from the United Kingdom unless he is a parent or guardian of the child.
> **87.** . . . (2) While a person not having legal custody of a child has actual custody of the child he has the like duties in relation to the child as a custodian would have by virtue of his legal custody . . .'

Thus a legal custodian and actual custodian for so long as the child is in his actual custody has, it is recognised, all the parental rights and duties relating to the person of the child including specifically the place at which and manner in which his time is spent. For the purposes of the 1975 Act a child is, in effect, a minor (see s 107(17)).

On the face of it, if there is a right and duty to determine the place and manner in which a child's time is spent, such right or duty must cover the right and duty completely to control the child subject of course always to the intervention of the court. Indeed there must, it seems to me, be such a right from birth to a fixed age unless whenever, short of majority, a question arises it must be determined, in relation to a particular child and a particular matter, whether he or she is of sufficient understanding to make a responsible and reasonable decision. This alternative appears to me singularly unattractive and impracticable, particularly in the context of medical treatment. If a child seeks medical advice the doctor has first to decide whether to accept him or her as a patient. At this stage, however, unless the child is going to his or her own general practitioner, which in the present context is unlikely, the doctor will know nothing about the child. If he decides to accept the child as a patient then, it is said, there is an inviolable duty of confidence and the parent cannot be informed or his or her consent sought without the child's permission. The doctor is entitled to decide what advice or treatment to administer.

Finally in this section it is necessary to mention s 48 of the Education Act 1944. Subsection (3) places a duty on every local education authority to make arrangements for seeing that comprehensive facilities for free medical treatment should be available to pupils in attendance at every school or county college maintained by it and empowers it to make such arrangements for senior pupils at any other educational establishment maintained by it. Subsection (4) places on every local education authority the further duty to make arrangements for encouraging and assisting pupils to take advantage of such facilities but contains the following proviso:

> 'Provided that if the parent of any pupil gives to the authority notice that he objects to the pupil availing himself of any medical treatment provided under this section the pupil shall not be encouraged . . . so to do.'

A senior pupil is by s 114 of the 1944 Act a person between the ages of 12 and 19. The age of majority was, at the time, 21.

This provision appears to me a plain recognition of the right of a parent to control the treatment provided for a child up to the age of 19.

Taken together, the statutory provisions in my opinion support the appellant's contentions.

(b) *The case law*

There are two classes of cases to be considered, first those cases which are specifically concerned with medical treatment and second those which are not.

In the first class of case I refer first to *Re D (a minor) (wardship: sterilisation)* [1976] 1 All ER 326, [1976] Fam 185. In that case a child, D, was severely handicapped and, for reasons which do not matter, her parents decided, when she was very young, to seek to have her sterilised when she reached about 18. She reached puberty at the age of 10 and her mother, who had over the years discussed the possibility of sterilisation with a consultant paediatrician, a Dr Gordon, raised the matter with him again. He and the mother agreed that the sterilisation operation should be performed provided that a Miss Duncan, a consultant gynaecologist, also agreed. Miss Duncan, did agree and D was accordingly booked into a hospital in order that a hysterectomy might be performed. The former and present headmasters of D's school, a social worker involved with the family and the plaintiff, Mrs Hamidi, an educational psychologist who had seen D on a number of occasions, disagreed with what was proposed. An attempt was made by them to secure a change of views but this failed. The plaintiff therefore instituted wardship proceedings and sought the ruling of the court as to what should be done. The matter was heard by Heilbron J in chambers but a full judgment was given in open court. There were two issues: (1) whether the wardship should be continued and (2) whether the proposed sterilisation should take place. Heilbron J decided that wardship should continue and that the operation should not take place. As to the first issue the judge said ([1976] 1 All ER 326 at 333, [1976] Fam 185 at 193–194):

> 'This operation could, if necessary, be delayed or prevented if the child were to remain a ward of court, and as Lord Eldon LC so vividly expressed it in *Wellesley's* case (1827) 2 Russ 1 at 18, 38 ER 236 at 242: "It has always been the principle of this Court, not to risk the incurring of damage to children which it cannot repair, but rather to prevent the damage being done." I think that is the very type of case where this court should "throw some care around this child", and I propose to continue her wardship, which, in my judgment, is appropriate in this case.'

And as to the second:

'In considering this vital matter, I want to make it quite clear that I have well in
mind the natural feelings of a parent's heart, and though in wardship proceedings
parents' *rights* can be superseded, the court will not do so lightly, and only in
pursuance of well-known principles laid down over the years. The exercise of the
court's jurisdiction is paternal, and it must be exercised judicially, and the judge
must act, as far as *humanly possible*, on the evidence, as a *wise parent would act*.' (My
emphasis.)

The first of these passages recognises explicitly that unless the wardship was continued
the mother could and would proceed with the proposed operation, and the second that
in refusing leave to have the operation performed the court was superseding the parents'
rights.

Two further matters require mention before I leave this case. First, Dr Gordon asserted
that provided he had the consent of the mother the decision whether the operation
should be performed was within his and Miss Duncan's sole clinical judgment. As to this
the judge said ([1976] 1 All ER 326 at 335, [1976] Fam 185 at 196):

'I cannot believe, and the evidence does not warrant the view, that a decision to
carry out an operation of this nature performed for non-therapeutic purposes on a
minor, can be held to be within the doctor's sole clinical judgment.'

It is to be noted that in the present case an even larger claim is asserted, namely on the
basis of clinical judgment alone to proceed *without the parents' consent* and contrary to her
known wishes and express prohibition.

Second, albeit it may not need stating since there is no dispute, the judge made it quite
clear that once a child is a ward of court no important step in the life of that child can be
taken without the consent of the court.

It was not seriously contended by counsel for the department that the giving of
contraceptive advice and treatment to a girl under 16 would be other than an important
step in her life. Assuming that it would be, it follows that, in the case of a ward, a doctor
who was approached for contraceptive advice and treatment in the case of such a person
would be obliged to inform the court and obtain its consent. Since, in wardship, the
court is under a duty to act as a wise parent would act it is submitted that, if there is no
wardship, parental consent must be sought in order that he or she should have the
opportunity to act wisely. Such contention appears to me to have considerable force.

The next case, *Re P (a minor)* (1982) 80 LGR 301, is a decision of Butler-Sloss J in
chambers, reported with her permission. P was aged 15 and had become pregnant for
the second time. She was in the care of the local authority. They and P were in favour of
an abortion but her parents, whose consent the local authority had, albeit not obliged to
do so, properly sought, objected strongly on religious grounds. When they objected, the
local authority instituted wardship proceedings. The parents' wishes were overridden
but since the child was in care this is not of particular significance. What is of some
importance however is that Butler-Sloss J not only ordered that an abortion should take
place against the parents' wishes, but ordered further that, with the approval and at the
request of the mother, she be fitted thereafter with a suitable internal contraceptive
device. As to this the judge said: 'I assume that it is impossible for this Local Authority
to monitor her sexual activities and, therefore, contraception appears to be the only
alternative.'

Butler-Sloss J stated that, in reaching her conclusions, she had found helpful what had
been said by the House of Lords about parental rights and obligations in a case much
relied on by counsel for the department, namely *J v C* [1969] 1 All ER 788, [1970] AC
668. That case, however, affords little assistance as to what rights and obligations (or
duties) are comprised in parental rights and obligations, for the question was whether s 1
of the Guardianship of Infants Act 1925 (which makes the welfare of the infant the first
and paramount consideration in proceedings in which custody or upbringing is in

question) applies only to disputes between parents or whether it also applies to disputes between parents and strangers. In so far as parental rights and obligations figured at all it was therefore in relation to the weight to be given to them in reaching a conclusion under the Act as to what was best for the child and not in relation to their extent. The department's reliance on this case is in my opinion misplaced.

*Re N (minors) (parental rights)* [1974] 1 All ER 126, [1974] Fam 40 was also relied on but that case also affords no real assistance.

The cases which do in my opinion assist are those cases relating to the age of discretion relied on by the appellant, all of which counsel for the department submits should be disregarded on the ground that they related to custody.

In *R v Howes* (1860) 3 E & E 332, 121 ER 467 the question was whether a father was, by habeas corpus, entitled to recover the custody of a child between 15 and 16 notwithstanding that the child did not desire to be in his custody. Cockburn CJ, giving the judgment of the court on the father's application for the return of the child to his custody, said (3 E & E 332 at 336–337, 121 ER 467 at 468–469):

> 'Now the cases which have been decided on this subject shew that, although *a father is entitled to the custody of his children till they attain the age of twenty-one, this Court will not grant a habeas corpus to hand a child which is below that age over to its father, provided that it has attained an age of sufficient discretion to enable it to exercise a wise choice for its own interests. The whole question is, what is that age of discretion?* We repudiate utterly, as most dangerous, the notion that any intellectual precocity in an individual female child can hasten the period which appears to have been fixed by statute for the arrival of the age of discretion; for that very precocity, if uncontrolled, might very probably lead to her irreparable injury. The *Legislature has given us a guide, which we may safely follow, in pointing out sixteen as the age up to which the father's right to the custody of his female child is to continue ; and short of which such a child has no discretion to consent to leaving him.*' (My emphasis.)

The repudiation of the notion that intellectual precocity can hasten the age at which a minor can be considered to be of sufficient discretion to exercise a wise choice for its own interests and the fixing of a single age is to be noted.

In *Re Agar-Ellis, Agar-Ellis v Lascelles* (1883) 24 Ch D 317 a father put restrictions on his 17-year-old daughter's intercourse with her mother. The girl was at the time a ward of court. Brett MR said (at 326): '. . . the father has the control over the person, education and conduct of his children until they are twenty-one years of age. That is the law.' It had been argued that, because in habeas corpus proceedings a girl of 16 or more would not be delivered up to her father if she was content to remain where she was, this showed that the father's right of custody and control terminated altogether at age 16, but this argument was rejected on the ground that habeas corpus was a special case. Cotton LJ, having quoted the passage from Cockburn CJ set out above, said (at 331):

> 'Therefore the Lord Chief Justice there most distinctly recognises what, having regard to the Act, I should have thought was beyond dispute, that during infancy and over sixteen the right of the father still continues.'

The Act referred to was the Tenures Abolition Act 1660, s 8 of which gave the father the right to dispose of the custody and tuition of his children up to the age of 21.

The judgment which, however, I find of most assistance is that of Bowen LJ, from which I quote at greater length (at 335–336):

> 'Now a good deal of this discussion has turned upon the exact limits of parental authority. As far as one can see, some little confusion has been caused by the use in earlier law books of distinctions by which the law now no longer strictly stands. The strict Common Law gave to the father the guardianship of his children during the age of nurture and until the age of discretion. The limit was fixed at fourteen years in the case of a boy, and sixteen years in the case of a girl; but beyond this, except in

the case of the heir apparent, if one is to take the strict terminology of the older law, the father had no actual guardianship except only in the case of the heir apparent, in which case he was guardian by nature till twenty-one. That was what was called guardianship by nature in strict law. But for a great number of years the term "guardian by nature" has not been confined, so far as the father is concerned, to the case of heirs apparent, but has been used on the contrary to denote that sort of guardianship which the ordinary law of nature entrusts to the father till the age of infancy has completely passed and gone. I do not desire to elaborate the matter more than is necessary. The history I think of the term "natural guardianship" and of its extension, more especially in Courts of Equity, to the father's natural custody and to the authority which a father has over his child up to the complete age of twenty-one, will be found in *Hargreave's* note to *Coke* (Co Lit 88b). There is, therefore, a natural paternal jurisdiction between the age of discretion and the age of twenty-one, which the law will recognise. It has not only been recognised by the Common Law and by the Court of Chancery but it has also been recognised by statute. The [Tenures Abolition Act 1660] enables the father by his will to dispose of the custody and tuition of his child or children until they attain the age of twenty-one years. It seems to me to follow that if a father can dispose of the custody and tuition of his children by will until the age of twenty-one, it must be because the law recognises, to some extent, that he has himself an authority over the children till that age is reached. To neglect the natural jurisdiction of the father over the child until the age of twenty-one would be really to set aside the whole course and order of nature, and it seems to me it would disturb the very foundation of family life.'

This case has been subject to some trenchant criticism since, but it makes it perfectly clear that the father had a legal right of custody until 21, the then age of majority, and that that right included a right of control over the person. It also specifies as being established *one* age of discretion for boys and *one* for girls.

The trenchant criticism above referred to appears in *Hewer v Bryant* [1969] 3 All ER 578 at 582, [1970] 1 QB 357 at 369, a case in which the matter for decision was the meaning of the words 'in the custody of a parent' in s 22(2)(*b*) of the Limitation Act 1939, as amended by the Law Reform (Limitation of Actions) Act 1954. In that section the court construed the words as covering a case where, as a matter of fact, the minor was in the effective care and control of the parent. There was, however, considerable discussion of the more general aspect of parental rights which is presently of assistance. The trenchant criticism appears in the judgment of Lord Denning MR:

'I would get rid of the rule in *Re Agar-Ellis* and of the suggested exceptions to it. That case was decided in the year 1883. It reflects the attitude of a Victorian parent towards his children. He expected unquestioning obedience to his commands. If a son disobeyed, his father would cut him off with 1s. If a daughter had an illegitimate child, he would turn her out of the house. His power only ceased when the child became 21. I decline to accept a view so much out of date. The common law can, and should, keep pace with the times. It should declare, in conformity with the recent report on the Age of Majority (Report of Committee on Age of Majority (Cmnd 3342)), that the legal right of a parent to the custody of a child ends at the eighteenth birthday; and even up till then, it is a dwindling right which the courts will hesitate to enforce against the wishes of the child, the older he is. It starts with a right of control and ends with little more than advice.'

The more general discussion appears in the judgment of Sachs LJ ([1969] 3 All ER 578 at 584–585, [1970] 1 QB 357 at 372–373) of which I quote only that part of it which says:

'In its wider meaning the word "custody" is used as if it were almost the equivalent of "guardianship" in the fullest sense—whether the guardianship is by nature, by nurture, by testamentary disposition, or by order of a court. (I use the words "fullest sense" because guardianship may be limited to give control only over the person or only over the administration of the assets of an infant.) Adapting the convenient phraseology of counsel, such guardianship embraces a "bundle of rights", or to be more exact, a "bundle of powers", which continue until a male infant attains 21, or a female infant marries. These include power to control education, the choice of religion, and the administration of the infant's property. They include entitlement to veto the issue of a passport and to withhold consent to marriage. They include, also, both the personal power physically to control the infant until the years of discretion and the right (originally only if some property was concerned) to apply to the courts to exercise the powers of the Crown as parens patriae. It is thus clear that somewhat confusingly one of the powers conferred by custody in its wide meaning is custody in its limited meaning, i.e., such personal power of physical control as a parent or guardian may have.'

Despite his views concerning *Re Agar Ellis*, Lord Denning MR was clearly of the view that the legal right to custody continues, and should continue, up to but not beyond the child's eighteenth birthday (which it does) albeit that the right was a dwindling one. This it clearly is, if only because a boy of 14 or a girl of 16 can give an adequate consent to being out of its father's custody or in that of another so as to defeat any claim of the father by habeas corpus to have it back. Furthermore, albeit there may remain until 18 a legal right of control, it may, as the child grows older, be necessary for the parents, because physical control is no longer practical, to seek the assistance of the court to buttress and support the legal right.

As to Sach LJ's observation it does not appear to me to matter whether one refers to the parent or guardian having a bundle of powers or a bundle of rights. What is important is the recognition of the wide area in which, subject always to intervention by the court, a parent or guardian is entitled (by the exercise of a power or right) to control a child.

The next in this group of cases which requires mention is *R v D* [1984] 2 All ER 449, [1984] AC 778, where the House of Lords had, in a criminal matter, to consider two certified questions, namely (a) whether the common law offence of kidnapping exists in the case of a child victim under the age of 14 years and (b) whether, in any circumstances, a parent may be convicted of such an offence where the child victim is unmarried and under the age of majority.

Both questions were answered in the affirmative. For present purposes it is only necessary to refer to it by reason of certain comments made by Lord Brandon (with whose speech all other members of the Appellate Committee agreed) concerning the Irish case *The People (A-G) v Edge* [1943] IR 115, a case in which the history of the parental right to custody is the subject of exhaustive discussion. With regard to the decision itself he said ([1984] 2 All ER 449 at 455, [1984] AC 778 at 803):

> 'There is, in my view, nothing in *Edge*'s case to show that the Irish Supreme Court was of the opinion that there did not exist any common law offence of kidnapping a child under 14. On the contrary, it is implicit in its decision that it considered that such an offence did exist, but that, in order to establish it, the taking or carrying away of such a child would have to be shown to have been without the consent of the child's parent or other lawful guardian, rather than without the consent of the child himself. It will be necessary to consider later whether this distinction, between a child over 14 and one under 14, accords with the English law of kidnapping.'

He reverted to this matter in these terms ([1984] 2 All ER 449 at 457, [1984] AC 778 at 806):

> 'In my opinion, to accept that doctrine as applicable under English law would not be consistent with the formulation of the third ingredient of the common law offence of kidnapping which I made earlier on the basis of the wide body of authority to which your Lordships were referred. That third ingredient, as I formulated it earlier, consists of the absence of consent on the part of the person taken or carried away. I see no good reason why, in relation to the kidnapping of a

child, it should not in all cases be the absence of the child's consent which is material, whatever its age may be. In the case of a very young child, it would not have the understanding or the intelligence to give its consent, so that absence of consent would be a necessary inference from its age. In the case of an older child, however, it must, I think, be a question of fact for a jury whether the child concerned has sufficient understanding and intelligence to give its consent; if, but only if, the jury considers that a child has these qualities, it must then go on to consider whether it has been proved that the child did not give its consent. While the matter will always be for the jury alone to decide, I should not expect a jury to find at all frequently that a child under 14 had sufficient understanding and intelligence to give its consent. I should add that, while the absence of the consent of the person having custody or care and control of a child is not material to what I have stated to be the third ingredient of the common law offence of kidnapping, the giving of consent by such a person may be very relevant to the fourth such ingredient, in that, depending on all the circumstances, it might well support a defence of lawful excuse.'

Although Lord Brandon is dealing with the criminal law and we are not, the opinion of the Appellate Committee that a child under 14 can in certain circumstances for the purposes of kidnapping give a valid consent may clearly be of significance and requires examination.

By way of preliminary I must, with respect, point out that in *Edge's* case the age of 14 was considered of significance because in that case the allegedly kidnapped child was a boy and for a boy the age of discretion was 14, whereas in the case of a girl it was 16. The passages which I have quoted must therefore be considered with appropriate amendments. to cover the two cases.

Lord Brandon envisages for the purposes of the criminal law three questions: (1) whether the child was so young that absence of consent would be a necessary or legal inference from its age; this he regards as a matter of ruling by the judge although he does not give any guidance as to how young a child must be before any such inference is drawn; (2) whether, if the judge does not rule that absence of consent is presumed, the particular child had at the time sufficient understanding and intelligence to give its consent; a question for the jury; (3) if the jury are satisfied that the particular child had such understanding and intelligence whether they are also satisfied that he or she did not give consent (see [1984] 2 All ER 449 at 457, [1984] AC 778 at 806).

It appears to me that if at some *age* there is a necessary inference that consent is absent that age must be a fixed age even for the purposes of the criminal law. The fixed age might be different for girls and boys but I am unable to see how it can vary as between individual girls and boys. It is apparent that Lord Brandon regarded the age as being below 14 and, since the child concerned was there aged 5, more than 5, but this leaves a nine-year gap which at some time will need to be resolved.

Whatever may be the case with regard to the criminal law and kidnapping however, and clearly very different considerations apply there, it still seems to be the case that consent of the child is no answer to habeas corpus unless the child has attained the age of either 14 or 16 as the case may be.

In relation to other aspects of custody and control there must also be a fixed age in order that parents, children and those dealing with children may know where they stand and what are their powers, rights, duties or obligations. It is difficult to see why any other age than the age of discretion should be applicable and there is nothing in the authorities to point to any lower age.

So far as kidnapping is concerned, if the victim is old enough for consent to be legally possible there can be no objection to an investigation at the trial and a finding of fact by the jury on the two questions mentioned. Indeed such findings would be essential before a person were convicted.

In the field which is presently under consideration however, I regard any such consideration as both impractical and undesirable. A child may be of sufficient understanding and intelligence to give a consent before, or not until after, it has attained whatever may be the fixed age, but if there be no such age then neither parent, child nor strangers will know what their respective positions are. In the present field I would not therefore, unless driven, accept that the position is as the House of Lords have held it to be for the purposes of a charge of kidnapping. I am not so driven.

It is important to remember that, wherever a child is concerned, the court is in the background in order that, in the event of dispute, it may override, in effect, everyone, in the interests of the child. In the case of medical treatment, contraceptive or otherwise, it cannot exercise its jurisdiction to protect children unless the doctor either seeks the court's ruling himself or informs the parent of what he proposes to do, so that the parent may either consent or himself or herself seek the court's ruling. If the doctor takes either course the parent is necessarily informed. It is however a vital part of the department's case that, save with the child's permission, the parent shall not be told but that the matter must be left to the clinical judgment of the doctor, who may for example have been told, 'If dad knew he'd beat me up.'

Talk of clinical judgment is in my view misplaced. I can see nothing particularly clinical in a decision to fit an interuterine device in a Roman Catholic girl aged 13 on the ground that she wishes to *start* having sexual intercourse with a boyfriend and because attempts with a sheath have been a disastrous failure, even if the girl or boy or both assert that they will otherwise proceed without any contraceptive measures.

The doctor in such circumstances cannot help taking into account his views on the moral, social, religious etc aspects.

I fully appreciate that information to the parent may lead to family trouble and that knowledge that going to the doctor involves disclosure to parents may deter others from seeking advice and treatment with, possibly, highly undesirable or even tragic results. A parent who, for example, had fought hard for the rights which the appellant seeks and had won the battle might thereafter wish that she had never fought it, for it might lead to pregnancy, a backstreet abortion and even death. Such matters are, however, matters for debate elsewhere. If it be the law that until a girl is 16 no one may, save by the intervention of the court, afford advice or treatment without the parent's consent, then that law must be observed until it is altered by the legislature. The common law must, it is true, move with the times or keep up to date whenever it legitimately can but, if, as the law presently stands, the relevant age is 16, then it cannot in my opinion legitimately change that position. Even if the case went to the House of Lords and all the judges were unanimous, the decision would be one of nine men only without the materials on which to act.

I have mentioned the foregoing wider aspects in order that it should be clear that I have not forgotten them. Before passing to another subject I mention one further matter. If a child can, without a parent's knowledge and consent, seek and receive contraceptive advice and treatment, he or she can, logically, also presumably do so in respect of other treatment. There are clearly inherent dangers in this. A mother who, for example, does not know that her child has had some particular injection or is taking some form of drug may, if the child is in an accident and unconscious, assure the doctor that she has not had that injection and is not taking any drugs. This may have serious and possibly fatal consequences. I give this particular example because it is, I hope and believe, free from the strong feelings aroused by the particular advice and treatment here under consideration.

So far as civil law is concerned I have not found anything in any case which supports the view that at *least* up to the age of discretion either a child itself or anyone dealing with the child can lawfully interfere with the parents' rights flowing from custody.

That such rights (and duties) exist cannot be doubted. Nor can it be doubted that up to *some* age no one save the court is entitled to interfere. The only question it seems to me to be determined is what that age is.

Under the common law it appears to me to be plain that, in general, that age is the age of majority so far as outsiders are concerned, albeit that in habeas corpus proceedings someone who has reached the age of discretion may give a consent which will prevent a parent recovering custody and that for the purposes of a defence to a common law charge of kidnapping the consent of someone under the age of discretion may suffice.

I am of opinion that the present law is that, save in so far as changed by statute or by such recognised exceptions as marriage or joining the armed forces, the age of majority prevails. Indeed, if it does not, the jurisdiction of the court which lasts till the age of majority can be stultified, for decisions can be taken which may be against the interests of the child without the parents knowing and thus having the opportunity to resort to the court for its assistance.

### The criminal aspects

#### (a) Statutory provisions

Before Woolf J, consideration of the question of the possible criminal liability of a doctor providing contraceptive advice and treatment to a girl under 16 was much canvassed, the appellant contending that a doctor who did so would be committing an offence under s 28 of the Sexual Offences Act 1956 or aiding and abetting an offence under s 6 of that Act.

Whether in an individual case a doctor who followed the guidance notes would commit a criminal offence of either kind must depend on the circumstances. Counsel for the appellant conceded that in some cases he would not and counsel for the department conceded that in some cases he would. Both of these concessions were inescapable. They make it both unnecessary and undesirable to consider the direct impact of the criminal law on the position of doctors proceeding in accordance with the notes of guidance. However, the provisions already referred to and other provisions of the Act remain of importance, as providing a clear indication of public policy. Furthermore, some assistance is to be found in this connection from other sections and from both earlier and later statutory history.

Sections 50 and 51 of the Offences against the Person Act 1861 created the offences of having unlawful carnal knowledge respectively of a girl under the age of 10 years and a girl between the ages of 10 and 12 years. The former offence was a felony carrying a minimum sentence of 3 years' penal servitude and a maximum of penal servitude for life or a maximum of two years' imprisonment with or without hard labour. The latter offence was a misdemeanour carrying a sentence of three years' penal servitude or imprisonment with or without hard labour for a term not exceeding two years.

By the Offences against the Person Act 1875 the foregoing sections were repealed and re-enacted with amendments, (1) substituting the ages of 12 and 13 for the ages of 10 and 12, (2) raising the minimum term of penal servitude for the graver offence from three to five years, (3) removing the possible sentence of penal servitude in the case of the lesser offence and (4) expressly stating in the case of the lesser offence that it was committed 'whether with or without her consent'. This last specific provision was presumably because by raising the age, there were being brought within the criminal law cases in which hitherto consent would have prevented any offence existing at all.

Ten years later, the Criminal Law Amendment Act 1885 repealed the 1875 Act and by ss 4 and 5 re-enacted the earlier provision with amendments, (1) raising the respective ages to 13 and 16, (2) making attempts to commit either of the offences offences in themselves and (3) providing in the case of the lesser offence the defence that the person charged had reasonable cause to believe that the girl was of or above the age of 16 years.

The 1885 Act remained in force until it was repealed by the 1956 Act, the relevant sections being replaced by ss 5 and 6 of the new Act. Under the new sections the graver offence remained a felony carrying a maximum sentence of imprisonment for life and the lesser offence remained a misdemeanour carrying a maximum sentence of two years' imprisonment. The respective ages remained unchanged. Attempts were, in both cases, preserved as separate offences in themselves, carrying maximum sentences of two years' imprisonment in both cases. As before there were no special defences in respect of the graver offence but in the case of the lesser offence there were two special defences provided by ss 6(2) and (3), which provided

> '(2) Where a marriage is invalid under section two of the Marriage Act, 1949, or section one of the Age of Marriage Act, 1929 (the wife being a girl under the age of sixteen), the invalidity does not make the husband guilty of an offence under this section because he has sexual intercourse with her, if he believes her to be his wife and has reasonable cause for the belief.
>
> (3) A man is not guilty of an offence under this section because he has unlawful sexual intercourse with a girl under the age of sixteen, if he is under the age of twenty-four and has not previously been charged with a like offence, and he believes her to be of the age of sixteen or over and has reasonable cause for the belief. In this subsection, "a like offence" means an offence under this section or an attempt to commit one, or an offence under paragraph (1) of section five of the Criminal Law Amendment Act 1885 (the provision replaced for England and Wales by this section).'

Since 1956 there have been two changes of importance. First by the Indecency with Children Act 1960 the maximum penalty for an attempt to commit the graver offence was increased from two years to seven years. Second, in 1967, as a result of the abolition of the distinction between felony and misdemeanour, certain procedural changes were made. An incidental result of this was that concealment of the graver crime, which previously would itself have constituted a crime, namely misprision of felony, ceased to be a crime.

So far as these two particular offences are concerned it will thus be seen that from 1861 to 1960 Parliament has seen fit, by way of the criminal law, progressively to increase the protection to the young, raising the ages at which their consent would prevent intercourse from being a crime from 12 to 13 to 16 and that, as late as 1960, additional protection was accorded to the under-thirteens by raising the maximum penalty for an offence of attempt from two years to seven years. It will also be seen that in the case of the lesser offence the defence provided by the 1885 Act was severely limited by the 1956 Act.

As to the graver crime, until 1967 anyone who was aware that an offence had been committed would have been under a positive duty to report it to the police or other lawful authority and would have been guilty of a common law offence if he failed to do so. Whether this applied also in the case of contemplated felonies had not been decided when the offence ceased to exist. In *Sykes v DPP* [1961] 3 All ER 33, [1962] AC 528 Lord Denning suggested that there might be exceptions to the general rule, including amongst such possible exceptions a doctor and his patient. He recognised, however, that parent and child was not an exception.

For present purposes the precise limits of the offence are of no importance. What is or may be of some importance however is that the graver crime was, until 1967, considered so serious that there was a public duty to report it.

Other sections of the 1956 Act which have some bearing are (1) s 14, which provides that it is an offence (subject to a special exception) to commit an indecent assault on a woman and also that a girl under 16 'cannot in law give any consent which would prevent an act being assault for the purposes of this section', (2) s 19 which, subject to an exception, makes it an offence to take an unmarried girl under the age of 18 out of the possession of her parent or guardian against *his* will, (3) s 20, which creates the like offence, but without the exception in the case of a girl under 16, and (4) ss 25 and 26, which provide, in the case respectively of girls under 13 and those between 13 and 16, that it is an offence for the owner of premises and certain others to permit the girl to resort to or be on the premises for the purpose of having unlawful sexual intercourse with men or a particular man. The former offence was originally a felony subject to a maximum sentence of life imprisonment. It still is so subject. The latter offence was and is subject to a maximum sentence of two years.

As to s 14, a normal preliminary to contraceptive advice and treatment is a vaginal examination, and some contraceptive devices involve in their fitting that which would, without consent, prima facie be indecent assaults. It may be that a doctor who, without *a* the consent of a woman, examines her vagina for medical purposes commits no indecent assault, but there are clearly strong arguments the other way. In my view a doctor who, for example, examines a ten year old, is at least at risk of prosecution unless he has the consent of a parent and this is so up to the age of 16 when, if the child consents the consent is valid by statute and the offence ceases. Moreover, it has always been the law that for a plain civil trespass to a child a parent had his own right to sue in certain *b* circumstances.

Section 19 affords a parent greater protection than habeas corpus, for in that case, if a girl is 16, she can in that connection give a valid consent. The position with regard to girls under 16 is in like case for both crime and habeas corpus, but between 16 and 18, although habeas corpus will not avail if the child consents, her consent is irrelevant to the crime. However, between 18 and 21, which was the then age of majority, the parent was *c* unprotected either by habeas corpus or by the criminal law. This does not, however, mean that the right to custody ceased at 18, merely that from then on, albeit the child was under age, her consent was valid for criminal and habeas corpus purposes.

Since by ss 25 and 26 anyone who allowed sexual intercourse with a girl under 16 to take place on his premises would commit an offence and, if the girl were under 13, would until 1967 have committed a felony, it would, as it seems to me, be odd to say the *d* least if it was perfectly lawful to take action which would go some way to lessen the inhibitions of a girl under 16 and a man against sexual intercourse by protecting them from any ensuing undesirable consequences.

These sections are the successors of like provisions in the 1885 Act under which a mother was convicted for allowing her 14-year-old illegitimate daughter to have intercourse with a man in their joint home: see *R v Webster* (1885) 16 QBD 134. A *e* mother or father, therefore, clearly has a duty to prevent the act of intercourse where by virtue of ownership of premises she or he can control the situation.

The provisions of the criminal law all appear to me to support the view which I have already expressed. It is true that prior to 1885 the consent of a girl under 16 would prevent intercourse with her being a crime, but since then girls under 16 have been consistently treated as being unable to give consent. *f*

It appears to me that it is wholly incongruous, when the act of intercourse is criminal, when permitting it to take place on one's premises is criminal and when, if the girl were under 13, failing to report an act of intercourse to the police would up to 1967 have been criminal, that either the department or the area health authority should provide facilities which will enable girls under 16 the more readily to commit such acts. It seems to me equally incongruous to assert that doctors have the right to accept the young, down, *g* apparently, to any age, as patients, and to provide them with contraceptive advice and treatment without reference to their parents and even against their known wishes.

It may well be that it would be highly unlikely that, in the case of a girl aged, say, 10, a doctor would do any such thing, but that is in my view irrelevant. The question is simply whether a doctor is entitled to do so or whether in doing so he would infringe the parents' legal rights. *h*

I can find no additional cases on the criminal aspect which assist in relation to the limited area in which for present purposes it is relevant.

In the final analysis the position is in my view as follows. (1) It is clearly established that a parent or guardian has, as such, a parcel of rights in relation to children in his custody. (2) By statute, subject to an exception, such rights can be neither abandoned nor transferred. (3) Such rights include the right to control the manner in which and the *j* place at which the child spends his or her time. (4) Those rights will be enforced by the courts subject to the right of the court to override the parental rights in the interests of the child. (5) There is no authority of any kind to suggest that anyone other than the court can interfere with the parents' rights otherwise than by resort to the courts, or pursuant to specific statutory powers or exceptions. (6) It is clearly recognised that there is some age below which a child is incapable as a matter of law of giving any valid consent or making any valid decision for itself in regard to its custody or upbringing. (7) The authorities indicate that this age is 16 in the case of girls and 14 in the case of boys, at all events for the purposes of habeas corpus. (8) So far as girls are concerned, the provisions of the criminal law show that Parliament has taken the view that the consent of a girl under 16 in the matter of sexual intercourse is a nullity.

In the light of the above, I conclude that as a matter of law a girl under 16 can give no valid consent to anything in the areas under consideration which apart from consent would constitute an assault, whether civil or criminal, and can impose no valid prohibition on a doctor against seeking parental consent.

I conclude further that any doctor who advises a girl under 16 as to contraceptive steps to be taken or affords contraceptive or abortion treatment to such a girl without the knowledge and consent of the parent, save in an emergency which would render consent in any event unnecessary, infringes the legal rights of the parent or guardian. Save in emergency, his proper course is to seek parental consent or apply to the court.

I express no view whether 16 should or should not be the age below which a girl can give no valid consent and make no valid decision in the two fields under consideration. I express only the view that in law it is presently such age.

I express my gratitude to both counsel for their assistance and for eschewing the sort of arguments which will doubtless follow the judgments given today.

I would allow the appeal and grant the second declaration sought amended so as to add at the end, 'save in cases of emergency or with the leave of the court'.

As to the first declaration, it cannot be granted in the terms sought, but it is clear that the result of what I have concluded is that the issue and subsequent maintenance of both the original and revised form of section G were and are contrary to law. I would therefore assume that the department and the local health authority would withdraw the latter whether or not a declaration were granted. Nevertheless, by reason of the far-reaching nature of this problem, it is in my view desirable that there should be a formal declaration by this court, and I would propose that it be declared: that the notice issued by the department in December 1980 setting out a revised form of section G of the memorandum of guidance issued in May 1974 is contrary to law.

**FOX LJ.** In January 1981 the appellant wrote to the local health authority demanding an assurance that in no circumstances would any of her daughters be given contraceptive or abortion treatment while they are under 16 in any of the family planning clinics under the control of the health authority without her (the appellant's) consent. That assurance was not forthcoming. These proceedings are the consequence. They require an investigation of the rights, if any, of parents to be informed of and to control medical treatment to their children. I say 'parents' because although the appellant is the sole plaintiff, she and her husband are of the same mind in relation to the case, and no point arises as to his absence. Nor, I may say, is any point taken on the fact that the proceedings take the form which they do and are not by way of judicial review.

Counsel for the Department of Health and Social Security questions the propriety of the use of the word 'rights' at all in relation to the position of parents in these matters. He says that, if parents can be said to have any rights in relation to their child, it is only a right to carry out the duties which the parents owe to the child. Parents, he says, have no 'free-standing' rights at all. For that he relies on the decision of the House of Lords in *J v C* [1969] 1 All ER 788, [1970] AC 668. The statutory background to that decision was s 1 of the Guardianship of Infants Act 1925, which is as follows:

'Where in any proceeding before any court (whether or not a court within the meaning of the Guardianship of Infants Act, 1886) the custody or upbringing of an infant, or the administration of any property belonging to or held on trust for an infant, or the application of the income thereof, is in question, the court, in deciding that question, shall regard the welfare of the infant as the first and paramount consideration, and shall not take into consideration whether from any other point of view the claim of the father, or any right at common law possessed by the father, in respect of such custody, upbringing, administration or application is superior to that of the mother, or the claim of the mother is superior to that of the father.'

These provisions are re-enacted in the Guardianship of Minors Act 1971, s 1.

Whether the 'welfare' principle enacted by the 1925 Act did anything more than re-state the existing Chancery doctrine in wardship cases I need not consider, but one would have thought that the language of the section was clear enough and that in any proceedings of the kind mentioned in the section, whether between parents or between a parent and a stranger, the welfare of the child is the first and paramount consideration. However, in *Re Carroll* [1931] 1 KB 317, [1930] All ER Rep 192 a dispute arose about an illegitimate child between her mother and an adoption society to whom she had, in the past, handed over the child and who, in that time, had handed the child over to persons who wished to adopt her. The mother now wished to recover the child and place her in an institution of a particular religious denomination. The child was made a ward. The High Court and the Divisional Court both decided that it was in the best interests of the child to leave her where she was. The Court of Appeal, however, by a majority reversed those decisions. Scrutton LJ said that there had been no material change in the law in the preceding 40 years save that the mother's wishes had been put on an equality with the father, that there was no case in which the court had disregarded the view of an only parent and that the wishes of the mother as the sole parent should prevail (see [1931] 1 KB 317 at 337, [1930] All ER Rep 192 at 202). Slesser LJ was of the opinion that s 1 of the 1925 Act was irrelevant. He said ([1931] 1 KB 317 at 355–356, [1930] All ER Rep 192 at 211):

'This statute, however, in my view, has confined itself to questions as between the rights of father and mother which I have already outlined—problems which cannot arise in the case of an illegitimate child . . . it is difficult to see . . . how it can be said from a consideration of that [statute] . . . that there has been a development of thought between 1891 and 1926 . . .'

In *J v C* the essence of the matter was the submission of the parents that united parents were prima facie entitled to the custody of their infant child and that the court would only deprive them of care and control if they were unfitted by character, conduct or otherwise to have care and control. And it was asserted that s 1 of the 1925 Act only applied to disputes between parents and not to disputes between parents and strangers (which was the position in *J v C*). The House of Lords held that s 1 applied to all disputes, whether between parents themselves or between parents and strangers, that the section requires that in any such dispute the welfare of the child is the paramount consideration, that *Re Carroll* was wrong in so far as it decided to the contrary and that since the judge had not misdirected himself in fact or law there was no ground for interfering with his decision that the welfare of the child in that case required that the child should be committed to the care of the foster parents and not to the parents. I do not think that the case is of assistance. No doubt, if a child is a ward of court and a question arises whether it should or should not receive particular medical treatment, the court will determine that question as it thinks best for the welfare of the child even though that determination conflicts with the honestly held views of responsible parents. But that does not really assist in deciding whether, when there is no wardship, the parents have any rights in relation to the giving of medical advice and treatment to their children. Most children are not the subject of litigation and, simply as a matter of convenience and ordered living, some rules have to be established for regulating their affairs even though the court, in the last resort, can in the exercise of its wardship or other jurisdiction impose its own view, on the particular facts of the individual case, as to what is best for the welfare of the child. A statutory example of that is marriage. A child who is over 16 but under 18 cannot, generally, marry without the consent of both parents (see the Marriage Act

1949, s 3 and Sch 2, as amended by the Family Reform Act 1969, s 2). The court can however override the refusal of the parents to consent (see s 3(1)(b) of the 1949 Act).

In short, I see no reason why the decision in *J v C* and the welfare principle to which it gives effect should be regarded as necessarily inconsistent with prima facie working rules which can be applied without prejudice to the ultimate authority of the court. The welfare principle as formulated in the statutes assumes the existence of a dispute before the court and, therefore, that there is an arbiter (the court) which can finally determine in the individual case what is best for the welfare of the child, even though reasonable persons may hold strongly differing views as to what is best. I appreciate that general rules may, in an individual case, work unsatisfactorily. There is, however, in the background, the ultimate control of the court if recourse is had to that.

I come then to the question whether parents have any relevant rights in the present case. Parliament seems clearly to have accepted that parents do have 'rights' in relation to their children. Thus, the Children Act 1975, s 85(1) provides that unless a contrary intention appears 'the parental rights and duties' means as respects a particular child (whether legitimate or not) 'all the rights and duties' which by law the mother and father have in relation to a legitimate child and his property. Further, except under the provisions of certain separation agreements between husband and wife, a person cannot surrender or transfer any parental right or duty which he has as respects a child (see s 85(2)).

And s 86 of the Children Act 1975 provides that in the Act, unless the contrary appears, 'legal custody' means as respects a child 'so much of the parental rights and duties as relate to the person of the child (including the place and manner in which his time is spent) . . .'

For the purpose of identifying any relevant rights I think one must start with custody. At common law the father had a right to custody of his legitimate child during minority. That right seems to have been more or less absolute in the absence of evidence that the father would abuse it to the detriment of the child. Thus in *R v De Manneville* (1804) 5 East 221, 102 ER 1054 the father, on a habeas corpus, obtained custody of his eight-month-old child from its mother. Lord Ellenborough CJ said (5 East 221 at 223, 102 ER 1054 at 1055): 'Then he [the father] having a legal right to the custody of his child, and not having abused it, was entitled to have it restored to him.' This doctrine was mitigated to some extent by two factors. First, the principle that habeas corpus would not go to compel a child who had attained the 'age of discretion' to return to the father against the child's wishes. The age of discretion was 16 for girls and 14 for boys (see *Thomasset v Thomasset* [1894] P 295 at 298, [1891–4] All ER 308 at 310 per Lindley LJ). The age of 16 seems to have derived from the Act 4 & 5 Phil & Mar c 8 (Abduction (1557)), which related to the abduction of girls (see *R v Howes* (1860) 3 E & E 332 at 334, 337, 121 ER 467 at 468–469). The second mitigating factor was the development in Chancery of the principle of the welfare of the child. The fusion of law and equity, with the rules of equity prevailing, which was enacted by the Supreme Court of Judicature Act 1875 does not, however, seem to have diminished the inclination of the courts to enforce the wishes of the father. The *Agar-Ellis* cases, *Re Agar-Ellis, Agar-Ellis v Lascelles* (1878) 10 Ch D 49 and *Re Agar-Ellis, Agar-Ellis v Lascelles* (1883) 24 Ch D 316, are extreme examples of this attitude. In the 1883 case Cotton LJ said (at 334):

> 'It has been said that we ought to consider the interest of the ward. Undoubtedly. But this Court holds this principle—that when, by birth, a child is subject to a father, it is for the general interest of families, and for the general interest of children, and really for the interest of the particular infant, that the Court should not, except in very extreme cases, interfere with the discretion of the father, but leave to him the responsibility of exercising that power which nature has given him by the birth of the child.'

The father in that case had put restrictions on contact between his 16-year-old daughter and her mother. The court refused to interfere.

In the 1878 case Bacon V-C said (at 56):

'The father is the head of his house, he must have the control of his family . . . and this Court never does interfere between a father and his children unless there be an abandonment of the parental duty . . .'

It seems that even in their own day the *Agar-Ellis* cases not surprisingly aroused strong feelings and were probably one of the causes which led to s 5 of the Guardianship of Infants Act 1886, which provided that the court might—

'upon the application of the mother of any infant . . . make such order as it may think fit regarding the custody of such infant and the right of access thereto of either parent, having regard to the welfare of the infant, and to the conduct of the parents . . .'

(See per Scrutton LJ in *Re Carroll* [1931] 1 KB 317 at 335, [1930] All ER Rep 192 at 201.)

Lord Denning MR in *Hewer v Bryant* [1969] 3 All ER 578 at 582, [1970] 1 QB 357 at 369 said that we should 'get rid of the rule in *Re Agar-Ellis*'. The principle of the virtual supremacy of the parents' wishes stated by Cotton LJ and Bacon V-C in the passages which I have cited represent, I agree, far too extreme a notion of the parents' rights and is unacceptable; it is indeed inconsistent with the provisions of s 1 of the Guardianship of Infants Act 1925 and its successor, the 1971 Act. I do not, however, think that the common law right to custody has been abrogated. We have not been referred to any statute or authority which does that. The right has been subjected to the control of the court and, in effect, no longer belongs to the father alone: it belongs to both parents. But, subject to any order of the court in relation to the individual child, it seems to me that the parents have custody. And further the custody continues during minority (see the observations of Bowen LJ in *Re Agar-Ellis* 24 Ch D 317 at 335–336). Lord Denning MR in *Hewer v Bryant* despite his criticism of *Re Agar-Ellis* did not doubt that legal custody should continue to 18 though as the child gets older it may, in practice, be a waning right unless the court is prepared to support it for the child's welfare.

The next question is: what does custody involve? I think that its central feature is control. No doubt it involves care of the child but, without control, the care may be hindered. It is significant that in defining 'legal custody' s 86 of the Children Act 1975 includes, among the rights therein comprised, the rights relating to 'the place and manner in which [the child's] time is spent'. These matters depend on control of the child's person and indeed the section refers to the child's person. If the parents are effectively to determine the place and manner in which the child's time is spent, it seems to me that the law must give them complete control of the child's person. Against that background, we have to consider first of all whether it is permissible, as the department asserts, for a doctor to give contraceptive treatment to a girl under 16 without informing the child's parents. I do not think it is. To provide contraceptive treatment to a girl of such an age must, it seems to me, be regarded as a matter of major importance in the child's life. And to do so without informing the parents is, I think, a serious interference with parental responsibility and the rights involved in custody. It seems to me to be an interference with the control of matters relative to the child and its person which the law (subject to the ultimate discretion of the court in individual cases) gives to the parents. It was accepted by counsel for the department that if a doctor was aware that a child was a ward of court it would not be proper for him to provide contraceptive treatment without the authority of the court. I think that concession was rightly made. The court's jurisdiction is, however, essentially parental, and it does not set out to do more than a wise and caring parent would (see *R v Gyngall* [1893] 2 QB 232 at 341 per Lord Esher MR). Exercising such jurisdiction it would certainly expect that no major decision regarding a girl under 16 should be made without reference to the court. And I think that most parents would certainly expect, in the case of a girl under 16, that they would be informed also. Such expectations in my view are fully supported by the legal rights of parents. Further, if the decision can be made by the doctor without informing the parents, the consequences may be to remove from the parents the right to obtain the court's ruling on whether it is for the child's welfare or not. The decision will have been taken and the treatment given. The parents may not learn of it until long afterwards. The position in relation to a girl under 16 is rendered even less acceptable by the fact that the contraceptive treatment is to enable the girl to embark on or continue sexual relations which, for the man, will normally constitute a criminal offence under s 6 of the Sexual Offences Act 1956 (ie unlawful sexual intercourse with a girl under 16).

The circular refers to the 'clinical judgment of the doctor'. On the evidence before us I am not clear that 'clinical judgment' will normally be a factor of real consequence. The girl generally is not ill: she is coming for contraceptive treatment to enable her to have sexual intercourse without risk of pregnancy. The problem, it seems to me, is in most cases more moral or social than clinical.

It is said that, if a doctor cannot give contraceptive treatment to a girl under 16 without the knowledge of the parents, some girls may be afraid to come to the doctor at all and will risk pregnancy. I see the force of that, but all we can do in this case is to endeavour to state the existing law. If the law as it stands is thought to involve more risks to young girls than it avoids (as to which opinions may differ), Parliament may have to intervene. But to cut out the parents from knowledge of the intended treatment, bearing in mind that one is dealing with girls of 15 and under, would be an important matter of public policy.

I have not so far examined the question whether a girl under 16 could herself give consent to contraceptive treatment and so override any parental rights. Section 8(1) and (3) of the Family Law Reform Act 1969 provides as follows:

'(1) The consent of a minor who has attained the age of sixteen years to any surgical, medical or dental treatment which, in the absence of consent, would constitute a trespass to his person, shall be as effective as it would be if he were of full age; and where a minor has by virtue of this section given an effective consent to any treatment it shall not be necessary to obtain any consent for it from his parent or guardian . . .

(3) Nothing in this section shall be construed as making ineffective any consent which would have been effective if this section had not been enacted.'

It is said on behalf of the appellant that sub-s (1) enables a consent to be given by a minor which otherwise could not be given and that sub-s (3) merely removes any doubt that the parents' consent could still be effective. The department, however, contends that a minor of sufficient understanding can give consent, and that sub-s (1) merely provides an irrebuttable presumption of sufficient understanding in the case of a person over 16. Subsection (3), it is said, merely allows proof of sufficient understanding in the individual case below 16.

That the common law developed a principle enabling a child to override parental wishes and to consent to the taking of major decisions concerning him provided it could be shown that he was of sufficient understanding seems to be unlikely. It is inconvenient in practice in that it may give rise to subsequent doubts, and difficulties of proof, whether the child does have sufficient understanding. The degree of such understanding might vary considerably according to the nature of the matter to be decided. The authorities in the civil law show no tendency to encourage such a rule. Thus in relation to the age of discretion Cockburn CJ said in R v Howes (1860) 3 E & E 332 at 336–337, 121 ER 467 at 468:

'We repudiate . . . the notion that any intellectual precocity in an individual female child can hasten the period which appears to have been fixed by statute for the arrival of the age of discretion; for that very precocity, if uncontrolled, might very probably lead to her irreparable injury.'

The statute referred to is the Act 4 & 5 Phil & Mar c 8 (Abduction (1557)), which I have already mentioned.

Again, in R v Gyngall [1893] 2 QB 232 at 250 Kay LJ said:

'Because the Court cannot inquire into every particular case the law has now fixed upon certain ages—as to boys the age of fourteen, and as to girls the age of sixteen— up to which, as a general rule, the Court will not inquire upon a habeas corpus, as between the father and the child, as to the consent of the child to the place wherever it may be.'

These quotations are dealing with habeas corpus but I think they state general objections to investigation of the varying capacities of understanding in individual children. I can see nothing in the authorities which supports, much less establishes, that, at common law, a decision (not in emergency) regarding the provision of medical treatment to a girl under 16 could have been taken without the consent of the father. As I have indicated the paternal rights at law were very wide, and I see no indication that decisions on major matters regarding the welfare of a girl under 16 could have depended on her consent. The only relevant statutory intervention is that contained in s 8 of the Family Law Reform Act 1969, which relates only to persons over 16.

The result, in my view, is that a girl under 16 cannot give a valid consent to contraceptive treatment and is not entitled to prohibit a doctor from seeking the consent of her parents.

A possible approach to the whole matter is that, while the doctor should be bound to inform the parents of his intention to provide contraceptive treatment, if the parents do not consent within a reasonable time he should be at liberty to proceed without their consent even though consent has been refused. This would enable the parents to make an application to the court to determine the matter. I do not think that is in line with the legal position. It reverses the existing legal position which, subject to the ultimate power of the court, gives the final decision to the parents and not to the doctor. That is the consequence of the right of control which, as I have indicated, seems to me to follow from the right to custody. And I do not think that persons not having custody can take on themselves the right to give consent. I appreciate that this may produce an unsatisfactory position if, for example, the parents cannot be found or the doctor profoundly disagrees, on the particular facts of the individual case, with their refusal to give consent. In such cases the local authority can, if it thinks fit, seek to have the matter determined by the court.

In dealing with this case I would not, in any way, wish to underrate the value of the part which an experienced doctor can play in the practical resolution of the problems with which we are concerned. Nor should one underrate the value of the parents' part. They know the child and they know its history. In most cases, whatever the civil law may be, the best outcome is likely to be that which is the consequence of full co-operation between the parents and the doctor in deciding what is in the child's interest.

In so far as we are concerned, for the purposes of s 1 of the Guardianship of Minors Act 1971, with the welfare of particular children, namely the daughters of the appellant now under the age of 16, we are dealing with children of a united family and with parents who are concerned for their well-being. That such children, while under 16, should be given contraceptive treatment without the knowledge of their parents seems to me, on the balance of probability, to be likely to be disruptive of family relationships and inimical to the children's welfare. Nor am I satisfied, on any facts before us, that it would be for their welfare that they should be given such treatment after notice to the parents but against the parents' wishes. The parents in this family are likely to know the child very well. Accepting that they may have strong views on these matters which may not be shared by others, I am not persuaded that, in relation to children of so young an age, their views should necessarily be overridden by those of the doctor (I am not referring to emergencies). It seems to me that, if the parents' wishes are to be overridden, that should be done by the court in relation to the particular circumstances of the time.

Looking at the whole matter, I think that in substance the appellant is entitled to the relief which she seeks. I should add that while the writ refers to abortion as well as contraceptive treatment the argument before us was directed to the latter. It is not, however, suggested that there is any difference in principle between the two for the present purposes.

I have not in this judgment examined the criminal law. The judge dealt with it in order to dispose of an argument that a doctor who provided contraceptive treatment to a girl under 16 might be guilty of a criminal offence. As regards any comparison with the criminal law as regards capacity to consent, the criminal law is concerned with different problems (including, in particular, the liberty of the subject) and different considerations apply. Accordingly I do not think that one can safely determine the civil law except on the basis of the civil law authorities, more particularly in view of the use made in the common law of the age of discretion.

I agree with the conclusions (1) to (8) in the judgment of Parker LJ, which I have read in draft, and with the order which he proposes. I would allow the appeal accordingly.

**EVELEIGH LJ.** We are concerned with two specific issues. Firstly, whether it is lawful for the area health authority to issue instructions to the effect that contraceptive aids may be given to children under 16 years of age without involving the parent in the decision to do so, even against the parent's wishes. Secondly, whether contraceptive and/or abortion advice and/or treatment may be given to any child of the plaintiff below the age of 16 without the prior knowledge and/or consent of the child's parent or guardian. Basically these issues involve the responsibility for major decisions in relation to a child's upbringing. As appears from the judgment of Parker LJ, which I have had the advantage of reading, the first and paramount consideration in such matters is the child's welfare. There is no difference in law in relation to contraception or any other major decision, for example education or religious upbringing.

As a matter of common sense and from the authorities to which Fox and Parker LJJ have referred, the authority to make such decisions rests with the person having custody of the child. The appellant is such a person and I shall use the word 'parent' to cover all persons who have custody. It follows that the parent's decision must prevail unless displaced by the child's welfare. Where a court awards custody to a person, it does so on the basis that that person is capable of making the right decision and, in consequence of the order, that person is the proper person to make the decision. A natural parent must be in the same position in the absence of a court order to the contrary. In some areas the parent's freedom to decide is circumscribed by statute, for example in education. Where this is not so, the parent's decision must be treated prima facie as being in the child's best interests. Anyone who interferes with the parent's decision must be prepared to demonstrate that the decision is not in the child's best interests. In the present case the area health authority has taken the attitude that whatever the parent's wishes or decision any child, and the appellant's three children in particular, must be free to obtain contraceptive treatment.

I shall deal with the second declaration first. The appellant contends that in relation to abortion or contraception she should be consulted. She wishes to have a say. She also wishes to ensure that as between herself and the doctors employed by the area health authority she shall have the deciding voice.

The appellant's children are not to be free to consult a doctor in confidence and to receive treatment in confidence. However, she clearly recognises that any decision of hers must be subject to review by the court.

The appellant's decision in this regard cannot be supported if in relation to each the child's welfare demands that it should be otherwise. There are two ways of showing this: first, on the general proposition that, irrespective of the particular child, such a parental decision must be wrong; second, that in relation to each of these children considered separately there are personal considerations to make the decision wrong.

As to the first approach to this question, it is tempting to answer it by saying that many reasonable people hold opposing views on the overall question of the desirability of providing contraceptive aids, and therefore it is impossible, as a generalisation, to say that aids should be available no matter what the personal circumstances of the child. Those who say that aids should be freely available do so on the grounds of public policy, as they see it, that the risk of illegitimate children should be avoided. Some say that those who put the opposite view do so because of outdated inborn prejudice which fails to accord the welfare of the child the first and paramount consideration. I shall therefore briefly list some points in the argument in order to see if the choice between them points inexorably in one direction.

It is said that public policy demands that unwanted illegitimate births must be avoided. If children think that their parents will be involved they will not come for help. Not only will they not seek contraceptive advice but they will hesitate, and thus delay, to seek advice if pregnant or after contracting a disease.

On the other side it is said that there is another way to avoid pregnancy, namely by abstinence; and that is the only 100% guarantee against pregnancy and disease. The availability of secret medical advice undermines the efforts of the parent to bring the child up with proper moral standards and encourages promiscuity. If a local authority is permitted to let it be known that it is proper for a child to obtain secret medical advice irrespective of the parents' wishes, the authority of the parent is undermined and the stability of family life threatened.

On the one side it is said that the child must be protected against the stress which pregnancy will cause. On the other side it is pointed out that the girl who indulges in sexual intercourse may suffer from remorse not only for having herself transgressed but for involving a man who may find himself charged with a criminal offence. One would like to think that a great majority of girls would not take part in unlawful sexual intercourse if it were not made easier to do so with impunity and if they did not feel that they would be seen to be standing apart from their less inhibited associates. A parent should be helped not hindered in providing the assurance and the comfort and the advice which such a child might need.

It is accepted that the provision of a contraceptive device is preceded by a careful medical examination. The doctor concerned will have no knowledge of the child's medical history. The decision to provide a device ought not simply to be regarded as a clinical one, for it involves the character of the child and her whole well-being. This is not a matter to be decided by one who does not know the child.

It is further argued that the courts have always lent their assistance to the parent who seeks to prevent harmful associations between the child and an undesirable man. The provision of a contraceptive device by a doctor who knows nothing of the girl or her companions may be furthering such an association.

The responsibility of a parent for the upbringing of the child is emphasised by the fact that the parent may be made to answer in the criminal courts for a child's misbehaviour. Home background and parental indifference are frequently pleaded as the reason that the child is a delinquent. Parental authority should not be undermined.

I am conscious that I have set out at greater length the case for those who oppose the scheme operated by the area health authority. It is inevitable because the health authority's case is simplicity itself, namely that public policy dictates its conduct. The opponents retort that public policy demands the stability of family life.

In some families, even where the members are closely united and where the parents try to maintain high standards, the parents may prefer not to know. They are best able to understand the relationship between themselves and their children and to decide what is best. A mother may wish to protect her child against the wrath of a puritanical father should he learn that a child has sought contraceptive help.

The above observations satisfy me that it is impossible to say that a parent who adopts the attitude of the appellant is not acting in the best interests of the child. On the other hand, I cannot say that a parent who does not seek to be involved will always be wrong. The question cannot be answered by a generalisation. I must therefore consider each of the appellant's children individually.

It happens that, apart from the age, the evidence before the court in relation to each child is the same. Each is being brought up by capable and responsible parents in a home which seeks to maintain high religious and moral standards and the happiness of the family. We have no other evidence relevant to our inquiry. In those circumstances I find it impossible to say that the appellant is wrong in her decision. Indeed on the evidence before us I must assume that she knows best and I think that she is right. I therefore would grant the second declaration with the minor amendment suggested by Parker LJ.

The notice referred to in the first declaration authorises the doctor employed by the area health authority to defy the wishes of a parent like the appellant. As I find that the appellant is entitled to the second declaration, I hope that I am not being too simplistic when I say that it must follow that, to the extent that it authorises such a course, the notice is unlawful. However, the declaration claimed is in somewhat wide and loose terms. I do not think that we should do more than grant the declaration which Parker LJ has drafted.

On my above approach to this case and the conclusion which I have reached, I do not think it necessary to examine jurisprudentially the nature of a parent's 'rights'. I am aware that it is sometimes argued that statutory provisions speak of 'rights' but do so only in the sense of powers. In the present case the welfare of children is our first and paramount consideration, and, if a declaration of the court will serve to promote that welfare, it is not useful to investigate the distinction betwen 'rights' and powers. I do not see why the parent should be denied relief, even if it is correct to say that a parent has no rights. In truth, however, I do not think it accurate to say that a parent has no rights. The rights may vary in their nature. Some may be only rights of imperfect obligation, but it is too sweeping a statement to say that a parent has no rights, as the judgments just delivered show.

I would emphasise the role of the court as Parker LJ has done. We have to decide the case according to law. The relevant authorities have been referred to, and in my judgment they lead to the orders which we propose to make. I do not seek to express my own views on the wider questions which the subject of birth control provokes. I would also emphasise that I do not intend to lay down a rule that in every case, no matter what the question is, no matter who the child is, the parent must be consulted before any important decision can ever be arrived at in relation to the child. A person who may be involved in such a situation will have three courses open to him. He may do nothing, he may consult the parent, he may make the decision himself and act independently if constrained to do so. Each case must depend on its own facts, and consequently I cannot say that there will never be a case where it is permissible to act in spite of the parent's wishes. Such cases, however, will be extremely rare and almost impossible to conceive when the parents are thoroughly responsible people.

I would add a word on confidentiality. A doctor's position is not an easy one. The courts recognise this. At the same time in law there is no such right which can justify silence at all times by a doctor, particularly when the welfare of a child is involved. A child may be contemplating doing something, for example something criminal or dangerous, which any sensible person would feel obliged to bring to the parent's attention for the child's protection. There is no law of confidentiality which would command silence when the welfare of the child is concerned. Because of this, I do not think that anything that I have said in relation to contraception should be influenced by arguments which we have heard as to the difficulty which the duty of confidentiality imposes on a doctor. The alleged duty must be subject to exceptions, and, if a doctor feels that he cannot recognise this in relation to contraceptive matters, he can avoid his dilemma by not accepting a child as a patient in the first place.

I have deliberately avoided a discussion of the criminal law. It is enough to say that in my opinion a doctor who prescribes a contraceptive device for a child under the age of 16 years will not necessarily be breaking the law. I think that it would be solving the problem by a sidewind if the appellant's case were to succeed only on the basis that such treatment would be a breach of the criminal law. We are concerned with the welfare of children from all aspects.

*Appeal allowed. Declarations made. Leave to appeal to the House of Lords granted on terms that orders for costs in the Court of Appeal and below be not disturbed and that costs are not asked for in the House of Lords.*

Solicitors: *Ollard & Bentley,* March (for the appellant); *Treasury Solicitor.*

Celia Fox    Barrister.

# Kavanagh v Lyroudias

COURT OF APPEAL, CIVIL DIVISION
SIR JOHN ARNOLD P AND HOLLINGS J
19, 27 MAY 1983

*Rent restriction – Possession – Protected tenancy – Occupation of dwelling house as residence – Occupation of two dwelling houses – Tenant using one house for sleeping in – Tenant using adjoining house for normal living purposes and meals – Whether tenant occupying adjoining house as residence – Whether tenant's user of adjoining house extending to all activities essential to exhibit characteristics of complete home – Rent Act 1977, s 2(1)(a).*

The defendant had been in occupation of a small dwelling house as tenant since 1955. He shared the house with a friend but the accommodation, which comprised a kitchen/dining room in the basement, a living room on the ground floor and a double bedroom and bathroom on the first floor, was inadequate for both of them. In 1973 the landlord granted the defendant the tenancy of the adjoining house, which was basically identical. Thereafter the defendant slept in that house but did not use its bathroom, there being no hot water. Occasionally he brought home work from his place of business to the house but he never cooked or ate his meals there. The other house provided the living room which was occupied by the defendant for normal living purposes, and he prepared and ate his meals in the kitchen/dining room of that house. In 1982 the plaintiff, the landlord's successor in title, terminated the defendant's tenancy of the adjoining house by a notice to quit and claimed possession of it. The defendant resisted the claim on the ground that he was the statutory tenant by virtue of s 2(1)(a)[a] of the Rent Act 1977 since he occupied the premises as his residence. The judge held that the defendant was in occupation of the adjoining house sufficiently to afford him the protection of the 1977 Act. The plaintiff appealed.

**Held** – The test to be applied in determining whether the premises of which it was sought to retain possession were part of a larger home was whether the use of the premises concerned extended to all those activities which were essential to enable them to exhibit the characteristics of a complete home. Since the defendant did not occupy the premises in question as a complete home in itself, he was not entitled to the protection of the 1977 Act in respect of them. The appeal would therefore be allowed (see p 562 *d* to *g* and *j* to p 563 *b* and *h*, post).

**Notes**

For the meaning of statutory tenancy and the effect of tenant having another house, see 27 Halsbury's Laws (4th edn) paras 590, 594.

For the Rent Act 1977, s 2, see 47 Halsbury's Statutes (3rd edn) 396.

**Cases referred to in judgment**

*Beck v Scholz* [1953] 1 All ER 814, [1953] 1 QB 570, [1953] 2 WLR 651, CA.
*Carega Properties SA (formerly Joram Developments Ltd) v Sharratt* [1979] 2 All ER 1084, [1979] 1 WLR 928, HL.
*Herbert v Byrne* [1964] 1 All ER 882, [1964] 1 WLR 519, CA.
*Langford Property Co Ltd v Athanassoglou* [1948] 2 All ER 722, sub nom *Langford Property Co Ltd v Tureman* [1949] 1 KB 29, CA.

---

*a* Section 2(1), so far as material, provides: 'Subject to this Part of this Act—(*a*) after the termination of a protected tenancy of a dwelling-house the person who, immediately before that termination, was the protected tenant of the dwelling-house shall, if and so long as he occupies the dwelling-house as his residence, be the statutory tenant of it . . .'

*Metropolitan Properties Co (FCG) Ltd v Barder* [1968] 1 All ER 536, [1968] 1 WLR 286, CA.
*Wigley v Leigh* [1950] 1 All ER 73, [1950] 2 KB 305, CA.
*Wimbush v Cibulia, Wimbush v Levinski* [1949] 2 All ER 432, [1949] 2 KB 564, CA.

**Appeal**
The plaintiff, Amanda Kavanagh, appealed against the decision of his Honour Judge Paiba in the West London County Court on 3 February 1983 refusing her claim for possession of premises known as 23 Rutland Street, London SW7, of which she was the landlord and the defendant, George Lyroudias, was the tenant, on the ground that the defendant was entitled to the protection afforded by s 2(1)(a) of the Rent Act 1977. The facts are set out in the judgment of the court.

*Robert Reid QC* for the plaintiff.
*Nicholas Davidson* for the defendant.

*Cur adv vult*

27 May. The following judgment of the court was delivered.

**SIR JOHN ARNOLD P.** This is an appeal from the order of his Honour Judge Paiba which he made on 3 February 1983 at the West London County Court. The claim which the judge had to consider was a claim for possession of the dwelling house, 23 Rutland Street, London SW7, and the judge dismissed the claim. The claim was based on the determination of a contractual tenancy by notice expiring on 15 October 1982. It was specifically pleaded that the defendant could not claim the protection of the Rent Acts as he was not in occupation of the property and there was an alternative pleading that reasonable alternative accommodation was available to the defendant.

The defendant had been in occupation of 21 Rutland Street, next door to the subject premises, since about 1955, and until 1973 that was the only relevant property which he had. He shared that property for the most part with Mr Coles, his friend, although Mr Coles was from time to time away living in the country. Mr Coles retired from his work in about 1973 and took up full-time residence in no 21. He was at the time sufficiently ill to impose on the defendant some responsibility for looking after his friend. The defendant was also, as he was getting older, anxious to have a bedroom of his own, which had not been possible in the restricted accommodation which the two men shared at no 21. So it was that when in 1973 the landlord of no 21 offered to the defendant the tenancy of no 23, which he also owned, the defendant was glad to accept the offer. Accordingly, the tenancy of no 23 was granted by the landlord to the defendant. It was that tenancy which was terminated contractually by the notice to quit. The plaintiff is in respect of no 23 the successor in title of the landlord who granted the tenancies and her claim for possession in these proceedings is resisted in reliance on the provisions of the Rent Act 1977. A different successor in title is now the reversionary owner of no 21.

The accommodation at 21 and 23 Rutland Street is basically identical. Each of them comprises a basement, ground floor and first floor. This accommodation, in no 21, is arranged as a kitchen/dining room in the basement, a living room on the ground floor and a double bedroom and bathroom on the first floor. At no 23 there is a storeroom with a gas cooker in a working condition in the basement, a study with a telephone extension from no 21 on the ground floor and bedroom and bathroom on the first floor, the bathroom having no hot water facility. The two houses are wholly separate. Each has a garden; they are together used as a single garden, the gate of no 23 having been blocked up. The judge found that it would not be a difficult matter to replace the gate if it became necessary.

During the material period the defendant has been sleeping for the most part in the bedroom in no 23. He has been keeping his clothes for the most part in no 21 but has some clothes in no 23; he has been using the bathroom at no 21 to bath, there being no hot water in no 23. Number 21 provides the living room which is occupied by the defendant for normal living purposes and the kitchen/dining room where are prepared and eaten all his meals. He uses the study at no 23 on occasions when he brings home work from his place of business, which is the Greek Embassy. He has never used no 23 for cooking or eating. On one occasion his sister, who was staying for a short while in no 23, baked some cakes there and it appears that on two other occasions she or another member of the defendant's family stayed at no 23. Those are the salient features of the relevant users of the two houses.

The first question which has to be decided is whether the defendant is the statutory tenant of no 23, his contractual tenancy having been effectively terminated as the judge held and as is not disputed on this appeal. Whether he is a statutory tenant depends on the provisions of s 2(1)(a) of the Rent Act 1977, which provides that a protected tenant, as was the defendant immediately before the termination of the tenancy, should be the statutory tenant if and so long as he occupies the dwelling houses as his residence. This matter has been considered in earlier authorities.

The particular provision now contained in s 2(1)(a) of the 1977 Act was first enacted in s 3 of the Rent Act 1968. This circumstance is not however important in relation to the continuing authority of the earlier cases as by reason of s 3(2) of the 1968 Act, continued by s 2(3) of the 1977 Act, the same qualifications for entitlement to retain possession have to be fulfilled by the tenant as was the case before the new statutory provision came into effect for the first time in 1968.

It is plain from the earlier cases that the right to retain possession is dependent on the tenant establishing that the premises are used by him as a home. Much consideration has been given to the effect on this requirement of there being more than one home and it has been held that when it is established that the property in question is used as a home the circumstance that the tenant has another home is not necessarily fatal to his claim to retain possession. Such a case was *Langford Property Co Ltd v Athanassoglou* [1948] 2 All ER 722, [1949] 1 KB 29, where a flat in London was held to qualify as a home of which the tenant was entitled to retain possession notwithstanding that he had another home in Buckinghamshire (as to this case, see *Beck v Scholz* [1953] 1 All ER 814, [1953] 1 QB 570). In *Wigley v Leigh* [1950] 1 All ER 73, [1950] 2 KB 305 and *Herbert v Byrne* [1964] 1 All ER 882, [1964] 1 WLR 519 a dwelling house was held to be one that was entitled to be retained although not currently used as a home because of an intention so to use it. These cases are in our view distinct in conception from those in which the issue is whether the premises of which it is sought to retain possession are a part of a larger home, that is a home including premises other than those concerned, or are in themselves a complete home. In such cases the test which is to be applied is whether the use of the premises concerned extends to all those activities which are essential to enable them to exhibit the characteristics of a complete home. In *Wimbush v Cibulia, Wimbush v Levinski* [1949] 2 All ER 432, [1949] 2 KB 564 the cases were concerned with premises in which all normal daytime activities were carried on while sleeping took place in adjoining premises. In those cases it was held, on the basis that the two sets of premises were comprised in separate tenancies, that the premises concerned did not constitute by themselves a home of which the tenant was entitled to retain possession. In the present case the judge held that there were two separate tenancies of nos 21 and 23 respectively. In *Metropolitan Properties Co (FCG) Ltd v Barder* [1968] 1 All ER 536, [1968] 1 WLR 286 the premises in question were used for sleeping only, while the whole of the daytime activities took place in the adjoining premises. Again the right of retention was rejected.

In the present case the judge noted the plaintiff's argument as including the proposition that the tenant had not been occupying no 23 as a residence and said: 'The expression used is "not being used as a home". The plaintiff's counsel called it "persistent partial user".' In the event the judge having considered the circumstances of the occupation concluded 'that the defendant is in occupation of no 23 sufficiently to afford him protection of the Rent Act'. In arriving at this conclusion the judge did not, as it seems to us, give any consideration to the question whether no 23 was occupied separately from the adjoining premises as a complete home in itself and in the light of the cases to which we have referred this in our view is the question which he should have asked himself. If he had done so, we find it impossible to avoid the conclusion that in the light of those cases he would have come to the conclusion that no 23 was not a complete home. In our judgment this appeal should be allowed and the right of retention of possession of no 23 denied to the defendant for lack of the character of a statutory tenant.

If this be the right view, the question whether suitable alternative accommodation was available for the defendant pursuant to s 98(1)(a) of the Rent Act 1977 does not strictly arise. The matter was considered by the judge and he was invited to deal with the matter irrespective of his decision on the point discussed above. It seems to us to be right that we should do so. The alternative accommodation said to be suitable was no 21. The judge rejected it as suitable alternative accommodation on the ground that, although ten years earlier the defendant and Mr Coles had been content to occupy no 21 together, the situation had changed and it was perfectly proper for the defendant now to wish to live in the larger premises comprehending nos 21 and 23. What has to be considered under s 98 is whether suitable alternative accommodation is available for the tenant. By the provisions of paras 4 and 5 of Pt IV of Sch 15 to the Act the matter which requires to be considered in relation to whether this condition is fulfilled is whether the accommodation is reasonably suitable to the needs of the tenant and his family. It cannot, as it seems to us, be doubted that no 21 alone is reasonably suitable to the needs of the defendant. The unsuitability found by the judge had relevance to the needs of the defendant and Mr Coles together. This is valid only, as it seems to us, if Mr Coles can be regarded as being of the family of the defendant. We can see no distinction between this question and that concerning the meaning of the word 'family' in the different provision of the Rent Act considered by the House of Lords in *Carega Properties SA (formerly Joram Developments Ltd) v Sharratt* [1979] 2 All ER 1084, [1979] 1 WLR 928. The House decided that 'family' was not a term of art but was used in its ordinary popular meaning and that in that meaning it requires at least a broadly recognisable de facto familial nexus. In the light thrown on the problem by the speeches in that case we find it impossible to say that Mr Coles could properly be regarded as a member of the family of the defendant. Accordingly, we would hold that the alternative accommodation at no 21 is relevantly suitable. However, the requirement of s 98 is not concerned only with the suitability of alternative accommodation said to be available: there is also the requirement that before making an order the court must consider it reasonable to do so where the order is one for possession of a dwelling house subject to a statutory tenancy. If it were right to regard no 23 as being subject to a statutory tenancy, we would agree with the judge that it would not be reasonable to make an order for possession. It would be in relation to this matter that we should think it necessary to give consideration to the position of the defendant and Mr Coles together and it would in our view be unreasonable to place the defendant in the position of having either to occupy cramped accommodation with Mr Coles or in effect to eject his old sick friend. But, as it is, we allow the appeal.

*Appeal allowed. Leave to appeal to House of Lords granted.*

Solicitors: *Blakeney's* (for the plaintiff); *Davenport Lyons & Co* (for the defendant).

Mary Rose Plummer    Barrister.

# Hampstead Way Investments Ltd v Lewis-Weare and another

HOUSE OF LORDS

LORD FRASER OF TULLYBELTON, LORD ELWYN-JONES, LORD KEITH OF KINKEL, LORD BRANDON OF OAKBROOK AND LORD TEMPLEMAN

26, 27 NOVEMBER 1984, 24 JANUARY 1985

*Rent restriction – Possession – Protected tenancy – Occupation of dwelling house as residence – Occupation of two dwelling houses – Tenant occupying one room of flat for sleeping five days a week – Tenant occupying dwelling house elsewhere at all other times – Remainder of flat occupied by member of tenant's family – Whether tenant occupying flat as residence – Rent Act 1968, s 3(2) – Rent Act 1977, s 2(1)(a).*

In May 1970 the tenant was granted a three-year lease of a flat which comprised two living rooms, two bedrooms and a small box-room. Living with him in the flat from July 1970 were his wife, stepson, stepdaughter and, after her birth in November 1971, daughter. In 1978 the tenant and his wife bought a three-bedroom house half a mile from the flat and, except for the stepdaughter (who went abroad), the family moved there and occupied it as their home. The tenant was employed by a night-club and worked five nights a week. In order not to disturb his wife when he returned from work early in the morning, the tenant retained a room in the flat to which he returned after work to sleep five days a week until the afternoon, after which he went to the house and had a light meal prepared by his wife. On Sundays and Mondays when he was off work he was at the house. The remainder of the flat was occupied for all usual living activities by the stepson. The tenant kept his working clothes at the flat and had his mail addressed there. He had no meals there nor did he entertain his friends there; all entertaining was done at the house. The tenant paid all the outgoings of the flat except for the gas bill, which his stepson paid. The landlords sought possession of the flat on the ground that the tenant had ceased to occupy it as his residence after the move to the house and, by virtue of s 2(1)(a)[a] of the Rent Act 1977 as construed with s 3(2)[b] of the Rent Act 1968, was no longer a protected tenant. The county court judge dismissed the landlords' claim for possession on the ground that the house and flat constituted one unit of living accommodation. The landlords appealed to the Court of Appeal, which allowed their appeal and granted them an order for possession against the tenant and his stepson on the ground that the judge had not considered whether the tenant occupied the flat separately from the house as a complete home in itself and that on the evidence the tenant was using the accommodation in the stepson's home as casual accommodation separately from the family home. The tenant and the stepson appealed to the House of Lords.

**Held** – Where a person owned one house which he occupied as his home for most of the time and at the same time was the tenant of another which he occupied for limited purposes, the question whether he occupied the second dwelling house as a second home was a question of fact and degree. In determining that question the court should consider not only whether the second home was occupied separately as a complete home in itself but also whether the tenant occupied both homes as a combined unit. Since the house and flat were half a mile from each other they could not possibly be regarded as constituting together a single unit of living accommodation, and since the tenant made very limited use of the flat his occupation of it was insufficient to make the flat his second home. It followed that he was not occupying it as his residence within s 3(2) of the 1968 Act, and the tenancy was therefore not a protected tenancy for the purposes of the 1977

---

*a*    Section 2(1), so far as material, is set out at p 567 *b*, post

*b*    Section 3(2), so far as material, is set out at p 567 *d*, post

Act. Accordingly, the possession order had been rightly made and the appeal would be dismissed (see p 565 *h j*, p 568 *g* to *j*, and p 569 *j* to p 570 *a* and *d* to *h*, post).

*Kavanagh v Lyroudias* [1985] 1 All ER 560 considered.

### Notes

For statutory tenancies and the effect of the tenant's absence and of having another house, see 27 Halsbury's Laws (4th edn) paras 590, 592, 594.

For the Rent Act 1968, s 3, see 18 Halsbury's Statutes (3rd edn) 788.

For the Rent Act 1977, s 2, see 47 ibid 396.

As from 29 August 1977 the 1968 Act was repealed by s 155(5) of and Sch 25 to the 1977 Act, and the provisions formerly contained in s 3 of the 1968 Act were replaced by s 2 of the 1977 Act. Note, however, that, by s 2(3) of the 1977 Act, the expression 'if and so long as he occupies the dwelling-house as his residence' in s 2(1)(*a*) of and Pt I of Sch 1 to the 1977 Act is to be construed in accordance with s 3(2) of the 1968 Act.

### Cases referred to in opinions

*Beck v Scholz* [1953] 1 All ER 814, [1953] 1 QB 570, [1953] 2 WLR 651, CA.
*Kavanagh v Lyroudias* [1985] 1 All ER 560, CA.
*Langford Property Co Ltd v Athanassoglou* [1948] 2 All ER 722, sub nom *Langford Property Co Ltd v Tureman* [1949] 1 KB 29, CA.
*Regalian Securities Ltd v Scheuer* (1982) 263 EG 973, CA.
*Roland House Gardens Ltd v Cravitz* (1975) 29 P & CR 432.
*Skinner v Geary* [1931] 2 KB 546, [1931] All ER Rep 302, CA.
*Wimbush v Cibulia, Wimbush v Levinski* [1949] 2 All ER 432, [1949] 2 KB 564, CA.

### Appeal

Courtney Lewis-Weare (the tenant) and Nishith Pandya (his stepson) appealed with leave of the Appeal Committee of the House of Lords granted on 24 May 1984 against the decision of the Court of Appeal (Eveleigh and May LJJ) on 24 February 1984 allowing an appeal by the respondents, Hampstead Way Investments Ltd (the landlords), against the decision of his Honour Judge Hill-Smith in the Willesden County Court on 4 July 1983 dismissing the respondents' claim against the appellants for possession of a flat, 5 Meadway Court, Meadway, London NW11 on the ground that the first appellant was a statutory tenant. The Court of Appeal made an order for possession against the appellants. The facts are set out in the opinion of Lord Brandon.

*Paul de la Piquerie* for the appellants.
*Ronald Bernstein QC* and *Nicholas Dowding* for the respondents.

Their Lordships took time for consideration.

24 January. The following opinions were delivered.

**LORD FRASER OF TULLYBELTON.** My Lords, I have had the advantage of reading in draft the speech of my noble and learned friend Lord Brandon. I agree with it, and for the reasons stated in it I would dismiss this appeal.

**LORD ELWYN-JONES.** My Lords, I have had the benefit of reading, in advance, the speech to be delivered by my noble and learned friend Lord Brandon. I agree with it, and for the reasons he gives I would dismiss the appeal.

**LORD KEITH OF KINKEL.** My Lords, I have had the benefit of reading in advance the speech to be delivered by my noble and learned friend Lord Brandon. I agree with it, and for the reasons he gives would dismiss the appeal.

**LORD BRANDON OF OAKBROOK.** My Lords, in this appeal Courtney Lewis-Weare (the tenant) and Nishith Pandya (the stepson) are the appellants and Hampstead Way Investments Ltd (the landlords) are the respondents.

On or shortly before 13 January 1982 the landlords began an action against the tenant and the stepson in the Willesden County Court, in which they claimed possession of a flat, 5 Meadway Court, Meadway, London NW11 (the flat). On 4 July 1983 his Honour Judge Hill-Smith dismissed the claim for possession on the ground that the tenant was protected by the Rent Act 1977. The landlords appealed against that decision and on 24 February 1984 the Court of Appeal (Eveleigh and May LJJ) allowed the appeal and made an order for possession in favour of the landlords. The Court of Appeal refused the tenant and the stepson leave to appeal to your Lordships' House, but leave for them to do so was later given by the Appeal Committee.

The material facts, as found by Judge Hill-Smith or appearing from uncontradicted evidence, are these. The flat had two living rooms, two bedrooms and a small box-room. At some previous date the tenant had been granted by the landlords or their predecessors in title a lease of the flat for three years from 1 May 1970 to 1 May 1973. In July 1970 the tenant married and his wife came to live with him at the flat. She already had two children by a previous marriage, a girl called Cheha and the stepson. In November 1971 the tenant's wife had a further child by the tenant, a girl called Naomi.

At all material times the tenant was employed as director and general manager of a night-club in the West End of London. In this employment he was required to work during the night five times a week from Tuesday to Saturday. He finished that work at 4 am.

From the time of the marriage until 1978 the tenant, his wife and first the two older children and later Naomi occupied the flat as their home. In that year the tenant and his wife bought jointly, with the assistance of a mortgage, a house, 113 Erskine Hill, NW11 (the house). The house had two living rooms and three bedrooms, one of which was very small and inconvenient. It was situated about half a mile from the flat. A certain amount of furniture was removed from the flat to the house, but the rest remained there, and the family then moved to the house and occupied it as their home. By then Cheha had left and gone to America, so that the persons to be housed were the tenant, his wife, the stepson and Naomi.

After the move the wife and Naomi lived entirely at the house. The tenant on the other hand retained a room in the flat for limited use by him. His routine following the nights on which he worked was to sleep in the one room retained by him in the flat from about 5 am when he got back to it from his work, until well into the afternoon. He then went to the house and had a light meal there prepared for him by his wife. After that, except on Sundays and Mondays, he went to the night-club and later ate his principal meal of the 24 hours there. The purpose of his sleeping at the flat, rather than at the house, was to avoid disturbing his wife and Naomi when he returned from work at about 5 am. The tenant kept his clothes in his room at the flat and had his mail addressed to him there. He never had any meals at the flat, nor did he entertain any of his friends there.

On Sunday and Monday, when the tenant was off work, he spent his time at the house, sleeping and eating there. In so far as he received and entertained friends, he did so at the house.

While the tenant retained the limited use of one room at the flat as described above, the stepson, who was a self-employed computer programmer and engineer, occupied the rest of the flat for all usual living activities.

The tenant paid all outgoings relating to the house. He also paid the outgoings relating to the flat, including the rent, but excluding the cost of gas, which was paid by the stepson. The telephones at both the house and the flat were rented by the tenant, the telephone accounts were paid by him, and both numbers were shown in the telephone directory as his.

It is not in dispute that the right of the tenant to remain in possession of the flat depends on the application to the particular circumstances of the case of the provisions contained in ss 1 and 2 of the Rent Act 1977. Those sections read:

'**1.** Subject to this Part of this Act, a tenancy under which a dwelling-house (which may be a house or part of a house) is let as a separate dwelling is a protected tenancy for the purposes of this Act. Any reference in this Act to a protected tenant shall be construed accordingly.

**2.**—(1) Subject to this Part of this Act—(a) after the termination of a protected tenancy of a dwelling-house the person who, immediately before that termination, was the protected tenant of the dwelling-house shall, if and so long as he occupies the dwelling-house as his residence, be the statutory tenant of it . . .

(3) In subsection (1)(a) above . . . the phrase "if and so long as he occupies the dwelling-house as his residence" shall be construed as it was immediately before the commencement of this Act (that is to say, in accordance with section 3(2) of the Rent Act 1968) . . .'

Section 3(2) of the Rent Act 1968, to which reference is there made, provides:

'In paragraph (a) of subsection (1) above . . . the phrase "if and so long as he occupies the dwelling-house as his residence" shall be construed as requiring the fulfilment of the same, and only the same, qualifications (whether as to residence or otherwise) as had to be fulfilled before the commencement of this Act to entitle a tenant, within the meaning of the Increase of Rent and Mortgage Interest (Restrictions) Act 1920, to retain possession, by virtue of that Act and not by virtue of a tenancy, of a dwelling-house to which that Act applied.'

It is common ground in the present case that the flat, when it was first let to the tenant, was let as a separate dwelling house within the meaning of s 1 of the Rent Act 1977. The result of that is that, when the lease for three years expired on 1 May 1973, the tenant became, and remained, so long as he occupied the flat as his residence, the statutory tenant of it within the meaning of s 2(1)(a) of the 1977 Act. The question in dispute between the parties is whether, after the move from the flat to the house in 1978, the tenant continued to occupy the flat as his residence. The tenant contends that he did; the landlords contend that he did not.

My Lords, the result of s 2(1)(a) of the Rent Act 1977, together with s 3(2) of the Rent Act 1968, is that the question whether the tenant continued to occupy the flat as his residence after the move has to be decided by reference to the case law on the subject which grew up during the period after the coming into force of the Increase of Rent and Mortgage Interest (Restrictions) Act 1920 and before the coming into force of the Rent Act 1968. It follows that, in order to decide the question in dispute, it is necessary to consider some of the relevant authorities forming part of that case law.

My Lords, the case which the tenant sought to make at the trial in the county court was that he occupied two dwelling houses as his residences: one was the house and the other was the flat. As will appear when I come to examine the authorities, there is no principle of law to prevent a person occupying two dwelling houses as his residences at the same time, and being a statutory tenant of either or both. Judge Hill-Smith, however, did not accept the tenant's contention in this respect. Instead he reached a different conclusion, which might aptly be called a halfway-house conclusion, which it does not appear that he was invited to do. He expressed his findings and conclusion as follows:

'The view I take on the evidence is that the flat at Meadway Court is ancillary to and part of the home itself. No doubt if Erskine Hill had four or five bedrooms no question would arise. It is clear that the size of Meadway Court was such as to make the acquisition of additional accommodation very desirable for the first defendant. I come to the conclusion that, viewing the evidence as a whole, at the time of acquisition there was no intention by the first defendant to abandon 5 Meadway Court or to give up occupation, and indeed nor, it would seem, in view of the age of the second defendant, would it have been possible for him to occupy Erskine Hill. I am satisfied that he was a member of the first defendant's family.'

On the basis of these findings and conclusion, Judge Hill-Smith held, in effect, that the tenant still occupied the flat as his residence, and was therefore a statutory tenant protected by the Rent Act 1977.

The first judgment in the Court of Appeal was delivered by May LJ. He expressed sympathy with the tenant's case, but he considered himself bound by a 1983 decision of the Court of Appeal, *Kavanagh v Lyroudias* [1985] 1 All ER 560, which he regarded in any case as having been correctly decided, to allow the appeal and give judgment for the landlords. Eveleigh LJ, following, put his decision in favour of the landlords on two grounds. First, he said that, on a true view of the facts, it appeared to him that the tenant was using accommodation in the stepson's home as casual accommodation quite separate from the family home which he shared with his wife and daughter at the house. Second, he said that, like May LJ, he considered himself bound by *Kavanagh v Lyroudias* to decide the case against the tenant.

My Lords, in order to determine this appeal, it is necessary to examine the more important cases decided between 1920 and 1968 on what is meant by the occupation of a dwelling house by a person as his residence, or, as it is put in many of the cases (without, in my view, any difference of meaning) the occupation of a dwelling house by a person as his home. It will further be necessary to consider the nature and scope of the Court of Appeal's decision in *Kavanagh v Lyroudias*, and whether it was rightly regarded by the Court of Appeal as applying to, and governing their decision in, the present case.

Until the coming into force of the Rent Act 1968 the principle that a person could only be a protected tenant of a dwelling house so long as he occupied it as his home was one which was not expressly laid down in any of the earlier Rent Acts. It was, rather, one which had been developed by judges as a matter of case law. The leading case on the existence of such a requirement is *Skinner v Geary* [1931] 2 KB 546, [1931] All ER Rep 302.

That requirement having been laid down in *Skinner v Geary*, there followed a series of decisions on what was meant by occupation of a dwelling house by a person as his home. Those decisions all depended on the particular facts of each case, and, as might be expected, are not always easy to reconcile. That being so, I do not consider that it would serve any useful purpose to examine each of such decisions in detail. In view of the terms of s 3(2) of the Rent Act 1968, it seems to me that the only useful course to take is to see to what extent it is possible to derive, from the decisions concerned, any propositions of general application with regard to the qualifications which have to be fulfilled, as to residence or otherwise, in order to create a situation in which a person is occupying a dwelling house as his home.

Approaching the matter on that basis, it seems to me that the following propositions of general application, relevant to the present case, can be derived from the decisions concerned. (1) A person may have two dwelling houses, each of which he occupies as his home, so that, if either of them is let to him, his tenancy of it is protected by the Rent Act 1977 (see *Langford Property Co Ltd v Athanassoglou* [1948] 2 All ER 722, [1949] 1 KB 29). (2) Where a person is a tenant of two different parts of the same house under different lettings by the same landlord, and carries on some of his living activities in one part of the house and the rest of them in the other part, neither tenancy will normally be protected. If, however, the true view of the facts is that there is, in substance, a single combined or composite letting of the two parts of the house as a whole, then the tenancies of both parts together will, or anyhow may, be protected (see *Wimbush v Cibulia, Wimbush v Levinski* [1949] 2 All ER 432, [1949] 2 KB 564). (3) Where a person owns one dwelling house which he occupies as his home for most of his time and is at the same time the tenant of another dwelling house which he only occupies rarely or for limited purposes it is a question of fact and degree whether he occupies the latter dwelling house as his second home (see *Langford Property Co Ltd v Athanassoglou* [1948] 2 All ER 722, [1949] 1

KB 29, *Beck v Scholz* [1953] 1 All ER 814, [1953] 1 QB 570). That principle has been followed and applied in cases since 1968: see *Roland House Gardens Ltd v Cravitz* (1975) 29 P & CR 432 and *Regalian Securities Ltd v Scheuer* (1982) 263 EG 973.

I turn now to examine *Kavanagh v Lyroudias* [1985] 1 All ER 560, on the authority of which both members of the Court of Appeal in the present case considered themselves bound to give judgment for the landlords. The facts of that case, which were somewhat unusual, were these. The landlord of a dwelling house, 23 Rutland Street, London SW7, brought an action for possession of it in the West London County Court. His main case was that the tenant of it could not claim the protection of the Rent Acts because he no longer occupied the dwelling house as his home. The tenant had occupied the next-door house, no 21, from about 1955, and until 1971 that was the only relevant property which he had. He shared it for the most part with a friend, C, although the latter was from time to time away living in the country. C retired from work in about 1973 and took up full-time residence at no 21. C was at that time sufficiently ill to impose on the tenant some responsibility for looking after him. The tenant himself was also anxious to have a bedroom of his own, which he did not have in no 21. In 1973 the landlord of no 21 offered the tenant a lease of no 23, which he also owned, and the tenant accepted the offer gladly. Subsequently, the reversions of nos 21 and 23 passed into the hands of different landlords.

The accommodation in nos 21 and 23 was basically the same. Each house had a basement, a ground floor and a first floor. At no 21 the basement was used as a combined kitchen and dining room, the ground floor was used as a living room, and the first floor had a double bedroom and a bathroom. At no 23 the basement contained a gas cooker in working condition, the ground floor was used as a study with a telephone extension from no 21, and the first floor had a bedroom and a bathroom, the latter without any hot water supply. Each house was physically entirely separate. Each house had a garden, but the two gardens were used as one single garden. In this connection the garden gate of no 23 had been blocked up, but the blocking up was readily removable if it should be desired to remove it.

During the material period before the action for possession was brought, the tenant had been sleeping for the most part in no 23. He had been keeping his clothes for the most part in no 21, but had some clothes also in no 23. He had been using the bathroom at no 21 to bathe, because of the absence of hot water in the bathroom at no 23. The tenant had been using the living room at no 21 and also the combined kitchen and dining room there, where all his meals were prepared and eaten. He had been using the study at no 23 on occasions when he brought work home from his business at the Greek Embassy. He had never used no 23 for cooking or eating. On one occasion his sister, who was staying for a short time in no 23, baked some cakes there, and on two other occasions she or another member of the tenant's family had stayed at no 23.

On these facts the county court judge concluded that the tenant was in occupation of no 23 sufficiently to afford him the protection of the Rent Acts. On an appeal by the landlords the Court of Appeal (Sir John Arnold P and Hollings J) took the view that the county court judge had not given any consideration to the question whether no 23 was occupied separately from no 21 as a complete home in itself, and that, if he had done so, he would have found it impossible to answer the question otherwise than in the negative. In these circumstances the Court of Appeal held that the tenant's tenancy of no 23 was not protected, and that the landlords were accordingly entitled to possession of that house.

Your Lordships were invited by counsel for the appellants in the present case to hold that *Kavanagh v Lyroudias* had been wrongly decided. In my opinion it is not necessary for your Lordships to decide that question, because the facts in *Kavanagh v Lyroudias* differ materially from those in the present case. Although the Court of Appeal in *Kavanagh v Lyroudias* considered that the proper question to be asked and answered was whether no 23 was occupied separately from no 21 as a complete home in itself, it seems to me that, on the authorities referred to earlier, there was a further question which needed to be asked and answered. That further question was whether the defendant tenant occupied nos 21 and 23 as a combined or composite home of the kind contemplated in *Wimbush v Cibulia* [1949] 2 All ER 432, [1949] 2 QB 564, bearing in mind that the leases of both houses had originally been granted to the tenant by a person who was the owner of both, and that it was only subsequently that the reversions of the two houses had passed into different hands. If I am right about this, the Court of Appeal in *Kavanagh v Lyroudias* reached their decision by asking and answering only one of the two relevant questions. It does not, however, follow that the decision itself was wrong, for the further question which I consider should have been asked and answered would obviously have been an extremely difficult one, on which it would be wrong to express an opinion without having first heard full argument on it. In fact the point was hardly raised before your Lordships at all.

It is, in my view, essential to bear in mind that all these Rent Act cases turn on their particular facts, and it is seldom helpful to decide one case with one set of facts by reference to another case with a different set of facts. On the view which I have expressed with regard to *Kavanagh v Lyroudias*, there is no real parallel between the facts of that case and those of the present case. Numbers 21 and 23 in the former case were next door to each other, and were treated by the tenant, for all practical purposes, as one unit of living accommodation, in one half of which he carried out some of his living activities, and in the other half of which he carried out the rest of those activities. By contrast, in the present case, since the house and the flat were half a mile away from each other, they could not possibly be regarded as constituting together a single unit of living accommodation.

That the house and flat together constituted together one unit of living accommodation was nevertheless the conclusion reached by Judge Hill-Smith in the present case. For the reason which I have just given, however, I do not consider that that conclusion can be supported. In my opinion, on the facts of the present case, there is one, and only one, question to be asked and answered in relation to it. That question is whether the tenant occupied the flat as a second home.

My Lords, I set out earlier in detail the very limited use made of the flat by the tenant, and it is unnecessary to rehearse these matters again. If one treats the question as one of fact and degree, as the authorities require that a court should do, it is, in my opinion, impossible to conclude that that limited use of the flat made by the tenant was sufficient to make the flat his second home. The flat was in truth the home, not of the tenant, who slept there on five nights a week and kept his clothes there, but that of the adult stepson, who carried out all an ordinary person's living activities there. On that ground, I would hold that the tenant was not occupying the flat as his residence within the meaning of s 3(2) of the Rent Act 1968, as incorporated into s 2(3) of the Rent Act 1977, and that his tenancy of the flat was not, therefore, protected by the latter Act.

It follows that I would affirm the judgment of the Court of Appeal, though not on the ground that the case is governed by *Kavanagh v Lyroudias*, and dismiss the appeal.

**LORD TEMPLEMAN.** My Lords, for the reasons given by my noble and learned friend Lord Brandon, I too would dismiss the appeal.

*Appeal dismissed.*

Solicitors: *Sears Tooth & Co* (for the appellants); *Grangewoods* (for the respondents).

Mary Rose Plummer    Barrister.

# R v Beck

COURT OF APPEAL, CRIMINAL DIVISION
WATKINS LJ, KENNETH JONES J AND SIR JOHN THOMPSON
21 JUNE, 15 AUGUST 1984

*Criminal law – Procuring execution of valuable security by deception – Execution – Acceptance of security – Series of acceptances – Final acceptance within jurisdiction – Earlier acceptances abroad – Forged traveller's cheques issued by English bank cashed abroad – Final payment on cheques occurring in England – Stolen credit card issued in England used abroad – Issuing company paying bills in respect of use of card in England – Whether 'execution' of securities occurring within jurisdiction – Theft Act 1968, s 20(2).*

*Criminal law – Procuring execution of valuable security by deception – Procuring – Stolen traveller's cheques and credit card – Cheques and card used to obtain money and goods from agents and traders – Agents and traders presenting cheques and bills to issuing bank and credit card company for payment – Bank and company paying cheques and bills – Bank and company paying for legal or commercial reasons though aware cheques and card stolen – Whether execution of valuable security 'procured' by defendant – Theft Act 1968, s 20(2).*

Stolen traveller's cheques issued by an English bank came into the possession of the appellant, who forged them and cashed them in France with agents of the bank. When the agents, who had acted in good faith in cashing the cheques, presented them to the bank in England for payment, the bank, though aware that the cheques had been stolen and though not legally obliged to honour them, nevertheless paid on the cheques because commercial considerations compelled them to do so. A stolen credit card issued by a company in England also came into the appellant's possession. He used the card in France to purchase goods from traders. When the traders, who had acted in good faith in accepting the card as payment for the goods, presented the bills so incurred to the credit card company in England for payment, the company, though aware that the card had been stolen, considered that it was contractually obliged to pay the bills. The appellant was charged with three counts of dishonestly procuring the execution of a valuable security by deception, contrary to s 20(2)[a] of the Theft Act 1968, which provided that 'acceptance' of a valuable security was to be treated as if it were 'execution' of the security. The trial judge ruled that the court had jurisdiction because the final acceptance of a traveller's cheque occurred when it was paid by the issuing bank and the final acceptance of the credit card bills was when the credit card company paid them and that execution of the traveller's cheques and the credit card bills had been 'procured' if what had been done was a cause which had had some effect on the actions of the bank and the credit card company in paying on the cheques and bills. The appellant was convicted. He appealed, contending that since his actions had been carried out in France he had committed no offence within the jurisdiction of the English courts and that there was no evidence to establish that he had procured, ie 'produced by endeavour', the bank and the credit card company to pay money to anyone else in respect of the traveller's cheques or the credit card.

**Held** – The appeal would be dismissed for the following reasons—

(1) Since 'execution' within s 20(2) of the 1968 Act was, by the terms of that subsection, extended to include 'acceptance', it followed that when a valuable security was accepted as genuine by a payer who paid the monetary value of it to the holder the payer thereby 'executed' the security within s 20(2). Furthermore, there could be more than one acceptance of a valuable security for the purpose of s 20(2), and accordingly, where the

final acceptance of a valuable security occurred in England, even though there had bee:
an earlier acceptance abroad, that final acceptance constituted execution of the securit
within the jurisdiction for the purpose of s 20(2). Since, therefore, final payment on th
traveller's cheques and the credit card bills had been made in England, the English court
had jurisdiction to deal with the offences (see p 574 h to p 575 d and p 576 h, post).

(2) The word 'procure' in s 20(2) bore the common meaning of 'causing' or 'bringing
about'. Accordingly, since the appellant's dishonesty in France had caused or brough
about a situation in England where the bank and the credit card company had had n
alternative, for legal and/or commercial reasons, but to pay on their valuable securities
ie the traveller's cheques and the credit card bills, the appellant had 'procured' the
execution of those securities (see p 576 a b and f to h, post); dicta of Lord Widgery CJ ii
A-G's Reference (No 1 of 1975) [1975] 2 All ER at 686 and of Cusack J in R v Broadfoo
[1976] 3 All ER at 755–756 applied.

**Notes**

For procuring the execution of a valuable security by deception, see 11 Halsbury's Law
(4th edn) para 1281.

For the Theft Act 1968, s 20, see 8 Halsbury's Statutes (3rd edn) 795.

**Cases referred to in judgment**

A-G's Reference (No 1 of 1975) [1975] 2 All ER 684, [1975] QB 773, [1975] 3 WLR 11, CA
R v Broadfoot [1976] 3 All ER 753, CA.

**Case also cited**

R v Thornton [1963] 1 All ER 170, [1964] 2 QB 176, CCA.

**Appeal**

On 7 October 1983 in the Crown Court at Manchester before his Honour Judge Hardy
and a jury the appellant, Brian Beck, was convicted of three counts of procuring the
execution of a valuable security by deception, contrary to s 20 of the Theft Act 1968. He
was sentenced to 18 months' imprisonment on each count to run concurrently. 428
similar offences were taken into consideration. He appealed against the convictions on a
point of law and the trial judge granted a certificate for an appeal on the point of law (see
out at letter j, below) stated therein. The facts are set out in the judgment of the court.

Benet Hytner QC and Mukhtar Hussain for the appellant.
John Alan Price QC and Michael Shorrock for the Crown.

Cur adv vuli

15 August. The following judgment of the court was delivered.

**WATKINS LJ.** On 7 October 1983 in the Crown Court at Manchester before his
Honour Judge Hardy the appellant was by jury convicted on three counts of procuring
the execution of a valuable security by deception contrary to s 20(2) of the Theft Act
1968. He was sentenced to 18 months' imprisonment on each count concurrent. No less
than 428 similar offences were at his request taken into consideration.

He appeals against conviction on a point of law. The trial judge granted a certificate
for this purpose in the following terms:

'The deception alleged in each count was not practised on the person who
executed the valuable security as they then knew of its falsity but upon someone
with whom their legal or commercial obligations were such that the jury could
nevertheless decide it caused them to execute it.'

The facts have in some measure a familiar modern ring about them. On 8 July 1981
fifteen packets of substantial quantities of Barclays Bank Visa traveller's cheques were

sent to branches of the Allied Irish Bank in Eire on behalf of Barclays Bank International Ltd, Lombard Street, London, who are one of the issuers of traveller's cheques under the Visa International system. They were dispatched through the post by their printers, Thomas De La Rue & Co. They were all stolen in the course of transmission, but by whom, where and how we do not know.

Between 14 August and 8 September 1981 a very large number of the stolen traveller's cheques had been unlawfully cashed in the south of France in the names of Robert Young and R Chew, 400 of which were presented to Barclays Bank International Ltd, through normal banking channels in France and in this country, for payment. The value of the sterling cheques amounted altogether to £7,860.

All the cheques had been forged by the appellant, who was by this deception and by the use of false passports (a very large number of British visitors' passports had been stolen early in 1981) enabled to considerably enrich himself in a very short space of time.

One of the cheques (count 1) had been cashed in Nice on 24 July in the name of Robert Augustine Young. Another of them (count 2) had been cashed in Cannes on the following day in the name of R Chew.

Although Barclays Bank International Ltd were aware that all the cheques presented to them for payment were forgeries, they honoured them. They did this, so the jury were informed, because, whilst they could not claim to be legally obliged to, they considered themselves liable to pay the agents and correspondents who had handled them, providing, in the case of a forged traveller's cheque, it was revealed on inquiry that the person who had encashed it had acted prudently. There is no suggestion in any of the relevant transactions that persons had acted imprudently. A witness from the bank explained that liability in this way: 'If we did not pay we would have all sorts of acceptability problems. Commercially, we have very little choice.'

In the ordinary and lawful way of dealing, a traveller's cheque is purchased from Barclays Bank or one of its agents. At the time of purchase, to comply with the condition of sale, the purchaser must sign each cheque with his usual signature in the presence of a servant or agent of the seller. When the purchaser wishes to cash a cheque he must put his signature on it once again in the space marked 'counter signature' in the presence of the person asked to encash it at a bank or other appropriate place either here or abroad. What should happen then is described on the back of each cheque thus:

> 'When countersigned by the purchaser whose signature appears on the face in the presence of the person cashing the issuer will pay in the United Kingdom ten pounds sterling, elsewhere negotiable at current rates of exchange.'

When the money is paid to the purchaser the payer has received a good title to the traveller's cheque and will receive the value of it at some point as it is returned or when it is returned through normal banking channels to, if it is for example a Barclays Bank Visa sterling traveller's cheque, the head office, for this purpose, of Barclays Bank International Ltd in Poole, Dorset.

On 22 July 1981, in Cannes, goods to the value of 1,000 French francs were purchased by the unlawful use of a Diners Club card (count 3). This had previously been stolen from the Mr Robert Young previously mentioned when his home in England had been burgled. The card was used in this way on 28 separate occasions in the space of a week for the purpose of obtaining money and goods.

The evidence against the appellant consisted of fingerprints on the traveller's cheques, his handwriting on them and his handwriting on bills rendered to Diners Club Ltd (Diners Club). For his unavailing defence he relied on an alibi which, by their verdicts, the jury obviously rejected. For the time when he was arrested in 1982 until after his convictions on the indictment the appellant protested his innocence. Immediately following conviction he admitted that he had forged all the cheques and cashed them and also that he had used the Diners Club card of Mr Young and had forged Mr Young's signature on bills at stores and banks where he had obtained goods and money.

The Diners Club, when presented with bills from Diners Club (France), to where they had been sent by the holders of them, amounting to a total of £1,713, knew that Mr

Young's card had been stolen and used unlawfully. They claimed to be under a legally
enforceable agreement to pay bills which have been incurred by the use of one of their
stolen cards providing there has been by the trader compliance with their conditions. It
is not said that any trader involved in the relevant transactions failed to thus comply.

The grounds of appeal are (1) that no offence was committed by the appellant within
the jurisdiction of the Crown Court, (2) that the judge was wrong in law (a) in ruling
that the final acceptance of a valuable security when it is a traveller's cheque is when it is
paid, (b) in directing the jury that 'procured' is only another word for 'caused' and that it
would be sufficient to bring the appellant's act within s 20(2) of the 1968 Act if it was a
cause which had some effect on the actions of Barclays Bank International Ltd and the
Diners Club, and (3) that the judge ought to have directed the jury that (a) 'procure'
meant 'produce by endeavour' and (b) there was no evidence to establish that the appellant
had endeavoured to produce the action of the bank or the club in paying money to
anyone else in respect of a traveller's cheque or Diners Club card.

Section 20 of the 1968 Act, so far as material, provides by sub-s (2) that a person who
'dishonestly, with a view to gain for himself . . . by any deception procures the execution
of a valuable security' shall on indictment be liable to a maximum term of seven years
imprisonment and that the subsection shall apply in relation to the 'making, acceptance,
indorsement, alteration, cancellation or destruction . . . of a valuable security . . . as if that
were the execution of a valuable security'. Subsection (3) defines by reference to s 15 of
the 1968 Act 'deception' as any deception, deliberate or reckless, by words or conduct as
to fact or law.

It is not in issue now that the appellant had in France, dishonestly with a view to gain
for himself by deceiving people there, obtained money or goods by the unlawful use of
valuable securities, namely traveller's cheques and a Diners Club card. Had he so behaved
in this country, it is acknowledged that his convictions could not, save possibly on the
issue of execution, have been challenged. But, it is argued, he deceived neither Barclays
Bank International Ltd nor the Diners Club (there is no dispute about that) and he did
not procure the execution, ie the acceptance by either, of a valuable security. All
acceptances within s 20(2) of valuable securities took place exclusively, counsel for the
appellant submits, in France. It is impermissible to so regard acceptance of the traveller's
cheques and bills for payment here which, in any event, was not procured by him. Not
surprisingly, the bank and the club and others who provide similar facilities for their
customers await with apprehension the outcome of this appeal.

We heard much argument about the definition properly to be given to the word
'execution'. It is a term of art, counsel for the appellant contended. It bears the meaning
it would bear in relation to a legal instrument. It means the due performance of all
formalities necessary to give validity to a document. Seeing that the traveller's cheques
were all forged, none of them could be said to have been executed. If that, he submits,
be wrong, it was beyond doubt that all acts of execution were performed in France.

Counsel for the Crown argued that execution in this context means no more than
giving effect to. The terms of s 20(2) of the 1968 Act envisage more than one kind of
execution. A shopkeeper executes, in other words gives effect to, a valuable security,
namely a bill arising out of the use of a Diners Club card, by demanding payment of the
bill. A forged traveller's cheque is a valuable security, forged or not, and capable of being
executed.

In our view, having regard only to the facts of this case, execution bears one of the
extended meanings given to it in s 20(2). Thus it is clear that, for example, the alteration,
cancellation or destruction of a valuable security can amount to an execution of it. So
may an acceptance of it. To attribute to the word the very restricted meaning counsel for
the appellant would have us accept and even to the somewhat more expansive definition
provided by counsel for the Crown would be, in our judgment, to fail to recognise the
plain indication of its meaning in the subsection itself. Thus, when a traveller's cheque is
accepted as genuine by a payer who pays the monetary value of it to the holder, he
executes it. Likewise, when Diners Club (France) accepts a bill for payment signed by the
actual or ostensible holder of a club card and pays it, execution takes place.

What we have found more troublesome with regard to the traveller's cheques is whether there can be more than one execution of a cheque for the purpose of s 20(2) and, if so, assuming the final execution to be in this country whether therefore this ingredient of the offence has taken place within the jurisdiction. The judge ruled that this was the effect of the subsection in the circumstances of the case. He was provided with no authority for the proposition; nor were we. But, like him, we see no good reason why there should not be a series of acceptances, i e executions, in respect of a traveller's cheque and provided the last of them, namely when the final act of payment on the cheque is made, occurs here, the Crown Court has jurisdiction to deal with the offence. We use the expression 'final act of payment' because when Barclays Bank International Ltd have paid the eventual holders the traveller's cheque becomes valueless; it is no longer a valuable security as a traveller's cheque.

In this respect the bill rendered to the Diners Club poses no difficulty. It was merely passed through Diners Club (France) and presented for payment here to Diners Club (UK). There seems to have been no act committed by Diners Club (France) which could be said to be an execution. If that be right, execution can only have occurred when the bill was accepted and paid here. If that be wrong and Diners Club (France) paid the bill to the original holder, we would apply the same reasoning to that situation as we think it sensible to apply to traveller's cheques.

Counsel for the appellant further relied on what he submitted was a wholly wrong definition attached by the judge to the word 'procures'. To procure does not, he says, mean to cause. It means to obtain by endeavour. He referred us in this connection firstly to *A-G's Reference (No 1 of 1975)* [1975] 2 All ER 684, [1975] QB 773. This was about aiding and abetting or procuring an offence under s 6(1) of the Road Traffic Act 1972 by lacing a drink. In the judgment of the court Lord Widgery CJ said ([1975] 2 All ER 684 at 686, [1975] QB 773 at 779):

> 'To procure means to produce by endeavour. You procure a thing by setting out to see that it happens and taking the appropriate steps to produce that happening. We think that there are plenty of instances in which a person may be said to procure the commission of a crime by another even though there is no sort of conspiracy between the two, even though there is no attempt at agreement or discussion as to the form which the offence should take. In our judgment the offence described in this reference is such a case.'

And, second, to *R v Broadfoot* [1976] 3 All ER 753. This concerned a charge of procuring a woman to become a common prostitute. Cusack J, having quoted from Lord Widgery CJ, went on (at 756):

> 'There is another expression which can be used as guidance in determining what should be decided on particular facts. During the course of argument in this court Shaw LJ suggested that "procuring" could perhaps be regarded as bringing about a course of conduct which the girl in question would not have embarked on spontaneously or of her own volition. It is essential, as I have said, that the interpretation of the word should be a matter of common sense for the jury concerned, and this court can see nothing wrong in the judge having suggested to the jury the word "recruited" as being a useful expression to consider in deciding what they thought on this particular issue.'

He had said (at 755):

> '[Counsel's] first complaint is that the learned judge told the jury that the word "procure" was really equivalent to the word "recruit". Let it be said at an early stage that the word "procure" in the 1956 Act is not a term of art. It is a word in common usage and a word which a jury is well able to understand. Each case in which it is alleged that there has been a procurement or attempted procurement must be related to the facts of that particular case. It is essential for a jury to make up their minds, when they have heard the evidence and decided what to accept, whether what they do accept does amount to "procuring". Counsel has quoted to the court several decisions dealing with the interpretation of the word "procure", in cases

involving quite different facts. The court does not find those references, though no doubt attention has properly been drawn to them, particularly helpful in this case; nor, indeed, do the dictionary definitions of the word have much bearing on what has to be decided.'

We agree with the general tenor of those observations. It is a word in common usage which, in our view, a jury can be relied on safely to understand. The most common meaning attached to it in our experience is to cause or to bring about. It has no special meaning for the purpose of s 20(2) of the 1968 Act and none, in our view, should be attributed to it by reference to its use in other enactments.

It is further submitted that the appellant did not cause or bring about the payments made by Barclays Bank International Ltd and Diners Club. On this issue the judge directed the jury as follows:

'The next point is that by doing what he did with the card and with the traveller's cheques he procured in England the execution of those valuable securities. "Procured" is only another word for caused. About that there is some dispute. I direct you, members of the jury, that it does not have to be the only cause of the execution, the execution that I have described, but it has to be a cause and a cause which has some effect on the actions of Barclays Bank and Diners Club. The way the prosecution put that is that, but for the person cashing the traveller's cheques and using the Diners Club card in France, Barclays Bank and Diners Club would never had had to consider paying out the money. Therefore, they cause the payment of the money. The point taken in respect of certainly the traveller's cheques when the witness was cross-examined by [counsel for the appellant] was that in a sense payment by the bank is voluntary because they were not bound to pay. I will remind you of what the witness said about that in due course, but, "In our eyes," he said, "we were legally bound to pay as commercial sense of good practice. We had no option." You may find, members of the jury, that the actions of the person in France using the traveller's cheques did cause the payment by Barclays Bank in this country, and payment by Barclays Bank in this country I have decided amounts to an execution.'

He is strongly, but unjustifiably we think, criticised in this regard. The appellant's dishonesty did not, it is said, deceive the bank or the Diners Club. They knew they were completing transactions which were dishonest at source. They need not, therefore, have made the payments demanded of them. We do not agree. There was evidence of obligations to do so before them on which the jury were entitled to act and to find that the appellant caused or brought about a situation in which both bank and club had no alternative for legal and/or commercial reasons but to pay for their valuable securities. This was an aspect of the matter which could properly and usefully have been, but was not, adverted to in the judge's direction. As it was however, the direction, we think, properly and sufficiently assisted the jury to reach a decision on the issue of procuring. The fact is that the appellant by his dishonesty set off a chain of events with inevitable consequences. To say that he did not procure them seems to us to disregard the evidence and to defy logic.

For these reasons we dismiss this appeal.

*Appeal dismissed.*

25 February 1985. The Court of Appeal (Purchas LJ, Kenneth Jones and Leonard JJ) refused leave to appeal to the House of Lords but certified, under s 33(2) of the Criminal Appeal Act 1968, that the following point of law of general public importance was involved in the decision: can the execution of a valuable security within s 20(2) of the Theft Act 1968 include the final payment by the issuing bank on a traveller's cheque?

Solicitors: *Millers*, Manchester (for the appellant); *D S Gandy*, Manchester.

Martine Kushner   Barrister.

# Lodwick v Sanders

QUEEN'S BENCH DIVISION
WATKINS LJ AND WEBSTER J
5, 6 JULY, 27 NOVEMBER 1984

*Police – Powers – Power to detain stopped vehicle – Vehicle stopped for purpose of investigating possible road traffic offences – Police officer suspecting vehicle stolen and attempting to detain it – Driver assaulting police officer – Whether police officer having power to detain vehicle – Whether police officer acting in execution of duty – Road Traffic Act 1972, s 159.*

The respondent, who was driving a lorry showing no vehicle excise licence, index plate or brake-lights, was stopped by police officers for the purpose of investigating the lorry. The respondent would not say whether he owned the vehicle and when asked about the excise licence he stated his name and address, then started the engine and tried to drive away. Because of the respondent's unsatisfactory answer about ownership of the lorry, the police officers suspected it may have been stolen and one of them entered the cab and took the ignition keys, whereupon the respondent grabbed the officer's hand, forced it against the steering wheel and made him drop the keys. He was arrested for assaulting a police officer in the execution of his duty. The incident was over in 30 seconds and before the officers were able to complete their inquiries. The respondent was subsequently acquitted of the assault charge on the ground that the officer who had taken the keys had not been acting in the execution of his duty. The magistrates held that, although s 159[a] of the Road Traffic Act 1972 obliged a driver to stop his vehicle when required and to remain at rest for a reasonable period, it did not empower a police officer to do any act which was an interference with the individual's liberty or property for the purpose of causing the vehicle to stop or remain at rest, and that, although the respondent had committed an offence in failing to give full particulars to the officers, the officer had had no right to detain him for that reason alone. On appeal by the prosecutor, the question arose whether a police officer who required a vehicle to stop under s 159 was acting in the execution of his duty if, believing the vehicle to have been stolen, he detained it to make further inquiries from the driver to establish its true ownership.

**Held** – Where a police officer, acting reasonably on a genuine inquiry into the suspected commission of a crime, required a motor vehicle to stop, pursuant to his power at common law or under s 159 of the 1972 Act, he was entitled to detain it for such reasonable time as to enable him, if he suspected it to have been stolen, to effect an arrest and explain to the driver the reason for the arrest. Accordingly, the police officer had acted lawfully in trying to detain the lorry, since he had been given no opportunity either to formulate the road traffic offences into which he was inquiring or to tell the respondent of his suspicion that the lorry had been stolen and, if necessary, to arrest him on that suspicion. The appeal would therefore be allowed (see p 581 e to p 582 a and d to j, p 583 b c and p 584 c and g to j, post).

## Notes
For assaulting or obstructing a constable in the execution of his duty, see 11 Halsbury's Laws (4th edn) para 962, and for cases on the subject, see 15 Digest (Reissue) 985–991, 8546–8590.

For power of police to stop a motor vehicle see 36 Halsbury's Laws (4th edn) para 328, 40 ibid para 267, and for cases on the subject, see 37(1) Digest (Reissue) 342, 346, 2186–2187, 2201–2203.

For the Road Traffic Act 1972, s 159, see 42 Halsbury's Statutes (3rd edn) 1803.

---

a   Section 159, so far as material, is set out at p 580 f g, post

**Cases referred to in judgments**

Beard v Wood [1980] RTR 454, DC.
Christie v Leachinsky [1947] 1 All ER 567, [1947] AC 573, HL.
Pedro v Diss [1981] 2 All ER 59, DC.
R v Waterfield [1963] 3 All ER 659, [1964] 1 QB 164, [1963] 3 WLR 946, CA.
Rice v Connolly [1966] 2 All ER 649, [1966] 2 QB 414, [1966] 3 WLR 17, DC.
Steel v Goacher [1983] RTR 98, DC.
Winter v Barlow [1980] RTR 209, DC.

**Cases also cited**

Ghani v Jones [1969] 3 All ER 1700, [1970] 1 QB 693, CA.
Kenlin v Gardiner [1966] 3 All ER 931, [1967] 2 QB 510, DC.
Lee v Knapp [1966] 3 All ER 961, [1967] 2 QB 442, DC.
R v Lemsatef [1977] 2 All ER 835, [1977] 1 WLR 812, CA.
Ward v Rawson [1978] RTR 498, DC.

**Case stated**

John Arthur Lodwick, a chief inspector of police, appealed by way of case stated by the justices for the petty sessional division of Peterborough in respect of their adjudication as a magistrates' court sitting at Peterborough on 19 August 1983 whereby they dismissed an information preferred by the appellant against the respondent, Neville Buckle Sanders, of assaulting Pc Roderick Alexander Cairns while in the execution of his duty, contrary to s 51(1) of the Police Act 1964. The facts are set out in the judgment of Watkins LJ.

Desmond Fennell QC and Richard Latham for the appellant.
Richard Daniel for the respondent.

*Cur adv vult*

27 November. The following judgments were delivered.

**WATKINS LJ.** On 19 August 1983 the justices for the petty sessional division of Peterborough dismissed an information laid by the appellant, a chief inspector of police, against the respondent who, it was alleged, on 29 May 1983 assaulted Pc Cairns while in the execution of his duty, contrary to s 51(1) of the Police Act 1964.

They found these facts. On 29 May at about 12.30 pm Pc Cairns and another police officer in a van saw the respondent driving an articulated motor lorry. It was not displaying a vehicle excise licence. The trailer seemed to have neither index plate nor brake-lights. They caused the respondent to stop the lorry. He switched off the engine, but stayed in the cab. Following questions about the state of the lorry, Pc Cairns asked. 'Do you own the vehicle?' The respondent replied: 'Maybe, maybe not, I am in a hurry.' It was, so we were told in this court, his lorry and it contained a tachograph which was out of order. Pc Cairns asked him about the excise licence. The respondent's response was to state his name and address. As he did so he started the engine and put the lorry in gear, intending to move off.

Pc Cairns was understandably not satisfied with the equivocal answer he was given about ownership of the lorry, the inspection of which neither he nor the other constable had completed. So he entered the cab and took possession of the ignition key to prevent the respondent driving away until all their inquiries had been made.

The respondent grabbed the constable's hand and pushed it tightly against the steering wheel, so causing him to release the key. Pc Cairns then arrested the respondent for assaulting him.

If the respondent had answered questions satisfactorily he would have been reported for motoring offences only. He was in any event, so we were told, reported for and convicted of such offences. If Pc Cairns had remained dissatisfied with them he would have arrested the defendant on suspicion of theft of the lorry. When the constable took the keys he did not know the respondent; and, although he did not say so, he already suspected the lorry had been stolen. If, which he did not, he had had the opportunity to do so he would have asked the respondent to produce driving documents under the Road Traffic Act 1972, Pt VII, and further examined the lorry and trailer.

The whole incident was over in about 30 seconds. These findings gave me the clear impression that not only did the justices conclude that Pc Cairns had no opportunity of informing the respondent that he wished to see driving documents, but also none of saying that he had in that very short time formed the suspicion that the respondent was at the wheel of a stolen lorry and that he, the constable, proposed to arrest the respondent on suspicion of having stolen it.

The justices were of the opinion that (a) the respondent's action in grabbing and pushing the officer's hand, if unlawful, amounted to an assault, (b) although s 159 of the Road Traffic Act 1972 obliged a driver when required under the section to stop, and further to remain at rest for a reasonable period, and provided he would be guilty of an offence if he failed to do so, the section did not empower a police officer to do any act which was an interference with a person's liberty or property to cause that vehicle to stop or remain at rest, (c) although the defendant had undoubtedly committed an offence of failing to give full particulars to the police officer, this was not an arrestable offence, and the officer had no right to prevent him from moving off for that reason alone, and (d) the officer was not therefore acting within the execution of his duty to restrict the freedom of the respondent by removing his vehicle key. Accordingly, they dismissed the information.

They ask the following questions of this court. (1) Is the driver of a motor vehicle, who stops it pursuant to a requirement made by a constable acting under s 159 of the 1972 Act, obliged under the section to cause the same to remain at rest for a reasonable period to enable the constable to complete any lawful inquiries under that Act? (2) Is a constable who has stopped a motor vehicle pursuant to a requirement made under s 159 of the 1972 Act, acting in the execution of his duty in preventing for a reasonable period the movement of such a vehicle before any lawful inquiries under the Act had been completed? (3) Is a constable acting in the execution of his duty in preventing the movement of such a vehicle if he reasonably believes that the vehicle or the driver of the vehicle is contravening the 1972 Act in such a way that a moving traffic offence will be committed if the vehicle is driven off by the driver? (4) Is a constable who has stopped a motor vehicle pursuant to a requirement made under s 159 of the Road Traffic Act 1972 acting in the execution of his duty in preventing for a reasonable period the movement of such a vehicle if he reasonably believes the vehicle may be stolen and wishes to make further inquiries of the driver and/or further independent investigations to establish the true ownership of the vehicle and the then driver's right to possession of the same?

From the exhaustive and helpful arguments addressed to us by counsel for the appellant and counsel for the respondent, and the many authorities to which they referred, it is unfortunately all too clear that in the absence of statutory power the right of a constable who has lawfully, by common law or statutory power, caused a motor vehicle to stop, to detain that vehicle and its driver while inquiries into the suspected commission of offences proceeds, lacks precise judicial definition.

In *Rice v Connolly* [1966] 2 All ER 649 at 651, [1966] 2 QB 414 at 419 Parker LJ stated:

> 'It is also in my judgment clear that it is part of the obligations and duties of a police constable to take all steps which appear to him necessary for keeping the peace, for preventing crime or for protecting property from criminal injury. There is no exhaustive definition of the powers and obligations of the police, but they are at least those, and they would further include the duty to detect crime and to bring an offender to justice.'

In the context of the present case it is the duty of the police to detect crime and to bring an offender to justice which is of particular significance. One of the questions which arises is how far a police constable is entitled to go in questioning and detaining for that purpose a suspect and detaining the motor vehicle of which he is the driver. In *R v Waterfield* [1963] 3 All ER 659 at 661–662, [1964] 1 QB 164 at 171–172 Ashworth J stated:

> 'Thus, while it is no doubt right to say in general terms that police constables have a duty to prevent crime and a duty, when crime is committed, to bring the offender to justice, it is also clear from the decided cases that when the execution of these general duties involves interference with the person or property of a private person, the powers of constables are not unlimited . . . It was contended that the two police constables were acting in the execution of a duty to preserve for use in court evidence of crime, and in a sense they were, but the execution of that duty did not in the view of this court authorise them to prevent removal of the car in the circumstances. In the course of argument instances were suggested where difficulty might arise if a police officer were not entitled to prevent removal of an article which had been used in the course of a crime, for example, an axe used by a murderer and thrown away by him. Such a case can be decided if and when it arises; for the purposes of the present appeal it is sufficient to say that in the view of this court the two police constables were not acting in the due execution of their duty at common law when they detained the car. Apart however from the position at common law, it was contended that Pc Willis was acting in the execution of a duty arising under s 223 of the Road Traffic Act, 1960. That section [the forerunner of s 159 of the 1972 Act], so far as material, provides that "a person driving a motor vehicle on a road . . . shall stop on being so required by a police constable in uniform." That argument, however, assuming that the car park is a road, involves considerable difficulties. In the first place its validity depends on a construction of the section which would enable the constable not merely to require a moving vehicle to stop but to require a stationary vehicle not to move. The court finds it unnecessary to reach a conclusion on that because, in the second place, it is to be observed that the section is merely giving a power as opposed to laying down a duty. It seems to the court that it would be an invalid exercise of the power given by the section if, as here, the object of its exercise was to do something, namely to detain a vehicle, which as already stated the constable had in the circumstances no right to do.'

Pc Cairns in requiring the respondent to stop used, so it is said, the power given to him by s 159 of the 1972 Act, which provides, so far as it is necessary to quote it:

> 'A person driving a motor vehicle on a road . . . shall stop the same on being so required by a constable in uniform, and if he fails to do so he shall be guilty of an offence.'

In respectful agreement with Ashworth J, I think that s 159 is to be construed as conferring a power on a constable to require a vehicle to stop. In my view, on being required to do so the driver of the vehicle is under a duty to stop. Whether the constable has lawfully used that power is a matter which the driver is afterwards entitled to challenge; likewise if it be contended that a constable acted unlawfully in what ever he did while the vehicle was at a standstill. If a constable was acting lawfully when requiring him to stop and thereafter, and the driver assaulted him, he would be liable to be found to have committed an offence against s 51(1) of the Police Act 1964, which provides that any person who assaults a constable in the execution of his duty shall be guilty of an offence punishable by imprisonment, fine, or both.

Unquestionably the respondent assaulted Pc Cairns but, so the justices found, he was not guilty of an offence because the constable had no right to prevent him from driving away; it was an act outwith the execution of the constable's duty.

It is well established that the police have no general power to detain any person for questioning. A constable may ask a question of a person, but he cannot (a) require that person to stop to be questioned, and (b) he cannot demand an answer to any question;

the right to silence in such a circumstance is predominant. There are statutory exceptions to this hallowed right of the citizen: see s 232 of the Road Traffic Act 1960 and ss 161 and 162 of the 1972 Act, which create offences in respect of persons refusing to answer a constable's proper questions.

A constable is given statutory power in some circumstances to detain a motor vehicle which he has cause to stop (see, inter alia, ss 82 and 99 of the Transport Act 1968) so that he may enter and inspect the vehicle and inspect records and other documents. There is, however, no such express power in Pt VII of the 1972 Act, which contains ss 159, 161, and 162.

Accordingly, counsel for the respondent submits that the constable having no power at common law to detain the lorry and to further question the respondent, the latter was entitled to drive away, as he in fact attempted to do.

Counsel for the appellant's response to that is that the respondent stopped the vehicle in performance of a duty so to do. It is a necessary inference of the creation of that duty, he contends, that the respondent should remain at a standstill until the constable, assuming he did not act capriciously and did not ask improper questions, had completed his inquiries. Moreover, a constable has the power to ensure that the duty is observed by, if necessary, detaining the vehicle.

It would, I agree, be likely to appear to the average person to be an unsatisfactory law which permitted a lorry which has, on lawful request, been stopped because two constables with good reason suspected it contravened the law in not displaying or having a vehicle excise licence, an index plate and brake-lights, to be driven away again with impunity before inquiries into these matters are completed. And, furthermore, the constables are able to do what the provisions of Pt VII of the 1972 Act empower them to do, namely, among other things, to require production of evidence of insurance and so forth.

In my view, it is a necessary inference of the existence of the power in s 159 and its conjunction with ss 161 and 162 that a driver is under a duty to keep the vehicle at a standstill while, at the very least, a constable has a reasonable opportunity of exercising his powers under those sections. Neither constable in the present case had come near to exhausting those powers, as the findings of the justices show.

Furthermore, I would regard it as unthinkable that a vehicle which seems to have no brake-lights, and for that reason may constitute a danger to others users of the road, should not be examined so that that and other possible defects may be verified. This process was still under way when the respondent tried to drive off. As I have said, a driver is not, save in circumstances created by statute, obliged to answer a constable's questions; but it seems to me, that does not entitle him to drive away a vehicle which a constable seeks for good reason (namely that at least one defect is apparent), to inspect, and following inspection to inform the driver of it, if he so decides, that the driver will be reported for one or more offences, including possibly an offence arising out of the defective state of a tachograph.

But there is a vital distinction between a duty owed by a driver to keep his vehicle at a standstill and a power, if such exists, in a constable to detain the vehicle against the driver's will. I am in no doubt that there are circumstances in which at common law a constable has that power.

Consonant with his duty to detect crime, Pc Cairns had, within the limited opportunity allowed him by the driver before the assault, unsuccessfully endeavoured to obtain the identity of the owner of the lorry. It was this failure which made him suspect that it had been stolen. There were questions unasked, the answers to which could either have confirmed or allayed the constable's suspicions, questions which the constable was empowered by ss 161 and 162 to ask, relating to production of documents, including driving licence, insurance certificate, statement of birth, and so on. With those answers his suspicion of theft may have hardened into a belief. True it is that the questions I have referred to are not, in the 1972 Act, designed to be asked for the purpose of ascertaining whether an offence of theft has been committed. But the fact that they are asked with the twin objectives of what the power to ask them is granted for, and an inquiry into a suspicion of theft, cannot in my judgment render either the asking of the question or, subject to what I am about to say on this essential matter, the detention of the vehicle unlawful.

Let it be supposed that the constable was not minded to ask further questions which by ss 161 and 162 he was empowered to ask, but was concerned further only with an inquiry into a suspected theft of the lorry. If he had a reasonable suspicion of theft was he powerless in law to prevent the lorry from being driven away? In *Steel v Gocher* [1983] RTR 98 at 103 Griffiths LJ said:

'For a multitude of reasons the police will, from time to time, wish to question motorists in the course of their duty to detect and prevent crime. I find nothing oppressive in police officers wishing to satisfy themselves, by inquiry, that a strange car being driven by two men after midnight through a good class residential area was there for an innocent purpose. If the public wish the police to contain and detect the ever increasing amount of crime and, in particular, the burglary of dwellinghouses, they must be prepared, from time to time, to put up with the occasional inconvenience of being stopped and questioned. They do not have to answer the questions but they must stop, as section 159 of the Road Traffic Act 1972 requires a motorist to stop if required to do so by a constable in uniform. I would add that one hopes that the public will co-operate with the police in answering their questions, albeit they are under no legal duty to do so.'

I wholly and respectfully agree with that, and say further that in my opinion a constable acting reasonably on a genuine inquiry into the suspected commission of crime, who has under his undoubted power either at common law or under s 159 required a motor vehicle to stop, is entitled to take reasonable steps to detain it for such reasonable time as will enable him, if he suspects it to have been stolen, to effect an arrest and to explain to the driver the reason for the arrest.

I am not aware of anything which indicates that Pc Cairns acted otherwise than reasonably throughout a proper inquiry, assuming, of course, that he acted lawfully in detaining the lorry.

If the justices had properly directed themselves in law, then on their findings of fact they must, so I think, have held that the constable in that respect acted lawfully. They concluded that such conversation as there was between him and the driver took no more than 30 seconds, which gave the constable no opportunity either to formulate the road traffic offences which he was inquiring into and to inform the driver of them, or, which is of particular relevance, to tell the driver of his suspicion that the lorry had been stolen and to arrest him on that suspicion.

In *Christie v Leachinsky* [1947] 1 All ER 567 at 573, [1947] AC 573 at 588 Viscount Simon said:

'The person arrested cannot complain that he has not been supplied with the above information as and when he should be, if he himself produces the situation which makes it practically impossible to inform him, *e.g.*, by immediate counter-attack or by running away.'

Those considerations apply here. Pc Cairns was, as I have explained, lawfully detaining an article which he suspected had been stolen. The respondent cannot complain that he had not been so informed before he attacked the constable. He should have been convicted of an offence under s 51(1) of the Police Act 1964. I would therefore allow the appeal and remit the case to the justices with a direction to convict the respondent.

In so doing I would thus answer the questions asked: (1) yes; (2) this does not arise; (3) this does not arise; (4) a constable who suspects a vehicle to have been stolen by the driver of it is entitled in the execution of this duty to detain and seize the vehicle and arrest the driver.

**WEBSTER J.** In my view, it is important in the context of this section to distinguish between a constable's powers and the citizen's duties, and between requiring a driver to stop his vehicle and stopping or physically stopping it. There is no doubt that a person driving a motor vehicle on a road is under a duty to stop when required to do so by a constable in uniform; and failure to perform the duty constitutes a criminal offence. And I agree with Watkins LJ that, having stopped if he does so, he is under a similar duty to remain at a standstill while the constable exercises whatever power he seeks to exercise. But, in my view, it does not follow from that duty on the part of the citizen that the constable has a power to detain him or his vehicle.

Considering the question simply as one of language and construction of the section and without regard to authority, there seems to me to be no doubt but that the constable has a power to 'require' a person to stop his motor vehicle; but I see nothing in the language of the section which justifies a construction of it having the effect that the constable has any power to do more than to 'require' the citizen to stop. Moreover, this construction of the section seems to me consistent with authority.

Watkins LJ has cited the relevant passage from the judgment of Ashworth J in *R v Waterfield* [1963] 3 All ER 659 at 661–662, [1964] 1 QB 164 at 171–172. Although I respectfully agree with Watkins LJ that in that passage Ashworth J can be taken to construe s 159 as conferring a power on a constable to require a vehicle to stop, the judge does not, in my view, express the opinion that a constable has a power to detain a vehicle: on the contrary, it seems to me that the last sentence of the passage cited is wholly inconsistent with that view.

In *Beard v Wood* [1980] RTR 454 at 458, Wien J cited the same passage of the judgment of Ashworth J and added:

'With respect, Ashworth J was clearly right in making the observations he did about the ambit of section 223. There is no question of detaining the vehicle in the instant appeal.'

It seems to me that Wien J also was rejecting the suggestion that a constable has a power to detain a vehicle.

But in *Winter v Barlow* [1980] RTR 209 at 213 Eveleigh LJ, in a judgment with which Kilner Brown J agreed, said:

'It is not necessary to go into the precise effect of s 159. It may be thought and may be argued that that section does not give a direct power as such anyway, but it simply imposes a duty on a person in the circumstances therein referred to, namely, when required to stop by a constable in uniform.'

In *Steel v Goacher* [1983] RTR 98 at 103 Griffiths LJ, in a judgment with which Forbes J agreed, and in a passage which followed that cited by Watkins LJ, said:

'That section [s 159] imposes a duty on a motorist to stop when required to do so by a constable in uniform. It does not follow that a constable in uniform must be deemed to have acted lawfully when, for whatever reason, he requires a motorist to stop. For purely practical reasons, there must be a rule that motorists stop when called upon to do so by a constable in uniform. The motorist must assume for the purpose of stopping that he is being lawfully required to stop, otherwise a dangerous and chaotic state of affairs would result. But once the motorist has stopped he can, thereafter, challenge the constable's right to stop him, for *nothing in the wording of the section gives any power to the constable to stop the motorist*. It is a section designed to ensure safety and good order *rather than to confer any specific power on a police constable*. I respectfully prefer the obiter observations of Eveleigh LJ to this effect in *Winter v Barlow* . . . to those of Ashworth J in *Reg v Waterfield* . . . in which he said of section 223 of the Road Traffic Act 1960, the forerunner of Section 159: ". . . the section is merely giving a power as opposed to laying down a duty".' (My emphasis.)

Griffiths LJ, while agreeing with the decision in *Beard v Wood*, dissented (at 104)—

'from that part of the reasoning in the judgment of Wien J in which he adopts and approves of the interpretation of the section suggested by Ashworth J in *Reg v Waterfield . . .*'

I respectfully agree with Griffiths LJ's opinion that the section confers no power on a constable to stop the driver of a motor vehicle, as distinct from requiring him to stop; but I do not, with respect, read the judgment of Ashworth J as expressing the view that a constable has a power to stop the driver of a motor vehicle, as distinct from requiring him to stop. In my view, with respect to Eveleigh and Griffiths LJJ, a constable has power to require a driver to stop his vehicle. But in any event, considering those authorities as a whole, although none of them is more than persuasive in this court, they all of them seem to me to be quite inconsistent with the proposition that the section confers on a constable a power physically to detain a motor vehicle once it has stopped.

I too would therefore answer the first question for our opinion in the affirmative, (substituting the word 'obliged' for the word 'required'). I agree that the second and third questions do not arise. But in the present case that does not seem to me to be the end of the matter, and there remains the fourth question.

Watkins LJ has already referred to the facts found, which include the fact that, if the defendant had not answered the constable's questions satisfactorily, the constable would have arrested him on suspicion of theft and taking without consent. After the constable had begun to ask questions the defendant simply replied with his full name and address, started the engine, and put the vehicle in gear to move off. It was at that point that the constable grabbed the ignition key. The constable took the keys, as the justices found, 'because he did not know the defendant and suspected that the vehicle may have been stolen'. I conclude that it is an inescapable inference that the suspicion, namely that the vehicle was or *might* have been stolen, must have hardened into a suspicion or belief that it *had* been stolen, and that the defendant had stolen it, or received it knowing it to be stolen, when the defendant began to drive it away.

A constable must give his reasons for detaining someone when he does so, just as he must give his reasons for arresting him: see *Pedro v Diss* [1981] 2 All ER 59; and I have no doubt that the same considerations would apply when a constable exercises his undoubted right to seize something which he suspects to be stolen from a person whom he believes to have stolen it or to have received it knowing it to have been stolen (see 36 Halsbury's Laws (4th edn) para 323). Watkins LJ has cited the dictum of Viscount Simon in *Christie v Leachinsky* [1947] 1 All ER 567 at 573, [1947] AC 573 at 588 where he said:

'The person arrested cannot complain that he has not been supplied with the above information as and when he should be, if he himself produces the situation which makes it practically impossible to inform him, *e.g.,* by immediate counter-attack or by running away.'

In my view, similar considerations apply in the present case. If, as I conclude, the constable suspected or believed that the vehicle was stolen immediately the defendant began to drive it away, and if, as I conclude, he suspected or believed that the defendant had stolen it or received it knowing it to be stolen, he thereupon became entitled to detain the vehicle; and if, as is apparent from the facts found, he had no time to explain that he was detaining it for that reason before he grabbed the ignition key, then, he was acting in the execution of this duty when he did so.

For these reasons, therefore, I agree that this appeal should be allowed, and that the case should be remitted to the justices with a direction to convict the respondent; and I agree with Watkins LJ's answer to the fourth question.

*Appeal allowed. Case remitted with direction to convict.*

Solicitors: *Sharpe Pritchard & Co*, agents for *D C Beal*, Huntingdon (for the appellant); *Southwell Dennis & Land*, Wisbech (for the respondent).

Raina Levy    Barrister.

# Willett v Wells

FAMILY DIVISION
HOLLINGS J
31 OCTOBER 1984

*Affiliation – Application for order – Time for application – Payment by putative father – Payment for child's maintenance within three years of its birth – Gift of clothing for child – Whether gift of clothing constituting 'money paid for [child's] maintenance' – Affiliation Proceedings Act 1957, s 2(1)(b).*

The mother of an illegitimate child sought an affiliation order against the respondent more than three years after the birth of the child. In order to entitle her to bring the claim the mother was required, by s 2(1)(b)ᵃ of the Affiliation Proceedings Act 1957, to prove that in the three years following the child's birth the respondent had 'paid money for its maintenance'. The respondent had not given the mother any money in that period but he had given the child a gift of a jumper and a pair of trousers. The magistrates dismissed the mother's claim. She appealed.

**Held** – Money expended by a putative father, or an alleged putative father, of a child on items such as food or clothing which would normally be paid for out of maintenance payments for the child constituted the payment of 'money for its maintenance' within s 2(1)(b) of the 1957 Act. Since it was to be inferred that the respondent had paid for the clothing himself, it followed that his gift of clothing to the child constituted money paid for the child's maintenance and that the mother was entitled to bring the claim and to have a maintenance order made against the father. The appeal would therefore be allowed (see p 588 *f* to *j*, post).

*Camrud v Hendry* [1935] 2 WWR 655 and *Roberts v Roberts* [1962] 2 All ER 967 considered.

## Notes

For the time for application for an affiliation order, see 1 Halsbury's Laws (4th edn) para 623.

For the Affiliation Proceedings Act 1957, s 2, see 1 Halsbury's Statutes (3rd edn) 77.

## Cases referred to in judgment

*Camrud v Hendry* [1935] 2 WWR 655.
*Roberts v Roberts* [1962] 2 All ER 967, [1962] P 212 [1962] 3 WLR 448.

## Case stated

The mother appealed by way of case stated by the justices for the county of Humberside, acting in and for the petty sessional division of Grimsby and Cleethorpes, in respect of their adjudication as a magistrates' court sitting at Grimsby whereby they dismissed a complaint by the mother of an illegitimate child under s 1 of the Affiliation Proceedings Act 1957 for an affiliation order against the alleged father on the ground that she was not entitled to make the complaint more than three years after the child's birth. The question for the opinion of the High Court was whether a gift of clothing given by the father to the mother for the child during the three years following its birth was 'money paid for [the child's] maintenance' within s 2(1)(b) of the 1957 Act as amended so as to entitle the mother to make a complaint more than three years after the birth. The facts are set out in the judgment.

---

*a*   Section 2, as amended, so far as material, is set out at p 586 *c d*, post

*Paul Genney* for the mother.
The father did not appear.

**HOLLINGS J.** This is an appeal by case stated from the decision of a magistrates' court for the petty sessional division of Grimsby and Cleethorpes sitting in Grimsby under the Affiliation Proceedings Act 1957. The magistrates were adjudicating on a complaint preferred by the mother against the father that he was the father of her illegitimate child born to her on 8 March 1981; and for an order that he pay her appropriate maintenance pursuant to the 1957 Act for that child.

The magistrates first heard the application on 2 April 1984, but the complaint was not issued until a date not long before that, on 9 March 1984; that is three years and one day after the birth of the child.

The Affiliation Proceedings Act 1957, s 2(1), as amended by the Affiliation Proceedings (Amendment) Act 1972, provides that a complaint for payments under s 1 of the 1957 Act may be made—

'(*a*) at any time within three years from the child's birth [and that condition was not complied with in the present case by one day]; or (*b*) at any subsequent time, upon proof that the man alleged to be the father of the child has within the three years next after the birth paid money for its maintenance . . .'

There is a third alternative with which this court is not concerned.

The mother was represented by a solicitor; the father was not represented. The mother gave evidence and as a result of that evidence the magistrates were able to make certain findings of fact which are set out in the case stated. They are as follows: that the mother gave birth to a child, on 8 March 1981; that the father was the father of the child; and they further found that during the three years following the birth of the child the father, to use their words, 'paid no maintenance to the [mother] for the child', neither did he cohabit with her, though he visited her when she was in the maternity home and they registered the birth of the child together. They also found that before the birth of the child the father paid to the mother half the cost of a pram. They finally found that the only contribution, to use their words, made by the father to the mother on behalf of the child during the three years following the birth was a present of a jumper and a pair of trousers.

The time limit was of course well in the minds of the court, and as the case stated goes on to say:

'It was contended by the [mother] that an order could be made because the present of a jumper and trousers during the 3 years following the birth of the child amounted to the payment of money for his maintenance pursuant to Section 2(1)(*b*) of the Affiliation Proceedings Act 1957.'

The father gave no evidence and made no submissions. The mother referred the magistrates to *Roberts v Roberts* [1962] 2 All ER 967, [1962] P 212.

The magistrates then set out at para 6 of the case stated their opinion:

'(a) that the case of *Roberts v Roberts* was irrelevant to these proceedings [and I will refer to that case at a later stage] . . . (b) that, because it was not made clear in the evidence how the [father] had acquired the jumper and trousers (whether by him purchasing them or having received them himself as a gift), the gift to the [mother] for the child was insufficient to constitute the payments of money for its maintenance pursuant to Section 2(1)(*b*) Affiliation Proceedings Act, 1957.'

The magistrates go on to say in their case stated that if it had been shown that the father had purchased the clothes himself for the child—

'we would have concluded that that amounted to the payment of money for its maintenance and, coupled with his prior contribution to the cost of the pram, an acknowledgment by him that he had a liability to maintain the child. The [mother] would then have been successful in her application for an order.'

They conclude: 'However, this was not made clear, and accordingly the application was dismissed.'

The question for the opinion of the High Court which the court is asked to answer is: however they (that is the jumper and trousers) were acquired by the father, was the one present of a jumper and trousers to the mother for the child during the three years following the birth of the child the payment of money for its maintenance, referred to in s 2(1)(*b*) of the 1957 Act?

The decision in *Roberts v Roberts* was not on this point. It was a decision in the Probate, Divorce and Admiralty Division under the Matrimonial Proceedings (Magistrates' Courts) Act 1960, whereby a wife claimed maintenance from her husband for the child of the wife by another man. It was held on appeal, the magistrates having ordered the husband to pay maintenance for the wife and £1 for the maintenance of the child, first, that the husband, by accepting the child as one of the family, thereby assumed full responsibility for the child's maintenance within the 1960 Act, and, second, that the child having formed part of the household of her putative father during the 12 months after the birth, there was evidence that the father had paid money for the child's maintenance as to render him liable for her maintenance in affiliation proceedings.

The relevant part of the judgment is that of Simon P where he said ([1962] 2 All ER 967 at 969–970, [1962] P 212 at 216):

> 'It is argued for the wife that there was no evidence that Mr. Wright paid money for Sandra's maintenance. It is true that the wife and Sandra were living in his house, and it is reasonable to suppose that what they lived on came from Mr. Wright; but, it is contended, that was paid by Mr. Wright to the wife in her capacity as housekeeper, and it was out of her earnings that the child was maintained. This seems to us to be an unrealistic approach. The wife may originally have been engaged as Mr. Wright's housekeeper; but after a short time she became his kept mistress, and it was their common child, not a stranger, for whom food and clothes and shelter were provided. This was not provided gratuitously like manna: it has to paid for; and the source of the payment, whoever did the actual shopping, was Mr. Wright. We consider that where it is proved that an illegitimate child forms part of the household of the child's father, there is prima facie evidence that he has paid money for the child's maintenance.'

I think the value of that decision for the purposes of this appeal is in the last two sentences, and especially the last one, that is that, if an illegitimate child forms part of the household of its father, that is prima facie evidence that he has paid money for its maintenance. To that extent and to that extent only that case is of assistance in the present case.

However, as a result of researches which were instituted this morning, a decision from the Western Provinces of Canada has been found: *Camrud v Hendry* [1935] 2 WWR 655. It was a decision of Knowles J in the King's Bench Division of Saskatchewan on an appeal in affiliation proceedings under the Child Welfare Act 1930, which had similar provisions with regard to the time within which a claim should be made. Section 114 of that Act reads:

> 'No filiation proceedings shall be commenced . . . after the expiration of twelve months from the date of birth, save that if the alleged father has paid money for the maintenance of the child after its birth . . .'

In that case, although there was evidence that the mother had continued living with the appellant as a housekeeper, and that for an indefinite time the child was maintained in the home of the appellant, the decision seems to have turned on the fact that after they had separated the appellant made a gift or some gifts to the infant, or to the mother for the infant. Knowles J said (at 656):

'Outstandingly the evidence along this line showed the purchase by the appellant of a pair of shoes which he brought on an occasion when he visited the respondent. Counsel for the respondent submits that this constituted a payment of money by the appellant for the maintenance of the child. In my opinion it does not. The words of the statute are so explicit to the effect that the limitation of 12 months is removed only if, in the words of the statute, "the father has paid money for the maintenance of the child". The respondent is entitled only to a strict interpretation of the statute. Any rights which are hers are not common-law rights. The law-makers did not say that the limitation would be removed by the donating of a gift, or the making of any present, but said most explicitly that there must be payment of money by the alleged father for the maintenance of the child. If the law-makers had intended to say that the limitation would be removed on the making of a gift they would no doubt have said so. I do not think the presenting of a pair of shoes for an infant is included in the words of the statute "if the alleged father paid money for the maintenance of the child". What he did was donate a pair of shoes for the maintenance of the child.'

That is a clear decision in favour of the father and against the mother's contention in this case, but it is of course only of persuasive authority. Investigation has also been made to see how long this phrase 'money for its maintenance' has been is use; and it can be traced back as far as 1844 (see the Poor Law Amendment Act 1844, s 69). The first Act making provision for affiliation payments was the Poor Law Amendment Act 1834, and this particular provision does not appear in it. But in the Poor Law Amendment Act 1844 one sees the phrase for the first time. Apart from the increase in the period from 12 months to three years by the 1957 Act, that phrase has remained in the relevant Acts throughout, but there are apparently no other decisions relative to it.

It is a comparatively short point, but one of course which has considerable importance. First, although this does not form part of the question which has been given to the court for its opinion, I can say at once that the magistrates' indication that there was not evidence that the father had bought the jumper and trousers himself, and therefore that was a further reason for saying he had not paid money, does not from my understanding of the evidence that was before them appear to be justified. If, as it appears, the evidence before them was that he had (that is the father had) given a jumper and trousers and there was no evidence whether he had been given those by somebody else or whether he paid for them himself, the proper inference to be drawn was that he had paid for those himself.

So the basis, the finding of fact, on which this question is founded is that the father did, within the three-year period (apparently about the first birthday of this child it seems) made a present of a jumper and trousers. The assumption is inevitable in the absence of other evidence that he paid money for those himself.

The phrase is 'paid money for its maintenance', that is a complaint may be made if at any time the father has paid money for its maintenance. It is not said that it must be shown that he has 'maintained the child', which may involve consideration of a number of payments over a period of time to see whether those payments did, as a jury point as it were, amount to maintenance. The phrase itself is 'paid money for its maintenance'. This is apt to cover one payment. Does that money have to be handed over in specie, or can it be paid for something which in itself is something which would properly be paid for out of maintenance payments, such as, as here, clothing? The answer is plainly that it can.

In my opinion, if a putative father, or an alleged putative father, expends money on food or clothing or such other items as would normally be paid for out of maintenance payments, then that is the payment of money for the maintenance of that child, and the magistrates ought to have so found.

For those reasons, I direct that the case should go back to the magistrates for them to find that the father has paid money for the child's maintenance, and thereupon to proceed to consider the evidence as to means and decide the appropriate financial order to make. I order accordingly.

I have come to this conclusion notwithstanding the decision in *Camrud v Hendry* which, as I have said, is only of persuasive effect, but assisted by the approach of Simon P in *Roberts v Roberts*.

*Appeal allowed ; case remitted to magistrates.*

Solicitors: *Wilkin & Chapman*, Cleethorpes (for the mother).

Bebe Chua      Barrister.

# R v HM Treasury, ex parte Smedley

COURT OF APPEAL, CIVIL DIVISION

SIR JOHN DONALDSON MR, SLADE AND LLOYD LJJ

12, 13, 19 DECEMBER 1984

*European Economic Community – Treaty provisions – Ancillary treaty – Ancillary – Financing of Community – Decision that Community be financed from own resources incorporated into community treaties – Member states subsequently undertaking to contribute to Community finances – Whether undertaking conflicting with decision incorporated into treaties – Whether undertaking capable of being 'ancillary' to treaties – European Communities Act 1972, ss 1(3), 2(3).*

*Judicial review – Declaration – Locus standi – Sufficient interest – United Kingdom undertaking to finance supplementary budget of European Community from Consolidated Fund – Undertaking purporting to be a treaty 'ancillary' to Community treaties – United Kingdom taxpayer seeking judicial review of determination that undertaking ancillary to Community treaties – Whether taxpayer having sufficient locus standi.*

*Statutory instrument – Draft statutory instrument – Draft Order in Council – Draft of order required to be approved by Parliament – Applicant seeking judicial review of validity of draft order – Applicant contending that order would be ultra vires – Whether court having jurisdiction to grant relief before draft of order approved by Parliament.*

By s 1(3)[a] of the European Communities Act 1972 Her Majesty was empowered to declare that an international agreement specified in an Order in Council was to be regarded as one of the 'Community Treaties', ie treaties etc under which the various European Communities and institutions had been established and treaties relating to the United Kingdom's accession to those Communities (including the Act of Accession (1972)) and any treaty or agreement 'ancillary' thereto. A treaty or international agreement could not be so specified unless a draft of the Order in Council had been approved by a resolution of each House of Parliament. Amounts required to meet obligations under Community treaties were, by s 2(3)[b] of the 1972 Act, to be charged on and issued out of the Consolidated Fund. By an EEC Council decision which had been incorporated into the Act of Accession and was therefore part of a Community treaty, it had been declared that from 1 January 1975 the Community budget was to be financed entirely from the Community's own resources. In 1984 a supplementary and amending Community budget was produced and the member states made an undertaking that the expenditure contemplated by that budget would be met out of funds provided by the member states in the form of reimbursable advances, and not out of the Community's own resources. In order to implement the undertaking, a draft Order in Council specifying the

---

a   Section 1, so far as material, is set out at p 592 *d* to *g*, post
b   Section 2(3), so far as material provides: 'There shall be charged on and issued out of the Consolidated Fund ... the amounts required to meet any Community obligation to make payments to any of the Communities ...'

undertaking as a treaty required to be regarded as a Community treaty was laid before each House of Parliament. The applicant, who was a United Kingdom taxpayer, applied (i) for an order of certiorari to quash the determination or intended determination of the Treasury that the undertaking was to be regarded as a Community treaty within s 1(2), or (ii) alternatively, a declaration that the determination was ultra vires. The applicant contended that since the purpose of the undertaking was to enable the Community to budget for expenditure in 1984 in excess of its own resources, and accordingly would result in the Community exceeding the limit of expenditure imposed by the Community treaties, the undertaking was in contravention of the treaties and could not be regarded as 'ancillary' to them. The Treasury contended (i) that the applicant had no sufficient locus standi within RSC Ord 53, r 3(7) to entitle him to apply for judicial review, (ii) that it would be an unjustifiable interference with the proceedings of Parliament to grant relief since at that stage neither House of Parliament had considered the draft order and therefore no order had been or could be made, and (iii) that the draft order was not contrary to the Community treaties, but ancillary to it. The judge dismissed the application. The applicant appealed.

**Held** – (1) (Per Slade and Lloyd LJJ) Since the application raised a serious question as to the powers of Her Majesty in Council to make an Order in Council in the form of the draft before Parliament, and since the making of the order would be followed by the expenditure of substantial sums from the Consolidated Fund in reliance on s 2(3) of the 1972 Act, the applicant, as a taxpayer, had sufficient locus standi to raise the question by way of judicial review (see p 595 *h j* and p 599 *c d*, post); *IRC v National Federation of Self-Employed and Small Businesses Ltd* [1981] 2 All ER 93 considered.

(2) Where an administrative order or regulation was required by statute to be approved by resolution of both Houses of Parliament, the court could in an appropriate case intervene by way of judicial review before the Houses had given their approval, even though in most cases the only appropriate form of relief, if any, would be by way of declaration. That jurisdiction was, however, to be exercised with great circumspection and with close regard to the dangers of usurping or encroaching on any function which statute had specifically conferred on Parliament or on the functions of Parliament in general. Since the function conferred on the two Houses of Parliament by s 1(3) of the 1972 Act in relation to the undertaking was to decide whether to approve the draft Order in Council, it followed that a decision by the court on the application at a time when Parliament had not considered the draft order would not involve any usurpation or encroachment on the functions of Parliament, and there was accordingly no reason why the court should not consider the application (see p 593 *h* to p 594 *b*, p 597 *b* to p 598 *a* and p 599 *c d*, post); *R v Electricity Comrs, ex p London Electricity Joint Committee Co (1920) Ltd* [1923] All ER Rep 150 applied.

(3) Although s 1(3) of the 1972 Act did not empower Her Majesty in Council to purport to bring within the ambit of the 'Community Treaties' an international agreement which demonstrably had no connection with those treaties, it did confer a power to make an Order in Council in relation to an agreement which was capable of being properly regarded as a treaty 'ancillary' to the Community treaties. Furthermore, the existence of a conflict between an agreement and provisions of the Community treaties would not necessarily disqualify that agreement from being properly regarded as ancillary to the treaties. On the facts, there was no such inconsistency between the undertaking and the Community treaties, since, although it was an expressed principle of the treaties that the Community budget should so far as possible (and usually) be entirely financed out of the Community's own resources, it did not follow that it had in all circumstances to be so financed. In the circumstances, since the very purpose of the undertaking was to provide money which the Community considered necessary in order to fulfil its essential functions and since the undertaking did not conflict with the Community treaties when read as a whole, the undertaking could properly be described as 'ancillary' to the Community treaties. It followed that the Order in Council if made

would not be ultra vires the power conferred by s 1(3) of the 1972 Act. The appeal would accordingly be dismissed (see p 594 *h j*, p 595 *a* to *e* and p 598 *e* to p 599 *d*, post).

## Notes
For declaratory judgments, see 1 Halsbury's Laws (4th edn) paras 185–187, and for cases on the subject, see 30 Digest (Reissue) 189–194, *202–234*.

For the European Communities Act 1972, ss 1, 2, see 42 Halsbury's Statutes (3rd edn) 79, 80.

For the Act of Accession (1972), see 42A ibid passim.

## Cases referred to in judgments
*Associated Provincial Picture Houses Ltd v Wednesbury Corp* [1947] 2 All ER 680, [1947] 1 KB 223, CA.

*Bulmer (HP) Ltd v J Bollinger SA* [1974] 2 All ER 1226, [1974] 1 Ch 401, [1974] 3 WLR 202, CA.

*Edwards v Bairstow* [1955] 3 All ER 48, [1956] AC 14, [1955] 3 WLR 410, HL.

*Hoffman-La Roche (F) & Co AG v Secretary of State for Trade and Industry* [1974] 2 All ER 1128, [1975] AC 295, [1974] 3 WLR 104, HL.

*IRC v National Federation of Self-Employed and Small Businesses Ltd* [1981] 2 All ER 93, [1982] AC 617, [1981] 2 WLR 722, HL.

*Midgley, Re, Barclays Bank Ltd v Midgley* [1955] 2 All ER 625, [1955] 1 Ch 576, [1955] 3 WLR 119.

*R v Boundary Commission for England, ex p Gateshead BC, R v Boundary Commission, ex p Foot* [1983] 1 All ER 1099, [1983] QB 600, [1983] 2 WLR 458, CA.

*R v Electricity Comrs, ex p London Electricity Joint Committee Co (1920) Ltd* [1924] 1 KB 171, [1923] All ER Rep 150, CA.

*R v Minister of Health, ex p Davis* [1929] 1 KB 619.

## Cases also cited
*A-G v West Gloucestershire Water Co* [1901] 2 Ch 339.

*Council of Civil Service Unions v Minister for the Civil Service* [1984] 3 All ER 935, [1984] 3 WLR 1174, HL.

## Appeal
William Oliver Smedley appealed against the decision of Woolf J, hearing the Crown Office List, on 7 December 1984 whereby he dismissed an application for judicial review by way of (i) an order for certiorari to remove into the Queen's Bench Division and quash the determination or intended determination of the Chancellor of the Exchequer that the undertaking referred to in the schedule to the draft statutory instrument entitled the European Communities (Definition of Treaties) (Undertaking on Supplementary Finance for the Community) Order 1984 could properly be regarded and specified as a Community treaty as defined by s 1(2) of the European Communities Act 1972, and (ii) alternatively, a declaration that the determination or intended determination was made ultra vires. The facts are set out in the judgment of Sir John Donaldson MR.

*Leolin Price QC, J B W McDonnell QC* and *Michael Ashe* for Mr Smedley.
*John Laws* for the Treasury.

*Cur adv vult*

19 December. The following judgments were delivered.

**SIR JOHN DONALDSON MR.** Mr William Oliver Smedley is, I am sure, a man of many parts. Today he seeks the assistance of the court in his capacity as Mr Smedley, British taxpayer and elector. What troubles him is an expressed intention by HM Treasury to pay the European Community a sum in excess of £121·5m out of the

Consolidated Fund and to do so without seeking the authority of Parliament in the form of an Appropriation Act or other similar statute. Instead, it would seem that the Treasury proposes to operate the special procedure provided by s 1 of the European Communities Act 1972, which involves laying a draft Order in Council before Parliament and, if that draft order is approved by affirmative resolution of both Houses of Parliament and an Order in Council is in fact made in those terms, to make the payment on the authority of s 2(3) of that Act.

On 28 November 1984 Mr Smedley obtained leave from Hodgson J to apply for relief by way of judicial review. His application came before Woolf J on 6 December and was dismissed on 7 December. His appeal to this court was heard on 12 and 13 December and, but for the fact that we received a message to the effect that a judgment given today would be as satisfactory as one given earlier and we welcomed the opportunity to put our judgments in writing, we had intended to give judgment on 14 December. Bearing in mind that at each stage the matter has been fully argued, there can be and is no complaint that the courts or the practitioners have been dilatory. Indeed in some other jurisdictions the timetable would be regarded with some surprise, not to say envy. I mention the matter not in any spirit of complacency, but merely in order to counterbalance the well-justified complaints which are sometimes made of the law's delays.

Section 1(2) of the 1972 Act defines the expressions 'the Treaties' and 'the Community Treaties' as they appear in the Act. It does so by referring to certain scheduled pre-accession treaties and to three other categories of treaty. Two of these three categories cover respectively the United Kingdom Accession Treaty and the Council Accession Decision, both of 22 January 1972. The third category is—

'any other treaty entered into by any of the Communities, with or without any of the member States, or entered into, as a treaty ancillary to any of the Treaties, by the United Kingdom'.

Section 1(3) of the Act then provides as follows:

'If Her Majesty by Order in Council declares that a treaty specified in the Order is to be regarded as one of the Community Treaties as herein defined, the Order shall be conclusive that it is to be so regarded; but a treaty entered into by the United Kingdom after the 22nd January 1972, other than a pre-accession treaty to which the United Kingdom accedes on terms settled on or before that date, shall not be so regarded unless it is so specified, nor be so specified unless a draft of the Order in Council has been approved by resolution of each House of Parliament.'

The word 'treaty' as distinct from 'the Treaties' is defined for the purposes of sub-ss (2) and (3) as including 'any international agreement, and any protocol or annex to a treaty or international agreement'.

Section 2(3) provides the Treasury with authority to charge on and issue out of the Consolidated Fund or, as the case may be, the National Loans Fund the amounts required to meet any Community obligation to make payments to any of the Communities or member states. In this context the expression 'Community obligation' means any obligation created or arising under the treaties.

It follows that if Her Majesty by Order in Council, the draft of which had previously been laid before and approved by resolution of each House of Parliament, were to declare that an international agreement is to be regarded as one of the Community treaties the Treasury would without further authority be entitled to make any payments called for by that agreement.

The Treasury took the first step down this procedural path when on or about 19 November 1984 a draft Order in Council was laid before both Houses of Parliament. This draft specified—

'Undertaking made by the Representatives of the Governments of the Member States, meeting within the Council on 2nd and 3rd October 1984, to make payments to the Community in 1984 to finance supplementary and amending budget No. 1, (Cmnd 9395).'

as being a treaty to be regarded as a Community treaty as defined in s 1(2) of the 1972 Act.

Before considering Mr Smedley's objections to this course and to the obvious intention to advise Her Majesty to make an Order in Council in the same terms if the draft is approved by both Houses of Parliament, I think that I should say a word about the respective roles of Parliament and the courts. Although the United Kingdom has no written constitution, it is a constitutional convention of the highest importance that the legislature and the judicature are separate and independent of one another, subject to certain ultimate rights of Parliament over the judicature which are immaterial for present purposes. It therefore behoves the courts to be ever sensitive to the paramount need to refrain from trespassing on the province of Parliament or, so far as this can be avoided, even appearing to do so. Although it is not a matter for me, I would hope and expect that Parliament would be similarly sensitive to the need to refrain from trespassing on the province of the courts.

Against that background, it would clearly be a breach of the constitutional conventions for this court, or any court, to express a view, let alone take any action, concerning the decision to lay this draft Order in Council before Parliament or concerning the wisdom or otherwise of Parliament approving that draft. Equally, as I made clear during the course of the argument, so far as I can see there can be no possible constitutional objection to Parliament debating this draft merely because this court is seised of Mr Smedley's complaint. The exercise on which Parliament would be engaged and that on which we are engaged are essentially different. That much is, I think, common ground.

However, counsel for the Treasury took the matter a little further when he submitted that, at the present stage when no Order in Council has been or could yet be made, it is premature for the court to consider Mr Smedley's application. There is obvious force in this submission, but it requires some further examination. It is the function of Parliament to legislate and legislation is necessarily in written form. It is the function of the courts to construe and interpret that legislation. Putting it in popular language, it is for Parliament to make the laws and for the courts to tell the nation, including members of both Houses of Parliament, what those laws mean. Furthermore, whilst Parliament is entirely independent of the courts in its freedom to enact whatever legislation it sees fit, legislation by Order in Council, statutory instrument or other subordinate means is in a quite different category, not being Parliamentary legislation. This subordinate legislation is subject to some degree of judicial control in the sense that it is within the province and authority of the courts to hold that particular examples are not authorised by statute, or as the case may be by the common law, and so are without legal force or effect.

At the present moment, there is no Order in Council to which Mr Smedley can object as being unauthorised. All that can be said is that it seems likely that, if both Houses of Parliament approve the draft Order in Council, Her Majesty will be advised to make and will make an order in the terms of the draft, whereupon the courts would without doubt be competent to consider whether or not the order was properly made in the sense of being intra vires.

In many, and possibly most, circumstances the proper course would undoubtedly be for the courts to invite the applicant to renew his application if and when an order was made, but in some circumstances an expression of view on questions of law which would arise for decision if Parliament were to approve a draft may be of service not only to the parties, but also to each House of Parliament itself. This course was adopted in *R v Electricity Comrs, ex p London Electricity Joint Committee Co (1920) Ltd* [1924] 1 KB 171, [1923] All ER Rep 150. In that case an inquiry was in progress, the cost of which would have been wholly wasted if, thereafter, the minister and Parliament had approved the scheme only to be told at that late stage that the scheme was ultra vires.

Similar considerations apply in the present case. It is apparent from the terms of the undertaking that the provision of the money is considered a matter of urgency. If we defer consideration of Mr Smedley's application until after both Houses of Parliament have considered the somewhat different question of whether each approves the draft Order in Council, we shall only have contributed an avoidable period of delay should the correct view be that an Order in Council in the terms of the draft would be valid and should only have contributed to what might be thought to be a waste of parliamentary time if the correct view is that such an Order in Council would be invalid.

One further point should be mentioned before turning to the substance of Mr Smedley's application. This is a submission by counsel for the Treasury that Mr Smedley has no sufficient interest within the meaning of RSC Ord 53, r 3(7). Woolf J did not find it necessary to decide this point and neither do I, although I agree with the judge that I should be extremely surprised to find myself obliged to uphold that submission.

The essence of Mr Smedley's complaint is that the undertaking to make the payment to the European Community is not 'a treaty ancillary to any of the Treaties' within the meaning of that phrase in s 1(2) of the 1972 Act and that for an Order in Council to declare that such a treaty is to be regarded as one of the Community treaties is ultra vires.

The factual background is that over the period 1970–75 the Community moved from a system whereby it was financed from contributions by member states to one whereby it was financed by what was known as its 'own resources'. The distinction is made clear in Council Decision 70/243 of 21 April 1970, art 4(1) of which declares that 'From 1 January 1975 the budget of the Communities shall, irrespective of other revenue, be financed entirely from the Communities' own resources'. This decision was incorporated into the Act of Accession (1972) by art 127. However this year a supplementary and amending budget has been produced and the member governments have thought it right that the expenditure contemplated by this budget, or by the original budget as amended, shall be met in part not out of the Community's own resources, but out of funds provided by the member states in the form of 'reimbursable advances'. This phrase is not defined, but is explained by para 3 of the undertaking, which records that—

> 'The Representatives of the Governments of the Member States take the view that the Council will adopt a regulation under Article 235 as the basis for the reimbursement of the above amounts to the Member States.'

The only other provisions of Community legislation which are or may be relevant are art 199 of the EEC Treaty, which provides that the revenue and expenditure shown in the budget should be in balance and art 1(5) of the Council Financial Regulation of 21 December 1977 (OJ L 356, p 1), which provides for supplementary or amending budgets in the event of unavoidable, exceptional or unforeseen circumstances, a situation which apparently arose in 1984.

Counsel for Mr Smedley submits that the international undertaking contravenes the requirement of art 127 of the Act of Accession (1972) and Council Decision 70/243 there referred to and, accordingly, is a departure from the Community treaties and so is incapable of being regarded as 'ancillary' to any of those treaties. That being so, any order declaring that it is to be so regarded is ultra vires.

In my judgment there is a simple answer to this submission. The concept of one treaty being 'ancillary' to another is not one of precision. There may be more than one view on whether a particular international agreement is or is not 'ancillary'. It is no doubt for this reason, amongst others, that Parliament has provided in s 1(3) of the 1972 Act for a system whereby an Order in Council shall be conclusive of what treaties are to be regarded as Community treaties and that no treaty entered into by the United Kingdom after 22 January 1972 shall be so regarded unless it is so characterised by an Order in Council. Furthermore, quite apart from whether a particular instrument would otherwise be regarded as 'ancillary' to the Community treaties, Parliament has retained the right to prevent it being so regarded by refusing to approve the draft Order in Council designed to achieve this result.

In that situation, the sole question for the court is whether the Order in Council, if made, would or would not be intra vires the power conferred by Parliament on those who would make it. This power does not derive from the affirmative resolution of the Houses of Parliament which, as I have explained, is a power of veto. It derives from a pre-existing power to be inferred from s 1 of the 1972 Act. In accordance with familiar principles of law, that power must be assumed to be limited to making an Order in Council in relation to an agreement which *could* properly be regarded as ancillary to the Community treaties.

And so I ask myself whether the undertaking *could* be so regarded. I do not ask myself whether I would so regard it. The only real challenge, as I have explained, is based on the submission that the undertaking conflicts with some of the provisions of the Community treaties. For my part I think that it may be open to doubt whether such a conflict would necessarily and in all circumstances disqualify an instrument from being regarded as ancillary to the Community treaties. However, I do not consider that there is any such inconsistency between the undertaking and the treaties. As was pointed out by Lord Denning MR in *H P Bulmer Ltd v J Bollinger SA* [1974] 2 All ER 1226, [1974] 1 Ch 410, Community instruments are not expressed against the background of English canons of construction and should not be so construed. As I read the Community treaties, they are designed to express principles. The relevant principle, so expressed, is that the Community budget should so far as possible, and thus usually, be entirely financed out of the Community's own resources, but this is not to say that it must in all circumstances be so financed. It is clear that, in the view of the member states, unusual circumstances have arisen in 1984 which have given rise to the need for a supplementary and amending budget. A temporary departure from the guiding principle set out in the Community treaties does not seem to me to be in any way inconsistent with the undertaking being properly regarded as ancillary to the Community treaties.

That objection apart, nothing could be more ancillary to the Community treaties than the provision of funds to enable the Community to fulfil its essential functions. Accordingly I am quite unable to hold that an Order in Council in the terms of the draft would be ultra vires the order-making power. On the contrary, I think that it would quite plainly be intra vires. I would dismiss the appeal.

**SLADE LJ.** The facts of this case have been stated in the judgment of Sir John Donaldson MR and I need not recapitulate them.

A preliminary question that arises on this appeal is whether or not Mr Smedley has 'sufficient interest' within the meaning of RSC Ord 53, r 3(7) to entitle him to apply for judicial review. Though counsel for the Treasury has not pressed this particular point very hard, he has submitted that Mr Smedley has no such interest. If this submission is correct, the appeal must fail in limine.

The speeches of their Lordships in *IRC v National Federation of Self-Employed and Small Businesses Ltd* [1981] 2 All ER 93, [1982] AC 617 well illustrate that there has been what Lord Roskill described as a 'change in legal policy' (see [1981] 2 All ER 93 at 116, [1982] AC 617 at 656), which has in recent years greatly relaxed the rules as to locus standi. Lord Diplock referred to a 'virtual abandonment' of the former restrictive rules as to the locus standi of persons seeking prerogative orders against authorities exercising governmental powers (see [1981] 2 All ER 93 at 104, [1982] AC 617 at 640). If the court had taken the view that Mr Smedley's application was of a frivolous nature, the wide discretion given to it by RSC Ord 53 would have enabled it to dispose of it appropriately. There has, however, been no suggestion that it is of this nature. It raises a serious question as to the powers of Her Majesty in Council to make an Order in Council in the form of the draft now before Parliament. The making of any such order would be likely to be followed automatically by the expenditure by the government of substantial sums from the Consolidated Fund in reliance on s 2 of the European Communities Act 1972. I do not feel much doubt that Mr Smedley, if only in his capacity as a taxpayer, has sufficient locus standi to raise this question by way of an application for judicial review; on the present state of the authorities, I cannot think that any such right of challenge belongs to the Attorney General alone.

The next question that arises is whether or not it is right that the court should pronounce on the question put to it by Mr Smedley at the present stage at a time when a draft Order in Council is before the Houses of Parliament and has not yet been considered by them. This is the issue which has caused me the greatest difficulty on this appeal. It is common ground that if and when the Order in Council has been laid before and approved by the two Houses no questions of parliamentary sovereignty or privilege would prevent the court from declaring, if it thought this right, that an Order in Council in these terms was invalid as having been made ultra vires the power conferred on Her Majesty in Council by s 1 of the 1972 Act (see, for example, *F Hoffman-La Roche & Co AG v Secretary of State for Trade and Industry* [1974] 2 All ER 1128 at 1145, [1975] AC 295 at 354 per Lord Wilberforce).

Counsel for the Treasury, however, has submitted in effect that, while there would be nothing to prevent the court (as did the judge) from expressing an opinion *adverse* to Mr Smedley's submissions of law in the course of dismissing his application, it would be wrong for it at this stage to grant him any relief, by way of declaration or otherwise, if it were to consider these submissions well founded. To grant any such relief as matters stand, counsel for the Treasury suggested, would constitute an unjustifiable interference with the procedures of Parliament; on no footing, he suggested, should relief be granted to the applicant at the present time.

However, if this court were of the opinion that the present parliamentary position prevented it from expressing any opinion as to the legal position in support of Mr Smedley's submissions, the same considerations would in my judgment inevitably prevent us from expressing any opinion to the contrary effect. If we were to take this view as to the effect of the parliamentary position, the proper course would be for us (and would have been for the judge) simply to dismiss the application on the grounds that it was premature, even though this would not have prevented Mr Smedley from making any new application if and when the Order in Council had been approved by both Houses of Parliament.

I therefore think it inevitable that this court should carefully address its mind to the question whether or not a decision on the legal issues now before it, given at this present moment, would constitute an interference with the functions of Parliament. If it would, this court should simply dismiss the appeal on the grounds that this application was premature and say nothing further on the interesting and important legal issues involved.

The answer to this question must, I think, depend on an analysis of the respective functions of Parliament, Her Majesty in Council and the courts in the context of s 1 of the 1972 Act and the proposed Order in Council. The operative part of the draft Order in Council simply provides:

'The treaty specified in the Schedule to this Order is to be regarded as a Community Treaty as defined in section 1(2) of the European Communities Act 1972.'

The schedule refers to—

'Undertaking made by the Representatives of the Governments of the Member States, meeting within the Council on 2nd and 3rd October 1984, to make payments to the Community in 1984 to finance supplementary and amending budget No. 1, (Cmnd 9395).'

The reasons why an Order in Council is considered necessary are these. In view of the wording of s 1(2) of the 1972 Act the undertaking can qualify as a Community Treaty within that subsection *only* if it amounts to 'any other treaty . . . entered into, as a treaty ancillary to any of the Treaties, by the United Kingdom'.

Section 1(3) of the 1972 Act provides:

'If Her Majesty by Order in Council declares that a treaty specified in the Order is to be regarded as one of the Community Treaties as herein defined, the Order shall be conclusive that it is to be so regarded; but a treaty entered into by the United Kingdom after the 22nd January 1972, other than a pre-accession treaty to which the United Kingdom accedes on terms settled on or before that date, shall not be so regarded unless it is so specified, nor be so specified unless a draft of the Order in Council has been approved by resolution of each House of Parliament.'

It follows that by virtue of s 1 the undertaking, not being a pre-accession treaty within this exception, (a) is incapable of being regarded as one of 'the Community Treaties' unless it is specified in an Order in Council, (b) is incapable of being specified in an Order in Council unless a draft of the Order in Council has first been approved by resolution of each House of Parliament.

The function conferred on the two Houses of Parliament by s 1(3) in relation to the undertaking will be, in effect, simply that of deciding whether or not to approve the draft Order in Council. If Parliament were to give a negative decision by withholding its approval, that would be that: the Order in Council could not be made. If, however, Parliament were to give its approval, then, at least according to the wording of s 1 of the 1972 Act, two consequences would follow: (1) Her Majesty by Order in Council would have the power to specify the undertaking as one which was to be regarded as a Community treaty as defined in s 1(2); (2) any such Order in Council would be 'conclusive' that the undertaking was to be so regarded.

I have somewhat laboured these distinctions between the respective functions of Parliament and Her Majesty in Council in the present case, for the purpose of demonstrating the somewhat limited role which is allotted to Parliament by s 1(3) of the 1972 Act. This role is analogous to a power of veto. If it withholds its approval from the draft Order in Council, the order cannot be made. If, however, the approval of Parliament is given, Her Majesty in Council is left with a discretion whether or not to make the order. There is no possible question of the court seeking or being able to control the exercise of the parliamentary power of veto. However, I can see no reason why the exercise of the last-mentioned discretion given to Her Majesty in Council should not be open to attack in the courts by the process of judicial review, subject to the stringent restrictions on any such attack imposed by what has come to be known as the *Wednesbury* principle (see *Associated Provincial Picture Houses Ltd v Wednesbury Corp* [1947] 2 All ER 680, [1947] 1 KB 223). Equally, if the analysis of the position set out earlier in this judgment is correct, I can see no good reason why a decision by the courts given at the present stage and relating to the proposed exercise of the discretion of Her Majesty in Council should be said to usurp or interfere with what I conceive to be the function of Parliament in this present context, namely that of deciding whether or not to exercise what is in substance a power of veto over the proposed Order in Council. Indeed, if this court were to consider that the proposed order would be beyond the legal powers of Her Majesty in Council, I would anticipate that, to echo the words of Younger LJ in *R v Electricity Comrs, ex p London Electricity Joint Committee Co (1920) Ltd* [1924] 1 KB 171 at 213, [1923] All ER Rep 150 at 165—

'the interference of the Court in such a case as this, and at this stage, so far from being even in the most diluted sense of the words a challenge to its supremacy, will be an assistance to Parliament.'

The latter decision seems to me good authority for the proposition that, where some administrative order or regulation is required by statute to be approved by resolution of both Houses of Parliament, the court can in an appropriate case intervene by way of judicial review before the Houses have given their approval, even though I conceive that in at least most such cases the only appropriate form of relief (if any) could be by way of declaration. This is a jurisdiction which must of course be exercised with great circumspection and with close regard to the dangers of usurping or encroaching on any function which statute has specifically conferred on Parliament or on the functions of Parliament in general. In the present case, however, I am satisfied that a decision on Mr Smedley's application will involve no such usurpation or encroachment. I should add that it is common ground that the mere existence of these present proceedings need place no fetter on the course of the impending debate in Parliament. For these reasons, I would reject the submission of counsel for the Treasury that the application is premature and that no decision should be made in relation to it at the present stage.

However, from what has already been said, two points are in my opinion clear. First, any attack by Mr Smedley on the proposed Order in Council has to be based on the proposed exercise of the discretion of Her Majesty in Council. Second, if it is to succeed, it must be shown that it falls within the *Wednesbury* principle.

Counsel in his argument on behalf of Mr Smedley has implicitly accepted this burden. He has submitted that as a matter of law the undertaking is *incapable* of being properly regarded as a 'treaty ancillary to any of the Treaties' within the meaning of those words as used in s 1(2) of the 1972 Act. It must follow, in his submission, that Her Majesty in Council would be acting subject to a misdirection in law and beyond the powers conferred by s 1(3) of the 1972 Act in making a declaration in the form embodied in the draft Order in Council.

If the premise of this argument were correct, I think that the conclusion would inevitably follow; and indeed counsel for the Treasury has not contended to the contrary. He has not submitted in such circumstances that the 'conclusive' provision at the beginning of s 1(3) would preclude the intervention of the court by way of judicial review. However, I am not able to accept the premise.

In the present context, it seems to me particularly significant that the phrase 'ancillary to', as used in s 1(2) of the 1972 Act, is an imprecise expression of wide and somewhat uncertain import. It is clear that one of the legislative purposes of the opening sentence of s 1(3) was to eliminate any uncertainty that might otherwise exist in relation to the status of a particular 'treaty' by the making of an appropriate Order in Council. The word 'treaty' is itself given a wide meaning by s 1(4) which defines it, for the purposes of sub-s (2) and (3), as including 'any international agreement, and any protocol or annex to a treaty or international agreement'. I do not suggest that s 1(3) would empower Her Majesty in Council to purport to bring into the ambit of the 'Community Treaties' an international agreement which demonstrably had no connection whatever with 'the Treaties' as defined in s 1(2). However, I do not think that the legislature can have contemplated that the courts would intervene in a case where Her Majesty by Order in Council had seen fit to make a declaration in regard to a particular treaty which was *capable* of being properly regarded as being 'a treaty ancillary to any of the Treaties', whether or not the contrary view might be arguable on the particular facts. One of the very purposes of the wide discretion given to Her Majesty in Council, linked to the somewhat imprecise description 'ancillary to', must have been to avoid any such dispute in borderline cases.

In his very able argument in the present case, counsel for Mr Smedley, having taken us through the relevant provisions of the 1972 Act, 'the Treaties' and the undertaking, has failed to persuade me that as a matter of law the undertaking is incapable of being properly regarded as a 'treaty ancillary to any of the Treaties' in the relevant sense. At first sight, indeed as I think he frankly recognised, there are formidable obstacles in the way of any such submission, since the very purpose of the undertaking is to provide money which the Community consider that they require to expend for the purpose of achieving the objectives of the EEC Treaty and the other treaties mentioned in s 1. There is therefore at least a very close connection between the undertaking and the existing treaties.

Nevertheless, counsel for Mr Smedley forcefully supported his submission by reference to a number of points of which I think the following were the essential features. He submitted: (1) the purpose of the undertaking was to enable the institutions of the Community to budget for expenditure in 1984 in excess of the Communities' 'own resources'; (2) the undertaking would result in the Communities exceeding the limits of expenditure imposed by the combined effect of the Community treaties; (3) the undertaking, being thus entered into in contravention of the Community treaties, could not be regarded as 'ancillary' to them.

For the reasons given by Sir John Donaldson MR, I am not convinced that the undertaking would necessarily conflict with the provisions of the Community treaties, when read as a whole. But, even if in some respects they did conflict, I cannot accept that this would necessarily prevent this international agreement from being properly described as 'ancillary' to the Community treaties. Counsel for Mr Smedley, while not attempting an exhaustive definition of the word 'ancillary', has submitted that the phrase 'as ancillary' connotes 'assistance of a subordinate or subservient kind'. Even accepting this submission for present purposes, any agreement which is ancillary to an earlier agreement in this sense may well involve some variation of that agreement and thus, in one sense, a measure of conflict with it. However, the fact that such variation may be thought in some respects to involve a departure from the terms of the earlier agreement, even on a point of principle, does not in my view inevitably prevent the subsequent agreement from being properly described as 'ancillary' to the earlier agreement, according to the ordinary meaning of words. This, I think, must be a question of degree according to the particular facts of each case. It is just the sort of point which the legislature by the 1972 Act has seen fit to leave to Her Majesty in Council to decide, subject to the parliamentary power of veto.

For these reasons, and the other reasons given by Sir John Donaldson MR, I can see no good reason for concluding that the proposed order if made by Her Majesty in Council would be ultra vires the power conferred by s 1(3) of the 1972 Act. I would accordingly dismiss this appeal.

**LLOYD LJ.** I agree.

*Appeal dismissed. Leave to appeal to the House of Lords refused.*

Solicitors: *Bower Cotton & Bower* (for Mr Smedley); *Treasury Solicitor.*

Frances Rustin    Barrister.

# R v Hampshire County Council, ex parte Ellerton

COURT OF APPEAL, CIVIL DIVISION
O'CONNOR, MAY AND SLADE LJJ
2 NOVEMBER, 20 DECEMBER 1984

*Fire brigade – Discipline – Exercise of disciplinary power – Standard of proof – Fireman charged with corrupt practice – Hearing before appeal tribunal of fire authority – Whether charge to be decided on civil or criminal standard of proof – Fire Services (Discipline) Regulations 1948.*

The applicant, a fire officer, was found guilty of two charges of corrupt practice, laid against him under the Fire Services (Discipline) Regulations 1948 and he appealed to an appeal tribunal of the fire authority. The appeal tribunal held that the case should be decided on the civil standard of proof and dismissed the appeal. The applicant applied for an order of certiorari to bring up and quash the tribunal's decision on the ground that it had wrongly applied the civil standard of proof. He contended that in disciplinary proceedings the criminal standard of proof, namely beyond reasonable doubt, should apply, and that since the fire service was a force which had a statutory code of discipline, namely the 1948 regulations, drafted in the language of the criminal law, the tribunal should have applied the criminal standard of proof. The judge dismissed the application. The applicant appealed.

**Held** – The appeal would be dismissed for the following reasons—
(1) A disciplinary tribunal which had a procedure for adjudicating on issues which arose from the contractual relationship of employer and employee was by its nature a

tribunal concerned with civil and not criminal matters and the appropriate standard of proof was therefore the civil standard, although the discharge of that burden varied according to the nature and seriousness of the allegation in issue (see p 602 *h* to p 603 *b*, p 604 *f*, p 607 *c* and *e* to *j* and p 608 *h j*, post); *Hornal v Neuburger Products Ltd* [1956] 3 All ER 970 and *Khawaja v Secretary of State for the Home Dept* [1983] 1 All ER 765 applied; dictum of McNeill J in *R v Police Complaints Board, ex p Madden* [1983] 2 All ER at 371 considered.

(2) Although the provisions of the 1948 regulations were drafted in the language of the criminal law they laid down procedures for adjudication on a series of offences, none of which (with one possible exception) was a criminal offence, and the penalties imposed for those offences related solely to the employee's terms of employment and were not sanctions of the criminal law. It followed that since the appeal tribunal of the fire authority was a domestic tribunal, and in the absence of any express provisions in the 1948 regulations or the Fire Services Act 1947, the appropriate standard of proof was the civil standard (see p 602 *h j*, p 604 *e f*, p 607 *c* to *j* and p 608 *h j*, post).

### Notes

For disciplinary procedure in the fire services, see 18 Halsbury's Laws (4th edn) para 585.

For the Fire Services Act 1947, see 13 Halsbury's Statutes (3rd edn) 696.

For the Fire Services (Discipline) Regulations 1948, see 9 Halsbury's Statutory Instruments (5th reissue) 8.

### Cases referred to in judgments

*Bhandari v Advocates Committee* [1956] 3 All ER 742, [1956] 1 WLR 1442, PC.
*Blyth v Blyth* [1966] 1 All ER 524, [1966] AC 643, [1966] 2 WLR 634, HL.
*Hornal v Neuburger Products Ltd* [1956] 3 All ER 970, [1957] 1 QB 247, [1956] 3 WLR 1034, CA.
*Khawaja v Secretary of State for the Home Dept* [1983] 1 All ER 765, [1984] AC 74, [1983] 2 WLR 321, HL.
*Maynard v Osmond* [1977] 1 All ER 64, [1977] 1 QB 240, [1976] 3 WLR 711, CA.
*R v Police Complaints Board, ex p Madden, R v Police Complaints Board, ex p Rhone* [1983] 2 All ER 353, [1983] 1 WLR 447.
*Wright v Wright* (1948) 77 CLR 191.

### Appeal

Ronald Andrew Ellerton appealed against the decision of McCullough J, hearing the Crown Office List, on 23 February 1984 whereby the judge dismissed an application for judicial review by way of an order of certiorari to bring up and quash the decision of the respondents, Hampshire County Council, in their capacity as a fire authority made on 1 September 1983 dismissing an appeal by the appellant pursuant to reg 8(5) of the Fire Services (Discipline) Regulations 1948 against findings of guilt by the chief fire officer in relation to charges proffered against the appellant on 24 February 1983. The facts are set out in the judgment of O'Connor LJ.

*Anthony Scrivener QC* and *Andrew Bano* for the appellant.
*Robert Reid QC* and *J S Gibbons* for the respondents.

*Cur adv vult*

20 December. The following judgments were delivered.

**O'CONNOR LJ.** The appellant is a divisional officer in the Hampshire Fire Brigade. On 18 April 1983 he was before the chief fire officer on six disciplinary charges. He was found guilty of two charges arising out of the use of a fire brigade vehicle to move a load of tree cuttings from his house to the local authority dump. He was acquitted of the other four charges. The penalty imposed was £40 stoppage of pay. The appellant appealed to the respondent fire authority, that is the Hampshire County Council, by virtue of reg 8(5) of the Fire Services (Discipline) Regulations 1948, SI 1948/545. The appeal is a rehearing under reg 9.

The appeal was heard by an appeal panel of the fire authority composed of five councillors on 1 September 1983. The appeal was dismissed and the punishment increased to £100 stoppage of pay. The facts giving rise to this appeal were set out by McCullough J:

> 'The hearing of [the appellant's] appeal was to take place before a panel of five members of the Hampshire County Council acting on behalf of the County Council as the fire authority. The chief fire officer was to be represented by Mr A L Webb, assistant county secretary of Hampshire County Council. He would present the case against [the appellant]. [The appellant] was to conduct his own defence with the assistance of Mr T Garland acting as the accused's friend. Mr J L Edgell, personnel services manager of the Manpower Services Unit of the Hampshire County Council, was to act as clerk to the panel. On 19 August 1983 Mr Webb wrote to each of the five members of the panel. A copy of his letter was sent to [the appellant]. This set out, inter alia, the procedure which Mr Webb suggested the panel might care to adopt. He said: "The issue open to the Members will be to decide whether or not the charges as alleged have been made out and in the absence of any authority within the Regulations themselves Members may care to adopt the civil proceedings onus of proof, namely the balance of probabilities." [The appellant] took the view that this set the standard too low and that proof beyond reasonable doubt was appropriate. The proceedings were opened by Mr Edgell confirming that the hearing would proceed in accordance with the procedure laid down in Mr Webb's letter. Mr Garland submitted that the charges should be proved beyond all reasonable doubt rather than on the balance of probabilities. In support he referred to a passage in Pain *Manual of Fire Service Law* (1951) p 137 which read: "In deciding the question of guilt, the tribunal should bear in mind that the accused is to be treated as innocent, unless the evidence shows him to have been guilty beyond all reasonable doubt." He referred also to guidance to the same effect in some Fire Service College training notes. Mr Webb made submissions in accordance with his letter. After the panel had taken advice from Mr Edgell it decided "that it was appropriate for the case to be decided on the balance of probabilities, as was customary in employment tribunals of this nature".'

The judge held that the civil standard of proof was the right standard for this domestic tribunal, and refused judicial review. The appellant appeals to this court. Counsel for the appellant has submitted that the judge was wrong to hold as he did and that in disciplinary proceedings in the fire service the criminal standard of proof should be used. He submitted that the fire service is a disciplined force with a statutory code of discipline drafted in the language of the criminal law and that the criminal standard of proof was appropriate.

The general rule is that in criminal cases the criminal standard of proof beyond reasonable doubt is required, while in civil cases the civil standard of proof on the balance of probabilities is sufficient. Sometimes the same facts can give rise to criminal and civil liability. For example, in *Hornal v Neuberger Products Ltd* [1956] 3 All ER 970, [1957] 1 QB 247 the defendant falsely represented that goods sold had been factory reconditioned. He could have been charged with the criminal offence of obtaining money by false pretences, in which event the prosecution would have had to prove that he had made the representation beyond reasonable doubt, whereas in the civil action for fraud the Court of Appeal held that proof on the balance of probabilities was sufficient. Denning LJ said ([1956] 3 All ER 970 at 973, [1957] 1 QB 247 at 258):

> '[The judge] reviewed all the cases and held rightly that the standard of proof depends on the nature of the issue. The more serious the allegation the higher the degree of probability that is required; but it need not, in a civil case, reach the very high standard required by the criminal law.'

*Hornal* was approved by the House of Lords in *Blyth v Blyth* [1966] 1 All ER 524, [1966] AC 643.

More recently the question of the standard of proof was considered by the House of Lords in *Khawaja v Secretary of State for the Home Dept* [1983] 1 All ER 765, [1984] AC 74. It is as well to remember the context in which this matter fell for decision. Where a person detained as an illegal immigrant seeks judicial review of the decision of the Secretary of State it is for the applicant to make a prima facie case; thereafter the burden shifts for '. . . in cases where the exercise of executive discretion interferes with liberty or property rights the burden of justifying the legality of the decision is on the executive' (see [1983] 1 All ER 765 at 782, [1984] AC 74 at 112 per Lord Scarman quoting Lord Atkin). Paragraph (3) of the headnote reads ([1984] AC 74 at 76):·

> 'That on an application for judicial review of an order detaining a person as an illegal entrant it was for the executive to prove to the satisfaction of the court on the balance of probabilities the facts relied on by the immigration officer as justifying his conclusion that the applicant was an illegal entrant.'

Lord Scarman considered the question of standard of proof, and reviewed the cases (see [1983] 1 All ER 765 at 782–784, [1984] AC 74 at 112–114). Three other members of the House expressly agreed with him on this topic. I need only quote two passages from his speech which give valuable guidance on how to approach the problem. He said ([1983] 1 All ER 765 at 783, [1984] AC 74 at 112):

> '. . . I have come to the conclusion that the choice between the two standards is not one of any great moment. It is largely a matter of words. There is no need to import into this branch of the civil law the formula used for the guidance of juries in criminal cases. The civil standard as interpreted and applied by the civil courts will meet the ends of justice.'

He concluded by saying ([1983] 1 All ER 765 at 784, [1984] AC 74 at 114):

> 'Accordingly, it is enough to say that, where the burden lies on the executive to justify the exercise of a power of detention, the facts relied on as justification must be proved to the satisfaction of the court. A preponderance of probability suffices; but the degree of probability must be such that the court is satisfied. The strictness of the criminal formula is unnecessary to enable justice to be done; and its lack of flexibility in a jurisdiction where the technicalities of the law of evidence must not be allowed to become the master of the court could be a positive disadvantage inhibiting the efficacy of the developing safeguard of judicial review in the field of public law.'

Although the House of Lords was considering the burden and standard of proof in the proceedings for judicial review, it follows of necessity that the immigration officer in making up his mind to detain a person as an illegal immigrant should use the same standard in assessing the evidence available to him.

If the flexibility of the civil standard is desirable in cases of judicial review, then a fortiori it is desirable in proceedings before domestic tribunals, particularly those deciding disputes arising out of a person's employment.

I have no doubt that proceedings under the provisions of the 1948 regulations are not criminal proceedings. The disciplinary tribunal and the fire authority are domestic tribunals, and in the absence of any express provision in the Act or regulations prima facie the civil standard of proof is appropriate. Counsel for the appellant recognised this, but advanced two reasons for saying that we should declare that offences under these regulations must be proved beyond reasonable doubt.

Firstly, he submitted that this statutory code is couched in the language of the criminal law for the 1948 regulations talk about 'offences', 'the accused', 'charges', 'punishments', and that this language used in relation to a disciplined force is enough to take proof of 'offences' out of the civil standard into the criminal. I cannot accept this submission. It is only necessary to look at the schedule to the regulations, which sets out the 'Code of

Offences against Discipline'. As the offences may lead to dismissal, reduction in rank, stoppage of pay, reprimand or caution, one would expect them to be of varying degrees of seriousness. There is a long list of offences, none of which are necessarily criminal, save perhaps wilful damage to clothing. Some crimes might also involve breaches of the code, for example a fireman who stole property while fighting a fire would offend against para 7(a) 'improperly using his position as a member of the fire brigade for his private advantage' and probably para 11(c) as well, '[acting] in a manner likely to bring discredit on the reputation of the fire brigade'. The fact that the language of the criminal law is used to lay down the procedure for adjudicating on a whole series of activities which form no part of the criminal law, but do form part of the relationship between master and servant, does not persuade me that we should depart from the prima facie rule.

Secondly, counsel for the appellant submitted that it was recognised that the criminal standard was used in disciplinary proceedings under the Police (Discipline) Regulations 1977, SI 1977/580 and that by analogy the same standard should be used for firemen. Broadly speaking, the code of offences found in Sch 2 to those regulations are not all that different to the 1948 regulations, but I do not wish to say more on the topic of the 1977 regulations, since we have not heard argument from the Police Federation, beyond saying that I doubt that the proposition asserted by McNeill J in *R v Police Complaints Board, ex p Madden* [1983] 2 All ER 353, [1983] 1 WLR 447 is correct. In that case the issue was whether the Police Board could bring disciplinary proceedings in respect of alleged criminal conduct where the Director of Public Prosecutions had refused to prosecute. McNeill J said ([1983] 2 All ER 353 at 371, [1983] 1 WLR 447 at 467):

'In dealing with the argument of counsel for the applicants on double jeopardy, counsel for the board contended that this principle, or a necessary extension of or gloss on it, rendered unfair a second attempt, on the same evidence and in the same circumstances, to put a police officer at risk of sanctions even if under the disciplinary and not under the criminal code. Indeed, he said, repeated investigation of the same facts could be oppressive and could bring the scheme into disrepute. One should remember that the standard of proof of police disciplinary charges is the same as that of criminal offences. He said the board ought not to be able to say on a point of sufficiency or reliability of evidence that the Director of Public Prosecutions may have got it wrong. I accept that the criminal standard of proof does apply to disciplinary charges. This seems to follow from cases such as *Bhandari v Advocates Committee* [1956] 3 All ER 742, [1956] 1 WLR 1442 and *Maynard v Osmond* [1977] 1 All ER 64, [1977] QB 240 and from the wording of the Police (Discipline) Regulations 1977, SI 1977/580, which reflects a "criminal style" approach to disciplinary charges. I do not think that such charges can properly be established on a "reasonable belief in guilt" basis such as may be acceptable in the "unfair dismissal" aspect of employment law . . .'

In *Bhandari v Advocates Committee* [1956] 3 All ER 742, [1956] 1 WLR 1442 the Privy Council were concerned with disciplinary proceedings against an advocate in Kenya. At the end of their advice their Lordships said ([1956] 3 All ER 742 at 744–745, [1956] 1 WLR 1442 at 1452):

'With regard to the onus of proof, the Court of Appeal said: "We agree that in every allegation of professional misconduct involving an element of deceit or moral turpitude a high standard of proof is called for, and we cannot envisage any body of professsional men sitting in judgment on a colleague who would be content to condemn on a mere balance of probabilities." This seems to their Lordships an adequate description of the duty of a tribunal such as the Advocates Committee, and there is no reason to think that either the committee or the Supreme Court applied any lower standard of proof.'

I do not think that the requirement that something more than the 'mere balance of probabilities' is required is to be read as requiring proof beyond reasonable doubt. It is just another way of saying what has been said in *Hornal* and *Khawaja* that the civil standard is flexible.

In *Maynard v Osmond* [1977] 1 All ER 64, [1977] QB 240 one of the issues was whether disciplinary proceedings against a police officer should await the determination of a civil action. Lord Denning MR said ([1977] 1 All ER 64 at 78–79, [1977] QB 240 at 251–252):

> 'The determination of that issue will not in law be binding in the disciplinary proceedings, but it is sure to have a considerable effect on them. It is plain that *either* Pc Maynard *or* Sergeant Hewitson has been guilty of attempting to pervert the course of justice: *either* Pc Maynard by making false charges against Sergeant Hewitson *or* Sergeant Hewitson by making false charges against Pc Maynard and getting the other officers to join in making those false charges. At present only Pc Maynard has been charged with disciplinary offences. But if he is acquitted of them, it may well be thought that Sergeant Hewitson should be charged in his turn. Nor need the matter stop at disciplinary charges. One or other may have to face a charge of perjury. In these circumstances, arrangements have been made for the trial in October of the civil action by David O'Connor against Sergeant Hewitson. But it may not be decisive. Much may turn on the burden of proof which would not be the same as in the disciplinary charges. Or, there may be an appeal, and it would not be desirable for the disciplinary charges to be delayed pending an appeal. So we must decide that question whether or not Pc Maynard is entitled to be legally represented at the hearing of the disciplinary charges.'

I see no reason to think that when Lord Denning MR spoke of 'burden of proof' he meant other than what he said, and I find nothing in this case which touches on the standard of proof. I am not persuaded by these cases that there is any reason for departing from the prima facie position.

Lastly, counsel for the appellant submitted that even if the civil standard of proof is the appropriate standard there was no evidence that the tribunal appreciated that the standard is flexible. Like the judge I see no reason to think that the members of the tribunal would not have realised that the more serious the alleged offence against discipline so the greater the degree of probability required to tip the balance.

I would dismiss this appeal.

**MAY LJ.** This is an appeal from an order of McCullough J of 23 February 1984 dismissing an application by the appellant for judicial review in the nature of certiorari to bring up and quash the decision of the Hampshire County Council in their capacity as a fire authority dismissing on 1 September 1983 the appellant's appeal against the decision of the chief fire officer that he had committed two offences of corrupt practice contrary to para (7) of the schedule to the Fire Services (Discipline) Regulations 1948, SI 1948/545.

At all material times the appellant was a divisional officer in the Hampshire Fire Brigade. On 18 April 1983 he faced six charges laid against him on 24 February 1983 by his assistant chief fire officer under the 1948 regulations. He was found guilty of two of the charges against him, the other four were dismissed. By a memorandum to the chief fire officer dated 21 April 1983 the appellant invoked his right of appeal against the chief fire officer's decision under reg 8(5) of the 1948 regulations.

The hearing of the appellant's appeal was arranged to take place before a panel of five members of the Hampshire County Council acting on behalf of that council as the fire authority. The chief fire officer was to be represented by a Mr Webb, assistant county secretary of the county council. He was to present the case against the appellant. The latter intended to conduct his own defence with the assistance of a Mr Garland acting as the accused's friend. A Mr Edgell, personnel services manager of the Manpower Services Unit of the Hampshire County Council, was to act as clerk to the panel.

On 19 August 1983 Mr Webb wrote to each of the five members of the panel, sending a copy of his letter to the appellant. In his letter Mr Webb suggested the procedure which the panel might care to adopt at the hearing of the appeal and said:

'The issue open to the Members will be to decide whether or not the charges as alleged have been made out and in the absence of any authority within the Regulations themselves Members may care to adopt the civil proceedings onus of proof, namely the balance of probabilities.'

The appellant has throughout been advised and taken the view that the proper standard of proof in relation to charges under the regulations is the criminal standard of proof, namely proof beyond reasonable doubt.

Accordingly, when the hearing of the appeal started, Mr Garland submitted on the appellant's behalf that the criminal standard of proof should indeed be applied. Mr Webb submitted in his turn that the standard of proof should be that applied in ordinary domestic disciplinary proceedings, that is to say the civil burden of proof. After taking advice from Mr Edgell, the panel decided 'that it was appropriate for the case to be decided on the balance of probabilities, as was customary in employment tribunals of this nature'. Having then heard the evidence in the case, the panel upheld the decision of the chief fire officer and dismissed the appellant's appeal. It is that decision which the appellant now seeks to have quashed in these proceedings for judicial review.

Before the judge below two main points were taken on the appellant's behalf. First, that in reaching their decision the panel of the authority wrongly applied the standard of proof applicable to civil proceedings. They ought, it was said, to have applied the standard of proof applicable to criminal proceedings, that is to say proof beyond reasonable doubt. The second point, which was based on the suggestion that in considering their sentence the panel had information before them about the appellant which they ought not to have had, was not persisted in before us. The judge thought, and I respectfully agree, that within the first point there are in truth two questions which have to be considered. First, were the panel correct in applying the civil rather than the criminal burden of proof? Second, did the panel appreciate that in cases where the civil burden is appropriate, there will nevertheless be degrees of probability within that standard which would depend on the subject matter of the case under consideration?

The judge held that the panel had been correct in dealing with the appeal on the basis of the civil burden of proof. He also held that the panel would certainly have appreciated that the relative seriousness of the allegations was a matter to be taken into account in coming to a conclusion whether that burden had been discharged.

Before us counsel for the appellant referred to s 1 of the Fire Services Act 1947 and the obligations imposed thereby on a fire authority. He submitted that in order that a fire service should be so organised and able to comply with the statutory duties imposed on them, it had to be what he described as a 'disciplined force', like the police. This is a phrase which, speaking for myself, I have heard on a number of occasions before this case, for instance in relation to prison officers. I think that it is difficult to give it any special meaning. Experience in industrial matters shows that it is necessary in most, if not all, organisations to have a disciplined work-force, to a greater or less extent. In the context of this application I think that the phrase can mean no more than that a particular fire service will have recognised ranks, each of them with recognised responsibilities, and that orders will be given on duty and at fires which will have to be obeyed promptly and without question in order that the fire services' job should be done properly.

Counsel then drew our attention to the 1948 regulations made under s 17(1) of the 1947 Act, to which I have already referred. He relied in particular on the terminology used in those regulations: for instance, the references in regs 2 and 3 to a 'charge'; the reference in reg 4 to 'the accused'; and the fact that, if the chief officer is not satisfied with any explanation that he might offer, he can be ordered to appear at the hearing of his case. Counsel went on to refer to the 'punishments' provided for by reg 13 and also to the schedule to the regulations, which is headed 'Code of Offences against Discipline'. He submitted that the 1948 regulations taken as a whole clearly have the flavour of criminal proceedings. They provided for what was in truth an adversarial trial under the code imposed by the 1948 regulations, which were themselves made pursuant to statutory powers. He suggested that the situation thereunder was very different from the usual contractual situation that rises in the normal master/servant relationship.

He compared the similarity between the 1948 Regulations and the corresponding Police (Discipline) Regulations 1977, SI 1977/580, and cited the dictum in *R v Police Complaints Board, ex p Madden* [1983] 2 All ER 353 at 371, [1983] 1 WLR 447 at 467, where McNeill J said:

'I accept that the criminal standard of proof does apply to disciplinary charges. This seems to follow from cases such as *Bhandari v Advocates Committee* [1956] 3 All ER 742, [1956] 1 WLR 1442 and *Maynard v Osmond* [1977] 1 All ER 64, [1977] QB 240 and from the wording of the Police (Discipline) Regulations 1977, SI 1977/580, which reflects a "criminal style" approach to disciplinary charges.'

That dictum in effect encapsulated the submissions of counsel for the appellant to us in the instant appeal.

Counsel also referred us to a brief passage from Pain *Manual of Fire Service Law* (1951) p 137 in which the author expressed the view that in deciding the question of guilt in these disciplinary cases the tribunal should bear in mind that the accused is to be treated as innocent, unles the evidence shows him to have been guilty beyond all reasonable doubt. In other words, that the criminal burden of proof was the appropriate one. We were told that such a view is also taken by the Fire Service College training notes in general use.

Counsel for the appellant also referred the court to the recent decision of the House of Lords in *Khawaja v Secretary of State for the Home Dept* [1983] 1 All ER 765 esp at 782–784, [1984] AC 74 esp at 112–114 per Lord Scarman where he considered this question of the appropriate burden of proof in the circumstances of that case, which, it will be remembered, was one concerning an alleged illegal immigrant. In considering the various earlier authorities Lord Scarman directed particular attention to the words of Morris LJ in *Hornal v Neuburger Products Ltd* [1956] 3 All ER 970 at 978, [1957] 1 QB 247 at 266 and said ([1983] 1 All ER 765 at 783–784, [1984] AC 74 at 113–114):

'The court held that the standard was the balance of probabilities. But, since the degree of probability required to tip the balance will vary according to the nature and gravity of the issue—"no real mischief results from an acceptance of the fact that there is some difference of approach in civil actions ... the very elements of gravity become a part of the whole range of circumstances which have to be weighed in the scale when deciding as to the balance of probabilities." (See [1956] 3 All ER 970 at 978, [1957] 1 QB 247 at 266 per Morris LJ.) ... The flexibility of the civil standard of proof suffices to ensure that the court will require the high degree of probability which is appropriate to what is at stake. "The nature and gravity of an issue necessarily determines the manner of attaining reasonable satisfaction of the truth of the issue" (see Dixon J in *Wright v Wright* (1948) 77 CLR 191 at 210).'

Counsel then posed the rhetorical question in the context of the present case: where on the civil scale does the burden lie? He stressed that this will necessarily vary from offence to offence. I agree that this may well be so; but I do not think that there is any good reason why this should not be so; is it not appropriate that in this field serious 'offences' should require stricter proof than relatively minor ones?

In so far as some professional bodies are concerned, the only relevant case is that of *Bhandari v Advocates Committee* [1956] 3 All ER 742, [1956] 1 WLR 1442 which was concerned with alleged professional misconduct on the part of an advocate of the Supreme Court of Kenya, and in which the Privy Council approved the approach of the Eastern Africa Court of Appeal which had been in these terms ([1956] 3 All ER 742 at 744–745, [1956] 1 WLR 1442 at 1452):

'We agree that in every allegation of professional misconduct involving an element of deceit or moral turpitude a high standard of proof is called for, and we cannot envisage any body of professional men sitting in judgment on a colleague who would be content to condemn on a mere balance of probabilities.'

We were told, for instance, that in proceedings before the General Medical Council, this dictum is relied on as authority for the proposition that the relevant burden of proof in proceedings against a medical practitioner for alleged misconduct is the criminal one. It is unnecessary for us to decide the point on this appeal, but for my part I doubt whether that dictum is indeed adequate authority for that proposition. In my judgment the emphasis in that quotation is to be placed on the word 'mere' and if this is done then the dictum is entirely consistent with the application of the civil standard of proof, albeit varying having regard to the nature of the matter in issue.

Counsel for the appellant also referred to the second aspect of the principal issue which arises in this appeal in the course of his submissions to the court, but I did not understand him to pursue the point with any substantial enthusiasm.

In answer, counsel for the respondents submitted that the proceedings the subject matter of the instant application and appeal were civil proceedings before a domestic tribunal and thus ones in which it was appropriate to apply the civil burden of proof and not the criminal one. The 1948 regulations themselves could have stipulated that the latter should apply but they did not. There was, he submitted, nothing unusual about this internal domestic tribunal, even though set up ultimately pursuant to statute. Further, when one considered the schedule to the 1948 regulations, it was quite clear that the tribunal's jurisdiction extended over a very wide range of offences.

Counsel for the respondents also pointed out a matter to which I have already referred, namely that many work-forces have to be disciplined. One immediately thinks of prison officers, those working on the railways and indeed many fields of employment in which some form of discipline must exist. Further, in my experience there is nothing very extraordinary in the disciplinary code with which this case is concerned. Similar ones are provided pursuant to other statutory powers elsewhere in the public sector: in many instances in the private sector not only similar, but indeed somewhat more complicated and detailed codes have been negotiated between employers and trade unions.

For my part I agree with the view taken by the judge below and with the submissions put before us by counsel on behalf of the respondents. We were shown no authority which supports the appellant's contentions in this appeal. Indeed if the civil burden of proof was appropriate in the circumstances and context of *Khawaja*'s case, I can see no reason why a similar burden of proof should not be appropriate in this case. Although the point is not strictly in issue on the present appeal, I would also respectfully reserve my view about the correctness of the dictum of McNeill J in *Madden*'s case to which I have referred.

For these reasons I am wholly satisfied that the judge below was correct and I would dismiss this appeal.

**SLADE LJ.** I respectfully agree with the two judgments which have been delivered and only wish to add a few observations of my own.

In support of the first of the two main points taken on behalf of the appellant, counsel emphasised that the disciplinary provisions to which he was subject were not the product of a mere contractual relationship between employer and employee: they were the product of subordinate legislation contained in the Fire Service (Discipline) Regulations 1948, SI 1948/545, albeit enacted after negotiation between the interested bodies. I do not think that this makes any material difference. The nature of the proceedings before the fire authority was unquestionably civil rather than criminal. As counsel pointed out on behalf of the respondents, it would have been possible for the 1948 regulations to provide that on the hearing of any appeal to the fire authority under reg 8(5) the criminal standard of proof should apply. They contained no express provision to this effect. Nor, in my opinion, can any such provision be implied from the 1948 regulations. The mere use of certain expressions which in some other contexts would reflect the language of the criminal law, such as 'charge' or 'the accused', in my opinion gives rise to no such implication. I can see no way in which the criminal standard of proof can be imported to the civil proceedings in the present case. I too would respectfully reserve any opinion about the correctness of the dictum of McNeill J in *R v Police Complaints Board, ex p*

*Madden* [1983] 2 All ER 353, [1983] 1 WLR 447 cited by O'Connor and May LJJ concerning the standard of proof under the Police (Discipline) Regulations 1977, SI 1977/580.

The second of the two main points raised, though not stressed, on behalf of the appellant has caused me slightly greater difficulty. The passages from the speech of Lord Scarman in *Khawaja v Secretary of State for the Home Dept* [1983] 1 All ER 765, [1984] AC 74 which have already been cited by May LJ well illustrate that the civil standard of proof on the balance of probabilities is a 'flexible' one and that, the graver the issue involved, the higher is the degree of probability which the court should require. The very fact that all of their Lordships in that case thought it necessary, albeit in rather different forms of words, to stress this point for the guidance of lower courts gives rise to the question whether the disciplinary appeal panel of the fire authority gave itself a sufficient direction in deciding that 'it was appropriate for the case to be decided on the balance of probabilities, as was customary in employment tribunals of this nature'.

The judge grasped this nettle in his judgment. He specifically asked himself the question whether the five members of the panel 'would automatically have appreciated that a less serious allegation is more easily proved to the required standard than is a more serious one'. He gave his answer to this question as follows:

'I have reminded myself of the nature of the allegations here, allegations of corrupt practice, the particulars of which, I think, can be summarised as "using a fire brigade vehicle to carry a private load and pretending to the man then in charge of the civil amenity tip to which the load was taken that it had come from the fire brigade". I have been influenced too by my belief that, as a matter of ordinary human experience, a person is less easily satisfied that a serious allegation is made out than that a trivial one is made out. Consider a parent anxious to decide whether one of his children stole a sum of money and whether another had the light on in his bedroom after it had been put out and he had been told to go to sleep . . . Taking all of these factors into account, I am unable to say that the panel applied to the case before it a lower standard of proof than the law required. In any event, to speak more generally, I believe that a tribunal of fact will automatically take the relative seriousness of an allegation into account as one of the factors bearing on the question of whether the civil burden of proof has been discharged.'

A number of the speeches in the *Khawaja* case use phrases such as a 'high degree of probability' or corresponding phrases (see, for example, [1983] 1 All ER 765 at 772, 784, 792, 794, [1984] AC 74 at 97, 113, 124, 128 per Lord Fraser, Lord Scarman, Lord Bridge and Lord Templeman). Lord Scarman referred to the 'flexibility of the civil standard of proof'. However, my understanding of the concept of the flexible standard of proof reflected in the speeches in the *Khawaja* case is *not* that it involves proof on, say, a 51:49 balance of probabilities in some cases and, say, a 75:25 balance in others; any sliding scale of this nature would lead to intolerable uncertainty in application. My understanding of the concept, which I think was that of the judge, is simply that the relative seriousness of the allegation is a relevant factor, on occasions a highly relevant factor, in considering whether or not the civil burden of proof on the balance of probabilities has been discharged in any given case. This, as I understand it, was essentially the point which their Lordships thought it right to spell out in the *Khawaja* case in the particular context of an allegation of illegal entry. However, in other cases, of which I think the present was one, the point may be so obvious that it does not need to be put into words.

For these reasons and the further reasons given by O'Connor and May LJJ I would dismiss this appeal.

*Appeal dismissed. Leave to appeal to the House of Lords refused.*

Solicitors: *Robin Thompson & Partners* (for the appellant); *R A Leyland*, Winchester (for the respondents).

Frances Rustin    Barrister.

# Re E (mental health patient)

COURT OF APPEAL, CIVIL DIVISION
STEPHENSON, FOX AND PURCHAS LJJ
15, 16 OCTOBER, 1 NOVEMBER 1984

*Mental health – Legal proceedings brought on behalf of patient – Ownership of papers in legal proceedings – Action brought on behalf of patient by Official Solicitor as next friend – Patient's father wishing to appeal against judgment – Whether papers 'property' of patient – Whether father as new next friend entitled to possession of papers in existence as result of proceedings – Whether Official Solicitor entitled to withhold papers – Mental Health Act 1983, ss 95, 96, 112.*

*Mental health – Legal proceedings brought on behalf of patient – Functions of next friend in legal proceedings – Appeal – Waiver of right of appeal – Whether patient bound by next friend's waiver of right of appeal.*

In 1975 E, then aged 28 but with a mental age of 3 as the result of a cerebral haemorrhage when she was five months old, suffered another haemorrhage and, as a result of not receiving prompt treatment at the hospital to which she was admitted, she became a quadriplegic. In 1978, acting by the Official Solicitor on her behalf, she successfully brought a claim for damages for negligence against the relevant area health authority and the two doctors employed by it who were responsible for the delay in treating her. In February 1981 judgment was given in E's favour and the damages which were awarded were thereafter administered by the Court of Protection under the Mental Health Act 1959, and subsequently under the Mental Health Act 1983. E's parents lodged an appeal against the award, but in December 1981, as a result of counsel's opinion that the appeal was very unlikely to succeed, the appeal was dismissed by consent. In 1983 the parents consulted new solicitors with a view to appealing out of time, and in March 1983 those solicitors wrote to the Official Solicitor and the solicitors instructed by him in the claim for damages, requesting the release of all the papers which were in existence as a result of the proceedings, in order to enable them to advise the parents not only on the prospects of the success of an appeal out of time but also on whether proceedings for negligence lay against those who had been advising and acting for E at the time. The Official Solicitor refused to release any papers other than a copy of the judgment and the pleadings. In July 1983 E's father sought an order from the Court of Protection that the papers relating to E's litigation be released to the new solicitors. Under s 95(1)[a] of the 1983 Act the court could, in regard to 'the property and affairs' of a patient, do anything which appeared to be necessary or expedient for the maintenance or other benefit of the patient or for administering the patient's affairs and under s 96(1)[b] the court could make orders and give directions and authorities in that regard, in particular for the conduct of legal proceedings in the name of the patient or on his behalf. By s 112[c] property was defined as including 'any thing in action, and any interest in real or personal property'. The master made an order for the production of certain documents on the ground that the papers were the 'property' of the patient and therefore the court was empowered under s 95(1) to order their production. The Official Solicitor appealed. The judge

---

a   Section 95(1), so far as material, provides: 'The judge may, with respect to the property and affairs of a patient, do or secure the doing of all such things as appear necessary or expedient—(a) for the maintenance or other benefit of the patient . . . or (d) otherwise for administering the patient's affairs.'

b   Section 96(1), so far as material, provides: 'Without prejudice to the generality of section 95 above, the judge shall have power to make such orders and give such directions and authorities as he thinks fit for the purposes of that section and in particular may for those purposes make orders or give directions or authorities for . . . (i) the conduct of legal proceedings in the name of the patient or on his behalf . . .'

c   Section 112, so far as material, is set out at p 614 j, post

dismissed the appeal, holding that a patient's rights in papers used by his next friend in litigation on his behalf were part of the patient's 'property' for the purpose of the 1983 Act, subject to the rights of others, eg solicitors instructed by the next friend who had a claim for costs, and accordingly the papers used by the Official Solicitor in litigation on E's behalf were E's property which the Official Solicitor had no right to retain as against E or anyone else properly acting on her behalf. The Official Solicitor appealed to the Court of Appeal.

**Held** – (1) The paramount consideration of the court in exercising its statutory jurisdiction under the 1983 Act over papers in the Official Solicitor's custody in connection with litigation in which he had acted as next friend of the patient was the interest, benefit and requirements of the patient. Furthermore, the benefit of the patient, and of his family, was not confined to material benefit but extended to whatever might be in their true interests (see p 615 a to c, post); dicta of Lord Macnaghten in *A-G v Marquis of Ailesbury* (1887) 12 App Cas at 688 and of Ungoed-Thomas J in *Re W* [1970] 2 All ER at 505 applied.

(2) Regardless of whether the action was dead or whether the Official Solicitor had ceased to be the patient's next friend, he was in a different position from an ordinary or lay next friend in that there might come into his possession, in connection with litigation when he was acting as next friend, confidential reports which a parent had no absolute right to see and which should not be inspected by anyone but the court itself in the performance of its statutory duty to consider the benefit of the patient, and it was important to preserve the confidence of those who gave information, often in writing, to the Official Solicitor which they might not give if they feared it might not be kept secret (see p 616 e to h, post); *Official Solicitor v K* [1963] 3 All ER 191 applied.

(3) It therefore followed that, where papers which a patient sought to inspect were in the custody of the Official Solicitor in connection with legal proceedings which he was authorised by the Court of Protection under the 1983 Act to conduct on behalf of the patient, or in which he was, under the Rules of the Supreme Court, the next friend of the patient whose property was being administered by the Court of Protection, the parent of that patient had no absolute right to see those papers, although they were the property of the patient, but instead had to obtain the authority of the Court of Protection for their disclosure as necessary or expedient for the benefit of the patient. However, the court should only rarely exercise its discretion to withhold disclosure of confidential documents from a patient or parent and then only where the court was fully satisfied that real harm to the patient would ensue from the disclosure. In the circumstances the proper course was for the court to inspect the papers itself and thereafter to allow inspection by the father's solicitors of those papers which were not harmful to the patient. The appeal would accordingly be allowed and the case remitted to the judge to inspect the papers (see p 616 h to p 617 a and d to f, post); dictum of Lord Evershed in *Official Solicitor v K* [1963] 3 All ER at 197 applied.

Per curiam. Although a next friend conducts litigation on behalf of a patient, the waiver of a right of appeal is beyond the ordinary conduct of the action and must be approved by the court, and accordingly the patient is not bound by a next friend's waiver of his right of appeal if in the opinion of the court the waiver is not for his benefit. Furthermore, that requirement cannot be circumvented by withdrawing or abandoning the appeal, because even parties who are sui juris need leave to withdraw their appeal (see p 615 f to h and p 617 j, post); *Rhodes v Swithenbank* (1889) 22 QBD 577, *Tod-Heatly v Barnard* [1890] WN 130 and dictum of Willmer LJ in *Re L* [1968] 1 All ER at 32 applied.

Decision of Sir Robert Megarry V-C [1984] 1 All ER 309 varied.

**Notes**

For parties and proceedings relating to mental disorder and legal incapacity, see 30 Halsbury's Laws (4th edn) paras 1017–1019, and for cases on the subject, see 34 Digest (Reissue) 28–29, 240–249.

For legal proceedings by a next friend, see 37 Halsbury's Laws (4th edn) para 240, and for cases on the subject, see 37(2) Digest (Reissue) 396–397, 2441–2446.

For the Mental Health Act 1983, ss 95, 96, 112, see 53 Halsbury's Statutes (3rd edn) 1129, 1130, 1143.

**Cases referred to in judgment**

A-G v Marquis of Ailesbury (1887) 12 App Cas 672, HL.

L, Re [1968] 1 All ER 20, [1968] P 119, [1967] 3 WLR 1645, CA.

Official Solicitor v K [1963] 3 All ER 191, [1965] AC 201, [1963] 3 WLR 408, HL.

Rhodes v Swithenbank (1889) 22 QBD 577, CA.

Scott v Scott [1913] AC 417, [1911–13] All ER Rep 1, HL.

Tod-Heatly v Barnard [1890] WN 130, CA.

W, Re [1970] 2 All ER 502, [1971] Ch 123, [1970] 3 WLR 87.

Walsh v George Kemp Ltd [1938] 2 All ER 266, CA.

**Appeal**

By a summons dated 5 July 1983 the father of E, a patient under the Mental Health Act 1959, and subsequently under the Mental Health Act 1983, applied to the Court of Protection for an order that the papers relating to E's claim for damages for negligence brought by the Official Solicitor acting as her next friend against the relevant area health authority and two doctors be released to the father's solicitors. On 1 August 1983 the master of the Court of Protection made an order for the production of all the documents sought, requiring them to be produced to the solicitors acting for E's father within 21 days. On 9 August the Official Solicitor appealed against the order, seeking its total discharge or alternatively that he should be directed to produce the documents only if the Queen's Bench Division so ordered. On 18 August a stay of the order of the Court of Protection pending the determination of the appeal was made by consent. By an order dated 11 November 1983 Sir Robert Megarry V-C ([1984] 1 All ER 309, [1984] 1 WLR 320) ordered that the Official Solicitor's appeal be dismissed and that certain specified documents requested by the father and in the possession of the Official Solicitor be made available for inspection and copying by the father's solicitors. By a notice of appeal dated 22 December 1983 the Official Solicitor appealed. The facts are set out in the judgment of the court.

Joseph Jackson QC and Dirik Jackson for the Official Solicitor.
K L May for the patient's father.

*Cur adv vult*

1 November. The following judgment of the court was delivered.

**STEPHENSON LJ.** This appeal raises a short, novel and important point: is the Official Solicitor bound to disclose all documents in his possession which relate to a claim which he brought as next friend on behalf of a patient, whose property and affairs were and are being administered by the Court of Protection, for inspection by solicitors representing the patient's father?

The master of the Court of Protection by order dated 1 August 1983 allowed inspection of all but one of nine documents or classes of documents which the patient's father applied by summons in the Court of Protection to inspect, namely:

'1. Pleadings.

2. Proofs of Evidence of all Witnesses.

3. Medical Reports.

4. Instructions to Counsel.

5. Solicitors Notes and Memoranda (if any).

6. Counsel's Advices.

7. Correspondence passing between the Official Solicitor and the Solicitors acting for the Plaintiff . . . at any time.

8. All Correspondence passing between the Official Solicitor and the Court of Protection.

9. All Correspondence passing between the Patient's relations and the Solicitors acting for the Patient and/or the Official Solicitor.'

The claim to inspect no 8 was not pursued.

Sir Robert Megarry V-C by order dated 11 November 1983 dismissed the Official Solicitor's appeal with costs (see [1984] 1 All ER 309, [1984] 1 WLR 320). (His order omits no 1, which had already been disclosed.) Counsel on behalf of the Official Solicitor asks this court to discharge the Vice-Chancellor's order (save as to costs) and to direct the master of the Court of Protection to examine the documents requested to be disclosed and to determine which if any of them should be made available for inspection and copying by the father's solicitors.

The patient is a woman now 37 years of age but with a mental age of 3 as a result of a cerebral haemorrhage which she suffered at the age of five months. In 1975 she suffered a further haemorrhage which was negligently treated. As a result she became quadriplegic. In 1978 she sued doctors and the relevant area health authority by the Official Solicitor as her next friend. At the trial of her action in January 1981 negligence was admitted and by a late reamendment of her statement of claim she alleged that it was desirable and beneficial for her—

'to be nursed at home, that a new home should be purchased by her parents and adapted for that purpose, that nurses be employed to attend her at an annual cost of up to £21,934 per annum, that her consultant physician and physiotherapist be paid to attend her at home, etc; alternatively that she should be nursed at a private institution such as Eastside House, London N.W.11 at an annual cost of £19,345 per annum and her parents should move house to be near her.'

In a reserved judgment on 23 February 1981 Wien J awarded her £43,912·01 damages, which were paid into the Court of Protection.

The patient's parents are devoted to her and wanted to care for her at home. The judge heard their evidence and declined to award damages for future care at home or in a private institution. He found that her parents' proposal to look after her at home was unrealistic and impractical, that they paid no heed to expert medical advice and gave her harmful massage, that there was no private hospital which treated the mentally subnormal who were seriously handicapped, a fact not in issue, and that Bromham Hospital where she was (and is) living without charge as a national health service patient under the care of Dr Fleming, whose evidence he heard, was 'the best and most suitable place for the treatment and care' of the patient.

Her parents were deeply dissatisfied with the judgment, the judge's comments on them and their evidence, and the amount of his award. So the Official Solicitor was instructed to give notice of appeal and counsel's advice was taken on the prospects of getting this court to increase the award. The advice of experienced leading counsel, given in November after seeing the parents with the Official Solicitor, in consultation with junior counsel who had conducted the case before the judge, was that an appeal would not succeed. In their joint opinion they stated that the award of £2,000 for reduced expectation of life was high, and that of £25,000 for pain, suffering and loss of amenities not excessively low having regard to the patient's pre-existing condition, that the refusal to award anything for private nursing care was based on a finding which could not be upset, that the expenses of such care would probably never be incurred. They were of opinion that the judge's treatment of special damage and future expenditure by which he arrived at the balance of his award was 'extraordinary', particularly in setting off the expenses of the parents' future visits to the patient against the patient's special damage, or, counsel would now add on behalf of the parents, against their savings on feeding her at home. But the judge had felt driven to take a broad view of the matter 'in view of the unsatisfactory state of not only the evidence but of the way it was argued'; and counsel considered that the Court of Appeal was unlikely to interfere with the result of that part of the judgment. Bearing in mind the danger of the damages awarded being depleted by an unsuccessful appeal (on a legal aid certificate), counsel advised against it, the parents accepted his advice, the Official Solicitor, who had been appointed receiver of the patient's property in November but remained her next friend, on 18 December 1981 instructed her solicitors to 'arrange for her appeal to be withdrawn forthwith' and to notify the Law Society, and also informed the Court of Protection of his position, including his instructions to the patient's solicitors.

On 22 February 1982 the solicitors for the appellant patient and the respondent doctors and authority signed and lodged a request in the form required by the Practice Direction of 21 February 1938 ([1938] WN 89) (now amended: see [1983] 1 All ER 448, [1983] 1 WLR 85) stating:

'All parties being sui juris we hereby consent to this appeal being dismissed with costs.'

The request in that form should not have been made, or accepted, as on the face of the document the appellant was not sui juris, a matter to which we refer again at the end of this judgment.

At the beginning of 1983 the Official Solicitor was replaced as receiver by the principal officer of the Management Division of the Court of Protection. The patient's parents still longed to take her home out of the care of Dr Fleming in Bromham Hospital and to get the money which would enable them to meet the expense of so doing. There appeared to be two ways of getting enough money, either by an increase of the damages awarded her by the judge or by an award of damages for professional negligence against her legal advisers. The first of these means would require the pursuit of the 'withdrawn' or 'dismissed' appeal. On 10 March 1983 different solicitors instructed by the parents formally requested the release of all the Official Solicitor's papers in the action in which he had acted as the patient's next friend, so that they could advise the parents on the prospects of success in seeking to appeal out of time. The Official Solicitor offered to provide a copy of the judgment of Wien J and of the pleadings, but no more.

On 10 April 1983 the Official Solicitor wrote to the father's solicitors that the Law Society's discharge certificate in respect of legal aid had been issued in March 1982, that he was functus officio and that application for the papers should be made to the Court of Protection.

On 5 July 1983 the patient's father took out a summons in the Court of Protection, asking for an order that the papers appertaining to the civil claim for damages brought by the Official Solicitor acting as next friend on behalf of the patient, and listed under the nine heads which we have already set out, be released to his solicitors. On 1 August 1983 the master of the Court of Protection heard his application and after a short adjournment granted it. She was willing to assume, after considering the provisions of RSC Ord 80, that the Official Solicitor's position as next friend had lapsed; and she did not accept his arguments that the Court of Protection had no jurisdiction or as a matter of principle should not produce them and that only the Queen's Bench Division, which appointed him to act as next friend, could authorise production of the papers in his litigation file. The master was told that the main purpose for which inspection was desired was to enable the appeal to be reconsidered and the other object was to enable a claim for professional negligence to be considered. She said that, if it was only the claim for negligence that was in question, she might take a different view. She was not told that the appeal had been 'dismissed by consent'; nor was she asked to inspect the documents herself before ordering production of them for inspection.

On 9 August 1983 the Official Solicitor gave notice of appeal to the nominated judge, asking either that no order for production of the documents be made or that he be directed, if the Queen's Bench Division so ordered, to produce the documents.

Before the appeal was heard by Sir Robert Megarry V-C the patient's sister acting as her next friend made an unsuccessful attempt to obtain production from a master of the Queen's Bench Division. On 19 October her summons of 21 September was dismissed by the master on procedural grounds, though he indicated that he would have dismissed it on the merits, rejecting the Official Solicitor's argument that as a matter of principle the documents should not be produced. He was not asked to adjourn the application or told the appeal had been dismissed.

On 11 November 1983 Sir Robert Megarry V-C gave his judgment dismissing the appeal. He was not told that the appeal had been dismissed by consent; he was told that it had been 'abandoned'. He was not asked by the Official Solicitor to examine the documents or to direct the master to examine them; he was asked to discharge the master's order. It was not until the successful application for a stay was heard on 21 December 1983 that the father and his advisers heard that the Official Solicitor's notice of appeal, dated the next day, was going to ask this court to discharge the Vice-Chancellor's order and to direct the master of the Court of Protection to examine the documents.

Sir Robert Megarry V-C held that the documents in question were the property of the patient, that even if she was not the absolute owner of them she had rights of property in them, perhaps enforceable only on indemnifying the Official Solicitor if still her next friend, and subject to the rights of others, whether he was still her next friend or had ceased to be her next friend, that the Official Solicitor had no right to retain them as against the patient or someone else properly acting on her behalf, that the Court of Protection had jurisdiction to order production of them to the father's solicitors and that it was for the benefit of the patient that the Official Solicitor should produce them.

In reaching his conclusion the Vice-Chancellor considered the relevant statutory provisions and a number of rules, authorities and textbooks relating to the position of a next friend and the ownershop of papers, but could find no clear authority on the ownership of papers brought into existence on behalf of a patient. His conclusion that these litigation papers are the patient's is, in our respectful judgment, plainly right and is now common undisputed ground. It is also common ground that the Court of Protection has jurisdiction to do what is for the benefit of the patient with respect to her papers. What is disputed is (1) whether production of these papers to her father's solicitors is for her benefit, (2) whether they have a right to inspect the papers, even if that would not be for her benefit, (3) whether, even if it is for her benefit, the Official Solicitor should refuse production because of his special position. The third question is not mentioned in the Official Solicitor's notice of appeal, or indeed in his counsel's skeleton argument, though put by Mr Jackson QC in the forefront of his appeal.

The relevant statutory powers are to be found in Pt VIII of the Mental Health Act 1959, now re-enacted in Pt VII of the Mental Health Act 1983. Since 1959 the old jurisdiction in lunacy under which a patient's property was administered under earlier statutes and the royal prerogative has been exercised by judges of the Supreme Court nominated by the Lord Chancellor, and by the master and deputy master of the Court of Protection, which is not a court in the usually accepted sense but an office of the Supreme Court for the protection and management of the property of persons (patients) incapable, by reason of mental disorder, of managing and administering their property and affairs (see ss 100 and 101 of the 1959 Act and ss 93 and 94 of the 1983 Act).

By s 102(1) of the 1959 Act (s 95(1) of the 1983 Act) the master, in exercising the functions of the judge—

'may, with respect to the property and affairs of the patient, do or secure the doing of all such things as appear necessary or expedient—(a) for the maintenance or other benefit of the patient, (b) for the maintenance or other benefit of members of the patient's family . . . or (d) otherwise for administering the patient's affairs.'

Subsection (2) of the same section provides that:

'In the exercise of the powers conferred by this section regard shall be had first of all to the requirements of the patient . . .'

By s 103(1)(h) of the 1959 Act (replaced with the omission of a qualification not material to this case by s 96(1)(i) of the 1983 Act) the judge or master may make such orders and give such directions and authorities as he thinks fit for 'the conduct of legal proceedings in the name of the patient or on his behalf'. By s 112 of the 1983 Act (replacing s 119(1) of the 1959 Act), '"property" includes any thing in action, and any interest in real or personal property'.

As we have already said, the court, in deciding what to do about the papers in the

Official Solicitor's file in the action in which he acted as next friend, is admittedly dealing
with the patient's property. In the exercise of that jurisdiction 'the leading principle, the
paramount consideration' is, and it has always been, the interest and benefit and
requirements of the patient (see *A-G v Marquis of Ailesbury* (1887) 12 App Cas 672 at 688
per Lord Macnaghten). That is the 'overriding principle' on which the court exercises its
paternal and now statutory jurisdiction as both administrator and judge, alike over the
affairs of its wards and of its patients (see *Scott v Scott* [1913] AC 417 at 437, [1911–13] All
ER Rep 1 at 9 per Viscount Haldane LC).

The benefit of the patient, and of his or her family, is not confined to material benefit
but extends to whatever may be meant by their true interests (see *Re W* [1970] 2 All ER
502 at 505, [1971] Ch 123 at 135 per Ungoed-Thomas J). It was for the patient's benefit
in every way that the Official Solicitor brought the action on her behalf and obtained a
large sum of money for her. If it is in her best interests that she should remain in the
Bromham Hospital, as the judge found, it is hard to see how it can be for her benefit that
she should be awarded more money to enable her parents to move her to their home.
But it is her father's case that home is the best place for her. He seeks to support that case
by a letter dated 8 May 1975 from a doctor to one of the defendants to the action set out
in a report of the Medical Service Committee of the Bedfordshire Family Practitioner
Committee, and by a copy of a 'strictly confidential' letter dated 14 June 1980 from Dr
Fleming to a fourth doctor. We looked at this material de bene esse, though it was not
supported by any notice of motion to adduce fresh evidence or exhibited to any affidavit.
It advances the father's case little, if at all, but looking at the judge's comments on the
evidence and argument before him, we think it impossible to assume that there might
not be evidence in any of the papers which the father wants his solicitors to inspect that
might advance his case further and so be of benefit to the patient, and, as was we think
properly argued, to her family.

There is force in the submission of counsel for the patient's father that the patient's
parents are entitled to know the worst about their daughter (unless their knowledge of it
can hurt her) and that inspection of some of these papers may, as he put it, 'draw the
poison' out of the family, to the lasting benefit of them all. However, if the judge may
have been wrong to accept Dr Fleming's evidence, uncontradicted as it was by any
medical evidence, any withdrawal, abandonment or agreement to the dismissal of any
appeal against his decision must be shown to be for the benefit of the patient and the
court must be convinced that in consenting to its withdrawal, abandonment or dismissal
the next friend is acting for her benefit. An infant is not bound by a next friend's waiver
of his right of appeal if in the opinion of the court the waiver is not for his benefit; the
next friend (or guardian ad litem) conducts the litigation, but such a thing as that waiver
of a right of appeal is 'beyond the ordinary conduct of the action' and must be approved
by the court (see *Rhodes v Swithenbank* (1889) 22 QBD 577; see also *Re L* [1968] 1 All ER
20 at 32, [1968] P 119 at 168 per Willmer LJ).

That must apply to require the Court of Protection's approval of a dismissal by consent
of a next friend's appeal on behalf of a patient (see *The Supreme Court Practice 1985*, vol 1,
p 1145, para 80/2/15). That requirement cannot be circumvented by withdrawing or
abandoning the appeal, for even parties who are sui juris need leave to withdraw their
appeals (see *Tod-Heatley v Barnard* [1890] WN 130).

If this understanding of the power, and indeed duty, of the Court of Protection is
right, then it ought to examine these papers in order to see whether they contain material
likely to benefit the patient by enabling her father to obtain more money for her (and
for her family); and it ought to disclose to his solicitors any material which is not harmful
to the patient or against her interest, unless (1) the court has no jurisdiction to do so
because the father has a right to inspect all the papers or (2) the court has a discretion and
ought to exercise it as a matter of principle against inspection because they are in the
possession of the Official Solicitor and not of a lay member of the public acting as next
friend, eg a parent.

It is counsel's contention on behalf of the father that the Official Solicitor is, or was, in
exactly the same position as any other next friend. The action is still alive because it is

subject to leave to appeal out of time. The Official Solicitor contends that he is still the next friend in the action because he has never been removed or replaced by a substitute as required by the rules. RSC Ord 80, r 3 provides:

> '... (3) Where a person is authorised under Part VII of the Act to conduct legal proceedings in the name of a patient or on his behalf, that person shall be entitled to be next friend or guardian ad litem, as the case may be, of the patient in any proceedings to which his authority extends unless, in a case to which paragraph (4) or (5) or rule 6 applies, some other person is appointed by the Court under that paragraph or rule to be next friend or guardian ad litem, as the case may be, of the patient in those proceedings.
> (4) Where a person has been or is next friend or guardian ad litem of a person under disability in any proceedings, no other person shall be entitled to act as such friend or guardian, as the case may be, of the person under disability in those proceedings unless the Court makes an order appointing him such friend or guardian in substitution for the person previously acting in that capacity ...'

Paragraph (5) of r 3 and r 6 do not apply.

The editors of *The Supreme Court Practice* treat the rule as not merely entitling but binding a next friend to continue to act as next friend unless and until the court or a judge by order substitutes another person to act in that capacity (see *The Supreme Court Practice 1985*, vol 1, p 1148, para 80/3/3). We incline to agree with them and to hold that the view of counsel for the patient's father, the master's assumption to the contrary and the Official Solicitor's original opinion that he was functus officio were wrong, unless the action is dead beyond hope of resurrection to new life by leave to renew the appeal out of time.

However, like Sir Robert Megarry V-C, we do not think that we need decide anything on this vexing question because, whether or not the action is dead or the Official Solicitor has ceased to be the patient's next friend, he is, in our opinion, in a different position from what we may term an ordinary or lay next friend, in a most important respect. There may come into his possession in connection with litigation, when he is acting as next friend (or guardian ad litem), confidential reports which a parent has no absolute right to see and which should not be inspected by anyone but the court itself in the performance of its statutory duty to consider the benefit of a patient or the welfare of an infant (see *Official Solicitor v K* [1963] 3 All ER 191, [1965] AC 201). It must be most important to preserve the confidence of those who give information, often in writing, to the Official Solicitor which they might not give if they feared it might not be kept secret. But the cases in which the court should exercise its discretion to withhold disclosure of a confidential report or other confidential documents from a party or parent must be rare, and where the court is fully satisfied judicially that real harm to the patient must ensue from disclosure see what Lord Evershed said in *Official Solicitor v K* [1963] 3 All ER 191 at 197, [1965] AC 201 at 219.

But we are not concerned with the position of the Official Solicitor in respect of discovery of documents in any other case, as, for instance, cases where he acts or has acted for infants who have attained their majority, or for patients who have ceased to be incapable of managing and administering their own property and affairs. All we are deciding is that where, as here, the papers of which the patient seeks inspection are in the custody of the Official Solicitor in connection with litigation in which he has been authorised by the Court of Protection under what is now Pt VII of the Mental Health Act 1983 to conduct legal proceedings on behalf of a patient, or in which he is, as he is entitled to be under the Rules of the Supreme Court, the next friend of a patient whose property is being administered by the Court of Protection, a parent of this patient has no absolute right to see those papers, although they are the patient's property, but must obtain the authority of the Court of Protection to order disclosure of them as necessary or expedient for the benefit of the patient. The right course is in this case for the Vice-Chancellor to do what he undoubtedly has power to do (without the aid of r 73 of the Court of Protection Rules 1982, SI 1982/322) and would probably have done had he been

asked after such argument as we have heard from counsel for the Official Solicitor and
counsel for the patient's father in this court: to inspect the papers himself, thereafter
allowing inspection by the father's solicitors of any papers not really harmful to the
patient. And Sir Robert Megarry V-C may be right in stating that that exception cannot
arise in the present case, where there is no hope of this patient recovering from her grave
disability.

Like Sir Robert Megarry V-C, we can see little prospect on either head, the appeal or
the proceedings for negligence. He said ([1984] 1 All ER 309 at 314, [1984] 1 WLR 320
at 326):

> 'But an examination of the papers might produce a different view, and if that
> examination is to be conducted on the footing that none of the cost will fall on E's
> estate, unless, indeed, it is found to be in the interest of E that the claim should be
> pursued, then it seems to me that it is for the benefit of E that this examination
> should be made. It may be a long shot, but it is a free long shot. On being assured
> that the examination will be made on that footing (and I think that it is desirable
> for this to be made explicit), I propose to dismiss the appeal.'

With that we respectfully agree, subject to the power and duty of the court to satisfy
itself by examination of each listed document that disclosure to the father's solicitors is
for the patient's benefit and not against her interest.

We would accordingly allow the appeal and set aside Sir Robert Megarry V-C's order
(except as to costs) and order the Vice-Chancellor to inspect the papers and give directions
in accordance with this judgment and with his decision that none of the costs should fall
on the patient's estate. We think that the master would have herself referred the
application to the Vice-Chancellor under r 45 of the Court of Protection Rules 1982
(which gives to her power to refer proceedings to the judge nominated by the Lord
Chancellor to act for the purposes of Pt VII of the 1983 Act), if she had not wished to
avoid the consequent delay. In our judgment the Vice-Chancellor himself should carry
out the inspection.

We must add a comment on the dismissal by consent of the appeal, a document which
was not before the master or the judge and was only produced as fresh evidence at the
hearing of this appeal by leave of the court. Clearly the solicitors should not have signed,
and the court should not have accepted, that request. It was made in a form for dismissal
by consent, 'DBC', authorised by the Practice Direction of 21 February 1938 ([1938]
WN 89) and now amended to read (see [1983] 1 All ER 448, [1983] 1 WLR 85). This
convenient method of dismissing an appeal without the expense of appearing in court
applied only 'Where an appellant is sui juris', but the plaintiff was, as appeared correctly
on the face of the request, not sui juris. The leave to withdraw an appeal to which we
referred earlier is now obtained by the 'DBC' procedure under the practice direction, but
it cannot be obtained in the case of an infant without the approval of the Court of Appeal
after a hearing (see *Walsh v George Kemp Ltd* [1938] 2 All ER 266 and *The Supreme Court
Practice 1985*, vol 1, p 1155, para 80/10–11/7). There seems to be no authority clearly
deciding that the settlement of a patient's claim under appeal by dismissal or other
compromise requires the same approval. The decision of this court in *Rhodes v Swithenbank*
(1889) 22 QBD 577 shows that the next friend of the patient requires the approval of the
Court of Protection (the nominated judge or the master exercising his powers) for the
dismissal or compromise.

We have not been shown any authority from the Court of Protection approving the
dismissal, or indeed any authority from the Court of Protection relating to the conduct
of the proceedings to the Official Solicitor. But the Court of Protection was in control of
her property, including the money obtained by the legal proceedings on her behalf, by
the time the appeal was dismissed; so its consent was necessary, and, as at present advised,
we think the Court of Appeal's consent was also necessary.

We do not have to decide what effect, if any, the 'DBC' in this case has on those
proceedings; but we would suggest that the necessity for approval of a consent in such

proceedings as these by the Court of Appeal as well as by the Court of Protection is a
matter for consideration by the Rule Committee, and perhaps for a practice direction.

*Appeal allowed; Vice-Chancellor's order of 11 November 1983 set aside; Vice-Chancellor to
inspect papers in accordance with judgment of Court of Appeal.*

28 January 1985. Sir Robert Megarry V-C, having inspected the documents concerned in
accordance with the Court of Appeal's direction, gave judgment in chambers stating that
he had failed to find anything, whether confidential or not, which in his view, if disclosed
to the father, would be capable of being harmful to E or of being against her interest.
His Lordship made a fresh order in substantially the same terms as his previous order but
directed that it was not to take effect until the father had undertaken to the court that
none of the costs of carrying out the order would fall on E's estate.

Solicitors: *Official Solicitor; Evill & Coleman* (for the patient's father).

Diana Brahams  Barrister.

# Re West Anstey Common

COURT OF APPEAL, CIVIL DIVISION
SIR JOHN DONALDSON MR, SLADE AND LLOYD LJJ
5, 6, 18 DECEMBER 1984

*Commons – Registration – Disputed claims – Reference to commons commissioner – Extent of
inquiry by commissioner – Objection taken to registration of part of land – No objection taken to
registration of remainder of land – Whether commissioner bound to inquire into validity of
registration of whole of land – Whether appellant eligible to be heard at inquiry despite failing to
object to registration – Commons Registration Act 1965, ss 5(6), 6(1).*

A local authority provisionally registered, under s 4 of the Commons Registration Act
1965, an area of land as common land. N objected, under s 5[a] of the 1965 Act, to part of
the land being included in the area provisionally registered, on the ground that he was
the owner and that there were no rights of common over it. His objection was referred
to a commons commissioner in accordance with s 5(6) of the 1965 Act, which provided
that 'Where . . . an objection is made . . . the registration authority shall refer the matter
to a Commons Commissioner'. By s 6(1)[b] of that Act the commissioner had a duty to
inquire into the 'matter' referred to him and could either confirm the registration, with
or without modification, or refuse to do so. At the hearing, N reached agreement with
interested parties claiming rights over his land whereby they accepted the validity of his
objection. H, who had not previously objected to the registration of the land as common
land, and who claimed to be the owner of certain other parts of the land, informed the
commissioner that he wished to challenge the registration so far as it affected his land.
The commissioner refused to hear him on the grounds that he was only bound to inquire
into that part of the land to which objection had been taken and that, in failing to object,
H was disentitled from being heard. In the light of N's agreement with the interested
parties, and without hearing evidence, the commissioner held that N's objection was
valid and excluded his land from the area provisionally registered. He then confirmed
the registration of the remainder as common land and, having accepted further
agreements made between the interested parties, made certain modifications to grazing
rights over that land. H appealed against the commissioner's decision, contending that
once an objection had been made to the registration of part of an area of land as common
land the status of the whole area was put in question. The judge upheld the commissioner's

a  Section 5, so far as material, is set out at p 621 *a* to *d*, post
b  Section 6(1), so far as material, is set out at p 623 *g*, post

decision. H appealed to the Court of Appeal. At the hearing of the appeal, the respondents, who had registered grazing rights over H's land, contended that it was open to a person to object to part only of a registration and that the 'matter' referred to in ss 5(6) and 6(1) of the 1965 Act was the particular dispute arising from the particular objection to a registration.

**Held** – An objection to the registration of any land as common land necessarily put in issue the validity of the entire registration since it was the act of registration to which objection was taken and it did not matter that the grounds of objection only related to part of the land comprised in the registration. Therefore, on the true construction of ss 5(6) and 6(1) of the 1965 Act, the 'matter' into which the commissioner had had a duty to inquire was the alleged status as common land of the whole area which had been put in question by N's objection and not merely the particular dispute between the parties, since (per Slade LJ), having regard to the policy of the 1965 Act, the duty of inquiry imposed on the commissioner was not intended to be regarded solely as a piece of civil litigation between individuals: the public also had an interest in its outcome. Furthermore, N's objection was in effect an objection to any rights registered over the area, so that at the time of the hearing all the grazing rights were merely provisional and required confirmation by the commissioner, and the onus of proof was on persons who had or who claimed registration of those rights to prove their case against H. By acceding to the agreements reached at the hearing and by modifying the grazing rights, the commissioner had in effect confirmed registrations without prior inquiry, and had treated H as bound by a compromise to which he was not a party. It followed that, although H had had no absolute right to be heard, the commissioner had had a discretion to hear him and, in the circumstances, should have exercised that discretion in H's favour. The appeal would therefore be allowed (see p 624 *c d* and *h* to p 625 *g*, p 626 *c*, p 627 *c* to p 628 *a* and *f g*, p 629 *d* to *f* and p 630 *g h*, post).

*Re Sutton Common, Wimborne* [1982] 2 All ER 376 approved.
Decision of Whitford J [1984] 1 All ER 161 reversed.

### Notes
For referral of the registration of common land to a commons commissioner, see 6 Halsbury's Laws (4th edn) para 673, and for the hearing before the commissioner, see ibid paras 695–696.

For the Commons Registration Act 1965, ss 4, 5, 6, see 3 Halsbury's Statutes (3rd edn) 922, 923, 924.

### Cases referred to in judgments
*Central Electricity Generating Board v Clwyd CC* [1976] 1 All ER 251, [1976] 1 WLR 151.
*Corpus Christi College, Oxford v Gloucestershire CC* [1982] 3 All ER 995, [1983] QB 360, [1982] 3 WLR 849, CA.
*Hales v Bolton Leathers Ltd* [1950] 1 All ER 149, [1950] 1 KB 493, CA; *affd* [1951] 1 All ER 643, [1951] AC 531, HL.
*Ilkley and Burley Moors, Re* (1983) 47 P & CR 324.
*Jackson v Hall* [1980] 1 All ER 177, [1980] AC 854, [1980] 2 WLR 118, HL.
*R v Commons Comr, ex p Winnington* (1982) Times, 26 November.
*Sutton Common, Wimborne, Re* [1982] 2 All ER 376, [1982] 1 WLR 647.

### Case also cited
*Box Parish Council v Lacey* [1979] 1 All ER 113, [1980] Ch 109, CA.

### Appeal
Hugh Michael James Harrison appealed with the leave of Whitford J against the decision of the judge ([1984] 1 All ER 161, [1984] Ch 172) on 12 October 1983 whereby he dismissed the appellant's application for an order pursuant to s 18 of the Commons Registration Act 1965 that all matters relating to the registration of common land and of

rights of common in the register of common land maintained by the Devon County Council under register unit CL 143 be remitted to a commons commissioner for rehearing. The grounds of appeal were, inter alia, (1) that the judge erred in concluding that the objection made by E J Nicholls and G E Nicholls to part of the land, only put in issue that part; (2) that the judge erred in concluding (a) that the commons commissioner was right in not putting the registrants of both land and rights to proof on the ground that the question of the burden of proof did not arise, (b) that the commissioner was right in refusing to hear the appellant notwithstanding that, as a result of the agreements he accepted between the registrants and E J Nicholls and G E Nicholls, there was an increase in the quantum of rights exercisable over the appellant's land. The facts are set out in the judgment of Slade LJ.

*Sir Frederick Corfield QC* and *Anne Williams* for the appellant
*Sheila Cameron QC* and *Frank Hinks* for the respondents.

*Cur adv vult*

18 December. The following judgments were delivered. ·

**SLADE LJ** (giving the first judgment at the invitation of Sir John Donaldson MR). This is an appeal by Mr H M J Harrison from a judgment of Whitford J given on 12 October 1983 on a case stated for the decision of the court under s 18(1) of the Commons Registration Act 1965. Though his judgment is reported ([1984] 1 All ER 161, [1984] Ch 172) and helpfully summarises the facts, I will attempt a summary of my own, since I think that a proper understanding of the facts is essential to a resolution of the legal issues arising in this rather unusual case.

On 15 August 1967 a tract of land comprising in all some 74 acres in North Devon and commonly known as West Anstey Common was provisionally registered as common land in the land section of the Register of Common Land on the application of the West Anstey Parish Meeting, under s 4 of the 1965 Act. The unit number of this registration was CL 143. This tract of land included areas commonly known as Anstey Rhiney Moor, Guphill Common, Anstey Money Common, Woodland Common and a part of Twitchen Common.

This registration of the 714 acres in the land section of the register was followed by four provisional registrations in the ownership section made in 1967 or 1968. Entry no 1 was made on the application of Mr J W J Milton and affected an area shown lettered 'A' on the register map and known as Anstey Money Common. Entry no 2 was made on the application of the appellant's father, Mr E M Harrison, and roughly affected the areas known as Anstey Rhiney Moor and Guphill Common. The sections of land concerned were shown lettered 'D' on the register map and comprised rather more than half of the land comprised in CL 143. I will refer to them as 'the Harrison land'. Entry no 3 was made on the application of the Badgworthy Land Co Ltd and related to a small area shown lettered 'E' on the register map. Entry no 4 was made on the application of Mr E J Nicholls and Mr G E Nicholls and related to the area shown lettered 'F' on the register map, known as Woodland Common. This area, though much smaller than that lettered 'D', was not insubstantial. Since entries 1 and 2 to a small extent related to the same intermediate area of land, each of these fell to be treated as an objection to the other to the extent of the conflict. The same applied to entries 2 and 3. However, no objection was made to the registration of entry no 4 which, by virtue of s 7 of the 1965 Act, had become final long before the commons commissioner gave his decision in this case.

The registration in the land section of the register was also followed by ten provisional registrations in the rights section made in 1967 or 1968. I need only refer to two of them. Entry no 1 recorded a claim by W S Whitmore 'to graze 220 sheep and 40 cattle over the whole of the land comprised in this register unit, except that portion east of the track from Badlake Gate to Ridge Road . . .' Entry no 7 recorded a claim by Fred Davey 'To graze:—270 breeding ewes plus lambs, 90 hogs, 4 rams, 30 cattle, 12 ponies over the whole of the land comprised in this register unit'.

All ten entries in the rights section of the register affected all or part of the Harrison land, together in most instances with other land.

Section 5 of the 1965 Act contains provisions for the notification of and objections to registration. Subsections (4) to (7) provide:

'(4) Where an objection to a registration under section 4 of this Act is made, the registration authority shall note the objection on the register and shall give such notice as may be prescribed to the person (if any) on whose application the registration was made and to any person whose application is noted under section 4(4) of this Act.

(5) Where a person to whom notice has been given under subsection (4) of this section so requests or where the registration was made otherwise than on the application of any person, the registration authority may, if it thinks fit, cancel or modify a registration to which objection is made under this section.

(6) Where such an objection is made, then, unless the objection is withdrawn or the registration cancelled before the end of such period as may be prescribed, the registration authority shall refer the matter to a Commons Commissioner.

(7) An objection to the registration of any land as common land or as a town or village green shall be treated for the purposes of this Act as being also an objection to any registration (whenever made) under section 4 of this Act of any rights over the land.'

There were only two objections to the entries in the land section. One of them was subsequently withdrawn. The other, objection no 529, was submitted in 1971 by Mr E J and Mr G E Nicholls on the form prescribed by reg 5(1) of the Commons Registration (Objections and Maps) Regulations 1968, SI 1968/989. The relevant register unit number was expressed in the form as being 'CL 143 (part)'. The registration objected to was expressed as appearing in the land section of the register. The 'grounds of objection' were therein stated as being:

'The land edged red on the attached plan is part of Woodlands Farm and is the private property of the objectors. No rights of common thereover have ever been granted by deed nor have they been acquired by prescription.'

The land thus edged red comprised merely Woodland Common. The grounds of objection themselves thus did not relate to the rest of the land comprised in CL 143.

There was only one actual objection to the entries in the ownership section of the register. Objection no 642 made by the executors of W S Whitmore in 1970 related to entry no 1 in the ownership section. There were, however, also four deemed objections arising by virtue of the conflicting entries in this section to which I have already referred.

There were four actual objections to the entries in the rights section of the register, all made in 1970 or 1971. One of them was subsequently complied with. Of the other three, objection no 603, made by Mr L J Earl, related to entry no 1 in the rights section; objection no 604, made by Mr J W J Milton, related to entries nos 1 and 7, objection no 584, made by Mr O P J Weaver, related to entry no 1. However, by virtue of s 5(7) of the 1965 Act, objection no 529 submitted by the Nichollses to the entry in the land section fell to be treated for the purposes of that Act as being also 'an objection . . . to any registration . . . under section 4 . . . of any rights over the land'.

No objections were made by the appellant or by his father, Mr E M Harrison, to any of the registrations either in the land, rights or ownership sections of the register, within the time allowed under the 1965 Act for the making of such objections.

However, by the beginning of 1981, a number of objections had been made and were still unresolved. These fell into three categories. (1) *Land* section: objection no 529 made by Mr E J and Mr G E Nicholls. (2) *Ownership* section: (a) objection no 642 made by the executors of W S Whitmore to entry no 1; (b) the four deemed objections arising from the conflicting entries of Mr J W J Milton, Mr E M Harrison and the Badgworthy Land Co Ltd. (3) *Rights* section: (a) objection no 603 made by Mr L J Earl to entry no 1; (b) objection no 604 made by Mr J W J Milton to entries nos 1 and 7; (c) objection no 584 made by Mr O P J Weaver to entry no 1; (d) the deemed objections made by Mr E J and Mr G E Nicholls (arising by virtue of objection no 529 in the land section).

These various objections gave rise to a reference to a commons commissioner, Mr L J Morris Smith, pursuant to s 5(6) of the 1965 Act. He held a hearing on 25 November 1981 at which a large number of the interested parties were present or legally represented.

In relation to objection 529 to the entry in the land section, evidence was given on behalf of the Parish Meeting, of Mr George (successor to the applicant for rights entry no 1), and of Mr Burton (the applicant for rights entry no 8) and on behalf of the objectors (the Nichollses). Miss P J Tuckett, the applicant for rights entry no 4, was not present or represented and, in the absence of evidence to establish her right, the commissioner treated the deemed objection to this entry as successful in its application to her right.

At some stage in the hearing, the solicitor appearing for the appellant, as successor to Mr E M Harrison, informed the commissioner that the appellant wished to challenge the entries in the land section and the rights section so far as they affected the Harrison land. The commissioner declined to accede to this application on grounds to which I will refer later.

At the hearing, the interested parties *other than the appellant* (and Miss Tuckett) came to a mutual agreement under which they all accepted the validity of objection no 529 so far as it extended to Woodland Common.

In the result the commissioner, when he came to give his decision, excluded Woodland Common from the land registered in the land section.

As regards the objections to entries in the ownership section, there was no appearance on behalf of the objectors in the case of objection no 642. In the absence of evidence to support it, the commissioner held that it did not succeed. This left merely the four deemed objections arising from the conflicting entries of Mr J W J Milton, the appellant's father, and Badgworthy Land Co Ltd. These boundary disputes were resolved by agreement of the three interested parties. Pursuant to this agreement, the commissioner confirmed entry no 3 in the ownership section and also confirmed entries nos 1 and 2 with small modifications of the respective boundaries. The effect of these modifications was, inter alia, to exclude the relatively small section lettered 'E' from the land shown in the register as being in the ownership of the appellant.

As regards the objections to entries in the rights section, the deemed objections made by the Nichollses had already been dealt with by the exclusion of Woodland Common from the land registered in the land section. In relation to objections 603, 604 and 584, which related to one or more of entries nos 1 and 7, agreement was again reached between all the interested parties *other than the appellant* (and Miss Tuckett). Pursuant to the terms of this agreement, the commissioner: (1) confirmed the registration at entry no 1 in the rights section of the register modified so as (a) to reduce the grazing rights to 110 sheep and 15 cattle (instead of 220 sheep and 40 cattle), and (b) to exclude from the land over which the right is exercisable the area lettered 'A' and 'B' on the register map (Woodland Common and Anstey Money Common); (2) confirmed the registration, with the modification that the grazing rights were to be exercisable only over Anstey Rhiney Moor, ie the areas lettered 'E' and 'D' on the register map lying north of Ridge Road, all of which, with the exception of the relatively small area lettered 'E', belong to the appellant.

By an originating notice of motion dated 26 May 1983, to which there were 23 respondents, the appellant sought an order pursuant to s 18 of the 1965 Act that all matters relating to the registration of common land relating to unit CL 143 be remitted to a commons commissioner for rehearing. The grounds of appeal were that the decision of the commissioner was wrong in law in that (i) he refused to hear relevant evidence tendered by or on behalf of the appellant on the issues whether he should confirm or refuse to confirm the provisional registration of common land and rights of common in respect of that unit, (ii) he refused to allow the appellant's solicitors to participate at the hearing of the inquiry into those issues, (iii) he determined those issues in accordance with the terms agreed between those present and entitled to be heard at the inquiry without making any finding on the evidence submitted to him.

Whitford J dismissed this appeal. He said ([1984] 1 All ER 161 at 164, [1984] Ch 172
at 178–179):

> 'The point as I see it in the end falls within a relatively small compass, for the
> question I have got to decide is whether the commissioner was bound on the
> Nichollses objection to inquire into the validity of the whole of the registration . . .
> or whether his duty was the rather more limited duty . . . of giving a decision in
> relation only to the objection made by the Nichollses namely to the inclusion of
> Woodland Common within the land registration.'

The judge, after reference to a number of sections of the 1965 Act, concluded that the
commissioner's duty was of the more limited nature. He considered that the language of
the 1965 Act did not exclude the making of objection to part only of a registration in the
land section of the register. Accordingly, he considered that the mere fact that the
Nichollses had made an objection to the entry in the land section of part of the land
comprised in CL 143 (Woodland Common) did not automatically put in issue, and
indeed would not even have entitled the commissioner to consider, the validity of the
registration of the land as a whole or of the rights of common claimed over the remainder
of the land comprised in the register unit (see [1984] 1 All ER 161 at 167, [1984] Ch 172
at 183). He distinguished the decision of Walton J in *Re Sutton Common, Wimborne* [1982]
2 All ER 376, [1982] 1 WLR 647 and considered that the only question before the
commissioner was ([1984] 1 All ER 161 at 167, [1984] Ch 172 at 183): 'Should Woodland
Common be included or should it not?'

Before this court counsel for the respondents, in seeking to uphold the judge's decision,
has very properly focussed much attention on the meaning of the word 'matter' in s 5(6)
of the 1965 Act. Her attractively simple argument runs on the following lines. The need
for the reference to a commissioner envisaged by that subsection presupposes that a
dispute has arisen between two parties because there has been a registration under s 4,
that registration has been objected to but not cancelled, and the objection has not been
withdrawn. In these circumstances, it is suggested, the 'matter' which falls to be referred
to the commissioner under s 5(6) is the resolution of the particular dispute arising from
the particular objection, no more and no less. Correspondingly, it is submitted, the 1965
Act leaves it open to a person to object to part only of a registration; if an entry in the
land section refers to adjoining properties Blackacre and Whiteacre, it is open to him to
object merely to the entry referring to Blackacre and the sole 'matter' which will fall to
be decided by the commissioner as a result of any such objection will be the dispute
relating to Blackacre.

Counsel for the respondents seeks to derive support for this construction of the word
'matter' in s 5(6) from the opening words of s 6(1):

> 'The Commons Commissioner to whom any matter has been referred under
> section 5 of this Act shall inquire into it and shall either confirm the registration,
> with or without modifications, or refuse to confirm it . . .'

The fact that a registration may be confirmed 'with modifications' in her submission
supports the contention that an objection may be made to part only of a registration.
Furthermore, she has drawn our attention to reg 5 of the 1968 regulations, which
prescribes Form 26 and other provisions relating to the manner of making objections.
Reg 5(4)(*a*) states:

> 'Where an objection is of a type mentioned in sub-paragraph (*b*) below, the
> objection form must be accompanied by a plan clearly defining by distinctive
> colouring the land to which the objection relates . . .'

Sub-paragraph (*b*) lists the types of objection to which sub-para (*a*) applies. The list begins
as follows:

> '(i) an objection to the registration of land as common land or as a town or village
> green relating to part only of the land comprised in a register unit . . .'

There are other similar references to 'part only' in succeeding sub-paragraphs.

No doubt with due regard to this provision, objection no 529 made by the Nichollses to the entry in the land section was accompanied by a plan defining the land to which the objection related.

I think it very doubtful whether the 1968 regulations can be used in any way as an aid to the construction of the provisions of the 1965 Act relating to the manner of making and dealing with objections to registration (see *Hales v Bolton Leathers Ltd* [1951] 1 All ER 643, [1951] AC 531 and also *Jackson v Hall* [1980] 1 All ER 177, [1980] AC 854, a decision which was not cited to us in argument). However, lest I should be thought to agree with counsel for the respondent's contrary submission I should say that the wording of reg 5(4)(*b*) appears to me to contemplate that while an objection to an entry in the land section may *relate* to part only of the land comprised in a register unit, it will nevertheless be an objection to '*the registration of* [*the whole*] *land as common land*'.

This is entirely consistent with the way in which I read the relevant provisions of the 1965 Act. Irrespective of the form of the regulations, I think that an objection made under s 4 to the registration of any land as common land necessarily puts in issue the entire registration. It is the act of registration to which objection is taken; and that act is indivisible. It matters not that the *grounds* of objection relate only to part of the land comprised in the registration. The 'registration of land as common land' which was objected to in the present case was, in my view, the registration of the unit no CL 143 as common land.

This leads to a consideration of the meaning of the word 'matter' in s 5(6) of the 1965 Act. In this context we have the benefit of some authority, though it is not binding on this court. In *Central Electricity Generating Board v Clwyd CC* [1976] 1 All ER 251, [1976] 1 WLR 151 a provisional registration of certain land as common land had been made by the respondent authority. The appellants, who were owners of the greater part of the area, objected to the registration. Goff J, in commenting on the function of the commissioner, said ([1976] 1 All ER 251 at 256, [1976] 1 WLR 151 at 157):

'What is referred to him under s 5(6) is "the matter" and the matter in my view is whether or not the land is common land.'

In *Re Sutton Common, Wimborne* [1982] 2 All ER 376 at 379, [1982] 1 WLR 647 at 652 Walton J made observations to the like effect (though the contrary view does not appear to have been argued):

'. . . what is referred to a commissioner is not the dispute arising from the making of any objection but "the matter", that is to say, the validity of the registration which has been put into question by the objection.'

At least until the decision in the *Sutton Common* case, different commissioners held differing views as to the 'matter' which was before them in circumstances such as the present (see the examples given by Walton J ([1982] 2 All ER 376 at 383, [1982] 1 WLR 647 at 656)).

Counsel for the respondents in her very persuasive argument has failed to persuade me that the approach of Walton J to the construction of s 5(6) is wrong. On the contrary, I think it is correct. The provisions of s 5(6) which envisage a 'matter' being referred to the commissioner and those of s 6(1) which envisage him 'inquiring into it' presuppose that he must address his mind to a question. That question is, I think, *what is to be done about the registration to which objection has been taken*? That is the matter which is referred to him. This construction is, I think, fully supported by a reference to the duties imposed on him by s 6(1) after he has conducted his inquiry. He must either 'confirm the registration with or without modifications or refuse to confirm it'. It is also supported by a consideration of the general policy of the 1965 Act. Of course, the duty of inquiry imposed on the commissioner must necessarily involve, inter alia, an inquiry into and adjudication on the proprietary rights of individuals. But I do not think the legislature would have intended it to be regarded solely as a piece of civil litigation between such individuals; the public also clearly has an interest in its outcome.

In my opinion, therefore, with great respect to both of them, the commissioner and the judge erred in regarding the matter which fell to be dealt with by the commissioner as being simply a dispute concerning Woodland Common, which could properly be dealt with merely by giving effect to a compromise entered into between the Nichollses, as owners of Woodland Common, and those persons who had registered rights over it and had chosen to be represented at the hearing. The objection made by the Nichollses to the entry CL 143 in the land section had raised wider issues. It had put in question the alleged status as common land of the whole of the land comprised in that entry, which was thereby alleged to be common land, even though the stated grounds of objection related only to Woodland Common itself. Furthermore, by virtue of s 5(7) of the 1965 Act, that objection fell to be treated as an objection to any registration under s 4 of any rights over that land, in other words as an objection to entries 1 to 10 inclusive in the rights section of the register.

Counsel for the respondents drew our attention to the strict timetable embodied in the 1965 Act, and regulations made thereunder, which governs the registration of land as common land and rights over such land and for the lodging of objections to any such registrations. She emphasised that finality is of the utmost importance to the interested parties. She submitted that, if by the last date for lodging an objection a registered right of common has not been objected to and the registrant has received no notice of objection, the registrant is entitled to assume that his right is not challenged; indeed, by virtue of ss 7(1) and 10 of the 1965 Act the registration in such circumstances becomes final and conclusive. She submitted that in the present case the Harrisons, who did not object to the entries in the rights section themselves, are now effectively trying, long out of time, to mount an objection on the back of the objection by the Nichollses.

The answers to these points are, I think, as follows. As I have already indicated, objection no 529 by the Nichollses to the entry in the land section fell to be treated as an objection to all the entries in the rights section; and the Harrisons would have been entitled to take this into account in omitting to lodge any objection on their own behalf. By virtue of objection no 529, none of those entries in the rights section had become conclusive by the time when the hearing before the commissioner began; none of them was more than provisional; all of them were subject to known challenge. In these circumstances the registration of *all* the rights provisionally registered in the rights section, in my opinion, required confirmation by the commissioner.

Once a registration of rights under the 1965 Act requires confirmation by a commissioner, it appears to me that the onus of proving his case inevitably falls on the person making the registration. This was the opinion expressed by Walton J in the *Sutton Common* case [1982] 2 All ER 376 at 383, [1982] 1 WLR 647 at 656. Though Lord Denning MR expressed a contrary view in *Corpus Christi College, Oxford v Gloucestershire CC* [1982] 3 All ER 995 at 1000, [1983] QB 360 at 367, the opinion of Walton J was indorsed by Oliver LJ in that case ([1982] 3 All ER 995 at 1009, [1983] QB 360 at 367). The same approach to the matter has subsequently been adopted by Nourse J in *Re Ilkley and Burley Moors* (1983) 47 P & CR 324 and by Woolf J in *R v Commons Comr, ex p Winnington* (1982) Times, 26 November. Whitford J in his judgment in the present case ([1984] 1 All ER 161 at 167, [1984] Ch 172 at 183) accepted that if, contrary to his view, there had been a need for the commissioner to inquire into the validity of the registration in the land section as a whole the onus would have rested on the original registrant. And indeed I do not think counsel for the respondents contended to the contrary.

On the particular facts of the *Sutton Common* case the information placed before the commissioner should have indicated that the registration, by a Mrs Colyer, in the land section, so far as it related to a part of the land of which Robert Thorne Ltd (Thorne) claimed to be the owner, was questionable. The reason was that during the course of the hearing the only outstanding claim to a right of common over the Thorne land, by a Mr Butler, had disappeared 'in a puff of smoke' (see [1982] 2 All ER 376 at 381, [1982] 1 WLR 647 at 654). The only remaining question was whether the registration in the land section could and should be confirmed on the basis that the land was 'waste land of a manor'. (In view of the definition of 'common land' in s 22(1) of the 1965 Act there could be no other possible basis.) However, the commissioner was faced with evidence that cast grave doubts on the possibility of the land comprised in the relevant unit being waste land of a manor. In these circumstances, Walton J held that he had erred in not insisting that Mrs Colyer should discharge the burden of proof as to the validity of the registration, and in excluding Thorne's available and relevant evidence, even though Thorne had not objected to the registration and therefore had no right to be heard under the Commons Commissioners Regulations 1971, SI 1971/1727.

The facts of the present case differ from those in the *Sutton Common* case, since, so far as I am aware, during the course of the hearing before Whitford J nothing occurred so as to cause the outstanding claims to rights over the land comprised in unit CL 143 to disappear 'in a puff of smoke'. However, with this qualification, I think, the present case is in all relevant essentials on all fours with the *Sutton Common* case. Following mutatis mutandis the reasoning of Walton J, it appears to me that at the hearing before the commissioner the onus fell on (a) the Parish Meeting to prove its case against the appellant in relation to entry no 1 in the land section of the register and (b) the registrants of entries in the rights section of the register to prove their respective cases against him.

What then was required in the way of proof? In this context I do not think I can do better than cite a passage from the judgment of Walton J in the *Sutton Common* case [1982] 2 All ER 376 at 383, [1982] 1 WLR 647 at 657–657:

> 'Of course, in many situations extremely little in the way of proof will be required. To take an example used at the hearing in this case, if there is a large area of land which is registered as a common, and an objection is taken as to a small piece on the fringes of the land, which happens to be somebody's back garden, then although the objection of that person theoretically puts in question the status of the whole of the area, provided that nothing else arises to cast the slightest doubt on the status of the remainder of the land, the commissioner will, I think, be fully entitled to rely on the original statutory declarations made by the registrant pursuant to reg 8(1) of the Commons Registration (General) Regulations 1966, SI 1966/1471, as discharging the necessary burden of proof. I do not, of course, intend to lay down any general rules as to how the burden of proof is to be satisfied in any case where the matter is not so simple. That must depend on precisely how the matter presents itself to the commissioner in any particular set of circumstances, which may, of course, vary almost infinitely. But if it is borne in on the commissioner, as the result of information which is either before him or which is sought to be placed before him and which, if correct, is relevant, that the registration is questionable, then he should, in my view, insist that the burden of proof is properly discharged to his satisfaction so as to establish (if possible) that the registration has, in fact, been properly made.'

I respectfully agree with every word in this passage, though I think Walton J may possibly have expressed himself a litle more widely than he would really have intended in saying a little later in his judgment ([1982] 2 All ER 376 at 384, [1982] 1 WLR 647 at 657):

> '. . . but that he [the commissioner] should not exclude any relevant evidence appears to me to be quite plain, no matter from what quarter that evidence may come.'

Should the commissioner have heard the appellant in the present case? Regulation 19(1) and (2) of the 1971 regulations sets out categories of persons who are 'entitled to be heard' at the hearing of any dispute as to the registration of any land as common land or as to the registration of any right of common. The appellant, not having lodged any objection to the relevant registrations, was not included in these categories. He therefore had no absolute right to be heard under the regulations.

However, reg 14(1) not only obliges the commissioner to give notice of a hearing to each of the persons entitled to receive such notice under the detailed provisions of reg 14(2), (3) and (4) (who roughly correspond with the persons entitled to be heard under reg 19); it also obliges him, at least ten days before the hearing is due to take place, to—

'cause a notice giving particulars of the hearing to be published in one or more local newspapers circulating in the area in which the land the subject of the dispute is situated.'

The 1971 regulations thus clearly recognise, as one would expect, that persons who are not 'entitled to be heard' may have an interest in attending the hearing. Most important of all, reg 23(5) provides:

'At the hearing of a dispute as to the registration of land as common land . . . the Commissioner may, if he thinks fit, take evidence from any person present who gives his name and address and volunteers to give evidence.'

It is therefore indisputable that the commissioner would have had a discretion to admit the evidence of the appellant before deciding whether or not to confirm the registrations in the land section and the rights section with or without modifications. I can well understand why he did not see fit to permit him to give evidence in relation to these registrations, taking the view, as he clearly did, that the matter before him was a limited dispute whether Woodland Common should or should not be included in the land registration. However, with respect to him, for reasons which I have attempted to explain, I think that he clearly erred in taking this view and that this led him wrongly to refuse to permit the appellant to adduce evidence.

The fact that the commissioner and the judge himself adopted an incorrect approach to the matter is, in my opinion, well illustrated by a point forcefully stressed by counsel for the appellant. The very modifications of entries nos 1 and 7 in the rights section of the register, sanctioned and directed by the commissioner, themselves substantially affected the appellant. In the case of both entries, they had the effect of switching the grazing rights claimed to much smaller areas, which still included the appellant's land. It is true that in the case of entry no 1 the number of permitted sheep and cattle was at the same time considerably reduced. Nevertheless, in default of any proper inquiry into the matter, it had to be assumed that the modifications by themselves might substantially prejudice and reduce the value of the Harrison land. The commissioner, in confirming the registrations at entries nos 1 and 7 with modifications of this nature, did so effectively without any prior inquiry; he did not hear the appellant, but for practical purposes treated him as bound by a compromise to which he was not a party.

Counsel for the appellants submitted in effect that there is nothing in the 1965 Act or the regulations made thereunder which compels or justifies a procedure such as this, which would appear to produce a result rather unfair to the appellant. I agree. His point well illustrates the difficulties in accepting the view that the Nichollses' objection to the registration in the land section of the register merely put in question the status of Woodland Common as common land or that Woodland Common could properly be looked at in isolation at the inquiry before the commissioner. For reasons which I have attempted to explain, I think these difficulties were insuperable. Though it was a matter for his discretion, the commissioner should, in my opinion, undoubtedly have permitted the appellant to adduce evidence relevant to the validity of the relevant entries in the land section and the rights section in so far as they affect the Harrison land.

To sum up my conclusions: (1) with great respect to him, the judge in my opinion erred in law in concluding that objection no 529 only put in issue the status of Woodland Common as common land and did not put in issue the status of the Harrison land as common land or the rights provisionally registered thereover and the quantum thereof in accordance with s 5(7) of the 1965 Act; (2) the judge, in my opinion, likewise erred in law in concluding that the commissioner was right (a) in failing to put the respective registrants of entries in the land section and the rights section of the register to proof, (b) in refusing to permit the appellant to adduce evidence of the nature already mentioned and (c) in treating the matter referred to him as being solely a dispute between the Nichollses and the registrants of rights registered in the register which was capable of being finally resolved by an agreement to which the appellant was not a party.

For these reasons, I would allow this appeal and remit the matter for a rehearing by the Chief Commons Commissioner or some other commissioner other than Mr Morris

Smith with a direction to hear and determine the validity of the registrations in the land
section and rights section under CL 143 in so far as these respective registrations affect
the Harrison land and to hear evidence and submissions on behalf of the appellant in
relation to such registrations.

**SIR JOHN DONALDSON MR.** The scheme of the Commons Registration Act 1965
involves, as a first stage, the provisional registration of land alleged to be common land
as defined in the Act and of rights of common alleged to be enjoyed over such land. The
second stage allows of objections to the provisional registrations. If the applicant for
provisional registration then withdraws his application with the consent of any other
person who has applied for provisional registration of that land or right, the entry is
expunged. If, on the other hand, the objections are withdrawn, the entry becomes final
(see s 7). These various steps are subject to a statutory timetable and if neither the
application for registration nor all the objections to it have been withdrawn before the
appropriate time, the registration authority is required by s 5(6) to 'refer the matter to a
Commons Commissioner'. This appeal concerns the duties of the commons commissioner, Mr L J Morris Smith, on such a reference.

The unit of common land provisionally registered consisted of 'West Anstey Common
including Anstey Rhiney Moor, Guphill Common, Anstey Money Common, Woodland
Common and part of Twitchen Common' in North Devon. It was registered as a single
unit and given the number CL 143. I refer to this area of land as 'the unit land'. Mr
Harrison, the appellant, is the owner of Anstey Rhiney Moor and Guphill Common,
which together appear to amount to a little more than half the unit land.

Woodland Common, a much smaller part of the unit land, but by no means
inconsiderable, was owned by the Nichollses. Various claimants to rights of common
applied to have their alleged rights registered and some of these rights extended to the
whole of the unit land. For example, Mr Whitmore claimed the right to graze 220 sheep
and 40 cattle over the whole of the unit land, Mrs Tuckett claimed a similar right in
respect of 15 ponies and 15 cattle, Mr Burton 65 cattle, 390 sheep and lambs and 10
horses, Mr Earl 20 bullocks and 100 sheep and the Nichollses 30 bullocks and 200 sheep.

The Nichollses objected to the entry of their part of the unit land as being common
land and this objection was registered. For the reasons given by Slade LJ this constituted
an objection to the registration of the whole of the unit land, albeit their complaint
related only to their own land. By s 5(7) this objection was deemed to extend to all rights
of common over the unit land, albeit the complaint again related only to such rights over
their land. Various other objections were registered, but are immaterial for present
purposes. However, the appellant failed to register any objection, probably due to an
oversight or misunderstanding. The issue in the appeal is whether, having failed to
register any objections within the statutory time limits, the appellant was entitled to be
heard at the commons commissioner's inquiry on the question of whether his land was
common land capable of being subject to the various rights of common which had been
claimed.

At the hearing the Nichollses reached a settlement with the various claimants to rights
over their land on the basis that their land was not common land and could therefore be
subject to no rights of common. What consideration they provided for this agreement,
if any, has not been revealed. The commissioner without hearing any evidence excluded
the Nichollses' land from the unit land and confirmed the registration of the remainder
of the unit land as common land. This was of course a quite different unit from that
which had been provisionally registered. He refused to hear the appellant in opposition.

The duties of the commons commissioner at such an inquiry are set out in s 6(1) of the
1965 Act:

> 'The Commons Commissioner to whom any matter has been referred under
> section 5 of this Act shall inquire into it and shall either confirm the registration,
> with or without modifications, or refuse to confirm it; and the registration shall, if
> it is confirmed, become final, and, if the confirmation is refused, become void . . .'

The commissioner took the view that 'the matter' referred to him was the provisional registration of the unit land and rights over it in so far only as there were extant objections. There being no objections to the registration of the appellant's land as common land or to rights of common over that land, neither that land nor those rights were comprised in the reference. If this is right, there can be no criticism of his actions once the registered objections had been disposed of by agreement. Nothing remained for him to do, save to give effect to those agreements. Whitford J, who considered the special case stated by the commissioner, upheld the commissioner's decision. From that decision the appellant now appeals.

Whitford J was referred to a decision of Walton J in *Re Sutton Common, Wimborne* [1982] 2 All ER 376, [1982] 1 WLR 647 that an objection to a registration of common land put in issue the validity of the whole of the entry and not just that part to which the objection related. He also held that the onus of proof then lay on the person who had applied for registration. Whitford J appears to have concluded that the *Sutton Common* case was distinguishable, but I do not understand on what basis. Counsel for the respondents submitted that the distinction lay in the fact that in the *Sutton Common* case, all claims to rights of common having been disposed of, the land had to be 'waste land of a manor, not subject to rights of common', if it was to be held to be common land. But this, as I see it, was not the basis of Walton J's decision and it does not appear to me to constitute a valid distinction.

There are two schools of thought. Whitford J considered that 'the matter' referred to the commissioner was limited to claims to which formal objections had been made and not withdrawn. Walton J considered that 'the matter' was the whole provisional registration. I have no doubt that Walton J was right. Section 6(1) shows that what is referred to the commissioner under s 5(6) is 'the registration'. The commissioner has to inquire into it and either confirm it with or without modification or refuse to confirm it. If, for example, an objector contends that the eastern half of whatever has been provisionally registered as common land should be excluded from registration, he is objecting to the registration of the land as provisionally registered and all of it and is contending that a different parcel of land should be registered, namely that which had been provisionally registered less the eastern half.

Thus far I accept the appellant's arguments. But if the commissioner has known of Walton J's decision, which he quite probably did not, and had applied it, he could have sought to justify the course which he adopted on a different basis. He could have said that (a) he was justified in excluding the evidence and representations which the appellant wanted to put forward and (b) that without that evidence and those representations, the only materials before him were the statutory declarations made in support of the applications for registration and the agreement between the applicants for registration and the objectors that the Nichollses' land should be excluded. Accordingly the crucial question is whether the commissioner was justified in excluding the appellant's proposed contribution to the debate, not on the ground that he did not have to consider the status of the appellant's land and rights of common over it, but for some other reason.

That other reason is said to be provided by the Commons Commissioners Regulations 1971, SI 1971/1727, to which the commissioner in fact referred. These are procedural rules governing the conduct of commons inquiries. Under reg 18 the procedure is to be such as the commissioner in his discretion shall determine, subject to the other regs in Pt II. Regulation 19 gives various people, such as the person on whose application the registration was made and the objectors, an entitlement to be heard. Regulation 23(5) entitles the commissioner to take evidence from any person present at the inquiry, if the matter referred concerns the registration of land as common land. Regulation 26 confines objectors to relying on grounds put forward in their formal objections, unless the commissioner thinks it just in all the circumstances to allow them to put forward additional grounds which appear to be material.

The commissioner seems to have construed reg 19 as if it provided that the appellant was not entitled to be heard. This was an error. Regulation 19 gave him no right to be heard, since he was not in any of the specified categories, but it did not disentitle him to be heard. The commissioner had a discretion to take his evidence under reg 23(5) and also, I am inclined to think, a general discretion if satisfied that the appellant could make a serious and sensible contribution and that it would be unjust to exclude him.

More impressive is an argument based on reg 26. If someone who has formally objected is, prima facie, to be confined to the four corners of his formal objection, why should someone who has not objected be able to put forward evidence and submissions without any limitation? There was a stage in the hearing when I was minded to accept this argument, but I have come to the conclusion that it cannot be sustained on the facts of this case. Whatever the real reason why the appellant did not make any formal objection, his inaction is consistent with his acceptance of the whole of the unit land as being common land and the various people who claimed rights of common over the whole of the land as having those rights. But if, subsequent to the reference to the commissioner, those who applied to register the whole of the unit land and those who claimed rights of common over that land are to be allowed, by agreement, to alter their contention in fundamental respects and thereafter to contend that (a) the Harrison land is common land but the Nichollses' land is not and (b) there are rights to graze 980 sheep and lambs, 4 rams, 150 cattle, 20 bullocks, 90 hogs, 27 ponies and 10 horses on half the area originally put forward as the grazing ground, it seems to me that the appellant was faced with an entirely new case and that he was entitled to ask the commissioner to hear him in the exercise of discretion.

Had these revised boundaries and rights been registered originally, the appellant might well have sought to have the Nichollses' land registered or his own land excluded on the basis that the position of the two holdings was indistinguishable and that if one was common land, so was the other or alternatively neither was common land. He might also have objected to all the rights being claimed as relating solely to his own land and that of owners other than the Nichollses, on the basis that if such rights existed at all, the burden of them had always been spread over the whole of the unit land. As things now are, the Nichollses can fence the various animals out of their land and confine them to the remainder of the unit land which is predominantly owned by the appellant. It also means that where common rights exist over a large area, the owner of a part of that area can, by doing a deal with the objectors, in effect transfer rights of common from his land on to the owners of the remainder of the unit land. This cannot be right.

Counsel for the respondents then treated us to the familiar 'floodgates' argument and submitted that no commons inquiry had ever been conducted on this basis. She went on to suggest that to allow the appeal on this ground would cast doubt on the validity of countless inquiries which had already taken place. I am not persuaded. Our concern is with this particular inquiry. The commissioner had a discretion to permit the appellant to be heard, but he was unaware of this fact and so never considered exercising it. We must therefore do so for him. I have no doubt that Mr Harrison should be heard. Indeed, in the circumstances of this case, I do not see how the commissioner's discretion could properly have been exercised in any other way.

I would allow the appeal and concur in the order proposed by Slade LJ. The commissioner concerned will no doubt consider whether in the interests of justice the appellant should not be required to particularise his objections, thus giving the other parties the chance to call evidence additional to the formal evidence which has already been submitted.

**LLOYD LJ.** I agree.

*Appeal allowed. Leave to appeal to the House of Lords refused.*

Solicitors: *Robbins Olivey & Blake Lapthorn*, agents for *Barrow & Chapman*, Dulverton (for the appellant); *Crosse Wyatt & Co*, South Molton (for the respondents).

Diana Procter    Barrister.

# Stearn and others v Twitchell

CHANCERY DIVISION
WARNER J
22, 23 NOVEMBER, 7 DECEMBER 1984

*Sale of land – Contract – Contract by correspondence – Whether contract resulting from acceptance by letter of an oral offer referring to written document not itself a letter constituting a 'contract by correspondence' – Law of Property Act 1925, s 46.*

On the true construction of s 46[a] of the Law of Property Act 1925, a 'contract by correspondence' does not include a contract arising out of the acceptance by letter of an oral offer to buy or sell land (even where that oral offer refers to a written document not itself a letter), since a single letter does not constitute 'correspondence' and there is a difference between correspondence which brings a contract into existence and correspondence which merely evidences a contract made by other means. Similarly, an oral acceptance of an offer made by letter will not, without more, constitute a 'contract by correspondence' (see p 634 *a b* and *e* to *h*, post).

### Notes
For offer and acceptance in contracts for the sale of land, see 42 Halsbury's Laws (4th edn) para 21, and for cases on the subject, see 40 Digest (Reissue) 17–24, 16–84.

   For the Law of Property Act 1925, s 46, see 27 Halsbury's Statutes (3rd edn) 421.

### Appeal
The plaintiffs, Edward William Stearn, Anita Stearn, Mere Hall Estates Ltd, James Francis Ruddy and Edward Douglas Simons, appealed against the order of Master Barratt dated 2 October 1984 whereby he determined that the agreement for the sale of certain land between the plaintiffs and the defendant, William James Twitchell, was a contract by correspondence and that therefore the rate of interest applicable on the purchase price was 5% per annum in accordance with condition 5 of the Statutory Form of Conditions of Sale 1925, SR & O 1925/779, made under s 46 of the Law of Property Act 1925. The hearing was in chambers but judgment was given by Warner J in open court. The facts are set out in the judgment.

*A J Bateson QC* and *D McConville* for the plaintiffs.
*Sally Finn* for the defendant.

*Cur adv vult*

7 December. The following judgment was delivered.

**WARNER J.** This is an appeal against an order of Master Barratt. In accordance with the new procedure, I heard the appeal in chambers, but I am delivering judgment in open court because the case gives rise to a question of interpretation of s 46 of the Law of Property Act 1925 on which, as counsel both told me, and as is confirmed by the textbooks to which I was referred, there is no existing judicial authority.

   The plaintiffs in this action were between them the freehold owners of an estate near Ludlow in Shropshire, called the Whitton Court Estate. The first two plaintiffs are Mr and Mrs E W Stearn (the vendors). Whitton Court was their home. The third plaintiff, Mere Hall Estates Ltd (formerly Whitton Court Estates Ltd), is a private company of which the vendors are directors and shareholders. The fourth and fifth plaintiffs, Mr Ruddy and Mr Simons, are the trustees of a family trust for the vendors' children.

   On 22 December 1982 the vendors, acting or purporting to act on behalf of the

---

*a*   Section 46 is set out at p 633 *e f*, post

company and of the trustees as well as on their own behalf, entered into a contract for the sale of a large part of the estate to Mr W J Twitchell, the defendant, for £125,000. It was a written contract, prepared without benefit of legal advice on either side, but nothing turns on it.

On the same day the vendors granted the defendant an option to purchase the rest of the estate for £115,000. The relevant document (which I shall call 'the option document') was handwritten by one of the vendors on Whitton Court writing paper, that is to say on a sheet of writing paper headed with the address and telephone number of Whitton Court. It is undated. The text of it is as follows:

'This document gives an option to purchase the remaining property known as the Whitton Court Estate to Mr. W. J. Twitchell until 15/1/83 for the sum of £115,000 [and that is repeated in words] to be completed on or before 31/3/83.'

The vendors each signed the document twice, the second time as directors of the company.

No problem arises from the circumstance that some of the land comprised in the option belonged to the company and some to the trustees.

As soon as those documents had been brought into existence, solicitors were instructed on both sides: Mr Attwood of William Attwood & Son for the vendors and Mr Brooks of Woolley & Weston for the defendant.

On 14 January 1983, which was a Friday, the defendant telephoned Mr Attwood to say that he, the defendant, was exercising the option. However, on the following Monday morning, 17 January, Mr Attwood received from the defendant through the post a letter dated 14 January in which he confirmed that he was taking up the option but subject to conditions, in particular a condition as to the sale and purchase by third parties of a strip of land adjoining land comprised in the option and a condition postponing completion until 1 May 1983.

On receipt of that letter Mr Attwood telephoned Mr Brooks, informed him of the contents of the letter and told him that the option must be exercised on the written terms or not at all. He gave the defendant an extra 48 hours, expiring at midnight on Tuesday, 18 January, to say which of a number of possible courses he wished to adopt. There were, on 17 January, further telephone conversations between Mr Attwood and Mr Brooks, and between them and their respective clients, but nothing was said during the course of those conversations that materially altered the situation, except that, in the late afternoon, Mr Brooks informed Mr Attwood that the defendant unconditionally exercised the option.

On the same day, 17 January, Mr Attwood and Mr Brooks wrote letters to each other which crossed in the post. Mr Attwood must have dispatched his letter before hearing from Mr Brooks that the defendant had decided to exercise the option unconditionally because he did not mention that fact in the letter. He confined himself to enclosing a copy of the defendant's letter of 14 January and to repeating what he, Mr Attwood, had told Mr Brooks on the telephone as to the courses open to the defendant, including of course the 48 hour extension of time for exercising the option. I must read the first three sentences of Mr Brooks's letter. They were as follows:

'Re Whitton Court, Whitton near Ludlow.

We refer to our telephone conversations today during which you informed us that the purported exercise by our client of the option to purchase certain parts of the above estate was a nullity. You did, however, agree to extend the option period for a further 48 hours to enable our client to reconsider and to exercise the option on the terms as stated in the written memorandum if he still wished to do so. We have taken instructions and as we informed you on the telephone late this afternoon, our client does now so exercise his option . . .'

I need not, I think, read any more of the letter.

Disputes arose between the parties, and the writ in this action was issued on 17 March

1983. Eventually the action was tried by Goulding J and he delivered judgment on 9 May 1984. He granted the plaintiffs specific performance of the agreement evidenced by the option document, the defendant's letter of 14 January 1983 and Mr Attwood's and Mr Brooks's letters of 17 January 1983. Goulding J directed that minutes should be prepared of his order. That took a little time and his order was not in fact made until 20 June 1984. It directed, among other things, an inquiry into—

'what rate of interest (if any) beyond 5 per centum per annum should be allowed for on the sum of £115,000 the purchase moneys for the property comprised in the said agreement from 31st March 1983 when the purchase ought to have been completed according to the terms of the agreement.'

What lies behind that is a contention advanced on behalf of the defendant that the agreement in question was a 'contract by correspondence' within the meaning of those words in s 46 of the Law of Property Act 1925, so that the statutory form of conditions of sale prescribed by the Lord Chancellor under that section applies (see the Statutory Form of Conditions of Sale 1925, SR & O 1925/779). Those conditions were in fact prescribed as long ago as 7 August 1925 and the rate of interest for which they provide is only 5%.

The summons for the inquiry came before Master Barratt on 2 October 1984. He was persuaded that the agreement was 'a contract by correspondence' and he held accordingly that the rate of interest payable on the purchase price of £115,000 was 5%. The present appeal is against that decision. It is agreed between the parties that I should decide only the question whether the agreement is indeed a contract by correspondence within the meaning of the section and that, if I hold that it is not, I should send the case back to the master to determine what rate of interest should apply.

Section 46 reads as follows:

'The Lord Chancellor may from time to time prescribe and publish forms of contracts and conditions of sale of land, and the forms so prescribed shall, subject to any modification, or any stipulation or intention to the contrary, expressed in the correspondence, apply to contracts by correspondence, and may, but only by express reference thereto, be made to apply to any other cases for which the forms are made available.'

There is no relevant statutory definition of the phrase 'contracts by correspondence'. The question is therefore simply what that phrase means in the context of the section.

I was referred to the definition of 'correspondence' in the Oxford English Dictionary. The relevant definition there is no 6: 'Intercourse or communication by letters.' I was also referred to two textbooks. The first was Professor J T Farrand's *Emmet on Title* (18th edn, 1983) p 83, where there is the following passage about s 46:

'The Act contains no definition of the word "correspondence". The popular meaning of the word is a contract arrived at by the parties by letters through the post or by hand. It would probably apply to the case where an offer was made by word of mouth and accepted by a letter through the post or by hand delivery, and to the case where the offer was made by letter through the post or by hand and accepted by word of mouth. Sometimes a contract is made by word of mouth, and by arrangement each of the parties writes to the other referring to the contract so made and confirming the terms in writing. It is doubtful whether the expression would cover this case.'

The other textbook to which I was referred was Professor J T Farrand's own book *Contract and Conveyance* (4th edn, 1983) p 81. I do not think that what Professor Farrand says there, in so far as it is material to this case, adds anything to the passage in *Emmet*, except that he points out the undesirability for a vendor of entering into a contract for the sale of land without the shelter of conditions and suggests that, for that reason, the widest possible application should be given to the statutory form of conditions.

I agree that letters confirming an oral contract would not constitute a 'contract by correspondence' within the meaning of the section. There is to my mind a difference between correspondence that brings a contract into existence and correspondence that merely evidences a contract made by other means.

I disagree, however, with the proposition that the phrase 'contract by correspondence' is apt to describe a contract resulting from the oral acceptance of an offer made by letter or from the acceptance by letter of an offer made orally. I do not think that a single letter can constitute 'correspondence'. I think that for there to be 'correspondence' there has to be at least an exchange of letters. It is noteworthy that the definition of 'correspondence' in the Oxford English Dictionary refers to 'letters' in the plural. I leave aside and say nothing about cases where telegrams or telexes are used.

Nor do I think that it would be proper for this court to give an artificially extended meaning to the phrase 'contracts by correspondence' in s 46 for fear of leaving vendors without the shelter of conditions. The section itself provides that the statutory form of conditions of sale may be made to apply to contracts other than those made by correspondence 'but only by express reference thereto', which does not seem to me consistent with an intention that those conditions should be given the widest possible application. The section also refers, in the case of a contract by correspondence, to 'any modification, or any stipulation or intention to the contrary, expressed in the correspondence' which suggests that the authors of the section envisaged that, in the case of such a contract, all its terms would be found in the correspondence, or at all events would be ascertainable from it.

I am prepared to assume in the defendant's favour that, in the present case, the acceptance that caused the relevant contract to come into existence was contained in Mr Brooks's letter of 17 January 1983. Counsel for the defendant drew my attention to a passage in *Emmet* p 91, which suggests that a merely oral exercise of the option would or might not have been effective. It does not seem to me, however, that the offer that was thereby accepted was contained in anything that can be described as a letter. Counsel for the defendant submitted that the option document itself had enough of the features of a letter to be treated as one. But the only features that that document had of a letter were that it was written on a sheet of headed writing paper and that it was signed. I think that it would be a plain misuse of language to describe it as a letter. In any case the irrevocable offer that it contained lapsed on 15 January 1983, the defendant's conditional acceptance of that offer by his letter of 14 January having been ineffective, or at most operating as a counter-offer, which was rejected by Mr Attwood on the telephone on the morning of 17 January 1983. The offer that was accepted by Mr Brooks's letter was the offer then made by Mr Attwood. That was an oral offer, albeit that it referred to the option document. Mr Attwood's letter of 17 January did not form part of the contract. It merely confirmed that oral offer and it reached Mr Brooks after the contract had been concluded by the posting of Mr Brooks's letter. At best, therefore, from the defendant's point of view, the case is one of a contract resulting from the acceptance by letter of an oral offer referring to a written document not itself a letter.

For the reasons I have already indicated, I do not think that such a contract is a 'contract by correspondence' within the meaning of s 46. I accordingly propose to allow this appeal and to send the case back to the master for further consideration by him.

*Appeal allowed. Leave to appeal to the Court of Appeal granted.*

Solicitors: *Cameron Markby* (for the plaintiffs); *Woolley & Weston*, St Albans (for the defendant).

Vivian Horvath    Barrister.

# Maynard v West Midlands Regional Health Authority

HOUSE OF LORDS

LORD FRASER OF TULLYBELTON, LORD ELWYN-JONES, LORD SCARMAN, LORD ROSKILL AND LORD TEMPLEMAN

14, 15, 16, 17, 21, 22, 23 MARCH, 5 MAY 1983

*Medical practitioner – Negligence – Diagnosis and treatment – Decision to operate – Operation involving risk to patient – Conflicting medical opinion as to necessity of operation – Whether negligence if operation supported by body of competent professional opinion.*

*Appeal – Evidence – Medical evidence – Conflicting medical evidence – Trial judge preferring medical evidence called by plaintiff to that called by defendant – Interference with judge's preference – Principles on which appellate court should act.*

Two consultants employed by the defendant health authority who were treating the plaintiff for a chest complaint thought she was suffering from tuberculosis, but also considered the possibility that she might be suffering from Hodgkin's disease. Accordingly, before obtaining the result of a test which would have determined whether she was suffering from tuberculosis, they decided to perform an exploratory operation to determine whether she was suffering from Hodgkin's disease. One of the consultants carried out the operation, which showed her in fact to be suffering from tuberculosis and not Hodgkin's disease. However as a result of the operation the plaintiff suffered damage to a nerve affecting her vocal cords which caused her speech to be impaired, such damage being an inherent risk of the operation. The plaintiff brought an action for negligence against the defendant health authority claiming that the consultants had been negligent in deciding to carry out the operation before obtaining the result of the tuberculosis test. At the trial of the action, expert medical evidence was called on both sides concerning whether the operation should have been carried out. The judge preferred the plaintiff's expert evidence and accordingly gave judgment to the plaintiff. On appeal, the Court of Appeal reversed the judge's decision, holding that there had been no negligence. The plaintiff appealed to the House of Lords.

**Held** – Where a plaintiff's claim was based on an allegation that the fully considered decision of two consultants in the field of their special skill was negligent, it was not sufficient for the plaintiff to show that there was a body of competent opinion which considered that that decision was wrong if there also existed a body of professional opinion, equally competent, which supported the decision as being reasonable in the circumstances. Furthermore, it was not sufficient for the plaintiff to show that subsequent events demonstrated that an operation need not have been performed if the decision to operate was reasonable at the time, in the sense that a responsible body of medical opinion would have accepted it as being proper. It had to be recognised that differences of opinion and practice existed in the medical profession and that there was seldom any one answer exclusive of all others to problems of professional judgment and therefore although the court might prefer one body of opinion to the other that was not a basis for a conclusion that there had been negligence on the part of the defendant doctor. On the evidence, the Court of Appeal had been right to reverse the judge's finding of negligence and the appeal would accordingly be dismissed (see p 636 *f g*, p 638 *d e g h*, p 639 *d e h*, p 640 *c d* and p 642 *a* to *c*, post).

Dicta of the Lord President (Clyde) in *Hunter v Hanley* 1955 SLT at 217, of Lord Bridge in *Whitehouse v Jordan* [1981] 1 All ER at 286 and of Brandon LJ in *Joyce v Yeomans* [1981] 2 All ER at 26–27 applied.

**Notes**

For the standard of care required of doctors, see 34 Halsbury's Laws (4th edn) para 12, and for cases on the subject, see 33 Digest (Reissue) 262–288, 2162–2330.

**Cases referred to in opinions**
*Bolam v Friern Hospital Management Committee* [1957] 2 All ER 118, [1957] 1 WLR 582.
*Hunter v Hanley* 1955 SLT 213.
*Joyce v Yeomans* [1981] 2 All ER 21, [1981] 1 WLR 549, CA.
*Watt (or Thomas) v Thomas* [1947] 1 All ER 582, [1947] AC 484, HL.
*Whitehouse v Jordan* [1981] 1 All ER 267, [1981] 1 WLR 246, HL.

**Case also cited**
*Onassis and Calogeropoulos v Vergottis* [1968] 2 Lloyd's Rep 403, HL.

**Appeal**
Blondell Agatha Maynard appealed, with leave of the Appeal Committee of the House of
Lords granted on 17 June 1982, against the decision of the Court of Appeal (Cumming-
Bruce LJ and Sir Stanley Rees, Dunn LJ dissenting) on 21 December 1981 allowing an
appeal by the respondents, West Midland Regional Health Authority, against the
judgment of Comyn J dated 28 July 1980 whereby he gave judgment for the appellant
for damages to be assessed in her action against the respondents for damages for
negligence by themselves their servants or agents in the performance of an operation or
treatment on her at East Birmingham Hospital between 20 July and 14 October 1970.
The facts are set out in the opinion of Lord Scarman.

*Richard Rougier QC* and *Raymond Walker* for the appellant.
*Philip Cox QC* and *Conrad Seagroatt* for the respondents.

Their Lordships took time for consideration.

5 May. The following opinions were delivered.

**LORD FRASER OF TULLYBELTON.** My Lords, I have had the advantage of
reading in draft the speech of my noble and learned friend Lord Scarman, and I agree
with it. For the reasons that he gives I would dismiss this appeal.

**LORD ELWYN-JONES.** My Lords, I have had the benefit of reading in draft the
speech to be delivered by my noble and learned friend Lord Scarman. I agree with it and
for the reasons he gives I would dismiss the appeal.

**LORD SCARMAN.** My Lords, the question in this appeal is whether a physician and
a surgeon, working together in the treatment of their patient, were guilty of an error of
professional judgment of such a character as to constitute a breach of their duty of care
towards her. The negligence alleged against each, or one or other, of them is that contrary
to the strong medical indications which should have led them to diagnose tuberculosis
they held back from a firm diagnosis and decided that she should undergo the diagnostic
operation, mediastinoscopy. It was an operation which carried certain risks, even when
correctly performed, as it is admitted that it was in this case. One of the risks, namely
damage to the left laryngeal recurrent nerve, did, as the judge has found and the
respondent authority now accepts, unfortunately materialise with resulting paralysis of
the left vocal chord. Comyn J, the trial judge, held that the two doctors were negligent.
The Court of Appeal (Cumming-Bruce LJ and Sir Stanley Rees, Dunn LJ dissenting) held
that they were not. The only issue for the House is whether the two medical men, Dr
Ross who was the consultant physician and Mr Stephenson the surgeon, were guilty of
an error of judgment amounting to a breach of their duty of care to their patient. Both
accept that the refusal to make a firm diagnosis until they had available the findings of
the diagnostic operation was one for which they were jointly responsible.
    The issue is essentially one of fact; but there remains the possibility, which it will be
necessary to examine closely, that the judge, although directing himself correctly as to
the law, failed to apply it correctly when he came to draw the inferences on which his

conclusion of negligence was based. Should this possibility be established as the true interpretation to be put on his judgment, he would, of course, be guilty of an error of law.

In English law the appeal process is a rehearing of fact and law. But the limitations on an appellate court's ability to review findings of fact are severe, and well established. Lord Thankerton stated the principles in *Watt (or Thomas) v Thomas* [1947] 1 All ER 582, [1947] AC 484; and recently the cases and the principles have been reviewed by this House in *Whitehouse v Jordan* [1981] 1 All ER 267, [1981] 1 WLR 246, itself a medical negligence case. It is, therefore, unnecessary now to restate them. I would, however, draw attention to some observations by Lord Bridge in *Whitehouse's* case and by Brandon LJ in a Court of Appeal case, *Joyce v Yeomans* [1981] 2 All ER 21, [1981] 1 WLR 549, since they are directly relevant to the problems facing your Lordships in this appeal. Lord Bridge said ([1981] 1 All ER 267 at 286, [1981] 1 WLR 246 at 269):

> '. . . I recognise that this is a question of pure fact and that, in the realm of fact, as the authorities repeatedly emphasise, the advantages which the judge derives from seeing and hearing the witnesses must always be respected by an appellate court. At the same time the importance of the part played by those advantages in assisting the judge to any particular conclusion of fact varies through a wide spectrum from, at one end, a straight conflict of primary fact between witnesses, where credibility is crucial and the appellate court can hardly ever interfere, to, at the other end, an inference from undisputed primary facts, where the appellate court is in just as good a position as the trial judge to make the decision.'

The primary facts in this case are undisputed. But there are gaps in our knowledge of some details of the medical picture due to a loss of hospital notes. These gaps occur in the critical period during which the two doctors made the decision which is said to be negligent. The gaps have to be bridged by inference. In this task, the trial judge, it must be recognised, had the advantage of seeing and hearing the two medical men whose professional judgment, reached during that period, is impugned. We are not, therefore, at the extreme end of Lord Bridge's 'wide spectrum', though we are near it. There is room for a judgment on credibility for the reasons given by Brandon LJ in *Joyce v Yeomans* [1981] 2 All ER 21 at 26–27, [1981] 1 WLR 549 at 556 where, speaking of expert evidence, he made this comment:

> 'There are various aspects of such evidence in respect of which the trial judge can get the "feeling" of a case in a way in which an appellate court, reading the transcript, cannot. Sometimes expert witnesses display signs of partisanship in a witness box or lack of objectivity. This may or may not be obvious from the transcript, yet it may be quite plain to the trial judge. Sometimes an expert witness may refuse to make what a more wise witness would make, namely proper concessions to the viewpoint of the other side. Here again this may or may not be apparent from the appellate court, although plain to the trial judge. I mention only two aspects of the matter, but there are others.'

These are wise words of warning, but they do not modify Lord Thankerton's statement of principle, nor were they intended to do so. The relevant principle remains, namely that an appellate court, if disposed to come to a different conclusion from the trial judge on the printed evidence, should not do so unless satisfied that the advantage enjoyed by him of seeing and hearing the witnesses is not sufficient to explain or justify his conclusion. But if the appellate court is satisfied that he has not made a proper use of his advantage, 'the matter will then become at large for the appellate court' (see [1947] 1 All ER 582 at 587, [1947] AC 484 at 488).

The only other question of law in the appeal is as to the nature of the duty owed by a doctor to his patient. The most recent authoritative formulation is that by Lord Edmund-Davies in the *Whitehouse* case. Quoting from the judgment of McNair J in *Bolam v Friern Hospital Management Committee* [1957] 2 All ER 118 at 121, [1957] 1 WLR 582 at 586 he said ([1981] 1 All ER 267 at 277, [1981] 1 WLR 246 at 258):

'"The test is the standard of the ordinary skilled man exercising and professing to have that special skill." If a surgeon fails to measure up to that standard in *any* respect ("clinical judgment" or otherwise) he has been negligent . . .' (Lord Edmund-Davies's emphasis.)

The present case may be classified as one of clinical judgment. Two distinguished consultants, a physician and a surgeon experienced in the treatment of chest diseases, formed a judgment as to what was, in their opinion, in the best interests of their patient. They recognised that tuberculosis was the most likely diagnosis. But in their opinion, there was an unusual factor, viz swollen glands in the mediastinum unaccompanied by any evidence of lesion in the lungs. Hodgkin's disease, carcinoma, and sarcoidosis were, therefore, possibilities. The danger they thought was Hodgkin's disease; though unlikely, it was, if present, a killer (as treatment was understood in 1970) unless remedial steps were taken in its early stage. They therefore decided on mediastinoscopy, an operative procedure which would provide them with a biopsy from the swollen gland which could be subjected to immediate microscopic examination. It is said that the evidence of tuberculosis was so strong that it was unreasonable and wrong to defer diagnosis and to put their patient to the risks of the operation. The case against them is not mistake or carelessness in performing the operation, which it is admitted was properly carried out, but an error of judgment in requiring the operation to be undertaken.

A case which is based on an allegation that a fully considered decision of two consultants in the field of their special skill was negligent clearly presents certain difficulties of proof. It is not enough to show that there is a body of competent professional opinion which considers that theirs was a wrong decision, if there also exists a body of professional opinion, equally competent, which supports the decision as reasonable in the circumstances. It is not enough to show that subsequent events show that the operation need never have been performed, if at the time the decision to operate was taken it was reasonable in the sense that a responsible body of medical opinion would have accepted it as proper. I do not think that the words of the Lord President (Clyde) in *Hunter v Hanley* 1955 SLT 213 at 217 can be bettered:

'In the realm of diagnosis and treatment there is ample scope for genuine difference of opinion and one man clearly is not negligent merely because his conclusion differs from that of other professional men ... The true test for establishing negligence in diagnosis or treatment on the part of a doctor is whether he has been proved to be guilty of such failure as no doctor of ordinary skill would be guilty of if acting with ordinary care . . .'

I would only add that a doctor who professes to exercise a special skill must exercise the ordinary skill of his speciality. Differences of opinion and practice exist, and will always exist, in the medical as in other professions. There is seldom any one answer exclusive of all others to problems of professional judgment. A court may prefer one body of opinion to the other, but that is no basis for a conclusion of negligence.

[His Lordship then considered the facts and evidence in detail and continued:]

At the trial and in the Court of Appeal there were two issues: causation and negligence. The judge decided both in favour of the plaintiff appellant. The Court of Appeal had no hesitation in upholding the judge on causation but reversed him on negligence. Thus it is that the only issue now is negligence. On this the judge's conclusions were that the operation was unnecessary, wrong, and in the circumstances unreasonable and a breach of the duty of care. He found that Dr Ross instigated the operation and that Mr Stephenson in failing to object to it and in sharing the decision was also in breach of his duty of care. The judge accepted the evidence of Dr Hugh-Jones, the appellant's principal expert witness, that it was almost certainly a case of tuberculosis from the outset and should have been so diagnosed, and that it was wrong and dangerous to undertake the operation. His detailed findings against Dr Ross were that he should not have used the operation where the right diagnosis was almost certainly tuberculosis, and that he should at the very least have waited for the pathological reports on the sputum, which in fact turned out to be positive. Dr Ross's defence that because of the risk of Hodgkin's disease he could not delay was rejected by the judge on the grounds that a delay of four to six weeks, up to ten at maximum, would not have mattered and that the fear of Hodgkin's disease being present was not a reasonable fear in the circumstances. The judge recognised that the defence had called a formidable number of distinguished experts, amongst whom it was legitimate to include Dr Ross and Mr Stephenson themselves, all of whom expressed a contrary view to his and approved the course of action taken in deferring diagnosis and performing the operation. The judge accepted not only the expertise of all the medical witnesses called before him but also their truthfulness and honesty. But he found Dr Hugh-Jones 'an outstanding witness; clear, definite, logical and persuasive'. The judge continued:

> 'I have weighed his evidence against that of the distinguished contrary experts. I do not intend or wish to take away from their distinction by holding that in the particular circumstances of this particular case I prefer his opinions and his evidence to theirs.'

My Lords, even before considering the reasons given by the majority of the Court of Appeal for reversing the findings of negligence, I have to say that a judge's 'preference' for one body of distinguished professional opinion to another also professionally distinguished is not sufficient to establish negligence in a practitioner whose actions have received the seal of approval of those whose opinions, truthfully expressed, honestly held, were not preferred. If this was the real reason for the judge's finding, he erred in law even though elsewhere in his judgment he stated the law correctly. For in the realm of diagnosis and treatment negligence is not established by preferring one respectable body of professional opinion to another. Failure to exercise the ordinary skill of a doctor (in the appropriate speciality, if he be a specialist) is necessary.

My Lords, it would be doing an injustice to the careful and detailed reasoning elsewhere evident in the judgment of the trial judge to dismiss this appeal on the basis of this one passage. But, to borrow a telling phrase from Cumming-Bruce LJ in the Court of Appeal, it certainly suggests that his finding of negligence is 'vulnerable to attack'. It gives rise to doubt whether he succeeded in making proper use of his advantage of seeing and hearing the witnesses who gave oral evidence.

The majority of the Court of Appeal developed a devastating attack on certain parts of the trial judge's judgment. They found that: (1) he failed to understand why Dr Ross expected the sputum tests to be negative; (2) he misunderstood Dr Ross's reason for not attaching diagnostic importance to the strongly positive Mantoux test; (3) he failed to understand the reasons in the medical history of the case for Dr Ross's cautious approach to diagnosis; (4) mistakenly finding that the respondent's experts were wrong in attributing the palsy of the right laryngeal nerve to the disease, he relied to some extent on this finding to discredit their opinion as to the wisdom and appropriateness of Dr Ross's course of action; (5) he mistakenly believed that an enlarged spleen (which the appellant did not have) was commonly an early indication of Hodgkin's disease.

My Lords, I will not take up time by explaining in detail why in my judgment each of these criticisms is justified. On points (4) and (5) the judge misunderstood the relevant evidence. On point (3) in preferring the opinion of Dr Hugh-Jones he utterly rejected the evidence of Dr Ross, Mr Stephenson and Dr Davies that the first cause for anxiety in the medical history was the X-ray of 2 July 1970 which showed an enlargement of the mediastinal glands. Dr Ross described it as puzzling, Mr Stephenson as 'alarming'. And Dr Shieff had noted on 2 July that perhaps there had been a recession followed by an enlargement of the glands. It was, of course, the contrast between the X-ray of 1968 and the X-ray of 2 July 1970 which led Dr Ross, when at a much later date he was discussing the case with the appellant's husband, to describe her condition as one of an 'enlarging' gland. The judge made the point that all the X-ray showed was an enlarged gland. This is perfectly true but Dr Ross in July 1970 had no means of knowing whether the enlargement had developed slowly over two years or recently and rapidly: and serial X-rays beginning in July, as was suggested he should have required, would not have given him the answer and might have led to delay which, if she was suffering from Hodgkin's disease, could have been fatal.

On point (2) Cumming-Bruce LJ pointed out, as is the fact, that Hodgkin's disease in a considerable proportion of cases does not convert a positive Mantoux reaction to negative. Though Dr Hugh-Jones's view, that a strongly positive Mantoux was very strong corroboration of tuberculosis was reasonable, there was room for the other view held by Dr Ross and others that it would not necessarily exclude Hodgkin's disease. Indeed it is plain, if I may make my own comment at this stage, that the judge consistently under-rated the possibility and the dangers of Hodgkin's disease.

And so far as sputum tests were concerned, the judge seems to have misunderstood why it was a reasonable view of Dr Ross that in the absence of any evidence of lesion in the lungs (and there was none, even though the possibility of hidden lesions remained) it was unlikely that the sputum tests would be positive. It was simply that in the absence of ulceration the infection would not make its way from mediastinum to bronchi or lungs.

None of these points are, however, decisive against the judge's finding of negligence. But they strongly suggest that this is a case in which, since the primary facts are not in dispute, the appellate court should review the trial judge's finding.

The Court of Appeal was, therefore, justified, I think, to treat the issue of negligence as being at large for it to draw the appropriate inferences and to reach its own conclusion. This it did: and I find the reasoning of the majority compelling. Cumming-Bruce LJ put it in this way. (1) Dr Hugh-Jones thought the appellant's case was a straightforward one of glandular tuberculosis in a West Indian lady: 'a typical case'. Dr Ross thought the case was not as obvious as Dr Hugh-Jones thought. Dr Ross accepted that glandular tuberculosis without any obvious lesion in the lungs, though very rare in persons of Caucasian origin, was not unexpected in West Indians, though he thought it unusual. He was supported by Mr Drew, a surgeon called for the defence (a witness whom the judge rejected on a ground (point 4) which was clearly mistaken). (2) Hodgkin's disease was certainly unlikely, as Dr Hugh-Jones argued. But, if present, its menace was so great that Dr Ross was not unreasonable in seeking to establish whether it was present or not. (3) Dr Ross was not unreasonable in refusing to wait for the sputum results before proceeding with the operation. Dr Hugh-Jones appeared to think that a few weeks delay would not matter. But he recognised, as did Dr Ross, that Hodgkin's was an extremely dangerous disease. Dr Ross was strongly supported by the evidence in his belief that, if it was present, treatment was urgent and should be begun before the disease began to spread. The caution of Dr Ross was as reasonable as the confidence of Dr Hugh-Jones. (4) The operation of mediastinoscopy was considered and acknowledged to be a reasonably safe procedure. Like all operations, it has its hazards, both general and particular. One of its particular hazards, by no means frequent, is permanent damage to the left laryngeal nerve, as sadly happened in the case of the appellant. Mr Stephenson had met with no complications in the 30 or more operations he had performed before July 1970.

The final conclusion, as expressed by Cumming-Bruce LJ, was that the judge's finding that the decision to operate was unreasonable could not be supported. Had the House not had the benefit of a fine, sustained argument by counsel for the appellant, I would at this stage have concluded my speech by expressing agreement with the views of the majority of the Court of Appeal. I hope I shall be doing no injustice to his argument, presented with a wealth of detail and an understanding of medical problems which I know won the admiration of the House, if I confine myself to a short statement of the reasons which compel me to reject it.

Before addressing himself to the medical issues, counsel submitted that it was wrong of the Court of Appeal to interfere with the findings of fact of the trial judge, and that it would be equally wrong of this House to review them. I have already given my reasons for rejecting this submission. It is certainly true that only rarely will the House itself review questions of fact. But the duty to do so does occasionally arise. Cases of professional negligence, where the primary facts are not in dispute, do sometimes require a review of the inferential findings, particularly in a case such as this where there are grounds for believing that the judge misunderstood some of the expert evidence.

It will be convenient to consider counsel's six medical points in the order in which he developed them. First, he stressed what he called the 'risk-benefit' ratio. The difficulty in the way of this point is the existence of a substantial body of professional opinion supporting Mr Stephenson's view that mediastinoscopy was, and is, a reasonably safe procedure. Its particular risks, haemorrhage and palsy of the left laryngeal nerve, were accepted, but their incidence is not high. Benefit from the operation could not be assured in advance: but it did provide the opportunity of direct visual observation of the swollen tissue and the procuring of a biopsy for analysis. These might well have proved to be of great value in either establishing or excluding the existence of Hodgkin's disease in this case. In the event, the operation was inconclusive: but it did enable Dr Ross to decide to proceed with anti-tuberculosis therapy.

Counsel described his second medical point as the 'cardinal question in the case'. It was based on Dr Hugh-Jones's opinion that enlargement of the mediastinal glands without necessarily a lesion in the lung was a typical presentation of tuberculosis in persons of Afro-Asian stock, though rare in persons of Caucasian stock. It was alleged that Dr Ross should have seen the appellant as a 'classic' case of Afro-Asian tuberculosis and should have proceeded to a firm diagnosis without calling for a mediastinoscopy. Dr Ross was not unaware of this difference between the two stocks, even though he refused to describe the presentation as a 'typical presentation' in a West Indian. His view he expressed in these words:

'In the West Indian and in some of the Asian and some of the African patients there may or may not be a lesion in the lung. She was unusual in that an adult should present with this [but] it was not unexpected in a West Indian because they do this more often than you would get it in an English person, but, even so, it is an unusual presentation to have enlarged glands like that with an adult.'

Dr Ross was not alone in his view. He was described by the judge as a careful, skilful, highly experienced consultant. And his experience lay in Birmingham where there was a substantial 'Afro-Asian' population. It cannot be said, therefore, that he was unaware of the presentation, even though he preferred to describe it as 'not unexpected' rather than as 'typical' or 'classic'. In this he was displaying, in contrast to Dr Hugh-Jones, a cautious approach to his problem of diagnosis. On the evidence adduced at trial his cautious approach cannot be said to be unreasonable.

Counsel's third point related to the three possibilities other than tuberculosis for the appellant's illness which had been mooted in evidence: sarcoid, carcinoma, Hodgkin's disease. Sarcoid and carcinoma could be ruled out, he submitted, as a justification in this case for deferring diagnosis until after a mediastinoscopy. He was, I think, plainly right.

He was left with the possibility of Hodgkin's disease. His fourth and fifth points dealt with this. Tuberculosis, he submitted, was almost certain, while Hodgkin's disease was no more than a remote possibility which should not have prevented a firm diagnosis of tuberculosis. Certainly this was Dr Hugh-Jones's view: it is not, therefore, to be considered unreasonable. But neither Dr Ross nor Mr Stephenson agreed: nor did the experts called for the defence. Dr Davies, a distinguished consultant physician, a Fellow of the Royal college of Physicians with continuous experience of tuberculosis over a period of 30 years, said that he would have called in this case for a mediastinoscopy for diagnostic purposes. It cannot, therefore, be said that Dr Ross, faced as he was with the contrast between the 1968 and 1970 X-rays, and aware of the menace of Hodgkin's disease if it were present, which was admittedly unlikely but by no means impossible, was unreasonable in his cautious approach to diagnosis. Further, there were very real differences of opinion amongst the experts as to the significance of some of the matters on which Dr Hugh-Jones relied for his confident diagnosis: notably the 'strongly positive' Mantoux test and the absence of an enlarged spleen. Finally, counsel submitted that Dr Ross, if uncertain, should have resorted to other diagnostic aids before using the mediastinoscopy operation. In particular why not wait for the sputum results? Why not arrange for serial X-rays? The answer of Dr Ross, which cannot on the evidence be said to be unreasonable, was that, if Hodgkin's disease should be present, speed was essential.

The judge thought that Dr Ross might have had an 'ideé fixe' about the possibility of

Hodgkin's disease. This, with respect, is not a possible view of his evidence read as a whole, especially in the light of the judge's own appraisal of him as a witness. Nor is it consistent with the existence of a strong body of evidence given by distinguished medical men supporting and approving of what he did in the circumstances of this case as they presented themselves to him at the time when he made his decision.

My Lords, the House in this case has reviewed the evidence. The review has led me to the clear conclusion that the Court of Appeal was right to reverse the judge's finding of negligence. I would dismiss the appeal.

**LORD ROSKILL.** My Lords, I have had the advantage of reading in draft the speech delivered by my noble and learned friend Lord Scarman. I entirely agree with it and for the reasons he gives I would dismiss this appeal.

**LORD TEMPLEMAN.** My Lords, I have had the advantage of reading in draft the speech of my noble and learned friend Lord Scarman, and I agree with it. For the reasons that he gives I would dismiss this appeal.

*Appeal dismissed.*

Solicitors: *Halls*, agents for *Rees Edwards Maddox & Co*, Birmingham (for the appellant); *Hempsons* (for the respondent).

Mary Rose Plummer    Barrister.


# Practice Direction

## COURT OF PROTECTION

*Mental health – Court of Protection – Practice – Application to the court – Matters requiring formal application – Trustee Act 1925, ss 36(9), 54 – Variation of Trusts Act 1958, s 1(3) – Mental Health Act 1983, ss 96(1)(d)(e)(k), 99 – Court of Protection Rules 1984, r 6, Form B.*

1. Rule 6 of the Court of Protection Rules 1984, SI 1984/2035, coming into operation on 1 February 1985, provides that any application to the court, other than a first application for the appointment of a receiver, may be by letter unless the court directs that a formal application shall be made, in which case it shall be made in Form B.

2. In some cases, decisions as to the need for a formal application will be made when the particular case is considered. However, application for the following relief will always require a formal application in Form B: (i) the settlement or gift of any property of a patient pursuant to s 96(1)(d) of the Mental Health Act 1983, other than gifts of amounts falling within the current annual limits for exemption from capital transfer tax, or qualifying for the exemptions for gifts in consideration of marriage or within the patient's normal expenditure; (ii) the execution for the patient of a will or codicil (s 96(1)(e) of the 1983 Act); (iii) the exercise of any power (including a power to consent) vested in the patient (s 96(1)(k) of the 1983 Act); (iv) the appointment of a new receiver (s 99 of the 1983 Act); (v) the appointment of new trustees under s 36(9) of the Trustee Act 1925 where the application is made subsequent to or separately from the first application for the appointment of a receiver; (vi) the appointment of new trustees under s 54 of the 1925 Act; (vii) orders for the execution of deeds of family arrangement (s 1(3) of the Variation of Trusts Act 1958).

A B Macfarlane
Master.

31 January 1985

# Sidaway v Bethlem Royal Hospital Governors and others

HOUSE OF LORDS

LORD SCARMAN, LORD DIPLOCK, LORD KEITH OF KINKEL, LORD BRIDGE OF HARWICH AND LORD TEMPLEMAN

3, 4, 5 DECEMBER 1984, 21 FEBRUARY 1985

*Medical practitioner – Negligence – Test of liability – Risk of misfortune inherent in treatment proposed by doctor – Doctor's duty to warn of inherent risk of misfortune – Operation to relieve persistent pain in neck resulting in serious disablement of patient – Doctor warning patient of material risks but not of all risks inherent in operation – Whether standard of care required of doctor in giving advice before operation the same as that normally required of medical practitioner in course of diagnosis and treatment – Whether higher standard requiring full disclosure to patient of all details and risks before operation.*

The plaintiff, who suffered from persistent pain in her neck and shoulders, was advised by a surgeon employed by the defendant hospital governors to have an operation on her spinal column to relieve the pain. The surgeon warned the plaintiff of the possibility of disturbing a nerve root and the possible consequences of doing so but did not mention the possibility of damage to the spinal cord even though he would be operating within three millimetres of it. The risk of damage to the spinal cord was very small (less than 1%) but if the risk materialised the resulting injury could range from the mild to the very severe. The plaintiff consented to the operation, which was carried out by the surgeon with due care and skill. However, in the course of the operation the plaintiff suffered injury to her spinal cord which resulted in her being severely disabled. She brought an action against the hospital governors and the surgeon's estate (the surgeon having died in the mean time) claiming damages for personal injury. Being unable to sustain a claim based on negligent performance of the operation, the plaintiff instead contended that the surgeon had been in breach of a duty owed to her to warn her of all possible risks inherent in the operation with the result that she had not been in a position to give an 'informed consent' to the operation. The trial judge applied the test of whether the surgeon had acted in accordance with accepted medical practice and dismissed the claim. On appeal the Court of Appeal upheld the judge, holding that the doctrine of informed consent based on full disclosure of all the facts to the patient was not the appropriate test under English law. The plaintiff appealed to the House of Lords.

**Held** – (1) (Per Lord Diplock, Lord Keith and Lord Bridge, Lord Scarman dissenting) The test of liability in respect of a doctor's duty to warn his patient of risks inherent in treatment recommended by him was the same as the test applicable to diagnosis and treatment, namely that the doctor was required to act in accordance with a practice accepted at the time as proper by a responsible body of medical opinion. Accordingly, English law did not recognise the doctrine of informed consent. However (per Lord Keith and Lord Bridge), although a decision on what risks should be disclosed for the particular patient to be able to make a rational choice whether to undergo the particular treatment recommended by a doctor was primarily a matter of clinical judgment, the disclosure of a particular risk of serious adverse consequences might be so obviously necessary for the patient to make an informed choice that no reasonably prudent doctor would fail to disclose that risk (see p 658 *b* to *d*, p 659 *c* to *f*, p 660 *c d f g* and p 662 *a b f g* and *j* to p 663 *d*, post); *Bolam v Friern Hospital Management Committee* [1957] 2 All ER 118 applied; *Canterbury v Spence* (1972) 464 F 2d 772 not followed; *Reibl v Hughes* (1980) 114 DLR (3d) 1 considered.

(2) (Per Lord Templeman) When advising a patient about a proposed or recommended treatment a doctor was under a duty to provide the patient with the information necessary to enable the patient to make a balanced judgment in deciding whether to

submit to that treatment, and that included a requirement to warn the patient of any dangers which were special in kind or magnitude or special to the patient. That duty was, however, subject to the doctor's overriding duty to have regard to the best interests of the patient. Accordingly, it was for the doctor to decide what information should be given to the patient and the terms in which that information should be couched (see p 664 *j* and p 665 *c* and *g* to p 666 *g*, post).

(3) Since (per Lord Diplock, Lord Keith and Lord Bridge) the surgeon's non-disclosure of the risk of damage to the plaintiff's spinal cord accorded with a practice accepted as proper by a responsible body of neuro-surgical opinion and since (per Lord Scarman and Lord Templeman) the plaintiff had not proved on the evidence that the surgeon had been in breach of duty by failing to warn her of that risk the defendants were not liable to the plaintiff. The appeal would accordingly be dismissed (see p 645 *a b g*, p 655 *f* to *h*, p 656 *j*, p 659 *e*, p 663 *d* to *f*, p 665 *a b* and p 666 *g*, post).

Per Lord Keith, Lord Bridge and Lord Templeman. When questioned specifically by a patient of apparently sound mind about the risks involved in a particular treatment proposed, the doctor's duty is to answer both truthfully and as fully as the questioner requires (see p 659 *e*, p 661 *d* and p 665 *b*, post).

Decision of the Court of Appeal [1984] 1 All ER 1018 affirmed.

### Notes

For the standard of care required of doctors, see 34 Halsbury's Laws (4th edn) para 12, and for cases on the subject, see 33 Digest (Reissue) 262–288, 2162–2330.

### Cases referred to in opinions

*Bly v Rhoads* (1976) 222 SE 2d 783.
*Bolam v Friern Hospital Management Committee* [1957] 2 All ER 118, [1957] 1 WLR 582.
*Canterbury v Spence* (1972) 464 F 2d 772, US App DC; *cert denied* 409 US 1064.
*Chatterton v Gerson* [1981] 1 All ER 257, [1981] QB 432, [1981] 3 WLR 1003.
*Crain v Allison* (1982) 443 A 2d 558.
*Derry v Peek* (1889) 14 App Cas 337, [1889–90] All ER Rep 1, HL.
*Donoghue (or M'Alister) v Stevenson* [1932] AC 562, [1932] All ER Rep 1, HL.
*Hills v Potter* [1983] 3 All ER 716, [1984] 1 WLR 641.
*Hunter v Hanley* 1955 SLT 213.
*McLoughlin v O'Brian* [1982] 2 All ER 298, [1983] 1 AC 410, [1982] 2 WLR 982, HL.
*Maynard v West Midlands Regional Health Authority* [1985] 1 All ER 635, HL.
*Nocton v Lord Ashburton* [1914] AC 932, [1914–15] All ER Rep 45, HL.
*Reibl v Hughes* (1980) 114 DLR (3d) 1, Can SC.
*Slater v Baker* (1767) 2 Wils 359, 95 ER 860.
*Whitehouse v Jordan* [1981] 1 All ER 267, [1981] 1 WLR 246, HL.

### Appeal

The plaintiff, Amy Doris Sidaway, appealed with leave of the Court of Appeal against the decision of that court (Sir John Donaldson MR, Dunn and Browne-Wilkinson LJJ) ([1984] 1 All ER 1018, [1984] QB 493) on 23 February 1984 dismissing her appeal against the decision of Skinner J on 19 February 1982 whereby he dismissed the appellant's action against the first respondents, the Board of Governors of the Bethlem Royal and Maudsley Hospitals, and the second respondents, Coutts & Co and Mrs Valda Helen Falconer, the executors of the estate of Murray A Falconer deceased, for damages for personal injury suffered by the appellant as a result of an operation carried out on her by Mr Falconer while employed by the first respondents. The facts are set out in the opinion of Lord Scarman.

*Leslie Joseph QC* and *Gerald Rabie* for the appellant.
*Adrian Whitfield QC* and *Nicola Davies* for the respondents.

Their Lordships took time for consideration.

21 February. The following opinions were delivered.

**LORD SCARMAN.** My Lords, the state of the evidence in this case compels me to the conclusion that the appellant has not made out a case of negligence against her surgeon, the late Mr Murray A Falconer. I regret profoundly that after a trial in the course of which the judge listened with great care to a substantial and complex volume of medical evidence and delivered a meticulous and detailed judgment, and after two appellate hearings (by the Court of Appeal and your Lordships' House), the conclusion should be that the plaintiff has failed to prove her case.

Such a result is, I believe, inevitable for a number of reasons. The issue is whether Mr Falconer failed to exercise due care (his skill was not challenged) in the advice which he gave his patient when recommending an operation; I use the word 'advice' to cover information as to risk and the options of alternative treatment. Whatever be the correct formulation of the applicable law, the issue cannot be settled positively for or against the doctor without knowing what advice, including any warning of inherent risk in the operation, he gave his patient before she decided to undergo it and what was his assessment of the mental, emotional and physical state of his patient. The trial judge derived no help on these two vital matters from the evidence of the appellant. Mr Falconer was not an available witness, having died before trial, and the medical records afforded no sure guide on either matter. Regrettable though a 'non-proven' verdict is, it is not, therefore, surprising. Where the court lacks direct evidence as to the nature and extent of the advice and warning (if any) given by the doctor and as to his assessment of his patient the court may well have to conclude that the patient has failed to prove her case.

This lack of evidence is unsatisfactory also from a purely legal point of view. I am satisfied, for reasons which I shall develop, that the trial judge and the Court of Appeal erred in law in holding that, in a case where the alleged negligence is a failure to warn the patient of a risk inherent in the treatment proposed, the Bolam test, (see *Bolam v Friern Hospital Management Committee* [1957] 2 All ER 118, [1957] 1 WLR 582), to which I shall refer in detail at a later stage of my speech, is to be applied. In my view the question whether or not the omission to warn constitutes a breach of the doctor's duty of care towards his patient is to be determined not exclusively by reference to the current state of responsible and competent professional opinion and practice at the time, though both are, of course, relevant consideration, but by the court's view whether the doctor in advising his patient gave the consideration which the law requires him to give to the right of the patient to make up her own mind in the light of the relevant information whether or not she will accept the treatment which he proposes. This being my view of the law, I have tested the facts found by the trial judge by what I believe to be the correct legal criterion. In my view the appellant has failed to prove that Mr Falconer was in breach of the duty of care which he owed to her in omitting to disclose the risk which the trial judge found as a fact he did not disclose to her.

I turn now to the detailed facts and issues in the case.

This is an appeal by the plaintiff, Mrs Sidaway, from the dismissal by the Court of Appeal ([1984] 1 All ER 1018, [1984] QB 493) of her appeal from the judgment of Skinner J given on 19 February 1982 whereby he dismissed her action for damages in respect of the personal injuries which she suffered as a result of a surgical operation performed on her by a neuro-surgeon on 29 October 1974. The first defendants are the governing body of the Maudsley Hospital, where she was treated and where she underwent the operation. The second defendants are the executors of Mr Falconer, the distinguished neuro-surgeon who advised and performed the operation. Mr Falconer died in August 1977, some five years before the trial of the action. Mrs Sidaway does not allege negligence in the performance of the operation. Her case is that she was not informed of a risk inherent in the operation, that the risk materialised with the result that she suffered, and continues to suffer, serious personal injury, and that, had she been warned, she would not have consented to the operation. Damages are agreed at £67,500 subject to liability.

The case is plainly of great importance. It raises a question which has never before been considered by your Lordships' House: has the patient a legal right to know, and is the doctor under a legal duty to disclose, the risks inherent in the treatment which the doctor recommends? If the law recognises the right and the obligation, is it a right to full disclosure or has the doctor a discretion as to the nature and extent of his disclosure? And, if the right be qualified, where does the law look for the criterion by which the court is to judge the extent of the disclosure required to satisfy the right? Does the law seek guidance in medical opinion or does it lay down a rule which doctors must follow, whatever may be the views of the profession? There is further a question of law as to the nature of the cause of action. Is it a cause of action in negligence, i e a breach of the duty of care, or is it based on a breach of a specific duty to inform the patient which arises not from any failure on the part of the doctor to exercise the due care and skill of his profession but directly from the patient's right to know?

Before attempting to answer these questions it is necessary to set out the facts of the case. At once a formidable difficulty arises. Mr Falconer was dead before the trial. The judge was not prepared to accept Mrs Sidaway's evidence that he gave no warning. The judge was, therefore, without any direct evidence as to the extent of the warning given. Further, the judge lacked evidence which Mr Falconer alone could have given as to his assessment of his patient with especial reference to his view as to what would be the effect on her of a warning of the existence of a risk, albeit slight, of serious personal injury arising from the operation however skilfully and competently it was performed. Such being the limitations on the availability of critically important evidence, I confess that I find it surprising that the trial judge felt able to reach the detailed findings as to the extent of the warning given which are a striking feature of his judgment. There is, however, no appeal against his findings; and I have no doubt that your Lordships' House must proceed on the basis of the facts as found. Nevertheless, the lack of knowledge of Mr Falconer's assessment of his patient reduces to some extent the guidance which your Lordships can give for the assistance of judges in future cases. It also presents difficulties for the appellant.

Mrs Sidaway was 71 years of age at the time of the trial in 1982. She was severely disabled by a partial paralysis resulting from her operation. The relationship of doctor and patient between Mr Falconer and herself had been long-standing prior to the operation. In 1958 she had injured an elbow at work and as a result had suffered persistent pain. Treatment failed to relieve pain. In July 1960 she was referred to the Maudsley Hospital, where Mr Falconer discovered that the second and third cervical vertebrae were congenitally fused and that there was a significant narrowing of the spinal column between the fifth and sixth vertebrae. Mr Falconer diagnosed the deformity in this area as the cause of her pain. He decided to operate. He removed the disc between the fifth and sixth vertebrae of the neck and fused the two vertebrae by a bone graft. Although pain persisted for another two years, it eventually disappeared. Mr Falconer's diagnosis was proved correct and his operation ultimately succeeded in relieving his patient's pain.

Mr Falconer annually reviewed his patient's progress between 1960 and 1970. In 1973 he wrote to Mrs Sidaway asking how she was. She replied, complaining of very persistent pain 'in the right arm and shoulder', which was the same area as before, and now also of pain in the left forearm. Mr Falconer saw her in the early months of 1974. After some delays, she was admitted to hospital on 11 October 1974. Her pain in the mean time had got progressively worse.

On admission Mrs Sidaway was thoroughly examined by Dr Goudarzi, a junior member of Mr Falconer's team. On 17 October she underwent a myelogram which revealed a partial block at the level of the C4/5 disc space, a posterior ridge in the same area which appeared to have, at least in part, a bony structure, and a narrowing of the subarachnoid space in the same area. Mr Falconer diagnosed that pressure on a nerve root was the cause of her pain and decided to operate. The operation, which he performed on 29 October 1974, and its risks were, if I may respectfully say so, admirably and lucidly described by the trial judge, from whose judgment I take the following description:

'The operation consisted of a laminectomy of the fourth cervical vertebra and a facetectomy or foraminectomy of the disc space between the fourth and fifth cervical vertebrae. A laminectomy is an excision of the posterior arch of the vertebra. It gives the surgeon access to the foramen or channel through which nerves travel from the spine laterally. Randomly placed in the foramina, running alongside the nerves, are small blood vessels known as the radicular arteries. These supply blood to the cord and are extremely vulnerable because of (a) their size and (b) the unpredictable nature of their siting. In one foramen, there may be one, two or more radicular arteries. Their rupture or blockage may cause damage to the cord by depriving it temporarily or permanently of its blood supply at the relevant level. At the operation, Mr Falconer freed the fourth cervical nerve root by removing the facets, or small bony protruberances, from the fourth vertebra and used a dental drill to free the nerve within the foramen.'

It was common ground between all the neuro-surgeons who gave evidence that the operation involved specific risks beyond those inherent in all operations under general anaesthetic. So far as the general risks are concerned, the judge commented that Mrs Sidaway was a healthy woman apart from her cervical spine, and no medical witness had suggested that any special warning as to the existence of those risks needed to be given.

The two specific risks of injury were (1) damage to a nerve root in the area of the operation and (2) damage to the spinal cord either by direct contact or by some interference, which might be slight and of short duration or very much more serious, of the radicular arteries running through a foramen. The risk of either sort of damage occurring was not great: one surgeon estimated the degree of risk at between 1% and 2%. But, if either risk materialised, the injury could be severe. Mr Uttley, the distinguished surgeon called on behalf of Mrs Sidaway, said that the possible effects of the damage ranged from a sensation of pins and needles in the hand to paraplegia, ie a partial paralysis. All the surgeons who were called as expert witnesses accepted that the risk of damage, though slight, was a real one. They distinguished between the two categories of specific risk, the effect of damage to a nerve root being in all probability that the operation would fail to relieve and might increase pain, while damage to the spinal cord might cause a partial paralysis. The risk of damage to the spinal cord was, however, in their opinion less than 1%.

There is no challenge to the judge's findings (1) that Mr Falconer's diagnosis was correct, (2) that his recommendation in favour of operative treatment was one which he could reasonably and properly have made to his patient and (3) that he performed the operation with due care and skill.

The issue between the parties arises solely in respect of the warning, if any, which Mr Falconer gave his patient of the specific risks inherent in the operation. None of the medical witnesses suggested that his decision to recommend the operation was itself wrong. And no one has ever suggested that the operation was carried out otherwise than competently and skilfully. The one criticism, made and pursued on behalf of Mrs Sidaway throughout this litigation, is that Mr Falconer was in breach of his duty as her medical adviser in failing to warn her of the risk of damage to the spinal cord.

Mrs Sidaway consented to the operation. She signed the usual consent form, in which she declared that the nature and purpose of the operation had been explained to her by Dr Goudarzi. Dr Goudarzi confirmed that he had given her this explanation; but he made it clear in his evidence that he would have left warning of the risks to Mr Falconer. And we know from the hospital records that Mr Falconer saw his patient before he operated. It would have been his practice to give a warning; but a finding as to what warning he gave faces the formidable difficulty to which I have already referred, that Mr Falconer was not available to give evidence. Nevertheless, the judge, while refusing to accept Mrs Sidaway's evidence that she was given no warning, made the following findings on the balance of probabilities. He said:

'On the evidence . . . the probabilities are that . . . on the day before the operation he [Mr Falconer] followed his usual practice . . . it is probable that he explained the nature of the operation [to his patient] in simple terms . . . As to the risks, I think it is probable that he mentioned the possibility of disturbing a nerve root and the consequences of doing so, but I am satisfied that he did not refer to the danger of cord damage or to the fact that this was an operation of choice rather than necessity.'

The medical witnesses were agreed that they would give a patient some warning of the specific risks involved before performing an operation of this kind. They would explain the nature and purpose of the operation, and that there was a small risk of untoward consequences and of an increase of pain instead of relief. Mr Uttley would go further: he would warn of the possible risk of some weakness of the legs resulting from the operation. Two answers in his cross-examination were of great importance. When asked whether he would question the judgment of a surgeon that it was not in his patient's interest to frighten her by talking about death or paralysis, he replied, 'Not at all'; and he agreed that such a judgment would be in accordance with a practice accepted as proper by a responsible body of competent neuro-surgeons. The existence of such a practice was also recognised by the other medical witnesses. Their view may be summarised as being that the extent of the warning is a matter for medical judgment with especial importance attached to the doctor's assessment of his patient.

This being the state of the evidence, the question for the House is whether the omission by Mr Falconer to warn his patient of the risk inherent in the operation of damage to the spinal cord with the possible result of a partial paralysis was a breach of duty owed by him to his patient. The duty of a doctor to warn was considered in *Bolam v Friern Hospital Management Committee* [1957] 2 All ER 118, [1957] 1 WLR 582, where it was treated as one to be answered within the context of the duty of care and skill owed by a doctor to his patient. In that case the plaintiff, a voluntary patient in the defendants' mental hospital, sustained fractures in the course of electroconvulsive therapy (ECT). The plaintiff claimed damages alleging negligence (1) in failing to administer a relaxant drug prior to the treatment, (2) in failing to provide some form of manual restraint during the passing of electric current through his brain and (3) in failing to warn him of the risks involved in the treatment. The case was heard by McNair J and a jury. The judge included in his summing up to the jury a number of directions as to the standard of care required of a doctor in advising and treating his patient. He said ([1957] 2 All ER 118 at 121, [1957] 1 WLR 582 at 586):

'The test is the standard of the ordinary skilled man exercising and professing to have that special skill . . . it is sufficient if he exercises the ordinary skill of an ordinary competent man exercising that particular art.'

He referred, without any critical comment, to the defence submission that the jury had to make up its mind on 'each of the three major topics' (these included the duty to warn of the risks of treatment) whether the defendants were acting 'in accordance with *a* [my emphasis] practice of competent respected professional opinion' (see [1957] 2 All ER 118 at 121, [1957] 1 WLR 582 at 587). And he concluded by directing the jury that a doctor is not guilty of negligence if he acts 'in accordance with a practice accepted as proper by a responsible body of medical men skilled in that particular art'. When the judge dealt with the facts, he reminded the jury of the differing evidence of the doctors as to the extent of warning which they believed to be proper before a patient decided to undergo a surgical operation. They all treated the question as one for medical judgment. There was, however, this difference of opinion among them: the doctor who recommended the ECT said that he did not agree that a patient should be warned of all the risks of the operation: he should be told that 'there were some slight risks, but not told of the risks of catastrophe' (see [1957] 2 All ER 118 at 124, [1957] 1 WLR 582 at 590. Others who were called to give independent expert evidence gave it as their opinion that a warning should be given, but its extent was a matter of medical judgment with especial importance attached to the character of the patient: 'Every patient has to be considered as an individual' (Dr Page) and 'Giving the full details may drive a patient away' (Dr Baker).

McNair J put the issue thus to the jury ([1957] 2 All ER 118 at 124, [1957] 1 WLR 582 at 590):

> '... having considered [the evidence on this point], you have to make up your minds whether it has been proved to your satisfaction that when the defendants adopted the practice they did (namely, the practice of saying very little and waiting for questions from the patient), they were falling below a proper standard of competent professional opinion on this question of whether or not it is right to warn.'

The jury found for the defendants. The judge clearly directed the jury to treat the test of negligence which he formulated as exclusively applicable in medical cases. The *Bolam* principle may be formulated as a rule that a doctor is not negligent if he acts in accordance with a practice accepted at the time as proper by a responsible body of medical opinion even though other doctors adopt a different practice. In short, the law imposes the duty of care; but the standard of care is a matter of medical judgment.

The *Bolam* principle has been accepted by your Lordships' House as applicable to diagnosis and treatment: see *Whitehouse v Jordan* [1981] 1 All ER 267, [1981] 1 WLR 246 (treatment) and *Maynard v West Midlands Regional Health Authority* [1985] 1 All ER 635 (diagnosis). It is also recognised in Scots law as applicable to diagnosis and treatment; indeed, McNair J in the *Bolam* case cited a Scottish decision to that effect, *Hunter v Hanley* 1955 SLT 213 at 217 per the Lord President (Clyde).

But was the judge correct in treating the 'standard of competent professional opinion' as the criterion in determining whether a doctor is under a duty to warn his patient of the risk, or risks, inherent in the treatment which he recommends? Skinner J and the Court of Appeal have in the instant case held that he was correct. Bristow J adopted the same criterion in *Chatterton v Gerson* [1981] 1 All ER 257, [1981] QB 432. The implications of this view of the law are disturbing. It leaves the determination of a legal duty to the judgment of doctors. Responsible medical judgment may, indeed, provide the law with an acceptable standard in determining whether a doctor in diagnosis or treatment has complied with his duty. But is it right that medical judgment should determine whether there exists a duty to warn of risk and its scope? It would be a strange conclusion if the courts should be led to conclude that our law, which undoubtedly recognises a right in the patient to decide whether he will accept or reject the treatment proposed, should permit the doctors to determine whether and in what circumstances a duty arises requiring the doctor to warn his patient of the risks inherent in the treatment which he proposes.

The right of 'self-determination', the description applied by some to what is no more and no less than the right of a patient to determine for himself whether he will or will not accept the doctor's advice, is vividly illustrated where the treatment recommended is surgery. A doctor who operates without the consent of his patient is, save in cases of emergency or mental disability, guilty of the civil wrong of trespass to the person; he is also guilty of the criminal offence of assault. The existence of the patient's right to make his own decision, which may be seen as a basic human right protected by the common law, is the reason why a doctrine embodying a right of the patient to be informed of the risks of surgical treatment has been developed in some jurisdictions in the United States of America and has found favour with the Supreme Court of Canada. Known as the 'doctrine of informed consent', it amounts to this: where there is a 'real' or a 'material' risk inherent in the proposed operation (however competently and skilfully performed) the question whether and to what extent a patient should be warned before he gives his consent is to be answered not by reference to medical practice but by accepting as a matter of law that, subject to all proper exceptions (of which the court, not the profession, is the judge), a patient has a right to be informed of the risks inherent in the treatment which is proposed. The profession, it is said, should not be judge in its own cause; or, less emotively but more correctly, the courts should not allow medical opinion as to what is best for the patient to override the patient's right to decide for himself whether he will submit to the treatment offered him. It will be necessary for the House to consider in this appeal what is involved in the doctrine and whether it, or any modification of it, has any place in English law.

*The appellant's submissions*

The appellant's first submission is that, even if (which she does not accept) the *Bolam* principle determines whether a warning of risk should or should not be given, the facts found establish liability. My Lords, the submission is untenable. It is not possible to hold that the appellant has shown negligence in the *Bolam* sense on the part of Mr Falconer in advising or treating her. His decision not to warn her of the danger of damage to the spinal cord and of its possible consequences was one which the medical witnesses were agreed to be in accordance with a practice accepted as proper by a responsible body of opinion among neuro-surgeons. Further, the medical evidence also emphasised that in reaching a decision whether or not to warn his patient a competent and careful surgeon would attach especial importance to his assessment of the character and emotional condition of his patient, it being accepted that a doctor acting in the best interests of his patient would be concerned lest a warning might frighten the patient into refusing an operation which in his view was the best treatment in the circumstances. Nobody knows what Mr Falconer's assessment of Mrs Sidaway's character, state of mind and emotion was before her operation. There is no evidence to justify an inference that this careful and compassionate man (the history of the case, which I have related, shows that he merited both adjectives) would have failed to consider what was in the best interests of his patient. He could well have concluded that a warning might have deterred her from agreeing to an operation which he believed to be the best treatment for her.

The appellant's second submission is that she has a cause of action which is independent of negligence in the *Bolam* sense. The submission is based on her right to decide for herself whether she should submit to the operation proposed. In effect, she invokes the transatlantic doctrine of informed consent.

*The law*

The doctrine is new ground in so far as English law is concerned. Apart from the judgment of Bristow J in *Chatterton v Gerson* [1981] 1 All ER 257, [1981] QB 432, I know of only one case prior to the present appeal in which an English court has discussed it. In *Hills v Potter* [1983] 3 All ER 716, [1984] 1 WLR 641 Hirst J followed Skinner J in this case, adding a comment, with which I respectfully agree, that it would be deplorable to base the law in medical cases of this kind on the torts of assault and battery. He did, however, carefully and helpfully devote part of his judgment to a consideration of the transatlantic cases which accept a doctrine of informed consent. He was, if I may say so, right to refuse to follow them: he was sitting at first instance and was faced with formidable English authority accepting the *Bolam* test (Skinner J in the present case and Bristow J in respect of advice; and this House in respect of diagnosis and treatment). But the circumstance that this House is now called on to explore new ground is no reason why a rule of informed consent should not be recognised and developed by our courts. The common law is adaptable; it would not otherwise have survived over the centuries of its existence. The concept of negligence itself is a development of the law by the judges over the last hundred years or so. The legal ancestry of the tort of negligence is to be found in the use made by the judges of the action on the case. Damage is the gist of the action. The action on the case was sufficiently flexible to enable the judges to extend it to cover situations where damage was suffered in circumstances which they judged to call for a remedy. It would be irony indeed if a judicial development for which the opportunity was the presence in the law of a flexible remedy should result now in rigidly confining the law's remedy to situations and relationships already ruled on by the judges.

Counsel for the appellant referred to *Nocton v Lord Ashburton* [1914] AC 932, [1914–15] All ER Rep 45 in an attempt to persuade your Lordships that the relationship between a doctor and patient is of a fiduciary character entitling a patient to equitable relief in the event of a breach of fiduciary duty by the doctor. The attempt fails: there is no

*a* comparison to be made between the relationship of doctor and patient with that of solicitor and client, trustee and cestui qui trust or the other relationships treated in equity as of a fiduciary character. Nevertheless, the relationship of doctor and patient is a very special one, the patient putting his health and his life in the doctor's hands. Where *Nocton v Lord Ashburton* does throw light is on the approach of our law to new or special situations and relationships not previously considered by the judges. In that case the House had to

*b* consider the field covered by *Derry v Peek* (1889) 14 App Cas 337, [1889–90] All ER Rep 1, the famous case in which the House had held that in an action of deceit it is necessary to prove actual fraud. Viscount Haldane LC had this to say ([1914] AC 932 at 947, [1914–15] All ER Rep 45 at 49):

> 'My Lords, the discussion of the case by the noble and learned Lords who took
> part in the decision appears to me to exclude the hypothesis that they considered
*c* > any other question to be before them than what was the necessary foundation of an
> ordinary action for deceit. They must indeed be taken to have thought that the facts
> proved as to the relationship of the parties in *Derry v. Peek* were not enough to
> establish any special duty arising out of that relationship other than the general duty
> of honesty. But they do not say that where a different sort of relationship ought to
> be inferred from the circumstances the case is to be concluded by asking whether
*d* > an action for deceit will lie. I think that the authorities subsequent to the decision
> of the House of Lords shew a tendency to assume that it was intended to mean more
> than it did. In reality the judgment covered only a part of the field in which
> liabilities may arise. There are other obligations besides that of honesty the breach
> of which may give a right to damages. These obligations depend on principles
> which the judges have worked out in the fashion that is characteristic of a system
*e* > where much of the law has always been judge-made and unwritten.'

This remains the approach of the judges to new or as yet unconsidered situations. Unless statute has intervened to restrict the range of judge-made law, the common law enables the judges, when faced with a situation where a right recognised by law is not adequately protected, either to extend existing principles to cover the situation or to

*f* apply an existing remedy to redress the injustice. There is here no novelty, but merely the application of the principle ubi jus ibi remedium. If, therefore, the failure to warn a patient of the risks inherent in the operation which is recommended does constitute a failure to respect the patient's right to make his own decision, I can see no reason in principle why, if the risk materialises and injury or damage is caused, the law should not recognise and enforce a right in the patient to compensation by way of damages.

*g* For the reasons already given, the *Bolam* principle does not cover the situation. The facts of this very case expose its limitation. Mr Falconer lacked neither care for his patient's health and well-being nor professional skill in the advice and treatment which he offered. But did he overlook or disregard his patient's right to determine for herself whether or not to have the operation? Did he fail to provide her with the information necessary for her to make a prudent decision? There is, in truth, no evidence to answer

*h* these questions. Mrs Sidaway's evidence was not accepted; and Mr Falconer was dead. Assume, however, that he did overlook this aspect of his patient's situation. Since neither his advice nor his treatment could be faulted on the *Bolam* test, his patient may have been deprived of the opportunity to exercise her right of decision in the light of information which she, had she received it, might reasonably have considered to be of importance in making up her mind. On the *Bolam* view of the law, therefore, even if she established

*j* that she was so deprived by the lack of a warning, she would have no remedy in negligence unless she could also prove that there was no competent and respected body of medical opinion which was in favour of no warning. Moreover, the tort of trespass to the person would not provide her with a remedy, for Mrs Sidaway did consent to the operation. Her complaint is that her consent resulted from ignorance of a risk, known by the doctor but not made known by him to her, inherent in the operation. Nor would the law of contract offer her a sure way forward. Medical treatment, as in her case, is frequently given today under arrangements outside the control of the law of contract.

One point is clear, however. If failure to warn of risk is actionable in English law, it must be because it is in the circumstances a breach of the doctor's duty of care; in other words, the doctor must be shown to be negligent. English law has not accepted a 'no fault' basis for the liability of a doctor to compensate a patient for injury arising in the course of medical treatment. If, however, the *Bolam* principle is to be applied to the exclusion of any other test to advice and warning, there will be cases in which a patient who suffers injury through ignorance of a risk known to the doctor has no remedy. Is there any difficulty in holding that the doctor's duty of care is sufficiently extensive to afford a patient in that situation a remedy, if as a result she suffers injury or damage? I think not. The root principle of common law negligence is to 'take reasonable care to avoid acts or omissions which you can reasonably foresee would be likely to injure your neighbour': see *Donoghue (or M'Alister) v Stevenson* [1932] AC 562 at 580, [1932] All ER Rep 1 at 11 per Lord Atkin. If it be recognised that a doctor's duty of care extends not only to the health and well-being of his patient but also to a proper respect for his patient's rights, the duty to warn can be seen to be part of the doctor's duty of care.

It is, I suggest, a sound and reasonable proposition that the doctor should be required to exercise care in respecting the patient's right of decision. He must acknowledge that in very many cases factors other than the purely medical will play a significant part in his patient's decision-making process. The doctor's concern is with health and the relief of pain. These are the medical objectives. But a patient may well have in mind circumstances, objectives and values which he may reasonably not make known to the doctor but which may lead him to a different decision from that suggested by a purely medical opinion. The doctor's duty can be seen, therefore, to be one which requires him not only to advise as to medical treatment but also to provide his patient with the information needed to enable the patient to consider and balance the medical advantages and risks alongside other relevant matters, such as, for example, his family, business or social responsibilities of which the doctor may be only partially, if at all, informed.

I conclude, therefore, that there is room in our law for a legal duty to warn a patient of the risks inherent in the treatment proposed, and that, if such a duty be held to exist, its proper place is as an aspect of the duty of care owed by the doctor to his patient. I turn, therefore, to consider whether a duty to warn does exist in our law and, if it does, its proper formulation and the conditions and exceptions to which it must be subject.

Some American courts have recognised such a duty. They have seen it as arising from the patient's right to know of material risks, which itself is seen to arise from the patient's right to decide for himself whether or not to submit to the medical treatment proposed. This is the doctrine of informed consent, to which I have already briefly referred. The landmark case is a decision of the United States Court of Appeals, District of Columbia Circuit, *Canterbury v Spence* (1972) 464 F 2d 772. This case, which has now been approved by the District of Columbia Appeal Court in *Crain v Allison* (1982) 443 A 2d 558, is discussed learnedly and lucidly in an article by Mr Gerald Robertson 'Informed Consent to Medical Treatment' (1981) 97 LQR 102, on which I have drawn extensively in reaching my opinion in this appeal. I wish to put on record my deep appreciation of the help I have derived from the article. The author deals so comprehensively with the American, Canadian and other countries' case law that I find it unnecessary to refer to any of the cases to which our attention has been drawn, interesting and instructive though they are, other than *Canterbury v Spence* and a case in the Supreme Court of Canada, *Reibl v Hughes* (1980) 114 DLR (3d) 1, in which the judgment of the Supreme Court came too late to be considered by Mr Robertson in his article. I have also been greatly assisted by the note on the present case by Professor Ian Kennedy ((1984) 47 MLR 454).

It is necessary before discussing the doctrine to bear in mind that it is far from being universally accepted in the United States of America, or indeed elsewhere. Speaking of the position as it was in 1981 Mr Robertson said (97 LQR 102 at 108):

'The present position in the United States is one of contrast between the minority of States which have chosen to follow the lead given by *Canterbury* by adopting the objective "prudent patient" test . . . and the majority of States which have been content to adopt the traditional test and determine the question of disclosure of risks by applying the "reasonable doctor" test.'

There can be little doubt that policy explains the divergence of view. The prolification of medical malpractice suits in the United States of America has led some courts and some legislatures to curtail or even to reject the operation of the doctrine in an endeavour to restrict the liability of the doctor and so discourage the practice of 'defensive medicine', by which is meant the practice of doctors advising and undertaking the treatment which they think is legally safe even though they may believe that it is not the best for their patient.

The danger of defensive medicine developing in this country clearly exists, though the absence of the lawyer's 'contingency fee' (a percentage of the damages for him as his fee if he wins the case but nothing if he loses) may make it more remote. However that may be, in matters of civil wrong or tort courts are concerned with legal principle; if policy problems emerge, they are best left to the legislature: see *McLoughlin v O'Brian* [1982] 2 All ER 298, [1983] 1 AC 410.

In *Canterbury v Spence* the court enunciated four propositions. (1) The root premise is the concept that every human being of adult years and of sound mind has a right to determine what shall be done with his own body. (2) The consent is the informed exercise of a choice, and that entails an opportunity to evaluate knowledgeably the options available and the risks attendant on each. (3) The doctor must, therefore, disclose all 'material risks'; what risks are 'material' is determined by the 'prudent patient' test, which was formulated by the court (464 F 2d 772 at 787):

'[a] risk is . . . material when *a reasonable person*, in what the physician knows or should know to be the patient's position, would be likely to attach significance to the risk or cluster of risks in deciding whether or not to forego the proposed therapy.' (My emphasis.)

(4) The doctor, however, has what the court called a 'therapeutic privilege'. This exception enables a doctor to withhold from his patient information as to risk if it can be shown that a reasonable medical assessment of the patient would have indicated to the doctor that disclosure would have posed a serious threat of psychological detriment to the patient.

In Canada, in *Reibl v Hughes* (1980) 114 DLR (3d) 1, Laskin CJC expressed broad approval of the doctrine as enunciated in *Canterbury v Spence*, though it would seem that approval of the doctrine was not necessary to a decision in the case. I find no difficulty in accepting the four propositions enunciated in *Canterbury*'s case. But with two notable exceptions they have not yet been considered, so far as I am aware, by an English court. In *Chatterton v Gerson* [1981] 1 All ER 257, [1981] QB 432 Bristow J did consider whether there is any rule in English law comparable with the doctrine of informed consent. He held that a doctor ought to warn of what may happen by misfortune however well the operation may be carried out 'if there is a *real* risk of a misfortune inherent in the procedure' (see [1981] 1 All ER 257 at 266, [1981] QB 432 at 444; my emphasis). He held that whether or not a warning should have been given depended on what a reasonable doctor would have done in the circumstances; and he applied the *Bolam* test to determine the reasonableness of what the doctor did. In *Hills v Potter* [1984] 3 All ER 716, [1984] 1 WLR 641 Hirst J, after discussing the doctrine, also applied the *Bolam* test.

In my judgment the merit of the propositions enunciated in *Canterbury v Spence* (1972) 464 F 2d 772 is that without excluding medical evidence they set a standard and formulate a test of the doctor's duty the effect of which is that the court determines the scope of the duty and decides whether the doctor has acted in breach of his duty. This result is achieved, first, by emphasis on the patient's 'right of self-determination' and, second, by the 'prudent patient' test. If the doctor omits to warn where the risk is such that in the court's view a prudent person in the patient's situation would have regarded it as significant, the doctor is liable.

The *Canterbury* propositions do indeed attach great importance to medical evidence, though judgment is for the court. First, medical evidence is needed in determining whether the risk is material, ie one which the doctor should make known to his patient. The two aspects of the risk, namely the degree of likelihood of it occurring and the seriousness of the possible injury if it should occur, can in most, if not all, cases be assessed only with the help of medical evidence. And, second, medical evidence would be needed to assist the court in determining whether the doctor was justified on his assessment of his patient in withholding the warning.

My Lords, I think the *Canterbury* propositions reflect a legal truth which too much judicial reliance on medical judgment tends to obscure. In a medical negligence case where the issue is as to the advice and information given to the patient as to the treatment proposed, the available options and the risk, the court is concerned primarily with a patient's right. The doctor's duty arises from his patient's rights. If one considers the scope of the doctor's duty by beginning with the right of the patient to make his own decision whether he will or will not undergo the treatment proposed, the right to be informed of significant risk and the doctor's corresponding duty are easy to understand, for the proper implementation of the right requires that the doctor be under a duty to inform his patient of the material risks inherent in the treatment. And it is plainly right that a doctor may avoid liability for failure to warn of a material risk if he can show that he reasonably believed that communication to the patient of the existence of the risk would be detrimental to the health (including, of course, the mental health) of his patient.

Ideally, the court should ask itself whether in the particular circumstances the risk was such that this particular patient would think it significant if he was told it existed. I would think that, as a matter of ethics, this is the test of the doctor's duty. The law, however, operates not in Utopia but in the world as it is; and such an inquiry would prove in practice to be frustrated by the subjectivity of its aim and purpose. The law can, however, do the next best thing, and require the court to answer the question, what would a reasonably prudent patient think significant if in the situation of this patient? The 'prudent patient' cannot, however, always provide the answer for the obvious reason that he is a norm (like the man on the Clapham omnibus), not a real person; and certainly not the patient himself. Hence there is the need that the doctor should have the opportunity of proving that he reasonably believed that disclosure of the risk would be damaging to his patient or contrary to his best interest. This is what the Americans call the doctor's 'therapeutic privilege'. Its true analysis is that it is a defence available to the doctor which, if he invokes it, he must prove. On both the test and the defence medical evidence will, of course, be of great importance.

The 'prudent patient' test calls for medical evidence. The materiality of the risk is a question for the court to decide on all the evidence. Many factors call for consideration. The two critically important medical factors are the degree of probability of the risk materialising and the seriousness of possible injury if it does. Medical evidence will be necessary so that the court may assess the degree of probability and the seriousness of possible injury. Another medical factor, on which expert evidence will also be required, is the character of the risk. In the event of an operation is the risk common to all surgery, eg sepsis, cadiac arrest, and the other risks associated with surgery and the administration of an anaesthetic? Or is it specific to the particular operation under consideration? With the worldwide development and use of surgical treatment in modern times the court may well take the view that a reasonable person in the patient's situation would be unlikely to attach significance to the general risks; but it is not difficult to foresee circumstances particular to a patient in which even the general risks of surgery should be the subject of a warning by his doctor, eg a heart or lung or blood condition. Special risks inherent in a recommended operational procedure are more likely to be material. The risk of partial paralysis, as in this case where the purpose of the operation was not to save

life but merely to relieve pain, illustrates the sort of question which may face first the
doctor and later the court. Clearly medical evidence will be of the utmost importance in
determining whether such a risk is material; but the question for the court is ultimately
legal, not medical, in character.

If the doctor admits or the court finds that on the prudent patient test he should have
disclosed the risk, he has available the defence that he reasonably believed it to be against
the best interest of his patient to disclose it. Here also medical evidence, including the
evidence of the doctor himself, will be vital. The doctor himself will normally be an
essential witness; and the reasonableness of his assessment may well need the support of
independent medical testimony.

My conclusion as to the law is therefore this. To the extent that I have indicated, I
think that English law must recognise a duty of the doctor to warn his patient of risk
inherent in the treatment which he is proposing; and especially so if the treatment be
surgery. The critical limitation is that the duty is confined to material risk. The test of
materiality is whether in the circumstances of the particular case the court is satisfied
that a reasonable person in the patient's position would be likely to attach significance to
the risk. Even if the risk be material, the doctor will not be liable if on a reasonable
assessment of his patient's condition he takes the view that a warning would be
detrimental to his patient's health.

*Conclusion*

Applying these principles to the present case, I ask first: has the appellant shown the
risk of damage to the spinal cord to have been a material risk? The risk was slight, less
than 1%; but, if it were to materialise, it could result in severe injury. It was for the
appellant, as plaintiff, to establish that the risk was so great that the doctor should have
appreciated that it would be considered a significant factor by a prudent patient in the
appellant's situation deciding whether or not to have the operation. The medical evidence
even of Mr Uttley, the appellant's expert witness, gets nowhere near establishing the
materiality of the risk in the sense just outlined. It is, of course, possible that Mr Uttley's
evidence was not directed to anything other than negligence in the *Bolam* sense. If so, the
appellant, who now relies on the principle of informed consent, must accept the
consequences: it was up to her to prove such a case, if she were seeking to establish it.
Further, we do not know Mr Falconer's assessment of his patient. It is possible that, had
he lived, he could have enlightened the court on much that would have been relevant.
After an anxious consideration of the evidence I do not find it possible to say that it has
been proved that Mr Falconer failed in his duty when he omitted, as we must assume
that he did, to warn his patient of the risk of injury to the spinal cord.

At the end of the day, therefore, the substitution of the *Canterbury* propositions for the
*Bolam* test of duty and breach of duty does not avail the appellant because the evidence
does not enable her to prove that Mr Falconer was in breach of his duty when he omitted
the warning. Lack of evidence was always her difficulty; and it remains so, even though,
contrary to the submission of the respondents, the law, in my view, recognises a right of
a patient of sound understanding to be warned of material risks save in the exceptional
circumstances to which I have referred. Accordingly, I would dismiss the appeal.

**LORD DIPLOCK.** My Lords, such facts as emerged in evidence at the trial of the
action that is the subject of this appeal have been set out by my noble and learned friend
Lord Scarman. They are characterised by their extreme paucity. We know nothing of
the emotional idiosyncrasies of the plaintiff, Mrs Sidaway (the patient), even in ordinary
health let alone under stress of ill-health and the prospects of waiting for surgical
treatment at the hands of Mr Falconer (the neuro-surgeon); and yet a doctor's duty of
care, whether he be general practitioner or consulting surgeon or physician, is owed to
that patient and none other, idiosyncrasies and all. Inevitably all treatment, medical or
surgical, involves some degree of risk that the patient's condition will be worse rather
than better for undergoing it. Statistically, the chances of any risk of the proposed

treatment going awry at all may be small, but, particularly if surgery is involved (though this is by no means confined to surgery), it is never totally absent and the degree of possible worsening involved may cover a whole spectrum of disabilities from mild occasional discomfort to what might justify the epithet 'catastrophic'. All these are matters which the doctor will have taken into consideration in determining, in the exercise of his professional skill and judgment, that it is in the patient's interest that he should take the risk involved and undergo the treatment recommended by the doctor.

There is no evidence in the instant case that the patient asked the neuro-surgeon a single question about whether there were any risks involved in undergoing the operation that he was proposing for her, or, if there were, what were the consequences of those risks or the chances of their occurring. So there are eliminated from our consideration matters of clinical judgment of the neuro-surgeon as to how to conduct a bilateral discussion with the patient in terms best calculated not to scare her off from undergoing an operation which, in the exercise of the paramount duty of care he owed to her individually to exercise his skill and judgment in endeavouring to heal her, he is satisfied that it is in her interests to undergo despite such risks as may be entailed.

Likewise, we do not know, save in vaguest terms which amount to little more than speculation but which the trial judge was prepared to hold on balance of probabilities to be a fact, what risks the neuro-surgeon did mention to the patient. The risks which it is contended the neuro-surgeon ought to have drawn to the attention of the patient, even though unasked, were damage to the nerve roots and damage to the spinal cord. The occurrence of these were possible however skilfully the intended operation was carried out; and the consequences of such damage might cover a whole spectrum of mishaps ranging from localised numbness or pins and needles to, in the worst cases, some degree of paraplegia, as unfortunately happened in the patient's case. Because of the physical area of the body in which the operation takes place, these are closely related risks, one or other of which may occur. The combined chance of one or other occurring was put by the neurological experts at something below 2%, of which injury to the spinal cord was rather more likely to have serious consequences if it were to happen, but the chances of its happening were less than half the chance of damage to the nerve roots, ie less than one in a hundred.

These two risks are specific to operations on the spinal column; but in addition there are involved the risks inherent in any general surgery, especially if conducted under anaesthesia. As in the case of spinal column surgery, the consequences of these other risks may be minor and evanescent or may be gravely and permanently disabling or even result in death itself. I find it significant that no common law jurisdiction either American or Canadian which has espoused the doctrine of 'informed consent' appears to have suggested that the surgeon was under a duty to warn his patient of such general risks which, rare though they may be, do happen and they are real risks.

We are dealing in the present appeal with a patient who has expressed to the neuro-surgeon no anxiety about any risks of the proposed operation going wrong; and we are likewise confronted with a neuro-surgeon whose practice, in the absence of specific questioning, was to mention to patients to whom he recommended such an operation for relief of pain, as he was proposing to undertake on the patient in the instant case, the risk of damage to the nerve roots with deleterious effect of varying degrees of discomfort or more serious disability, if the one in fifty chance occurred and despite the utmost operating skill something went wrong.

What we do know, however, and this is in my view determinative of this appeal, is that all the expert witnesses specialising in neurology (including the patient's own expert witness, Mr Uttley, who would not himself have undertaken a similar operation without waiting a period of time, after October 1974, to see what developed as to the persistence of the patient's pain) agreed that there was a responsible body of medical opinion which would have undertaken the operation at the time the neuro-surgeon did and would have warned the patient of the risk involved in the operation in substantially the same terms as the trial judge found on the balance of probabilities the neuro-surgeon had done, ie without specific reference to risk of injuring the spinal cord.

My Lords, it is the very paucity of facts in evidence that makes it possible, in my view, to treat this appeal as raising a naked question of legal principle. It falls within a pattern of frequently occurring cases, which involve no consideration of the idiosyncracies of an exceptional patient. For the last quarter of a century the test applied in English law whether a doctor has fulfilled his duty of care owed to his patient has been that set out in the summing up to the jury by McNair J in *Bolam v Friern Hospital Management Committee* [1957] 2 All ER 118, [1957] 1 WLR 582. I will call this the *Bolam* test. At any rate, so far as diagnosis and treatment are concerned, the *Bolam* test has twice received the express approval of this House.

The *Bolam* test is far from new; its value is that it brings up to date and re-expresses in the light of modern conditions in which the art of medicine is now practised an ancient rule of common law. The original rule can be traced to the maxim spondet peritiam artis et imperitia culpae adnumeratur. It goes back to the origin of assumpsit; it applied to all artificers and was firmly founded in 'case' (moderniter negligence) although it may be of interest to note that as long ago as 1767 in *Slater v Baker* 2 Wils 359, 95 ER 860 a suggestion that where injury was caused by surgery the form of action lay in trespass vi et armis was rejected with scant sympathy by the Court of King's Bench.

The standard of skill and judgment in the particular area of the art of medicine in which the doctor practised that was called for by the expression peritia was the standard of ordinary skill and care that could be expected to be shown by a doctor who had successfully completed the training to qualify as a doctor, whether as general practitioner or as consultant in a speciality if he held himself out as practising as such, as the case might be. But, unless the art in which the artificer claims to have acquired skill and judgment is stagnant so that no improvement in methods or knowledge is sought (and of few is this less true than medicine and surgery over the last half-century), advances in the ability to heal resulting from the volume of research, clinical as well as technological, will present doctors with alternative treatments to adopt and a choice to select that treatment (it may be one of several) that is in their judgment likely at the time to prove most efficacious or ameliorating to the health of each particular patient committed to their care.

Those members of the public who seek medical or surgical aid would be badly served by the adoption of any legal principle that would confine the doctor to some long-established, well-tried method of treatment only, although its past record of success might be small, if he wanted to be confident that he would not run the risk of being held liable in negligence simply because he tried some more modern treatment, and by some unavoidable mischance it failed to heal but did some harm to the patient. This would encourage 'defensive medicine' with a vengeance. The merit of the *Bolam* test is that the criterion of the duty of care owed by a doctor to his patient is whether he has acted in accordance with a practice accepted as proper by a body of responsible and skilled medical opinion. There may be a number of different practices which satisfy this criterion at any particular time. These practices are likely to alter with advances in medical knowledge. Experience shows that, to the great benefit of humankind, they have done so, particularly in the recent past. That is why fatal diseases such as smallpox and tuberculosis have within living memory become virtually extinct in countries where modern medical care is generally available.

In English jurisprudence the doctor's relationship with his patient which gives rise to the normal duty of care to exercise his skill and judgment to improve the patient's health in any particular respect in which the patient has sought his aid has hitherto been treated as a single comprehensive duty covering all the ways in which a doctor is called on to exercise his skill and judgment in the improvement of the physical or mental condition of the patient for which his services either as a general practitioner or as a specialist have been engaged. This general duty is not subject to dissection into a number of component parts to which different criteria of what satisfy the duty of care apply, such as diagnosis, treatment and advice (including warning of any risks of something going wrong however skilfully the treatment advised is carried out). The *Bolam* case itself embraced failure to advise the patient of the risk involved in the electric shock treatment as one of the allegations of negligence against the surgeon as well as negligence in the actual carrying out of treatment in which that risk did result in injury to the patient. The same criteria were applied to both these aspects of the surgeon's duty of care. In modern medicine and surgery such dissection of the various things a doctor has to do in the exercise of his whole duty of care owed to his patient is neither legally meaningful nor medically practicable. Diagnosis itself may involve exploratory surgery, the insertion of drugs by injection (or vaccination) involves intrusion on the body of the patient and oral treatment by drugs, although it involves no physical intrusion by the doctor on the patient's body, may in the case of particular patients involve serious and unforeseen risks.

My Lords, no convincing reason has in my view been advanced before your Lordships that would justify treating the *Bolam* test as doing anything less than laying down a principle of English law that is comprehensive and applicable to every aspect of the duty of care owed by a doctor to his patient in the exercise of his healing functions as respects that patient. What your Lordships have been asked to do, and it is within your power to do so, is to substitute a new and different rule for that part only of the well-established *Bolam* test as comprises a doctor's duty to advise and warn the patient of risks of something going wrong in the surgical or other treatment that he is recommending.

The juristic basis of the proposed substitution, which originates in certain state court jurisdictions of the United States of America and has found some favour in modified form by the Supreme Court of Canada, appears to me, with great respect, to be contrary to English law. Its foundation is the doctrine of 'informed consent' which was originally based on the assumption made in the United States Court of Appeals, District of Columbia Circuit, in *Canterbury v Spence* (1972) 464 F 2d 772, where the cynic might be forgiven for remarking that it enabled a defence under the state statute of limitations to be outmanoeuvred, that prima facie the cause of action in a case of surgery was trespass to the person unless 'informed consent' to the particular battery involved in the surgical operation could be proved. From a period long before American independence this, as I have pointed out, has never been so in English law. The relevant form of action has been based in negligence, ie in assumpsit, alone.

The Supreme Court of Canada, after some initial vacillation, rejected trespass to the person, ie battery, as the cause of action in cases of surgery but endeavoured to transfer the concept of 'informed consent' to a patient's cause of action in negligence, into which, in my opinion, it simply cannot be made to fit. Consent to battery is a state of mind personal to the victim of the battery and any information required to make his consent qualify as informed must be relevant information either actually possessed by him or which he is estopped from denying he possessed, because he so acted towards the defendant as to lead to the latter reasonably to assume the relevant information was known to him. There is no room in the concept of informed consent for the 'objective' patient (as he is referred to at one point by the Supreme Court of Canada) to whom the doctor is entitled, without making any inquiry whether it is the fact or not, to attribute knowledge of some risks but not of others. It may be that most patients, though not necessarily all, have a vague knowledge that there may be some risk in any form of medical treatment; but it is flying in the face of reality to assume that all patients from the highest to the lowest standard of education or intelligence are aware of the extent and nature of the risks which, notwithstanding the exercise of skill and care in carrying out the treatment, are inevitably involved in medical treatment of whatever kind it be but particularly surgical. Yet it is not merely conceded but specifically asserted in the Canadian cases that it is no part of the duty of care on the part of the doctor to go out of his way to draw the attention of his patient to these. On what logical or juristic basis can the need for informed consent be confined to some risks and not extended to others that are also real, and who decides which risk falls into which class?

My Lords, I venture to think that in making this separation between that part of the doctor's duty of care that he owes to each individual patient, which can be described as a duty to advise on treatment and warn of its risks, the courts have misconceived their functions as the finders of fact in cases depending on the negligent exercise of professional skill and judgment. In matters of diagnosis and the carrying out of treatment the court is not tempted to put itself in the surgeon's shoes; it has to rely on and evaluate expert evidence, remembering that it is no part of its task of evaluation to give effect to any preference it may have for one responsible body of professional opinion over another, provided it is satisfied by the expert evidence that both qualify as responsible bodies of medical opinion. But, when it comes to warning about risks, the kind of training and experience that a judge will have undergone at the Bar makes it natural for him to say (correctly) it is my right to decide whether any particular thing is done to my body, and I want to be fully informed of any risks there may be involved of which I am not already aware from my general knowledge as a highly educated man of experience, so that I may form my own judgment whether to refuse the advised treatment or not.

No doubt, if the patient in fact manifested this attitude by means of questioning, the doctor would tell him whatever it was the patient wanted to know; but we are concerned here with volunteering unsought information about risks of the proposed treatment failing to achieve the result sought or making the patient's physical or mental condition worse rather than better. The only effect that mention of risks can have on the patient's mind, if it has any at all, can be in the direction of deterring the patient from undergoing the treatment which in the expert opinion of the doctor it is in the patient's interest to undergo. To decide what risks the existence of which a patient should be voluntarily warned and the terms in which such warning, if any, should be given, having regard to the effect that the warning may have, is as much an exercise of professional skill and judgment as any other part of the doctor's comprehensive duty of care to the individual patient, and expert medical evidence on this matter should be treated in just the same way. The *Bolam* test should be applied.

I agree with your Lordships that this appeal should be dismissed.

**LORD KEITH OF KINKEL.** My Lords, I have had the advantage of reading in draft the speech to be delivered by my noble and learned friend Lord Bridge. I agree with it, and for the reason which he gives would dismiss the appeal.

**LORD BRIDGE OF HARWICH.** My Lords, the facts giving rise to this appeal have been fully recounted by my noble and learned friend Lord Scarman. I draw attention in briefest summary only to those which seem to me central to the issue of law arising for decision.

The appellant underwent at the hospital for which the first respondents are the responsible authority an operation on her cervical vertebrae performed by a neuro-surgeon, since deceased, whose executors are the second respondents. The nature of the operation was such that, however skilfully performed, it involved a risk of damage to the nerve root at the site of the operation or to the spinal cord. The trial judge described that risk as 'best expressed to a layman as a 1% or 2% risk of ill-effects ranging from the mild to the catastrophic'. The appellant in fact suffered, without negligence on the surgeon's part in the performance of the operation, a degree of damage to the spinal cord of which the effects, if not catastrophic, were certainly severe. Damages have been agreed, subject to liability, in the sum of £67,500.

The appellant denied that she had seen the surgeon at all before the operation was performed. This evidence the judge rejected. He found that, before the appellant consented to undergo the operation, the surgeon explained the nature of the operation to her in simple terms and warned her of the possibility and likely consequences of damage to the nerve root, but did not refer to the risk of damage to the spinal cord. Most unfortunately, the surgeon who performed the operation died before these proceedings were instituted. Accordingly, the trial judge, the Court of Appeal and your Lordships' House have all been denied the advantage of what would clearly have been vital evidence on the issue of liability, not only the surgeon's own account of precisely what he had told this appellant, but also his explanation of the reasons for his clinical judgment that, in her case, the information he gave her about the operation and its attendant risks was appropriate and sufficient. The judge was thus driven to base the finding, to which I have earlier referred, in part on inference from documents, but mainly on the evidence of other doctors as to what they knew of the deceased surgeon's customary practice when discussing with patients an operation of the kind the appellant was to undergo. The result is that liability falls to be considered, in effect, in relation to that customary practice, independently of the vitally important individual doctor/patient relationship which must play so large a part in any discussion of a proposed operation with a patient. That introduces an element of artificiality into the case which we may deplore but cannot avoid.

There was a difference of opinion between the neuro-surgeons called as expert witnesses whether they themselves would, in the circumstances, have warned the appellant specifically of the risk of damage to the spinal cord. But the one expert witness called for the appellant agreed readily and without reservation that the deceased surgeon, in omitting any such warning, would have been following a practice accepted as proper by a responsible body of competent neuro-surgeons.

Broadly, a doctor's professional functions may be divided into three phases: diagnosis, advice and treatment. In performing his functions of diagnosis and treatment, the standard by which English law measures the doctor's duty of care to his patient is not open to doubt. 'The test is the standard of the ordinary skilled man exercising and professing to have that special skill.' These are the words of McNair J in *Bolam v Friern Hospital Management Committee* [1957] 2 All ER 118 at 121, [1957] 1 WLR 582 at 586, approved by this House in *Whitehouse v Jordan* [1981] 1 All ER 276 at 277, [1981] 1 WLR 246 at 258 per Lord Edmund-Davies and in *Maynard v West Midlands Regional Health Authority* [1985] 1 All ER 635 per Lord Scarman. The test is conveniently referred to as the *Bolam* test. In *Maynard's* case Lord Scarman, with whose speech the other four members of the Appellate Committee agreed, further cited with approval the words of the Lord President (Clyde) in *Hunter v Hanley* 1955 SLT 213 at 217:

> 'In the realm of diagnosis and treatment there is ample scope for genuine difference of opinion and one man clearly is not negligent merely because his conclusion differs from that of other professional men ... The true test for establishing negligence in diagnosis or treatment on the part of a doctor is whether he has been proved to be guilty of such failure as no doctor of ordinary skill would be guilty of if acting with ordinary care...'

The language of the *Bolam* test clearly requires a different degree of skill from a specialist in his own special field than from a general practitioner. In the field of neuro-surgery it would be necessary to substitute for the Lord President's phrase 'no doctor of ordinary skill', the phrase 'no neuro-surgeon of ordinary skill'. All this is elementary and, in the light of the two recent decisions of this House referred to, firmly established law.

The important question which this appeal raises is whether the law imposes any, and if so what, different criterion as the measure of the medical man's duty of care to his patient when giving advice with respect to a proposed course of treatment. It is clearly right to recognise that a conscious adult patient of sound mind is entitled to decide for himself whether or not he will submit to a particular course of treatment proposed by the doctor, most significantly surgical treatment under general anaesthesia. This entitlement is the foundation of the doctrine of 'informed consent' which has led in certain American jurisdictions to decisions and, in the Supreme Court of Canada, to dicta on which the appellant relies, which would oust the *Bolam* test and substitute an 'objective' test of a doctor's duty to advise the patient of the advantages and disadvantages of undergoing the treatment proposed and more particularly to advise the patient of the risks involved.

There are, it appears to me, at least theoretically, two extreme positions which could be taken. It could be argued that, if the patient's consent is to be fully informed, the doctor must specifically warn him of *all* risks involved in the treatment offered, unless he has some sound clinical reason not to do so. Logically, this would seem to be the extreme to which a truly objective criterion of the doctor's duty would lead. Yet this position finds no support from any authority to which we have been referred in any jurisdiction. It seems to be generally accepted that there is no need to warn of the risks inherent in all surgery under general anaesthesia. This is variously explained on the ground that the patient may be expected to be aware of such risks or that they are relatively remote. If the law is to impose on the medical profession a duty to warn of risks to secure 'informed consent' independently of accepted medical opinion of what is appropriate, neither of these explanations for confining the duty to special as opposed to general surgical risks seems to me wholly convincing.

At the other extreme it could be argued that, once the doctor has decided what treatment is, on balance of advantages and disadvantages, in the patient's best interest, he should not alarm the patient by volunteering a warning of any risk involved, however grave and substantial, unless specifically asked by the patient. I cannot believe that contemporary medical opinion would support this view, which would effectively exclude the patient's right to decide in the very type of case where it is most important that he should be in a position to exercise that right and, perhaps even more significantly, to seek a second opinion whether he should submit himself to the significant risk which has been drawn to his attention. I should perhaps add at this point, although the issue does not strictly arise in this appeal, that, when questioned specifically by a patient of apparently sound mind about risks involved in a particular treatment proposed, the doctor's duty must, in my opinion, be to answer both truthfully and as fully as the questioner requires.

The decision mainly relied on to establish a criterion of the doctor's duty to disclose the risks inherent in a proposed treatment which is prescribed by the law and can be applied independently of any medical opinion or practice is that of the District of Columbia Circuit Court of Appeals in *Canterbury v Spence* (1972) 464 F 2d 772. The judgment of the court (Wright, Leventhal and Robinson JJ), delivered by Robinson J, expounds the view that an objective criterion of what is a sufficient disclosure of risk is necessary to ensure that the patient is enabled to make an intelligent decision and cannot be left to be determined by the doctors. He said (at 784):

'Respect for the patient's right of self-determination on particular therapy demands a standard set by law for physicians rather than one which physicians may or may not impose upon themselves.'

In an attempt to define the objective criterion it is said (at 787) that—

'the issue on non-disclosure must be approached from the viewpoint of the reasonableness of the physician's divulgence in terms of what he knows or should know to be the patient's informational needs.'

A risk is required to be disclosed—

'when a reasonable person, in what the physician knows or should know to be the patient's position, would be likely to attach significance to the risk or cluster of risks in deciding whether or not to forego the proposed therapy.'

The judgment adds (at 788): 'Whenever non-disclosure of particular risk information is open to debate by reasonable-minded men, the issue is for the finder of facts.'

The court naturally recognises exceptions from the duty laid down in the case of an unconscious patient, an immediate emergency or a case where the doctor can establish that disclosure would be harmful to the patient.

Expert medical evidence will be needed to indicate the nature and extent of the risks and benefits involved in the treatment (and presumably of any alternative course). But the court affirms (at 792): 'Experts are unnecessary to a showing of the materiality of a risk to a patient's decision on treatment, or to the reasonably, expectable effect of risk disclosure on the decision.' In English law, if this doctrine were adopted, expert medical opinion whether a particular risk should or should not have been disclosed would presumably be inadmissible in evidence.

I recognise the logical force of the *Canterbury* doctrine, proceeding from the premise that the patient's right to make his own decision must at all costs be safeguarded against the kind of medical paternalism which assumes that 'doctor knows best'. But, with all respect, I regard the doctrine as quite impractical in application for three principal reasons. First, it gives insufficient weight to the realities of the doctor/patient relationship. A very wide variety of factors must enter into a doctor's clinical judgment not only as to what treatment is appropriate for a particular patient, but also as to how best to communicate to the patient the significant factors necessary to enable the patient to make an informed decision whether to undergo the treatment. The doctor cannot set out to educate the patient to his own standard of medical knowledge of all the relevant factors involved. He may take the view, certainly with some patients, that the very fact of his volunteering, without being asked, information of some remote risk involved in the treatment proposed, even though he describes it as remote, may lead to that risk assuming an undue significance in the patient's calculations. Second, it would seem to me quite unrealistic in any medical negligence action to confine the expert medical evidence to an explanation of the primary medical factors involved and to deny the court the benefit of evidence of medical opinion and practice on the particular issue of disclosure which is under consideration. Third, the objective test which *Canterbury* propounds seems to me to be so imprecise as to be almost meaningless. If it is to be left to individual judges to decide for themselves what 'a reasonable person in the patient's position' would consider a risk of sufficient significance that he should be told about it, the outcome of litigation in this field is likely to be quite unpredictable.

I note with interest from a learned article entitled 'Informed Consent to Medical Treatment' (1981) 97 LQR 102 at 108 by Mr Gerald Robertson, a lecturer in law in the University of Leicester, that only a minority of states in the United States of America have chosen to follow *Canterbury* and that since 1975 'there has been a growing tendency for individual states to enact legislation which severely curtails the operation of the doctrine of informed consent'. I should also add that I find particularly cogent and convincing the reasons given for declining to follow *Canterbury* by the Supreme Court of Virginia in *Bly v Rhoads* (1976) 222 SE 2d 783.

Having rejected the *Canterbury* doctrine as a solution to the problem of safeguarding the patient's right to decide whether he will undergo a particular treatment advised by his doctor, the question remains whether that right is sufficiently safeguarded by the application of the *Bolam* test without qualification to the determination of the question what risks inherent in a proposed treatment should be disclosed. The case against a simple application of the *Bolam* test is cogently stated by Laskin CJC, giving the judgment of the Supreme Court of Canada in *Reibl v Hughes* (1980) 114 DLR (3d) 1 at 13:

'To allow expert medical evidence to determine what risks are material and, hence, should be disclosed and, correlatively, what risks are not material is to hand over to the medical profession the entire question of the scope of the duty of disclosure, including the question whether there has been a breach of that duty. Expert medical evidence is, of course, relevant to findings as to the risks that reside in or are a result of recommended surgery or other treatment. It will also have a bearing on their materiality but this is not a question that is to be concluded on the basis of the expert medical evidence alone. The issue under consideration is a different issue from that involved where the question is whether the doctor carried out his professional activities by applicable professional standards. What is under consideration here is the patient's right to know what risks are involved in undergoing or foregoing certain surgery or other treatment.'

I fully appreciate the force of this reasoning, but can only accept it subject to the important qualification that a decision what degree of disclosure of risks is best calculated to assist a particular patient to make a rational choice whether or not to undergo a particular treatment must primarily be a matter of clinical judgment. It would follow from this that the issue whether non-disclosure in a particular case should be condemned as a breach of the doctor's duty of care is an issue to be decided primarily on the basis of expert medical evidence, applying the *Bolam* test. But I do not see that this approach involves the necessity 'to hand over to the medical profession the entire question of the scope of the duty of disclosure, including the question whether there has been a breach of that duty'. Of course, if there is a conflict of evidence whether a responsible body of medical opinion approves of non-disclosure in a particular case, the judge will have to resolve that conflict. But, even in a case where, as here, no expert witness in the relevant medical field condemns the non-disclosure as being in conflict with accepted and responsible medical practice, I am of opinion that the judge might in certain circumstances come to the conclusion that disclosure of a particular risk was so obviously necessary to an informed choice on the part of the patient that no reasonably prudent medical man would fail to make it. The kind of case I have in mind would be an operation involving a substantial risk of grave adverse consequences, as for example the 10% risk of a stroke from the operation which was the subject of the Canadian case of *Reibl v Hughes* (1980) 114 DLR (3d) 1. In such a case, in the absence of some cogent clinical reason why the patient should not be informed, a doctor, recognising and respecting his patient's right of decision, could hardly fail to appreciate the necessity for an appropriate warning.

In the instant case I can see no reasonable ground on which the judge could properly reject the conclusion to which the unchallenged medical evidence led in the application of the *Bolam* test. The trial judge's assessment of the risk at 1% or 2% covered both nerve root and spinal cord damage and covered a spectrum of possible ill-effects 'ranging from the mild to the catastrophic'. In so far as it is possible and appropriate to measure such risks in percentage terms (some of the expert medical witnesses called expressed a marked and understandable reluctance to do so), the risk of damage to the spinal cord of such severity as the appellant in fact suffered was, it would appear, certainly less than 1%. But there is no yardstick either in the judge's findings or in the evidence to measure what fraction of 1% that risk represented. In these circumstances, the appellant's expert witness's agreement that the non-disclosure complained of accorded with a practice accepted as proper by a responsible body of neuro-surgical opinion afforded the respondents a complete defence to the appellant's claim.

I would dismiss the appeal.

**LORD TEMPLEMAN.** My Lords, the appellant patient, Mrs Sidaway, claims £67,500 damages against the estate of the deceased neuro-surgeon, Mr Murray A Falconer, for his failure to warn her of the risk that the operation which he recommended and performed with the consent of Mrs Sidaway might cause the damage to her spinal cord which in fact occurred and the disability from which she is now suffering.

Between 1958 and 1960 Mrs Sidaway suffered pain as a result of deformity in the region of her fifth and sixth cervical vertebrae. Conservative treatment, including collar, traction and manipulation failed to effect a cure. In 1960 Mr Falconer removed the disc between the affected vertebrae and fused them with a bone graft. After some time the pain disappeared. Mrs Sidaway's condition was reviewed annually until 1970 and in 1973 Mr Falconer's secretary wrote to Mrs Sidaway inquiring after her health. The evidence is that Mr Falconer was experienced, competent, conscientious and considerate in his practice and in his attitude to his patients, including Mrs Sidaway. In 1973 Mrs Sidaway complained again of persistent pain. She was examined by Mr Falconer, went into hospital on 11 October, and was operated on by Mr Falconer on 29 October. Mr Falconer has since died. Mr Sidaway said that during her 18 days in hospital prior to the operation Mr Falconer did not examine or speak to her. The trial judge rightly assumed that Mrs Sidaway's recollection was understandably at fault and that she was seen and advised by Mr Falconer.

Mrs Sidaway was suffering increasing pain as a result of pressure on the fourth cervicle nerve root. The operation proposed and carried out by Mr Falconer required the excision of part of a vertebra in order to obtain access to the channel through which the affected nerve travelled. This would enable the removal of boney excrescences from the fourth vertebra and the freeing of the nerve within its channel by the use of a dental drill. The operation involved working within 3 mm of the spinal cord, exposing the cord and interfering with the nerve root.

Basing himself on evidence of the usual practice of Mr Falconer and apparently assuming that Mr Falconer's explanation to every patient followed the same practice, the trial judge, without the benefit of any direct evidence from Mr Falconer or Mrs Sidaway, made the confident finding that Mr Falconer probably explained the nature of the operation to Mrs Sidaway in simple terms and the reasons for performing the operation and mentioned the possibility of damage to a nerve root and the consequences of doing so, but the judge was 'satisfied that he did not refer to the danger of cord damage or to the fact that this was an operation of choice rather than necessity'. The judge was also satisfied that 'even if the surgeon exercised proper care and skill, the spinal cord might be damaged causing weakness or paralysis . . . and that the nerve root might be damaged causing pain and/or weakness . . .' Mrs Sidaway's spinal cord was in fact damaged inadvertently without negligence on the part of Mr Falconer, the performer of the operation.

In my opinion a simple and general explanation of the nature of the operation should have been sufficient to alert Mrs Sidaway to the fact that a major operation was to be performed and to the possibility that something might go wrong at or near the site of the spinal cord or the site of the nerve root causing serious injury. If, as the judge held, Mr Falconer probably referred expressly to the possibility of damage to a nerve root and to the consequences of such damage, this warning could only have reinforced the possibility of something going wrong in the course of a delicate operation performed in a vital area with resultant damage. In view of the fact that Mr Falconer recommended the operation, Mrs Sidaway must have been told or could have assumed that Mr Falconer considered that the possibilities of damage were sufficiently remote to be ignored. Mrs Sidaway could have asked questions. If she had done so, she could and should have been informed that there was an aggregate risk of between 1% and 2% of some damage either to the spinal cord or to a nerve root resulting in injury which might vary from irritation to paralysis. But to my mind this further information would only have reinforced the obvious, with the assurance that the maximum risk of damage, slight or serious, did not exceed 2%. Mr Falconer may reasonably have taken the view that Mrs Sidaway might be confused, frightened or misled by more detailed information which she was unable to evaluate at a time when she was suffering from stress, pain and anxiety. A patient may prefer that the doctor should not thrust too much detail at the patient. We do not know how Mr Falconer explained the operation to Mrs Sidaway and we do not know the reasons for the terms in which he couched his explanation.

On the assumption that Mr Falconer explained that it was necessary to remove bone and free a nerve root from pressure near the spinal cord, it seems to me that the possibility of damage to a nerve root or to the spinal cord was obvious. The operation was skilfully performed but by mishap the remote risk of damage to the spinal cord unfortunately caused the disability from which Mrs Sidaway is now suffering. However much sympathy may be felt for Mrs Sidaway and however much in hindsight the operation may be regretted by her, the question now is whether Mr Falconer was negligent in the explanation which he gave.

In my opinion, if a patient knows that a major operation may entail serious consequences, the patient cannot complain of lack of information unless the patient asks in vain for more information or unless there is some danger which by its nature or magnitude or for some other reason requires to be separately taken into account by the patient in order to reach a balanced judgment in deciding whether or not to submit to the operation. To make Mr Falconer liable for damages for negligence, in not expressly drawing Mrs Sidaway's attention to the risk of damage to the spinal cord and its consequences, Mrs Sidaway must show, and fails to show, that Mr Falconer was not entitled to assume, in the absence of questions from Mrs Sidaway, that his explanation of the nature of the operation was sufficient to alert Mrs Sidaway to the general danger of unavoidable and serious damage inherent in the operation but sufficiently remote to justify the operation. There is no reason to think that Mr Falconer was aware that, as Mrs Sidaway deposed, a specific warning and assessment of the risk of spinal cord damage would have influenced Mrs Sidaway to decline the operation although the general explanation which she was given resulted in her consenting to the operation.

There is no doubt that a doctor ought to draw the attention of a patient to a danger which may be special in kind or magnitude or special to the patient. In *Reibl v Hughes* (1980) 114 DLR (3d) 1 a surgeon advised an operation on the brain to avoid a threatened stroke. The surgeon knew or ought to have known that there was a 4% chance that the operation might cause death and a 10% chance that the operation might precipitate the very stroke which the operation was designed to prevent. The patient ought to have been informed of these specific risks in order to be able to form a balanced judgment in deciding whether or not to submit to the operation.

When a patient complains of lack of information, the court must decide whether the patient has suffered harm from a general danger inherent in the operation or from some special danger. In the case of a general danger the court must decide whether the information afforded to the patient was sufficient to alert the patient to the possibility of serious harm of the kind in fact suffered. If the practice of the medical profession is to make express mention of a particular kind of danger, the court will have no difficulty in coming to the conclusion that the doctor ought to have referred expressly to this danger as a special danger unless the doctor can give reasons to justify the form or absence of warning adopted by him. Where the practice of the medical profession is divided or does not include express mention, it will be for the court to determine whether the harm suffered is an example of a general danger inherent in the nature of the operation and if so whether the explanation afforded to the patient was sufficient to alert the patient to the general dangers of which the harm suffered is an example. If a doctor conscientiously endeavours to explain the arguments for and against a major operation and the possibilities of benefiting and the dangers, the court will be slow to conclude that the doctor has been guilty of a breach of duty owed to the patient merely because the doctor omits some specific item of information. It is for the court to decide, after hearing the doctor's explanation, whether the doctor has in fact been guilty of a breach of duty with regard to information.

A doctor offers a patient diagnosis, advice and treatment. The objectives, sometimes conflicting, sometimes unattainable, of the doctor's services are the prolongation of life, the restoration of the patient to full physical and mental health and the alleviation of pain. Where there are dangers that treatment may produce results, direct or indirect, which are harmful to the patient, those dangers must be weighed by the doctor before he recommends the treatment. The patient is entitled to consider and reject the recommended treatment and for that purpose to understand the doctor's advice and the possibility of harm resulting from the treatment.

I do not subscribe to the theory that the patient is entitled to know everything or to the theory that the doctor is entitled to decide everything. The relationship between doctor and patient is contractual in origin, the doctor performing services in consideration for fees payable by the patient. The doctor, obedient to the high standards set by the medical profession, impliedly contracts to act at all times in the best interests of the patient. No doctor in his senses would impliedly contract at the same time to give to the patient all the information available to the doctor as a result of the doctor's training and experience and as a result of the doctor's diagnosis of the patient. An obligation to give a patient all the information available to the doctor would often be inconsistent with the doctor's contractual obligation to have regard to the patient's best interests. Some information might confuse, other information might alarm a particular patient. Whenever the occasion arises for the doctor to tell the patient the results of the doctor's diagnosis, the possible methods of treatment and the advantages and disadvantages of the recommended treatment, the doctor must decide in the light of his training and experience and in the light of his knowledge of the patient what should be said and how it should be said. At the same time the doctor is not entitled to make the final decision with regard to treatment which may have disadvantages or dangers. Where the patient's health and future are at stake, the patient must make the final decision. The patient is free to decide whether or not to submit to treatment recommended by the doctor and therefore the doctor impliedly contracts to provide information which is adequate to enable the patient to reach a balanced judgment, subject always to the doctor's own obligation to say and do nothing which the doctor is satisfied will be harmful to the patient. When the doctor himself is considering the possibility of a major operation the doctor is able, with his medical training, with his knowledge of the patient's medical history and with his objective position, to make a balanced judgment whether the operation should be performed or not. If the doctor making a balanced judgment advises the patient to submit to the operation, the patient is entitled to reject that advice for reasons which are rational or irrational or for no reason. The duty of the doctor in these circumstances, subject to his overriding duty to have regard to the best interests of the patient, is to provide the patient with information which will enable the patient to make a balanced judgment if the patient chooses to make a balanced judgment. A patient may make an unbalanced judgment because he is deprived of adequate information. A patient may also make an unbalanced judgment if he is provided with too much information and is made aware of possibilities which he is not capable of assessing because of his lack of medical training, his prejudices or his personality. Thus the provision of too much information may prejudice the attainment of the objective of restoring the patient's health. The obligation of the doctor to have regard to the best interests of the patient but at the same time to make available to the patient sufficient information to enable the patient to reach a balanced judgment if he chooses to do so has not altered because those obligations have ceased or may have ceased to be contractual and become a matter of duty of care. In order to make a balanced judgment if he chooses to do so, the patient needs to be aware of the general dangers and of any special dangers in each case without exaggeration or concealment. At the end of the day, the doctor, bearing in mind the best interests of the patient and bearing in mind the patient's right to information which will enable the patient to make a balanced judgment, must decide what information should be given to the patient and in what terms that information should be couched. The court will award damages against the doctor if the court is satisfied that the doctor blundered and that the patient was deprived of information which was necessary for the purposes I have outlined. In the present case on the judge's findings I am satisfied that adequate information was made available to Mrs Sidaway and that the appeal should therefore be dismissed.

*Appeal dismissed.*

Solicitors: *Armstrong & Co* (for the appellant); *Trower Still & Keeling* (for the first respondents); *Le Brasseur & Bury* (for the second respondents).

Mary Rose Plummer    Barrister.

# R v Cambridge Justices, ex parte Fraser

QUEEN'S BENCH DIVISION

KERR LJ AND WEBSTER J

27 JUNE 1984

*Magistrates – Summary trial – Offence triable summarily or on indictment – Committal proceedings – Defendant charged with indictable offence – Magistrates deciding evidence only supporting lesser offence triable either way – Whether magistrates entitled to try lesser offence summarily – Whether magistrates obliged to commit defendant for trial – Magistrates' Courts Act 1980, ss 2(4), 6(1), 25(3).*

The applicant appeared before a magistrates' court on committal proceedings charged with the indictable offence of causing grievous bodily harm, contrary to s 18 of the Offences against the Person Act 1861. The magistrates decided that although the evidence did not support a prima facie case of that offence it did support a prima facie case of the lesser offence of wounding under s 20 of the 1861 Act, that offence being triable either summarily or on indictment. The magistrates decided that, although the wounding charge was suitable for summary trial, the fact that it could be tried on indictment meant that they were obliged by s 6(1)[a] of the Magistrates' Courts Act 1980 to commit the applicant for trial in the Crown Court. The applicant applied for judicial review of the magistrates' decision, contending that since s 6(1) was expressed to be subject to 'the provisions of this . . . Act relating to the summary trial of indictable offences' the requirement in s 6(1) to commit the applicant for trial in the Crown Court was subject to the power which magistrates had under s 2(4)[b] of the 1980 Act to try summarily any offence which was triable either way, and accordingly that the magistrates could have proceeded under s 25(3)[c] of the 1980 Act to try the wounding charge summarily.

**Held** – On the true construction of s 6(1) of the 1980 Act, if a defendant appeared before magistrates charged with an offence triable on indictment only and the magistrates, sitting as examining justices, found that the evidence only disclosed a prima facie case of a lesser offence which was triable either way, the magistrates were nevertheless required by s 6(1) to commit the defendant for trial in the Crown Court and were not entitled to try the lesser offence summarily, because the mandatory requirement in s 6(1) that the magistrates commit the accused 'for any indictable offence' applied also to offences triable either way. The magistrates could not exercise their power under s 2(4) of the 1980 Act to try summarily an offence which was triable either way since, by referring to s 18 of that Act, s 2(4) required the magistrates to decide, before any evidence was heard, that an offence triable either way should be tried summarily and accordingly s 2(4) had no application after the magistrates, as examining justices, had heard the evidence in the case. Furthermore, if as examining justices the magistrates decided that the evidence only disclosed a prima facie case of an offence triable either way they could not then offer the defendant summary trial under s 25(3) of the 1980 Act, because s 25(3) only applied if the defendant had appeared before the magistrates at the outset of their inquiry as examining justices on a charge triable either way. Since the magistrates had heard the evidence before deciding that there was a prima facie case of an offence triable either way (so that s 2(4) had no application) and since the applicant had appeared before the magistrates at the outset charged with an offence triable only on indictment (so that s 25(3) did not apply to the case), the magistrates had been obliged by s 6(1) to commit the applicant for trial on the lesser offence of wounding. The application would therefore be dismissed (see p 670 *b* to *e* and *j* to p 671 *g* and p 672 *b* to *f*, post).

---

a   Section 6(1), so far as material, is set out at p 668 *j* to p 669 *a*, post

b   Section 2(4) is set out at p 670 *e f*, post

c   Section 25(3), so far as material, is set out at p 669 *b c*, post

Per curiam. If a defendant appears before magistrates in committal proceedings charged with an offence triable either way and the magistrates find that the evidence *a* does not support a prima facie case of that offence but does support an offence triable summarily, they have jurisdiction under s 25(3) of the 1980 Act to try the lesser offence summarily (see p 671 *h j* and p 672 *a* to *c*, post).

### Notes

For changing the mode of trial after commencement of an inquiry by examining justices *b* into an information, see 29 Halsbury's Laws (4th edn) para 306.

For justices' decision to commit for trial or to discharge a defendant, see 11 ibid, para 156.

For the Offences against the Person Act 1861, ss 18, 20, see 8 Halsbury's Statutes (3rd edn) 152, 154.

For the Magistrates' Courts Act 1980, ss 6, 25, see 50(2) ibid 1446, 1466. *c*

### Application for judicial review

David Martin Alexander Fraser applied , with the leave of Nolan J granted on 23 January 1984, for judicial review by way of (i) an order of certiorari to quash an order made by the South Cambridgeshire justices sitting as a magistrates' court at Cambridge on 11 July 1983 that the applicant be committed for trial to the Crown Court at Cambridge on a *d* charge of wounding, contrary to s 20 of the Offences against the Person Act 1861 and (ii) an order of mandamus requiring the justices to proceed to hear the charge of wounding contrary to s 20 of the 1861 Act summarily. The facts are set out in the judgment of Webster J.

*Jonathan Haworth* for the applicant. *e*
*John Farmer* for the justices.

**WEBSTER J** (delivering the first judgment at the invitation of Kerr LJ). This is an application for judicial review by way of orders of certiorari and mandamus by David Fraser, by which he applies to the court for orders quashing an order made by the justices of the petty sessional division of South Cambridgeshire, sitting at Cambridge on 11 July *f* 1983, by which they committed the applicant for trial on a charge of wounding contrary to s 20 of the Offences against the Person Act 1861 and ordering those justices to hear that charge by way of summary trial.

The application arises in the following circumstances. On that date, 11 July, the applicant appeared before the magistrates on one charge, namely that he on 10 June 1983 at Melbourn in the County of Cambridge, unlawfully and maliciously wounded Patricia *g* May Cooper with intent to do her grievous bodily harm, contrary to s 18 of the Offences against the Person Act 1861.

It is necessary to interpose here to observe that an offence under s 18 of the 1861 Act is an offence which is triable on indictment only, whereas an offence under s 20 of the 1861 Act is an offence which is triable either summarily or on indictment, an offence which is described hereafter, and in the legislation to which I will refer, as an offence triable either *h* way. It is also necessary to remind oneself of the well-known rule of law, namely that a person charged with an offence under s 18 can be found guilty of an offence under s 20 when tried on indictment.

The statutory background to this application, to which I should refer before I recite the further history of the matter, consists primarily of ss 6(1) and 25 of the Magistrates' Courts Act 1980. Section 6(1) is in these terms: *j*

'Subject to the provisions of this and any other Act relating to the summary trial of indictable offences, if a magistrates' court inquiring into an offence as examining justices is of opinion, on consideration of the evidence and of any statement of the accused, that there is sufficient evidence to put the accused on trial by jury for any indictable offence, the court shall commit him for trial; and, if it is not of that opinion, it shall . . . discharge him.'

Section 25(1) provides:

'Subsections (2) to (4) below shall have effect where a person who has attained the age of 17 appears or is brought before a magistrates' court on an information charging him with an offence triable either way.'

I need not recite the provisions of sub-s (2), but sub-s (3) provides:

'Where the court has begun to inquire into the information as examining justices, then, if at any time during the inquiry it appears to the court, having regard to any representations made in the presence of the accused by the prosecutor, or made by the accused, and to the nature of the case, that the offence is after all more suitable for summary trial, the court may, after doing as provided in subsection (4) below, ask the accused whether he consents to be tried summarily and, if he so consents, may proceed to try the information summarily . . .'

The provisions of sub-s (4) require that the implications of summary trial be explained to the accused. I need not recite that subsection.

I return to the facts which give rise to this application. On 11 July 1983 the magistrates began to inquire into the charge under s 18 of the 1861 Act as examining justices, in accordance with s 6 of the 1980 Act. The evidence adduced by the prosecution was read to the court and, after that had been done and submissions made, the magistrates determined that the evidence failed to disclose a prima facie case as charged, that is to say of an offence under s 18, but that it did disclose a prima facie case of wounding contrary to s 20 of the 1861 Act. That charge was then written down by the court clerk. Mr Wilson, who was the prosecutor, and Mr Masters, who is the solicitor who appeared before the magistrates on behalf of the applicant, then made submissions to the court as to the mode of the trial. In particular, it was submitted by Mr Masters that the matter could and should proceed by way of summary trial in exercise by the magistrates of their powers under s 25(3) of the 1980 Act. After those submissions were made the magistrates retired and on their return to the court announced that they had determined that the charge was suitable for summary trial.

Mr Wilson then asked the magistrates to adjourn, which they did. When they returned to court he made submissions which have been made again by counsel for the justices to us in this court, that the provisions of s 6 of the 1980 Act were mandatory in their terms and that they obliged the magistrates to commit the applicant for trial on the charge of wounding contrary to s 20 of the 1861 Act. Mr Masters argued that that was not the case, that the justices had followed the correct procedure and that the applicant should be tried summarily; but the magistrates, having been advised by their clerk, committed the applicant to the Crown Court at Cambridge for trial on the charge of wounding.

The grounds on which the applicant seeks judicial review in this court are that the justices, having determined as examining justices that the evidence before them disclosed a prima facie case of an offence of wounding under s 20 of the 1861 Act, having caused the charge to be written down and having determined in accordance with s 25 of the 1980 Act that the charge was suitable for summary trial, thereupon wrongly considered themselves bound by s 6 of the 1980 Act to commit the applicant for trial when, in fact, they should have proceeded to a summary trial of the charge.

It is necessary, therefore, to look back again to the provisions of ss 6 and 25 of the 1980 Act, and to draw attention to and emphasise some of those provisions. Counsel for the applicant emphasises the opening words of sub-s (1) of s 6, 'Subject to the provisions of this and any other Act relating to the summary trial of indictable offences', and in connection with those words he draws attention to the fact that the expression 'indictable offences', though not defined in the 1980 Act, is defined in the Criminal Law Act 1977, by s 64(1)(a), to mean 'an offence which, if committed by an adult, is triable on

indictment, whether it is exclusively so triable or triable either way'. It seems to me that
the expression 'indictable offences' where it appears in s 6 of the 1980 Act is to be given    *a*
that definition; but for my part (and I will return in a moment to those opening words
which I have just quoted) it is necessary to read the provisions of s 6 as they are written,
and for the purpose of forming a view about the point to give some of them an emphasis.
Subsection (1) continues with these words:

> '. . . if a magistrates' court inquiring into *an* offence as examining justices is of
> opinion, on consideration of the evidence and of any statement of the accused, that    *b*
> there is sufficient evidence to put the accused on trial by jury for *any* indictable
> offence, the court shall commit him for trial . . .'

In my view the distinction between the words 'an offence' towards the beginning of
those words and the words 'any indictable offence' towards the end is a material
distinction which cannot be overlooked. I, for my part, can see no reason for giving the    *c*
words 'any indictable offence' any meaning other than their apparent meaning, that is to
say any offence triable either on indictment only or either way. Applying the provisions
of that subsection to the facts of this case the justices were inquiring into an offence,
namely an offence under s 18 of the 1861 Act, as examining justices. On consideration
of the evidence they were of the opinion that there was sufficient evidence to put the
accused on trial by jury for an offence under s 20 of the 1861 Act, which, being an offence    *d*
triable either way, was in my view, for the reasons I have given, an offence within the
meaning of those words 'any indictable offence' in that subsection. Accordingly they
were compelled, by the mandatory word 'shall' which follows, to commit the applicant
for trial unless there be something in the opening words of the subsection which qualifies
or removes the mandatory effect of that word.

Counsel for the applicant submits that those opening words do qualify the apparently    *e*
mandatory effect of that word 'shall'. He submits that the opening words of the subsection
are to be construed as referring to s 2(4) of the 1980 Act, which provides:

> 'Subject to sections 18 to 22 below and any other enactment (wherever contained)
> relating to the mode of trial of offences triable either way, a magistrates' court shall
> have jurisdiction to try summarily an offence triable either way in any case in which
> under subsection (3) above it would have jurisdiction as examining justices.'    *f*

His submission is that in the present case the justices, having decided that there was
no prima facie case of an offence under s 18 but that there was sufficient evidence to go
to a jury on an offence under s 20, had jurisdiction to try the offence under s 20
summarily, by virtue of their jurisdiction under s 2(4) of the 1980 Act, that that power
conferred by that subsection is inconsistent with the apparently mandatory effect of the
word 'shall' in s 6(1) of the 1980 Act, and, therefore, that that mandatory effect is to be    *g*
taken as being qualified by the power conferred by s 2(4). He says that in the present case
the justices should have tried the matter summarily and that they were not obliged to
commit the applicant for trial on the lesser offence under s 20 of the 1861 Act.

In my view there are two difficulties about that approach. The first difficulty appears
to me to be this. Section 2(4) is expressly made subject to ss 18 to 22 of the 1980 Act, and    *h*
s 18 provides:

> '(1) Sections 19 to 23 below shall have effect where a person who has attained the
> age of 17 appears or is brought before a magistrates' court on an information
> charging him with an offence triable either way.
> (2) Without prejudice to section 11(1) above, everything that the court is required
> to do under sections 19 to 22 below [which are the sections which lay down the    *j*
> procedure for embarking on a summary trial of an offence triable either way] must
> be done before any evidence is called and, subject to subsection (3) below and section
> 23 below, with the accused present in court . . .'

It seems to me that, since the very terms of s 6 of the 1980 Act contemplate that the magistrates will do nothing, either by way of committal of the defendant or by way of discharging him, until after they have considered and therefore heard the evidence, it is difficult to see how it can be reasonably suggested that the qualifying words at the beginning of that subsection are to be taken to refer back to the provisions of s 2(4), which can only have effect where the magistrates make a decision and embark on a summary trial *before* any evidence is called.

The second difficulty which in my view lies in the path of counsel for the applicant is that it is necessary for him to submit, as I understand it, not only that the magistrates were not obliged to commit the applicant for trial by virtue of the provision of s 6(1) of the 1980 Act but that they also had a power to embark on the summary trial of the offence under s 20 of the 1861 Act by virtue of the powers conferred by s 25(3) of the 1980 Act. In my view, a reading of the clear words of that section, particularly in the context of sub-s (1) of s 25, really makes that submission unarguable.

I have already recited the provisions of sub-ss (1) and (3) of s 25 of the 1980 Act. I go back to them again to note that, under sub-s (1), sub-s (3) has effect where a person 'appears or is brought before a magistrates' court on an information charging him with an offence triable either way'. Subsection (3) begins with the words: 'Where the court has begun to inquire into the information as examining justices . . .' As it seems to me, the words 'the information' can only refer back to the words 'an information charging him with an offence triable either way'.

If, therefore, the magistrates were to have had power in this case to have embarked on the summary trial of the offence under s 20 of the 1861 Act, it seems to me that it would have been necessary to show that the applicant was a person who appeared or was brought before them on an information charging him with an offence triable either way. But he clearly was not, such a person. He was a person appearing or brought before the court on an information charging him with an offence triable on indictment only. Counsel for the applicant, with some bravery in my view, sought to argue that, once the court had decided that there was no case sufficient to commit him on the s 18 offence but that there was a case sufficient to convict him of an offence under s 20 of the 1861 Act, then in those circumstances the applicant became, for the purpose of this section, a person who, at that stage, appeared or was brought before the magistrates on an information charging him with an offence triable either way. For my part I do not think that those words can be read in that way. In my view the words 'appears or is brought before a magistrates' court' refer, and refer only, to his appearance or his being brought before the court at the outset of the inquiry, and the information that is relevant to the existence of their powers under that section is the information with which he was charged when he appeared or was brought before the court.

In my view those reasons are sufficient to dispose of this application and to dispose of the submissions of counsel for the applicant. I only add one point. So far, according to my reasoning, it might appear that the opening words of s 6(1) of the 1980 Act, 'Subject to the provisions of this and any other Act relating to the summary trial of indictable offences', have no meaning. That, of course, would be an unsatisfactory position in which to leave this Act. But, in my view, it is only necessary, in order to give a meaning to those words, to look to s 25, which I have just been considering. It seems to me that those words are intended to, and that they do as a matter of construction, refer if not to other provisions then at the very least to the powers conferred by s 25 and, in particular, to the power conferred by s 25(3) on a court which has begun to inquire into an information charging a person with an offence triable either way to proceed to try the matter summarily if, at any time during the inquiry, it appears to the court to be suitable to take that course.

It is true that this construction of the 1980 Act leads to one anomaly, that is that if a person who appears before the magistrates for committal appears on an information which lays an offence which is triable on indictment only, as was the case here, then, if the court finds there is no sufficient evidence to put him on trial before a jury on that offence but that there is sufficient evidence to put him on trial before a jury on a lesser offence, being an indictable offence triable either way, the court may not proceed to try that lesser offence summarily but is bound to commit him for trial on it; whereas if he is brought before the court for committal on an information charging an offence which is triable either way, then, by virtue of the provisions of s 25(3), the justices may, if they find that offence not sufficiently made out to justify committal but find some other offence which is triable summarily made out, try that other offence summarily. That may be an anomaly. If so, as it seems to me, it is simply a consequence of the statutory provisions, and it does not deter me from arriving at the conclusion to which, in my view, one is compelled by the clear words of the two sections in question, namely ss 6(1) and 25 of the 1980 Act. For those reasons I would refuse the application.

**KERR LJ.** I agree. I have not found it an easy matter but counsel for the justices has convinced me that the proper interpretation of the opening words of s 6(1) of the Magistrates' Courts Act 1980, 'Subject to the provisions of this and any other Act relating to the summary trial of indictable offences', is to put on one side, for the purposes of construing the remainder of s 6(1), any charges of offences triable either way. Having put those on one side the section proceeds to consider the situation where the justices, as in the present case, are inquiring into an offence as examining justices and, since it is not an offence triable either way, as examining justices inquiring into an offence triable on indictment only. Having embarked on that process in relation to such an offence, they are then bound to commit for trial if the evidence before them discloses a case which is sufficient to be placed before a jury. If that is so, then they are bound to commit even if the offence disclosed by that evidence is one which is also triable summarily.

The note to the words 'any indictable offence' in *Stone's Justices' Manual*, (116th edn, 1984) vol 1, p 281, note (d) is, in my view, correct when it says that these words—

> 'contemplate committal for trial either for the offence of which the accused has been formally charged or some other indictable offence as disclosed by the evidence of the witnesses in the depositions.'

Accordingly, I agree that this application for judicial review fails.

*Application refused.*

Solicitors: *Masters & Co*, Cambridge (for the applicant); *D C Beal*, Huntingdon (for the justices)

N P Metcalfe Esq     Barrister.

# R v Spencer and others
# R v Smails and others

COURT OF APPEAL, CRIMINAL DIVISION
MAY LJ, DRAKE AND ANTHONY LINCOLN JJ
4, 5 OCTOBER, 2 NOVEMBER 1984

*Criminal evidence – Corroboration – Direction to jury – Mental patient with criminal conviction detained in special hospital – Patient sole witness for prosecution – Whether full warning to be given to jury of danger of acting on patient's uncorroborated evidence – Whether direction to approach patient's evidence with great caution adequate.*

*Jury – Juror – Discharge during trial – Discretion to discharge juror – Exercise of discretion – Juror's wife having same occupation as defendants – Juror making known anti-defence views – Juror discharged – Whether entire jury should be discharged – Test to be applied.*

The appellants, who were nursing staff at a special hospital, were charged with ill-treating patients, contrary to s 126 of the Mental Health Act 1959. In two separate trials before the same judge, the prosecution relied wholly on the uncorroborated evidence of patients who had criminal convictions or were suffering from mental disorders. At the first trial it became apparent that one of the jurors had formed a definite view of the case and appeared to be biased against the appellants. On the day before the trial ended, during the course of the judge's summing up, the court was informed that the juror's wife worked at another mental hospital which had been referred to in evidence at the trial and that the juror had discussed the case on several occasions with three jurors to whom he gave lifts to and from the court. The judge discharged the juror and the other jurors were directed not to discuss the case with him. The judge refused an application by the appellants that the remaining jurors be discharged, on the ground that it had not been shown that there was a high degree of risk that the jury were prejudiced by their discussions with the discharged juror. At both trials the judge directed the jury to approach the evidence of the patients with great caution but did not warn them that it would be dangerous to convict on the patients' uncorroborated evidence. The appellants were all convicted. Subsequently the Court of Appeal, Criminal Division allowed an appeal concerning similar allegations of ill-treatment at the same hospital on the ground that the trial judge had not given a full warning that it would be dangerous to convict on the patients' uncorroborated evidence. The appellants appealed, relying on the previous Court of Appeal decision.

**Held** – The appeals would be dismissed for the following reasons—

(1) There was no difference between the Civil and Criminal Divisions of the Court of Appeal in the application of the principle of stare decisis, save that in the Criminal Division the court might be dealing with the liberty of the subject and it might be necessary in the interests of justice to an appellant for the court not to follow a previous decision (see p 677 *e* to *g* and p 678 *a b*, post); *Young v Bristol Aeroplane Co Ltd* [1944] 2 All ER 293 and *R v Newsome* [1970] 3 All ER 455 applied; *R v Gould* [1968] 1 All ER 849 considered.

(2) The evidence of patients at a secure hospital did not fall into the category of evidence of witnesses where a full warning was necessary. Accordingly, the judge had not been required to give a full warning and in the circumstances his direction to the jury was adequate. The previous Court of Appeal decision to the contrary was either per incuriam or not binding and would not be followed (see p 681 *f g*, post); *R v Beck* [1982] 1 All ER 807 applied; dictum of Lord Hailsham LC in *DPP v Kilbourne* [1973] 1 All ER at 447 and *R v Bagshaw* [1984] 1 All ER 971 not followed.

(3) In exercising his discretion whether to discharge the jury, the judge had to consider

whether there was a real danger that the defendant's position had been prejudiced or that an injustice had been done. Although the judge had applied the wrong test, the question remained whether, if he had applied the correct test, he would have reached the opposite conclusion and discharged the jury. The fact that the three jurors had discussed the case with the discharged juror did not mean that the jury had been prejudiced or biased against the appellants when they had considered their verdict and therefore it had not been shown that the appellants' position had been prejudiced or that an injustice had been done (see p 683 c d, p 684 f to h and p 685 j to p 686 d, post); R v Twiss [1918] 2 KB 853, R v Prime (1973) 57 Cr App R 632 and R v Sawyer (1980) 71 Cr App R 283 applied.

Quaere. Whether in practice there is any difference between telling a jury that it is dangerous to convict on uncorroborated evidence and warning the jury that for fully explained reasons certain evidence should be approached with great caution (see p 682 j, post).

### Notes
For corroboration in criminal proceedings, see 1 Halsbury's Laws (4th edn) paras 453–457, and for cases on the subject, see 14(2) Digest (Reissue) 618–621, 5026–5078.

For discharge of a juror for misconduct, see 26 Halsbury's Laws (4th edn) para 637, and for cases on the subject, see 30 Digest (Reissue) 330–331, 446–449.

For the Mental Health Act 1959, s 126, see 25 Halsbury's Statutes (3rd edn) 149.

As from 30 September 1983 s 126 of the 1959 Act was replaced by s 127 of the Mental Health Act 1983.

### Cases referred to in judgment
Arthurs v A-G for Northern Ireland (1970) 55 Cr App R 161, HL.
DPP v Hester [1972] 3 All ER 1056, [1973] AC 296, [1972] 3 WLR 910, HL.
DPP v Kilbourne [1973] 1 All ER 440, [1973] AC 729, [1973] 2 WLR 254, HL.
People, The v Casey (No 2) [1963] IR 33.
R v Bagshaw [1984] 1 All ER 971, [1984] 1 WLR 477, CA.
R v Beck [1982] 1 All ER 807, [1982] 1 WLR 461, CA.
R v Evans, R v Allen [1964] 3 All ER 401, [1965] 2 QB 295, [1964] 3 WLR 1173, CCA.
R v Gould [1968] 1 All ER 849, [1968] 2 QB 65, [1968] 2 WLR 643, CA.
R v Holland, R v Smith [1983] Crim LR 545, CA.
R v Ketteridge [1915] 1 KB 467, [1914–15] All ER Rep 482, CCA.
R v Long (1973) 57 Cr App R 871, CA.
R v Newsome, R v Browne [1970] 3 All ER 455, [1970] 2 QB 711, [1970] 3 WLR 586, CA.
R v O'Reilly [1967] 2 All ER 766, [1967] 2 QB 722, [1967] 3 WLR 191, CA.
R v Prater [1960] 1 All ER 298, [1960] 2 QB 464, [1960] 2 WLR 343, CCA.
R v Price (Herbert) [1968] 2 All ER 282, [1969] 1 QB 541, [1968] 2 WLR 1397, CA.
R v Prime (Melvyn John) (1973) 57 Cr App R 632, CA.
R v Riley (1979) 70 Cr App R 1, CA.
R v Russell (1968) 52 Cr App R 147, CA.
R v Sawyer (1980) 71 Cr App R 283, CA.
R v Stannard (1962) [1964] 1 All ER 34, [1965] 2 QB 1, [1964] 2 WLR 461, CCA.
R v Taylor [1950] 2 All ER 170, [1950] 2 KB 368, CCA.
R v Turnbull [1976] 3 All ER 549, [1977] QB 224, [1976] 3 WLR 445, CA.
R v Twiss [1918] 2 KB 853, CCA.
R v Whitaker (1976) 63 Cr App R 193, CA.
Young v Bristol Aeroplane Co Ltd [1944] 2 All ER 293, [1944] KB 718, CA; affd [1946] 1 All ER 98, [1946] AC 163, HL.

### Cases also cited
Colchester Estates (Cardiff) v Carlton Industries plc [1984] 2 All ER 601, [1984] 3 WLR 693.
R v Knowlden (1981) 77 Cr App R 94, CA.

### Applications for leave to appeal
On 24 June 1983 in the Crown Court at Nottingham before his Honour Judge Hopkin

and a jury the appellants, Alan Widdison Spencer, Kenneth Ball and Michael Dennis
Mason, were convicted of ill-treating certain patients contrary to s 126 of the Mental
Health Act 1959. The appellant Spencer was sentenced to twelve months' imprisonment
on each count, suspended for two years, and the appellants Ball and Mason were each
sentenced to six months' imprisonment, suspended for eighteen months. On 12 October
1983 also in the Crown Court at Nottingham and before Judge Hopkin and a jury, the
appellants, George Glenville Smails, Paul White and Kenneth Ball, were each convicted
of an offence under s 126 of the 1959 Act and were each sentenced to six months'
imprisonment, suspended for eighteen months. Each of them applied for leave to appeal
against conviction. The court granted leave to appeal and, with the consent of counsel,
treated the hearing as the hearing of the appeals. The facts are set out in the judgment of
the court.

*Wilfred Steer QC* and *Brian Sommerville* for the appellants.
*Jeremy Roberts QC* and *Richard Dixon* for the Crown.

*Cur adv vult*

2 November. The following judgment of the court was delivered.

**MAY LJ.** On 24 June 1983 in the Crown Court at Nottingham before his Honour
Judge Hopkin and a jury, the three defendants, Spencer, Ball and Mason, were convicted,
as to Spencer, of six counts of ill-treating a patient, contrary to s 126 of the Mental Health
Act 1959 and as to Ball and Mason, each on one similar count. Spencer was sentenced to
twelve months' imprisonment on each count concurrent, suspended for two years. Ball
and Mason were each sentenced to six months' imprisonment, suspended for eighteen
months.

On 12 October 1983 also in the Crown Court at Nottingham and before the same
judge, the defendants White, Smails and Ball again were each convicted of one similar
offence contrary to the provisions of the same section of the 1959 Act. On 19 October
1983 they were each sentenced to six months' imprisonment suspended for eighteen
months.

We heard the applications of each of these defendants for leave to appeal against their
convictions on 4 and 5 October 1984 and reserved our decision, which this now is. In the
course of the hearing of these applications it became apparent that an important point of
at least mixed law and fact arose, and we thought it right, if leave to appeal was strictly
required, that this should be granted. Counsel for the five defendants was content that
we should treat the hearing of the applications as his clients' several appeals against their
convictions and we did so. We accordingly refer to them hereafter in this judgment as
the appellants.

These prosecutions were two of a series of 14 trials which concerned a number of
allegations of ill-treatment of patients at Rampton Hospital by the nursing staff, of which
each of these five appellants were themselves members. The prosecutions followed on a
television programme in 1979, which made a substantial number of allegations of ill-
treatment over the years at Rampton. Police inquiries were started after the programme
had been televised and led to the series of trials, of which these two were part. The
allegations against the five appellants were all of some form of assault against a patient or
patients at the hospital which was alleged to have occurred between September 1974 and
November 1976.

In most of the 14 trials, and certainly in the two with which we are concerned, the
prosecution case depended wholly on the evidence of patients or ex-patients of Rampton,
who were plainly 'suspect' witnesses. Each judge who has tried any of these Rampton
prosecutions has had this matter well in mind and in the course of his summing up has
given the jury a substantial warning about the approach that they should adopt to the
evidence of such witnesses.

In the first of the instant cases the judge's direction to the jury on this point was in
these terms:

'You must, ladies and gentlemen, approach the evidence of Mr Hosein, Mr Firth, Mr Evan Glyn Hughes, Mr William Hughes, Mr Aldred, and Mr Nugent with great caution. Why? Well for three reasons. Firstly, because they are all persons of bad character. The law, in rules which are formulated over many years, requires me to tell you even if they were merely persons of bad character and nothing else, that you must approach their evidence with great caution. It goes further than that of course in this case. The second reason is this, that at the time of these events thay were all persons suffering from some form of mental disorder. Thirdly, they may of course have all conspired together to make false allegations. People make false allegations as we know for all sorts of reasons, some of which have been suggested in this case, but apart from that your own experience no doubt tells you that people do on occasions make false allegations. So therefore I must tell you that as far as all those patients are concerned you must approach their evidence with great caution. You would be wise to look for support for their evidence for those reasons. I tell you at once, [counsel for the appellants] is right, and [counsel for the Crown] does not argue to the contrary, that there is no support for their allegations at all because as far as they are concerned even where you have two or three of them giving evidence on one particular count, one witness of this type cannot support another. But, if, ladies and gentlemen, having seen them and having heard them and borne in mind the warning which I have given you come to the conclusion that you are sure in all or any of their cases that they are telling the truth, then you may convict on their evidence without there being any support at all. It is, as I say, for you to judge the facts. When I say the facts I mean also the importance which you attach to any particular witness and whether or not he is telling the truth.'

The terms of the judge's direction in the second of the instant trials were substantially the same.

Another of the series of trials relating to the alleged treatment of patients at Rampton Hospital was *R v Bagshaw* [1984] 1 All ER 971, [1984] 1 WLR 477, which was tried also in the Crown Court at Nottingham before Judge Hopkin and a jury on 11 May 1982, and subsequently reached the Court of Appeal, Criminal Division.

In his summing up in that case the trial judge warned the jury about the evidence of similar witnesses in very much the same terms. The only possibly relevant difference was that his direction in the cases presently appealed from included the phrase: 'You would be wise to look for support for their evidence for those reasons', whereas the direction in *Bagshaw*'s case did not.

In that earlier case another division of this court held that the trial judge's direction had been inadequate and allowed appeals against conviction. The court held that with witnesses of the nature and having the disabilities of Rampton patients, to which the judge referred, nothing short of a full warning that it is dangerous to convict on their uncorroborated evidence will suffice.

In *Bagshaw*'s case [1984] 1 All ER 971 at 977, [1984] 1 WLR 477 at 484 O'Connor LJ, giving the considered judgment of the court, said:

'Patients in hospital under the Mental Health Act 1959 are not a category like accomplices or complainants in sexual cases, nor would we wish to make them into an additional category. Patients detained in a special hospital after conviction for an offence or offences, even if they are not a category, may well fulfil to a very high degree the criteria which justify the requirement of the full warning in respect of witnesses within accepted categories. It seems to us that in such cases nothing short of the full warning that it is dangerous to convict on the uncorroborated evidence of the witness will suffice. The cases recognise that there is a difference between a warning that the jury should approach the evidence of a witness with caution and a warning that it is dangerous to convict. Indeed, the difference is obvious (see *R v Price* [1968] 2 All ER 282, [1969] 1 QB 541, *R v Riley* (1979) 70 Cr App R 1 and *R v Holland, R v Smith* [1983] Crim LR 545). We are in no doubt that the three complainants in the present case were shown to be persons in respect of whom the full warning was essential. It follows that in our view these convictions are unsafe and must be quashed.'

Counsel's first submission on behalf of the appellants in the appeals before us was therefore that we were bound by the decision in *Bagshaw's* case, that the former could not be distinguished from the latter and that consequently these appeals should also be allowed.

On behalf of the Crown Mr Roberts submitted that the court's decision in *Bagshaw's* case was reached per incuriam, in that it was inconsistent with earlier decisions of this court which were not cited to it, that in such circumstances it was not only open to, but indeed the duty of, this present court to choose between two inconsistent lines of authority, that having done so we should respectively conclude that *Bagshaw's* case was wrongly decided, that the direction given by the judge in the instant case was wholly adequate and that accordingly these appeals should be dismissed.

Mr Roberts himself appeared for the Crown in *Bagshaw's* case. He told us, and we accept, that the question of the adequacy of the trial judge's direction in that case was not originally raised in the appellant's grounds of appeal. This ground was only raised by way of an amendment of the original grounds allowed by the court in the course of the hearing of the appeal (see [1984] 1 All ER 971 at 973, [1984] 1 WLR 477 at 479). It is quite clear that the relevant amendment was made during the opening submissions of counsel for the appellants at the suggestion of the court, and that although counsel for the Crown sought to deal with the fresh ground as adequately as he could in his reply, he confessed that he now realises that he ought to have dealt with the point far more fully, as indeed he did in his submissions before us.

Counsel accepted that in general the Criminal Division of the Court of Appeal is bound to follow its own decisions in the same way as the Civil Division of the court. He referred us to the well-known decision of *Young v Bristol Aeroplane Co Ltd* [1944] 2 All ER 293, [1944] 1 KB 718, and we accept that the principles laid down in that case apply, subject to the one point with which we deal hereafter, to any decision of the Court of Appeal, whether sitting in its civil or criminal jurisdiction.

Although it may not be necessary to decide the point in the instant appeals, we appreciate that in *R v Taylor* [1950] 2 All ER 170, [1950] 2 KB 368 a Court of Criminal Appeal comprising seven members departed from a previous view assumed by the court and declined to follow an earlier authority. In our respectful opinion the ratio of that decision was that to which Widgery LJ first referred in the case of *R v Newsome, R v Browne* [1970] 3 All ER 455 at 458, [1970] 2 QB 711 at 716, namely that the court justified its action to a very large degree by the fact that in that case a departure from authority was necessary in the interests of the appellant. Lord Goddard CJ, in giving the judgment of the court, took a robust view that if a man be in prison and in the judgment of the court wrongly in prison, it should not allow such matters as stare decisis to stand in the way.

However in *R v Gould* [1968] 1 All ER 849, [1968] 2 QB 65 this court prima facie appears to have gone further. In giving the judgment of the court Diplock LJ said ([1968] 1 All ER 849 at 851, [1968] 2 QB 65 at 68):

'In its criminal jurisdiction, which it has inherited from the Court of Criminal Appeal, the Court of Appeal does not apply the doctrine of stare decisis with the same rigidity as in its civil jurisdiction. If on due consideration we were to be of opinion that the law had been either misapplied or misunderstood in an earlier decision of this court, or its predecessor the Court of Criminal Appeal, we should be entitled to depart from the view as to the law expressed in the earlier decision notwithstanding that the case could not be brought within any of the exceptions laid down in *Young v. Bristol Aeroplane Co., Ltd....*'

On the facts of that case the court was not in truth going further than it went in *Taylor*. However, Widgery LJ had been a member of the court in *Gould*, and in his judgment in *Newsome* expressed the view that the dictum which we have quoted should not be regarded as being qualified by the decision in *Taylor*. However *Newsome* was a case which was concerned with the exercise of discretion in sentencing and not with any previous decision on a point of law of the Court of Appeal sitting in its criminal jurisdiction.

As a matter of principle we respectfully find it difficult to see why there should in general be any difference in the application of the principle of stare decisis between the Civil and Criminal Divisions of this court, save that we must remember that in the latter we may be dealing with the liberty of the subject and if a departure from authority is necessary in the interests of justice to an appellant, then this court should not shrink from so acting. In our opinion the dictum from *Gould* must be read in this sense and subject to this the principles laid down in *Young v Bristol Aeroplane Co Ltd* should apply.

Against this background counsel for the Crown submitted that this court's decision in *Bagshaw's* case [1984] 1 All ER 971, [1984] 1 WLR 477 conflicted with the decision of another division in *R v Beck* [1982] 1 All ER 807, [1982] 1 WLR 461, and that accordingly we were required to decide which of those two conflicting decisions we should follow. Further, in the circumstances we have outlined, counsel also submitted that the decision in *Bagshaw* was given per incuriam in that, following the late amendment of the grounds of appeal, the court was not referred to earlier inconsistent decisions and that if it had been so referred, its decision would have been different.

In developing his submissions counsel for the Crown took us first to the actual judgment in *Bagshaw's* case. After stating the facts and details of that case the court then referred to, and clearly founded itself on, a passage from the speech of Lord Hailsham LC in the well-known case of *DPP v Kilbourne* [1973] 1 All ER 440 at 447, [1973] AC 729 at 740, which we think we should set out in full:

'But side by side with the statutory exceptions is the rule of practice now under discussion by which the judges have in fact warned juries in certain classes of case that it is dangerous to found a conviction on the evidence of particular witnesses or classes of witness unless that evidence is corroborated in a material particular implicating the accused, or confirming the disputed items in the case. The earliest of these classes to be recognised was probably the evidence of accomplices 'approving' for the Crown, no doubt, partly because at that time the accused could not give evidence on his own behalf and was therefore peculiarly vulnerable to invented allegations by persons guilty of the same offence. By now the recognised categories also include children who give evidence under oath, the alleged victims, whether adults or children, in cases of sexual assault, and persons of admittedly bad character. I do not regard these categories as closed. A judge is almost certainly wise to give a similar warning about the evidence of any principal witness for the Crown where the witness can reasonably be suggested to have some purpose of his own to serve in giving false evidence (cf *R v Prater* [1960] 1 All ER 298, [1960] 2 QB 464 and *R v Russell* (1968) 52 Cr App R 147). The Supreme Court of the Republic of Ireland has apparently decided that at least in some cases of disputed identity a similar warning is necessary (*People v Dominic Casey (No 2)* [1963] IR 33 at 39, 40). This question may still be open here (cf *R v Williams* [1956] Crim LR 833 and *Arthurs v A-G for Northern Ireland* (1970) 55 Cr App R 161 at 169).'

Counsel submitted, and we agree, that this passage from Lord Hailsham LC's speech in *DPP v Kilbourne* was clearly obiter. In that case the accused had been convicted of offences of buggery, attempted buggery and indecent assault on two groups of boys. In such a case it is clear law that a trial judge must warn the jury that it is dangerous to convict on the uncorroborated evidence of a complainant. We shall refer to such a direction hereafter as the 'full warning'. The issue for decision in *DPP v Kilbourne* was whether the evidence of one group of boys, if otherwise accepted by the jury, could in law be capable of being corroboration of the evidence of the other group of boys.

With equal respect counsel for the Crown went further and submitted that Lord Hailsham LC's opinion as expressed in this passage is not supported by the authorities to which he referred nor by other subsequent decided cases in the same field. For the reasons to which we refer later, we have been driven to agree.

In its judgment in *Bagshaw's* case this court said that it had in mind, without setting them out, certain passages from the speeches of Lord Morris and Lord Diplock in *DPP v Hester* [1972] 3 All ER 1056, [1973] AC 296. As we have been asked to hold that the decision in the former case was reached per incuriam we think that it is desirable now to set out those passages from those speeches to which we think that the court must have been referring.

In *Hester's* case ([1972] 3 All ER 1056 at 1059–1060, [1973] AC 296 at 309) Lord Morris said:

> 'The accumulated experience of courts of law, reflecting accepted general knowledge of the ways of the world, has shown that there are many circumstances and situations in which it is unwise to found settled conclusions on the testimony of one person alone. The reasons for this are diverse. There are some suggestions which can readily be made but which are only with more difficulty rebutted. There may in some cases be motives of self-interest; or of self-exculpation; or of vindictiveness. In some situations the straight line of truth is diverted by the influences of emotion or of hysteria or of alarm or of remorse. Sometimes it may be that owing to immaturity or perhaps to lively imaginative gifts there is no true appreciation of the gulf that separates truth from falsehood. It must, therefore, be sound policy to have rules of law or of practice which are designed to avert the peril that findings of guilt may be insecurely based.'

Lord Morris then pointed out that it was for these reasons that various statutes do impose the necessity in some cases for more than one witness before there can be a conviction. He went on to say that it has similarly come about 'that in other instances the courts have given guidance in terms which have become rules'. Instances to which he referred were those which are well known, namely where charges of sexual offences are made and cases in which children are witnesses.

The relevant passage, as we think, from Lord Morris's speech ends with this paragraph ([1972] 3 All ER 1056 at 1060, [1973] AC 296 at 309):

> 'All the rules which have been evolved are in accord with the central principle of our criminal law that a person should only be convicted of a crime if those in whose hands decision rests are sure that guilt has been established. In England it has not been laid down that such certainty ought never to be reached in dependence on the testimony of but one witness. It has, however, been recognised that the risk or danger of a wrong decision being reached is greater in certain circumstances than in others. It is where those circumstances exist that rules based on experience, wisdom and common sense have been introduced.'

We think that in these passages to which we have referred Lord Morris was explaining the reasons why the rules relating to the necessity for corroboration had developed to lay the ground for his subsequent discussion of the particular point which did arise for their Lordship's decision in *Hester's* case. It is noteworthy in our view that he spoke of categories in which the common law had prior to the time when he was speaking laid down the rule of practice which had become a rule of law, but he did not suggest that there were likely to be other categories in the future in which the similar full warning would have to be given.

The relevant parts of Lord Diplock's speech in the same case are we think to the same effect (see [1972] 3 All ER 1056 at 1072–1074, [1973] AC 296 at 324–326). Lord Diplock stated the three categories in which the full warning is certainly required, but we do not find any suggestion in his speech in *Hester's* case that there may be, still less that there are likely to be, other categories of witnesses requiring the full warning than those three to which he refers (see [1972] 3 All ER 1056 at 1073, [1973] AC 296 at 325). The passage from his speech which was quoted by this court in the judgments in *Bagshaw's* case seems to us with respect to go to the question of how the full warning on corroboration is to be phrased so that a jury may easily understand it, rather than to the actual circumstances in which such a warning has at common law been held to be necessary.

On this analysis there is in our opinion nothing in the speeches in *Hester's* case to support the suggestion that the categories of case requiring the full warning are still open. Indeed, if there were, we respectfully think that it too would be obiter. Nevertheless there is no doubt that in the past 25 years suggestions to this effect have been made. On a consideration of the authorities and textbooks it is clear that they have been based on dicta in *R v Prater* [1960] 1 All ER 298, [1960] 2 QB 464, *People v Casey (No 2)* [1963] IR 33 and *Kilbourne's* case [1973] 1 All ER 440, [1973] AC 729, the last of which we have already quoted in this judgment.

In *Prater's* case a man by the name of Welham was a co-defendant with the appellant on an indictment charging them with six counts of conspiracy to defraud and uttering forged documents with that intent. Welham gave evidence on his own behalf adverse to the appellant Prater. It was argued on Prater's behalf that Welham was in truth an accomplice and that accordingly the full warning ought to have been given, but was not. The Court of Criminal Appeal did not decide this point, but in giving the judgment of the court Edmund Davies J said ([1960] 1 All ER 298 at 299–300, [1960] 2 QB 464 at 466):

> 'For the purposes of this present appeal, this court is content to accept that, whether the label to be attached to Welham in this case was strictly that of an accomplice or not, in practice it is desirable that a warning should be given that the witness, whether he comes from the dock, as in this case, or whether he be a Crown witness, may be a witness with some purpose of his own to serve . . . This court, in the circumstances of the present appeal, is content to found itself on the view which it expresses that it is desirable that, in cases where a person may be regarded as having some purpose of his own to serve, the warning against uncorroborated evidence should be given.'

However, as was subsequently said in *R v Whittaker* (1976) 63 Cr App R 193 at 196, *Prater* has not remained a wholly unqualified decision. Indeed it was the subject of strong comment in the Court of Criminal Appeal in *R v Stannard* [1964] 1 All ER 34 at 40, [1965] 2 QB 1 at 14, where Winn J said:

> 'The rule, if it be a rule, enunciated in *R v Prater* ([1960] 1 All ER 298, [1960] 2 QB 464), is no more than a rule of practice. I say deliberately "if it be a rule" because, reading the passage of the judgment as I have just read it, it really seems to amount to no more than an expression of what is desirable and what, it is to be hoped, will more usually than not be adopted, at any rate where it seems to be appropriate to the learned judge. It certainly is not a rule of law . . .'

In *R v Russell* (1968) 52 Cr App R 147 this court approved the decision in *Stannard* and in giving the judgment of the court Diplock LJ adopted the words of Salmon LJ in *R v O'Reilly* [1967] 2 All ER 766 at 768–769, [1967] 2 QB 722 at 727, to this effect:

> 'The rule that the jury must be warned does not mean, however, that there has to be some legalistic ritual to be automatically recited by the judge, that some particular form of words or incantation has to be used and, if not used, the summing-up is faulty and the conviction must be quashed. The law, as this court understands it, is that there should be a solemn warning given to the jury, in terms which a jury can understand, to safeguard the accused. In this case the learned deputy chairman gave such a warning although he never used the magic word "corroboration"; and it is doubtful if the jury would have understood what it meant if he had. Indeed, when the actual word is used it is necessary for the court to tell the jury what it does mean.'

Finally, in *R v Whittaker* this court specifically approved the approach to *Prater* in the subsequent cases to which we have just referred.

We turn shortly to *The People v Casey (No 2)* [1963] IR 33, to which Lord Hailsham LC

referred in the dictum from *Kilbourne*'s case on which this court appears to have relied in
a   *R v Bagshaw* [1984] 1 All ER 971, [1984] 1 WLR 477. *Casey* was a case concerning visual
identification and the Supreme Court held, earlier than the courts of this country in *R v
Turnbull* [1976] 3 All ER 549, [1977] QB 224, that juries should be very carefully warned
when the correctness of an identification is challenged. In considering the nature of the
warning to be given and whether indeed there should be any direction relating to
corroboration, the Supreme Court continued in its judgment in these terms ([1963] IR
b   33 at 40):

> 'This direction is not meant to be a stereotyped formula. It may be too condensed
> to be fully appreciated by a jury without some further explanation and the facts of
> an individual case may require it to be couched in stronger or more ample terms, as
> when the witness or witnesses had no previous acquaintance with the appearance of
> the accused or had only an indifferent opportunity for observation. It does, however,
c   > contain a minimum warning which should be given in any case which depends on
> visual identification. No specific reference is made to "corroboration in a material
> particular implicating the accused". An item of evidence falling within this formula
> may, according to its nature, have very little or very great probative value. This
> consideration is meant to be covered by the words, "in the light of all the
> circumstances, and with due regard to all the other evidence in the case", and it is
d   > for the judge to deal with the lesser or greater probative value of any item of
> corroborative evidence.'

Finally, we have neither been referred to nor discovered in our own researches any
authority to support the suggestion made in the dictum from Lord Hailsham LC's speech
in *Kilbourne* that the full warning is required in respect of witnesses who are persons of
e   admittedly bad character. Judges always warn juries about the evidence of such witnesses,
in whatever terms they think appropriate to the case, but we respectfully do not think
that such witnesses do form one of the recognised categories in which the full warning
has to be given and in which, if the jury are not warned in so many words of the dangers
of acting on the uncorroborated evidence of such witnesses, an appeal against conviction
would be bound to succeed, subject to the application of the proviso to s 2(1) of the
Criminal Appeal Act 1968.

In the circumstances we agree with the submission of counsel for the Crown that none
of the dicta to which we have referred can be treated as any authority for any extension
of the rule of practice or law which requires the full corroboration warning in other than
the well-known but limited categories of case. Indeed we also agree that the attitude of
our courts over recent years has in fact been to refuse to increase the number of categories
in which the full warning, with all the complications it involves, has to be given, but to
f   emphasise the duty of a trial judge in appropriate cases to warn the jury of a 'special need
for caution' in relation to the evidence of certain witnesses, in terms appropriate to the
particular case under consideration: see *R v Evans, R v Allen* [1964] 3 All ER 401, [1965]
2 QB 295, *R v Long* (1973) 57 Cr App R 871 and *R v Turnbull*.

It is against this background that we turn to the recent case of *R v Beck* [1982] 1 All ER
g   807, [1982] 1 WLR 461. We do not think it necessary to set out the facts of that case in
any detail. It is sufficient to say that in so far as is relevant for present purposes the first
ground of appeal in that case was that the judge wrongly failed to direct the jury that it
would be dangerous to act on the uncorroborated evidence of three witnesses 'since they
had a purpose of their own to serve in giving evidence, namely to cover up false
representations made or acceded to by them in the insurance claim'.

The argument on behalf of the appellant on this point was based essentially on *Prater*
which the court reiterated had been the subject of strong comment in *Stannard* and also
in *Whittaker*, to both of which cases we have referred. Counsel for the appellant in *Beck*'s
case apparently accepted that a full warning could not be required in every case where a
witness may be regarded as having some purpose of his own to serve, but submitted that
where a witness has a 'substantial interest' of his own for giving false evidence, then the

full warning should be given. Where one drew the line, counsel argued, was a matter of degree, but once the boundary had been crossed the obligation to give such a warning was not thereafter of discretion.

In dealing with this contention this court said ([1982] 1 All ER 807 at 812–813, [1982] 1 WLR 461 at 467–468):

'We cannot accept this contention. In many trials today, the burden on the trial judge of the summing up is a heavy one. It would be a totally unjustifiable addition to require him, not only fairly to put before the jury the defence's contention that a witness was suspect, because he had an axe to grind, but also to evaluate the weight of that axe and oblige him, where the weight is "substantial", to give an accomplice warning with the appropriate direction as to the meaning of corroboration together with the identification of the potential corroborative material ... In short, the phrase [taken from *Prater*] "it is desirable that in cases where a person may be regarded as having some purpose of his own to serve, the warning against uncorroborated evidence should be given" is related to cases where witnesses may be participants or involved in the crime charged.'

A little later in their judgment the court said ([1982] 1 All ER 807 at 813, [1982] 1 WLR 461 at 469):

'While we in no way wish to detract from the obligation on a judge to advise a jury to proceed with caution where there is material to suggest that a witness's evidence may be tainted by an improper motive, and the strength of that advice must vary according to the facts of the case, we cannot accept that there is any obligation to give the accomplice warning with all that entails, when it is common ground that there is no basis for suggesting that the witness is a participant or in any way involved in the crime the subject matter of the trial.'

In our view the ratio of this court's decision in *Beck's* case was that, apart from those cases where statute so requires and the special instances of cases involving allegations of sexual offences or the evidence of young children, the full warning is only required where a witness is in truth an accomplice of the defendant, or so thought to be by the jury.

With respect, the ratio of the decision in *Bagshaw's* case in the passage from the judgment which we quoted does not seem to us to be entirely clear. Either the court took the view that patients detained in a special hospital after a conviction for an offence or offences are to be considered a special category in respect of whose evidence the full warning must be given: if this were so, then we do not think that this can be reconciled with *Beck's* case. Alternatively, the court in *Bagshaw* was of the opinion that on the view they took of the witnesses and their evidence, the direction given by the trial judge was inadequate: if this were so, then, although we must treat and have treated that opinion as extremely persuasive, it was not, we respectfully think, a decision on the relevant law which is in the end binding on us. As we have said, the court in *Bagshaw's* case did not have the benefit of the full argument on the point which has been addressed to us: in particular on the validity of the dictum quoted from Lord Hailsham LC's speech in *Kilbourne*. We respectfully think that had this court in *Bagshaw* had the benefit of full argument, and especially had the decision in *Beck's* case been drawn to its attention, it might well have reached a different conclusion.

We fully appreciate that there is a difference between telling a jury that it is dangerous to convict on the uncorroborated evidence of a particular witness or witnesses on the one hand and warning them that for fully explained reasons they should approach and consider that evidence with great caution on the other. From a practical point of view however we wonder whether to a jury the one is any more forceful or restraining than the other. It is our combined experience, both from sitting at first instance and also in this court, that where the full warning has to be given as a matter of law it is very difficult to direct the jury in terms which thay can clearly understand, particularly when one has to go on and direct them about which part of the other evidence can or cannot be considered to be corroborative. To warn a jury appropriately of a special need for caution

*a* in respect of the evidence of a particular witness, explaining to them if necessary why such caution is required, is in our respectful opinion a clearer and better way of approaching this problem than, in effect, creating an additional category of witness in respect of whom the full warning must be given, with all its complications and which, if not given will of itself lead to the quashing of the conviction concerned.

We should add that in the first of the series of trials of nursing staff at Rampton to

*b* which we have referred, and which was presided over by Stephen Brown J, the judge gave very much the same, though perhaps not so full a warning as did the judge in the instant case, without any direction in respect of the need for corroboration. So also did Webster J in another of the trials, although in that case the jury acquitted. Finally, we were told that in yet another case the same trial judge as in the instant cases indicated to counsel in advance the form of direction he proposed to give and on neither side was it

*c* submitted that this was in any way inadequate.

For all these reasons we do not think that the judge's summing up in the cases before us can be validly criticised on the ground that he failed to warn the jury of the danger of convicting on the uncorroborated evidence of the patients. In our opinion the warning which the trial judge gave the jury about their evidence was entirely adequate. We add, as did this court in *Bagshaw*'s case, that in our view the judge's summing up in the instant

*d* cases were also lucid and fair in the extreme.

In the first of the two cases which were before us, counsel argued a second ground in support of his clients' appeal. During their trial it became clear to both the judge and counsel that one male juror, a Mr Peat, had early on formed a definite view of the case and on occasions appeared to be biased against the defendants and in favour of the prosecution. There is some information in the papers before us to suggest that his attitude

*e* during the trial had on one or two occasions annoyed some of his fellow jurors.

During the short adjournemnt on the day before the trial ended and after the judge had begun his summing up, a court usher was told by another juror that Mr Peat's wife worked at a mental hospital other than Rampton but which figured in the evidence in the trial. Counsel told the judge of this when he sat after the adjournment and, having confirmed the information with Mr Peat in court, the judge, with the agreement of both

*f* prosecution and defence, discharged him.

At this point Mr Peat asked the judge whether it would be all right for him to wait in the ante-room because 'I have got three to take back to Newark'. Possibly because the judge and counsel were at that stage of the trial concentrating on the summing up, the full significance of Mr Peat's question was not appreciated by anyone. Indeed the judge then turned to the remaining members of the jury and said:

*g*
> 'Members of the jury, you realise of course, I am sure, how very careful we have to be. Who he is giving a lift back to Newark, I know not. If it is any of you I must enjoin you please do not discuss this case with Mr Peat any further.'

By the next morning all counsel had had the opportunity of thinking rather more fully about what Mr Peat had said the previous day. Counsel for the appellants had also

*h* found out that he had been in the habit of giving three of his fellow jurors in the same case a daily lift to and from their homes in Newark, which was near where he himself lived. In those circumstances the probabilities were that Mr Peat would have aired his anti-defence opinions during those car journeys and possibly given his passengers other information prejudicial to the three defendants. Counsel therefore applied to the judge for the discharge of the remaining eleven jurors and a retrial.

Counsel on behalf of the Crown resisted the application. He pointed out that if there were to be a retrial the witnesses would have to be recalled. Concern had already been expressed by doctors and others about the effect that giving evidence and being cross-examined had had on the Rampton patients involved. He submitted that the test which the judge should apply was one which counsel for the Crown now accepts was too strict, namely that the jury should not be discharged unless it could be shown that there was a very high risk that the apparently biased juror had influenced any of his fellows.

The judge rejected the application of counsel for the appellants. He said that he took into account that the case was then in its tenth day, that so far as the appellants were concerned, through no fault of anyone, years had passed since they had first been seen about the allegations made, and that it could cause considerable concern if the witnesses who had been patients at Rampton, and who were mentally disturbed, had to be recalled to give evidence. The judge then rightly held that it was a matter for his discretion whether to discharge the jury or not and gave his ruling in these terms:

'Weighing the matter as best I can I exercise my discretion in this matter by saying that in my view there is not a high degree of risk that this jury is going to be prejudiced in any way by anything they may or may not have heard and in those circumstances in so far as this case is concerned I shall allow them to continue.'

The appellants' original application for leave to appeal, which referred to these incidents involving Mr Peat, was received by the Registrar of Criminal Appeals on 19 July 1983. On 8 August 1983 a statement was taken from Mr Peat by a representative of the Director of Public Prosecutions. In that statement he confirmed that he had been in the habit of giving three of his fellow jurors a lift to and from court and that he had done so on the afternoon on which he himself had been discharged, when the court ultimately rose for the day. He went on to say that 'during the journey we discussed the case and also how it came to light about my wife working at [the other mental] hospital'. Other parts of this statement made it quite clear that Mr Peat had formed a clear view about the guilt of the appellants but nothing to suggest that he had expressed this view to the three juror passengers in his car when he was giving them a lift home on that last occasion. Nevertheless, on all the material that there is before us we think we must conclude that in the course of that journey he did do just that.

As we have said, counsel for the Crown accepted before us that the test of a 'high degree of risk that the jury had been prejudiced' was wrong. In these circumstances, although counsel for the appellants accepted that the decision whether or not to discharge the jury was one for the exercise of the trial judge's discretion, and that this court should be slow to interfere with a judge's decision on this point, he submitted that once the judge had been shown to have exercised his discretion on a wrong principle there had been a material irregularity in the course of the trial and that consequently his clients' appeal should be allowed.

We do not think that that is the right approach. In our view the proper approach is to ask ourselves whether, if the judge had applied the correct test, he would or might have reached the opposite conclusion and discharged the jury. Both counsel agreed that that correct test was the one stated in *R v Sawyer* (1980) 71 Cr App R 283, namely whether there was a 'real danger' that the appellants' position had been prejudiced in the circumstances we have outlined. Each of us has no doubt that if at that stage the judge had asked himself whether there was in truth a real danger that the appellants' position had been prejudiced by the conversations which the three jurors had had in the car with Mr Peat prior to the latter's discharge, he would have reached the same conclusion and would have rejected the application of counsel for the appellants. Further, we think that he would have been entitled to do so on the grounds to which he referred in his ruling and that, having done so, his decision could not have been criticised in this court.

We must however take this point a little further, because there is available to us the information which was not available to the judge, namely that despite his warning to the jury after he had discharged Mr Peat, the three of them had talked to the latter about the case in the car that evening. Counsel for the appellants submitted that in those circumstances the verdicts of the jury thereafter must be considered to have been unsafe or unsatisfactory. Counsel for the Crown, on the other hand, contended that this by no means followed and that we should not leap to the conclusion that the three jurors were not on the following day entirely conscientious in the consideration which they gave to this case.

In addition to *R v Sawyer*, to which we have already referred, there are we think two a    other authorities to which we can draw attention, The first of these is *R v Twiss* [1918] 2 KB 853. In that case it transpired that one or more of the jurymen, during the short adjournment on the first day of the trial, had had conversations with certain witnesses for the Crown, including the boys with whom it was alleged that the appellant had committed various acts of gross indecency. In giving the judgment of the court Darling J said ([1918] 2 KB 853 at 858):

b       'The Juries Detention Act, 1897 (60 & 61 Vict. c. 18), allows the Court to permit jurymen to separate in cases of felony, except on a charge of murder, treason, or treason felony. Can it be supposed that when the Legislature passed that statute it thought that jurymen, when they leave the Court (the case being part heard) and go to luncheon, never mention the case to any one?'

c    The judge then referred to *R v Ketteridge* [1915] 1 KB 467, [1914–15] All ER Rep 482, which he said was a different case, and subsequently continued ([1918] 2 KB 853 at 859):

      'The whole solemn procedure of the Court had been violated in that case; whereas in the present case the trial was proceeded with and the juryman did that which we know, and the Legislature knows, jurymen must constantly do ... In those circumstances it is necessary for us to consider whether what the juryman did was of such a character as to lead us to think that there may have been an injustice done to the prisoner.'

d    A case whose facts were closer to those of the instant case is that of *R v Prime* (1973) 57 Cr App R 632. In that case a man called Earl had been called as juror for the trial but apparently on his own initiative had said that he knew the appellant and that he did not think that it was right he should serve on the jury. He was accordingly excused from jury service on that count. He remained in court and during the mid-day adjournment he was seen by the appellant's mother and wife walking in the street in company with two of the jurors. The two women both said that Earl jokingly turned to them and said 'He is guilty'.

e    In giving the judgment of the court on this point Lord Widgery CJ echoed what had been said in *Twiss*, pointing out that jurors today are not segregated in the way that they were: they leave the jurybox and walk out through the same entrances as everyone else; very often they have lunch sitting on the next stool to a witness in the case. Lord Widgery CJ then went on (57 Cr App R 632 at 636):

f       '... we are now prepared to accept that contact between a juror and someone else is not necessarily fatal to the validity of the trial, and it must be taken that we have accepted, and the public have accepted, that jurors are better educated than they were, and that if they are told by the judge not to talk about the case outside, there is a reasonable prospect that they will not do so ... If the matter goes further than that, and it can be shown that somebody tries to tamper with the juror in the sense that he has tried to pass him information which should not be passed, that is a different matter; but it has got to be proved by acceptable evidence, and it is not to be inferred nowadays merely because by force of circumstances a juror and an outsider have been put in close company one with the other. It is with those principles in mind that one turns to look at the facts of this case. Is there anything which suggests that the conviction is unsafe to be derived from the simple fact that Earl and those jurors were talking together?'

g

h    In our judgment the effect of each of these three cases is that in this type of circumstance this court must ask itself whether it thinks there is anything in the events which ex hypothesi should not have occurred which leads it to the conclusion that an injustice may have been done, or that there is a real danger that the appellant may have been prejudiced by what has gone on. In the instant case, we do not think that we should come to that conclusion. It was apparent to both the judge and counsel that Mr Peat had made his views clear to all his fellow jurors over a period of some ten days during which he had been one of their number. Nevertheless when the connection of Mrs Peat with the associated hospital became apparent, the judge exercised his discretion only to   *a* discharge Mr Peat and not the whole jury.

The three jurors to whom Mr Peat gave the final lift home had been specifically warned by the judge immediately after Mr Peat had been discharged that they should not talk to him about the case, just as no doubt they had been warned on earlier occasions. It is quite true that these jurors did not comply with that warning and direction from the judge and their failure to do so is to be deplored. Nevertheless we do not think that   *b* in the circumstances there is any realistic chance that those three jurors, or any of them, carried with them into the deliberations of themselves and their fellow jurors, when the judge finished his summing up the following morning, any prejudice or bias which they had acquired from Mr Peat the afternoon before. We do not forget that the convictions in this case were by majority verdicts reached after the jury had been out considering their verdicts for over 5½ hours. We think that this is readily explicable by the nature of   *c* the evidence which the jury had heard, and by the type of witness by whom that evidence had been given, and about whom and their evidence the judge had so fully warned the jury in the course of his summing up.

In the result each of these appeals will be dismissed.

*Appeals dismissed.*   *d*

*The court refused leave to appeal to the House of Lords but certified, under s 33(2) of the Criminal Appeal Act 1968, that the following point of law of general public importance was involved in the decision: in a case where the evidence for the Crown is solely that of a witness who is not in one of the accepted categories of suspect witnesses, but who, by reason of his particular mental condition and criminal connection, fulfilled the same criteria, must the judge warn the jury that it is*   *e* *dangerous to convict on his uncorroborated evidence?*

*18 December. The Appeal Committee of the House of Lords granted the appellants leave to appeal.*

Solicitor: *Tracey Barlow Furniss & Co,* Worksop (for the appellants); *Director of Public Prosecutions.*   *f*

Richard Willett Esq   Barrister.

# Reed (Inspector of Taxes) v Nova Securities Ltd   *g*

HOUSE OF LORDS

LORD KEITH OF KINKEL, LORD EDMUND-DAVIES, LORD BRIDGE OF HARWICH, LORD BRANDON OF OAKBROOK AND LORD TEMPLEMAN

2, 3, 4 OCTOBER, 29 NOVEMBER 1984, 31 JANUARY 1985   *h*

*Income tax – Company – Group relief – Appropriation of assets to trading stock – Transfer between members of group – Company dealing in shares and securities acquiring shares and debts from parent at small market value – Parent company having acquired assets for large sum – Acquiring company electing to have assets brought into its trading account at value equal to cost of assets to parent company – Whether assets acquired as trading stock – Finance Act 1965, Sch 7,*   *j* *para 1(1)(3) – Income and Corporation Taxes Act 1970, ss 137(4), 274(1).*

In March 1973 the taxpayer company, which had traded in shares and securities since 1955, was acquired by another company, L. On 17 August 1973 L disposed of certain assets, consisting of shares and bank debts, to the taxpayer company for £30,000, which represented their market value. The shares alone were valued at only £10. The assets had not formed part of L's trading stock and had been acquired by L for £3,936,765. The taxpayer company claimed that the assets had been acquired by it as 'trading stock' within ss 137(4)[a] and 274(1)[b] of the Income and Corporation Taxes Act 1970 and made an election under the Finance Act 1965, Sch 7, para 1(3)[c] that, in computing the profits of its trade for the purposes of corporation tax, the market value of the assets acquired should be treated as being increased by £3,906,765, being what would have been the amount of the allowable loss accruing to the taxpayer company under para 1(1)[d] of Sch 7 to the 1965 Act had no such election been made. The Revenue rejected the taxpayer company's claim. At the hearing of an appeal before the General Commissioners the Revenue agreed to the issue being determined not by oral evidence but on the basis of an agreed statement of facts which did not investigate the intentions of either the taxpayer company or L regarding trading at any time with the acquired assets. The commissioners found as a fact that the taxpayer company had acquired all the assets in the course of its trading in shares and securities and that the assets had been acquired as trading stock and accordingly allowed the taxpayer company's appeal. The judge dismissed an appeal by the Crown, holding that the commissioners had been entitled to reach the conclusion that the assets had been acquired by the taxpayer company in the course of its trade and had thus been acquired as trading stock. The Court of Appeal found that it was proper for the commissioners to have concluded as they did and dismissed an appeal by the Crown. The Crown appealed to the House of Lords, contending that s 274(1) of the 1970 Act did not apply because the taxpayer company had acquired the assets not as trading stock but for the purpose of obtaining a fiscal advantage.

**Held** – For a company to acquire an asset as trading stock it not only had to be of a kind which was sold in the ordinary course of that company's trade but also had to be acquired with a view to resale at a profit. On the facts, the commissioners had been justified in concluding that the taxpayer company, whose trade was that of dealing in shares and securities, had acquired the bank debts as trading stock. However, the taxpayer company's acquisition of the shares, which had no value, was without commercial justification and no reasonable body of commissioners could have concluded that, although acquired in connection with the debts, the shares had been acquired by the taxpayer company as trading stock. The appeal would therefore be allowed so far as the claim to relief related to the acquisition of the shares by the taxpayer company (see p 688 f to h, p 689 b, p 692 h j and p 694 b to j, post).

Per curiam. (1) A company which acquires an asset for purposes other than trading does not acquire it as trading stock even though the company habitually trades in similar assets (see p 688 f to h, p 689 b and p 692 j, post); *Coates (Inspector of Taxes) v Arndale Properties Ltd* [1985] 1 All ER 15 applied.

(2) The practice of the Revenue of not instructing counsel to appear on its behalf at hearings before the commissioners in cases where millions of pounds are at stake and where the law is complex should be reviewed (see p 688 f to j, p 689 b and p 692 e to g, post).

Per Lord Bridge. In a case where the facts are unusual and a difficult issue of fact arises for decision, it is essential that the taxpayer be left to prove his entitlement to tax relief before the commissioners by calling oral evidence and not be allowed to proceed on an exiguous agreed statement of facts (see p 688 j, post).

**Notes**

For transfer of trading stock between members of groups of companies, see 5 Halsbury's Laws (4th edn) para 206.

For the Finance Act 1965, Sch 7, para 1, see 34 Halsbury's Statutes (3rd edn) 949.

For the Income and Corporation Taxes Act 1970, ss 137, 274, see 33 ibid 192, 375.

---

a   Section 137(4), so far as material, is set out at p 692 g, post
b   Section 274(1), so far as material, is set out at p 690 j to p 691 a, post
c   Paragraph 1(3), so far as material, is set out at p 691 d e, post
d   Paragraph 1(1), so far as material, is set out at p 691 b c, post

With effect from 6 April 1979 para 1 of Sch 7 to the 1965 Act was replaced by s 122 of the Capital Gains Tax Act 1979.

**Cases referred to in opinions**

Coates (Inspector of Taxes) v Arndale Properties Ltd [1985] 1 All ER 15, [1984] 1 WLR 1328, HL.

Edwards (Inspector of Taxes) v Bairstow [1955] 3 All ER 48, [1956] AC 14, [1955] 3 WLR 410, HL.

FA & AB Ltd v Lupton (Inspector of Taxes) [1971] 3 All ER 948, [1972] AC 634, [1971] 3 WLR 670, HL.

Furniss (Inspector of Taxes) v Dawson [1984] 1 All ER 530, [1984] AC 474, [1984] 2 WLR 226, HL.

Southard & Co Ltd, Re [1979] 3 All ER 556, [1979] 1 WLR 1198, CA.

**Appeal**

The Crown appealed by leave of the Court of Appeal against an order of that court (Fox and Kerr LJ, Lawton LJ dissenting) ([1984] STC 124) on 6 December 1983 dismissing the Crown's appeal from a decision of Walton J ([1982] STC 724) on 29 July 1982 whereby he dismissed the Crown's appeal by way of case stated (set out at [1982] STC 725–727) from the determination of the General Commissioners for the division of Holborn, Greater London, finding that the taxpayer, Nova Securities Ltd (Nova), had acquired certain assets in the course of its trade as trading stock and qualified for stock relief pursuant to para 1 of Sch 7 to the Finance Act 1965. The facts are set out in the opinion of Lord Templeman.

*Jonathan Parker QC, John Mummery* and *Peter Goldsmith* for the Crown.
*C N Beattie QC* and *C J F Sokol* for Nova.

Their Lordships took time for consideration.

31 January. The following opinions were delivered.

**LORD KEITH OF KINKEL.** My Lords, I have had the benefit of reading in advance the speech to be delivered by my noble and learned friend Lord Templeman. I agree that, for the reasons which he states, the appeal should be allowed in part and an order made in the terms which he proposes.

**LORD EDMUND-DAVIES.** My Lords, I am in agreement with the speech prepared by my noble and learned friend Lord Templeman. I would accordingly allow the appeal in part and make the order proposed by him.

**LORD BRIDGE OF HARWICH.** My Lords, I have had the advantage of reading in draft the speech of my noble and learned friend Lord Templeman. I fully agree with it and with the order he proposes allowing the appeal in part.

I add a word only to express my own emphatic opinion, in concurrence with that of my noble and learned friend, that this was a case where the Inland Revenue owed it to the general body of taxpayers to ensure that their case was competently conducted before the General Commissioners. A claim to tax relief on nearly £4m turned on the result. The facts were, to say the least, unusual and a difficult issue of fact arose for decision. In these circumstances any competent advocate experienced in tax matters would have realised that, if the Revenue were to succeed on the grounds unsuccessfully argued before Walton J and the Court of Appeal, it was essential to leave the taxpayers to prove their case before the commissioners by oral evidence. The background to the transactions in question could then have been thoroughly explored in cross-examination. This might very well have elicited material to support the conclusion of fact reached in the dissenting judgment of Lawton LJ.

Instead the Revenue allowed the case to proceed before the commissioners on an
exiguous agreed statement of facts. In the result the Revenue have only themselves to
blame that, so far as the debts are concerned, neither Walton J nor the majority of the
Court of Appeal, nor any of your Lordships feel able to interfere with the inference
which the commissioners drew from the facts so agreed.

**LORD BRANDON OF OAKBROOK.** My Lords, I have had the advantage of
reading in draft the speech prepared by my noble and learned friend Lord Templeman.
I agree with it, and for the reasons which he gives I would allow the appeal in part only
as proposed by him.

**LORD TEMPLEMAN.** My Lords, the respondent taxpayer company, Nova Securities
Ltd (Nova), claims to have sustained a trading loss for corporation tax purposes amounting
to £3,905,915 for the accounting period 6 April 1973 to 31 December 1973. The
appellant, the Inland Revenue, denied that Nova had sustained a trading loss and raised
an assessment on an admitted trading profit of £850.

By s 238 of the Income and Corporation Taxes Act 1970 corporation tax is charged on
the profits of a company and profits means income and chargeable gains. By s 265(2) the
total amount of chargeable gains to be included in the profits of a company for the
purposes of corporation tax shall, save as otherwise provided, be computed in accordance
with the principles applying for capital gains tax. By s 265(1) the amount to be included
in respect of chargeable gains in a company's total profits for any accounting period shall
be the total amount of chargeable gains accruing to the company in that period after
deducting any allowable losses accruing to the company in that period and any remaining
allowable losses previously accruing to the company while it has been within the charge
to corporation tax. Thus an allowable capital loss sustained by a company may only be
set off in the computation of the corporation tax payable by that company and in respect
of capital gains, if any, made by that company. On the other hand, by s 258, for the
purposes of corporation tax, relief from a trading loss may be surrendered by a company
which is a member of a group of companies in favour of other companies included in
that group. By s 274 of the 1970 Act and para 1 of Sch 7 to the Finance Act 1965 group
relief may be made available by converting a capital loss sustained by one company in
the group into a trading loss sustained by another member of that group provided certain
conditions are fulfilled, in particular provided that an asset pregnant with loss is
transferred within the group to a trading company which acquires the 'asset as trading
stock'. In *Coates (Inspector of Taxes) v Arndale Properties Ltd* [1985] 1 All ER 15, [1984] 1
WLR 1328 your Lordships decided that a group of companies failed to obtain group
relief because the asset responsible for the loss was not acquired by a trading company
pursuant to s 274(1) 'as trading stock'. In the present case Nova asserts and the Inland
Revenue deny that Nova acquired certain debts and shares as trading stock.

The Littlewoods Organisation Ltd (Littlewoods) acquired the whole of the issued share
capital of a West German company, Medaillon Mode GmbH (Medaillon). The acquisition
cost to Littlewoods of the Medaillon shares amounted to £1,512,599. Littlewoods also
guaranteed payment of certain of Medaillon's bank overdrafts. This venture by
Littlewoods into the Federal Republic appears to have been a disaster. Littlewoods were
called on to pay under their guarantees and took assignments of the debts owed by
Medaillon to the banks. The acquisition cost to Littlewoods of the bank debts amounted
to £2,424,166. In addition, Littlewoods advanced to Medaillon sums amounting in the
aggregate to a further £4·8m. Thus Littlewoods were faced, subject to any possibility of
recovery from Medaillon, with the prospect of a capital allowable loss of £1·5m in respect
of Medaillon shares and a capital allowable loss of £2·4m in respect of Medaillon's bank
debts. Littlewoods could not claim an allowable loss in respect of the advances of £4·8m
which Littlewoods had made directly to Medaillon because by para 11 of Sch 7 to the
1965 Act and s 23(2) of that Act the loss suffered by an original creditor is not an allowable
loss for capital gains purposes. The prospective allowable loss of £1·5m attributable to
the shares of Medaillon and £2·4m attributable to the Medaillon bank debts could only

be set off against capital gains (if any) made by Littlewoods and could not be transferred to the group of companies of which Littlewoods were the parent.

With the object, no doubt, of converting their allowable losses into trading losses available for group relief, Littlewoods on 15 March 1973 acquired the whole of the issued share capital of Nova, which thus became a member of the group of companies headed by Littlewoods. Nova had been in existence since 1955 as a company dealing in shares and securities, capable therefore of sustaining trading losses in respect of shares and debts. In the year ended 5 April 1973 Nova traded in shares and securities to the extent of £20,615 and made a trading profit of £1,048.

By a letter dated 17 August 1973 Littlewoods, whose board of directors included two out of the three directors of Nova, offered to sell the Medaillon shares and the Medaillon bank debts to Nova for £30,000. The letter contained the following explanation (see [1982] STC 724 at 729):

> 'The only asset of Medaillon and its subsidiary is a building in Offenbach owned by Medaillon and which is being offered for sale . . . It is impossible to give any estimate or warranty as to the net amount that may be realised on the sale of the building after repayment of [certain secured loans], but after providing for disbursements and other expenses it is thought it may be of the order of £150,000 to £200,000. On the basis that the net proceeds amounted to £150,000 this would produce the sum of approximately £55,000 towards repayment of the [bank debts] . . .'

The balance, namely £95,000 of the net proceeds, would be repayable to Littlewoods in part payment of Littlewoods's advances of £4·8m to Medaillon. Thus the shares which Littlewoods had acquired for £1·5m and the bank debts which Littlewoods had acquired for £2·4m were offered to Nova for £30,000 and might produce for Nova £55,000, more or less, depending on the sale price of the building at Offenbach. Nova accepted the offer; subsequently, the Medaillon shares were transferred by Littlewoods to Nova for the apportioned price of £10 and the bank debts were assigned by Littlewoods to Nova for the apportioned price of £29,990. In the result Littlewoods sustained an actual capital loss of £1,512,589 resulting from the purchase and sale of the Medaillon shares and £2,394,176 resulting from the purchase and sale of the Medaillon bank debts. For corporation tax purposes, however, the sale by Littlewoods to Nova of the Medaillon shares and Medaillon bank debts did not produce an allowable loss to Littlewoods. Section 273(1) of the 1970 Act provides:

> '. . . where a member of a group of companies [Littlewoods] disposes of an asset to another member of the group [Nova], both members shall . . . be treated, so far as relates to corporation tax on chargeable gains, as if the asset acquired by [Nova] were acquired for a consideration of such amount as would secure that on [Littlewoods'] disposal neither a gain nor a loss would accrue to [Littlewoods]. . .'

Thus for corporation tax purposes Littlewoods, having acquired the Medaillon shares for £1,512,599, are deemed to have sold those shares and Nova is deemed to have purchased those shares not for the actual price of £10 but for the price of £1,512,599. Similarly, Littlewoods, having acquired the Medaillon bank debts for £2,424,166, are deemed to have sold those bank debts and Nova is deemed to have purchased those bank debts not for the actual price of £29,990 but for the price of £2,424,166. If s 273 had stood alone the potential allowable loss of Littlewoods in respect of the Medaillon shares and bank debts amounting in the aggregate to £3,906,765 would simply have been transferred to and become the potential allowable loss of Nova. But if Nova, a trading company, acquired the Medaillon shares and the Medaillon bank debts as 'trading stock' then Nova became in a position to convert the potential capital allowable loss into a trading loss. By s 274(1) of the 1970 Act:

> 'Where a member of a group of companies [Nova] acquires an asset as trading stock from another member of the group [Littlewoods], and the asset did not form

part of the trading stock of any trade carried on by [Littlewoods], the member acquiring it [Nova] shall be treated for purposes of paragraph 1 of Schedule 7 to the Finance Act 1965 as having acquired the asset otherwise than as trading stock and immediately appropriated it for the purposes of the trade as trading stock.'

As will appear, the effect of para 1 of Sch 7 to the 1965 Act on the appropriation which Nova is deemed to make by s 274(1) of the 1970 Act is to convert the potential allowable loss of Nova in respect of the Medaillon shares and bank debts into an actual allowable loss for corporation tax purposes unless Nova elects to treat the loss as a trading loss. By para 1(1) of Sch 7 to the 1965 Act as amended:

'Subject to sub-paragraph (3) below, where [a trader appropriates an asset] for the purposes of the trade as trading stock . . . and, if he had then sold the asset for its market value, a chargeable gain or allowable loss would have accrued to him, he shall be treated as having thereby disposed of the asset by selling it for its then market value.'

Thus, if sub-para (1) had applied, Nova would have been deemed to have sold the Medaillon shares and the Medaillon bank debts for £30,000 (assuming that £30,000 was the market value of the assets) after having been deemed to have purchased those assets for £3,936,765. In the result Nova would have sustained an allowable loss of £3,906,765. Sub-paragraph (3) provides that sub-para (1) shall not apply in relation to an appropriation of an asset for the purposes of a trade if the trader—

'elects that instead the market value of the asset at the time of the appropriation [£30,000] shall, in computing the profits of the trade for purposes of tax, be treated as . . . increased by the amount of the allowable loss referred to in that sub-paragraph, and . . . the profits of the trade shall be computed accordingly . . .'

Thus, provided Nova in fact acquired the Medaillon shares and Medaillon bank debts as trading stock, Nova could elect to treat Littlewoods' capital loss of £3,906,765 as Nova's trading loss of £3,906,765 for the purposes of corporation tax. By a letter dated 15 August 1974 Nova wrote to the inspector of taxes referring to its acquisition of the Medaillon shares and bank debts from Littlewoods and claiming that—

'We acquired these shares and debts as trading stock, and pursuant to section 274 Taxes Act 1970, and paragraph 1(3) of Schedule 7 to the Finance Act 1965, we hereby elect that in computing the profits of the trade for purposes of tax the market value of these shares and debts shall be treated as increased by £3,906,765 the amount which would have been the amount of the allowable loss under sub-paragraph (1) of this paragraph if this election had not been made.'

Thus Nova claimed to have converted an allowable loss of £3,906,765 into a trading loss of £3,906,765. It is common ground that, if Nova acquired the Medaillon shares and Medaillon bank debts as trading stock, it is deemed to have made a trading loss of £3,906,765 reduced by £850 profit on other transactions during the accounting period of 6 April 1973 to 31 December 1973 to a net trading loss of £3,905,915. That trading loss is available for group relief.

By s 258(1) of the 1970 Act, relief from trading losses—

'may . . . be surrendered by a company . . . which is a member of a group of companies . . . [to] . . . another company . . . which is a member of the same group [and] may be allowed to the claimant company by way of a relief from corporation tax called "group relief".'

On 4 September 1975 Nova surrendered one-third of its trading loss for the accounting period ending 31 December 1973 to each of three claimant companies, members of the group of companies which included Littlewoods and Nova.

On 5 October 1979 Nova received on the sale of the Offenbach premises the sum of £35,447·54 in part repayment of the Medaillon bank debts amounting to £2·4m. It does not appear that Nova has sold or disposed of the Medaillon shares or the Medaillon bank debts or any part of them.

The Revenue resisted the claim by Nova to have sustained a trading loss of £3,905,915 for corporation tax purposes for the period ending 31 December 1973. The question is whether Nova acquired from Littlewoods the Medaillon shares and bank debts 'as trading stock' as required by s 274 of the 1970 Act. This question was referred to the General Commissioners. The Revenue allowed the question to be determined not by oral evidence but on the basis of an agreed statement of facts which exhibited the relevant documents, but was wholly silent as to the reasons and intentions of Littlewoods and Nova and as to the possibility at any time of trading with the assets acquired by Nova. The Revenue chose to appear before the General Commissioners by an official from the solicitors' office of the department. Nova was represented by a London firm of solicitors, junior counsel and leading counsel experienced in the field of fiscal litigation. Before the General Commissioners the onus of proving that the Medaillon shares and bank debts were acquired by Nova as trading stock lay with Nova. The General Commissioners did not deliver a reasoned decision but in their stated case contented themselves with finding—

'as facts that the share capital and debts of Medaillon as set out in paragraph 6 of the Agreed Statement of Facts were acquired by Nova Securities Ltd in the course of their trading in shares and securities and that they were acquired as trading stock. Accordingly we . . . determine the assessment as profits £850 less losses £850 on the Assessment as raised . . . The question of law for the opinion of the High Court is whether our decision was justified on the evidence before us.'

(See [1982] STC 724 at 726.)

The Revenue having lost the battle before the commissioners can only succeed before the court if they can show that the commissioners committed an error of law or if they can show, pursuant to the test laid down by this House in Edwards (Inspector of Taxes) v Bairstow [1955] 3 All ER 48, [1956] AC 14, that no person, if properly instructed in the law and acting judicially, could have reached the determination of the commissioners.

The Revenue handicapped themselves by omitting to instruct counsel to appear at the hearing before the commissioners. A similar mistake was made in Coates (Inspector of Taxes) v Arndale Properties Ltd [1985] 1 All ER 15, [1984] 1 WLR 1328. Despite ample warnings in the past, the Revenue appear to be persisting in the practice of appearing by a departmental official in cases where millions of pounds are at stake and the law is complex. In my opinion that practice should be reviewed in the interests of the general body of taxpayers.

On appeal by the Revenue by case stated, Walton J held that the decision of the commissioners was correct (see [1982] STC 724). Nova was a company whose trade was that of dealing in shares and securities. Trading stock as defined by s 137(4)(a) of the Income and Corporation Taxes Act 1970 means property 'such as is sold in the ordinary course of the trade'. The Medaillon shares and bank debts were, therefore, trading stock. As to the unusual features of the transaction 'it is not for the Revenue to tell people how they shall conduct their business' (see [1982] STC 724 at 731).

The Court of Appeal by a majority affirmed the order of Walton J (see [1984] STC 124). The members of the Court of Appeal were, however, unanimously of the view that property could only be acquired 'as trading stock' if it was acquired for the purpose of being used in the course of trade.

I agree. If a company is to acquire an asset as trading stock, the asset must not only be of a kind which is sold in the ordinary course of the company's trade but must also be acquired for the purposes of that trade with a view to a resale at a profit. A company which acquired an asset for purposes other than trading would not, in my opinion, acquire the asset as trading stock even though the company habitually traded in similar assets. Thus, in the Arndale case, the Arndale company traded in property and acquired a lease. By a contemporaneous and pre-arranged sale, the Arndale company transferred the lease to another company in the same group. The object of these manoeuvres was to obtain the benefit of s 274, which applies to property acquired as trading stock, while ensuring at the same time that the lease was never in fact traded. Your Lordships held that Arndale did not acquire the lease as trading stock.

In the instant case the members of the Court of Appeal were divided as to the result. Lawton LJ, dissenting, would have allowed the appeal. He considered that the transaction was abnormal; the circumstances in which the agreement between Littlewoods and Nova was made were not those of normal trading; had the commissioners viewed the transaction as a whole they could not reasonably have come to the conclusion, as they did, that Nova had acquired the Medaillon shares and the Medaillon bank debts as trading stock (see [1984] STC 124 at 133–134).

Fox LJ agreed that the transaction must be viewed as a whole but declined to draw the inference that the sole purpose of the acquisition by Nova was to obtain a fiscal benefit for the Littlewoods group of companies. He said (at 138):

'... if the Revenue wanted so fundamental a finding as that the sole or paramount purpose of the acquisition was fiscal, they should have insisted on oral evidence before the commissioners and sought a finding of fact to that effect.'

Kerr LJ agreed with Fox LJ and held that there was insufficient material to entitle the court to overturn the commissioners' finding that Nova acquired the Medaillon shares and Medaillon bank debts as trading stock (at 139). Both Lawton and Fox LJJ relied on the principle to be deduced from the dividend-stripping cases and particularly on the decision of this House in *FA & AB Ltd v Lupton (Inspector of Taxes)* [1971] 3 All ER 948, [1972] AC 634.

In *Lupton's* case a dealer in stocks and shares purchased shares in a company worth £1·7m. The purchase price depended on the success or failure of a tax recovery claim which the purchaser undertook to make. After the purchase the purchaser received from the purchased company a dividend of £800,000 and claimed that they suffered a loss when the value of the purchased shares after payment of the dividend of £800,000 fell by £800,000. The purchaser claimed relief under s 341 of the Income Tax Act 1952, which afforded relief 'Where any person sustains a loss in any trade'. This House held that relief was not to be granted because the object of the transaction was to obtain a fiscal advantage and the purchase did not form part of the trading activities of a dealer in stocks and shares. Viscount Dilhorne said ([1971] 3 All ER 948 at 963, [1972] AC 634 at 657):

'... if a transaction viewed as a whole is one entered into and carried out for the purpose of establishing a claim against the Revenue under s 341, I for my part would have no hesitation in holding that it does not form part of the trading activities of a dealer in stocks and shares. When I say "viewed as a whole", I mean that regard must be had not only to the inception of the transaction, to the arrangements made initially, but also to the manner of its implementation.'

Lord Simon said ([1971] 3 All ER 948 at 965, [1972] AC 634 at 660):

'... what is in reality merely a device to secure a fiscal advantage will not become part of the trade of dealing in shares just because it is given the trappings normally associated with a share-dealing within the trade of dealing in shares ...'

In a dividend-stripping case, such as *Lupton's* case, an artificial loss is artificially created and the artificial transaction does not constitute trading but constitutes the manufacture of a tax advantage. In the present case Littlewoods sustained a real loss.

My Lords, the theoretical independent existence of every corporation enables a group of companies to escape liability at common law for the losses of an individual member of the group: see *Re Southard & Co Ltd* [1979] 3 All ER 556 at 565, [1979] 1 WLR 1198 at 1208. The theoretical independent existence of every corporation inspired a tax avoidance industry which has only partly been brought under control by the principles summarised by Lord Brightman in *Furniss (Inspector of Taxes) v Dawson*, [1984] 1 All ER 530 at 543, [1984] AC 474 at 527. Nevertheless the legislature, recognising for the purpose of inflicting tax that group companies do not lead an independent existence, has invented group relief which enables a group of companies to shuffle its losses between members of the group to obtain a tax advantage. The legislature has not extended group relief to allowable losses, but has conferred on a group of companies power to convert an allowable loss into a trading loss which can then be shuffled to secure a tax advantage. The Revenue cannot complain that Littlewoods have secured a fiscal advantage by the statutory method presented by s 274 of the 1970 Act and para 1 of Sch 7 to the 1965 Act. The only requirement in these circumstances is that, apart from s 274 considerations, there must be an acquisition by a trading company 'as trading stock'.

So far as the Medaillon bank debts are concerned. I agree with Fox LJ ([1984] STC 124 at 138) that the court cannot—

'conclude that no reasonable tribunal, properly instructed, could have decided, on the evidence, that the property was acquired by Nova "as trading stock" . . . Nova was a trading company. It bought property of a kind in which it was authorised to deal . . . Before deciding to buy the property the board of Nova considered what, in ordinary commercial terms, was the profit which Nova was likely to make on the transaction.'

It is conceivable that Nova might have decided to acquire similar bank debts from a source unconnected with the group and in the hope of making a profit either by waiting until the realisation of the debts or by resale.

Different considerations apply, however, to the Medaillon shares. Medaillon's assets were valued at not more than £200,000. Medaillon's debts amounted to £8·7m. The shares were worthless. There was no commercial justification for the acquisition of the shares by Nova. There was no conceivable reason, apart from s 274, why the shares should change hands at all. In my opinion no reasonable tribunal could have concluded that the shares were acquired by Nova as trading stock.

The distinction between the Medaillon bank debts and the Medaillon shares arose in the course of argument before your Lordships. The Revenue were given leave to argue the point after an adjournment of some weeks to enable Nova to consider its position. Counsel for Nova urged that the shares were purchased as part of a package deal: Nova could not acquire the Medaillon bank debts without also acquiring the Medaillon shares. But, assuming this to be so, the shares were not acquired as trading stock just because they were acquired in connection with bank debts which were so acquired.

The Medaillon shares may have been acquired in order that Nova might acquire the Medaillon bank debts as trading stock. But s 274 only applies to the shares if the shares were acquired by Nova as trading stock, namely with a view to the resale of the shares at a profit. The shares were not commercially saleable at any price. Nova only acquired the right to share certificates which represented nothing in view of the insolvency of Medaillon and the right to be the latest and last entry in the register of a defunct company. Counsel for Nova suggested that a purchaser of the bank debts might have been willing to offer a price for the shares in order to control the disposal of the Offenbach premises. In the light of the facts and the terms of the offer letter, dated 17 August 1973, the suggestion was ingenious but fanciful.

In the circumstances in my opinion the assessment made on Nova for the accounting period 6 April 1973 to 31 December 1973 on the basis of a trading profit of £850 should remain discharged. The claims to group relief, however, based on the trading loss of £3,906,765 sustained as a result of the acquisition of the Medaillon bank debts and the Medaillon shares ought only be allowed on the basis of a trading loss of £2,394,176 based on the acquisition of the Medaillon bank debts as trading stock. On this appeal the order of Walton J should be varied and the question posed by the stated case should be answered by declaring that the decision of the commissioners was justified in respect of the acquisition by Littlewoods of the Medaillon bank debts but not in respect of the acquisition of the Medaillon shares.

In view of the failure of the Revenue to differentiate between the shares and the bank debts until a late stage, I suggest that the orders of the courts below with regard to costs should stand and that there should be no order for the costs of the appeal to your Lordships' House.

*Appeal allowed in part. Orders as to costs in the Court of Appeal and below to stand. No order as to costs in the House of Lords.*

Solicitors: *Solicitor of Inland Revenue; Allen & Overy* (for Nova).

Rengan Krishnan Esq    Barrister.


# The Antonis P Lemos

HOUSE OF LORDS

LORD SCARMAN, LORD DIPLOCK, LORD ROSKILL, LORD BRANDON OF OAKBROOK AND LORD TEMPLEMAN

14 JANUARY, 21 FEBRUARY 1985

*Admiralty – Jurisdiction – Action in rem – Claim arising out of agreement relating to carriage of goods in a ship or to use or hire of ship – Agreement – Whether 'agreement' must be agreement between plaintiff and defendant – Whether claim in tort can be a claim 'arising out of' agreement relating to carriage of goods in or use or hire of a ship – Supreme Court Act 1981, s 20(2)(h).*

By a time charter dated 22 February 1980 the defendant shipowners chartered a vessel to S Ltd, who, by a sub-charter dated 16 October 1981, sub-chartered the vessel to the plaintiffs, who by a voyage charter dated 21 September 1981 (the sub-sub-charter) had chartered to A Ltd a ship to be nominated to carry a cargo of corn from a port in North America to Alexandria, it being an express term of the sub-sub-charter that that ship's maximum draught on arrival at the port of discharge would not exceed 32 feet in salt water. The plaintiffs nominated the defendants' vessel for the purposes of the sub-sub-charter. When the vessel arrived at Alexandria its draught exceeded 32 feet, with the consequence that the plaintiffs incurred costs for lightening and delay. The plaintiffs alleged that the master or a servant of the defendants had been negligent in permitting the vessel to overload and that the defendants were liable for such negligence. Subsequently the plaintiffs brought an action in rem against the vessel in the Admiralty Court for damages and obtained a warrant of arrest against the vessel. Under s 20(2)(h)[a] of the Supreme Court Act 1981 the court had Admiralty jurisdiction to hear a claim 'arising out of any agreement relating to the carriage of goods in a ship or to the use or hire of a ship', and s 20 was in substantially the same terms as a provision enacted to give effect to the International Convention relating to the Arrest of Sea-going Ships made on 10 May 1952. The defendants moved to have the writ and warrant of arrest set aside on the ground that the court had no jurisdiction to entertain the plaintiffs' claim because (i) s 20(2)(h) applied only to claims of a purely contractual character and did not extend to claims founded on tort and (ii) in any event, even if s 20(2)(h) did extend to claims in tort, it only applied to claims which were directly connected with an agreement made between the two parties to the action themselves. The judge made the order sought by the defendants, holding that the court had no jurisdiction. On appeal by the plaintiffs, the Court of Appeal reversed the judge's order, holding that in order for a claim to fall within s 20(2)(h) of the 1981 Act it was irrelevant that the agreement in question was not an agreement between the plaintiffs and the defendants. The defendants appealed to the House of Lords.

a   Section 20(2), so far as material, is set out at p 698 j, post

**Held** – The appeal would be dismissed for the following reasons—

(1) Although the words 'arising out of' were capable of meaning 'arising under', they could also have a wider meaning of 'connected with', and the question whether they were to be given a wide or narrow meaning in a particular case depended on the context in which they were used. On the true construction of s 20(2)(h) of the 1981 Act the words 'arising out of' were to be given the wide interpretation of meaning 'connected with', under the principle that a domestic statute designed to give effect to an international convention was in general to be given a broad and liberal construction, and because that was clearly the meaning indicated by art 1(1) of the 1952 convention, to which s 20(2) of the 1981 Act was intended to give effect. Accordingly the plaintiffs' claim, even though founded on tort, fell within the court's jurisdiction under s 20(2)(h) because the claim was connected with an agreement relating to the carriage of goods in, or the use or hire of, a ship, namely either the sub-charter or the sub-sub-charter, notwithstanding that the defendants were not a party to either agreement (see p 697 *a* to *c*, p 700 *d* to *j*, p 702 *a* to *h*, p 703 *a b* and *d* to *g* and p 704 *f g*, post); *The St Elefterio, Schwarz & Co (Grain) Ltd v St Elefterio ex-Arion (owners)* [1957] 2 All ER 374 and *The Sennar* [1983] 1 Lloyd's Rep 295 followed; *The Nuova Raffaelina* (1871) LR 3 A & E 483, *Union of India v E B Aaby's Rederi A/S* [1974] 2 All ER 874 and *Gatoil International Inc v Arkwright-Boston Mutual Insurance Co* [1985] 1 All ER 129 distinguished.

(2) Section 20(2)(h) of the 1981 Act was not expressly or by necessary implication restricted to agreements made directly between the parties to the action, and in the absence of authority to the contrary there was no good reason for importing into s 20(2)(h) restrictive words to that effect. Accordingly the plaintiffs' claim fell within s 20(2)(h) and the court had Admiralty jurisdiction to hear and determine it (see p 697 *a* to *c* and p 703 *h* to p 704 *g*, post); *The St Elefterio, Schwarz & Co (Grain) Ltd v St Elefterio ex-Arion (owners)* [1957] 2 All ER 374 and *The Sennar* [1983] 1 Lloyd's Rep 295 distinguished.

Decision of Court of Appeal [1984] 2 All ER 353 affirmed.

### Notes

For the Admiralty jurisdiction of the High Court, see 1 Halsbury's Laws (4th edn) paras 307–312, and for cases on the subject, see 1(1) Digest (Reissue) 219–223, 1240–1251.

For the Supreme Court Act 1981, s 20, see 1 Halsbury's Statutes (4th edn) 18.

### Cases referred to in opinions

*Gatoil International Inc v Arkwright-Boston Mutual Insurance Co* [1985] 1 All ER 129, [1985] 2 WLR 74, HL.

*Nuova Raffaelina, The* (1871) LR 3 A & E 483.

*St Elefterio, The, Schwarz & Co (Grain) Ltd v St Elefterio ex-Arion (owners)* [1957] 2 All ER 374, [1957] P 179, [1957] 2 WLR 935.

*Sennar, The* [1983] 1 Lloyd's Rep 295.

*Union of India v E B Aaby's Rederi A/S* [1974] 2 All ER 874, [1975] AC 797, [1974] 3 WLR 269, HL.

*West of Scotland Ship Owners Mutual Protection and Indemnity Association (Luxembourg) v Aifanourios Shipping SA, The Aifanourios* [1980] 2 Lloyd's Rep 403, Ct of Sess.

*Zeus, The* (1888) 13 PD 188.

### Interlocutory appeal

The owners of the ship Antonis P Lemos appealed, with leave of the Court of Appeal, against the decision of that court (Cumming-Bruce and Parker LJJ) ([1984] 2 All ER 353, [1984] 2 WLR 825) on 14 February 1984 allowing the appeal of the respondents, Samick Lines Co Ltd, against the order of Sheen J dated 27 May 1983 setting aside the writ in rem issued on 20 May 1983 by the respondents against the ship and the warrant of arrest in respect of it. The facts are set out in the opinion of Lord Brandon.

*Mark O Saville QC* and *Jonathan Gaisman* for the appellants.
*Bernard Rix QC* and *Peter Hayward* for the respondents.

Their Lordships took time for consideration.

21 February. The following opinions were delivered.

*a* **LORD SCARMAN.** My Lords, I have had the advantage of reading in draft the speech to be delivered by my noble and learned friend Lord Brandon. I agree with it, and for the reasons he gives I would dismiss the appeal.

**LORD DIPLOCK.** My Lords, I have had the advantage of reading in draft the speech of my noble and learned friend Lord Brandon. I agree with it, and for the reasons which *b* he gives I would dismiss this appeal.

**LORD ROSKILL.** My Lords, I have had the advantage of reading in draft the speech to be delivered by my noble and learned friend Lord Brandon. I agree with him, and for the reasons which he gives I would dismiss the appeal.

*c* **LORD BRANDON OF OAKBROOK.** My Lords, this appeal raises a question of statutory construction relating to the Admiralty jurisdiction of the High Court.

The case concerns a Greek-registered ship, the Antonis P Lemos (the vessel), which is and was at all material times wholly owned by the appellants.

By a time charter dated 22 February 1980 (the head charter) Containerbank Corp, acting as managers of the vessel for the appellants, chartered her to Sammisa Ltd (the *d* head charterers) for a period of ten to twelve months, later extended by agreement for a further six to twelve months, both periods at the head charterers' option. The head charter contained a provision allowing the head charterers to sub-charter the vessel, subject to an obligation to inform Containerbank Corp of their doing so.

By a sub-time-charter dated 16 October 1981 (the sub-charter) the head charterers sub-chartered the vessel to the respondents, Samick Lines Co Ltd (the sub-charterers), for one *e* time charter trip. The sub-charter contained a provision similar to that in the head charter, allowing the sub-charterers to sub-sub-charter the vessel, subject to an obligation to inform the sub-charterers of their doing so.

Nearly a month before the making of the sub-charter the respondents had already, by a voyage charter dated 21 September 1981 (the sub-sub-charter), chartered to Agri *f* Industries (the sub-sub-charterers) a ship to be nominated to carry a full cargo of heavy grains and/or sorghums and/or soya beans from a North American port to Alexandria or Port Said, at the sub-sub-charterers' option. Later, after the making of the sub-charter, the respondents nominated the vessel for the purposes of the sub-sub-charter, and the sub-sub-charterers chose Alexandria as the port of discharge. The sub-sub-charter contained an express guarantee by the respondents that the vessel's maximum draught on arrival at the port of discharge would not exceed 32 feet in salt water.

*g* In performance of the sub-sub-charter, the vessel on 20 and 21 October 1981 loaded a full cargo of corn at Houston, Texas, for carriage to Alexandria. When the vessel arrived at the latter port on 11 November 1981, however, her draught exceeded 32 feet in salt water, in consequence of which she had to be lightened before berthing, and delay in her discharge occurred. By reason of these matters, the respondents had to pay the cost of *h* lightening, which they would not otherwise have had to do, and incurred certain other expenses and losses.

In order to recover the cost, expenses and losses so incurred, the respondents on 20 May 1983 began an action in rem against the vessel in the Admiralty Court, and arrested her in that action in order to obtain security for their claim.

The indorsement on the back of the writ by which such action was begun reads:

*j*     'The Plaintiffs, as sub-charterers of the Defendants' ship ANTONIS P LEMOS under a time charter dated 16 October 1981 made between Sammisa Co Ltd as Owners and the Plaintiffs as charterers, claim damages for the loss suffered by them by reason of the negligence of the Defendants, their servants or agents in causing permitting or suffering the said ship to load a quantity of corn at Houston, Texas, USA on 20 and 21 October 1981 such that her draft on arrival at Alexandria, Egypt on 11 November 1981 exceeded 32 feet rendering her unable to berth without lightening.'

The claim so indorsed is, as your Lordships will have observed, founded solely on the tort of negligence, and is not founded on any breach of any contract made directly between the two parties to the action.

By notice of motion dated 24 May 1983 the appellants (defendants in the action) applied to the Admiralty Court for an order that the writ and warrant of arrest be set aside and the vessel released, on the ground that the Admiralty Court had no Admiralty jurisdiction, and therefore no jurisdiction in rem against the vessel, in respect of the claim.

On 27 May 1983 Sheen J, having heard the appellants' motion, decided the question raised by it in their favour, and made an order substantially in the terms sought by them. He gave the respondents leave to appeal to the Court of Appeal, and, in order to protect the position of both parties in the event of an appeal being brought, made his order conditional on (1) the appellants giving security for the claim in an acceptable form and (2) the respondents undertaking to pay the appellants' costs of giving such security in the event of any appeal brought by the former proving unsuccessful.

By notice of appeal dated 19 August 1983 the respondents appealed to the Court of Appeal against the order of Sheen J. The Court of Appeal (Cumming-Bruce and Parker LJJ) heard the appeal on 30 and 31 January 1984, and on 14 February 1984 Parker LJ delivered a reserved judgment ([1984] 2 All ER 353, [1984] 2 WLR 825), with which Cumming-Bruce LJ agreed, allowing the appeal and reversing the order of Sheen J. The Court of Appeal further gave leave to the appellants to appeal to your Lordships' House.

My Lords, it is common ground that the sole question for determination in this appeal is whether the respondents' claim, having regard to its nature and the facts on which it is based, comes within that part of the Admiralty jurisdiction of the High Court which is derived from s 20(2)(h) of the Supreme Court Act 1981. For the purpose of determining that question, it is necessary to assume, without deciding, that the respondents have an arguable case in law in respect of their claim.

If, on the one hand, the claim does not come within s 20(2)(h) of the 1981 Act, the Admiralty Court, to which the Admiralty jurisdiction of the High Court is assigned, has no Admiralty jurisdiction, as distinct from any other jurisdiction which it may have, to hear and determine it, and accordingly no power to arrest the vessel as security for such claim. On that view, which Sheen J took, the respondents' action was not properly brought, and the vessel was not properly arrested in it. The result of that would be that the writ by which the action was begun should be set aside, and the security substituted for the vessel given up and cancelled.

If, on the other hand, the claim comes within s 20(2)(h) of the 1981 Act, the Admiralty Court has Admiralty jurisdiction to hear and determine it, and further, by virtue of s 21(4) of the same Act, has power to exercise such jurisdiction in rem against the vessel. On that view, which the Court of Appeal took, the respondents' action was properly brought, the warrant of arrest was properly issued and the vessel was properly arrested as security for the claim. The result of that would be that the appellants' attempt to have the writ by which the action was begun set aside, and the security substituted for the vessel given up and cancelled, must fail.

Your Lordships have now to choose between these two contrary views. In order to do this, it is first necessary to set out the relevant terms of s 20 of the Supreme Court Act 1981. That sections provides:

'(1) The Admiralty jurisdiction of the High Court shall be as follows, that is to say—(a) jurisdiction to hear and determine any of the questions and claims mentioned in subsection (2) . . .

(2) The questions and claims referred to in subsection (1)(a) are . . . (h) any claim arising out of any agreement relating to the carriage of goods in a ship or to the use or hire of a ship . . .'

My Lords, the appellants put forward two alternative contentions with regard to the construction of s 20(2)(h) of the 1981 Act. Their primary contention was that s 20(2)(h)

applied only to claims of a purely contractual character, founded on some agreement of
the kinds referred to in it and made directly between the two parties to an action, and
that the paragraph did not extend to other claims founded on tort, even though such
claims were connected, directly or indirectly, with such an agreement. Their second and
alternative contention was that, even if s 20(2)(h) extended also to claims in tort, it only
did so if they were directly connected with some agreement of the kinds referred to in it,
and provided further (and this was the crucial limitation) that the agreement concerned
was one made between the two parties to the action themselves. In terms of the present
case this would mean some agreement made directly between the appellants and the
respondents relating to the carriage of goods in the vessel, or to the use or hire of the
vessel, which it is common ground was never made. If either of these two contentions is
accepted as correct, the respondents' claim would plainly not come within s 20(2)(h).
Sheen J rejected the first contention but accepted the second. Hence his decision in favour
of the appellants. The Court of Appeal rejected the first contention, and also rejected
what I have described as the crucial limitation in the second contention. Hence the
decision of that court in favour of the respondents.

Before considering whether the decision of the Court of Appeal was right or not, it is
necessary to draw attention to certain preliminary matters. The first matter is that the
provisions of the 1981 Act which deal with the Admiralty jurisdiction of the High Court
are the successors of earlier provisions in the Administration of Justice Act 1956 and are,
so far as material, in substantially the same terms. The second matter is that Pt I of the
1956 Act was, as has long been recognised, enacted in order to give effect in England to
the adherence of the United Kingdom to the International Convention relating to the
Arrest of Sea-going Ships (Brussels, 10 May 1952; TS 47 (1960); Cmnd 1128) (the
convention). Parker LJ, in his judgment in the Court of Appeal, accepted the proposition
put forward by the respondents that, since the provisions of the 1981 Act relating to the
Admiralty jurisdiction of the High Court was designed to give domestic effect to an
international convention, a broad and liberal construction should be given to them.
There is ample authority to support this as a general proposition, to some of which Parker
LJ referred in his judgment. I have no doubt that the proposition is, in general, correct,
and that Parker LJ was right to accept it.

So far as the appellants' first contention is concerned, it is clear from the judgment of
Sheen J that it was argued before him and that, following authority to which I shall refer
shortly, he declined to accept it. It appears from the judgment of Parker LJ in the Court
of Appeal that the contention was only faintly argued before that court, so that,
understandably enough, it was more or less brushed aside by him. Before your Lordships
the contention was fully developed by counsel for the appellants, and it follows that it is
necessary for your Lordships to examine it fully yourselves.

Such authorities as there are on this question, both at first instance in the Admiralty
Court, are against the appellants' contention. In *The St Elefterio, Schwarz & Co (Grain) Ltd
v St Elefterio ex-Arion (owners)* [1957] 2 All ER 374, [1957] P 179 the question arose
whether a claim for damages caused by the ante dating of bills of lading, which was
founded on the tort of deceit or possibly negligence, was within s 1(1)(h) of the 1956 Act,
which was the predecessor of, and in the same terms as, s 20(2)(h) of the 1981 Act. It was
held by Willmer J that the claim was within that provision. He said ([1957] 2 All ER 374
at 375, [1957] P 179 at 183):

'In my judgment the words of s. 1(1)(h) of the Act of 1956 . . . are . . . wide enough
to cover claims whether in contract or in tort arising out of any agreement relating
to the carriage of goods in a ship.'

That decision stood unchallenged for some 26 years until the present case, having been
followed by Sheen J, in relation to s 20(2)(h) of the 1981 Act, in *The Sennar* [1983] 1
Lloyd's Rep 295, another case of a claim in tort in respect of the antedating of a bill of
lading.

In his able address to your Lordships, counsel for the appellants recognised that these authorities were against the first contention for the appellants, and would have to be overruled if that contention was accepted. He relied, however, on six points, which he *a* developed under three main heads, as supporting the view that the contention was, despite these authorities, correct. These six points, in the sequence in which I think that it is convenient to state them, were as follows. The first point was that the expression 'arising out of', as contained in s 20(2)(*h*) of the 1981 Act, was, on the ordinary and natural meaning of the words used, the equivalent of the narrower expression 'arising under' and not of the wider expression 'connected with'. The second point was that, if *b* the expression 'arising out of', as contained in s 20(2)(*h*) of the 1981 Act, was given the wider meaning of 'connected with', a number of later paragraphs of s 20(2) would be unnecessary, because their subject matter would already be covered by para (*h*). The third point was that the narrower construction of the expression 'arising out of' was supported by *The Nuova Raffaelina* (1871) LR 3 A & E 483. The fourth point was that there was authority in your Lordships' House for the proposition that, in one context at least, the *c* expression 'arising out of' had the same meaning as the expression 'arising under'. The fifth point was that your Lordships' House had, in a recent appeal from Scotland, given a narrow rather than a wide construction to another expression contained in s 20(2)(*h*) of the 1981 Act, namely the expression 'relating to'. The sixth point was that the French text of the convention was, equally with the English text, the official text of it, that, if the expression 'arising out of', as contained in the English text, was ambiguous it was *d* legitimate to look at the French text in order to resolve the ambiguity; and that, if the French text was looked at, it supported the appellants' case. I shall consider each of these points in turn.

With regard to the first point, I would readily accept that in certain contexts the expression 'arising out of' may, on the ordinary and natural meaning of the words used, be the equivalent of the expression 'arising under', and not that of the wider expression *e* 'connected with'. In my view, however, the expression 'arising out of' is, on the ordinary and natural meaning of the words used, capable, in other contexts, of being the equivalent of the wider expression 'connected with'. Whether the expression 'arising out of' has the narrower or the wider meaning in any particular case must depend on the context in which it is used.

With regard to the second point, it is necessary to bear in mind that the list of claims *f* in s 20(2) of the 1981 Act is derived from art 1(1) of the convention, which contains a list of what are there called 'maritime claims'. Paragraph (*h*) of s 20(2) is derived from sub-paras (*d*) and (*e*) of art 1(1), although the arrangement and wording of s 1(1) of the 1956 Act, and s 20(2) of the 1981 Act, do not, as I shall have reason to point out again later, correspond with the arrangement and wording of art 1(1) itself. It was clearly the agreed policy of the states which negotiated the convention to have, in art 1(1) of it, a full and complete list of specific maritime claims or kinds of claim, rather than a few general *g* formulations comprehending them all. Having regard to this policy, some degree of overlap between the specific claims and kinds of claim listed in art 1(1) seems to me to have been natural and inevitable, and this overlap is reproduced in s 20(2) of the 1981 Act. In relation to this it was rightly conceded by counsel for the appellants that, even if the expression 'arising out of' in para (*h*) of s 20(2) of the 1981 Act was given the narrower meaning for which he contended, there would still be some overlap between different *h* paragraphs of s 20(2). In view of these considerations I do not think that this second point has any real force.

With regard to the third point, I do not think that, on a proper understanding of *The Nuova Raffaelina*, it supports the appellants' contention. In that case it was held by the High Court of Admiralty, affirming the Liverpool Court of Passage, that a claim by *j* chartering brokers, brought in rem against a ship, to recover commission payable by the owners of such ship under the terms of a charter effected by such brokers, was not a claim 'arising out of any agreement made in relation to . . . [a] ship, or in relation to the carriage of goods in [a] ship' within the meaning of s 2 of the County Courts Admiralty Jurisdiction Amendment Act 1869. In my view the ground on which that case was

decided was simply that chartering brokers, who had negotiated the charter of a ship
a  containing a stipulation for the payment by the owners of such ship of a commission to
them, were not entitled to enforce that stipulation, because they were not themselves
parties to the charter, although, if the charterers had sued as trustees for the brokers, the
claim might have been properly brought under the section of the 1869 Act relied on. On
that view of the case, it does not lay down any principle with regard to the construction
of the expression 'arising out of', as used in that much earlier statutory provision
b  comparable to s 20(2)(h) of the 1981 Act.

With regard to the fourth point, reliance was placed on the observations of two of their
Lordships in Union of India v E B Aaby's Rederi A/S [1974] 2 All ER 874, [1975] AC 797.
That case concerned the scope of the expression 'arising out of', as used in the Centrocon
arbitration clause in a charter, which provided that 'all disputes arising out of this
contract' should be referred to arbitration in London. Viscount Dilhorne and Lord
c  Salmon both said that the expression 'arising out of', as there used, meant the same as the
expression 'arising under' (see [1974] 2 All ER 874 at 885, 886–887, [1975] AC 797 at
814, 817). As I indicated earlier, I do not doubt that, in some contexts, such as an
arbitration clause in a commercial contract, it would be right to treat the first of these
two expressions as the equivalent of the second. It does not follow, however, that it
would be right to do so in all contexts, and in particular in the context of provisions
d  derived from, and intended to give domestic effect to, an international convention,
which require, in general, to be given a broad and liberal construction. For these reasons
I do not consider that the observations of two of their Lordships in the case referred to
should be taken as applicable to the construction of the expression 'arising out of' in
s 20(2)(h) of the 1981 Act.

With regard to the fifth point, the decision of your Lordships' House relied on was
e  Gatoil International Inc v Arkwright-Boston Mutual Insurance Co [1985] 1 All ER 129, [1985]
2 WLR 74. That case raised the question whether a claim by insurers and an insurance
broker for the recovery of premiums due under a marine insurance policy on cargo was
a claim arising out of 'any agreement relating to the carriage of goods in any ship whether
by charterparty or otherwise', as used in s 47(2)(e) of the 1956 Act, which is in Pt V of
that Act dealing with Admiralty jurisdiction and arrestment of ships in Scotland. Your
f  Lordships' House, reversing the Second Division of the Inner House of the Court of
Session, held that the words in question did not cover such a claim. In so doing, your
Lordships' House preferred to give the expression 'relating to', as used in s 47(2) of the
1956 Act, the narrower, rather than the wider, of the two meanings which it was accepted
that it was capable of having. Lord Keith, with whom all the other members of the
Appellate Committee agreed (although Lord Wilberforce gave additional reasons for the
g  decision, based on an examination of the travaux préparatoires preceding the conclusion
of the convention), examined a considerable number of English authorities, beginning
with those concerned with the construction of s 2 of the 1869 Act, and going on to more
modern authorities on s 1(1)(h) of the 1956 Act and s 20(2)(h) of the 1981 Act itself.
Having reviewed these authorities, he regarded two of them as strongly supporting the
conclusion that the expression 'relating to', as used in s 47(2) of the 1956 Act, should be
h  given its narrower, rather than its wider, construction. These two authorities were The
Zeus (1888) 13 PD 188 in England and West of Scotland Ship Owners Mutual Protection and
Indemnity Association (Luxembourg) v Aifanourios Shipping SA, The Aifanourios [1980] 2
Lloyd's Rep 403 in Scotland. In The Zeus Hannen P had to deal with the question whether
a claim under a contract to load a ship with coals was within s 2 of the 1869 Act. He held
that it was not. In The Aifanourios Lord Wylie had to deal with the question whether a
j  claim by an insurance association for the payment of release calls under a contract of
insurance on a ship and her cargo was within either para (d) or para (e) of s 47(2) of the
1956 Act, which together corresponded in Scotland with s 1(1)(h) of the same Act in
England. He held that it did not.

It is, no doubt, tempting to say that, because your Lordships' House in the Gatoil case
gave a narrow, rather than a wide, meaning to the expression 'relating to', as used in paras

(d) and (e) of s 47(2) of the 1956 Act, it should likewise give a narrow, rather than a wide, meaning to the expression 'arising out of' in s 20(2)(h) of the 1981 Act. In my view, however, this temptation should be resisted, on the ground that there are two significant differences between the two expressions.

The first difference is this. In art 1(1) of the convention the expression 'arising out of' is placed so as to govern all the maritime claims, or kinds of claim, which are listed in the succeeding paras (a) to (q). This arrangement was followed in s 47(2) of the 1956 Act applying to Scotland. So far as England is concerned, however, and also Northern Ireland (see s 55 of the 1956 Act), the arrangement and wording of art 1(1) of the convention were not, for reasons which I have never understood, similarly followed in s 1(1) of the Act. On the contrary, there are to be found in s 1(1) of the 1956 Act a rearrangement and rewording of the claims as set out in art 1(1) of the convention, as a result of which the expression 'arising out of' no longer governs all the claims listed in paras (a) to (q), but is transferred so that it appears in only three of those paragraphs: para (h), the subject matter of which has already been discussed, para (q), which deals with claims in general average, and para (r), which deals with claims in bottomry.

With the arrangement and wording of art 1(1) of the convention, as followed in s 47(2) of the 1956 Act applicable in Scotland, the expression 'arising out of' governs, as I have already indicated, all the claims listed in paras (a) to (q). If one substitutes in art 1(1) the expression 'arising under' for the expression 'arising out of', it is immediately apparent that the former expression simply makes no sense in relation to most of the claims set out in paras (a) to (q). Indeed, it only makes any real sense in relation to paras (d) and (e). By contrast, if one substitutes in art 1(1) the expression 'connected with' for the expression 'arising out of', it makes complete sense in relation to all the claims listed in paras (a) to (q), including paras (d) and (e), which are the crucial paragraphs in this case. These considerations make it abundantly clear that, in art 1(1) of the convention, as followed in s 47(2) of the 1956 Act applicable in Scotland, the expression 'arising out of' cannot have the narrower meaning of 'arising under', but must rather have the wider meaning of 'connected with'. It cannot have been the intention of the legislature, as a result of the rearrangement and rewording of art 1(1) of the convention in s 1(1) of the 1956 Act applicable in England and Northern Ireland, involving the transfer of the expression 'arising out of' so that it no longer governs all the claims listed in paras (a) to (s) of s 1(1) but only those in paras (h), (q) and (r), to give a meaning to the expression 'arising under' in those two paragraphs different from, and narrower than, the meaning which it has in art 1(1) of the convention and s 47(2) of the same Act. To attribute such an intention to the legislature would mean that the latter, when giving domestic effect to the adherence of the whole of the United Kingdom to the convention, had enacted provisions applicable in England and Northern Ireland which differed materially from those applicable in Scotland. I do not consider that it can be right to attribute to the legislature any such bizarre intention.

By contrast, the expression 'relating to' was used in the same way in para (h) of s 1(1) of the 1956 Act as in paras (d) and (e) of art 1(1) of the convention and in s 47(2) of the same Act, and there is nothing in the arrangement or wording of art 1(1) of the convention, of the kind which there is in respect of the expression 'arising out of', to indicate whether the former expression is to be given the wider or the narrower of the two meanings which it is capable of having.

The second difference concerns the authorities on the construction of the expression 'arising out of', as used in para (h) of both s 1(1) of the 1956 Act and s 20(2) of the 1981 Act. As the review of the authorities made by Lord Keith in the Gatoil case shows, the English authorities (The St Elefterio [1957] 2 All ER 374, [1957] P 179 and The Sennar [1983] 1 Lloyd's Rep 295) support a wide construction of the expression 'arising out of' as so used. By contrast, both English authority (The Zeus) and Scottish authority (The Aifanourios) support a narrow construction of the expression 'relating to', as used in s 2 of the 1869 Act in the former case and in paras (d) and (e) of s 47(2) of the 1956 Act in the latter case. These authorities tilt the balance in favour of giving a narrow meaning to the

expression 'relating to', where it occurs in the 1956 and 1981 Acts, which, in the absence
of such authorities, it might not be right to give it.

For these reasons I do not regard the decision of your Lordships' House in the *Gatoil*
case on the construction of the expression 'relating to' contained in para (*e*) of s 47(2) of
the 1956 Act as being determinative of the construction of the different expression
'arising out of' contained in para (*h*) of s 20(2) of the 1981 Act.

With regard to the sixth point, the expression in the French text of art 1(1) of the
convention corresponding to the expression 'arising out of' in the English text of it is
'ayant l'une des causes'. If the expression 'arising out of' is to be regarded as ambiguous,
which in the context of art 1(1) of the convention I do not, for the reasons given when
discussing the *Gatoil* case, think that it is, I accept that it would be open to your Lordships
to look at the French text in order, if possible, to resolve the ambiguity. The difficulty,
however, is that your Lordships have no evidence to show what meaning, as a matter of
French law, the expression 'ayant l'une des causes' has. It may well be a term of art in
French law, in which case it is impossible to ascertain its meaning without expert
evidence from a qualified French lawyer as to what that meaning is. No such expert
evidence was put before your Lordships and, in its absence, I do not consider that any
assistance can be derived from a comparative examination of the French text.

My Lords, having considered the six points argued by counsel for the appellants, I am
not persuaded that any one of those points singly, or any combination of them together,
leads to the conclusion that the expression 'arising out of' in s 20(2)(*h*) of the 1981 Act
should be given the narrow meaning of the expression 'arising under', rather than the
wider meaning of the expression 'connected with'. On the contrary, I am satisfied, on
four main grounds, that the expression 'arising out of' should be given the second and
wider meaning. The first ground is the principle, referred to earlier, that a domestic
statute designed to give effect to an international convention should, in general, be given
a broad and liberal construction. The second ground is that, for the reasons given when
discussing the *Gatoil* case [1985] 1 All ER 129, [1985] 2 WLR 74, I think that there is a
clear indication in the arrangement and wording of art 1(1) of the convention that the
expression 'arising out of' is there used in the wider of the two meanings of which it is
capable. The third ground is that, on the basis that the second ground is correct, the
rearrangement and rewording of art 1(1) of the convention contained in s 1(1) of the
1956 Act, and followed in s 20(2) of the 1981 Act, cannot have been intended to substitute
a narrow meaning for the expression 'arising out of' in those two subsections for the
wide meaning which it clearly has in art 1(1) of the convention. The fourth ground is
that the English authorities, *The St Elefterio* [1957] 2 All ER 374, [1957] P 179 and *The
Sennar* [1983] 1 Lloyd's Rep 295, support the wider meaning of the expression 'arising
out of' in s 1(1)(*h*) of the 1956 Act and s 20(2)(*h*) of the 1981 Act. *The St Elefterio*, as I said
earlier, stood unchallenged for some 26 years until the present case, and, in the interval,
the legislature saw fit, in the 1981 Act, to re-enact the provision construed in that case in
the same terms as before.

My Lords, having dealt, somewhat at length, I fear, with the first contention for the
appellants, I now turn to deal with the second. With regard to this part of the case your
Lordships have the great assistance of the clear and cogent judgment of Parker LJ in the
Court of Appeal, which makes it possible for me to deal with it much more briefly than
I have thought it necessary to deal with the first.

The reasoning on which Parker LJ proceeded in rejecting the appellants' second
contention can be formulated as follows. Firstly, there were, in the factual context of the
case, a number of agreements falling within the classes of agreements specified in
s 20(2)(*h*) of the 1981 Act. Parker LJ was there referring to the head charter, the sub-
charter and the sub-sub-charter. Secondly, unless the agreements referred to in s 20(2)(*h*)
of the 1981 Act were limited to agreements made directly between the two parties to an
action, the only question for consideration was whether the respondents' claim was one
arising out of one or more of those agreements. Thirdly, s 20(2)(*h*) of the 1981 Act
contained no words which, either expressly or by necessary implication, restricted the

agreements referred to in it to agreements made directly between the two parties to an action. Fourthly, there was no good reason, in the absence of authority to the contrary, for importing into s 20(2)(h) restrictive words having that effect. Fifthly, there was no such authority to the contrary, both *The St Elefterio* and *The Sennar* having been cases in which the relevant agreement had in fact been made between the two parties to the action, so that the question did not arise for decision in them. Sixthly, having regard to these matters, the right view was that, if the respondents could establish that their claim arose out of an agreement of the relevant kind, ie an agreement relating to the carriage of goods in a ship or to the use of hire of a ship, then, even if such agreement was not one made directly between the respondents and the appellants, that claim fell with s 20(2)(h). Seventhly, the respondents were, in the action brought by them, asserting negligence of the appellants, their servants or agents in loading at Houston such a quantity of corn that the vessel's draught on arrival at Alexandria exceeded 32 feet in salt water. Eighthly, if that claim was sustainable, a matter which did not presently arise, it could only be because (a) it had been guaranteed in the sub-sub-charter that the vessel's draught on arrival would not exceed 32 feet in salt water, (b) the master or the appellants were aware of that guarantee and, probably, (c) the sub-charter included provisions that the master should be under the supervision of the appellants as regards employment and that loading should be under the supervision of the master (with comparable provisions also in the head-charter.) To that catalogue I would add: (d) that it was reasonably foreseeable that, if the vessel's draught on arrival exceeded the maximum draught guaranteed in the sub-sub-charter, the respondents would suffer damage in that they would incur additional costs and expenses. Ninethly, in the absence of authority to the contrary, the right view was that a claim based on the matters set out above plainly arose out of the sub-sub-charter, or the sub-charter, or both. This was so because, in the absence of the guarantee in the sub-sub-charter, and the master's or the appellants' awareness of it, it appeared impossible to contend that the latter owed a duty to the respondents to load only such a quantity of cargo as would enable the vessel to arrive at Alexandria with a draught not exceeding 32 feet in salt water. Tenthly, there was again no authority to the contrary.

I find myself in complete agreement with the reasoning of Parker LJ with regard to this second part of the case. On the grounds stated by him I am of opinion that the second contention for the appellants should be rejected.

My Lords, for the reasons which I have given, I conclude that the judgment of the Court of Appeal, reversing that of Sheen J and deciding in favour of the respondents, should be affirmed, and that the appeal should be dismissed with costs.

**LORD TEMPLEMAN.** My Lords, for the reasons given by my noble and learned friend Lord Brandon, I would dismiss this appeal.

*Appeal dismissed.*

Solicitors: *Richards Butler & Co* (for the appellants); *Holman Fenwick & Willan* (for the respondents).

Mary Rose Plummer   Barrister.

# Curling v Law Society

COURT OF APPEAL, CIVIL DIVISION
OLIVER, PURCHAS LJJ AND NEILL J
5, 6, 21 DECEMBER 1984

*Legal aid – Charge on property recovered for deficiency of costs – Property recovered or preserved in proceedings – Property adjustment order in matrimonial proceedings – Husband conceding wife's share to half interest in property but wishing to postpone sale – Title to property not in issue in proceedings – Consent order that wife transfer her interest to husband in return for sum representing her half share – Whether charge for benefit of legal aid fund extending to sum so received notwithstanding that title to property never in issue in proceedings – Legal Aid Act 1974, s 9(6)(7).*

The husband and wife were married in 1968 and subsequently bought a matrimonial home in their joint names. In 1981 the husband petitioned for divorce, seeking, inter alia, custody of the children and a property adjustment order in respect of the home. The wife, who was legally aided, also sought custody of the children and an order that the house be sold. The husband did not dispute the wife's entitlement to a half share of the property but wished to remain in the house. He applied for an injunction requiring the wife to vacate the home but as the result of negotiations between the parties a consent order was made whereby the husband abandoned his application for the injunction and agreed to pay to the wife a sum representing her half share in the property in return for her transferring her half share to him. The wife subsequently sought a declaration that the Law Society was not entitled to a charge under s 9(6)[a] of the Legal Aid Act 1974 in respect of the sum received by her under the consent order, because title to the property had never been in issue in the proceedings and therefore the sum which she had received as representing her share of the property could not be regarded as 'property . . . recovered or preserved' for the purposes of s 9(6). The judge refused to make the declaration. The wife appealed.

**Held** – Where, even though title to a property was not in issue, proceedings were necessary to obtain possession of the property, the property was 'recovered . . . in the proceedings' for the purposes of s 9(6) of the 1974 Act. Accordingly, since by the consent order the wife had obtained possession of the amount which represented her share in the former matrimonial home, the Law Society was entitled under s 9(6) to a charge in respect of the sum received by the wife, notwithstanding that title to the property had never been in issue. The wife's appeal would accordingly be dismissed (see p 711 *b* to *e*, p 715 *e g h* and p 716 *a*, post).

Dicta of Lord Simon and Lord Scarman in *Hanlon v Law Society* [1980] 2 All ER at 209, 214 followed.

Per Oliver LJ. (1) The criterion applicable in deciding what is property 'recovered or preserved' is the same for both s 9(6) and s 9(7) of the 1974 Act and therefore if property is held to be 'recovered or preserved' for the purposes of s 9(6) it must equally be 'recovered or preserved' for the purposes of s 9(7) (see p 714 *g h*, post); dictum of Sir John Arnold P in *Jones v Law Society* (1983) 4 FLR at 740–741 disapproved.

(2) Since in the vast majority of cases the matrimonial home constitutes the only family asset of any value, the sensible division of property within the limits of slender resources can be seriously affected by the attachment of a charge for legal aid costs and there is therefore an urgent need to reconsider the legislative provisions (see p 715 *j* to p 716 *a*, post).

**Notes**

For charges for the benefit of the legal aid fund on property recovered or preserved, see

---

*a* Section 9, so far as material, is set out at p 709 *g* to *j*, post

37 Halsbury's Laws (4th edn) para 938, and for cases on the subject, see 37(3) Digest (Reissue) 350–353, 5056–5063.

For financial provision and property adjustment orders on divorce and the matters to which the court must have regard, see 13 Halsbury's Laws (4th edn) paras 1052–1053.

For the Legal Aid Act 1974, s 9, see 44 Halsbury's Statutes (3rd edn) 1048.

**Cases referred to in judgments**

*Doherty v Doherty* [1975] 2 All ER 635, [1976] Fam 71, [1975] 3 WLR 1, CA.

*Foxon v Gascoigne* (1874) LR 9 Ch App 654, LJJ.

*Hanlon v Law Society* [1980] 1 All ER 763, [1981] AC 124, [1980] 2 WLR 756, CA; *affd in part* [1980] 2 All ER 199, [1981] AC 124, [1980] 2 WLR 756, HL.

*Harris v Goddard* [1983] 3 All ER 242, [1983] 1 WLR 1203, CA.

*Jones v Law Society* (1983) 4 FLR 733.

*Mesher v Mesher and Hall* (1973) [1980] 1 All ER 126, CA.

*Pelsall Coal and Iron Co v London and North Western Rly Co (No 3)* (1892) 8 TLR 629.

*Philippine, The* (1867) LR 1 A & E 309.

*R v Law Society, ex p Sexton* [1984] 1 All ER 92, [1984] QB 360, [1983] 3 WLR 830, CA.

*Simmons v Simmons* [1984] 1 All ER 83, [1984] Fam 17, [1983] 3 WLR 818, CA.

*Till v Till* [1974] 1 All ER 1096, [1974] QB 558, [1974] 2 WLR 447, CA.

*Van Hoorn v Law Society* [1984] 3 All ER 136, [1984] 3 WLR 199.

**Cases also cited**

*Browne (formerly Pritchard) v Pritchard* [1975] 3 All ER 721, [1975] 1 WLR 1366, CA.

*Cooke v Head (No 2)* [1974] 2 All ER 1124, [1974] 1 WLR 972, CA.

*de Lasala v de Lasala* [1979] 2 All ER 1146, [1980] AC 546, PC.

*Dean v Dean* [1978] 3 All ER 758, [1978] Fam 161.

*Martin v Martin* [1977] 3 All ER 762, [1978] Fam 12, CA.

**Appeal**

The plaintiff, Lesley June Curling (the wife), appealed from the order of Anthony Lincoln J made on 27 June 1984 whereby he refused to grant the wife declarations (i) that the wife did not recover or preserve any property within the meaning of s 9(6) of the Legal Aid Act 1974 in proceedings for divorce between herself and Anthony George Kattenhorn (the husband), and in particular as a consequence of an order made by consent in those proceedings dated 26 January 1982, and (ii) that the defendant, the Law Society, was not entitled to a charge pursuant to s 9(6) of the 1974 Act and the Legal Aid (General) Regulations 1980 in respect of the sum of £15,201·92 payable to the wife as a consequence of the consent order. The facts are set out in the judgment of Neill J.

*Nicholas Wall* for the wife.
*Duncan Matheson* for the Law Society.

*Cur adv vult*

21 December. The following judgments were delivered.

**NEILL J** (giving the first judgment at the invitation of Oliver LJ). This is an appeal by the plaintiff in the action, Mrs Lesley June Curling, against the decision of Anthony Lincoln J given on 27 June 1984 where he refused to make certain declarations sought by her against the Law Society.

These declarations, as set out in the originating summons dated 23 November 1983, were in these terms:

'(1) A declaration that the Plaintiff did not recover or preserve any property within the meaning of Section 9(6) of the Legal Aid Act 1974 in proceedings for divorce between herself and Anthony George Kattenhorn in the Divorce Registry under number 10453 of 1981 and in particular as a consequence of an order made by consent in these proceedings on 26th January 1982.

(2) A declaration that the Defendant is not entitled to a charge pursuant to Section 9(6) of the Legal Aid Act 1974 and the Legal Aid (General) Regulations 1980 in respect of the sum of £15,201·92 payable to the Plaintiff as a consequence of the order made in the aforesaid proceedings on 26th January 1982 . . .'

Mrs Curling, then Lesley June Corder, was married to Anthony George Kattenhorn on 20 July 1968. In 1971 the matrimonial home was bought in joint names at 23 Greenvale Road, Eltham. They lived there for the next ten years and had two daughters, Louise (now 11) born in 1973 and Emily (now 8) born in 1976.

In April 1981, however, Mrs Kattenhorn (as she then was) committed adultery with Mr Richard Curling, whom she later married. In September 1981 Mr Kattenhorn moved out of the matrimonial bedroom and on 17 September he presented his petition for divorce. In his petition Mr Kattenhorn sought the following relief: (1) dissolution of the marriage; (2) custody of the two children of the family; (3) 'A property adjustment order in respect of the matrimonial home 23 Greenvale Road, Eltham, S.E.9' (I quote the words of the prayer in the petition).

It will be remembered that in the subsequent proceedings against the Law Society which led to the judgment of Anthony Lincoln J, Mrs Curling sought a declaration that she did not recover or preserve any property within the meaning of s 9(6) of the Legal Aid Act 1974 in the divorce proceedings brought against her by Mr Kattenhorn. It is therefore important to start by investigating the attitudes which the two parties took up at the outset of the divorce proceedings and then to trace how the question of the matrimonial home was eventually dealt with. I shall hereafter call the parties respectively 'the husband' and 'the wife'.

On 14 September 1981 (three days before the petition was presented) the wife's solicitors wrote to the husband (omitting parts of the letter which are not material) as follows:

'Our client invites you to file a petition for divorce within the course of the next month which proceedings will not be defended either by herself or Mr. Curling in default of which she has instructed us to file a petition on her behalf based on your unreasonable behaviour . . . In the divorce proceedings our client will claim and will undoubtedly be granted custody of Louise and Emily but our client will be willing to afford you generous access to the children as from the date that you separate . . . It is our client's intention to remain living at 23, Greenvale Road with the children until such time as the marriage has been dissolved and matters ancillary to the divorce have been resolved. However, it seems clear that sooner or later 23, Greenvale Road will have to be sold and the proceeds of sale divided between you and our client and it seems to us that the sooner the property is placed on the market for sale the better since this is necessarily a difficult time for you and our client with a consequent effect upon the children and the sooner matters are brought to a conclusion the better. Accordingly, we would invite you immediately to place 23, Greenvale Road on the market for sale with a firm of estate agents and at a price to be discussed with our client with a view to the property being sold and the proceeds divided at about the same time that the marriage is dissolved. Entirely without prejudice to her position should proceedings become necessary on ancillary matters, our client would presently be prepared to agree the net proceeds of sale of the property being divided equally between you. Our client's intention is once 23 Greenvale Road has been sold to purchase another property using her share of the net proceeds of sale and a fresh mortgage advance and to move into her new home with Louise and Emily and with Mr. Curling . . . our client has no present intention of claiming any maintenance for herself whatsoever nor any lump sum other than her proper share in the net proceeds of sale of 23, Greenvale Road. Our client, however, will require a fair proportion of the contents of 23 Greenvale Road as and when the property is sold to include all such items as are necessary to ensure the future wellbeing of the children . . .'

On 17 September the husband's solicitors replied:

'We are . . . instructed at this moment that the house is not to be put on the market for sale.'

Further correspondence between the solicitors followed. On 27 November the husband swore a further affidavit in support of an application for directions. In para 3 of this affidavit he said:

'The matrimonial home 23, Greenvale Road, Eltham S.E.8. is a 3 bedroomed house, with 2 living rooms and kitchen etc, jointly owned by the Parties. I refuse to move out of the matrimonial home and the [wife] refuses to do so until custody of the children is settled.'

Meanwhile (according to affidavits sworn by the wife's solicitor and by the husband in the present proceedings against the Law Society) the husband had begun to consider the possibility of buying the wife's interest in the matrimonial home. He had in mind that in due course he would be paying the wife a lump sum equivalent to one-half of the equity of the property.

On 21 December the decree nisi was granted. By that time the wife had been granted legal aid limited to access and custody and to ancillary relief. On 24 December the wife swore an affidavit in support of her proposed application for the custody of the two children. In paras 26 and 27 of this affidavit she referred to the matrimonial home:

'26. As I see it, the main problem incidental to the future care of the children is the accommodation that will be provided for them. I have suggested to the [husband] that the property at 23 Greenvale Road aforesaid should be sold and the proceeds of sale divided between us. I am advised and verily believe that if the property were sold as two self-contained flats each flat would have a value of about £22,500 whereas if the building were sold as one unit it would probably be worth about £40,000. There is a mortgage on the property in favour of the Anglia Building Society to secure an outstanding mortgage loan of about £5,100 so that depending upon the actual value of the property there is equity therein of about £34,900 to £39,000.
27. I am about to make application to this Honourable Court for ancillary relief to include application for an Order that 23 Greenvale Road should be sold and the proceeds of sale divided between myself and the [husband] as may to this Court seem just. Assuming that I were granted at least 50% of the net proceeds of sale I would have a lump sum of about £17,500 to £20,000 which I could utilise as a deposit on the purchase of alternative accommodation for myself and the children . . .'

In January 1982 the husband applied for an injunction to exclude the wife from the matrimonial home. This application was supported by an affidavit sworn on 15 January. In this affidavit the husband reiterated his refusal to move out of the matrimonial home and asked the court to grant him an injunction ordering the wife to vacate it. On 21 January the wife's legal aid certificate was amended to include the injunction proceedings.

On 22 January the wife swore her affidavit in opposition to the husband's application. Towards the end of this affidavit she repeated her belief that the interests of the children would best be served by them remaining in her custody and that the matrimonial home should be sold and the proceeds of sale divided so that she should be in a financial position to purchase a suitable alternative home for herself and her children.

On 26 January the wife's application for custody and the husband's cross-application for an injunction to exclude the wife from the matrimonial home and for interim custody were due to be heard. Before the hearing took place, however, the husband was advised by counsel that his application for custody was hopeless and, on accepting this advice, the husband gave instructions that negotiations should take place to try to negotiate a settlement of the financial matters.

The husband's account of what then happened is set out in the affidavit which he swore in the present proceedings on 11 April 1984. He said this:

'11. . . . I told my Counsel that I considered the gross value of the property to be about £37,000 and that after taking into account the outstanding mortgage of £5,100 and the expenses on a sale of about £1,000 there was equity in the property of about £30,900. I instructed my Counsel that I considered the [wife] to have a half interest in the equity in the property but my ability to pay the full value of the [wife's] half share was limited by my borrowing capacity.

12. My Counsel then engaged in negotiations with the [wife's] solicitor and she reported back to me at various stages in the negotiations to the effect that there was some argument about the true value of the [wife's] half share in the equity and there was also some argument about the time scale for my paying any lump sum that was agreed and what would happen in the event of my not paying the agreed sum in the agreed time scale. Finally, however, agreement was reached that I would pay the [wife] a lump sum of £15,000 (being rather less that the full value of the [wife's] half share in the equity) within three months thereafter in consideration of which the [wife] would transfer to me her interest in the property. It was agreed that this lump sum payment and transfer of the property would be in full and final settlement of all claims for ancillary relief. It was agreed that if I did not pay the lump sum within three months then the property would be sold and the proceeds of sale would be divided equally between the [wife] and myself . . .'

Following the conclusion of these negotiations the terms of the settlement were put in writing and were then incorporated into a consent order made by his Honour Judge Aron Owen. It is plain from the terms of the order that the consent order was made in respect of the husband's application for an injunction. A separate order was made dealing with the custody of and access to the children.

There was then some delay before the agreed sum of £15,000 was paid to the wife. On 14 June 1982, however, the husband's cheque for £15,000 and £291·92 for interest was cleared and a deed of transfer was handed over which enabled the husband to become the owner of the whole equity in the house. It is these two sums representing capital and interest which form the subject matter of the present proceedings. The Law Society contends that the wife recovered these sums in the divorce proceedings and that they are therefore subject to the statutory charge imposed by s 9(6) of the Legal Aid Act 1974. Section 9(6) is in these terms:

'Except so far as regulations otherwise provide, any sums remaining unpaid on account of a person's contribution to the legal aid fund in respect of any proceedings and, if the total contribution is less then the net liability of that fund on his account, a sum equal to the deficiency shall be a first charge for the benefit of the legal aid fund on any property (wherever situated) which is recovered or preserved for him in the proceedings.'

I should also refer to s 9(7), which provides:

'The reference in subsection (6) above to property recovered or preserved for any person shall include his rights under any compromise arrived at to avoid or bring to an end the proceedings and any sums recovered by virtue of an order for costs made in his favour in the proceedings . . .'

In the present case it is common ground that there is a deficiency within the meaning of s 9(6) of the 1974 Act, but it is contended on behalf of the wife that neither of the sums paid by the husband constitute 'property . . . recovered or preserved' for her in the divorce proceedings.

Counsel developed his argument on behalf of the wife on the following lines. (a) The wife's beneficial interest in the former matrimonial home was not in issue in the divorce proceedings: the husband had at all material times acknowledged that she had an equal interest with him in the jointly owned property. (b) The realisation of a beneficial interest in property by turning it into money did not equal the recovery of property within the meaning of s 9(6) of the 1974 Act; in the instant case the wife exchanged her interest for a sum of money worth slightly less than her beneficial interest. (c) For a person to recover property in matrimonial proceedings he or she has to emerge from the proceedings with a net tangible benefit which he or she did not have before the proceedings commenced. (d) The correct approach to what constituted property recovered or preserved in proceedings under s 24 of the Matrimonial Causes Act 1973 was to be found in the speeches in *Hanlon v Law Society* [1980] 2 All ER 199 esp at 206–210, [1981] AC 124 esp at 176–182 per Lord Simon. The earlier cases under the Solicitors Acts have now to be looked at afresh in the light of the decision in *Hanlon's* case. (e) The only benefit which the wife gained from the consent order made on 26 January 1982 was an acceleration of her right to be paid for her interest in the jointly owned property. Such a benefit was incapable of forming the subject matter of a charge under s 9(6).

On behalf of the Law Society on the other hand it was argued that the claim for a property adjustment order in the petition, which referred in terms to the matrimonial home, put in issue the wife's interest in the property. Furthermore, in the ancillary proceedings the wife successfully stopped the husband obtaining a *Mesher* order (see *Mesher v Mesher and Hall* (1973) [1980] 1 All ER 126) which would or might have postponed the sale of the house and her right to obtain her share of the proceeds. In the context of this case the realisation of her interest was in a very real sense a recovery by the wife.

In seeking to deal with the similar arguments which were addressed to him in the court below the judge defined the first task of the court as being to find out what was at issue in the proceedings. He referred in this context to the speech of Lord Simon in *Hanlon v Law Society* [1980] 2 All ER 199 at 209, [1981] AC 124 at 180 where he said:

'In property adjustment proceedings, in my view, it is only property the ownership or transfer of which has been in issue which has been "recovered or preserved" so as to be the subject of a legal aid charge. What has been in issue is to be collected as a matter of fact from pleadings, evidence, judgment and/or order. I can see no reason for extending the words to items of property the ownership or possession of which has never been questioned.'

It seems to me that the judge was clearly right in adopting this approach, which was also in line with what Lord Scarman said ([1980] 2 All ER 199 at 214, [1981] AC 124 at 187):

'A person recovers or preserves in legal proceedings only what is in issue between the parties; and one discovers what was in issue by looking to the pleadings and the evidence.'

What then was in issue in the divorce proceedings apart from the question of the custody of the children?

It was submitted on behalf of the Law Society that the husband put in issue the wife's entitlement to a share in the matrimonial home merely by including in his petition a claim for a property adjustment order in respect of the house. That claim, however, has to be looked at in the light of the other evidence and in particular of the husband's concession that *as a matter of prior entitlement* the wife should have a half share in the net proceeds of the sale of the house.

I would therefore accept the submission of counsel for the wife that at no material time was there an issue in the divorce proceedings as to the *ownership* of the matrimonial home.

But in my judgment the ownership of the house cannot be looked at in isolation in considering whether the wife has recovered any property in the proceedings.

I have already made reference to the correspondence and to the affidavits which throw light on the dispute between the parties about the matrimonial home in the period between September 1981 and January 1982. The husband wished to remain in the house and to postpone the sale, at any rate for the time being. In addition he wished to exclude the wife from the house. The wife for her part wanted the house to be sold so that she could receive her share of the proceeds and use it towards the purchase of a new house. The wife achieved her aim by the compromise which was reached on 26 January 1982 and by the consent order which was made on the same day.

It is true that the sum of £15,000 merely represented her agreed share of the proceeds of sale (or indeed perhaps rather less than her full share), but the fact that a party to legal proceedings recovers in the proceedings that to which he or she is in law already entitled cannot by itself prevent the attachment of the statutory charge.

The question is whether the party's right to recover the property has been in issue in the proceedings and for this purpose I can see no reason to limit the relevant issue to that of ownership alone.

The judge took the view that the wife recovered the £15,000 in the proceedings because she achieved an immediate or at any rate an accelerated right to her share of the proceeds of sale. He referred to the mention made by Lord Simon in *Hanlon's* case of both ownership and possession.

I agree with the judge. In my opinion the recovery of possession of property may constitute the recovery of property within s 9(6), just as the defeat of a claim by another party to a possessory interest in property may constitute the preservation of property.

I would dismiss the appeal.

**OLIVER LJ.** I agree. In his judgment the judge adverted to the absence of any dispute between the parties as to their respective beneficial entitlements to the property, but he summarised the contest between them thus:

'The [wife] wanted her half of the proceeds out of an immediate sale to be paid to her as custodian of the children no longer living at the matrimonial home. The [husband] wished to postpone the receipt by her of those proceeds by interposing the trust for sale on the home itself, retaining the home as custodian of the children. That was an obstacle which the [wife] had to surmount if she was to obtain a lump sum in exchange for the transfer of her interest to the husband. In the compromise, the obstacle became surmountable with the surrender by the husband of the custodianship of the children.'

The judge then reviewed certain authorities and, after analysing the effect of the compromise, concluded: 'She [that is the wife] gained, or made an advance, in relation to the possessory issue and therefore she recovered property.' He accordingly refused the declaration sought.

In submitting that this conclusion was wrong counsel for the wife bases himself primarily on the speech of Lord Simon in *Hanlon v Law Society* [1980] 2 All ER 199, [1981] AC 124. That case established that the concept of property being 'recovered or preserved' was as applicable to proceedings culminating in a property adjustment order under s 24 of the Matrimonial Causes Act 1973 as it was to any other proceeding in which property is in issue, but counsel for the wife relies particularly on two passages from Lord Simon's speech, in the first of which he dealt with the ambit of the words 'property recovered or preserved' and in the second of which he considered their application to proceedings under s 24 of the 1973 Act.

Lord Simon, having referred to the words of s 9(6) of the Legal Aid Act 1974 observed ([1980] 2 All ER 199 at 206, [1981] AC 124 at 176):

'These words in the Legal Aid Act 1974 were undoubtedly taken from a succession of Solicitors Acts, which gave courts power to award solicitors a charge on "property recovered or preserved" (in later Acts, "through their instrumentality"). There are numerous cases dealing with these words in the Solicitors Acts; the more relevant were reviewed by Reeve J and Arnold P. The words in the Solicitors Acts have been liberally construed, consonant with the obvious parliamentary intention of promoting the interest of a solicitor whose activity has resulted in a proprietary benefit to his client. But the same liberal approach to construction is not appropriate in a measure imposing a charge for a social service: the words should certainly not be extended beyond the ordinary sense which is appropriate in the context. I think *Till v Till* [1974] 1 All ER 1096, [1974] QB 558 must be read with this caution in mind. Moreover, proceedings in a divorce suit for financial relief under s 23 and for property adjustment under s 24 differ in many ways from the ordinary lawsuit. In consequence, circumspection is required in using the authorities under the Solicitors Acts, though some are certainly illuminating in showing how the words "property recovered or preserved" struck judicial minds in that different context, and can with caution be used analogically.'

The second passage on which counsel for the wife places particular reliance is where Lord Simon cited the following passage from the judgment of Jessel MR in *Foxon v Gascoigne* (1874) LR 9 Ch App 654 at 657:

'... where the Plaintiff claims property, and establishes a right to the ownership of the property in some shape or other, there the property has been recovered ... where a Defendant's right to the ownership of property is disputed, and that right has been vindicated by the proceedings, there the property has been preserved.'

Lord Simon continued ([1980] 2 All ER 199 at 209, [1981] AC 124 at 180):

'Jessel MR's explanation may be too narrow for all the cases decided under the liberally construed Solicitors Acts. But it seems to me to explain the words in their ordinary sense and thus to be applicable analogically to a case like the instant. In other words, property has been recovered or preserved if it has been in issue in the proceedings: recovered by the claimant if it has been the subject of a successful claim, preserved to the respondent if the claim fails. In either case it is a question of fact, not of theoretical "risk". In property adjustment proceedings, in my view, it is only property the ownership or transfer of which has been in issue which has been "recovered or preserved" so as to be the subject of a legal aid charge. What has been in issue is to be collected as a matter of fact from pleadings, evidence, judgment and/or order. I can see no reason for extending the words to items of property the ownership or possession of which has never been questioned.'

A similar view was expressed by Lord Scarman ([1980] 2 All ER 199 at 214, [1981] AC 124 at 187):

'But the question now arises: what property did the appellant recover, when she obtained her order? Like my noble and learned friend Lord Simon, I accept the view expressed by Arnold P as to the law, but reject his analysis of the facts. A person recovers or preserves in legal proceedings only what is in issue between the parties; and one discovers what was in issue by looking to the pleadings and the evidence. Had there been in this case a clear concession or admission that, *as a matter of prior entitlement*, ie before the exercise of the court's discretion under ss 24 and 25 of the 1973 Act, the husband's beneficial interest in the house was limited to a half share, I would have agreed that by her proceedings the appellant "recovered", ie got, his half share, but was not engaged in "preserving" hers, which was not in dispute. But I am satisfied that no such concession or admission was made by the husband. The whole house was in issue.' (Lord Scarman's emphasis.)

The reference in that passage to the views of Sir John Arnold P was, I think, a reference to this short passage from his judgment in the same case in this court ([1980] 1 All ER 763 at 777, [1981] AC 124 at 155):

'None of these cases seems to me to decide that the proprietor of an equitable interest in property who claims in an action a further equitable interest in that property and whose equitable interest is not in that action disputed can be said to have recovered or preserved his own equitable interest or anything in respect of it, and indeed Jessel MR's dictum in *Foxon v Gascoigne* contradicts such a proposition. Nor in my view does any of those cases embody or express a principle whereby anything more can be seen to have been recovered or preserved than the additional equitable interest successfully claimed by the plaintiff.'

In essence the submissions which counsel for the wife makes, basing himself on these passages, may be summarised by saying that the judge went wrong in two respects, that is to say (a) he failed to appreciate that *Hanlon* established that the only relevant consideration was whether the beneficial ownership of the property was in issue, which it never was in this case, and (b) he wrongly extended to the concept of 'property' for the purpose of the statutory charge the same broad and benevolent interpretation accorded to a lien under the Solicitors Act by treating as 'property recovered' what was no more than an accelerated realisation of an undisputed interest.

Now as regards what was in issue in the proceedings, counsel for the Law Society has attached some importance to the fact that in the petition the husband had sought a property adjustment order not just generally but specifically in respect of the matrimonial home. In that respect the case was substantially indistinguishable from the decision of Sir John Arnold P in *Jones v Law Society* (1983) 4 FLR 733, where there was a similar specific claim in relation to the house and its contents. That was a case where, as in the instant case, the husband and wife had (or would have had if their joint tenancy was severed) equal beneficial interests in the matrimonial home. At the stage of presentation of the petition there was, so far as appears from the report, no indication of what form of order the wife was seeking, but after the petition had been served discussions ensued as a result of which it was agreed that she should buy out the husband's interest for £4,000, a sum substantially less than the actual value of the husband's half share. That having been done, the Law Society claimed a charge on the £4,000 in respect of the husband's costs. Sir John Arnold P found that that claim succeeded. The claim in the petition, he held, raised an issue which, until either accepted or abandoned, remained in being as a live claim and it was not a necessary ingredient of its being an issue that there should have been a notice to proceed on that claim. He said (at 740):

'Unlimited as that is in form, it must mean that the petitioner was claiming by way of a property adjustment order a transfer to her of the entirety or, if the court so thought, something less than the entirety, of the husband's interest in the property of and the contents at 61 Coral Avenue. Therefore, it seems to me that it set up a claim and, correspondingly, an issue relating to the entirety of the husband's interest in that property and in those contents.'

In the result, Sir John Arnold P held that nothing was recovered or preserved under s 9(6) of the 1974 Act but that the £4,000 was property recovered or preserved under s 9(7) by virtue of the compromise at which the parties had arrived.

Counsel for the wife has submitted that we should not follow *Jones v Law Society* for two reasons. In the first place, he submits that, in so far as it might be thought to be authority for the proposition that a mere specific claim for a property adjustment order necessarily puts the whole of the respondent's interest in the property in issue, it is wrong. Secondly, he submits that Sir John Arnold P was wrong in concluding that the £4,000 there recovered was 'property recovered or preserved' for the purpose of s 9(7) although he was right in concluding that it was not such property for the purpose of s 9(6).

Speaking for myself I agree with counsel for the wife as regards the first point to this extent, that I do not think that *Jones v Law Society* can be used as an authority for the proposition that a claim to a property adjustment order in relation to specific identified property can by itself be treated as conclusive of the question whether the respondent's interest in the property is in issue in the proceedings. Nor do I think that Sir John Arnold P sought so to suggest for he said (4 FLR 733 at 740): 'It seems to me, therefore, that, *subject to what may have happened afterwards*, the making of that claim in the petition raised an issue.' (My emphasis.)

Moreover, he had already referred to the passage from Lord Simon's speech in *Hanlon* where he emphasised the need to look beyond the mere pleadings in order to find what had been at issue in the proceedings. All I think can be said is that it raised an issue in that case. Counsel for the wife has referred us to *Doherty v Doherty* [1975] 2 All ER 635, [1976] Fam 71 and to *Harris v Goddard* [1983] 3 All ER 242, [1983] 1 WLR 1203 for the proposition that the claim in the petition is not the definition of an issue but merely the necessary preliminary to the making of a claim which will (and in many cases can only) be formulated when notice of the application is given under r 68 of the Matrimonial Causes Rules 1977, SI 1977/344. Moreover, it is the fact, as was submitted, that the mere claim for an order under s 24 of the 1973 Act does not necessarily impugn the respondent's title to the property. It may, for instance, involve a *Mesher v Mesher* order, which merely postpones the immediate enjoyment of an acknowledged interest (see *Mesher v Mesher and Hall* (1973) [1980] 1 All ER 126), or it may even involve the bare vesting of a legal estate to give effect to a subsisting equitable interest. For my part, therefore, I think that little or nothing turns on the pure pleading point that the petitioner or his or her advisers have chosen to identify in the necessary claim in the petition a particular property as being one in respect of which an order under s 24 is sought.

As to the second point of counsel for the wife regarding *Jones v Law Society*, I confess that I have found the passage in the judgment in *Jones v Law Society* (1983) 4 FLR 733 at 740–741 which distinguishes between sub-s (6) and sub-s (7) very difficult to follow. As regards sub-s (6), Sir John Arnold P regarded the matter in issue as being the husband's 'Interest in the house'. That he held had not been preserved, because he transferred it to the wife. Equally, it had not been recovered 'because what was obtained by him was recovered as being a consideration . . . for the transfer away from him of his interest in the house'. This, I think, is counsel's point that, where an interest in property (or, to be strictly accurate, in the proceeds of sale of property) is compounded for money, there is an 'equation' of the money and the interest. I do not, for my part, quarrel with that and nor does counsel for the Law Society. But on that reasoning Sir John Arnold P must, with respect, have been wrong in saying that the husband had not 'preserved' anything. His whole interest had been in issue. He came away with that interest (on the 'equation' principle) to the extent of £4,000 and it really mattered not at all whether that was preserved to him as a result of the proceedings or of the compromise in the proceedings. Speaking only for myself, therefore, I would hold with respect that the extempore judgment of Sir John Arnold P in *Jones v Law Society* was wrong on this point and that (apart from such unusual circumstances as one finds, for instance in *Van Hoorn v Law Society* [1984] 3 All ER 136, [1984] 3 WLR 199) there is no different criterion applicable to what is property recovered or preserved for the purposes of sub-s (6) from that which is applicable to such property for the purposes of sub-s (7).

Having said that, however, I do not find the case of great assistance in the context of the instant case, where it is quite clear on the facts that there was never an issue as to the wife's ultimate entitlement to her share of the proceeds of sale nor any claim to deprive her permanently of it. What clearly was in issue in this case was whether the house should be sold or retained by the husband as his residence, or, to put it another way, whether the wife was going to receive her share of any money representing her share before the children attained full age. That, as the judge said, was the obstacle which she overcame as a result of the consent order made in the proceedings. What was potentially a distant project of receiving her share at some time in the future was translated into an immediate entitlement.

It is at this point that counsel for the wife seeks to escape from nineteenth century cases on solicitors' liens to which the judge referred and which Lord Simon warned can be referred to 'with caution' and 'used analogically'. The significance of those cases, and particularly *The Philippine* (1867) LR 1 A & E 309 and *Pelsall Coal and Iron Co v London and*

*North Western Rly Co (No 3)* (1892) 8 TLR 629, is that the lien of the solicitor was there
a held to attach to property not itself in issue in the proceedings to the extent that as a
result of the solicitor's work the value of the property had increased.

Counsel for the wife submits, first, that the wide and benevolent approach to the
solicitor's lien which led to that result has no application even analogically to the Law
Society's charge under the statute and, second, that in any event the enhancement in the
value of the property to the plaintiff represented by the element of acceleration is
b incapable of valuation. In my judgment there is a fallacy here. The shares in *The Philippine*
and the wagons in the *Pelsall Coal and Iron Co* case were not the subject matter of the suits
in which the solicitors claiming the lien had acted, so that there is no exact parallel
between those cases and the present. They are merely illustrative of the liberal approach
to what, for the purposes of the Solicitors Acts, may be considered to have been
'recovered'. Whilst they suggest that that word may, in some circumstances, be widely
c construed, they do not, as it seems to me, bear at all on the question of recovery in a case
where the very property in respect of which the lien is claimed is reduced into possession
as a result of the suit. In my judgment it is wrong to deduce from *Hanlon v Law Society*
the proposition that property is only recovered if the title to it is in issue. It has to be
remembered that what Lord Simon said was ([1980] 2 All ER 199 at 209, [1981] AC 124
at 180): '. . . it is only property the ownership *or transfer* of which has been in issue which
d has "recovered or preserved" . . . I can see no reason for extending the words to
items of property the ownership *or possession* of which has never been questioned'. (My
emphasis.)

Where, even though the *title* to property may not be in issue, the proceedings are
necessary in order to reduce it into or restore it to the possession of its owner, it seems to
me that, quite literally, the property has been 'recovered'. For instance, a landlord seeking
e to forfeit a lease or a landowner seeking to evict a squatter who claims no title but merely
refuses to move is pursuing property the title to which is not in issue. But I find it
unarguable that the property reduced to possession by the judgment has not been
'recovered' by the proceedings. Equally, if a trustee for sale wrongly refuses to concur in
selling so that proceedings are necessary under s 30 of the Law of Property Act 1925 to
compel a sale and the distribution of proceeds, I would have thought it quite clear that,
f as a result of the proceedings, the beneficiary had 'recovered' his share. It seems to me
entirely inappropriate and irrelevant in such a case to seek to assess the increment to the
plaintiff of the value of his interest. He has, quite literally, recovered (ie got into his
hands) property which he would not have in his hands had it not been for the proceedings.

That, as it seems to me, equally applies in the instant case. The wife's interest, though
undisputed, was effectively locked away from her by the husband's insistence on
g remaining in possession and his seeking, by the threatened ouster, to convert his
possession into sole possession, unless and until she either obtained an order in the
proceedings for the property to be sold and its proceeds distributed or prevailed on the
husband to pay her the monetary equivalent of her interest.

In my judgment, therefore, the judge rightly concluded that the Law Society's charge
attached to the moneys paid to her under the consent order and I too would dismiss the
h appeal.

I would only add a word of regret that the hope expressed in their Lordships' house in
*Hanlon v Law Society* (perhaps most forcibly in the speech of Lord Lowry (see [1980] 2 All
ER 199 at 226, [1981] AC 124 at 204)) echoed by Sir John Arnold P in *Jones v Law Society*
(1983) 4 FLR 733 and re-echoed by this court in *Simmons v Simmons* [1984] 1 All ER 83,
[1984] Fam 17 and in *R v Law Society, ex p Sexton* [1984] 1 All ER 92, [1984] QB 360 has
still not been fulfilled.

In the vast majority of cases the matrimonial home constitutes the only family asset of
any value. Time and again sensible division of property within the limits of the
frequently slender resources available founders on the rock of the attachment of the
charge for legal aid costs. That is no criticism at all of the Law Society, which has to
administer the legal aid scheme within the framework of the 1974 Act and the

regulations as they stand. But in *Hanlon v Law Society* [1980] 2 All ER 199 at 212, [1981]
AC 124 at 184 Lord Simon described the desirability for reconsideration of these    a
provisions as urgent. Now, over four years later, it is certainly no less urgent.

**PURCHAS LJ.** I agree that this appeal must be dismissed for the reasons given in the
judgments of Oliver LJ and Neill J.

*Appeal dismissed. No order for costs. Leave to appeal to the House of Lords refused.*    b

Solicitors: *James & Charles Dodd* (for the wife); *David Edwards*, Secretary, Legal Aid (for
the Law Society).

Diana Procter    Barrister.

c

# Re Asbestos Insurance Coverage Cases

HOUSE OF LORDS

LORD FRASER OF TULLYBELTON, LORD WILBERFORCE, LORD KEITH OF KINKEL, LORD ROSKILL AND
LORD BRIDGE OF HARWICH    d

6, 7, 11, 28 FEBRUARY 1985

*Evidence – Foreign tribunal – Examination of witness in relation to matters pending before foreign
tribunal – Evidence . . . for purpose of civil proceedings – Production of documents – Particular
documents specified in order – Letters rogatory requesting specimen insurance policies – Whether
request referring to specified documents – Whether documents merely falling within class of*    e
*documents – Evidence (Proceedings in Other Jurisdictions) Act 1975, s 2(4).*

*Evidence – Foreign tribunal – Examination of witness in relation to matters pending before foreign
tribunal – Evidence . . . for purpose of civil proceedings – Oral examination – Whether English
court will determine in advance whether evidence of witness is relevant to issue before foreign
court – Evidence (Proceedings in Other Jurisdictions) Act 1975, s 2(2)(a).*    f

The respondents, four United States corporations who were manufacturers of asbestos,
had insurance policies with various insurers to cover asbestos-related claims. The
appellants were S Ltd, who were insurance brokers who had effected certain of the
respondents' insurance policies in England, and three directors of S Ltd. The respondents,
who were faced with numerous claims from persons seeking compensation for asbestos-    g
related injuries, brought proceedings in California seeking, inter alia, declarations and
damages against the insurers in respect of the claims. In the course of the Californian
proceedings a number of issues arose in relation to the respondents' insurance cover,
causing them to seek and obtain letters rogatory from the Californian court addressed to
the appellants, requesting the testimony of the three directors and production by S Ltd
of certain documents, in particular (i) under para (b) of the letters rogatory, written    h
instructions from the respondents to S Ltd to obtain specimen insurance policies referred
to in the letters rogatory, (ii) under para (g), written instructions from the respondents to
S Ltd to obtain certain other specimen insurance policies, and (iii) under the first part of
para (j), 'exemplars' of certain excess comprehensive personal injury and property damage
'umbrella' liability policies in use in the London insurance market during the period
1950–66. On an application to the High Court by the respondents, an order was made    j
by a master pursuant to s 1[a] of the Evidence (Proceedings in Other Jurisdictions) Act
1975 requiring the three directors to attend before examiners to give testimony pursuant
to s 2(2)(a)[b] of that Act. A summons by the appellants to set aside the master's order was

_____

a   Section 1, so far as material, is set out at p 719 h j, post
b   Section 2, so far as material, is set out at p 720 a to c, post

dismissed by the judge, who ordered the directors to attend before examiners to give oral
*a* testimony, and further ordered S Ltd to give effect to all requests in the letters rogatory
for the production of documents. On appeal, the Court of Appeal dismissed appeals by
the directors but allowed in part S Ltd's appeal against the order relating to the production
of documents. The court nevertheless ordered production of the documents specified in
paras (b) and (g) and the first part of para (j) of the letters rogatory. The appellants
appealed to the House of Lords, contending (i) that by virtue of s 2(4) of the 1975 Act the
*b* court could only order production of a document if the document was individually
particularised and identified, which the documents ordered to be produced were not, (ii)
that the request in respect of para (j) was a 'fishing' expedition, and (iii) that, although
the three directors were in a position to give some evidence relevant to the Californian
proceedings, it was likely that they would be asked to give evidence which they were not
qualified to give. Under s 2(4) of the 1975 Act an order made under s 1 could not require
*c* a person to produce any documents other than 'particular documents specified in the
order' which appeared to the court to be likely to be in his possession.

**Held** – (1) Having regard to the purpose of s 2(4) of the 1975 Act, which was to preclude
pre-trial discovery, the words 'particular documents specified in the order' were to be
construed strictly, in order to preclude requests which were merely 'fishing' expeditions.
*d* The test to be applied in relation to the production of documents was whether 'particular
documents' were specified, i e individual documents separately described, although it was
permissible to have a compendious description of several documents provided that the
exact documents were actual documents evidence of which could be produced to satisfy
the judge that they did exist or at least had existed. On the facts, paras (b) and (g) of the
letters rogatory did not refer to particular documents but in effect merely to all or any
*e* documents falling within the class of written instructions and were therefore a request
for conjectural documents which might or might not exist, and there was no evidence
that there was usually a single document or set of documents by which written
instructions for policies from the respondents were transmitted to the appellants.
Furthermore, in para (j) the 'exemplars' referred to the standard forms of 'umbrella'
policies developed by the appellants in conjunction with others and which were varied
*f* from time to time, and para (j) gave no indication of the dates on which the exemplars
were amended or different exemplars came into use, and therefore its effect was to call
for all exemplars of umbrella policies that were in use at the time of the period from
1950 to 1966. It followed that paras (b) and (g) and the first part of para (j) of the letters
rogatory described a class of documents and not particular documents. Accordingly the
appeal in respect of the production of documents would be allowed (see p 719 *e f*, p 720 *c*
*g* *d*, p 721 *a* to *j*, p 722 *c* to *g* and p 723 *f* to *j*, post); dicta of Lord Wilberforce and Lord
Diplock in *Rio Tinto Zinc Corp v Westinghouse Electric Corp* [1978] 1 All ER at 442, 463
applied.

(2) It was inappropriate for an English court to determine in advance the matters
relevant to issues before a foreign court on which a witness was in a position to give
evidence. It followed that since the directors had acknowledged that they were in a
*h* position to give some evidence that was relevant to the Californian proceedings they
should be required to attend to give oral testimony. The appeals relating to the oral
testimony would accordingly be dismissed (see p 719 *e f* and p 722 *j* to p 723 *a d* and *f* to
*j*, post).

**Notes**
For evidence for proceedings in other jurisdictions, see 17 Halsbury's Laws (4th edn)
*j* paras 326–330, and for cases on the subject, see 22 Digest (Reissue) 665–668, 7111–7123.
For the Evidence (Proceedings in Other Jurisdictions) Act 1975, ss 1, 2, see 45
Halsbury's Statutes (3rd edn) 483, 484.

**Cases referred to in opinions**
*Radio Corp of America v Rauland Corp* [1956] 1 All ER 549, [1956] 1 QB 618, [1956] 2
  WLR 612, DC.

*Rio Tinto Zinc Corp v Westinghouse Electric Corp, RTZ Services Ltd v Westinghouse Electric Corp* [1978] 1 All ER 434, [1978] AC 547, [1978] 2 WLR 81, HL.          *a*

**Appeal**
Sedgwick Group plc, Sedgwick Overseas Group Ltd, Sedgwick North America Ltd (Sedgwick), Philip Gerald Crane, William Ernest Parton and David Murray Thistleton-Smith appealed, with leave of the Appeal Committee of the House of Lords granted on 5 December 1984, against the decision of the Court of Appeal (Eveleigh, O'Connor and *b* Slade LJJ) dated 20 November 1984 whereby it allowed in part the appellants' appeal against the order of McNeill J on 25 July 1984 that, inter alia, (i) the appellants' summons seeking to set aside or discharge the order of Master Lubbock made ex parte on the application of the respondents, Johns-Manville Corp, Fibreboard Corp, GAF Corp and Armstrong World Industries Inc, on 16 December 1983 ordering Mr Philip Crane to attend and give testimony be dismissed on terms, (ii) the appellants' summons seeking to *c* set aside or discharge the order of Master Hodgson made ex parte on the respondents' application on 13 February 1984 ordering Mr William Parton to attend to give testimony be dismissed, (iii) the appellants' summons seeking to set aside or discharge the order of Master Bickford-Smith made ex parte on the respondents' application on 30 March 1984 ordering Mr David Thistleton-Smith to attend to give testimony be dismissed and (iv) the appellants produce those documents requested in the letters rogatory addressed to *d* Sedgwick as described in paras (a) to (h) and the first part of para (j) thereof. The facts are set out in the opinion of Lord Fraser.

*Nicholas Phillips QC* and *Christopher Symons* for the appellants.
*Michael Burton QC* for the respondents.

*e*

At the conclusion of the argument their Lordship allowed the appeal in respect of the production of documents and dismissed the appeal in respect of oral testimony stating that they would give reasons later.

28 February. The following opinions were delivered.

*f*

**LORD FRASER OF TULLYBELTON.** My Lords, these appeals raise two questions under s 2 of the Evidence (Procedure in Other Jurisdictions) Act 1975. The questions relate to letters rogatory issued out of the Superior Court of California for the City of San Francisco requesting the assistance of the High Court in England, and to orders made by the High Court in response to that request. One question relates to orders for witnesses to attend before an examiner in England for oral examination. The other relates to an *g* order for production of documents.
    The respondents are four American corporations, or groups of corporations, who manufacture asbestos. They are engaged in litigation in the United States of America against insurers with whom they had a large number of insurance policies to cover asbestos-related claims. Five actions have been raised in the Superior Court of California in San Francisco and they are collectively referred to as 'the co-ordination proceedings'. *h* The insurers named in the titles to the five actions are merely a few of the many insurers involved and in each action certain underwriters at Lloyd's of London are also parties. In four of the actions, one or other of the respondents is the plaintiff and the defendants are insurers or, in one case, American insurance brokers. In the fifth action one of the insurers is the plaintiff and one of the respondents is the defendant. But nothing turns on the forms of the particular actions. The appellants are Sedgwick Group plc and two of *j* its subsidiary companies (collectively referred to as 'Sedgwick'), who together represent, as a result of amalgamations or otherwise, the final brokers through whom all the relevant policies with Lloyd's underwriters in London were arranged, and three individuals who are or were at the material time directors of those brokers.
    Each of the respondents is faced with claims from persons who say that they are

suffering from asbestos-related injuries, and who seek compensation for these injuries
a and in some cases for damage to property. In the co-ordination proceedings the
respondents seek declarations and damages and in some cases injunctive relief and
rectification against the insurers, including Lloyd's underwriters. There are many
thousands of claims and their total amount is very large. The respondents allege that the
insurers have failed or declined to defend actions brought by the claimants for
compensation, or to idemnify the respondents against the claims.

b     The issues in the co-ordination proceedings include the following: (1) whether certain
of the policies which are alleged to exist, dating back as far as 1920, exist at all; (2) the
extent of the cover actually placed by the respondents with Sedgwick and in particular
whether the insurance cover extends only to claims based on asbestos-related disease
which manifested itself during the policy period or is provided only under policies which
relate to the period of inhalation or ingestion; (3) the construction of certain of the
c policies issued by Lloyd's underwriters to the respondents through the agency of
Sedgwick, including the level of loss at which liability of 'excess' underwriters arises; and
(4) whether the respondents failed to disclose to the underwriters the extent of their
knowledge of the risk of asbestos-related injury.

    The orders now under appeal were made by McNeill J on 25 July 1984. He ordered
the three individual appellants to attend before examiners to give oral testimony. As
d regards the production of documents, he made an order against Sedgwick giving effect
to all the requests in the letters rogatory, except those in two paragraphs and certain
others which were not pursued by the pursuant respondents. The Court of Appeal
(Eveleigh, O'Connor and Slade LJJ) unanimously dismissed the appeals by the three
individual appellants against the orders relating to oral testimony, and allowed in part
Sedgwick's appeal against the order relating to production of documents. Slade LJ gave a
e dissenting judgment in respect of the documents and would have allowed Sedgwick's
appeal in relation to all the documents in issue. The appellants have now appealed by
leave of his House.

    On 11 February 1985 the House allowed the appeal in respect of documents and
dismissed the appeal in respect of oral evidence. The reasons for the decision were not
stated on that day, owing to the urgency of announcing the decision so that it could be
f carried into effect before the trial began in California early in March. We intimated that
the reasons would be given later, and that we now do.

    The 1975 Act was passed in order, inter alia, to give effect to the principles of the
Convention on the Taking of Evidence abroad in Civil or Commercial Matters (The
Hague, 18 March 1970; TS 20 (1977); Cmnd 6727) which was ratified by the United
Kingdom in 1976. The 1975 Act was fully considered by this House in *Rio Tinto Zinc*
g *Corp v Westinghouse Electric Corp* [1978] 1 All ER 434 at 444, [1978] AC 547 at 612, where
Lord Wilberforce said:

    '. . . I am of opinion that following the spirit of the 1975 Act which is to enable
    judicial assistance to be given to foreign courts, the letters rogatory ought to be
    given effect to so far as possible . . .'

h I respectfully agree and I approach the present appeal with that admonition in mind.
    Section 1 of the 1975 Act (reading it short) provides:

    'Where an application is made to the High Court . . . for an order for evidence to
    be obtained in [England], and the court is satisfied—(a) that the application is made
    in pursuance of a request issued by or on behalf of a court or tribunal ("the
    requesting court") exercising jurisdiction . . . in a country or territory outside the
    United Kingdom; and (b) that the evidence to which the application relates is to be
    obtained for the purposes of civil proceedings which either have been instituted
    before the requesting court or whose institution before that court is contemplated,
    the High Court . . . shall have the powers conferred on it by the following provisions
    of this Act.'

Section 2(1) provides that the High Court shall have power by order to make such
provision for obtaining evidence in England as may appear to the court to be appropriate    *a*
for the purpose of giving effect to the request in pursuance of which an application has
been made under s 1. Subsection (2) of s 2, so far as relevant, provides that an order under
the section 'may . . . make provision—(a) for the examination of witnesses, either orally
or in writing; (b) for the production of documents . . .'
Subsection (3) is not material in the present appeal. Subsection (4) is the subsection
which is directly in point here and I must quote it in full as follows:                       *b*

> 'An order under this section shall not require a person—(a) to state what
> documents relevant to the proceedings to which the application for the order relates
> are or have been in his possession, custody or power; or (b) to produce any documents
> other than particular documents specified in the order as being documents appearing
> to the court making the order to be, or to be likely to be, in his possession, custody
> or power.'                                                                                  *c*

Two preliminary observations fall to be made on sub-s (4). It was evidently passed in
order to give effect to the United Kingdom government's reservation, made in accordance
with art 23 of the convention when it ratified the convention, declaring that 'the United
Kingdom will not execute letters of request issued for the purpose of obtaining pre-trial
discovery of documents'. While that is the explanation for the presence of sub-s (4) in the   *d*
1975 Act, I do not consider that it assists directly in the construction of the subsection so
far as this appeal is concerned. The wide-ranging nature of pre-trial discovery in the
United States of America was explained by Lord Wilberforce in *Westinghouse*, but there is
no question of the letters of request which are before the House in this appeal having
been issued for the purpose of obtaining pre-trial discovery. The time for such discovery
is long past, the trial is due to begin in California about one month after the date on       *e*
which we heard the appeal. Secondly, counsel for the appellants drew our attention to
what appears to be a drafting error in para (b) of sub-s (4). Paragraph (b) refers to 'particular
documents specified in the order *as* being documents appearing to the court' etc. The
effect of the word 'as', read literally, would be to require that the order itself must specify
that the documents appear to the court etc. But that is, apparently, not the usual practice,
and the order against Sedgwick does not so specify. Counsel did not take any objection to   *f*
the order on that ground and I think he was wise not to do so.

*Production of documents*
It will be convenient to consider first Sedgwick's appeal against the order for production
of documents. This appeal is limited to the order so far as it gives effect to paras (b) and
(g) and the first part of para (j) of the letters of request. (McNeill J had already refused     *g*
the request for documents under the second part of para (j).) These paragraphs are in the
following terms:

> '. . . (b) The written instructions from the plaintiffs or their agents to Sedgwick to
> obtain the insurance policies set forth in exhibit 1 hereto . . .
> (g) The written instructions to Sedgwick from the plaintiffs or their agents to
> obtain the insurance policies referred to in (f) above . . .                               *h*
> (j) The exemplars of Price, Forbes & Co. Ltd.'s excess comprehensive personal
> injury and property damage 'umbrella' liability policies in use in the London
> insurance market during the period 1950 through 1966 . . .'

Paragraphs (b) and (g) raise exactly the same point and can be considered together.
Exhibit 1 referred to in para (b) is a list of policies identified by their numbers and by the    *j*
numbers of brokers' slips. Paragraph (g) refers back to para (f) which in turn refers to
exhibit 4 where the dates during which predecessors of certain of the respondents are
said to have effected policies are stated. The question is whether paras (b) and (g) of the
letters specify 'particular documents' and thus comply with s 2(4)(b) of the 1975 Act.
McNeill J held that they did so. The majority of the Court of Appeal upheld that view,
but Slade LJ dissented, holding that they did not particularise the documents.

The meaning of the expression 'particular documents specified in the order' in sub-s (4)(b) was considered by several of the noble and learned Lords who took part in the Westinghouse decision. They were all emphatic that the expression should be given a strict construction. Having regard to the purpose of sub-s (4), which, as I have already mentioned, is to preclude pre-trial discovery, it is to be construed so as not to permit mere 'fishing' expeditions. Lord Wilberforce said ([1978] 1 All ER 434 at 442, [1978] AC 547 at 609):

> 'These provisions, and especially the words "particular documents specified in the order" (replacing "documents to be mentioned in the order" in the [Foreign Tribunals Evidence Act 1856]) together with the expressed duty of the English court to decide that the documents are or are likely to be in the possession, custody or power of the person called on to produce, show in my opinion that a strict attitude is to be taken by English courts in giving effect to foreign requests for the production of documents by non-party witnesses. They are, in the words of Lord Goddard CJ, not to countenance "fishing" expeditions: Radio Corpn of America v Rauland Corpn [1956] 1 All ER 549 at 554, [1956] 1 QB 618 at 649.'

Lord Diplock expressed perhaps an even more restrictive view of the effect of sub-s (4)(b) where he said ([1978] 1 All ER 434 at 463, [1978] AC 547 at 635):

> 'The requirements of s 2(4)(b), however, are not in my view satisfied by the specification of classes of documents. What is called for is the specification of "particular documents" which I would construe as meaning individual documents separately described.'

I do not think that by the words 'separately described' Lord Diplock intended to rule out a compendious description of several documents provided that the exact document in each case is clearly indicated. If I may borrow (and slightly amplify) the apt illustration given by Slade LJ in the present case, an order for production of the respondents' 'monthly bank statements for the year 1984 relating to his current account' with a named bank would satisfy the requirements of the paragraph, provided that the evidence showed that regular monthly statements had been sent to the respondent during the year and were likely to be still in his possession. But a general request for 'all the respondent's bank statements in 1984' would in my view refer to a class of documents and would not be admissible.

The second test of particular documents is that they must be actual documents, about which there is evidence which has satisfied the judge that they exist, or at least that they did exist, and that they are likely to be in the respondents' possession. Actual documents are to be contrasted with conjectural documents, which may or may not exist. In Westinghouse [1978] 1 All ER 434 at 470, [1978] AC 547 at 644 I said:

> 'The reference to "any" documents in the sweeping-up words in the schedule to the letters rogatory suggests to me that the draftsmen did not know whether such documents were in existence or not. Accordingly the words seem to be an attempt to circumvent s 2(4)(a) of the 1975 Act, an attempt which should not be allowed to succeed.'

In my opinion the terms of paras (b) and (g) of the letters rogatory in the present case fail both these tests. They fail the second test because there was no evidence that there was usually a single document or set of documents by which written instructions for policies from the plaintiffs or their agents were transmitted to Sedgwick. The only document to which our attention was called as being a specimen of such instruction related to the renewal of a policy and it is certainly not a definite instruction. It is addressed to one of the firms now represented by Sedgwick and it includes the following paragraph:

> 'We would ask you specifically to remove from the renewal [a particular provision] as this is not in keeping with the umbrella form as now written. We look forward

to hearing from you on this subject by cable as soon as possible, after the receipt of this memorandum.'

That appears to be a request or inquiry which might well have led to correspondence and discussion about the terms of the final policy. Moreover, for all that appears from the evidence, it is possible that instructions for some policies may have been given verbally and that there were no written instructions for those policies. In an affidavit sworn by the attorney for one of the respondents, he states his belief that—

> 'it is necessarily the case that Sedgwick must have received instructions [NB not 'written instructions'] to proceed as it did and *on this basis* have reason to believe that Sedgwick possesses the documents. . . referred to in [para (b) of the letters rogatory].' (My emphasis.)

In the light of the evidence as a whole paras (b) and (g) are in effect calls for production of 'written instructions *if any*', that is to say for conjectural documents which may or may not exist. In *Westinghouse* Lord Wilberforce was willing to extend 'particular documents specified' to include replies to letters 'where replies must have been sent' (see [1978] 1 All ER 434 at 443, [1978] AC 547 at 611). I would go that far with him, but I would not extend the expression to documents which may or may not exist.

For much the same reasons I am of opinion that these paragraphs of the letters rogatory also fail the first test in respect that they do not refer to particular documents at all. In effect they refer to 'all or any documents falling within the class consisting of written instructions'. The class is ill-defined and in my view there is room for some doubt whether the specimen document that I have mentioned relating to renewal of a policy falls within the class or not. I would therefore hold that paras (b) and (g) should not be made the subjects of the order for production of documents.

With regard to para (j) the words 'exemplars' is not one that is in common use and its meaning is not altogether clear to me. For the present purpose the evidence shows that 'exemplars' is used to describe the standard forms of what were called 'umbrella' policies which were developed by Sedgwick in conjunction with others, and which varied from time to time. The first part of para (j) gives no indication of the dates on which the exemplars were amended or different exemplars of umbrella policies that were in use at any time during the period from 1950 to the end of 1966. That is in my opinion clearly a description of a class of documents and not of particular documents. Moreover, the class is not clearly defined by the opening words of para (j), which refer to 'exemplars of Price, Forbes & Co. Ltd.'s . . . "umbrella" . . . policies'. There is nothing to show how their policies are to be distinguished from policies of other firms; the distinction might be important having regard to evidence that they 'and . . . other Sedgwick companies' were responsible, 'in conjunction with one or more North American brokers, for developing, drafting and marketing these umbrella policies'. This paragraph therefore fails the first test.

*Oral testimony*
The appeals from the three individual appellants against orders to give oral evidence were presented on the basis that the California judge who issued the letters rogatory had been misled into overestimating the evidence that these appellants could give. For example, it is said that Mr Crane, whose experience of insurance is limited to dealing with claims, has been asked to give evidence about placement of risks, underwriting, drafting and interpretation of policies and other matters of which he has no direct knowledge. I am not impressed by this argument. Each of these three appellants admits that he is in a position to give some evidence that is relevant to the co-ordination proceedings. It may be that they will be asked for evidence about matters which are outwith their experience, and which they are not qualified to deal with. If so, they can say so. It would be quite inappropriate, even if it were possible, for this House or any English court to determine in advance the matters relevant to the issues before the

Californian courts on which each of these witnesses is in a position to give evidence. As Lord Keith said in *Westinghouse* [1978] 1 All ER 434 at 478, [1978] AC 547 at 654:

'In the face of a statement of letters rogatory that a certain person is a necessary witness for the applicant, I am of opinion that the court of request should not be astute to examine the issues in the action and the circumstances of the case with excessive particularity for the purpose of determining in advance whether the evidence of that person will be relevant and admissible. That is essentially a matter for the requesting court.'

Counsel for the appellants appreciated the difficulty in the way of his House if it tried to determine the matters on which oral evidence would be relevant and admissible in the Californian proceedings, and, in order to meet the difficulty, he suggested that the letters rogatory should be sent back to the Californian court to be reconsidered by the judge there with a view to their being amended and restricted. I am not in favour of that course. It would cause delay, which is an important matter as the trial in California is due to begin early in March 1985. Quite apart from the delay, the Californian judge might not be persuaded to restrict the scope of the letters rogatory to the extent that would satisfy the appellants, or at all, and there would be no satisfactory way of resolving any difference between his view and the views of the English court. I would refuse the appeals against the orders relating to oral evidence.

*Costs*

The appellants at first contended that no orders at all should be made in response to the letters rogatory, and it was therefore necessary for the respondents to bring the matter before McNeill J. The respondents should therefore have their costs up to the end of the proceedings before McNeill J. So far as the appeals to the Court of Appeal and this House are concerned, success has been divided and no order for costs either in the Court of Appeal or in this House should be made.

**LORD WILBERFORCE.** My Lords, I have had the benefit of reading in advance the text of the speech delivered by my noble and learned friend Lord Fraser. In concurrence with him I find myself in agreement with the judgment of Slade LJ in the Court of Appeal. I agree with the disposal of the appeals suggested by my noble and learned friend.

**LORD KEITH OF KINKEL.** My Lords, I agree that, for the reasons set out in the speech of my noble and learned friend Lord Fraser, the appeal relating to documents should be allowed and that relating to oral evidence dismissed.

**LORD ROSKILL.** My Lords, I have had the advantage of reading in draft the speech delivered by my noble and learned friend Lord Fraser. I agree with it, and for the reasons which he gives I would allow the appeal relating to documents and dismiss the appeal to oral evidence.

**LORD BRIDGE OF HARWICH.** My Lords, I have had the advantage of reading the speech of my noble and learned friend Lord Fraser explaining the reasons for the order of the House made on 11 February last that the appeal in respect of documents be allowed and the appeal in respect of oral evidence be dismissed. I agree with it. I also agree with his proposals with respect to costs.

*Appeal in relation to documents allowed. Appeal in relation to oral evidence dismissed.*

Solicitors: *Herbert Smith & Co* (for the appellants); *Coward Chance* (for the respondents).

Mary Rose Plummer    Barrister.

# Faccenda Chicken Ltd v Fowler and others
# Fowler v Faccenda Chicken Ltd

CHANCERY DIVISION

GOULDING J

27–30 JUNE, 1, 4–8, 11–15, 18–22, 26–29 JULY, 6, 7, 10–14, 17–21, 24 OCTOBER, 8 NOVEMBER 1983

Master and servant – Duty of servant – Confidential information – Confidential information acquired by employee in course of employment – No express agreement restricting disclosure by employee – Information forming part of skill and knowledge acquired by employee – Employee's employment terminated – Employee using information as principal or disclosing information in service of new employer – Whether abuse of confidential information.

Master and servant – Conspiracy – Conspiracy to injure employer's goodwill – Circumstances in which conspiracy actionable.

The plaintiff company was engaged in the business of marketing fresh chickens. In 1973 it employed F as its sales manager and at his suggestion adopted a method of selling fresh chickens from refrigerated vans which travelled through particular routes within a defined area. Each van salesman acquired sales information regarding the customers' names and addresses, the general limits of the routes, the quantity and quality of goods sold and the prices charged. In November 1980 F left the plaintiff's employment and subsequently set up his own business of selling fresh chickens from refrigerated vans. He conducted his business in the same area as the plaintiff, his vans operated on the same routes as the plaintiff and served the same type of customers. Five of the plaintiff's van salesmen and three other employees left the plaintiff's employment and joined F's business. None of the former employees was subject to an express agreement restricting his or her services after leaving the plaintiff's employment. The plaintiff brought an action against F and the other former employees claiming (i) damages for breach of their contracts of employment by using the plaintiff's sales information to the disadvantage or detriment of the plaintiff and (ii) damages for conspiracy to injure the plaintiff's goodwill and connection by abuse of confidential information.

**Held** – The action would be dismissed for the following reasons—

(1) Confidential information of an employer's business acquired by an employee in the course of his service, which necessarily became part of the employee's skill and knowledge applied in the course of the employer's business and which was not subject to any relevant express agreement, could be used by the employee after the lawful termination of his employment for his own benefit in competition with his former employer either where he traded as a principal making personal use of such information or where, having entered new employment, he disclosed such information to further the business of his new employer. It followed that in the absence of an express agreement restricting the use of sales information, the former employees were not in breach of their contracts by using such information to further F's business (see p 729 g, p 731 b to d and f to h, p 732 e f and p 733 g h, post); Wessex Dairies Ltd v Smith [1935] All ER Rep 75, Printers and Finishers Ltd v Holloway [1964] 3 All ER 731 applied; Terrapin Ltd v Builders' Supply Co (Hayes) Ltd [1960] RPC 128 considered.

(2) A combination of persons whose acts resulted in damage to the plaintiff was an actionable conspiracy if (a) the acts done in pursuance of the combination would have been actionable if done by one person alone and/or (b) the sole or predominant purpose of the combination was to injure the plaintiff. On the facts, the wrongful act alleged was the abuse of confidential information and, since that allegation had not been established, there were no grounds for holding that there had been a conspiracy by F and the other employees to injure the goodwill of the plaintiff. Accordingly, the claim for damages for

conspiracy failed (see p 729 *g*, p 733 *j* and p 734 *a b*, post); *Lonrho Ltd v Shell Petroleum Co Ltd* [1981] 2 All ER 456 considered.

**Notes**
For employees' duty not to disclose confidential information after termination of employment, see 16 Halsbury's Laws (4th edn) para 549, and for cases on the subject, see 20 Digest (Reissue) 284–288, *2618–2633*.

For the tort of conspiracy, see 45 Halsbury's Laws (4th edn) paras 1526–1528, and for cases on the subject, see 45 Digest (Repl) 299–302, *162–191*.

**Cases referred to in judgment**
*Amber Size and Chemical Co Ltd v Menzel* [1913] 2 Ch 239.
*Cranleigh Precision Engineering Ltd v Bryant* [1964] 3 All ER 289, [1965] 1 WLR 1293.
*Leng (Sir W C) & Co Ltd v Andrews* [1909] 1 Ch 763, CA.
*Lonrho Ltd v Shell Petroleum Co Ltd* [1981] 2 All ER 456, [1982] AC 173, [1981] 3 WLR 33, HL.
*Printers and Finishers Ltd v Holloway* [1964] 3 All ER 731, [1965] 1 WLR 1.
*R v Ardalan* [1972] 2 All ER 257, [1972] 1 WLR 463, CA.
*Robb v Green* [1895] 2 QB 315, [1895–9] All ER Rep 1053, CA.
*Saltman Engineering Co Ltd v Campbell Engineering Co Ltd* (1948) [1963] 3 All ER 413, CA.
*Terrapin Ltd v Builders' Supply Co (Hayes) Ltd* [1960] RPC 128, CA.
*United Indigo Chemical Co Ltd v Robinson* (1931) 49 RPC 178.
*Wessex Dairies Ltd v Smith* [1935] 2 KB 80, [1935] All ER Rep 75, CA.
*Worsley (E) & Co Ltd v Cooper* [1939] 1 All ER 290.

**Cases also cited**
*Baker v Gibbons* [1972] 2 All ER 759, [1972] 1 WLR 693.
*Coco v A N Clark (Engineers) Ltd* [1969] RPC 41.
*Crofter Hand Woven Harris Tweed Co Ltd v Veitch* [1942] 1 All ER 142, [1942] AC 435, HL.
*Drane v Evangelou* [1978] 2 All ER 437, [1978] 1 WLR 455, CA.
*Irish, Re, Irish v Irish* (1888) 40 Ch D 49.
*Littlewoods Organisation Ltd v Harris* [1978] 1 All ER 1026, [1977] 1 WLR 1472, CA.
*Louis v Smellie* (1895) 73 LT 226, [1895–9] All ER Rep 875, CA.
*Marshall (Thomas) (Exports) Ltd v Guinle* [1978] 3 All ER 193, [1979] Ch 227.
*Morris (Herbert) Ltd v Saxelby* [1916] 1 AC 688, [1916–17] All ER Rep 305, HL.
*Quinn v Leathem* [1901] AC 495, [1900–3] All ER Rep 1, HL.
*R v Griffiths* [1965] 2 All ER 448, [1966] 1 QB 589, CCA.
*Reid Sigrist Ltd v Moss Mechanism Ltd* (1932) 49 RPC 461.
*Reuter's Telegram Co v Byron* (1874) 43 LJ Ch 661.
*Seager v Copydex Ltd* [1967] 2 All ER 415, [1967] 1 WLR 923, CA.
*Stratford (J T) & Son Ltd v Lindley* [1964] 3 All ER 102, [1965] AC 269, HL.
*Thomson (D C) & Co Ltd v Deakin* [1952] 2 All ER 361, [1952] Ch 646, CA.
*Vandervell's Trusts, Re (No 2), White v Vandervell Trustees Ltd* [1974] 3 All ER 205, [1974] Ch 269, CA.
*Ware & De Freville Ltd v Motor Trade Association* [1921] 3 KB 40, [1920] All ER Rep 387, CA.
*White v Riley* [1921] 1 Ch 1, [1920] All ER Rep 371, CA.

**Action**
On 10 September 1981 the plaintiff, Faccenda Chicken Ltd, commenced an action in the Chancery Division of the High Court against the first defendant, Barry Fowler, and nine other defendants, all former employees of Faccenda Chicken Ltd, seeking damages for breach of contract of employment and for conspiracy to injure Faccenda's goodwill and connection. On 16 September 1982 Mr Fowler commenced an action in the Queen's Bench Division against Faccenda Chicken Ltd claiming outstanding commission and

interest thereon. Faccenda Chicken Ltd counterclaimed for breach of contract, wrongful disposal or conversion. On 15 March 1983 the Queen's Bench action was transfered to the Chancery Division, and on 27 June 1983 both actions came before Goulding J. The facts are set out in the judgment.

*John Trench* and *William Hunter* for Faccenda Chicken Ltd.
*Peter Crawford QC* and *James Gibbons* for Mr Fowler and the other defendants.

*Cur adv vult*

8 November. The following judgment was delivered.

**GOULDING J.** I have to deliver judgment in two actions arising out of the same events. The first, which I shall call 'the Chancery action', was begun on 10 September 1981. The plaintiff is a company called Faccenda Chicken Ltd, and there are ten defendants. Nine of them are individuals. They were formerly in the employment of Faccenda Chicken Ltd but subsequently became employed by the tenth defendant, a company called Fowler Quality Poultry Products Ltd, which I shall refer to as 'the Fowler company', I shall call the other action 'the Queen's Bench action' for it was commenced in the Queen's Bench Division on 16 September 1982, and was transferred on 15 March 1983 to the Chancery Division. It is an action by Barry Fowler, who is the first-named defendant in the Chancery action, against Faccenda Chicken Ltd. Faccenda Chicken Ltd has pleaded a counterclaim in the Queen's Bench action which I must also deal with in my judgment. When hereafter I speak of 'the defendants' without further explanation, I mean (unless the context otherwise requires) the defendants in the Chancery action other than the Fowler company.

Faccenda Chicken Ltd called a large number of witnesses in support of its case, and they were cross-examined at great length. Robin Michael Faccenda, its chairman and managing director, suffers from a reluctance, which in my experience is not uncommon among successful businessmen, to accept facts as they are and not as he would like them to be. Otherwise I hold the evidence of witnesses for Faccenda Chicken Ltd to be honest and credible within the limits set by the respective witnesses' levels of intelligence and means of knowledge. I must make an exception for one minor witness named Hussein Hassan, whose testimony was patently worthless, and for Mr R C Franklin, a chicken producer called as an expert, who appeared to me to be unintelligent and to be prejudiced against Mr Fowler.

All the defendants gave evidence. I regard their testimony critically for several reasons. In the first place it seemed apparent to me that there had been a good deal of collaboration between them in preparing what they were to say. That is natural enough, as the defendants did not sever in their defence and appeared by the same solicitors and counsel. Such collaboration does not of itself suggest any lack of truth or candour, but in my opinion it necessitates particular caution in evaluating the evidence. A second reason for caution is to be found in the serious discrepancies between certain passages in the defendants' affidavits sworn for the purposes of early interlocutory proceedings and their oral testimony now given in court. I also bear in mind the strong loyalty which Mr Fowler evidently commands, the circumstances of a newspaper advertisement that I shall have to mention, and the false statements made by the defendants to colleagues at Faccenda Chicken Ltd regarding their intentions on leaving that company's service. I had the opportunity to observe for a considerable time the two most important persons in the defendants' organisation, Mr Fowler and Mr Finch. Mr Fowler appeared to me a highly strung and nervous individual, but in the end I formed the opinion that he was a truthful witness. Of Mr Finch I feel more doubt, and I observe caution in accepting facts on his uncorroborated assertion alone.

Faccenda Chicken Ltd is a company which carries on the business of breeding, rearing, slaughtering, preparing and selling chickens. They are known as fresh chickens, meaning that they are chilled in refrigerators until sale but are not actually frozen. Faccenda

Chicken Ltd carries on business under the direction of its chairman and managing director, the aforesaid Robin Michael Faccenda. In or about 1973 it engaged Mr Fowler as its sales manager. At that time, and for some time afterwards, the company sold its chickens to wholesalers, and did not approach retailers directly. Mr Fowler, who is agreed to be a businessman of considerable ability, proposed to Mr Faccenda the establishment of what he called a van sales operation, whereby itinerant refrigerated vehicles would daily offer fresh chickens to such traders as butchers, supermarkets and catering establishments. Starting at first in a small way, Mr Fowler built up this branch of the business until it came to represent a substantial part, though always the smaller part, of the company's trade. There were in all ten refrigerated vehicles, each driven by a salesman and travelling in a particular sector of the Midlands. The sectors radiated in different directions from Brackley in Northamptonshire, where Faccenda Chicken Ltd has its factory. Each salesman followed a different round within his sector on each of the five working days of the week, some customers receiving a call once a week and others twice a week, according to their requirements and the possibilities of the van sales organisation. Thus, the whole operation was based on 50 journeys or rounds, one for each vehicle on each working day of the week. The journeys were, of course, not rigidly fixed, but variable from time to time as particular customers were gained or lost or their requirements changed. It is clear from the evidence that the weekly standing orders of customers were not contractually binding on them. The evidence shows in my judgment that each customer was freely permitted to take less than his standing order when the salesman called, or to increase, or vary the composition of his order if the goods he wanted on the particular day were available in the van when it called. Firm orders were placed on special occasions or by large customers by telephoning to the office of Faccenda Chicken Ltd at Brackley, but the van salesman played no part in their negotiation.

Each of the van salesmen, after a few weeks' employment in a particular area, knew well the names and addresses of the customers in his area, the general limits of the area and the detailed routes which he took on the several days of the working week to supply the customers. He also knew their usual requirements, both as to quantity and quality of the goods supplied, the timing of deliveries, and the prices which they respectively paid. The last item was of much importance because Faccenda Chicken Ltd was accustomed to quote different prices to different customers buying similar goods, depending on their individual circumstances. All this information I shall refer to collectively as 'the sales information'. It is the subject-matter of the Chancery action and of the counterclaim in the Queen's Bench action, Faccenda Chicken Ltd alleging that it was confidential information and was, in the circumstances I shall have to recount, abused by the defendants, including the Fowler company. It is clear from the evidence of witnesses on both sides that the sales information would be of value to a competitor in the trade. Counsel for Faccenda Chicken Ltd, in the course of evidence and argument, paid special attention to the importance of knowing the prices paid by the respective customers, possibly because of the phrase 'trade secrets, such as prices, etc.' used by Farwell LJ in his judgment in *Sir W C Leng & Co v Andrews* [1909] 1 Ch 763 at 774. There has been much controversy regarding the extent to which one trader's prices are generally known to his rivals in the fresh chicken market. I find that an experienced salesman quickly acquires a good idea of the prices obtained by his employer's competitors, but usually such knowledge is only approximate; and in this field accurate information is valuable, because a difference of even a penny a pound may be important. It was also plainly established by evidence on both sides that a salesman quickly commits the whole of the sales information relating to his own area to memory. It is information which he must necessarily acquire and keep up to date in order to do his job, and in applying it day by day he soon knows it without referring to any memorandum.

Late in November 1980 Mr Faccenda received certain information which he forthwith imparted to the police. As a result Mr Fowler and one Lloyd, who was an employee of a customer of Faccenda Chicken Ltd, were arrested on 11 December. While at the police station on that day Mr Fowler offered in writing his resignation as sales manager of Faccenda Chicken Ltd, and Mr Faccenda, who was at the police station, accepted it. Mr

Fowler also signed a confession of his alleged crime. He was released from custody later that evening. Early in January both he and Lloyd were charged with the theft of 45 cases of chicken, now valued at £435. On 4 March they were committed for trial at the Crown Court at Northampton.

The resignation of Mr Fowler dealt a serious blow to the business of Faccenda Chicken Ltd. I think that Mr Faccenda, whatever view he took of the alleged theft, must have regarded the loss of his sales manager with mixed feelings. He had become discontented with the large sums that Fowler was earning by way of commission, and had tried in vain to persuade him to take his remuneration, or the greater part thereof, by way of a fixed salary.

Mr Fowler and his wife negotiated after his resignation for the purchase of an hotel at East Looe in Cornwall, but that project fell through at the end of March 1981. At some point of time Mr Fowler decided to set up a new business of selling fresh chickens from refrigerated vehicles. He had no source of supply under his own control, but it appears that fresh chickens are generally abundant on the market and he seems to have had no great difficulty in buying them in bulk. He advertised for employees under a box number in a local newspaper, but I do not doubt that his former colleagues knew very well who was behind the advertisement. Five of the ten van salesmen of Faccenda Chicken Ltd, their supervisor, Graham William Finch, and two ladies employed in the offices of Faccenda Chicken Ltd, gave notice and subsequently entered the employment of the Fowler company, which Mr Fowler incorporated for the purposes of his new trade. Mr Finch is the second-named defendant in the Chancery action, the two ladies (Linda Farmer and Susan Dennis) are the third and fourth defendants, and the five van salesmen are the fifth to ninth defendants therein.

Mrs Dennis is in a slightly different position from the others in that she had given notice before the advertisement appeared, and I accept her statement that she had then no knowledge of Mr Fowler's plans. The defendants, while working out their notices, did not disclose their intention to join Mr Fowler, and made various false statements to colleagues about their future plans.

The newspaper advertisement and the letters subsequently passing between Mr Fowler and the other defendants have been attacked as a sham, but I think that that is too harsh a term. Mr Fowler certainly desired to man his new enterprise with employees from Faccenda Chicken Ltd whom he knew to be experienced and competent, and loyal to himself. The other defendants had received knowledge of his intentions before the advertisement appeared and knew who had inserted it. Mr Finch had already helped him by giving information of his project to five others among the defendants: Pellatt, the two Uptons, Carter and Petts. But so far as I can see, there is no evidence that any of the defendants had agreed the terms on which he or she would serve Mr Fowler, or the defendant company when incorporated, before such terms were put in writing by Mr Fowler on receiving replies to the advertisement, and I think his definite offer of profit-sharing bonuses may well have helped to decide them. Nor do I doubt that Mr Fowler was interested to see what replies to the advertisement he would receive from other applicants, though in the event he employed none of them. Thus I do not myself stigmatise the advertisement as a sham, though there is certainly a strong flavour of insincerity in the defendants' replies.

The Fowler company's business was and is conducted from Brackley. The business commenced on 6 July 1981, although the Fowler company was not legally incorporated until the following month. Its refrigerated vehicles operate in some of the sectors visited by those of Faccenda Chicken Ltd and the two companies serve the same type of customer. They are in direct competition, and I have no doubt that Mr Fowler intended to compete with Faccenda Chicken Ltd, and also with other traders, from the outset. None of the defendants was subject to any express agreement restrictive of his or her activities after leaving the service of Faccenda Chicken Ltd. In those circumstances Mr Fowler took legal advice on their position and, to put it shortly, he endeavoured to sail as near the wind as possible without actual illegality. I shall have to judge whether he has succeeded. I feel sure on the evidence as a whole that all the defendants proposed to use such sales information as they respectively possessed in the promotion of the new enterprise. I also think, on the evidence as a whole, that if such use was unlawful there was a sufficient combination between the defendants to sustain a single claim in conspiracy against them all, assuming for the moment the other essential elements of that tort to be present. It is quite unreal, in my view, to treat the commencement of the new Fowler business as involving merely a number of bilateral contracts of employment, each made between Mr Fowler (later the Fowler company) and a single individual. In the words used by the trial judge (who was his Honour Judge Trapnell) in *R v Ardalan* [1972] 2 All ER 257 at 262, [1972] 1 WLR 463 at 470 they were all in the same plan together. The promise of profit-sharing, which I have already mentioned, is not immaterial in this connection.

Before I go on to consider the conduct of the new enterprise on and after 6 July when, as I have already said, the operation began, I must deal with allegations made by Faccenda Chicken Ltd of wrongful acts by three of the defendants before that date. On 1 June 1981 Mr Finch, as supervisor at Faccenda Chicken Ltd, called on all van salesmen to let him have a set of journey sheets showing the customers' average orders and the prices they were paying. It is contended that he did this in order to obtain information for use in the business about to be set up by Mr Fowler and that he took away or copied the journey sheets for that purpose.

Secondly, an exercise book containing the names, addresses and telephone numbers of certain customers of Faccenda Chicken Ltd and of some other persons was in the possession of Mrs Farmer at her home when her employment came to an end. It was returned to Faccenda Chicken Ltd when a demand was made for it on or about 9 July 1981. It is alleged that Mrs Farmer used or copied the contents of the book for the purposes of Fowler's new enterprise.

The third accusation relates to a customer of Faccenda Chicken Ltd called Walter Smith (or perhaps Walter Smith Ltd), who operates a number of butchers' shops in the Midlands. Three of the shops habitually bought Faccenda chickens each Wednesday, and Walter Smith's manager expressed a wish that they should have a second weekly delivery on Friday. The request was orally conveyed to Finch by one of the Faccenda salesmen, but he did not respond to it. This probably happened about the end of May or beginning of June 1981. It is asserted that Finch deliberately refrained from obliging the customer in the hope of obtaining the business for Fowler's new enterprise.

The parties concerned have sworn to innocent explanations of all these three matters. I have considered the evidence on each, and have sought to apply the ordinary civil test of the balance of probability. I find that Faccenda Chicken Ltd has failed to prove any of the three charges to my satisfaction.

A great deal of documentary and oral evidence was devoted to the description and analysis of the trading activities both of the Fowler business and of Faccenda Chicken Ltd during the weeks (and especially the first week) that followed the commencement of the former. Faccenda Chicken Ltd claims that it was the particular target of the operation. It alleges that Mr Fowler and his confederates deliberately arranged to call on its customers on the same days of the week as its own salesmen, and generally at a somewhat earlier hour. It is also strongly contended that the defendants pursued a deliberate policy of undercutting Faccenda prices. I regard these allegations as greatly exaggerated. It is certainly true that the majority of the customers of the new business had previously been customers of Faccenda Chicken Ltd, and that in many, though not all, cases they ceased to be so. It is difficult to know what significance to attach to this fact without knowing to what extent Faccenda Chicken Ltd had acquired the whole of the available market in the larger towns within a radius of, say, 50 miles from Brackley. My impression is that a large proportion of the relevant retailers were buying Faccenda chickens, many of them also purchasing chickens (probably of lower quality) from one or more of Faccenda's competitors. As to the timing of calls on customers, it was inevitable that the Fowler salesmen should use the knowledge of customers' requirements that they had acquired as Faccenda salesmen, but I do not find that routes and times were deliberately planned and organised in the comprehensive way that Faccenda Chicken Ltd would have me believe.

As to undercutting, I accept the defendants' explanation of their pricing policy. It was to obtain a minimum gross profit on chickens of 4p per pound. Prices yielding a lower profit were quoted as a temporary inducement, or introductory offer, for a period of two or three weeks to potential customers thought to be of value. They were also accepted when it was necessary, at the approach of the weekend, to get rid of perishable stock in danger of deterioration. The result, in cases where a fair comparison can be made, is that Fowler prices generally undercut Faccenda prices, but there are also many examples where they were the same or higher.

The experience of the van sales division of Faccenda Chicken Ltd in the second half of 1981 was unhappy, exacerbating a decline which had already been experienced during the first half of the year. The accountant of Faccenda Chicken Ltd has furnished figures relating to three periods which are approximately the second half of 1980, the first half of 1981 and the second half of 1981. The average weekly profit of the van sales division, calculated in a conventional way, was £2,497 in the first period and £511 in the second period; there was an average weekly loss of £2,539 in the third. The average weekly turnover in the second period was about 116%, and in the third period about 106% of that in the first period. The average weekly selling price per pound of chicken in the three periods respectively was 47·3p, 45·0p and 45·5p. The deterioration of the trade in 1981 was very largely due, in my opinion, not to the activities of the defendants, but rather to their defection from the service of Faccenda Chicken Ltd. The company's own evidence showed that the loss of Mr Fowler's management had an adverse effect on the volume of its wholesale trade. The consequence was a real danger of loss through the deterioration of accumulated stock. For that reason Mr Faccenda urged an increase in the volume of van sales, even if that required the reduction of prices. Thus we see some increase of turnover, at the expense of profits, in the first half of 1981. It must plainly have become impossible to sustain such increased turnover in the second half of 1981 when half of the experienced van salesmen of Faccenda Chicken Ltd had left its service, whether or not they were engaging in that of a competitor. Thus in the last of the three periods turnover sinks almost to that in the first, but with only a slight recovery of prices. I believe also that general market conditions, not peculiar to the parties, must have played some part in the varying fortunes of Faccenda Chickens Ltd, but I have not heard evidence that enables me to make any findings on that subject.

Mr Fowler or the Fowler company had been trading for just two months when, on 8 September 1981, his trial began at the Crown Court at Northampton. Mr Lloyd had pleaded guilty. The judge ruled that the purported confession of Mr Fowler was not admissible in evidence before the jury, and Mr Fowler was acquitted.

The writ in the Chancery action was issued, as I have said, on 10 September 1981, the date, it would appear, of Mr Fowler's acquittal. In that action Faccenda Chicken Ltd alleges in the first place that the defendants have broken their contracts of employment by using the sales information to the disadvantage or detriment of the company. Injunctions were originally claimed but in view of the lapse of time the claim for breach of contract is now rightly restricted to damages. As a second cause of action sounding in damages, Faccenda Chicken Ltd alleges a conspiracy by the defendants (including the Fowler company) to injure its goodwill and connection by such abuse of confidential information and also by inducing breaches of contract by the customers of Faccenda Chicken Ltd. The statement of claim in the Chancery action also contains the allegations that I have already rejected regarding the journey sheets called for by Mr Finch and the exercise book in Mrs Farmer's possession.

The Queen's Bench action was commenced on 16 September 1982. In it Mr Fowler claims £22,975 for outstanding commission said to be due to him, and interest on that sum. The counterclaim of Faccenda Chicken Ltd sought damages under three heads. The first is breach of contract by abuse of confidential information, in effect a repetition

(so far as regards Mr Fowler) of the claim in the Chancery action. The second is the
alleged wrongful disposal or conversion of chickens in November 1980 which founded
the criminal proceedings. As to that, in order to shorten the matter Mr Fowler's counsel
made a concession (during the evidence-in-chief of Mr Faccenda) agreeing to pay £435
without admission of liability. I therefore need not consider the point further. The third
head of the counterclaim is an alleged conspiracy between Mr Fowler and Mrs Dennis
and/or Mrs Farmer to obtain the disclosure to Mr Fowler of certain weekly costings of
Faccenda Chicken Ltd. This third matter is not now pursued, so that in effect the
counterclaim, so far as is in dispute, is comprised in the claim made in the Chancery action.

Let me now deal with the alleged abuse of confidential information. I must make it
clear that anything I say about the law is intended to apply only to cases of master and
servant. In my view information acquired by an employee in the course of his service,
and not the subject of any relevant express agreement, may fall as regards confidence into
any of three classes. First there is information which, because of its trivial character or its
easy accessibility from public sources of information, cannot be regarded by reasonable
persons or by the law as confidential at all. The servant is at liberty to impart it during
his service or afterwards to anyone he pleases, even his master's competitor. An example
might be a published patent specification well known to people in the industry concerned.
This class of information, however, must not be extended too readily. Lord Greene MR
indicated its limits when he said in *Saltman Engineering Co Ltd v Campbell Engineering Co
Ltd* (1948) [1963] 3 All ER 413 at 415:

> 'I think that I shall not be stating the principle wrongly, if I say this with regard
> to the use of confidential information. The information, to be confidential, must, I
> apprehend, apart from contract, have the necessary quality of confidence about it,
> namely, it must not be something which is public property and public knowledge.
> On the other hand, it is perfectly possible to have a confidential document, be it a
> formula, a plan, a sketch, or something of that kind, which is the result of work
> done by the maker on materials which may be available for the use of anybody; but
> what makes it confidential is the fact that the maker of the document has used his
> brain and thus produced a result which can only be produced by somebody who
> goes through the same process.'

Second, there is information which the servant must treat as confidential, either because
he is expressly told it is confidential, or because from its character it obviously is so, but
which once learned necessarily remains in the servant's head and becomes part of his
own skill and knowledge applied in the course of his master's business. So long as the
employment continues, he cannot otherwise use or disclose such information without
infidelity and therefore breach of contract. But when he is no longer in the same service,
the law allows him to use his full skill and knowledge for his own benefit in competition
with his former master; and (in spite of words used obiter by Bennett J in a passage that I
am about to cite) there seems to be no established distinction between the use of such
information where its possessor trades as a principal, and where he enters the employment
of a new master, even though the latter case involves disclosure and not mere personal
use of the information. If an employer wants to protect information of this kind, he can
do so by an express stipulation restraining the servant from competing with him (within
reasonable limits of time and space) after the termination of his employment. An
example of such information is the manufacturing process in question in *United Indigo
Chemical Co Ltd v Robinson* (1931) 49 RPC 178 at 187, where Bennett J said:

> 'In those circumstances it seems to me to be almost impossible, in justice to the
> servant, to restrain him when he leaves his master's employment from using—not
> disclosing—information which he could not help acquiring. It seems to me that to
> try to restrain him by injunction from using knowledge, which in that way has
> become his own, is to try to do something which the Court really has no power to
> do, or rather it has no power to enforce the injunction if one could be granted.'

A second example is the trade information described in *E Worsley & Co Ltd v Cooper*

[1939] 1 All ER 290. The following passage from Maugham LJ's judgment in *Wessex Dairies Ltd v Smith* [1935] 2 KB 80 at 89, [1935] All ER Rep 75 is also material:

> 'First, after the employment terminates, the servant may, in the absence of special stipulation, canvass the customers of the late employer, and further he may send a circular to every customer. On the other hand, it has been held that while the servant is in the employment of the master he is not justified in making a list of the master's customers, and he can be restrained, as he was in *Robb* v. *Green*, from making such a list, or if he has made one, he will be ordered to give it up. But it is to be noted that in *Robb* v. *Green* ([1895] 2 QB 315, [1895–9] All ER Rep 1053) the defendant was not restrained from sending out circulars to customers whose names he could remember. Another thing to be borne in mind is that although the servant is not entitled to make use of information which he has obtained in confidence in his master's service he is entitled to make use of the knowledge and skill which he acquired while in that service, including knowledge and skill directly obtained from the master in teaching him his business. It follows, in my opinion, that the servant may, while in the employment of the master, be as agreeable, attentive and skilful as it is in his power to be to others with the ultimate view of obtaining the benefit of the customers' friendly feelings when he calls upon them if and when he sets up business for himself. That is, of course, where there is no valid restrictive clause preventing him doing so.'

Third, however, there are, to my mind, specific trade secrets so confidential that, even though they may necessarily have been learned by heart and even though the servant may have left the service, they cannot lawfully be used for anyone's benefit but the master's. An example is the secret process which was the subject matter of *Amber Size and Chemical Co Ltd v Menzel* [1913] 2 Ch 239.

Chancery action falls into my second class, and cannot be protected in the absence of an express restrictive stipulation. The defendants being free to compete with Faccenda Chicken Ltd and to solicit its customers, it is impossible, in my judgment, to say they must not use their own knowledge of the whereabouts and requirements of those customers, the prices they have been paying, and the routes by which they are conveniently visited.

Much was made in argument of the so-called springboard doctrine, stated in the following terms by Roxburgh J in *Terrapin Ltd v Builders' Supply Co (Hayes) Ltd* [1960] RPC 12 as set out in *Cranleigh Precision Engineering Ltd v Bryant* [1964] 3 All ER 289 at 301, [1965] 1 WLR 1293 at 1317–1318:

> 'As I understand it, the essence of this branch of the law, whatever the origin of it may be, is that a person who has obtained information in confidence is not allowed to use it as a spring-board for activities detrimental to the person who made the confidential communication, and spring-board it remains even when all the features have been published or can be ascertained by actual inspection by any member of the public.'

The *Terrapin* case was not one between master and servant, but the spring-board doctrine is nevertheless, in my opinion, applicable in proper circumstances to such a case. The *Cranleigh Precision* case is itself an example. However, the sphere in which it can be applied as between master and servant is considerably limited by the servant's freedom, after lawful termination of his employment, to compete with his former employer and to solicit the latter's customers, unless, of course, he has been restrained by express contract from doing so. The present case, in my judgment, is analogous to *Printers and Finishers Ltd v Holloway* [1964] 3 All ER 731 at 736, [1965] 1 WLR 1 at 6, where Cross J said:

> 'If [the managing director] is right in thinking that there are features in his process which can fairly be regarded as trade secrets and which his employees will inevitably carry away with them in their heads, then the proper way for the plaintiffs to protect themselves would be by exacting covenants from their employees

a
restricting their field of activity after they have left their employment, not by asking the court to extend the general equitable doctrine to prevent breaking confidence beyond all reasonable bounds.'

It is interesting to observe that Mr Faccenda himself said in cross-examination that any of the van salesmen would take away confidential information in his head which he was not at liberty to use. In Mr Faccenda's view the salesman was therefore not at liberty to join a competing enterprise. He said that although he had not caused them to be told,
b
'You won't be able to work for anybody else in this area in this line of business,' it seemed to him obvious that they must not do so, so obvious that fairness did not require its express mention. He would not object, he said, to a former van salesman working in the same trade in a completely different area. That evidence confirms my view that Faccenda Chicken Ltd is inviting me to strain the proper limits of the law regarding abuse of confidential information in order to make good its own omission to impose restrictive
c
stipulations on those who serve it.

In deciding the Chancery action in this way I have had to give careful consideration to the state of the pleadings. Paragraph 3 of the statement of claim, in all its successive versions, has been in the following terms:

d
'In each of the contracts of employment of the first nine Defendants with the Plaintiffs, there were terms implied by law, that those Defendants would faithfully serve the Plaintiffs and would not use confidential information and/or trade secrets gained by them and each of them whilst in the Plaintiffs' employment to the disadvantage or detriment of the Plaintiffs, whether during the currency of such employment or after its cessation.'

The defence contains a simple admission of para 3, along with other paragraphs of the
e
statement of claim. It is arguable that the admission precludes the defendants from contending that the sales information falls into the second class in my classification already explained. Grammatically, para 3 of the statement of claim seems to imply that if information is confidential when gained it cannot ever be used to the employer's disadvantage, even after cessation of the employment. It appears that I mentioned this point in an observation that I made on the 20th day of the trial, when Faccenda Chicken
f
Ltd had closed its case and the defendants' witnesses were about to be called. Having forgotten that intervention, I referred to the point again on the 39th (and last) day of the trial, and an application was then made to amend the defence, which application at that late stage I refused. On reflection I think that so literal and strict a construction of the defendants' admission would be unfair to them. It was not developed in argument on behalf of Faccenda Chicken Ltd, and I think it is probably right to say that para 3 of the
g
statement of claim was intended and understood to mean no more than that the defendants were subject to such obligations of confidence as the law imposes on an employee in the absence of express agreement. I think, therefore, that I am not precluded from accepting the defendants' arguments by a technical point of pleading. The claim for damages for breach of contract accordingly fails.

I turn to the allegation of conspiracy made in the Chancery action. Its final version
h
reads thus:

'12. Further or in the alternative, the Defendants and each of them unlawfully conspired together to injure the Plaintiffs' goodwill and connection by unlawfully making use of the said confidential information and/or trade secrets of the Plaintiffs gained by the individual Defendants whilst in the Plaintiffs' employment in manner aforesaid and by knowingly or recklessly persuading procuring or inducing
j
customers of the Plaintiffs to break their contracts with the Plaintiffs for the purchase of chickens, with intent to procure such breaches.'

On my interpretation of the authorities a combination of persons resulting in damage to the plaintiff is an actionable conspiracy if either or both of the following conditions is fulfilled: (a) that acts done pursuant to the combination would be actionable if done by one person alone, or (b) that the sole or predominant purpose of the combination was to injure the plaintiff. It was indeed argued before me that the sufficiency of the former condition alone has been denied by the recent decision of the House of Lords in *Lonrho Ltd v Shell Petroleum Co Ltd* [1981] 2 All ER 456, [1982] AC 173, but I do not so understand their Lordships' speeches. Now in counsel's closing address for Faccenda Chicken Ltd it was conceded, in my view necessarily, that the evidence failed to establish a predominant purpose of injuring that company rather than of promoting the interests of the alleged conspirators. Accordingly it is only the first-mentioned condition that need be considered. Here the wrongful acts alleged by the statement of claim are the abuse of confidential information and the inducement of breaches of contract. The first I have already held not to be established, and the second was rightly, in view of the evidence, abandoned in counsel's closing address. The Chancery action therefore fails and is dismissed.

In case I am held to be wrong in my conclusions regarding confidential information, I will shortly consider what damage was suffered by Faccenda Chicken Ltd from the hypothetically unlawful use thereof. As the defendants insist, it is impossible to disentangle the effects of such improper competition from those of other influences, in particular the mere resignation of the individual defendants from their several positions with Faccenda Chicken Ltd and their replacement with inexperienced persons. If Mr Fowler and the other defendants had left the company at the dates they respectively did in fact leave, and had then disappeared from the scene, most of the loss complained of by the company would inevitably have been sustained. But that the defendants' knowledge and use of the sales information did cause some loss of orders, and some otherwise avoidable reduction of prices, I am persuaded. I do not think the damage to Faccenda Chicken Ltd justly attributable to that cause was very large. I feel sure it was less than £10,000. If I were a juryman, I would, assuming of course that the defendants' liability was established, propose to give Faccenda Chicken Ltd £5,000 damages in the Chancery action. It would be a single verdict against all the defendants on the basis of conspiracy. I ought to mention that it has not been argued that the Fowler company is in a different position from the (individual) defendants, nor has application been made to withdraw the inaccurate admission in the defence that it was incorporated on 6 July 1981.

Finally, I must dispose of the Queen's Bench action. When the trial began, there was a dispute between Faccenda Chicken Ltd and Mr Fowler as to the right method of calculating his outstanding commission. In his address on the 34th day, however, counsel for Mr Fowler accepted the method favoured by the company. At an earlier stage he had stated that, so calculated, the commission would amount to £17,608, subject to a deduction of £5,282 in respect of Sch E income tax at 30%. I will give judgment therefore in the Queen's Bench action for £12,326 or such other figure as may be agreed between counsel. On the counterclaim I give judgment for £435, the sum conceded as I have already mentioned. I hope that counsel may be able to agree what ought to be adjudged for interest on the two sums aforesaid. If not, it will probably be best for me to refer the question to chambers.

I will myself hear argument as to costs. It is my duty to say that in my opinion this litigation could have been fairly disposed of with much less time and expense than have in fact been incurred. My criticism is directed against both sides. Faccenda Chicken Ltd must, I think, be principally responsible for the large (and in my opinion partly unnecessary) bulk of the documents placed before the court. On the other hand, the defendants were to my mind more prolix in the examination and cross-examination of witnesses and in legal argument.

While I think it right to make those observations, I am none the less grateful for the patience of counsel on both sides in conducting this lengthy trial.

*Order accordingly.*

Solicitors: *Penningtons*, agents for *Shoosmiths & Harrison*, Banbury (for Faccenda Chicken Ltd); *Johnson & Gaunt*, Banbury (for Mr Fowler and the other defendants).

Evelyn M C Budd    Barrister.

# R v Nottingham County Court, ex parte Byers

QUEEN'S BENCH DIVISION (CROWN OFFICE LIST)

LATEY J

23 NOVEMBER, 3 DECEMBER 1984

*Divorce – Practice – Undefended causes – Special procedure – Disposal of cause – Certification of satisfaction with contents of petition – Registrar refusing to give certificate – Whether refusal of certificate constituting an 'order or decision' – Whether appeal from registrar's refusal lying to judge – Correct approach to special procedure divorces – Matrimonial Causes Rules 1977, rr 48(1), 124.*

Where in an undefended divorce suit under the special procedure system the registrar decides to grant or refuse a certificate under r 48(1)(a)[a] of the Matrimonial Causes Rules 1977 to the effect that he is satisfied that the contents of the petition are sufficiently proved and that the petitioner is entitled to a decree, his decision is in substance a judicial determination because it involves the registrar considering whether the procedural requirements of the special procedure system have been complied with and whether there are any defects in the petition, as well as whether there is sufficient proof of the ground alleged in the petition. Accordingly, although the form notifying the refusal of a registrar's certificate of satisfaction is not described therein as an 'order', it amounts in substance to an interlocutory order within r 124[b] of the 1977 rules and therefore an appeal lies to the judge from the registrar's refusal (see p 738 *g h* and p 739 *d e*, post); dictum of Lord Halsbury LC in *Lane v Esdaile* [1891] AC at 211 applied.

The objectives of the special procedure system are simplicity, speed and economy. Accordingly, a registrar should not approach a special procedure divorce in an over-meticulous or over-technical manner and should prefer substance to mere form. Provided that the petition and affidavit in support fulfill the essential requirements of the 1977 rules it is irrelevant that there are surplus matters in the petition or affidavit (see p 737 *e* to *g*, post).

### Notes

For the disposal of causes in the special procedure list, see 13 Halsbury's Laws (4th edn) para 848.

For the Matrimonial Causes Rules 1977, rr 48, 124, see 10 Halsbury's Statutory Instruments (4th reissue) 255, 289.

### Cases referred to in judgment

*Day v Day* [1979] 2 All ER 187, [1980] Fam 29, [1979] 2 WLR 681, CA.

*Lane v Esdaile* [1891] AC 210, HL.

*Mitchell v Mitchell* [1983] 3 All ER 621, [1984] Fam 1, [1983] 3 WLR 666, CA.

### Application for judicial review

Kathleen Georgina Byers applied, with leave of Forbes J granted on 15 May 1984, for (i) an order of mandamus directing the registrar of the Nottingham County Court (a) to certify under r 48 of the Matrimonial Causes Rules 1977 that the applicant was entitled to a decree of divorce under s 1(2)(c) of the Matrimonial Causes Act 1973 and (b) to set down the applicant's divorce petition in the special procedure list, and (ii) alternatively, an order of mandamus directing his Honour Judge Heald to hear and determine the

---

a    Rule 48(1), so far as material, is set out at p 738 *e f*, post

b    Rule 124, so far as material, provides '. . . any party may appeal from . . . an order or decision [made or given by the registrar in matrimonial proceedings pending in a divorce county court] to a judge . . .'

applicant's appeal from the registrar's decision. The respondent to the application was the Nottingham County Court. The facts are set out in the judgment.

*Richard Slowe* for the applicant.
The respondent did not appear.

*Cur adv vult*

3 December. The following judgment was delivered.

**LATEY J.** This is an application for judicial review, after leave granted by Forbes J.
It brings to the fore difficulties of some general concern in the operation of the special procedure system for undefended divorce suits.
His Honour Judge Heald, a judge of great experience, in a judgment to which I will return a little later said this:

'This is an appeal of the greatest importance to the profession and the registrars in the Nottingham and Derby group of courts. It raises a number of matters, which I know have been troubling the solicitors' branch of the profession for a long period. It concerns the so-called 'Special Procedure' system of divorce.'

And he concluded:

'I would make this comment. This is a matter of great importance and I would be happy if the matter were taken to the Court of Appeal for a more definitive judgment so that the profession generally throughout the country could discover how they can overcome the situation which often arises whereby a special procedure divorce comes to a halt because of an impasse between the solicitor for the petitioner and the registrar. Further, this matter is of such importance that with the consent of the solicitor for the petitioner I have given this judgment in open court so at least the profession locally may be aware of my views on the matter.'

Counsel for the applicant for what seem to me to be good reasons advised that the correct course was not to appeal to the Court of Appeal but to go by way of judicial review, for mandamus.
Counsel for the applicant informed me that these difficulties or similar ones are not peculiar to Nottingham but have been arising in other parts of the country. Mr Registrar Kenworthy-Browne believed this to be so in some parts. He sat with me throughout the hearing and has given valuable help to counsel and myself. He confirmed, on the authority of the senior registrar, that there have been no complaints of this nature from practising solicitors or the Law Society in the principal registry.
Legal aid is not available in special procedure cases. Counsel informed me that the Law Society, as the body representing practising solicitors, is concerned that solicitors are being expected unnecessarily to do too much in too many cases under the Green Form system due to these procedural difficulties.
The facts can be shortly stated. The applicant is the petitioner in an undefended special procedure divorce suit. She filed her petition and swore the affidavit of evidence required by the Matrimonial Causes Rules 1977, SI 1977/344.
When asked to give his certificate as required by r 48 of the rules the registrar refused to do so but directed that three matters first be dealt with by the petitioner's solicitors. The first was that a statement in the petition that no agreement or arrangement had been made or was proposed to be made between the parties for the support of the petitioner should be deleted as it was only required when the suit was brought under the Matrimonial Causes Act 1973, s 1(2)(e) and this was not such a suit. The second was that a child born to the petitioner was prima facie a child of the family and the registrar required full details as to why it was said that the child was not. The third was this: the

petition alleged desertion for two years and in para 2 alleged that the petitioner and the
respondent had never lived together as husband and wife. The registrar's comment was:
'If Para 2 of Petition is literally true, why not non consummation.' The form (D79) in
which the registrar notified the petitioner's solicitors is headed 'Notice of refusal of
registrar's certificate (Special Procedure).' It goes on to say: 'Please note that the Registrar,
having considered the evidence filed, is not satisfied that the Petitioner is entitled to the
decree. . . sought, because:—' there then followed the three objections already mentioned.
The form concludes: 'The Petitioner should file further evidence [deal with the above
matters] and renew the request for directions for trial.'

The petitioner's solicitors wrote to the registrar contending that his objections were
misconceived, giving their reasons, and asked him to grant his certificate. The registrar
refused.

The petitioner appealed. The judge, Judge Heald, dealt with the registrar's three points
and rejected them on the grounds that the first two were related to matters in the petition
which were no more than surplusage to requirement; and that the third was misconceived
because even if the petitioner had grounds for nullity on the ground, not of 'non-
consummation', but of non-consummation due to incapacity or wilful refusal, the
marriage would be voidable and not void and there would be nothing to prevent the
petitioner electing to sue for divorce, if she preferred, as her solicitors had correctly
pointed out to the registrar.

The judge's reasoning and conclusions on those matters are so plainly correct that I
need not repeat them.

So this particular case shows a certificate being withheld for three reasons: the first two
because there were included in the petition matters which need not have been; the third
because the registrar queried the choice of remedy when the choice of remedy was not
for him but for the petitioner.

It was a wholly mistaken approach by the registrar. The objectives of the special
procedure are simplicity, speed and economy. This does not mean that the essentials of
the petition and proof of its contents should not be satisfied. They must be. It does mean,
unless those objectives are to be set at nought, that there should be no room for over-
meticulousness and over-technicality in approach. For example, provided that the
essentials are satisfied, what does it matter if there is something in the petition or affidavit
evidence which is unnecessary and so surplus? Again, there is nothing that I am aware of
in this jurisdiction which excludes that salutary maxim de minimis non curat lex. It is
true that, before the introduction of the special procedure, minor irregularities were
simply and easily and inexpensively put right at the hearing before the judge, and in this
respect the registrars' function now is not always an easy one. But to my mind the
registrars can properly exercise their function by preferring substance to mere form,
though one must accept that there are cases where the line may be a difficult one to draw.
That is one reason why I single out at the end of this judgment one particular suggestion
which has been made.

It should not be thought that the mistaken approach in this case is typical. I am sure
that it is not. But from what Judge Heald has said, and from what counsel has informed
this court of the information accumulated by the Law Society, there is substantial cause
for concern in some parts of the country.

The judge then went on to consider what a petitioner's solicitor can do in circumstances
such as these. He said:

> 'The problem is in these cases, and I understand they arise frequently, what does
> the petitioner's solicitor then do? The special procedure has grave disadvantages
> where this type of situation arises. There is no appearance before the registrar or the
> judge. In the old days of oral hearings the petitioner could explain to the judge the
> various matters and the judge could then come to a decision on which there was an
> appeal. In the present case the solicitor does not know where to go. He therefore has
> appealed to me. Is he entitled to do so?'

The judge came to the conclusion that the registrar had not made any 'order or decision' within r 124 of the 1977 rules and that therefore there was nothing to appeal from.

The petitioner applies for an order of mandamus either (1) directed to the registrar to grant the certificate or (2) to the judge to hear and determine the appeal. The judge made it abundantly plain that if he had jurisdiction to hear the appeal he would have allowed it.

Counsel for the applicant has, if I may say so, presented an admirably clear and thorough argument and has put to the court anything which might militate against his submissions. He contends that the judge was in error in concluding that he had no jurisdiction to hear the appeal and asks for mandamus accordingly. If that does not succeed, he asks for mandamus directed to the registrar.

Where a petitioner and registrar reach this kind of impasse it would beyond question be expedient that an appeal lie to the judge. It would be far quicker, simpler and cheaper. There is, of course, a third course open and that is to remove the case from the special procedure list. But that runs counter to the objectives of the special procedure which are, I repeat, to achieve simplicity, speed and economy.

Is there then anything from which an appeal can lie? Counsel for the applicant conceded from the start that there is no 'final decision'. But he contends that there is an 'interlocutory order'.

He went through the relevant parts of rr 33, 48, 128. This was helpful, indeed necessary, but I do not think it necessary to review it all in this judgment. What it amounts to is this. In theory, before consideration of the grant of the certificate, the cause has to be entered in the special procedure list which means that at that stage the procedural requirements of r 33 have to have been complied with. In practice the two matters are dealt with together and this is clearly a sensible and time-saving practice. Any defects in the petition pertain to the entering of the cause. As to the certificate itself, the relevant provisions (omitting immaterial words) of r 48(1) are these:

'. . . the registrar shall consider the evidence filed by the petitioner and—(a) if he is satisfied that the petitioner has sufficiently proved the contents of the petition and is entitled to a decree, the registrar shall make and file a certificate to that effect; (b) if he is not so satisfied he may either give the petitioner an opportunity of filing further evidence or remove the cause from the special procedure list whereupon rule 33(3) shall cease to apply.'

Counsel for the applicant argued that in considering the grant or withholding of the certificate the registrar should concern himself solely with proof of the alleged ground for the divorce. On that point I disagree. The petitioner has sufficiently to prove the contents of the petition and that he is entitled to a decree. For example, he has to prove that there is a marriage to dissolve. This reinforces the view that procedural requirements, possible defects in the petition and proof of the ground for divorce should all be considered together.

The rest of r 48 deals with what is to happen after the grant of a certificate.

So all the registrar is concerned with is: does the evidence satisfy him that the procedural requirements have been complied with, that the petitioner has sufficiently proved the contents of the petition and that he is entitled to a decree? Supposing the registrar is not so satisfied but the petitioner believes that he is in error and wishes to demonstrate it, is there no appeal? Or must the petitioner proceed by way of judicial review and mandamus? Or have the suit removed from the special procedure list?

To put it another way, in refusing to grant the certificate has the registrar made an interlocutory 'order'? If he has, the rules (r 124) prescribe that there is an appeal to the judge.

Whether or not this jurisdiction is sui generis, it is certainly an unusual one. In the light of the decision of the Court of Appeal in Day v Day [1979] 2 All ER 187, [1980] Fam 29, the rules have effectively removed the adjudication from the judge to the registrar. If there are late or last-minute developments, as there not infrequently are, the

judge can do little other than grant a short postponement to enable application to be
made to the registrar. In *Mitchell v Mitchell* [1983] 3 All ER 621, [1984] Fam 1 the Court
of Appeal observed that there is then a right of appeal from the registrar to the judge.

In considering whether or not what has happened or been done is or is not an
'interlocutory order' the courts over the years have found themselves in muddied waters.
On the authorities it seems to me to be impossible or at all events unwise to generalise,
but each particular category has to be considered separately.

For myself, I do not think that there is any better starting point than that described by
Lord Halsbury LC in *Lane v Esdaile* [1891] AC 210 at 211:

> 'I confess myself I should hesitate if it was only to turn upon the question of
> language, because although a thing might be called an order, or might be called a
> judgment, or might be called a rule, or might be called a decree, it might well be
> that nevertheless by reason of the context it would come within the obvious
> meaning and purpose of the statute; so that although it was no one of those things
> in name it might be one of those things in substance, and therefore would come
> within the general provision that an appeal should lie.'

When the registrar refuses the certificate no piece of paper emerges described as an
order. What emerges in form is described as a 'Notice of refusal of registrar's certificate'.
But in substance he has judicially considered the matter and judicially determined that
there be no grant of a certificate. The paper could just as appropriately be described as
'Notice of registrar's order refusing the certificate'. It must, I think, be a matter of
impression to some extent, but, in my judgment, in substance though not in name the
registrar makes an order in these circumstances and does so also if he grants the certificate.

That order is an interlocutory one and so an appeal lies from it to the judge. On that
matter and that only I differ from Judge Heald's decision.

Accordingly there will be an order for mandamus directed to Judge Heald as asked for
in the notice of motion.

I should add that during the hearing a number of matters were touched on peripheral
to this appeal where there might, I do not say would, with advantage be alterations in the
rules or practice. Mr Registrar Kenworthy-Browne has taken a note of them and will
bring them to the attention of those concerned.

One that I will mention is the suggestion that instead of the certifying process there be
substituted a report and recommendation process to the judge.

I was impressed by counsel's suggestion that this might meet many of the difficulties
petitioners and their advisers encounter. But I do no more than mention it as I am aware
that it and other kindred matters are under active consideration by those concerned
elsewhere.

*Order of mandamus requiring the judge to hear and determine the appeal.*

Solicitors: *Ellis-Fermor*, Beeston (for the applicant).

Bebe Chua    Barrister.

# Westminster City Council v Croyalgrange Ltd and another

QUEEN'S BENCH DIVISION
ROBERT GOFF LJ AND McCULLOUGH J
29 NOVEMBER 1984

*Sex establishment – Control – Licensing – Offence – Knowingly using or causing or permitting use of premises as sex establishment except under and in accordance with terms of licence – Knowingly – What knowledge must be proved – Whether sufficient to prove knowledge of use of premises as sex establishment – Whether prosecution must prove that defendant knew premises were used other than under and in accordance with terms of a licence – Local Government (Miscellaneous Provisions) Act 1982, Sch 3, paras 6(1), 20(1)(a).*

To establish that a person has, in any area in which Sch 3 to the Local Government (Miscellaneous Provisions) Act 1982 is in force, knowingly used, or knowingly caused or permitted the use of, any premises as a sex establishment otherwise than under and in accordance with the terms of a licence granted under that schedule, contrary to paras 6(1)[a] and 20(1)(a)[b] thereof, it is necessary to prove not merely that that person knew the premises were used as a sex establishment but that he knew the use which he made, or which he caused or permitted to be made, of the premises was otherwise than under and in accordance with the terms of such a licence. Moreover, such knowledge may be proved not only by proving actual knowledge but also by showing that the defendant deliberately shut his eyes to obvious means of knowledge or deliberately refrained from making inquiries (see p 743 *c* to *f*, p 744 *e* to *j* and p 745 *a* to *c*, post).

Dictum of Devlin J in *Roper v Taylor's Central Garages (Exeter) Ltd* [1951] 2 TLR at 288 applied.

*Brooks v Mason* [1902] 2 KB 743 distinguished.

## Notes
For the requirement for licences for sex establishments and for using sex establishments other than in accordance with a licence, see 45 Halsbury's Laws (4th edn) paras 1020–1023.

For the Local Government (Miscellaneous Provisions) Act 1982, Sch 3, paras 6, 20, see 52 Halsbury's Statutes (3rd edn) 1820, 1825.

## Cases referred to in judgment
*Brooks v Mason* [1902] 2 KB 743.
*R v Edwards* [1974] 2 All ER 1085, [1975] QB 27, [1974] 3 WLR 285, CA.
*Roper v Taylor's Central Garages (Exeter) Ltd* [1951] 2 TLR 284, DC.

## Cases also cited
*Grant v Borg* [1982] 2 All ER 257, [1982] 1 WLR 638, HL.
*Nimmo v Alexander Cowan & Sons Ltd* [1967] 3 All ER 187, [1968] AC 107, HL.
*R v Oliver* [1943] 2 All ER 800, [1944] KB 68, CCA.

## Case stated
Westminster City Council (Westminster) appealed by way of a case stated by Ronald Bartle Esq, a stipendiary magistrate for the petty sessional division of South Westminster, in respect of his adjudication at Bow Street Magistrates' Court on 29 December 1983 whereby he dismissed (1) two informations laid by Westminster against the first

---

*a*   Paragraph 6(1) is set out at p 741 *j*, post
*b*   Paragraph 20(1), so far as material, is set out at p 742 *a*, post

respondents, Croyalgrange Ltd (Croyalgrange), alleging (i) that on 8 February 1983 they
*a* knowingly permitted the use of premises at 4 Peter Street, London W1 as a sex
establishment without the grant of a licence by Westminster under Sch 3 to the Local
Government (Miscellaneous Provisions) Act 1982, contrary to s 2 of and paras 6(1) and
20(1)(a) of Sch 3 to the 1982 Act and (ii) a like offence on 24 February 1983 and (2) two
informations laid by Westminster against the second respondent, Charles Grech, alleging
(i) that the first offence alleged against Croyalgrange was committed with his connivance,
*b* he being a director of Croyalgrange, and (ii) a similar charge against Mr Grech in relation
to the second offence alleged against Croyalgrange. The facts are set out in the judgment
of Robert Goff LJ.

*John E A Samuels* QC and *Roger McCarthy* for Westminster.
*John W Rogers* QC for the respondents.

*c*
**ROBERT GOFF LJ.** There is before the court an appeal by way of case stated, the case
being stated by Mr Bartle, a stipendiary magistrate sitting in South Westminster.

The case is concerned with what is called a sex establishment in Soho. Two informations
were laid against each of the two respondents, Croyalgrange Ltd and Mr Charles Grech.
They were laid against them by the solicitor acting for and on behalf of the prosecuting
*d* authority, which is the Westminster City Council. The first information, as against
Croyalgrange, was that on 8 February 1983 they did knowingly permit the use of
premises at 4 Peter Street, London W1 as a sex establishment without the grant of a
licence by Westminster City Council under Sch 3 to the Local Government (Miscellaneous
Provisions) Act 1982, contrary to s 2 of and paras 6(1) and 20(1)(a) of Sch 3 to the 1982
Act. The second information against Croyalgrange related to a like offence committed
*e* on a different date, 24 February 1983.

The first information alleged against Mr Grech was that the offence set out, being the
first offence alleged as against Croyalgrange, was committed with his connivance, he
being a director of Croyalgrange, whereby he, as well as that company, was guilty of the
offence, contrary to s 2 of and paras 6(1), 20(1)(a) and 26(1) of Sch 3 to the 1982 Act. The
second information charged against him was a like offence in relation to the second
*f* offence alleged against Croyalgrange.

I must first refer to the relevant statutory provisions. The Act in question is the Local
Government (Miscellaneous Provisions) Act 1982. We are concerned with Pt II, which is
entitled 'Control of Sex Establishments'. Section 2(1) provides:

> 'A local authority may resolve that Schedule 3 to this Act is to apply to their area;
> and if a local authority do so resolve, that Schedule shall come into force in their area
> *g* on the day specified in that behalf in the resolution [subject to a period of time
> which has to elapse between the date of the resolution and the specified day].'

Westminster City Council, having within its area the part of London we all know as
Soho, did make such a resolution in respect of the whole of its area. That resolution was
passed in December 1982, and it came into effect for the whole area, including Soho, as
*h* from 1 February 1983.

I turn next to Sch 3 to the Act. There is a definition of what is called a sex establishment,
but I need not set that out for the purposes of this judgment. Then there is a provision,
in para 6(1) of Sch 3, which is concerned with the requirement for licences for sex
establishments. It reads as follows:

> 'Subject to the provisions of this Schedule, no person shall in any area in which
> this Schedule is in force use any premises, vehicle, vessel or stall as a sex establishment
> except under and in accordance with the terms of a licence granted under this
> Schedule by the appropriate authority.'

I can go straight to para 20(1) of Sch 3, which, under the heading 'Enforcement',
provides:

'A person who—(a) knowingly uses, or knowingly causes or permits the use of, any premises, vehicle, vessel or stall contrary to paragraph 6 above . . . shall be guilty  a of an offence.'

It appears from para 22 of Sch 3 that the maximum penalty for the offence is a fine not exceeding £10,000. Finally, I must refer to para 26(1), which is concerned with offences by bodies corporate. It provides:

'Where an offence under this Schedule committed by a body corporate is proved  b to have been committed with the consent or connivance of, or to be attributable to any neglect on the part of, any director, manager, secretary or other similar officer of the body corporate, or any person who was purporting to act in any such capacity, he, as well as the body corporate, shall be guilty of the offence.'

In the present case Croyalgrange was charged under para 20(1) and Mr Grech was  c charged under para 26(1) of Sch 3.

I do not propose to go in any great detail into the facts set out in the case, because the question which is posed for our consideration is a question of law on the construction of the 1982 Act, and in particular of Sch 3. It was found by the magistrates that there was a certain establishment in Soho at 4 Peter Street which, on the facts found in the case, was plainly being used as a sex establishment. The premises were owned by Croyalgrange.  d There was in existence a lease to a Mr Buttigieg and it appears that there may at the relevant time have been a subtenancy by him to a Mr Thomas. At all events the premises were owned by Croyalgrange and Mr Grech was a director of that company. I understand that Mr Buttigieg was convicted of an offence under para 20(1) of Sch 3 of using the premises as a sex establishment without a licence.

I read the case as containing an implicit finding of fact by the stipendiary magistrate  e that at the material times Mr Grech did indeed know that the premises were being used as a sex establishment, but the crucial submission made on behalf of the two respondents was that, for a person to be guilty of an offence under para 20(1) or para 26(1), he must have known on the relevant dates not only that the premises were being used as a sex establishment but also that no licence was then in force for the premises granted by the Westminster City Council following its resolution making the whole of its area, including  f Soho, an area in respect of which the provisions of the 1982 Act applied, and further that they did not in fact know that no such licence was then in force for the premises in question.

The magistrate concluded that, although he had grounds for suspicion as to the knowledge of Mr Grech and through him of Croyalgrange, it was not proved to his satisfaction on the criminal burden of proof that there was knowledge on his part or on  g the part of Croyalgrange that there was no such licence then in force. However, it was also the submission of the prosecution that, on a true construction of the 1982 Act, all the prosecution had to prove was (1) that on the relevant date the premises in question were being used as a sex establishment and that there was no licence in force and (2) that the accused knew that the premises were being used as a sex establishment. The submission for the prosecution was that the element of knowledge specified in para 20  h of Sch 3 did not include knowledge of the absence of a licence.

The question we have to decide on this case is whether or not that submission is well founded. I have to say, with great respect to the magistrate, that the question posed for our consideration in the case, which was intended to raise that question, was not very aptly drawn. In this court, we have, by agreement, exercised our power to amend that question by deleting the question as posed by him and substituting the following  j question for our consideration:

'To constitute an offence contrary to paragraph 20(1)(a) of Schedule 3 of the Local Government (Miscellaneous Provisions) Act 1982, is it necessary for the prosecution to prove that the defendant knew that the use which he was making of the premises (or the use which he was causing or permitting others to make of the premises) was other than under and in accordance with the terms of a licence granted under the said Schedule 3 ?'

The submission of counsel for Westminster was to the effect that the word 'knowingly' in para 20(1)(a) of Sch 3 to the Act was directed towards the element in para 6(1) of the fact of the premises in question being used as a sex establishment. He submitted, as he had done before the magistrate, that it was not necessary for the prosecution to prove knowledge of the absence of a licence. He submitted that the purpose of the introduction of the requirement of knowledge in para 20(1)(a) was to prevent persons being held responsible for permitting the use of premises in circumstances when, unknown to them, acts had been committed on the premises which caused the premises to fall within the words 'sex establishment' as defined in the Act. For example, a person might run a perfectly innocent newsagent's business and unknown to him the manager of one of his shops might be selling pornographic literature or videos over, or rather under, the counter. Counsel submits that that was in reality the kind of matter towards which the requirement of knowledge in the statute was directed.

I approach the matter as follows. Here we have an offence which expressly includes the word 'knowingly'. The word 'knowingly' in para 20(1)(a) is attached not only to the words 'causes or permits the use of, any premises, vehicle, vessel or stall contrary to paragraph 6 above', but also to the word 'uses'. Prima facie, as a matter of ordinary construction, when the word 'knowingly' is so introduced in a provision of this kind, it required knowledge by the accused of each of the facts constituting the actus reus of the offence. On that basis, it would follow that, in the present case, a person who is accused of an offence under para 20(1)(a) must have knowledge not only of the fact that the premises in question are being used as a sex establishment but also that they are unlicenced. Furthermore, I feel bound to say that this strikes me as being a perfectly sensible construction to place on this paragraph. It seems to me that, if there is indeed an honest belief on the part of a defendant, eg a landlord, that there is in force a valid licence for the premises in question, it is not at all unreasonable that Parliament should have decided that he should not be guilty of an offence under the sub-paragraph.

However, counsel for Westminster urged us to look at para 6(1). He drew our attention to the fact that it provides:

'No person shall in any area in which this Schedule is in force use any premises . . . as a sex establishment except under and in accordance with the terms of a licence granted under this Schedule by the appropriate authority.'

Counsel submitted that this is a case where the actus reus is the use of the premises as a sex establishment, but that there is engrafted on that an exception in the case of circumstances where a licence has been granted.

Counsel also reminded us of those cases where offences are drawn in this way and in consequence the prosecution does not have to produce prima facie evidence of the absence of a licence for advancing its case in court, the burden resting on the defence to produce evidence of the existence of the licence. He referred us in particular to *R v Edwards* [1974] 2 All ER 1085, [1975] QB 27, in which the whole of that topic was considered at length by Lawton LJ in delivering the judgment of the Court of Appeal, Criminal Division.

It may well be that the present is such a case, although probably that does not now matter very much for the simple reason that, now the licensing system is under way, the question whether a licence is or is not in force for the relevant premises will be well known to, for example, the Westminster City Council, which is both the licensing authority and the prosecuting authority. But, assuming that to be so, in my judgment it does not have any impact on the question of construction with which we are concerned in the present case. We are not concerned here with the burden of proof, but with the question whether, as a matter of construction, the requirement of knowledge applies to both elements, ie the fact of use and the absence of a licence. I for my part do not find those cases of assistance.

We also had our attention drawn to *Brooks v Mason* [1902] 2 KB 743. That case arose under the Intoxicating Liquors (Sale to Children) Act 1901 and was concerned with the question whether on the facts of that case an offence had been committed under a section which prohibited persons from knowingly selling or delivering intoxicating liquor to a child under 14 except where such intoxicating liquor was sold or delivered in a vessel corked and sealed in the prescribed manner. The point in the case was whether a publican, who had delivered intoxicating liquor to a child under 14 in a vessel which was corked and which he believed to be sealed but which had not in fact been sealed in accordance with the manner prescribed in the statute, was guilty of an offence, despite his lack of knowledge of the fact that the vessel was not sealed. It was held that, on a true construction of that particular statute, he was guilty because, as Lord Alverstone CJ put it (at 747):

'I think the Act only intended to except intoxicating liquors sold or delivered in vessels which were in fact properly sealed and secured.'

I for my part feel that that case is not of assistance to us in the present case. We have in each case to construe the particular Act of Parliament in question, and I do not feel that the construction placed by the court on the different provisions of an Act of Parliament concerned with the sale or delivery of intoxicating liquor to children provides us with useful guidance on the problem of construction now before us. It is understandable that, in *Brooks v Mason*, the court should have considered that Parliament intended that a publican who delivered intoxicating liquor to a child must ensure that the container was corked and sealed in the prescribed manner, and the words in the relevant statute were so drafted as to be susceptible of being read in that sense. But, when I turn to the provisions of Sch 3 to the 1982 Act, I find the position to be different. The primary offence is established in para 20(1)(a), in which the word 'knowingly' appears: a person commits an offence if he knowingly uses, or knowingly causes or permits the use of, premises contrary to para 6. Premises are used contrary to para 6 if they are used as a sex establishment except under and in accordance with the terms of a licence. To me, on a natural reading of the words of Sch 3, the prohibited use is not just use as a sex establishment, but use as an unlicenced sex establishment; and only if a person knowingly so uses premises, or causes or permits such use of them, will he be guilty of an offence under para 20(1)(a). My reading of the words in these paragraphs of the schedule is consistent with the opinion I have already expressed, that I do not find it surprising that Parliament should have intended that, only if the defendant knew not only of the fact that the premises were being used as a sex establishment but also that they lacked the requisite licence, would he be guilty of an offence under the schedule. For my part therefore, I can see nothing in this Act of Parliament to persuade me that we should not apply the ordinary principle that, where it is required that an offence should have been knowingly committed, the requisite knowledge must embrace all the elements of the offence. I can see no reason here for departing from that ordinary approach as a matter of construction.

I would only add this. It is well established that, in cases where knowledge is required, knowledge may be proved not only by showing actual knowledge, but also by showing that the defendant in question has deliberately shut his eyes to obvious means of knowledge or deliberately refrained from making inquiries, the results of which he might not care to know. We were referred, very helpfully, by counsel for the respondents to the judgment of Devlin J in *Roper v Taylor's Central Garages (Exeter) Ltd* [1951] 2 TLR 284 at 288, in which in the course of his judgment he reaffirmed that proposition, and treated deliberately shutting one's eyes to obvious means of knowledge as being equivalent to actual knowledge. In a case such as the present, it is open to the prosecution, if there is difficulty in establishing actual knowledge, to rely where appropriate on that alternative type of knowledge. In many cases of the present kind, I cannot help but think that magistrates may have no difficulty in drawing the inference of actual knowledge or holding that there was a deliberate refraining by the defendant from making inquiries or shutting his eyes to obvious means of knowledge.

a However, we are not concerned with the question whether or not in the present case the magistrate was right to conclude that the prosecution had not proved the requisite knowledge on the part of the defendants. We are simply concerned to answer the question of law. I for my part, for the reasons I have given, would answer the question in its amended form in the affirmative. I would, therefore, dismiss the appeals.

**McCULLOUGH J.** I agree and for the same reasons. I would only add this, if it is not
b out of order to do so, having regard to the fact that neither counsel referred to the provision, that since the conclusion of the argument I have observed that para 20(1)(c) of Sch 3 to the Local Government (Miscellaneous Provisions) Act 1982 is so worded that, where a term or condition of a licence is contravened, the licence holder does not commit an offence unless he knew of the contravention. I believe that the requirement that knowledge be proved in that case supports the view that knowledge of the absence of any
c licence at all must be proved where the allegation is of an offence against para 20(1)(a).

*Appeal dismissed.*

*The court refused leave to appeal to the House of Lords but certified, under s 1(2) of the Administration of Justice Act 1960, that the following point of law of general public importance
d was involved in the decision: to constitute an offence contrary to para 20(1)(a) of Sch 3 to the Local Government (Miscellaneous Provisions) Act 1982, is it necessary for the prosecution to prove that the defendant knew that the use which he was making of the premises himself (or the use of which he was causing or permitting others to make of the premises) was other than under and in accordance with the terms of a licence granted under the said Sch 3?*

e *4 February 1985. The Appeal Committee of the House of Lords granted Westminster leave to appeal.*

Solicitors: *Terence F Neville* (for Westminster); *Irwin Shaw* (for the respondents).

Michael Wall Esq     Barrister.

f

# Re M (a minor)

COURT OF APPEAL, CIVIL DIVISION
CUMMING-BRUCE AND SLADE LJJ
g 8, 9, 10 OCTOBER, 9 NOVEMBER 1984

*Child – Care – Local authority – Wardship proceedings – Jurisdiction of High Court to make wardship order where child already subject of care order – Application by mother for child to be made ward of court – Local authority intending to terminate mother's access to child and to place child with long-term foster parents with a view to adoption – Whether grounds for invoking High
h Court's wardship jurisdiction – Whether powers of juvenile court adequate – Children Act 1975, s 14 – Child Care Act 1980, ss 12A to 12G.*

In May 1984 a mother gave birth to a boy who, because of the mother's condition, had to be placed in the charge of the local authority. When the child was a month old the local authority applied to a juvenile court for a care order. The authority informed the court
i that in its opinion there was no realistic prospect of the child being rehabilitated with the mother and that if the care order were granted it intended to terminate access by the mother and place him with long-term foster parents with a view to adoption. However, the social worker who had been appointed the boy's guardian ad litem stated that, although she was in favour of him remaining with the authority for the time being, she recommended that there should be a future assessment of the mother's condition and a programme aimed at gradually rehabilitating her with the child. The mother applied in

the proceedings for the child to be returned to her forthwith. The juvenile court dismissed her application and made the care order. The mother applied to the High $a$ Court to have the child made a ward of court. The question arose whether the High Court could assume jurisdiction because there was a lacuna in the powers of the juvenile court making it necessary for the High Court to supplement the juvenile court's powers. The mother contended that the juvenile court was unable to give effect to the guardian ad litem's recommendations because it only had power to make or refuse a care order and could not impose conditions in a care order. The judge dismissed the mother's $b$ application on the ground that the juvenile court had adequate powers to deal with the situation under ss 12A to 12G$^a$ of the Child Care Act 1980 since, if after the care order had been made the local authority served on the mother notice to terminate access under s 12B, she would have the right under s 12C to ask the juvenile court for an access order and that court would have power to make an order giving her access to the child. The mother appealed, contending that the judge had been wrong to equate the powers of the $c$ juvenile court under ss 12A to 12G with the powers of the High Court in wardship, because, inter alia, (i) the juvenile court could not make an order under s 12C if such an order would frustrate a local authority's long-term plans for a child in its care and (ii) the juvenile court had no power of control over the local authority's decision to place the child with long-term foster parents with a view to adoption.

$d$

**Held** – There were no grounds for invoking the High Court's wardship jurisdiction, since the juvenile court had adequate powers to deal with the situation under ss 12A to 12G of the 1980 Act and s 14$^b$ of the Children Act 1975, in that it could, under s 12C of the 1980 Act, if it considered it appropriate, make an access order contrary to the wishes of the local authority, and by virtue of s 14 of the 1975 Act the child could not be freed for adoption until the local authority had obtained the consent of the magistrates' court. $e$ Accordingly the mother's appeal would be dismissed (see p 750 $f$ to $h$, p 752 $f g$, p 755 $a$ to $e$ and p 756 $a b$ and $d$ to p 757 $a$, post).

M v Humberside CC [1979] 2 All ER 744 and A v Liverpool City Council [1981] 2 All ER 385 considered.

**Notes**

For wardship jurisdiction, local authority powers and magistrates' courts' powers, see 24 $f$ Halsbury's Laws (4th edn) paras 580–581, and for cases on wardship jurisdiction, see 28(2) Digest (Reissue) 911–916, 2220–2247.

For the Children Act 1975, s 14, see 45 Halsbury's Statutes (3rd edn) 687.

For the Child Care Act 1980, ss 12A to 12G (as inserted by the Health and Social Services and Social Security Adjudications Act 1983, s 6, Sch 1, Pt I), see 53 ibid 698. $g$

**Cases referred to in judgments**

A v Liverpool City Council [1981] 2 All ER 385, [1982] AC 363, [1981] 2 WLR 948, HL.

E (S A) (a minor) (wardship), Re [1984] 1 All ER 289, [1984] 1 WLR 156, HL.

F (wardship: adoption), Re [1984] FLR 60, CA.

J (a minor) (wardship: jurisdiction), Re [1984] 1 All ER 29, [1984] 1 WLR 81, CA. $h$

M v Humberside CC [1979] 2 All ER 744, [1979] Fam 114, [1979] 3 WLR 234.

---

$a$   Sections 12A to 12G, so far as material, are set out at p 754 $b$ to $j$, post
$b$   Section 14, so far as material, provides:
     '(1) Where, on an application by an approved adoption society or local authority, an authorised court is satisfied in the case of each parent or guardian of the child that—(a) he freely, and with $j$ full understanding of what is involved, agreed generally and unconditionally to the making of an adoption order, or (b) his agreement to the making of an adoption order should be dispensed with on a ground specified in section 12(2), the court shall, subject to subsection (5), make an order declaring the child free for adoption.
     (2) No application shall be made under subsection (1) unless—(a) it is made with the consent of a parent or guardian of the child . . .'

**Interlocutory appeal**

*a* On 28 May 1984 a place of safety order was obtained by the Berkshire County Council (the local authority) in respect of a baby boy born on that day. The mother was allowed supervised access. On 18 July 1984 magistrates sitting at Reading Juvenile Court made a care order under s 1(2)(b) of the Children and Young Persons Act 1969 in favour of the local authority. By an originating summons dated 8 August 1984 the mother applied to have the child made a ward of court. The local authority opposed the application. On 24 *b* August 1984 Bush J dismissed the summons and dewarded the child. The mother appealed. The facts are set out in the judgment of Cumming-Bruce LJ.

*Lionel Swift QC* and *Diane Barnett* for the mother.
*Mhairi McNab* for the local authority.

*c*                                                                  *Cur adv vult*

9 November. The following judgments were delivered.

**CUMMING-BRUCE LJ.** This is an appeal by a mother of a minor born on 28 May 1984 against the order of Bush J, who decided in wardship proceedings instituted by the mother that the minor should be dewarded. The minor was in the care of the local *d* authority, which gave an undertaking to the judge not to remove the minor to long-term foster parents pending the appeal of the mother to this court.

*The general law*
In this court the appellant accepts that the judge accurately summarised the law governing the conditions in which the court will assume its jurisdiction so as to intervene *e* in the way in which a local authority exercises the powers conferred on it by statute in relation to a minor whom it has in its care. Bush J, after referring to *A v Liverpool City Council* [1981] 2 All ER 385, [1982] AC 363, correctly summarised the relevant passages in the judgment of Baker P in *M v Humberside CC* [1979] 2 All ER 744 at 751, [1979] Fam 114 at 123, where the President said:

*f*      'Now ... it seems to me that the High Court will assume jurisdiction only in limited circumstances. First, if the powers of the lower court require to be supplemented, that is to say, where its powers are inadequate. Second, if there has been some irregularity or excess in the exercise of the powers of the local authority, and, third, the composite head, if there is something exceptional, something really unusual about the case which necessitates the intervention of the High Court.'
*g*
For the next five years the wardship jurisdiction was exercised in cases in which a parent was seeking rehabilitation of a child who clearly had to remain for the present in the care of a local authority. If there was an issue whether rehabilitation was practicable, the juvenile court had no power to impose conditions as to access. Wardship proceedings were necessary to supplement the powers of the magistrates. These cases became known *h* as 'lacuna' cases.
The judge decided in the instant case that there was no lacuna in the powers of the juvenile court, and that there was no exceptional feature calling for his intervention in the wardship jurisdiction. The mother appeals on the grounds that both decisions were wrong.

*j* *Are the powers of the juvenile court still inadequate?*
This issue arose because the social worker appointed as guardian ad litem of the minor recommended to the juvenile court that the present condition of the mother, considered in the light of her history, pointed to the solution that the child should remain in the care of the local authority, but that there should be a further assessment of the mother's condition and capacity, and a programme aimed at gradual rehabilitation with increasing

access commensurate with the mother's prospects of recovery. This recommendation was, in the view of the guardian ad litem, supported by psychiatric evidence called on her behalf. The local authority, on the other hand, had declared at the beginning of the case in the juvenile court that its plan for the baby was to place him with long-term foster parents with a view to adoption and to terminate access to his mother. Its case before the magistrates was that there was really no prospect of rehabilitating the child with his mother. The mother's case was that the child should return to her forthwith. The magistrates simply announced their decision that the child should remain in the care of the local authority without giving any indication of their view about the recommendations of the guardian ad litem as to the prospects of rehabilitation, access, or postponement of placement of the baby with long-term foster parents.

Before Bush J it was argued on behalf of the mother that this was just the kind of situation in which there was a lacuna in the powers of the juvenile court of the kind illustrated in a number of decisions in the Family Division and this court, and by the decision and reasoning of the House of Lords in *Re E (S A) (a minor) (wardship)* [1984] 1 All ER 289, [1984] 1 WLR 156. The judge decided that there was no longer any lacuna in the powers of the court because it had been filled by the legislation about parents' rights on termination of access, which gave new powers to the juvenile court and, on appeal, to the High Court and which was brought into force on 30 January 1984 (see the Health and Social Services and Social Security Adjudications Act 1983 (Commencement No 2) Order 1983, SI 1983/1862). The judge added that there is another protection for a parent in this position provided by the 'Code of Practice, Access to Children in Care' laid before Parliament on 16 December 1983.

Counsel for the mother (the appellant) has submitted that the judge was wrong in his conclusion that the new powers added, as ss 12A to 12G to the Child Care Act 1980, by the Health and Social Services and Social Security Adjudications Act 1983, Sch 1, Pt I, and accompanied by the guidance given by the Departments in the code of practice, have the practical effect of giving the juvenile court the same effective powers as could be wielded by the High Court in the wardship jurisdiction. He rested this submission on three main grounds for regarding the new provisions as inadequate to enable the juvenile court, or the High Court on appeal, to protect and to promote the welfare of the child as effectively as the High Court in its wardship jurisdiction. (1) As a matter of construction ss 12A to 12G of the Child Care Act 1980 are only intended to deal with access consistent with the local authority's plan for long-term care of the minor. The new provisions were not intended to be applied in such a way as to frustrate a local authority's plans for the child. Therefore a juvenile court would not contemplate ordering access in a situation in which the local authority regarded rehabilitation as impracticable. (2) Even if this is wrong, a parent's right to apply to the juvenile court only arises after the local authority has first given notice of termination of access, and there is no such right as long as some access continues, however inadequate, to prepare the child for rehabilitation. Further, by the statutory form of the notice of termination of access that the local authority now has to give, the parent has six months in which to apply. This interval of time may have a crucial and prejudicial effect on the child for whom long-term plans may be postponed for a length of time inconsistent with his needs. (3) The arrangements for preparing a child for adoption by placing him with long-term foster parents with a view to adoption raise issues wider than those dealt with by ss 12A to 12G of the Child Care Act 1980.

On the first point I can see no reason, as a matter of construction, to accept the restricted meaning advanced by counsel for the mother. In their natural meaning the words are wide enough to contemplate refusal of access for any reason, including the reason that future rehabilitation has to be recognised as impracticable having regard to the needs of the child. The Health and Social Services and Social Security Adjudications Act 1983 was given the royal assent on 13 May 1983. By that date there had been a series of judicial decisions in which the existence of a lacuna in the powers of the juvenile court had been explained in the sense that the court had no power, when making an order committing the care of a child to a local authority, to control in any way the decision of a the local authority to terminate access, thus preventing a parent from getting any judicial control over a programme for future rehabilitation of a child with his parents, save by resort to the wardship jurisdiction. In my view there is a strong presumption that by 1983 Parliament was well aware of this line of judicial pronouncement, continuing unabated since Baker P's judgment in 1979 in M v Humberside CC [1979] 2 All ER 744, [1979] Fam 114, and decided to increase the powers of the juvenile court in order to lose the well-recognised gap in existing powers. And these judicial pronouncements

b amounted to a call for new legislation designed to confer on the juvenile court powers enabling that court to take the decision when a parent took issue with a local authority on rehabilitation as a reason for continued access. As an aid to construction I would also think it right if it were necessary to have regard to para 4 of the code of practice for access to children in care, which specifically envisages that a parent may apply to the juvenile court after notice to terminate access, because there is no realistic hope of rehabilitation.

c The code of practice was prepared by the Secretaries of State pursuant to a duty imposed on them by s 12G(1). By s 12G(3) provision is made for laying copies of the code and of any alteration before Parliament, and either House of Parliament may require them to withdraw it. The current code was placed before Parliament on 16 December 1983, and the new ss 12A to 12G were brought into force by statutory instrument on 30 January 1984, save for s 12F(3) and (4) dealing with appointment of, and rules for, the

d guardian ad litem, which came into force on 27 May 1984 (see SI 1983/1862). In these circumstances it is unlikely that Parliament would have allowed the code of practice to be published in the form laid before it if the right of a parent to apply to the juvenile court on receipt of notice of termination of access did not arise in the circumstances which most urgently called for judicial control, ie the case of the parent seeking access with a view to rehabilitation.

e As to the second point taken by counsel for the mother, the provisions of ss 12B and 12C are evidently framed by the legislature so as to impose on the local authority the duty to take formal steps giving notice to a parent, guardian or custodian of a decision to terminate or to refuse to make arrangements for access, and thereafter to give the parent the right to a judicial decision.

The serious content of the proceedings is underlined by the provision that an appeal

f from the juvenile court is not to the Crown Court but to the High Court. The period of six months running from the date of service of notice of termination is evidently contemplated as the period which reconciles, as far as practicable, the urgency of the needs of the child with the reasonable requirement of the parents for time to decide on their course of action. On the facts of the instant appeal, this time period could not be a reason for intervention by the wardship judge. The local authority announced its

g intention to refuse access if the juvenile court confirmed its care of the child. The care order having been made, the local authority has served notice of termination dated 6 September 1984 on the mother. The fact that she might decide to wait for six months before applying to the juvenile court against the refusal could not possibly be a ground for continuing the wardship. Whether it could ever be a good ground in another case it is unnecessary for us to speculate. I should think it very unlikely.

h Counsel for the mother is right in his submission that the new legislation dealing with access does not itself clothe the juvenile court and the High Court on appeal with all the powers which effectively give them the powers of a wardship judge. The court also needs powers over a decision of a local authority to place a child with long-term foster parents with a view to adoption. In the case of a child who is a ward of court the local authority must obtain the leave of the wardship judge before so placing the child (see the decision

i of this court in Re F (wardship: adoption) [1984] FLR 60). But the answer is simply that since 27 May 1984 the court has had the relevant power. On that day s 14 of the Children Act 1975 at last was brought into force after lying dormant on the statute book for nine years. It may be that Bush J referred only to ss 12A to 12G of the Child Care Act 1980 merely by inadvertence. It is more likely that he was directing his mind specifically to the legislation dealing with access because that was the issue most prominently before him for consideration. The law now clearly imposes two duties on a local authority which intends, as does this local authority, to place the child as soon as possible with *a* foster parents with a view to adoption. It must bring access to an end if, as in this case, that is a condition precedent to successful adoption of a very young child. To that end it must comply with s 12B of the Child Care Act 1980. It must also, before placing the child with long-term foster parents with a view to adoption, comply with s 14 of the Children Act 1975.

That section was brought into force by the Children Act 1975 and the Adoption Act *b* 1976 (Commencement Order) 1983, SI 1983/1946. By para 8 of Sch 2 thereto the words 'approved adoption society or local authority' are to be substituted for the words 'adoption agency' in s 14, and for the word 'agency' there is substituted the words 'society or authority'. The local authority therefore has to make application to an authorised court. 'Authorised court' is construed by s 100 of the 1975 Act to be—

> '(a) the High Court; (b) the county court within whose district the child is, and, *c* in the case of an application under section 14, any county court within whose district a parent or guardian of the child is; (c) any other county court prescribed by rules made under section 102 of the County Courts Act 1959; (d) a magistrates' court within whose area the child is and, in the case of an application under section 14, a magistrates' court within whose area a parent or guardian of the child is.'

*d*
(See sub-s (2).)

The procedure is prescribed by the Magistrates' Courts (Adoption) Rules 1984, SI 1984/611, which came into operation on 27 May 1984. The proceedings are domestic proceedings within the meaning of s 65 of the Magistrates' Courts Act 1980, and the court must be composed in accordance with the provisions of that Act which relate to a court hearing domestic proceedings.

*e*
There is nothing to lead me to expect that a local authority will be dilatory in making an application to free a child in its care for adoption. The code of practice emphasises the importance of speed in the administration of business relating to children. I see no reason why the new powers of the courts should not be invoked and exercised without undue periods of delay.

My conclusion on this ground of appeal is that the combined effect of Pt I of Sch 1 to *f* the Health and Social Services and Social Security Adjudications Act 1983 and the statutory instrument bringing into operation the provisions of s 14 of the Children Act 1975 confer on the courts all the powers necessary to fill the lacuna which before 28 May 1984 gave rise to judicial concern. It is unlikely that it will again be necessary, in the absence of some really exceptional factor, to exercise the wardship jurisdiction in order to afford judicial control over decisions or action taken by local authorities in connection *g* with the termination of access or preparation for placing a child in care with long-term foster parents with a view to adoption. Counsel for the mother submitted that a case might occur in which a local authority might continue access, but only at long intervals and so give rise to a situation in which the parent might be frustrated in seeking access of the frequency appropriate to a programme for rehabilitation which the local authority thought quite impracticable. That is not this case. If it arises, the facts might have to be *h* considered in wardship proceedings.

*Is this an exceptional case requiring intervention of the wardship court?*
The other ground on which the mother relies rests on submissions particular to the conduct of the proceedings before the juvenile court. Before the juvenile court the infant *j* was legally represented by a solicitor. The guardian ad litem had submitted her report in writing to the juvenile court. Therein she restricted herself to a provisional recommendation, because she had not at the date of submitting her report seen the most recent psychiatric reports on the mother. She provisionally recommended that the child should be offered an opportunity for rehabilitation with his mother at that early stage of

his development, whilst retaining certain safeguards, rather than undergo a further move
a   to a long-term foster home with a view to adoption.
    The proceedings were heard over four days. We have admitted a note, taken by counsel
for the mother before the magistrates, of the oral representations made by the guardian
ad litem personally after the evidence had ended. She then stated that she would prefer a
care order in favour of the local authority with a view to future assessment of the
prospects of rehabilitation. She did not favour long-term fostering at that stage. She said
b   that the door should not be closed completely on the mother. I would interpret these
recommendations as pointing to a continuation of some access. When the solicitor for
the infant addressed the magistrates, we are told, and accept that he said, that he opposed
the mother's application for return of the child to her forthwith, and accepted on the
evidence that the child should remain in local authority care. He made no submission
about rehabilitation, in spite of the recommendation of the guardian ad litem. Counsel
c   for the mother submitted that therein his conduct was irregular, as, under the rules,
where the infant is legally represented, the solicitor must accept the instructions of the
guardian ad litem. Counsel for the mother submits that the solicitor should have
represented to the magistrates that the guardian ad litem opposed a care order involving
placement of the child with long-term foster parents, and that was the only plan that the
local authority had announced to the magistrates as their intention if a care order was
d   made. This irregularity by the solicitor is said to have created an exceptional situation in
that it contributed to the outcome, when the bench simply stated that the child was to
remain in the care of the local authority without saying anything about the guardian ad
litem's recommendation in favour of short-term, but against long-term, fostering.
    The rules which prescribe the rights and duties of a guardian ad litem appointed under
r 14A of the Magistrates' Courts (Children and Young Persons) Rules 1970, SI 1970/1792
e   (as added by SI 1976/1769) or under s 32B(1) of the Children and Young Persons Act 1969
(as added by the Children Act 1975, s 64) are the Magistrates' Courts (Children and
Young Persons) (Amendment) Rules 1984, SI 1984/567, which substituted new paras (2),
(4), (6) and (7) in r 14A (as added), and which came into operation on 27 May 1984. By
paras (6) and (7) of r 14A it is provided:

f         '(6) The guardian *ad litem* appointed under this rule or section 32B(1) of the Act
      of 1969, with a view to safeguarding the interests of the relevant infant before the
      court shall—(a) so far as is reasonably practicable, investigate all circumstances
      relevant to the proceedings and for that purpose shall interview such persons, inspect
      such records and obtain such professional assistance as the guardian *ad litem* thinks
      appropriate; (b) regard as the first and paramount consideration the need to safeguard
g         and promote the infant's best interests until he achieves adulthood, and shall take
      into account the wishes and feelings of the infant, having regard to his age and
      understanding, and shall ensure that those wishes and feelings are made known to
      the court; (c) except where a solicitor has been instructed to represent the infant
      before the appointment of the guardian *ad litem* or a direction has been given in
      accordance with paragraph (4) of this rule that a solicitor be instructed, obtain the
h         views of the court as to whether the infant should be legally represented and, unless
      the court otherwise directs, instruct a solicitor to represent the infant; (d) consider
      how the case should be presented on behalf of the infant, acting in conjunction with
      the solicitor in a case in which one has been instructed (whether by the guardian *ad
      litem* or otherwise) to represent the infant; and shall, in such a case, instruct the
      solicitor (unless the solicitor considers, having taken into account the views of the
      guardian *ad litem*, that the infant wishes to give instructions which conflict with
      those of the guardian *ad litem* and that he is able, having regard to his age and
      understanding, to give such instructions on his own behalf); (e) seek the views of
      the court in any case where difficulties arise in relation to the performance of his
      duties; (f) as soon as practicable make a report in writing to the court for the
      purposes of rule 20(1)(a); (g) perform such other duties as the court may direct.

(7) When the court has finally disposed of the case the guardian *ad litem* shall consider, acting in conjunction with the solicitor in a case in which the infant is *a* legally represented, whether it would be in the infant's best interests to appeal to the Crown Court and, if it is considered that it would be, he shall ensure that notice of appeal is given on behalf of the infant (unless the solicitor, in a case in which the infant is legally represented, considers, having taken into account the views of the guardian *ad litem*, that the infant wishes to give instructions which conflict with those of the guardian *ad litem* and that he is able, having regard to his age and *b* understanding, to give such instructions on his own behalf).'

The guardian ad litem had in her concluding oral representation recommended that she would prefer a care order in favour of the local authority with a view to future assessment of the prospects of rehabilitation, and short-term as opposed to long-term fostering. Counsel for the mother submits that on a proper construction of r 14A(6)(d) it was the duty of the solicitor for the infant to submit to the magistrates that he opposed *c* the application of the local authority for a care order because the only care order that the guardian ad litem recommended was one that included conditions designed to provide for future assessment of prospects of rehabilitation and for short-term fostering. I observe that this allegation that the solicitor for the infant failed to accept the instructions of the guardian ad litem is not made by the guardian ad litem.

The solicitor for the infant had inquired whether it would be necessary for him to *d* appear in the wardship proceedings, but neither he nor the guardian ad litem took part in them. The guardian ad litem is not a party to this appeal. If this court considered that she ought to have been a party, it would have taken the appropriate action. In my view the submission to this court that the solicitor failed to act on the instructions of the guardian ad litem is misconceived. The solicitor for the infant and not the social worker appointed as guardian ad litem had the responsibility of deciding on the infant's behalf *e* how to reconcile the recommendations of the guardian ad litem with the statutory powers of the juvenile court. In the proceedings before it the juvenile court could only make or refuse a care order. An adjournment in order to assess the prospects of rehabilitation would have been quite wrong, having regard to the new powers of the juvenile court in proceedings brought before it under s 12B of the Child Care Act 1980 and s 14 of the Children Act 1975. The solicitor for the infant carried out the instructions *f* of the guardian ad litem correctly, and there is no material before us to suggest the contrary. There is nothing exceptional about this case.

For these reasons I would move that the appeal be dismissed.

**SLADE LJ.** I respectfully agree with the judgment of Cumming-Bruce LJ, but will add *g* something of my own since this case seems to me to raise issues of some general interest and importance in cases where disputes arise between a local authority and a parent concerning the care of a child.

In June and July 1984 the juvenile court heard an application by the respondent local authority seeking a care order in respect of the minor who was then just over one month old. At the hearing the local authority indicated to the magistrates that in its view there *h* was no realistic prospect of rehabilitating the child with the mother, and that, if the order was granted, it intended to terminate access and to place him with long-term foster parents with a view to adoption. However, the guardian ad litem of the child in her oral evidence indicated her personal opinion that, while the child should for the time being remain with the local authority, there should be a phased programme aimed at eventual rehabilitation with the mother. The mother herself sought an order for the return of the *j* child to her, coupled with a supervision order.

On 18 July 1984 the magistrates made the care order sought by the local authority. I think that on this appeal three points have been common ground. Firstly, if the magistrates had expressly stated that they had considered the guardian ad litem's representations and rejected them on their merits, there could have been no question of any party thereafter seeking to challenge the magistrates' decision by way of wardship proceedings, though the ordinary right of appeal to the Crown Court would have been available. Secondly, if, before the magistrates gave their decision, the local authority had not indicated to them its future intentions with regard to the child, the mother could not have successfully invoked wardship proceedings to challenge a subsequently announced intention by the local authority to place the child with long-term foster parents with a view to adoption. Any such challenge would have been met by the decision in *A v Liverpool City Council* [1981] 2 All ER 385, [1982] AC 363, which ordinarily precludes the invocation of wardship proceedings as a means of interfering with the exercise by local authorities of discretions entrusted to them by statute relating to the welfare of children within their care.

Thirdly, however, there are at least two well-recognised qualifications to the general principle stated in *A v Liverpool City Council*. The High Court may be prepared to assume jurisdiction in wardship if either (1) there is a 'lacuna' in the powers of the lower court, which renders it appropriate that those powers should be supplemented by the exercise of the wardship jurisdiction, or (2) there is something exceptional about the case which necessitates the intervention of the High Court. In this context Cumming-Bruce LJ has already referred to a well-known passage from the judgment of Baker P in *M v Humberside CC* [1979] 2 All ER 744 at 751, [1979] Fam 114 at 123.

On 8 August 1984 the mother issued an originating summons seeking to make the child a ward of court. Bush J by his order of 24 August 1984 dewarded the child and dismissed the mother's application. On this appeal the mother's submissions in essence are that he was wrong to do so because this is a lacuna case and/or an exceptional case in the senses described above. Cumming-Bruce LJ in his judgment has already explained the reasons why it is submitted on behalf of the mother that this is an exceptional case requiring the intervention of the wardship court. I do not wish to add to his reasons for rejecting that submission, with which I agree. My own observations will be directed to the submission that this is a 'lacuna' case.

It is clear that when the magistrates came to give their decision on 18 July 1984 the choice of courses open to them was a limited one. On the facts as they then stood, there was no practical possibility of sending the child back to the mother without a supervision order. Even if they had entirely agreed with the guardian ad litem's views that the child should remain with the local authority but a phased rehabilitation should be attempted, they would have had no power to make directions designed to achieve that end. For practical purposes there were only two courses open to them, namely, either to send the child back to the mother under the protection of a supervision order or to make the care order sought by the local authority.

Counsel for the mother, in his very persuasive argument, has submitted that there was a relevant lacuna in the powers of the juvenile court. For it might be that the magistrates agreed with the opinion of the guardian ad litem as to the desirability of a rehabilitation, but found themselves fettered by the lack of any power to give practical effect to her recommendations. In this context he drew our attention to the decision of this court in *Re J (a minor) (wardship: jurisdiction)* [1984] 1 All ER 29, [1984] 1 WLR 81, on the facts of which it was accepted that, in respect of an application to a juvenile court for the discharge of a care order, there was a lacuna in the statutory scheme, because if the magistrates thought it right in principle to discharge the order, they had no statutory power to impose conditions relating to the return of the child to its parents. Sir George Baker, in his judgment in the latter case ([1984] 1 All ER 29 at 35, [1984] 1 WLR 81 at 88), stressed that—

> 'It would be quite different ... if [the magistrates] decided, and appeared to decide, to dismiss the application on the true merits of the mother's case.'

In the present case counsel for the mother pointed out that the magistrates gave no indication that they rejected the guardian ad litem's views as to an attempted rehabilitation. For the purposes of this appeal I am content to assume that the magistrates did *not* reject these views on their merits.

On this assumption there would, in any opinion, have been considerable force in the submission that there was a relevant lacuna in the power of the magistrates in the present case, if it had not been for the new provisions relating to access to children in care inserted after s 12 of the Child Care Act 1980 by the Health and Social Services and Social Security Adjudications Act 1983. The new provisions came into force on 30 January 1984 (see SI 1983/1862) and, as I understand them, were specifically intended to introduce a significant exception to the general principle stated in *A v Liverpool City Council* [1981] 2 All ER 385, [1982] AC 363, as I have described it above.

It is perhaps worth setting out a few of these new provisions. Section 12A makes the provisions applicable 'to any child in the care of a local authority in consequence . . . of a care order' otherwise than 'in consequence of an order made by the High Court'. Section 12B (so far as material) provides:

'(1) A local authority may not terminate arrangements for access to a child to whom this Part of this Act applies by its parent, guardian or custodian, or refuse to make such arrangements unless they have first given the parent, guardian or custodian notice of termination or refusal in a form prescribed by order made by the Secretary of State.

(2) A notice under this section shall contain a statement that the parent, guardian or custodian has a right to apply to a court for an order under section 12C below.

(3) A notice terminating access shall state that access will be terminated as from the date of service of the notice.

(4) A local authority are not to be taken to terminate access for the purpose of this section in a case where they propose to substitute new arrangements for access for existing arrangements.

(5) A local authority are not to be taken to refuse to make arrangements for access for the purposes of this section in a case where they postpone access for such reasonable period as appears to them to be necessary to enable them to consider what arrangements for access (if any) are to be made . . .'

Section 12C provides:

'(1) A parent, guardian or custodian on whom a notice under section 12B above is served may apply for an order under this section (in this Part of this Act referred to as an "access order").

(2) An application under subsection (1) above shall be made by way of complaint to an appropriate juvenile court.

(3) An access order shall be an order requiring the authority to allow the child's parent, guardian or custodian access to the child subject to such conditions as the order may specify with regard to commencement, frequency, duration or place of access or to any other matter for which it appears to the court that provision ought to be made in connection with the requirement to allow access.

(4) A juvenile court is an appropriate juvenile court for the purposes of this Part of the Act if it has jurisdiction in the area of the authority serving the notice under section 12B above.

(5) An appeal shall be to the High Court against any decision of a juvenile court under this Part of this Act.'

Section 12G provides that the Secretary of State shall prepare and lay before Parliament 'a code of practice with regard to access to children in care'. Pursuant to this section, a code of practice was duly prepared, laid before Parliament and came into force on 30 January 1984.

It must be assumed that in making their order of 18 July 1984 the magistrates would have been well aware of the provisions of the Child Care Act 1980 to which I have referred and of the events which could reasonably be expected to follow the making of a care order. Thus, in my opinion, they could reasonably have anticipated that the following consequences would be likely to ensue. (1) Pursuant to s 12B, the local authority would be likely to serve a notice terminating the subsisting arrangements for access to the child by the mother. (2) The mother would then be likely to apply to the juvenile court for an 'access order' under s 12C. (3) The juvenile court, on hearing that application, would have full power in the proper exercise of its discretion, if it thought fit, to override the wishes of the local authority by making an order requiring it to allow the mother access 'subject to such conditions as the order may specify with regard to commencement, frequency, duration or place of access or to any other mattter for which it appears to the court that provision ought to be made in connection with the requirement to allow access' (s 12C(3)). (4) The magistrates would thus be in a position on an application for an access order, if they thought fit, effectively to scotch any plans of the local authority for long-term fostering with a view to adoption (subject to any appeal to the High Court under s 12C(5)).

Prima facie, therefore, I can see no reason why for practical purposes the magistrates should have regarded themselves as being hampered by any lacuna in their powers when making the care order, even if they had been in sympathy with the guardian ad litem's views regarding the desirability of an attempt at rehabilitation (as, for present purposes, I am content to assume they may possibly have been). Prima facie they could have anticipated that these views could be given practical effect, so far as appropriate, on a subsequent application by the mother for an access order.

Counsel for the mother, however, has suggested that the juvenile court, on considering an application for an access order relating to a child in care, will be bound to proceed on the basis that an unappealed care order is in force and, accordingly, on the assumption that it cannot properly introduce access arrangements if these will frustrate the long-term care planned for a child by a local authority. This suggestion raises what seems to me an important question of principle. If well-founded, it would impose an important limit on the powers of juvenile courts when dealing with applications for access orders under s 12C. In my opinion, however, it is not well founded. First, the discretion conferred on the court by s 12C(3) is in terms very wide and by its very nature exercisable contrary to the wishes of the local authority. Second, the code of practice itself expressly contemplates that an application for an access order by a parent may be made, and may succeed, in a case where the intention of the local authority is to place a child with 'a permanent substitute family'. Thus, para 4 of the code reads as follows:

'There will, however, be some circumstances in which local authorities conclude after careful consideration that access is not in the child's best interests. This may happen because there are clear indications that access is damaging to the child or because it must be recognised that there is no realistic hope of rehabilitation and the child's future lies with a permanent substitute family. The local authority may conclude that termination of access is an essential part of such a plan for a child. Where a decision is made to terminate access—or, exceptionally, to refuse access from the outset—the local authority is required by section 12B of the Child Care Act 1980 to serve notice on the parents before access is terminated. The parents have a right to apply to the juvenile court for an order requiring the local authority to grant access.'

Since the publication of this code is envisaged by s 12G of the 1980 Act and it has been laid before Parliament in accordance with that section, it is, in my opinion, permissible to refer to it as an aid in the construction of s 12C. Thus, it reinforces my opinion that, in exercising the wide discretion given to it under s 12C on an application for an access order, the juvenile court should not regard itself as inhibited by the fact that a care order has already been made. The views and wishes of the local authority as regards the child's future are, of course, entitled to great respect, but all other relevant factors brought to the court's attention must be given due weight. In short, the juvenile court, in exercising the discretion conferred on it by the 1980 Act, is not inhibited by the principle stated in *A v Liverpool City Council* [1981] 2 All ER 385, [1982] AC 363. A legislative purpose of the section, I infer, was to provide a specific exception to that principle. I therefore cannot accept the suggestion that a juvenile court could not properly make an access order in a case where the local authority regards rehabilitation as impracticable.

Counsel for the mother made a number of penetrating observations on the wording of the new provisions of s 12 of the 1980 Act. He questioned whether the wording of s 12c(3) would be wide enough to give the magistrates the power to make all the particular directions which they might wish to make in any given case (for example, in regard to psychiatric assistance for a parent). He pointed out that, under the prescribed form of 'notice of termination' (see s 12B), a parent has six months within which to apply for an access order, so that delays and uncertainties prejudicial to the child might be occasioned during the period before it was known whether or not the parent intended to apply. He observed that the rights conferred by s 12c are conferred only on a 'parent, guardian or custodian' and are not available, for example, to grandparents. He observed that the parent's right to apply under s 12c only arises after he or she has received a notice terminating access and that in view of s 12B(4) a local authority might conceivably be able to avoid the need to serve any such notice by proposing new arrangements for quite minimal access.

I appreciate that all or any of these points might in other cases conceivably give rise to problems which might justify the intervention of the High Court by way of wardship, on the grounds that a relevant lacuna existed. With all respect to counsel for the mother's argument, however, I am not persuaded that any relevant lacuna has yet been shown on the facts of the present case. The local authority, as anticipated, has served its notice terminating access on the mother. She accordingly has her right to apply for an access order under s 12c. If, contrary to my present expectation, the parties' respective legal advisers, or indeed the magistrates themselves in the light of the circumstances which exist when that application falls to be determined, were to take the view that a new lacuna situation had arisen which made it necessary to invoke the wardship jurisdiction of the High Court, the application could be made at that stage. Meantime, I see no sufficient grounds for invoking the wardship jurisdiction in a situation such as the present which Parliament, in the new provisions of ss 12A to 12G of the Child Care Act 1980, has envisaged will normally be dealt with by the juvenile court.

Though adoption is contemplated in the present case, I do not think that this factor will make it necessary to invoke the jurisdiction of the High Court in wardship, since sub-ss (1) to (4) and (6) to (8) of s 14 of the Children Act 1975 have at long last been brought into force as from 27 May 1984 by SI 1983/1946. Until s 1 of the 1975 Act comes into force, which I understand has not yet occurred, s 14 has effect with the substitution of the words "approved adoption society or local authority' for the words 'adoption agency' and of the words 'society or authority' for the word 'agency' where that word occurs alone (see SI 1983/1946, Sch 2, para 8).

Under s 100(2) of the 1975 Act, the 'magistrates' court' is an 'authorised court' for the purpose of s 14 of that Act. Thus, under s 14, it will in my opinion be open to the local authority to invoke the jurisdiction of the magistrates' court without necessarily invoking the wardship jurisdiction for this purpose, to free the child for adoption. The judge did not expressly advert to these statutory provisions, but, in my opinion, they prevent the adoption envisaged by the local authority from, by itself, giving rise to a lacuna situation which renders necessary the intervention of the court by way of wardship.

Counsel for the mother made somewhat gloomy prognostications of the delays that would be likely to ensue in practice if matters proceeded before the magistrates instead of a judge in wardship. I do not wish to add anything to what Cumming-Bruce LJ has said in this context. For the reasons given by him, and for the further reasons which I have attempted to state, I think that the judge was right in concluding that this is not a case where any relevant lacuna has been shown.

I would accordingly dismiss this appeal.

*Appeal dismissed.*

Solicitors: *Meaden & Griffiths*, Reading (for the mother); *Sharpe Pritchard & Co*, agents for *D C H Williams*, Reading (for the local authority).

Bebe Chua    Barrister.

# Chapman v Chapman and others

CHANCERY DIVISION

SIR ROBERT MEGARRY V-C SITTING WITH CHIEF MASTER HORNE AND MR H M CRUSH AS ASSESSORS

1, 2, 5 NOVEMBER, 4 DECEMBER 1984

*Costs – Taxation – Delay – Delay in commencement of taxation proceedings – Delay of more than a year – Inordinate and inexcusable delay – Prejudice to other parties – No notice of intention to proceed given – Taxing master allowing only nominal sum by way of penalty – Whether failure to commence taxation a 'failure to proceed with taxation' – Effect of failure to give notice of intention to proceed – Whether receiving party proving prejudice arising out of delay – Whether merely nominal allowance appropriate – RSC Ord 2, r 1, Ord 3, r 6, Ord 62, rr 7(5), 8(6), 16.*

The plaintiff, a widow, succeeded in actions she brought against the defendants, the trustees of her husband's will, and by consent new trustees were appointed. By two orders for costs made in the proceedings the defendants were ordered to pay personally the plaintiff's costs in the actions and her costs of applying for the appointment of new trustees. The orders for costs were perfected on 7 May 1980 and 30 April 1982 respectively, and by RSC Ord 62, r 21(3) the plaintiff was required, if she wished her costs to be taxed, to commence the taxation within three months of the costs orders being perfected. The plaintiff did not in fact commence taxation until 5 August 1983, when she lodged a composite bill of costs for £10,000 in respect of both orders. The plaintiff also failed, before commencing the taxation, to give the defendants the notice of her intention to proceed that Ord 3, r 6[a] required. The taxing master held that there had been inordinate and inexcusable delay on the plaintiff's part in commencing the taxation which had prejudiced the defendants, and he allowed the plaintiff's costs at a nominal £5 under Ord 62, r 7(5)[b], on the grounds that the plaintiff had failed 'to proceed with taxation' and the allowance of a nominal amount would 'prevent [the] other parties being prejudiced' by the plaintiff's delay. The plaintiff applied for a review of the taxation, contending (i) that Ord 3, r 6 did not apply to a taxation of costs, (ii) that Ord 62, r 7(5) did not apply to delay in commencing a taxation, as opposed to delay in proceeding with a taxation once commenced, and (iii) that, even if Ord 62, r 7(5) did apply, the plaintiff's delay in commencing the taxation had not been inordinate and inexcusable and had not prejudiced the defendants.

**Held** – (1) RSC Ord 3, r 6 applied to the taxation of costs because r 6 was quite general in its terms, and Ord 62 could not be regarded as being a self-contained code since it could not be made to work properly without reference to other Rules of the Supreme Court. After a year's delay, a notice to proceed was therefore needed, even after judgment, so

---

*a*   Rule 6, so far as material, is set out at p 762 j, post

*b*   Rule 7(5) is set out at p 761 c, post

long as any matters remained in controversy. However, failure to serve a notice to proceed before commencing taxation was merely an irregularity which did not affect the validity of the taxation until such time as the taxation was set aside under Ord 2, r 1$^c$. The plaintiff's failure to serve notice of her intention to proceed therefore had no practical effect on the taxation except to give the court jurisdiction to set aside the taxation under Ord 2, r 1, for irregularity, and no such order had been made or even sought (see p 762 g h and p 763 a e f and h j, post); *MacFoy v United Africa Co Ltd* [1961] 3 All ER 1169 applied; dictum of Parker J in *Pamplin v Fraser (No 2)* [1984] 2 All ER at 697 not followed.

(2) The taxing officer's power under Ord 62, r 7(5) to allow only a nominal amount on taxation, although not appropriate to deal with a failure to give notice of intention to proceed with taxation, was wide enough to cover actual delay in commencing the taxation if the delay had been inordinate and inexcusable and had prejudiced other parties to the proceedings. Although the plaintiff's delay in commencing the taxation was, in respect of both costs orders, inordinate and inexcusable, the defendants had adduced no sufficient evidence to establish that they had been prejudiced by the delay, and the court would not infer prejudice from the mere fact of delay. It followed that Ord 62, r 7(5) did not apply and that the master's order would be discharged (see p 761 j to p 762 a, p 764 a b, p 765 e to g, p 766 f to h, p 767 c to e and p 768 b, post); *Drake & Fletcher Ltd v Clark* (1968) 112 SJ 95 applied; dicta of Parker J in *Pamplin v Fraser (No 2)* [1984] 2 All ER at 698–699 not followed.

Per curiam. (1) The proper consideration in deciding whether to apply Ord 62, r 7(5) by allowing the receiving party only a 'nominal or other sum for costs' is what discount from the bill of costs will prevent the paying party from being prejudiced by the receiving party's inordinate and inexcusable delay, rather than what punishment should be meted out to the receiving party for the delay. While substantial evidence of real prejudice might result in only a 'nominal sum' being allowed for costs, flimsy evidence of prejudice ought to result in the allowance of something more than a nominal sum. Furthermore, in many cases the paying party will derive financial advantage from the delay since he will have the use of the money during that period and will be able to earn interest on it, and that advantage has to be set against whatever disadvantage he suffers from the delay (see p 762 b to d, post).

(2) Once the three months' time limit for commencing a taxation expires without a solicitor lodging a bill for taxation and obtaining an extension of time, the second limb of Ord 62, r 8(6)$^d$ bites, so that the solicitor's fees for drawing the bill and attending a subsequent taxation are automatically disallowed (unless the taxing officer otherwise directs) even if subsequently the taxing officer extends the time for lodging the bill under Ord 62, r 16$^e$ (see p 764 e to g, post).

**Notes**

For the requirement of notice of intention to proceed after a year's delay in the proceedings, see 37 Halsbury's Laws (4th edn) para 34, and for cases on the subject, see 37(2) Digest (Reissue) 203–205, 1345–1354.

For the powers and discretion of taxing officers, see 37 Halsbury's Laws (4th edn) paras 731–732, and for cases on the subject, see 37(3) Digest (Reissue) 293–296, 4666–4680.

---

c   Rule 1, so far as material, provides:
    '(1) Where ... there has ... been a failure to comply with the requirements of these rules, whether in respect of time ... or in any other respect, the failure shall be treated as an irregularity and shall not nullify the proceedings ... or any ... order therein.
    (2) ... the Court may, on the ground that there has been such a failure as is mentioned in paragraph 1 ... set aside ... the proceedings in which the failure occurred ... or any ... order therein ...'
d   Rule 8(6) is set out at p 760 g to j, post
e   Rule 16, so far as material, provides: 'A taxing officer may—(a) extend the period within which a party is required ... to begin proceedings for taxation or to do anything in or in connection with proceedings ...'

For the time for beginning taxation proceedings, see 37 Halsbury's Laws (4th edn) para
733.

**Cases referred to in judgment**
Biss v Lambeth Southwark and Lewisham Area Health Authority [1978] 2 All ER 125, [1978] 1
    WLR 382, CA.
Blakey v Latham (1889) 43 Ch D 23, CA.
Deighton v Cockle [1912] 1 KB 206, [1911–13] All ER Rep 133, CA.
Drake & Fletcher Ltd v Clark (1968) 112 SJ 95, [1968] CA Bound Transcript 5.
MacFoy v United Africa Co Ltd [1961] 3 All ER 1169, [1962] AC 152, [1961] 3 WLR 1405,
    PC.
May v Wooding (1815) 3 M & S 500, 105 ER 698.
Metroinvest Ansalt v Commercial Union Assurance Co (1984) Times, 12 November, CA.
Pamplin v Fraser (No 2) [1984] 2 All ER 693, [1984] 1 WLR 1385.
Tabata v Hetherington (1983) Times, 15 December, [1983] CA Bound Transcript 511.
Taylor v Roe (1893) 62 LJ Ch 391.

**Summons to review taxation**
The plaintiff, Mrs Rose Anne Chapman, applied for a review of the taxation of her costs
of (i) consolidated actions brought by her against the defendants, Cecil Alfred Chapman,
George Allan Chapman and Albert Edward Hancock, the trustees of her husband's will,
and (ii) an application for the appointment of new trustees, under two orders for the
payment of those costs by the defendants personally, whereby the deputy taxing master,
Master Matthews, allowed the plaintiff's costs at £5, pursuant to RSC Ord 62, r 7(5), in
place of the sum of over £10,000 appearing in the bill of costs the subject of the taxation.
The summons was heard in chambers but the judgment was given by Sir Robert Megarry
V-C in open court. The facts are set out in the judgment.

Mr Michael Cook, solicitor, for the plaintiff.
Nigel Davis for the second defendant.
The first and third defendant did not appear.

                                                                    Cur adv vult

4 December. The following judgment was delivered.

**SIR ROBERT MEGARRY V-C.** In this review of taxation a number of points of law
arose during the three days of argument; and at the request of all parties I am delivering
judgment in open court. The basic facts may be recounted quite shortly. The plaintiff is
the widow of a testator whose will and codicil gave her, inter alia, a life interest in residue.
The first defendant is the testator's brother, and the second defendant is the testator's son
by a first marriage. These two defendants have agreed to indemnify the third defendant,
a stranger, against any liability for costs, damages or other awards. All three were trustees
of the testator's estate. Two actions were brought, one in 1975 and the other in 1977, and
these were consolidated. The claims were, inter alia, for damages for breach of trust and
for the removal of the defendants as trustees of the testator's estate; and the claims
succeeded. The first order in the consolidated actions was made on 18 January 1980, and
on 7 May 1980 that order was perfected. Under the order the defendants were ordered
personally to pay the plaintiff her costs of the consolidated actions, the costs to be taxed.
Under a summons dated 20 August 1981, the court made a consent order on 26
November 1981, appointing new trustees in place of the defendants, making a vesting
order, and so on, and ordering the defendants personally to pay the plaintiff her costs of
and incidental to the application, the costs to be taxed if not agreed. The second order
was perfected on 30 April 1982.
    On 5 August 1983 the plaintiff's composite bill of costs in respect of both orders was

lodged for taxation. Under RSC Ord 62, r 21(3), proceedings for taxation must be begun within three months after the order has been perfected. For order no 1, time expired on 7 August 1980, and so the taxation was begun almost exactly three years late. For order no 2, time expired on 30 July 1982, and so the taxation was begun a few days more than one year late. The bill was for a little over £10,000.

The taxation came before Deputy Master Matthews on 14 December 1983. The master, who had before retirement been chief taxing master, referred the plaintiff's representative to Ord 62, r 8(6), which in cases of delay in taxation provides for the costs of drawing the bill and attending the taxation to be disallowed unless otherwise ordered. The defendants' representative thereupon invoked Ord 62, r 7(5), and sought to have the bill itself assessed at a nominal sum by reason of inexcusable and unconscionable delay which had caused prejudice to the defendants: I shall turn to this rule in due course. The plaintiff's representative thereupon sought an adjournment in order to consider his position; and in granting this, the master drew attention to *Drake & Fletcher Ltd v Clark* (1968) 112 SJ 95 and *Pamplin v Fraser (No 2)* [1984] 2 All ER 693, [1984] 1 WLR 1385 (I add the references to the more ample reports now available).

The matter was then argued before the master at the adjourned hearing on 21 February 1984. The master had two affidavits before him, one for the defendants sworn on 16 February and the other for the plaintiff sworn on 17 February. After considering the arguments and evidence, the master decided to apply Ord 62, r 7(5), and assessed the costs payable to the plaintiff at £5 in place of the sum of over £10,000 appearing in the bill; and on 29 March 1984 the master announced this decision and gave reasons for it. On the same day the plaintiff delivered an objection to this assessment, on the ground that the delay had not been so inordinate as to cause prejudice to the defendants or to any of them; and the defendants, also on the same day, answered the plaintiff's objection by in effect asserting that the master had been right. On 3 April the master gave his written answers to the plaintiff's objection. The master's answers are given in a 12-page document which, if I may say so, admirably sets out the issues and the reasons for the decision. On 25 April the plaintiff took out a summons for review of the taxation; and, sitting with assessors, I heard argument on this by Mr Michael Cook for the plaintiff and Mr Nigel Davis, counsel for the defendants. Strictly speaking, Mr Davis, I should say, appeared only on behalf of the second defendant; but he told me that the first defendant supported the second defendant. The third defendant, cushioned by his indemnity, took no part in the proceedings, though I understand that he is well aware of them.

Order 62 contains various provisions which explicitly relate to delay in taxation. Rule 8(6) contains, first, a discretionary power for the taxing officer to direct a solicitor who is guilty of delay to pay costs personally to any party. Second, if a solicitor fails to proceed to taxation within the fixed time, or otherwise delays the taxation, he has his fees for drawing the bill and attending the taxation automatically disallowed unless the taxing officer otherwise directs. Perhaps I had better quote r 8(6) in full:

> 'Where in any proceedings before a taxing officer the solicitor representing any party is guilty of neglect or delay or puts any other party to any unnecessary expense in relation to those proceedings, the taxing officer may direct the solicitor to pay costs personally to any of the parties to those proceedings; and where any solicitor fails to leave his bill of costs (with the documents required by this Order) for taxation within the time fixed by or under this Order or otherwise delays or impedes the taxation, then, unless the taxing officer otherwise directs, the solicitor shall not be allowed the fees to which he would otherwise be entitled for drawing his bill of costs and for attending the taxation.'

Third, there is r 8(1). This applies where costs are, inter alia, wasted by undue delay; and it allows the court to make an order against any solicitor considered to be responsible for the delay, subjecting him to certain liabilities in respect of costs. This power is given not to the taxing officer but to the court, a term which, by the combined effect of Ord 1, r 4(1), and Ord 62, r 1(1), does not include a taxing officer. Again I had better quote r 8(1) in full:

'Subject to the following provisions of this rule, where in any proceedings costs are incurred improperly or without reasonable cause or are wasted by undue delay or by any other misconduct or default, the Court may make against any solicitor whom it considers to be responsible (whether personally or through a servant or agent) an order—(a) disallowing the costs as between the solicitor and his client; and (b) directing the solicitor to repay to his client costs which the client has been ordered to pay to other parties to the proceedings; or (c) directing the solicitor personally to indemnify such other parties against costs payable by them.'

With that, I turn to Ord 62, r 7(5). This reads as follows:

'Where a party entitled to costs fails to procure or fails to proceed with taxation, the taxing officer in order to prevent any other parties being prejudiced by that failure, may allow the party so entitled a nominal or other sum for costs or may certify the failure and the costs of the other parties.'

It will be seen that this is drafted in terms not of delay but of failure: it applies where a party entitled to costs 'fails to procure or fails to proceed with taxation', and so applies if a party does nothing, or, having initiated taxation, does nothing further. Unaided by authority, I would have hesitated to say that it applied to a case in which there is delay in initiating taxation, but thereafter no delay in proceeding with it. The draftsmen of the rules have shown themselves to be fully capable of using the word 'delay' when they mean delay. Where there are many persons entitled to costs in the same proceedings, as where multiple defendants have succeeded in Chancery proceedings, such a provision prevents one defendant from obstructing the other defendants by failing to lodge his bill for taxation: for under the rule the taxing officer may proceed to tax the bills of all the defendants, allowing merely a nominal sum to the laggard defendant.

That, however, must be considered in the light of *Drake & Fletcher Ltd v Clark* (1968) 112 SJ 95, as further revealed by the transcript in the Supreme Court Library ([1968] CA Bound Transcript 5): for the report in the Solicitors' Journal is abbreviated. In that case, the successful plaintiffs did not lodge their bill of costs for 3½ years after they had obtained a consent order in their favour. The defendant, a retired solicitor who acted in person, then contended that he had been prejudiced by the delay, and applied for costs to be assessed at a nominal sum under r 7(5). The district registrar agreed that the defendant had been prejudiced and did not tax the bill, which was for £950, but instead of allowing a nominal sum, allowed £720. On appeal, the judge substituted an order for taxation. In the Court of Appeal, the defendant, Mr Clark, contended that he had been prejudiced because he could no longer remember things which he would have been able to remember if the bill had been taxed promptly; and his affidavit also said that his financial position had deteriorated and he had become less able to discharge the costs. The Court of Appeal held that the defendant had been prejudiced by 'prolonged and inexcusable delay', that the defendant was entitled to know where he stood, and that the plaintiff should be allowed only the nominal sum of 40 shillings for the costs. The conclusion of Lord Denning MR (at p 4 of the transcript) was that 'In view of the delay and the prejudice to Mr Clark, the case falls exactly within Ord 62, r 7(5)'. Salmon and Edmund Davies LJJ concurred. The sentence that I have quoted does not appear in the report in the Solicitors' Journal, I may say.

It is impossible to discover from the transcript what arguments were advanced and considered on the point; but the conclusion is inescapable. I do not think that the case decides anything on the words 'fails to procure . . . taxation' in r 7(5), for the plaintiffs had brought in their bill for taxation, late though they were. I think that it must be the words 'fails to proceed with taxation' that the court held were wide enough to include 'failing to initiate taxation without such delay as suffices to prejudice the other party', or words to that effect. Nothing is said about the provisions in Ord 62 which expressly

relate to delay, and the absence of any mention of delay in r 7(5). Unguided, I would
have found it difficult to construe the paragraph in this way; but, like the master, I think
that I am bound to give it this meaning. In saying that, I bear in mind the severity with
which r 7(5) is capable of operating. The matter is not merely one of disallowing the
costs of taxation: the penalty for delay in bringing in a bill for taxation may, if the other
party has been prejudiced, be the disallowance of virtually the whole of a bill for tens of
thousands of pounds.

I also find considerable difficulty in perceiving the basis on which a merely nominal
sum was allowed. The district registrar had allowed £720 in respect of a bill for £950,
but the Court of Appeal allowed only £2. As I read the words 'in order to prevent any
other parties being prejudiced by that failure' in r 7(5), what the taxing officer must
normally do is to allow such a sum as will prevent any other parties from being prejudiced
by the failure. The language of the rule points to the question being not what punishment
for delay ought to be meted out to the receiving party, but what discount from the bill
will prevent the paying party from being prejudiced. In many cases, delay will bring a
real financial advantage to the paying party, since he will have the use of the money and
can keep what it earns, without being exposed to any liability to pay interest on the costs
for any period prior to the master's certificate; and whatever disadvantages the paying
party suffers, this advantage may have to be set against them. I can see little in the *Drake
& Fletcher* case that provides guidance on whether the sum is to be nominal or otherwise,
and, if otherwise, how much.

I turn to *Pamplin v Fraser (No 2)* [1984] 2 All ER 693, [1984] 1 WLR 1385. This was
much discussed during argument. A Queen's Bench Divisional Court had dismissed an
appeal against three convictions for minor offences in a magistrates' court, and had
ordered the appellant to pay the respondent's taxed costs. The respondent did not lodge
his bill for taxation until some 13 months after the appeal had been dismissed, so that he
was some 10 months late. The bill was taxed at about £500, and the appellant applied
for a review by a taxing master. He objected to the whole bill, contending that as over a
year had elapsed since the appeal had been dismissed, Ord 3, r 6, required the respondent
to give a notice to proceed. He had not done this, and so the taxation was invalid, and the
whole bill should be disallowed.

On a review of taxation, Parker J held that a notice to proceed under Ord 3, r 6 was
required, but that the result of the failure to give such a notice was not that the taxation
should be set aside. He said that in his view 'the consequences of a failure to give notice
under Ord 3, r 6 fall to be dealt with under Ord 62, r 7(5)...' (see [1984] 2 All ER 693 at
697, [1984] 1 WLR 1385 at 1389). The judge based his decision that a notice to proceed
was required on what Lord Ellenborough CJ said in *May v Wooding* (1815) 3 M & S 500
at 501, 105 ER 698. While a matter is still in controversy, after the elapse of a year
without any proceedings the party concerned should be given notice so that he can
prepare himself. This does not apply to the mere enforcement of a judgment or order,
nor to signing judgment after an order for judgment has been obtained (*Deighton v Cockle*
[1912] 1 KB 206, [1911–13] All ER Rep 133); but it does apply, even after judgment, if
matters still remain in controversy. To the authorities cited in the *Pamplin* case I may add
*Blakey v Latham* (1889) 43 Ch D 23 at 25 and *Taylor v Roe* (1893) 62 LJ Ch 391 at 392. The
relevance of this is that in the case before me the plaintiff gave the defendants no notice
to proceed before lodging the bill for taxation. The plaintiff did indeed ultimately give
the defendants such a notice, but this was not until over four months after the bill had
been lodged for taxation and the *Pamplin* case had been reported; and there is no
suggestion that this affects anything that I have to decide.

This decision came as a surprise to many. The rule itself (Ord 3, r 6) is quite general:

'Where a year or more has elapsed since the last proceeding in a cause or matter,
the party who desires to proceed must give to every other party not less than one
month's notice of his intention to proceed...'

The only argument against the application of this rule to a taxation of costs that seems to

me to have any weight is that Ord 62 is intended to be, and very nearly is, a self-contained
*a* code for the taxation of costs. Yet Ord 62 cannot be made to work properly without
resorting to some of the other orders in the Rules of the Supreme Court, such as Ord 1, r
4, and Mr Cook has failed to persuade me that Parker J was wrong in his conclusion.
Whether the action is proceeding towards judgment, or whether judgment has been
given but the progress is towards taking accounts or inquiries or taxing costs, after a
year's inactivity a due warning that what had seemed to be dead is to be restored to life
*b* seems equally desirable.

On the other hand, I have been puzzled about the consequences of not giving a notice
to proceed. In the *Pamplin* case Parker J said that the consequences of a failure to give the
notice fell to be dealt with under Ord 62, r 7(5); but I find it difficult to follow this. The
paragraph deals with cases where a party 'fails to procure or fails to proceed with taxation',
and not with procuring it or proceeding with it without first giving due warning. Order
*c* 2, r 1 (which was not mentioned in the *Pamplin* case) seems to me to be much more in
point. Put shortly, this provides that failures to comply with the rules are to be treated as
irregularities, and not as nullifying what has been done, but that the court is to have a
very wide power to set aside, wholly or in part, what has been done, and to make such
orders dealing with the proceedings as it thinks fit. Order 2, r 2, provides for any
applications to set aside what has been done to be made by summons or motion, and
*d* prohibits such applications unless made within a reasonable time and before the applicant
has taken any fresh step after becoming aware of the irregularity. These provisions
replace provisions in the former Ord 70, and were plainly intended to remove the former
distinction between acts which were nullities and so were void ab initio, and those that
were mere irregularities and were not thus void.

During the argument, I took the view that a failure to comply with the rules, including
*e* a failure to serve a notice to proceed, did not by itself invalidate the proceedings or any
step taken in them, despite the irregularity. Until anything has been set aside, it remains
valid, despite being irregular. Indeed, unless it remains valid, it is difficult to see what
there would be for the court to 'set aside'; and Ord 2, r 1(2) is drafted in terms of setting
aside the valid, rather than validating the invalid. I do not think that this view is affected
by the general words at the end of the paragraph which gives the court power to 'make
*f* such order (if any) dealing with the proceedings generally as it thinks fit'.

In taking this view, I was unaware of *Metroinvest Ansalt v Commercial Union Assurance
Co* (1984) Times, 12 November, a Court of Appeal decision which was shortly reported
after I had reserved judgment. This appeared to indicate, on a quite different subject
matter, that an irregular step or document was not valid inter partes until the matter was
brought before the court, and the court had decided how to exercise its jurisdiction. On
*g* this footing, the whole process of taxation in this case seemed to be invalid, and so I had
to consider restoring the case for further argument. However, the revised transcript of
the judgment of Cumming-Bruce LJ does not contain this particular passage in that
form; and although difficulties still remain, I do not think that the decision prevents me
from applying the view taken by the Privy Council in *MacFoy v United Africa Co Ltd*
[1961] 3 All ER 1169 at 1176, [1962] AC 152 at 160 that, until avoided, an irregularity
*h* remains 'good and a support for all that has been done under it', and 'is good until
avoided'. On this footing, in the present case the failure to serve a notice to proceed
before referring the bill to taxation, though an irregularity, does not invalidate or affect
the reference, but merely opens the jurisdiction for the court to make an order under
Ord 2; and no such order has been made or even sought.

I pause there. It does not seem to me that the failure to give a notice to proceed before
making a reference to taxation after a year's inactivity has much practical effect. True,
the paying party may apply to the court (not to the taxing master) under Ord 2 to set
aside the reference, and the court may do so. But until such an application is made and
decided, the reference, though irregular, is an effective reference. True also that in the
*Pamplin* case the judge said that the failure to give the notice to proceed fell to be dealt
with under Ord 62, r 7(5); yet as I have said, I find it difficult to see in what way the

taxing officer can deal with it, since ex hypothesi the receiving party is proceeding with the taxation, and there is nothing in the rule to say that it applies where a party is proceeding with a taxation without first giving due warning. In the end, counsel for the defendants accepted this view. I cannot see that in the *Pamplin* case the judge in fact gave effect in any way to the failure to give a notice to proceed; and in so far as he said that the failure should be dealt with under r 7(5), I would respectfully but firmly disagree.

Let me add that under Ord 62, r 22(1), where proceedings for taxation have been 'duly begun' in accordance with r 21, the 'proper officer' is to give not less than seven days' notice to all parties entitled to be heard in the taxation, and so at least that warning will be given, despite the absence of any notice to proceed. Of course, on the face of it, proceedings for taxation will not have been 'duly begun' under r 21 if they are commenced outside the three months' period from the perfection of the order for taxation; and a fortiori if more than a year has run. But r 16 authorises a taxing officer to extend the period within which proceedings for taxation must be begun; and the practice is that no formal application for an extension of time need be made on taking a reference, though on the substantive hearing this may be raised as a preliminary point: see *Practice Direction* [1984] 1 All ER 873, [1984] 1 WLR 520. The practical effect seems to be that there is an automatic extension of time for taking the reference, subject to any objection to the extension that may thereafter be made; for otherwise the reference ought to be rejected in limine.

I think that I should also say something about another point. I have already set out r 8(6), with its provision in the second limb for the automatic disallowance of the fee for taxation if the solicitor fails to lodge his bill for taxation within the specified time. In the *Pamplin* case [1984] 2 All ER 693 at 698, [1984] 1 WLR 1385 at 1390 the judge says that 'there is an inconsistency between extending the time and then disallowing the fee for taxation under r 8(6). Once the time was extended the bill was in time.' I find this a little difficult to follow. Once the three months have run without the bill being left for taxation, and without time being extended, the second limb of r 8(6) bites, and the solicitor's fee for taxation is automatically disallowed unless the taxing officer otherwise directs. If subsequently time is extended, that does not undo what has already happened: the fee for taxation stands disallowed, and remains so, despite any extension of the time for referring the bill for taxation under r 16. The disallowance can be reversed only if 'the taxing officer otherwise directs' under r 8(6). True, once the extension has been made it can be said that the bill was lodged 'within the time fixed by or under this Order'. But there is nothing in this to undo the disallowance that has already occurred; and this disallowance was automatic, so that there is no question of 'then disallowing the fee'.

I turn to the question of delay. Initially, Mr Cook accepted that the three years' delay in respect of order no 1 was inordinate delay; but when he came to reply, he sought to withdraw that concession, and counsel for the defendants made no objection to him doing this. Mr Cook's contention was that although there was delay, it was not inordinate; and he relied on *Tabata v Hetherington* (1983) Times, 15 December. Brevity in reporting could scarcely be carried farther, since the entire report is in two sentences: the transcript ([1983] CA Bound Transcript 511) is 17 pages long. The defendants had applied to have an action for libel dismissed for want of prosecution, based on inordinate and inexcusable delay to the prejudice of the defendants, or making a fair trial impracticable. There were two periods of delay after writ issued, each of about 19 months, and although these were held to be inordinate, the application failed because the delay had produced no substantial risk of prejudice or inability to have a fair trial. In the course of the leading judgment, at p 7 of the transcript, Cumming-Bruce LJ said:

> '"Inordinate" means a period of time which has elapsed which is materially longer than the time which is usually regarded by the court and the profession as an acceptable period of time.'

It is this sentence, transposed into oratio obliqua, which appears in the report in The Times.

Mr Cook relied on a variety of factors to support his contention that in the present case
there was no inordinate delay. The defendants made no complaint of it until they got to
taxation; there had been attempts at a settlement; the defendants had on occasion
grumbled when the plaintiff's solicitors said that they were going to proceed to taxation;
and the delay had in fact been ended by the plaintiff and not by the defendants, who
could, if they wished, have referred the matter to taxation: see *Practice Direction* [1974] 2
All ER 1248, [1974] 1 WLR 1035. In the atmosphere which existed prior to the *Pamplin*
decision, extensions of time were almost invariably granted, said Mr Cook, however
great the delay. Then there were the problems of the papers in respect of order no 1
being required for the purpose of obtaining order no 2, and so not being available for the
costs draftsmen. On top of that, the solicitor in charge of the proceedings on the plaintiff's
behalf was beset by all the problems of the amalgamation of two firms of solicitors.
However, this took place on 1 April 1981, so that the amalgamation was over 2¼ years
old when the composite bill was finally lodged. In addition, Mr Cook ingeniously
attempted to whittle down the period of delay by dividing it into two periods, one before
22 July 1981 and the other after that date. That date is the date when the plaintiff's
solicitors wrote to the defendants' solicitors saying that unless the costs were agreed
within 14 days, the plaintiff would proceed to taxation; and this was met with a reply six
days later asking the plaintiffs to wait 'rather longer' before referring the matter to
taxation, language which on no footing could mean waiting for two years. However, I
do not think that the attempted division really affects the matter, and I agree with the
contention of counsel for the defendants that one must look at the totality of the delay.

Mr Cook's tally was impressive: yet three years' delay, even against this background, is
far too long to be acceptable. Mr Cook's persuasive submissions could account for some
of this period, but, like the master, I cannot see how they could possibly account for it all,
even if the general atmosphere prior to the *Pamplin* decision was as lax as is suggested. It
must be remembered that drafting a bill of costs does not have to be done by the solicitor
personally, and that there are many costs draftsmen. It seems to me that the three years
is plainly a delay that is both inordinate and inexcusable; and in this the assessors concur.

The one year's delay for order no 2 is, of course, much less; but the matters dealt with
by that order were considerably less complex and voluminous. On 20 April 1982 the
plaintiff's solicitors had submitted to the defendants' solicitors a draft bill (on a solicitor
and own client basis) for £1,252·63 in respect of order no 2, to which the charges of their
London agents had to be added, so that over 15 months before the composite bill was
finally lodged, a draft bill with most of the material required for conversion into a party
and party bill was in existence; and to this some of the factors on which Mr Cook relied
no longer had any application. I would therefore hold that the one year's delay in respect
of order no 2 was also inordinate and inexcusable; and again the assessors concur.

That brings me to the issue of prejudice. Have the defendants been prejudiced by the
plaintiff's inordinate and inexcusable delay? Counsel for the defendants contended that
any prejudice, however small, sufficed for his purpose, subject to excluding any prejudice
which was merely de minimis. He said that in the present case there was a sufficiency of
prejudice to the defendants, both inferential and express. Prejudice, he said, was to be
inferred from mere delay; and he cited a sentence in the *Pamplin* case [1984] 2 All ER
693 at 699, [1984] 1 WLR 1385 at 1391 where the judge referred to the application of
r 7(5) to cases 'where the delay has been inordinate and inexcusable and where either
specific prejudice is established or the delay is so long that prejudice can be inferred'. In
the *Drake & Fletcher* case, where there were 3½ years of delay, Lord Denning MR (at p 3
of the transcript) referred to the paying party having forgotten things that he would have
remembered had the taxation been held within a reasonable time, and also to the
deterioration of his financial position over the years; and he said that the paying party
was entitled to know where he stood. On the evidence before the Court of Appeal, this
delay had prejudiced him. Counsel for the defendants also cited *Biss v Lambeth Southwark
and Lewisham Area Health Authority* [1978] 2 All ER 125 at 131, 134, [1978] 1 WLR 382 at
389, 393; but the reference to the sword of Damocles brings out the very real difference

between having an action hanging over one's head and, on the other hand, knowing that one is liable for costs and merely being uncertain about the amount.

Counsel for the defendants further referred to the express evidence of prejudice. In the main this consists of assertions in an affidavit by the defendants' solicitor (a) that the 'First Defendant has apparently suffered further prejudice in that the protracted delay in proceeding with the taxation of costs has caused his health to suffer'; and (b) that the second defendant's 'financial position has worsened in the period of 18 months between the Order of January 1980 and service of the plaintiff's first bill of costs'. A schedule 'setting out details of the Second Defendant's financial position during the relevant period' is then exhibited. In addition, the solicitor says that his knowledge and clear recollection of the facts of the case has diminished over the period and he is not in such a strong position as he might otherwise have been to challenge the costs being claimed.

The direct evidence of prejudice could scarcely be less impressive. Not a word further is said about how, or how far, the first defendant's health has suffered; and counsel for the defendants could add nothing, even on instructions. Not a word further is said about the extent to which the second defendant's financial position has worsened for any period. The exhibit is an unsigned and undated manuscript document recording the changes in the second defendant's employment. Probably it was written by the second defendant, though counsel could not tell me why neither the exhibit nor the affidavit said so, or why the affidavit did not verify the exhibit. The second defendant, it seems, had held the positions of chairman and managing director or director in various companies which in early 1981 fell on hard times. In July or August 1981 the second defendant lost his jobs, his holiday pay entitlement, and his pension rights, as well as his capital in one company, and received only his statutory redundancy payment; and he had to pay up £4,500 on a personal guarantee. In the autumn of 1981 he was unemployed, in November 1981 he obtained a consultancy job with two companies, and in November or December 1982 one of these terminated. In March 1983 he became self-employed, though it does not appear what the result of this was. From first to last not a single figure is mentioned, apart from the £4,500 that he had to pay on the guarantee; and there is not a word about his capital resources. Furthermore, on 13 October 1983, some six months after he became self-employed, his solicitors wrote to the plaintiff's solicitors making an increased offer to pay £8,000 to the plaintiff in order to avoid a taxation of costs. This replaced offers of £6,750 and £7,000 made respectively in January and March of that year.

If a paying party contends that he has been prejudiced by the receiving party's delay, I think that it is for the paying party to establish the prejudice, and not for the receiving party to establish that there has been none. I do not think that it is normally open to the paying party to adduce either no evidence of prejudice, or else miserably feeble evidence of it, and then say that from mere delay, however gross and inordinate, the court should infer prejudice. I say nothing of a case in which there is some good reason (e g death) why no express evidence of prejudice under some particular head, or at all, can be put forward: in such a case it may well be right to conclude on the facts that there was prejudice. But where there is no reason why the paying party should not establish just what prejudice he has suffered, I do not think that it would be right to infer prejudice from delay. Indeed, from that party's omission to demonstrate any prejudice, I would infer that there has been none.

I have stressed this point in view of what was said in the *Pamplin* case. 'No particular prejudice was shown, but it is clear that mere delay can amount to prejudice . . .' (see [1984] 2 All ER 693 at 698, [1984] 1 WLR 1385 at 1390). The power under r 7(5) may be exercised in appropriate cases, and these (in words that I have already quoted) will normally 'only be those where the delay has been inordinate and inexcusable and where either specific prejudice is established or the delay is so long that prejudice can be inferred' (see [1984] 2 All ER 693 at 699, [1984] 1 WLR 1385 at 1391). I would read these references to delay which suffices to establish prejudice as referring only to cases where it has become impossible to adduce evidence of the prejudice and not as enabling a paying party to refrain from putting forward such evidence and rely on prejudice being inferred from mere delay. If I am wrong in reading the dicta thus, then with all due respect I must say that I disagree with them.

In the present case, I can see no reason why in an affidavit expressly dealing with prejudice to the defendants, a word or two might not have been said about how the first defendant's health had been affected, or how the amount of the second defendant's capital and income had changed, or how it was that the delay had affected the defendants' solicitors' recollection of the facts of a case mainly depending on documents so as to impair his ability to contest the question of costs. Something, too, might have been said to explain why any prejudice that arose was not offset by the financial advantage of being able to pay late rather than promptly, or why, instead of pressing for taxation, the defendants' solicitors from time to time had been seeking to delay it (as in their letter of 28 July 1981) or were making offers in an attempt to avoid taxation (as in their letters of 27 January, 21 March and 13 October 1983).

From what I have said, it must be plain that I do not think that this is a case in which r 7(5) applies. Although I entirely agree with the master about the delay being inordinate and inexcusable, I cannot, on the evidence, concur in his conclusion that the delay has prejudiced the defendants. In addition to the matters to which I have referred, he said of the first defendant that 'it is also stated that he is now over 70 years of age and has retired'; but even if this had been established by evidence, I do not think that it would have altered my conclusion. I appreciate that I am differing from the opinion of a most experienced master, but I am fortified in my view by the conclusions of the assessors coinciding with mine after what I think must have been a more detailed examination of the matter than that which took place before the master. Even if any degree of prejudice that is not merely de minimis suffices for the purposes of r 7(5), as counsel for the defendants contended, I cannot see that any such prejudice to the defendants or any of them has been established.

That conclusion makes it unnecessary for me to say much about another difficulty that I feel about the master's conclusion that he should assess the plaintiff's costs at £5. In his reasons the master said that he had considered whether he could properly assess the costs at some higher amount without causing prejudice to the defendants, but that in view of *Drake & Fletcher*, 'and upon considering the effect on the defendants inter se I felt unable to do so'. He then said that he assessed the costs at £5 'with considerable misgivings because until the decision in *Pamplin v Fraser* delays in taxation proceedings, rightly or wrongly, rarely resulted in so harsh a penalty'.

In saying that, I am not sure whether the master was taking the view that *Drake & Fletcher* compelled him to reject a higher sum. If he was, I would not, with respect, agree with him; for no decision of the courts can spirit away the words nominal 'or other sum' in r 7(5). I am also a little puzzled by the words 'effect on the defendants inter se' in relation to the very flimsy evidence of prejudice that was before the master. The power under r 7(5) is a power 'to prevent any other parties being prejudiced' by the failure to procure or proceed with the taxation, not a power to confer a bonus on them; and without some process of assessing the prejudice I do not see how a proper decision can be reached under the rule. If a taxing officer reaches the conclusion that there is enough prejudice to invoke the rule, I would have thought that while substantial evidence of real prejudice might well result in only a nominal sum being allowed, flimsy evidence that barely sufficed to satisfy the rule ought to result in the allowance not of a similar nominal sum but something more substantial.

The master's concluding words must, I think, refer not so much to the need for a notice to proceed as to the refusal in *Pamplin* to extend the time for taxation, and the reduction of the sum allowed to £5. The judge had said that it was 'clear that mere delay can amount to prejudice', and that with no possible excuse the effect of the delay was to keep hanging over the appellant's head an unquantified debt which might be enforced by imprisonment, and which by the delay he could justifiably consider was regarded by the respondent as being too small to be worth proceeding with (see [1984] 2 All ER 693 at 698, [1984] 1 WLR 1385 at 1390); the amount, as I have mentioned, was some £500. However, these considerations do not apply to the present case, where there is no risk of imprisonment and the sum certainly could not be regarded by anyone as being too small to be worth proceeding with. Furthermore, the delay in *Pamplin*, though less than in the present case, seems to have been totally unexplained (see [1984] 2 All ER 693 at 697–698, [1984] 1 WLR 1385 at 1389–1390), whereas in the present case there is at least some degree of explanation, even though it does not suffice to prevent the delay from being inexcusable. My conclusion is that on reviewing the taxation I should discharge the master's order or certificate.

The question, then, is what order I should make. Order 62, r 35, gives me all the powers and discretions of the master. In his affidavit the plaintiff's solicitor had duly sought an extension of time for the taxation under r 16. This appears not to have been specifically dealt with by the master, no doubt because he was applying r 7(5) and assessing the plaintiff's costs at £5. Yet if, as I have held, r 7(5) does not apply, and time is not extended, the result would be that the plaintiff would not recover even a nominal sum for costs.

During argument, little was said about this. If time is extended, I think, for the reasons that I have given, that the second limb of Ord 62, r 8(6), would still operate automatically so as to disallow the fees of the plaintiff's solicitor for drawing the bill and attending the taxation; and as at present advised I would not give any direction to the contrary. But I do not think that I ought to decide whether to extend the time, or whether to give a direction, without hearing any submissions on these points that either side wishes to put forward; and for this purpose I shall adjourn into chambers so that the points may be argued either forthwith, or, if the parties so request, after they have been able to consider this judgment. At the same time I shall also consider the form of the order that is to be made.

Let me add one further point. It is general knowledge that a thoroughgoing revision of Ord 62 has been under consideration for some while. I venture to express the hope that in that revision, if not before, consideration will be given to a number of points that this case has brought to the fore. First, there is the question whether, in view of other provisions expressly referring to delay, r 7(5) is really intended to apply to cases of delay in lodging a bill of costs for taxation, especially if thereafter there is no delay in proceeding with the taxation. Second, there is the question whether Ord 3, r 6, does, or ought to, apply to the taxation of costs. Third, if Ord 3, r 6, is intended so to apply, there is the question of what are the consequences of failing to give the requisite notice to proceed. In particular, does it have any effect (and if so, what) in relation to r 7(5)? Fourth, in relation to a failure to comply with the rules in respect of taxation of costs, ought any of the powers under Ord 2, r 1, to be conferred on taxing officers, or ought any exercise of those powers to continue to require a separate application by summons or motion to the court, and not a taxing officer? These questions are far from being exhaustive; but if they are resolved, that ought at least to do something towards relieving a number of practitioners from some of the invincible repugnance (I borrow a phrase from another division) with which they now approach Ord 62.

*Master's order discharged.*

Solicitors: *Ward Bowie*, agent for *Donne Mileham & Haddock*, Brighton (for the plaintiff); *Compton Carr* (for the defendants).

Vivian Horvath　Barrister.

# Smalley v Crown Court at Warwick and others

HOUSE OF LORDS
LORD FRASER OF TULLYBELTON, LORD DIPLOCK, LORD KEITH OF KINKEL, LORD BRIDGE OF
HARWICH AND LORD BRIGHTMAN
23, 24, 28 JANUARY, 28 FEBRUARY 1985

*Crown Court – Supervisory jurisdiction of High Court – Trial on indictment – High Court having no supervisory jurisdiction in matters relating to trial on indictment – Relating to trial on indictment – Estreatment by Crown Court of surety's recognisance – Recognisance provided by surety to secure defendant's attendance at Crown Court for trial – Whether order estreating surety's recognisance an order made in 'a matter relating to trial on indictment' – Whether Divisional Court having jurisdiction to hear application for certiorari to quash order – Supreme Court Act 1981, s 29(3).*

The appellant stood as surety for his brother, who was committed to stand trial on indictment in the Crown Court for certain Customs offences. Subsequently the appellant was given notice under r 21[a] of the Crown Court Rules 1982 that default had been made by his brother in performing the conditions of the recognisance, and the Crown Court judge ordered the whole amount of the appellant's recognisance be estreated. The appellant applied for an order of certiorari to quash the order of the Crown Court. The Commissioners of Customs and Excise, the respondents, contended that by virtue of s 29(3)[b] of the Supreme Court Act 1981 the High Court had no jurisdiction to grant judicial review of the order of the Crown Court because it was an order made 'in a matter relating to trial on indictment'. The Divisional Court dismissed the appellant's application, holding that it had no jurisdiction. The appellant appealed to the House of Lords.

**Held** – An order estreating the recognisance of a surety for a defendant who failed to surrender to his bail at the Crown Court when committed for trial was not 'a matter relating to trial on indictment' for the purposes of s 29(3) of the 1981 Act, since it was not an order which affected the conduct of the trial in any way. Accordingly, the jurisdiction of the High Court to grant judicial review in the case of an aggrieved surety for bail was not excluded by s 29(3) of the 1981 Act. The appeal would accordingly be allowed (see p 771 *b* to *e*, p 779 *e* to *g* and p 780 *g* to *j*, post); *R v Smith (Martin)* [1974] 1 All ER 651, *R v Southampton Justices, ex p Green* [1975] 2 All ER 1073 and *R v Crown Court at Sheffield, ex p Brownlow* [1980] 2 All ER 444 considered; dictum of Shaw LJ in *R v Crown Court at Sheffield, ex p Brownlow* [1980] 2 All ER at 454 disapproved.

Per curiam. It is not inconsistent with the status and dignity of a Crown Court judge that his decisions should be subject to judicial review (see p 771 *b* to *e*, p 777 *j*, p 778 *f* to *h* and p 780 *h j*, post); dictum of Shaw LJ in *R v Crown Court at Sheffield, ex p Brownlow* [1980] 2 All ER at 455 disapproved.

Semble. Where the Crown Court orders the recognisance of a surety for a defendant committed for trial in the Crown Court to be estreated the surety is 'a party to the proceedings' in which the Crown Court's order is made against him and he is therefore entitled to question the order of the Crown Court by way of a case stated for the opinion of the High Court under s 28(1)[c] of the 1981 Act (see p 771 *c e*, p 773 *f* to p 774 *b* and p 780 *h j*, post).

### Notes
For the supervisory jurisdiction of the High Court over the Crown Court, see 10 Halsbury's Laws (4th edn) paras 710, 870.

*a*   Rule 21 is set out at p 771 *g h*, post
*b*   Section 29(3) is set out at p 772 *e f*, post
*c*   Section 28(1) is set out at p 772 *d e*, post

For the Supreme Court Act 1981, ss 28, 29, see 51 Halsbury's Statutes (3rd edn) 623, 624.

**Cases referred to in opinions**

*Amand v Secretary of State for Home Affairs* [1942] 2 All ER 381, [1943] AC 147, HL.

*Gatoil Inc v Arkwright-Boston Manufacturers Mutual Insurance Co* [1985] 1 All ER 129, [1985] 2 WLR 74, HL.

*Meredith, Ex p* [1973] 2 All ER 234, [1973] 1 WLR 435, DC.

*R v Assistant Recorder of Kingston-upon-Hull, ex p Morgan* [1969] 1 All ER 416, [1969] 2 QB 58, [1969] 2 WLR 246, DC.

*R v Central Criminal Court, ex p Binji* (25 May 1979, unreported), DC.

*R v Collier* (7 December 1972, unreported), DC.

*R v Crown Court at Cardiff, ex p Jones* [1973] 3 All ER 1027, [1974] QB 113, [1973] 3 WLR 497, DC.

*R v Crown Court at Chichester, ex p Abodundrin* (1984) 79 Cr App R 293, DC.

*R v Crown Court at Sheffield, ex p Brownlow* [1980] 2 All ER 444, [1980] QB 530, [1980] 2 WLR 892, CA.

*R v Deputy Chairman of Inner London Quarter Sessions, ex p Metropolitan Police Comr* [1969] 3 All ER 1537, [1970] 2 QB 80, [1970] 2 WLR 95, DC.

*R v Grondkowski and Malinowski* [1946] 1 All ER 559, [1946] KB 369, CA.

*R v Hayden* [1975] 2 All ER 558, [1975] 1 WLR 852, CA.

*R v Lambeth Metropolitan Stipendiary Magistrate, ex p McComb* [1983] 1 All ER 321, [1983] QB 551, [1983] 2 WLR 259, CA.

*R v London County Quarter Sessions (Chairman), ex p Downes* [1953] 2 All ER 750, [1954] 1 QB 1, [1953] 3 WLR 586, DC.

*R v Norfolk Quarter Sessions, ex p Brunson* [1953] 1 All ER 346, [1953] 1 QB 503, [1953] 2 WLR 294, DC.

*R v Oxfordshire Justices* (1953, unreported), DC.

*R v Smith (Martin)* [1974] 1 All ER 651, [1975] QB 531, [1974] 2 WLR 495, CA.

*R v Southampton Justices, ex p Green* [1975] 2 All ER 1073, [1976] QB 11, [1975] 3 WLR 277, CA.

*Sydall v Castings Ltd* [1966] 3 All ER 770, [1967] 1 QB 302, [1966] 3 WLR 1126, CA.

**Appeal**

The appellant, John Herbert Smalley, applied with leave of Woolf J granted on 7 September 1983 for an order of certiorari to quash the decision of his Honour Judge Harrison-Hall made at the Crown Court of Warwick on 15 July 1983 estreating a recognisance in the sum of £100,000 entered into by the appellant to secure the attendance for trial at the Crown Court of the appellant's brother, Ian Smalley. On 14 March 1984 the Divisional Court of the Queen's Bench Division (Kerr LJ and Glidewell J) dismissed the application on the preliminary point taken by the respondents, the Commissioners of Customs and Excise, that the High Court had no jurisdiction to review the decision of the Crown Court having regard to the terms of s 29(3) of the Supreme Court Act 1981. On 2 April 1984 the Divisional Court certified pursuant to s 12 of the Administration of Justice Act 1969 (in the event that the proceedings were civil proceedings) that a point of law of general public importance was involved in its decision, namely whether the High Court had jurisdiction to conduct judicial review of the order of a Crown Court judge estreating the recognisance of a surety provided for the purpose of securing the attendance of a defendant committed for trial on indictment, and that the point of law related wholly or mainly to the construction of s 29(3) of the 1981 Act and was one in respect of which the Divisional Court was bound by the decision of the Court of Appeal in *R v Crown Court at Sheffield, ex p Brownlow* [1980] 2 All ER 444, [1980] QB 530; alternatively (in the event that the proceedings were a criminal cause or matter), the Divisional Court certified pursuant to s 1(2) of the Administration of Justice Act 1960 that the aforesaid point of law involved in the decision was a point of law of general

public importance, but it refused leave to appeal to the House of Lords. On 6 June 1984
the Appeal Committee of the House of Lords granted the appellant leave to appeal against
the decision of the Divisional Court. The facts are set out in the opinion of Lord Bridge.

*Roger Henderson QC* and *Edmund Lawson* for the appellant.
*John Laws* for the respondents.

Their Lordships took time for consideration.

28 February. The following opinions were delivered.

**LORD FRASER OF TULLYBELTON.** My Lords, I have had the advantage of
reading in draft the speech of my noble and learned friend Lord Bridge. I agree with it,
and for the reasons given by him I would allow this appeal and remit the appellant's
application to the Divisional Court.

**LORD DIPLOCK.** My Lords, I have had the advantage of reading in draft the speech
of my noble and learned friend Lord Bridge. I agree with it, and for the reasons which
he gives I would allow the appeal.
    I express no view whether an application to the Crown Court to have the case stated
by that court for the opinion of the High Court under s 28(1) would be an alternative
though a roundabout way of securing the same result as an application under s 29(3).

**LORD KEITH OF KINKEL.** My Lords, I agree that, for the reasons given in the
speech to be delivered by my noble and learned friend Lord Bridge, this appeal should be
allowed.

**LORD BRIDGE OF HARWICH.** My Lords, on 28 June 1982 Ian Smalley, having
been charged with offences under s 68(2) of the Customs and Excise Management Act
1979, was committed by the Warwick magistrates' court for trial at the Crown Court at
Warwick. He was granted bail on condition, inter alia, of providing one surety in the
sum of £100,000. Ian's brother, John Herbert Smalley, the appellant before your
Lordships, agreed to provide that surety and duly entered into a recognisance in the
required sum on the same day.
    Rule 21 of the Crown Court Rules 1982, SI 1982/1109, provides as follows:

> '(1) Where a recognizance has been entered into in respect of a person granted bail
> to appear before the Crown Court and it appears to the Court that a default has been
> made in performing the conditions of the recognizance, the Court may order the
> recognizance to be estreated.
>     (2) Where the Crown Court is to consider making an order under paragraph (1)
> for a recognizance to be estreated, the appropriate officer of the Court shall give
> notice to that effect to the person by whom the recognizance was entered into
> indicating the time and place at which the matter will be considered; and no such
> order shall be made before the expiry of 7 days after the notice required by this
> paragraph has been given.'

    Having been given due notice pursuant to that rule, the appellant appeared on 15 July
1983 in the Crown Court at Warwick where, in the event, his Honour Judge Harrison-
Hall made an order that the whole amount of the appellant's recognisance be estreated.
    My Lords, I have quite deliberately refrained from giving any account of the events
leading to the making of the Crown Court's order, lest the language I use should be
thought to reflect in any way on the merits of the matter. Those merits do not arise for
consideration in the present appeal, which is concerned solely with the issue whether the
Divisional Court had jurisdiction to entertain an application for judicial review seeking
an order of certiorari to quash the Crown Court's order. On 7 September 1983 the

appellant obtained leave from Woolf J to make such an application. The application was heard by the Divisional Court (Kerr LJ and Glidewell J) on 14 March 1984. The *a* preliminary objection having been taken on behalf of the Commissioners of Customs and Excise as respondents that the court had no jurisdiction to entertain the application, their Lordships, with undisguised reluctance, held themselves bound by the authority of the Court of Appeal's decision in *R v Crown Court at Sheffield, ex p Brownlow* [1980] 2 All ER 444, [1980] QB 530 to uphold the respondents' objection. On 2 April 1984 the Divisional Court, recognising that it would be open to argument in your Lordships' *b* House that their judgment was in 'a criminal cause or matter', in which case the jurisdiction of the Court of Appeal would be ousted by s 18(1)(*a*) of the Supreme Court Act 1981, granted two certificates to enable an appeal to be brought direct to your Lordships' House, one under the leapfrog procedure provided by s 12 of the Administration of Justice Act 1969 for civil appeals, the other certifying that a point of law of general public importance was involved in their decision pursuant to s 1 of the *c* Administration of Justice Act 1960, being the certificate necessary to give this House jurisdiction to entertain the appeal if it was in a criminal cause or matter. Your Lordships' House granted leave to appeal on 6 June 1984.

The presently applicable statutory provisions are to be found in the Supreme Court Act 1981. The Crown Court is declared by s 45 to be a superior court of record. The relevant parts of ss 28 and 29 of the Act provide as follows: *c*

'**28.**—(1) Subject to subsection (2), any order, judgment or other decision of the Crown Court may be questioned by any party to the proceedings, on the ground that it is wrong in law or is in excess of jurisdiction, by applying to the Crown Court to have a case stated by that court for the opinion of the High Court.

(2) Subsection (1) shall not apply to—(*a*) a judgment or other decision of the Crown Court relating to trial on indictment . . .

**29** . . . (3) In relation to the jurisdiction of the Crown Court, other than its jurisdiction in matters relating to trial on indictment, the High Court shall have all such jurisdiction to make orders of mandamus, prohibition or certiorari as the High Court possesses in relation to the jurisdiction of an inferior court . . .'

All these provisions were originally enacted by the Courts Act 1971. Though cast in a *f* different form the provisions of s 28(1) and (2)(*a*) of the 1981 Act reproduce unchanged in effect the provisions of s 10(1)(*a*), (2) and (3) of the 1971 Act and s 29(3) of the 1981 Act re-enacts verbatim s 10(5) of the 1971 Act.

Ultimately the decision of this appeal must turn on the construction of the exclusionary clause in s 29(3) 'other than its jurisdiction in matters relating to trial on indictment'. But, before turning to that central issue and the authorities which bear on it directly, it is appropriate to advert to some more peripheral matters which were canvassed in argument.

In *R v Southampton Justices, ex p Green* [1975] 2 All ER 1073, [1976] QB 11 the applicant was a surety for her husband's bail. On his failing to surrender as required, the wife's recognisance was ordered by justices to be estreated. The Divisional Court refused her leave to move for an order of certiorari to quash the justices' order. On her appeal to the Court of Appeal, the preliminary point was taken that no appeal lay, since the order of the Divisional Court was made in 'a criminal cause or matter'. The court rejected this view. Lord Denning MR, with whose judgment Browne LJ and Brightman J agreed, said ([1975] 2 All ER 1073 at 1076, [1976] QB 11 at 15–16):

'A recognisance is in the nature of a bond. A failure to fulfil it gives rise to a civil debt. It is different from the ordinary kind of civil debt, because the enforcement is different. It is enforceable like a fine . . . But that method of enforcement does not alter the nature of the debt. It is simply a civil debt on a bond and as such it is not a criminal cause or matter.'

In the instant case Kerr LJ found it impossible to reconcile that decision with the conclusion which he nevertheless felt himself bound by *Brownlow*'s case to reach that the order estreating the appellant's recognisance was here made in 'a matter relating to trial on indictment'. Conscious that *Green's* case presents a formidable obstacle to his arguments for the respondents, counsel for the respondents invited us to overrule it. He drew our attention to the doubts expressed in *R v Lambeth Metropolitan Stipendiary Magistrate, ex p McComb* [1983] 1 All ER 321 at 329, 332, [1983] QB 551 at 563, 567 by Sir John Donaldson MR and May LJ whether *Green's* case had been rightly decided. In *Green's* case Lord Denning MR relied on a passage from the speech of Viscount Simon LC in *Amand v Secretary of State for Home Affairs* [1942] 2 All ER 381 at 385, [1943] AC 147 at 156 in support of his conclusion. Sir John Donaldson MR and May LJ in the passages referred to above, thought that the speeches of Viscount Simon LC and Lord Wright in *Amand's* case pointed the other way. *Amand's* case was concerned with an application for a writ of habeas corpus by an alleged absentee without leave from the Netherlands army, who was liable by virtue of the Allied Forces Act 1940 and an Order in Council made thereunder, applying to visiting forces the relevant provisions of the Army Act applicable to the home forces, to be delivered into military custody of the Netherlands authorities. Your Lordships' House held that to be 'a criminal cause or matter'. I must frankly confess that I can find nothing in the speeches in that case which throws any light one way or the other on the totally different question whether an order estreating the recognisance of a surety for a defendant admitted to bail in criminal proceedings is covered by the same language. I do not find it necessary for present purposes to give a concluded answer to that question. It follows that I am not prepared to hold that *Green's* case was wrongly decided.

Counsel for the respondents argued as what he described as his 'fall-back' position that, if the appellant had any remedy, it was not by way of application for judicial review under s 29(3) of the 1981 Act but by way of an appeal by case stated under s 28(1). The first question this argument raises is whether the appellant was 'a party to the proceedings' in which the order to estreat his recognisance was made. Since no application was made on the appellant's behalf to have a case stated by the Crown Court for the opinion of the High Court, the question is strictly academic in relation to the present appeal. But in view of the manifestly close relationship between the exclusionary clauses in ss 28(2)(a) and 29(3), consideration of the question may throw light on the point of construction which is directly in issue.

What were 'the proceedings' in which the order estreating the appellant's recognisance was made? Were they part and parcel of the criminal proceedings against his brother Ian? If so, the only parties to the proceedings were the prosecutor and Ian. But the decision in *Green's* case clearly implies, and quite apart from *Green's* case it seems to me strongly arguable, that the proceedings in which the Crown Court's order against the appellant was made were separate proceedings instituted by the notice given to the appellant under r 21(2) of the 1982 rules. If that is the right view, it is plain that the appellant was a party to those separate proceedings, by which he was clearly affected, but his brother Ian was not.

As I have said, it is strictly unnecessary to decide whether the appellant was 'a party to the proceedings' in which the Crown Court's order was made against him; but it is illuminating to consider the position which would arise if he was such a party and sought to appeal by case stated under s 28(1). The question would then arise under s 28(2)(a) whether the order estreating the recognisance amounted to 'a judgment or decision of the Crown Court relating to trial on indictment'. It is very strange that, whereas s 28(1) refers to 'any order, judgment or other decision', s 28(2)(a) omits the word 'order'. I hesitate to attach any significance to this oddity of drafting, since it surely cannot have been Parliament's intention that any 'order' of the Crown Court, properly so called, eg an order for the payment of costs by one party to the other at the conclusion of a trial on indictment, should be open to challenge in the High Court by case stated. That apart, however, counsel for the respondents, as I understand him, submits that the exclusion of 'a judgment or other decision of the Crown Court relating to trial on indictment' by s 28(2)(a) may be narrower in its scope than the exclusion of the Crown Court's 'jurisdiction in matters relating to trial on indictment' by s 29(3). Counsel for the respondents sought to attach significance to the presence in s 29(3) of the words 'its jurisdiction in matters' which are absent from s 28(2)(a). I reject this line of argument. The language of the exclusionary clause in s 29(3) is aptly chosen to cover not only orders, judgments or decisions of the Crown Court which could be quashed by order of certiorari, but also inaction or threatened action susceptible to orders of mandamus and prohibition respectively. It is this which accounts for the difference in language between ss 28(2)(a) and 29(3). The difference cannot affect the construction of the critical phrase 'relating to trial on indictment', which, in my opinion, must mean the same thing in both subsections. It would be absurd that a decision liable to be questioned by case stated under s 28(1) on the ground of error of law should not equally be liable to review under s 29(3) on the ground of, say, bias in the court.

The authorities directly bearing on the construction of s 29(3) of the 1981 Act and its predecessor s 10(5) of the 1971 Act begin with Ex p Meredith [1973] 2 All ER 234, [1973] 1 WLR 435. The applicant, who had been acquitted at his trial on indictment by the Crown Court but refused any order for the payment of his costs either by the prosecution or out of central funds, sought leave to apply for an order of mandamus. The hearing appears to have proceeded on the basis that the application was for an order of certiorari to quash the order refusing costs. After referring to s 10 of the 1971 Act, Lord Widgery CJ said ([1973] 2 All ER 234 at 234–235, [1973] 1 WLR 435 at 436):

> 'Counsel [for the applicant]... faces the initial difficulty of whether, in view of s 10 of the Courts Act 1971, certiorari can go to the Crown Court in respect of an order relative to costs following a trial on indictment. It seems to us clear that it cannot, and although it may seem a little illogical that before the Courts Act 1971 this case would probably have gone to quarter sessions, whence the decision would have been open to review on certiorari, now, by virtue of the amalgamation of assizes and quarter sessions in the single Crown Court, it seems to us that certiorari cannot go in respect of a judgment or other decision of that court relating to trial on indictment, and if one reaches that conclusion, it is inescapable that the order complained of here was an order relating to trial on indictment.'

In R v Crown Court at Cardiff, ex p Jones [1973] 3 All ER 1027, [1974] QB 113 an unsuccessful attempt was made to distinguish, in relation to s 10(5) of the 1971 Act, an order of the Crown Court that an acquitted defendant make a contribution to his own costs of defence under a legal aid order from an order directly relating to the payment of costs of trial. The attempt failed. The Divisional Court held that the order was one 'relating to trial on indictment'. Boreham J expressed the view that 'one of the ordinary incidents of a trial on indictment is the question of costs' (see [1973] 3 All ER 1027 at 1035, [1974] QB 113 at 122). He added ([1973] 3 All ER 1027 at 1036, [1974] QB 113 at 123):

> 'At the end of the day I would approach the matter thus: the words in the subsection "matters relating to trial on indictment" are words of common usage, they are simple words, and this is one of those occasions which frequently arise in construing an Act of Parliament where either further definition or an attempted paraphrase is likely to confuse rather than to clarify. I prefer to apply as best I can those words to the questions that the judge had to resolve: was the exercise, if I may call it that, on which he was about to embark aptly described as a matter relating to trial on indictment? When the question is put thus, the answer in my judgment is clearly, Yes...'

In R v Smith (Martin) [1974] 1 All ER 651, [1975] QB 531 a trial on indictment at the Crown Court had been necessarily adjourned at the outset because an essential defence witness was too ill to attend. The defendant's solicitors, acting under a legal aid order, had given no advance notice to the court of the difficulty. The Crown Court judge thought that they were at fault and ordered them personally to pay the costs of both the prosecution and the defence thrown away by the adjournment. The solicitors appealed to the Court of Appeal. The court (Lord Denning MR, Megaw LJ and Sir Eric Sachs)

unanimously held that they had no jurisdiction to entertain the appeal. All three
members of the court, however, considered whether the solicitors would have had any
remedy by application for an order of certiorari to the Divisional Court. It is to be noted
that both counsel for the appellant solicitors and counsel appearing as amicus curiae
argued that the remedy was excluded by s 10(5) of the 1971 Act. Accordingly, the
relevant observations were both obiter and made without the benefit of bilateral
argument. Lord Denning MR said ([1974] 1 All ER 651 at 656, [1975] QB 531 at 542):

> 'Then what about the present order on the solicitors to pay the costs personally?
> Is that order one "relating to trial on indictment"? The words "relating to" are very
> wide. They are equivalent to "connected with" or "arising out of". So interpreted,
> they cover the present case. The order against the solicitors arose out of a trial by
> indictment. It related to the adjournment of it. It was, therefore, an order "relating
> to trial on indictment".'

Megaw LJ said ([1974] 1 All ER 651 at 658, [1975] QB 531 at 544–545):

> '... both counsel as amicus curiae and counsel for the appellants submitted that
> s 10 would provide no effective remedy because the present case would come within
> the same line of reasoning as led the Queen's Bench Division Divisional Court in *Ex
> parte Meredith* [1973] 2 All ER 234, [1973] 1 WLR 435 and in *R v Crown Court at
> Cardiff, ex parte Jones* [1973] 3 All ER 1027, [1974] QB 113 to the conclusion that it
> had no jurisdiction to determine the challenges made in those cases to orders of the
> Crown Court. It may be so. For myself, I am not so sure. However, I should not
> wish to be taken as expressing any concluded view whether or not the present case
> would be distinguishable, for the purposes of s 10, from the two cases above cited.
> But I am by no means convinced that an order made by the Crown Court against a
> solicitor, in the exercise of its inherent disciplinary jurisdiction over an officer of the
> court (if that be the true nature of the order) is properly to be described as an order
> "relating to trial on indictment", merely because an order against a defendant in a
> trial on indictment in respect of costs incurred in that trial is an order "relating to
> trial on indictment". I think that the title which has been given to this appeal, *R v
> Smith*, is inaccurate and misleading. Neither the Crown as prosecutor nor Mr Martin
> Smith are in any way concerned. The appeal is, and should be entitled as, an appeal
> by the solicitors concerned.'

Sir Eric Sachs cited with approval the passage I have already set out from the judgment
of Boreham J in the *Jones* case [1973] 3 All ER 1027 at 1036, [1974] QB 113 at 123 and
expressed the opinion that 'the solicitors cannot here resort to any of the remedies
provided in s 10 of the 1971 Act' (see [1974] 1 All ER 651 at 660, [1975] QB 531 at 547).

The very question now before your Lordships was considered by a Divisional Court
constituted by Geoffrey Lane LJ and Ackner J in *R v Central Criminal Court, ex p Binji* (25
May 1979, unreported). The court had asked the Treasury Solicitor to instruct counsel as
amicus to assist the court on the question of jurisdiction. Mr Simon Brown, fulfilling
that role, said to the court:

> 'There are a number of cases where a Divisional Court, in connection with
> attempted applications for supervisory orders in respect of costs, has declined
> jurisdiction on the footing that that is connected with or relating to a trial on
> indictment. But this, with respect, clearly falls on the other side of any dividing
> line, and one would shrink from finding to the contrary unless one were driven to
> do so because of the manifest effect of so doing, which would be to say that such an
> order by the Crown Court was simply not open to review anywhere else at all.
> Unless one were driven to that unhappy conclusion, one would not seek to arrive at
> it and one is not bound by the authorities to do any such thing.'

Giving judgment, with which Geoffrey Lane LJ agreed, Ackner J said:

> 'Therefore, the matter which concerned us and which caused us to adjourn for
> the advantage of an amicus was whether this matter related to the jurisdiction of

the Crown Court in matters relating to trial on indictment. Having heard argument from Mr Jennings, and having had the brief and characteristically frank admission *a* from Mr Brown that he did not consider that this touched or concerned the jurisdiction of the Crown Court in the sense to which I have referred quoting from the Act, we think this is a proper case in which we should grant leave to move.'

The question at issue in *Brownlow's* case [1980] 2 All ER 444, [1980] QB 530 was very far removed from the question which the present appeal raises. Two police officers had been committed for trial at the Crown Court at Sheffield charged with assault occasioning *b* actual bodily harm. A few days before their trial was due an application was made on behalf of the defendants to the judge who was to try the case for an order that the prosecution inform the defence whether any members of the jury panel had criminal convictions and give details of such convictions. The judge ordered that the chief constable be supplied with a copy of the panel of jurors from which the jury in the case would be drawn, and that he should supply to the solicitors for the defence and the *c* prosecution full details of any criminal convictions recorded against any member of the panel. The chief constable applied for an order of certiorari to quash the judge's order. The Divisional Court held that they had no jurisdiction in the matter. The chief constable's appeal to the Court of Appeal was dismissed by a majority (Shaw and Brandon LJJ, Lord Denning MR dissenting). Lord Denning MR said ([1980] 2 All ER 444 at 451–452, [1980] QB 530 at 539–540): *d*

'So I approach the two words "relating to" fully appreciating that others may interpret them differently from me. They are two words in common use but they are not clear or specific. Like many English words or phrases they are flexible enough to be capable of two or more interpretations. You can see that by looking again at a case in this court about "relations" and "descendants": see *Sydall v Castings* *e* *Ltd* [1966] 3 All ER 770, [1967] 1 QB 302. So here, just as one person may be *closely* related to, or *distantly* related to, another: so may one matter be *closely* related to, or *distantly* related to, another. There is a choice before the judges: either to give the words "relating to" a wide interpretation or a narrow interpretation. My choice is plain. I think the words "relating to" should be interpreted as "closely relating to". So close indeed that the words "relating to trial on indictment" should be read as *f* equivalent to "in the course of trial on indictment". By giving the words this interpretation the law becomes sensible and consistently, and any erroneous order can be put right by a higher court. There is no gap left without a remedy. In this way, when a judge of the Crown Court makes an interlocutory order *in the course of a trial on indictment*, there is no appeal at that stage to a higher court. The trial judge should have the final word on such matters as adjournments, joint or several trials, particulars and so forth. The only remedy is this: in case a trial judge should make a *g* mistake on an interlocutory matter, such as to cause injustice, the man can appeal against his conviction, and it will be taken into account at that stage: see *R v Grondkowski and Malinowski* [1946] 1 All ER 559, [1946] KB 369. When a judge of the Crown Court makes an order, *not* in the course of a trial on indictment, but before it has started or after it has finished, preparatory to it or subsequent to it, *h* there is no appeal from him to a higher court. But if his order is erroneous, there is recourse to the Divisional Court by way of mandamus or certiorari. The Divisional Court can intervene so as to put right that which has gone wrong.'

The crucial passage from the leading majority judgment of Shaw LJ must be cited in full. He said ([1980] 2 All ER 444 at 454–455, [1980] QB 530 at 543–545): *j*

'It seems plain that any decision of a Crown Court which appertains to or arises in connection with its jurisdiction to try cases on indictment comes within the exclusory provisions contained in sub-ss (1) and (5) of s 10 of the 1971 Act. The closeness or remoteness of the relationship of the decision in question to the jurisdiction to try cases on indictment is wholly irrelevant. It is the fact that the decision is so related to or arises in connection with trial on indictment that excludes it from the supervisory jurisdiction of the High Court. Neither sub-s (1) nor sub-s (5) of s 10 refers to "a trial on indictment". The phrase used is "trial on indictment" which is a general reference not to a specific event or occasion but to a jurisdiction. Any decision as to a matter which arises out of or incidentally to or in the course of that jurisdiction whether it relates to a proximate trial or a remote one falls, as I see it, inescapably and inevitably into the immunity from review by the High Court. Apart from the basic question of construction, there are formidable historical and practical justifications for this immunity. The Courts Act 1971 abolished the courts of assize and the courts of quarter sessions. It established in their place the Crown Court which embodies both their jurisdictions. One was that of a superior court of record while the other was that of an inferior court. The Crown Court is declared by s 4 of the Act to be a "superior court of record"; but its composite jurisdiction is still subject to the historical distinctions which existed before the Act came into operation. In its jurisdiction relating to trial on indictment, the Crown Court is the direct heir of the assize courts wherein the judges held the commission of the Sovereign to hold courts of general gaol delivery and of oyer and terminer. It would have been a derogation of their status and function in this judicial office of high consequence to be subject to the review of any court. The verdict of a jury if adverse to an accused might be reviewed in the Court of Criminal Appeal when that court was created by the Criminal Appeal Act 1907 which made possible appeals against conviction or sentence. Apart from this statutory intervention there was only a consultative recourse to the Court of Crown Cases Reserved. The authority of judges of assize in the trial of cases on indictment was paramount and their decisions could not be questioned. Nor can the authority of Crown Court judges be questioned now in matters relating to their jurisdiction to try cases on indictment. Theirs must be not only the first but also the last word. A judge of assize could revoke or review or modify any order or decision he had made before the trial of an accused had been finally disposed of; but he was not subject to external oversight. It would have been inconsistent with the status and dignity of judges who presided over and controlled the trial of persons indicted for criminal offences to be subject to external control at every stage from committal until verdict. It would be no less invidious and inappropriate in the case of a judge of the Crown Court in the discharge of those same functions which have devolved on him. On the practical side, if decisions made by a judge of the Crown Court as to matters which are related to trial on indictment were subject at any stage to review by the High Court, the trial of a particular cause might be interminably delayed by incidental applications which could then be taken to the High Court by way of case stated or an application for judicial review. The 1971 Act does not, in s 10, make reference to matters closely or remotely related to trial on indictment. It is general and unspecific in this regard. It is difficult to think of any matter more closely related to trial on indictment than an order which may, in due course, affect the composition or constitution of a jury which will try alleged offenders already committed for trial.'

I complete this review by noting that the Divisional Court (Ackner LJ and Taylor J) in *R v Crown Court at Chichester, ex p Abodundrin* (1984) 79 Cr App R 293 held that a decision of the Crown Court refusing to grant legal aid to defendants for their trial on indictment was 'in a matter relating to trial on indictment' and was accordingly not reviewable.

I must begin my consideration of the question of construction on which this appeal depends by respectfully rejecting the historical approach which played so large a part in the reasoning of Shaw LJ in *Brownlow*'s case. I cannot accept that the role of the Crown Court as heir of the assize courts of the 'status and dignity' of judges and commissioners of assize are significant, let alone decisive, in construing the provisions of ss 28 and 29 of the 1981 Act which re-enact the provisions of s 10 of the 1971 Act. The Crown Court is a single court which has inherited the combined functions of both the former courts of quarter sessions and assize courts. Courts of quarter sessions were subject to the supervisory jurisdiction of the High Court exercised by the prerogative writs and orders;

assize courts, as superior courts of record, were not. There was no judge whose learning
in this field was more respected than Lord Goddard CJ. In *R v London County Quarter*
*Sessions (Chairman), ex p Downes* [1954] 1 QB 1 at 7; cf [1953] 2 All ER 750 at 752 he said:

'This court has on several occasions sent an order of mandamus to sessions where
they have declined to proceed. A recent instance was *Rex* v. *Oxfordshire Justices*
(1953), which is not reported, but I was a member of the court, where the sessions
held that they had no power to try a charge of dangerous driving on indictment as
the defendant had not elected to go for trial, and in *Rex* v. *Norfolk Quarter Sessions;*
*Ex parte Brunson* ([1953] 1 All ER 346, [1953] 1 QB 503), where the court declined
to proceed because some inadmissible evidence had been given before the
committing justices. In both those cases the court, by order of mandamus, directed
the sessions to hear and determine. With regard to certiorari, the question is by no
means so clear, and I may refer to a recent note by Mr. D. M. Gordon in the Law
Quarterly Review (69 LQR 175). It seems that when sessions are sitting as a court of
oyer and terminer to try prisoners on indictment certiorari will not lie to bring up a
judgment either of acquittal or conviction. The quashing of an indictment is not a
judgment of acquittal, nor a fortiori of conviction. It is true that in the *Norfolk* case,
where this point was not taken, this court did order certiorari to issue both for the
order quashing the indictment and for the order as to costs. It may be that had this
point been taken the court would have confined the certiorari to the order for costs.
But in truth I do not think that any certiorari is necessary, so that we need not
consider the cases and learning on this subject. The court by its order of mandamus
will direct the sessions to try the indictments, so it would be eminently futile to take
the objection that they have made an order quashing them. It is just because they
have made that order that the court directs them to try the case, thus in effect
directing them to ignore the order they have made.'

Later decisions to the like effect are *R v Assistant Recorder of Kingston-upon-Hull, ex p*
*Morgan* [1969] 1 All ER 416, [1969] 2 QB 58 and *R v Deputy Chairman of Inner London*
*Quarter Sessions, ex p Metropolitan Police Comr* [1969] 3 All ER 1537, [1970] 2 QB 80. It
must follow that the effect of s 10 of the 1971 Act was to change the law in one direction
or the other. It either curtailed the High Court's supervisory powers over the jurisdiction
formerly exercised by courts of quarter sessions or it enlarged those powers over the
jurisdiction formerly exercised by the assize courts.

I see no inconsistency with the 'status and dignity' of a judge of the Crown Court that
his decisions should be subject to judicial review. A Crown Court judge may be the Lord
Chief Justice, a High Court judge, a circuit judge, a recorder or an assistant recorder. A
Divisional Court called on to review a decision of the Crown Court will normally be
constituted by a Lord Justice of Appeal and one or two High Court judges. From 1907 to
1966 whenever the Lord Chief Justice went on circuit and presided at assizes, as he
frequently did, any appeal against conviction or sentence in a case tried before him lay to
the old Court of Criminal Appeal, which was in such a case necessarily constituted by
three puisne judges. I have never heard it suggested that this was inconsistent with the
status and dignity of the Lord Chief Justice.

The passage cited above from the dissenting judgment of Lord Denning MR in
*Brownlow's* case [1980] 2 All ER 444 at 451–452, [1980] QB 530 at 539–540 suggests that
the words 'relating to', in any context, are imprecise and may be given a broad or a
narrow interpretation. That view finds support in the recent decision of your Lordship's
House in *Gatoil Inc v Arkwright-Boston Manufacturers Mutual Insurance Co* [1985] 1 All ER
129, [1985] 2 WLR 74. The question there was whether the words in s 47(2)(e) of the
Administration of Justice Act 1956 'any agreement relating to the carriage of goods in
any ship whether by charterparty or otherwise' covered an agreement to pay premiums
on a policy of insurance under a war risk open cover on cargo. Lord Keith, delivering the
main speech, expressed the conclusion that the contract of insurance in question was 'not
connected with the carriage of goods in a ship in a sufficiently direct sense to be capable
of coming within para (e)' (see [1985] 1 All ER 129 at 137, [1985] 2 WLR 74 at 84–85).

a
    This conclusion was unanimously indorsed by the other members of the appellate committee. Lord Wilberforce said in terms (see [1985] 1 All ER 129 at 131, [1985] 2 WLR 74 at 77), that 'the courts are left with a choice of a broad or a narrow interpretation' and gave his own reasons reinforcing the conclusion of Lord Keith that a narrow construction should be adopted.

    It is, of course, obvious that the phrase 'relating to trial on indictment' in ss 28(2)(a) and 29(3) is apt to exclude appeal or judicial review in relation to the verdict given or

b
sentence passed at the conclusion of a trial on indictment, both of which are subject to appeal as provided by the Criminal Appeal Act 1968. I accept the submission of counsel for the respondents that in this context, as in ss 76 and 77 of the 1981 Act, the words 'trial on indictment' must include the 'trial' of a defendant who pleads guilty on arraignment. Beyond this it is not difficult to discern a sensible legislative purpose in excluding appeal or judicial review of any decision affecting the conduct of a trial on

c
indictment, whether given in the course of the trial or by way of pre-trial directions. In any such case to allow an appellate or review process might, as Shaw LJ pointed out in *Brownlow's* case [1980] 2 All ER 444 at 455, [1980] QB 530 at 544–545, seriously delay the trial. If it is the prosecutor who is aggrieved by such a decision, it is in no way surprising that he has no remedy, since prosecutors have never enjoyed rights of appeal or review when unsuccessful in trials on indictment. If, on the other hand, the defendant

d
is so aggrieved, he will have his remedy by way of appeal against conviction under the Criminal Appeal Act 1968 if he has suffered an injustice in consequence of a material irregularity in the course of the trial, which, I apprehend, may well result not only from a decision given during the trial, but equally from a decision given in advance of the trial which affects the conduct of the trial, eg a wrongful refusal to grant him legal aid.

    I can, however, discover no intelligible legislative purpose which would be served by

e
giving to the words 'relating to trial on indictment' a wider operation than indicated in the foregoing paragraph. An order estreating the recognisance of a surety for a defendant who fails to surrender to his bail at the Crown Court to which he was committed for trial cannot affect the conduct of any trial on indictment in any way. If such an order is wrongly made, for example by denying the surety the right to be heard, I can see no sensible reason whatever why the aggrieved surety should not have a remedy by judicial

f
review. Still less can I see any reason for distinguishing in this respect between the position of a surety, on the one hand, for a defendant committed on bail to the Crown Court for trial and a surety, on the other hand, for a defendant committed on bail to the Crown Court either for sentence after conviction by a magistrates' court, or on appeal to the Crown Court against conviction and sentence by a magistrates' court. If, therefore, the phrase 'relating to trial on indictment' may be construed broadly or narrowly, a

g
purposive approach points, to my mind, unmistakably to a construction sufficiently narrow, at all events, to avoid the exclusion of judicial review in such a case as this.

    Reverting to the judgments in *Brownlow's* case, I am of opinion, with all respect, that Lord Denning MR took too narrow a view when he suggested that the words 'relating to trial on indictment' should be read as equivalent to 'in the course of trial on indictment', thus enabling him to conclude that review should be allowed of any order made which

h
was preparatory to a trial on indictment. I think the decision of the majority in that case was right that the order in question, potentially affecting, as it did, the composition of a jury for a forthcoming trial, was, as Shaw LJ put it, 'closely related to trial on indictment', or as I would prefer to say, was an order affecting the conduct of the trial. There are, however, two sentences in the judgment of Shaw LJ from which I must express my respectful but emphatic dissent. He said ([1980] 2 All ER 444 at 454, [1980] QB 530 at

j
544):

    'The closeness or remoteness of the relationship of the decision in question to the jurisdiction to try cases on indictment is wholly irrelevant ... Any decision as to a matter which arises out of or incidentally to or in the course of that jurisdiction whether it relates to a proximate trial or a remote one falls, as I see it, inescapably and inevitably into the immunity from review by the High Court.'

I can find nothing in the language or the policy of the legislation to support these sweeping statements.

It must not be thought that in using the phrase 'any decision affecting the conduct of a trial on indictment' I am offering a definition of a phrase which Parliament has chosen not to define. If the statutory language is, as here, imprecise, it may well be impossible to prescribe in the abstract a precise test to determine on which side of the line any case should fall and, therefore, necessary to proceed, as counsel for the appellant submitted that we should, on a case by case basis. But it is obviously desirable that your Lordships' House should give as clear guidance as the statutory language permits, and I hope the criterion I have suggested may provide a helpful pointer to the right answer in most cases.

The Court of Appeal, Criminal Division, decided in *R v Hayden* [1975] 2 All ER 558, [1975] 1 WLR 852 that an order that a convicted defendant pay a sum towards the costs of the prosecution is subject to appeal under the Criminal Appeal Act 1968 as falling within the definition of 'sentence' in s 50(1) of that Act. But the court, at the same time, followed and affirmed an earlier decision (*R v Collier* (7 December 1972, unreported on this point) that an order that the defendant make a contribution to his own legal aid costs is not appealable. That being so, I feel considerable unease that a defendant tried on indictment and ordered by the Crown Court to contribute to his own legal aid costs, no matter how gravely flawed by errors of law or procedure the order may be, should have no remedy available to question it. This is not the occasion to overrule the decision of the Divisional Court in *R v Crown Court at Cardiff, ex p Jones* [1973] 3 All ER 1027, [1974] QB 113, since we have not heard the point argued. I observe, however, that the relevant statutory criterion applicable is to order the defendant in receipt of legal aid 'to make such contribution . . . as appears to the court making the order reasonable having regard to his resources and commitments': see the Legal Aid Act 1974, s 32(1). This is quite a different criterion from such as would govern the discretion whether or not to make any of the orders for costs which may be made under s 3(1)(a) or s 4(1) of the Costs in Criminal Cases Act 1973. The exercise of that discretion is intimately related to the conduct of the trial; indeed, it may be said to be an integral part of the trial process. A legal aid contribution order, on the other hand, seems to be unaffected by any consideration arising from the conduct of the trial, and is certainly no part of the trial process. There appears to me, therefore, to be much to be said for the view that it is not 'relating to trial on indictment' within the meaning of s 28(2)(a) or s 29(3) of the 1981 Act.

Finally, as regards the solicitor who is ordered to pay personally the costs thrown away by the adjournment of a trial on indictment, it would again be inappropriate to express a concluded view. But, for my part, having considered the obiter dicta in the passages I have cited above from *R v Smith (Martin)* [1974] 1 All ER 651, [1975] QB 531, I much prefer the doubts of Megaw LJ to the confident assertions of Lord Denning MR and Sir Eric Sachs.

My Lords, I would accordingly allow this appeal and remit the appellant's application for judicial review to the Divisional Court to be heard on its merits. I propose that the respondents be ordered to pay the appellant's costs of the appeal to this House, but that all questions relating to the costs of the proceedings in the Divisional Court be left for determination by that court when it finally disposes of the appellant's application.

**LORD BRIGHTMAN.** My Lords, I would allow this appeal for the reasons given in the speech of my noble and learned friend Lord Bridge. In particular, I gratefully adopt his criterion, 'any decision affecting the conduct of a trial on indictment', as a helpful pointer to the interpretation of the exclusionary clause in s 29(3) of the 1981 Act.

*Appeal allowed.*

Solicitors: *Kingsley Napley & Co* (for the appellant); *Solicitor for the Customs and Excise.*

Mary Rose Plummer   Barrister.

# Lee v Walker

COURT OF APPEAL, CIVIL DIVISION
CUMMING-BRUCE, DILLON LJJ AND SIR DENYS BUCKLEY
19, 20, 21 NOVEMBER, 5 DECEMBER 1984

*Contempt of court – Committal – Breach of injunction – Jurisdiction – County court – Suspension of committal – Judge ordering committal order to be suspended on condition that defendant comply with certain conditions – Whether county court having jurisdiction to suspend order – County Courts Act 1984, s 38.*

*Contempt of court – Committal – Breach of injunction – Jurisdiction – County court – Consecutive sentences of imprisonment for contempt – Defendant committed to prison for contempt – Order suspended providing defendant comply with certain conditions – Defendant in breach of conditions – Judge ordering removal of suspension of committal order – Judge finding defendant in further breach of injunction and ordering defendant to prison for further period to run consecutive to period of original committal – Whether county court having power to impose consecutive sentences of imprisonment for civil contempt – County Courts Act 1984, s 38.*

*Contempt of court – Committal – County court – Application – Notice of committal – Whether notice to be signed by 'proper officer' of court – Whether notice signed by solicitor of party seeking committal a valid notice – CCR 1981 Ord 29, r 1(4).*

On 14 September 1984 in the county court the defendant was found to have breached certain injunctions and was committed to prison for 28 days for contempt of court, that order to be suspended for two months providing he complied with certain conditions. On 24 October 1984 a different judge of the county court held that the defendant was in breach of the conditions imposed by the order of 14 September and ordered that the suspension of the committal order be removed and that the defendant be committed to prison for 28 days. The judge also found that the defendant had committed further breaches of the injunctions and ordered that in respect of that contempt he be committed to prison for three months consecutive to the period of 28 days. The Official Solicitor appealed on behalf of the defendant, contending (i) that the county court had no jurisdiction to suspend committal of a contemnor for breach of an order of the court because, although s 38[a] of the County Courts Act 1984 had conferred on county courts the same ancillary jurisdiction as the High Court had, a county court was an inferior court and as such could not have the statutory jurisdiction to suspend committal orders conferred by RSC Ord 52, r 7(1)[b] only on the High Court, (ii) that neither the High Court nor, a fortiori, the county court had power to impose consecutive sentences of imprisonment where a contemnor was found to have committed acts of contempt of court of a civil nature, ie by failure to comply with orders of the court made in civil proceedings, and (iii) that because of certain irregularities, in that all three notices of committal had been signed by the plaintiff's solicitors and not by a 'proper officer' as required by CCR 1981 Ord 29, r 1(4)[c], the committal orders were bad and should be quashed.

**Held** – (1) The High Court's jurisdiction to suspend committal orders in contempt proceedings was not statutory but was founded on common law. Moreover on its true construction RSC Ord 52, r 7 did not confer a new jurisdiction on the High Court to suspend orders, but merely prescribed the procedure for the exercise of that power. Since by virtue of s 14(4A)[d] of the Contempt of Court Act 1981 the county court was to be

---

a   Section 38 is set out at p 783 j to p 784 b, post
b   Rule 7(1) provides: 'The Court by whom an order of committal is made may by order direct that the execution of the order of committal shall be suspended for such period or on such terms as it may specify.'
c   Rule 1(4), so far as material, is set out at p 786 b, post
d   Section 14(4A) is set out at p 783 h, post

treated as a superior court, and since s 38 of the 1984 Act conferred on the county court the same powers as the High Court had, it followed that the county court had power to   *a* suspend a committal order conditional on compliance with certain conditions (see p 784 *c* to *g*, post); Re Lumley, ex p Cathcart [1894] 2 Ch 271 distinguished.

(2) The High Court had an inherent jurisdiction to impose consecutive sentences of imprisonment in appropriate cases where the court had power to imprison. Furthermore the inherent jurisdiction of the court to punish contempt of court had not been affected by statutes dealing with imprisonment. It followed that under s 38 of the 1984 Act the   *b* county court also had power to impose consecutive sentences for contempt (see p 785 *e* to *j*, post); dictum of Wilmot CJ in Wilkes v R [1558–1774] All ER Rep at 575 and Morris v Crown Office [1970] 1 All ER 1079 applied.

(3) However, although the court could overlook a defect which could properly be regarded as insignificant, the defects in the notices of committal were not insignificant since the requirement that the notice was to be signed by an officer of the court was   *c* designed for the protection of the person on whom the notice was to be served, and compliance with that requirement was important and to be observed. The committal orders would accordingly be quashed and the appeal allowed (see p 786 *f* to p 787 *a*, post).

**Notes**

For suspension of committal orders, see 9 Halsbury's Laws (4th edn) para 9, and for cases   *d* on conditional orders, see 16 Digest (Reissue) 106–107, 1072–1079.

For the Contempt of Court Act 1981, s 14(4A) (as inserted by the County Courts (Penalties for Contempt) Act 1983, s 1), see 53 Halsbury's Statutes (3rd edn) 55.

**Cases referred to in judgments**

Burrows v Iqbal (7 June 1984, unreported), CA.
Danchevsky v Danchevsky (No 2) (1977) 121 SJ 796, [1977] CA Bound Transcript 416A.   *e*
Dent v Dent and Hall [1962] 1 All ER 746, [1962] P 187, [1962] 2 WLR 793.
Gordon v Gordon [1946] 1 All ER 247, [1946] P 99, CA.
Head v Head [1982] 3 All ER 14, [1982] 1 WLR 1186.
Lumley, Re, ex p Cathcart [1894] 2 Ch 271, CA.
McIlraith v Grady [1967] 3 All ER 625, [1968] 1 QB 468, [1967] 3 WLR 1331, CA.   *f*
Morris v Crown Office [1970] 1 All ER 1079, [1970] 2 QB 114, [1970] 2 WLR 792, CA.
R v Cutbush (1867) LR 2 QB 379.
R v Wilkes (1769) 4 Burr 2527, [1558–1774] All ER Rep 570, 98 ER 327, HL.

**Appeal**

By an order dated 9 March 1984 made in the Worthing County Court, the plaintiff,   *g* Tracey Louise Lee, was granted injunctions restraining the defendant, Peter Walker, (i) from assaulting, molesting or otherwise interfering with the plaintiff and (ii) from, inter alia, entering on the plaintiff's property known as North Flat, 417 Brighton Road, Lancing, West Sussex. On 14 September 1984 in the Worthing County Court his Honour Judge John Ward ordered that the defendant be committed for contempt to prison for 28 days and further ordered that the order for committal should not be put into force   *f* provided that the defendant complied with certain conditions for a period of two months. On 24 October 1984 his Honour CJ Cunliffe sitting as a deputy circuit judge in Worthing County Court held that the defendant was in breach of the suspended order of committal dated 14 September and ordered (i) that the suspension of that order be removed and that the defendant be committed to prison for 28 days and (ii) that the defendant be committed for contempt to prison for three months, that period to run consecutive to   *f* the period of 28 days' imprisonment. The Official Solicitor appealed on behalf of the defendant. The facts are set out in the judgment of the court.

James Munby for the Official Solicitor.
Joseph Hamed for the plaintiff.

*a* At the conclusion of the argument the court announced that the appeal would be allowed for reasons to be given later.

5 December. The following judgment of the court was delivered.

**CUMMING-BRUCE LJ.** On 21 November 1984 we allowed appeals moved by the Official Solicitor on behalf of the defendant, and quashed a committal order made against
*b* him by his Honour Judge Ward in Worthing County Court on 14 September 1984 and two committal orders made against him by his Honour CJ Cunliffe sitting as a deputy circuit judge in the same court on 24 October 1984. We now give reasons for those decisions.

By his order of 14 September 1984 Judge Ward ordered that the defendant be committed for his contempt in certain breaches of injunction to prison for 28 days, and
*c* further ordered that the committal order should not be put into force provided that the contemnor should for a period of two months as from that date comply with two conditions.

On 24 October 1984 Deputy Judge Cunliffe held that he was in breach of a condition imposed by the order of the county court of 14 September and ordered that the suspension of the order of committal of 14 September be removed and that the contemnor be
*d* committed for contempt to prison for 28 days or until sooner discharged by due course of law.

On the same day Deputy Judge Cunliffe found that the defendant had committed further contempt by breaches of injunction since 14 September, and ordered that for that contempt he should be committed to prison for three months and that the three month period do run consecutive to the period of 28 days' imprisonment ordered on
*e* removal of the suspension of the committal order made by Judge Ward on 14 September.

The grounds of appeal fall under three distinct heads. First, that the county court has no jurisdiction to suspend committal of a contemnor to prison for contempt by breach of an order of the court in the manner purported to be ordered by the county court judge on 14 September.

Second, that the county court had no jurisdiction to order on 24 October that the three
*f* month period of imprisonment imposed by the second committal order on that day should run consecutive to the period of 28 days ordered by the first committal order made on that day.

Third, that all three committal orders were bad and must be quashed as all the orders were fatally tainted by procedural irregularities arising from all three notices of application for committal and on the face of all three orders of committal.
*g* We deal with those contentions in that order.

*Has the county court power to suspend a committal order made for contempt by breach of an order of the court?*

Counsel for the Official Solicitor submitted that the county court is an inferior court of record and as such cannot have any jurisdiction to commit for contempt unless such jurisdiction has been conferred by statute. Whatever the validity of this proposition in
*h* earlier years, it cannot survive the year 1983, when by the Contempt of Court Act 1981, s 14(4A) as inserted by the County Courts (Penalties for Contempt) Act 1983, which came into force on 13 May 1983, it was enacted that 'For the purposes of the preceding provisions of this section a county court shall be treated as a superior court and not as an inferior court'. However his next submission was that the power of the High Court was statutory, and conferred by RSC Ord 52, r 7. Order 52 replaced Ords 59 and 44. He
*i* submits that Ord 52, r 7 conferred on the High Court express statutory power and s 38 of the County Courts Act 1984 cannot as a matter of construction extend to confer on the county court a power which the relevant statute only confers on the High Court. We do not accept the submission. Section 38 reads:

'(1) Every county court, as regards any cause of action for the time being within its jurisdiction—(a) shall grant such relief, redress or remedy or combination of remedies, either absolute or conditional; and (b) shall give such and the like effect to every ground of defence or counterclaim equitable or legal, as ought to be granted or given in the like case by the High Court and in as full and ample a manner.

(2) For the purposes of this section it shall be assumed (notwithstanding any enactment to the contrary) that any proceedings which can be commenced in a county court could be commenced in the High Court.'

There was in the instant case a cause of action within the jurisdiction of the county court, namely the proceedings in which on 9 March 1984 the plaintiff obtained injunctions against the defendant. The injunctions ordered were relief, redress or remedy or combination of remedies within the meaning of the rule, and the order for committal was an order ancillary to the enforcement of that relief. By the terms of the section relief, redress or remedy or combination of remedies may be either absolute or conditional and the jurisdiction is such as ought to be granted or given in the like case by the High Court pursuant to the powers conferred by Ord 52, r 7. We do not accept that Ord 52, r 7 conferred a new jurisdiction on the High Court. In our view the content of the rule was procedural, and prescribed the procedure for the exercise of a power of suspension of committal orders which has never been doubted. As a matter of practice, the procedure usually followed was to direct that the order should lie in the office for a stated time and should not issue if the contemnor within that time complied with stated conditions, as a way of tempering justice with mercy, to use the language of Scarman J when sentencing the contemnor in *Dent v Dent and Hall* [1962] 1 All ER 746, [1962] P 187. The common law way of giving a suspended sentence was explained by Lord Denning MR in *Morris v Crown Office* [1970] 1 All ER 1079 at 1083, [1970] 2 QB 114 at 125. Order 52, r 7 now prescribes the procedure for exercising the ancient common law power. The rule does not confer jurisdiction, but prescribes the method of its exercise. Counsel for the Official Solicitor submitted that the decision of this court in *Re Lumley, ex p Cathcart* [1894] 2 Ch 271 was inconsistent with this view of the jurisdiction. But the judgments in that case make it plain that the court was not doubting the jurisdiction to make a penal order and to give days of grace before the order came into operation. It was the form of the order that was incorrect as a means of exercising the jurisdiction. The decision of the Divisional Court in *Head v Head* [1982] 3 All ER 14, [1982] 1 WLR 1186 is not material to the powers of the High Court as it is concerned with the extent of the statutory powers conferred by s 63 of the Magistrates' Courts Act 1980.

For these reasons we find it unnecessary to examine other authorities cited by both counsel, to whose industry and argument we are none the less indebted. We hold that the county court had power on making an order of committal to prison to suspend the order conditional on compliance with stated conditions.

*Has the county court power to impose consecutive sentences for contempt?*

The second point on jurisdiction taken by counsel on behalf of the Official Solicitor is that he submits that neither the High Court nor, a fortiori, the county court has any power to impose consecutive sentences of imprisonment where a contemnor is found to have committed acts of contempt of court of the nature of civil contempt, ie by failure to comply with orders of the court made in civil proceedings. It is submitted that, if it is necessary or desirable to impose separate sentences for separate acts of contempt, then all those sentences must be concurrent.

It is submitted as a general proposition that there is no inherent power in the court to pass a consecutive sentence, because any sentence of imprisonment must take immediate effect. This general proposition is said to be illustrated by *Head v Head*, a decision of a Divisional Court of the Family Division. As we have stated earlier, *Head v Head* was, however, merely a decision under a particular statute, the Magistrates' Courts Act 1980 under the definition section in which, s 150, the term sentence expressly did not include a committal for contempt. We do not find that decision relevant to the present case.

As we see it, the position at common law was that before 1827 the court had no power
*a* to pass a sentence of imprisonment for felony because the sentence for felony was death,
and therefore there was no occasion for passing consecutive sentences for felony. But the
court had power to pass a sentence of imprisonment for misdemeanour, and in *R v Wilkes*
(1769) 4 Burr 2527 at 2577, [1558–1774] All ER Rep 570 at 575 Wilmot CJ in giving the
opinion of the judges to the House of Lords explained most lucidly that a judgment of
imprisonment against a defendant to commence from and after the determination of an
*b* imprisonment to which he was before sentenced for another offence was good in law. If
that were not so, either the offender would receive no punishment at all for the second
offence, or, by the imposition of an unduly long sentence for the second offence, the
principle that the sentence for each offence should be what is appropriate for that offence
as a separate offence would be flouted. Counsel for the Official Solicitor submits that
*Wilkes's* case only applies where a man has been tried for misdemeanour on indictment
*c* or information. But the reasoning of Wilmot CJ is directed throughout not to the form
of the proceedings, but to the justice of the sentence and his conclusion is that the
imposition of a consecutive sentence of imprisonment is the only form, consistent with
justice, whereby a man who is imprisoned already for one offence can be properly
punished for another offence meriting imprisonment.

We note at this juncture that it was stated by Lawton LJ in *Danchevsky v Danchevsky*
*d* (No 2) [1977] CA Bound Transcript 416A that civil contempt of court is a common law
misdemeanour, and we have heard no argument to show that Lawton LJ was wrong. We
note also that in *R v Cutbush* (1867) LR 2 QB 379 at 382 Cockburn CJ, in giving the
judgment at the Court of Queen's Bench, referred to right and justice requiring that,
when a man has been guilty of separate offences for each of which a separate term of
imprisonment is a proper form of punishment, he should not escape from the
*e* punishment due to the additional offence merely because he is already sentenced to be
imprisoned for another offence.

We conclude that the High Court has always had inherent jurisdiction to impose
consecutive sentences of imprisonment in any appropriate case where the court had
power to imprison.

Counsel for the Official Solicitor submits that, even if that was the case in the days of
*f* Wilmot CJ it is not so now, because the powers of the High Court to imprison are now
governed by statute, and there is no statute giving that court power to impose consecutive
sentences for civil contempt. In essence his submission is that as the legislature has
stepped in and prescribed the court's powers to imprison there is no inherent jurisdiction
left in the High Court to do what might otherwise have been permissible at common
law. *Morris v Crown Office* [1970] 1 All ER 1079, [1970] 2 QB 114 shows, however, in our
*g* judgment, that the inherent jurisdiction of the court to punish contempt of court
subsists, and is not cut down by statutes dealing generally with imprisonment for crime.
Counsel for the Official Solicitor cited *Morris v Crown Office* on a different limb of this
appeal, to show that the special provisions laid down by general statutes about sentencing
for offences under the criminal law had no application to sentencing for contempt of
court. It must follow that these statutes do not abolish or cut down the inherent powers
*h* of the High Court to punish for contempt of court.

If the High Court has power to impose consecutive sentences for contempt of court,
has the county court such a power? A county court is now a 'superior court' for the
purposes of s 14 of the Contempt of Court Act 1981 and can under that section commit
a contemnor to prison for as long a period as the High Court can. We would find it
surprising if the county court did not have the same power as the High Court to impose
*i* a consecutive sentence of imprisonment for contempt. We have already held that s 38 of
the County Courts Act 1984 gives the county court power to suspend a sentence of
imprisonment imposed for contempt. The same reasoning leads us to the conclusion
that under s 38 the county court has power to impose a consecutive sentence of
imprisonment for contempt. We cannot regard the prescribed form of warrant for

committal, Form N80, or the prescribed form of order of committal for breach of or
neglect to obey an order, Form N79, as sufficient to override this conclusion, which is    *a*
founded, as already indicated, on right and justice.

*The procedural irregularities*
Finally we must deal with certain admitted irregularities relating to the three
committal orders.
CCR 1981 Ord 29, r 1(4) provides:                                                          *b*

'If the person served with the judgment or order fails to obey it, the proper officer
shall, at the request of the judgment creditor, issue a notice calling on that person to
show cause why a committal order should not be made against him . . .'

The meaning of the term 'proper officer' is defined in Ord 1, r 3. It includes the registrar
and the chief clerk of the relevant court as well as certain other authorised persons.       *c*
The defendant having disobeyed the injunction made on 9 May 1984, a notice which
purported to be pursuant to Ord 29, r 1(4) was served on him on 7 September 1984. That
notice, however, was irregular by reason of the fact that it was not signed by a proper
officer of the court but by the plaintiff's solicitors. It was accordingly defective. The
suspended committal order was, however, made on that application on 14 September
1984.                                                                                        *d*
The defendant having committed further breaches of the injunction as well as of the
condition of suspension contained in the suspended committal order, a further notice
purporting to be pursuant to Ord 29, r 1(4) was served on him on 22 October 1984. On
that application being heard the suspension of the suspended committal order was
removed and the defendant was committed to prison for the period specified in the
suspended order, namely 28 days. On the same application the judge committed the         *e*
defendant to prison for the further period of three months to run consecutively to the 28
days. The notice served on 22 October 1984 suffered from a precisely similar defect to
that of the earlier notice. Regrettably these defects were not detected at the hearing of
either of the applications.
Counsel for the plaintiff has admitted the defects and has not disputed the consequent
invalidity of the three committal orders. This was a proper course. Where a man's liberty    *f*
is at stake every requirement of the law must be strictly complied with (see *Gordon v
Gordon* [1946] 1 All ER 247, [1946] P 99 per Lord Greene MR, *McIlraith v Grady* [1967]
3 All ER 625 at 627, [1968] 1 QB 468 at 477 per Lord Denning MR). This does not mean
that, if in the circumstances of a particular case a defect can properly be regarded as
insignificant, a court cannot disregard it. This court did so in *Burrows v Iqbal* (7 June
1984, unreported) (Sir John Donaldson MR and Griffiths LJ), where the suggested          *g*
irregularity was a failure to state in a committal order the date on which the only relevant
contempt of court was found to have been committed and the circumstances were such
that the contempt could only have occurred on a particular day, which was easily
identifiable, and could in any event have been identified by reference to the judge's note.
We do not consider, however, that the defects in the present case can be regarded as
insignificant. The requirement that the notice must be signed by an officer of the court    *h*
must, we think, be designed for the protection of the person on whom the notice is to be
served, and compliance should be insisted on.
The reference in Ord 29, r 1(4) to 'the judgment creditor' appears to us to be an oddity.
No point has been taken in this case on these words and we have heard no argument
about them, but we are inclined to the view that they be a consequence of a slip of the
pen or an oversight on the parts of the draftsman and of the rule making authority. The     *j*
context suggests that the person intended to be referred to is the person entitled to the
benefit of the judgment or order which is alleged not to have been obeyed.
As soon as the defects in the notices in the present case and the consequent invalidity
of the committal orders were admitted we directed that the defendant should be released
on unconditional bail. When the arguments of the other points had been completed, we

indicated that we would allow the appeal for reasons to be given later. Therefore we
a discharged the defendant from custody.

*Appeal allowed. Committal orders quashed; defendant discharged from custody. No order for
costs.*

Solicitors: *Official Solicitor; Gates & Co,* Steyning (for the plaintiff).

b
                                                                    Bebe Chua    Barrister.

# Williams v Fawcett

c COURT OF APPEAL, CIVIL DIVISION
SIR JOHN DONALDSON MR, DILLON LJ AND MUSTILL J
13, 14 FEBRUARY 1985

*Contempt of court – Committal – County court – Application – Notice of committal – Breach of
undertaking – Notice to respondent to show cause why committal order should not be made –*
d *Whether notice to be signed by 'proper officer' of court – Whether notice to specify alleged breaches
of undertaking – County Court (Forms) Rules 1982, Form N78.*

*Contempt of court – Committal – County court – Application – Notice of committal – Breach of
undertaking – Notice to respondent to show cause why committal order should not be made –
Whether notice to be addressed to proper officer of court – Whether notice to be signed by
e applicant's solicitor without qualification – County Court (Forms) Rules 1982, Form N78.*

*Precedent – Court of Appeal – Binding effect of previous decisions of court – Power of court to
depart from previous decision – Exceptional circumstances in which court will depart from
previous decision – Case unlikely to reach House of Lords and concerning liberty of subject.*

The respondent gave an undertaking in court not to molest the applicant nor to return
to her house for a specified period. The applicant subsequently alleged that the respondent
had breached the undertaking on a number of occasions, and she applied for an order
committing the respondent for contempt. Notice was accordingly given to the respondent
in Form N 78 of the County Court (Forms) Rules 1982 to show cause why he should not
be committed to prison. The notice failed to specify particulars of the breaches alleged
f and was signed only by the applicant's solicitor. The particulars of the alleged breaches
were not provided until the day of the hearing and at the hearing the respondent
requested an adjournment. The judge refused the request and made the committal order
sought. The respondent appealed, contending, inter alia, that the notice was defective
because it failed to specify the alleged breaches and it was required to be signed by a
'proper officer' of the court.

g **Held** – (1) There was no requirement that a notice in Form N 78 of the 1982 rules
requiring the respondent to show cause why he should not be committed for contempt
had to be signed by a 'proper officer' of the court. In the circumstances there were
exceptional circumstances for not following, as being per incuriam, previous decisions of
the Court of Appeal which held that a proper officer was required to sign the notice,
those circumstances being (a) that the growth of the error in the previous cases could be
clearly detected, (b) that the cases concerned the liberty of the subject and (c) that the
cases were of such a nature that it was unlikely that any of them would reach the House
of Lords, so giving the House an opportunity of correcting the error which had crept
into the law. Accordingly the previous decisions of the Court of Appeal would not be
followed (see p 795 *f* to *j* and p 796 *a e* and *g*, post); dicta of Lord Greene MR in *Young v*

*Bristol Aeroplane Co Ltd* [1944] 2 All ER at 300 and of Evershed MR in *Morelle Ltd v Wakeling* [1955] 1 All ER at 718 applied; *Gagnon v Macdonald* (1984) Times, 14 November and *Lee v Walker* [1985] 1 All ER 781 not followed.

(2) However, it was wholly wrong to ask the respondent to answer allegations as serious as were breaches of an undertaking given to the court without giving him reasonable notice, and the offer of an adjournment could not cure that defect. Accordingly, on that ground and on the ground that the ˙notice had failed to specify the breaches alleged, the appeal would be allowed and the committal order quashed (see p 791 *d e* and p 796 *c* to *e* and *g*, post).

*Per curiam.* It is undesirable, but not fatal, for a notice to be addressed to the registrar or other proper officer of the court, or for the notice to be signed by the applicant's solicitor unless he qualifies his signature with a statement to the effect that the notice is made on the application of the applicant or his solicitor, thereby removing any ambiguity whether the notice was an order of the court. The County Court Rules Committee should consider amending Form N 78 to accommodate applicants' solicitors whose practice is to sign the forms (see p 792 *d* to *f* and p 796 *a* to *e* and *g*, post).

(2) Form N 79, the committal form, should be amended in order to provide an appropriate space for recording any dispensation pursuant to CCR 1981 Ord 29, r 1(6) and (7)[a] (see p 796 *d e* and *g*, post).

**Notes**

For breach of undertaking given to the court, see 9 Halsbury's Laws (4th edn) para 75, and for cases on the subject, see 16 Digest (Reissue) 81–84, 796–816.

For the binding effect of Court of Appeal decisions, see 26 Halsbury's Laws (4th edn) para 578, and for cases on the subject, see 30 Digest (Reissue) 269–273, 763–793.

**Cases referred to in judgments**

*Gagnon v Macdonald* (1984) Times, 14 November, CA.
*Lakin v Lakin* (19 December 1984, unreported), CA.
*Lee v Walker* [1985] 1 All ER 781, CA.
*McIlraith v Grady* [1967] 3 All ER 625, [1968] 1 QB 468, [1967] 3 WLR 1331, CA.
*Morelle Ltd v Wakeling* [1955] 1 All ER 708, [1955] 2 QB 379, [1955] 2 WLR 672, CA.
*Nguyen Thi An v Phung Chan Phi* [1984] FLR 773, CA.
*Payne v Payne* (28 March 1979, unreported), CA.
*Young v Bristol Aeroplane Co Ltd* [1944] 2 All ER 293, [1944] KB 718, CA; affd [1946] 1 All ER 98, [1946] AC 163, HL.

**Cases also cited**

*D v A & Co* [1900] 1 Ch 484.
*Mancaster Motor Co (London) Ltd v Bremith Ltd* [1941] 2 All ER 11, [1941] 1 KB 75, CA.

**Appeal**

The respondent, William Edwin Fawcett, appealed against the order of his Honour Judge Forrester-Paton QC sitting at Middlesbrough County Court on 9 January 1985 whereby the respondent was committed to prison for four months for breaches of an undertaking given by him to his Honour Judge S S Gill on 3 August 1984 not to molest the applicant, Angela Williams, and not to return to her house, 60 Tennyson Avenue, Grangetown, Middlesbrough. The facts are set out in the judgment of Sir John Donaldson MR.

*James Munby* for the respondent.
*Quintin Iwi* for the applicant.

**SIR JOHN DONALDSON MR.** This is an appeal by Mr William Fawcett (the respondent) against an order made by his Honour Judge Forrester-Paton QC on 9 January 1985 committing him to prison for various terms, totalling in all four months, for five breaches of an undertaking not to molest the respondent to this appeal, Angela Williams

---

*a*	Rule 1, so far as material, is set out at p 790 *d* to *f*, post

a (the applicant), and not to return to her house at 60 Tennyson Avenue, Grangetown, Middlesbrough.

The appeal raises two issues. First, should the committal order be set aside for procedural errors? Second, is there any requirement that a notice to show cause why a respondent should not be committed to prison be signed by 'the proper officer' of the court? At the conclusion of the argument we quashed the order, and I now give my reasons for that decision.

b The matter starts with CCR 1981 Ord 29, r 1, which is the governing order concerning committals for breaches of injunctions. Although in this case the complaint was of a breach of an undertaking, an undertaking is of course always treated as being the equivalent of an injunction in the like terms. I need not read para (1) of Ord 29, r 1, but I must read most of the other paragraphs. Paragraph (2) provides:

c 'Subject to paragraphs (6) and (7), a judgment or order shall not be enforced under paragraph (1) unless (a) a copy of the judgment or order has been served personally on the person required to do or abstain from doing the act in question and also, where that person is a body corporate, on the director or other officer of the body against whom a committal order is sought, and (b) in the case of a judgment or order requiring a person to do an act, the copy has been so served before the expiration of the time within which he was required to do the act and was d accompanied by a copy of any order, made between the date of the judgment or order and the date of service, fixing that time.'

That paragraph shows that, subject to the exercise of the dispensing power which is contained in paras (6) and (7), the order containing the injunction, or recording the undertaking, must be served personally on the person who is bound by it. Further, if it e involves a positive injunction or a positive undertaking, it has to be served before the time when the act is to be done.

Paragraph (3) reads:

'Where a judgment or order enforceable by committal order under paragraph (1) has been given or made, the proper officer shall, if the judgment or order is in the nature of an injunction, at the time when the judgment or order is drawn up, and in any other case on the request of the judgment creditor, issue a copy of the judgment, or order, indorsed with or incorporating a notice as to the consequences of disobedience, for service in accordance with paragraph (2).'

That paragraph refers to what is known as a 'penal notice' and it is to be observed that the court has no discretion whether to issue it. It must be issued at the time when the order or judgment is drawn up if that order or judgment is in the nature of an injunction or, in any other case, if and when the judgment creditor so requests.

I now turn to para (4), which is the paragraph with which we have been principally concerned. That reads:

'If the person served with the judgment or order fails to obey it, the proper officer shall, at the request of the judgment creditor, issue a notice calling on that person to show cause why a committal order should not be made against him, and subject to paragraph (7) [that is one of the dispensing paragraphs] the notice shall be served on him personally.'

I get from that rule the following propositions. First, it is 'the proper officer' who has to issue the notice to show cause, and he does so at the request of the judgment creditor. 'The proper officer' is a term of art, which is defined in Ord 1, r 3 as follows:

'... "proper officer" means the registrar or, in relation to any act of a formal or administrative character which is not by statute the responsibility of the registrar, the chief clerk or any other officer of the court acting on his behalf in accordance with directions given by the Lord Chancellor ...'

Similarly that rather strange expression in this context, 'the judgment creditor', is a term of art, which is defined in Ord 25, r 1 as meaning 'the person who has obtained or is entitled to enforce a judgment or order'.

Second, I get from this rule that the notice has to call on the respondent to show cause why a committal order should not be made, and that, on the authorities, this is a condition precedent to the exercise of the power of committal.

Third, the notice must be served personally, subject to the dispensing power in para (7), which would no doubt be exercised where somebody, having been present in court and having had an injunctive order made against him, committed a breach of the injunction before there was any opportunity to serve him, and there may well be other cases.

The fourth matter I get not directly from the paragraph, but from the paragraph read in conjunction with the County Court (Forms) Rules 1982, SI 1982/586. This is that the notice must be in Form N 78, since by r 2(1) of the 1982 rules it is provided that:

'The forms contained in the Schedule to these Rules [which include Form N 78] shall be used in connection with proceedings in county courts to which the County Court Rules 1981 apply, subject to and in accordance with the provisions of this rule.'

I should mention that that form contains a space for the seal of the court, and it is also provided under r 2(5) of the 1982 rules that: 'Every form in the Schedule marked with the word "Seal" shall bear the seal of the court.' The only remaining paragraphs of r 1 of Ord 29 to which I need refer are paras (6) and (7). Paragraph (6) provides:

'A judgment or order requiring a person to abstain from doing an act may be enforced under paragraph (1) notwithstanding that service of a copy of the judgment or order has not been effected in accordance with paragraph (2) if the judge is satisfied that, pending such service, the person against whom it is sought to enforce the judgment or order has had notice thereof either—(a) by being present when the judgment or order was given or made, or (b) by being notified of the terms of the judgment or order whether by telephone, telegram or otherwise.'

Paragraph (7) provides:

'Without prejudice to its powers under Order 7, rule 8, the court may dispense with service of a copy of a judgment or order under paragraph (2) or a notice to show cause under paragraph (4), if the court thinks it just to do so.'

If those powers of dispensation are exercised, this fact has to be stated in the committal order. The authority for that proposition is *Nguyen Thi An v Phung Chan Phi* [1984] FLR 773. The ratio of this decision appears to be that since Form N 79, which is the committal order form and is also a compulsory form, makes provision in the text for recording when notice of the order was served on the contemnor, if the order was not served on the contemnor, it should be so stated on the form.

I now return to Form N 78. As I have already mentioned, it must be sealed, but it is important to note the limited effect of sealing such a notice. Section 134 of the County Courts Act 1984 states:

'(1) All summonses issuing out of a county court, and all such other documents so issuing as may be prescribed, shall be sealed or stamped with the seal of the court.

(2) All such summonses and other documents purporting to be so sealed shall, in England and Wales, be received in evidence without further proof.'

So the only effect of the seal is that the document is admissible in evidence without further proof as being what it purports to be.

It is of some significance in the context of Form N 78 and the suggestion that it has to be signed by 'the proper officer' that there is no space on the form for his signature. By contrast, Form N 76, which is a certificate to be indorsed on a duplicate warrant of committal issued for the rearrest of a debtor, does contain a place where the certificate would be signed by the registrar. It seems, therefore, that, where these forms are intended

to be signed by someone, there will be a space for them to append their signature. No
*a* such space occurs in form N 78 so far as the proper officer is concerned, although in the
rather curious layout of the prescribed form there is, as it were, an appendix with space
for the bailiff to certify that he has served the notice and for him to sign that certificate.
In practice this part of the form is not reproduced when the notice is served otherwise
than by the bailiff.

   I now turn briefly to the facts of this case. The undertaking was given by the
*b* respondent in court on 3 August 1984, and was expressed to remain in force for a period
of six months expiring on 2 February 1985. The notice to show cause why he should not
be committed to prison for breach of that undertaking was given on 20 November and
called on him to appear in court on 26 November. The notice was essentially in Form N
78, but it failed to show any particulars of the breach or breaches of the undertaking
alleged against him. It was addressed to him and it was signed by the solicitors for the
*c* applicant.

   The matter was stood over by consent until 9 January, and on that day the respondent
duly attended at court. Then, for the first time, he was provided with particulars of the
five breaches of the undertaking which were alleged. Not surprisingly, counsel appearing
on his behalf applied for an adjournment. That adjournment was refused, and evidence
was called. There is some doubt in the minds of those who recollect the proceedings
*d* whether or not there was an indication by the judge that the application for an
adjournment could be renewed; but, in my judgment, that is plainly immaterial, because
to ask somebody to respond to allegations as serious as are breaches of an undertaking
without any reasonable notice is wholly wrong. It could not be cured by offering him an
adjournment after the evidence had been taken or partly taken, both because it was then
too late and because the rules require that particulars of the breach or breaches alleged
*e* appear in the notice to show cause.

   So on the grounds both that he was denied an adjournment and that the notice failed
to specify the breaches (either would have sufficed) the order must be quashed.

   I therefore turn to the matters of more general interest. They are, first, the penal
notice, second, whether a notice to show cause why someone should not be committed
to prison has to be signed by the proper officer, third, what the effect is of addressing
*f* such a notice to the registrar as well as to the respondent, and, fourth, what the effect is
of the notice being signed by the applicant's solicitor.

   So far as the penal notice is concerned, it does not arise in this case because the
respondent's undertaking was incorporated in an order, and that order did carry a penal
notice. There was therefore no need to exercise any dispensing power or to record that
dispensation in the committal order. But I advert to the matter because we have been
*g* told in the course of the argument that it is not uncommon for courts to fail and, on
occasion, to refuse to attach a penal notice to an injunction given in a matrimonial
context. We have not been told quite why courts should be adopting this attitude, but it
may very well be that it is thought that there should be some middle position between
'inviting', in fairly strong terms, a party to a matrimonial dispute to refrain, for example,
from going near the matrimonial home and ordering him not to do so with the added
*h* threat of immediate imprisonment. It may be thought in some cases that whilst it is one
thing for the court to assist the wife by requiring the husband not to molest her, it is
another thing to give the wife the weapon of being, as it were, able to taunt him by
saying, 'One step further and you go to prison.'

   That is speculation. But the fact is that if this is being done on a fairly wide scale, it
must be that the courts concerned think that there is good reason for adopting this line.
But I have to say that, as the law stands, there is no warrant for their doing so. The rule is
mandatory, and the court is required, when issuing an order containing an injunction or
an undertaking to the like effect, to indorse a penal notice. That is quite clear from Ord
29, r 1. However, the County Court Rule Committee may wish to consider whether
there should be some relaxation of this requirement, and, if so, what the effect of such a
relaxation should be on the liability to imprisonment of the person to whom the
injunction is addressed, bearing in mind that the penal notice is intended to put him on

notice of just that risk. It may be thought that some balance has to be achieved between, on the one hand, raising the temperature of the matrimonial dispute and, on the other, not allowing a situation to be reached in which somebody is committed to prison in circumstances in which he did not have fair warning.

Now I turn to the question of the signature of the applicant's solicitor. The problem really arises, as was pointed out in argument, from the fact that Ord 29, r 1(4) contemplates a request by the applicant to the court to issue a notice and the issue of a notice by the court. There are no separate forms for the request and the notice, and the two processes seem in practice to have become elided. As a result, so we are told, it is comparatively common for the applicant's solicitors to draw up the *draft* order, as it then is, in Form N 78, and to sign it, thereby warranting that the draft is correct and that there are reasonable grounds for issuing the order. The proper officer of the court then looks at what is, at that stage, only a request and a draft. If he is satisfied that it appears to be in order, he stamps it with the court's seal, and it is issued, either being returned to the solicitors in order that they may arrange for its service or given to the court bailiff so that the bailiff may serve it. That is why the signature of the solicitor appears. It is also why in a minority of cases we have seen notices which, in addition to being addressed to the respondent, which is essential, are also addressed to the registrar. The solicitors completing Form N 78 address it to the registrar, as the senior officer of the court, because at that stage the form is still a request to issue a notice to the respondent in the like terms.

This is, of course, unfortunate, because it might lead an alleged contemnor to believe that he is being required to show cause by the applicant or the applicant's solicitors rather than by the court. I suggest that it would be better if Form N 78 ended with some such rubric as 'This order was made on the application of', leaving a space for the inclusion of the name either of the judgment creditor or the judgment creditor's solicitor. If precedent is required for such an amendment, it is to be found in Form N 37, which relates to an order for the oral examination of a judgment debtor. This is dated at the bottom of the order, and continues: 'This order was made on the application of [a name and address] (Solicitor(s) for) the Plaintiff'.

However, those amendments have yet to be considered, let alone brought into effect. Meanwhile, if solicitors are to sign these forms at all, and it is probably better that they should not, it is highly desirable that they should include some such sentence as I have already indicated, namely 'This order was made on the application of', putting in their own name or the name of their client, as the case may be.

So far I have not referred to the authorities, and there are four decisions of this court which require consideration. The first is *Payne v Payne* (28 March 1979, unreported), the court consisting of Orr and Brandon LJJ. We have seen a copy of the notice to show cause, which was a somewhat remarkable document. At that time the relevant Order was not Ord 29, r 1, but Ord 25, r 68(2), the only material difference being that the notice had to be issued by the registrar and not by the proper officer. It is a remarkable notice because it says: 'Take notice that we intend to apply to the Registrar of this Court . . . for an Order that the Respondent be committed . . . for breach of the Order made herein on the 9th February, 1979 and served on him on the 9th February, 1979.' It tells you nothing whatever about what that order said. It tells you nothing whatever about the alleged breach. It gives no indication whatsoever to the respondent that he is required to show cause why he should not be committed to prison. Indeed, since it is in form merely notice of an intended application by the applicant, there is no indication that it was issued by the court other than the court seal and that is commonly impressed on all sorts of documents. In those circumstances, it is not surprising that the court set aside the subsequent committal order. However, in the course of his judgment, Orr LJ, after referring to Ord 25 r 68(2), said:

> 'The form of notice which is before us is clearly not in the form required by that section, Form 194, and there are certain features of the form which require to be mentioned. Form 194 makes it clear that the application is to be made to the court and not to the registrar. In the present case the form we have before us purports to be addressed to the registrar. A second feature is that the form with which we are

concerned does not purport to be issued by the registrar. Moreover, it does not contain, and this is the third point, words "requiring the husband to attend and show cause why he should not be committed".'

The next is an authority for which I must accept responsibility. It is *Gagnon v Macdonald* (1984) Times, 14 November, on which I sat with Oliver LJ. The notice in that case was again unusual. It was on one of the printed forms appropriate to proceedings under the Matrimonial Causes Rules 1977, SI 1977/344. It had been subject to extensive amendment to try to bring it into line with Form N 78, but I must say that it did not look like Form N 78. It invited the respondent to take notice that the petitioner intended to apply to the judge for an order—

'that the Respondent be committed to prison for being in breach of the Order of this Court made on the 18th September 1984. The breach alleged is that the Respondent is still in occupation of [a particular house] as stated in the Affidavit of William Stowe sworn 12th October 1984.'

It then went on to add, somewhat gratuitously, 'The probable length of the hearing of this application is 20 minutes', but it did not condescend to tell the respondent that he was required to show cause why he should not be committed to prison. It was addressed to the registrar, who otherwise did not appear to be involved in the proceedings at all since the notice foreshadowed an application to the judge. It was addressed to the respondent, and was signed by the solicitors for the petitioner.

The only objection taken by counsel instructed by the Official Solicitor on behalf of the respondent Mr Macdonald was that the form failed to require the respondent to show cause. But in the course of the argument we were referred to *Payne v Payne*. I then raised the question of whether it was not an additional defect that this notice was addressed to the registrar and also signed by the petitioner's solicitor. In my judgment I referred to the terms of the notice, and continued:

'Then, after dealing with the probable length of the application, it is dated and signed by the solicitors and addressed to the registrar and the respondent. So this is quite clearly a notice issued by a party to the proceedings.'

Then, after referring to Ord 29, r 1(4), I continued:

'The notice to which I have referred failed to comply with that rule in at least two respects. First, it was not issued by the proper officer, who would of course be an officer of the county court; and, secondly, although it was served on Mr MacDonald personally in accordance with the rule, it failed to call on him to show cause why a committal order should not be made against him.'

My judgment did not say in terms that the form should have been signed by the proper officer, but there was a plain implication that, it having been signed by the solicitors, it was not issued by the proper officer, and that it required the signature of the proper officer in order that it might be valid. The decision to set aside the committal order was fully justified in that the notice failed to call on the respondent to show cause why a committal order should not be made against him. However, any implication that the notice had to be signed by the proper officer or that it was invalidated by being signed by the petitioner's solicitors was plainly unjustified.

The next case was *Lee v Walker* [1985] 1 All ER 781. There the court consisted of Cumming-Bruce, Dillon LJJ and Sir Denys Buckley. There were no less than three notices to show cause why there should not be a committal. The court was told, and we have been told, that there were a number of procedural irregularities on which the court could have relied in quashing the committal. However Cumming-Bruce LJ, delivering the judgment of the court, said (at 786):

'The defendant having disobeyed the injunction made on 9 May 1984, a notice which purported to be pursuant to Ord 29, r 1(4) was served on him on 7 September 1984. That notice, however, was irregular by reason of the fact that it was not signed

by a proper officer of the court but by the plaintiff's solicitors. It was accordingly
defective . . . [A further] notice served on 22 October 1984 suffered from a precisely    a
similar defect to that of the earlier notice. Regrettably these defects were not
detected at the hearing of either of the applications. Counsel for the plaintiff, has
admitted the defects and has not disputed the consequent invalidity of the three
committal orders. This was a proper course. Where a man's liberty is at stake every
requirement of the law must be strictly complied with (see *Gordon v Gordon* [1946]
1 All ER 247, [1946] P 99 per Lord Greene MR, *McIlraith v Grady* [1967] 3 All ER    b
625 at 627, [1968] 1 QB 468 at 477 per Lord Denning MR).'

In fairness to counsel, it should be said that he had not seen the transcript of the
judgment in *Gagnon v Macdonald* before he arrived in court and had no real opportunity
of detecting the error in my reasoning.

So there we see the growth of the doctrine that the notice has to be signed by the    c
proper officer coming to full fruition and stated expressly as opposed to impliedly as in
*Gagnon's* case.

The matter ends so far as the authorities are concerned, and they are all very recent
authorities, with *Lakin v Lakin* (19 December 1984, unreported), in which this court
consisted of Watkins LJ and Neill J. The notice in that case was in form N 78, but it failed
to require the respondent to show cause why he should not be committed to prison, and    d
it failed to specify the breaches alleged save by reference to affidavits of the petitioner.
This is not a compliance with the rules. There were other curious features in that the
Form N 78 had been adapted to ask the judge to issue a penal notice and simultaneously
to commit the respondent to prison. Either the penal notice was not needed or it was
wrong to commit to prison immediately after issuing it. The notice was addressed to the
registrar as well as to the respondent and was signed by the plaintiff's solicitor. Watkins    e
LJ, with whom Neill J agreed, said:

'Unhappily, this notice of application was as ineffective as was the order of 23
March. That is because primarily, though not entirely, there was no proper notice
within the body of the application to the respondent to show cause why he should
not be committed to prison, nor was the notice, such as it was, provided by a proper    f
officer of the court. The notice was in fact signed by the petitioner's solicitor's,
whereas in order to be effective in this respect the notice should have been given to
the respondent by the registrar of the county court. One observes that not only was
the application signed by the solicitors, but it is in fact addressed to the registrar, in
addition of course to the respondent.'

If we are bound by these decisions, and we are unless they can be treated as having    g
been reached per incuriam, they represent a very considerable change in the law for
which, so far as I can see, there is absolutely no warrant. The change to which I refer is,
of course, a requirement that these notices shall be signed by the proper officer. The rule
of stare decisis is of the very greatest importance, particularly in an appellate court, such
as this, which sits in six or seven divisions simultaneously. But for this rule, the law
would not only bifurcate; it would branch off in six or seven different directions.    h

That of course has been stresed over and over again. It was emphasised in the classic
case of *Young v Bristol Aeroplane Co Ltd* [1944] 2 All ER 293, [1944] KB 718 and in *Morelle
Ltd v Wakeling* [1955] 1 All ER 708, [1955] 2 QB 379, which considered *Young's* case. But
in each of those cases, as I will demonstrate briefly, the court retained the power in an
exceptional case to depart from its previous decisions. Thus in *Young's* case [1944] 2 All
ER 293 at 300, [1944] KB 718 at 729 Lord Greene MR said:    j

'Where the court has construed a statute or a rule having the force of a statute, its
decision stands on the same footing as any other decision on a question of law. But
where the court is satisfied that an earlier decision was given in ignorance of the
terms of a statute or a rule having the force of a statute the position is very different.

*a* It cannot, in our opinion, be right to say that in such a case the court is entitled to disregard the statutory provision and is bound to follow a decision of its own given when that provision was not present to its mind. Cases of this description are examples of decisions given *per incuriam*. We do not think that it would be right to say that there may not be other cases of decisions given *per incuriam* in which this court might properly consider itself entitled not to follow an earlier decision of its own. Such cases would obviously be of the rarest occurrence and must be dealt with

*b* in accordance with their special facts.'

*Morelle's* case was a five-judge Court of Appeal, although I hasten to add that it is now well-established that a five-judge Court of Appeal has no more authority than a three-judge Court of Appeal. It consisted of Evershed MR, Denning, Jenkins, Morris and Romer LJJ. I read from the judgment ([1955] 1 All ER 708 at 718, [1955] 2 QB 379 at

*c* 406):

'As a general rule the only cases in which decisions should be held to have been given per incuriam are those of decisions given in ignorance or forgetfulness of some inconsistent statutory provision or of some authority binding on the court concerned: so that in such cases some part of the decision or some step in the reasoning on which it is based is found, on that account, to be demonstrably wrong.

*d* This definition is not necessarily exhaustive, but cases not strictly within it which can properly be held to have been decided per incuriam must, in our judgment, consistently with the stare decisis rule which is an essential feature of our law, be, in the language of LORD GREENE, M.R., of the rarest occurrence. In the present case, it is not shown that any statutory provision or binding authority was overlooked . . .

As we have already said, it is, in our judgment, impossible to fasten on any part of

*e* the decision under consideration, or on any step in the reasoning on which the judgments were based, and to say of it: "Here was a manifest slip or error".'

In my judgment, one *can* say that in so far as the authorities which I have cited decide that a notice to show cause must be signed by 'the proper officer' there was a manifest slip or error. There is no warrant for that proposition whatsoever either in the rules or in the statute. So I ask myself: is this case exceptional? I remind myself of the dangers of

*f* treating a decision as given per incuriam simply on the ground that it can be demonstrated to be wrong, even if the error is fairly clear on an examination of the authorities. However, for my part I think there are very exceptional features about the four decisions of this court to which I have referred and they are these.

There is, first of all, the clearness with which the growth of the error can be detected if the decisions are read consecutively. Second, these cases are all concerned with the liberty

*g* of the subject. It is true that if we were to leave the law as it has been declared to be, namely that these notices have to be signed by the proper officer, there are a number of subjects who would have to be released forthwith, because it is almost unknown for any notice to show cause to be signed by the proper officer. The change would, therefore, be beneficial to some subjects. But the other side of the coin is that these cases are also concerned with the maintenance of the authority of the courts to insist on obedience to

*h* their orders. They are therefore in a very special category. They are also, as I have said, cases which appear to be by no means unusual. Unfortunately there are a number of committals for contempt, particularly in the field of domestic violence. They are cases which are most unlikely to reach the House of Lords, which, if we do not act, is alone able to correct the error which has crept into the law.

*i* I say that such a case is unlikely to reach the House of Lords because if the law is to be left as it has evolved, then this court would quash the committal order and it would be for the respondent to take the case to the House of Lords. I doubt whether any respondents would take that course, bearing in mind that there would be a substantial delay before the appeal to the House of Lords was heard and that he or she would, probably rightly, consider it unlikely that the House of Lords would require the contemnor to return to prison to complete his sentence.

I would like to conclude by summarising the position as I see it. First, a notice in form N 78 does not have to be signed by the proper officer and, in so far as decisions of this court suggest the contrary, they should not be followed. Second, the notice has to be addressed to the respondent, but it is undesirable that it should be addressed in addition to the registrar or to the proper officer. On the other hand, if this is done, it should not be regarded as fatal but should be accepted as a reflection of the fact that these documents start life as, in effect, requests to the court to issue the notice. It is an undesirable practice, but it is not a ground for refraining from making a committal order. Third, I think that it is equally undesirable, for the same reason, namely that it may cause the respondent to wonder whether or not the notice is the order of the court, that the notice should be signed by the applicant's solicitor unless he qualifies his signature with some such rubric as 'This order is made on the application of'. But, again, I do not think his failure so to qualify his signature is a ground for refusing to make a committal order. Fourth, particulars of the alleged breaches must appear in the notice. This has been said over and over again by this court, and I mention it merely to reaffirm it. Fifth, the notice must be in Form N 78 and must call on the respondent to show cause why he should not be committed to prison. Again, that is merely a reaffirmation of the law as it has been stated on many occasions. Sixth, I think that the County Court Rule Committee should consider amending Form N 78 to accommodate the many applicant's solicitors whose practice is to sign these forms. I do not suggest that solely for the convenience of those solicitors, but because I believe that the practice may be a convenience to respondents. If they have any objection to the notice, they can take it up with the applicants' solicitors straight away, and it may in some cases save further proceedings. Seventh, and last, I would invite the County Court Rule Committee to consider amending Form N 79, which is the committal form itself, in order to provide an appropriate space for recording any dispensation pursuant to Ord 29, r 1(6) or (7).

**DILLON LJ.** I agree. I feel that it would be very desirable in view of the amount of uncertainty in the differences in practice in the field that Form N 78 should be amended by the addition of some such wording as Sir John Donaldson MR suggested. It is ironic that very similar wording was suggested by his Honour Judge Forrester-Paton QC himself in a Practice Direction for the Middlesbrough County Court, unfortunately issued too late for the notice to show cause in the present case, in which he suggested that there should be added at the foot of the notice a note to the following effect: 'This notice was issued on the application of [blank] of [blank], solicitors for the [blank].' This would make the situation clear in all cases and would have the advantage of bringing the solicitors' name on to the face of the notice without any confusion as to their function, so that the recipient of the notice can take any necessary steps to put forward his defence or secure an adjournment without difficulty.

**MUSTILL J.** I agree with both judgments which have been given.

*Appeal allowed.*

Solicitors: *Official Solicitor* (for the respondent); *Appleby Hope & Matthews*, Normanby (for the applicant).

Frances Rustin    Barrister.

# Bonalumi v Secretary of State for the Home Department and another

COURT OF APPEAL, CIVIL DIVISION
STEPHENSON, LLOYD LJJ AND SIR DAVID CAIRNS
21, 22 NOVEMBER 1984

*Criminal law – Appeal – Criminal cause or matter – Order of High Court – Order for inspection of banker's books – Order made for purpose of providing evidence in extradition proceedings and pending criminal proceedings abroad – Whether order for inspection of books order in a 'criminal cause or matter' – Whether appeal lying from order to Court of Appeal – Bankers' Books Evidence Act 1879, s 7 – Supreme Court Act 1981, s 18(1)(a).*

Criminal proceedings for fraud were pending against the appellant in a Swedish court. The Home Secretary made an order under s 5[a] of the Extradition Act 1873 directing a magistrate to take evidence for transmission to the Swedish court. The Swedish government requested assistance from the Home Secretary in obtaining evidence of an account kept by the appellant at a London bank. Accordingly, the Home Secretary sought and obtained an order from the High Court under s 7[b] of the Bankers' Books Evidence Act 1879 for inspection of the appellant's accounts at the bank. The appellant appealed against the order to the Civil Division of the Court of Appeal. The question arose whether the appeal was from a judgment of the High Court in a 'criminal cause or matter' so that no appeal lay to the Court of Appeal by virtue of s 18(1)(a)[c] of the Supreme Court Act 1981. The appellant contended that proceedings for an order under s 7 of the 1879 Act were not a criminal cause or matter, because (i) those proceedings could not of themselves result in a criminal trial of the appellant since his pending trial abroad would proceed whatever the outcome of the proceedings for an order under s 7, (ii) the order under s 7 would not subject him to the Swedish criminal jurisdiction since he was already subjected to that jurisdiction and (iii) alternatively, the proceedings for an order under s 7 were a cause or matter separate from both the criminal proceedings in the magistrates' court under the 1873 Act and the criminal proceedings in Sweden.

**Held** – An order made under s 7 of the 1879 Act was an order in a 'criminal cause or matter' for the purposes of s 18(1)(a) of the 1981 Act if it was sought and made in criminal proceedings. Since the order had been sought and made for the purposes of both the magistrates' court proceedings under the 1873 Act and the criminal proceedings in Sweden, both of which were criminal proceedings, the order had been made in a criminal cause or matter and no appeal lay to the Court of Appeal against the making of the order (see p 800 j to p 801 b, p 8905 d to h and p 806 g h, post).

*Ex p Woodhall* (1888) 20 QBD 832, dictum of Viscount Cave in *Re Clifford and O'Sullivan* [1921] 2 AC at 580 and *Amand v Secretary of State for Home Affairs* [1942] 2 All ER 381 applied.

*R v Grossman* (1981) 73 Cr App R 302 not followed.

**Notes**
For statutory restrictions on appeals to the Court of Appeal, see 37 Halsbury's Laws (4th edn) para 681.
For the Extradition Act 1873, s 5, see 13 Halsbury's Statutes (3rd edn) 271.
For the Bankers' Books Evidence Act 1879, s 7, see 12 ibid 849.
For the Supreme Court Act 1981, s 18, see 51 ibid 608.

---

a  Section 5, so far as material, is set out at p 799 *f g*, post
b  Section 7 is set out at p 799 *h j*, post
c  Section 18(1), so far as material, is set out at p 800 *e f*, post

**Cases referred to in judgments**

*Amand v Secretary of State for Home Affairs* [1942] 2 All ER 381, [1943] AC 147, HL.
*Chief Constable of Hampshire v A* [1984] 2 All ER 385, [1984] 2 WLR 954, CA.
*Chief Constable of Kent v V* [1982] 3 All ER 36, [1983] QB 34, [1982] 3 WLR 462, CA.
*Clifford and O'Sullivan, Re* [1921] 2 AC 570, HL.
*Malone v Comr of Police of the Metropolis* [1979] 1 All ER 256, [1980] QB 49, [1978] 3 WLR
    936, CA.
*R v Brixton Prison (Governor), ex p Savarkar* [1910] 2 KB 1056, [1908–10] All ER Rep 603,
    CA.
*R v DPP, ex p Raymond* (1979) 70 Cr App R 233, CA.
*R v Fletcher* (1876) 2 QBD 43, [1874–80] All ER Rep 543, CA.
*R v Grossman* (1981) 73 Cr App R 302, CA.
*R v Hull Prison Board of Visitors, ex p St Germain* [1979] 1 All ER 701, [1979] QB 425,
    [1979] 2 WLR 42, CA.
*R v Southampton Justices, ex p Green* [1975] 2 All ER 1073, [1976] QB 11, [1975] 3 WLR
    277, CA.
*R v Steel* (1876) 2 QBD 37, CA.
*Seaman v Burley* [1896] 2 QB 344, CA.
*Woodhall, Ex p* (1888) 20 QBD 832.
*Young v Bristol Aeroplane Co Ltd* [1944] 2 All ER 293, [1944] KB 718, CA; *affd* [1946] 1 All
    ER 98, [1946] AC 163, HL.

**Appeal**

The Secretary of State for the Home Department and the government of Sweden applied
to the High Court for an order under the Bankers' Books Evidence Act 1879 for liberty
to inspect bank accounts held by Sergio Bonalumi at the London branch of the Banco di
Roma for the purpose of obtaining evidence in criminal proceedings in Sweden against
Mr Bonalumi. In a judgment given on 16 November 1984 Macpherson J ordered that
the applicants should be at liberty to inspect the accounts. Mr Bonalumi wished to appeal
from that judgment to the Civil Division of the Court of Appeal but there was doubt
whether the Court of Appeal had jurisdiction to entertain an appeal. On 19 November
1984 the Registrar of Civil Appeals directed that an appeal should be set down for hearing
but that before the appeal was heard on the merits the preliminary point whether
Macpherson J's judgment was a judgment in a 'criminal cause or matter' within s 18(1)(a)
of the Supreme Court Act 1981, so that no appeal lay to the Court of Appeal under
s 18(1)(a), should be decided. The facts are set out in the judgment of Stephenson LJ.

*J G Ross* for Mr Bonalumi.
*Alan Moses* for the applicants.

**STEPHENSON LJ.** This is an appeal by Mr Bonalumi from an order made by
Macpherson J on 16 November 1984 under s 7 of the Bankers' Books Evidence Act 1879.
The order is in this form:

    '. . . that the Applicants be at liberty to inspect and take copies of all statements of
    account, confirmations, vouchers, copies of which have been produced for Sergio
    Bonalumi, cheques received and other documents recording or evidencing deposits
    made or receipts received by or on behalf of Sergio Bonalumi at Banco di Roma,
    London Branch, between 1st June 1978 and 30th April 1982. This Order refers to
    accounts held in the sole name of Sergio Bonalumi or joint accounts held by Sergio
    Bonalumi with other parties . . .'

And then there is a provision which is not relevant to this appeal.

    That order was required for evidence to be used in criminal proceedings in Sweden
against Mr Bonalumi, who is, we understand, in this country at the moment. There was
a request from the government of Sweden to the Secretary of State for the Home

Department in which what was asked for was assistance in obtaining from the Banco di
*a* Roma in London a statement of account held by Sergio Bonalumi at that bank, I think
from the year 1976 to 1982. That request stated that the account was needed, or might
be needed, by the prosecutor as evidence in the case against Sergio Bonalumi concerning
an offence described as 'gross disloyalty to a principal', which is now pending in the
District Court of Helsinborg.

In compliance with that request, the Secretary of State made an order under s 5 of the
*b* Extradition Act 1873, giving a direction to the Guildhall justices. That order is in these
terms:

'Whereas it is desired to obtain evidence in this country for the purposes of a
certain criminal matter now pending in a Court or Tribunal at Helsingborg in
Sweden NOW I, by virtue of the power conferred on me by Section 5 of the
Extradition Act, 1873, do hereby authorize and require you to take and transmit to
*c* me in the manner prescribed by the said enactment such evidence in furtherance of
the Commission Rogatoire hereunto annexed, as you may be able to gain from any
witness or witnesses within your jurisdiction.'

That was directed to the justices sitting at the Guildhall Justice Room.

That order was abortive in the sense that in February 1984 a justice sitting in the
*d* Guildhall Justice Room was not satisfied that there was evidence of any criminal
proceeding in Sweden; but that defect was remedied when a further order was made
under the section and considered by a justice in the Guildhall Justice Room in November,
this very month. As was natural and proper, the Banco di Roma was not prepared to
volunteer inspection of the confidential accounts of one of its clients without an order
from the court, so the Secretary of State sought an order from the High Court, as he was
*e* empowered to do. He could have sought an order from a magistrates' court, but he chose
to apply to the High Court for the order under the Bankers' Books Evidence Act 1879
without, as counsel for the applicants has told us, having any idea or suspicion that by
choosing that court he might be depriving Mr Bonalumi of any power of appeal.

I should read the relevant sections. The Extradition Act 1873 provides by s 5, which is
still in force (though the same ground appears now to be covered by the provisions of the
Evidence (Proceedings in Other Jurisdictions) Act 1975):

'A Secretary of State may, by order under his hand and seal, require a police
magistrate or a justice of the peace to take evidence for the purpose of any criminal
matter pending in any court or tribunal in any foreign state; and the police
magistrate or justice of the peace, upon the receipt of such order, shall take the
evidence of every witness appearing before him for the purpose in like manner as if
*f* such witness appeared on a charge against some defendant for an indictable offence,
and shall certify at the foot of the depositions so taken that such evidence was taken
before him, and shall transmit the same to the Secretary of State; such evidence may
be taken in the presence or absence of the person charged, if any, and the fact of
such presence or absence shall be stated in such deposition . . .'

*g* Section 7 of the Bankers' Books Evidence Act 1879 provides:

'On the application of any party to a legal proceeding a court or judge may order
that such party be at liberty to inspect and take copies of any entries in a banker's
book for any of the purposes of such proceedings. An order under this section may
be made either with or without summoning the bank or any other party, and shall
be served on the bank three clear days before the same is to be obeyed, unless the
court or judge otherwise directs.'   .

Such an order may be made in any legal proceedings, whether those proceedings are
criminal or civil.

Macpherson J heard the application, which was an application by the Secretary of State.
He pointed out that the Secretary of State was not a party to the criminal proceedings in

which it was sought to use evidence which might be provided by the bank accounts, and
there was a short adjournment in order that the government of Sweden might be joined    a
as an applicant. Having achieved that joinder, the judge was then satisfied that justice
and comity, as he put it, required the order to be made and that he had power to make
it, and he made the order.

From that order there was an appeal to the Divisional Court, which was heard by
Glidewell J. He was moved, not by an appeal but by an application for leave to apply for
judicial review. He heard the application and he refused leave to apply for that remedy.    b
In the course of doing so, he pointed out that he had no jurisdiction, and that there might
be difficulties in finding jurisdiction in the Court of Appeal because it might be a
criminal cause or matter, with which the Civil Division would have no jurisdiction to
deal, and it might not be within the statutory powers of the Criminal Division either.
That led counsel for Mr Bonalumi to appeal to the Civil Division of this court.

The point indicated by Glidewell J was taken by the Registrar of Civil Appeals. It was    c
pointed out by counsel that there was a decision of this court in R v Grossman (1981) 73
Cr App R 302, in which a court consisting of Lord Denning MR, Shaw and Oliver LJJ
had entertained an appeal from an order made under the Bankers' Books Evidence Act
1879 in support of a prosecution in a Welsh magistrates' court for tax evasion and had
discharged the order that had been made. In those circumstances the registrar, in my
opinion rightly, decided that the appeal ought to be considered and be listed for hearing    d
in this court, but that before the appeal was heard on the merits the preliminary point
should be decided, whether the appeal lay at all to this court, on the ground that it was
an appeal in a criminal cause or matter. Ever since the Court of Appeal was set up over
100 years ago, its statutory jurisdiction has been limited to exclude criminal causes or
matters. Section 47 of the Supreme Court of Judicature Act 1873 was repeated in s 31 of
the Supreme Court of Judicature (Consolidation) Act 1925, and the same restriction now    e
appears in s 18(1)(a) of the Supreme Court Act 1981. That provides as follows:

> 'No appeal shall lie to the Court of Appeal—(a) except as provided by the
> Administration of Justice Act 1960 [that relates to contempt of court and has
> nothing to do with this case], from any judgment of the High Court in any criminal
> cause or matter . . .'                                                                       f

Macpherson J's judgment in this case is alleged on behalf of the Secretary of State and
the government of Sweden to be clearly a judgment in a criminal cause or matter. It is
therefore submitted that this court has no jurisdiction to hear, and is prevented by
s 18(1)(a) of the 1981 Act from hearing, the appeal at all. It is pointed out by counsel on
behalf of those two parties that the judgment of Macpherson J was a judgment in relation
to evidence to be taken in a court of criminal jurisdiction, namely the justices' court at    g
Guildhall, according to criminal rules of evidence for the purpose of a criminal case
which is known to be taking place in Sweden. The reason why this appeal has been
brought urgently before this division of this court is that the Guildhall justice was going
to complete, or continue, the hearing of the evidence under the direction of the Secretary
of State's order yesterday, and will resume the hearing tomorrow dependent on the result
of this appeal, and that the proceedings against Mr Bonalumi are due to start in Sweden    h
on Tuesday of next week. In my judgment we are not concerned with the nature of
those proceedings, or with exactly what is comprised in the offence of disloyalty to a
principal; but it is plain from affidavits and from what the judges below have been told
that this is a case of fraud on an employer, and fraud producing allegedly ill-gotten gains
which it is suspected may have found their way into the bank account of which inspection
has been ordered by Macpherson J.

Is this judgment of Macpherson J a judgment in a criminal cause or matter? I am    j
tempted to say that it is too plain for argument to the contrary. If you take those words
in their natural and ordinary meaning and consider the position (proceedings in train
before the Guildhall justices and proceedings starting next week in Sweden) it is quite
clearly an order which could have been made in civil proceedings but has in fact been

made in criminal proceedings both in a magistrates' court in this country and in a district
court in Sweden. Indeed, I go further and say that, if the procedure of the Evidence
(Proceedings in Other Jurisdiction) Act 1975 and RSC Ord 70 had been used to obtain
this order, or this evidence, so that there would have been no proceedings in a criminal
court but only in a civil court, in this country, it would be difficult to argue that the
order was none the less not made in criminal proceedings in a criminal cause or matter,
namely the criminal cause or matter which is to be litigated in Sweden.

We have listened to an admirable argument from counsel for Mr Bonalumi seeking to
persuade us that s 18(1)(a) of the 1981 Act does not mean what in my judgment it plainly
says, or at any rate that on its natural and ordinary meaning it does not apply to the facts
of this case and to the judgment which is sought to be put under appeal.

Counsel for Mr Bonalumi is able to point out that, if this is a judgment in a criminal
cause or matter, so was the order made in *R v Grossman*; and he has also referred us to a
number of other authorities which he submits indicate that this court has exercised
jurisdiction to hear appeals from orders which would appear to be orders made in
criminal causes or matters.

He begins by stressing the fact, which has to be conceded to be the fact, that, if the
submission of counsel for the applicants is right, there is no appeal from this order.
Glidewell J has rightly said that the Divisional Court has no jurisdiction to review the
order; the Criminal Division has no jurisdiction under the Criminal Appeal Act 1968 to
hear an appeal against the order, and the Civil Division of this court has no jurisdiction.
That may be the intention of Parliament, but if so it is an intention of Parliament which
has apparently surprised the Secretary of State and his advisers; but neverthelesss it is
plain that, if this is a judgment in a criminal cause or matter, Macpherson J's order is
final.

Then counsel for Mr Bonalumi sought to rely on the submission that, perhaps
unexpectedly, the preference of the High Court over a magistrates' court, to which the
application could have been made, has the effect of depriving the parties of a right of
appeal, but it also takes the application in some way out of the criminal cause or matter
to which on the face of it it relates. In that connection he relies on three recent decisions
of this court (particularly the last two): *Malone v Comr of Police of the Metropolis* [1979] 1
All ER 256, [1980] QB 49, *Chief Constable of Kent v V* [1982] 3 All ER 36, [1983] QB 34
and *Chief Constable of Hampshire v A* [1984] 2 All ER 385, [1984] 2 WLR 954.

In the first of those cases there was an action for detinue against the Metropolitan
Police Commissioner by the plaintiff Malone, who had been charged with eight other
persons and committed for trial on charges of conspiracy and handling stolen property.
Wien J granted the commissioner an injunction, ordering him to deliver up bank notes
and foreign currency which had been seized in a search of the plaintiff's premises. This
court allowed an appeal against that injunction. There was, as I have reason to remember,
long and detailed argument by counsel in the case, but it did not include any suggestion
that the injunction which Wien J had granted was made in a criminal cause or matter
and that therefore the court had no jurisdiction to hear the appeal. The reason may be,
and I hope it was, as counsel for the applicants points out, that the injunction had been
granted in civil proceedings, namely in an action for detinue, although undoubtedly the
subject of the injunction was required for use at one stage or another in criminal
proceedings.

In the two later cases chief constables of police had taken out summonses. In the first
of them a defendant had been arrested and charged with forgery and obtaining money
by deception in respect of sums which had been drawn on stolen cheques and were
believed to have been paid into his bank account. Beldam J held that he had no
jurisdiction to grant an injunction on an originating summons taken out by the Chief
Constable of Kent to restrain the defendant from withdrawing money from his bank
accounts. On an appeal by the chief constable it was held by a majority that there was
power to grant such an injunction, and such an injunction was granted.

Roughly the same thing happened in the last case, in which the Chief Constable of

Hampshire had taken out an originating summons for an interlocutory injunction
restraining another defendant, a company, from withdrawing money from its bank    *a*
accounts. There the injunction, which Sir Neil Lawson had granted, was upheld by this
court.

In neither of those two cases was the point taken that the injunctions granted or
refused were orders made in a criminal cause or matter, and it may be, again as counsel
for the applicants has submitted, that those appeals were entertained on the basis that
what the chief constables were doing was seeking to exercise their common law right    *b*
and duty to seize and detain goods stolen or unlawfully obtained and to restore them to
their true owners, as indicated in the judgment of Oliver LJ in the last case (see [1984] 2
All ER 385 at 388, [1984] 2 WLR 954 at 957).

So it may be that those three cases, *Malone v Comr of Police of the Metropolis*, *Chief
Constable of Kent v V* and *Chief Constable of Hampshire v A*, were all rightly decided. What
is plain is that they are no authority against the order under appeal in this case being an    *c*
order in a criminal cause or matter, because they did not decide a point which was never
taken. The same is true, in my judgment, of *R v Grossman* (1981) 73 Cr App R 302.

Counsel for Mr Bonalumi has rightly stressed the difficulty of believing that a court
constituted as it was in that case did not appreciate that, sitting in its civil division, it had
no jurisdiction to entertain an appeal from an order made in a criminal cause or matter,
particularly in view of the fact that Lord Denning MR had been a party to decisions in    *d*
two cases, *R v Southampton Justices, ex p Green* [1975] 2 All ER 1073, [1976] QB 11 and *R
v DPP, ex p Raymond* (1979) 70 Cr App R 233, and Shaw LJ had been a party to *R v Hull
Prison Board of Visitors, ex p St Germain* [1979] 1 All ER 701, [1979] QB 425.

But I think the history of judicial decisions is littered with cases in which points that
appear later to be obvious have not been taken, even by the most eminent counsel, for
reasons which are not clear; it may be from mere human fallibility. The obstinate fact    *e*
remains that in *R v Grossman* the point was never taken, and I have been able to confirm
with Oliver LJ that his recollection accords with what one would assume from the report,
namely that it was not taken or considered by counsel or by any member of the court.

In those circumstances the decision is clearly not binding on this court. Failure to
consider a statutory provision is one of the clearest cases in which, on the principles laid
down in *Young v Bristol Aeroplane Co Ltd* [1944] 2 All ER 293, [1944] KB 718, this court is    *f*
not bound to follow its own decisions. So therefore the matter must be looked at de novo
now that the point has been clearly taken.

That leaves counsel for Mr Bonalumi, I think, only with the comfort that he derives,
or seeks to derive, from observations of the Law Lords in *Amand v Secretary of State for
Home Affairs* [1942] 2 All ER 381, [1943] AC 147.

Before turning to that case and two cases which preceded it, I remind myself that what    *g*
the court has to do is to construe the words of the statute, and it must start by applying
Lord Wensleydale's golden rule (put bluntly) of giving the words their natural and
ordinary significance unless there is some compelling reason to the contrary. I start from
this, that it seems to me that the words of s 18(1)(a) of the 1981 Act quite plainly hit the
order of Macpherson J in this case. The court should be wary of imposing glosses on plain
words, however eminent the judges who appear to be imposing them. It should also be    *h*
wary (all this is elementary) of treating observations of judges, even when they look like
statements of principle, as statutory definitions, and as statutory definitions made without
regard to the facts of the particular case with which the judges were dealing.

That said, I begin, as counsel for Mr Bonalumi began, with *Ex p Woodhall* (1888) 20
QBD 832, a decision of this court. In that case the Queen's Bench Division had refused an
application for a writ of habeas corpus made on behalf of a person who had been
committed to prison under s 10 of the Extradition Act 1870 as a fugitive criminal accused    *j*
of an extradition crime. This court held that that decision was given in a criminal cause
or matter within the meaning of s 47 of the Supreme Court of Judicature Act 1873, to
which I have already referred. Lord Esher MR in giving the first judgment said (at 835):

'The result of all the decided cases is to shew that the words "criminal cause or

matter" in s. 47 should receive the widest possible interpretation. The intention was
that no appeal should lie in any "criminal matter" in the widest sense of the term,
this Court being constituted for the hearing of appeals in civil causes and matters.'

Then he referred to a number of cases and cited from the judgment of Mellish LJ in *R v
Fletcher* (1876) 2 QBD 43 at 44, [1874–80] All ER Rep 543 at 544. There Mellish LJ said:

> 'In *Reg v. Steel* ((1876) 2 QBD 37) we held that clause [ie the last clause of s 47 of
> the 1873 Act] was not confined, as was contended, to the High Court when sitting
> as the Court to hear points reserved in criminal cases, but extended to all criminal
> cases in the High Court, and therefore to criminal cases in the Queen's Bench
> Division. The question here is somewhat wider, whether the exemption from
> appeal extends to a proceeding in the Queen's Bench Division, which might be said
> to be not strictly a criminal proceeding in that court, but was a proceeding taken in
> that court for the purpose of quashing a conviction before justices, which was clearly
> a criminal proceeding. Was that proceeding in the Queen's Bench Division "a
> proceeding in a criminal matter?" Now, the intention of the legislature appears to
> me clearly to have been to leave the procedure in criminal cases substantially
> unaltered.'

Then Mellish LJ went on to hold that the proceeding was in a criminal matter, and he
had no doubt that the clause was intended to refer to all criminal matters whatever
coming before the High Court.

Lord Esher MR (then Brett JA) had said in *R v Fletcher* (2 QBD 43 at 46):

> 'I should read the clause as meaning "no appeal shall lie from any decision of the
> High Court by way of judgment in any criminal cause or matter."'

And in *Ex p Woodhall* he dismissed the appeal for want of jurisdiction.

Lindley LJ also cited the words of Mellish LJ, and followed them (see 20 QBD 832 at
837); he was in favour of putting a wide construction on the words. Of course, the facts
of that case, as is perhaps particularly demonstrated by the remaining judgment of
Bowen LJ, were stronger, I think it is right to say, than those in this case. Nevertheless,
any suggestion that the words should be given a restricted meaning, if there is an
ambiguity in them, is clearly not open to this court in view of the judgments in *Ex p
Woodhall* particularly as Lord Esher MR's statement has since been approved in their
Lordships' House.

In *Re Clifford and O'Sullivan* [1921] 2 AC 570 the House of Lords held that the order
appealed from was not made in a criminal cause or matter because it did not relate to
proceedings in any court, but only to proceedings of a military investigation on the
authority of the Commander-in-Chief in Ireland. But the question of a criminal cause or
matter was considered, in particular by Viscount Cave, where he said (at 580):

> '. . . but in order that a matter may be a criminal cause or matter it must, I think,
> fulfil two conditions which are connoted by and implied in the word "criminal." It
> must involve the consideration of some charge of crime, that is to say, an offence
> against the public law (Imperial Dictionary, tit. "Crime" and "Criminal"); and that
> charge must have been preferred or be about to be preferred before some Court or
> judicial tribunal having or claiming jurisdiction to impose punishment for the
> offence or alleged offence. If these conditions are fulfilled, the matter may be
> criminal, even though it is held that no crime has been committed, or that the
> tribunal has no jurisdiction to deal with it [and he cites two cases for that, one of
> which is *R v Fletcher*], but there must be at least a charge of crime (in the wide sense
> of the word) and a claim to criminal jurisdiction.'

If that is restricting in any way the wide meaning of the words, it restricts them in a
way which does not take this order out of their ambit. Nor in my judgment does
anything said about this statutory restriction in *Amand v Secretary of State for Home Affairs*
[1942] 2 All ER 381, [1943] AC 147. There, as in *Ex p Woodhall*, the court was concerned

with habeas corpus; in *Amand's* case the applicant had been arrested, under the Allied
Forces Act 1940 and under an order made under that Act, to be dealt with by the army    *a*
of the Netherlands, then in this country. There was no actual certainty that he would be
charged, prosecuted and tried by the Netherlands forces; this was a preparatory
proceeding of arrest under the statutory power. That, I think, is made reasonably plain,
particularly by the speech of Lord Wright (see [1942] 2 All ER 381 at 386, [1943] AC 147
at 158).

In the leading speech Viscount Simon LC referred to a number of authorities and said    *b*
([1942] 2 All ER 381 at 385, [1943] AC 147 at 156, 157):

> 'It will be observed that these decisions, which I accept as correct, involve the view
> that the matter in respect of which the accused is in custody may be "criminal"
> although he is not charged with a breach of our own criminal law; and (in the case
> of the Fugitive Offenders Act, 1881) although the offence would not necessarily be
> a crime at all if committed here. It is the nature and character of the proceeding in    *c*
> which *habeas corpus* is sought which provide the test. If the matter is one the direct
> outcome of which may be trial of the applicant and his possible punishment for an
> alleged offence by a court claiming jurisdiction to do so, the matter is criminal. This
> is the true effect of the "two conditions" formulated by VISCOUNT CAVE in *Re Clifford
> and O'Sullivan* ([1921] 2 AC 570 at 580) . . . The proceedings in the present case are
> for the direct purpose of handing the appellant over so that he may be dealt with on    *d*
> these charges. Whether they are hereafter withdrawn or disproved does not affect
> the criminal character of the matter in the least . . .'

It is on those words, 'If the matter is one the direct outcome of which may be trial of
the applicant and his possible punishment for an alleged offence by a court claiming
jurisdiction to do so, the matter is criminal', on which counsel for Mr Bonalumi strongly    *e*
relies. He also relies on what was said by Lord Wright ([1942] 2 All ER 381 at 388, [1943]
AC 147 at 162):

> 'The principle which I deduce from the authorities [he had just referred to *Re
> Clifford and O'Sullivan* as the last of them] which I have cited and the other relevant
> authorities which I have considered is that, if the cause or matter is one which, if
> carried to its conclusion, may result in the conviction of the person charged and in a    *f*
> sentence of some punishment, such as imprisonment or fine, it is a criminal cause
> or matter. The person charged is thus put in jeopardy. Every order made in such a
> cause or matter by an English court, is an order in a criminal cause or matter, even
> though the order, taken by itself, is neutral in character and might equally have
> been made of a cause or matter which is not criminal. The order may not involve
> punishment by the law of this country, but, if the effect of the order is to subject by    *g*
> means of the operation of English law the persons charged to the criminal
> jurisdiction of a foreign country, the order is, in the eyes of English law for the
> purposes being considered, an order in a criminal cause or matter, as is shown by *Ex
> p. Woodhall* and *R* v. *Brixton Prison (Governor), Ex p. Savarkar* ([1910] 2 KB 1056,
> [1908–10] All ER Rep 603). These conditions are fulfilled by the order in the present
> case.'

Counsel for Mr Bonalumi says that in this case the matter is not one the direct outcome    *h*
of which may be trial of the applicant, because the applicant is already about to be tried
and that position is not in the least affected by the order under the Bankers' Books
Evidence Act 1879 whether it is made or not. Similarly he says that the effect of the
order is not to subject by means of the operation of English law Mr Bonalumi to the
criminal jurisdiction of Sweden, because he is already subjected to that. That seems to
me to be violating, or to be ignoring, the caution with which one has to approach the    *j*
statements of judges, however eminent. It is only if one takes those two sentences away
from the case with which their Lordships were dealing and supposes that they are setting
out exclusive principles (for instance, supposing Viscount Simon LC, when he says, 'If

the matter is one the direct outcome of which' and so on, means 'if and only if', and
a giving too little effect to his use of the word 'may' ('which *may* be the trial of the applicant
and his possible punishment')), it is only by such a method of interpretation that one
finds any support for the contention of counsel for Mr Bonalumi that this order is outside
s 18(1)(*a*). Although Viscount Simon LC's judgment was agreed with by Lord Thankerton,
Lord Wright and Lord Atkin (who did not give a separate judgment), Lord Porter does
not in any way support such a restriction as counsel seeks to derive from those passages
b in the speeches of Viscount Simon LC and Lord Wright which I have read.

Lord Porter said ([1942] 2 All ER 381 at 389, [1943] AC 147 at 164):

> . . . 'in any given case it must be determined whether or not the proceeding [he is
> speaking of mandamus, but it would apply to habeas corpus and it applies, I think,
> to proceedings for an order under the Bankers' Books Evidence Act 1879] is criminal.
c > This does not mean that the matter in order to be criminal must be criminal
> throughout: it is enough if the proceedings in respect of which *mandamus* is asked is
> criminal, e.g., the recovery of a poor rate is not of itself a criminal matter, but its
> enforcement by magistrates by warrant of distress is; and, if a case be stated by them
> as to their right so to enforce it and that case is determined by the High Court, no
> appeal lies (see *Seaman v. Burley* ([1896] 2 QB 344)) . . . The proceeding from which
d > the appeal is attempted to be taken must be a step in a criminal proceeding, but it
> need not itself of necessity end in a criminal trial or punishment. It is enough if it
> puts the person brought before the magistrate in jeopardy of a criminal charge . . .'

And he referred to two authorities in support of that.

I find nothing in the speeches in that case, or indeed in any of the other judgments to
which we have been referred, to cut down what is to me the plain meaning of the words
e in such a way as to exclude this order from the statutory restriction. This is a case in
which proceedings have actually been started in two criminal courts, in London and in
Sweden; and this order, made for the purpose of putting evidence before first one of
those courts and then the other, seems to me as plainly as possible to be an order in a
criminal cause or matter.

I would have liked to have taken time to put what I recognise may be a judgment in
an important matter into better shape, but the urgency of the case has led me to do my
best now. Forming, as I have, a clear view that we have no jurisdiction to entertain this
appeal, in my judgment we must refuse to entertain it accordingly.

**LLOYD LJ.** I agree.

Once it was conceded that the expression 'criminal cause or matter' is not confined to
f offences against English criminal law, as appears from *Ex p Woodhall* (1888) 20 QBD 832,
or even to offences which would be criminal if committed in England, as appears from
*R v Brixton Prison (Governor), ex p Savarkar* [1910] 2 KB 1056, [1908–10] All ER Rep 603,
both of which decisions were approved by the House of Lords in *Amand v Secretary of
State for Home Affairs* [1942] 2 All ER 381, [1943] AC 147, the consequence in this case
appears to me to be inevitable: we must decline jurisdiction.

g Counsel for Mr Bonalumi seeks to distinguish all previous decisions in this field on the
ground that the application under the Bankers' Books Evidence Act 1879 will not of itself
result in a criminal trial; for the trial in Sweden will proceed whatever the result of that
application. In support of that ground he relies on a sentence from Viscount Simon LC's
speech in *Amand's* case [1942] 2 All ER 381 at 385, [1943] AC 147 at 156, which
Stephenson LJ has read already:

> 'If the matter is one the direct outcome of which may be trial of the applicant and
> his possible punishment for an alleged offence by a court claiming jurisdiction to do
> so, the matter is criminal.'

But, if the argument of counsel for Mr Bonalumi were correct, it would involve this:
that in the case of foreign criminal proceedings it is only the first step taken in this

country which would ever be caught by the expression 'criminal cause or matter', not any subsequent step in the course of the selfsame proceedings. I can see no possible *a* ground for so confining the words.

In support of the same argument counsel for Mr Bonalumi also relies on what Lord Wright said ([1942] 2 All ER 381 at 388, [1943] AC 147 at 162):

'The order may not involve punishment by the law of this country, but, if the effect of the order is to subject by means of the operation of English law the persons charged to the criminal jurisdiction of a foreign country, the order is, in the eyes of *b* English law for the purposes being considered, an order in a criminal cause or matter . . .'

But a little earlier Lord Wright had said: 'Every order made in such a cause or matter by an English court, is an order in a criminal cause or matter . . .' not, be it noted, the first order only.

The second argument of counsel for Mr Bonalumi was that the application under the Bankers' Books Evidence Act 1879 should be regarded as a separate cause or matter, distinct from the proceedings before the Guildhall justices; and still further distinct, I think he would say, from the criminal proceedings in Sweden. But so to hold would in my judgment be contrary to the decision in *Ex p Woodhall* (1888) 20 QBD 832. In that case Mr Finlay QC argued as follows (at 833): 'An application for a writ of habeas corpus *d* is a collateral matter, not necessarily having reference to any criminal proceeding.' That argument, which was rejected, is very similar to the argument advanced in the present case.

The argument of counsel for Mr Bonalumi would also be contrary to the decision of the House of Lords in *Amand's* case. In that case Viscount Simon LC, in the sentence immediately before the passage on which counsel for Mr Bonalumi relied, said ([1942] 2 *e* All ER 381 at 385, [1943] AC 147 at 156): 'It is the nature and character of the proceeding in which *habeas corpus* is sought which provide the test.' To the same effect is what Lord Wright said ([1942] 2 All ER 381 at 387, [1943] AC 147 at 160):

'In the present case, the immediate proceeding in which the order was made was not the cause or matter to which the section refers. The cause or matter in question was the application to the court to exercise its powers under the Allied Forces Act, *f* 1940, and [the order made under that Act], and to deliver the appellant to the Netherlands military authorities. It is in reference to the nature of that proceeding that it must be determined whether there was an order made in a criminal cause or matter.'

Here, by parity of reasoning, the cause or matter is the proceeding under s 5 of the *g* Extradition Act 1873.

I have nothing to add to what Stephenson LJ has said on the recent cases, including *R v Grossman* (1981) 73 Cr App R 302, in which the present point was not taken. I too would decline jurisdiction.

**SIR DAVID CAIRNS.** I agree that this court must decline jurisdiction to hear this appeal for the reasons which have been given in the two judgments already delivered, to which I have nothing of my own to add.

*Appeal dismissed on ground of lack of jurisdiction to entertain it. Leave to appeal to House of Lords refused.*

Solicitors: *Pothecary & Barratt*, agents for *Hawkins & Co*, Hitchin (for Mr Bonalumi); *Treasury Solicitor*.

Diana Brahams	Barrister.

# R v Tonner and others
# R v Evans

COURT OF APPEAL, CRIMINAL DIVISION
WATKINS LJ, KENNETH JONES AND WATERHOUSE JJ
25, 26, 28 JUNE 1984

*Criminal law – Conspiracy – Fraud – Conspiracy to defraud – Conspiracy to evade payment of value added tax – Some acts of conspiracy constituting substantive offences and some not – Whether Crown entitled to charge common law conspiracy – Whether complexity of offence and greater penalties at common law entitling Crown to charge common law conspiracy – Criminal Law Act 1977, ss 1(1), 5.*

*Criminal law – Trial – Commencement of trial – Whether trial begins on arraignment or only when jury sworn and seised of issue – Criminal Justice Act 1982, s 72.*

The appellants conspired by diverse and complex transactions to evade paying to the Revenue large sums of value added tax. The Crown did not charge the appellants with conspiracy contrary to s 1(1)[a] of the Criminal Law Act 1977, as it could have done by alleging conspiracy to cheat the Revenue contrary to s 32(1) of the Theft Act 1968 or conspiracy to commit acts contrary to s 38(1) of the Finance Act 1972, but with common law conspiracy to defraud, that being the only form of common law conspiracy not abolished by s 5[b] of the 1977 Act. The trial judge ruled that the Crown could properly proceed with the charges as laid. The appellants were convicted of common law conspiracy. They appealed, contending that the charges were improperly laid because the appropriate charges were conspiracy to commit substantive offences contrary to s 1(1) of the 1977 Act. The Crown contended that the purpose of conspiracy to defraud at common law being preserved by s 5(2) of the 1977 Act was to enable prosecuting authorities to charge common law conspiracy to defraud not only where the agreement in question was to perform conduct which did not constitute any substantive offence at all but also where the agreement was to perform a combination of acts some of which would constitute substantive offences and some of which would not, or where the conduct agreed on was so diverse and complicated as to warrant laying an all-embracing charge of common law conspiracy to defraud which a jury could more easily understand than a series of charges alleging conspiracies to commit various substantive offences arising out of the same circumstances. The Crown further contended that it was legitimate for the Crown to have regard to the seriousness of the defendants' conduct and to charge common law conspiracy to defraud in order to attract the greater penalties available for that offence.

One of the appellants, E, had been arraigned for trial in April 1983 but in June jury were discharged and a retrial was ordered. On 24 May 1983 s 72[c] of the Criminal Justice Act 1982 abolished the right of an accused to make an unsworn statement from the dock, but the abolition was not to apply to 'a trial ... which began before' s 72 came into force. The appellant's retrial commenced in October 1983 and the question arose whether his trial began before s 72 came into force so that he was entitled to make an unsworn statement from the dock at his retrial.

**Held** – (1) If a conspiracy involved the commission of any substantive offence the only charge that could be brought was conspiracy contrary to s 1(1) of the 1977 Act, even if some of the conduct involved in the conspiracy would not amount to a substantive

---

a   Section 1(1) is set out at p 811 *h*, post
b   Section 5, so far as material, is set out at p 811 *j*, post
c   Section 72 is set out at p 815 *e* to *g*, post

offence and even though the charge might result in serious criminal conduct being
inadequately punished. Furthermore there were, in the circumstances, no grounds for $a$
the court to apply the proviso to s 2(1)$^d$ of the Criminal Appeal Act 1968 and dismiss the
appeal on the basis that the evidence established the offence of cheating the Revenue
contrary to common law, since the appellants had not had the opportunity of meeting
such a charge and the jury had not been directed on it. Accordingly, the convictions of
common law conspiracy to defraud would be quashed. However, the court would
exercise its power under s 3$^e$ of the Criminal Appeal Act 1968 to substitute of its own $b$
accord convictions for conspiring to act contrary to s 38(1) of the 1972 Act (see p 813 $j$,
p 814 $b c e f$ and $j$ to p 815 $b$, p 819 $e$ and p 820 $g$, post); R v Ayres [1984] 1 All ER 619
applied.

(2) A trial only began when the jury had been sworn and were seised of the issue, and
not when the accused was arraigned to plead to the indictment. It followed that E's trial
began in October 1983, when the jury at the retrial were sworn, and that he had therefore $c$
not been entitled to make an unsworn statement from the dock at the retrial (see p 818 $g$
to $j$, post); dicta of Ritchie CJ in Morin v R (1890) 18 SCR at 415, of Scarman LJ in R v
Vickers [1975] 2 All ER at 948 and of Shaw LJ in R v Williams (Roy) [1977] 1 All ER at 879
applied.

### Notes
For conspiracy to defraud, see 11 Halsbury's Laws (4th edn) para 61, and for cases on the $d$
subject, see 15 Digest (Reissue) 1398–1403, 12236–12297.

For unsworn evidence of a defendant, see 11 Halsbury's Laws (4th edn) para 465.

For the Criminal Appeal Act 1968, ss 2, 3, see 8 Halsbury's Statutes (3rd edn) 690, 691.

For the Theft Act 1968, s 32, see ibid 802.

For the Criminal Law Act 1977, ss 1, 5, see 47 ibid 145, 151.

For the Criminal Justice Act 1982, s 72, see 52 ibid 580. $e$
Justice Act 1982, s 72, see 52 ibid 580.

As from 27 August 1981, s 1(1) of the 1977 Act was substituted by s 5(1) of the
Criminal Attempts Act 1981.

### Cases referred to in judgment
*Catherwood v Thompson* [1958] OR 326, Ont CA. $f$
*Morin v R* (1890) 18 SCR 407, Can SC.
*R v Ayres* [1984] 1 All ER 619, [1984] AC 447, [1984] 2 WLR 257, HL.
*R v Duncalf* [1979] 2 All ER 1116, [1979] 1 WLR 918, CA.
*R v Ellis* (1973) 57 Cr App 571, CA.
*R v Hudson* [1956] 1 All ER 814, [1956] 2 QB 252, [1956] 2 WLR 914, CCA.
*R v Lovelock* [1956] 3 All ER 223, [1956] 1 WLR 1217, CCA. $g$
*R v Paling* (1978) 67 Cr App R 299, CA.
*R v Quinn* [1978] Crim LR 750.
*R v Vickers* [1975] 2 All ER 945, [1975] 1 WLR 811, CA.
*R v Walters* (1979) 69 Cr App R 115, CA.
*R v Williams (Roy)* [1977] 1 All ER 874, [1978] QB 373, [1977] 2 WLR 400, CA. $h$

### Cases also cited
*R v Jones* (1974) 59 Cr App R 120, CA.
*R v McCarthy* [1981] STC 298, CA.
*R v McLaughlin* (1982) 76 Cr App R 42, CA.
*R v McVitie* [1960] 2 All ER 498, [1960] 2 QB 483, CCA.
*R v Molyneux* (1980) 72 Cr App R 111, CA. $j$
*R v Nelson* (1977) 65 Cr App R 119, CA.
*R v Parker and Bulteel* (1916) 25 Cox CC 145.

---

$d$  Section 2(1), so far as material, provides: '. . . Provided that the Court may, notwithstanding that
   they are of opinion that the point raised in the appeal might be decided in favour of the appellant,
   dismiss the appeal if they consider that no miscarriage of justice has actually occurred.'
$e$  Section 3, so far as material, is set out at p 819 $d$, post.

R v Simmonds [1967] 2 All ER 399, [1969] 1 QB 685, CA.
a  R v Welham [1960] 1 All ER 260, [1960] 2 QB 445, CCA; affd [1960] 1 All ER 805, [1961]
   AC 103, HL.

**Appeals**

*R v Tonner and others*

On 6 May 1983 in the Central Criminal Court before his Honour Judge Lowry QC and a
b  jury the appellants, Gordon Campbell Tonner, Wilfrid Haydn Rees and William Harding,
were convicted on an indictment charging Tonner with two counts of conspiracy to
defraud contrary to common law and Rees and Harding with one count of conspiracy to
defraud contrary to common law. Further counts in the indictment charging the
appellants with conspiracy contrary to s 1(1) of the Criminal Law Act 1977 were ordered
to be left on the file. Tonner was sentenced to a total of 7½ years' imprisonment and fined
c  a total of £400,000, Rees was sentenced to 2½ years' imprisonment and Harding was
sentenced to 2 years' imprisonment. The appellants appealed against the convictions on
a point of law, namely that the judge erred in law in failing to direct the Crown that the
conspiracies to defraud contrary to common law were wrongly charged and that in the
counts in question the statement of offence should have been conspiracy contrary to
s 1(1) of the 1977 Act. The appellants also applied for leave to appeal against sentence.
d  The facts are set out in the judgment of the court.

*R v Evans*

On 14 January 1984 in the Central Criminal Court before his Honour Judge Lowry QC
and a jury the appellant, Ronald Evans, was convicted, following a retrial which
commenced in October 1983, of conspiracy to defraud contrary to common law and was
sentenced to 3½ years' imprisonment. He appealed against his conviction on the ground
e  that the indictment should have charged conspiracy contrary to s 1(1) of the Criminal
Law Act 1977 and not conspiracy to defraud contrary to common law. He also appealed
against conviction on the further ground that the trial judge erred in law in ruling that
his trial began when the second jury were sworn, in October 1983, and that therefore, by
virtue of s 72 of the Criminal Justice Act 1982, he was not entitled to make an unsworn
f  statement from the dock, submitting that the judge should have ruled that his trial
began when he was arraigned, in April 1983, prior to the first, abortive, trial, so that his
trial began before the commencement of s 72 of the 1982 Act, and s 72 did not apply to
him. Evans also appealed against sentence. The facts are set out in the judgment of the
court.

g  *Stephen Leslie* (assigned by the Registrar of Criminal Appeals) for Tonner, Rees and
   Harding.
*Anthony Arlidge QC* and *Peter Rook* for the Crown in the appeals of Tonner, Rees and
   Harding.
*William Clegg* and *Richard Whittam* (assigned by the Registrar of Criminal Appeals) for
   Evans.
h  *Paul Purnell QC, Anthony Glass* and *Peter Finnigan* for the Crown in the appeal of Evans.

**WATKINS LJ** delivered the following judgment of the court. The appellants Tonner,
Rees and Harding on 6 May 1983 in the Central Criminal Court, after a trial lasting 41
days, were convicted and sentenced by his Honour Judge Lowry QC as follows: Tonner,
for conspiracy to defraud, seven years' imprisonment and a fine of £300,000; on a second
count for a like offence, seven years' imprisonment concurrent and a fine of £100,000.
He was also ordered to pay £20,000 prosecution costs and £10,000 legal aid costs. Those
fines were ordered to be paid by 5 November 1983, with 12 months' imprisonment
consecutive in default. A suspended sentence of 18 months' imprisonment imposed on
5 June 1981 for handling stolen property was ordered to take effect as six months'
imprisonment consecutive. That meant a total term of imprisonment of 7½ years. Rees,
for conspiracy to defraud, was sentenced to two years' and six months' imprisonment
consecutive to a sentence which he was then serving. His parole licence, which had been
effective until then, was revoked, and by order he was deprived of two roughcast fine

gold bars. Harding, for conspiracy to defraud, was sentenced to two years' imprisonment, and he too was by order deprived of two rough-cast fine gold bars.

A number of counts on the indictment were left, by order of the judge, on the file. They were: count 3, conspiracy to defraud, against Tonner alone of these appellants; count 5, conspiracy to contravene s 38(1) of the Finance Act 1972; count 6, a like offence, those two counts being laid against all three appellants; and count 7, conspiracy to contravene the provisions of s 170(2) of the Customs and Excise Management Act 1979, against Tonner alone. All three appellants appeal against conviction.

There were a number of co-accused. One Bingham was found not guilty of conspiracy to defraud and of other conspiracies, as also was a man called Falco. One Furness was sick; the judge discharged the jury from returning a verdict in respect of him. Stahl pleaded guilty to count 1, conspiracy to defraud, and was sentenced to two years' imprisonment, 12 months of which was suspended. Another man, Tryniszewski, was not to be found, despite the issue of a bench warrant, so he was not tried.

The facts are these. Between June 1981 and April 1982 the three appellants were involved in a conspiracy to evade payment of value added tax by obtaining gold without paying tax on it and selling it and charging tax on the sale. That tax they failed to account for to the Customs and Excise. It was asserted that Tonner was the prime mover and succeeded in respect of a few companies in depriving the Revenue of a total of £3m in value added tax. Rees and Harding co-operated effectively to the extent of playing notable roles in the operation of one company.

This was an extremely well-conceived, artful and daring plan to deprive the Revenue of vast sums of money. In effect, they or someone on their behalf smuggled into this country gold on which no tax was paid, melted it down and sold it on to bullion dealers in Hatton Garden. In addition, they bought a substantial number of Krugerrand and Canadian coins which they also melted down into gold bars and sold at very substantial cost to bullion dealers in Hatton Garden.

As for some of the transactions, a scheme of self-invoicing was resorted to by the buyers, and as for others there was direct invoicing to one or more of the three companies to which reference has already been made. In relation to part of the very substantial amount of gold which was dealt with in those different ways false invoices were created. An account was rendered to the Revenue by the use of false invoices relating to the buying of gold on which it was said that value added tax had been paid. The amount of that was set off against value added tax on true invoices given by bullion dealers in Hatton Garden. That set-off falsely revealed that the companies owed the Revenue a very trifling sum of money.

In relation to another and quite substantial part of value added tax kept away from the Revenue the intention was that one or more of the appellants, and others, would abscond with the money, no doubt leaving this country to spend the rest of their lives in a sunnier clime.

The respective roles played by the appellants and others were canvassed at length before the jury. There can be no doubt whatever that it was for a time a very successful enterprise. It was enabled to be effective because the companies created for the purpose were properly registered for the purposes of value added tax, and had therefore numbers on that register. The third company was however brought into life principally by Rees and Harding, who, using false names, managed to register that company for the purposes of value added tax and improperly thereby to obtain a number on the register, which was thereafter used to further the success of the unlawful enterprise. That was how those three men busied themselves for a number of months in 1982 and early in 1983.

Turning now to the appellant Evans, on 14 January 1984 in the Central Criminal Court, after a retrial which lasted three months, he was convicted and sentenced by Judge Lowry to 3½ years' imprisonment for conspiracy to defraud. He appeals against conviction by leave of Beldam J. On the indictment he had co-accused, seven men and a limited company. He alone was convicted. There was a failure to agree in respect of one co-defendant, Wilson, and verdicts of not guilty in respect of the others including the limited company.

a   The facts as far as Evans is concerned were these. Four of the men who were found not guilty were directors of a company, Illuminate Ltd, which was formed as a jewellery business, with premises in Hatton Garden. A man called Rajnikant Unadkat ('Raj' for short) and his brother traded as jewellery importers and engaged in buying and selling gold.

b   On 2 November 1981 a company named D Roberts Ltd, with an office in Shoreditch High Street, was registered for value added tax. On 4 and 5 November David Roberts, its so-called director, opened a number of bank accounts in the company's name. Between early November 1981 and early January 1982 nearly 60,000 gold coins were bought by or on behalf of David Roberts at a cost of £17m. No value added tax was paid on those coins. They were delivered to the premises of the company, Illuminate, where they were melted into bars and sold on the open market by Raj, who charged and received value added tax at 15%. The value of the bars was less than the equivalent weight of the coins.

c   The profit which was pocketed by those unlawfully dealing in this way was made by not handing over the value added tax charged on the sale to the Customs and Excise. The loss to the commissioners through the dealings of these men was about £2½m.

This fraud was concealed for some time by the production of false invoices. Raj produced invoices to show that he had purchased gold at a slightly lower rate from Illuminate. The rate of profit was running at something like 8% of the value added tax

d   imposed on sale and purchase. The investigation into this fraud was hindered for a considerable time because no one was able to find Roberts. He it was, whoever he was, who had registered the business of the company, D Roberts Ltd. He it was who arranged for payment of the coins and had transactions, at any rate on paper, with Raj.

Eventually Roberts was unmasked. A man was arrested on 30 June 1982. His name was not Roberts at all: it was Evans. He had been wearing a wig, a commonplace device

e   to try to hide one's identity. It was effective for some while but eventually it was taken off in the manner which has been very briefly outlined. He too therefore stood his trial and was convicted as already mentioned.

This court heard the appeals against conviction simultaneously, at the invitation of counsel for the appellants and with the consent of counsel for the Crown We acceded to the invitation because the main ground of appeal of all four appellants is identical in one

f   respect. Much time has been saved by avoiding duplication. That ground of appeal is that the conspiracies to defraud contrary to common law were all wrongly charged, that the statement of offence in each material count should have alleged a conspiracy contrary to s 1(1) of the Criminal Law Act 1977 (see R v Ayres [1984] 1 All ER 619, [1984] AC 447). Consequently, subject to the exercise by this court of its power to apply the proviso to s 2(1) of the Criminal Appeal Act 1968, all convictions must, so it is said, be quashed.

g   When these appellants were convicted R v Ayres had not been heard in the House of Lords. There existed at that time an unresolved controversy as to the precise effects of the provisions of ss 1(1) and 5 of the 1977 Act. The terms of s 1(1) are:

'Subject to the following provisions of this Part of this Act, if a person agrees with any other person or persons that a course of conduct shall be pursued which will

h   necessarily amount to or involve the commission of any offence or offences by one or more of the parties to the agreement if the agreement is carried out in accordance with their intentions, he is guilty of conspiracy to commit the offence or offences in question.'

Section 5, so far as material, provides:

j   '(1) Subject to the following provisions of this section, the offence of conspiracy at common law is hereby abolished.

(2) Subsection (1) above shall not affect the offence of conspiracy at common law so far as it relates to conspiracy to defraud, and section 1 above shall not apply in any case where the agreement in question amounts to a conspiracy to defraud at common law . . .'

R v Walters (1979) 69 Cr App R 115, approving as it did a ruling in R v Quinn [1978]

Crim LR 750, and *R v Duncalf*[1979] 2 All ER 1116, [1979] 1 WLR 918 produced in this
court solutions to the problem which seemingly could not be reconciled. Consequently *a*
some judges adopted what might be called the *Walters* solution and others that of *Duncalf*.
Despite submissions in the joint trials of Tonner, Rees and Harding and in the trial of
Evans, Judge Lowry declined to follow *R v Duncalf*. Accordingly he permitted the Crown
in both trials to proceed with charges of conspiracy to defraud contrary to common law.

In *R v Ayres* [1984] 1 All ER 619, [1984] AC 447, the defendant had been charged on
an indictment with the common law offence of conspiracy to defraud, the particulars of *b*
the offence being that he had conspired with his co-defendant and other persons to obtain
money from an insurance company by falsely claiming that a lorry and its contents had
been stolen while in transit. He was convicted and he appealed on the ground, inter alia,
that he had been improperly charged with conspiracy to defraud at common law and
that he should have been charged with conspiracy to obtain property by deception
contrary to s 1(1) of the 1977 Act. The House of Lords held, dismissing the appeal ([1984] *c*
AC 447 at 447–448):

'(1) that upon the true construction of the Act of 1977 common law conspiracy
to defraud and statutory conspiracy contrary to section 1 were mutually exclusive
offences; that "conspiracy to defraud" within the meaning of section 5(2) was limited
to those exceptional fraudulent agreements which, if carried into effect, would not
necessarily result in the commission of any substantive criminal offence by any of *d*
the conspirators and that whenever the evidence supported the commission of a
substantive criminal offence if the agreement constituting the conspiracy had been
performed, the only proper charge was conspiracy contrary to section 1; that since
the evidence against the defendant supported an attempt to obtain property by
deception if the conspiracy had been performed, the charge of conspiracy to defraud
was improper and that was a material irregularity in the course of the trial... *Reg.* *e*
*v. Duncalf* ([1979] 2 All ER 1116, [1979] 1 WLR 918), approved ... But (2)
dismissing the appeal, that in all the circumstances of the case there had been no
actual miscarriage of justice because the particulars of offence in the indictment and
the judge's directions to the jury made it plain that the crime alleged against the
defendant was conspiracy to obtain money by deception, and accordingly, the
conviction would be upheld under the proviso to section 2(1) of the Criminal Appeal *f*
Act 1968...'

I shall return to the speech of Lord Bridge in *R v Ayres* a little later.

Counsel for the appellants submit that in both their cases there is no room for doubt
whether common law conspiracy or statutory conspiracy should be charged. The
particulars in each of the material counts make it abundantly plain that either the alleged *g*
unlawful agreements were to commit substantive offences or, if not, as they contend
cannot possibly be the position, they were designed to set in being the unlawful process
of defrauding the Revenue, that is to say the public, in which event they would have
acted contrary to common law. All the conduct complained of, they submit, must have
been within the contemplation of Parliament when it enacted the provisions of s 38(1) of
the Finance Act 1972 or those of s 170(1) of the Customs and Excise Management Act *h*
1979. Section 38(1) provides:

'If any person is knowingly concerned in, or in the taking of steps with a view to,
the fraudulent evasion of tax by him or any other person, he shall be liable to a
penalty of £1,000, or three times the amount of the tax, whichever is the greater, or
to imprisonment for a term not exceeding two years, or to both.'

The maximum penalties for acting contrary to not only s 38(1) but also s 170(1), which *j*
we see no need to quote, and of course for acting contrary to s 1(1) of the 1977 Act by
conspiring to do so, which are identical, are almost trifling compared with the maximum
penalties which can be and were imposed in these cases for the common law conspiracy.

The Crown, not surprisingly, having regard to the scale of the frauds here, had this

factor very much in mind when laying the charges at common law. But both counsel for
a the appellants argue that Parliament cannot possibly have overlooked the consequences
of enacting ss 1(1) and 5 of the 1977 Act. Moreover, in hearing the appeal in R v Ayres
the House of Lords must have had them in contemplation. A copy of the indictment in
Evans's case was produced to their Lordships during the hearing of the appeal in R v
Ayres.

Regardless of that, both counsel for the appellants argue that the clear terms of the two
b sections cannot be expanded into an interpretation that they cannot sensibly bear merely
because the conduct complained of was on a uniquely serious scale. And finally they
maintain that, if the unlawful conduct agreed on contains a mixture of that which
amounts to a statutory offence and that which does not, then the conspiracy is caught by
s 1(1) of the 1977 Act.

During the trial of Tonner, Rees and Harding counsel for the Crown revealed to the
c judge why he had drafted the material counts in the indictment as he did. We have a
transcript of what passed between counsel and the judge in relation to this matter.
Counsel is recorded as having explained to the judge his reasons for deliberately refraining
from charging the three appellants and others with the common law offence of conspiracy
to cheat the Revenue. Counsel for the appellants Tonner, Rees and Harding pricked up
his ears at that and said that if counsel for the Crown had indicted his clients in that way
d he would have addressed legal argument on it. At the conclusion of the argument the
judge concluded that it was right for the Crown to proceed with the trial against the
three appellants on the indictment as presented.

Counsel for the Crown, whose submissions in this court have been supported by
counsel for the Crown in Evans's case, opened his argument by posing the rhetorical
question: what does a lacuna in this context mean? He submitted that s 5 of the 1977
e Act was designed to provide the prosecuting authority with the means of charging a
defendant with the common law offence of conspiracy in cases where s 1(1) of the 1977
Act could not be applied. He contended that it covers, obviously, unlawful conduct
agreed to be performed which does not constitute an offence within the meaning of s 1
of the 1977 Act, where, in sub-s (4), the offence is defined thus:

f 'In this Part of this Act "offence" means an offence triable in England and Wales,
except that it includes murder . . .'

There is a lacuna also, he submits, in two other circumstances not considered by the
House of Lords in R v Ayres: firstly, where the agreement is to perform a combination of
conduct which constitutes an offence or offences within the meaning of s 1(1) and that
g which does not. Here some of the conduct contemplated was clearly contrary to s 38(1)
of the Finance Act 1972 and possibly to s 170(1) of the Customs and Excise Management
Act 1979. But there was much else to be done. Some of it admittedly amounted to
cheating the public revenue, which by s 32(1) of the Theft Act 1968 is retained as an
offence.

Secondly, he says, what is agreed on is so diverse and complicated as to warrant alleging
h against a defendant or defendants one all-embracing conspiracy charge which a jury
could more easily understand than were it to be faced with a series of conspiracies in
different counts all arising out of the same circumstances. Furthermore, he continued,
the seriousness of the conduct agreed on, measured against the punishment available to
penalise it, is a legitimate consideration.

If counsel for the Crown is right it must follow, in our judgment, that the decision in
j R v Ayres left a considerable area of uncertainty as to what constitutes a lacuna, and
consequently substantially failed to achieve its purpose, which must have been to remove
the doubts which existed about the effects of ss 1(1) and 5 of the 1977 Act.

Regrettable though it may be that serious criminal conduct may appear to be
inadequately punished consequent on the decision in R v Ayres, we do not accept that it
left in its wake a lacuna of the nature contended for by counsel for the Crown. We would

cite Lord Bridge's conclusion, with which all of their Lordships agreed ([1984] 1 All ER 619 at 625, [1984] AC 447 at 459):

'For these reasons, and for those expressed in the extract quoted above from the judgment of the count in *R v Duncalf* [1979] 2 All ER 1116 at 1120–1121, [1979] 1 WLR 918 at 922–923, which which I respectfully agree, I conclude that the phrase "conspiracy to defraud" in s 5(2) of the 1977 Act must be construed as limited to an agreement which, if carried into effect, would not necessarily involve the commission of any substantive criminal offence by any of the conspirators. I would accordingly answer the certified question in the affirmative.'

That, effectively and precisely, we think, draws the line between what can and what cannot be regarded as conspiracy to defraud at common law. It is now, we think, beyond doubt that, if a conspiracy involves the commission of *any* substantive offence, it can be charged only under s 1(1) of the 1977 Act. We therefore find that these appellants were wrongly charged.

This leads us directly to the application of the proviso to s 2(1) of the Criminal Appeal Act 1968, on which we have heard argument, a great deal of which has been directed to the definition of cheating the Revenue contrary to common law. Counsel for the appellants Tonner, Rees and Harding, and counsel for the appellant Evans too, submit that only positive acts will suffice for this purpose, that if there is one act among a number of positive acts which is passive (in other words, a failure to do this or that) a cheat is not established. In this context we were referred to a number of authorities, including *R v Hudson* [1956] 1 All ER 814, [1956] 2 QB 252, and to some statutory provisions and old textbooks, which it is submitted establish that proposition. We are not persuaded that any one of them has that effect.

We do not however have to go so far as to decide that point, nor do we have positively to conclude, as we would if we had had to do so, that here were committed barefaced cheats on the Revenue on a substantial scale. This is because we cannot accede to the joint invitation of counsel for the Crown and counsel for the Crown in Evans's case to apply the proviso as was done in *R v Ayres*. In relation to this matter Lord Bridge proposed a test which we adopt. He said ([1984] 1 All ER 619 at 626, [1984] AC 447 at 460–461):

'If the statement and particulars of the offence in an indictment disclose no criminal offence whatever or charge some offence which has been abolished, in which case the indictment could fairly be described as a nullity, it is obvious that a conviction under that indictment cannot stand. But, if the statement and particulars of offence can be seem fairly to relate to and to be intended to charge a known and subsisting criminal offence but plead it in terms which are inaccurate, incomplete or otherwise imperfect, then the question whether a conviction on that indictment can properly be affirmed under the proviso must depend on whether, in all the circumstances, it can be said with confidence that the particular error in the pleading cannot in any way have prejudiced or embarrassed the defendant.'

Counsel for the Crown and counsel for the Crown in Evans's case submit that there would be no miscarriage of justice here if we were to apply the proviso on the basis that the misdescribed statement of offence were to read, 'Cheating the Revenue contrary to common law', that the particulars of the offence as set out in the indictment are apposite to cover the charge, and that the evidence amply established it.

If we felt able to accept those submissions, the power to punish would be unaffected. In the sense that the punishment should fit the crime, this is probably what ought to happen. But we are with regret driven to find that there would truly be a miscarriage of justice if we did so. The proviso was not intended to be used in circumstances such as these, where (1) in the case of Tonner, Rees and Harding, the Crown could have charged but refrained from charging these appellants with cheating the Revenue. We have no criticism to make of counsel for the Crown in this respect; he had a difficult decision to make at the time of drafting the indictment; (2) there would have been legal argument

at the trial on the definition of 'cheating'. This did not take place, as has already been
a made plain. If it had, the appellants may have benefited from it; (3) the jury were never
directed on the issues arising from the offence of cheating; (4) issues involving the
admissibility of evidence may have arisen on a charge of cheating which did not arise in
either trial; (5) in the trial of Evans the offence of cheating was never envisaged. We
accept that it is probably wrong in principle to apply the proviso in that circumstance;
(6) it is not known what evidence either jury accepted. In the trial of Evans there were
b wholesale acquittals; and (7) no appellant had the opportunity to meet the allegations
arising from the offence of cheating.

We turn now to the other ground of appeal which is relied on by Evans alone. It has
been argued before the court by his counsel, supported by Mr Nicholas Brandt, counsel
for an appellant called Rhiney whose appeal is to be heard hereafter[1]. The decision on
this particular ground of appeal will govern Rhiney's appeal against conviction, since the
c circumstances on which it was founded and the law on which it was based are identical.
Thus it was that we allowed counsel for Rhiney to make his submissions in support of
counsel for the appellant Evans.

The facts which need to be stated as a preliminary to exploring what is undoubtedly
an important matter for the appellant Evans, and of course for Rhiney, are these. He was
first of all arraigned at the Crown Court at Southwark on 11 April 1983. After some
d while, and when the prosecution had concluded its case, there were submissions to the
judge conducting the trial, as a result of which the jury were discharged from giving a
verdict. That was on 22 June 1983. On 19 October 1983 there was a retrial of Evans.
That concluded in the manner I have already stated. Between arraignment on 11 April
and the retrial commencing on 19 October, s 72 of the Criminal Justice Act 1982 came
into force on 24 May. That section provides:

e
'(1) Subject to subsections (2) and (3) below, in any criminal proceedings the
accused shall not be entitled to make a statement without being sworn, and
accordingly, if he gives evidence, he shall do so on oath and be liable to cross-
examination; but this section shall not affect the right of the accused, if not
represented by counsel or a solicitor, to address the court or jury otherwise than on
oath on any matter on which, if he were so represented, counsel or a solicitor could
f address the court or jury on his behalf.
(2) Nothing in subsection (1) above shall prevent the accused making a statement
without being sworn—(a) if it is one which he is required by law to make personally;
or (b) if he makes it by way of mitigation before the court passes sentence upon him.
(3) Nothing in this section applies—(a) to a trial; or (b) to proceedings before a
magistrates' court acting as examining justices, which began before the commence-
g ment of this section.'

Judge Lowry was addressed at the commencement of the trial of Evans in October
1983 on the effect of s 72. The contention of counsel for the appellant was and remains
that the trial of Evans had commenced when he was arraigned as long ago as April 1983,
and that accordingly, having regard to s 72(3) of the 1982 Act, it was self-evident that
h that section did not apply, that the trial was, as it were, in midstream. The judge, who
took considerable care to listen to those submissions directed to the question when a trial
by jury can properly be said to commence, came to the conclusion that it commences at
the time when the jury are sworn and the defendant is put in the charge of that jury. It
did not begin, and never has begun, he said, with the arraignment of a defendant.

---

j   1   Neville Rhiney appealed against his conviction on a retrial in the Crown Court at St Albans before
McCowan J and a jury on 20 July 1983 on two counts of robbery and one of attempted robbery,
contrary to s 8 of the Theft Act 1968, in which the trial judge ruled that s 72 of the Criminal
Justice Act 1982 applied so as to disentitle Rhiney from making an unsworn statement from the
dock. The Court of Appeal, Criminal Division (Watkins LJ, Kenneth Jones and Waterhouse JJ), in
a judgment of the court delivered by Kenneth Jones J immediately following the above-reported
decision, dismissed the appeal for the same reasons as it gave in respect of Evans's appeal

Accordingly, the trial proceeded and Evans was denied the right which he claimed to make a statement from the dock. In the event, he did not give evidence and, having been forbidden to do so, made no statement from the dock.     *a*

The point of counsel for the appellant Evans, made here with commendable brevity and clarity, rests on a number of provisions in various statutes and certain decided cases. Counsel for Rhiney adopted the argument of counsel for the appellant Evans and supplemented it by citing a Canadian case to which we will make reference in due course. Beginning, then, with the argument of counsel for the appellant Evans and referring to     *b* some of the statutory provisions to which he has drawn our attention, we look at the Criminal Evidence Act 1898. That Act for the first time gave an accused the right to give evidence on his own behalf. It further provided that the right of an accused to make a statement from the dock was not to be affected. So until 1982 there never had been any doubt that a defendant had the right to make a statement from the dock. The exercise of that right, scarcely used 20 or 30 years ago, had become very fashionable and this     *c* doubtless led Parliament to enact s 72 of the 1982 Act. So much, then, for the origins of this state of affairs.

We have been referred to the Courts Act 1971, s 7(1) of which provides for committal for trial on indictment. Counsel for the appellant Evans submits that the words therein, 'committing a person for trial', can only mean that, from the time a person is committed for trial, nowadays to the Crown Court, that trial is in being. We do not find that in the     *d* least convincing. We go further into the section and look at sub-s (4)(i), which reads:

'. . . For the purposes of this subsection—(i) "the prescribed period" means such period for the respective purposes of paragraphs (a) and (b) of this subsection as may be prescribed by Crown Court rules, and the rules may make different provision for different places of trial, or for other different circumstances . . .'     *e*

What this part of s 7 intended to provide was a time limit within which a defendant was to be brought to trial once he had been committed to the Crown Court. It cannot, so it seems to us, be said that by enacting s 7 Parliament intended to lay down a rule that a trial begins, for example, on arraignment, because it went on to state in sub-s (4)(ii) that: 'the trial shall be deemed to begin when the defendant is arraigned'. If there had been     *f* any doubt when a trial begins it would not have been necessary for Parliament to state in that subsection that a trial begins when the defendant is arraigned. It is quite clear that the intention was to ensure that Crown Court officials, and judges too, should have a clear yardstick which would govern them in determining whether a person had been brought to trial within the prescribed period; it had no other function. So it seems to us that the provisions of s 7 cannot possibly be of assistance in deciding when, legally     *g* speaking, a trial by jury can properly be said to begin.

We were referred also to certain provisions in s 4(4)(a) of the Criminal Procedure (Insanity) Act 1964. This clearly was a special provision to determine the circumstances in which a person should be found unfit to plead. It is a procedure which is well known to our courts. It takes place inevitably before arraignment, because the whole purpose of endeavouring to discover whether a person is fit to plead is to decide whether or not the     *h* charge should be put to him and that he should be required to answer that charge.

We were referred to s 12 of the Juries Act 1974, where the expression 'In proceedings for the trial . . .' is used. The argument is that that expression can only mean that it was envisaged by the legislature that a trial was in being in the circumstances contemplated in s 12, which deals with challenges to jurors and so on. We do not take that view of it; we cannot see how it could possibly mean that.     *j*

That leads us to look at *R v Vickers* [1975] 2 All ER 945, [1975] 1 WLR 811. In that case there had been a ruling on a question of law before the commencement of the trial. I use the words 'the commencement of the trial' in the loosest possible sense for the moment. That was sought to be challenged in the Court of Appeal. In the course of the judgment Scarman LJ said ([1975] 2 All ER 945 at 948, [1975] 1 WLR 811 at 814):

'After a short adjournment, the charge was then put to the appellant, who pleaded guilty to the conspiracy. We think it clear that the proceedings in which the ruling was given were not part of the trial. Arraignment is the process of calling an accused forward to answer an indictment. It is only after arraignment, which concludes with the plea of the accused to the indictment, that it is known whether there will be a trial and, if so, what manner of trial. Hale (2 Hale PC 219), describing arraignment, says that, if the prisoner pleads not guilty—"the clerk joins issue with him . . . and enters the plea: then he demands how he will be tried, the common answer is 'by God and the country' and thereupon the clerk enters 'po. se.' [Ponit se in patriam]." In Hale's time trial by compurgation or battle were possible alternatives to trial by jury. Not so today; but even today there is no trial on a plea of guilty; for "an express confession . . . is the highest conviction that can be": Hawkins, Pleas of the Crown (ch 31, s 1). Thus it still remains true that there is no trial until it is known whether one is necessary; on a plea of guilty, no trial is needed for the entering of the plea is the conviction.'

It might be said that for the purpose of the determination of the issue in that appeal what Scarman LJ there said was obiter dicta. But obiter or not we find it to be a very comprehensive and accurate statement of the law as to the commencement of trial.

We have been referred to and have very carefully examined the decisions in a number of other cases, namely, R v Paling (1978) 67 Cr App R 299, R v Ellis (1973) 57 Cr App R 571, R v Williams (Roy) [1977] 1 All ER 874, [1978] QB 373. It is to R v Williams (Roy) that we turn to look in a little detail at the judgment of Shaw LJ. The question when a trial can truly be said to begin having been canvassed, Shaw LJ observed ([1977] 1 All ER 874 at 878, [1978] QB 373 at 381):

'He submitted that there was no trial at all, for there was no proper beginning to a trial. This proposition in an abstruse and abstract sense has an appearance of validity. The fact is however that the proceedings which began on 25th May had all the elements of a duly constituted trial by jury and followed in all particulars the course of such a trial. If on some earlier occasion the appellant had been arraigned, no question could have arisen as to the regularity of the proceedings on 25th May. There was a mutual assumption between the Crown and the appellant that the prosecution were put to proof of their accusation so that a trial of the issues was necessary.'

It should be interpolated here that the charge had never been put; there had been no arraignment. Shaw LJ continued ([1977] 1 All ER 874 at 879, [1978] QB 373 at 381):

'Counsel for the Crown has conducted extensive research into the literature relating to the function and significance of arraignment in a criminal trial. The court is much indebted to him for the very helpful results of his labours. They support the view which this court has formed. Counsel for the Crown referred to Roscoe's Criminal Evidence (16th edn, 1952) p 242, where arraignment is dealt with as coming within the proceedings "before trial". The author states that "A person indicted for felony must in all cases appear in person and be arraigned . . ." . . .'

Later Shaw LJ made it plain that the court was accepting the proposition that the trial began when the jury were seised of the issue.

We were referred to a Canadian case, Catherwood v Thompson [1958] OR 326. It arose from a civil action in the county court, and the Court of Appeal held (at 331–332):

'When a trial may be said actually to have commenced is often a difficult question but, generally speaking, this stage is reached when all preliminary questions have been determined and the jury, or a judge in a non-jury trial, enter upon the hearing and examination of the facts for the purpose of determining the questions in controversy in the litigation.'

Counsel for Rhiney has made an exploration (it would be a disservice to him to describe it in any other way) into the judgments of the Supreme Court of Canada in *Morin v R* (1890) 18 SCR 407, in an appeal from the Court of Queen's Bench for Lower Canada (Appeal Side). That case concerned the right of the Crown to stand aside jurors when the panel had already been gone through. The issue before the Court of Appeal was whether or no that matter could be the subject of appeal. It could only be the subject of appeal, so it was said, if the trial had not commenced. That court, constituted of six judges, and presided over by Ritchie CJ, reached the conclusion, as to three of them, that the trial started when the jury were seised of the matter, and, as to the other three, to the contrary, that the trial started probably at about the time of arraignment.

Counsel for Rhiney seeks to persuade us, by an examination of the judgment of Strong J in that case, that, although that judge came down on the side of Ritchie CJ and another judge in saying that the trial started at the time when the defendant was put in the charge of the jury, he really did so under the duress of what he called authority binding on him. The result, therefore, said counsel for Rhiney very engagingly, was not 3:3 but 4:2 in his favour. Examining law reports in that way is a legitimate forensic exercise and, as we found, a welcome diversion. But the plain fact of the matter is that Strong J came to the conclusion that he was bound by authority. Accordingly, as I have said, the Canadian court was in an inconclusive state as a result of the decision of those six distinguished judges.

The judgment of Ritchie CJ is, we think, worthy of very careful study. It is instructive in that the Chief Justice examined a large number of authorities, most of them English. He relied quite heavily on the work of *Chitty on Criminal Law* (2nd edn, 1826) in reaching this very clearly stated final conclusion (18 SCR 407 at 415):

'Until a full jury is sworn there can be no trial, because until that is done there is no tribunal competent to try the prisoner. The terms of the jurymen's oath seem to show this. And as is to be inferred as we have seen even from what Lord Campbell says that all that takes place anterior to the completion and swearing of the jury is preliminary to the trial. How can the prisoner be tried until there is a court competent to try him? And how can there be a court until there is a judge on the bench and a jury in the box duly sworn? Until there is a court thus constituted there can be no trial, because there is no tribunal competent to try him. But when there is a court duly constituted the prisoner being present and given in charge to the jury his trial in my opinion commences, and not before.'

That expresses more aptly and clearly than we think we could what we deem to be the true position. We go further and say that our experience as judges in the criminal courts leads us inevitably to the conclusion, unassisted by the authorities to which we have referred in the course of this judgment, that it would be wholly insensible to speak of the commencement of a trial as being other than when the jury have been sworn and take the prisoner into their charge, to try the issues and, having heard the evidence, to say whether he is guilty or not of the charge against him, always remembering that it is inevitably a trial by jury, not by a judge. A trial can take place only if the defendant himself demands it by pleading not guilty. If he pleads guilty there is no issue to be tried.

Counsel for the appellant Evans at one stage submitted that there is an issue to be tried on a plea of guilty when there is a matter to be resolved which may affect sentence, a question of fact relating to a state of affairs, for example. It is true of course that a judge sometimes goes to the extent of calling evidence before him on a plea of guilty, to be sure that he has the essential facts established before he passes sentence. To that extent it may be said that there is an issue to be resolved. But it is not the kind of issue which is in contemplation when considering trial by jury; it is a wholly different matter.

For those reasons we are firmly of the opinion that, as was stated so eloquently by Ritchie CJ, a trial starts at the time he adumbrated.

Evans did not give evidence in his trial. Before the trial started he knew the legal position. We are sure that he had been advised on the law as it stood. He must have

heard the legal argument which took place before the judge about the time of the
a commencement of the trial. In Rhiney's case it needs to be said that Rhiney not only
gave evidence himself but called various witnesses on his plea of alibi. We fail to see what
hardship there was to either of these two men as a result of the enactment of s 72 of the
1982 Act.

That, however, is not a matter that can affect our judgment. We have to interpret the
effect of the plain provisions of s 72. This we have done, with the result that I have
b already stated.

As that ground of appeal fails, we turn to look at the effect of the other main ground
of appeal. It must inevitably lead to the quashing of the convictions of Tonner, Rees,
Harding and Evans on the charge of conspiracy at common law. This court has however
a power to substitute of its own accord a conviction of one or more of these appellants of
another offence if it deems it right and just so to do. Counsel for the appellants Tonner,
c Rees and Harding and counsel for the appellant Evans are aware of the intention of the
court in this respect, because we invited argument by them on it. Both counsel made it
absolutely clear that they could not resist, in the whole of the circumstances, the use by
the court of the provisions of s 3 of the Criminal Appeal Act 1968. For present purpose
those provisions are contained in sub-s (1):

> d    'This section applies on an appeal against conviction, where the appellant has been
> convicted of an offence and the jury could on the indictment have found him guilty
> of some other offence, and on the finding of the jury it appears to the Court of
> Appeal that the jury must have been satisfied of facts which proved him guilty of
> the other offence.'

The other offence, as is acknowledged by both counsel for the appellants, is that of acting
e contrary to s 38(1) of the Finance Act 1972. We quash the convictions, as we have said,
and substitute for them in every instance in respect of every appellant a verdict of guilty
of conspiring to act contrary to the provisions of s 38(1) of the 1972 Act, and such
convictions will therefore be recorded.

We turn therefore to the only remaining matter in these appeals. In doing so we are
of course aware that we are circumscribed in our powers by the provisions of s 1(1) of the
Criminal Justice Act 1977, and we bear them carefully in mind. The maximum sentence
under s 38(1) of the Finance Act 1972 is two years' imprisonment, but the fines which
can be levied are very heavy, as is manifest from the fact that the court has power to
impose a fine three times the amount of the value of the tax kept away from the Revenue.

Turning to the individuals concerned here, we look first at Tonner. He is 51 years of
age, and he has a criminal record. He has been to borstal for office-breaking and larceny.
f That was a long time ago, it is true. He has further been convicted of receiving stolen
jewellery, and in 1980 of conspiracy to utter counterfeit gold coins. In 1981 he was first
convicted of dishonestly handling stolen jewellery. That conviction was the result of
information having been passed to police officers by what is nowadays called a 'super-
grass'. The conduct which brought about that conviction was committed as long ago as
1974. That was said to be why, in passing a sentence of 18 months' imprisonment, the
court suspended it for two years. Doubtless it was with that fact in mind that Judge
Lowry in activating that sentence reduced it to six months. We think it is an important
feature of Tonner's conduct that it was not very long after the imposition of that
suspended sentence that he began the activities which have been of so much concern to
this court in these appeals. Clearly he paid very little heed to the fact that he was subject
to a suspended sentence.

Counsel has urged on us that in those circumstances we should impose on Tonner
concurrent sentences regardless of the heavy sentences imposed by the judge below. It is,
he submitted, wrong in principle to make them consecutive. In that regard he has
referred us to R v Lovelock [1956] 3 All ER 223, [1956] 1 WLR 1217. We think that that
case is opposed to the principle which counsel would have us believe exists. He has said
that it exists in his own head. It may be none the worse for that; but we should prefer

other assistance before coming to the belief that it really does exist. We are sure that he will not regard that comment as discourteous. We see no reason, having regard to the gravity of the matter, why consecutive sentences should not be passed in this case. This was indeed a very serious affair.

We fully note the terms of the sentences which were imposed by the judge and we bear in mind of course the submissions made to us of Tonner's involvement in the second count. For his part in the conspiracy as found by this court we think there should be a sentence of two years' imprisonment on count 1 and of two years' imprisonment on count 2, those sentences to run consecutively, and moreover also to run consecutively to the six months' imprisonment which was activated by Judge Lowry, making overall a term of 4½ years' imprisonment.

Finally, as the costs are not challenged, we look at the fines. Counsel very frankly has conceded that he cannot launch an attack on the fines imposed on the first count. He has therefore confined his attack to the fine on the second count, which he submits is grossly excessive, having regard to a number of factors, notable amongst which is the role played by his client in that count.

We bear those matters in mind, but cannot accept that Tonner was not at the centre of the web and not heavily engaged in what Rees and Harding were doing, as a result of the conviction of the company. We see no reason whatever to reduce the fine of £100,000. This appeal therefore in respect of that must fail.

Accordingly, in relation to the offences for which we deal with Tonner, we fine him £300,000 on the first count and £100,000 on the second count, and order him to pay £20,000 towards the costs of the prosecution and £10,000 towards legal aid costs. So much, then, for Tonner.

Rees is 43 and Harding 45 years of age. Both have criminal records, and they are a pair of scoundrels. They did not receive a day too long. In fact it could be said that the sentences imposed on them were lenient. We do not regard either of them as deserving of the slightest sympathy or consideration from the point of view of leniency. They it was who deceived the registrar into accepting the false names they used for the purposes of value added tax, and they it was who sold the gold on to buyers in Hatton Garden.

We should not, we think, be doing our duty unless we were to impose on Rees and Harding the maximum sentence it is in our power to pass, that is two years' imprisonment.

We regard Evans as a man of hitherto good character. He has some spent convictions, of which we take no notice. He is now 42 years of age. He played for very high stakes indeed and was quite ingenious. As we have already said, it took a considerable time to unclothe Mr Roberts of his wig and to reveal Mr Evans. But we cannot accede to his counsel's invitation to this court, and Evans will also go to prison for two years.

For the reasons we have given we allow the appeals to the extent of quashing the convictions for conspiracy to defraud at common law and substituting convictions as already stated.

*Appeals allowed to extent of quashing convictions for common law conspiracy to defraud and substituting therefor convictions for conspiracy to act contrary to s 38(1) of Finance Act 1972. Appeals against sentence allowed in part.*

Solicitors: *Solicitor for the Customs and Excise.*

Raina Levy     Barrister.

# National Westminster Bank plc v Morgan

HOUSE OF LORDS

LORD SCARMAN, LORD KEITH OF KINKEL, LORD ROSKILL, LORD BRIDGE OF HARWICH AND LORD BRANDON OF OAKBROOK

10, 11, 12, 13 DECEMBER 1984, 7 MARCH 1985

*Equity – Undue influence – Presumption of undue influence – Banker and customer – Customer relying on bank's advice – Wife executing mortgage to bank over matrimonial home – Bank not advising wife to obtain independent legal advice – Bank suing to recover possession of home for mortgage arrears – Wife seeking to set aside mortgage – Whether confidential relationship necessarily giving rise to presumption of undue influence – Whether transaction required to be manifestly disadvantageous before court can set it aside.*

The husband, who was in difficulties with his business, was unable to meet the repayments due under a mortgage secured over the home which he owned jointly with his wife. As a result the then mortgagee commenced proceedings to take possession of the home, and to avert that possibility the husband made refinancing arrangements with a bank, the refinancing being secured by a legal charge in favour of the bank. The bank was made aware of the urgency of the matter and the bank manager called at the home to get the wife to execute the charge. In the course of the bank manager's brief visit to the home the wife made it clear that she had little faith in her husband's business ventures and that she did not want the legal charge to cover his business liabilities. The bank manager assured her in good faith but incorrectly that the charge only secured the amount advanced to refinance the mortgage. In fact the charge was by its terms unlimited in extent and therefore could extend to all the husband's liabilities to the bank, although it was the bank's intention to treat it as limited to secure the amount required to refinance the mortgage. The wife did not receive independent legal advice before signing the charge. The bank subsequently obtained an order for possession of the home after the husband and wife fell into arrears with payments. Soon afterwards the husband died without owing any indebtedness to the bank for business advances. The wife appealed against the order for possession, contending that she had signed the charge because of undue influence from the bank and that therefore it should be set aside. The bank contended that the defence of undue influence could only be raised when a defendant had entered into a transaction which was manifestly disadvantageous to him and, since the husband had died without business debts owing to the bank, the wife was not manifestly disadvantaged but in fact had benefited under the transaction because it had averted the proceedings for possession by the prior mortgagee. The Court of Appeal allowed the wife's appeal, holding that a special relationship had been created which raised the presumption of undue influence which the bank was unable to rebut because it had failed to advise the wife to seek independent legal advice. The bank appealed to the House of Lords.

**Held** – A transaction could not be set aside on the grounds of undue influence unless it was shown that the transaction was to the manifest disadvantage of the person subjected to the dominating influence. The basis of the principle was not public policy but the prevention of the victimisation of one party by another, and therefore a presumption of undue influence would not necessarily arise merely from the fact that a confidential relationship existed between the parties, and although undue influence was not restricted to gifts but could extend to commercial transactions, e g between a banker and a customer, it was not based simply on inequality of bargaining power. On the facts, the bank manager had not crossed the line between on the one hand explaining an ordinary banking transaction in the course of a normal business relationship between banker and customer and on the other hand entering into a relationship in which he had a

dominating influence, and, furthermore, the transaction was not unfair to the wife. The
bank had therefore not been under a duty to ensure that she had independent advice.  a
Accordingly, the appeal would be allowed and the order for possession sought by the
bank would be granted (see p 825 *g h*, p 826 *e* to *j*, p 827 *g* to p 828 *a* and *j*, p 829 *g h*,
p 830 *b* to *d* and p 831 *b* to *j*, post).

Dicta of Lindley LJ in *Allcard v Skinner* [1886–90] All ER Rep at 99–101, of Lord
Macnaghten in *Bank of Montreal v Stuart* [1911] AC at 137, of Lord Shaw in *Poosathurai v
Kannappa Chettiar* (1919) LR 47 Ind App at 3, 4 and of Sir Eric Sachs in *Lloyds Bank Ltd v  f
Bundy* [1974] 3 All ER at 772 applied.

Decision of the Court of Appeal [1983] 3 All ER 85 reversed.

**Notes**
For the relation of banker and customer, see 3 Halsbury's Laws (4th edn) para 40, and for
cases on the subject, see 3 Digest (Reissue) 553–561, 3587–3625.

For persons in a confidential relationship, see 16 Halsbury's Laws (4th edn) para 1454.

**Cases referred to in opinions**
*Allcard v Skinner* (1887) 36 Ch D 145, [1886–90] All ER Rep 90, CA.
*Bank of Montreal v Stuart* [1911] AC 120, PC.
*Huguenin v Baseley* (1807) 14 Ves 273, [1803–13] All ER Rep 1, 33 ER 526, LC.
*Lloyds Bank Ltd v Bundy* [1974] 3 All ER 757, [1975] QB 326, [1974] 3 WLR 501, CA.
*Ormes v Beadel* (1860) 2 Giff 166, 66 ER 70; *rvsd* 2 De G F & J 333, 45 ER 649, LC.
*Poosathurai v Kannappa Chettiar* (1919) LR 47 Ind App 1, PC.
*Rhodes v Bate* (1866) LR 1 Ch App 252, [1861–73] All ER Rep 805, LJJ.

**Appeal**
National Westminster Bank plc (the bank) appealed with leave of the Appeal Committee
of the House of Lords granted on 10 November 1983 against the decision of the Court of
Appeal (Dunn and Slade LJJ) ([1983] 3 All ER 85) on 29 June 1983 allowing an appeal by
Mrs Janet Morgan (the wife) against an order made by Mr C S Rawlins sitting as an
assistant recorder in Bridgwater County Court on 5 November 1982 whereby he
adjudged that the bank was entitled to recover against the wife possession of the property
known as Crossmoor Meadows, East Lyng, Taunton, Somerset. The facts are set out in
the opinion of Lord Scarman.

*Peter Scott QC, Charles Falconer* and *Philip Brook Smith* for the bank.
*Leolin Price QC* and *Peter St J Langan QC* for the wife.

Their Lordships took time for consideration.

7 March. The following opinions were delivered.

**LORD SCARMAN.** My Lords, the appellant, the National Westminster Bank plc (the
bank), seeks against Mrs Janet Morgan (the wife), the respondent in the appeal, an order
for the possession of a dwelling house in Taunton. The house is the wife's family home.
She acquired it jointly with her husband, and since his death on 9 December 1982 has
been the sole owner. The bank relies on a charge by way of legal mortgage given by her
and her husband to secure a loan granted to them by the bank. The manner in which the
wife came to give this charge is at the heart of the case. The only defence to the bank's
action with which your Lordships are concerned is the wife's plea that she was induced
to execute the charge by the exercise of undue influence on the part of the bank. The
bank, she says, procured the charge by bringing to bear undue influence on her at an
interview at home which Mr Barrow, the bank manager, sought and obtained in early
February 1978.

The action was heard in the Bridgwater County Court in November 1982. The assistant
recorder, Mr C S Rawlins, delivered a careful judgment in which after a full review of

the facts he rejected the defence of undue influence and made the possession order sought
by the bank. He also rejected the wife's counterclaim for equitable relief.

The wife appealed. The Court of Appeal reversed the judge, dismissed the bank's
claim, and granted the wife relief in the shape of a declaration that the legal charge was
not a good and subsisting charge (see [1983] 3 All ER 85).

The bank appeals with the leave of the House. Two issues are said to arise: the first, the
substantive issue, is whether the wife has established a case of undue influence; the
second, said to be procedural, is whether, if she has, she ought properly to be granted
equitable relief, and the nature of any such relief. The two issues are, in truth, no more
than different aspects of one fundamental question: has the wife established a case for
equitable relief? For there is no longer any suggestion that she has a remedy at law.
Unless the transaction can be set aside on the ground of undue influence, it is
inimpeachable. The House is not concerned with the claim for damages for negligence
raised by the wife in her counterclaim but not pursued by her in the Court of Appeal;
nor has any case of misrepresentation been advanced.

In the appeal the bank invites the House to review the decision of the Court of Appeal
in *Lloyds Bank Ltd v Bundy* [1974] 3 All ER 757, [1975] QB 326. The case, it would appear,
has been widely misunderstood, though not, I hasten to add, by the judges of our courts.
The majority of the court in that case addressed themselves to its very special facts and
held that the customer's banking transaction (a legal charge on the home, as in this case)
was procured by undue influence exercised by the bank manager; but Lord Denning
MR preferred to base his judgment on inequality of bargaining power. Because this
difference of approach may have led to some confusion, I have no doubt that the House
should accede to the bank's invitation. Whether the bank is correct in its submission that
the majority decision was wrong in law is, however, another matter, to which I shall
return later in my speech.

*The facts of the case*

There is no dispute as to the primary facts; they were agreed by counsel in the county
court. Mr and Mrs Morgan, the husband and the wife, bought the house on 17 September
1974 with the assistance of two loans secured by a first and a second mortgage. The first
was a charge by way of legal mortgage to the Abbey National Building Society to secure
a loan of £12,800; the second was a legal charge to an investment company to secure a
loan of £4,200. The total of £17,000 thus borrowed almost certainly approximated at
the time to the value of the property; and the consequence of the two loans was to saddle
the property with a burden of debt, the servicing of which was to cause the husband
great difficulty. The mortgage repayments soon fell into arrears.

The husband was in business as an earth-moving contractor, a business which he
conducted first through a company, Highbell Ltd, and later through a company named
D A Morgan Contracts Ltd. The business was undercapitalised and subject to alarming
fluctuations of fortune. Highbell ceased to trade in July 1975.

Between 1975 and 1977 the husband banked at the Basingstoke branch of the National
Westminster Bank, though he and his family were living in Taunton. He was frequently
in overdraft on his personal account, so that Basingstoke asked the North Street, Taunton
branch to try to collect what was due. On at least six occasions Mr Barrow, the North
Street manager, visited the Morgan house in an attempt to collect the debt. Certainly on
one occasion he had a discussion with the wife when she told him that the house was on
the market and that the debt would be repaid. The trial judge found as a fact that during
this period the wife's relationship with the bank was a business one, that the family was
in financial difficulty, and that husband and wife were concerned about their inability to
maintain the mortgage repayments.

In June 1977 the husband put a proposal to Basingstoke: it was to borrow from the
bank sufficient to pay off the second mortgage, and to set up a new company (D A
Morgan Contracts Ltd) which he declared to have a rosy future.

The bank agreed subject to a legal charge to be given by both owners of the property, ie by the wife as well as the husband. The bank suggested, very wisely and fairly, that the wife should take legal advice, which she did and for which the bank paid. The advice was that the amount to be secured should be limited to £6,000; and the bank accepted the limit.

A few days later (end of June 1977) the bank discovered that a possession order in respect of the house had been made by a court in favour of the second mortgagee. The trial judge found that the wife knew of this order when she executed the legal charge in favour of the bank.

The bank now had second thoughts. In the result it did not make the loan to the husband, who was rescued by the generosity of his father who paid off the second mortgagee. The charge to secure £6,000 stood, however; and it continued as a support for the husband's borrowing, subject to the limit demanded and obtained by the wife. During these unhappy events husband and wife were, the judge found, desperately anxious not to lose their home.

In October 1977 a crisis arose on the first mortgage. The Abbey National warned the bank that they were starting proceedings for possession in default of payment of mortgage instalments. On 19 October 1977 the husband transferred his personal account (in overdraft £588) to North Street. The Abbey National began their proceedings, alleging a debt of over £13,000. On 12 December 1977 the wife transferred her account to North Street. From this date onward the husband and the wife's banking transactions were with Mr Barrow, the North Street manager.

A bank rescue operation was decided on by the husband and the wife, if they could arrange it. On 30 January 1978 the husband asked the bank 'to refinance' the Abbey National Loan. By this time the society had obtained a possession order. The husband told the bank that all he needed was a bridging loan of £14,500 for some five weeks. If the bank would pay off the society, he would arrange for the bank's repayment by his company, which it would appear was currently in a prosperous phase and had, it was then believed, good prospects.

The bank accepted the proposal on the recommendation of Mr Barrow. He was informed of the approval by his area office by letter of 31 January 1978 in these terms:

'D. A. A. Morgan and another: In reply to your letter of 30 Janaury 1978 the following limit has been granted; £14,500 on current account to 7.3.78 on the short term bridging basis submitted, subject to completion of a new unlimited legal mortgage on NWB 1016 over Crossmoor Meadow to replace the existing limited second mortgage.'

The 'existing limited second mortgage' was the 1977 legal charge limited to £6,000. In place of it Mr Barrow was being instructed to obtain an *unlimited* mortgage to secure a *loan limited* to £14,500. There was considerable discussion by counsel as to the true meaning of this approval. But is is really quite simple: the debt to be secured was the loan of a sum which Abbey National required to be paid if they were to call off their proceedings for possession and to discharge their mortgage; the security for the loan limited to £14,500 was to be a mortgage without express limit. The document of approval sent by the area office and quoted above limited the mortgage to the Abbey National debt and did not authorise Mr Barrow to use the security to support any other lending transaction.

On 1 February 1978 the husband and the wife signed an authority to the bank to pay off the Abbey National and to charge the husband's personal account. The bank, however, required the mortgage to secure the loan to be in joint names (the property being in joint ownership). Between 3 and 6 February a joint account was opened. The details of the transaction were these. In the first week of February the debit of £14,207·22 was transferred from the husband's personal account to the joint account, being the sum which the bank had paid to the Abbey National, and the husband and the wife signed the legal charge, which is the transaction which the wife seeks in these proceedings to have declared null and void on the ground that it was procured by the bank's exercise of undue influence on her. The charge bears the date 8 March 1978; no point arises on the discrepancy between this date and the date early in February when it was signed, the delay being attributable to the fact that the bank did not receive from the Abbey National the deeds of the property until the end of February.

There can be no doubt as to the terms of the charge: it was a charge to secure 'all present or future actual or contingent liabilities' of the husband to the bank. The wife had, therefore, signed a charge the terms of which were without limit and covered *all* the liabilities of the husband to the bank. It was, however, plainly the intention of the bank, as it was also its instruction to Mr Barrow, to treat the security as limited to the bridging finance (capital and interest) needed by the joint owners of the house to pay off the Abbey National and to obtain a period of time (about five weeks) in which to repay the bank. The bank had at no time sought to use the security for any other purpose.

I now come to the heart of the case. It is not suggested, nor could it be, that prior to the interview at which the wife signed the charge the relationship between the bank and its two customers, the husband and the wife, had been other than the normal business one of banker and customer. It was business for profit so far as the bank was concerned; it was a rescue operation to save their house so far as the two customers were concerned.

But it is said on behalf of the wife that the relationship between the bank and herself assumed a very different character when in early February Mr Barrow called at the house to obtain her signature to the charge; the husband had already signed.

The trial judge set the scene for the critical interview by these findings of fact: husband and wife were looking for a rescue operation by the bank to save the home for themselves and their children; they were seeking from the bank only a breathing space of some five weeks; and the wife knew that there was no other way of saving the house.

Mr Barrow's visit to the house lasted 15 to 20 minutes. His conversation with the wife lasted only five minutes. The wife's concern was lest the document which she was being asked to sign might enable the husband to borrow from the bank for business purposes. She wanted the charge confined to paying off the Abbey National and to the provision of bridging finance for about five weeks. She told Mr Barrow that she had no confidence in her husband's business ability and did not want the mortgage to cover his business liabilities. Mr Barrow advised her that the cover was so limited. She expressed her gratitude to the bank for saving their home. The judge found that the bank was not seeking any advantage other than to provide on normal commercial terms but at extremely short notice the bridging finance necessary to secure their home. He rejected the suggestion that the wife had any misgivings on the basis that she would prefer the house to be sold. He accepted that it was never the intention of Mr Barrow that the charge should be used to secure any other liability of the husband.

The atmosphere in the home during Mr Barrow's visit was plainly tense. The husband was in and out of the room, 'hovering around'. The wife made it clear to Mr Barrow that she did not want him there. Mr Barrow did manage to discuss the more delicate matters when he was out of the room.

Such was the interview in which it is said that Mr Barrow crossed the line which divides a normal business relationship from one of undue influence. I am bound to say that the facts appear to me to be a far cry from a relationship of undue influence or from a transaction in which an unfair advantage was obtained by one party over the other. The trial judge clearly so thought, for he stated his reasons for rejecting the wife's case with admirable brevity. He made abundantly clear his view that the relationship between Mr Barrow and the wife never went beyond that of a banker and customer, that the wife had made up her own mind that she was ready to give the charge, and that the one piece of advice (as to the legal effect of the charge) which Mr Barrow did give, though erroneous as to the terms of the charge, correctly represented his intention and that of the bank. The judge dealt with three points. First, he ruled on the submission by the bank that the transaction of loan secured on the property was not one of manifest disadvantage to the wife since it provided what to her was desperately important, namely the rescue of the house from the Abbey National. He was pressed, of course, with the contrast between the unlimited terms of the legal charge and the assurance (to which at all times the bank adhered) by Mr Barrow that the charge was limited to paying off the Abbey National and the bridging finance. He considered the balance to be between the 'enormous' advantage of preserving the home from the Abbey National and the 'essentially theoretical' disadvantage of the terms of the written charge, and accepted the submission that the transaction was not manifestly disadvantageous to the wife.

Second, he rejected the submission made on behalf of the wife that Mr Barrow put pressure on her. In his view the pressure on her was the knowledge that Abbey National were on the point of obtaining possession with a view to the sale of her home. It was, however, suggested that Mr Barrow had made a mistake in the advice which he gave her as to the nature of the charge. Mr Barrow's mistake was not as to the bank's intentions but as to the wording of the charge. He accurately stated the bank's intention and events have proved him right. I would add in passing that no case of misrepresentation by Mr Barrow was sought to be developed at the trial and the case of negligence is not pursued.

The judge recognised that Mr Barrow did not advise her to take legal advice; but he held that the circumstances did not call for any such advice and that she was not harried into signing. She was signing to save her house and to obtain short-term bridging finance. 'The decision,' the judge said, 'was her own.'

Third, he rejected the submission that there was a confidential relationship between the wife and the bank such as to give rise to a presumption of undue influence. Had the relationship been such as to give rise to the presumption, he would have held, as counsel for the bank conceded, that no evidence had been called to rebut it. He concluded that the wife had failed to make out her case of undue influence.

The Court of Appeal disagreed. The two Lords Justices who constituted the court (Dunn and Slade LJJ) (surely it should have been a court of three) put an interpretation on the facts very different from that of the judge; they also differed from him on the law.

As to the facts, I am far from being persuaded that the trial judge fell into error when he concluded that the relationship between the bank and the wife never went beyond the normal business relationship of banker and customer. Both Dunn and Slade LJJ saw the relationship between the bank and the wife as one of confidence in which she was relying on the bank manager's advice. Each recognised the personal honesty, integrity, and good faith of Mr Barrow. Each took the view that the confidentiality of the relationship was such as to impose on him a 'fiduciary duty of care'. It was his duty, in their view, to ensure that the wife had the opportunity to make an independent and informed decision; but he failed to give her any such opportunity. They, therefore, concluded that it was a case for the presumption of undue influence.

My Lords, I believe that Dunn and Slade LJJ were led into a misinterpretation of the facts by their use, as is all too frequent in this branch of the law, of words and phrases such as 'confidence', 'confidentiality', 'fiduciary duty'. There are plenty of confidential relationships which do not give rise to the presumption of undue influence (a notable example is that of husband and wife: see Bank of Montreal v Stuart [1911] AC 120); and there are plenty of non-confidential relationships in which one person relies on the advice of another, eg many contracts for the sale of goods. Nor am I persuaded that the charge, limited as it was by Mr Barrow's declaration to securing the loan to pay off the Abbey National debt and interest during the bridging period, was disadvantageous to the wife. It meant for her the rescue of her home on the terms sought by her: a short-term loan at a commercial rate of interest. The Court of Appeal has not, therefore, persuaded me that the judge's understanding of the facts was incorrect.

But, further, the view of the law expressed by the Court of Appeal was, as I shall endeavour to show, mistaken. Dunn LJ, while accepting that in all the reported cases to which the court was referred the transactions were disadvantageous to the person influenced, took the view that in cases where public policy requires the court to apply the presumption of undue influence there is no need to prove a disadvantageous transaction (see [1983] 3 All ER 85 at 90). Slade LJ also clearly held that it was not necessary to prove a disadvantageous transaction where the relationship of influence was proved to exist. Basing himself on the judgment of Cotton LJ in Allcard v Skinner (1887) 36 Ch D 145 at 171, [1886–90] All ER Rep 90 at 93, he said ([1983] 3 All ER 85 at 92):

'Where a transaction has been entered into between two parties who stand in the *a*  relevant relationship to one another, it is still possible that the relationship and influence arising therefrom has been abused, even though the transaction is, on the face of it, one which, in commercial terms, provides reasonably equal benefits for both parties.'

I can find no support for this view of the law other than the passage in Cotton LJ's judgment in *Allcard v Skinner* to which Slade LJ referred. The passage is as follows:

*b*      'The question is—Does the case fall within the principles laid down by the decisions of the Court of Chancery in setting aside voluntary gifts executed by parties who at the time were under such influence as, in the opinion of the Court, enabled the donor afterwards to set the gift aside? These decisions may be divided into two classes—First, where the Court has been satisfied that the gift was the result of influence expressly used by the donee for the purpose; second, where the relations *c*      between the donor and donee have at or shortly before the execution of the gift been such as to raise a presumption that the donee had influence over the donor. In such a case the Court sets aside the voluntary gift, unless it is proved that in fact the gift was the spontaneous act of the donor acting under circumstances which enabled him to exercise an independent will and which justifies the Court in holding that the gift was the result of a free exercise of the donor's will. The first class of cases *d*      may be considered as depending on the principle that no one shall be allowed to retain any benefit arising from his own fraud or wrongful act. In the second class of cases the Court interferes, not on the ground that any wrongful act has in fact been committed by the donee, but on the ground of public policy, and to prevent the relations which existed between the parties and the influence arising therefrom being abused.'

*e*  The transactions in question in *Allcard v Skinner* were gifts; it is not to be supposed that Cotton LJ was excluding the applicability of his observations to other transactions in which disadvantage or sacrifice is accepted by the party influence. It is significant for the proper understanding of his judgment that gifts are transactions in which the donor by parting with his property accepts a disadvantage or a sacrifice, and that in *Allcard v Skinner* the donor parted with almost all her property. I do not, therefore, understand Cotton LJ, *f*  when he accepted that Miss Allcard's case fell into the class where undue influence was to be presumed, to have treated as irrelevant the fact that her transaction was manifestly disadvantageous to her merely because he was concerned in the passage quoted to stress the importance of the relationship. If, however, as Slade LJ clearly thought, Cotton LJ in the last sentence quoted should be understood as laying down that the transaction need not be one of disadvantage and that the presumption of undue influence can arise in *g*  respect of a transaction which provides 'reasonably equally benefits for both parties', I have with great respect to say that in my opinion Cotton LJ would have erred in law; principle and authority are against any such proposition.

Like Dunn LJ, I know of no reported authority where the transaction set aside was not to the manifest disadvantage of the person influenced. It would not always be a gift: it can be a 'hard and inequitable' agreement (see *Ormes v Beadel* (1860) 2 Giff 166 at 174, 66 *h*  ER 70 at 74); or a transaction 'immoderate and irrational' (see *Bank of Montreal v Stuart* [1911] AC 120 at 137) or 'unconscionable' in that it was a sale at an undervalue (see *Poosathurai v Kannappa Chettiar* (1919) LR 47 Ind App 1 at 3–4). Whatever the legal character of the transaction, the authorities show that it must constitute a disadvantage sufficiently serious to require evidence to rebut the presumption that in the circumstances of the relationship between the parties it was procured by the exercise of undue influence. *i*  In my judgment, therefore, the Court of Appeal erred in law in holding that the presumption of undue influence can arise from the evidence of the relationship of the parties without also evidence that the transaction itself was wrongful in that it constituted an advantage taken of the person subjected to the influence which, failing proof to the contrary, was explicable only on the basis that undue influence had been exercised to procure it.

The principle justifying the court in setting aside a transaction for undue influence

can now be seen to have been established by Lindley LJ in *Allcard v Skinner*. It is not a
vague 'public policy' but specifically the victimisation of one party by the other. It was    ***a***
stated by Lindley LJ in a famous passage (36 Ch D 145 at 182–183, [1886–90] All ER
Rep 90 at 99):

> 'The principle must be examined. What then is the principle? Is it that it is right
> and expedient to save persons from the consequences of their own folly? or is it that
> it is right and expedient to save them from being victimised by other people? In
> my opinion the doctrine of undue influence is founded on the second of these two    ***b***
> principles. Courts of Equity have never set aside gifts on the ground of the folly,
> imprudence, or want of foresight on the part of donors. The Courts have always
> repudiated any such jurisdiction. *Huguenin* v. *Baseley* ((1807) 14 Ves 273, [1803–13]
> All ER Rep 1) is itself a clear authority to this effect. It would obviously be to
> encourage folly, recklessness, extravagance and vice if persons could get back
> property which they foolishly made away with, whether by giving it to charitable    ***c***
> institutions or by bestowing it on less worthy objects. On the other hand, to protect
> people from being forced, tricked or misled in any way by others into parting with
> their property is one of the most legitimate objects of all laws; and the equitable
> doctrine of undue influence has grown out of and been developed by the necessity
> of grappling with insidious forms of spiritual tyranny and with the infinite varieties
> of fraud.'    ***d***

When Lindley LJ came to state the circumstances which give rise to the presumption, he
put it thus (36 Ch D 145 at 183, [1886–90] All ER Rep 90 at 99–100):

> 'As no Court has ever attempted to define fraud so no Court has ever attempted
> to define undue influence, which includes one of its many varieties. The undue
> influence which Courts of equity endeavour to defeat is the undue influence of one    ***e***
> person over another; not the influence of enthusiasm on the enthusiast who is
> carried away by it, unless indeed such enthusiasm is itself the result of external
> undue influence. But the influence of one mind over another is very subtle, and of
> all influences religious influence is the most dangerous and the most powerful, and
> to counteract it Courts of Equity have gone very far. They have not shrunk from
> setting aside gifts made to persons in a position to exercise undue influence over the    ***f***
> donors, although there has been no proof of the actual exercise of such influence;
> and the Courts have done this on the avowed ground of the necessity of going this
> length in order to protect persons from the exercise of such influence under
> circumstances which render proof of it impossible. The Courts have required proof
> of its non-exercise, and, failing that proof, have set aside gifts otherwise
> unimpeachable.'    ***g***

And in a later passage he returned to the critical importance of the nature of the
transaction (36 Ch D 145 at 185, [1886–90] All ER 90 at 100–101):

> 'Where a gift is made to a person standing in a confidential relation to the donor,
> the Court will not set aside the gift if of a small amount simply on the ground that
> the donor had no independent advice. In such a case, some proof of the exercise of    ***h***
> the influence of the donee must be given. The mere existence of such influence is
> not enough in such a case; see the observations of Lord Justice *Turner* in *Rhodes* v.
> *Bate* ((1866) LR 1 Ch App 252 at 258, [1861–73] All ER Rep 805 at 809). But if the
> gift is so large as not to be reasonably accounted for on the ground of friendship,
> relationship, charity, or other ordinary motives on which ordinary men act, the
> burden is upon the donee to support the gift.'    ***j***

Subsequent authority supports the view of the law as expressed by Lindley LJ in
*Allcard v Skinner*. The need to show that the transaction is wrongful in the sense explained
by Lindley LJ before the court will set aside a transaction whether relying on evidence or
the presumption of the exercise of undue influence has been asserted in two Privy
Council cases. In *Bank of Montreal v Stuart* [1911] AC 120 at 137 Lord Macnaghten,
delivering the judgment of the Board, said:

'It may well be argued that when there is evidence of overpowering influence and
the transaction brought about is immoderate and irrational, as it was in the present
case, proof of undue influence is complete. However that may be, it seems to their
Lordships that in this case there is enough, according to the recognized doctrine of
Courts of Equity, to entitle Mrs. Stuart to relief. Unfair advantage of Mrs. Stuart's
confidence in her husband was taken by Mr. Stuart, and also it must be added by
Mr. Bruce.'

In *Poosathurai v Kannappa Chettiar* (1919) LR 47 Ind App 1 at 3 Lord Shaw, after
indicating that there was no difference on the subject of undue influence between the
Indian Contract Act 1872 and English law quoted the Indian statutory provision, s 16(3):

'Where a person who is in a position to dominate the will of another enters into a
contract with him, and the transaction appears on the face of it, or on the evidence,
to be unconscionable, the burden of proving that such contract was not induced by
undue influence shall lie upon the person in the position to dominate the will of the
other.'

He then proceeded to state the principle in a passage of critical importance, which,
since, so far as I am aware, the case is not reported elsewhere, I think it helpful to quote
in full (at 4):

'It must be established that the person in a position of domination has used that
position to obtain unfair advantage for himself, and so to cause injury to the person
relying upon his authority or aid. Where the relation of influence, as above set forth,
has been established, and the second thing is also made clear, namely, that the
bargain is with the "influencer," and in itself unconscionable, then the person in a
position to use his dominating power has the burden thrown upon him, and it is a
heavy burden, of establishing affirmatively that no domination was practised so as
to bring about the transaction, but that the grantor of the deed was scrupulously
kept separately advised in the independence of a free agent. These general
propositions are mentioned because, if laid alongside of the facts of the present case,
then it appears that one vital element – perhaps not sufficiently relied on in the
Court below, and yet essential to the plaintiff's case – is wanting. It is not proved as
a fact in the present case that the bargain of sale come to was unconscionable in itself
or constituted an advantage unfair to the plaintiff; it is, in short, not established as a
matter of fact that the sale was for undervalue.'

The wrongfulness of the transaction must, therefore, be shown: it must be one in
which an unfair advantage has been taken of another. The doctrine is not limited to
transactions of gift. A commercial relationship can become a relationship in which one
party assumes a role of dominating influence over the other. In *Poosathurai's* case the
Board recognised that a sale at an undervalue could be a transaction which a court could
set aside as unconscionable if it was shown or could be presumed to have been procured
by the exercise of undue influence. Similarly, a relationship of banker and customer may
become one in which the banker acquires a dominating influence. If he does and a
manifestly disadvantageous transaction is proved, there would then be room for the
court to presume that it resulted from the exercise of undue influence.

This brings me to *Lloyds Bank Ltd v Bundy* [1974] 3 All ER 757, [1975] QB 326. It was,
as one would expect, conceded by counsel for the wife that the relationship between
banker and customer is not one which ordinarily gives rise to a presumption of undue
influence; and that in the ordinary course of banking business a banker can explain the
nature of the proposed transaction without laying himself open to a charge of undue
influence. This proposition has never been in doubt, though some, it would appear, have
thought that the Court of Appeal held otherwise in *Lloyds Bank Ltd v Bundy*. If any such
view has gained currency, let it be destroyed now once and for all time (see [1974] 3 All
ER 757 at 763, 766, 767, [1975] QB 326 at 336, 340, 341–342 per Lord Denning MR,
Cairns LJ and Sir Eric Sachs). Your Lordships are, of course, not concerned with the
interpretation put on the facts in that case by the Court of Appeal; the present case is not

a rehearing of that case. The question which the House does have to answer is: did the court in *Lloyds Bank Ltd v Bundy* accurately state the law?

Lord Denning MR believed that the doctrine of undue influence could be subsumed under a general principle that English courts will grant relief where there has been 'inequality of bargaining power' (see [1974] 3 All ER 757 at 765, [1975] QB 326 at 339). He deliberately avoided reference to the will of one party being dominated or overcome by another. The majority of the court did not follow him; they based their decision on the orthodox view of the doctrine as expounded in *Allcard v Skinner* (1887) 36 Ch D 145, [1886–90] All ER Rep 90. This opinion of Lord Denning MR, therefore, was not the ground of the court's decision, which has to be found in the view of the majority, for whom Sir Eric Sachs delivered the leading judgment.

Nor has counsel for the wife sought to rely on Lord Denning MR's general principle; and, in my view, he was right not to do so. The doctrine of undue influence has been sufficiently developed not to need the support of a principle which by its formulation in the language of the law of contract is not appropriate to cover transactions of gift where there is no bargain. The fact of an unequal bargain will, of course, be a relevant feature in some cases of undue influence. But it can never become an appropriate basis of principle of an equitable doctrine which is concerned with transactions 'not to be reasonably accounted for on the ground of friendship, relationship, charity, or other ordinary motives on which ordinary men act . . .' (see *Allcard v Skinner* 36 Ch D 145 at 185, [1886–90] All ER Rep 90 at 100–101 per Lindley LJ). And even in the field of contract I question whether there is any need in the modern law to erect a general principle of releif against inequality of bargaining power. Parliament has undertaken the task (and it is essentially a legislative task) of enacting such restrictions on freedom of contract as are in its judgment necessary to relieve against the mischief: for example, the hire-purchase and consumer protection legislation, of which the Supply of Goods (Implied Terms) Act 1973, the Consumer Credit Act 1974, the Consumer Safety Act 1978, the Supply of Goods and Services Act 1982 and the Insurance Companies Act 1982 are examples. I doubt whether the courts should assume the burden of formulating further restrictions.

I turn, therefore, to consider the ratio decidendi of Sir Eric Sachs's judgment.

In so far as Sir Eric appears to have accepted the 'public policy' principle formulated by Cotton LJ in *Allcard v Skinner*, I think for the reasons which I have already developed that he fell into error if he is to be understood as also saying that it matters not whether the transaction itself was wrongful in the sense explained by Lindley LJ in *Allcard v Skinner*, by Lord Macnaghten in *Bank of Montreal v Stuart* and by Lord Shaw in the *Poosathurai* case. But in the last paragraph of his judgment where Sir Eric turned to consider the nature of the relationship necessary to give rise to the presumption of undue influence in the context of a banking transaction, he got it absolutely right. He said ([1974] 3 All ER 757 at 772, [1975] QB 326 at 347):

> 'There remains to mention that counsel for the bank, whilst conceding that the relevant special relationship could arise as between banker and customer, urged in somewhat doom-laden terms that a decision taken against the bank on the facts of this particular case would seriously affect banking practice. With all respect to that submission, it seems necessary to point out that nothing in this judgment affects the duties of a bank in the normal case where it obtains a guarantee, and in accordance with standard practice explains to the person about to sign its legal effect and the sums involved. When, however, a bank, as in the present case, goes further and advises on more general matters germane to the wisdom of the transaction, that indicates that it may—not necessarily must—be crossing the line into the area of confidentiality so that the court may then have to examine all the facts including, of course, the history leading up to the transaction, to ascertain whether or not that line has, as here, been crossed. It would indeed be rather odd if a bank which vis-à-vis a customer attained a special relationship in some ways akin to that of a "man of affairs"—something which can be a matter of pride and enhance its local reputation—should not, where a conflict of interest has arisen as between itself and

a

the person advised be under the resulting duty now under discussion. Once, as was inevitably conceded, it is possible for a bank to be under that duty, it is, as in the present case, simply a question for "meticulous examination" of the particular facts to see whether that duty has arisen. On the special facts here it did arise and it has been broken.'

This is good sense and good law, though I would prefer to avoid the term 'confidentiality' as a description of the relationship which has to be proved. In truth, as

b

Sir Eric recognised, the relationships which may develop a dominating influence of one over another are infinitely various. There is no substitute in this branch of the law for a 'meticulous examination of the facts'.

A meticulous examination of the facts of the present case reveals that Mr Barrow never 'crossed the line'. Nor was the transaction unfair to the wife. The bank was, therefore, under no duty to ensure that she had independent advice. It was an ordinary banking

c

transaction whereby the wife sought to save her home; and she obtained an honest and truthful explanation of the bank's intention which, notwithstanding the terms of the mortgage deed which in the circumstances the trial judge was right to dismiss as 'essentially theoretical', was correct; for no one has suggested that Mr Barrow or the bank sought to make the wife liable, or to make her home the security, for any debt of her husband other than the loan and interest necessary to save the house from being taken

d

away from them in discharge of their indebtedness to the building society.

For these reasons, I would allow the appeal. In doing so, I would wish to give a warning. There is no precisely defined law setting limits to the equitable jurisdiction of a court to relieve against undue influence. This is the world of doctrine, not of neat and tidy rules. The courts of equity have developed a body of learning enabling relief to be granted where the law has to treat the transaction as unimpeachable unless it can be held

e

to have been procured by undue influence. It is the unimpeachability at law of a disadvantageous transaction which is the starting point from which the court advances to consider whether the transaction is the product merely of one's own folly or of the undue influence exercised by another. A court in the exercise of this equitable jurisdiction is a court of conscience. Definition is a poor instrument when used to determine whether a transaction is or is not unconscionable: this is a question which depends on the particular facts of the case.

I propose, therefore, that the House order as follows: (1) that the appeal be allowed; (2) that possession of the house be given within 28 days of the date of judgment in this House; (3) that no order be made as to costs in the Court of Appeal or in this House save for a legal aid taxation of the wife's costs.

**LORD KEITH OF KINKEL.** My Lords, I agree that this appeal should be allowed for the reasons set out in the speech of my noble and learned friend Lord Scarman.

**LORD ROSKILL.** My Lords, I have had the advantage of reading in draft the speech of my noble and learned friend Lord Scarman. I respectfully and entirely agree with it and for the reasons he gives I would allow this appeal.

**LORD BRIDGE OF HARWICH.** My Lords, for the reasons given in the speech by my noble and learned friend Lord Scarman, with which I fully agree, I would allow this appeal.

**LORD BRANDON OF OAKBROOK.** My Lords, I have had the advantage of reading in draft the speech prepared by my noble and learned friend Lord Scarman. I agree with it, and for the reasons which he gives I would allow the appeal.

*Appeal allowed.*

Solicitors: *Wilde Sapte,* agents for *Osborne Clarke,* Bristol (for the bank); *Park Nelson & Doyle Devonshire,* agents for *Clarke Willmott & Clarke,* Taunton (for the wife.)

Mary Rose Plummer    Barrister.

# Practice Directions

## FAMILY DIVISION

*Administration of estates – Practice – Service – Notice to quit – Estate vested in President of Family Division – Address for service – Administration of Estates Act 1925, s 9.*

*Landlord and tenant – Notice to quit – Service – Intestacy – Service on President of Family Division – Address for service.*

When an estate has vested in the President of the Family Division and it is necessary to serve on him a notice to quit, the notice should be sent by post to him c/o The Treasury Solicitor, Queen Anne's Chambers, 28 Broadway, London SW1H 9JS.

Persons serving notices are particularly requested not to send them addressed to the President at the Royal Courts of Justice nor to him at his private address.

The Practice Direction of 30 July 1965 ([1965] 3 All ER 230, [1965] 1 WLR 1237) is hereby cancelled.

13 February 1985

B P TICKLE
Senior Registrar.

## FAMILY DIVISION

*Minor – Psychiatric examination – Wardship cases and matrimonial causes – Costs of examination.*

It is a firmly established principle in wardship cases that the minor should not be subjected to psychiatric examination without leave of the court. The Court of Appeal in *B (M) v B (R)* [1968] 3 All ER 170, [1968] 1 WLR 1182 considered that this principle should also apply to children in matrimonial causes.

Where the court has given such leave, the costs of the examination and report will normally be allowed on taxation, either inter partes or out of the legal aid fund as appropriate, subject to the taxing officer's discretion as to amount.

Where no such leave has been obtained the court may refuse to admit the report in evidence and may direct that the costs of obtaining any examination and report should be disallowed.

21 February 1985

B P TICKLE
Senior Registrar.

# Nancollas v Insurance Officer
# Ball v Insurance Officer

COURT OF APPEAL, CIVIL DIVISION

SIR JOHN DONALDSON MR, DILLON LJ AND MUSTILL J

20 FEBRUARY, I MARCH 1985

*Industrial injury – Disablement benefit – Accident arising out of and in course of employment – Accident occurring while claimant travelling from home to place where work to be undertaken – Relevant considerations – Whether injury 'arising out of and in the course of employment' – Social Security Act 1975, s 50(1).*

Where a claim is made for industrial injury benefit under s 50(1)[a] of the Social Security Act 1975 in respect of injuries sustained in a road accident the question whether the accident is one 'arising out of and in the course of . . . employment' is largely an issue of fact for the adjudicating officer or, on appeal, for the local tribunal and the commissioner. In applying the words of s 50(1) those adjudicating on the issue should adopt a broad approach in weighing all factors material to a particular claim and should then consider the aggregate of such factors in the final evaluation, no one factor being so decisive as to outweigh the others. Since the incidents of employment are so varied, there is no conclusive test or proposition of law that is binding on those adjudicating on the issue, and in particular there is no test based on whether a claimant was at the material time acting in the course of his contractual obligations to his employers (see p 835 *b c*, p 836 *c* to *f* and p 840 *d* to *f*, post).

Dicta of Lord Carson in *St Helens Colliery Co Ltd v Hewitson* [1923] All ER Rep at 269 and of Ormrod LJ in *Paterson v Costain & Press (Overseas) Ltd* [1979] 2 Lloyd's Rep at 207–208 applied.

*Weaver v Tredegar Iron and Coal Co Ltd* [1940] 3 All ER 157 considered.

Dictum of Lord Denning MR in *Vandyke v Fender* [1970] 2 All ER at 340 doubted.

## Notes

For accidents arising out of or in the course of employment, see 33 Halsbury's Laws (4th edn) paras 486–497, and for cases on the subject, see 35 Digest (Reissue) 683–707, 6723–6840.

For the Social Security Act 1975, s 50, see 45 Halsbury's Statutes (3rd edn) 1138.

## Cases referred to in judgment

*Allen v Siddons* (1932) 25 BWCC 350, CA.

*Edwards (Inspector of Taxes) v Bairstow* [1955] 3 All ER 48, [1956] AC 14, [1955] 3 WLR 410, HL.

*Evans v Postmaster General* (1924) 17 BWCC 378, CA.

*Netherton v Coles* [1945] 1 All ER 227, CA.

*Paterson v Costain & Press (Overseas) Ltd* [1979] 2 Lloyd's Rep 204, CA.

*St Helens Colliery Co Ltd v Hewitson* [1924] AC 59, [1923] All ER Rep 249, HL.

*Stewart (John) & Son (1912) Ltd v Longhurst* [1917] AC 249, HL.

*Vandyke v Fender* [1970] 2 All ER 335, [1970] 2 QB 292, [1970] 2 WLR 929, CA.

*Weaver v Tredegar Iron and Coal Co Ltd* [1940] 3 All ER 157, [1940] AC 955, HL.

## Cases also cited

*Elleanor v Cavendish Woodhouse Ltd and Comerford* [1973] 1 Lloyd's Rep 313, CA.

*R v Industrial Injury Benefit Tribunal, ex p Fieldhouse* (1974) 17 KIR 63, DC.

*R v National Insurance Comr, ex p Reed* (1980) App to Decision R (I) 7/80, DC.

---

a   Section 50(1), so far as material, provides: '. . . where an employed earner suffers personal injury . . . by accident arising out of and in the course of his employment, being employed earner's employment, there shall be payable to or in respect of him . . . industrial injuries benefits . . .'

**Appeals**

*Nancollas v Insurance Officer*

Frederick Douglas Nancollas appealed against the decision of the Social Security
Commissioners (I O Griffiths QC (Chief Commissioner), Mr J G Monroe, and Mr D G
Rice) given on 8 September 1981 whereby they allowed an appeal by the respondent
insurance officer, against the decision of the Worthing local tribunal given on 16
February 1981, and held that at the time of the accident in which the appellant sustained
personal injuries he was not acting in the course of his employment within the meaning
of s 50(1) of the Social Security Act 1975. The facts are set out in the judgment of the
court.

*Ball v Insurance Officer*

Peter Donald Ball appealed against the decision of the Social Security Commissioner (Mr
J G Monroe) given on 17 June 1983 whereby he dismissed the appellant's appeal from
the majority decision of the Wakefield local tribunal dated 22 June 1982 upholding the
decision of the respondent insurance officer, that the appellant had not been acting in the
course of his employment within the meaning of s 50(1) of the Social Security Act 1975
at the time of his accident. The facts are set out in the judgment of the court.

*John Tanzer* for Mr Nancollas.
*Frederic Reynold QC* and *Peter Latham* for Mr Ball.
*David Latham* for the Department of Health and Social Security.

*Cur adv vult*

1 March. The following judgment of the court was delivered.

**SIR JOHN DONALDSON MR.**

*Introduction*

   Mr Frederick Nancollas was a senior disablement resettlement officer employed by the
Department of Employment. Mr Peter Ball was a police officer employed by the West
Yorkshire Metropolitan Police. Both were involved in road accidents and both claimed
industrial injury benefit under s 50(1) of the Social Security Act 1975, on the basis that
they were employed earners who had suffered personal injury by accident arising 'out of
and in the course of' their respective employments. In each case the sole issue was
whether the accidents occurred in the course of their employments. The claim of Mr
Nancollas was disallowed by the insurance officer, now known as an adjudicator,
unanimously allowed by the local tribunal, but disallowed by a tribunal of commissioners
(Mr I O Griffiths QC (the chief commissioner), Mr J G Monroe and Mr D G Rice). The
claim of Mr Ball was disallowed by the insurance officer, disallowed by a majority
decision of the local tribunal and disallowed by the commissioner (Mr J G Monroe). Mr
Nancollas and Mr Ball now appeal to this court.

   Although the claims have heretofore been considered separately, the central issue was
the same in both and accordingly the two appeals have been heard together. The two
claims have one other factor in common and one which is to be deplored. That factor is
inordinate delay. Claims for industrial injury benefit are not large, but, if there is any
entitlement, the benefit is needed promptly. Furthermore, in the rare case where the
claim raises an issue fit for consideration by this court, it is likely that a number of other
pending claims will be similarly affected. In each case the greater part of the delay has
occurred between the decision of the appeal to the commissioner and the hearing in this
court. In the case of Mr Nancollas this was nearly 3½ years, the notice of appeal having
been given 20 months after the commissioners' decision. In the case of Mr Ball it was 20
months. Measures can and will be taken within the Civil Appeals Office to try to ensure
that such delays do not occur again, but it cannot be too strongly emphasised that it is
the primary responsibility of the parties and perhaps, in particular, that of the Department

of Health and Social Security which is indirectly concerned with all such appeals, to bring
a them to the attention of the Civil Appeals Office and to co-operate in arrangements
which will enable the appeals to be heard speedily.

*'In the course of his employment'*
    These apparently clear and simple words gave rise to endless litigation in the context
of the Workmen's Compensation Acts and have proved no less prolific in their present
b context. None of these authorities purports to construe the words other than in their
natural meaning. None provides a simple formula which, on application to the facts,
provides a ready answer to the question, 'Did he suffer the accident in the course of his
employment?' and, in the nature of things, none could do so, because the incidents of
employment are so varied. All that they can and do attempt is to draw attention to factors
which are material and should be taken into account and balanced one against the other
c in answering the question. The authorities have, therefore, to be studied for guidance as
to the approach to be adopted, rather than as providing any answer in particular cases.
Furthermore, since many of the authorities are of some antiquity and date from a period
when the employment relationship was not inaccurately described as that of master and
servant, the importance attached to the orders or instructions of the employer and the
search for contractual duties may no longer be so appropriate. The concept is unchanged,
d but, in a changed social matrix, the foundation of the employment relationship is no
longer so much based on orders and instructions as on requests and information and
contractual rights and duties are supplemented by mutual expectations of co-operation.
    Both the instant appeals are concerned with whether the claimant was at the relevant
time engaged on an activity which was in the course of his employment or whether he
was going from his home to another place in order to resume the course of his
e employment. Whilst at home, neither was acting in the course of his employment. Had
each completed the journey successfully, they would thereafter without doubt have been
acting in the course of their employment. The issue concerns where the line is to be
drawn in between. Somewhat similar problems engaged the attention of the House of
Lords in *St Helens Colliery Co Ltd v Hewitson* [1924] AC 59, [1923] All ER Rep 249 and
*Weaver v Tredegar Iron and Coal Co Ltd* [1940] 3 All ER 157, [1940] AC 955. It is tempting
to include extensive citations from those appeals in order to illustrate the truth of Lord
Carson's dictum in the *St Helens* case [1924] AC 59 at 98, [1923] All ER Rep 249 at 269
that—

> 'ambiguous as the words of the statute are, I doubt if the authorities give any
> great assistance in elucidating them; nor do I feel certain that any definition can be
> framed, apart from the particular facts of each case, which will be found helpful to
f solve the meaning of the statute.'

    What emerges from those authorities and others is that, in given situations, claimants
have been held to have been acting in the course of their employment and that,
accordingly, in similar, but not identical, situations, and such is the rich variety of real
life that truly identical situations are comparatively rare, a claimant could, *not should
inevitably*, be held to be so acting. They also show clearly the correctness of the dictum of
Ormrod LJ in *Paterson v Costain & Press (Overseas) Ltd* [1979] 2 Lloyd's Rep 204 at 208.
In support of his view, Ormrod LJ referred to the speech of Lord Wright in *Weaver's* case
[1940] 3 All ER 157 at 170, [1940] AC 955 at 975:

> 'The words of the Act are very general, no doubt designedly so. Experience has
> shown how infinitely various may be the facts to which the words are to be applied.
> In [*John Stewart & Son (1912) Ltd v Longhurst* [1917] AC 249 at 259], LORD
> BUCKMASTER uttered a warning against the mistake involved in attempting to define
> a fixed boundary between the cases which are within the statute and those which
> are without. He said: "This it is almost impossible to achieve. No authority can with
> certainty do more than decide whether a particular case upon particular facts is or is
> not within the meaning of the phrase." The realities of each case must be regarded.'

Ormrod LJ went on to conclude ([1979] 2 Lloyd's Rep 204 at 208):

'I do not myself think that we can resolve this in terms of duty, in terms of  *a*
ownership of premises or by any of the other various tests which have been used in
other judgments. These are not tests so much as explanations for holding yea or nay
whether the particular incident occurred in the course of the employment. The
question has to be decided one way or another way and reasons have to be given;
and it is very difficult to give reasons, as Lord Buckmaster demonstrated.'

These authorities also cast doubt on the correctness of the importance which Lord  *b*
Denning MR attached in *Vandyke v Fender* [1970] 2 All ER 335 at 340, [1970] 2 QB 292
at 305 to the claimant being unable to show that he was obliged by the terms of his
employment to travel in a particular vehicle. That case was in fact concerned with the
same words, but in the context of motor insurance and may be distinguishable on that
ground. However, the reality is that none of the authorities purports to lay down any  *c*
conclusive test and none propounds any proposition of law which, as such, binds other
courts. They do indeed approve an approach which requires the court to have regard to
and to weigh in the balance every factor which can be said in any way to point towards
or away from a finding that the claimant was in the course of his employment. In the
context of the present appeals, there are a number of such factors to which we must have
regard, but none is of itself decisive.                                                  *d*

*The roles of the adjudicating officer and, on appeal, the local tribunal and the commissioner*
None of these decision-takers can act as if the claim with which he is concerned is the
first such claim under the 1975 Act. They must have regard to previous decisions, if only
in order to do justice between claimants and to provide some consistency of decision.
This is particularly true of the function of the adjudicating officer, who must reach the  *e*
majority of his decisions on the basis of guidelines derived from his knowledge of
previous decisions. But they are only guidelines. In the end his decision must stand or
fall on the correctness of his appreciation of the particular facts and of their interrelation
and, having weighed those facts, the correctness of his conclusion, which is very largely
one of fact, that the claimant was or was not in the course of his employment.           *f*

*The role of the courts*
The jurisdiction of the courts is confined to questions of law arising out of the decision.
As such they have to adopt the approach approved in *Edwards (Inspector of Taxes) v
Bairstow* [1955] 3 All ER 48, [1956] AC 14, intervening only if it is clear that there has
been a self-misdirection by the commissioner or if the only reasonable conclusion on the
facts found is inconsistent with that decision. This again makes it all the more dangerous  *g*
to attempt to decide particular claims on the footing that a decision on a similar claim
was upheld by this court or by the House of Lords. Bearing in mind the limited
jurisdiction of the courts, a contrary decision might also have been upheld.

*Mr Nancollas's claim*
The primary facts are found and stated in para 2 of the tribunal of commissioners'  *h*
reasons:

'The claimant is a senior disablement resettlement officer of the Department of
Employment who lives at West Worthing and whose employment involves, in
addition to work at his main base office at Worthing, calling at other job centres and
paying domiciliary visits to disabled persons in his area (which covers Sussex and
Surrey and extends at least as far as Aldershot). He does not work fixed hours but
adjusts them to the duties that he has to perform. On 30 October 1980 his work  *j*
took him to Guildford, where he attended a case conference about a particular
disabled person and a decision was taken that he (the claimant) should see the
disabled person concerned. Arrangements were then made that the claimant should

interview him at the Aldershot employment office on the following day. He
returned home that evening with or without calling back at his Worthing office.
On the following morning he started out by car for Aldershot ... He did not get
there, however, because at a roundabout at Broadbridge Heath (on a direct route
from Worthing to Aldershot) his stationary car was struck in the rear by a following
vehicle. He sustained injuries to his head and neck.'

The reasoning which led them to reject the claim is long and detailed but the substance
sufficiently appears from what follows in this judgment. The starting point is a
proposition of law which the commissioners derived from the judgment of Lord
Denning MR in *Vandyke v Fender* [1970] 2 All ER 335, [1970] 2 QB 292 that 'The journey
to and from work is not a journey in the course of employment unless the claimant is
fulfilling a duty to his employer in undertaking it at the time or in the manner in which
he is doing so', coupled with references to the *St Helens Colliery* and *Weaver* cases. With
the greatest respect to the commissioners, this discloses what may be a misreading and
certainly a misapplication of the authorities. In all three cases the employees concerned
each had only one regular work place, a mine or a factory, and the courts proceeded on
the basis that the journeys were between home and the work place. They then considered
whether any and, in the *St Helens* and *Weaver* cases, how much of that journey could
properly be said to be in the course of the employment. In Mr Nancollas's case, the issue
was different. He had indeed a regular work place in his Worthing office, but on the day
in question he was going somewhere else for the purposes of his work. The issue was
whether the journey was not only in the course of, but part of, his work: whether at the
material time the road was his work place. More specifically, it was whether Mr Nancollas
was employed, inter alia, to drive to places in his area at which disabled persons could be
interviewed and there interview them or whether he had a number of work places which
he had to reach in order to work at them.

Mr Nancollas lived in Worthing. He had his main base office in Worthing. He was
sufficiently senior to decide for himself when and in what manner to travel to outstations
and, if he had set out for Aldershot from his Worthing office instead of from his home,
there can be no doubt that the whole of his journey from that office would have been
undertaken in the course of his employment. It cannot, in principle, make any difference
that, no doubt for sensible reasons such as that there would be no time to undertake any
worthwhile work at the Worthing base office, he drove straight to Aldershot from his
home. This was not a case of a man who one day worked at a Guildford office, on another
at an Aldershot office and on a third at a Worthing office, travelling by car from home to
the relevant 'work place' each day. He was an itinerant officer who, in the course of his
employment, had to roam his area calling at appropriate offices and, no doubt, private
homes to attend case conferences and to interview disabled people. In driving to
Aldershot, Mr Nancollas was not going to work. That was part of his work.

In para 8 of their reasons the commissioners produce a sophisticated analysis of their
own previous decisions, based on a nice appreciation of the contractual arrangements
governing the transport, the extent of the discretion of the employee, whether he carried
working tools or papers with him and how far he had to travel. No doubt these and other
matters are part of the factual matrix. They are the brush strokes which go to make up
the full picture. But the decision will not turn on how many brush strokes there are or
the nature of those strokes regarded individually. It will depend on whether or not it is
proper to add a rubric to the finished picture, viewing it as a composite whole, reading
'He (or she) was in the course of his employment'.

Paragraph 9 deals with calls made on the employer's business on the way between
home and a fixed place of work. The making of a call may well cause part or the whole
of the journey to be in the course of the employment. It would probably be only part,
namely that part between the intermediate port of call and the work place, if little or no
deviation was involved. But it could be the whole journey if the port of call was in the
opposite direction. In any event this would only be one factor in a complex mosaic taking

in the nature of all other aspects of the employee's employment. The decision-taker must
avoid the dangers and temptations of being myopic. He must stand back and look at the     *a*
picture as a whole.

Paragraphs 10 to 12 deal with situations in which there is a break in the course of
employment, as there was of course in this case at least when Mr Nancollas reached his
home on the previous evening. In saying that 'it is impracticable in the light of the
authorities binding on us to lay down hard and fast rules', it seems that the commissioners
were saying that their own previous decisions compelled them to decide claims in     *b*
particular ways, albeit they could not be analysed and reformulated as 'hard and fast
rules'. This is a misappreciation of the position and can involve a sophistication of
distinction between the detailed facts of individual claims which is not only confusing,
but is not warranted by the words of the statute. The statute calls for a 'Yes' or 'No' answer
to a broad question. The approach should be that of a jury. On all the relevant evidence,
is it 'Yes' or 'No'?     *c*

In the current state of the authorities, self-misdirection is not difficult and we are
satisfied that there was misdirection in this case. On a proper direction, we are also
satisfied that the only decision consistent with the facts found by the commissioners was
that when Mr Nancollas met with his accident he was in the course of his employment.

*Mr Ball's claim*

Mr Ball was a police officer. He was also a fingerprint expert. He lived at Wakefield
and normally worked at a Wakefield police station, although he no doubt travelled to
scenes of crime. However he also had another relevant talent. He was a sailing instructor
and, in the course of his duties, instructed police cadets on Embsay reservoir, which is
some 40 miles from Wakefield. The sailing courses normally lasted for 48 hours and he
used to stay overnight at Embsay. When he was detailed to instruct police cadets, he used
to travel to Embsay using a motor cycle which was his own personal property. This
method of transport was approved by his superior officers and he was paid a mileage
allowance. He was required to telephone his station in the morning before leaving for
Embsay, in order to find out whether his orders had been changed, because, for example,
he was required for finger print duties. His employment called for the performance of
an agreed number of hours' work each week and time for this purpose began to run
when he telephoned to the police station and continued throughout the journey to
Embsay.

The commissioner, having referred to the facts, began by directing himself as follows:

'In Decision R(I) 18/55 at para 10 the commissioner stated the question to be
determined as follows:—"The question at issue is whether on the particular journey
he was travelling in the performance of a duty, or whether the journey was
incidental to the performance of that duty and not merely preparatory to the
performance of it." This is no doubt an impeccable statement of the rule, but it is
useless as a guide to the way in which the question should be answered.'

We respectfully disagree. That was not the question at issue. The question at issue was
whether the particular journey was performed in the course of Mr Ball's employment.
Whether it was or was not undertaken in the performance of a duty is but one of the
factors to be taken into account in answering that question, albeit no doubt an important
factor. His formulation of the issue is more accurate if 'duty' is to be interpreted as being
synonymous with 'employment'. If, as may well have been the case, the commissioner
was using the word in this sense, his formulation suggests that he accepted the
proposition, powerfully criticised by Lord Atkin in *Weaver's* case, that the limits of
employment are conclusively defined by the scope of the employee's contractual duty to
his employer, unless 'duty' is given an extremely wide meaning (see [1940] 3 All ER 157
at 163–164, [1940] AC 955 at 966).

The commissioner then built on this foundation, saying:

'Some of the circumstances in which a person travelling to or from work is to be
regarded as being on a journey in the performance of or incidental to the
performance of a duty were listed in paras 8 and 9 of Decision R(I) 14/81 (from
which there is to be an appeal to the Court of Appeal) while in paragraph 12 of the
same decision there are listed certain factors that ought not of themselves to be
regarded as converting a journey into one in the performance of a duty. Among
such factors present in this case are the fact that the journey is undertaken in
working hours, that its cost is borne by the employer (see also *Allen v Siddons* (1932)
25 BWCC 350, *Netherton v Coles* [1945] 1 All ER 227), that the claimant is at the
time carrying with him tools or papers (or I think equipment of any sort) to be used
by him in the performance of his duties (see also *Evans v Postmaster-General* (1924)
17 BWCC 378), or that the journey is a long one (in the present case it was about 40
miles). It is also I consider clear that it is not sufficient that the journey is one that
would not have been undertaken at all but for the employment.'

This formulation invites a consideration of individual factors as being decisive of the
issue and of other individual factors as not being of themselves decisive. Factors can have
very different weights, but it is doubtful if any factor can be so decisive that it is incapable
of being outweighed by others. Furthermore, stressing a consideration of the factors
individually, rather than in the aggregate, invites a mental discarding of non-decisive
factors, whereas they all play their part in the final evaluation.

In a later part of his reasoning the commissioner refers to—

'the rule that a person who is employed to work without a break (other than that
required for the intervening journey) first at one place and then at another makes
the journey from the one place to the other in performance of a duty (see decision
R(I) 2/67 at para 13). Whereas, if there is a break such as an overnight break between
the two duties, this is not necessarily so (see decision R(I) 3/71, where a claimant
normally employed to work at St Helens was for a time detached on Thursdays and
Fridays to work at Barrow in Furness 100 miles away and was injured in a road
accident while returning from Barrow to his home near St Helens one Friday, and
the accident was held not to have arisen in the course of his employment).'

There is no such rule or, if there is, it largely begs the question, since, as stated, the
workman is employed to work at A, to travel to B and to work at B. The journey must
therefore, almost necessarily, be in the course of his employment. Again he refers to the
rule that—

'where a claimant was under an obligation to his employer to use the method of
transport to his work that he is using then if he meets with an accident while using
such transport the accident arises in the course of his employment.'

This he founds on *Vandyke v Fender* [1970] 2 All ER 335, [1970] 2 QB 292 which, if it
purports to establish any rule, the rule so established is the converse, namely, that if the
employee is not under any such obligation he is not acting in the course of his
employment.

The truth of the matter is that there are no rules. There are only factors pointing one
way or the other.

The commissioner's conclusion was that—

'there is nothing in the facts of the present case that differentiates it from other
cases relating to accidents on journeys to and from work, so as to bring the claimant
into the course of his employment.'

We are unable to accept that conclusion or the premise on which it is based. As with
Mr Nancollas's claim, the principal issue was whether this was a journey to work or
whether the journey was itself part of his work.

Mr Ball had a primary place of work in Wakefield and a primary occupation as a fingerprint expert. His secondary activity, as a sailing instructor, was undoubtedly undertaken in the course of his employment and it involved him in a journey of 40 miles    *a* from his home instead of his usual journey of a mile or so. Time spent on the journey was regarded as counting towards his weekly quota of hours on duty, for which he was paid. The expense of the journey was paid for by his employers. Embsay was not an alternative work place in any normal sense of the word. It was simply a place to which he was sent on this particular occasion. We can, I think, take judicial notice of the fact that once a policeman reports for duty, he is liable to be sent anywhere within the area of   *b* his force. Mr Ball reported in by telephone, and the fact that previous instructions to go to Embsay were then confirmed did not make undertaking the journey any less one which was part of, and thus necessarily undertaken in the course of, his employment. In riding his motor cycle to Embsay Mr Ball was not going to work. That was part of his work.

This again is a case in which we are driven to say that the commissioner misdirected   *c* himself and that the only decision consistent with the facts is that at the time of the accident the claimant was in the course of his employment.

*General*

We cannot overemphasise the importance of looking at the factual picture as a whole and rejecting any approach based on the fallacious concept that any one factor is   *d* conclusive. The addition or subtraction of one factor in a given situation may well tip the balance. In another, the addition or subtraction of the same factor may well make no difference. We appreciate that it would assist if we could lay down rules or even guidelines. However, there are no rules, other than that which is contained in the statute: if, looking at the whole factual picture, the claimant suffered the accident whilst in the course of his employment, he is eligible for benefit, assuming all other conditions are   *e* satisfied. As to guidelines, it would be possible to point to material factors: was he being paid for what he was doing? Was it the employer's car? If not, was he paid mileage allowance? Was it of any concern to the employer that he was where he was? Had he a fixed place of work and was he going to it? Had he more than one fixed place of work and was he travelling between them? But any such list would mislead, if, as is almost inevitable, it was once thought to be comprehensive. We could list factors which are   *f* irrelevant, but again any examples would have to be so extreme as to be unhelpful, because otherwise we might be dismissing a factor which, in exceptional circumstances which we had not envisaged, might nevertheless have had some weight.

For these reasons both appeals will be allowed.

*Appeals allowed.*                                                        *g*

Solicitors: *Kingsford Dorman*, agents for *Marsh & Ferriman*, Worthing (for Mr Nancollas); *Russell Jones & Walker* (for Mr Ball); *Solicitor to the Department of Health and Social Security*.

Diana Procter    Barrister.

# Practice Note

COURT OF APPEAL, CIVIL DIVISION
SIR JOHN DONALDSON MR AND MAY LJ
4 MARCH 1985

*Court of Appeal – Practice – Documents to be lodged by appellant – Preparation of bundles of documents – Judge's note of judgment – Pagination of bundles – Legibility of documents.*

**SIR JOHN DONALDSON MR** made the following statement at the sitting of the court. I would like to remind solicitors of the Practice Note of 18 May 1983 ([1983] 2 All ER 416, *The Supreme Court Practice 1985* vol 1, para 59/9/8, p 827). It relates to the preparation of bundles of documents for the use of the Court of Appeal.

Documentation is dull work, but it is of very considerable importance if delay in hearing appeals is to be avoided. At present far too much of the time of the Civil Appeals Office is devoted to pointing out errors in the documentation. In particular there have recently been a spate of cases in which documents have not been bundled.

Other common errors are:

(1) Failure to appreciate, in the case of county court appeals, that concluding lines in the judge's notebook reading 'Judgment for the defendant with costs on scale 2' or the like are not 'the judge's own note of his judgment'. What is required is a note of the reasons for the decision. In the majority of cases, the judge gives an extempore judgment and will not usually have a note of it. In such circumstances, it is incumbent on those representing the appellant to have a note of judgment prepared, agreed with those representing the respondent and submitted to the judge for his approval. In order to avoid delay, this should be put in hand as soon as the appeal is set down. In those cases where the appellant acts in person, counsel or solicitors for the other side must make available their notes of judgment even though the appellant has himself made no note of the reasoned judgment. This applies equally to those cases heard in the High Court for which no official transcript of judgment is available.

(2) Failure to paginate documents properly. At present, many bundles are numbered merely by document. This is incorrect. Each page should be numbered individually and consecutively.

(3) Failure to ensure that all documents are legible. In particular, care must be taken to ensure that the edges of pages are not cut off by the photocopying machine. If it proves impossible to produce adequate copies of individual documents or if manuscript documents are illegible, typewritten copies of the relevant pages should also be interleaved at the appropriate place in the bundle.

It seems likely that the work of documentation is often delegated to very junior members of the solicitors' staff, often without referring them to the Practice Note. Delegation is not, as such, objectionable, but (a) the member of staff must be fully instructed on what is required and be capable of ensuring that these requirements are met and (b) the solicitor in charge of the case must personally satisfy himself that the documentation is in order before it is delivered to the court. London agents too have a responsibility. They are not just postmen. They should check the sufficiency of the documentation before delivering it to the court and be prepared to answer any questions which may arise.

Diana Procter    Barrister.

# Banin v MacKinlay (Inspector of Taxes)

COURT OF APPEAL, CIVIL DIVISION
OLIVER, PURCHAS LJJ AND NEILL J
I 3 DECEMBER 1984

*Income tax – Appeal – Hearing – Natural justice – Duty to hear parties – Appeal to Special Commissioners – Taxpayer in person – Taxpayer not attending hearing – Taxpayer seeking to conduct hearing by presenting written argument – Taxpayer sending documents to commissioners – Commissioners refusing to read or admit documents – Whether breach of rules of natural justice – Whether commissioners exercising discretion to admit documents properly – Whether privilege to plead before commissioners by writing extending to litigants in person – Taxes Management Act 1970, s 50(5).*

The inspector of taxes raised assessments on the taxpayer for the years 1975–76 to 1981–82 and the taxpayer's appeals against them were listed for hearing before the Special Commissioners on a Monday. On the Friday before that date a bundle of documents marked 'Pleadings and Affidavit' was handed in to the commissioners on the taxpayer's behalf. The taxpayer did not attend the hearing and his representative, an employee of his accountant, stated that he was not familiar with the case and had attended solely in order to read a statement by the taxpayer to the commissioners and to note their decision. The Special Commissioners refused to admit the taxpayer's statement, and decided the appeals solely on the evidence and arguments put forward by the Crown. The taxpayer appealed, contending (i) that, although the procedure at the hearing was regulated by s 50[a] of the Taxes Management Act 1970, the commissioners were subject to the rules of natural justice and in particular the rule that they should hear both sides, and that that rule entitled a litigant to put his case before the court in writing, (ii) that the privilege granted to lawyers by s 50(5) of the 1970 Act that they might plead in writing extended to litigants in person and (iii) that the commissioners had had a discretion to look at the 'pleading' (the affidavit being admittedly inadmissible) and in refusing to do so had failed to exercise their discretion properly. The judge dismissed the taxpayer's appeal, holding that the commissioners had not acted contrary to the rules of natural justice, that s 50(5) conferred a special privilege on the legal profession which did not extend to litigants in person and that in refusing to look at the taxpayer's documents the commissioners had not failed to exercise their discretion properly. The taxpayer appealed to the Court of Appeal.

**Held** – The appeal would be dismissed for the following reasons—
(1) A litigant had no basic right to conduct his case in writing without attending the hearing and the entitlement to plead in writing conferred on barristers and solicitors on behalf of a litigant under s 50(5) of the 1970 Act was a special privilege which did not extend to the litigant himself (see p 846 *b* to *d* and *f g*, p 847 *c* to *g* and p 849 *b c* and *h j*, post).
(2) Where a tribunal was presented with a document which admittedly contained inadmissible material, it was not under a duty to read the whole of the document in order to see whether there was anything admissible in it. Accordingly, since the commissioners had not been under a duty to read the taxpayer's 'Pleadings and Affidavit', it could not be said that they had improperly exercised their discretion in not reading them (see p 848 *d* to *f* and p 849 *a b* and *h j*, post).
Per curiam. The General Commissioners and the Special Commissioners are entitled to regulate the proceedings before them within the terms of the 1970 Act in the way which is most convenient for them, and that includes a discretion, if they think it right, to look at any written representation to which a taxpayer might wish to refer (see p 847 *h* and p 849 *j*, post).
Decision of Harman J [1984] 1 All ER 1116 affirmed.

---

*a* Section 50, so far as material, is set out at p 846 *f g*, post

**Notes**

a For a person's right to be heard, see 1 Halsbury's Laws (4th edn) paras 74–77, and for cases on the subject, see 1(1) Digest (Reissue) 200–201, 1172–1176.

For the procedure on appeals to the commissioners, see 23 Halsbury's Laws (4th edn) paras 1607–1617, and for cases on the subject, see 28(1) Digest (Reissue) 555–562, 2024–2059

For the Taxes Management Act 1970, s 50, see 34 Halsbury's Statutes (3rd edn) 1296.

b

**Cases referred to in judgments**

*Noble v Wilkinson (Inspector of Taxes)* (1958) 38 TC 135.

*R v Income Tax Special Comrs, ex p Elmhirst* [1936] 1 KB 487, [1935] All ER Rep 808, CA.

**Appeal**

c Mayer Menahem Banin (the taxpayer) appealed against an order of Harman J ([1984] 1 All ER 1116) dated 8 February 1984 dismissing his appeal against a determination of the Special Commissioners (set out at [1984] 1 All ER 1117–1123) whereby assessments to income tax and class 4 national insurance contributions for the years 1975–76 and 1981–82 were confirmed. The grounds of the taxpayer's appeal were that the commissioners were in breach of the rules of natural justice and the provisions of s 50(5) of the Taxes d Management Act 1970 and failed to exercise their discretion properly in that they refused to read a bundle of documents marked 'Pleadings and Affidavit' which had been deposited with them on the taxpayer's behalf, regarding them as inadmissible because the taxpayer was not present or properly represented at the hearing. The facts are set out in the judgment of Oliver LJ.

e *C W Koenigsberger* for the taxpayer.
*Robert Carnwath* for the Crown.

**OLIVER LJ.** This is an appeal from a judgment of Harman J ([1984] 1 All ER 1116) delivered on 8 February 1984, dismissing the taxpayer's appeal from a determination of the Special Commissioners determining certain assessments which had been made on f the taxpayer.

As the judge observed, the appeal is a somewhat unusual one, because it is not an appeal which raises any point of law as regards the correctness, or otherwise, of the assessments which were determined by the Special Commissioners; it is based entirely on the assertion that the Special Commissioners, in hearing the case, went wrong in law as a matter of procedure as regards the hearing, and that the error of law lies not so much g in the result of the proceedings, as in the way in which the proceedings were conducted.

The taxpayer is, as I understand it, a manufacturing jeweller, and in respect of the years 1975–76 to 1981–82 inclusive he appears to have preserved a degree of reticence with regard to his financial affairs which prompted the inspector of taxes concerned with his tax affairs to raise estimated assessments on him for those years, both in respect of the business of manufacturing jeweller and in respect of certain properties, or the income h from certain properties, of which apparently the taxpayer was possessed.

Certain accounts were submitted on behalf of the taxpayer, but the inspector had a number of queries, and the taxpayer was invited to attend, with his accountant, to clear up those queries, but it seems that he elected not to do so. There were queries about the introduction of a largish capital sum in the business; there were queries about the taxpayer's drawings; there were queries about the absence of balance sheets; and there were queries about travelling expenses and about curious and unexplained increases in turnover, and also with regard to the taxpayer's general dealings in property.

On 24 November 1981 the Revenue wrote to the taxpayer, setting out their views and stating their intention of listing appeals against the assessments for hearing before the General Commissioners. That letter, as I understand it (and I get this from the stated case (set out at [1984] 1 All ER 1117–1123)), contains a list of the figures of assessment which they proposed to ask the commissioners to determine on the appeal, together with a full explanation and analysis. The accountants were invited to indicate what figures were challenged, and to put forward appropriate alternative figures, and to support those figures with evidence. That appears to have produced no response, so accordingly the appeals were listed for 25 October 1982 before the Special Commissioners, the General Commissioners, it appears, having relinquished jurisdiction.

On the Friday before the hearing date, that is on 22 October, the accountants delivered to the office of the Special Commissioners a bundle of documents which was described, so it appears, somewhat delphically as 'Pleadings and Affidavit', apparently prepared by the taxpayer himself. That deposit appears to have been accompanied by no other explanation of what the documents were there for, what use was intended to be made of them or any letter explanatory of their contents.

The accountants were immediately telephoned by the clerk to the Special Commissioners and were told that the commissioners, in accordance with their usual practice, would not look at those documents before the hearing, and suggested that the taxpayer be present in person, or at least by somebody who was prepared to present the appeal on his behalf.

The account of this is to be found in para 5 of the case stated, which states:

'Mr Davis [who was the accountant concerned, when he was telephoned apparently by the clerk] told our clerk that the [taxpayer] had no money and was "on Social Security". Mr Davis did not himself attend the appeal meeting, but sent Mr De Silva, a member of his staff. Mr De Silva knew nothing of the case other than what he had learned from a partial reading of [the taxpayer's] statement, and attended the hearing merely with a view to read that statement to us and to note the outcome of the appeals, not to argue [the taxpayer's] case. Mr De Silva was unable to tell us why [the taxpayer] had not come himself to the hearing to give evidence, but referred to the statement which, he said, mentioned that the [taxpayer] was inarticulate and unable to speak well.'

Then they go on to say, in para 6:

'No postponement of the hearing had been sought. The [taxpayer's] failure to attend the hearing, a failure for which no satisfactory explanation was offered, meant that he could not be examined on any evidence which he might offer, whether written or oral. We therefore decided not to admit his statement.'

Later, in para 10 of the case stated, the commissioners, having set out the facts in relation to the assessments under appeal, say:

'We took the view that the [taxpayer's] accountants had been made sufficiently aware, both from the extended correspondence with the Revenue, and in particular the letter of 24 November 1981 . . . of the case that had to be met. It appears to us that the [taxpayer] was content to leave the handling of the matters in issue to the accountants. The accountants, on being told of the desirability of sending a representative to the appeal meeting, complied in form only, Mr De Silva being empowered only to read (should we admit it) the [taxpayer's] statement and to note our decision.'

As I have said, the bundle of documents appears to have been unaccompanied by any letter of explanation or indication that the documents were those on which the taxpayer was proposing to rely in the opening of his appeal.

The stated case goes on at para 11:

'We decided, upon the facts found by us [and they refer to a certain authority], that the Inspector had made out a *prima facie* case that there had been omissions from the accounts for the year to 30 April 1974 which formed the basis of assessment for the year 1975/76. In the absence of representations before us on behalf of the [taxpayer] that there was no *prima facie* case to answer, it was open to us to find that there had been wilful default or neglect.'

They concluded:

'Upon the facts found by us, and in the absence of any representations before us on behalf of the [taxpayer], or any response by the Accountants to the figures put before them in the Inspector's letter of 24 November 1981, we determined these assessments in accordance with the Inspector's figures as follows [and they then set them out].'

They finally conclude:

'The questions of law for the opinion of the court were: (1) Whether our decision not to admit the document submitted on behalf of the [taxpayer] and described as "Pleadings and Affidavit" was correct. (2) Whether, given our finding that the inspector had made out a *prima facie* case that there had been omissions from the account which formed the basis of the further assessment for 1975/76, and in the absence of any representations on behalf of the [taxpayer] it was open to us (a) to confirm the further assessment for 1975/76 and (b) to grant a certificate under s 70(3) of the Taxes Management Act 1970 in respect of the tax charged by that assessment. (3) Whether it was correct, given the findings of fact, for us to increase the assessment for 1976/77.'

Though those are stated as three separate questions for the court, counsel for the taxpayer before us has not contended that, assuming that the facts found by the Special Commissioners were properly found, their conclusion was not a correct one, and the case has proceeded purely and simply on the question of whether it was right for the commissioners to proceed without reference to the documents which had been lodged by the accountant on the taxpayer's behalf, and headed 'Pleadings and Affidavit'.

The grounds urged in the appeal before us, and indeed before the judge who rejected the appeal to him, are threefold: first of all, it is said the refusal to look at the documents is contrary to natural justice; second, it is said that it was contrary to an express provision contained in s 50(5) of the Taxes Management Act 1970, to which I shall have to refer; and, third, it is said that, if both of those grounds are rejected, nevertheless there was a discretion in the commissioners to look at these documents (and I should mention at this stage that it is not in issue that there is such a discretion) but that their failure to look at them was not a proper exercise of that discretion.

On the first point, what counsel for the taxpayer says is this, that in para 6 of the stated case, to which I have referred, which says 'No postponement of the hearing had been sought', what the commissioners then say is that, because the taxpayer could not be examined on his evidence, they would not look at the statement which he had lodged. In other words, says counsel for the taxpayer, they assumed that the statement headed 'Pleadings and Affidavit' contained only evidence. He submits that that was a wrong assumption on their part; that the reference to 'Pleadings' indicated that the document contained a certain amount of argument and that it is contrary to natural justice for a tribunal, or a court of law, not to take account of an argument put forward by a party. He says that they should at least have looked to see what was in the document. He points out that these are proceedings where, as he says, a taxpayer cannot obtain his costs and if he is incapable, either physically or intellectually, of presenting his case he should be permitted to put forward his arguments in writing.

In his judgment in this case the judge dealt with that submission thus (and I will read only a short extract from his judgment) ([1984] 1 All ER 1116 at 1124):

'The basic submission put by counsel for the taxpayer is that s 50, although it is the procedural section [and that relates to the other point to which I will come in a moment], is subject to and supplemented by the rules of natural justice. With that counsel for the Crown does not quarrel. Counsel for the taxpayer goes on to assert that it is a rule of natural justice that every person may put before the body deciding his cause his arguments in any such form as he pleases: by film, by tape recording, by writing or by any sort of method. In my judgment, there is no such rule of natural justice. The rule of natural justice that will apply is that well-known and basic proposition, audi alteram partem: each side has a right to be heard.'

Then later on he said:

'Of course litigants may well be allowed to supplement their arguments, which they may be afraid they have expressed badly or which they may wish to clarify because they are inarticulate, by summarising them in writing and putting down the points, even developing them in writing, and handing them in, saying, "There is the basis of my argument; will you, the tribunal, read it?" But that is a very different thing from the proposition that there is a basic right to conduct your case in any such manner as you choose, and, in particular, to conduct your case in writing without your own attendance. In my judgment there is no such right, and there is no entitlement as a matter of natural justice to present cases in writing. I therefore reject the taxpayer's first argument.'

If I may say so, I think that is the pith of the judge's judgment. Counsel for the taxpayer submits that this is wrong because he says the Special Commissioners ought at least to have looked at the documents de bene esse; but I am bound to say that, against the background of this case, I see no reason why they were bound to. On their face the documents did not reveal what they contained except that they indicated they were there by way of evidence. There was no covering letter to explain them, and it does not appear that Mr De Silva was able to offer any explanation except to make a statement that he apparently culled from the documents that the taxpayer claimed to be inarticulate, whatever that means.

In my judgment, so far as the point of natural justice is concerned, the judge was entirely right.

So I then turn to the second submission which counsel for the taxpayer made, which is that the Special Commissioners, in declining to admit these documents and to look at them, were in breach of a statutory provision contained in the Taxes Management Act 1970, and the particular provision on which he relies is that which is contained in s 50(5), which reads as follows:

'Upon any appeal the Commissioners shall permit any barrister or solicitor to plead before them on behalf of any party to the appeal, either orally or in writing, and shall hear any accountant, that is to say, any person who has been admitted a member of an incorporated society of accountants: Provided that on an appeal against an assessment under Schedule B the Commissioners shall permit any agent appointed by the appellant to plead before them on his behalf.'

That standing alone might perhaps suggest that there was some right to make written submissions, because counsel for the taxpayer submits that, if a barrister or a solicitor appearing is entitled, as the subsection says, to put written submissions or written particulars before the Special Commissioners, it would be illogical to assume that the appellant himself did not have a similar right. An agent would not ordinarily, he suggests, be thought of as having a right which did not subsist in the principal.

But I think for a start that one has to look at sub-s (5) in the context of the section as a whole, and I think one must read the whole of the section. Subsection (1) provides: 'The Commissioners shall cause notice of the day for hearing appeals to be given to every appellant . . .' Subsection (2) deals with the notice to be given to the Board; sub-s (3) deals with attendance of officers of the Board. Subsection (4) I think is important in the context of the instant case, and that reads as follows:

'If it is shown to the satisfaction of the Commissioners that owing to absence, sickness or other reasonable cause any person has been prevented from attending at the hearing of an appeal on the day fixed for that purpose, they may postpone the hearing of his appeal for such reasonable time as they think necessary, or may admit the appeal to be made by any agent, clerk or servant on his behalf.'

Subsection (6) is in these terms:

'If, on an appeal, it appears to the majority of the Commissioners present at the hearing, by examination of the appellant on oath or affirmation, or by other lawful evidence, that the appellant is overcharged by any assessment, the assessment shall be reduced accordingly, but otherwise every such assessment shall stand good.'

One of the difficulties which counsel for the taxpayer faces in the context of this submission is the difficulty that does appear on the face of sub-s (4), namely that there was nothing on which the commissioners could be satisfied that the taxpayer had been prevented from attending, so hearing Mr De Silva as they did was an act of grace on their part.

Second, he is in this difficulty that, under sub-s (5), it is I think quite clear that the privilege of pleading orally or in writing is confined to barristers and solicitors, and that the accountant has no such right. Counsel for the taxpayer tries to deal with that by suggesting that, since this is a matter of litigation, the right of representation is restricted in some way to people who might otherwise be thought to have rights of audience before a court (solicitors or barristers); but of course he has to deduce from that also that the right exists also in the taxpayer himself.

The judge dealt with the matter thus in his judgment ([1984] 1 All ER 1116 at 1124–1125):

'His second argument was that to refuse to allow argument to be presented in writing was contrary to the express statutory provision in s 50(5). In my judgment that is to reverse the whole nature of s 50(5), which confers a special privilege on the legal profession, granted, I suppose, because it was hoped that their pieces of paper would be relevant and adequately expressed, a hope which I fear is too often not realised. None the less, it is a privilege granted, and it is drawn by express contrast to what is allowed to accountants. In my view it is completely inconsistent with the proposition that all litigants have a right to present their cases in writing and that this subsection is some extension to the legal profession of that right. This is a special privilege granted, and it carries no wider or more general right.'

That came after a historical review of the provisions of s 50(5) in which it appears that this section, as it now stands, was a total reversal of the original position where, under s 57(9) of the Taxes Management Act 1880—

'No barrister, solicitor, attorney, or any person practising the law shall be allowed to plead before the said Commissioners on such appeal for the appellant . . . either vivâ voce or by writing.'

I do not think I can improve on the judgment of the judge; in my judgment he was entirely right in the conclusion to which he came, and this point has no substance in it.

I turn then to the third point on which counsel for the taxpayer relies, and that is the question of discretion. Now one accepts straight away that the commissioners are entitled to regulate the proceedings before them within the terms of the Taxes Management Act 1970 in the way which is most convenient for them, and that will include, I apprehend, a discretion (if they thought it right) to look at any written representations to which the taxpayer might wish to refer.

In his judgment the judge says this about the matter ([1984] 1 All ER 1116 at 1125):

'The difficulty here is: on what grounds am I, as a matter of law, to say that the commissioners, who considered the matter and who set out in para 6 of the case stated their decision not to admit the document, erred in law? What did they fail to take into account which they should have taken into account, or what principle of law did they not consider? Counsel for the taxpayer submits that it must in every case be that you should read the document which you are asked to exercise your discretion to admit before you decide whether or not to admit it. In my judgment that is to seek to put the cart before the horse. The question is: should you admit it? If you do, then you read it. And the reasons why you should admit it will be *a* properly urged in a letter or in some other form of representation, or by an employee, in this case Mr De Silva, who attended on this occasion and who could have been instructed to submit that matter.'

Counsel for the taxpayer says that this is totally illogical because why should you look at one document rather than another? The judge concedes that you might look at a letter which explains what is in the document, but it is illogical to look at the letter if you *b* cannot look at the document itself. You cannot, says counsel for the taxpayer, exercise a discretion as to the admission of the document until you know the nature of the document which you are asked to admit, and you can only ascertain the nature of the document which you are asked to admit by reading it.

The judge goes on in his judgment to say ([1984] 1 All ER 1116 at 1125–1126): *c*

'It seems to me that the commissioners were placed in a difficult and unenviable state, with a document which is admittedly now partly if not wholly inadmissible and irregular, and that in looking at the document and considering the history they were entitled to come to the conclusion, and no error of law is demonstrated in their so doing, that they would not admit the bundle into the hearing. It seems to me that they acted in a way in which I confess I think I would have been likely to act, *c* and certainly not in a way which demonstrates any error which I, sitting here, could possibly correct.'

The reference there to the document which is 'admittedly now partly if not wholly inadmissible and irregular' was to the concession of counsel for the taxpayer made before the judge, and to this court, that if and in so far as the document consisted of an affidavit or evidence it was not lawful evidence which could properly be admitted before the *e* commissioners.

But that does not really touch the primary point of counsel for the taxpayer, where he says that, where a tribunal is presented with a document which admittedly contains inadmissible material, there is nevertheless a duty to read the whole of the document in order to see whether there is something admissible in it. With very great respect, that *f* seems to me a quite impossible contention.

Counsel for the Crown has referred us to *Noble v Wilkinson (Inspector of Taxes)* (1958) 38 TC 135, which shows that in a case of this sort one has to demonstrate an error of law, and where an application had been made by letter to the commissioners for an adjournment but where they decided, nevertheless, to proceed with the hearing, against the background of a lengthy delay and failure to deal with queries. Wynn-Parry J said (at *g* 143–144):

'The General Commissioners were sitting in a judicial capacity, and it is not to be doubted that they had complete control over the conduct of the cases before them and that they had a discretion either to grant or to refuse to grant an application for an adjournment of each case. The Commissioners' Court, if I may so call it, is entitled to every respect by an appellate Court on the question of whether or not *h* that Court has properly exercised the discretion to agree to an adjournment or to refuse it, and an appellate Court should only interfere in a case where it is clearly established that there has been through the refusal to grant an adjournment a miscarriage of justice; but the onus thrown upon the party who alleges that such a miscarriage of justice has taken place is to my mind a very heavy onus. I cannot see that there was any duty on the Commissioners or their Clerk to communicate with *j* the solicitors to the Appellants, either for the purpose of saying whether or not they wished the attendance of the Appellants or the solicitors or for the purpose of intimating whether or not they would be inclined to grant the adjournment asked for. It appears to me that they were correct in taking the view that it was the duty of the solicitors to decide in the best interests of their client whether they would attend the hearing or not and that in those circumstances the solicitors and the a      Appellant act at the peril of the Appellant if the decision is taken not to attend the hearing.'

There of course the circumstances of the case were rather different from those in the present case, but I think the principle is clear, that the onus (and it is a heavy onus) lies on the appellant to show that there was some miscarriage of justice. There being, as in my judgment there clearly is, no duty on the tribunal to read the documents, where, in this case, did they go wrong in the exercise of their discretion?

b      In that context, I think the background is important. The general rule, as clearly appears from s 50(4), is that the appellant should attend personally. As counsel for the Crown has pointed out, the commissioners are an investigatory body (that I think appears from *R v Income Tax Special Comrs, ex p Elmhirst* [1936] 1 KB 487, [1935] All ER Rep 808, which is referred to in *Noble v Wilkinson*) and it is important that they should have the taxpayer before them; they have no power to summon him, although, under s 52(2) they c      have power to summon other witnesses.

Counsel for the Crown points here to a number of matters which indicate that the issues before the Special Commissioners were inevitably going to be primarily issues of fact, because one sees, on the facts, the commissioners came to a particular conclusion, and indeed counsel for the taxpayer does not quarrel with their conclusion on the facts d      which they found. The issue was: were those facts correct? And that was primarily a matter of evidence.

Second, he points to the fact that there was no explanation offered of what these documents were, and why they were there, and why it was that the taxpayer could not attend, nor, indeed, any explanation tendered to the tribunal as to what was meant by the somewhat obscure reference to the documents as 'Pleadings and Affidavit'.

e      There was a person there who was at least capable of indicating (as a representative of the taxpayer) why it was that the taxpayer could not be there, and why the Special Commissioners should entertain the documents which had been deposited with them as the taxpayer's opening of an appeal which it was his burden to present, but, as they pointed out in para 6 of the case stated (to which I have referred), there was no explanation and no application for any adjournment.

f      Their reasoning is stated in para 6; but, as counsel for the Crown has pointed out, they went further and considered, in para 10 of the case stated (to which I have already referred), whether it was proper for them, in the circumstances, to proceed with the hearing of the appeal. I repeat again the words which they use:

g      'It appeared to us that the [taxpayer] was content to leave the handling of the matters in issue to the accountants. The accountants, on being told of the desirability of sending a representative to the appeal meeting, complied in form only, Mr De Silva being empowered only to read (should we admit it) the [taxpayer's] statement and to note our decision.'

That was done at the taxpayer's choice, and it seems to me that it is far too late to complain now about it, or to complain that the commissioners, in declining to allow the h      appeal to be opened by consulting this obscure and ill-identified document, were in any way in error in the exercise of their discretion.

It seems to me therefore that all three grounds on which this appeal has been urged fail, and I would accordingly dismiss the appeal.

**PURCHAS LJ.** I agree.

j      **NEILL J.** I also agree.

*Appeal dismissed with costs. Order for costs not to be enforced without leave of the court.*

Solicitors: *Kean & Kean* (for the taxpayer); *Solicitor of Inland Revenue.*

Clare Mainprice    Barrister.

# R v Hollinshead and others                                                            *a*

COURT OF APPEAL, CRIMINAL DIVISION
STEPHEN BROWN LJ, HODGSON AND GLIDEWELL JJ
14, 21 DECEMBER 1984

*Criminal law – Conspiracy – Conspiracy to defraud – Agreement to manufacture devices enabling
fraud on electricity board – Devices to be sold to stranger – Whether agreement a common law* **b**
*conspiracy to defraud.*

*Criminal law – Conspiracy – Conspiracy to defraud – Agreement to manufacture device enabling
fraud on electricity board – Devices to be sold to stranger – Whether aiding and abetting
commission of offence by stranger – Whether conspiracy to aid and abet an offence known to law
– Accessories and Abettors Act 1861, s 8 – Criminal Law Act 1977, s 1(1).*                     **c**

The appellants agreed to make and sell to a third party 19 devices for altering electricity
meters to show that less electricity had been used than was actually the case. The
appellants expected the third party, a casual acquaintance, to sell the devices to others for
use in defrauding electricity boards. The third party was in fact a policeman, who
subsequently caused the appellants to be arrested. The appellants were charged with two **d**
counts of conspiracy, count 1 alleging that they had conspired to aid, abet, counsel or
procure persons unknown to commit offences of deception against an electricity board
(which was an offence under s 2 of the Theft Act 1978) and charging conspiracy contrary
to s 1(1)[a] of the Criminal Law Act 1977, which provided that it was an offence for persons
to agree to pursue a course of conduct which would necessarily amount to or involve the
commission of any offence by one or more of them if the agreement was carried out in **e**
accordance with their intentions. Count 2 charged them with conspiracy to defraud,
contrary to common law. The indictment stated nothing about the means by which the
fraud was to be perpetrated. The trial judge decided that the trial should proceed only on
count 2, and ordered that count 1 be left to lie on the file. The appellants were convicted
on count 2. They appealed against their conviction on count 2, and the Crown sought
the leave of the court to proceed on count 1 in the event that the appeal against conviction **f**
on count 2 were allowed. At the hearing of the appeals the Crown contended that, since
the inevitable consequence of the appellants' activities was fraud on electricity boards,
their activities amounted to conspiracy to defraud.

**Held** – (1) There had been a material irregularity in the indictment charging the
appellants with conspiracy to defraud at common law since an indictment for conspiracy
to defraud had always to state the means by which the fraud was to be carried out. The **g**
statement of the offence in the indictment on count 2 should therefore have included
and culminated with the dishonest affixing of a device to an electricity meter; and, since
that would have amounted to at least two substantive offences under the 1978 Act, the
charge under count 2 should have been laid as conspiracy contrary to s 1 of the 1977 Act.
The appeals against conviction on count 2 would therefore be allowed and the convictions
quashed (see p 855 *j* to p 856 *b* and *e* and p 857 *c*, post); *R v Ayres* [1984] 1 All ER 619 **h**
followed.
    (2) Furthermore conspiracy to aid and abet an offence was not an offence known to
law, since (a) s 8[b] of the Accessories and Abettors Act 1861, which stated that a person
who aided, abetted, counselled or procured an offence was 'liable to be tried' rather than
'guilty of an offence', was merely in the nature of a deeming provision and did not itself
create an offence, and (b) on the true construction of s 1(1) of the 1977 Act 'the **j**
commission of any offence or offences by one or more of the parties to the agreement'
referred to commission by a principal in the first degree and did not include an offence
by a secondary party, so that an agreement to aid and abet an offence was not a conspiracy
under the 1977 Act. In any event, it could not be said that the appellants had agreed to

a   Section 1(1) is set out at p 853 *e f*, post
b   Section 8 is set out at p 857 *f g*, post

a  procure the commission of an offence under s 2 of the 1978 Act since they had merely
agreed to procure the supply of the devices to a wholesaler who was then expected to deal
with them himself, with the result that their course of conduct fell short of the
commission of any offence by any of them. It followed that count 1 did not disclose an
offence, and leave to proceed on that count would therefore be refused (see p 857 g to j
and p 858 c to g, post).

Per curiam. There is no authority or justification for the proposition that an agreement
b  between two or more persons to carry out a course of conduct which is not in itself
unlawful but which will very probably result in the commission of a fraud by a stranger
to the agreement amounts to the common law offence of conspiracy to defraud (see p 856
h j, post).

### Notes

c  For conspiracy to defraud and indictments in conspiracy, see 11 Halsbury's Laws (4th
edn) paras 58–62, and for cases on the subject, see 15 Digest (Reissue) 1398–1403, 12236–
12297.

For the Accessories and Abettors Act 1861, s 8, see 8 Halsbury's Statutes (3rd edn) 114.

For the Criminal Law Act 1977, s 1, see 47 ibid 690.

For the Theft Act 1978, s 2, see 48 ibid 313.

d  As from 27 August 1981 s 1(1) of the 1977 Act was substituted by s 5(1) of the Criminal
Attempts Act 1981.

### Cases referred to in judgment

DPP v Bhagwan [1970] 3 All ER 97, [1972] AC 60, [1970] 3 WLR 501, HL.

DPP v Nock [1978] 2 All ER 654, [1978] AC 979, [1978] 3 WLR 57, HL.

e  Haughton v Smith [1973] 3 All ER 1109, [1975] AC 476, [1974] 2 WLR 1, HL.

Hyam v DPP [1974] 2 All ER 41, [1975] AC 55, [1974] 2 WLR 607, HL.

R v Ayres [1984] 1 All ER 619, [1984] AC 447, [1984] 2 WLR 257, 78 Cr App R 232, HL.

R v Duncalf [1979] 2 All ER 1116, [1979] 1 WLR 918, CA.

R v Peck (1839) 9 Ad & El 686, 112 ER 1372.

R v Po Koon-tai [1980] 3 HKLR 492.

f  Scott v Comr of Police for the Metropolis [1974] 3 All ER 1032, [1975] AC 819, [1974] 3
WLR 741, HL.

### Case also cited

R v Allsop (1976) 64 Cr App R 29, CA.

### Appeals

g  On 23 May 1984 in the Crown Court at Bristol before his Honour Judge Fallon QC the
appellants, Peter Gordon Hollinshead, Stefan Dettlaff and Kenneth David Griffiths, were
convicted on indictment of conspiracy to defraud, after the appellants had changed their
original pleas of guilty following a ruling by the trial judge. Hollinshead and Dettlaff
were sentenced to nine months imprisonment, three months' suspended, and Griffiths
was sentenced to eighteen months' imprisonment, six months suspended. They appealed
h  against their convictions on the grounds, inter alia, that an agreement to manufacture
and supply to a wholesaler devices which might ultimately be used to defraud one or
more electricity boards was not a conspiracy to defraud the electricity boards because (i)
the acts themselves fell short of any substantive offence and conspiracy to aid and abet
was not an offence known to law and (ii) the ultimate victims (the electricity boards)
were too remote from the agreement, and accordingly a limited agreement to
j  manufacture and supply to a wholesaler was not an agreement to defraud as it was not
'aimed' at any contemplated victim of fraud. The facts are set out in the judgment of the
court.

Graham Jones (assigned by the Registrar of Criminal Appeals) for Hollinshead.
Ian Glen (assigned by the Registrar of Criminal Appeals) for Dettlaff and Griffiths.
Adrian Palmer for the Crown.

Cur adv vult

21 December. The following judgment of the court was delivered.

**HODGSON J.** On 22 May 1984 at the Crown Court at Bristol the appellants, after submissions at the end of the prosecution case, changed their original pleas to ones of guilty and were sentenced, on a count charging them with conspiracy to defraud, to terms of imprisonment. Hollinshead was sentenced to nine months' imprisonment, three months suspended, Dettlaff to the same punishment and Griffiths to eighteen months' imprisonment, six months suspended. The trial judge certified that the case was fit for appeal on the ground that the conviction of each defendant turns on a point of law of some complexity and on which there is no direct authority.

The facts are not in dispute and can be briefly stated. Griffiths knew how to make a device which, fitted in a certain way to a domestic electricity meter, has the effect of reversing the flow of current, so making it appear that less electricity has been used than is the case. These devices are contained in black boxes and have no other useful purpose. Any use to which they may be put will thus inevitably constitute a fraud on an electricity board.

Dettlaff supplied two of these boxes to Hollinshead. On 12 September 1983 Hollinshead met a man in a public house and agreed to sell him 20 of the boxes at £100 each. Unknown to Hollinshead that man was a policeman. Hollinshead telephoned Dettlaff who arranged with Griffiths that he would make the boxes. He made 19. Hollinshead had arranged for the boxes to be delivered on the following day at a service station on the M5. All three appellants went to the rendezvous and the boxes were handed over to the policeman. The three appellants were promptly arrested by other police officers.

The prosecution was then faced with the problem of what charges to bring against the appellants. No doubt bearing in mind what Lord Bridge had said in the then recently reported *R v Ayres* [1984] 1 All ER 619, [1984] AC 447 the appellants were charged with two conspiracy charges. The two counts in the indictment, as finally settled, were: count 1, 'Conspiracy, contrary to Section 1 of the Criminal Law Act 1977'. The particulars of offence are that—

'on a day or days unknown between the 1st day of July and the 19th day of September 1983 [they] conspired together to aid, abet, counsel or procure persons unknown by deception and with intent to make permanent default in whole or in part on an existing liability dishonestly to induce the South Western Electricity Board to wait for or to forgo payment for electricity supplied.'

Count 2, 'Conspiracy to defraud, contrary to common law'. The particulars of offence are that—

'on a day or days unknown between the 1st day of July and the 19th day of September 1983, [they] conspired together to defraud one or more Electricity Boards by the manufacture and/or sale of devices to alter electricity meters.'

It was those counts which the appellants faced on 22 May 1984. There were two other people charged in the same indictment, a Miss Halewood, with whom Hollinshead lived, and a man called Nelson. One of these boxes had been found at Miss Halewood's home. She was originally included in the conspiracy counts but she and Nelson also faced counts charging substantive offences of deception under s 2 of the Theft Act 1978. To these offences each pleaded guilty and they were sentenced to suspended terms of imprisonment. It was not established that the boxes in the possession of Halewood and Nelson came from Griffiths; they appeared to have come from some other source.

We have no transcript of what occurred between the judge and counsel before the trial began, but we are told that the judge was, understandably as we think, concerned as to how he could sum up count 1 to the jury and he decided that the trial should proceed on the count charging the common law offence of conspiracy to defraud; he ordered count 1 to lie on the file not to be proceeded with save with the leave of the Crown Court or this court.

At the end of the prosecution evidence, which went, as we understand, almost

unchallenged, there were lengthy submissions by counsel for the three appellants. It was
submitted that count 2 did not disclose an offence. Having heard counsel for the Crown,
the judge ruled against the submissions. The appellants, as I have said, then changed
their pleas and were sentenced.

We have been provided by counsel for Dettlaff and Griffiths and counsel for the Crown
with very helpful skeleton arguments, but before turning to the detailed submissions
which have been made to us it will be convenient if we sketch the development of the
law of conspiracy which has taken place in recent years culminating in R v Ayres.

In 1970 in DPP v Bhagwan [1970] 3 All ER 97 at 104, [1972] AC 60 at 79 Lord Diplock
said this of conspiracy:

'The least systematic, the most irrational branch of English penal law it still rests
on the legal fiction that the offence lies not in the overt acts themselves which are
injurious to the common weal but in an inferred anterior agreement to commit
them.'

Following the publication of the Law Commission's Report on Conspiracy and Criminal
Law Reform (Law Com no 76) the Criminal Law Act 1977 was passed. In R v Ayres
[1984] 1 All ER 619 at 624, [1984] AC 447 at 458 Lord Bridge said that he—

'read the report as identifying the defect in the previous law of criminal conspiracy
as arising from the uncertainty as to what might constitute the subject matter of an
agreement amounting to a criminal conspiracy, which, in general terms, could only
be eliminated by restricting criminal conspiracies to agreements to commit
substantive criminal offences.'

It was this result which the legislation sought to achieve in s 1(1) of the Criminal Law
Act 1977 which (before its amendment by s 5 of the Criminal Attempts Act 1981)
provided:

'Subject to the following provisions of this Part of this Act, if a person agrees with
any other person or persons that a course of conduct shall be pursued which will
necessarily amount to or involve the commission of any offence or offences by one
or more of the parties to the agreement if the agreement is carried out in accordance
with their intentions, he is guilty of conspiracy to commit the offence or offences in
question.'

But there was a complication. One of the peculiarities of the common law offence of
conspiracy was that some courses of conduct which would not amount to criminal
offences if pursued by one person would be criminal if more than one person agreed
together to pursue them. And by this means conduct in several fields of the law was
brought within the criminal law. In Working Paper no 56 (1974) on Criminal Law,
Conspiracy to Defraud, the Law Commission dealt in detail with the common law
offence of conspiracy to defraud and identified a number of such situations. The stated
object of the Law Commission is that these situations shall where necessary be dealt with
by the creation of new substantive criminal offences, but at the time when the provisions
of the Criminal Law Act 1977 were to come into force this had not been done. The effect
of s 1(1) of the 1977 Act would therefore have been to remove from the criminal law
conduct which should be prohibited and punished. Accordingly, s 5 of the 1977 Act
provided, so far as it is relevant:

'(1) Subject to the following provisions of this section, the offence of conspiracy at
common law is hereby abolished.
(2) Subsection (1) above shall not affect the offence of conspiracy at common law
so far as relates to conspiracy to defraud, and section 1 above shall not apply in any
case where the agreement in question amounts to a conspiracy to defraud at
common law . . .'

This led to a difference of judicial opinion as to the relationship between ss 1 and 5.
Lord Bridge in R v Ayres [1984] 1 All ER 619 at 622, [1984] AC 447 at 455 summarised

the controversy. He said:

'One school of judicial thought with regard to the construction of ss 1 and 5 of  **a**
the 1977 Act holds that any conspiracy to commit an offence involving an element
of fraud in the sense explained in the foregoing paragraph is properly indicated as a
common law conspiracy to defraud. The contrary view is that, whenever the
conspiracy, if carried into execution, would involve the commission of a substantive
offence, notwithstanding that the offence involves an element of fraud, the offence
committed is a statutory conspiracy under s 1 of the 1977 Act and should be indicted  **b**
as such.'

Lord Bridge, after considering all the authorities and expressing agreement with the
'closely reasoned and careful reserved judgment of the court' delivered by Roskill LJ in *R
v Duncalf* [1979] 2 All ER 1116, [1979] 1 WLR 918, concluded ([1984] 1 All ER 619 at
625, [1984] AC 447 at 459):                                                                                  **c**

'For these reasons, and for those expressed in the extract quoted above from the
judgment of the court in *R v Duncalf* [1979] 2 All ER 1116 at 1120–1121, [1979] 1
WLR 918 at 922–923, with which I respectfully agree, I conclude that the phrase
"conspiracy to defraud" in s 5(2) of the 1977 Act must be construed as limited to an
agreement which, if carried into effect, would not necessarily involve the
commission of any substantive criminal offence by any of the conspirators. I would  **d**
accordingly answer the certified question in the affirmative.'

Lord Bridge then went on to consider what the effect of this ruling would be. He said
([1984] 1 All ER 619 at 625–626, [1984] AC 447 at 459–460):

'The effect of this ruling should not, I believe, create undue difficulty for  **e**
prosecutors or judges. In the overwhelming majority of conspiracy cases it will be
obvious that performance of the agreement which constitutes the conspiracy would
necessarily involve, and frequently will in fact have already involved, the commission
of one or more substantive offences by one or more of the conspirators. In such cases
one or more counts of conspiracy, as appropriate, should be charged under s 1 of the
1977 Act. Only the exceptional fraudulent agreements will need to be charged as  **f**
common law conspiracies to defraud, when either it is clear that performance of the
agreement constituting the conspiracy would not have involved the commission by
any conspirator of any substantive offence or it is uncertain whether or not it would
do so. In case of doubt, it may be appropriate to include two counts in the indictment
in the alternative. It would then be for the judge to decide how to leave the case to
the jury at the conclusion of the evidence, bearing always in mind that the crucial  **g**
issue is whether performance of the agreement constituting the conspiracy would
necessarily involve the commission of a substantive offence by a conspirator. If it
would, it is a s 1 conspiracy. If it would not, it is a common law conspiracy to
defraud.'

The decision is summarised in the headnote (78 Cr App R 232):

'The appellant was charged on indictment with one W. with conspiracy to defraud  **h**
at common law. The substantive fraud alleged was an intention to obtain money
from an insurance company by deception contrary to section 15 of the Theft Act
1968, i.e., by a false representation that a load of scallops had been stolen while in
transit. He was convicted and appealed against conviction on the ground, *inter alia*,
that the indictment should have been laid as a conspiracy to obtain property by  **j**
deception contrary to section 1(1) of the Criminal Law Act 1977 and not as
conspiracy to defraud contrary to common law. The Court of Appeal dismissed the
appeal holding that on the clear wording of section 5(2) of the Act of 1977 the
appellant had been properly charged with conspiracy to defraud and that Court
rejected a submission that the indictment was defective. On appeal therefrom to
the House of Lords. *Held*, that (1) on the true construction of the Criminal Law Act

a
1977 an offence which amounted to a common law conspiracy must be charged as such and not as a statutory conspiracy under section 1; conversely a section 1 conspiracy could not be charged as a common law conspiracy, i.e., the two offences were mutually exclusive; the phrase 'conspiracy to defraud' in section 5(2) of the Act of 1977 must be construed as limited to an agreement which, if carried into effect, would not necessarily involve the commision of any substantive criminal offence by any of the conspirators. Accordingly, a conspiracy to defraud at common law could

b
only be charged when the evidence did not support any statutory, substantive conspiracy, and the evidence in the instant case supported an attempt to obtain property by deception if the conspiracy had been carried out, the appellant had been convicted upon an indictment which did not charge him accurately with the only offence for which he could properly be convicted, and there had thus been a material irregularity in the trial.'

c
It is important that one fallacy should be refuted, a fallacy which somewhat confused the submissions made to the trial judge. Reference was made on a number of occasions to the classic, if imprecise, definition of conspiracy at common law as 'an agreement to do an unlawful act or a lawful act by unlawful means'. This definition has no longer any place in the law. The only common law conspiracies which still exist are conspiracy to defraud and conspiracy to corrupt public morals or outrage public decency and, as we

d
have seen, conspiracy to defraud is now limited to agreements to defraud where the fraud perpetrated does not itself amount to a crime. (The other two conspiracies were retained from caution rather than necessity, corrupting morals and outraging decency being almost certainly themselves substantive offences.)

The submissions of the appellants on count 2 (the only count of course with which we are directly concerned) can be summarised. First, it is said that, to constitute a conspiracy to defraud, the course of conduct agreed on by the parties, if carried out, must be an act

e
which directly affects the proposed victim of the fraud. Although the manufacture and sale of one of these boxes might in certain circumstances result in the manufacturer and vendor becoming a secondary party to an offence (or perhaps, as suggested in argument by Glidewell J, to being guilty of incitement) these activities cannot amount to a fraud in themselves. This is put another way in the first proposition in the skeleton argument of

f
counsel for Dettlaff and Griffiths. He says:

'The actus reus of conspiracy lies in the agreement. The question is "What did the Appellants agree to do?" If the execution of their agreement would not involve any unlawful act in the fraudulent sense, they cannot be guilty of conspiracy to defraud.'

g
We think that that proposition would be more accurately stated thus: 'If the execution of their agreement would not involve any act of fraud . . .'

Second, it is submitted that, if the course of conduct agreed can in some way be extended to the fraud which was the only fraud which could be perpetrated on an electricity board, the connection of one of these devices to the meter, then that would clearly be the commission of a substantive offence either under s 2 of the Theft Act 1978

h
or, more simply, false accounting under s 17 of the Theft Act 1968. It should therefore have been charged under s 1 of the Criminal Law Act 1977 (see R v Ayres).

Third, it is submitted that the requirement in s 1(1) of the 1977 Act that the agreement that the course of conduct agreed on shall amount to or involve the commission of an offence by one or more of the parties to the agreement is in effect no more than a restatement of the common law and that, for an agreement to amount to a conspiracy to defraud, the course of conduct agreed must necessarily amount to the performance of an

j
act of fraud by one or more of the parties to the agreement if the agreement is carried out in accordance with their intentions. It is pointed out that in all the examples of conspiracy to defraud cited in argument or discovered by counsel in their researches this has been the case. Here, the course of conduct agreed on would not result in any of the appellants himself defrauding an electricity board.

It has been the law for well over a hundred years that an indictment for conspiracy to defraud should state the means by which the fraud is to be carried out (see *R v Peck* (1839) 9 Ad & El 686, 112 ER 1372). At an early stage in his submissions counsel for the Crown *a* conceded that count 2 did not do this, adding that he had never been asked for particulars. But that answer does not go to the root of the matter. For a count in the indictment to comply with this requirement it would, it seems to the court, inevitably have to include and culminate with the dishonest affixing of the box to the meter and that would clearly amount to at least two substantive Theft Act offences. The charge should therefore plainly have been laid under s 1 of the Criminal Law Act 1977.                                      *b*

This objection to the validity of these proceedings is made clearer if one compares the indictment in this case (however extended to comply with the requirement of particularity) with that in *Scott v Comr of Police for the Metropolis* [1974] 3 All ER 1032 at 1034, [1975] AC 819 at 834:

'1ST COUNT                    STATEMENT OF OFFENCE

                              CONSPIRACY TO DEFRAUD                                   *c*

                              PARTICULARS OF OFFENCE

[Named people] on divers days between the 1st day of January 1971 and the 30th day of December 1972 conspired together and with other persons to defraud such companies and persons as might be caused loss by the unlawful copying and distribution of films the copyright in which and the distribution rights of which *d* belonged to companies and persons other than the said persons so conspiring and by divers other subtle crafty and fraudulent means and devices.'

That clearly sets out an agreement to pursue a course of conduct, in which one or more of the conspirators would participate, which would be a fraud but would not (copyright law apart) amount to an offence if committed by an individual.

Counsel for the Crown was not, in our judgment, ever able to meet successfully this *e* preliminary objection to the validity of the proceedings. To charge these appellants with conspiracy to defraud was therefore a material irregularity.

Counsel for the Crown's answer to the first attack made on these convictions is summarised in his skeleton argument in propositions 3, 5 and 6. Proposition 3 is:

'In determining whether the evidence disclosed a conspiracy to defraud:— (a) It *f* is unnecessary to categorise the Appellants' activities, whether as aiders and abettors, or otherwise. (b) The sole issue is whether the Appellants' activities were capable of being described as a "conspiracy to defraud".'

Proposition 5 states:

'(a) The word "defraud" has a very wide meaning. (b) In determining whether *g* certain activities amount to an agreement to defraud, a Jury is entitled to look at the consequences of those activities.'

Proposition 6 states:

'(a) The inevitable consequence of the Appellants' activities (if uninterrupted) was fraud on one or more of the Electricity Boards. (b) Therefore the Appellants' *h* activities could amount to a conspiracy to defraud.'

In developing his argument counsel for the Crown leant heavily on the decision of the House of Lords in *Hyam v DPP* [1974] 2 All ER 41, [1975] AC 55. His argument can be summarised thus. If two or more people agree on a course of conduct which is not in itself unlawful but which will probably (or very probably) have the consequence that someone will be defrauded, even though the fraud contemplated will be perpetrated by *j* a stranger to the agreement, then that agreement is a conspiracy to defraud. He did not make any suggestion how remote the consequence would have to be before the agreement ceased to be criminal. Any such statement of the law would, in our judgment, be wholly without justification. It is unsupported by any authority and merely to state it in those terms demonstrates, we think, that it would represent an extension of the law of conspiracy wholly unsupported by authority and unjustified on general principles.

Finally, so far as the participation of at least one of the conspirators in the actual course
of conduct agreed is concerned, we do not think that there is any difference between the
old common law and the new statutory conspiracy. No authority has been cited to us
and we know of none which is authority for any other conclusion. With the difference
that the new statutory offence is limited to agreements to commit substantive offences it
otherwise does no more than restate the common law. It is to be noticed in this
connection that Lord Bridge, in the passage from his speech in *R v Ayres* [1984] 1 All ER
619 at 625, [1984] AC 447 at 460 already cited, said:

> 'Only the exceptional fraudulent agreements will need to be charged as common
> law conspiracies to defraud, when either it is clear that performance of the agreement
> constituting the conspiracy would not have involved the commission *by any
> conspirator* of any substantive offence or it is uncertain whether or not it would do
> so.' (Our emphasis.)

It follows that these convictions must be quashed because it is not and cannot be
suggested that there is any room for the application of the proviso to s 2(1) of the
Criminal Appeal Act 1968, particularly as the prosecution's attempt to frame a charge
under s 1 of the Criminal Law Act 1977 has not yet been finally disposed of. But the
quashing of these convictions does not end the matter. Count 1 remains on the file. The
prosecution ask the leave of this court to proceed on that count if, as they have done, they
fail to sustain the conviction on count 2. The defence on the other hand, have asked this
court to direct the entry of verdicts of not guilty on count 1.

In cases where, the trial having proceeded either on s 1 of the 1977 Act or on the
common law, a verdict of not guilty on the facts is returned it would clearly be the
proper course to direct verdicts of not guilty on the other count. But that, of course, is
not the position in this case. The appellants, who have no merits, have succeeded on
count 2 purely on a point of law, and in a proper case it might be the correct course to
give leave to proceed on the alternative count. But before this court took that course it
would have to be satisfied that the alternative count did itself disclose an offence. It is
therefore necessary to examine count 1 in the context of the facts of this case. That raises
the general question whether a conspiracy to aid and abet an offence is itself an offence
known to the law.

Section 8 of the Accessories and Abettors Act 1861, as amended by the Criminal Law
Act 1977, provides:

> 'Whosoever shall aid, abet, counsel, or procure the commission of any indictable
> offence, whether the same be an offence at common law or by virtue of any Act
> passed or to be passed, shall be liable to be tried, indicted, and punished as a principal
> offender.'

Counsel for the Crown says that the word he relies on in this case is 'procure'. That
section does not itself create an offence but is in the nature of a deeming provision which
also permits the use of a shortened form of indictment. The wording is 'shall be liable to
be tried etc' not 'shall be guilty of an offence'. It has, we think, to be compared with s 1
of the 1977 Act, which requires the course of conduct agreed to amount to or involve the
commission of 'any offence or offences'. In our judgment the plain meaning of the two
sections when placed side by side is that a conspiracy to aid, abet, counsel or procure an
offence is not itself an offence.

In Smith and Hogan *Criminal Law* (5th edn, 1983) pp 234–235 the authors deal
specifically with this question. Under the heading 'Agreement to do acts of secondary
participation' they say:

> 'Persons may agree to do an act which would render them liable to conviction as
> secondary parties if that offence were committed. Is an agreement to aid and abet
> an offence a conspiracy? The Criminal Attempts Act 1981 makes it clear that there
> can be no attempt to aid and abet an offence but it leaves open the question whether
> there can be a conspiracy to do so. D1 and D2, knowing that E intends to commit a

burglary, agree to leave a ladder in a place where it will assist him to do so. E is not
a party to that agreement. If E uses the ladder and commits burglary, D1 and D2 *a*
will be guilty of aiding and abetting him to do so. Are they guilty of conspiracy to
commit burglary? If the course of conduct is placing the ladder, it seems clear that
they are not. Placing the ladder is not an offence, not even an attempt to aid and
abet burglary, since the Criminal Attempts Act 1981 makes it clear that this is not
an offence known to the law. It has been argued above that "course of conduct"
should be interpreted to include the consequences intended to follow from the *b*
conduct agreed upon, including the action of a third party to the agreement—in
that example, P, who takes up the poisoned tea and drinks it. So it might be argued,
consistently with that, the course of conduct ought to include E's use of the ladder
in committing burglary. If that should be accepted, the next question would be
whether the burglary is "the commission of any offence by one or more of the
parties to the agreement". E is not a party to the agreement, so the question becomes, *c*
do the words "commission of any offence" include participation in the offence as a
secondary party? Since all the parties to a conspiracy to commit an offence will be
guilty of that offence if it is committed, but s. 1(1) [of the 1977 Act] contemplates
that it may be *committed* by only one of them, it is clear that "commission" means
commission by a principal in the first degree. It is submitted therefore that an
agreement to aid and abet an offence is not a conspiracy under the Act. This *d*
conclusion rests on the interpretation of the Act.' (The authors' emphasis.)

(The authors then go on to consider *R v Po Koon-tai* [1980] 3 HKLR 492, to which it is not
necessary for us to refer.) We are in complete agreement with the reasoning of the
authors in the passage cited.

Apart however from this objection on a point of law there seems to be another fatal
flaw in this count. We do not think that it can be said that on the facts of this case these *e*
appellants agreed to procure the commission of an offence under s 2 of the Theft Act
1978. What they agreed to do was to procure the supply of these boxes to a wholesaler
who was expected thereafter to deal in them. It is not always clearly understood that, if
conspirators bring to a conclusion the course of conduct agreed and that involves the
commission of an offence, they then all become, whether actually participants or not, *f*
liable under the 1861 Act to conviction as principals. Here the course of conduct agreed
fell short and would always have fallen short of the commission of any offence. It was
this difficulty which no doubt led the trial judge to doubt whether he could find a way
of leaving this count, on a proper direction in law, to the jury.

It follows that we have concluded that count 1 does not disclose an offence. We do not
therefore give leave to proceed on that count. However, we think that we have no
jurisdiction to direct verdicts of not guilty. *g*

At a late stage the appellants were given leave to add a further ground of appeal:

'(c) The devices in this case were always destined for the Police Officers' lawful
custody. The Police Officers had placed an order for them. In the circumstances
fraud was impossible. Impossibility is a defence to common law conspiracy.'

This submission was not made to the trial judge. It is founded on the fact that the *h*
amendment of s 1 of the 1977 Act by s 5 of the Criminal Attempts Act 1981 operates
only on statutory conspiracies and not on conspiracy to defraud. It is submitted therefore
that the doctrine of impossibility in attempted crime laid down in *Haughton v Smith*
[1973] 3 All ER 1109, [1975] AC 476 and applied to conspiracy to defraud in *DPP v Nock*
[1978] 2 All ER 654, [1978] AC 979 invalidates count 2. Because we have reached clear
conclusions on other grounds as to these two counts, we have not thought it necessary to *j*
hear argument on or decide this question. It remains open to the appellants.

We are told that Griffiths is not on his own as a manufacturer of these boxes and that
the result of our decision will seriously hamper the police in their efforts to bring to
justice manufacturers and suppliers. We think and hope that these fears are exaggerated.
It is not for this court to postulate hypothetical situations and supply theoretical answers

to them from the prosecution point of view, but we think that in the vast majority of
cases detected by the police it will be possible to frame charges which will disclose either
an offence or complicity in an offence. We think that prosecutors would do well to bear
in mind that incitement is itself a substantive offence and that therefore a charge of
conspiracy to incite can be laid under s 1 of the 1977 Act.

*Appeals allowed. Convictions on count 2 quashed. Leave to proceed on count 1 refused.*

*The court adjourned an application for leave to appeal to the House of Lords but certified, under s
33(2) of the Criminal Appeal Act 1968, that the following point of law of general public
importance was involved in the decision: (1) if parties agree (i) to manufacture devices whose only
use is fraudulently to alter electricity meters and (ii) to sell those devices to a person who intends
merely to resell them (and not himself to use them), does that agreement constitute a common law
conspiracy to defraud? (2) alternatively, is such an agreement properly charged as a statutory
conspiracy to aid, abet, counsel or procure persons unknown to commit offences under s 2 of the
Theft Act 1978?*

*14 January 1985. The Court of Appeal (Stephen Brown LJ, Heilbron and Leggatt JJ) refused
leave to appeal to the House of Lords.*

*28 February. The Appeal Committee of the House of Lords granted leave to appeal.*

Solicitors: *R O M Lovibond*, Bristol (for the Crown).

Sophie Craven    Barrister.


# R v Millward

COURT OF APPEAL, CRIMINAL DIVISION

LORD LANE CJ, RUSSELL AND KENNEDY JJ

14, 25 JANUARY 1985

*Criminal law – Perjury – Mens rea – Witness wilfully making statement in judicial proceeding
knowing it to be false – Statement material in that proceeding – Material – What knowledge
prosecution must prove – Whether prosecution need prove that witness knew or believed the
statement was 'material in that proceeding' – Perjury Act 1911, s 1(1)(6).*

In order to establish that a person charged with perjury, contrary to s 1(1)[a] of the Perjury
Act 1911, has the requisite mens rea for the commission of the offence, the prosecution
merely has to show that in the judicial proceeding in which he was a witness he wilfully
(ie deliberately and not inadvertently or by mistake) made on oath a statement which he
knew to be false or did not believe to be true. The prosecution does not have to show that
he knew or believed the statement to be material in that proceeding, for the materiality
of the statement is a matter which, by virtue of s 1(6)[b], is to be decided objectively by the
judge (see p 861 j, p 862 a b and d to h and p 863 f g, post).

A false statement may be considered 'material' within the meaning of s 1(1) of the
1911 Act if it might have affected the outcome of the proceedings (see p 863 a to f, post);
*R v Lavey* (1850) 3 Car & Kir 26 applied; *R v Sweet-Escott* (1971) 55 Cr App R 316
considered.

---

a    Section 1(1), so far as material, provides: 'If any person lawfully sworn as a witness . . . in a judicial
     proceeding wilfully makes a statement material in that proceeding, which he knows to be false or
     does not believe to be true, he shall be guilty of perjury . . .'
b    Section 1(6) is set out at p 862 d, post

**Notes**

For the meaning of perjury, and the materiality of a statement, see 11 Halsbury's Laws *a* (4th edn) paras 938, 941, and for cases on the subject, see 15 Digest (Reissue) 945, 952–955, 8150–8154, 8206–8243.

For the Perjury Act 1911, s 1, see 8 Halsbury's Statutes (3rd edn) 241.

**Cases referred to in judgment**

R v Holden (1872) 12 Cox CC 166, Assizes.
R v Lavey (1850) 3 Car & Kir 26, 175 ER 448, NP. *b*
R v Murray (1858) 1 F & F 80, 175 ER 635, NP.
R v Sweet-Escott (1971) 55 Cr App R 316, Assizes.

**Case also cited**

R v Ryan (1914) 10 Cr App R 4, CCA. *c*

**Appeal**

On 24 November 1983 in the Crown Court at Stafford before Drake J and a jury the appellant, Neil Frederick Millward pleaded not guilty to a charge of perjury, contrary to s 1(1) of the Perjury Act 1911. He admitted that he had made certain false statements while giving evidence on oath as a principal witness in a judicial proceeding, but *d* submitted that he could not be guilty of perjury (i) because the false statements were not made with the mens rea necessary for the commission of the offence, and (ii) because, in any event, the statements were not, within the meaning of s 1(1), 'material' to the proceedings. Drake J rejected both submissions. The appellant thereupon changed his plea to one of guilty. He was sentenced to three months' imprisonment, suspended for one year. He appealed against conviction on the ground that the judge had erred in *e* rejecting both his submissions. The facts are set out in the judgment of the court.

*Richard Tucker QC* and *Simon Brown* (both assigned by the Registrar of Criminal Appeals) for the appellant.
*Peter Stretton* for the Crown.

*f*

*Cur adv vult*

25 January. The following judgment of the court was delivered.

**LORD LANE CJ.** In November 1983 in the Crown Court at Stafford before Drake J and a jury the appellant, who was at all material times a police officer, was charged with *g* perjury. He pleaded not guilty. At the close of the prosecution case submissions were made by counsel on his behalf. The judge rejected those submissions. The effect of that rejection was to render the appellant's proposed defence ineffective. He was thereupon advised, and correctly advised, to change his plea to guilty, which he did.

He was sentenced to three months' imprisonment suspended for 12 months and ordered to pay £500 towards his legal aid costs. The only issue in this appeal is whether *h* the judge was correct in law in the rulings which he made.

The facts were as follows. On 10 June 1982 the appellant had reason to stop a car containing two Indian men. He considered that certain offences had been committed by the driver. He knew the driver by sight but not by name. The driver gave his name as Parshan Singh. The appellant asked the driver for his driving licence and other documents, but these were not forthcoming and accordingly the appellant served Form *j* HORT 1 on the driver requiring him to produce the necessary documents at the police station. These documents relating to Parshan Singh (hereinafter called Parshan) were produced by Parshan at the police station in due course.

On 14 July the appellant saw Parshan at the police station and told him that he, the appellant, was satisfied that Manjit Singh (hereinafter called Manjit) and not Parshan had been the driver of the car on 10 June and that Manjit had given a false name at the scene

(presumably because he held no proper driving licence); Parshan had accordingly also
a   been guilty of deception when he produced the documents in answer to the HORT 1 and
when he claimed to have been the driver.
  On 10 January 1983 Parshan and Manjit duly appeared at Walsall Magistrates' Court.
Manjit was charged with driving offences and both defendants were charged with
offences allegedly committed on 13 June in connection with the production of the
driving documents.
b     Whilst the two Indians were waiting outside the court for the case to be called on, they
saw the appellant talking to another police officer, Pc Revelle. Revelle, it should be said,
had no connection with the trial of the two Indians at all. Revelle left the appellant, came
over to the two Indians and asked to see their driving licences. Parshan produced his.
Manjit did not. The incident struck the two Indians as being somewhat odd and they
reported it to their solicitor.
c     The hearing started soon afterwards. The prosecution case depended principally (if not
entirely) on the evidence of the appellant to the effect that Manjit and not Parshan was
the driver of the car which he had stopped on 10 June. He was cross-examined on behalf
of the two Indians to suggest that his identification of the driver was mistaken. He was
then asked the following questions:

d     Q. Have you spoken to Pc Revelle this morning? A. Yes.
      Q. Are you aware that Pc Revelle approached my clients this morning and asked
    to see their driving licences and inspected Parshan's driving licence, but could not
    inspect Manjit Singh's driving licence because he didn't have it with him? A. No.
    [That was a lie.]
      Q. Did you ask Pc Revelle to see my clients? A. No. [That was also a lie.]
      Q. Did Pc Revelle talk to you after he had spoken to my clients? A. No. [That was
e     also a lie.]
      Q. Is it not the case that you asked Pc Revelle to see my clients so that you could
    find out which one was Manjit Singh and which one was Parshan Singh because you
    were not sure? A. No.
      Q. [This was in re-examination.] Has there been any sort of conversation between
f     you and Pc Revelle even remotely resembling that suggested to you? A. No. [That
    also was a lie.]'

  The matter was investigated. The appellant eventually admitted the lies and the
charges against the two Indians were therefore quite properly dropped.
  During the subsequent inquiries the appellant gave as his reason for enlisting the help
of Pc Revelle that he suspected Parshan and Manjit were going to try in some way to
g   deceive the magistrates by switching their identities. It seems that there was some basis
for that suspicion. He wanted to be sure who they were saying they were on that
particular day. When questioned he panicked, hence the lies.
  The submissions made to the learned judge were twofold: (1) that there was no prima
facie case that the admittedly false statements were made with the requisite guilty mind
and (2) that in any event the false statements were not 'material' to the proceedings. As
h   already indicated the judge rejected both submissions. These submissions have now been
repeated before this court.
  The basis of counsel's first submission is that the word 'wilfully' requires proof by the
prosecution of knowledge or belief by the accused man that the question asked and the
answer to be given are material. No offence is committed, it is submitted, if a person
makes a statement even though he knows it to be false and even though it is in law
i   material, if he does so in the honest though mistaken belief that it is not material in that
proceeding. The appellant, it is suggested, believed or may have believed, that the lying
answers that he gave were immaterial to the proceedings and if so, it would follow that
no offence would have been committed. In other words the submission is that the
prosecution must prove not only that the false statement was made with knowledge of
its falsity or lack of belief in its truth, but also that the appellant knew or believed that
the false statement was material in the proceeding.

Counsel for the appellant concedes that he has no authority directly bearing on this problem and that this is a point which does not seem to have occurred to anyone in the *a* past. However that is no reason on its own for rejecting the submission. It does not seem to us that as a matter of construction the words of s 1(1) of the Perjury Act 1911 can properly bear the meaning which counsel seeks to ascribe to them. If Parliament had intended that result, it would have been simple to say so, for example by providing that if any person sworn as a witness in a judicial proceeding wilfully makes a statement *which he knows to be* material in that proceeding and which he knows to be false *b* or does not believe to be true, he shall be guilty of the offence. Indeed words to this effect can be found in s 1A of the Perjury Act 1911, which was added by Sch 1 to the Evidence (Proceedings in Other Jurisdictions) Act 1975. It is noteworthy that under s 1A(b) of the Perjury Act a person giving testimony which is false in a material particular commits an offence if he does not believe the testimony to be true whether or not he knows of its materiality. So, when setting the standard in 1975 for those giving evidence otherwise *c* than on oath, Parliament did not recoil from saying that the materiality of the false statement was something which, at least on occasions, could be viewed objectively.

When seeking to discover the intentions of Parliament in their use of the word 'wilfully', it is perhaps instructive to look at s 1(6) of the 1911 Act. This provides as follows:

> 'The question whether a statement on which perjury is assigned was material is a *d* question of law to be determined by the court of trial.'

Looking at s 1 of the Act as a whole, it is clear that the question to which s 1(6) refers can only arise out of s 1(1). If that subsection means that a statement is only material when the person making it believes it to be so, then s 1(6) is meaningless. It would be surprising, to say the least, if Parliament intended to say that it was for the judge to decide if the *e* statement was in fact material, and then for the jury to decide if the person making the statement was aware of the materiality. In other words it seems to us to be unlikely that Parliament should have expressly provided that the question of materiality should be decided as a matter of law by the judge without stating in terms, if such is what they intended, that it would be for the jury to decide whether the defendant believed the statement was material. *f*

Counsel for the appellant did invite our attention to the construction which other courts and some academic writers have attributed to the word 'wilfully' when it has been used in connection with other offences such as obstructing a police officer in the execution of his duty (see s 51(3) of the Police Act 1964). We have carefully considered the various authorities to which our attention has been invited but we do not derive assistance therefrom. *g*

In our judgment the use of the word 'wilfully' in this section of the 1911 Act requires the prosecution to prove no more than that the statement was made deliberately and not inadvertently or by mistake.

The second submission is that the lying statements made by the appellant were not material in the proceeding before the justices. Counsel for the appellant contends that it is the materiality of the truth, if told, which is the question to be decided and that it is *h* only where the truth, if told, would have affected the decision of the magistrates that the requirement of materiality is satisfied. Here again he cites a number of decisions which he concedes, and we agree, provide examples rather than guidance: for instance, *R v Murray* (1858) 1 F & F 80, 175 ER 635 and *R v Holden* (1872) 12 Cox CC 166.

He also draws our attention to *R v Sweet-Escott* (1971) 55 Cr App R 316. This was a decision at Devonshire Assizes by Lawton J on the question of materiality in a case *j* brought under the same section of the 1911 Act. He has this to say (at 320–321):

> 'What then is the principle upon which the judge should draw the line? . . . The question arises whether this cross-examination would have affected the decision of the Okehampton Magistrates to commit Miss X for trial had this defendant admitted that he had had those convictions. In my judgment, it is inconceivable that they

would have refused to commit because over twenty years before as a young man he had got into trouble . . .'

This passage is cited by counsel for the appellant as support for his contention that a statement is only material if the truth *would* have affected the outcome and not if it merely *might* have done so. Lawton J was plainly not concerned with that particular distinction in the case he was deciding.

The matter in our judgment was correctly stated by Lord Campbell CJ in *R v Lavey* (1850) 3 Car & Kir 26 at 30, 175 ER 448 at 450, where he directed the jury as follows (it should be noted that this was of course before the provisions of s 1(1) and (6) of the 1911 Act came into existence):

'You can, I think, have no doubt that she was tried at the Central Criminal Court, and on the question, whether what she falsely swore was material or not, you will consider whether her evidence in this respect might not influence the mind of the judge of the County Court in believing or disbelieving the other statements she made in giving her evidence . . .'

Nor do we subscribe to the view that it is the materiality of the truth, if told, which is in issue, though that in some cases may help to throw light on the materiality of the false statement. The section is clear. It is the statement which is made which must be material, in this case the denial that the appellant had enlisted Pc Revelle to make inquiries of the Indians. Whatever may have been the true reason for that request, the lies told effectively brought to a halt that line of cross-examination, which undoubtedly went to the heart of the case, namely the appellant's expressed belief that the driver had been Manjit. The fact that further cross-examination was prevented might very well, it is clear, have affected the outcome of the case. Even looked at as the appellant asked that we should, the answer would remain the same. The truth if told would have entailed the admission that the appellant was indeed making inquiries about the respective identity of the two Indians. Whatever explanation he might have given for this would not alter the fact that the admission itself might very well have affected the justices' determination of guilt or innocence.

In our judgment in cases under s 1(1) of the Perjury Act 1911 the prosecution have the burden of proving to the requisite standard the following matters: (1) that the witness was lawfully sworn as a witness; (2) in a judicial proceeding; (3) that the witness made a statement wilfully, that is to say deliberately and not inadvertently or by mistake; (4) that that statement was false; (5) that the witness knew it was false or did not believe it to be true; (6) that the statement was, viewed objectively, material in the judicial proceeding. This last requirement is, by virtue of s 1(6) of the 1911 Act, a matter to be decided by the judge.

In our judgment the decision of the judge in the present case was correct and this appeal must accordingly be dismissed.

*Appeal dismissed.*

Solicitors: *Director of Public Prosecutions* (for the Crown).

N P Metcalfe Esq    Barrister.

# Société United Docks and others v Government of Mauritius
# Marine Workers Union and others v Mauritius Marine Authority and others

PRIVY COUNCIL

LORD DIPLOCK, LORD KEITH OF KINKEL, LORD BRANDON OF OAKBROOK, LORD BRIGHTMAN AND LORD TEMPLEMAN

I MAY, 16, 17, 18 JULY, 25 OCTOBER 1984

*Mauritius – Constitutional law – Human rights and freedoms – Right not to be deprived of property without compensation – Statute creating corporation having monopoly to store and load sugar – Consequent loss of business by dock and stevedore companies – No provision in statute for payment of compensation – Whether companies deprived of property without compensation – Constitution of Mauritius 1968, ss 3(c), 8(1) – Mauritius Sugar Terminal Corporation Act 1979, s 5.*

*Mauritius – Constitutional law – Human rights and freedoms – Right not to be deprived of property without compensation – Pay dispute between marine authority and workers referred to arbitration – Arbitrator recommending increases of salary and allowances – Minister directing authority not to implement award – Minister authorised to give directions in the public interest to authority 'in relation to the exercise of the powers of the Authority' – Attorney General authorised to object to enforcement of arbitration award – Whether minister exceeding powers – Whether Attorney General's objection to enforcement of award depriving workers of property without compensation – Constitution of Mauritius 1968, ss 3(c), 8(1) – Ports Act 1975 (Mauritius), s 9(1) – Code of Civil Procedure (Amendment) Act 1981 (Mauritius).*

In two separate appeals from Mauritius the question arose whether the respective appellants had suffered 'deprivation of property without compensation' contrary to s 3(c)ᵃ of the Constitution of Mauritius

In the first appeal the appellants were dock companies and stevedores who had over a long period been engaged to handle, store and load sugar for export by the syndicate of sugar growers and millers who controlled Mauritian sugar exports. The appellants used manual labour for loading and their methods required the sugar to be bagged. In 1970 the growers and millers syndicate proposed that a bulk terminal with mechanised loading facilities be constructed to handle the loading of sugar and that the appellants should be adequately compensated for the consequent loss of almost all their business. The syndicate were unable to raise the necessary finance for the new terminal and in 1979 the government of Mauritius decided that it should be constructed by, and vest in, a statutory corporation established by the Mauritius Sugar Terminal Corporation Act 1979. By s 5ᵇ of that Act the new corporation was given a monopoly over the storage and loading of sugar. There was no provision in the Act for compensation to be paid to the appellants. The bulk terminal commenced operating in 1980, causing the appellants to be put out of business almost completely. Both the government and the syndicate refused to pay compensation to the appellants, who then instituted proceedings against the government alleging that they had been deprived of property without compensation, contrary to s 3(c) of the Constitution because, inter alia, the statutory monopoly under s 5 of the 1979 Act prevented the appellants from competing with the new statutory corporation and they had been deprived of the compensation which the syndicate had promised in

---

ᵃ Section 3 is set out at p 867 *d* to *f*, post

ᵇ Section 5, so far as material, is set out at p 869 *f g*, post

1970 to pay. The Supreme Court of Mauritius held that the appellants were not entitled
*a* to redress under the Constitution. The appellants appealed to the Privy Council. At the
hearing of the appeal the government contended that s 3, being in the nature of a
preamble giving general recognition to rights, was subject to subsequent sections of the
Constitution which spelt out those rights in detail, including in particular s 8(1)*c*, which
in relation to property rights restricted protection against loss without compensation to
the compulsory acquisition of property. The government contended that although the
*b* appellants' business may have been destroyed it had not been compulsorily acquired and
therefore they had no right to compensation.

In the second appeal the appellants were workers employed by the Mauritius ports
authority and trade unions representing those workers. Following a pay dispute the
authority and the unions agreed to submit the dispute to an arbitrator, whose award
would under the Code of Civil Procedure of Mauritius be enforceable by the Supreme
*c* Court. When the arbitrator made an award providing for wage increases which the
government considered to be excessive, the appropriate minister, in the purported
exercise of his power under s 9(1)*d* of the Ports Act 1975 to give such directions to the
authority 'in relation to the exercise of the powers of the Authority' as he considered to
be in the national interest, directed the authority not to implement the award. The
government also procured the enactment of the Code of Civil Procedure (Amendment)
*d* Act 1981, which provided that an objection lodged by the Attorney General would bar
the enforcement of an arbitration award by the Supreme Court. The Attorney General
lodged such an objection when the appellants sought to enforce the award. The appellants
instituted proceedings complaining that the 1981 amending Act had deprived the
authority's workers of property without compensation, contrary to ss 3(*c*) and 8 of the
Constitution. The Supreme Court of Mauritius dismissed the proceedings and refused to
*e* enforce the award. The appellants appealed to the Privy Council.

**Held** – (1) In the first appeal, on the true construction of the Constitution of Mauritius
s 3 was not merely a preamble, either in form or in substance, but an enacting provision,
and therefore in relation to compensation for loss of property rights the Constitution was
*f* not restricted to providing protection under s 8 against loss caused by compulsory
acquisition but extended to the protection granted by s 3 against loss caused by
deprivation and destruction. Accordingly, although the appellants' business had not been
compulsorily acquired, that did not of itself prevent the appellants claiming compensation.
However, the appellants were not able to show that they had been deprived of property
or goodwill by the coercive actions of the government, since their business had simply
become irrelevant and non-existent, and the Constitution did not afford protection
*g* against progress or provide compensation for a business which was lost as the result of
technological advance. Furthermore, the setting up of a statutory monopoly under s 5 of
the 1979 Act did not deprive the appellants of property or goodwill, since they remained
free to offer their services to the new corporation and the fact that the corporation chose
not to use those services because they were out of date was not a ground for compensation;
*h* nor had the appellants been deprived of the compensation which the syndicate had
promised to pay, because that promise had been conditional on the syndicate building
the terminal. The first appeal would therefore be dismissed (see p 870 *c d* and *h* to
p 871 *a e f* and p 873 *d* to p 874 *b* and *d* to *j*, post); *Olivier v Buttigieg* [1966] 2 All ER 459
and *Government of Malaysia v Selangor Pilot Association* [1978] AC 337 distinguished.

(2) In the second appeal, the minister had no power under s 9(1) of the 1975 Act to
*j* direct the authority not to give effect to the arbitrator's award, because he could only give
directions to the authority 'in relation to the exercise of the powers' of the authority and
could not therefore direct the authority to exercise a power which it did not possess,

---

*c*   Section 8(1) is set out at p 867 *g* to *j*, post
*d*   Section 9(1) is set out at p 875 *e f*, post

namely the power lawfully to commit a breach of contract by refusing to be bound by
the award. Furthermore, the 1981 amending Act was a coercive action of the government   a
which deprived the appellants of property without compensation, contrary to s 3 of the
Constitution, because the Act and the Attorney General's objection given thereunder
making the award unenforceable deprived the workers employed by the authority of a
chose in action, namely the right to sue and recover damages for breach of their contracts
of employment by the authority. The appellants were therefore entitled to redress under
the Constitution, the appropriate redress for each worker being compensation equal to   b
the increased salary and allowances to be paid by the port authority or the government.
The second appeal would therefore be allowed (see p 876 e to p 877 c and g to j, post).

## Notes

For the Constitution of Mauritius, see 6 Halsbury's Laws (4th edn) para 982.

## Cases referred to in judgment

A-G v Antigua Times Ltd [1975] 3 All ER 81, [1976] AC 16, [1975] 3 WLR 232, PC.
A-G of The Gambia v Momodou Jobe [1984] AC 689, [1984] 3 WLR 174, PC.
Burmah Oil Co (Burma Trading) Ltd v Lord Advocate [1964] 2 All ER 348, [1965] AC 75,
    [1964] 2 WLR 1231, HL.
France Fenwick & Co Ltd v R [1927] 1 KB 458.
Government of Malaysia v Selangor Pilot Association [1978] AC 337, [1977] 2 WLR 901, PC.
Hinds v R [1976] 1 All ER 353, [1977] AC 195, [1977] 2 WLR 366, PC.
Jaundoo v A-G of Guyana [1971] AC 972, [1971] 3 WLR 13, PC.
Liyanage v R [1966] 1 All ER 650, [1967] 1 AC 259, [1966] 2 WLR 682, PC.
Maharaj v A-G of Trinidad and Tobago (No 2) [1978] 2 All ER 670, [1979] AC 385, [1978]
    2 WLR 902, PC.
Manitoba Fisheries Ltd v R [1979] 1 SCR 101, Can SC.
Olivier v Buttigieg [1966] 2 All ER 459, [1967] 1 AC 115, [1966] 3 WLR 310, PC.
Thornhill v A-G of Trinidad and Tobago [1981] AC 61, [1980] 2 WLR 510, PC.

## Appeal

*Société United Docks and others v Government of Mauritius*
The plaintiffs in two consolidated actions, Société United Docks, Desmarais Bros Ltd,
Taylor & Smith Ltd and D'Hotman & Sons Ltd, appealed with leave granted by the
Supreme Court of Mauritius on 4 July 1983 against the judgment of that court (Moollan
CJ and Glover J) on 11 November 1982 dismissing their claims against the defendant,
the Government of Mauritius, for declaratory relief and compensation for loss of part of
their businesses. The facts are set out in the judgment of the Board.

*Marine Workers Union and others v Mauritius Marine Authority and others*
The applicants in two connected actions, the Marine Workers Union and three of its
members, Premananda Ponamballum, Clement Moutou and Maurice Paruit, and the
Mauritius Marine Authority Employees Union and three of its members, Percy Derek
Lingaya, Moossa Ibrahim and Narainsamy Valayden, appealed with leave granted by the
Supreme Court of Mauritius on 28 June 1982 against the decision of that court (Rault CJ
and Glover J) on 21 December 1981, exercising original jurisdiction and dismissing the
appellants' application to enforce an award made by an arbitrator (Francis J Lefebvre),
assisted by two assessors (Fee Sian Young Kiang Young and Roger Requin), on 2 August
1980 by which, inter alia, the arbitrator reorganised the structure of the Mauritius
Marine Authority (the respondent) and laid down new pay structures for most of the
employees. The respondent had failed to implement the award. The co-respondent to
the appeals was the Ministère Public (the Attorney General) in the presence of the co-
respondents, the two above-named assessors. The facts are set out in the judgment of the
Board.

The appeals were heard together because they raised the question whether the

appellants in both appeals had suffered injury which entitled them to redress under the
*a* Constitution of Mauritius.

*Sydney Kentridge QC* and *J Raymond Hein QC* (of the Mauritius Bar) for the appellants in
the Société United Docks appeal.
*Madun Gujadhur QC* and *M Dulloo* (both of the Mauritius Bar) for the appellants in the
Marine Workers Union appeal.
*b* *George Newman QC* and *Mark Strachan* for the respondents in both appeals.


25 October. The following judgment of the Board was delivered.


**LORD TEMPLEMAN.** These two appeals were heard together because they both
*c* involved consideration of the question whether the appellants have suffered injury which
entitles them to redress under the Constitution of Mauritius.
Chapter II of the Constitution dated 12 March 1968 is headed 'Protection of
Fundamental Rights and Freedoms of the Individual' and comprises ss 3 to 19 inclusive.
Section 3 is in these terms:

*d*  '*Fundamental rights and freedoms of the individual.* It is hereby recognised and
declared that in Mauritius there have existed and shall continue to exist without
discrimination by reason of race, place of origin, political opinions, colour, creed or
sex, but subject to respect for the rights and freedoms of others and for the public
interest, each and all of the following human rights and fundamental freedoms,
namely—(*a*) the right of the individual to life, liberty, security of the person and
*e* the protection of the law; (*b*) freedom of conscience, of expression, of assembly and
association and freedom to establish schools; and (*c*) the right of the individual to
protection for the privacy of his home and other property and from deprivation of
property without compensation, and the provisions of this Chapter shall have effect
for the purpose of affording protection to the said rights and freedoms subject to
such limitations of that protection as are contained in those provisions, being
*f* limitations designed to ensure that the enjoyment of the said rights and freedoms
by any individual does not prejudice the rights and freedoms of others or the public
interest.'

Section 8 is entitled 'Protection from deprivation of property' and sub-s (1) provides as
follows:

*g*  'No property of any description shall be compulsorily taken possession of, and no
interest in or right over property of any description shall be compulsorily acquired,
except where the following conditions are satisfied, that is to say—(*a*) the taking of
possession or acquisition is necessary or expedient in the interests of defence, public
safety, public order, public morality, public health, town and country planning or
the development or utilisation of any property in such a manner as to promote the
public benefit; and (*b*) there is reasonable justification for the causing of any hardship
*h* that may result to any person having an interest in or right over the property; and
(*c*) provision is made by a law applicable to that taking of possession or acquisition—
(i) for the prompt payment of adequate compensation; and (ii) securing to any
person having an interest in or right over the property a right of access to the
Supreme Court, whether direct or on appeal from any other authority, for the
determination of his interest or right, the legality of the taking of possession or
*i* acquisition of the property, interest or right, and the amount of any compensation
to which he is entitled, and for the purpose of obtaining prompt payment of that
compensation.'

Section 17 is entitled 'Enforcement of protective provisions' and sub-s (1) is in these
terms:

'If any person alleges that any of the foregoing provisions of this Chapter has
been, is being or is likely to be contravened in relation to him, then without  *a*
prejudice to any other action with respect to the same matter that is lawfully
available, that person may apply to the Supreme Court for redress.'

On any such application for redress, the Supreme Court, by s 17(2), may—

'make such orders, issue such writs and give such directions as it may consider
appropriate for the purpose of enforcing, or securing the enforcement of, any of  *b*
[the provisions of sections 3 to 16] to the protection of which the person concerned
is entitled: Provided that the Supreme Court shall not exercise its powers under this
subsection if it is satisfied that adequate means of redress for the contravention
alleged are or have been available to the person concerned under any other law.'

The appellants claim that they have been subjected by the government of Mauritius to  *c*
'deprivation' of property without compensation in contravention of s 3 of the Constitution
and they seek redress under s 17. The respondents assert that s 3 does not confer rights
more extensive than the rights specified in s 8, which applies only where property has
been 'compulsorily taken possession of' or 'compulsorily acquired'. The respondents
have not compulsorily taken possession of or compulsorily acquired any property
belonging to the appellants and therefore, it is said, the appellants are not entitled to any  *d*
redress.

*The Société United Docks appeal*

The export of sugar from Mauritius has long been organised by an association of
growers and millers known as the Mauritius Sugar Syndicate. The appellant dock
companies were engaged by the syndicate to handle and store bagged sugar in warehouses  *e*
belonging to the dock companies. The appellant stevedore companies were engaged by
the syndicate to load the sugar on board ships by manual labour. As early as 1954 there
were proposals for the construction of a bulk terminal to replace the warehouses of the
dock companies and for the installation of mechanised loading to replace the manual
labour of the stevedores. At first the dock companies envisaged that they would provide
the bulk terminal themselves. Reports and estimates were commissioned but the dock  *f*
companies made no progress, because they lacked either the will or the means. The
syndicate then decided to pursue the project. The minutes of a meeting held at the
Chamber of Agriculture on 21 January 1970 attended by representatives from the
Chamber of Agriculture, from the syndicate, from the dock companies and from the
stevedore companies recorded that:

'All sugar associations, grouping millers and planters had agreed that the most  *g*
appropriate way of settling the problem of financing and administering the sugar
bulk terminal would be the setting up of a non-profit company run along the lines
of a producers' co-operative society and operating as an offspring of the Mauritius
Sugar Syndicate. This would have the merit of allowing all sugar producers to reap
the full benefit of the anticipated economies since the new company would claim
from the Mauritius Sugar Syndicate—which would be financing the project—the  *h*
actual net cost of storage and loading.'

It was recognised that this development would put the dock companies and the stevedore
companies out of business except for the storage and loading of small quantities of
demerara sugar and domestic supplies which would not be handled by the bulk terminal.
In these circumstances it was further recorded in the minutes of the meeting that:  *j*

'The sugar industry had emphatically agreed that the dock and stevedore
companies should be adequately compensated in some form or other having regard
to the valuable and competent services which they had provided in the handling of
Mauritian sugar over a great number of years. The actual terms of such compensation

could be discussed at some later stage as there were other pressing matters to deal
with, namely the labour redundancy aspect . . .'

This decision of the syndicate, announced on 21 January 1970, tolled the death-knell
of the main business of the dock companies and stevedore companies, solacing them only
with the hope of receiving some mark of gratitude from the syndicate for past services.
In order to finance the construction of the bulk terminal, the syndicate sought and
obtained government measures which raised levies on the proceeds of sale of the 1974
and 1975 sugar crops. The moneys thus raised proved insufficient and further levies or
other sources of capital were required. Finally, in 1979 the government decided that the
bulk terminal should be constructed by and should be vested in a statutory corporation
which, despite the protests of the syndicate, would be controlled by a majority of
representatives of the government. The government's decision resulted in the Mauritius
Sugar Terminal Corporation Act 1979 (the Sugar Terminal Act) which came into force
on 30 June 1979. By s 3 the Act established the Mauritius Sugar Terminal Corp as a body
corporate. By s 4 the corporation was directed to provide, operate and maintain facilities
for the storage, sampling, bagging, packing, loading and unloading of sugar. By s 7 the
administration and control of the affairs of the corporation were vested in a board
consisting of a majority of members of government departments. The minority included
representatives of planters and millers, a representative of the syndicate and representatives
of employees of the corporation. All these representatives are, however, appointed by the
minister to whom responsibility for the corporation is assigned. By s 17 of the Sugar
Terminal Act, the initial capital of the corporation was established at 300m rupees made
up of over 126m rupees being the proceeds of the levies on the sugar crops for the years
1974 and 1975 and interest earned thereon, and over 173m rupees being the amount
contributed by the government. By s 19 the revenue of the corporation was directed to
be applied in payment of certain costs, charges and expenses, including compensation
payable to employees of the dock companies and to employees of the stevedore companies
and any balance of revenue of the corporation was directed to accrue 'to such persons in
such manner and in such proportion as the Board may determine'.

Section 5(1) conferred an express monopoly on the corporation in these terms:

'. . . no person, other than the Corporation or an authorised body, shall—(a) as
from the appointed day store or load into ships any sugar manufactured in Mauritius
. . .'

By s 5(2):

'. . . as from the appointed day—(a) every miller shall cause all sugars manufactured
by him to be delivered to the Corporation or, with the approval of the Corporation,
to an authorised body . . .'

By s 2 the appointed day was defined as a day to be appointed by the minister for the
purposes of s 5 and 'authorised body' was defined as any person authorised by the minister
to receive or store sugar. No formal appointment of the appointed day has been made
but by an order dated 28 February 1980 the minister appointed the syndicate to be an
authorised body. The bulk terminal was constructed and began operations in July 1980.
The services of the dock companies and the stevedore companies for the export of sugar
from Mauritius forthwith became redundant. The corporation and the syndicate as an
authorised body will no doubt continue to avail themselves of the services of warehouses
and stevedores, if offered by the appellants, so far as is necessary for the storage and
loading of demerara sugar and domestic supplies which are not handled by the bulk
terminal. But the main business of the dock companies and the stevedore companies
came to an end when the bulk sugar terminal began its operations in July 1980.

Although the Sugar Terminal Act provided for compensation to be paid to the
redundant workers of the dock companies and the stevedore companies, no provision
was made for compensation to be paid to those companies themselves. The syndicate had

offered in 1970 to pay compensation in gratitude for past services. The offer was made
when the syndicate expected to become the owner of the bulk terminal but the syndicate
is no longer willing to pay compensation now that the bulk terminal is owned and
controlled by the corporation. In December 1980 the dock companies and the stevedore
companies instituted these present proceedings. In their plaint with summons dated 23
December 1980 the appellant dock companies assert that the Sugar Terminal Act—

> '(a). . . in so far as it creates a monopoly in favour of the Mauritius Sugar Terminal
> Corporation with regard to the storage and loading of sugar involves a compulsory
> acquisition or taking of possession of property . . . (b) that the effect of [the Act] has
> been to deprive the [appellants] of that part of its property consisting in its business
> of storing and handling of sugar, without payment of compensation. (c) that such
> deprivation amounts to a violation of the [appellants'] fundamental right to
> protection against such deprivation guaranteed by section 3(c) and 8 of the
> Constitution of Mauritius . . .'

The appellants accordingly applied for redress under s 17 of the Constitution.

Their Lordships consider that the business of the appellants was not compulsorily
taken possession of or compulsorily acquired by the government, the corporation or
anyone else. Once the bulk terminal was constructed the business of the dock companies
in providing warehouses for the storage of sugar for export from Mauritius and the
business of the stevedore companies in providing stevedores to load sugar manually
simply became irrelevant and ceased to exist. The appellants contend that even so they
are entitled to redress under the Constitution; they contend that the effect of the Sugar
Terminal Act was to deprive them of their business without compensation in breach of
the rights granted to them by s 3 of the Constitution. The government of Mauritius
deny that the Sugar Terminal Act deprived the appellants of any property but if it did so
the appellants, it is said, are not entitled to redress because they cannot prove that their
property was compulsorily taken possession of or compulsorily acquired. The Constitution
offers redress where, in the words of s 8, property is compulsorily taken possession of or
compulsorily acquired but not otherwise. Section 3 of the Constitution only contains a
general recognition and acceptance of rights and freedoms and only affords protection in
the circumstances specified in the subsequent sections of Chapter II of the Constitution.
The relevant subsequent section is s 8, which only enables an individual to claim
protection and to obtain redress if property is compulsorily taken possession of or
compulsorily acquired without compensation. The appellants reject the government's
narrow construction of the Constitution and deny that s 8 has a limiting effect on s 3.
The appellants contend that s 3 has effect in accordance with its terms and in suitable
cases, such as the present, provides protection beyond the ambit of s 8. Alternatively, s 8
must be construed in the light of s 3 and so construed applies not only when property is
compulsorily taken possession of or compulsorily acquired but also when property is
destroyed.

Their Lordships have no doubt that all the provisions of Chapter II, including s 8, must
be construed in the light of the provisions of s 3. The wording of s 3 is only consistent
with an enacting section; it is not a mere preamble or introduction. Section 3 recognises
that there has existed, and declares that there shall continue to exist, the right of the
individual to protection from deprivation of property without compensation, subject to
respect for others and respect for the public interest. Section 8 sets forth the circumstances
in which the right to deprivation of property can be set aside but it is not to curtail the
ambit of s 3. Prior to the Constitution the government could not destroy the property of
an individual without payment of compensation. The right which is by s 3 of the
Constitution recognised and declared to exist is the right to protection against deprivation
of property without compensation. A constitution concerned to protect the fundamental
rights and freedoms of the individual should not be narrowly construed in a manner
which produces anomalies and inexplicable inconsistencies. Loss caused by deprivation
and destruction is the same in quality and effect as loss caused by compulsory acquisition.

If by the Sugar Terminal Act the appellants were deprived of property without
*a* compensation they are entitled to claim redress under the Constitution.
Counsel for the government of Mauritius relied on the decision of Wright J in *France
Fenwick & Co Ltd v R* [1927] 1 KB 458. That case, however, only decided that a direction
given pursuant to regulations made under the Emergency Powers Act 1920 that a vessel
should not be unloaded did not amount to a requisition of the vessel and did not entitle
the owner of the vessel to compensation for requisition or to compensation at common
*b* law. The case is not authority for the proposition that at common law compensation is
not payable for deprivation or destruction of property. Indeed, in *Burmah Oil Co (Burma
Trading) Ltd v Lord Advocate* [1964] 2 All ER 348, [1965] AC 75 the House of Lords by a
majority held that there was a legally enforceable general right at common law to
compensation for damage or destruction done in the exercise of the royal prerogative in
relation to war.
*c* Counsel for the government of Mauritius next relied on *Olivier v Buttigieg* [1966] 2 All
ER 459, [1967] 1 AC 115. In that case Lord Morris, delivering the judgment of the
Board, described s 5 of the Constitution of Malta, which contains provisions similar in
many respects to s 3 of the Constitution of Mauritius, as—

'an introduction to and in a sense a prefatory or explanatory note in regard to the
sections which are to follow . . . The section appears to proceed by way of explanation
*d* of the scheme of the succeeding sections'.

(See [1966] 2 All ER 549 at 461, [1967] 1 AC 115 at 128.)
As Lord Morris also pointed out, s 5 of the Constitution of Malta—

'begins with the word "Whereas". Though the section must be given such
declaratory force as it independently possesses, it would appear in the main to be of ·
*e* the nature of a preamble.'

Section 3 of the Constitution of Mauritius on the other hand is not a preamble in form
or in substance but is an enacting provision. In *Olivier v Buttigieg* government employees
were forbidden to introduce a specified newspaper into government hospitals and this
prohibition was held to be an unconstitutional hindrance of the newspaper editor in the
*f* enjoyment of his freedom to impart ideas and information without interference,
although the editor was not thereby debarred from expressing and circulating his view
to the public. The Board were clearly not prepared to give a narrow construction to the
freedoms granted by the Constitution of Malta.
In *Jaundoo v A-G of Guyana* [1971] AC 972 the Board held that redress under art 19 of
the Constitution of Guyana, similar in terms to s 17 of the Constitution of Mauritius,
*g* could be obtained under the usual practice and procedure of the High Court and included
redress by way of an award of compensation for damages. The same principles apply to
the Constitution of Mauritius, although on the present appeals the contrary was faintly
argued.
In *A-G v Antigua Times Ltd* [1975] 3 All ER 81, [1976] AC 16 it was argued that the
redress given by the Constitution of Antigua to a 'person' was not available to a
*h* corporation. Lord Fraser, delivering the judgment of the board, said ([1975] 3 All ER 81
at 84, [1976] AC 16 at 25):

'Having regard to the important place in the economic life of society occupied by
corporate bodies, it would seem natural for such a modern constitution, dealing
with inter alia rights to property, to use the word "person" to include corporations.'

*j* On the present appeals it was suggested on behalf of the government of Mauritius that a
different result should follow in the present case because s 3 of the Constitution of
Mauritius referred to the right of 'the individual'. But no logical distinction can be drawn
between the individual protected by s 3 and 'the person' protected by the remaining
sections of Chapter II of the Constitution. Both expressions include a corporation where
the context so allows, as it does in the present instance.

Counsel for the government of Mauritius relied on the decision of the Board in
*Government of Malaysia v Selangor Pilot Association* [1978] AC 337 for the argument that    a
the Constitution of Mauritius only entitled an individual to redress if his property was
compulsorily taken possession of or compulsorily acquired. In the *Selangor* case an
association of licensed pilots providing piloting services in Port Swettenham enjoyed a
monopoly. By the Port Authorities (Amendment) Act 1972 and regulations made
thereunder the power to grant licences was transferred from the pilot board of Port
Swettenham to a pilotage committee appointed by the port authority. Licensed pilots    b
could only lawfully provide pilotage if employed by the port authority. The port
authority offered employment to all the licensed pilots including the members of the
association and began to operate a pilot service. Article 13 of the Constitution of Malaysia
provided:

> '(1) No person shall be deprived of property save in accordance with law.
> (2) No law shall provide for the compulsory acquisition or use of property without    c
> adequate compensation.'

It was held that the rights of licensed pilots to provide pilotage services and to employ
others as pilots were not rights of property within art 13(1) and (Lord Salmon dissenting)
that there had been no compulsory acquisition or use of the goodwill or business of the
association. There are significant differences for present purposes between the Constitution    d
of Malaysia and the Constitution of Mauritus. Article 13(1) of the Constitution of
Malaysia affords no protection against the deprivation of property 'in accordance with
law' and the necessary law was passed. Article 13(2) provided compensation only for
compulsory acquisition or use. Section 3 of the Constitution of Mauritius on the other
hand recognises and declares the right to compensation for deprivation of property in
accordance with law.                                                                      e
    In *Maharaj v A-G of Trinidad and Tobago (No 2)* [1978] 2 All ER 670 at 676–677, [1979]
AC 385 at 395–396 the Board considered s 1 of the Constitution of Trinidad and Tobago
entitled the individual to the 'protection or non-interference under the law as it existed
immediately before the Constitution came into effect' but—

> 'the protection afforded was against contravention of those rights or freedoms by
> the state or by some other public authority endowed by law with coercive powers.    f
> The chapter is concerned with public law, not private law.'

    The victim of coercive powers exercised by the government was entitled under the
Constitution to redress by way of an award of damages. The question in the present case
is whether the appellants are the victims of the exercise of coercive power by the
government of Mauritius.                                                                  g
    In *Manitoba Fisheries Ltd v R* [1979] 1 SCR 101 under the Canadian Freshwater Fish
Marketing Act 1970 the Freshwater Fish Marketing Corp was granted the commercial
monopoly in the export of fish from Manitoba and as a direct result of that grant a
company engaged in the business of exporting fish from Manitoba was then unable
lawfully to continue its business. It was held that the corporation had not taken or
acquired the business of the company but that the Act had deprived the company of its    h
business and for such deprivation the company was entitled to compensation at common
law. The Supreme Court of Canada rejected the argument that compensation was only
payable where a business had been compulsorily acquired.
    In *Thornhill v A-G of Trinidad and Tobago* [1981] AC 61 at 69 Lord Diplock again dealt
with the Constitution of Trinidad and Tobago. He said that the existing rights and
freedoms which 'shall continue to exist' were—                                           j

> 'not described with the particularity that would be appropriate to an ordinary Act
> of Parliament nor are they expressed in words that bear precise meanings as terms
> of legal art. They are statements of principles of great breadth and generality,
> expressed in the kind of language more commonly associated with political
> manifestos or international conventions . . .'

Lord Diplock went on to reaffirm that the protection afforded to the individual was
against contravention of rights and freedoms by the state or by some other public
authority endowed by law with coercive powers and not by another private individual.
And he continued (at 70):

> 'The lack of all specificity in the descriptions of the rights and freedoms protected
> . . . may make it necessary sometimes to resort to an examination of the law as it
> was at the commencement of the Constitution in order to determine what limits
> upon freedoms that are expressed in absolute and unlimited terms were nevertheless
> intended to be preserved in the interests of the people as a whole and the orderly
> development of the nation; for the declaration that the rights and freedoms
> protected by that section already existed at that date may make the existing law as it
> was then administered in practice a relevant aid to the ascertainment of what kind
> of executive or judicial act was intended to be prohibited by the wide and vague
> words used in those paragraphs . . .'

Finally, in *A-G of The Gambia v Momodou Jobe* [1984] AC 689 at 700 Lord Diplock,
dealing with the Constitution of The Gambia, said:

> 'A constitution, and in particular that part of it which protects and entrenches
> fundamental rights and freedoms to which all persons in the state are to be entitled,
> is to be given a generous and purposive construction.'

On the true construction of the Constitution of Mauritius and on authority their
Lordships conclude that if the dock companies and the stevedore companies have been
deprived of property by the coercive actions of the government then they are entitled to
compensation. The dock companies and the stevedore companies have undoubtedly
sustained a loss. They can no longer derive profit from or sell the goodwill of a business
which consisted of providing warehouses and manual labour for the storage and loading
of sugar for export. That loss would not have occurred if the bulk terminal had not been
built. The Sugar Terminal Act authorised and procured the construction of the bulk
terminal. But the dock companies and the stevedore companies have no right to complain
about the erection of a bulk terminal.

The Constitution does not afford protection against progress or provide compensation
for a business which is lost as a result of technological advance. At some time between
1954 and 1970 the syndicate and the appellants recognised that an efficient sugar industry
required a bulk terminal. By 1970 everyone connected with the industry recognised that
the bulk terminal once erected would put an end to the main business of the appellants.
The dock companies and the stevedore companies could not complain of the effect of the
construction of the bulk terminal by the syndicate, by the government or by anyone else.
The bulk terminal was eventually erected by the corporation as a result of government
insistence. The government did not act in order to ruin the appellants but in order to
preserve an efficient sugar industry in the national interest. The main business of the
appellants was doomed once it became clear that an efficient sugar industry required a
bulk terminal. The appellants point to s 5 of the Sugar Terminal Act, which conferred a
monopoly on the corporation, and claim compensation because s 5 prohibits the
warehouse companies and the stevedore companies from loading and storing sugar. But
the monopoly granted by s 5 did not in the event inflict any damage on the appellants.
The statutory monopoly was unnecessary to prevent competition by the appellants with
the bulk terminal. The appellants' business could not compete with the bulk terminal
because the business of the appellants no longer provided an efficient service for the sugar
industry. There is no reason to think and no evidence to support any argument that the
subsidiary business of the appellants dealing with demerara sugar and domestic supplies
has suffered because of the Sugar Terminal Act or because of the monopoly granted by
s 5 of that Act. Where the services of the appellants remain relevant and useful they will
no doubt be employed by the corporation or by the syndicate as an authorised body.

If the Act had deprived the appellants of any goodwill, then the appellants would have been entitled to compensation equal to the value lost. The appellants remained free to offer their services to the corporation and to the syndicate as an authorised body. But, so  *a* far as those services were offered in respect of the export of sugar, these had long ceased to be relevant to a sugar industry which was free to modernise and was forced to modernise its operations by the use of a bulk terminal. The Act did not deprive the appellants of their goodwill attached to the services offered by the appellants in connection with export sugar. The Act did not deprive the appellants of the goodwill attached to the services offered by the appellants in connection with the handling of demerara sugar and  *b* domestic supplies. The appellants remained free to offer those services to the corporation and to the syndicate as an authorised body. Those services remained relevant to the sugar industry and were unaffected by the Act.

Counsel for the appellants recognised the difficulty of attributing the loss of the appellants' business to the effect of the Sugar Terminal Act. He argued in the alternative that the appellants lost the compensation which in 1970 the syndicate had been willing  *c* to pay. The appellants may have been disappointed but they have not been deprived. It is possible that, if the syndicate had constructed the bulk terminal, the syndicate would have honoured or could have been obliged by the law of Mauritius to honour its 1970 promise to pay something, doubtfully quantifiable by the court, in recognition of the past services of the dock companies and the stevedore companies. The government decided, in good faith and in the national interest, to construct the bulk terminal; that  *d* decision did not deprive the appellants of anything. The indirect result, possibly unknown to the government at the time, was that the syndicate never became under a duty to pay anything to the appellants. The syndicate had promised to pay something if the syndicate built the terminal. The syndicate did not build the terminal and therefore the syndicate never became bound to pay anything.

The government's decision to build the terminal may have had many repercussions;  *e* the government are not responsible for all those repercussions but only for depriving an individual of property by coercive action. The syndicate, who were never in a position to construct the bulk terminal, never became bound to pay anything to the appellants. The syndicate were dependent on the government making available to the syndicate the moneys raised by the 1974 and 1975 sugar levies. The syndicate were dependent on the government imposing further levies and making the proceeds available to the syndicate.  *f* The government were not bound to finance the syndicate by imposing and making available levies on sugar or by any other means. The government refused to finance the syndicate. That refusal made it effectively impossible for the syndicate to construct the bulk terminal and the syndicate never came under an obligation to honour the promise made in 1970 to the appellants.

It is true that, if the government had financed the syndicate and if the bulk terminal  *g* had been constructed by the syndicate, then the appellants would have expected the syndicate to honour the promise made in 1970. But the refusal of the government to finance the syndicate did not deprive the appellants of anything. The refusal of a bank to lend money to a purchaser does not deprive the vendor's estate agent of his commission, although the result of that refusal is that the estate agent is disappointed and is never in a position to enforce the promise of the vendor to pay commission in the event of a sale.  *h* The government decided not to finance the syndicate; the government decided to construct the bulk terminal. The government passed the Sugar Terminal Act to give effect to the decisions reached by the government and not with the object of coercing the appellants. The government owed no duty to the syndicate or to the appellants not to reach the decisions which were made or to make any other decisions.

The Supreme Court of Mauritius (Moollan CJ and Glover J) decided that the dock  *j* companies and the stevedore companies were not entitled to redress under the Constitution. Their Lordships agree and it follows that the appeal from the Supreme Court must be dismissed. Their Lordships will humbly advise Her Majesty accordingly. There will be no order as to costs.

*The Marine Works Union appeal*

a    The facts relevant to this appeal are not in dispute. The Ports Act 1975, which came into force on 1 July 1976, established the respondent, the Mauritius Marine Authority (the MMA) as a body corporate charged, inter alia, with the operation of ports in Mauritius. By 1979 the MMA employed some 569 workers divided into 105 pay grades. The appellants are either workers employed by the MMA or trade unions representing workers employed by the MMA. Following industrial action designed to secure

b    improvements in pay and allowances, there took place on 29 July 1979 a meeting attended by the Prime Minister and other ministers, by representatives of the MMA and by representatives of the trade unions. At the meeting the MMA and the trade unions agreed that industrial action would cease and that the dispute should be submitted to arbitration.

By the Code of Civil Procedure an arbitration award, subject to any challenge to its

c    legality or validity, is enforceable by an order of a judge of the Supreme Court. Accordingly, at the meeting which agreed on arbitration, the Prime Minister, according to the minutes of the meeting provided by the Ministry of Labour and Industrial Relations, stressed that 'both parties would have no alternative than to abide by the decision of the arbitrator'. Pursuant to the agreement, terms of reference were agreed, an arbitrator and assessors were appointed and evidence was submitted. The principal task

d    of the arbitrator was to examine and review the salary scales and allowances of employees of the MMA. The arbitrator made his award dated 2 August 1980 and on 12 December 1980 application was made by summons to the court for the award to be made executory and enforced. No challenge was mounted to the legality or the validity of the award but the government took the view that the increases of salary and allowances awarded by the arbitrator would have undesirable repercussions on the level of wages in the public sector and would have grave inflationary effects on the national economy. In these circumstances

e    the minister responsible for ports made an order under s 9(1) of the Ports Act 1975 directing the MMA not to implement the award. Section 9(1) provides:

'The Minister may, in relation to the exercise of the powers of the Authority under this Act, after consultation with the Authority, give such specific and general directions to the Authority, not inconsistent with this Act, as he considers necessary

f    in the public interest and the Authority shall comply with those directions.'

The authority is the MMA, which, on receiving the order from the minister, opposed the application to the court to make the award of the arbitrator executory on the grounds that the minister had directed the MMA not to implement the award. Before the court gave a decision on the application to make the arbitration award enforceable, the government, perhaps conscious of the difficulties of taking effective action under s 9 of

g    the Ports Act, took further legislative action.

By the Code of Civil Procedure (Amendment) Act 1981, which came into force on 8 April 1981, the Code of Civil Procedure relating to arbitration was amended by the insertion of a power for the Attorney General to object to the enforcement of any arbitration award which in his opinion was contrary to the public interest. Notice of the

h    objection was required to be served on the parties and copies of the notice were required to be lodged in the Registry of the Supreme Court. It was expressly provided that the objection of the Attorney General should constitute a bar to any application for the enforcement of the award and, where the objection was lodged during the pendency of the hearing of an application to make the award executory, the judge or, in the case of an appeal, the Supreme Court should not proceed with the hearing of the application or

j    appeal.

Finally, s 3 of the amending Act provided that the amendment should apply to any arbitration award made or given before the commencement of the Act whether or not judicial proceedings had been instituted for the enforcement of the award. Although the amending Act is of general application, it is common ground that the Act was

intentionally passed for the express purpose of preventing the enforcement of the
arbitration award dated 2 August 1980 relating to the employees of the MMA.

 On 9 April 1981 the Attorney General served and lodged notice of objection to the
execution of the arbitration award dated 2 August 1980 relating to the employees of
MMA on the ground that the execution of the award was, in the opinion of the Attorney
General, contrary to the public interest. That objection prevented the court from making
an order enforcing the award.

 The appellants filed affidavits complaining that the retrospective provisions of the
amending Act deprived the appellants, and were intended to deprive the appellants, of
the benefit of the arbitration award and complaining that the retrospective provisions
interfered with the exercise of judicial power. The appellants also complained that the
amending Act was contrary to the provisions of s 8 of the Constitution. These complaints
were referred to the Supreme Court pursuant to s 84 of the Constitution, which directs
that any question as to the interpretation of the Constitution involving a substantial
question of law shall be referred to the Supreme Court.

 On 21 December 1981 the Supreme Court (Rault CJ and Glover J) rejected the
appellants' application to make the award executory on the grounds that the minister
responsible for ports had lawfully exercised his powers under s 9 of the Ports Act to
prevent the MMA from enforcing the award and on the alternative ground that the
objection of the Attorney General pursuant to the amending Act lawfully prevented the
award being made enforceable. The Supreme Court held that the minister responsible
for ports had not exceeded his jurisdiction under s 9 of the Ports Act, that the amending
Act did not offend the Constitution and that the actions of the minister, of the
government and of the Attorney General were justified in view of the public interest
involved. By leave of the Supreme Court the appellants now appeal to the Board.

 Although no doubt the minister responsible for ports considered that he possessed the
power and was under a duty in the public interest to forbid the MMA to give effect to
the award, their Lordships cannot accept that s 9(1) of the Ports Act 1975 conferred on
the minister the requisite authority. The minister can only give directions to the MMA
'. . . in relation to the exercise of the powers of [the MMA] . . .' By the agreement for
arbitration which resulted in the award the MMA became contractually bound to accept
and give effect to the award. The MMA is not authorised by statute and has no power
lawfully to commit a breach of contract. The minister cannot direct the MMA to exercise
a power which the MMA does not possess. The minister cannot direct the MMA to
commit a breach of contract.

 The amending Act and the Attorney General's objection given thereunder made the
award unenforceable and deprived the appellants and all the workers employed by the
MMA of the benefit of the award. The award improved the gross salaries of employees
of the MMA from 1 January 1980 and their allowances from 1 July 1980. These
improvements were directed to endure until 30 June 1983. The amending Act and the
objection of the Attorney General thereunder prevented the implementation of the
award and deprived each worker employed by the MMA at any time or times between 1
January 1980 and 30 June 1983 of the difference between the salary and allowances in
fact paid to him and the increased salary and allowances payable to him pursuant to the
award.

 Prior to the amending Act the appellants were entitled to an order of the court making
the award executory and enforceable and each relevant employee was entitled to sue the
MMA for, and to recover, the difference between the salary and allowances in fact paid to
him and the salary and allowances to which he was entitled pursuant to the award during
the duration of the award. The amending Act has thus deprived and was intended to
deprive each worker of a chose in action, namely the right to sue for and recover damages
for breach by the MMA of its contract of employment.

 Section 3 of the Constitution of Mauritius recognises and declares, inter alia, the right
of the individual to protection from deprivation of property without compensation. The
Board have already determined in connection with the contemporaneous case of the
*Société United Docks v Government of Mauritius* that the protection afforded by s 3 is not

confined to property which has been compulsorily taken possession of or compulsorily
a  acquired within the meaning of s 8. The appellants rightly complained on behalf of the
workers employed by the MMA that the workers have been deprived of property, namely
their right to sue for and recover damages for breach by the MMA of its contract of
employment, contrary to s 3 of the Constitution. Section 17(2) confers on the Supreme
Court original jurisdiction to—

b        'make such orders, issue such writs and give such directions as it may consider
appropriate for the purpose of enforcing, or securing the enforcement of, any of the
foregoing provisions of this Chapter to the protection of which the person is
entitled.'

The appropriate redress for each worker is compensation equal to the increased salary
and allowances of which that worker has been deprived by the amending Act.
c        The attention of the Supreme Court was not directed to the provisions of ss 3 and 17
of the Constitution but to the question whether the retrospective provisions of the
amending Act, aimed specifically at the award, constituted an unconstitutional
infringement by the legislature of the judicial powers. In *Liyanage v R* [1966] 1 All ER
650, [1967] 1 AC 259 the Parliament of Ceylon passed Acts pursuant to a legislative plan
ex post facto to secure the conviction and enhance the punishment of particular
d  individuals, legalising their imprisonment while they were awaiting trial, making
admissible statements which had been inadmissibly obtained, altering the fundamental
rules of evidence so as to facilitate their conviction and altering ex post facto the
punishment to be imposed on them. The Board held that the Acts involved the
usurpation and infringement by the legislature of judicial powers inconsistent with the
written constitution of Ceylon which, though not in express terms, manifested an
e  intention to secure to the judiciary freedom from political, legislative and executive
control. Similarly, in *Hinds v R* [1976] 1 All ER 353 at 360, [1977] AC 195 at 213 the
Board affirmed the principle that—

'implicit in the very structure of a constitution on the Westminster model is that
judicial power, however it be distributed from time to time between various courts,
is to continue to be vested in persons appointed to hold judicial office in the manner
f        and on the terms laid down in the chapter dealing with the judicature, even though
this is not expressly stated in the constitution . . .'

In the present case the Board have not heard full argument and do not pronounce on
the submission by the appellants that the amending Act was an unconstitutional
interference with the rights of the Supreme Court.
g        It suffices that the amending Act was a coercive act of the government which alone
deprived and was intended to deprive the appellants of property without compensation
and thus infringed the Constitution. The Supreme Court reached the opposite conclusion
and the appeal must therefore be allowed and a declaration made that each worker
employed by the MMA at any time or times between 1 January 1980 and 30 June 1983
is entitled by way of redress under s 17 of the Constitution to be paid by the MMA or the
h  government of Mauritius the difference between the salary and allowances in fact paid to
him and the increased salary and allowances which would have been payable to him
pursuant to the award. Their Lordships will humbly advise Her Majesty accordingly.
The respondent must pay the costs of the appellants here and below.

*Société United Docks appeal: appeal dismissed.*
i  *Marine Workers Union appeal: appeal allowed.*

Solicitors: *Bernard Sheridan & Co* (for the appellants in the Société United Docks appeal);
*Slaughter & May* (for the appellants in the Marine Workers Union appeal); *Charles Russell
& Co* (for the respondents in both appeals).

Mary Rose Plummer   Barrister.

# Gloucestershire County Council v Farrow and others

COURT OF APPEAL, CIVIL DIVISION

EVELEIGH, FOX AND PARKER LJJ

26, 27 NOVEMBER 1984

*Highway – Dedication – Presumption – Public use for prescribed period – Existing private right not asserted in derogation of highway during prescribed period – Manorial market right – Land originally dedicated subject to market right – Whether user for prescribed period without assertion of market right effecting rededication free from market right and extinguishing right – Highways Act 1980, s 31(1).*

A lord of the manor owned an ancient market franchise under royal charter which entitled him to hold a weekly market in a market square owned by him. By the late nineteenth century the square had been dedicated as a highway in connection with the market and in consequence a public right of way had been created over the square, subject to the lord of the manor's right to use the square for the weekly market. The surface of the square, being a highway maintainable by the public at large, became vested in the local highway authority. In about 1900 the weekly market ceased to be held and since then had never been held. In August 1979 the lord of the manor leased his market rights and privileges to a company which wished to revive the weekly market. The highway authority brought an action against the lord of the manor and the company seeking (i) a declaration that because the square was a highway they were not entitled to obstruct it by exercising the manorial market right and (ii) an injunction restraining them from doing so. The highway authority alleged that the square had been continuously enjoyed as a highway by the public as of right for a period of over 20 years, during which period the right to hold the market had not been asserted, and therefore by virtue of s 31(1)[a] of the Highways Act 1980 the public had a right of way over the square unqualified by the manorial market right, which was in effect extinguished by s 31(1). The defendants submitted that s 31 was not intended to deprive a landowner of the right to exercise on his own land a subsisting legal privilege vested in him such as the market right. The judge granted the declarations sought, holding that by virtue of s 31(1) of the 1980 Act the square had been rededicated as a highway free from the market right, and accordingly the market right had been extinguished. The company appealed.

**Held** – Where a way over land had been 'actually enjoyed by the public as of right and without interruption for a full period of 20 years' within the first part of s 31(1) of the 1980 Act, then the effect of the second part of s 31(1), namely that 'the way [was] to be deemed to have been dedicated as a highway', was to convert the way into a highway that was a free right of way which could not be interfered with. Since the public had enjoyed a right of way to cross and recross the square without any interruption for more than 20 years, and since during that period that right of enjoyment had not been interfered with by the holding of markets in the square, s 31(1) operated to rededicate the existing way over the square as a highway free from any interruption and therefore not subject to any right to hold a market in the square. Furthermore, since the effect of the rededication under s 31(1) was not to extinguish the lord of the manor's right to hold markets over other land in the manor but merely to prevent that right being exercisable over the square, the absence of compensation for removal of the market rights over the square was not a material consideration. The appeal would accordingly be dismissed (see p 881 j to p 882 b and e to p 883 e and g to p 884 b, post).

Decision of Goulding J [1983] 2 All ER 1031 affirmed.

---

*a*   Section 31(1) is set out at p 880 h j, post

**Notes**

a   For creation of a highway by the statutory presumption of dedication of a way over land, see 21 Halsbury's Laws (4th edn) paras 61, 72, 78, and for cases on the subject, see 26 Digest (Reissue) 472–475, 3190–3198.

For the Highways Act 1980, s 31, see 50(1) Halsbury's Statutes (3rd edn) 497.

**Cases referred to in judgments**

b   A-G v Honeywill [1972] 3 All ER 641, [1972] 1 WLR 1506.

A-G v Horner (1885) 11 App Cas 66, HL; affg (1884) 14 QBD 245, CA.

**Cases also cited**

A-G v Horner (No 2) [1913] 2 Ch 140, CA.

A-G and Newton Abbot RDC v Dyer [1946] 2 All ER 252, [1947] Ch 67.

c   Copestake v West Sussex CC [1911] 2 Ch 331.

Fairey v Southampton CC [1956] 2 All ER 843, [1956] 2 QB 439, CA.

Jones v Bates [1938] 2 All ER 237, CA.

Lewis v Thomas [1950] 1 All ER 116, [1950] 1 KB 438, CA.

Merstham Manor Ltd v Coulsdon and Purley UDC [1936] 2 All ER 422, [1937] 2 KB 77.

R v Charlesworth (1851) 16 QB 1012, 117 ER 1169.

d

**Appeal**

Bisbey Properties Ltd, the third defendant in an action brought against them and against the first and second defendants, Michael Farrow, trading as Stow-on-the-Wold Market Co, and Kenneth Hugh de Courcy, by the plaintiff, Gloucestershire County Council, appealed against the decision of Goulding J ([1983] 2 All ER 1031, [1984] 1 WLR 262)

e   whereby he, inter alia, granted the plaintiff declarations (i) that the land known as Market Square, Stow-on-the-Wold, Gloucestershire, constituted a highway within s 34 of the Highways Act 1959, as amended by s 31 of the Highways Act 1980, (ii) that the defendants were not entitled either jointly or severally to exercise or to cause or permit to be exercised on the highway in the Market Square any weekly Thursday market rights derived from any franchise granted under the terms of any royal charter and (iii) an order

f   restraining the defendants and each of them whether by themselves, their servants or agents or otherwise howsoever from causing, permitting, aiding or abetting the holding on the highway at the Market Square of a weekly Thursday market so as to obstruct the right of the public to pass and repass and to park their vehicles on the highway or otherwise interfere with the right of the public to the use and enjoyment of the highway or so as to cause a public nuisance. The first and second defendants took no part in the

g   appeal. The facts are set out in the judgment of Fox LJ.

Simeon Maskrey for the third defendant.

Michael Burke-Gaffney QC and G S Lawson Rogers for the plaintiff.

**FOX LJ** (delivering the first judgment at the invitation of Eveleigh LJ). This is an appeal

h   from a decision of Goulding J ([1983] 2 All ER 1031, [1984] 1 WLR 262) and it is concerned with the attempts of the third defendant, Bisbey Properties Ltd, to revive the weekly Thursday market in the market place at Stow-on-the-Wold. That is objected to by the plaintiff, the Gloucestershire County Council, which is the highway authority. The second defendant, Mr de Courcy, who I hope will not think I am discourteous if I do not use the full style by which he is sued, claims as the lord of the manor of Stow and the owner of a market franchise granted in the reign of Henry I. The first defendant is a director of Bisbey Properties Ltd and, as I understand, trades as Stow-on-the-Wold Market Co. The judge declared (1) that the market place is a highway for the purposes of s 34 of the Highways Act 1959, as amended by s 31 of the Highways Act 1980, and that the defendants are not entitled to exercise or to permit to be exercised thereon any weekly Thursday market rights derived under the terms of any royal charter, (2) that the second and third defendants be restrained from holding any such market on the market place,

(3) that the counterclaims between the second defendant and the plaintiff and between the third defendant and the plaintiff be dismissed. Those counterclaims sought *a* declarations as to the exercise of market rights and also fair rights on the market place.

The market, so the judge found, began before the commencement of legal memory, having been granted to the Abbey of Evesham by a charter of Henry I. For the purposes of this case it is common ground that the market ceased about the year 1900. The exact date when it was last held is not known, nor is it known why it ceased. The second defendant claims to be the owner of the market franchise and also the owner of a *b* franchise granted to the Abbey of Evesham by Edward IV to hold a fair at Stow twice yearly.

The claims are admitted for the purposes of this action. Bisbey Properties Ltd has a lease granted in 1979 by the second defendant of the market franchise rights and privileges for seven years from 20 September 1979. The market place is an open space in the centre of Stow. It is about 500 feet long from north to south, and it is about 200 feet *c* wide at its widest point. The width in fact varies. The judge found that the market place was originally waste of the manor of Stow. He also found, for the purposes of the action, that it belonged to the second defendant except to the extent or for the purposes for which it might be vested in the plaintiff as the highway authority. The judge was satisfied that the Thursday market was in fact held in the market place, though specific positive evidence of that was scarce. *d*

As to the character of the market place as a highway, it was conceded, apparently after some days of hearing at the trial, that the whole of the market place is and has been, beyond the memory of persons now living, a public highway. The ordnance survey map of 1885 shows the whole surface, apart from that occupied by a building now long since demolished, as metalled road. The judge was of the opinion ([1983] 2 All ER 1031 at 1036, [1984] 1 WLR 262 at 268): *e*

'... I ought to infer that what was being done was being lawfully done. Accordingly, if the question had been raised before a court at that time [that is to say, in the last century], I would expect the court to have held that the market place was dedicated as a highway in connection with the market and with a view to utilising the franchise, and that consequently the dedication created a public right *f* of way subject to the right of the lord of the manor to use the market place for a market and fairs. The House of Lords reached a similar conclusion regarding a modern highway in A-G v Horner (1885) 11 App Cas 66. I have seen no evidence which would enable the court to limit the inference to any particular part of the market place. That, however, is not the end of the matter because it comes to be litigated not in the latter part of the nineteenth century but in the latter part of the *g* twentieth century.'

At that point I should refer to the provisions of s 31 of the Highways Act 1980, which it is accepted we can take as applicable for the purposes of the present case. Those provisions replaced s 34 of the 1959 Act without, as I understand it, significant alterations for present purposes. The provisions of s 31 are of crucial importance to the issues in the present case. The material provisions are sub-s (1) and (2), and they are as follows: *h*

'(1) Where a way over any land, other than a way of such a character that use of it by the public could not give rise at common law to any presumption of dedication, has been actually enjoyed by the public as of right and without interruption for a full period of 20 years, the way is to be deemed to have been dedicated as a highway unless there is sufficient evidence that there was no intention during that period to dedicate it. *j*
(2) The period of 20 years referred to in subsection (1) above is to be calculated retrospectively from the date when the right of the public to use the way is brought into question, whether by a notice such as is mentioned in subsection (3) below or otherwise.'

Since the end of the nineteenth century it is clear, on the judge's findings, that the

public has been enjoying a general right of way over the market place. The defendants
a  concede that beyond living memory it has been used as a public highway. It is the
plaintiff's case that the market place has been enjoyed by the public as of right and
without interruption for a relevant period of 20 years within s 31, and that accordingly
it is deemed by the section to have been dedicated as a highway. The section places, it is
said, no limits or restrictions on the assumed dedication. Accordingly, the market place,
it is submitted, is now a highway freed and discharged from any rights of the second
b  defendant and his successors to hold a Thursday market on it.

The judge's conclusion on that was as follows. In his judgment, after referring to the
decision in A-G v Honeywill [1972] 3 All ER 641, [1972] 1 WLR 1506, the judge continued
([1983] 2 All ER 1031 at 1038, [1984] 1 WLR 262 at 270):

> 'In his judgment, Bristow J said ([1972] 3 All ER 641 at 644, [1972] 1 WLR 1506
> c  at 1510): "It is not disputed, and I take it to be clear law, that if a right of way was
> originally dedicated for use on foot it can subsequently be dedicated for use with
> vehicles as well." Similarly, urges counsel for the council, a highway originally
> dedicated subject to the right to use the land for a periodic market, can subsequently
> be dedicated free from that reservation, and that is what the 1980 Act compels one
> to presume in this case. Counsel was, however, unable to point to any instance in
> which such a rededication of land used under a franchise had occurred, or to explain
> d  the means by which it would be effected. Thus I am left to decide the matter as best
> I can on principle alone. On the whole I am of opinion that Parliament enacted s 31
> of the Highways Act 1980, and its statutory predecessor, in order to avoid the need
> for lengthy and expensive antiquarian investigations when highway rights are called
> in question. That being so, I ought to give the section a broad interpretation and to
> accept the submission on the effect of 20 years' user which (though framed in my
> e  own language) I just now attributed to counsel for the council. Accordingly, I must
> hold that the manorial right to have a weekly market in the market place has been
> lost by the lapse of a 20-year period without such market being held.'

If that conclusion is right, it disposes of the case. If it is wrong, further matters arise on
the respondent's notice which asks for the judgment to be upheld on other grounds.
f  None of those grounds are abandoned by counsel for the plaintiff council. He specifically
reserves all of them.

The second defendant, I should mention for completeness, appealed also, we are told,
on costs, but abandoned that appeal and advances no argument in support of the present
appeal and, indeed, does not appear in person or by counsel.

The defendants' case, put broadly, is this: (1) s 31 of the Highways Act 1980 should
g  not be construed as interfering with or injuring individuals' rights without compensation
unless there is no other possible interpretation of it. That being so, s 31 should have been
given an interpretation which did not remove the right of the third defendant to hold a
weekly market, and (2) the purpose of s 31 is to simplify proof that a right of way over
land has been dedicated as a highway. It is not the function of the section to dedicate as a
highway a way over land that is already a highway. As the square has been dedicated as a
h  highway, subject to the right to hold the fair and market, s 31 does not operate to
rededicate it and extinguish those rights.

I come now to the detailed language of the s 31 of the 1980 Act. Omitting words
which are not applicable, sub-s (1) starts as follows:

> 'Where a way over any land . . . has been actually enjoyed by the public as of right
> and without interruption for a full period of 20 years . . .'

j  There must, therefore, be a way enjoyed by the public. 'Way' I take to mean a route or a
course. In the present case it is, as it seems to me, a quite general route or course over any
part of the market place.

It is then necessary to consider the nature of the enjoyment, that is to say is it on foot
only, or some other limited enjoyment, or is it a general right to pass and repass? In this
case the enjoyment was that of a general right to pass and repass. Further, the enjoyment

during this century was in no way affected by any exercise of market rights. Thus far, therefore, the public has been enjoying a general right of passage to and fro across the  *a* whole of the market place. So far as the period of enjoyment is concerned, it appears to have been for the greater part of this century.

Next, the enjoyment must be as of right and without interruption. The public user was never questioned, at any rate until this dispute began. As regards interruption, it is suggested that there has been interruption from two sources: first, the twice-weekly fair which interfered with passage over the market place. The judge found against the  *b* defendants on this, and no point is taken on the matter in the notice of appeal. Counsel for the plaintiff tells us that counsel then appearing for the defendants did not press an argument on the interruption point. It is, as it seems to me, not necessary to investigate the legal aspects of the matter, but there may have been very good reasons why counsel took the course which he did. In the circumstances, it seems to me that the point is not open to the defendants in this court, and counsel for the plaintiff indeed did not come  *c* here ready to argue it, though he did in fact give us some assistance with it.

The second interruption put forward is interruption by the parking which the plaintiff, as the highway authority, in exercise of its statutory power, permits and controls on the market place. The point was evidently not thought worth taking below and it does not feature in the notice of appeal. In this court I think it originated from the Bench. Again, I do not think that the point is open to the defendants in this court, and again there may  *d* well have been very good reasons why counsel did not think it worth putting forth below; but I express no view one way or the other on the legal issues which it would involve.

The requirements of the first part of sub-s (1) of s 31, to which I have referred, are therefore satisfied. The result is that the final part of the subsection applies, and I quote:

'... the way is to be deemed to have been dedicated as a highway unless there is  *e* sufficient evidence that there was no intention during that period to dedicate it.'

There is, in my view, no evidence of any intention during the relevant period not so to dedicate, and accordingly the way is deemed to have been dedicated as a highway.

Now, what is deemed to have been dedicated is a free right of passage to and fro across the market place. Such a right of passage, I think, is quite inconsistent with the co-  *f* existence of a right to interrupt that right of passage by holding Thursday markets. It would be a quite different right to that which the statute says it is to be. The statute contains no limitations on the deemed right of way, and I find it impossible to read them in. It is necessary to remember that the enjoyment referred to in sub-s (1) was in the present case an enjoyment quite without interference by markets. There were no markets in any relevant period, and it is what I may call the 'uninterfered with' right of way that  *g* the statute is deeming to have been dedicated. It is said, however, that if that is right, then Parliament is taking away rights without compensation, and that that is not to be lightly inferred. We were referred to A-G v Horner (1884) 14 QBD 245 at 257; but one has, it seems to me, to consider the question in the context of the particular statute. So considered, I do not think that there is substance in the objection here. I draw attention to the following points. (1) Parliament is, to some extent at least, certainly evincing an  *h* intention in this statute to take away property rights without compensation. Thus, the statute is designed to produce certainty. It may very well deem a right of way to be dedicated where none could have been proved without the aid of the statute. That is an interference with the rights of the owner of the servient tenement and is uncompensated. (2) In the context of s 31 (1) of the 1980 Act, the complaint of loss of rights in the sort of cases with which the section is dealing has, I think, some unreality. The rights will not  *j* have been exercised for 20 years at least. If they had been exercised, they would normally constitute an interruption and prevent the section applying. In the present case nobody has thought it worth exercising for nearly a century. (3) The right to hold a Thursday market is not in fact being extinguished. The right still exists. It is not a right which is annexed simply to the market place. It can be exercised over any land in Stow within the

boundaries which may be limited by the proper construction of the franchise. The
*a* judge's decision only prevents it being exercised on the market place. In the circumstances,
I would reject the argument based on absence of compensation.

The further argument is advanced that a public right of way existed from the later
years of the nineteenth century at the latest. Section 31, it is said, does not apply to the
case where there is already an admitted right of way. But the point about the present
case, I think, is that the admitted right of way is a right subject to a right of market and
*b* to the interference which that involves. I see no reason, any more than did Goulding J,
why the right of way should not by the operation of the statute subsequently be
rededicated free from that right of interference. It is the creation of a different right of
way.

Lastly, a point is taken on sub-s (2) of s 31 in relation to the period of 20 years which
that subsection says 'is to be calculated retrospectively from the date when the right of
*c* the public to use the way is brought into question . . .' What is said is that the letters of
10 May 1973 and 6 July 1979 from the second defendant to the plaintiff and the Chief
Constable of Gloucestershire do not question the right of the public to use the right of
way, and these are the letters relied on by the plaintiff to limit the 20-year period. But
the letter of 10 May says that the market place is not a highway in any respect, and the
letter of 6 July also denies that the market place is a highway. The denial continued until,
*d* as I understand it, the eighth day of the trial. In any event the defendants have always
denied the existence of the unfettered right of way now being asserted by the plaintiff.
Accordingly, I do not see any force in that argument.

The result, in my view, looking at the whole matter, is that Goulding J reached the
right conclusion; and I would dismiss the appeal.

*e* **PARKER LJ.** I agree and have very little to add. Under s 31 of the Highways Act 1980,
the enjoyment of a way is the matter which first has to be asserted. The way being
asserted may be a way which is restricted or unrestricted. If it is restricted, the restriction
need not amount to an interruption. On the facts of this case, what was enjoyed in the
last 20 years was a way subject to the restriction twice a year entailed in the holding of a
fair, but to no restriction during that period entailed by the holding of a market. There
*f* was a further possible restriction in the existence of the car park. The use of the restriction
entailed by the fair as an interruption and by the car park as either an interruption or a
mere restriction in aid of the defendants' argument is, I agree, not open. It might have
been possible, but no doubt for good reason was not advanced, to say that the way which
had been enjoyed by the public over the period in question was a way subject to those
two restrictions and thereby preserve the right to hold the fair, which is not in issue, and
*g* also the right to hold the market so long as it was held on the car park area and involved
no greater restriction than did the car park. But, inasmuch as what was enjoyed was a
way unrestricted by the market, and the car park point is not open, then that is what is
shown to have been enjoyed for 20 years, and the nature of the highway created is
thereby defined.

The only other matter that I would wish to mention is that under sub-s (2), the
*h* reference to 'the right of the public to use the way is brought into question' is a clear
reference back to 'the way' referred to in s 31(1). Whatever else was not in dispute, it is
perfectly clear that there was disputed and is disputed the right of the public to use the
way unrestricted by the market, and there is therefore an additional reason for saying
that the matter was brought into question from a defined date.

Apart from those two short points, I have nothing to add, and would agree with the
*j* result.

**EVELEIGH LJ.** Section 34 of the Highways Act 1959 refers, as does s 31 of the 1980
Act, to a way which 'has actually been enjoyed for 20 years'. The effect is to convert such
a way, that is, the way which has been actually enjoyed (and I would emphasise the word
'actually') into a highway. It has been found as a fact that the public has enjoyed a way

which was subject to no such limitation as is claimed by the defendants. Consequently, there can be no such limitation on the highway. This seems to me to be the simple and direct approach to this case which the statute compels us to adopt. To accede to the defendants' argument would involve deeming the way to be a highway of a different character from that which was actually enjoyed.

I agree with Fox and Parker LJJ that this appeal should be dismissed.

*Appeal dismissed. Leave to appeal to the House of Lords refused.*

Solicitors: *E P Rugg & Co & W Norris Bazzard & Co*, agents for *Dennis Faulkner & Alsop*, Daventry (for the third defendant); *R I M Wotherspoon*, Gloucester (for the plaintiff).

Celia Fox   Barrister.

# Practice Direction

COURT OF PROTECTION

*Mental health – Court of Protection – Practice – Costs – Solicitors' costs – Fixed costs – Extension of categories of work – Certifying accounts.*

Fixed costs for solicitors for three categories of work in the Court of Protection were introduced in 1983, by agreement with the Law Society and the Chief Taxing Master: see the Practice Direction of 1 September 1983 ([1983] 3 All ER 192). The amounts available in the three categories were increased with effect from 1 November 1984 (see [1984] LS Gaz 3221).

As regards category I (work up to and including completion of the directions contained in the First General Order), the former practice whereby the court could direct taxation even if the solicitor sought fixed costs will no longer apply.

It has now been further agreed with the Law Society and the Chief Taxing Master that category II work (work in respect of the preparation and lodgment of a receivership account) will be extended. Where a solicitor prepares an account, or it is prepared by his firm, and it is certified by a partner in the firm by the prescribed indorsement on the back of the account form (see the Practice Direction of 13 September 1984 ([1984] 3 All ER 320, [1984] 3 WLR 1210), the fixed costs in category II are increased to £70 (plus VAT) in respect of accounts received by the court on or after 1 March 1985.

For avoidance of doubt, the court does not require every receivership account prepared by solicitors to be certified, but if the solicitor concerned chooses to certify the account the provisions of the Practice Direction of 13 September 1984 are to apply.

Whether or not a solicitor certifies the account, it must be signed by the receiver and it remains the receiver's account.

If a solicitor who is also a receiver prepares his own account, it may be certified by a partner of his, but, if he is practising on his own, then the account may only be certified (if at all) by a solicitor in a separate firm.

5 March 1985

A B MACFARLANE
Master, Court of Protection.

# Re Hastings (a bankrupt)

CHANCERY DIVISION
WARNER AND PETER GIBSON JJ
23, 24 OCTOBER, 8 NOVEMBER 1984

*Bankruptcy – Petition – Amendment – Amendment made out of time – Different dates of service of bankruptcy notice and of act of bankruptcy substituted for those appearing in original petition – Whether misdescription of dates constituting a defect of substance – Whether petition can be amended more than three months after alleged act of bankruptcy – Bankruptcy Act 1914, s 4(1)(c).*

On 20 June 1983 a bankruptcy notice was issued on the application of petitioning creditors who were owed £1,668 by the debtor. The notice, which required the debtor to pay the sum owing within ten days of service, was served on him on 29 July. However, the affidavit of service filed by the petitioning creditors stated 29 June 1983 as the date of service of the bankruptcy notice. On 7 September the petitioning creditors presented their petition alleging that within three months before the date of the presentation of the petition the debtor had committed an act of bankruptcy by failing to comply before 12 July 1983 with the requirements of a bankruptcy notice served on him on 29 June 1983. Under s 4(1)(c)[a] of the Bankruptcy Act 1914 a creditor was not entitled to present a bankruptcy petition unless the act of bankruptcy on which the petition was founded occurred 'within three months before the presentation of the petition'. A receiving order was made against the debtor, who applied to the registrar for its rescission on the ground that he had not committed the act of bankruptcy relied on in the petition. The petitioning creditors applied for leave to amend the petition, and on 13 April 1984, more than eight months after the act of bankruptcy had been committed, the registrar allowed the petition to be amended by the substitution of 29 July 1983 for 29 June, and 12 August for 12 July, and dismissed the debtor's application for rescission of the order. The debtor appealed, contending, inter alia, that s 4(1)(c) and the three-month time limit specified therein applied to an application for leave to amend a petition and that therefore the registrar had erred in allowing the petition to be amended so as to introduce an act of bankruptcy which occurred more than three months prior to the application for leave to amend. The petitioning creditors contended that the incorrect dates were mere defects of form and that the only act of bankruptcy relied on had in fact occurred within the three months prior to the petition being presented.

**Held** – Where the description of the act of bankruptcy relied on in a bankruptcy petition included erroneous but consistent dates of service of the bankruptcy notice and of the completion of the acts of bankruptcy and where there was nothing else in the petition from which the debtor could infer that the creditor was relying on an act of bankruptcy occurring at a different date, the misdescription was a defect of substance and not mere form, since the debtor was entitled to know from the petition itself the act of bankruptcy relied on by the creditor. Accordingly, the registrar had erred in allowing amendments which introduced a wholly different date for the act of bankruptcy relied on, since those amendments introduced, outside the period of three months prior to the petition, a new act of bankruptcy (see p 888 *g* to p 889 *b*, post).

**Notes**

For amendment of a bankruptcy petition, see 3 Halsbury's Laws (4th edn) para 337, and for cases on the subject, see 4 Digest (Reissue) 166–168, 1471–1490.

For the Bankruptcy Act 1914, s 4, see 4 Halsbury's Statutes (4th edn) 518.

---

*a*  Section 4(1), so far as material, provides: 'A creditor shall not be entitled to present a bankruptcy petition against a debtor unless . . . (c) the act of bankruptcy on which the petition is grounded has occurred within three months before the presentation of the petition . . .'

**Cases referred to in judgments**

Debtor (No 49 of 1932), Re a, ex p the debtor v The petitioning creditor and Official Receiver (1933) 102 LJ Ch 143.

Debtor (No 31 of 1969), Re a, ex p the debtor v Triggs Turner & Co [1970] 1 All ER 920, DC.

Dunhill, Re, ex p Dunhill [1894] 2 QB 234, DC.

Johnson, Re, ex p Johnson (1883) 25 Ch D 112, CA.

Maund, Re, ex p Maund [1895] 1 QB 194, DC.

Skelton, Re, ex p Coates (1877) 5 Ch D 979, CA.

**Appeal**

The appellant debtor, David Clive Hastings, appealed against an order of Mr Registrar Keyes made in the Slough County Court on 13 April 1984 whereby it was ordered (i) that the application by the debtor dated 16 February 1984 for an order to rescind the receiving order of 17 October 1983 made against him under s 108 of the Bankruptcy Act 1914 be dismissed; (ii) that the petitioning creditors be given leave to amend the petition by substituting 29 July 1983 and 12 August 1983 in the place of 29 June 1983 and 12 July 1983 respectively as being the date of service of the bankruptcy notice and the date before which the debtor failed to comply with the requirements of the bankruptcy notice; and (iii) that the debtor be adjudged bankrupt. The respondent creditors were Geoffrey S Beccle & Co. The facts are set out in the judgment of Peter Gibson J.

Martin Spencer for the appellant debtor.
R Fawls for the respondent creditors.

Cur adv vult

8 November. The following judgments were delivered.

**PETER GIBSON J** (giving the first judgment at the invitation of Warner J). This is an appeal by the bankrupt against three orders made by Mr Registrar Keyes in the Slough County Court on 13 April 1984 whereby he (1) allowed certain amendments to the bankruptcy petition, (2) refused to rescind the receiving order, and (3) made an order of adjudication. By those amendments different dates in respect of the act of bankruptcy were substituted for the dates appearing in the original petition. The substantial question before us is whether the registrar erred in allowing those amendments more than three months after the act of bankruptcy relied on in the petition.

The respondents, the petitioning creditors, are solicitors, Messrs Geoffrey S Beccle & Co (the creditors). They obtained judgment in February and April 1983 against the bankrupt, and on 20 June 1983 were owed the sum of £1,668·13, the balance of the judgment debt. On that date a bankruptcy notice was issued on the creditors' application. The notice was in the statutory form requiring the bankrupt within ten days after service to pay that sum or to secure or compound it or to satisfy the court that he had a sufficient counterclaim, set-off or cross-demand. The creditors filed an affidavit of service. In it a process server, Mr Harper, deposed to serving the bankruptcy notice on Friday, 29 June 1983 which was in fact a Wednesday. The 29 July, the actual date of service, as the registrar subsequently held, was a Friday. On 7 September 1983 the creditors presented their petition. In it they alleged that the bankrupt within three months before the date of the presentation of the petition committed the following act of bankruptcy: that he failed to comply before 12 July 1983 with the requirements of a bankruptcy notice served on him on 29 June 1983.

The petition was served on the bankrupt and on 17 October 1983 the receiving order was made at a hearing at which the bankrupt did not appear and was not represented. The order recited that it appeared to the court that the act of bankruptcy relied on in the petition had been committed. After being served with the receiving order the bankrupt applied for a stay of the advertisement of the order on the ground, inter alia, that he had not been served personally with the bankruptcy notice. He also applied for rescission of the order and that application was heard by the registrar on 13 January 1984. Mr Harper a gave evidence orally but instead of confirming what he had said in his affidavit of service he stated that he had served the bankruptcy notice on 29 July 1983. The bankrupt also gave oral evidence denying service. Although the bankrupt complains that he was taken by surprise by Mr Harper's oral evidence and has been denied the opportunity of obtaining evidence as to his whereabouts on 29 July 1983 there appears to have been no application for an adjournment. The registrar preferred the evidence of Mr Harper, held that the bankrupt had been duly served and dismissed the application for rescission.

b There has been no appeal against that order.

On 16 February 1984 the bankrupt applied again for rescission of the receiving order on the ground that it had been based on an allegation in the petition as to an act of bankruptcy which had not been committed. At a preliminary hearing the registrar suggested to the creditors that the petition should be amended. Accordingly, the creditors on 29 March 1984 gave notice of their intention to apply for leave to amend the petition

c by substituting 29 July 1983 for 29 June 1983 as the date of service of the bankruptcy notice and 12 August 1983 for 12 July 1983 as the date before which the bankrupt failed to comply with the requirements of the bankruptcy notice. In respect of the last date the creditors miscalculated the statutory ten days after service of the notice, 11, and not 12, August being the correct date. But this error was not observed by the registrar when on 13 April 1984, more than eight months after the act of bankruptcy, he allowed the

d amendment, dismissed the application for rescission and made the adjudication order.

It appears from the registrar's notes that in allowing the amendments he proceeded thus in his reasoning: only one act of bankruptcy occurred, the petition was presented within three months from the act, the error in the date of service was a simple misprint in the affidavit of service which was carried into the petition, the bankrupt knew when in fact he had been served, the amendment of such a misprint in the petition is not an

e amendment of substance and no injustice has been done.

Counsel for the bankrupt submitted that the registrar thereby erred in law. He referred to s 4(1)(c) of the Bankruptcy Act 1914 which provides that a creditor is not entitled to present a petition unless the act of bankruptcy on which the petition is grounded has occurred within three months before the presentation of the petition and submitted that the registrar should not have allowed an amendment alleging as the act

f of bankruptcy relied on in the petition a new act of bankruptcy committed well outside the period of three months before the application for leave to amend.

Counsel for the creditors, while stressing that the statutory power of amendment conferred by s 109(3) of the 1914 Act was in unfettered terms and expressly exercisable at any time, accepted that the power of amendment should not be exercised to introduce into a petition a new act of bankruptcy occurring outside the three months' period. He

g was plainly right so to accept. It is now well established that in determining whether to exercise the power of amendment the court will have regard to the time limit contained in s 4(1)(c): see Re Maund, ex p Maund [1895] 1 QB 194 and Re a debtor (No 31 of 1969), ex p the debtor v Triggs Turner & Co [1970] 1 All ER 920. As Ungoed-Thomas J said in the latter case (at 922):

h 'It is clearly the intention of the legislature as expounded in the authorities that any act of bankruptcy should be relied on within the three months' period which it prescribes, and it seems to me to be as contrary to this to allow an amendment which would introduce an act of bankruptcy out of time, whether such act at some time previously appeared on the petition or not.'

Counsel for the creditors submitted that that principle was inapplicable in the present

j case because here only one act of bankruptcy had occurred and that within three months of the presentation of the petition. Here, he submitted, there had been a mere defect in form, a misdescription of the one act of bankruptcy by reference to incorrect dates. He said that as the registrar had ascertained on the oral evidence, including that of the bankrupt, when service of the bankruptcy petition had been effected, there was no injustice to the bankrupt in allowing the amendment to the petition, a document which, as he rightly said, the court is readier to amend than a bankruptcy notice.

I accept that there was only one act of bankruptcy on which the creditors intended to rely. But the question whether, for the purposes of the application of the principle relating to amendments outside the three months' period, there was one act or there were two acts of bankruptcy cannot, in my judgment, be answered subjectively by the creditors in subsequent evidence received by the court.

Counsel for the creditors referred us to *Re a debtor* (No 49 of 1932) (1933) 102 LJ Ch 143 as justifying the proposition that a court is not precluded from considering what had in fact occurred. In that case the petition alleging an act of bankruptcy had been presented, and the affidavit verifying the position had been sworn, the day before the act of bankruptcy did in fact occur, but at the hearing all the facts alleged in the petition were duly proved and the receiving order was held to have been duly made. That was a case of a true irregularity which had caused no injustice. There no amendment to the petition was called for and the debtor knew from the petition what case he had to meet. It does not follow from that case that the court should consider what in fact occurred in a case where an amendment of the petition is necessary.

The form of petition prescribed by r 143 of the Bankruptcy Rules 1952, SI 1952/2113, is plainly designed to tell the debtor precisely what it is that is alleged to found the bankruptcy proceedings. The prescribed form requires a statement that the debtor within three months before the date of the presentation of the petition has committed the following act of bankruptcy, and then, as the notes on the statutory form indicate, the creditor is required to set out the nature and date of the act of bankruptcy relied on. In *Re Skelton, ex p Coates* (1877) 5 Ch D 979 the act of bankruptcy alleged in the petition was that the debtor departed from his dwelling house or otherwise absented himself, but there was no allegation that the debtor had done so with intent to defraud or delay his creditors. On appeal to the Court of Appeal it was contended by the creditor that this omission was cured by the statutory predecessor of s 147(1), which provides that no preceedings in bankruptcy shall be invalidated by any formal defect or by any irregularity unless the court is satisfied that substantial injustice has been caused thereby and that the injustice cannot be remedied by an order of the court. The Court of Appeal rejected that contention. James LJ said (at 982):

> 'To allow this appeal would be an encouragement to slovenly procedure. The forms ought to be adhered to. This is really not a mere matter of form. The Act says you must tell the debtor what the act of bankruptcy is which you allege against him, so that he may have the opportunity of contesting it in the first instance.'

Similarly in *Re Johnson, ex p Johnson* (1883) 25 Ch D 112 at 116 Cotton LJ, after referring to *Re Skelton, ex p Coates*, commented: 'The petition ought to show what charge the debtor has to come and meet.' It is not sufficient to say, as the registrar did, that the bankrupt knew when he was served, thereby implying that the bankrupt would know what act of bankruptcy was being referred to by the creditors. The bankrupt was entitled to know from the petition what was the act of bankruptcy relied on by the creditors.

The date of the commission of the act of bankruptcy relied on is an important part of its description. It may be that the omission to state the date of completion of the act of bankruptcy will not be fatal if it is possible to ascertain that date from elsewhere in the petition. For example, if the date of service of the bankruptcy notice is alleged, it is a mere matter of calculation to ascertain the date of the act of bankruptcy (see *Re Dunhill, ex p Dunhill* [1894] 2 QB 234). It is possible that an error in such date would be remediable even outside the three months' period if the true date was ascertainable from elsewhere in the petition. But, where, as in the present case, the erroneous description of the act of bankruptcy relied on in the petition includes dates for service of the bankruptcy notice and for the completion of the act of bankruptcy which are entirely consistent and there is nothing elsewhere in the petition from which the debtor can infer that the creditor is relying on an act of bankruptcy occurring at a different date, in my judgment it is wrong to treat such misdescription as a mere defect in form and as not being a defect of substance. Whatever may be the position as to an amendment within the three months' period, and I say nothing as to that, it cannot be right to allow an application made *a* outside that period for an amendment which introduces wholly different dates for the act of bankruptcy relied on, even though the creditors always intended to refer to one and the same act of bankruptcy. From the viewpoint of the debtor such an amendment introduces a new act of bankruptcy relied on by the creditors, and that cannot be allowed outside the three months' period.

For these reasons therefore I conclude that the registrar erred in allowing the amendments to the petition. Counsel for the creditors did not dispute that if the *b* amendments should not have been allowed, neither the receiving order nor the adjudication should stand. I would allow the appeals against all three orders made on 13 April 1984.

**WARNER J.** I agree.

*Appeal allowed.*

*c*

Solicitors: *Piper Smith & Basham* (for the appellant debtor); *Geoffrey S Beccle & Co* (for the respondent creditors).

Vivian Horvath    Barrister.

*d*
# Practice Direction

QUEEN'S BENCH DIVISION

*Practice – Post – First and second class mail – Affidavit of service – Interpretation Act 1978, s 7
*e* – RSC Ord 10, r 1(3).*

With effect from 16 April 1985 the Practice Direction issued on 30 July 1968 ([1968] 3 All ER 319, [1968] 1 WLR 1489) is hereby revoked and the following substituted therefor.

*f* 1. Under s 7 of the Interpretation Act 1978 service by post is deemed to have been effected, unless the contrary has been proved, at the time when the letter would be delivered in the ordinary course of post.

2. To avoid uncertainty as to the date of service it will be taken (subject to proof to the contrary) that delivery in the ordinary course of post was effected (a) in the case of first class mail, on the second working day after posting, (b) in the case of second class mail, *g* on the fourth working day after posting. 'Working days' are Monday to Friday, excluding any bank holiday.

3. Affidavits of service shall state whether the document was dispatched by first or second class mail. If this information is omitted it will be assumed that second class mail was used.

4. This direction is subject to the special provisions of RSC Ord 10, r 1(3) relating to *h* the service of originating process.

J R BICKFORD SMITH
8 March 1985                                                    Senior Master.

*Explanatory note*
*i* It is no longer safe to assume that letters posted by first class mail will always be delivered on the following day. To reduce the number of applications by companies to set aside default judgments on the grounds of late service, more realistic assumptions are now prescribed.

This direction does not affect the provisions of RSC Ord 10, r 1(3) relating to the postal service of originating process; these generally prescribe the seventh calendar day after posting by first class mail as the date of deemed service on individuals and firms.

# X v Commissioner of Police of the Metropolis

CHANCERY DIVISION
WHITFORD J
12 OCTOBER 1984

*Rehabilitation – Rehabilitation of offenders – Spent conviction – Disclosure of spent conviction – Disclosure in course of official duties – Official duties – Disclosure of spent convictions by London office of Interpol to foreign Interpol office in response to request about plaintiff's criminal activities – Plaintiff suspected of planning crimes abroad – Whether information disclosed by London Interpol office in course of 'official duties' – Whether duties of English police extending to suppression of crime abroad – Rehabilitation of Offenders Act 1974, s 9(2).*

The plaintiff was convicted of various offences in 1966 but by 1975 he had become a 'rehabilitated person' for the purposes of the Rehabilitation of Offenders Act 1974 and he was therefore entitled under s 4(1)[a] to 'be treated for all purposes in law as a person who has not committed or been . . . convicted of' the offences. Subsequently the London office of the International Criminal Police Commission (Interpol) received a request from the Paris office of Interpol for information about the plaintiff's criminal record and activities because he was suspected of planning to commit crimes in Andorra. A police officer at the London office of Interpol complied with the request and transmitted to the Paris office information from official records regarding the plaintiff's spent convictions. The plaintiff sought a declaration that the officer's disclosure of that information was unauthorised, and constituted an offence under s 9(2)[b] of the 1974 Act, because the officer had disclosed the information 'otherwise than in the course of [his official] duties', since the official duties of the police in England did not include the prevention of crime abroad.

**Held** – Since the suppression of international crime was as important to the inhabitants of England as the suppression of domestic crime, the police in England had an obligation to prevent the commission of crime abroad. Accordingly, the disclosure of information about the plaintiff's spent convictions by the officer at the London office of Interpol had been made in the course of the officer's 'official duties' and the disclosure was therefore authorised under s 9(2) of the 1974 Act. It followed that the plaintiff was not entitled to the declaration sought (see p 895 c to f, post).

Dictum of Viscount Cave LC in *Glasbrook Bros Ltd v Glamorgan CC* [1924] All ER Rep at 582 applied.

## Notes

For the disclosure of spent convictions in the course of official duties, see 11 Halsbury's Laws (4th edn) para 934.

For the Rehabilitation of Offenders Act 1974, ss 4, 9, see 44 Halsbury's Statutes (3rd edn) 151, 162.

## Cases referred to in judgment

*Glasbrook Bros Ltd v Glamorgan CC* [1925] AC 270, [1924] All ER Rep 579, HL.
*Hoffman v Thomas* [1974] 2 All ER 233, [1974] 1 WLR 374, DC.
*R v Waterfield* [1963] 3 All ER 659, [1964] 1 QB 164, [1963] 3 WLR 946, CCA.
*Rice v Connolly* [1966] 2 All ER 649, [1966] 2 QB 414, [1966] 3 WLR 17, DC.

## Preliminary issue

On the hearing of a summons dated 14 October 1983 issued in an action brought by the

---

a   Section 4(1), so far as material, is set out at p 891 h, post
b   Section 9(2) is set out at p 893 a b, post

a
plaintiff, X, against the defendants, the Home Office and the Commissioner of Police of the Metropolis, seeking declarations regarding the defendants' duties to the plaintiff under the provisions of the Rehabilitation of Offenders Act 1974, Master Dyson, by an order dated 15 December 1983, ordered that the following question be tried as a preliminary issue in the action, namely whether the plaintiff was entitled to the following declarations claimed in the statement of claim: that is (1) a declaration that the defendants by virtue of s 4(1) of the 1974 Act were under a duty to treat the plaintiff for all purposes

b
of law as a person who had not committed or been charged with or prosecuted for or convicted of or sentenced for certain offences under the Companies Act 1948 which were the subject of his conviction in 1966; (2) a declaration that the defendants by virtue of s 4(1) and/or s 9 of the 1974 Act were under a duty not to disclose to the police force of a foreign state the fact that the plaintiff was a person who had been convicted of and sentenced for those offences; and (3) a declaration that the defendants by disclosing to

c
Interpol and the police forces of Andorra and Monaco the fact that the plaintiff had committed, been charged with, been prosecuted for and convicted of and sentenced for the offences which were the subject of his conviction in 1966 acted in breach of the aforesaid duty or duties imposed by s 4(1) and/or s 9 of the 1974 Act. By the same order Master Dyson by consent ordered that the proceedings against the Home Office be discontinued. The facts are set out in the judgment.

d
*Richard Slowe* for the plaintiff.
*Charles Gray QC* for the commissioner.

**WHITFORD J.** I have to consider a preliminary point in an action brought by the plaintiff against the Home Office and the Metropolitan Police Commissioner. The

e
plaintiff was convicted in 1966 of certain offences under the Companies Act 1948 and he was sentenced to a term of six months' imprisonment. Pursuant to the provisions of the Rehabilitation of Offenders Act 1974, in 1975 he became a rehabilitated person. Now, as the matter was originally put in the statement of claim, what was being said was that having regard to the provisions of s 4(1) of the 1974 Act he thereafter had to be treated for all purposes in law as a person who had not committed, or been charged with, or

f
prosecuted for, or convicted of, the offences in question, and furthermore, as I understood the matter as it was originally pleaded, having regard to the provisions of the Act, the defendants were under a duty so to treat the plaintiff.
   As matters have developed, the question finally to be decided on this preliminary point has narrowed down. In the course of the argument it was accepted by counsel for the plaintiff that so far as the 1974 Act is concerned there is no positive duty imposed in

g
general terms on persons not to disclose what are conveniently referred to as spent convictions, and in the light of the way in which the matter has developed I do not need to spend a great deal of time on s 4 of the Act, which is entitled 'Effect of rehabilitation', but I will have just to look at it. It provides by sub-s (1), subject to certain other sections, that—

h
   'a rehabilitated person for the purposes of this Act in respect of a conviction shall be treated for all purposes in law as a person who has not committed or been charged with or prosecuted for or convicted of or sentenced for the offence or offences which were the subject of that conviction . . .'

Then it provides in s 4(1)(a) that no evidence shall be admissible in proceedings, and it also provides that nobody shall be required to answer questions relating to his past if the

j
answer given to those questions would refer to spent convictions or circumstances ancillary thereto.
   There is a provision under sub-s (2) of s 4 in these terms:

   'Subject to the provisions of any order made under subsection (4) below, where a question seeking information with respect to a person's previous convictions, offences, conduct or circumstances is put to him or to any other person otherwise

than in proceedings before a judicial authority—(a) the question shall be treated as not relating to spent convictions or to any circumstances ancillary to spent convictions, and the answer thereto may be framed accordingly . . .'

Not it is to be observed (and this was, of course, accepted by counsel for the plaintiff) 'must be framed accordingly'; and then there is a provision that the person in question does not undergo any liability if he fails to acknowledge or disclose any spent conviction.

So, quite plainly, so far as the general provisions of the Act are concerned, what is being done (and it is obviously in accordance with the protection which it was intended should be afforded to certain classes of offenders) is the making of provision to ensure that, in the sort of circumstances envisaged, these spent convictions are not, in fact, going to be disclosed. Now, the question which I have got to determine arises on the construction of but one subsection of one section of the Act, and that is s 9(2), to which I will be coming.

It is, I think, convenient at this stage to deal briefly with the facts on which the plaintiff's claim is based, because whatever the present state of the pleading, or indeed the present state of the parties, matters which, if necessary, could be cured by amendment, the complaint that is now being made is that there has been a commission of a criminal offence contrary to s 9, and the plaintiff's claim, which is based essentially on requests for declarations and damages, is going to rest on the correctness of the assertion that the relevant events amounted to the commission of a criminal offence pursuant to the provisions of s 9. I should say that this is not (and counsel for the plaintiff made this quite plain in the course of his reply) a case in which it is in any way being suggested that there was some gross impropriety in what the police may have done, and quite plainly that must be right. Counsel, as I understand it, put it on the failure of the authorities to realise the limitations placed on their freedom of disclosure of information by the provisions of s 9 and, indeed, said that it might well be, having regard to the provisions of one subsection of s 9 that if, in fact, that which is the subject of complaint was, as he submits, unlawfully done, but none the less was something which it would have been appropriate to make special provision for, that can be done, for all that is going to be required is the making of some appropriate order by the Secretary of State.

What was done was this. At a time when the plaintiff had become a rehabilitated offender, a request was sent by the Paris office of the International Criminal Police Commission, conveniently referred to throughout the proceedings as Interpol, to London for all relevant information which London might possess or be able to acquire about the plaintiff, in particular about his criminal record, true identity and criminal activities because he was suspected of planning swindles in Andorra. In response to that request, information relating to his spent convictions was sent to Paris, transmitted onwards to Andorra, and, indeed, although we know nothing about this, one of the points that counsel for the plaintiff makes is that once it had passed to Paris control of further dissemination of the information had passed out of the hands of London, although evidence was given that great care is taken in forwarding information in response to requests. Indeed, on the evidence of Detective Superintendent Thompson, in the case of a request such as I am concerned with it is never forwarded except on the giving of adequate reason. It is a matter of trust so far as further dissemination is concerned. Interpol is widespread (I think there are about 36 member countries now) and so the matter stands.

Well, the information was sent, and I come to the short point arising under s 9 of the 1974 Act. It is entitled 'Unauthorised disclosure of spent convictions'. It was suggested by counsel for the commissioner that the heading to this section, on the face of it, appears to contemplate that there might be authorised disclosure of spent convictions; and indeed I did not understand counsel for the plaintiff to be arguing that there might not be authorised disclosure of spent convictions, but I am not concerned with the heading; I am concerned with the section. In sub-s (1) 'official records' are defined, 'specified information' is defined. There is no point in reading out these subsections. There is no doubt in the circumstances of this case that the information which was transmitted came from an official record, and there is no doubt that it was specified information as defined. Subsection (2), which is the relevant part of s 9, is in these terms:

'Subject to the provisions of any order made under subsection (5) below [and no such order has been made, though sub-s (5) is the subsection under which counsel for the plaintiff suggested an order might be made if it was thought appropriate], any person who, in the course of his official duties, has or at any time has had custody of or access to any official record or the information contained therein, shall be guilty of an offence if, knowing or having reasonable cause to suspect that any specified information he has obtained in the course of those duties is specified information, he discloses it, otherwise than in the course of those duties, to another person.'

I do not think it is known, and I am not certain whether it could be known, exactly who was responsible for the transmission of the information to Paris pursuant to the request relating to the plaintiff, but there can be no doubt that it was a person who, in the course of his official duties, had access to official records and he must at least have had reasonable cause to suspect that this information was specified information. He disclosed it. The question is: was it disclosed in the course of the discloser's official duties?

I have been referred to a certain amount of authority on both sides which it was suggested might be of assistance in coming to a conclusion as to exactly what is meant by the words 'official duties'.

The cases which were relied on by counsel for the plaintiff were both cases in which the words that were, in fact, being considered were in the one case, R v Waterfield [1963] 3 All ER 659, [1964] 1 QB 164, the words 'in the due execution of their duty', and in the other case, Hoffman v Thomas [1974] 2 All ER 233, [1974] 1 WLR 374, 'in the course of the execution of his duty'. These were both cases concerned with facts wholly differing from the facts which I have to consider, but counsel for the plaintiff placed particular reliance on the approach of Ashworth J, who was sitting with Lord Parker CJ in the Court of Appeal in R v Waterfield [1963] 3 All ER 659 at 661, [1964] 1 QB 164 at 170–171, where Ashworth J said:

'In the judgment of this court it would be difficult, and in the present case it is unnecessary, to reduce within specific limits the general terms in which the duties of police constables have been expressed. In most cases it is probably more convenient to consider what the police constable was actually doing and in particular whether such conduct was prima facie an unlawful interference with a person's liberty or property. If so, it is then relevant to consider whether (a) such conduct falls within the general scope of any duty imposed by statute or recognised at common law and (b) whether such conduct, albeit within the general scope of such a duty, involved an unjustifiable use of powers associated with the duty.'

I am bound to say I do not find that this or, indeed, any of the other authorities of direct assistance to me. Counsel for the commissioner submitted that if you adopt the approach formulated by Ashworth J it does not assist the plaintiff in this case, because what the police officer in question was doing (it would have been somebody that had been seconded to the Interpol department at New Scotland Yard) was not prima facie anything that could be said to be an unlawful interference with this plaintiff's liberty or with his property. Counsel for the plaintiff suggested that those words must not be read too narrowly. He submits that the whole purpose of the 1974 Act is to give this much protection to an offender who has been rehabilitated that, in his particular case, the slate is wiped clean, and that was not done, or rather was undone by the communication of the information from London to Paris.

If I do not go to Hoffman v Thomas in detail it is only because it does not appear to me to take the matter very much further. Counsel for the commissioner referred me to a case in the House of Lords, Glasbrook Bros Ltd v Glamorgan CC [1925] AC 270, [1924] All

ER Rep 579. This case was essentially concerned with questions whether, in fact, the making of a charge for the protection of a colliery by a local police force was permissible.   *a* The observations with regard to duty are couched in very general terms. Viscount Cave LC speaks of—

'an absolute and unconditional obligation binding the police authorities to take all steps which appear to them to be necessary for keeping the peace, for preventing crime, or for protecting property from criminal injury . . .'

*b*

(See [1925] AC 270 at 277, [1924] All ER Rep 579 at 582.)

It was a case in which there was dissent. I do not think I need go into the other speeches in detail. Viscount Finlay and Lord Shaw approached the matter in the same broad way as Viscount Cave LC did. The dissenting judgment of Lord Carson, which was referred to by counsel for the commissioner, refers to the observations of Viscount Cave LC, which I have cited, with approval. Lord Carson says ([1925] AC 270 at 292, [1924] All   *c* ER Rep 579 at 589–590):

'If I might with respect offer any criticism on the Lord Chancellor's statement, I would myself prefer to lay down that it is the duty of the police to take all steps that are necessary for the purposes mentioned by the Lord Chancellor.'

So that puts it very broadly; and in *Rice v Connolly* [1966] 2 All ER 649 at 651, [1966]   *d* 2 QB 414 at 419 Lord Parker CJ, speaking of the obligations and duties of a police constable, puts it in the same sort of broad terms in a passage in his judgment.

I do not think I am really very much assisted by dictionary definitions. Citing the Oxford English Dictionary, counsel for the plaintiff relied on the definition of 'duty' under definition 4, taking the relevant synonym to be 'obligation', and counsel for the commissioner suggested that definition 5 might be equally applicable, where duty is   *e* defined as 'The action which one's position or station directly requires'. The comment of counsel for the plaintiff was that there was no direct requirement resting on the officer who transmitted the information so to do. Furthermore, in relation to the very broad expressions of opinion as to what police duties may comprehend, he had this much to say, that, although there is no expression limiting the obligations in the authorities to which I have referred to an obligation to prevent crime in the United Kingdom, it could   *f* scarcely be said that there is an obligation resting on the police in this country to prevent crime in Andorra.

Now, Interpol has been at work for a good many years, and this country has accepted obligations which have involved transmitting information for the assistance of forces in other parts of the world, and receiving information which may assist in the detection and suppression of crime in this country in return. I have had the advantage of being   *g* taken through the constitution of Interpol by counsel for the plaintiff, and I have had the advantage of hearing the evidence of Detective Superintendent Thompson, who is at present in charge of the London end of Interpol, though he was not there at the time when the events the subject of complaint took place. I have already referred to the evidence which he gave relating to the way in which inquiries are dealt with, to the fact that it is not just a question of a request being made and an answer being given without   *h* any further inquiry at all, as I think counsel for the plaintiff may, at least, at one time have thought, for at the start of his cross-examination he was putting questions to Detective Superintendent Thompson whether inquiries were in fact made. Apparently there had been no discovery so there was no particular reason why he should have seen the relevant paper, but it is a matter which might have been made clear before. I think counsel for the plaintiff was perhaps a little surprised when the relevant inquiry, coupled   *j* with the reason why it was being made, was produced. Certainly Detective Superintendent Thompson was under no doubt that, if he had been there when the inquiry had come in and he had had the responsibility of answering it, he would have considered that it was his duty to ascertain the reason for the inquiry. The question, I think quite understandably, *a*  was not pursued with Detective Superintendent Thompson in cross-examination, and indeed his view as to what he might have thought was his duty could not be conclusive.

To reach a proper conclusion on the true construction of s 9 of the 1974 Act it is, I think, proper to approach the matter in this way. Under s 9 improper disclosure of information properly required may be a criminal offence. What is the mischief against which the section is being directed? Quite plainly, in my view (and s 9, of course, must be considered in the context of the Act as a whole, and I think I have been taken to all the relevant sections), it is concerned with situations in which persons, who quite rightly *b*  become aware of specified information in the course of their official duties, may, for some reason or another, and in no sense in any way in connection with any duty arising out of their station or office, communicate to some third party that specified information. Of course, there is a specific provision in sub-s (4) of s 9 penalising persons who obtain specified information from official records by means of fraud, dishonesty or bribe, but *c*  under s 9, in circumstances in which the disclosure is a disclosure in the course of the duties of the person disclosing, no criminal offence is committed.

One has to consider in the circumstances of this case the police officer who has been sent to Interpol, London, who receives a request for information of this kind, and one has to consider what his duty must be. The position of Interpol, as I have said, was gone into in some detail, and it is quite plain that under its constitution and, indeed, in *d*  accordance with the practice, as I have said, for a good many years this country as a member of Interpol has accepted obligations relating to the transmission of information following requests received, with as it appears on the evidence as I have heard it, this safeguard, that information is just not broadcast on request without reason being given. The House of Lords in 1925, when it was speaking in very general terms about police duties, may not, in the state of the world as it then was, have been considering the duties *e*  of the police in connection with the combating of international crime. As matters stand today, international crime has assumed a significance which, so far as this country is concerned, makes its suppression as important to the inhabitants of this country, and perhaps in some cases more important, as the suppression of domestic crime.

I have come to the conclusion that it cannot possibly be said that the disclosure which was in fact made was made otherwise than in the course of the duties of the person *f*  making that disclosure, and the preliminary point must be answered in this sense.

*Order accordingly.*

Solicitor: *Slowes* (for the plaintiff); *D M O'Shea* (for the commissioner).

Evelyn M C Budd      Barrister.

# Practice Direction

FAMILY DIVISION

*Family Division – Appeal – Appeal from registrar – Notes of evidence and registrar's judgment.*

1. As from 11 March 1985 on entering an appeal to a judge from a judgment, order or decision of a registrar exercising jurisdiction in the Family Division of the High Court or in a divorce county court the following procedure will apply.

2. Where the appellant is represented, and either party wishes to bespeak a copy of the registrar's notes of evidence, the appellant's solicitor shall (a) within 21 days from the date on which the appeal is lodged, certify that either the appellant or the respondent considers that notes of evidence taken before the registrar are necessary for the purpose of appeal and that notes of evidence will be lodged and (b) if he has so certified, unless otherwise directed, not less than 21 days prior to the hearing of the appeal lodge a copy of the notes of evidence (which can be bespoken from the registrar) and of judgment (being notes prepared by the appellant's solicitor, and where the respondent is represented agreed by his legal advisers, and approved by the registrar).

3. Where the appellant is acting in person and the respondent is represented, the respondent's solicitor shall, after service of the notice of appeal, comply with the obligations imposed by para 2(a) and (b) above (save as to the agreement as to notes of judgment) as if he were acting for the appellant, and inform the appellant of the lodging of such notes and (if so required) supply to him a copy thereof on payment of the usual charge.

4. Where either party is represented but neither party wishes to bespeak a copy of the registrar's notes of evidence, a copy of the notes of judgment shall be (a) prepared by the appellant's solicitor and, if the respondent is represented, agreed by his solicitor or (b) prepared by the respondent's solicitor if the appellant is not represented, and in any case shall be approved by the registrar, and not less than 21 days prior to the hearing a copy of the notes shall be lodged by the solicitor who prepared them.

5. Where both parties to the appeal are acting in person the appellant shall notify the registrar of the appeal and the registrar shall, where possible, make a note for the assistance of the judge hearing the appeal and shall furnish each party with a copy of that note or certify that no note can be made.

6. This direction supersedes the Practice Direction of 26 February 1979 ([1979] 1 All ER 813, [1979] 1 WLR 284) and is issued with the approval of the President and the concurrence of the Lord Chancellor.

B P TICKLE
Senior Registrar.

21 February 1985

# Westminster City Council v Select Managements Ltd

COURT OF APPEAL, CIVIL DIVISION
EVELEIGH, FOX AND PARKER LJJ
19, 20 DECEMBER 1984, 8 FEBRUARY 1985

*Health and safety at work – Non-domestic premises – Statutory duty of persons having control of such premises – Duty owed to persons who are not their employees but who use non-domestic premises made available to them as place of work etc – Person having control of block of flats – Whether lifts and electrical installations serving common parts of block are 'non-domestic premises' – Whether lifts and electrical installations 'made available as place of work' etc to persons repairing and maintaining them – Whether person having control of block of flats owing statutory duty to such persons – Health and Safety at Work etc Act 1974, ss 4, 53(1).*

Three improvement notices were served on a company by a council under the Health and Safety at Work etc Act 1974. The notices related to two lifts and an electrical installation serving the common parts of a residential block of flats managed by the company, and alleged that the company was contravening s 4[a] of the 1974 Act, which required persons in control of premises to ensure that the premises were 'safe and without risks to health'. Under s 4(1) that duty was owed to persons who '(a) are not their employees; but (b) use non-domestic premises made available to them as a place of work or as a place where they may use plant . . . provided for their use there . . .' The company's appeal against the notices was allowed by an industrial tribunal but on appeal the judge reversed that decision. The company appealed to the Court of Appeal, contending that the common parts of the block of flats were not 'non-domestic' premises within s 4(1)(b) because either (i) the whole of the block of flats, including the common parts, were 'domestic premises' or (ii) the common parts were not 'premises'.

**Held** – (1) The common parts of a block of flats were 'non-domestic premises' as defined by s 53(1)[b] of the 1974 Act since they were either a 'place' or an 'installation on land', and were therefore 'premises', and they were not 'domestic' since they were used in common by the occupants of more than one private dwelling (see p 899 *b* to *h*, p 901 *b* to *d* and p 904 *c d*, post).

(2) (Sir Edward Eveleigh dissenting). Furthermore, the common parts were made available as a 'place of work' to persons who were not employees of the company but who came to repair and maintain the premises, or, alternatively, the lifts and electrical installations in the common parts were 'plant' provided for the use of such persons. Accordingly, for the purposes of s 4 the common parts of the flats were non-domestic premises made available to persons not employed by the company as a place of work or where they could use plant provided for their use, and the company was under a duty, in accordance with s 4, to ensure that they were kept safe. The company's appeal would therefore be dismissed (see p 900 *b* to *h* and p 901 *j* to p 902 *f*, post).

Decision of Taylor J [1984] 1 All ER 994 affirmed.

**Notes**
For improvement notices, see 20 Halsbury's Laws (4th edn) para 473.
For the Health and Safety at Work etc Act 1974, ss 4, 53, see 44 Halsbury's Statutes (3rd edn) 1090, 1136.

**Cases cited**
*Benabo v Wood Green BC* [1945] 2 All ER 163, [1946] KB 38.

---

*a*   Section 4 is set out at p 903 *b* to *e*, post
*b*   Section 53(1), so far as material, is set out at p 899 *a b*, post

*Cox v H C B Angus Ltd* [1981] ICR 683.
*Field v Perrys (Ealing) Ltd* [1950] 2 All ER 521.

**Appeal**

Select Managements Ltd appealed against the decision of Taylor J ([1984] 1 All ER 994, [1984] 1 WLR 1058) hearing the Crown Office list on 20 December 1983 whereby an appeal by Westminster City Council was allowed, and the majority decision of an industrial tribunal sitting at London (Central) (chairman Lady E Mitchell) on 28 January 1983 and registered on 9 March 1983 allowing appeals by the appellants against three improvement notices served on them by the council relating to the common parts of a block of flats at 6 Hall Road, London NW8, which the appellants managed, was reversed. The facts are set out in the judgment of Parker LJ.

*Anthony Scrivener QC* and *Richard Nussey* for the company.
*James Goudie QC* and *A F Wilkie* for the council.

*Cur adv vult*

8 February. The following judgments were delivered.

**PARKER LJ** (giving the first judgment at the invitation of Fox LJ). The appellants manage a block of flats at 6 Hall Road, London NW8. They are in control of the common parts of the block in connection with the carrying on by them of the business or undertaking of managing the block. The common parts include two lifts, staircases, landings and a ground-floor hall or foyer.

Three questions arise for determination on this appeal. (1) Are the common parts 'non-domestic premises' within the meaning of s 4(1) of the Health and Safety at Work etc Act 1974? which provides:

'This section has effect for imposing on persons duties in relation to those who—
(a) are not their employees; but (b) use non-domestic premises made available to them as a place of work or as a place where they may use plant or substances provided for their use there, and applies to premises so made available and other non-domestic premises used in connection with them.'

(2) If so, are such common parts made available to persons not in the appellants' employment as a place of work and so used by them? (3) Are such common parts made available to such persons as a place where they may use plant and substances provided for their use there and so used by them?

Owing to the manner in which the matter has reached this court, very little is known of the persons who are not employed by the appellants but who use the common parts of the block. There is a resident caretaker but it is not known by whom he is employed or what his duties are. Persons not employed by the appellants attend at the block from time to time for the purpose of inspecting, maintaining and repairing the lifts and the electrical installations in the common parts. No more was established by evidence. It may be inferred, however, that the common parts are regularly cleaned and from time to time decorated. The persons who do the cleaning and decorating, however, may or may not be the appellants' employees. It may also be inferred that the lifts, landings, staircases and hall are used both by the tenants of the flats and those visiting them. Such visitors will, no doubt, include some who visit in the course of their employment such as delivery men or doctors.

With this preliminary I turn to the three questions.

*(1) Are the common parts 'non-domestic premises'?*

Part I of the 1974 Act contains in s 53 its own definition section. For the purposes of the present question two of the definitions only are relevant. I set them out:

'... "domestic premises" means premises occupied as a private dwelling (including any garden, yard, garage, outhouse or other appurtenance of such premises which is not used in common by the occupants of more than one such dwelling), and "non-domestic premises" shall be construed accordingly ...

"premises" includes any place and, in particular, includes—(a) any vehicle, vessel, aircraft or hovercraft, (b) any installation on land (including the foreshore and other land intermittently covered by water), any offshore installation, and any other installation (whether floating, or resting on the seabed or the subsoil thereof, or resting on other land covered with water or the subsoil thereof), and (c) any tent or movable structure ...'

It is clear that each flat is a place and is occupied as a private dwelling. Each of the flats is therefore within the definition of 'domestic premises'. It is equally clear that the lifts and other common parts are not within the definition for, since they are used in common by the occupants of more than one private dwelling, they are, even if appurtenances of each of the flats, excluded from being domestic premises. If the common parts are not domestic premises then, by the concluding words of the definition, they are, if premises at all, non-domestic premises.

Counsel for the appellants submitted that the common parts were not premises at all. This submission might have had substance were it not for the fact that the definition of 'premises' is so wide as to include things which one would not ordinarily consider to be within the meaning of the word. When, however, the definition brings within that meaning any 'place' and then particularises as being within that meaning vehicles, vessels, aircraft and hovercraft, installations on land and offshore, tents and movable structures, there can, in my view, be no doubt that the hall, landing and staircases of a block of flats are places and thus within the definition of 'premises'. As to the lifts (in which I include the lift cages, shafts, gates, wells and motor rooms) they are also, in my view, within the definition either specifically as being installations on land or generally as being places. The judge held that the electrical installation for the common parts was in a like position. For myself, albeit it makes no difference to the end result, I cannot accept this. The electrical installation is merely a collection of wires, fittings, switches, plug sockets etc for lighting the common parts and enabling such things as vacuum cleaners and floor polishers to take electric power from the sockets. To describe such a collection or any part of it as a 'place' is, in my view, quite unreal. It can, no doubt, be described as an installation as can anything which has been installed, such as an entry-phone, inter-communication system or television line system. 'Installations' within the definition of 'premises' do not, however, in my view, cover such systems. If an electrician is working on a switch or length of wire in the hall of a block, the 'place' where he is working is, in my view, the hall and not the switch.

Before turning to the second of the three questions, I should refer to a further argument of counsel for the appellants, namely that the block of flats should be considered as a whole and that, so considered, it fell within the definition of 'domestic premises'. This argument I reject. The block consists of a number of places occupied as separate dwellings and thus of a number of domestic premises and of certain common parts which, by reason of their common use, are excluded from the definition. Counsel for the appellants was constrained to accept that, if on the ground floor there was a movable stall for selling goods, this would be a movable structure and thus premises within the definition, but non-domestic premises. It is, in my view, wholly artificial to construe the definition so that the entire block would be domestic premises if there was no such stall but not domestic premises if there were such a stall.

(2) *Are the common parts made available to persons not employed by the appellants as a place of work?*

'Place of work' is not defined in the Act but there are definitions of 'work' and 'at work' in s 52(1). This subsection provides:

'For the purposes of this Part—(a) "work" means work as an employee or as a self-

employed person; (b) an employee is at work throughout the time when he is in the
course of his employment, but not otherwise; and (c) a self-employed person is at    a
work throughout such time as he devotes to work as a self-employed person; and,
subject to the following subsection, the expressions "work" and "at work", in
whatever context, shall be construed accordingly.'

When lift engineers or electricians attend at the block to inspect, maintain or repair
the lifts or electrical installations they are, when carrying out inspection, maintenance or
repair, plainly 'at work' within the definition. If the lift engineers spend three weeks    b
working on the lifts or electricians spend three weeks working in or on the hall, landings
and staircases, it appears to me that the common parts are made available to them as a
place of work. Such parts are for the duration of the three weeks, as a matter of plain
language, their place of work and one made available to them by the appellants, who
might, for example, give notice to all tenants that no 1 lift was out of use for the period
in order that the work might be carried out. In the same way, if the common parts are    c
redecorated by a firm of contractors, such parts are made available to the contractor's
employees as their place of work.

It was submitted that the common parts were not made available as a place of work to
maintenance men. I cannot see why not. Electricians and lift engineers are, it seems to
me, within the ambit of this section just as much as the employees of a cleaning
contractor who attend daily to clean the common parts. It may be that, in the case of    d
maintenance men, the duty imposed by s 4(2) will, in some cases, afford them less
protection, but that is a separate matter.

(3)  *Are the common parts made available to persons not employed by the appellants as a place*
*where they may use plant or substances provided for their use there?*

By s 53, plant includes any machinery, equipment or appliance. The lifts and electrical    e
installation are, in my judgment, within the definition of 'plant' and are provided for the
use of all persons lawfully using the common parts, be they tenants, visitors in the course
of their employment and thus 'at work', maintenance men, cleaners, decorators and so
on. Such plant is made available for the use of all such persons and, in so far as such
persons are not employees of the appellants, s 4 will apply. If they are such employees,
the appellants will have similar duties under s 2.    f

In reaching the above conclusions I have not found it necessary to rely on the provisions
of s 1 of the Act, for I have felt no doubt about the meaning of the particular provisions
which fall to be construed. Had I felt any such doubt, it would, however, have been set
at rest by those provisions. The objects of the Act are, so far as immediately material, to
secure the health, safety and welfare of persons at work and to protect persons not at
work against risks to health and safety arising in connection with the activities of persons    g
at work, which risks are to be treated as including risks attributable to the manner of
conducting an undertaking (see s 1(1)(a) and (b) and s 1(3)). The lift engineers and
electricians are persons at work. If the appellants' manner of conducting their undertaking
is to allow the lifts and electrical installations to become dangerous, all persons, whether
or not at work, will be exposed to risks and the object of the Act will be defeated if a
narrow construction is given to the succeeding sections.    h

I would dismiss the appeal.

**FOX LJ.** We are concerned with three improvement notices served by the Westminster
City Council on Select Managements Ltd (the appellants) under the Health and Safety at
Work etc Act 1974 in respect of the common parts of a block of flats in London. Two of
the notices relate to lifts in the block of flats; and the other relates to electrical installations    j
in the common parts. The appellants manage the block.

Section 4 of the 1974 Act is applicable only to 'non-domestic premises'. The first matter
to be determined is whether the common parts of the block are 'non-domestic premises'
within s 4. The expression is defined, by s 53 of the Act, by reference to the expressions
'domestic premises' and 'premises' as follows:

'. . . "domestic premises" means premises occupied as a private dwelling (including any garden, yard, garage, outhouse or other appurtenance of such premises which is not used in common by the occupants of more than one such dwelling), and "non-domestic premises" shall be construed accordingly . . .

"premises" includes any place and, in particular, includes . . . (b) any installation on land . . .'

In my opinion, the common parts of the block, whether halls, stairs, corridors, lifts or other parts, are plainly 'non-domestic premises' within the definition since they are used in common by the occupants of more than one private dwelling, namely the occupants of the individual flats, and are therefore not 'domestic premises' within the definition. The contention was advanced that, while the common parts are indeed used in common by the occupants of the flats, they are not 'premises' at all. I need not consider the ambit of the word 'premises' apart from statutory definition. The word is, in fact, defined by s 53 as including, inter alia, 'any place' and 'any installation on land'. Halls, corridors and stairs are certainly 'places'; and the lift complexes are 'installations on land' and parts of them at least are 'places'. A further argument was advanced that to direct the question to the status of the common parts is wrong. One should consider the block as a whole; and the block as a whole, it is said, must be domestic premises. I do not think that is right. The plain fact is that the block consists of a number of domestic premises, the individual flats, plus the common parts.

Now, s 4 of the Act imposes obligations on persons in control of premises. It is not in dispute that the appellants is in control of any relevant non-domestic premises for present purposes. Section 4 imposes liability on the persons having control in relation to persons who—

'(a) are not their employees; but (b) use non-domestic premises made available to them as a place of work or as a place where they may use plant or substances provided for their use there . . .'

Since, as it seems to me, there are non-domestic premises under the control of the appellants, the question then is whether those premises are made available to, and used by, persons not employed by the appellants as a place of work or as a place where such persons may use plant or substances provided for their use.

At this point I should refer to the factual position. We have scanty information about user. It is accepted that there is a caretaker in the block of flats, though it does not appear by whom he is employed. Further, as I understand it, it is accepted that persons who are not in the employ of the appellants do from time to time go to the block for purposes of lift maintenance and attending to electrical installations. It seems that the repairs required by the council have, in fact, been done and what the parties are concerned about now is not the form or content of the improvement notices but determination of the question of principle relating to the position of a lift engineer or other workman who is engaged in repairs or other works to the common parts of the block.

I consider then whether common parts are 'made available' to persons not employed by the company 'as a place of work'.

Section 52(1) of the Act is in the following terms:

'. . . (a) "work" means work as an employee or as a self-employed person; (b) an employee is at work throughout the time when he is in the course of his employment, but not otherwise; and (c) a self-employed person is at work throughout such time as he devotes to work as a self-employed person; and, subject to the following subsection, the expressions "work" and "at work", in whatever context, shall be construed accordingly.'

This provision seems to me to resolve any question whether a lift engineer or electrician who is engaged on lift maintenance or repair or on repair or maintenance of electrical installations is at 'work'. I think he is; and that is so whether he is employed or self-employed. The employed person will be engaged in the course of his employment. And the self-employee will be in the course of his work as a self-employed person. But are the common parts a place of work? In my opinion, they are. It seems to me that, if an engineer is working in the lift shaft or is doing work on a piece of mechanism in a hallway or landing, then the lift shaft or the hallway or landing can, without misuse of language be called a place. Similarly, it seems to me that, if a contractor's workman comes to the flats to plaster a wall on a common stairway, he is engaged in work in a place in the common parts of the block. And I see no serious difficulty about the use of the words 'made available'. The place in the common parts, e g hall or landing or stairway, where a lift engineer, electrician or plasterer does his work is made available to him as a place for use in the course of his employment. And if, for example, a lift engineer has to mend a piece of equipment, he may take it away or he may mend it on the premises. If he mends it on the premises, such as a hall or landing adjoining the lift, that place is made available to him.

There remains, however, the question whether the common parts are 'made available' to persons who are not the company's employees 'as a place where they may use plant or substances provided for their use there'. Section 53(1) of the Act provides that 'plant' 'includes any machinery, equipment or appliance'. I see no reason to doubt that both the lifts and the electrical installations in the common parts come within that definition. Further, in my view, such lifts and electrical installations are properly described in the ordinary use of English, as provided for the use of all those persons who lawfully use the common parts, including contractors, builders, decorators, electricians and delivery men. If such persons are not in the employment of the company, they are within s 4(1).

The Act contains, by way not merely of preamble but of express enactment, a statement of what its provisions are intended to secure (see s 1). The conclusions which I have reached do not seem to me to be in conflict with that. One of the purposes of the Act is to secure 'the health, safety and welfare of persons at work' (see s 1(a)). The reduction of lifts and electrical installations to a dangerous condition does put at risk the safety of persons at work in the common parts, be they decorators or lift engineers doing maintenance work.

I would dismiss the appeal.

**SIR EDWARD EVELEIGH**[1]. The appellants control 6 Hall Road, London NW8, a residential block of flats. Three improvement notices were served on them by the council's inspector under s 21 of the Health and Safety at Work etc Act 1974. The notices related to the common parts of the block and they alleged that the appellants were:

'Contravening in circumstances that make it likely that the contravention will continue or be repeated, Section 4 of the Health and Safety at Work etc. Act 1974.'

Two notices specified work which was required to be done to each of two lifts in the building. The third notice required the common parts of the premises to be rewired and required renewal of any fittings found to be defective. For the purpose of this appeal, no distinction need be drawn between any of the three notices. There was an appeal against the notices to the industrial tribunal under s 24 of the 1974 Act. The tribunal allowed the appeal but their decision was reversed on appeal to the High Court ([1984] 1 All ER 994, [1984] 1 WLR 1058). From that decision the appellants, now appeal. The issue is whether the premises fell within s 4 of the 1974 Act, for if they did not there could be no contravention and therefore no basis for the serving of a notice under s 21. Section 21 reads:

'If an inspector is of the opinion that a person—(a) is contravening one or more of the relevant statutory provisions; or (b) has contravened one or more of those provisions in circumstances that make it likely that the contravention will continue or be repeated, he may serve on him a notice (in this Part referred to as "an improvement notice") stating that he is of that opinion, specifying the provision or provisions as to which he is of that opinion, giving particulars of the reasons why he

---
1  Sir Edward Eveleigh retired as a Lord Justice of Appeal on 21 December 1984

is of that opinion, and requiring that person to remedy the contravention or, as the case may be, the matters occasioning it within such period (ending not earlier than the period within which an appeal against the notice can be brought under section 24) as may be specified in the notice.'

The relevant statutory provision is contained in s 4, which reads:

'(1) This section has effect for imposing on persons duties in relation to those who—(a) are not their employees; but (b) use non-domestic premises made available to them as a place of work or as a place where they may use plant or substances provided for their use there, and applies to premises so made available and other non-domestic premises used in connection with them.

(2) It shall be the duty of each person who has, to any extent, control of premises to which this section applies or of the means of access thereto or egress therefrom or of any plant or substance in such premises to take such measures as it is reasonable for a person in his position to take to ensure, so far as is reasonably practicable, that the premises, all means of access thereto or egress therefrom available for use by persons using the premises, and any plant or substance in the premises or, as the case may be, provided for use there, is or are safe and without risks to health.

(3) Where a person has, by virtue of any contract or tenancy, an obligation of any extent in relation to—(a) the maintenace or repair of any premises to which this section applies or any means of access thereto or egress therefrom; or (b) the safety of or the absence of risks to health arising from plant or substances in any such premises; that person shall be treated, for the purposes of subsection (2) above, as being a person who has control of the matters to which his obligation extends.

(4) Any reference in this section to a person having control of any premises or matter is a reference to a person having control of the premises or matter in connection with the carrying on by him of a trade, business or other undertaking (whether for profit or not).'

There was no evidence that any working person had been on the premises other than the residential caretaker. As he was an employee of the appellants, it was necessary for the council to show that there was some other person, not an employee, who used the premises and to whom the premises were made available as a place of work. The council contended that anyone who might come and work on the premises would bring into operation s 4, for example, a window cleaner, and it was also contended that the lift repairer would be such a person. There was no evidence that there was or ever had been any person in relation to whom a duty existed under s 4(1) at any time when the premises were defective. Consequently, I find it difficult to see how the foundation can be laid for the service of a notice under s 21. It is interesting to note that the notices do not allege a past contravention. They use a formula that is a mixture of s 21(a) and s 21(b). To rely on the future lift repairer as the person to whom the duty is owed seems to me to produce an absurdity. If there has been no breach in the past and if there is no one who currently has a workplace there, it follows that, on the council's argument, s 4 can only be brought into play when steps are taken to repair the lift in obedience to the notice. It would be tempting to say that the way to avoid the consequences of the 1974 Act would be for the appellants to do nothing. What the consequences would be under the Occupiers Liability Act 1957 to visitors on the premises is another matter.

In so far as the council have relied on visits by the milkmen and the postmen, I do not think that they help. There are many people who have no place of work, for example, travellers and hawkers, unless perhaps they have a base from which they operate. The milkman's depot and the postman's sorting office may be their place of work, but not every place at which they happen to be during the course of their employment will be a place of work.

I gather that the repairs have now been done. The parties none the less seek a ruling on the proper interpretation of s 4 of the 1974 Act. Consequently, bearing in mind the difficulties on the facts which I have mentioned, the argument before this court has concentrated on the position of a lift repairer or other workman who is engaged in repairing common parts of a block of flats. The appellants contend that those common parts are domestic premises and, further or alternatively, that they are not used or made available as a place of work.

By s 53(1) of the 1974 Act it is provided that:

'... "domestic premises" means premises occupied as a private dwelling (including any garden, yard, garage, outhouse or other appurtenance of such premises which is not used in common by the occupants of more than one such dwelling), and "non-domestic premises" shall be construed accordingly ...
"premises" includes any place and, in particular, includes—(a) any vehicle, vessel, aircraft or hovercraft ... and (c) any tent or movable structure ...'

I agree with the judge that the common parts are non-domestic premises. They are clearly premises. They are not occupied as a private dwelling but as part of a building which provides a facility used in common by the occupants of more than one private dwelling. I cannot accept the argument that the whole building must be looked at from the point of view of the landord and treated as a private dwelling occupied by him.

The question that remains, therefore, is whether a person who carries out repairs to non-domestic premises can be said to 'use non-domestic premises made available to him as a place of work'. To say that he does so is, in my opinion, straining the English language. I understand the words to mean that the premises are provided for the purpose of affording a place at which a person may carry out his work. There is contemplated a situation where a person has work to do but requires a place in which to do it. The statute and cases which are concerned with the safety of workers reveal many niceties of expression in relation to places where work is performed. We speak of working place, working platform, any place at which any person has at any time to work and also workplace or place of work. The council seek to equate a 'place of work' with a 'place at which any person has at any time to work'. To my mind, a place of work usually has a degree of permanence or continuity. It is not the object of the work but the place which is used to carry out work which has an end product quite separate from the place itself. The above was my immediate reaction to the meaning of s 4 of the 1974 Act. However, I turned to the meaning of 'available' in the Shorter Oxford Dictionary as a check. I think it is interesting to reproduce the entry: '1. Capable of producing a desired result (arch. or Obs.) 1502. 2.Of advantage (to, unto) (arch.) 1474. 3. Capable of being turned to account; hence at one's disposal, within one's reach 1827.' I find the entry wholly consistent with the interpretation for which the appellants contend.

In the phrase under consideration I think it right to treat the words 'as a place of work' as governed by the word 'use' as well as the words 'made available to them'. As I mentioned above, the word 'premises' includes a vehicle. I find it extremely difficult to regard a mechanic working inside a motor car as using it as a place of work and more difficult still to regard the owner as having made it available to the mechanic as a place of work.

This is a penal statute. Subject to the minister's power to limit the penalty, a contravention of a requirement imposed by an improvement notice was made punishable by a term of imprisonment for a period up to two years. No doubt s 4 of the 1974 Act will apply to a wide variety of cases. It has been possible to avoid the responsibilities which an employer has to his employees by entering into agreements which do not result in an employer/employee relationship. There are many cases where people are engaged as independent contractors and use premises and facilities provided for them in circumstances where the person in control of those premises has not come within the penal provisions of the Factories Act 1961 and other safety regulations. I do not say this with any intention of laying down boundaries for the application of s 4 of the 1974 Act.

I mention it, however, because I feel that the present case is far from anything that the
*a* legislature had in mind.

I would allow this appeal.

*Appeal dismissed. Leave to appeal to the House of Lords refused.*

Solicitors: *Penningtons* (for the appellants); *Terence F Neville* (for the council).
*b*

Celia Fox    Barrister.

# Miles v Wakefield Metropolitan District Council

*c*

COURT OF APPEAL, CIVIL DIVISION

EVELEIGH, FOX AND PARKER LJJ

17, 18 DECEMBER 1984, 8 FEBRUARY 1985

*Registrar – Superintendent registrar of births, deaths and marriages – Remuneration – Registrar*
*d* *paid by local authority – Powers of dismissal for breach of statutory duty exercisable by Registrar*
*General – Whether registrar employed by local authority – Whether office-holder or employee –*
*Whether local authority bound to pay full salary despite registrar's breach of statutory duties –*
*Registration Service Act 1953, s 6(3)(4).*

The plaintiff was a superintendent registrar of births, deaths and marriages in the
*e* defendant council's area. By s 6(3)[a] of the Registration Service Act 1953 the council was
responsible for paying the appellant's salary. Section 6(4) provided that superintendent
registrars held office 'during the pleasure of the Registrar General'. The plaintiff's hours
of work were 37 hours per week including 3 hours on Saturday mornings. From August
1981 until October 1982, as part of industrial action and in breach of his statutory duties,
the plaintiff refused to conduct marriage ceremonies on Saturday mornings, although he
*f* carried out other duties normally on that morning. The council refused to pay the
plaintiff for Saturday morning work and withheld part of his salary. An action by the
plaintiff to recover the amount withheld was dismissed and he appealed to the Court of
Appeal, contending that he was an office-holder and not an employee of the council and
therefore his salary was a reward for the tenure of that office rather than for the carrying
out of the functions of that office. The council contended that the plaintiff was both an
*g* office-holder and an employee of the council under a contract of employment, which
meant that the council did not have an unqualified obligation to pay the plaintiff and
they could not be required to pay his full salary irrespective of wilful refusal by him to
perform all or part of his duties.

**Held** – Under the 1953 Act a superintendent registrar was a statutory office-holder and
*h* accordingly the plaintiff was not an employee of the council, nor had he any contractual
relationship with the council. Furthermore (Sir Edward Eveleigh dissenting), under
s 6(3) of that Act the council had an unqualified obligation to pay the appellant's salary
for as long as he held office and if the appellant was in breach of any of his statutory
duties the council was not entitled to take what was, in effect, disciplinary financial action
against him, the only remedy for such breach lying in the Registrar General's power of
*j* dismissal. Accordingly, the appellant was entitled to recover the salary which had been
withheld. The appeal would therefore be allowed (see p 909 *b*, p 910 *c* to *e*, p 911 *g* to *j*, p
912 *c d*, p 913 *b* to *j*, p 914 *a* and p 915 *h j*, post).

---

*a*    Section 6, so far as material, is set out at p 915 *c*, post

**Notes**
For employee's right to remuneration, see 16 Halsbury's Laws (4th edn) paras 532–535, *a* and for cases on the subject, see 20 Digest (Reissue) 290–295, 2645–2668.

For the appointment and remuneration of superintendent registrars, see 39 Halsbury's Laws (4th edn) para 1072.

For the Registration Service Act 1953, s 6, see 27 Halsbury's Statutes (3rd edn) 1057.

**Cases referred to in judgments** *b*
*Barthorpe v Exeter Diocesan Board of Finance* [1979] ICR 900, EAT.
*Cuckson v Stones* (1858) 1 E & E 248, [1843–60] All ER Rep 390, 120 ER 902.
*Cutter v Powell* (1795) 6 Term Rep 320, [1775–1802] All ER Rep 159, 101 ER 573.
*Flarty v Odlum* (1790) 3 Term Rep 681, 100 ER 801.
*Gorse v Durham CC* [1971] 2 All ER 666, [1971] 1 WLR 775.
*Liverpool Corp v Wright* (1859) 28 LJ Ch 868. *c*
*102 Social Club and Institute Ltd v Bickerton* [1977] ICR 911, EAT.
*Palmer v Vaughan* (1818) 3 Swan 173, 36 ER 818.
*R v Barratt (George)* [1976] 3 All ER 895, [1976] 1 WLR 946, CA.
*Secretary of State for Employment v Associated Society of Locomotive Engineers and Fireman (No 2)* [1972] 2 All ER 949, [1972] 2 QB 455, [1972] 2 WLR 1370, NIRC and CA.
*Slingsby's Case* (1680) 3 Swan 178, 36 ER 821. *d*
*Wells v Foster* (1841) 8 M & W 149, [1835–42] All ER Rep 549, 151 ER 987.

**Cases also cited**
*Apthorpe v Apthorpe* (1887) 12 PD 192.
*Boston Deep Sea Fishing and Ice Co v Ansell* (1888) 39 Ch D 339, [1886–90] All ER Rep 65.
*Button v Thompson* (1869) LR 4 CP 330. *e*
*Healey v SA Française Rubastic* [1917] 1 KB 946.
*Henthorne and Taylor v Central Electricity Generating Board* [1980] IRLR 361, CA.
*Royle v Trafford BC* [1984] IRLR 184.

**Appeal**
Henry Gladstone Miles appealed against the order and judgment of Nicholls J given on 9 *f* November 1983 dismissing his claim for £774·06 plus interest pursuant to s 35A of the Supreme Court Act 1981 as money had and received by the respondents, the Wakefield Metropolitan District Council, to the appellant's use, or as a debt owed by the respondents to the appellant. The facts are set out in the judgment of Parker LJ.

*Stephen Sedley QC* for the appellant.
*Alexander Irvine QC* and *M R Taylor* for the respondents. *g*

*Cur adv vult*

8 February. The following judgments were delivered.

*h*
**PARKER LJ** (giving the first judgment at the invitation of Fox LJ). The appellant is, and at all material times was, a superintendent registrar of births, deaths and marriages, appointed and entitled to be paid by the respondent council pursuant to the provisions of the Registration Service Act 1953. His normal hours of work per week were 37, three of which were from 9.00 am to 12.00 noon on Saturdays. His functions included the performance of marriage ceremonies. Saturday mornings were the most popular times *j* with the public for the performance of this particular function and, until about August 1981, the appellant regularly performed a number of such ceremonies at those times. From August 1981 to October 1982, however, the appellant refused to carry out this particular function on Saturday mornings. He did so on the instructions of his union with the deliberate intention, as part of industrial action, of causing inconvenience to the public. Such action was aimed at securing increased remuneration and it was no doubt hoped that, in order to avoid the inconvenience, the public would exert pressure on the

a respondents and others in a like position to accord such increased remuneration. The respondents' response to the appellant's refusal to perform marriage ceremonies on Saturday mornings was to withhold 3/37ths of his salary, that is to say not to pay him at all for Saturday mornings, notwithstanding that on such mornings he carried out other of his functions. The total amount withheld was £774·06. It is now accepted that, in refusing to perform his marriage function on Saturday mornings, the appellant was in breach of his obligations. His claim to recover the amount withheld was instituted in the
b county court but was rightly transferred to the High Court, where it was dismissed by Nicholls J. From that dismissal he now appeals.

With regard to the appellant's conduct the judge found as follows:

c
'Throughout the period of industrial action Mr Miles continued to attend his office and work during his normal hours of work each week, the only difference being in the pattern in which he chose to discharge his various functions over a weekly period. He refused to conduct any marriage ceremonies on Saturday mornings, but on that morning he undertook other work instead. He continued to conduct weddings for all those who wished to avail themselves of his services, but only from Monday to Friday.'

d For present purposes it is unnecessary to go further into the facts. As to the basis on which the appellant's claim was dismissed, the position may also be stated very shortly. Section 5 of the 1953 Act provides that, for the purposes of the Registration Acts, there is to be, in every non-metropolitan county and metropolitan district, one or more districts and that for each district there is to be a superintendent registrar. Section 6 of the 1953 Act provides that every superintendent registrar shall (subject to a proviso to be mentioned later) be appointed by the council of the non-metropolitan county and
e metropolitan district in which his district is situated and shall be a salaried officer paid by such council.

The respondents were thus under a statutory obligation to appoint and to pay the appellant. As to the statutory obligation to pay, the judge said:

f
'In my view, it is implicit in the Wakefield Council's obligation to pay Mr Miles that the council is so obliged only when Mr Miles is duly carrying out his statutory obligations. If he declines to carry out all or a part of his obligations, he cannot require the council to pay all or an appropriate part of his salary.'

He then concluded that the deduction or withholding of 3/37ths of the appellants salary was appropriate and 'was a fair measure of the extent to which Mr Miles was failing to
g carry out his statutory obligations week by week'. The principal contention of counsel for the apellant was that the appellant was the holder of an office and that his salary was a reward for the tenure of that office and not for the carrying out of the functions of that office. Hence, no matter that he was in breach of his duties or even that he wrongfully refused to work, he was entitled to be paid in full, the only remedy for misconduct lying in the power of the Registrar General to remove him from office.

h For the respondents, counsel's argument amounted in substance to no more than the assertion that Parliament cannot, when imposing on councils the obligation to pay, have intended that such obligation was unqualified and required them to pay full salary irrespective of wilful refusal by a superintendant registrar to perform all or part of his functions for any period however long so long as he was not removed from office by the Registrar General.

j The arguments on both sides expanded during the course of the hearing partly because, although (1) it was not alleged in the pleadings that the appellant was an employee of the respondents, (2) it was common ground before the judge that the appellant was not such an employee, (3) there was no cross-notice seeking to raise any such point and (4) both the relevant statutes and the documents indicated that, although superintendent registrars were appointed and paid by the relevant councils, they were not employees of such councils, counsel for the respondents sought leave to contend that the appellant was both the holder of an office under the Crown or statute and an employee of the respondents under a contract of employment. The development of the arguments was also in part due to the fact that it appeared to us that it was or might be material when considering *a* the construction of the statute to know what would have been the position had the appellant been employed under a contract of employment.

There can, in my opinion, be no doubt that it is much too late to permit the respondents to contend that the appellant was employed by the respondents under a contract of employment, or indeed was in any contractual relationship with the respondents such as by a contract for services. There was, for example, no investigation *b* before the judge concerning the circumstances of the appellant's initial appointment which would, if a contract was being asserted, have been essential. Counsel for the appellant submitted that leave to take the point should also be refused on the simple ground that, having regard to the provisions of the 1953 Act, it was unarguable. For reasons which will presently appear, this submission is, in my judgment, well founded. Accordingly, this case must be determined on the basis that there is and was no *c* contractual relationship between the parties.

*The statutory provisions*

Nicholls J having proceeded on the basis that the matter turned on the construction of the 1953 Act, it is convenient to consider next the relevant provisions. It is first necessary to note that the registration service is by ss 1 to 4 of the 1953 Act headed by a Registrar *d* General who is appointed by Her Majesty, who holds office during Her Majesty's pleasure and who is paid out of moneys provided by Parliament. The 1953 Act then provides by ss 5 to 12 for the general organisation of the service.

In general terms this is to be by superintendent registrars in districts and by registrars in sub-districts. These officers are to be, in general, appointed and paid by the relevant councils but by s 6(4) it is provided that they shall hold office during the pleasure of the *e* Registrar General. However, if a vacancy occurs in either office and the relevant council refuses to fill the vacancy or fails, after notice given by the Registrar General, to do so within the time specified in the notice, the Registrar General is to make the necessary appointment. In such a case, the relevant council, although it will neither have appointed nor have any power of dismissal, will still be obliged to pay the salary.

Although at present we are directly concerned only with superintendent registrars, it *f* is necessary to consider also certain other officers. By s 7 of the 1953 Act the Registrar General and a superintendent registrar, with the approval of the Registrar General, may from time to time appoint additional registrars of marriages. Such persons will hold office during the pleasure of the Registrar General if appointed by him. If appointed by a superintendent registrar they will hold office during his pleasure but will also be removable by the Registrar General. However appointed, such additional registrars are *g* entitled to retain fees received by or payable to them under the Marriage Act 1949, subject to the proviso that at such times and in such manner as may be prescribed they must pay to the relevant council so much of the total sums received or payable to them such amount as the Registrar General may certify to be equal to one-third of such total sums less any amount that the Registrar General may allow as remuneration for the trouble and expense of collecting and accounting for such third parts. *h*

The council's interest in the case of additional registrars is thus only in the receipt of one-third of the fees. They neither appoint nor pay nor dismiss. Nevertheless, any refusal on the part of any additional registrar to perform marriages may clearly affect the council financially, for it may result in a reduction in the fees collected and thus of the fraction payable to the council.

Sections 8 and 9 of the 1953 Act provide for deputy and interim superintendent *j* registrars and registrars. Deputies must be appointed by all superintendent registrars and registrars. They hold office during the pleasure of the officers appointing them but are removable by the Registrar General. In broad terms their function is to carry out the duties of those appointing them when such persons are not available.

An interim officer of either kind is to function where the relevant permanent officer ceases to hold office. In such a case, if the permanent officer has only one deputy, that

deputy automatically takes over as interim officer. If he has more than one deputy, the
a clerk of the relevant council is to determine which one shall be interim officer. If he has
no deputy the clerk of the relevant council is to appoint an interim officer. An interim
officer, until a new permanent officer is appointed, has all the powers and duties of the
office. The sections make no provision for the remuneration of either deputies or interim
officers.

The provisions of the 1953 Act mentioned thus far appear to me to point strongly to
b the conclusion that all officers in the registration service are statutory office-holders and
are not in contractual relationship with the relevant council. I should also mention one
further provision. Some superintendent registrars and registrars in office at the date of
the commencement of the 1953 Act were not then salaried officers but were remunerated
by way of a portion of the fees collected by them in the same way as additional registrars
appointed under the 1953 Act. Such a person would by s 18 remain unsalaried unless
c and until he applied to become a salaried officer. When and if he applied he would
become a salaried officer under s 6 whether or no the relevant council desired it. The
council's only freedom of action would lie in the ability of the clerk to specify the date,
which must not be later than the beginning of the next financial year, when the change
should become operative. This too indicates that the position cannot be contractual.

Having dealt with general organisation, the 1953 Act provides for local organisation
d in ss 13 and 14. Section 13 provides for there to be a scheme or schemes known as local
schemes for each non-metropolitan county or metropolitan district and requires each
local scheme to make provision for a number of specified matters including, by sub-s
(2)—

'. . . (e) fixing, subject to such power of revision as may be provided by the scheme,
e the salary and other remuneration, if any, to be attached to each office, and the
allowances, if any, to be paid for travelling, for the provision of office accommodation
and for other expenses; (f) fixing, subject to such power of revision as may be
provided by the scheme, the conditions on which an office is to be held, so, however,
that nothing in the scheme shall affect the power of the Registrar General to remove
from office an officer in any case in which the Registrar General is satisfied that the
f officer has been guilty of serious default in the performance of the duties imposed
on him by the Registration Acts or any regulations made thereunder; (g) applying
with any necessary modifications, adaptations and exceptions the provisions of the
Local Govenment Act, 1929, relating to the transfer, superannuation and
compensation of officers; (h) conferring on the proper officer of the non-metropolitan
county or metropolitan district powers with respect to—(i) the fixing of the hours
g of attendance of officers; (ii) the distribution of business between officers; (iii) the
transfer of superintendent registrars and registrars of births and deaths within or
between districts.'

It also provides that a local scheme may in addition make provision for certain further
matters which it is unnecessary to specify.

Local schemes are to be proposed by the relevant councils and submitted to the
h minister for approval. They do not take effect unless and until approved by him.

There are thus in s 13, albeit subject to the approval of the minister, wide powers in
the relevant council with regard to the amount of salary payable to salaried officers and
as to the conditions on which an office is held. However, it is noteworthy that the
Registrar General's power of removal for serious default of any officer in the performance
of the duties imposed by the 1953 Act or any regulations is not to be affected. It is also to
j be noted that the Local Government Act 1929 does not apply to officers unless the
scheme so provides.

Finally, so far as the 1953 Act is concerned, I refer to s 20, under which the Registrar
General, with the approval of the minister, may make regulations, inter alia—

'(a) prescribing the duties of superintendent registrars, registrars of births and
deaths and registrars of marriages in the execution of any enactment relating to

their functions; (b) prescribing the duties under the Registration Acts of proper officers of non-metropolitan counties and metropolitan districts, and such other officers as may be appointed in pursuance of any local scheme . . .'

It is therefore, as one might expect since he has the power of dismissal and is the head of the entire service, the Registrar General who is given the power to prescribing the duties both of officers of the service and of clerks to relevant councils.

We were referred to the Registration of Births, Deaths and Marriage Regulations 1968, SI 1968/2049, made by the Registrar General, reg 10(3) of which provides:

'An officer shall comply with any instruction or direction, whether particular or general, given to him by the Registrar General in any matter relating to the due performance by the officer of his duties in the execution of any enactment relating to his functions (not being a matter for which specific provision is made).'

We were further referred to the Local Government Superannuation Regulations 1974, SI 1974/520, by reg A6 of which, registration officers are for the purposes of those regulations deemed to be officers in the employment of the relevant councils.

In my judgment the appellant is, in the light of the statutory provisions, clearly not an employee or officer of the council by whom he is paid and is in no contractual relationship with it. I regard the contrary as unarguable.

What then is the consequence of the conclusion that the appellant is a statutory office-holder and has no contractual relationship with the respondents, albeit the respondents are obliged to pay his salary?

Counsel for the appellant submits that it is the simple one that the appellant is entitled to his full salary unless and until the Registrar General dismisses him. In support of this proposition he relies on four cases which, in chronological order, are *Flarty v Odlum* (1790) 3 Term Rep 681, 100 ER 801, *Wells v Foster* (1841) 8 M & W 149, [1835–42] All ER Rep 549, *Palmer v Vaughan* (1818) 3 Swan 173, 36 ER 818 and *Liverpool Corp v Wright* (1859) 28 LJ Ch 868.

Neither *Flarty v Odlum* nor *Wells v Foster* is, in my opinion, of any assistance. The first concerned the assignability of half pay by an army officer, and the second the assignability of a pension granted to a retired audit clerk. Neither was, at the material time, obliged to do any work. *Palmer v Vaughan* concerned the assignability of the profits of the office of a clerk of the peace, but no decision on that point was made. The case was cited by counsel for the appellant solely for a note of *Slingsby's Case* (1680) 3 Swan 178, 36 ER 821 extracted from Lord Nottingham's manuscripts which appears as a footnote to *Palmer's* case (1818) 3 Swan 173 at 178, 36 ER 818 at 821. The issue in that case was whether the Master of the Mint could be suspended from office and it was held that he could. The office carried what was described as 'a mere salary'. Lord Nottingham in his note, having observed that other high officers had previously been suspended and that he would seal the patent of suspension, said (3 Swan 178 at 179, 36 ER 821):

'. . . nor do I do this because I am so required, but because I think the law allows it; for it is expressly within the difference of all the books, it being an office without any profits but the mere salary, which must be continued . . .'

*Slingsby's Case* is, in so far as it is authority for anything other than the right of the Crown to suspend, authority only for the proposition that, if the holder of an office is suspended when he is ready and willing to perform his office, he is entitled to be paid during his suspension. It is of little, if any, assistance to counsel for the appellant, whose contention is that, if an office holder wrongfully refuses to perform the functions of his office, he is nevertheless entitled to his salary.

There remains the *Liverpool Corp* case, which concerned a clerk of the peace whose office was held during good behaviour and whose remuneration was by way of fees attached to the office. He expressly agreed on his appointment to accept a fixed salary of £500 and to account to the council for any fees received beyond this amount. The matter for determination was whether the agreement was valid. It was held that it was not on

two grounds, one of which only is presently relevant. As to this, Page Wood V-C said (28
LJ Ch 868 at 871):

> 'Then there is a second ground of public policy, for which the case of *Palmer* v.
> *Vaughan* is the leading authority, which is this, that independently of any corrupt
> bargain with the appointor, nobody can deal with the fees of a person who holds an
> office of this description, because the law presumes, with reference to an office of
> trust, that he requires the payment which the law has assigned to him for the
> purpose of upholding the dignity and performing properly the duties of that office;
> and therefore it will not allow him to part with any portion of those fees either to
> the appointor or to anybody else.'

There was no question in that case of the clerk of the peace doing anything other than
performing properly the duties of his office, and it is no authority for the proposition
that an office holder is entitled to receive moneys payable for properly performing his
duties when he is refusing to do any such thing.

The authorities on which counsel for the appellant relies do not, therefore, assist him.
If they do not, then the only means of determining the question before us is the means
adopted by the judge, namely as a question of the true construction of the 1953 Act.

The conclusion arrived at by the judge that, if the appellant declines to carry out part
of his statutory obligations, an appropriate part of his salary may be withheld appears to
me to present great difficulty. This is particularly so in a case such as the present when
the refusal related only to the pattern of work and when the recalcitrant officer worked
his full hours. It is difficult to accept that when Parliament imposed the obligation on a
council to pay the salary, it intended that the council should be entitled to withhold some
part of his salary for any and every breach of duty. When, as here, no complaint was
made to the Registrar General and, as the judge found, the Registrar General's inspector
who visited Wakefield in January 1982 while the industrial action was in operation not
only made no adverse comment on the appellant's refusal but congratulated him on the
excellent way in which the service was run in the district, to withhold all pay for Saturday
mornings appears on the face of it unjust and thus unlikely to have been within the
parliamentary intent.

In my judgment, it was not within such intent. Clearly, where officers are remunerated
by way of fees, as are additional registrars of marriages and as were those superintendent
registrars and registrars who were so remunerated at the date of commencement of the
1953 Act and who had not elected to become salaried, no deduction could be made. It
might or might not be that, in that case, a refusal to perform marriages on Saturdays
would result in less fees being collected and thus the council's proportion being less, but
this would not give any right to increase the proportion and then withhold some of the
fees remaining in the hands of the officer. I cannot think that Parliament can have
intended that superintendent registrars who were appointed or had become salaried
officers under the 1953 Act should have been exposed to what is, in effect, disciplinary
financial action not available against additional registrars of marriages or existing non-
salaried officers before they changed. Such an intention would result, if the appellant had
been remunerated by fees for the first six months of the industrial action, in his being
subject to no financial sanction such as is contended for, but, on his change to salaried
officer, in his becoming at once so subject. I cannot accept this. In my judgment, the
obligation to pay is, while the officer holds office, unqualified. This does not mean that
the paying council are without remedy. For a serious breach the Registrar General would
no doubt dismiss. If it be the case that this puts officers in a better position than if they
were employees in this respect, this does not, in my judgment, affect the matter. If in
this respect they are in a better position, in others they are in a worse position. It is, for
example, common ground that they are not entitled to the benefits of the employment
protection legislation.

I find it unnecessary to decide whether, if the appellant had been an employee of the
respondents, they would have been entitled to withhold part of his salary, but I do not

accept that they would. Had that been the case, the respondents would no doubt have
had a claim for any damages they could prove but, in the absence of a breach amounting *a*
to a repudiation accepted by dismissal or a specific right to suspend, there appear to me
strong grounds for saying there is no right to withhold payment and take the benefit of
all work in fact done during the period in which the refusal to perform a particular
function was operative. *Gorse v Durham CC* [1971] 2 All ER 666, [1971] 1 WLR 775
appears to me to be authority for the proposition that there is no such right. The right is
asserted on the basis that an employee, in order to recover unpaid salary, must show that *b*
in the relevant period he was ready and willing to perform his contract and that, if he
was not, he can recover nothing even if his unwillingness did not go to the root of the
contract or, albeit that it did, it was not accepted as a repudiation. The validity of this
proposition may have to be decided in the future. As it was not fully argued before us
and does not require decision now, I say only that I regard the proposition as being of
doubtful validity.                                                                   *c*

In my judgment, officers such as the appellant are not, on the true construction of the
1953 Act, liable to have salary withheld for breach of their statutory obligations. The
remedy for such breach lies only in the Registrar General's power to dismiss. I would
allow this appeal, set aside the judgment of Nicholls J and enter judgment for the amount
claimed, with interest in such amount as may be agreed or, in default of agreement, as
may be determined by a master of the Chancery Division.                             *d*

**FOX LJ.** It was common ground before the judge that the appellant was not an employee
of the respondents. And the contrary was neither pleaded nor raised by notice on this
appeal. It is now asserted by the respondents, however, that the appellant was not merely
the holder of an office but also an employee of the respondents. I am not satisfied that *e*
the point is open to the respondents, but, in any event, I do not feel able to accept it.

The significant matters in relation to the respondents assertion, are, in my view, as
follows.

(i) Although the relevant local authorities appoint superintendent registrars, they hold
office only during the pleasure of the Registrar General (see s 6 of the Registration Service
Act 1953), who is the head of the registration service, is paid out of moneys provided by *f*
Parliament and holds office at the pleasure of the Crown. The Registrar General is quite
independent of the local authorities.

Local schemes (approved by the minister) may, inter alia, fix the conditions on which
an office may be held, but nothing is to affect the power of the Registrar General to
dismiss an officer for serious default.

(ii) On the occurrence of a vacancy in the office of superintendent registrar, if the local *g*
authority refuses, or fails after request by the Registrar General, to fill the vacancy, the
appointment may be made by the Registrar General (see s 6 of the 1953 Act).

(iii) A superintendent registrar may, with the consent of the Registrar General, appoint
additional registrars of marriages who will hold office during the pleasure of the
superintendent registrar but be removable by the Registrar General. A person so
appointed will keep the fees payable to him under the Marriage Act 1949 subject to the *h*
payment of a specified part to the local authority. Such additional registrars are thus
neither appointed nor dismissed by the local authority (see s 7 of the 1953 Act).

(iv) Deputy superintendent registrars, and deputy registrars, are appointed by the
superintendent registrar, or the registrar, as the case may be, and hold office during the
pleasure of the appointing officer but are removable by the Registrar General (see s 8 of
the 1953 Act).                                                                       *j*

(v) The Registrar General may, with the approval of the minister, make regulations
prescribing the duties of superintendent registrars in the execution of any enactment
relating to their functions (see s 20 of the 1953 Act). The Registration of Births, Deaths
and Marriages Regulations 1968, SI 1968/2049, reg 10(3) requires that an officer shall
comply with any instruction or direction of the Registrar General in any matter relating
to the performance of his specific statutory duties.

(vi) A superintendent registrar is 'a salaried officer paid by [the local authority]'. But he must account to the Registrar General for fees which he receives from the public in the execution of his duties and, on the direction of the Registrar General, will pay to the local authority such sums as the Registrar General certifies is due to the authority in respect of such fees (see s 6 of the 1953 Act).

(vii) The position of superintendent registrar is referred to in the statute as an 'office' (see for example, ss 6(1), 9(1), 15(1) and 18(1) of the 1953 Act).

In my opinion, a superintendent registrar is the holder of an office and is not employed by the local authority. It is true that the local authority will, normally, appoint him and will pay him and will provide the premises in which he works. But he holds office not at the will of the local authority but of the Registrar General. Further, his duties may be prescribed by the Registrar General with the consent of the minister. He has the power, with the consent of the Registrar General, of appointing additional registrars of marriage who hold office during the pleasure of but removable by the Registrar General; and the position as to the appointment of deputy superintendent registrars is similar. All these provisions seem to me to point against the degree of control one would expect to belong to the local authority if a master and servant relationship existed. I do not think that the relationship of a superintendent registrar with the local authority is contractual at all. It seems to me that the superintendent registrars are part of a national service, at the head of which is a person quite independent of the local authorities and that, although the service has in some respects a close contact with the local authorities, it is designedly kept at a distance from them in other, and important, respects. In general, I think that the respective obligations of the local authority and the superintendent registrar are wholly statutory in their origin and they can be given full effect to without imputing any contractual basis at all. I do not find assistance in the fact that the statute provides that a registrar shall be a 'salaried officer'. I think that is merely a formal recognition of the fact that superintendent registrars under the 1953 Act are not remunerated out of fees as were their statutory predecessors.

I proceed then on the basis that the superintendent registrar is an office-holder and no more. He was required under his conditions of service to work for 37 hours per week, including three hours on Saturday mornings. The judge held that the respondents were entitled to withhold 3/37ths of his salary as representing the three hours on Saturday mornings when he refused to conduct marriage ceremonies. I do not think that can be justified. The judge was of opinion that, while the statute does not expressly give the local authority any power to withhold payment of remuneration if the superintendent registrar does not make himself available to carry out the full range of his functions for any particular period, such power must be implied. In my view, the statute imposes on the local authority an obligation to pay the salary of superintendent registrars. There is no limitation on that obligation and it is not contractual. It is simply an unqualified statutory obligation. In particular, I see no warrant in the statute for any power in the local authority to make what, in some instances, would be deductions of salary computed on a somewhat arbitrary basis. The present case provides a sharp example of the sort of difficulties that the implied power would produce. Thus, the appellant was obliged under the local scheme to work 37 hours a week and did in fact work 37 hours a week. In respect of the relevant three hours on Saturdays, the position was not that he did not perform the functions of his office but that he did not perform these functions which the respondents desired him to perform on Saturday mornings. He did other work comprised in his duties as a superintendent registrar. There is no finding that such work was not necessary or was not properly performed or that what he was doing was not genuine work at all but was some sort of sham. And neither the Registrar General nor his inspector has made any complaint against the appellant in relation to the performance of his duties. He is therefore, under the order appealed from, suffering a deduction on a time basis computed in respect of a period when in fact, he worked the full time. I do not feel able to accept that Parliament can have intended that. It seems to me that the only remedy available in such a case is not by way of a reduction of salary but for the Registrar General to invoke his powers of dismissal.

I express no view as to the position if there had been a contract, since that does not arise.

I would allow the appeal.

**SIR EDWARD EVELEIGH**[1]. It was accepted by the respondents that the appellant was not their employee. It was further accepted on the authority of *R v Barrett (George)* [1976] 3 All ER 895, [1976] 1 WLR 946 that he was serving under the Crown. The judge found that, when the appellant rearranged his weekly work schedule, he did so not with a view the better to discharge his duties, but with the intention, in compliance with his union's instructions, of disrupting the smooth discharge of those duties and consequently he was not duly fulfilling his statutory obligations. There has been no attempt in this court to challenge any of the above matters although it has been contended on behalf of the respondents that there was a contractual relationship between them and the appellant.

On behalf of the appellant it has been submitted that he is the holder of an office and that his salary is an entitlement which goes with that office and is not payment for work done or services rendered in performance of the duties of that office. We have been referred to a number of cases in which the remuneration of an office-holder has been considered. For the reasons stated by Parker LJ I do not think that those authorities are of any assistance. Because the remuneration for one office is treated as being paid for the purpose of maintaining the status of that office, it does not follow that the salary of every office-holder is to be treated in the same way. Each case must depend on its own facts.

In *Barthorpe v Exeter Diocesan Board of Finance* [1979] ICR 900 it was held that the fact that the complainant as a stipendiary reader was an office-holder did not itself prevent him from being employed under a contract of service. Slynn J said (at 904):

'The primary submission made to us is that the complainant is an office holder. As such, it follows that he is not employed under any contract of service. We do not accept this. Merely to say that someone holds an office does not seem to us to decide the question which has to be decided under this Act. Some office holders may well not be employed under a contract of service. It does not follow that an office holder cannot be employed under a contract of service. The question, as we see it, under the Act is whether the office he holds is one the appointment to which is made by, or is coexistent with, a contract of service.'

It could equally well be said that it does not follow that a person is an office-holder that his salary is an entitlement of the office and not a payment for work done. Moreover, it does not follow that there cannot be conditions affecting the right to receive that salary which may be imposed by contract, by statute or which are in some other way attached to the office.

In *102 Social Club and Institute Ltd v Bickerton* [1977] ICR 911 it was held that the industrial tribunal should have considered the question whether the secretary in his capacity of an office-holder was merely a member of the club who received an honorarium for the work he did for the club, or whether he rendered the services to the club as an employee in return for the payment of a salary. Phillips J said (at 919):

'So the question is whether the payment was made contractually for the services, and whether the services were rendered in return for the payment, or whether it was a mere grant or solatium.'

The above two cases provide no direct answer to the question which we have to decide, but they and the cases referred to in them indicate clearly that each case has to be considered on its own facts. Decisions relating to the assignability of an army officer's pay or pension in the nineteenth century provide no assistance in considering the nature of a superintendent registrar's right to a salary payable in consequence of Registration Service Act 1953.

1 Sir Edward Eveleigh retired as a Lord Justice of Appeal on 21 December 1984

Before that Act was passed a superintendent registrar's remuneration came from the
*a* fees payable to him in respect of the execution of his duties. If he earned no fees he would
receive no pay. We are being asked to say that, in one respect at least, the superintendent
registrar's position has improved since the 1953 Act in that his salary must now be paid
to him whether or not he performs his duties provided he continues to hold the office.

It is argued that, as the Registrar General is the only person who can dismiss a
superintendent registrar, the salary is payable until he is thus dismissed. I cannot see that
*b* the power of dismissal must necessarily influence the terms on which the salary is payable
or be an indication of its nature. Such a line of reasoning merely sidesteps the vital
question, namely: is the remuneration an absolute entitlement of the office or is it a
salary which is paid in consideration of services rendered?

To answer this question one must go straightaway to the 1953 Act. Section 6 provides:

*c*
'(1) Every superintendent registrar and every registrar of births and deaths shall
be appointed by the council of the non-metropolitan county or metropolitan district,
in which his district or sub-district is situated . . .

(3) Every superintendent registrar and every registrar of births and deaths shall
be a salaried officer paid by the council of the non-metropolitan county or
metropolitan district, in which his district or sub-district is situated . . .

*d*
(4) Every superintendent registrar and every registrar of births and deaths shall
hold office during the pleasure of the Registrar General.'

Section 5 of the 1953 Act provides that there should be a superintendent registrar for
each district. Section 13 provides that there should be in force a local scheme in which
provision is made for a number of matters. These include the location of offices, the
number of superintendent registrars and other officers, the salary and other remuneration,
*e* if any, to be attached to each office and fixing conditions on which an office is to be held.
It is specifically provided that nothing in the scheme should affect the power of the
Registrar General to remove an officer. It also provided that the local scheme could confer
on the proper officer of the non-metropolitan county or metropolitan district general
powers of supervising the administration of the provisions of the Registration Acts. By
s 14 of the 1953 Act the minister's approval is required for the provisions of the local
*f* scheme.

By these provisions the 1953 Act is placing the initiative and the responsibility on the
local authority to see that registration services are available in their district. Not only is
the appointment of the superintendent registrar primarily the local authority's
responsibility but also, once appointed, he is to be a salaried officer paid by the local
authority. There is a marked contrast in the way in which provision is made for the
*g* salary of the Registrar General. Section 4 of the 1953 Act provides that the salary and the
expenses of the Registrar General are to be paid out of moneys provided by Parliament.

I must confess that on reading s 6(3), it seemed to me that the superintendent registrar,
when appointed, would become an officer of the council and that his remuneration
would be a salary in the same way that the remuneration of other officers of the council
was their salary. I would have gone a stage further and thought that the superintendent
*h* registrar was to be an employee of the council. The fact that he could be dismissed only
by the Registrar General and the fact that he would have a considerable measure of
independence in the performance of his duties need not necessarily have prevented this
conclusion. However, the concession made by counsel on behalf of the respondents
would seem to be well founded and is supported by the provisions of s 20 which
empowers the Registrar General with the approval of the minister to make regulations
*j* prescribing the duties of superintendent registrars. It is also supported by the Local
Government Superannuation Regulations 1974, SI 1974/520, which provide that for the
purpose of the regulations, registration officers shall be 'deemed' to be in the employment
of the local authority.

However, the fact that the superintendent registrar is an office-holder and is not in the
employment of the council will not inevitably lead to the conclusion that his

remuneration is the reward for the tenure as opposed to the discharge of his office. If
s 6(3) stood on its own, which it does not, I would still regard it as saying that the $a$
superintendent registrar's remuneration was payable by the council on the basis that he
was an officer of that council and that he should receive his salary on that basis. Precisely
what the salary would be and the terms on which it would be payable would, of course,
have to be determined. The council has to determine the salary and conditions of service
of its officers. By s 13 of the 1953 Act it is required to do this in relation to the
superintendent registrar but, in his case, it is necessary for the minister's approval to be $b$
obtained. It is, therefore, necessary to consider the local scheme.

Paragraph 5 of the local scheme is important and I set it out in full:

> '(1) Subject to the provisions of this Scheme, the extent of service for each
> principal office shall be that specified in the tables in schedule 2 and each principal
> officer shall be remunerated on the scale of salary determined in accordance with
> article 10 for the extent of service as from time to time amended of the principal $c$
> office or offices to which he is appointed: Provided that—(a) no principal officer
> shall be remunerated for more than whole-time service notwithstanding that he
> may be appointed to two or more principal offices any one of which is within or
> without the area; (b) where the extent of service for a principal office or offices
> exceeds whole-time service, the Council or the Councils of the areas in which those
> offices are held shall provide for assistance to be given to the extent of the excess: so, $d$
> however, that where a single office is held by more than one principal officer, the
> excess shall be calculated as the difference between the extent of service of that office
> and the combined whole-term service of the officers holding the office.
> (2) Where, after consultation with the Proper Officer, the Registrar General is
> satisfied that the extent of service for any principal office requires amendment, he
> may by notice in writing to the Council amend that extent from such date $e$
> subsequent to the consultation as he may determine: Provided that no reduction in
> the extent of service of any principal office shall be effective to reduce the service
> required to be given by the holder of that office at the time the reduction is made.'

'Extent of service' is defined as being average number of hours of service per week
required for the proper performance of the duties of a principal office. Consequently, we $f$
see in para 5 that the salary is related to the number of hours required for the proper
performance of the duties.

'Whole-time service' is defined as service amounting on average to a working week of
the number of hours specified from time to time in the scheme of conditions of service
as the normal hours of duty in offices of local authorities. In the present case the current
number was 37 hours. Consequently, the effect of para 5 is that, where the hours of $g$
service for the proper performance of the duties of the principal office is more than 37
hours, the superintendent registrar is to be given assistance.

The final proviso to para 5 is important. It shows that the 37 hours which is the basis
of the superintendent registrar's remuneration are required to be served and may still be
required of him even if the extent of service of the principal office is reduced.

The affinity of the registrar's salary with that of a local government officer is marked $h$
in para 10 of the local scheme, which provides:

> 'The scale of salary of principal officer or of a deputy designated by the Proper
> Officer shall be the scale from time to time determined by the National Joint
> Council as appropriate to the group in which the officer or deputy is included and
> the salary weighting provisions of the Scheme of Conditions of Service from time to
> time applicable shall apply as if the officer or deputy were a local government $j$
> officer.'

By para 12 of the local scheme it is provided that the National Joint Council's scheme of
conditions of service shall apply to each principal officer for the purposes of the grant of
ordinary, sick and maternity leave, the payment of travelling expenses and the payment
of removal expenses when transferred under the provisions of the local scheme.

a
The appellant's appointment was authorised by the 1953 Act. The provisions in the local scheme relating to his conditions of service and salary were drawn up pursuant to the provisions of the same Act. It is from the 1953 Act and the local scheme that we must determine the entitlement of the appellant to his salary. I find it unnecessary and strictly irrelevant to have regard to the history of the office, although I confess that I find it difficult to ignore the fact that, before the 1953 Act, the registrar was paid according to the fees he earned. To my mind, the local scheme indicates that a superintendent
b
registrar's salary is like most other salaries payable for work which he is required to do according to the terms of his appointment. The first definition of salary in *Stroud's Judicial Dictionary* (4th edn, 1974) vol 5, p 2426 commends itself to me for the purpose of the present case:

c
'"'Salarie' is a word often used in our bookes, and it signifies a recompence or consideration given unto any man for his paines bestowed upon another mans business" (*Termes de la Ley, Salarie*).'

This claim was made as a test case. As often happens when the parties seek to have a particular point determined, other matters, which might be relevant to the claim, are not dealt with with the thoroughness which one would expect if the recovery of the sum of money claimed was the principal or sole consideration. It was only when the question
d
was raised by the court that counsel addressed themselves to the right of an employer to withhold part of a salary when an employee absented himself from work. It was only when the matter was raised by the court that counsel adverted to the possibility of there being a contractual relationship of some kind between the parties, even though it was conceded that the relationship was not one of employer and employee.

The respondents delivered to the appellant a document containing the conditions of
e
his service. Acceptance of this document does not mean that there was a contract between the parties. The truth probably is that they never intended to enter into a formal contractual relationship seeing that their relationship was governed by statute. However, it does not matter. The relevant provisions are in the statute and local scheme and there is no need to invoke the document. As to the right of an employer to withhold part of the salary when an employee does not work, I find it impossible to lay down a general
f
rule other than there is no rule of law to prevent him from so doing. Each particular case, however, must depend on the terms of the particular engagement. As I have said, the local scheme is to the effect that the salary is payable in respect of services rendered and I see nothing in this case to show that the respondents are required to pay when services were not rendered.

In *Secretary of State for Employment v Associated Society of Locomotive Engineers and*
g
*Fireman (No 2)* [1972] 2 All ER 949 at 967, [1972] 2 QB 455 at 492 Lord Denning MR said:

'. . . is a man to be entitled to wages for his work when he, with others, is doing his best to make it useless? Surely not. Wages are to be paid for services rendered, not for producing deliberate chaos. The breach goes to the whole of the consideration, as was put by Lord Campbell CJ in *Cuckson v Stones* (1858) 1 E & E 248 at 255,
h
[1843–60] All ER Rep 390 at 392, and with other cases quoted in Smith's Leading Cases (13th edn 1929) vol 2, p 48, the notes to *Cutter v Powell* (1795) 6 Term Rep 320, [1775–1802] All ER Rep 159.'

I therefore would dismiss this appeal.

i
*Appeal allowed. Leave to appeal to the House of Lords refused.*

*1 April. The Appeal Committee of the House of Lords granted the respondent leave to appeal.*

Solicitors: *Penelope Grant* (for the appellant); *Lawrence A Tawn*, Wakefield (for the respondents).

Celia Fox    Barrister.

# Harrison v Michelin Tyre Co Ltd

QUEEN'S BENCH DIVISION

COMYN J

12, 13 JULY 1984

*Vicarious liability – Master and servant – Act within course of employment – Test to be applied in determining whether act done 'in course of employment' – Employee playing practical joke on fellow employee at work – Fellow employee injured – Whether employer vicariously liable.*

The plaintiff, a tool grinder employed by the defendants, was injured in the course of his employment while standing on the duck-board of his machine talking to a fellow employee. The injury occurred when S, another employee, while pushing a truck along a passageway (indicated by chalk lines) in front of the plaintiff, decided to indulge in some horseplay by suddenly turning the truck two inches outside the chalk lines and pushing the edge of it under the plaintiff's duck-board. The duck-board tipped up and the plaintiff fell off it and was injured. He brought an action for damages for personal injuries against the defendants, claiming that S had been acting in the course of his employment, and that therefore they were vicariously liable for his negligence. The defendants denied liability, contending that at the time of the incident S had embarked on a frolic of his own.

**Held** – For the purpose of determining vicarious liability, the test whether an employee was acting in the course of his employment was whether a reasonable man would say either that the employee's act was part and parcel of his employment (in the sense of being incidental to it) even though it was unauthorised or prohibited by the employer, in which case the employer was liable, or that it was so divergent from his employment as to be plainly alien to his employment, and wholly distinguishable from it, in which case the employer was not liable. Applying that test, a reasonable man would say that, even though S's act was of a kind which would never have been countenanced by the defendants, it was none the less part and parcel of his employment. Accordingly the defendants were vicariously liable for S's negligence (see p 920 *d* to *f* and p 922 *c* to *e* and *j* to p 923 *c*, post).

*Century Insurance Co Ltd v Northern Ireland Road Transport Board* [1942] 1 All ER 491 and *Canadian Pacific Rly Co v Lockhart* [1942] 2 All ER 464 followed.

*Hudson v Ridge Manufacturing Co Ltd* [1957] 2 All ER 229 and *Coddington v International Harvester Co of GB* (1969) 6 KIR 146 distinguished.

## Notes

For the liability of an employer in tort for the acts of his employee, see 16 Halsbury's Laws (4th edn) paras 742–744, and for cases on the subject, see 20 Digest (Reissue) 526–534, 4085–4141.

## Cases referred to in judgment

*Canadian Pacific Rly Co v Lockhart* [1942] 2 All ER 464, [1942] AC 591, PC.

*Century Insurance Co Ltd v Northern Ireland Road Transport Board* [1942] 1 All ER 491, [1942] AC 509, HL.

*Coddington v International Harvester Co of GB* (1969) 6 KIR 146.

*Hudson v Ridge Manufacturing Co Ltd* [1957] 2 All ER 229, [1957] 2 QB 348, [1957] 2 WLR 948.

*Joel v Morison* (1834) 6 C & P 501, 172 ER 1338, NP.

*Lloyd v Grace Smith & Co* [1912] AC 716, [1911–13] All ER Rep 51, HL.

*Smith v Crossley Bros* (1951) 95 SJ 655.

## Action

The plaintiff, Frederick Gerald Harrison, brought an action against the defendants,

Michelin Tyre Co Ltd, claiming damages for personal injuries sustained, and losses and
expenses incurred, as a result of an accident which occurred on or about 9 December
1977 at the defendants' premises at Campbell Road, Stoke-on-Trent, arising out of the
negligence of their servant or agent. The facts are set out in the judgment.

*Stephen Sedley QC* for the plaintiff.
*Henry De Lotbiniere* for the defendants.

**COMYN J.** The issue I have to resolve here is liability only. If liability is established
damages are agreed at an all inclusive sum of £4,000; the case being an accident case.

It is exactly 150 years ago that Parke B spoke the memorable words about liability of
an employer, that he was not liable if the employee was on a frolic of his own. That was
in *Joel v Morrison* (1834) 6 C & P 501 at 503, 172 ER 1338 at 1339. That is just what this
case is about and that memorable phrase has been the subject matter of innumerable
questions in law examinations for the last 150 years: it now, unfortunately, becomes a
question for me in 1984 in circumstances not covered, so far as I can find, by any decided
case before or since; and, in fact, this particular case is singular also in the fact that it is
literally a frolic which the defendants rely on.

The relevant facts can be shortly stated. The incident giving rise to this claim involves
two fellow employees of the defendants, the Michelin Tyre Co Ltd: they were the
plaintiff, Mr Harrison and a man named Mr Smith. Both were employed as grinders at
the defendants' factory at Stoke-on-Trent. On 9 December 1977 the plaintiff was at his
machine, standing on its duck-board but with his back to the machine because he was
talking to a fellow employee. There was, in front of the plaintiff's machine and the row
of machines beside it, a passageway which was indicated by chalk lines, a fairly wide
passageway. Mr Smith was, in the course of his employment, pushing an empty two-
wheeled hand truck along the passageway when he suddenly and for no apparent reason
turned the hand truck a matter of literally a couple of inches and pushed its edge or ledge
under the plaintiff's duck-board which had the result of tipping the duck-board, felling
the plaintiff and injuring the plaintiff. Now this action by Mr Smith was done while he
was in the middle of doing what he was supposed to be doing, namely, pushing the truck
from point A to point B. It was not, on his part, an accident at all in the sense of being
unexpected or unplanned; it was done purposely and intended by him and I quote from
his evidence, which indeed the plaintiff accepted, it was done by him as a joke, hence, of
course, the frolic. It was a joke which hardly merits the description 'joke' in even the
most extended meaning of that word, but I am satisfied on the joint evidence of the
plaintiff and Mr Smith that it was so intended. It was not a matter in respect of which
the employers would be exercising any supervision, nor is there any personal claim made
against the employers for personal liability on their part; the claim is made for vicarious
liability for Mr Smith's undoubted negligence. It was no accident so far as Mr Smith was
concerned, but it was an accident and a serious accident so far as the plaintiff, Mr
Harrison, was concerned.

Now, what is said on behalf of the defence is, that in doing what he did, Mr Smith was
embarking on a frolic of his own and was doing something wholly outside the course of
his employment. To find for the plaintiff I have to find that what he was doing was 'in
the course of his employment'. It is to be noted that up to that very moment Mr Smith
was acting in the course of his employment and doing precisely what his employment
required him to do, namely to push the truck. It is to be noted that the truck was one
provided for him by the defendants and was their truck, that this happened in their
factory and happened only a couple of inches off the chalked passageway.

As so often happens in the law, the simplest of facts give rise to the most complex
questions of law. I have had the advantage from counsel on both sides of reference to a
number of textbooks and to a number of cases, the principal textbook cited to me being
that well-known work, *Charlesworth and Percy on Negligence* (7th edn, 1983). Having had
the opportunity of considering my judgment overnight, I have been through all the
other leading textbooks on tort and have followed up as many of the cases cited in them
as seemed to me relevant and I say with some confidence that, between us, counsel and I

have made a comprehensive search into this subject from the days of Parke B onwards. There are a number of lines of cases on this question of the course of employment, for example, a considerable body of case law deals with the use of vehicles from the days of horse buses onwards to motor cars and ordinary omnibuses. Some of the cases deal with incidents which occurred away from the actual place of work; either, for example, in regard to lorry driving or else purposeful deviation from the place of work by the employees to somewhere either far or near: far, for example, in the case of a luncheon at a public house; near, for example, in regard to a local playing field. Another line of cases deals with incidents which have been specifically prohibited by the employers in many of which, nevertheless, the employer has been held vicariously liable. Another line of cases deals with conduct of such a bizarre nature that one would not think at first sight any employer could be held liable for and yet in many cases have been, and then yet another line of cases deals with completely extraneous activities by employees which it would be hard to categorise as conceivably coming within the scope of employment.

I have searched through these cases for two things: (1) for some case which would decide this one for me (that is a judge's perpetual and lazy search) but it was unrewarding in this case for I found no case which would decide this one for me and I have to decide it for myself getting such help from the cases as I can; and (2) for some basic principle running through the cases; that is an activity which I say somewhat cynically could have occupied me for many weeks if not months because the large body of case law which I have looked at is notable for one thing, its inconsistency very often with an immediately preceding case; the cases are very hard to reconcile in a number of instances.

I will come to a few cases in a moment but, in searching for a principle, I have presumptuously invented one of my own and I have done it in the form of two questions: one which if answered Yes makes the employer liable; the other if answered Yes renders him not liable. The first question: was the incident part and parcel of the employment in the sense of being incidental to it although and albeit unauthorised or prohibited? The test, of course, for that question as for the other, being a reasonable approach. The alternative question is: or was it so divergent from the employment as to be plainly alien to and wholly distinguishable from the employment? If it was, then the employer is not liable.

One is constantly surprised in the law at reading the facts of a reported case and jumping ahead, as one will, to guessing the answer that the court gave; in no field has it proved more surprising than in this. I was given by the defendants, for example, a decision by Pearce J, overruled by the Court of Appeal, in *Smith v Crossley Bros* (1951) 95 SJ 655. The facts there were that the plaintiff was a boy of 16, an apprentice in an apprentice training school with the defendants. When he was working there another apprentice approached him from behind and placed a compressed air pipe near his rectum and signalled to a third apprentice to turn on the compressed air; the result was that the plaintiff sustained rupture of the colon. The point was taken that these two malevolent apprentices were acting in the course of their employment; the defence was that they were on a frolic of their own so that the employers were not liable. Pearce J held in favour of the seriously injured apprentice and against the employers but was overruled on appeal, Singleton LJ saying that the defendants had no reason whatever to anticipate that the two apprentices in question would use the compressed air pipe in the way they did; the duty of an employer was to take reasonable care for the safety of an employee and the evidence did not show any negligence by the defendants. The injury to the plaintiff resulted from what was wilful misbehaviour by the other two boys and a wicked act which the defendants had no reason to foresee. Now, that marks a landmark in the defendants' case before me because, though the frolic, as it is called here, was nothing like so serious and was not intended wickedly, nevertheless, the defendants say that that is a case directly in point.

They also rely on a decision of Ormrod J given at Sheffield Assizes in 1969 called *Coddington v International Harvester Co of GB* (1969) 6 KIR 146; this was the case of a practical joker and, very shortly, the facts were that there was a man who had an unblemished record, had been in the employ of the defendants for 16 years but was a a practical joker although his conduct had not caused actual or reasonably apprehended danger. There then occurred an incident in regard to furnaces where fire got kicked from man to man and the so called practical joker gave a kick which brought fire on the plaintiff and injured him. Ormrod J gave judgment for the employers, saying that there was nothing in the man's previous conduct which suggested that he might endanger the safety of others; that they could not have foreseen that he might be a potential danger and could not have foreseen any accident such as the one that had happened. The basic

b facts did not raise a prima facie case that the events which occurred arose out of, or within the scope of, the employment of the persons concerned. The onus was on the plaintiff to establish the acts were within the scope of this man's employment and the plaintiff had failed to do so. That again forms part of the platform of the defendants' case.

Then in 1957 there was the decision of Streatfeild J in *Hudson v Ridge Manufacturing Co Ltd* [1957] 2 All ER 229, [1957] 2 QB 348. Again the facts were short: for nearly four

c years one of the defendants' employees had made a nuisance of himself to his fellow employees, including the plaintiff, a cripple, by persistently engaging in skylarking, such as tripping them up. Many times he had been reprimanded by the foreman and warned that he would hurt someone but without effect; no further steps were taken to check this conduct by dismissal or otherwise and then, in his horseplay, there came a day when he tripped up the plaintiff and injured him. The plaintiff claimed against the defendant

d employers for damages on the ground they had failed to maintain such discipline as would protect the plaintiff from dangerous horseplay. It was held as a matter of fact that the judge regarded the case as potentially one of difficulty; that the dangerous misbehaviour potential of this man had been known to the employers for a long time; they had failed to prevent it or remove the source of it so they were liable to the plaintiff for failing to take proper care of his safety and *Smith v Crossley* was distinguished. I draw

e attention to that last fact to show that the last 150 years show in this field a ready susceptibility of distinguishing cases where I, as the judge of this case, would wish to see a series of cases nearer the point to here being followed year by year and case by case. But I think that the plaintiff succeeds in his contentions here on the principles which I have stated as elaborated and illustrated by two cases which to my mind give me the most help and point the right pointer for a decision of this case.

f The first is a well-known case, *Century Insurance Co Ltd v Northern Ireland Road Transport Board* [1942] 1 All ER 491, [1942] AC 509, and the facts of that case are almost unbelievable. The employee in question was employed on a petrol tanker to fill a petrol tank at a garage. He went through all the proper motions and acted in the course of his employment in driving his tanker up to the right point and in connecting his tanker to the tank. He then, as was said for his own comfort and pleasure, lit a cigarette and threw

g the lighted match on the ground. One cannot, I venture to think, imagine a more unauthorised act by any employer, a more reckless act by any employee or a more prohibited act by almost every standard one could think of and probably prohibited by regulations too. In that case the point was strongly taken in the Irish courts that he was on a frolic of his own. That perhaps is an instance where the word 'frolic' is an understatement: I would have thought on a 'madness' of his own. But I confess this with

h great diffidence to the Irish courts and the House of Lords, they appear to have found no difficulty whatsoever in finding that what he did was within the course of his employment. I say I confess to respectful surprise but the reasoning is there and is, I hope, reflected in the two principles which I endeavoured to state earlier. Lord Wright said ([1942] 1 All ER 491 at 497, [1942] AC 509 at 519):

j      'On the ... question ... whether Davison's negligence was in the course of his employment, all the decisions below have been against the appellants. I agree with them and need add little. The act of a workman in lighting his pipe or cigarette is an act done for his own comfort and convenience and at least, generally speaking, not for his employer's benefit. That last condition, however, is no longer essential to fix liability on the employer (*Lloyd v Grace Smith & Co.* ([1912] AC 716, [1911–13] All ER Rep 51)). Nor is such an act *prima facie* negligent. It is in itself both innocent and harmless. The negligence is to be found by considering the time when and the circumstances in which the match is struck and thrown down. The duty of the $a$ workman to his employer is so to conduct himself in doing his work as not negligently to cause damage either to the employer himself or his property or to third persons or their property, and thus to impose the same liability on the employer as if he had been doing the work himself and committed the negligent act.'

He and Viscount Simon LC, who delivered the other speech in the case, found no $b$ difficulty about it at all; the other Law Lords concurred (they were Lord Romer and Lord Porter). I emphasise that the case occasioned no difficulty to the courts in Ireland and none to the House of Lords and I am fortified in that view in finding in the report, which I have read and reread, that counsel for the plaintiff were not called on. I may confess respectful surprise at that case, but it of course binds us and expresses the law. I ask rhetorically: if employers are to be liable for that, what real distinction is there between $c$ that and the two-inch deviation from the passageway by Mr Smith, who does something unauthorised and foolish and negligent by pushing the edge or ledge of his trolley under the plaintiff's duck-board? I find it hard, in principle, to see any distinction. On the other hand, the line of cases represented by those cited to me by the defendants I do find distinguishable because they were essentially cases where personal liability was alleged against the employers for failure to supervise. I stress, and cannot stress too strongly, that $d$ the present case is not one of an allegation of personal liability against the employers but is of vicarious liability against them, which, indeed, in its very meaning, exonerates them from a personal liability but fixes them with a representative liability for the negligence of their servant. There was, after all, here, virtually all one movement by Mr Smith from the passageway, a quick right turn of about two inches at most and the placing of the edge or ledge of the trolley under the duck-board, all done in the course, as I see it, truly, $e$ fairly and reasonably of his employment.

The only other case I will refer to is Canadian Pacific Rly Co v Lockhart [1942] 2 All ER 464, [1942] AC 591, an appeal from the Supreme Court of Canada. It was a Privy Council decision, of course, coming from Canada; the members of the board were Viscount Maugham, presiding, Lord Thankerton, Lord Russell, Lord Macmillan and Lord Romer. The headnote reads as follows ([1942] AC 591): $f$

'Where a servant of the appellant company, in disregard of written notices prohibiting employees from using privately owned motor-cars for the purposes of the company's business unless adequately protected by insurance, used his uninsured motor car on a journey for the purpose of, and as a means of execution of, work which he was ordinarily employed to do, and by negligent driving injured the $g$ respondent: Held, that the means of transport was incidental to the execution of that which he was employed to do, and that the prohibition of the use of an uninsured motor-car merely limited the way in which, or by means of which, he was to execute the work, and that breach of the prohibition did not exclude the liability of the company to the respondent.'

A statement in Salmond on Torts (9th edn, 1936) p 95 approved. That case again, like $h$ all the other cases I have considered, does not meet the actual situation that I have to meet face on but the principle there stated accords fully with the earlier case of Century Insurance and falls within, in my view, the first of the two questions of principle which I postulated earlier.

I would only end this judgment by saying that I have read and reread not only the passages in Charlesworth and Percy cited to me but also the chapters in Salmond, Winfield $j$ and Jolowicz on Torts (12th edn, 1984), Clerk and Lindsell on Torts (15th edn, 1982) and the collection of cases in Bingham's Modern Cases on Negligence (3rd edn, 1978) which stretch over the years and are summarised there. I have also looked at various decisions cited in those textbooks and it seems to me in the end that the vital thing is what the principle is. I have endeavoured to state it; I do not think this is purely a question of fact except, in so far as applying the principles, one has got to be reasonable.

In my judgment, for the reasons which I have given, Mr Smith was acting in the
*a* course of his employment in doing what he did (prank or joke or practical joke or gesture
or whatever one cares to call it) and that the defendants are liable for his obvious
negligence and are liable (this I stress) not personally but vicariously as being the
employers of a man who, in the middle of his employment, for a matter of literally
seconds, did something which was quite wrong and which they would never have
countenanced, of course they would never have countenanced, and which he himself
*b* regards now (I heard him in the witness box) as an act of complete folly. He says it was
all really part of a day of general skylarking which had been taking place, a day of banter
between the employees. In my judgment it matters not and, though this may be regarded
as a frolic and a very nasty type of frolic, it was not a frolic of his own within the meaning
of Parke B's words and the defendants are not excused from liability. In the result I give
judgment for the plaintiff in the agreed sum of £4,000 damages.

*c*
*Judgment for the plaintiff; stay of execution in the sum of £2,500, on the usual terms.*

Solicitors: *Brian Thompson & Partners* (for the plaintiff); *Thompson & Co* (for the
defendants).

*d*
K Mydeen Esq    Barrister.

# Beeston Shipping Ltd v Babanaft
# International SA
*e*
# The Eastern Venture

COURT OF APPEAL, CIVIL DIVISION
DUNN AND WATKINS LJJ
10 AUGUST 1983

*f*
*Contempt of court – Committal – Debtor – Attendance for examination – Adjournment of date
for attendance – Debtor served with original notice for attendance – Debtor not served with notice
of adjourned date – Debtor failing to attend examination on adjourned date – Whether debtor in
contempt – Whether notice enforceable by committal proceedings – Whether relevant that debtor's
legal representatives were aware of adjourned date – RSC Ord 48, r 1.*

*g*
Where an order is made under RSC 48, r 1[a] requiring a judgment debtor to attend for
oral examination on his debts at such time and place as may be appointed and the
examination is subsequently adjourned to an appointed date, then, if the debtor is not
served with an amended order indorsed with the new date of examination, his failure to
attend on the new date will not constitute contempt of court, because there must be strict
*h* compliance with the rules of court before an order can be enforced by committal
proceedings. Service of the original order indorsed merely with a penal notice is therefore
not sufficient to put the debtor in contempt if he fails to attend the adjourned hearing.
Furthermore, the fact that the debtor's legal representatives are themselves aware of the
adjourned date and of the consequences of non-attendance is not of itself sufficient to
render the debtor liable to committal for contempt for non-attendance. Committal is an
*j* extreme remedy concerning the liberty of the subject, and proceedings for committal
will be bad unless the rules are strictly complied with (see p 927 *a* to *c*, p 928 *b c h j* and
p 929 *f* to *h*, post).
    *Re Tuck, Murch v Loosemore* [1906] 1 Ch 692 applied.
    *Rendell v Grundy* [1895] 1 QB 16 distinguished.

_____
*a*    Rule 1, so far as material, is set out at p 929 *e*, post

**Notes**

For examination of a judgment debtor, see 17 Halsbury's Laws (4th edn) para 440, and  *a*
for cases on the subject, see 21 Digest (Reissue) 327–328, 2140–2152.

**Cases referred to in judgments**

*Harvey's Estate, Re* [1907] P 239.
*Hyde v Hyde* (1888) 13 PD 166, CA.
*Protector Endowment Co v Whitlam* (1877) 36 LT 467.                                   *b*
*Rendell v Grundy* [1895] 1 QB 16, CA.
*Tuck, Re, Murch v Loosemore* [1906] 1 Ch 692, CA.

**Interlocutory appeal**

Mr Bahaedine Bassatne, a director of the defendants, Babanaft International SA, appealed
against the judgment of Nolan J given on 8 August 1983 holding that Mr Bassatne was   *c*
in contempt of court in failing to attend an oral examination on 4 August 1983, pursuant
to orders made under RSC Ord 48 on 17 March 1983 by Master Grant for the purpose of
inquiring into the debts owed by the defendants. The grounds of the appeal were, inter
alia, that the judge erred in law in holding (1) that Mr Bassatne was in contempt of court
in failing to attend the examination on 4 August because the judge erred in holding that
service on Mr Bassatne of the original orders dated 17 March requiring him to attend for  *d*
examination on 7 April 1983, which were indorsed with a penal notice that he would be
in contempt of court if he did not attend at the time appointed, covered adjourned dates
for his oral examination without service on him of an amended order giving the
adjourned date, and (2) that the words contained in a telex message dated 28 March 1983
from the plaintiffs' solicitors to the defendants' solicitors were a sufficient offer of conduct
money to attend the adjourned examination on 4 August. The facts are set out in the  *e*
judgment.

*Anthony Thompson QC* for the defendants.
*Charles Haddon-Cave* for the plaintiffs.

**DUNN LJ.** This is an appeal from an order of Nolan J made on 8 August 1983 whereby  *f*
he held that Mr Bahaedine Bassatne was in contempt of court in that he failed to attend
an oral examination on 4 August 1983 in breach of orders of Master Grant dated 17
March for an oral examination pursuant to RSC Ord 48. The orders of the master arose
out of a judgment which had been obtained by the plaintiffs against the defendants on
21 October 1982, under RSC Ord 14, for a sum of something over $US705,000 in respect
of a repudiation of a time charter. Pursuant to that judgment there was an arbitration in  *g*
which the plaintiffs' claim is something over $US9,000,000.

Mr Bassatne is a director of the defendant company. We were told that he is a Lebanese
national based in Greece with worldwide international business interests. On 17 March
Master Grant made an order which is the foundation of these proceedings and, because
of its importance, I will read it. The order was—

'that Bahaedine Bassatne of 15 Stanhope Gate, London W.1., an officer of the  *h*
above-named debtor company [Babanaft International SA] attend and be orally
examined as to whether any and what debts are owing to the judgment debtor
company, and whether the said judgment debtor company has any and what other
property or means of satisfying the judgment signed herein, on the 21st day of
October 1982, before one of the officers of the High Court of Justice, [and these are
the important words:] at such time and place as he may appoint, and that the said  *j*
Bahaedine Bassatne produce any books or documents in his possession or power
relating to the same before the said officer at the time of the examination . . .'

In accordance with the practice, the order was taken by the plaintiffs' solicitors to the
master's secretary's office where the appointment was given. It was stamped on the back

with a rubber stamp in common form. The officer of the court appoints the day for the
*a* judgment debtor to attend in room 81, Royal Courts of Justice, and the time and the date
are recorded on the backsheet of the order. In this case the date appointed and recorded
on the order was 7 April 1983. The order was then indorsed with a penal notice, and an
unsuccessful attempt was made to serve it on Mr Bassatne personally. It is unnecessary to
recite the details of that: they are set out in an affidavit of an articled clerk of the plaintiffs'
solicitors who failed to effect personal service, although Mr Bassatne was apparently
*b* present in the office when he went there with the order. As a result, on 24 March Lloyd
J made an order for service of the order by post to Mr Bassatne's address in London.

By agreement between the solicitors the date was then changed to 20 April, and on
that date the oral examination took place. Mr Bassatne produced no documents and the
examination was adjourned until 6 June, when inspection was envisaged. It appears that
most of the defendants' documents were in Athens. Between 18 and 28 July there was
*c* inspection of, we have been told, a large number of documents in Athens. There had
previously been made to the master an ex parte application for discovery of further
documents and an order had been made on that occasion. By consent the hearing was
further adjourned until 4 August.

It appears from the original documents which we have before us that, although the
adjourned dates of 20 April and 4 August were duly stamped on the back of the original
*d* order of 17 March, the orders as amended were never served on Mr Bassatne and,
although the penal notice was attached to the original order giving the date of 7 April,
no subsequent penal notice was drawn to the attention of Mr Bassatne.

It is right to say that throughout this time Mr Bassatne was represented by experienced
solicitors: first of all by the same firm as were representing the defendants in the action,
and subsequently he was separately represented.

*e* We have been referred to numerous telexes which indicate that the solicitors at any
rate were well aware of the dates of the adjourned hearings and, according to their
telexes, were in communication with Mr Bassatne, their client. Indeed, on 3 June 1983
Messrs Simmons & Simmons, who were acting for Mr Bassatne personally, telexed the
plaintiffs' solicitors saying:

*f*      'We confirm our telcon with Mr Bush when we advised you that our client Mr
Bassatne had now instructed us that arrangements will be made for you to inspect
the documents in Athens on Monday 18th July. Mr Bassatne has further agreed to
an adjournment of the hearing on 6th June in favour of a return date of 4th August,
when he will attend court once more.'

*g* On the same day they telexed:

      'Further to our telephone conversations this afternoon and to our telex of
confirmation we confirm that it will not be necessary for Mr Bassatne to be re-served
with the order adjourning the hearing.'

On 2 August Mr Bassatne's solicitors applied to the master for the hearing date of 4
*h* August to be vacated and the hearing adjourned. That application was refused. On 4
August Mr Bassatne failed to appear. His counsel and solicitors were there. The
examination was adjourned until 2 pm and he still did not appear. So that evening the
plaintiffs applied ex parte to Nolan J for a suspended committal order. Not surprisingly,
the judge refused that application. It is extremely rare for a court to consider an ex parte
application for a committal order, even a suspended committal order; and such
*j* applications are rightly only granted in very exceptional circumstances. What the judge
did was to give leave to serve short notice on Mr Bassatne and he said that the notice
should be served by telex, which was sent on the following day.

The hearing took place on 8 August 1983 and the judge declared that Mr Bassatne was
in contempt and adjourned the hearing to consider the appropriate penalty, indicating
that he was thinking in terms of a fine.

The two points which were taken before the judge and which were taken in this court on behalf of Mr Bassatne may be shortly stated as follows. The first, and perhaps *a* fundamental, point was that the order, properly construed, was an order to appear for examination on 4 August and that that order had never been served on Mr Bassatne, nor had he been tendered conduct money for the hearing on 4 August. For those two reasons it was said that the necessary foundation to enable him to be found guilty of contempt of court had not been laid and that, as this was a matter of the liberty of the subject, the rules must be strictly observed and accordingly the order should not be made.          *b*

We have been provided with a note of the judgment and the judge dealt with the first point in this way. He said:

'. . . the critical matter is what was actually said in the order of Master Grant. This was that Mr Bassatne should "attend . . . before one of the officers of the High Court of Justice, at such time and place as he may appoint". In my judgment those words include "at such times" as that officer might appoint. They are not limited to initial *c* appointment. They cover adjournment(s) of that appointment. There has been no further order or note of further order because there was no need for a further order. It follows that the penal notice served on Mr Bassatne in relation to the first hearing carries through to any adjourned hearing of the examination.'

The relevant rules which are material are contained in RSC Ords 42 and 45. Order 42, *d* r 1(3) provides that any order must be marked with the name of the judge, referee or master by whom it was made and must be sealed. Order 42, r 2(1) provides that a judgment or order which requires a person to do an act must specify the time after service of the judgment or order, or some other time, within which the act is to be done. Order 45, r 6 provides in effect that, where an order does not specify the time, the court may subsequently specify the time. That is the effect of r 6(2) of Ord 45.          *e*

The question of enforcement is dealt with by Ord 45, r 5. Rule 5 provides:

'(1) Where—(a) a person required by a judgment or order to do an act within a time specified in the judgment or order refuses or neglects to do it within that time . . . or (b) a person disobeys a judgment or order . . . then, subject to the provisions of these rules, the judgment or order may be enforced by one or more of the following means . . . (iii) . . . an order of committal against that person . . .'          *f*
(2) Where a judgment or order requires a person to do an act within a time therein specified and an order is subsequently made under rule 6 requiring the act to be done within some other time, [then one refers back to para (1) of the rule and effectively the order must specify the time when the act is to be done] . . .'

So in this case the original order of Master Grant provided simply that Mr Bassatne was *g* to attend court at such time and place as the officer may appoint.

The officer appointed, first of all, 7 April and then the subsequent dates, and the relevant one so far as we are concerned is 4 August. That became under Ord 45, r 6(2) the time specified in the order, and failure to comply with that time, namely the time specified in the order of 4 August, fell to be dealt with, so far as committal proceedings were concerned, under Ord 45, r 5, and if there was any neglect, as there was, to appear *h* on 4 August, then the provisions of Ord 45, r 5 became applicable. Order 45, r 7 deals with service of copies of judgments prerequisite to enforcement under r 5. Rule 7(2)(b) requires that—

'an order shall not be enforced under rule 5 unless . . . (b) in the case of an order requiring a person to do an act, the copy has been so served before the expiration of *j* the time within which he was required to do the act'.

The expression 'so served' means served personally.

Paragraph (4) of r 7 provides that the order must be indorsed with a penal notice. Paragraph (5) provides that with the copy of an order required to be served there must be served the previous order, ie in this case the order stating the original time followed

by the extended time. Paragraph (6) provides the well-known exception in the case of
*a* prohibitions or negative restraining orders, but those are not applicable to this case
because this is a case under r 7 of Ord 45 whereby Mr Bassatne was required to do a
positive act.

I mention these rules at some length because there has been a suggestion, or more than
a suggestion, by counsel for the plaintiffs that, where the person sought to be committed
is represented by solicitors and where, as here, the evidence is that the solicitors are
*b* perfectly well aware of the various orders that have been made, committal proceedings
can be instituted without strict adherence to the rules. Nothing could be further from
the truth: committal for contempt of court is an extreme remedy and, whatever the
relationship between the solicitors may be and whatever knowledge in fact the person to
be proceeded against for contempt of court has, none the less the committal proceedings
will be bad unless the rules are strictly complied with. The reason for this of course is
*c* that committal proceedings are not like civil actions for breach of contract: they concern
the liberty of the subject.

There are many authorities to this effect. The one that was referred to us was *Re Tuck,
Murch v Loosemore* [1906] 1 Ch 692, where a writ of attachment was refused where there
had been an order directing a trustee to pay money into court. The order had not been
personally served on him. In fact the order was made by consent and the trustee was in
*d* court when it was made and he even initialled one of the briefs. Even so, it was held that
personal service was necessary. Cozens-Hardy LJ referred to a dictum of Cotton LJ in
*Hyde v Hyde* (1888) 13 PD 166 at 171–172 which suggested that, if the person was
actually in court at the time the order was made, personal service would be unnecessary.
Cozens-Hardy LJ distinguished that case, where it was a negative act which was the
subject of the order, from a case such as our present case where the order requires a
*e* person to do a positive act, and in such a situation, before committal proceedings can be
started, the order with a penal notice attached must be personally served.

Counsel for the plaintiffs referred us to *Rendell v Grundy* [1895] 1 QB 16, which was a
case in which objection had been taken because on the motion for committal the affidavit
in support had not been served on the respondent. The judge adjourned the matter and
gave the respondent and his solicitors an opportunity of dealing with the affidavit. They
*f* indicated apparently at the adjourned hearing that the respondent could not answer the
affidavit and the committal order was made. In the Court of Appeal Lord Esher MR,
having recited the facts, said (at 21–22):

> 'Every purpose for which the law as to service of copies of the affidavits was made
> has been satisfied. The defendant has not been injured in the smallest degree by
> what has taken place. I am prepared to say that, under the circumstances of this case,
*g* > though the defendant might be entitled to have copies of the affidavits served upon
> him with the summons, and that has not been done, yet, having been offered what
> was exactly equivalent, and having accepted it, he cannot afterwards set up this
> objection to the application for an attachment. He has in reality had everything to
> which he was entitled, and therefore I do not think we ought to entertain this
*h* > objection.'

Counsel for the plaintiffs says that in this case Mr Bassatne, although the amended
order was not served on him, has had everything to which he could have been entitled
and has not in any way been prejudiced or injured by the failure to serve the amended
order. He submitted that the observations of Lord Esher MR in *Rendell v Grundy* to
which I have just referred were quite general and wide enough to cover the circumstances
*j* of this case. I cannot accept that submission. Quite a different point was being dealt with
in *Rendell v Grundy*. It was a procedural matter concerned with the hearing of the motion
to commit. The defendant in that case was given an opportunity, through an
adjournment, of considering the allegations in the affidavit, but that is entirely different
to a situation where the whole basis of the contempt alleged is the breach of an order of
the court.

In this case the motion for committal is for an order that Mr Bassatne be committed to prison on the grounds that he is in contempt of court 'for that he failed to attend an oral examination on 4th August 1983 in breach of the Orders of Master Grant dated 17th March 1983 for such oral examination'. That is the order on which this motion for committal was based.

Where does one find the order? One finds it partly in the original order of Master Grant and partly in the indorsements of the officer of the court. Before that order can be enforced by way of proceedings for committal, it must be served personally on Mr Bassatne and conduct money must have been tendered. In my view the judge fell into error in accepting that, because the original order with 7 April indorsed on it was served, that was good service for any subsequent hearing. In my view it was not. If the plaintiffs desired to enforce attendance at the subsequent hearing, then they should have served the order which directed him to attend at the subsequent hearing.

The question of conduct money remains to be considered. It is the invariable practice when persons are summoned before examiners that they should be tendered conduct money, and, although the practice is not contained in the rules, it clearly emerged from *Protector Endowment Co v Whitlam* (1877) 36 LT 467, where the Court of Queen's Bench refused an order of attachment, partly on the ground that no conduct money had been paid. Lush J said:

'. . . a reasonable sum of money to defray the expenses of coming and attending to give evidence, and of returning from giving such evidence, must be tendered to a witness.'

That has been the invariable practice.

Gorrell Barnes P in *Re Harvey's Estate* [1907] P 239 refused to make an order of attachment because conduct money had not been tendered for a witness who had been ordered to attend for examination. It is interesting to see that counsel for the petitioner had submitted that conduct money was not necessary because the witness had admitted means. I only mention that because there was a submission by counsel for the plaintiffs that Mr Bassatne is a man of substantial means, but there is no indication in any of the cases that have been referred to us that conduct money is not required if the examinee has sufficient means to attend at court.

The question in this case is essentially one of fact, because it is said that there was in this case a sufficient tender of conduct money which was contained in a telex from Messrs Holman Fenwick & Willan, the plaintiffs' solicitors, dated 28 March. They say: 'You will appreciate that Mr Bassatne is entitled to conduct money. Please let us know by return whether our undertaking to you would be satisfactory in this regard.' In fact there was never any reply to that telex and, although Mr Bassatne appeared on 20 April, apparently no conduct money was paid to him.

Counsel for the defendants has submitted that that telex does not constitute a tender of conduct money. It is no more than an invitation to treat and there must be a firm offer of conduct money before it can be said to have been tendered. Speaking for myself, I would regard that telex as a sufficient tender of conduct money for the hearing in question, namely the hearing of 7 April which was subsequently adjourned to 20 April, but I could not construe it as, so to speak, a blanket offer of conduct money for any hearing that might be held pursuant to the order of Master Grant. So I do not think that it was a sufficient tender of conduct money for the hearing on 4 August, but, however that may be, in my judgment this application fails in limine because the order for Mr Bassatne to attend and be examined on 4 August was never personally served on him. There was no order for substituted service so far as that order was concerned and that order was never indorsed with a penal notice.

Counsel for the defendants raised a question as to the form of the indorsement. The officer of the court appoints the day for the judgment debtor to attend and counsel for the defendants points out that Mr Bassatne was not the judgment debtor. The judgment debtor was the company of which Mr Bassatne was an officer. The rule provides that the *a* court has power to order either the judgment debtor or, if the judgment debtor is a body corporate, an officer thereof to attend before the master for examination, and, for the avoidance of doubt, I would think it advisable that there should be two rubber stamps to be used appropriately when the judgment debtor is an individual or when it is a corporate body. In the latter case the order should be directed to an officer of the judgment debtor, but it is not necessary to decide whether that itself makes this order bad, because, for the reasons that I have given, I am satisfied that on other grounds it cannot be supported,

*b* and, accordingly, I would allow the appeal and dismiss the application for committal for contempt of court.

**WATKINS LJ.** A person who seeks to commit another to prison for contempt of court takes a very serious step with possibly grave consequences. In order to justify it, that person has to establish that the order sought could have been obeyed, that the order is a

*c* valid one that it was brought to the notice of the person who should have obeyed it, and that that person disobeyed it. In this case Mr Bassatne, though described as a judgment debtor and about whom the plaintiffs in the two actions with which this case is concerned entertain very grave suspicions, is only a judgment debtor in the sense that he is either the president or a director or both of the defendant company. None the less he fell, properly in my opinion, to be ordered to attend to be examined according to the

*d* provisions of RSC Ord 48. Rule 1(2) of Ord 48 provides:

'An order under this rule must be served personally on the judgment debtor and on any officer of a body corporate ordered to attend for examination.'

In the note to Ord 48, r 1 in *The Supreme Court Practice 1982* vol 1 para 48/1–3/2, p799 it is stated that—

*e* 'A copy of the order and appointment must be served personally on the debtor or on the particular officer of the body corporate ordered to attend for examination; but in a proper case an order for substituted service may be made.'

There is no denying that there is a good and valid order in existence calling for the attendance of Mr Bassatne at these courts for the purpose of being orally examined. The

*f* issue therefore is whether that order needed to be served on Mr Bassatne and whether it has in fact been served in accordance with Ord 48. In my judgment this issue can be tested in this rather simple and direct way: the original order was made as long ago as March 1983 and obeyed eventually in the circumstances which Dunn LJ has outlined, but the relevant order and appointment for Mr Bassatne to come to these courts on 4 August was made at a much later time and by another person, namely Mrs Tanner. I

*g* take the proper practice to be that which is laid down in *The Supreme Court Practice*, which has, I think, the force of law.

Accordingly, no order of this kind can be used for the purpose of asserting that a person is in contempt of court for disobeying it unless it is served on the person who is called on to obey it, so that he, by that service, is made aware of the whole content of the order, the appointment made for his attendance in particular.

*h* With those few words it only needs to be added, so far as my judgment is concerned, that I agree entirely with what Dunn LJ has said and I, too, would allow this appeal.

*Appeal allowed; declaration that Mr Bassatne was not in contempt of court in failing to attend for oral examination on 4 August 1983. Leave to appeal to the House of Lords refused.*

Solicitors: *Simmons & Simmons* (for the defendants); *Holman Fenwick & Willan* (for the plaintiffs).

Carolyn Toulmin    Barrister.

# Auty and others v National Coal Board                                    a

COURT OF APPEAL, CIVIL DIVISION
WALLER, OLIVER AND PURCHAS LJJ
5, 6, 7, 8, 9, 27 MARCH 1984

*Damages – Personal injury – Loss of future earnings – Pension – Mineworkers' pension scheme –*
*Pensions index-linked and earnings related – Allowance for inflation – Plaintiffs' pension rights*   b
*diminished because of loss of earnings following injuries – Whether allowance should be made for*
*inflation – Whether actuarial evidence of future inflation admissible.*

*Damages – Personal injury – Loss of future earnings – Pension – Mineworkers' pension scheme –*
*Discount for accelerated capital payment for future loss – Appropriate rate of discount.*        c

*Fatal accident – Damages – Lost opportunity of widow's post-retirement pension – Mineworker*
*killed while employed – Widow receiving widow's pension based on husband's death while*
*employed – If husband had predeceased widow in retirement widow would have been entitled to*
*post-retirement pension – Whether lost opportunity of post-retirement pension to be taken into*
*account in assessing widow's dependency.*                                              d

A mineworkers' pension scheme funded by contributions from workers and the National
Coal Board provided members of the scheme with guaranteed earnings-related pension
rights on retirement at the age of 65 and also pension rights on the occurrence of other
contingencies, such as death while employed, premature retirement due to incapacity
and termination of employment for redundancy. Under r 16(2) of the scheme, pensions
were payable to a member's widow if 'one or more of the following conditions' were       e
satisfied, including (a) death of the member while employed or (b) death of the member
in retirement. Rule 26 of the scheme attempted to protect pensions against inflation by
index-linking pensions payable under the scheme, but there was no guaranteed fund for
the payment of index-linked increases and therefore payment of such increases was
dependent on the rate of inflation and the government of the day providing the coal       f
board with the necessary funds. The first three plaintiffs were mineworkers who were
injured in accidents at work and in consequence had to do work that was less well paid
than formerly, thereby suffering loss of earnings which would affect their earnings-
related retirement pensions. The fourth plaintiff was the widow of a mineworker killed
in an accident at work five years before he was due to retire. She accordingly became
entitled to a widow's pension under r 16(1)(a). All four plaintiffs brought actions in
negligence against the board claiming damages, including loss of future pension rights,   g
the fourth plaintiff's claim being under the Fatal Accidents Act 1976. The first three
plaintiffs claimed that their pension rights on retirement at 65 would be diminished
because of the loss of earnings consequent on their injuries, while the fourth plaintiff
claimed that her dependency should include both the value of her husband's retirement
pension on his assumed death in retirement and, on the same assumption, the value of
her lost chance of a widow's post-retirement pension under r 16(2)(b) of the scheme. The  h
fourth plaintiff contended that under s 4(1)[a] of the 1976 Act her widow's pension under
r 16(2)(a) was to be ignored in assessing her dependency. The judge, in assessing damages,
valued the lost pension rights of the first three plaintiffs and the lost retirement pension
of the fourth plaintiff's deceased husband on the basis of the present-day value of a
guaranteed retirement pension without making any allowance for index-linked increases,
because he regarded it as highly speculative whether any such increases would be paid.    i
He also adopted the conventional approach to the assessment of compensation for future
loss when assessing the amount to be awarded as compensation for the lost pension rights
and rejected actuarial evidence on future inflation adduced by the plaintiffs, on the
grounds that such evidence was unsuitable, if not inadmissible, and accordingly made no
allowance for future inflation. He also applied low multipliers based on a 5% discount

---

*a*   Section 4(1) is set out at p 942 *d*, post

rate of the capital awards to take account of the accelerated payment of a capital sum for
a future loss. The judge also rejected the fourth plaintiff's claim for loss of the prospect
of a widow's post-retirement pension. The plaintiffs appealed, contending that as a
general rule an allowance for inflation should be made in assessing compensation for
future loss, or, alternatively, that such an allowance ought to be made because the
mineworkers' pension scheme was in effect an insurance scheme providing cover against
(a) specified contingencies on the occurrence of which benefit was payable and (b)
inflation (having regard to r 26). The plaintiffs further contended that the judge ought
to have applied a lower discount rate of 2% (and an appropriately increased multiplier) in
line with the conventional rate of interest of 2% awarded for pre-trial interest on damages
already accrued at the date of trial. The fourth plaintiff also appealed against the rejection
of her claim for loss of the prospect of a widow's post-retirement pension.

**Held** – The appeal would be dismissed for the following reasons—

(1) The general rule that inflation should not affect the assessment of compensation
for loss in personal injury cases (except to the extent that the value of the loss should be
taken as at the date of trial and not at the date of the injury) applied to the assessment of
compensation for a lost future capital payment such as a pension right. The fact that the
mineworkers' pension scheme provided for the index-linking of future benefits payable
under the scheme did not, in all the circumstances, prevent that rule applying or provide
an exception to it, because it was highly speculative whether the provisions of r 26 would
ever be applied and it was therefore impossible to put a value on the element of insurance
cover against inflation intended to be provided by r 26. Furthermore, actuarial evidence
was not a reliable guide either to future inflation or to future political events, such as
whether a future government would decide to provide the coal board with funds to meet
index-linked increases. It followed that the judge had been right to make no allowance
for future inflation (see p 936 *e* to *j*, p 938 *a* to *d*, p 939 *b* and *e* to *j*, p 940 *f* to *j*, p 942 *c*, p
945 *f* to *j* and p 946 *a b*, post); dictum of Edmund Davies LJ in *Mitchell v Mulholland (No
2)* [1971] 2 All ER at 1214, *Cookson v Knowles* [1978] 2 All ER 604 and *Lim Poh Choo v
Camden and Islington Area Health Authority* [1979] 2 All ER 910 applied.

(2) The question of the appropriate discount rate when assessing compensation for
future loss was quite different from the question of pre-trial interest on accrued damages,
since in compensation for future loss the discount rate was based on the future, post-trial,
interest which a plaintiff could earn on the capital sum awarded to him for his future loss
whereas interest on accrued damages was awarded to a plaintiff to compensate him for
having been kept out of money to which he had been entitled between the date of the
writ and the date of the trial. Accordingly, the rate of 2% applied in awarding pre-trial
interest was not appropriate in the case of assessment of compensation for future loss.
Instead, the appropriate discount was 4% or 5%, in the judge's discretion (unless there
were special reasons for departing from that rule), even though those figures were based
on the interest rates which could be earnt on capital in a time of stable currency, since it
had to be taken into account that in times of high inflation and high interest rates a
plaintiff could protect his capital award against inflation by prudent investment. It
followed that in all the circumstances, the court would not interfere with the discount
rate of 5% used by the judge (see p 937 *b* to *f*, p 938 *a* to *d*, p 939 *b e*, p 941 *a* to *j*, p 945 *f
g*, p 947 *b* to *d*, p 948 *b* to *e* and p 949 *b c*, post); dicta of Lord Diplock and Lord Fraser in
*Cookson v Knowles* [1978] 2 All ER at 611, 615 applied; *Birkett v Hayes* [1982] 2 All ER 710
and *Wright v British Rlys Board* [1983] 2 All ER 698 distinguished; *Todorovic v Waller*
(1981) 56 ALJR 59 considered.

(3) The fourth plaintiff was not entitled to claim as part of her dependency the value
of the lost opportunity of a widow's post-retirement pension under r 16(2)(b) of the
scheme because the conditions for payment of a widow's pension specified in r 16(2)
were mutually exclusive and therefore, once the fourth plaintiff had become entitled to
a widow's pension under r 16(2)(a) on the death of her husband while employed, she
could not become entitled to a widow's post-retirement pension under r 16(2)(b).
Accordingly the prospect of a widow's post-retirement pension was not something which
she had 'lost' as a result of her husband's death (see p 938 *h* to p 939 *b*, p 942 *h*, p 943 *d* to

*f*, p 944 *c* to *e* and *g* to *j*, p 945 *e f* and p 949 *j* to p 950 *b*, post); *Parry v Cleaver* [1969] 1 All
ER 555 applied; *Davies v Whiteways Cider Co Ltd* [1974] 3 All ER 168 distinguished.

**Notes**
For the measure of damages in personal injuries cases, see 12 Halsbury's Laws (4th edn)
paras 1145–1158.
   For damages under the Fatal Accidents Act 1976, see 34 Halsbury's Laws (4th edn)
paras 94–98, and for cases on the subject, see 36(1) Digest (Reissue) 360–362, *1456–1469.*
   For the Fatal Accidents Act 1976, s 4, see 46 Halsbury's Statutes (3rd edn) 1122.
   As from 1 January 1983 s 4 of the 1976 Act was substituted by s 3(1) of the
Administration of Justice Act 1982 in respect of causes of action accruing on or after that
date.

**Cases referred to in judgments**
*Birkett v Hayes* [1982] 2 All ER 710, [1982] 1 WLR 816, CA.
*Cookson v Knowles* [1978] 2 All ER 604, [1979] AC 556, [1978] 2 WLR 978, HL.
*Davies v Whiteways Cider Co Ltd* [1974] 3 All ER 168, [1975] QB 262, [1974] 3 WLR 597.
*Humphrey v Ward Engineering Services Ltd* (1975) 119 SJ 461
*Jefford v Gee* [1970] 1 All ER 1202, [1970] 2 QB 130, [1970] 2 WLR 702, CA.
*Lea v Owen* (22 January 1980) referred to in Kemp and Kemp *The Quantum of Damages* vol
   1, Pt III, para 27–314.
*Lim Poh Choo v Camden and Islington Area Health Authority* [1979] 2 All ER 910, [1980] AC
   174, [1979] 3 WLR 44, HL.
*Mallett v McMonagle* [1969] 2 All ER 178, [1970] AC 166, [1969] 2 WLR 767, HL.
*Mitchell v Mulholland (No 2)* [1971] 2 All ER 1205, [1972] 1 QB 65, [1971] 2 WLR 1271,
   CA.
*O'Brien v McKean* (1968) 42 ALJR 223, Aust HC.
*Parry v Cleaver* [1969] 1 All ER 555, [1970] AC 1, [1969] 2 WLR 821, HL.
*Taylor v O'Connor* [1970] 1 All ER 365, [1971] AC 115, [1970] 2 WLR 472, HL.
*Todorovic v Waller, Jetson v Hankin* (1981) 56 ALJR 59, Aust HC.
*Wright v British Rlys Board* [1983] 2 All ER 698, [1983] 2 AC 773, [1983] 3 WLR 211, HL.
*Young v Percival* [1974] 3 All ER 677, [1975] 1 WLR 17, CA.

**Appeal**
The plaintiffs, Harry Auty, Lawrence Sidney Mills, Douglas Rogers and Kathleen Popow
(widow and administratrix of the estate of Alexander Popow deceased) (the appellants)
appealed against the judgment of Tudor Evans J given on 19 June 1981 and entered on 8
October 1981 ordering the defendants, the National Coal Board (the respondents) to pay
the following sums to the respective appellants as damages for loss of potential pension
rights and benefits under the Mineworkers' Pension Scheme (the scheme) consequent on
injuries suffered by Auty, Mills and Rogers in the course of their employment with the
respondents and the death of Mrs Popow's husband in the course of his employment
with the respondents: namely £1,000 to Auty, £1,598 to Mills, £825 to Rogers and
£607·50 to Mrs Popow. The appellants sought an order increasing the awards on the
grounds, inter alia, that the judge misdirected himself in law (1) in valuing the loss of
the pension rights in that he failed to take sufficient account of the provisions of the
scheme as a whole, in particular, that the nature of the scheme was to provide insurance
cover and that the benefits payable under the scheme were index-linked for protection
against inflation, (2) in failing to distinguish a claim for loss of benefits under a scheme
providing insurance cover from a claim for future loss of earnings, and adopting, in
assessing the awards, the conventional method of assessment by applying a multiplier
based on average life expectancy discounted by 5% to take account of accelerated payment
of a capital sum for the future loss in question which could be invested and earn interest;
(3) in rejecting the expert evidence of an actuary as providing criteria for assessing the
present value of the future loss of pension rights under the scheme on the ground that
the actuary's evidence was inadmissible as being hearsay evidence, or was of no evidentiary
value, (4) in assessing at too low a figure the present value of the future loss of pension

rights and benefits; and (5) in the case of Mrs Popow, in taking no account of the fact that
*a* the retirement benefits she would have received if her husband had survived to
retirement age and died thereafter, were lost to her as a result of his premature and
tortious death. By a respondent's notice the respondents sought variation of so much of
the judge's judgment as adjudged that the appellants Auty, Mills and Rogers were
entitled to recover damages for loss of the value of a widow's pension payable on their
death in retirement or in service. The facts are set out in the judgment of Waller LJ.

*b*
*Barry Mortimer QC* and *Simon Grenfell* for the appellants.
*T R A Morison QC, Peter Goldsmith* and *Nicholas Underhill* for the respondents.

*Cur adv vult*

*c* 27 March. The following judgments were delivered.

**WALLER LJ.** This appeal is concerned with the assessment of damages for the loss of
pension rights by the appellants when injured or killed whilst working for the National
Coal Board (the respondents). Liability and the assessment of general damages has already
been determined in actions tried separately, but in these four cases the assessment relating
to partial loss of pension rights was reserved so that the four cases could be dealt with as
*d* test cases concerning the method of determining the injury to the appellants' rights
under the Mineworkers' Pension Scheme (the scheme). The amounts at stake are not
very great, and in each case form a very small proportion of the total damage. The appeals
have been brought so that the parties may have guidance for future cases, the appellants
seeking to show that the judge's figures were too low, and the respondents, with the
exception of one item, supporting the figures fixed by the judge. Tudor Evans J heard
*e* evidence and argument in the Sheffield Crown Court, and gave judgment in London on
19 June 1981.
    The scheme was originally formed in 1952 but was amended and converted into an
earnings-related scheme in 1975. These four claims all arise after 1975. Membership of
the scheme is obligatory on mineworkers employed by the respondent. Contributions
are at the rate of $5\frac{1}{4}\%$ of the gross weekly taxable earnings, and the respondents as
*f* employers also contribute $5\frac{1}{4}\%$. The benefits explained by the judge in his judgment as
follows:

'*Members' benefits*
        (i) Pension and a lump sum are payable at the normal retirement age of 65.
        (ii) It is open to a member to defer retirement for not more than five years. If he
*g* so elects, he ceases to pay contributions but the pension and lump sum are increased
if he continues in the scheme for at least one year after the age of 65. The pension
and the lump sum become payable when the member eventually retires and not
later than the age of 70. The relevance of this part of the scheme in the present cases
is whether the plaintiffs (Auty, Mills and Rogers) might remain at work until they
are 70 and whether the deceased might have done so.
*h*       (iii) There is a provision for voluntary early retirement. A member may elect to
take very early retirement at the age of 60 but not before. If he does, his benefits
will not be payable until he reaches the age of 65. I shall consider the rules relating
to the calculation of the benefit in cases of very early retirement later. An issue of
fact arises in the cases of Auty, Mills and Rogers, whether any of them is likely to
elect to take very early retirement and whether the deceased (Mr Popow) might
*i* have done so.
        (iv) There are provisions for incapacity retirement provided that the member is
medically certified as unfit for any work with the respondents. In that event he
receives an immediate retirement pension as for normal age retirement and a lump
sum. There is no claim for the potential loss of this benefit.
        (v) Members who are made redundant are entitled to benefits. There are detailed
provisions but it is not necessary to refer to them. Later I shall have to consider
whether there is any possibility of Auty, Mills and Rogers being made redundant,

or whether the deceased might have been. If so, it will act as a discount against proved losses. There is also no claim in any of the cases for the loss in the value of a pension payable on redundancy.

(vi) If a member's service is terminated (other than for incapacity, redundancy or for very early retirement) the pension and lump sum are preserved to the age of 65. The amount depends on the age and length of scheme service of the member.

(vii) If a member leaves the scheme and takes other work, he may transfer his pension rights to his new employers if they have an approved pension scheme. Conversely, a man joining the scheme is able to transfer to the scheme an approved pension from his previous employment.

(viii) Finally, in order to show the comprehensive nature of the scheme, I mention without stating any detail that benefits are payable on the death of a member to a woman who was living with him, or who had care of his children; they are also payable to adult dependants and to the children of a deceased member up to the age of 16.

*Widow's benefits*

(i) As I have already mentioned, if a member dies in service, from whatever cause, his widow receives two-thirds of the pension which would have been payable to the member if he had retired on grounds of incapacity at the date of his death. She also receives a lump sum, which is the highest of either one year's pensionable earnings or 156 times the weekly rate of what would have been the member's incapacity pension or £300.

(ii) When a member dies after normal age retirement or after very early retirement or as a result of incapacity or following redundancy, his widow receives a pension equal to two-thirds of his pension. Should death occur within five years of age or incapacity retirement or very early retirement (but not redundancy) the widow receives the balance of five years' pension in a lump sum.'

I also take the calculation of benefits from the judge's judgment as follows:

'*The calculation of benefits*

(i) The weekly pension on retirement is calculated by taking 1/90th of the weekly pensionable earnings and multiplying the sum by the number of years for which the member has contributed to the scheme. The years are counted from 6 April 1975. The pensionable earnings are the average weekly earnings taken over the best three consecutive years of the last 13 years of membership of the scheme [each of these three years is however up-dated and increased by reference to the cost of living index up to the last of the 13 years] . . . Thus, on retirement at 65, the 13-year period begins at the age of 52. If a member elects to take very early retirement, the period for the calculation of benefit begins at 47 and the pension and lump sum is fixed at the age of 60 but will not be payable until 65. All pensions are subject to tax on a PAYE basis. The lump sum is tax-free . . .

(ii) If a member elects to take very early retirement at 60, his years of pensionable service are reduced by five. Thus, if any of the plaintiffs Auty, Mills and Rogers are likely to take very early retirement, their pension benefits will be reduced. The same consideration applies to the deceased.

(iii) The lump sum payable on retirement is 156 times the weekly rate of pension as I have already mentioned.

(iv) In the case of a deferred pension up to the maximum age of 70 the pension and lump sum is calculated as in (i) above, but for each additional year worked after 65 the pension is increased by a further 1/90th of pensionable earnings.

(v) All other members' pensions, whether for incapacity, redundancy or if payable in any other circumstances, are calculated in accordance with the method described in (i) above.'

The claims of the three appellants other than the widow Mrs Popow were all based on similar considerations, and I will first consider the appellant Auty. His claim was for the loss of rights under the scheme which he had suffered as a consequence of his accident.

His injury prevented him from doing his job as a face-worker, and consequently he
a suffered a loss of £35·29 per week until he reached the age of 50. Thereafter he would
suffer no loss because he had intended to stop face work then in any event. This loss was
agreed and the effect of it would be that the pension payable at age 65 would be £633
less than if he had not had the accident. The judge's calculation of damage can
conveniently be set out as follows:

b

| | | |
|---|---|---|
| Net annual loss of pension after tax (£633—30%) | | £443 |
| Plaintiff's expectation of life beyond 65 | 6·68 years | |
| ⅔rds of plaintiff's wife's expectation beyond | | |
| plaintiff's (5·58 years) | 3·72 years | |
| Total years of loss | | 10·4 years |
c | Appropriate multiplier applied by judge | | 7 |
| | | |
| Pension loss at age 65 | £3,101 | |
| Lump sum payment at 65 | £1,899 | |
| | | £5,000 |
| | | |
d | Discounted at 5% to give present-day value of pension | | |
| payable in 31 years' time | £1,100 | |
| | | |
| Less further discount to cover contingencies | £300 | |
| | | £800 |
| Add to this for loss of death in service benefit | | £200 |
e | Total | | £1,000 |

The appellants' case was: (1) that the judge paid insufficient attention to the effects of
inflation; in particular (a) although he rejected the actuarial evidence, there were some
parts of it to which he should have paid attention, (b) even adopting the conventional
approach, the judge's discount should have been 2% and not 5%, (c) even if inflation
f should not normally be taken into account, this case was one of those exceptional cases
where it should be taken into account, (d) since the scheme was intended to pay attention
to increases in cost of living, the judge should have given effect to this; (2) that the judge
had taken seven years' purchase when it should have been higher, and that the judge had
discounted twice for risk of death and had discounted too heavily for contingencies; (3)
g that the award for loss of the right to a widow's pension from death in service was too
low; (4) that in the case of Mrs Popow the judge should have awarded a sum for loss of
the opportunity for obtaining a post-retirement widow's pension.
   (1) On the general question of how far future inflation should be taken into account
in assessing damages, there have been a number of authorities in which observations
have been made as to the impact of inflation on the award of damages. I need only refer
to one, Cookson v Knowles [1982] 2 All ER 604, [1979] AC 556. There Lord Diplock,
h having said that the loss of earnings should be based on the rate at the time of trial and
not at the date of the accident, said ([1978] 2 All ER 604 at 611, [1979] AC 556 at 571–
572):

   'The conventional method of calculating it has been to apply to what is found on
   the evidence to be a sum representing "the dependency", a multiplier representing
i  what the judge considers in the circumstances particular to the deceased to be the
   appropriate number of years' purchase. In times of stable currency the multipliers
   that were used by judges were appropriate to interest rates of four per cent to five
   per cent whether the judges using them were conscious of this or not. For the
   reasons I have given I adhere to the opinion Lord Pearson and I had previously
   expressed [ie Lord Pearson in Taylor v O'Connor [1970] 1 All ER 365 at 378, [1971]
   AC 115 at 142–143 and Lord Diplock in Mallett v McMonagle [1969] 2 All ER 178
   at 190, [1970] AC 166 at 176], which was applied by the Court of Appeal in Young v

*Percival* [1974] 3 All ER 677 at 686–688, [1975] 1 WLR 17 at 27–29, that the likelihood of continuing inflation after the date of trial should not affect either the figure for the dependency or the multiplier used. Inflation is taken care of in a rough and ready way by the higher rates of interest obtainable as one of the consequences of it and no other practical basis of calculation has been suggested that is capable of dealing with so conjectural a factor with greater precision.'

And Lord Fraser said ([1978] 2 All ER 604 at 615, [1979] AC 556 at 576–577):

'The multipliers which are generally adopted in practice are based on the assumption (rarely mentioned and perhaps rarely appreciated) that the principal sum of damages will earn interest at about four or five per cent, which are rates that would be appropriate in time of stable currency, as my noble and learned friend, Lord Diplock, pointed out in *Mallett v McMonagle* [1969] 2 All ER 178 at 190, [1970] AC 166 at 176. But in times of rapid inflation the rate of interest that can be earned by prudent investment in fixed interest securities tends to be high, as investors seek to protect their capital and also to obtain a positive rate of interest. At the date of the trial in this case (May 1976) it was possible to obtain interest at a rate of approximately 14 per cent in gilt-edged securities, and so long as inflation continues at its present rate of approximately 10 per cent, experience suggests that the interest element in the widow's assumed annuity will be appreciably higher than the four or five per cent on which the multiplier is based. What she loses by inflation will thus be roughly equivalent to what she gains by the high rate of interest, provided she is not liable for a high rate of income tax.'

The other members of the House agreed with the speeches of Lord Diplock and Lord Fraser. In that case, unlike the present one, the court was concerned with valuing the prospective annual loss for the remaining working life of the deceased, ie the present capital value of annual payments over a number of years. Where they are future payments, the limit to which inflation should influence the assessment of future loss is to take the loss at the date of trial and not at the date of the accident, and no more, save where the plaintiff is liable to pay a high rate of income tax.

In the present case the question is different, namely what is the present-day value of a capital payment to be made in 31 years' time?

(a) The actuarial evidence called by the appellants indicated that considerable allowance should be made for inflation. The judge, in his judgment, set out fully and with the greatest care the evidence of Mr Gooch, the actuary. The judge was concerned about the number of assumptions made by Mr Gooch. These included future inflation and the rate at which it would occur, the personal future of each individual plaintiff in relation to marriage, work in the community and possible date of retirement, and certain other matters. I do not here repeat all the assumptions or the effect of the answers that Mr Gooch gave in cross-examination. The judge regarded many of them as pure speculation. After pointing out that Mr Gooch was an actuary and not an economist, the judge came to the conclusion that his evidence was inadmissible as being 'based on hearsay' and 'speculative in its nature'. I wholly agree with the judge. Even if it were admissible, I would myself strongly discourage it. I agree with the observations of Edmund Davies LJ in *Mitchell v Mulholland (No 2)* [1971] 2 All ER 1205 at 1214, [1972] 1 QB 65 at 79:

'With deference, these views as to the inadmissibility of such evidence in general commend themselves strongly to me. But Sir Garfield Barwick CJ conceded that in a special case an exception might be made to such inadmissibility, continuing the passage just quoted by saying (see *O'Brien v McKean* (1968) 42 ALJR 223 at 227): "Where sound and precise evidence can be given as to the probable rate of increase in cost of some specific item becoming greater than the probable rate of benefit by the use of the capital sums to be awarded, the matter may possibly be different: though as at present advised I should consider such a possibility remote".'

(b) Counsel for the appellants, relying on certain cases decided since *Cookson v Knowles* a [1978] 2 All ER 604, [1979] AC 556 and since the trial of this action, submitted that there were grounds for taking a lower rate than 4% to 5%. These cases were *Birkett v Hayes* [1982] 2 All ER 710, [1982] 1 WLR 816 and *Wright v British Rlys Board* [1983] 2 All ER 698, [1983] 2 AC 773. It is true that in the latter case Lord Diplock referred to his observations in *Cookson v Knowles* [1978] 2 All ER 604 at 611, [1979] AC 556 at 571 and said ([1983] 2 All ER 698 at 704, [1983] 2 AC 773 at 783):

b 'It does not follow from this, however, that in times of highly unstable currency, the part of the interest rate that represents the reward obtained for foregoing the use of money still remains at 4% to 5%.'

But both these cases were dealing with pre-trial interest and not, as in *Cookson v Knowles* and the present case, interest in the future. Counsel for the appellants also referred to an Australian case, *Todorovic v Waller, Jetson v Hankin* (1981) 56 ALJR 59, but that was a case c dealing with laying down a guiding rule in Australian conditions and has no application here. In my judgment these cases do not affect the principle which I have already stated.

(c) Nor can it be said, as counsel for the appellants sought to argue, that this is a special case for departing from the general rule as contemplated by Lord Fraser in *Cookson v Knowles* [1978] 2 All ER 604 at 616, [1979] AC 556 at 577–578, when he excepted the possibility of cases with a high rate of income tax.

d (d) Finally on this part of the appellants' case, this court does not have to consider the question of whether or not the judge should have made a different award because the scheme took into account the cost of living index. The judge held, as a question of fact, that the assumption that the fund would be able to make payments increased in line with increases in the cost of living was not justified and was based on pure speculation.

Accordingly, the judge was faced with a somewhat different assessment from *Cookson* e *v Knowles* and other cases to which the judge was referred. Having decided that he could make no allowance for the possibility of increased pension payments because of the increased cost of living index, he had to decide the present-day value of a fixed sum payable in 31 years' time. He chose a 5% discount rate table, and in my opinion nobody could fault such a choice.

(2) It was submitted (a) that the judge in taking a multiplier of seven to compensate f for 10·4 years' loss was taking a figure that was too low and (b) that in applying a substantial discount for other imponderables he was discounting twice over for early death.

(a) The judge did not explain the use of seven as a multiplier, but it is not suggested that such a calculation should be done with complete accuracy, and using a 5% table the judge was faced with choosing between seven and eight. He chose seven, and in my g opinion this court should not interfere.

(b) The discount for imponderables which the judge made in Auty's case was 27%. The judge said that the imponderables included voluntary wastage, redundancy, dismissal, supervening ill-health, disablement or death before 65, and said that death was the major discount. It was submitted that the risk of death was already taken into consideration in the expectation of life. This is a misunderstanding. The expectation of h life is an average, and assumes everybody lives to that age and then dies, but in fact some die before and some after. Those who die before are the important ones.

Sir Gordon Willmer in *Mitchell v Mulholland (No 2)* [1971] 2 All ER 1205 at 1219–1220, [1972] 1 QB 65 at 85–86, after saying that actuarial calculations were based on the performance of the average man, went on:

j 'The average man has an expectation of life of a certain number of years. This is a matter of probability, but for purposes of actuarial calculation it has to be treated as a certainty. Yet nobody can say whether an individual plaintiff is an average man, or that he will live for the expectation of life of an average man of his age. Any actuarial calculation must, therefore, be discounted to allow for the chance that he may only live for a shorter period. The chances, and not the probabilities, are what the judge has to evaluate in any given case. It is true that there is also a chance that the individual plaintiff may live longer than the average expectation of life. The chances are equal either way, but as a matter of calculation it can be shown that the impact of the chance of shorter life is of greater significance than that of longer life.'

I agree with this; indeed, when making the calculation which the judge had to make, those who die early are the only ones which matter because the fact of living longer than the expectation is immaterial.

The question of a discount for imponderables is very much a question for the trial judge, and in my opinion he was perfectly entitled to make the discount which he made for each of the three appellants in this case.

(3) Counsel for the appellants submitted that the figure awarded by the judge for death in service was too low. He prayed in aid some calculations prepared by Mr Gooch, which he submitted would afford guidance on the question. But these figures involve making a number of assumptions. Would the appellant be one of those who would die before reaching the age of 65? If so, when would he die, because the pension would vary according to that time. If it were after age 63, the amount would be less than if it were earlier. The greater probability would be that the appellant would not die before age 65, in which case no widow's pension from death in service would be payable. The judge, correctly in my opinion, did not make any calculation. He made his own assessment. In my opinion he was right to do so and I agree with the figure that he found. I should add that a cross-appeal on this point was not pursued.

The observations which I have made in relation to the case of Auty apply equally to the two other appellants, Mills and Rogers.

(4) Finally I come to the claim by Mrs Popow. Mr Popow was aged 55 when he was killed. The judge found that he had a normal expectation of life and would have retired at 60. If he had not been killed and had died in service or before 65, his widow would have been entitled to a widow's pension. If he had died after he retired, his widow would also have been entitled to a widow's pension. Counsel for the appellants has put forward the rather startling proposition that although the widow is in receipt of a widow's pension, she is nevertheless entitled to claim as part of her dependency a sum representing the loss of the chance of a post-retirement widow's pension. He submits that she has lost that chance and that she is entitled to some amount as part of the dependency for that lost chance because s 4 of the Fatal Accidents Act 1976 provides that a benefit or pension paid as the result of the death shall not be taken into account in assessing damages.

The Fatal Accidents Act 1976 was a consolidating Act, and s 1 provided for the right of action for wrongful acts causing death. Section 3(1) provided:

'In the action such damages may be awarded as are proportioned to the injury resulting from the death to the dependants respectively . . .'

Section 4(1) provided:

'In assessing damages in respect of a person's death . . . there shall not be taken into account any insurance money, benefit, pension or gratuity which has been or will or may be paid as a result of the death.'

On the death of her husband, it is clear that Mrs Popow qualified for, and received, a widow's pension. Furthermore, her dependency was assessed by ignoring the amount of that pension. No part of her dependency either then or thereafter could arise from lack of a widow's pension because she continued to be in receipt of one. Put another way, she cannot claim for loss of an opportunity to obtain a widow's pension at a later date when she has not lost the opportunity of a widow's pension because she is already in receipt of a widow's pension.

This conclusion is, in my opinion, consistent with the decision of the House of Lords in Parry v Cleaver [1969] 1 All ER 555, [1970] AC 1, where the House was considering whether or not a pension to an injured policeman should be brought into account in a personal injury claim. The majority held that it should not be brought into account against loss of wages, but should be brought into account against the police pension when

he reached retiring age. Lord Reid expressed his reasoning in the passage from his speech
*a* ([1969] 1 All ER 555 at 563–564, [1970] AC 1 at 20–21) quoted in the judgment of
Oliver LJ. It follows that in my judgment there was no loss of dependency at the date of
the deceased's death in relation to the loss of a chance after his hypothetical death in
retirement. The pension was already being paid and therefore there was nothing lost.

In my opinion the very full and admirable judgment of the judge arrived at the correct
conclusions in relation to each of the issues in this case, and I would dismiss this appeal.

*b*
**OLIVER LJ.** I agree that this appeal fails.

The appellants' criticisms of the judge's conclusions in the case of Auty, Mills and
Rogers fall in substance under two heads, both of which stem from the nature of the
Mineworkers' Pension Scheme as a scheme which seeks to introduce an index-linking
element into the future and contingent benefits payable thereunder. It is said that the
*c* judge failed to appreciate, or to give sufficient weight, to what is described as the
'insurance element' in the scheme, and thus to attribute any weight to the only evidence
which could assist him in evaluating such element, that is to say the evidence of Mr
Gooch, the actuary called by the appellants in the court below. Secondly, it is said that
even applying a conventional approach to the assessment of the present value of the
future and contingent benefits of the scheme, he gave no or insufficient weight to the
*d* inflation-proof nature of the scheme, and thus misled himself either into applying too
low a multiplier, or into adopting too high a discount for present payment. There are, in
addition, a number of aspects in which it is claimed that the judge was in error in
applying the conventional basis of valuation of the appellants' claims.

For the reasons which Waller LJ has given, I agree that these criticisms are not well-
founded. The proposition that an interest in an index-linked scheme must have a higher
*e* value than an interest in a non-index-linked scheme and that therefore the court ought
to search for some method of valuation which will give effect to the advantage of index-
linking is one which has, on the face of it, some attraction, until one appreciates the
essentially tenuous nature of the index-linking in this case.

The so-called 'inflation-proof' element arises from the provisions of r 26, whose
language the judge described as 'complicated'. It is no necessary criticism of the
*f* draftsman, who had a formidable task to perform, but speaking for myself, I have found
that perhaps an understatement. Indeed I confess that the rule has appeared to me as
something of a minor masterpiece of opacity. What does emerge from it, however, with
tolerable clarity, is that there is no guaranteed fund from which increased pensions are to
be provided, and that the index-linking is founded rather in hope than in confidence.
Pensionable earnings and pensions in payment will be increased in accordance with the
*g* cost of living index if funds are available from normal contributions (which they are
never in the least likely to be) or if the board is prepared to make extra deficiency
payments. Thus what the judge found himself being invited to do was to take a view
about what the rates of future inflation were likely to be and whether, in some twenty to
thirty years' time, the government of the day would be able or willing to provide funds
to the board to make deficiency payments in order to protect benefits under the scheme
*h* from whatever degree of inflation had by then occurred or was likely to occur in the
future. He did not, in fact, find Mr Gooch a reliable witness and that really is the end of
the matter so far as this court is concerned. But I am not in the least surprised that the
judge, even if he had felt able to accept the reliability of the witness, found the evidence
that he was able to give less than helpful. Actuarial evidence is no doubt of the greatest
assistance where one is seeking to value interests in a fund of ascertained amount for the
*j* purposes of purchase, sale or exchange. Indeed, such valuations are the foundation of
virtually all schemes propounded under the Variation of Trusts Act 1958. But as a
method of providing a reliable guide to individual behaviour patterns, or to future
economic and political events, the predictions of an actuary can be only a little more
likely to be accurate (and will almost certainly be less entertaining) than those of an
astrologer. The judge was, in my judgment, right to reject evidence of this type as
admissible for the purposes for which it was sought to adduce it in the case before him.

Nevertheless counsel for the appellants submits that, even accepting the highly speculative nature of the benefits capable of arising from the index-linking provisions of the scheme, and even approaching the problem on a conventional basis, the judge should nevertheless have made allowance for inflation in his award of compensation for loss of pension rights, although he accepts that no such allowance falls to be made in assessing loss of future wages. The argument as I understand it rests on two bases, which may be either cumulative or alternative. First it is said that, whatever may be the right approach to the problem of inflation in relation to claims for loss of future wages, special allowance for it ought to be made in the assessment of damages for depreciation in the value of future pension rights under this scheme because the scheme is essentially an insurance scheme.

The scheme, it is argued, not only provides the member with a guaranteed pension on retirement, but also provides him and his dependants with effective insurance cover against other vicissitudes, including redundancy and, in particular, death in service, all benefits being, like the retirement pension, index-linked so far as funds will permit.

Thus, for instance, if a plaintiff dies before retirement but at a time when his pensionable earnings have been reduced by reason of the lapse of the 13 years from the date of his optimum earnings, his widow will receive a smaller death-in-service pension than she would have done if he had been able to continue to do the work which he was doing before the accident occurred. Theoretically he ought to be compensated for this by an award of a sum which would enable him to buy, in the market, insurance cover to protect his widow against loss by providing for her, on his death in service, a sum equal to the difference between what she will actually receive in this event and what she would have received if he had continued to work normally. But there is no such equivalent cover available in the insurance market and in the absence, therefore, of any available yardstick and on the footing that actuarial evidence is rejected, this element in the scheme ought to be recognised and allowed for, it is suggested, in the discount which has to be made for accelerated payment.

Further or alternatively, although counsel for the appellants recognises that a chain of authorities over the past 15 years, culminating with *Lim Poh Choo v Camden and Islington Area Health Authority* [1979] 2 All ER 910, [1980] AC 174, support the proposition that damages generally require no special protection against inflation, since actual interest rates can normally be expected to exceed the rate of inflation, he submits that the approach both of this court and of the House of Lords in two more recent cases justifies a different rule in the case of damages awarded to compensate for a future payment.

As regards the former of these criticisms, there appear to me to be two answers. In so far as the appellants complain that the judge failed to appreciate that the scheme provided a form of insurance cover against various eventualities, the complaint appears to me to be ill-founded. He appears clearly to have had this aspect of the scheme in mind, and indeed his judgment reflects a most careful analysis of the various risks against which protection was to be provided. In so far as the complaint is that the 'insurance' was an insurance against inflation, the very fact that there is no market by reference to which the cost of the benefits can be assessed provides its own answer, for it demonstrates the essentially speculative nature of the index-linking which is said to be the insured benefit. The only value of such an insurance lies in the ability of the insurance fund to meet claims, and the absence of a market quotation for such risks may be assumed to be an indication of the market's lack of confidence in the prospect of such risks being capable of being met. Thus one is brought back to the question of how far one can rely on some future government being prepared to fund the conditionally contracted benefits.

The judge did not feel that he could be called on, first to speculate about this, and then to back his speculation with an award based on its presumed accuracy. I agree with him.

As regards the alternative way in which the case is argued, counsel for the appellants relies on *Birkett v Hayes* [1982] 2 All ER 710, [1982] 1 WLR 816 and *Wright v British Rlys Board* [1983] 2 All ER 698, [1983] 2 AC 773, as indicating that an appropriate rate of discount is no more than 2%.

During the hearing of these appeals I expressed myself as unable to understand how either of these cases is of any assistance at all in arriving at the proper discount to be made in assessing damages for future loss. Further argument has done nothing to relieve my lack of understanding. Those cases, unless I have misread them, are concerned with the question of how a successful plaintiff is to be compensated for the fact that the compensation for non-pecuniary loss, which theoretically he ought to have received the moment he issued his writ, has in fact been withheld from him until the trial. Against the disadvantage that he has theoretically been kept out of his money has to be balanced the fact that the award which is made to him at the trial is made in the money of the day, so that it takes into account any inflation which has occurred since the date of the writ. Thus any interest awarded to him need not take into account a risk element, but is concerned solely with the amount which the plaintiff may reasonably be said to have been deprived of, for the use, without risk of depreciation, of his money in the interim period.

It was this process of reasoning which led this court to the figure of 2% as an appropriate figure. Thus in *Birkett v Hayes* [1982] 2 All ER 710, [1982] 1 WLR 816, if one adopts Lord Denning MR's supposition that the award in that case, if made at the date of the writ, would have been £20,000 as opposed to the £30,000 awarded at the trial, and adds back the difference in the form of interest to cover the risk element, the actual rate of interest which the plaintiff received on his money was something approaching 17% compound. I find myself entirely unable to comprehend how it can be argued from this that where the court is concerned with the quite different problem of the discount to be made for the fact that the plaintiff is receiving here and now a capital sum to compensate him for a loss of future income, that discount should be at a similarly low rate. In the *Birkett v Hayes* situation, the assumption is that the risk element has already been taken care of in the award of compensation and that the court is concerned only with what I may call the 'reward' element in interest. Here the assumption is that the plaintiff is put into possession of a capital sum which he can employ to provide for both the risk and the reward element in the future. Indeed the logic of counsel for the appellants' submissions, if carried to their conclusion, would be the adoption of a discount rate of 17%, or thereabouts.

I find myself, therefore, quite unable to accept the argument for a 2% discount rate based on these cases.

A further persuasive authority relied on by counsel for the appellants in support of his contentions was *Todorovic v Waller* (1981) 56 ALJR 59, where the High Court of Australia, by a majority, adopted a 3% rate of discount. Counsel for the appellants bases himself on the supposition that Australian interest rates are generally higher than those in the United Kingdom, and accordingly prays this case in aid as support for the 2% which he claims to be the appropriate rate.

But that case, in the first place, is not binding on us, and in part rejects the reasoning of Lord Scarman in *Lim Poh Choo v Camden and Islington Area Health Authority* [1979] 2 All ER 910, [1980] AC 174, which does bind us, and, secondly, it was concerned with the practice in Australia, where economic and market conditions are not necessarily the same as they are here. So far as this country is concerned, the judge felt himself bound, after a very careful review of the authorities, to follow the guidance provided by a series of cases in the House of Lords, and he was clearly right to do so. His adoption of a 5% rate as opposed to a 4% or 4½% rate was a matter well within his discretion, and I am certainly not prepared to say that this was too high. It is said, similarly, that he was too ungenerous in the multipliers which he applied. For instance, in the case of Auty where the life expectancy tables produced a joint expectation of 10·40 years on full pension (allowing for a reduction to two-thirds on the prior death of the husband) the judge applied a multiplier of seven. It is said that he should have applied eight. But in an assessment which is admittedly not an exact science, I can see no obvious reason for saying that he was wrong or too ungenerous, and certainly, speaking for myself only, no reason for substituting out of my own inexperience a different figure from that adopted as a matter of judgment by a judge whose experience in this field is almost unrivalled.

The other specific criticisms which have been made are that the judge made, in effect, a double discount for contingencies, in that he based his figure largely on the possibility *a* of death before 65, a possibility which, it is argued, is already taken into account in the average life expectancy. For the reasons which Waller LJ has given, there is nothing in that point.

Equally, I can for my part find nothing wrong with the judge's valuation of the possibility of the widow receiving a pension on the death of her husband in service. As already mentioned, it is quite impossible to find any reliable yardstick by which this can *b* be measured, and the judge was compelled, as judges frequently are in matters of this sort, to do his best to make an assessment with virtually no material to help him. For my part, I am wholly unprepared to say that his estimate was wrong or ought to be interfered with.

The case of Popow raises the same question as regards the extent to which inflation is to be taken into account in valuing the deceased's right to a pension on retirement as that *c* which arises in the cases of Auty, Mills and Rogers, and must, as regards this point, receive the same answer. But it also raises a separate and unique question with regard to the application of s 4 of the Fatal Accidents Act 1976. That Act, like its predecessors dating back to 1846, preserves the right of action of a person who dies as a result of tortious injury but, by s 3, relates the damages recoverable to the injury suffered by the deceased's dependants as a result of his death. Section 4(1) is in the following terms: *d*

> 'In assessing damages in respect of a person's death in an action under this Act, there shall not be taken into account any insurance money, benefit, pension or gratuity which has been or will or may be paid as a result of the death.'

Now, in the instant case, Mr Popow's widow became entitled, as a result of his death, to a lump sum and an immediate pension under the provisions of the scheme. She also *e* became entitled to damages under the Fatal Accidents Act 1976 calculated by reference to her loss of dependency on his future earnings and his future retirement pension on the footing that, but for the accident, he could, subject to conventional discounts, be expected to live for the normal life-span of a man of his age. Clearly, in assessing that loss, the widow's lump sum and present pension entitlement fell to be excluded from the computation by reason of s 4(1) of the Act. *f*

But it is argued that, in addition to the injury inflicted on the widow by the loss of her dependency during the deceased's lifetime if he had lived for his normal life expectancy, the widow has been deprived, by his death, of the widow's pension which she would have received under the scheme if her husband had survived to retirement age and died thereafter. Thus, the argument proceeds, notwithstanding that she receives in the present a widow's pension as a result of his actual death, she is entitled to be compensated in *g* addition for the pension which she would have received in the future on his hypothetical death in retirement, because s 4(1) tells us that, for the purpose of assessing her damages, we are to ignore her present actual pension entitlement even though it will continue to be payable throughout the period during which the hypothetical pension on death in retirement would have become payable, if it ever arose.

The proposition is a startling one, for the necessary consequence of any man's death *h* before retirement is that he does not die in retirement. A man who dies this year cannot die next year. Thus in every case it can be said that the actual death deprives the widow of the pension which she would have got on her husband's hypothetical death in the future. During the residue of his normal life expectancy, she in fact suffers no loss because the compensation which she receives for her loss of dependency during his lifetime covers also the sum which she might be expected to receive by way of pension *j* on the hypothetical death of her husband during that period. But on the expiry of that period there is, it is argued, nothing to be set against the pension to which she would become entitled on her husband's death at that time, since her dependancy ceases and the pension which she is actually receiving has to be ignored.

Counsel for the respondents conjures up an awesome vision of a flood of widows' claims, hitherto unthought of, for loss of future hypothetical pension rights, but although

a
such a prospect may cause one to question the reasoning which produces the result, it cannot affect the value of the nugget which counsel for the appellants has uncovered and which has lain undetected since 1959 (when what is now s 4 was first introduced) if, on its true construction, that is what the section means.

In an extremely careful and helpful judgment the judge dealt with this point very shortly as follows:

b
'With respect to the claim by Mrs Popow for the loss in value of a widow's pension on the assumed death of her late husband in retirement, I consider that the loss would be the result of a natural death and not the result of a tortious death.'

He then considered and distinguished the case of *Davies v Whiteways Cider Co Ltd* [1974] 3 All ER 168, [1975] QB 262 and, if I may say so respectfully, was clearly right in distinguishing it, for that was a case where the widow was able to show a direct and immediate pecuniary loss to herself as a result of her husband's death. This is the only c part of the judge's judgment with which I do not find myself wholly in agreement, for I have not been able to follow, and counsel for the respondents has not been able to explain how, assuming that there was a loss of the widow's expectation, that loss can be said to be attributable to a natural death which, ex hypothesi, has not occurred. I suspect that the sentence from the judgment quoted above may conceal some ellipsis of the actual process d of reasoning.

Nevertheless, for my part, I find myself wholly unpersuaded by counsel for the appellants' submission on behalf of Mrs Popow that the result which he claims does indeed follow ineluctably from the provisions of the statute and that the judge therefore reached the wrong conclusion. It seems to me that the answer to counsel's proposition lies, as is so often the case where absurdity results, in an examination of the major e premise on which the proposition is based. The starting point is the scheme. It is a consequence of counsel's categorisation of the scheme as an insurance scheme insuring the member and his family against a variety of misfortunes, that he treats the benefits provided for in each event as separate and distinct rights. Thus he speaks of a 'death-in-service pension' and a 'death-after-retirement pension'. The scheme, however, in fact provides simply for 'a pension' payable on one event, namely widowhood, which may f occur in any one or more of a series of different circumstances, some of which are mutually exclusive and some of which (for instance, death in service and death as a result of an industrial accident) are not.

It is, of course, the case that the amount of the pension will vary according to the date on which and the circumstances in which it becomes payable. Thus, for instance, if the pension becomes payable as a result of death in service, it is likely to be at a lower rate g than it would be if the deceased had lived and retired, because his years of service would be greater. Similarly, if his death is the result of industrial accident or disease, the scheme provides for certain minima which are not otherwise applicable. It has, however, to be borne in mind that what counsel for the appellants claims for the widow is not the future loss represented by the difference between the actual rate of pension which she receives and the hypothetical rate which she would receive if her husband had died after h retirement. Indeed, he would be in great difficulty in claiming that because he could not do it without doing what s 4(1) of the 1976 Act says is not to be done. What he claims is a sum to compensate her for a total loss of pension on a hypothetical death after retirement.

Turning now to the scheme, widow's benefit is dealt with in r 16, para (1) of which provides:

j
'Subject as hereinafter provided, where any member or other person (in this Rule called "the deceased") dies on or after 6th April 1975 benefit shall be payable to his Widow by reference to him under and in accordance with this Rule.'

Paragraph (2) goes on to provide:

'Benefit shall be payable under paragraph (3) of this Rule by reference to the deceased if any one or more of the following conditions are satisfied [there follows an enumeration of a number of conditions which include (inter alia) death of the deceased in service and death of the deceased after retirement].'

Paragraph 3(a) then provides:

'The benefit payable under this paragraph shall be a pension calculated in accordance with whichever shall be applicable of paragraphs (4), (5), (5A) and (5AA) of this Rule.'

The applicable paragraph in the cases of death in service before 65, death in service after 65 and death after retirement is para 4. In the two former cases the pension is to be two-thirds of the amount of the pension which would have been payable to the deceased himself if he had retired immediately before his death, and in the third case two-thirds of the deceased's actual pension payable in retirement.

It is, of course, inherent in this that, in so far as the conditions on which it becomes payable are mutually exclusive, it is payable once only on the first of those conditions to occur; but it would, in my judgment, be a misuse of language to say that, by the occurrence of the actual condition which triggers the benefit of the scheme, the widow has 'lost' the benefit which might have been triggered by an event which can no longer occur. On that footing, a widow whose husband dies naturally whilst in service 'loses' the 'death by industrial injury' benefit because the opportunity to suffer industrial injury and thus to achieve the appropriate minimum pension has been denied to him by his earlier natural death. The correct analysis, as it seems to me, is merely that the condition for the operation of the widow's benefit part of the scheme has occurred so that she has gained her appropriate entitlement. She has lost nothing.

Turning then to the 1976 Act, the key section appears to me to be not s 4, but s 3. Section 3(1) provides:

'In the action such damages may be awarded as are proportioned to the injury resulting from the death to the dependants respectively, and the amount so recovered, after deducting the costs not recovered from the defendant, shall be divided among the dependants in such shares as may be directed.'

There are thus two stages in the inquiry. Firstly there must be ascertained what 'injury . . . to the dependants' has resulted from the death. Secondly, there must be assessed the damages which are to be awarded for that injury. No doubt in ascertaining the extent of the injury suffered (for instance, the loss of dependency or of the estate duty advantage with which *Davies v Whiteways Cider Co Ltd* [1974] 3 All ER 168, [1975] QB 262 was concerned) you do not take into account any countervailing advantage which may have resulted to the dependant from the death in the form of pension or insurance benefit. In other words, it is no doubt right to observe the provisions of s 4(1) at both stages of the inquiry.

But it is still necessary to establish that the dependant has in fact suffered an injury (ie lost something) as a result of the death. Here what is claimed as the injury is the loss of the very thing (ie a widow's pension) that the widow in fact has gained as a result of the fulfilment of the conditions of the scheme earlier rather than later, and whilst s 4 precludes setting the benefit of the pension against damage suffered under some other head, there is nothing in that section which requires one to assume, in ascertaining whether there has been any injury at all, that that which has happened in fact has not happened.

The fallacy of the appellant's reasoning is, in my judgment, that it premises a loss which has not occurred and which cannot be substantiated either in fact or in law.

The point raised by counsel for the appellants on Mrs Popow's behalf is a novel one and it is, perhaps, not altogether surprising that it has not previously received judicial consideration. *Humphrey v Ward Engineering Services Ltd* (1975) 119 SJ 461, to which we were referred, is concerned with a rather different point, namely whether pension and insurance benefits are to be taken into account initially for the purpose of seeing whether the dependants are generally better off or worse off as a result of the death. Similarly *Lea v Owner* (22 January 1980, referred to in Kemp and Kemp *The Quantum of Damages*, vol 1, Pt III, para 27–314) does not help in the present context, since it was concerned with the loss by the widow, as a result of her husband's death, of a separate and individual retirement pension to which she would have been entitled in her own right so long as both she and her husband were alive.

Some guidance, however, can I think be obtained from the decision of the House of Lords in *Parry v Cleaver* [1969] 1 All ER 555, [1970] AC 1, where their Lordships, by a majority, followed the analogy of the Fatal Accidents Act in refusing to treat a sickness pension which the plaintiff received as a result of his injuries as an offset against damages for loss of earnings up to retirement age, but nevertheless took it into account as an offset in assessing the amount to be awarded for loss of the retirement pension benefit arising under the same scheme. The matter is aptly summed up by Lord Reid ([1969] 1 All ER 555 at 563–564, [1970] AC 1 at 20–21):

'As regards police pension, his loss after reaching police retiring age would be the difference between the full pension which he would have received if he had served his full time and his ill-health pension. It has been asked why his ill-health pension is to be brought into account at this point if not brought into account for the earlier period. The answer is that in the earlier period we are not comparing like with like. He lost wages but he gained something different in kind, a pension. But with regard to the period after retirement we are comparing like with like. Both the ill-health pension and the full retirement pension are the products of the same insurance scheme; his loss in the later period is covered by his having been deprived of the opportunity to continue in insurance so as to swell the ultimate product of that insurance from an ill-health to a retirement pension. There is no question as regards that period of a loss of one kind and a gain of a different kind.'

To put it another way, to the extent of the ill-health pension payable after retirement age, the plaintiff had suffered no loss. That is, in my judgment, precisely what has happened here. As a result of her husband's death, the widow has become entitled to a widow's pension under the scheme, and it is impossible to say that she has 'lost' the pension which in fact she is receiving merely because one of the other events on which it would have become payable has not occurred and never can now occur. Accordingly, I am satisfied, albeit for somewhat different reasons, that the judge also reached the right conclusion as regards this head of damage claimed. I too would dismiss the appeal.

**PURCHAS LJ.** The four test cases involved in this appeal can, I hope not unfairly, be described as a skirmish late in a campaign which has been waged for two decades or more to inject into the art of assessment of compensation for future loss the techniques of the actuary. This is not to say that actuarial evidence is inadmissible. Unhappily, where compensation for future loss is involved, its value is almost invariably diminished if not extinguished by uncertainties. These difficulties were highlighted in the cross-examination by counsel for the respondents of Mr Gooch, the actuary called in support of the appellants' cases, and need not be repeated here. No amount of calculation can make good deficiencies in the basic data on which the actuarial projections are based. This, with respect to counsel for the appellants, also indicates the fallacy in his submissions which were aimed at distinguishing cases under this pension scheme from those involving the assessment of damages for future loss. These have been considered in the judgments already delivered.

As to the suitability of actuarial computations, however, the matter hardly admits of further discussion. For my part, I can see no material distinction between the problems encountered in the assessment of future loss invariably found in serious injury cases such as the cost of future care and attention, future loss of earnings, or the loss of contingent financial rights, from the assessment of damages for the future contingent loss of benefits under this pension scheme. In form the distinction is that the court must assess the sums required at the date of trial to provide the appropriate sums in the future, but the problems are indistinguishable from those considered in *Lim Poh Choo v Camden and Islington Area Health Authority* [1979] 2 All ER 910, [1980] AC 174. As Oliver LJ has already pointed out, the 'inflation-proof' provisions of r 26 of the scheme are by no means a sure foundation. Not the least of the uncertainties arising in this case to which reference is made by the judge is that to date the funds in the scheme have proved inadequate to enable payments to keep pace with inflation without the so-called deficiency payments which have hitherto been made jointly by the union, the coal board and the government. This introduces an element of political speculation into the problem.

The four cases were selected as representing different but typical problems arising in claims under the pensions scheme entered into by both the coal board and the National Union of Mineworkers. However, the principles involved are common to three of them. The fourth case raises questions of its own. It is not to deny the importance of the problems involved to comment that the amounts of compensation in dispute are small in comparison with the total awards for the main injuries and loss in each case agreed or already awarded by Tudor Evans J, who had, in three of the cases, dealt with the main question of compensation.

Before Tudor Evans J counsel for the appellants presented the case for the three male plaintiffs on the basis that the conventional approach could not be used to assess the proper compensation for the diminution of the prospective rights under the scheme in four respects: (i) reduction in value of the pension payable on retirement; (ii) reduction in value of a lump sum; (iii) reduction in value of a widow's pension payable on death in retirement; (iv) reduction in value of a widow's pension payable on death in service. The unsuitability of the conventional approach, counsel submitted, was a justification for resorting to actuarial methods.

*Reduction in value of pension and lump sum payable on retirement*

Mr Gooch produced arithmetical projections on which he based calculations of the present-day value of the reduction in the various pension rights. His evidence was the subject of careful and detailed consideration by the judge, and was roundly rejected by him.

Although by their notice of appeal the appellants adhere to the actuarial approach, counsel for the appellants has not attempted to argue its validity before us with any degree of force. He submitted that in adopting the conventional approach, the judge failed to adapt this to take into account the particular aspects of the pension scheme, namely the protection against inflation intended under the scheme which he described as being in the nature of an insurance cover. Counsel for the appellants submitted that this justified a departure from the standard method of discounting at 4% or 5% in respect of present compensation for future loss. In particular counsel for the appellants relied on three cases, *Birkett v Hayes* [1982] 2 All ER 710, [1982] 1 WLR 816, *Wright v British Rlys Board* [1983] 2 All ER 698, [1983] 2 AC 773, and *Todorovic v Waller* (1981) 56 ALJR 59.

The decisions in *Birkett v Hayes* and *Wright v British Rlys Board* need some consideration in this context. The history of the courts' attempts to deal with the question of interest to be allowed under s 3 of the Law Reform (Miscellaneous Provisions) Act 1934 (as amended) on a sum of damages awarded at trial to compensate the plaintiff for having been kept out of his money is set out in the speech of Lord Diplock in *Wright's* case [1983] 2 All ER 698 at 701–706, [1983] 2 AC 773 at 779–786, and needs no repetition here. The courts were attempting to produce a formula which would do justice to both sides in the particular circumstances of that problem.

The short-term investment rate applied in *Jefford v Gee* [1970] 1 All ER 1202, [1970] 2 QB 130 was proving too high. The Court of Appeal recognised this and moved too far in the other direction, namely to award no interest on damages at all. Finally the matter was resolved at an interest rate per annum of 2% which was approved in *Wright's* case. In arriving at this figure, the House of Lords were dealing with a different problem from the problem which arises when assessing what is the appropriate figure by which to discount for a future loss. The interest awarded under the 1934 Act is in the form of a single payment which is a percentage of the damages awarded at the time of trial. Since a the Finance Act 1971, this interest is not subject to tax, and the sum on which it is based represents damages assessed at the date of trial and, therefore, includes an inflationary element related to the period between the service of the writ and the date of trial (see *Birkett v Hayes* [1982] 2 All ER 710 at 713, [1982] 1 WLR 816 at 820–821 per Lord Denning MR). The progress of inflation in these circumstances is established, and the computation is a retrospective one without imponderables. It must, therefore, be a low figure for interest (see *Birkett v Hayes* [1982] 2 All ER 710 at 716–717, [1982] 1 WLR 816

b at 824–825 per Eveleigh LJ).

With respect to his argument, I am unable to follow counsel for the appellants' submission that *Birkett v Hayes* and *Wright's* case support a discount rate as low as 2% or 3% in assessing damages for future loss. I agree that, in line with the citations already given from *Cookson v Knowles* [1978] 2 All ER 604, [1979] AC 556, the figure of 4% to 5% as applicable in times of stable currency reflects the real value of money, the risk involved

c in lending it as well as the incidence of taxation. It does not involve by definition the risk of future inflation; but taken in conjunction with the higher interest rates available in times of inflation, the method will afford, on prudent investment, a reasonable degree of protection against the uncertainties of inflation and risk in lending, so as to counteract the drop in the purchasing power of money during the period over which the damages must be discounted.

d Mr Gooch's contentions, which were rejected by the judge, were that investment at current rates of interest could not protect the fund and that, therefore, there should be no discount at all. With respect, I do not find it surprising that the judge rejected this submission, as it would mean the collapse of the existing money market as it is known at present.

The decision in the Australian High Court in *Todorovic v Waller* (1981) 56 ALJR 59 is,

e of course, not binding on us, but the judgments are of importance, save in so far as they reject the speech of Lord Scarman in *Lim Poh Choo v Camden and Islington Area Health Authority* [1979] 2 All ER 910, [1980] AC 174. In particular, we were referred to the judgment of Gibbs CJ and Wilson J, who were two of the majority of five, the whole court consisting of seven judges. After a careful review of the authorities, including the English cases, recognition is given to the importance of certainty leading to the settlement

f of claims and the lack of any justification for using a method of an actuarial or mathematical nature in assessing damages because of the numerous imponderables involved where future loss is concerned. I would wish to quote only one short paragraph without wishing to be discourteous to a long and carefully reasoned judgment (56 ALJR 59 at 66):

g 'We consider that in future the courts in Australia, in States where the question is not governed by statute, should, in assessing damages, arrive at the present value of a future loss by discounting at a fixed rate which will be applied in all cases and which will in itself reflect the effect of notional tax on notional income from the invested fund. To take this course may seem to involve some sacrifice of accuracy in the interests of predictability, but the whole process involves so much speculation that it is impossible to pretend to accuracy. In fixing the discount rate, the fact that

h for so long the rates applied by the courts in Australia have been at a level of five per cent and above should not be disregarded. Some downward adjustment is necessary to take account of notional tax. The actuaries' tables show that if the assumption is, as it must be, that the income is earned at the discount rate the necessary adjustment is quite small, particularly when the assumed income is within the range within which most employees' incomes fall in Australia. Now that the effect of inflation

j has become more apparent, it seems right to make a further moderate downward adjustment to the rate. Our own choice would be to adopt a discount rate of four per cent, but all that we have said indicates how arbitrary any choice must be and for that reason it is necessary for individual members of the Court to adjust their views in the interests of achieving a final and authoritative decision. We therefore concur in the view, to which we understand a majority of the Court is prepared to subscribe [this means the other three of the majority of five], that until this Court otherwise decides, a discount rate of three per cent should in future be applied and that no further allowance should be made for notional tax.'

I do not find this authority any cause to depart from the guidelines already established in the cases cited by the judge on which he based his decision to use a discount rate of 5%. It might be arguable that in matters of the choice of discount factors or other mathematical or even actuarial data, this court is not bound by its own earlier decisions, or indeed by the House of Lords, as it would be in matters of law, but that having been said, for my part I agree, with respect, that the attraction of adopting a figure in the 4% to 5% range is that it achieves predictability and a rough and ready protection against the greater excesses of inflation, provided that the exceptional case can be dealt with individually, e g if there is a high incidence of income tax or other special features.

The High Court of Australia appears to have been attempting to choose a figure relative to the incidence of income tax, and acknowledging the development of inflation in a more predictable manner. The English courts do not ignore inflation: they recognise its existence and acknowledge the impossibility of adopting a mathematical or actuarial approach to it, being content with the formula which, being based on a normal stable economy, is to a degree self-regulatory. In times of high inflation and, therefore, high interest rates, the sum invested will show a yield far greater than 4% to 5% which will compensate for the drop in the value of money over the period of the notional investment.

Incidentally, the flexible approach of Gibbs CJ and Wilson J in *Todorovic v Waller* permitted them to reduce from 4% to 3%, in the interests of agreement with the other judges forming the majority of the court. This in itself shows how arbitrary the approach to this problem has to be. I do not, therefore, find myself able to accede to counsel for the appellants' submission that the judge adopted too high a discount rate in assessing the present value of the future capitalised loss related to the depreciation of the pension rights. The choice between two discount figures is very much a matter of judgment for the trial judge, and one with which this court should be slow to interfere unless one of the well-known reasons to do so appears.

Counsel for the appellants also submitted that the result of calculating the periods of expectation of life from the age at trial and then discounting the overall figure for day-to-day contingencies was that there was a double discount for the period between ages 34 to 65. To eliminate this, he submitted that the expectation of life figures should be taken to be those for the plaintiff's 65th birthday. This was based on the fact that life tables are averages anyway.

As Waller LJ has already explained, by reference to the judgment of Sir Gordon Willmer in *Mitchell v Mulholland (No 2)* [1971] 2 All ER 1205, [1972] 1 QB 65, this argument was misconceived. The judge used a multiplier of seven for the computation of the value of loss of pension as at 65, and then discounted this figure in Auty's case by 27%. I agree that both these figures were well within the range of his discretion and this court should, therefore, not interfere. The same applies to the figures adopted in the cases of Mills and Rogers.

*Reduction in value of widow's pension payable on death in retirement or death in service*

Counsel for the appellants suggested that claims for reduction in the value of the widow's pension arising on death either in service or in retirement were not susceptible to computation by the conventional method and that, therefore, resort must be had to actuarial computations. He complained that the judge had 'plucked a figure out of the air', and that he was wrong in so doing. Counsel submitted that the proper measure of damage would be the cost of obtaining insurance cover to meet the shortfall in prospect of the pensions available to the widow. With respect to counsel, this submission has a clear fallacy in it, namely that it is buying the damage suffered in fact by the widow, whereas the injury in respect of which damages can be awarded is that suffered by the plaintiff. In effect the only loss recoverable is the loss of opportunity to continue to provide a higher widow's pension in either event. The judge, in his judgment, came to the following conclusions:

a
'In one sense the loss can only arise on death, but the plaintiffs, as a consequence of the tort, have lost the right to contribute to the same extent from their wages in order to confer a benefit in the event of their predeceasing their wives. Is that loss recoverable by the plaintiffs and, if so, how is it to be valued. I think that the plaintiffs are able to recover damages for this consequence of the tort? After all, the rights under the scheme attach to the member.'

b
With respect, I agree entirely with the judge's approach to this problem. The value of the right to contribute to an enhanced widow's pension is not susceptible to any mathematical computation and must be one of impression. In my judgment the judge approached this head of damage in a perfectly proper manner. I can see no ground at all for interfering with his assessments in any of the three cases.

c
*Claim by the widow*
The single issue arising out of the fourth case, that of the widow Mrs Popow, is difficult. The judge distinguished her case from *Davies v Whiteways Cider Co Ltd* [1974] 3 All ER 168, [1974] 3 WLR 597, on the ground that her claim was not a result of the tortious death, whereas the widow in *Davies's* case suffered a loss in the form of estate
d duty payable directly as a result of the death. With great respect to the judge, I must agree that he was wrong in this conclusion. The wording of s 3(1) of the Fatal Accidents Act 1976 is '. . . such damages may be awarded as are proportioned to the injury resulting from the death to the dependants respectively . . .' and extends obviously to the widow who is a person injured, and the injuries sustained, namely the loss of a widow's pension which would in due course become payable on the natural death, cannot be said to result
e from that natural death. It must result from the tortious death. The question that remains is whether the widow's pension that is in fact being paid under the scheme as a result of her husband's death in service must be ignored when considering her rights to a hypothetical pension on death in retirement because of the provisions of s 4 of the 1976 Act.
It is necessary to look back to the terms of the scheme itself. Widow's benefit is a topic
f covered by rr 16 to 19. These occupy the best part of 26 pages in the bundle before us. They cover widows of miners, colliery workers and former mineworkers. Rule 16(2) reads:

'Benefit shall be payable under paragraph (3) of this Rule by reference to the deceased if any one or more of the following conditions are satisfied – (a) He dies while he is in Eligible Employment; or (b) He has prior to the date of his death
g retired from Eligible Employment in such circumstances that a pension is or would had he survived have become payable to him under any of [a number of rules there set out].'

Thereafter, there are a number of further conditions which are not relevant to this appeal.
h
Were it not for the inclusion of the words 'or more', the problem arising under the Popow claim would cause no difficulty. The benefit, namely a pension and lump sum provided under para (3) of r 16, would become payable as a result of the tortious death. This would have brought into operation the provisions of r 6 of the scheme, which would not be assumed to refer to more than one death, by virtue of the facts of nature.
The fact that r 16(2) refers to 'one or more of the following conditions' in my mind
j does not have the effect of allowing the rule to be used as a basis for a loss of a widow's pension in another hypothetical situation as well as the factual situation which has brought the operation of the rule into effect. In my judgment the widow has no subsisting claim to a widow's pension under r 16(2)(b), because she has already benefited under r 16(2)(a). She has, therefore, no right and has suffered, therefore, no injury within the meaning of s 3 of the 1976 Act. The fact that s 4 of the 1976 Act precludes 'In assessing damages . . . [the taking] into account [of] any insurance money, benefit,

pension or gratuity which has been or will or may be paid as a result of the death ...' does not have the effect of reviving a right which has lapsed under r 16(2)(a) of the pension scheme. To put the matter another way, s 4 of the 1976 Act merely precludes the court from taking into account any (sic) 'benefit'; but it does not provide that the death itself must be ignored. The established fact of death in service precludes the possibility of death in retirement, and without the condition precedent of such a death being established, the possibility of a widow's pension on death in retirement.

    I should like to add my tribute to those of my brethren to the detail and clarity with which the judge dealt with a large number of complicated issues.

*Appeal dismissed. Leave to appeal to House of Lords refused.*

*28 June. The Appeal Committee of the House of Lords (Lord Scarman, Lord Brandon of Oakbrook and Lord Templeman) dismissed a petition by the appellants for leave to appeal.*

Solicitors: *Raley & Pratt*, Barnsley (for the appellants); *C T Peach* (for the respondents).

Sophie Craven    Barrister.

# Robertson v Lestrange and another

QUEEN'S BENCH DIVISION

WEBSTER J

23, 24, 26, 27, 31 JULY 1984

*Fatal accident – Damages – Inflation – Discount for accelerated capital payment for future loss – Effect of availability of index-linked securities for investment of award – Whether conventional discount rate of 4% or 5% still appropriate – Whether discount rate should be related to return on index-linked securities – Whether discount rate of 2% appropriate – Whether value of pension rights should be disccounted at more than conventional rate if pension rights would not have accrued for many years.*

The fact that index-linked securities, which are inflation-proof and currently yielding a net return of 2%, are now available to a widow for the investment of an award made to her under the Fatal Accidents Acts 1976 is not sufficient reason for altering the practice or convention of not taking inflation into account when assessing damages under that Act, which practice is reflected in the conventional discount rate of 4% or 5% for accelerated payment of a capital sum as compensation for future loss of an annual dependency. Accordingly, the discount rate for accelerated payment of a capital sum to represent a lost future annual dependency should still be 4% or 5%, and the appropriate multiplier should be consistent with that rate, except where the assumed annuity (equalling the amount of the dependency) by which the capital sum awarded is measured is so large as to attract a high rate of income tax or, possibly, where there is some other feature peculiar to the particular case which would make the conventional approach unjust. It is not open to a court of first instance to consider departing from the conventional approach unless the evidence before it is that all competent advice recommends investing the award in such a way that, given current and estimated future interest rates and other relevant economic factors, the capital sum awarded would be exhausted before the end of the period of the dependency (see p 957 *h* to p 958 *b*, post); *Cookson v Knowles* [1978] 2 All ER 604 applied.

    Where a deceased husband's pension rights would not have accrued until 35 years after his actual death, then in order to take account of that fact the value of his pension rights

should, for the purpose of assessing damages under the 1976 Act, be discounted by a
*a*  considerably greater discount than the conventional discount of 4% or 5% (see p 958 *e* to
*g*, post); *Lim Poh Choo v Camden and Islington Area Health Authority* [1979] 2 All ER 910
applied.

### Notes

For damages under the Fatal Accidents Act, see 34 Halsbury's Laws (4th edn) paras 94–
*b*  98, and for cases on the subject, see 36(1) Digest (Reissue) 360–362, *1456–1469*
    For the Fatal Accidents Act 1976, see 46 Haslsbury's Statutes (3rd edn) 1115.

### Cases referred to in judgment

*Bulmer v Bulmer* (1883) 25 Ch D 409.
*Cookson v Knowles* [1978] 2 All ER 604, [1979] AC 556, [1978] 2 WLR 978, HL; *affg*
*c*    [1977] 2 All ER 820, [1977] QB 913, [1977] 3 WLR 279, CA.
*Eifret v Holt's Transport Co Ltd* [1951] 2 All ER 655n.
*Graham v Dodds* [1983] 2 All ER 953, [1983] 1 WLR 808, HL.
*Harris v Empress Motors Ltd* [1983] 3 All ER 561, [1984] 1 WLR 212, CA.
*Kircher v West* (12 January 1961) referred to in Kemp and Kemp *The Quantum of Damages*
    vol 1, Pt II, para 23–005.
*d*  *Lim Poh Choo v Camden and Islington Area Health Authority* [1979] 2 All ER 910, [1980] AC
    174, [1979] 3 WLR 44, HL; *varying* [1979] 1 All ER 332, [1979] QB 196, [1978] 3
    WLR 44, CA.
*Mallett v McMonagle* [1969] 2 All ER 178, [1970] AC 166, [1969] 2 WLR 767, HL.
*Sanderson v Sanderson* (1877) 36 LT 847.
*Wright v British Rlys Board* [1983] 2 All ER 698, [1983] 2 AC 773, [1983] 3 WLR 211, HL.
*e*  *Young v Percival* [1974] 3 All ER 677, [1975] 1 WLR 17, CA.

### Action

By a writ issued on 24 February 1983 the plaintiff, Yvonne Myfanwy Robertson, suing as
the administratrix of the estate of George Robertson deceased, claimed against the
defendants, Harry Edward Lestrange and B & A Britton Ltd, damages under the Fatal
*f*  Accidents Act 1976 for herself and her children and damages under the Law Reform
(Miscellaneous Provisions) Act 1934 consequent on the death of the deceased on 14 May
1982 as a result of a road accident on 11 May 1982. The facts are set out in the judgment.

*Roy McAulay QC* and *Charles Bennett* for the plaintiff.
*Piers Ashworth QC* and *John Leighton Williams* for the defendants.

*g*                                                            *Cur adv vult*

31 July. The following judgment was delivered.

**WEBSTER J.** This is a claim by Yvonne Myfanwy Robertson, the administratrix of the
*h*  estate of George Robertson deceased, against Harry Edward Lestrange and B & A Britton
Ltd for damages under the Fatal Accidents Act 1976 and the Law Reform (Miscellaneous
Provisions) Act 1934, the claim under the Fatal Accidents Act being a claim for herself
and the dependants of the deceased husband which arises out of the death of her husband
on 14 May 1982 as the result of an accident which he sustained on 11 May. I gave
judgment on the issue of liability in this matter on 14 July and, as I said, when the trial
*j*  proceeded on the next day, I wished to add two things to the judgment that I then gave,
which I repeat in case they have got lost somewhere in the transcribing system. The first
is that in my judgment the first defendant's speed was too fast by about 10 mph and the
second is that had he not been travelling at a speed of between 30 and 35 mph it is
probable that Mr Robertson would have been able to reach the south side of Christopher
Street without thinking that he had to take evasive action, and that even if he had taken

some evasive action it is probable that he would not have turned or moved so quickly, and that the first defendant would have been able to avoid him or to stop before hitting *a* him.

I now turn to the issue of quantum. Mr Robertson was born in October 1952; he was just over 29½ years old when he died in May 1982. The plaintiff, his widow, was born in March 1953, and she was just under 29 at that date. There are three children: a girl who was born in October 1973, so that she was then aged 8½ years; a boy born in March 1978 was aged 4; and a boy born in March 1980 was aged 2. After Mr Robertson left school he *b* studied at Strathclyde University and obtained a BA honours degree in economics. He was then employed by the Scottish Office for five years and joined Esso Petroleum Co on 10 November 1980 as an energy economist in their corporate planning department. He was in good health, and he could have been expected to have worked until his retirement at the age of 65, 35½ years after the date of his death.

I turn first to consider his projected earnings. He had been recruited by Esso from *c* outside the group. There were 40 applicants for the appointment and he and one other were chosen. He was chosen, as was the other, for his high management potential. Between the date of that appointment and his death he was well thought of, perhaps indeed highly thought of, and he was thought to have justified his selection and appointment. I am satisfied that he was regarded as being in the top 10% of his salary group in terms of merit and performance. His gross basic salary at the date of his death *d* was £12,750. I am quite satisfied from the evidence of Mr Senior and Mr Corrish (Mr Senior was employed by the group at the date of Mr Robertson's death and Mr Corrish is still employed by them) that between 1982 and 1989 his earnings would have been as follows:

| | |
|---|---|
| from 1 July 1982 | £14,660 | *e* |
| from 1 July 1983 | £16,600 |
| from 1 July 1984 | £20,000 (he having achieved one promotion by that date). |
| from 1 July 1985 | £20,500 (in 1984 money) |
| from 1 July 1986 (and all figures hereafter are in 1984 money) | £21,015 | *f* |
| from 1 July 1987 | £21,540 |
| from 1 July 1988 | £22,080 |
| from 1 July 1989 | £23,750 (having achieved one further promotion by that date). |

In my view, the first seven of those eight figures can be treated as certainties, subject *g* to the vicissitudes of life. The eighth, which is dependent on his having achieved a second promotion in 1989, is not so certain. None the less, in my view, it has a very high degree of probability.

There are two views how to approach the rest of Mr Robertson's working life. One, which is expressed in Kemp and Kemp *The Quantum of Damages* vol 1, Pt II, para 21–002, *h* is that I should take into account any good promotion prospects by applying a higher multiplier than I otherwise would apply. The other, of which an example is to be found in the decision in *Young v Percival* [1974] 3 All ER 677, [1975] 1 WLR 17, is that I should make an attempt to assess his future earnings, taking into account the prospects of promotion.

In the present case, where there is evidence which makes possible an assessment of his *j* prospects and of the result of those prospects on his earnings, I choose the latter course, noting that in assessing his future earnings I cannot do so on the simple basis of a balance of probability, but only on the basis of an estimate 'as to what are the chances' or 'what is the degree of likelihood' that a particular thing will or would have happened (see Lord Diplock in *Mallett v McMonagle* [1969] 2 All ER 178 at 190–191, [1970] AC 166 at 176

and in *Cookson v Knowles* [1978] 2 All ER 604 at 608, [1979] AC 556 at 568). If Mr
a   Robertson had been promoted in 1990, then aged 37, there would have been two further
salary groups, to each of which he might have been promoted. Thereafter, he might
have been promoted above those groups so as to join those employees whose emoluments
are shown in the group accounts. If Mr Robertson had achieved only one further
promotion after 1989, he would have ended in a group with a maximum basic salary of
about £29,000 in 1984 money. If he had achieved a second promotion into the top
b   group, his salary would in practice, in view of his earlier history, have been between
about £27,000 and £32,500. Most of the employees who were appointed above that
group were paid £30,000 or £35,000 in 1983. I will assume an average of £35,000 in
1994. In 1983 about 60 out of 4,000 non-unionised employees were promoted to those
levels or above, that is to say about one in 65. If Mr Robertson had remained in the top
10% of his salary group from time to time his chances of reaching that level on a crude
c   statistical basis would have been about one in six or seven. In these circumstances I assess
his chances of salary promotion as follows: an evens chance of being promoted in about
1994 at age about 42 to a salary of about £26,000 rising to about £29,000, that is to say
averaging about £27,500 if he had remained in that group; one chance in three of rising
to the next group in about 2000 aged then about 48, at a salary of about £28,000 rising
to about £32,000, that is to say averaging about £30,000 if he had remained in that
d   group; and one chance in six or seven of promotion in about 2005 aged then 53 to a
salary of about £35,000 for the remainder of his working life. All these figures are in
1984 money terms and all these chances reflect his performance during his few years
with the group and do not take into account the risks to life or health or the possibility
that his performance after his death might not have been as good as it had been before;
nor, however, do they take into account a possibility that it might have been better.
e   Those last two possibilities, in my view, cancel each other out.
      Because it is common ground that the children would have ceased to be dependent in
1997, it is necessary to arrive at two separate figures for average earnings, that is to say
the average from the date of trial until that date ie 1997, and the average from 1997 until
retirement. Those averages in turn can only be arrived at with reasonable accuracy by
taking in turn: (1) the average of each of the years 1984 to 1988; (2) the year from 1 July
f   1989; (3) the years from 1 July 1990 to 1 July 1993; (4) the years from 1 July 1994 to 1
July 1996; (5) the years from 1 July 1997 to 1 July 2004; (6) the years from 1 July 2005
to retirement.
      The average of period (1), a period of five years, is £21,027, say £21,025. I take the
year from 1 July 1989 as £23,500. I treat the next period as four years at £25,500, that is
to say £23,500 plus a half of £4,000 being the difference between £23,500 and £27,500.
g   I treat the next, fourth, period as three years at £27,000, that is to say £25,500 plus a
third of £4,500, the difference between £25,500 and £30,000. The average over those
13 years to 30 June 1997 is £23,970. The fifth period is eight years, also at £27,000; and
the sixth and last period is 12 years at £28,500, that is to say £27,000 plus about one-
sixth of £8,000, the difference between £27,000 and £35,000. The average over those
last 20 years is £27,900.
h       I break off here to say that I am sure that all these figures of mine will be checked and,
if necessary, corrected before a final judgment is drawn up.

*Other receipts*
      At the date of his death Mr Robertson was receiving a London allowance for working
in London of over £1,000 a year. In principle that allowance, if paid, would simply
j   reflect higher expenditure on housing or travelling or a mixture of both attributable to
the location of his place of work. But he might well have moved from London, had he
been promoted, and he would probably have moved from London in any event within
the next few years if, as is likely, the group headquarters move to Leatherhead. It seems
to me a fair approach to this benefit is to bring it into the gross receipts until trial, but
not thereafter. The same applies to the holiday bonus which would have terminated in

any event in 1984. A meal allowance was also given, which from 1986 would have amounted to £555 per annum. I have assumed that the whole of the meal allowance is to be added to his gross receipts until trial, but that thereafter I should add just less than half of it, that is to say £250, to his average gross receipts, making them £24,220 until 1997 and £28,150 thereafter.

The plaintiff claims also a sum representing the benefit of a company car and the use of the group's discount at shops. It is impossible to quantify either of those benefits. As will be seen, I am not going to reduce the dependency as projected earnings increase, and in those circumstances it seems fair for me to take no account of these matters in assessing gross earnings. The same consideration applies to Mr Robertson's projected business of buying cars in Scotland and selling them in England, in partnership with his wife and a married couple in Scotland. Even if that business had been set up, it seems to me unlikely that it would have continued so far as he was concerned if he went higher up the ladder of promotion with Esso; and it seems to me that a fair solution is to ignore that matter again as part of the decision not to decrease the dependency with the projected increase in his future earnings.

Finally, the same considerations apply to the possibility that Mrs Robertson might have earned in the future. That possibility was a long way off at the date of Mr Robertson's death: she was working for an O level preparatory to taking a higher education qualification, preparatory in turn to becoming a teacher. Though I certainly do not regard those possibilities as purely speculative, they are in my view sufficiently taken into account in the same way.

*Deductions from gross earnings*

Mr and Mrs Robertson are Mormons. Mr Robertson paid 10% of his gross receipts from his employment to the church as a tithe, although he was not doing so in the year of his death because of financial stringency that year. He intended, none the less, to make up that lost year and any other lost years later, and Mrs Robertson is paying 10% of her gross income in the same way. The effect of her evidence, as it seems to me, is that payment of that tithe is in the nature of spiritual or afterlife insurance paid for the benefit of the whole family. Counsel on her behalf asks me to treat the whole of that tithe as a family expense. Counsel on behalf of the defendants asks me to deduct the whole of it from the gross receipts as being a payment to charity. I conclude that although technically the payment is a payment to charity it is one of a very unusual nature, representing a continuous obligation as seen by Mr and Mrs Robertson. I conclude that a fair solution is to deduct 5% from Mr Robertson's gross projected income from trial, and to treat the other 5% as part of the family expenses. I do not take the tithe into account from the date of death to the date of trial, because it was not being paid at the date of death. The deduction of 5% therefore reduces the average gross receipts to 1997 from £24,220 to £23,010, say £23,000, and it reduces the gross receipts thereafter from £28,150 to £26,742, say £26,750.

*The possibility of early retirement*

All the figures that I have given so far have been based on a retirement at 65. Counsel for the defendants has urged me to take into account the present trend towards early retirement. On the other hand, early retirement at 60 instead of 65 is often accompanied by handsome inducements, sometimes of quite large capital sums. I conclude that I should give some effect to this possibility by rounding down the average for the last 20 years from £26,750 to £26,500.

*The risk of losing his employment*

In my view this case is no different from any ordinary case, despite some evidence of Esso's contractions since 1982. If it differs at all, it seems to me that it is less likely that Mr Robertson would lose his job than the ordinary man, in view of the circumstances of his recruitment from outside the group as a person with higher management potential,

and in view of the fact that until his death he was making good the reasons for appointing
*a* him on that basis. I treat, therefore, the risk of losing his employment, as it is
conventionally treated, as one of the facts to be taken into account in the multiplier.

### Tax and other deductions

Figures have been prepared on the assumption of a continuing mortgage of £25,000
at 13% interest, a historically fairly high rate. Those figures reduce a gross income of
*b* £23,000 to a net disposable income of about £15,600 for the years to 30 June 1997. For
the remaining years they reduce the gross income of £26,500 to about £17,700.

### Loss of services

To each of these figures is to be added £750 per annum for the loss of services from
the date of Mr Robertson's death, an agreed figure, which produces final net figures of
*c* £16,350 to 30 June 1997, and £18,450 thereafter.

### Dependency

It is common ground that all of the children can be treated as ceasing to be dependent
in 1997. The proportion of net disposable income which should be taken as representing
the dependency of Mrs Robertson and the children on Mr Robertson was at first agreed
*d* but then became an issue. But, having considered the evidence, including some detailed
figures relating to one year only, I conclude that there is nothing to justify me from
departing from what is now the conventional apportionment, in a normal case of this
kind, of 75% while the children are dependent and 66⅔% thereafter. Counsel for the
defendants submitted that I should decrease this net dependency as the net disposable
income increases; but the increase in that net disposable income is not dramatic, even
*e* though I have taken account of and tried to allow for Mr Robertson's chances of reaching
the top of the managerial tree and, in any event, I am satisfied that he did not smoke,
drink or gamble, and that his interests other than his work were centred on his home
and family. I therefore treat those percentages as constant.

### The multiplier

*f* The plaintiff through her counsel first asked for a multiplier of 21½ for 35½ years,
although it was reduced to an unquantified extent after the plaintiff's expert witness, Mr
Paul, had given evidence. The defendants through their counsel, who would have been
content with the 'conventional' multiplier of 15 or 16, asked in the light of the plaintiff's
contentions for a multiplier of 13½. The plaintiff's argument went as follows. The object
of an award is to compensate the widow and family for the loss of dependency year by
*g* year sustained as a result of the husband and father's death until the end of the relevant
dependency. Until recently this has been done in practice by adopting discount rates of
4½%, which produce the 'conventional' multiplier, in this case, of 15 or 16, or which are
consistent with those 'conventional' multipliers. Where a dependency is calculated in
that way there is always a risk that an award might become progressively of less value in
real terms because of inflation and because, if it is invested in equities, the capital might
*h* be at risk. In *Wright v British Rlys Board* [1983] 2 All ER 698, [1983] 2 AC 773 the House
of Lords has adverted to the existence of the recently established index-linked, that is to
say inflation-proof, bonds. Counsel for the plaintiff adopted as part of his argument the
monograph in the Stop Press Supplement for February 1984 in *Kemp and Kemp* vol 2, and
in particular the statement there (at pp 3–4) that—

*j* 'Surely . . . the discount rate to be adopted by the courts should be the rate of
interest representing the yield currently obtainable from index-linked securities,
after deduction of such tax as the plaintiff would have to pay on income from such
investment . . .'

and that 'the logical consequence' would be that 'there should be a substantial increase in
the multipliers which the court currently applies to the relevant multiplicand . . .'

Counsel for the plaintiff adduced evidence to support his contention, namely the evidence of Mr Paul, a partner in Binder Hamlyn. According to his written evidence, taking into account the availability of index-linked securities, a fair discount rate in the case of a large award for the future should now be not more than 3% net, which in the present case would produce a multiplier of 21½. Counsel for the defendants resisted this contention, and he in turn adduced evidence through Mr Aldous, a partner in Robson Rhodes, that in investing a large award today—

'Investment management policy would be to secure a proportion of income and cash realisation from suitably maturing gilts, which would also protect the investor against short term set backs and falling interest rates. The remaining money, and most of the money, should go into mixed equity stocks for capital growth to be converted later into higher yielding stocks and gilts as the fund became more of an annuity scheme. It is reasonable to suppose therefore that a well managed portfolio should yield a gross income return to the investor of something between 6% and 7%.'

In addition, according to Mr Aldous, history shows that such investment would show real growth, that is to say growth over and above the rate of inflation, of 2%, and that taking into account capital and income such a sum would generate distributable income and capital of 6½% net, which would indicate a multiplier of 13½ for 35 years.

In considering this issue, I adopt, first, the objective of the award under the Fatal Accidents Act 1976 as described in non-contentious but highly authoritative terms by Lord Fraser, in a speech with which Viscount Dilhorne, Lord Salmon and Lord Scarman agreed, in *Cookson v Knowles* [1978] 2 All ER 604 at 615, [1979] AC 556 at 576–577, where Lord Fraser said:

'The measure of the proper award to a widow (who is generally the main dependant and to whom alone I refer, brevitatis causa) is a sum which, prudently invested would provide her with an annuity equal in amount to the support that she has probably lost through the death of her husband, during the period that she would probably have been supported by him. The assumed annuity will be made up partly of income on the principal sum awarded, and partly of capital obtained by gradual encroachment on the principal. The income element will be at its largest at the beginning of the period and will tend to decline, while the capital element will tend to increase until the principal is exhausted. The multipliers which are generally adopted in practice are based on the assumption (rarely mentioned and perhaps rarely appreciated) that the principal sum of damages will earn interest at about four or five per cent, which are rates that would be appropriate in time of stable currency, as my noble and learned friend, Lord Diplock, pointed out in *Mallett v McMonagle* [1969] 2 All ER 178 at 190, [1970] AC 166 at 176.'

But in achieving that objective I have to recognise that I am carrying out an exercise which has more than once been described as 'artificial' (for instance, Lord Diplock in *Cookson v Knowles* [1978] 2 All ER 604 at 608, [1979] AC 556 at 568, 'artificial and conjectural'). Moreover, it is not entirely clear whether the exercise is to be regarded as one of fact finding (see Lord Bridge in *Graham v Dodds* [1983] 2 All ER 953 at 960, [1983] 1 WLR 808 at 817) or, at least where multipliers are concerned, as one of impression, common sense, estimation, selection, choice, convention, discretion or practice, since each one of those words have been used, most of them, I think, in the House of Lords in the last few years in the cases which I have already mentioned and in *Lim Poh Choo v Camden and Islington Area Health Authority* [1979] 2 All ER 910, [1980] AC 174. In particular, it seems to me that the selection of the appropriate multiplier has become to a considerable extent a matter of impression and discretion, taking into account all the circumstances, but circumscribed by the range of multipliers adopted in practice by the courts. As to that range, I note that Lord Diplock in *Mallett v McMonagle* [1969] 2 All ER 178 at 191, [1970] AC 166 at 177 said that the courts have seldom exceeded a multiplier

of 16. As I understand it, evidence of interest rates and appropriate discount rates has
a rarely until recently been given at first instance, although such evidence has been adduced
on appeal in a number of cases where it has been used to test the appropriateness of a
particular multiplier. But I note that Lord Diplock in *Mallett v McMonagle* [1969] 2 All
ER 178 at 190, [1970] AC 166 at 176 said:

b
'In estimating the amount of the annual dependency in the future, had the
deceased not been killed, money should be treated as retaining its value at the date
of the judgment, and in calculating the present value of annual payments which
would have been received in future years, interest rates appropriate to times of stable
currency such as 4 per cent. to 5 per cent. should be adopted.'

I emphasise those last words 'should be adopted'. It perhaps suggests that a court should
derive the appropriate multiplier from the appropriate discount rate, rather than that it
c should select what it regards as the appropriate multiplier, and then test it against the
correct discounted rate.

It does not seem to me that the decision in *Wright v British Rlys Board* [1983] 2 All ER
698, [1983] 2 AC 773 affects the position under the Fatal Accidents Act at all. It is true
that in that case Lord Diplock said ([1983] 2 All ER 698 at 703–704, [1983] 2 AC 773 at
782):

d
'The first route by which an informed choice of the appropriate rate of interest
can be reached has only been accessible since the United Kingdom government
started to issue index-linked (ie inflation-proof) bonds . . .'

And he later said ([1983] 2 All ER 698 at 704, [1983] 2 AC 773 at 783):

e
'. . . medium- and long-term index-linked issues of 2% or 2½% have latterly been
made available to private individuals who, if liable to income tax, obtain a net return
of 2% to 2½% less tax, and even now are currently traded at around about par.'

But that case was concerned with a wholly different exercise, namely the award of interest
on damages which had already accured to compensate a plaintiff for having been kept
out of money to the receipt of which he or she had been entitled over a period which had
f passed at the date of the award.

As to the monograph in *Kemp and Kemp*, it is said that the conclusion which I have
already quoted followed logically from the court assuming that the damages awarded
will be invested 'in the only type of security which will give certain protection against
inflation'. But I cannot see why the court should make any such assumption. Even Mr
Paul, the expert called on behalf of the plaintiff, did not go so far as to say that he would
g advise investing the whole of the award in index-linked bonds, and Mr Aldous said that
he would not advise that any part of it be invested in that way: he would only advise
such an investment when it was essential to provide for the realisation of a precise sum
on a precise date, and in his opinion a portfolio of the kind to which I have already
referred would give sufficient protection against inflation and would be a prudent
investment, even taking into account the risk of a 40% collapse in capital values, such as
h occurred in 1974. If I had to choose between the evidence of Mr Aldous and that of Mr
Paul, I would choose that of Mr Aldous. Mr Paul's evidence in a number of respects did
not impress me. But I conclude that since *Cookson v Knowles* [1978] 2 All ER 604, [1979]
AC 556, which reaffirms the principle that no account should be taken of inflation in
assessing damages under the Fatal Accidents Act, there have been no changes which
necessitate the re-examination of that principle, at any rate for a court of first instance.
j The only changes have been the abolition of the investment surcharge and the
introduction of index-linked bonds. Neither of those changes lead me to the conclusion
that the principle should be re-examined, at any rate by myself. I conclude, therefore,
that the practice or convention remains unaltered and that the conventional multiplier
consistent with a discount rate of 4½% should still be applied, except where 'the annuity
is large enough to attract income tax at a higher rate' (see Lord Fraser in *Cookson v Knowles*

[1978] 2 All ER 604 at 616, [1979] AC 556 at 577), which is not so in the present case, or, possibly, where there is some other feature peculiar to the particular case which would make such an approach unjust. But there is no such peculiar feature in this case. Moreover, I conclude that a court at first instance should not consider departing from the existing convention unless the evidence before it were to be that all competent advice would recommend investing the award in such a way that, given current and estimated future interest rates and other relevant economic factors, the fund would be exhausted before the end of the period or periods of dependency. I have nothing like such evidence before me in this case.

It is common ground that the actuarial expectation of life of Mr Robertson was 72 at the date of his death, and that his working life, as I have said, is to the age of 65. He had no hobbies or activities which carried risk, and in my view the appropriate multiplier in his case, which reflects many of the factors to which I have already specifically adverted so far, is 16 years from the date of death.

Before calculating the Fatal Accidents Act award it is necessary to make a distinction between the award up to the date of trial, that is for past losses, and the award thereafter for future losses. The figures for remuneration which Mr Robertson would have earned for the period up to trial are agreed; and, as I have indicated, I include for that period, but not thereafter, the London allowance, the holiday bonus and the meal allowance. Those figures produce a total net remuneration of £28,643, say £28,645. To that sum is to be added £750 for two years and two months, that is to say £1,625, making a total of £30,270. Seventy-five per cent of that sum is £22,700 to the nearest £5, without taking into account interest, and that is the award for past loss of dependency until the date of trial. The Fatal Accidents Act award from date of trial leaves a multiplier of 14, which I apportion as to 7½ up to 1997 and as to 6½ thereafter. Thus the award under the Fatal Accidents Act for the future losses till 1997 will be £16,350 × 75% × 7½, namely £91,968, say £91,970; and the award from 1997 will be £18,450 × 66⅔% × 6½, namely £79,949, producing a total of £171,919 for future losses. Two further sums are to be added to this figure. First, there is an agreed lump sum of £2,000 for funeral expenses and the loss of Mr Robertson's services in doing certain repairs to the house. Finally, there is a claim for the loss of Mr Robertson's pension rights. The actuarial value of those rights discounted to 4½% is £14,270; but in my view a considerably greater discount must be applied so as to take into account the fact that the pension, which would have generated about £38,000 gross receipts till actuarial age of death at 72, would not accrue until 35 years after Mr Robertson's actual death. In *Lim Poh Choo v Camden and Islington Area Health Authority* [1979] 1 All ER 332, [1979] QB 196, Bristow J awarded £8,000 for a pension worth about £50,000 in gross receipts, accruing 24 years later, of which the discounted value at the trial was £18,500, and this award was not disturbed by the House of Lords [see 1979] 2 All ER 910, [1980] AC 174. In my judgment, the proper award under this head is £5,000. Thus the total Fatal Accidents Act award is £178,910 in respect of future losses from the date of trial. So that the total Fatal Accidents Act award is: past loss £22,700, plus interest of 14%, namely £3,178 = £25,878; future loss £178,919; total £204,797, say £204,790.

I will return to the apportionment of this award between the dependants later in this judgment, and turn first to the claims under the Law Reform (Miscellaneous Provisions) Act 1934, under which the first head of claim is that for Mr Robertson's lost years of earnings. It follows from the conclusions which I have already reached that Mr Robertson's prospective net loss of earnings from the date of trial over the remainder of his working life is £15,600 per annum unitl 1997 and £17,700 thereafter.

In *Harris v Empress Motors Ltd* [1983] 3 All ER 561 at 575–576, [1984] 1 WLR 212 at 229 O'Connor LJ said:

'I think one can say in relation to a man's net earnings that any proportion thereof that he saves or spends exclusively for the maintenance or benefit of others does not form part of his living expenses. Any proportion that he spends exclusively on a himself does. In cases where there is a proportion of the earnings expended on what may conveniently be called shared living expenses, a pro rata part of that proportion should be allocated for deduction.'

The analysis of one year of family expenditure which I have already mentioned shows that the family expenditure constituted about twice the total expenditure attributed individually to Mr Robertson, his wife and the children, and that that balance was equally distributed between Mr Robertson, his wife and his three children. In the light of those

b facts and of that dictum of O'Connor LJ, it seems necessary to deduct only 2/7ths of those net earnings till 30 June 1997 and 50% thereafter. Thus the claim for the lost years' earnings will be: (1) 5/7ths of £28,643, namely £20,460 till trial, plus (2) 7½ × 5/7ths of £15,600, namely £83,570 till 1997, plus 6½ × 50% of £17,700, namely £57,525, plus 50% of £5,000, the value of pension rights, namely £2,500, making a total of £164,055.

c In addition, the estate has an agreed claim for £1,500 loss of expectation of life, and a claim for Mr Robertson's pain and suffering for four days from the accident until his death, which I assess at £150. These further awards totalling £1,650 bring the award for Mr Robertson's estate under the Law Reform Act to £165,705.

*Apportionment*

d The particular problem of apportionment in a Fatal Accidents Act award and the result of that apportionment flowing from the interaction of the Law Reform Act and the Fatal Accidents Act awards, which I am about to describe, only affects awards relating to deaths occurring before January 1983, because the law has been changed for deaths on or after that date. Mr Robertson died intestate, and consequently and by virtue of the provisions of s 46 of the Administration of Estates Act 1925 (as amended) the respective interests of

e Mrs Robertson and the three children in the Law Reform award of £165,705 are £100,056 to the widow, and £21,883 to each of the three children, these figures being agreed between the parties. If, therefore, the total Fatal Accidents Act claim of £204,790 were to be apportioned as to £10,000 for each of the three children, and as to the balance of £174,790 to Mrs Robertson, the awards would be as follows: to the widow, Mrs Robertson, £174,790, her Fatal Accidents Act exceeding her Law Reform interest; and

f to the children £21,883 × 3 namely £65,649, their Law Reform interests exceeding their Fatal Accidents Act apportionments. The total of £240,439 would produce a windfall of £35,649, the amount by which that total award would exceed the Fatal Accidents Act award.

Counsel for the defendants submits that this is a windfall which has the effect of compensating the family for more than the loss which it has suffered at the expense of

g the defendants. He points out, quite rightly, that until the introduction of the recovery of damages for lost years earnings after death the defendant had no interest in the apportionment of Fatal Accident Act awards, which have been matters for concern only to the plaintiffs and the dependants and the courts. He submits that in making that apportionment in this case, where the defendants are acutely interested in it, I should make such an apportionment as will eliminate any difference between the two awards,

h so that there is no windfall at all. Were I to apportion the Fatal Accidents Act award in that way, it would involve apportioning £100,056 to Mrs Robertson and £21,883 to each of the three children, a total of £65,649, so that their share of the total award would represent about one-third of the total award. There has been at least one apportionment as high as this in recent years, even when the defendants had no interest in an apportionment: see *Kircher v West* (12 January 1961) referred to in *Kemp and Kemp* vol 1,

j Pt II, para 23–005.

In recent years the children's shares of total Fatal Accident Act awards has varied between about one-third and about one-twentieth of the total according to the number of children, their ages and the varying circumstances of each case; but counsel for the defendants points out that much higher apportionments have been made to children in the past, and he cites as examples *Sanderson v Sanderson* (1877) 36 LT 847 (deceased aged 64, four children 16 and under, where the apportionment was one-third to the widow *a* and two-thirds to the children), *Bulmer v Bulmer* (1884) 25 Ch D 409 (a quarter to the widow and three-quarters to six children) and *Eifret v Holt's Transport Co Ltd* [1951] 2 All ER 655n (where the Court of Appeal refused to interfere with an apportionment of one-third to the widow and two-thirds to the children because it was no concern to the defendants how the total award was apportioned).

Counsel for the defendants submits that I should not depart from the ordinary practice *b* of apportionment and that I should take into account in particular the fact that it is the mother's obligation to care and provide for her children, and that in the nature of things she will have to have the management of the funds available for their keep, maintenance and education; and accordingly, he submits, the bulk of the award should go to her. Section 3(1) of the Fatal Accidents Act 1976 provides that the amount recovered should be divided amongst the dependants but 'in such shares as may be directed'. The matter *c* appears, therefore, to be one of discretion but of a discretion, of course, which is to be exercised in accordance with the law and taking into account the relevant considerations. I must, therefore, try and direct myself as to the relevant considerations which seem to me, without attempting to be exhaustive and confining myself to the facts of this case, as follows: (1) the relevant proportions of the loss suffered, that is to say the respective interests of the dependants in the dependency; (2) the possibility that if the funds are left *d* in the widow's hands they might, because of a series of accidents, devolve in such a way that they would not inure to the benefit of the children; (3) the fact that any funds apportioned to the children should be administered on the basis that they were to be spent on their care, maintenance and education and exhausted by the end of the dependency; (4) the obligation of the mother to care for the children, and the likelihood of her doing so responsibly; and I should add in the present case that I have no doubt *e* whatsoever at all about Mrs Robertson's sense of responsibility; and (5) the possibly windfall effect of the apportionment, not as a conclusive factor but as a material factor, being the only factor in which the defendants are interested and one, therefore, to be given at least as much weight as the considerations which might favour a lower apportionment for the children.

Directing myself in this way, I conclude that I should attempt to apportion the Fatal *f* Accidents Act award to the children so as to reduce as far as possible, or if possible eliminate, any windfall effect provided that the award reasonably reflects the loss of dependency suffered by them. I also conclude, of course, that I can only apportion in this way that part of the award which represents the loss which affects the children, in this case the past loss £25,880, plus the future loss to 1997, £91,970, that is to say £117,850. If I were to give Mrs Robertson a 2/5ths share in that sum and each of the children a *g* 1/5th share, each share would be worth £23,570. To reduce those shares to £21,883, that is to say slightly below 1/5th, seems to me to be perfectly compatible with the loss of dependency suffered. I, therefore, apportion the total Fatal Accidents Act award of £204,790 as to £139,141 to the plaintiff mother and as to £21,883 to each of the children, making a total of £65,649. So the final awards will be under the Law Reform Act to the widow £100,056, to the children £21,883 each, making a total of £165,705; *h* under the Fatal Accidents Act to the widow £39,085, to the children nil, making a total of £39,085; and making a grand total between the two awards of £204,790.

*Judgment for the plaintiff for £39,085 under the Fatal Accidents Act and for £165,705 under the Law Reform Act. Stay as to 50% of total award for 28 days.*

*j*

Solicitors: *Devonshire & Co* (for the plaintiff); *Joynson-Hicks & Co* (for the defendants).

K Mydeen Esq    Barrister.

a                              **L v K**

FAMILY DIVISION AT LIVERPOOL
EWBANK J
29 JANUARY 1985

b   *Affiliation – Putative father – Boy under age of 14 – Whether irrebuttable presumption of criminal law that boy under 14 incapable of having sexual intercourse applying in civil law – Whether presumption applying in paternity cases.*

*Affiliation – Evidence – Putative father – Evidence of putative father that he was not fertile and was incapable of fathering child.*

c   The rule of the criminal law that there is an irrebuttable presumption that a boy under the age of 14 is not able to have sexual intercourse is not a rule that applies in the civil law. Accordingly, paternity cases relating to boys under 14 should be decided on a commonsense basis on the facts in the particular case, and without any preconceived notions or presumptions. In such cases, if a mother gives evidence which is corroborated that sexual intercourse took place at the relevant time, it will be for the putative father
d   himself to show, if it be the case, that he was not fertile and that he was incapable of fathering the child (see p 962 *j* to p 963 *b* and *g h*, post).

**Notes**
For evidence in affiliation proceedings, see 1 Halsbury's Laws (4th edn) paras 633–634.
    For the irrebuttable presumption of the criminal law that a boy under the age of 14 is
e   incapable of having sexual intercourse, see 11 ibid para 33, and for cases on the subject, see 14(1) Digest (Reissue) 66, 362–368.

**Cases referred to in judgment**
*R v Brimilow* (1839) 9 C & P 366, 173 ER 871, NP.
*R v Eldershaw* (1828) 3 C & P 396, 172 ER 472, NP.
f   *R v Groombridge* (1836) 7 C & P 582, 173 ER 256, NP.
*R v Jordan and Cowmeadow* (1839) 9 C & P 118, 173 ER 765, NP.
*R v Philips* (1839) 8 C & P 736, 173 ER 695, NP.
*R v Waite* [1892] 2 QB 600, CCR.
*R v Williams* [1893] 1 QB 320, CCR.

g   **Case stated**
L appealed by way of a case stated by the Blackpool magistrates in respect of their decision on 29 June 1984 whereby, on a complaint made by K (the mother) under s 1 of the Affiliation Proceedings Act 1957, they made an affiliation order against L under s 4 of that Act. The facts are set out in the judgment.

h   *Robert Brown* for L.
*Leslie Portnoy* for the mother.

**EWBANK J.** This is an appeal by way of case stated from a decision of the Blackpool magistrates dated 29 June 1984. The magistrates had before them a complaint under s 1
j   of the Affiliation Proceedings Act 1957 by a young woman who had given birth to a child on 15 October 1982. She brought the action against L, whom she alleged was the father of the child.
    The magistrates heard the evidence of the mother. She asserted that L had had sexual intercourse with her on several occasions at about the time of the conception of the child. She produced the evidence also of her mother, to whom L had admitted that he had had

sexual intercourse with the mother at the relevant time. So that in accordance with the statute there was evidence before the magistrates, and corroboration of that evidence, on which in ordinary circumstances they could have come to the conclusion that L was the father. And that is the conclusion they came to.

There had been a blood test of L, of the mother and of the child. The blood test indicated that L could not be excluded from being the father of the child. But L himself did not give evidence.

He was 13¾ at the time of the conception of the child and his case, as presented to the magistrates, was that there was an irrebuttable presumption of law that he was incapable of being the father of the child and that therefore the complaint against him should be dismissed.

The case stated asks the High Court whether there is such a presumption and, if there is, whether the presumption is rebuttable or irrebuttable. If it is rebuttable, the further question is asked whether the evidence of the mother, which is corroborated in respect of sexual intercourse, is sufficient evidence to prove the paternity.

The basis of the case put forward on behalf of L is that in a court of law a boy under 14 cannot be convicted of rape or unlawful carnal knowledge, and the basis of that rule is a presumption of law that a boy under 14 is to be presumed to be impotent. I have been referred to a passage in Hale's Pleas of the Crown (1 Hale PC 630):

'An infant under the age of fourteen years is presumed by law unable to commit a rape, and therefore it seems cannot be guilty of it, and tho in other felonies *malitia supplet ætatem* in some cases as hath been shewn, yet it seems as to this fact the law presumes him impotent, as well as wanting discretion.'

I have been taken through a number of cases: R v Groombridge (1836) 7 C & P 582, 173 ER 256, R v Brimilow (1839) 9 C & P 366, 173 ER 871, R v Jordan and Cowmeadow (1839) 9 C & P 118, 173 ER 765, R v Philips (1839) 8 C & P 736, 173 ER 695 and R v Eldershaw (1828) 3 C & P 396, 172 ER 472. These cases all establish this principle. The matter was considered again in R v Waite [1892] 2 QB 600 at 601, where Lord Coleridge CJ, dealing with rape, said: '. . . a boy under fourteen is under a physical incapacity to commit the offence. That is a presumptio juris et de jure . . .' And in the following year, in R v Williams [1893] 1 QB 320 at 321, also in the Court for Crown Cases Reserved, Lord Coleridge CJ said in relation to charge of rape that the boy had been proved to be under the age of 14, 'and therefore could not by law be convicted of rape; nor could he, in my opinion, be convicted of attempting to do that which the law says he was physically incapable of doing'.

The position in criminal law is that there is an irrebuttable presumption that a boy under 14 is not able to have sexual intercourse, whatever the actual facts may be. I have been invited to consider the reasons for the original rule. It is said that perhaps it was due to the severity of the penalty on a charge of rape in respect of a young boy. It is said that it perhaps is connected with the original minimum age of parties to a marriage contract, which was 14. It perhaps does not matter why the rule came into existence. The rule has been in existence for hundreds of years, and it is quite clear that a charge of rape cannot be made against a boy who is under 14 at the time of the alleged offence.

It is said on behalf of L that that rule ought to be applied to affiliation proceedings, and the magistrates ought to regard themselves as bound to find, irrespective of the facts, that a boy under 14 at the time of complaint was incapable of fathering a child. It has to be pointed out that there is a distinction between what has to be proved on a charge of rape and on a complaint under the Affiliation Proceedings Act 1957. In rape the ingredient relevant to the matters I am considering is penetration by the man. In paternity cases the ingredient is the impregnation of the woman. This will usually involve penetration and fertilisation, but penetration is not an essential ingredient. There have been cases of what is called conception ab extra. So that the ingredients of the two matters are not necessarily the same. Usually fatherhood will be proved on proof of sexual intercourse at the time of the conception, and usually it will be for the man who has had intercourse at the time of

a
the conception to show that he was not the father, and if it be his case to show that his semen was not fertile.

It is clearly not necessarily the case that the rule of criminal law applies to paternity cases, although some authorities suggest that this may be so. It is said on behalf of L that it is wrong that there should be different rules in relation to the criminal law and the civil law, and therefore the rule of the criminal law ought to be imported into the civil law. I do not find that that is a compelling argument, particularly when the rule of

b
criminal law is, as has been described in Smith and Hogan *Criminal Law* (5th edn, 1983) p 412, absurd. It may be a rule of law that a boy under 14 cannot be guilty of rape, but it by no means follows that a boy under 14 is not capable of having sexual intercourse.

I have been referred, surprisingly, to the Perpetuities and Accumulations Act 1964. Section 2(1) of that Act provides:

c
'Where in any proceedings there arises on the rule against perpetuities a question which turns on the ability of a person to have child at some future time, then—(*a*) subject to paragraph (*b*) below, it shall be presumed that a male can have a child at the age of fourteen years or over, but not under that age, and that a female can have a child at the age of twelve years or over, but not under that age . . . (*b*) in the case of a living person evidence may be given to show that he or she will or will not be able to have a child at the time in question.'

d
It is pointed out on behalf of the mother that if indeed there was a general rule which had been merged into the civil law that a boy under 14 could not father a child, or alternatively could not have sexual intercourse, because of an irrebuttable presumption of law that he was incapable, then it would not have been necessary to have para (*a*) of sub-s (1) of this section. And it is pointed out that in this type of civil action evidence

e
may be given to show that a particular person may or may not be able to have a child at a particular time, and that as far as concerns individuals who are alive, it is the actual evidence that is available which is going to be acted on.

The magistrates, having heard the evidence of the mother and the grandmother of the child, decided that the mother's evidence satisfied them, together with the corroboration which was afforded by the grandmother's evidence, that L was the father. The evidence

f
they heard was evidence of sexual intercourse at the time of the conception, and in the absence of any other evidence, in my judgment, they were fully entitled to come to the conclusion that L was the father. Indeed, they could have come to no other conclusion on the evidence they had.

In my judgment paternity cases relating to boys under 14 have to be considered without any preconceived notions, or any presumptions: each case must be decided on a

g
commonsense basis on the facts in that particular case. Of course, there could be some cases where the magistrates would say, 'This boy could not have been the father because he is so young.' But otherwise, if a mother gives evidence which is corroborated, that sexual intercourse has taken place at the relevant time, it will be for the putative father himself to show, if it be the case, that he was not fertile, and that he was incapable of fathering the child. This appeal is dismissed.

h
*Appeal dismissed.*

Solicitors: *W & H Alker*, Blackpool (for L); *Slater Atkinson & Co*, Blackpool (for the mother).

Bebe Chua    Barrister.

# Re Williams (deceased)
# Wiles and another v Madgin and others

*a*

CHANCERY DIVISION

NICHOLLS J

7, 10 DECEMBER 1984

*b*

*Will – Construction – Ambiguity – Extrinsic evidence – Admissibility of extrinsic evidence to assist construction – Will ambiguous – Will listing 25 names in three separate groups with no indication as to purpose of grouping – Letter written by testatrix to solicitors asking them to 'organise' contents of will – Whether letter admissible to assist in construing will – Whether letter of assistance in construction – Administration of Justice Act 1982, s 21(1)(b) (2).*

*c*

On 30 March 1983, seven days before she died, the testatrix executed a home-made will in which after stating that it was her last will and testament she merely listed 25 names divided into three groups, which were unequal in size and included a mixture of next of kin, other relatives and three organisations. There was nothing in the will to indicate the purpose of the groupings and there were no words of gift. The will concluded with instructions as to what was to happen in the event of 'any beneficiaries' predeceasing the *d* testatrix. The day before the will was executed the testatrix wrote to her solicitors asking them to 'organise' the bequests of her will and explaining that 'I have divided the recipients into three categories and wish that the first, for example, should receive, say, £2,000 each; the second £1,000, and the third £500'. The executrices of the will issued a summons to determine, inter alia, whether, if there was an effective disposition by the testatrix, her estate should be divided equally between the 25 persons named in the will *e* or whether the estate should be divided into three shares, one for each of the listed groups, and then each share divided equally between the beneficiaries listed in that group. The question arose whether the testatrix's letter could be admitted as extrinsic evidence under s 21(1)(b) and (2)[a] of the Administration of Justice Act 1982, which provided for extrinsic evidence, including evidence of the testator's intention, to be admitted to assist in the interpretation of a will 'in so far as the language used in any part *f* of [the will] is ambiguous on the face of it'.

**Held** – (1) Although the testatrix had made an effective disposition of her estate to the 25 named persons as beneficiaries, her will was ambiguous in that there was no indication of the purpose for which the beneficiaries had been divided into three groups, and at least two possible meanings could be attached to the division into groups. Accordingly, *g* the letter was admissible under s 21(1)(b) and (2) of the 1982 Act to assist in interpreting the testatrix's will (see p 967 *e* to p 968 *b*, post).

(2) However, the letter was of no assistance in construing the will, since—

(a) the purpose of admitting extrinsic evidence under s 21(1)(b) and (2) of the 1982 Act was to assist in the construction of a will by showing which of two or more possible meanings a testator had attached to a particular word or phrase, and, although the true *h* meaning of the word or phrase might not be apparent until extrinsic evidence was admitted, the word or phrase read in its context had to be capable of bearing that meaning, since otherwise the court would in effect be rewriting part of the will. Accordingly, the gifts to the 25 named persons could not be construed primarily as pecuniary legacies or as gifts of proportional shares in the estate, since such constructions were outside any meaning which the simple division made in the will was capable of *j* bearing (see p 969 *e* to p 970 *e* and *f g*, post);

(b) if extrinsic evidence showed a testator was unclear or undecided about what he meant by an ambiguous word or phrase, that did not enable or require the court to reject the word or phrase altogether if the will could be construed without the aid of the

*a*    Section 21 is set out at p 966 *f g*, post.

extrinsic evidence, and therefore the rejection of the letter as an aid to construing the will
*a* did not mean that the gifts to the 25 named persons failed altogether (see p 969 *h j* and p
970 *f g*, post);
    (c) the letter was merely a letter of instruction to the testatrix's solicitors and offered no
explanation of what she had meant by the divisions in the will (see p 970 *a b* and *f g*,
post).
    (3) Accordingly the will would be construed without the assistance of the letter and
*b* since there was no indication in the will itself why the beneficiaries were divided into
three groups the estate would be divided equally between the 25 named persons (see
p 970 *b* to *f*, post).

### Notes
For the law as to admissibility of evidence in the interpretation of wills, see 50 Halsbury's
*c* Laws (4th edn) paras 378–384, and for cases on the subject, see 50 Digest (Reissue) 581–
619, 5838–6379.
    For presumption against intestacy, see 50 Halsbury's Laws (4th edn) paras 440–442,
and for cases on the subject, see 50 Digest (Reissue) 515–523, 5026–5100.
    For the Administration of Justice Act 1982, s 21, see 52 Halsbury's Statutes (3rd edn)
1977.

*d* ### Cases cited
*Barrance, Re, Barrance v Ellis* [1910] 2 Ch 419.
*Harrison, Re, Turner v Hellard* (1885) 30 Ch D 390, CA.
*Robertson v Fraser* (1871) LR 6 Ch App 696.
*Salusbury v Denton* (1857) 3 K & J 529, 69 ER 1219.
*Stevens (decd), Re, Pateman v James* [1952] 1 All ER 674, [1952] Ch 323.
*e* *Turner, Re, Carpenter v Staveley* [1949] 2 All ER 935.

### Adjourned summons
By an originating summons dated 3 July 1984, as amended on 2 November and 6
December 1984 pursuant to orders of Master Chamberlain and subsequently reissued,
the plaintiffs, Denise May Wiles and Kathleen Joyce Muir, the executrices appointed by
*f* the will made on 30 March 1983 by Enid Florence Emily Williams (otherwise Cook)
deceased (the testatrix), sought, inter alia, the determination of the following questions:
whether on the true construction of the will of the testatrix her estate was (a) divisible in
equal shares between 22 named individuals, Hitchin Hospital, the National Trust and
the charitable purpose (cancer research) or (b) was divisible into three equal parts
corresponding with three groups referred to in the will or (c) if the estate was divisible
*g* between the 22 named individuals, Hitchin Hospital, the National Trust and the
charitable purpose (cancer research) in some other and, if so, what shares or (d) whether
the estate devolved as on the partial intestacy of the testatrix. The defendants to the
summons were or represented the beneficiaries named in the will (other than the next of
kin of the testatrix), the next of kin of the testatrix and Her Majesty's Attorney General.
The facts are set out in the judgment.
*h*
*Geoffrey Jaques* for the plaintiffs.
*Mark Blackett-Ord* for the group 1 beneficiaries.
*Roger Kaye* for the group 2 beneficiaries.
*Kenneth Farrow* for the next of kin.
*Peter Crampin* for the Attorney General.
*j* *Frank Hinks* for the group 3 beneficiaries.

*Cur adv vult*

10 December. The following judgment was delivered.

**NICHOLLS J.** Mrs Enid Florence Emily Williams died on 6 April 1983. She executed
a short, home-made will seven days earlier, on 30 March 1983. The will began:

'This is the last Will and Testament of Enid F. E. Williams of 94 Fairview Road, Stevenage, my executrix being Denise Wiles, 41 Berkley Crescent and Kathleen   *a* Muir, 92 Fairview Road.'

There followed a list of the names of 22 individuals with their addresses, and of three organisations or purposes: Hitchin Hospital, the National Trust and Cancer Research. The 25 names were divided into three groups, prefaced respectively by the numbers 1, 2 and 3. The groups were unequal in size: group 1 consisted of eight individuals, including   *b* the two executrices, and Cancer Research; group 2 consisted of four individuals; and group 3 consisted of ten individuals, Hitchin Hospital and the National Trust.

The will concluded:

'In the event of any beneficiaries predeceasing me, their share to be added to the residue of my estate. John Kings is to have the choice of furniture and ornaments   *c* before the house and contents are sold.'

From this summary it will be seen that the list of 25 persons (for brevity I will treat the two organisations and Cancer Research as persons) was not accompanied by any words of gifts: there is no express statement in the will of why these persons were named in the will or, if they were intended beneficiaries, of what they were to receive from the   *d* testatrix's estate.

Probate was duly granted to the two named executrices, and questions have now arisen on the interpretation and effect of the will. The approximate net capital of the estate, after payment of all expenses other than the costs of these proceedings, is about £57,000.

Summonses raising questions on the construction of wills are not now as common as they were but, this apart, the only feature which makes this application at all unusual is   *e* that this is, apparently, the first occasion on which a court has had to consider the effect of s 21 of the Administration of Justice Act 1982. That section concerns the admissibility of extrinsic evidence, including evidence of a testator's intention, to assist in interpretation of a will. The section provides:

'(1) This section applies to a will—(a) in so far as any part of it is meaningless; (b)   *f* in so far as the language used in any part of it is ambiguous on the face of it; (c) in so far as evidence, other than evidence of the testator's intention, shows that the language used in any part of it is ambiguous in the light of surrounding circumstances.
(2) In so far as this section applies to a will extrinsic evidence, including evidence of the testator's intention, may be admitted to assist in its interpretation.'   *g*

The section applies to deaths on or after 1 January 1983 (see ss 73(6) and 76(11)) and, accordingly, it applies in this case. On 29 March 1983 the testatrix wrote a letter addressed to her solicitors, and before me some of the parties sought to have that letter admitted in evidence by virtue of s 21 on one or other of the points of construction in issue.

Three points were in issue on the construction of the will. First, apart from the specific   *h* gift of furniture and ornaments, was there an effective disposition by the testatrix of her estate? Second, if there was a gift of the estate to the 25 listed persons, was the estate to be divided between them equally, or was it to be divided into three shares, one for each of the listed groups, with those named in each group sharing equally in their group's one-third share? I will call the first of these two possibilities 'the personal equality construction' and the second 'the group equality construction'. On the personal equality construction,   *j* each of the 25 persons was given a 1/25th share in the estate. On the group equality construction, those listed in groups 1, 2 and 3 were given 1/27th, 1/12th and 1/36th shares respectively. Third, whichever of the two constructions on the second question is right, do the beneficiaries take as tenants in common or joint tenants? This third question arises from the fact that, although all 25 persons survived the testatrix, one of them (Mrs Chan, who was in group 3) died subsequently.

The proceedings before me took the following course. Initially, counsel representing
a  the various groups or interests presented their arguments in support of the answers to
the three questions for which they were contending, urging me that the answers were so
clear that no question arose of any part of the will being meaningless (s 21(1)(a)) or of the
language used in any part of it being ambiguous on its face (s 21(1)(b)). It was not
suggested by anyone that s 21(1)(c), concerned with what are sometimes called latent
ambiguities, was in point in this case. Counsel's fallback positions were that if their
b  primary arguments were wrong, and if their opponents might be right, then the
conditions specified in para (a) or para (b) of s 21(1) were satisfied here, and the testatrix's
letter was admissible and should be admitted. Having heard these arguments, I ruled
that the language of the will was on its face ambiguous on one point, namely the use of
the numerals 1, 2 and 3 to divide the list of 25 persons into three groups without any
clear indication of the purpose of such grouping. The letter, which until then I had not
c  read, was produced and read, and I heard further submissions on the questions of
construction in the light of that evidence, and also submissions on the purpose for which
evidence admitted under s 21 may be used.

To make these two-stage arguments intelligible, I must start with the arguments
addressed to me at the first stage, namely before the letter was admitted in evidence. On
the first of the three questions counsel for the testatrix's next of kin submitted that, there
d  being no dispositive words (save as to the furniture and ornaments), no intelligible
meaning could be given to the list of 25 names. He submitted that, although the will
refers to the 'share' of a predeceasing beneficiary, the direction then given (that the share
was to be added to 'the residue of my estate') suggests that the share given was not a share
of residue, but was a share of some other, wholly unspecified, nature. I cannot accept
this. The will has been admitted to probate as a testamentary document. In it the testatrix
e  appointed two executrices. She then listed 25 names, and followed the list with words
which make plain that she envisaged that those in that list were 'beneficiaries' who, if
they survived, would be entitled to a share. In my view, donative intent in favour of
those persons is obvious, and I can see nothing in the will to suggest that those persons
were not intended to share the whole of the balance of the estate between them. In
particular, I do not think that the direction that the shares of predeceasing beneficiaries
f  were to be added to the residue is sufficiently clear to raise a serious doubt on this point.
I also note that the testatrix envisaged that the house and contents would be sold; Mr
Kings was to have the choice of furniture and ornaments before the sale, but the will
made no provision regarding the proceeds of sale. I think this tends to suggest that she
assumed that Mr Kings having made his choice, and the house and the rest of the contents
having been sold, the proceeds (like the rest of her estate) would be going to the 25 listed
g  persons.

The answer to the second question of construction is not so clear. The testatrix placed
her 25 beneficiaries into three groups, but her purpose in so doing is not apparent on the
face of the will. The basis of the classification, if not the intended result, might have been
apparent if the testatrix had, for example, placed her relations in one group, charities in
another group and friends in a third group, but she has not done this. It seems that the
h  testatrix was married three times but was not married when she died. She had no
children. Her surviving blood relations included two aunts and several cousins. Each of
the testatrix's three groups included relations; each of the three groups included statutory
next of kin; each of the three groups included individuals who were not relations; and
charitable gifts were included in group 1 and in group 3. From this the inference seems
to me that the testatrix may have intended the grouping to be related, in some
j  unexplained way, to the size of the benefits that the groups or the members of the groups
were to receive. Turning to s 21, I do not think that the numbering 1, 2 and 3 can be
regarded as meaningless within s 21(1)(a), namely without meaning. The difficulty is a
different one, namely which of at least two possible meanings is to be attributed to the
use of the numerals 1, 2 and 3 in the context of this unusual will, wholly devoid as it is
of any relevant express dispositive words. One possible meaning being contended for
was that by the use of these numerals the testatrix intended to say that her *estate* should

be divided into three equal shares, one share to go to the members of each group. Another meaning was that the testatrix was intending thereby to divide her list of *beneficiaries* into three parts and that she failed to spell out what the consequences of that division were to be (and hence the beneficiaries should take equal shares). Thus the problem is one of ambiguity, not of meaninglessness. Moreover, I do not think that the choice between the group equality construction and the personal equality construction is so clear that it can be said there is no real doubt or ambiguity. On this basis the letter was admitted in evidence under para (*b*).

The letter was dated 29 March 1983, which was the day before the will was executed. It was addressed to the testatrix's solicitors, and received by them through the post in the usual way, in an envelope which also contained the original will. It must be probable that the letter and the will were placed in the envelope after the will had been executed, either by the testatrix or someone acting on her instructions. Wednesday, 30 March 1983 was the Wednesday in Holy Week, and the testatrix died a week later on the Wednesday after Easter. The letter was in manuscript and headed with the testatrix's home address, and signed by her. It read:

'Dear Sir,
    I would be glad if you could "organise" the bequests of my will before the actual document is made out. I have no idea what the final amount of my assets will be. My decease may not be far off, in which case there will be savings accounts to add to the house value; at least perhaps I consider an amount of £40,000. I have divided the recipients into three categories and wish that the first, for example, should receive, say, £2,000 each; the second £1,000, and the third £500.
    The share of anybody who predeceases me would be added to the residue. No doubt before final settlements are made adjustments will be necessary, but I wish the 2nd and 3rd groups to receive the same, and the residue left spread over group one. I understand debts, expenses, cremation costs and costs will be be deducted from the residue, together with charge for entry of death in the Book of Remembrance at Stopsley.
    I should be glad if you could deal with the copy as soon as possible, or the original if possible, from these details so that the will can be signed and witnessed.
                                                                    Yours truly . . .'

Counsel advanced a wide range of submissions and alternative submissions in the light of the contents of that letter. The summary which follows is not intended to be comprehensive. Counsel for the beneficiaries listed in group 1 submitted that although extrinsic evidence was admissible only to assist in construing a meaningless or ambiguous part of a will, when admitted in the case of an ambiguity, the extrinsic evidence can throw up a construction not evident from the will alone so long as such construction is consistent with the terms of the will. He then submitted that the letter showed that the testatrix intended that the persons in groups 1, 2 and 3 were to receive the whole estate in the proportions of 4:2:1 respectively, the second paragraph of the letter being concerned with the share of a predeceasing beneficiary. Alternatively, the persons in group 1 were to receive pecuniary legacies of £2,000 each, those in group 2 £1,000 each, and those in group 3 £500, the residue belonging to the group 1 beneficiaries.

Counsel for the group 2 beneficiaries argued that extrinsic evidence admitted to assist in construing an apparent ambiguity could not let in a new construction not apparent from the will. He also submitted that the letter itself did not assist at all, having been written the day before the will was executed. Alternatively, it showed only that the testatrix intended to divide her beneficiaries into three categories, and in the absence of any clear or admissible alternative the inference was that the estate should be divided into three equal shares or (in the further alternative) into three shares in the proportions of 4:2:1.

Counsel for the next of kin submitted that if extrinsic evidence, admitted because of uncertainty on which of two constructions of the relevant language in the will is the

a correct one, showed that a testator intended neither of those constructions, it was not
then open to the court to reject the evidence and find for one or other of those
constructions. Here, he submitted, the letter outlined a scheme different from either the
personal equality construction or the group equality construction. The testatrix envisaged
pecuniary legacies of differing amounts for the members of the three groups, and then a
division of residue in terms which are not clear. So both the personal equality construction
and the group equality construction must be wrong and the testatrix's intention not
b being clear, her estate (other than the furniture and ornaments chosen by Mr Kings) is
undisposed of and passes as on an intestacy.

Counsel for the Attorney General submitted that one of the purposes for which
extrinsic evidence is admitted is to allow the 'dictionary' principle to apply, and that once
a word of uncertain meaning lets in extrinsic evidence, that evidence may lead to a
construction of the will not otherwise apparent. He submitted that the letter assists
c because it negatives the group equality construction and showed that the purpose of the
numerals was only to guide the solicitors when preparing a new will for the testatrix.

Counsel for the group 3 beneficiaries contended that if the letter failed to assist in
showing what was the testatrix's intention on the ambiguous provision in the will, the
court should not treat that provision as ineffectual and failing, but it should reject the
letter as an aid and construe the will without regard to it. To this summary I add that at
d an early stage a further argument was advanced to the effect that, once extrinsic evidence
was admitted, it was admissible for all purposes and its use was not confined to the
meaningless or ambiguous parts of the will which made the evidence admissible.
Subsequently this argument was abandoned, and in my view rightly so.

I have found the letter to be of no assistance, for several reasons. First, the letter does
not support either the group equality construction or the personal equality construction.
e Second, as to other possible constructions, it is necessary to keep in mind the purpose of
s 21. Section 21 is concerned with the admission of evidence as an aid to construction.
Subsection (2), when read with the material paragraph (para (b)) of sub-s (1), provides
that, in so far as the language used in any part of a will is ambiguous on the face of it,
extrinsic evidence, including evidence of the testator's intention, may be admitted to
assist in its interpretation. The evidence may assist by showing which of two or more
f possible meanings a testator was attaching to a particular word or phrase. 'My effects' and
'my money' are obvious examples. That meaning may be one which, without recourse
to the extrinsic evidence, would not really have been apparent at all. So long as that
meaning is one which the word or phrase read in its context is capable of bearing, then
the court may conclude that, assisted by the extrinsic evidence, that is its correct
construction. But if, however liberal may be the approach of the court, the meaning is
g one which the word or phrase cannot bear, I do not see how, in carrying out a process of
construction (or interpretation, to use the word employed in s 21), the court can declare
that meaning to be the meaning of the word or phrase. Such a conclusion, varying or
contradicting the language used, would amount to rewriting part of the will, and that is
a result to be achieved, if at all, under the rectification provisions in s 20. (In passing, I
note that there is no claim for rectification in the present case. It was suggested in the
h course of argument that s 20 could not apply to a home-made will such as the one before
me, because 'clerical error' in s 20(1)(a) suggests a clerk. I do not accept this. A testator
writing out or typing his own will can make a clerical error just as much as someone else
writing out or typing a will for him.) Again, if extrinsic evidence shows that a testator
was unclear, or undecided, on what he meant by the ambiguous word or phrase, I do not
see how that can require or enable the court to reject the word or phrase altogether if the
j court is able to construe the word or phrase without the aid of extrinsic evidence.

Applying that approach to the evidence admitted under s 21(1)(b) in this case, I reject
the submission that the contents of the letter can lead to the conclusions that the gift to
the 25 beneficiaries fails altogether. Likewise, I do not accept the contention that the gifts
are to be construed primarily as pecuniary legacies, or as gifts to individuals or groups of
shares in the estate in the proportions of 4:2:1. Even if the contents of the letter clearly

supported these constructions (which I do not think they do), such constructions seem to me to be outside any meaning which the simple division in this will is capable of bearing.   *a*

My third reason for rejecting the letter as an aid is that I do not think that in any event it is or affords an explanation of what the testatrix meant by what she had written in her will. It was a letter of instruction to solicitors to prepare a new will, telling them what were the provisions she wished them to include in her new will regarding the three categories of beneficiaries. What the letter did not do is to explain, nor does it assist in understanding, what the testatrix meant to be achieved by the divisions she had made in   *b* the will she had already executed when the letter was posted to the solicitors.

So I return to construe the will without the benefit of any assistance from the letter. The division of the list of the 25 beneficiaries into three groups of unequal sizes does suggest that the testatrix intended to differentiate between the beneficiaries in some way on the benefits they were to receive. But I do not think that the will gives any indication of what form that differentiation was to take. In particular, I do not think that one can   *c* spell out from the division a direction that the estate was to be divided into three equal shares so as to achieve equality between the groups. There being no such indication, in my view, the gift must be taken as one to all 25 beneficiaries equally.

The third question which arises is whether the beneficiaries take as tenants in common in equal shares or as joint tenants. All counsel dealt with this point briefly, and I shall do the same. In my view, the gift to this heterogeneous collection of 22 individuals, Hitchin   *d* Hospital, the National Trust and Cancer Research, was to them in equal shares, namely as tenants in common. Hence Mrs Chan's estate is entitled to a 1/25th share.

Finally, I mention one further point on the scope of s 21(1)(*b*). Obviously, numerals can be language used in a will just as much as words or letters or other symbols. The applicability of s 21(1)(*b*) cannot depend on whether a testator or the draftsman of his will has used words such as one, two and three rather than numerals 1, 2 and 3, or the   *e* letters a, b and c or other symbols. But it seems to me that the ambiguity apparent on the face of this testatrix's will is not as to the meaning which the testatrix was ascribing to the numerals 1, 2 and 3; rather, the ambiguity is as to the purpose for which those numerals were inserted in the will at all, dividing as they did the list of beneficiaries into three groups. This can be illustrated by noting that the problem would be the same if instead of using the first three numerals the testatrix had used words or letters or simply   *f* separated the groups by drawing horizontal lines across the page at the appropriate places. The testatrix has failed to explain the purpose for which she has made the division. Rejecting as I have the extrinsic evidence as of no assistance, its admission has made no difference to the outcome of this case. But I am not to be taken as deciding that an ambiguity such as I have just described is an ambiguity of language within s 21(1)(*b*). The point was not referred to in the arguments before me, and should it arise for decision   *g* in another case, one of the matters which may need to be considered is the ambit of the mischief intended to be remedied by s 21(1)(*b*).

*Declaration accordingly.*

Solicitors: *Brignall White & Orchard*, Stevenage (for the plaintiffs); *Hawkins & Co*, Hitchin (for the group 1 beneficiaries); *Woolley & Weston*, Hitchin (for the group 2 beneficiaries); *Hamiltons*, Stevenage (for the next of kin and group 3 beneficiaries); *Treasury Solicitor*.

Jacqueline Metcalfe   Barrister.

# R v O'Brien and another

QUEEN'S BENCH DIVISION
HOBHOUSE J
19 NOVEMBER, 20 DECEMBER 1984

*Legal aid – Criminal cases – Representation by counsel – Joint defendants – Defendants' right to separate representation – Defendants assigned same solicitor – Whether solicitor having right to select separate counsel to represent defendants – Whether each counsel entitled to be paid out of legal aid fund – Legal Aid in Criminal Proceedings (General) Regulations 1968, regs 9, 14.*

Two defendants were committed by magistrates for trial on a charge of affray. When they applied for legal aid the magistrates made legal aid orders providing for joint representation by solicitor and counsel and assigned the same solicitor to act for both defendants. Under reg 14[a] of the Legal Aid in Criminal Proceedings (General) Regulations 1968 a solicitor or counsel could be assigned to two or more legally assisted persons whose cases were to be heard together, unless the interests of justice required that such persons be separately represented. The solicitor was entitled under reg 9[b] on the 1968 regulations to 'instruct any counsel who is willing to act'. The solicitor instructed separate counsel to appear for the two defendants, but on taxation after the trial the taxing officer allowed the costs of only one counsel and disallowed the costs of the applicant, the other counsel. On appeal, the taxing master upheld the taxing officer's decision on the ground that the relevant legal aid order did not authorise the applicant's costs. The applicant appealed to High Court against the taxing master's decision.

**Held** – On the true construction of regs 9 and 14 of the 1968 regulations, where the same solicitor was assigned by the court under a legal aid order to represent two legally aided defendants, that solicitor was not restricted to appointing the same counsel to represent both defendants, since his discretion under reg 9 to appoint any counsel willing to act was not fettered by reg 14. Although the court had power to assign the solicitor, it did not also have power to assign the counsel to be instructed by that solicitor and therefore could not by means of the legal aid order fetter the right of the solicitor to select counsel. The magistrates' orders could be construed as allowing the solicitor to appoint different counsel and both counsel were accordingly entitled to be paid out of the legal aid fund. The appeal would therefore be allowed (see p 975 *c* to *j*, post).

## Notes
For legal representation under legal aid in criminal proceedings, see 11 Halsbury's Laws (4th edn) para 753.

For the Legal Aid in Criminal Proceedings (General) Regulations 1968, regs 9, 14, see 6 Halsbury's Statutory Instruments (4th reissue) 33, 34.

## Case referred to in judgment
*Cope v United Dairies (London) Ltd* [1963] 2 All ER 194, [1963] 2 QB 33, [1963] 2 WLR 926.

## Appeal
The applicant, Thomas Staten Culver, a barrister, appealed against the order of the taxing master, Master Devonshire, made on 2 February 1984 whereby he upheld an order disallowing the applicant's fee for representing a defendant, Joseph Edward Ollife, at the

---

*a*   Regulation 14 is set out at p 975 *a b*, post
*b*   Regulation 9 is set out at p 974 *g*, post

Central Criminal Court. The appeal was heard in chambers but judgment was given by
Hobhouse J in open court. The facts are set out in the judgment.          *a*

*Stephen Sedley QC*, the applicant with him, for the applicant.

*Cur adv vult*

20 December. The following judgment was delivered.          *b*

**HOBHOUSE J.** This appeal under reg 12 of the Legal Aid in Criminal Proceedings
(Costs) Regulations 1982, SI 1982/1197, raises an important point under the Legal Aid in
Criminal Proceedings (General) Regulations 1968, SI 1968/1231. It is an important point
because the criminal courts in England and Wales are at present adopting different and
inconsistent interpretations of the 1968 regulations. This is creating confusion and needs   *c*
to be resolved.

The situation concerned is an everyday one. Two or more defendants are charged
under one or more indictments which are going to be tried together. They each apply
for legal aid. The court making the legal aid orders sometimes forms a view whether
both defendants should be represented by the same solicitor and counsel, or whether
separate representation is justified. If both can properly be jointly represented it is   *d*
desirable that they should be: the charge on the legal aid fund is less; the trial or
proceedings on sentence will be more expeditious and satisfactory.

Joint representation in court obviously involves the same barrister being instructed on
behalf of each defendant. But just as a single barrister may be instructed by two different
firms of solicitors if the defendants have different solicitors, so also a single firm of
solicitors acting for two defendants may choose to instruct a different barrister to appear   *e*
for each of them. Even if there is no conflict of interest, the interests of justice may
require separate advocates to appear.

In some parts of the country the courts take the view that the question whether there
should be one or two counsel to appear on behalf of two defendants being tried together
should be governed by the legal aid order (or amendment to that order). On this approach
the question is conveniently determined before the trial or other hearing and is not left   *f*
to the discretion of the solicitor or the taxing officer. In other parts of the country the
view is taken that the 1968 regulations do not allow the courts to make a legal aid order
which directs what counsel shall appear for the applicant. The order can state whether
there is to be a single solicitor, but it is that solicitor who decides whether or not to
instruct a single counsel to represent both defendants, and it is for the taxing officer to
decide whether the expense of instructing separate counsel is justified, and therefore to   *g*
be allowed on the legal aid taxation.

In the present matter there were two defendants, Mr O'Brien and Mr Ollife. They had
originally been charged with murder, but they were committed by Camberwell Green
Magistrates' Court on an indictment charging affray. They each applied for legal aid. On
20 October 1982 the magistrates made two legal aid orders, one for O'Brien and the other
for Ollife. That for Ollife included the following words material to the present appeal:   *h*

'In accordance with the provisions of section 28 and 29 of the Legal Aid Act, 1974,
the above-named court hereby grants legal aid to *Joseph Edward Ollife* for . . .
Proceedings before the Central Criminal Court in connection with *his trial* . . .
Except as otherwise provided above, the legal aid granted shall consist of
representation by solicitor and counsel jointly with *C. W. P. O'Brien* including advice
on the preparation of the case for the proceedings.   *j*
The solicitor assigned is *B. Rose-Smith, 135 Stockwell Rd SW9 . . .*'

That for O'Brien was in identical terms, except that it was granted to Christopher
William Peter O'Brien, and the printed words 'jointly with' were followed by the typed
words '*J. E. Ollife*'.

Mr Rose-Smith, in preparing for the trial at the Old Bailey, instructed Mr Longstaffe *a*  of counsel. Mr Longstaffe advised that the two men should be represented by separate counsel, and accordingly Mr Rose-Smith instructed Mr Longstaffe to appear for Mr O'Brien, and Mr Culver to appear for Mr Olliffe. At the trial, pleas of not guilty were accepted to the affray charges, and pleas of guilty to other charges were accepted and the two men were duly sentenced.

On the legal aid taxation, the fees of Mr Longstaffe were allowed but those of Mr Culver disallowed. Mr Culver took it to the taxing master, Master Devonshire, who also *b*  disallowed Mr Culver's fees. The reasons given by Master Devonshire were very simple and clear. A taxing master can only allow fees which are authorised by a legal aid order. The legal aid order in favour of Mr Ollife does not authorise separate counsel to be instructed for the two defendants. Therefore, even though he was satisfied that the instruction of separate counsel was justified in the interests of justice having regard to the facts of the case, he held that he had no power to allow the fees. He certified that his *c*  decision related to a point of principle of general importance.

The first step in the reasoning of Master Devonshire is clearly correct, and so is the third if the second step is also correct. The taxing master's jurisdiction and function is governed by the terms in which the legal aid order has been made. He cannot go outside or vary the terms of the order; he cannot disregard the order, or any part of it, on the ground that it is in his opinion ultra vires or improper. As was said by Megaw J in *Cope v* *d*  *United Dairies (London) Ltd* [1963] 2 All ER 194 at 196, [1963] 2 QB 33 at 38:

'The defendants submit that the senior taxing master exceeded his jurisdiction. They say that the order made by Master RITCHIE was clear and unambiguous; and that, even if the taxing master thought that it was wrong or ultra vires, he had no option but to comply. He was not entitled to disallow certain items on the ground that they were wrongly or irregularly made the subject of taxation. If the order *e*  were wrong, the only remedy would have been by way of appeal from that order to the judge in chambers. No such appeal has been made. The defendants further submitted that Master RITCHIE's order was not wrong, irregular or ultra vires. Counsel for the Law Society agreed that the taxing master could not properly refuse to carry out an order for taxation, in whole or in part, because he considered it to be wrong or ultra vires, and that the same applies to this court on a review. With that *f*  proposition, I agree.'

If Master Devonshire was correct in his reading of the order made, then it is not now disputed that his decision was right. But Mr Culver has appealed to the High Court. He is represented by leading counsel; his appeal is supported in a written submission on behalf of the Lord Chancellor. It is said that the second step in the reasoning of Master *g*  Devonshire is wrong. The order must be read with the provisions of the regulations under which it was made. When this is done, it will be seen that it should not be read so as to contradict the solicitor's right to select counsel.

At this stage, it is convenient to note that s 39 of the Legal Aid Act 1974 confers a power to make regulations which include a power to prescribe forms. The 1968 regulations prescribe certain forms for use 'with such variation as the circumstances may *h*  require' (reg 33) and reg 6 provides that 'A legal aid order shall be in Form 6 . . .' The prescribed form of order differs from the printed form used in the present case; the prescribed form does not include the words 'jointly with'. The amendments made in 1983 (SI 1983/1863) do not affect this or any other question I have to decide.

Criminal legal aid is dealt with in Pt II of the 1974 Act. The drafting of the Act makes it clear that the application for and the grant or refusal of legal aid is done on an individual *j*  basis. It is the individual applicant who is granted or refused legal aid. Section 28(7) authorises the grant of legal aid to a person, such as Mr Ollife, who is committed for trial at the Crown Court.

Section 30(1) of the 1974 Act provides:

'For the purposes of the Part of this Act legal aid, in relation to any proceedings to which a person is a party, shall be taken, subject to the following provisions of this

section, as consisting of representation by a solicitor and counsel assigned by the
court, including advice on the preparation of that person's case for those proceedings.'    *a*

This subsection introduced the phrase 'representation by a solicitor and counsel assigned
by the court.' The word 'assigned' is used a number of times in the section. It clearly
contemplates that any legal representative, whether solicitor or barrister, acting for an
assisted person should be appointed by the court.

Section 38(1) states that 'Any practising barrister or solicitor may be assigned to act for
a legally assisted person' unless on the list of unfit practitioners. This, again, contemplates    *b*
assignment.

The critical provision, s 37(2), which enables a practitioner to recover his fees from the
legal aid fund is similarly drafted:

> 'Subject to regulations under section 39 below, the costs of legal aid ordered to be
> given to a legally assisted person for the purpose of any proceedings shall include    *c*
> sums on account of the fees payable to any counsel or solicitor assigned to him and
> disbursements reasonably incurred by any such solicitor for or in connection with
> those proceedings.'

This subsection refers to the rule-making power in s 39, which includes the power to
make regulations to 'make provision with respect to the manner in which counsel and
solicitors are to be assigned to legally assisted persons in pursuance of legal aid orders' (see    *d*
s 39(1)(e)). It follows that, if the necessity for any given counsel to show that he has been
assigned by the court to represent the assisted person is to be dispensed with, such
dispensation must be found in the regulations.

I therefore turn to the 1968 regulations. In discussing them, I will leave on one side
the question of representation by assigned counsel in the House of Lords and the Court
of Appeal and confine myself to the Crown Court.    *e*

Regulation 8 provides:

> '*Assignment of solicitor*
> Subject to the provisions of Regulations 11 and 14 of these Regulations, any
> person in respect of whom a legal aid order is made, entitling him to the services of
> a solicitor, may select any solicitor who is willing to act and such solicitor shall be    *f*
> assigned to him.'

Regulation 9 provides:

> '*Selection of counsel*
> Where a legal aid order is made in respect of the services of solicitor and counsel,
> the solicitor may instruct any counsel who is willing to act: Provided that in the case    *g*
> of proceedings in the Court of Appeal or House of Lords, counsel may be assigned
> by the court or person making or amending the legal aid order.'

Regulation 10, so far as material, provides:

> '*Assignment of counsel only*
> (1) Where a legal aid order in respect of proceedings in [the Crown Court] is    *h*
> made or amended so as to provide for representation by counsel only, counsel shall
> be assigned by the court or person making or amending the legal aid order . . .'

The scheme which these provisions follows is clear. In the Crown Court where an order
is made for solicitor and counsel, it is only the solicitor who must be, and is to be,
assigned; counsel is not to be assigned by the court, but under reg 9 is to be selected by
the assigned solicitor. This effect of the 1968 regulations is put further beyond doubt by    *j*
the provisions for assignment of counsel, where only counsel is to represent the assisted
person, or where the proceedings are in the Court of Appeal or the House of Lords.
Regulation 13, although given the heading 'Assignment of two counsel', is drafted so as
to recognise that what may happen is that, even in this situation, the order may allow
two counsel for one assisted person without counsel being assigned by the court.

However, when one comes to the point with which this appeal is concerned, where
*a* the same representatives may be acting for two or more assisted persons, the intention of
the 1968 regulations is again in a form which makes the intention clear. The regulation
which deals with this situation is reg 14:

> '*Assignment of one solicitor or counsel to more than one legally assisted person*
> A solicitor or counsel may be assigned to two or more legally assisted persons
> whose cases are heard together, unless the interests of justice require that such
> *b* persons be separately represented.'

Regulation 8 (assignment of a solicitor) is expressly made subject to this regulation,
whereas reg 9 (selection of counsel) is not. Regulation 14 deals with assignment of legal
representatives. Where a solicitor is assigned, the same solicitor can in appropriate cases
be assigned to more than one person. Where a counsel is assigned, the same enabling
*c* power exists. But the fact that a single solicitor has been assigned successively to two
assisted persons under reg 8, possibly having overridden the wishes of one or more of
those persons, does not affect the discretion of the solicitor under the first part of reg 9.

The court has the power to assign the solicitor; it does not as well have the power to
assign the counsel to be instructed by that solicitor to appear in the Crown Court; it
cannot by its order fetter the right of the solicitor to select counsel. It is wrong to construe
*d* reg 14 as giving a power to assign counsel when that power is not to be found in some
other regulation; still less should it be construed as giving the court the power to make a
legal aid order which requires two assisted persons to be represented by the same counsel
when the authority making the order has not even got the power to assign counsel at all.

It follows that any court which construes reg 14 as giving it the power, when making
an order for representation of an assisted person in the Crown Court by solicitor and
*e* counsel, to direct that the same counsel should appear for that person as for another is
mistaken in law, and any such order is ultra vires.

If the orders made for these two defendants on 20 October 1982 have to be construed
as such orders, they are both ultra vires and invalid. I see no valid basis for treating one
order as less invalid than the other. If they each require the same counsel to appear for
Mr O'Brien as for Mr Ollife, the fee of Mr Longstaffe is as unauthorised as that of Mr
*f* Culver. On this reading, there was no order which authorised Mr Culver's fees and the
appeal would have to be dismissed.

However, I consider that when one reads these orders, having in mind the terms of
the 1968 regulations, it is possible to read the words 'jointly with' as explanatory rather
than as imposing a limitation. The words which restrict the use which can be made of
the order are the words which assign Mr B Rose-Smith as solicitor. If either of the
*g* defendants should object that Mr B Rose-Smith is not the solicitor he himself has selected,
the words 'jointly with' his co-defendant explain that the court has exercised its power
under reg 14 to restrict the defendant's right to select a solicitor under reg 8. The orders
do not purport to assign any counsel and, although they are open to such a construction,
there is no need to construe them as invalidly seeking to exclude the solicitor's right of
selection under reg 9. Where it is possible to construe an order as being intra vires, not
*h* ultra vires, that is the construction which should be adopted.

The relevant order is therefore one which can be construed as authorising the
instruction of Mr Culver to appear for Mr Ollife, and I therefore allow this appeal with
costs, which I assess at £575, and remit the matter to the taxing officer for him to tax the
fee of Mr Culver in the criminal proceedings.

Before leaving this matter I must mention two further points. The first is that this
*j* question of the correct understanding of the 1968 regulations, and in particular reg 14,
having now been argued before the High Court and become the subject of judicial
decision in open court, all courts should now adopt the interpretation which I have held
to be correct, and desist from making orders which purport to limit the right of selection
of counsel under reg 9, or which might be thought so to do. Secondly, I recognise that
from considerations of convenience it would in many ways have been more satisfactory

if the 1968 regulations had given the court making or amending the order the power to
determine in advance of the trial the question of separate or joint representation by   *a*
counsel. Counsel and solicitors would then know without risk where they stood in
relation to the legal aid fund. But the 1968 regulations do not permit this desirable
certainty to be achieved in that manner. It should accordingly be further considered by
those responsible for the regulations whether there is sufficient provision in the
regulations as now amended in 1983 (the 1983 amendments not having affected the
question of law which I have decided) to enable solicitors and counsel to obtain guidance   *b*
in advance in cases where the increased cost of instructing separate counsel might
subsequently be challenged on taxation.

The order I make on this appeal is: under reg 12(7) of the Legal Aid in Criminal
Proceedings (Costs) Regulations 1982 it is ordered that the determining officer of the
Central Criminal Court determine the fees of Mr T Culver of counsel under reg 8 and
that the time limit specified in reg 7(1) be extended and it is further ordered that the   *c*
sum of £575 being the reasonable costs incurred in connection with the appeal be
allowed in addition.

*Order accordingly.*

Solicitors: *Mackenzie Patten* (for the applicant).   *d*

K Mydeen Esq   Barrister.

# Sharneyford Supplies Ltd v Edge (Barrington Black Austin & Co (a firm), third party)

CHANCERY DIVISION   *f*
MERVYN DAVIES J
10–14, 17–20 DECEMBER 1984, 18 JANUARY 1985

*Sale of land – Damages for breach of contract – Vendor's inability to show good title – Limitation
on damages if vendor's inability to show good title not attributable to his default – Contract for
purchase of farm with vacant possession on completion – Farm occupied by persons asserting that*   *g*
*they were tenants – Vendor failing to take proceedings against occupants of farm – Whether
vendor doing all he reasonably could to get vacant possession – Whether damages to be assessed in
accordance with general law – Whether purchaser only entitled to limited damages.*

*Misrepresentation – Innocent misrepresentation – Sale of land – Damages – Limitation of damages
– Innocent misrepresentation by vendor of land – Claim by purchaser for damages under statute*   *h*
*– Damages recoverable in tort – Whether statutory cause of action having effect of removing
limitation on damages recoverable in contract – Misrepresentation Act 1967, s 2(1).*

By a contract dated 14 November 1979 the defendant agreed to sell a maggot farm to the
plaintiff company for £8,500. It was a condition of the sale that the defendant give
vacant possession. The farm was, however, occupied by two business tenants on a periodic   *j*
or yearly tenancy and the defendant was unable to give vacant possession. The plaintiff
brought an action against the defendant for breach of contract and misrepresentation in
not giving vacant possession on the date fixed for completion or thereafter. The master
ordered, inter alia, that there be tried as a preliminary issue the question whether, if the
plaintiff was entitled to damages, its damages in contract were limited to its expenses,

*a* under the rule that where a vendor of realty was unable to make good title the purchaser was not entitled to damages for the loss of his bargain but was limited to recovering his expenses. The question also arose whether the plaintiff was entitled, under s 2(1)$^a$ of the Misrepresentation Act 1967, to recover damages for innocent misrepresentation.

**Held** – (1) Applying the principle that where a vendor entered into a contract for the sale of land knowing that he had no title and no means of acquiring title the purchaser's *b* damages for breach of contract were limited to his expenses incurred in the abortive sale, the plaintiff's damages in contract were prima facie limited to the expenses it had incurred and it was not entitled to damages for the loss of its bargain. Furthermore, although a vendor was under a duty to take reasonable steps towards obtaining a good title where it was within his power to do so, the vendor was not obliged to go to the extent of entering into litigation, and accordingly the defendant was not obliged to take *c* proceedings for possession against the tenants. Since there was nothing, short of litigation, which the defendant could reasonably have done to enable him to give vacant possession and since there had been no bad faith on his part, the defendant was entitled to rely on the rule excluding damages for the loss of the plaintiff's bargain and limiting the plaintiff's damages in contract to its expenses (see p 987 *b* to *e* and p 989 *b c*, post); *Bain v Fothergill* [1874–80] All ER Rep 83, *Williams v Glenton* (1866) LR 1 Ch App 200 and *Wroth* *d* *v Tyler* [1973] 1 All ER 897 applied; *Day v Singleton* [1899] 2 Ch 320 and *Malhotra v Choudhury* [1979] 1 All ER 186 considered.

(2) The rule that a purchaser's damages in contract were limited to his expenses if the vendor of realty was unable to make good title applied even where there was innocent misrepresentation, since the only exception to the rule was where deceit was proved. However, where a separate claim (ie apart from any claim in contract) was made for *e* damages for innocent misrepresentation under s 2(1) of the 1967 Act such damages could be awarded but would be measured in tort and did not operate to remove any restriction limiting the purchaser's damages in contract (see p 990 *g h* and p 991 *a b*, post); dictum of Graham J in *Watts v Spence* [1975] 2 All ER at 536 not followed.

(3) The plaintiff was accordingly entitled to damages for breach of contract, which would be limited to its expenses, and to damages for innocent misrepresentation pursuant *f* to the 1967 Act (see p 984 *j* and p 991 *b* to *d*, post).

**Notes**

For actions for damages by purchasers of realty, see 42 Halsbury's Laws (4th edn) para 267, and for cases on the subject, see 40 Digest (Reissue) 391–403, 3452–3579.

For damages under the Misrepresentation Act 1967, see 31 Halsbury's Laws (4th edn) *g* para 1103, and for cases on the subject, see 34 Digest (Reissue) 380–381, 3103–3105.

For the Misrepresentation Act 1967, s 2, see 22 Halsbury's Statutes (3rd edn) 676.

**Cases referred to in judgment**

*Bain v Fothergill* (1874) LR 7 HL 158, [1874–80] All ER Rep 83.
*Braybrooks v Whaley* [1919] 1 KB 435, DC.
*h* *Cumberland Consolidated Holdings Ltd v Ireland* [1946] 1 All ER 284, [1946] KB 264, CA.
*Daniel, Re, Daniel v Vassall* [1917] 2 Ch 405, [1916–17] All ER Rep 654.
*Day v Singleton* [1899] 2 Ch 320, CA.
*Engell v Fitch* (1869) LR 4 QB 659, Ex Ch.
*Flureau v Thornhill* (1776) 2 Wm Bl 1078, [1775–1802] All ER Rep 91, 96 ER 635.

*j*   *a*  Section 2(1) provides: 'Where a person has entered into a contract after a misrepresentation has been made to him by another party thereto and as a result thereof he has suffered loss, then, if the person making the misrepresentation would be liable to damages in respect thereof had the misrepresentation been made fraudulently, that person shall be so liable notwithstanding that the misrepresentation was not made fraudulently, unless he proves that he had reasonable ground to believe and did believe up to the time the contract was made that the facts represented were true.'

*Keen v Mear* [1920] 2 Ch 574, [1920] All ER Rep 147.
*Lehmann v McArthur* (1868) LR 3 Ch App 496.
*Malhotra v Choudhury* [1979] 1 All ER 186, [1980] Ch 52, CA.
*Minister of Health v Bellotti, Minister of Health v Holliday* [1944] 1 All ER 238, [1944] KB 298, CA.
*Royal Bristol Permanent Building Society v Bomash* (1887) 35 Ch D 390, [1886–90] All ER Rep 283.
*Watts v Spence* [1975] 2 All ER 528, [1976] Ch 165, [1975] 2 WLR 1039.
*Williams v Glenton* (1866) LR 1 Ch App 200.
*Wroth v Tyler* [1973] 1 All ER 897, [1974] Ch 30, [1973] 2 WLR 405.

**Cases also cited**
*Alltrans Express Ltd v CVA Holdings Ltd* [1984] 1 All ER 685, [1984] 1 WLR 394, CA.
*Anglo-Cyprian Trade Agencies Ltd v Paphos Wine Industries Ltd* [1951] 1 All ER 873.
*Baron v Phillips* (1979) 38 P & CR 91, CA.
*Barton v London and North Western Rly Co* (1888) 38 Ch D 144, CA.
*Caballero v Henty* (1874) LR 9 Ch App 447.
*Cohen v Nessdale Ltd* [1981] 3 All ER 118; *affd* [1982] 2 All ER 97, CA.
*Doe d Tucker v Morse* (1830) 1 B & Ad 365, 109 ER 822.
*Doe d Pennington v Taniere* (1848) 12 QB 998, 116 ER 1144.
*Doyle v Olby (Ironmongers) Ltd* [1969] 2 All ER 119, [1969] 2 QB 158, CA.
*D'Silva v Lister House Development Ltd* [1970] 1 All ER 858, [1971] Ch 17.
*Edwards v Wickwar* (1865) LR 1 Eq 68.
*Errington v Martell-Wilson (decd)* (1980) 130 NLJ 545.
*Harvey v Pratt* [1965] 2 All ER 786, [1965] 1 WLR 1025, CA.
*Holder v Holder* [1966] 2 All ER 116, [1968] Ch 353; *affd* [1968] 1 All ER 665, [1968] Ch 353, CA.
*Hollington Bros v Rhodes* [1951] 2 All ER 578.
*Huddersfield Police Authority v Watson* [1947] 2 All ER 193, [1947] KB 842, DC.
*Jones v Gardiner* [1902] 1 Ch 191.
*Lewis v MTC (Cars) Ltd* [1974] 3 All ER 423, [1974] 1 WLR 1499; *affd* [1975] 1 All ER 874, [1975] 1 WLR 457, CA.
*Longrigg Burrough & Trounson v Smith* (1979) 251 EG 847, CA.
*McConnel v Wright* [1903] 1 Ch 546, CA.
*Pilkington v Wood* [1953] 2 All ER 810, [1953] Ch 770.
*Sherbrooke v Dipple* (1981) 41 P & CR 173, CA.
*Thomas v Kensington* [1942] 2 All ER 263, [1942] 2 KB 181.
*Walker v Boyle* [1982] 1 All ER 634, [1982] 1 WLR 495.

**Preliminary issues**
By a writ of summons issued on 29 November 1980 the plaintiff, Sharneyford Supplies Ltd (formerly Flinthall Farms Ltd), sought as against the defendant, Philip Michael Edge, specific performance of an agreement made between the parties on 14 November 1979 for the purchase of a farm at Monk Bretton in the parish of Royston near Barnsley in the county of South Yorkshire, damages in addition to or in lieu of specific performance, alternatively a declaration that the plaintiff was entitled to the return of the deposit of £850 and interest thereon, the cost of investigating title to the farm and interest thereon and damages for misrepresentation and/or breach of warranty and/or breach of contract. On 21 March 1984 the plaintiff amended its pleading to restrict its claim to damages and a return of its deposit. On 15 March Master Dyson ordered, inter alia, that the following questions be tried as preliminary issues: (i) whether the defendant was liable to the plaintiff and (ii) in the event that the defendant was held so liable, whether the quantum of damages recoverable by the plaintiff was to be assessed in accordance with (a) the general law or (b) the rule in *Bain v Fothergill* (1874) LR 7 HL 158, [1874–80] All ER Rep 83. By a third party notice the defendant sought to be indemnified by the third party,

Barrington Black Austin & Co (sued as Barrington Black & Co), the defendant's former
a solicitors, against the plaintiff's claims and costs. The facts are set out in the judgment.

*J M Chadwick QC* and *Terence Mowschenson* for the plaintiff.
*J M Collins* for the defendant.
*W D Ainger* for the third party.

b                                                                              *Cur adv vult*

18 January. The following judgment was delivered.

**MERVYN DAVIES J.** I have before me two preliminary issues in an action for
damages for breach of a contract for the sale of land, for the return of a deposit and for
c damages for misrepresentation. The plaintiff is a company called Sharneyford Supplies
Ltd, formerly known as Flinthall Farms Ltd. The defendant is Mr Philip Michael Edge.
The defendant has an indemnity third party claim against a firm of solicitors who
formerly acted for him. They are Messrs Barrington Black Austin & Co.
   The contract sued on is dated 14 November 1979 and is made on a Law Society
Contract of Sale form (1973 revision). The vendor is Mr Edge and the purchaser is the
d plaintiff company. The land sold is specified in the particulars as—

> 'All That plot of land containing ·592 acres or thereabouts situate at Monk Bretton
> in the parish of Royston near Barnsley in the County of South Yorkshire and also all
> those buildings now erected thereon together with but subject to the matters
> referred to in the Charges Register under Title Number SYK 44697.'

e    Interestingly enough the land is used as a maggot farm. Indeed the purchase price of
£8,500 was to be accompanied by a covenant on the part of the plaintiff to supply the
defendant free of charge with 30 gallons of maggots every week for 20 years determinable
in circumstances which I need not mention. The retail price of maggots was £3·25 a
gallon in 1979, so the contract was worth about £100 a week to the vendor. The date
fixed for completion was 12 December 1979, the contract stating that the vendor was
f registered with absolute title under the title number already mentioned. The contract
incorporated the Law Society's General Conditions. General Condition 3(1) reads: 'Unless
the Special Conditions otherwise provide the property is sold with vacant possession on
completion.'
   Completion did not take place on the date fixed nor has completion taken place since
that date. The plaintiff's complaint is that on 12 December 1979 the defendant was, and
g still is, unable to give vacant possession because the land sold is and has been in the
occupation of third parties, namely Mr Brian Meek and Mr Denis Holt.
   On 29 November 1980 the plaintiff issued a writ claiming specific performance with
damages. However the plaintiff then found other premises for the maggot trade which
it had proposed to carry on at Monk Bretton, and so on 21 March 1984 it amended its
pleading to restrict its claim to damages and a return of its deposit.
h    The damages claimed are put under two heads: (a) cost of investigating title etc in the
sum of £472·05 and (b) loss of profits from December 1979 to 30 June 1982, the latter
date being the date when the plaintiff company was able to begin trading at the other
premises that I have mentioned. The loss of profits claim is made in the sum of £131,544
with interest.
   On 15 March 1984 Master Dyson, among other orders, ordered in para 7 that the
j plaintiff be at liberty to administer interrogatories and that there be tried as preliminary
issues the following questions:

> '(i) whether the Defendant is liable to the Plaintiff (ii) in the event that the
> Defendant is held to be so liable whether the quantum of damages recoverable by
> the Plaintiff is to be assessed in accordance with (a) the general law or (b) the rule in
> Bain v. Fothergill ((1874) LR 7 HL 158, [1874–80] All ER Rep 83).'

So I confine myself to those two questions. On 4 July 1984 the master made another order. He ordered that the third party be at liberty to appear at the trial of the preliminary issues and that the question of liability of the third party be tried at the trial but subsequent thereto. The third party put in a notice of appeal dated 6 July 1984 against that order.

This appeal by the third party was listed for hearing before me together with the hearing of the preliminary issues and third party proceedings. It has not, I think, been necessary to consider the appeal separately. In any event my judgment in the third party proceedings follows this disposal of the two preliminary issues in the action that I have already mentioned.

The pleadings of all parties have been extensively amended, including amendments made in the course of the trial.

During the trial counsel for the defendant conceded that the defendant was liable to the plaintiff for the sum of £472·05 already mentioned. That concession was made in the light of the fact that the defendant had contracted to sell with vacant possession and had failed to give such possession. In these circumstances counsel for the plaintiff went on to contend that the defendant's liability was not limited to that sum. Referring to preliminary issue (ii) in the action he submitted that the plaintiff's damages were to be assessed in accordance with the general law and not limited by the rule in *Bain v Fothergill*.

I proceed to set out the facts. In 1970 the defendant agreed to buy the maggot farm I have mentioned from a Mr Bywater. The purchase price was to be paid over a period of years. The defendant went into possession. Payment was made within about six years. On 8 December 1976 the defendant was registered as proprietor of the farm. It seems that the defendant did not find his own activities at the farm profitable. He allowed Mr Brian Meek and Mr Denis Holt to go into possession. There is a letter dated 22 April 1976 written by the defendant's solicitors to Mr Meek's solicitors. The defendant's solicitors were then known as Austin & Co; there was later a change of name to Barrington Black Austin & Co. The letter reads:

'We act for Mr Edge the proposed landlord in this case and understand your client is Mr Brian Meek of 23, Robin Terrace, Featherstone. We believe your client has agreed subject to contract to take a lease of our client's maggot farm at Monk Bretton, Barnsley for 10 years with 5 yearly review. We gather the payment to be made by your client for the first 5 years is to be by way of 30 gallons of maggots per month delivered to out client's premises at Kirkgate Anglers, 95, Kirkgate, Leeds. Please confirm that you have instructions whereupon we will send you a draft lease for approval.'

It is accepted that the words above 'per month' should be 'per week'.

In due course Messrs Shaw & Ashton on 30 April 1976 said they awaited a draft lease. However no draft lease was sent. On 23 September 1976 Austin & Co informed Shaw & Ashton that they had difficulty in expressing the proposed maggot rent in the terms of the lease. In the event no lease was ever executed, but Messrs Meek and Holt remained in occupation of the farm and maintained a supply of maggots to the defendant. They have done so, as I understand, up to the present time.

On 7 November 1977 the defendant, together with Messrs Meek and Holt and another gentleman who was then working with Meek and Holt at the farm, one Hughes, were summoned before the magistrate for nuisance at the farm. All four defendants were fined £5 each. In a latter dated 2 September 1977 Austin & Co wrote to the prosecuting local authority a letter in the course of which it was stated that Mr Edge was the freeholder of the farm and that the other defendants (to the summonses) were his tenants. It is material to mention this because an issue arises whether or not Messrs Meek and Holt are tenants or licensees at the farm.

One then arrives at the entry on the scene of the plaintiff company, then known as Flinthall Farms Ltd. On 1 June 1979 Messrs Ray & Vials, solicitors acting for the plaintiff company, wrote to Austin & Co. The letter has these words:

*a*
'We should be grateful if you would let us have a draft contract for our approval. Naturally, the sale would have to be with vacant possession. We particularly stress this as we understand that the property may be occupied at the present time by tenants. We look forward to hearing from you.'

This letter followed conversations between Mr Anthony John Mitchell, a director of the plaintiff company, and the defendant. Mr Mitchell said that the defendant was interested in selling, and that the defendant had said that the farm was occupied but that
*b* he (the defendant) had checked with his solicitor and there would be no trouble with getting vacant possession. Mr Mitchell said the farm was of no use to him without vacant possession and he stressed the importance of that point. The defendant's evidence was to the same effect. He said, as well, that, before consenting to negotiations with Mr Mitchell, he asked his solicitor Mr Hill (of Austin & Co) about the position of the occupants of the farm.

*c*
He said that Mr Hill had told him that he (Hill) could get the occupants off at any time. The defendant said he was anxious about vacant possession because he did not want to let down the people he was selling to.

Following the letter dated 1 June 1979 there was correspondence between the solicitors culminating in the contract dated 14 November 1979 above mentioned. In the course of the correspondence inquiries before contract were sent. I set out two of them with Mr
*d* Hill's answers:

*e*
'13. *Completion* How long after exchange of contracts will the vendor be able to give vacant possession for the whole of the property *Answer* Hopefully 4 weeks *Additional enquiry 7* We believe that the premises are at present occupied. Vacant possession must be given at completion. Can you please say what steps the vendor will take to obtain vacant possession and whether the present occupants come within the protection of Part II of the Landlord and Tenant Act 1954 *Answer* The vendor is already arranging for the property to be vacated and we are informed that the tenants cannot rely on the protection of the Act.'

The defendant said that he did not supply those answers. They were sent by Mr Hill. The answer to (7) was untrue in the sense that the defendant was not then arranging for
*f* a vacating of the property. He said he first saw the inquiries and answers in 1981 after he had changed his solicitors and after the writ in the action had been issued.

When Mr Hill informed the defendant that contracts had been exchanged he asked the defendant in a letter dated 14 November 1979 to let him know 'the position regarding the tenants at the property'. This surprised the defendant. He had supposed that Mr Hill was getting the occupants out. The defendant spoke to Mr Holt. Mr Holt told him that
*g* he and Meek were not leaving the farm. So the defendant again spoke to Mr Hill. Mr Hill told the defendant to leave the matter to him. This the defendant did and so he (the defendant) took no steps himself towards securing the removal of the occupants. The telephone messages of 19 November and 11 December 1979 accord with this evidence. The completion date of 12 December 1979 came and went without completion and with Messrs Meek and Holt still in possession. Mr Hill's assurances that the occupants could
*h* be removed were not made good and indeed on 28 December 1979 we see Mr Hill writing to the defendant to say that papers had been sent to counsel.

At this time the plaintiff was content to wait, albeit with some impatience, and inquiring on 21 January 1980 whether or not possession proceedings had been commenced. It was not until 6 February 1980 that Mr Hill at last wrote to Mr Holt. He said:

*j*
'We understand that you and a Mr. Meek occupy the property as licensees of our client and have done so on an informal basis for some time. We believe you are aware that our client now requires possession of the property and have already written to you in this respect without having any reply from you. Will you please indicate as quickly as possible the earliest date on which you will be able to give vacant possession.'

I did not see the letter therein said to have been written 'already'. The solicitors acting
for Messrs Meek and Holt replied on 15 February 1980. Messrs Shaw & Ashton wrote:

> 'Your letter of the 6th February addressed to Mr. D. Holt of 54 Weeland Road,
> Knottingley, has been handed to us for our attention and we are instructed to
> represent Mr. Holt and his partner Mr. Meek. The third paragraph of your letter
> refers to previous correspondence but Mr. Holt has informed us that this is the first
> letter he has received from anyone in respect of this matter. Our clients do not
> accept that they occupy the premises as Licensees whether on an informal or formal
> basis. There were negotiations between our respective clients before April 1976 at
> which time it was agreed that our clients should have a 10 year lease of the premises
> at a rental for the first five years of 30 gallons of maggots per week which were to be
> delivered to [the defendant's] premises at Kirkgate, Wakefield or were to be collected
> by [the defendant]. In the event a formal written lease was never entered into by
> the parties but in reliance upon the agreement our clients entered into the occupation
> in April 1976 and have continued in exclusive occupation of the premises since that
> date. Our clients have also maintained payment of the agreed rental and continue
> to do so. In addition our clients have carried out repairs and renovations to the
> premises at a cost of approximately £1,000. When Notices were served by the
> Health Department of the local authority, our clients carried out the work that was
> demanded. In the light of these acts of part performance we have advised our clients
> that they have enjoyed the benefit of a business tenancy within the terms of the
> Landlord and Tenant Act 1954 and look forward to hearing from you with your
> agreement in due course.'

This unpalatable letter was followed by a disappointing opinion of counsel dated 28
February 1980. An extract from the opinion reads:

> 'I have settled a pleading but I hold out no hopes whatsoever for their success and
> if the stakes were not as high as they are my advice to my client would ordinarily
> have been that these pleadings could amount to no more than an attempt to remove
> Meek by bluff and that he really ought to think twice about spending any money
> on them at all.'

In the event no possession proceedings were launched, but attempts were made to
negotiate a removal of the occupants. There is a letter dated 29 February 1980 written by
Mr Hill to Messrs Shaw & Ashton. The defendant was said to be willing to consider
reimbursing the occupants with a sum of £1,000 said to have been spent by them on
repairs and there was talk of a payment as well of twice the rateable value of the farm, a
sum between £200 and £300 a year. The letter then itemised five complaints against the
occupants for the purpose of suggesting that even if a tenancy existed there were grounds
for having the tenants removed. Messrs Shaw & Ashton replied on 4 March 1980. They
said:

> 'Thank you for your letter of the 29th February. We have taken our client's
> instructions in the matter and they do not accept as genuine any of the matters
> specified as breaches of the terms of the tenancy. They are, however, prepared to
> consider vacating the premises if compensated in the sum of £12,000. This is a
> figure which is not negotiable. We are instructed to accept service of any proceedings
> your client may care to issue.'

It is fair to say that as respects the complaints of tenancy breaches by Messrs Meek and
Holt the defendant said in chief that he did not complain about the state of the farm to
Mr Hill or to Mr Meek or to anyone. He said he hardly ever went to the farm. As to the
letter dated 4 March 1980 the defendant never saw it until 1984. In 1980 the defendant
knew nothing of the £12,000. In fact the defendant was away on a holiday in March
1980. There was evidence from the defendant's father. Mr Edge senior is a partner with
his son. He said he heard at the time from Mr Hill of the £12,000 suggestion. He told
Hill that his son had not got £12,000.

About the end of May 1980 Mr Hill left the firm of Barrington Black Austin & Co. Mr
*a*  I C Percy of that firm took over the Edge sale.

The defendant went through 'the whole story', as he put it, with Mr Percy. The
defendant told Mr Percy that he had told Mr Hill that there were people in the farm and
that Mr Hill had said that he (Hill) could get them off. Mr Percy suggested that the
defendant should think about separate advice. In the event the defendant consulted his
present solicitors, Messrs Saffman & Co.

*b*   Mr Percy of course sought Mr Hill's views on the matter. Mr Hill wrote to Mr Percy a
long letter dated 11 June 1980. I think I should set it out although it is perhaps more
relevant to the third party claim:

*c*
'Thank you for your letter of 5th June 1980. I have of course acted for Mr. Philip
Edge and his father for a number of years and appreciate the present problem. As
far as I am concerned, this property has been occupied over the years since the
purchase thereof by a variety of people. Mr. Edge worked it himself for a fair period,
the details of which I do not know, but I am aware that for a number of years the
premises have been occupied by a succession of employees, partners or licensees.
Mr. Edge has never as far as I can say created any tenancy, but has always received
rather than any rent or money payment a supply of maggots for resale at Kirkgate
*d*       Anglers. I was aware that deliveries in this respect for a long time had been irregular
and spasmodic, and that the arrangement was not very satisfactory but it was one
with which Mr. Edge persisted.

I recall that there was a time when the current occupants whose identity I do not
know but who were represented by Messrs. Shaw & Ashton of Pontefract wished to
enter into a formal lease of the premises, which Mr. Edge was prepared to agree.
*e*       You will note the correspondence on the file in this respect and no conclusion was
reached—this being from their side not mine. I also recall that at the time Mr. Edge
was by no means happy as to the reliability of the people he was dealing with
because of their conduct on the premises, but he allowed the irregular situation to
continue.

I also recall that on the file there are details of enforcement notices served by the
*f*       local authority upon Mr. Edge and the occupants. These presumably resulted from
complaints about smell etc from local occupants of adjacent houses. This was a
matter which gave Mr. Edge grave cause for concern as the proprietor of the
premises, and I recall that the problem was settled by the premises being put in
order by him and the occupants.

When the matter of the proposed sale to Flint Hall Farms Ltd. arose, I clearly
*g*       discussed with Mr. Edge very carefully before a contract was even despatched the
problem of vacant possession of the premises being given. Mr. Edge told me at the
outset that the present occupants whose identity I did not know, would move
without difficulty and at short notice on his say so, and I proceeded accordingly,
relying upon what he told me.

We did discuss the position of the occupants of the premises and I did indicate
*h*       that there might be problems, but that providing they were prepared to vacate as I
had been informed, the sale could proceed. The occupants had no formal lease or
agreement to occupy the premises, but had been there for some time and I said that
this might well cause difficulty. Mr. Edge was quite certain that they would leave
at his request and he repeated to me initially a history of the unsatisfactory nature
of the occupancy of the premises for many years and I told him that in the last
*j*       resort, subject to proof of the matters he mentioned, vacant possession should be
available after Court proceedings.

I exchanged contracts on Mr. Edge's instructions to do so when it was in my view
well known to him that there was a risk over the matter of vacant possession of the
premises. This was a risk which he was prepared at the time to take, indeed to
assume and something which was not considered a major difficulty. There was of
course difficulty and I was then required formally to require the occupants to leave.

Their reaction from the file is quite apparent, although I recall that one out of three did go after I wrote. Having reported the position, only after some delay did Mr. Edge Snr. arrange to see me, and after discussion at which my version of the position with regard to vacant possession was repeated and accepted, I did telephone Messrs. Shaw & Ashton in Mr. Edge's presence. They initially reacted in apparent full awareness of their client's position and with instructions to the effect that their clients would vacate the premises on payment of twice the [net annual value] for rating of the premises. This was clearly not what was said later, but Mr. Edge Snr. will no doubt confirm what I told him at the time, and indeed he expressed to me a willingness to pay more than twice the [net annual value] for rating and a sum he described as "reasonable compensation" to secure possession, leaving it to me to try to negotiate accordingly. I asked him at the time and subsequently for full details of breaches complained of against the occupants with a view to pursuing proceedings in case no settlement could be reached (as we envisaged might well be the case) and though such information was promised in detail it was not forthcoming.

I do appreciate the problem in the matter, but repeat that exchange of contracts was effected quite simply on the basis that the occupants of the premises would leave forthwith on being requested to do so by Mr. Edge. These were his instructions, and when the problem of vacant possession became apparent my advice was that Court proceedings would have to be taken. I did take Counsel's opinion on fairly scant information in my possession, but from what I recall of what was said in the opinion, upon proof of complaints made being provided in detail (which was requested and as far as I know not provided) possession proceedings stand more than a fair chance of success.

I cannot add much more at this stage, but will clearly amplify any aspect of the matter so far as I can if required.'

The defendant in his evidence criticised the letter in the strongest terms. He said the remarks on occupancy in the first paragraph were a complete fabrication in that Mr Hill knew that Messrs Holt and Meek were running the farm. As well it was not right to say, as in the second paragraph, that he (the defendant) was 'by no means happy'. The defendant described as a complete lie the statement in the fourth paragraph that 'Mr. Edge told me at the outset . . .' As well there was untruth in the fifth paragraph where it reads 'Mr. Edge was quite certain . . .' The same evidence was given as respects the whole of the sixth paragraph. In this connection Mr Edge senior, while confirming that he saw Mr Hill, denied that he 'accepted' as suggested in the sixth paragraph. The consistent and convincing evidence throughout of the defendant was that if there had been any indication that Mr Hill could not get the occupants out he would never have gone on with the contract. On the contrary he was assured by Mr Hill that he (Hill) would get the occupants off. Whatever Mr Hill told him to do he did.

I do not think I need recount the facts further save to say that the writ was issued on 29 November 1980 and the third party notice on 16 January 1981.

I turn now to the plaintiff's claim for damages for breach of contract. The farm was sold with vacant possession on completion: see General Condition 3(1). The defendant was not able to give such possession to the plaintiff on the date fixed for completion or thereafter. The defendant is therefore liable in damages for breach of contract: see *Royal Bristol Permanent Building Society v Bomash* (1887) 35 Ch D 390 at 394, [1886–90] All ER Rep 283 at 285 and *Cumberland Consolidated Holdings Ltd v Ireland* [1946] 1 All ER 284 at 287, [1946] KB 264 at 270. The defendant's counsel accepted that the defendant was so liable but contended that in light of the rule in *Bain v Fothergill* (1874) LR 7 HL 158, [1874–80] All ER Rep 83 this liability in damages was limited to the plaintiff's expenses incurred in investigating title (and an obligation to return the deposit). The expenses incurred were agreed in the sum of £472·05. Accordingly one answers preliminary issue (i) in the affirmative and I proceed to (ii), that is whether the quantum of damages recoverable by the plaintiff is to be assessed in accordance with (a) the general law or (b) the rule in *Bain v Fothergill*.

The rule in *Bain v Fothergill* derives from *Flureau v Thornhill* (1776) Wm Bl 1078,
a    [1775–1802] All ER Rep 91 at 91–92, where De Grey CJ said:

> 'Upon a contract for a purchase, if the title proves bad, and the vendor is (without
> fraud) incapable of making a good one, I do not think that the purchaser can be
> entitled to any damages for the fancied goodness of the bargain, which he supposes
> he has lost.'

b    In *Bain v Fothergill* LR 7 HL 158 at 207, [1874–80] All ER Rep 83 at 87 Lord Chelmsford
put the matter in this way:

> 'If a person enters into a contract for the sale of a real estate knowing that he has
> no title to it, nor any means of acquiring it, the purchaser cannot recover damages
> beyond the expenses he has incurred by an action for the breach of the contract; he
> can only obtain other damages by an action for deceit.'

c
*Bain v Fothergill* shows that the rule as originally laid down in 1776 applies even when
the vendor (if not fraudulent) knows when he signs the contract that his title is defective.
On the other hand Lord Hatherley in *Bain v Fothergill* LR 7 HL 158 at 209; cf [1874–80]
All ER Rep 83 at 88 said:

> 'Whenever it is a matter of conveyancing, and not a matter of title, it is the duty
d    of the vendor to do everything that he is enabled to do by force of his own interest,
> and also by force of the interest of others whom he can compel to concur in the
> conveyance.'

See also *Day v Singleton* [1899] 2 Ch 320 at 329. Megarry J in *Wroth v Tyler* [1973] 1 All
ER 897 at 916, [1974] Ch 30 at 53 regarded the rule as conveniently stated in *Williams on*
e    *the Contract of Sale of Land* (1930) p 128 in this way:

> 'Where the breach of contract is occasioned by the vendor's inability, without his
> own fault, to show a good title, the purchaser is entitled to recover as damages his
> deposit, if any, with interest, and his expenses incurred in connection with the
> agreement, but not more than nominal damages for the loss of his bargain.'

f    In light of these authorities it is, I think, convenient first to consider whether the
defendant's failure to convey in this case was due to an inability to show a good title. If
the occupants of the farm were trespassers or licensees it was within the defendant's
power to have them removed so as to be able to give vacant possession; so that there was
no inability to show a good title. But if the occupants were tenants, for a term of years or
yearly, then it was not within the defendant's power to have them removed by 12
g    December 1979; so that there was an inability to show a good title. In this connection
see *Williams on Vendor and Purchaser* (4th edn, 1936) vol 1, p 201, which states:

> 'So also, where land is expressly or impliedly sold with vacant possession, a good
> title is not shown if it is subject to any tenancy for years or less, which will not
> expire before the day fixed or the proper time for completion.'

h
The defence Mark IV, as it emerged during the trial, eventually alleged a tenancy in
favour of Messrs Meek and Holt for ten years, alternatively a tenancy from year to year. I
am unable to conclude that there was any ten-year term, if only because the date of the
commencement of the term is not specified. On the other hand I think that the only
reasonable conclusion to make as to the Meek/Holt occupancy is that they are at least
business tenants holding on a periodic or yearly tenancy. There was no evidence from
j    the occupants themselves, but it seems clear that they have been in exclusive occupation
of the farm since 1976, during that time carrying on the business of a maggot farm.
They have paid a periodic rent, not, it is true, in money, but in the way of making a
regular 30-gallon a week supply of maggots to the defendant. The defendant in his
evidence said that in 1976 he told Mr Hill that there was to be a lease of the farm. His
evidence was that from 1976 onward Messrs Meek and Holt used the farm and that he

(the defendant) did not use it. By and large he received his regular maggot supply. The
correspondence before me shows the occupants referred to as tenants.                    *a*

Since I hold that the occupants of the farm were in occupation under a tenancy it
follows that the defendant had an 'inability . . . to show a good title' and thus makes part
of the way towards establishing his claim to a *Bain v Fothergill* limitation of damages (cf
*Wroth v Tyler*, where, as I understand, there was held to be no defect of title).

I move on to consider whether or not the defendant can make the rest of the way. He
has to show that it was without his fault that he could not show a good title. It is plain    *b*
that it was not within his power to compel the tenants to vacate, at any rate by any
relevant date. The matter therefore stands outside those cases where the vendor can as a
matter of conveyancing (as opposed to title) assure a good title, albeit at some expense or
difficulty to himself. I refer to such cases as *Engell v Fitch* (1869) LR 4 QB 659 and *Re
Daniel, Daniel v Vassall* [1917] 2 Ch 405, [1916–17] All ER Rep 654.

However, such words as those of Lord Hatherley that I have quoted from *Bain v*    *c*
*Fothergill* LR 7 HL 158 at 209 have led to the rule that when it is within the power of the
vendor to make a good title (albeit without title at the time of contract) then it is his duty
to take reasonable steps towards the obtaining of a good title. One may start with *Day v
Singleton* [1899] 2 Ch 320. There Lindley MR says (at 329):

> 'Neither Lord Chelmsford's speech nor Lord Hatherley's is an authority for the
> application of that exceptional rule [ie *Bain v Fothergill*] to the case of a vendor who    *d*
> can make good title but will not, or will not do what he can do and ought to do in
> order to obtain one.'

This sentiment is clearly explained in *Malhotra v Choudhury* [1979] 1 All ER 186,
[1980] Ch 52. That was a case where a husband contracted to sell a house belonging to
himself and his wife; his wife refused to join in the sale so that the defendant's title was    *e*
defective. Stephenson LJ said that it was the duty of the husband 'to use his best
endeavours to carry out his contractual obligations, in this case by obtaining his wife's
consent' (see [1979] 1 All ER 186 at 199, [1980] Ch 52 at 71). He said this ([1979] 1 All
ER 186 at 204, [1980] Ch 52 at 76):

> 'There is, on the authorities, a plain duty, in my judgment, to try for consent in a
> case like this, whether it is a matter of conveyancing or a defect of title which you    *f*
> seek to remove.'

Cumming-Bruce LJ said ([1979] 1 All ER 186 at 204, [1980] Ch 52 at 77):

> 'For the reasons stated by Stephenson LJ, it is quite clear that on the ratio of *Day v
> Singleton* the vendor who seeks to avail himself of the protection afforded to what is
> described as the rule in *Bain v Fothergill* must go to the length of satisfying the court    *g*
> that he has done all that he reasonably can to mitigate the effects of his breach of
> contract by trying to remove such fault on the title as appears.'

In these circumstances it seems to me that the question for consideration is whether
there were taken by the defendant or on his behalf those steps towards the removal of
the occupants of the farm which the law requires of him. More precisely, did the    *h*
defendant by himself or his solicitor do what he reasonably could do to try to acquire
vacant possession of the farm?

The cases afford some guidance for the answering of this question. Subject to that
guidance the question is a question of fact to be decided on the evidence. *Bain v Fothergill*
was excluded in *Day v Singleton* because the vendor was inactive in the matter of seeking
a consent to assign (see [1899] 2 Ch 320 at 328). *Bain v Fothergill* was excluded in *Malhotra
v Choudhury* because there was inactivity in seeking the wife's concurrence (see [1979] 1    *j*
All ER 186 at 204, [1980] Ch 52 at 77); cf *Keen v Mear* [1920] 2 Ch 574 at 581, [1920] All
ER Rep 147 at 152). Here the position is that there was some activity by the defendant
or on his behalf. There is then the consideration that here the defendant did not go to
the length of taking proceedings to put out the occupiers of the farm. In *Williams v
Glenton* (1866) LR 1 Ch App 200 at 208–209 Turner LJ said:

*a*
'I am not aware of any case in which the Court has gone the length of saying that a vendor shall be compelled to enter into litigation with an adverse claimant in order to perfect his title, and so enable himself to complete a contract which he has entered into for sale of the property. The vendor, however, is bound to complete the contract, and if he does not take the steps which are necessary to enable him to do so, he is liable for damages upon the contract; and heavy damages would be given if, having the means of completing the sale, he should decline to take the
*b*
proceedings necessary for that purpose.'

The defendant did not decline to take proceedings while 'having the means of completing the sale'. The defendant has never had such means. In that any litigation by the defendant would have been to perfect his title, the words quoted show, as I understand, that the defendant was not obliged to enter into any litigation. See also
*c*
*Lehmann v McArthur* (1868) LR 3 Ch App 496. Megarry J discusses this topic in a wider context in *Wroth v Tyler* [1973] 1 All ER 897 at 910–913, [1974] Ch 30 at 47–51. I think I may found myself on this quotation from *Williams on Vendor and Purchaser* (4th edn, 1936) vol 2, 1020:

*d*
'. . . although a vendor who has contracted to give vacant possession is bound at his peril to eject a tenant by sufferance, a tenant at will or a trespasser who refuses to give up possession, he is not obliged to engage in litigation with persons asserting in good faith and with apparent or reasonably possible right, claims adverse to his title.'

There is no doubt that at all material times Messrs Meek and Holt were asserting in good faith that they were tenants of the farm. It follows that the defendant does not lose the protection of *Bain v Fothergill* by having failed to take proceedings against Messrs
*e*
Meek and Holt.

There remains the question of what the defendant could and should reasonably have done, short of litigation, with a view to enabling him to give vacant possession to the plaintiff. I will summarise what the defendant, or his solicitor Mr Hill, did do. I will be repeating some of the facts already set out because in considering this particular question it is convenient to extract the following chronological facts.
*f*
(i) Early in 1979 the defendant told Mr Mitchell (of the plaintiff company) that he would not talk about a sale of the farm. He said there were people on the farm and he did not know if he could get them off.

(ii) Next day he rang up Mr Hill. He told him of a possible sale and said he did not wish to negotiate until he knew the position concerning the people on the farm. Mr Hill, having been told that nothing had been signed, said that he (Hill) could get them off at
*g*
any time.

(iii) The defendant rang up Mr Mitchell. He told him what Mr Hill had said and so bargaining ensued between the defendant and Mr Mitchell.

(iv) On 1 June 1979 correspondence began between Mr Hill and Messrs Ray & Vials the plaintiff's solicitors. Messrs Ray & Vials's letter is set out above. In the course of the correspondence the answers to preliminary inquiries that I have mentioned were given.
*h*
Otherwise the pre-contract correspondence does not allude to vacant possession nor did Mr Hill raise the matter in correspondence with his client, the defendant. On the other hand the defendant in his evidence said that he was again assured by Mr Hill that there was no problem about vacant possession.

(v) Contracts were exchanged and dated 14 November 1979. On the same day Mr Hill wrote to the defendant and his letter has, as I have said, this sentence: 'Please let us
*j*
know the position regarding the tenants at the property . . .' The defendant said that he did not understand the letter. He supposed that Mr Hill was getting vacant possession and here now was Mr Hill asking him (the defendant) about vacant possession. So the defendant rang Mr Holt. He asked when he was going out. Mr Holt said: 'We are not going.' I do not regard the defendant's evidence in this regard as inconsistent with his answers to interrogatory 2(i). The defendant informed Mr Hill of this conversation. Mr Hill said: 'Leave it to me.' On that footing the defendant took no action.

(vi) There was then, I think, some conversation between Mr Mitchell and the defendant. In any event on 19 November 1979 a record taken at Mr Hill's office shows that the defendant sought to speak to Mr Hill on that day. He left a message. It was: 'Can you write to people on maggot farm as Mr. Edge has had a word with them and they say they won't move out.'

(vii) On 10 December 1979 Messrs Ray & Vials inquired what steps were being taken to remove the occupants of the farm.

(viii) On 11 December 1979 the defendant again tried to speak to Mr Hill. There is then a letter dated 28 December 1979 from Mr Hill to the defendant in which he said this:

'We confirm we have now sent the papers to Counsel for urgent proceedings to be settled, and will let you know as soon as we have them back. We enclose a copy of a letter sent to the purchaser's solicitors today for your information. We have spoken to them by telephone and they have agreed to await the outcome of the proceedings.'

In fact Mr Hill had not sent papers to counsel. However he did so on 2 January 1980.

(ix) Before counsel's opinion arrived Mr Hill wrote to Mr Holt. I have already set out the terms of the letter and of the reply dated 15 February 1980 received from Messrs Shaw & Ashton.

(x) Counsel's opinion is dated 28 February 1980 and was to the discouraging effect that I have already mentioned.

(xi) The final steps respecting the attempts to obtain vacant possession appear in the letters dated 29 February 1980 and 4 March 1980 that I have already referred to.

One concludes from a consideration of these events that there was no bad faith on the part of the defendant, or, indeed, on the part of Mr Hill, although Mr Hill's conduct vis-à-vis his client was unsatisfactory. One also concludes that the defendant was advised that proceedings would be unsuccessful and that on 6 February 1980, albeit at no prompt stage, it was indicated to the farm occupiers that vacant possession was required. Then on 4 March 1980 it was learned that the price of possession was a non-negotiable figure of £12,000.

Although the defendant said that he did not see the letter with the £12,000 offer until 1984 it is, I think, to be presumed in the plaintiff's favour that the offer was made to the defendant, since it is plain that the offer went to his solicitor. On that footing, was the offer something which the defendant could and ought reasonably to have accepted? In so far as it is relevant it was explained to me that the defendant had not the means to pay £12,000, and even if the £8,500 purchase price is taken into account, so that only £3,500 remained to be paid, he would have had difficulty in raising such a sum since he had only a half share with his wife in the house in which he lives. On the other hand, £12,000 might not be an unreasonable sum to pay to preserve for the defendant £8,500 and a maggot supply worth about £100 a week for 20 years. Counsel for the plaintiff pointed out that the letter dated 6 February 1980 was no proper notice to determine the occupants' licence, if licence it was. It may be said that the letter was defective as a notice to determine. Nevertheless it was a plain indication of a wish to bring occupation to an end. In this connection see *Minister of Health v Bellotti, Minister of Health v Holliday* [1944] 1 All ER 238, [1944] 1 KB 298. Counsel also drew attention to the fact that the defendant continued to accept a maggot supply from the occupants at all material times.

I do not think that fact material since the maggots were being produced and had to be used, and, more importantly, Messrs Meek and Holt were in no way misled by the defendant's acceptance of maggots into thinking that the defendant was content that they should stay on the farm. I am satisfied that at all times after the defendant spoke to Mr Holt soon after 14 November 1979 both Meek and Holt knew that at all times the defendant was anxious to see their departure. Counsel for the plaintiff further submitted that the defendant's activities in seeking to bring about vacant possession ought to have been initiated, if not completed, prior to the date fixed for completion, ie 12 December 1979.

The defendant was active before that date. He spoke to Mr Holt soon after 14
a November 1979. In any event it seems to me that time was not of the essence of
completion and there having been no notice to complete served by the purchaser the
defendant was entitled to complete on the completion date or within a reasonable time
thereafter.

I have found the question I have posed, ie did the defendant by himself or his solicitor
do what he reasonably could do to try to acquire vacant possession, very difficult. Giving
b my best consideration to the circumstances that I have set out above, I have come to the
conclusion that the answer is in the affirmative. In taking this view I have taken account
of the suggestion that the £12,000 offer ought to have been pursued, at any rate in the
sense that there should have been negotiations to reduce that figure.

However, in view of the intimation that the figure was not negotiable, I do not think
that the defendant was obliged to take that course. It follows that in my view the damages
c for breach of contract for which the defendant is accountable are limited by the rule in
*Bain v Fothergill*.

I must now consider *Watts v Spence* [1975] 2 All ER 528, [1976] Ch 165. Counsel for
the plaintiff submitted that (i) the defendant had by his solicitor made to the plaintiff a
misrepresentation which induced the plaintiff to enter into the contract of sale and (ii)
that being so, the *Bain v Fothergill* limitation on damages does not apply. It was admitted
d by counsel for the defendant that there was indeed a misrepresentation by the defendant
(in answer to additional inquiry no 7). The misrepresentation was innocent in the sense
that the misrepresentation was not made fraudulently either by the defendant or by Mr
Hill. In these circumstances, after a reading of *Watts v Spence*, the submissions of counsel
for the plaintiff seem very well founded. In that case the defendant was a joint owner
with his wife of the family house. He agreed to sell the house to the plaintiff. The wife
e refused to concur in the sale. Graham J found that the defendant had made a false
representation to the plaintiff that he was the owner of the house (see [1975] 2 All ER
528 at 534, [1976] Ch 165 at 175). The misrepresentation was not pleaded as a fraudulent
misrepresentation. The judge held that damages were recoverable without any *Bain v
Fothergill* limitation. The judgment reads as follows ([1975] 2 All ER 528 at 536, [1976]
Ch 165 at 177–178):

f
'If the [Misrepresentation Act 1967] had been in force at the time of *Bain v
Fothergill*, it seems at least probable that the vendor's immunity against damages for
loss of bargain ought to have been confined to cases where there was no
misrepresentation innocent or fraudulent which induced the contract: for example,
where the defect in title was something which was unknown at the time of entering
into the contract and which was only found out on investigation. In that event Lord
g Chelmsford's words (LR 7 HL 158 at 207, [1874–80] All ER Rep 83 at 87): "If a
person enters into a contract for the sale of real estate knowing that he has no title to
it, nor any means of acquiring it", and, so on, down to the words "other damages by
an action for deceit", might well have read: "In those cases where a person enters
into a contract for the sale of real estate knowing that he has no title to it and has
h made no representation, innocent or fraudulent, that he will be able to acquire it by
the time for completion, thereby inducing the purchaser to enter into the contract,
the purchaser cannot recover damages beyond the expenses he has incurred by an
action for the breach of the contract; he can only obtain other damages by an action
based on innocent misrepresentation or deceit where such exists." The law should I
think be so stated now the 1967 Act is in force, and I so hold. The truth of the
j matter is that *Bain v Fothergill* limits the damages for breach of contract; it does not
limit damages for fraudulent misrepresentation. The 1967 Act for the first time
enables a plaintiff to sue for innocent misrepresentation, a cause of action now made
akin to an action for damages for fraud. The 1967 Act has thus created a new cause
of action, one with which *Bain v Fothergill* never had anything to do. The practical
effect is, however, that some purchasers who would have been caught by *Bain v
Fothergill* if the 1967 Act had not been passed can now, by suing on the new statutory

right, get damages for loss of bargain which they could not have recovered before. It follows that in my judgment the present case falls outside the restrictive rule of *a* *Bain v Fothergill* as that rule should now be limited in the light of the 1967 Act. If the representation here had been treated as fraudulent, the plaintiff would, on the authority of *Bain v Fothergill* itself, have been entitled to recover for loss of his bargain, and in my judgment he is equally outside the case and equally entitled to recover for the loss of his bargain on the ground that there was a representation which was in fact false and which the defendant, Mr Spence, had no ground for *b* believing to be true and which he did not in fact believe to be true.'

Three observations occur to me as to the basis from which the judge proceeded to that conclusion in his judgment. (1) The judge appeared to be satisfied that the defendant had acted fraudulently, albeit that fraud was not pleaded and that the judge said it was not necessary to deal with the case on the basis of fraud (see [1975] 2 All ER 528 at 535, [1976] Ch 165 at 176). In this case it is quite plain that the defendant, who was the most *c* honest of witnesses, was in no sense at all fraudulent. His solicitor was careless but I do not think that the solicitor was in any sense fraudulent. (2) *Day v Singleton* [1899] 2 Ch 320 was not cited in *Watts v Spence*. That fact perhaps led the judge to say ([1975] 2 All ER 528 at 533, [1976] Ch 165 at 174):

> 'It follows, I think, that the words "without default" in *Bain v Fothergill* must be *d* taken to mean "without fraud" and that, on the authority of that case, the purchaser must be able to go as far as proving fraud before he can recover for the loss of his bargain.'

That is not so. As I understand, loss of bargain damages can be recovered without showing fraud if the defendant does not show that he has done what he reasonably ought to have done to perfect his title: see, e g, *Day v Singleton, Braybrooks v Whaley* [1919] 1 KB *e* 435 and (since *Watts v Spence*) *Malhotra v Choudhury* [1979] 1 All ER 186, [1980] Ch 52. (3) I refer to the first sentence in the long extract from Graham J's judgment quoted above. The sentiment there expressed is, to my mind, difficult to square with the fact that *Bain v Fothergill* decided that, fraud apart, damages were to be limited even if the vendor knew of defects in his title.

In light of those three observations, and particularly having regard to the lack of *f* authority cited to Graham J, it is, I think, permissible to approach the judge's final conclusion with some circumspection. His final conclusion was ([1975] 2 All ER 528 at 536, [1976] Ch 165 at 178):

> 'The practical effect is, however, that some purchasers who would have been caught by *Bain v Fothergill* if the 1967 Act had not been passed can now, by suing on *g* the new statutory right, get damages for loss of bargain which they could not have recovered before.'

I do not assent to that conclusion. An action on the new statutory right is an action in which damages will be measured as in tort, not contract; and in tort, as I understand, loss of bargain damages may not, in every case, be recoverable.

I respectfully agree with the criticisms of the judgment in *Watts v Spence* made by the *h* author of *McGregor on Damages* (14th edn, 1980) paras 1486–1489. One sees that in *Bain v Fothergill* LR 7 HL 158 at 207, [1874–80] All ER Rep 83 at 87 Lord Chelmsford said:

> 'If a person enters into a contract for the sale of a real estate knowing that he has no title to it, nor any means of acquiring it, the purchaser cannot recover damages beyond the expenses he has incurred by an action for the breach of the contract; he *j* can only obtain other damages by an action for deceit.'

So where there was deceit Lord Chelmsford contemplated an action for 'other' damages for deceit. Since the Misrepresentation Act 1967 there may be an action for 'other' damages for innocent misrepresentation. This new cause of action has nothing to do with the rule in *Bain v Fothergill*. Indeed Graham J expressly says so (see [1975] 2 All ER a 528 at 536, [1976] Ch 165 at 178). The new cause of action gives rise to damages in tort (measured as in tort, not contract). But it does not operate to remove any *Bain v Fothergill* limitation on damages in contract. It follows, in my opinion, that there is not such 'practical effect' as Graham J mentions above. I appreciate that, under *Bain v Fothergill*, if the tort of deceit is proved then there is a removal of the *Bain v Fothergill* limitation on contractual damages. But *Bain v Fothergill* does not allow of any other tort having that effect. It follows that a new statutory tort cannot have that effect. In expressing the views b that I do, I do so with much reluctance because I am of course aware of my duty, if possible, to follow Graham J.

The true position appears to be that in this case the plaintiff is entitled to damages for breach of contract limited by the rule in *Bain v Fothergill* and, as well, to damages for innocent misrepresentation pursuant to the 1967 Act. I do not decide whether or not such damages for innocent misrepresentation embrace any element for loss of bargain c because in the course of the preliminary issues discussed before me that question was not pursued to an extent which justifies any present decision on my part. I should add that the statement of claim included a claim for damages for misrepresentation. There was no reference to the 1967 Act. But if and in so far as any reference ought to have been made I am satisfied that the defendant had every opportunity to deal with the misrepresentation claim as being based on that Act.

d The answer to the preliminary issues set out in the order dated 15 March 1984 therefore are: 7(i): yes; 7(ii): the quantum of damages is to be assessed in accordance with the rule in *Bain v Fothergill*; but the plaintiff is, as well as to those damages, also entitled to damages for innocent misrepresentation.

*Judgment in third party proceedings*

e I turn now to the defendant's claim against the third party. This judgment in the third party proceedings should be read with the findings in the action in mind, so that any reading of this third party judgment should follow a reading of the judgment in the action. The third party is the firm of solicitors in which Mr Hill was a partner up to June 1980. The defendant's claim appears in its final form in the third party notice that was served on 12 December 1984 in the course of the trial. In general the defendant of course f seeks to be indemnified against the plaintiff's claims and the costs of the action. For evidence against the third party the defendant relied on the evidence given in the action. The defendant was recalled to the witness box and cross-examined by counsel for the third party. In the course of the cross-examination the defendant maintained consistently and clearly that Mr Hill was at all material times aware of the presence of Messrs Holt and Meek at the farm, that he (the defendant) stressed that Mr Hill was told he (the g defendant) did not wish to negotiate with Mr Mitchell unless and until it was clear that Messrs Holt and Meek could be removed and that Mr Hill assured him (the defendant) that Messrs Holt and Meek could be removed.

The defendant made plain that he took no part and was not consulted about the answer sent to inquiry no 7. It was only after receiving the letter dated 14 November 1979 that the defendant, by his own inquiries, learned that Mr Hill had by then done nothing h about removing the farm occupiers and that the occupiers were determined not to go. There is no occasion for doubting the defendant's evidence in any way. He was plainly a witness of truth and as well there was no evidence at all given on behalf of the third party. Mr Hill was conspicuous by his absence.

The defendant's evidence was, as I have said, that Mr Hill's long letter dated 11 June 1980 was full of inaccuracies.

j The third party notice alleges that Mr Hill was negligent in several respects between March and December 1979. I do not think that I need particularise the negligence alleged. The negligence is spelt out at length in the third party notice. As an example I will quote para 18:

'You were negligent in the drafting of the said contract and/or when submitting the same to the Defendant for signature in that:—(a) at a time when you knew or ought to have known there was no prospect or no reasonable prospect of vacant possession being given by the Defendant to the Plaintiff on completion of the sale of the said farm you included or permitted the inclusion of terms in the contract of sale of the said farm which provided for:—(i) completion of the said sale to take place 28 days from exchange of contract, and (ii) vacant possession of the said farm to be given to the Plaintiff on completion of the said sale when you fully intended exchanging the Defendant's contract for the Plaintiff's contract of sale as soon as the Defendant had signed and returned to you his contract. (b) you failed to inform the Defendant of the aforesaid terms of the said contract of sale. (c) further, you failed to inform the Defendant of there being no prospect or no reasonable prospect of vacant possession being given to the Plaintiff on completion of the said sale. (d) alternatively, you failed to inform the Defendant of the risk of him not being able to give vacant possession of the said farm to the Plaintiff on completion of the said sale. (e) further, you failed to advise the Defendant as to his probable and/or possible liabilities to the Plaintiff in the event of vacant possession of the said farm not being given on completion of the said sale.'

The alleged negligence all stems from the fact that Mr Hill, knowing that the farm was occupied, ought plainly to have realised that some occupation rights might be raised and yet he answered inquiry no 7 as he did and allowed the defendant to sign the contract. There is a reamended defence to the third party notice dated 14 December 1984. In so far as the facts there asserted are at variance with the defendant's evidence I discount them altogether. Having listened to the evidence and read the correspondence and documents I am satisfied that negligence against Mr Hill is established.

Counsel for the third party sought to say that Mr Hill could not be held to be negligent if the farm occupants were licensees and not tenants. To that end counsel sought to show that Messrs Meek and Holt were at all times licensees. I do not think that the occupants' status on the farm affects the question whether or not Mr Hill was negligent. The complaint against him is that he allowed the defendant to bind himself to give vacant possession without in any way, on any reasonable grounds, satisfying himself that the defendant could give vacant possession; and one bears in mind that Mr Hill acted in this way in a situation where the purchaser had stressed that he wanted vacant possession and the defendant had stressed that he did not wish to negotiate a sale unless and until he (the defendant) was sure that he could give vacant possession.

In fact I have held, in the action, if and so far as it is necessary to take a view as to the status of the occupants, that they were yearly tenants. Paragraph 4 of the reamended defence to the third party notice contends that during various alternative periods of time after the defendant consulted his new solicitors on or about 13 June 1980 the defendant was under a duty to mitigate by seeking possession of the farm by proceedings or by negotiating a surrender. I have already decided that the defendant sufficiently discharged any such duties as he has in those respects. Paragraph 5 of the reamended defence has a contention that takes effect if—

'it should be determined that the defendant is not entitled to rely on the rule commonly known as the rule in *Bain v Fothergill* on the ground that he did not use his best endeavours to give or obtain vacant posession of the farm'.

Since I have found that the defendant did use his best endeavours, this contention does not arise.

Accordingly I find the third party is liable to indemnify the defendant in respect of the claims in the action and of his costs in the action.

*Order accordingly.*

Solicitors: *Ray & Vials*, Northampton (for the plaintiff); *Godlove Saffman Lyth & Goldman*, Leeds (for the defendant); *Willey Hargrave*, Leeds (for the third party).

Jacqueline Metcalfe   Barrister.

a
# Re St Michael and All Angels, Great Torrington

COURT OF ECCLESIASTICAL CAUSES RESERVED

SIR HUGH FORBES, SIR ANTHONY LLOYD, THE BISHOP OF ROCHESTER, THE BISHOP OF CHICHESTER
AND RT REV KENNETH WOOLLCOMBE

b   18 DECEMBER 1984, 18 FEBRUARY 1985

*Ecclesiastical law – Court of Ecclesiastical Causes Reserved – Appeal – Review of exercise of
discretion – Faculty proceedings – Approach of court in reviewing chancellor's exercise of
discretion.*

c   *Ecclesiastical law – Faculty – Confirmatory faculty – Discretion – Exercise of discretion –
Matters to be considered – Pastoral considerations – Views of those who approbate or reprobate
change – Introductions to church – Removal of memorial.*

*Ecclesiastical law – Faculty – Ornaments – Addition of ornaments – Ornaments lawful and
ordered – Ornaments lawful but not specifically ordered – Books – What things are ornaments –*
d   *Whether faculty required for ornaments lawful and ordered – Whether faculty required for
ornaments lawful but not specifically ordered – Revised Canons Ecclesiastical, Canon F 13, para 3.*

*Ecclesiastical law – Faculty – Archdeacon – Duty of archdeacon in faculty proceedings – Faculty
Jurisdiction Measure 1964, s 9.*

e   *Ecclesiastical law – Court of Ecclesiastical Causes Reserved – Appeal – Certificate whether
question of doctrine, ritual or ceremonial is involved – Application for certificate – Procedure –
Ecclesiastical Jurisdiction Measure 1963, s 10(3).*

*Ecclesiastical law – Appeal – Transfer of appeal – Transfer to and from Court of Ecclesiastical
Causes Reserved – Transfer to and from Arches Court of Canterbury and Chancery Court of*
f   *York – Need for machinery for facilitation of transfer.*

The attitude of the Court of Ecclesiastical Causes Reserved when asked to interfere with
the exercise of a discretion by a diocesan chancellor in faculty proceedings should
correspond with that adopted by the Court of Appeal and will differ according to the
circumstances of the case. It will normally be in favour of upholding the judgment
g   where the chancellor's decision is based on the credibility of witnesses he has seen; but,
where the credibility or reliability of witnesses is not in question or where the point in
dispute is the proper inference to be drawn from proved facts, it is generally in as a good
a position to evaluate the evidence as the chancellor (see p 996 *a* to *f*, post); dictum of
Lord Reid in *Benmax v Austin Motor Co Ltd* [1955] 1 All ER at 329 applied; dictum of the
Dean of the Arches in *Re St Edburga's, Abberton* [1961] 2 All ER at 430–431 approved.

h     In exercising the discretion to grant a confirmatory faculty, the proper approach is to
determine whether, on weighing the pastoral considerations involved, the balance is in
favour of or against the retention of the introductions. In applying that test proper
weight is to be given to the views of those who approbate or reprobate the change.
Where a proposal involves the removal of one article and its replacement by another,
both matters should be set out in any petition for a faculty, since, particularly in the case
j   of a confirmatory faculty, both the diocesan advisory committee and the chancellor may
be unaware that anything has been or is to be removed. Such a course is especially
important when the item to be removed is or is part of a memorial, since the chancellor
is unlikely to grant a faculty for that purpose without considering what might be the
reaction of the family of the deceased (see p 998 *a* to *f*, post).

    Canon F13, para 3 of the Revised Canons Ecclesiastical, which requires a faculty for
the addition of any ornament (which includes vestments, books, cloths, chalices and

patens) into a church, is subject to two qualifications: (i) a faculty is not generally required
for the introduction of an ornament ordered by the canons of the Church, eg a Bible of *a*
large size for the use of the minister; and (ii) although a faculty may strictly be required
for the addition of anything which is not ordered though lawful, minor matters may
often be introduced without a faculty, since the ecclesiastical courts are not eager to
assume jurisdiction. The range of books which fall into the category of those which are
lawful but not specifically ordered is very large, and includes the Alternative Service
Book 1980, translations of the Bible other than the Authorised Version and a large variety *b*
of hymn books. Chancellors are entitled to repose confidence in the incumbent and
churchwardens in relation to the introduction of some of those books, but in cases of
doubt inquiries should be made of the diocesan registry whether a faculty should be
sought (see p 998 *j* to p 999 *f*, post); dictum of T Pemberton Leigh in *Liddell v Westerton*
(1857) 29 LTOS at 55 adopted.

The purpose of s 9 of the Faculty Jurisdiction Measure 1964, by which the archdeacon *c*
of the archdeaconry in which the parish concerned is situated is deemed to have an
interest in faculty proceedings, is to enable the archdeacon to offer assistance to the
chancellor, particularly with respect to the consideration of the pastoral questions
involved. Archdeacons should accordingly be ready to intervene in faculty suits so that
they may be of service to the chancellor (see p 1000 *a b*, post); dictum of the Deputy
Dean of the Arches in *Re St Gregory's, Tredington* [1971] 3 All ER at 271 approved. *d*

Since s 10(3) of the Ecclesiastical Jurisdiction Measure 1963 does not require an
application for a certificate whether or not a question of doctrine, ritual or ceremonial is
involved in an appeal from a judgment, order or decree of a consistory court to be made
orally, the sensible course is for any intending applicant to make written application (see
p 995 *h j*, post).

Consideration should be given to providing machinery whereby appeals could be *e*
readily transferred, if appropriate, from the Court of Ecclesiastical Causes Reserved to the
Arches Court of Canterbury or the Chancery Court of York, and vice versa (see p 995 *j* to
p 996 *a*, post).

**Notes**
For the Court of Ecclesiastical Causes Reserved, see 14 Halsbury's Laws (4th edn) paras *f*
1289–1290.

For confirmatory faculties, see ibid para 1311, and for cases on the subject, see 19
Digest (Reissue) 444, 3524–3525.

For ornaments, see 14 Halsbury's Laws (4th edn) paras 960–961, and for cases on the
subject, see 19 Digest (Reissue) 347–350, 2673–2682.

For the archdeacon's functions, see 14 Halsbury's Laws (4th edn) para 499. *g*
For the Ecclesiastical Jurisdiction Measure 1963, s 10, see 10 Halsbury's Statutes (3rd
edn) 253.

For the Faculty Jurisdiction Measure 1964, s 9, see ibid 310.

**Cases referred to in judgment**
*Benmax v Austin Motor Co Ltd* [1955] 1 All ER 326, [1955] AC 370, [1955] 2 WLR 418, *h*
HL.
*Liddell v Westerton* (1857) 29 LTOS 54, PC.
*St Edburga's, Abberton, Re* [1961] 2 All ER 429, [1962] P 10, [1961] 3 WLR 87, Ct of
Arches.
*St Gregory's, Tredington, Re* [1971] 3 All ER 269, [1972] Fam 236, [1971] 2 WLR 796, Ct
of Arches. *j*

**Appeal**
The petitioners, Jeremy David Hummerstone, the rector of the Church of St Michael and
All Angels in the Parish of Great Torrington in the Diocese of Exeter, and James William
Bastin and John Ivor Downing, churchwardens, appealed to the Court of Ecclesiastical
Causes Reserved against the judgment of the Chancellor, Mr David Calcutt QC, sitting

in the Consistory Court of Exeter on 7 June 1983 whereby he dismissed the petitioners'
*a* petition and allowed the cross-petition by the party opponent, Eric Herbert Trimm. By a
certificate dated 7 June 1983 the chancellor certified that the cause involved a question of
doctrine, ritual or ceremonial. The facts are set out in the judgment of the court.

*Florence O'Donoghue* for the rector and churchwardens.
The party opponent did not appear.

*b*
*Cur adv vult*

18 February. The following judgment of the court was delivered.

**SIR HUGH FORBES.** This is an appeal by the rector and churchwardens of the Parish
*c* of Great Torrington against a decision of the Chancellor of the Diocese of Exeter (Mr
David Calcutt QC) given in his faculty jurisdiction on 7 June 1983. The cause which was
before him involved, first, a petition by the rector and churchwardens for a confirmatory
faculty for the retention in the church of St Michael and All Angels and in the Chapel of
St James therein of (a) a photographic reproduction of an icon of the Blessed Virgin Mary
and the Child Jesus, the original of which, in the church of Czestochowa in Poland, has
*d* acquired the title of 'the Black Madonna', (b) a portable candle-stand with money box
attached intended for the lighting of candles in front of the icon and (c) two hessian
covered screens or notice-boards each about six feet square when assembled. There was,
secondly, before the chancellor a cross-petition by the party opponent, a Mr Trimm,
asking for a faculty (a) to remove the icon and candle-stand, (b) to replace a painting of
the Blessed Virgin Mary and the Child Jesus, which had been removed to accommodate
*e* the icon, together with two rows of chairs which had been removed to accommodate the
candle-stand (both the picture and the chairs formed part of a memorial to a former
Archdeacon of Barnstaple, the late Mr Jones), (c) to remove the hessian screens and (d) to
remove a Roman Lectionary which had been placed on a portable stand also in St James's
Chapel.

In the event the chancellor granted a faculty for the retention of the screens but
*f* rejected the petition for the retention of the icon and candle-stand; he granted the party
opponent a faculty for the removal of the icon, the candle-stand and the Roman
Lectionary and for the replacement of the painting and the two rows of chairs.

Against that decision the rector and churchwardens appealed and have appeared by
counsel. The respondent Mr Trimm has not appeared or been represented.

The petition and cross-petition undoubtedly raised matters of doctrine, ritual or
*g* ceremonial; in his judgment the chancellor determined all such matters in favour of the
rector and churchwardens. He rejected their petition however, except in regard to the
screens, in the exercise of his discretion. As there was no cross-appeal no question
involving doctrine, ritual or ceremonial has to be determined by this court. Nevertheless
the chancellor was right to certify that the cause he was trying was one which did raise
such matters, for that is what is required by s 10 of the Ecclesiastical Jurisdiction Measure
*h* 1963. Had there been a cross-appeal the appeal would then have involved such matters
also. There are, however, two points which we think we should make. First, although it
was undoubtedly convenient that the chancellor should have given this certificate in his
judgment, a step he took with the laudable intention of saving costs, s 10 of the measure
makes it clear that the duty of the chancellor to certify arises only on the application of
the party desiring to appeal. There is nothing in the section which requires this
*j* application to be made orally and we think that the sensible course is for any intending
applicant to make written application. Second, as the appeal in this case does, in the
event, not involve matters of doctrine, ritual or ceremonial it is one which might
conveniently have been heard by the Arches Court of Canterbury. It seems to us that
consideration might be given to providing some machinery whereby appeals could be
readily transferred, if appropriate, from this court to the Arches Court. Similar machinery
for transfer from the Arches Court to this court might also be considered if, for instance,

an appellant to the Arches Court had overlooked the necessity to obtain a certificate from
the chancellor and the appeal to that court on examination was found to involve matters    *a*
of doctrine, ritual or ceremonial.

We now turn to consider the main grounds of appeal. These have been set out in the
notice of appeal but in reality they all amount to one main complaint: that the chancellor
exercised his discretion wrongly in rejecting the petition. We should look therefore at
what should be the proper attitude of this court when asked to interfere with the exercise
of a discretion by a diocesan chancellor in faculty proceedings.                            *b*

The leading authority on this point is the judgment of Sir Henry Willink QC, Dean of
the Arches, in *Re St Edburga's, Abberton* [1961] 2 All ER 429 at 430–431, [1962] P 10 at
15:

> 'Counsel were in agreement that the attitude of this court should correspond with
> that adopted by the Court of Appeal and I accept this as correct. What this attitude
> should be has been recently described with the highest authority by the House of    *c*
> Lords in *Benmax* v. *Austin Motor Co., Ltd.* ([1955] 1 All ER 326, [1955] AC 370). It
> will differ according to the circumstances of the case. For example, it will be strongly
> affected in favour of upholding the judgment of the trial judge where his decision
> is based on the credibility of witnesses whom he has seen. In the circumstances of
> the present appeal the proper attitude for the court is thus defined by LORD REID
> ([1955] 1 All ER 326 at 329, [1955] AC 370 at 376): "But in cases where there is no    *d*
> question of the credibility or reliability of any witness, and in cases where the point
> in dispute is the proper inference to be drawn from proved facts, an appeal court is
> generally in as good a position to evaluate the evidence as the trial judge . . . though
> it ought, of course, to give weight to his opinion." Elsewhere in the speeches in that
> case a distinction is drawn between the finding of primary facts and their evaluation
> when so found. A faculty case gives rise to the exercise of discretion, but if it appears    *e*
> to this court that the discretion of the chancellor has been based on an erroneous
> evaluation of the facts taken as a whole, it is within the jurisdiction of this court to
> allow an appeal.'

We agree with this statement of the law and consider that it should guide us in our
approach to this appeal.                                                                     *f*

It is now time to turn to the judgment of the chancellor. In order to understand how
he exercised his discretion one should start at the middle of that judgment:

> 'I now turn to consider the question of discretion. How should that be exercised?
> In this case it seems to me that a proper exercise of that discretion turns on a proper
> evaluation of the pastoral situation within the parish. If more good than harm is
> likely to be done by retaining the various items (or some of them) within the    *g*
> church, then they should be allowed to stay; but, if more harm than good, then they
> should be allowed to be removed. In assessing these matters, a priest should be
> encouraged to lead his people, and, within reasonable and proper limits, he should
> be given some leeway. In approaching my assessment of the evidence I must always
> bear in mind that Mr Hummerstone is supported by both of his churchwardens and
> by a majority of the parochial church council; and normally these are considerations    *h*
> which would carry considerable weight. In this case, however, the point has been
> taken that the petition is, in truth, no more than the petition of Mr Hummerstone
> himself. It therefore becomes necessary for me, however regrettable this may be, to
> start with a consideration of the view which I have formed of Mr Hummerstone.
> Sadly, Mr Hummerstone is, in my judgment, high-handed in his dealings with
> those who happen not to agree with him, is intolerant of their views and is    *j*
> contemptuous of institutions and of people in positions of authority. This conclusion,
> which I have only reached after anxious reflection, was borne in on me not only by
> my close observation of Mr Hummerstone throughout the hearing, but also by the
> evidence of many of the witnesses, and also by some of the documentary evidence.
> A startling but clear illustration of this last matter occurred when the parish news-

sheet for 16 January 1983 was introduced into evidence. One item (for which Mr Hummerstone admitted authorship) was in these terms: "*To perpetuate the name of a loved one* . . . a Michelmore is one of those flexible strips with which you tie up plastic bags, and also one of those stretchy objects with which you fasten a girl's hair. It stands for anything which can rightly be called a twister." Mr Hummerstone explained to me, in evidence, that this was an intended reference to the person who is, in fact, the diocesan registrar, but he asserted that it was a reference to him not in his capacity as registrar but as secretary of the diocesan parsonages board; and accordingly, so Mr Hummerstone contended, it was irrelevant to the present proceedings. In my judgment, to publish to the parish at large a notice in those terms throws a flood of light on the character of the incumbent. I was told by Mr Trimm, in evidence, that Mr Hummerstone regards the annual meeting of the parochial church council [sic] as a joke, describing it as a palace of varieties. I accept Mr Trimm's evidence, and I believe that Mr Hummerstone so regards the meeting. I was also told in evidence (given on behalf of the petitioners) that one of the churchwardens was not consulted before the icon and candle-stand were introduced in to the church, and also that neither of them was consulted before the lectionary was so introduced. In the result I am not prepared to place the weight which would normally be placed on the views of the churchwardens and of the parochial church council. Wherever the evidence given on behalf of the petitioners differs from that given on behalf of Mr Trimm and his various witnesses, I prefer the latter. In my judgment the evidence persuades me that there is a very considerable body of opinion within the worshipping congregation, and indeed within the parish generally, which disapproves of the various changes which are the subject matter of these proceedings, and which would wish to see the church as it was before those changes were made. That body of opinion is out of sympathy with the standard of churchmanship which has been imposed on them suddenly and without proper consultation; and they see at least the introduction of the icon and candle-stand and the lectionary as tangible instances of the changes which have been made and of which they disapprove. In my judgment so far as the icon and candle-stand and the Roman Lectionary are concerned more harm than good is likely to be done if those particular items are retained in the church.'

Applying the principles enunciated by Sir Henry Willink in the St Edburga's case we would not wish to interfere with the chancellor's view of the credibility of the witnesses. On the evidence which he accepted he was entitled to find, as he did, that there was a considerable body of opinion within the worshipping congregation which disapproved of the introduction of these items. It is plain from his judgment that he formed an unfavourable opinion of the incumbent. Of course he had the opportunity of seeing and hearing Mr Hummerstone not only when he gave evidence but also while he conducted the case on behalf of the petitioners, including the cross-examination of the witnesses called for the party opponent, a process which can often be revealing of the character of a litigant in person. But, accepting as we do that the chancellor, having seen and heard Mr Hummerstone, was entitled to form a view of the character and attitudes of the incumbent, we cannot see that such a view entitled him to give less than the normal weight to the fact that the incumbent was supported by both churchwardens and by a majority of thirteen to one of the parochial church council. There was clearly a lack of consultation before these items were introduced: one churchwarden knew nothing about the icon and the other nothing about the lectionary, while the parochial church council was consulted about neither. The fact however remains that despite such lack of prior consultation they did support the incumbent on the petition. The chancellor's view of the personality of the incumbent might have been relevant if the cause of the lack of consultation were an issue in the case, but it was not. We cannot accept that the incumbent's personality and attitudes could be said legitimately to detract from the almost unanimous support of the churchwardens and parochial church council or to invalidate the natural inference to be drawn from that support that there must exist at

least a considerable body of opinion within the worshipping congregation which
approved of these introductions.

In approaching the exercise of a discretion in circumstances such as these we think
that the proper test is one not dissimilar from that adopted by the chancellor: it is
whether, on weighing the pastoral considerations involved, the balance is in favour of or
against the retention of these introductions. In applying that test proper weight must of
course be given to the views of those who approbate or reprobate the change. We do not
think that in this case proper weight was given to the views of those who supported the
petition. It may be that the chancellor's natural distaste for the gratuitously offensive
attack on the diocesan registrar in the parish news-sheet led him into error in this respect.
But, whatever the reason may have been, we think that the discretion was, to use Sir
Henry Willink's words, 'based on an erroneous evaluation of the facts taken as a whole'
and was therefore wrongly exercised. In our view we are therefore entitled to look
ourselves at the pastoral situation, so far as it is disclosed in the facts found by the
chancellor and the inferences which we are entitled to draw from those facts.

In the argument before us, as in the petition itself, one matter has escaped mention. It
is clear from the terms of the letter from Mr Trimm, which was treated as a cross-
petition, that the first thing he complained of was not the introduction of the icon but
the fact that the painting of the Madonna and Child had been removed. Similarly he
appeared particularly exercised about the removal of the two rows of chairs to
accommodate the candle-stand. In both cases the items removed were part of a memorial
to the late Archdeacon Jones of Barnstaple.

Now there is nothing in the petition to indicate that the painting and chairs had been
removed to accommodate the icon and candle-stand. It would not therefore be apparent
to anyone not conversant with the previous appearance and history of the church that
anything had been removed at all. A proposal which involves removal of one article and
its replacement by another requires both matters to be set out in any petition for a
faculty, otherwise, particularly in the case of a confirmatory faculty, both the diocesan
advisory committee and the chancellor may be unaware that anything has been or is to be
removed. It becomes even more important that this should be done when the item to be
removed is or is part of a memorial. No chancellor is likely to grant a faculty involving
removal of a memorial without pausing to consider what might be the reaction of the
family of the deceased. Here there is nothing to indicate that any attempt was made by
the petitioners to find out whether there were any living members of the family of
Archdeacon Jones and if so what their views might be.

In the circumstances, we see no justification for the removal of the painting and the
chairs. These should in our view be replaced in their old position in St James's Chapel.
At the same time, giving full weight to the fact that the retention of the icon and candle-
stand is supported by both churchwardens and the majority of the parochial church
council, while mindful also of the fact that there is a considerable body of opinion
opposed to their retention, we think that, on balance, the icon and the candle-stand
should be retained in the church. A new site for the icon and candle-stand should be
found and one which is approved by the archdeacon and the diocesan advisory committee.

We find ourselves in some difficulty about the lectionary. From its description this
appears to be the book containing the text of the Scripture readings authorised for use on
weekdays by the Alternative Service Book 1980, Table 4, pp 1071–1091. Counsel for the
rector and churchwardens seemed inclined to accept that a faculty would be required for
its introduction but clearly came unprepared to argue the point whether a faculty is
required for the placing in a church of a book authorised for use in services in that
church. We are left, therefore, without assistance in the matter.

Despite such lack of assistance we feel we can go thus far in suggesting what the
position is in relation to the introduction of books into churches. It is clear that Canon
F13, para 3 of the Revised Canons Ecclesiastical requires a faculty for the addition of any
ornament. As to what is an ornament we consider that the definition given by the Right
Hon T Pemberton Leigh delivering the judgment of the Privy Council in *Liddell v
Westerton* (1857) 29 LTOS 54 at 55 still holds good today:

a

'The term "ornaments", in ecclesiastical law, is not confined, as by modern usage, to articles of decoration or embellishment, but it is used in the larger sense of the word "*Ornamentum*," which, according to the interpretation of Forcellini's Dictionary, is used *pro quocunque apparatu seu implemento*. All the several articles used in the performance of the services and rites of the church are ornaments. Vestments, books, cloths, chalices, and patens are among the church ornaments . . .'

b

A book must therefore be regarded as an ornament.

We think however that Canon F13, para 3 is subject to two qualifications which have long been part of the law relating to faculties. The first is that a faculty, in general, is not required for the introduction of an ornament ordered by the canons of the Church. Thus a faculty should not be required for the introduction of a Bible of large size for the use of the minister, for this is ordered to be provided by Canon F9. The second is that, although a faculty may strictly be required for the addition of anything which is not ordered

c

though lawful, we consider that in the law appertaining to faculties it is still right to say that ecclesiastical courts are not eager to assume jurisdiction. Minor matters therefore may be introduced without a faculty. In Sir Alfred Kempe's memorandum as to the Law of Faculties, printed as appendix to the Report of the Archbishops' Committee on Ancient Monuments (Churches) (July 1914) it is said:

d

'Moreover, the ecclesiastical courts repose confidence in the incumbent and churchwardens, and in matters of small moment will not regard them as liable to censure for having acted without the express authority of the faculty. The courts are not eager for jurisdiction in such cases. But if any doubt exists they should inquire of the registry whether they may safely proceed without a faculty.'

e

It is plain that the range of books which fall into the category of those which are lawful but not specifically ordered by the canons of the Church is very large. The Alternative Service Book, translations of the Bible other than the Authorised Version, a very large variety of hymn books are instances which spring readily to mind. The extent to which the introduction of some of these might legitimately be regarded as matters of small moment in relation to which chancellors are entitled to repose confidence in the incumbent and churchwardens would no doubt always be in the minds of ecclesiastical

f

judges, as should, in the minds of incumbents and churchwardens, Sir Alfred Kempe's wise warning that in case of doubt they should inquire of the registry whether they may safely proceed without a faculty.

Although we believe that the general law relating to faculties for ornaments is as we have stated we would not wish to give a definitive ruling on the introduction of this book and its lectern in this case. This is a problem which we do not attempt to solve and

g

for good reason. Not only have we heard no argument on these points but there was no petition before the chancellor for the retention of these two items though there was a cross-petition for their removal. In the circumstances we think that the matter should go back to the chancellor for him to determine, after such argument, if any, as the petitioner and party opponent may consider to be required, whether a faculty is in law necessary for the introduction of this lectionary and its portable stand. If the chancellor determines

h

that a faculty is required then it should in our view be granted, because we should have granted such a faculty ourselves had there been a petition for such a faculty and had we been satisfied that one was necessary.

We have considered whether we should ourselves grant a faculty for the icon and candle-stand. We are in no doubt that we have the power to do so in appropriate cases, but in this case something still requires to be done, namely the choice of a new site and

j

the approval of that site by the archdeacon and the diocesan advisory committee. It would therefore be more appropriate in our view to remit the matter to the chancellor for him to grant the faculty, as we direct should be done, without the necessity for citation, when the new site is found and approved. This course seems all the more desirable as the matter of the lectionary will have to be reconsidered by the chancellor also. In view of the nature of the icon and candle-stand we think that the faculty for those items should be 'until further order'.

Finally we would wish to reiterate the point made in *Re St Gregory's, Tredington* [1971] 3 All ER 269 at 271, [1972] Fam 236 at 239–240 by the Deputy Dean of the Arches, Mr George Newsom QC, that s 9 of the Faculty Jurisdiction Measure 1964 exists to enable the archdeacon to offer assistance to the chancellor in faculty cases. Whilst archdeacons have many duties they should be ready to give priority to a case of this character where they can be of considerable help to a chancellor, particularly perhaps in that judge's consideration of the pastoral questions involved. We think it important that archdeacons should bear in mind this part of their duties and be ready to intervene in faculty suits so that they may be of service to the chancellor.

The orders which we make are therefore these: (1) that the order of the chancellor granting Mr Trimm a faculty for the restoration to its former position of the painting and the chairs should stand, subject to the stay of execution for 28 days to enable the petitioners to restore them if they themselves wish to carry out the instructions of this court; (2) that the remainder of the chancellor's order, granting a faculty to Mr Trimm to remove the icon, the candle-stand and the Roman Lectionary should be revoked; (3) that the chancellor should himself, without further citation, grant a faculty to the petitioners for the stationing of the icon and candle-stand in some suitable part of the church when the approval of the archdeacon and the diocesan advisory committee is available; (4) that the chancellor should consider whether a faculty is necessary for the placing of the lectionary and its lectern in the church, after such argument as he may require and the parties may think fit to put before him, and if, after such consideration, he concludes that a faculty is necessary that he should grant such faculty.

So far as costs are concerned, we would not disturb the chancellor's order for costs below; these items were introduced without a faculty and therefore, a faculty had to be obtained. The party opponent did not appear on the appeal, and we think therefore that there should be no order for costs on the appeal.

*Order accordingly.*

Solicitors: *Pethybridges & Best*, Torrington (for the rector and churchwardens).

N P Metcalfe Esq    Barrister.

a

# Re W (a minor) (wardship: jurisdiction)

COURT OF APPEAL, CIVIL DIVISION
OLIVER, PURCHAS AND NEILL LJJ
4, 5 DECEMBER 1984, 17 JANUARY 1985

b    *Child – Care – Local authority – Wardship proceedings – Jurisdiction of court to review decision of local authority – Care order – Local authority proposing application to free child for adoption – Parents consenting to proposal but relatives opposing application – Wardship proceedings commenced by relatives – Whether High Court should exercise wardship jurisdiction – Children and Young Persons Act 1969, s 1 – Children Act 1975, s 14.*

c    At the request of the parents, the local authority placed their child with temporary foster parents and applied to the juvenile court for a care order under s 1[a] of the Children and Young Persons Act 1969 in contemplation of making a further application to the court under s 14(1)[b] of the Children Act 1975 to free the child for adoption. The aunt, uncle and paternal grandparents (the relatives) were opposed to the application but had no right under the 1975 Act to appear before the juvenile court. They therefore applied to d    the High Court for the child to be made a ward of court and for the uncle and aunt to be given care and control. They contended that in view of their inability to take part in the proceedings under s 14(1) of the 1975 Act and because of the parents' consent to the decision of the local authority there would be no challenge to the local authority's application and no proper consideration of the relatives' wishes that the uncle and aunt have care of the child. The judge held that in the exceptional circumstances of the case, including the unusual position of the parents and the practical difficulty facing the e    relatives in bringing their case before the court, the child should be made a ward. The local authority appealed to the Court of Appeal.

**Held** – (1) Where a care order had been made under s 1 of the 1969 Act, or a child had been received into care under s 2 of the Child Care Act 1980, the welfare of the child became the responsibility of the local authority, and accordingly the High Court would f    not exercise its wardship jurisdiction in respect of the child save in exceptional circumstances, namely (a) where there was a challenge to a decision of the local authority on the basis of unreasonableness or by way of judicial review, (b) where there was a lacuna in the statutory scheme under the 1969 and 1975 Acts so that the local authority, alone or in conjunction with the juvenile court, had no power or no sufficient power to take a certain course of action and (c) where an exceptional situation made the g    intervention by the High Court imperative (see p 1007 g h, p 1017 g to p 1018 c and f to j, p 1020 b and p 1021 b c, post); A v Liverpool City Council [1981] 2 All ER 385 applied.

---

(2) (Purchas LJ dissenting). The statutory scheme provided by Parliament in the 1969 and 1975 Acts, although not providing for participation by persons (such as relatives) other than the parents, nevertheless did contain safeguards, for example the appointment of an independent guardian ad litem under s 20 of the 1975 Act. Therefore, so long as the local authority properly exercised its powers, there was no reason to suppose that the child's best interests would be prejudiced. It could not therefore be said that failure to provide for representations by the relatives constituted a lacuna in the statutory scheme which necessitated the intervention of the High Court, nor were the facts so exceptional as to justify the exercise of the wardship jurisdiction. Accordingly, since there had been no challenge to the reasonableness of the local authority's actions or by way of judicial review, the appeal would be allowed (see p 1017 *d e*, p 1019 *b c* and *g* to *j*, p 1020 *a b* and p 1024 *a b e f* and *h j*, post); *Re E (minors) (wardship: jurisdiction)* [1984] 1 All ER 21 and *Re J (a minor) (wardship: jurisdiction)* [1984] 1 All ER 29 applied.

**Notes**

For the care of a child by a local authority and its duty towards a child in care, see 24 Halsbury's Laws (4th edn) paras 787, 797.

For wardship jurisdiction, see ibid paras 576–583, and for cases on the subject, see 28(2) Digest (Reissue) 911–916, 2220–2247.

For the Children and Young Persons Act 1969, s 1, see 40 Halsbury's Statutes (3rd edn) 849.

For the Children Act 1975, ss 14, 20, see 45 ibid 687, 693.

For the Child Care Act 1980, s 2, see 50(1) ibid 1058.

**Cases referred to in judgments**

*A v Liverpool City Council* [1981] 2 All ER 385, [1982] AC 363, [1981] 2 WLR 948, HL.

*Associated Provincial Picture Houses Ltd v Wednesbury Corp* [1947] 2 All ER 680, [1948] 1 KB 223, CA.

*B (a minor) (wardship: child in care), Re* [1974] 3 All ER 915, [1975] Fam 36, [1975] 2 WLR 302.

*Council of Civil Service Unions v Minister for the Civil Service* [1984] 3 All ER 935, [1984] 3 WLR 1174, HL.

*E (minors) (wardship: jurisdiction), Re* [1984] 1 All ER 21, [1983] 1 WLR 541, Fam D and CA.

*H (a minor) (wardship: jurisdiction), Re* [1978] 2 All ER 903, [1978] Fam 65, [1978] 2 WLR 608, Fam D and CA.

*J (a minor) (wardship: jurisdiction), Re* [1984] 1 All ER 29, [1984] 1 WLR 81, CA.

*M v Humberside CC* [1979] 2 All ER 744, [1979] Fam 114, [1979] 3 WLR 234.

*M (an infant), Re* [1961] 1 All ER 788, [1961] Ch 328, [1961] 2 WLR 350, CA.

*Y (a minor) (child in care: access), Re* [1975] 3 All ER 348, [1976] Fam 125, [1975] 3 WLR 342, Fam D and CA.

**Appeal**

The defendant, Hertfordshire County Council, appealed against the order of Ewbank J dated 7 November 1984 whereby he granted the application of the plaintiffs (the relatives) that the child in question be made a ward of court and dismissed the council's application that the child should cease to be a ward of court. The appeal was heard in camera but judgment was given in open court. The facts are set out in the judgment of Purchas LJ.

*Heather Pope* for the relatives.
*David Bodey* for the council.

*Cur adv vult*

17 January. The following judgments were delivered.

*a*

**PURCHAS LJ** (giving the first judgment at the invitation of Oliver LJ). This is an appeal by the Hertfordshire County Council from an order made on 7 November 1984 by Ewbank J sitting in the Family Division. It concerns a minor aged four, to whom I shall refer as 'Sarah', and raises an important point touching on the wardship jurisdiction exercised by the Family Division. The judge dismissed an application by the council to *b* de-ward Sarah. At the same time, he made orders in wardship committing Sarah's care to the council under s 7(2) of the Family Law Reform Act 1969, granting access to Sarah's aunt, uncle and grandparents, with a view to assessing whether a bond could be formed between Sarah and her extended family, giving leave to the council to issue an application under s 14 of the Children Act 1975, for freeing Sarah for adoption to be heard in January 1985, together with the originating summons in wardship. He ordered a welfare report *c* to be prepared for the hearing in January, and ordered that the officer making the report should also act as the reporting officer in the freeing for adoption application. It is difficult to imagine a more expeditious and efficient way of keeping all options open to ensure that Sarah's welfare is safeguarded.

But the council object. They want to obtain a care order under s 1 of the Children and Young Persons Act 1969. This they will do in the juvenile court under r 13 of the *d* Magistrates' Courts (Children and Young Persons) Rules 1970, SI 1970/1792 (as amended). They can make their own arrangements free from the supervision of the Family Division, and subsequently make another application to the domestic court under r 3 of the Magistrates' Courts (Adoption) Rules 1976, SI 1976/1768 (as amended), to free Sarah for adoption under the provisions of s 14 of the 1975 Act. They say that under the authority of *A v Liverpool City Council* [1981] 2 All ER 385, [1982] AC 363, they are entitled to do *e* this, and that the judge was wrong to make the orders which he did. They may well be right.

The history discloses a tragic family story, some details of which it is necessary to rehearse in this judgment. For reasons which will become apparent, neither Sarah's mother nor father were parties to the wardship application. The first and second plaintiffs are the uncle and aunt of Sarah, being respectively the brother of Sarah's father and the *f* sister of Sarah's mother. The third and fourth plaintiffs are Sarah's paternal grandparents. I shall refer to the plaintiffs collectively as 'the relatives'. The council's social services department (the department) have been involved with Sarah and with her mother since about 1977.

Sarah has two brothers: Tony, born on 20 August 1979, and Alan, born on 26 October 1983. Sarah was born on 11 November 1980. The uncle and aunt have three children: *g* Tara who is eight; Amanda who is six and Darren who is nearly four. This family live only two miles away from the father and mother and their family, but contact between Sarah and them has been limited to occasional social events, such as birthdays and Christmas parties, etc. There is no reason to think that the uncle and aunt's family is not a satisfactory and happy one.

The father is an engineer and has, during the past five years, been managing director *h* of his own business, which is a design and sales firm. He appears to be very hard working and successful but there is a suggestion that this has affected his relationship with his extended family, including the relatives. The mother's father died when she was four years of age. Her elder sister is mentally handicapped and continues to live with her mother.

In adolescence the mother was exposed to pressures thought to be too much for her, *j* with the result that she threatened to take an overdose on more than one occasion. In 1978 she was referred to the department when care proceedings were considered. There was a psychiatrist's assessment of her during this period, which indicated that she was not mentally ill although she presented as a disturbed adolescent.

Tony was conceived when the mother was 16 years of age. She married the father just before Tony's birth. There has been a normal bonding between the mother and Tony.

During this time there was trouble between the mother and her sister Gillian, which
resulted in the mother and father leaving the home of the mother's mother to find      *a*
accommodation of their own. However, they continued keeping in close touch with the
mother's mother.

From the outset there has been no natural bonding between the mother and Sarah.
Quoting from the welfare report:

> 'The natural bonding process between mother and child does not seem to have
> occurred, and [the mother] has strong negative feelings for Sarah. The situation over   *b*
> the last eighteen months has deteriorated to a point where the mother feels very
> rejecting of Sarah with feelings of wanting to hurt her.'

The mother's psychiatric condition deteriorated during her pregnancy with Alan to
the extent that she became so depressed that in September 1983 the family as a whole
were referred to the department by the nursing officer for child care, as a result of Sarah   *c*
being kicked by the mother. From that moment the mother and the family received
considerable support from her general practitioner and health visitor, and were clearly
the subject of attention from various members of the department. There was a psychiatric
report from Princess Alexandra Hospital dated 8 October 1984 before the judge, from
which it is clear that, by October 1983, the mother was—

> '. . . clearly suffering from a moderately severe depressive illness (depression of   *d*
> her mood, with gloomy preoccupation, excessive crying and a feeling that she did
> not care what happened to her or those around her).'

During the latter part of 1983 and the first part of 1984 the department were resisting
the mother's wishes to 'get rid of' Sarah and were 'trying by various means to help the
mother overcome her rejection of Sarah but without success'. On 6 August 1984 the   *e*
mother and father asked the department to remove Sarah from their home. Officers of
the department discussed the implications of the request, and came to the conclusion
that Sarah should be removed for her own safety and emotional needs. She had already
been placed on the departments 'at risk' register after a case conference in April 1984.
During investigations it came to light that Sarah had been bruised and bitten by the
mother.                                                                                  *f*

On 9 August 1984 a place of safety order under s 28 of the 1969 Act was obtained by
the council in respect of Sarah. In view of the wishes expressed by the mother and father,
the council could have received Sarah into care under s 2 of the Child Care Act 1980. No
reason is given in the evidence filed by the council for their decision to make applications
under the 1969 Act. On the evidence available there would not appear to be any reason
for either a place of safety order or a care order. The position could at any time be   *g*
safeguarded by a resolution under s 3 of the 1980 Act, but in view of the decision to
apply under s 14 of the 1975 Act, this would also appear to be unnecessary.

Nevertheless the council commenced proceedings to obtain a care order under s 1 of
the 1969 Act. On 4 September the Cheshunt Juvenile Court made an interim order and
adjourned the application to 2 October. It was, from an early stage, the council's intention
to apply subsequently to the domestic court for an order freeing Sarah for adoption, it   *h*
being the request of the mother and father that such an application should be made. In
the meanwhile, the relatives became alerted to what was occurring, and took steps of
their own. They issued an originating summons dated 25 September 1984 making Sarah
a ward of court. In this summons the uncle and aunt claimed that Sarah be made a ward
of court and that they should be granted her care and control. The grandparents claimed
access to Sarah.                                                                         *j*

Not unnaturally, the relatives expressed surprise and regret that they had not been
approached by the department over the question of Sarah's care. I understand this feeling,
obviously held genuinely by them. On the other hand, it must be remembered that
during the first half of 1984 those responsible in the department were bending their best
endeavours to support the mother and father and to dissuade them from rejecting Sarah.

a   Most probably, because of a sense of guilt felt by the mother and father in relation to their proposed release of Sarah, they would not have reacted favourably if, on their own initiative, the department had involved the rest of the family. Indeed, it would almost certainly have been counter-productive. However, after the decision in August 1984, in view of the provisions of s 2(3)(b) of the 1980 Act, it is not clear why the department did not investigate the option of placing Sarah with the uncle and aunt.

b   Since the making of the interim care order, Sarah has been with short-term foster parents with whom she cannot stay in the long term. Unfortunately she is becoming increasingly attached to them and is indicating a wish to stay with them. The longer the situation is allowed to continue, the stronger this bonding will become and the greater the disruption when an eventual move has to be made. The department, therefore, were anxious to proceed to a long-term solution of Sarah's problems without any delay.

c   In their affidavits, the relatives made detailed complaints about the conduct of a Mr Lothian, a senior social worker with the department. The uncle said that Mr Lothian was told that the relatives would only be too happy to look after Sarah and have her with them until the situation in the father and mother's family had been resolved, but that he refused to allow them to see Sarah or to tell them where she was.

The grandfather deposed at para 5 of his affidavit, sworn on 26 September 1984:

d   'My wife and I have contacted the Local Authority and in fact had a meeting with them and my son and his wife on the 12 September. However, we have failed to get any satisfaction from the Local Authority with regards access to Sarah or knowledge of her whereabouts. [The father and mother] have not consulted us before the action as regards to Sarah and have not asked for our help. However, my family feel that we cannot allow this to happen if we can do something to prevent Sarah being e   adopted. As a result of the lack of co-operation and help from the Local Authority, I would submit to this Honourable Court that Sarah should be made a Ward of Court and in the Wardship proceedings my wife and I can apply for access to Sarah and also support my son [the uncle] in his application for care and control of Sarah. We would give him all the support he needed and all members of my family would support him.'

f   In his affidavit sworn on 23 October 1984, the father said:

'. . . 7. I am aware that my brother . . . and his wife . . . would like to care for Sarah and that my parents would like to see her. Sarah has only seen them infrequently. We are not a close family and we only visit my parents who live in Suffolk approximately twice a year. The visits last about five hours but there is little real contact. There has been little real contact with [the uncle] and his family either. g   We met at Christmas 1983 and on one or two occasions since then. At these infrequent family gatherings my parents and [the uncle] and his wife have given Sarah more attention than they have given our two sons possibly because the feelings of my wife and I towards Sarah were so obvious . . .

10. I believe that my wife and I are too biased to be able to make the right h   decision about Sarah's placement. In asking the Hertfordshire County Council's Social Services Department to take Sarah into care we are also asking them to decide on the best place for her. If it is felt that Sarah should be adopted by [the uncle] and his wife we would not oppose that application. If in fact Sarah should be placed outside the family we would not oppose that either.'

Mr Lothian, in his affidavit sworn on 23 October 1984, said:

j   '. . . 3. I deny the Plaintiffs' allegations that the Defendant has been uncooperative in its response to the Plaintiffs' expressed interest in Sarah. I have spoken with the 1st Plaintiff on the telephone on two occasions and met him at my office on two occasions including a meeting on 12 September 1984 which the other three Plaintiffs attended. I have spoken with the 3rd Plaintiff on two occasions on the telephone and have met him on the one occasion. My only contact with the 2nd and 4th Plaintiffs was at the meeting on 12 September when the 2nd Plaintiff had little to say. I have also spoken with the Plaintiffs' solicitors on two occasions. My experience of the Plaintiffs is thus limited but in the course of it I have found them unable or unwilling to discuss Sarah's position objectively. They have appeared intolerant of the views of anyone who disagreed with their own assessment of the situation, be it Sarah's own parents, my Department or the General Practitioner who has been treating [the mother]. On 12 September 1984 the Divisional Social Services Officer Mr Scott and I were to have discussed Sarah's situation with the 3rd and 4th Plaintiff. The time of that meeting, namely 10.00 a.m. was for the convenience of the 3rd and 4th Plaintiffs who had an appointment to see their legal advisers later that morning. To my surprise, the 3rd and 4th Plaintiffs arrived for the meeting accompanied by the 1st and 2nd Plaintiffs. Mr Scott and I were quite prepared to see the 3rd and 4th Plaintiffs as arranged and to see the 1st and 2nd Plaintiffs at a subsequent meeting but we declined to see all four together. Our experience in the past has been that emotions can tend to run high at such meetings and can be counter-productive at least to start with . . .'

Finally there was an affidavit sworn on 7 November 1984 by the managing clerk of the firm of solicitors acting for the relatives, to the effect that, when he tried to arrange a meeting between his clients, himself and Mr Lothian to discuss Sarah, Mr Lothian said to him: 'This matter is getting out of hand', and went on to refuse to allow a meeting with legal advisers present.

I have cited extracts from the affidavits to demonstrate the unfortunate position which has arisen between the department and the relatives. This continued up to the hearing before the judge, and was never resolved, the last round of affidavits being sworn by the relatives and their solicitor just before the hearing, leaving no time for a further affidavit from Mr Lothian, nor was he called, although he was present at the hearing. The judge, however, in his judgment made no findings adverse to the department in relation to their conduct and, therefore, it would not be right for me to come to any conclusion or express any views on this topic. I, therefore, do not do so.

I now turn to the judgment of the judge. On the point which had been taken before him, namely that the instant case was distinguishable from other cases to which reference will shortly be made, because there was only an interim order rather than a final care order, the judge ruled in favour of the council, referring to the case of *Re E (minors) (wardship: jurisdiction)* [1984] 1 All ER 21, [1983] 1 WLR 541, in these terms:

'It is clear, however, from *Re E* that the approach of the High Court is the same whether there is in fact a care order in existence or whether there is merely an application for a care order.'

This was clearly right and has not been challenged in any way on this appeal. The basic issue on which the judge decided this application is:

'The father and the mother have expressed the wish that Sarah should be placed for adoption, and it is the intention of the local authority to apply for an order that the child should be freed for adoption. They would intend to consider various possible adoptive parents, and they would not rule out the uncle and aunt in looking for adoptors. The uncle and aunt are concerned that the child has been whisked away from the family. They have had no contact with the child since the place of safety order, and they fear that [what] they can offer the child is not going to be fully looked at by the local authority. They say that the best thing might be for Sarah to come to live with them and for the mother and father to have more time to consider whether they really wish to take such a decisive step as adoption. They say two things. First of all, that the mother is not in a fit mental state to make long-term decisions relating to her child. Secondly, that the father is giving in to the mother's wishes and is not himself making a free choice.'

a    The plaintiffs reinforce their contention that the department will not properly consider the solution they offer, namely that Sarah should live with the uncle and aunt, by pointing out that under the proceedings involved in the care order made under the provisions of the 1969 Act, or the application under s 14 of the 1975 Act, they have no right of audience. The judge was clearly impressed with the point that the special feature in this case is that the mother and father are the only people who qualify as parents who can be heard in either set of proceedings. There will, therefore, be no opportunity for

b   Sarah's future to be considered in adversarial proceedings before either the juvenile or the domestic courts. The judge sets out this aspect in the judgment:

> 'In this case, however, the parents are not opposing the care order, and would have no interest in trying to invoke the wardship proceedings. They do not oppose the care order, and the uncle and aunt point out that since the local authority otherwise will have an unopposed application for a care order before the magistrates,
>
> c   how can it be said that the welfare of the child is going to be given the importance that it should have? They point out that the merits of the possibility of the child going into the care and control of the uncle and aunt is simply not going to be considered, and that the magistrates' court in reality is not going to hear the case on its merits, and certainly not going to hear the point of view that they wish to put forward.'

d    After referring to an extract from the speech of Lord Wilberforce in *A v Liverpool City Council* [1981] 2 All ER 385 at 388–389, [1982] AC 363 at 373, the judge continued in these terms:

> 'On behalf of the uncle and aunt it is said that they are not asking this court to supervise the exercise of the discretion which would be committed to the local
>
> e   authority if and when the care order is made. They are asking that their case should be heard and the court should be satisfied that the proposal for freeing the child for adoption is in the interests of the child and that the consent to the freeing for adoption is freely given by the mother in particular, and by the father. This, in my view, is an exceptional case. It is a case where the High Court ought to exercise its wardship powers and, in those circumstances the child will become a ward of court.'

f    Counsel for the council submitted that the judge had erred in deciding that this was 'an exceptional case' so as to bring it within Lord Wilberforce's speech ([1981] 2 All ER 385 at 388–389, [1982] AC 363 at 373):

> 'The court's general inherent power is always available to fill gaps or to supplement
>
> g   the powers of the local authority; what it will not do . . . is to supervise the exercise of discretion within the field committed by statute to the local authority.'

   Lord Wilberforce emphasised that the court will not supervise, except by way of judicial review, the exercise of discretion by a local authority within the field committed to it by statute. In areas where Parliament has provided for a review by the court, whether it be the High Court, the county court or the juvenile or domestic court,

h   different considerations may apply and in those circumstances the general inherent power exercised by the Family Division may be available to supplement the powers or fill gaps. To this extent I cannot agree with the submissions of counsel for the council.

   In considering the statements of policy contained in the speeches in *A v Liverpool City Council*, it is helpful to remember the factual background. The infant involved was a

j   young boy aged about two years who was the subject of a care order made some months before his mother issued proceedings in wardship. He was living with foster parents. Although formally seeking care and control in her wardship application, the mother of the child was in fact seeking to oppose a restriction of the access which had hitherto been afforded to her by the local authority. She had previously been enjoying access each week to the child at the home of the foster parents. This was reduced to one hour's supervised

access each month, to take place at a day nursery run by the council. The reason given
was—

> 'that rehabilitation of the mother and the child (ie restoration to his mother's care)
> was not in the child's best interest and that, therefore, there was no point in
> maintaining regular access.'

It must be noticed that *A v Liverpool City Council* was decided before the coming into force
of s 6 of and Sch 1 to the Health and Social Services and Social Security Adjudications Act
1983, which dramatically curtailed the powers of the local authority to withhold access
from a parent. However, by s 12B(4) of the 1980 Act, as introduced by the 1983 Act, the
Liverpool City Council would not have been subject to this restriction as long as they
intended merely to vary the arrangements for access rather than bring access to an end.

I refer to some further extracts from the speech of Lord Wilberforce as follows ([1981]
2 All ER 385 at 387, [1982] AC 363 at 371):

> 'The point which I desire to emphasise is that, against a background of continual
> social changes, within and beyond the family, the object of intervention by the
> courts, whether the courts of Chancery, or their predecessor the Court of Wards and
> Liveries, or their present successors, the courts of the Family Division of the High
> Court, is to promote the welfare of the child.'

After referring to some statistics, Lord Wilberforce continued ([1981] 2 All ER 385 at
387, [1982] AC 363 at 371):

> 'It is obvious that this situation called for a large delegation of power to local
> authorities and a large measure of discretion for them, and this has been conferred
> by the (consolidating) Child Care Act 1980 and by the surviving portion of the
> Children and Young Persons Act 1969.'

After emphasising that the general principle guiding both the authorities and the
courts, namely the welfare of the child, is the same, Lord Wilberforce said ([1981] 2 All
ER 385 at 388, [1982] AC 363 at 372):

> 'It must, however, be borne in mind that, whereas the duties and powers of local
> authorities and of juvenile courts are defined and limited by statute, there is no
> similar limitation on those of the High Court. This leads to the next and decisive
> question: given that both the High Court and the local authority have responsibilities
> for the welfare of the child, what is the relationship, or dividing line, between
> them? I think that there is no doubt that the appellant, the child's mother, is arguing
> for a general reviewing power in the court over the local authority's discretionary
> decision; she is, in reality, asking the court to review the respondent's decision as to
> access and to substitute its own opinion on that matter. Access itself is undoubtedly
> a matter within the discretionary power of the local authority. In my opinion the
> court has no such reviewing power. Parliament has by statute entrusted to the local
> authority the power and duty to make decisions as to the welfare of children without
> any reservation of reviewing power to the court. There are, indeed, certain limited
> rights of appeal as to the care order itself: under s 2(12) of the 1969 Act there is an
> appeal to the Crown Court against the care order; the appellant did not exercise this
> right and is now long out of time. Or the appellant could apply to the juvenile court
> under s 21 of the 1969 Act to discharge the care order or to vary it; this she has not
> done, and any such application would not be likely to succeed. Furthermore, if the
> facts so permitted, she could apply to the High Court for judicial review of the care
> order or the local authority's actions under it; there is no suggestion of any ground
> on which this would be possible in the present case. Nowhere is there any suggestion
> in the legislation that the High Court was to be left with a reviewing power as to
> the merits of local authorities' decisions.'

A little further on in his speech, Lord Wilberforce comes to a statement on which the
*a* council place great reliance ([1981] 2 All ER 385 at 388–389, [1982] AC 363 at 373):

> 'In my opinion Parliament has marked out an area in which, subject to the
> enacted limitations and safeguards, decisions for the child's welfare are removed
> from the parents and from supervision by the courts. This is not to say that the
> inherent jurisdiction of the High Court is taken away. Any child, whether under
> care or not, can be made a ward of court by the procedure of s 9(2) of the Law
> *b* reform (Miscellaneous Provisions) Act 1949. In cases (and the present is an example)
> where the court perceives that the action sought of it is within the sphere of
> discretion of the local authority, it will make no order and the wardship will lapse.
> But in some instances there may be an area of concern to which the powers of the
> local authority, limited as they are by statute, do not extend. Sometimes the local
> authority itself may invite the supplementary assistance of the court. Then the
> *c* wardship may be continued with a view to action by the court. The court's general
> inherent power is always available to fill gaps or to supplement the powers of the
> local authority; what it will not do (except by way of judicial review where
> appropriate) is to supervise the exercise of discretion within the field committed by
> statute to the local authority.'

*d* It appears from the speech of Lord Roskill that the mother's case was that the decision
of the local authority was '"wholly unreasonable" and "arbitrary"' (see [1981] 2 All ER
385 at 390, [1982] AC 363 at 374) . On this basis the mother sought to challenge the
decision of the local authority on the basis of the well-known principles enunciated in
*Associated Provincial Picture Houses Ltd v Wednesbury Corp* [1947] 2 All ER 680, [1948] 1
KB 223. Lord Roskill was of the opinion that there was no evidence which could possibly
justify such a challenge, and that the trial judge rightly rejected it. The challenge was not
*e* renewed in argument in their Lordships' House. Lord Roskill referred to part of the
judgment of Lord Evershed MR in *Re M (an infant)* [1961] 1 All ER 788 at 795 , [1961]
Ch 328 at 345, saying ([1981] 2 All ER 385 at 391–392, [1982] AC 363 at 376):

> 'Lord Evershed MR, with whom Upjohn and Pearson LJJ expressly concurred,
> stated his first two conclusions thus: "(i) The prerogative right of the Queen as
> *f* parens patriae in relation to infants within the realm is not for all purposes ousted
> or abrogated as the result of the exercise of the duties and powers by local authorities
> under the Children Act, 1948: in particular the power to make an infant a ward of
> court by invocation of s. 9 of the Act of 1949 is unaffected. (ii) But even where a
> child is made a ward of court by virtue of the Act of 1949, the judge in whom the
> prerogative power is vested will, acting on familiar principles, not exercise control
> *g* in relation to duties or discretions clearly vested by statute in the local authority,
> and may, therefore, and in a case such as the present normally will, order that the
> child cease to be a ward of court." The statutory codes which existed in 1958 and in
> 1961 have been elaborated and extended and amended several times since these
> decisions as the social needs of our society have changed and, unhappily, the number
> of deprived children in the care of local authorities has tragically increased. It cannot
> *h* possibly be said that the massive volume of legislation since 1961 culminating in
> the Child Care Act 1980, a consolidating Act which, though repealing the whole of
> the 1948 Act, left intact the early part of the 1969 Act has lessened the responsibilities
> of local authorities. This hardly suggests an intention by Parliament to restrict the
> scope of the statutory control by local authorities of child welfare in favour of the
> use by the courts of the prerogative wardship jurisdiction. On the contrary, the
> *j* plain intention of this legislation is to secure the continued expansion of that
> statutory control.'

*A v Liverpool City Council* has been considered by this court in two recent judgments:
*Re E (minors) (wardship: jurisdiction)* [1984] 1 All ER 21, [1983] 1 WLR 541 and *Re J (a
minor) (wardship: jurisdiction)* [1984] 1 All ER 29, [1984] 1 WLR 81. In the former, this

court upheld a decision of the trial judge to de-ward the minor, although Dunn LJ agreed to this course with obvious anxiety and reluctance. In the latter, on facts not very *a* dissimilar, Cumming-Bruce LJ, with whom Sir George Baker agreed, found that there were exceptional circumstances in which the court should intervene.

In *Re E* the local authority had obtained a place of safety order in respect of three children, and had applied to the juvenile court for a care order in relation to each, pursuant to s 1 of the 1969 Act. Before that application was heard, however, the mother commenced wardship proceedings in which she sought care and control of the children, *b* with supervision to the local authority. The children were twin boys aged two and a girl aged one. When the matter came on for hearing before Balcombe J, the position was analogous to that reached in the instant case, namely an application for a care order under the 1969 Act had been initiated but adjourned because of wardship proceedings issued by the parents.

Balcombe J, following *A v Liverpool City Council*, refused to continue the wardship. The *c* parents appealed. One of the grounds on which the appellant in *Re E* sought to distinguish *A v Liverpool City Council* was that the procedure under the 1969 Act did not allow the juvenile court (or the Crown Court on appeal) to make provision for, or control, a phased return to the parent or an experimental period of increasing contact by way of access.

Another ground of appeal in *Re E* was that it was unfair that the local authority could have recourse to wardship as recommended by Lord Wilberforce in *A v Liverpool City* *d* *Council*, whereas the natural parents could not. Dunn LJ said ([1984] 1 All ER 21 at 26–27, [1983] 1 WLR 541 at 555):

'In this case the only ground on which it is suggested that the court should exercise the wardship jurisdiction is because, if the court in wardship made a care order under s 7(2) of the Family Law Reform Act 1969, the court would have power to grant access to the natural mother with a view to the children being rehabilitated *e* and ultimately returned to her care (see *Re Y (a minor) (child in care: access)* [1975] 3 All ER 348, [1976] Fam 125). If, on the other hand, a care order is made by the juvenile court, then under s 1 of the Children and Young Persons Act 1969 the justices would have no power to order access, and the decision whether or not the children should be rehabilitated with their natural mother would rest with the local authority without supervision from any court except by judicial review, which *f* would almost certainly not be appropriate. The difficulty I find with that argument is, as counsel for the local authority pointed out, that Parliament has set up a statutory scheme which gives wide powers to local authorities to provide for the welfare of children. Under that scheme, once a care order has been made by the juvenile court, the decision whether the child should be rehabilitated with its natural parents, and consequently whether there should be access to that end, is a *g* matter for the discretion of the local authority and not for the court. In my view, it is not for the High Court in its wardship jurisdiction to say that it should take over a discretion which has been vested in local authorities by Parliament.'

Dunn LJ then went on to review the position generally in which mothers particularly find anxiety and dissatisfaction with the operation of the statutory code, but pointing out *h* the practical difficulties of allowing a resort to wardship in cases of this kind. Like Lord Wilberforce in *A v Liverpool City Council*, Dunn LJ referred to statistics to show the size of the problem if resort were, in all such cases, to be allowed to the High Court.

Dunn LJ expressed views which, with respect, I entirely indorse ([1984] 1 All ER 21 at 28, [1983] 1 WLR 541 at 557):

'If that course were adopted [i e drawing a distinction between infants in care as a *j* result of misbehaviour of their own, and infants in care as a result of the inadequacy of their parents] an appeal would lie from the domestic court to the Divisional Court of the Family Division instead of to the Crown Court, which is a wholly inappropriate tribunal for this purpose. In a proper case the Divisional Court could direct that the

child should be made a ward of court. The existing procedures undoubtedly give
grounds for a sense of grievance by many parents involved in care proceedings in
the juvenile court but so far, despite judicial urging, Parliament has done nothing
about it. This, I think, is why there are so many applications in wardship, because
the parents feel that they have a fairer and more satisfactory trial in the High Court
than in the juvenile court. But we have to accept the law as it stands and, looking at
the situation as we must, from the point of view of the welfare of the children as
opposed to the rights and feelings of parents, I cannot think it right that the High
Court should interfere with a statutory scheme which, in effect, places the
responsibility for the children's welfare in the hands of local authorities and gives
local authorities what Parliament considers to be adequate powers to safeguard the
children's welfare ... In my view, before the court can exercise its jurisdiction in
wardship, it must be satisfied that such exercise is in the interests of the child and,
in considering that question, the court will, in an appropriate case, consider whether
the child's welfare is likely to be adequately safeguarded under the statutory scheme
or whether, in the particular circumstances of the case, the welfare of the child
requires the exercise of some additional remedy open to the High Court but not
available through the statutory scheme. In order to determine this question it is not
necessary for the court to hear all the evidence.'

Since Re E was decided, amendments to the statutory code restricting a local authority's
right to terminate access to a child in care have come into force. These have, in some
measure, met the points made by Dunn LJ, including a provision for an appeal by the
parent from a decision of the juvenile court directly to the Family Division. A new Pt IA
to the 1980 Act has been inserted under the provisions of s 6 of and Sch 1 to the 1983
Act. Section 12A of the 1980 Act applies the provisions of ss 12B to 12F, inter alia, to 'care
orders'. These sections provide for the service of a notice on the parent, guardian or
custodian, by a local authority who intends either to terminate access or to refuse to grant
access with a right to the parent, guardian or custodian, to apply to the court to challenge
the decision of the local authority, or to vary any access order which has been made.
Section 12G provides for the preparation of a code of practice by the Secretary of State
with regard to access to children in care.

The current code of practice introduced by Local Authority Circular LAC (83)19, dated
16 December 1983, provides, inter alia:

'The Wider Family. 8. Consideration of access should take into account the child's
wider family. The access arrangements should include relatives—siblings, grandparents, putative fathers, for example—with whom contact should be preserved. In
some cases it may be appropriate to identify relatives, who may include a non-
custodial parent, with whom contact has lapsed and to follow up the prospects of re-
establishing contact.'

Counsel for the council submits that, in restricting these rights to parents, guardians
or custodians, Parliament has indicated that they should not be extended to the extended
family. With respect to counsel, his submission may well beg the question whether, in
an exceptional case, there may or may not be a need to supplement the powers of
supervision given by statute, even if there is no obvious lacuna in the statutory code. In
this respect, with considerable diffidence and regret, I find myself in disagreement with
Oliver and Neill LJJ, whose judgments in draft I have had the privilege of reading.

In Re J (a minor) (wardship: jurisdiction) [1984] 1 All ER 29, [1984] 1 WLR 81 it was
held that there was a lacuna in the statutory code which justified the court exercising its
jurisdiction in wardship. In that case, in December 1981, the local authority obtained a
care order in respect of a girl aged eight months pursuant to s 1 of the 1969 Act, and
thereafter held the child in care, reviewing from time to time the position of the child
and the mother. For a little over two months, after taking the infant into care, the
mother was granted access. In March 1982 the local authority exercising their statutory

powers, moved the child to a long-term foster home having decided that successful
rehabilitation with the mother was improbable. Having placed the child with long-term   *a*
foster parents, the local authority decided that access by the mother was not in the child's
best interest and thereafter access ceased. By November 1982 the mother had married
and her circumstances changed dramatically. She had formed a stable relationship and
was to produce a child. During the winter of 1982–83, the mother set about the recovery
of her child. On 8 December 1982 she issued a complaint to the juvenile court for the
discharge of the care order. Realising that a period of rehabilitation would be necessary,   *b*
the mother asked the local authority to give an undertaking to make the infant a ward of
court if the magistrates discharged the care order. The local authority refused to give the
undertaking. The mother issued an originating summons in wardship on 14 March. As
a result of this, the proceedings in the juvenile court were adjourned, and the local
authority applied for directions to the High Court, seeking the de-warding of the child.

    Cumming-Bruce LJ distinguished that case from the case of *Re E* on the basis that the   *c*
juvenile court was able only to discharge the care order, or order its continuation, and
had no supervisory powers in relation to the future conduct of the local authority.
Cumming-Bruce LJ said ([1984] 1 All ER 29 at 33–34, [1984] 1 WLR 81 at 87):

> 'In these proceedings the mother's legal representative asked the local authority's
> solicitor if he would give an undertaking to make the child a ward of court if the
> justices discharged the care order, which shows a very responsible attitude on the   *d*
> part of the mother. The solicitor of the local authority felt unable to commit
> himself, and I know not and make no observation about the merits of the stance
> that he took up. That was the background of the mother herself trying to make the
> child a ward of court because the local authority would not, or at any rate had not
> given any undertaking to do so. The object of the mother's application to ward the
> child was to fill the lacuna in the statute because she could not be confident that the   *e*
> local authority was prepared to do so. Had the local authority felt able to commit
> itself to making the child a ward of court immediately on the contingency of the
> discharge of the care order, the mother would never have applied at all. In these
> circumstances I take the view that had the local authority applied to make the child
> a ward in order to protect the child during the transitional period by enabling the
> wardship judge to exercise power which the juvenile court I would think ought to   *f*
> have, but certainly has not got, such an application by the local authority would be
> exactly the kind of application contemplated by Lord Wilberforce at the end of his
> speech, to fill a gap in the statutory scheme, not in this case a gap in the powers of
> the local authority but a gap in the powers of the juvenile court. If the wardship
> does not continue, there is a real risk that the justices may feel compelled to refuse
> the care order simply because they do not know what is going to happen to the   *g*
> child, but are confident that it would be wrong for the child to be transferred before
> the mother had got to know her. The purpose of the wardship proceedings, as I
> understand it, is to enable the justices to discharge their jurisdiction without the
> inhibition, anxiety and uncertainty flowing from the fact that otherwise they cannot
> know whether the child will be protected on the discharge of the order.'

    Had ss 12A to 12C of the 1980 Act been introduced by the 1983 Act at the material   *h*
time, events in *Re J* might well have been different. Before terminating access early in
1982, the local authority would have been obliged to serve a notice under s 12B(1). The
mother would then have qualified, under s 12C(1), to apply to the juvenile court, who on
the application could have made the order considered to be appropriate. If they had failed
to do this, the mother could have appealed to the Family Division under s 12C(5).   *j*

    At this stage it is probably useful to consider the speeches of *A v Liverpool City Council*
[1981] 2 All ER 385, [1982] AC 363, and the judgments of this court to which I have just
referred, in the context of the statutory provisions currently existing. There have, of
course, come into operation a number of important statutory developments since May
1981 (when the speeches in *A v Liverpool City Council* were delivered), introduced, inter

alia, by s 6 of and Sch 1 to the 1983 Act. One main change seems to be a recognition by
Parliament that the total deprivation of access to a parent is not a matter to be left entirely
to the administrative discretion of the local authority, and is to be distinguished from the
day-to-day management of access, and is made subject to an appeal to the High Court
rather than the Crown Court. With some diffidence, as I have the misfortune to differ in
some respects from the views of Oliver and Neill LJJ, I would suggest the following
general principles on which a judge of the Family Division should approach the exercise
of wardship jurisdiction.

I share the doubt to be expressed by Oliver LJ that the parts of the speech of Lord
Wilberforce which have been cited were intended by their Lordships to be definitions;
but they do provide important guidelines binding on this court. With these qualifications,
these considerations appear to apply. (a) If it appears that the purpose of the application
is merely to effect a review of, or control over, the exercise by a local authority of its
administrative discretion in fields committed exclusively to the local authority by statute,
then the judge should dismiss the application and deward the child without further
inquiry. This was the course taken by Balcombe J in *Re E* [1984] 1 All ER 21, [1984] 1
WLR 541, when the matter was taken quite correctly in the form of a preliminary point.
(b) There are many questions affecting the welfare of a child either in care or proposed to
be taken into care, which have not been left exclusively to the administrative discretion
of the local authority. Generally speaking these involve decisions of greater importance
than those under (a) above, which affect the longer-term management of the child and
even his or her status. These issues range widely from decisions whether the child should
be taken into care, or whether an existing care order should be discharged, or varied, to
decisions whether the child should be adopted against the wishes of the parent or
guardian. In these cases the statutes provide for control by the courts in varying ways and
by various courts, depending on the particular matters in issue.

Without in any way detracting from the admirable way in which social services
departments generally shoulder the immense burden placed on them, the need for
control in these areas is obviously necessary to guard against the rare but possibly
irreversible error which might arise from an idiosyncratic and mistaken decision on the
part of single, or small groups of, social workers acting within the large administrative
structure involved. (c) In cases where Parliament has decreed that there should be
intervention by the courts, then the judge should inquire to see whether, by continuing
the wardship, he will achieve both the intention of the statute and the best interests of
the child, or whether these will be better served by dismissing the application and de-
warding the child. An example will illustrate this point.

On an application in wardship by a mother: when an application under s 1 of the 1969
Act has been initiated by the local authority against the wishes of the mother, if it appears
that all that the mother seeks to do is to challenge the making of the care order or to
obtain a care order under s 7(2) of the Family Law Reform Act 1969, the judge would
probably dismiss the application. The effect of an order under s 7(2) would merely be to
achieve an ongoing supervision over the exercise by the local authority of their
administrative discretion, and would be contrary to the spirit and intention of the statute.
In such a case Parliament has decreed that the matter should be decided by the juvenile
court, with a restricted right of appeal to the Crown Court.

On the other hand, if the purpose of the local authority's application to the juvenile
court under s 1 of the 1969 Act appears to be to prepare for an application to the domestic
court under s 14 of the 1975 Act, without the obligations otherwise imposed on them to
consider returning the child to its family or friends under s 2 of the 1980 Act, then it
would be open to the judge to conclude that the intention of Parliament and the best
interests of the child would be best served by continuing the wardship so that all matters
could be considered in one forum at the same time.

In the case of an application under s 14, Parliament has decreed that the matter should
be dealt with by 'an authorised court', which includes the Family Division of the High
Court, and has further given powers to the magistrates to refuse to deal with a difficult

case if they consider it would be better dealt with in the High Court. There are intermediate situations in which the statute provides that questions are to be decided in the first instance by the magistrates' court, but that these decisions are to be subject to a direct appeal to the Family Division of the High Court. In considering whether or not to continue wardship, the judge should take into account the statutory provisions for supervision by the courts and the particular circumstances of each case before exercising his discretion in deciding on the most expeditious course in the interests of the child. This is what Ewbank J did in the instant case, and in my judgment he was correct to do so.

(d) There will also be exceptional cases in which it appears to the judge that the best interests of the child cannot be achieved within the provisions of the statutory code, and where the wardship jurisdiction is required in the manner envisaged in the speech of Lord Wilberforce. As was emphasised in that speech, these cases must lie outside the field in which Parliament has given to the local authority freedom of administrative decision. Apart from this qualification, it would not be profitable to attempt to categorise the sort of cases envisaged. Their identification must depend on an investigation by the judge of all the circumstances of each case. These will include the declared intention of all the parties involved, and their relationship with the child.

In the instant case, the judge was obviously impressed by the fears expressed by the relatives that their case might never be properly considered unless this was done in wardship. This was a matter on which the judge was, in my judgment, entitled to reach the conclusion he did on the limited evidence before him, and was correct in continuing the wardship until the hearing of the summons, so as to enable further inquiries to be made before finally deciding whether or not to confirm the wardship.

The issues, therefore, which arise in the instant appeal are whether there were any indications which would justify Ewbank J's decision that Sarah's welfare required that the wardship should be continued pending an application under s 14 of the 1975 Act, and that both matters should be considered together in the High Court.

Counsel for the council submitted that once the infant was subject to care proceedings under the 1969 Act, jurisdiction in the council under the statutory code was established, and that the court should not continue wardship so as to interfere with the exercise of that jurisdiction. Counsel relied on the following facts, namely that Sarah had been the subject of a place of safety order, that she was, de facto, in the care of the department and placed with short-term foster parents, that there had been an application under s 1 of the 1969 Act and that an interim care order had been made by the juvenile court.

Counsel for the council submitted that the department had beaten the relatives to the procedural post. He relied on both *A v Liverpool City Council* [1981] 2 All ER 385, [1982] AC 363 and *Re E* [1984] 1 All ER 21, [1983] 1 WLR 541 for the proposition that where Parliament had provided a statutory code, it was not for the court to intervene. This principle has been clearly stated, albeit with just a hint of logistical pragmatism, in the speech of Lord Wilberforce and the judgment of Dunn LJ. In the field where statute has given administrative discretion free from supervision by the court, this proposition is clearly correct. With respect to the submission of counsel for the council that the future welfare of the infant should depend on a jurisdictional race, this is to my mind not logically supportable. If the infant's welfare can be ensured under the administrative discretion granted to the local authority under the statutory code, their powers should not be prejudiced by a pre-emptive application in wardship, as would appear to be the logical result of the submissions of counsel for the council. Whichever process is started first on an application, in the wardship proceedings to de-ward the infant, the result ought to be the same.

Counsel for the council conceded that had the relatives established or were they able in the future to establish that the department had never properly considered and assessed the course proposed by them, namely the possibility of establishing Sarah in the long-term with the uncle and aunt, then they would be able to present a case for judicial review. As members of the extended family compared with strangers, other things being

equal, the relatives would appear at least to have a strong case. Had Sarah been taken into
a care under s 2 of the 1980 Act, there would have been a positive obligation on the
department under s 2(3)(b) to 'endeavour to secure that the care of the child is taken over
... (b) by a relative ...' In any event, the department would be obliged to observe the
principle of audi alteram partem so as to escape an allegation of 'procedural impropriety':
see per Lord Diplock in *Council of Civil Service Unions v Minister for the Civil Service* [1984]
3 All ER 935 at 951, [1984] 3 WLR 1174 at 1196.

b        As I have already said, this issue was not considered by the judge. If he had considered
it and come to the conclusion that the relatives' case had not been properly considered
and was unlikely to be so considered in the future by the department, then rather than
wait for a proven failure to justify judicial review, as I understand the submission of
counsel for the council, he conceded that it would have been open to the judge to
continue the wardship, provided that the standards he applied would be the same as
c those appropriate to an application for a grant of certiorari. Instead, he continued the
wardship in order to review the matter himself.

The statutory code to be considered in the instant case embraces the 1969 Act, the
1975 Act, the 1980 Act and the 1983 Act, not only as regards the provisions dealing with
children in care, but also the provisions for freeing for adoption. In the latter case the
code makes extensive provisions for access to the courts. Under s 14 of the 1975 Act, an
d application may be made to an authorised court. By s 100, the following are authorised
courts: The High Court, relevant county courts and magistrates' courts within whose
area a parent or guardian of the child is.

Under s 101(1) of the 1975 Act (as amended) at the instance of any party to an
application under s 14 made in the county court, the High Court may order the removal
of the application to the High Court; under s 101(2), there is an appeal from the
e magistrates' court to the High Court. Under s 101(3), if the application is made to a
magistrates' court and that court considers that the matter is one which would more
conveniently be dealt with in the High Court, the magistrates' court shall refuse to make
an order, and in that case no appeal to the High Court lies.

Parliament has, in the case of s 14 applications, clearly envisaged that in appropriate
cases the High Court shall become involved, and in so doing has not restricted its inherent
f jurisdiction in this respect.

Section 104 provides:

> 'Saving for powers of High Court. Nothing in this Act shall restrict or affect the
> jurisdiction of the High Court to appoint or remove guardians, or otherwise in
> respect of children.'

g In cases where the statutory code provides for supervision by the High Court by way of
original or appellate jurisdiction, there must be ground for thinking that Parliament did
not intend to exclude wardship jurisdiction where this would prove more expeditious or
in the better interest of the child. Had Parliament intended this, nothing would have
been easier than to have said so.

The relatives have no right of resort to the juvenile or domestic courts to question the
h exercise by the local authority of their functions under the statutory code. They are at
the mercy of the department. It is at least arguable that there is a lacuna in the statutory
code if it is established that it is in the interests of the infant that the possibility of
rehabilitation with her extended family is one which should be guarded by a right to
have the question considered by a court. The attitude of the council in this regard appears
from the affidavit of Mr Lothian sworn on 23 October 1984:

j
> '4 ... (2) It is unlikely that Sarah will receive from her own parents the care and
> love she needs and consequently consideration must be given to find substitute
> parents willing and best able to care for her on a permanent basis ...
> 4(7) The department has been and still is prepared to discuss with the 1st and 2nd
> Plaintiffs their offer of a home for Sarah but the department would be seeking the

family best able to meet her needs. The fact that the 1st and 2nd Plaintiffs are related to Sarah does not necessarily mean they are the best family for her. Further, according to [the father], Sarah has only had limited contact up to now with any of the Plaintiffs.'

Before the judge, and on appeal before us, however, counsel for the council frankly accepted that the department had in mind an application to free Sarah for adoption. It is not clear, however, whether such an application would be postponed to a consideration of establishing a home with the uncle and aunt short of adoption, or whether (as appears from the summary in the report from the social worker, Mrs Anna Murison) the department had already taken the preliminary steps to make an application under s 14, and intend to consider the relatives' claim alongside other prospective adopters, but no more. The judge was clearly concerned that the s 14 proceedings would be initiated without any opportunity to the relatives to be heard, and without at least some trial access to determine whether Sarah would settle down with the uncle and aunt in their family.

In the instant case the position of the relatives is much strengthened by reason of the intended application under s 14 of the 1975 Act. It cannot be denied that an important matter to be considered in deciding Sarah's future is the possibility of her making her home with the uncle and aunt. If the application is made in the domestic court, the only opportunity the relatives have is to persuade the court to make them respondents to the application under r 4(3) of the Magistrates' Courts (Adoption) Rules 1984, SI 1984/611; but this might not be an appropriate course, since they would not necessarily be opposing the application.

By far the more likely course for the magistrates' court to take would be to refuse to make the order under s 101(3) of the 1975 Act. In a complex case of this nature, it is to be hoped that a responsible adoption agency would make the application under s 14 to the High Court in the first place. In this event the High Court would be able to ensure that the relatives would be heard within the s 14 proceedings or, if necessary, cause wardship proceedings to be issued to be heard concurrently with the s 14 proceedings.

The instant case is also unusual because of the attitude of the mother and father, who are positively supporting adoption but appear to be neutral as to whether this should be done within or without their extended family. The attitude of the mother and father results in a lack of adversarial contest before the juvenile court, both in the application under s 1 of the 1969 Act, and subsequently in the domestic court under s 14 of the 1975 Act, if the latter application is to be made to the magistrates' court.

Counsel for the council submitted that the statutory code has committed the total management of the infant to the discretion of the local authority, provided this discretion is properly exercised. This is certainly the case so far as the day-to-day decisions are concerned. However, as I have already said in this judgment, where more fundamental decisions are concerned, the administrative discretionary powers are subject to the overriding supervision of the court. Moreover, in the case of applications under s 14 of the 1975 Act, the statutory code is very far from leaving matters to the unfettered administrative discretion of the local authority, as appears from the statutory provisions already cited in this judgment.

It would appear from the parts of his judgment cited earlier in this judgment that the ratio on which the judge came to the conclusion that this case showed special circumstances which would indicate that the wardship should continue in the interests of the ward, were the complex features of the case, including the unusual position of the natural parents, the importance of considering the opportunity of placing Sarah with her uncle and aunt, and the practical difficulties facing the relatives in bringing their case before any court, unless it be the High Court (or possibly the county court) under s 14 of the 1975 Act or in wardship which, in the way that the judge made his order, amounts very much to the same thing.

In the particular circumstances of this case, namely the absence of any realistic opportunity of a balanced consideration of the best interests of the child taking place, the

judge came to the conclusion that, in order to achieve this, the wardship proceedings
a  should remain on foot, at least until there had been a proper investigation and report by
a welfare officer.

At the same time, by his order (to which I referred at the beginning of this judgment)
the judge made provision for the preliminary steps towards a declaration under s 14 of
the 1975 Act to take place simultaneously with his order committing Sarah into the care
of the council. This could only be done in the High Court and was a course which was
b  demanded by the urgency inherent in Sarah's particular circumstances. After a very
careful review of the position disclosed in the evidence before him, the judge, having
considered the appropriate authorities, came to the conclusion that Sarah's case was
exceptional and in order to ensure her welfare, it was necessary to invoke the inherent
jurisdiction of the court. I cannot say that he erred in principle.

For these reasons I find it impossible to accede to the submissions of counsel for the
c  council that this court should put into reverse those steps provided for in the judge's
order, and accordingly I would dismiss this appeal.

**NEILL LJ.** It is with great diffidence that I feel obliged to take a different view of this
case from that taken by Purchas LJ. In addition I feel anxiety about coming to a different
conclusion from that reached by the experienced judge who heard the matter at first
d  instance and who exercised his discretion to make the child a ward of court after a careful
review of the evidence and the authorities.

I find myself quite unable, however, to regard the present case as one of those
comparatively rare cases where, though a local authority is involved, the court is entitled
to invoke its wardship jurisdiction.

The application which is presently in existence before the juvenile court is an
e  application for a care order under s 1 of the Children and Young Persons Act 1969. For
the purpose of the wardship proceedings, however, it is right to consider not only this
application but also the probability that the local authority will shortly make an
application under s 14 of the Children Act 1975 to free the child for adoption, and that if
such an order is made, adoption proceedings will follow in due course. I must look at the
matter as a whole.

f  Guidance on the difficult relationship between the statutory powers of local authorities
under the 1969 Act and the Child Care Act 1980, on the one hand, and the jurisdiction
of the High Court in wardship, on the other hand, has been provided by the House of
Lords in *A v Liverpool City Council* [1981] 2 All ER 385, [1982] AC 363.

Purchas LJ has already set out the most important passages from the speeches of Lord
Wilberforce and Lord Roskill in that case. He has also referred to the judgments in two
g  subsequent cases in this court: *Re E (minors) (wardship: jurisdiction)* [1984] 1 All ER 21,
[1983] 1 WLR 541 and *Re J (a minor) (wardship: jurisdiction)* [1984] 1 All ER 29, [1984] 1
WLR 81.

It is not necessary for me to repeat these passages again, but before I attempt to state
what appear to me to be the principles which are to be applied in a case such as the
present, I should mention three matters.

h  (a) In *Re E (minors)* the Court of Appeal declined to treat as a lacuna in the statutory
scheme sufficient to justify the assumption of the court's wardship jurisdiction the fact
that the justices had no power where a care order had been made under the 1969 Act to
order that a natural parent should have access to the child. This 'gap' in the scheme was
later filled by legislation: see the new s 12A of the 1980 Act which was inserted by s 6 of
and Sch 1 to the Health and Social Services and Social Security Adjudications Act 1983.

j  (b) In *Re J (a minor)* the Court of Appeal upheld the decision to continue the wardship
despite the objections of the local authority, but in that case the effect of a successful
application by the mother for the discharge of the care order would have meant that
(unless the operation of the discharge had been temporarily suspended which, it seems,
was not suggested) neither the local authority nor the juvenile court would have retained
*any* supervisory powers during a period when the child, who was only two years of age

and who had not seen her mother for a year, would be re-establishing her links with her mother. The mother herself recognised the difficulties of the transitional period and the wardship filled the vacuum which would otherwise have existed.

(c) In *A v Liverpool City Council* [1981] 2 All ER 385 at 392–393, [1982] AC 363 at 378 Lord Roskill suggested that the decision of the Court of Appeal in *Re H (a minor) (wardship: jurisdiction)* [1978] 2 All ER 903, [1978] Fam 65 could be supported on the basis that it was only by the invocation of the wardship jurisdiction that the result could be achieved which was in the best interests of the child, being a result which the local authority and the juvenile court, within the limit of their powers, were unable to achieve. This passage in Lord Roskill's speech seems to me further to underline the fact that the High Court will, in general, only intervene if the facts disclose some gap in the *powers* of the local authority, or the *powers* of the local authority and the juvenile court combined.

I turn next to try to formulate the principles which I believe I should seek to apply in the instant case.

(1) In every case the welfare of the child is the paramount consideration. But it is to be remembered that the local authority in exercising its statutory powers is guided, or should be guided, by the same general principle as the court.

(2) Where a care order has been made under s 1 of the 1969 Act, or the child has been received into care under s 2 of the 1980 Act, the welfare of the child becomes the responsibility of the local authority. Thereafter, subject to the rights of appeal and other safeguards provided as part of the statutory code, it is the local authority which is to be the general arbiter of what is in the interests of the child. In any particular case, the court's perception of what is in the interests of the child may differ from the perception of the local authority but, subject to the exceptions which I shall turn to in (4), it is the view of the local authority which is to prevail. Accordingly, subject to these exceptions, the court will not exercise its wardship jurisdiction in respect of a child in the care of a local authority.

(3) The principles in (2) apply not only where the child is already in care but also where an application for a care order has been made by a local authority: see *Re E (minors)*.

(4) Nevertheless, the power of the High Court to protect any child by the exercise of its wardship jurisdiction is not taken away. But it is a jurisdiction which, in the case of a child in care, is to be invoked with circumspection. Indeed, though future cases may disclose other categories, the modern authorities suggest that the High Court will not exercise any of its powers to safeguard the welfare and interests of a child for whom a local authority has assumed, or is seeking to assume, responsibility unless one or more of the following conditions are satisfied. (a) The evidence discloses that the decision or decisions of the local authority can be challenged on the basis of the principles enunciated in *Associated Provincial Picture Houses Ltd v Wednesbury Corp* [1947] 2 All ER 680, [1948] 1 KB 223, or by way of judicial review in accordance with RSC Ord 53. (b) The evidence discloses that a certain course of action should be taken or a certain result achieved in the interests of the child, but the local authority, whether alone or in conjunction with the lower court, has no *power* or no sufficient *power* to take that action or to achieve that result. In such a case the High Court can intervene to supplement the powers of the local authority, and indeed the local authority itself may invite the assistance of the court. (c) The evidence discloses something exceptional which requires the intervention of the High Court. I have included this residual category in deference to the views of Baker P as expressed in *M v Humberside CC* [1979] 2 All ER 744 at 751, [1979] Fam 114 at 123 and repeated by him in *Re J (a minor)* [1984] 1 All ER 29 at 34, [1984] 1 WLR 81 at 87–88. I venture to think, however, that if full effect is to be given to the speeches in *A v Liverpool City Council* this residual category should be confined to the really unusual case where the interests of the child make the court's intervention imperative.

(5) The court should take account of the fact that it is now over 35 years since the Children Act 1948 was enacted. As Lord Roskill pointed out in *A v Liverpool City Council* [1981] 2 All ER 385 at 391–392, [1982] AC 363 at 377, it is the plain intention of the

**a** legislation passed since 1948 to secure the continued expansion of the statutory control by local authorities of child welfare. Moreover, the volume of this legislation and the number of amending provisions cover so much ground that in my view a court should exercise great care before coming to the conclusion that a feature which the court may regard as a flaw in the legislation is in fact an omission or lacuna sufficient to justify the invocation of the wardship jurisdiction.

**b** I come now to the facts of the instant case. As Purchas LJ pointed out, the judge made no adverse findings against the local authority in his judgment. Accordingly we are not dealing with a case which might fall within the *Wednesbury* principles or be a candidate for judicial review. As I see it, the question for our consideration is whether the High Court should intervene in the interests of the child, either because a gap has been revealed in the statutory scheme, or because on the exceptional facts the intervention of the court is otherwise imperative.

**c** In support of the case that the child should be made and should remain a ward of court, great attention has been directed to the fact that the natural parents are content to play a passive role. Accordingly, it is said, the juvenile court is not going to have the benefit of argument on the merits of the possibility of the child going into the care and control of the uncle and aunt, or on the question whether the parents (and in particular the mother) are in a state of mind to appreciate the importance of the decision involved

**d** in giving their consent to a freeing for adoption order.

Speaking for myself, I see great force in the contention that where the parents of a child are themselves unwilling or unable to care for him, members of the extended or wider family, if willing to help, are often in a unique position to help with his care and upbringing. Indeed it could be argued that it would be desirable that members of the wider family should be given a statutory right to be heard in proceedings involving

**e** infant children to whom they are closely related. But that is not the position under the existing legislation. In cases which fall within the 1969 or the 1980 Acts, the statutory scheme places the responsibility for the welfare of children on local authorities.

It is to be noted that s 2(3) of the 1980 Act refers to a child being placed in the care of 'a relative or friend of his', and that para 8 of the current code of practice (see LAC (83)19 dated 16 December 1983) provides that 'consideration of access should take into account

**f** the child's wider family'.

But these provisions are directed to the exercise by the local authority of *its* discretion, and in no way derogate from the principle that it is the local authority which has the responsibility, under the statutory scheme, to make the decisions relating to the welfare of the child.

The question then arises whether there is any gap or lacuna in the statutory scheme

**g** which prevents or inhibits the local authority from considering the importance or suitability of the wider family, either in relation to the care of or access to the child, or in relation to adoption. Assuming, as I do, that the local authority is prepared to exercise its powers properly, I can find no gap in its powers. Moreover, it is to be observed that Parliament has made provision for specific machinery to try to ensure that the consent of parents to an adoption is given freely and after due consideration.

**h** Accordingly, though I can well understand the motives which have led the relatives to make an application for wardship, I am quite unable to find any gap in the statutory scheme or in the powers in the local authority which require the intervention of the High Court.

Nor, with all due respect to those who take a different view, can I regard the facts of this case as so exceptional that such intervention can be justified on some wider principle.

**j** Lord Wilberforce and Dunn LJ have drawn attention to the numbers of children in care throughout the country. I am not prepared to assume, without clear evidence, that there are not many cases, perhaps thousands of cases, where the parents do not oppose a care order but where members of the wider family would wish to urge some different solution for the child's future from that proposed by the local authority.

For these reasons I am satisfied that this is not a case where the court should intervene by exercising its wardship jurisdiction.

In my judgment the judge erred in principle in exercising his discretion to continue the wardship. I would allow the appeal.

**OLIVER LJ.** I too have the misfortune to have arrived at a different conclusion from that reached by Purchas LJ. I have had the opportunity of reading the judgment delivered by Neill LJ, and agree that the appeal should be allowed for the reasons which he gives. I add some words of my own only because of the importance of the case.

The general principles on which the High Court should proceed in exercising its inherent jurisdiction in wardship cases where a local authority has obtained, or is in process of applying for, a care order are not in doubt. They were laid down by their Lordships' House in *A v Liverpool City Council* [1981] 2 All ER 385, [1982] AC 363, and reiterated by this court in *Re E (minors) (wardship: jurisdiction)* [1984] 1 All ER 21, [1983] 1 WLR 541. But this is an unusual case, and the difficulty lies in the application of those principles in the peculiar circumstances with which the court is confronted here. It is clear from *A v Liverpool City Council* that the High Court has no general power to review decisions of the local authority within the framework of the statutory scheme for the care of minors which Parliament has established.

The position was succinctly expressed by Lord Wilberforce in these words ([1981] 2 All ER 385 at 388–389, [1982] AC 363 at 373):

'The court's general inherent power is always available to fill gaps or to supplement the powers of the local authority; what it will not do (except by way of judicial review where appropriate) is to supervise the exercise of discretion within the field committed by statute to the local authority.'

I doubt, however, whether this can have been intended by their Lordships as a definition, for Lord Roskill (with whom Lord Fraser and Lord Keith agreed, as they did with Lord Wilberforce) observed ([1981] 2 All ER 385 at 393, [1982] AC 363 at 379):

'. . . the wardship jurisdiction of the court is never extinguished merely because the child is in the care of a local authority. Its exercise must, however, be closely circumscribed. I do not think that any useful purpose would be served by your Lordships attempting to define the limits within which that circumscription must exist, for cases of this class vary infinitely. Clearly the jurisdiction can be invoked by a local authority when its own powers are inadequate to make the welfare of the child paramount or when it is necessary to this end to take action against some stranger. But the courts must not, in purported exercise of wardship jurisdiction, interfere with those matters which Parliament has decided are within the province of a local authority to whom the care and control of a child has been entrusted pursuant to statutory provisions.'

Now it is quite clear that in the passages to which I have referred, their Lordships were pointing to particular circumstances in which the wardship jurisdiction could and could not properly be invoked. It must not be invoked for the purpose of challenging or exercising supervision over those discretions which, by statute, are given to the local authority. It may properly be invoked by the local authority itself to supplement its statutory powers. But I cannot read these passages as intended either to lay down a rule that, once the statutory procedure has been invoked, the only person who can ever be permitted to invoke the court's inherent power is the local authority itself (which seemed to be the direction in which the argument of counsel for the council was tending) or to suggest that because the invocation of the inherent power necessarily puts the court in the position of supervising decisions otherwise by statute left to the local authority, that is necessarily a fatal objection to the continued exercise of the jurisdiction if it is properly invoked for some other and legitimate purpose.

The matter is put thus in the judgment of Dunn LJ in *Re E* [1984] 1 All ER 21 at 28, [1983] 1 WLR 541 at 557:

a

'In my view, before the court can exercise its jurisdiction in wardship, it must be satisfied that such exercise is in the interests of the child and, in considering that question, the court will, in an appropriate case, consider whether the child's welfare is likely to be adequately safeguarded under the statutory scheme or whether, in the particular circumstances of the case, the welfare of the child requires the exercise of some additional remedy open to the High Court but not available through the statutory scheme.'

b

In whatever terms the principles are expressed, however, the authorities concur in indicating that once care has been assumed by a local authority under the statutory scheme, the jurisdiction should be invoked only where it is required to supply some lacuna in the scheme, some gap which the welfare of the child demands should be made good.

c

The question raised by the present appeal is whether, in the very unusual circumstances of this case, the judge was filling such a lacuna, or whether in fact he was seeking to supervise those discretions which, by statute, are vested in the appellants.

I do not propose to rehearse again the facts of the case before the court, which have been fully set out in the judgment of Purchas LJ, but one cannot help being struck at the outset by two curious features. In the first place, the case is one in which, from first to last, there has never been any contest between the parents of this little girl and the local authority, and where in fact the end result which the local authority is now seeking to achieve, and which, it seems, the parents have all along been willing, if not anxious, to embrace, that is to say, her ultimate adoption, is a result which could have been achieved without the local authority being involved at all and with the willing assistance of the relatives with whom, unhappily, the authority appears now to be at issue.

d

e

The second unusual feature is that, despite the existence of a body of close, respectable and affectionate relatives, no attempt has been made to involve or even to inform them of what was proposed for Sarah's future until the decision had been taken to set in train the steps leading to her adoption.

In the course of the hearing I asked counsel for the council whether, as a matter of ordinary practice and common sense, a local authority invested with the case of a child of this age and with close relatives in the vicinity, would not, as a first avenue, seek to explore the possibility of invoking the assistance of the extended family. He was able to give an affirmative answer to this, but to explain, on instructions, that this elementary step had not been taken in the instant case because the parents, being sensitive to what other members of their family might think of them, had requested that they be not informed.

f

g

The consequent failure to pursue the matter with interested relatives is, I can see, readily intelligible in these circumstances, for so long as the local authority was seeking to rehabilitate Sarah with her parents, it was obviously important that their confidence should not be forfeited by informing the family against their wishes. Factually, however, it has meant that it is only at a very late stage that the plaintiffs have had an opportunity even of seeking to express a view about whether all her existing family ties should be severed. I have said that this is a curious feature, and it is so, not solely because of the unusual circumstances, but because it highlights the anomalous distinction between the two sets of statutory powers under the 1969 Act and the 1980 Act respectively.

h

I entirely agree with Purchas LJ that it would be absurd if the result of this case were made to depend on the accident of who went to court first, but it seems almost equally absurd that the existence of a duty to attempt to rehabilitate a child in care with his or her relations should depend on whether the authority elects to proceed to obtain a care order under s 1 of the Children and Young Persons Act 1969 or to receive the child into care under s 2 of the Child Care Act 1980. Had the latter course been taken in the instant case, the council would have been under a specific statutory duty at least to consider rehabilitating Sarah with her extended family before setting in train the procedure for freeing her for adoption.

j

That said, however, it is, I think, of only historical relevance in the instant case, in that it serves further to explain how it came about that the decision to apply to free Sarah for adoption was taken without any consultation with the plaintiffs, or any other members of the family, apart from her parents. *a*

Parliament has deliberately provided these two parallel methods of proceedings and this circumstance does not, in itself, point to a lacuna which requires to be filled by the court.

It is, however, plain from Mr Lothian's affidavit, that the decision to move for adoption had been taken even before the making of the interim care order, and, if there is a feature *b* of the instant case which is capable of distinguishing it from, for instance, *Re E*, it can I think be only this. Once the child is in care, the local authority is, of course, statutorily in the position of the parent. It operates under the statutory discretions which are not subject to the supervision of the High Court, and as long as matters stand thus, its decisions as regards care, access and so on, are not open to challenge except by way of judicial review, and it is not contended that, at the moment, any circumstances exist in *c* the instant case justifying such a review.

Once, however, the decision is made to apply to an authorised court under s 14 of the Children Act 1975 to free the child for adoption, the argument is that the authority is moving into a sphere where the statute itself provides for the court to become involved. The court is, of course, not necessarily the High Court. It may be, and in the present case but for the wardship summons would have been, the domestic bench of the magistrates' *d* court. It may be the county court. But it could be the High Court, which is equally an 'authorised court' for the purposes of s 14.

If, therefore, so the argument runs, the statutory code is one which is in any event going to involve a supervisory role in the court at the stage of making the order freeing the child for adoption, and if the matter is (as it is) one in which the High Court has jurisdiction, it is at least permissible to invoke that supervisory jurisdiction at the stage *e* where the decision has been taken, instead of waiting until the moment when the substantive application is actually made.

The difficulty that I feel about this is that the supervisory role of the court in an application under s 14 is of the most limited order. The court has only to satisfy itself that the parent or guardian understands what is involved, and agrees to the making of an adoption order, or that his agreement can be dispensed with on one or other of the *f* statutory grounds. Once that is accomplished, the section provides that the court *shall* make the order declaring the child free, although this is subject to the general duty in s 3 to promote the welfare of the child.

There is, of course, a provision in s 104 to the effect that the 1975 Act does not restrict or affect the jurisdiction of the High Court in respect of children, but that does not, in my judgment, assist here. That jurisdiction still has to be exercised in accordance with *g* the principles now laid down in *A v Liverpool City Council*.

The invocation of the wardship jurisdiction cannot, therefore, in any sense be treated as if it were a mere anticipation of a role which the court is later to assume in any event. It is in fact just the reverse, for the object is not to ensure that the relatives are represented on the application to free Sarah for adoption, where any representations on their part must be largely irrelevant, but to seek to impose a supervision either on the discretion of *h* the local authority to apply for such an order at all, or on the conduct of the authority as the statutory parent after such an order has been made.

That this is so is, I think, plain from the evidence which the relatives filed in support of the summons. When one looks at that evidence as a whole, it becomes clear that there were three motivating factors behind the summons. First, the relatives and the other members of the family were shocked and surprised when they found out about the *j* interim care order, and incensed that they were being refused access to Sarah and kept in the dark about her whereabouts. Their initial purpose was, therefore, to obtain access and to obtain an order committing care and control to the first and second plaintiffs.

Second, they challenged the appropriateness of an adoption order at all, their view being that the parents' decision had been made under stress and that, given time and a

a

release from the day-to-day burden of looking after Sarah, they would be prepared to consider the possibility of receiving her back into her immediate family.

Third, they wished (on the assumption that, contrary to their view, adoption was considered as the right solution) to propose themselves as the obvious front runners as prospective adopters.

b

As regards the first and the third of these objectives, I find inescapable the conclusion that what the summons was seeking to do was to remove to the court those parental decisions which are, by statute, entrusted to the authority having the care of the child. The same, it seems to me, goes for the second, save for one matter to which I will refer in a moment. Whether the right course for the welfare of the child is short-term fostering, long-term fostering or moving towards adoption is, as it seems to me, pre-eminently a question falling within the ambit of the discretion conferred on the authority, and the authority alone, under the statutory scheme. For better or for worse the only check which the legislature has thought fit to impose on the process is that of either obtaining consent from the parents, or satisfying the court that the case is one where the consent of the parents can be dispensed with.

c

The one matter, as it seems to me, which does not come under the heading of day-to-day discretion, is the question which the plaintiffs raised by their evidence whether there was really, in any true sense, parental consent in this case.

d

Sarah's mother had a considerable history of depressive illness which had prompted her to attempt suicide. She had in fact attempted to kill herself in May 1984, only three months before the making of the interim care order. In October 1984, when the psychiatrist saw her, she was 'suffering from a moderately severe depressive illness', and was only 'beginning to manage all right'. The decision to move for adoption had been taken in September 1984.

e

The relatives did not accept the psychiatrist's view that she was fit to make a reasoned and responsible decision about her daughter's future. They also felt convinced that the father's consent was not freely given in any real sense, but was dictated by the need to placate his wife and keep his marriage from foundering. His own evidence was that 'my wife and I do not feel competent because of our obvious bias to be involved in deciding where Sarah lives or who she visits', and that 'my wife and I are too biased to be able to make the right decision about Sarah's placement'.

f

The relatives complained that they had not been able to obtain the views of the mother's general practitioner, and that their information about the circumstances in which consent to adoption was given emanated from Mr Lothian, for whom they clearly entertain some distrust.

g

It was this aspect of the matter which seems particularly to have impressed the judge and which as I read his judgment, played a key part in his decision. He said:

'The uncle and aunt point out that the agreement has to be freely given with a full understanding of what is involved, and they ask whether the court could come to a proper decision on that aspect, without at least allowing a contrary view to be put forward. The uncle and aunt point out, as is the case, that relations have no right to be heard in care proceedings.'

h

Then a little later he postulated the question:

'. . . since the local authority will otherwise have an unopposed application for a care order before the magistrates, how can it be said that the welfare of the child is going to be given the importance that it should have?'

j

The plaintiffs, he said, were simply—

'. . . asking that their case should be heard and the court should be satisfied that the proposal for freeing the child for adoption is in the interests of the child and that the consent to the freeing for adoption is freely given by the mother in particular, and by the father.'

It was that, as I read his judgment, which finally drove the judge to conclude that the case was an exceptional one, justifying the continuation of the wardship.

Now although I see the force of this, the fact is that Parliament has not, and presumably deliberately has not, seen fit to provide for the representation of persons other than parents on the making of care orders. It may be that that is a defect in the legislation, but I do not think that it can properly be described as a lacuna. Indeed, the judge himself quoted this passage from the judgment of Lane J in *Re B (a minor) (wardship: child in care)* [1974] 3 All ER 915 at 920, [1975] Fam 36 at 42):

'. . . if a court will not interfere with a local authority's care of a child at the behest of a parent, it is even less likely to do so on behalf of a grandparent, even though the one has, and the other has not, a means other than by way of a wardship order, of seeking to obtain the care of a child.'

Whether, then, the judge's decision can be upheld comes down in the end, in my judgment, to the narrow point of whether, having regard to the intended application under s 14 of the 1975 Act, such representation is necessary in order to secure that the interests of the child are properly protected before the court, whether it be a bench of magistrates or the High Court, and to ensure that the question of whether consent is given freely and with full understanding is properly investigated.

But in fact both these matters have been thought of and provided for in the statutory scheme itself. Section 20 of the 1975 Act provides in terms for the appointment of an independent guardian ad litem to safeguard the interests of the child, and of an independent reporting officer to provide the court with satisfactory evidence that consent is given freely and with full understanding.

If there is a serious issue about the validity of the parents' consents, there is, as it seems to me, no reason why the relatives should not bring to the notice of the reporting officer any views which they may have on the subject, but I find difficulty in seeing how it can be said that the absence of any provision for attendance or representation at the hearing of persons desirous of challenging the consents constitutes a lacuna in the scheme, which requires the intervention of the High Court in the exercise of its inherent jurisdiction.

In my judgment, therefore, the judge ought not, consistently with the principles laid down by their Lordships in *A v Liverpool City Council*, to have ordered the wardship to continue, and the appeal must be allowed.

I confess that this is a conclusion to which I have been driven with some reluctance, for I well understand the wisdom and good sense which impelled the judge to take the course that he did. The duties and powers in relation to children which Parliament has imposed and conferred on local authorities (and frequently that means the individual social worker as the only person having personal knowledge of the child) are enormously wide-ranging. In a case where the parents themselves have expressed and demonstrated indifference, the importance of the views of those other persons with whom the child is connected by bonds both of affection and kinship receiving a careful and unprejudiced consideration is, I should have thought, obvious. There is no reason to believe that they will not receive it, but the unhappy differences which have evidently arisen between the council and the plaintiffs, for which I do not attempt to allocate responsibility, understandably create an anxiety in the plaintiffs' minds.

For my part, however, I feel compelled by authority to hold that no ground has been demonstrated on which the statutory discretion of the council can properly be subjected to the supervision of the court.

*Appeal allowed. Leave to appeal to the House of Lords granted.*

Solicitors: *Curwen Carter & Evans*, Hoddesdon (for the relatives); *W J Church*, Hertford (for the council).

Diana Procter   Barrister.

# R v Moloney

*a*

HOUSE OF LORDS

LORD HAILSHAM OF ST MARYLEBONE LC, LORD FRASER OF TULLYBELTON, LORD EDMUND-DAVIES,
LORD KEITH OF KINKEL AND LORD BRIDGE OF HARWICH

28, 29 JANUARY, 21 MARCH 1985

*b* *Criminal law – Murder – Intent – Intent distinguished from foresight of consequences – Intention to kill or cause really serious injury – What prosecution must prove to establish intention to murder.*

*Criminal law – Intention – Crimes of specific intent – Foresight of consequences – Relevance of foresight of consequences – Appropriate direction to be given to jury.*

*c*

The mental element in murder consists of an intention to kill or cause really serious injury, and not merely foresight that death or serious injury will be a probable consequence of the accused's voluntary act. Accordingly, when prosecuting a charge of murder, or any crime of specific intent, the Crown cannot prove intention merely by showing either (i) that the accused desired a certain consequence to happen, whether or *d* not he foresaw that it would probably happen, or (ii) that he foresaw that it would probably happen, whether he desired it or not (see p 1026 e and j to p 1027 a and f to j, p 1032 j, p 1036 j and p 1038 c d, post); R v Vickers [1957] 2 All ER 741, DPP v Smith [1960] 3 All ER 161 and Hyam v DPP [1974] 2 All ER 41 considered.

Knowledge or foresight of consequences is at best material from which the jury, properly directed, may infer intention when considering a crime of specific intent. The *e* trial judge should normally avoid any elaboration or paraphrase of what is meant by intent (except where he considers it necessary to explain that it is quite distinct from motive or desire) and should leave to the jury's good sense the question whether the accused acted with the necessary intent. In the few cases where it is necessary to direct the jury by reference to the foresight of consequences, the judge should do no more than *f* invite the jury to consider (i) whether the relevant consequence which must be proved (eg death or really serious injury in murder) was a natural consequence of the accused's voluntary act and (ii) whether the accused foresaw that it would be a natural consequence of his act, and then direct the jury that, if so, it is proper for them to draw the inference that the accused intended that consequence (see p 1026 e, p 1027 f to j, p 1032 j, p 1036 j to p 1037 d, p 1038 h j and p 1039 e f, post); dicta of Lord Goddard CJ in R v Steane [1947] 1 All ER at 816 and of Lord Hailsham in Hyam v DPP [1974] 2 All ER at 43 applied.

*g*

**Notes**

For the mental element of murder and other crimes of specific intent, see 11 Halsbury's Laws (4th edn) paras 15–16, 360, 1157, and for cases on the subject, see 15 Digest (Reissue) 1109–1111, 9313–9338.

*h* **Cases referred to in opinions**

*Cunliffe v Goodman* [1950] 1 All ER 720, [1950] 2 KB 273, CA.
*DPP v Smith* [1960] 3 All ER 161, [1961] AC 290, [1960] 3 WLR 546, HL.
*Hyam v DPP* [1974] 2 All ER 41, [1975] AC 55, [1974] 2 WLR 607, HL; *affg* [1973] 3 All ER 842, [1974] QB 99, [1973] 3 WLR 475, CA.
*Leung Kam-kwok v R* (17 December 1984, unreported), PC.
*j* *R v Beer* (1976) 63 Cr App R 222, CA.
*R v Belfon* [1976] 3 All ER 46, [1976] 1 WLR 741, CA.
*R v Cunningham* [1981] 2 All ER 863, [1982] AC 566, [1981] 3 WLR 223, HL.
*R v Lawrence* [1981] 1 All ER 974, [1982] AC 510, [1981] 2 WLR 524, HL.
*R v Steane* [1947] 1 All ER 813, [1947] KB 997, CCA.
*R v Vickers* [1957] 2 All ER 741, [1957] 2 QB 664, [1957] 3 WLR 326, CCA.

*Southern Portland Cement Ltd v Cooper* [1974] 1 All ER 87, [1974] AC 623, [1974] 2 WLR 152, PC.
*Woolmington v DPP* [1935] AC 462, [1935] All ER Rep 1, HL.

**Appeal**
Alistair Baden Roy Moloney appealed with leave of the Appeal Committee of the House of Lords granted on 25 July 1984 against the decision of the Court of Appeal, Criminal Division (May LJ, Boreham and Nolan JJ) on 16 December 1983 dismissing his appeal against his conviction on 17 September 1982 in the Crown Court at Birmingham before Stephen Brown J and a jury of the offence of murder, for which he was sentenced to life imprisonment. On 7 June 1984 the Court of Appeal, Criminal Division refused the appellant leave to appeal to the House of Lords but certified, under s 33(2) of the Criminal Appeal Act 1968, that a point of law of general public importance (set out at p 1029 *h j*, post) was involved in the decision to dismiss the appeal. The facts are set out in the opinion of Lord Bridge.

*Louis Blom-Cooper QC* and *Rupert Massey* for the appellant.
*Desmond Perrett QC* and *Jonathan Woods* for the Crown.

Their Lordships took time for consideration.

21 March. The following opinions were delivered.

**LORD HAILSHAM OF ST MARYLEBONE LC.** My Lords, for the reasons which appear in the speech about to be delivered by my noble and learned friend Lord Bridge, which I have had the privilege of reading in draft and with which I agree, the disposal of this case cannot be in doubt. The appeal must be allowed. The verdict of murder must be set aside. A verdict of manslaughter must be substituted. The case must be remitted to the Court of Appeal, Criminal Division to determine the appropriate sentence. The case must be listed for hearing at the earliest possible date. The appellant has been in custody since November 1981, since the date of his conviction on a life sentence for murder, which, on any view, must be treated as unsafe and unsatisfactory.

I agree with my noble and learned friend that the certified question must be answered in the negative owing to the presence of para (b) in the question as certified, and I agree with the reasons which have lead my noble and learned friend to that conclusion.

I do, however, feel constrained to add the sense of deep distress I feel at the course which this unhappy and cautionary tale has taken in order to reach your Lordships' House. It has only come here by leave of your Lordships. That leave could not have been given had the Court of Appeal not certified a point of law of general public importance to have been involved.

Strictly speaking that question, though now, I hope, about to be satisfactorily answered, did not arise. It did not arise because, as my noble and learned friend has demonstrated, the verdict was already unsafe and unsatisfactory for a simpler and more fundamental reason. On a true analysis of the evidence, the real defence was never properly left to the jury with an appropriate *Woolmington* direction (see *Woolmington v DPP* [1935] AC 462, [1935] All ER Rep 1).

This gives rise to all the more concern because the committing justices, men and women unqualified in the law, had already come to the conclusion that, on a true analysis of the facts, only a committal for manslaughter and not murder was justified, and, on arraignment, the appellant had given the prosecution and the court yet another opportunity to analyse the matter correctly by tendering a plea of guilty to manslaughter which, it seems, was not acceptable, and in any event not accepted.

I do not wish to qualify in any way what my noble and learned friend is about to say in answer to the certified question. It had already been pointed out by Wien J in *R v Belfon* [1976] 3 All ER 46 at 51–52, [1976] 1 WLR 741 at 747 that it is not foresight but intention which constitutes the mental element in murder, and the undesirability of

elaborating unnecessarily on the meaning of intention in all but exceptional cases had
*a* already been emphasised by Lawton LJ in *R v Beer* (1976) 63 Cr App R 222 at 225. In the
same place Lawton LJ had also emphasised the very unusual nature of the facts in *Hyam
v DPP* [1974] 2 All ER 41, [1975] AC 55, to which I had ventured to draw the attention
of the House (see [1974] 2 All ER 41 at 55–56, [1975] AC 55 at 78). At this point I feel
that I should insert a word of personal explanation. The innocent victims who perished
in the fire caused by Mrs Hyam were not the target of the appellant's malice, which was
*b* solely directed, or to use Viscount Kilmuir LC's phrase 'aimed', at her rival in love who
was asleep upstairs and who, with a small boy, was, in the event, unharmed. It was for
this reason that I made reference to Viscount Kilmuir's speech in *DPP v Smith* [1960] 3
All ER 161 at 167, [1961] AC 290 at 327. Further, the intention of the appellant in *Hyam
v DPP* was made apparent by two separate sets of facts (see [1974] 2 All ER 41 at 55–56,
[1975] AC 55 at 78). These were (1) that, prior to setting in train her criminal plan, Mrs
*c* Hyam first ascertained that her former lover was not in the house and therefore safe, thus
making it plain that her intention was to expose those who were in the house to danger
to their lives, and (2) that she took elaborate precautions to make sure that her actions did
not awake the sleepers in the house, thus making it doubly clear that her intention was
to expose them to whatever danger would be involved in the fire. I certainly did not
intend by my observations to fall either into the trap exposed in this case by my noble
*d* and learned friend of opening up a charge of murder in 'motor manslaughter' cases
which are the result of criminal negligence or recklessness and not intention, or to excuse
the hypothetical terrorist in my noble and learned friend's bomb disposal case whose
intention may well prove to have been obvious. However, as I am content to accept my
noble and learned friend's formulation in the present appeal, these observations are now,
I suppose, of purely historical interest. I do not think I fell into either error. But, if I did,
*e* I would clearly have been wrong.
    In the end justice in this case will have been done, but, in my view, at the end of an
unduly long and circuitous route. It would have been done at the trial if the court and
the prosecution had followed the very sensible course taken by the committing justices,
or accepted the very proper plea tendered on behalf of the defence. It would have been
done on appeal had the court analysed correctly the true nature of the defence emerging
*f* from the evidence and noticed the fact that it had not been properly put to the jury. I
conclude with the pious hope that your Lordships will not again have to decide that
foresight and foreseeability are not the same thing as intention although either may give
rise to an irresistible inference of such, and that matters which are essentially to be treated
as matters of inference for a jury as to a subjective state of mind will not once again be
erected into a legal presumption. They should remain what they always should have
*g* been, part of the law of evidence and inference to be left to the jury after a proper
direction as to their weight, and not part of the substantive law.

**LORD FRASER OF TULLYBELTON.** My Lords, I have had the advantage of
reading in draft the speech of my noble and learned friend Lord Bridge. I agree with it
and for the reasons given by him I would allow the appeal and make the other orders
*h* which he suggests.

**LORD EDMUND-DAVIES.** My Lords, I have had a like advantage, and I too would
allow the appeal and make the orders indicated in the speech of my noble and learned
friend Lord Bridge, with which I am in respectful and total agreement.

*j* **LORD KEITH OF KINKEL.** My Lords, I have had the benefit of reading in draft the
speech of my noble and learned friend Lord Bridge. I agree with it, and for the reasons
he gives I too would allow the appeal.

**LORD BRIDGE OF HARWICH.** My Lords, in the early hours of 22 November 1981
the appellant fired a single cartridge from a 12-bore shotgun. The full blast of the shot
struck the appellant's stepfather, Patrick Moloney, in the side of the face at a range of

about six feet and killed him instantly. According to the police surgeon, who was on the scene within an hour of the shooting, the whole of the skull had in fact been destroyed, leaving just the root of the neck.

Behind this shocking event lies a tragic story. In November 1981 the appellant was aged 22. He was a serving soldier in the Gordon Highlanders, and was at the material time on leave at the home of his mother and stepfather, having returned from duty in Belize in South America. He had been in the army since November 1978 and had served in Northern Ireland, in this country and finally in South America.

There is no doubt that the appellant was one of a united, happy family. His mother had married the victim, Patrick Moloney, when the appellant was a very small boy. The appellant, at some stage, changed his name to Moloney. To all intents and purposes Patrick Moloney acted as a father to the appellant and was treated by the appellant as such. The undisputed evidence at the appellant's trial was that the stepfather and stepson enjoyed a happy and loving relationship with each other.

On 21 November 1981 there was a dinner party at the home of Mr and Mrs Moloney to celebrate the ruby wedding anniversary of Mrs Moloney's father and mother, the appellant's maternal grandparents. The party was a convivial one. Drink flowed freely. Both Patrick Moloney and the appellant drank a great deal of wine and spirits. By 1 am on 22 November all the members of the family had retired to bed except the appellant and his stepfather. They were heard downstairs laughing and talking in an apparently friendly way.

Shortly before 4 am on 22 November the grandfather was awakened by the sound of a shot. He immediately came downstairs and found the appellant already on the telephone to the police station. The appellant said to the police officer who answered his call: 'I've just murdered my father.' He gave the address of the Moloney home.

Two police patrol officers arrived on the scene at 4.09 am. The appellant's breath smelt strongly of alcohol, his eyes were bloodshot and he was unsteady on his feet, but his manner was calm and collected.

The police officers looked into the room where the shooting had taken place and saw the body of the deceased in an armchair by the fireplace. There was a double-barrelled shotgun positioned between the dead man's knees; it was broken and pointing down towards the floor. The barrels appeared to be unloaded. It is appropriate to add at this point that later investigation revealed that the deceased had a live cartridge on his knee. A second shotgun, obviously that from which the fatal shot had been fired, was lying on the couch on the opposite side of the room.

The appellant was taken to the police station. At about 4.30 am he was in the detention room in the company of one of the police patrol officers, a Pc Dighton, not a CID officer. According to Pc Dighton, at about this time, the appellant made two oral statements which were to play some significant part in his trial. At first he said: 'I didn't want to kill him. It was kill or be killed. I loved him, I adored him.' A little later, he said:

> 'It all started because I wanted to leave the army. I went and got the guns and took the cartridges out of the cupboard. We both started to load the guns. I was quicker than him. He's got a bad arm; I should have realised. I loaded the gun before him and pointed it to him. I said: "You've lost." He said: "You wouldn't dare pull the trigger." I did and he's dead. If I hadn't, he would have done and he would have been sitting here instead of me.'

It is right to emphasise that neither of these statements was in writing. A note purporting to record his recollection of what had been said was made by Pc Dighton some time after the event. As will be seen, these two very brief statements by no means accorded with the full account which the appellant shortly afterwards gave to two detective officers in a form which was recorded and signed by him.

At 5.45 am the appellant was examined by a doctor. His breath smelt strongly of alcohol and his tongue was dry and furred. His co-ordination was poor; he had difficulty in unbuttoning his shirt, and he tended to sway on his feet and to walk with an unsteady gait. At 5.50 am the doctor took a sample of blood from the appellant. This revealed on

later analysis that the proportion of alcohol in the blood at that time was 157 mg of
a  alcohol per 100 ml of blood, ie almost twice the permitted limit of alcohol in the blood
above which it becomes an offence to drive a motor vehicle.

Following his examination by the doctor, the appellant was interviewed by the acting
detective chief superintendent, Superintendent Cole, and Det Sgt Fletcher. Sergeant
Fletcher made a full written record of this interview which the appellant in due course
signed as correct. It is in the course of this record that one reads the appellant's full
b  account of the tragic events at his family home on the morning of 22 November. He has,
in all essentials, adhered to that account ever since. The material part of the statement
reads as follows:

'It started with a dinner party which was thrown for my grandparents' fortieth
wedding anniversary. Towards the end, we all had a lot to drink and our guests had
left and I told me Dad I wanted to leave the army. He disagreed with me and started
c  to outline his reasons for disagreeing with me. It was obviously set for being a long
discussion so my mother, my sister and grandparents went to bed. We had a couple
more drinks while the discussion went on and I was very drunk, and I suspect he
was as well. At this point I have to become vague because the conversation came
round to personal prowess and in particular with a shotgun. Me Dad claimed that
he could not only outshoot me but outload me, outdraw me, i.e. he was faster than
d  me, and claimed even with a crippled left arm he was still faster than me. I disagreed
with him and said: "Don't be silly" or words to that effect. In fact we were swearing
at each other at this time. So he said: "We'll prove it. Go and get two of the
shotguns." He has four, I have one. So I went upstairs and got my shotgun and I got
his shotgun. I gave him his shotgun and he told me to get two cartridges out of a
box in the cupboard. I gave him one and took the other myself. He opened his gun
and started to remove his snap caps. I opened my gun and removed two empty
e  cartridges which I use as snap caps as I don't have any. I inserted the cartridge in the
right hand barrel, closed the gun, took off the safety catch and pulled the trigger of
the left hand barrel, and told him he'd lost. By this time I don't think he'd even
cleared his barrel of the snap caps. He looked at me and said: "I didn't think you'd
got the guts, but if you have pull the trigger." I didn't aim the gun. I just pulled the
f  trigger and he was dead. I then went and called the police and told the operator I
had just murdered my father, and that's the story.'

The appellant was in the due course charged with murder, and brought before the St
Neots Magistrates' Court to be committed for trial. On 12 February 1982 that court
found that there was no prima facie case of murder and committed the appellant to stand
g  his trial at the Crown Court on a charge of manslaughter. The indictment, however,
preferred against the appellant charged him with murder. A plea of guilty to
manslaughter tendered by the appellant was not acceptable to the Crown. The trial took
place before Stephen Brown J and a jury in the Crown Court at Birmingham. On 17
September 1982 the appellant was convicted of murder. His appeal against conviction
was dismissed by the Court of Appeal, Criminal Division (May LJ, Boreham and Nolan
h  JJ) on 16 December 1983. The court certified that a point of law of general public
importance was involved in the decision in the following terms:

'Is malice aforethought in the crime of murder established by proof that when
doing the act which causes the death of another the accused either: (a) intends to kill
or do serious harm; or (b) foresees that death or serious harm will probably occur,
whether or not he desires either of those consequences?'

i  Your Lordships' House granted leave to appeal.

Before turning to the substantial issues which the appeal raises, it is appropriate to
refer to a subordinate issue, which was canvassed at the trial and which, at best, can have
done nothing but confuse the jury and add an unnecessary burden to the judge's task in
summing up. As already stated, the appellant had offered a plea of guilty to manslaughter
and had at no stage contested his guilt of that offence. He said in evidence that he had no

recollection of having spoken the words attributed to him by Pc Dighton, in particular the two sentences, 'It was kill or be killed' and 'If I hadn't, he would have done and he would have been sitting here instead of me.' The implication of these two sentences, if they were ever spoken, was wholly inconsistent not only with the detailed account of events in the written statement which the appellant signed and the evidence he gave in support of that account but also with the objective evidence that the deceased was found after the event with his gun broken and unloaded. Counsel who appeared for the appellant at the trial (not the counsel who appeared in the Court of Appeal or before your Lordships) nevertheless invited the jury to acquit the appellant of any offence, on the ground that he acted in self-defence. In the circumstances the judge, very prudently no doubt, felt it proper to leave this issue to the jury with appropriate directions, though on a true analysis it will be apparent that there was not a scintilla of evidence to discharge the evidential burden on the appellant necessary to raise any issue of self-defence at all. It is difficult to dispel a lurking anxiety that the argument that he acted in self-defence may have operated on the minds of the jury adversely to the appellant.

The true and only basis of the appellant's defence that he was guilty not of murder but of manslaughter was encapsulated in the two sentences in his statement: 'I didn't aim the gun. I just pulled the trigger and he was dead.' The appellant amplified this defence in two crucial passages in his evidence. He said: 'I never deliberately aimed at him and fired at him intending to hurt him or to aim close to him intending to frighten him.' A little later he said he had no idea in discharging the gun that it would injure his father: 'In my state of mind I never considered that the probable consequence of what I might do might result in injury to my father. I never conceived that what I was doing might cause injury to anybody. It was just a lark.'

This being the evidence, the issue for the jury was a short and simple one. If they were sure that, at the moment of pulling the trigger which discharged the live cartridge, the appellant realised that the gun was pointing straight at his stepfather's head, they were bound to convict him of murder. If, on the other hand, they thought it might be true that, in the appellant's drunken condition and in the context of this ridiculous challenge, it never entered the appellant's head when he pulled the trigger that the gun was pointing at his father, he should have been acquitted of murder and convicted of manslaughter.

The judge correctly directed the jury that, in order to prove the appellant guilty of murder, 'the prosecution have to prove that he intended either to kill his stepfather or to cause him some really serious bodily injury'. But he had earlier given the following direction on intent:

'When the law requires that something must be proved to have been done with a particular intent, it means this: a man intends the consequences of his voluntary act (a) when he desires it to happen, whether or not he foresees that it probably will happen, and (b) when he foresees that it will probably happen, whether he desires it or not.'

That part of the direction following the colon is given in the precise terms of the so-called definition of intent set out in *Archbold's Pleading, Evidence and Practice in Criminal Cases* (40th edn, 1979) p 948, para 1441a. The textbook places this definition in inverted commas although it does not purport to be a quotation from any judgment or work of authority. The text then continues: 'As will be seen, this definition is in accordance with the great preponderance of authority.' Finding such a passage in the standard textbook, which is every judge's vade-mecum when on circuit, no one can possibly blame the judge for relying on it.

Before considering the criticisms levelled at this direction, it is necessary to examine two later passages in the summing up and a supplementary direction given to the jury in answer to a question which they asked. The judge, when he came to set out the case for the defence, quoted what I have described above as the two crucial passages in the appellant's evidence amplifying the sentence in his statement: 'I didn't aim the gun.' The judge did not relate these passages to his direction on intent, as many judges, I think, might have done, by saying to the jury: 'Members of the jury, if you believe that may be

true, you should acquit of murder and convict of manslaughter.' Moreover, only a few
sentences further on he quoted an answer given by the appellant under cross-examination
as follows:

> 'There is no doubt that when I fired that gun it was pointing at my father's head
> at a distance of about six feet, and at this distance there is no doubt it would cause
> death. It is a lethal weapon.'

It is clear that this answer must have been intended to acknowledge what the appellant
recognised to be the fact *with hindsight*; it cannot have been intended as an admission of
his state of mind at the time of the shooting. It may be that the context made this clear
to the jury, and I hesitate to criticise such an experienced judge, but the possibility of the
jury misunderstanding the significance of these passages in the appellant's evidence
imposed, as it seems to me, a special duty on the judge to give the jury a direction which
placed the real issue before them in unmistakable terms, when, as happened in the event,
the jury returned four hours after their initial retirement and asked for 'clarification of
intent'.

Having reminded the jury that the necessary intent was either to kill or to cause really
serious bodily harm, the judge continued in a passage which it is only fair to quote in
full. He said:

> 'In deciding the question of the accused man's intent, you will decide whether he
> did intend or foresee that result by reference to all the evidence, drawing such
> inferences from the evidence as appear proper in the circumstances. Members of
> the jury, it is a question of fact for you to decide. As I said I think when I was
> directing you originally you cannot take the top of a man's head off and look into
> his mind and actually see what his intent was at any given moment. You have to
> decide it by reference to what he did, what he said and all the circumstances of the
> case. An intent may be an impulsive intent or it may be premeditated. Nobody has
> suggested in this case that there was that element of premeditation. What the
> prosecution have said is that when he pulled the trigger of that gun it must have
> been pointing at the deceased and that the accused knew that it was pointing at him,
> knew it was loaded, and when he by a deliberate act pulled the trigger and fired the
> live barrel of that gun at his stepfather then, say the Crown, he must have intended
> at the very least to have caused him some really serious bodily injury. The defendant
> denies that he had that intent, and in considering the question of his intent it is
> right that you should take into account the evidence relating to the drink that he
> had taken. As I have already endeavoured to explain to you, drink of itself is no
> defence for any unlawful action which may be committed, but it is one of the
> factors which you should have regard to in considering whether this accused man
> did have that necessary intent when he pulled that trigger. A drunken intent is still
> an intent, but you must be satisfied that he did intend either to kill or to do really
> serious bodily injury before you can return a verdict of guilty of murder.'

It will be observed that in this passage foresight of probable consequences, as an
alternative to intent, has become mere foresight. The Crown's case of what it was
contended the appellant *must* have known is recapitulated at some length. The defence is
stated baldly as a denial of intent, without reference to the appellant's evidence to the
effect that he did not realise the gun was aiming at his father.

Delivering the judgment of the Court of Appeal in this case, May LJ said:

> 'We respectfully accept [counsel for the appellant's] submission, based on the
> dictum of Lawton LJ in *R v Beer* (1976) 63 Cr App R 222 at 225, that in most cases
> there is no need, indeed it is undesirable, to give a jury any definition of intent or
> intention in a murder case. It is usually sufficient to direct them, as indeed did the
> learned judge after the passage to which I have already referred, that intent or
> intention is a question of fact for them to determine, taking into account all the
> circumstances of the case.'

May LJ then quoted the trial judge's initial direction on intent by reference to foresight of probable consequences. He continued:

'We think it is quite clear why the learned judge did, in this particular case, go further than is usual in most cases of murder. Intent or intention, in common parlance at least, involves the existence of a state of mind comprising the decision at least to attempt to achieve the intended result.'

May LJ then referred to the approval by Lord Hailsham in *Hyam v DPP* [1974] 2 All ER 41 at 51–52, [1975] AC 55 at 74 of the famous definition of intention given by Asquith LJ in *Cunliffe v Goodman* [1950] 1 All ER 720 at 724, [1950] 2 KB 237 at 253, and added:

'On the facts of the present case, as they appear from the papers, we are certainly prepared to accept that [the appellant] never intended to kill or cause serious bodily injury to his father, using the word "intended" in that limited sense. Nevertheless, in the present case there was also ample material on which a jury could conclude that [the appellant] had deliberately discharged his gun when it was pointing in the direction of his father and at a distance of only six feet.'

The dictum of Lawton LJ in *R v Beer* to which May LJ refers now has the indorsement of the Judicial Committee of the Privy Council in the judgment delivered by Lord Roskill in *Leung Kam-kwok v R* (17 December 1984, unreported).

My Lords, I have to say, with all respect, that I have difficulty in following the reasoning in the passage I have cited from the judgment of May LJ if he was saying, as he seems to have been, that this was a case where it was appropriate to direct the jury that foresight of probable consequences was equivalent to intent. It seems to me, on the contrary, to have been a prime example of a case where this was, in the language of Lawton LJ in *R v Beer* 63 Cr App R 222 at 225, an 'irrelevant direction, which may cause confusion for the jury'. The fact that, when the appellant fired the gun, the gun was pointing directly at his stepfather's head at a range of about six feet was not, and could not be, disputed. The sole issue was whether, when he pressed the trigger, this fact and its inevitable consequence were present to the appellant's mind. If they were, the inference was inescapable, using words in their ordinary, everyday meaning, that he intended to kill his stepfather. The undisputed facts that the appellant loved his stepfather and that there was no premeditation or rational motivation could not, as any reasonable juror would understand, rebut this inference. If, on the other hand, as the appellant was in substance asserting, it never crossed his mind, in his more or less intoxicated condition and when suddenly confronted by his stepfather's absurd challenge, that by pulling the trigger he might injure, let alone kill, his stepfather, no question of foresight of consequences arose for consideration. Whatever his state of mind, the appellant was undoubtedly guilty of a high degree of recklessness. But, so far as I know, no one has yet suggested that recklessness can furnish the necessary element in the crime of murder.

If the jury had not demonstrated, by the question they asked after four hours of deliberation, that the issue of intent was one they did not understand, there might be room for further argument as to the outcome of this appeal. As it is, the jury's question, the terms of the judge's further direction and the jury's decision, just over an hour later, to return a unanimous verdict of guilty of murder leave me in no doubt, with every respect to the trial judge, and the Court of Appeal, that this was an unsafe and unsatisfactory verdict.

That conclusion would be sufficient to dispose of this appeal. But, since I regard it as of paramount importance to the due administration of criminal justice that the law should indicate the appropriate direction to be given as to the mental element in the crime of murder, or indeed in any crime of specific intent, in terms which will be both clear to judges and intelligible to juries, I must first examine the present state of the law on that subject, and, if I find that it leads to some confusion, I must next consider whether it is properly within the judicial function of your Lordships' House to attempt some

clarification and simplification. I emphasise at the outset that this is in no sense an
*a* academic, but is essentially a practical, exercise.

I could not, however hard I tried, hope to emulate the outstanding erudition with
which the speeches in your Lordships' House in *Hyam v DPP* [1974] 2 All ER 41, [1975]
AC 55 studied the history and development of, and the authorities relevant to, the
concept of 'malice aforethought', to use the anachronistic and now wholly inappropriate
phrase which still lingers on in the definition of murder to denote the necessary mental
*b* element. It will be sufficient for my purposes to consider, as shortly as may be, the most
significant developments in this field within the past thirty years.

The Homicide Act 1957, by s 1(1), abolished what used to be called constructive
malice, but not what used to be called implied malice. It was so held and the implications
of the change in the law were made clear by a particularly strong Court of Criminal
Appeal (Lord Goddard CJ, Hilbery, Byrne, Slade and Devlin JJ) in *R v Vickers* [1957] 2 All
*c* ER 741, [1957] 2 QB 664. Lord Goddard CJ, delivering the unanimous judgment of the
court, explained that killing in the course of committing another felony, e g theft or rape,
('constructive malice') was no longer murder. To constitute murder what had now to be
proved was either an intention to kill ('express malice') or an intention to do grievous
bodily harm ('implied malice'). The admirably clear and simple directions to the jury
given by Hinchcliffe J, the trial judge, were expressly approved as 'impeccable'. Those
*d* directions several times indicated that to support a conviction for murder an intention to
kill or do grievous bodily harm must be proved, but contained no paraphrase or
elaboration of what the concept of intention involved.

The next case I must consider is *DPP v Smith* [1960] 3 All ER 161, [1961] AC 290. The
case is important for three reasons. The first is that the House, reversing the Court of
Criminal Appeal, approved a direction by the trial judge, Donovan J, in a capital murder
*e* case, in the following terms ([1960] 3 All ER 161 at 165–166, [1961] AC 290 at 325):

'The intention with which a man did something can usually be determined by a
jury only by inference from the surrounding circumstances including the
presumption of law that a man intends the natural and probable consequences of
his acts . . . If you feel yourselves bound to conclude from the evidence that the
accused's purpose was to dislodge the officer, then you ask yourselves this question:
*f* Could any reasonable person fail to appreciate that the likely result would be at least
serious harm to the officer? If you answer that question by saying that the reasonable
person would certainly appreciate that, then you may infer that that was the
accused's intention, and that would lead to a verdict of guilty on the charge of capital
murder.'

*g* The effect of this decision was to declare the presumption that a man intends the natural
and probable consequences of his acts to be irrebuttable, or, put in other language, to
require juries, in deciding whether a person accused of murder had the necessary
intention to kill or cause grievous bodily harm, to apply the objective test of the
reasonable man, not the subjective test of what was in the mind of the accused man. In
this respect the decision was never popular with the profession. It is said to have been
*h* widely disregarded by trial judges, directing juries in murder cases, until it was eventually
overruled by s 8 of the Criminal Justice Act 1967, which provides:

'A court or jury, in determining whether a person has committed an offence,—
(a) shall not be bound in law to infer that he intended or foresaw a result of his
actions by reason only of its being a natural and probable consequence of those
actions; but (b) shall decide whether he did intend or foresee that result by reference
*j* to all the evidence, drawing such inferences from the evidence as appear proper in
the circumstances.'

The second and third reasons why *DPP v Smith* is important sufficiently appear by two
short citations from the speech of Viscount Kilmuir LC, with which Lord Goddard, Lord
Tucker, Lord Denning and Lord Parker all agreed. He said ([1960] 3 All ER 161 at 167,
[1961] AC 290 at 327):

'The jury must of course in such a case as the present make up their minds on the evidence whether the accused was unlawfully and voluntarily doing something to *a* someone. The unlawful and voluntary act must clearly be aimed at someone in order to eliminate cases of negligence or of careless or dangerous driving.'

He said ([1960] 3 All ER 161 at 171, [1961] AC 290 at 334):

'My Lords, I confess that, whether one is considering the crime of murder or the statutory offence [sc s 18 of the Offences against the Person Act 1861], I can find no *b* warrant for giving the words "grievous bodily harm" a meaning other than that which the words convey in their ordinary and natural meaning. "Bodily harm" needs no explanation and "grievous" means no more and no less than "really serious".'

My Lords, between 1957, when *R v Vickers* [1957] 2 All ER 741, [1957] 2 QB 664 was decided, and the decision of *Hyam v DPP* [1974] 2 All ER 41, [1975] AC 55, in 1974, I do *c* not believe it was ever the practice of trial judges to equate intent with foresight of probable consequences. To invite a jury in effect, whatever the precise terms used in summing up, to apply the rule of evidence, or for that matter of common sense, that a man may ordinarily be presumed to intend the natural and probable consequences of his acts is a different matter altogether.

So I must turn to consider *Hyam v DPP* and discover, if I can, just what it decided. Mrs *d* Hyam was jealous of a Mrs Booth. Mrs Hyam feared that Mr Jones, her former lover, was about to marry Mrs Booth. Mrs Hyam went to Mrs Booth's house at night (having first assured herself that Mr Jones would not be there) where Mrs Booth and her three children were sleeping. Taking care to disturb no one, Mrs Hyam set the house on fire with petrol. Mrs Booth and one of her children escaped, the other two children died in the fire. Mrs Hyam was tried for murder before Ackner J and a jury. She was convicted. *e*

The direction which Ackner J gave to the jury in written form on the question of intent was in the following terms ([1974] 2 All ER 41 at 44 [1975] AC 55 at 65):

'The prosecution must prove, beyond all reasonable doubt, that the accused intended to (kill or) do serious bodily harm to Mrs Booth, the mother of the deceased girls. If you are satisfied that when the accused set fire to the house she knew that it *f* was highly probable that this would cause (death or) serious bodily harm then the prosecution will have established the necessary intent. It matters not if her motive was, as she says, to frighten Mrs Booth.'

The Court of Appeal, Criminal Division dismissed Mrs Hyam's appeal, but gave her leave to appeal to this House and certified that the following point of law of general public importance was involved in the decision: *g*

'Is malice aforethought in the crime of murder established by proof beyond reasonable doubt that when doing the act which led to the death of another the accused knew that it was highly probable that the act would result in death or serious bodily harm?'

*h*

Your Lordships' House dismissed the appeal by a majority of three (Lord Hailsham, Viscount Dilhorne and Lord Cross) to two (Lord Diplock and Lord Kilbrandon). Lord Hailsham gave a qualified negative answer to the certified question expressed in the following propositions ([1974] 2 All ER 41 at 56, [1975] AC 55 at 79):

'(1) Before an act can be murder it must be "aimed at someone" as explained in *j* *Director of Public Prosecutions v Smith* [1960] 3 All ER 161 at 167, [1961] AC 290 at 327, and must in addition be an act committed with one of the following intentions, the test of which is always subjective to the actual defendant: (i) The intention to cause death; (ii) The intention to cause grievous bodily harm in the sense of that term explained in *Director of Public Prosecutions v Smith* [1960] 3 All ER 161 at 172, [1961] AC 290 at 335, ie really serious injury; (iii) Where the defendant knows that *a*  there is a serious risk that death or grievous bodily harm will ensue from his acts, and commits those acts deliberately and without lawful excuse, the intention to expose a potential victim to that risk as the result of those acts. It does not matter in such circumstances whether the defendant desires those consequences to ensue or not, and in none of these cases does it matter that the act and the intention were aimed at a potential victim other than the one who succumbed. (2) Without an intention of one of these three types the mere fact that the defendant's conduct is

*b*  done in the knowledge that grievous bodily harm is likely or highly likely to ensue from his conduct is not by itself enough to convert a homicide into the crime of murder.'

Viscount Dilhorne said ([1974] 2 All ER 41 at 57, [1975] AC 55 at 80):

'It is to be observed that Ackner J in his direction to the jury said that such

*c*  knowledge [sc that it was highly probable that the act would cause death or serious bodily harm] establishes the necessary intent. The question certified asked whether it constituted malice aforethought. If it did, it does not follow that it established an intent to do grievous bodily harm.'

He went on to express the opinion that the question certified should be answered in the affirmative. He added, however ([1974] 2 All ER 41 at 59, [1975] AC 55 at 82):

*d*  'I think, too, that if Ackner J had left the question of intent in the way in which it is left in the vast majority of cases, namely, was it proved that the accused had intended to kill or to do grievous bodily harm, no reasonable jury could on the facts of this case have come to any other conclusion than that she had intended to do grievous bodily harm, bearing in mind her knowledge and the fact that, before she set fire to the house, she took steps to make sure that Mr Jones was not in it as she

*e*  did not want to harm him. If the normal direction had been given, much litigation would have been avoided.'

Lord Diplock, in his dissenting opinion, said this with regard to the law of intent generally ([1974] 2 All ER 41 at 63, [1975] AC 55 at 86):

*f*  '. . . I agree with those of your Lordships who take the uncomplicated view that in crimes of this class no distinction is to be drawn in English law between the state of mind of one who does an act because he desires it to produce a particular evil consequence, and the state of mind of one who does the act knowing full well that it is likely to produce that consequence although it may not be the object he was seeking to achieve by doing the act.'

*g*  However, he developed an elaborate argument for limiting the 'particular evil consequence' in the definition of murder which an accused must have intended, in the sense indicated in the passage cited, to the death of the victim, and consequentially for excluding from the definition an intention to cause injury, no matter how serious, which was not likely to cause death. This view would result in a conveniently simple definition of the mental element in murder as an intention to cause death or to endanger life. It

*h*  would also, of course, involve overruling *R v Vickers* [1957] 2 All ER 741, [1957] 2 QB 664.

Lord Kilbrandon delivered a short speech agreeing with Lord Diplock that—

'to kill with the intention of causing grievous bodily harm is murder only if grievous bodily harm means some injury which is likely to cause death: if murder

*j*  is to be found proved in the absence of an intention to kill, the jury must be satisfied from the nature of the act itself or from other evidence that the accused knew that death was a likely consequence of the act and was indifferent whether that consequence followed or not.'

(See [1974] 2 All ER 41 at 72, [1975] AC 55 at 98.)

Lord Cross, although voting with the majority, effectively sat on the fence on the main issue which divided the rest of their Lordships. Having reviewed their differences, he concluded his speech by saying ([1974] 2 All ER 41 at 72, [1975] AC 55 at 97–98):          *a*

> 'All that I am certain of is that I am not prepared to decide between them without having heard the fullest possible argument on the point from counsel on both sides—especially as a decision that *R v Vickers* was wrongly decided might have serious repercussions since the direction approved in that case must have been given in many homicide cases in the last 17 years. For my part, therefore, I shall content myself with saying that *on the footing that R v Vickers was rightly decided* the answer          *b*
> to the question put to us should be "Yes" and that this appeal should be dismissed.' (Lord Cross's emphasis.)

The Criminal Law Revision Committee in its Fourteenth Report entitled Offences against the Person (Cmnd 7844 (1980)) pp 8ff drew attention under the heading 'The mental element in murder' to the suggested effect of *Hyam v DPP*, but pointed out three          *c*
uncertainties which the decision left unresolved. One of these has been finally settled by the unanimous decision of this House in *R v Cunningham* [1981] 2 All ER 863, [1982] AC 566, affirming *R v Vickers* and making clear that the restricted definition of the mental element in murder favoured in *Hyam v DPP* by Lord Diplock and Lord Kilbrandon, could now only be adopted by legislative, not by judicial, action. The other two uncertainties remain.          *d*

First, is it a necessary ingredient in the crime of murder which helps to distinguish it from the crime of manslaughter that the action of the accused should be 'aimed' at someone in the sense intended by Lord Hailsham in *Hyam v DPP* [1974] 2 All ER 41 at 56, [1975] AC 55 at 79, relying on a passage in the speech of Viscount Kilmuir LC in *DPP v Smith* [1960] 3 All ER 161 at 167, [1961] AC 290 at 327? If so, what exactly does this involve? Second, if foresight of probable consequences is to be treated either as equivalent          *e*
to intent or as evidence from which intent may (or must?) be inferred, how is the degree of probability in homicide cases, where some risk of death or serious injury is foreseen, to be defined in a way that will distinguish murder from manslaughter?

Before attempting to grasp these nettles, I would make some general observations. The definition of intent on which Stephen Brown J based his initial direction to the jury in this case and which first appeared in the 40th edition (1979) but now appears virtually          *f*
unchanged in the current edition of *Archbold's Pleading, Evidence and Practice in Criminal Cases* (41st edn, 1982) p 995, para 17–13 is, as previously stated, clothed with the spurious authority of quotation marks. I will repeat it here for clarity:

> 'In law a man intends the consequence of his voluntary act, (*a*) when he desires it to happen, whether or not he foresees that it probably will happen, or (*b*) when he foresees that it will probably happen, whether he desires it or not.'          *g*

Although in its terms applicable to any offence of specific intent, this so-called definition must be primarily derived from *Hyam v DPP*. The text embodies a reference to Viscount Dilhorne's opinion, implicit in the passage cited above from the report ([1974] 2 All ER 41 at 59, [1975] AC 55 at 82), that in *Hyam v DPP* itself, as in the vast majority of cases, an explanation of intent was unnecessary and notes the indorsement of this view to          *h*
which I have already referred in *R v Beer* (1976) 63 Cr App R 222. Apart from copious references to *Hyam v DPP*, the ensuing citation in support of the claim that the definition 'is in accordance with the great preponderance of authority' refers to many decided cases in which there are to be found obiter dicta on the subject. But looking on their facts at the decided cases where a crime of specific intent was under consideration, including *Hyam v DPP* itself, they suggest to me that the probability of the consequence taken to          *j*
have been foreseen must be little short of overwhelming before it will suffice to establish the necessary intent. Thus, I regard the *Archbold* definition of intent as unsatisfactory and potentially misleading and one which should no longer be used in directing juries.

The golden rule should be that, when directing a jury on the mental element necessary in a crime of specific intent, the judge should avoid any elaboration or paraphrase of what is meant by intent, and leave it to the jury's good sense to decide whether the

accused acted with the necessary intent, unless the judge is convinced that, on the facts
a   and having regard to the way the case has been presented to the jury in evidence and
argument, some further explanation or elaboration is strictly necessary to avoid
misunderstanding. In trials for murder or wounding with intent, I find it very difficult
to visualise a case where any such explanation or elaboration could be required, if the
offence consisted of a direct attack on the victim with a weapon, except possibly the case
where the accused shot at A and killed B, which any first year law student could explain
b   to a jury in the simplest of terms. Even where the death results indirectly from the act of
the accused, I believe the cases that will call for a direction by reference to foresight of
consequences will be of extremely rare occurrence. I am in full agreement with the view
expressed by Viscount Dilhorne that, in *Hyam v DPP* itself, if the issue of intent had been
left without elaboration, no reasonable jury could have failed to convict. I find it difficult
to understand why the prosecution did not seek to support the conviction, as an
c   alternative to their main submission, on the ground that there had been no actual
miscarriage of justice.

I do not, of course, by what I have said in the foregoing paragraph, mean to question
the necessity, which frequently arises, to explain to a jury that intention is something
quite distinct from motive or desire. But this can normally be quite simply explained by
reference to the case before the court or, if necessary, by some homely example. A man
d   who, at London airport, boards a plane which he knows to be bound for Manchester,
clearly intends to travel to Manchester, even though Manchester is the last place he wants
to be and his motive for boarding the plane is simply to escape pursuit. The possibility
that the plane may have engine trouble and be diverted to Luton does not affect the
matter. By boarding the Manchester plane, the man conclusively demonstrates his
intention to go there, because it is a moral certainty that that is where he will arrive.

e   I return to the two uncertainties noted by the Criminal Law Revision Committee in
the report referred to above as arising from *Hyam v DPP* which still remain unresolved. I
should preface these observations by expressing my view that the differences of opinion
to be found in the five speeches in *Hyam v DPP* have, as I believe, caused some confusion
in the law in an area where, as I have already indicated, clarity and simplicity are, in my
view, of paramount importance. I believe it also follows that it is within the judicial
f   function of your Lordships' House to lay down new guidelines which will achieve those
desiderata, if we can reach broad agreement what they should be.

In one sense I should be happy to adopt in its entirety the qualified negative answer
proposed by Lord Hailsham to the certified question in *Hyam v DPP* [1974] 2 All ER 41
at 56, [1975] AC 55 at 79, because, if I may say so, it seems to me to be supported by the
most convincing jurisprudential and philosophical arguments to be found in any of the
g   speeches in *Hyam v DPP*. But I have to add at once that there are two reasons why I cannot
regard it as providing practical guidance to judges who have to direct juries in the rare
cases where foresight of probable consequences must be canvassed with the jury as an
element which should affect their conclusion on the issue of intent.

First, I cannot accept that the suggested criterion that the act of the accused, to amount
to murder, must be 'aimed at someone' as explained in *DPP v Smith* [1960] 3 All ER 161
h   at 167, [1961] AC 290 at 327 by Viscount Kilmuir LC is one which would be generally
helpful to juries. The accused man in *DPP v Smith* was driving a car containing stolen
goods. When told to stop by a police constable he accelerated away. The constable clung
to the side of his car and the accused, in busy traffic, pursued an erratic course in order to
shake the constable off. When finally shaken off, the constable fell in front of another car
and was killed. In this context it was, no doubt, entirely apposite to say, as Viscount
j   Kilmuir LC did: 'The unlawful and voluntary act must clearly be aimed at someone in
order to eliminate cases of negligence or of careless or dangerous driving.' But what of
the terrorist who plants a time bomb in a public building and gives timely warning to
enable the public to be evacuated? Assume that he knows that, following evacuation, it
is virtually certain that a bomb disposal squad will attempt to defuse the bomb. In the
event the bomb explodes and kills a bomb disposal expert. In our present troubled times,
this is an all too tragically realistic illustration. Can it, however, be said that in this case

the bomb was 'aimed' at the bomb disposal expert? With all respect, I believe this criterion would create more doubts than it would resolve.

Second, I believe that Lord Hailsham's inclusion in the mental element necessary to a conviction of murder of 'the intention to expose a potential victim', inter alia, to 'a serious risk that . . . grievous bodily harm will ensue from his acts' (see [1974] 2 All ER 41 at 56, [1975] AC 55 at 79) comes dangerously near to causing confusion with at least one possible element in the crime of causing death by reckless driving, and by inference equally of motor manslaughter, as identified by Lord Diplock in the later case of *R v Lawrence* [1981] 1 All ER 974 at 982, [1982] AC 510 at 526–527, where the driving was such 'as to create an obvious and serious risk of causing physical injury to some other person' and the driver 'having recognised that there was some risk involved, had nonetheless gone on to take it'. If the driver, overtaking in a narrow country lane in the face of an oncoming cyclist, recognises and takes not only 'some risk' but a serious risk of hitting the cyclist, is he to be held guilty of murder?

Starting from the proposition established by *R v Vickers* [1957] 2 All ER 741, [1957] 2 QB 664, as modified by *DPP v Smith* [1960] 3 All ER 161, [1961] AC 290, that the mental element in murder requires proof of an intention to kill or cause really serious injury, the first fundamental question to be answered is whether there is any rule of substantive law that foresight by the accused of one of those eventualities as a probable consequence of his voluntary act, where the probability can be defined as exceeding a certain degree, is equivalent or alternative to the necessary intention. I would answer this question in the negative. Here I derive powerful support from the speech of Lord Hailsham in *Hyam v DPP* [1974] 2 All ER 41 at 52, [1975] AC 55 at 75, where he said:

> 'I do not, therefore, consider, as was suggested in argument, that the fact that a state of affairs is correctly foreseen as a highly probable consequence of what is done is the same thing as the fact that the state of affairs is intended.'

And again ([1974] 2 All ER 41 at 54, [1975] AC 52 at 77):

> '. . . I do not think that foresight as such of a high degree of probability is at all the same thing as intention, and, in my view, it is not foresight but intention which constitutes the mental element in murder.'

The irrationality of any such rule of substantive law stems from the fact that it is impossible to define degrees of probability, in any of the infinite variety of situations arising in human affairs, in precise or scientific terms. As Lord Reid said in *Southern Portland Cement Ltd v Cooper* [1974] 1 All ER 87 at 94, [1974] AC 623 at 640:

> 'Chance probability or likelihood is always a matter of degree. It is rarely capable of precise assessment. Many different expressions are in common use. It can be said that the occurrence of a future event is very likely, rather likely, more probable than not, not unlikely, quite likely, not improbable, more than a mere possibility, etc. It is neither practicable nor reasonable to draw a line at extreme probability.'

I am firmly of opinion that foresight of consequences, as an element bearing on the issue of intention in murder, or indeed any other crime of specific intent, belongs not to the substantive law but to the law of evidence. Here again I am happy to find myself aligned with Lord Hailsham in *Hyam v DPP* [1974] 2 All ER 41 at 43, [1975] AC 55 at 65, where he said: 'Knowledge or foresight is at the best material which entitles or compels a jury to draw the necessary inference as to intention.' A rule of evidence which judges for more than a century found of the utmost utility in directing juries was expressed in the maxim, 'A man is presumed to intend the natural and probable consequences of his acts'. In *DPP v Smith* [1960] 3 All ER 161, [1961] AC 290 your Lordships' House, by treating this rule of evidence as creating an irrebuttable presumption and thus elevating it, in effect, to the status of a rule of substantive law, predictably provoked the intervention of Parliament by s 8 of the Criminal Justice Act 1967 to put the issue of intention back where it belonged, viz in the hands of the jury, 'drawing such inferences from the evidence as appear proper in the circumstances'. I do not by any

*a* means take the conjunction of the verbs 'intended or foresaw' and 'intend or foresee' in that section as an indication that Parliament treated them as synonymous; on the contrary, two verbs were needed to connote two different states of mind.

I think we should now no longer speak of presumptions in this context but rather of inferences. In the old presumption that a man intends the natural and probable consequences of his acts the important word is 'natural'. This word conveys the idea that

*b* in the ordinary course of events a certain act will lead to a certain consequence unless something unexpected supervenes to prevent it. One might almost say that, if a consequence is natural, it is really otiose to speak of it as also being probable.

Section 8 of the Criminal Justice Act 1967 leaves us at liberty to go back to the decisions before that of this House in *DPP v Smith* and it is here, I believe, that we can find a sure, clear, intelligible and simple guide to the kind of direction that should be given to a jury

*c* in the exceptional case where it is necessary to give guidance how, on the evidence, they should approach the issue of intent.

I know of no clearer exposition of the law than that in the judgment of the Court of Criminal Appeal (Lord Goddard CJ, Atkinson and Cassels JJ) delivered by Lord Goddard CJ in *R v Steane* [1947] 1 All ER 813 at 816, [1947] KB 997 at 1004 where he said:

*d*
> 'No doubt, if the prosecution prove an act the natural consequences of which would be a certain result and no evidence or explanation is given, then a jury may, on a proper direction, find that the prisoner is guilty of doing the act with the intent alleged, but if, on the totality of the evidence, there is room for more than one view as to the intent of the prisoner, the jury should be directed that it is for the prosecution to prove the intent to a jury's satisfaction, and if, on a review of the whole evidence, they either think that the intent did not exist or they are left in
*e* doubt as to the intent, the prisoner is entitled to be acquitted.'

In the rare cases in which it is necessary to direct a jury by reference to foresight of consequences, I do not believe it is necessary for the judge to do more than invite the jury to consider two questions. First, was death or really serious injury in a murder case (or whatever relevant consequence must be proved to have been intended in any other

*f* case) a natural consequence of the defendant's voluntary act? Second, did the defendant foresee that consequence as being a natural consequence of his act? The jury should then be told that if they answer Yes to both questions it is a proper inference for them to draw that he intended that consequence.

My Lords, I would answer the certified question in the negative. I would allow the appeal, set aside the verdict of murder, substitute a verdict of manslaughter and remit

*g* the case to the Court of Appeal, Criminal Division to determine the appropriate sentence. Having regard to the time the appellant has already spent in custody, the case should be listed for hearing at the earliest possible date.

*Appeal allowed. Verdict of murder set aside and verdict of manslaughter substituted; case remitted to Court of Appeal, Criminal Division to determine appropriate sentence.*

Solicitors: *Wild Hewitson & Shaw*, Cambridge (for the appellant); *Director of Public Prosecutions*.

Mary Rose Plummer    Barrister.

# Practice Direction

CHANCERY DIVISION

*Practice – Consent order – Chancery Division – Order sought going outside relief claimed in notice of motion or writ – Procedure – Written consent required – Respondent's undertaking.*

1. Where the respondent to a motion does not appear either by counsel or in person, the applicant sometimes asks the court to make a consent order, relying on a letter of consent from the respondent or his solicitors, or sometimes on draft minutes of order signed by the respondent's solicitors.

2. If the relief sought by the applicant falls wholly within the relief claimed in the notice of motion, no difficulty normally arises, for the court is able to grant the relief even if there is no effective consent by the respondent.

3. Where, however, the order sought goes outside the relief claimed in the notice of motion, or even in the writ, or when undertakings are proffered by the respondent, the practice has varied; and it has become desirable to establish a simple and uniform procedure and so save costs. In future, and subject always to the discretion of the judge, no order will normally be made in such cases unless a consent signed by or on behalf of the respondent is put before the court in accordance with the following provisions. (1) Where there are solicitors on the record for the respondent, the court will normally accept as sufficient a written consent signed by those solicitors on their headed notepaper. (2) Where there are solicitors for the respondent but they are not on the record, the court will normally accept as sufficient a written consent signed by those solicitors on their headed notepaper only if in the consent (or in some other document) the solicitors certify that they have fully explained to the respondent the effect of the order and that the respondent appeared to have understood the explanation. (3) Where there is a written consent signed by a respondent who is acting in person, the court will normally not accept it as being sufficient unless the court is satisfied that the respondent understands the effect of the order, either by reason of the circumstances (eg that the respondent is himself a barrister or solicitor) or by means of other material, eg that the respondent's consent is given in reply to a letter to him which sufficiently explained the effect of the order in simple language. (4) Where the respondent offers any undertaking to the court (a) the letter or other document offering the undertaking must be signed by the respondent personally, (b) solicitors must certify on their headed notepaper that the signature is the signature of the respondent and (c) the solicitors must similarly certify, if the case falls within sub-para (2) or sub-para (3) above, that they have explained to the respondent the consequences of giving the undertaking and that the respondent appeared to understand the explanation.

4. This procedure will apply generally to all applications in court in the Chancery Division, whether by motion or otherwise; and it will apply, mutatis mutandis, whether the order is sought by a plaintiff or a defendant or (on motion) by the applicant or the respondent.

By direction of the Vice-Chancellor.

EDMUND HEWARD
Chief Master.

22 March 1985

# Rabin and others v Gerson Berger Association Ltd and others

CHANCERY DIVISION
HARMAN J
14 JANUARY 1985

*Document – Admissibility in evidence – Extrinsic evidence – Trust deed – Construction – Extrinsic evidence of intention of person executing trust deed – Counsel's opinion given at or prior to execution of trust deed – Whether opinion admissible as evidence in construction of deed.*

Evidence of counsel's opinion given at or prior to the execution of a trust deed is not admissible on a summons concerning the construction of the deed, because the opinion merely amounts to evidence of the intention of the party executing the will or settlement and accordingly admission of such evidence would be a breach of the parol evidence rule (see p 1042 c to h, post).

### Notes
For admission of extrinsic evidence, see 12 Halsbury's Laws (4th edn) paras 1478–1501, and for cases on the subject, see 17 Digest (Reissue) 349–398, 1167–1626.

### Cases referred to in judgment
*Prenn v Simmonds* [1971] 3 All ER 237, [1971] 1 WLR 1381, HL.
*Reardon Smith Line Ltd v Hansen-Tangen, Hansen-Tangen v Sanko Steamship Co* [1976] 3 All ER 570, [1976] 1 WLR 989, HL.
*River Wear Comrs v Adamson* (1877) 2 App Cas 743, [1874–80] All ER Rep 1, HL.

### Interlocutory application
In the course of the hearing of a preliminary issue concerning the construction of certain charitable trust deeds, the plaintiffs, Mortimer Rabin and six others, made an interlocutory application for liberty to refer to the opinions of counsel made at or prior to the execution of the trust deeds. The defendants, Gerson Berger Association Ltd and five others, opposed the application.

*Michael Lyndon-Stanford QC* and *David Rowell* for the plaintiffs.
*Andrew Morritt QC* and *David Unwin* for the defendants.

**HARMAN J.** I have before me a preliminary issue directed by an order made in February 1983 concerning construction or other issues arising on the trusts of three charitable trust deeds.

In opening the matter, counsel for the plaintiffs has sought to refer to documents, in particular the opinions of well-known tax counsel, given at or shortly before the time of the execution of the charitable trust deeds, which was on All Fools' Day 1968. Counsel for the defendants has resisted the court looking at those documents on the ground that they are not admissible evidence at all.

Counsel for the plaintiffs puts to me the well-known line of authority (in modern times at least) of *Prenn v Simmonds* [1971] 3 All ER 237, [1971] 1 WLR 1381 and *Reardon Smith Line Ltd v Hansen-Tangen, Hansen-Tangen v Sanko Steamship Co* [1976] 3 All ER 570, [1976] 1 WLR 989: see Lord Wilberforce's speech in both authorities. He points to Lord Wilberforce's formulation of the proposition, which Lord Wilberforce asserted was in no way new and went back at least to *River Wear Comrs v Adamson* (1877) 2 App Cas 743, [1874–80] All ER Rep 1, that documents are not to be construed in a vacuum but in the context of the factual matrix in which they came to be made. That is, in my understanding, and always has been the basis on which written documents are construed.

Lord Wilberforce also asserted that evidence of intention may not be given expressly and
that there is no possible way of resorting to such evidence for construction purposes.

Counsel for the plaintiffs starts his proposition with the admission, as it were, that the
whole practice of this court for at least the last hundred years has been against him. There
have been multitudinous originating summonses for the construction of settlements and
clauses in wills, which settlement or will was executed by the settlor or testator following
on and frequently in accordance with the draft settled by the advice of counsel. Never,
says counsel for the plaintiffs, and in my belief he is entirely right in this, have such
opinions been referred to on the summonses which have come before this court over the
last hundred years. None the less, he says, that is no reason why this settlement should
not be construed as any commercial document would be construed, bearing in mind its
particular circumstances, of course, such as that many of the terms in a settlement or will
settled by a skilled draftsman will be terms of art and will not stand naked to the world
as a business document made between businessmen without skilled assistance may well
do.

Counsel for the defendants challenges the admission on a simple proposition. He
asserts that to admit counsel's opinion amounts to a straight breach of the parol evidence
rule and to nothing more than what Lord Wilberforce in *Prenn v Simmonds* said was not
possible or permissible, the giving of express evidence about the intention of the party.
The fact that counsel has advised and settled a draft is a fact and is no doubt admissible,
although, since it leads nowhere, nobody will bother to give it in evidence or debate it.

The content of the opinion and the ideas which it asserts in the draft annexed to or
settled at the same time as that opinion are really no more than setting out how counsel
has interpreted the intention of the settlor within the limits set by the law, and what
they come to is counsel's intentions in carrying out the purposes set out in his instructions
and deriving from the testator's or settlor's instructions to his solicitor.

The point in the end is a short one. In my judgment, counsel for the defendants is
right. In my judgment, the fact that the matter is unprecedented is explained by the
proposition that, although there are no different rules for construing documents drawn
by skilled draftsmen as compared with documents expressed in the rude vigour of
commercial language, yet the rule is the same for both, that parol evidence of the
intention of the party is not admissible in either. Thus the practice has been correct in
not citing counsel's opinions on summonses for the construction of wills and settlements,
and such evidence is not admissible because it does amount to evidence of the intention
of the party executing the will or settlement. Indeed it may well be that such evidence
should be the more carefully kept out where the document is unilateral and where
considerable dangers might arise if one were to try and construe a document according
to an opinion and a draft settled which had only partially carried out the intention of the
draftsman and, therefore, of the settlor.

However that may be, it seems to me quite clear that the argument of intention is
right and that these opinions cannot be admitted.

*Application refused.*

Solicitors: *Norton Rose Botterell & Roche* (for the plaintiffs); *Heald Nickinson* (for the
defendants).

Evelyn M C Budd    Barrister.

# Chellaram and others v Chellaram and others

CHANCERY DIVISION
SCOTT J
14, 15, 18, 19, 20, 21, 22, 25 JUNE, 13 JULY 1984

*Trust and trustee – Removal of trustee – Jurisdiction – Settlement – Settlement made abroad – Trust property situated abroad – Removal of trustees and appointment of new trustees – Settlements made by Indian settlors – Trust property consisting of shares in Bermudian companies – Beneficiaries domiciled in India – Trust deeds kept in London and trust administered in London – Whether English court having jurisdiction to administer settlements – Whether English courts having jurisdiction to remove and replace trustees – Whether English court forum non conveniens.*

In 1975 two brothers who were members of an Indian trading family and who were domiciled in India set up discretionary settlements for the benefit of other members of the family. The settlements were drawn up in Bombay by a member of the Indian Bar as a means of avoiding Indian taxation and exchange control regulations. The terms of the settlements were similar to the terms of settlements in common usage in England. The assets of the settlements consisted of shares in two companies incorporated in Bermuda which were holding companies for the family's trading businesses throughout the Far East and West Africa, each local business being run by means of an operating company. The six trustees of the settlements were all born in India and had Indian domicile although they lived in different parts of the world. Four had British passports, two resided permanently in London and nearly everyone connected with the settlements had some residential connection with London, although most of the beneficiaries resided permanently in India. The settlement deeds were held by London solicitors and such administration as there had been had taken place in London. Despite the considerable value of the settlements' assets no distribution of capital or income had ever been made to the beneficiaries, who commenced an action in England seeking the removal of the trustees and the appointment of new trustees. The trustees each accepted service of the writ in England and applied for the action to be stayed, on the grounds (i) that the court had no jurisdiction, because the removal of foreign trustees of a foreign settlement was a matter for the proper law of the settlement, which was Indian law in respect of the settlements in question, (ii) that any order made by the court would be ineffective, since the assets of the settlements were situated abroad, and (iii) the forum conveniens was the court in Bombay.

**Held** – The trustees' application for a stay of proceedings would be dismissed, for the following reasons—

(1) Although the court had no jurisdiction to determine the existence or extent of rights under a foreign trust, since those were matters to be determined under the proper law of the trust, the court did have inherent jurisdiction to administer a foreign trust for the purpose of enforcing or protecting undisputed rights of the beneficiaries that were binding on the trustees, and to make an in personam order against the trustees for that purpose if the trustees were subject to the jurisdiction of the court. In respect of the enforcement of undisputed rights of the beneficiaries it was irrelevant whether the trust assets were situated in England or whether the proper law of the trust was English law. Furthermore, in the exercise of its jurisdiction to enforce such rights the court could make an in personam order against the trustees requiring them to resign and to vest the trust assets in new trustees. Accordingly, since the trustees had voluntarily submitted to the court's jurisdiction by accepting service of the writ, the court had jurisdiction to order their removal and replacement (see p 1052 d e, p 1053 b e and j to p 1054 f, p 1055 a, p 1057 d to g, p 1058 b and p 1060 f to h, post); *Ewing v Orr Ewing* (1883) 9 App Cas 34 and *Letterstedt v Broers* [1881–5] All ER Rep 882 applied.

(2) The trustees had not made out a defence of forum non conveniens in respect of the English court's jurisdiction, since the fact that there was some uncertainty whether the Bombay court would accept jurisdiction and that there would in any event be a very long

delay before the case could be heard in Bombay outweighed the settlements' and
beneficiaries' connection with India, and therefore the court would not exercise its      *a*
discretion to order a stay of the English proceedings (see p 1053 *b*, p 1058 *f* to *h*, p 1059 *e*
to *h* and p 1060 *a* to *e* and *g h*, post); *MacShannon v Rockware Glass Ltd* [1978] 1 All ER
625, dictum of Robert Goff J in *Trendtex Trading Corp v Crédit Suisse* [1980] 3 All ER at
734, *Amin Rasheed Shipping Corp v Kuwait Insurance Co, The Al Wahab* [1983] 2 All ER 884
and dictum of Lord Diplock in *The Abidin Daver* [1984] 1 All ER at 476 applied; *Ewing v
Orr Ewing* (1883) 9 App Cas 34 not followed.      *b*

Per curiam. In determining the law which governs a foreign trust there is no
distinction between the validity, interpretation and effect of the trust on the one hand
and its administration on the other. All matters affecting the determination of the duties
and rights of the trustees and the beneficiaries arising out of the settlement (including
the right to remove and replace trustees if that right is conferred by the trust instrument)
are governed by the proper law of the trust and not by any so-called law of the place of      *c*
administration of the trust; it is merely the enforcement of such rights and duties, once
determined, that may take place under a different law (see p 1056 *j* to p 1057 *c*, post);
*Wynn NO and Westminster Bank Ltd NO v Oppenheimer, Re Pollak's Estate* [1937] TPD 91
considered.

**Notes**      *d*
For the power of the court to remove trustees, see 48 Halsbury's Laws (4th edn) paras
774–775, and for cases on the subject, see 47 Digest (Repl) 232–234, *2036–2062.*

For the jurisdiction of the English court to enforce trusts relating to foreign
immovables, see 8 Halsbury's Laws (4th edn) para 645, and for cases on the subject, see
11 Digest (Reissue) 401–402, 404–410.

For the jurisdiction of the English court in actions in personam and for refusal to      *e*
exercise the jurisdiction, see 8 Halsbury's Laws (4th edn) paras 406–407.

**Cases referred to in judgment**
*Abidin Daver, The* [1984] 1 All ER 470, [1984] AC 398 [1984] 2 WLR 196, HL.
*Amin Rasheed Shipping Corp v Kuwait Insurance Co, The Al Wahab* [1983] 2 All ER 884,
  [1984] AC 50, [1983] 3 WLR 241, HL.      *f*
*Atlantic Star, The, Atlantic Star (owners) v Bona Spes (owners)* [1973] 2 All ER 175, [1974]
  AC 436, [1973] 2 WLR 795, HL.
*Ewing v Orr Ewing* (1883) 9 App Cas 34, HL.
*Kehr (decd), Re, Martin v Foges* [1951] 2 All ER 812, [1952] Ch 26.
*Ker's Settlement Trusts, Re* [1963] 1 All ER 801, [1963] Ch 553, [1963] 2 WLR 1210.
*Letterstedt v Broers* (1884) 9 App Cas 371, [1881–5] All ER Rep 882, PC.      *g*
*MacShannon v Rockware Glass Ltd* [1978] 1 All ER 625, [1978] AC 795, [1978] 2 WLR
  362, HL.
*Marlborough (Duke) v A-G (No 1)* [1945] 1 All ER 165, [1945] Ch 78.
*Trendtex Trading Corp v Crédit Suisse* [1980] 3 All ER 721; *affd* [1980] 3 All ER 721,
  [1980] QB 629, [1980] 3 WLR 367, CA; *affd* [1981] 3 All ER 520, [1982] AC 679,
  [1981] 3 WLR 766, HL.      *h*
*Wilks, Re, Keefer v Wilks* [1935] Ch 645, [1935] All ER Rep 787.
*Wynn NO and Westminster Bank Ltd NO v Oppenheimer, Re Pollak's Estate* [1937] TPD 91.

**Cases also cited**
*Baroda (Maharanee) v Wildenstein* [1972] 2 All ER 689, [1972] 2 QB 283, CA.
*Cook Industries Inc v Galliher* [1978] 3 All ER 945, [1979] Ch 439.      *j*
*Courtney Re, ex p Pollard* (1840) Mont & Ch 239, [1835–42] All ER Rep 415.
*Iveagh v IRC* [1954] 1 All ER 609, [1954] Ch 364.
*Jones v Jones* (1894) 30 NYS 177.
*Paget's Settlement, Re* [1965] 1 All ER 58, [1965] 1 WLR 1046.
*Penn v Lord Baltimore* (1750) 1 Ves Sen 444, [1558–74] All ER Rep 99.
*Perpetual Executors and Trustees Association of Australia Ltd v Roberts* [1970] VR 732.
*Razelos v Razelos (No 2)* [1970] 1 All ER 386, [1970] 1 WLR 392.

*St Pierre v South American Stores (Gath & Chaves) Ltd* [1936] 1 KB 382, [1935] All ER Rep
a   408, CA.
*Weckstrom v Hyson* [1966] VR 277.

**Interlocutory application**

By a writ issued on 14 December 1983 the plaintiffs, Harish Shewakram Chellaram,
Radhika Harish Chellaram, Vishal Harish Chellaram (a minor) and Ashwin Harish
Chellaram (a minor), beneficiaries under certain discretionary settlements, sought as
b   against the defendants, Lal Lokumal Chellaram, Sham Lokumal Chellaram, Ram
Tahilram Chellaram, Murli Tahilram Chellaram, Hotchand Gopaldas Advani, Lokumal
Kishinchand Chellaram and Pishu Tahilram Chellaram, trustees of the settlements, the
following orders: (1) that the defendants provide the plaintiffs with copies of, or permit
the plaintiffs to inspect and take copies of, all trust documents relating to two of the
settlements, namely Mohan's settlement and Harish's settlement, (2) that the defendants
c   provide the plaintiffs with full and proper accounts of those settlements from the dates
of their respective creation, (3) that the defendants provide the plaintiffs with (i) accounts
of Kayshewak Bermuda Ltd, Eskay (Bermuda) Ltd, Kaycee (Bermuda) Ltd and Chellsons
(Bermuda) Ltd, (ii) minutes of the general meetings of those companies, (iii) copies of
directors' service contracts relating to those companies and (iv) copies of registers
maintained by those companies from and after 14 February 1975, and (4) an order
d   removing the defendants as trustees of Mohan's and Harish's settlements and appointing
some fit and proper persons to be trustees in their place. By a notice of motion dated 11
January 1984 the defendants applied for the following relief, namely an order under RSC
Ord 12, r 8 and/or under the inherent jurisdiction of the court that the writ in the action
be set aside, alternatively that all further proceedings in the action be stayed, on the
grounds that the action was not proper to be brought in the English High Court and was
e   frivolous and vexatious and an abuse of the court's process. At the hearing of the motion
the defendants indicated that they would not seek to have the writ set aside but only
sought a stay so far as related to the prayer for the removal of trustees and the appointment
of new ones. The facts are set out in the judgment.

f   *Michael Miller QC* and *Francis Barlow* for the defendants.
*Michael Lyndon-Stanford QC* and *Nicholas Warren* for the plaintiffs.

*Cur adv vult*

13 July. The following judgment was delivered.

**SCOTT J.** The plaintiffs in this action are beneficiaries under certain discretionary
g   settlements of which the defendants are trustees. By specially indorsed writ dated 14
December 1983 the plaintiffs sought under paras 1, 2 and 3 of the prayer, orders that the
defendants provide them with copies of all relevant trust documents, with trust accounts,
with accounts of certain companies with which the settlements are connected, and with
copies of certain other documents. Under para 4 of the prayer the plaintiffs sought an
order removing the defendants as trustees of the settlements and appointing other
h   trustees in their places.

By notice of motion dated 11 January 1984 the defendants sought an order that the
writ be set aside or, alternatively, that all further proceedings in the action be stayed on
the grounds that the action was not proper to be brought in this court and was frivolous,
vexatious and an abuse of the process of the court. That application is now before me.

Notwithstanding the wide terms of the relief sought by the notice of motion, counsel
j   for the defendants opened the application on the footing that he did not seek to have the
writ set aside and sought a stay of the action only so far as the prayer for the removal of
trustees and the appointment of new trustees was concerned. As to the rest, the
defendants take the position that since the date of the writ they have made available to
the plaintiffs copies of all trust accounts, and have supplied the plaintiffs with all available
or appropriate information: if the plaintiffs wish to continue the action in order to obtain
additional documents or information, or for the purposes of costs, the defendants will
not argue against the plaintiffs' rights to do so. They do, however, contend that the claim

for their removal as trustees and for the appointment of others in their places, should be
stayed. This contention of the defendants is based on two alternative grounds. First, it is
submitted that the proper law of the settlements is the law of India and that this court
has no jurisdiction or, alternatively, no power to remove trustees of foreign settlements
and to appoint new ones in their places. Second, it is submitted that the issue between
the plaintiffs and the defendants has no, or no sufficient, connection with this country,
that India is the forum conveniens in which the issue should be litigated, and, as a matter
of discretion, this court should decline to permit the issue to be litigated here.

Each of these contentions requires that I should carefully consider the circumstances
relevant to the settlement and to this litigation. The litigation concerns the affairs and
fortunes of the Chellaram family, a well-known Bombay trading family. The family
trading enterprise was started by the grandfather of the first plaintiff, one Kishinchand
Chellaram. He has been, for many years deceased. He had three sons: Shewakram,
Lokumal and Tahilram. Since the surname of practically everyone involved in the
present case is Chellaram, I hope I will not be thought guilty of any discourtesy if, from
time to time, for convenience I refer to the members of the family simply by their
respective given names.

Shewakram died in 1949 and was survived by his widow, Lachmibai, who is now 74
years of age. Shewakram and Lachmibai had two sons: Mohan and Harish (the first
plaintiff). The second plaintiff, Radhika Chellaram, is the wife of Harish. They have two
children, the third and fourth plaintiffs, both of whom are minors. Mohan is unmarried.
I have been told that his capacity to manage his own affairs may be open to doubt.
Shewakram and Lachmibai had also daughters who are now married.

Kishinchand's second son, Lokumal, is the sixth defendant. He is now 70 years of age.
Lokumal has two sons, namely Lal and Sham, the first and second defendants.

Kishinchand's third son, Tahilram is now deceased. Tahilram had three sons, namely
Murli (the fourth defendant), Pishu (the seventh defendant) and Ram (the third
defendant).

Following the death of Kishinchand Chellaram, the family trading business was carried
on by his three sons. Shewakram, for a time, left the family business but subsequently
returned to it. The business consisted, as to part, of trading enterprises carried on within
India and, as to part, of trading enterprises carried on outside India. The trading business
outside India was carried on in a large number of countries, mainly in the Far East and
in West Africa, and generally in each of these countries through the medium of an
operating company incorporated under the laws of the country in question. The shares
of the several operating companies were held by a Bermudian holding company, Kaycee
(Bermuda) Ltd. There has been no evidence before me as to the manner in which the
trading enterprise in India was organised.

At the time of his death, Shewakram Chellaram held a 30% interest in the Bermudian
holding company, and thereby in the family trading enterprises outside India. This 30%
interest was, on his death, inherited by his widow, Lachmibai. In 1973 the Chellaram
family, following some years of discussions, decided to effect a separation of the trading
interests of the Lokumal branch of the family from those of the Tahilram branch of the
family. Accordingly, a new Bermudian company was incorporated, Chellsons (Bermuda)
Ltd. Kaycee (Bermuda) Ltd was to own the operating companies of the Lokumal branch;
Chellsons (Bermuda) Ltd was to own the operating companies of the Tahilram branch.
Lachmibai decided to retain her 30% interest in both holding companies. Accordingly,
after the division and reorganisation had been effected, Kaycee was owned as to 70% by
Lal and Sham and as to 30% by Lachmibai: Chellsons was owned as to 70% by Murli,
Pishu and Ram, and as to 30% by Lachmibai.

At about the same time as this division and reorganisation was finally effected,
Lachmibai gave her 30% interest to her two sons, Mohan and Harish. I am not clear
whether or not this gift was made before or after the division. Nothing, however, turns
on this. They each became absolutely entitled to a 15% shareholding in Kaycee and a
15% shareholding in Chellsons.

At this stage I should describe in a little more detail the location of some of the
*a* operating companies. In Singapore there was a Chellsons operating company, K
Chellaram and Sons (Far East) Ltd. This company had also a branch in Kuala Lumpur. In
Hong Kong there were two Kaycee companies and one Chellsons company. Both Kaycee
and Chellsons had operating companies in Nigeria. Kaycee had companies in Ghana and
Sierra Leone. Chellsons had companies in Gambia, Upper Volta and Niger. Both had
companies in Spain and Gibraltar. Both also had companies in London incorporated
*b* under the Companies Act 1948. The Kaycee London company was K Lokumal & Sons
(London) Ltd. The Chellsons London company was K Chellaram & Sons (London) Ltd.
These London companies served a rather different function from that served by the other
operating companies. They were used for providing financial and administrative services
to the other members of their respective groups. London served, to some extent, as a post
office through which material which needed to be distributed among the group would
*c* be sent for that purpose. These were the groups owned by the Bermudian holding
companies in which Harish and Mohan held their shares.

On 14 February 1975 Mohan and Harish each made a discretionary settlement of his
shares in Kaycee (Bermuda) Ltd and Chellsons (Bermuda) Ltd. These settlements were
made on the advice of the fifth defendant, Mr Advani. Mr Advani is an eminent lawyer
practising in Bombay. He was described to me by counsel for the defendants as the doyen
*d* of the Bombay Bar. He drafted these two settlements. They are in identical terms, save
for the class of beneficiaries, and are broadly in terms with which any practitioner at the
Chancery Bar in England would be familiar. Each settlement was made between the
settlor of the one part and three trustees of the other part. The three trustees were Ram
Chellaram, a Mr K Rupchand and a Mr G R Bharwani. In Harish's settlement the class of
beneficiaries was described as comprising the following: his mother, Lachmibai; his
*e* wife, Radhika; his two children; his brother, Mohan; the wife and any children of
Mohan; the children and remoter issue of the father and mother of the settlor; the
spouses of any of those persons, and the spouse of any adopted child of the settlor. There
were, however, expressly excluded from the class of beneficiary, the settlor, the spouse of
the settlor and the husbands of any female issue of Lachmibai.

The class of beneficiaries under Mohan's settlement is the same, save that Mohan is
*f* excluded and Harish is included. Accordingly, Harish and Radhika are beneficiaries
under Mohan's settlement; Mohan is a beneficiary under Harish's settlement; Lachmibai
and Harish's two children are beneficiaries under both settlements. In addition, Mohan
and Harish's sisters are beneficiaries under both settlements.

The settlements confer on the trustees wide powers to apply income or capital for the
benefit of any of the relevant class of beneficiaries, and in each there is an ultimate trust
*g* for the issue of the settlor. Each settlement contains, in addition, the following relevant
provisions: a very wide power of investment of trust money authorising investment in,
inter alia, 'property of whatever nature and wheresoever situated'; a charging clause for
'any trustee who may be a Trust Corporation Accountant and who is a Barrister-at-Law';
a power for the trustees by deed to declare that the settlement shall 'take effect in
accordance with the Law of some other place in any part of the World and that the forum
*h* for the administration hereof shall thenceforth be the Courts of that place'; finally, a
power of appointment of new trustees vested in 'the Trustees of the executors or
administrators (or the liquidator) of the last surviving Trustee'. In Harish's settlement,
his address is given as 102 High Street, Singapore, and the settlement was signed by him
in Singapore. In Mohan's settlement, his address is given as 54 Marina, Lagos, and the
settlement was signed by him in Lagos. In neither settlement is any address given for
*j* any of the three trustees. However, both Mr Rupchand and Mr Bharwani were, at the
date of the settlements, permanently resident in London. Mr Rupchand was chairman
and Mr Bharwani was a director of K Chellaram & Sons (London) Ltd, the Chellsons
London company.

There is some dispute between the parties as to the residence at the time of the
settlements of the third trustee, Ram Chellaram. In his affidavit he deposes to a residence

in Las Palmas, Canary Islands, since 1974. However, it is common ground that he or the Chellsons London company maintained (and still maintains) a house in London available for his use, and that he has always spent some months in London each year. Moreover, Ram held, at the date of the settlement, a British passport issued in London on 27 September 1972, in which his country of residence is given as England. There is evidence that the settlement signed by Harish was returned by him, duly signed, to Mr Advani. It is a fair inference that it was then taken or sent by Mr Advani to London and there signed by the three trustees. I infer that the same process was followed in the case of Mohan's settlement.

It appears from the evidence that the two settlements were kept in London in the custody of Messrs Norton Rose Botterell & Roche, solicitors. Each settlement purported to settle the shares of the settlor in Kaycee (Bermuda) Ltd and in Chellsons (Bermuda) Ltd. The share certificates relating to these shares were at all material times held in Bermuda by Bermudian solicitors, Messrs Conyers Dill & Pearman, who acted for the Chellaram family in connection with the Bermudian company affairs. By letter dated 25 March 1975 addressed to Conyers Dill & Pearman, and written from London, Harish enclosed a copy of his discretionary settlement and a copy of Mohan's discretionary settlement, but requested that the shares be allowed to remain for the time being registered in the names of himself and Mohan respectively. He concluded by saying that when it was desired that the shares should be transferred into the names of the trustees of the settlement, Conyers Dill & Pearman would be so informed. It is not so stated in the evidence, but I infer that this letter, like the settlements, was drafted by Mr Advani. Accordingly, the trust shares remained vested in the respective settlors.

However, on 22 October 1976 a new Bermudian holding company, Eskay (Bermuda) Ltd (which I will call Eskay 1) was incorporated by Conyers Dill & Pearman, with an issued share capital of 180,000 shares of $Bd2·40 each. Of these, 89,998 were transferred to Mohan, and 89,997 to Harish. The five remaining shares were held by partners or employees of Conyers Dill & Pearman in order to comply with Bermudian law, in trust for the trustees of the two settlements. The holdings of Mohan and of Harish in Kaycee (Bermuda) Ltd and Chellsons (Bermuda) Ltd were transferred to Eskay 1. In order to document that the new shares in Eskay 1 were subject to the trusts of the settlements, Mohan signed two letters addressed to the trustees of his settlement: one letter referred to his Kaycee (Bermuda) Ltd shares; the other to his Chellsons (Bermuda) Ltd shares. By each letter, Mohan confirmed that 'the shares of Eskay are trust property and that those shares of Eskay registered in my name are being held by me for the trustees of the settlement.' These two letters were signed by Mohan in London before a notary public on 29 March 1977. Two similar letters to the trustees were signed by Harish in Singapore before a notary public on 24 March 1977. By two letters dated 7 June 1978, one addressed to the trustees of Mohan's settlement, and the other addressed to the trustees of Harish's settlement, Mr Rupchand and Mr Bharwani purported to resign their respective trusteeships. These letters purported to be written from 16–26 Banner Street, London EC1, the officers of the Chellsons London company. To whom they were actually sent is uncertain. They appear to have been left in the custody of Norton Rose Botterell & Roche in London. Since no new trustees were appointed in place of the two retiring trustees, it is not clear whether the retirements were of any legal effect.

However, effective deeds of retirement and appointment of trustees were made dated 12 May 1981. The parties thereto were Mr Rupchand and Mr Bharwani of the first part, Ram Chellaram of the second part and Lal Chellaram, Sham Chellaram, Murli Chellaram and Mr Advani of the third part. By one of these deeds Lal, Sham, Murli and Mr Advani were appointed trustees of Harish's settlement jointly with Ram, and in place of Mr Rupchand and Mr Bharwani. By the other deed, the same appointment was made in respect of Mohan's settlement. Each of the deeds was executed by the parties thereto in London and was then sewn up in the settlement to which it related and kept by Norton Rose Botterell & Roche in London.

There is in evidence before me a document dated 27 March 1981 signed by Harish and witnessed by Mr Advani, in which Harish purported to transfer to the trustees of his settlement the 89,997 shares in Eskay 1 which stood in his name. Presumably, Mohan

*a*  signed a similar document. There is, however, no evidence whether or not the shares were then formally registered in the names of the trustees.

Later during 1981 an important company reconstruction took place. The background to this was the desire by the Lokumal and Tahilram branches of the family that each should conduct its overseas trading business without any participation therein by the other. This had been achieved in the main by the Kaycee/Chellsons division effected in

*b*  1973. However, the settlement trustees held, through Eskay 1, interests both in Kaycee (Bermuda) Ltd and in Chellsons (Bermuda) Ltd, and the settlement trustees included both Lokumal representatives, namely Lal and Sham, as well as Tahilram representatives, namely Ram and Murli. It was desired to remove this fiduciary participation by Lokumal trustees in Chellsons' affairs and by Tahilram trustees in the affairs of Kaycee. In addition, the decision was reached, although by whom and in what circumstances is not clear, that

*c*  the settlement holdings in Kaycee and Chellsons respectively should be represented by a different class of share from the shares held by the Lokumal or Tahilram shareholders, as the case may be. So, the following steps were taken.

(1) On 9 June 1981 Kaycee and Chellsons each held a special general meeting converting the shares held by Eskay 1 into B shares with a minimum guaranteed and preferential dividend of 6%, and with restricted voting rights. The meetings were held

*d*  in Bermuda. At each company meeting the chairman, Sir Bayard Dill, a partner in Conyers Dill & Pearman, held the proxy from Eskay 1. The proxy forms had been signed by Mr John Ellison, another partner in Conyers Dill & Pearman (as a director of Eskay 1), and by Mr Younie, also a partner in that firm (as assistant secretary of Eskay 1). The evidence before me does not reveal in what manner the approval of the settlement trustees to this conversion of the trust shares into the B shares was obtained, or how that

*e*  approval was communicated to Conyers Dill & Pearman. (2) Eskay 1 was put into liquidation. (3) On 26 June 1981 two new Bermudian companies were formed: Eskay 'K' (Bermuda) Ltd, which subsequently became Kayshewak Ltd (Kayshewak), and Eskay 'C' (Bermuda) Ltd, which subsequently became Eskay (Bermuda) Ltd, (and which I will call 'Eskay 2'). Each company had an issued share capital of 150,000 shares of £1 each. In the case of Kayshewak, 149,995 of the issued shares were allotted to the trustees of the

*f*  two settlements, and in the case of Eskay 2, 149,995 shares were allotted to a nominee Bermudian company, Pembroke Ltd, to hold for the trustees. The remaining shares in each of the two companies were allotted to individual members of Conyers Dill & Pearman, on trust, I infer, for the trustees of the settlements. The consideration for the allotment of the Kayshewak shares was the Kaycee shares held by Eskay 1. The consideration for the allotment of the Eskay 2 shares was the Chellsons shares held by

*g*  Eskay 1.

(4) By deed of appropriation and appointment dated 24 May 1982, supplemental to Harish's settlement, first, two funds were constituted: an 'A' fund comprising the settlement's Kayshewak shares, and a 'B' fund comprising the settlement's Eskay 2 shares. Second, the Tahilram trustees, that is, Ram and Murli, and also Mr Advani, retired as trustees of the Kayshewak shares and Lokumal Chellaram was appointed in their place.

*h*  So Lal, Sham and Lokumal became trustees of the Kayshewak shares, Kayshewak being the company which held the shares in Kaycee. Third, the Lokumal trustees, that is Lal and Sham, retired as trustees of the 'B' fund and Pishu Chellaram was appointed in their place. So Ram, Murli, Pishu and Mr Advani became trustees of the Eskay 2 shares, Eskay 2 being the company which held the shares in Chellsons.

A deed of the same date between the same parties and to the same effect was made

*j*  supplemental to Mohan's settlement. Both these deeds were drawn up by Norton Rose Botterell & Roche in London, and were executed by the respective parties thereto in London. These deeds were kept in London by Norton Rose Botterell & Roche.

In summary, by the process I have mentioned, each settlement held Kayshewak shares of which the trustees were the first, second and sixth defendants, and Eskay 2 shares, of which the trustees were the third, fourth, fifth and seventh defendants. Kayshewak held B class shares in Kaycee (Bermuda) Ltd, representing 30% of its issued share capital. Eskay

2 held B class shares in Chellsons (Bermuda) Ltd, representing 30% of the issued share capital of that company. There are no other trust assets.

The plaintiffs have two particular complaints arising out of the reorganisation to which I have referred. Firstly, complaint is made of the acceptance of the B class non-voting shares in substitution for the ordinary shares previously held. The trustees, it is said, ought never to have agreed to this. Secondly, it is said that the reorganisation involved the family trustees (that is to say, all the trustees bar Mr Advani), being placed in a position in which they had conflicting interests and duties. I need not, for the purposes of this application, further consider these complaints; but they represent some of the matters which the court may have to consider if the action proceeds.

Accounts of Kaycee (Bermuda) Ltd and of Chellsons (Bermuda) Ltd have recently been supplied to the plaintiffs and are in evidence. Kaycee's balance sheet, as at 30 June 1983, shows it as having a net worth of £4,246,699. Chellsons' balance sheet as at 30 June 1982 shows it as having a net worth of £2,849,866. These accounts, however, are not consolidated accounts, and each company is simply a holding company. It is possible that consolidated accounts may show a different picture. However, these are the companies in each of which the settlements hold a 30% interest and, on any basis, the settled assets are substantial in worth.

It is, therefore, a matter of some surprise to discover that the settlements have not, from the date on which they were made to the present time, received any income whatever from these assets. So far as appears from the evidence before me, in the period up to the incorporation of Eskay 1, no dividend was ever paid by Kaycee or Chellsons to Mohan or to Harish. After the incorporation of Eskay 1, Eskay 1 received no such dividends. Since the reorganisation in 1981, Kayshewak and Eskay 2 have respectively received the minimum 6% dividend from Kaycee and Chellsons, but neither Kayshewak nor Eskay 2 has ever declared a dividend, so no income has ever been received by the trustees of the settlements. It follows that no distribution of trust income or trust capital to any of the beneficiaries under the settlements has ever been made.

Having thus reviewed the settlements and their history, I should now return to the individual members of the Chellaram family. Their respective circumstances are relevant both to a consideration of what is the proper law of the settlements, and also to counsel for the defendants forum conveniens argument.

Mohan is Indian by birth and domicile. At the date of the settlements he was resident in Lagos. He is now, and has for some time, been resident in Bombay.

Harish is also Indian by birth. He has a domicile of origin in India. In 1972, or thereabouts, he went with his wife and children to live in Singapore and manage the Singapore company, K Chellaram & Sons (Far East) Ltd. In order to do so, he was required under Singaporean law to bring into Singapore a substantial capital sum and to acquire the status of a permanent resident. He did both. He has since retained that status. Both he and his wife, Radhika, have deposed that on moving to Singapore they had no intention of ever returning to live in India and had acquired a Singaporean domicile at the time the settlements were made. No cross-examination has taken place of them or of any other deponent, notwithstanding a number of disputes of fact which appear from the affidavits. I bear that in mind, but nevertheless, addressing myself to the objective facts, I am unable to conclude that Harish has lost his domicile of origin, let alone that he had lost it by 14 February 1975. He has always held an Indian passport. I have seen copies of his passport issued in 1973, and of his current passport which was issued in 1980. In both his domicile is given as India. In both he gives as his permanent address in India his mother's Bombay address at which, it is common ground, rooms are permanently available for his and his family's occupation. His wife's successive passports and his children's passports likewise claim an Indian domicile with a permanent address in India at the home of Mrs Lachmibai Chellaram. The family regularly visit Bombay. I do not see any prospect that Harish, in the face of these facts, could establish that he had abandoned his Indian domicile of origin. The evidence, in my view, shows that when he made his settlement he was domiciled in India.

Mrs Lachmibai Chellaram is, and has always been, domiciled in India and resident in

Bombay. The sisters of Harish and Mohan are beneficiaries under the settlements; they
all live in India.

I now come to the trustees. I have already described the residence of the original
trustees at the date of the settlements. The present trustees are scattered around the
world. They are all Indian-born and domiciled in India. Lokumal is resident in India;
Lal is resident in Hong Kong; Sham is resident in Lagos. Of the Tahilram family, Ram is
resident in Las Palmas; Pishu is resident in India; Murli is resident part of the time in
Bombay and partly in West Africa. All of the Chellarams appear to have London
addresses, houses where they or their respective families stay when in England. These
houses stand in the names of their respective London companies. They all appear to visit
England with some regularity.

Mr Advani, the only non-family trustee, practises law in Bombay but visits England
regularly, usually in May of each year.

The bedrock of counsel for the defendants' case is that these two settlements are foreign
settlements, the proper law of which is the law of India. Counsel for the plaintiffs
contends, on the contrary, that the proper law is the law of England.

It is important to be clear at the outset as to the relevance of this issue on the present
application. The application seeks to prevent the plaintiffs from prosecuting in England
a claim for the removal of the trustees and for the appointment of new trustees. Counsel
for the defendants argues that the law by which the proposition that the trustees should
be removed must be tested, and by which the question of who should be appointed in
their places must be answered, is the proper law of the settlement. Counsel for the
plaintiffs submits, however, that it is not the proper law of the settlement but the law of
the place of administration that should govern such issues as removal of trustees and
appointment of new ones. The place of administration, he submits, is London.

The proper law of the settlement is, per Lord Greene MR in *Duke of Marlborough v A-G
(No 1)* [1945] 1 All ER 165 at 168, [1945] Ch 78 at 83, the law which governs the
settlement. He went on:

'This law can only be the law by reference to which the settlement was made and
which was intended by the parties to govern their rights and liabilities.'

In *Dicey and Morris on the Conflict of Laws* (10th edn, 1980) p 678, r 120 states:

'The validity, the interpretation and the effect of an *inter vivos* trust of movables
are governed by its proper law, that is, [r 120 identifying the proper law of the
settlement as:] in the absence of any express or implied selection of the proper law
by the settlor, the system of law with which the trust has its closest and most real
connection.'

When counsel for the defendants first opened the case to me, I was strongly inclined
to regard the law of India as the obvious proper law of these two settlements, but as
argument progressed I found myself progressively less certain. The beneficiaries are an
Indian family. The trustees were all Indian in origin although one or other may have
held a British passport. The settlements were drawn up in Bombay by Mr Advani, an
Indian practitioner, acting apparently in the course of his profession. The settlors were
Indian in origin and Indian-domiciled at the date of the settlement. All these factors
point, and I think point strongly, to the law of India being the proper law.

Mr Advani has sworn an affirmation in which he has stated in terms that he intended
Indian law to apply to these settlements which he drafted. This evidence is inadmissible
as evidence of the intentions of the parties to the settlements, but I may, I think, take it
as indicating that the settlements are appropriate in form for the purposes of Indian law.
Nevertheless, I am left with doubts. The trust property was Bermudian. The underlying
assets, in the form of the operating companies, were all situated outside India. The
purpose of the settlements was, it seems, in part to escape Indian taxation and, in part, to
escape Indian exchange control regulations. But most important of all, it seems to me, is
the identity of the three original trustees. Two, Mr Rupchand and Mr Bharwani, were
permanently resident in England. The third, Ram Chellaram, was the member of the

family who, in 1975, appeared to have the closest connection with England. The
inference is inescapable that the parties to the settlements contemplated that *a*
administration thereof would take place in London. Indeed, counsel for the defendants
accepted that this was an inference which was open to be drawn.

The question why, if the parties intended the settlements to be governed by Indian
law they should have arranged for an English administration, is a difficult one to answer.
The parties' contemplation of an English administration seems to me to point strongly
in favour of an English proper law. For the moment, however, I propose to leave the *b*
question open and to assume that counsel for the defendants is right that the law of India
is the proper law of the settlement and to see where that leads. It leads, counsel for the
defendants submitted, to the conclusion that the English courts should have nothing to
do with the plaintiffs' claim for the removal of the trustees. You cannot have, he said,
English courts removing foreign trustees of foreign settlements any more than you can
have foreign courts removing English trustees of English settlements. Tied up in this cri *c*
de cœur are, in my view, three separate points. First, there is the question of jurisdiction.
Does an English court have jurisdiction to entertain such a claim? Second, there is the
question of power. If an English court does have jurisdiction, can it make an effective
order removing foreign trustees of foreign settlements? Third, there is the forum
conveniens point. Is this an action which an English court ought to be trying?

I start with jurisdiction. In a sense, there is no doubt at all but that the court has *d*
jurisdiction. Each of the defendants was either served personally or service was effected
on Norton Rose Botterell & Roche who had authority to accept service. No question
arises as to the application of RSC Ord 11. By reason of due service of the writ, the court
has jurisdiction over each of the defendants in respect of each of the issues raised by the
writ.

As to subject matter, also there is in my judgment no doubt that the court has *e*
jurisdiction. In *Ewing v Orr Ewing* (1883) 9 App Cas 34 it was held by the House of Lords
that the English courts had jurisdiction to administer the trusts of the will of a testator
who died domiciled in Scotland. The will was proved in Scotland by executors, some of
whom resided in Scotland and some in England. The assets, the subject of the trusts,
consisted mainly of hereditable and personal property in Scotland. An infant beneficiary
resident in England brought an action in England for the administration of the trusts of *f*
the will by the English courts. It was clear that the proper law of the trusts was the law
of Scotland. None the less, the House of Lords, affirming the Court of Appeal, upheld
the jurisdiction of the English courts. The Earl of Selborne LC said (at 40–41):

> '. . . the jurisdiction of the English Court is established upon elementary principles.
> The Courts of Equity in England are, and always have been, Courts of conscience,
> operating in personam and not in rem; and in the exercise of this personal *g*
> jurisdiction they have always been accustomed to compel the performance of
> contracts and trusts as to subjects which were not either locally or ratione domicilii
> within their jurisdiction. They have done so as to land, in Scotland, in Ireland, in
> the Colonies, in foreign countries . . . A jurisdiction against trustees, which is not
> excluded ratione legis rei sitae as to land, cannot be excluded as to moveables,
> because the author of the trust may have had a foreign domicil; and for this purpose *h*
> it makes no difference whether the trust is constituted inter vivos, or by a will, or
> mortis causâ deed.'

Lord Blackburn agreed (at 45–46):

> 'It was argued that the domicil of the testator being Scotch, the Court of Chancery
> had no jurisdiction at all; that the jurisdiction depended on the domicil of the *j*
> testator, or at least on the probate in England, and was therefore confined to the
> comparatively small part of the property that was obtained by means of the English
> probate. I do not think that there is either principle or authority for this contention.
> The jurisdiction of the Court of Chancery is in personam. It acts upon the person
> whom it finds within its jurisdiction and compels him to perform the duty which
> he owes to the plaintiff.'

*a*  Both the Earl of Selborne LC and Lord Blackburn went on to say that the jurisdiction of the court to administer the foreign trust was not truly discretionary and that the plaintiff was entitled to the order sought ex debito justitiae (see 9 App Cas 34 at 41–42, 47–48).

That view cannot, in my judgment, stand with more recent pronouncements in the House of Lords (see eg Lord Diplock in *The Abidin Daver* [1984] 1 All ER 470 at 476, [1984] AC 398 at 411–412). Current authority establishes that the court does have a discretion to decline jurisdiction on forum conveniens or forum non conveniens grounds.

*b*  But the principle that the English court has jurisdiction to administer the trusts of foreign settlements remains unshaken. The jurisdiction is in personam, is exercised against the trustees on whom the foreign trust obligations lie, and is exercised so as to enforce against the trustees the obligations which bind their conscience.

The jurisdiction which I hold the court enjoys embraces, in my view, jurisdiction to remove trustees and appoint new ones. In *Letterstedt v Broers* (1884) 9 App Cas 371 at

*c*  385–386, [1881–5] All ER Rep 882 at 886 Lord Blackburn, giving the judgment of the Privy Council in a case on appeal from the Supreme Court of the then colony of the Cape of Good Hope, referred to a passage in *Story's Equity Jurisprudence* (12th edn, 1877) § 1289, which reads:

'. . . Courts of equity have no difficulty in interposing to remove trustees who have abused their trust . . .'

*d*
Lord Blackburn then continued:

'It seems to their Lordships that the jurisdiction which a Court of Equity has no difficulty in exercising under the circumstances indicated by Story is merely ancillary to its principal duty, to see that the trusts are properly executed.'

*e*  Accordingly, in my judgment, the courts of this country, having jurisdiction to administer the trusts of the two settlements, have jurisdiction ancillary thereto to remove the trustees.

The argument of counsel for the defendants that the court did not have jurisdiction to remove the trustees of a foreign settlement was based in part on the proposition that an order of removal would be ineffective to divest the present trustees of the fiduciary duties

*f*  they owed under the proper law of the settlements. To some extent, this submission was based on the form of the relief sought in para 4 of the writ. It seeks:

'An order removing the Defendants as trustees of Mohan's Settlement and Harish's Settlement and appointing some fit and proper persons to be trustees in their place.'

An order in that form would not of itself, however, divest existing trustees and vest trust

*g*  property in new trustees. Consequently, such an order would usually be accompanied by a vesting order under s 44 (in the case of land) or s 51 (in the case of stocks and shares) of the Trustee Act 1925. It could not, in my opinion, sensibly be suggested (and counsel for the plaintiffs has not suggested) that a vesting order under s 51 could divest the defendants of the trust shares in the Bermudian holding companies or could vest those shares in new trustees. A vesting effect could be achieved by a vesting order only in respect of stocks

*h*  and shares situated within the territorial jurisdiction of the court. Further, so long as the trust shares remain vested in the defendant trustees, their fiduciary obligations in respect thereof must remain. So, counsel for the defendants submitted, the court lacks the power to grant the relief sought by para 4 of the writ.

This argument is, in my judgment, based on a point of form and not of substance. The jurisdiction of the court to administer trusts, to which the jurisdiction to remove

*j*  trustees and appoint new ones is ancillary, is an in personam jurisdiction. In the exercise of it, the court will inquire what personal obligations are binding on the trustees and will enforce those obligations. If the obligations are owed in respect of trust assets abroad, the enforcement will be, and can only be, by in personam orders made against the trustees. The trustees can be ordered to pay, to sell, to buy, to invest, whatever may be necessary to give effect to the rights of the beneficiaries, which are binding on them. If the court is satisfied that, in order to give effect to or to protect the rights of the beneficiaries, trustees

ought to be replaced by others, I can see no reason in principle why the court should not
make in personam orders against the trustees requiring them to resign and to vest the
trust assets in the new trustees. The power of the court to remove trustees and to appoint
new ones, owes its origin to an inherent jurisdiction and not to statute, and it must follow
that the court has power to make such in personam orders as may be necessary to achieve
the vesting of the trust assets in the new trustees. This is so, in my judgment, whether or
not the trust assets are situated in England, and whether or not the proper law of the
trusts in question is English law. It requires only that the individual trustee should be
subject to the jurisdiction of the English courts. It does not matter, in my view, whether
they have become subject to the jurisdiction by reason of service of process in England
or because they have submitted to the jurisdiction, or because under RSC Ord 11 the
court has assumed jurisdiction. In every case, orders in personam are made by the courts
on the footing that those against whom they are made will obey them.

Accordingly, and for these reasons, I do not accept counsel for the defendants'
submission that the English courts have no power to remove the defendants as trustees
of these two settlements. Since, however, such removal would have to be effected by in
personam orders, the plaintiffs have put before me an amended statement of claim which
seeks such orders. In my judgment, the court would have power, if it thought it right to
do so, to make those orders.

There are two other associated points which I should now deal with. As an adjunct to
his submission that the English courts lack the power to remove trustees of foreign
settlements, counsel for the defendants submitted that if such an order in the in personam
form were made the defendants could not safely obey the order without first obtaining
confirmation from the Indian courts that it would be proper for them to do so. Further,
he submitted, his clients ought not to be subjected to such an order unless it were clear
that Indian law would regard them, if they did obey, as discharged from their fiduciary
obligations under the settlement.

It would be a matter entirely for the defendants and their advisers what steps they take
in the Indian courts, but for my part I am not impressed by the proposition that such
confirmation would be necessary. The English courts have jurisdiction over these
defendants. An objection to the exercise of jurisdiction on forum conveniens grounds
has been taken and I must deal with it, but, if in the end the case continues in England, I
would expect that the Indian courts, for reasons of comity would afford the same respect
to orders of this court as in like circumstances and for the same reasons English courts
would afford to theirs.

Counsel for the defendants suggested to me that I would give short shrift to an order
of a foreign court removing a trustee of an English trust; but if the English trustee had
been subject to the jurisdiction of the foreign court exercised in like circumstances to
those in which English courts claim and exercise jurisdiction, I can see no reason why I
should recoil from an order in personam made by the foreign court against an English
trustee. And if the order had been given effect to by, for example, the trustee transferring
trust assets in England into the names of new trustees, I can see no reason why an English
court should question the efficacy of the transfer. All of this assumes, of course, that
there were no vitiating features in the manner in which the foreign order was obtained.

As to the point that the defendants might, notwithstanding that they had transferred
the Bermudian shares to new trustees, still owe fiduciary duties under the settlements,
there is, in my view, no substance in that point. Firstly, no party to the English action
could so contend. Mohan and Lachmibai Chellaram are not parties to the action but
could easily be joined, as also could any of the sisters who wished to be joined. This does
not therefore seem to me to be a practical problem. Secondly, the point could be raised
as a defence to the plaintiffs' claim for the removal of trustees, and, if the court were
satisfied that the point was a sound one, I cannot imagine that the defendants would be
ordered to transfer the shares. Thirdly, the status of trustee and the burden of the
fiduciary obligations arising therefrom have, as it seems to me, no reality except in
relation to assets which are vested in or under the control of the trustee. If a trustee is
divested of the trust assets, I do not understand how it can be supposed that he can retain

any fiduciary obligation thereafter in respect of those assets or in respect of the income derived from them.

I do not, therefore, think, there is anything in counsel for the defendants' objections to the efficacy of the in personam orders, if such orders were made.

I have dealt with counsel for the defendants' submission on jurisdiction and on the power of an English court to make the orders sought on the footing that Indian law is the proper law of the settlements. As an adjunct to his arguments on those matters, counsel for the defendants submitted that, if Indian law was the proper law of the settlements, then Indian law was the system of law which ought to be applied to the matter of removal of trustees of the settlements, and to the appointment of new ones. He drew my attention to the relevant provisions of the Indian Trusts Act 1882, as amended up to 1969, and commented, rightly in my opinion, that the various provisions in that Act relevant to the removal and appointment of trustees by the Indian court could not be applied by an English court in the present case.

Counsel for the defendants wielded this point as part of his argument on jurisdiction and also as relevant to his forum conveniens point. Counsel for the plaintiffs has contended that the proper law of the settlement is English law but he has submitted that, even if that is wrong, England is the place where the trusts were intended to be administered and the place where, in fact, the trusts have been administered, that the administration of a trust is governed not by the proper law of the trust but by the law of the place where administration takes place, and that the removal of trustees and the appointment of new ones is a matter of administration. It is a feature of the history of these settlements that there has been remarkably little administration. The reason for this is that the trust property has been represented simply by shares in Bermudian holding companies, and no trust income has been derived therefrom. Until recently, when in response to the plaintiffs' demand trust accounts were prepared, there were no such accounts. However, counsel for the plaintiffs is, in my view, right in pointing out that such administration as there has been has taken place in London. It was in London that the deeds of retirement and appointment of new trustees were prepared and executed; such legal advice as has been taken by the trustees seems to have been taken by Mr Advani from Norton Rose Botterell & Roche in London, and there seems to me to be no room for any real doubt that the parties to the settlement contemplated that the administration would take place in London.

Accordingly, in my judgment, the factual basis on which counsel for the plaintiffs makes his submission is sound. As to law, counsel for the plaintiffs relies on the proposition stated in *Dicey and Morris* p 683, r 121 that:

'The administration of a trust is governed (*semble*) by the law of its place of administration.'

Among the matters classified in the notes to r 121 as matters of administration is 'the question who can appoint a new trustee and what persons may be so appointed'. If this rule correctly states the law, it would seem to follow that the issue regarding removal of the trustees of these settlements should be governed by the law of the place of administration of the settlements. However, the tentative manner in which the rule is expressed is justified, in my view, by the lack of clear authority provided by the cases cited in the footnotes.

There are two categories of case which must be distinguished from cases as the present case. Firstly, there are cases which establish that the administrative powers conferred on personal representatives by the Administration of Estates Act 1925 can be exercised by English personal representatives in relation to assets in England, whether or not the deceased died domiciled in England (see *Re Wilks, Keefer v Wilks* [1935] Ch 645, [1935] All ER Rep 787). These cases exemplify the well-settled proposition that the administration of a deceased's assets is governed by the law of the country from which the administrator derives his authority.

Secondly, there are cases which support the view that the provisions of English trust legislation apply to trust property situated in England whether or not the trusts on which the trust property is held are the trusts of foreign settlements (see *Re Kehr (decd), Martin v Foges* [1951] 2 All ER 812, [1952] Ch 26, although Danckwerts J doubted 'whether trustees constituted by the law of a foreign country would have the powers conferred on trustees regulated by English law' (see [1951] 2 All ER 812 at 814, [1952] Ch 26 at 30); see also *Re Ker's Settlement Trusts* [1963] 1 All ER 801, [1963] Ch 553. But neither of these lines of cases supports the proposition in *Dicey and Morris*, r 121 when applied to a foreign settlement which is being administered in England but where the trust property is not in England.

More cogent support is provided by *Wynn NO and Westminster Bank Ltd NO v Oppenheimer, Re Pollak's Estate* [1937] TPD 91. In that case the testator was domiciled in the Transvaal. He left moveables in England and in South Africa as well as in other countries. By his will he appointed as his executor and trustee an English bank which had no branch in South Africa and left his residuary estate on trust for beneficiaries, the majority of whom were domiciled in England. A number of questions were raised for the decision of the Transvaal court, including a question as to the law which should determine the rights and duties of the bank as trustee in the execution of the testamentary trust. Since the testator was domiciled in the Transvaal, South African law governed the construction of the will, but the court concluded that the testator had intended the trust to be administered in England, and Davis J, with whose judgment Greenberg J concurred, said (at 101):

'I have no doubt that in appointing an English bank . . . to administer a trust fund wherein the great majority of the persons interested were at the time domiciled in England, the testator . . . intended English law to govern.'

He cited with approval this passage in the American Law Institute's Restatement of the Law of Conflict of Laws (see [1937] TPD 91 at 101–102):

'If the testator appoints as trustee a trust company of another state, presumptively his intention is that the trust should be administered in the latter state; the trust will therefore be administered according to the law of the latter state.'

Accordingly, the court held that the rights and duties of the bank as trustee were to be governed by English law, notwithstanding that the essential validity of the trust and the construction of the will were governed by the law of South Africa, the domicile of the testator. The reasoning which led the Transvaal court to this decision I respectfully accept. The court concluded that the testator in establishing a settlement to be administered in England must have intended English law to govern its administration. The court gave effect to that intention. But it does not follow from *Wynn NO and Westminster Bank Ltd NO v Oppenheimer, Re Pollak's Estate* that the law of the place of the administration of a trust would govern the rights and duties of the trustee in a case where the circumstances did not enable the inference to be drawn that such was the testator's or settlor's intention. *Wynn NO and Westminster Bank Ltd NO v Oppenheimer, Re Pollak's Estate* was a case of testamentary trust. It is well-established English law that the essential validity of a testamentary trust of movables is governed by the law of the testator's domicile. But there is no reason why a testator should not by will establish a trust to be governed by some law other than the law of his domicile. His ability to create the trust may be subject to the law of his domicile but subject thereto he is, in my view, as able by will to make a foreign settlement as he is able to do so inter vivos. *Wynn NO and Westminster Bank Ltd NO v Oppenheimer, Re Pollak's Estate* supports the proposition that a testator can do so. It does not, in my view, support anything further and does not really support r 121.

As a matter of principle, I find myself unable to accept the distinction drawn by rr 120 and 121 in *Dicey and Morris* between 'validity, interpretation and effect' on the one hand and 'administration' on the other hand. The rights and duties of trustees, for example, may be regarded as matters of administration but they also concern the effect of the settlement. The rights of the trustees are enjoyed as against the beneficiaries; the duties of the trustees are owed to the beneficiaries. If the rights of the beneficiaries are to be

ascertained by applying the proper law of the settlement, I do not understand how the
*a*   duties of the trustees can be ascertained by applying a different law, and vice versa. In
my judgment, a conclusion that the law of the place of administration of a settlement
governs such matters as the rights and duties of the trustees can only be right if that law
is the proper law governing the settlement.

But the right of beneficiaries to have trustees removed and new ones appointed is a
right of a rather special nature. It is not, at least in the usual case, a right conferred by the
*b*   settlement. If it were the case that a settlement conferred on particular beneficiaries or
on a particular person such as the settlor the right to remove trustees and appoint new
ones, that right (like any other rights conferred by the settlement on beneficiaries or
trustees) would, in my view, require to be given effect in accordance with the proper law
of the settlement. That would, in my view, be so, regardless of where the settlement was
being administered. But no such right is conferred by the two settlements with which I
*c*   am concerned.

The plaintiffs' claim for the removal of trustees and the appointment of new ones is,
in this case, as in most cases, not an attempt to enforce a corresponding right conferred
by the settlements, but is an appeal to the inherent jurisdiction of the court to which
Lord Blackburn referred in *Letterstedt v Broers* (1884) 9 App Cas 371 at 385–386,
[1881–5] All ER Rep 882 at 886. The function of English courts in trust litigation is to
*d*   enforce or protect the rights of the beneficiaries which bind the conscience of the trustee
defendants. The identification and extent of those rights is a matter for the proper law of
the settlement, but the manner of enforcement is, in my view, a matter of machinery
which depends on the powers enjoyed by the English courts. Among the powers available
to English courts is the power to order the removal of trustees and the appointment of
new ones. This power is, in my view, machinery which, under English domestic law,
*e*   can be exercised by English courts where necessary in order to enable the rights of
beneficiaries to be enforced or protected. The exercise of the domestic power does not, in
my view, depend on whether the rights of the beneficiaries are enjoyed under domestic
settlements or foreign settlements, or on whether the trust property is situated in
England or abroad. The locality of the trust property will, however, determine whether
the removal can be achieved by an in rem order or whether an in personam order is
*f*   appropriate. Accordingly, except where rights conferred by the settlement are under
consideration, the removal of trustees and the appointment of new ones is not, in my
judgment, a matter to be governed by the proper law of the settlement. Nor, in my
opinion, is it a matter governed by the law of the place where the administration of the
settlement has taken place. It is, in my judgment, a matter to be governed by the law of
the country whose courts have assumed jurisdiction to administer the trusts of the
*g*   settlement in question.

In the view of the matter I take, therefore, I do not think that the identification of the
proper law of the settlement is a critical issue on this application. Any court before which
the plaintiffs' case is litigated will have to consider the rights of the beneficiaries under
these discretionary settlements in order to form an opinion whether the enforcement or
protection of those rights requires the removal of the present trustees but no one has
*h*   suggested that the nature of those rights is going to be different if tested under Indian
law than if tested under English law. Any such difference is likely to be marginal only
and to be immaterial for the purposes of the plaintiffs' claim for the removal of the
trustees.

Counsel for the defendants argued that, if the proper law of the settlements were the
law of India, the identity of any new trustees should be decided on by the application of
*j*   criteria relevant to an Indian discretionary trust established for the benefit of an Indian
family, and that this could not well be done by an English court. I hope I have the
argument correctly, and if I have I am bound to say that I think there is nothing in it.
On any footing, these discretionary settlements are Indian settlements, in a descriptive
and not a proper law sense, intended for the benefit of an Indian family, and English
courts if they came to appoint new trustees, would apply criteria to their selection which
would reflect that character of the settlements. I do not accept that the criteria which

would be applied by an Indian court would be any different from those applied by an English court, and I do not accept that in either jurisdiction those criteria would be any *a* different if English law or Indian law were the proper law of the settlements.

It is, therefore, not necessary for me to decide on this application whether Indian law or English law is the proper law of the settlements. I am dealing with an interlocutory application. The relevant evidence has not been tested by cross-examination. In these circumstances, I would, I think, be unwise to express a conclusion on the proper law question and I do not do so. *b*

I have held, contrary to counsel for the defendants' submission, that the English courts have both jurisdiction and power to deal with the plaintiffs' claim for the removal of trustees and for the appointment of new ones. In that event, counsel for the defendants submits that the court ought nevertheless to decline to exercise that jurisdiction on the ground, shortly stated, that there is another competent jurisdiction, India, in which justice can be done between the parties, and that by comparison with India, England is a *c* forum non conveniens. I have been referred to a number of decisions in which the criteria to be applied by a court which is asked to stay an action on, in effect, forum non conveniens grounds, have been discussed. Counsel for the defendants referred me to *The Atlantic Star, Atlantic Star (owners) v Bona Spes (owners)* [1973] 2 All ER 175 at 181, 200, [1974] AC 436 at 454, 475 to Lord Reid's dictum that the plaintiff should offer some reasonable justification for his choice of forum, and Lord Kilbrandon's comments that *d* conveniens is to be read as meaning 'appropriate' rather than 'convenient'.

In *MacShannon v Rockware Glass Ltd* [1978] 1 All ER 625 at 636, 644, [1978] AC 795 at 818–819, 828 Lord Salmon expressed the test as being whether the defendants could show that to refuse a stay would produce injustice and Lord Keith said that a defendant seeking a stay must show good reason why the court's discretion should be exercised in his favour. I was referred to *Amin Rasheed Shipping Corp v Kuwait Insurance Co, The Al* *e* *Wahab* [1983] 2 All ER 884 at 893, [1984] AC 50 at 68, where Lord Diplock referred to excessive costs or excessive delay likely to be occasioned by the foreign proceedings as factors to be taken into account, and to the most recent House of Lords authority on the subject, *The Abidin Daver* [1984] 1 All ER 470 at 476, [1984] AC 398 at 411, where Lord Diplock commented that there was no longer any discernible difference between the English law approach and the Scottish doctrine of forum non conveniens. Counsel for *f* the plaintiffs referred me to the principles set out by Robert Goff J in *Trendtex Trading Corp v Crédit Suisse* [1980] 3 All ER 721 at 734.

These authorities establish that the old rule expressed by Lord Blackburn in *Ewing v Orr Ewing* (1883) 9 App Cas 34 that an English court has no discretion, where defendant trustees are properly before it, to decline to administer the trust of a foreign settlement, is no longer good law. On the positive side, the authorities establish that in all cases *g* where, on forum conveniens grounds a stay is sought, the court must strike a balance between the right of the plaintiff to choose his forum and the right of the defendant that he should not be required to take part in litigation before a court inappropriate for that litigation. In striking the balance, all the circumstances relevant to the parties and to the litigation are proper to be taken into account.

The circumstances on which counsel for the defendants most heavily relied was that *h* these are Indian settlements made for the benefit of an Indian family. I accept his adjectives if used in a descriptive sense, and I accept that this is a factor in favour of litigation in India rather that in England. The point is, however, a rather more precise one. Although litigation in India and the jurisdiction of the Indian courts have been mentioned, it is in fact litigation in Bombay and the jurisdiction of the Bombay courts for which counsel for the defendants is contending. The Chellaram family is a Bombay *j* family. The evidence adduced before me has concerned the jurisdiction of, and the incidents of, litigation in the Bombay courts. There has been no evidence relating to litigation in any other courts in India.

Counsel for the plaintiffs has sought to meet counsel for the defendants' point by questioning whether the Bombay court would accept jurisdiction in this case, and I have had expert evidence as to this from Bombay lawyers. Mr Mehta, for the plaintiffs, has

given his opinion that the Bombay court would not have jurisdiction. Mr Munim, for
the defendants, has concluded that it would. Both views depend on certain assumptions
which Mr Mehta and Mr Munim respectively make. Having considered this evidence,
the position, in my view, can be summarised thus: the Bombay court has the jurisdiction
conferred on it by the letters patent which created it; it does not enjoy, as does the
English court, an inherent jurisdiction. The Bombay court has, as I understand it,
jurisdiction if the defendants are resident or carry on business within its territorial area.
This requirement is satisfied so far as Mr Advani, Lokumal Chellaram and Pishu
Chellaram are concerned. As to the others, Lal, Ram, Sham and Murli, each of them
retains in Bombay both a business and residential connection which I would expect to be
sufficient to satisfy the jurisdictional requirements. It is, however, on the evidence,
possible that there might be some difficulty in the case of Lal who resides generally in
Hong Kong, and in the case of Sham, who is generally in Nigeria, in establishing the
requirement.

In addition, the Bombay court has jurisdiction whenever the cause of action in question
arises within the jurisdiction. This test of jurisdiction is a little difficult to apply to a case
where administration of a trust, or a facet thereof such as the removal of the trustees, is
sought. This is particularly so where, as here, the trust property is not situated within the
jurisdiction.

Although on the evidence before me, I think it likely that the Bombay court would
accept jurisdiction, I am left with a measure of doubt whether it would, under the terms
of its letters patent, have jurisdiction to entertain this case. It is true, as counsel for the
defendants pointed out, that all the defendants, having asserted before me that the
Bombay court would have jurisdiction, would be in a poor position to assert before the
Bombay court that it did not. But neither of the experts has commented on this point,
and I am not sure that I can make any assumptions as to how the Bombay court would
be likely to receive it. Under English law, a statutory jurisdiction cannot normally be
enlarged by an estoppel.

I think, therefore, that the lack of certainty about the jurisdiction of the Bombay court
goes some way to counteracting counsel for the defendants' reliance on the Indian nature
of the settlements and the beneficiaries.

There is, however, a further important point regarding litigation in Bombay. The
evidence before me was that the usual delay in the Bombay court between the
commencement of an action and the date of hearing is from seven to ten years. Counsel
for the defendants accepted that that was so but suggested that the plaintiffs could bring
their claim by means of a petition instead of by writ, and that an action commenced by
petition would be far more expeditious than an action commenced by writ. However,
nothing in the expert evidence supported either suggestion. Mr Advani, Mr Mehta and
Mr Munim discussed the likely delay in the case of writ actions. None mentioned the
possibility of a petition. I cannot believe that one or other would not have done so had a
petition represented a practicable and preferable alternative. I must, therefore, approach
the present application for a stay on the footing that if the plaintiffs are required to
litigate in India they must expect a minimum delay of seven years before obtaining a
hearing. Such delay might expose the plaintiffs to considerable hardship. I have already
observed that no income has ever been produced by the trust shareholdings and that no
distributions under the settlements have ever been made. This circumstance, whether or
not a matter of legitimate complaint by the plaintiffs, has never in the past been
complained about. Harish Chellaram and his family have in the past been in receipt of
very substantial periodic payments from family sources. The evidence before me does
not indicate the precise source of these payments, nor whether the payment had any, and
if so, what connection with the interests of the plaintiffs under the settlements. However,
in May 1983 the payments ceased. I need not explore the reasons why the payments
ceased; the evidence put before me on that matter is highly controversial and is untested
by any cross-examination. It is, however, common ground that the payments have ceased
and that the financial position of Harish and his family has correspondingly worsened.
Substantial assets potentially available for the support of Harish and his family are tied

up in the settlements, but those assets are controlled by the defendants and are not producing any income at all. In these circumstances, I think that counsel for the plaintiffs is entitled to say that a minimum seven-year and a possible ten-year delay before a hearing can be obtained, might represent a serious injustice to the plaintiffs.

I bear in mind that, if the English action continues, there will be some delay in England before the case is heard, but I do not believe the delay will approach anywhere near the minimum seven-year delay which, it seems, must be expected in Bombay. This, in my view, represents a heavy factor in the balance against a stay.

The personal circumstances of the parties and any witnesses are relevant. As to this, I accept that India would be a more convenient locality in which to litigate than England would be. This is certainly so for the defendants who live in India, namely Mr Advani, Lokumal and Pishu. It is probably so for Murli, Sham and Lal, although I find it difficult to see why it should be so for Ram. For the plaintiffs too, who live in Singapore, Bombay would seem, objectively speaking, to be a more convenient locality for litigation than London. For Mrs Lachmibai Chellaram and Mohan Chellaram, both of whom are probable witnesses and possible additional parties, Bombay would be far more convenient than London. However, all the defendants have establishments in London at which they reside from time to time with their respective families. I infer that there would be no difficulty in Mrs Lachmibai Chellaram and Mohan obtaining accommodation in London in a family environment. Moreover, the Chellaram family, although properly described as a Bombay family, are in many respects an international family. London is familiar to them. They visit London relatively regularly and, at least to some extent, organise their business affairs from London. I do not, therefore, regard the geographic convenience of Bombay as a factor of very much weight.

Taking into account all the various factors, the balance comes down, in my opinion, firmly on the side of allowing the litigation in England to continue. The commencement of the action in England was not, in my view, an exercise in 'forum shopping': there always was, and is, a strong connection between England and the settlements, and between England and the Chellaram family. Administration of the settlements was intended at the date of the settlements to take place in England. Such administration thereof as there has been since the date of the settlements, has taken place in England. four of the defendants hold British passports. All the defendants as well as the plaintiffs regularly spend time in England. In these circumstances, the pejorative epithet of 'forum shopping' is not, in my judgment, aptly applied to the commencement by the plaintiffs of this action in England. Further relevant factors are that this is not a lis alibi pendens case and that it is a case in which each of the defendants was either served personally in England or gave instructions to Norton Rose Botterell & Roche to accept service on his behalf, and thereby voluntarily submitted to the jurisdiction.

In my judgment, the defendants have failed to cast England as a forum non conveniens. It is settled on authority that the onus lies on the defendants to satisfy me that I ought, in my discretion, to grant a stay. They have not done so, and I therefore refuse a stay and dismiss their application.

*Application dismissed.*

Solicitors: *Norton Rose Botterell & Roche* (for the defendants); *Macfarlanes* (for the plaintiffs).

Jacqueline Metcalfe    Barrister.

# Chief Supplementary Benefit Officer v Leary

COURT OF APPEAL, CIVIL DIVISION

LAWTON, KERR AND SLADE LJJ

17 SEPTEMBER, 18 OCTOBER 1984

*Precedent – Social security commissioners – Decisions binding on commissioners – Previous decisions of High Court given when exercising jurisdiction subsequently conferred on commissioners – Whether such decisions binding on commissioners – Tribunals and Inquiries Act 1971, s 13 – Tribunals and Inquiries (Supplementary Benefit Appeal Tribunals) Order 1977 – Tribunals and Inquiries (Supplementary Benefit Appeal Tribunals) (Revocation) Order 1980.*

*Supplementary benefit – Overpayment – Recovery – Misrepresentation or non-disclosure – Recovery after death of claimant – Calculation of sums overpaid – Sum of cash and moneys in bank account discovered after death of claimant – Whether such sums are 'capital resources' – Whether such sums more properly 'resources not specified [elsewhere] in ... provisions' – Supplementary Benefit Act 1976, Sch 1, paras 20, 27.*

From 1970 until his death in 1981 the claimant was in receipt of payments of supplementary benefit made under the Supplementary Benefits Act 1976. Such payments were calculated on the basis that the claimant's only capital resources were a small sum in a savings bank and a premium bond. After his death it was found that the claimant had also had moneys in two bank accounts and a sum of cash. The supplementary benefit officer claimed, pursuant to s 20[a] of the 1976 Act, a sum from the respondent, the claimant's personal representative, in respect of the overpayment made consequent on the claimant's non-disclosure, the amount claimed being calculated on the basis that the moneys were to be treated as 'capital resources' under para 20[b] of Sch 1 to the 1976 Act. The respondent appealed to a supplementary benefit appeal tribunal, which dismissed the appeal, and then to the Tribunal of Social Security Commissioners, contending that the sums were to be treated as 'resources not specified' elsewhere in the schedule, in accordance with para 27[c] of Sch 1. The commissioners held that they were not bound to follow previous decisions of the High Court on points of law made between 1 January 1978 and 24 November 1980 under the jurisdiction conferred on it by the Tribunals and Inquiries Act 1971, s 13 and the Tribunal and Inquiries (Supplementary Benefit Appeal Tribunals) Order 1977, since during that period the High Court had exercised a jurisdiction which had subsequently been vested in the commissioners by the Tribunals and Inquiries (Supplementary Benefit Appeal Tribunals) (Revocation) Order 1980. Accordingly they declined to follow a decision of the High Court when that court was exercising such jurisdiction and they allowed the appeal. The benefit officer appealed to the Court of Appeal.

**Held** – The appeal would be dismissed for the following reasons—

(1) Although an inferior court was not entitled to disregard a decision of a superior court, a distinction was to be drawn between decisions of the High Court exercising its supervisory jurisdiction, which was wide and discretionary, and which was binding on the commissioners, and the particular jurisdiction conferred on the High Court by the 1976 Act and the 1977 order, which was much more narrow and not discretionary. The effect of the 1980 order was that the narrower jurisdiction exercised by the High Court between 1 January 1978 and 24 November 1980 was subsequently to be exercised by the commissioners and in those circumstances it could not have been intended that when exercising the same jurisdiction the commissioner should be bound by earlier decisions

---

*a*   Section 20, so far as material, is set out at p 1064 *e*, post

*b*   Paragraph 20 is set out at p 1064 *a*, post

*c*   Paragraph 27 is set out at p 1063 *j*, post

of the High Court. Accordingly the commissioners had been entitled to decide that the
earlier decision of the High Court was not binding on them (see p 1065 e to j, post).    **a**

(2) Paragraphs 20 and 27 of Sch 1 to the 1976 Act were not mutually exclusive and
accordingly there was no reason why cash sums or other moneys should not be considered
under para 27 merely because they were 'capital resources' for the purposes of para 20.
On its true construction para 27 required the Department of Health and Social Security,
in calculating the claimant's resources, to disregard the specific resources, set out in paras
17 to 19 but to take into account those resources specified in paras 21 to 26 relating to    **b**
income and pensions. Accordingly the department had a discretion to treat other
resources, including capital resources not specifically mentioned elsewhere in the
schedule, as reduced by such amount as would be reasonable in the particular
circumstances of a case. Furthermore there was no reason to restrict the ambit of para 27
to casual receipts of money, such as gifts (see p 1064 j to p 1065 d and h, post).

### Cases referred to in judgment
    **c**

*Farrell v Alexander* [1976] 2 All ER 721, [1977] AC 59, [1976] 3 WLR 145, HL.
*Musgrove v Secretary of State for Social Services* (3 July 1981, unreported), QBD.

### Cases also cited

*Bland v Chief Supplementary Benefit Officer* [1983] 1 All ER 537, [1983] 1 WLR 262, CA.
*Chapman v Goonvean and Rostowrack China Clay Co Ltd* [1973] 1 All ER 218, [1972] 1 WLR    **d**
    1634, NIRC; *affd* [1973] 2 All ER 1063, [1973] 1 WLR 678, CA.
*R v National Insurance Comr, ex p Stratton* [1979] 2 All ER 278, [1979] QB 361, CA.
*R v Social Security Commission, ex p Butler* (16 December 1983, unreported), QBD.
*Racal Communications Ltd, Re* [1980] 2 All ER 634, [1981] AC 374, HL.

### Notes
    **e**
For the right of recovery of supplementary benefit on misrepresentation or non-
disclosure, see 33 Halsbury's Laws (4th edn) paras 834–851, and for cases on the subject,
see 35 Digest (Reissue) 733–734, 6982–6986.

For appeals from supplementary benefit appeal tribunals, see 33 Halsbury's Laws (4th
edn) para 819.

For the Tribunals and Inquiries Act 1971, s 13, see 41 Halsbury's Statutes (3rd edn)    **f**
258.

For the Supplementary Benefit Act 1976, s 20, Sch 1, Pt III (paras 17–30), see 46 ibid
1065, 1083.

As from 24 November 1980 (subject to a saving) Sch 1 to the 1976 Act was substituted
by para 30 of Sch 2 to the Social Security Act 1980. For the purpose of ascertaining the
amount of supplementary benefit to which a person is entitled, his resources are now
calculated in accordance with the Supplementary Benefit (Resources) Regulations 1981,    **g**
SI 1981/1527, made under para 1(2)(b) of Sch 1 (as substituted) to the 1976 Act.

### Appeal

The Chief Supplementary Benefit Officer appealed with leave against the decision of the
Tribunal of Social Security Commissioners (Mr I O Griffiths QC, Mr V G H Hallett and
Mr D G Rice) given on 25 July 1983 whereby it held (i) that the amount to be repaid to    **h**
the Department of Health and Social Security by the respondent, A J Leary, the personal
representative of the deceased claimant, Timothy Leary, in respect of the sums held in
bank accounts and in cash constituted 'resources not specified in the foregoing provisions
of this Schedule' as set out in para 27 of Sch 1 to the Supplementary Benefits Act 1976
and not 'capital resources' within para 20 of Sch 1, and (ii) that it was not bound by a
previous decision of the High Court to the contrary effect. The facts are set out in the    **j**
judgment of the court.

*Robert Carnwath* for the appellant.
*Richard Drabble* for the respondent.

*Cur adv vult*

18 October. The following judgment of the court was delivered.

**LAWTON LJ.** This is the judgment of the court on an appeal by the chief supplementary benefit officer against a decision of the Tribunal of Social Security Commissioners given on 25 July 1983 whereby they adjudged that the decision of the Supplementary Benefit Appeal Tribunal given on 18 December 1981 was erroneous in point of law and should be set aside and the claim for benefit reheard. The appellant did not submit that the decision was not erroneous in point of law. What has concerned him is the directions which the commissioners gave as to how a differently constituted tribunal was to treat the claim when it was reheard. The appellant submitted that in giving these directions the commissioners misconstrued Pt III of Sch 1 to the Supplementary Benefits Act 1976 and failed to follow a decision of the High Court which was binding on them.

*The facts*

On 2 March 1970 the late Mr Timothy Leary (the deceased) began to receive supplementary benefit. This was on the basis that his only capital consisted of a National Savings Bank account and one premium bond. He went on receiving supplementary benefit until his death on 11 May 1981. After his death it was discovered that he had had £1,589·14 cash in his possession and current and deposit accounts with the Midland Bank which were in credit in a total sum of £3,513·31. Had the Department of Health and Social Security (the DHSS) known these facts, the deceased would not have been paid the amounts of supplementary benefit which were paid. The overpayment was alleged to be £4,383. This sum was claimed, pursuant to s 20 of the 1976 Act, from the deceased's personal representative, the respondent to this appeal. He appealed to the Supplementary Benefit Appeal Tribunal. That tribunal dismissed the appeal on the ground that 'he could not provide evidence of how the cash in the house accrued'. The commissioners adjudged, and the appellant has accepted, that the tribunal misdirected themselves as to the burden of proof. This was the main reason why a rehearing was ordered. The commissioners, in paras 5 and 6 of their decision, set out their reasons for deciding as they did about the burden of proof. Neither party in this court has criticised their reasons. When the case is reheard by a new appeal tribunal there will be an issue as to the origin of the cash sum of £1,589·14 and when it was acquired by the deceased. Another issue before the commissioners was the method by which the DHSS had calculated the alleged overpayment. It was accepted in this court that a wrong method of calculating the overpayment had been used and that the correct method would take into account the fact that any financial resources the deceased had would have diminished as time went by because he would have had to use some of them to get the money which he would have required week by week to live. We do not find it necessary to say anything more about how, as a matter of accounting, the overpayment (and there was clearly some) should be calculated. What is relevant for the purposes of this appeal is the statutory basis for adopting this accounting method.

*The appeal issues*

The commissioners thought the statutory basis was derived from para 27 of Sch 1 to the 1976 Act, which is in these terms:

'Any resources not specified in the foregoing provisions of this Schedule may be treated as reduced by such amount (if any) as may be reasonable in the circumstances of the case.'

The appellant has submitted that the agreed accounting method involves nothing more than the application of the arithmetical principle of diminishing returns to para 20 of that schedule, which provides as follows:

'The capital resources taken into account, together with any income derived from
them, shall be treated as equivalent to a weekly income of 25p for each complete     *a*
£50 of the excess of the value of the capital resources over £1,200.'

He submitted that para 27 of that schedule is wholly irrelevant in the present case, on the
grounds that the cash sum of £1,589·14 and the moneys totalling £3,513·31 standing in
the two bank accounts, while constituting 'capital resources' within para 20, do not
constitute 'resources not specified in the foregoing provisions of this Schedule' within     *b*
para 27. On the facts of this case in terms of money it will probably matter little to the
respondent whether para 20 or para 27 applies; but to the DHSS it matters a great deal
because cases of overpayment involve millions of pounds of public money.

In deciding as they did about the construction and relevance of para 27, the
commissioners adjudged that they were not bound by a decision of Sir Douglas Frank
QC, sitting as a deputy judge of the High Court in *Musgrove v Secretary of State for Social
Services* (3 July 1981, unreported), which was to the contrary effect. Counsel for the     *c*
appellant submitted that they were bound by that decision. He told us that this problem
of precedence was of importance to the administration of the supplementary benefit
legislation because between 1 January 1978 and 24 November 1980 appeals from appeal
tribunals went to the High Court, not as now to the commissioners. The DHSS want to
know whether such High Court judgments as were given during this period on appeal
from appeal tribunals are binding on the commissioners. It was not in dispute before us     *d*
that all judgments given by the High Court under its supervisory jurisdiction are binding
on the commissioners.

As we have said, the appellant's claim was made under s 20(1) of the 1976 Act, which
is in these terms:

> 'If, whether fraudulently or otherwise, any person misrepresents, or fails to     *e*
> disclose, any material fact, and in consequence of the misrepresentation or failure—
> (a) the Secretary of State incurs any expenditure under this Act . . . the Secretary of
> State shall be entitled to recover the amount thereof from that person.'

The DHSS did incur expenditure because the deceased had failed to disclose material
facts, namely his two bank accounts and possibly the cash found in his house. What the     *f*
DHSS can recover will depend on the expenditure it would have incurred had the
deceased made the disclosures he should have made. Supplementary benefit to which a
person is entitled is the amount by which his resources fall short of his requirements: see
para 1(1) of Pt I of Sch 1 to the Act. The method of calculating requirements is set out in
Pt II of that schedule and of calculating resources in Pt III. The word 'resources', however,
is not defined. It includes assets of all kinds. Some resources, however, are to be     *g*
disregarded: interest in a dwelling house (para 17), maternity and death grants and sums
payable to a person as holder of the Victoria Cross or the George Cross (para 18) and the
value of capital resources which do not exceed £1,200 (para 19). Capital resources which
are to be taken into account are to be treated as equivalent to a weekly income of 25p for
each complete £50 of the excess of the capital resources over £1,200: see para 20. If the
capital resources to be taken into account are in the form of bank or building society     *h*
credits, as they usually are, para 20 is easy to apply; but if they are in the form of movable
property such property will have to be valued, and if it is owned jointly by the claimant
with someone else who refuses to agree to a sale there will be difficulty as to how much,
if any, of the value is to be taken into account. Even if the claimant is the sole owner of
movable property, it may be unreasonable to take particular items into account in
applying para 20. For example, he may be a disabled person, unable to earn, who needs a     *j*
motor car to get about. It would be surprising in such a case if the DHSS had to give a
value to the motor car and take it into account when making the calculation required
under para 20. Part III of Sch 1 sets out in paras 17 to 19 and 21 to 26 how particular
kinds of resources are to be dealt with. In so far as these paragraphs apply in any particular
case the DHSS is left with no discretion.

Then comes para 27. We construe this paragraph as meaning that, when assessing the
amount of the claimant's resources, the DHSS *must* disregard the specific resources
mentioned in paras 17 to 19 but *must* take into account those specified in paras 21 to 26.
Any other resources (and they would include capital resources not specifically mentioned
in paras 17 to 19 and 21 to 26) may be treated as reduced by such amount, if any, as may
be reasonable in all the circumstances of the case. If the DHSS has this discretion (as we
adjudge it has) the calculation required by para 20 becomes easier and more reasonable.
The value of the motor car for example used by the disabled person can be disregarded,
as can interest in a valuable asset jointly owned. On the other hand, such discretion as
there is in the DHSS would be used unreasonably if the official exercising it disregarded
the intention of the Act, namely that those persons who have resources over the
prescribed limits should use them for their own requirements. We can find nothing in
Sch 1 to justify the DHSS's submission that para 27 cannot apply to the cash sum and
other moneys in question merely because they are 'capital resources' within para 20.
Paragraphs 20 and 27, in our judgment, are not mutually exclusive. It was suggested that
para 27 should be construed as applying to casual receipts such as birthday presents and
money won by gambling and was a 'long stop'. This was based on what Sir Douglas
Frank had said in *Musgrove*. We can find nothing in Pt III of Sch 1 to justify this restricted
construction. In our judgment Sir Douglas Frank misconstrued para 27 and the
commissioners construed it correctly. We should add that para 27 has been repealed by
the amendments made to the 1976 Act by the Social Security Act 1980; but it is still
applicable to overpayments made before 24 November 1980.

*The problem of precedence*

Were the commissioners entitled to treat *Musgrove* as not binding them? An inferior
court is not entitled to disregard a decision of a superior court, however sure it may be
that it has been wrongly decided: see *Farrell v Alexander* [1976] 2 All ER 721, [1977] AC
59. The commissioners considered that they were entitled to treat as having no more
than persuasive force the decisions of the High Court on points of law made between 1
January 1978 and 24 November 1980 under the jurisdiction conferred on that court by
the combined operation of the Tribunals and Inquiries Act 1971 and the Tribunals and
Inquiries (Supplementary Benefit Appeal Tribunals) Order 1977, SI 1977/1735, because
during that period the High Court was exercising a jurisdiction which since 24 November
1980 has been vested in them by the Tribunals and Inquiries (Supplementary Benefit
Appeal Tribunals (Revocation)) Order 1980, SI 1980/1601.

A distinction has to be drawn between decisions of the High Court exercising its
supervisory jurisdiction which are, and always have been, binding on the commissioners
and the particular jurisdiction conferred on the High Court by the Act and the statutory
instrument to which we have referred. The supervisory jurisdiction of the High Court is
wide and discretionary. That given to the High Court between 1 January 1978 and 24
November 1980 was much narrower and was not discretionary. The effect of the 1980
order was to transfer the narrow jurisdiction from the High Court to the commissioners,
probably for reasons of convenience. In these circumstances, it cannot, in our judgment,
have been intended that when exercising this same jurisdiction the commissioners
should be bound by earlier decisions of the High Court. In our judgment the
commissioners were entitled to decide, as they did, that the decision in *Musgrove* was not
binding on them.

We dismiss the appeal.

*Appeal dismissed. No order as to costs.*

Solicitors: *Solicitor to the Department of Health and Social Security*; *R J G Smith* (for the
respondent).

Diana Procter      Barrister.

# Re Sinclair (deceased)
# Lloyds Bank plc v Imperial Cancer Research Fund and another

COURT OF APPEAL, CIVIL DIVISION
O'CONNOR, SLADE LJJ AND BRISTOW J
26, 27 FEBRUARY 1985

*Will – Lapse – Divorce – Effect of divorce on testamentary gift – Testator bequeathing entire estate to wife and in the event of wife predeceasing him or failing to survive him for one month estate to pass to research fund – Marriage dissolved before testator's death and wife surviving him by one month – Whether divorce causing gift to lapse in same way as death of legatee would have – Wills Act 1837, s 18A.*

By cl 3 of his will dated 8 November 1958 the testator bequeathed all his estate to his wife and by cl 4 directed that in the event of his wife predeceasing him or failing to survive him for a period of one month the estate was to pass to a named research fund. In 1962 the testator and his wife were divorced. The testator died in October 1983. His former wife was still alive but the bequest to her was invalidated by s 18A[a] of the Wills Act 1837, which provided that after a decree of dissolution of marriage any devise to a former spouse was to 'lapse' except in so far as a contrary intention appeared by the will. The question arose whether the estate passed to the research fund under cl 4 of the will or whether the will had made no effective gift and the estate therefore passed to the person entitled on an intestacy. The judge held that the estate passed to the person entitled on an intestacy. The research fund appealed, contending, inter alia, that the true meaning of s 18A was that in the event of a divorce a devise or bequest to a former spouse was deemed to have failed as if the former wife had predeceased the testator and with the same consequences as regards the remainder of the will.

**Held** – On the true construction of s 18A of the 1837 Act, if a devise or bequest to a testator's spouse 'lapsed' by reasons of the parties' divorce it failed without qualification and irrespective of the consequences. In particular, the devise or bequest was not deemed to have failed as if the former wife had predeceased the testator, and gifts in the will contingent on the former wife predeceasing the testator did not take effect if the former wife was still alive at the date of the testator's death. Furthermore, the word 'lapse' in s 18A could not be construed as a deeming provision designating in relation to the other provisions of the will the consequences which would ensue in the event of the former spouse being prevented from receiving the gift. Accordingly, the gift to the wife failed by reason of the divorce, and since neither of the exact contingencies specified in cl 4 of the will had occurred the gift over to the research fund did not take effect. The appeal would therefore be dismissed (see p 1069 g h, p 1070 g to p 1071 a and p 1072 b to e and j to p 1073 c, post).

*Re Cherrington (decd)* [1984] 2 All ER 285 overruled.

Decision of Michael Wheeler QC sitting as a deputy judge of the High Court [1984] 3 All ER 362 affirmed.

**Notes**

For the effect of dissolution or annulment of the marriage of a testator who dies on or after 1 January 1983, see 50 Halsbury's Laws (4th edn) para 281.

For the Wills Act, s 18A (as inserted by the Administration of Justice Act 1982, s 18(2)), see 52 Halsbury's Statutes (3rd edn) 1972.

---

a    Section 18A is set out at p 1068 a to c, post

**Cases referred to in judgments**

Andrew v Andrew (1845) 1 Coll 686, 63 ER 598.
Cherrington (decd), Re [1984] 2 All ER 285, [1984] 1 WLR 772.
Elliot v Davenport (1705) 1 P Wms 83, 24 ER 304.
Fox's Estate, Re, Dawes v Druitt, Phoenix Assurance Co Ltd v Fox [1937] 4 All ER 664, CA.
Jones v Westcomb (1711) Prec Ch 315, 24 ER 149.
Levy, Re, ex p Walton (1881) 17 Ch D 746, [1881–5] All ER Rep 548, CA.

**Case also cited**

Bailey (decd), Re, Barrett v Myder [1951] 1 All ER 391, [1951] Ch 407, CA.

**Appeal**

The first defendants, Imperial Cancer Research Fund, appealed against the order of Michael Wheeler QC sitting as a deputy judge of the High Court on 30 July 1984 ([1984] 3 All ER 362, [1984] 1 WLR 1240) whereby on the application of the plaintiff, Lloyds Bank plc, the executor and trustee of a will dated 8 November 1958 of Edgar Charles Rowan Sinclair (the testator), he declared that on the true construction of the will and of s 18A of the Wills Act 1837 and in the events which had happened, the net residuary estate of the testator ought to be paid to the second defendant, William Arthur Rowan Sinclair, on the footing that the will made no effective gift to the fund under cl 4 of the will. The facts are set out in the judgment of Slade LJ.

Peter Rawson for the fund.
Philip Rossdale for the executor.
Angus Nicol for the second defendant.

**SLADE LJ** (delivering the first judgment at the invitation of O'Connor LJ). This is an appeal by the Imperial Cancer Research Fund (which I will call 'the fund') from a judgment of Michael Wheeler QC, sitting as a deputy judge of the High Court, which was given on 30 July 1984 ([1984] 3 All ER 362, [1984] 1 WLR 1240). The judgment concerned the construction of a will dated 8 November 1958 of the late Edgar Charles Rowan Sinclair (whom I will call 'the testator').

The appeal raises a question as to the effect of his divorce on his testamentary dispositions.

At the date of his will he had a wife, Mrs Eileen Sinclair (whose present name, we were told, is now Mrs Clayton). By the will he began by revoking all former testamentary instruments and appointed Lloyds Bank Ltd (which I will call 'the executor') to be the executor and trustee. Having made provision for the executor's remuneration, the will proceeded as follows:

'3. I GIVE DEVISE and BEQUEATH the whole of my estate both real and personal and wheresoever situate unto my Wife Eileen Sinclair absolutely provided she survives me for the period of one month.

4. If my said Wife shall predecease me or fail to survive me for the period aforesaid then I Give Devise and Bequeath the whole of my estate both real and personal and wheresoever situate unto the Imperial Cancer Research Fund [and then the address is given] absolutely and I declare that the receipt of the Treasurer for the time being or any other proper officer shall be a sufficient receipt to my Executor for this bequest.'

The testator and Mrs Eileen Sinclair had married on 11 March 1953, but some four years after the will was made, namely on 10 September 1962, their marriage was dissolved by decree absolute of divorce. As the law stood up to the end of 1982, the dissolution of the marriage would not by itself have affected the gift in favour of Mrs Eileen Sinclair. However, on 1 January 1983 the new s 18A of the Wills Act 1837, which had been introduced into that section by s 18(2) of the Administration of Justice Act 1982, came

into force. Section 18A, the sidenote to which reads 'Effect of dissolution or annulment
of marriage on wills', provides as follows:

> '(1) Where, after a testator has made a will, a decree of a court dissolves or annuls
> his marriage or declares it void,—(a) the will shall take effect as if any appointment
> of the former spouse as an executor or as the executor and trustee of the will were
> omitted; and (b) any devise or bequest to the former spouse shall lapse, except in so
> far as a contrary intention appears by the will.
> (2) Subsection (1)(b) above is without prejudice to any right of the former spouse
> to apply for financial provision under the Inheritance (Provision for Family and
> Dependants) Act 1975.
> (3) Where—(a) by the terms of a will an interest in remainder is subject to a life
> interest; and (b) the life interest lapses by virtue of subsection (1)(b) above, the
> interest in remainder shall be treated as if it had not been subject to the life interest
> and, if it was contingent upon the termination of the life interest, as if it had not
> been so contingent.'

After the new section had come into force, the testator died on 26 October 1983,
without having revoked the will. On 14 December 1983 probate was granted to the
executor. Mrs Eileen Sinclair survived the period of one month specified in cll 3 and 4 of
the will. There was no doubt that the new s 18A of the Wills Act 1837 caused the gift of
the residuary estate in her favour to fail. Doubts, however, arose whether, in the events
which had happened, the combined effect of the will and of s 18A was to cause the
residuary estate of the testator on the one hand to devolve on the fund under cl 4 of the
will or, on the other hand, to devolve as on the testator's intestacy. The only person
interested on the footing of an intestacy was the testator's brother, Mr William Arthur
Rowan Sinclair. In these circumstances, the executor, for the purpose of resolving these
doubts, issued an originating summons, joining as defendants the fund and Mr William
Sinclair.

Two principal points were argued before the deputy judge on behalf of the fund. The
first (which I will call the s 18A point) is to be found summarised in para 1 of the notice
of appeal as follows:

> 'On the true construction of section 18A of the Wills Act 1837 (as amended)
> where, after a testator has made a will, a decree of a court dissolves or annuls his
> marriage, any devise or bequest to the former spouse lapses on the basis that the
> former spouse is deemed to have predeceased the testator.'

The second principal point argued on behalf of the fund in the court below (which I
will call 'the *Jones v Westcomb* point' (see (1711) Prec Ch 315, 24 ER 149)) is summarised
in para 2 of the notice of appeal as follows:

> 'Alternatively and notwithstanding that the testator's wife did not predecease him
> or fail to survive him by the period of one month, on the true construction of clause
> 4 of the said Will and by reason of the rule known as the Rule in *Jones v. Westcomb*
> the gift therein of the said residuary estate in favour of the Defendant Imperial
> Cancer Research Fund was effective.'

The deputy judge rejected both these arguments and accordingly held that the
testator's residuary estate ought to be paid to Mr William Sinclair on the footing that the
will had made no effective gift of it. The fund now appeals from this decision.

At the start of his opening of the appeal, counsel for the fund indicated that he did not
feel it right to pursue any further the *Jones v Westcomb* point, which he accordingly
abandoned. His submissions in this court have therefore been confined to the s 18A
point, to which I now turn.

This argument at the end of the day depends on the meaning of the single word 'lapse'
in the context of s 18A(1)(b). I think that the word 'lapse', as appearing in a will, is capable
of bearing a variety of meanings according to the context. This variety is illustrated by
the following passage from *Stroud's Judicial Dictionary* (4th edn, 1973) vol 3, p 1489:

'(2) A legacy is said to "lapse" when the legatee dies in the lifetime of the testator, or when something happens in such lifetime which prevents the intended legatee from being entitled to the legacy, or (it is submitted) when the legatee dies after the testator but before becoming entitled to the legacy.'

The variety of possible meanings is also illustrated by the decision of this court in *Re Fox's Estate* [1937] 4 All ER 664, where it was held that, in the particular context of the will in that case, the word 'lapse' was apt to refer to the failure of a gift by reason of the death of a beneficiary after the testator's death without having had any children.

Counsel for the fund accepted that, in an appropriate context, the word 'lapse' is perfectly capable of referring to any event which happens in a testator's lifetime and which prevents an intended legatee from becoming entitled to his gift. He accepted that, in an appropriate context, the word is capable of bearing the simple meaning of 'fail' or 'shall be of no effect'. Nevertheless, he submitted that the primary meaning of the word 'lapse' is 'fail by reason of the death of the beneficiary in the lifetime of the testator'. In this context he prayed in aid *Jarman on Wills* (8th edn, 1951) vol 1, p 438, note (a), where the editors say: 'The term "lapse" is generally applied to failure by the death of the devisee or legatee in the testator's lifetime', though they do go on to add, 'but it is sometimes used in a wider sense, as for instance in the case of a failure of a contingent gift by reason of the event not taking place'.

We were also referred to *Elliott v Davenport* (1705) 1 P Wms 83 at 86, 24 ER 304 at 305 and to *Roper on Legacies* (4th edn, 1847) p 462 as illustrating the use of the word 'lapse' in what counsel for the fund submits is its primary sense.

Our attention was also drawn to a passage from the judgment of Knight Bruce V-C in *Andrew v Andrew* (1845) 1 Coll 686 at 691, 63 ER 598 at 600–601, where he appears to have regarded the word 'lapse' as not strictly appropriate to cover the failure of a gift owing to the marriage during a testator's lifetime of a beneficiary to whom a bequest had been made so long as she should remain unmarried. We were also referred to a passage from the judgment of Greene MR in *Re Fox's Estate* [1937] 4 All ER 664 at 667, where he used the phrase 'strict technical sense' of the word 'lapse' in the context of a will as referring to the failure of a testamentary gift by reason of the death of the donee during the testator's lifetime.

Counsel for the fund further pointed out that s 18(2) of the Administration of Justice Act 1982 expressly incorporates the new s 18A in the 1837 Act. He drew our attention to ss 25, 32 and 33 of the 1837 Act, in each case as amended by the Statute Law Revision (No 2) Act 1888. He submitted that in the sidenote to s 25 and in the body of s 32 and also in the body of s 33 (before a new s 33 was substituted by s 19 of the 1982 Act) and in the sidenote to the new s 33 the word 'lapse' was used in each case in the strict technical sense. As the very first of his written submissions to this court, and in the light of those other provisions of the 1837 Act, he contended (as he had contended before the deputy judge) that the word 'lapse' in the new s 18A 'must have been intended to have the same meaning as it bears in the original Act', that is to say so as to refer to failure by reason of the death of the legatee during the lifetime of the testator.

This submission, in this simple form, cannot in my view on any footing be well founded. On no possible footing can one read the opening words of the new s 18A(1)(b) as meaning simply 'any devise or bequest to the former spouse shall fail by reason of the death of the legatee during the testator's lifetime'. For, in the cases dealt with by s 18A(1)(b), the former spouse is ex hypothesi still alive at the date of the testator's death.

In the more developed stages of his argument, counsel for the fund therefore had to contend and did contend that, in the context of s 18A(1)(b), the word 'lapse' means something more than this. He contended that (unlike the word as used in the other provisions of the 1837 Act) the single word 'lapse' in this context is in truth a *deeming* provision. He submitted that the opening words of s 18A(1)(b) should be read as meaning 'any devise or bequest to the former spouse shall fail with the same consequences as if the former spouse had died in the testator's lifetime'. It is thus an essential part of the fund's case on this appeal that the single word 'lapse' in s 18A(1)(b) should be read as not only importing a failure of the relevant gift in favour of the former spouse, but as designating also the *consequences* of such failure in relation to the *other* provisions contained in the will.

The most direct support for this submission is to be found in the recent decision of Butler-Sloss J in *Re Cherrington (decd)* [1984] 2 All ER 285, [1984] 1 WLR 772. The facts of that case were as follows. By cl 2 of a will made in 1966 a testator had appointed his wife to be sole executrix. By cl 3 he gave her all his real and personal estate with a proviso that if she predeceased him the clauses following should have effect. By cl 4 he appointed his son, together with an informally adopted son, and a solicitor to be executors. By cl 5 he left the residue of his estate to the two sons equally. The marriage was subsequently dissolved by decree of divorce made absolute on 28 January 1983. The testator died on 28 March 1983. The estate was a small one, and the division had been agreed by the interested parties (see [1984] 2 All ER 285 at 286, [1984] 1 WLR 772 at 774) but a problem arose as to who should take the grant in respect of the estate, whether it should be to the executors named in cl 4, on the footing that the contingency envisaged by cl 3 had occurred and cl 4 accordingly was in operation, or whether there was now no appointment under the will of an executor.

On an unopposed application, Butler-Sloss J was urged by counsel for the applicant to equate 'lapse' with 'predecease', having regard to the provisions of s 18A. In her judgment she referred to the note from *Jarman* which I have already quoted. She accepted that sub-s (3) of s 18A was somewhat difficult to follow if 'lapse' was intended to refer to 'predecease', since on this footing the second part of the subsection would be unnecessary. But she expressed the view that the subsection was set out for the avoidance of doubt. She considered that to interpret 'lapse' as meaning 'shall be of no effect' would, in the case of the will before her, cause a residual intestacy and defeat the purpose of the testator and would be likely to do so in many other wills. She concluded ([1984] 2 All ER 285 at 287, [1984] 1 WLR 772 at 775):

> 'For the purposes of simplicity, certainty, and to give effect to the intentions of the testator, I propose to interpret s 18A(1)(*b*) of the 1982 Act as referring to the former spouse predeceasing the testator and hold, therefore, that the proviso to cl 3 of the will takes effect. In those circumstances, the appointment of the executors under cl 4 takes effect.'

Like the deputy judge, I have, if I may say so, considerable sympathy with the decision of Butler-Sloss J, who did not have the advantage of adversarial argument and was clearly, and understandably, influenced by a desire to provide a sensible definitive answer to the question which had been posed to her, with the minimum of expense and delay to the estate. Nevertheless, with great respect to her, I share his opinion that the construction which she placed on s 18A(1)(*b*) was wrong.

As I have already pointed out, though this important point was not specifically referred to in her judgment, the construction of the relevant wording of the subsection favoured by her in that case in truth involves reading it as meaning 'any devise or bequest to the former spouse shall fail with the same consequences as if the former spouse had died in the testator's lifetime'. It involves reading it as a deeming provision. For my part, I find it impossible to read the opening words of s 18A(1)(*b*) in this manner. First, as I have said, it must be and is accepted that the word 'lapse' is, in an appropriate context, perfectly apt to cover the happening of any event in a testator's lifetime which prevents the intended legatee from being entitled to the legacy, and thus to mean nothing more than 'fail'. In my opinion, the natural meaning of the word 'lapse' in the context of s 18A(1)(*b*) is to refer to the happening of an event, namely divorce, in the testator's lifetime which is to prevent the intended legatee, the former spouse, from becoming entitled to the legacy. The natural meaning of the word 'lapse' in this particular context is that, in the relevant contingency, the devise or bequest to the former spouse shall fail, no more and no less.

Second, if the legislature had intended that s 18A(1)(*b*) should have the effect, not only of preventing the former spouse from receiving the gift in cases such as this, but also of designating the consequences which would ensue in relation to the other provisions of the will, it would in my opinion inevitably have said so. To spell out a deeming provision

a from this one word 'lapse' would in my opinion be impermissible according to any proper principles of statutory construction.

Third, the conclusion that the legislature did not regard s 18A(1)(b) as designating the consequences that would ensue from the failure of the gift to the former spouse, in relation to the other provisions of the will, is in my opinion clearly supported by the presence of sub-s (3). For this subsection does designate such consequences in those cases

b where the will has given the former spouse a life interest. The provisions of sub-s (3) would have been wholly unnecessary if s 18A(1)(b) had itself been intended to provide that the effect of the failure of the gift on all the other provisions of the will was to be the same as if the former spouse had died in the testator's lifetime. I am not at all convinced by the submission of counsel for the fund that sub-s (3) was inserted by the legislature merely for the avoidance of doubt. If the legislature had intended 'lapse' in s 18A(1)(b) to

c bear the deeming sense suggested by him, no possible doubt, as I see the position, could have arisen.

As to the other sections of the 1837 Act to which reference has been made, ss 32 and 33 deal with situations which have arisen by reason of the death of a testamentary beneficiary during the testator's lifetime. If one reads the word 'lapse' in these sections as meaning 'fail', no more and no less, it makes perfect sense in its context. Likewise, if one

d reads the word 'lapsed' in the sidenote to s 25 as meaning 'failed', no more and no less, it makes perfect sense in its context. Furthermore, there is no question of the word 'lapse' or 'lapsed' in any of these other statutory provisions bearing a deeming sense. I do not therefore think that these provisions give any support to the construction of s 18A(1)(b) which is submitted on behalf of the fund.

Counsel for the fund further submitted that if the word 'lapse' in s 18A(1)(b) had been

e intended by the legislature to mean no more than 'fail', s 18A(1) could have been more simply drafted so as to read as follows:

> 'Where, after a testator has made a will, a decree of a court dissolves or annuls his marriage or declares it void, the will shall take effect as if (a) any appointment of the former spouse as an executor or as the executor and trustee of the will and (b) any devise or bequest to the former spouse were omitted, except in so far as a contrary

f intention appears by the will.'

I have two comments to make on this submission. First, I am by no means convinced that the suggested alternative wording would have achieved satisfactory clarity. To provide for a will to take effect as if the devise or bequest to the former spouse had been omitted could well make a verbal nonsense of other provisions of the will which were

g expressed to follow on that particular devise or bequest. Second, para (a) of s 18A(1), as it stands, is prefaced by the words 'as if'. This undoubtedly is a deeming provision. Its wording is in marked contrast with that of para (b).

The general criticism which was made of the drafting of the new s 18A(1) would, I think, be well deserved if it bore the sense which counsel for the fund seeks to place on it, but not, in my view, on the construction placed on it by the deputy judge.

h Finally, in this context, counsel for the fund mentioned that, as is no doubt the case, in many instances testators, who leave gifts to their husbands or wives, also provide for substitutional gifts in the event of their spouses predeceasing them. Echoing the comment of Butler-Sloss J in the *Cherrington* case, he submitted that in many cases their intentions would be wholly frustrated if the construction which the deputy judge placed on s 18A(1)(b) were correct. He referred us to the judgment of Jessel MR in *Re Levy, ex p*

j *Walton* (1881) 17 Ch D 746 at 750, [1881–5] All ER Rep 548 at 549–550 in which he referred to the rule of construction as laid down by Lord Selborne LC in these words:

> 'The more literal construction ought not to prevail if (as the court below has thought) it is opposed to the intentions of the legislature, as apparent by the statute, and if the words are sufficiently flexible to admit of some other construction by which that intention will be better effectuated.'

Counsel for the fund submitted that the construction of s 18A(1)(*b*) favoured by the deputy judge would be likely to lead to absurdity or injustice and therefore should not be supported. I am not persuaded by these submissions. This does not seem to me to be a case where it can be said that the intention of the legislature, as apparent from the statute, was anything more than to cause the gift to the former spouse to fail in the relevant contingency. As the deputy judge pointed out, the truth of the matter is that both marriage and divorce are events of such moment as to require the parties at least to reconsider their testamentary dispositions (see [1984] 3 All ER 362 at 367, [1984] 1 WLR 1240 at 1246). I see no reason why the legislature should not have contemplated that this would continue to be the case, notwithstanding the enactment of the new section.

For all these reasons, I am driven to the conclusion that the learned deputy judge was right in thinking that the word 'lapse' in s 18A(1)(*b*) of the 1837 Act means simply 'fail' and that the s 18A point fails accordingly.

Since the wording of this section itself does not assist the fund, I should revert to the provisions of the will itself.

Clause 4, which contains the gift over in favour of the fund, begins with the words: 'If my said Wife shall predecease me or fail to survive me for the period aforesaid', that is to say the period of one month. Thus the gift over contained in cl 4 is expressed to take effect on two alternative contingencies only, namely that of Mrs Eileen Sinclair predeceasing the testator or failing to survive him for one month. Neither of these two contingencies in fact occurred.

The general principle is that, where there is a gift over on certain alternative contingencies, it will not take effect unless one or other of those exact contingencies happens. What is sometimes referred to as the rule in *Jones v Westcomb* (1711) Prec Ch 316, 24 ER 149 affords an exception to the general principle. This rule, as I understand it, may be invoked if it can be shown that, though none of the exact contingencies on which the gift over is specified to take effect has happened, yet the gift over must a fortiori have been intended to take effect in the event which has actually happened. Though the rule in *Jones v Westcomb* was invoked on behalf of the fund before the deputy judge, counsel for the fund, as I have indicated, has not thought the argument worth submitting on this appeal. If I may say so, I for my part think he was right to take this course.

In this context I would add these very brief observations. I am bound to say that I have some sympathy with the fund, because, like the deputy judge, I have more than a sneaking suspicion that, if the testator had addressed his mind to the contingency which in the event happened, he would have wished the estate to go to the fund. However, one cannot, I think, possibly say with any certainty that, merely because this testator in 1958 intended that his estate should go over to the fund if his wife should predecease him, he would necessarily and a fortiori have intended that the same results should ensue if his marriage ended by divorce during his lifetime. As the deputy judge pointed out, the truth of the matter is that, when he made his will, he clearly did not address his mind in any way to the unhappy contingency of a future divorce. It would not, I think, be open to the court to rewrite the will by adding other specific contingencies to those clearly expressed in cl 4 on the basis of mere intelligent speculation as to what the testator might have intended if his marriage were to end in divorce. It could only be done, if at all, by a process of necessary implication, though I should mention that counsel for the executor drew our attention to s 20 of the Administration of Justice Act 1982, which enables the court in certain limited circumstances to rectify the provisions of a will and to s 21, which expands the general rules as to the admission of evidence in their interpretation. Neither of these sections, however, have been invoked in argument in the present case.

I have merely added these obiter observations on the *Jones v Westcomb* point, which has not been argued before us, to indicate at least my support, as a matter of first impression, for the decision of the court below on this point, and for the course which the fund's legal advisers have taken in this context.

For the purpose of deciding this appeal, it suffices to say that in my opinion the deputy a judge reached the right conclusion on the s 18A point essentially for the right reasons. The consequences must be that, while the gift to Mrs Eileen Sinclair under cl 3 of the will must fail, the gift over to the fund in cl 4 cannot take effect and the testator's estate must pass to Mr William Sinclair as on the testator's intestacy.

Despite the valiant and sustained argument of counsel for the fund I would accordingly dismiss this appeal.

b **BRISTOW J.** I agree.

**O'CONNOR LJ.** I also agree, and I only wish to add a few words as we are overruling the decision of Butler-Sloss J in *Re Cherrington (decd)* [1984] 2 All ER 285, [1984] 1 WLR 772. Like her, had I felt able to construe s 18A(1)(*b*) as counsel for the fund would have us do, I would have been happy to do so, because it seems to me that in a very great many c cases the result of this decision will be that the true intention of the testator may well be defeated. But I can find no ambiguity in s 18A(1)(*b*). It seems to me that the use of the words 'lapse' in that subsection can only be construed in the sense of 'fail'.

For the reasons given by Slade LJ I agree that this appeal must be dismissed.

*Appeal dismissed.*

d
Solicitors: *Wilde Sapte* (for the fund); *Keene Marsland*, Tunbridge Wells (for the executor); *H Kennard & Son* (for the second defendant).

Frances Rustin    Barrister.

e

# R v Diggines, ex parte Rahmani and others

COURT OF APPEAL, CIVIL DIVISION
f STEPHENSON, FOX AND PURCHAS LJJ
7 NOVEMBER, 20 DECEMBER 1984

*Natural justice – Hearing – Duty to hear parties etc – Immigration adjudicator – Applicant not given hearing through fault of her own advisers – Adjudicator not at fault – Whether breach of rules of natural justice – Whether adjudicator's decision reviewable.*

g
The applicant was an Iranian citizen whose request for an extension of her stay in the United Kingdom had been refused by the Home Secretary. The applicant wished to appeal to an immigration adjudicator and consulted the Immigrants Advisory Service, which lodged an appeal on her behalf. The notice of appeal stated that she wished to have an oral hearing and to call witnesses. She later notified the advisory service of a change of h address but they failed to keep a record of her new address and when the appeal came on for hearing they wrongly informed the adjudicator that her absence was due to her own fault and invited the adjudicator to proceed and decide the appeal on the papers. The applicant's appeal was then dismissed without a hearing. She applied for and was granted certiorari to quash the adjucator's decision. The adjudicator appealed.

j **Held** – Where an applicant was denied a hearing by a tribunal through no fault of the applicant or the tribunal but because of the fault of the applicant's advisers, there was nevertheless a breach of the audi alteram partem rule which entitled the applicant to judicial review of the tribunal's decision if it was adverse to the applicant. Applying that principle, the appeal would be dismissed (see p 1082 *a* and *e* to p 1083 *a* and *j* to p 1084 *d*, p 1086 *d e* and p 1087 *j*, post).

*R v Leyland Magistrates, ex p Hawthorn* [1979] 1 All ER 209 and *R v Blundeston Prison Board of Visitors, ex p Fox-Taylor* [1982] 1 All ER 646 applied.

*a*

*R v Immigration Appeal Tribunal, ex p Enwia* [1983] 2 All ER 1045 considered.

Per Stephenson LJ. The court has power to review and quash a decision made in breach of the rules of natural justice even where the breach is the result of the applicant's own fault, although it will seldom be right in such circumstances for the court to quash the decision (see p 1082 *a* to *c*, post).

*b*

**Notes**

For the principles of natural justice and certiorari for breach of those principles, see 1 Halsbury's Laws (4th edn) paras 64, 74, 87.

**Cases referred to in judgments**

*c*

*A-G v Ryan* [1980] AC 718, [1980] 2 WLR 143, PC.

*Anisminic Ltd v Foreign Compensation Commission* [1969] 1 All ER 208, [1969] 2 AC 147, [1969] 2 WLR 163, HL.

*Ashrafi v Immigration Appeal Tribunal* [1981] Imm AR 34.

*Chief Constable of the North Wales Police v Evans* [1982] 3 All ER 141, [1982] 1 WLR 1155, HL.

*d*

*Council of Civil Service Unions v Minister for the Civil Service* [1984] 3 All ER 935, [1984] 3 WLR 1174, HL.

*Daganayasi v Minister of Immigration* [1980] 2 NZLR 130, NZ CA.

*Hoffman-La Roche (F) & Co AG v Secretary of State for Trade and Industry* [1974] 2 All ER 1128, [1975] AC 295, [1974] 3 WLR 104, HL.

*Mehta v Secretary of State for the Home Dept* [1975] 2 All ER 1084, [1975] 1 WLR 1087, CA.

*e*

*R v Ashford (Kent) Justices, ex p Richley (No 2)* [1955] 3 All ER 604, [1956] 1 QB 167, [1955] 3 WLR 778, CA.

*R v Blundeston Prison Board of Visitors, ex p Fox-Taylor* [1982] 1 All ER 646, DC.

*R v Gillyard* (1848) 12 QB 527, 116 ER 965.

*R v Glamorganshire (Inhabitants)* (1700) 1 Ld Raym 580, 91 ER 1287.

*R v Hull Prison Board of Visitors, ex p St Germain (No 2)* [1979] 3 All ER 545, [1979] 1 WLR 1401, DC.

*f*

*R v Immigration Appeal Tribunal, ex p Enwia, R v Immigration Appeal Tribunal, ex p AS* [1983] 2 All ER 1045, [1984] 1 WLR 117, CA.

*R v Immigration Appeal Tribunal, ex p Jusoh* (28 July 1976, unreported), DC.

*R v Immigration Appeal Tribunal, ex p Mawji* [1984] CA Bound Transcript 435.

*R v Leicester Recorder, ex p Wood* [1947] 1 All ER 928, [1947] KB 726, DC.

*g*

*R v Leyland Magistrates, ex p Hawthorn* [1979] 1 All ER 209, [1979] QB 283, [1979] 2 WLR 28, DC.

*R v Northamptonshire Justices, ex p Nicholson* [1974] RTR 97, DC.

*R v Northumberland Compensation Appeal Tribunal, ex p Shaw* [1951] 1 All ER 268, [1951] 1 KB 711, DC; *affd* [1952] 1 All ER 122, [1952] 1 KB 338, CA.

*R v Stafford Justices, ex p Stafford Corp* [1940] 2 KB 33, CA.

*h*

*R v University of Cambridge* (1723) 1 Str 557, 93 ER 698.

*R v West Sussex Quarter Sessions, ex p Albert & Maud Johnson Trust Ltd* [1973] 3 All ER 289, [1974] QB 24, [1973] 3 WLR 149, CA.

*R (Burns) v Tyrone County Court Judge* [1961] NI 167.

*Ridge v Baldwin* [1963] 2 All ER 66, [1964] AC 40, [1963] 2 WLR 935, HL.

*j*

**Appeal**

Mahnaz Rahmani, Koorosh Saroui and Katayon Saroui applied, with the leave of McCullough J granted on 13 September 1982, for judicial review of the determination dated 16 December 1981 of C E Diggines, an adjudicator under the Immigration Act

a
1971 dismissing the applicants' appeal against the Secretary of State's refusal to extend their leave to stay in the United Kingdom. The applicants sought certiorari to quash the determination and mandamus directing the adjudicator to rehear the appeal. By a judgment given on 16 June 1983 Taylor J allowed the application and issued certiorari to quash the determination and mandamus directing the adjudicator to rehear the applicants' appeal by way of an oral hearing. The adjudicator appealed. The grounds of the appeal were (1) that the judge erred in law in deciding he was entitled to grant

b
judicial review of the adjudicator's determination when it was accepted there had been no error, unfairness or fault of any sort on the part of the adjudicator, the Secretary of State or anyone acting on his behalf, (2) that the judge erred in finding that a mistake or error made by the applicants' advisers constituted a breach of the rules of natural justice so as to enable the applicants to obtain the relief they sought, and (3) that the judge ought not to have granted relief to the applicants because on the facts it was clear that even if

c
they had had an oral hearing dismissal of their appeal was inevitable. The facts are set out in the judgment of Stephenson LJ.

*Andrew Collins* for the adjudicator.
*Sir Charles Fletcher-Cooke QC* and *George Warr* for the applicants.

*Cur adv vult*

d
20 December. The following judgments were delivered.

**STEPHENSON LJ.** On 16 December 1981 an adjudicator dismissed, unheard, an appeal by the applicants against a refusal by the Secretary of State to extend their stay in the United Kingdom. What is meant by describing the appeal as unheard will be

e
explained below, as will the circumstances which led the adjudicator quite properly to dismiss it. The applicants did not appeal against the dismissal to the Immigration Appeal Tribunal; they applied for judicial review to quash it. On 13 September 1982 they were given leave to apply for judicial review and on 16 June 1983 Taylor J quashed the determination of the adjudicator and commanded him to hear the applicants' appeal by an oral hearing. From the judge's decision the adjudicator appeals to this court.

f
The facts are fully set out in the judgment of the judge. The principal applicant is a married woman nearly 30 years of age. She has travelled on an Iranian passport from Iran, where her husband is, to this country moving from one to the other since 1978, the second time on 8 December 1978 when she brought her two small children, who are the other two applicants. On her second visit she enrolled at the Wimbledon Language Centre to study English, and when she returned to this country on 28 September 1979

g
she was admitted as a student with leave to stay for seven months, subsequently extended to September 1980. On 16 September 1980 she applied for a further extension, giving as her reason 'so that I can look after my children while they are at school here'. The Secretary of State refused her application and the application of her children on 11 November 1980. Their appeals from this refusal were consolidated and were dismissed by the adjudicator in the circumstances which have now to be described.

h
The children's applications were refused because their mother's application was refused. In notifying her (hereafter referred to as 'the applicant') of his decision the Secretary of State said:

'You have applied for leave to remain in the United Kingdom, in order to look after your children, but there is no provision in the Immigration Rules entitling you to an extension of stay for this purpose.'

j
He also told her:

'The United Kingdom Immigrants Advisory Service, a voluntary organisation independent of the Government, will advise you, if you wish, about the decision which has been made against you and on whether to exercise your right of appeal ... free of charge [giving the London address of the service].'

The applicant wisely consulted the service, which has been of the greatest value to immigrants, but this time, as the judge found, it 'let her down rather badly', giving rise to this appeal.

The applicant has sworn an affidavit in which she says that the reason she gave in her last application for an extension was erroneous, and it is right to say that she had stated in her earlier application that she was going to take a one-year course in September (1979) and intended to go back to Iran after she had finished her studies. The relevant parts of the rest of her affidavit, which deal with events after she decided to consult the immigrants advisory service (the UKIAS), are summarised with the other material facts by the judge as follows:

'According to her affidavit, she saw a Mr Moss. She indicated that she wished to appeal against the refusal. He agreed to act on her behalf. He suggested that she should produce various documents relating to the financial support from her husband. On 8 December, she went to see Mr Moss. She took with her the documents for which he had asked. She had a short discussion with him in the course of which (she says on oath) she informed him that she had changed her address and had gone to live with her mother at 53 Alexandra Road, London SW19. She asked Mr Moss whether he required her passport but he said that it was not required at that stage. He said that he would contact her if he required it or anything else. He indicated that he had already lodged the notice of appeal on behalf of the applicant and the two children and gave her the rather gloomy news that it would be at least another nine months before her appeal would be heard in the ordinary course of events. After that meeting, the applicant continued with her studies at the Wimbledon Language Centre and took the view that so far as this appeal was concerned, the ball was very much in the advisory service's court. She thought that they would contact her when they wanted any other information or when anything was going to transpire. There was a specific request on the notice of appeal for an indication as to whether a hearing was or was not requested. That was positively dealt with and the notice showed that a hearing was requested. Furthermore, on the next page of the notice of appeal, it was indicated that approximtely three witnesses would be called in support of the appeal. The next thing, so far as the applicant was concerned, was that she decided to go and see what was happening in March 1982 as she had heard nothing from the advisory service. By that time, she had completed her course at the Wimbledon Language Centre and she wished to go on and obtain a professional qualification. She therefore applied to the London Electronics College and was offered a place on their TEC course leading to a TEC certificate. Before embarking on that, she decided to go and see Mr Moss. She did so on 22 March 1982. It then became apparent that, in the interim, her appeal had been heard by an adjudicator on 16 December 1981. There had been no hearing as such but he had dealt with the matter on the papers and had dismissed her appeal. It must be said, in the clearest possible terms, that no criticism can be attached to the adjudicator in any way for dealing with the matter in the way in which he did. The advisory service indicated to the adjudicator that they had not been able to make any contact with the applicant at what had been her address and therefore that as they had no instructions from her, they specifically invited the adjudicator to deal with the matter on the documents. Why the advisory service did that remains obscure, but there is an affidavit from Mr Moss which shows that he delegated the handling of the applicant's case to someone else in the advisory service. It is quite clear that the change of address which the applicant said that she communicated to them on 8 December 1980 was not acted on by the advisory service and the documents that she said she left there have also not turned up. In his affidavit, Mr Moss says: "Although I had no written record of the said meeting in December 1980 and could not trace the papers the first applicant said she had left with me she impressed me as a straightforward truthful person and I saw no reason to doubt what she said".'

Mr Moss accepted the applicant's statement that she had given the UKIAS her change a  of address with documentary evidence from her bank that they had received a remittance from her husband; he apologised to her for the way the UKIAS had handled her case and tried vainly to get the Secretary of State to alter his decision. The Secretary of State, after correspondence with the applicant's member of Parliament, refused to alter his decision and, on 16 December 1982, decided to make a deportation order against the applicant, a decision which is the subject of another appeal awaiting the outcome of this.

b  The adjudicator's determination and reasons were, in the absence of any oral evidence, or indeed any written submissions or argument on the applicant's behalf, short and right. I quote two of its four paragraphs:

c  '2. The grounds of appeal, which was lodged by United Kingdom Immigrants Advisory Service on 12 November 1980, were stated at that time as "to follow after detail consultation with UKIAS". However, no further grounds of appeal have in fact been submitted, and in a letter dated 12 November 1981 the U.K.I.A.S. said that their letter to the appellant at her last known address had been returned. Since they had no further instructions from the appellants and no knowledge of their whereabouts, the U.K.I.A.S. therefore requested that the Adjudicator decide this case in such manner as he may deem proper. I am therefore determining it under Rule 12 . . .

d  4. No evidence has been submitted to prove that the appellant had the necessary means to support herself and her children, even if the extension requested had been otherwise permissible under the rules, and she has failed to instruct her representative. In these circumstances I can only accept the Secretary of State's reasons for refusing the application, and the appeal is accordingly dismissed.'

e  The 'Rule 12' to which he refers is r 12 of the Immigration Appeals (Procedure) Rules 1972, SI 1972/1684, which in effect requires an oral hearing except in five cases, of which I quote the first three:

f  'An appellate authority may determine an appeal without a hearing if—(a) no party to the appeal has requested a hearing; or (b) the appellate authority has decided, after giving every other party to the appeal an opportunity of replying to any representations submitted in writing by or on behalf of the appellant, to allow the appeal; or (c) the appellate authority is satisfied that the appellant is outside the United Kingdom or that it is impracticable to give him notice of a hearing and, in either case, that no person is authorised to represent him at a hearing.'

g  Accepting that the condition in para (a) was not satisfied because in the notice of appeal lodged by the UKIAS on her behalf, to which the adjudicator referred, she had requested a hearing of the appeal and stated that approximately three witnesses would be called to give evidence in support of her appeal, the condition in para (b) was not satisfied because no representations were submitted in writing on her behalf: the adjudicator had only the Home Office statement of facts and reasons required by r 8 of the same rules. The condition in para (c) might seem to have been satisfied but was not because the notice given to the UKIAS was by rr 26(1) and 44(1) deemed to have been given to the applicant.

h  The conditions in paras (d) and (e) of r 12 have no application. If, therefore, there had been nothing further, the adjudicator would have exceeded his jurisdiction in determining the appeal without a hearing and would presumably have adjourned the appeal for inquiries to be made before determining it. But the request of the UKIAS representative to which the adjudicator refers made it difficult, if not impossible, for him to do otherwise than answer the request by dismissing the appeal there and then on the

j  supposition that the applicant had abandoned her appeal.

Counsel for the adjudicator has indicated that he would be willing for this court to decide the appeal on the basis that the adjudicator was at fault in acting as he did. But in my judgment he cannot now challenge the judge's finding that no criticism can be attached to the adjudicator. We have to decide the appeal on the basis that the adjudicator acted properly and without fault, and indeed that the applicant acted properly and without fault in respect of the appeal to the adjudicator, and that the only fault lies with the UKIAS and theirs is the sole responsibility for depriving her of her right to an oral hearing. We have only to consider two grounds of appeal in this court:

'(1) That the learned Judge erred in law in deciding that he was entitled to grant judicial review to the Applicant when it was accepted that there had been no error or unfairness or fault of any sort on the part of the Respondent or the Secretary of State or anyone acting on his behalf.
(2) That the learned Judge erred in finding that a mistake or error made by the Applicants' advisers constituted a breach of the rules of natural justice so as to enable the Applicants to obtain relief in the form of certiorari and/or mandamus.'

A third ground, that on the facts dismissal of the applicant's appeal to the adjudicator was inevitable, has been rightly abandoned. In *R v Immigration Appeal Tribunal, ex p Mawji* [1984] CA Bound Transcript 435 this court decided very recently that the tribunal should rehear an appeal on the facts which they had never heard and decided because they misunderstood what was meant by an immigrant establishing himself here for the purpose of setting up in business. The court refused to dismiss the appeal on the ground that the immigrant would inevitably have failed on the facts if they had been given in evidence: the immigrant had been deprived of his statutory right to have his appeal on the facts decided by the tribunal. It would be even more obviously wrong for this court to decide what would have been the result of the applicant's appeal to the adjudicator if she had not been deprived of her statutory right to an oral hearing.

We are then here concerned with what would strike not only a lawyer but any fair-minded person as a failure of elementary justice. 'Natural justice', said Geoffrey Lane LJ, giving the judgment of the Divisional Court in *R v Hull Prison Board of Visitors, ex p St Germain (No 2)* [1979] 3 All ER 545 at 552, [1979] 1 WLR 1401 at 1408, 'requires that the procedure before any tribunal which is acting judicially shall be fair in all the circumstances.' Not only has the applicant not had a fair hearing: she has not had a hearing at all.

An important question has been decided against a person who has not been heard or put her side of her case. Audi alteram partem is a principle of natural justice which has not been complied with. It has been violated, 'never mind who by', runs the argument of counsel for the applicant; and certiorari and mandamus are the only adequate means available to the applicant if she is to have natural justice. There is no other means available, for there is no power to enlarge the time for the necessary application for leave to appeal from the determination of the adjudicator which is laid down by r 15 of the Immigration Appeals (Procedure) Rules 1972 (see *Ashrafi v Immigration Appeal Tribunal* [1981] Imm AR 34). That there is no such power counsel for the adjudicator cannot dispute; he can only point to the power of the Secretary of State to take full account of the relevant circumstances, including domestic and compassionate circumstances, in considering whether deportation is the right course on the merits and before making a deportation order, under paras 154, 156 and 158 in Pt XII of the Statement of Changes in Immigration Rules (HC Paper (1982–83) no 169). Any claim the applicant might have for damages for negligence against the UKIAS or its officers would not, of course, give her a right or permission to remain in the United Kingdom (cf *Mehta v Secretary of State for the Home Dept* [1975] 2 All ER 1084 at 1088, [1975] 1 WLR 1087 at 1091 per Lord Denning MR).

The judge, after reviewing a number of authorities to which I must refer, and after considering counsel for the adjudicator's submission that to grant certiorari to a party who could prove no fault on the part of anyone except her own advisers would be an unjustifiable extension of the remedy with dangerous consequences in encouraging unscrupulous applicants to obtain second hearings, said this:

'I do not consider it is a proper approach in this matter to be frightened by the spectre of successful, unscrupulous applicants manipulating the court's procedures to their advantage. Obviously, the court would have to deal in each case with the facts as they appear. In the present case, there has been no suggestion of mala fides

a at all. I have to look at this application to see whether, on the principles of natural justice and the principles on which judicial review is available, this is a proper case in which to grant the remedy. I find it incongruous to say, on the one hand, that one is concerned with the principles of natural justice and, on the other, to say one can only grant the remedy if natural justice is breached from a particular direction. In my judgment, it cannot be a proper test whether the remedy should be granted, in a case where the aggrieved party is wholly innocent, to ask whether the breach of
b natural justice has come from the court, the adjudicator, the opposition or from some fault on the part of the applicant's legal advisers. The test whether natural justice has been breached cannot turn, when the aggrieved party is wholly innocent, on whose fault it is that there was a breach. The court is concerned whether the proceedings as to the decision-making process are in natural justice properly open for review.'

c

    Counsel for the adjudicator submits that nevertheless the court has no power to make the orders the judge made because judicial review is restricted to three categories and ought not to be extended beyond them. Those three categories are: (1) errors of law on the face of the record; (2) acts in excess of jurisdiction, including breaches of natural justice; (3) decisions obtained by fraud, perjury or collusion.
d     The first category has been generally recognised at least since the judgment of Lord Goddard CJ in *R v Northumberland Compensation Appeal Tribunal, ex p Shaw* [1951] 1 All ER 268, [1951] 1 KB 711; *affd* [1952] 1 All ER 122, [1952] 1 KB 338, CA. But there is no error on the face of the adjudicator's determination and reasons. It has long been the court's duty to keep those whose proceedings the court supervises to acting within the powers which they have and to quash their decisions where they are reached by exceeding
e jurisdiction. And the House of Lords and the Privy Council have now reaffirmed that an order made contrary to natural justice is outside jurisdiction and void (see *Anisminic Ltd v Foreign Compensation Commission* [1969] 1 All ER 208, [1969] 2 AC 147, *F Hoffman-La Roche & Co AG v Secretary of State for Trade and Industry* [1974] 2 All ER 1128, [1975] AC 295, *A-G v Ryan* [1980] AC 718 at 727, where Lord Diplock said that it was a necessary implication that a minister, who had legal authority to determine the rights of
f individuals, is required to observe the principles of natural justice when exercising that authority, and if he fails to do so his purported decision is a nullity). But it stands valid until set aside or quashed (see H W R Wade *Administrative Law* (5th edn, 1982) pp 312–314, 469–470). Counsel for the adjudicator's trinity of categories may not be up to date, as in the very recent speeches in the House of Lords in *Council of Civil Service Unions v Minister for the Civil Service* [1984] 3 All ER 935, [1984] 3 WLR 1174, there appears a
g revised version of the categories which puts breach of natural justice, equated with failure to act fairly, under the head of procedural impropriety.
    Here there was a failure to observe a most important principle of natural justice, but the failure, even if it can be said to be a failure by the adjudicator who had authority to determine the applicant's rights, was caused by the applicant's advisers. In every reported case of such a failure (says counsel for the adjudicator) except two, the failure has been
h the fault of the court or tribunal exercising authority to determine rights. The first of those exceptions was a decision which is not binding on this court and unless it is distinguishable from this case should be overruled by this court; the second was a decision which this court overruled on the facts, leaving open the question whether such a failure caused by an applicant's own advisers could entitle an applicant to judicial review.
j     Before going into this question and examining the authorities, there is the third category established in 1848 by the decision of the Court of Queen's Bench in *R v Gillyard* 12 QB 527, 116 ER 965. There Gillyard had been convicted by justices of an offence against the excise laws on the information of his employer, a maltster named Haigh, who had collusively procured Gillyard's conviction in order to avoid the penalties for which he himself was liable and would have been found liable if he had not prosecuted the

apparently innocent Gillyard to conviction. Lord Denman CJ was willing, 'If it were
necessary . . . to create a precedent'; Coleridge J considered that the rule for quashing the          *a*
conviction was being made absolute on the ground that it was 'a fraud and mockery, the
result of conspiracy and subornation of perjury'; and Erle J said that in quashing the
conviction, the court was 'exercising the most salutary jurisdiction which this Court can
exercise', namely authority 'to correct all irregularities in the proceedings of inferior
tribunals'. It is noteworthy that the court, undeterred by lack of precedent, quashed
proceedings, regular on the face of them, of a court which had been misled, in order to          *b*
do justice, one judge regarding the fraud practised on the court as constituting or causing
an irregularity in its proceedings. That decision created an exception to any rule that
might be thought to limit the power of the High Court to quash the decisions of tribunals
that had themselves been at fault. It has been followed in such cases of perjury in
affiliation proceedings as *R v Leicester Recorder, ex p Wood* [1947] 1 All ER 928, [1947] KB
726, *R v Ashford (Kent) Justices, ex p Richley (No 2)* [1955] 3 All ER 604, [1956] 1 QB 167          *c*
and *R (Burns) v Tyrone County Court Judge* [1961] NI 167. But it has not yet been extended
to cases where a tribunal has failed to observe a principle of natural justice by an innocent
mistake; and counsel for the adjudicator submits that it should not be so extended, at
any rate when the mistake is induced by fault on the part of the agents of the party
complaining of the failure.

The observations of Lord Reid in *Ridge v Baldwin* [1963] 2 All ER 66 at 71, [1964] AC          *d*
40 at 64–65 on the principle audi alteram partem, and of Lord Hailsham LC in *Chief
Constable of the North Wales Police v Evans* [1982] 3 All ER 141 at 143–144, [1982] 1 WLR
1155 at 1160–1161 on fair treatment, cannot be read out of context as warranting the
application of those principles to cases which they were not considering. Nor is this court
free to follow the dissenting judgment of Lord Denning MR in *R v West Sussex Quarter
Sessions, ex p Albert & Maud Johnson Trust Ltd* [1973] 3 All ER 289 at 294–296, [1974] QB          *e*
24 at 35–36 and to admit fresh evidence on applications for judicial review to correct the
decision of an inferior court or tribunal: we must follow the decision of the majority in
that case, as did the Divisional Court in *R v Northamptonshire Justices, ex p Nicholson*, [1974]
RTR 97. There are, however, the two reported attempts, one successful, to quash
decisions reached without fault or error on the part of the court or tribunal, to which I
have already referred.          *f*

The first is the decision of the Divisional Court in *R v Leyland Magistrates, ex p
Hawthorn* [1979] 1 All ER 209, [1979] QB 283. There justices had convicted the applicant
for judicial review of driving without due care and attention on adequate evidence
without any procedural error. But there was a procedural error on the part of the
prosecution in failing to disclose to the applicant the names and addresses of two material
witnesses who had given information to the police but were not called to give evidence          *g*
by the prosecution. That error deprived the applicant of an elementary right to be
notified of those witnesses, which the Divisional Court held entitled him to have his
conviction quashed. In giving judgment, with which the other judges agreed, Lord
Widgery CJ, after referring to *R v West Sussex Quarter Sessions, ex p Albert & Maud Johnson
Trust Ltd* said ([1979] 1 All ER 209 at 210–211, [1979] QB 283 at 286):

> 'There is no doubt that an application can be made by certiorari to set aside an          *h*
> order on the basis that the tribunal failed to observe the rules of natural justice.
> Certainly if it were the fault of the justices that this additional evidentiary
> information was not passed on, no difficulty would arise. But the problem, and one
> can put it in a sentence, is that certiorari in respect of breach of the rules of natural
> justice is primarily a remedy sought on account of an error of the tribunal, and here,
> of course, we are not concerned with an error of the tribunal: we are concerned with          *j*
> an error of the police prosecutors. Consequently, amongst the arguments to which
> we have listened an argument has been that this is not a certiorari case at all on any
> of the accepted grounds. We have given this careful thought over the short
> adjournment because it is a difficult case in that the consequences of the decision
> either way have their unattractive features. However, if fraud, collusion, perjury

a
and such like matters not affecting the tribunal themselves justify an application for certiorari to quash the conviction, if all those matters are to have that effect, then we cannot say that the failure of the prosecutor which in this case has prevented the tribunal from giving the defendant a fair trial should not rank in the same category. We have come to the conclusion that there was here a clear denial of natural justice. Fully recognising the fact that the blame falls on the prosecutor and not on the tribunal, we think that it is a matter which should result in the conviction being
b
quashed.'

Counsel for the applicant had referred to *R v Gillyard* and *R v Leicester Recorder, ex p Wood* among other cases. Counsel for the prosecution submitted that certiorari would not lie for a miscarriage of justice based on a failure of professional duty and that the applicant might have a remedy by applying to the Crown Court for leave to appeal out of time, an application which would be positively supported by the prosecution. This
c
possibility, not noticed in the judgment of the Lord Widgery CJ, makes me doubt whether the court was right to exercise its discretion in the applicant's favour. But I do not doubt that the court has a discretionary jurisdiction to quash the decision of a court or tribunal which has been misled to its decision by misconduct of the proceedings on the part of the respondent to the application to quash (see *R v Blundeston Prison Board of Visitors, ex p Fox-Taylor* [1982] 1 All ER 646).
d
Is this true of mistake or misconduct on the part of the applicant's agents or even of the applicant himself? Comyn J held that it was, but this court reversed his decision on the facts and left the question open in *R v Immigration Appeal Tribunal, ex p Enwia* [1983] 2 All ER 1045, [1984] 1 WLR 117. There the facts as the judge found them were not very different from the undisputed facts of the instant case. The applicant claimed, and the judge found, that the UKIAS took it on themselves to notify the adjudicator that they
e
wanted a paper judgment, but the applicant had in fact always wanted an oral hearing to enable him to give and hear evidence; and, although he had himself contributed a great deal to the adjudicator's assumption that he did not want an oral hearing and although there was no criticism of the adjudicator or of the appeal tribunal which refused him leave to appeal, the judge quashed the tribunal's determination so as to give him an opportunity to be heard.
f
This court, however, held that the applicant had never asked (unlike the applicant in this case) for an oral hearing, but had authorised the UKIAS to submit the appeal to the adjudicator on the papers; and on the evidence before the judge he had, on advice from the UKIAS, never wanted one until after his application to the tribunal for leave to appeal had been dismissed. In the course of giving the judgment of the court I said this ([1983] 2 All ER 1045 at 1052–1053, [1984] 1 WLR 117 at 130):
g
'We have considered also the four or five categories of case to which judicial review applies, which counsel for the tribunal submits, contrary to the judgment of Comyn J, are exhaustive, and the possibility that they may be extended in a proper case to cover errors in law, not only of the decision-making body, but of the other party, for which *R v Leyland Justices, ex p Hawthorn* [1979] 1 All ER 209, [1979] QB
h
283 is an authority, and even of the party complaining of the decision by way of judicial review, for which there is no authority. Bearing in mind the judgments of Orr and Lawton LJJ in *R v West Sussex Quarter Sessions, ex p Albert and Maud Johnson Trust Ltd* [1973] 3 All ER 289 at 298–299, 301, [1974] QB 24 at 39, 42, and of Lord Hailsham LC and Lord Brightman in *Chief Constable of the North Wales Police v Evans* [1982] 3 All ER 141 at 143–144, 155, [1982] 1 WLR 1155 at 1160–1161, 1174–
j
1175, we can see that it might be permissible to quash a decision seriously affecting a person who by mistake or misunderstanding due to his own defects or those of his advisers was deprived of the opportunity of being fully heard before the decision was reached. However, we find it unnecessary and undesirable to decide whether judicial review would lie in such a case, because we are clearly of opinion that this is not such a case.'

We have now to decide whether it is permissible to quash such a decision when the applicant is wholly innocent and it is the applicant's advisers who are at fault. I have come to the conclusion that it is. Taylor J thought so, and I agree with him for the reasons he gives in the passage which I have already quoted from his judgment. We do not have to consider, and the judge very properly did not consider, whether it is ever permissible to grant judicial review to an applicant who is not wholly innocent. Where the mistake or misunderstanding which leads to the denial of natural justice is the applicant's own, it may seldom, if ever, be right for the court to exercise its discretion in his or her favour; for in most, if not all, cases of that kind there could be no unfairness towards the author and only begetter of the procedural defect. But I would hold, if necessary, that the court has the discretionary power to review and quash a decision reached as a result of an applicant's own fault.

The remedy of judicial review and the jurisdiction to quash decisions of lower courts and tribunals have their lines of limitation which do not extend beyond defects or irregularities at the trial and which will leave hard cases beyond the lines: see *R v West Sussex Quarter Sessions, ex p Albert & Maud Johnson Trust Ltd* [1973] 3 All ER 289 at 298–299, [1974] QB 24 at 39, 42 per Orr and Lawton LJJ; and natural justice is not to be confused with a vague sense of unfairness, as counsel for the adjudicator submitted that the judge had confused it. But the remedy and the jurisdiction are not to be confined too rigorously by precedent, and I respectfully agree with the observation of Lord MacDermott LCJ in *R (Burns) v Tyrone County Court Judge* [1961] NI 167 at 172 that—

> 'Though the main branches of certiorari have long since been shaped and fixed by precedent, they are still alive and capable of growth in the furtherance of their established purposes.'

But as Orr LJ pointed out, fraud and perjury cases illustrate circumstances in which fresh evidence may be admissible in support of an application for certiorari; and I am of the opinion, in agreement with the judge, that the denial of a hearing to the applicant, in the circumstances proved by evidence accepted as true, is a defect or irregularity which entitles and requires the High Court to put it right. It is a breach of a basic rule of natural justice, incorporated in the Immigration Appeals (Procedure) Rules 1972, which vitiates the proceedings before the adjudicator, and no less a breach because the adjudicator when making his decision did not know of the facts which constituted the breach.

I do not need to get support for that conclusion from the opinion of Cooke J in the New Zealand case of *Daganayasi v Minister of Immigration* [1980] 2 NZLR 130, on which counsel for the applicant relied, that a mistake of fact which misleads a decision-making body (in that case a minister) into producing an injustice may be a ground for judicial review. I would prefer to join the other two judges in that case, Richmond and Richardson JJ, in leaving open the question Cooke J answered in what they described as a difficult and developing area of the law as yet in a far from settled state.

I am content to accept what Taylor J said at the conclusion of a judgment in which I can detect no confusion or error.

> 'It seems to me that there is a clear distinction to be drawn between the situation in the present case, which must be rare indeed, where there has been no oral hearing at all in a case which gravely affects the applicant's future, and cases on the other side of the line where there has been an oral hearing but subsequently some further evidence has emerged which it is suggested might have made a difference to the outcome. In the former case, which is the present case, it seems to me that there has been a basic failure in the rules of natural justice. There has been an irregularity in the sense that a wholly different type of determination has been carried out, namely, a determination purely on paper evidence as against a full oral hearing.'

I cannot put it better than that, and I would only add that there was nothing wrong with the adjudicator's decision, which may turn out to be right after all, on the accepted facts, but there was a fundamental flaw in the decision-making process. I would affirm a the judge's judgment and dismiss the appeal, but must not be taken to be giving any encouragement to immigrants to absent themselves when their appeals come up for an oral hearing and then to blame their advisers or the adjudicator for dismissing their appeals.

**FOX LJ.** The essential features of the case are these.

The applicant was entitled to an oral hearing before the adjudicator if she asked for b one. She did ask for one. She did not receive an oral hearing; her appeal was dismissed in her absence without one. The fact that she did not get an oral hearing was not through any fault of her own or of the adjudicator.

Counsel for the adjudicator, rightly anxious to avoid unfairness to the applicant but equally anxious that the allowing of this appeal should not lead to abuse by the unscrupulous, would not be unhappy if we were to interpret what occurred as an c irregularity of the adjudicator and allow the appeal accordingly. I do not think however that we can so deal with the matter. It would be quite contrary to the facts. The adjudicator did nothing wrong and there is no irregularity by him. Indeed, I do not see that he could have done other than he did. He was told by the applicant's representatives (the advisory service) that they had no instructions and they invited the adjudicator to deal with the cases on the documents alone.

d Counsel for the adjudicator submits that judicial review is only available in three familiar cases, namely (1) error of law on the face of the record, (2) acts in excess of jurisdiction and (3) order obtained by fraud or perjury or collusion.

There is here no ex facie error of law. And there was no fraud, perjury or collusion. But it has been accepted that an order made contrary to natural justice is in excess of jurisdiction and void (see *Anisminic Ltd v Foreign Compensation Commission* [1969] 1 All ER e 208, [1969] 2 AC 147 and *A-G v Ryan* [1980] AC 718) though the precise categorisation may need revision (see *Council of Civil Service Unions v Minister for the Civil Service* [1984] 3 All ER 935, [1984] 3 WLR 1174).

What happened here was that, without any fault by the adjudicator or the applicant, the adjudicative process failed and the applicant was wholly denied the oral hearing which she had asked for and to which she was entitled. It is difficult to regard that as f other than a deprival of justice.

In *R v Leyland Magistrates, ex p Hawthorn* [1979] 1 All ER 209, [1979] QB 283 the trial was conducted by the court with complete propriety. The applicant was found guilty of a motoring offence by the justices. After the trial it was discovered that the police were aware of witnesses whom they did not call and whose existence they did not disclose to the defence. Whether it was necessary to deal with the matter by prerogative order at all g or whether it could have been dealt with by a consent application for leave to appeal out of time I need not consider. Certiorari was granted. The Divisional Court recognised that there was no error by the tribunal. There was simply an error by the prosecutors. 'Consequently', said Lord Widgery CJ, 'amongst the arguments to which we have listened an argument has been that this was not a certiorari case at all on any of the accepted grounds' (see [1979] 1 All ER 209 at 210–211, [1979] QB 283 at 288). Nevertheless the h Divisional Court accepted that, if fraud, perjury and collusion, none of which affects the tribunal itself, are sufficient for certiorari, it could not be said that the failure of the prosecution to disclose the names of the witnesses was not in the same category if it prevents the tribunal from giving the defendant a fair trial. In that case, as in this, there was denial of justice by the conduct of the proceedings not through any failure by the tribunal or by the applicant but from another source. Again, in *R v Blundeston Prison* j *Board of Visitors, ex p Fox-Taylor* [1982] 1 All ER 646 there had been no failure by the Board of Visitors. The failure was by the prison authorities to inform the accused of the existence of the witness and that failure led to the failure in the investigating process by the prison visitors.

Apart from the point which I have mentioned in relation to the alternative remedy in the *Leyland* case I see no reason to suppose that these two cases were wrongly decided. If a breach of the rules of natural justice is to be a ground for certiorari I do not see why one should stop short at a breach caused in a particular way. The real question is whether there was, in truth, a breach of the rules of natural justice. That requires in each case an examination of the facts, including the conduct of the applicant. If one concludes that there was, I do not see why the court cannot grant certiorari if it thinks fit, even if the tribunal itself did not err.

It seems to me that the present case does not take the principle beyond that accepted in the *Leyland* and *Blundeston* cases, and since it seems to me that there has in fact been a denial of natural justice for which the applicant was in no way responsible I think that the decision of Taylor J was correct. The case is not on all fours with any of the preceding cases but this is not a static branch of the law (see for example the observations of Lord Diplock in *Council of Civil Service Unions v Minister for the Civil Service* [1984] 3 All ER 935 at 950, [1984] 3 WLR 1174 at 1196) and if there has been a failure of natural justice I think that the court should correct it.

I should however emphasise that we are dealing with the case of a wholly innocent applicant. If the failure of the adjudicative process had been the consequence of a failure or misconduct by her, different considerations would apply.

I would dismiss the appeal.

**PURCHAS LJ.** The facts against which this appeal is brought by the Secretary of State are fully set out in the judgments already delivered and need not be repeated here. The question raised by this appeal may be shortly stated but is of importance. I would pose it in this form: in the presence of an established failure by an inferior statutory body to hear and determine in accordance with natural justice a question referred to it under statutory powers, are the courts powerless to give a remedy to the persons aggrieved unless it can be shown that the statutory body itself has been at fault? The framing of the question in this manner involves of necessity that the failure has arisen from some cause extraneous to the tribunal itself. This poses a second question, namely: is there a distinction to be drawn from the nature of that cause, e g acts or omissions on the part of the statutory body, by the applicant, by the respondent, or the intervention of some supervening outside factor?

In my judgment it is important to distinguish between the determination of the scope of the jurisdiction and restrictions arising from precedent in the exercise of judicial discretion within that jurisdiction. Effectively judicial control would, in my view, call for maximum scope to be given to the jurisdiction itself in association with flexibility of discretion within certain guidelines as might be established: see the judgment of Greene MR in *R v Stafford Justices, ex p Stafford Corp* [1940] 2 KB 33 at 43:

'Now, in my opinion, the order for the issue of the writ of certiorari is, except in cases where it goes as of course, strictly in all cases a matter of discretion. It is perfectly true to say that if no special circumstances exist, and if all that appears is a clear excess of jurisdiction, then a person aggrieved by that is entitled ex debito justitiae to his order. That merely means this, in my judgment, that the Court in such circumstances will exercise its discretion by granting the relief. In all discretionary remedies it is well known and settled that in certain circumstances—I will not say in all of them, but in a great many of them—the Court, although nominally it has a discretion, if it is to act according to the ordinary principles upon which judicial discretion is exercised, must exercise that discretion in a particular way, and if a judge at a trial refuses to do so, then the Court of Appeal will set the matter right. But when once it is established that in deciding whether or not a particular remedy shall be granted the Court is entitled to inquire into the conduct of the applicant, and the circumstances of the case, in order to ascertain whether it is proper or not proper to grant the remedy sought, the case must in my judgment be one of discretion.'

In the instant case it is accepted that through no fault of the applicant or of the a   adjudicator, the applicant's case was never put before the adjudicator either in the form of written submissions or, as the applicant had requested at an earlier stage, in the form of oral submissions. Nor for the purposes of this appeal can it be said that the adjudicator was wrong in proceeding to determine the matter on the documents provided by the Secretary of State. It is common ground that in the instant appeal there was a failure to observe the basic principle of natural justice, audi alteram partem, and that this was caused by shortcomings on the part of the agents, the UKIAS. For the purposes of this

b   appeal we were invited to ignore any suggestion that the applicant herself might have contributed to the failure through what has been described during argument as 'inertia'.

The problem, therefore, becomes neatly defined. The principle of audi alteram partem is one of the most fundamental concepts of natural justice known to the law. It may be excessive to have resort to the 'Garden of Eden' as Fortescue J did in *R v University of Cambridge* (1723) 1 Str 557 at 567, 93 ER 698 at 704, but the whole history of natural justice demonstrates the fundamental importance of this principle. Nor in this case is the

c   court required to consider the distinctions between judicial and other administrative acts, since the statute and regulations made thereunder provide that the applicant is entitled to a hearing (see r 12 of the Immigration Appeals (Procedure) Rules 1972, SI 1972/1684, already cited by Stephenson LJ). The question is one of jurisdiction only. It is accepted that if the jurisdiction exists this is a case in which the court ought to exercise

d   its discretion and grant relief.

Counsel for the adjudicator submitted that the court's powers to grant an order for certiorari are restricted to certain defined situations which he listed under three categories: (i) errors of law on the face of the record; (ii) acts in excess of jurisdiction, with which he included a failure to act within the rules of natural justice; (iii) decisions obtained by fraud, perjury or collusion. There are a number of difficulties with this submission.

e   Although the prerogative writs stemmed from the right assumed by the royal courts to 'examine the proceedings of all jurisdictions erected by Act of Parliament' (see per Holt CJ in *R v Glamorganshire Inhabitants* (1700) 1 Ld Raym 580, 91 ER 1287 at 1288) the areas over which the courts regularly exercise their powers of review extend far beyond these original boundaries. In the recent case of *Council of Civil Service Unions v Minister for the Civil Service* [1984] 3 All ER 935 at 950, [1984] 3 WLR 1174 at 1196, Lord Diplock said:

f           'Judicial review has I think developed to a stage today when without reiterating any analysis of the steps by which the development has come about, one can conveniently classify under three heads the grounds on which administrative action is subject to control by judicial review. The first ground I would call "illegality", the second "irrationality" and the third "procedural impropriety". That is not to say that further development on a case by case basis may not in course of time add further

g           grounds. I have in mind particularly the possible adoption in the future of the principle of "proportionality" which is recognised in the administrative law of several of our fellow members of the European Community; but to dispose of the instant case the three already well-established heads that I have mentioned will suffice.'

h   The tenor of this speech runs contrary to counsel for the adjudicator's submission that the list of categories is closed. The 'dramatic and, indeed . . . radical change in the scope of judicial review' was also described in the speech of Lord Roskill (see [1984] 3 All ER 935 at 953, [1984] 3 WLR 1174 at 1199).

For my part I cannot accept that this fundamental jurisdiction can be restrained in an

j   arbitrary or general way and believe that this is recognised by Lord Diplock in the passage just cited. There are, of course, well-defined areas in which the courts will not interfere, such as that under review in the House of Lords decision just mentioned; but these are not relevant in the instant appeal.

Another difficulty with which counsel for the adjudicator is faced is that he is obliged to submit that *R v Leyland Magistrates, ex p Hawthorn* [1979] 1 All ER 209, [1979] QB 283 is wrongly decided. He may also have overlooked the judgment of Lord Widgery CJ, with whom the other members of the Divisional Court agreed, in *R v Immigration Appeal Tribunal, ex p Jusoh* (28 July 1976, unreported). In this case the applicant was refused leave to appeal from the adjudicator because the grounds of appeal in fact considered by the tribunal were correctly thought to raise no arguable point of law (see r 14 of the Immigration Appeals (Procedure) Rules 1972). There had, however, been submitted another set of grounds of appeal which for reasons never determined were not supplied to the tribunal. Lord Widgery CJ said:

'The normal practice, and I think the one we ought to follow here, is that if it is once accepted, as it is, that there was an error in the procedure, and that the proper grounds of appeal were never before the tribunal, I think the proper answer myself is that certiorari should go to quash the refusal of the application for leave to appeal, thus clearing the way for a further application for leave to appeal.'

The final difficulty in the submissions of counsel for the adjudicator is to justify what might be called his third 'special category'. In these cases the decision-making body has behaved with absolute propriety and no patent error appears on the face of the record. Yet there has occurred a breach of the rules of natural justice induced by the conduct of some third party. It is not easy to see why in logic the availability of the remedy should depend on the quality of the conduct of the third party.

With respect to the able argument of counsel for the adjudicator, I cannot agree that in the presence of an established breach on the part of an inferior tribunal of the rules of natural justice, eg a failure to obey the principle audi alteram partem, the court has no jurisdiction to grant an order of certiorari, notwithstanding that the failure has arisen through no fault of the tribunal itself. Whether or not the court should exercise its discretion will depend on ascertaining the cause of the failure in relation to the conduct of the applicant.

Cases in which the question of jurisdiction arose in relation to a decision made by an inferior tribunal have been mentioned by Stephenson LJ. *R v Gillyard* (1848) 12 QB 527, 116 ER 965 was a case in point. The facts of this case have already been described by Stephenson LJ; but I venture to cite in slightly more detail the judgment of Lord Denman CJ (12 QB 527 at 529, 116 ER 965 at 966):

'He [the maltster] urges that he ought not to be called upon to purge himself by affidavit of an indictable offence, and that certiorari does not lie in this case. Such an answer clenches the accusation. Is this conviction, then, to stand because some other Court may have jurisdiction? Suppose some person had personated Gillyard, and the conviction had been procured by such a trial; must we say that such a shadow shall prevail? In so holding we should be doing away with a most useful jurisdiction. If it were necessary, we ought, in such a case, to create a precedent, in order that persons who have set the law in motion for fraudulent purposes may understand that, if they are charged with such an offence, they will be expected to answer the accusation.'

The attitude of the court in *R v Gillyard* is reflected in the more recent cases of *R v Leyland Magistrates, ex p Hawthorn*, [1979] 1 All ER 209, [1979] QB 283 and *R v Blundeston Prison Board of Visitors, ex p Fox-Taylor* [1982] 1 All ER 646, to which reference has already been made by Stephenson LJ. In the *Leyland* case evidence favourable to the defendant in the magistrates' court had been withheld by the prosecution. I cite one short extract from the judgment of Lord Widgery CJ ([1979] 1 All ER 209 at 210–211, [1974] QB 283 at 286):

'But the problem, and one can put it in a sentence, is that certiorari in respect of breach of the rules of natural justice is primarily a remedy sought on account of an error of the tribunal, and here, of course, we are not concerned with an error of the tribunal: we are concerned with an error of the police prosecutors. Consequently, amongst the arguments to which we have listened an argument has been that this a  is not a certiorari case at all on any of the accepted grounds. We have given this careful thought over the short adjournment because it is a difficult case in that the consequences of the decision either way have their unattractive features. However, if fraud, collusion, perjury and such like matters not affecting the tribunal themselves justify an application for certiorari to quash the conviction, if all those matters are to have that effect, then we cannot say that the failure of the prosecutor which in this case has prevented the tribunal from giving the defendant a fair trial

b  should not rank in the same category.'

With respect to Lord Widgery CJ I would venture to comment that the correct approach should have been that the tribunal had failed to try the case according to the rules of natural justice but through no fault of theirs. The fault lay with the prosecution. A further step along the path was taken by Phillips J in *R v Blundeston Prison Board of*
c  *Visitors* [1982] 1 All ER 646 at 649–650:

'Certiorari in cases of this kind is based on a failure by the adjudicating body. As has been pointed out, there has been no failure by the board of visitors. The failure as I have found is by the authorities of the prison. Therefore, it can be said it would be pushing certiorari very far, he would say too far, away from its essential base, which must be a failure of the adjudicating authority going to jurisdiction. The
d  answer to that, I think, is that that is precisely what the Divisional Court in *Leyland* did, justifying it for the reasons I have given. In effect, as I understand what is said is this: that albeit the failure was by the prosecution in that case it led to a failure of the process of the adjudicating justices, albeit they were not responsible for it, nor did they cause it. But none the less, proceedings before them were vitiated and their jurisdiction impugned. It does not mean that this case takes the principle any
e  further, once one accepts, as I have found, that there was a breach of natural justice whereby the existence of a potentially relevant witness was not brought to the attention of the board of visitors.'

This approach also supports the comments made by this court when acknowledging the possibility (but not deciding) that the court would grant an order of certiorari on judicial
f  review even though the failure arose from the acts of the applicant himself (see *R v Immigration Appeal Tribunal, ex p Enwia* [1983] 2 All ER 1045 at 1052–1053, [1984] 1 WLR 117 at 130, to which reference has been made by Stephenson LJ.

Counsel for the adjudicator further submitted that if the judge's judgment were upheld it would have widespread and unwelcome repercussions, the so-called floodgates argument. This submission was robustly dealt with by the judge in the extract from his
g  judgment already cited by Stephenson LJ. However, I would like to add that the spectre to which he refers can be exorcised by two restrictions inherent in the judicial review process. Firstly, the breach of natural justice must first be established within the well-known criteria laid down in *Chief Constable of the North Wales Police v Evans* [1982] 3 All ER 141, [1982] 1 WLR 1155, which appear in the passages cited in the judge's judgment. This distinguishes cases such as *R v West Sussex Quarter Sessions, ex p Albert & Maud*
h  *Johnson Trust Ltd* [1973] 3 All ER 289, [1974] QB 24. Secondly, even where jurisdiction exists as a result of an established failure on the part of an inferior tribunal to achieve natural justice, the court will not exercise its discretion to grant relief if the conduct of the application has conduced to that failure or if other conditions exist in which it would not be proper for the court to exercise its discretion to grant an order of certiorari. In the instant appeal there are no reasons to inhibit the exercise of discretion in the applicant's
j  favour and in my judgment the court has jurisdiction to grant the relief sought.

I would therefore indorse the reasoning of Taylor J in his lucid and careful judgment, and agree that this appeal should be dismissed.

*Appeal dismissed. Leave to appeal to the House of Lords refused.*

21 February. The Appeal Committee of the House of Lords allowed a petition by the adjudicator for leave to appeal.

*a*

Solicitors: *Treasury Solicitor*; *Egerton Sandler* (for the applicants).

Diana Brahams    Barrister.

*b*

# Practice Note

COURT OF APPEAL, CIVIL DIVISION,
SIR JOHN DONALDSON MR, BROWNE-WILKINSON LJ AND MUSTILL J
18 MARCH 1985

*c*

*Court of Appeal – Practice – Civil Division – Applications to single judge – Documents to be lodged – Notification of hearing date.*

*d*

**SIR JOHN DONALDSON MR** gave the following direction at the sitting of the court. At present, single judge applications are heard on Fridays by two nominated Lords Justices. This system suffers from certain drawbacks, in particular the uneconomic use of judge-power, and it is therefore proposed that, as from the beginning of the Easter Term, a new system will be introduced on an experimental basis. This will involve the following changes to current procedures.

*e*

1. On setting down an application for hearing by a single Lord Justice, the following documents are to be lodged *in triplicate*: (a) the summons or, where the application is ex parte, the notice setting out the nature of the application; (b) the order under appeal; (c) in the case of an application for leave to appeal, the order of the court below refusing such leave; (d) the affidavit in support of the application, containing, in the case of an application for leave to appeal, the grounds of the proposed appeal.

*f*

2. A hearing date will no longer be given at the time of setting down. In the case of an inter partes application, notice of application should be served on the respondent(s) indorsed 'Date and time to be notified by the Civil Appeals Office'.

3. Any further documents in support of the application must be lodged with the Civil Appeals General Office (room 246) within ten days of the date on which the application is set down, after which, unless the court directs that any further documents are to be filed, a hearing date will be fixed.

*g*

4. The Civil Appeals Office will notify the applicant and, in the case of inter partes applications, the respondent(s) of the time and date on which the application is to be heard.

Diana Procter    Barrister.

End of Volume 1